DATE DUE FOR RETURN

GUIDE TO
American Foreign Relations since *1700*

Editor

RICHARD DEAN BURNS

Contributing Editors

Edward M. Bennett
Robert S. Bothwell
Albert Hall Bowman
Thomas A. Bryson
Thomas H. Buckley
Richard Dean Burns
Raymond A. Esthus
Robert H. Ferrell
John Lewis Gaddis
Lawrence E. Gelfand
Scott R. Hall
George C. Herring
Gary R. Hess
Larry D. Hill
Paul S. Holbo
Michael H. Hunt
Akira Iriye
Howard Jones
Lawrence S. Kaplan
Warren F. Kimball
Warren F. Kuehl
Bruce Kuniholm
Lester D. Langley
Thomas M. Leonard
Frank J. Merli
Thomas Noer
Thomas G. Paterson
Bradford Perkins
David M. Pletcher
Forrest C. Pogue
Armin Rappaport
Gary M. Ross
John H. Schroeder
Martin Sherwin
Joseph M. Siracusa
William Stinchcombe
David F. Trask
Roger R. Trask
Russell F. Weigley
Joan Hoff Wilson
Louis Wilson

Contributors

Henry S. Albinski
David L. Anderson
John Duke Anthony
Glen St. John Barclay
Sharon L. Bollinger
Gene M. Brack
Alan S. Brown
Peter H. Buckingham
Richard Dean Burns
John C. Campbell
John Chay
Edward W. Chester
Anthony Cheung
Christopher Chipello
John Gary Clifford
Bruce Cumings
Calvin D. Davis
Charles DeBenedetti
R. Hrair Dekmejian
Roger Dingman
Robert A. Divine
Justus D. Doenecke
Steven Dorr
Carolyn Eisenberg
Thomas H. Etzold
Wilton Fowler
John Gimbel
Mary Gormly
Ross Gregory
Robert Griffith
Fraser Harbutt
George Harris
Robert A. Hart
Alan K. Henrikson
Richard Herr
Peter P. Hill
Michael Hudson
James H. Hutson
Richard H. Immerman
Ronald J. Jensen
Howard Jones
William Kamman
Allen H. Kitchens
Marvin W. Kranz
Mary V. Kuebel
Walter LaFeber

David C. Lawson
Melvyn P. Leffler
Ann M. Lesch
James R. Leutze
Steven I. Levine
David Long
Mark M. Lowenthal
Michael Lutzker
William H. Masterson
Robert E. May
Robert Messer
Aaron Miller
Jean-Donald Miller
James A. Nathan
Arthur Ned Newberry III
Arnold A. Offner
John Offner
Alison G. Olson
Gary B. Ostrower
Carl P. Parrini
Rouhollah Ramazani
James Reardon-Anderson
Bernard Reich
David Reynolds
Barry R. Rigby
Gary M. Ross
Michael Schaller
Mary K. Schenck
Thomas Schoonover
Louise Sieminski
William Z. Slany
Ronald H. Spector
Mark A. Stoler
Roland N. Stromberg
Edwin B. Strong
Sandra C. Taylor
Eugene P. Trani
Nancy Bernkopf Tucker
Michael Van Dusen
Robert H. Van Meter, Jr.
William O. Walker III
Samuel F. Wells, Jr.
Mira Wilkins
Lawrence S. Wittner
Lawrence A. Yates
Marvin R. Zahniser

GUIDE TO
American Foreign Relations since *1700*

Edited by Richard Dean Burns
The Society for Historians of American Foreign Relations

ABC–CLIO, INC.
Santa Barbara, California
Oxford, England

**Library of Congress Cataloging in
Publication Data**

Main entry under title:

Guide to American foreign relations since 1700.

Bibliography: p.
Includes index.
1. United States—Foreign relations—
Bibliography.
I. Burns, Richard Dean.
Z6465.U5G84 1982 [E183.7] 016.32773 82-13905
ISBN 0-87436-323-3

10   9   8   7   6   5   4   3   2   1

ABC-Clio, Inc.
2040 Alameda Padre Serra, Box 4397
Santa Barbara, California 93103

Clio Press Ltd.
Woodside House, Hinksey Hill
Oxford, OX1 5BE, England

This book is printed on acid-free paper, Smyth
sewn, and covered in Holliston Roxite Vellum.

Manufactured in United States of America.

Contents

1
Reference Aids

2
Overviews: Diplomatic Surveys, Themes, and Theories

3
Colonial and Imperial Diplomacy to 1774

4
The American Revolution, 1775–1783

5
The Confederation and Federalist Era, 1781–1801

6
The Jeffersonian Era, 1801–1815

7
Florida, Hispanic America, and the Monroe Doctrine

8
American Diplomatic and Commercial Relations with Europe, 1815–1861

9
United States and Mexico, 1821–1861

10
Canadian-American Boundary, 1783–1872

11
Civil War Diplomacy

12
Expansionist Efforts
after the Civil War, 1865–1898

13
The Spanish-American War, 1898–1900

14
The United States and Europe, 1867–1914

15
The United States
and Latin America, 1861–1919

16
Peace, Arbitration, and
Internationalist Movements to 1914

17
United States and
East and Southeast Asia to 1913

18
United States, Turkey, Middle East, and Africa to 1939

19
World War I and Peace Settlement, 1914–1920

20
Internationalism, Isolationism, Disarmament, and Economics, 1920–1937

21
Interwar Diplomacy, 1920–1937

22
Prelude to World War II, 1936–1941

23
Wartime Diplomacy, 1941–1945

24
U.S. Cold War Diplomacy:
Overviews, Historiography, and Personalities

25
Anglo-American-Soviet Diplomacy
for the Postwar World, 1941–1945

26
United States and the Soviet Union, 1946–1953

27
United States and East Asia, 1941–1953

28
United States and Europe after 1945

29
United States and the Soviet Union after 1953

30
United States, Southeast Asia,
and the Indochina Wars since 1941

31
United States and East Asia after 1953

32
The United States, Australia, New Zealand,
and the Central Pacific

33
The United States and the Middle East since 1941

34
United States, Caribbean, and Central America after 1941

35
United States, Mexico, and South America since 1941

36
Canadian-American Relations since 1941

37
United States, South Asia, and Sub-Saharan Africa since 1941

38
International Organization, Law, and Peace Movements since 1941

39
Economic Issues and Foreign Policy

40
The Armed Forces, Strategy, and Foreign Policy

Appendixes

Indexes

List of Illustrations

How to Use This Guide

The *Guide* contains important features and aids designed to enhance researcher access to, and use of, the information it contains. It offers both a standard table of contents at the beginning of the volume and a separate contents listing at the opening of each chapter. Subject and author indexes also are provided.

Users searching for episodes or themes with fixed chronological boundaries are advised to turn first to the general table of contents, which lists the major sections of each chapter. Because the *Guide* takes a largely chronological approach to America's diplomatic experiences, this aid will frequently direct the researcher immediately to the chapter(s) of interest. The detailed chapter contents then provides convenient access to the material that follows.

The *Guide*'s enlarged subject index enables the reader to track themes and topics through several chapters and to accumulate information about specific individuals. It is divided into two major sections—*Topics* and *Individuals*. The first major section provides access to such topics or themes as the open door, manifest destiny, monetary policy, commerce, international law, and containment policy, and as to such episodes as the *Trent* affair, the Second Front issue, and the Marshall Plan. Subdivisions of this section include reference groupings by nation, region, and state, and by war, crisis, and conference.

The second major section of the subject index is divided into two subsections—Americans and foreigners. The individuals listed here consist of historical figures, famous and obscure, and of historians and writers whose names have appeared either in titles or annotations. Henry A. Kissinger appears because of his activities and policies as secretary of state, but the author index should also be checked to locate his writings. A special effort has been made to list in the various sections of the subject index those chapters of collected essays, often lost from bibliographical control, that relate to important diplomats or to significant diplomatic topics.

The extensive cross-reference system, which adds some 3,000 entries to the *Guide*, consists of reference notes given under the various subject headings, as well as individually cited cross-reference entries. These aids direct researchers to other potentially useful sections of the volume, and point out specific books, essays, documents, and reference aids on similar or related topics. For example, when researchers turn to Chapter 2 to locate materials on the "Monroe Doctrine," they will discover reference notes leading them to related sections of other chapters, such as "The Monroe Doctrine to 1861" (Chapter 7); "The Monroe Doctrine 1861–1919" (Chapter 15); and "Good Neighbor Policy/Monroe Doctrine" (Chapter 21). Abbreviated cross-reference entries within these chapter sections direct the user to additional relevant items in other chapters.

The cross-referencing system avoids duplication of entries while still providing comprehensive coverage to each major theme or era covered by a particular work. Each full citation within a chapter is numbered consecutively, in **bold face,** with the chapter number followed by the individual citation number. For example, George F. Kennan's *Memoirs* constitute the 124th full citation in Chapter 24, and is identified as **24:124.** Other citations to the same work are unnumbered cross-references to this numbered citation, with the citation number appearing in parentheses after the title. The original annotations of these cross-references are unchanged and thus retain the explanation of the work's special significance for that particular chapter. The numbered citation in Chapter 24 for both volumes of the Kennan *Memoirs* emphasizes Kennan's role in the early cold war years. An annotated, unnumbered cross-reference to Kennan's volume appears in Chapter 22 with an annotation stressing its significance for the prewar years, while the second volume's cross-reference annotation in Chapter 29 stresses Kennan's later diplomatic roles and political views. Judicious use of the cross-reference system not only will provide researchers with the ready location of a variety of works, but may suggest new questions and different approaches as well.

Special sections in each chapter provide guidance for the specialist, researcher, instructor, and student. Chapter introductions highlight key issues, suggest general surveys on particular themes or issues, and provide insight into the historiographical treatment of important episodes and topics. Scholars in search of topics for study will find the introductions especially valuable. The "Resources and Overviews" sections of Chapters 3 through 40 maintain the connections between particular periods and topics and the citations to general studies and basic reference aids contained in Chapters 1 and 2. Similarly, biographies, autobiographies, memoirs, and other works by or relating to American and foreign diplomats and statesmen have been collected within the "Personalities" section of the appropriate chapter.

Other useful features of the *Guide* include 12 maps, which appear in the appropriate chapters throughout the volume, and two appendixes on major American policymakers since 1781. Appendix I is a chronological chart of presidents, secretaries of state, chairmen of the Senate Foreign Relations Committee, secretaries of defense, and national security advisers. Appendix II provides brief biographical sketches of American secretaries of state.

Preface

BIBLIOGRAPHICAL GUIDES are tools essential to the pursuit of the historian's craft. Every field of historical instruction and scholarly investigation claims its special bibliographical apparatus. Such aids guide the established scholar as well as the fledgling student launching a career. Because they are so vital to the effective performance of teaching and research, bibliographical guides invariably appear as a new historical field gains substantial academic recognition and a respectable group of active practitioners. In this century, bibliographical tools have appeared at about the same moment as the earliest classroom texts for that field.

It is axiomatic that each succeeding generation reinterprets its history. Allowing for some exaggeration, even the most successful bibliographical guide cannot expect to enjoy any greater longevity than a generation. Their useful life span is limited not only by the continuous proliferation of new historical literature and the increasing abundance of both printed and manuscript sources, but also by the continuous process of dynamic change that every field of historical inquiry undergoes as it responds to an influx of fresh theories, concepts, methods, and appraisals. A bibliographical guide should, therefore, reflect the prevalent values of its scholarship. It should also suggest the issues and questions that scholars have been addressing, and, at least by implication, those significant questions that still elude historical scholarship.

As a special field for instruction and investigation, American diplomatic historiography emerged in the aftermath of World War I. The first generation to give form, substance, and leadership to the field during its formative decade of the 1920s contained men who had observed the deprivations of the war at close range while serving either in the military forces or as members of the numerous wartime governmental agencies. Such organizations as the Inquiry and the later American Commission to Negotiate Peace at Paris in 1918–1919 recruited historians, among other academicians, exposing them to the harsh realities of international politics, and occasionally to direct participation in the treaty negotiations. Many of these men caught the spirit of Wilsonian internationalism but soon came to realize that the American government and public were not yet ready to assume the responsibilities of leadership in the world community. Rejection of the Treaty of Versailles, including American membership in the League of Nations and the World Court, prompted many historians to advocate special training in international historiography within the curricula of American colleges and universities. Now, after six decades, and with the preparation of this new *Guide to American Foreign Relations since 1700,* the pioneering efforts of such early leaders in the field as Ephraim D. Adams, George H. Blakeslee, Archibald Cary Coolidge, Tyler Dennett, John H. Latane, and Charles Seymour should be remembered along with the work of Samuel Flagg Bemis and Dexter Perkins.

In 1935, the *Guide to the Diplomatic History of the United States, 1775–1921* was published by the Government Printing Office. Its editors, Samuel Flagg Bemis and Grace

Gardner Griffin, the bibliographer, emphasized in their prefatory comments that the project was intended to be a guide rather than a mere bibliography. What Bemis and Griffin compiled was not just another good bibliographical volume; their *Guide* sought to suggest significant and insightful research to the interested scholarly community. Literally an entire generation of historians concerned with international diplomacy benefited from and exploited the numerous suggestions found in the *Guide*. Bemis and Griffin limited their project to the national period beginning with the American Revolution and terminating with the close of the first world war (a brief section of Chapter 7 treats the Washington Conference of 1921–1922). They frankly admitted that within the chronological limitations imposed, their *Guide* remained far from complete. Excluded were "things of ephemeral, insignificant or useless nature, and we have presumed to draw a line that would exclude works not pertinent to the diplomatic history of the United States." Moreover, where bibliographical aids for special topics already existed, the editors decided that the *Guide* would not list their contents but would only refer readers to such sources. Textbooks as a genre were likewise excluded and biographical works were cited "only in exceptional instances" because of the anticipated publication of the *Dictionary of American Biography,* then already in preparation. Editors Bemis and Griffin were obliged to make numerous editorial judgments which directly affected the dimensions and utility of their *Guide*.

Not the least important of these judgments was how the editors defined diplomatic history. They perceived diplomacy in the narrow terms common to the 1920s, as the execution, or implementation, of the American government's foreign policy. Concepts such as *manifest destiny, mission, isolationism, imperialism, navalism, national security, the open door, pacificism,* and *militarism* fell outside the editors' criteria. Public opinion and the role of special interest groups in influencing foreign policy decisions also received short shrift. International economics, intelligence operations, and international cultural relations were implicitly considered beyond the purview of their *Guide*. Diplomacy as traditionally conceived placed emphasis on the legal and political relations between and among sovereign states, and it was this restricted definition that was utilized by editors Bemis and Griffin.

During the four and a half decades since Bemis and Griffin published their *Guide,* American diplomatic historiography has undergone a vast metamorphosis. The field is now commonly referred to as American foreign relations, reflecting the recent concern among historians with the international dynamics involved in the formulation as well as the execution of foreign policy. Today the number of persons engaged in teaching, researching, and studying the history of American foreign relations is enormous; courses are offered at nearly all colleges and universities in the United States. The number of serious publications, including specialized journals, pertaining to U.S. foreign relations and international history has grown proportionately. Correspondingly, the proliferation and dispersal of sources has reached such a critical point that scholars often experience deep feelings of inadequacy when endeavoring to use this documentation. Besides collections of printed documents, scholars in our generation must wade through masses of archival records pertaining to various American governmental bureaus and departments that now share the State Department's importance in shaping and conducting the nation's foreign policy. We have become increasingly aware—as Bemis himself always was—that basic research in foreign relations must become multinational, or as translated into the language of the researcher, multiarchival, often requiring systematic investigation of records in several countries. When Bemis and Griffin were compiling their *Guide* during the 1920s and early 1930s, few scholars studying American relations with eastern Asia and what we presently call the Third World possessed competence in Chinese, Japanese, Korean, or other non-European languages. Command of languages often regarded as exotic will allow historians to use a wider range of the documents within their research and thus address questions which an earlier generation of scholars could not have attempted. As the interrelatedness of numerous problems in the world is recognized by the historical community, we become increasingly aware of American foreign relations as the study of international history.

From its beginnings in the 1960s, The Society for Historians of American Foreign Relations (SHAFR) has acknowledged the need for a new bibliographical guide. As the Bemis and Griffin *Guide* served the requirements of an earlier generation of diplomatic historians, so a new guide would be the indispensable tool for scholars in the late twentieth century. A committee of editors under the direction of Professor Richard Dean Burns accepted the challenge to compile this new bibliographical work. While following many of the valuable features of the older work, this new *Guide* also contains thousands of annotated entries. Although it continues to be selective, its entries nearly double the number contained in the Bemis and Griffin *Guide,* which it supersedes. The enlarged chronological boundaries extend from the international experience of the Anglo-American colonies prior to independence to the international relations of the United States since the early 1920s. Most important, this new *Guide* reflects the state of the historiography of American foreign relations as of 1981.

Our hope is that a new generation of students and scholars will make use of the new reference tool and exploit its historiographic riches to the extent that it replaces Bemis and Griffin as the invaluable aid to study and research in the field. If the hopes of the editors of this volume are realized, the need to compile a successor within the next decade should be fully expected.

LAWRENCE E. GELFAND
University of Iowa

Acknowledgments

THE APPEARANCE of this volume will undoubtedly come as a surprise to those well-meaning colleagues with previous experience in directing collaborative ventures who at the outset warned me that, while the idea of having 40 to 50 specialists develop their own chapters was fine, it would be impossible to obtain the promised work. Fortunately, they were wrong; indeed, the cooperative spirit displayed by the participants is mainly responsible for the appearance of the completed *Guide*.

The new *Guide* is truly the result of a team effort. The contributing editors played a particularly significant role. We worked together to balance the quest for coherent individual chapters with the need for an integrated volume. I deeply appreciate the courtesy these professionals displayed (although I suspect they often felt otherwise) as we meshed differing perspectives. A special acknowledgment is merited by those contributing editors who volunteered for assignments "above and beyond" their initial commitments. Among them was Thomas Bryson, who regretfully did not live to see the *Guide* completed; we will all miss this hard-working colleague.

Many other individuals assisted in the development of the *Guide*. One unsung group is the band of reviewers, also including some contributing editors, who spent many hours checking manuscript pages. Of this group, I would especially like to recognize the valuable assistance of Thomas Campbell, Alexander DeConde, Clifford Egan, James Field, Raymond O'Connor, and David Patterson. The SHAFR Council, although frequently changed in membership, has always been extraordinarily supportive. Paul Varg, former president of SHAFR, obtained the financial support of The Bentley Foundation. Financial grants from the Alvin M. Bentley Foundation and the National Endowment for the Humanities were essential in providing the time for reviewing and editing some 5,000 pages of manuscript.

Various individuals helped to nurture the *Guide*. Unfortunately, I can here acknowledge the efforts of only a few of them. Lawrence E. Gelfand, University of Iowa, gave extensively of his time for nearly five years prior to 1975 as chairman of a special SHAFR committee. His search for funding, while unsuccessful, led to extensive consideration of the size and scope of the project. Warren F. Kuehl, University of Akron, negotiated for and found a publisher, which provided incentive to proceed. I shall always be indebted to him for his support and encouragement extended during the early stages of organizing the *Guide*. Also in these early days, members of a SHAFR-appointed Advisory Committee, especially David Fletcher, Wayne Cole, and Norman Graebner, were most helpful in selecting contributing editors. Wayne Cole generously allowed us to use the maps from his *An Interpretive History of American Foreign Relations* (Rev. ed., Dorsey, 1974) as the basis for the illustrations in this volume. Thomas Paterson and D. C. Heath and Company granted us permission to reprint (in Appendix I) the "Makers of American Foreign Policy" from

American Foreign Policy: A History, 2d ed. Beverly Wachel, who typed the various drafts of the *Guide,* and Richard D. Burns III, my son, who gave of his weekends to perform many tedious tasks, provided additional energy and skills necessary to the *Guide*'s completion.

In the formative stages, Susan Hoffman Hutson assisted in the preparation of style guides and other information for the contributing editors, and in making design decisions. Subsequently, Mary Gormly, a reference librarian at California State University, Los Angeles, joined me in the processing of individual chapters. Mary deserves special recognition for the long hours she spent tracking down errant bibliographical citations and for her efforts to ensure that the citations in the *Guide* conform to those employed by the Library of Congress, and thus used in catalog cards.

Several representatives of Clio Books deserve recognition for their help in the development of the *Guide.* From the beginning, Dr. Eric Boehm lent his considerable support to the idea of a SHAFR bibliographical guide. Bonnie Simrell, Editor-in-Chief, has spent many hours devising the best means of transforming the bulky manuscript into its present printed form. Editor Barbara Pope mastered the challenge of coordinating the efforts of a virtual army of editors, contributors, proofreaders, and others through the complex process of production. And I must acknowledge a special debt on behalf of all of us to Paulette Wamego, who copyedited the entire manuscript and greatly improved its message and utility.

Even with the assistance of all these people, I would not have been able to complete the *Guide* without the unselfish assistance provided by Frances R. Burns. During the last year alone, Frances worked with me—proofreading, numbering entries, and indexing—through 32 consecutive weekends so that we would keep pace with the production schedule. It is because of Fran's and Mary Gormly's willingness to spend long unrewarded hours, including weekends, performing tedious but vital tasks that the *Guide* was completed.

Finally, while I greatly appreciate the assistance I have received from many individuals, it should be understood that none is responsible for errors of commission or omission. For these I alone am responsible.

RICHARD DEAN BURNS
Claremont, California

Introduction

FOREIGN AFFAIRS today commands academic attention on a scale, and in dimensions, scarcely imagined a half-century ago. When Samuel Flagg Bemis and Grace Gardner Griffin prepared their *Guide to the Diplomatic History of the United States* during the 1930s, they regarded as outside their purview such concepts as *manifest destiny, mission, isolationism, navalism,* and *national security.*[1] As Professor Gelfand notes in his *Preface* to this volume, the editorial criteria applied by Bemis and Griffin narrowly defined American diplomacy as the execution of governmental policies.

Since then, diplomatic historians have greatly expanded their field of inquiry. In the past three decades, much research has been devoted to assessing the impact of public opinion, domestic politics, and military and economic factors on the formulation of American foreign policy. More recently, diplomatic historians have recognized the vital importance of cultural and geographical perceptions, as well as international economic factors, to an understanding of relationships among nations.

Diplomatic historians nevertheless have been criticized for an excessive concentration on archival materials at the expense of new interpretations that deal with large and imponderable questions.[2] This criticism may be valid, but a review of the writings collected in this volume demonstrates that diplomatic historians (as well as other students of international affairs) have made considerable progress during the past 50 years in identifying and understanding the determinate factors in international relationships. This *Guide* offers the twofold service of illuminating the paths diplomatic historians have trod and suggesting the ones still to be investigated.

Objectives of the Guide

This volume directs the user to helpful sources of information on American foreign relations. It provides comprehensive coverage of America's international affairs with the inclusion of selected references to scores of themes and episodes. The teacher and researcher will find the *Guide* a ready introduction to basic printed (and occasionally microfilmed) books, monographs, essays, documents, and reference works related to the topics that made up America's diplomatic record. We have not included all the entries that appeared in Bemis and Griffin's *Guide to the Diplomatic History of the United States,* nor have we duplicated their design. Consequently, the Bemis and Griffin *Guide* retains value, especially for its references to manuscript collections of interest to researchers working with eighteenth- and nineteenth-century topics.

Professors and students seeking fresh research possibilities, as well as those with projects already under way, will welcome this new *Guide,* but the books' usefulness goes beyond initiating or directing research. For instance, a specialist in American Revolutionary War diplomacy will find comprehensive, current coverage of that subject in Chapter 4; more important, however, if he or she is preparing a lecture or directing a seminar on nineteenth-century American–East Asian diplomacy, Chapter 17 will provide useful references for any unfamiliar ground. Similarly, the researcher concerned with United States–Latin American relations may uncover new investigative approaches, as well as additional references, by browsing through material on the "Monroe Doctrine" and "Pan-Americanism and Hemispheric Security" in Chapter 2, "The Monroe Doctrine to 1861" in Chapter 7, and "Good Neighbor Policy/Monroe Doctrine" in Chapter 21.

Finally, we number among our objectives the education of our colleagues. Many librarians and social scientists have resigned themselves to the expectation that historians—especially those investigating foreign affairs—are probably unaware of the usefulness of specialized bibliographies, various periodical indexes, and other reference aids. Through this *Guide,* and its subsequent revisions or supplements, diplomatic historians and their students may gradually discover and utilize many more of the valuable reference aids available.

Design of the Guide

Contributing editors developed each chapter as a single unit; once the entire manuscript was assembled, the editor then shaped the individual chapters into an integrated work by reassigning specific citations (and occasionally entire sections) from one chapter to another in order to eliminate duplication and to concentrate related items in the most appropriate chapters.

Although the decisions of each contributing editor were influenced by several differing criteria, all the contributors generally used the following guidelines for determining which items merited serious review for possible inclusion:
1. works employing archival or multiarchival research
2. works interpreting general trends, providing differing views, or offering contradictory assumptions
3. works synthesizing previous research

The contributing editors also included as many specialized bibliographies, bibliographical essays, and other aids as possible. Unusually complete or analytical bibliographies within monographs are highlighted by mention within the annotation for that monograph. Many of the contributing editors and contributors faced the problem of having either too much or too little material. Certain chronological periods and subject themes generated extensive lists of books and essays (e.g., World War II), and in such cases, competition for inclusion was strong. In other cases, there was difficulty in locating enough titles to provide adequate coverage.

The inclusion or exclusion of foreign-language titles was a much debated problem. The final criteria called for such titles to be included if they were unavailable in English and if the contributing editor believed them worthy of translation, but foreign-language titles were not to constitute more than ten percent of any chapter. In most instances, the number actually included fell far below that level, the major exception being Spanish titles relating to Latin America. For the rendering of Asian names, the *Guide* follows the suggestion by Raymond Esthus to give the family name first in accord with the style used in Asia and employed by most Asian specialists. The chief exception to this rule is an author who has adopted the Western style or has Westernized his or her name.

Supplementary Research Tools

All finding aids become dated before they can be published. This *Guide* is no exception, but there are a number of tools by which the materials in the *Guide* can be supplemented and updated. A review of Chapter 1 will direct the researcher to several periodical indexes that collect (and frequently annotate) journal articles dealing with American diplomatic experiences. Among these basic indexes are *America: History and Life* (Part A), *Historical Abstracts,* and the American Historical Association's *Recently Published Articles.* Each of these tools has advantages and disadvantages.

America: History and Life (Part A) uses annotated entries to provide comprehensive coverage of journals publishing articles related to American and Canadian history, but frequently the articles are not listed until 18 months after publication. *Historical Abstracts* provides wide coverage of foreign-language journals, but distance and the preparation of English-language annotations obviously mean some delay before an article can be listed. Both *America: History and Life* and *Historical Abstracts* have author and subject indexes; the subject indexes are perhaps the most thorough of any similar reference tool. *Recently Published Articles* provides a more current listing of published journal articles, but does not include annotations. Unfortunately, the usefulness of *Recently Published Articles* is greatly reduced by the lack of a subject index or cross-reference system.

Chapter 1 also lists specialized indexes and abstracts dealing with the Middle East, Latin America, and other regions. Basic indexes and abstracts, such as the *Sociological Abstracts* and the *International Political Science Abstracts,* which essentially serve other disciplines, are also valuable to diplomatic historians and international relations specialists. Those who deal with more contemporary issues should take note of *ABC POL SCI,* a listing of the current tables of contents of prominent foreign relations and political science journals. While not annotated, *ABC POL SCI* provides access to articles that have been published within the past few months and indexes them by author and subject.

Locating newly published books presents another problem. No readily available serial publication lists recently printed scholarly books, but *America: History and Life* (Parts B and C) can be useful. Part B *(Index to Book Reviews)* has a title index, which makes it much easier to locate a particular volume. Part C *(American History Bibliography)* is the most useful because it arranges books, dissertations, and articles by chronological stages and subject themes. *Reviews in American History* is a relatively new quarterly journal devoted exclusively to lengthy reviews of books dealing with American history. The journal is useful because it gathers together titles on similar topics for comparative review essays, but it fails to meet the need for an adequate current listing of recently published books on American foreign relations.

Information about current dissertations is more readily available. The best known and most frequent consulted listing is the *Dissertation Abstracts International,* which indexes, with lengthy annotations, doctoral dissertations from American, Canadian, and Mexican universities. Also readily at hand, especially to members of SHAFR, is the annual essay "Doctoral Dissertations in U.S. Foreign Affairs," prepared by Calvin L. Christman and printed annually in *Diplomatic History.* Part C of *America: History and Life* also lists current dissertations; Warren F. Kuehl's two-volume *Dissertations in History* indexes dissertations completed at American and Canadian universities between 1873 and 1970.

Where Do We Go from Here?

It is hoped that diplomatic historians will not need to wait another half-century for a revision of the *Guide*. Plans are under way to update the *Guide* in about five years, either with a supplement or a complete revision. In addition to searching out new materials, the next revision will be retrospective and seek to include items that were unintentionally overlooked during the preparation of this first edition.

During the interim, it may be possible to develop bibliographical articles or pamphlets corresponding to the various themes in the *Guide*. These essays could treat such chronological topics as the Interwar Years, 1920–1939 or The Cold War Years, and such themes as U.S.–East Asian Relations, U.S.–Middle Eastern Affairs, or Political Economics in American Foreign Relations. Any comments and suggestions for improving the *Guide* would be welcomed by the publisher and by SHAFR's Bibliographic Committee.

RICHARD DEAN BURNS
Editor

Notes

1. Samuel Flagg Bemis and Grace Gardner Griffin, *Guide to the Diplomatic History of the United States, 1775–1921* (Washington, D.C.: GPO, 1935).

2. See, for example, Charles S. Maier, "Marking Time: The Historiography of International Relations," in Michael Kammen, ed., *The Past Before Us: Contemporary Historical Writing in the United States* (Ithaca, N.Y.: Cornell University Press, 1980), pp. 355–87. Maier's criticisms are discussed in "Responses to Charles S. Maier . . . ," *Diplomatic History* 5 (Fall 1981): 353–82; also see the "Introduction" to Chapter 2 of this *Guide*.

1

Reference Aids

Contributing Editor
DAVID F. TRASK
*Chief Historian, U.S. Army
Center of Military History*

Contributors
Mary Gormly
*California State University
Los Angeles*

Allen H. Kitchens
Department of State

Marvin W. Kranz
Library of Congress

William Z. Slany
*The Historian,
Department of State*

Contents

1

Introduction

The reference material listed here is by no means exhaustive, but it should provide a starting point for research on almost any aspect of American foreign relations. Reading the introduction or preface of each source will inform the researcher of the criteria the author used and the coverage included. Students unfamiliar with American foreign relations should study the material in this chapter before beginning research. General background information and basic bibliographies are a starting point for research.

Major sections are "Bibliographies;" "Biographical Data, Atlases, Encyclopedias, Dictionaries, and Yearbooks;" "Indexes and Directories to Periodicals, Newspapers, Book Reviews, Dissertations, Oral Histories, and Microforms;" "Guides to Archives and Manuscript Collections;" and "Guides to Public Documents and Document Collections."

Bibliographies are divided, for convenience, into two categories: "functional" or "topical" subjects such as international law and peace research; and "geographic," covering either a country or region, for example, Germany or Southeast Asia. Bibliographies are guides to the subject or area under investigation and may be either retrospective or current in focus. For example, *Foreign Affairs Bibliography: A Selected and Annotated List of Books on International Relations* (1:15) is an annotated books list on foreign affairs since 1919; it is worldwide in scope. On the other hand, *Communism in the United States: A Bibliography* (1:75), also annotated, covers a specific subject with a narrower time-span (1919–1959). By using a bibliography compiled by an expert in the subject, the researcher is led from general to specific sources.

Biographical Data, Atlases, Encyclopedias, Dictionaries, and Yearbooks give basic facts and little or no analysis. Researchers frequently must acquire or verify special data found in "fact books."

Biographical dictionaries and the various "Who's Who" books will be helpful in gathering facts on well-known personalities. The *National Cyclopaedia of American Biography* (1:187) and the *Dictionary of American Biography* (1:182) are multivolume sets which cover important personages in some detail. *Current Biography* (1:178), is used for contemporary personalities. Biographical dictionaries such as *Who's Who in Government* (1:193) and *Latin American Government Leaders* (1:194) are oriented to a specific area or subject, and data may be detailed or cursory.

Atlases are of several types: geographical, political, and historical. They will help the researcher locate specific towns, countries, and regions throughout history. These are very important since boundaries have changed frequently in recent decades.

Encyclopedias often provide an overview of a subject and a selected bibliography on specific topics. Encyclopedia articles are usually written by experts and often contain useful bibliographies of books, articles, and other resources. Multisubject and one-subject encyclopedias are available. An example of the former is the *Encyclopedia of American Foreign Policy* (1:164), which, in three volumes, cover at some length subjects such as "Intervention," "Monroe Doctrine," "Nationalism," and provides pertinent bibliographies. An example of a one-subject encyclopedia is the *Encyclopedia of Latin America* (1:165), which contains articles on all aspects of Latin American history, politics, and culture, with selected bibliographies.

There are dictionaries other than those which define the terms used in a specific subject and/or field. The *Dictionary of American History* (1:173), a multivolume work encyclopedic in form, defines events, dates, and people important in United States history.

Yearbooks and weekly/monthly digests are important for keeping up with current events. The *African Recorder: A Fortnightly Record of African Events, with Index* (1:149) and the *Asian Recorder: A Weekly Digest of Asian Events with Index* (1:150) are weekly/monthly digests. Yearbooks and annuals may be less current, but they offer more analyses of events. *The Annual Register of World Events: A Review of the Year* (1:142) has been reviewing world events since 1758, concentrating on Great Britain and the Commonwealth. A more specific type of annual is the *Far Eastern Economic Review: Yearbook* (1:143), which sums up important economic events and trends in the Far East for a particular year.

Annual reviews of various types are an excellent

source for updating knowledge in a subject or becoming acquainted with unfamiliar areas of study. Many contain essays on trends and occasionally survey important publications in a particular field of study.

Indexes and Directories to Periodicals, Newspapers, Book Reviews, Dissertations, Oral Histories, and Microforms are the keys to non-book material.

The best, and at times the only, way to approach the tremendous number of journal articles available is through periodical indexes and abstracts. While indexes only list titles of periodicals, abstracts also briefly summarize articles. Two of the more useful periodical indexes are *America: History and Life* (1:214) and the *Historical Abstracts* (1:218); the former covers all aspects of American history, including foreign relations, while the latter covers aspects of modern history from 1450 and is worldwide in coverage.

Other indexes are more specialized in subject coverage. The *Public Affairs Information Service Bulletin* (1:226), better known as PAIS, covers current literature on subjects such as government, political science, and economics. Unlike other periodical indexes, it also lists government documents and some books. It, too, is worldwide in coverage.

An important directory dealing with periodicals is *Ulrich's International Periodicals Directory: A Classified Guide to Current Periodicals, Foreign and Domestic* (1:212). It lists, by subject, journals and periodicals worldwide and gives publisher, place of publication, price, circulation, and, most important, where each periodical is indexed.

Newspapers are an excellent source for current material, historical research in any field, and opinions from earlier eras on once-controversial matters. The greatest difficulty in researching newspapers is the relative scarcity of indexing.

The best-known indexes for newspapers are the *New York Times Index* (1:231), which covers the period from 1851 to the present, and the *Index to the Times* (London), which covers the years since 1906, and its forerunner, Palmer's *Index to the Times Newspaper* (1:232), with coverage from 1790 to 1941. All of these indexes, as well as others, are subject oriented and need careful reading.

Book reviews are an excellent way to stay current on literature published on a subject or field. While some book review digests or indexes are oriented to a specific field, for example, *Index to Book Reviews in Historical Periodicals* (1:235), others have much broader scope. The best known is the *Book Review Digest* (1:233), which is an index and digest of selected book reviews in American and English periodicals. Another source of book reviews that should not be overlooked is professional journals.

Much scholarly research is available in the form of master theses and doctoral dissertations. Since the majority of these have not been published, they must be located through indexes, of which the most useful, and probably the best known, is *Dissertation Abstracts International* and its various predecessors (1:240). It indexes, and provides lengthy abstracts of, doctoral dissertations from American and, in recent years, Canadian and Mexican universities.

Some indexes list dissertations on specific subjects or areas, such as "Doctoral Dissertations in U.S. Foreign Affairs" (1:245), *Doctoral Dissertations in Military Affairs: A Bibliography* (1:246), updated annually, and *Latin America and the Caribbean: A Dissertation Bibliography* (1:249). These usually do not contain abstracts.

One source not to be overlooked, particularly for contemporary history, is oral histories, such items as interviews, speeches, lectures, and memoirs of prominent diplomats and others involved in American foreign relations. Many of these oral histories are on tape and are housed in presidential and university libraries, and there are increasing efforts to provide typescript texts. The key to location and contents is *Oral History in the United States: A Directory* (1:255), which is a guide to major oral history repositories in the United States and their holdings.

In the last decade or two microfilm records ranging from diplomatic material in the U.S. National Archives to out-of-print newspapers have increased tremendously. The guides and directories listed here (1:256–264) are useful for identifying and locating microfilms.

Guides to Archives and Manuscript Collections list materials, usually in manuscript form, in various governmental and societal archives. So voluminous are these materials that guides are necessary to locate both collections and items in them. Fortunately, in some cases archival material is available on microfilm. The U.S. National Archives has microfilmed much of its material, particularly diplomatic and consular reports. The *Catalogue of National Archives Microfilm Publications* (1:259) will aid in locating these.

There are also guides to manuscript collections in other than national archives. *A Guide to the Manuscript Collections of the Bancroft Library* (1:279) contains material on the Pacific Coast and the West as well as Mexico and Central America.

An index to manuscript collections in general is the *National Union Catalog of Manuscript Collections* (1:282), which includes data on more than 29,000 manuscript collections in 850 repositories and on the availability of microfilm copies.

Guides to Public Documents and Document Col-

4

lections lead researchers to one of the greatest sources on American foreign relations—the documents of the United States and foreign governments, the United Nations, the League of Nations, and various international agencies. There are guides not only to the collections themselves but also on how to use the documents.

Among the guides to U.S. government publications ("government publications" and "government documents" are often used interchangeably) are *United States Government Publications* (1:301), which lists and describes typical publications of all branches of the government, and *Government Publications and Their Use* (1:310), one of the most up-to-date guides to the use of U.S. government publications and their indexes. These would be extremely valuable to the student unfamiliar with the publishing record of the U.S. government.

A Guide to the Use of United Nations Documents (1:327) serves the same function for that organization. It is an excellent guide in that it includes information on methods of research, basic aids and guides, and a selected subject guide. Another useful source is *Publications of the United Nations System: A Reference Guide* (38:11) which presents an overview of the organizations of the United Nations and their publications, together with a comprehensive list of their periodicals and selected other serials.

A comparable guide to League of Nations documents is *Guide to League of Nations Publications: A Bibliographical Survey of the Work of the League, 1920–1947* (20:6). It also lists publications of affiliated organizations, such as the International Labor Office and the Permanent Court of International Justice.

The major source for all of the U.S. government publications is the *Monthly Catalog of United States Government Publications* (1:319) and its various predecessors, which has been coming out monthly since 1895 and is the best source for current information. There are also indexes to public documents of Congress since 1789, indexes to documents relating to foreign affairs, indexes to various congressional hearings and so forth—all of which will make the task of research a little easier. (See 1:299–320 for other guides to these U.S. documents.)

A comparable guide to United Nations publications is the *United Nations Documents Index* (1950–1962) and its successor, *United Nations Documents Index: Cumulative Checklist* (1963–1973) (1:334). Other UN document indexes are listed by either subject or country. Indexes to the official records of both the UN and UNESCO are also noted.

Also in this section are some representative major document collections pertaining to American foreign relations. A few titles show the range of material available to researchers. *Documents on American Foreign Relations* (1:339) is a compilation, published annually, of major public documents on the subject. *Documents on International Affairs* (1:340), covering 1928 to 1963, is a useful source for the official documents and public statements of foreign leaders. *Diplomatic Correspondence of the United States, Canadian Relations, 1784–1860* (1:343), *Diplomatic Correspondence of the United States Concerning the Independence of the Latin American Nations (1809–1830)*, (7:4), and *The Diplomatic Correspondence of the United States: Inter-American Affairs, 1831–1860* (7:5) are major sources for diplomatic history.

The *American State Papers* (1:349) and the various debates and proceedings of the U.S. Congress, known popularly as the *Annals of Congress* (1:351), the *Congressional Globe* (1:353), and the *Congressional Record* (1:354), and covering 1789 to the present, are major primary sources. The *British and Foreign State Papers* (1:363), covering 1812 to 1925, and the *Parliamentary Debates* (1:365), covering 1803 to the present, are the British equivalent of the U.S. material cited.

Listed also are documents on public opinion, very important for a country's point-of-view, and material on international law and arbitration—both major resources.

Treaties and international agreements of various kinds are another important source of documents. *United States Treaties and Other International Agreements* and its cumulative indexes (1:378) is an ongoing set that is very current in scope.

The sources cited here are only a few of the reference aids, useful for research on all aspects of American foreign relations, contained in this chapter.

Guides to Reference Aids

See also "Bibliographies of Bibliographies," below.

1:1 American Historical Association. *The American Historical Association's Guide to Historical Literature*. New York: Macmillan, 1961. Successor to George M. Dutcher, *A Guide to Historical Literature* (1:5), it contains, with numerous annotations, references to bibliographies, library and museum holdings, encyclopedias and reference works, gazetteers, and atlases, anthropological, demographic, and linguistic studies, printed sources, general and specialized secondary works, government publications, periodicals, and publications of academies, universities, and learned societies.

1:2 *American Reference Books Annual.* Ed. by Bohdan S. Wynar. Littleton, Colo.: Libraries Unlimited, 1970– . This reference aid is of great value because it reviews virtually all new reference books printed in the United States, and is especially useful for locating new bibliographies. Its classified arrangement, together with author-title-subject index, makes it easy to use. A five-year (1975–1979) index pulls together recent reference aids.

1:3 Conover, Helen F. *A Guide to Bibliographical Tools for Research in Foreign Affairs.* 2d rev. ed. Washington, D.C.: Library of Congress, 1958. Essentially a bibliography of bibliographies, most of the reference works cited were published in the first half of the 1950s, and emphasize contemporary events in international relations for that time period. One of its three major divisions includes specialized sources for regional studies, including early United Nations material. All items are annotated and many economic monographs and references to general economic reference sources are included.

1:4 Coulter, Edith M., and Gerstenfeld, Melanie. *Historical Bibliographies: A Systematic and Annotated Guide.* Berkeley: University of California Press, 1935. Reprint 1965. Older work; still useful. Now seriously outdated in most sections but can be used in conjunction with AHA's *Guide to Historical Literature* (1:1).

1:5 Dutcher, George M., et al., eds. *A Guide to Historical Literature.* New York: Macmillan, 1931. Long a standard work, it is superseded by AHA's *Guide to Historical Literature* (1:1).

1:6 Harvard University. Henry Adams History Club. *A Select Bibliography of History.* 4th ed. Cambridge: Harvard University, the Club, Department of History, 1970. Introduction to bibliography for many historical fields, it is useful for orienting the historian who is beginning study in one of these fields.

1:7 Holler, Frederick L., ed. *Information Sources of Political Science.* 3d ed. (5 vols. in 1). Santa Barbara,

Calif.: ABC-Clio, 1981. This wide-ranging volume is an extremely useful aid to locating references to international relations (1776–1975), and related issues.

1:8 International Committee of Historical Sciences. *International Bibliography of the Historical Sciences.* Paris: Librairie Armand Colin, 1926– . Reprint (vols. 1–14), 1963. Extensive rather than comprehensive, it contains materials on U.S. diplomatic history from European as well as American authors. Interrupted during World War II, volume 15 (1940–1946) has not been published.

1:9 Poulton, Helen J. *The Historian's Handbook: A Descriptive Guide to Reference Works.* Norman: University of Oklahoma Press, 1972. This volume provides a description of basic reference works and is useful in introducing the beginning student to the various types of aids available.

1:10 Sheehy, Eugene P.; Keckeissen, Rita G.; and McIlvaine, Elaine. *Guide to Reference Books.* 9th ed. Chicago: American Library Association, 1976. Latest edition of work previously edited by Constance Winchell; it is convenient for citations to all types of basic reference materials. Section D covers history and area studies.

1:11 Stanford University. Hoover Institution on War, Revolution, and Peace. *The Library Catalogs of the Hoover Institution . . . : Catalog of the Western Language Collections.* 63 vols. Boston: Hall, 1969. These volumes reproduce the catalog cards for the Western-language books, pamphlets, and special collections which include many items on foreign affairs.

1:12 Walford, Albert J. *Guide to Reference Material.* 3 vols. 2d ed. London: Library Association, 1966–1970. It covers all fields; parallel to the American work compiled by Eugene P. Sheehy (1:10). A new edition is being prepared. Only volume 2 (1968) covers history and political science.

Bibliographies

Specialized bibliographies also appear throughout the *Guide* under their various topics.

DIPLOMACY AND FOREIGN RELATIONS

1:13 Council on Foreign Relations. *Catalog of the Foreign Relations Library.* 9 vols. Boston: Hall, 1969. The 148,000 cards listed in this catalog cross-reference some 55,000 books, documents, and pamphlets in Western languages. Subject headings generally are those of the Library of Congress. This valuable catalog covers all phases of international relations since 1918.

1:14 Dexter, Byron, with Bryant, Elizabeth H., and Murray, Janice L., eds. *The Foreign Affairs Fifty-Year Bibliography: New Evaluation of Significant Books on International Relations, 1920–1970,* New York: Bowker, 1972. A selective but unusually full set of appraisals of some 2,100 significant books on international relations (1920–1970), it is useful as a supplement to, but not a cumulation of, *Foreign Affairs Bibliography.*

1:15 *Foreign Affairs Bibliography: A Selected and Annotated List of Books on International Relations.* 5 vols. to date. New York: Harper, 1933– . The most thorough annotated bibliography of books on all aspects of international affairs, with good coverage of foreign-language titles, it lists only 10 percent of items published. The five volumes published to date cover 1919 to 1932, 1932 to 1942, 1942 to 1952, 1952 to 1962, and 1962 to 1972. These volumes are based on the book notes in each issue of *Foreign Affairs,* which in turn provide a convenient supplement for the post-1972 period.

1:16 Groom, A. J. R., and Mitchell, C. R., eds. *International Relations Theory: A Bibliography.* New York: Nichols, 1978. This collection of 14 essays reviews various subfields of international relations. These critical and selective essays cite nearly 1,000 publications, but do not include basic reference aids. This volume complements the Pfaltzgraff guide (1:21).

1:17 Hannigan, Jane A., comp. *Publications of the Carnegie Endowment for International Peace, 1910–1967, Including International Conciliation, 1924–1967.* New York: Carnegie Endowment for International Peace, 1971. The endowment published and distributed vast amounts of materials on foreign affairs. These included its *Yearbooks,* with extensive information on peace activities, its pamphlet series, monographs from its sponsored research, and reprints of classic works on peace and international law. This is a valuable guide to more than endowment efforts.

1:18 Harmon, Robert B. *The Art and Practice of Diplomacy: A Selected and Annotated Guide.* Metuchen, N.J.: Scarecrow, 1971. This briefly annotated list of nearly 900 articles, books, and documents reflects the nature and objectives of modern diplomacy. Included are the historical evolution of diplomacy and the diplomatic and consular services of various nations. Indexes.

1:19 LaBarr, Dorothy F., and Singer, J. David. *The Study of International Politics: A Guide to the Sources for the Student, Teacher, and Researcher.* Santa Barbara, Calif.: ABC-Clio, 1976. A bibliography of major books and articles on the study of contemporary international relations, especially useful for its listing of the contents of edited volumes, symposia, and major journals in the field. Unannotated.

1:20 Mossa, Farag. *Diplomatie contemporaine: Guide bibliographique.* Geneva: Centre Europeen de la Donation Carnegie pour la Paix Internationale, 1964. This useful work, which includes a wide range of Western- and non-Western-language volumes, deals with contemporary diplomacy throughout the world. References are placed under topical headings; all items are also indexed by country. Also published by Taplinger (1964).

1:21 Pfaltzgraff, Robert L., Jr. *The Study of International Relations: A Guide to Information Sources.* Detroit: Gale, 1977. A useful annotated bibliography of some 360 major books, it deals with the nature of the postwar international system and methods of studying it. The author provides brief introductory essays for each chapter, and includes a list of recommended books for a small personal library and a list of major journals in the field of international affairs. It serves as a good supplement to the *Foreign Affairs Fifty-Year Bibliography* (1:14), which covers works only through 1970.

1:22 Wright, Moorhead; Davis, Jane; and Clarke, Michael. *Essay Collections in International Relations: A Classified Bibliography.* New York: Garland, 1977. This is an index of 1,600 essays which have appeared in 240 books between 1945 and 1975. It indexes these often overlooked essays under 22 subclassifications.

1:23 Zawodny, J. K. [Janusz Kazimierz]. *Guide to the Study of International Relations.* San Francisco:

Chandler, 1966. A good place to start for basic statistical abstracts, archives, documents, atlases, films, and general bibliographical information in English (1945–1966).

RELATED TOPICS

1:24 Doenecke, Justus D., ed. *The Literature of Isolationism: A Guide to Non-Interventionist Scholarship, 1930–1972.* Colorado Springs: Myles, 1972. This is a useful, if occasionally eclectic, guide to materials.

Arms Control, Disarmament, and Peace Research

1:25 Burns, Richard Dean. *Arms Control and Disarmament: A Bibliography.* War/Peace Bibliography Series, no 6. Santa Barbara, Calif.: ABC-Clio, 1977. An exceptionally comprehensive bibliography, it includes a large number of articles. Although its coverage ranges beyond American experiences, and even further distant in time than 1700, it does provide sources for the Rush-Bagot agreement (1817), the Hague conferences (1899, 1907), the interwar treaties and negotiations, and post-1945 efforts. It concentrates on arms control/disarmament themes and negotiations; it also arranges conferences and treaties in chronological order according to type—e.g., arms limitation, demilitarization, outlawing of weapons, arms traffic, and rules of war.

1:26 Carroll, Berenice A.; Fink, Clinton F.; and Mohraz, Jane E. *Peace and War: A Guide to Bibliographies.* War/Peace Bibliography Series, no. 16. Santa Barbara, Calif.: ABC-Clio, forthcoming. This guide is useful for locating 19th- and 20th-century views of the nature and composition of peace and war.

1:27 Clemens, Walter C., Jr. *Soviet Disarmament Policy, 1917–1963: An Annotated Bibliography of Soviet and Western Sources.* Stanford, Calif.: Hoover Institution, 1965. Clemens provides a comprehensive list of basic documents, books, and articles covering the ideological, economic, legal, strategic, and historical dimensions of arms control and disarmament in Soviet policy.

1:28 Cook, Blanche Wiesen, ed. *Bibliography on Peace Research in History.* Santa Barbara, Calif.: ABC-Clio, 1969. Listing 1,129 archival sources, guides to peace research literature, journals and institutions related to peace studies, monographs, general studies, bibliographical works, dissertations, and works in progress, this is the most comprehensive, but not entirely accurate compilation in the field. Several of the sections deal with materials related to peace groups. Those entries not easily identified by their titles are annotated.

[The Hague. Peace Palace. Library]. "Card Catalogue of the Peace Palace at The Hague [1800–1970]" (16: 2) is a microfiche edition of approximately 600,000 cataloged holdings which is especially useful because of the arrangement of its periodical reference guide.

Pickus, R., and Woito, R. *To End War: An Introduction to the Ideas, Books, Organizations, Work . . .* [1776–1970] (38: 4).

1:29 United Nations. Dag Hammarskjöld Library. *Disarmament: A Select Bibliography.* New York: United Nations, 1965–. A useful compilation of English- and foreign-language monographs and articles that focus on contemporary issues, it also lists selected UN documents. Thus far four volumes have been issued: volume 1, *1962–1964* (1965); volume 2, *1962–1967* (1968); volume 3, *1967–1972* (1973); and volume 4, *1973–1977* (1978).

Economics, Multinational Corporations, and Trade

1:30 Ball, Nicole. *World Hunger: A Guide to the Economic and Political Dimensions.* War/Peace Bibliography Series, no. 15. Santa Barbara, Calif.: ABC-Clio, 1981. Although unannotated, this extremely useful volume is an analytical survey of the literature. Ball provides a valuable introduction which outlines the basic issues and interpretations of the problem; her comments under the various subheadings compare differing viewpoints.

Healy, D. *Modern Imperialism: Changing Styles in Historical Interpretation* (12:3) emphasizes the late 19th century.

1:31 Hernes, Helga. *The Multinational Corporation: A Guide to Information Sources.* Detroit: Gale, 1977. Most of the references listed here deal with the post-1945 era.

1:32 Lall, Sanjaya. *Foreign Private Manufacturing and International Corporations: An Annotated Bibliography.* New York: Praeger, 1975. Most of the references deal with the post-1945 era.

1:33 Molineu, Harold, comp. *Multinational Corporations and International Investment in Latin America: A Selected and Annotated Bibliography, with an Annotated Film Bibliography.* Athens: Ohio University, Center for International Studies, Latin American Program, 1978. This is a useful introduction to a wide range of economic sources.

1:34 Wheeler, Lora Jeanne. *International Business and Foreign Trade: Information Sources.* Detroit: Gale, 1968. Although dated, this bibliography is very useful for basic references.

International Law and Organizations

Atherton, A. L., comp. *International Organizations: A Guide to Information Sources* (16:1).

1:35 Grieves, Forest L. *International Law, Organization, and the Environment: A Bibliography and Research Guide.* Tucson: University of Arizona Press, 1974. A specialized guide that is valuable in revealing the range of research possibilities in the international field. Lacks any classification by nation, so U.S. policy is not easy to locate. Author index.

1:36 Harvard University. Law School Library. *Catalog of International Law and Relations.* Ed. by Margaret Moody. 20 vols. Cambridge: Harvard University, Law School Library, 1965–1967. These volumes reproduce a card catalog containing about 360,000 entries.

1:37 Haas, Michael, comp. *International Organization: An Interdisciplinary Bibliography.* Stanford, Calif.: Hoover Institution Press, 1971. This massive guide contains sections on bibliographies, textbooks, documentary sources, the early history of international organizations, the League of Nations system and the United Nations, regional bodies, and nonpolitical and "transcontinental nonuniversal international organizations." The arrangement is conducive to locating subjects and items. Subject index.

1:38 Johnson, Harold S., and Singh, Baljit, comps. *International Organization: A Classified Bibliography.* East Lansing: Michigan State University Press, 1969. A list of book and article titles according to a subject classification devised by the compilers, there is no breakdown on a national level of relations with the UN and no indexes.

1:39 Lewis, John R. *Uncertain Judgment: A Bibliography of War Crimes Trials.* War/Peace Bibliography Series, no. 8. Santa Barbara, Calif.: ABC-Clio, 1979. This volume is valuable for appropriate 19th- and 20th-century treaties and trials. Extensive coverage is provided for the Nuremburg tribunal, the Far East tribunals, and Vietnam trials and charges.

Robinson, J., comp. *International Law and Organization: General Sources of Information* [1776–1978] (38:2).

1:40 Szladits, Charles. *Bibliography on Foreign and Comparative Law: Books and Articles in English.* New York: Columbia University, Pasken School, 1955. This volume lists about 14,000 titles but does not cover the Anglo-American system.

Military Affairs and Intelligence Operations

Bibliographies relating to specific U.S. wars are listed in appropriate chapters.

1:41 Albion, Robert G. *Naval and Maritime History: An Annotated Bibliography.* 4th ed. Mystic, Conn.: Marine Historical Association, 1972. A listing of works published, as well as some unpublished, on all aspects of naval affairs. The sections that touch upon the period of the Revolution are thin but still useful.

Albrecht, U., et al. *A Short Research Guide on Arms and Armed Forces* (40:1) concentrates on weapons and armed forces in Europe, the Third World, and the United States.

1:42 Anderson, Martin. *Conscription: A Select and Annotated Bibliography.* Stanford, Calif.: Hoover Institution Press, 1976. This work interprets its subject very broadly and includes not only the all-volunteer military and universal military training questions but delves into the economic, legal, philosophical, racial, and political aspects of the issue. Its historical dimensions extend from the American Revolution to the 1970s.

1:43 Blackstock, Paul W., and Schaf, Frank L., Jr., eds. *Intelligence, Espionage, Counterespionage, and Covert Operations: A Guide to Information Sources.* Detroit: Gale, 1978. This highly selective bibliography, emphasizing books and articles in English, provides a fine introduction to American and Soviet intelligence agencies. While it emphasizes the dramatic, it also provides a great deal of guidance to the political and diplomatic dimensions of intelligence gathering and covert operations. Annotations and introductions are very helpful.

1:44 Burt, Richard, comp. and ed., and Kemp, Geoffrey, ed. *Congressional Hearings on American Defense Policy, 1947–1971: An Annotated Bibliography.* Lawrence: University Press of Kansas, 1974. Burt and Kemp provide a list of the hearings held on foreign policy and national defense issues for the 80th through the 92d Congresses. Also included is a list of those testifying and brief summaries of subjects dealt with; they do not cover executive session testimony.

1:45 Greenwood, John, comp. *American Defense Policy since 1945: A Preliminary Bibliography.* Lawrence: University Press of Kansas, 1973. A "preliminary" bibliography of books, articles, and government documents, it deals with U.S. postwar defense policy, but excludes foreign policy, arms control, and civil-military relations. It includes sections on bibliographies, data and descriptive material, strategic thought and military doctrine, the defense policymaking process, defense output, weapons systems, and military programs, and the domestic effects of defense policies.

Higham, R., ed. *Official Histories: Essays and Bibliographies from All Over the World* (23:5) emphasizes military histories since World War I.

1:46 Higham, Robin, ed. *A Guide to the Sources of British Military History.* Berkeley: University of California Press, 1971. A collection of bibliographical essays that survey essentially military affairs from prehistoric Britain to the post–World War II era. There are many nuggets, here and there, for the diplomatic historian with the patience to comb the essays and the appended lists of references; a subject index would have vastly improved the volume's utility.

1:47 Higham, Robin, ed. *Guide to the Sources of United States Military History.* Hamden, Conn.: Shoe

String Press, 1975. A fine collection of bibliographical essays by 18 specialists in American military history; unfortunately it is not indexed. These essays feature, in addition to strategy and tactics, books and articles about American military and naval officers involved in the making and carrying-out of foreign policy from 1607 to the 1970s.

1:48 Jessup, John E., Jr., and Coakley, Robert W., eds. *A Guide to the Study and Use of Military History.* Washington, D.C.: Center of Military History, 1979. This is an indispensable bibliography of world military history, with emphasis on the United States. In addition to the bibliography, chapters by both U.S. Army historians and civilian academics treat the history of the writing of military history. The bibliography lists relevant journals.

1:49 Lang, Kurt. *Military Institutions and the Sociology of War: A Review of the Literature with Annotated Bibliography.* Beverly Hills, Calif.: Sage, 1972. This useful volume includes such headings as "The Profession of Arms," "Military Organizations," "The Military System," "Civil-Military Relations," and "War and Warfare."

Larson, A. D. *Civil-Military Relations and Militarism* (40:4) places military institutions in their political and social context (20th century).

Larson, A. D. *National Security Affairs: A Guide to Information Sources* (40:5).

1:50 Miller, Samuel D., comp. *An Aerospace Bibliography.* Rev. ed. Washington, D.C.: G.P.O., 1978. An upgraded and expanded edition of earlier bibliography by M. A. Cresswell and C. Berger (1971), this edition covers air and space topics from early in the 20th century to the present.

1:51 Smith, Myron J., Jr. *The Secret Wars: A Guide to Sources in English.* 3 vols. War/Peace Bibliography Series, nos. 12–14. Santa Barbara, Calif.: ABC-Clio, 1980–1981. These volumes catalog, without annotation, books, articles, and documents related to intelligence, covert operations, propaganda, psychological warfare, and international terrorism (1939–1980).

1:52 U.S. Department of the Army. *Nuclear Weapons and NATO: [An] Analytical Survey of Literature.* Rev. ed. DA PAM 50-1. Washington, D.C.: G.P.O., 1975. This survey, prepared by Harry Moskowitz and Jack Roberts, contains 800 abstracts of articles, books, documents, and studies relating to the many issues confronting NATO.

1:53 U.S. Department of the Navy. *United States Naval History, Naval Biography, Naval Strategy and Tactics: A Selected and Annotated Bibliography.* 3d ed. Washington, D.C.: G.P.O., 1962. This little pamphlet contains a number of useful hints about research in naval history. It lists what might be called the standard works in its field and, in some cases, offers cautions about their shortcomings.

1:54 U.S. Department of the Air Force. Office of Air Force History. *A Guide to Documentary Sources.* Ed. by Lawrence J. Paszek. Washington, D.C.: G.P.O., 1973. A guide to documents—personal and official—dealing with air force history.

Revolution, Terrorism, and Guerrilla Warfare

1:55 Blackey, Robert, ed. *Modern Revolutions and Revolutionists: A Bibliography.* 2d ed. War/Peace Bibliography Series, no. 5. Santa Barbara, Calif.: ABC-Clio, 1982. This volume is useful owing to its scope and organization: a large section is devoted to concepts and aspects of revolution, while others are given to works on early and modern Europe, North and Latin America, Asia, Africa, India, and the Middle East.

Burns, R. D., and Leitenberg, M. *War in Vietnam, 1941–1980* (30:2) contains references to revolution and guerrilla warfare in Southeast Asia. This volume updates M. Leitenberg and R. D. Burns, *The Vietnam Conflict* (1973).

1:56 Norton, Augustus R., and Greenburg, Martin H. *International Terrorism: An Annotated Bibliography and Research Guide.* Boulder, Colo.: Westview, 1979. This guide contains some 1,000 items related to modern international terrorism. Also, see Myron J. Smith, Jr., *The Secret Wars,* volume 3, for additional references (1:51).

Sable, M. H. *The Guerrilla Movement in Latin America since 1950: A Bibliography* [1950–1976] (35:9).

COUNTRIES AND REGIONS

Specialized bibliographies and guides are located in appropriate chapters.

United States

1:57 Bemis, Samuel Flagg, and Griffin, Grace Gardner, eds. *Guide to the Diplomatic History of the United States, 1775–1921.* Washington, D.C.: G.P.O., 1935. Reprint 1963. The predecessor to the present volume, it is still indispensable for 18th and 19th century printed and manuscript materials.

1:58 Boyce, Richard F., and Boyce, Katherine Randall. *American Foreign Service Authors: A Bibliography.* Metuchen, N.J.: Scarecrow, 1973. This volume lists books written by foreign service officers and other American personnel who served abroad in some diplomatic post. It is based upon Library of Congress catalog and replies to inquiries; but does not include articles or books by non-foreign service personnel which discuss the foreign service.

Cronon, E. D., and Rosenof, T. D., comps. *The Second World War and the Atomic Age, 1940–1973.* (24:1) contains 2,769 serially numbered unannotated citations to books, articles, and dissertations relating to U.S. domestic and foreign affairs.

1:59 DeConde, Alexander, ed. *American Diplomatic History in Transformation.* Washington, D.C.: American Historical Association, 1976. This is a useful pamphlet with suggestions for research. It updates his *New Interpretations in American Foreign Policy* (1957).

1:60 Fowler, Wilton B. *American Diplomatic History since 1890.* Northbrook, Ill.: AHM, 1975. These 3,000 unannotated entries are usefully arranged by chronological periods, geographic regions, and topical themes. Includes some items not cited in the *Guide.*

1:61 Graebner, Norman A. *American Diplomatic History before 1900.* Arlington Heights, Ill.: AHM, 1978. This collection of judiciously chosen items includes some not cited in the *Guide.*

1:62 Haines, Gerald K., and Walker, J. Samuel, eds. *American Foreign Relations: A Historical Review.* Westport, Conn.: Greenwood, 1981. These seventeen essays by diplomatic history specialists discuss the changing interpretations of specific historical episodes and themes. While most of the essays treat chronological periods, separate chapters are devoted to critical geographical regions—Asia, Africa, the Middle East, and Latin America.

1:63 Plischke, Elmer, ed. *U.S. Foreign Relations: A Guide to Information Sources.* Detroit: Gale, 1980. This extensive compilation is concerned essentially with "the foreign policy process," rather than diplomatic history. It focuses on such topics as negotiation and negotiating style, protocol, privileges and immunities, the president and foreign relations, Congress and foreign relations, the foreign service. Chapter 6 contains bibliographical guides, and Chapter 22 lists government publications. Chapter 23 lists memoirs and biographical literature. Unfortunately, there is no subject index; but the extensive table of contents is quite useful.

Smith, D. M. "Rise to Great World Power, 1865–1918" (13:4) provides a historiographical survey of recent interpretations.

General Guides

1:64 American Historical Association. *Writings on American History, 1902–1903, 1906–1948–.* Ed. by Grace G. Griffin, et al. Princeton, N.J.: Publisher varies, 1905–. This "on and off" series provides useful references on diplomatic issues. For the period since 1961, see James J. Dougherty, et al., *Writings on American History, 1962–1973: A Subject Bibliography of Articles* (1:216). Volumes are appearing for the years after 1973.

1:65 Basler, Roy P., et al., eds. *A Guide to the Study of the United States of America.* Washington, D.C.: Library of Congress, 1960. This wide-ranging work contains a brief but useful section on diplomatic history and foreign affairs; it is easy to consult and contains good descriptive summaries of the works it lists. There is also a supplement for the years 1956 to 1965, published in 1976 (1:69).

1:66 Beers, Henry P., ed. *Bibliographies in American History: Guide to Materials for Research.* New York: Wilson, 1942. Reprint 1959, 1973. This is a standard work on the subject.

1:67 Freidel, Frank, ed. *Harvard Guide to American History.* 2 vols. Cambridge: Harvard University Press, 1974. A useful guide to all aspects of U.S. history, it includes materials on the history of foreign relations. Additionally, Freidel updates Edward Channing et al., *Guide to the Study and Reading of American History* (Boston: Ginn, 1912), and Oscar Handlin et al., *Harvard Guide to American History* (Cambridge: Harvard University Press, 1954).

1:68 Larned, Josephus N. *Literature of American History: A Bibliographical Guide.* Boston: American Library Association Publication Board, 1902. Reprint 1973. An annotated bibliography, it is not up-to-date but may be occasionally useful for source materials, selection of titles, and critical notes.

1:69 Orr, Oliver H., Jr., *A Guide to the Study of the United States of America: Supplement 1956–1965.* Washington, D.C.: Library of Congress, 1976. This volume supplements Roy P. Basler et al., *A Guide to the Study of the United States of America* (1:65).

Special Topics

1:70 Billington, Ray A., ed. *The American Frontier.* 2d ed. Washington, D.C.: American Historical Association, 1965. This "Service Center for Teachers" pamphlet is useful for research suggestions. See also Billington's *Westward Expansion: A History of the American Frontier,* 4th ed. (New York: Macmillan, 1974), "Bibliography," pp. 663–805, which is a comprehensive bibliography of western history as a whole.

1:71 Fehrenbacher, Don E., ed. *Manifest Destiny and the Coming of the Civil War.* New York: Appleton-Century-Crofts, 1970. This volume lists unannotated secondary materials relating to foreign policy issues.

1:72 Ferguson, E. James, comp. *Confederation, Constitution, and Early National Period, 1781–1815.* Arlington Heights, Ill.: AHM, 1975. This volume is an unannotated listing of published books and articles on the period (1781–1815). There is a section on foreign affairs in chapter 1, "Guides and General Sources," and chapter 2, "National Public Affairs," has a foreign affairs section for the Confederation period. Sections for the Federalist era also included cover foreign relations.

1:73 Monaghan, Frank. *French Travellers in the United States, 1765–1932: A Bibliography: With Supplement by Samuel J. Marino.* New York: Antiquarian, 1961. An annotated list of 1,800 published accounts of French, Belgian, Swiss, and French-Canadian travellers in the United States, it does not include accounts in journals and newspapers. Items are arranged alphabetically by author, with appropriate cross-references, and a note where the account is located. An indispensable guide.

1:74 Paul, Rodman W., and Etulain, Richard W., comps. *The Frontier and the American West.* Arlington Heights, Ill.: AHM, 1977. Although largely unannotated, this work is an extensive bibliography treating all aspects of the westward movements, such as manifest destiny, the Mexican War, all ethnic groups, and border problems.

1:75 Seidman, Joel, comp. *Communism in the United States: A Bibliography.* Ithaca, N.Y.: Cornell University Press, 1969. A thorough, annotated bibliography of some 7,000 books and articles dealing with communism in the United States (1919–1959), it is an updated and expanded version of the Fund for the Republic's *Bibliography on the Communist Problem in the United States* (1955).

1:76 Smith, Dwight L., ed. *Indians of the United States and Canada: A Bibliography.* Clio Bibliography Series, no. 3. Santa Barbara, Calif.: ABC-Clio, 1974. This volume may be of assistance to those who are looking into U.S.-Indian relationships during the formative years of the Republic.

1:77 Winther, Oscar O., and Van Orman, Richard A., comps. *A Classified Bibliography of the Periodical Literature of the Trans-Mississippi West, 1811–1967.* Westport, Conn.: Greenwood, 1973. This reprint combines two previous works: O. O. Winther's *A Classified Bibliography of the Periodical Literature of the Trans-Mississippi West (1811–1957)* (Bloomington: Indiana University Press, 1961); and O. O. Winther and R. A. Van Orman's *A Classified Bibliography of the Periodical Literature of the Trans-Mississippi West: A Supplement (1957–1967)* (Bloomington: Indiana University Press, 1970).

Europe, Canada, and Australia

1:78 Remington, Robin A. *International Relations of Eastern Europe: A Guide to Information Sources.* Detroit: Gale, 1978. Collected here are citations to over 1,000 monographs and journals, articles on post–World War II communist Eastern Europe. Brief annotations and author, title, and subject indexes.

Australia

Hudson, W. J., ed. "Australia's External Relations: Towards a Bibliography of Journal Articles (Section I: Asia)" (32:1) is a selective list chosen from materials published from 1945 to 1970.

Hudson, W. J., ed. "Australia's External Relations: Towards a Bibliography of Journal Articles (Section

II)" (32:2) emphasizes non-Asian matters in essays printed from 1945 to 1970.

Launitz-Schurer, L., and Siracusa, J. M. "The State of United States History in Australia" (32:6) is a full bibliography of Australian-American relations

Canada

Granatstein, J. L., and Stevens, P., eds. *Canada since 1867: A Bibliographical Guide* (36:1) covers national politics, foreign and defense policy, and other topics.

Page, D. M. *A Bibliography of Works on Canadian Foreign Relations, 1945–1970* (36:3) arranges unannotated items under a broad range of topics. A volume exists for 1971 to 1975, and other five-year updates are planned.

France

1:78a *Bibliographie annuelle de l'histoire de France du cinquième siècle à 1939.* Paris: Comité Français des Sciences Historiques and the Centre National de la Recherche Scientifique, 1956–.

1:79 Bowditch, John, and Grew, Raymond, eds., assisted by Geiger, Roger. *A Selected Bibliography on Modern French History, 1600 to the Present.* Ann Arbor, Mich: University Microfilms, 1974. The 112 pages of this slim volume are arranged chronologically by periods and topically within periods.

Germany

1:80 Carlson, Andrew R. *German Foreign Policy, 1890–1914, and Colonial Policy to 1914: A Handbook and Annotated Bibliography.* Metuchen, N.J.: Scarecrow, 1970. Carlson lists diplomatic histories, dissertations, archival and printed document collections, and reference aids, many of which relate to Germany's relations with the United States.

1:81 Price, Arnold H. *East Germany: A Selected Bibliography.* Washington, D.C.: Library of Congress, 1978. The 833 items are concerned with conditions in East Germany as well as with external relations; begins in 1945 but with special emphasis for the period after 1958.

1:82 Price, Arnold H. *The Federal Republic of Germany: A Selected Bibliography of English Language Publications.* Washington, D.C.: Library of Congress, 1978. Price lists 1,325 items for the period 1945 to 1976.

Great Britain

Brown, L. M., and Christie, I. R., eds. *Bibliography of British History, 1789–1851* (6:1).

Hanham, H. J., ed. *Bibliography of British History, 1851–1914* (8:1).

Pargellis, S. M., and Medley, D. J. *Bibliography of British History . . . , 1714–1789* (3:11) contains chapters dealing with foreign relations.

Soviet Union (Russia)

1:83 Hammond, Thomas T., comp. and ed. *Soviet Foreign Relations and World Communism: A Selected, Annotated Bibliography of 7,000 Books in Thirty Languages.* Princeton, N.J.: Princeton University Press, 1965. The most thorough English-language bibliography of primary sources and secondary works on Soviet foreign policy and international communism (1917–1961), it contains some items through 1964. It is valuable for its critical annotations and the unusually extensive coverage of foreign-language material.

1:84 Horak, Stephan M., ed. *Russia, the USSR and Eastern Europe: A Bibliographic Guide to English Language Publications, 1964–1974.* Littleton, Colo.: Libraries Unlimited, 1978. The 1,611 carefully annotated items in this volume continue the bibliography of Horecky below.

1:85 Horecky, Paul L., ed. *Russia and Soviet Union: A Bibliographic Guide to Western Language Publications.* Chicago: University of Chicago Press, 1965. The 1,960 items in this carefully organized bibliography are thoroughly described and evaluated.

Hunter, B. *Soviet-Yugoslav Relations, 1948–1972: A Bibliography of Soviet, Western and Yugoslav Comment and Analysis* (28:2).

1:86 Jones, David L. *Books in English on the Soviet Union, 1917–73: A Bibliography.* New York: Garland, 1975. Soviet foreign relations—including those with the United States are given considerable attention in this unannotated bibliography.

1:87 Kanet, Roger E. *Soviet and East European Foreign Policy: A Bibliography of English- and Russian-Language Publications, 1967–1971.* Santa Barbara, Calif.: ABC-Clio, 1974. This work, designed to update Hammond's work (1:83), contains over 3,000 citations of books and articles on the foreign policy of the Soviet Union and of the eight East

European countries. Its unfortunate organization tends to discourage researchers, but the persistent will find it quite useful.

1:88 Morley, Charles. *Guide to Research in Russian History.* Syracuse, N.Y.: Syracuse University Press, 1951. This bibliography contains 840 carefully described items in all languages; foreign titles are translated. It is the basic aid in the study of Russian history.

Okinshevich, L., comp. *United States History and Historiography in Postwar Soviet Writings, 1945–1970* (24:2) lists books and articles dealing with all aspects of U.S. history published in the Soviet Union (1945–1970), with pp. 218–76 covering U.S. history since 1945. Titles are given in both Russian and English; brief annotations are included where title does not convey content.

1:89 Thompson, Anthony, ed. *Russia/U.S.S.R.* World Bibliography Series, no. 6. Santa Barbara, Calif.: ABC-Clio, 1979. Twelve hundred English-language books are cited for this clear and readable presentation of Russian and Soviet geography, foreign relations, politics, law, and human rights.

Spain

1:90 Cortada, James W., ed. *A Bibliographical Guide to Spanish Diplomatic History, 1460–1977.* Westport, Conn.: Greenwood, 1977. This bibliography does not include information on manuscript materials, although it does list various guides to the archives. In his introduction, Cortada notes with regret the paucity of general surveys of Spanish diplomacy and of specialized works covering many areas, including the early 19th century, but he nevertheless is able to list a substantial number of useful accounts.

Wilgus, A. C. *Latin America, Spain and Portugal: A Selected and Annotated Bibliographical Guide to Books Published in the United States, 1954–1974* (1:125).

Asia

1:91 Association of Asian Studies. *Bibliography of Asian Studies.* In *Journal of Asian Studies* pt. 5 (Sept. 1957–). Formerly entitled "Far Eastern Bibliography," appearing in the *Far Eastern Quarterly* (1936–1955) (title varies slightly), it is now issued individually as an annual.

1:92 *Cumulative Bibliography of Asian Studies, 1941–1965.* Author Bibliography. 4 vols.; Subject Bibliography, 4 vols. Boston: Hall, 1969–1970.

1:93 *Cumulative Bibliography of Asian Studies* [*Supplement*], *1966–1970.* Author Bibliography; Subject Bibliography. 6 vols. Boston: Hall, 1972–1973. These volumes cumulate the entries from the *Bibliography of Asian Studies* and its predecessor, "Far Eastern Bibliography," which appeared in the *Far Eastern Quarterly,* 1941 to 1965.

May, E. R., and Thomson, J. C., Jr., eds. *American-East Asian Relations: A Survey* (2:334) surveys the literature on American-East Asian relations from 1784 through the 1960s. Most of the essays treat China and/or Japan, but there is one on the Philippines to 1946. The essays on the years since World War II provide some coverage of material on U.S. relations with Korea and Southeast Asia, as well as relations with China and Japan.

1:94 Nunn, G. Raymond. *Asia: A Selected and Annotated Guide to Reference Works.* Cambridge, Mass.: MIT Press, 1971. A useful reference aid, this guide lists primarily books and periodicals published in English and Japanese.

1:95 Onorato, Michael P., ed. *Philippine Bibliography (1899–1946).* Santa Barbara, Calif.: ABC-Clio, 1968. This is a useful, brief introduction to the Philippines under American rule containing some 400 items.

China

Berton, P., and Wu, E. *Contemporary China: A Research Guide* [1945–1966] (31:1).

1:96 Dial, Roger. *Studies on Chinese External Affairs: An Instructional Bibliography of Commonwealth and American Literature.* Halifax: Dalhousie University, Center for Foreign Policy Studies, 1973. This is a valuable analytical bibliography of monographs and articles.

1:97 Hucker, Charles O. *China: A Critical Bibliography.* Tucson: University of Arizona Press, 1962. This selected, annotated list of books, articles, and individual chapters in books contributes significantly to the academic study of both traditional and modern China. Although dated, it is useful for background material.

1:98 McCutcheon, James M., comp. *China and America: A Bibliography of Interactions, Foreign and Domestic.* Honolulu:University of Hawaii Press, 1973. This is a highly selective bibliography of secondary literature in English on Sino-American interactions from the 18th century to the present. It includes books, articles, and dissertations arranged by subjects such as foreign policy and public opinion, economics, missionaries, and immigration.

Saran, V. *Sino-Soviet Schism: A Bibliography, 1956–1964* (31:4).

1:99 Tsien Tsuen-Hsuin, comp., with Cheng, James K. M. *China: An Annotated Bibliography of Bibliographies.* Boston: Hall, 1978. This is a comprehensive, annotated list of bibliographies in Western as well as Chinese and Japanese languages. Material on foreign relations is prominent.

Japan and Korea

1:100 Morley, James W., ed. *Japan's Foreign Policy, 1868–1941: A Research Guide.* New York: Columbia University Press, 1974. This is a massive and indispensable volume of mainly Japanese-language research aides, sponsored by the East Asian Institute of Columbia University.

1:101 Silberman, Bernard S. *Japan and Korea: A Critical Bibliography.* Tucson: University of Arizona Press, 1962. This selected, annotated guide to the most authoritative and available works on Japan and Korea (as of 1962) is excellent for background materials. It is divided by subject, with a short introductory essay to each section.

South Asia

1:102 Chand, Attar. *Bibliography of Indo-Soviet Relations, 1947–1977.* New York: Sterling, 1978.

Mahar, J. Michael. *India: A Critical Bibliography* (37:4) is useful for background data. Mahar has selected and annotated the most authoritative works on India.

Southeast Asia

Burns, R. D., and Leitenberg, M. *War in Vietnam, 1941–1980* (30:2) contains many general references to the problems and nations of Southeast Asia.

1:103 Hay, Stephen N., and Case, Margaret H. *Southeast Asian History: A Bibliographic Guide.* New York: Praeger, 1962. This comprehensive, well-annotated bibliography listing scholarly books, articles, and dissertations on Southeast Asian history is one of the best introductions to the literature.

1:104 Pelzer, Karl J. *West Malaysia and Singapore: A Selected Bibliography.* New Haven, Conn.: Human Relations Area Files Press, 1971. This is a comprehensive, although unannotated, bibliography.

Thombley, W. G., and Stiffin, W. J. *Thailand: Politics, Economy, and Socio-Cultural Setting: A Selected Guide to the Literature* (30:6).

Trager, F. N. *Burma: A Selected and Annotated Bibliography* (30:7).

Tregonning, K. G. *Southeast Asia: A Critical Bibliography* (30:8).

Middle East and North Africa

Atiyeh, G. N., comp. *The Contemporary Middle East, 1948–1973: A Selective and Annotated Bibliography* (33:3).

1:105 Bryson, Thomas A. *United States-Middle East Diplomatic Relations, 1784–1978: An Annotated Bibliography.* Metuchen, N.J.: Scarecrow, 1979. This aid provides a checklist of about 1200 items—books, articles, dissertations, documentary collections, bibliographical guides and treaty collections. It arranges these items both topically and chronologically, providing a ready reference to materials related to a given decade or country.

1:106 DeNovo, John A. "Researching American Relations with the Middle East: The State of the Art, 1970." In Milton O. Gustafson, ed., *The National Archives and Foreign Relations Research.* Athens: Ohio University Press, 1974, pp. 243–64. In addition to providing numerous areas of research that the scholar might pursue, this essay also furnishes a comprehensive list of books, articles, dissertations, and papers that updates the recent work of scholars.

1:107 Littlefield, David W. *The Islamic Near East and North Africa: An Annotated Guide to Books in English for Non-Specialists.* Littleton, Colo.: Libraries Unlimited, 1977. Much of its contents commend this volume to the attention of the specialist. The guide is divided into two main parts: general works and individual countries, which encompasses bibliographies and reference works, the disciplines of history, politics, religion, language, and literature, and country studies. The annotations are uneven in length and may be both evaluative and descriptive. Overall

this work is a useful companion volume to the Atiyeh bibliography (33:3). Indexes.

1:108 Howard, Harry N., et al. *Middle East and North Africa: A Bibliography for Undergraduate Libraries.* Williamsport, Pa.: Bro-Dart, 1971. A list of basic books by country and subject, it is designed essentially for libraries in undergraduate colleges and universities.

Schulz, A. *International and Regional Politics in the Middle East and North Africa: A Guide to Information Sources* (33:14) is a useful, annotated bibliography of books in English. It concentrates on foreign affairs and covers a wide range of topics, from theory to specific issues.

1:109 Simon, Reeva S. *the Modern Middle East: A Guide to Research Tools in the Social Sciences.* Boulder, Colo.: Westview, 1978. This volume emphasizes pertinent reference works. Its primary stress is on modern history, political science, sociology, and anthropology; its secondary focus is on geography, economics, psychology, and education. Subject index.

Tamkoç, M. *A Bibliography on the Foreign Relations of the Republic of Turkey, 1919–1967: And Brief Biographies of Turkish Statesmen* (33:18) is prepared for English speakers, for titles in Turkish are translated. This collection contains primary sources and secondary works and lists journal articles and dissertations as well as documents.

1:110 U.S. Department of State. *Point Four: Near East and Africa: A Selected Bibliography on Economically Underdeveloped Countries.* Washington, D.C.: G.P.O., 1951. Reprint 1969. This bibliography is aimed primarily at assistance in the planning and development of the Point Four Program. References are, for the most part, basic economic studies published in the 1940s.

Sub-Saharan Africa

1:111 DeLancey, Mark W. *Bibliography on African International Relations.* Boulder, Colo.: Westview, 1980. Concentrating on African states and organizations, this bibliography briefly annotates books and articles in English, French, German, and other languages.

1:112 Duignan, Peter, ed. *Guide to Research and Reference Works on Sub-Saharan Africa.* Stanford,

Calif.: Hoover Institution Press, 1976. In addition to listing general reference works, this guide has chapters on references to history and international relations, as well as chapters treating individual African states.

1:113 el-Khawas, Mohamed A., and Kornegay, Francis A., Jr., eds. *American-Southern African Relations: Bibliographic Essays.* Westport, Conn.: Greenwood, 1975. These essays cover Angola, Mozambique, Southern Rhodesia [Zimbabwe], Namibia, black America, as well as U.S.-South African relations.

1:114 Pollak, Oliver, and Pollak, Karen., eds. *Rhodesia/Zimbabwe.* World Bibliography Series, no. 4. Santa Barbara, Calif.: ABC-Clio, 1979. A selected, annotated survey of the literature of Rhodesia focusing on racism, paternalism, and colonialism. The 500 entries include geography and politics.

U.S. Department of State. *Africa: Problems and Prospects: A Bibliographic Survey* (37:7) annotates literature on contemporary problems. It lists all types of material, popular and scholarly, friendly and unfriendly. Included are national profiles, as well as basic reference works.

Latin America

Bartley, R. H., and Wagner, S. L. *Latin America in Basic Historical Collections: A Working Guide* [1492–1970] (1:265).

1:115 Bayitch, S. A. *Latin America and the Caribbean: A Bibliographical Guide to Works in English.* 2 vols. Coral Gables, Fla.: University of Miami Press, 1967. Revised and augmented from a 1961 edition, this guide is classified by general topics and separated by countries. It lists books, pamphlets, and articles in English in a great variety of disciplines, and includes a list of periodicals. Despite its comprehensive nature, the lack of an author index and introduction limits its usefulness.

Chilcote, R. H. *Revolution and Structural Change in Latin America: A Bibliography on Ideology, Development and the Radical Left, 1930–1965* (35:2).

1:116 Gormly, Mary. *Resources for Latin American Studies.* Los Angeles: California State University, Center for Latin American Studies, 1977. An annotated bibliography of major sources for Latin Ameri-

can studies in all disciplines. Of particular importance are the chapters on the National Archives microfilms of diplomatic reports, mostly consular, from U.S. officials stationed in Latin America to the Department of State (1806–1929).

1:117 Gropp, Arthur E. *A Bibliography of Latin American Bibliographies Published in Periodicals.* 2 vols. Metuchen, N.J.: Scarecrow, 1976. Gropp presents bibliographic information published in Latin American periodicals and in periodicals published elsewhere with special reference to Latin America through 1965. He covers all fields of knowledge, subdivided by country. This is an important source for data that is usually hard to obtain.

1:118 Griffin, Charles C., ed. *Latin America: A Guide to the Historical Literature.* Austin: University of Texas Press, 1971. One of the most recent and most comprehensive guides to writings on Latin American history, including some works on U.S.-Latin American relations. Part 7 covers international relations since 1830. Extensive index.

1:119 Meyer, Michael C., ed. *Supplement to a Bibliography of United States-Latin American Relations since 1810.* Lincoln: University of Nebraska Press, 1979. Meyer follows the organization of original volumes edited by Trask, Meyer, and Trask, with a few new subsections reflecting new trends and events; it essentially adds material published since 1967, plus additional older materials.

1:120 Trask, David F.; Meyer, Michael C.; and Trask, Roger R., eds. *A Bibliography of United States-Latin American Relations since 1810: A Selected List of Eleven Thousand Published References.* Lincoln: University of Nebraska Press, 1968. This is the only comprehensive guide to publications in English, Spanish, Portuguese, French, and other languages, in the field of U.S.-Latin American relations. Organized chronologically and topically, with country chapters. Updated by Meyer, immediately above.

1:121 Trask, Roger R. "Inter-American Relations." In Roberto Esquinazi-Mayo and Michael C. Meyer, eds., *Latin American Scholarship since World War II: Trends in History, Political Science, Literature, Geography, and Economics.* Lincoln: University of Nebraska Press, 1976, pp. 203–21. This bibliographical essay reviews the historiography of inter-American relations. Schools of historians are categorized and described. The additional bibliography alone makes this piece worthwhile.

1:122 U.S. Department of the Army. *Latin America and the Caribbean: Analytic Survey of the Literature.* Rev. ed. Washington, D.C.: G.P.O. (1969), 1975. This work contains chapters on a wide range of subjects: political, military, economic, and social; regional aspects; country-by-country surveys; and reference works. The emphasis is on contemporary popular and scholarly books, articles, and documents.

1:123 U.S. Library of Congress. Hispanic Division. *Handbook of Latin American Studies.* Cambridge: Harvard University Press; Gainesville: University of Florida Press, 1936–1951, 1951–. The items listed are well annotated, and they include works in progress as well as published material. There is a short essay for each subject discussing current trends.

1:124 Wilgus, A. Curtis. *Historiography of Latin America: A Guide to Historical Writing, 1500–1800.* Metuchen, N.J.: Scarecrow, 1975. It contains selective bibliographical accounts of important writers. Extensive bibliography and index.

1:125 Wilgus, A. Curtis. *Latin America, Spain and Portugal: A Selected and Annotated Bibliographical Guide to Books Published in the United States, 1954–1974.* Metuchen, N.J.: Scarecrow, 1977. This annotated list is organized by region, then country, with subsections on history, politics, foreign relations, biography, bibliography, etc. The user must rely on the analytical table of contents. Author index.

Monroe Doctrine

1:126 Bradley, Phillips. *A Bibliography of the Monroe Doctrine, 1919–1929.* London: London School of Economics, 1929. This pamphlet supplements H. H. B. Meyer's 1919 bibliography. See D. F. Trask, M. C. Meyer, and R. R. Trask, eds., *A Bibliography of United States-Latin American Relations since 1810* (1:120), and Meyer's subsequent volume (1:119) for additional references.

1:127 U.S. Library of Congress. *List of References on the Monroe Doctrine.* Comp. by Herman H. B. Meyer. Washington, D.C.: G.P.O., 1919. Meyer provides very broad coverage of a wide variety of diplomatic questions involving the Americas.

1:128 U.S. Senate. *Selected Bibliography on the Monroe Doctrine.* Washington, D.C.: G.P.O., 1941. It deals mostly with the modern aspects of the Monroe Doctrine.

Caribbean and Central America

Bray, W. D. *Controversy over a New Canal Treaty between United States and Panama: Selective Annotated Bibliography of United States, Panamanian, Colombian, French, and International Organization Sources* (34:2) is an invaluable guide which contains extensive annotations.

Comitas, L. *The Complete Caribbeana, 1900–1975: A Bibliographical Guide to the Scholarly Literature* (34:4) has the most comprehensive coverage.

1:129 California State University. Latin American Studies Center. *Central America: A Bibliography.* 2d ed. Latin American Bibliography Series, no. 2. Los Angeles: California State University, 1980. It lists nearly 2,000 English and Spanish general references.

1:130 Griffith, William. "The Historiography of Central America since 1830." *Hispanic American Historical Review* 40:4 (1960), 548–69. It emphasizes works published since 1920. Excellent for background data, especially U.S. relations with and intervention in various countries.

Pérez, L. A., Jr. *The Cuban Revolutionary War, 1953–1958: A Bibliography* (34:8) is an exhaustive list of works, without annotations, on a range of topics, including U.S. policy. Most references are in Spanish.

1:131 Pérez Cabrera, José M. *Historiografía de Cuba* [Cuban historiography]. Mexico, D.F.: Instituto Panamericano de Geografía e Historia, 1962. A one-volume history of Cuban historical writing from the early chroniclers to about 1900; it is also valuable for the Greater Antilles.

Ragatz, L. J., comp. *A Guide for the Study of British Caribbean History, 1763–1834* (7:3).

Valdes, N. P., and Lieuwen, E. *The Cuban Revolution: A Research-Study Guide, 1959–1969* (34:9) is an indispensable bibliographical guide; U.S. libraries holding significant collections are indicated. It has detailed subject categories.

National Bibliographies

1:132 Arnade, Charles W. "The Historiography of Colonial and Modern Bolivia." *Hispanic American Historical Review* 42:3 (1962), 333–84. A discussion of Bolivia's leading historians and trends in Bolivian historical writing that reveals Bolivia has had few research historians.

1:133 Cosío Villegas, Daniel, comp. *Cuestiones Internacionales de México: Una Bibliografía* [The international affairs of Mexico: A bibliography]. Mexico, D.F.: Secretaría de Relaciones Exteriores, 1966. This is a comprehensive bibliography of Mexican and, to some degree, other Latin American foreign relations; relations with the United States form a large part. It includes all types of published materials, primary and secondary.

Feigin de Roca, E., and Gaer de Sabulsky, A., comps. *Historiografía Argentina, 1930–1970* [Argentine historiography, 1930–1970] (35:3) is an extensive listing of books and articles published in Argentina.

Harmon, R. M., and Chamberlain, B. J. *Brazil: A Working Bibliography in Literature, Linguistics, Humanities, and the Social Sciences* (35:5) emphasizes basic works published since 1960.

Lombardi, J. V.; Damas, G. C.; and Adams, R. E., comps. *Venezuelan History: A Comprehensive Working Bibliography* (35:7) lists over 4,000 items in English and Spanish. Emphasizing books and articles published since 1945, it is useful for background information.

Norris, R. E. *Guía Bibliografía para el Estudio de la Historia Ecuatoriana* [Bibliographical guide for the study of Ecuadorian history] (35:8) is organized by historical periods and major themes.

1:134 Stein, Stanley J. "The Historiography of Brazil, 1808–1889." *Hispanic American Historical Review* 40:2 (1960), 234–78. This thorough summary emphasizes the major interpretations of 19th-century Brazilian history.

1:135 Watson, Gayle H. *Colombia, Ecuador, and Venezuela: An Annotated Guide to Reference Materials in Humanities and Social Sciences.* Metuchen, N.J.: Scarecrow, 1971. This is a critical analysis of reference materials (1498–1970) for the three countries that once comprised the Viceroyalty of New Granada. A bibliographical essay and the subject and main entry indexes serve as a guide to the listings.

BIBLIOGRAPHIES OF BIBLIOGRAPHIES

1:136 Boehm, Eric H., ed. *Bibliographies on International Relations and World Affairs: An Annotated Directory.* Santa Barbara, Calif.: ABC-Clio, 1965. This bibliography of bibliographies includes standard works and information about journals on international affairs and library accessions lists. It is analytic as well as substantive.

Gropp, A. E. *A Bibliography of Latin American Bibliographies* (1:117) is an essential and important source on Latin American bibliographies; updated with a 1971 supplement by Gropp.

Tsien Tsuen-Hsuin, comp., with Cheng, J. K. M. *China: An Annotated Bibliography of Bibliographies* (1:99).

General

1:137 Besterman, Theodore. *A World Bibliography of Bibliographies and of Bibliographical Catalogues, Calendars, Abstracts, Digests, Indexes, and the Like.* 4th ed., rev. 5 vols. Lausanne: Societas Bibliographia, 1965–1966. This massive work is the most comprehensive of its kind, listing 117,000 citations.

1:138 *Bibliographic Index: A Cumulative Bibliography of Bibliographies, 1937–.* New York: Wilson, 1938–. This series supplements Besterman's work; it is arranged by subject.

1:139 Collison, Robert L. *Bibliographies, Subject and National: A Guide to Their Contents, Arrangement and Use.* 3d ed., rev. and enl. London: Crosby, Lockwood, 1968. A selective listing of the most important works, the handbook contains 400–500 carefully selected and annotated references to bibliographies.

1:140 Courtney, William P. *A Register of National Bibliography: With a Selection of the Chief Bibliographical Books and Articles Printed in Other Countries.* 3 vols. London: Constable, 1905–1912. Courtney lists British materials through 1912, and also those of other countries. Volumes 1–2 list the bibliographies published before 1905; volume 3 is a supplement containing about 10,000 additional references, principally to bibliographies published 1905 to 1912.

1:141 United Nations. Educational, Scientific and Cultural Organization [UNESCO]. *Guide to National Bibliographical Information Centers.* 3d ed. Paris: UNESCO, 1970. It lists 186 centers in 77 countries.

Yearbooks, Atlases, Encyclopedias, Dictionaries, and Biographical Data

YEARBOOKS AND OTHER DIGESTS

1:142 *The Annual Register of World Events: A Review of the Year.* London: Longmans, Green, 1758–. This annual reviews world events; it is especially useful for Britain and the Commonwealth countries.

China Yearbook (31:5) is the official annual of the Taipei government, since 1951.

1:143 *Far Eastern Economic Review: Yearbook.* Hong Kong: Far Eastern Economic Review, 1950–. It supersedes the special Christmas issue of the *Review*, and features such themes as politics, economics, and trade for various countries. Comprehensive and up-to-date.

Greenwood, G., and Harper, N., eds. *Australia in World Affairs* 1950– (32:12) is a quinquennial survey of Australian foreign policy and contains many essays useful to American diplomatic historians.

1:144 *Political Handbook and Atlas of the World.* New York: Harper & Row, 1927–. A valuable annual reference guide to world governments, listing officials in power, political parties, names of major newspapers, summaries of the year's events, and, since 1963, maps.

1:145 *The Statesman's Year Book: Statistical and Historical Annual of the States of the World.* New York: St. Martin's Press, 1864–. An annual yearbook providing basic factual information on countries of the world and major international organizations, it provides more factual and statistical information than its American counterpart, the *Political Handbook and Atlas of the World* (1:144), but lacks the latter's review of recent events in each country.

1:146 *Survey of International Affairs* [1920–1963]. 45 volumes. New York: Oxford University Press, 1925–1977. A distinguished series of essays—sometimes whole volumes—on specific aspects of international affairs, written soon after the events described. Together, they provide a valuable detailed narrative of international diplomacy through 1963. Intended to be used with its accompanying documentary series, *Documents on International Affairs* (1:340); useful also in conjunction with its American counterpart, *The United States in World Affairs* (1:147).

1:147 *The United States in World Affairs, 1931–.* New York: Simon & Schuster, 1932–. An indispensable annual review of American foreign policy, which, despite being written immediately after the events described, manages to attain a level of analysis and balance that gives it lasting value. Each volume contains an excellent chronology and bibliography. Unfortunately, publication is now suspended—the last volume published was for 1970, and the years 1968 and 1969 have yet to be covered.

Year Book of World Affairs [1947–] (24:3).

1:148 *Yearbook on International Communist Affairs.* Stanford, Calif.: Hoover Institution, 1967–. This annual provides a country-by-country profile of Communist parties, together with information on international communist activities.

Weekly/Monthly Digests

1:149 *African Recorder: A Fortnightly Record of African Events, with Index.* New Delhi: Recorder Press, 1962–. Fortnightly, with semiannual and annual indexes. Summaries of events are entered under country, with an added section for events relating to "Africa outside Africa."

1:150 *Asian Recorder: A Weekly Digest of Asian Events with Index.* New Delhi: Recorder Press, 1955–. This weekly summary of events in all Asian countries, arranged alphabetically by country, places considerable emphasis on Indian affairs.

Current Digest of the Soviet Press (29:4) presents English translations of current articles from Soviet publications.

1:151 *Facts on File: A Weekly Digest with Cumulative Index.* New York: Facts on File: 1940–. This is a convenient weekly summary of major news events, domestic and foreign, with cumulative indexes.

1:152 *Keesing's Contemporary Archives: Weekly Diary of World Events*. London: Keesing's, 1931–. The British equivalent of *Facts on File*, but it is somewhat stronger in its coverage of international events than its American counterpart. Also weekly, it includes some documents, speeches, etc.; with cumulative index.

1:153 *Vital Speeches of the Day*. New York: City News, 1934–. This journal collects speeches by the great and near-great, which often are not reported elsewhere.

Arms Control and Disarmament Yearbooks

Stockholm International Peace Research Institute. *SIPRI Yearbook of World Armaments and Disarmament* [1968–] (40:9) is an exceptionally informative annual survey of military and disarmament issues. See U. Albrecht et al., *A Short Research Guide on Arms and Armed Forces* (40:1) for critical review.

United Nations. *The United Nations Disarmament Yearbook* [1976–] (38:102) is an annual survey of disarmament activities of the United Nations. It updates *The United Nations and Disarmament, 1945–1970* (38:103).

Military Yearbooks

1:154 *Brassey's Annual: The Armed Forces Year-Book*. New York: Macmillan, 1886–. For those needing specific information about armies and weapons, this annual is one of several that may be helpful. The *Jane's* series, with specific annual editions on navies, air forces, etc., may be used to supplement *Brassey's Annual*.

International Institute for Strategic Studies. *The Military Balance* [1961–] (40:8) is a quantitative assessment of defense expeditures and military forces throughout the world. See also IISS, *Strategic Survey* (1967–). See U. Albrecht et al., *A Short Research Guide on Arms and Armed Forces* (40:1) for critical review.

ATLASES, ENCYCLOPEDIAS, AND DICTIONARIES

1:155 *Government Reference Books*. Littleton, Colo.: Libraries Unlimited, 1970–. It lists bibliographies, directories, dictionaries, statistical works, handbooks, almanacs, and similar reference sources published by the U.S. government. Published biennially and annotated. Coverage began 1968–1969.

1:156 Wynkoop, Sally, ed. *Subject Guide to Government Reference Books*. Littleton, Colo.: Libraries Unlimited, 1972. An introductory guide to reference works published by the U.S. Government Printing Office and government agencies. *Government Reference Books* (see above) serves as a continuing supplement.

Atlases

1:157 Chew, A. F. *An Atlas of Russian History: Eleven Centuries of Changing Borders*. Rev. ed. New Haven, Conn.: Yale University Press, 1970. The maps depict important changes in Russia's boundaries and possessions from the 9th century to recent changes resulting from World War II.

1:158 Esposito, Vincent J., ed. *The West Point Atlas of American Wars*. 2 vols. New York: Praeger, 1959. These volumes contain battlefield and strategic maps, as well as accompanying text.

1:159 Fullard, H. *Soviet Union in Maps*. London: Philip, 1972.

1:160 Hall, Peter. *The New Penguin World Atlas*. 2d ed. Baltimore: Penguin, 1979. This is a useful reference with increased attention to the Middle East and Southern Africa.

1:161 Herrman, Albert. *An Historical Atlas of China*. Rev. ed. Chicago: Aldine, 1966. This is a new edition of a standard reference, it includes maps and text.

McEvedy, C. *Atlas of African History* (37:10) is useful in revealing tribal enmity and European conquest, as well as more contemporary events.

1:162 McEvedy, Colin, and Jones, Richard. *Atlas of World Population History*. New York: Facts on File, 1978. Containing nearly 200 tables, maps, and historical time graphs, this work is useful for comparing national populations.

1:163 Shepherd, William R. *Shepherd's Historical Atlas.* 9th ed., rev. New York: Barnes & Noble, 1973. This is an excellent general reference work.

Encyclopedias

1:164 DeConde, Alexander, ed. *Encyclopedia of American Foreign Policy: Studies of the Principal Movements and Ideas.* 3 vols. New York: Scribner's, 1978. This huge, selective reference work contains ninety-five topical essays of conceptual analysis of themes of American foreign policy by diplomatic historians and other specialists. Many of the essays deal with themes covering the whole span of American foreign policy; titles include "Alliances, Coalitions, and Ententes," "Armed Neutralities," "Isolationism." Others deal with more traditional episodes; see also "King Cotton Diplomacy," "Truman Doctrine." For a critical review, see Bradford Perkins, "Rating DeConde's Stable of Diplomatic Historians." *Diplomatic History* 3:4 (1979), 439–42.

1:165 Delpar, Helen, ed. *Encyclopedia of Latin America.* New York: McGraw-Hill, 1974. This offers a broad and comprehensive overview of Latin American history, economics, politics, arts, and so forth. Emphasis is on the national periods; it contains much biographical information.

1:166 Florinsky, Michael T., ed. *McGraw-Hill Encyclopedia of Russia and the Soviet Union.* New York: McGraw-Hill, 1961. Although dated, this double-columned volume is a useful reference. Among its offerings are biographies of Soviet leaders, descriptions of treaties, and surveys of central issues in Soviet foreign policy.

1:167 Langer, William L. *The New Illustrated Encyclopedia of World History.* 6th ed. 2 vols. New York: Abrams, 1975. This is the latest edition of the most useful work of its kind.

1:168 Maxwell, Robert, ed. and comp. *Information U.S.S.R.: An Authoritative Encyclopedia about the Union of Soviet Socialist Republics.* New York: Macmillan, 1962. Much of this volume is translated from volume 50 of the *Great Soviet Encyclopedia.*

1:169 Morris, Richard B., ed. *Encyclopedia of American History.* Bicentennial ed. New York: Harper & Row, 1976. Organized both chronologically and topically, it provides comprehensive coverage of dates, events, achievements, and persons.

1:170 Prokhorov, A. M., ed. *Great Soviet Encyclopedia.* New York: Macmillan, 1973. This English translation of the third edition of the multivolume Soviet publication provides a wealth of information about the U.S.S.R. and its leaders. The index is an essential guide to the entries.

1:171 Wieczynski, Joseph L., ed. *The Modern Encyclopedia of Russian and Soviet History.* Gulf Breeze, Fla.: Academic International Press, 1976–. An ongoing, multivolume project, beginning in 1976 with "A," this encyclopedia includes references to and entries on key Soviet diplomatic personalities and events and is written by leading scholars. Major entries carry brief bibliographies.

Dictionaries

1:172 Adams, James Truslow. *Dictionary of American History.* 2d ed., rev. 6 vols. New York: Scribner's, 1942–1961. This series covers all aspects of American history except biography.

1:173 *Dictionary of American History.* Rev. ed. 8 vols. New York: Scribner's, 1976. This edition updates Adams's earlier *Dictionary of American History.*

1:174 Palmer, Alan. *The Facts on File Dictionary of 20th Century History.* New York: Facts on File, 1979. An alphabetically arranged reference guide of more than 600 articles about peoples and events from 1900 to 1978; with cross references.

1:175 Rossi, Ernest E., and Plano, Jack C. *The Latin American Political Dictionary.* Santa Barbara, Calif.: ABC-Clio, 1980. This dictionary provides definitions for concepts, institutions, and events basic to the politics and economics of Latin America.

1:176 Williams, E. Neville. *The Facts on File Dictionary of European History, 1485–1789.* New York: Facts on File, 1980. Substantial articles on important personalities and topics, following the mainstream of political history. Comprehensive subject index.

BIOGRAPHICAL DATA

See also, in Chapter 2, "Diplomats, Agents, and Diplomatic Service."

1:177 Armin, Max. *Internationale Personalbibliographie, 1800–1943* [International person bibliography, 1800–1943]. 2 vols. Leipzig: Hiersemann, 1944–1952. This useful series is supplemented by a third volume covering 1944 to 1959 (Stuttgart: Hiersemann, 1961–1963).

1:178 *Current Biography*. New York: Wilson, 1940–. The most useful single source for detailed biographies of living contemporary figures. Published monthly with annual cumulations, this source provides biographical sketches of two to three pages each on both national and international personalities, based on newspaper and periodical material. The sketches are updated.

1:179 *International Who's Who*. London: Europa, 1935–. The major source for basic biographical information on living world leaders, providing dates of birth, titles, decorations, publications, and addresses. Published annually.

1:180 *Who's Who in the World*. Chicago: Marquis, 1970–. This is the American counterpart to the *International Who's Who*.

American

Boyce, R. F., and Boyce, K. R. *American Foreign Service Authors: A Bibliography* (1:58).

1:181 Dargan, Marion. *Guide to American Biography*. 2 vols. Albuquerque: University of New Mexico Press, 1947–1952. Selection guide to books and articles on "representative Americans": volume 1 covers the period 1607 to 1815; volume 2 covers 1815 to 1933. Name and subject indexes.

1:182 *Dictionary of American Biography*. 21 vols. New York: Scribner's, 1946. A basic authority for biographical information, it has supplements 1-4, published between 1944 and 1974, which update the work to include people who lived through 1950. For a brief survey see *Concise Dictionary of American Biography* (New York: Scribner's, 1964).

1:183 Freidel, Frank, ed. "Biographies and Writings." *Harvard Guide to American History*. Rev. ed. Cambridge: Harvard University Press, vol. 1, pp. 154–274. Chapter 10 lists, by subject's name, the major biographies and selected writings of prominent American figures. It is not complete, but nonetheless is a handy reference for secondary figures.

1:184 Garraty, John A., and Sternstein, Jerome L., eds. *Encyclopedia of American Biography*. New York: Harper & Row, 1974. A quick reference tool, it contains biographical sketches and brief interpretive essays about prominent people in American history, including foreign affairs.

1:185 Kaplan, Louis A., et al. *A Bibliography of American Autobiographies*. Madison: University of Wisconsin Press, 1961. It includes 6,377 entries listed by author; the subject index indicates occupations, locale, and important historical events.

1:186 Matthews, William, with Peares, Roy H. *American Diaries: An Annotated Bibliography of American Diaries Written Prior to the Year 1861....* Berkeley: University of California Press, 1945. Reprint 1959. A chronological list of diaries written prior to 1861 with annotations giving full name, occupation, dates and home, author, and brief notes as to subject content of diary and record of printed source. Manuscript sources are listed in a companion volume, below.

1:187 *National Cyclopaedia of American Biography*. 59 vols. New York: White, 1892–1971. The most comprehensive American work, it's less limited and selective than the *Dictionary of American Biography* (1:182), and more up to date than *Appleton's Cyclopaedia of American Biography*.

1:188 *National Cyclopaedia of American Biography: Current Volumes, A-M*. New York: White, 1930–1978 (in progress). Includes living persons only, the biographies given being considerably longer than those in *Who's Who in America*. Each volume is separately indexed, and all are cumulatively indexed in the general index (see below).

1:189 *National Cyclopaedia of American Biography: Revised Index, Permanent and Current Series*. Comp. by H. A. Harvey and Raymond D. McGill. New York: White, 1975. Indexes not only the main biographical articles but also names, institutions, events, and other subjects mentioned in the articles.

1:190 *Political Profiles.* 5 vols. to date. New York: Facts on File, 1978–. These volumes contain biographies of the various men and women who were and are prominent in American politics since World War II. These initial volumes cover the Truman years to the Nixon/Ford years.

1:191 U.S. Department of State. *The Biographic Register, 1870–.* Washington, D.C.: G.P.O., 1870–. An annual publication, its title varies; some years are omitted. Since 1944, it includes only the biographical section, and in recent years has provided information on personnel of the State Department and other federal government agencies in the field of foreign affairs.

1:192 *Who's Who in America: A Biographical Dictionary of Notable Living Men and Women, 1899–.* Chicago: Marquis, 1899–. Published biennially, the 41st edition covers 1980–1981, and includes about 73,000 people. For sketches of individuals now deceased, see *Who Was Who in America: Historical Volume, 1607–1896* (Chicago: Marquis, 1963). For sketches of deceased people who were listed in *Who's Who,* see *Who Was Who in America* (Chicago: Marquis, 1942–).

1:193 *Who's Who in Government.* Chicago: Marquis, 1972–. This biographical directory lists key figures in United States federal, state, and local government.

Latin American

Camp, R. A. *Mexican Political Biographies, 1935–1976* (35:76).

1:194 Foster, David W., ed. *Latin American Government Leaders.* 2d ed. Tempe: Arizona State University, Center for Latin American Studies, 1975. Foster includes short biographical sketches of important government leaders listed by country. Updates Tambs (1:200).

1:195 Hilton, Ronald, ed. *Who's Who in Latin America.* 7 vols. 3d ed. Palo Alto, Calif.: Stanford University Press, 1945. A "Biographical Directory of Notable Living Men and Women of Latin America," it is much out of date for contemporary figures.

1:196 Iguíniz, Juan Bautista. *Bibliografía and Biográfica Mexicana.* Mexico, D.F.: UNAM, Instituto de Investigaciones Históricas, 1969. The 1,314 well-annotated items (books, articles, pamphlets) contain biographical data on important Mexican personalities.

1:197 Martínez, Rufino. *Diccionario biográfico-histórico dominicano, 1821–1930* [Biographical-historical Dominican dictionary, 1821–1930]. Santo Domingo: Universidad Autónoma de Santo Domingo, 1971. This volume contains valuable biographical information on the most prominent figures in Dominican history.

1:198 Peraza Sarausa, Fermín. *Diccionario Biográfico Cubano* [Cuban biographical dictionary]. 14 vols. Havana: Biblioteca del Bibliotecario, 1952–1962. Reprint 1965–1967. A major Cuban biographical dictionary, it includes only deceased persons. A cumulative index to the set is provided in volume 12.

1:199 Peraza Sarausa, Fermín. *Personalidades Cubanas* [Cuban personalities]. 10 vols. Havana: Biblioteca del Bibliotecario, 1957–1968. Supplement to the *Diccionario Biográfico Cubano,* it includes only living persons.

1:200 Tambs, Lewis A., et al., eds. *Latin American Government Leaders.* Tempe: Arizona State University, Center for Latin American Studies, 1970. Short biographical sketches of important government leaders are listed by country.

1:201 Taplin, Glen W., comp. *Middle American Governers.* Metuchen, N.J.: Scarecrow, 1972. Taplin covers Central America as well as Mexico, from prehistoric times to 1970. Major events and important people, other than rulers, are also listed. Organized by country and then chronologically. Index.

Soviet

1:202 Institut zur Erforschung der U.S.S.R. *Party and Government Officials of the Soviet Union, 1917–1967.* Metuchen, N.J.: Scarecrow, 1969.

1:203 *Prominent Personalities in the U.S.S.R.: A Biographic Directory.* Metuchen, N.J.: Scarecrow, 1968.

1:204 *The Soviet Diplomatic Corps, 1917–1969.* Metuchen, N.J.: Scarecrow, 1970.

1:205 *Who Was Who in the Soviet Union: A Biographical Dictionary of Prominent Soviet Historical Personalities.* Metuchen, N.J.: Scarecrow, 1972. These volumes are useful in providing biographical data on individuals who are not normally in the headlines.

Others

1:206 *Dictionary of Canadian Biography.* 10 vols. to date. Toronto: University of Toronto Press, 1966–. Volume 10 brings this project to 1880.

1:207 Lewytzkyj, Borys, ed. *Who's Who in the Socialist Countries: A Biographical Encyclopedia of 10,000 Leading Personalities in Sixteen Communist Countries.* New York: Saur, 1978. Although there are obvious gaps in its coverage, out of 10,000 biographical sketches, at least half are of Soviet personalities, primarily government officials, party functionaries, and some prominent scholars. The coverage is uneven, and biographical sketches vary in length, depending on the relative importance of the personalities discussed.

1:208 Perleberg, Max. *Who's Who in Modern China, from the Beginning of the Chinese Republic to the End of 1953.* Hong Kong: Ye Olde Printerie, 1953. This volume contains information about the rulers of Nationalist and Communist China, with index in Chinese and English.

1:209 Robert, Adolphe; Bourloton, Edgar; and Cougny, Gaston, eds. *Dictionnaire des parlementaires français, comprenant tous les membres des assemblées françaises et tous les ministres français depuis le 1 mai 1789 jusqu'au 1 mai 1889, avec leurs noms, état civil, états de services, actes politiques, votes parlementaires, etc.* [Dictionary of French parliamentarians, comprising all the members of the French Assembly and all the French members from 1 May 1789 to 1 May 1889, with their names, civil status, state of service, political activities, parliamentary votes, etc.]. 5 vols. Paris: Bourloton, 1891. These volumes are particularly valuable for good but brief biographical profiles of ministers and members of parliament.

Indexes and Directories to Periodicals, Newspapers, Book Reviews, Dissertations, Oral Histories, and Microforms

Gregory, W., ed. *List of the Serial Publications of Foreign Governments, 1815–1931* (1:321) lists holdings in 85 U.S. libraries.

1:210 Hubbard, Harlan P. *Hubbard's Newspaper and Bank Directory of the World.* 2 vols. New Haven, Conn.: Hubbard, 1882–1884. Hubbard describes over 33,000 newspapers and 15,000 books.

1:211 Stewart, James D.; with Hammond, Muriel E., and Saenger, Erwin, eds. *British Union Catalogue of Periodicals: A Record of the Period of the World, from the 17th Century to the Present Day, in British Libraries.* New York: Academic, 1955–1958. This catalogue includes more than 140,000 titles found in nearly 440 libraries. It was supplemented by 991 pages by same editors (London: Butterworths, 1962).

1:212 *Ulrich's International Periodicals Directory: A Classified Guide to Current Periodicals, Foreign and Domestic.* New York: Bowker, 1932–. This volume appears biennially and under various previous titles; *Ulrich's Periodical Directory, 1943–1963.*

1:213 Union of International Associations. *Directory of Periodicals Published by International Organizations.* 3d ed. Brussels: The Union, 1969.

PERIODICALS

1:214 *America: History and Life.* Santa Barbara, Calif.: ABC-Clio, 1964–. *Part A: Article Abstracts and Citations* (three times per year) provides a most useful survey of articles published on the history of the United States and Canada. *Part B: Index to Book Reviews* (semiannual); *Part C: American History Bib-*

liography (Books, Articles and Dissertations) (annual); and *Part D: Annual Index,* a cumulative index to Parts A, B, and C comprise the annual volume. Five-year indexes.

1:215 American Historical Association. *Recently Published Articles.* Washington, D.C.: AHA, 1976–. This series replaces the "Recently Published Articles" section of the *American Historical Review.* It contains many references to U.S. foreign affairs and policy, sometimes listed under other geographic headings. The lack of a subject index greatly reduces these volumes' utility.

1:216 Dougherty, James T., et al. *Writings on American History, 1962–1973: A Subject Bibliography of Articles.* 4 vols. Washington, D.C.: American Historical Association, 1967. These volumes, complemented by *America: History and Life* (1:214), fill a gap in American historical bibliography. The lack of annotations will prove a hindrance; many of the titles give no indication of contents.

1:217 Dushing, Harriet G., and Morris, Adah V., eds. *Nineteenth Century Readers' Guide to Periodical Literature, with Supplementary Indexing, 1900–1922.* 2 vols. New York: Wilson, 1944–. Included are materials from 51 periodicals, mainly in the period from 1890 to 1899.

1:218 *Historical Abstracts.* Santa Barbara, Calif.: ABC-Clio, 1955–. This useful reference aid provides abstracts and bibliographic citations of articles, books, and dissertations on world history and related topics, except the United States and Canada (see 1:214). *Part A: Modern History Abstracts (1450–1914)* and *Part B: Twentieth Century Abstracts (1914–present)* represent the format since the publication was divided into two parts in 1971. Prior to 1971, the abstracts covered the period 1775 to 1945. Books and dissertations are covered beginning with volume 31 (1980). Five-year indexes.

1:219 *Humanities Index.* New York: Wilson, 1974–. This index continues in part *Social Science and Humanities Index and International Index to Periodicals.* It covers more scholarly journals than the *Readers' Guide* (1:227). Historical journals are indexed here.

1:220 *Index Bibliographicus.* 4th ed. 2 vols. (2 vols. in preparation). The Hague: Federation Internationale de Documentation, 1959–1964. Volume 2 covers the social sciences, volume 1 being science and technol-

ogy. Forthcoming are volume 3, humanities, and volume 4, general bibliographies. The 4th edition is a completely revised listing of currently published abstracting and bibliographic services arranged by the Universal Decimal Classification.

1:221 *An Index to Legal Periodical Literature.* 5 vols. Boston and Indianapolis: Publisher varies, 1888–1924. This index covers 1888 to 1924. It is supplemented by the *Index to Legal Periodicals.*

1:222 *Index to Legal Periodicals, 1908–.* New York: Wilson, 1909–. Published for the American Association of Law Libraries; it has annual cumulations with some exceptions. Printed under one cover with the *Law Library Journal* (volumes 1–28, 1908–1935).

1:223 *Peace Research Abstracts Journal.* Oakville, Canada: Canadian Peace Research Institute, 1964–. This monthly covers books and articles, with earliest entries back to 1954. The range of subjects is broad under a ten-heading classification system. These include "International Law, Economics, and Diplomacy," "International Institutions and Regional Alliances," "Ideology and Issues," "Nations and National Policies," "Limitations of Arms," and "Decision Making and Communications." Users must familiarize themselves with the coding index.

1:224 *Poole's Index to Periodical Literature, 1802–81.* 2 vols. Rev. ed. Boston: Houghton, 1891. Reprint 1938. Originally edited by William Frederick Poole for the American Library Association. Continued by *Reader's Guide to Periodical Literature.* Still an important index to American and English periodicals since it covers 105 years and indexes a total of 590,000 articles in 12,241 volumes of 479 periodicals. Subject index only.

1:225 *Poole's Index to Periodical Literature, Supplements, Jan. 1882–Jan. 1, 1907.* Boston: Houghton, 1887–1908.

1:226 Public Affairs Information Service. *Public Affairs Information Service Bulletin.* New York: PAIS, 1915–. This is an index to current literature in fields such as government, political science, and economics. It also indexes government documents and some books as well as periodicals. Popularly known as PAIS.

1:227 *Reader's Guide to Periodical Literature.* New York: Wilson, 1905–. This was the first modern index (volume 1, 1900–). Beginning with volume 19, 1953,

Reader's Guide indexes U.S. periodicals of broad, general, and popular character representing all the important scientific and humanistic subjects. About 160 periodicals are included.

1:228 Sears, Minnie, and Shaw, Marian, eds. *Essay and General Literature Index, 1900–1933*. New York: Wilson, 1934–. An index to about 40,000 essays and articles in 2,144 volumes of collections of essays and miscellaneous works. Supplements include: (1) seven-year cumulations (1934–1940, 1941–1947, 1948–1954); (2) five-year cumulation (1955–1959); (3) semiannual and annual cumulations. Indexes for 1900 to 1969; annual indexes 1970–.

Winther, O. O., and Van Orman, R. A., comps. *A Classified Bibliography of the Periodical Literature of the Trans-Mississippi West, 1811–1967* (1:77).

Latin America

Cox [Vagt], B. C. *HAPI: Hispanic American Periodicals Index* (35:10) reviews more than 200 Latin American periodicals. It continues *Indice General de Publicaciones Latino-Americanos* 1961–1970 (35:13) and *Index to Latin American Periodical Literature 1929–1960*.

Pan American Union. Columbus Memorial Library. *Index to Latin American Periodical Literature, 1929–1960* (35:12) is a quarterly publication that is supplemented by the *Index to Latin American Periodical Literature, 1929–1960*. It has been superseded by the *Hispanic American Periodical Index* (HAPI). Titles in both Spanish and English.

NEWSPAPERS

1:229 Charno, Steven M., comp. *Latin American Newspapers in United States Libraries: A Union List*. Austin: University of Texas Press, 1969. This detailed listing of some 5,500 titles from Latin American countries and Puerto Rico held in 70 U.S. libraries is arranged by country and their cities. Included are details on reported holdings of each title and, whenever possible, the dates of commencement and cessation of publication. There is a selected bibliography of works concerning the press, journalism, and related matters.

1:230 *New York Daily Tribune Index* [1875–1906]. 31 vols. New York: Tribune Association, 1876–1907.

A much briefer index than the *New York Times Index,* but it is useful for the period covered.

1:231 *New York Times Index*. New York: Times, 1913–. It is issued semimonthly with annual cumulations. *New York Times Index Prior Series,* 12 vols. (reprint New York, 1966–1977) is designed to provide coverage from 1851 to 1912; some volumes are reprinted from indexes originally prepared for staff use.

1:232 Times. London. *Index to the Times*. London: Times, 1906–. This series indexes the London *Times*. Entitled *The Annual Index* from 1906 to 1913, and *The Official Index* from 1914 to 1957; it is monthly (1906–1914), quarterly (1914–1956), and bimonthly (after 1956). Palmer's *Index to the Times Newspaper* (London, 1868–1943; reprint 1965) covers the period 1790 to June 1941; it is much briefer than the official index, but it is useful because of the longer period covered.

BOOK REVIEWS

America: History and Life (1:214) indexes book reviews beginning in 1974, *Part B. Part C* is a subject index to these book reviews (as well as dissertations).

1:233 *Book Review Digest*. New York: Wilson, 1905–. A digest and index of selected book reviews in about 75 English and American periodicals, it is general in character. Arranged alphabetically by author of book reviewed, with subject and title index, it is published monthly, with semiannual and annual cumulations.

1:234 *Book Review Index*. Detroit: Gale, 1965–. This index has an author listing with alphabetical citations to reviews. Published bimonthly.

1:235 Brewster, John W., and McCleod, Joseph H. *Index to Book Reviews in Historical Periodicals*. Metuchen, N.J.: Scarecrow, 1975–. It is arranged in alphabetical order by author of book under review; covers 1972, 1973 (published 1976), 1974 (published 1975), 1975 (published 1976), 1976 (published 1977). About 97 percent of the better known scholarly journals and historical society organs are represented.

1:236 *Index to Book Reviews in the Humanities*. Detroit: Thomson, 1960–. Published annually, it indexes several hundred periodicals, originally all in English, although a number of foreign-language titles were added in the 1970 volume. With volume 11

(1970), periodical titles in the field of history and related areas were dropped from this index.

DOCTORAL DISSERTATIONS/MASTER'S THESES

1:237 *American Doctoral Dissertations.* Ann Arbor, Mich.: University Microfilms, 1957–. This is the successor to *Doctoral Dissertations Accepted by American Universities* (1:241); it is issued annually as no. 13 of the monthly issues of *Dissertation Abstracts* beginning with volume 16, no. 13. It consolidates in one list the dissertations for which doctoral degrees were granted in Canada and the U.S. during the year covered, as well as those available on microfilm from University Microfilms. (Title varies: *Index to American Doctoral Dissertations.* 1955/56–963/64; *American Doctoral Dissertations* 1964/65–.)

1:238 Bilboul, Roger R., ed. *Retrospective Index to Theses of Great Britain and Ireland, 1716–1950.* 5 vols. Santa Barbara, Calif.: ABC-Clio, 1975–1977. Volume 1, "Social Sciences and Humanities," provides the existence, location, availability, and conditions of use of theses from twenty universities. Subject and author index.

1:239 *Comprehensive Dissertation Index.* 37 vols. Ann Arbor, Mich.: University Microfilms, 1973. This index covers the years 1861 to 1972: volume 27, law and political science; and volume 28, history. It supersedes earlier partial indexes of the Library of Congress and *Dissertation Abstracts.* It is a computer-generated index that attempts to list all dissertations of U.S. and some foreign universities.

1:240 *Dissertation Abstracts International.* Ann Arbor, Mich.: University Microfilms, 1938–. Title varies: volume 1–11 (1938–1951) issued as *Microfilm Abstracts*; volume 12–29 (1952–June 1969) as *Dissertation Abstracts*; and from volume 30, no. 1 (July 1969) with current name. A compilation of abstracts of doctoral dissertations submitted to University Microfilms by a varying number of cooperating universities, including, with volume 30, some foreign schools.

1:241 *Doctoral Dissertations Accepted by American Universities.* No. 1–22. New York: Wilson, 1934–1955. This series covers the period 1933/34–1954/55

and is a list of dissertations (U.S. and Canada) arranged by subject and then by university. Continued by *American Doctoral Dissertations.*

1:242 Kuehl, Warren F. *Dissertations in History: An Index to Dissertations Completed in History Departments of United States and Canadian Universities.* 2 vols. Lexington: University of Kentucky Press, 1965–1972. Lists about 13,500 dissertations by author. The volumes have a subject index.

1:243 *Masters Abstracts: Abstracts of Selected Masters Theses on Microfilm.* Ann Arbor, Mich.: University Microfilms, 1962–. This series consists of semiannually published abstracts of a selected list of master's theses, from various universities, available on microfilm.

1:244 U.S. Library of Congress. Catalog Division. *List of American Doctoral Dissertations Printed in 1912–38.* 26 vols. Washington, D.C.: G.P.O., 1913–1940. The volumes do not include unpublished items; includes the printed theses of about 45 colleges and universities.

Special Topics

1:245 Christman, Calvin L., comp. "Doctoral Dissertations in U.S. Foreign Affairs." *Diplomatic History* 3:2 (1979), 231–48. This valuable list is to appear annually; it divides the references into subject categories. Not annotated.

Dossick, J. J. *Doctoral Research on Russia and the Soviet Union, 1960–1975* (29:2) is a list of American, Canadian, and British doctoral dissertations in a variety of fields, including Soviet-American relations. Dissertations are listed by subject, with no annotations. It is a companion volume to Dossick's 1960 publication with the same title, which covered dissertations written to 1960.

1:246 Millett, Allan R., and Cooling, B. Franklin, III, comps. *Doctoral Dissertations in Military Affairs: A Bibliography.* Manhattan: Kansas State University Library, 1972. A groundbreaking effort in the military history field, it includes dissertations in related academic disciplines as well. Published dissertations are conveniently marked with asterisks. This initial volume has been updated annually since 1973 in *Military Affairs.*

Asia

Gordon, L. H. D., and Shulman, F. J., comps. *Doctoral Dissertations on China: A Bibliography of Studies in Western Languages, 1945–1970* (17:7) is kept up-to-date by listings in *Asian Studies Professional Newsletter.*

Shulman, F. J., comp. *Doctoral Dissertations on Japan and Korea, 1969–1974: A Classified Bibliographical Listing of International Research* (17:8).

Shulman, F. J., comp. *Japan and Korea: An Annotated Bibliography of Doctoral Dissertations in Western Languages, 1877–1969* (17:9) is supplemented by lists of recently completed dissertations and dissertations in progress appearing in the Association for Asian Studies *Newsletter* beginning 14:4 (1969).

1:247   Shulman, Frank J., comp. *Doctoral Dissertations on Asia: An Annotated Bibliographical Journal of Current International Research.* Ann Arbor, Mich.: University Microfilms, 1975–. This is a semiannual compilation published for the Association for Asian Studies. It lists recently accepted and in-progress dissertations.

1:248   Stucki, Curtis W., comp. *American Doctoral Dissertations on Asia, 1933–June 1966.* Ithaca, N.Y.: Cornell University, Department of Asian Studies, 1968. This compilation includes many dissertations on U.S.-Asian relations. The China section has a subsection on relations with the United States that lists 61 dissertations. The section on Japan's foreign relations incudes 46 dissertations on relations with the United States. It also includes an appendix listing Master's theses at Cornell University (1933–1968).

Latin America

Baa, E. M., comp. *Theses on Caribbean Topics* (34:1) a list of doctoral and master's theses dating from the 19th century, but emphasizing the years 1945 to 1967.

Chaffee, W. A., Jr., and Griffin, H. M. *Dissertations on Latin America by United States Historians, 1960–1970: A Bibliography* (35:1).

1:249   Deal, Carl W., ed. *Latin America and the Caribbean: A Dissertation Bibliography.* Ann Arbor, Mich.: University Microfilms, 1978. Deal lists 7,200 dissertations, mainly for the 1962 to 1977 period. The chapters titled "History" and "Law and Political Science" list many dissertations on U.S.-Latin American

relations. Taken directly from *Dissertations Abstracts International* but without the annotations.

Kantor, H. *A Bibliography of Unpublished Doctoral Dissertations and Masters Theses Dealing with the Governments, Politics and International Relations of Latin America* (34:7) has entries dating from 1911, but emphasizes 1940 to 1952.

1:250   Snarr, D. Neil, and Brown, E. Leonard. "An Analysis of Ph.D. Dissertations on Central America, 1960–1974." *Latin American Research Review* 12:2 (1977), 187–202. The authors conclude that doctoral dissertations on Central American topics have rarely made their way into advanced research. The bibliography contains a list of 140 dissertations on Central American social change and development.

Middle East

1:251   Selim, George D., comp. *American Doctoral Dissertations on the Arab World, 1883–1974.* Rev. ed. Washington, D.C.: Library of Congress, 1976. Selim includes dissertations on the Middle and Near East that deal with foreign affairs issues. Author listing and subject index.

1:252   Shulman, Frank J. *American and British Doctoral Dissertations on Israel and Palestine in Modern Times.* Ann Arbor, Michigan: University Microfilms, 1973. A listing of dissertations that includes materials on foreign affairs.

ORAL HISTORY DIRECTORIES

1:253   Mason, Elizabeth B., and Storr, Louis M., eds. *The Oral History Collection of Columbia University.* New York: Columbia University, Oral History Research Office, 1973. This directory lists 2,697 transcripts of memoirs, speeches, and lectures arranged alphabetically by name or subject. Many of these "histories" pertain to foreign affairs issues.

1:254   Meckler, Alan M., and McMullin, Ruth. *Oral History Collections.* New York: Bowker, 1975. Numerous interviews of prominent American diplomats have been conducted under the auspices of projects such as the Eisenhower Administration Project (Columbia University) and the Dulles Oral History Project (Princeton University). These oral histories, as well as those at other institutions like the presidential libraries, can be located through this guide, which indicates the length (hours or pages) and restrictions on access.

1:255   Shumway, Gary L. *Oral History in the United States: A Directory*. New York: Oral History Association, 1971. A guide to major oral history repositories in the United States, listing objectives, size, and major topics.

MICROFILM AND PHOTOCOPIED MATERIALS

1:256   Hale, Richard W., comp. *Guide to Photocopied Historical Materials in the United States and Canada*. Ithaca, N.Y.: Cornell University Press, 1961. Although now dated due to the tremendous proliferation of microfilm records since 1961, this volume continues to provide an introduction to such documentation.

1:257   U.S. Library of Congress. *National Register of Microfilm Masters*. Washington: Library of Congress, 195–. Published annually, it lists only master microforms, those from which copies are made. Included are foreign and domestic books, pamphlets, serials, foreign doctoral dissertations. Newspapers are listed in the *Newspapers in Microform* (1:262), and archival materials are listed in *National Union Catalog of Manuscript Collections* (1:282).

1:258   U.S. National Archives Microfilm Publications. *Purport Lists for the Department of State Decimal File, 1910–1944*. Washington, D.C.: National Archives and Records Service, 1976. An explanatory pamphlet for the use of diplomatic records in the National Archives. Although records are now available through 1949, the decimal system remains the same as described herein.

1:259   U.S. National Archives and Records Service. *Catalogue of National Archives Microfilm Publications*. Washington, D.C.: National Archives and Records Service, 1974. This volume supersedes the agency's earlier *List of National Archives Microfilm Publications, 1947–1968*.

1:260   *Union Library Catalogue of the Philadelphia Metropolitan Area: Committee on Microphotography: Union List of Microfilms*. 2 vols. Ann Arbor, Mich.: Edwards, 1961. Supplement to the basic lists published in 1942 and 1951, it includes more than 52,000 entries for the period 1949 to 1959.

Newspapers

1:261   Brayer, Herbert O. "Preliminary Guide to Indexed Newspapers in the United States, 1850–1900." *Mississippi Valley Historical Review* 33:2 (1946), 237–58. Arranged by state and then by library or other depository, Brayer's guide indicates indexes to files of newspapers, dates covered, and physical nature of the index.

1:262   U.S. Library of Congress. *Newspapers in Microform*. Washington, D.C.: Library of Congress, 1973–. This annual supplements *Newspapers in Microform: United States, 1948–1972* and *Newspapers in Microform: Foreign Countries, 1948–1972*.

1:263   U.S. Library of Congress. *Newspapers in Microform: Foreign Countries, 1948–1972*. Washington, D.C.: Library of Congress, 1973. This is the latest cumulation in a continuing series.

1:264   U.S. Library of Congress. Union Catalog Division. *Newspapers on Microfilm*. 6th ed. Washington, D.C.: Library of Congress, 1967. It lists over 17,000 U.S. and over 4,600 foreign newspapers found in U.S. and Canadian libraries on microfilm. Superseded by the Library of Congress' *Newspapers on Microfilm: United States, 1948–1972* (1973).

Guides to Archives and Manuscript Collections

1:265   Bartley, Russell H., and Wagner, Stuart L. *Latin America in Basic Historical Collections: A Working Guide* [1492–1970]. Stanford, Calif.: Hoover Institution, 1972. This indispensable aid describes the nature and contents of library holdings relating to Latin America. It is arranged by institution within country and contains a detailed table of contents, classified list of institutions, and country index.

1:266   Carnegie Institution of Washington. [Guides to Manuscript Material for the History of the United States. 23 vols.] Washington, D.C.: Carnegie Institution, 1906–1943. A series of volumes compiled to help the research worker find material for the history of the United States located in foreign archives and libraries. Still useful, although in some cases more recent inventories have been made. Some of these guides have been listed separately in this Guide.

1:267   Duignan, Peter. *Handbook of American Resources for African Studies.* Stanford, Calif.: Hoover Institution, 1967. Duignan's valuable compilation surveys the holdings of 95 library and manuscript collections, 108 church and missionary libraries and archives, 95 art and ethnographic collections, and 4 business archives. There was no systematic attempt to cover North Africa, and the discussions of the holdings vary in depth. An index is included.

In the United States

1:268   Bhatt, Purnima Mehta. *Scholar's Guide to Washington, D.C. for African Studies.* Washington, D.C.: Smithsonian Institution Press, 1980. This is a detailed listing of libraries, archives, manuscript and film collections, and government agencies. The scope of each collection is outlined.

1:269   Billington, Ray A. *Guides to American History Manuscript Collections in Libraries of the United States.* New York: Peter Smith, 1952. This essay was reprinted from the *Mississippi Valley Historical Review* 38:3 (1951).

1:270   Carman, Harry J., and Thompson, Arthur W. *A Guide to the Principal Sources for American Civilization, 1800–1900, in the City of New York: Printed Materials.* New York: Columbia University Press, 1962. This guide contains an extensive bibliography.

1:271   Grant, Steven A. *Scholar's Guide to Washington, D.C. for Russian/Soviet Studies.* Washington, D.C.: Smithsonian Institution Press, 1977. A detailed listing of libraries, archives, manuscript and film collections, museums, data banks, publications, and government agencies. The scope of each collection is outlined.

1:272   Griffin, Grace G., ed. *A Guide to Manuscripts Relating to American History in British Repositories Reproduced for the Library of Congress.* Washington, D.C.: Library of Congress, 1946. A compilation of the manuscripts reproduced and available at the Library of Congress. Most of the collections are pertinent for the Revolution, including the Carlisle manuscripts and many others. The collection has been greatly increased since the publication of this guide, however.

1:273   Grow, Michael. *Scholar's Guide to Washington, D.C. for Latin American and Caribbean Studies.* Washington, D.C.: Smithsonian Institution Press, 1979. A detailed listing of libraries, archives, manuscripts and film collections, plus institutions and government agencies. The scope of each collection is outlined.

1:274   Gustafson, Milton O., ed. *The National Archives and Foreign Relations Research.* Athens: Ohio University Press, 1974. This volume includes essays on the manuscript holdings of the National Archives and Records Service relating to foreign relations. Extensive bibliography.

1:275   Hamer, Philip M., ed. *A Guide to Archives and Manuscripts in the United States.* New Haven: Yale University Press, 1961. Prepared under the auspices of the U.S. National Publications Commission, it has been superseded by *Directory of Archives and Manuscript Repositories* (1:284).

1:276   Harrison, John T. *Guide to Materials on Latin America in the National Archives.* Washington, D.C.: National Archives and Records Service, 1961. Harrison covers the period from 1774 to the first half of the 20th century, including material from the General Records of the United States, which pertain to topics such as boundary commission and boundary disputes, and records of the Department of State, Treasury, War and Navy.

1:277   Lowenstein, Linda, comp. *Government Resources Available for Foreign Affairs Research.* Washington, D.C.: G.P.O., 1965. This directory records unclassified resources available to scholars in 59 different government offices.

1:278   Matthews, William. *American Diaries in Manuscript, 1580–1954: A Descriptive Bibliography.* Athens: University of Georgia Press, 1974. A chronological listing of more than 5,000 unpublished diaries, including those published only in part, it gives name, date of diary, brief statement of contents if known, and location. Author index.

1:279   Morgan, Dole L., and Hammond, George P., eds. *A Guide to the Manuscript Collections of the Bancroft Library.* 2 vols. to date. Berkeley: University of California Press, 1963–. Volume 1 covers the entire West from Alaska to Arizona and from Texas to Hawaii, excluding California. The manuscripts are arranged by states and annotated. Volume 2 (1972) contains many important manuscripts and collections of manuscripts pertaining to the history and politics of Mexico and Central America, from the pre-Columbian era to the late 19th century. These are arranged alphabetically by author and/or title and are well annotated, with an index. Presumably, volume 3 will cover California.

1:280 O'Neill, James E. "Copies of French Manuscripts for American History in the Library of Congress." *Journal of American History* 51:4 (1965), 674–91. A listing of the rapidly growing collection at the Library of Congress, which includes many copies of collections critical to the American Revolution. In addition, the microfilming of the complete *Correspondance Politique* for the period has been finished. The author notes that most of the works listed are available on interlibrary loan. See also Nasatir and Monell (1:295).

1:281 Ulibarri, George S., and Harrison, John P. *Guide to Materials on Latin America in the National Archives of the United States.* Washington, D.C.: National Archives and Records Service, 1974. This guide covers all branches and departments of the U.S. government, with a name and subject index. The appendixes include lists of National Archives publications relating to Latin America, diplomatic and consular records from Latin America. This is definitive work. Updates Harrison's *Guide* (1:276).

1:282 U.S. Library of Congress. *The National Union Catalog of Manuscript Collections.* Hamden, Conn.: Shoe String Press, 1962. Published annually for the period 1959 to 1971, it includes cards for more than 29,000 manuscript collections in 850 repositories and indicates availability of microfilm copies.

1:283 U.S. National Archives. *Records in the National Archives Relating to the Russian Empire and the Soviet Union.* National Archives Reference Information Paper no. 1. Washington, D.C., Aug., 1952. This guide describes the contents of record groups; arranged topically and chronologically. Index.

1:284 U.S. National Historical Publications and Records Commission. *Directory of Archives and Manuscript Repositories.* Washington, D.C.: National Archives, 1978. It provides a comprehensive finding aid to 3,200 archives and manuscript repositories, and has name-subject index and lists of types of repositories, e.g., public libraries. Replaces all previous listings of this nature, including Hamer's guide (1:275).

In Latin America and the Caribbean

1:285 Bell, Herbert C. F., and Parker, D. W. *Guide to British West Indian Archives Materials in London and in the Islands, for the History of the United States.* Washington, D.C.: Carnegie Institution, 1926. A guide to a body of widely scattered materials for the history of the British colonial empire in America and the United States before 1815 (earliest date is 1711). It covers the Colonial Office Papers preserved in the Public Record Office, London, as well as material in West Indian archives.

1:286 Bolton, Herbert E. *Guide to Materials for the History of the United States in the Archives of Mexico.* Washington, D.C.: Carnegie Institution, 1913. Reprint 1965. Materials cover all phases of Spanish exploration, settlement, wars, etc., in what is now the United States. It also covers all aspects of Mexican-U.S. relations. Essential for the researcher working with Mexican archival material. Unfortunately, individual citations are not given, on the index to the various volumes, and these are all listed in English. See also Chapman below.

1:287 Chapman, Charles E. *Catalogue of Materials in the Archivo General de Indias for the History of the Pacific Coast and the American Southwest.* Berkeley: University of California Press, 1919. Covers the Spanish period as well as the Mexican period in the western part of the United States. Its arrangement is similar to Bolton above, but the citations here are to specific items and are listed in Spanish. Many copies of the items in the Archivo General de Indias, Seville, are to be found in the Archivo General de la Nación in Mexico.

1:288 Hill, Roscoe R. *Descriptive Catalogue of the Documents Relating to the History of the United States in the "Papeles Procedentes de Cuba," Deposited in the Archivo General de Indias in Seville.* Washington, D.C.: Carnegie Institution, 1916. Reprint 1965. The 2,375 *legajos* of the *Papeles de Cuba* (1767–1865) came from the Archivo General de Cuba (Havana), which accessioned them in 1888–1889. Many of these documents were originally from Louisiana and Florida. Some went to the United States and were deposited in the Library of Congress in 1905. (See also Pérez, below). Most cover the history of the southern United States from 1761 to 1821. The catalog includes material on phases of Spanish administration, internal and external political history, relations with the United States, the Indian problem, and relationship with the capitan-general of Cuba. Bibliography. General Index.

1:289 Pérez, Luis Marino. *Guide to Materials for American History in Cuban Archives.* Washington, D.C.: Carnegie Institution, 1907. This description and history of the Havana archives includes a special section on Florida, one on the Louisiana Papers and also relations between Cuba and the United States, and on the administration of Cuba. Appendix lists documents in the Library of Congress and transcripts at Georgetown University as of 1907. See also Hill (1:288) for more on these documents.

In Europe

Beers, H. P., ed. *The French in North America: A bibliographical guide to French Archives, Reproductions, and Research Missions* (3:2) is a textual account of the bibliographical activities of institutions and individuals in obtaining reproductions of French documents relevant to American (primarily U.S.) history. Extensive bibliography of archival materials and detailed index.

1:290 Bonnel, Ulane, et al., eds. *Guide des Sources de l'histoire des Etats-Unis dans les Archives Françaises* [Guide of the sources of United States history in the French archives]. Paris: France Expansion, 1976. This project in honor of the U.S. bicentennial was conceived as an expansion of the invaluable *Guide to the Material for American History in the Libraries and Archives of Paris, Vol. II: Archives of the Ministry of Foreign Affairs* (1:294).

1:291 Crick, Bernard R., and Alman, Miriam, eds. *A Guide to Manuscripts Relating to America in Great Britain and Ireland.* London: Oxford University Press, 1961. The collections, 18th to 20th century, are listed by dates and general descriptions but without a complete breakdown of their extent and value. The work includes information on how to use the public and private archives and often if special permission is needed.

1:292 Golder, Frank A. *Guide to Materials for American History in Russian Archives.* 2 vols. Washington, D.C.: Carnegie Institution, 1917–1937. This annotated inventory of documents, primarily correspondence between the foreign ministry in St. Petersburg and the Russian ministry in Washington,

often summarizes the content of the messages in addition to noting the subject of the dispatch. Thus it is more than an archival directory.

Great Britain. Public Record Office. *The Second World War: A Guide to Documents in the Public Record Office* (25:6) is invaluable to the researcher who wishes to consult British records dealing with the diplomacy of World War II and includes much information on the Anglo-American relationship.

1:293 Horecky, Paul L., and Kraus, David H., eds. *East Central and Southeast Europe: A Handbook of Library and Archival Resources in North America.* Santa Barbara, Calif.: ABC-Clio, 1976. This long-needed guide profiles 43 research libraries, archives, and special institutions in North America with major East Central and Southeast European collections in the humanities, socioeconomic, and political sciences.

1:294 Leland, Waldo G., ed. *Guide to the Material for American History in the Libraries and Archives of Paris.* 2 vols. Washington, D.C.: Carnegie Institution, 1932–1943. Volume 2 of this series covers in detail the *fonds* of the Ministry of Foreign Affairs. Although dated, this work is indispensable for research in France in the manuscript collections for this period. An extensive summary of the contents of primary collections is included. In Paris and at the Library of Congress is an unpublished third volume of the series covering the *Correspondance Politique* with the United States to 1830. See Bonnel, et al. (1:290).

1:295 Nasatir, Abraham P., and Monell, Gary E., eds. *French Consuls in the United States: A Calendar of Their Correspondence in the Archives Nationales.* Washington, D.C.: Library of Congress, 1967. A useful volume containing information on commerce, loans, and trade between the two nations. The editors have calendared many of the more important documents. This work should be used in conjunction with O'Neill's (1:280) description of French manuscripts at the Library of Congress. It supplements Leland (1:294) and Bonnel (1:290). Indexed.

1:296 Robertson, James A. *List of Documents in Spanish Archives Relating to the History of the United States Which Have Been Printed or of Which Transcripts Are Preserved in American Libraries.* Washington, D.C.: Carnegie Institution, 1910. Material from Mexican archives, as well as Spanish, is given, since such data were often found in both archives. Listed in chronological order and divided in two sections: published documents and transcripts. Bibliography and index.

1:297 Shepherd, William R. *Guide to the Materials for the History of the United States in the Spanish Archives.* Washington, D.C.: Carnegie Institution, 1907. The material is taken from the general archives of Simancas, the Archivo Histórico Nacional, and the Archivo de Indias, Seville, and covers Nueva España [New Spain], Mexico, Cuba, Santo Domingo, and the southern part of the United States.

1:298 Thomas, Daniel H., and Case, Lynn M., eds. *Guide to the Diplomatic Archives of Western Europe.* Philadelphia: University of Pennsylvania Press, 1959. In separate articles, this volume offers descriptions of the archival collections of Austria, Belgium, Denmark, France, Germany, Great Britain, Italy, the Netherlands, Norway, Portugal, Spain, Sweden, Switzerland, Vatican City, and Bavaria, from the 18th century to the near mid-20th century. Appended to each chapter are lists of printed documentary materials and guides to manuscripts.

Guides to Public Documents and Document Collections

GUIDES TO PUBLIC DOCUMENTS

1:299 Brown, Everett S. *Manual of Government Publications: United States and Foreign.* New York: Appleton-Century-Crofts, 1950. Reprint 1964. A brief manual that discusses the government publications of the United States and various countries of the world and emphasizes international organizations and U.S. and British publications. It also covers the British Commonwealth and France, Germany, Austria, Russia, Italy, Ireland, Latin America, Near and Middle East, Japan, and China. Out-of-date, but still useful.

1:300 Childs, James B., ed. *Government Document Bibliography in the United States and Elsewhere.* 3d ed. Reprint 1964. Washington, D.C.: G.P.O., 1942.

Reprint 1964. Childs lists catalogs, indexes, and guides to the documents of each country, sometimes with brief annotations, in five sections: U.S., Confederate States of America, states, foreign countries, and the League of Nations.

U.S. Government

1:301 Boyd, Anne Morris, and Rips, Rae E., eds. *United States Government Publications.* 3d ed. rev. New York: Wilson, 1949. This volume includes information on the nature, distribution, and catalogs and indexes of U.S. government publications. It lists and describes important typical publications of the legislative, judicial, and executive branches.

1:302 *Cumulative Subject Index to the Monthly Catalog of United States Government Publications, 1900–1971.* Comp. by William W. Buchan and Edna M. Kanely. 15 vols. Washington, D.C.: Carrollton, 1973–1975. This index merges the numerous annual indexes of the *Monthly Catalog* with the two decennial and one six-month index (July–December 1934), plus new indexing for the previously unindexed issues (June 1906–December 1908), providing a subject approach in one alphabet to over 800,000 government publications from a 72-year period.

Declassified Documents Quarterly (24:4) is a quarterly guide to recently declassified government documents, cumulatively indexed and keyed to microfiche copies of the documents themselves.

1:303 Greely, Adolphus W., ed. *Public Documents of the First Fourteen Congresses, 1789–1817.* Washington, D.C.: G.P.O., 1900. This is a chronological listing by Congress number, then by type, with index of names. Supplement published in 1904.

1:304 Hasse, Adelaide R., ed. *Index to United States Documents Relating to Foreign Affairs, 1828–1861.* 3 vols. Washington, D.C.: G.P.O., 1914–1921. This index is essential for locating U.S. documents on foreign affairs from 1828 to 1861, for the years surveyed fall between the *American State Papers* and the Foreign Relations series. The index covers the reports of Congress, *Senate Executive Journal, Opinions of the Attorney General, Statutes-at-Large,* and *Congressional Globe,* and uses place (e.g., Cuba), name (e.g., John Forsyth), and subject (e.g., canals).

1:305 Hirschberg, H. S., and Melinat, Carl H., eds. *Subject Guide to United States Government Publica-*

tions. Chicago: American Library Association, 1947. This is a selection of materials considered most generally useful in libraries. Arranged by subject. Updated by Jackson, below.

1:306 Jackson, Ellen P., ed. *Subject Guide to Major United States Government Publications*. Chicago: American Library Association, 1968. Arranged by subjects, it is highly selective, covering the period from earliest times to 1967 and confined largely to books and serial publications.

1:307 Leidy, William P. *A Popular Guide to Government Publications*. 3d ed. New York: Columbia University Press, 1968. Leidy has information on about 3,000 titles, arranged by broad subject, a high percentage of them published between 1961 and 1966. Previous editions cover titles published between 1940 and 1962.

1:308 New York: Public Library. Research Libraries. *Catalog of Government Publications in the Research Libraries*. 40 vols. Boston: Hall, 1972. A photoreproduction of the catalog cards for more than a million volumes of government publications or public documents, it is arranged by political jurisdiction.

1:309 Poore, Benjamin P., ed. *A Descriptive Catalogue of the Government Publications of the United States, September 5, 1774–March 4, 1881.* 2 vols. Washington, D.C.: G.P.O., 1885. Reprint 1953. It lists and briefly describes the contents of the documents contained in the Serial Set: *House Documents, Senate Documents, Executive Documents,* and *House Reports.* The materials are cited in chronological order, and there is a general index. This catalogue contains valuable information but is difficult to use for quick reference because the index is incomplete, and not detailed or specific.

1:310 Schmeckebier, Lawrence F., and Eastin, Roy B. *Government Publications and Their Use*. 2d rev. ed. Washington, D.C.: Brookings Institution, 1961. This is a useful guide to government publications with descriptions, including classification and distribution, of catalogs and indexes, bibliographies, congressional publications, constitutions, court decisions, administrative regulations, presidential papers, foreign affairs, reports, organization and personnel, and maps. It includes a list of government periodicals, and microfacsimile editions of government publications. Most up-to-date source for explanations of the use of U.S. government publications and their indexes.

1:311 U.S. Department of the Interior. Division of Documents. *Comprehensive Index to the Publications of the United States Government, 1881–1893*. Ed. by John G. Ames. 2 vols. in 1. Washington, D.C.: G.P.O., 1905. This index bridges the gap between Poore's *Descriptive Catalogue* (1:309) and the first volume of the *Catalogue of the Public Documents of Congress and of Other Departments . . . 1893–1940* (1:317). It covers both congressional and departmental series for its period.

1:312 U.S. Department of State. *Publications of the Department of State: A Cumulative List from October 1, 1929 to January 1, 1953*. Washington, D.C.: G.P.O., 1954. Supplements published by the Government Printing Office in 1958 and 1961 cover the periods January 1, 1953, to December 31, 1957, and January 1, 1958, to December 31, 1960. Arranged alphabetically by subject, with an index by series.

1:313 U.S. House. Library. *Index to Congressional Committees Hearings in the Library of the United States House of Representatives Prior to January 1, 1951.* Washington, D.C.: G.P.O., 1954. The Senate and House lists differ, neither being complete; they include only the hearings in their respective libraries. However, coverage, especially for recent years, is fairly complete.

1:314 U.S. House. Library. *Supplemental Index to Congressional Committee Hearings, January 3, 1949 to January 3, 1955; 81st, 82d and 83d Congresses, in the Library of the United States House of Representatives.* Washington, D.C.: G.P.O., 1956.

1:315 U.S. Senate. Library. *Cumulative Index of Congressional Committee Hearings (Not Confidential in Character) from 74th Congress (Jan. 3, 1935) through 85th Congress (Jan. 3, 1959) in the United States Senate Library.* Washington, D.C.: G.P.O., 1959. The list is not complete. The three quadrennial supplements published by the G.P.O. in 1963, 1967, and 1971 cover the years 1959 (86th Congress) to 1971 (91st Congress).

1:316 U.S. Senate. Library. *Index of Congressional Committee Hearings (Not Confidential in Character) Prior to January 3, 1935 in the United States Senate Library.* Washington, D.C.: G.P.O., 1935. This list is not complete, includes hearings in Senate Library only.

1:317 U.S. Superintendent of Documents. *Catalog of the Public Documents of Congress and of Other*

Departments of the Government of the United States for the Period March 4, 1893 –December 31, 1940. 25 vols. Washington, D.C.: G.P.O., 1896–1945. This index, generally referred to as the *Document Catalog,* forms for the years 1893 to 1940 the permanent and complete catalog of all government publications both congressional and departmental. A dictionary catalog in form, listing all documents under author (governmental or personal), subject, and, when necessary, title; gives full catalog information for each book or pamphlet included.

1:318   U.S. Superintendent of Documents. *Checklist of United States Public Documents, 1789–1909.* 3d ed. rev. and enl. Washington, D.C.: G.P.O., 1911. An approximately complete checklist (not a catalog) that covers congressional documents through the 60th Congress, and department and bureau publications to the end of 1909. Replaces *Tables and Index* (1:320), but not its index section.

1:319   U.S. Superintendent of Documents. *Monthly Catalog of United States Government Publications.* Washington, D.C.: G.P.O., 1895–. Published monthly, this is a current bibliography of publications issued by all branches of the government, including both the congressional and the department and bureau publications. Supplements were published by the G.P.O. in 1947–1948 (3 vols.) for the years 1941–1942, 1943–1944, and 1945–1946.

1:320   U.S. Superintendent of Documents. *Tables of and Annotated Index to the Congressional Series of United States Public Documents (1817–1893).* Washington, D.C.: G.P.O., 1902. This table of American state papers and documents of the 15th through the 52d Congress includes an alphabetical subject index to these documents.

Foreign Governments

1:321   Gregory, Winifred, ed. *List of the Serial Publications of Foreign Governments, 1815–1931.* New York: Wilson, 1932. A union list of about 30,000 government serials in 85 U.S. libraries, it is arranged alphabetically by country.

1:322   Great Britain. *Index to Foreign Office Correspondence, 1920–1946.* 111 vols. London: Nendeln, 1969–1977. These indexes, made within the Foreign Office, refer to subjects, persons, and places. Also included within this set are indexes to "green" or "secret" papers.

1:323   International Committee for Social Sciences Documentation. *Etudes des Bibliographies Courantes des Publications Officielles Nationales: Guide Sommaire et Inventaire. A Study of Current Bibliographies of Official National Publications: Short Guide and Inventory.* Paris: UNESCO, 1958. It lists national bibliographies, official journals, document bibliographies, and legislative publications of all independent states. Introductory matter is in French and English; annotation sometimes in French and sometimes in English.

Mesa, Rosa Quintero, comp. *Latin American Serial Documents: A Holding List* (35:18) is a guide to accessible published documents (1808–1972) of Latin American countries, with a list of holdings in the United States.

International Organizations

1:324   Gregory, Winifred, ed. *International Congresses and Conferences, 1804–1937: A Union List of Their Publications Available in Libraries of the United States and Canada.* New York: Wilson, 1938. Arranged alphabetically by name of congress or conference, it excludes diplomatic congresses and conferences, and those held under the auspices of the League of Nations.

League of Nations

Aufricht, H. *Guide to League of Nations Publications: A Bibliographical Survey of the Work of the League, 1920–1947* (20:6) is arranged by broad subject with index. It is selective, but includes some confidential items and some not sold publicly, and also lists publications of affiliated organizations, such as the International Labor Office and the Permanent Court of International Justice.

1:325   Ghébali, Victor Y., and Ghébali, Catherine. *A Repertoire of League of Nations Serial Documents, 1919–1947.* 2 vols. Dobbs Ferry, N.Y.: Oceana, 1973. This is not an inventory of individual documents, but a survey of all the known series of documents covering league institutional structure and league activities in connection with the implementation of peace treaties, the maintenance of international peace and security, and the promotion of functional cooperation.

Reno, E. A. Jr., ed. *League of Nations Documents, 1919–1946: A Descriptive Guide and Key to the Microfilm Collection* (20:7) is for use with the microfilm edition of League of Nations documents published by Research Publications, but independently useful.

1:326   United Nations. Library. Geneva. *Repertoire des Données Publiées Reguliérement dans les Journaux Officials.* [Analysis of materials published regularly in official gazettes]. Geneva: The Library, 1958. This revised and expanded edition of an earlier list published by the League of Nations Library (1935) includes an inventory of the league's entire collection of official gazettes.

United Nations

1:327   Brimmer, Brenda; Wall, Linwood R.; Chamberlin, Waldo; and Hovet, Thomas, Jr. *A Guide to the Use of United Nations Documents (Including Reference to the Specialized Agencies and Special U.N. Bodies).* Rev. ed. Dobbs Ferry, N.Y.: Oceana, 1962. This excellent guide for the researcher using UN documents includes information on methods of research, basic tools and guides, and a selected subject guide. It is a vastly enlarged version of Carol C. Moor and Waldo Chamberlin's *How to Use United Nations Documents* (New York: New York University Press, 1952).

1:328   United Nations. Dag Hammarskjöld Library. *UNDEX: United Nations Documents Index: Series A: Subject Index.* New York: United Nations, 1970–. Published monthly, except July and August, it provides the information needed for locating a document on a given topic through its UN document symbol. It includes references to the subject matter of documents and publications issued by the UN for which analytical annotations have been stored in computer-based files.

1:329   United Nations. Dag Hammarskjöld Library. *UNDEX: United Nations Documents Index: Series B: Country Index.* New York: United Nations, 1970–. Published monthly, except July and August, it lists member states alphabetically, indicating participation in UN activities. It gives type of action or participation, subject on which action was taken, and document symbol.

1:330   United Nations. Dag Hammarskjöld Library. *UNDEX: United Nations Documents Index: Series C: List of Documents Issued.* New York: United Nations, 1974–. Published monthly, except July and August, it contains a listing and the bibliographical description of all documents and publications of the UN, except restricted material and internal papers, and all printed publications of the International Court of Justice.

1:331   United Nations. Dag Hammarskjöld Library. *UNDIS: The United Nations Documentation Information System: A Handbook of Products and Services.* New York: United Nations, 1974. Provides information on the computer-based information storage and retrieval system designed to facilitate access to official documents and publications of the UN, and describes the UNDEX series and its use. The *Index to Proceedings* series and *Index to Resolutions* series are available from *UNDIS.*

1:332   United Nations. Dag Hammarskjöld Library. *Checklist of United Nations Documents, 1946–1949.* New York: United Nations, 1949–1953. Issued in parts, each one is devoted to the documents of a particular organ of the United Nations. Detailed subject index.

1:333   United Nations. Dag Hammarskjöld Library. *Government Gazettes: An Annotated List of Gazettes Held in the Dag Hammarskjöld Library* New York: United Nations, 1964. This is an alphabetical list, by country, of gazettes held as of September 1964.

1:334   United Nations. Dag Hammarskjöld Library. *United Nations Documents Index.* 24 vols. New York: United Nations, 1950–1973. Published monthly (January 1950–December 1973), this index continues the *Checklist of United Nations Documents* (vol. 1–13, 1950–1962). It includes an annual cumulative index which supersedes indexes of the monthly issues. Beginning with volume 14 (1963), index and the *United Nations Documents Index: Cumulative Checklist* supersede monthly issues. Reprint 1974.

1:335   United Nations. Dag Hammarskjöld Library. *United Nations Documents Index: Cumulative Checklist.* 11 vols. New York: United Nations, 1964–1975. An annual publication (volumes 14–24, 1963–1973), it supersedes the monthly issues of the *United Nations Documents Index* and contains consolidated lists of all documents and publications issued by the United Nations and the International Court of Justice during the year. Now superseded by *UNDEX: United Nations Documents Index.*

1:336   United Nations. Economic and Social Council. *The United Nations System: International Bibliography.* Vol. 2A (1965–1970), vol. 2B (1971–1975). Munich: United Nations Economic and Social Council, 1977.

1:337   United Nations. Office of Conference Services. *United Nations Official Records, 1948–1962.*

New York: United Nations, 1963. This is a complete listing of the official records by year, or by series.

1:338 United Nations. Office of Conference Services. *United Nations Publications: Catalogue, 1945/63 –*. New York: United Nations, 1964–. Arranged in 17 categories, each title is preceded by an identifying sales number.

Winton, H. N. M., ed. *Publications of the United Nations System: A Reference Guide* (38:11) presents a brief overview of the organizations of the UN and their publications, indicates a number of valuable reference works published by these organizations, and provides a comprehensive list of their periodicals and selected other recurrent publications.

Document Collections

Annual Series

1:339 *Documents on American Foreign Relations.* New York: Simon & Schuster, 1939–. A compilation of major public documents on American foreign policy, published annually by the Council on Foreign Relations and intended to accompany its *United States in World Affairs* volumes (1:147). Beginning in 1971, the title changed to *American Foreign Relations, 19–: A Documentary Record.*

1:340 *Documents on International Affairs.* 31 vols. New York: Oxford University Press, 1929–1973. For the years covered (1928–1963), this is the best source for the official documents and public statements of foreign leaders. Designed as a supplement to its *Survey of International Affairs* (1:146); publication was suspended with the year 1963.

Other Collections

1:341 Challener, Richard D., ed. *From Isolation to Containment, 1921–1952: Three Decades of American Foreign Policy from Harding to Truman.* New York: St. Martin's Press, 1970. Included are short excerpts from speeches, diplomatic documents, books dealing with policy during the period.

1:342 Ferrell, Robert H., ed. *America as a World Power, 1872–1945.* Columbia: University of South Carolina, 1971. The documentary history of American policy during the above years, with introduction, headnotes and/or endnotes.

Manning, W. R., ed. *Diplomatic Correspondence of the United States Concerning the Independence of the Latin-American Nations* (7:4) consists of three volumes arranged by country for the period 1809 to 1830.

Manning, W. R., ed. *The Diplomatic Correspondence of the United States: Inter-American Affairs, 1831–1860* (7:5) consists of 12 volumes organized by countries.

1:343 Manning, William R., ed. *Diplomatic Correspondence of the United States: Canadian Relations, 1784–1860.* 4 vols. Washington, D.C.: Carnegie Endowment for International Peace, 1940–1945. These volumes contain documents relating to the relations of the United States with Britain and France, as well as with British Canada.

1:344 Richardson, James D., ed. *A Compilation of the Messages and Papers of the Presidents.* 11 vols. New York: Bureau of National Literature, 1896–1910. These volumes contain the official papers of the presidents (1789–1900).

Schlesinger, A.M. Jr., ed. *The Dynamics of World Power: A Documentary History of U.S. Foreign Policy, 1945–1973.* (24:6) consists of five volumes, most of which have been cited separately in the *Guide.*

1:345 U.S. Senate. Committee on Foreign Relations. *The Legislative Origins of American Foreign Policy: The Senate Foreign Relations Committee in Executive Session, 1913–1933, 1947–1950.* 10 vols. New York: Garland, 1979. This set reprints the proceedings of the Foreign Relations Committee from 1913 to 1933, and after a period when transcripts of executive sessions were discontinued, continues with the committee's "Historical Series" for the early cold war years. The later years are valuable for the origins of the Truman Doctrine, NATO, Marshall Plan, and other economic aid programs.

Public Opinion

1:346 Cantril, Hadley, and Strunk, Mildred, eds. *Public Opinion, 1935–1946.* Princeton, N.J.: Princeton University Press, 1951. This volume collects many of the early efforts to poll public opinion. It contains much material relating to foreign affairs.

1:347 Columbia Broadcasting System (CBS News). *Face the Nation: The Collected Transcripts from CBS Radio and Television Broadcasts, 1954–1971.* 14 vols. New York: Holt Information Systems, 1972–. The complete, unedited transcripts of the television and radio interviews beginning in 1954. Included are such people as John Foster Dulles, Nikita Khrushchev, and Henry A. Kissinger. Indexed.

1:348 Gallup, George H. *The Gallup Poll: Public Opinion, 1935–1971.* 3 vols. New York: Random House, 1972. These volumes include data from some 7,000 polls dealing with all aspects of national life, with considerable attention paid to foreign affairs. Arranged chronologically; indexed. Updated for 1972 to 1977 (1978), for 1978 (1979), and for 1979 (1980).

National Collections

United States

1:349 *American State Papers.* Ed. by Walter Lowrie and Matthew St. C. Clarke. 38 vols. Washington, D.C.: Gales & Seaton, 1832–1861. These volumes, published by direction of Congress, contain a mass of documentary material bearing upon the early history of the United States. The six volume subseries, *Class I: Foreign Relations,* is of course most directly useful to diplomatic historians, but others, notably *Class II: Indian Affairs* and *Class IV: Commerce and Navigation* also repay examination. Unfortunately, the editing is not only careless but consciously distorted, so that the volumes must be used with extreme care.

1:350 Claussen, Martin P., ed. *The National State Papers of the United States: Texts of Documents (1789–1817).* 24 vols. to date. Wilmington, Del.: Glazier, 1980–. This set is to cover the administrations of Washington to Madison, and will contain the full text of all extant bills, legislative resolutions, amendments, petitions, presidential messages, Senate and House committee reports, as well as all known supplementary material. The initial 24 volumes cover the Adams administration.

Declassified Documents Quarterly [1975–] (24:4) lists abstracts of recently declassified documents of various agencies of the U.S. government. Abstracts are keyed to a microfiche collection of copies of the declassified documents. A retrospective collection was published in 1977, with cumulative indexes for each year, and containing over 8,000 documents.

U.S. Arms Control and Disarmament Agency. *Documents on Disarmament* [1960–] (40:14) is a basic collection, it supplements U.S. Department of State *Documents on Disarmament, 1945–1959* (40:15).

1:351 U.S. Congress. *The Debates and Proceedings in the Congress of the United States, 1st to 18th Con-* gresses, *March 3, 1789–May 27, 1824.* 42 vols. Washington, D.C.: Gales & Seaton, 1834–1856. This series, usually called and often footnoted as the *Annals of Congress,* is neither complete nor accurate. Nevertheless, there is no substitute to which one can turn for accounts of congressional debates.

1:352 U.S. Congress. *Register of Debates in Congress: 18th-25th Congress, 6 December 1824–16 October 1837.* 14 vols. in 29. Washington, D.C.: Gales & Seaton, 1825–1937.

1:353 U.S. Congress. *The Congressional Globe: 23rd Congress to 42nd Congress, 2 December 1833–3 March 1873.* 46 vols in 109. Washington, D.C.: The Globe, 1834–1873.

1:354 U.S. Congress. *Congressional Record: Proceedings and Debates of the Congress: 43rd Congress, 4 March 1873–.* Washington, D.C.: G.P.O., 1873–. The above three sets contain texts of debates and speeches as well as the details of congressional proceedings that have been reported in official and unofficial publications since 1824.

1:355 U.S. Department of State. *American Foreign Policy, 1950–1955: Basic Documents.* 2 vols. Pub. no. 6446. Washington, D.C.: G.P.O., 1957. Designed as a supplement to *A Decade of American Foreign Policy: Basic Documents, 1941–1949* (23:20), this collection includes principal messages, addresses, statements, reports, diplomatic notes, and treaties.

1:356 U.S. Department of State. *American Foreign Policy: Current Documents, 1956–1967.* 12 vols. Washington, D.C.: G.P.O., 1959–1969. This is an official compendium. See also its predecessor, *American Foreign Policy, 1950–1955: Basic Documents* (1:355).

1:357 U.S. Department of State. *Department of State Bulletin.* Washington, D.C.: G.P.O., 1939–. The bulletin publishes important statements and documents relating to U.S. foreign relations. For its predecessor, *Press Releases,* see 1:361.

1:358 U.S. Department of State. *Foreign Relations of the United States.* Washington, D.C.: G.P.O., 1861–. A massive official series containing several hundred volumes, *Foreign Relations* prints selected materials from State Department archival files. Volumes contain correspondence, notes, memoranda, documents, etc., produced during one calendar year, although from time to time special volumes dealing with specific diplomatic episodes are issued. Volumes related to the early 1950s are currently being released. For a general review of the series, focusing on the volumes for 1943 to 1946, see Richard W. Leopold's "The Foreign Relations Series Revisited: One Hundred Plus Ten," *Journal of American History* 59:4 (1973), 935–57 and William Z. Slany's "History of the Foreign Relations Series," Society for Historians of American Foreign Relations *Newsletter* 12:1 (1981), 10–19.

1:359   U.S Department of State. "General Records of the Department of State, RG 59 and RG 84." Microfilmed. Washington, D.C.: National Archives, n.d. These microfilmed records, available at many universities and regional offices of the National Archives, are arranged in several sets. For a description of these various sets, see the most recent National Archives' *List of National Archives Microfilm Publications.* Record Group 84 includes records of foreign service posts to the year 1912.

1:360   U.S. Department of State. *Press Conferences of the Secretaries of State, 1922–1974.* 15 microfilm reels. Wilmington, Del.: Scholarly Resources, n.d. A typescript, verbatim record of the press conferences of the secretaries of state, microfilmed from the collections of the library of the Office of Press Relations, Department of State, it also includes various Department of State press releases. An important source for research on the views of department officials.

1:361   U.S. Department of State. *Press Releases.* Washington, D.C: Department of State, 1929–1939. From October 5, 1929 to June 24, 1939, the Department of State issued weekly *Press Releases* which carried information about current policy, major speeches of the president or secretary of state on foreign policy, and like information. These are bound in volumes by year in major libraries. This publication was replaced on July 1, 1939, by the *Department of State Bulletin* (1:357), with an expanded format and more analysis of the government policy.

1:362   U.S. President. *Public Papers of the Presidents of the United States.* Washington, D.C.: G.P.O., 1960–. These volumes constitute an official compilation of the public messages, speeches, and statements of the presidents. Especially valuable are the recapitulations of presidential press conferences. Each volume is indexed separately and there are several volumes for each presidency. The presidency of Harry S Truman was the first for which these volumes were prepared, and all subsequent presidents' public papers have been

published in this official format. *The Cumulated Indexes to the Public Papers of the Presidents,* 5 vols. (Millwood, N.Y.: KTO, 1977), cover Truman through Nixon.

Great Britain

1:363   Great Britain. *British and Foreign State Papers.* London: Ridgway, 1812–. Compiled and indexed by the librarian and keeper of the papers in the British Foreign Office, these annual papers include correspondence between Britain and the United States since 1812. Volume 64 indexes volumes 1–63; volume 93 indexes volumes 65–92; volume 115 indexes volumes 94–114; volume 138 indexes volumes 116–137.

1:364   Great Britain. *House of Commons: Sessional Papers, 1801–1900.* London: H.M.S.O., n.d. Available on microprint cards and in typescript, these papers include correspondence of Canadian officials with both England and the United States.

1:365   Great Britain. *Parliamentary Debates.* Vols. 1–41 (1803–1820); 2d ser., vols. 1–25 (1820–1830); 3d ser., vols. 1–356 (1830–1890/91); 4th ser., vols. 1–199 (1892–1908); 5th ser., Commons, vol. 1– (1909–), Lords, vol. 1– (1909–). Publisher varies. The first through fourth series are unofficial, nor do they contain complete or verbatim accounts of the debates—they are generally known and cited as *Hansard* or *Debates* (Hansard). In 1909, with the fifth series, the *Parliamentary Debates* became official, complete, and verbatim; H.M. Stationery Office became the publisher.

1:366   Irish University Press Series on British Parliamentary Papers. *United States of America* [1802–1899]. 60 vols. Shannon: Irish University Press, n.d. These volumes collect official British "sessional and command" papers that relate to three topics: (1) diplomatic correspondences, negotiations, treaties, etc.: the War of 1812, the Canadian boundary, slavery issues, the Civil War, and the Treaty of Washington; (2) economic information and statistics, especially investment and trade; and (3) special studies, education, labor relations, etc.

Stock, L. F. *Proceedings and Debates of the British Parliaments Respecting North America* (3:22) covers 1542 to 1754.

Webster, C. K., ed. *Britain and the Independence of Latin America, 1812–1830: Select Documents from the Foreign Office Archives* (7:6) includes communications between London, European governments, and the United States.

Others

Australia. Department of Foreign Affairs. *Documents on Australian Foreign Policy, 1937–1949* (32:9–32:10) has published the initial volumes, dealing with 1937 to 1939. These volumes are indispensable.

Hurewitz, J. C., ed. *The Middle East and North Africa in World Politics: A Documentary Record* (18:3) is one of the most authoritative document collections for this region.

1:367 *Los Presidentes de México ante la nación: Informes, manifiestos y documentos de 1821 á 1966* [The presidents of Mexico before the nation: decrees, statements and documents, 1821–1966]. 5 vols. Mexico, D.F.: Presidente, 1966. These volumes contain an extensive collection of presidential decrees, statements, and documents from 1821 to 1966.

1:368 [U.S.S.R.]. *Milestones of Soviet Foreign Policy, 1917–1967.* Trans. David Skvirsky. Moscow: Progress Publishers, 1967. Fifty years after the Russian Revolution the Soviets present 73 important documents on foreign policy, including a lengthy narrative summary of events.

International Law

1:369 Deák, Francis, ed. *American International Law Cases, 1783–1968.* 19 vols. Dobbs Ferry, N.Y.: Oceana, 1971–1978. A full and continuing compilation of cases arranged under general categories of international law, with special emphasis on executive and judicial influences. Editorial introductions, indexing, and explanatory footnotes are minimal.

1:370 Friedman, Leon., comp. *The Law of War: A Documentary History.* 2 vols. New York: Random House, 1972. The documents in this collection range from Hugo Grotius's *The Law of War and Peace* to the courts-martial of William L. Calley, Jr., and Ernest Medina (1600–1972). The foreword by Telford Taylor and Friedman's introduction are helpful surveys of the history of international law.

1:371 Hackworth, Green H., ed. *Digest of International Law.* 8 vols. Washington, D.C.: G.P.O., 1940–1944. Hackworth, as legal adviser of the State Department, compiled this series as a supplement to John Bassett Moore's eight-volume set. It contains

portions of diplomatic exchanges, rulings, treaties, and other data on recognition, expansion, neutrality, intervention, the Monroe Doctrine, extradition, nationality, and diplomatic codes (1789–1940). Volume 8 is an index. See M. M. Whiteman (38:24).

Moore, J. B., ed. *History and Digest of International Arbitrations . . .* [1795–1898] (16:11).

Moore, J. B., ed. *International Adjudications, Ancient and Modern: History and Documents: Modern Series* (16:12).

1:372 Moore, John Bassett. *A Digest of International Law.* 8 vols. Washington, D.C.: G.P.O., 1906. Reprint 1970. These volumes cover law as revealed through discussions, treaties, agreements, awards, precedents, and policies enunciated by government officials. The emphasis is on the U.S. role. Moore's work was the third such compilation; the first was prepared by John L. Cadwalader, *A Digest . . .* (1877), and the second by Francis Wharton, *Digest of International Law of the United States,* 3 vols. (1886).

Whiteman, M. M. *Digest of International Law* (38:24) is a successor to the work of Green H. Hackworth (1:371).

Treaties

1:373 Bevans, Charles I., comp. *Treaties and Other International Agreements of the United States of America, 1776–1949.* 12 vols. Washington, D.C.: G.P.O., 1968–. Here is the definitive compilation of U.S. treaties prior to the year 1950, superseding the collection compiled by William M. Mallory et al. (1:375). The first four volumes of the series are for multilateral treaties, and thereafter the bilateral treaties are alphabetical by country.

Davenport, F., C. O. Paullin, and eds. *European Treaties Bearing on the History of the United States and Its Dependencies* [1455–1697] (3:16).

1:374 League of Nations. *Treaty Series: Publication of Treaties and International Engagements Registered with the Secretariat of the League.* 205 vols. London: Harrison, 1920–1946. These volumes print treaties no. 1 to 4834, September 1920 to 1944/1946.

1:375 Mallory, William M., et al., comps. *Treaties, Conventions, International Acts, Protocols, and Agreements between the United States and Other Powers, 1776–1937.* 4 vols. Washington, D.C.: G.P.O., 1909–1938. Published in four volumes under varying editorship, this treaty set is still useful, but the treaty texts soon will all be superseded by the treaties published in the series compiled by Charles I. Bevans (1:373).

1:376 Miller, David Hunter, ed. *Treaties and Other International Acts of the United States of America, 1776–1863*. 8 vols. Washington, D.C.: G.P.O., 1931–1948. Dated but still useful, this collection was the standard reference for years.

1:377 United Nations. *Treaty Series: Treaties and International Agreements Registered or Filed and Re-* *corded with the Secretariat of the United Nations, 1946/1947–*. New York, 1947–.

1:378 *United States Treaties and Other International Agreements*. Washington, D.C.: G.P.O., 1950–. This is the only major set that is a continuing and up-to-date register of official American agreements. Volumes 1–30, to 1980 are in 85 volumes. A 5-volume cumulative index exists for 1950 to 1975, *UST Cumulative Index* (Buffalo, N.Y.: William S. Hein, 1973–1977). The cumulative index also has a subject index (volume 4).

2

Overviews:
Diplomatic Surveys,
Themes, and Theories

Contributing Editor

RICHARD DEAN BURNS

California State University
Los Angeles

Contributors

Wilton Fowler

University of Washington

Alan K. Henrikson

Tufts University

Contents

Introduction

During the past half-century diplomatic historians have come to focus less on ambassadors and foreign secretariats, and more on the forces shaping foreign policy, the implications of foreign relations, and the nature of global affairs. They have scrutinized, with varying degrees of success, domestic factors such as the impact of public opinion, economic influences, strategic planning, and cultural values for their role in the formulation of America's various foreign policies. Diplomatic historians also have expanded their study of the United States' relations with areas other than Europe, although Sub-Saharan Africa and South and Southeast Asia are still inadequately treated.

This chapter (and Chapter 24 for the post-1945 era) collects many of the broad thematic studies and geographical surveys, which often overlap several chapters, in order to provide here a convenient and coherent sampling of the basic accounts. Many of the references cited here were extracted from the lists of annotated works submitted by other contributing editors as part of their original manuscripts. Thus, much of the credit for this broad survey of themes and geographical works belongs to these perceptive contributors.

Reviewing diplomatic history's vitality is an ongoing exercise. Among the many essays which attempt to gauge its vigor and ills, two are particularly useful for a quick diagnosis. Alexander DeConde's AHA pamphlet, *American Diplomatic History in Transformation* (1:59), examines the corpus by briefly surveying the standard literature. Richard W. Leopold's article, "The History of United States Foreign Policy: Past, Present, and Future" (2:3), reviews growth of the profession from its infancy and offers an insightful discussion of the shortcomings of its practitioners. One seeking a more extensive diagnosis than offered by these essays (and the ones listed below) should peruse the Society for Historians of American Foreign Relations *Newsletter*. Past issues have carried such examinations as A. DeConde's "What's Wrong with American Diplomatic History" (1:2 [1970], 1–16),

N. A. Graebner's "The State of Diplomatic History" (4:1 [1973], 2–12), D. S. Patterson's "What's Wrong (and Right) with American Diplomatic History? A Diagnosis and Prescription" (9:3 [1978], 1–14), B. Perkins "What's Good for the United States is Good for the World, and Vice Versa: Reflections of a Diplomatic Historian" (6:1 [1975], 2–12), and J. H. Wilson's "Foreign Policy Trends since 1920" (8:3 [1977], 1–17).

Most recently *Diplomatic History* (5:4 [Fall 1981], 353–82) printed a "symposium" in which a half-dozen members of SHAFR expressed their views on the current state of diplomatic history. This soul-searching was prompted by Charles S. Maier's essay "Marking Time: The Historiography of International Relations," which appeared in Michael Kammen, ed., *The Past before Us: Contemporary Historical Writing in the United States* (Ithaca, N.Y.: Cornell University Press, 1980), 355–87. These various opinions on Maier's critical assessment, taken together, provide an excellent view of the "state of the art" at the beginning of the 1980s.

Topics and items appearing in the "Themes and Theory" segment have been arbitrarily chosen and thus may appear to be rather eclectic. Obviously many other topics could have been listed, such as "Progressivism and Foreign Policy," "Dependency Theory," and "Manifest Destiny and Social Darwinism," for example, which appear in Chapters 13, 35, and 12 respectively. (For an introduction to themes not listed in the *Guide*, one should consult A. DeConde's *Encyclopedia of American Foreign Policy* [1:164]). The criteria for selecting the topics included here grew out of the realization, during the editing of the *Guide*, that these particular topics were being duplicated in several chapters. Thus, the more general treatments of "themes and theory" were grouped here and cross-referenced to specific chapters. Specific references to works which address these topics, but which relate them to a particular historical episode or era, have generally been left in the chapter that covers that chronological period or deals with that theme. Consequently, the reader is advised to check each subtopic for cross-reference suggestions.

The theme "Geographical Ideas and Context" was suggested, and subsequently developed, by Alan K. Henrikson, who believes that diplomatic historians have generally neglected the policymaker's perception of distances and terrain. His essay, "America's Changing Place in the World: From 'Periphery' to 'Centre'?" (2:35), focuses on these spatial complexities. Also included under this topic are H. J. Mackinder's *Diplomatic Ideals and Reality* (2:38) and C. S. Gray's *The Geopolitics of the Nuclear Era* (2:45), which seek to examine the geopolitical aspects of policy.

The nineteenth-century concept of manifest destiny is well surveyed in F. Merk's *Manifest Destiny and Mission in American History* (2:52); however, America's role in support of internationalism has not received similar coverage. W. F. Kuehl's "Internationalism" (2:59) and B. C. Shafer's "Webs of Common Interests: Nationalism, Internationalism and Peace" (2:61) provide fine introductions to internationalism. Isolationism has come in for more thorough study. Of the works collected here, S. Adler's *The Isolationist Impulse* (20:121) is the basic study. Although there are many fine accounts of the immigrant's hazards of passage and difficulties in establishing a new home in America, there appears to be little consideration of immigration policy as it relates to American foreign relations generally. M. T. Bennett (2:70) and R. A. Divine (2:71) examine the debates over more recent immigration restrictions, yet this field should be a fertile one for the student who views the issue more broadly. Missionaries and philanthropists have come under considerable criticism of late. Often they have been seen as advance agents of American entrepreneurship or American governmental interests, and, indeed, often they were. But they did not always stand in the way of indigenous nationalism. Studies which survey the role of American missionaries, philanthropists, and educators include M. Curti's *American Philanthrophy Abroad* (2:72), Curti and Birr's *Prelude to Point Four* (2:73), and P. A. Varg's "Missionaries" (2:81).

Any attempt to identify and delineate schools of diplomatic history and the "theories" that have influenced them is bound to evoke criticism, especially regarding the references selected, the groups used, and the labels employed. As several contributing editors have wrestled with this problem, see for example the introductions to Chapters 24 and 39, any attempt here to elaborate on such classifications would be redundant. However, it is hoped that these references and subsections are generally representative of two basic approaches to the study of foreign relations. H. Magdoff's *The Age of Imperialism* (2:91) and W. A. Williams's *The Tragedy of American Diplomacy* (2:99) emphasize economic considerations,

while G. F. Kennan's *American Diplomacy, 1900 – 1950* (2:111) and H. J. Morgenthau's *Politics among Nations* (2:112) stress politico-military factors.

Political scientists have long focused on the problems of policymaking; consequently, the sections dealing with special studies and policy formation have drawn upon many of their works. However, no attempt has been made to provide here more than a sampling of these efforts; for more references on these themes (and several others), see Elmer Plischke's recent *U.S. Foreign Relations: A Guide to Information Sources* (1:63).

Some diplomatic historians have sought to employ various of these analytical methods in a multidisciplinary approach. For example, Roger Dingman profitably used the "bureaucratic politics" model in his *Power in the Pacific* (20:153), while several others have successfully utilized multidisciplinary techniques in studying public opinion. Akira Iriye (2:121 – 122) offers some advice to historians desiring to study diplomacy as a process of intercultural relations, that is, to examine national domestic desires in relationship to the nation's foreign policy as well as international relations as interaction among cultural systems. Thus while multiarchival research and language skills are important, many of these analytical techniques suggested by other disciplines could and should also be incorporated by diplomatic historians into their studies.

Diplomatic History: Surveys

STATE OF THE ART

DeConde, A., ed. *American Diplomatic History in Transformation* (1:59) briefly surveys the standard literature. Earlier editions are entitled *New Interpretations in American Foreign Policy.*

2:1 Dennis, Donnie L. "A History of American Diplomatic History." Ph.D. diss., University of California, Santa Barbara, 1971. Dennis reviews the historiography and interpretative "schools" of American diplomatic history, and casts some light upon the development of diplomatic history as an academic discipline.

2:2   Evans, Laurence. "The Dangers of Diplomatic History." In Herbert J. Bass, ed., *The State of American History*. Chicago: Quadrangle, 1970, pp. 142–56. Evans analyzes what he believes are several weaknesses in diplomatic history as a field of independent study and finds that inherent limitations of historians' present approach to the study of foreign policy have affected historical writing.

2:3   Leopold, Richard W. "The History of United States Foreign Policy: Past, Present, and Future." In C. F. Delzell, ed. *The Future of History*. Nashville, Tenn.: Vanderbilt University Press, 1977, pp. 231–46. Leopold, one of the founding fathers of American diplomatic history, reviews its evolution since 1938. Practising historians will find his many observations insightful, and novices will find them most instructive.

2:4   May, Ernest R. "Emergence to World Power." In John Higham, ed., *The Reconstruction of American History*. New York: Harpers, 1962, pp. 180–96. May analyzes how the emergence of the United States to world power has affected the writing of American diplomatic history.

2:5   McCormick, Thomas J. "The State of American Diplomatic History." In Herbert J. Bass, ed., *The State of American History*. Chicago: Quadrangle, 1970, pp. 119–41. McCormick argues for a conception of diplomatic history as the study of the total impact of societies upon other societies and implies that diplomatic historians should also be social historians.

2:6   Neu, Charles E. "The Changing Interpretive Structure of American Foreign Policy." In John Braeman, Robert H. Bremner, and David Brody, eds., *Twentieth-Century American Foreign Policy*. Columbus: Ohio State University Press, 1971, pp. 1–57. Neu analyzes the changing assumptions and presuppositions underlying the writing of American diplomatic history from the 1920s to the present.

2:7   Trask, David F. "Writings on American Foreign Relations: 1957 to the Present." In John Braeman, Robert H. Bremner, and David Brody, eds., *Twentieth-Century American Foreign Policy*. Columbus: Ohio State University Press, 1971, pp. 59–118. Trask surveys the major scholarly works on American foreign policy and diplomacy.

DIPLOMATIC HISTORIES

2:8   Anderson, George L., ed. *Issues and Conflicts: Studies in Twentieth Century American Diplomacy*. Lawrence: University Press of Kansas, 1959. Reprint 1969. This collection of essays focuses on such themes as China, the Middle East, Palestine, revisionism between the two world wars, collective security, immigrants, the Kellogg Pact. Many of the essays are cited separately through the *Guide*.

2:9   Bailey, Thomas A. *A Diplomatic History of the American People*. 10th ed. Englewood Cliffs, N.J.: Prentice-Hall, 1980. The most popular textbook in the field, it is detailed, episodic, and witty. An accessible book for beginners, while veterans have come to rely on its extensive and updated bibliographical entries. Bailey concludes that the "level of American foreign policy, which sooner or later feels the impact of public opinion, cannot rise substantially higher than the masses will let it."

2:10   Bartlett, Ruhl J. *Policy and Power: Two Centuries of American Foreign Relations*. New York: Hill & Wang, 1963. This book is an extended essay by a longtime student of American diplomacy. The detail is not so full as that in other texts, but the learning and insight are full indeed. The writing is graceful and occasionally witty; the opinions judicious. Bibliography.

2:11   Bemis, Samuel Flagg. *A Diplomatic History of the United States*. 4th ed. New York: Holt, 1955. This authoritative text remains the single best work on the first century of American diplomacy. The 20th century portions are outdated. Bibliography.

2:12   Blake, Nelson M., and Barch, Oscar T., Jr. *The United States in Its World Relations*. New York: McGraw-Hill, 1960. A chronological survey, it tries to relate all sides of controversies. Along the way, the authors comment on ways in which the diplomatic institutions of the country might be improved. Bibliography.

2:13   Cole, Wayne S. *An Interpretive History of American Foreign Relations*. 2d ed. Homewood, Ill.: Dorsey, 1974. A compact survey, it repeatedly compares the domestic with external influences on American foreign policy.

2:14   Davids, Jules. *America and the World of Our Time: United States Diplomacy in the Twentieth Cen-*

tury. 3d ed. New York: Random House, 1970. A detailed treatment of developments for the New Deal, World War II, and cold war years, it is less satisfactory for the early years of the century. A special feature is the tabular chronology of important developments since 1898.

2:15 DeConde, Alexander. *A History of American Foreign Policy*. 3d ed. New York: Scribner's, 1978. A detailed synthesis, in two volumes, it frequently essays explanation of foreign policy formulation by reference to social, economic, or cultural developments. Fuller than usual attention is given to immigration questions. Supplementary readings.

2:16 Dulles, Foster Rhea. *America's Rise to World Power 1898–1954*. New York: Harper & Row, 1954. Dulles disclaims any attempt to tell the full story of America's rise to world power. Rather, his survey depicts the continuing struggle between those forces in the nation which favor taking on international responsibilities and those which oppose. Bibliography.

2:17 Ferrell, Robert H. *American Diplomacy: A History*. 3d ed. New York: Norton, 1975. A full and judicious survey by an accomplished historian whose fondness for a good story makes the book lively. Excerpts from contemporary documents follow each chapter. The bibliography is extensive and annotated.

2:18 Gardner, Lloyd C.; LaFeber, Walter F.; and McCormick, Thomas J. *Creation of the American Empire*. Chicago: Rand-McNally, 1976. These essays are noteworthy for emphasis on the domestic motivations—especially economic and ideological—behind American foreign policy. The book occasionally surprises: for instance, only two pages are devoted to the diplomacy of the Civil War because, the authors say, "diplomatic historians habitually over-study crisis events."

2:19 Graebner, Norman A., ed. *Ideas and Diplomacy: Readings in the Intellectual Tradition of American Foreign Policy*. New York: Oxford University Press, 1964. This documentary history focuses on the relationship between ideas and American foreign policy. Thoughtful interpretative commentaries to each of the twelve chapters make this study a survey of the intellectual milieu in which foreign policy is formulated and conducted.

2:20 Lens, Sidney. *The Forging of the American Empire*. New York: Crowell, 1971. Lens sets out to revise the "myth of morality" in the history of American foreign policy: "America the benevolent . . . does not exist and never has existed." Much emphasis on Wall Street's influence and, for later years, on the military-industrial complex. Bibliography.

2:21 Leopold, Richard W. *The Growth of American Foreign Policy: A History*. New York: Knopf, 1962. This account is an impressive example of historical craftsmanship. Unfortunately not revised, it remains for the period 1889 to 1960 a most learned study. The analysis of themes and influences in American foreign policy is exceptional. Extensive bibliography.

2:22 May, Ernest R. *"Lessons" of the Past: The Use and Misuse of History in American Foreign Policy*. New York: Oxford University Press, 1973. This analysis of how policymakers have misused history, both as a guide to and justification for action, concentrates on World War II, the origins of the cold war, Korea, and Vietnam. It concludes with guidelines for a more effective relationship between history and policy.

2:23 Paterson, Thomas G.; Clifford, J. Garry; and Hagan, Kenneth J. *American Foreign Policy: A History*. Lexington, Mass.: Heath, 1977. Profusely illustrated, briskly written, this text by three younger scholars embodies fair amounts of revisionism which became conspicuous during the 1960s. But the treatment is balanced, and the bibliography is both helpful to the reader and indicative of the authors' labors.

2:24 Pratt, Julius W.; De Santis, Vincent P.; and Siracusa, Joseph M. *A History of United States Foreign Policy*. 4th ed. Englewood Cliffs, N.J.: Prentice-Hall, 1980. This text is noteworthy for its conciseness and for the care taken to specify such details as Senate votes on treaties and the dates of important decisions. Bibliography.

2:25 Smith, Daniel M. *The American Diplomatic Experience*. Boston: Houghton Mifflin, 1972. A straightforward, lucid chronology of the major episodes in American diplomatic history, its emphasis is on events and persons rather than on institutions or theories. Bibliography.

2:26 Strauss, W. Patrick. *Isolation and Involvement: An Interpretive History of American Diplomacy*. Waltham, Mass.: Xerox, 1972. This is a competent synthesis, embellished by some photographs, anecdotes, and extracts from key documents. The didacticism is low key and balanced. Bibliography.

2:27 Van Alstyne, Richard W. *American Diplomacy in Action: A Series of Case Studies*. Stanford, Calif.: Stanford University Press, 1944. The case studies are arranged under the headings of security, expansion, and neutrality. It concludes with the plea—in 1944—for collective security and the reign of law throughout the world. Bibliography.

2:28 Wells, Samuel F., Jr.; Ferrell, Robert H.; and Trask, David F. *The Ordeal of World Power: American Diplomacy since 1900*. Boston: Little, Brown, 1975. The book is tightly organized and graphically illustrated. At the end of each of the three sections there is a table of significant statistics. The point of view is middle-of-the-road.

2:29 Williams, William A., ed. *From Colony to Empire: Essays in in the History of American Foreign Relations*. New York: Wiley, 1972. Representing a revisionist point of view, these ten essays provide a new version of American foreign policy. The authors, among them Walter LaFeber, Richard Van Alstyne, Lloyd Gardner, Robert Freeman Smith, contend that the United States has been aggressive and exploitive in its foreign relations.

Themes and Theory

2:30 Alexander, Charles C. *Nationalism in American Thought, 1930–1945*. Chicago: Rand-McNally, 1969. Although this volume deals with much broader ramifications of nationalism than simply its foreign policy context, it is useful because it develops a chronological account of nationalism as it affects Americans' views of themselves and the external world. Extensive bibliography.

2:31 Basiuk, Victor. *Technology, World Politics and American Policy*. New York: Columbia University Press, 1977. This book suggests the future impact of technology on international relations and societies for the next 75 years, and speculates on what changes will result.

2:32 Ekirch, Arthur A., Jr. *Ideas, Ideals, and American Diplomacy: A History of Their Growth and Interaction*. New York: Appleton-Century-Crofts, 1966. This book is a study of such themes as mission,

manifest destiny, and overseas expansion which guided the implementation of American foreign policy. Bibliography.

2:33 Graber, Doris A. *Crisis Diplomacy: A History of United States Intervention Policies and Practices*. Washington, D.C.: Public Affairs Press, 1959. A solid, well-researched summary, this volume includes chapters on American intervention during the 19th and 20th centuries.

THEMES

Geographical Ideas and Context

2:34 Boggs, S. Whittemore. "Global Relations of the United States." *U.S. Department of State Bulletin* 30 (June 14, 1954), 903–12. A former State Department geographer questions, with novel illustrative devices, some of the geographical assumptions on which U.S. foreign policy has been based—e.g., the division of the world into hemispheres.

2:35 Henrikson, Alan K. "America's Changing Place in the World: From 'Periphery' to 'Centre'?" In Jean Gottmann, ed., *Centre and Periphery: Spatial Variation in Politics*. Beverly Hills, Calif.: Sage, 1980, pp. 73–100. From being on the "periphery" of the Atlantic world in the late 18th century, the United States gradually became a "center" in its own right, in ever larger and more complex spatial contexts. Maps and references.

2:36 Herz, John H. "Rise and Demise of the Territorial State." *World Politics* 9:4 (1957), 473–93. Herz, a political theorist, points out that a basic advantage of the modern territorial state—its "impermeability"— is being eroded by the factors of economic, psychological, aerial, and, especially, nuclear warfare.

2:37 Kristof, Ladis K. D. "The Origins and Evolution of Geopolitics." *Journal of Conflict Resolution* 4:1 (1960), 15–51. This is a learned, cosmopolitan, and incisive analysis of the development of the basic concepts of geopolitics, as distinct from pure geography and politics, from Aristotle to the present. Extensive bibliography.

2:38 Mackinder, Halford J. *Democratic Ideals and Reality*. Ed. by Anthony J. Pearce. Rev. ed. New York: Norton (1919), 1962. This classic of political geography, remembered mainly for its simple formula that control of East Europe brought command of the heartland, world-island, and world, is a work of complexity, imagination, and power. It repays careful reading, especially in light of Mackinder's own reconsiderations (1943) included in this volume.

2:39   Nicks, Oran W., ed. *This Island Earth*. Washington, D.C.: National Aeronautics and Space Administration, 1970. A collection of vivid satellite images, with an interesting text, this volume supports astrophysicist Fred Hoyle's prophecy (1948): "Once a photograph of the Earth, taken from the outside, is available—once the sheer isolation of the Earth becomes plain—a new idea as powerful as any in history will be let loose."

2:40   Schwartz, Seymour I., and Ehrenberg, Ralph E. *The Mapping of America*. New York: Abrams, 1980. This lavishly illustrated work is the newest and most comprehensive analytical history of American cartography. Including maps by Mitchell, Melish, and other cartographic authorities relied upon by statesmen, it documents a medium which gave the changing image of the American land its known shape.

2:41   Sprout, Harold, and Sprout, Margaret. *Toward a Politics of the Planet Earth*. New York: Van Nostrand Reinhold, 1971. The Sprouts, pioneers in the adaptation of geographical concepts to the study of international relations, apply their distinctive "ecological perspective" to the new issues of overpopulation and limited global resources.

To 1941

2:42   Bowman, Isaiah. *The New World: Problems in Political Geography*. Yonkers-on-Hudson, N.Y.: World, 1921. Bowman, America's most distinguished political geographer, surveys in meticulous detail the territorial changes in Europe and elsewhere associated with World War I. Numerous maps, extensive bibliography, and list of treaties.

Goetzmann, W. H. *Exploration and Empire: The Explorer and the Scientist in the Winning of the American West* (10:71) is a comprehensive portrait of the "romantic horizon" of American history, and of the actors and agencies engaged in reconnoitering it. Maps, photographs, and bibliographical note.

2:43   Mahan, Alfred T. *The Interest of America in Sea Power, Present and Future*. Boston: Little, Brown, 1897. This collection of Mahan's more popular writings—on "Looking Outward" and the strategic importance to the United States of Hawaii,

the Isthmus of Darien, and the islands of the Caribbean—provides a good introduction to this most influential of all American strategic thinkers.

May, R. E. *The Southern Dream of a Caribbean Empire, 1854–1861* (7:116) is a corrective to the traditional view of American expansion as ever-westward. May explores the activities of filibusters in the tropics in the context of the sectional conflict over slavery.

Vevier, C. "American Continentalism: An Idea of Expansion, 1845–1910" (10:76) departs from the convention of examining American expansionism in terms of conflicting mercantile and agrarian interests. Vevier effectively shows that both of these interests were unified by a larger vision of American world "geopolitical centralism," according to which domination of the North American continent was a vital stage in linking Europe and Asia.

Weinberg, A. K. *Manifest Destiny: A Study of Nationalist Expansionism in American History* (2:55) analyzes the various "justificatory doctrines" accompanying, and sometimes motivating, American movement across the continent and beyond. Weinberg's many quotations from primary sources make the book a useful guide to expansionist literature.

Whitaker, A. P. *The Western Hemisphere Idea: Its Rise and Decline* (2:284) traces the historical evolution of the Pan-American sense of solidarity, based partly on geography and partly on culture.

Since 1941

2:44   Cohen, Saul B. *Geography and Politics in a World Divided*. New York: Random House, 1963. A leading political geographer summarizes in introductory fashion the work of Guyot, Ratzel, Mahan, Mackinder, Haushofer, Spykman, de Seversky, and other forerunners. Focusing on major "power cores"—the United States, the Soviet Union, and maritime Europe—he applies geopolitical concepts to the cold war. Appendix on theoretical approaches to international relations. Bibliography.

Conant, M. *The Long Polar Watch: Canada and the Defense of North America* (36:99) is a study of American-Canadian continental military arrangements from the 1940 Ogdensburg agreement to the establishment of the Distance Early Warning (DEW) line.

2:45   Gray, Colin S. *The Geopolitics of the Nuclear Era: Heartland, Rimlands, and the Technological*

Revolution. New York: Crane, Russak, 1977. A defense analyst forcefully argues that, despite the advent of missile-borne nuclear weapons, the old concepts of grand geopolitical theory—focusing on the historic struggle between virtually landlocked Eurasian powers and maritime-dependent insular powers—are more relevant than ever.

2:46 Harrison, Richard E. *Look at the World: The FORTUNE Atlas for World Strategy*. New York: Knopf, 1944. Harrison's bird's-eye view and orthographic maps of the theaters of World War II helped American military planners and the American public form a new "global" perspective. This atlas is a work of art and influence, and is of continuing relevance.

Henrikson, A. K. "The Map as an 'Idea': The Role of Cartographic Imagery during the Second World War" (23:157) is a detailed examination of the military and diplomatic bearings of the revolution that occurred in the early 1940s in the way Americans visually imagined the world and represented it cartographically.

2:47 Henrikson, Alan K. "The Geographical 'Mental Maps' of American Foreign Policy Makers." *International Political Science Review* 1:4 (1980), 495–530. Statesmen respond to the world as they perceive and imagine it—which may not be the way the world really is. This illustrated theoretical analysis of the "mental maps," or cognitive geographical frameworks, of recent U.S. foreign policy officials suggests a new, more psychological approach to the study of diplomatic history.

2:48 Lippmann, Walter. *U.S. Foreign Policy: Shield of the Republic*. Boston: Little, Brown, 1943. Lippmann's cogent essay, noted for its argument that the "solvency" of foreign policy depends on maintaining a balance between purpose and power, is also an analysis of the structure of the world political-geographical situations of the United States. Critical of previous American overextensions, Lippmann urges concentration on a defense of the "Atlantic Community."

2:49 Seversky, Alexander P. de. *Air Power: Key to Survival*. New York: Simon & Schuster, 1950. The author, a Russian-born aviator and air planner, urges abandonment of the American World War II "stepping stone" strategy, which required overseas bases, and adoption of a strategy of direct intercontinental warfare—a doctrine that has been criticized as "air isolationism."

2:50 Staley, Eugene. "The Myth of Continents." *Foreign Affairs* 19:3 (1941), 481–94. Staley, an international economist, attempts to debunk the semi-isolationist notion of Pan-American "continental" unity by arguing that, especially in terms of cost-distance, the then-imperilled nations of Western Europe are closer to the United States than are most of those of the western hemisphere.

2:51 Wohlstetter, Albert. "Illusions of Distance." *Foreign Affairs* 46:2 (1968), 242–55. Wohlstetter counters Vietnam War–induced American isolationism by arguing in effect that, because of the technological revolution in transportation and communication, there are no "far-away countries" any more.

Manifest Destiny

See also Chapter 9, "American Expansionism"; Chapter 10, "Manifest Destiny"; Chapter 12, "Manifest Destiny and Social Darwinism"; and Chapter 13, "Progressivism and Foreign Policy."

Graebner, N. A., ed. *Manifest Destiny* (10:72) is a useful collection of documentary materials (1844–1860).

2:52 Merk, Frederick, with Merk, Lois Bannister. *Manifest Destiny and Mission in American History: A Reinterpretation*. New York: Knopf, 1963. A comparison of the two concepts which lay behind expansionism (1830–1898): mission and manifest destiny. Merk considers the first good and the second evil. The first is idealistic, self-denying and totally American; the second is oppressive, aggressive, and un-American. Mission involves the spread of American ideals by example; manifest destiny is the extension of those ideals by force. Extensive bibliography.

Pratt, J. W. "The Origin of 'Manifest Destiny'" (10:74) identifies the first usage of the term.

2:53 Van Alstyne, Richard W. "The Significance of the Mississippi Valley in American Diplomatic History, 1686–1890." *Mississippi Valley Historical Review* 36:1 (1949), 215–38. In viewing the Mississippi Valley as the core of the American empire and the basis for American expansionism in several directions, this article provides useful background to U.S. relations with England and Europe in the 19th century.

Vevier, C. "American Continentalism: An Idea of Expansion, 1845–1910" (10:76).

2:54 Vevier, Charles. "Brooks Adams and the Ambivalence of American Foreign Policy." *World Affairs Quarterly* 30:1 (1959), 3–18. Adams believed that the continentalism of the Monroe Doctrine, which stood for the development of America first, was being changed in 1898 with the formulation of the open door policy.

2:55 Weinberg, Albert K. *Manifest Destiny: A Study of Nationalist Expansionism in American History.* Baltimore: Johns Hopkins Press, 1935. The author relates moral ideas to expansionism from America's republican beginnings to its position as world leader by the turn of the 20th century. Though many have believed that moral justification was a rationalization for the nation's self-interest, Weinberg argues that America's moral ideology was genuine. He admits, however, that the country's nationalism often took on the appearance of self-aggrandizement when it encountered the territorial demands of other nations.

Internationalism

See also Chapters 16, 20, and 38 for additional references.

Cheever, D. S., and Haviland, H. F., Jr. *Organizing for Peace: International Organization in World Affairs* [1815–1954] (38:33).

2:56 Claude, Inis L., Jr. "American Attitudes towards International Organization." In Ken Booth and Moorehead Wright, eds., *American Thinking about Peace and War: New Essays on American Thought and Attitudes.* New York: Barnes & Noble, 1978, pp. 207–22. By examining the thought and policy of peace groups, advocates of world federation and government, and lawyers since 1920, Claude characterizes Americans as legalistic and institutionally oriented, pragmatic and idealistic, and not consistent in pursuing objectives.

2:57 Claude, Inis L., Jr. "International Organization." In Alexander DeConde, ed., *Encyclopedia of American Foreign Policy.* New York: Scribner's, 1978, vol. 2, pp. 473–81. This essay emphasizes conceptual developments rather than concrete bodies, showing the tendency of the United States to be supportive of ideas and organizations despite isolationist tendencies. It also contains a valuable elaboration on sovereignty. Bibliography.

2:58 Deák, Francis. "Neutrality Revisited." In Wolfgang Friedmann, Louis Henkin, and Oliver J. Lissitzyn, eds., *Transnational Law in a Changing Society.* New York: Columbia University Press, 1972, pp. 137–54. Deák reviews changes in the international system, new attitudes, and historical events since the 1930s to show how these have modified worldwide and U.S. concepts of neutrality.

2:59 Kuehl, Warren F. "Internationalism." In Alexander DeConde, ed., *Encyclopedia of American Foreign Policy.* New York: Scribner's, 1978, vol. 2, pp. 443–54. A succinct summary of efforts by individuals and groups to move the United States toward a more internationalist perspective from colonial times to 1978. It also examines ideas and proposals. Bibliography.

2:60 Mangone, Gerard J. *The Idea and Practice of World Government.* New York: Columbia University Press, 1951. A general history (ancient times to 1951) which notes the impact of the American federal system as a model and, also, perceives a danger to any organization which the United States dominates. Extensive bibliography.

2:61 Shafer, Boyd C. "Webs of Common Interests: Nationalism, Internationalism, and Peace." *Historian* 36:3 (1974), 403–33. This thoughtful essay by a noted scholar of nationalism examines the growth of internationalist thought from 1600 to 1970, with references to American writers. Shafer perceives a greater interrelationship between nationalism and internationalism than historians have recognized.

2:62 U.S. Department of State. *International Organization and Conference Series.* Washington, D.C.: G.P.O., 1945–. The department periodically issues pamphlets on international organizations of special interest: *General Series* (S.1.70/1), *Regional Series* (S.1.70/2), *United Nations and its Commissions* (S.1.70/3), *Specialized Agencies* (S.1.70/4), and *Irregular Series* (S.1.70/5). They provide information on the history of each organization covered, its work, plans, and the nature of U.S. participation.

2:63 U.S. Department of State. *Participation of the United States Government in International Conferences.* Washington, D.C.: G.P.O., 1932–1962. This State Department compilation includes data on the official participation of the United States in conferences, meetings, and expositions for the fiscal year covered by each volume. Contains lists of delegates and a brief summary of actions and deliberations. Includes subject and name indexes. These originated in 1932 and appeared in combined volumes until 1946; thereafter they cover the fiscal year. Titles vary.

U.S. Department of State. *United States Contributions to International Organizations* (38:21) is an annual record, since 1945, showing U.S. contributions as well as those of other governments.

Wasson, D., comp. *American Agencies Interested in International Affairs* [1931–1964] (38:32).

2:64 Wynner, Edith, and Lloyd, Georgia. *Searchlight on Peace Plans: Choose Your Road to World Government.* New York: Dutton, 1944. Revised 1949. This impressive summary of hundreds of plans for an international organization contains many proposals by Americans. It also reflects the popular effort to influence thinking in favor of a world government. Index.

Isolationism

See also Chapter 20, "Isolationism," and Chapter 22, "Isolation and Intervention," for additional references.

Adler, S. *The Isolationist Impulse: Its Twentieth Century Reaction* (20:121) is a basic study.

2:65 Billington, Ray A. "The Origins of Middle Western Isolationism." *Political Science Quarterly* 60:1 (1945), 44–64. Changing socioeconomic conditions and the turbulent politics of the 1890s help to account for the shift to isolationism in the Middle West in the 20th century. Republican Middle Westerners mistrusted the expansionism of Democratic presidents, eastern bankers, and large corporations, preferring instead to advocate a continuation of the isolationist tradition.

2:66 DeConde, Alexander. "On Twentieth-Century Isolationism." In Alexander DeConde, ed., *Isolation and Security: Ideas and Interests in Twentieth-Century American Foreign Policy.* Durham, N.C.: Duke University Press, 1957, pp. 3–32. DeConde sees American isolationism rooted in a complex of emotions and ideas that derive from tradition.

2:67 Esthus, Raymond A. "Isolationism and World Power." *Diplomatic History* 2:2 (1978), 117–29. Esthus accepts the idea that between 1898 and 1914, the United States came of age as a world power. But he finds that this new status did not usher in any dramatic change in U.S. foreign policy: "The forces of isolationism and internationalism were in contention, but for the most part isolationism had the upper hand."

2:68 Fensterwald, Bernard. "The Anatomy of American 'Isolationism' and Expansionism." *Journal of Conflict Resolution* 2:2 (1958), 111–39; 2:4 (1958), 280–309. Part 1 analyzes the history of these concepts, while part 2 examines the psychological factors underlying American attitudes toward the problems of foreign policy.

2:69 Weinberg, Albert K. "The Historical Meaning of the American Doctrine of Isolation." *American Political Science Review* 34:3 (1940), 539–47. Weinberg states that isolation is not a theory of American foreign policy, it is a theory about a theory of American foreign policy. He feels that the concept of isolation is useful only in so far as it indicates the misunderstanding of an ideology, serves as a point of departure for investigation, and contains in its connotation certain suggestive half-truths.

Immigration

See also Chapter 14, "Immigration Policies and Problems," and Chapter 17, "Immigration and the Crises with Japan."

2:70 Bennett, Marion T. *American Immigration Policies.* Washington, D.C.: Public Affairs Press, 1963. Bennett provides a substantiated account of U.S. debates over immigration restrictions, mostly since 1941.

Corwin, A. F., ed. *Immigrants and Immigrants: Perspectives on Mexican Labor Migration to the United States* [1848–1976] (35:187) traces the historical evolution of Mexican immigration.

Daniels, R. *The Politics of Prejudice: The Anti-Japanese Movement in California and the Struggle for Japanese Exclusion* (17:259).

2:71 Divine, Robert A. *American Immigration Policy, 1924–1952.* New Haven, Conn.: Yale University Press, 1957. This account reviews U.S. policy from the establishment of the quota system to the McCarran-Walter Act. Bibliography. For a criticism of the McCarran-Walter Act (1952), see J. C. Bruce,

The Golden Door: The Irony of Our Immigration Policy (New York: Random House, 1954).

Freidel, F., ed. *Harvard Guide to American History* (1:67) contains, in chapter 20, an extensive list of books and articles related to immigration and ethnicity.

Shalloo, J. P. "United States Immigration Policy, 1882–1948" (14:31).

Philanthropy and Missionaries

2:72 Curti, Merle E. *American Philanthropy Abroad: A History.* New Brunswick, N.J.: Rutgers University Press, 1963. This volume presents a thorough summary of American philanthropy (primarily nongovernmental) abroad. In examining this topic, Curti provides useful background information to diplomatic historians. Bibliography.

2:73 Curti, Merle, and Birr, Kendall. *Prelude to Point Four: American Technical Missions Overseas, 1838–1930.* Madison: University of Wisconsin Press, 1954. This history of American technical missions overseas examines the problems that arose in the early efforts to bring technological advancement to countries in Asia and Africa.

2:74 Daniel, Robert L. *American Philanthropy in the Near East, 1820–1960.* Athens: Ohio University Press, 1970. Daniel focuses on the role that American missionaries, philanthropists, and educators had in the Arab cultural awakening. American missionary, educational, and philanthropic elements did not always receive full diplomatic protection from American diplomatic officials. Yet they did provide technical assistance and education which furnished an example later employed by the United States in its post–World War II Point Four programs.

Hoover, H. C. *An American Epic: Famine in Forty-Five Nations: The Battle on the Front Line, 1914–1923* (19:41) focuses on relief efforts during and immediately after World War I.

Missionaries
See also Chapter 17, "U.S. Missionaries [China, Japan, Korea];" and Chapter 18, "U.S. Missionaries and Arab Nationalism."

2:75 Anderson, Rufus. *History of the Missions of the American Board of Commissioners for Foreign Missions to the Oriental Churches.* 2 vols. Boston: Congregational Publication Society, 1873. A foreign secretary of the ABCFM provides a lengthy narrative account of the missions based on correspondence from missionaries in the field.

2:76 Bliss, E. M., ed. *Encyclopaedia of Missions.* 2 vols. New York: Funk & Wagnalls, 1891. This is a useful work which furnishes the student with historical sketches of missionary boards, mission fields, mission stations, and missionaries.

Drummond, R. H. *A History of Christianity in Japan* [1549–1970] (17:209) is a comprehensive survey of missionary efforts in Japan.

2:77 Fairbank, John K., ed. *The Missionary Enterprise in China and America.* Cambridge: Harvard University Press, 1974. This is a collection of twelve essays by leading authorities on the missionary movement in China. Topics include a comparison of missionary activities in China and the Near East, the role of lay businessmen in large mission boards, the student volunteer movement, the impact of liberal theology on missions, efforts to establish greater cohesion among missionary sects, the first church newspaper in China, the Chinese "Christian" reformers, and the missionary justification of the use of force in 19th-century China.

2:78 Gingerich, Melvin. "North American Mennonite Overseas Outreach in Perspective, 1890–1965." *Mennonite Quarterly Review* 39:4 (1965), 262–79. The number of missionaries on foreign soil, besides many others on furlough, had increased from none in 1890 to nearly 800 by 1965.

Grabill, J. L. *Protestant Diplomacy and the Near East: Missionary Influence on American Policy, 1810–1927* (18:20) emphasizes the missionary influence during the Wilson era on American diplomacy with Turkey.

Jones, M. H. *Swords into Plowshares: An Account of the American Friends Service Committee, 1917–1937* (20:108).

Liu, Kwang-Ching. *American Missionaries in China* [1827–1939] (17:201).

2:79 Lutz, Jessie G. *China and the Christian Colleges, 1850–1950.* Ithaca, N.Y.: Cornell University Press, 1971. This study evaluates the role of the Christian colleges in the development of modern, revolutionary, and nationalistic China. The author concludes that the educational endeavor of the missionaries had a much greater impact on China than did the evangelical endeavor. Extensive bibliography. Also see Philip West, *Yenching University and Sino-American Relations, 1916–1952* (Cambridge: Harvard University Press, 1976); and Mary E. Ferguson, *China Medical Board and Peking Union Medical College* (New York: China Medical Board of New York, 1970).

2:80   Phillips, Clifton J. *Protestant America and the Pagan World: The First Half Century of the American Board of Commissioners for Foreign Missions, 1810–1860.* Cambridge: Harvard University Press, 1969. The ABCFM was founded by New England Congregationalists but also represented for a time the Presbyterian and Dutch Reformed churches. The study recounts its activities in the Middle East, Africa, South Asia, East Asia, and the Pacific.

Varg, P.A. *Missionaries, Chinese, and Diplomats: The American Protestant Missionary Movement in China, 1890–1952* (17:206).

2:81   Varg, Paul A. "Missionaries." In Alexander DeConde, ed., *Encyclopedia of American Foreign Policy.* New York: Scribner's, 1978, vol. 2, pp. 567–74. This general survey describes the great expansion of activity in the 1890s. Bibliography.

THEORY

2:82   Bennett, John C. *Foreign Policy in Christian Perspective.* New York: Scribner's, 1966. This small book, by a professor from Union Theological Seminary, is a good place to begin on the connection between morality and foreign policy.

2:83   Kennedy, Thomas C. *Charles A. Beard and American Foreign Policy.* Gainesville: University Presses of Florida, 1975. Kennedy argues that there was a logical consistency in his thinking. Beard shifted from an internationalist position to an isolationist when he came to believe that domestic reform would be endangered by extensive foreign commitments, particularly commercial commitments.

2:84   Kratochwil, Friedrich V. *International Order and Foreign Policy: A Theoretical Sketch of Post-War International Politics.* Boulder, Colo.: Westview, 1978. A theoretical analysis of the nature of the international order, using the cold war as a case study, it argues that the characteristics of that order depend

largely on the extent to which major national participants in it share common intellectual assumptions, perceptions of each other, and "rules of the game."

2:85   Lauren, Paul G., ed. *Diplomacy: New Approaches in History, Theory and Policy.* New York: Free Press, 1979. These original essays by historians and political scientists combine the different perspectives, cases and styles to demonstrate ways in which they may learn from each other.

2:86   Lefever, Ernest W. *Ethics and United States Foreign Policy.* New York: Meridian, 1957. The author seeks to assess the role of Judaeo-Christian values in the development of American foreign policy. Bibliography. His subsequent *Ethics and World Politics* (Baltimore, 1972) includes his views on the Vieunam conflict.

2:87   Osgood, Robert E. *Ideals and Self-Interest in America's Foreign Relations: The Great Transformation of the Twentieth Century.* Chicago: University of Chicago Press, 1953. While focusing on idealist-realist approaches to foreign policy, Osgood analyzes peace movements, internationalism, and the growing responsibility of the United States as a world power.

Tarlton, C. D. "The Styles of American International Thought: Mahan, Bryan, and Lippmann" (14:16) is an analysis of three styles of American political thought which expanded during 1898 to 1914 to include international affairs.

Imperialism

See also Chapter 35, "Dependency Theory," for a Latin American version of imperialism.

2:88   Amin, Samir, et al. *La Crise de l'Imperialisme* [The crisis of imperialism]. Paris: Les Editions de Minuit, 1975. Essays by Amin, Alexandre Faire, Gustave Massiah, and Mahmoud Hussein discuss the problems inherent in imperialism based on the Marxist assumption that there are basic structural defects in contemporary capitalism. The focus is on the United States, Europe, and Japan and nationalistic movements in the Third World.

2:89   Brown, Michael B. *The Economics of Imperialism.* Baltimore: Penguin, 1974. This is a good introduction to several, often conflicting Marxist theories about imperialism. Numerous tables provide statistical information dating from 1710 to 1970. Material on the United States is interspersed throughout.

2:90 Cohen, Benjamin J. *The Question of Imperialism: The Political Economy of Dominance and Dependence.* New York: Basic Books, 1973. Describing himself as believing that capitalism can be reformed, Cohen sceptically analyzes Marxist and radical theories of imperialism. In the final chapter he suggests an alternative explanation of imperialism based on "the anarchic organization of the international system of states" which drives nations to become preoccupied with national security. Bibliography.

2:91 Magdoff, Harry. *The Age of Imperialism.* New York: Monthly Review Press, 1969. The author examines the connections between the American business community and American foreign policy, and asserts that American business seeks to control as many sources of raw materials as possible, to monopolize manufacturing processes, and to dominate all markets.

2:92 Magdoff, Harry. *Imperialism: From the Colonial Age to the Present.* New York: Monthly Review Press, 1978. In this series of essays, Magdoff discusses three neglected areas of imperialism: the power conflict at various levels of the hierarchy of nations; the struggle for hegemony in the international monetary system; and the role of the periphery in the interpower struggles at the core. Throughout he attempts to focus on misconceptions and false issues which exist among Marxists and non-Marxists alike about the nature of imperialism.

U.S. Imperialism/Economic Determinism

See also Chapter 12, "Economic Influences"; Chapter 13, "Progressivism and Foreign Policy" and "The Debate on Imperialism, 1898–1900"; Chapter 15, "Taft and Dollar Diplomacy, 1909–1913"; Chapter 17, "Spheres and the Open Door"; Chapter 20, "Reciprocal Trade Agreements"; and Chapter 26, "The Marshall Plan" and "Point Four Program," for related economic themes.

Gardner, L. C. *Economic Aspects of New Deal Diplomacy* (21:12) is the only general study dealing exclusively with foreign economic policy of the first two Roosevelt administrations. Unfortunately this pioneering work is disjointed and inadequately documented and thus needs to be supplemented by monographs dealing with specific topics, such as reciprocal trade and monetary policy.

Kolko, G. *The Politics of War: The World and United States Foreign Policy, 1943–1945* (25:19) is one of the most detailed revisionist accounts of American economic aims at the end of World War II. One does not have to agree with all aspects of the interpretation to benefit from the abundance of factual material. Also see J. Kolko and G. Kolko, *Limits of Power . . . 1945–1954* (24:40).

2:93 Kolko, Gabriel. *The Roots of American Foreign Policy: An Analysis of Power and Purpose.* Boston: Beacon, 1969. Kolko argues that postwar American foreign policy has been dominated by large economic interests that have determined who holds power and how it is wielded. He dismisses "superfluous notions of capriciousness, accident and chance as causal elements in American foreign and military policy."

LaFeber, W. *The New Empire: An Interpretation of American Expansion, 1860–1898* (12:84) is one of the most comprehensive of the economic-determinist interpretations.

2:94 May, Ernest R. *American Imperialism: A Speculative Essay.* New York: Atheneum, 1968. This book combines fair-minded historiographical analysis, intelligent questions about the process and timing of expansionism, insights from social science about public opinion and elite influence, and the use of nontraditional sources. The thesis is that foreign fashions helped cause a shift from anticolonialism to imperialism in the United States. The interpretation and evidence deserve further testing.

2:95 Nearing, Scott, and Freeman, Joseph. *Dollar Diplomacy: A Study in American Imperialism.* New York: Huebsch, 1925. This study remains the most thorough and best-known indictment of U.S. economic penetration of Latin America in the early 20th century. Although subsequent scholarship disagrees over the issue of imperialism as Nearing and Freeman describe it, newer treatments of the topic, stressing the interplay of government and business, have benefited from their endeavor.

2:96 Van Alstyne, Richard W. *The Rising American Empire.* New York: Oxford University Press, 1960. This book, which is meant to be a history of the growth of the American nation-state (1613–1960), portrays the United States as unrelentingly expansionist until the early 20th century.

Williams, W. A. "Confessions of an Intransigent Revisionist" (24:89) states his purposes as a revisionist historian, replies to critics, and remains (mostly) unrepentant. Williams acknowledges his debt to Beard in his "A Note on Charles Austin Beard's Search for a General Theory of Causation," *American Historical Review* 62 (Oct. 1956), 59–80.

2:97 Williams, William A. "The Age of Mercantilism: An Interpretation of the American Political Economy, 1763–1828." *William and Mary Quarterly* 3d ser. 15:4 (1958), 419–37. An arresting article in which the author attempts to shape major elements of American economic and political thought into a synthesis. Mercantilists are defined as those Americans who sought self-sufficiency through increased domestic production and a favorable balance of trade. James Madison, not Alexander Hamilton, is seen as the central figure in the development of mercantilism and the Monroe Doctrine as the mature statement of this policy.

2:98 Williams, William A. *The Roots of the Modern American Empire: A Study of the Growth and Shaping of Social Consciousness in a Marketplace Society.* New York: Random House, 1969. Williams argues that strains of evangelism ran through U.S. growth as a nation and pushed Americans from the original concept of "City on a Hill" to that of "Empire of the Globe." Bibliography.

2:99 Williams, William A. *The Tragedy of American Diplomacy.* Rev. ed. New York: Dell, 1972. This book is considered by some to be the most influential volume written on American diplomatic history during the past two decades. It is not a history of U.S. foreign policy but rather a search for its roots, which the author sees in the open door policy — the conviction, shared by American leaders since the turn of the century, that prosperity at home required economic expansion overseas, which in turn restricted the legitimate revolutionary aspirations of other countries.

Critics of "U.S. Imperialism" Thesis

Becker, W. H. "American Manufacturers and Foreign Markets, 1870–1900: Business Historians and the 'New Economic Determinists'" (12:87) seeks to refute the thesis about overproduction and a business consensus on the need for foreign markets.

Becker, W. H. "Foreign Markets for Iron and Steel, 1893–1913: A New Perspective on the Williams School of Diplomatic History" (14:18) questions the validity of the thesis, propounded by William A. Williams and other scholars, that trade expansion was a necessary condition for the economic well-being of the United States from the 1890s to World War I. Becker makes an able case for iron and steel, but readers are directed to the rejoinder in the same issue (pp. 245–55) by Howard Schonberger, "William H. Becker and the New Left Revisionists: A Rebuttal."

2:100 Etherington, Norman. "Theories of Empire and Modern American Imperialism." *Australian Journal of Politics and History* 20:2 (1974), 210–22. The author challenges Harry Magdoff's New Left interpretation of modern American foreign policy in *The Age of Imperialism* (2:91), by reexamining alternative explanations of imperialism: Schumpeter's "objectless" imperialism, Fieldhouse's emphasis on colonial counters to European power rivalries, and the role ascribed to nationalism by Hobson, Van Alstyne, and others.

2:101 Field, James A., Jr. "American Imperialism: The Worst Chapter in Almost Any Book." *American Historical Review* 83:3 (1978), 644–83. This article continues the demolition of the social Darwinian thesis by Holbo and others, raises questions about naval development, recalls the country's Atlantic orientation, and portrays the lack of shipping and naval strength in the Pacific. The author poses a new technological explanation for imperialism based on the communications revolution and stresses the role of historical accident. An exchange of opinion follows with Walter LaFeber and Robert L. Beisner.

Holbo, P. S. "Economics, Emotion, and Expansion: An Emerging Foreign Policy" (12:89) criticizes the arguments and evidence of earlier interpretations, especially those stressing foreign markets, social Darwinism, and foreign example.

Hunt, M. H. "Americans in the China Market: Economic Opportunities and Economic Nationalism, 1890s–1931" (39:54) looks beyond the contemporary rhetoric and the debate among historians to assess the reality of the China Market. Government support for trade expansion made little difference in the volume of trade. What did matter were local conditions in

China and the domestic strength of the American manufacturer.

2:102 Melanson, Richard A. "The Social and Political Thought of William Appleman Williams." *Western Political Quarterly* 31:3 (1978), 392–409. Melanson praises Williams for undertaking grand syntheses in an age of monographic specialization, but faults his "simplistic theory of human nature, his inability to specify the ultimate sources of American expansion, his failure to deal with the problem of American exceptionalism, and his unwillingness to provide a sense of perspective through which to view the American experience."

2:103 Seltzer, Alan L. "Woodrow Wilson as 'Corporate Liberal': Toward a Reconsideration of Left Revisionist Historiography." *Western Political Quarterly* 30:2 (1977), 183–212. This is a critical analysis of New Left historiography; for another view that focuses on Wilson, see L. E. Ambrosius, "The Orthodoxy of Revisionism: Woodrow Wilson and the New Left" (19:67).

2:104 Slater, Jerome. "Is United States Foreign Policy 'Imperialist' or 'Imperial'?" *Political Science Quarterly* 91:1 (1976), 63–87. Slater critically examines the increasingly common view that the United States has been either an "imperialist" or an "imperial" power. After scrutinizing the distinctions between these two views, he argues that both are misleading about the intentions of policymakers and the actual capacity of the United States to control other nations.

2:105 Staley, Eugene. *War and the Private Investor*. New York: Doubleday, Doran, 1935. Reprint 1967. Staley argues that private investors almost always appear after the political desire for war has arisen, rather than the other way around. Other works which criticize the "economic cause of war" thesis include Lionel Robbins, *The Economic Causes of War* (London: Cape, 1939, reprint 1968); and Jacob Viner, "Finance and Balance of Power Diplomacy," *Southwestern Political and Social Science Quarterly* 9:4 (1929).

Thompson, J. A. "William Appleman Williams and the 'American Empire' " (12:90) disputes the interpretations of American foreign policy by William A. Williams and his "disciples," most notably Walter LaFeber. The views of Williams and his "school" derive from the theoretical framework outlined by Williams in his pioneering work, *The Tragedy of*

American Diplomacy (2:99) and several more recent writings.

Wilkins, M. "The Role of U.S. Business" (22:97) systematically analyzes the key American business groups affected by developments in East Asia in the 1930s. She emphasizes the different interests among these groups (business pluralism). She suggests that business groups tended to have a small impact on the course of diplomatic events. The essay is part of the growing literature on business pluralism and the policymaking process.

Wilson, J. H. *American Business and Foreign Policy, 1920–1933* (20:185) tests the theories of William A. Williams, by analyzing both government and business organizational structures and influence on one another, and shows that American business opinion toward U.S. foreign policy was not monolithic and that often various sectors opposed one another on international economic issues. Wilson coins the term *independent internationalism* to describe the combination of open and closed door economic practices pursued by the United States in the 1920s.

Balance of Power

2:106 Butterfield, Herbert. "The Balance of Power." In Herbert Butterfield and Martin Wright, eds., *Diplomatic Investigations: Essays in the Theory of International Politics*. Cambridge: Harvard University Press, 1966, pp. 132–48. Butterfield seeks, within a historical context, to examine the basic principles of the balance of power system. His focus is pre–World War I, as is M. S. Anderson's in "Eighteenth-Century Theories of the Balance of Power," in R. Hatton and M. S. Anderson, eds., *Studies in Diplomatic History: Essays in Memory of David Bayne Horn* (London: Longmans, 1970), pp. 183–98.

2:107 Campbell, A. E. "Balance of Power." In Alexander DeConde, ed., *Encyclopedia of American Foreign Policy*. New York: Scribner's, 1978, vol. 1, pp. 58–65. This is a useful survey of the balance of power idea and its relationship to U.S. foreign policy.

2:108 Haines, Richard L. "The Balance-of-Power System in Europe." In LeRoy Graymer, ed., *Systems and Actors in International Politics*. Scranton, Pa.: Chandler, 1971, pp. 9–32. Haines reviews the functioning of the balance of power system in European politics during the 18th and 19th centuries. His account is useful as a background survey.

2:109   Wright, Martin. "The Balance of Power and the International Order." In Alan James, ed., *The Bases of International Order: Essays in Honour of C. A. W. Manning.* New York: Oxford University Press, 1973, pp. 85–115. This essay both describes the history of the balance of power idea and analyzes its theoretical contents. Also see his earlier essay in H. Butterfield and M. Wright, eds., *Diplomatic Investigations: Essays in the Theory of International Politics* (Cambridge: Harvard University Press, 1966), pp. 149–75.

"Realist" Thesis

2:110   Halle, Louis. *Dream and Reality: Aspects of American Foreign Policy.* New York: Harper, 1959. A former member of the State Department's policy planning staff, Halle reflects on the history of American foreign policy from the realist perspective. He is essentially concerned about policy goals (often illusions) and national means. For another statement of his view of realist foreign policy principles see his *Civilization and Foreign Policy* (New York: Harper, 1955).

2:111   Kennan, George F. *American Diplomacy, 1900–1950.* Chicago: University of Chicago Press, 1951. In these brief essays Kennan reviews the assumptions underlying 50 years of U.S. foreign policy. In providing a sharp critique of America's "legalistic-moralistic" approach to foreign policy issues, he endorses the realist view.

2:112   Morgenthau, Hans J. *Politics among Nations: The Struggle for Power and Peace.* 5th rev. ed. New York: Knopf, 1978. A leading exponent of post–World War II realism, Morgenthau grounds his thesis on historical and philosophical principles emanating from the balance of power concept. A useful bibliography. For endorsement and criticism, see such accounts as T. I. Cook and Malcolm Moos, *Power through Purpose: The Realism of Idealism as a Basis for Foreign Policy* (Baltimore: Johns Hopkins Press, 1954); J. H. Hertz, *Political Realism and Political Idealism* (Chicago: University of Chicago Press, 1951): and R. Niebuhr, *Christian Realism and Political Problems* (New York: Scribner's, 1953).

2:113   Spykman, Nicholas J. *America's Strategy in World Politics: The United States and the Balance of Power.* New York: Harcourt, Brace, 1942. In this controversial early treatise of foreign policy realism, Spykman stresses the dependence of American security upon the balance of power, especially in Europe. Additionally, he analyzes the history of U.S. foreign relations with reference to the American geographical position. Maps and bibliography.

2:114   Thompson, Kenneth W. "The Limits of Principle in International Politics: Necessity and the New Balance of Power." *Journal of Politics* 20:3 (1958), 437–67. Thompson discusses the problem of morality in international relations, and briefly presents the viewpoints of Herbert Butterfield, Charles de Visscher, Reinhold Niebuhr, and Hans J. Morgenthau on the problem of principle and necessity in politics.

2:115   Thompson, Kenneth W. "Moral Reasoning in American Thought on War and Peace." *Review of Politics* 39:3 (1977), 386–99. Most American moral reasoning on war and peace has been largely monistic—based on single theories which tend to cancel each other out because they are "insufficient." Four American thinkers, Reinhold Niebuhr, Hans Morgenthau, Walter Lippman, and George Kennan, have manifested a "pluralistic" approach to such ponderings.

Critics of "Realist" Thesis

Gardner, L. C. "American Foreign Policy, 1900–1921: A Second Look at the Realist Critique of American Diplomacy" (14:11) takes a hard look at George Kennan's "realistic" critique of American foreign policy as applied to the first two decades of the 20th century.

2:116   Haas, Ernst B. "The Balance of Power: Prescription, Concept or Propaganda?" *World Politics* 5:4 (1953), 442–77. The purpose of this article is the clarification, not only of the *verbal* differences in meaning, but also of the *applied meaning* of the balance of power phrases as they vary in accordance with the intention of the users. Examples are cited.

2:117   Speer, James P., II. "Hans Morgenthau and the World State." *World Politics* 20:2 (1968), 207–27. Speer concludes that the final inadequacy of Morgenthau's world state is "that he depends upon the slender reed of diplomacy, rather than upon government, to create the order out of which a sense of community can grow."

SPECIAL STUDIES

Bureaucratic Politics

2:118 Ball, Desmond J. "The Blind Men and the Elephant: A Critique of Bureaucratic Politics Theory." *Australian Outlook* 28:1 (1974), 71–92. A recent theory, crediting bureaucracies with total control of American foreign policy, is criticized, using the works of Graham T. Allison and Morton H. Halperin.

2:119 Halperin, Morton H.; with Clapp, Priscilla, and Kanter, Arnold. *Bureaucratic Politics and Foreign Policy.* Washington, D.C.: Brookings Institution, 1974. This is a useful overview of current thinking regarding the impact of bureaucracies on foreign policy, with examples drawn from the postwar period. It argues that the behavior of states cannot be understood apart from the interests of the bureaucracies charged with implementing it.

Intercultural Relations

2:120 Heald, Morrell, and Kaplan, Lawrence S. *Culture and Diplomacy: The American Experience.* Westport, Conn.: Greenwood, 1977. This significant study seeks to trace the "cultural setting" of U.S. foreign policy from colonial days to present, on the assumption that in order to understand American diplomacy it is necessary to understand the culture within which policy is formed.

2:121 Iriye, Akira. "Culture and Power: International Relations as Intercultural Relations." *Diplomatic History* 3:2 (1979), 115–28. Iriye explores the problems involved in relating domestic desires (culture) to a nation's foreign policy. He argues the utility of examining "international relations as interactions among cultural systems and among systems of power."

2:122 Iriye, Akira. "Intercultural Relations." In Alexander DeConde, ed., *Encyclopedia of American Foreign Policy.* New York: Scribner's, 1978, vol. 2, 428–42. Intercultural history is defined as the history of relations between America and non-Western cultures. Iriye demonstrates his point with a brief summary of America's intercultural relations. Bibliography.

National Interest

2:123 Beard, Charles A., and Smith, George H. E. *The Idea of National Interest: An Analytical Study in American Foreign Relations.* New York: Macmillan, 1934. This is a brilliant if flawed effort to trace the evolution of the idea of national interest, throughout American history. In general, Beard sees the national interest as arising out of conflicts among domestic economic interest groups.

2:124 Ekirch, Arthur A., Jr. "Charles A. Beard and Reinhold Niebuhr: Contrasting Conceptions of National Interest in American Foreign Policy." *Mid-America* 59:2 (1977), 103–16. Beard believed the United States should confine itself to the defense of the western hemisphere to preserve national interest. Niebuhr concluded that realism demanded American intervention in world affairs.

2:125 Good, R. C. "National Interest and Political Realism: Niebuhr's 'Debate' with Morgenthau and Kennan." *Journal of Politics* 22:4 (1960), 597–619. Debates on national interest proceed from two perspectives: one tends to be policy oriented; the other, ethically oriented. These two perspectives overlap in real situations. The second perspective provides the subject of this study, that is, the national interest as a problem in political ethics.

2:126 Morgenthau, Hans J. "Another 'Great Debate': The National Interest of the United States." *American Political Science Review* 46:4 (1952), 961–89. This debate concerned the nature of all politics, including the utopias and realist points of view. What separates the utopian from the realist position cannot be so sharply expressed in terms of alternative foreign policies. What sets them apart is not necessarily a matter of practical judgment, but of philosophies and standards of thought.

2:127 Morgenthau, Hans J. "The Mainsprings of American Foreign Policy: The National Interest vs Moral Abstraction." *American Political Science Review* 44:4 (1950), 833–54. Morgenthau believes that a foreign policy derived from national interest is in fact morally superior to a foreign policy inspired by universal principles. In this context he discusses the history of American foreign policy from the days of the founding fathers to post–World War II.

2:128 Wolfers, Arnold. "'National Security' as an Ambiguous Symbol." *Political Science Quarterly*

47:4 (1952), 481–502. Wolfers feels that when political formulas such as national interest or national security gain popularity, they need to be scrutinized with particular care. They may not mean the same things to different people; they may not have any precise meaning at all.

Self-Determination

2:129 Cobban, Alfred. *National Self-Determinism.* Rev. ed. Chicago: University of Chicago Press, 1948. The standard, historical treatment of the growth of this idea.

2:130 Lent, Ernest S. "American Foreign Policy and the Principle of Self-Determination." *World Affairs* 133:4 (1971), 293–303. Lent focuses on the consistency with which practice in American diplomacy has conformed to the principle of self-determination. "National self-determination" is applied to nationality groups as in Europe; "colonial self-determination" refers to overseas dependencies of major powers; and "secessionist self-determination" refers to the rights claimed by groups within the borders of independent nations.

2:131 Plischke, Elmer. "Self-Determination: Reflections on a Legacy." *World Affairs* 140:1 (1977), 41–57. The tenet of self-determination, with deep roots from the American Revolution, is analyzed to show its strength as a principle in UN-U.S. relations.

2:132 Unterberger, Betty Miller. "National Self-Determination." In Alexander DeConde, ed., *Encyclopedia of American Foreign Policy.* New York: Scribner's, 1978, vol. 2, 635–50. Unterberger traces American attitudes and U.S. policy toward national self-determination, particularly since the Spanish-American War. Bibliography.

Wright, T. P., Jr. "The Origins of the Free Elections Dispute in the Cold War" (26:33).

2:133 Wright, Theodore P., Jr. *American Support of Free Elections Abroad.* Washington, D.C.: Public Affairs Press, 1964. A critical, although uneven, treatment of the U.S. experience in eight Central American and Caribbean countries, which questions the goals and techniques of U.S. policy. Extensive bibliography.

2:134 Wright, Theodore P., Jr. "Free Elections in the Latin American Policy of the United States."

Political Science Quarterly 74:1 (1959), 89–112. Wright examines the Latin American policy of the United States during the first third of the 20th century and finds it replete with examples of unsuccessful intervention in support of free elections.

Policy Formation

2:135 Bailey, Thomas A. *The Art of Diplomacy: The American Experience.* New York: Appleton, 1968. A dean of American diplomatic history develops a series of maxims, based on U.S. experiences, in his renowned witty fashion.

2:136 Divine, Robert A. "War, Peace, and Political Parties in 20th Century America." Society for the History of American Foreign Relations *Newsletter* 8:1 (1977), 1–6. Divine discusses the correlation between the tendencies for the Republican party to be in office during times of peace and the Democratic party to be in power during times of war in the 20th century.

2:137 Etheredge, Lloyd S. "Personality Effects on American Foreign Policy, 1898–1968: A Test of Interpersonal Generalization Theory." *American Political Science Review* 72:2 (1978), 434–51. Whether personality characteristics of American leaders crucially affect major American foreign policy decisions has been a matter of considerable disagreement. A test of two hypotheses drawn from interpersonal generalization theory shows such influences have probably been crucial in a number of cases in American foreign policy between 1898 and 1968.

2:138 Henkin, Louis. *Foreign Affairs and the Constitution.* Mineola, N.Y.: Foundation Press, 1972. Reprint 1975. This is one of the best analyses of the connections between provisions in the federal Constitution and the conduct of foreign policy (1789–1972). It is also important for its discussion of the American approach to international law and tribunals.

2:139 Janis, Irving. *Victims of Groupthink: A Psychological Study of Foreign-Policy Decisions and Fiascoes.* Boston: Houghton Mifflin, 1972. An attempt to differentiate the characteristics of effective and ineffective decisionmaking in national security affairs, it is based on case studies dealing with Pearl

Harbor, the Marshall Plan, Korea, the Bay of Pigs, the Cuban missile crisis, and Vietnam.

PRESIDENTIAL ROLE

2:140   Chai, Jai Hyung. "Presidential Control of the Foreign Policy Bureaucracy: The Kennedy Case." *Presidential Studies* 8:4 (1978), 391–403. The passive leadership of Secretary of State Dean Rusk prompted Kennedy to take personal control of American foreign policy.

2:141   Divine, Robert A. *Foreign Policy and U.S. Presidential Elections, 1940–1960.* 2 vols. New York: New Viewpoints, 1974. In thorough discussion of the role of foreign policy in each of six presidential elections (1940–1960), Divine argues that campaign commitments have generally not significantly affected subsequent diplomacy, but that presidential aspirants have oversimplified foreign policy issues in the interests of getting elected. Bibliography.

2:142   Landecker, Manfred. *The President and Public Opinion: Leadership in Foreign Affairs.* Washington, D.C.: Public Affairs Press, 1968. The author reviews Roosevelt's and Truman's administrations in an effort to determine how these leaders assessed and mobilized public support for their foreign affairs policies.

2:143   Neustadt, Richard E. *Presidential Power: The Politics of Leadership.* New York: Wiley, 1960. This classic analysis of the nature of presidential power has important implications for foreign policy. The main point is that the president's power is more that of persuasion than command, even within the executive branch of the government; that much depends on the avidity with which the president seizes and wields the reins of power. Neustadt includes case studies on the Chinese intervention in Korea and the MacArthur dismissal.

2:144   Schlesinger, Arthur M., Jr. *The Imperial Presidency.* New York: Houghton Mifflin, 1974. A history of presidential involvement in the making of foreign policy since the writing of the Constitution, it places particular emphasis on the post–World War II era. Schlesinger argues that postwar presidents have assumed far more power with regard to the conduct of foreign affairs than was intended in the American Constitution.

CONGRESSIONAL ROLE

2:145   Carroll, Holbert N. *The House of Representatives and Foreign Affairs.* Pittsburgh: University of Pittsburgh Press, 1958. This comprehensive study, focusing on the post-1945 era, examines the enlarged role of the lower house in foreign affairs.

2:146   Dahl, Robert A. *Congress and Foreign Policy.* New York: Harcourt, 1950. A leading political scientist examines the Congress' role in shaping U.S. foreign policy, and includes useful statistical data.

2:147   Dennison, Eleanor E. *The Senate Foreign Relations Committee.* Stanford, Calif.: Stanford University Press, 1942. This useful study reviews the organization, influence, and operations of the committee. It may be supplemented by J. W. Gould's "The Origins of the Senate Committee on Foreign Relations," *Western Political Quarterly* 12 (1959), 67–82.

2:148   Farnsworth, David N. *The Senate Committee on Foreign Relations.* Urbana: University of Illinois Press, 1961. The volume has a great deal of illustrative material from 1940 to the late 1950s. It is especially good on foreign aid issues. Bibliography.

2:149   Grassmuck, George L. *Sectional Biases in Congress on Foreign Policy.* Baltimore: Johns Hopkins Press, 1951. This statistical analysis of roll call votes for two periods (1921–1932 and 1933–1941) on selected foreign policy legislation is useful for comparing regional interests.

2:150   Holt, W. Stull. *Treaties Defeated by the Senate: A Study of the Struggle between President and Senate over the Conduct of Foreign Relations.* Baltimore: Johns Hopkins Press, 1933. This pioneering monograph contains descriptions of many treaties and their fate at the hands of the Senate. The author assesses ratification votes, focusing on the factor of partisanship. His footnotes contain many useful citations.

2:151   Johnson, Loch, and McCormick, James M. "The Making of International Agreements: A Reappraisal of Congressional Involvement." *Journal of Politics* 40:2 (1978), 468–78. This analysis of U.S. foreign policy (1946–1972) indicates the predominance of statutory agreements; executive agreements are used rarely and treaties are used least of all. Congress has played a greater procedural, if not substantive, role than conventional wisdom would suggest.

2:152　Lerche, Charles O., Jr. *The Uncertain South: Its Changing Patterns of Politics in Foreign Policy.* Chicago: Quadrangle, 1964. Concentrating on roll call votes (1953–1962), the author, a longtime student of southern politics, finds that the South has been willing to go against the tide of national opinion, and suggests that its role is disruptive in matters involving foreign policy.

Pastor, R. A. *Congress and the Politics of U.S. Foreign Economic Policy, 1929–1976* (39:30) focuses on trade policy (1929–1976), aid policy (1945–1976), and investment policy (1960–1976).

2:153　Rieselbach, Leroy N. *The Roots of Isolationism: Congressional Voting and Presidential Leadership in Foreign Policy.* Indianapolis: Bobbs-Merrill, 1966. The central question posed is which members of congress, specifically of the House of Representatives, are likely to support and which to oppose the international policies suggested by the president? Valuable tables, bibliography.

2:154　Stennis, John C., and Fulbright, J. William. *The Role of Congress in Foreign Policy.* Washington, D.C.: American Enterprise Institute for Public Policy Research, 1971. While Stennis believes that the balance between Congress and the executive is adequate, Fulbright finds the executive usurping the Congress' role.

2:155　Westerfield, H. Bradford. *Foreign Policy and Party Politics: Pearl Harbor to Korea.* New Haven, Conn.: Yale University Press, 1955. Despite its age, this book remains one of the few comprehensive analyses of the interaction between foreign policy and party politics (1941–1950). The author concludes that bipartisanship reached its high point with the 1948 election, and declined thereafter.

2:156　Westphal, Albert C. F. *The House Committee on Foreign Affairs.* New York: Columbia University Press, 1942. Reprinted 1968. Although the study is on the Foreign Affairs Committee, Westphal also deals with the House in a broad way, notably when discussing the questions of embargo and neutrality legislation.

2:157　Wilcox, Francis O. *Congress, the Executive and Foreign Policy.* New York: Harper & Row, 1971. Wilcox examines the impact of the separation of powers upon U.S. foreign affairs.

STATE DEPARTMENT

2:158　Barnes, William, and Morgan, John M. *The Foreign Service of the United States: Origins, Development, and Functions.* Washington, D.C.: U.S. Department of State, 1961. Prepared by the State Department's Historical Office, this account surveys its themes in descriptive fashion.

Beichman, A. *The "Other" State Department: The United States Mission to the United Nations—Its Role in the Making of Foreign Policy* (38:197) is an informative study of the organization, activities, and individuals of the U.S. mission to the United Nations.

2:159　Bloomfield, Lincoln P. "Planning Foreign Policy: Can It Be Done?" *Political Science Quarterly* 93:3 (1978), 369–91. Bloomfield reviews the experience of policy planning staffs in the U.S. State Department and in foreign governments and sharply questions their effectiveness. He concludes with suggestions of how to improve the incorporation of long-range thinking into foreign policy planning.

2:160　Brady, Linda P. "Planning for Foreign Policy: A Framework for Analysis." *International Journal* 32:4 (1977), 829–48. Brady traces the successes and failures of the policy planning staff of the U.S. Department of State from its formation through subsequent transformation and rejuvenation.

2:161　Campbell, John F. *The Foreign Affairs Fudge Factory.* New York: Basic Books, 1971. The former editor of *Foreign Policy* provides an informative critique of the State Department's bureaucratic methods. I. M. Destler's *Presidents, Bureaucrats, and Foreign Policy* (Princeton, N.J.: Princeton University Press, 1972) critically reviews the many proposals to reform the department.

2:162　Chittick, William O. *State Department, Press and Pressure Groups: A Role Analysis.* New York: Wiley-Interscience, 1970. Chittick analyzes the roles of individuals and "actors" in and around the department, and how they influence the making of policy.

2:163　DeConde, Alexander. *The American Secretary of State: An Interpretation.* New York: Praeger, 1962. This examination of the office of secretary of state focuses on the responsibilities, influences, and vulnerabilities in the American political system. For a more contemporary and equally critical emphasis, see

N. L. Hill's *Mr. Secretary of State* (New York: Random House, 1963), and Henry M. Jackson, ed., *The Secretary of State and the Ambassador* (New York: Praeger, 1964).

2:164   DeSantis, Hugh. *Diplomacy of Silence: The American Foreign Service, The Soviet Union and the Cold War, 1933–1947.* Chicago: University of Chicago Press, 1980. This is a "psycho-social" analysis of the influence of professional foreign service officers on the course of America's Soviet relations from recognition to the Truman Doctrine. The author makes extensive use of interviews with former officers and State Department records, and concludes that foreign service officers contributed significantly to the disintegration of American-Soviet postwar relations. Bibliography.

2:165   Leacaces, John P. *Fires in the In-Baskets: The ABC's of the State Department.* Cleveland: World, 1968. This is a useful, balanced study of the department's operations. See also Graham H. Stuart's *The Department of State: A History of Its Organization, Procedure, and Personnel.* (New York: Macmillan, 1949).

Diplomats, Agents, and Diplomatic Service

See also Chapter 1, "Biographical Data."

2:166   Bemis, Samuel Flagg, ed. *The American Secretaries of State and Their Diplomacy.* 10 vols. New York: Knopf, 1928. Reprint 1958. These dated but still useful sketches, prepared by different historians, cover the secretaries from 1789 to 1925.

2:167   Bemis, Samuel Flagg, and Ferrell, Robert, eds. *The American Secretaries of State and Their Diplomacy.* New series. 9 vols. to date. New York: Cooper Square, 1963–. These volumes (11–19) continue the themes and scope of the original series, beginning with Frank B. Kellogg and Henry L. Stimson and continuing thus far to Dean Rusk.

Burns, R. D., and Bennett, E. M., eds. *Diplomats in Crisis: United States-Chinese-Japanese Relations, 1919–1941* (22:42) contains vignettes of 13 diplomats of varying influence.

2:168   Graebner, Norman A., ed. *An Uncertain Tradition: American Secretaries of State in the Twentieth*

Century. New York: McGraw-Hill, 1961. These essays, covering John Hay to John Foster Dulles, are particularly useful summaries of the careers of the pre-1945 secretaries; the later essays need to be revised in light of new data which has become available.

2:169   Merli, Frank J., and Wilson, Theodore A., eds. *Makers of American Diplomacy from Benjamin Franklin to Henry Kissinger.* 2 vols. New York: Scribner's, 1974. Twenty-five biographical essays on formal and informal American diplomatists, covering the spectrum of diplomatic history. Bibliographical notes appended to each chapter.

2:170   Wriston, H. M. *Executive Agents in American Foreign Relations.* Baltimore: Johns Hopkins Press, 1929. This massive volume surveys the American practice and opinion of using executive agents for various purposes. The book includes chapters on the use of executive agents to open diplomatic relations with a nation, to negotiate with an unrecognized government, to communicate with a colonial state, and to deal with a government which had terminated formal diplomatic relations with the United States.

Diplomatic Corps

2:171   Davis, Robert R., Jr. "Diplomatic Plumage: American Court Dress in the National Period." *American Quarterly* 20:2 (1968), 164–79. A survey of the dilemma which American diplomats faced regarding the wearing of court attire in foreign countries.

2:172   Davis, Robert R., Jr. "Republican Simplicity: The Diplomatic Costume Question, 1789–1867." *Civil War History* 15:1 (1969), 19–29. This article traces the evolution of formal dress for American diplomats from 1789 to 1867. The move toward simple, "democratic" dress began under President Jackson and reached a high point in the 1850s under Secretary of State William Marcy.

2:173   Downing, Margaret B. "The Diplomatic Corps at the Federal Capital, 1789–1929." *Records* [Columbia Historical Society] 33/34 (1931), 25–39. Downing summarizes, in anecdotal style, the significant milestones in the operations of the foreign diplomatic corps in the United States.

2:174   Harr, John E. *The Professional Diplomat.* Princeton, N.J.: Princeton University Press, 1969. Harr provides a detailed examination of the foreign service corps, and recommends certain changes. H. S. Villard, a career diplomat, defends the corps, suggests why morale occasionally falls, and urges a number of changes in his *Affairs at State* (New York: Crowell, 1965). See also Elmer Plischke, *United States Diplomats and Their Missions: A Profile of American Diplomatic Emissaries since 1778* (Washington, D.C.: American Enterprise Institute for Policy Research, 1975).

2:175 Ilchman, W. F. *Professional Diplomacy in the United States, 1779–1939.* Chicago: University of Chicago Press, 1961. This study of the administrative history of the American diplomatic corps focuses on the development of professionalism in the foreign service. Bibliography.

2:176 Kennedy, Charles S., Jr. "Foreign Consuls in the United States." *Foreign Service Journal* 52:9 (1975), 19–23. This is a brief survey of the history (1778–1979) of foreign consuls in the United States which discusses their various functions and problems.

Paterson, T. G. "American Businessmen and Consular Service Reform, 1890's to 1906" (14:22).

2:177 Paullin, Charles O. *Diplomatic Negotiations of American Naval Officers, 1778–1883.* Baltimore: Johns Hopkins Press, 1912. Reprint 1967. Organized by country and geographic area, this volume includes a useful survey of diplomatic activities carried on by naval officers. The book concentrates on negotiations with the Barbary States, Turkey, China, and Japan.

2:178 Schulzinger, Robert. *The Making of the Diplomatic Mind: The Training, Outlook and Style of United States Foreign Service Officers, 1908–1931.* Middletown, Conn.: Wesleyan University Press, 1975. The author attempts to trace the professionalization of the foreign service after about 1900. This trend, he believes, reflected the enlarged role of the United States in world politics as well as aspirations and anxieties of professional diplomats. Annotated bibliography.

Stock, L. F. "American Consuls to the Papal States, 1797–1867" (8:104).

2:179 Stuart, Graham H. *American Diplomatic and Consular Practice.* 2d ed. New York: Appleton, 1952. This analytical review of the diplomatic bureaucracy through which U.S. foreign affairs are conducted is updated with the use of post-1945 materials.

2:180 Werking, Richard H. *The Master Architects: Building the United States Foreign Service, 1890–1913.* Lexington: University of Kentucky Press, 1977.

This book analyzes the bureaucratic determinants of American foreign policy. The thesis is that young, aggressive, ambitious officials in the State Department, abetted by businessmen and reformers, utilized the argument of foreign trade expansion in order to develop and reform the foreign service and especially the consular service. The bureaucrats, who are described usefully, enjoyed little success before 1898. Bibliography.

2:181 Willson, Beckles. *America's Ambassadors to England, 1785–1928: A Narrative of Anglo-American Diplomatic Relations.* New York: Stokes, 1929. Reprint 1969. This volume contains a brief summary of each American minister to the Court of St. James from 1785 to 1925. The style and presentation are popular not scholarly; its analysis is dated.

2:182 Willson, Beckles. *America's Ambassadors to France (1777–1927): A Narrative of Franco-American Diplomatic Relations.* London: Murray, 1928. Reprint 1969. This volume contains a brief summary of each American minister to France. The style and presentation are popular not scholarly.

U.S. Overseas Information Programs

2:183 Bogart, Leo. *Premises for Propaganda: The United States Information Agency's Operating Assumptions in the Cold War.* New York: Free Press, 1976. This is an abridgement of an official five-volume report written in 1954 but not declassified until 1974. It demonstrates the problem that plagued the agency: should the USIA inform or propagandize?

2:184 Elder, Robert E. *The Information Machine.* Syracuse, N.Y.: Syracuse University Press, 1968. Elder provides an analytical study of the USIA and its role in American foreign affairs.

Handlery, G. "Propaganda and Information: The Case of U.S. Broadcasts to Eastern Europe" (28:166) is a careful comparison of broadcasts during 1973 which concludes that Radio Free Europe is relatively objective and that its activity is in the enlightened interests of America.

2:185 Rubin, Ronald I. *The Objectives of the U.S. Information Agency: Controversies and Analysis.* New York: Praeger, 1968. Rubin examines the role of the USIA in the American political structure. See also

John W. Henderson, *The United States Information Agency* (New York: Praeger, 1969), for a factual, and generally favorable, account.

2:186 Sorensen, Thomas C. *The World War: The Story of American Propaganda.* New York: Harper & Row, 1968. In a good history of the U.S. Information Agency, stressing the Edward R. Murrow years, Sorensen argues that it is not enough to just inform with the facts—one must make a case for American views.

2:187 Stephens, Oren. *Facts to a Candid World: America's Overseas Information Program.* Stanford, Calif.: Stanford University Press, 1955. This useful account of official American efforts to influence world opinion, from World War I to the 1950s—through its overseas offices—focuses on the difficulties involved. Wilson P. Dizard, a veteran USIA official, describes post-1945 efforts in his *The Strategy of Truth: The Story of the U.S. Information Service* (Washington, D.C.: Public Affairs Press, 1961).

Cultural Diplomacy

For U.S.-U.S.S.R. exchanges, see Chapter 29, "Cultural and Scientific Relations."

Barghoorn, F. C. *The Soviet Cultural Offensive: The Role of Cultural Diplomacy in Soviet Foreign Policy* (29:198) is a study of the purposes and techniques of Soviet "cultural" diplomacy, which the author closely equates with messianic propaganda. Discussed are such topics as student exchanges, tourist travel, exhibitions, and historical research in the 1950s.

2:188 Braisted, Paul J., ed. *Cultural Affairs and Foreign Relations.* Rev. ed. Washington, D.C.: Columbia, 1968. These essays review several aspects of international cultural relations, education, and science.

Byrnes, R.F. *Soviet-American Academic Exchanges, 1958–1975* (29:199) gives special attention to the Inter-University Committee (of which he was a founder and chairman) and its administration of the principal Soviet-American exchange programs.

2:189 Coombs, Philip H. *The Fourth Dimension of Foreign Policy: Educational and Cultural Affairs.* New York: Harper & Row, 1964. A former State Department official reviews past U.S. efforts to employ cultural contacts to strengthen basic foreign policy objectives.

2:190 Espinosa, J. Manuel. *Inter-American Beginnings of U.S. Cultural Diplomacy, 1936–1948.* Washington, D.C.: G.P.O., 1976. Authored by a historian and State Department official active in cultural programs, this work demonstrates that such efforts originated as a result of perceived Axis threat to the Americas. Envisioned as more than propaganda, the program sought to promote better understanding within the hemisphere by the exchange of students, artists, musicians, intellectuals, educators, and businessmen.

Fairbank, W. *America's Cultural Experiment in China, 1942–1949* (27:71) chronicles the activities of the State Department's International Educational and Cultural Exchange Program in China.

Kellermann, H. J. *Cultural Relations as an Instrument of U.S. Foreign Policy: The Educational Exchange Program between the United States and Germany, 1945–1954* (28:84).

2:191 McMurry, Ruth, and Lee, Muna. *The Cultural Approach: Another Way in International Relations.* Chapel Hill, N.C.: University of North Carolina Press, 1947. They survey the cultural relations programs undertaken by France, Germany, Japan, Russia, Latin America, and the United States. It is descriptive rather than analytical.

2:192 Ninkovich, Frank. "The Currents of Cultural Diplomacy: Art and the State Department, 1938–1947." *Diplomatic History* 1:3 (1977), 215–37. Initially, the department looked to the private sector for cultural contributions to its program. After the war, however, it purchased examples of modern art and exhibited them around the world. This display of avant garde forms occasioned congressional protest.

2:193 Thomson, Charles A., and Laves, Walter H. C. *Cultural Relations and U.S. Foreign Policy.* Bloomington: Indiana University Press, 1963. The authors discuss the objectives of a cultural relations program, and the evolution of such programs from 1938 to 1962.

DOMESTIC INFLUENCES

2:194 Hero, Alfred O., Jr., and Starr, Emil. *The Reuther-Meany Foreign Policy Dispute: Union Lead-*

ers and Members View World Affairs. Dobbs Ferry, N.Y.: Oceana, 1970. The authors discuss the foreign policy split that came out in the open in 1966 between the more liberal forces of Reuther and the more conservative forces of Meany.

2:195　Mills, C. Wright. *The Power Elite.* New York: Oxford University Press, 1956. A pioneering analysis of what would later become known as the American "establishment," this book influenced a considerable number of revisionist critiques of U.S. foreign policy in the 1960s. Mills argues that American society is run by elites (corporate, political, military, and social) who are not representative of the American public generally.

2:196　Rosenau, James N., ed. *Domestic Sources of Foreign Policy.* New York: Free Press, 1967. This useful, but uneven collection of essays, seeks to demonstrate the supremacy of domestic factors in the shaping of American foreign policy.

2:197　Shepherd, George W., Jr., ed. *Racial Influence on American Foreign Policy.* New York: Basic Books, 1971. One of the few books to deal with the influence of racial considerations on U.S. foreign policy, this volume concentrates on relations with Asia, Africa, and Latin America. See also R. F. Weston, *Racism in U.S. Imperialism: The Influence of Racial Assumptions on American Foreign Policy, 1893–1946* (Columbia, S.C., 1972).

2:198　Shoup, Laurence H., and Minter, William. *Imperial Brain Trust: The Council on Foreign Relations and United States Foreign Policy.* London: Monthly Review Press, 1977. Described as a work of "Marxian historical sociology" in the preface, this volume develops a theory of how monopoly capitalists on the CFR led the United States down the imperialist path. Extensive bibliography.

Public Opinion and Foreign Policy

Many chapters have sections related to public opinion.

2:199　Alger, Chadwick F. "'Foreign' Policies of U.S. Publics." *International Studies Quarterly* 21:2 (1977), 227–318. U.S citizens, slightly informed about global, social, and economic processes, generally defer to experts on foreign policy issues. Alger analyzes reasons for this attitude and suggests that

people can develop competence in matters of foreign policy.

2:200　Almond, Gabriel A. *The American People and Foreign Policy.* New York: Praeger (1950), 1960. This analysis of public opinion and foreign policy, drawing on studies done in the immediate postwar years, constituted a methodological breakthrough. The concepts of elites and moods, which it pioneered, are now part of the political science lexicon; its generalizations about public opinion are of lasting value in understanding American foreign policy.

2:201　Bailey, Thomas A. *The Man in the Street.* New York: Macmillan, 1948. Reprint 1964. Bailey examines the power of public opinion in the United States, with examples from the time of the American Revolution to the present, although the emphasis is on the 20th century.

2:202　Baker, Roscoe. *The American Legion and American Foreign Policy.* New York: Bookman, 1954. Between 1920 and 1950, the legion favored tighter restrictions on immigration, consistently saw communism as a danger, favored national defense measures, opposed disarmament programs, and until the late 1930s endorsed isolationist policies. This is a detailed account of its efforts to influence responses to these issues. Bibliography.

2:203　Gerson, Louis L. *The Hyphenate in Recent American Politics and Diplomacy.* Lawrence: University Press of Kansas, 1964. This study examines the influence of immigrant Americans on U.S. foreign policy.

Hero, A. O., Jr. "The American Public and the UN, 1954–1966" (38:188) analyzes the numerous polls taken by the Gallup, Harris, and Roper organizations over the past thirty years. American public opinion on the UN has been consistently favorable despite criticism of specific UN developments.

2:204　Hero, Alfred O., Jr. *Americans in World Affairs.* Boston: World Peace Foundation, 1959. How do Americans feel about, and react to, world affairs? What motivates this interest? These questions and others are discussed on the basis of statistical surveys. Extensive bibliographical notes.

2:205　Hero, Alfred O., Jr. "American Negroes and U.S. Foreign Policy: 1937–1967." *Journal of Conflict Resolution* 13:2 (1969), 220–51. Large amounts of opinion-survey data have been collated for this study in order to obtain more accurate information about racial differences in foreign policy opinions in this country.

2:206 Hero, Alfred O., Jr. *American Religious Groups View Foreign Policy: Trends in Rank-and-File Opinion, 1937–1969.* Durham, N.C.: Duke University Press, 1973. Hero attempts to systematically examine the impact of the churches and the public stances of their national and international leadership upon church members. Vast statistical tables.

2:207 Hero, Alfred O., Jr. *The Southerner and World Affairs.* Baton Rouge: Louisiana State University Press, 1965. In one of the few comprehensive efforts to study regional views concerning recent foreign policy issues, Hero concludes that the South's view shifted, from the end of World War II to the mid-1960s, from enthusiasm for international cooperation to measured skepticism. Should be read in conjunction with a parallel study, C. O. Lerche, Jr., *The Uncertain South: Its Changing Pattern of Politics in Foreign Policy* (2:152).

2:208 Hilderbrand, Robert C. *Power and the People: Executive Management of Public Opinion in Foreign Affairs, 1869–1921.* Chapel Hill: University of North Carolina Press, 1981. Hilderbrand here considers the question: how important has public opinion been perceived by officials charged with the formulation of foreign policy? In the process of answering this question, he emphasizes the procedures, personal and institutional, utilized by the White House and the executive branch.

Hohenberg, J. *Between Two Worlds: Policy, Press, and Public Opinion in Asian-American Relations* (31:25) is a study of the relationship between foreign correspondence and foreign policy from 1941 to the mid-1960s. The author finds that the exchange of news, ideas, and opinion between the United States and Asia is often political in character, involving governments and their struggle with the independent news media for control.

2:209 Leopold, Richard W. "The Mississippi Valley and American Foreign Policy, 1890–1941: An Assessment and an Appeal." *Mississippi Valley Historical Review* 37:4 (1951), 625–42. This article provides a historiographical appraisal of scholarship bearing on the midwestern sectionalism and world affairs, and is filled with suggestions for further research.

May, E. R. *American Imperialism: A Speculative Essay* (2:94) contains a valuable chapter on the uses of public opinion in foreign policy.

2:210 Miscamble, Wilson D. "Catholics and American Foreign Policy from McKinley to McCarthy: A Historiographical Survey." *Diplomatic History* 4:3 (1980), 223–40. This useful survey (1898–1950s) reviews the literature relating to American Catholic efforts to influence U.S. foreign policy.

2:211 Paterson, Walfred H. "The Foreign Policy of the Socialist Party of America before World War I." *Pacific Northwest Quarterly* 65:4 (1974), 176–83. The author reviews the foreign policy expressions of the Socialist party, and concludes that the Socialists were content to minimize foreign policy issues until after the start of World War I.

2:212 Rappaport, Armin. *The Navy League of the United States.* Detroit: Wayne State University Press, 1962. This book asserts that the league had little influence during most of its existence. When legislation that it backed was passed, outside factors—not its own propaganda—were responsible. Rappaport demolishes the myth that the league served as a front for munitions and shipbuilding lobbies.

2:213 Stuhler, Barbara. *Ten Men of Minnesota and American Foreign Policy, 1898–1968.* St. Paul: Minnesota Historical Society, 1973. This study shows again the dangers of stereotyping foreign policy attitudes in the Middle West. It examines one imperialist—Cushman Davis; three isolationists—Charles Lindbergh, Sr., Harold Knutson, and Henrik Shipstead; and six internationalists—Frank Kellogg, Joseph Ball, Harold Stassen, Walter Judd, Hubert Humphrey, and Eugene McCarthy.

Bilateral and Regional Studies

These general studies have been collected here to provide easy access to individual background information. More specialized accounts, both in terms of chronology and specific themes, will be found in the appropriate chapters below.

2:214 American University. Foreign Area Studies. Area Handbook Series. Washington, D.C.: G.P.O., 1951– . These area handbooks (which are country studies on a world wide basis) provide a useful introduction as they address such issues as history, traditions, culture, education, as well as data on economics and military, political, and social institutions. Each handbook contains extensive bibliographies as well as maps, charts and tables, usually in appendixes.

2:215 Chester, Edward W. *The United States and Six Atlantic Outposts: The Military and Economic Considerations.* Port Washington, N.Y.: Kennikat, 1980. This account reviews American contacts with Iceland, Greenland, the Azores, Bermuda, Jamaica, and the Bahamas. By the time of World War II, both U.S. merchants and investors had shown an interest in these Atlantic outposts; military activities date from the 1770s. Extensive bibliography.

EUROPE AND CANADA

2:216 Akenson, Donald H. *The United States and Ireland.* Cambridge: Harvard University Press, 1973. This book covers Irish history, but concentrates on the 20th century and the 1960s in particular. This is a useful starting point for students. Extensive bibliography.

McNeill, W. H. *The Metamorphosis of Greece since World War II* [1945–1977] (28:139) is an important starting point for anyone who wants to understand modern Greece.

2:217 Wandycz, Piotr. *The United States and Poland.* Cambridge: Harvard University Press, 1979. By an outstanding expert on Polish foreign relations, this volume is the best single book on its topic. It will be the basic starting point for years to come. Bibliography.

Canada

Brebner, J. B. *North Atlantic Triangle: The Interplay of Canada, the United States and Great Britain* [1490s–1940s] (2:233) is useful on U.S.-Canadian border differences.

2:218 Callahan, James M. *American Foreign Policy in Canadian Relations.* New York: Macmillan, 1937. Callahan includes accounts of America's involvement in the Canadian rebellion of 1837–1838, the formation of the Webster-Ashburton Treaty in 1842, and the negotiation of the Treaty of Washington of 1871. It is still useful for background information.

2:219 Craig, Gerald M. *The United States and Canada.* Cambridge: Harvard University Press, 1968. Craig surveys U.S.-Canadian relations from the early 17th century to the 1960s, and argues that one of their biggest problems has been American unwillingness to show more than mild concern for Canadian interests. Extensive bibliography.

2:220 Deener, David R., ed. *Canada-United States Treaty Relations.* Durham, N.C.: Duke University Press, 1963. This collection of papers discusses the significance of their mutual treaties concerning boundaries, defense, and trade. Though not meant to be a balanced survey, the writers touch upon agreements ranging from the 1780s through 1960. Extensive bibliography.

2:221 Glazebrook, George P. DeT. *A History of Canadian External Relations.* New York: Oxford University Press, 1950. A major work on Canadian diplomatic history, this volume is useful for its view of U.S.-Canadian realations.

Granatstein, J. L., ed. *Canadian Foreign Policy since 1945: Middle Power or Satellite?* (36:23).

Jordan, F. J. E. "The International Joint Commission and Canada-United States Boundary Relations" [1909–1974] (36:180).

2:222 McInnis, Edgar W. *The Unguarded Frontier: A History of American-Canadian Relations.* Garden City, N.Y.: Doubleday, Doran, 1942. This narrative covers the whole range of Canadian-American border disputes. Bibliography.

2:223 Willoughby, William R. *The St. Lawrence Waterway: A Study in Politics and Diplomacy.* Madison: University of Wisconsin Press, 1961. A Great Lakes-St. Lawrence waterway has long been an important issue in U.S.-Canadian relations, and this volume traces the dream for 250 years.

France

2:224 Blumenthal, Henry. *France and the United States: Their Diplomatic Relations, 1789–1914.* Chapel Hill: University of North Carolina Press, 1970.

This diplomatic survey concentrates on the policy development in Franco-American relations rather than public attitudes in the two nations toward one another. The judgments are clear, thoughtful, and moderate. Bibliography.

2:225 Brinton, C. Crane. *The Americans and the French*. Cambridge: Harvard University Press, 1968. Brinton concentrates on the period after 1945, and finds more faults with Americans than with the French. Bibliography.

Carmor, G. de. *The Foreign Policies of France* (28:122) is a detailed survey covering 1944 to 1968.

2:226 Duroselle, Jean-Baptiste. *France and the United States: From the Beginnings to the Present*. Trans. by Derek Coltman. Chicago: University of Chicago Press, 1978. This is an examination of American relations with France in the context of French perceptions and responses. Bibliography.

2:227 White, Elizabeth B. *American Opinion of France from Lafayette to Poincaré*. New York: Knopf, 1927. This general survey is based on the writings of prominent American diplomats and intellectuals rather than on newspapers and periodicals. Bibliography.

2:228 Zahniser, Marvin R. *Uncertain Friendship: American-French Relations through the Cold War*. New York: Wiley, 1975. An excellent brief survey (1523–1970), it is more reliable for the early period than Jean-Baptiste Duroselle (2:226). Bibliography.

Germany (Prussia)

Adams, H. M. *Prussian-American Relations, 1775–1871* (5:152) contains a brief descriptive survey of these relations, but lacks an introduction, a conclusion, or any analytical framework.

2:229 Gatzke, Hans W. *Germany and the United States: A "Special Relationship"?* Cambridge: Harvard University Press, 1980. This is a general survey of German-American relations from 1776 to the 1970s. It is useful as an introduction to diplomatic issues. Bibliography.

2:230 Knapp, Manfred; Link, Werner; Schröder, Hans-Jürgen; and Schwabe, Klaus. *Die USA and Deutschland, 1918–1975: Deutsch-amerikanische Beziehungen zwuschen Rivakität und Parnerschaft* [The

USA and Germany, 1918–1975: German-American relations, between rivalry and partnership]. Munich: Beck, 1978. Knapp, Link, and Schröder summarize their previously published works, all of which have been well received. Concentrating on 1918–1919, Schwabe examines the gap between Wilson's new diplomacy rhetoric and his acceptance of a victor's peace. Link analyzes the deteriorating German-American relationship during the Weimar era, while Schröder looks at the developing rivalry during the 1930s. An original essay by Knapp surveys relations after World War II.

Morgan, R. *The United States and West Germany, 1945–1973* (28:86) is a solid short survey which provides an introduction to U.S.-Germany interests and issues since World War II.

Great Britain

2:231 Allen, Harry C. *Conflict and Concord: The Anglo-American Relationship since 1783*. New York: St. Martin's Press, 1959. Allen argues that social, political, and economic factors prevailed over the issues threatening the Atlantic relationship. He holds that, because "there was no deep, inherent antagonism" between the nations after the War of 1812, "Anglo-American cordiality" developed quickly after 1814.

2:232 Allen, Harry C. *Great Britain and the United States: A History of Anglo-American Relations (1783–1952)*. New York: St. Martin's Press, 1955. This work, the standard modern survey of its subject, demonstrates the vagaries of the transatlantic connection between the United States and Great Britain. The book reflects the author's commitment to the need for cordial relations between the two nations, and displays his sympathetic understanding of the American problem in British affairs.

2:233 Brebner, John B. *North Atlantic Triangle: The Interplay of Canada, the United States and Great Britain*. New Haven, Conn.: Yale University Press, 1945. Reprint 1966. Brebner discusses the major factors involved in American-British-Canadian relations in North America from the 1490s through the 1940s. Extensive bibliography.

2:234 Campbell, Charles S., Jr. *From Revolution to Rapprochement: The United States and Great Britain, 1783–1900*. New York: Wiley, 1974. A brief survey; the author's thesis is that a real Anglo-American rapprochement was not realized until the end of the 19th century. Bibliography.

2:235 Gordon, Michael R. *Conflict and Consensus in Labour's Foreign Policy, 1914–1965*. Stanford, Calif.: Stanford University Press, 1969. In a valuable analysis of internal Labour debate over foreign policy, the author argues that in 1945 the Atlee government repudiated the commitment to a distinctively socialist foreign policy — in favor of the Anglo-American collaboration. This realignment divided the party. The author examines the ideas and attitudes expressed in the ensuing struggle. Extensive bibliography.

2:236 Medlicott, W. N., ed. *From Metternich to Hitler: Aspects of British and Foreign History, 1814–1939*. New York: Barnes & Noble, 1963. This collection of essays is useful for understanding the basis of British foreign policy.

2:237 Nicholas, Herbert G. *The United States and Britain*. Chicago: University of Chicago Press, 1975. This book provides a useful introduction to this bilateral relationship.

2:238 Pelling, Henry. *America and the British Left: From Bright to Bevin*. New York: New York University Press, 1957. Pelling traces the views of the British Left toward the United States and American foreign affairs. The author argues that after 1945 socialist suspicions of America were tempered by more pragmatic British trade union leadership which, in effect, saved the Anglo-American relationship from serious disruption.

2:239 Willson, Beckles. *Friendly Relations: A Narrative of Britain's Ministers and Ambassadors to America (1791–1930)*. Boston: Little, Brown, 1934. Reprint 1969. This is a series of brief portraits of the subjects. The treatment is popular and short on analysis and, inevitably, dated. The author also performed a similar service for *America's Ambassadors to England (1785–1928)* (2:181).

2:240 Windrich, Elaine. *British Labour's Foreign Policy*. Stanford, Calif.: Stanford University Press, 1952. An approving study that argues the Labour party has maintained continuity in the principles of its foreign policy over the past 50 years. It has worked for peace, security, independence, and prosperity, as opposed to the balance of power and imperialism. Although the work has little to say on Anglo-American relations directly, it is useful for understanding the foreign policies of the British Left.

Italy

DeConde, A. *Half Bitter, Half Sweet: An Excursion into Italian-American History* (8:101) is a broad, cultural survey of the interaction of Italy and the United States as well as Italians and Americans on a very broad canvass. Diplomatic relations are clearly part of this story.

2:241 Hughes, Henry S. *The United States and Italy*. 3d ed. Cambridge: Harvard University Press, 1979. This account remains a basic starting point for studying U.S.-Italian relations. As Hughes has noted, most Americans think they are very familiar with Italy when in fact they know very little. Bibliography.

Scandinavia

2:242 Fogdall, Soren J. M. P. *Danish-American Diplomacy, 1776–1920*. Iowa City: University of Iowa Press, 1926. Despite limited documentation, Fogdall covers many topics of interest, including extradition arrangements, the status of the Danish West Indies, trade and tariff matters, Mormon missionaries in Denmark, claims settlements, and arbitration conventions.

Hovde, B. J. *Diplomatic Relations of the United States with Sweden and Norway, 1814–1905* (8:106) briefly treats Swedish responses to French intervention in Mexico, the problem posed by Mormon immigrants from the Scandinavian countries, and extradition and naturalization treaties.

2:243 Scott, Franklin D. *Scandinavia*. Rev. ed. Cambridge: Harvard University Press, 1975. This volume is an excellent starting point for the American student and covers all the Scandinavian countries. Bibliography.

Spain

Cortada, J. W., ed. *Spain in the Twentieth-Century World: Essays on Spanish Diplomacy, 1898–1978* (28:155) provides a useful background to U.S.-Spanish relations.

2:244 Cortada, James W. *Two Nations over Time: Spain and the United States, 1776–1977*. Westport, Conn.: Greenwood, 1978. The author analyzes the diplomatic relations between the two nations by examining economic and cultural factors as well as the domestic politics of both nations. Bibliography.

Watson, W., et al. *Spain: Implications for United States Foreign Policy* [1945–1975] (28:159) focuses on U.S.-Spanish military relations.

Soviet Union (Russia)

2:245 Bailey, Thomas A. *America Faces Russia: Russian-American Relations from Early Times to Our Day.* Ithaca, N.Y.: Cornell University Press, 1950. Bailey's survey dwells thematically on the superficial nature of American-Russian "friendship" and on the similarities of recurrent diplomatic problems. The work is highly anecdotal. Bibliography.

2:246 Bray, William G. *Russian Frontiers: From Muscovy to Khrushchev.* Indianapolis: Bobbs-Merrill, 1963. The author sees Soviet communism as the latest vehicle for Russian imperialism. The Soviet Union has carried out traditional expansionist policies, many of which date back to the Muscovite era. Bray compares the techniques and goals, the successes and failures of czarist and Soviet expansionism.

2:247 Dulles, Foster Rhea. *The Road to Teheran: The Story of Russia and America, 1781–1943.* Princeton, N.J.: Princeton University Press, 1944. This volume traces relations between the United States and Russia from 1776 to 1940s. It is a general, pre-cold war introduction.

2:248 Gaddis, John Lewis. *Russia, the Soviet Union and the United States: An Interpretive History.* New York: Wiley, 1978. This brief account surveys American relations with Russia from before the American Revolution to the Ford administration. It is useful as an introduction to themes and episodes affecting this relationship, particularly prior to World War II. Extensive bibliographical essay.

2:249 Kennan, George F. "The United States and the Soviet Union, 1917–1976." *Foreign Affairs* 54:4 (1976), 671–90. This article constitutes a useful brief overview of its subject. Kennan argues that the United States was ill prepared to understand the Russian revolutions and slow to recognize the possibility of common interests with the new Soviet regime.

2:250 Laserson, Max M. *The American Impact on Russia: Diplomatic and Ideological, 1784–1917.* New York: Macmillan, 1950. This volume examines diplomatic, as well as socioeconomic, political, and cultural contacts, between the nations. The author concludes that the American impact on Russia in this period was much more substantial than generally recognized. Bibliography.

2:251 Ponomaryov, B.; Gromyko, A.; and Khvostov, V., eds. *History of Soviet Foreign Policy, 1917–1945.* Trans. by David Skvirsky. Moscow: Progress Publishers, 1969. Using "scientific" Marxist analysis "to expose the predatory policy of imperialism," the Soviet authors use the theme of socialism in one country to flay the perfidious West in general and the United States in particular, while emphasizing the ideas of Lenin and all but ignoring the role of Stalin.

2:252 Rogger, Hans. "America in the Russian Mind—Or Russian Discoveries of America." *Pacific Historical Review* 47:1 (1978), 27–51. The Russian image of America in the 19th and 20th centuries has been ambivalent and contradictory. America has been criticized as materialistic, despiritualized, cut off from tradition, exploitative, and egotistic, and complimented for political liberty, technical ingenuity and energy, religious toleration, and lack of formal social distinctions.

2:253 Sivachev, Nikolai V., and Yakovlev, Nikolai N. *Russia and the United States: U.S.-Soviet Relations from the Soviet Point of View.* Trans. by Olga Adler Titelbaum. Chicago: University of Chicago Press, 1979. This book interprets and summarizes relations from 1776 to the present. Based on Marxist methodology, as well as American and Soviet unpublished and published materials, it is extraordinarily interesting. This stimulating book should be read by every serious student of Soviet-American affairs.

Sutton, A. C. *Western Technology and Soviet Economic Development, 1917–1965* (20:204).

Triska, J. F., and Finley, D. D. *Soviet Foreign Policy* [1917–1968] (29:25) is a useful starting point for the fundamental issues in the study of Soviet diplomatic behavior.

2:254 Ulam, Adam B. *Expansion and Coexistence: Soviet Foreign Policy, 1917–1973.* 2d ed. New York: Holt, Rinehart & Winston, 1974. The most reliable work on the general course of Soviet foreign policy, this book is essential for study of its subject.

2:255 Whelan, Joseph G., comp. "Soviet-American Relations, 1933–60: A Brief Selective

Chronology with Interpretive Commentary." *Congressional Record* (Senate) 106:12 (July 1, 1960), 15317–34. Prepared by the Library of Congress and published separately by the library, the report was conveniently reprinted here. It is useful for its chronology, the commentary has much less value.

2:256 Williams, William Appleman. *American-Russian Relations, 1781–1947.* New York: Rinehart, 1952. Williams anticipates the revisionist writings now so much a part of Soviet-American historiography. Its appearance early in the cold war caused a mild sensation because of its critique of the policy of containment, its suggestion that American leaders of the 1920s, 1930s, and the war years mishandled relations, and its contention that Soviet-American antagonism had long roots in prerevolutionary relations.

Switzerland

2:257 Meier, Heinz K. *Friendship under Stress: U.S.-Swiss Relations, 1900–1950.* Bern: Lang, 1970. If nothing else, this book demonstrates the paucity of literature dealing with prewar diplomacy between the United States and such lesser powers as Switzerland. The author focuses on U.S.-Swiss relations during the two world wars, exploring economic relations and Switzerland's importance as a neutral nation.

2:258 Meier, Heinz K. *The United States and Switzerland in the Nineteenth Century.* The Hague: Mouton, 1963. This study traces the generally friendly relations which existed between these two nations to the outbreak of World War I. Bibliography.

LATIN AMERICA

2:259 Aguilar Monteverde, Alonso. *Pan Americanism from Monroe to the Present: A View from the Other Side.* Trans. by Asa Zatz. New York: Monthly Review Press, 1969. This revised English edition presents a sweeping view of U.S.-Latin American relations. The author sees U.S. policy in various eras as designed to promote weak and dependable allies in the western hemisphere and to exploit Latin America. Bibliography contains other critical works.

Arévalo, J. J. *The Shark and the Sardines* [1900–1954] (34:35) is a classic polemic, highly critical of U.S. policies.

2:260 Bemis, Samuel Flagg. *The Latin American Policy of the United States: An Historical Interpretation.* New York: Harcourt, Brace, 1943. A classic, still useful account, but it doesn't reflect recent research and interpretations. Bibliography.

Blasier, C. *The Hovering Giant: United States Responses to Revolutionary Change in Latin America* [1910–1964] (35:26) examines U.S. responses to social revolutions in Mexico, Bolivia, Guatemala, and Cuba.

Callcott, W. H. *The Western Hemisphere: Its Influence on United States Policies to the End of World War II* [1789–1945] (35:83).

2:261 Connell-Smith, Gordon. *The United States and Latin America: An Historical Analysis of Inter-American Relations.* New York: Wiley, 1974. This recent analysis, generally critical of U.S. policy, by a prominent British Latin Americanist is constructed as a counterbalance to the orthodox accounts of Samuel Flagg Bemis and J. Lloyd Mecham. Modestly footnoted, with no formal bibliography.

Davis, H. E.; Finian, J. J.; and Peck, F. T. *Latin American Diplomatic History: An Introduction* [1493–1975] (35:21) is a general survey which provides a valuable overview.

Davis, H. E., and Wilson, L. C., eds. *Latin American Foreign Policies: An Analysis* [1810–1974] (35:22) examines the foreign policies of Latin American states.

2:262 Gantenbein, James W., ed. *The Evolution of Our Latin American Policy: A Documentary Record.* New York: Columbia University Press, 1950. A large collection of documents, it is arranged topically and chronologically, from the 18th century to 1949.

2:263 Gardner, James A. *Legal Imperialism: American Lawyers and Foreign Aid in Latin America.* Madison: University of Wisconsin Press, 1980. This book offers a scholarly and carefully documented history of the role of American lawyers in legal assistance for Latin America, and an analysis of the American legal models that informed and were carried abroad as part of this process.

Gil, F. G. *Latin American-United States Relations* [1821–1970] (35:30) is a brief survey which perceives cycles in inter-American relations.

2:264 Karnes, Thomas L., ed. *Readings in the Latin American Policy of the United States.* Tucson: University of Arizona Press, 1972. A very useful collection of original documents, arranged chronologically and topically, it is well edited and connected with introductions providing historical contexts. Bibliography.

Lieuwen, E. *United States Policy in Latin America* [1810–1965] (35:31) emphasizes the more recent years, when he finds U.S. policy influenced by strategic considerations.

2:265 Mecham, J. Lloyd. *A Survey of United States-Latin American Relations.* Boston: Houghton Mifflin, 1965. Frequently consulted for its orthodox interpretations, this is one of the basic surveys in the field. The volume is arranged by chapters dealing with general policies in various periods, followed by chapters on bilateral relations with the various Latin American nations. Mecham maintains that over the years, while means to an end have changed from time to time, the most consistent objective of U.S. policy in Latin America has been to protect its own national security. Extensive bibliography.

2:266 Mörner, Magnus. *Race and Class in Latin America.* New York: Columbia University Press, 1970. This is a useful overview to the internal determinants of foreign policy in Latin American.

Needler, M. C. *The United States and the Latin American Revolution* [1823–1976] (35:33) argues that U.S. understanding of these revolutions has been hampered by narrow preoccupation with private interests, false security concerns, and outdated ideological fixations.

2:267 Pike, Frederick B. *The United States and the Andean Republics: Peru, Bolivia, and Ecuador.* Cambridge: Harvard University Press, 1977. A synthesis based primarily on secondary works, this volume provides an analysis of the political and economic developments in Peru, Ecuador, and Bolivia that have taken place under the patronage of the United States. Pike demonstrates that U.S. leaders, stressing such principles as competitive independence, have never fully comprehended the Andean culture, which emphasizes corporate (patron-client) value systems. Extensive bibliography.

2:268 Stuart, Graham H., and Tigner, James L. *Latin America and the United States.* 6th ed. Englewood Cliffs, N.J.: Prentice-Hall, 1975. A com-

prehensive textbook, arranged by topics and by countries, it is useful for facts and information. Bibliography.

2:269 Whitaker, Arthur P. *The United States and South America: The Northern Republics.* Cambridge: Harvard University Press, 1948. A general survey, it has more information on the history of the nations in northern South America than on their relationships with the United States.

2:270 Whitaker, Arthur P., ed. *The United States and the Southern Cone: Argentina, Chile, and Uruguay.* Cambridge: Harvard University Press, 1976. A history of the three nations and their relations with the United States, stressing the 20th century, which argues that U.S. imperialism, earlier restricted to the Caribbean, was gradually extended to the southern cone nations. Lengthy bibliographical essay.

Monroe Doctrine

For additional references, see Chapter 7, "The Monroe Doctrine, to 1861," Chapter 15, "The Monroe Doctrine, 1861–1919," and Chapter 21, "Good Neighbor Policy/Monroe Doctrine."

2:271 Dozer, Donald M., ed. *The Monroe Doctrine: Its Modern Significance.* New York: Knopf, 1965. These reprinted selections represent both American and Latin American views. The editor provides an introductory essay which puts the selections in perspective.

Fabela, I. *Intervención* [1865–1954] (35:42) discusses the law of intervention in an inter-American setting.

2:272 Logan, John A. *No Transfer: An American Security Principle.* New Haven: Yale University Press, 1961. From the beginning of the nation, Logan believes, Americans have opposed the transfer of colonial possessions in this hemisphere from one European power to another (stronger) one. This principle is closely allied to the Monroe Doctrine although not at first formally connected to it.

2:273 Perkins, Dexter. *A History of the Monroe Doctrine.* Rev. ed. Boston: Houghton Mifflin, 1963. The classic survey of the history of the Monroe Doctrine; Perkins ranges from the doctrine's origins during the colonial and revolutionary periods through the first decade of the post–World War II era.

2:274 Thomas, Ann Van Wynen, and Thomas, A. J., Jr. *Non-Intervention: The Law and Its Import in the Americas.* Dallas: Southern Methodist University Press, 1956. The authors' purpose was to clarify the meaning of the terms *intervention* and *nonintervention* as they applied to U.S. relations with Latin America and to actions by the OAS and United Nations. The point of view is almost wholly legal, and the treatment is based upon elucidation of treaties and rulings of international law. It discusses various forms of intervention.

2:275 Van Alstyne, Richard W. "The Monroe Doctrine." In Alexander DeConde, ed., *Encyclopedia of American Foreign Policy.* New York: Scribner's, 1978, vol. 2, pp. 584–96. An interpretive survey of the history of the Monroe Doctrine by a leading scholar of U.S. expansion. Bibliography.

Pan-Americanism and Hemispheric Security

2:276 Ball, Mary M. *The Problem of Inter-American Organization.* Stanford, Calif.: Stanford University Press, 1944. This concise introduction to the development of the Pan-American system contains the clearest descriptions of the various organs of the system extant at the time of publication. The carefully prepared index and list of agencies add to its usefulness. Bibliography.

2:277 Connell-Smith, Gordon. *The Inter-American System.* New York: Oxford University Press, 1966. This study by an English scholar is of special value because it provides a view from outside the western hemisphere. The author is adept in pointing out the gap between the exaggerated claims made by the United States for the success of the system and its modest achievements. This volume provides a contrast to J. Lloyd Mecham's laudatory account (2:283). Extensive bibliography.

2:278 Dávila, Carlos G. *We of the Americas.* Chicago: Ziff-Davis, 1949. Essentially the same as a Spanish version published in Santiago de Chile the following year, this treatise decries the failure of Pan-Americanism (1790–1948) and calls for greater attention by the United States to its neighbors of the south. The author maintains that Pan-Americanism was being subordinated to world policies and that the

result was danger to the western hemisphere. He was also an early advocate of inter-American economic integration.

2:279 Duggan, Laurence. *The Americas: The Search for Hemisphere Security.* New York: Holt, 1949. Written by a Latin American specialist in the State Department, the work (covering 1823–1948) treats realistically the good neighbor policy, wartime relations, and the postwar period. It serves to answer critics of Truman's policies. It also contains a summary of the social and historical background of Latin America and concludes with synopses of the inter-American conferences through 1948.

2:280 Inman, Samuel G. *Inter-American Conferences, 1826–1954: History and Problems.* Washington, D.C.: University Press of Washington, D.C., 1965. An uncritical and optimistic history of the inter-American system, from Bolívar's Panama Congress to the tenth meeting at Caracas in 1954, it is valuable for the personal insights and experiences of the author.

2:281 Karnes, Thomas L. "Pan-Americanism." In Alexander DeConde, ed., *Encyclopedia of American Foreign Policy.* New York: Scribner's, 1978, vol. 2, pp. 730–41. A brief synthetic survey, it incorporates recent research and interpretations. Bibliography.

2:282 Martz, John D., and Schoulty, Lars, eds. *Latin America, the United States, and the Inter-American System.* Boulder, Colo.: Westview, 1980. This collection of original essays focuses on the workings of the contemporary inter-American system, with emphasis on the changes in the hemispheric political economy, U.S. control over the behavior of Latin American governments, and the human rights issue.

2:283 Mecham, J. Lloyd. *The United States and Inter-American Security, 1889–1960.* Austin: University of Texas Press, 1961. The author, with emphasis on development of the Monroe Doctrine and the inter-American system, is not overly critical of U.S. policy, and sees security concerns as important in the development of U.S. policy. Bibliography.

2:284 Whitaker, Arthur P. *The Western Hemisphere Idea: Its Rise and Decline.* Ithaca, N.Y.: Cornell University Press, 1954. This volume includes eight essays on the European origins of the western hemisphere idea to modern interpretations of the concept. Bibliography.

Argentina

Haring, C. H. *Argentina and the United States* [18th century to 1941] (15:201) is a useful short survey.

2:285 Levene, Ricardo. *A History of Argentina.* Trans. by William Spence Robertson. Chapel Hill: University of North Carolina Press, 1937. This volume, by a distinguished Argentine historian, is useful for U.S.-Argentina affairs (1500–1930).

2:286 Milenky, E. S. *Argentina's Foreign Policies.* Boulder, Colo.: Westview, 1978. Chapter 4 treats U.S.-Argentine relations.

2:287 Peterson, Harold F. *Argentina and the United States, 1810–1960.* Albany: State University of New York Press, 1962. This work contains considerable information on the diplomatic relationship between two antagonists in the inter-American system. Peterson emphasizes the misunderstandings and misperceptions between Argentina and the United States and is especially detailed in covering the Falkland Islands dispute (1830s), Argentina's opposition to the United States in the Pan-American system, and the Perón era. Extensive bibliography.

2:288 Whitaker, Arthur P. *The United States and Argentina.* Cambridge: Harvard University Press, 1954. A short overall survey, stressing Argentine history (1810–1953) as well as relations with the United States.

Bolivia

Malloy, J. M. *Bolivia: The Uncompleted Revolution* (35:200).

Wilkie, J. W. *The Bolivian Revolution and U.S. Aid since 1952: Financial Background and Context of Political Decisions* (35:203).

Brazil

2:289 Burns, E. Bradford. *A History of Brazil.* 2d ed. New York: Columbia University Press, 1980. Burns has prepared an excellent scholarly history of Brazil; it covers a wide array of topics, including military and diplomatic policy through 1978.

2:290 Burns, E. Bradford. *Nationalism in Brazil: A Historical Survey.* New York: Praeger, 1968. This study of Brazilian nationalism—from its origins through the 20th century—is a useful overview. Critical bibliographical essay.

2:291 Fontaine, Roger W. *Brazil and the United States: Toward a Maturing Relationship.* Washington, D.C.: American Enterprise Institute for Public Policy Research, 1974. This study examines the strains imposed on the traditional relationship of the two countries by Brazil becoming the "other major power" in the western hemisphere. The author maintains that two issues—development of the Amazon Basin and Brazil's ambitious nuclear energy program—will dominate relations in the future.

2:292 Hill, Lawrence F. *Diplomatic Relations between the United States and Brazil.* Durham, N.C.: Duke University Press, 1932. This is a standard diplomatic survey, organized thematically and chronologically, which covers the subject from earliest contacts to the 1930s. The author, a Brazilian specialist, takes both an American and Brazilian perspective. Bibliography.

Chile

2:293 Evans, Henry C., Jr. *Chile and Its Relations with the United States.* Durham, N.C.: Duke University Press, 1927. This older study is still useful, mostly because Frederick Pike's survey of U.S.-Chilean relations begins with the 1880s, and because Evans's account goes beyond standard diplomatic history to comment on Chilean politics. Bibliography.

2:294 Galdames, Luís. *A History of Chile.* Trans. by Isaac J. Cox. Chapel Hill: University of North Carolina Press, 1941. A standard Chilean text, written in the Liberal tradition, it contains excellent biographical sketches of 19th-century Chilean political figures. Bibliography.

2:295 Pike, Frederick B. *Chile and the United States, 1880–1962: The Emergence of Chile's Social Crisis and the Challenge to United States Diplomacy.* Notre Dame, Ind.: University of Notre Dame Press, 1963. This is a detailed analysis of the development of social problems in Chile and their effects on relations with the United States. The author argues that the United States typically supported the upper classes in Chile.

2:296 Sherman, William R. *The Diplomatic and Commercial Relations of the United States and Chile, 1820–1914.* Boston: Badger, 1926. Less adequate than volume on same topic by Evans (2:293), it is still useful for its attention to commercial relations.

Colombia

Galbraith, W. O. *Colombia: A General Survey* (35:230).

2:297 Parks, E. Taylor. *Colombia and the United States, 1765–1934.* Durham, N.C.: Duke University Press, 1935. This work, a general survey of American-Colombian diplomatic relations, provides a good account of Colombian political history. The emphasis is on American canal policy in the 19th century. Bibliography.

Randall, S. J. *The Diplomacy of Modernization: Colombian-American Relations, 1920–1940* (21:287).

Mexico

2:298 Callahan, James M. *American Foreign Policy in Mexican Relations.* New York: Macmillan, 1932. Callahan places heavy emphasis on political relations and diplomatic correspondence; he is more factual than interpretive.

Carreño, A. M. *La diplomacía extraordinaria entre México y Estados Unidos* [1789–1947] (9:16) is a survey by a prominent Mexican author. The author's interpretation, stressing U.S. territorial expansion, is hostile.

2:299 Cline, Howard F. *The United States and Mexico.* 3d ed. Cambridge: Harvard University Press, 1963. A classic, it is somewhat mistitled because most of the book deals with Mexican history since 1910.

2:300 Rippy, J. Fred. *The United States and Mexico.* Rev. ed. New York: Knopf, 1931. This survey of Mexican-American relations emphasizes political and diplomatic activities, and the content is more factual than interpretive. Extensive bibliography.

Ross, S. R., ed. *Views across the Border: The United States and Mexico* [1848–1975] (35:173) focuses on mutual cultural and social issues.

2:301 Schmitt, Karl M. *Mexico and the United States, 1821–1973: Conflict and Coexistence.* New York: Wiley, 1974. This overall survey, reflecting recent research, develops two basic themes: the economic dependency of Mexico on the United States, and the power differential between the two nations. Bibliography.

2:302 Zorrilla, Luis G. *Historia de las relaciones entre México y los Estados Unidos de América, 1800–1958* [The history of relations between Mexico and the United States]. 2 vols. Mexico, D. F.: Editorial Porrúa, 1965–1966. The two volumes cover 1821 to 1963, and are good for the Mexican side of controversies and for its use of Mexican materials. Rather anti-American, the author makes insufficient use of American materials. Bibliography.

Peru

2:303 Carey, James C. *Peru and the United States, 1900–1962.* Notre Dame, Ind.: University of Notre Dame Press, 1964. While not of the quality of some other studies of U.S. bilateral relations with South American nations, this is a reliable account which emphasizes private business and financial affairs. Also included are a comprehensive treatment of U.S. aid programs and perhaps the single best analysis of Vice-President Nixon's 1958 misadventures in Lima.

2:304 Pike, Frederick B. *The Modern History of Peru.* New York: Praeger, 1967. A readable, concise history of Peru since independence, it stresses political considerations. It is useful for background information.

2:305 Wagner de Reyna, Alberto. *Historia diplomática del Perú, 1900–1945* [Diplomatic history of Peru, 1900–1945]. 2 vols. Lima: Ediciones Peruanas, 1964. A diplomatic history of Peru from 1900 to 1945 by an eminent Peruvian historian and diplomat, with useful bibliographies, indexes of treaties, and chronologies.

Venezuela

2:306 Liss, Sheldon B. *Diplomacy and Dependence: Venezuela, the United States and the Americas.*

Salisbury, N.C.: Documentary Publications, 1978. This is a detailed survey of bilateral relations (1810–1977); despite the title, there is little treatment of inter-American relations. Although the author's purpose was to test dependency theory, most of the account is orthodox diplomatic history. Yet the author is convincing in demonstrating that the United States has had considerable impact on Venezuela's economic growth, political liberalism, and maldistribution of wealth, especially after the early days of petroleum development. Extensive bibliography.

CARIBBEAN AND CENTRAL AMERICA

2:307 Karnes, Thomas L. *The Failure of Union: Central America, 1824–1960*. Chapel Hill: University of North Carolina Press, 1961. Using Central American archives, the author traces the ill-fated attempts at union. The work's strength is with the post-1871 period. Extensive bibliography.

2:308 Langley, Lester D. *Struggle for the American Mediterranean: United States-European Rivalry in the Gulf-Caribbean, 1776–1904*. Athens: University of Georgia Press, 1976. This is a synthesis of the international history of the Caribbean in the 19th century which deals with various episodes of American-European rivalry. The author concludes that American interventionist policy of the 20th century was deeply rooted in the 19th century. Bibliography.

2:309 Langley, Lester D. *The United States and the Caribbean, 1900–1970*. Athens: University of Georgia Press, 1980. This volume continues the synthesis of the international history of the Caribbean begun in Langley's work cited immediately above, with the major focus on the United States' role. It is a useful survey of 20th-century episodes and themes. Bibliography.

2:310 Parker, Franklin D. *The Central American Republics*. New York: Oxford University Press, 1964. A broad survey, it focuses on political, social, cultural, and economic themes which are useful for background. Bibliography.

2:311 Perkins, Dexter. *The United States and the Caribbean*. 2d ed. Cambridge: Harvard University Press (1947), 1966. Perkins examines 20th-century U.S.-Caribbean relations, including economic inter-

ests in the second edition. The author contends that changing conditions make maintenance of good relations much more difficult.

2:312 Woodward, Ralph L. *Central America: A Nation Divided*. New York: Oxford University Press, 1976. Contains excellent summaries of the isthmus' relation to the world; it supersedes the volume on Central America by F. D. Parker (2:310).

Cuba

Foner, P. S. *A History of Cuba and Its Relations with the United States* (13:20) focuses on U.S. efforts to annex Cuba and the filibusting episodes of the 1850s, Cuba's wars for independence, and ends (1492–1898) before the United States joined the final campaign. Foner is highly critical of U.S. policies.

2:313 Johnson, Willis F. *The History of Cuba*. 5 vols. New York: Buck, 1920. The emphasis in this account is on the Cuban economy; thus it is useful for U.S.-Cuban commercial relations.

2:314 Langley, Lester D. *The Cuban Policy of the United States: A Brief History*. New York: Wiley, 1968. This is a general survey of U.S. policy toward Cuba (1776–1962) with two chapters on the years 1808 to 1861, one on the Ten Years' War (1868–1878), one on the war with Spain, one on the protectorate era (1898–1934), and the final chapter on the United States and Batista and Castro. The theme of the book is that Castro fulfilled U.S. dreams of a "progressive" Cuba but did so in a socialist, anti-U.S. framework. Bibliography.

Portell Vilá, H. *História de Cuba en sus relaciones con los Estados Unidos y España* (13:23) is a well-documented, well-balanced work by a prominent Cuban historian who is critical of both Cuba and the United States.

2:315 Thomas, Hugh. *Cuba: The Pursuit of Freedom*. New York: Harper & Row, 1971. A monumental work covering Cuban society, economics, politics, and especially the island's international history (1762–1968). The author's emphasis is frankly political, but the narrative "pauses" at convenient places to comment on Cuban society. The theme of the 20th century is the failure of the republic created after the Spanish-American War. It contains data on the Cuban economy. Extensive bibliography.

Dominican Republic (Santo Domingo) and Haiti

2:316 Atkins, G. Pope, and Wilson, Larman C. *The United States and the Trujillo Regime*. New Brunswick, N.J.: Rutgers University Press, 1972. An excellent survey of U.S.-Dominican Republic relations (1904–1960s), with an emphasis upon the Trujillo era. The authors conclude that the United States should recognize that democracy cannot be imposed from the outside.

2:317 Clausner, Marlin D. *Rural Santo Domingo: Settled, Unsettled and Resettled*. Philadelphia: Temple University Press, 1973. A general survey of the agrarian situation and its impact on the politics of the Dominican Republic (1850–1960). Bibliography.

2:318 Fagg, John E. *Cuba, Haiti and the Dominican Republic*. Englewood Cliffs, N.J.: Prentice-Hall, 1965. This is a useful brief introduction to the history of the Dominican Republic and its neighbors. Bibliography.

2:319 Heinl, Robert D., and Heinl, Nancy G. *Written in Blood: The Story of the Haitian People, 1492–1971*. Boston: Houghton Mifflin, 1978. This is a political-military history of Haiti, with considerable reference to U.S.-Haitian relations, but it ignores the nation's socioeconomic problems.

2:320 Hoetink, Hermannus. *El Pueblo Dominicano 1850–1900: Apuntes para so sociología histórica* [The Dominican people 1850–1900: notes for historical sociology]. Santiago, Dominican Republic: Universidad Católica Madre y Maestra, 1971. A systematic analysis of the Dominican Republic's society and economic development, it has valuable sections on foreign influence. Bibliography.

Logan, R. W. *The Diplomatic Relations of the United States with Haiti, 1776–1891* (5:121) this is the standard diplomatic study of Haitian relations with the United States. Perhaps the most important contribution of the work is the impact of racial factors in the Haitian-American relationship. Bibliography.

2:321 Logan, Rayford W. *Haiti and the Dominican Republic*. New York: Oxford University Press, 1968. A general introduction to the history of the Dominican Republic (1750–1960), which emphasizes its troubled relations with Haiti. Bibliography.

2:322 Rotberg, Robert I., with Clague, Christopher K. *Haiti: The Politics of Squalor*. Boston: Houghton Mifflin, 1971. There is a short rendering of Haitian history from 1492 to the election of Duvalier, but the chapters on Haitian economy by Clague are most valuable. Bibliography.

Tansill, C. C. *The United States and Santo Domingo, 1798–1873: A Chapter in Caribbean Diplomacy* (5:123) traces the development of American interest in the island, especially the lure of the West Indian commercial market and the strategic worth of Samana Bay. Unfortunately, in the absence of a bibliography, scholars who wish to follow Tansill's trail must carefully examine the footnotes.

2:323 Welles, Sumner. *Naboth's Vineyard: The Dominican Republic, 1844–1924*. 2 vols. New York: Payson & Clarke, 1928. This is a comprehensive account with good coverage of U.S.-Dominican relations. Welles was one of the architects and practitioners of the good neighbor policy during the presidency of Franklin D. Roosevelt.

Panama

2:324 Ealy, Lawrence O. *The Republic of Panama in World Affairs, 1903–1957*. Philadelphia: University of Pennsylvania Press, 1957. While it deals with other topics, the most persistent foreign policy issue affecting Panama is, of course, the canal.

Panama Canal

See Chapters 7, 15, and 34 for additional references.

2:325 Anguizola, Gustave A. *The Panama Canal: Isthmian Political Instability*. 2nd ed. Washington, D.C.: University Press of America, 1977. A Panamanian scholar, employing Panamanian documents, adds a different dimension to the discussion of U.S. construction and operation of the canal. Bibliography.

2:326 Ealy, Lawrence O. *Yanqui Politics and the Isthmian Canal*. University Park: Pennsylvania State University Press, 1971. Ealy discusses U.S. canal politics from the 1840s to the 1970s: chronologically to 1914 and topically thereafter. It is a broad study which is informative on political debates in the United States. Bibliography.

2:327 LaFeber, Walter. *The Panama Canal: The Crisis in Historical Perspective*. New York: Oxford

University Press, 1978. After describing pre-1903 Panamanian nationalism, the author discusses the 1903 Panamanian revolution and U.S.-Panama relations in the ensuing seventy-five years. LaFeber sees the 1978 treaties as a "diplomatic triumph" for the United States. Extensive bibliography.

2:328 Liss, Sheldon B. *The Canal: Aspects of United States-Panamanian Relations.* Notre Dame, Ind.: University of Notre Dame Press, 1967. This general survey develops the "canal relationship" from 1903 to 1967.

2:329 Mack, Gerstle. *The Land Divided: A History of the Panama Canal and Other Isthmian Canal Projects.* New York: Knopf, 1944. Mack has written a detailed study of the 19th-century isthmian canal dream. Bibliography.

2:330 Williams, Mary W. *Anglo-American Isthmian Diplomacy, 1815–1915.* Washington, D.C.: American Historical Association, 1916. Williams provides a detailed account of the disputes over the Clayton-Bulwer Treaty in the 1850s, as well as later episodes. This old, but still useful study, emphasizes the canal as a persistent issue in Anglo-American relations. Bibliography.

AFRICA AND ASIA

For general accounts related to the United States and South Asia, see Chapter 37; for the United States and Southeast Asia, see Chapter 30.

2:331 Coox, Alvin D., and Conroy, Hilary, eds. *China and Japan: Search for Balance since World War I.* Santa Barbara, Calif.: ABC-Clio, 1978. A collection of new essays tracing the Sino-Japanese relationship from the late-19th-century disintegration of China's Confucian international system to the 1972 breakthrough with Japan. The final chapter makes an effort at analyzing two triangular relationships: China-Japan-United States and China-Japan-Soviet Union.

2:332 Iriye, Akira. *Across the Pacific: An Inner History of American-East Asian Relations.* New York: Harcourt, Brace & World, 1967. This study examines the images that Americans, Chinese, and Japanese had of one another (1780–1963). While giving new estimates of the leaders and diplomats and their policies, the author attempts to penetrate the surface of diplomacy to analyze the misperceptions and misunderstandings resulting from the differing cultural milieu of those leaders and statesmen. Bibliography.

2:333 Isaacs, Harold R. *Images of Asia: American Views of China and India.* New York: Harper, 1972. This is a valuable study of American images and ideas of China and India (1700s–1957) based on books and popular literature but mainly on intensive interviews of a selected group of 181 persons conducted in the mid-1950s. The author describes the wide spectrum of impressions, attitudes, and feelings, tracing their sources within individual experience as well as the related historical background. Originally published as *Scratches on Our Minds* (1958), the 1972 edition includes a new preface.

2:334 May, Ernest R., and Thomson, James C., Jr., eds. *American-East Asian Relations: A Survey.* Cambridge: Harvard University Press, 1972. This chronological survey of American diplomatic, commercial, and military relations with East Asia, with emphasis on China and Japan, consists of seventeen essays organized under four periods (18th–19th centuries, 1900–1922, 1922–1941, and 1941–1969). As a fundamental work, it provides a stimulating basis for further studies and research in the field.

Africa

2:335 Bohannan, Paul, and Curtin, Philip. *Africa and Africans.* Garden City, N.Y.: Natural History Press, 1971. Written by an anthropologist and an historian, this slim book is an excellent summary of traditional African religion, values, and social structure. It is essential in understanding the clash between the West and Africa.

2:336 Chester, Edward W. *Clash of Titans: Africa and U.S. Foreign Policy.* Maryknoll, N.Y.: Orbis, 1974. This is the first comprehensive survey (1783–1974) of the subject. It touches on economic, religious, and cultural contacts, as well as political. All of the pertinent material in the Foreign Relations series has been examined and included. The volume is probably most valuable for the years from 1783 to 1945. Indexes, tables, and extensive bibliography.

2:337 Curtin, Philip D. *African History.* Boston: Little, Brown, 1978. This brief survey, from prehistory to postcolonial decades, is a good starting point for those who are interested in white contacts with the continent.

2:338   Fage, J. D., and Oliver, Roland, eds. *The Cambridge History of Africa*. 2 vols. Cambridge: At the University Press, 1975–1978. These volumes provide a detailed summary of African history which incorporates the most recent scholarship.

2:339   Howe, Russell Warren. *Along the African Shore: An Historic Review of Two Centuries of U.S.-African Relations*. New York: Barnes & Noble, 1975. Only 40 percent of this thin volume deals with the years from 1766 through 1935; the third chapter covers the Italo-Ethiopian War and World War II, and the final 40 percent encompasses the post–World War II period. Howe finds no coherent policy for much of the period under review. Index.

Australia and New Zealand

See Chapter 36 for references.

Reese, T. R. *Australia, New Zealand and the United States: A Survey of International Relations, 1941–1968* (32:140) is an extremely full and substantially documented study.

China

2:340   Cohen, Warren I. *America's Response to China: An Interpretative History of Sino-American Relations*. New York: Wiley, 1971. This is a concise and imaginative interpretation of Sino-American relations in the 19th and 20th centuries which focuses on American perceptions and response to China that are rested on fluctuating sentiments and the lack of reality. The author deals with Ch'ing China's tribute and treaty systems, and traces the course of relations through successive developments in China to the 1960s. In examining American attitudes toward the growth of communism, he points out that obsessive fear of it and involvement in the Chinese civil war constitute the "great aberration."

2:341   Cohen, Warren I. *The Chinese Connection: Roger S. Greene, Thomas W. Lamont, George E. Sokolsky, and American-East Asian Relations*. New York: Columbia University Press, 1978. Cohen traces U.S.-China relations through three Americans connected with policy and events. Bibliography.

2:342   Dulles, Foster Rhea. *China and America: The Story of Their Relations since 1784*. Princeton, N.J.: Princeton University Press, 1946. This brief survey is both critical and colorful. The author excells in assimilating the best work of other scholars while at the same time adding perspectives from other sources such as newspapers and magazines.

2:343   Etzold, Thomas H., ed. *Aspects of Sino-American Relations since 1784*. New York: New Viewpoints, 1978. The authors generally find American policy in Asia (1784–1970s), particularly China, ambiguous and hazy. The essays are arranged chronologically. William Brinker surveys the first century of Sino-American cultural relations; Frederick Hoyt and Eugene Trani examine 19th-century Chinese immigration to the United States; Raymond Esthus discusses the open door policy (1899–1922); David Trask and Etzold, respectively, deal with American policy at the 1919 Paris Peace Conference and American Far Eastern strategy in 1948 to 1951. In the last chapter, Jerome Holloway and Etzold describe America's relations with Chinese Communist leaders since the 1920s.

Fairbank, J. K. *China: The People's Middle Kingdom and the U.S.A.* [1900–1960s] (31:39) is an introductory reader to contemporary China and its relations with the United States. It consists of eleven published essays, of which three offer perspectives on the Chinese Revolution, two treat the problem of Taiwan, and six discuss other aspects of American policy toward Communist China.

Fairbank, J. K. *China Perceived: Images and Policies in Chinese-American Relations* [1800–1972] (31:23) focuses on perceptions and policies in Sino-American relations.

2:344   Fairbank, John K. *The United States and China*. 3d ed. Cambridge: Harvard University Press, 1971. The bulk of this study is an analysis of China's history and culture, though two chapters deal directly with U.S. China policy and provide a thoughtful commentary on the nature of that policy in the 19th and 20th centuries. Bibliography.

2:345   Gittings, John. *The World and China, 1922–1972*. New York: Harper & Row, 1974. An important introduction to Chinese Communist foreign policy, this sympathetic and vigorously argued work is notable for its treatment of Mao's thinking and of the Chinese adaptation to a changing international situation. Chapters 4–9 are particularly important for their treatment of the China-U.S.-U.S.S.R. triangle (1939–1953).

2:346 Neumann, William L. "Determinism, Destiny, and Myth in the American Image of China." In George L. Anderson, ed., *Issues and Conflicts: Studies in Twentieth Century American Diplomacy.* Lawrence: University Press of Kansas, 1959, pp. 1–22. A study of the role played by unreality (myth, irrationality, and unquestioned assumptions) in the shaping of foreign policies, this essay shows the roots of America's emotional attachment to China, upon which resistance to Japan was often premised. Included are the sense of special proximity, the faith in the China market, and the concept of American destiny.

2:347 Spence, Jonathan. *The China Helpers: Western Advisers in China, 1620–1960.* London: Bodley Head, 1969. Of the sixteen advisers dealt with in this study, eight are American. They are Peter Parker, commissioner to China; Frederick Townsend Ward, commander of the Ever Victorious Army; W. A. P. Martin, missionary and educator; Edward Hume, head of Yale in China; O. J. Todd, an engineer; and the American generals Claire Chennault, Joseph Stilwell, and Albert Wedemeyer. The analyses are perceptive but based entirely on published sources.

Japan

Blaker, M. *Japanese International Negotiating Style* [1895–1941] (22:207) uses 18 case studies to deduce a peculiarly Japanese bargaining style.

2:348 Neu, Charles E. *The Troubled Encounter: The United States and Japan.* New York: Wiley, 1975. An analytical survey (1853–1972), it is a useful account from which to obtain a general perspective.

2:349 Neumann, William L. *America Encounters Japan: From Perry to MacArthur.* Baltimore: Johns Hopkins Press, 1963. This narrative survey is based on published American sources.

2:350 Nish, Ian H. *Japanese Foreign Policy, 1869–1942: Kasumigaseki to Miya Kezaka.* London: Routledge & Kegan Paul, 1977. Basing his biographical approach on documents heretofore unavailable in English, a leading authority on Anglo-Japanese relations probes the motives and ideas of the Japanese foreign ministry. Bibliography.

Reischauer, E. O. *The Japanese* (31:118) is the best single-volume introduction to Japanese politics and society.

2:351 Reischauer, Edwin O. *The United States and Japan.* 3d ed. Cambridge: Harvard University Press, 1965. This introductory work studies U.S.-Japanese relations (1500s–1964). Reischauer provides an overview of the problem and a discussion of Japan's physical environment, prewar economy, and the characteristics of its people. The American occupation, its immediate effects, postwar developments, and the prospects of American-Japanese relations are carefully examined.

2:352 Titus, David A. *Palace and Politics in Prewar Japan.* New York: Columbia University Press, 1974. This indispensable study of the prewar imperial institution (1868–1941) and its relationship to government emphasizes the "privatizing" whereby the palace through court advisers concealed political disharmonies and thereby distanced itself from Western democracy. Bibliography.

Korea

See Chapters 17 and 31 for additional references.

Baldwin, F., ed. *Without Parallel: The American-Korean Relationship since 1945* (27:147).

Philippines

Abueva, J. V. "Filipino Democracy and the American Legacy" [1898–1975] (30:110) is a provocative study of intercultural relations.

2:353 Grunder, Garel A., and Livezey, William E. *The Philippines and the United States.* Norman: Oklahoma University Press, 1951. An older but still useful study, it contains an extensive but somewhat outdated bibliography.

2:354 Lansang, Jose A. "The Philippine-American Experiment: A Filipino View." *Pacific Affairs* 25:3 (1952), 226–34. A critical assessment by a Filipino journalist which argues that American tutelage brought to the Philippines the forms and symbols of democracy but not the substance.

2:355 Owen, Norman G., ed. *Compadre Colonialism: Studies on the Philippines under American Rule.* Ann Arbor: University of Michigan Press, 1971. The general theme of this collection is that the United States early reached a tacit modus vivendi with the traditional elements of the ruling class, thus preventing hopes for genuine social and economic reforms.

2:356   Stanley, Peter W. *A Nation in the Making: The Philippines and the United States, 1899–1921.* Cambridge: Harvard University Press, 1974. A readable and detailed account of the efforts by the Americans to win over the Philippine elite and the relationship of these efforts to the development and modernization of the islands and to their eventual independence. It is probably the best survey of U.S.-Philippine relations. Bibliography.

2:357   Storey, Moorefield, and Lichauco, M. P. *The Conquest of the Philippines by the United States, 1898–1925.* New York: Scribner's, 1926. A severe indictment of American policy, this account remains a useful source.

MIDDLE EAST

See Chapters 18 and 33 for additional references.

2:358   Adler, Cyrus, and Margolith, A. M. *With Firmness in the Right: American Diplomatic Action Affecting Jews, 1840–1945.* New York: American Jewish Committee, 1946. This study examines the intercession on behalf of Jews in U.S. diplomatic correspondence. The authors present the facts associated with each diplomatic action in a clear and concise manner.

Baram, P. J. *The Department of State in the Middle East, 1919–1945* (33:82) discusses the makeup of the department's Near Eastern section.

2:359   Bryson, Thomas A. *American Diplomatic Relations with the Middle East, 1784–1975: A Survey.* Metuchen, N.J.: Scarecrow, 1977. Bryson surveys U.S. relations with Middle Eastern states and discusses the growth of commercial intercourse and missionary activities in shaping U.S. policy. The author suggests that American policymakers pursued policy that followed certain guiding principles and the concept of the national interest. The work is based on English-language sources. Bibliography.

2:360   Bryson, Thomas A. *Tars, Turks, and Tankers: The Role of the U.S. Navy in the Middle East, 1800–1979.* Metuchen, N.J.: Scarecrow Press, 1980. The author treats the role of the U.S. Navy in supporting American foreign policy objectives in the Middle East. While the bulk of this work deals with the era following World War II, the period prior to the war is given ample treatment.

2:361   Davison, Roderic H. "Where Is the Middle East?" *Foreign Affairs* 38:4 (1960), 665–75. Davison discusses the confusion relative to the proper definition of the territory that constitutes the geographic Middle East and traces the use of the terms *Near East* and *Middle East* from the late 19th century to the mid-20th century.

Field, J. A., Jr. *America and the Mediterranean World, 1776–1882* (18:6) is an elegantly written account which treats the American missionary and educational efforts and their consequences for modernization and Arab nationalism, the problems of missionary protection, and the naval and diplomatic responses. Also included are brief treatments of the naval exploration of the Dead Sea and the Koszta affair; the beginnings of Palestinian archaeology; early American Zionism and Palestinian settlements; and the efforts of technicians and merchants.

2:362   Howard, Harry N. *Turkey, the Straits and U.S. Policy.* Baltimore: Johns Hopkins University Press, 1974. The former State Department official and university professor traces American interest in the Turkish Straits beginning in the 19th century, when U.S. sailing vessels began to pass through the Bosphorus and Dardanelles on a regular basis. The "basic consistency" in American policy has been the continuing insistence on freedom for commercial traffic and keeping the Black Sea as an open area. Extensive bibliography.

2:363   Malone, Joseph J. "America and the Arabian Peninsula: The First Two Hundred Years." *Middle East Journal* 30:3 (1976), 406–24. In 1833, the Uscat-American Treaty of Amity and Commerce was signed, which facilitated American entry into the controversial Middle Eastern armaments trade.

Iran (Persia)

2:364   Ramazani, Rouhollah K. *The Foreign Policy of Iran, 1500–1941.* Charlottesville: University Press of Virginia, 1966. The author surveys Iranian diplomacy from the 16th century to World War II. He asserts that the Persians wanted the United States to serve as a counterweight to the British and Russians. Bibliography.

2:365 Ramazani, Rouhollah K. *Iran's Foreign Policy, 1941–1973: A Study of Foreign Policy in Modernizing Nations.* Charlottesville: University Press of Virginia, 1975. A comprehensive empirical analysis of Iran's foreign policy which draws on primary sources as well as on extensive field research and observation to provide the best single volume on Iran's foreign policy in the postwar period. Extensive bibliography.

North Africa

Gallagher, C. F. *The United States and North Africa: Morocco, Algeria and Tunisia* [1784–1963] (18:8).

Hall, L. J. *The United States and Morocco, 1776–1956* (18:10).

3

Colonial and Imperial Diplomacy to 1774

Contributing Editor
Lawrence S. Kaplan
Kent State University

Contributors
Alan S. Brown
Western Michigan University

James H. Hutson
Manuscript Division
Library of Congress

Alison G. Olson
University of Maryland

Contents

Introduction

American diplomacy before 1776 represents a relatively new conception of American diplomatic history. It was not found in the original *Guide*. Bemis and Griffin conceded a colonial presence only to the extent that the chronological beginning of their work was in 1775.

There was wisdom in their decision. The subject of American diplomacy in the colonial years is as synthetic as it is amorphous. On the other hand, there was obviously no nation-state in existence and no formal diplomacy to be conducted. On the other, there is the problem of definition in the absence of normal criteria. Can American diplomacy be appropriately identified under the rubric of European colonial powers dealing with or operating in the Americas? Can relations between colonies and the mother country, informal and formal, be considered diplomacy even if the terms of the relationship were not so considered by either party? Similarly, do the relations between colony and colony fit into the category in the absence of firm control from the Board of Trade or Parliament? Should British treaties or colonial dealing with the Indians be considered diplomatic relations?

All these questions and more confront the diplomatic historian attempting to find a place for American diplomacy before 1776. Fortunately, a few scholars in the years since Bemis and Griffin compiled their guide have examined the area and have created a subfield out of colonial diplomacy where none existed before. Foremost among them is Max Savelle, who has contributed a quantity of vitally important essays and books ranging from a detailed monograph on the Canadian boundary between 1749 and 1753 to far-reaching essays on the nature of American ideas of the outside world in the eighteenth century, to a monumental summa on American diplomacy from 1492 to 1763—*The Origins of American Diplomacy: The International History of Angloamerica, 1492–1763* (3:46).

Another scholar, Felix Gilbert, a European intellectual historian, has influenced a generation of American diplomatic historians by pointing out the European, particularly the English, origins of the American idea of isolationism in his *To the Farewell Address: Ideas of Early American Foreign Policy* (5:165). Two younger scholars, Jack Sosin, *Agents and Merchants: British Colonial Policy and the Origins of the American Revolution, 1763–1775* (3:192), and Michael Kammen, *A Rope of Sand: The Colonial Agents, British Politics, and the American Revolution* (3:191), have rationalized and extended studies on colonial agents in such a way that they may be seen as proto-diplomats of a nation in the making.

Supported by such pioneering efforts, the historian can look at diplomacy in the colonial period with a different eye and with a broader perspective. There is still the question, however, of just how broadly the range legitimately should be. In this chapter the range encompasses two broad themes which characterize colonial diplomacy as presented below: First, the relationships among the colonial powers, great and small, as they were played out in the North American and Atlantic arenas. Occasionally a book or article concerned primarily with diplomacy in the European continent is cited if it has important implications for America. The second theme is the slow growth of colonial experience in statecraft, as expressed in reactions among colonies and between colony and mother country. Increasingly, these connections took the form of quasi-diplomatic relations reflecting the autonomous life led by the colonies, with the colonial movement toward union assuming a major role by 1774.

Within these broad categories the initial problems evolve from the issue of inclusiveness. There can be no identification of diplomacy among the colonies without including the diplomacy of the colonial powers. The temptation here is to touch any aspect of English or French diplomacy that remotely deals with the American colonies. To succumb to this temptation would distort the pattern of this volume and obscure the genuine role colonial diplomacy should play in the *Guide*. Hence, we have tried to restrict the list to the most significant figures and issues in European diplomacy in which the Americas are involved. The sub-topics themselves were not difficult to locate: Anglo-Spanish and Anglo-French diplomacy predominate logically. For the former, a further breakdown chronologically is useful; 1713, the end of the War of the Spanish Succession, divides the list. For the latter, three categories are used, since the material is more plentiful. As the bulk of the subjects are in the eighteenth century, 1749 marks the chronological division. Canada, particularly colonial relations between the French colony and the American colony, is considered as a theme by itself.

The growth of colonial self-awareness in relations with the mother country is an enormous topic potentially filling all the space allotted to this chapter. The articles and books on relations between the colonies are more manageable. To maintain a balance, we have excluded more than we would have liked from the subtopic of Anglo-American relations while including most of the important contributions on intercolonial relations. The colonial agency, which involves both categories, has sufficient literature and is of sufficient importance to warrant separate topic status.

One area in particular has not found a clear place in colonial diplomacy: Indian-European relations. Indian relations appear peripherally, for the most part, in the bibliography of this chapter. They deserve more attention and will probably benefit from the revival of Indian studies in other areas of American history. There is room for diplomatic historians to explore, along the lines of John Phillip Reid, *A Better Kind of Hatchet: Law, Trade, and Diplomacy in the Cherokee Nation during the Early Years of European Contact* (3:172).

The most important materials inevitably address the decade before the Revolution, with many of the monographs in this period overlapping into the revolutionary period. Given their significance and their quantity, three subtopics have been allotted to this decade, and one or two more might have been added. Indeed, the reader may make a case for reordering all the topics and recasting the criteria employed. Such is the nature of a subject that belongs essentially to another subdiscipline of history, colonial history.

The challenge was made manageable by the willingness of colleagues in colonial and British history to participate in the project. They do not share in whatever errors of organization readers might observe, but their advice and their contributions have made the task much lighter for the contributing editor than it would have been otherwise.

Resources and Overviews

RESEARCH AIDS

While pertinent bibliographies and reference aids are listed here, there are more extensive lists in Chapter 1.

Bibliographies

3:1   Adams, Thomas R., comp. *American Independence: The Growth of an Idea.* Providence, R.I.: Brown University Press, 1965. This is a bibliographic study of American political pamphlets printed between 1764 and 1776 dealing with disputes between Great Britain and the colonies. A good view of ideology, particularly Whig, exploited by the colonists.

American Historical Association. *Writings on American History, 1902 –* (1:64) contains a number of references to works in colonial diplomacy, although under a variety of categories.

3:2   Beers, Henry P., ed. *The French in North America: A Bibliographical Guide to French Archives, Reproductions, and Research Missions.* Baton Rouge: Louisiana State University Press, 1957. Beers has prepared a description of work by American and Canadian historians and institutions in the French archives, including documentary compilations and reproductions. A particularly interesting chapter, "Historians of American Diplomacy," begins with Jared Sparks's initial investigations.

Bibliographie annuelle de l'histoire de France (1:78a) is more convenient than other guides to the yearly output of French scholarship.

3:3   *Books about Early America: A Selected Bibliography.* 5th ed. Williamsburg, Va.: Institute of Early American History and Culture, 1976. More than half the entries deal with the colonial period from 1749 to 1775.

3:4   Coker, William S., and Holmes, Jack D. F. "Sources for the History of the Spanish Borderlands." *Florida Historical Quarterly* 49:4 (1971), 380–93.

This article describes the abundance of source materials, published, microcopied, and in manuscript, located in Spain, France, and various U.S. collections, relating particularly to Spanish Florida and Spanish Louisiana.

Cortada, J. W., ed. *A Bibliographical Guide to Spanish Diplomatic History, 1460–1977* (1:90).

3:5 Davies, Godfrey, and Kesler, Mary F. *Bibliography of British History: Stuart Period, 1603–1714*. 2d ed. Oxford: Clarendon Press, 1970. There are entries for diplomatic history under the sections "Political History" and "Colonial History."

Dippel, H. *Americana Germanica, 1770–1800* (4:2).

3:6 Gipson, Lawrence H. *A Bibliographical Guide to the History of the British Empire*. New York: Knopf, 1958.

3:7 Gipson, Lawrence H., ed. *A Guide to Manuscripts Relating to the History of the British Empire, 1748–1776*. New York: Knopf, 1958. These last two volumes, 14 and 15, of the author's history of the British empire (3:31), reflect the prodigious work that went into his thirteen-volume opus.

3:8 Greene, Jack P., comp. *The American Colonies in the 18th Century, 1689–1763*. New York: Appleton-Century-Crofts, 1969. Emphasizing Britain and its colonies in his bibliography, Greene includes sections on diplomatic relations among the European empires and between Britain and the colonies.

3:9 Leach, Douglas E. "Colonial Forces, 1607–1766." In Robin Higham, ed., *A Guide to the Sources of United States Military History*. Hamden, Conn.: Shoe String Press, 1975, pp. 70–99. A bibliographical essay, with 366 references appended, which examines British military policy and actions through the Seven Years' War; also see Higham's bibliography on the British army (1:46).

3:10 McDermott, John F., ed. *The Spanish in the Mississippi Valley, 1762–1804*. Urbana: University of Illinois Press, 1974. Three of these essays are of a bibliographical nature useful to the diplomatic historian: Charles E. O'Neill's "The State of Studies on Spanish Colonial Louisiana," A. Otis Herbert's "Resources in Louisiana Repositories for the Study of Spanish Activities in Louisiana," and C. Harvey Gardiner's "The Mexican Archives and the Historiog-

raphy of the Mississippi Valley in the Spanish Period"; see especially Gardiner's extensive footnotes.

Monaghan, F. *French Travellers in the United States, 1765–1932: A Bibliography* (1:73).

3:11 Pargellis, Stanley M., and Medley, D. J. *Bibliography of British History: The Eighteenth Century, 1714–1789*. 2d ed. Totowa, N.J.: Rowman (1961), 1977. In addition to materials found in chapters dealing with foreign relations, there is a special section on the American colonies; a number of citations include annotations.

3:12 Read, Conyers. *Bibliography of British History: Tudor Period, 1485–1603*. 2d ed. Oxford: Clarendon Press, 1959. There is a section on foreign affairs as well as on discovery and colonization.

Thomas, D. H., and Case, L. M., eds. *Guide to the Diplomatic Archives of Western Europe* [1400–1959] (1:298) contains lists of printed documents.

3:13 Vaughan, Alden T. *The American Colonies in the 17th Century*. New York: Appleton-Century-Crofts, 1971. A section on the "Imperial Matrix" as well as sections on political and military conflicts among the empires are included.

Atlases and Other Aids

Cappon, L. J. and Petchenik, B. B., eds. *Atlas of Early American History . . . , 1760–1790* (4:9).

Clark, D. S. *Index to Maps of the American Revolution in Books and Periodicals . . . , 1763–1789* (4:10).

3:14 Wheat, James C., and Brun, Christian F., eds. *Maps and Charts Published in America before 1800: A Bibliography*. New Haven, Conn.: Yale University Press, 1969. A listing that notes locations, whether printed or in manuscript collections, of over nine hundred maps identified as having been produced in the United States before 1800. Many military maps made during the American Revolution are not included.

Document Collections

More general collections are listed in Chapter 1, and other collections are found in "Personalities," below.

3:15 Boyd, Julian P. *The Susquehanna Company Papers.* 11 vols. Ithaca, N.Y.: Cornell University Press, 1962. Six of the volumes are concerned with the years 1750 to 1774, and involve conflict between the Connecticut sponsors and the Pennsylvania Colony. It is a classic example of intercolonial diplomacy.

3:16 Davenport, Frances, and Paullin, Charles O., eds. *European Treaties Bearing on the History of the United States and Its Dependencies.* Washington, D.C.: Carnegie Institution, 1917. This useful collection of documents (1455–1697), deals not only with the major colonial powers but includes Brandenberg and Denmark. The Treaty of Ryswick in 1697 concludes the volume.

3:17 Great Britain. Public Record Office. *Acts of the Privy Council of England, Colonial Series.* 6 vols. London: H.M.S.O., 1908–1912. The Privy Council, advisers to the crown, had formal authority over the colonies until the Revolution, although the Board of Trade took over most of its functions in the 18th century.

3:18 Great Britain. Public Record Office. *Journals of the Commissioners for Trade and Plantations, 1704–1782.* 14 vols. London: H.M.S.O., 1920–1938.

3:19 Kinnaird, Lawrence, ed. and trans. *Spain in the Mississippi Valley, 1765–1794.* 3 vols. In the Annual Report of the American Historical Association for the Year 1945. Washington, D.C.: G.P.O., 1946–1949, vols. 2–4. These translations of French and Spanish documents from Spanish governmental files for Louisiana and West Florida are deposited at the Bancroft Library. Although incomplete, the volumes (2: 1765–1781; 3: 1782–1791; 4: 1792–1794) offer material not frequently used, including many of Oliver Pollock's letters.

3:20 Labaree, Leonard W., ed. *Royal Instructions to British Colonial Governors, 1670–1776.* 2 vols. New York: Appleton-Century, 1935. The interesting chapters deal with the Indians, with external affairs, and with the governor's relations with council and assembly.

3:21 Pennsylvania Provincial Council. *Minutes of the Provincial Council of Pennsylvania.* 10 vols. Philadelphia: Severns, 1851–1852. Council dealings with the proprietor, the assembly, and the mother country are included in these volumes (1683–1776).

3:22 Stock, Leo F., ed. *Proceedings and Debates of the British Parliaments Respecting North America.* 5 vols. Washington, D.C.: Carnegie Institution, 1924–1941. The volumes cover the period from 1542 to 1754.

3:23 Symcox, Geoffrey. *War, Diplomacy, and Imperialism, 1618–1763.* New York: Harper & Row, 1973. These documents, with a 38-page introduction, stress the colonies' importance in 18th-century European diplomacy because of their increasing economic significance and the growing ability of European nations to control their colonies. Also the difficulty of nations to make significant territorial acquisitions in Europe projected European rivalries overseas.

OVERVIEWS

Colonial/Imperial Experience

3:24 Abbot, William W. *The Colonial Origins of the United States, 1607–1763.* New York: Wiley, 1975. In an effort to identify and describe the emergence of the constituent elements of American nationalism, the author contends that the colonies had little in common until well into the 18th century.

3:25 Andrews, Charles M. *The Colonial Background of the American Revolution: Four Essays in American Colonial History.* Rev. ed. New Haven, Conn.: Yale University Press, 1931. A splendid overview of Britain's relations with its colonies over a period of a century and a half by the master of the imperial school of Anglo-American historians, it emphasizes the mutual advantages in the relationship. With regret, Andrews finds Britain unable to adjust to the changing society of its colonies, although the fanaticism of the "Boston radicals" much more than the incompetence of British officials receive his measured blame.

3:26 Andrews, Charles M. *The Colonial Period of American History.* 4 vols. New Haven, Conn.: Yale University Press, 1934–1938. British colonial relations (1500–1763) as seen through the eyes of Whitehall.

3:27 Beer, George Louis. *The Old Colonial System, 1660–1754.* New York: Macmillan, 1912. A classic study of the development of the British empire, it presents a sympathetic view of British mercantilism and its effects.

3:28 Bridenbaugh, Carl. *The Spirit of '76: The Growth of American Patriotism before Independence.* New York: Oxford University Press, 1975. The author investigates intercolonial bonds formed by trade, religion, learning, politics, and culture. He concludes that a national consciousness, a feeling of "Americanism," was present as early as 1700 and grew stronger with each passing year.

3:29 Brown, Richard M., and Olson, Alison G., eds. *Anglo-American Political Relations, 1675–1775.* New Brunswick, N.J.: Rutgers University Press, 1970. These eleven essays on relations between Britain and the colonies in the 18th century focus on politics. The essays reflect the most recent trends in historical thinking about Anglo-American politics during the first half of the 18th century.

3:30 Curti, Merle. *The Roots of American Loyalty.* New York: Atheneum, 1968. The early chapters are informative about the development of American national consciousness, what Curti calls "the beginnings of American patriotism." Bibliography.

3:31 Gipson, Lawrence H. *The British Empire before the American Revolution.* 15 vols. 2d ed. New York: Knopf (1939–1958), 1958–1970. This monumental work is an exhaustive survey of the areas of intercolonial cooperation and conflict for 1748 to 1776. It is an indispensable source for intercolonial relations. Volumes 1–3 have been revised. Extensive bibliography, volume 14.

3:32 Leach, Douglas E. *Arms for Empire: A Military History of the British Colonies in North America, 1607–1763.* New York: Macmillan, 1973. The fullest, most balanced interpretation of its major theme, it also stresses the growth of tensions between England and America as a result of the colonial wars. The English became increasingly disdainful of American culture and irritated at the intractability of colonial legislatures, while the colonists became increasingly convinced of their own ability to outfight the "repressive" British regulars. Extensive bibliography.

3:33 Morison, Samuel Eliot. *The Northern Voyages, A.D. 500–1600.* Vol. 1 in *The European Discovery of America.* New York: Oxford University Press, 1971.

3:34 Morison, Samuel Eliot. *The Southern Voyages, A.D. 1492–1616.* Vol. 2 in *The European Discovery of America.* New York: Oxford University Press, 1974. This magisterial treatment, the fruition of a lifetime's labor, is by the foremost maritime historian of his generation.

3:35 Osgood, Herbert L. *The American Colonies in the Eighteenth Century.* 4 vols. New York: Columbia University Press, 1924. Though old, Osgood's magisterial work is still perhaps the best account of intercolonial cooperation and conflict from 1700 to 1763. The detail is encyclopedic and accurate.

3:36 Osgood, Herbert L. *The American Colonies in the Seventeenth Century.* 3 vols. New York: Columbia University Press, 1904–1907. Its theme is the colonizing process of the British empire, with emphasis on the development of institutions.

3:37 Peckham, Howard H. *The Colonial Wars, 1689–1762.* Chicago: University of Chicago Press, 1964. The colonial wars ultimately drove a wedge between England and America, partly because the wars led to intercolonial cooperation and partly because the encounters between English and American troops led Americans to regard the English as "foreign." Bibliography.

3:38 Rose, John H.; Newton, A. P.; and Benian, E. A. *The Old Empire from the Beginnings to 1783.* Vol. 1 in *Cambridge History of the British Empire.* New York: Macmillan, 1929. The emphasis in this volume is on the West Indies and North America, with close attention to British rivalry with France, Holland, and Spain.

3:39 Savelle, Max. *Seeds of Liberty: The Genesis of the American Mind.* New York: Knopf, 1948. An ambitious, broadly conceived intellectual and cultural history of the colonies, it shows the growth from Old World roots of a distinctive American mentality between 1650 and 1750. Savelle contends that this mentality, developed in the colonies by 1750, was an important factor in producing the American Revolution. Bibliography.

3:40 Simmons, R. C. *The American Colonies: From Settlement to Independence.* New York: McKay, 1976. The most useful of recent colonial textbooks as far as the international history of America is concerned. Extensive bibliographical essay.

3:41 Van Alstyne, Richard W. *The Genesis of American Nationalism.* Waltham, Mass.: Blaisdell, 1970. Van Alstyne's first chapter is valuable in showing how a shared belief in the idea of empire created a common patriotism in colonial Americans from 1700 to 1750.

Origins of American Diplomacy

Gilbert, F. *To the Farewell Address: Ideas of Early American Foreign Policy* (5:165) argues that early American ideas on foreign policy, particularly on isolationism, drew their vitality from English isolationism and the ideas of French philosophes.

3:42 Kaplan, Lawrence S. *Colonies into Nation: American Diplomacy, 1763–1801.* New York: Macmillan, 1972. In an interpretation of American diplomacy, Kaplan incorporates recent contributions. The colonial agent is seen as the precursor of the American diplomat. It is one of the few surveys to place the origins of American diplomacy in the colonial period. Bibliographical essay.

3:43 Savelle, Max. "The American Balance of Power and European Diplomacy, 1713–78." In Richard B. Morris, ed., *The Era of the American Revolution.* New York: Columbia University Press, 1939, pp. 140–69. The balance of colonial power became more and more important until, by the American Revolution, the balance of European power was assumed to rest on the balance of power in America.

3:44 Savelle, Max. "Colonial Origins of American Diplomatic Principles." *Pacific Historical Review* 3:3 (1934), 334–50. The conceptions of isolationism, of the two spheres, and of peaceful settlement of disputes have colonial origins; consequently, the permanent bases of American diplomacy are rooted in the geography of North America.

3:45 Savelle, Max. "The International Approach to Early Anglo-American History, 1492–1763." In Ray Billington, ed., *The Reinterpretation of Early American History: Essays in Honor of John Edwin Pomfret.* San Marino, Calif.: Huntington Library, 1966. Savelle discusses the divergence between the English approach to foreign policy, in which the colonies were entirely subordinate to the mother country, and the colonial approach, in which local free trade, local isolation, and local expansion (all of them basic interests of the United States after the Revolution) were uppermost.

3:46 Savelle, Max. *The Origins of American Diplomacy: The International History of Angloamerica, 1492–1763.* New York: Macmillan, 1967. The most

authoritative work on the colonial background of American diplomacy, it emphasizes the role of the Americas in the foreign policy of the European colonial powers. As a product of Savelle's lifetime labors, it is more noteworthy for its breadth than for its depth of treatment. Extensive bibliography.

3:47 Viner, Jacob. "Power versus Plenty as Objectives of Foreign Policy in the Seventeenth and Eighteenth Centuries." *World Politics* 1:1 (1948), 1–29. Viner argues that, for the mercantilists, power and plenty were regarded as fundamentally harmonious, coexisting ends of national policy.

Williams, W. A. "The Age of Mercantilism: An Interpretation of the American Political Economy, 1763–1828" (2:97).

Personalities

Additional references on individuals may be found in Chapter 1, "Biographical Data."

EUROPEAN

Edmund Burke

See also Chapter 4, "Personalities," for King George III and Lord North.

Burke, E. *The Correspondence of Edmund Burke* (4:82) is a useful collection. The first two volumes (volume 1, edited by T. W. Copeland; volume 2, by L. S. Sutherland) take Burke's career up to 1774.

3:48 Hoffman, Ross J. S. *Edmund Burke: New York Agent.* Memoirs, vol. 41. Philadelphia: American Philosophical Society, 1956. This study centers on Burke, as colonial agent for New York (1761–1774), who served the interests of empire at the expense of the colony. Burke doubted the wisdom, not the power, of Parliament to legislate for America.

Lord Dartmouth
3:49 Barger, Bernard D. *Lord Dartmouth and the American Revolution.* Columbia: University of South Carolina Press, 1965. A defense of Dartmouth's role as American secretary (1772–1775), in which the au-

thor claims that Dartmouth sought conciliation but failed to convince Lord North. It includes details of efforts to negotiate with various colonial agents, especially Franklin. Extensive bibliography.

3:50 Great Britain. Historical Manuscripts Commission. *The Manuscripts of the Earl of Dartmouth, with a New Introduction and Preface by George A. Billias.* 3 vols. Boston: Gregg (1887–1889), 1972. These volumes drew materials from the Historical Manuscripts Commission concerning the Dartmouth family in the 17th and 18th centuries. The second earl of Dartmouth was secretary of state for the colonies (1772–1775).

George III
See Chapter 4, "Personalities," for references.

George III. *The Correspondence of King George the Third, 1760–1783* (4:88) covers, in volumes 1–3, the period through 1774 and deals increasingly with American problems.

Lord North
See Chapter 4, "Personalities," for references.

William Pitt
3:51 Pitt, William. *Correspondence of William Pitt, Earl of Chatham.* Ed. by William S. Taylor, et al. 4 vols. London: John Murray, 1838–1840. Volumes 2 to 4 contain letters of the 1760s and 1770s during Pitt's leadership of the Opposition in the British Parliament.

3:52 Williams, Basil. *The Life of William Pitt, Earl of Chatham.* 2 vols. London: Longmans, Green, 1913. A reverential treatment of a great figure who united Britain in the major crisis of the 18th century, it focuses on England and the empire in the 1760s rather than America in the 1770s.

Lord Rockingham
3:53 Hoffman, Ross J. S. *The Marquis: A Study of Lord Rockingham, 1730–1782.* New York: Fordham University Press, 1973. This is a study of Rockingham as a pillar of the Old Whigs and their defense of the British Constitution against Tory encroachment. At the same time, Rockingham's deficiencies as a leader are not overlooked. Bibliography.

3:54 Langford, Paul. *The First Rockingham Administration, 1765–1776.* New York: Oxford University Press, 1973. Langford presents the various forces at work, in the Namierist manner, that led to the repeal of the Stamp Act in 1766. He claims that the fall of

Rockingham's ministry was caused less by Bute and the royal party's machinations than by its own blunders. Extensive bibliography.

Others
3:55 Bellot, Leland J. *William Knox: The Life and Thought of an Eighteenth-Century Imperialist.* Austin: University of Texas Press, 1977. A colonial agent for Georgia and undersecretary of state in the American Department under Lord North, Knox was a central figure in the transformation of the Navigation Acts after the French and Indian War. He appears as a consistent supporter of imperial government over the colonies, but a subordinate rather than a policymaker. Bibliography.

3:56 Eccles, William J. *Frontenac: The Courtier Governor.* Toronto: McClelland & Stewart, 1959. Highly critical of Frontenac, Eccles suggests that his reputation for repelling British assault on Canada, humbling the Iroquois, and extending French power to the West during 1675 to 1700 was largely undeserved. Extensive bibliography.

3:57 Forster, Cornelius P. *The Uncontrolled Chancellor: Charles Townshend and His American Policy.* Providence: Rhode Island Bicentennial Foundation, 1978. Following the approach of Lewis Namier and John Brooke, *Charles Townshend* (3:62), Forster portrays Townshend as a mixture of charm and ambition, using any ally in his pursuit of power. But he identifies a consistency that to some extent redeems Townshend's character: a vision of a new and better organized British empire in which the American colonies, subject to more orderly controls, would play a vital role. Bibliography.

3:58 Grenville, George. *The Grenville Papers.* 4 vols. Ed. by William J. Smith. London: John Murray, 1852–1853. Volumes 2 to 4 deal with George Grenville's role as chancellor of the exchequer from 1763 to 1765, and with the defense of his American policy during the balance of that decade.

3:59 Hall, Michael G. *Edward Randolph and the American Colonies, 1676–1703.* Chapel Hill: University of North Carolina Press, 1960. Randolph appears here both as an architect and a symbol of British imperial policy in the late 17th century. Extensive bibliography.

3:60 Jacobsen, Gertrude A. *William Blathwayt: A Later Seventeenth Century English Administrator.* New Haven, Conn.: Yale University Press, 1932. This is a useful biography of a Stuart administrator who held a variety of public offices (1668–1717), most of them related to the colonies (plantations, war, state). Blathwayt's career illustrates the primacy of the mother country in the relationship. Extensive bibliography.

3:61 Lodge, Sir Richard. "Sir Benjamin Keene, K.B.: A Study in Anglo-Spanish Relations." *Transactions of the Royal Historical Society* 4th ser. 15 (1932), 1–43. As English ambassador to Madrid (1746–1757), Keene revealed so much personal charm with Spanish ministers that his own personality should be considered an important factor in the friendly Anglo-Spanish relations existing on the eve of the Seven Years' War.

3:62 Namier, Lewis B., and Brooke, John. *Charles Townshend.* New York: St. Martin's Press, 1964. This political biography traces Townshend's rise from Parliament to the Board of Trade to chancellor of the exchequer in 1767. It emphasizes his conviction that Britain held constitutional authority to tax colonies.

Norris, J. M. *Shelburne and Reform* (4:93) deals, in the early part, with Shelburne's efforts in the 1760s as president of the Board of Trade and secretary of state for the Southern Department.

3:63 Pargellis, Stanley M. *Lord Loudon in America.* New Haven, Conn.: Yale University Press, 1933. The British commander in the colonies during the French and Indian Wars (1750–1765), devoted as much time to persuading colonies to cooperate as he did in fighting the French. Extensive bibliography.

3:64 Plumb, John H. *Sir Robert Walpole: The King's Minister.* Boston: Houghton Mifflin, 1961. Six chapters deal with Walpole's management of foreign relations from 1715 to 1740 under George I; see also A. M. Wilson (3:123). Extensive bibliography.

3:65 Schutz, John A. *Thomas Pownall, British Defender of American Liberty: Study of Anglo-American Relations in the Eighteenth Century.* Glendale, Calif.: A. H. Clark, 1951. Governor of Massachusetts in the critical period of the French and Indian War, Pownall urged a course of compromise between colonial subordination and colonial liberty. Extensive bibliography.

3:66 Soltau, Roger H. *Duke de Choiseul: The Lothian Essay, 1908.* Oxford: Blackwell, 1909. In a favorable interpretation of the career of France's

foreign minister during the Seven Years' War, Soltau emphasizes the duke's role in the Family Compact of 1761. Bibliography.

AMERICAN

See also "Colonial Agents," below, for additional references.

John Adams
See Chapters 4 and 5, "Personalities," for additional references.

3:67 Adams, John. *The Papers of John Adams, 1755–1775.* 2 vols. Ed. by Robert J. Taylor. Cambridge: Harvard University Press, 1977. The definitive edition of the John Adams Papers begins with Adams in 1755 and brings his career to 1775.

Samuel Adams
3:68 Adams, Samuel. *The Writings of Samuel Adams.* 4 vols. Ed. by Henry A. Cushing. New York: Putnam's, 1904. The first three volumes of this collection of Adams's papers deal with the period from 1764 to 1775.

3:69 Miller, John C. *Sam Adams: Pioneer in Propaganda.* Boston: Little, Brown, 1936. Adams's success lay in capitalizing on the blunders of his opponents in Boston and London to obtain his goals.

Robert Dinwiddie
3:70 Dinwiddie, Robert. *Robert Dinwiddie: Official Records of Robert Dinwiddie, Lieutenant-Governor of the Colony of Virginia, 1751–1758.* Ed. by Robert A. Brock. 2 vols. Richmond: Virginia Historical Library, 1883–1884.

3:71 Koontz, Louis K. *Robert Dinwiddie: His Career in American Colonial Government and Westward Expansion.* Glendale, Calif.: A. H. Clark, 1941. In Koontz's apologia, which seeks to correct misinterpretations of others, Dinwiddie is seen as agent of empire in the Ohio Valley (1751–1759). Such advantages as he may have derived from alliances with prominent Virginian interests were incidental to his larger goal. Bibliography.

Benjamin Franklin
See Chapter 4, "Personalities," for additional references.

3:72 Franklin, Benjamin. *The Papers of Benjamin Franklin*. 21 vols. to date. Ed. by Leonard W. Labaree, et al. New Haven, Conn.: Yale University Press, 1959–. The first twenty-one volumes have appeared in this authoritative edition. Volume 5, documenting efforts to promote colonial union in the mid-1750s, culminating in the Albany Plan of Union in 1754, is particularly important. Exhaustive footnotes and headnotes make this volume an indispensable source for intercolonial relations in the 1750s.

3:73 Hawke, David F. *Franklin*. New York: Harper & Row, 1976. This is a good modern political biography which should be read in conjunction with Labaree's definitive edition of Franklin's papers.

Stourzh, G. *Benjamin Franklin and American Foreign Policy* (4:52) is a careful inquiry into the sources of Franklin's ideas on foreign policy.

Van Doren, C. *Benjamin Franklin* (4:53) is the best biography.

Zimmerman, J. J. "Benjamin Franklin: A Study of Pennsylvania Politics and the Colonial Agency, 1755–1775" (3:186).

Sir William Johnson

3:74 Flexner, James T. *Mohawk Baronet: Sir William Johnson of New York*. New York: Harper, 1959. As superintendent of Indian affairs for the Northern Department during the French and Indian Wars, Johnson was an influential diplomat in dealing with Indians, particularly the Iroquois. Bibliography.

3:75 Johnson, Sir William. *The Papers of Sir William Johnson*. 14 vols. Ed. by James Sullivan and Alexander C. Flick. Albany: University of the State of New York Press, 1921–1962. This is primarily correspondence of the superintendent of Indian affairs for the Northern Department during the French and Indian Wars.

Alexander Spotswood

3:76 Dodson, Leonidas. *Alexander Spotswood: Governor of Colonial Virginia, 1710–1722*. Philadelphia: University of Pennsylvania Press, 1932. In this topical examination of Virginia during his administration as governor, Spotswood balances his functions as royal representative fulfilling imperial policies and service to his colonial constituents. His claim to fame as an empire builder, is in encouraging migration movement which would benefit both colony and empire.

3:77 Spotswood, Alexander. *Alexander Spotswood: The Official Letters of Alexander Spotswood, Governor of Virginia, 1710–1722*. 2 vols. Ed. by Robert A. Brock. Richmond: Virginia Historical Society, 1882–1885. A revealing picture of an imperial-minded colonial governor, it pays special attention to the mutual benefits, for colony and mother country, which westward expansion would bring.

Others

3:78 Alden, John R. *John Stuart and the Southern Colonial Frontier*. Ann Arbor: University of Michigan Press, 1944. In an authoritative study of the leading colonial negotiator with Indians of the South, Alden credits Stuart, after 1762, with coping with jealous governors and avaricious traders as well as with hostile Spanish and French agents. Extensive bibliography.

3:79 Bailyn, Bernard. *The Ordeal of Thomas Hutchinson*. Cambridge: Harvard University Press, 1974. This is a sympathetic appreciation of the last civilian governor of the Massachusetts Bay Colony, who was torn between his loyalty to his native land and his duties as royal representative. This study of a conservative caught up in a time of radical upheaval highlights the ideological crisis on the eve of the Revolution. Bibliography.

3:80 Byrd, William. *William Byrd, William Byrd's Histories of the Dividing Line betwixt Virginia and North Carolina*. Ed. by William K. Boyd. Raleigh: North Carolina Historical Commission, 1967. This is a view of the dispute between the two colonies from the vantage point of a member of one of Virginia's most distinguished families—a Byrd's-eye view.

3:81 Colden, Cadwallader. *The Letters and Papers of Cadwallader Colden, 1711–1755*. 7 vols. New York: New York Historical Society, 1918–1937. Volumes 6 and 7 deal with his service as lieutenant governor of New York from 1761 to 1775 and with his role as manager of Indian affairs and defender of the Grenville legislation.

3:82 Ettinger, Amos A. *James Edward Oglethorpe: Imperial Idealist*. London: Oxford University Press, 1936. This balanced account of Oglethorpe shows him as the leader of Georgia in campaigns against the Spanish over the Florida boundary.

3:83 Illick, Joseph, ed. *William Penn, the Politician: His Relations with the English Government*. Ithaca, N.Y.: Cornell University Press, 1965. A monograph that emphasizes the importance of British politics to colonial welfare as well as the specific importance of the colonial agent in maintaining the autonomy of the colony. Pennsylvania under Penn's guidance from England was successful because of his function as a lobbyist. Extensive bibliography.

3:84 Leder, Lawrence H. *Robert Livingston, 1654–1728, and the Politics of Colonial New York.* Chapel Hill: University of North Carolina Press, 1961. A biography of the founder of one of the two most important families of colonial New York, it finds its subject's private ambitions coincided with British imperial interest in Indian and French affairs. Extensive bibliography.

3:85 Lee, Richard Henry. *Life of Arthur Lee.* 2 vols. Boston: Wells & Lilly, 1829. An uncritical portrait of the colonial agent of Massachusetts in the 1770s; includes valuable letters.

3:86 Meade, Robert. *Patrick Henry: Patriot in the Making.* Philadelphia: Lippincott, 1957. This is the most authoritative contemporary biography of the Virginia burgess who challenged British authority in 1765. This initial volume, of a two-volume study, deals with the prerevolutionary years.

3:87 Murdock, Kenneth B. *Increase Mather: The Foremost American Puritan.* Cambridge: Harvard University Press, 1925. The Puritan divine as colonial agent of Massachusetts is the main theme. Considerable attention is given to Mather's relatively brief role as diplomat in London after the Glorious Revolution. Bibliography.

3:88 Schutz, John A. *William Shirley: King's Governor of Massachusetts.* Chapel Hill: University of North Carolina Press, 1961. An able imperialist in mid-18th-century Massachusetts, Shirley combined his talents as a spoilsman with those of an administrator. Bibliography.

3:89 Wainwright, Nicholas B. *George Croghan: Wilderness Diplomat.* Chapel Hill: University of North Carolina Press, 1959. Croghan was a leading diplomat (and fur trader) with Indians and a valuable adviser on Indian affairs in Pennsylvania and New York in mid-18th-century America. Bibliography.

3:90 Zimmerman, John J. "Charles Thomson, 'The Sam Adams of Philadelphia.' " *Mississippi Valley Historical Review* 45:3 (1958), 464–80. Thomson's selection as secretary of the First Continental Congress marked a high point in the radicals' attempts to control the revolutionary movement. Alone among Pennsylvanians, Thomson is seen as the most consistent supporter of the radical cause from the Stamp Act crisis to the Declaration of Independence.

Colonial Empires and Their Diplomacy to 1763

See "Document Collections," especially Symcox (3:23).

ANGLO-SPANISH RELATIONS

See "Personalities," especially Sir Benjamin Keene, under "Others"; also "Bibliographies," especially Coker and Holmes (3:4) and McDermott (3:10).

3:91 Bannon, John F. *The Spanish Borderlands Frontier, 1513–1821.* New York: Holt, Rinehart & Winston, 1970. Bannon ranges across the continent as he explores the economic, political, religious, and military impacts of Spain's tenuous and always defensive presence in North America. He concludes that the Spanish borderlanders were also pioneers, whose achievements in opening the frontier have too long been overlooked. The author's outstanding bibliography merits the attention of any scholar working in Spanish-American relations in the period prior to 1821.

3:92 Bourne, Edward G. *Spain in America, 1450–1580.* New York: Harper, 1904. One-half of this old, but useful, general account is devoted to Spain's colonial administration in America, with a favorable interpretation of the Spanish role. Bibliography.

Chatelain, V. E. *The Defenses of Spanish Florida, 1565–1763* (7:39) deals almost exclusively with St. Augustine.

Cook, W. L. *Flood Tide of Empire: Spain and the Pacific Northwest, 1543–1819* (5:180).

3:93 Crane, Verner W. *The Southern Frontier, 1670–1732.* Durham, N.C.: Duke University Press, 1928. This major work emphasizes Indian trade as the dynamic force in Britain's conflict with Spain and France on the southern frontier as the fur trade, not farming, dominated the economy. Bibliography.

3:94 Gibson, Charles. *Spain in America*. New York: Harper & Row, 1966. The work has a chapter, "Imperial Readjustments," that encapsulates Spain's imperial problems with her European rivals in the 17th century. Extensive bibliography.

3:95 Madariaga, Salvador de. *The Rise of the Spanish American Empire*. Westport, Conn.: Greenwood (1947), 1975. The author attributes Spain's shrinking empire (1492–1764) to its loss of sea power by 1700; this in turn was due to a failure of Spanish national character, "a tendency to leisure and idleness, and a tendency to neglect craftsmanship." Bibliography.

3:96 McLachlan, Jean O. *Trade and Place with Old Spain, 1667–1750: A Study of the Influence of Commerce on Anglo-Spanish Diplomacy in the First Half of the Eighteenth Century*. New York: Octagon Books (1940), 1974. In the early 18th century, British trade with Spain and the Mediterranean outweighed that with New Spain and the West Indies. McLachlan believes the Wars of the Spanish Succession and of Jenkins' Ear were fought primarily for the control of Old Spanish and Mediterranean trade, rather than for New World territory. Extensive bibliography.

3:97 Means, Philip A. *The Spanish Main: Focus of Envy, 1492–1700*. New York: Scribner's, 1935. This survey of Spanish, French, and English competition emphasizes that, to 1700, the "very largely successful" Spanish had lost little territory in the Caribbean and none on the American continent.

3:98 Parry, John H. *The Spanish Seaborne Empire*. New York: Knopf, 1966. Chapters 13–15 discuss the increasing claims of the British, Dutch, and French to trade and to territory within the Spanish West Indies in the 17th and 18th centuries, and unrealistic Spanish claims to a trade monopoly and a general lordship over America. Extensive bibliography.

3:99 Quinn, David B. *England and the Discovery of America, 1481–1620*. New York: Knopf, 1974. Portuguese as well as Spanish relations play a large role in this account, with access to fisheries as important as territorial conflict. Bibliography.

3:100 TePaske, John J. *The Governorship of Spanish Florida, 1700–1763*. Durham, N.C.: Duke University Press, 1964. Despite the almost absolute powers of ten colonial governors in the 18th century, their energies were dissipated in the defense of the territory from foreign encroachment. Spain failed to provide adequate means to protect the colony, which for this period was a neglected outpost of its empire. Bibliography.

3:101 Wright, Irene. "Spanish Policy towards Virginia, 1606–1612: Jamestown, Ecya, and John Clark of the Mayflower." *American Historical Review* 25:3 (1920), 448–79. The Spanish government, though well informed of British aims toward Virginia, did nothing to stop the settlement because it underestimated the potential menace and believed Virginia a waste of English money.

3:102 Wright, J. Leitch, Jr. *Anglo-Spanish Rivalry in North America*. Athens: University of Georgia Press, 1971. Wright argues that Spain (1492–1821) saw its North American colonies, especially Florida and Louisiana, as buffers to protect Mexico and safeguard strategic sailing routes. Nine chapters relate to the period before 1763. Extensive bibliography.

3:103 Wright, J. Leitch, Jr. "Spanish Reaction to Carolina." *North Carolina Historical Review* 41:4 (1964), 464–76. The author contrasts Spanish indifference to early-17th-century English settlements in Virginia with their growing concern in Carolina after 1670; but even when alarmed, the Spanish were unable to contest the British. They lacked an adequate navy, were unable to attract Spanish settlers, and could not use the Indians effectively.

War of Jenkins' Ear, 1739

3:104 Hildner, Ernest G. "The Role of the South Sea Company in the Diplomacy Leading to the War of Jenkins' Ear, 1729–1739." *Hispanic American Historical Review* 18:3 (1938), 322–41. The South Sea Company was largely responsible for the War of Jenkins' Ear. Engaging in quarrels of its own with the Spanish and refusing to pay its debts to the Spanish government, the company demanded that the British government support its demands.

3:105 Lanning, John T. *The Diplomatic History of Georgia: A Study of the Epoch of Jenkins' Ear*. Chapel Hill: University of North Carolina Press, 1936. This revisionist study (1730–1750) minimizes Oglethorpe's philanthropism and emphasizes instead his interest in promoting British influence over the

Creeks and Cherokees at the expense of the Spanish. Bibliography.

3:106 Reese, Trevor. "Georgia in Anglo-Spanish Diplomacy, 1736–1739." *William and Mary Quarterly* 3d ser. 15:2 (1958), 168–90. Based largely on British sources, the article suggests that Georgia was only a subsidiary issue in the quarrels leading to war in 1739.

3:107 Temperley, Harold W. V. "The Causes of the War of Jenkins' Ear, 1739." *Transactions of the Royal Historical Society* 3d ser. 3 (1909), 197–236. British fear of a Franco-Spanish alliance was a main cause of war in 1739. Before then, Anglo-Spanish cooperation to exclude France from America was possible; after 1739, Franco-Spanish cooperation to exclude England became inevitable. Jenkins' Ear was the first war waged for the balance of trade rather than for the balance of power.

ANGLO-FRENCH RELATIONS

See "Bibliographies," especially Beers (3:2).

3:108 Andrews, Charles M. "Anglo-French Commercial Rivalry, 1700–1750: The Western Phase." *American Historical Review* 20:3 (1915), 539–56; 20:4 (1915), 761–80. English pamphlets (on which the article is mainly based) stressed that from 1700 to 1750, France exceeded England in worldwide commerce. In reality, the only French threat lay with the sugar islands that were trading with British mainland colonies.

3:109 Cole, Charles W. *Colbert and a Century of French Mercantilism.* 2 vols. New York: Columbia University Press, 1939. A monumental work, it has useful chapters on French colonies and emphasizes the international character of French mercantilism. The weaknesses of France's colonial policies vis-à-vis Britain's are apparent. Bibliography.

3:110 Davenport, Frances G. "American and European Diplomacy to 1648." In the Annual Report of the American Historical Association for the Year 1915. Washington, D.C.: G.P.O., 1917, pp. 151–61. Davenport surveys a century of French and British diplomacy aimed at breaking the Spanish-Portuguese monopoly in the Americas; the end of the Thirty Years' War marked the Iberian split and concessions to France and Britain.

3:111 Davies, Kenneth G. *The North Atlantic World in the Seventeenth Century.* Minneapolis: University of Minnesota Press, 1974. An important part of this survey deals with the North Atlantic in the 17th-century wars; the advantage ultimately fell to the British. Extensive bibliography.

3:112 Eccles, William J. *France in America.* New York: Harper & Row, 1972. France's relations with England (1500–1774) dominate a volume in which New France appears to be an instrument in the larger 17th- and 18th-century imperial struggle between England and France. Extensive bibliography.

3:113 Gipson, Lawrence. "A French Project for Victory Short of a Declaration of War, 1755." *Canadian Historical Review* 26:4 (1945), 361–71. The French memorial, printed in 1755, demanded British abandonment of the Ohio. The very publication of this memorial suggests that the French had clear objectives regarding colonial territories.

3:114 Graham, Gerald S. *Empire of the North Atlantic: The Maritime Struggle for North America.* 2d ed. Toronto: University of Toronto Press, 1958. In a discussion of the navy in British politics, Graham starts with the assumption that the British development of naval superiority (and correspondingly, the French failure to develop adequate sea power under Louis XIV) was responsible for the expansion of the British empire.

3:115 Guttridge, George H. *The Colonial Policy of William III in America and the West Indies.* Hamden, Conn.: Shoe String Press, 1966. The French wars of William III pointed up the failure of the older imperial system in which the colonies were regarded as trading stations; yet the task of creating a new political framework for British imperialism was evaded.

3:116 Jacobs, Wilbur R. *Diplomacy and Indian Gifts: Anglo-French Rivalry along the Ohio and Northwest Frontiers, 1748–1763.* Stanford, Calif.: Stanford University Press, 1950. Gifts were given so extensively that some Indian tribes, which held the balance of power between France and Britain in America, became virtually dependent upon European goods. After British conquest of Canada, these presents were markedly reduced; a lack of presents was a significant cause of Pontiac's rebellion. Bibliography.

3:117 Morgan, William T. "English Fear of 'Encirclement' in the Seventeenth Century." *Canadian His-*

torical Review 10:1 (1929), 4–22. By the accession of William III, the Ohio Territory had become of interest to foreign powers in large part because of the "visionary efforts" of colonial leaders like Frontenac and La Salle, Coxe, Dengan, and Berkeley.

3:118 Mulkearn, Lois. "The English Eye the French in North America." *Pennsylvania History* 21:4 (1954), 316–37. The Anglo-French rivalry from 1613 to the Seven Years' War saw warfare in which the British and the French relied primarily on their Indian allies shift to warfare in which the main fighting was between British and French troops.

3:119 Pares, Richard. "American versus Continental Warfare, 1739–63." *English Historical Review* 51:3 (1936), 429–65. France and England were undecided in 1739, and again in 1755, whether to wage primarily a commercial or a continental war; both initially leaned to commercial war but came to lay greater stress on continental action. One can see this shift in William Pitt, who strongly defended a German war by 1763.

3:120 Price, Jacob M. *France and the Chesapeake: A History of the French Tobacco Monopoly 1694–1791 and Its Relations to the British and American Tobacco Trades.* 2 vols. Ann Arbor: University of Michigan Press, 1973. This is a superb economic and political history of the tobacco trade. In his well-written and extensively researched work, Price covers the important role of Scottish merchants as intermediaries in selling American tobacco to the monopolistic French Farmers General. Extensive bibliography.

3:121 Priestley, Herbert I. *France Overseas through the Old Regime: A Study in European Expansion.* New York: Appleton-Century, 1939. This survey covers the development of all French colonies from the Crusades to Napoleon. Chapters 3, 6–7, 10, 12–13, and 19 pertain to French colonies in America. Bibliography.

3:122 Sosin, Jack M. "Louisburg and the Peace of Aix-la-Chapelle, 1748." *William and Mary Quarterly* 3d ser. 14:4 (1957), 516–35. Sosin argues that Louisburg was returned to France in 1748 in exchange for French evacuation of the Flemish Barrier towns and the Austrian Netherlands, rather than for Madras.

3:123 Wilson, Arthur M. *French Foreign Policy during the Administration of Cardinal Fleury, 1726–1743.* Cambridge: Harvard University Press, 1936. The first complete study of Fleury's foreign policies, it emphasizes his successful statecraft vis-à-vis Walpole on the Continent. Extensive bibliography.

Canada

3:124 Biggar, H. P. *The Early Trading Companies of New France: A Contribution to the History of Commerce and Discovery in North America.* Toronto: University of Toronto Library (1901), 1972. The book narrates the history of trade in New France from the earliest settlements to 1632. Bibliography is good, but dated.

3:125 Eccles, William J. *The Canadian Frontier, 1534–1760.* New York: Holt, Rinehart & Winston, 1969. A general survey, it emphasizes the fur trade and the role of French merchants in the expansion of New France. Extensive bibliography.

3:126 Eccles, William J. *Canada under Louis XIV, 1663–1701.* New York: Oxford University Press, 1964. Eccles claims that the rapid consolidation of French power on the St. Lawrence between 1663 (when the very survival of French settlements was in doubt) and 1701 (when Louis XIV decided to seize and hold the whole interior of North America) was due primarily to Louis XIV's administrative ability. Extensive bibliography.

3:127 Parkman, Francis. *France and England in North America.* 9 vols. Boston: Little, Brown, 1865–1892. The epic account of the Anglo-French struggle (1600–1763) for North America, with emphasis upon the American scene rather than on the European sponsors.

3:128 Pilgrim, Donald G. "France and New France: Two Perspectives on Colonial Security." *Canadian Historical Review* 55:4 (1974), 381–407. Counters W. J. Eccles's view (3:126) that the defensive weaknesses of New France in the 1680s were the responsibility of Sugnelay, the French secretary of state. Pilgrim argues that the secretary found his own authority limited, French resources overextended, and other French leaders eager to develop cooperation with the Stuart monarchs.

3:129 Rule, John C. "The Old Regime in America: A Review of Recent Interpretations of France in America." *William and Mary Quarterly* 3d ser. 19:4 (1962), 575–600. He discusses "French Imperialist," "British Imperialist," "French Canadian," and

"Anglo-Canadian" schools of French imperial history, and calls for more biographies, family studies, and administrative histories.

3:130 Rutledge, Joseph F. *Century of Conflict: The Struggle between the French and British in North America.* Garden City, N.Y.: Doubleday, 1956. This Parkmanesque attempt at creating "the glowing human story of France and England on this continent" seeks to "find flesh and blood and a sense of immediacy in the crowding events" in a lengthy narrative.

3:131 Savelle, Max. *Diplomatic History of the Canadian Boundary, 1749–1763.* New Haven, Conn.: Yale University Press, 1940. Preservation of British dominance in northeastern fisheries, control of the fur trade, and the rapid expansion of British settlements westward all pushed England and France into conflict. The inferior position of France, particularly in the West, helped to assure its diplomatic defeat in 1763. Colonial interests joined British mercantilist interests to press for the removal of France from Canada. Bibliography.

3:132 Wrong, George M. *The Rise and Fall of New France.* 2 vols. New York: Macmillan, 1928. Wrong's Parkmanesque interpretation of the conflict between the "dependent" French and the self-reliant (and inevitably victorious) English, from the earliest settlements to 1760. Volume 2 is most useful to diplomatic historians. Bibliography.

3:133 Zoltvany, Yves F. "New France and the West, 1701–1713." *Canadian Historical Review* 46:4 (1965), 301–22. Between 1701 and 1713, Pontchartrain, French minister of the marine, attempted to modify French commitments in the Great Lakes and Mississippi Valley by linking the beaver trade, encouraging missions, and preventing the westward progress of the English.

Seven Years' War, 1756–1763

See "Personalities," especially Sir William Johnson, and, under "Others," Duc de Choiseul, Lord Loudon, Thomas Pownall; also see "Bibliographies," especially Leach (3:9).

3:134 Christelow, Allan. "The Economic Background of the Anglo-Spanish War of 1762." *Journal of Modern History* 18:1 (1946), 22–36. Friendly Anglo-Spanish relations early in the Seven Years' War ended in 1759 with the accession of Charles III to the Spanish

throne. The new king opposed existing trade treaties with Britain and favored French pleas for cooperation to limit British continental influence.

3:135 Dorn, Walter L. *Competition for Empire, 1740–63.* New York: Harper, 1940. Dorn argues that the essential characteristics of the mid-18th-century state system were first, expansionism, and second, preventing domination by any one power. Bibliography.

3:136 Gipson, Lawrence H. "British Diplomacy in the Light of Spanish New World Issues, 1750–1757." *American Historical Review* 51:4 (1945), 627–48. Gipson discusses the "consummate skill" of the Pelham-Newcastle ministry in playing down Anglo-Spanish differences on the eve of the Seven Years' War.

Gold, R. L. *Borderland Empires in Transition: The Triple-Nation Transfer of Florida* (7:40) is a thoroughly researched examination of the transfer of the Floridas from Spanish and French to British control in the Treaty of Paris in 1763. Bibliography.

3:137 Grant, William L. "Canada versus Guadeloupe, an Episode of the Seven Years' War." *American Historical Review* 17:3 (1912), 735–43. A summary of English pamphlet arguments (1760–1763) stressing a common emphasis on an empire commercially self-contained.

3:138 Hamer, Philip M. "Anglo-French Rivalry in the Cherokee Country, 1754–1757." *North Carolina Historical Review* 2:3 (1925), 303–22. English efforts on behalf of the Cherokees helped to cement Anglo-Cherokee relations early in the Seven Years' War.

3:139 Higonnet, Patrice Louis-René. "The Origins of the Seven Years' War." *Journal of Modern History* 40:1 (1968), 57–90. Neither British nor French leaders wanted war; they were pulled into it by aggressive colonial governors urging shows of force. These in turn produced mutual suspicion, which was far more important than possible tangible gains in bringing war.

Lyon, E. W. *Louisiana in French Diplomacy, 1759–1804* (6:94).

Pares, R. *Colonial Blockade and Neutral Rights, 1739–1763* (16:154).

3:140 Pease, Theodore C., ed. *Anglo-French Boundary Disputes in the West, 1749–1763.*

Springfield: Illinois State Historical Library, 1936. The issues presented in these disputes were the substance of the Seven Years' War in America. Documents.

3:141 Rashed Zenab Esmat. *The Peace of Paris, 1763.* Liverpool: University of Liverpool Press, 1951. A full examination of the peace negotiations ending the Seven Years' War, from 1759 to 1763, which blames British appetite for conquest for continuing a war that might have ended with the fall of Canada in 1760.

3:142 Savelle, Max. "Diplomatic Preliminaries of the Seven Years' War in America." *Canadian Historical Review* 20:1 (1939), 17–36. This discussion of delimiting French and English possessions concludes that among the six major areas—Rupert's Land, Acadia, St. Lawrence, Great Lakes Basin, Ohio Valley, Mexican Gulf Coastal Plain, and West Indies—disagreement arose only over the St. John River valley in Acadia.

THE NETHERLANDS, SWEDEN, AND OTHERS

3:143 Boxer, Charles R. *The Dutch Seaborne Empire, 1600–1800.* London: Hutchinson, 1965. Dutch policy necessarily steered between a preoccupation with European trade and a preoccupation with colonial quarrels which sucked European powers into wars. There is very little on the colonies themselves. Bibliography.

3:144 Boxer, Charles R. *The Portuguese Seaborne Empire, 1415–1825.* London: Hutchinson, 1969. As the first modern colonial empire, Portugal was a foil for the competing empires of Holland, Spain, France, and England. Bibliography.

3:145 Johnson, Amandus. *The Swedish Settlements on the Delaware, 1638–1664.* 2 vols. Philadelphia: Swedish Colonial Society, 1911. A general survey in which chapters 36–37 and 46–47 cover English-Dutch relations in the 1640s and 1650s.

3:146 Julien, C.-Andre. *Les voyages de découverte et les premiers établissements* [The voyages of discovery and the first settlements]. Paris: Presses Universitaires de France, 1948. A survey of French overseas expansion, it explains France's failure to establish permanent holdings in the 16th century. The opposi-

tion of Spain's Philip II and his influence with the French crown helped to account for colonization failures in Florida and Brazil.

3:147 Kupp, Jan. "Could the Dutch Commercial Empire Have Influenced the Canadian Economy during the First Half of the Eighteenth Century?" *Canadian Historical Review* 52:4 (1971), 367–87. More research might show that through credit, capital, and trade in cheap goods, Dutch merchants were important to the economy of France (and Canada) from the early 17th century to at least 1760.

3:148 Wilson, Charles H. *Profit and Power: A Study of England and the Dutch Wars.* London: Longmans, Green, 1957. The colonies were minor pawns in a struggle (1650–1675) which found the pacific Dutch trying to hold a precarious trade advantage against the nationalistic challenges of France and England.

Growth of Colonial Statecraft to 1763

RELATIONS WITH ENGLAND

See "Document Collections," especially Stock (3:22).

View from England

See "Personalities," especially, under "Others," Edward Randolph, William Blathwayt, Sir Robert Walpole; also see Brown and Olson. (3:29).

3:149 Barrow, Thomas C. *Trade and Empire: The British Customs Service in Colonial America, 1660–1775.* Cambridge: Harvard University Press, 1967. A study of the customs service in the governance of the British empire in America, which stresses mid-18th-century changes. Extensive bibliography.

3:150 Clark, Dora M. *The Rise of the British Treasury: Colonial Administration in the Eighteenth Century.* New Haven, Conn.: Yale University Press, 1960. The British Treasury was the most powerful 18th-century colonial policymaking body and, hence, the agency primarily responsible for colonial unrest. Financial problems were the most pressing during wars and Grenville was a product of this pressure. The study also illustrates bureaucratic struggles between the Treasury, the secretary of state for the Southern Department and the Board of Trade. Extensive bibliography.

3:151 Dickerson, Oliver M. *American Colonial Government, 1696–1765: A Study of the British Board of Trade in Its Relation to the American Colonies, Political, Industrial, Administrative.* Cleveland: A. H. Clark, 1912. A pioneer study of the one agency with nominal supervision over the colonies; as such the Board of Trade inspired colonial diplomacy. Bibliography.

Gipson, L. H. *The British Empire before the American Revolution* (3:31) contains, in virtually every volume, information about "negotiations" between American and British officials both in Great Britain and the colonies. Volumes 1–10 should be consulted for any aspect of the pre-1763 period.

3:152 Harper, Lawrence A. *The English Navigation Laws: A Seventeenth-Century Experiment in Social Engineering.* New York: Columbia University Press, 1939. In this classic account, the Navigation System is seen as a successful form of British colonial management. Extensive bibliography.

3:153 Henretta, James A. *"Salutary Neglect": Colonial Administration under the Duke of Newcastle.* Princeton, N.J.: Princeton University Press, 1972. The author carefully examines British policy toward America during the years of "salutary neglect," roughly 1721 to 1754. He finds British policy conservative, lethargic, and shortsighted, the result of a political bureaucracy chosen for patronage rather than for expertise and industry. Bibliography.

3:154 Labaree, Leonard W. *Royal Government in America: A Study of the British Colonial System before 1783.* New Haven, Conn.: Yale University Press, 1930. The central theme is the relationship of the colonial governor to the council, assembly, and to his royal superiors in England. His difficulties in securing a permanent revenue underscore the balance of power between governor and assembly.

3:155 Olson, Alison G. *Anglo-American Politics, 1660–1775: The Relationship between Parties in England and Colonial America.* New York: Oxford Uni-

versity Press, 1973. In the relationship between the colonies and the British political parties, Olson sees 1689 to 1714 as a high-water mark of imperial cooperation; thereafter, the difficulty of Americans establishing enduring and productive relationships with British political groups is stressed.

3:156 Steele, I. K. *Politics of Colonial Policy: The Board of Trade in Colonial Administration, 1696–1720.* New York: Oxford University Press, 1968. A thorough study of the Board of Trade's early-18th-century role in administering the colonies, it takes a Namierist approach, emphasizing the board's personnel and personalities rather than its institutional aspects. Bibliography.

3:157 Thomas, Robert P. "A Quantitative Approach to the Study of the Effects of British Imperial Policy upon Colonial Welfare: Some Preliminary Findings." *Journal of Economic History* 25:4 (1965), 615–38. Thomas concludes that the trade acts imposed no hardships upon the American colonies before 1763.

3:158 Wickwire, Franklin B. "John Pownall and British Colonial Policy." *William and Mary Quarterly* 3d ser. 20:4 (1963), 543–54. This account of the "perennial" secretary (1740–1776) to its Board of Trade describes the formulation of colonial policy within the board.

View from America

See "Personalities," especially Robert Dinwiddie, Benjamin Franklin, Alexander Spotswood, and, under "Others," William Byrd, James Oglethorpe, William Penn, Robert Livingston, William Shirley; also see Leach (3:32) and Peckham (3:37).

3:159 Barnes, Viola. *The Dominion of New England.* New Haven, Conn.: Yale University Press, 1923. The Dominion of New England is described as the most complete expression of 17th-century British colonial policy. Bibliography.

3:160 Buffinton, Arthur H. "The Isolationist Policy of Colonial Massachusetts." *New England Quarterly* 1:2 (1928), 158–79. The isolation from European affairs which early Massachusetts enjoyed could not be sustained over the 17th century. It became endangered by French power in Canada and Acadia, interested in trade, and engulfed in balance of power problems.

3:161 Greene, Jack P. *The Quest for Power: The Lower Houses of Assembly in the Southern Royal Colonies, 1689–1763.* Chapel Hill: University of North Carolina Press, 1963. A seminal study in the beginnings of American statecraft, it views how colonial legislatures manipulated political power and colonial governors. Extensive bibliography.

3:162 Kammen, Michael G. *Empire and Interest: The American Colonies and the Politics of Mercantilism.* Philadelphia: Lippincott, 1970. This study ranges from 1696 to 1776, but 1763 is seen as inaugurating mercantilism as serving the specific interests of British mercantilists, as opposed to its earlier serving the whole empire. Extensive bibliography.

3:163 Katz, Stanley N. *Newcastle's New York: Anglo-American Politics, 1732–1753.* Cambridge: Harvard University Press, 1968. Katz studies the corrosion of the governor's position and crown prerogatives as New York advanced as an 18th-century maritime center. The coming of war impelled imperial interests to limit colonial autonomy, and to end the fruitful Anglo-American collaboration that characterized Newcastle's tenure as secretary of state. Extensive bibliography.

3:164 Rogers, Alan. *Empire and Liberty: American Resistance to British Authority, 1755–1763.* Berkeley: University of California Press, 1975. Increased British governmental powers set in motion by the Seven Years' War sparked American defiance. Resistance to what was seen as arbitrary rule in America is pushed back from the 1760s to the French and Indian War. Bibliography.

3:165 Root, Winfred T. *The Relations of Pennsylvania with the British Government, 1695–1765.* Philadelphia: University of Pennsylvania Press, 1912. The key to this study is the role of the Board of Trade. While the shortcomings of the Pennsylvania Charter disturbed both London and Philadelphia, there was no serious response in Whitehall to the call for centralization. The author equates this failure to respond with "salutary neglect." Bibliography.

3:166 Sachse, William L. *The Colonial American in Britain.* Madison: University of Wisconsin Press, 1956. Sachse describes the British milieu in which 18th-century colonial Americans operated, including colonial dealings with British bureaucrats.

COLONY VERSUS COLONY

See Bridenbaugh (3:28), Curti (3:30), and Savelle (3:39); also "Document Collections," especially Boyd (3:15).

3:167 Gipson, Lawrence H. "Thomas Hutchinson and the Framing of the Albany Plan of Union, 1754." *Pennsylvania Magazine of History* 74:1 (1950), 5–35. The author ascribes a major role in devising the Albany Plan of Union, 1754, to Thomas Hutchinson, later the royal governor of Massachusetts.

3:168 Hutson, James H. "Tentative Moves toward Intercolonial Union." In *Aspects of American Liberty.* Philadelphia: American Philosophical Society, 1977, pp. 81–94. Hutson surveys efforts to unite the colonies politically from 1630 to 1776.

3:169 Leach, Douglas E. *Flintlock and Tomahawk: New England in King Philip's War.* New York: Norton, 1958. Leach discusses the war's effect on New England society and emphasizes local conditions rather than imperial relations. Extensive bibliography.

3:170 Leach, Douglas E. *The Northern Colonial Frontier, 1607–1763.* New York: Holt, Rinehart & Winston, 1966. This book looks at frontier conflicts more from the standpoint of the colonist than that of the imperial powers. Extensive bibliography.

3:171 Newbold, Robert C. *The Albany Congress and Plan of Union of 1754.* New York: Vantage, 1955. A balanced treatment of the Albany Congress of 1754, the most important 18th-century attempt to forge an intercolonial union. Bibliography.

3:172 Reid, John P. *A Better Kind of Hatchet: Law, Trade, and Diplomacy in the Cherokee Nation during the Early Years of European Contact.* University Park: Pennsylvania State University Press, 1976. In a perceptive study of Cherokee-English relations in South Carolina, Reid employs tools of ethnohistory and comparative law to examine the effect of trade upon both the English and the Indians from the 17th century to the end of the colonial period. The loss of Cherokee autonomy through trade dependency was matched by colonial impatience with treaties with chieftains who lacked the power to enforce them.

3:173 Ward, Harry M. *Unite or Die: Intercolony Relations 1690–1763.* Port Washington, N.Y.: Kennikat, 1971. This is among the most thorough studies of intercolonial relations from 1690 to 1763. Chapter 11 has a good summary of the many intercolonial boundary disputes. Bibliography.

3:174 Ward, Harry M. *The United Colonies of New England, 1643–1690*. New York: Vantage, 1961. An exhaustive account of the New England colonies' attempt to forge a union for the conduct of Indian relations and trade. The work is marred by the author's efforts to make the united colonies scheme a precursor of all later attempts at union, including the Constitution. Bibliography.

COLONIAL AGENTS

See "Personalities," especially Benjamin Franklin, and, under "Others," Arthur Lee, Increase Mather; also see Kammen (3:191) and Sosin (3:192).

3:175 Appleton, Marguerite. "Richard Partridge: Colonial Agent." *New England Quarterly* 5:3 (1932), 293–309. Partridge, an agent for Rhode Island (1715–1759) and periodically for other colonies, was called "a clearing house for the colonies." He deserves closer study.

3:176 Bond, Beverly W., Jr. "The Colonial Agent as a Popular Representative." *Political Science Quarterly* 35:3 (1920), 372–92. This study stresses the contention and discord between various branches of the colonial government (1700–1763) over the selection of an agent to represent the colony at the British court.

3:177 Burns, James J. *The Colonial Agents of New England*. Washington, D.C.: Catholic University of America, 1935. Burns claims agents successfully adjusted problems which did not touch on Britain's right to govern the colonies. This book has inaccuracies and must be used with care. Bibliography.

3:178 Freiberg, Malcolm. "William Bollan, Agent of Massachusetts." *More Books: The Bulletin of the Boston Public Library* 23:2 (1948), 43–220ff. This is a thorough study of the career of Massachusetts's colonial agent (1745–1762), and agent of the Massachusetts Council (1762–1776).

3:179 Gipson, Lawrence H. *Jared Ingersoll: A Study of American Loyalism in Relation to British Colonial Government*. New Haven, Conn.: Yale University Press, 1920. As a Connecticut agent, the best among American representatives of the British imperial administrative system, Ingersoll attempted to serve as a bridge between the colonies and the mother country. Extensive bibliography.

3:180 Lilly, Edward P. *The Colonial Agents of New York and New Jersey*. Washington, D.C.: Catholic University of America, 1936. A competent study of these two middle colonies' agents, it emphasizes local political conflicts provoked by the agents' selection. Bibliography.

3:181 Lonn, Ella. *The Colonial Agents of the Southern Colonies*. Chapel Hill: University of North Carolina Press, 1945. This is a thorough, well-researched account of the activities of the agents of the southern colonies. Bibliography.

3:182 Sanford, Charles L. "The Days of Jeremy Dummer, Colonial Agent." Ph.D. diss., Harvard University, 1952. This is the best study of Dummer of Massachusetts and Connecticut, who was the most successful of early-18th-century colonial agents. Extensive bibliography.

3:183 Tanner, Edwin P. "Colonial Agencies in England during the Eighteenth Century." *Political Science Quarterly* 16:1 (1901), 24–49. In an old but still useful survey, Tanner reviews the agencies' operations in Great Britain.

3:184 Varga, Nicholas. "Robert Charles: New York Agent, 1748–1770." *William and Mary Quarterly* 3d ser. 18:2 (1961), 211–35. Varga provides as exhaustive a study as we are likely to have of Charles and the New York agency.

3:185 Wolff, Mabel P. *The Colonial Agency of Pennsylvania, 1712–1757*. Philadelphia, 1933. A reliable study of the Pennsylvania agency during this period. Bibliography.

3:186 Zimmerman, John J. "Benjamin Franklin: A Study of Pennsylvania Politics and the Colonial Agency, 1755–1775." Ph.D. diss., University of Michigan, 1956. There are any number of works on Franklin as a colonial agent. For the fullest understanding of this aspect of his career, a modern political biography, such as Hawke (3:73), should be compared with Labaree's definitive edition of Franklin's papers (3:72).

Anglo-American Confrontation, 1763–1774

See "Personalities," especially John Adams, Samuel Adams, George III; also see "Bibliographies," especially Adams (3:1).

GENERAL

England

3:187 Alvord, Clarence W. *The Mississippi Valley in British Politics.* 2 vols. Cleveland: A. H. Clark, 1917. The origins of the American Revolution lie as much in the West as in the East. Vacillating British policy from the Proclamation of 1763 to the Quebec Act of 1774 accounts for much of the sentiment that erupted in 1775. Extensive bibliography.

3:188 Christie, Ian R., and Labaree, Benjamin W. *Empire or Independence, 1760–1776: A British-American Dialogue on the Coming of the American Revolution.* New York: Norton, 1976. A good blend of Anglo-American scholarship, this account is based on a great variety of materials recent and contemporary. Extensive bibliography.

3:189 Dickerson, Oliver M. *The Navigation Acts and the American Revolution.* Philadelphia: University of Pennsylvania Press, 1951. Dickerson interprets the Revolution as a by-product of British efforts to convert the successful and mutually beneficial mercantile system prevailing before 1763 into a revenue-raising exploitation of colonial wealth. He emphasizes the corruption of British customs officials and naval officers linked with the enforcement of the Navigation Acts. His evidence is impressive but not wholly convincing. Excellent bibliography.

3:190 Gipson, Lawrence H. *The Coming of the Revolution, 1763–1775.* New York: Harper, 1954. This encapsulated version of Gipson's magisterial study of the British empire before the Revolution presents the coming of the Revolution from Britain's imperial perspective. The basic cause of the Revolution, in Gipson's survey, is the coming of age of the American colonies and their consequent demands for an autonomy within the empire that England was not willing to grant. Excellent bibliography.

3:191 Kammen, Michael G. *A Rope of Sand: The Colonial Agents, British Politics, and the American Revolution.* Ithaca, N.Y.: Cornell University Press, 1968. The first two chapters provide a valuable survey of American agents in pre-1763 Britain. Kammen's appendix contains a roster of colonial agents active in London from 1755. Extensive bibliography.

3:192 Sosin, Jack M. *Agents and Merchants: British Colonial Policy and the Origins of the American Revolution, 1763–1775.* Lincoln: University of Nebraska Press, 1965. Additionally, the first chapter supplies useful information on the American agents and the British bureaucracy of the pre-1763 period. Bibliography.

3:193 Sosin, Jack M. *Whitehall and Wilderness: The Middle West in British Colonial Policy, 1760–1775.* Lincoln: University of Nebraska Press, 1961. In his revision of Alvord (3:187), Sosin finds a coherence and an intelligence to British imperial authority that Alvord failed to locate. Extensive bibliography.

3:194 Stout, Neil R. *The Royal Navy in America, 1760–1775: A Study of Enforcement of British Colonial Policy in the Era of the American Revolution.* Annapolis, Md.: Naval Institute Press, 1973. The British navy mainly enforced the Navigation Acts because of the custom service's inefficiency. The British cabinet's failure to provide sufficient ships restricted the navy's suppression of smuggling; furthermore, naval officers' insensitivity to civilian sensibilities raised colonial passions generally against British authority. Extensive bibliography.

3:195 Ubbelohde, Carl *The Vice-Admiralty Courts and the American Revolution.* Chapel Hill: University of North Carolina Press, 1960. This essential work stresses the role these juryless courts played after 1763, in developing friction between British officials and colonial Americans. Extensive bibliography.

America

See "Colonial/Imperial Experience," above, for the development of an "American consciousness."

3:196 Jensen, Merrill. *The Founding of a Nation: A History of the American Revolution, 1763–1776*. New York: Oxford University Press, 1968. A major work, it details political life in each of the colonies, with emphasis to 1770, as Americans respond to British parliamentary measures. Bibliographical notes.

3:197 Kraus, Michael. *Intercolonial Aspects of American Culture on the Eve of the Revolution, with Special Reference to the Northern Towns*. New York: Columbia University Press, 1928. This is a thorough survey of many areas—science, business, art, religion, medicine—in which the 18th-century colonies interacted. Bibliography.

3:198 Maier, Pauline. *From Resistance to Revolution: Colonial Radicals and the Development of American Opposition to Great Britain, 1765–1776*. New York: Knopf, 1972. Maier's important work places American leaders and violence within the "Real Whig" tradition, and shows its importance in developing a revolutionary ideology.

3:199 Merritt, Richard L. *Symbols of American Community, 1735–1775*. New Haven, Conn.: Yale University Press, 1966. The author attempts to show, by quantitative symbol analysis, that a "growing colonial interaction" evolved a distinct political community with a sense of nationality in America by 1770.

Palmer, R. R. *The Age of the Democratic Revolution . . . , 1760–1790* (4:32).

3:200 Savelle, Max. "The Appearance of an American Attitude toward External Affairs, 1750–1775." *American Historical Review* 52:4 (1947), 655–66. Savelle uses newspapers and pamphlets to show the growing national self-consciousness of the colonies; these reflected a changing view of France from hated enemy in 1750 to potential ally in 1775.

3:201 Schlesinger, Arthur M. *The Colonial Merchants and the American Revolution, 1763–1776*. New York: Longmans, 1918. In a landmark study of the origins of the American Revolution, Schlesinger identifies—through newspapers, letter-books, diaries, correspondence, and official records—the important role merchants played in staving off radical measures of Parliament and colonials until 1776. Bibliography.

3:202 Schlesinger, Arthur M. *Prelude to Independence: The Newspaper War on Great Britain, 1764–1776*. New York: Knopf, 1958. This solid work reveals the role of newspapers and their editors in keeping issues alive between the British and colonial Americans. Bibliography.

Sosin, J. M. *Revolutionary Frontier, 1763–1783* (4:155).

3:203 Tate, Thad W. "The Coming of the Revolution in Virginia: Britain's Challenge to Virginia's Ruling Class, 1763–1776." *William and Mary Quarterly* 3d ser. 19:3 (1962), 323–43. Planters opposed Britain's imperial policies in Virginia because they saw threats to traditional constitutional rights, especially to self-government.

France and Spain

Ketcham, R. L. "France and American Politics, 1763–1793" (4:39) focuses on James Madison to survey the role of France in American political thinking after the Seven Years' War.

3:204 Loughrey, Mary E. *France and Rhode Island, 1686–1800*. New York: King's Crown, 1944. The author traces the influences of migration, intellectual currents, and the French military presence, concentrating on the last half of the 18th century. The research is thorough and the analysis is sufficient to establish that there was French influence, but whether Rhode Islanders perceived this or whether they considered all Europeans in the same way remains unanswered.

Lyon, E. W. *Louisiana in French Diplomacy, 1759–1804* (6:94).

McDermott, J. F., ed. *The Spanish in the Mississippi Valley, 1762–1804* (3:10).

Nasatir, A. P. *Borderland in Retreat: From Spanish Louisiana to the Far Southwest* (5:136).

Renault, F. *Le Pacte de famille et l'Amérique . . . de 1760 à 1792* (4:139).

Sagnac, P. *La Fin de l' Ancien Régime et la Révolution Américaine, 1763–1789* (4:34).

Tarrade, J. *Le Commerce colonial de la France à la fin de l' Ancien Régime . . . de 1763 à 1789* (4:151).

CONFRONTATION: FIRST PHASE, 1763–1768

See "Personalities," especially Edmund Burke, George Grenville, William Knox, William Pitt, Lord Rockingham, Charles Townshend; also, Cadwallader Colden, Patrick Henry, Thomas Hutchinson.

3:205 Barrow, Thomas C. "Background to the Grenville Program, 1757–1763." *William and Mary Quarterly* 3d ser. 23:1 (1965), 93–104. This study revises older views of the Grenville measures, mainly designed to solve problems of finance and imperial defense, by showing that Treasury Board figures called for policy changes "as a means to achieve the final and effective subordination of the commercial interests of the Americans to the requirements of the Mother Country."

3:206 Chaffin, Robert J. "The Declaratory Act of 1766: A Re-appraisal." *Historian* 37:1 (1974), 5–25. Chaffin argues, effectively, that the Declaratory Act was not passed solely as the price for repeal of the Stamp Act, but had been planned several weeks prior to repeal to placate parliamentary supporters.

3:207 Chaffin, Robert J. "The Townshend Acts of 1767." *William and Mary Quarterly* 3d ser. 27:1 (1970), 96–121. This detailed background study of these measures reveals that Townshend had considered American revenues many years prior to 1767 and that, in the main, his proposals were less severe than those supported by Shelburne and others.

3:208 Ernst, Joseph A. "The Currency Act Repeal Movement: A Study of Imperial Politics and Revolutionary Crisis, 1764–1767." *William and Mary Quarterly* 3d ser. 25:2 (1968), 177–211. Ernst presents the complex details of efforts by colonial agents to enlist British merchants and politicians for repeal of the

Currency Act, and in the process reveals how the issue of repeal gradually merged with the crisis over parliamentary taxation of the colonies.

3:209 Gipson, Lawrence H. "The American Revolution as an Aftermath of the Great War for Empire, 1754–1763." *Political Science Quarterly* 65:1 (1950), 86–104. Gipson argues that great wars breed revolution; the removal of the French threat, colonial wartime violations of trade regulations, and general imbalance of imperial relations produced by the war set the stage for the American Revolution.

3:210 Johnson, Allen S. "The Passage of the Sugar Act." *William and Mary Quarterly* 3d ser. 16:4 (1959), 507–14. The first American taxation measure by the Grenville ministry (1764) was insignificant in anticipated revenues but of major importance in its constitutional implications.

3:211 Knollenberg, Bernhard. *Origin of the American Revolution: 1759–1766.* New York: Macmillan, 1960. Stricter British policies began in 1759 with measures advocated by the Earls of Grenville and Halifax. The concentration of unpopular measures in a short time stimulated colonial discontent and prepared the way for revolution. Extensive bibliography.

3:212 Morgan, Edmund S. "Colonial Ideas of Parliamentary Power, 1764–1766." *William and Mary Quarterly* 3d ser. 5:3 (1948), 311–41. Morgan suggests that the colonies did not make a distinction between "internal" and "external" taxation, but simply opposed all taxation with/without representation.

3:213 Morgan, Edmund S. "The Postponement of the Stamp Act." *William and Mary Quarterly* 3d ser. 7:3 (1950), 353–92. Grenville's offer of postponement was not only insincere, but it actually set the tone for, and influenced, British policy and negotiations with the Americans until 1778, when genuine concessions were offered belatedly.

3:214 Morgan, Edmund S., and Morgan, Helen M. *The Stamp Act Crisis: Prologue to Revolution.* Chapel Hill: University of North Carolina Press, 1953. The Stamp Act crisis (1765–1766) caused Americans to work out techniques of resistance, organization, and, especially, ideas concerning parliamentary power.

They did not extend to Parliament the right of taxing them whether internal or external. Bibliographical notes.

3:215 Thomas, P. G. D. "Charles Townshend and American Taxation in 1767." *English Historical Review* 83:1 (1968), 33–51. Thomas downgrades the idea that American revenue was a central issue in British politics in 1767 or that Townshend had wanted such revenue for years. He does offer a detailed account of passage of Townshend duties.

CONFRONTATION: SECOND PHASE, 1768–1774

See "Personalities," especially Edmund Burke, Lord Dartmouth, Lord North, William Pitt, and, under "Others," William Knox, Lord Shelburne; also Americans, under "Others," Cadwallader Colden, Patrick Henry, Thomas Hutchinson, Charles Thomson.

3:216 Ammerman, David. *In the Common Cause: American Response to the Coercive Acts of 1774.* Charlottesville: University Press of Virginia, 1974. This detailed study focuses on the Continental Congress after passage of Britain's Coercive Acts, and reveals a high degree of American unity in resistance to the acts. Bibliography.

3:217 Brown, Richard D. *Revolutionary Politics in Massachusetts: The Boston Committee of Correspondence and the Towns, 1772–1774.* Cambridge: Harvard University Press, 1970. Brown studies the relationships of the Boston Committee with town committees and offers insights into revolutionary ideology and political behavior in the crises of imperial relations. Extensive bibliography.

3:218 Clark, Dora M. "The American Board of Customs, 1767–1783." *American Historical Review* 45:4 (1940), 777–806. Clark ably discusses a "significant but fatal experiment in colonial administration" which not only failed as an administrative reform, but succeeded in exacerbating the strained relations between England and the colonies.

3:219 Donoughue, Bernard. *British Politics and the American Revolution, the Path to War, 1773–75.* London: Macmillan, 1964. The best general account of ministerial politics and the American question for 1773 to 1775; it shows how British political beliefs and practices prevented any real understanding of the American position. Bibliography.

3:220 Greene, Jack P. "Bridge to Revolution: The Wilkes Fund Controversy in South Carolina, 1769–1775." *Journal of Southern History* 29:1 (1963), 19–52. Greene reveals how quarrels over the assembly's right to dispose funds caused a breakdown of royal authority in South Carolina before 1775.

3:221 Greene, Jack P., and Jellison, Richard M. "The Currency Act of 1764 in Imperial-Colonial Relations, 1764–1776." *William and Mary Quarterly* 3d ser. 18:4 (1961), 485–518. The colonies considered this act a serious grievance; even after a British concession (1773) the First Continental Congress believed that the Currency Act demonstrated that little faith could be placed in the British government to remedy problems.

3:222 Labaree, Benjamin W. *The Boston Tea Party.* New York: Oxford University Press, 1964. This major work reveals how the Tea Act crisis (1773) produced responses on both sides of the Atlantic which brought Anglo-American affairs close to the breaking point; it also affirms that the principle of taxation was the real issue behind the Tea Party. Extensive bibliography.

3:223 Lovejoy, David S. "Rights Imply Equality": The Case against Admiralty Jurisdiction in America, 1764–1776." *William and Mary Quarterly* 3d ser. 16:4 (1959), 459–84. Many Americans came to feel that Admiralty Court jurisdiction "reduced them below the rank of Englishmen."

3:224 Metzger, Charles H. *The Quebec Act: A Primary Cause of the American Revolution.* New York: Catholic Historical Society, 1936. The colonists included the 1774 act as one of the Coercive Acts, since it seemed to favor French Roman Catholics over Protestant colonials. Bibliography.

3:225 Shy, John W. *Toward Lexington: The Role of the British Army in the Coming of the American Revolution.* Princeton, N.J.: Princeton University Press,

1965. A notable work that focuses on how the presence, and eventual use, of troops (1763–1779) contributed to the prerevolutionary crisis, reinforcing colonial attitudes that viewed all British actions with suspicion. Extensive bibliography.

3:226 Zobel, Hiller B. *The Boston Massacre*. New York: Norton, 1970. The massacre (1770) is seen as much the product of the radicals' escalation of violence as of British oppression. Samuel Adams appears as the master manipulator of the event. Bibliography.

4

The American Revolution, 1775–1783

Contributing Editor
WILLIAM STINCHCOMBE
Syracuse University

Contents

Introduction

The revolutionary era has been the subject of many excellent and varied works in the years since Samuel F. Bemis and Grace G. Griffin published their comprehensive guide to diplomatic history. The total number of books and articles for the Revolution has grown enormously, although it can scarcely equal the number available on many topics in twentieth-century diplomatic history. The most important change in scholarship since World War II has been the advent of microfilm editions and complete letterpress editions for the leading participants in the Revolution. The papers of Thomas Jefferson and Alexander Hamilton are complete for the Revolution, and in the near future those of Benjamin Franklin, John Adams, Henry Laurens, and Robert Morris will also be finished. A new edition of the Washington Papers is being prepared which will replace the Fitzpatrick edition.

Francis Wharton's *The Revolutionary Diplomatic Correspondence of the United States* (4:24) is inadequate because of omissions and the failure to decipher many documents. There are no prospects for publication of a modern edition of this correspondence. Alternatives are available in the microfilm edition of the papers of the Continental Congress and the relevant microfilm from the State Department records, but these collections do not offer a complete solution. Of the important figures, John Jay and Robert R. Livingston still lack complete microfilm or letterpress editions. A relatively complete microfilm edition of the Lee Family Papers is available, but, surprisingly, we still lack comprehensive biographies of Richard Henry and Arthur Lee. The emphasis in scholarship has been on American figures, and despite an expanded and improved duplication of foreign archives by the Library of Congress, multiarchival research in European libraries is indispensable, as the many works listed below indicate.

The dominant interpretation of revolutionary diplomacy in the last generation has stressed the realism of the founding fathers, an emphasis perhaps reflecting the tensions and ideology arising from the cold war. As a corollary to this we have seen a more thorough examination of leadership, often using the methodology of other disciplines, to explain the continuation of the eight-year struggle against Great Britain and the success in the peace negotiations with France and Great Britain in 1782. As the older nationalistic Whig interpretation has waned, more attention has been paid to the role of the American colonies in the European balance of power. The previous view of treating the Revolution as a disruption of the English imperial system has gained only a few adherents recently. Likewise, the post–World War I isolationist image of a pristine America and a corrupt Europe has faded. The current emphasis is to explain foreign policy not just from the American viewpoint but from the perspective of allies, adversaries, and neutrals. Domestic influences on each country's foreign policy, moreover, are now considered an integral part of any comprehensive understanding of the policies of the Continental Congress, Lord North, or Count de Vergennes.

The realist interpretation was rarely challenged until the early 1960s, but the amoral and anti-intellectual side of this approach was certain to be contested. Felix Gilbert's seminal work, *To the Farewell Address: Ideas of Early American Foreign Policy* (5:165), marks the transition to new interpretations. Gilbert argues that idealism and realism were contending ideas in foreign policy from the nation's inception. But each theory had to be studied within the European diplomatic background and the context of late-eighteenth-century intellectual beliefs. Gilbert also stressed, however, the rapid adaptation that Americans made to the realities of the European state system, leading to a quick abandonment of militia diplomacy and many of the utopian ideas contained in Thomas Paine's *Common Sense*. Since Gilbert's work, the importance of the intellectual climate has been widely accepted, but this interpretation has modified, not supplanted, the realist view. Most recently the intellectual emphasis has received its strongest statement in Garry Wills' *Inventing America: Jefferson's Declaration of Independence* (New York, 1978). Wills offers an imaginative reconstruction of Jefferson's thought, noting Jefferson's deep dependence on the works of the Scottish enlightenment rather than the continental philosophies or particularly John Locke.

The interplay between the intellectual and realist interpretations seems likely to persist.

The international implications of the Revolution have also received increased attention in the last two decades. This research has been more often by European history specialists than by American historians. Robert R. Palmer's *The Age of the Democratic Revolution* (4:32) has probably been the most influential study locating the American Revolution within the larger European political context from 1760 to 1800. Almost paradoxically, Palmer's work has contributed greatly to the prevailing belief in the distinctiveness of the American Revolution, although the author clearly establishes that this revolution was part of a wider political movement.

Despite repeated exhortations, diplomatic historians and other specialists have done little to use comparative history or an international context to examine the West Indies. An often-cited example would call for a comparison of the drive for autonomy and independence from 1760 to 1800 in Haiti and the United States. A number of older works deal with the limited diplomatic connections between the United States and particular West Indian islands, but little has been done within an international framework on the scale that Palmer used in depicting the European background to the Revolution. American historians have produced substantial scholarship comparing slavery and colonial societies in the West Indies, but still needed are comparative studies of the commercial, political, and intellectual effects of the interrelationship between the United States and the West Indies in the revolutionary era.

Publications in diplomatic history amount to only a small portion of the vast scholarship on the American Revolution, and most of the recent literature deals with domestic aspects of the subject. The growing popularity of social history has produced detailed studies of the Revolution's effects on a particular town or country, but it is difficult to incorporate these works in diplomatic history, a field in which the emphasis is on national issues and the focus almost inevitably on elite decisionmaking by congressmen and diplomats. Two good examples of the recent trends in social history are Robert Gross's *The World of the Minuteman* (New York, 1977) and Richard Ryerson's *The Revolution is Now Begun* (Philadelphia, 1978), which study the local social and political composition of Concord and Philadelphia for this period.

Some perennial questions that interest students of diplomacy can best be considered by assimilating the approaches and the material contained in these and many other works. How far, for example, did national leaders' beliefs on diplomatic alliances, isolationism,

and commercial ties penetrate into the general population's consciousness? In addition to measuring the depth of ideological commitment, we might also assess the rise of American nationalism, which was certainly aided by the war, but in what ways? Did American national goals change the focus of politics in the cities and states? Was the key to the Revolution republicanism, religion, or merely political separation from Great Britain? To answer these questions requires a dependence on a multitude of local studies, often without a direct connection to diplomacy, and some integration of the findings and research methods should be attempted. Social and diplomatic history have more often tended to be on parallel rather than intersecting lines. It would be profitable, however, to study revolutionary figures with a surer knowledge of their local political origins as well as the social world in which they lived. Was Benjamin Franklin better understood by his contemporaries in Congress from other states than by his fellow citizens in Philadelphia? Did the controversy over Silas Deane have its origins in his repudiation by revolutionary colleagues in Connecticut? The answer to each of these questions is probably not contained in any study of diplomacy but in auxiliary fields of American history.

Any limited listing of works on the Revolution involves some method of selection. The following list concentrates more on guides to primary sources, secondary literature, and printed documents rather than on valuable older monographs and articles that have been superseded in scope and research.

Resources and Overviews

RESEARCH AIDS

While pertinent bibliographies and reference aids are listed here, there are more extensive lists in Chapter 1.

Bibliographies

Beers, H. P., ed. *The French in North America: A Bibliographic Guide to French Archives, Reproductions, and Research Missions* (3:2) lists materials for 1775 to 1783.

4:1 Beers, Henry P., ed. *The French and the British in the Old Northwest: A Bibliographical Guide to Archive and Manuscript Sources.* Detroit: Wayne State University Press, 1964. Although not specifically on the revolutionary war, this guide lists published and unpublished primary sources for American and Canadian participation in the American midwest and Upper Canada during the Revolution. Its excellent bibliography adds to the value of this guide.

Bibliographie annuelle de l'histoire de France (1:78a) is more convenient than other guides to French scholarship.

Coker, W. S., and Holmes, J. D. F. "Sources for the History of the Spanish Borderlands" (3:4).

Cortada, J. W., ed. *A Bibliographical Guide to Spanish Diplomatic History, 1460–1977* (1:90) lists more than fifty Spanish works on the American Revolution that are not repeated in this chapter.

4:2 Dippel, Horst. *Americana Germanica, 1770–1800* [German works on the United States, 1770–1800]. Stuttgart: Bibliographie Deutscher Amerikaliteratur, 1976. This is a precise and exacting companion volume to the author's work *Germany and the American Revolution* (4:142). It reveals that German interest in the Revolution was much more extensive than previously believed.

Gipson, L. H. *A Bibliographical Guide to the History of the British Empire* (3:6).

Gipson, L. H., ed. *A Guide to Manuscripts Relating to the History of the British Empire, 1748–1776* (3:7)—although these two volumes are most useful for the period before the Revolution, many of the materials that Gipson used are relevant for the entire war.

McDermott, J. F., ed. *The Spanish in the Mississippi Valley, 1762–1804* (3:10).

Monaghan, F. *French Travellers in the United States, 1765–1932: A Bibliography* (1:73).

Pargellis, S. M., and Medley, D. J. *Bibliography of British History . . ., 1714–1789* (3:11) includes sections on political, economic, and military history for the revolutionary period.

4:3 Rankin, Hugh F. "The American Revolution." In Robin Higham, ed., *A Guide to the Sources of*

United States Military History. Hamden, Conn.: Shoe String Press, 1975, pp. 100–124. An excellent selection and introduction to the military aspects of the war, the listing is primarily by American military events. It ignores the interrelationship of military events, strategy, diplomacy, and the Atlantic context.

4:4 Shy, John W., comp. *The American Revolution.* Northbrook, Ill.: AHM, 1973. Shy lists books, essays, and other items on a wide range of topics relating to the Revolution.

4:5 Smith, Dwight L., and Simmerman, Terry A., eds. *Era of the American Revolution: A Bibliography.* Clio Bibliography Series, no. 4. Santa Barbara, Calif.: ABC-Clio, 1975. Sections on diplomacy and foreign affairs are thin in this annotated bibliography (1763–1789), but the introduction to the entire subject is good.

4:6 Smith, Myron J., Jr. *Navies in the American Revolution: A Bibliography:* Metuchen, N.J.: Scarecrow, 1973. A sound guide that features naval affairs; there are items relevant to revolutionary war diplomacy. The work emphasizes American and English sources and is very lightly annotated.

Thomas, D. H., and Case, L. M., eds. *Guide to the Diplomatic Archives of Western Europe* [1400–1959] (1:298) contains, additionally, lists of printed commentary materials.

4:7 U.S. Library of Congress. *The American Revolution: A Selected Reading List.* Washington, D.C.: G.P.O., 1968. A general reading list aimed at the undergraduate, it covers all phases of the American Revolution, including many works on diplomacy.

Atlases and Other Aids

4:8 Boatner, Mark M. *Encyclopedia of the American Revolution.* New York: McKay, 1968. This handy, well-organized reference work includes entries on major persons, battles, and political events.

4:9 Cappon, Lester J., and Petchenik, Barbara B., eds. *Atlas of Early American History: The Revolutionary Era, 1760–1790.* Princeton, N.J.: Princeton University Press, 1976. This well-researched and elaborately produced work covers many phases of the Revolution, including city maps for different periods, population maps for 1760 and 1790, economic patterns, and cultural activity. It also has detailed military and alliance maps for different periods of the war, including Spanish Borderlands and West Indies. Extensive bibliography.

4:10 Clark, David S. *Index to Maps of the American Revolution in Books and Periodicals: Illustrating the Revolutionary War and Other Events of the Period, 1763–1789*. Westport, Conn.: Greenwood, 1974. The sources are clearly indicated and the coverage is extensive and careful. The index is superb, a great asset in reference books of this kind. Military, naval, state, and population maps are among those indexed.

4:11 Marshall, Douglass W., and Peckham, Howard H., eds. *Campaigns of the American Revolution: An Atlas of Manuscript Maps*. Ann Arbor: University of Michigan Press, 1976. This atlas of 58 battle maps (1775–1781) is drawn primarily from the Sir Henry Clinton Papers. They are clearly reproduced as originally drawn. The research and notes on sources are concise and scholarly.

Wheat, J. C. and Brun, C. F., eds. *Maps and Charts Published in America before 1800: A Bibliography* (3:14) does not include the military maps made during the American Revolution.

DOCUMENT COLLECTIONS

More general collections are listed in Chapter 1, and other collections may be found in "Personalities," below.

4:12 Burnett, Edmund C., ed. *Letters of Members of Continental Congress*. 8 vols. Washington, D.C.: Carnegie Institution, 1921–1936. Burnett has long been a standard source, his decision to print a letter depended on whether the member was attending Congress at the time. Because of space limitations, Burnett excerpts many letters and inevitably omits information critical to scholars. See Smith (4:21).

4:13 Butler, John P., comp. *Index: The Papers of the Continental Congress*. 5 vols. Washington, D.C.: G.P.O., 1978. This is an exhaustive alphabetical and chronological index to all of the papers of the Continental Congress. All items refer to microfilm series and reel numbers for convenient use. Used with the *Index: Journals of Continental Congress, 1774–1789* (Washington, D.C.: National Archives and Records Service, 1976), any document of the Continental Congress can be quickly located.

4:14 Chinard, Gilbert, ed. *The Treaties of 1778 and Allied Documents*. Baltimore: Johns Hopkins Press, 1928. This is a complete edition of the treaties of alliance in both English and French. The accompanying documents are selective but well chosen.

4:15 Doniol, Henri. *Histoire de la participation de la France à l'établissement des Etats-Unis d'Amérique* [French participation in United States independence]. 5 vols. Paris: Imprimerie Nationale, 1885–1892. A massive compilation of documents from many ministries, it describes the increased French involvement with the Americans. This work should be used with caution since, for example, omissions in the documents appear without notice. Doniol sought to prove the closeness of the two nations.

4:16 Ford, Worthington C., ed. *The Journals of Continental Congress*. 34 vols. Washington, D.C.: G.P.O., 1904–1937. This soundly edited work includes the debates that were available, resolutions, and rollcall votes. Although not totally complete, this is a reliable guide to the actions of Congress.

4:17 Great Britain. Historical Manuscripts Commission. *Report on American Manuscripts in the Royal Institution of Great Britain*. 4 vols. London: H.M.S.O., 1904–1909. These documents focus on British military reports and letters regarding the conduct of the war in the colonies. The work's value is somewhat limited except for the logistics of military planning and execution.

Kinnaird, L., ed. and trans. *Spain in the Mississippi Valley, 1765–1784* (3:19).

4:18 Murdoch, David H. *Rebellion in America: A Contemporary British Viewpoint, 1765–1783*. Santa Barbara, Calif.: ABC-Clio, 1979. This collection has over 900 facsimile pages from Burke's *Annual Register*, coupled with identification of key people and editorial commentary.

4:19 Paullin, Charles O., ed. *Outletters of the Continental Marine Committee and Board of Admiralty: August 1776–September 1780*. 2 vols. New York: Naval Historical Society, 1914. The editing is careful but without elaborate annotation; a good source but of somewhat limited value for diplomacy.

4:20 Rice, Howard C., Jr., and Brown, Anne S. K., eds. and trans. *The American Campaigns of Rochambeau's Army: 1780–1781, 1782, 1783*. 2 vols. Princeton, N.J.: Princeton University Press, 1972. The journals of three French officers, the Comte de Clermont-Crevecoeur, Jean B. P. A. de Verger, and Louis-Alexandre Berthier give some idea of how French officers viewed the Revolution and the alliance. Volume 2 includes many reproductions of French maps and views of the United States. The editing is impeccable. Bibliography.

4:21　Smith, Paul H., ed. *Letters of Delegates to Congress, 1774–1779.* 8 vols. to date. Washington, D.C.: Library of Congress, 1976–. This will be a definitive edition of the letters, more than doubling the number of letters printed in Burnett (4:12). It is annotated lightly but with sure scholarship.

4:22　Stevens, Benjamin, ed. *Facsimiles of Manuscripts in European Archives Relating to America, 1775–1783.* 25 vols. London, 1889–1898. The wide variety of documents from British, French, and Spanish archives, and their exact reproduction, make this series an invaluable source. It is incomplete, but the editor has demonstrated care and intelligence in his selection.

4:23　U.S. Department of Navy. Naval History Division. *Naval Documents of the American Revolution.* Ed. by William B. Clark. 8 vols. to date. Washington, D.C.: G.P.O., 1964. This continuing edition of naval affairs provides information often unobtainable elsewhere, but the absence of a consistent editorial policy and occasional failure to consult original documents have been justly criticized. A useful but not thorough documentation of the navy's role in the American Revolution.

4:24　Wharton, Francis, ed. *The Revolutionary Diplomatic Correspondence of the United States.* 6 vols. Washington, D.C.: G.P.O., 1889. Wharton is the standard collection of American diplomatic correspondence for the Revolution. He omits some documents and others are only printed in part, because Wharton did not decode the letters. The complete editions of the Adams, Franklin, and Laurens papers, along with the microfilm of the Lee Family Papers, will fill in most of the missing documents. The editor's hostile attitude toward the Lee Family lessens the value of the work.

Whitaker, A. P., ed. *Documents Relating to the Commercial Policy of Spain in the Floridas with Incidental Reference to Louisiana* (6:2).

OVERVIEWS

Books

4:25　Bemis, Samuel Flagg. *American Foreign Policy and the Blessings of Liberty and Other Essays.* New Haven, Conn.: Yale University Press, 1962. Of value for the Revolution are "The British Secret Service and the French-American Alliance," "The Rayneval Memoranda of 1782 on Western Boundaries and Some Comments on the French Historian Doniol," and "Canada and the Peace Settlement of 1782–1783." Based on extensive research, these articles by one of the foremost diplomatic historians have not been surpassed in their total contribution.

4:26　Bemis, Samuel Flagg. *The Diplomacy of the American Revolution.* 3d ed. Bloomington: Indiana University Press (1937), 1957. In the best summary of the diplomacy of the American Revolution in Europe, Bemis skillfully exploits archives and offers a Whig interpretation of an innocent America dealing with corrupt Europe. The interpretation has been challenged but not the coverage and detailed analysis.

Bourguignon, H. J. *The First Federal Court: The Federal Appellate Prize Court of the American Revolution, 1775–1787* (16:151).

4:27　Burnett, Edmund C. *The Continental Congress.* New York: Norton, 1941. This general work on Congress is by the original editor of the *Letters of Members of Continental Congress* (4:12). Although challenged in recent literature, this work still remains the best book for studying how the Congress functioned and for evaluating its limited success.

Gilbert, F. *To the Farewell Address: Ideas of Early American Foreign Policy* (5:165) analyzes the intellectual origins of American foreign policy from the Model Treaty to the Farewell Address; see also Hutson (5:166).

4:28　Goodwin, Albert, ed. *The American and French Revolutions, 1763–93.* Vol. 8 in *The New Cambridge Modern History.* Cambridge: At the University Press, 1965. The best chapters are Robert R. Palmer, "Social and Psychological Foundations of the Revolutionary Era," and Esmond Wright, "American Independence in its American Context: Social and Political Aspects."

4:29　Higginbotham, Don. *The War of American Independence: Military Attitudes, Policies, and Prac-*

tice, 1763–1789. New York: Macmillan, 1972. An excellent, well-written survey of the military history of the Revolution, it is based on substantial primary sources as well as a prodigious amount of secondary literature. The author has succeeded very well in widening the scope of traditional military history. Extensive bibliography.

Kaplan, L. S. *Colonies into Nation: American Diplomacy, 1763–1801* (3:42).

4:30   Kaplan, Lawrence S., ed. *The American Revolution and "A Candid World."* Kent, Ohio: Kent State University Press, 1977. This is a good series of articles on diverse topics of diplomacy, including the reasons for the failure of reconciliation by the North cabinet, two appraisals of the Model Treaty, a fine article on Catherine the Great and her shrewd appraisal of the American Revolution and the British government. Wider themes include the location of the American Revolution in the Law of Nations and the movement toward isolation from 1775 to 1801.

Lint, G. L. "The Law of Nations and the American Revolution" (16:153).

4:31   Mackesy, Piers. *The War for America, 1775–1783.* Cambridge: Harvard University Press, 1964. It is perhaps the finest description of British military objectives and successes. Based on massive research, the work presents the complicated struggle in the West Indies among France, Spain, and Great Britain. The author concludes that, in the final analysis, the war was lost there, and Yorktown was the result of that failure. Bibliography.

4:32   Palmer, Robert R. *The Challenge.* Vol. 1 in *The Age of the Democratic Revolution: A Political History of Europe and America, 1760–1790.* Princeton, N.J.: Princeton University Press, 1959. In perhaps the most influential, intellectual, and political history of the last generation, the author argues that there was a widespread democratic movement in Europe, of which the United States was a part and to which Americans made their own distinct contributions. The scope, research, and analysis of this volume make it the most appropriate book with which to begin a study of the diplomacy of the Revolution.

4:33   Rakove, Jack N. *The Beginnings of National Politics: An Interpretive History of the Continental Congress.* New York: Knopf, 1979. The subtitle reveals the scope of a book that touches in many places on foreign affairs. The author studies the Continental

Congress as an institution and the rise of politics as a profession, in contrast to Burnett's treatment of debates, bills, and finances (4:27).

Rose, J. H.; Newton, A. P.; and Benian, E. A. *The Old Empire from the Beginnings to 1783* (3:38).

4:34   Sagnac, Philippe. *La Fin de l'Ancien Régime et la Révolution Americaine, 1763–1789* [The end of the Old Regime and the American Revolution]. Paris: Presses Universitaires de France, 1947. This is a wide-ranging, integrated study that reveals several critical differences in the study of history by French scholars as compared to American. The thesis is not new, but it does try to cover changes in secular life and material conditions as well as political and diplomatic developments.

4:35   Stinchcombe, William C. *The American Revolution and the French Alliance.* Syracuse, N.Y.: Syracuse University Press, 1969. The author analyzes the domestic reaction to the French alliance in the United States. Americans clearly realized the advantages of the alliance and suspended their traditional anti-French and anti-Catholic beliefs to make it a success. Extensive bibliography.

Essays

4:36   Barrow, Thomas. "The American Revolution as a Colonial War for Independence." *William and Mary Quarterly* 3d ser. 25:3 (1968), 452–64. By comparing the American Revolution and the later French and Russian revolutions historians have not reached a better understanding of the American Revolution. The drive for independence and autonomy makes the American Revolution different from classical revolutions. Interesting, but the author does not answer Palmer's thesis (4:32).

4:37   Burrows, Edwin, and Wallace, Michael. "The American Revolution: The Ideology and Psychology of National Liberation." *Perspectives in American History* 6 (1972), 167–308. The emphasis is on psychology rather than ideology and comparisons are drawn to 20th-century national liberation struggles. The mother-child analogy is heavily used, and the authors conclude that Americans came to equate national liberation with personal liberation.

4:38   Hutson, James H. "The Partition Treaty and the Declaration of American Independence." *Journal of American History* 58:2 (1972), 877–96. The timing of the Declaration of Independence is related to many reports suggesting a partitioning of the New World between England and France which would allow England an unfettered hand in crushing the rebellion. This careful analysis shows a more sensitive reaction by members of the Continental Congress to the international arena than previously believed.

4:39 Ketcham, Ralph L. "France and American Politics, 1763–1793." *Political Science Quarterly* 78:2 (1963), 198–223. Although James Madison and many of his political allies could be considered pro-French, the author rightly argues that many of these men regarded France as the only counterweight to Britain, particularly after the Declaration of Independence. The same considerations affected foreign policy long after the Revolution.

Williams, W. A. "The Age of Mercantilism: An Interpretation of the American Political Economy, 1763–1828" (2:97) is a good analysis of the major elements of American economic and political thought.

Personalities

Additional references on individuals may be found in Chapter 1, "Biographical Data."

AMERICANS

John Adams
See Chapter 5, "Personalities," for additional references.

4:40 *The Adams Papers*. Ser. 2: *Adams Family Correspondence*. 4 vols. Ed. by Lyman H. Butterfield. Cambridge: Harvard University Press, 1963–1973. The letters among the members of the Adams family are of equal importance to the diary, particulary John Adams's description of his two missions to France, his negotiations in the Netherlands, and his part in the peace negotiations of 1782.

4:41 *The Adams Papers*. Ser. 1: *Diary and Autobiography of John Adams*. 4 vols. Ed. by Lyman H. Butterfield, et al. Cambridge: Harvard University Press, 1961. John Adams's diary (1755–1804) offers a great deal of material on the Revolution and diplomacy. The autobiography shows Adams trying to re-

write the history of the Revolution, as in his treatment of the Model Treaty. The editing is beyond reproach, and the notes offer, in addition to biographical information, a commentary on scholars' interpretations.

4:42 Cappon, Lester J., ed. *The Adams-Jefferson Letters: The Complete Correspondence between Thomas Jefferson and Abigail and John Adams*. 2 vols. Chapel Hill: University of North Carolina Press, 1959. This well-edited and astutely annotated edition is more useful for diplomacy of the later period when both men served in Europe, yet their views and those of Abigail Adams are important. In the latter part of their lives, both men reviewed the meaning and significance of the American Revolution.

4:43 Hutson, James H. *John Adams and the Diplomacy of the American Revolution*. Lexington: University of Kentucky Press, 1980. Hutson argues that Adams's erratic and often contradictory and self-defeating actions were due to a paranoia which caused him to view all those he encountered, colleagues and adversaries alike, as involved in conspiracies against him.

The Papers of John Adams, 1755–1775 (3:67).

4:44 Shaw, Peter. *The Character of John Adams*. Chapel Hill: University of North Carolina Press, 1976. Shaw's superior study does an outstanding job analyzing Adams's actions in times of stress, such as in his argument with Vergennes in 1781, and in clarifying what Adams said about his role in the American Revolution.

Silas Deane
4:45 Deane, Silas. *The Deane Papers: Correspondence between Silas Deane, His Brothers, and Their Business and Political Associates, 1771–1795*. Hartford: Connecticut Historical Society, 1930. Really a supplement to the New York Historical Society's volumes, it includes political letters but deals most with Deane's business affairs. This should be used with other printed Deane papers and important documents still in manuscript collections.

4:46 Deane, Silas. *Papers of Silas Deane*. 5 vols. Ed. by Charles Isham. New York: New York Historical Society, 1886–1890. Very useful for Deane's activities up to the signing of the French alliance in 1778, the papers also include Deane's attempts to be exonerated by the Continental Congress, which recalled him under unclear circumstances. They are also useful for

Deane's extensive business activities, for the government and for his own private interest.

Benjamin Franklin

See Chapter 3, "Personalities," for additional references.

4:47 Aldridge, Alfred O. *Franklin and His French Contemporaries.* New York: New York University Press, 1957. Franklin's reputation as a scientist was already widely known in Paris before his arrival, and Franklin exploited this fame to win converts to the American cause.

4:48 Currey, Cecil B. *Code Number 72: Benjamin Franklin, Patriot or Spy?* Englewood Cliffs, N.J.: Prentice-Hall, 1972. The author presents a suggestive and not conclusive case that Benjamin Franklin spied for the British while American minister to France. There was a grey area in which men acted as intermediaries used by all powers during the Revolution. Franklin was lax about protecting secrets and had around him a number of men who combined the role of spy and intermediary.

4:49 Henderson, H. James. "Congressional Factionalism and the Attempt to Recall Benjamin Franklin." *William and Mary Quarterly* 3d ser. 27:2 (1970), 246–67. Congressional politics, essentially sectional, nearly led to Franklin's recall in 1779. The article's analysis is sound but perhaps emphasizes sectional voting too much, overlooking the continuing skepticism about Franklin by many members of Congress.

4:50 Lopez, Claude A. *Mon Cher Papa: Franklin and the Ladies of Paris.* New Haven, Conn.: Yale University Press, 1966.

4:51 Lopez, Claude A., and Herbert, Eugenia W. *The Private Franklin: The Man and His Family.* New York: Norton, 1975. Franklin was the most important American diplomat of the Revolution. The previous editions of his writings will be superseded by the Yale edition (3:72). These two works by Lopez (and Herbert) contain new information pertaining to diplomacy. They show more convincingly than previously Franklin's deep hostility toward Great Britain, as highlighted in his relationship with his Tory son, William Franklin. Bibliographies.

4:52 Stourzh, Gerald. *Benjamin Franklin and American Foreign Policy.* Chicago: University of Chicago Press, 1954. This is a sound, penetrating analysis of the intellectual origins of Franklin's thoughts about foreign policy. Despite overtones of the cold war realist school, this is the best book on Franklin and foreign policy.

4:53 Van Doren, Carl. *Benjamin Franklin.* New York: Viking (1938), 1973. Of the books under consideration, Van Doren's biography is still unsurpassed for understanding the man.

Alexander Hamilton

See Chapter 5, "Personalities," for additional references.

4:54 Flexner, James T. *The Young Hamilton: A Biography.* Boston: Little, Brown, 1978. Although dealing only with the first half of Hamilton's life, the author ranges widely to support his thesis that his subject's career was prefigured by young manhood. The most perceptive and unbiased of Hamilton biographies.

4:55 Mitchell, Broadus. *Alexander Hamilton: Youth to Maturity, 1755–1788.* New York: Macmillan, 1957. The first volume of this masterly (two-volume) biography finds the precocious Hamilton not only involved in politics as Washington's aide, but also independently during the Revolution. Although largely tangential to diplomacy, this is the best place to begin studying Hamilton's role. Extensive bibliography.

John Jay

See Chapter 5, "Personalities," for additional references.

Monaghan, F. *John Jay: Defender of Liberty* (5:33).

4:56 Morris, Richard B., and Shumway, Floyd, eds. *John Jay: The Making of a Revolutionary— Unpublished Papers, 1745–1780.* New York: Harper & Row, 1975. This work covers John Jay's presidency of the Continental Congress and his appointment as minister to Spain. A second volume will presumably cover Jay's activities in the Paris peace negotiations. While the editors decided not to print much of Jay's diplomatic correspondence, they do attempt to list all of the diplomatic correspondence and its location.

Thomas Jefferson

Cappon, L. J., ed. *The Adams-Jefferson Letters* (4:42).

Jefferson, Thomas. *The Papers of Thomas Jefferson* (5:34)—edited by Boyd—is the definitive edition.

4:57 Malone, Dumas. *Jefferson the Virginian.* Vol. 1 in *Jefferson and His Time.* Boston: Little, Brown, 1948. Malone's extensively researched and well-written volume describes Jefferson's intellectual background, his sporadic interest in foreign affairs, and his appointment as a peace commissioner. The treatment of the intellectual influences and Jefferson's role in drafting the Declaration of Independence have been superseded by Garry Wills's *Inventing America* (New York, 1978). Still, this is the best biography for Jefferson's entire revolutionary career.

Henry and John Laurens

4:58 "Correspondence between Honorable Henry Laurens and His Son, John, 1777–1780." *South Carolina Historical and Genealogical Magazine* 6:1–4 (1905), passim. This correspondence covers Henry Laurens as president of Continental Congress until his resignation in the Deane-Lee controversy. Father and son spoke their minds about a great number of national and international issues. This work will be replaced by *The Papers of Henry Laurens* (Columbia: University of South Carolina Press, 1968– [7 vols. to date]). See also "Letters from Marquis de Lafayette to Hon. Henry Laurens, 1777–1780" (4:106).

4:59 "Mission of John Laurens to Europe in 1781." *South Carolina Historical and Genealogical Magazine* 1:1–4 (1900), passim; 2:1–2 (1901), passim. John Laurens was sent to France in 1781 to press for increased military and financial aid. These articles include all of the important documents, but they fail to cover French reaction or Franklin's dismay at young Laurens's style. Laurens successfully returned with the necessary money and promise of supplies just before Yorktown.

4:60 Wallace, David D. *The Life of Henry Laurens, with a Sketch of the Life of Lt. Col. John Laurens.* New York: Russell & Russell (1915), 1967. This biography is still the best work on Laurens as president of the Continental Congress, his subsequent capture and imprisonment in London, and his token participation in the 1782 peace negotiations. The microfilm edition of the Laurens Papers and the limited letterpress edition of his letters, however, allow for a new assessment.

James Madison

See Chapter 5 and 6 for additional references.

4:61 Brant, Irving. *James Madison: The Nationalist, 1780–1787.* Indianapolis: Bobbs-Merrill, 1948. This volume by Madison's best-known modern biographer delves deeply into Madison's career in

Congress. Madison participated in many of the formal and informal decisions concerning foreign policy during the last years of the war. It was at this time that Madison gained his lifelong reputation of being pro-French.

4:62 Madison, James. *The Papers of James Madison.* 13 vols. to date. Ed. by William T. Hutchinson, et al. Chicago: University of Chicago Press, 1962–. Madison's papers offer the finest record of a politically active congressman. The French understood Madison's attachment to them and cultivated him carefully. The series is excessively annotated, sometimes losing Madison but illuminating many obscure incidents and figures.

John Sullivan

4:63 Sullivan, John. *Letters and Papers of Major-General John Sullivan of the Continental Army.* 3 vols. Ed. by Otis G. Hammond. Concord: New Hampshire Historical Society, 1930–1939. After inflaming French-American relations by his ill-chosen remarks following the failure at Newport, Sullivan later, while in the Continental Congress, became a paid agent of the French minister, Luzerne. Edited with care and useful; it does not contain all of Sullivan's papers.

4:64 Whittemore, Charles P. *A General of the Revolution: John Sullivan of New Hampshire.* New York: Columbia University Press, 1961. This is a well-researched biography of the controversial general known for his swagger and conceit. Sullivan was deeply involved in French-American relations. His activities as a paid agent of the French in the Continental Congress are minimized. The book is otherwise objective in treating Sullivan's performance and failings. Bibliography.

George Washington

See Chapter 5, "Personalities," for additional references.

4:65 Flexner, James T. *George Washington: In the American Revolution.* Boston: Little, Brown, 1968. The second volume of a well-written four-volume biography presents much more analysis of Washington's motives, politics, and pride than does Freeman. Using his evidence carefully, the author presents a different picture of Washington's personality than available elsewhere. The research is adequate.

4:66 Freeman, Douglas S. *Leader of the Revolution.* Vol. 4 in *George Washington, A Biography.* 7 vols. New York: Scribner's, 1952.

4:67 Freeman, Douglas S. *Victory with the Help of France*. Vol. 5 in *George Washington, A Biography*. 7 vols. New York: Scribner's, 1951. These two volumes (of seven volumes) detail Washington's military exploits and his dealings with the French and British. The scholarship is first-rate, with extensive research, but Freeman is hesitant in analyzing Washington's political actions. Even so these volumes remain the best biography for this period.

4:68 Institut Français de Washington, ed. *Correspondence of General Washington and Comte de Grasse*. Washington, D.C.: G.P.O., 1931. De Grasse and Washington letters cover the Yorktown campaign (August 17–November 4, 1781). In contrast to many wartime allied contacts, De Grasse cooperated fully with both Washington and Rochambeau.

4:69 Washington, George. *The Writings of George Washington*. 39 vols. Ed. by John C. Fitzpatrick. Washington, D.C.: G.P.O., 1931–1944. The standard edition of Washington's letters is done with skill, but since it does not print Washington's incoming letters, the Library of Congress microfilm edition should be consulted until the new edition published by the University of Virginia is completed. Washington had many contacts with Frenchmen and with members of Congress, which make this an exceptionally good source.

Others
4:70 Alberts, Robert C. *The Golden Voyage: The Life and Times of William Bingham, 1752–1804*. Boston: Houghton Mifflin, 1970. The opening chapters of this well-written work cover Bingham's rise as a wealthy merchant during the Revolution. As congressional agent in Martinique, he enriched himself and his business partners while fulfilling his public duties. The biography is soundly based on the Bingham Papers but thin in analysis. Bibliography.

4:71 Coe, Samuel G. *The Mission of William Carmichael to Spain*. Baltimore: Johns Hopkins Press, 1928. This is the best available work on the minor diplomat. It does not cover Carmichael's earlier activities, which were as important as the mission. Carmichael was involved in the Silas Deane controversy, and later in Spain he broke with John Jay. We probably will not learn more about Carmichael as his papers apparently were destroyed.

4:72 Cresson, William P. *Francis Dana: A Puritan Diplomat at the Court of Catherine the Great*. New York: Dial, 1930. An undistinguished biography of the U.S. minister to Russia, who earlier served as John Adams's secretary in Europe. The section on Russian politics and diplomacy is superficial; see Griffiths's article (4:146). Yet this is the only work on Dana himself that is worthy of note.

4:73 Dangerfield, George. *Chancellor Robert R. Livingston of New York, 1746–1813*. New York: Harcourt, Brace, 1960. As secretary of foreign affairs from 1781 to 1784, Livingston was not reticent about giving instructions to American diplomats. Livingston's pro-French proclivities are fairly treated and his position clearly presented. The writing is excellent and the research faultless. Extensive bibliographical notes.

4:74 Greene, Nathanael. *The Papers of General Nathanael Greene*. Ed. by Richard B. Snowman, et al. Chapel Hill: University of North Carolina Press, 1976. One of Washington's most trusted aides, Greene had many contacts with Frenchmen, which will make this series valuable for the study of diplomacy. Greene worked to mend Franco-American differences after their joint failure at Newport in 1778. The editing and notes are exemplary.

4:75 James, James A. *The Life of George Rogers Clark*. Chicago: University of Chicago Press, 1929. The best biography of the mediocre general who is credited with winning the old Northwest. The author, who edited Clark's papers for the revolutionary period, has extensively researched Clark's dealings with Spanish and later French officials, but tends to excuse Clark's faults. This work, together with Clark's papers, is the best place to begin a study of the Mississippi Valley during the Revolution.

4:76 Lee, Richard Henry. *The Letters of Richard Henry Lee*. 2 vols. Ed. by James C. Ballagh. New York: Macmillan, 1911–1914. Lee's letters are critical because of his extensive interest in foreign affairs, as reflected in his correspondence with his brothers in Europe and with Massachusetts figures. While this edition is fairly complete, it should be used in conjunction with the Lee Family Papers (microfilm).

4:77 Lee, William. *Letters of William Lee*. 3 vols. Ed. by Worthington C. Ford. Brooklyn, N.Y.: Historical Printing Club, 1891. These papers of one of four politically active brothers include materials on Lee's trips to Prussia and on the divisive Lee-Deane quarrel. The Lee Family Papers (microfilm) includes a few items not printed here, but this work retains its value.

4:78 Morison, Samuel Eliot. *John Paul Jones: A Sailor's Biography.* Boston: Little, Brown, 1959. The research is thorough, and the author knows his subject and the sea very well. The book is written with grace and verve. The author does not dwell on the political and financial aspects of the American navy in France, but this is a minor quibble about the best biography of John Paul Jones.

4:79 Morris, Robert. *The Papers of Robert Morris, 1781–1784.* 5 vols. to date. Ed. by E. James Ferguson and John Cantanzariti. Pittsburgh: University of Pittsburgh Press, 1973–. The superintendent of finance's activities included arranging European loans and handling the disintegrating American finances. Morris was as deeply involved in foreign policy as was Robert R. Livingston. The editing and notes are first-rate.

4:80 Paine, Thomas. *The Complete Writings of Thomas Paine.* 2 vols. Ed. by Philip Foner. New York: Citadel, 1945. In addition to strongly stating his views on foreign policy in *Common Sense* in 1776, Paine served as secretary of the congressional committee handling foreign affairs and became involved in the Deane-Lee controversy in 1778–1779. The editor has succeeded in bringing together the works and letters of this important man.

4:81 Rush, Benjamin. *The Letters of Benjamin Rush.* 2 vols. Ed. by Lyman H. Butterfield. Princeton, N.J.: Princeton University Press, 1951. Rush was not only involved in many events touching upon foreign affairs, he entertained opinions on every happening. He argued with New England delegates over the ultimatum to be included in the peace commissioners' instructions, urged a larger American navy, and later reflected a moderate's view of the French alliance. Well edited.

BRITISH

Edmund Burke

4:82 Burke, Edmund. *The Correspondence of Edmund Burke.* Ed. by Thomas W. Copeland. Chicago: University of Chicago Press, 1961–1965, vols. 3–5. One of the most prominent members of the opposition to Lord North's American policy, Burke grew more reticent as violence erupted. He was as interested in showing that the American War of Independence demonstrated the North coalition's inability to govern as he was in discerning the nature of the Revolution. Well edited by successive editors.

4:83 Cone, Carl B. *The Age of the American Revolution.* Vol. 1 in *Burke and the Nature of Politics.* Lexington: University of Kentucky Press, 1957. Indirectly the author gives an excellent sense of the nature of American policy in British politics. This first volume, which goes to the downfall of the North cabinet in 1782, shows Burke to be a pragmatic politician believing in reconciliation with the United States but maintaining the supremacy of Parliament. Volume 2, on the French Revolution, is 5:98.

Lord Carlisle

Brown, W. A. *Empire or Independence . . . , 1774–1783* (4:130).

4:84 Great Britain. Historical Manuscripts Commission. *The Manuscripts of the Earl of Carlisle.* London: H.M.S.O., 1897. As the head of the commission for negotiations with the United States in 1778, offered in response to the French alliance, Carlisle quickly became disillusioned with the possibility of success. This volume reveals some of the problems the British had in seriously considering accommodation after 1776.

Sir Henry Clinton

4:85 Willcox, William B. *Portrait of a General: Sir Henry Clinton in the War of Independence.* New York: Knopf, 1964. The finest biography of any British military leader or minister that we have. The author analyzes his subject's personality, leadership during the war, and ultimate failure, drawing a perceptive psychological portrait. This work is the place to begin in understanding the British position in the American Revolution.

4:86 Willcox, William B., ed. *The American Rebellion: Sir Henry Clinton's Narrative of his Campaigns, 1775–1782.* New Haven, Conn.: Yale University Press, 1954. After the Yorktown disaster, Clinton was dismissed, and his request for a parliamentary inquiry was refused. Clinton wrote a long defense of his role as head of the British forces. The document, although repetitive, is interesting and valuable.

George III

4:87 Brooke, John. *King George III.* New York: McGraw-Hill, 1970. In a work based on extensive research, Brooke correctly depicts George III as a good Whig king who accepts the limitations placed upon him by the British political system. But the king persistently refused to compromise and fought the recognition of American independence to the very last.

4:88 George III. *The Correspondence of King George the Third, 1760–1783*. Ed. by John W. Fortescue. 6 vols. London: Macmillan, 1928. The exchanges between Lord North and George III cover many areas, including English spies in France and military efforts against the Americans. The king encouraged compromise and accommodation in 1778 at the time of the Carlisle Commission and reluctantly acknowledged American independence in 1782. A well-edited and informative source.

Lord North

George III. *The Correspondence of King George the Third, 1760–1783* (4:88) contains exchanges with Lord North.

Hoffman, R. J. S. *The Marquis: A Study of Lord Rockingham, 1730–1782* (3:53) studies the leader of the opposition to North.

4:89 Valentine, Alan. *Lord North*. 2 vols. Norman: University of Oklahoma Press, 1967. Although short on analysis of the relationship between politics in the House of Commons and the issues of the war, this biography gives a fine account of the partnership between Lord North and the king. North was more inclined to compromise, while the king remained intransigent toward the Americans. See (4:87).

Others

Bellot, L. J. *William Knox: The Life and Thought of an Eighteenth-Century Imperialist* (3:55) adds new details on Knox's contributions during the peace negotiations and his dealings with the Earl of Shelburne. This sensible book on a career civil servant reflects adequate research in the William Knox Papers.

4:90 Brown, Gerald S. *The American Secretary: The Colonial Period of Lord George Germain, 1775–1778*. Ann Arbor: University of Michigan Press, 1963. Germain has deservedly had the reputation for being stubborn and less than brilliant. The author does very well in placing him within the 18th-century context and in clearly depicting the frustrations and eventual failure of Germain's American policy.

4:91 Curwen, Samuel. *The Journal of Samuel Curwen, Loyalist*. 2 vols. Ed. by Andrew Oliver. Cambridge: Harvard University Press, 1972. The diary of a Loyalist exile in Great Britain during the war which traces the optimism and more often the pessimism that Loyalists felt toward the North government. Curwen

offers interesting observations about American leaders. He did not have a government position as did Thomas Hutchinson, so his diary is even more valuable. The editing and introduction are first-rate.

4:92 Gruber, Ira D. *The Howe Brothers and the American Revolution*. New York: Atheneum, 1972. This provocative work, based on all available Howe material, argues, not altogether convincingly, that the Howes had a dual commission to plan the war and make peace with the Americans, and that this ambiguity led to their failure.

Hoffman, R. J. S. *The Marquis: A Study of Lord Rockingham, 1730–1782* (3:53) examines the leader of the opposition to Lord North during the war. Rockingham held office briefly in 1782, when the Earl of Shelburne took the leadership. The author shows a mastery of parliamentary politics and British manuscript sources, and he defines the entire problem in terms of English politics.

4:93 Norris, John M. *Shelburne and Reform*. London: Macmillan, 1963. A good monograph on one of the most puzzling and distrusted British political leaders during the era of the American Revolution. The work includes a good chapter on the Shelburne ministry. An appendix clearly explains the complicated vote on the peace treaty.

4:94 Reid, Loren D. *Charles James Fox: A Man for the People*. Columbia: University of Missouri Press, 1969. This is an acceptable biography of the leader of the opposition to the king and Lord North in the House of Commons. The subtitle to the contrary, Fox, like many 18th-century Whigs, did not believe in the cause of the people or in democracy. In foreign policy Fox remained more concerned about the European balance of power than the war in America. Bibliography.

4:95 Rodney, Lord. *Letter Books of Lord Rodney, 1780–1782*. 2 vols. Ed. by Dorothy C. Barck. New York: Naval Historical Society, 1932. This is a very good source for the West Indian campaign of 1782. The preface contains a good description of the other Rodney papers at the British Public Record Office. The editing is good and the index superb.

4:96 Sandwich, Earl of. *The Private Papers of John, Earl of Sandwich, First Lord of the Admiralty, 1771–1782*. 4 vols. Ed. by G. R. Barnes and J. H. Owen. London: Naval Records Society, 1932–1938. The editors argue that Sandwich, the ineffective and often-criticized First Lord of the Admiralty during the

American Revolution, has been unjustly criticized by Whig historians, but in recent years non-Whig scholars have been just as harsh. The editing is very sparse; the work should be used in conjunction with Mackesy (4:31).

4:97 Wickwire, Franklin, and Wickwire, Mary. *Cornwallis: The American Adventure.* Boston: Houghton Mifflin, 1970. A sound work covering the most talented and aggressive British general, it is particularly good on the southern campaigns leading to the Yorktown debacle. The writing is graceful and the research solid, but Cornwallis's attitudes toward the Revolution's political issues remain elusive.

FRENCH

François Barbé-Marbois
4:98 Barbé-Marbois, François. *Our Revolutionary Forefathers: Letters of François Marquis de Barbé-Marbois.* Ed. and trans. by Eugene P. Chase. New York: Duffield, 1929. The diary of Barbé-Marbois, first secretary to the French minister, Chevalier de la Luzerne (1779–1785), is an interesting document. Barbé-Marbois certainly edited it later in his life, and parts were omitted at his family's request. The diary reflects more on the mores of American society than on the Revolution's politics.

4:99 Lyon, E. Wilson. *The Man Who Sold Louisiana: The Career of François Barbé-Marbois.* Norman: University of Oklahoma Press, 1942. This biography is by one of the foremost students of the Louisiana question in French-American diplomacy. The research has not been superseded, and the author shows that the American Revolution made the careers of men such as Barbé-Marbois just as it did for their American counterparts.

Conrad Alexandre Gérard
4:100 Gérard, Conrad Alexandre. *Conrad Alexandre Gérard: Despatches and Instructions.* Ed. by John J. Meng. Baltimore: Johns Hopkins Press, 1935. The dispatches of the first French minister to the United States in 1778–1779. Gérard was also the diplomat who negotiated the French-American alliance. An indispensable source for French policy, it is enhanced by a good introduction.

Meng, J. J. "French Diplomacy in Philadelphia, 1778–1779" (4:123).

Comte de Grasse
Institut Français de Washington, ed. *Correspondence of General Washington and Comte de Grasse* (4:68).

4:101 Lewis, Charles L. *Admiral De Grasse and American Independence.* Annapolis, Md.: Naval Institute Press, 1945. This biography of De Grasse, which contains some useful information, strives mightily to exonerate De Grasse from his disgrace in 1782, but is not altogether successful. For material on De Grasse during the revolutionary era, the author relies far too heavily on Doniol.

Scott, J. B. *De Grasse à Yorktown* (4:169).

Marquis de Lafayette
Burnett, E. C., and Leland, W. G., eds. "Letters from Lafayette to Luzerne, 1780–1782" (4:108).

4:102 Gottschalk, Louis R. *Lafayette Comes to America.* Chicago: University of Chicago Press, 1935.

4:103 Gottschalk, Louis R. *Lafayette Joins the American Army.* Chicago: University of Chicago Press, 1937.

4:104 Gottschalk, Louis R. *Lafayette and the Close of the American Revolution.* Chicago: University of Chicago Press, 1942. This is the outstanding biography of Lafayette by the acknowledged authority on the subject. The range of research, level of analysis, and detachment with which the author views the subject and the issues all make this a first-rate biography. In the popular mind as well as in official circles, Lafayette was the foremost Frenchman in the American Revolution. These volumes are the place to begin any study of Lafayette, French-American relations, the battle of Newport, and the campaign leading to Yorktown.

4:105 Idzerda, Stanley J., ed. *Lafayette in the Age of the American Revolution.* 4 vols. to date. Ithaca, N.Y.: Cornell University Press, 1977–. This is a limited edition of the more important documents concerning Lafayette's role in the American Revolution. This work supersedes any other source, particularly Lafayette's multivolume memoirs, as well as the articles containing Lafayette's letters to Luzerne and Henry Laurens.

4:106 Lafayette, Marquis de. "Letters from Marquis de Lafayette to Hon. Henry Laurens, 1777–1780." *South Carolina Historical and Genealogical*

Magazine 7/9:1–4 (1906–1908), passim. Lafayette was an incorrigible patronage-seeker for his friends, and many of the letters in this work concern this issue. The letters are from the Laurens Papers, and will be superseded with the publication of the Lafayette Papers and Laurens Papers.

4:107 Lafayette, Marquis de. *The Letters of Lafayette to Washington: 1777–1799.* 2d ed. Ed. by Louis R. Gottschalk, and Bill, Shirley. Philadelphia: American Philosophical Society, 1976. An edition of the complete correspondence between the two men, it is important for Lafayette's role at Newport in 1778 and in Virginia in 1781. Well edited.

Chevalier de la Luzerne

4:108 Burnett, Edmund C., and Leland, Waldo G., eds. "Letters from Lafayette to Luzerne, 1780–1782." *American Historical Review* 20:2 (1915), 341–76; 20:3 (1915), 577–612. More often than not, Lafayette urged the French to be more active in supporting the Americans. Luzerne had to try to control his often impetuous countryman and allow decisions by the commander of the French forces in the United States, General Rochambeau. A useful source.

4:109 O'Donnell, William E. *The Chevalier de la Luzerne: French Minister to the United States, 1779–1784.* Louvain: Bibliothèque de l'Université, 1938. O'Donnell was given access to the Luzerne Papers while they were still in private hands, and he skillfully exploits this source. Because the author is the only scholar to see this entire collection, his work on Luzerne should be consulted.

Sioussat, St. G. L. "The Chevalier de la Luzerne and the Ratification of the Articles of Confederation in Maryland, 1780–1781" (4:125).

Comte de Rochambeau

Kennett, L. *The French Forces in America, 1780–1783* (4:157).

4:110 Rochambeau, Comte de. *Memoires militaires, historiques, et politiques de Rochambeau, ancien maréchal de France* [Military, historical and political memoirs of Rochambeau]. 2 vols. Paris: Fain, 1809. The memoirs of the general who commanded the French army at Yorktown has all of the faults of memoirs written many years after the event, but it does show Rochambeau's appreciation of Washington and the sacrifices that Americans were willing to make to defeat the British. It also reveals Rochambeau's ability to work in harmony with Americans in difficult situations.

Comte de Vergennes

4:111 Doniol, Henri. "Le Ministère des Affaires Étrangères de France sous le Comte de Vergennes" [The French Ministry of Foreign Affairs under Count de Vergennes]. *Revue d'Histoire Diplomatique* 7 (1893), 528–60. This description of the office of foreign affairs under Count de Vergennes includes an account of his assistants carrying out his American policy. Murphy's work (4:113) on Vergennes supersedes this, but it is a good summary of Doniol's many years of labor in French-American relations.

Dull, J. R. *The French Navy and American Independence . . . , 1774–1787* (4:119).

4:112 Faÿ, Bernard. "Portrait de Comte de Vergennes" [Portrait of Count de Vergennes]. *Franco-American Review* 1:3 (1936), 143–48. This very brief sketch is by a recognized scholar on the influence of the American Revolution on France. Faÿ is not uncritical of Vergennes but the reader should also consult Murphy's article.

4:113 Murphy, Orville T. "Charles Gravier de Vergennes: Portrait of an Old Regime Diplomat." *Political Science Quarterly* 83:3 (1968), 400–418. An astute examination of the foreign minister's motives and personality which argues that Vergennes's commitment to duty, discipline, and honor distinguishes him more than his intellectual ability or insight in French-American affairs. A necessary corrective to the portrait of Vergennes as a cynical, *realpolitik* diplomat.

Others

4:114 Beaumarchais, Caron de. *Correspondance [de] Beaumarchais* [Correspondence of Beaumarchais]. 4 vols. Ed. by Brian N. Morton. Paris: Nizet, 1969–. These first three volumes deal with Beaumarchais's controversial intermediary service between Americans in France and the French government before the French-American alliance; this role diminished greatly after 1778. This is the best source for French involvement with the United States before 1778.

4:115 Chastellux, Marquis de. *Travels in North America in the Years 1780, 1781, and 1782 by Marquis de Chastellux.* 2 vols. Ed. and trans. by Howard C. Rice, Jr. Chapel Hill: University of North Carolina

Press, 1963. Second in command of the French army in the United States, Chastellux traveled throughout the country during the winter season. His comments are usually intelligent, but he overrates the simplicity and republican nature of the United States. This edition includes the notes of the original translator, George Grieve, who also toured the United States during the Revolution; thus it has two different views. A well-edited work with exceptionally informative notes.

4:116 Von Closen, Baron Ludwig. *The Revolutionary Journal of Baron Ludwig Von Closen, 1780–1783.* Ed. and trans. by Evelyn Acomb. Chapel Hill: University of North Carolina Press, 1958. Von Closen offered many descriptions of American officials and soldiers whom he met, and he also reported Rochambeau's reactions to events. This fine and complete journal is supplemented by an excellent biographical directory; also the translating and editing are superb.

Europe and the American Revolution

FRANCE

See "Personalities," especially Silas Deane, Benjamin Franklin, John Laurens, James Madison, John Sullivan, and, under "Others," Robert R. Livingston; see "Document Collections," especially Chinard (4:14) and Doniol (4:15).

4:117 Aulard, Albert. "La Dette Americaine envers la France" [The American debt toward France]. *Revue de Paris* 32:11 (1925), 319–38; 32:12 (1925), 524–50. Obviously inspired by the controversy over World War I Allied debts to the United States, the author analyzed French loans to the United States during and after the American Revolution and their repayment. He emphasized the patience and generosity of France, noting that the debt constituted the only really tangible connection between the two countries.

4:118 Corwin, Edward S. *French Policy and the American Alliance of 1778.* Hamden, Conn.: Shoe String Press (1916), 1962. A sound account of the

reasons for French intervention set in a European framework, it has been superseded by Dull's work. Vergennes's demand for a more assertive role by France to redress British preponderance is now widely accepted as a result of this work.

4:119 Dull, Jonathan R. *The French Navy and American Independence: A Study of Arms and Diplomacy, 1774–1787.* Princeton, N.J.: Princeton University Press, 1976. From exacting research in French archives, Dull contends that Vergennes set French policy and guided Louis XVI and the cabinet. If the author overemphasizes the naval buildup's role in the 1778 intervention, he nonetheless has written one of the finest political-military studies of French intervention. Extensive bibliography.

4:120 Echeverria, Durand. *Mirage in the West: A History of the French Image of American Society to 1815.* Princeton, N.J.: Princeton University Press, 1957. An intriguing book that suggests the French saw in the United States the kind of society that they desired for France. The revolutionary period abounds in comments by Frenchman and French visitors to the United States who often wrote from little knowledge. The research is exquisite, but it is the subtle analysis of both French and American reactions that makes the work a significant contribution.

4:121 Faÿ, Bernard. *The Revolutionary Spirit in France and America: A Study of Moral and Intellectual Relations between France and the United States at the End of the Eighteenth Century.* Trans. by Ramon Guthrie. New York: Harcourt, Brace, 1927. An intellectual history of the Enlightenment's influence on 18th-century revolutions. The author is a recognized scholar of American influence on France, and his research is still acceptable. The economic aspects of the American Revolution and their effects on France are unexplored; nor does the author examine American influence outside of the intellecutal elite. Bibliography.

4:122 Godechot, Jacques. *France and the Atlantic Revolution of the Eighteenth Century, 1770–1799.* Trans. by Herbert Rowen. New York: Free Press, 1965. This work offers a thesis commonly advanced about the late 18th century: an Atlantic revolution, including the rapid development of French ports such as Nantes and Bordeaux to accommodate expanding commerce from the West Indies. The American Revolution and in part the French Revolution are seen in this larger context. Godechot's thesis is provocative and his comments on the American Revolution shrewd, although not supported by elaborate research.

Jones, H. M. *America and French Culture, 1750–1848* (5:108).

4:123 Meng, John J. "French Diplomacy in Philadelphia, 1778–1779." *Catholic Historical Review* 24:1 (1938), 39–57. After he had negotiated the alliance with the United States, Gérard was instructed to maintain the alliance and assure French rights to the Newfoundland fishery, which he accomplished with ease. The author downplays the hostility to Gérard and to France because of his 1779 intervention on behalf of Silas Deane.

4:124 Murphy, Orville T. "The Battle of Germantown and the Franco-American Alliance of 1778." *Pennsylvania Magazine of History* 82:1 (1958), 55–64. The author contends that historians have overlooked this battle as a precipitating cause of French intervention. This article redresses the balance, although it may be that Germantown demonstrated that Washington's army could not be annihilated, which with the victory at Saratoga, prompted Vergennes to recognize the United States.

4:125 Sioussat, St. George L. "The Chevalier de la Luzerne and the Ratification of the Articles of Confederation in Maryland, 1780–1781." *Pennsylvania Magazine of History* 60:4 (1936), 391–418. Luzerne and Barbé-Marbois intervened to assure Maryland's ratification of the Articles of Confederation. Financial and military inducements caused several opponents of ratification to be absent from the critical vote. Accompanying documents validate the author's thesis.

4:126 U.S. Library of Congress. *List of Works Relating to the French Alliance in the American Revolution.* Washington, D.C.: G.P.O., 1907. Now badly out of date, its remaining value is the listing of articles and documents published in obscure and now nonexistent American periodicals.

4:127 Van Tyne, Claude. "French Aid before the Alliance of 1778." *American Historical Review* 31:1 (1925), 20–40. The research and the thesis of this article on French supplies before 1778 has stood the test of subsequent scholarship. The supplies and particularly the gunpowder from the Netherlands and France were invaluable to the American armies. A more detailed explanation is now available; see Mor-

ton's work on Beaumarchais (4:115) and from Dull's monograph (4:119).

GREAT BRITAIN

See "Personalities" for additional references.

4:128 Bemis, Samuel Flagg. *The Hussey-Cumberland Mission and American Independence.* Princeton, N.J.: Princeton University Press, 1931. The best account in English of British efforts, never seriously pursued, to reach separate peace terms with Spain without Spanish recognition of United States independence. The author's research is extensive, but his anti-European bias leads to a number of overstated conclusions about Spain and European diplomacy.

4:129 Bonwick, Colin. *English Radicals and the American Revolution.* Chapel Hill: University of North Carolina Press, 1977. This is a study of the small group of English radicals concentrated in Dissenter groups. They came to see the American Revolution as vital to the cause of preserving liberties in Britain. But this group did not penetrate the upper or lower classes and had only minimal effects on policy. Bibliography.

4:130 Brown, Weldon A. *Empire or Independence: A Study in the Failure of Reconciliation, 1774–1783.* Baton Rouge: Louisiana State University Press, 1941. This careful study of ill-fated British negotiations with the colonies concentrates on the Carlisle Commission in 1778. The author points out that Great Britain offered compromises only when forced to do so, and then too little and too late. See Gruber's work on the Howe brothers (4:92) and Lord Carlisle's papers (4:84). Bibliography.

4:131 Christie, Ian R. *The End of North's Ministry, 1780–1782.* London: Macmillan, 1958. A well-researched account of the last years of the North ministry, this is an astute analysis of the 1780 parliamentary election and its relationship to the growth of party. The competition between the king, ministers, and shifting factions in the House of Commons is well presented.

4:132 Clark, Dora M. "British Opinion of Franco-American Relations: 1775–1795." *William and Mary Quarterly* 3d ser. 4:3 (1947), 305–16. This article, based on English newspapers during and after the Revolution, found the British so convinced of the virtues of their form of government and religion, they could not believe that the Americans would betray them by signing an alliance with France. The author is unable to determine how deeply the opinions expressed in the newspapers penetrated the British middle class or influenced the ruling class.

4:133 Norton, Mary B. *The British Americans: The Loyalist Exiles in England, 1774–1789*. Boston: Little, Brown, 1972. A well-researched account of Loyalists who chose exile in England; it nicely complements Smith's study (4:162). While her analysis of the American community and its influence on British policy is sound, Norton may understate the problem of merchants who chose exile to maintain their commercial position.

EUROPE

The Netherlands

See Chapter 5 for additional references. Also see 'Personalities," above, for John Adams.

Boxer, C. R. *The Dutch Seaborne Empire, 1600–1800* (3:143).

4:134 Edler, Friedrich. *The Dutch Republic and the American Revolution*. Baltimore: Johns Hopkins Press, 1911. A political account of the role of the Netherlands in the American Revolution. Although none of the author's conclusions has been challenged, the work has been superseded by those of Winter (5:150) and Schama (4:136).

4:135 Renault, Francis. *La Neutralité hollandaise durant la guerre d'Amérique* [Dutch neutrality during the American war]. Paris: Graouli, 1925. This extensively researched monograph still makes many worthwhile observations.

4:136 Schama, Simon. *Patriots and Liberators: Revolution in the Netherlands, 1780–1815*. New York: Knopf, 1977. Although this social and political history of the Netherlands extends beyond the Revolution, the author's opening chapters add new material on the American Revolution's influence on the patriot party in the Netherlands. He finds the influence of John Adams (1781–1782) to be as profound as Adams proclaimed it to be. A first-rate analysis treating both internal Dutch affairs and international politics, it

should be combined with Winter's work (5:150). Extensive bibliography.

Russia

See "Personalities" for American Francis Dana (under "Others"); also see Kaplan (4:30) for essay on Catherine the Great and U.S. foreign policy.

Bailey, T. A. *America Faces Russia: Russian-American Relations from Early Times to Our Day* [1776–1950] (2:245).

4:137 Bolkhovitinov, Nikolai N. *The Beginnings of Russian-American Relations, 1755–1815*. Trans. by Elena Levin. Cambridge: Harvard University Press, 1976.

4:138 Bolkhovitinov, Nikolai N. *Russia and the American Revolution*. Trans. by C. Jay Smith. Tallahassee, Fla.: Diplomatic Press, 1976. These works by a Russian specialist emphasize the ambiguity of Catherine's response to America because of Russian interests in Turkey. The author has used a wide variety of Russian and American sources; his footnotes and bibliographical essay illustrate current Russian research on the American Revolution. Although useful, Griffiths (4:146) provides better insight into the interplay between the United States and Russia.

Dulles, F. R. *The Road to Teheran: The Story of Russia and America, 1781–1943* (2:247).

Spain

See "Personalities" for John Jay and, under "Others," William Carmichael.

4:139 Renault, Francis. *Le Pacte de famille et l'Amérique: La Politique coloniale Franco-Espagnole de 1760 à 1792* [The family pact and America: colonial politics of France and Spain from 1760 to 1792]. Paris: Leroux, 1922. As with the author's numerous monographs on France, Spain, and the Netherlands during the Revolution, this one reveals extensive research in European archives and provides a clear, straightforward interpretation that still contains many worthwhile observations.

4:140 Yela Utrilla, Juan F. *España ante la independencia de los Estados Unidos* [Spain before United States independence]. 2 vols. Lerida: Graficos Academía Mariana, 1925. This sound interpretation of Spain's contributions to U.S. independence contains an accurate listing of Spanish aid. The title is so worded because Spain did not recognize the United States until after Great Britain accepted the Treaty of Paris in 1783. Volume 2 prints a number of important documents from Spanish archives dealing with American, French, and Spanish diplomacy.

Other Nations

4:141 Barton, H. A. "Sweden and the War of American Independence." *William and Mary Quarterly* 3d ser. 23:3 (1966), 408–30. A reexamination of the role of Sweden, particularly of Swedish soldiers who fought in the American Revolution. The author finds, contrary to previous scholars, that more Swedish soldiers enlisted in the British army and navy than in the American, and the next largest contingent served in the French forces.

4:142 Dippel, Horst. *Germany and the American Revolution.* Trans. by Bernard A. Uhlendorf. Chapel Hill: University of North Carolina Press, 1977. The research is deep but the analysis is not always clear. This exhaustive study does show that the influence of the American Revolution was far greater in Germany than previously believed even though Prussia, and to a lesser extent Austria, pursued a policy of neutrality and showed little sympathy for Americans. Extensive bibliography.

4:143 Libiszowska, Zofia. "L'Opinion polonaise et la Révolution américaine au XVIIIe siècle" [Polish opinion of the American Revolution in the eighteenth century]. *Revue d'Histoire Moderne et Contemporaine* 17:4 (1970), 984–98. After the partition of Poland in 1773, the Poles were responsive to the influences of the American Revolution. In addition to their own anti-Russian nationalism, the Poles adapted from the Revolution a desire for political reforms based on parliamentary practices. A good study but it does not supersede Palmer's treatment (4:32).

4:144 Madariaga, Isabel de. *Britain, Russia, and the Armed Neutrality of 1780: Sir James Harris's Mission to St. Petersburg during the American Revolution.* New Haven, Conn.: Yale University Press, 1962. This is an excellent study of the League of Armed Neutrality under the guidance of Catherine and supported by France. The research is outstanding and the conclusions fair. Perhaps there is an undue emphasis on Harris's role to the detriment of the indigenous Russian pressures for continued trade with all belligerents.

Special Topics

ECONOMIC AFFAIRS

See "Personalities" for William Bingham (under "Others").

4:145 Godechot, Jacques. "Les Relations économiques entre la France et les États-Unis de 1778 à 1789" [Economic relations between France and the United States, 1778–1789]. *French Historical Studies* 1:1 (1958), 26–39. This article on economic relations updates the traditional view that the United States and France did not have complementary trade relations. A sound article, but it underplays the importance of Bordeaux in the American trade and understates the amount of trade between the French West Indies and the United States.

4:146 Griffiths, David M. "American Commercial Diplomacy in Russia: 1780–1783." *William and Mary Quarterly* 3d ser. 27:3 (1970), 379–410. The best-researched piece on relations with Russia, it additionally provides more information about the mysterious but important role of Stephen Sayre in American diplomacy. Catherine would not alienate Great Britain because of problems with Turkey; thus commercial diplomacy failed because of overriding Russian concerns, not because of the anti-U.S. policies of the British and French ambassadors in Russia.

4:147 Jameson, J. Franklin. "St. Eustatius in the American Revolution." *American Historical Review* 8:4 (1903), 683–703. This article demonstrates the value of neutrality in wartime. St. Eustatius, a Dutch possession, was an entrepôt for Dutch and French powder and other war supplies to reach the United States. After the French entry into the war, the role of St. Eustatius declined, and it was finally destroyed by Admiral Rodney when the Dutch entered the war in 1780.

4:148 Luthy, Herbert. *La Banque Protestante en France de la Révocation d'Edit de Nantes à la Révolution: De la Banque aux Finances, 1730–1794* [The Protestant Bank in France from the revocation of the Edict of Nantes to the revolution: from bankers to financiers, 1730–1794]. 2 vols. Paris: S.E.V.P.E.N., 1961. The second volume of this wide-ranging and excellent work has many details on the effects of the American Revolution on the financial situation in Europe. The author traces interconnected banking families and their involvement in all aspects of trade and politics, including the financing of American loans and French credit policy.

4:149 Martin, Gaston. "Commercial Relations between Nantes and the American Colonies." *Journal of Economic and Business History* 4:4 (1932), 812–29. The author has extensively mined the records of the important port of Nantes. Trade with the United States increased from 1775 to 1778; but with French intervention and subsequent British blockade, trade declined rapidly, and Bordeaux remained the most important port for French-American commerce.

Price, J. M. *France and the Chesapeake: A History of the French Tobacco Monopoly 1694–1791* . . . (3:120) finds that the Farmers General, during the revolutionary period, was instrumental in supporting aid and loans to the United States. It offers new information on Benjamin Franklin's and Robert Morris's tobacco connection.

4:150 Setser, Vernon G. *The Commercial Reciprocity Policy of the United States, 1774–1829*. Philadelphia: University of Pennsylvania Press, 1937. The author follows American efforts to institute new, liberal commercial programs upon independence. All failed, owing to the closed imperial economic systems maintained by European powers. Bibliography.

4:151 Tarrade, Jean. *Le Commerce colonial de la France à la fin de l'Ancien Régime: L'Evolution de régime de "l'Esclusif" de 1763 à 1789* [French colonial commerce at the end of the Old Regime]. 2 vols. Paris: Presses Universitaires de France, 1972. In a meticulous account of France's relaxation of its mercantilist policy in its West Indian colonies, the author shows the political difficulties in gaining the consent of French merchants. The war caused an ever-increasing colonial demand for foodstuffs, which allowed local officials to relax the ban against American traders. Bibliography.

Ubbelohde, C. *The Vice-Admiralty Courts and the American Revolution* (3:195).

Winter, P. J. van. *American Finance and Dutch Investment, 1780–1805, with an Epilogue to 1840* (5:150) details, in minute and exacting fashion, the commercial and financial connections between the United States and the Netherlands during the war.

AMERICAN WEST IN THE REVOLUTION

See "Personalities" for George Rogers Clark (under "Others"); also see "Document Collections" for Kinnaird (3:19).

4:152 Abernethy, Thomas P. *Western Lands and the American Revolution.* New York: Russell & Russell (1937), 1959. The role of speculators and the development of congressional policy toward the frontier are the subjects of this richly researched study written in the mode of the Progressive era. This is the best study of the national and international connections of the Indiana, Vandalia, Illinois, and Wabash land companies that we have. Extensive bibliography.

Bannon, J. F. *The Spanish Borderlands Frontier, 1513–1821* (3:91).

4:153 Caughey, John W. *Bernardo de Galvez in Louisiana, 1776–1783.* Gretna, La.: Pelican (1934), 1972. This impressive piece of research remains the best monograph available in English on the Spanish efforts in the Lower Mississippi Valley during the Revolution. The author puts in perspective the genuine Spanish contributions to the victory in the American west. Bibliography.

Lyon, E. W. *Louisiana in French Diplomacy, 1759–1804* (6:94) relies on the now questionable assumption the France continued to desire Louisiana after cession to Spain in 1763.

McDermott, J.F., ed. *The Spanish in the Mississippi Valley, 1762–1804* (3:10).

Nasatir, A. P. *Borderland in Retreat: From Spanish Louisiana to the Far Southwest* [1762–1822] (5:136).

4:154 Phillips, Paul C. *The West in the Diplomacy of the American Revolution.* New York: Russell & Russell (1913), 1967. The struggle for the Mississippi Valley during the Revolution is viewed from Philadelphia and Paris. Using Doniol and Stevens extensively but failing to exploit appropriate Spanish sources, the author depicts Spain as grasping, while the United States sought only what rightfully belonged to it.

4:155 Sosin, Jack M. *Revolutionary Frontier, 1763–1783*. New York: Holt, Rinehart & Winston, 1967. A succinct, clear account which challenged the Turner thesis on the frontier's leveling tendency and points out that established institutions were critical of the region's development. The Continental Congress disposed of land similarly to the British policy of 1774. Sosin also presents a clear account of the role of Indians during the Revolution. Extensive bibliography.

Starr, J. B. *Tories, Dons, and Rebels: The American Revolution in British West Florida* (7:44).

MILITARY AFFAIRS

See "Overviews," especially Higginbotham (4:29) and Mackesy (4:31); also see "Personalities" for Sir Henry Clinton, and, under "Others," Lord Cornwallis, the Howe brothers; Marquis de Lafayette, Comte de Rochambeau; George Washington, and, under "Others," Nathanael Greene. For additional references, see "Bibliographies," especially Rankin (4:3); also see "Atlases and Other Aids" for maps, especially Marshall and Peckham (4:11).

4:156 Graymont, Barbara. *The Iroquois in the American Revolution*. Syracuse, N.Y.: Syracuse University Press, 1972. White settlers split the Six Nations, as some tribes supported the British and others the Americans. The Iroquois backed the British and paid dearly when the British lost in 1779. A well-written, adequately researched book that concludes the Iroquois were doomed, whichever side they chose, but that a British victory would have slowed the process.

4:157 Kennett, Lee. *The French Forces in America, 1780–1783*. Westport, Conn.: Greenwood, 1977. The finest account of Rochambeau's army in the United States, it examines the interactions of French and American cultures during the Revolution. The research is excellent, the conclusions just and reasonable. The professional behavior exhibited by French officers offered a contrast to British and American performance.

4:158 Kite, Elizabeth S. *Brigadier-General Louis Lebègue Duportail: Commandant of Engineers in the Continental Army*. Baltimore: Johns Hopkins Press, 1933. Duportail was recruited because of his engineering background, and throughout the Revolution the Americans had to rely on such French assistance to sustain their campaigns. Vergennes secured approval for a number of French-paid officers, including De-Kalb and Duportail, to help the Americans.

4:159 Lawrence, Alexander A. *Storm over Savannah: The Story of Count d'Estaing and the Siege of the Town*. Athens: University of Georgia Press, 1951. Count d'Estaing attempted two joint ventures with the Americans, and they both ended as military and political failures. The first was at Newport in 1778, the next was an effort to dislodge the British from Savannah. This work is a well-written and -documented study of that campaign, although wider strategic ramifications are ignored.

4:160 O'Donnell, James H. *Southern Indians in the American Revolution*. Knoxville: University of Tennessee Press, 1973. British and American policies toward the southern Indians, particularly the Cherokees, are examined. The United States sought through friendship or, more often, war to ensure that the Indians did not side with the British. This concise work shows the decline of British influence and the ascendancy of American settlers.

4:161 Patterson, A. Temple. *The Other Armada: The Franco-Spanish Attempt to Invade Britain in 1779*. Manchester: Manchester University Press, 1960. The work adequately explains the failure, but does not probe deeply into French policy. Because Spain insisted on this invasion, no substantial aid was given to the Americans during 1779. This in turn had consequences for British strategy. This study has been superseded by Dull (4:119).

4:162 Smith, Paul H. *Loyalists and Redcoats: A Study in the British Revolutionary Policy*. Chapel Hill: University of North Carolina Press, 1964. After the defeat at Saratoga, the British increasingly relied on Loyalists to maintain British forces in the colonies. This well-researched study is a model of policy analysis and the best place to begin a study of the complicated problem of the Loyalists.

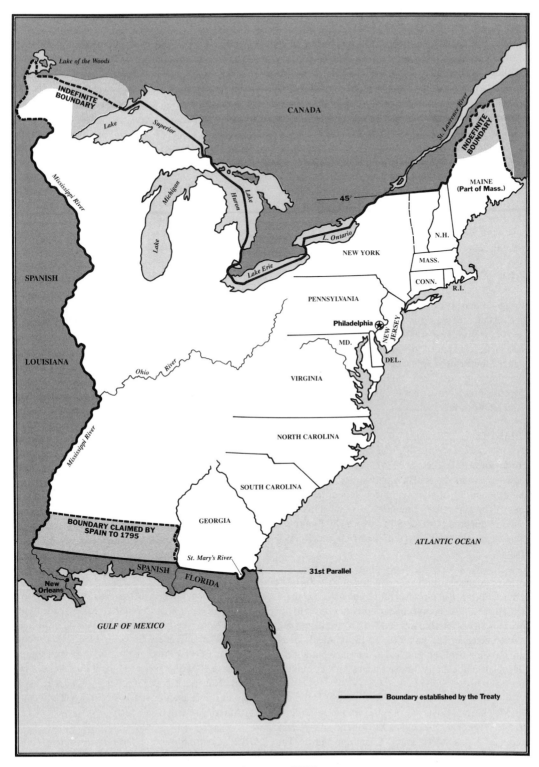

The United States after the Treaty of Paris, 1783

NAVAL AFFAIRS

See "Document Collections" for Clark (4:23) and Paullin (4:19); also see "Personalities" for Comte de Grasse, American John Paul Jones (under "Others"), and Britons Lord Sandwich, Lord Rodney (under "Others"). For additional references, see "Bibliographies," especially Rankin (4:3) and Smith (4:6).

4:163   Allen, Gardner W. *A Naval History of the American Revolution*. 2 vols. Williamstown, Mass.: Corner House (1913), 1970. An old, but still eminently useful, account of American naval activities during the Revolution. Battles and exploits are stressed, so this work should be used in conjunction with others dealing more directly with diplomatic aspects.

4:164   Clark, William B. *Ben Franklin's Privateers: A Naval Epic of the American Revolution*. Baton Rouge: Louisiana State University Press, 1956. An account of American privateers in French ports before and after the alliance was signed with France. Franklin had nominal control of the legalized pirate raids against the British. This work should be used in conjunction with the Deane and Lee papers, however, because Franklin was not as involved as many other Americans in the operations.

4:165   James, William M. *The British Navy in Adversity: A Study of the War for Independence*. New York: Russell & Russell (1926), 1970. It is based on extensive work in British archives and gives a sustained narrative of all major encounters of the British navy. The appendixes contain lists of the ships of all sides in important battles. Still a worthwhile source, it can be supplemented by the Sandwich and Rodney papers.

4:166   Johnson, Ruth Y. "American Privateers in French Ports." *Pennsylvania Magazine of History* 53:4 (1929), 352–74. This account of privateers, up to the French-American alliance in 1778, is useful but not comprehensive. The author covers the political side of the question between England and France but not the financial implications for Americans or the implications for British shipping.

4:167   Lacour-Gayet, G. *La Marine militaire de la France sous le règne de Louis XVI* [French navy in the reign of Louis XVI]. Paris: Champion, 1905. The author has mined the French archives effectively, and this edition, unlike the 1910 edition, contains a number of pertinent documents. A useful summary of French

naval participation in the war, but it is superseded by Dull (4:119).

4:168   Rankin, Hugh F. "The Naval Flag of the American Revolution." *William and Mary Quarterly* 3d ser. 11:3 (1954), 339–53. This article reveals the use of the navy in the early years of the Revolution to show the first recognition, in naval terms, of the United States as an independent country. As usual, the author's research is excellent and his analysis and conclusions judicious.

4:169   Scott, James B. *De Grasse à Yorktown*. Baltimore: Johns Hopkins Press, 1931. The author relied excessively on Doniol and the old edition of Lafayette's *Mémoires,* now superseded by a new edition. The author is enamored of the idea of close French-American relations which detracts from his assessment of De Grasse and the motives underlying allied actions.

4:170   Syrett, David. *Shipping and the American War, 1775–1783: A Study of British Transport Organization*. London: Athlone, 1970. A study of the Naval Board and the multitude of problems that it faced. After 1779 the Naval Board was responsible for all supplies to America and other theaters of war. The author is judicious, and his careful study draws primarily from the British Public Record Office.

PEACE NEGOTIATIONS, 1782

See "Personalities" for John Adams, Benjamin Franklin, John Jay.

Bemis, S. F. "Canada and the Peace Settlement of 1782–83" (10:32) suggests why the United States did not obtain Canada during peace negotiations.

4:171   Brown, Marvin L., ed. and trans. *American Independence through Prussian Eyes: A Neutral View of the Peace Negotiations of 1782–1783*. Durham, N.C.: Duke University Press, 1959. These excerpts from materials by Prussian diplomats on the progress and success of the peace negotiations are soundly edited. Not much new information is added, as the Prussians were as surprised as the French at how much the Americans achieved.

4:172   Conn, Stetson. *Gibraltar in British Diplomacy in the Eighteenth Century*. New Haven, Conn.: Yale University Press, 1942. Spain made repeated attempts to regain Gibraltar from 1776 to 1779, first by peaceful means and later, after Spain entered the war, by military means. After 1782 the British did not seriously consider ceding Gibraltar to Spain.

4:173 Harlow, Vincent T. *The Founding of the Second British Empire: Discovery and Revolution.* New York: Longmans, Green, 1952. Backed by massive research, the author argues convincingly that Great Britain started to pursue a new colonial policy when the loss of the American colonies became apparent. This indispensable work is the only one to explore Lord Shelburne's efforts to see that the United States was not permanently alienated from Great Britain.

4:174 Klingelhofer, Herbert E. "Matthew Ridley's Diary during the Peace Negotiations of 1782." *William and Mary Quarterly* 3d ser. 20:1 (1963), 95–133. An American merchant in Paris, Ridley had close contacts with John Adams and John Jay. This is an important, well-informed diary, carrying the gossip of the day, and gives a different picture of American negotiations.

4:175 Morris, Richard B. *The Peacemakers: The Great Powers and American Independence.* New York: Harper & Row, 1965. The standard account of Henry Laurens, John Adams, Benjamin Franklin, and particularly John Jay who negotiated the peace with Great Britain in 1782. This well-researched work is marred by the author's excessive distrust of Vergennes and Europeans in general.

4:176 Murphy, Orville T. "The Comte de Vergennes, the Newfoundland Fisheries and the Peace Negotiations of 1783: A Reappraisal." *Canadian Historical Review* 46:1 (1965), 32–46. This author examines the issue of the fisheries, and charges of later historians that Vergennes sought to exclude the Americans. Murphy shows convincingly that Vergennes was far more concerned with maintaining French rights and sought to make sure that England and the United States would not exclude France.

4:177 Smith, Paul H. "Sir Guy Carleton, Peace Negotiations, and the Evacuation of New York." *Canadian Historical Review* 50:3 (1969), 245–64. Carleton, who succeeded Clinton as commander of the British forces in North America in 1782, deliberately sought to undermine the peace talks in Paris by delaying the evacuation of New York. The article demonstrates the British commander's stubbornness and also the new administration's determination to abide by parliamentary resolutions and peace agreements.

The Confederation and Federalist Era, 1781–1801

Contributing Editor
ALBERT HALL BOWMAN
University of Tennessee at Chattanooga

Contributors
Marvin R. Zahniser
Ohio State University

Peter P. Hill
George Washington University

William H. Masterson
University of Tennessee at Chattanooga

Contents

Introduction

Foreign affairs have exercised a dominating influence during two widely separated eras in the history of the United States: at the beginning, following the American Revolution, and recently, in the aftermath of the Second World War. In the last two decades of the eighteenth century, the new republic struggled to establish its sovereignty in a world dominated by European monarchies; in the mid-twentieth century the United States was the most powerful nation on earth, attempting to restore order in a war-torn world and protect its and its allies' traditional values against a perceived new threat. The contrasts between the United States positions could hardly have been greater. For a variety of reasons, therefore, it is not surprising that students of diplomatic history have been drawn in the recent past to the Confederation and Federalist era in greater numbers than ever before.

That era witnessed the efforts of the Confederation to gain international recognition, the establishment of a new polity under the Constitution of 1787, and the struggles of the new federal government to maintain American sovereignty and security during the wars spawned by the French Revolution, while the two great antagonists, Great Britain and France, each sought to use the United States against its enemy.

Any survey of the historiography of the era will inevitably discover the paramount importance of the French Revolution for American foreign policy. Consequently, the attention of students has centered more on United States relations with France than on those with other nations, and that concentration has been abetted by the intrinsic fascination of the French Revolution itself. This is implicit in Lawrence S. Kaplan's *Colonies into Nation* (3:42), the best interpretive survey of the era, and in two books by Alexander DeConde, *Entangling Alliance* (5:158) and *The Quasi-War* (5:206); it is explicit in Albert H. Bowman, *The Struggle for Neutrality* (5:156). American relations with Great Britain and with Spain were also important, but more often than not as counterpoints to the Franco-American relationship. In addition, it is not too much to say that the impact of the French Revolution on American domestic politics profoundly affected the development of political parties in the United States.

There exists no general diplomatic history of the Confederation. Although we ought to know more about American commercial relations with France, Great Britain, Spain, and other parts of the world during that time, the main outlines of American foreign relations of the 1780s have long been generally accepted. Controversy has been limited for the most part to the debate over the meaning of the period, although a rough consensus exists that the Confederation failed and that a principal cause was the weakness of American influence abroad, especially in regard to Great Britain and the expansion of American commerce. Merrill Jensen argues the case for the Confederation in *The New Nation* (5:159), while Richard B. Morris summarizes the historiography of the controversy in "The Confederation Period and the American Historian" (5:3).

The onset of the French Revolution and especially the outbreak of war in 1793 compelled the attention of the federal government. Because of the Franco-American treaties of 1778, America's reaction was an immediate issue. It was resolved in President Washington's Neutrality Proclamation, opposed by Secretary of State Jefferson, who wanted to use the question of neutrality to bargain with both sides for American advantage. That episode has not been analyzed in detail since Charles M. Thomas, *American Neutrality in 1793* (5:172), in 1931. The Genet mission, on the other hand, owing in part to the masses of materials published by Frederick Jackson Turner, especially *Correspondence of the French Ministers* (5:11), has received periodic attention since the end of the nineteenth century. The same cannot be said of succeeding French missions, Fauchet's and Adet's, except in the case of the latter in connection with Washington's Farewell Address. The traditional view of the address as a timeless guide for American foreign policy was forcefully stated by Samuel Flagg Bemis almost half a century ago, in "Washington's Farewell Address: A Foreign Policy of Independence" (5:173), but more recent interpretations, such as Alexander

DeConde, "Washington's Farewell, the French Alliance, and the Election of 1796" (5:174), have emphasized its immediate, partisan purposes.

The impact of Jay's Treaty with Great Britain on France and the response of the French Directory likewise have received recent attention which clarifies better than heretofore the reasons for and the purposes of French policy. Joseph Charles, *The Origins of the American Party System* (5:169), and Jerald A. Combs, *The Jay Treaty* (5:195), deal with the treaty's domestic implications. Recent writers have pointed to the fact that, whether or not the treaty prevented war with Great Britain, it did lead to the "quasi-war" with France. In a kind of addendum to the debate over Jay's Treaty, historians have generally exonerated Edmund Randolph of Federalist charges of treason—Irving Brant, "Edmund Randolph, Not Guilty!" (5:59)—but President Washington's role in that affair has not yet been adequately explained.

The XYZ affair has received much recent attention, with the principal result that French motives and policies are better understood than under the traditional, nationalistic interpretation. In addition to writers already mentioned, William Stinchcombe, in *The XYZ Affair* (5:213) has contributed to the revision of stereotypical accounts still widely repeated. In particular, Talleyrand's position under the Directory and his role in averting open hostilities with the United States are better appreciated. The Franco-American quasi-war and the Franco-American Convention of 1800 have been studied anew, and scholars' use of French archival sources has supplied an essential dimension hitherto lacking. Historians still disagree on the meaning of the Convention of 1800 and on President Adams's tactics, but it is safe to say that Franco-American relations during the Federalist decade, as reconstructed by the scholarship of the past generation, are better understood than United States relations with other nations.

Anglo-American relations during this period have provided a literature which, although formidable, is less extensive than that of the Franco-American connection. In *Aftermath of Revolution* (5:130), Charles R. Ritcheson carries the story to 1795 from the viewpoint of Whitehall, while Bradford Perkins deals in a more restrained way with *The First Rapprochement* (6:10) initiated by the Jay Treaty. Problems of actual British recognition of American independence and of the implementation of the Peace of 1783 dominated diplomacy under the Confederation, while the relations of the United States with Great Britain and France were so intertwined in the Federalist period that they cannot meaningfully be separated. The same is true to a lesser degree of American relations with Spain, which centered almost exclusively on the navigation of the Mississippi River. The Mississippi question, of which the (Pinckney) Treaty of San Lorenzo (1795) was an end and a beginning, has been intensively studied, notably by Samuel Flagg Bemis in *Pinckney's Treaty* (5:201). Perhaps because that treaty has traditionally been counted such an American triumph, other aspects of Spanish-American relations, commerce, for example, have been relatively neglected.

The triangular relationship between the United States, Great Britain, and France dominated the foreign policies of the early republic, with the issue of the navigation of the Mississippi occasionally playing a separate role, less dangerous to the United States because of Spain's weakness. Relations with the Dutch Republic were important, although chiefly in the economic and financial spheres, and they have not yet received the systematic attention they deserve. Since the late 1940s, early Russian-American relations have received some attention, owing, one assumes, to contemporary concerns, and there has been some work on Prussian-American relations and those of the United States with the Barbary States of North Africa.

Biographical literature for this period has been significantly enriched in recent years. Magisterial biographies of George Washington by Douglas Southall Freeman (5:65) and James T. Flexner (4:65), Thomas Jefferson by Dumas Malone (5:36, 5:37), and James Madison by Irving Brant (5:42) have appeared or are in progress, and the several recent biographies of Alexander Hamilton attest to a fuller and more objective appreciation of his seminal contributions to American history. Nor have lesser figures such as James Monroe, Rufus King, Charles Cotesworth Pinckney, Elbridge Gerry, and Timothy Pickering, to mention only a few, been neglected. No student of the period can afford to ignore these valuable resources. Unfortunately, however, extended biographical treatment of foreign representatives in the United States is relatively scarce, and biographies of major foreign figures, Talleyrand, Robespierre, and Napoleon, for example, and Lord Hawkesbury, Lord Grenville, and the younger Pitt, usually pay scant attention to American affairs. Inevitably, or course, relations with America were minor concerns of European statesmen in this era of revolutionary upheaval.

Historians have increasingly recognized, not only that American foreign relations were inextricably bound up with domestic policies, but that foreign policy also depends on the larger social, economic, cultural, and intellectual contexts of American society. Perhaps to a slightly lesser degree, the same recognition has been extended to the domestic influences affecting the governments with which the United States interacted. Although written from the European perspective, Robert R. Palmer's *The Age of the Democratic Revolution* (4:32) is a brilliant example of this eclecticism.

The student of the Confederation and Federalist era has an unusually large base on which to build, but much work of synthesis, interpretation, and of topical research remains to be done. United States relations, particularly economic, with the Netherlands and Spain are relatively unexplored for the entire era and, as also already noted, little has been written of foreign relations under the Confederation. A study of Anglo-American relations under the Confederation would be valuable, as would be a study based on both American and British sources of the whole subject of impressment, which was more important in the 1790s than is usually assumed. The last word obviously has not been written concerning the Jay Treaty, nor of many other episodes of the Federalist period. While the Genêt mission has its own literature, less attention has been devoted to those of the Fauchet commission and of Adet. In short, while foreign affairs in the era have been intensively studied, there remain many research opportunities. The student should approach them, however, with the understanding that most topics have multinational implications and should be treated in an international context.

Resources and Overviews

RESEARCH AIDS

While pertinent bibliographies and reference aids are listed here, there are more extensive lists in Chapter 1.

Bibliographies

5:1 Berwick, Keith B. *The Federalist Age, 1789–1829*. Washington, D.C.: American Historical Association, 1961. This pamphlet of bibliographical essays contains a brief pertinent section, "The Foundations of American Foreign Policy." Coverage is very limited but with judicious comments.

Bibliographie annuelle de l' histoire de France (1:78a) is more convenient than other guides to the yearly output of French scholarship.

Brown, L. M., and Christie, I. R., eds. *Bibliography of British History, 1789–1851* (6:1).

Coker, W. S., and Holmes, J. D. F. "Sources for the History of the Spanish Borderlands" (3:4).

5:2 Cooke, Jacob E. "The Federalist Age: A Reappraisal." In George A. Billias and Gerald N. Grob, eds., *American History: Retrospect and Prospect.* New York: Free Press, 1971, pp. 85–153. Essentially a bibliographical essay that emphasizes conflicting interpretations of the age. The author deals with foreign affairs largely in terms of the continuing Jefferson-Hamilton controversy and the more recent realist versus idealist historiographical argument.

Dippel, H. *Americana Germanica, 1770–1800* (4:2).

Ferguson, E. J., comp. *Confederation, Constitution and Early National Period, 1781–1815* (1:72) lists domestic as well as foreign affairs items for the Confederation and Federalist era.

McDermott, J. F., ed. *The Spanish in the Mississippi Valley, 1762–1804* (3:10).

Monaghan, F. *French Travellers in the United States, 1765–1932: A Bibliography* (1:73).

5:3 Morris, Richard B. "The Confederation Period and the American Historian." *William and Mary Quarterly* 3d ser. 13:1 (1956), 139–56. This often-reprinted essay reviews the historiography of the Confederation. Morris sides with the traditional view of the 1780s as a "critical period" and concludes that the adoption of the Constitution precipitated a greater revolution in American life than had the separation from England.

5:4 Nichols, Roger L. "From the Revolution to the Mexican War." In Robin Higham, ed., *A Guide to the Sources of United States Military History.* Hamden, Conn.: Shoe String Press, 1975, pp. 125–51. This essay contains a few items on the quasi-war, but it is most valuable on the establishment of the peacetime army after the Revolution.

5:5 Smith, Myron J., Jr., ed. *The American Navy, 1789–1860: A Bibliography*. Metuchen, N.J.: Scarecrow, 1974. Smith's bibliographies deal largely with naval matters, but there are items referring to the quasi-war and other incidents that affected diplomacy.

5:6 Stewart, John H. *The French Revolution: Some Trends in Historical Writing, 1945–1965*. Washington, D.C.: American Historical Association, 1967. A pamphlet in the American Historical Association's Service Center for Teachers of History series whose coverage is restricted to the period indicated in the title.

Thomas, D. H., and Case, L. M., eds. *Guide to the Diplomatic Archives of Western Europe* [1400–1959], (1:298) contains, additionally, lists of printed commentary materials.

Atlases and Other Aids

Cappon, L. J. and Petchenik, B. B., eds. *Atlas of Early American History . . ., 1760–1790* (4:9) contains information bearing on foreign relations during the Confederation period.

Document Collections

More general collections are listed in Chapter 1, and other collections may be found in "Personalities," below.

American State Papers (1:349).

5:7 Cunningham, Noble E., Jr., ed. *Circular Letters of Congressmen to Their Constituents, 1789–1829*. 2 vols. Chapel Hill: University of North Carolina Press, 1978. This valuable collection, most of which is letters from representatives from the southern and western states, contains a wealth of information on national concerns as expressed in congressional debates. The editor notes that "from the First Congress to the end of the War of 1812, the most striking feature of the circulars as a group is the emphasis given to foreign affairs." A thorough index.

5:8 Gebhardt, Adam G., comp. *State Papers Relating to the Diplomatic Transactions between the American and French Governments, from the Year 1793, to the Conclusion of the Convention, on the 30th of September, 1800*. 3 vols. London: Vogel, 1807. Reprint 1816. This collection of official correspondence was assembled from American newspapers and U.S. government publications for the benefit of British readers. Publication may have been inspired by the storm over the *Chesapeake* affair.

Kinnaird, L., ed. and trans. *Spain in the Mississippi Valley, 1765–1794* (3:19).

5:9 Knox, Dudley W., ed. *Naval Documents Related to the Quasi-War between the United States and France*. 7 vols. Washington, D.C.: G.P.O., 1935–1938. This collection includes diplomatic, commercial, and military documents from February 1797 to December 31, 1801. These materials relate to establishment of the Navy Department, to American armed merchant vessels, and to encounters between American and French vessels.

Manning, W. R., ed. *Diplomatic Correspondence of the United States: Canadian Relations, 1784–1860* (1:343) contains, in volume 1, a valuable collection of documents relating to U.S. affairs with Britain and France.

5:10 Mayo, Bernard, ed. *Instructions to the British Ministers to the United States, 1791–1812*. In the Annual Report of the American Historical Association for the year 1936. Washington, D.C.: G.P.O., 1941, vol. 3. This volume reproduces with scrupulous accuracy every one of the instructions from the foreign secretaries and their deputies to British representatives in the American capital. Mayo's editorial contributions include the content footnotes which identify personalities, summarize reports and developments, and sometimes point to the location of other important materials.

5:11 Turner, Frederick Jackson, ed. *Correspondence of the French Ministers to the United States, 1791–1797*. In the Annual Report of the American Historical Association for the Year 1903. Washington, D.C.: G.P.O., 1904, vol. 2. Reprint 1972. Volume 2 includes the diplomatic correspondence of French ministers to the United States from Jean de Ternant through Joseph Philippe Létombe, who took over the correspondence when Pierre Auguste Adet suspended his functions in May 1797 on the eve of the quasi-war. The correspondence is in French.

U.S. Congress. *The Debates and Proceedings in the Congress of the United States, 1st to 18th Congresses, March 3, 1789–May 27, 1824* (1:351) is commonly referred to as *Annals of Congress*.

Whitaker, A. P., ed. *Documents Relating to the Commercial Policy of Spain in the Floridas with Incidental Reference to Louisiana* (6:2).

Personalities

OVERVIEWS

5:12 Brinton, Crane. *A Decade of Revolution, 1789–1799*. New York: Harper, 1934. Given the importance of European affairs to this period in American history, this volume provides a useful overview. Bibliography. A more recent survey is George Rudé, *Revolutionary Europe, 1783–1815* (Cleveland: World, 1964).

Crawley, C. W., ed. *War and Peace in an Age of Upheaval, 1793–1830* (6:7).

5:13 Darling, Arthur B. *Our Rising Empire, 1763–1803*. New Haven, Conn.: Yale University Press, 1940. Reprint 1962. A standard work which is still useful; its title states the thesis. Based on wide research in American and foreign archives, it follows generally the view that America benefited from Europe's distresses. Bibliography.

Kaplan, L. S. *Colonies into Nation: American Diplomacy, 1763–1801* (3:42) provides a balanced assessment of Vergennes and Jay in the Confederation period, as well as perceptive comments on Jay's Treaty, the quasi-war, and other diplomatic concerns of the Federalist administrations.

5:14 Miller, John C. *The Federalist Era, 1789–1801*. New York: Harper, 1960. This volume is still probably the best summary of the era, although the author's pro-Federalist bias is apparent. Extensive bibliography.

Setser, V. G. *The Commercial Reciprocity Policy of the United States, 1774–1829* (4:150).

5:15 Varg, Paul A. *Foreign Policies of the Founding Fathers*. East Lansing: Michigan State University Press, 1963. Varg's basic theme is useful: the interplay of ideals and reality, especially economic reality, is the reason this extended essay is sometimes a stimulating book. As a work of interpretation, the study understandably' rests almost entirely on secondary resources; more serious is the apparent failure to consult many important historical studies.

Additional references on individuals may be found in Chapter 1, "Biographical Data."

AMERICAN

John Adams

See Chapter 4, "Personalities," for additional references.

5:16 Adams, John. *The Works of John Adams*. 10 vols. Ed. by Charles Francis Adams. Boston: Little, Brown, 1850–1856. Long a standard reference for Adams materials (1735–1826), the usefulness of this set has been diminished by publication of Butterfield's edition (4:40) and by the microfilming of the Adams Papers deposited in the Massachusetts Historical Society, now available on 608 reels.

5:17 Brown, Ralph A. *The Presidency of John Adams*. Lawrence: University Press of Kansas, 1975. This book offers a favorable assessment of John Adams as president and concludes that Adams had greater popular support in 1800 than in 1796. Bibliography.

5:18 Smith, Page. *John Adams*. 2 vols. Garden City, N.Y.: Doubleday, 1962. Adams's career as peace commissioner to negotiate an end to the revolutionary war, as minister to England during the Confederation, and as vice-president and president are recounted in volume 2. Smith treats Adams's presidential term sympathetically, including his negotiating strategy with France, but almost no foreign research materials are used. Bibliography.

John Quincy Adams

See Chapter 6, "Personalities," for additional references.

Bemis, S. F. *John Quincy Adams and the Foundations of American Foreign Policy* (6:16) relates, in chapter 4, Adams's awkwardness during a brief mission to London (1795–1796) in the aftermath of the Jay-Grenville negotiations, and chapter 5 records his success in negotiating a new commercial treaty with Prussia in 1799.

John Brown
See also James Wilkinson, below.

5:19 Warren, Elizabeth. "Senator John Brown's Role in the Kentucky Spanish Conspiracy." *Filson Club Historical Quarterly* 36:1 (1962), 158–76. Warren clears John Brown of any serious complicity in General James Wilkinson's Spanish conspiracy (1787–1792), contending that historians have read too much into Brown's conversations with Diego de Gardoqui and given too much credence to Wilkinson's readiness to identify Brown as an enthusiastic separatist.

5:20 Watlington, Patricia. "John Brown and the Spanish Conspiracy." *Virginia Magazine of History and Biography* 75:1 (1967), 52–68. The author alleges that this prominent Kentucky legislator was "definitely involved in the plot to separate Kentucky from the United States and ally it with Spain." Brown, the author maintains, gradually abandoned his advocacy of Spanish ties when he found his fellow Kentuckians unenthusiastic.

Benjamin Franklin
See Chapters 3 and 4, "Personalities," for references.

Elbridge Gerry
See also "The XYZ Affair," below.

5:21 Billias, George A. *Elbridge Gerry: Founding Father and Republican Statesman.* New York: McGraw-Hill, 1976. Gerry, one of the XYZ diplomats, has received harsh treatment from historians. Rather than viewing Gerry as a political chameleon, Billias sees him as a man constantly guided by principle. This study focuses on Gerry in the American Revolution, at the Federal Constitutional Convention, and in the administrations of Washington and Adams. Based upon widely scattered materials, this volume is now the standard account of Gerry's life. Bibliography.

5:22 Gerry, Elbridge. *Elbridge Gerry: Letterbook, Paris, 1797–1798.* Ed. by Russell W. Knight. Salem, Mass.: Essex Institute, 1966. Gerry's letters, most of them to his wife, during his mission to France are reprinted.

5:23 Morison, Samuel Eliot. "Elbridge Gerry, Gentleman-Democrat." *New England Quarterly* 2:1 (1929) 6–33. This affectionate but critical sketch of Gerry's career (1744–1814) finds that Gerry "was

always changing sides," but no one ever questioned his sincerity and integrity.

Alexander Hamilton
See Chapter 4, "Personalities," for additional references.

5:24 Boyd, Julian P. *Number 7: Alexander Hamilton's Secret Attempts to Control American Foreign Policy.* Princeton, N.J.: Princeton University Press, 1964. The author presents evidence that Hamilton, through his covert relations with British secret agent Major George Beckwith and British minister George Hammond, used deceit and treachery to frustrate Secretary of State Jefferson and dominate American foreign policy. The book stirred considerable controversy.

5:25 Earle, Edward Mead. "Adam Smith, Alexander Hamilton, and Friedrich List: The Economic Foundations of Military Power." In Edward M. Earle, ed., *Makers of Modern Strategy: Military Thought from Machiavelli to Hitler.* Princeton, N.J.: Princeton University Press, 1943, pp. 117–54. An analysis of Hamilton's "Report on Manufactures" shows, according to the author, that Hamilton advocated diversified economy to ensure self-sufficiency which could provide defensive military strength. Earle calls Hamilton "an American Colbert or Pitt or Bismarck."

5:26 Hamilton, Alexander. *The Papers of Alexander Hamilton.* 25 vols. Ed. by Harold C. Syrett, et al. New York: Columbia University Press, 1961–1977. The definitive edition of Hamilton's papers (1768–1804), superseding earlier editions of Hamilton's *Works* edited by Henry Cabot Lodge and J. C. Hamilton. Notes are generally economical, revealing editorial balance and great erudition.

5:27 Hendrickson, Robert. *Hamilton.* 2 vols. New York: Mason/Charter, 1976. A detailed biography highly favorable to Hamilton, but John C. Miller, *Alexander Hamilton: Portrait in Paradox* (New York: Harper, 1959), is briefer and better balanced. Forrest McDonald's *Alexander Hamilton: A Biography* (New York: Norton, 1979) is frankly partisan, but is especially good on the background of Hamilton's financial policies.

5:28 Lycan, Gilbert L. *Alexander Hamilton and American Foreign Policy: A Design for Greatness.* Norman: University of Oklahoma Press, 1970. This volume lauds Hamilton's excursions into foreign policy and denounces his critics. The tone is adulatory, but not as uncritical as that of Helene Johnson Looze, *Alexander Hamilton and the British Orientation of American Foreign Policy, 1783–1803* (The Hague: Mouton, 1969). Bibliography.

5:29 Malone, Dumas. "Discussion: Hamilton on Balance." *Proceedings of the American Philosophical Society* 102:2 (1958), 129–35. Hamilton was "a Colossus and his works remain as his enduring monument," but he is censured for his "intermeddling" in foreign affairs, especially for his intimate relations with British agents, "the least savory part of Hamilton's record as a responsible official in these early years."

5:30 Stourzh, Gerald. *Alexander Hamilton and the Idea of Representative Government.* Stanford, Calif.: Stanford University Press, 1970. The author concludes that Hamilton regarded himself as the founder of an empire. He differed from his American contemporaries in rejecting the philosophy of John Locke in favor of Hume and Hobbes and the political economy of Adam Smith. His foreign policy was directed toward the power and the glory of the state, based on an aristocratic society and a partnership with Britain.

John Jay
See Chapter 4 "Personalities" for additional references; also "Jay's Treaty," below.

5:31 Boyd, Julian P. "Two Diplomats between Revolutions: John Jay and Thomas Jefferson." *Virginia Magazine of History and Biography* 66:2 (1958), 131–46. The author documents the obstructionist tactics of John Jay, secretary for foreign affairs, in defeating the 1784 consular treaty with France and his acceptance of England's violations of the peace treaty. Jay's sharing of secrets with the British consul, Boyd says, amounted to "malfeasance in office." Jefferson meanwhile successfully negotiated a consular convention even more liberal toward France.

5:32 Jay, John. *The Correspondence and Public Papers of John Jay.* 4 vols. Ed. by Henry P. Johnston. New York: Putnam's, 1890–1893. Reprint 1968. A leading Federalist, collaborator on the Federalist Papers with Hamilton and Madison, chief justice of the United States, and governor of New York, Jay is mainly important during the Federalist era for Jay's Treaty. A new edition of Jay's writings is being edited by Richard B. Morris and Floyd Shumway (4:56).

5:33 Monaghan, Frank. *John Jay: Defender of Liberty.* Indianapolis: Bobbs-Merrill, 1935. In the only full-length biography of Jay (1745–1829), Monaghan favorably views Jay's diplomacy (1780s–1790s) as secretary of foreign affairs and minister to England. Monaghan used Jay papers not included in Johnston's collection. Samuel F. Bemis's study of Jay, in volume 1 of *The American Secretaries of State and Their Diplomacy* (2:166), is still useful. Bibliography.

Thomas Jefferson
See Chapters 4 and 6, "Personalities," for additional references.

Cappon, L. J., ed. *The Adams-Jefferson Letters* (4:42) is useful for the period both men served in Europe.

5:34 Jefferson, Thomas. *The Papers of Thomas Jefferson.* 19 vols. to date. Ed. by Julian P. Boyd, with Lyman H. Butterfield and Mina R. Bryan. Princeton, N.J.: Princeton University Press, 1950–. Only nineteen volumes of the definitive edition of Jefferson's papers have thus far appeared, taking the story to March 1791. Scholars who rely on printed materials must continue to use older editions, such as Lipscomb and Bergh (6:26) and Ford (6:27). Boyd's edition is superbly edited; noted are often models of erudition. Alexander Hamilton's manipulations are not viewed favorably.

5:35 Kaplan, Lawrence S. *Jefferson and France: An Essay on Politics and Political Ideas.* New Haven, Conn.: Yale University Press, 1967. Jefferson is presented as an ardent nationalist, yet a Francophile who wanted strong national connections with France and on occasion took questionable steps to ensure the bond. The work is well argued and based on primary sources, but at variance with recent Jefferson biographies. Bibliography.

5:36 Malone, Dumas. *Jefferson and the Rights of Man.* Vol. 2 in *Jefferson and His Time.* Boston: Little, Brown, 1951.

5:37 Malone, Dumas. *Jefferson and the Ordeal of Liberty.* Vol. 3 in *Jefferson and His Time.* Boston: Little, Brown, 1962. These two volumes of one of the most distinguished biographies in American literature carry Jefferson from the revolutionary war to his election to the presidency. Jefferson is treated respectfully but not uncritically.

5:38 Palmer, Robert R. "Dubious Democrat: Thomas Jefferson in France." *Political Science Quarterly* 72:3 (1957), 388–404. While American minister to France (1784–1789), Jefferson was frequently consulted by French reformers. Jefferson advised his French friends to direct their efforts toward the model of the British government; he did not believe that the French could "manage" much liberty.

5:39   Peterson, Merrill D. "Thomas Jefferson and Commercial Policy, 1783-1793." *William and Mary Quarterly* 3d ser. 22:4 (1965), 584–610. Jefferson's attempts in the 1780s to weaken links with Great Britain, chiefly through encouragement of trade with France, were unsuccessful. French commercial nationalism, Hamilton's orientation of American trade policy toward England, and Genet's mission combined to wreck Jefferson's commercial plan.

5:40   Woolery, William K. *The Relation of Thomas Jefferson to American Foreign Policy, 1783–1793.* Baltimore: Johns Hopkins Press, 1927. An old study, it credits Thomas Jefferson with solving the problems of American neutrality.

Rufus King

Ernst, R. *Rufus King* (6:37) is a biography of a leading Federalist and lieutenant of Alexander Hamilton.

5:41   King, Rufus. *The Life and Correspondence of Rufus King.* 6 vols. Ed. by Charles R. King. New York: Putnam's, 1894–1900. A close friend and confidant of Alexander Hamilton, King was sent as minister to Great Britain in 1796 and was so effective that Jefferson retained him at that post after 1801. His quoted correspondence (1755–1827), by far more useful than the connecting narrative, provides essential information on Anglo-American relations, as well as on the thinking of Federalist leaders.

James Madison

See Chapters 4 and 6, "Personalities," for additional references.

5:42   Brant, Irving. *James Madison.* 6 vols. Indianapolis: Bobbs-Merrill, 1941–1961. In this six-volume biography, written almost entirely from original sources, the author attempts with considerable success to revise the traditional perception of Madison as a pale reflection of Jefferson. Of interest here are the second volume, *James Madison: The Nationalist, 1780–1787* (4:61), and the third, *James Madison: Father of the Constitution, 1787–1800.* Other individual volumes are cited in Chapter 6 of the *Guide.* Brant condensed his six volumes into one, *The Fourth President* (Indianapolis: Bobbs-Merrill, 1970).

Koch, A. *Jefferson and Madison* (6:30).

Madison, James. *The Papers of James Madison* (4:62) will be the definitive edition when Hutchinson finished, but the volumes published thus far extend only to March 1789. For subsequent years one must turn to Hunt's edition (6:45).

5:43   McCoy, Drew R. "Republicanism and American Foreign Policy: James Madison and the Political Economy of Commercial Discrimination, 1789–1794." *William and Mary Quarterly* 3d ser. 31:4 (1974) 633–46. This article examines Madison's commercial discrimination against Great Britain in the context of his approach to internal American economic development. The author maintains that both flowed from Madison's republican ideology and aimed at economic independence for the United States.

John Marshall
See also "The XYZ Affair," below.

5:44   Baker, Leonard. *John Marshall: A Life in Law.* New York: Macmillan, 1974. "Book Three: Diplomat" relates the experiences of Marshall and his colleagues during the XYZ affair in Paris in 1797. Although based on manuscript collections, French sources are not among them. The author revises Beveridge's account in many particulars and is less admiring of Marshall, although his treatment is highly favorable. Bibliography.

5:45   Beveridge, Albert J. *The Life of John Marshall.* 4 vols. Boston: Houghton Mifflin, 1916–1919. Volume 2 (1789–1801) covers Marshall's part in the XYZ mission and his service as secretary of state. Bibliography. Also laudatory of Marshall is Andrew J. Montague's study of Marshall in volume 2 of *The American Secretaries of State and Their Diplomacy* (2:166).

5:46   Marshall, John. *The Papers of John Marshall.* 3 vols. to date. Chapel Hill: University of North Carolina Press, 1974–. A major portion of volume 3 (1796–1798) concerns Marshall's mission to France and the XYZ affair; diplomatic editor William C. Stinchcombe's inclusion of Marshall's Paris journal makes this a superb contribution.

James Monroe
5:47   Ammon, Harry. *James Monroe: The Quest for National Identity.* New York: McGraw-Hill, 1971. Monroe is depicted as very political in his judgments,

shrewd, and sensitive to criticism. His missions to France and England are treated with maturity and balance. This biography, now the definitive one, is based upon manuscript collections, which are on microfilm. Extensive bibliography.

5:48 Bond, Beverly W., Jr. "The Monroe Mission to France, 1794–1796." *Johns Hopkins University Studies in Historical and Political Science* 25:2–3 (1907), 9–103. This old study, long a standard, is seriously dated. Of Monroe, Bond concludes: "His mistakes are to be ascribed rather to lack of judgment than to any intention of wrongdoing."

5:49 Brown, Stuart G., ed. *The Autobiography of James Monroe.* Syracuse, N.Y.: Syracuse University Press, 1959. An introduction and notes are supplied by the editor to long fragments of this unfinished autobiography. Written between 1827 and 1830, they reflect a faulty memory and the mellowing of old age. Monroe deals with his missions to France, 1794–1797 and 1803; the account ends with his mission to Britain in 1806.

5:50 Monroe, James. *The Writings of James Monroe.* 7 vols. Ed. by Stanislaus M. Hamilton. New York: Putnam's, 1898–1903. Because Monroe was not as fecund a writer as Madison and, especially, Jefferson, Hamilton chose to omit a large proportion of his correspondence and public papers. In addition to being incomplete, the work is sometimes inaccurate, in part because of Hamilton's misreading of what must be almost the most difficult handwriting of any early American statesman.

Gouverneur Morris

5:51 Davenport, Beatrix Cary, ed. *A Diary of the French Revolution, by Gouverneur Morris.* 2 vols. Boston: Houghton Mifflin, 1939. Less inhibited than the edition of Morris's granddaughter, Anne Cary Morris, *The Diary and Letters of Gouverneur Morris,* 2 vols. (New York, 1888), this is Morris's account of his European wanderings from the beginning of the French Revolution through his first eight months as minister to France, to January 1793.

5:52 Mintz, Max M. *Gouverneur Morris and the American Revolution.* Norman: University of Oklahoma Press, 1970. This sound, but brief and somewhat episodic biography, is more reliable than Howard Swiggett's *The Extraordinary Mr. Morris* (Garden City, N.Y.: Doubleday, 1952). Extensive bibliography.

William Vans Murray

See also "The Convention of 1800," below.

5:53 Ford, Worthington C., ed. "Letters of William Vans Murray to John Quincy Adams, 1797–1803." In the Annual Report of the American Historical Association for the Year 1912. Washington, D.C.: G.P.O., 1913, pp. 341–715. Letters are drawn from the Adams Papers, Pickering Papers, and Murray Papers in the Pennsylvania Historical Society, the Morgan Library in New York, Library of Congress, as well as Murray's official dispatches in the Department of State. They are helpful in understanding Murray's role as peacemaker following the XYZ affair.

5:54 Hill, Peter P. *William Vans Murray, Federalist Diplomat: The Shaping of Peace with France, 1797–1801.* Syracuse, N.Y.: Syracuse University Press, 1971. Murray, a Federalist congressman from Maryland, was appointed U.S. minister to the Batavian Republic (Netherlands) in 1797. Although the author focuses principally on Murray's role in ending the Franco-American quasi-war, Murray's mission found him reporting the frequent upheavals in Dutch revolutionary politics and the problems of Dutch-American commerce. Bibliography.

Timothy Pickering

5:55 Clarfield, Gerald H. *Timothy Pickering and American Diplomacy, 1795–1800.* Columbia: University of Missouri Press, 1969. Secretary of State Pickering's hatred of the French Revolution is depicted, as is his preference by 1798 for an Anglo-American military alliance. The author somewhat modifies the harsh views of Pickering in most recent scholarship. Still useful is Edward H. Phillips, "The Public Career of Timothy Pickering, Federalist, 1745–1802" (Ph.D. diss., Harvard University, 1950).

5:56 Pickering, Octavius, and Upham, Charles, eds. *The Life of Timothy Pickering.* 4 vols. Boston: Little, Brown, 1867–1873. The correspondence of Timothy Pickering (1745–1829), with particular attention to his career as secretary of state and later as U.S. senator.

Thomas Pinckney

See also "Pinckney's Treaty, 1795," below.

5:57 Bemis, Samuel Flagg. "The London Mission of Thomas Pinckney, 1792–1796." *American Historical Review* 28:2 (1923), 228–47. Pinckney's mission to London was unimportant and overshadowed by his negotiation of the treaty of 1795 with Spain which bears his name. He was the first U.S. minister received by the British government and resigned after President Washington's special envoy, John Jay, concluded the Jay Treaty.

5:58 Cross, Jack L. *London Mission: The First Critical Years.* East Lansing: Michigan State University Press, 1968. The author finds more accomplishments in Pinckney's mission (1794–1796) than does Bemis. Pinckney "swallowed his injured pride" and aided John Jay; also, he is credited with securing the repeal of the obnoxious order of November 8, 1793, barring American trade with the West Indies. The argument is not altogether convincing. Bibliography.

Edmund Randolph

5:59 Brant, Irving. "Edmund Randolph, Not Guilty!" *William and Mary Quarterly* 3d ser. 7:2 (1950), 179–98. This is a definitive exoneration of the secretary of state (1794–1795), whom the author shows to have been the victim of his cabinet colleagues, Pickering and Wolcott, and of the intermeddling of the British government.

5:60 Conway, Moncure D. *Omitted Chapters of History Disclosed in the Life and Letters of Edmund Randolph.* New York: Putnam's, 1888. Reprint 1971. A very sympathetic biography, it fails, however, to present adequately Randolph's case concerning the Fauchet dispatches.

5:61 Randolph, Edmund. *A Vindication of Mr. Randolph's Resignation.* Philadelphia: Samuel H. Smith, 1795. Randolph's famous "vindication" failed to achieve its purpose: his explanation of the Fauchet dispatches satisfied almost no one, friend or enemy, and his bitter attack on President Washington injured only himself.

5:62 Reardon, John J. *Edmund Randolph: A Biography.* New York: Macmillan, 1974. In this solid biography sympathetic to Randolph (1753–1813), the author agrees with the judgment of James Madison: "His best friend can't save him from the self-condemnation of his political career, as explained by himself." Extensive bibliography.

William Short

5:63 Boyce, Myrna. "The Diplomatic Career of William Short." *Journal of Modern History* 15:2 (1943), 97–119. This concise sketch examines all major aspects of Short's diplomatic career (1786–

1798). Most fully treated are Short's functions as legation secretary to Jefferson and later as chargé d'affaires in Paris.

5:64 Shackelford, George G. "William Short: Diplomat in Revolutionary France, 1785–93." *Proceedings of the American Philosophical Society* 102:6 (1958), 596–612. Short served in France as chargé d'affaires (1785–1789) and became minister at The Hague when Gouverneur Morris arrived as minister to France. The author suggests that Short might have averted later French-American contentions if he had been minister at Paris.

George Washington

See Chapter 4, "Personalities," for additional references.

Flexner, J. T. *George Washington* (4:65) is a gracefully written interpretive biography; volumes 3 and 4 have the same time divisions as Freeman's biography, volumes 6 and 7.

5:65 Freeman, Douglas S. *George Washington: A Biography.* 7 vols. New York: Scribner's, 1948–1957. This magisterial biography contains every known fact concerning Washington (1732–1799). Volume 6, *Patriot and President* (1954), traces Washington's career from the Peace of 1783 to the end of his first term as president; volume 7, *First in Peace* (1957), was written from Freeman's voluminous notes by John A. Carroll and Mary W. Ashworth. The book is long on detail and short on interpretation, an indispensable resource. Extensive bibliography.

5:66 McDonald, Forrest. *The Presidency of George Washington.* Lawrence: University Press of Kansas, 1974. In this imaginative, provocative tour de force, the author confronts the "Washington myth" and concludes that the first president (1789–1797) was "indispensable, but only for what he was, not for what he did." Bibliography.

James Wilkinson

See also John Brown, above.

5:67 Hay, Thomas R. "Some Reflections on the Career of General James Wilkinson." *Mississippi Valley Historical Review* 21:4 (1935), 471–94. Hay suggests that Wilkinson found no incongruity between self-interest and national interest, that he was an expansionist ahead of his time. The author points out that the general deceived Spanish officials as readily as he did Americans.

5:68 Jacobs, James R. *Tarnished Warrior: Major-General James Wilkinson*. New York: Macmillan, 1938. Jacobs portrays Wilkinson (1757–1825) not unsympathetically as a frontier extrovert who unquestionably gave major impetus to Kentucky's separatist intrigues with Spain in the late 1780s and early 1790s. Although this study is more narrative than analytical, readers will find it adequately documented. Bibliography.

Others

Bemis, S. F., ed. *The American Secretaries of State and Their Diplomacy* (2:166) includes in volume 1 sketches of the secretaries who served under the Confederation, Robert R. Livingston and John Jay; volume 2 treats the secretaries of the Federalist era, Thomas Jefferson, Edmund Randolph, Timothy Pickering, and John Marshall.

5:69 Bernhard, Winfred E. A. *Fisher Ames: Federalist and Statesman, 1758–1808*. Chapel Hill: University of North Carolina Press, 1965. A devoted guardian of New England mercantile interests, and one of the most extreme of the Massachusetts High Federalists, Ames was a sour, vituperative partisan who detested democracy. The standard printed source is Seth Ames, ed., *Works of Fisher Ames*, 2 vols. (Boston: Little, Brown, 1854; reprint 1969). Bibliography.

5:70 Cox, Joseph W. *Champion of Southern Federalism: Robert Goodloe Harper of South Carolina*. Port Washington, N.Y.: Kennikat, 1972. Harper was a leading southern Federalist and Hamilton lieutenant in the House of Representatives.

Dangerfield, G. *Chancellor Robert R. Livingston of New York, 1746–1813* (4:73) is a widely acclaimed biography of the first foreign minister of the United States (under the Confederation Congress) and minister to France under President Jefferson.

5:71 Gibbs, George. *Memoirs of the Administrations of Washington and John Adams, Edited from the Papers of Oliver Wolcott, Secretary of the Treasury*. 2 vols. New York: Printed for the Subscribers, 1846. These volumes contain a wealth of correspondence (1789–1801) of Oliver Wolcott with numerous Federalist leaders. With a highly partisan narrative connecting the documents, the work furnishes a detailed view of the thinking of the Federalists, particularly the Hamiltonian wing.

5:72 Jameson, J. Franklin, ed. "Letters of Stephen Higginson, 1783–1804." In the Annual Report of the American Historical Association for the Year 1896. Washington, D.C.: G.P.O., 1897, vol. 7, pp. 704–841. Higginson was a leader of the New England Federalists who desperately wanted war with France in 1798. He represented the Anglophile Boston merchant elite.

5:73 Lodge, Henry Cabot. *The Life and Letters of George Cabot*. Boston: Little, Brown, 1877. This is a biography of a leading New England Federalist (1751–1801), perhaps the most highly respected of the New England merchant princes. The volume is valuable for Cabot's letters.

5:74 Morison, Samuel Eliot. *The Life and Letters of Harrison Gray Otis, Federalist, 1765–1848*. 2 vols. Boston: Houghton Mifflin, 1913. A leading Massachusetts Federalist of the second generation, Otis was generally more moderate than most of his elders. Morison adopts a generally sympathetic but not uncritical attitude toward his ancestor; his narrative and extensive selections from Otis's correspondence are presented separately.

5:75 Robinson, Blackwell P. *William R. Davie*. Chapel Hill: University of North Carolina Press, 1957. A prominent North Carolina Federalist, Davie, together with Oliver Ellsworth and William Vans Murray, followed the XYZ mission and concluded the Treaty of Mortfontaine. Robinson's analysis of the mission, although based on manuscript sources, adds little information or insight. Davie's role in the negotiation remains unclear. Bibliography.

5:76 Rogers, George C. *Evolution of a Federalist: William Loughton Smith of Charleston (1758–1812)*. Columbia: University of South Carolina Press, 1962. For loyally supporting Hamiltonian causes during his congressional career, Smith was appointed minister to Lisbon in 1797. Chapter 13 describes his four years as ringside observer of the XYZ affair, the advent of Bonaparte, and the Ellsworth mission; Smith also figured peripherally in U.S. diplomacy with the Barbary powers. Bibliography.

5:77 Steiner, Bernard C., ed. *The Life and Correspondence of James McHenry: Secretary of War under Washington and Adams*. Cleveland: Burrows, 1907. Despite a sympathetic editor, the contemporary and historical judgment concerning McHenry's incompetence is amply illustrated. Alexander Hamilton's most slavish follower, McHenry was eventually dismissed by President Adams for disloyalty. Bibliography.

5:78 Tolles, Frederick B. *George Logan of Philadelphia*. New York: Oxford University Press, 1953. Tolles follows Quaker physician Logan on his self-appointed peace mission to France following the XYZ affair. No evidence is presented that Logan's actions in any way influenced the French government, though Logan's intervention led to passage of the Logan Act.

5:79 Welch, Richard E., Jr. *Theodore Sedwick, Federalist: A Political Portrait*. Middletown, Conn.: Wesleyan University Press, 1965. Sedwick was an important Massachusetts Federalist (1746–1813), a member of the Hamiltonian wing. Bibliography.

5:80 Zahniser, Marvin R. *Charles Cotesworth Pinckney, Founding Father*. Chapel Hill: University of North Carolina Press, 1967. Pinckney, minister to France succeeding Monroe, was originally sympathetic to the French Revolution, but his experiences as minister and XYZ commissioner embittered him toward France and the Revolution. He used his powerful family and state connections to ensure South Carolina's support of the Adams administration in the quasi-war. Bibliography.

FRENCH

Napoleon Bonaparte

See Chapter 6, "Personalities," for additional references.

5:81 Bonaparte, Napoleon. *Correspondance de Napoléon Ier publiée par ordre de l'empéreur Napoléon III* [Correspondence of Napoleon I published by order of the emperor Napoleon III]. 32 vols. Paris: Plon, 1858–1870. Provides very useful table of contents ("Table des Pièces") which lists all items by number, gives the date on all documents, indicates for whom the item is intended, and gives a brief summary of contents.

5:82 Cronin, Vincent. *Napoleon Bonaparte: An Intimate Biography*. New York: Morrow, 1972. The collapse of the Directory allowed Bonaparte's 1799 accession to power, and he negotiated the Convention of 1800. Biographies of Napoleon, however, rarely mention the United States and this one is no exception. Another authoritative biography is André Castelot, *Napoleon,* trans. by Guy Daniels (New York: Harper & Row, 1971). Bibliography.

Edmond Charles Genêt

See also "The Genêt Mission, 1793–1794," below.

5:83 Didier, L. "Le Citoyen Genêt [Citizen Genêt]." *Revue des Questions Historiques* 92 (1912), 62–90; 93 (1913), 5–25, 423–49. This old essay by a French historian is still useful. The author states that Genêt's plan was to involve the United States in the European war, but his plans to invade Canada, Louisiana, and the Floridas all miscarried through his ignorance and incompetence.

5:84 Minnigerode, Meade. *Jefferson: Friend of France, 1793*. New York: Putnam's, 1928. The title is ironic: the book is a biography of Genêt, with emphasis on his 1793 mission. Written from Genêt's private papers, Jefferson is portrayed as the principal author of "a tale of perfidy" directed against Genêt. It provides virtually the only defense of Genêt's conduct.

Comte d'Hauterive

5:85 Childs, Frances S. "The Hauterive Journal." *New York Historical Society Quarterly* 33:2 (1949), 69–86. Comte d'Hauterive, later a confidant of Talleyrand, was very critical of Genêt's grandiose schemes. A genuine friend of America, he included in his journal (1793–1794) sage advice to Americans.

5:86 Childs, Frances S. "A Secret Agent's Advice on America, 1797." In Edward M. Earle, ed., *Nationalism and Internationalism*. New York: Columbia University Press, 1950, pp. 18–44. The secret agent was Hauterive, French consul at New York. His dispatches warned of a Federalist intent to form an alliance with England and counseled measures that the Directory should take to prevent this alliance.

Louis-Guillaume Otto

5:87 Chinard, Gilbert, ed. "Considérations sur la conduite du gouvernement des États Unis envers la France, depuis 1789 jusqu'en 1797, par Louis-Guillaume Otto" [Considerations of the conduct of the government of the United States toward France, 1789 to 1797, by Louis-Guillaume Otto]. *Bulletin de l'Institut Français de Washington,* no. 16 (1943). Otto criticized successive French ministers for sending misleading reports to France of American affairs. He analyzed American political parties and concluded with a plea for mutually beneficial relations, commercial and political, between the two nations.

5:88 O'Dwyer, Margaret M., ed. "A French Diplomat's View of Congress, 1790." *William and Mary Quarterly* 3d ser. 21:3 (1964), 408–44. These lengthy and perceptive dispatches from Louis-Guillaume Otto, French chargé d'affaires at New York (1785–1791), reviewed the debates and actions of the second session of the First Congress. They were dated from January 12 to August 12, 1790, when Congress adjourned.

Prince Talleyrand

5:89 Huth, Hans, and Pugh, Wilma J., trans. and eds. "Talleyrand in America as a Financial Promoter, 1794-96." In the Annual Report of the American Historical Association for the Year 1941. Washington, D.C.: G.P.O., 1942, vol. 2, pp. 1–181. This collection includes previously unpublished letters and memoirs of Talleyrand in America and contains, for the most part, correspondence with various land speculators.

5:90 Orieux, Jean. *Talleyrand: The Art of Survival.* Trans. by Patricia Wolf. New York: Knopf, 1974. The most recent biography of Talleyrand, which like all the others gives scant space to American affairs. Extensive bibliography. The most complete biography is Georges Lacour-Gayet, *Talleyrand,* 4 vols. (Paris: Payot, 1928–1934), which has not yet been translated. Others in English include Crane Brinton, *The Lives of Talleyrand* (New York: Norton, 1936); Duff Cooper, *Talleyrand* (London, 1932); and J. F. Bernard, *Talleyrand: A Biography* (New York: Putnam's, 1973).

5:91 Pallain, Georges, ed. *Le Ministère de Talleyrand sous le Directoire* [The ministry of Talleyrand under the Directory]. Paris: Plon, Nourrit, 1891. The editor provides an introduction to selections of Talleyrand's correspondence as foreign minister (1797–1799). Talleyrand's reports consistently urged reconciliation with the United States.

5:92 Stinchcombe, William C., ed. "A Neglected Memoir by Talleyrand on French-American Relations, 1793–1797." *Proceedings of the American Philosophical Society* 121:3 (1977), 195–208. A translation of a long overlooked memoir by Talleyrand of October 1797, it was intended to formulate the French position for negotiations with American commission-

ers John Marshall, Charles Cotesworth Pinckney, and Elbridge Gerry in 1797. Because of the vindictive attitude of the Directory toward the United States, however, it had little impact.

Others

5:93 Alméras, Henri d'. *Barras et son temps: Scènes et portraits* [Barras and his time: scenes and portraits]. Paris: Michel, 1930. Paul François Barras, member of the Executive Directory, is pictured far more interestingly in his own *Memoirs of Barras, Member of the Directorate,* ed. by Georges Duruy, trans. by C. E. Roche, 4 vols. (New York: Harper, 1895–1896).

5:94 Dupre, Huntley. *Lazare Carnot: Republican Patriot.* Oxford, Ohio: Mississippi Valley Press, 1940. Carnot, "organizer of victory," was elected to the Executive Directory but lost out in events surrounding 18th Fructidor. Carnot's interests were not directed toward the United States, but this scholarly, well-crafted biography reconstructs events during the early months of the Directory. Bibliography.

5:95 Fauchet, Joseph. "Mémoire sur les États-Unis d'Amérique par Joseph Fauchet" [Memoir concerning the United States of America by Joseph Fauchet]. Ed. by Carl L. Lokke. In the Annual Report of the American Historical Association for the Year 1936. Washington, D.C.: G.P.O., 1938, vol. 1, pp. 83–123. Fauchet succeeded Genet as minister to America, serving from February 1794 to June 1795. In the second part of this memoir, he recounts his extensive efforts to defeat the Jay Treaty and states that the purpose of the Jay Treaty may be frustrated if France plays a skillful political game in America. See also James (5:112).

5:96 Gottschalk, Louis R. *Lafayette between the American and the French Revolutions.* Chicago: University of Chicago Press, 1950. Gottschalk argues that American men and ideas had significance for French revolutionary developments. This volume (1781–1789) is particularly useful in explaining French-American commercial problems, and the commercial policy of Vergennes. Gottschalk's multivolume work on Lafayette is the most satisfying account available. Extensive bibliography.

5:97 Revellière-Lépeaux. *Mémoires de Revellière-Lépaux, membre du Directoire de la République* [Memoirs of Revellière-Lépeaux, member of the Directory of the Republic]. 3 vols. Paris: Plon, Nourrit,

Guide to American Foreign Relations since 1700

1895. A director from November 1795 to 1799, Revellière-Lépeaux was the high priest of the Theophilanthropists. This set contains an interesting memoir, written in late December 1798 by M. Rozier, the French consul-general at New York City, analyzing French-American relations.

BRITISH

Edmund Burke

See Chapters 3 and 4, "Personalities," for additional references.

5:98 Cone, Carl B. *The Age of the French Revolution*. Vol. 2 in *Burke and the Nature of Politics*. Lexington: University of Kentucky Press, 1964. Volume 1 of this two-volume work is entitled *The Age of the American Revolution*. For comment on both see (4:83).

Robert Liston

5:99 Kyte, George W. "Robert Liston and Anglo-American Cooperation, 1796–1800." *Proceedings of the American Philosophical Society* 93:3 (1949), 259–66. The author credits Liston with the high degree of Anglo-American cooperation, but "the temporary Anglo-American accord of 1796–1800" deteriorated because of the British government's refusal to change its policies toward neutrals, President Adams's successful policy with France, and Liston's succession by less able ministers.

5:100 Wright, Esmond. "Robert Liston, Second British Minister to the United States." *History Today* 11:2 (1961), 118–27. Liston was "a model diplomat of the old school," who returned to England at the end of 1800 with Anglo-American relations much more cordial than they had been on his arrival five years before.

Others
5:101 Great Britain. Historical Manuscripts Commission. *The Manuscripts of J. B. Fortescue, Esq., Preserved at Dropmore*. 10 vols. London: H.M.S.O., 1892–1927. This valuable collection also contains the papers of William Wyndham, Lord Grenville, who was British foreign secretary from 1791 to 1804. Volumes 1–5 cover the years 1782 to 1800.

5:102 Menk, Patricia Holbert, ed. "D. M. Erskine: Letters from America, 1798–1799." *William and Mary Quarterly* 3d ser. 6:2 (1949), 251–84. The young Erskine had been sent to America by his father.

His letters contain some shrewd comments about Americans and their generally hostile attitudes toward England. Erskine returned to the United States as British minister in 1806.

5:103 Neel, Joanne Loewe. *Phineas Bond: A Study in Anglo-American Relations, 1786–1812*. Philadelphia: University of Pennsylvania Press, 1968. Bond was a Loyalist who fled to England during the American Revolution and returned as British consul at New York (1786–1812). Always devoted to the British empire, he disliked the United States and was fearful of its growing power. Bibliography.

OTHER FOREIGN PERSONALITIES

5:104 Burson, Caroline M. *The Stewardship of Don Estéban Miro, 1782–1792: A Study of Louisiana Based Largely on the Documents in New Orleans*. New Orleans: American Printing, 1940. Although this work treats internal developments, the diplomatic historian may profit from the author's analysis of the governor's efforts to befriend the southwest tribes as a barrier to American encroachment, and from the account of Miro's colonization efforts, principally at New Madrid, and his dealings with Wilkinson and Gardoqui. Bibliography.

5:105 Chastenet, Jacques. *Godoy, Master of Spain*. Trans. by J. F. Huntington. Port Washington, N.Y.: Kennikat (1953), 1972. Manuel de Godoy, Spanish premier (1792–1798, 1801–1808) is portrayed as a well-meaning, occasionally skillful statesman. Although Chastenet dwells too much on court intrigue, this work accurately explains the fluctuating relations between Spain and France which, in turn, help to explain U.S. relations with both powers. The Kennikat reprint lacks footnotes and bibliography.

5:106 Holmes, Jack D. L. *Gayoso: The Life of a Spanish Governor in the Mississippi Valley, 1789–1799*. Baton Rouge: Louisiana State University Press, 1965. This biography of the first Spanish governor of the Natchez District complements any study of relations between Philadelphia and Madrid during the Federalist era. Gayoso negotiated the Indian treaties of Natchez (1792) and Nogales (1793), and ably provided for the defense of the Lower Mississippi. Extensive bibliography.

America and Europe, 1783–1801

FRANCE

See "Personalities" for additional references, especially Thomas Jefferson, James Monroe, Gouverneur Morris, Timothy Pickering, William Short and, under "Others," Robert Livingston; also "Document Collections," especially Gebhardt (5:8) and Turner (5:11); also "Bibliographies," especially Stewart (5:6).

5:107 Childs, Frances S. *French Refugee Life in America, 1790–1800*. Baltimore: Johns Hopkins Press, 1940. The book deals with French refugees who fled the French West Indies, Saint-Domingue (Santo Domingo) in particular, during the revolutionary upheavals there. Mostly destitute and torn by factional disputes, they were a constant source of trouble to successive French ministers and American authorities. Bibliography.

Echeverria, D. *Mirage in the West: A History of the French Image of American Society to 1815* (4:120) finds that events of the 1790s mark the beginning of an unfavorable view of things American.

5:108 Jones, Howard M. *America and French Culture, 1750–1848*. Chapel Hill: University of North Carolina Press, 1926. Jones presents detailed information on how French culture impacted American society and concludes that religious and other differences hindered the acceptance of French culture in America. Bibliography.

Impact of French Revolution

Faÿ, B. *The Revolutionary Spirit in France and America* (4:121).

Godechot, J. *France and the Atlantic Revolution... , 1770–1799* (4:122) offers a view similar to Palmer (4:32).

5:109 Lefebvre, Georges. *The French Revolution from Its Origins to 1793*. Trans. by Elizabeth Moss Evanson. New York: Columbia University Press, 1962. Lefebvre's works are indispensable guides to the social and political setting of the French Revolution. This work, together with his *The French Revolution from 1793 to 1799* (New York, 1964), *The Thermidorians* (London, 1964), and *The Directory* (London, 1965), present both overview and synthesis. Lefebvre's *Napoleon* (6:86 and 6:87) is also strong on synthesis and interpretation. Bibliographies.

Palmer, R. R. *The Age of the Democratic Revolution... , 1760–1790* (4:32) advances the thesis that the histories of Europe and America during this "age of the democratic revolution" are inseparable.

5:110 Sorel, Albert. *L'Europe et la Révolution française* [Europe and the French Revolution]. 2 vols. Paris: Plon, Nourrit, 1887–1908. This classic work on international aspects of the French Revolution supports the standard view that the great interests of states generally take precedence over ideological considerations.

Revolutionary France's Foreign Policy

See "Personalities," especially Frenchmen Paul F. Barras, Lazare Carnot, Revellière-Lépeaux (under "Others"), and Prince Talleyrand.

5:111 Guyot, Raymond. *Le Directoire et la Paix de l'Europe: Des Traités de Bâle à la deuxième coalition (1795–1799)* [The Directory and the Peace of Europe: from the treaties of Basel to the second coalition]. Paris: Librairie Felix Alcan, 1912. This is an exhaustive, indispensable study of the Directory's foreign policies. It devotes much more attention than is usual in French works to relations with the United States. Bibliography.

5:112 James, James A. "French Opinion as a Factor in Preventing War between France and the United States, 1795–1800." *American Historical Review* 30:1 (1924), 44–55. James recounts the peace representations with America by Louis-Guillaume Otto, Létombe, Victor DuPont, French businessmen, and others. Talleyrand's peace overtures were based on careful policy calculations, primarily to prevent a U.S.-British alliance that might seize Spanish Florida and Louisiana.

5:113 Lyon, E. Wilson. "The Directory and the United States." *American Historical Review* 43:3

(1938), 514–32. Long a standard work on Franco-American relations under the Directory (1795–1799), this article has been superseded by DeConde, *Entangling Alliance* (5:158) and *The Quasi-War* (5:206), and by Bowman, *The Struggle for Neutrality* (5:156).

5:114 Masson, Frédéric. *Le Département des Affaires Entrangères pendant la Révolution, 1787–1804* [The Department of Foreign Affairs during the Revolution, 1787–1804]. Paris: Plon, 1877. This volume is useful in following the twists in French foreign policy during the Revolution. Masson identifies no less than fifteen foreign ministers during the period, counting Talleyrand twice.

5:115 Rain, Pierre. *La Diplomatie française d'Henri IV à Vergennes* [French diplomacy from Henry IV to Vergennes]. Paris: Plon, 1945. In this volume, and in his *La Diplomatie française: De Mirabeau à Bonaparte* (Paris, 1950), Rain traces the Revolution's move away from pacifism to an assertiveness based upon the doctrines of natural frontiers, the liberation of oppressed peoples, and self-determination.

America and the Revolution

5:116 Appleby, Joyce. "America as a Model for the Radical French Reformers of 1789." *William and Mary Quarterly* 3d ser. 28:2 (1971), 267–86. Here is a discussion of the debate among French reformers over the relative merits of the American and British political systems as models for France.

5:117 Banning, Lance. "Jeffersonian Ideology and the French Revolution: A Question of Liberticide at Home." *Studies in Burke and His Time* 17:1 (1976), 5–26. Following intellectual and psychological interpretations of the revolutionary era advanced by Bernard Bailyn, Gordon S. Wood, and others, the author explains what he calls the emotional response in America to the French Revolution and the European war.

Goodwin, A., ed. *The American and French Revolutions, 1763–93*. Vol. 8 in *The New Cambridge Modern History* (4:28).

5:118 Hazen, Charles D. *Contemporary American Opinion of the French Revolution*. Baltimore: Johns Hopkins Press, 1897. This work is divided into two sections: the opinions of Americans abroad, primarily those of Gouverneur Morris, Monroe, and Jefferson;

and the opinions of Americans at home. An excellent analysis of an unfavorable American reaction setting in as atheism and terrorism marked the French Revolution.

5:119 James, James A. "French Diplomacy and American Politics, 1794–1795." In the Annual Report of the American Historical Association for the Year 1911. Washington, D.C.: G.P.O., 1913, vol. 1, pp.156–63. This article analyzes Joseph Fauchet's mission to the United States and concludes that the mission was a failure but that Fauchet's policies, and his successor Adet's, were "among the influences contributing to the triumph of the Republican Party."

Ketcham, R. L. "France and American Politics, 1763–1793" (4:39) finds many American leaders seeing France only as a counterweight to England after the Revolution.

5:120 Sears, Louis M. *George Washington and the French Revolution*. Detroit: Wayne State University Press, 1960. Sears includes most of the correspondence Washington received from American or French witnesses of the French Revolution together with Washington's replies. Washington is portrayed as enlightened and judicious on the issues. More sophisticated and balanced judgments are found in Freeman's final volume (5:65).

The Haitian Revolution, 1789–1804

See Chapter 6, "The Louisiana Purchase," for additional references.

5:121 Logan, Rayford W. *The Diplomatic Relations of the United States with Haiti, 1776–1891*. Chapel Hill: University of North Carolina Press, 1941. The first three chapters offer the most comprehensive treatment to date of U.S. relations with Haiti in the late 18th century. Logan includes the text of the Maitland Convention, but overlooks the formal role of American diplomacy in the Anglo-American-Haitian commercial arrangement. Extensive bibliography.

5:122 Ott, Thomas O. *The Haitian Revolution, 1789–1804*. Knoxville: University of Tennessee Press, 1973. Toussaint L'Ouverture, through the upheavals caused by the French Revolution, international war and domestic rebellion, and occupation by the British, vanquished all his rivals and enemies save one: Napoleon Bonaparte.

5:123 Tansill, Charles C. *The United States and Santo Domingo, 1798–1873: A Chapter in Caribbean Diplomacy.* Baltimore: Johns Hopkins Press, 1938. Tansill still offers the most detailed account of the British (Maitland) mission to Haiti in 1797–1798. This study is superseded by Rayford Logan's broader treatment and by Bradford Perkins's investigation of American diplomacy in British dealings with Toussaint.

Commerce

Godechot, J. "Les Relations économiques entre la France et les États-Unis de 1778 à 1789" (4:145).

5:124 Nussbaum, Frederick L. "American Tobacco and French Politics, 1783–1789." *Political Science Quarterly* 40:4 (1925), 497–516. The French Tobacco Farm's determination to control the importation of American tobacco, attempted in collusion with Robert Morris, assisted in preventing growth of a postwar French-American trade.

5:125 Nussbaum, Frederick L. *Commercial Policy in the French Revolution: A Study in the Career of G. J. A. Ducher.* Washington, D.C.: American Historical Association, 1923. Nussbaum explores the career of Ducher, who played a key part in developing exclusionist commercial legislation, and shows the differing commercial policies favored by French parties. A pioneering study of continuing value.

5:126 Nussbaum, Frederick L. "The French Colonial Arrêt of 1784." *South Atlantic Quarterly* 27:1 (1928), 62–78. Monarchial government tried to recast colonial mercantile regulations in order to attract American trade to the West Indies. Protests by French merchants, led by those in Bordeaux, and continued American evasions of the more generous French measures made it difficult to normalize trading relations between America and France.

Price, J. M. *France and the Chesapeake: A History of the French Tobacco Monopoly 1694–1791* . . . (3:120) analyzes the struggles within France and America to gain a share of this lucrative trade, and the temporary abandonment of the monopoly following the French Revolution.

5:127 Sée, Henri "Commerce between France and the United States, 1783–1784."*American Historical Review* 31:4 (1926), 732–52. Letters and documents of the Chamber of Commerce of Nantes demonstrate that French officials and businessmen were aware of the opportunities and difficulties in establishing a sizable trade with America.

5:128 Stover, John F. "French-American Trade during the Confederation, 1781–1789." *North Carolina Historical Review* 35:4 (1958), 399–414. French-American commerce failed to reach its potential as direct trade favored America by a ratio of approximately five to one. From 1784 to 1790, French exports to the United States totaled under one-twentieth the exports of Great Britain to the United States. See the earlier work of Edmund Buron, "Statistics on Franco-American Trade, 1788–1806," *Journal of Economic and Business History* 4 (1931–1932), 571–80.

Tarrade, J. *Le Commerce colonial de la France à la fin de l' Ancien Régime . . . de 1763 à 1789* (4:151).

5:129 Toussaint, Auguste. "Early American Trade with Mauritius, 1778–1811."*Essex Institute Historical Collection* 87:4 (1951), 373–87. Written by the archivist of the island of Mauritius, this article not only examines the considerable American trade with the Ile de France, but also explains certain deviations from mercantilist policy which France permitted to American shipmasters. The author finds, for example, that American commerce with Mauritius was little affected by the Franco-American quasi-war.

GREAT BRITAIN

See "Personalities," especially Rufus King, Robert Liston, and James Monroe; also see "Jay's Treaty, 1794," below.

Burt, A. L. *The United States, Great Britain, and British North America from the Revolution to the Establishment of Peace after the War of 1812* (6:5) revises some traditional interpretations, for example, that the United States could not have gained better terms in the Jay Treaty, regardless of Hamilton's indiscretions.

Clark, D. M. "British Opinion of Franco-American Relations, 1775–1795" (4:132) describes British officials as "legalistic and conservative" and suggests that British merchants and press favored moderate treatment of Americans.

Graham, G. S. *Sea Power and British North America, 1783–1820* (6:109).

Perkins, B. *The First Rapprochement... , 1795–1805* (6:10) argues that the Jay Treaty (1794) ushered in a decade of improved Anglo-American relations.

5:130 Ritcheson, Charles R. *Aftermath of Revolution: British Policy toward the United States 1783–1795.* Dallas: Southern Methodist University Press, 1969. Reprint 1971. This important study forcefully presents the case for Great Britain's American policy. The view is from Whitehall. Extensive bibliography.

Ward, A. W., and Gooch, G. P., eds. *The Cambridge History of British Foreign Policy* (6:82) is dated but still useful; the first two chapters of volume 1 view relations with the United States in the context of British foreign policy. The Jay Treaty of 1794, for example, is described as "something of a triumph for British foreign policy."

Wright, J. L., Jr. *Britain and the American Frontier, 1783–1815* (5:182).

Commerce

5:131 Churchward, Lloyd G. "Rhode Island and the Australian Trade, 1792–1812." *Rhode Island History* 7:4 (1948), 97–104. Australian customs documents reveal a moderately active trade pattern that grew out of the more important U.S. commerce with Canton.

5:132 Furber, Holden. "The Beginnings of American Trade with India, 1784–1812." *New England Quarterly* 11:2 (1938), 235–65. Prior to 1792–1793, U.S. trade with such ports as Madras, Calcutta, and Bombay appeared to be merely ancillary to the China trade. The loose wording and lax enforcement of article 13 of Jay's Treaty gave Americans greater access to Indian markets than the company would otherwise have permitted.

5:133 Levi, Werner. "The Earliest Relations between the United States of America and Australia." *Pacific Historical Review* 12:4 (1943), 351–61. Levi explains that prevailing winds made Australia a con-

venient port of call for Canton-bound American merchantmen, touching at New South Wales (1792–1812) shortly after the first colonists were settled there.

5:134 Price, Jacob, M. "New Time Series for Scotland's and Britain's Trade with the Thirteen Colonies and States, 1740–1791." *William and Mary Quarterly* 3d ser. 32:2 (1975), 307–25. Anglo-American trade statistics for the period previously have not included Scotland. New Scottish figures revise the totals to some degree.

5:135 Toth, Charles W. "Anglo-American Trade and the British West Indies (1783–1789)."*Americas* 32:3 (1976), 418–36. American leaders in the peace negotiations, and consistently thereafter, sought commerce access to the British West Indies. Little was achieved until after the outbreak of war in Europe in 1793.

SPAIN

For efforts to involve the United States in revolutionary movements in Spanish America, see Robertson (7:64) and Smelser (7:76).

Bannon, J. F. *The Spanish Borderlands Frontier, 1513–1821* (3:91).

Cook, W. L. *Flood Tide of Empire: Spain and the Pacific Northwest, 1543–1819* (5:180).

McDermott, J. F., ed. *The Spanish in the Mississippi Valley, 1762–1804* (3:10).

5:136 Nasatir, Abraham P. *Borderland in Retreat: From Spanish Louisiana to the Far Southwest.* Albuquerque: University of New Mexico Press, 1976. Though not diplomatic history as such, Nasatir's study focuses on Spain's defensive posture in coping with British, French, and American pressures on six separate frontiers during the period 1762 to 1822. Bibliography.

5:137 Nasatir, Abraham P. *Spanish War Vessels on the Mississippi, 1792–1796.* New Haven, Conn.: Yale University Press, 1968. Although they never saw action, these vessels figured in Spain's plans to defend Louisiana, and gave moral support to Natchez, Nogales, and New Madrid when each was threatened by American attack. Pinckney's Treaty, Nasatir finds, deprived Spain of the Indian component of her defense. Bibliography.

Mississippi Valley

See Chapter 6, "Louisiana and the Spanish Empire," for additional references. Also see "Personalities," above, for John Brown and James Wilkinson; "Document Collections," especially Kinnaird (3:19); "Bibliographies," especially Coker and Holmes (3:4) and McDermott (3:10); and "The Genêt Mission, 1793–1794," below.

5:138 Caughey, John W. *McGillivray of the Creeks.* Norman: University of Oklahoma Press, 1938. Reprint 1959. This work remains the major study of Alexander McGillivray, the Creek leader whose diplomacy played a key role in U.S. and Spanish efforts to gain political ascendancy in the old Southwest. A 60-page biography is followed by 214 reproduced letters to and from McGillivray.

5:139 Echeverria, Durand. "General Collot's Plan for a Reconnaissance of the Ohio and Mississippi Valleys, 1796." *William and Mary Quarterly* 3d ser. 9:4 (1952), 512–20. General Victor Collot was commissioned by Adet in 1796 to survey the Mississippi and Missouri river valleys; captured by the British, he was exchanged just as France regained Louisiana. See also George W. Kyte, "A Spy on the Western Waters: The Military Intelligence Mission of General Collot in 1796" (*Mississippi Valley Historical Review* 34 [1947], 427–42).

Lyon, E. W. *Louisiana in French Diplomacy, 1759–1804* (6:94).

5:140 Turner, Frederick Jackson. "The Policy of France toward the Mississippi Valley in the Period of Washington and Adams." *American Historical Review* 10:2 (1905), 249–79. Turner demonstrates France's deep, continuing interest in controlling the Mississippi Valley to limit English influence, to have a granary for the French West Indies, to influence American policies, and to undercut Spain's New World influence.

5:141 Whitaker, Arthur P. *The Spanish American Frontier, 1783–1795: The Westward Movement and the Spanish Retreat in the Mississippi Valley.* Lincoln: University of Nebraska Press, 1927. Whitaker maintains that Thomas Pinckney's diplomatic triumph stemmed not so much from European events (the

Bemis thesis) as from Madrid's realization "that it had failed, and knew that it had failed, in its frontier conflict with the United States."

Wright, J. L., Jr. *Anglo-Spanish Rivalry in North America* [1607–1821] (3:102).

5:142 Wright, J. Leitch, Jr. "The Creek-American Treaty of 1790: Alexander McGillivray and the Diplomacy of the Old Southwest." *Georgia Historical Quarterly* 51:4 (1967), 379–400. The author untangles the commercial and territorial interests of Britain, Spain, the state of Georgia, and several Indian factions as he explains what McGillivray hoped to accomplish by the treaty of New York and why he failed.

Commerce

5:143 Bernstein, Harry. *Origins of Inter-American Interest, 1700–1812.* Philadelphia: University of Pennsylvania Press, 1945. Chapter 3 documents the growing commerce between the United States and Spanish America in the late eighteenth century. Later chapters explore the cultural exchanges and the formation of "political ties" which antedated Latin American independence. Extensive bibliography.

5:144 Coatsworth, John H. "American Trade with European Colonies in the Caribbean and South America, 1790–1812." *William and Mary Quarterly* 3d ser. 24:2 (1967), 243–66. This study describes the growth, distribution, and composition of American exports to the Caribbean possessions of Britain, France, and Spain.

5:145 Nichols, Roy F. "Trade Relations and the Establishment of the United States Consulates in Spanish America, 1779–1809." *Hispanic American Historical Review* 13:3 (1933), 289–313. Nichols deals almost exclusively with U.S. "consuls" at Havana, who enjoyed greatest success whenever Cuba's need for American commodities and American carriers reached a peak, usually when Spain and Britain were at war. The author draws on both Spanish and U.S. archival sources.

5:146 Ogden, Adele. *The California Sea Otter Trade, 1784–1848.* Berkeley: University of California Press, 1941. A commercial history with international policy ramifications, this work examines Spain's effort to regulate, control, and restrict the taking of sea otters on the California coast by Russian competitors and British and American interlopers.

OTHER NATIONS

The Netherlands

See also "Personalities" for William Vans Murray.

5:147 Buist, Marten G. *At Spes Non Fracta: Hope and Company, 1770–1815: Merchant Bankers and Diplomats at Work.* The Hague: Nijhoff, 1974. This minutely detailed study of a prominent Dutch banking family touches only randomly on American-Dutch finance and commerce of the pre-1801 period; nevertheless, it describes the important linkage between the Hopes and the Barings after 1795 that later facilitated the financing of the Louisiana Purchase. Extensive bibliography.

5:148 Riley, James C. "Foreign Credit and Fiscal Stability: Dutch Investment in the United States, 1781–1794." *Journal of American History* 65:3 (1978), 654–78. Riley establishes that Dutch loans enabled Hamilton to give first the appearance, and later the substance, of solvency to U.S. government finances. The result was to establish the credit of the new government swiftly, and to bridge the early gap between low tax revenue and heavy commitment to expenditure.

Schama, S. *Patriots and Liberators: Revolution in the Netherlands, 1780–1815* (4:136) explains why Dutch financial houses eagerly invested in U.S. government securities, how Dutch firms expected a major share of the Atlantic carrying trade, and how, instead, by the mid-1790s American carriers beat them out.

5:149 Westermann, Johannes C. *The Netherlands and the United States: Their Relations in the Beginning of the Nineteenth Century.* The Hague: Nijhoff, 1935. One of few specific treatments of early Dutch-American relations (1780–1821), this study examines the Treaty of 1782. Bibliography.

5:150 Winter, Pieter J. van. *American Finance and Dutch Investment, 1780–1805, with an Epilogue to 1840.* Adapted by James C. Riley. Trans. by C. M. Geyl and I. Clephane. 2 vols. New York: Arno, 1977. A revised, updated, and translated version of Winter's *Het aandeel van den Amsterdamschen handel . . .* , (1927–1933), this title investigates Dutch investment in the United States (trade, government loans, Bank of the United States, canal building, and unsettled land).

The research in Dutch and American sources is prodigious, and the work is the finest treatment of the subject in print. Extensive bibliography.

5:151 Winter, Pieter J. van. "De Amerikaanse Zaken van C. J. M. De Wolf" [The American affairs of C. J. M. De Wolf]. *Mededelingen van de Koninklijke Vlaamse Academie voor Wetenschappen, Letteren en Schone Kunsten van Belgie, Klasse der Letteren* 32:2 (1970), 1–30. Winter describes the activities of De Wolf, a Dutch financier and speculator, who dealt with Gouverneur Morris and William Short in facilitating payments of the U.S. debt to France.

Prussia

See "Personalities" for John Quincy Adams.

5:152 Adams, Henry M. *Prussian-American Relations, 1775–1871.* Cleveland: Press of Western Reserve University, 1960. Using German and English sources, Adams explains why Prussia, tenaciously neutral during the American Revolution, was moved to conclude the "liberal" commercial treaty with Adams in 1785. Bibliography.

5:153 Reeves, Jesse S. "The Prussian-American Treaties." *American Journal of International Law* 11:3 (1917), 475–510. An analysis of the Treaty of 1785, which Benjamin Franklin negotiated with Frederick the Great, and its several renewals. The 1785 treaty was "acclaimed at the time as setting a new standard of international conduct, realizing to the fullest extent the humanitarian aspirations of the eighteenth century."

Russia

See Chapters 6 and 7 for additional references.

Bailey, T. A. *America Faces Russia: Russian-American Relations from Early Times to Our Day* [1776–1950] (2:245).

Bolkhovitinov, N. N. *The Beginnings of Russian-American Relations, 1775–1815* (4:137) suggests, in part 2, a troubled but steadily expanding commerce. He also explores Russian interests in Alaska before and after the chartering of the Russian-American Company in 1799.

Dulles, F. R. *The Road to Teheran: The Story of Russia and America, 1781–1943* (2:247).

5:154 Gibson, James R. *Imperial Russia in Frontier America: The Changing Geography of Supply of Russian America, 1784–1867.* New York: Oxford University Press, 1976. Gibson recounts the supply problems which the Russian-American Company never fully overcame. Although this study deals principally with the company, its bibliography includes nearly all secondary works, published in Russian, English, and French prior to 1976, relating to Russian colonization in North America.

Kushner, H. I. *Conflict on the Northwest Coast . . . , 1790–1867* (8:92).

Laserson, M. M. *The American Impact on Russia: Diplomatic and Ideological, 1784–1917* (2:250) deals, in chapter 4, most specifically with the era 1784 to 1801.

5:155 Okun, Semen Bentsionovich. *The Russian-American Company.* Trans. by Carl Ginsburg. Cambridge: Harvard University Press, 1951. Chapter 2 describes the fierce domestic political battle which preceded the chartering of the Russian-American Company in 1799. Okun's use of Russian printed and manuscript sources (1784–1867) adds a dimension lacking in most other works on this subject.

Confederation and Federalist Years

See "Bibliographies," especially Ferguson (1:72) and Morris (5:3).

5:156 Bowman, Albert H. *The Struggle for Neutrality: Franco-American Diplomacy during the Federalist Era.* Knoxville: University of Tennessee Press, 1974. Federalist diplomacy (1789–1801) is viewed as not neutral toward France, a point highlighted by the Jay Treaty. Bowman makes a valuable contribution by showing how American policy was viewed by members of the French foreign office.

French desire to involve America in the European war is outlined, as are the views of Talleyrand.

5:157 Dauer, Manning J. *The Adams Federalists.* Baltimore: Johns Hopkins Press, 1953. President Adams is portrayed as an able political leader whose pursuit of a moderate course, recognizing the claims of both the agrarian and mercantile interests, isolated the Hamiltonians and provided continuity in American domestic and foreign policies. Extensive bibliography.

5:158 DeConde, Alexander. *Entangling Alliance: Politics and Diplomacy under George Washington.* Durham, N.C.: Duke University Press, 1958. Alexander Hamilton is presented as the major figure in shaping foreign policy, with Washington serving as a useful figurehead. Washington's diplomacy (1789–1797) was shaped by foreign trade needs, the strength of the British navy, and requirements of the Hamiltonian fiscal system. The Farewell Address is depicted as a partisan political document, shaped by Hamilton to help Federalists win the election of 1796. Bibliography.

5:159 Jensen, Merrill. *The New Nation: A History of the United States during the Confederation, 1781–1789.* New York: Knopf, 1950. A standard work on the Confederation, written from the viewpoint of the progressive school of historiography. The author rejects the traditional "critical period" interpretation of the Confederation.

5:160 Kurtz, Stephen G. *The Presidency of John Adams: The Collapse of Federalism, 1795–1800.* Philadelphia: University of Pennsylvania Press, 1957. This standard account of the Adams presidency is favorable to Adams and his decision to defy Federalist leaders in order to seek peace with France, but Adams's actions, particularly his nomination of envoys to France in 1799, remain controversial.

5:161 Marks, Frederick W., III. *Independence on Trial: Foreign Affairs and the Making of the Constitution.* Baton Rouge: Louisiana State University Press, 1973. In the only diplomatic survey of the Confederation period (1781–1789), Marks argues that high anxiety concerning foreign affairs, particularly British trade restrictions, and the ineffectiveness of Confederation government were important factors in demands for a new constitution. John Jay's diplomacy is treated sympathetically. Extensive bibliography.

5:162　Trescot, William H. *The Diplomatic History of the Administrations of Washington and Adams, 1789–1801*. Boston: Little, Brown, 1857. An old but balanced study, it argues that the French Revolution initially threatened to compromise American independence but in the end played "a most important, though unforeseen, part in accomplishing that very independence."

5:163　White, Leonard D. *The Federalists: A Study in Administrative History*. New York: Macmillan, 1948. Dated and occasionally mistaken in its political inferences, this book is useful on the workings of the Department of State (1789–1801) and on Hamilton's interference with Jefferson's conduct of foreign affairs. The author makes it clear that President Washington controlled his administration, while President Adams did not.

DEVELOPMENT OF AMERICAN FOREIGN POLICY

See "Personalities" for additional references, especially Alexander Hamilton, Thomas Jefferson, and James Madison.

5:164　Bowman, Albert H. "Jefferson, Hamilton, and American Foreign Policy." *Political Science Quarterly* 71:1 (1956), 18–41. After examining American foreign policy contests (1790–1794), Bowman concludes, contrary to the realist school, that Jefferson rather than Hamilton had the truer vision of U.S. interests.

5:165　Gilbert, Felix. *To the Farewell Address: Ideas of Early American Foreign Policy*. Princeton, N.J.: Princeton University Press, 1961. In one of the most influential books of the last thirty years, the author sees two contradictory tendencies in U.S. policy from its origin: the desire for commerce with Europe and a longing for isolation from European politics and wars. He concludes that American policy (1775–1783) has often been a blend of idealism and realism. Bibliography.

5:166　Hutson, James H. "Intellectual Foundations of Early American Diplomacy." *Diplomatic History* 1:1 (1977), 1–19. Differing sharply with Felix Gilbert, the author contends that Americans of the revolutionary generation (1776–1796) acted according to the same assumptions of power politics that dominated contemporary European statecraft. American ideas derived from English Opposition ideology rather than from the French philosophes.

5:167　Kaplan, Lawrence S. "The Consensus of 1789: Jefferson and Hamilton on American Foreign Policy." *South Atlantic Quarterly* 71:1 (1972), 91–105. This thoughtful essay seeks to transcend historiographical arguments concerning whether Jefferson or Hamilton was the "realist" or "idealist" and asserts that they shared, in 1789 and later, a consensus: "support of a strong central government capable of maintaining freedom from European entanglements and profits from European commerce."

5:168　Smelser, Marshall. "The Federalist Period as an Age of Passion." *American Quarterly* 10:4 (1958), 391–419. The author shows that the Federalist era, especially after 1793, was characterized by obsessive political passions: Federalists saw Jacobin plots everywhere, and Republicans believed that the Federalists intended to crush republicanism. In "The Jacobin Phrenzy: The Menace of Monarchy, Plutocracy, and Anglophilia, 1789–1798," *Review of Politics* 21 (1959), 239–58, Smelser concentrates on Republican obsessions; see also his "The Jacobin Phrenzy: Federalism and the Menace of Liberty, Equality, and Fraternity," ibid. 13 (1951), 457–82.

Sofaer, A. D. *War, Foreign Affairs and Constitutional Power: The Origins* (6:77) is a valuable study of the development of presidential power (1787–1820).

Stourzh, G. *Benjamin Franklin and American Foreign Policy* [1764–1784] (4:52) combines the history of ideas with foreign policy and finds that Franklin thought of foreign policy in terms of power politics.

Williams, W. A. "The Age of Mercantilism: An Interpretation of the American Political Economy, 1763–1828" (2:97).

Political Parties and Foreign Policy

See "Personalities" for additional references, especially James Madison and Louis-Guillaume Otto, and "Document Collections" for Cunningham (5:7).

Banner, J. M., Jr. *To the Hartford Convention: The Federalists and the Origins of Party Politics in Massachusetts, 1789–1815* (6:66).

Brown, S. G. *The First Republicans: Political Philosophy and Public Policy in the Party of Jefferson and Madison* [1775–1823] (6:67).

Chambers, W. N. *Political Parties in a New Nation, 1776–1809* (6:68).

5:169 Charles, Joseph. *The Origins of the American Party System: Three Essays*. New York: Harper, 1961. Three essays, "Hamilton and Washington," "Jefferson and Adams," and "The Jay Treaty," argue that the shifting positions of Federalists and Democratic Republicans toward the Anglo-French struggle in Europe from 1793 to 1800 were responsible for the creation of the American system of political parties.

Cooper, J. "Jeffersonian Attitudes toward Executive Leadership and Committee Development in the House of Representatives, 1789–1829" (6:69).

5:170 Cunningham, Noble E., Jr. *The Jeffersonian Republicans: The Formation of Party Organization, 1789–1801*. Chapel Hill: University of North Carolina Press, 1957. This standard work on the Democratic Republicans is especially useful on the influence of the French Revolution and the Anglo-French war on party development in the United States. Bibliography.

Neutrality Policy

5:171 Hyneman, Charles S. "The First American Neutrality: A Study of the American Understanding of Neutral Obligations during the Years 1792 to 1815." *Illinois Studies in the Social Sciences* 20:1–2 (1934), 1–178. The policy of neutrality developed by the United States in 1793 "represented by far the most advanced existing opinions" of the obligations of neutrals and "is identical with the standard of conduct which is now adopted by the community of nations."

Kaplan, L. S., ed. *The American Revolution and "A Candid World"* (4:30) contains essays with themes such as the movement toward isolation beyond 1783.

5:172 Thomas, Charles M. *American Neutrality in 1793: A Study in Cabinet Government*. New York: Columbia University Press, 1931. The author states that Washington's cabinet debates produced "a new, an American policy of neutrality" which established precedents for neutral duties (duties rather than rights) more than a century later. Bibliography.

Washington's Farewell Address

See Gilbert (5:165).

5:173 Bemis, Samuel Flagg. "Washington's Farewell Address: A Foreign Policy of Independence." *American Historical Review* 39:2 (1934), 250–68. Long the standard treatment, the author's claim that the address has "ever since [been] a polestar of American foreign policy" has increasingly been questioned in recent years.

5:174 DeConde, Alexander. "Washington's Farewell, the French Alliance, and the Election of 1796." *Mississippi Valley Historical Review* 43:4 (1957), 641–58. The Farewell Address is here viewed as a partisan campaign document shaped largely by Hamilton to influence the 1796 election. Washington's famous warnings were directed against the Democratic Republican opposition and the French alliance.

5:175 Fry, Joseph A. "Washington's Farewell Address and American Commerce." *West Virginia History* 37:4 (1976), 281–90. The author maintains that Alexander Hamilton was solely responsible for the section of the address devoted to foreign commerce which sought to guarantee close commercial ties with Great Britain.

5:176 Kaufman, Burton I., ed. *Washington's Farewell Address: The View from the 20th Century*. Chicago: Quadrangle, 1969. This collection of essays on the Farewell Address published from 1899 to 1969 provides a useful survey of changing interpretations. Bibliography.

5:177 Markovitz, Arthur A. "Washington's Farewell Address and the Historians: A Critical Review." *Pennsylvania Magazine of History and Biography* 44:2 (1970), 173–91. This essay reviews the historiography of the address and concludes: "Only a person lacking historical insight into the period would argue that Washington's valedictory was a noble and disinterested legacy to the nation."

5:178 Paltsits, Victor H., ed. *Washington's Farewell Address*. New York: New York Public Library, 1935. This work contains successive drafts of the address by Washington, Madison, and Hamilton, together with their correspondence and other supporting documents. Extensive bibliography.

5:179 Weinberg, Albert K. "Washington's 'Great Rule' in Its Historical Evaluation." In Eric F. Goldman, ed., *Historiography and Urbanization: Essays in American History in Honor of W. Stull Holt.* Baltimore: Johns Hopkins Press, 1941, pp. 109–38. Tracing the evolution of Washington's famous warning against permanent alliances to 1940, the author concludes that the purposely ambiguous "great rule" had come to mean maintenance of freedom of action for the United States in international affairs.

Diplomatic Episodes

NOOTKA SOUND CONTROVERSY, 1790–1794

5:180 Cook, Warren L. *Flood Tide of Empire: Spain and the Pacific Northwest, 1543–1819.* New Haven, Conn.: Yale University Press, 1973. The author details the Spanish interaction with British, Russian, American, and Indian interests on the Pacific Northwest Coast which culminated in the Nootka Sound controversy (1790–1794). More than half of this historical-anthropological study centers on the events at Nootka, but the outcome was decided in Europe and the United States. Extensive bibliography.

5:181 Manning, William R., ed. "The Nootka Sound Controversy." In the Annual Report of the American Historical Association for the Year 1904. Washington, D.C.: G.P.O., 1905, pp. 279–478. This classic study of the Anglo-Spanish conflict on the Pacific Northwest Coast provides a detailed account of events which had repercussions in Madrid and London, and raised serious questions for the Washington administration. Bibliography.

Whitaker, A. P. *The Spanish American Frontier, 1783–1795* (5:141).

5:182 Wright, J. Leitch, Jr. *Britain and the American Frontier, 1783–1815.* Athens: University of Georgia Press, 1975. The author omits no important interface among Britain, Spain, France, the United States, and the Indians. Wright clearly understands the dynamics of frontier encounters, whether in East and West Florida or in the old Northwest during the 1790–1794 Anglo-American crisis brought about by the Nootka Sound incident. Extensive bibliography.

THE GENÊT MISSION, 1793–1794

See "Personalities" for Edmond Charles Genêt.

5:183 Ammon, Harry. *The Genêt Mission.* New York: Norton, 1973. Ammon concludes that Genêt was unsuccessful mainly because of his ignorance of the American political system and his unusual capacity for self-deception. The work is based primarily upon printed documents and a skillful use of secondary literature. Bibliography. Still useful are two doctoral dissertations: Maude H. Woodfin, "Citizen Genêt and His Mission" (University of Chicago, 1928), and William F. Keller, "American Politics and the Genêt Mission, 1793–1794" (University of Pittsburgh, 1951).

5:184 Ammon, Harry. "The Genêt Mission and the Development of American Political Parties." *Journal of American History* 52:4 (1966), 725–41. The author contends that Genêt played a significant role in stimulating party organization in support of, and in opposition to, France and its revolution.

5:185 Murdock, Richard K. "Citizen Mangourit and the Projected Attack on East Florida in 1794." *Journal of Southern History* 14:4 (1948), 522–40. Mangourit, French consul in Charleston, served as Genêt's agent in an unsuccessful effort to raise forces to invade the Spanish Floridas. The article is based primarily upon Turner's edition of the French diplomatic correspondence (5:11).

5:186 Murdock, Richard K. "The Genesis of the Genêt Schemes." *French-American Review* 2:2 (1949), 81–97. This account is derived mainly from the essays and documents published by Frederick Jackson Turner (5:188–5:192).

5:187 Palmer, Robert R. "A Revolutionary Republican: M. A. B. Mangourit." *William and Mary Quarterly* 3d ser. 9:4 (1952), 483–96. A discussion of the activities of the French consul at Charleston who served enthusiastically as Genêt's agent in commissioning and arming privateers and attempting to raise forces for an attack on Spanish Florida.

5:188 Turner, Frederick Jackson, ed. "Documents on the Blount Conspiracy, 1795–1797." *American Historical Review* 10:3 (1905), 574–606. Records are printed from the British Public Record Office, the Department of State, and the Archives du Ministère des Affaires Étrangères to illustrate the plan for frontiersmen, Indians, and a British expedition from Canada to seize Louisiana and the Floridas from Spain before France did so.

5:189 Turner, Frederick Jackson, ed. "Documents on the Relations of France to Louisiana, 1792–95." *American Historical Review* 3:3 (1897), 490–516. Documents from the Archives du Ministère des Affaires Etrangères demonstrate Genêt's attempts to take Louisiana in 1793 and 1794. Turner also includes various analyses of Louisiana, its value to France, and plans to take it, and a description of Genêt's conduct and reception in the United States.

5:190 Turner, Frederick Jackson, ed. "The Mangourit Correspondence in Respect to Genêt's Projected Attack upon the Floridas, 1793–94." In the Annual Report of the American Historical Association for 1897. Washington, D.C.: G.P.O., 1898, pp. 569–679. Michel Ange Bernard de Mangourit, Minister Genêt, and others were involved in the plan to incite revolts and seize the Floridas and Louisiana. Documents also include an interesting analysis of the Genêt mission by Minister Adet.

5:191 Turner, Frederick Jackson. "The Origins of Genêt's Projected Attack on Louisiana and the Floridas." *American Historical Review* 3:4 (1898), 650–71. This article recounts the plans of the Girondist regime in France to extend the French empire of liberty in North America. The Spanish-American revolutionary, Francisco de Miranda, George Rogers Clark, and others were involved in the elaborate schemes.

5:192 Turner, Frederick Jackson, ed. "Selections from the Draper Collection in the Possession of the State Historical Society of Wisconsin, to Elucidate the Proposed French Expedition under George Rogers Clark against Louisiana in the Years 1793–94." In the Annual Report of the American Historical Association for the Year 1896. Washington, D.C.: G.P.O., 1897, vol. 1, pp. 930–1107. Includes the Clark-Genêt correspondence, as well as correspondence copied from the Spanish archives showing Spanish awareness of the French scheme against Louisiana and the Floridas. A brief historical introduction and a chronological index

to documents related to the Clark-Genêt venture also appear.

JAY'S TREATY, 1794

See "Personalities" for additional references, especially John Jay; for Joseph Fauchet's efforts to defeat the treaty, see James (5:112) and Fauchet (5:95).

5:193 Bemis, Samuel Flagg. *Jay's Treaty: A Study in Commerce and Diplomacy.* Rev. ed. New Haven, Conn.: Yale University Press (1923), 1962. The author concludes, in this still standard work, that the treaty would have been more acceptable without Alexander Hamilton's intervention; nevertheless, the treaty probably prevented war between the United States and Great Britain.

5:194 Clarfield, Gerald. "Postscript to the Jay Treaty: Timothy Pickering and Anglo-American Relations, 1795–1797." *William and Mary Quarterly* 3d ser. 23:1 (1966), 106–20. Secretary of State Timothy Pickering sought to arrive at a modus vivendi between Great Britain and the United States following the Jay Treaty. Pickering is credited with lessening tensions between the two nations.

5:195 Combs, Jerald A. *The Jay Treaty: Political Battleground of the Founding Fathers.* Berkeley: University of California Press, 1970. In this useful work, the struggle over Jay's Treaty is explained in terms of perceptions of power: Federalists saw their nation as weak and vulnerable and therefore feared provoking Great Britain; Republicans viewed the country as strong and geographically secure and so opposed compromising American principles.

5:196 Ford, Worthington C., ed. "Edmund Randolph on the Jay Treaty." *American Historical Review* 12:3 (1907), 587–99. Letters of the secretary of state to President Washington after Senate ratification, including note to British minister Hammond demanding withdrawal of provision order.

5:197 Newcomb, Josiah T. "New Light on Jay's Treaty." *American Journal of International Law* 18:4 (1934), 685–92. Newcomb discovered a British order-in-council of August 6, 1794, which rescinded an earlier prohibition against neutrals carrying grain to France. Significantly, John Jay was about to begin negotiations.

5:198 Ogg, Frederick A. "Jay's Treaty and the Slavery Interests of the United States." In the Annual Report of the American Historical Association for the Year 1901. Washington, D.C.: G.P.O., 1902, vol. 1, pp. 275–98. The British case concerning slaves carried off during the American Revolution "must be judged well-nigh impregnable."

5:199 Perkins, Bradford. "Lord Hawkesbury and the Jay-Grenville Negotiations." *Mississippi Valley Historical Review* 40:2 (1953), 291–304. Lord Hawkesbury, president of the Board of Trade, endorsed most of Foreign Secretary Grenville's concessions to the United States but successfully opposed any relaxation of British regulations concerning neutral rights.

5:200 Sterling, David L. "A Federalist Opposes the Jay Treaty: The Letters of Samuel Bayard." *William and Mary Quarterly* 3d ser. 18:3 (1961), 408–24. Bayard was a Delaware Federalist; his reasoned opposition to Jay's Treaty illustrates the divisions the treaty created within the party.

PINCKNEY'S TREATY, 1795

See "Personalities" for Thomas Pinckney.

5:201 Bemis, Samuel Flagg. *Pinckney's Treaty: A Study of America's Advantage from Europe's Distress.* Baltimore: Johns Hopkins Press, 1926. Bemis's still valid thesis, borrowed from Jefferson, is that European quarrels in this era could be relied upon to advance the purposes of American foreign policy. The author contends that the Treaty of San Lorenzo, highly acceptable to the United States, resulted from Spain's distress at the prospect of a French invasion and at possible implications of Jay's Treaty. Bibliography.

5:202 Riley, Franklin L. "Spanish Policy in Mississippi after the Treaty of San Lorenzo." In the Annual Report of the American Historical Association for the Year 1897. Washington, D.C.: G.P.O., 1898, vol. 1, pp. 177–92. The dilatory tactics of Spanish officials in carrying out the terms of the (Pinckney's) treaty are described.

5:203 Young, Raymond A. "Pinckney's Treaty: A New Perspective." *Hispanic American Historical Review* 43:4 (1963), 526–35. While ascribing Pinckney's success partly to Godoy's alarm at the implications of the Jay-Grenville Treaty and partly to the certainty that London would resent Spain's exit

from the First Coalition, the author insists on the critical importance of Pinckney's role as negotiator.

QUASI-WAR, 1797–1800

See "Personalities" for additional references, especially John Adams; also see "Document Collections" for Knox (5:9).

5:204 Allen, Gardner W. *Our Naval War with France.* Boston: Houghton Mifflin, 1909. The standard account of the naval operations of the undeclared war.

5:205 Bonnel, Ulane. *La France, les États-Unis et la guerre de course, 1797–1815* [France, the United States and the privateering war, 1797–1815]. Paris: Nouvelles Éditions Latines, 1961. This detailed study focuses upon American prizes and prisoners in French territories, as well as upon the problems raised by privateering. It shows that most French seizures occurred in the 1790s, primarily in the Caribbean. The author made good use of the proceedings before the Conseil des prises, and lesser courts. Bibliography.

Clauder, A. C. *American Commerce as Affected by the Wars of the French Revolution and Napoleon, 1793–1810* (6:107).

5:206 DeConde, Alexander. *The Quasi-War: The Politics and Diplomacy of the Undeclared War with France.* New York: Scribner's, 1966. DeConde demonstrates that peace was never beyond the reach of reasonable statesmen. Adams is depicted as wavering, while Talleyrand is viewed as persistently moving toward a peaceful resolution. Extensive bibliography.

5:207 Morison, Samuel Eliot, ed. "DuPont, Talleyrand, and French Spoliations." *Proceedings of the Massachusetts Historical Society* 49 (1915–1916), 63–79. This is a memoir addressed by Victor DuPont, former French consul in the United States, to Talleyrand, which argues that unauthorized depredations by French corsairs on American commerce threatened to enlarge French-American hostilities. The editor states that this memoir was decisive in reversing French policy and averting the war.

5:208 Scott, James Brown, ed. *The Controversy over Neutral Rights between the United States and France 1797–1800: A Collection of American State Papers and Judicial Decisions.* New York: Oxford

University Press, 1917. Scott includes messages of President Adams to Congress, congressional replies, acts of Congress, proclamations, Court of Claims records and judgments, as well as judgments of the U.S. Supreme Court, and treaties concluded between the United States and France (1778–1800).

5:209 Stinchcombe, William C. "Talleyrand and the American Negotiations of 1797–1798." *Journal of American History* 62:3 (1975), 575–90. The author believes that Talleyrand was a proponent of reconciliation throughout the troubles of 1796 to 1798. His demand for an explanation of President Adams's remarks to Congress was sincere, not motivated by greed or a desire to postpone negotiations unduly.

5:210 Tolles, Frederick B. "Unofficial Ambassador: George Logan's Mission to France, 1798." *William and Mary Quarterly* 3d ser. 7:1 (1950), 3–25. After he had left the presidency, John Adams gave some of the credit for his decision in 1799 to send a new mission to France to the information concerning French conciliation that Logan brought back. The congressional response to Logan's mission was the Logan Act.

The XYZ Affair

See "Personalities" for additional references, especially Elbridge Gerry, John Marshall, and under "Others," Charles C. Pinckney and Prince Talleyrand.

Bowman, A. H. *The Struggle for Neutrality: Franco-American Diplomacy during the Federalist Era* (5:156).

5:211 Kramer, Eugene. "John Adams, Elbridge Gerry, and the Origins of the XYZ Affair." *Essex Institute Historical Collections* 94:1 (1958), 57–68. A critical evaluation of President Adams's appointment of Gerry to the commission to France with John Marshall and Charles Cotesworth Pinckney. Gerry had had no prior contact with the State Department or with his colleagues on the objects of the mission, and entertained incompatible views.

5:212 Stinchcombe, William C. "The Diplomacy of the WXYZ Affair." *William and Mary Quarterly* 3d ser. 34:4 (1977), 590–617. "In the WXYZ Affair, John Adams realized that a settlement with France was essential" for the United States to extricate itself from

European entanglements. Federalist measures during the summer of 1798 were defensive, and the danger of war was already subsiding when Adams risked Federalist party unity by resuming negotiations with France. There were four, not three French agents, hence "WXYZ."

5:213 Stinchcombe, William C. *The XYZ Affair.* Westport, Conn.: Greenwood, 1981. For the first time the full story, based on new materials, is told. The author reviews not only foreign policy conflicts between Federalists and Republicans, but also differences within Adams's own cabinet. Even more important, French policies are fully explored and the role of Talleyrand and the French agents more fully explored.

THE CONVENTION OF 1800

See "Personalities" for additional references, especially William R. Davie (under "Others") and William Vans Murray.

5:214 Cooke, Jacob E. "Country above Party: John Adams and the 1799 Mission to France." In Edmund P. Wills, ed., *Fame and the Founding Fathers.* Bethlehem, Pa.: Moravian College, 1967, pp. 53–77. A highly critical analysis of President Adams's decision in 1799 to send a new mission to France, a decision which, the author says, unnecessarily and irreparably divided the Federalist party. A demurring "Comment" by Stephen G. Kurtz follows, pp. 78–79.

5:215 DeConde, Alexander. "Foreclosure of a Peacemaker's Career: A Criticism of Thomas Jefferson's Isolation." *Huntington Library Quarterly* 15:3 (1952), 297–304. President Jefferson was motivated by political expediency in appointing Robert R. Livingston to the Paris post instead of Murray, whom the author believes deserved it. Jefferson is also criticized for abolishing the ministry to The Hague.

5:216 DeConde, Alexander. "William Vans Murray and the Diplomacy of Peace: 1797–1800." *Maryland Historical Magazine* 48:1 (1953), 1–26. Murray constituted "the keystone to the fabric of Franco-American diplomacy that brought peace" between France and the United States, both in the discussions which led to Adams's new mission to France and in the negotiations resulting in the Convention of 1800. An earlier, shorter version of this essay appeared in the *Huntington Library Quarterly* 15:1 (1952), 185–94.

5:217   Du Casse, Albert. *Histoire des négociations diplomatiques relatives aux traités de Mortfontaine, de Lunéville et d'Amiens* [History of the diplomatic negotiations relative to the treaties of Mortfontaine, Luneville and Amiens]. 3 vols. Paris: Dentu, 1855. Volume 1 treats the Convention of 1800 (Treaty of Mortfontaine) in detail. This account was written from the memoirs of Joseph Bonaparte, formerly king of Naples and of Spain; the author regards the negotiations of these three treaties as his greatest service to France. Bibliography.

5:218   Kurtz, Stephen G. "The French Mission of 1799–1800: Concluding Chapter in the Statecraft of John Adams." *Political Science Quarterly* 80:4 (1965), 543–57. Adams's positive response to Talleyrand's peace overtures was governed by his desire to maintain peace, to defuse domestic tensions, and to squelch Federalist militarist adventurers. His leisurely appointment of negotiators was deliberate; Adams wished to strengthen the Caribbean fleet before negotiating.

5:219   Lyon, E. Wilson. "The Franco-American Convention of 1800." *Journal of Modern History* 12:3 (1940), 305–34. This is a standard work on the convention.

5:220   Richmond, Arthur A. "Napoleon and the Armed Neutrality of 1800." *Journal of the Royal United Service Institution* 104:614 (1959), 1–9. Bonaparte sought to foster a league of armed neutrals to counter Britain's naval preponderance. When American commissioners arrived at Paris in 1800 to negotiate a settlement of Franco-American disputes, he insisted on including in the Convention of 1800 the liberal maritime principles of the Treaty of Commerce of 1778, hoping thereby to maneuver the United States into the league.

THE BARBARY PIRATES

See Chapter 18 for references.

The Jeffersonian Era, 1801–1815

Contributing Editor

BRADFORD PERKINS
University of Michigan

Contents

Introduction

The major diplomatic challenges faced by Thomas Jefferson and James Madison during their successive presidencies were those which culminated in a declaration of war against Great Britain in June 1812. Understandably, historians have concentrated on them. The conflict with Tripoli, the Louisiana Purchase, ambitions regarding the Floridas, first contacts with a Latin America on the brink of revolution against Spain, the negotiations which ended the War of 1812—all of these, especially the Louisiana Purchase, have attracted scholarly attention. Still, the literature devoted to these subjects is, at least in amount, modest by comparison with that which, directly or indirectly, speaks to the causes of war.

In addition to its intrinsic importance, the interpretational challenges presented by this topic help to explain its fascination for scholars. Until about 1910, virtually all historians shared the view, powerfully expressed by Alfred T. Mahan, *Sea Power in Its Relations to the War of 1812* (6:9), that British assaults upon American maritime interests, particularly the seizure of ships and impressment of seamen, drove the United States to declare war. Then, struck by the fact that New England, the section most deeply involved in ocean commerce, had opposed war, while western congressmen—the "War Hawks"—had sought it, many historians struck out along a new path. Although they differed among themselves regarding western motivation, this group, among whom Julius W. Pratt, author of *The Expansionists of 1812* (6:140), was most influential, ascribed the coming of war to the political influence of the frontier. Despite occasional challenges, perhaps most notably by A. L. Burt, in *The United States, Great Britain, and British North America* (6:5), this interpretation became the predominant one.

Recent scholarship has challenged the western thesis on many grounds without restoring the maritime interpretation in its original form. Wider research has rendered suspect one of Pratt's key arguments, that the West sought the conquest and absorption of Canada. Moreover, Roger H. Brown, in *The Republic in Peril: 1812* (6:153) and other works, have argued that the vote for war reflected partisan rather than sectional influences, pointing out, for example, that Pennsylvania Republicans provided more votes for war than the entire West, and Brown, although not all of his contemporaries, even denies the existence of a War Hawk faction. Most of these writers agree that the spiritual challenge posed by British policies, as much as or more than their material impact, convinced many Americans, however reluctantly, that there was no honorable alternative to war. Many of these conclusions were also reached, or anticipated, in Bradford Perkins, *Prologue to War* (6:11), a work which, additionally, provides much information on the making of those British policies against which Americans protested.

Despite the recent outpouring, many opportunities remain open to scholars. We still know far too little about French policy and its impact on the Anglo-American controversy. There is no satisfactory modern treatment of the Embargo and other restrictions on commerce, both in terms of their impact on Europe and upon the American economy, although Burton I. Spivak, *Jefferson's English Crisis* (6:129), is a fine exploration of the president's thoughts and motives. No published treatment of impressment incorporates research in both British and American materials. The Federalists, and their attitude toward the great war in Europe, deserve more attention than they have received, even if only to show why their political stock fell so dismally. If Irving Brant, *James Madison: Secretary of State* (6:38) and *James Madison: The President* (6:39), and his respondents have exposed Madison's activities to view, the same cannot be said of those of all other important figures, including John Randolph. The Republican period is in some ways a particularly attractive one for research, since the sources are abundant but not so overwhelming as to be unmanageable, and the historian may hope that it will continue to evoke the lively scholarship that has marked recent years.

Resources and Overviews

Smith, M. J., Jr., ed. *The American Navy, 1789–1860: A Bibliography* (5:5) focuses primarily on naval matters between 1789–1815; however, there are also materials listed of interest to diplomatic historians.

Thomas, D. H., and Case, L. M., eds. *Guide to the Diplomatic Archives of Western Europe* [1400–1959], (1:298) contains, additionally, lists of printed documentary materials.

Trask, D. F.; Meyer, M. C.; and Trask, R. R., eds. *A Bibliography of United States–Latin American Relations since 1810* (1:120) has a few items that bear upon the period before 1810; see also Meyer (1:119), which updates the initial volume.

RESEARCH AIDS

While pertinent bibliographies and reference aids are listed here, there are more extensive lists in Chapter 1.

Bibliographies

Bibliographie annuelle de l'histoire de France (1:78a) is more convenient than other guides to the yearly output of French scholarship.

6:1 Brown, Lucy M., and Christie, Ian R., eds. *Bibliography of British History, 1789–1851.* Oxford: Clarendon Press, 1977. This masterful bibliography is the essential introduction to its subject. Guides to manuscripts are included, but the primary emphasis is upon printed, even secondary, material. This work demonstrates how many lacunae there are and how many of the standard treatments of British developments are far out of date.

Coker, W. S., and Holmes, J. D. F. "Source for the History of the Spanish Borderlands" (3:4).

Cortada, J. W., ed. *A Bibliographical Guide to Spanish Diplomatic History, 1460–1977* (1:90).

Egan, C. L. "The Origins of the War of 1812: Three Decades of Historical Writing" (6:102).

Ferguson, E. J., comp. *Confederation, Constitution and Early National Period, 1781–1815* (1:72) lists domestic as well as foreign affairs items for the Jefferson and Madison years.

Goodman, W. H. "The Origins of the War of 1812: A Survey of Changing Interpretations" (6:103).

Monaghan, F. *French Travellers in the United States, 1765–1932: A Bibliography* (1:73).

Nichols, R. L. "From the Revolution to the Mexican War" (5:4) focuses on military activities, but contains many references of interest to the diplomatic historian.

Document Collections

More general collections are listed in Chapter 2, and other collections may be found in "Personalities," below.

American State Papers (1:349).

Cunningham, N. E., Jr., ed. *Circular Letters of Congressmen to Their Constituents, 1789–1829* (5:7) finds that until 1815 considerable emphasis was given to foreign affairs.

Manning, W. R., ed. *Diplomatic Correspondence of the United States: Canadian Relations, 1784–1860* (1:343) contains important correspondence, in volume 1, bearing upon boundary disputes, relations with the Indians, and so forth. It also reproduces many of the documents bearing upon the Henry affair of 1812.

Manning, W. R., ed. *Diplomatic Correspondence of the United States Concerning the Independence of the Latin-American Nations* [1809–1830] (7:4) contains only a small proportion which bears upon the years prior to 1815, but this helps to elucidate developing American policy toward Spain's rebellious empire.

Mayo, B., ed. *Instructions to the British Ministers to the United States, 1791–1812* (5:10) is particularly valuable.

U.S. Congress. *The Debates and Proceedings in the Congress of the United States, 1st to 18th Congresses, March 3, 1789–May 27, 1824* (1:351) are commonly referred to as *Annals of Congress*.

Webster, C. K., ed. *Britain and the Independence of Latin America, 1812–1830* (7:6).

6:2 Whitaker, Arthur P., ed. *Documents Relating to the Commercial Policy of Spain in the Floridas with Incidental Reference to Louisiana*. De Land, Fla.: Florida State Historical Society, 1931. This collection (1778–1808) is a translation of thirty documents, mostly from the Archivo General de las Indias, printed in both English and Spanish. The documents reveal the special commercial problems facing the Spanish crown in a revolutionary era and show the concessions Spain made to trade between Pensacola and New Orleans and France, Great Britain, and the United States.

OVERVIEWS

6:3 Abernethy, Thomas P. *The South in the New Nation, 1789–1816*. Baton Rouge: Louisiana State University Press, 1961. Abernethy's account of the Burr conspiracy is more concise and somewhat different from his earlier monograph (6:19) on that subject. His treatment of the West Florida rebellion is extremely well done, and his examination of southern attitudes toward the War of 1812 is helpful. The "Critical Essay on Authorities" is a superb guide to material of all types.

6:4 Adams, Henry. *History of the United States during the Administrations of Jefferson and Madison*. 9 vols. New York: Scribner's, 1889–1891. This classic work is, unfortunately, more often praised than read. Adams includes masses of detail, but he sometimes mishandles his sources. These shortcomings are far outweighed by the breadth of his research, the vigor of his prose, and the often provocative judgments. For a sophisticated critique, see Merrill D. Peterson, "Henry Adams on Jefferson the President," *Virginia Quarterly Review* 39 (1963), 187–201.

6:5 Burt, Alfred L. *The United States, Great Britain, and British North America from the Revolution to the Establishment of Peace after the War of 1812*. New Haven, Conn.: Yale University Press, 1940. Reprint 1961. This long-standard work deals much more with the coming of the War of 1812 than with the Ghent negotiations. Burt relies chiefly on government published documents, rather than on archival material, although he incorporates the work of other scholars. Particularly noteworthy is his challenge, unusual for its time, to the emphasis on western ambitions as the major cause of the War of 1812.

6:6 Channing, Edward. *A History of the United States*. New York: Macmillan, 1917, vol. 4. Channing's *History* is neither as famous nor as provocative as Adams's, but it is a cool, thoughtful, and clearly written survey of politics and diplomacy. The treatment of what he calls "the Louisiana Procurement" is particularly useful. Regarding the origins of the War of 1812, his conclusions are indistinct, although he gives some attention to Canadian conquest as a war aim.

6:7 Crawley, Charles W., ed. *War and Peace in an Age of Upheaval, 1793–1830*. Vol. 9 in *The New Cambridge Modern History*. Cambridge: At the University Press, 1965. This cooperative work in European history contains chapters of very uneven merit. Still, it provides a useful, wide-ranging study of the background of diplomacy as well as of diplomacy itself.

6:8 Godechot, Jacques. *L'Europe et l'Amérique à l'époque napoléonienne* [Europe and America in the age of Napoleon]. Paris: Presses Universitaires de France, 1967. This is, for an American historian, both a rewarding and an irritating book. The portions on the western hemisphere are cursory and simplistic, but the treatment of the age is broad and imaginative. It is a fine introduction to the diplomacy of the period. The lengthy bibliographical essay includes a very capable discussion of French materials.

6:9 Mahan, Alfred Thayer. *Sea Power in Its Relations to the War of 1812*. 2 vols. Boston: Little, Brown, 1905. This famous spokesman for sea power considers maritime issues the sole cause of the War of 1812. While clearly an American nationalist, Mahan urges the reader to recognize the pressures forcing Britain to act as she did. He is very critical of Jefferson and Madison for their alleged supineness. In addition to a long section on the causes of the war, there is a short chapter on the Ghent negotiations, but most of this work is detailed military history.

6:10 Perkins, Bradford. *The First Rapprochement: England and the United States, 1795–1805*. Philadelphia: University of Pennsylvania Press, 1955. The last five chapters deal with Jefferson's first administration, with particular attention to England's role during the Louisiana controversy and to the growing tension after 1803. Extensive bibliography.

6:11 Perkins, Bradford. *Prologue to War: England and the United States, 1805–1812*. Berkeley: University of California Press, 1961. In this comprehensive treatment of the road to the War of 1812, Perkins is very critical of the leadership of Jefferson and Madison and perhaps excessively understanding of some

British figures. He ascribes the coming of the war primarily to maritime issues, as much for their psychological as their material impact, and downplays sectionalism as a factor. A "Note on the Sources" and extremely detailed footnotes.

6:12 Perkins, Bradford. *Castlereagh and Adams: England and the United States, 1812–1823*. Berkeley: University of California Press, 1964. The last of a trilogy on Anglo-American relations from 1795 to 1823, this volume includes the most recent, extended discussion of the Ghent negotiations. Perkins's analysis often revises traditional interpretations, most generally by arguing that the settlement owed at least as much to British weakness of purpose as to the firmness and talents of the American negotiators. A "Note on the Sources."

6:13 Smelser, Marshall. *The Democratic Republic, 1801–1815*. New York: Harper & Row, 1968. Essentially a work of synthesis, this study sometimes seems to meld rather than to compare or evaluate contradictory interpretations, and on other occasions it follows rather than builds upon standard accounts. All things considered, however, this is the best introduction to American politics and diplomacy in this period. Extensive bibliography and useful footnotes.

Van Alstyne, R. W. *The Rising American Empire* (2:96).

Varg, P. A. *Foreign Policies of the Founding Fathers* (5:15) is an interpretive work covering the period up to 1812.

Personalities

Additional references on individuals may be found in Chapter 1, "Biographical Data."

AMERICAN

John Quincy Adams
6:14 Adams, John Quincy. *Memoirs of John Quincy Adams*. 12 vols. Ed. by Charles Francis Adams.

Philadelphia: Lippincott, 1874–1877. The first three volumes contain Adams's account of his role during the Jefferson and Madison administrations, as senator from Massachusetts repudiated by his constituency because he refused to follow the Federalist line, as envoy to Russia, and as peace commissioner at Ghent. Passages describing the Ghent negotiations are particularly important, but Adams's nature frequently colored his understanding of the behavior of others.

6:15 Adams, John Quincy. *The Writings of John Quincy Adams*. 7 vols. Ed. by Worthington C. Ford. New York: Macmillan, 1913–1917. Ford was selective rather than complete, but the editing is sensible. This incomplete edition stops at 1823. Both official and private correspondence are included; among the latter are a series of marvelous letters to Adams's parents. Volume 5 contains nearly 250 pages on the negotiations which brought the War of 1812 to a close.

6:16 Bemis, Samuel Flagg. *John Quincy Adams and the Foundations of American Foreign Policy*. New York: Knopf, 1949. This sturdy volume is particularly important because of Bemis's use of the previously closed Adams manuscripts. The views are somewhat nationalistic, and John Quincy Adams (1767–1829) is pictured as an heroic figure, but Bemis is far too good a scholar to toy with the evidence or to conceal his own preconceptions.

James A. Bayard
6:17 Bayard, James A. *Papers of James A. Bayard, 1796–1815*. Ed. by Elizabeth Donnan. In the Annual Report of the American Historical Association for the Year 1913. Washington, D.C.: G.P.O., 1915, vol. 2. The main interest in Bayard's correspondence derives from his leadership of moderate southern Federalists.

6:18 Borden, Morton. *The Federalism of James A. Bayard*. New York: Columbia University Press, 1955. Borden's biography provides a useful, cool analysis of the behavior and attitudes of the Federalist congressman and senator from Delaware. Bayard, perhaps to a greater degree even than Rufus King, may be said to represent moderate opinion within the party. Borden provides no discussion of Bayard's role as commissioner at Ghent, but the role was a small one. Extensive bibliography.

Aaron Burr
6:19 Abernethy, Thomas P. *The Burr Conspiracy*. New York: Oxford University Press, 1954. This extensively researched account emphasizes the threat to the

union posed by the Burr conspiracy (1803–1808). Although the author concentrates on the domestic ramifications, including Burr's trial for treason, Spanish and British connections with the leading actors, notably Burr and General James Wilkinson, are also closely examined. Extensive bibliography.

6:20   Parmet, Herbert S., and Hecht, Marie B. *Aaron Burr: Portrait of an Ambitious Man.* New York: Macmillan, 1967. This study of Burr (1756–1836) incorporates the findings of recent scholarship as well as the fruits of research in primary materials. Unfortunately, Parmet and Hecht develop few strong or original judgments, and as a consequence this biography has limited utility, except as background.

6:21   Schachner, Nathan. *Aaron Burr.* New York: Stokes, 1937. This biography still remains the most interesting and perhaps the best study of Burr. Schachner conceals few of Burr's many faults, but his interpretation tends to be favorable—and therefore provocative. Extensive bibliography.

Henry Clay

See Chapter 7, "Personalities," for additional references; also see "The Decision for War," below.

6:22   Mayo, Bernard. *Henry Clay: Spokesman of the New West.* Boston: Houghton Mifflin, 1937. This extremely lively, readable study stresses Clay's importance and highlights the dramatics, especially, of the war session. Despite impressive research, Mayo does not appear to have been able to question traditional interpretations of the coming of war in 1812. Extensive bibliography.

Albert Gallatin

See also Chapter 10, "Personalities."

6:23   Balinkey, Alexander. *Albert Gallatin: Fiscal Theories and Policies.* New Brunswick, N.J.: Rutgers University Press, 1958. This highly detailed study is very critical of Republican fiscal policies (1801–1813), which, it is alleged, deprived the Treasury of the flexibility and strength required by the crises of the period, particularly the War of 1812. Useful primarily as background, Balinkey's study only occasionally speaks directly to the major diplomatic issues but is nonetheless helpful in understanding them.

6:24   Walters, Raymond, Jr. *Albert Gallatin: Jeffersonian Financier and Diplomat.* New York: Macmil-

lan, 1957. This biography is very favorable to its subject, whose manuscripts the author was the first to use since Henry Adams's *The Life of Albert Gallatin* (Philadelphia: Lippincott, 1879). The work is particularly useful for the treatment of Republican styles of government, the problems posed by the Embargo and the enervating effect of factionalism. The account of the Ghent negotiations is less satisfactory. Extensive bibliography.

Thomas Jefferson

See Chapters 4 and 5, "Personalities," for additional references.

6:25   Chinard, Gilbert. *Thomas Jefferson: The Apostle of Americanism.* Boston: Little, Brown, 1929. Until the appearance of Peterson's biography (6:34), Chinard's was the most successful one-volume study. Charmingly written and placing heavy emphasis on Jefferson's thought, it still is rewarding reading, although some of the interpretations have been vigorously challenged.

Honeywell, R. J. "President Jefferson and His Successor" (6:43).

6:26   Jefferson, Thomas. *The Writings of Thomas Jefferson.* 20 vols. Ed. by Andrew A. Lipscomb and Albert E. Bergh. Washington, D.C.: Thomas Jefferson Memorial Association, 1903–1905. Volumes 10 to 14 reproduce correspondence during the years from 1801 to 1815, although later volumes include some retrospective observations on that period. It is more complete but less accurate than the Ford edition.

6:27   Jefferson, Thomas. *The Writings of Thomas Jefferson.* 12 vols. Ed. by Paul L. Ford. New York: Putnam's, 1904–1905. Ford uses very little of modern editorial apparatus, making understanding sometimes difficult. In addition, he chose to delete an even higher proportion of Jefferson's writings while president than he did for earlier periods (volumes 9 to 11 contain material on 1801 to 1815). This and all other editions of Jefferson's writings will be rendered totally obsolete when Boyd's edition (5:34) is completed.

6:28   Johnstone, Robert M., Jr. *Jefferson and the Presidency: Leadership in the Young Republic.* Ithaca, N.Y.: Cornell University Press, 1978. This examination of Jefferson's leadership, employing approaches adapted from political science, concludes that he was an effective leader, in large part through his astute use of nonformal modes of influence. (The sole cited exception is the Embargo). The author's grasp of diplomacy is limited, and the research base is too insubstantial to give confidence in all of his findings, although many of them are shared by other scholars.

6:29 Kaplan, Lawrence S. "Jefferson, the Napoleonic Wars, and the Balance of Power," *William and Mary Quarterly* 3d ser. 14:2 (1957), 196–217. This vigorous article praises Jefferson for his understanding of the importance to America of a European balance of power (1805–1815), particularly so that the United States might pursue a course of isolationism. It criticizes Jefferson for tactical failures, for occasional duplicity, and for permitting rancor toward Great Britain to distort rational calculations. The themes foreshadow many of those in his *Jefferson and France* (5:35).

6:30 Koch, Adrienne. *Jefferson and Madison: The Great Collaboration.* New York: Oxford University Press, 1950. In this study of the relationship in terms of philosophy and political ideas, Koch emphasizes that Jefferson and Madison were equal partners, producing together an outlook too often ascribed largely to the older man. Little direct attention is paid to diplomacy, but the nature of the relationship of two men who directed foreign affairs at a critical time is illuminated.

6:31 Malone, Dumas. *Jefferson the President: First Term, 1801–1805.* Vol. 4 in *Jefferson and His Time.* Boston: Little, Brown, 1970. This magisterial biography is generally more temperate in tone, and is thus a more effective case for the defense, than Brant's comparable biography of Madison (6:38, 6:39). Malone's treatment is not free from bias, and at various points it is vulnerable to contradiction or argument. In this volume, except on the Louisiana question, there is relatively little attention to diplomacy. Extensive bibliography.

6:32 Malone, Dumas. *Jefferson the President: Second Term, 1805–1809.* Vol. 5 in *Jefferson and His Time.* Boston: Little, Brown, 1974. This volume by Malone is perhaps a shade more annalistic and slightly more defensive in tone than its predecessor. Much attention is paid to Burr's conspiracy and trial, and there is intensive treatment of the growing controversy with England and of the Embargo. Extensive bibliography.

6:33 Peterson, Merrill D. *The Jefferson Image in the American Mind.* New York: Oxford University Press, 1960. This masterful work evaluates American views

of Jefferson, from 1826 to 1956, tracing the ups and downs of his reputation among scholars and others. There is sufficient reference to Jefferson's diplomacy to make the volume a useful introduction. Extensive bibliography.

6:34 Peterson, Merrill D. *Thomas Jefferson and the New Nation: A Biography.* New York: Oxford University Press, 1970. By far the best one-volume biography of the third president, Peterson's work is insightful, well written, and comprehensive, interweaving treatments of Jefferson's thought and actions. The judgments are on the whole favorable to Jefferson, although Peterson is quite critical of the Embargo and often incorporates, while refuting, other negative assessments. Essentially, this is a work of high quality synthesis based upon a nearly exhaustive reading of earlier scholarly work, although at various points primary research strengthens the study and fills in gaps.

6:35 Stuart, Reginald C. *The Half-Way Pacifist: Thomas Jefferson's View of War.* Toronto: University of Toronto Press, 1978. This short, trenchant discussion of Jefferson's attitude toward war concludes that he was no pacifist and that he saw war as a legitimate instrument of policy. It criticizes him for failing to understand political and military realities that developed during his lifetime.

6:36 Wiltse, Charles M. *The Jeffersonian Tradition in American Democracy.* Chapel Hill: University of North Carolina Press, 1935. This dated but still useful study of Jefferson's thought is friendly, although not uncritical. Chapter 9, "The Family of Nations," explores the complexities and, sometimes inadvertently, exposes the inconsistencies in Jefferson's approach to international relations; it can usefully be read in conjunction with Kaplan (5:35).

Rufus King

6:37 Ernst, Robert. *Rufus King: An American Federalist.* Chapel Hill: University of North Carolina Press, 1968. This detailed narrative is particularly important for its treatment of King's mission to London, which included the first few years of the Jefferson administration. However, there is also helpful information on national and especially Federalist politics thereafter.

King, R. *The Life and Correspondence of Rufus King* [1755–1827] (5:41) includes material from 1801 to 1815 in volumes 3–5. Particularly valuable for King's mission in London, the volumes are thinner, but still useful, for the years after his return.

James Madison

See Chapters 4 and 5, "Personalities," for additional references.

6:38 Brant, Irving. *James Madison: Secretary of State, 1800–1809.* Indianapolis: Bobbs-Merrill, 1952. This study, volume 4 of a six-volume standard biography, argues forcefully, perhaps overly forcefully, the case for Madison at the expense of Jefferson and of diplomatic opponents. Although sometimes petulant in tone and made less effective by an annalistic organization, this is the starting point for any examination of Madison. Brant did very impressive research in materials in the United States, but his understanding of the international setting is incomplete.

6:39 Brant, Irving. *James Madison: The President, 1809–1812.* Indianapolis: Bobbs-Merrill, 1956. This volume, even more detailed and annalistic than Brant's others, provides an unmatched chronological account of this key period in Anglo-American relations. Not particularly interested in war causation, Brant is determined to demonstrate that Madison, not the so-called War Hawks, controlled and directed events. Subsequent scholarship has affirmed the downplaying of the War Hawks without ascribing to Madison the vigorous leadership which Brant portrays.

6:40 Brant, Irving. *James Madison: Commander-in-Chief, 1812–1836.* Indianapolis: Bobbs-Merrill, 1961. Most of this volume deals with Madison's second presidency, the remainder with his life in retirement. There is no formal bibliography, but this volume indicates the sources used; once again, the research in American materials is impressive, that in foreign sources somewhat unsatisfactory. The six volumes are condensed in Brant's *The Fourth President: A Life of James Madison* (Indianapolis: Bobbs-Merrill, 1970).

6:41 Brant, Irving. "Madison and the War of 1812." *Virginia Magazine of History and Biography* 74:1 (1966), 51–68. Brant vigorously and succinctly summarizes the themes in the two volumes listed immediately above.

6:42 Cunliffe, Marcus. "Madison (1812–1815)." In Ernest R. May, ed., *The Ultimate Decision: The President as Commander in Chief.* New York: Braziller, 1960, pp. 21–54. Cunliffe presents a thoughtful discussion of Madison's qualities of leadership during the War of 1812. Although no direct attention is paid to diplomacy, it is useful as background and as an exploration into Madison's patterns of executive leadership.

6:43 Honeywell, Roy J. "President Jefferson and His Successor." *American Historical Review* 46:1 (1940), 64–76. Honeywell demonstrates that Jefferson exercised only moderate influence over his successor. The two men drifted apart after Jefferson withdrew to Monticello, although they did not quarrel. Madison rarely asked advice and sometimes ignored that which was preferred, although he frequently informed his former chief of decisions after they had been taken.

Kaplan, L. S. "France and Madison's Decision for War, 1812" (6:160).

6:44 Ketcham, Ralph. *James Madison: A Biography.* New York: Macmillan, 1971. This recent biography of Madison admits a great debt to Irving Brant, but Ketcham has also derived assistance from other students of the period. A lengthy one-volume biography, it has utility, but the judgments tend to be conventional.

Koch, A. *Jefferson and Madison: The Great Collaboration* (6:30).

6:45 Madison, James. *The Writings of James Madison.* 9 vols. Ed. by Gaillard Hunt. New York: Putnam's, 1900–1910. Although more useful than other collections of Madison's writings, Hunt's edition has important drawbacks. Less than four volumes (6–9) cover the period from 1801 to 1815, and much important material is omitted. There is no editorial apparatus to clarify the context in which Madison's letters are written.

Madison, J. *The Papers of James Madison* (4:62) will be the definitive edition when Hutchinson's edition is completed; meanwhile one must turn to Hunt's edition.

6:46 Pancake, John S. "The 'Invisibles': A Chapter in the Opposition to President Madison." *Journal of Southern History* 21:1 (1955), 17–37. Pancake explores the activities from 1802 to 1812 of a Republican faction centered around Samuel Smith of Maryland, national legislator and brother of Madison's inept secretary of state. The group pressured Madison toward war, it is argued, because it felt deeply about maritime issues with Great Britain.

6:47 Smith, Abbot. "Mr. Madison's War: An Unsuccessful Experiment in the Conduct of National Policy." *Political Science Quarterly* 57:2 (1942), 229–46. Smith argues that Madison concluded, as early as 1809, that war with Britain was the proper policy but that his constitutional scruples prevented him from recommending or demanding it; he felt that Congress should make the decision for itself. That Madison had a circumscribed view of executive responsibility is beyond dispute, but Smith overargues his point.

James Monroe

Ammon, H. *James Monroe* (5:47) is a sophisticated, smooth-flowing biography based on extensive research; the judgments are careful rather than forceful, but perhaps because Monroe was a very private man who often did not reveal his thoughts, some puzzles in his behavior are left unsolved.

Monroe, James. *The Writings of James Monroe* (5:50) contains, in volumes 3–4, material for the period from 1801 to 1815.

Others

6:48 Brant, Irving. "Joel Barlow, Madison's Stubborn Minister." *William and Mary Quarterly* 3d ser. 15:4 (1958), 438–52. This article describes Barlow as a vigorous, perceptive representative in France at a difficult time (1810–1812), when Napoleon's tortuous but also neglectful policy toward the United States created difficulty for Madison's administration. Brant's article renders obsolete the very brief treatment of this episode in the standard biography, James Woodress, *A Yankee's Odyssey: The Life of James Barlow* (Philadelphia: Lippincott, 1958).

6:49 Bruce, William C. *John Randolph of Roanoke, 1773–1833*. 2 vols. New York: Putnam's, 1922. This tedious biography provides the most useful sketch of the life and political career of its subject. Randolph was an important, highly individualistic figure, nominally a Republican but often a splenetic opponent of the foreign policies of Jefferson and Madison, and Bruce's biography quotes much of his vigorous criticism.

6:50 Cassell, Frank A. *Merchant Congressman in the Young Republic: Samuel Smith of Maryland, 1752–1839*. Madison: University of Wisconsin Press, 1971. This solidly researched volume traces the career of an important Republican of the second rank, a factional leader who often caused difficulty for Jefferson and Madison. Because Smith was also an important commercial figure, the volume also provides insights into the relationship between business interests and the formulation of foreign policy. Cassell's verdicts should be compared with those in Pancake, "The 'Invisibles' " (6:46).

6:51 Cleaves, Freeman. *Old Tippecanoe: William Henry Harrison and His Time*. New York: Scribner's, 1939. Cleaves's well-researched biography of Harrison (1773–1841), American commander on the western front during the War of 1812, traces the gradual development of American military power culminating in the battle of Lake Erie and the Thames. Earlier portions of this work, following Harrison's prewar negotiations with the Indians, show the rising tension on the frontier. Bibliography.

Dangerfield, G. *Chancellor Robert R. Livingston of New York, 1746–1813* (4:73) contains a most important treatment of the negotiations about Louisiana. Dangerfield stresses the personal credit owing to Livingston, the minister to Paris who acted alone until James Monroe arrived for the denouement.

Hatfield, Joseph T. *William Claiborne: Jeffersonian Centurian in the American Southwest* (6:93) treats an important lieutenant of Jefferson.

6:52 Irwin, Ray W. *Daniel W. Tompkins, Governor of New York and Vice President of the United States*. New York: New York Historical Society, 1968. Tompkins (1774–1825), successor to Burr and Clinton as Republican leader in the state, is shown to have been an intense nationalist and, consequently, a supporter of the War of 1812. Irwin's grasp of developments within New York is more sure than his understanding of national and diplomatic issues.

Jacobs, J. R. *Tarnished Warrior: Major-General James Wilkinson* (5:68) is valuable chiefly because it presents the life of an important figure in the frontier intrigue of the time.

Morison, S. E. *The Life and Letters of Harrison Gray Otis, Federalist, 1765–1848* (5:74) helps to elucidate the ideas of New England Federalists, although Otis avoided the excesses of many of his coadjutors.

FOREIGN

George Canning

See Chapter 7, "Personalities," for additional references.

6:53 Hinde, Wendy. *George Canning.* London: Collins, 1973. Hinde's *Canning* has very little on American affairs. However, the personal characteristics which colored his American policy are clearly shown not to have been aberrations; the main objectives of his policy, which largely determined his attitude toward the United States while at the Foreign Office (1807–1809), are made clear. Even less attention to American affairs is paid in Peter Dixon, *Canning: Politician and Statesman* (London: Weidenfeld & Nicolson, 1976).

6:54 Temperley, Harold W. V. *Life of Canning.* London: Finch, 1905. This dated, essentially uncritical study of Canning's public career devotes only one chapter to his tenure at the Foreign Office (1807–1809), and that chapter does not delve into relations with the United States. The book, although considered a classic work, is useful to historians of American diplomacy only in providing background information.

Lord Castlereagh
See Chapter 7, "Personalities," for additional references.

6:55 Bartlett, Christopher J. *Castlereagh.* New York: Scribner's, 1966. The shortcomings of this biography are obvious: it does not rest on research in primary materials. Its merits are briskness, clarity, and judgment. Castlereagh's general outlook, the setting in which he worked, and the impact of his larger problems upon relations with the United States are made clear. Bibliographical note.

6:56 Castlereagh, Lord. *Correspondence, Despatches, and Other Papers of Viscount Castlereagh, Second Marquess of Londonderry, Third Series.* Ed. by Marquess of Londonderry. 4 vols. London: John Murray, 1853. Volumes 1 and 2 of this series, which reproduce letters to and from Lord Castlereagh, include some material dealing with the negotiations at Ghent in 1814. Although useful, the selections do not fully elucidate British policy during the negotiations.

Francisco de Miranda
6:57 Robertson, William S. *The Life of Miranda.* 2 vols. Chapel Hill: University of North Carolina Press, 1929. This biography, although old, is still the most useful life of the first important Latin American revolutionary. Francisco de Miranda (1750–1816) had many contacts with Americans and drew support from them, particularly for his 1806 filibustering expedition. Robertson's research is impressive, although it concentrates rather narrowly on Miranda rather than the setting in which he moved. Bibliography.

6:58 Robertson, William S., ed. "Francisco de Miranda and the Revolutionizing of Spanish America." In the Annual Report of the American Historical Association for the Year 1907. Washington, D.C.: G.P.O., 1908, vol. 1, pp. 189–550. This correspondence covers Miranda's career: his intrigues with both France and Great Britain to obtain aid in overthrowing Spanish rule in South America and his relations with Rufus King and other Americans in London in 1798.

Napoleon Bonaparte
See Chapter 5, "Personalities," for additional references.

6:59 Geyl, Pieter. *Napoleon: For and Against.* New Haven, Conn.: Yale University Press, 1949. This volume perceptively analyzes the literature on Napoleon written from 1815 to 1940, concentrating on important contributions and making no effort to be exhaustive. In addition, Geyl's work is useful because of the author's own comments on Napoleon and his career, including his foreign policy.

6:60 Heath, Phoebe A. *Napoleon I and the Origins of the Anglo-American War of 1812.* Toulouse: Privat, 1929. The theme of this old, somewhat naive work is almost unique. (A. Schalck de la Faverie, *Napoléon et l'Amérique* [Napoleon and America], [Paris: Librairie Payot, 1917], is far less satisfactory.) The conclusions, on balance unfavorable to Napoleon, are supported by modest research.

Lefebvre, G. *Napoleon* . . . . (6:86 and 6:87).

Others
6:61 Gray, Denis. *Spencer Perceval, the Evangelical Prime Minister, 1762–1812.* Manchester: Manchester University Press, 1963. This turgid yet impressive biography emphasizes that portion of Perceval's career (1807–1812) most important for American diplomatic historians. No other work more comprehensively deals with British factional politics, and there is extended treatment of the order-in-council. However, Gray's limited knowledge of American developments leads to some errors. Extensive bibliography.

6:62 Great Britain. Historical Manuscripts Commission. *Report on the Manuscripts of Earl Bathurst Preserved at Cirencester Park.* Ed. by Francis

Bickley. London: H.M.S.O., 1923. This volume, which reproduces selections from the correspondence of Lord Bathurst, an important member of the Perceval government with a particular interest in American affairs, includes a substantial amount of information regarding the order-in-council and the negotiations at Ghent in 1814.

6:63   Lester, Malcolm. *Anthony Merry Redivivus.* Charlottesville: University Press of Virginia, 1978. This effort to restore the reputation of the British minister to the United States from 1803 to 1806, universally excoriated by previous historians, is vigorous and provocative, if not entirely successful. Bibliography.

6:64   Rose, J. Holland. *William Pitt and the Great War.* London: Bell, 1911. Reprint 1971. Rose's old treatment of Pitt's role (1789–1806) during the Anglo-French wars will remain the standard work only until John Ehrman completes his multivolume biography of Pitt, now carried only to 1789. There is little bearing directly upon the United States in Rose's detailed, nationalistic account.

6:65   Wellington, Arthur, Duke of. *Supplementary Despatches, Correspondence, and Memoranda of Field Marshal Arthur Duke of Wellington, K.G.* Ed. by Arthur, Second Duke of Wellington. London: John Murray, 1862, vol. 9. This volume, which includes letters to and from the Duke of Wellington, contains important material bearing upon the Ghent negotiations, in particular the British decision, taken in the fall of 1814, to terminate the war at the expense of abandoning major British objectives.

The Setting:
Politics and Policy

AMERICAN POLITICS

See "Personalities" for additional references; also "Document Collections" for Cunningham (5:7), and "Bibliographies" for Ferguson (1:72).

6:66   Banner, James M., Jr. *To the Hartford Convention: The Federalists and the Origins of Party Politics*

in Massachusetts, 1789–1815. New York: Knopf, 1970. This thoroughly researched and forcefully argued study sheds much light on the setting for diplomacy. Banner not only exposes Federalist errors and inconsistencies, he makes their positions understandable and goes far to explain their rise and fall. Bibliography.

6:67   Brown, Stuart G. *The First Republicans: Political Philosophy and Public Policy in the Party of Jefferson and Madison.* Syracuse, N.Y.: Syracuse University Press, 1954. This short study provides a convenient introduction to the ideology and policy of the Republicans. On the whole, the judgments are conventional and/or sympathetic. Unfortunately, the research, both in primary and secondary materials, leaves a good deal to be desired, and the chief emphasis is on the period prior to 1801. Bibliographical note.

6:68   Chambers, William N. *Political Parties in a New Nation, 1776–1809.* New York: Oxford University Press, 1963. This account, already brief, devotes only a small portion of its attention to the period of Jefferson's presidency. Nevertheless, it is valuable for its treatment of the factors influencing party development and limiting the extent of party discipline.

6:69   Cooper, Joseph. "Jeffersonian Attitudes toward Executive Leadership and Committee Development in the House of Representatives, 1789–1829." *Western Political Quarterly* 18:1 (1965), 45–63. This article, based on a close reading of the *Annals of Congress* (1:351), would have been even more useful had the range of research been wider. Cooper shows how, during the presidencies of Jefferson and Madison, Republican theories of government led to a diminution of direct executive leadership. Although rarely dealing with political issues as such, Cooper clarifies congressional procedures regarding them, including the decision for war in 1812.

6:70   Cunningham, Noble E., Jr. *The Jeffersonian Republicans in Power, 1801–1809.* Chapel Hill: University of North Carolina Press, 1963. This sequel to a volume dealing with the foundation of the Republican party (5:170) concentrates in perhaps excessive detail upon organization and operation. Among its strengths are an exposure of the differences between states and an examination of the congressional caucus as an instrument of leadership. Bibliographical note.

6:71   Cunningham, Noble E., Jr. *The Process of Government under Jefferson.* Princeton, N.J.: Princeton University Press, 1978. This detailed study examines the administrative processes of the executive and legislative branches of government during Jefferson's administrations. While there is very little that bears directly upon American diplomacy, the volume is useful because it explores such things as the relationship between the president and his lieutenants, and the locations of influence in Congress. Bibliography.

6:72   Fischer, David H. *The Revolution of American Conservatism: The Federalist Party in the Era of Jeffersonian Democracy.* New York: Harper & Row, 1965. Fischer's stimulating, brief study examines patterns of party behavior. Fischer argues that, reluctantly and in self-defense, Federalists abandoned their deferential view of politics and embraced a majoritarian one.

6:73   Goodman, Paul. *The Democratic-Republicans in Massachusetts.* Cambridge: Harvard University Press, 1964. This well-written and well-researched study stresses the complexity of Massachusetts politics and the feebleness of party loyalties during the early national period, as well as the impact of diplomatic issues upon the latter. Extensive bibliography.

6:74   Graber, Doris A. *Public Opinion, the President, and Foreign Policy: Four Case Studies from the Formative Years.* New York: Holt, Rinehart & Winston, 1968. While pointing out that the president's concepts of public sentiment varied a good deal, Graber suggests that in the cases under review (Louisiana and the war decision of 1812 are included) the influence of public opinion was small. Interesting for methodology, the study suffers from a paucity of research and a lack of historical sophistication.

6:75   Hofstadter, Richard. *The Idea of a Party System.* Berkeley: University of California Press, 1969. This thoughtful study is a useful corrective to the tendency to view politics in the Jeffersonian era as a contest between clearly defined Republican and Federalist parties. From a different angle, it makes somewhat the same point as Young (6:79).

6:76   Risjord, Norman K. *The Old Republicans: Southern Conservatism in the Age of Jefferson.* New York: Columbia University Press, 1965. Although Risjord's primary purpose is to identify the "Old Republicans," a faction which resisted nationalizing tendencies, his discussion of Republican schisms, the nature of presidential leadership and the decision for

war in 1812 shed broad light on the period. Extensive bibliography.

6:77   Sofaer, Abraham D. *War, Foreign Affairs and Constitutional Power: The Origins.* Cambridge, Mass.: Ballinger, 1976. This ground-breaking study by a legal historian explores the extent of the president's powers regarding diplomacy and war. It discusses such issues as the Louisiana Purchase, the West Florida affair, the Embargo, and the War of 1812.

6:78   White, Leonard D. *The Jeffersonians: A Study in Administrative History, 1801–1829.* New York: Macmillan, 1951. Jefferson's managerial style, the methods of conducting diplomacy and Gallatin's difficulties in enforcing the Embargo are among the topics examined by White.

6:79   Young, James S. *The Washington Community, 1800–1828.* New York: Columbia University Press, 1966. This often intricate, occasionally overstated study argues that after a brief period of successful leadership by Jefferson, presidents lost control of Congress, partly because the Republican party was composed of uncontrollable blocs with little loyalty to its head or to its policies.

EUROPEAN POLITICS

Britain

See "Personalities" for additional references; also "Document Collections" for Mayo (5:10), and "Bibliographies" for Brown and Christie (6:1).

6:80   Feiling, Keith G. *The Second Tory Party, 1714–1832.* London: Macmillan, 1938. Despite its title, Feiling's book comes near to being a history of partisan or factional politics generally. Only a bit more than two chapters deal with the period from 1801 to 1815, but this is still a good introduction to the feebleness of British party ties. Extensive bibliography.

6:81   Roberts, Michael. *The Whig Party, 1807–1812.* London: Macmillan, 1939. Roberts's study, based on exemplary research, is organized topically. Unfortunately, chapter 3, "The Whigs and the War," has little to say about matters which concerned the United States; it virtually ignores the campaign against the order-in-council in which Whig leaders played an important, active role. Roberts stresses Whig difficulties, factionalism and—as far as the war is concerned—vacuity. Extensive bibliography.

6:82 Ward, Sir Adolphus W., and Gooch, George P., eds. *The Cambridge History of British Foreign Policy. Vol. 1: 1783–1815.* New York: Macmillan, 1922. Reprint 1977. This volume is now very much dated; nevertheless, it is still the best survey of its subject. The chapter on Anglo-American relations is thin, but other chapters develop British policies toward Europe in ways that make policy toward the United States more understandable.

6:83 Watson, J. Steven. *The Reign of George III, 1760–1815.* Oxford: Clarendon Press, 1960. Like others in this section, this book is valuable essentially for the background it provides. Internal politics in Great Britain and the problems of the French war, two matters of great importance for relations with the United States, are covered, the first more satisfactorily than the second. Bibliography.

France

See "Personalities" for additional references about Napoleon Bonaparte.

6:84 Bergeron, Louis *L'Épisode napoléonienne: Aspects extérieurs, 1799–1815* [The Napoleonic period: foreign developments, 1799–1815]. Paris: Editions de Seuil, 1972. This work is an able, if brief, work of synthesis. Much of it is devoted to military campaigns, although the treatments of diplomacy and particularly of the Continental System, frequently critical of Napoleon, help to make his American diplomacy understandable.

Blumenthal, H. *France and the United States: Their Diplomatic Relations, 1789–1914* (2:224) devotes a mere thirty pages to the years prior to 1815, yet it is the only modern treatment of its subject.

Echeverria, D. *Mirage in the West: A History of the French Image of American Society to 1815* (4:120) places most of its emphasis before 1799, but the last chapter, entitled "The Consulate and the Empire, 1799–1815," provides helpful material on the period of Jefferson and Madison.

6:85 Fugier, André. *La Révolution française et l'empire napoléonienne* [The French Revolution and the Napoleonic empire]. Paris: Hachette, 1954. Fugier provides an introduction, essentially a work of synthesis rather than research, to the diplomacy of the major nations in this turbulent age as well as the domestic underpinnings of that diplomacy. Probably most use-

ful to an American historian for its description of French policy, the volume also devotes substantial attention to American developments. Bibliography.

6:86 Lefebvre, Georges. *Napoleon: From 18 Brumaire to Tilsit, 1799–1807.* Trans. by Henry F. Stockhold. London: Routledge & Kegan Paul, 1969.

6:87 Lefebvre, Georges. *Napoleon: From Tilsit to Waterloo, 1807–1815.* Trans. by J. E. Anderson. London: Routledge & Kegan Paul, 1969. These two volumes are translations of portions of Lefebvre's classic study, *Napoléon,* first published in 1935. Lefebvre's research is prodigious although somewhat unobtrusive since there are no footnotes. The scope is broad, both geographically and topically; this is the study of an age even more than a biography. Bibliography of printed materials.

The Netherlands

See Chapters 4 and 5 for references to U.S.-Netherlands relations.

Russia

See Chapters 5 and 7 for additional references.

Bolkhovitinov, N. N. *The Beginnings of Russian-American Relations, 1755–1815* (4:137). Based on research in both countries; however, it is particularly important because of the author's intensive work in Russian materials.

6:88 Crosby, Alfred W. *America, Russia, Hemp and Napoleon: American Trade with Russia and the Baltic, 1783–1812.* Columbus: Ohio State University Press, 1965. While this book provides few insights into Russian policy, it does depict the nature of American trade with Russia and the economic warfare being conducted in Europe. Bibliographies.

Golder, F. A. "The Russian Offer of Mediation in the War of 1812" (6:176).

Kushner, H. I. *Conflict on the Northwest Coast . . . , 1790–1867* (8:92) covers, in chapter 1, the period to 1815; although very brief, the discussion complements Bolkhovitinov (4:137).

6:89 Ryan, A. N. "The Defense of British Trade with the Baltic, 1808–1813." *English Historical Re-*

view 74:292 (1959), 443–66. One of the principal leaks in the Continental System was the trade with the Baltic, a trade in which the Americans participated. This article describes British efforts to keep that trade open in the face of obstruction by Napoleon's satellites.

THE BARBARY STATES

For references, see Chapter 18.

Louisiana and the Spanish Empire

Chapter 7 contains additional references; see also "Bibliographies" for Coker and Holmes (3:4) and Trask (1:121); also see "Document Collections" for Manning (7:5).

See "Personalities," especially Francisco de Miranda.

Coatsworth, J. H. "American Trade with European Colonies in the Caribbean and South America, 1790–1812" (5:144).

Kaufmann, W. W. *British Policy and the Independence of Latin America, 1804–1828* (7:61).

Logan, J. A. *No Transfer: An American Security Principle* [1760–1945] (2:272) examines the Louisiana and Florida controversies in this light.

Madariaga, S. de. *The Fall of the Spanish American Empire* (7:63).

McDermott, J. F., ed. *The Spanish in the Mississippi Valley, 1762–1804* (3:10).

Nichols, R. F. "Trade Relations and the Establishment of the United States Consulates in Spanish America, 1779–1809" (5:145).

Peterson, H. F. *Argentina and the United States, 1810–1960* (2:287) deals with the period prior to 1815 in a single chapter, points out early American com-

mercial contacts, and describes the mission of the first commercial agent, Joel R. Poinsett.

6:90   Whitaker, Arthur P. *The United States and the Independence of Latin America, 1800–1830.* Baltimore: Johns Hopkins Press, 1941. The first three chapters of this classic account describe the early development of commercial contacts, the dispatch of commercial agents to serve in Latin America, and the "Large Policy of 1808," Jefferson's dreams of expansion. Bibliographical note.

THE LOUISIANA PURCHASE

For earlier French interest, see Chapter 5, "The Genet Mission, 1793–1794"; also see "Personalities" for additional references, especially Thomas Jefferson, Robert R. Livingston (under "Others"), and James Monroe.

6:91   Adams, Mary P. "Jefferson's Reaction to the Treaty of San Ildefonso." *Journal of Southern History* 21:2 (1955), 173–88. This article, drawn from a variety of primary sources, shows Jefferson's reactions to the retrocession of Louisiana. His attention to military preparations shows that the president was willing to consider, or at least to threaten, war if Napoleon persisted in his Louisiana adventure.

6:92   DeConde, Alexander. *This Affair of Louisiana.* New York: Scribner's, 1976. This volume, now the standard treatment of the Louisiana cession, rests upon extensive research. Although DeConde discusses and often incorporates the judgments of others, his emphasis is upon the drive for Louisiana as part of an expansionist, even imperialist, American tradition. Extensive bibliographical essay.

6:93   Hatfield, Joseph T. *William Claiborne: Jeffersonian Centurion in the American Southwest.* Lafayette: University of Southwestern Louisiana Press, 1976. Claiborne was an important lieutenant of Jefferson and an unvarying expansionist. This biography contributes to an understanding of the acquisition of Louisiana and West Florida as well as the coming of the War of 1812.

Hidy, R. W. *The House of Baring in American Trade and Finance* (8:155) is useful for the financing of the Louisiana Purchase.

Logan, R. W. *The Diplomatic Relations of the United States with Haiti, 1776–1891* (5:121) discusses, in

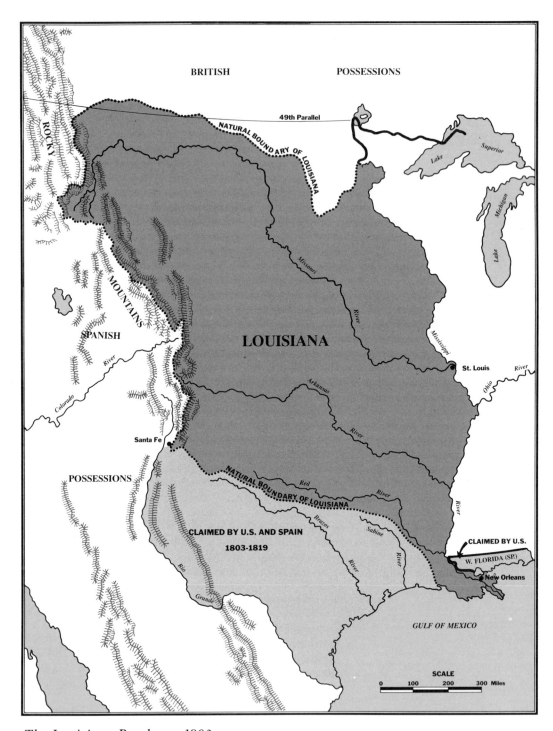

The Louisiana Purchase, 1803

chapters 4 and 5, the Jeffersonian period and, among other things, provides useful information on Napoleon's effort to put down the Haitian revolt and the American reaction thereto.

Lyon, E. W. *The Man Who Sold Louisiana: The Career of François Barbé-Marbois* (4:99) finds Barbé-Marbois playing a large role in the sale of Louisiana and, perhaps, in influencing the First Consul to make it.

6:94 Lyon, E. Wilson. *Louisiana in French Diplomacy, 1759–1804.* Norman: University of Oklahoma Press, 1934. Before publication of DeConde (6:92), this study and Whitaker (6:98) were the most important contributions to the history of the Louisiana Purchase. Both still retain great value, and they are complementary rather than rival studies, each stressing different aspects of the Louisiana affair. Lyon's emphasis is on the formulation of French policy, including a discussion of the motives which impelled Napoleon to abandon his Louisiana project. Extensive bibliography.

Ott, T. O. *The Haitian Revolution, 1789–1804* (5:122) is based on wide research but does not materially revise previous interpretations. Only a small portion of the volume deals with Napoleon's Haitian-Louisiana problems.

Perkins, B. *The First Rapprochement . . . , 1795–1805* (6:10).

6:95 Renaut, François P. *La Question de la Louisiane, 1796–1806* [The Louisiana question, 1796–1806]. Paris: Champion, 1918. This short summary of the Louisiana issue from the French point of view carries the story into the debate over the extent of the purchase. It is based very largely on French archival materials, although even here it suffers by comparison with Lyon (6:94).

6:96 Smith, Ronald D. "Napoleon and Louisiana: Failure of the Proposed Expedition to Occupy and Defend Louisiana, 1801–1803." *Louisiana History* 12:1 (1971), 21–41. Smith gracefully reviews the factors underlying Napoleon's policies toward Louisiana. His conclusion, the result of a careful study of French official documents, is that a combination of circumstances led the emperor to order the sale to the United States.

Tansill, C. C. *The United States and Santo Domingo, 1798–1873* (5:123) sheds light on Napoleon's policies

and the difficulties he faced and thus, in turn, upon one facet of the Louisiana question.

6:97 U.S. Department of State. *State Papers and Correspondence Bearing upon the Purchase of the Territory of Louisiana.* Washington, D.C.: G.P.O., 1903. At the direction of Congress, the Department of State prepared this volume, which contains correspondence (1800–1803) drawn almost exclusively from department archives. Virtually all of it is letters to and from American representatives in Europe, although enclosed material from foreign sources is included.

6:98 Whitaker, Arthur P. *The Mississippi Question, 1795–1803: A Study in Trade, Politics, and Diplomacy.* New York: Appleton-Century, 1934. Whitaker still provides the most complete study of the growth of American trade and interest in the area, and it offers a less intensive but thoughtful treatment of French and Spanish policy.

6:99 Whitaker, Arthur P. "The Retrocession of Louisiana in Spanish Policy." *American Historical Review* 39:3 (1934), 454–76. From a detailed examination of Franco-Spanish relations in the wake of Pinckney's Treaty, Whitaker concludes that Godoy began immediately to negotiate for the retrocession of Louisiana to France. In return, Godoy planned to recover Santo Domingo and to win French support for an attack on Gibraltar.

6:100 Winston, James E., and Colomb, R. W. "How the Louisiana Purchase Was Financed." *Louisiana Historical Quarterly* 12:2 (1929), 189–237. In 1803 the House of Baring cooperated with Amsterdam's Hope and Company in financing the United States' purchase of Louisiana from France.

SPANISH BORDERLANDS

See "Personalities" for additional references, especially Aaron Burr and, under "Others," James Wilkinson; also see Chapter 7, "The Florida Question."

Bannon, J. F. *The Spanish Borderlands Frontier, 1513–1821* (3:91).

6:101 Brooks, Philip C. "Spain's Farewell to Louisiana, 1803–1821." *Mississippi Valley Historical Review* 27:1 (1940–1941), 29–42. Brooks, author of the standard account of the Florida cession of 1819, shows that, foolishly, some Spanish officials continued to dream of recovering Louisiana until 1815.

Cook, W. L. *Flood Tide of Empire: Spain and the Pacific Northwest, 1543–1819* (5:180).

Cox, I. J. *The West Florida Controversy, 1798–1813* (7:47) criticizes almost every American leader involved in this affair, above all Jefferson.

Egan, C. L. "The United States, France, and West Florida, 1803–1807" (7:49) supplements Cox particularly as a consequence of his close examination of French archives. Jefferson emerges badly.

Nasatir, A. P. *Borderland in Retreat: From Spanish Louisiana to the Far Southwest* [1762–1822] (5:136).

Patrick, R. W. *Florida Fiasco: Rampant Rebels on the Georgia-Florida Border, 1810–1815* (7:51) is a vivacious account of efforts by George Matthews and others to filch Florida from Spain and deepens the account in Pratt.

Pratt, J. W. *The Expansionists of 1812* (6:140).

Coming of the War of 1812

6:102   Egan, Clifford L. "The Origins of the War of 1812: Three Decades of Historical Writing." *Military Affairs* 38:2 (1974), 72–75. This short article seeks to bring Goodman, below, up to date. The text discusses only a limited number of works, and the comments often are brisk. The footnotes, as lengthy as the article itself, provide a good guide to works published between 1940 and 1973.

6:103   Goodman, Warren H. "The Origins of the War of 1812: A Survey of Changing Interpretations." *Mississippi Valley Historical Review* 28:2 (1941–1942), 171–86. This able historiographical article, often considered a model, thoughtfully assesses the material available to 1941. Goodman's judgments are deft, and his suggestions for further work and speculations as to its likely outcome are impressive, especially since many have come true.

GENERAL

Burt, A. L. *The United States, Great Britain and British North America from the Revolution to the Establishment of Peace after the War of 1812* (6:5).

6:104   Carr, Albert Z. *The Coming of War*. Garden City, N.Y.: Doubleday, 1960. This lively, popular study refuses to weigh one presumed cause of war in 1812 against another, insisting instead that such factors were important only as a manifestation of a broader shift in the power equation between the two nations. Bibliography.

Dangerfield, G. *Era of Good Feelings* [1817–1825] (6:173).

6:105   Horsman, Reginald. *The Causes of the War of 1812*. Philadelphia: University of Pennsylvania Press, 1962. Horsman stresses the importance of maritime issues, reaching the rather commonsensical conclusion that, had there been no European conflict and thus no assault on American neutral rights, there would have been no war between the United States and Great Britain. His critical examination of the importance of the Indian problem and the presumed desire to conquer Canada is particularly impressive. Bibliography.

Perkins, B. *Prologue to War . . . , 1805–1812* (6:11).

6:106   White, Patrick C. T. *A Nation on Trial: America and the War of 1812*. New York: Wiley, 1965. This short study of the years from 1803 to 1815 has many minor errors and inconsistencies, and there are few original judgments. For the most part the author is content to meld the various interpretations of the coming of war and the peace of Ghent.

SOURCES OF CONTROVERSY

The War of Decrees and American Commerce

See "Personalities," under "Foreign," "Others," for Anthony Merry; also see references under "European Politics," "France" and "Russia."

Bonnel, U. *La France, les États-Unis et la guerre de course, 1797–1815* (5:205) sheds light on French seizures of American ships. The number of captures, the behavior and principles of French prize courts and the administrative details of French policy are examined.

Buck, N. S. *The Development of the Organization of Anglo-American Trade, 1800–1850* (8:153) sticks very narrowly to the subject of its title and does not consider trade in its political aspects, but it is still helpful.

6:107   Clauder, Anna C. *American Commerce as Affected by the Wars of the French Revolution and Napoleon, 1793–1810.* Philadelphia: University of Pennsylvania Press, 1932. This dissertation attempts only to weigh the impact on American trade of European restrictions, not the origins of those restrictions. Because the scene shifted so frequently, few clear and persistent themes emerge, but the data presented are important to an understanding of the period. Bibliography.

6:108   Crouzet, François. *L'Économie britannique et le Blocus Continental, 1806–1813* [The British economy and the Continental System, 1806–1813]. 2 vols. Paris: Presses Universitaires de France, 1958. This study is absolutely essential to an understanding of economic conditions in Britain and of the effectiveness of French policy toward commerce. It cannot be ignored by the student of Anglo-American relations, although only a small part deals directly with American commerce. The bibliography contains exhaustive lists of British governmental archives and the manuscripts of business figures and commercial houses.

6:109   Graham, Gerald S. *Sea Power and British North America, 1783–1820.* Cambridge: Harvard University Press, 1941. Part 4, "The Challenge of the United States," describes important aspects of Anglo-American commercial relations from a British vantage point.

6:110   Heckscher, Eli F. *The Continental System: An Economic Interpretation.* Oxford: Clarendon Press, 1922. Heckscher stresses the mercantilist aspects of Napoleonic and, to a lesser degree, British policy. Implicitly and sometimes explicitly, he contrasts those policies with the ones pursued by belligerents during World War I. A Swede cut off from foreign archives and libraries by the war, Heckscher wrote a volume which in some ways suffers by comparison with Melvin (6:113); however, its arguments are clearer.

Hidy, R. W. *The House of Baring in American Trade and Finance* (8:155) is useful for the picture it gives of the organization, the volume, and the vagaries of Anglo-American commercial intercourse during the European wars.

Hyneman, C. S. "The First American Neutrality . . . , 1792 to 1815" (5:171).

6:111   Jouvenel, Bertrand D. *Napoléon et l'économie dirigée* [Napoleon and the planned economy]. Brussels: Editions de la Toison d'Or, 1942. Although this work is not qualitatively the equal of Melvin (6:113), it sets the emperor's policies (1799–1815), of which it is frequently critical, in a broader context. Jouvenel emphasizes a determination to establish economic self-sufficiency as the core of Napoleon's policy.

6:112   Lingelbach, William E. "England and Neutral Trade." *Military Historian and Economist* 2:2 (1917), 153–78. This article is valuable chiefly for its interesting defense of the logic of the *Essex* decision of 1805, a landmark in the British treatment of American commerce, and is one of the best brief treatments of the problem in its legal aspects.

6:113   Melvin, Frank E. *Napoleon's Navigation System: A Study of Trade Control during the Continental Blockade.* New York: Appleton, 1919. Melvin examines the origins, the shifting impact and the political consequences of the Continental System. Admiration for Napoleon's talents and even for his economic perceptions is tempered by criticisms of various tactical moves. The trade of the United States is pictured as extremely important in the emperor's calculations. Extensive bibliography.

6:114   Parkinson, C. Northcote, ed. *The Trade Winds: A Study of British Overseas Trade during the French Wars, 1793–1815.* London: Allen & Unwin, 1948. Although only one chapter (Herbert Heaton, "The American Trade," pp. 194–226) deals directly with American commerce, this volume deserves to be read in full. There is probably no study which so clearly and economically describes the state of British trade, an important factor in British policy toward neutrals.

6:115   Perkins, Bradford. "George Joy, American Propagandist at London, 1805–1815." *New England Quarterly* 34:2 (1961), 191–210. Through a study of the activities and correspondence of a self-appointed propagandist for the United States, this article sheds some light on opposition to the order-in-council and, more generally, to British policies which exacerbated relations with the United States.

6:116   Perkins, Bradford. "Sir William Scott and the *Essex.*" *William and Mary Quarterly* 3d ser. 13:1 (1956), 169–83. This article, an expanded and reorganized version of the account in Perkins (6:11), examines the background and meaning of the *Essex* decision. It deserves to be read with Lingelbach, "England and Neutral Trade" (6:112), since some of the judgments directly conflict.

6:117 Phillips, W. Alison, and Reede, Arthur H. *The Napoleonic Period*. Vol. 2 in *Neutrality, Its History, Economics and Law*. New York: Columbia University Press, 1936. Although now somewhat out of date, this is a clear, well-constructed introduction to the problems of commerce during the period. It explicates the European policies which caused difficulty for the Americans.

Setser, V. G. *The Commercial Reciprocity Policy of the United States, 1774–1829* (4:150).

Impressment

6:118 Steel, Anthony. "Anthony Merry and the Anglo-American Dispute about Impressment, 1803–1806." *Cambridge Historical Journal* 9:2 (1947–1949), 331–51. This article, designed in part as an answer to Zimmerman (6:122), argues that from 1803 to 1806 impressment was an intrinsically unimportant issue. Steel makes little effort to understand the American point of view, which is pictured largely through the reports of Anthony Merry, British minister at Washington.

6:119 Steel, Anthony. "Impressment in the Monroe-Pinckney Negotiations, 1806–1807." *American Historical Review* 57:2 (1951–1952), 352–69. Reiterating themes presented in his other articles, Steel argues that impressment was vital to British security and indeed survival in the face of the Napoleonic challenge but, for the Americans, an essentially minor issue to be exploited or not, as politics suggested.

6:120 Steel, Anthony. "More Light on the *Chesapeake*." *Mariner's Mirror* 39:4 (1953), 243–65. While not denying that the attack on the *Chesapeake* in 1807 was "indefensible at law," Steel attempts to make it understandable. Basically, the argument is that the active recruitment of British sailors and deserters from the Royal Navy for service in the United States Navy created tension which was more the fault of the United States than Great Britain.

6:121 Tsiang I-Mien. *The Question of Expatriation in America Prior to 1907*. Baltimore: Johns Hopkins Press, 1942. The first chapter of Tsiang's slim monograph provides an introduction to the legal questions underlying the impressment issue. Among other things, it shows Jefferson's opposition to the doctrine of perpetual allegiance to have been established even before the Revolution.

6:122 Zimmerman, James F. *Impressment of American Seamen*. New York: Columbia University Press, 1925. The only monograph solely devoted to impressment, Zimmerman's work deserves examination. It is very much dated and it fails to place the issue in a broad context. However, this work provides a chronology and seeks to solve the vexing (perhaps insoluble) problem of the number of men taken by the Royal Navy. Zimmerman's study will be displaced when Scott T. Jackson, "Impressment and the Anglo-American Discord, 1787–1818" (Ph.D. diss., University of Michigan, 1976), is published.

Commercial Coercion and Its Effects

See "Personalities" for additional references, especially Thomas Jefferson.

6:123 Heaton, Herbert. "Non-Importation, 1806–1812." *Journal of Economic History* 1:2 (1941), 178–98. Heaton's study demonstrates that the Embargo and other legislation restricting American commerce left open far more trade than has often been assumed. He thus casts a negative light on the effectiveness of economic coercion as a means to procure satisfaction from the European powers.

6:124 Higham, Robin. "The Port of Boston and the Embargo of 1807–1809." *American Neptune* 16:3 (1956), 189–208. This useful article shows that, at least in Boston, the Embargo did not mean the death of commerce. An upsurge in coastal trade made the decline in overseas commerce less painful, and there were evasions and violations of the Embargo whose magnitude cannot be established.

6:125 Jennings, Walter W. *The American Embargo, 1807–1809*. Iowa City: University of Iowa Press, 1921. This old study is still valuable, particularly for its efforts to assess the Embargo's economic impact in the United States, on agriculture and especially industry as well as maritime commerce. This work suggests important questions even if it does not always answer them satisfactorily.

6:126 Labaree, Benjamin W. *Patriots and Partisans: The Merchants of Newburyport, 1764–1815*. Cambridge: Harvard University Press, 1962.

Labaree's study suggests important conclusions regarding the state of ocean trade and the impact of the Embargo which may have national or at least sectional applicability. The author also explores the rivalry between parties which was exacerbated by differences over foreign affairs, and he devotes some attention to the consideration of secession during the War of 1812. Extensive bibliography.

6:127 Reinoehl, John H. "Post-Embargo Trade and Merchant Prosperity: Experiences of the Crowninshield Family, 1809–1812." *Mississippi Valley Historical Review* 42:2 (1955–1956), 229–49. Reinoehl suggests that long-accepted generalizations about the basic healthiness of American overseas commerce must be reexamined. If the Crowninshields are typical, the Embargo seems merely to have concealed or speeded commercial decline, and prosperity did not return during the years of virtually open trade between 1809 and 1811.

6:128 Sears, Louis M. *Jefferson and the Embargo.* Durham, N.C.: Duke University Press, 1927. With Jennings (6:125) and the new work by Spivak (6:129), this is one of the essential works on the great Jeffersonian experiment (1807–1809). The underlying hypothesis—that Jefferson, a pacifist, sought to preserve peace by adopting the Embargo policy—is open to question. But Sears presents an argument that deserves to be considered.

6:129 Spivak, Burton I. *Jefferson's English Crisis: Commerce, Embargo, and the Republican Revolution.* Charlottesville: University Press of Virginia, 1979. This is the most satisfactory examination of Jefferson's thinking regarding the Embargo. He first conceived of it as a precautionary withdrawal from the ocean but subsequently came to hope that it would have a coercive impact upon Europe, especially Britain, and finally hoped that a cessation of foreign trade would help America turn away from "English" commercialism, which had a deleterious impact upon the nation's social and political mores. Bibliography.

The Decision for War

THE WEST AND THE INDIANS

See "Personalities" for additional references, especially William Henry Harrison, under "Others."

6:130 Anderson, Dice R. "The Insurgents of 1811." In the Annual Report of the American Historical Association for the Year 1911. Washington, D.C.: G.P.O., 1913, vol. 1, pp. 167–76. Anderson argues that Westerners sought war and the conquest of Canada, largely as a means of consolidating American control of Indians in the Northwest. It is a speculative essay rather than a piece of research, and important as an early statement of the thesis.

6:131 Byrd, Cecil K. "The Northwest Indians and the British Preceding the War of 1812." *Indiana Magazine of History* 38:1 (1942), 31–50. British policymaking officials desired good relations with the Indians and ordered subsidies to them, but they did not wish an Indian-American war to break out and sought to dissuade the tribes from starting one. Byrd's research is limited, but the thesis is now generally accepted.

6:132 Coleman, Christopher B. "The Ohio Valley in the Preliminaries of the War of 1812." *Mississippi Valley Historical Review* 7:1 (1920–1921), 39–50. Coleman argues, more on the basis of speculation than sound research, that the West led the demand for war, seeking Canada and seeking primarily to end British support for Indians who made American expansion difficult and dangerous.

6:133 Hacker, Louis M. "Western Land Hunger and the War of 1812: A Conjecture." *Mississippi Valley Historical Review* 10:4 (1924), 365–95. Hacker suggests that a greedy desire for fertile Canadian land explains western support for war in 1812. The argument was almost immediately demolished by Pratt (6:141), and the theme has not been since revived by any serious, attentive scholar.

6:134 Horsman, Reginald. "American Indian Policy in the Old Northwest, 1783–1812." *William and Mary Quarterly* 3d ser. 18:1 (1961), 35–53. Although only one-third of this article deals with the period after 1801, Horsman makes clear the ambiguities and contradictions of Jefferson's policy, a policy which produced the Indian reaction during the War of 1812.

6:135 Horsman, Reginald. "British Indian Policy in the Northwest, 1807–1812." *Mississippi Valley Historical Review* 45:1 (1958), 51–66. Horsman demonstrates that British Indian policy was essentially negative, precautionary, and defensive in purpose. Nevertheless, the acquisitiveness of Americans, the consequent Indian resistance, and the overzealousness of British agents created an explosive situation.

6:136 Horsman, Reginald. *Expansion and American Indian Policy, 1783–1812.* East Lansing: Michigan State University Press, 1967. The author describes the tension between expansionist pressures and the belief that the Indian tribes should be fairly treated, and he explains the development of difficulties on the frontier during the War of 1812.

6:137 Horsman, Reginald. *Matthew Elliott, British Indian Agent.* Detroit: Wayne State University Press, 1964. By concentrating on an important British agent around Detroit, Horsman develops themes he briefly discussed in "British Indian Policy" (6:135). British policy was complex, somewhat contradictory, and subject to easy American misunderstanding. Bibliography.

6:138 Horsman, Reginald. "Western War Aims, 1811–1812." *Indiana Magazine of History* 53:1 (1957), 1–18. Horsman here gathers together and summarizes the arguments, insofar as they deal with the West, later presented in *The Causes of the War of 1812* (6:105). Essentially, his conclusions challenge those presented in Pratt (6:140).

6:139 Lewis, Howard T. "A Re-Analysis of the Causes of the War of 1812." *Americana* 6 (1911), 506–16, 577–78. Lewis's article shares honors with Anderson (6:130) for having developed the view that the declaration of war in 1812 was essentially the product of a desire for the conquest of Canada and that the Indians were the chief western concern.

Patrick, R. W. *Florida Fiasco* (7:51).

6:140 Pratt, Julius W. *The Expansionists of 1812.* New York: Macmillan, 1925. Without question the most influential study of the coming of the War of 1812, this work argues that, at the behest of the West and South, the United States went to war in an effort to conquer Canada and Florida. Westerners sought to eradicate Indian interference, Southerners to acquire territory and to open trade routes. Much recent scholarship suggests corrections, but textbooks still follow his interpretation. Bibliography.

6:141 Pratt, Julius W. "Western Aims in the War of 1812." *Mississippi Valley Historical Review* 12:1 (1925), 36–50. This is an effective rebuttal of Hacker's argument (6:133) that the West sought the conquest of Canadian farmland. Pratt particularly stresses the existence of a "bargain" between western and southern expansionists.

6:142 Stagg, J. C. A. "James Madison and the Coercion of Great Britain: Canada, the West Indies, and the War of 1812." *William and Mary Quarterly* 3d ser. 38:1 (1981), 3–34. This article adds a new dimension to the discussion of American reasons for attacking Canada. Stagg argues that Madison sought its conquest so as to deprive the British empire, especially the West Indies, of goods exported (often illegally) through Canada from the United States and also of the increasing exports of Canada itself. Otherwise, Madison feared, his preferred policy of commercial restriction would be fatally undermined.

6:143 Taylor, George R. "Agrarian Discontent in the Mississippi Valley Preceding the War of 1812." *Journal of Political Economy* 39:4 (1931), 471–505. After an unstable boom, Taylor argues, the Mississippi Valley suffered a sharp series of economic setbacks after 1806. Ascribing depressed agricultural prices solely, but erroneously, to European interferences with trade, Westerners supported the Embargo in order to coerce Europe; when this failed, they endorsed war as an alternative. Taylor introduces a new element into the discussion of the West's war spirit, but he does not seek to assay the West's responsibility for the War of 1812.

6:144 Taylor, George R. "Prices in the Mississippi Valley Preceding the War of 1812." *Journal of Economic and Business History* 3:1 (1930), 148–63. This article is essential underpinning to Taylor's arguments in "Agrarian Discontent" (6:143). The author combines careful research with solid but imaginative economic concepts to demonstrate the fluctuations in prices and in economic conditions generally.

Tucker, G. *Tecumseh* (6:172).

Weinberg, A. K. *Manifest Destiny: A Study of Nationalist Expansionism in American History* [1775–1935] (2:55) has few direct references to the period of the War of 1812; however, several strands in American thought that are singled out could be tested in the Republican era.

Wright, J. L., Jr. *Britain and the American Frontier, 1783–1815* (5:182) stresses England's anti-American designs, while admitting that they were often complex, confused, and poorly executed. In the process, Wright challenges the views, among others, of Burt (6:5) and Horsman (6:105).

STATE AND LOCAL OPINION

See "Personalities" for additional references.

Abernethy, T. P. *The South in the New Nation, 1789–1816* (6:3).

Banner, J. M., Jr. *To the Hartford Convention: The Federalists and the Origins of Party Politics in Massachusetts, 1789–1815* (6:66).

6:145   Barlow, William R. "The Coming of the War of 1812 in Michigan Territory." *Michigan History* 53:2 (1969), 91–107. As early as 1807, Barlow argues, Michiganders were resigned to war with England. However, in an explicit refutation of Pratt (6:140), Barlow maintains that, far from seeking war as a solution to Indian problems, Michiganders feared that a conflict with England would touch off an Indian war for which they were unprepared.

6:146   Barlow, William R. "Ohio's Congressmen and the War of 1812." *Ohio History* 72:3 (1963), 175–94. This article extends Barlow's argument in the article immediately above. Ohio and its representatives in Washington were by no means unanimously for war in 1812; Canada was a target of opportunity rather than a war aim.

Goodman, P. *The Democratic-Republicans in Massachusetts* (6:73).

6:147   Haynes, Robert V. "The Southwest and the War of 1812." *Louisiana History* 5:1 (1964), 41–51. This brief examination of developments in the Mississippi and Orleans territories applies the interpretation of western sentiment expressed in Taylor, "Agrarian Discontent" (6:143). Southwesterners also had their eyes on the Floridas, since Spain's possession of them impeded access to the sea.

Labaree, B. W. *Patriots and Partisans* (6:126).

6:148   Latimer, Margaret K. "South Carolina—A Protagonist of the War of 1812." *American Historical Review* 60:4 (1956), 914–29. This article convincingly extends to South Carolina, and by implication to the entire South and perhaps even to all areas producing agricultural goods for export, Taylor's thesis in "Agrarian Discontent" (6:143). Many in South Carolina, suffering economically, blamed their problems on European interferences with trade and con-

cluded that war with Britain was the solution to their problems.

6:149   Lemmon, Sarah McCulloh. *North Carolina and the War of 1812*. Chapel Hill: University of North Carolina Press, 1973. This extremely intensive study examines North Carolina's attitudes toward a declaration of war and the war itself. There was significant opposition between 1812 and 1815. Lemmon emphasizes the importance of the national honor theme, downplaying the contributions of expansionism, fear of the Indians, and commercial depression. Bibliography.

6:150   Sapio, Victor A. *Pennsylvania and the War of 1812*. Lexington: University of Kentucky Press, 1970. This monograph confirms the recent emphasis on party considerations in the coming of the War of 1812. Outraged by British attacks upon American rights and convinced that peaceful coercion had failed, but not economically in distress, Pennsylvania Republicans supported war as an undesirable imperative.

6:151   Sears, Alfred B. *Thomas Worthington: Father of Ohio Statehood*. Columbus: Ohio State University Press, 1958. Chapters 6 through 9 (1803–1814) of this solid biography show that, as senator from Ohio, Worthington opposed war in 1812, in part because he feared the frontier was inadequately prepared for an Indian war. Sears believes that this position was shared by most of Worthington's constituents. Extensive bibliography.

6:152   Shulim, Joseph I. *The Old Dominion and Napoleon Bonaparte*. New York: Columbia University Press, 1952. This careful study traces attitudes toward Napoleon (1798–1809). It clearly demonstrates the falsity of the charge that either Jefferson or his followers had much use for Napoleon, whom they considered the betrayer of a republican experiment.

THE WAR SESSION: CONGRESS AND THE PRESIDENT

See "Personalities" for additional references, especially Henry Clay and James Madison.

6:153   Brown, Roger H. *The Republic in Peril: 1812*. New York: Columbia University Press, 1964. This important contribution stresses partisan as opposed to sectional considerations in the vote for war in 1812. Brown downplays the differences within the Republican party, denying for example that there were any real War Hawks. His study of Republican actions and attitudes in 1811–1812 is unmatched. Extensive bibliography.

Cooper, J. "Jeffersonian Attitudes toward Executive Leadership and Committee Development in the House of Representatives, 1789–1829" (6:69).

6:154   Fritz, Harry W. "The War Hawks of 1812: Party Leadership in the Twelfth Congress." *Capitol Studies* 5:1 (1977), 25–42. This article seeks to restore, in more sophisticated form, the War Hawk interpretation. Admitting the importance of partisan interest and Republican ideology, Fritz argues that they would have been insufficient to produce a declaration of war but for the leadership of the War Hawks. The argument is well worth considering.

6:155   Glover, Richard. "The French Fleet, 1807–1814: Britain's Problem and Madison's Opportunity." *Journal of Modern History* 39:1 (1967), 233–52. Glover argues that by 1812 Napoleon's rebuilt French naval power was nearly ready to challenge the Royal Navy's command of the seas. Glover seeks to demonstrate that French naval growth was an important factor in Madison's decision to support a war against Britain in 1812.

6:156   Hatzenbuehler, Ronald L. "Party Unity and the Decision for War in the House of Representatives, 1812." *William and Mary Quarterly* 3d ser. 29:3 (1972), 367–90. On the basis of roll call analysis, this article supports the argument that the vote for war is best explained in partisan rather than sectional terms. Hatzenbuehler's article is valuable to an understanding of the War Hawk Congress.

6:157   Hatzenbuehler, Ronald L. "The War Hawks and the Question of Congressional Leadership in 1812." *Pacific Historical Review* 45:1 (1976), 1–23. Hatzenbuehler differentiates between War Hawks and leaders, suggesting that without support from the latter, including Madison and Monroe, the War Hawks might not have had their way. Roll call analysis helps identify War Hawks, and the papers of Peter B. Porter, chairman of the House Foreign Affairs Committee, provide new details on the war session.

6:158   Horsman, Reginald; Brown, Roger; DeConde, Alexander; and Risjord, Norman. "The War

Hawks and the War of 1812." *Indiana Magazine of History* 60:2 (1964), 119–58. In this symposium, Horsman and Brown reiterate arguments for and against, respectively, the existence of a War Hawk faction in the Congress of 1811–1812. DeConde and Risjord comment. Taken together, the several contributions summarize the controversy.

6:159   Johnson, Leland R. "The Suspense Was Hell: The Senate Vote for the War of 1812." *Indiana Magazine of History* 55:4 (1969), 247–67. A detailed examination of the Senate during the war session, this article argues that the outcome in the upper chamber was even more problematical than in the House. Republican factionalism made a majority for war seem almost impossible, but party loyalty eked out a victory.

6:160   Kaplan, Lawrence S. "France and Madison's Decision for War, 1812." *Mississippi Valley Historical Review* 50:4 (1964), 652–71. Kaplan demonstrates that Madison and the Republicans had no love for Napoleonic France and never gave a moment's consideration to an alliance. They did hope that France would divert British resources and make America's task easier.

6:161   Morison, Samuel Eliot. "The Henry-Crillon Affair of 1812." *Proceedings of the Massachusetts Historical Society* 69 (1956), 207–32. A lively, scholarly treatment of a British secret agent, later a turncoat. President Madison sought to use John Henry's disclosures to influence the move toward war in 1812. The entire affair reflects little credit on anyone involved, least of all the president. (Morison's article adds much to E. A. Cruikshank, *The Political Adventures of John Henry* [Toronto: University of Toronto Press, 1936].)

Pancake, J. S. "The 'Invisibles'" (6:46).

6:162   Risjord, Norman K. "1812: Conservatives, War Hawks, and the Nation's Honor." *William and Mary Quarterly* 3d ser. 18:2 (1961), 196–210. Risjord argues that, faced with the alternatives of submission and war, Americans chose the latter as the only means to preserve the nation's honor. He downplays the importance of material factors such as ship seizures, economic depression, and expansionism.

6:163   Smith, Theodore C. "War Guilt in 1812." *Proceedings of the Massachusetts Historical Society* 64 (1932), 319–45. A shrewd examination of charges that War Hawks drove a reluctant Madison to endorse war in 1812 by threatening not to support his reelection, this article remains a useful contribution.

6:164 Stagg, J. C. A. "James Madison and the 'Malcontents': The Political Origins of the War of 1812." *William and Mary Quarterly* 3d ser. 33:4 (1976), 558–85. Stagg argues that, by working through congressional committees, Madison exercised much more leadership than has been generally recognized. Faced by challenges within the Republican party which threatened to deprive him of reelection and convinced that further negotiations with England were fruitless, he sought escape through a declaration of war.

The War of 1812

MILITARY AND POLITICAL DEVELOPMENTS

See "Personalities" for additional references, especially William Henry Harrison (under "Others") and James Madison; also see "Bibliographies" for Nichols (5:4).

6:165 Coles, Harry L. *The War of 1812*. Chicago: University of Chicago Press, 1965. This is essentially a work of military history, stronger in dealing with American than British developments. For diplomatic historians, Coles's study is useful only as background.

6:166 Gribbin, William. *The Churches Militant: The War of 1812 and American Religion*. New Haven, Conn.: Yale University Press, 1973. Both opponents and supporters of the war, of course, found justification for their positions in the Bible. The nation as a whole, however, believed that the successful conclusion of the war showed God's continued faith in the United States. Bibliography.

6:167 Horsman, Reginald. *The War of 1812*. New York: Knopf, 1964. This skillful narrative is particularly strong in reconstructing British policy and organization, although the interpretations tend to confirm rather than alter previous ones. The plan of the volume precludes much attention to diplomacy. Bibliographical note.

6:168 Kaplan, Lawrence S. "France and the War of 1812." *Journal of American History* 57:1 (1970), 36–47. Kaplan considers many of the same issues he discussed in "France and Madison's Decision for War" (6:160), extending the coverage forward to 1815. He shows how hopes and fears for Napoleon's success influenced American tactics, and he discusses the policies of the emperor and the restored Bourbons toward the United States.

Lemmon, S. M. *North Carolina and the War of 1812* (6:149).

6:169 Mahon, John K. *The War of 1812*. Gainesville: University of Florida Press, 1972. Longer than Coles's work (6:165) but with the same focus, this study provides a background to diplomacy.

6:170 Morison, Samuel Eliot. "Dissent in the War of 1812." In Samuel Eliot Morison; Frederick Merk; and Frank Freidel, *Dissent in Three American Wars*. Cambridge: Harvard University Press, 1970, pp. 3–31. This graceful essay contends that the War of 1812 was America's most unpopular war and suggests that civil war might have broken out in 1815 if the Ghent negotiations had not succeeded.

6:171 Pratt, Julius W. "Fur Trade Strategy and the American Left Flank in the War of 1812." *American Historical Review* 40:2 (1935), 246–73. This is almost purely an examination of the small-scale warfare west of the Great Lakes. The military situation there in 1814 would, on the basis of the principle of *uti possidetis,* have justified British title.

6:172 Tucker, Glenn. *Tecumseh: Vision of Glory.* Indianapolis: Bobbs-Merrill, 1956. Reprint 1973. This dated volume, although unreliable in some particulars, is still the most useful life of the Shawnee leader. Bibliography.

PEACE NEGOTIATIONS: THE TREATY OF GHENT

See "Personalities" for additional references, especially John Quincy Adams and Albert Gallatin.

6:173 Dangerfield, George. *The Era of Good Feelings*. New York: Harcourt, Brace, 1952. Despite its title, this book contains an extended discussion of the negotiations at Ghent and a shorter section dealing with the causes of the War of 1812. Dangerfield's judgments are not, in any real sense, revisionist, but they are so forcefully and colorfully presented as to reward the reader.

6:174 Engelman, Fred L. *The Peace of Christmas Eve*. New York: Harcourt, Brace & World, 1962. Engelman's lively study was the most complete account of the Ghent negotiations until publication of Perkins (6:12). The judgments, particularly regarding British policy, are usually conventional. Bibliography.

6:175 Gates, Charles M. "The West in American Diplomacy, 1812–1815." *Mississippi Valley Historical Review* 26:4 (1940), 499–510. Gates traces both American and British policy toward the West, showing in particular the brief rise and then, at Ghent, the fall of London's barrier state project.

6:176 Golder, Frank A. "The Russian Offer of Mediation in the War of 1812." *Political Science Quarterly* 31:3 (1916), 380–91. Despite its age, this article is, because of Golder's work in Russian archives, the only satisfactory account of the episode. He makes clear the tangle of conflicting motives behind the Russian offer to mediate between the United States and Russia's ally, Great Britain. The offer, embraced by the Americans, was rejected by the British.

6:177 Mills, Dudley. "The Duke of Wellington and the Peace Negotiations at Ghent in 1814." *Canadian Historical Review* 2:1 (1921), 19–33. Mills develops the now familiar point that Wellington warned the British ministry that military realities, notably failure to control the Great Lakes, did not justify demands for American territory. The Duke's intervention, it is suggested, was decisive.

Perkins, B. *Castlereagh and Adams . . . , 1812–1823* (6:12).

6:178 Updyke, Frank A. *The Diplomacy of the War of 1812*. Baltimore: Johns Hopkins Press, 1915. Although dated, this study is the most detailed account of the Ghent negotiations. Updyke used American and, to a lesser degree, British primary sources, but much more has become available, and many of his judgments are now questioned.

6:179 Webster, Charles K. *The Foreign Policy of Castlereagh, 1812–1815: Britain and the Reconstruction of Europe*. London: Bell, 1931. Although there is almost no mention of the United States, this volume provides the best understanding of Britain's position at the time of the Ghent negotiations. More than most background works, it should not be ignored.

Florida, Hispanic America, and the Monroe Doctrine

Contributing Editor
LESTER D. LANGLEY
University of Georgia

Contents

Introduction

The years from 1815 to 1860 saw fundamental changes in the evolution of American diplomacy, particularly in the development of United States policy toward the western hemisphere. In 1819 Secretary of State John Quincy Adams realized continentalist ambitions toward the southern frontier when the United States and Spain signed the Transcontinental Treaty, which finally settled the long and often acrimonious dispute along the Spanish-American frontier.

The salient issues of the Transcontinental Treaty related closely to another paramount question of the age—the posture a professedly revolutionary society should strike toward revolutionary movements in the Spanish empire, a debate that sharply divided American nationalists of these years, Adams, James Monroe, Henry Clay, Andrew Jackson, and other notable public figures. Recognition of the new Latin American governments was essentially a debate over tactics, whether the United States should move forthrightly, in keeping with its own revolutionary heritage, as Clay argued, or circumspectly, as Adams advocated, in order to settle the Florida question and avoid unwise political commitments.

In 1823 these issues were subsumed in a much more consequential debate over the British proposal for a joint statement affirming the independence of the new Latin American states. The response was Monroe's famous message to Congress of December 1823, drafted largely by Adams. In a profound statement that would eventually become known as the Monroe Doctrine, the message marked out a unilateral course for American policy *and* rejected alliance with the hemispheric republics or with Great Britain. In the ensuing years American relations with the new republics were typified by aggressive American commercial ambitions, interest in transisthmian routes, dreams of tropical empire, and, in the case of Mexico (as a subsequent chapter considers), a deterioration of diplomacy culminating in war.

The Florida question, the Monroe Doctrine, and American relations with Latin America from 1815 to 1861 are topics of continuing interest and debate among diplomatic historians. Yet, the most notable syntheses of these problems are works of an earlier generation of scholars: Arthur Whitaker, *The United States and the Independence of Latin America, 1800–1830* (6:90), a pioneering study which explains not only American policy but American impressions of the hemisphere from Thomas Jefferson to Andrew Jackson; Dexter Perkins's two volumes, *The Monroe Doctrine, 1823–1826* (7:132), and *The Monroe Doctrine, 1826–1867* (7:156), which have been rightly called a biography of a policy; and Samuel Flagg Bemis's monumental *John Quincy Adams and the Foundations of American Foreign Policy* (6:16), a classic biography and a major interpretation of American foreign relations from the Federalist era to the age of Jackson. The most recent effort to interpret the era has come from revisionist historians: William Appleman Williams, who argues the Monroe Doctrine culminated the American search for a definition of empire ("The Age of Mercantilism" [2:97]); and Richard Van Alstyne *The Rising American Empire* [2:96]), who integrates the salient events and disputes of the era into a coherent strategy for continental empire.

For the most part, historians have treated the Florida question, the Monroe Doctrine, and American relations with the hemispheric republics as related but separate issues. The scholarship on the Florida tangle, for example, generally divides on whether one considers the Transcontinental Treaty a result of Spanish imperial decline (Charles C. Griffin, *The United States and the Disruption of the Spanish Empire, 1810–1822: A Study of the Relations of the United States with Spain and the Rebel Spanish Colonies* [7:60]); frontier pressures (Philip C. Brooks, *Diplomacy and the Borderlands: The Adams-Onís Treaty of 1819* [7:57]); or, more recently, the imperial crusade of the archetypal continentalist (Robert Remini, *Andrew Jackson and the Course of American Empire, 1767–1821* [7:21]). Regrettably, the concept of the southern Indians as being more than pawns in the Florida dispute has not been fully integrated into diplomatic scholarship. And too much effort, perhaps, has been expended on inquiries into the authenticity of the Rhea letter and the authorization for Jackson's 1818 Florida raid.

Similarly, writings on the Monroe Doctrine have

often lapsed into endless squabbles over the origin of the timeless wisdom contained in Monroe's 1823 State of the Union address—the noncolonization doctrine, the concept of the two spheres, noninterference, etc.—to the detriment of other, more meaningful, issues. Books on the Monroe Doctrine abound; the Library of Congress card catalog lists more than 350 published works on the topic. The scholarship continues to be dominated by the superb multivolume history by Perkins (7:132, 7:156), a penetrating study based on multiarchival research, which insists that the origins of the doctrine lay in commercial pressures and that in fact European powers were not threatening intervention in the New World to restore the Spanish empire. The only serious challenge to Perkins's supremacy in the historiography on the doctrine is Ernest R. May's *The Making of the Monroe Doctrine* (7:131), which is less a history of the origins and meaning of Monroe's message than a penetrating discussion of political maneuvering by the leading presidential candidates in the Monroe cabinet. May, using quantitative techniques, challenges traditional approaches to the study of this diplomatic problem by suggesting that the primary motive of Monroe, Adams, and their cohorts in the great debate of autumn 1823 was not fear of European encroachment so much as political ambition.

As might be expected, scholarship on the Latin American revolutions and early hemispheric diplomatic relations has focused on the impact of these revolutions on the Florida treaty, and, later, on the Monroe Doctrine. Here, the pioneering work is Whitaker's *The United States and the Independence of Latin America* (6:90), which should be supplemented by rich scholarship on the same topic from the British perspective by William W. Kaufmann, *British Policy and the Independence of Latin America* (7:61); J. Fred Rippy, *Rivalry of the United States and Great Britain over Latin America* (7:11); Charles K. Webster, *The Foreign Policy of Castlereagh, 1815–1822* (7:34); and Harold Temperley, *The Foreign Policy of Canning, 1822–1827* (7:31).

There is much more to be done on the role of the American navy during the revolutions, though Edward Billingsley, *In Defense of Neutral Rights: The United States Navy and the Wars of Independence in Chile and Peru* (7:68), explores this topic. Most of the volumes published by Duke University Press in the 1930s on United States relations with individual hemispheric republics and later studies of a similar genre cover the revolutionary period in considerable detail. There are scores of scholarly articles focusing on the movement for recognition of the republics, the activities of American agents in Latin America and

Latin American agents in the United States, the economic rivalry of the United States and Great Britain for hemispheric trade, and the 1826 Panama Conference.

After the 1826 conclave, political though not commercial interest in Latin America (Mexico excepted) declined (and the scholarship has reflected this trend) until the isthmian question of the 1840s and the "Southern dream of tropical empire" in Cuba and Nicaragua in the 1850s. Much more could be done with American interest in Latin America in the 1830s, for the Jackson administration avidly pursued commercial expansion and an isthmian route. Indeed, the entire topic of American policy toward the hemisphere from the war of 1812 until the Civil War awaits a fresh synthesis that would equal the distinguished achievement of Arthur Whitaker's *The United States and the Independence of Latin America*.

Resources and Overviews

RESEARCH AIDS

While pertinent bibliographies and reference aids are listed here, there are more extensive lists in Chapter 1.

Bibliographies

7:1 Arnade, Charles W. "A Guide to Spanish Florida Source Material." *Florida Historical Quarterly* 35:4 (1957), 320–25. This article contains short commentary and lists sources; it is useful for background materials (1565–1819) on the Florida question.

Bradley, P. *A Bibliography of the Monroe Doctrine, 1919–1929* (1:126).

Brown, L. M., and Christie, I. R., eds. *Bibliography of British History, 1789–1851* (6:1).

Cortada, J. W., ed. *A Bibliographical Guide to Spanish Diplomatic History, 1460–1977* (1:90).

Griffin, C. C., ed. *Latin America: A Guide to the Historical Literature* [1776–1970] (1:118).

7:2   Harris, Michael H. *Florida History: A Bibliography.* Metuchen, N.J.: Scarecrow, 1972. A general bibliography (1519–1972) which has some references to the 1817 to 1821 era.

Pérez Cabrera, J. M. *Historiografía de Cuba* (1:131) lists early chroniclers to about 1900.

7:3   Ragatz, Lowell J., comp. *A Guide for the Study of British Caribbean History, 1763–1834: Including the Abolition and Emancipation Movements.* In the Annual Report of the American Historical Association for the Year 1930. Washington, D.C.: G.P.O., 1932, vol. 3. Reprint, 1970. This annotated bibliography, a major reference, includes manuscripts, official records of Great Britain, the United States, and the British West Indies, as well as secondary works.

Trask, D. F.; Meyer, M. C.; and Trask, R. R., eds. *A Bibliography of United States–Latin American Relations since 1810* (1:120); also see Meyer (1:119), which updates the initial volume.

U.S. Library of Congress. *List of References on the Monroe Doctrine* (1:127).

U.S. Senate. *Selected Bibliography on the Monroe Doctrine* [1823–1941] (1:128) deals mostly with 20th-century issues.

Document Collections

More general collections are listed in Chapter 2, and other collections may be found in "Personalities," below.

American State Papers (1:349).

Cunningham, N. E., Jr., ed. *Circular Letters of Congressmen to Their Constituents, 1789–1829* (5:7) contains comments to contemporary issues, for example, the Florida dispute.

7:4   Manning, William R., ed. *Diplomatic Correspondence of the United States Concerning the Independence of the Latin-American Nations.* 3 vols. New York: Oxford University Press, 1925. The selections in these volumes (1809–1830) are arranged by country, rather than chronologically. They include correspondence with European countries regarding Latin America as well as exchanges between the Department of State and Latin American and United States diplomats.

7:5   Manning, William R., ed. *The Diplomatic Correspondence of the United States: Inter-American Affairs, 1831–1860.* 12 vols. Washington, D.C.: Carnegie Endowment for International Peace, 1932–1939. These volumes, by a famous scholar of hemispheric relations, are an indispensable source for State Department material on inter-American affairs in the mid-19th century. The organization of the volumes is by country, and Manning favors coverage of the more important hemispheric nations (Argentina, Brazil, Chile, and Mexico) and slights the less important, for example, Bolivia. Index.

U.S. Congress. *Congressional Globe: Containing the Proceedings and Debates, 1834–1873* (1:353).

U.S. Congress. *The Debates and Proceedings in the Congress of the United States, 1st to 18th Congresses, March 3, 1789–May 27, 1824* (1:351) are commonly referred to as *Annals of Congress.*

U.S. Congress. *Register of Debates in Congress: 18th–25th Congress, 6 December 1824–16 October 1837* (1:352).

7:6   Webster, Charles K., ed. *Britain and the Independence of Latin America, 1812–1830: Select Documents from the Foreign Office Archives.* 2 vols. New York: Oxford University Press, 1938. A superb collection introduced by a summary of the policies of Castlereagh and Canning toward Latin America. Volume 1 contains communications between London and Latin American governments; volume 2, communications between London and European governments and the United States.

Indexes

Golder, F. A. *Guide to Materials for American History in Russian Archives* [1781–1917] (1:292).

Hasse, A. R., ed. *Index to United States Documents Relating to Foreign Affairs, 1828–1861* (1:304) refers to published documents, papers, correspondence, and legislation and decisions made concerning international questions. It uses place (i.e., Cuba), name (i.e., John Forsyth), and subject (i.e., canals).

7:7   "Preliminary Checklist of Floridiana, 1500–1865, in Libraries of Florida." *Florida Library Association Bulletin* 2:2 (1930), 4–16.

OVERVIEWS

7:8 Arciniegas, German. *Caribbean: Sea of the New World*. New York: Knopf, 1946. This work covers four centuries of Caribbean history (1492–1900); and is good on 19th-century isthmian canal ventures.

7:9 Becker, Jerónimo. *Historia de las relaciones exteriores de la España durante el siglo xix* [History of the foreign relations of Spain during the nineteenth century]. 3 vols. Madrid: Ratés, 1924–1926. Becker was archivist of the Spanish foreign office and based this history, considered a classic, on material from the Spanish archives.

7:10 Dangerfield, George. *The Awakening of American Nationalism, 1815–1828*. New York: Harper & Row, 1965. This is a well-written interpretation of America during the Monroe and Adams presidencies. The chapters on foreign affairs contain considerable insights on British reaction to the Florida dispute and the Monroe Doctrine. Bibliography.

Dangerfield, G. *The Era of Good Feelings* [1817–1825] (6:173) is an elegantly written account of the Monroe era. The chapter on the Monroe Doctrine argues that British "liberal" Tories were anxious for an understanding with the United States in order to promote commerce.

Langley, L. D. *Struggle for the American Mediterranean: United States–European Rivalry in the Gulf-Caribbean, 1776–1904* (2:308) contains chapters on the annexation of Florida and American policy toward the Caribbean (1800–1823).

7:11 Rippy, J. Fred. *Rivalry of the United States and Great Britain over Latin America, 1808–1830*. Baltimore: Johns Hopkins Press, 1929. Rippy's focus is on economic and political issues in assessing antagonism of the United States and Britain over Spanish Florida, Texas, Cuba, and the commercial rivalry in South America. He used archives in Britain and the United States.

Van Alstyne, R. W. *The Rising American Empire* (2:96).

7:12 Van Deusen, Glyndon G. *The Jacksonian Era, 1828–1848*. New York: Harper, 1959. A synthesis of the major forces in Jacksonian America; however there is little on foreign affairs before the 1840s. Bibliography.

Varg, P. A. *United States Foreign Relations, 1820–1860* (8:6) is a synthesis based on existing scholarship, which does a good job of summarizing the main issues and developments in American foreign policy during these four decades.

Williams, W. A. "The Age of Mercantilism: An Interpretation of the American Political Economy, 1763–1828" (2:97).

Personalities

Additional references on individuals may be found in Chapter 1, "Biographical Data."

AMERICAN

John Quincy Adams

Adams, J. Q. *The Memoirs of John Quincy Adams* (6:14) contains portions of his diary from 1795 to 1848. The diary is abridged by Allan Nevins, ed., *The Diary of John Quincy Adams, 1794–1845* (New York: Longmans, Green, 1928).

Adams, J. Q. *The Writings of John Quincy Adams* (6:15) admirably supplements Adams's memoirs. The years 1814 to 1823 are covered in volumes 5–7.

Bemis, S. F. *John Quincy Adams and the Foundations of American Foreign Policy* (6:16) gives Adams principal credit for the Monroe Doctrine and the Transcontinental Treaty.

7:13 Hackett, Charles W. "The Development of John Quincy Adams' Policy with Respect to an American Confederation and the Panama Congress, 1822–1825." *Hispanic American Historical Review* 8:4 (1928), 496–526. This detailed assessment of Adams's thought on hemispheric confederation is based heavily on Manning, *Diplomatic Correspondence* (7:4).

7:14 LaFeber, Walter, ed. *John Quincy Adams and American Continental Empire*. Chicago: Quadrangle, 1965. A handy source of readings, it reveals the continentalist vision of Adams.

Henry Clay

7:15   Clay, Henry. *Spanish America*. London: Wilson, 1829. This brief account focuses on Poinsett's mission to Mexico and relations generally with Latin America (1823–1828).

7:16   Eaton, Clement. *Henry Clay and the Art of American Politics*. Boston: Little, Brown, 1957. A compact biography, organized topically, it discusses Clay's public life from 1812 to 1850. Bibliography.

7:17   Hoskins, H. L. "The Hispanic American Policy of Henry Clay, 1816–1828." *Hispanic American Historical Review* 7:4 (1927), 460–78. According to Hoskins, Clay's interest in, and promotion of, hemispheric understanding derived naturally from his "western" ideals.

7:18   Van Deusen, Glyndon G. *The Life of Henry Clay*. Boston: Little, Brown, 1937. A favorable biography that sums up Clay's role in foreign affairs. It discusses Clay as a War Hawk during 1810 to 1812, as a delegate to the Ghent negotiations, as a proponent of an active Latin American policy and as secretary of state (1825–1829).

Andrew Jackson

See Chapter 8, "Personalities," for additional references.

7:19   Bassett, John S. *The Life of Andrew Jackson*. 2 vols. Garden City, N.Y.: Doubleday, Page, 1911. In an exhaustive, ponderously written narrative based on primary sources, Bassett discusses the Florida question in detail. He argues that Monroe was correct about the Rhea letter, which, allegedly, proved Jackson's claim that he was ordered into Spanish Florida.

7:20   James, Marquis. *Andrew Jackson: The Border Captain*. Indianapolis: Bobbs-Merrill, 1933. James has written a powerful historical narrative with rich detail on the Florida raid of 1818 and Jackson's governorship.

7:21   Remini, Robert V. *Andrew Jackson and the Course of American Empire, 1767–1821*. New York: Harper & Row, 1977. This is the first volume of a projected multivolume biography. One of its major themes is that Jackson's view of, and role in, American expansion virtually determined the course of American empire. Extensive bibliography.

James Monroe

See Chapters 5 and 6, "Personalities," for additional references.

Ammon, H. *James Monroe* (5:47) argues that Monroe deserves more credit for the diplomatic triumphs of his administration than does Adams.

Monroe, J. *The Writings of James Monroe* (5:50) covers, in volume 6, the years 1817 to 1823; the portion relating to the Monroe Doctrine has 49 letters, none by Monroe.

Joel R. Poinsett

See Chapter 9, "Personalities," for additional references.

Rippy, J. F. *Joel R. Poinsett* (9:41) includes an account of Poinsett's mission to Spanish-American rebels and his controversial mission to Mexico.

James K. Polk

See Chapter 9, "Personalities" for additional references.

McCormac, E. I. *James K. Polk: A Political Biography* (9:43).

Polk, J. K. *Diary of James K. Polk during His Presidency, 1845 to 1849* (9:46) contains an extraordinary record of a president's thoughts, which remains a basic source on American foreign affairs in the late 1840s.

Richard Rush

7:22   Powell, John H. *Richard Rush: Republican Diplomat, 1780–1859*. Philadelphia: University of Pennsylvania Press, 1942. A son of Dr. Benjamin Rush, Richard Rush served as comptroller of the U.S. Treasury (1811–1814), attorney general (1814–1817), secretary of state ad interim (1817), and secretary of the treasury (1825–1829). This scholarly treatment is his standard biography, including his important mission as minister to Great Britain (1817–1825) when the Monroe Doctrine was being formulated. Anthony M. Brescia has edited *The Letters and Papers of Richard Rush* (microfilm), which contains correspondence with most of the important figures of the first five decades of the 19th century.

7:23   Rush, Richard. *Memoranda of a Residency at the Court of London, 1819–1825*. 2 vols. Philadelphia: Lea & Blanchard, 1845. Rush, American minister to

Britain during the Monroe era (1817–1823), was an Anglophile. He published this lengthy, detailed diary in an era of Anglo-American antagonism to calm relations.

Others

Bemis, S. F., ed. *American Secretaries of State and Their Diplomacy* (2:166) contains, in volume 4, brief accounts of the following secretaries of state: John Quincy Adams, Henry Clay, Martin Van Buren; Edward Livingston, and John Forsyth. The Adams essay, by Dexter Perkins, is an excellent summary.

7:24 Nichols, Roy F. *Advance Agents of American Destiny.* Philadelphia: University of Pennsylvania Press, 1956. This work, a collection of ten essays, focuses on promoters of American overseas trade from the Revolution to the Civil War. Five of the chapters relate to Latin America. A prominent subject is William Shaler, American consul in North Africa and Havana. Two chapters deal with the "guano" promoters of the 1850s. Bibliography.

7:25 Wiltse, Charles M. *John C. Calhoun: Nationalist, 1782–1828.* Indianapolis: Bobbs-Merrill, 1944. Calhoun, according to Wiltse, was the "one true nationalist" of the era (1812–1828). This first of three volumes contains much information on Calhoun's role in the movement to censure Jackson after his 1818 Florida raid. Extensive bibliography.

FOREIGN

Simón Bolívar

7:26 Lecuna, Vicente, comp., and Bierck, Harold, ed. *Selected Writings of Bolívar.* Trans. by Lewis Bertrand. 2 vols. New York: Colonial Press, 1951. An indispensable source for the creator of the Pan-American movement, it includes an introductory essay on Bolívar's life and thought (1810–1830).

7:27 Madariaga, Salvador de. *Bolívar.* New York: Pelligrini & Cudahy, 1952. In a psychological biography representing prodigious research, the author argues that the Congress of Panama constituted Bolívar's effort to widen his authority. The biography by Gerhard Masur is more balanced.

7:28 Masur, Gerhard. *Simón Bolívar.* Albuquerque: University of New Mexico Press, 1948. This is considered the most thorough, balanced, and objective biography of Bolívar. Masur has obviously mastered

the enormous amount of Bolívar materials. Extensive bibliography.

7:29 Mendez, P. Octavio. *Bolívar y las relaciones interamericanas* [Bolívar and inter-American relations]. Panama City: Imprenta Nacional, 1960. Mendez presents an interpretive study of inter-American relations and the influence of Bolívar's thought. Bibliography.

7:30 Rippy, J. Fred. "Bolívar as Viewed by Contemporary Diplomats of the United States." *Hispanic American Historical Review* 15:3 (1935), 287–97. Rippy argues that diplomats sent to Gran Colombia (1820–1830) had preconceptions about Latin American leaders, and thus misunderstood Bolívar.

George Canning

See Chapter 6, "Personalities," for additional references.

7:31 Temperley, Harold W. V. *The Foreign Policy of Canning, 1822–1827: England, the Neo-Holy Alliance, and the New World.* London: Bell, 1925. The definitive study of Canning and his foreign policy, it is especially valuable for the Monroe Doctrine and British attitude. Temperley shows how Canning shaped a policy midway between militant liberalism and conservative Toryism. Extensive bibliography.

Lord Castlereagh

See Chapter 6, "Personalities," for additional references.

Perkins, B. *Castlereagh and Adams . . . , 1812–1823* (6:12) explains Anglo-American issues, from the peace of Ghent to the Monroe Doctrine, largely through the personalities of Castlereagh and Adams.

7:32 Webster, Charles K. "Castlereagh and the Spanish Colonies, 1815–1818." *English Historical Review* 27:105 (1912), 78–95.

7:33 Webster, Charles K. "Castlereagh and the Spanish Colonies, 1818–1822." *English Historical Review* 30:120 (1915), 631–45. In this two-part essay, Webster argues that Castlereagh accepted the inevitability of Latin American independence and was ready to recognize new governments at the time of his death, 1822.

7:34 Webster, Charles K. *The Foreign Policy of Castlereagh, 1815–1822: Britain and the European Alliance.* London: Bell, 1925. This is the definitive study of Castlereagh's foreign policy. Unfortunately, the New World is slighted in the author's portrayal of Castlereagh as a European statesman striving to restore the balance of power to a shattered continent.

Francisco de Miranda

See Chapter 6, "Personalities," for references.

Others

Bowman, C. H., Jr. "The Activities of Manuel Torres as Purchasing Agent, 1820–1821" (7:69).

Dusenberry, W. "Juan Manuel de Rosas as Viewed by Contemporary American Diplomats [1830–1851]" (7:91).

7:35   Rodríguez, Mario. *A Palmerstonian Diplomat in Central America: Frederick Chatfield, Esq.* Tucson: University of Arizona Press, 1964. Chatfield, British chargé d'affaires in Central America in the 1840s, used sometimes questionable tactics in his efforts to expand and protect British interests and deter American penetration. Bibliography.

7:36   Robertson, William S. "Metternich's Attitude toward Revolutions in Latin America." *Hispanic American Historical Review* 21:4 (1941), 538–58. Metternich opposed republican movements in Spanish America (1815–1824) and supported monarchy, but his views were not so severe as his beliefs about revolution in Europe. In the New World, he believed, European powers should act in their self-interest.

The Florida Question

Bannon, J. F. *The Spanish Borderlands Frontier, 1513–1821* (3:91).

7:37   Bowman, Charles H., Jr. "Vicente Pazos and the Amelia Island Affair, 1817." *Florida Historical Quarterly* 53:3 (1975), 273–95. This essay chronicles the efforts of Pazos, an Argentine exile, to establish a "republic of Florida" on Amelia island in 1817.

7:38   Bradley, J. W. "W. C. C. Claiborne and Spain: Foreign Affairs under Jefferson and Madison." *Louisiana History* 12:4 (1971), 287–314; 13:1 (1972), 5–26. Bradley's extended article deals with the unre-

mitting efforts of Claiborne, governor of two American territories contiguous to the Spanish empire, to shape a more forceful policy.

7:39   Chatelain, Verne E. *The Defenses of Spanish Florida, 1565–1763*. Washington, D.C.: Carnegie Institution, 1941. This study deals almost exclusively with St. Augustine, reflecting author's work as director of St. Augustine Historical Program; however, it goes beyond description of fortifications and offers insights into the administration of Spanish Florida.

Cook, W. L. *Flood Tide of Empire: Spain and the Pacific Northwest, 1543–1819* (5:180).

7:40   Gold, Robert L. *Borderland Empires in Transition: The Triple-Nation Transfer of Florida.* Carbondale: Southern Illinois University Press, 1969. The author focuses on the years 1763 to 1765, when the transfer of the Spanish colony to British jurisdiction brought widespread political and military change in the colony and untold hardship on the Spanish residents, many of whom were moved to Cuba. Bibliography.

7:41   Howard, Clinton N. *The British Development of West Florida, 1763–1764*. Berkeley: University of California Press, 1947. Howard studies both British administrative policy and the rush of settlers into the area. Bibliography.

7:42   Johnson, Cecil. *British West Florida, 1763–1783*. New Haven, Conn.: Yale University Press, 1943. This study has four chapters on political institutions, two on land use and settlement, and one on society, life, and labor, and an account of conquest during the Revolution. Extensive bibliography.

7:43   Mowat, Charles L. *East Florida as a British Province, 1763–1784*. Berkeley: University of California Press, 1943. This is a highly detailed administrative and political study. Extensive bibliography.

Nasatir, A. P. *Borderland in Retreat: From Spanish Louisiana to the Far Southwest* [1762–1822] (5:136).

7:44   Starr, J. Barton. *Tories, Dons, and Rebels: The American Revolution in British West Florida.* Gainesville: University of Florida Press, 1976. This is largely a military history of campaigns in West Florida (1776–1783). The British chose to garrison the area, thus using troops that might have been employed elsewhere.

Wright, J. L., Jr. *Anglo-Spanish Rivalry in North America* [1607–1821] (3:102) shows that after the War of 1812, Spain sought a British alliance to protect Florida from American designs.

Wright, J. L., Jr. *Britain and the American Frontier, 1783–1815* (5:182) argues that Britain aimed to frustrate American frontier expansion by fashioning alliances with various indigenous groups.

U.S., SPAIN, AND FLORIDA FRONTIER

See "Personalities" for John C. Calhoun (under "Others") and Andrew Jackson; also see Chapter 6, "Louisiana and the Spanish Empire," for additional references.

7:45   Cox, Isaac J. "The American Intervention in West Florida." *American Historical Review* 17:2 (1912), 290–311. The United States occupied West Florida (1810–1813) because of territorial ambition and frontier disturbances. The author argues that the United States had "plausible" claims to the territory between the Mississippi and Perdido.

7:46   Cox, Isaac J. "The Border Missions of General George Mathews." *Mississippi Valley Historical Review* 12:3 (1925), 309–33. Cox provides a brief biographical sketch of George Mathews, the ex-governor of Georgia, who seized East Florida in 1812. Moreover, he argues that Mathews served a "covetous and vacillating administration" in Washington.

7:47   Cox, Isaac J. *The West Florida Controversy, 1798–1813: A Study in American Diplomacy.* Baltimore: Johns Hopkins Press, 1918. This lengthy, even tedious study comes to life only when Cox engages, as he often does, in criticism of almost every American leader involved in this affair, above all Jefferson. The research in American and Spanish governmental archives is exemplary, but the French side is neglected, although during Jefferson's administration Paris was almost as important as Madrid.

7:48   Din, Gilbert C. "The Irish Mission to West Florida." *Louisiana History* 12:4 (1971), 315–34. Din deals with little-known effort of Spain to colonize West Florida with Irish Catholic priests in a campaign of Hispanicizing the Irish population. The program failed because of American cultural pressures.

7:49   Egan, Clifford L. "The United States, France and West Florida, 1803–1807." *Florida Historical Quarterly* 47:3 (1969), 227–53. Egan's article supplements Cox, *The West Florida Controversy* (7:47), particularly as a consequence of his close examination of French archives. Nicely written, it tells as much about this aspect of the controversy as readers will desire to know. Jefferson emerges very badly, primarily because his reading of developments in France was blindly optimistic.

7:50   Ellsworth, L. F., ed. *The Americanization of the Gulf Coast, 1803–1850.* Pensacola, Fla.: Historical Pensacola Preservation Board, 1972. This collection of ten essays by noted scholars deals with frontier economics, slavery, racism, and religion.

7:51   Patrick, Rembert W. *Florida Fiasco: Rampant Rebels on the Georgia-Florida Border, 1810–1815.* Athens: University of Georgia Press, 1954. This account of the effort by George Mathews and his coadjutors to filch Florida from Spain supplements and deepens the account in Pratt, *Expansionists of 1812* (6:140). Madison and Monroe are excoriated for their instigation of the affair but, rather surprisingly, their principal agent, Mathews, earns Patrick's sympathy. The research is substantial but narrow, and Patrick does not always understand the setting in which the Florida affair took place. Bibliography.

Pratt, J. W. *The Expansionists of 1812* (6:140) presents considerable detail on frontier pressures against Spanish Florida.

7:52   Waciuma, Wanjoni. *Intervention in Spanish Floridas, 1801–1813: A Study in Jeffersonian Foreign Policy.* Boston: Brandon, 1976. This highly critical work reviews American pressure against Spanish Florida from Jefferson's inaugural to the intervention of 1813. It covers the absorption of West Florida (1810–1813), the Mathews invasion of East Florida, and Mitchell's mission to Florida. Both Jefferson and Madison are portrayed as men of intrigue and duplicity in their efforts to acquire the Spanish colony.

7:53   White, David H. "The Forbes Conspiracy in Spanish Florida, 1801–1806." *Florida Historical Quarterly* 52:3 (1974), 274–85. The Forbes company assumed the trading interests of a British company holding a monopoly on the Indian trade in Spanish Florida. Spanish nationals complained that the Forbes company evaded Spanish trade regulations, but the company continued to operate until 1819.

7:54 Wyllys, R. K. "The East Florida Revolution of 1812–1814." *Hispanic American Historical Review* 9:4 (1929), 415–45. The various filibustering projects from American territory into East Florida during the War of 1812 are assessed. Wyllys argues that the United States did not profit by these invasions immediately, but did learn the technique of pressuring the Spanish to relinquish Florida.

THE TRANSCONTINENTAL TREATY, 1819

See "Personalities," especially John Quincy Adams.

7:55 Baker, Maury. "The Spanish War Scare of 1816." *Mid-America* 45:2 (1963), 67–78. United States–Spanish antagonism over Florida boundary, and the assault on an American ship, helped persuade Spain to sign the Transcontinental Treaty of 1819.

7:56 Bisceglis, Louis R. "The Florida Treaty and the Gallatin-Vives Misunderstanding." *Florida Historical Quarterly* 48:3 (1970), 247–63. The author deals with the mission of General Dionisio Vives to the United States in 1820 to discuss the misunderstandings arising over the Florida treaty. Vives indicated to Albert Gallatin that Florida could be transferred immediately if the United States pledged a policy of neutrality toward the Spanish rebellion.

7:57 Brooks, Philip C. *Diplomacy and the Borderlands: The Adams-Onís Treaty of 1819*. Berkeley: University of California Press, 1939. This is considered the standard diplomatic history of the Transcontinental Treaty, upon which Samuel Flagg Bemis drew heavily for his biography of John Quincy Adams (6:16). Exploiting American, French, and Spanish sources, the author explores the career of Don Luís de Onís in the United States (1809–1819), the negotiation of the 1819 treaty, and its ratification. Frontier historians and Spanish borderlanders have chided Brooks for emphasizing the Spanish side of the negotiations. Extensive bibliography.

7:58 Hyde de Neuville, J. G. *Memoirs of Baron Hyde de Neuville: Outlaw, Exile, Ambassador*. 2 vols. London: Sands, 1913. These memoirs offer a brief commentary on Hyde de Neuville's "good offices" between Adams and de Onís during Florida negotiations.

The Indian Question

See Chapter 6, "The West and the Indians."

Horsman, R. *Expansion and American Indian Policy* (6:136) is a superbly researched and succinct summary of American Indian policy (1783–1812); but there is less on the southern than northern tribes.

7:59 Rogin, Michael P. *Fathers and Children: Andrew Jackson and the Subjugation of the American Indians*. New York: Knopf, 1975. Rogin combines a Marxian analysis with Freudian psychology to argue that Jackson persecuted the Indians (1813–1837) to prove his manliness and to provide new cotton lands for agricultural capitalists.

U.S. and Latin America, 1815–1830

See "Personalities," especially Simón Bolívar, Henry Clay, George Canning, Lord Castlereagh, Francisco de Miranda, James Monroe, Joel R. Poinsett, and, under "Others," Manuel Torres.

7:60 Griffin, Charles C. *The United States and the Disruption of the Spanish Empire, 1810–1822: A Study of the Relations of the United States with Spain and the Rebel Spanish Colonies*. New York: Columbia University Press, 1937. In this standard work, based on multiarchival research, the author argues that impetus for recognition of the republics derived mostly from the prospect of commercial gain. Extensive bibliography.

7:61 Kaufmann, William W. *British Policy and the Independence of Latin America, 1804–1828*. New Haven, Conn.: Yale University Press, 1951. In a solid, traditional diplomatic history, Kaufmann assesses British actions and motives in the Latin American struggle for independence. Bibliography.

7:62 Lynch, John. *The Spanish-American Revolutions, 1808–1826*. New York: Norton, 1973. An informative and well-researched synthesis of Latin

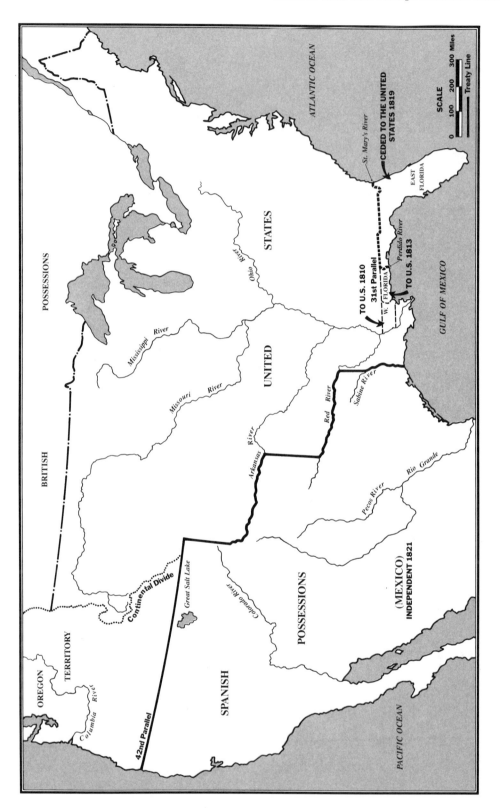

The Adams–Onís Treaty Boundary, 1819–21

America's struggle for independence (1808–1826), it demonstrates how the revolutions created new nations but did not change the basic social structure. Extensive bibliography.

7:63 Madariaga, Salvador de. *The Fall of the Spanish American Empire*. London: Hollis & Carter, 1947. This is an intellectual and psychological portrait of an empire in decline (1776–1824) by a noted Spanish historian. Bibliography.

7:64 Robertson, William S. *France and Latin American Independence*. Baltimore: Johns Hopkins Press, 1939. An extensively researched study, it shows how Napoleon, perhaps unintentionally, furthered the independence movement by his actions in Spain in 1808. Later, Napoleon realized that the independence of Latin America was inevitable. In the 1820s, France did not threaten that independence. Extensive bibliography.

Whitaker, A. P. *The United States and the Independence of Latin America, 1800–1830* (6:90) is an excellent assessment of the private, informal influences in the hemispheric relationship.

7:65 Zimmerman, A. F. "Spain and Its Colonies, 1808–1820." *Hispanic American Historical Review* 11:4 (1931), 439–63. Zimmerman discusses the events in Europe and how these affected the course of the Latin American independence movement.

U.S. AND REVOLUTIONS IN SPANISH AMERICA

7:66 Auchmuty, J. J. *The United States Government and Latin American Independence, 1810–1830*. London: King, 1937. The author argues that the United States failed to make friends among the republics. It is based on material in Manning's *Diplomatic Correspondence* (7:4); however, it contains errors of fact.

7:67 Bemis, Samuel Flagg. "Early Diplomatic Missions from Buenos Aires to the United States, 1811–1824." *American Antiquarian Society Proceedings* 49 (1939), 11–102. A highly factual account which argues that the United States contributed more than Great Britain to the cause of Latin American independence.

7:68 Billingsley, Edward B. *In Defense of Neutral Rights: The United States Navy and the Wars of Independence in Chile and Peru*. Chapel Hill: University of North Carolina Press, 1967. United States naval officers (1815–1824), though sympathetic to the Latin American revolutionaries, protected American commercial rights and opposed paper blockades. Naturally, the rebels sometimes resented such actions. Bibliography.

7:69 Bowman, Charles H., Jr. "The Activities of Manuel Torres as Purchasing Agent, 1820–1821." *Hispanic American Historical Review* 48:2 (1968), 234–45. Bowman explores the role of Torres as revolutionary agent in the United States before his acceptance as the first minister of Colombia to this country. The author exploits both American and Colombian sources.

7:70 Craine, Eugene R. "The United States and the Independence of Buenos Aires." Ph.D. diss., University of Oklahoma, 1954. Craine surveys American-Argentine relations (1810–1824) up to the time of diplomatic recognition.

7:71 Goebel, Dorothy B. "British-American Rivalry in the Chilean Trade, 1817–1820." *Journal of Economic History* 2:2 (1942), 190–207. American traders in Chile during these years suffered from royalist harassment, rebel hostility, and British competition.

7:72 Johnson, John J. "Early Relations of the United States with Chile." *Pacific Historical Review* 13:3 (1944), 260–70. From about 1790, Chilean-American trade had existed, although it was illegal until 1810. During Chile's struggle for independence, the United States became an important source of supplies.

7:73 Keen, Benjamin. *David Curtis DeForest and the Revolution of Buenos Aires*. New Haven, Conn.: Yale University Press, 1947. This is a biography of an early inter-Americanist who promoted American commercial interests, and the Argentine cause, in the United States.

7:74 Neumann, William L. "United States Aid to the Chilean Wars of Independence." *Hispanic American Historical Review* 27:2 (1947), 204–19. In this account of commercial and naval assistance from 1815 to 1820, supplied by individual Americans, the author de-emphasizes the British role in Chile's war of independence.

7:75 Pratt, E. J. "Anglo-American Commercial and Political Rivalry in the Plata, 1820–1830." *Hispanic American Historical Review* 11:3 (1931), 302–35. The shrewdness of British diplomats paved the way for Uruguayan independence under British protection. The British did not want a confrontation with the United States in the La Plata region in the 1820s. The American minister to Argentina (J. M. Forbes) advanced American interests, but his British counterpart was clearly his superior in dealing with the Argentineans and Brazilians. Based on British and American archival sources.

7:76 Smelser, Marshall. "George Washington Declines the Part of El Libertador." *William and Mary Quarterly* 3d ser. 11:1 (1954), 42–51. An account of the scheme, developed by Francisco de Miranda and Rufus King in 1797 to 1799, and subsequently supported by Alexander Hamilton, to liberate Spanish America. George Washington, as titular commander of the American army, declined to countenance it.

7:77 Street, John. *Artigas and the Emancipation of Uruguay*. Cambridge: At the University Press, 1959. In a scholarly analysis of the colonial era and the life of Artigas, Street paints a flattering portrait of the Uruguayan hero and an unflattering one of Argentine leaders. Extensive bibliography.

7:78 Vivian, James F. "The *Paloma* Claim in United States and Venezuelan-Colombian Relations, 1818–1826." *Caribbean Studies* 14:4 (1975), 57–72. Vivian explores the claims of American property owners against privateers acting ostensibly on behalf of rebel governments. He shows that Adams held out for strict accountability, while Monroe inclined toward flexibility, in U.S. settlement of such cases.

7:79 Worcester, Donald E. *Seapower and Chilean Independence*. Gainesville: University of Florida Press, 1962. This study, based mostly on published sources, extends beyond Chile's independence struggle (1815–1820) in its significance; it is also relevant for Peru.

EVOLUTION OF U.S. POLICY

Bernstein, H. *Origins of Inter-American Interest, 1700–1812* (5:143) focuses on commercial relations, and their cultural and political impact, between three cities—Boston, New York, and Philadelphia—and Spanish America.

7:80 Lockey, Joseph B. *Pan-Americanism: Its Beginnings*. New York: Macmillan, 1920. This is a thorough study, based on printed sources, which surveys the United States' reaction to the independence movements in Latin America (1810–1860). Extensive bibliography.

7:81 Robertson, William S. "The First Legations of the United States in Latin America." *Mississippi Valley Historical Review* 2:2 (1915), 183–212. From 1822 to 1827, the United States accredited diplomatic missions to six Latin American governments. Robertson argues that the main efforts of these missions were commercial, with little emphasis on political connection; yet he believes such efforts laid the basis for Pan-Americanism.

7:82 Robertson, William S. "The Recognition of the Hispanic American Nations by the United States." *Hispanic American Historical Review* 1:3 (1918), 239–69. A detailed study, it argues that recognition occurred (1821–1826) because of congressional pressure and presidential expedience.

7:83 Stewart, Watt. "The South American Commission, 1817–1818." *Hispanic American Historical Review* 9:1 (1929), 31–59. The U.S. commission consisted of Rodney, Graham, and Bland, and visited Rio de Janeiro, Buenos Aires, and Santiago de Chile. Inspiration for this mission came from the public's desire for information and, most important, from a presidential desire to stall the revolutionary governments in their quest for U.S. recognition. The commission's report argued for recognition of Buenos Aires and Chile.

Whitaker, A. P. *The Western Hemisphere Idea: Its Rise and Decline* [1600–1950] (2:284).

7:84 Winn, W. B. "The Issue of Religious Liberty in the United States Commercial Treaty with Colombia of 1824." *The Americas* 26:3 (1970), 291–301. The author suggests that article 11 of the 1824 treaty with Colombia served as a model for American treaties with other Latin American governments. It provided that non-Catholic U.S. citizens would not be forced to worship according to the Roman Catholic religion.

First Pan American Congress, 1826

7:85 Reinhold, Frances L. "New Research on the First Pan American Congress Held at Panama in 1826." *Hispanic American Historical Review* 18:3 (1938), 342–63. Reinhold discusses northern press reaction to the Panama Congress and compares editorial judgments with attitudes of policymakers and congressional leaders. The press was eager for involvement, largely for commercial reasons.

7:86 Sanders, Ralph. "Congressional Reaction in the United States to the Panama Congress of 1826." *The Americas* 11:2 (1954), 141–54. The United States refused to continentalize the Monroe Doctrine in 1826. Congressional interest was in promoting American trade, but it did recognize strategic importance of the Caribbean.

U.S. and Latin America, 1830–1861

U.S. AND SOUTH AMERICAN NATIONS

Books

7:87 Bernstein, Harry. *Making an Inter-American Mind*. Gainesville: University of Florida Press, 1961. A sequel (1812–1900) to the author's *Origins of Inter-American Interest, 1700–1812* (5:143), this volume deals with interplay between scientists, intellectuals, and scholars in the United States and their colleagues in Latin America and Iberia. Bibliography.

7:88 Calogeras, João P. *A History of Brazil*. Trans. by Percy A. Martin. Chapel Hill: University of North Carolina Press, 1939. This is an excellent translation of a classic in Brazilian history, which emphasizes war, politics, and diplomacy between 1815 and 1861.

Evans, H. C., Jr. *Chile and Its Relations with the United States* [1820–1927] (2:293) finds that in the 19th century the United States was mostly interested in trading with Chile.

Galdames, L. *A History of Chile* [1492–1925] (2:294) has excellent biographical sketches of 19th-century Chilean political figures.

Hill, L. F. *Diplomatic Relations between the United States and Brazil* [1824–1933] (2:292) finds most American diplomats in Brazil to be inept; exceptions were William Tudor and Louis Agassiz.

Levene, R. *A History of Argentina* [1500–1930] (2:285) devotes more than 100 pages to the struggle for independence.

7:89 Manchester, Alan K. *British Preeminence in Brazil: Its Rise and Decline: A Study in European Expansion*. Chapel Hill: University of North Carolina Press, 1933. Manchester demonstrates how the British exploited their relationship with Portugal to gain dominance over Brazilian economy from 1822 to about 1860. Extensive bibliography.

Parks, E. T. *Colombia and the United States, 1765–1934* (2:297) devotes five chapters to American canal policy in the 19th century.

Peterson, H. F. *Argentina and the United States, 1810–1960* (2:287) discusses the troubles between the United States and Argentina in the 1830s.

7:90 Rivas, Raimundo. *Historia diplomática de Colombia, 1810–1934* [Diplomatic history of Colombia, 1810–1934]. Bogotá: Imprenta Nacional, 1961. This is considered the best diplomatic history of Colombia; Rivas had access to materials in the Colombian foreign office.

Sherman, W. R. *The Diplomatic and Commercial Relations of the United States and Chile, 1820–1914* (2:296) pays little attention to commercial relations.

Essays

7:91 Dusenberry, William. "Juan Manuel de Rosas as Viewed by Contemporary American Diplomats." *Hispanic American Historical Review* 41:4 (1961), 495–514. American diplomats who served in Argentina during the era of Rosas (1830–1851) gradually become more critical; based mostly on State Department material.

7:92 Flickema, T. O. "Sam Ward's Bargain: A Tentative Reconsideration." *Hispanic American Historical Review* 50:3 (1970), 538–42. This brief article deals with the American naval expedition in Paraguay

(1858–1859), controversies with Paraguay, and the role of Sam Ward in the arbitral settlement of 1860.

7:93 Flickema, T. O. "The Settlement of the Paraguayan-American Controversy of 1859: A Reappraisal." *The Americas* 25:1 (1968), 49–69. In 1858–1859 an impressive American naval force entered the Rio de la Plata to deal with claims against Paraguay. The author contends that the conciliatory approach of American commissioner James Bowlin and Paraguayan president Carlos Antonio Lopez was significant in settling the issues.

7:94 Gray, William H. "American Diplomacy in Venezuela, 1835–1865." *Hispanic American Historical Review* 20:4 (1940), 551–74. Using Venezuelan and American sources, the author concentrates on major diplomatic issues: nonintervention, Pan-Americanism, naturalization problems, commerce, maritime questions, and claims. Though Venezuela was suspicious of American motives during the Mexican War, the two countries had forged a friendly relationship by 1865.

7:95 Harrison, John P. "Science and Politics: Origins and Objectives of Mid-Nineteenth Century Government Expeditions to Latin America." *Hispanic American Historical Review* 35:2 (1955), 175–202. Harrison discusses the U.S. Exploring Expedition (1838–1842); the Naval Astronomical Expedition to the Southern Hemisphere (1849–1852); the Amazon Exploration (1851–1852); and the Expedition to Rio de la Plata (1853–1856). These expeditions were inspired as much by manifest destiny as by science.

7:96 Langley, Lester D. "The Jacksonians and the Origins of Inter-American Distrust." *Inter-American Economic Affairs* 30:3 (1976), 3–21. Langley deals with the Jacksonian push for commercial treaties and economic concessions from Latin American republics. In negotiating with the republics, Jacksonian diplomats created considerable ill will.

7:97 Nolan, Louis C. "The Relations of the United States and Peru with Respect to Claims, 1822–1870." *Hispanic American Historical Review* 17:1 (1937), 30–66. The U.S. was insistent on Peru's admission of its obligation to pay claims advanced by private American citizens.

7:98 Nuermberger, Gustave A. "The Continental Treaties of 1856: An American Union Exclusive of the United States." *Hispanic American Historical Review* 20:1 (1940), 32–55. Latin Americans, fearful of U.S.

commercial expansion, failed to agree among themselves on a defensive federation, despite Chilean efforts.

U.S. AND CENTRAL AMERICAN/CARIBBEAN NATIONS

7:99 Foner, Philip S. *From the Conquest of Cuba to La Escalera.* Vol. 1 in *A History of Cuba and Its Relations with the United States.* New York: International Publishers, 1962. The first in a multivolume series based on Cuban and U.S. sources. Writing from a perspective sympathetic to Castro, Foner argues that expansion of slavery was the motivating force in U.S. policy toward Cuba from the 1820s to the 1840s. Bibliography.

Johnson, W. F. *The History of Cuba* [1509–1920] (2:313).

Karnes, T. L. *The Failure of Union: Central America, 1824–1960* (2:307) relates how the initial attempt in the late 1830s came to naught because of national jealousies and ambitions.

Langley, L. D. *The Cuban Policy of the United States* [1776–1962] (2:314) argues that U.S. policy was initially counterrevolutionary and, after 1848, opportunistic.

7:100 Lockey, Joseph B. "Diplomatic Futility." *Hispanic American Historical Review* 10:3 (1930), 265–94. An informative and entertaining article describing U.S. missions to Central America from 1824 to 1849. It demonstrates the ineptness of American policy before 1845.

Logan, R. W. *The Diplomatic Relations of the United States with Haiti, 1776–1891* (5:121).

Parker, F. D. *The Central American Republics* [1500–1960] (2:310).

Tansill, C. C. *The United States and Santo Domingo, 1798–1873* (5:123) discusses the early lure of the West Indian commercial market, and the strategic importance of Samaná Bay as viewed by the Adams to Grant administrations.

Thomas, H. *Cuba: The Pursuit of Freedom* [1762–1968] (2:315) contains chapters on the era of 1815 to

1848 which are very good assessments of the Cuban sugar economy.

Welles, S. *Naboth's Vineyard: The Dominican Republic, 1844–1924* (2:323).

Woodward, R. L. *Central America: A Nation Divided* (2:312) contains excellent summaries of Central American independence struggles.

U.S. Expansion in Caribbean/Central America, 1845–1861

ISTHMIAN DIPLOMACY

See Chapter 15, "The Panama Canal Question."

7:101 Allen, Cyril. *France in Central America: Felix Belly and the Nicaraguan Canal.* New York: Pageant, 1966. Felix Belly was a vigorous French publicist and promoter who tried to promote a French canal across Nicaragua from the 1850s. His activities were continuously frustrated by American diplomats. Bibliography.

DuVal, M. P. *Cadiz to Cathay: The Story of the Long Diplomatic Struggle for the Panama Canal* (15:110).

Ealy, L. O. *Yanqui Politics and the Isthmian Canal* (2:326).

7:102 Folkman, David I., Jr. *The Nicaragua Route.* Salt Lake City: University of Utah Press, 1972. This is an account of the intense commercial rivalry between promoters of the Nicaraguan and Panamanian routes (1850–1868) across the isthmus. The author emphasizes business concerns in the Nicaragua route, especially those of Cornelius Vanderbilt. Bibliography.

Mack, G. *The Land Divided: A History of the Panama Canal and Other Isthmian Canal Projects* [1513–1944] (2:329) contains a detailed study of 19th-century dreams.

7:103 Rippy, J. Fred. "Diplomacy of the United States and Mexico Regarding the Isthmus of Tehuántepec, 1848–1860." *Mississippi Valley Historical Review* 6:4 (1920), 503–21. Rippy has prepared a detailed account of treaty discussions and American entrepreneurs interested in developing the Tehuántepec route.

7:104 Schott, Joseph L. *Rails across Panama: The Story of the Building of the Panama Railroad, 1849–1855.* Indianapolis: Bobbs-Merrill, 1967. A vividly written popular history, it re-creates many of the now-debunked legends of the building of the railroad.

7:105 Stansifer, Charles L. "E. George Squier and the Honduras Interoceanic Railroad Project." *Hispanic American Historical Review* 46:1 (1966), 1–27. In the early 1850s Squier, Zachary Taylor's emissary to Central America in 1849, negotiated a contract with the Honduran government to construct a railroad. Later, the contract was sold to British investors and led to a series of poor loans contracted by Honduras.

U.S.-European Rivalries

7:106 Lockey, Joseph B. "A Neglected Aspect of Isthmian Diplomacy." *American Historical Review* 41:2 (1936), 295–305. Lockey examines the origins of the 1846 treaty with New Granada (Colombia) and traces the history of treaty negotiations with Colombia from 1824 to 1846. Colombia feared British pretensions in the isthmus and chose American guarantees.

7:107 Naylor, Robert A. "The British Role in Central America prior to the Clayton-Bulwer Treaty of 1850." *Hispanic American Historical Review* 40:3 (1960), 361–82. Naylor argues that the British role was commercially opportunistic despite the fact that Britain did not recognize the Central American federation nor establish normal diplomatic relations.

7:108 Van Aken, Mark. "British Policy Considerations in Central America before 1850." *Hispanic American Historical Review* 42:1 (1962), 54–59. Disputing the thesis of Robert A. Naylor, who argued that British interests were almost exclusively commercial (7:107), Van Aken contends that British aims in Central America before 1850 were highly political.

7:109 Van Alstyne, Richard W. "The Central American Policy of Lord Palmerston, 1846–1848." *Hispanic American Historical Review* 16:3 (1936), 339–59. The author focuses on British interests in the

Mosquitia in Nicaragua. Palmerston wanted a protectorate over the Mosquitia and, generally, British domination in Central America. Two documents are appended.

Williams, M. W. *Anglo-American Isthmian Diplomacy, 1815–1915* (2:330).

Clayton-Bulwer Treaty, 1850

7:110 Bourne, Kenneth. "The Clayton-Bulwer Treaty and the Decline of British Opposition to the Territorial Expansion of the United States, 1857–1860." *Journal of Modern History* 33:3 (1961), 287–91. The United States became resentful of the Clayton-Bulwer Treaty and insisted on greater prerogative in Central America. Britain finally acquiesced.

7:111 Hickson, G. E. "Palmerston and the Clayton-Bulwer Treaty." *Cambridge Historical Journal* 3:3 (1931), 295–303. A standard diplomatic account (1850–1860), it should be compared with Van Alstyne (7:114, 7:115).

7:112 Howe, George F. "The Clayton-Bulwer Treaty." *American Historical Review* 42:3 (1937), 484–90. Howe offers a brief interpretation of article 8 of the Clayton-Bulwer Treaty, dealing with Anglo-American protection of isthmian routes. Britain refused Colombia a guarantee of sovereignty over Panama.

7:113 Rodríguez, Mario. "The *Prometheus* and the Clayton-Bulwer Treaty." *Journal of Modern History* 36:3 (1964), 260–78. A British warship fired on the U.S. steamer in 1851 to enforce collection of port taxes at Greytown. The resulting crisis brought about a British apology.

7:114 Van Alstyne, Richard· W., ed. "Anglo-American Relations, 1853–1857." *American Historical Review* 42:3 (1937), 491–500. This is a collection of letters from the papers of the Earl of Clarendon, British foreign secretary (1853–1858), which relate to the Clayton-Bulwer Treaty.

7:115 Van Alstyne, Richard W. "British Diplomacy and the Clayton-Bulwer Treaty, 1850–1860." *Journal of Modern History* 11:2 (1939), 149–83. The Clayton-Bulwer Treaty satisfied British interests in Central America because it effectively curbed American territorial ambitions.

SLAVERY AND EXPANSION

See Chapter 8, "Suppression of the Slave Trade."

7:116 May, Robert E. *The Southern Dream of Caribbean Empire, 1854–1861*. Baton Rouge: Louisiana State University Press, 1973. This is an assessment of southern tropical imperialists of the 1850s, who dreamed that a tropical empire in the Caribbean would restore the South to its former political power in the Union. When the dream collapsed, the South seceded. Bibliography.

Cuba

7:117 Ambacher, Bruce. "George M. Dallas, Cuba, and the Elections of 1856." *Pennsylvania Magazine of History and Biography* 97:3 (1973), 318–32. Dallas was a critic of the Pierce administration's efforts to acquire Cuba. He was appointed minister to Great Britain in 1856 to remove him from the United States.

7:118 Ettinger, Amos A. *The Mission to Spain of Pierre Soulé, 1853–1855: A Study in the Cuban Diplomacy of the United States*. New Haven, Conn.: Yale University Press, 1932. An exhaustive study, based on American and European (but not Spanish) sources, it examines the Pierce administration's effort to purchase Cuba. Ettinger argues Soulé represented those southern slave interests who wanted Cuban annexation. Extensive bibliography.

7:119 Katz, Irving. "August Belmont's Cuban Acquisition Scheme." *Mid-America* 50:1 (1968), 52–63. Belmont was a Democratic party chieftain who continually intrigued in schemes to purchase Cuba in the 1850s. The author argues that Belmont played an important role in the origins of the Ostend Manifesto.

7:120 Portell Vilá, Hermínio. *Narciso López y su época* [Narciso López and his era]. 3 vols. Havana: Compañía Editora de Libros y Folletos, 1930–1958. A major work in Cuban history (1845–1851), it is based on a stupendous amount of source material. The author forcefully argues that López was neither an annexationist nor a dupe of southern expansionists.

7:121 Rauch, Basil. *American Interest in Cuba, 1848–1855*. New York: Columbia University Press, 1948. While this volume thoroughly covers the annexationist schemes of the era, the author used no works in Spanish. Unfortunately, the book is marred by errors. Bibliography.

7:122 Urban, C. Stanley. "The Africanization of Cuba Scare, 1853–1855." *Hispanic American Historical Review* 37:1 (1957), 29–45. The liberal policy of the Cuban governor-general, under British influence, convinced American Southerners that Cuban slavery would be abolished. This led to American efforts to purchase the island and, those failing, to the Ostend Manifesto, which advocated seizure of Cuba.

Filibustering

7:123 Brown, Charles H. *Agents of Manifest Destiny: The Lives and Times of the Filibusters.* Chapel Hill: University of North Carolina Press, 1980. A well-written narrative of the filibusters of the 1850s, this work focuses on American participation in the Cuban revolutionary expeditions of Narciso López and on William Walker's two great expeditions, to Mexico and Nicaragua. The filibusters of the fifties, the author concludes, dreamed of tropical empire. Bibliography.

7:124 Carr, Albert Z. *The World and William Walker.* New York: Harper & Row, 1963. Carr has written a psychological portrait of Walker, who ruled Nicaragua with his filibusters in the 1850s.

7:125 Feipel, Louis N. "The Navy and Filibustering in the Fifties." *U.S. Naval Institute Proceedings* 44:4 (1918), 767ff. A serialized account of the navy's efforts to deal with isthmian filibustering in the 1850s, it includes considerable material on the burning of Greytown in 1854.

7:126 Greene, Laurence. *The Filibuster: The Career of William Walker.* Indianapolis: Bobbs-Merrill, 1937. In a narrative account based heavily on the work on the filibusters by W. O. Scroggs, Greene argues that Walker was courageous but lacked the qualities of a statesman.

7:127 Langley, Lester D. "The Whigs and the López Expeditions to Cuba, 1849–1851: A Chapter in Frustrating Diplomacy." *Revista de Historia de América* 71:1 (1971), 9–22. Based mostly on U.S. State Department material, the article focuses on the troubles of the Taylor-Fillmore administration in enforcing the neutrality laws against filibustering expeditions to Cuba (1849–1851).

7:128 Scroggs, William O. *Filibusters and Financiers: The Story of William Walker and His Associates.* New York: Macmillan, 1916. A biography of William Walker and a dated account of filibustering in the 1850s, it denies that Walker was spreading slavery, though he contemplated conquest of Cuba and eventual union of Central America and Cuba with the southern states.

7:129 TePaske, John J. "Appleton Oaksmith: Filibuster Agent." *North Carolina Historical Review* 35:4 (1958), 427–47. Oaksmith served with Walker in Nicaragua. He became Walker's representative to the United States and promoted Nicaraguan securities in this country.

The Monroe Doctrine, to 1861

See "Personalities," especially John Quincy Adams, George Canning, Lord Castlereagh, James Monroe, Richard Rush, and, under "Foreign," "Others," Prince Metternich.

7:130 Alvarez, D. Alejandro, ed. *The Monroe Doctrine: Its Importance in the International Life of the States of the New World.* New York: Oxford University Press, 1924. This collection of essays by eminent Latin Americans and Americans assesses the impact of the Monroe Doctrine on the foreign relations of both the United States and Latin American nations.

Dozer, D. M., ed. *The Monroe Doctrine: Its Modern Significance* [1823–1963] (2:271).

Logan, J. A. *No Transfer: An American Security Principle* [1760–1945] (2:272).

7:131 May, Ernest R. *The Making of the Monroe Doctrine.* Cambridge: Harvard University Press, 1975. May argues that the origin of the message lay in the domestic political situation and the jockeying for position in the upcoming election of 1824. John Quincy Adams was motivated in large part by political opportunism and his realization that a stern warning in Monroe's message would enhance his presidential ambitions. Extensive bibliography.

7:132 Perkins, Dexter. *The Monroe Doctrine, 1823–1826*. Cambridge: Harvard University Press, 1927. Perkins concludes, in this standard work on the doctrine, that there were two principles: noncolonization and noninterference. After an exhaustive study of European archives, Perkins holds that there was no real threat to Spanish America by the continental powers. Extensive bibliography.

AMERICAN ORIGINS

7:133 Bornholdt, Laura. "The Abbé de Pradt and the Monroe Doctrine." *Hispanic American Historical Review* 24:2 (1944), 201–21. The author refutes the theory that Napoleon's aide influenced Jefferson's thinking on the concept of the two spheres, an integral part of the Monroe Doctrine.

7:134 Craven, W. R., Jr. "The Risk of the Monroe Doctrine." *Hispanic American Historical Review* 7:3 (1927), 320–33. Craven concludes that there was little danger of European intervention (1823–1824) in Spanish America and that Adams shrewdly recognized that British interests would thwart any interventionist plans.

7:135 Ford, Worthington C. "John Quincy Adams and the Monroe Doctrine." *American Historical Review* 7:4 (1902), 676–96. The author uses extensive quotations from Adams's writings to illustrate his decisive influence on the making of the Monroe Doctrine in the critical four months of 1823 before the message was delivered.

7:136 McGee, Gale W. "The Monroe Doctrine: A Stopgap Measure." *Mississippi Valley Historical Review* 38:2 (1951), 233–50. Canning's proposal to Rush for a joint statement on Latin America was in fact an American idea and Monroe's message of December 1823 anticipated further Anglo-American cooperation.

7:137 Perkins, Bradford. "The Suppressed Dispatch of H. U. Addington, Washington, November 3, 1823." *Hispanic American Historical Review* 37:4 (1957), 480–85. George Canning "suppressed" a memorandum on conversation between British chargé d'affaires in the United States and Adams about Canning's offer of the joint statement on Latin America made to Richard Rush.

7:138 Schellenberg, Thomas R. "Jeffersonian Origins of the Monroe Doctrine." *Hispanic American* *Historical Review* 14:1 (1934), 1–32. In this intellectual analysis of Jefferson's contribution to the Monroe Doctrine, the author argues that the concept of two spheres, implicit in Monroe's messages, comes from Jefferson's philosophy of the New World.

Whitaker, A. P. *The United States and the Independence of Latin America, 1800–1830* (6:90) argues that Monroe deserves most of the credit for the Monroe Doctrine.

Williams, W. A. "The Age of Mercantilism: An Interpretation of the American Political Economy, 1763–1828" (2:97) is an interpretative essay which sees the Monroe Doctrine as the ultimate expression of an American declaration of empire.

EUROPE AND THE RECONQUEST OF SPANISH AMERICA

7:139 Lawson, Leonard A. *The Relation of British Policy to the Declaration of the Monroe Doctrine*. New York: Longmans, Green, 1922. A summation of a familiar theme, though the work is useful in its analysis of the role played by commercial interests in Anglo-American relations in the 1820s.

7:140 Perkins, Dexter. "Europe, Spanish America, and the Monroe Doctrine." *American Historical Review* 27:2 (1922), 207–18. Perkins argues that European powers, in 1823–1824, never had a practical policy for reconquest of Spanish America. Monroe's message did not readily affect their policy.

7:141 Perkins, Dexter. "Russia and the Spanish Colonies, 1817–1818." *American Historical Review* 28:4 (1923), 656–72. The Russian czar sympathized with Spain about the loss of its New World empire, but he was unwilling to act without British approval. The Holy Alliance, then, was no threat to the republics.

7:142 Robertson, William S. "Russia and the Emancipation of Spanish America, 1816–1826." *Hispanic American Historical Review* 21:2 (1941), 196–221. Russia followed the policy of "legitimacy" and the principles of the Holy Alliance, but urged Spain to liberalize her colonial policy.

7:143 Robertson, William S. "The United States and Spain in 1822." *American Historical Review* 20:4 (1915), 781–800. Robertson deals with anticipation of the Monroe Doctrine in Spain, and Spanish warnings about a republican political system to Britain and other European powers.

7:144 Tatum, E. H., Jr. *The United States and Europe, 1815–1823: A Study in the Background of the Monroe Doctrine.* Berkeley: University of California Press, 1936. Tatum argues, from published sources, that the Monroe Doctrine was aimed at Great Britain to prevent possible British seizure of Spanish Cuba. He also offers an account of European impressions of the United States after 1815. Bibliography.

7:145 Temperley, Harold W. V., ed. "Documents Illustrating the Reception and Interpretation of the Monroe Doctrine in Europe, 1823–4." *English Historical Review* 39:156 (1924), 590–93. He offers several documents showing that Monroe's message met with more concern in Europe than has been otherwise believed.

THE RUSSIAN-AMERICAN DIMENSION

See Chapter 8, "Russia," "Northwest America," for additional references.

Bailey, T. A. *America Faces Russia: Russian-American Relations from Early Times to Our Day* [1776–1950] (2:245).

7:146 Bolkhovitinov, N. N. "Russia and the Declaration of the Non-Colonization Principle: New Archival Evidence." Trans. by Basil Dmytryshyn. *Oregon Historical Quarterly* 72:2 (1971), 101–26. This article, by a Soviet historian who has written extensively on Russian-American relations and the Monroe Doctrine, argues that the noncolonization principle of Monroe's message of 1823 originated in American expansionist ambitions in the Pacific Northwest. The famous Ukase of 1821 was only a pretext used by John Quincy Adams to justify the noncolonization principle, which was aimed primarily against the British.

Dulles, F. R. *The Road to Teheran: The Story of Russia and America, 1781–1943* (2:247).

Gibson, J. R. *Imperial Russia in Frontier America . . . , 1784–1867* (5:154) contains extensive bibliography on Russian colonization.

7:147 Hudsuhak, Mykhailo. *When Russia Was in America: The Alaska Boundary Treaty Negotiations, 1824–25, and the Role of Pierre de Poletica.* Vancouver, B.C.: Michell, 1971. Negotiations arose from the ukase promulgated in St. Petersburg in 1821, which endorsed broad Russian territorial claims. The United States and Great Britain rejected these claims and the resulting agreement restricted Russia to the Alaska region.

Kushner, H. I. *Conflict on the Northwest Coast . . . , 1790–1867* (8:92).

Manning, C. A. *Russian Influence in Early America* (8:93) holds that the Russian threat of expansion south from Alaska toward California was one of the factors which precipitated the noncolonization principle.

7:148 Mazour, Anatole G. "The Russian-American and Anglo-Russian Conventions, 1824–1825: An Interpretation." *Pacific Historical Review* 14:3 (1945), 303–10. This article analyzes why Russia was so lenient in negotiations of 1824 and 1825, concluding that Russia was more concerned with its rivalry in the Near East with Great Britain than in its claims on the remote northwest coast of North America.

7:149 Nichols, Irby C., Jr. "The Russian Ukase and the Monroe Doctrine: A Re-evaluation." *Pacific Historical Review* 36:1 (1967), 13–26. Nichols examines the Russian decree of 1821, closing off Alaskan waters to foreign commerce, and argues that the ukase was issued because of internal politics, not as an assertion of Russian imperialism.

EVOLUTION OF THE DOCTRINE, 1823–1861

7:150 Bingham, Hiram. *The Monroe Doctrine: An Obsolete Shibboleth.* New York: Da Capo (1913), 1976. A reprint of a classic account which condemned the use of the doctrine to justify American expansion.

7:151 Cady, J. F. *Foreign Intervention in the Río de la Plata, 1838–50.* Philadelphia: University of Pennsylvania Press, 1929. Cady covers the foreign rivalries of French, British, and American governments in the La Plata region during the era of Juan Manuel de Rosas, dictator of Argentina (1828–1852). Bibliography.

7:152 Davis, Thomas B., Jr. "Carlos de Alvear and James Monroe: New Light on the Origin of the Monroe Doctrine." *Hispanic American Historical Review* 23:4 (1943), 632–49. Davis assesses the impressions of the Monroe Doctrine on Argentina's first minister to the United States, who believed the doctrine pledged the United States to protection of South America.

7:153 Goebel, Julius. *The Struggle for the Falkland Islands: A Study in Legal and Diplomatic History.* New Haven, Conn.: Yale University Press, 1927. An exhaustive study, it specifically emphasizes the U.S.-Argentine squabble (1783–1835) caused by seizure of an American fishing vessel in the Falklands in 1831. Extensive bibliography.

7:154 Merk, Frederick, with Merk, L. B. *The Monroe Doctrine and American Expansionism, 1843–1849.* New York: Knopf, 1966. In his "study in the psychology of expansionism," Merk examined the American belief that European interference in North America retarded American manifest destiny. American leaders worried about European pressures because of public support for expansionism.

7:155 Manning, William R., ed. "Statements, Interpretations, and Applications of the Monroe Doctrine, etc., 1823–1845." *American Society of International Law Proceedings* 8 (1914), 34–59. This essay is a handy reference on the evolution of the Monroe Doctrine from Monroe to Polk. (This entire issue of the *Proceedings* is devoted to the evolution of the doctrine to 1914.)

7:156 Perkins, Dexter. *The Monroe Doctrine, 1826–1867.* Baltimore: Johns Hopkins Press, 1933. In the sequel to *The Monroe Doctrine, 1823–1826* (7:132), the author uses a vast array of published and unpublished sources to trace the evolution of the doctrine: forgotten in the 1830s, revived in the 1840s, exploited in the 1850s, and championed in the 1860s. Extensive bibliography.

7:157 Robertson, William S. "French Intervention in Mexico in 1838." *Hispanic American Historical Review* 24:2 (1944), 222–52. This is a detailed account of the diplomatic aspects of the "Pastry War."

7:158 Robertson, William S. "South America and the Monroe Doctrine, 1824–1828." *Political Science Quarterly* 30:1 (1915), 82–105. The author evaluates South America's reception of the Monroe Doctrine.

American Diplomatic and Commercial Relations with Europe, 1815–1861

Contributing Editor
JOHN H. SCHROEDER
University of Wisconsin—Milwaukee

Contributor
Howard Jones
University of Alabama

Contents

Introduction

The theme of diplomatic and commercial relations with Europe is not central to the history of American foreign policy in the period from 1815 to 1861. After 1815 the United States was far less preoccupied with European affairs than she had been in the first twenty-five years of the republic. Although the rivalry with England remained intense for decades, the focal point of United States foreign policy moved from the Old World to the New—to Florida, Texas, Oregon, California, Central America, and the Caribbean. Even in commercial matters Europe often was of less interest to politicians and publicists than newer areas of opportunity. In the years from 1815 to 1861 American trade with Europe was more extensive than that with South America, Asia, or the Pacific Islands, but Americans were fascinated by the vast potential of new regions. This emphasis has persisted among twentieth-century historians.

Although material on American diplomatic and commercial relations with Europe can be found in most general diplomatic and economic history texts, no study has attempted to synthesize the topic. Instead, the reader must rely on general histories of the antebellum United States to provide the economic, political, and intellectual background for American relations with Europe and then turn to books on specific aspects of the relationship. The most satisfactory synthesis is Paul Varg, *United States Foreign Relations, 1820–1860* (8:6). This study benefits from Varg's previous work on the foreign policy of the founding fathers by placing United States diplomacy after 1815 in a broad perspective and by summarizing the relationship of the new American republic to the Atlantic community. William Appleman Williams's *The Roots of the Modern American Empire* (2:98) traces, in the early chapters, the breakdown of American mercantilism and the increasing application of Adam Smith's liberal commercial doctrines to American foreign policy. Williams argues that a determining force in American foreign policy after Jackson's election in 1829 was a relentless and aggressive drive for new overseas markets for the American farmer.

Although the United States had begun to develop a competent diplomatic establishment by the Civil War, the diplomacy of the republic was characterized by a disdain for the traditional style and forms practiced by European diplomats between 1815 and 1860. The United States relied on an uneven mixture of amateurism, bluster, shrewdness, and opportunism in the conduct of its foreign policy. Such experienced and capable diplomats as John Quincy Adams, Albert Gallatin, Daniel Webster, and Edward Everett were few and far between. As a result, biographies of the individuals who conducted American diplomacy with Europe are almost invariably political studies which treat diplomatic episodes as passing phases in careers devoted to domestic politics. Among the exceptions are Samuel Flagg Bemis's two-volume biography of John Quincy Adams. *John Quincy Adams and the Foundations of American Foreign Policy* (6:16) covers the period through the end of Adams's presidency, and *John Quincy Adams and the Union* (8:7) examines Adams's long and productive post-presidential career from 1828 to 1848. The latter details virtually all of the leading American-European problems which Adams witnessed after 1829.

The foreign policy of the presidents who served between 1815 and 1860 is satisfactorily summarized in the various presidential biographies listed in this chapter. Their secretaries of state are treated individually in volumes 4, 5, and 6 of *The American Secretaries of State and Their Diplomacy* (2:166), edited by Samuel Flagg Bemis. *Daniel Webster* (8:25), by Irving Bartlett, includes solid sections on Webster's two productive terms as secretary of state. Robert Dalzell, in *Daniel Webster and the Trial of American Nationalism, 1843–1852* (8:26), has written an insightful study which relates Webster's nationalism and his views on American foreign policy to his personal ambitions. Of special note as biographies of secondary, but significant, figures in American diplomacy during the period are J. H. Powell, *Richard Rush: Republican Diplomat, 1780–1859* (7:22); David Lowenthal, *George Perkins Marsh: Versatile Vermonter* (8:32); George I. Oeste, *John Randolph Clay: America's First Career Diplomat* (8:35); and

Francis F. Wayland, *Andrew Stevenson: Democrat and Diplomat, 1785–1857* (8:39).

Although the United States had regular diplomatic relations with virtually every nation in Europe, those with Great Britain, France, and Russia were of the greatest importance. American diplomacy with the other nations in the Old World tended to focus narrowly on the negotiation of commercial agreements and the resolution of minor difficulties. Students in Anglo-American relations between 1815 and 1860 can begin their introduction to an extensive literature on the subject by reading Charles S. Campbell, *From Revolution to Rapprochement* (2:234). Campbell's broad survey can be supplemented by H. C. Allen, *Conflict and Concord: The Anglo-American Relationship since 1783* (2:231), and by Kenneth Bourne, *Britain and the Balance of Power in North America, 1815–1908* (8:55). While Allen emphasizes an underlying cordiality of Anglo-American relations after 1814, Bourne argues that there was basic hostility between the two nations. *To the Webster-Ashburton Treaty* (10:31), by Howard Jones, provides a thorough examination of the various complicated issues which Webster and Ashburton attempted to resolve in 1842. This study and its extensive bibliography offer an excellent starting point for students who wish to examine in greater detail such controversies as the neutrality crisis of the late 1830s, the slave trade, the *Creole* incident, and the *Amistad* affair.

Franco-American relations have been studied in detail by Richard A. McLemore and Henry Blumenthal. In *Franco-American Diplomatic Relations, 1816–1836* (8:85), McLemore explores the background and development of the French claims controversy of the mid-1830s. *A Reappraisal of Franco-American Relations, 1830–1871* (8:82), by Blumenthal, challenges the traditional view that nineteenth century relations between the two nations were cordial by presenting ample evidence of antagonism, suspicion, and misunderstanding. Although numerous surveys exist on Russian-American relations, they tend to provide little material on the nineteenth century. An exception is Benjamin P. Thomas's *Russo-American Relations, 1815–1867* (8:90), which is flawed by its strict reliance on American sources. More specialized are Walther Kirchner, *Studies in Russian-American Commerce, 1820–1860* (8:141), and Howard Kushner, *Conflict on the Northwest Coast: American-Russian Rivalry in the Pacific Northwest, 1790–1867* (8:92).

There are a number of specialized studies on American reaction to European revolutionary movements. American response to the move for Greek independence is perceptively summarized by James Field, *America and the Mediterranean World, 1776–1882* (18:6). Although his treatment is not so detailed as that of Myrtle Cline's outdated *American Attitude toward the Greek War of Independence, 1821–28* (8:110), Field's study superbly combines intellectual and diplomatic history. The only detailed, if dated, studies of the United States' response to the revolutions of 1848 and subsequent upheaval in Europe are A. J. May, *Contemporary American Opinion of the Mid-Century Revolutions in Central Europe* (8:120); H. R. Marraro, *American Opinion on the Unification of Italy, 1846–1861* (8:102); John G. Gazley, *American Opinion of German Unification, 1848–1871* (8:95); and Merle Curti, "Austria and the United States, 1848–1852" (8:108). Louis Kossuth's celebrated visit to the United States has been studied by Donald Spencer in *Louis Kossuth and Young America* (8:123). In spite of the excitement generated by the flamboyant Hungarian's tour of the United States, Spencer argues that actual support for American intervention in Hungary was never strong enough to make action by the federal government a possibility.

No detailed modern study of American commerce with Europe exists for this period. Convenient starting points for students are offered by Douglass North, *The Economic Growth of the United States, 1790–1860* (8:144), and by George Rogers Taylor, *The Transportation Revolution, 1815–1860* (8:149). Both books contain chapters on foreign commerce, statistical appendixes, and good bibliographies. John G. B. Hutchins, *The American Maritime Industries and Public Policy, 1789–1914* (39:50), is based on exhaustive research and contains an extensive bibliography on the shipping industry and government policy. Nonspecialists may wish to supplement Hutchins's work with Robert G. Albion, *Square-Riggers on Schedule* (8:133); Carl C. Cutler, *Greyhounds of the Sea* (8:136); and David B. Tyler, *Steam Conquers the Atlantic* (8:150).

A number of well-researched and detailed studies are available on specialized aspects of American trade with Europe. Norman S. Buck, *The Development of the Organization of Anglo-American Trade, 1800–1850* (8:153); Ludwig Beutin, *Bremen und Amerika* (8:135); Walther Kirchner, *Studies in Russian-American Commerce, 1820–1860* (8:141); and John W. Rooney, Jr., *Belgian-American Diplomatic and Consular Relationships, 1830–1850* (8:147) all provide excellent and extensive information on their subjects. Of special note is Ralph Hidy, *The House of Baring in American Trade and Finance* (8:155), which is a first-rate business history on the English banking house most heavily involved in American trade and finance.

A survey of the available literature indicates that substantial opportunity exists for research on American diplomatic and commercial relations with Europe between 1815 and 1861. The American diplomatic missions in Europe offer ample material for a study on American professional diplomacy before the Civil War. Such a study could focus on the numerous missions in Europe to determine the nature, characteristics, and quality of the diplomatic service. There is also a need for more specialized studies on the role of a number of individuals in shaping American foreign policy. The most notable are James Buchanan, Lewis Cass, Millard Fillmore, James K. Polk, and John Tyler. In addition, both Henry Clay and Edward Everett are without modern scholarly biographies of their long and rich careers.

Traditional, narrow diplomatic studies which detail relations with individual European nations could be effectively updated by research combining diplomatic, economic, and intellectual history. James Field has pointed the way in *America and the Mediterranean World, 1776–1882,* which examines and intertwines not only diplomatic and commercial contacts, but also the development of a missionary movement and the rise of secular attempts to transmit the values of freedom, self-determination, and modernization to the Mediterranean region. There is also need for additional research on the American response to European revolutionary movements, and the nation's internal debate on the extent to which the country should exert its influence to stimulate change in Europe.

Diplomatic historians of the twentieth century often concentrate on the relationship between overseas commercial interests and American foreign policy by examining the influence of lobbies and special interest groups. Unfortunately, scholars of the pre–Civil War era have not studied this influence. Research on the topic would significantly enhance our understanding of the influences which shaped American foreign policy in the period.

Resources and Overviews

RESEARCH AIDS

While pertinent bibliographies and reference aids are listed here, there are more extensive lists in Chapter 1.

Bibliographies

Albion, R. G. *Naval and Maritime History: An Annotated Bibliography* (1:41).

Bibliographie annuelle de l'histoire de France (1:78a).

Brown, L. M., and Christie, I. R., eds. *Bibliography of British History, 1789–1851* (6:1).

Cortada, J. W., ed. *A Bibliographical Guide to Spanish Diplomatic History, 1460–1977* (1:90).

Golder, F. A. *Guide to Materials for American History in Russian Archives* [1781–1917] (1:292).

8:1 Hanham, H. J., ed. *Bibliography of British History, 1851–1914.* Oxford: Oxford University Press, 1976. This mammoth compilation seeks "to list the major works which a student is likely to wish to consult, [to offer] a selection of other works which makes clear the scope of contemporary printed materials, and [to include] a selection of biographies and autobiographies." It is comprehensive through 1973. Extensive index.

Monaghan, F. *French Travellers in the United States, 1765–1932: A Bibliography* (1:73).

Smith, M. J., Jr., ed. *The American Navy, 1789–1860* (5:5).

Document Collections

More general collections are listed in Chapter 2, and other collections may be found in "Personalities," below.

American State Papers (1:349).

8:2 Catterall, Helen T., ed. *Judicial Cases Concerning American Slavery and the Negro.* 5 vols. Washington, D.C.: Carnegie Institution, 1926–1932. These volumes contain material on the legal questions involved in the domestic slave trade and other cases relating to slavery. The documents show that the question of slavery became so intricately involved in Anglo-American difficulties that it threatened settlement of seemingly unrelated matters such as the United States-Canadian boundary.

Hasse, A. R., ed. *Index to United States Documents Relating to Foreign Affairs, 1828–1861* (1:304).

8:3 Irish University Press Series on British Parliamentary Papers. *Slave Trade.* 95 vols. Shannon: Irish University Press, 1968–1971. This extensive collection consists of reprinted 19th-century British diplomatic correspondence, naval officers' reports, findings of mixed commissions in cases trying captured slavers, select committee reports, antislavery treaties, and much more material. Volume 24 contains correspondence dealing with the *Creole* case, while volumes 11, 14, 15, 20, 25, 39, 41, 43–48, and 50 are rich in correspondence concerning British efforts to gain U.S. agreement to antislavery treaties and joint patrol issues.

U.S. Congress. *Congressional Globe: Containing the Proceedings and Debates, 1834–1873* (1:353).

U.S. Congress. *The Debates and Proceedings in the Congress of the United States, 1st to 18th Congresses, March 3, 1789–May 27, 1824* (1:351). These are commonly referred to as *Annals of Congress.*

U.S. Congress. *Register of Debates in Congress: 18th–25th Congress, 6 December 1824–16 October 1837.* (1:352).

OVERVIEWS

Dangerfield, G. *The Awakening of American Nationalism, 1815–1828* (7:10) surveys the contest between economic nationalism and democratic nationalism in the United States after 1815. The study is useful to American diplomatic historians because it places commercial and foreign policy in a larger perspective.

Davis, R. R., Jr. "Republican Simplicity: The Diplomatic Costume Question, 1789–1867" (2:172) traces the evolution of formal dress for American diplomats from 1789 to 1867. The move toward simple, "democratic" dress began under President Jackson and reached a high point in the 1850s under Secretary of State William Marcy.

Ilchman, W. F. *Professional Diplomacy in the United States, 1779–1939* (2:175) includes an informative chapter on early diplomatic service in the United States between 1779 and 1889.

8:4 Potter, David. *The Impending Crisis, 1848–1861.* New York: Harper & Row, 1976. Potter's detailed survey of the coming of the Civil War includes excellent material on American diplomacy in the 1850s. A masterful work that manages to see old things in new ways. Extensive bibliography.

8:5 Strout, Cushing. *The American Image of the Old World.* New York: Harper & Row, 1963. Based on writings of American political and intellectual figures, this study provides an intellectual history of American images of Europe. The primary value of the book rests with its combination of historical and literary sources.

Van Alstyne, R. W. *The Rising American Empire* (2:96).

Van Deusen, G. G. *The Jacksonian Era, 1828–1848* (7:12) is a traditional survey of American political history which includes a useful summary of American foreign policy during these two decades.

8:6 Varg, Paul A. *United States Foreign Relations, 1820–1860.* East Lansing: Michigan State University Press, 1979. Varg relates America's foreign policy to Europe and Asia as well as to its expansionist concerns in North America. Commercial goals were vital to the United States, but numerous elements entered into its decisionmaking process. By 1860, the United States dominated North America and, though seriously threatened by the divisive issue of slavery, it had taken great steps toward becoming a world power. Bibliography.

Williams, W. A. *The Roots of the Modern American Empire: A Study of the Growth and Shaping of Social Consciousness in a Marketplace Society* (2:98) includes several chapters on the economic basis of American foreign policy prior to 1860. Williams stresses the rising influence of Adam Smith's liberal commercial doctrines and the drive for new markets as critical factors in American diplomacy between the Revolution and the Civil War.

Personalities

Additional references on individuals may be found in Chapter 1, "Biographical Data."

AMERICAN

John Quincy Adams

See Chapters 6 and 7 "Personalities," for additional references.

Bemis, S. F. *John Quincy Adams and the Foundations of American Foreign Policy* (6:16) includes discussions of Anglo-American controversies over the African slave trade.

8:7 Bemis, Samuel Flagg. *John Quincy Adams and the Union*. New York: Knopf, 1956. The second of a two-volume biography, this book treats the years from 1829 to 1848 in great detail. Because Adams served through almost all of this time in the House, the study concentrates primarily on domestic political issues; however, Bemis does discuss Adams's stand during the *Amistad* and *Creole* controversies.

James Buchanan

8:8 Buchanan, James. *Works of James Buchanan: Comprising His Speeches, State Papers and Private Correspondences*. Ed. by John B. Moore. 12 vols. Philadelphia, 1908–1911. Reprint, n.d. Although old and incomplete, this edition of Buchanan's papers is still very useful for students of American diplomacy. There are a large number of significant speeches, personal letters, and state papers from his career as diplomat, secretary of state and president.

8:9 Klein, Philip S. *President James Buchanan: A Biography*. University Park: Pennsylvania State University Press, 1962. Klein's comprehensive scholarly biography of Buchanan includes detailed information on Buchanan's service as secretary of state, minister to Russia, and minister to England as well as his one term as president. Bibliography.

Langley, L. D. "Two Jacksonian Diplomats in Czarist Russia" (8:89) discusses the activities of James Buchanan and John Randolph.

8:10 Smith, Elbert B. *The Presidency of James Buchanan*. Lawrence: University Press of Kansas, 1975. This book provides a straightforward scholarly account of Buchanan's presidency. Although it focuses on the domestic political crisis, the volume includes pertinent information about American foreign policy. Bibliography.

Lewis Cass

8:11 Spencer, Donald S. "Lewis Cass and Symbolic Intervention: 1848–1852." *Michigan History* 53:2 (1969), 1–17. This article analyzes the precise content and specific meaning of Lewis Cass's pleas for the United States to assume a more aggressive role in supporting the democratic revolutionary movements in Europe between 1848 and 1852.

8:12 Woodford, Frank B. *Lewis Cass: The Last Jeffersonian*. New Brunswick: N.J.: Rutgers University Press, 1950. Although the definitive biography of Cass remains to be written, this study provides a solid survey of Cass as a politician and diplomat—as minister to France (1836–1842) and as secretary of state (1857–1860). Woodford explains Cass's longtime opposition to British search policies in the suppression of the slave trade. Bibliography.

8:13 Young, William T. *Sketch of the Life and Public Services of General Lewis Cass: With the Pamphlet on the Right of Search, and Some of His Speeches on the Great Political Questions of the Day*. Philadelphia: E. H. Butler, 1853. This old account includes the correspondence of the American minister to France with leaders of the Tyler administration, as well as a reprint of Cass's anonymously written pamphlet opposing the British search policy as a step leading to impressment and thus to destruction of American honor.

Henry Clay

See Chapter 7, "Personalities," for additional references.

8:14 Clay, Henry. *Papers of Henry Clay, 1797–1826*. 5 vols. Ed. by J. F. Hopkins and M. W. Hopkins. Lexington, University Press of Kentucky, 1959–1973. Projected as the definitive edition of Clay's papers, these volumes include material collected from numerous sources and are accompanied by full editorial notes. Of particular interest here are volumes 4 and 5, which cover Clay's first 22 months as secretary of state (1825–1826).

Van Deusen, G. G. *The Life of Henry Clay* (7:18) remains the best single treatment of Clay and his long political career, which included service as secretary of state (1825–1829).

George Mifflin Dallas

8:15 Belohlavek, John M. *George Mifflin Dallas: Jacksonian Patrician*. University Park: Pennsylvania

State University Press, 1977. Belohlavek's account is a traditional biography of a Jacksonian politician and diplomat who served as a senator and vice-president as well as American minister to Russia (1837–1839) and Great Britain (1856–1861). Bibliography.

8:16 Dallas, Susan, ed. *Diary of George Mifflin Dallas while United States Minister to Russia, 1837–1839*. Philadelphia: Lippincott, 1892. Reprint 1970. This printed diary provides a good summary of Dallas's years as minister to Russia.

Donovan, T. A. "President Pierce's Ministers at the Court of St. James." (8:58).

8:17 Donovan, Theresa A. "Difficulties of a Diplomat: George Mifflin Dallas in London." *Pennsylvania Magazine of History* 92:4 (1968), 421–40. Donovan summarizes Dallas's frustrating years as American minister to England from 1856 to 1861.

Edward Everett

8:18 Frothingham, Paul R. *Edward Everett: Orator and Statesman*. Boston: Houghton Mifflin, 1925. This study is the only full account of Everett's long public career. It is based on the voluminous Everett manuscript collections and contains an adequate account of Everett's terms as minister to England (1841–1845) and as secretary of state (1852–1853). Everett's correspondence with Secretary of State Webster may be found in the microfilm edition of Webster's papers, see (10:17).

8:19 Geiger, John O. "A Scholar Meets John Bull: Edward Everett as United States Minister to England, 1841–1845." *New England Quarterly* 49:4 (1976), 577–95. Geiger summarizes and praises Everett's role as minister to Great Britain under President Tyler.

8:20 Kaplan, Lawrence S. "The Brahmin as Diplomat in Nineteenth Century America: Everett, Bancroft, Motley, Lowell." *Civil War History* 19:1 (1973), 5–28. Kaplan examines the role and significance of these four well-qualified ministers to the Court of St. James. He concludes that despite their considerable talents, the role of diplomatic ministers "mattered little or not at all" to American foreign policy in the 19th century.

Andrew Jackson

See Chapters 7 and 9, "Personalities," for additional references.

8:21 Davis, Burke. *Old Hickory: A Life of Andrew Jackson*. New York: Dial, 1977. In lieu of a comprehensive recent biography of Jackson's presidency, this volume provides a good summary of Jackson's life and career.

8:22 Jackson, Andrew. *Correspondence of Andrew Jackson*. Ed. by J. S. Bassett and J. F. Jameson. 7 vols. Washington, D.C.: Carnegie Institution, 1927–1935. Reprint, n.d. This edition provides an excellent collection of Jackson's personal correspondence, but is not complete and tends to focus on domestic politics. Volume 7 is an extensive index.

Thomas, R.C. "Andrew Jackson versus France: American Policy toward France, 1834–1836" (8:87) summarizes Jackson's policy during the French claims crisis.

Edward Livingston

Carossa, V. P., and Leder, L. H. "Edward Livingston and Jacksonian Diplomacy." (8:83).

8:23 Hatcher, William B. *Edward Livingston: Jeffersonian Republican and Jacksonian Democrat*. Baton Rouge: Louisiana State University Press, 1940. Livingston served as secretary of state from 1831 to 1833 and as minister to France from 1833 to 1835. This is a detailed scholarly treatment of his life and public career. Bibliography.

James Monroe

See Chapters 5 and 6 "Personalities" for additional references.

Ammon, H. *James Monroe* (5:47) includes a detailed treatment of foreign policy during Monroe's presidency.

James K. Polk

See Chapter 9, "Personalities," for additional references.

McCormac, E. I. *James K. Polk: A Political Biography* (9:43) is an outdated biography; nevertheless, it remains the one thorough account of Polk's presidency.

Sellers, C. G. *James K. Polk: Continentalist, 1843–1846* (9:48).

Richard Rush

See Chapter 7, "Personalities," for additional references.

Powell, J. H. *Richard Rush, Republican Diplomat, 1780–1859* (7:22) covers his years as minister to Great Britain (1817–1825) and to France (1847–1849).

John Tyler

See Chapter 10, "Personalities," for additional references.

Chitwood, O. P. *John Tyler: Champion of the Old South* (10:9).

8:24 Tyler, John. *The Letters and Times of the Tylers.* 3 vols. Ed. by Lyon G. Tyler. New York: Da Capo (1884–1896), 1970. This collection is valuable because most of Tyler's papers were destroyed in 1865. The compiler, the president's son, wrote his father's correspondents and secured copies of letters to and from the former president.

Daniel Webster

See Chapter 10, "Personalities," for additional references.

8:25 Bartlett, Irving H. *Daniel Webster.* New York: Norton, 1978. Because it provides an informed account of Webster and his varied public career, this biography presents an excellent starting point for anyone interested in pursuing the diplomatic aspects of Webster's career. The volume is organized chronologically and is based on exhaustive research in the voluminous manuscripts of Webster and his contemporaries.

8:26 Dalzell, Robert F. *Daniel Webster and the Trial of American Nationalism, 1843–1852.* Boston: Houghton Mifflin, 1973. The author concentrates on the ways in which Webster's attempt to advance his political career affected the nationalism in which he believed so strongly. Bibliography.

8:27 Shewmaker, Kenneth E. "Daniel Webster and the Politics of Foreign Policy, 1850–1852." *Journal of American History* 63:2 (1976), 303–15. The author argues that Webster accepted his appointment and used his position as secretary of state (1850–1852) primarily to promote the Compromise of 1850 and national unity. The article contends that Webster used the Hulsemann affair to this end, not as a device to advance his chances for the presidency in 1852.

Others

Bemis, S. F., ed. *The American Secretaries of State and Their Diplomacy* (2:166) covers, in volumes 4, 5, and 6, the years from 1817 to 1861 and contains a useful summary of each secretary of state's term in office.

8:28 Curtis, James C. *The Fox at Bay: Martin Van Buren and the Presidency, 1837–1841.* Lexington: University of Kentucky Press, 1970. Based on extensive research, this volume concentrates on Van Buren's presidency, but it also includes a useful summary of Van Buren's career prior to his election in 1836. Bibliography.

8:29 Duckett, Alvin L. *John Forsyth: Political Tactician.* Athens: University of Georgia Press, 1962. Forsyth was minister to Spain (1819–1823) and secretary of state (1834–1841). This detailed scholarly biography summarizes his career. Bibliography.

8:30 Hall, Claude H. *Abel Parker Upshur: Conservative Virginian, 1790–1844.* Madison: State Historical Society of Wisconsin, 1964. This traditional biography presents a detailed description of Upshur's life and public career, which included a significant term as secretary of the navy (1841–1843) and a brief tenure as secretary of state (1843–1844). Bibliography.

8:31 Hamilton, Holman. *Zachary Taylor: Soldier in the White House.* Indianapolis: Bobbs-Merrill, 1951. The second of a two-volume study (9:52), this book is based on extensive primary sources and presents a detailed summary of the diplomatic as well as the political aspects of Taylor's presidency. Extensive bibliography.

8:32 Lowenthal, David. *George Perkins Marsh: Versatile Vermonter.* New York: Columbia University Press, 1958. A thoroughly researched traditional biography, this volume provides a detailed account of the diplomatic as well as the intellectual activities of Marsh's career. Extensive bibliography.

8:33 Nichols, Roy F. *Franklin Pierce: Young Hickory of the Granite Hills.* 2d ed. Philadelphia: University of Pennsylvania Press (1958), 1964. A detailed, traditional biography, it includes a sound account of foreign policy questions during the presidency of Pierce. Bibliography.

8:34 Nye, Russel B. *George Bancroft: Brahmin Rebel.* New York: Knopf, 1944. Based primarily on the voluminous collection of Bancroft manuscripts, this study remains the standard biography of this historian, politician, and diplomat. Bancroft's career included service as minister to Great Britain (1846–

1849) and as minister to Germany (1867–1874). Bibliography.

8:35 Oeste, George I. *John Randolph Clay: America's First Career Diplomat*. Philadelphia: University of Pennsylvania Press, 1966. Oeste's scholarly biography of Clay traces his career as a diplomatic representative of the United States from 1836 to the late 1860s. Bibliography.

8:36 Rayback, Robert J. *Millard Fillmore: Biography of a President*. Buffalo, N.Y.: Buffalo Historical Society, 1959. This volume remains the only modern, scholarly biography of Fillmore and his public career. Bibliography.

8:37 Rooney, J. William, Jr. "The Diplomatic Mission of Henry Washington Hilliard to Belgium, 1842–1844." *Alabama Historical Quarterly* 30:1 (1968), 19–31. This article summarizes Hilliard's rather uneventful mission to Belgium. His main contribution was to stress the need for a commercial treaty between the two nations.

8:38 Spencer, Ivor D. *The Victor and the Spoils: A Life of William L. Marcy*. Providence, R.I.: Brown University Press, 1959. Based on the large collection of Marcy papers, this scholarly study presents a traditional account of Marcy's political career, including a summary of his term as secretary of state from 1853 to 1857.

Walters, R., Jr. *Albert Gallatin: Jeffersonian Financier and Diplomat* (6:24) provides a well-researched summary of his diplomatic services, including his years as minister to France (1816–1823) and minister to Great Britain (1823–1829).

8:39 Wayland, Francis F. *Andrew Stevenson: Democrat and Diplomat, 1785–1857*. Philadelphia: University of Pennsylvania Press, 1949. This extensively researched biography examines Stevenson's career as Speaker of the House of Representatives (1827–1834) and as minister to England (1836–1841). Stevenson was able to maintain amicable relations with England while upholding the American position on a series of sensitive issues, especially regarding the search controversy in the slave-trade suppression dispute. Extensive bibliography.

Willson, B. *America's Ambassadors to England, 1785–1928: A Narrative of Anglo-American Diplomatic Relations* (2:181).

8:40 Wiltse, Charles M. *John C. Calhoun: Sectionalist, 1840–1850*. Indianapolis: Bobbs-Merrill, 1951. This is the third in a three-volume biography of Calhoun and includes detailed treatment of Calhoun's term as secretary of state from 1844 to 1845. Extensive bibliography.

Ziegler, B. M. *The International Law of John Marshall* [1800–1835] (16:142).

BRITISH

George Canning
See Chapters 6 and 7, "Personalities," for additional references.

Temperley, H. W. V. *The Foreign Policy of Canning, 1822–1827* (7:31).

Lord Castlereagh
See Chapters 6 and 7, "Personalities," for additional references.

Perkins, B. *Castlereagh and Adams . . . , 1812–1823* (6:12).

Webster, C. K. *The Foreign Policy of Castlereagh, 1815–1822* (7:34).

Lord Palmerston
See Chapter 10, "Personalities," for additional references.

8:41 Ashley, Anthony Evelyn M. *The Life of Henry John Temple, Viscount Palmerston, 1846–1865: With Selections from His Speeches and Correspondence*. 2 vols. London: Bentley, 1879. These volumes essentially continue the life begun by Bulwer in 1870. It is much dated and, aside from its documents, has little to offer the modern student of Palmerstonian statecraft.

8:42 Bulwer, Sir Henry Lytton. *The Life of Henry John Temple, Viscount Palmerston: With Selections from His Diaries and Correspondence*. 3 vols. London: Bentley, 1870–1874. The third volume of this set, edited by Evelyn Ashley, added some letters and speeches from the period 1835 to 1847. The first "authorized" life has left much to be desired in the way of standards of historical editing.

8:43 Connell, Brian, ed. *Regina v. Palmerston: The Correspondence between Queen Victoria and Her*

Foreign and Prime Minister, 1837–1865. London: Evans, 1962. This collection of extracts on a wide range of subjects devotes relatively little material to American affairs. There are no notes, little in the way of scholarly apparatus, and the work is perhaps best described as a handy introduction to some difficult-to-get material.

8:44 Guedalla, Philip. *Palmerston*. London: Berlin, 1926. Perhaps the most vividly written of the Palmerston biographies, this was one of the first to appreciate and utilize the private papers at Broadlands. Whatever its defects—and professors and pedants have found many—this is biography as art, more interested in personality than in politics or policies.

8:45 Ridley, Jasper. *Lord Palmerston*. London: Book Club Associates, 1970. Despite this highly laudable and very readable attempt, Palmerston (1784–1865) still awaits a biographer who can do justice to both the man and his measures.

8:46 Southgate, Donald. *'The Most English Minister . . .': The Policies and Politics of Palmerston*. New York: St. Martin's Press, 1966. Though this study, not quite a biography, slights American affairs (and gets one or two things wrong when mentioning them), it has many acute observations about Palmerstonian statecraft.

8:47 Webster, Charles. *The Foreign Policy of Palmerston, 1830–1841: Britain, the Liberal Movement and the Eastern Question*. 2 vols. New York: Humanities Press (1951), 1969. By design, this masterwork omits American affairs, but it is required reading for any consideration of Palmerstonian statecraft. There is no reason to question that he disliked Yankees or distrusted the French, but, on occasion, he could subordinate distaste and distrust to the pursuit of British national interests, which he regarded as eternal.

Lord John Russell

See Chapter 11, "Personalities," for additional references.

8:48 Russell, Lord John. *The Later Correspondence of Lord John Russell, 1840–1878*. Ed. by G. P. Gooch. 2 vols. New York: Longmans, Green, 1925. Gooch has provided a good and representative selection of the correspondence of the British foreign secretary. While these volumes contain much that is valu-

able, they must be supplemented by the unpublished material in the British Public Record Office.

8:49 Walpole, Spencer. *The Life of Lord John Russell*. 2 vols. London: Longmans, Green, 1889. Reprint 1968. As much as possible it has been the author's intent to let Lord John (1792–1878) speak for himself and to quote documents not published elsewhere. Of course the student will wish to consult the Russell correspondence edited by G. P. Gooch (8:48).

Others

8:50 Argyll, George Douglas Campbell, 8th Duke of. *George Douglas Eighth Duke of Argyll (1823–1900): Autobiography and Memoirs*. Ed. by Dowager Duchess of Argyll. 2 vols. London: John Murray, 1906. Like other works in this genre, it is heavy in its use of extracts from private letters.

Jones, W. D. *Lord Aberdeen and the Americas* (8:60).

8:51 Lingelback, Anna L. "William Huskisson as President of the Board of Trade." *American Historical Review* 43:4 (1938), 759–74. This article summarizes Huskisson's term as president of the British Board of Trade from 1823 to 1827 and his role in setting a commercial policy which directly affected the United States.

8:52 Maxwell, Sir Herbert E. *The Life and Letters of George William Frederick, Fourth Earl of Clarendon*. 2 vols. London: Arnold, 1913. If little known in America, Lord Clarendon's influence on Anglo-American affairs, though muted, was often very strong. The above standard life may be supplemented with his grandson's more intimate, private biography: George Villiers, *A Vanished Victorian: Being the Life of George Villiers, Fourth Earl of Clarendon, 1800–1870* (London: Eyre & Spottiswoode, 1938).

Diplomatic Relations with Europe

GREAT BRITAIN

Also see "Personalities," especially George Bancroft (under "Others"), James Buchanan, George Mifflin Dallas, Edward Everett, and Richard Rush.

Allen, H. C. *Conflict and Concord: The Anglo-American Relationship since 1783* (2:231) argues that, because "there was no deep, inherent antagonism" between the nations after the War of 1812, "Anglo-American cordiality" developed quickly after 1814.

Allen, H. C. *Great Britain and the United States: A History of Anglo-American Relations (1783–1952)* (2:232) emphasizes themes similar to those in *Conflict and Concord*.

8:53 Barnes, James J. *Authors, Publishers and Politicians: The Quest for an Anglo-American Copyright Agreement, 1815–1854.* Columbus: Ohio State University Press, 1974. Barnes examines the struggle for a copyright law, an often-neglected divisive factor in Anglo-American relations.

8:54 Best, Geoffrey. *Mid-Victorian Britain, 1851–1875.* New York: Schocken, 1972. Best has fashioned "a minor classic" through an innovative and very personal combination of the Victorian literary humanist tradition with the concepts and methodology of recent social history. This work almost captures a sense of being alive in the period when Britain enjoyed a preeminence rarely achieved in world affairs. Extensive bibliography.

8:55 Bourne, Kenneth. *Britain and the Balance of Power in North America, 1815–1908.* Berkeley: University of California Press, 1967. Based on extensive research in British archives, this study examines the problems raised by the possibility of a future war with the United States and "their influence on official British policy toward the United States." The volume is useful because it concentrates on Anglo-American hostility in contrast to those studies which stress the use of cordial relations in the period.

8:56 Bourne, Kenneth. *The Foreign Policy of Victorian England, 1830–1902.* Oxford: Clarendon Press, 1970. The author's mastery of all facets of British diplomacy allows him to stress the interconnectedness of American and European affairs. The few items devoted to America in the documents section help convey the point that, to London, Europe and other parts of the world demanded more attention than America.

Brebner, J. B. *North Atlantic Triangle: The Interplay of Canada, the United States and Great Britain* (2:233).

Campbell, C. S., Jr. *From Revolution to Rapprochement: The United States and Great Britain, 1783–1900* (2:234) provides a solid introduction to the relationship.

8:57 Crook, D. P. *American Democracy in English Politics, 1815–1850.* Oxford: Clarendon Press, 1965. This work deals with the larger dimensions of American influence on British foreign policy and, as such, is useful in providing a background to Anglo-American diplomacy.

8:58 Donovan, Theresa A. "President Pierce's Ministers at the Court of St. James." *Pennsylvania Magazine of History and Biography* 91:4 (1967), 457–70. This essay traces the services of James Buchanan and George M. Dallas as ministers, and their efforts to interpret American policy to England and to reduce ill feeling toward the United States.

Jones, H. *To the Webster-Ashburton Treaty* (10:31) deals also with most of the issues which aggravated Anglo-American relations after 1815. As such, the book is an excellent starting point for students interested in the slave trade, the *Creole* incident, the *Amistad* affair, and the neutrality crisis of the late 1830s.

8:59 Jones, Wilbur D. *The American Problem in British Diplomacy, 1841–1861.* Athens: University of Georgia Press, 1974. Jones examines British policy toward the United States by placing the topic within the context of British domestic politics, British imperial problems, and British relations with other nations. Particularly useful for American historians, it explains how British leaders viewed the United States and the tactics they used.

8:60 Jones, Wilbur D. *Lord Aberdeen and the Americas.* Athens: University of Georgia Press, 1958. Based largely on the Aberdeen Papers, this volume focuses on Lord Aberdeen's diplomacy toward the United States from 1841 to 1846. The volume centers on four problems: the Webster-Ashburton Treaty, British plans in Texas, Anglo-French intervention in La Plata, and the Oregon question.

8:61 Kelley, Robert. *The Transatlantic Persuasion: The Liberal-Democratic Mind in the Age of Gladstone.* New York: Knopf, 1969. Although this intellectual history concentrates on the Age of Gladstone, it contains excellent chapters on the ideas and influence of Adam Smith, Edmund Burke, and

Thomas Jefferson. Accordingly, it provides appropriate background material for an understanding of Anglo-American relations prior to the Civil War.

8:62 Martin, Kingsley. *The Triumph of Lord Palmerston: A Study of Public Opinion in England before the Crimean War.* London: Hutchinson (1924), 1963. While the focus of this engaging little book is far from the American Civil War, it has much to say about two subjects necessary to understand that war's international dimension: Lord Palmerston and public opinion.

Nicholas, H. G. *The United States and Britain* (2:237) includes a chapter on the period from 1812 to 1860.

Perkins, B. *Castlereagh and Adams . . . , 1812–1823* (6:12) traces the rise of nationalism in American diplomacy from 1812 to 1823.

8:63 Thistlethwaite, Frank. *The Anglo-American Connection in the Early Nineteenth Century.* Philadelphia: University of Pennsylvania Press, 1959. These six lectures explore the types and extent of "communication" between the United States and Great Britain in the early 19th century. They provide an especially useful background to diplomatic and commercial relations between the two nations.

8:64 White, Laura A. "The United States in the 1850's as Seen by British Consuls." *Mississippi Valley Historical Review* 19:4 (1933), 509–36. This article summarizes the observations made by British consuls to the British Foreign Office concerning political and social conditions in the United States.

Suppression of the Slave Trade

See "Personalities," especially John Quincy Adams, Lewis Cass, and, under "Others," Andrew Stevenson; and see "Document Collections" for British Parliamentary Papers (8:3); also see Chapter 11, "Slavery and the Slave Trade" and Chapter 18, "The Slave Trade."

8:65 Booth, Alan R. "The United States African Squadron, 1843–1861." *Boston University Papers in African History* 1 (1964), 77–117. Booth discusses the ineffectiveness of the joint-squadron idea and concludes that the attitudes of America's secretaries of the navy, mostly Southerners or southern sympathizers, made the arrangement impossible. Instead of suppres-

sing the slave trade, they sought to build American commerce along the African coast, encouraged inadequate congressional funding of the plan, and authorized the use of unseaworthy ships.

8:66 Du Bois, W. E. B. *The Suppression of the African Slave-Trade to the United States of America, 1638–1870.* New York: Longmans, Green, 1896. Reprint 1965. Du Bois reviews the efforts made by Americans to limit and suppress the slave trade. It also discusses the slavers' illegal use of the American flag to avoid the British slave patrol, a matter of serious dispute in Anglo-American relations from the 1820s to the 1860s.

8:67 Duignan, Peter, and Clendenen, Clarence. *The United States and the African Slave Trade, 1619–1862.* Stanford, Calif.: Stanford University Press, 1962. A brief history of U.S. involvement in the slave trade, it well illustrates the ineffectual use of the joint-squadron plan established by the Webster-Ashburton Treaty (see Chapter 10). Bibliography.

8:68 Eaton, Clement. *The Freedom-of-Thought Struggle in the Old South.* New York: Harper & Row, 1964. Many times, especially during the 1830s, the lower South experienced great anxiety over the possibility of slave revolts. The implication drawn from his findings, though not argued by the author, is that this state of fear influenced Southerners to oppose any tampering with slavery—especially when British interference with the institution seemed imminent.

8:69 Fladeland, Betty. *Men and Brothers: Anglo-American Antislavery Cooperation.* Urbana: University of Illinois Press, 1972. Fladeland shows the effect of slavery and the African slave trade on Anglo-American relations from 1830 to 1860. She examines the *Creole* affair within the context of international law and the African slave-trade controversy, and also includes a discussion of the *Amistad* case. Extensive bibliography.

8:70 Howard, Warren S. *American Slavers and the Federal Law, 1837–1862.* Berkeley: University of California Press, 1963. This study contains information on the Webster-Ashburton Treaty's joint-cruising arrangement. Bibliography.

Jones, H. *To the Webster-Ashburton Treaty* (10:31) explains the Webster-Ashburton joint-squadron plan and the settlement of the *Creole* affair.

8:71 Mathieson, William L. *Great Britain and the Slave Trade, 1839–1865*. London: Longmans, Green, 1929. Mathieson provides a detailed analysis of British attempts to stamp out the slave trade and to induce other nations, especially the United States, to cooperate in the venture. The book refers incidentally to the Lyons-Seward Treaty of 1862 (see Chapter 11) for suppression of the trade.

8:72 Milne, A. Taylor. "The Slave Trade and Anglo-American Relations, 1807–1862." *Bulletin of the Institute of Historical Research* [Great Britain] 9 (1931–1932), 126–29. This brief piece, a synopsis of the author's thesis, sees slavery and the slave trade as a major factor in the "uneasy relationship" of the United States and Great Britain before the Civil War. Milne argues that American failure to suppress the slave trade antagonized influential people in England and slowed British efforts to eradicate the odious business. See the author's expansion of his theme (11:104).

8:73 Soulsby, Hugh G. *The Right of Search and the Slave Trade in Anglo-American Relations, 1814–1862*. Baltimore: Johns Hopkins Press, 1933. The right-of-search and African slave-trade questions intertwined to pose great problems for the Webster-Ashburton negotiations and other issues in Anglo-American relations. Bibliography.

8:74 Van Alstyne, Richard W. "The British Right of Search and the African Slave Trade." *Journal of Modern History* 2:1 (1930), 37–47. This essay emphasizes how the right-of-search question was involved in the African slave-trade debate, and admits to a theoretical distinction between the alleged right of "search" and the right of "visit"—as the Peel ministry claimed. The search controversy did not end until Britain and the United States adopted mutual search policies during America's Civil War.

Creole and Amistad Affairs

Adams, E. D. "Lord Ashburton and the Treaty of Washington" (10:56) includes Ashburton's instructions on the search issue, as well as material relating to the *Caroline* affair.

8:75 Barnes, Gilbert H. *The Antislavery Impulse, 1830–1844*. New York: American Historical Association, 1933. Barnes explains how abolitionists in the House of Representatives used the *Creole* slave revolt

to launch an attack on the gag rule and reopen the slavery question to debate on the floor. Bibliography.

Bemis, S. F. *John Quincy Adams and the Union* (8:7) includes an insightful discussion of the former president's views on slavery; during the debate over the *Creole* affair, he continued his long fight against the gag rule.

8:76 Fladeland, Betty. *James Gillespie Birney: Slaveholder to Abolitionist*. Ithaca, N.Y.: Cornell University Press, 1955. Birney used legal arguments during the *Creole* affair as well as strong protests against the gag rule in the House of Representatives. Bibliography.

8:77 Haines, Charles G., and Sherwood, Foster H. *The Role of the Supreme Court in American Government and Politics, 1835–1864*. Berkeley: University of California Press, 1957. The authors analyze the legal and constitutional differences between the *Amistad* and *Creole* cases. Bibliography.

8:78 Jones, Howard. "The Peculiar Institution and National Honor: The Case of the *Creole* Slave Revolt." *Civil War History* 21:1 (1975), 28–50. The insurrection on board the *Creole* affected the settlement of Maine's boundary (1841–1842) as the question of national honor threatened to elevate the revolt into an Anglo-American crisis. Not only did the emotional slavery issue pose a threat, but the lack of an Anglo-American extradition agreement forced Webster to appeal for return of the escaped slaves on the principle of comity.

Jones, W. D. "The Influence of Slavery on the Webster-Ashburton Negotiations" (10:61) argues that the problems of slavery and the *Creole* affair almost wrecked the Webster-Ashburton negotiations.

8:79 McClendon, R. Earl. "The *Amistad* Claims: Inconsistencies of Policy." *Political Science Quarterly* 48:3 (1933), 386–412. The damage claims resulting from the *Amistad* affair lingered for many years.

8:80 Wish, Harvey. "American Slave Insurrections before 1861." *Journal of Negro History* 22:3 (1937), 299–320. The *Creole* revolt was one of at least fifty-five insurrections at sea from 1699 to the 1840s. The result, Wish believes, was a "conspiracy of silence" in the South on the incidence of slave revolts, a strategy designed to stop their spread.

FRANCE

See "Personalities," especially Lewis Cass, Albert Gallatin (under "Others"), Andrew Jackson, Edward Livingston, and Richard Rush.

8:81 Barker, Nancy Nichols. *Distaff Diplomacy: The Empress Eugénie and the Foreign Policy of the Second Empire.* Austin: University of Texas Press, 1967. This book provides one of the rare glimpses of the influence of women on diplomacy (1850–1870).

Blumenthal, H. *France and the United States: Their Diplomatic Relations, 1789–1914* (2:224) concentrates on policy development in Franco-American relations.

8:82 Blumenthal, Henry. *A Reappraisal of Franco-American Relations, 1830–1871.* Chapel Hill: University of North Carolina Press, 1959. Blumenthal challenges the traditional assumption that Franco-American relations were friendly and cordial during this period. Instead, he concludes that relations were clouded by hostility, distrust, and misunderstanding. Extensive bibliography.

8:83 Carossa, Vincent P., and Leder, Lawrence H. "Edward Livingston and Jacksonian Diplomacy." *Louisiana History* 7:3 (1966), 241–48. This piece summarizes the French claims episode and reprints a letter from Livingston to Secretary of State John Forsyth dated June 21, 1835.

8:84 Curtis, Eugene N. "American Opinion of the French Nineteenth Century Revolutions." *American Historical Review* 29:2 (1924), 249–70. Curtis surveys the opinion of the American press and leading politicians toward the French revolutions of 1830, 1848, and 1870, respectively.

8:85 McLemore, Richard A. *Franco-American Diplomatic Relations, 1816–1836.* Baton Rouge: Louisiana State University Press, 1941. This study traces the rise and development of the "aggressive nationalism" manifested in American policy toward France during the claims controversy.

8:86 Rémond, René. *Les Etats-Unis devant l'opinion française, 1815–1852* [The United States in French opinion, 1815–1852]. 2 vols. Paris: Colin, 1962. These volumes contain an exhaustive study of

the evolution of French attitudes toward the United States in the first half of the 19th century, including coverage of Franco-American diplomatic relations. Extensive bibliography.

8:87 Thomas, Robert C. "Andrew Jackson versus France: American Policy toward France, 1834–1836." *Tennessee Historical Quarterly* 35:1 (1976), 51–64. Thomas summarizes Jackson's policy toward France in the crisis of 1834 to 1836. The author concludes that the lack of a strong, constructive domestic opposition permitted Jackson to pursue a dangerous policy which threatened a needless war.

8:88 Webster, Charles K. "British Mediation between France and the United States, 1834–1836." *English Historical Review* 42:1 (1927), 58–78. Although England was never an official mediator in this Franco-American dispute, Lord Palmerston played an important role in helping to resolve the crisis.

White, E. B. *American Opinion of France from Lafayette to Poincare* (2:227).

Willson, B. *America's Ambassadors to France (1777–1927): A Narrative of Franco-American Diplomatic Relations* (2:182).

Zahniser, M. R. *Uncertain Friendship: American-French Relations through the Cold War* (2:228) provides a good introduction to this period.

RUSSIA

See "Personalities," especially James Buchanan and George Mifflin Dallas.

Bailey, T. A. *America Faces Russia: Russian-American Relations from Early Times to Our Day* [1776–1950] (2:245) is a broad survey of this period.

Dulles, F. R. *The Road to Teheran: The Story of Russia and America, 1781–1943* (2:247).

8:89 Langley, Lester D. "Two Jacksonian Diplomats in Czarist Russia." *Research Studies* 45:2 (1977), 92–99. This article summarizes the diplomatic activities of Andrew Jackson's two appointees as minister to Russia: John Randolph and James Buchanan. The author emphasizes the importance of commercial rather than political relations.

Laserson, M. M. *The American Impact on Russia: Diplomatic and Ideological, 1784–1917* (2:250) concludes that the American impact on Russia during this period was more substantial than generally recognized.

8:90 Thomas, Benjamin P. *Russo-American Relations, 1815–1867.* Baltimore: Johns Hopkins Press, 1930. This early work contains a traditional survey of diplomatic relations between the United States and Russia, but it is based only on American sources.

Williams, W. A. *American-Russian Relations, 1781–1947* (2:256) has little material on 19th-century affairs.

Northwest America

See also Chapter 7, "The Monroe Doctrine, to 1861," and Chapter 12, "The Alaska Purchase, 1854–1867," for additional references.

8:91 Farrar, Victor J. "Background to the Purchase of Alaska." *Washington Historical Quarterly* 13:2 (1922), 93–104. Farrar traces Alaska's place in Russian-American relations (1820–1850), especially the fishing rights conflict and other issues raised by Russian presence in Alaska.

Gibson, J. R. *Imperial Russia in Frontier America..., 1784–1867* (5:154).

8:92 Kushner, Howard I. *Conflict on the Northwest Coast: American-Russian Rivalry in the Pacific Northwest, 1790–1867.* Westport, Conn.: Greenwood, 1975. Kushner emphasizes American-Russian relations leading to the United States' purchase of Alaska in 1867, but includes details on America's expansion into the Pacific Northwest. He shows that American traders in the 1790s sought the pelts of the sea otter to further their commercial interests in China. Bibliography.

8:93 Manning, Clarence A. *Russian Influence in Early America.* New York: Library Publishers, 1953. By focusing on the theme of Russian expansionism, this volume traces the Russian advance along the northwest coast of North America and subsequent Russian attempts to preserve their interests in the area to 1867.

Nichols, I. C., Jr. "The Russian Ukase and the Monroe Doctrine" (7:149).

Okun, S. B. *The Russian-American Company* [1784–1867] (5:155).

8:94 Wheeler, Mary E. "Empires in Conflict and Cooperation: The 'Bostonians' and the Russian-American Company." *Pacific Historical Review* 40:4 (1971), 419–41. This article analyzes the development of competition and cooperation between the Russian-American Company and the shippers of Boston along the northwest coast in the two decades prior to 1825.

OTHER EUROPEAN STATES

The German States

Adams, H. M. *Prussian-American Relations, 1775–1871* (5:152).

8:95 Gazley, John G. *American Opinion of German Unification, 1848–1871.* New York: Columbia University Press, 1926. Gazley's detailed survey is based primarily on American press opinion and the writings of American political and intellectual figures. Bibliography.

Holland and Belgium

8:96 Hoekstra, Peter. *Thirty-Seven Years of Holland-American Relations, 1803–1840.* Grand Rapids, Mich.: Eerdmans-Sevensina, 1916. This study provides a traditional survey of commercial relations and negotiations between the United States and Holland during these four decades.

8:97 Laurent, P. H. "Anglo-American Diplomacy and the Belgian Indemnities Controversy, 1836–1842." *Historical Journal* 10:2 (1967), 197–217. Laurent traces Anglo-American cooperation in the indemnities controversy which arose from the Revolution of 1830.

8:98 Laurent, P. H. "Belgium's Relations with Texas and the United States, 1839–1844." *Southwestern Historical Quarterly* 68:2 (1964), 220–36. This article summarizes commercial negotiations between Texas and Belgium and the attempt to establish a Belgian settlement in Texas. The author concludes that such negotiations stimulated expansionism in the United States by provoking a reaction against European interference in North America.

Rooney, J. W., Jr. *Belgian-American Diplomatic and Consular Relationships, 1830–1850: A Study in American Foreign Policy in the Mid-Nineteenth Century* (8:147) traces the continuous efforts by the United States and Belgium to develop mutually advantageous trade relations and to strengthen them through treaty provisions.

8:99   Wagner, Jonathan F. "Beaumont in Brussels: An American Response to the Revolution of 1830." *Studies in History and Society* 6:2 (1975), 46–59. The article summarizes Augustus Beaumont's observations and criticism of the Belgian Revolution of 1830. Beaumont was a doctrinaire, anti-British liberal who was born in Connecticut but had settled in Jamaica.

Westermann, J. C. *The Netherlands and the United States: Their Relations in the Beginning of the Nineteenth Century* (5:149) focuses on the development of commercial relations.

Winter, P. J. van. *American Finance and Dutch Investment, 1780–1805, with an Epilogue to 1840* (5:150).

Italy, the Papal States, and Sicily

8:100   Bárány, George. "A Note on the Prehistory of American Diplomatic Relations with the Papal States." *Catholic Historical Review* 47:4 (1961–1962), 508–13. This article traces the growth of interest in establishing formal diplomatic relations between the United States and the Papal States from 1844 to 1848.

8:101   DeConde, Alexander. *Half Bitter, Half Sweet: An Excursion into Italian-American History.* New York: Scribner's, 1971. DeConde includes a brief summary on early contacts between the United States and the Italian people. Extensive bibliography.

8:102   Marraro, H. R. *American Opinion on the Unification of Italy, 1846–1861.* New York: Columbia University Press, 1932. Marraro traces American opinion and diplomatic response toward the events leading to the unification of Italy.

8:103   Pagano, Luigi A. "Sicilia e Stati Uniti di America nel Risorgimento" [Sicily and the United States of America during the Risorgimento]. *Rassegna Storica del Risorgimento* 41:3 (1954), 484–93. Pagano focuses on the friendly attitudes which existed in 1848–1849 and 1860 between the Sicilian revolu-

tionary government and American diplomats and naval commanders.

8:104   Stock, Leo F. "American Consuls to the Papal States, 1797–1867." *Catholic Historical Review* 15:3 (1929), 233–51. This is a brief summary of various American consuls and their activities.

Scandinavia

8:105   Carlson, Knute E. *Relations of the United States with Sweden.* Allentown, Pa.: Haas, 1921. This brief volume concentrates on the cordial commercial relations between the United States and Sweden (1776–1827) which culminated with the ratification of the Treaty of 1827.

Fogdall, S. J. M. P. *Danish-American Diplomacy, 1776–1920* (2:242).

8:106   Hovde, B. J. *Diplomatic Relations of the United States with Sweden and Norway, 1814–1905.* Iowa City: University of Iowa Studies in Social Science, 1920. Based entirely on American sources, this brief study summarizes American diplomatic relations with Sweden and Norway between 1814 and 1905.

Scott, F. D. *Scandinavia* [1600–1945] (2:243).

Spain

Becker, J. *Historia de las relaciones exteriores de la España durante el siglo xix* (7:9).

8:107   Chadwick, French E. *The Relations of the United States and Spain: Diplomacy.* New York: Scribner's, 1906. This book is a detailed diplomatic history based on traditional diplomatic sources. Approximately one-quarter of the book deals with the period from 1815 to 1860.

Cortada, J. W. *Two Nations over Time: Spain and the United States, 1776–1977* (2:244) analyzes diplomatic relations by examining economic and cultural factors as well as domestic politics.

Ettinger, A. A. *The Mission to Spain of Pierre Soulé, 1853–1855* (7:118).

Other States

8:108 Curti, Merle. "Austria and the United States, 1848–1852: A Study in Diplomatic Relations." *Smith College Studies in History* 11:3 (1926), 141–206. This study is a traditional account of the diplomatic relations between the United States and Austria from the revolutions of 1848 through the Kossuth affair of 1851–1852.

Field, J. A., Jr. *America and the Mediterranean World, 1776–1882* (18:6).

8:109 Lerski, Jerzy J. *A Polish Chapter in Jacksonian America: The United States and the Polish Exiles of 1831*. Madison: University of Wisconsin Press, 1958. Lerski describes the plight of the Polish exiles who emigrated to the United States in 1831.

Meier, H. K. *The United States and Switzerland in the Nineteenth Century* (2:258) traces the generally friendly relations up to World War I.

Tatum, E. H., Jr. *The United States and Europe, 1815–1823* (7:144) examines American attitudes toward world affairs and the relationship of international politics to United States foreign policy, and relates them to the Monroe Doctrine.

Diplomatic Episodes

U.S. AND GREEK INDEPENDENCE

8:110 Cline, Myrtle A. *American Attitude toward the Greek War of Independence, 1821–28*. Atlanta, 1930. The most detailed account of the U.S. reaction to the Greek revolution against the Turks, it demonstrates the growth of public and congressional support for U.S. intervention. American commercial interests were among the opponents of intervention. Bibliography.

Curti, M. E. *American Philanthropy Abroad: A History* (2:72) devotes a chapter to the relief effort on behalf of the Greeks.

8:111 Dakin, Douglas. *The Greek Struggle for Independence, 1821–1833*. Berkeley: University of Cali-

fornia Press, 1973. This study provides a thorough examination of the movement for Greek independence. Although the author does not relate the Greek struggle to United States diplomacy, this book provides an excellent background. Bibliography.

Daniel, R. L. *American Philanthropy in the Near East, 1820–1960* (2:74) devotes a chapter to American philanthropic efforts on behalf of the Greek revolutionaries.

8:112 Earle, Edward Mead. "American Interest in the Greek Cause, 1821–1827." *American Historical Review* 33:1 (1927), 44–63. Earle demonstrates that American concern for the Greek cause could have had detrimental effects on the course of U.S.-Turkish relations leading up to the negotiation of the 1830 U.S.-Turkish treaty.

8:113 Earle, Edward Mead. "Early American Policy Concerning Ottoman Minorities." *Political Science Quarterly* 42:3 (1927), 337–67. This short account demonstrates the conflict (1821–1828) between popular sentiment and the national interest. The precedent of nonintervention set the course for later U.S. reaction to the pleas of Ottoman minorities.

Field, J. A., Jr. *America and the Mediterranean World, 1776–1882* (18:6) devotes half a chapter to the dichotomy between advocates of the national interest and the philanthropic lobby.

8:114 Larrabee, Stephen A. *Hellas Observed: The American Experience of Greece, 1775–1865*. New York: New York University Press, 1957. Based on English-language sources, this volume traces the extensive American interest in Greece and summarizes the American image of Greece.

Seaburg, C., and Paterson, S. *Merchant Prince of Boston: Colonel T. H. Perkins, 1764–1854* (8:148) finds that Perkins opposed U.S. aid to the Greeks because it would interfere with the lucrative Boston-Smyrna-China trade.

HUNGARIAN REVOLUTION, KOSSUTH, AND THE YOUNG AMERICA MOVEMENT

8:115 Curti, Merle. "George N. Sanders—American Patriot of the Fifties." *South Atlantic Quarterly* 27:1 (1928), 79–87. This article provides a summary of the life and career of one of the most aggressive proponents of the Young America doctrines. The revolutionary outbursts of 1848 in Europe stimulated some American idealists who inaugurated the Young America movement, which had as one of its goals active intervention against European despotisms.

8:116   Curti, Merle. "Young America." *American Historical Review* 32:1 (1926), 34–49. Although this article was written more than five decades ago, it still provides a good introduction and insights into the Young America movement.

8:117   Danbom, David B. "The Young America Movement." *Journal of the Illinois State Historical Society* 67:3 (1974), 294–306. Danbom provides a summary of the Young America movement, its composition, and attitudes on American foreign policy in the 1850s.

8:118   Deak, Istvan. *The Lawful Revolution: Louis Kossuth and the Hungarians, 1848–1849*. New York: Columbia University Press, 1979. Deak provides the fullest account in English of the 1848 Hungarian Revolution. The author focuses on Kossuth as a symbol of liberalism in America and elsewhere.

8:119   Komlos, John H. *Louis Kossuth in America, 1851–1852*. Buffalo, N.Y.: East European Institute, 1973. This monograph provides a summary of Kossuth's life, his career prior to 1851, and his visit to the United States in 1851 and 1852. Bibliography.

8:120   May, A. J. *Contemporary American Opinion of the Mid-Century Revolutions in Central Europe*. Philadelphia: University of Pennsylvania Press, 1927. May's survey is based on newspapers, magazines, and political correspondence. The study summarizes, but does not analyze, the positive American response to the revolutions. Bibliography.

8:121   Oliver, John W. "Louis Kossuth's Appeal to the Middle West, 1852." *Mississippi Valley Historical Review* 14:4 (1928), 481–95. Oliver provides a description of Kossuth's travels in the Middle West and a useful summary of the region's reaction to the Hungarian revolutionary leader.

8:122   Potts, E. Daniel, and Potts, Annette. *Young America and Australian Gold: Americans and the Gold Rush of the 1850's*. St. Lucia: University of Queensland Press, 1974. This study examines American migration to Australia during the gold rush of the 1850s. Although few Americans in Australia were

associated with the Young America movement, "most would have shared their beliefs in capitalistic progress and romantic individualism." Bibliography.

8:123   Spencer, Donald S. *Louis Kossuth and Young America: A Study of Sectionalism and Foreign Policy, 1848–1852*. Columbia: University of Missouri Press, 1977. Spencer describes Kossuth's visit to the United States in 1851–1852 and examines the subsequent decline in support among a variety of groups for Kossuth and his appeals for American intervention in Austria. Extensive bibliography.

8:124   Szilassy, Sandor. "America and the Hungarian Revolution of 1848–1849." *Slavonic and East European Review* 44:1 (1966), 180–96. Based on American State Department sources and contemporary published sources, this article traces the response of the United States government to the Hungarian Revolution of 1848.

U.S. AND THE CRIMEAN WAR

8:125   Dowty, Alan. *The Limits of American Isolation: The United States and the Crimean War*. New York: New York University Press, 1971. Dowty examines American opinion and policy toward the Crimean crisis to demonstrate that the United States played the role of an active neutral during this conflict rather than the role of an isolationist power. Bibliography.

8:126   Dvoichenko-Markov, Eufrosina. "Americans in the Crimean War." *Russian Review* 13:2 (1954), 137–45. This is a brief summary of those few Americans in the Crimean War who actively participated on the Russian side.

8:127   Golder, Frank A. "Russian-American Relations during the Crimean War." *American Historical Review* 31:3 (1926), 462–76. Based on Russian archival sources, this article examines American sympathy and support for Russia during the Crimean War.

8:128   Henderson, Galvin. "The Diplomatic Revolution of 1854." *American Historical Review* 43:1 (1937), 22–50. This article provides excellent background for understanding the United States and the Crimean War by focusing on the European powers in the crisis of 1854 and the breakdown of the system created in 1815.

8:129 Jones, Horace P. "Southern Opinion on the Crimean War." *Journal of Mississippi History* 29:2 (1967), 95–117. Jones surveys the response of a large number of southern newspapers and periodicals to the Crimean War. The author concludes that the South's deep hostility toward England resulted in a large majority of southern newspapers being pro-Russia during the crisis.

8:130 Oliva, L. Jay. "America Meets Russia: 1854." *Journalism Quarterly* 40:1 (1963), 65–69. This article surveys American press opinion at the outset of the Crimean War and finds that it was predominantly anti-Russian.

Commercial Relations

8:131 Adamson, Rolf. "Swedish Iron Exports to the United States, 1783–1860." *Scandinavian Economic History Review* 17:1 (1969), 58–114. Containing detailed charts, maps, and tables, this article summarizes the trade that flourished in the 1830s before declining significantly in the 1840s and 1850s.

8:132 Albion, Robert G. *The Rise of New York Port, 1815–1860*. New York: Scribner's, 1939. Albion's detailed study, based on exhaustive research, traces the rise of New York as the chief American seaport. The book contains thirty-one appendixes of commercial information and statistics. Extensive bibliography.

8:133 Albion, Robert G. *Square-Riggers on Schedule: The New York Sailing Packets to England, France, and the Cotton Ports*. Princeton, N.J.: Princeton University Press, 1938. Based on extensive primary research, this book is a fine study of this aspect of American commerce with England and France.

8:134 Bergquist, Harold E., Jr. "Russo-American Economic Relations in the 1820's: Henry Middleton as a Protector of American Interests in Russia and Turkey." *East European Quarterly* 11:1 (1977), 27–41. The article summarizes Middleton's activities as American minister to Russia in the 1820s in behalf of American commercial interests and his important role in negotiating the 1830 treaty with Turkey.

8:135 Beutin, Ludwig. *Bremen und Amerika: Zur Geschichte der Weltwirtschaft und der Beziehungen Deutschlands zu den Vereinigten Staaten* [Bremen and America: on the history of the world economy and of the relationship of Germany to the United States]. Bremen: Schunemann, 1953. A thorough study, it focuses on commercial relations between the United States and Bremen from 1800 to 1939, and explains how the economic life of Bremen was changed by its relations with the United States. Bibliography.

8:136 Cutler, Carl C. *Greyhounds of the Sea: The Story of the American Clipper Ship*. New York: Halcyon House, 1930. For the nonspecialist; this narrative offers a general account of the clipper ships, which were commercial carriers.

8:137 Frederickson, J. William. "American Shipping in the Trade with Northern Europe, 1783–1860." *Scandinavian Economic History Review* 4:2 (1956), 109–25. The author examines the comparatively small amount of trade between the United States, Russia and Scandinavia and includes an analysis of the economic and political factors which affected that trade.

8:138 Gregory, Frances W. *Nathan Appleton: Merchant and Entrepreneur, 1779–1861*. Charlottesville: University Press of Virginia, 1975. Gregory's detailed biography focuses on the business and commercial practices of an extremely successful 19th-century American entrepreneur.

8:139 Homans, J. Smith, ed. *An Historical and Statistical Account of the Foreign Commerce of the United States*. New York: Putnam's, 1857. Reprint 1975. This mid-19th-century volume includes a brief summary of American commerce with individual nations and geographic areas of the world with a useful statistical chart included for each.

Hutchins, J. G. B. *The American Maritime Industries and Public Policy, 1789–1914* (39:50).

8:140 Johnson, Emory, et al. *History of Domestic and Foreign Commerce of the United States*. 2 vols. New York: Franklin (1915), 1966. Although outdated in many respects, this work contains a useful narrative on aspects of American commerce as well as a wealth of statistical information.

8:141 Kirchner, Walther. *Studies in Russian-American Commerce, 1820–1860*. Leiden: Brill,

1975. This volume includes a considerable amount of statistical detail as well as information on how trade between the two nations was organized. The author finds no indication of any "colonial exploitation" of Russia by the United States.

8:142 McMaster, John B. *The Life and Times of Stephen Girard, Mariner and Merchant.* 2 vols. Philadelphia: Lippincott, 1918. Traditional life and times biography of Girard, whose career in business and commerce spanned decades from the 1770s to the 1820s.

8:143 Morison, Samuel Eliot. *The Maritime History of Massachusetts, 1783–1860.* Boston: Houghton Mifflin, 1941. This volume remains the classic history of maritime activity in Massachusetts. Thoroughly researched and well written, the study provides an insightful treatment of maritime activity in the state. Bibliography.

8:144 North, Douglass C. *The Economic Growth of the United States, 1790–1860.* Englewood Cliffs, N.J.: Prentice-Hall, 1961. The book contains several useful chapters on the role international trade played in the growth of the American economy. Bibliography.

8:145 Porter, Kenneth W. *The Jacksons and the Lees: Two Generations of Massachusetts Merchants, 1765–1844.* 2 vols. Cambridge: Harvard University Press, 1937. This book is a documentary study which includes a narrative of the commercial activities of the two families and an extensive collection of correspondence from each family.

8:146 Porter, Kenneth W. *John Jacob Astor, Business Man.* 2 vols. Cambridge: Harvard University Press, 1931. Based on extensive research, this detailed account of Astor's life and business activities remains the most complete treatment of this topic.

8:147 Rooney, John W., Jr. *Belgian-American Diplomatic and Consular Relationships, 1830–1850: A Study in American Foreign Policy in the Mid-Nineteenth Century.* Louvain: Universitaires de Louvain, Bureaux du Recueil, 1969. A detailed and thoroughly researched study which traces the continuous efforts by the United States and Belgium to develop mutually advantageous trade relations and to strengthen them through treaty provisions.

8:148 Seaberg, Carl, and Paterson, Stanley. *Merchant Prince of Boston: Colonel T. H. Perkins,*

1764–1854. Cambridge: Harvard University Press, 1971. A clearly written and well-documented study which focuses on the business, investment, and trading activities of Colonel Thomas Handasyd Perkins. Bibliography.

Setser, V. G. *The Commercial Reciprocity Policy of the United States, 1774–1829* (4:150).

8:149 Taylor, George R. *The Transportation Revolution, 1815–1860.* New York: Holt, Rinehart & Winston, 1951. This economic history of American business and commerce provides a detailed background for American commercial relations in the period and includes chapters on foreign trade and the American merchant marine. Extensive bibliography.

8:150 Tyler, David B. *Steam Conquers the Atlantic.* New York: Appleton-Century, 1939. Although dated, this narrative history provides a solid account for the nonspecialist of the rise and development of the Atlantic steamship in trade, mail service, and passenger service in the 19th century.

Wilkins, M. *The Emergence of Multinational Enterprise: American Business Abroad from the Colonial Era to 1914* (39:134) deals, in the first two chapters, with the period to 1860.

8:151 Willett, Thomas D. "International Specie Flows and American Monetary Stability, 1834–1860." *Journal of Economic History* 28:1 (1968), 28–50. This article concludes that the international movement of specie played a significant role in America's monetary disturbances.

Woodman, H. D. *King Cotton and His Retainers: Financing and Marketing the Cotton Crop of the South, 1800–1925* (11:174).

WITH GREAT BRITAIN

Barnes, James J. *Authors, Publishers and Politicians: The Quest for an Anglo-American Copyright Agreement, 1815–1854* (8:53) examines the struggle for a copyright law, an often-neglected divisive factor in Anglo-American relations.

8:152 Benns, F. Lee. *The American Struggle for the British West India Carrying Trade, 1815–1830.* Bloomington: Indiana University Studies, 1923. This thoroughly researched study details the American drive to win trade concessions from Great Britain in the West Indies, which culminated with the Reciprocity Treaty of 1830.

8:153 Buck, Norman S. *The Development of the Organization of Anglo-American Trade, 1800–1850.* New Haven, Conn.: Yale University Press, 1925. Reprint 1968. This topic-by-topic monograph examines in detail the "methods of buying and selling goods" between the United States and Great Britain. The volume concentrates on American cotton and English manufacturing goods. Bibliography.

8:154 Galbraith, John S. *The Hudson's Bay Company as an Imperial Factor, 1821–1869.* Berkeley: University of California Press, 1957. Galbraith relates the growth and decline of the British firm's fur trade to the political and diplomatic history of the period. Bibliography.

8:155 Hidy, Ralph W. *The House of Baring in American Trade and Finance.* Cambridge: Harvard University Press, 1949. This masterful exercise in business history traces the affairs, down to 1861, of what came to be the English banking house most heavily involved in American trade and finance. The research is exemplary, wide-ranging and deep, although primary reliance is understandably upon the records of the House of Baring itself.

8:156 Killick, John R. "Bolton Ogden and Company: A Case Study in Anglo-American Trade, 1790–1850." *Business History Review* 48:4 (1974), 501–19. The author concludes that many functions which had been discharged by general merchants in 1800 were divided by 1840 among specialists such as shipowners, manufacturers, bankers, speculators, and stockbrokers. Hence, vast increases in commerce were possible, but traditional firms such as Bolton Ogden and Company declined.

8:157 Martin, Thomas P. "Cotton and Wheat in Anglo-American Trade and Politics, 1846–1852." *Journal of Southern History* 1:3 (1935), 293–319. Summarizes the importance of American cotton and wheat to Great Britain between 1846 and 1852 and describes the effect this trade had on English policy toward the United States.

8:158 Martin, Thomas P. "The Upper Mississippi Valley in Anglo-American Anti-Slavery and Free Trade Relations: 1837–1842." *Mississippi Valley Historical Review* 15:2 (1928), 204–20. Traces alliance in Upper Mississippi Valley of antislave forces and wheat farmers to pressure England to reduce its restrictive Corn Laws.

8:159 Price, Jacob M. "One Family's Empire: The Russell-Lee-Clerk Connection in Maryland, Britain, and India, 1707–1857." *Maryland Historical Magazine* 72:2 (1977), 165–225. This detailed article examines the Russell-Lee-Clerk family cluster by examining aspects of their far-flung commercial and professional careers. The study is based on extensive manuscript and business records.

8:160 Sandberg, Lars G. "A Note on British Cotton Cloth Exports to the United States: 1815–1860." *Explorations in Economic History* 9:4 (1972), 427–28. This note presents value and volume of British cotton cloth exports to the United States from 1815 to 1860.

9

United States and Mexico, 1821–1861

Contributing Editor
DAVID M. PLETCHER
Indiana University

Contributors
Gene M. Brack
New Mexico State University

Robert E. May
Purdue University

Thomas Schoonover
University of Southwestern Louisiana

Contents

Introduction

The relations of the United States with Mexico from 1821 to 1861 parallel other strands of American diplomatic history. During most of these four decades Anglo-American relations were either bothersome or critical. The Canadian rebellions of 1837 to 1840 immediately followed the Texas Revolution of 1836, and both tested the inadequate American neutrality laws and opened possibilities for border expansion. More important, the Oregon crisis of 1845–1846 exactly coincided with the crisis in U.S.-Mexican relations that produced the Mexican War, and the two crises merged to create one of the most complicated years in nineteenth-century American diplomatic history. The relations of the United States with newly independent Mexico helped to determine the nature of American relations with other, more remote Latin American states. Finally, U.S.-Mexican relations and especially the Mexican War made possible the rise of the United States to the position of second-rank power—not yet a figure of world importance but nearly supreme in its own region.

Several general works, most of them recently published, will introduce the reader to the subject, and their comprehensive bibliographies will lead him to more specialized works. A good short survey of U.S.-Mexican relations, which devotes two chapters to this period, is Karl M. Schmitt, *Mexico and the United States* (2:301). A readable introduction to American expansionist impulses and motives is Norman A. Graebner, *Empire on the Pacific* (9:12). More detailed than either of these and giving some insight into rival interpretations of the Texas question and the Mexican War is David M. Pletcher, *The Diplomacy of Annexation* (9:13). A complementary volume which treats the military history of the war in similar detail is K. Jack Bauer, *The Mexican War, 1846–1848* (9:148). For the 1850s, few general surveys exist. A readable and up-to-date monograph is Robert E. May, *The Southern Dream of Caribbean Empire, 1854–1861* (7:116), although it devotes only one chapter solely to Mexico.

A casual glance over the bibliography on U.S.-Mexican relations (1821–1861) reveals at once the two principal trends in historiography—emphasis on the Mexican War and overwhelming attention to the regional history of the border area, especially Texas and California. Both trends, of course, are easily understood. In the first place, any major war, especially a completely victorious one, attracts historians. Second, regional history long ago proved its solidity as a bulwark to general American history, and in the whole country one cannot find two more chauvinistic states than Texas and California. Except for the Mexican War itself, the history of Texas from settlement to annexation has called forth more books and articles than any other subject covered in this chapter.

The question of the causes of the Mexican War is the only one in this chapter that has gone through a series of definable changes related to events of the period in which the historian happened to be writing. For several decades after the war, the question of its causes was polarized along political lines—Democrats believed Polk justified; Whigs thought him a tyrannical aggressor. At the same time the slavery question divided opinion sectionally—abolitionists opposed the war because it added potentially slave territory, while the proslavery South was inclined to defend the action, although with less unanimity. Between the Reconstruction period and World War I, opinion on the Mexican War changed little. After passions had cooled and documents had been published, historians such as George L. Rives, *The United States and Mexico, 1821–1848* (9:18), began to treat the subject with some scholarly objectivity.

In 1919, six years after Rives published his work, Justin H. Smith produced a two-volume study, *The War with Mexico* (9:140), which influenced writings on the Mexican War for at least half a century. Smith was less objective than Rives, but he combined a highly colored style with some of the most impressive documentation ever observed in the field of American diplomatic history. (His text, however, sometimes bore little relation to the facts and views of the cited sources.) Smith adopted a pejorative attitude toward Mexico inspired by nearly a decade of revolution in that country and by Wilsonian diplomacy. He reverted to the old Democratic, nationalistic view that the Mexican War was justified by Mexican actions and even that Mexico threatened the United States, instead of vice versa. There was, however, one difference between Smith and the Democrats of the 1840s—to him Polk was no hero but a mediocre timeserver who offered little true leadership.

Most studies of the Mexican War written between 1920 and about 1970 reflected Smith's interpretation of its causes in one way or another. To be sure, a small counterwave appeared, represented by the articles of Richard R. Stenberg, especially "The Failure of Polk's Mexican War Intrigue of 1845" (9:146), and by Glenn W. Price, *Origins of the War with Mexico* (9:145). Reacting at the opposite end of the scale from Smith, these writers saw in the coming of the war an elaborate plot by Polk, who deliberately planned the war to acquire territory and extricate himself from political difficulties. A third interpretation is that of Pletcher, *The Diplomacy of Annexation* (9:13). In this work Polk is presented as a dominant president and a skilled politician but one who did not plan for war until a few weeks before it broke out and then only as a last resort. At the same time, the book recognizes American aggressive intentions and minimizes the Mexican "threat."

The greatest contributions by recent historians of the Mexican War itself have been made in the areas of military history and public opinion. The monographs of K. Jack Bauer are well researched studies of the United States Army and Navy in the war, with some attention to the Mexican side. Public and press opinion on both sides is well studied (within the limitations of pre-poll quantitative analysis) in such monographs as John H. Schroeder, *Mr. Polk's War* (9:187); Norman E. Tutorow, *Texas Annexation and the Mexican War* (9:25); Gene M. Brack, *Mexico Views Manifest Destiny* (9:142); and Jesús Velasco Martínez, *La Guerra de 47 y la opinión pública* (9:193).

In the areas of border history both before and after the Mexican War, historiographical trends are more difficult to discern. One reason is that most works are general state histories or journal articles dealing with relatively narrow subjects. Older works, such as the articles and books of William R. Manning (early U.S.-Mexican relations), Eugene C. Barker (Texas), J. Fred Rippy (U.S.-Mexican relations), and the long-standing staple, Paul N. Garber, *The Gadsden Treaty* (9:210), consist largely of straight diplomatic history. This is also true of works by more recent Mexican writers, such as Carlos Bosch García (*Historia de las relaciones entre México y los Estados Unidos, 1819–1848* [9:15]) and Luis G. Zorrilla (*Historia de las relaciones entre México y los Estados Unidos de América, 1800–1958* [2:302]), almost as if they, in turn, had to go through the same phases of

development as the earlier generation of American historians. More recently, American historians who have essayed full books on the years before or after the war have paid more attention to social or economic implications of U.S.-Mexican relations.

If one asks what lines of research need to be followed in the future, one answer is obvious. Except perhaps for Mexican public opinion during the Mexican War, we need to know more about the Mexican side of the bilateral relationship throughout the period of this chapter—the connection between diplomacy and politics, public opinion in the 1850s, the contributions of Mexican leaders (even the much discussed Benito Juárez remains something of an enigma), and the role of the church and other interest groups. Charles A. Hale, *Mexican Liberalism in the Age of Mora, 1821–1853* (New Haven, 1968) is not listed because it deals little with the United States, but it presents a sympathetic view of Mexico that is indispensable to the historian of U.S.-Mexican relations. If applied to those relations (as Hale does in his article [9:190]), this view will supply a much needed element.

Apart from more books and articles on the Mexican side, there are other less glaring gaps in present historiography. In the period before the Mexican War one might well study and compare the Mexican problems in retaining Texas and California against American expansion. Was there ever a chance that Mexico might preserve its integrity? In the war period, we need a biography of Nicholas Trist which will emphasize his public career and especially the crucial months he spent in Mexico. This might well be combined with an analysis of Mexican politics during the peace negotiations. Other, more limited wartime subjects are the relationship between Americans and Mexicans during the United States occupation and the attitudes of the small population of New Mexico, a supposedly loyal territory that easily succumbed to American influence.

In the 1850s it would be useful to have a new study of the Gadsden Treaty, the events that led up to it, and its relationship to the developing sectional conflict in the United States. Such a study should emphasize economic and social factors more than Garber (9:210) did. Although the many articles and books about filibusters shed considerable light on specific expeditions, we still need research delineating the involvement of American adventurers with Mexican partisan rivalries and social questions. Also social and class studies of filibuster leaders and, wherever possible, their followers would be welcome.

There are a few attractive broader areas of research covering most or all of the period of this chapter. U.S.-Mexican trade patterns might be studied with newly developed techniques of quantitative analysis (although the paucity of reliable statistics should be kept in mind as an obstacle). It would be useful to have collective biographies or elite studies of persons involved in U.S.-Mexican relations: ministers, consuls, businessmen, and others. Finally, the period between 1821 and 1861 needs to be studied as a whole. Although the survey of Karl M. Schmitt (2:301) incorporates much recent research, it emphasizes the decades since 1867. The time has come for someone to attempt a more penetrating study of the earlier period, combining the diplomatic, political, economic, social, and cultural elements of a complex international triangle: the United States, Mexico, and Europe.

Resources and Overviews

RESEARCH AIDS

While pertinent bibliographies and reference aids are listed here, there are more extensive lists in Chapter 1.

Bibliographies

9:1 Beers, Henry P. *Spanish and Mexican Records of the American Southwest: A Bibliographical Guide to Archives*. Tucson: University of Arizona Press, 1979. This invaluable guide covers the whole sweep of history from Spanish rule to the present. There are four main geographical sections (New Mexico, Texas, California, and Arizona), each of which includes provincial and legal records, archival reproductions, documentary publications, manuscript collections, and land and ecclesiastical records. Each section is preceded by an account of history and government.

Brown, L. M., and Christie, I. R., eds. *Bibliography of British History, 1789–1851* (6:1).

Connor, S. V. "Attitudes and Opinions about the Mexican War, 1846–1970" (9:134).

Cosío Villegas, D., comp. *Cuestiones Internacionales de México: Una Bibliografía* (1:133) is a comprehensive bibliography of Mexican foreign relations.

9:2 Cumberland, Charles C. "The United States–Mexican Border: A Selective Guide to the Literature of the Region." *Rural Sociology* 25:2 (1960), supplement. A very useful list, it covers the whole history of the border and includes both documents and secondary works related to cultural, diplomatic, and border aspects.

9:3 Esquinazi-Mayo, Roberto. "Historiografía de la Guerra entre México y los EE UU" [Historiography of the war between Mexico and the U.S.]. *Duquesne Hispanic Review* 1:2 (1962), 33–48; 1:3 (1962), 7–35.

Fehrenbacher, D. E., ed. *Manifest Destiny and the Coming of the Civil War* (1:71) lists a wide variety of essays and books.

Graebner, N. A. "How Wars Begin: The Mexican War" (9:136) surveys recent interpretations.

Harstad, P. T., and Resh, R. W. "The Causes of the Mexican War: A Note on Changing Interpretations" (9:143).

Nichols, R. L. "From the Revolution to the Mexican War" (5:4) contains many references to military operations, but also lists some references of interest to diplomatic historians.

Paul, R. W., and Etulain, R. W., comps. *The Frontier and the American West* (1:74) is a useful bibliography with references to manifest destiny, the Mexican War, and related themes.

Smith, M. J., Jr., ed. *The American Navy, 1789–1860* (5:5) lists items pertaining mostly to naval matters, but contains references important to diplomatic historians.

9:4 Snoke, Elizabeth R. *The Mexican War: A Bibliography of MHRC* [Military History Research Collection] *Holdings for the Period 1835–1850*. Carlisle, Pa.: U.S. Army, Carlisle Barracks, Military History Research Collection, 1973. Although pertaining to a single collection, this is a convenient guide to secondary sources and printed primary sources on the war.

Trask, D. F.; Meyers, M. C.; and Trask, R. R., eds. *A Bibliography of United States–Latin American Relations since 1810* (1:120) is updated by M. C. Meyer's *Supplement* (1:119).

9:5 Tutorow, Norman E., comp. and ed. *The Mexican-American War: An Annotated Bibliography.* Westport, Conn.: Greenwood, 1981. An extensively annotated bibliography, this reference aid will be an essential guide to sources (both printed and archival) for many years. Its eight appendixes include a chronology, tables, graphs, and war maps; also included is a listing of military organizations, prominent politicians, and naval vessels.

9:6 Weber, David J. "Mexico's Far Northern Border, 1821–1845: A Critical Bibliography." *Arizona and the West* 19:3 (1977), 225–66. A guide to literature on Texas, New Mexico, Arizona, and California before the Mexican War. Some works cited relate indirectly to U.S.-Mexican diplomacy, which is valuable for indications of American/European penetration.

Document Collections

More general collections are listed in Chapter 1, and other collections may be found in "Personalities," below.

9:7 Bosch García, Carlos, ed. *Material para la historia diplomática de México* [Material for the diplomatic history of Mexico]. México, D.F.: Universidad y Sociales Nacional Autónoma de México, 1957. This collection of diplomatic documents, mostly Spanish translations of U.S. State Department communications, contains few documents from the Mexican archives.

9:8 Garrison, George P., ed. *Diplomatic Correspondence of the Republic of Texas.* 3 vols. In the Annual Report of the American Historical Association for the Years 1907, 1908. Washington, D.C.: G.P.O., 1908–1911. This standard source for diplomatic correspondence of Texas (1836–1845) contains all of the important materials from the manuscript archives.

Manning, W. R., ed. *Diplomatic Correspondence of the United States Concerning the Independence of the Latin-American Nations* (7:4).

Manning, W. R., ed. *Diplomatic Correspondence of the United States: Inter-American Affairs, 1831–1860* (7:5) covers, in volumes 8 and 9, Mexico.

9:9 México, Secretaría de Relaciones Exteriores. *La Diplomacia Mexicana* [Mexican diplomacy]. 3 vols. México, D.F.: Tipográfica Artística, 1910–1913. This

is roughly the equivalent for Mexico of the first Manning collection, and includes the first Mexican mission to the United States in the 1820s.

U.S. Congress. *Congressional Globe: 23rd Congress to 42nd Congress, 2 December 1833–3 March 1873* (1:353).

Indexes

Hasse, A. R., ed. *Index to United States Documents Relating to Foreign Affairs, 1828–1861* (1:304).

OVERVIEWS

American Expansionism

See also "Filibusters," below, and Chapter 10, "Manifest Destiny."

Billington, R. A. *The Far Western Frontier, 1830–1860* (10:2) surveys Americans' movement into Texas, California, and the Southwest, as well as the Mexican War.

9:10 García Cantú, Gastón. *Las Invasiones Norteamericanas en México* [The North American invasions of Mexico]. México, D.F.: Ediciones Era, 1971. This is a popular, Marxist, and nationalist exposition of U.S. aggression and formal threats of aggression against Mexican territory (1800–1918). Notes indicate extensive use of printed primary and secondary sources.

Goetzmann, W. H. *Exploration and Empire: The Explorer and the Scientist in the Winning of the American West* (10:71).

9:11 Goetzmann, William H. *When the Eagle Screamed: The Romantic Horizon in American Diplomacy 1800–1860.* New York: Wiley, 1966. The author provides a brief interpretation of American expansionist diplomacy from 1800 to 1850. He argues that the primary impulse for American expansion derived from European ideas, particularly the romantic and global ideas of grandeur and destiny.

9:12 Graebner, Norman A. *Empire on the Pacific: A Study in American Continental Expansion.* New York: Ronald, 1955. Graebner's study of American expansionism in both California and Oregon (1820–1848) emphasizes the maritime aspects of American expansion into California. Bibliography.

Merk, F., with Merk, L. B. *Manifest Destiny and Mission in American History: A Reinterpretation* [1830–1898] (2:52) uses the Oregon issue and the Mexican War to show that manifest destiny was the sordid side of American expansionism.

Merk, F., with Merk, L. B. *The Monroe Doctrine and American Expansionism, 1843–1849* (7:154) deals with alleged British designs and bona fide American expansionism in California, Yucatan, and Cuba and—at considerable length—with the Texas boundary question as a cause of the Mexican War.

9:13 Pletcher, David M. *The Diplomacy of Annexation: Texas, Oregon, and the Mexican War.* Columbia: University of Missouri Press, 1973. This study interrelates the three questions (1815–1848), emphasizing choices open to policymakers. Employing American, Texan, Mexican, British, French, Spanish sources, Pletcher suggests that Polk might have avoided the Mexican War but chose an aggressive style of diplomacy that brought about steady escalation of peacetime enmity and then fighting. Extensive bibliography.

Van Alstyne, R. W. *The Rising American Empire* (2:96) devotes chapters 5 and 6 partly to Texas and California.

9:14 Wallace, Edward S. *Destiny and Glory.* New York: Coward-McCann, 1957. Wallace has written a popular account of the Mexican War, U.S. interest in Yucatán, and filibuster expeditions into Sonora (1845–1860). Bibliography.

U.S.-Mexican Diplomatic Relations

9:15 Bosch García, Carlos. *Historia de las relaciones entre México y los Estados Unidos, 1819–1848* [History of relations between Mexico and the United States, 1819–1848]. México, D.F.: Escuela Nacional de Ciencias Políticas y Sociales, 1961. Useful primarily for the Mexican viewpoint of diplomatic problems, this account is based largely on American archival sources, with some use of Mexican documents and secondary works. Bibliography, with interesting comments on principal secondary works.

Callahan, J. M. *American Foreign Policy in Mexican Relations* [1808–1930] (2:298) covers the period 1821 to the 1860s, in chapters 1–9, with heavy emphasis on political relations and diplomatic correspondence.

9:16 Carreño, Alberto M. *La diplomacía extraordinaria entre México y Estados Unidos* [The extraordinary (i.e., confidential) diplomacy between Mexico and the United States]. 2 vols. 2d ed. México, D.F.: Editorial Jus, 1961. This survey (1789–1947), by a prominent Mexican author, has detailed treatment only to the accession of Porfirio Díaz (1876). It is most valuable for copious quotations from Mexican sources. Carreño is very suspicious of American activities, often with reason.

9:17 Dunn, Frederick S. *The Diplomatic Protection of Americans in Mexico.* New York: Columbia University Press, 1933. This account has useful footnote citations to published and manuscript correspondence; pages 1–90 cover the period to 1861.

Rippy, J. F. *The United States and Mexico* (2:300) surveys Mexican-American relations, with the period 1848 to 1860 occupying over one-third of the text.

9:18 Rives, George L. *The United States and Mexico, 1821–1848.* 2 vols. New York: Scribner's, 1913. Rives's detailed, balanced treatment is based on published sources and some State Department manuscripts. More conventional and less colorful than Justin Smith's volumes (9:140), it is still both readable and reliable, although modern research has added details and new interpretations. Extensive notes.

Schmitt, K. M. *Mexico and the United States, 1821–1973: Conflict and Coexistence* (2:301).

Zorrilla, L. G. *Historia de las relaciones entre México y los Estados Unidos de América, 1800–1958* (2:302) deals, in volume 1, with the period 1821 to the 1860s, and is good for the Mexican side of controversies.

Special Studies

9:19 Alessio Robles, Vito. *Coahuila y Texas, desde la consumación de la independencia hasta el Tratado de Paz de Guadalupe Hidalgo* [Coahuila and Texas, from the completion of independence to the Peace Treaty of Guadalupe Hidalgo]. 2 vols. México, D.F., 1945–1946. Thoroughly researched in archival and secondary sources of both Mexico and the United

States, this account concentrates on the diplomatic and military aspects of border rivalries (1821–1848). Extensive bibliography.

9:20 Blaisdell, Lowell L. "The Santangelo Case: A Claim Preceding the Mexican War." *Journal of the West* 11:2 (1972), 248–59. This is a well-written and fascinating case study of a claims case which complicated U.S.-Mexican relations in the decade before the Mexican War.

9:21 MacCorkle, Stuart A. *American Policy of Recognition towards Mexico.* Baltimore: Johns Hopkins Press, 1933. A comprehensive study that is useful for its treatment of early relations in the 1820s; but it is now somewhat outdated. Bibliography.

9:22 Schwartz, Rosalie. *Across the River to Freedom: U.S. Negroes in Mexico.* El Paso: Texas Western Press, 1975. This pamphlet conveniently traces the fugitive slave problem which complicated U.S.-Mexican relations (1820–1860).

9:23 Sepúlveda, César. "Sobre reclamaciones de Norteamericanos a México." [Concerning claims of Americans against Mexico]. *Historia Mexicana* 11:2 (1961), 180–206. A large part of this article is devoted to the period 1821 to 1861.

9:24 Silbey, Joel H. *The Shrine of Party: Congressional Voting Behavior, 1841–1852.* Pittsburgh: University of Pittsburgh Press, 1967. This is a quantitative study of U.S. congressional voting patterns on selected expansionist issues, including the Texas question and the Mexican War. Bibliography.

9:25 Tutorow, Norman E. *Texas Annexation and the Mexican War: A Political Study of the Old Northwest.* Palo Alto, Calif.: Chadwick House, 1978. A quantitative study of voting and editorial opinion (1843–1848), it covers issues in more detailed fashion than Silbey (9:24) but is limited to the states of Ohio, Indiana, Illinois, and Michigan. Extensive bibliography.

Personalities

Additional references on individuals may be found in Chapter 1, "Biographical Data."

AMERICAN

John Quincy Adams
See Chapters 6 and 7, "Personalities," for additional references.

Knapp, F. A., Jr. "John Quincy Adams ¿Defensor de Mexico?" (9:95) describes Adams's opposition to the annexation of Texas.

Anthony Butler
Mayo, B. "Apostle of Manifest Destiny" (9:86) is an account of Anthony Butler, who replaced Poinsett as minister to Mexico.

Stenberg, R. R. "Jackson, Anthony Butler and Texas" (9:87).

John C. Frémont
9:26 Nevins, Allan. *Frémont, Pathmarker of the West.* New York: Ungar, 1955. Nevins's second biography of Frémont (1813–1890), represents more up-to-date research than *Frémont, the World's Greatest Adventurer* 2 vols. (New York, 1928) and offers some revised conclusions. The enlarged 1955 edition deals with Frémont's activities in California. Bibliography.

9:27 Stenberg, Richard R. "Polk and Frémont, 1845–1846." *Pacific Historical Review* 7:3 (1938), 211–27. Stenberg's essay applies a "plot" thesis to Polk's secret instructions to Frémont; on slender evidence it assumes that Polk intended Frémont to seize California.

9:28 Tays, George. "Frémont Had No Special Instructions." *Pacific Historical Review* 9:2 (1940), 157–72. In essence, this is a reply to Stenberg's article. Although it is generally considered impossible to prove a negative proposition, Tays presents strong evidence.

9:29 Wiltsee, Ernest A. *The Truth about Frémont: An Inquiry.* San Francisco: Grabhorn, 1936. This anti-Frémont account insists that his move to revolutionize California (1845–1847) was part of a plot developed by Polk.

Samuel Houston
9:30 Friend, Llerena. *Sam Houston: The Great Designer.* Austin: University of Texas Press, 1954. The best of the biographies of Houston (1793–1863), it is balanced and readable. Extensive bibliography.

9:31 James, Marquis. *The Raven: The Story of Sam Houston.* Indianapolis: Bobbs-Merrill, 1929. In a romantic, colorful account, James emphasizes action rather than analysis. Bibliography.

9:32 Wisehart, M. K. *Sam Houston: American Giant.* Washington, D.C.: Luce, 1962. This is a very detailed, essentially a factual account, eschewing analysis. Extensive bibliography.

Andrew Jackson

See Chapters 7 and 8, "Personalities," for additional references.

Barker, E. C. "President Jackson and the Texas Revolution" (9:80).

Stenberg, R. R. "The Texas Schemes of Jackson and Houston" (9:88).

Mirabeau B. Lamar

9:33 Christian, Asa K. *Mirabeau Buonaparte Lamar.* Austin, Tex.: Von Boechmann-Jones, 1932. Lamar (1798–1859), the second president of Texas, greatly exacerbated relations with Mexico by his expansionist policies. This study devotes considerable attention to Texan foreign relations.

9:34 Gambrell, Herbert. *Mirabeau Buonaparte Lamar: Troubadour and Crusader.* Dallas: Southwest Press, 1934. This account is less impressive than the same author's biography of Anson Jones; moreover, Christian's biography has greater detail on foreign relations.

9:35 Lamar, Mirabeau B. *Papers.* Ed. by C. A. Gulick et al. 6 vols. Austin, Tex.: Baldwin, 1921–1927.

Thomas O. Larkin

See "The California Question, 1821–1847" below, for more about Larkin.

9:36 Larkin, Thomas O. *First and Last Consul: Thomas Oliver Larkin and the Americanization of California: A Selection of Letters.* Ed. by John A. Hawgood. San Marino, Calif.: Huntington Library, 1962. Larkin was the U.S. consul at Monterey, California, during the Mexican period. This volume is important for the background and events which led to the Bear Flag revolt. Larkin later eased the shift from Mexican to American control of California.

9:37 Larkin, Thomas O. *The Larkin Papers: Personal, Business and Official Correspondence of Thomas Oliver Larkin, Merchant and the United States Consul in California.* 10 vols. Ed. by George P. Hammond. Berkeley: University of California Press, 1951–1964. Index, 1968.

Joel R. Poinsett

9:38 Fuentes Mares, José. *Poinsett: Historia de una gran intriga* [Poinsett: history of a great intrigue]. México, D.F.: Editorial Jus, 1958. This account uses the Poinsett Papers and the published State Department correspondence to fully develop the Mexican case against Poinsett as the spearhead of American imperialism (1821–1829).

9:39 Parton, Dorothy R. *The Diplomatic Career of Joel Roberts Poinsett.* Washington, D.C.: Catholic University of America Press, 1934. This account is briefer but more balanced than Rippy's biography (9:41). Bibliography.

9:40 Putnam, Herbert E. *Joel Roberts Poinsett: A Political Biography.* Washington, D.C.: Mimeoform Press, 1935. Bibliography.

9:41 Rippy, J. Fred. *Joel R. Poinsett: Versatile American.* Durham, N.C.: Duke University Press, 1935. Rippy's biography, very pro-Poinsett, is a readable account of this diplomat and secretary of war (1779–1851).

9:42 Weber, Ralph E. "Joel R. Poinsett's Secret Mexican Dispatch Twenty." *South Carolina Historical Magazine* 75:2 (1974), 67–76. Weber deals with Poinsett's suspicions concerning French designs on Mexico.

James K. Polk

9:43 McCormac, Eugene I. *James K. Polk: A Political Biography.* Berkeley: University of California Press, 1922. About two hundred pages are devoted to Texas and the Mexican War; however, the work is largely superseded by the first two volumes of Sellers (9:48) for the period to 1846. The discussion of the causes of the Mexican War is brief but balanced. Bibliography.

9:44 McCoy, Charles A. *Polk and the Presidency.* Austin: University of Texas Press, 1960. McCoy's study focuses largely on Polk's administrative abilities and actions. In two chapters he discusses Polk's control of foreign affairs and conduct of the Mexican War. Extensive bibliography.

9:45 Polk, James K. *Polk: The Diary of a President.* Ed. by Allan Nevins. New York: Longmans, Green, 1929. While this volume contains only part of the Polk diary, it includes most of the important entries concerning diplomacy and the Mexican War. Also, Nevins has added a long introduction, analyzing Polk and the principal members of his government with much perceptiveness.

9:46 Polk, James K. *The Diary of James K. Polk during His Presidency, 1845 to 1849.* Ed. by Milo M. Quaife. Chicago Historical Society Collections, vols. 6–9. Chicago: McClurg, 1910. These volumes present a complete transcript of Polk's detailed and very revealing diary, beginning in August 1845 and covering nearly all his presidency. A considerable amount of the diary concerns foreign relations, the Oregon question, the settlement of Texas annexation, and the Mexican War.

9:47 Reeves, Jesse S. *American Diplomacy under Tyler and Polk.* Baltimore: Johns Hopkins Press, 1907. Although largely outdated, it is interesting for historiographical reasons. Notes.

9:48 Sellers, Charles G. *James K. Polk: Continentalist, 1843–1846.* Princeton, N.J.: Princeton University Press, 1966. This is the second volume of a projected three-volume biography. It is primarily political, but Sellers devotes more attention to diplomacy with Mexico and Britain. Polk's personal life, well developed in the first volume, is subordinated in this one. Extensive bibliography.

9:49 Van Horn, James. "Trends in Historical Interpretation: James K. Polk." *North Carolina Historical Review* 42:4 (1965), 454–64. Van Horn traces the controversies over Polk's capabilities as president and his responsibility for and conduct of the Mexican War, indicating the rising evaluation of Polk since World War I.

Winfield Scott

Castañeda, C. E. "Relations of General Scott with Santa Ana" (9:162).

9:50 Elliott, Charles W. *Winfield Scott: The Soldier and the Man.* New York: Macmillan, 1937. Elliott's detailed biography devotes several chapters to the Mexican war. Bibliography.

Scott, W. *Memoirs of Lieut.-General Scott, . . .* (10:8).

Zachary Taylor

9:51 Dyer, Brainerd. *Zachary Taylor.* Baton Rouge: Louisiana State University Press, 1946. This is a straightforward, uncritical account of Taylor's activities (1784–1850). Extensive bibliography.

9:52 Hamilton, Holman. *Zachary Taylor.* 2 vols. Indianapolis: Bobbs-Merrill, 1941–1951. Hamilton is a little more colorful than Dyer, but no more penetrating. Volume 1 deals with Taylor's military career; see 8:31 for volume 2. Bibliography.

Nicholas P. Trist

Chamberlin, E. K. "Nicholas Trist and Baja California" (9:163).

Farnham, T. J. "Nicholas Trist and James Freaner and the Mission to Mexico [1847]" (9:165).

Northup, J. "Nicholas Trist's Mission to Mexico: A Reinterpretation" (9:169).

Sears, L. M. "Nicholas P. Trist: A Diplomat with Ideals" (9:170).

Others

9:53 Barker, Eugene C. *The Life of Stephen F. Austin, Founder of Texas, 1793–1836: A Chapter in the Westward Movement of the Anglo-American People.* Nashville: Cokesbury, 1925. Barker argues that Austin "strove honestly to make Texas a model state in the Mexican system." A partial answer to the thesis that the Texas Revolution was a plot; it is more convincing for Austin than for his followers. Extensive bibliography.

9:54 Clarke, Dwight L. *Stephen Watts Kearny: Soldier of the West.* Norman: University of Oklahoma Press, 1961. Clarke has provided a good account of the conquest of Santa Fe and California. Extensive bibliography.

9:55 Gambrell, Herbert. *Anson Jones: The Last President of Texas.* 2d ed. Garden City, N.Y.: Doubleday, 1964. This is a sympathetic, yet fair account of an enigmatic man (1798–1858) who was a central figure in the last stages of the annexation struggle. Extensive bibliography.

9:56 Lander, Ernest M., Jr. *Reluctant Imperialists: Calhoun, the South Carolinians, and the Mexican War.* Baton Rouge: Louisiana State University Press, 1980. Senator John C. Calhoun of South Carolina was against sending American troops deep into Mexico and was a severe critic of President Polk's war policy. South Carolinians had mixed feelings about the war and, like other Southerners, were worried about the danger to slavery if additional territory were wrestled from Mexico. Extensive bibliography.

Spencer, I. D. *The Victor and the Spoils: A Life of William L. Marcy* (8:38) is a good biography of a leading policymaker in the Polk and Buchanan administrations; has chapters on the Mexican War and the Gadsden Purchase.

9:57 Wallace, Edward S. *General William Jenkins Worth: Monterey's Forgotten Hero*. Dallas: Southern Methodist University Press, 1953. This is a reasonably successful effort to rehabilitate Worth (1794–1849), based on many private papers as well as published sources. Bibliography.

MEXICAN

Antonio López de Santa Anna

9:58 Callcott, Wilfrid H. *Santa Anna: The Story of an Enigma Who Once Was Mexico*. Norman: University of Oklahoma Press, 1936. Callcott's is the best biography (in English) available. Extensive bibliography.

9:59 Hanighen, Frank C. *Santa Anna: The Napoleon of the West*. New York: Coward-McCann, 1934. A popular account, but well researched, it focuses on Santa Anna's relations with Texas.

9:60 Jones, Oakah L., Jr. *Santa Anna*. New York: Twayne, 1968. A brief but detailed biography, it resorts to judicious speculation about the many gaps in Santa Anna's recorded life. Extensive bibliography.

Others

9:61 Cotner, Thomas E. *The Military and Political Career of José Joaquín de Herrera, 1792–1854*. Austin: University of Texas Press, 1949. Cotner's research has resulted in a scholarly biography of a moderate Mexican leader who tried to avoid war with the United States. Extensive bibliography.

Hutchinson, C. A. "Valentín Gómez Farías and the 'Secret Pact of New Orleans'" (9:85).

Spell, L. M. "Gorostiza [Manuel de] and Texas" (9:110) describes the Mexican minister to Washington during the annexation movement.

BRITISH

9:62 Blake, Clagette. *Charles Elliot, R.N., 1801–1875: A Servant of Britain Overseas*. London: Cleaver-Hume, 1960. Elliot was the principal British diplomatic agent in Texas during the republic period (1838–1845) and did his best to prevent U.S. annexation of Texas. The work supplements E. D. Adams's monograph (9:92).

Texas: Settlement and Independence, 1820–1836

EARLY U.S.-MEXICAN RELATIONS

See "Personalities," especially Stephen Austin (under "Others") and Joel R. Poinsett.

9:63 Bosch García, Carlos. *Problemas diplomáticas del México independiente* [Diplomatic problems of independent Mexico]. México, D.F.: El Colegio de México, 1947. This account deals with foreign recognition of independent Mexico and related problems of the 1820s, but provides little on the Texas question. The emphasis is heavily political and diplomatic, based on Mexican archival documents and, for the United States, William R. Manning's collections (7:4 and 7:5). Bibliography.

9:64 Graebner, Norman A. "United States Gulf Commerce with Mexico, 1822–1848." *Inter-American Economic Affairs* 5:1 (1951), 36–51. Graebner provides a good account of early economic ties based on published original and secondary sources.

9:65 Manning, William R. *Early Diplomatic Relations between the United States and Mexico*. Baltimore: Johns Hopkins Press, 1916. This account extends to the end of Poinsett's mission (1821–1829), and provides a straightforward account of diplomacy, based on State Department archives. Bibliography.

Rippy, J. F. *Rivalry of the United States and Great Britain over Latin America, 1808–1830* (7:11) deals, in chapter 3, with the early stages of the Texas question; while chapter 7 examines the Poinsett mission to Mexico.

9:66 Salit, Charles R. "Anglo-American Rivalry in Mexico, 1823–1830." *Revista de Historia de América,* no. 16 (1943), 65–84. This is a more up-to-date account than Rippy (7:11) on the rivalry between Poinsett and Henry G. Ward.

9:67 Smith, Ralph A. "Indians in American-Mexican Relations before the War of 1846." *Hispanic American Historical Review* 43:1 (1963), 34–64. Indian raids multiplied Mexico's problems. Developments on both sides of the Rio Grande encouraged the Apache, Navajos, Utes, Comanche, and Kiowas in making raids. Bibliographical notes.

Weber, R. E. "Joel R. Poinsett's Secret Mission, Dispatch Twenty" (9:42) deals with Poinsett's suspicions concerning French designs on Mexico.

EARLY TEXAS-MEXICAN RELATIONS

9:68 Ashford, Gerald. "Jacksonian Liberalism and Spanish Law in Early Texas." *Southwestern Historical Quarterly* 57:1 (1953), 1–37. Ashford provides the background for some of the unrest in Texas during 1835–1836.

9:69 Bacarisse, Charles A. "The Union of Coahuila and Texas." *Southwestern Historical Quarterly* 61:3 (1958), 341–49. A prominent grievance of Texans against Mexico was that, in combining Texas and Coahuila, Mexico minimized control of local institutions and made Texans responsible to a faraway state capital.

9:70 Bancroft, Hubert H. *History of the North Mexican States and Texas.* 2 vols. San Francisco: The History Company, 1883–1889. Volume 2 has a detailed account of Texas-Mexican relations, the revolution of 1836, and events leading to Texas annexation; extensive use of American and Mexican archival sources. Some of its conclusions have been revised by later historians. Elaborate notes.

9:71 Barker, Eugene C. *Mexico and Texas, 1821–1835.* Dallas: Turner, 1928. As in all his works on the

subject, Barker emphasizes the largely unplanned character of the Texas Revolution, an interpretation with which most Mexicans and many Americans disagree. A good, brief survey, now somewhat superseded.

9:72 Cleaves, W. S. "Lorenzo de Zavala in Texas." *Southwestern Historical Quarterly* 35:1 (1932), 29–40. Zavala, a prominent Mexican liberal who served in early regimes and was driven into exile by Santa Anna in 1835, fled to Texas, and later became the republic's first vice-president. The Mexicans generally regard him as a traitor.

9:73 Harris, Helen Willits. "Almonte's Inspection of Texas in 1834." *Southwestern Historical Quarterly* 41:3 (1938), 195–211. This essay provides a Mexican view of Texas on the eve of revolution.

9:74 Howren, Allein. "Causes and Origin of the Decree of April 6, 1830." *Southwestern Historical Quarterly* 16:4 (1913), 378–422. The 1830 decree was a Mexican effort to avert the American threat to Texas by forbidding immigration and constructing a chain of forts.

9:75 Hutchinson, C. Alan. "General José Antonio Mexía and His Texas Interests." *Southwestern Historical Quarterly* 82:2 (1978), 117–42. Mexía was identified with Texas through the whole prerevolutionary period (1822–1839), as an impresario, then as a land company agent who worked to prevent the Mexican government from shutting off American colonization. However, he would not join the independence movement.

9:76 Lowrie, Samuel H. *Culture Conflict in Texas, 1821–1835.* New York: Columbia University Press, 1932. Lowrie attributes the Texas Revolution primarily to cultural differences between Americans and Mexicans, arising from misunderstandings and centering in questions concerning religion, slavery, and politics, the last of which finally precipitated the revolution. Bibliography.

9:77 McElhannon, Joseph C. "Imperial Mexico and Texas, 1821–1823." *Southwestern Historical Quarterly* 53:2 (1949), 117–50. The author discusses the political relations between Agustín de Iturbide (emperor of Mexico) and the early settlements of Texas.

9:78 Morton, Ohland. *Terán and Texas: A Chapter in Texas-Mexican Relations.* Austin: Texas State Historical Association, 1948. General Manuel Mier y Terán, military commandant of the northern provinces in the late 1820s, was most suspicious of American intentions and tried to erect a defense system to retain Texas as part of Mexico.

CAUSES OF THE TEXAS REVOLUTION

9:79   Barker, Eugene C. "Land Speculation as a Cause of the Texas Revolution." *Texas Historical Quarterly* 10:1 (1906), 76–95. Barker minimizes the importance of land speculation as a reason for American enlistment in the Texas army but admits its significance as a contributing cause of settlement and friction with Mexico (1821–1836).

9:80   Barker, Eugene C. "President Jackson and the Texas Revolution." *American Historical Review* 12:4 (1907), 788–809. Barker denies that Jackson (1829–1836) intrigued with Houston or anyone else to bring on the revolution; compare with the "conspiracy" articles of Stenberg.

9:81   Barker, Eugene C. "The United States and Mexico, 1835–1837." *Mississippi Valley Historical Review* 1:1 (1914), 3–30. A survey of events, consistent with Barker's other writings which offset Mexican criticism of Texans and Americans for deliberately planning the revolution; now largely superseded by more detailed accounts.

9:82   Binkley, William C. *The Texas Revolution.* Baton Rouge: University of Louisiana Press, 1952. An interpretive essay, it places the immediate responsibility for the revolution (1835–1836) on the Mexican government, while recognizing the underlying divergence between Texas and Mexico.

9:83   Gibson, Joe. "A. Butler: What a Scamp!" *Journal of the West* 11:2 (1972), 235–47. Gibson details Butler's efforts to exploit the troubled Mexican political situation (1832–1835) to the advantage of the United States, especially in the purchase of Texas.

9:84   Hutchinson, C. Alan. "Mexican Federalists in New Orleans and the Texas Revolution." *Louisiana Historical Quarterly* 39:1 (1956), 1–47. Hutchinson analyzes relations between a group of Mexican Federalist (i.e., anti-Santa Anna) exiles in New Orleans and Texans discontented with Mexican rule. The Federalists were interested only in opposing centralist

organization of Mexico, while Texans moved toward outright independence.

9:85   Hutchinson, C. Alan. "Valentín Gómez Farías and the 'Secret Pact of New Orleans.'" *Hispanic American Historical Review* 36:4 (1956), 471–89. This is a companion-piece to Hutchinson's article on Mexican Federalists. Gómez Farías was a Federalist leader who saw the Texans as potential allies against the rival Centralists in Mexico City. His disillusionment at the Texas Revolution was an important factor in stimulating his later strong anti-Americanism.

9:86   Mayo, Bernard. "Apostle of Manifest Destiny [Anthony Butler]." *American Mercury* 18:72 (1929), 420–26. Mayo has written a readable, popular account of the man who succeeded Joel Poinsett as minister to Mexico (1829–1834) and did more open intriguing for Texas annexation than Poinsett.

9:87   Stenberg, Richard R. "Jackson, Anthony Butler and Texas." *Southwestern Social Science Quarterly* 13:3 (1932), 264–86. Here Stenberg extends his "plot" thesis concerning U.S.-Mexican relations. He accuses Jackson of intending from the beginning of his administration to acquire Texas and of using Butler as his agent; the accusations against Butler are more convincing than those against Jackson.

9:88   Stenberg, Richard R. "The Texas Schemes of Jackson and Houston." *Southwestern Social Science Quarterly* 15:3 (1934), 229–50. Stenberg's sequel to his Jackson and Butler article develops the plot between Jackson and Houston (1829–1837) to split Texas from Mexico.

COURSE OF THE TEXAS REVOLUTION

See "Personalities," especially Samuel Houston and Antonio López de Santa Anna.

9:89   Barker, Eugene C. "The Finances of the Texas Revolution." *Political Science Quarterly* 19:4 (1904), 612–35. The Texas revolutionary government sought to defray the relatively small cost of the revolution by obtaining funds in the United States.

9:90   Presley, J. "Santa Anna in Texas: A Mexican Viewpoint." *Southwestern Historical Quarterly* 62:4 (1959), 489–512. Presley argues that Santa Anna could not have reconquered Texas in 1836 or even kept his army there for very long, even without the Battle of San Jacinto.

9:91 Valadés, José C. *México, Santa Anna y la Guerra de Texas* [Mexico, Santa Anna and the Texas War]. 3d ed. México, D.F.: Editores Mexicanos Unidos, 1965. The first edition was published in 1935, but the author claims to have substantially revised the second and third editions. A reasonably dispassionate, even resigned study of the loss of Texas from the Mexican viewpoint. Bibliography.

Texas: Republic and Annexation, 1836–1845

See "Personalities," especially Anson Jones (under "Others") and Mirabeau B. Lamar.

9:92 Adams, Ephraim D. *British Interests and Activities in Texas, 1838–1846*. Baltimore: Johns Hopkins Press, 1910. Almost entirely based on Foreign Office correspondence, Adams's account is still largely the accepted version of Anglo-Texan political relations, although others have added materials on British economic interests.

9:93 Barker, Eugene C. "The Annexation of Texas." *Southwestern Historical Quarterly* 50:1 (1946), 49–74.

Blake, C. *Charles Elliot, R.N., 1801–1875* (9:62) describes British efforts to prevent annexation.

9:94 Garrison, George P. "The First Stage of the Movement for the Annexation of Texas." *American Historical Review* 10:1 (1904), 72–96. Many details have been added, but this early account, based largely on U.S. and Texan diplomatic sources, is still a useful summary of the efforts.

9:95 Knapp, Frank A., Jr. "John Quincy Adams ¿Defensor de México?" *Historia Mexicana* 7:1 (1957), 116–23. Knapp describes Adams's stubborn opposition to the annexation of Texas, mostly manifested in the House of Representatives and in speeches attacking the motives of his opponents.

Laurent, P. H. "Belgium's Relations with Texas and the United States, 1839–1844" (8:98).

Merk, F. *Fruits of Propaganda in the Tyler Administration* (10:35) suggests that American movement into Texas functioned as a "safety valve" in the Southwest, and reprints Robert J. Walker's famous article advocating annexation of Texas.

9:96 Schmitz, Joseph W. *Texan Statecraft, 1836–1845*. San Antonio, Tex.: Naylor, 1941. In this study of Texas foreign relations negotiations with Europe and Mexico are given more attention than the annexation question. Extensive bibliography.

9:97 Smith, Justin H. *The Annexation of Texas.* Rev. ed. New York: Barnes & Noble, 1941. The original edition was published in 1911, and it has not been greatly changed since. It is a straightforward, balanced account, based on extensive research, that emphasizes the negotiation of the annexation treaty and its discussion by the American public and Congress. Though superseded in some areas, this is still a major work. Bibliography.

Tutorow, N. E. *Texas Annexation and the Mexican War* (9:25).

Special Studies
9:98 Vigness, David M. "Relations of the Republic of Texas and the Republic of the Rio Grande." *Southwestern Historical Quarterly* 57:3 (1954), 312–21. The Republic of the Rio Grande was a secessionist organization in Mexico. This article is closely related to another by Vigness on Texas raids into Mexico during 1840 (9:105).

BORDER FIGHTING AND NAVAL ACTIONS

9:99 Binkley, William C. *The Expansionist Movement in Texas, 1836–1850*. Berkeley: University of California Press, 1925. Binkley discusses Texas efforts to occupy the Rio Grande Valley, including Santa Fe, N. Mex., and congressional action on Texas affairs after the Mexican War.

9:100 Gailey, Harry A., Jr. "Sam Houston and the Texas War Fever, March–August 1842." *Southwestern Historical Quarterly* 62:1 (1958), 29–44. Gailey relates Houston's success in waging limited war against Mexico.

9:101 Hill, Jim Dan. *The Texas Navy in Forgotten Battles and Shirtsleeve Diplomacy.* Chicago: University of Chicago Press, 1937. The small Texas navy posed a threat to Mexico chiefly through an alliance with rebellious Yucatan. A colorful account.

9:102 McClendon, R. E. "Daniel Webster and Mexican Relations: The Santa Fe Prisoners." *Southwestern Historical Quarterly* 36:4 (1933), 288–311. Webster worked with eventual success for the release of Texans (1842–1843) captured during an ill-advised attack on Santa Fe and kept in Perote and other central Mexican prisons.

9:103 Nance, Joseph M. *After San Jacinto: The Texas-Mexican Frontier, 1836–1841.* Austin: University of Texas Press, 1963. This is a detailed account of the makeup of the Texas army during the revolution, fighting during the revolution, and border skirmishes during the first five years of Texas independence. Extensive bibliography.

9:104 Nance, Joseph M. *Attack and Counterattack: The Texas-Mexican Frontier, 1842.* Austin: University of Texas Press, 1964. A sequel to the preceding Nance monograph, this is an exhaustively detailed account of border fighting during the climactic year of Texas-Mexican border raids. Extensive bibliography.

9:105 Vigness, David M. "A Texas Expedition into Mexico, 1840." *Southwestern Historical Quarterly* 62:1 (1958), 18–28. Texas was invited to participate in local movements in northern Mexico against the central government. The Republic of the Rio Grande was established in Laredo, but Mexican government forces defeated its revolutionary army.

9:106 Wells, Tom H. *Commodore Moore and the Texas Navy.* Austin: University of Texas Press, 1960. Moore was a one-time officer of the U.S. Navy. The book covers much the same ground as Hill (9:101), though somewhat less colorfully and with more penetration. Extensive bibliography.

9:107 Wooster, Ralph A. "Texas Military Operations against Mexico, 1842–1843." *Southwestern Historical Quarterly* 67:4 (1964), 465–84.

ANNEXATION DIPLOMACY, 1843–1845

9:108 Bosch García, Carlos. "Dos diplomacias y un problema [Two diplomacies and a problem]." *Historia Mexicana* 2:1 (1952), 46–65. This general account of the annexation of Texas (1843–1845) is entirely based on U.S. State Department documents.

9:109 Middleton, Annie. "Donelson's Mission to Texas in Behalf of Annexation." *Southwestern Historical Quarterly* 24:4 (1921), 247–91. Donelson, Polk's official representative (1844–1845), joined several private propagandists and played a more vital role in annexation than Commodore Robert F. Stockton, whom he restrained. This article largely contradicts the "plot" thesis developed by Stenberg and Price regarding the annexation.

9:110 Spell, Lota M. "Gorostiza and Texas." *Hispanic American Historical Review* 37:4 (1957), 425–62. Manuel de Gorostiza, Mexican minister to Washington during part of the Texan annexation movement, confronted the State Department impotently on the subject, foreshadowing the later major crisis of 1845–1846.

The California Question, 1821–1847

9:111 Bancroft, Hubert H. *History of California.* 7 vols. San Francisco: The History Company, 1884–1890. Volumes 3 to 5 have a detailed account of events of 1825 to 1848, leading to American occupation of California; some of its conclusions have been revised by later historians. Extensive use of American and Mexican archival sources, as identified in copious footnotes, make this work still valuable.

9:112 Caughey, John W. *California.* New York: Prentice-Hall, 1940. Chapters 1–15 present an authoritative study of California history to 1848; but later editions of the work shorten this section considerably. Extensive bibliography.

9:113 Cleland, Robert G. *A History of California: The American Period.* New York: Macmillan, 1922. Chapters 1–16 cover the late empire and the Mexican periods in greater detail than Caughey's survey. Cleland's later *From Wilderness to Empire: A History of California,* a combined edition of his earlier *From Wilderness to Empire, 1542–1900* and *California in Our Time, 1900–1940* (edited and revised by Glenn S. Dumke, New York: Knopf, 1959), makes a good introduction to the subject.

9:114 Hittell, Theodore M. *History of California.* 4 vols. San Francisco: Stone, 1897. This account provides a useful bridge between Bancroft (9:111) and modern writers; volume 2 covers the 1840s.

9:115 Richman, Irving B. *California under Spain and Mexico, 1535–1847.* Boston: Houghton Mifflin, 1911. Chapters 12–16 cover Mexican rule, the coming of the war, and the American occupation.

RISING TENSIONS TO 1845

See "Personalities," especially Thomas O. Larkin.

9:116 Adams, Ephraim D. "English Interest in the Annexation of California." *American Historical Review* 14:4 (1909), 744–63. This article exploded the myth of a British plot to seize California; it is reprinted in the author's *British Interests and Activities in Texas, 1838–1846* (9:92).

9:117 Brooke, George M., Jr. "The Vest Pocket War of Commodore Jones." *Pacific Historical Review* 31:1 (1962), 217–33. This is a carefully documented account of events of Jones's occupation (1842).

9:118 Cleland, Robert G. "The Early Sentiment for the Annexation of California: An Account of the Growth of American Interest in California, 1835–1846." *Southwestern Historical Quarterly* 18:3 (1914), 1–40, 231–60. Cleland describes the events and the publications in the eastern United States, as well as in California itself, which supported annexation.

9:119 Coughlin, Magdalena. "California Ports: A Key to Diplomacy for the West Coast, 1820–1845." *Journal of the West* 5:2 (1966), 153–72. Coughlin basically agrees with Graebner, *Empire on the Pacific* (9:12).

9:120 Engelson, Lester D. "Proposals for Colonization of California by England in Connection with the Mexican Debt to British Bondholders, 1837–1846." *California Historical Society Quarterly* 18:2 (1939), 136–48. Whereas Adams established that England never seriously planned intervention (9:116), this article details the proposals made by private parties to the British Foreign Office.

9:121 Hatheway, C. G. "Commodore Jones's War." *History Today* 16:3 (1966), 194–201. Hatheway gives more attention to the aftermath of the occupation than the other accounts (9:117 and 9:123); no documentation.

9:122 Hawgood, John A. "The Pattern of Yankee Infiltration in Mexican Alta California, 1821–1846." *Pacific Historical Review* 27:1 (1958), 27–37. This account discusses the role of Thomas O. Larkin, U.S. consul at Monterey, California, in the American penetration of California and the events leading up to the Bear Flag revolt.

9:123 High, James. "Jones at Monterey, 1842." *Journal of the West* 5:2 (1966), 173–86. High emphasizes the California background and events; no notes but lists principal sources.

9:124 Kelsey, Rayner W. "The United States Consulate in California." *Academy of Pacific Coast History Publications* 1:5 (1910), 161–267. This extended essay concentrates on activities of Thomas O. Larkin during 1840 to 1847.

9:125 Knapp, Frank A., Jr. "The Mexican Fear of Manifest Destiny in California." In Thomas E. Cotner and Carlos E. Castañeda, eds., *Essays in Mexican History.* Austin: University of Texas Press, 1958, pp. 192–208. Knapp analyzes the rising concern for California (1838–1847) in Mexican press and Congress, and Mexican inability to do anything effective to resist the threat.

9:126 Underhill, Reuben L. *From Cowhides to Golden Fleece.* Stanford, Calif.: Stanford University Press, 1946. American influences in California (1821–1847) as a background to the war are described, with emphasis on Thomas O. Larkin. Bibliography.

EVENTS OF 1845–1848

See "Personalities," especially John C. Frémont and, under "Others," Stephen W. Kearny.

9:127 Hussey, John A. "The Origin of the Gillespie Mission." *California Historical Society Quarterly* 19:1 (1940), 43–58. Hussey traces the inception of the secret mission (1845–1846) to Larkin and Frémont from Polk's reception of Larkin's alarmist dispatch to Gillespie's departure.

9:128 Jones, Oakah L., Jr. "The Pacific Squadron and the Conquest of California, 1846–1847." *Journal of the West* 5:2 (1966), 187–202. Jones traces the movements of Sloat's squadron during the crisis leading up to the occupation of California and the Bear Flag revolution, and reviews accounts by Bancroft (9:111) and later writers concerning the myth of the British interventions to occupy California.

9:129 Kearney, Thomas. "The Mexican War and the Conquest of California: Stockton or Kearny Conqueror and First Governor?" *California Historical Society Quarterly* 8:3 (1929), 251–61. This study tries to settle the long-standing debate as to the credit for establishing American rule firmly in California after Sloat's original proclamation of occupation (1846–1847); the author favors Kearny.

9:130 Marti, Werner H. *Messenger of Destiny: The California Adventures, 1846–1847, of Archibald Gillespie, U.S. Marine Corps.* San Francisco: Howell, 1960. A detailed account of Gillespie's secret mission to John C. Frémont, 1846, and the ensuing Bear Flag revolution in California; Marti defends Frémont.

9:131 Wiltsee, Ernest A. "The British Vice Consul in California and the Events of 1846." *California Historical Society Quarterly* 10:2 (1931), 99–128. The British threat to California is examined.

The Mexican War, 1846–1848

See "Personalities," especially James K. Polk.

9:132 Alcaraz, Ramón, et al. *Apuntes para la historia de la guerra entre México y los Estados-Unidos* [Notes for the history of the war between Mexico and the United States]. México, D.F.: Tipográfica de M. Payno (Hijo), 1848. Reprint 1952. This account con-

tains partially eyewitness accounts by journalists, politicians, and other publicists; English translation published in the United States (New York, 1850).

9:133 Bill, Alfred H. *Rehearsal for Conflict: The War with Mexico, 1846–1848.* New York: Knopf, 1947. A popular account, it emphasizes the fighting of the war and focuses on the army officers who later served in the Civil War. Bibliography.

9:134 Connor, Seymour V. "Attitude and Opinions about the Mexican War, 1846–1970." *Journal of the West* 11:2 (1972), 361–66. Connor examined 766 works about the war and concluded that 75 percent of them neither tried to fix national guilt nor found a single cause, 6.7 percent saw the United States as an imperialist aggressor, 1.2 percent blamed Polk, 7.8 percent blamed Mexico, and 1 percent specifically blamed the Mexican attack.

9:135 Connor, Seymour V., and Faulk, Odie B. *North America Divided: The Mexican War, 1846–1848.* New York: Oxford University Press, 1971. A short, popular account, it echoes Justin Smith (9:140) in explaining the causes of the war. Extensive bibliography.

9:136 Graebner, Norman A. "How Wars Begin: The Mexican War." In David H. White and John W. Gordon, eds., *Proceedings of the Citadel Conference on War and Diplomacy.* Charleston, S.C.: Citadel Development Foundation, 1979, pp. 15–25. This brief survey of principal recent interpretations is more up to date, but less detailed, than other articles in this group.

9:137 Henry, Robert S. *The Story of the Mexican War.* Indianapolis: Bobbs-Merrill, 1950. Henry characterizes the war as "unsought" and "unescapable" by the United States. Most space is devoted to military events, but the work is largely superseded by Bauer (9:148).

Jay, J. *A Review of the Causes and Consequences of the Mexican War* (16:93) indicts the legal and moral justifications advanced for expansion into Texas and for the Mexican War.

Livermore, A. A. *The War with Mexico Reviewed* (16:94) emphasizes the criticisms of American peace movement.

9:138 Roa Barcena, José María. *Recuerdos de la invasión Norteamericana (1846–1848)* [Memories of

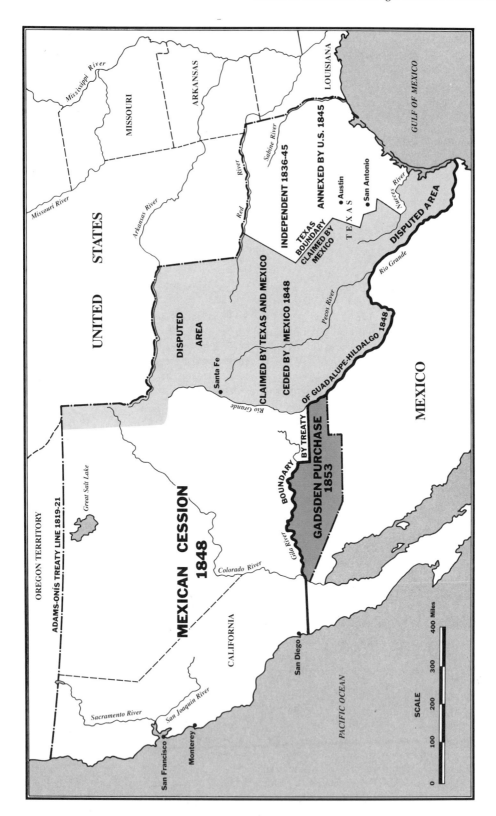

Texas, California, and the Southwest, 1845–53

the American invasion (1846–1848)]. Ed. by Antonio Castro Leal. 3 vols. México, D.F.: J. Buxo, 1883. Reprint 1947. This is an important source apparently derived from Mexican materials, many of which are contemporary with the events described, but the lack of documentation makes accurate attribution impossible.

9:139 Singletary, Otis A. *The Mexican War*. Chicago: University of Chicago Press, 1960. A survey account, especially good for understanding how partisan politics and interservice rivalry complicated the American war effort (1846–1848). Bibliography.

9:140 Smith, Justin H. *The War with Mexico*. 2 vols. New York: Macmillan, 1919. Awarded a Pulitzer Prize (1920), this work has dominated American attitudes toward the Mexican War for a half-century. Its account of the causes of the war is now recognized to be unduly biased against Mexico, and its account of military events is superseded by Bauer's two works (9:148 and 9:149). Based on exhaustive research, it is written in a purple style long out of fashion. Extensive bibliography.

9:141 Tyler, Ronnie C. "The Mexican War: A Lithographic Record." *Southwestern Historical Quarterly* 77:1 (1973), 1–84. This is a collection of contemporary lithographs of American military forces and Mexican scenes during the war, with brief accompanying text comparing the pictorial record of the war with that of other 19th-century wars.

CAUSES OF THE WAR

9:142 Brack, Gene M. *Mexico Views Manifest Destiny, 1821–1846: An Essay on the Origins of the Mexican War*. Albuquerque: University of New Mexico Press, 1975. Brack provides a useful account of rising Mexican suspicions of the United States. He suggests that few Mexicans desired war and especially refutes Justin Smith on this point. The most important sources used are Mexican newspapers and pamphlets. Extensive bibliography.

9:143 Harstad, Peter T., and Resh, Richard W. "The Causes of the Mexican War: A Note on Changing Interpretations." *Arizona and the West* 6:4 (1964), 289–302. A roughly chronological study of interpretations (1846–1974) which shows their progression and relationship.

9:144 Kohl, Clayton C. *Claims as a Cause of the Mexican War*. New York: New York University Press, 1914. A thorough treatment of a narrow subject (1821–1848), this account remains the standard monograph on an aspect of the causes which loomed large in Polk's war message but was deprecated by Polk's opponents and by most subsequent writers.

9:145 Price, Glenn W. *Origins of the War with Mexico: The Polk-Stockton Intrigue*. Austin: University of Texas Press, 1967. Price provides the fullest available exposition of the "plot" thesis—that Polk tried to provoke a war with Mexico in the spring of 1845, using Robert F. Stockton as his principal agent provocateur and the protection of Texas during the annexation process as "cover." It is based on extensive research but relies considerably on surmise. Extensive bibliography.

9:146 Stenberg, Richard R. "The Failure of Polk's Mexican War Intrigue of 1845." *Pacific Historical Review* 4:1 (1935), 39–68. This is the first full statement of the "plot" thesis of the causes of the Mexican War; later revived and amplified by Price, with the addition of new material on Robert F. Stockton.

9:147 Vázquez de Knauth, Josefina. *Mexicanos y Norteamericanos ante la guerra del 47* [Mexicans and Americans before the war of '47]. México, D.F.: Sep Setenta, 1972. This is a 50-page interpretive and synthetic essay followed by 225 pages of contemporary and secondary accounts interpreting the causes of the Mexican War (1845–1846).

MILITARY ACTION

See "Personalities," especially Antonio López de Santa Anna, Winfield Scott, and Zachary Taylor; also "Bibliographies" for military accounts.

9:148 Bauer, K. Jack. *The Mexican War, 1846–1848*. New York: Macmillan, 1974. This is a well-researched, balanced treatment of military events during the war and the occupation of Mexico, based on army sources little used by other writers. Bauer relates the campaigns to the state of the art of war during the early 19th century. Extensive bibliography.

9:149 Bauer, K. Jack. *Surfboats and Horse Marines: U.S. Naval Operations in the Mexican War, 1846–1848*. Annapolis: Md.: Naval Institute Press,

1969. Bauer covers naval operations more thoroughly here than in his more comprehensive military history (above), but the latter is more minutely documented. Bibliography.

9:150 Gerhard, Peter. "Baja California in the Mexican War, 1846–1848." *Pacific Historical Review* 14:4 (1945), 418–24. This is a detailed history of events based on original sources.

9:151 Houston, Donald E. "The Role of Artillery in the Mexican War." *Journal of the West* 11:2 (1972), 273–84. The war provided artillerymen with a laboratory for testing guns and tactics. According to Houston, the artillery frequently saved the American army from destruction.

9:152 Irey, Thomas R. "Soldiering, Suffering, and Dying in the Mexican War." *Journal of the West* 11:2 (1972), 285–98. Irey analyzes the unusually high mortality rate during the war.

9:153 Lavender, David. *Climax at Buena Vista: The American Campaigns in Northeastern Mexico, 1846–47.* Philadelphia: Lippincott, 1966. This is a good brief account of the first campaigns of the war, from Palo Alto to Buena Vista, that focuses on Taylor's army. Bibliography.

9:154 McCornack, Richard B. "The San Patricio Deserters in the Mexican War." *The Americas* 8:2 (1951), 131–142. A study of a group of American Catholics, many of them Irish, who served as a unit in the Mexican army during the war.

9:155 Nichols, Edward J. *Zach Taylor's Little Army.* Garden City, N.Y.: Doubleday, 1963. A colorful, popular account that reviews the war in northern Mexico.

9:156 Pohl, James W. "The Influence of Antoine Henri de Jomini on Winfield Scott's Campaign in the Mexican War." *Southwestern Historical Quarterly* 77:1 (1973), 85–110. Jomini's writings on Napoleonic strategy and tactics influenced several generations of American military leaders; Scott, who was a great student of the subject, furnishes one of the best examples of the influence.

9:157 Smith, Ralph A. "El Contrabando en la guerra con Estados Unidos" [Contraband in the war with the United States]. *Historia Mexicana* 11:3 (1962), 361–81. Smith has written a detailed study of a limited topic.

9:158 Vandiver, Frank E. "The Mexican War Experience of Josiah Gorgas." *Journal of Southern History* 13:3 (1947), 373–94. This is a useful analysis of American supply arrangements during the war. It shows the staff and bureaucratic frustrations that Scott faced.

9:159 Wallace, Edward S. "Deserters in the Mexican War." *Hispanic American Historical Review* 15:3 (1935), 374–83. Wallace covers much the same ground as McCornack on the San Patricio group (9:154).

9:160 Webb, Walter Prescott. *The Texas Rangers in the Mexican War.* Austin, Tex.: Jenkins Garrett, 1975. Webb's M.A. thesis, written in 1920, is well documented from published sources.

DIPLOMACY

See "Personalities," especially James K. Polk and Nicholas P. Trist.

9:161 Bravo Ugarte, José. "La Misión confidencial de Moses Y. Beach en 1847, y el clero Mexicano" [The confidential mission of Moses Y. Beach in 1847 and the Mexican clergy]. *Ábside* 12:4 (1948), 476–96. This overlaps the article of Anna Kasten Nelson (9:168) considerably but relies largely on Mexican sources and emphasizes Beach's machinations with the proclerical rebels.

9:162 Castañeda, Carlos E. "Relations of General Scott with Santa Anna." *Hispanic American Historical Review* 29:4 (1949), 455–73. Scott unsuccessfully sought in 1847 to avoid an attack on the Valley of Mexico by negotiating.

9:163 Chamberlin, Eugene K. "Nicholas Trist and Baja California." *Pacific Historical Review* 32:1 (1963), 49–63. Chamberlin blames Trist for the failure of the United States to acquire Baja California. Since Trist's instructions were flexible on this point, the objection seems captious.

9:164 De Armond, Louis. "Justo Sierra O'Reilly and Yucatan–United States Relations, 1847–1848." *Hispanic American Historical Review* 31:3 (1951), 420–36. O'Reilly bore an invitation for U.S. annexation of Yucatan at the end of the Mexican War, which precipitated an argument in Congress but led to no action.

9:165 Farnham, Thomas J. "Nicholas Trist and James Freaner and the Mission to Mexico." *Arizona and the West* 11:3 (1969), 247–60. Freaner served as courier (1847) between Trist in Mexico and Washington. Farnham believes that he may have been the deciding force in persuading Trist to disobey Polk's order and stay in Mexico to complete his peace negotiations. The argument is not wholly proved and is a small point at that.

9:166 Graebner, Norman A. "Lessons of the Mexican War." *Pacific Historical Review* 47:3 (1978), 325–42. The title is deceptive, for the essay deals with the dilemma facing Polk in late 1847 and early 1848 after the occupation of Mexico City, when he was caught between Whig and other opposition to the war and the developing all-Mexico movement.

9:167 Johnson, Kenneth M. "Baja California and the Treaty of Guadalupe Hidalgo." *Journal of the West* 11:2 (1972), 328–47. Johnson exonerates Trist for not securing the annexation of Baja California in the treaty; see Chamberlin (9:163).

9:168 Nelson, Anna Kasten. "Mission to Mexico: Moses Y. Beach, Secret Agent." *New York Historical Society Quarterly* 59:3 (1975), 227–45. This is an account of Beach's unsuccessful effort in 1847 to negotiate peace, and his efforts to exploit the proclerical revolt in Mexico City for his purposes.

9:169 Northup, Jack. "Nicholas Trist's Mission to Mexico: A Reinterpretation." *Southwestern Historical Quarterly* 71:3 (1968), 321–46. Northup faults Trist for not carrying out his instructions but does not take into consideration the exceedingly complicated political situation in Mexico.

9:170 Sears, Louis M. "Nicholas P. Trist: A Diplomat with Ideals." *Mississippi Valley Historical Review* 11:1 (1924), 85–98. Although the article is old, its appreciative view of Trist is closer to a just appraisal than the more critical articles of Chamberlin (9:163) and Northup (9:169).

9:171 Smith, Justin H. "La República de Río Grande" [The Republic of the Rio Grande]. *American Historical Review* 25:4 (1920), 660–75. There was an abortive attempt at secession in northeastern Mexico before and during the Mexican War. Smith is primarily concerned with its last phases, before it finally disappeared in 1847.

9:172 Williams, Mary W. "Secessionist Diplomacy of Yucatan." *Hispanic American Historical Review* 9:2 (1929), 132–43. Williams traces the efforts of a local regime in Yucatan to end a caste (actually race) war (1847–1848) with the Indians through secession from Mexico and annexation to the United States. The mission of O'Reilly, described in Louis De Armond's article (9:164), was the result.

REACTIONS TO THE WAR

American

9:173 Borit, G. S. "Lincoln's Opposition to the Mexican War." *Journal of the Illinois State Historical Society* 67:1 (1974), 79–100. As a Whig member of the House of Representatives, Lincoln offered partisan opposition in 1847 to the war. His stand would be worth, at most, no more than a paragraph but for his later career.

9:174 Boucher, Chauncey W. "In Re That Aggressive Slaveocracy." *Mississippi Valley Historical Review* 8:1 (1921), 13–79. A classic article, it exploded the myth that a unified South provoked and supported the war.

9:175 Brent, Robert A. "Reaction in the U.S. to Nicholas Trist's Mission to Mexico, 1847–1848." *Revista de Historia de América,* nos. 35–36 (1953), 105–18. The reactions to the Trist mission mirrored reactions to the war itself; that is, they were contradictory and they fluctuated.

9:176 Collins, John R. "The Mexican War: A Study in Fragmentation." *Journal of the West* 11:2 (1972), 225–34. This study of congressional voting on war issues (1846–1848) shows partisan and sectional fragmentation.

9:177 Curti, Merle. "Pacifist Propaganda and the Treaty of Guadalupe Hidalgo." *American Historical Review* 33:3 (1928), 596–98. In a footnote to the treaty, Curti demonstrates the United States was not responsible for article 21, a mild recommendation that disputes be settled by arbitration.

9:178 Davies, Thomas J., Jr. "Assessments during the Mexican War: An Exercise in Futility." *New Mexico Historical Review* 41:3 (1966), 197–216. The assessments or taxes were U.S.-forced contributions on the Mexican authorities during the occupation.

Davies discusses origins of the policy and obstacles to its implementation.

9:179 Dodd, William E. "The West and the War with Mexico." *Journal of the Illinois State Historical Society* 5:2 (1912), 159–72. Dodd finds that an alliance of South and West was responsible for the prosecution of the war. He blames Trist for his failure to take all of Mexico.

9:180 Ellsworth, Clayton S. "The American Churches and the Mexican War." *American Historical Review* 45:2 (1940), 301–26. Most religious groups supported the war, with the exception of many Catholics and most New England denominations.

9:181 Fuller, John D. P. *The Movement for the Acquisition of All Mexico, 1846–1848.* Baltimore: Johns Hopkins Press, 1936. This is a sound study of press and congressional opinion in the United States, with some consideration of its influence on Polk. Compare with F. Merk (2:52), pp. 157–201. Bibliography.

9:182 Goldin, Gurston. "Business Sentiment and the Mexican War, with Particular Emphasis on the New York Businessman." *New York History* 33:1 (1952), 54–70. Many business leaders opposed the war, both because they disliked the disturbance it caused and because they feared that it would encourage abolitionism and harm their profitable ties with the South.

9:183 Haun, Cheryl. "The Whig Abolitionists' Attitude toward the Mexican War." *Journal of the West* 11:2 (1972), 260–72. Haun analyzes the most determined opposition group.

9:184 Hinckley, Ted C. "American Anti-Catholicism during the Mexican War." *Pacific Historical Review* 31:1 (1962), 121–37. This essay focuses on a narrow but important segment of American sentiment toward the war.

9:185 Lambert, Paul F. "The Movement for the Acquisition of All Mexico." *Journal of the West* 11:2 (1972), 317–27. Lambert suggests that American peace sentiment might have prevailed on Polk to end the war even if Trist had not opportunely negotiated an acceptable treaty.

Lander, E. M., Jr. *Reluctant Imperialists: Calhoun, the South Carolinians, and the Mexican War* (9:56) is a careful analysis which supports the conclusions of Boucher (9:174) that the rampant expansionism of the

southern "slaveocracy" during the war was a myth. Instead, South Carolina was mildly expansionist, that is, only to the Rio Grande.

9:186 Merk, Frederick. "Dissent in the Mexican War." In Samuel Eliot Morison, Frederick Merk, and Frank Freidel, *Dissent in Three American Wars.* Cambridge: Harvard University Press, 1970, pp. 35–63. Mainly a review of antiwar newspapers, it is a useful supplement to Schroeder's more detailed book.

9:187 Schroeder, John H. *Mr. Polk's War: American Opposition and Dissent, 1846–1848.* Madison: University of Wisconsin Press, 1973. Schroeder's work covers some of the same ground as Merk's brief essay, but offers a more detailed study of the types and growth of American opposition to the war. Bibliography.

Mexican

9:188 Berge, Dennis E. "A Mexican Dilemma: The Mexico City Ayuntamiento and the Question of Loyalty, 1846–1848." *Hispanic American Historical Review* 50:2 (1970), 229–56. Berge offers one of a very few scholarly studies which discuss the Mexican side of an episode during the war.

9:189 Bosch García, Carlos. "Antecedentes históricos del principio de no intervención en torno a la Guerra de 1847" [Historical antecedents of the principle of non-intervention with respect to the War of 1847]. *Revista de Ciencias Políticos y Sociales* 8:1 (1962), 15–25.

9:190 Hale, Charles A. "The War with the United States and the Crisis in Mexican Thought." *The Americas* 14:2 (1957), 153–73. This is a penetrating study of Mexican liberalism before and during the war that draws from extensive Mexican sources and shows understanding of the dilemma facing liberals, who had formerly admired American institutions and could not repudiate them suddenly.

9:191 Moseley, Edward H. "The Religious Impact of the American Occupation of Mexico City, 1847–1848." In Eugene R. Huck and Edward H. Moseley, eds., *Militarists, Merchants and Missionaries: United States Expansion in Middle America.* University: University of Alabama Press, 1970, pp. 39–52. The effect of the occupation on Mexican religion was very slight, but the contact with Americans may have encouraged Mexican liberals to work for political reform.

9:192 Spell, Lota M. "The Anglo-Saxon Press in Mexico, 1846–1848." *American Historical Review* 38:1 (1932), 20–31. Spell deals with the newspapers sponsored by the American army which achieved modest success and became the foundation of the press in the postwar American Southwest.

9:193 Velasco Martínez, Jesús. *La Guerra de 47 y la opinión pública* [The War of 1847 and public opinion]. México, D.F.: Secretaría de Educación Pública, 1975. This account supplements the Brack study (9:142) of Mexican public opinion, using some of the same sources, and extends into the postwar period.

Other

9:194 D'Olwer, Luis Nicolau. "Santa Anna y la invasión vistos por Bermúdez de Castro" [Santa Anna and the invasion as seen by Bermúdez de Castro]. *Historia Mexicana* 4:1 (1954), 47–65. Bermúdez de Castro, the Spanish minister to Mexico, was not only a shrewd observer of the war but also the moving force in an intrigue to create a Mexican throne for a Spanish prince.

9:195 Mullins, William H. "The British Press and the Mexican War: Justin Smith Revised." *New Mexico Historical Review* 52:3 (1977), 207–27. Smith was wrong to think that the British press encouraged the Mexicans to fight. The British, to be sure, disliked the United States but they respected its strength.

Postwar U.S. Expansionism, 1848–1860

9:196 Berbusse, Edward J. "Two Kentuckians Evaluate the Mexican Scene from Vera Cruz, 1853–1861." *The Americas* 31:4 (1975), 501–12. This essay deals with two U.S. consuls, John T. Pickett and B. I. Twyman, who joined Minister John Forsyth in fishing in troubled Mexican waters.

9:197 Cue Canovas, Agustín. *El Tratado McLane-Ocampo: Juárez, los Estados Unidos y Europa* [The McLane-Ocampo Treaty: Juárez, the United States, and Europe]. 2d ed. México, D.F.: Ediciones Centenario, 1959.

9:198 Fuentes Mares, José. *Juárez y los Estados Unidos* [Juárez and the United States]. México, D.F.: Libro Mex Editores, 1960. This account deals with the negotiations leading to the McLane-Ocampo Treaty (1857–1860). Bibliography.

May, Robert E. *The Southern Dream of Caribbean Empire, 1854–1861* (7:116) deals, in Chapter 6, with filibuster attempts across the Mexican border.

9:199 Monaghan, J. *Chile, Peru and the California Gold Rush of 1849.* Berkeley: University of California Press, 1973. This account reviews the anti-Chilean demonstrations in California.

9:200 Pletcher, David M. "A Prospecting Expedition across Central Mexico, 1856–1857." *Pacific Historical Review* 21:1 (1952), 21–41. Led by Edward Lee Plumb, an important U.S.-Mexican agent and promoter during the 1860s and 1870s, the expedition sought and found exploitable iron deposits, but their supporting company lacked capital for development.

9:201 Tamayo, Jorge L. "El Tratado McLane-Ocampo" [The McLane-Ocampo Treaty]. *Historia Mexicana* 21:4 (1972), 573–613. After a lengthy background, this is primarily a diplomatic account (1848–1859). From the few notes, the author has apparently used only published sources.

9:202 Wilgus, A. Curtis. "Official Expression of Manifest Destiny Sentiment Concerning Hispanic America, 1848–1871." *Louisiana Historical Quarterly* 15:3 (1932), 486–506. This is largely a string of quotations from Congress and the press.

DIPLOMATIC ISSUES

Boundary and Indians Questions, 1848–1853

9:203 Goetzmann, William H. "The United States–Mexican Boundary Survey, 1848–1853." *Southwestern Historical Quarterly* 62:2 (1958), 164–90.

9:204 Lesley, Lewis B. "The International Boundary Survey from San Diego to the Gila River, 1849–1850." *California Historical Society Quarterly* 9:1 (1930), 3–15. This article partly overlaps the Goetzmann article.

9:205 Moseley, Edward H. "Indians from the Eastern United States and the Defense of Northeastern Mexico, 1855–1864." *Southwestern Social Science Quarterly* 46:3 (1965), 273–80. The Seminoles and Kickapoos migrated into Mexico with the encouragement of Governor Santiago Vidaurri and fought for the Mexicans.

9:206 Park, Joseph F. "The Apaches in Mexican-American Relations, 1843–1861: A Footnote to the Gadsden Treaty." *Arizona and the West* 3:2 (1961), 129–46. Park deals largely with actions on the American side of the border and uses mostly published sources.

9:207 Porter, Kenneth W. "The Seminole in Mexico, 1850–1861." *Hispanic American Historical Review* 31:1 (1951), 1–36. Seminoles voluntarily migrated from the Indian Territory because they opposed having the Creeks as neighbors. They and their Negro slaves fought for Mexico on the frontier.

Tehuántepec Question

9:208 Diket, A. L. "Slidell's Right Hand: Émile La Sère." *Louisiana History* 43:3 (1963), 177–205. La Sère was president of one of the rival Tehuantepec companies.

9:209 Fernández MacGregor, Genaro. *El Istmo de Tehuántepec y los Estados Unidos* [The Isthmus of Tehuántepec and the United States]. Mexico, D.F.: Editorial Elede, 1954. The efforts of the United States to build a railroad over the isthmus (1848–1865); they eventually came to naught.

Rippy, J. F. "Diplomacy of the United States and Mexico Regarding the Isthmus of Tehuántepec, 1848–1865" (7:103) is a fuller account, covering a longer time period, than his book (*The United States and Mexico*); it discusses U.S. efforts (1848–1865) to build a railroad across the isthmus to establish an interocean connection.

Gadsden Treaty, 1853

9:210 Garber, Paul N. *The Gadsden Treaty.* Philadelphia: University of Pennsylvania Press, 1923. This has long been the standard work on the subject, but it is now considerably outdated. Extensive bibliography.

9:211 Lesley, L. B. "The Negotiation of the Gadsden Treaty." *Southwestern Historical Quarterly* 27:1 (1923), 1–26.

Park, J. F. "The Apaches in Mexican-American Relations, 1843–1861: A Footnote to the Gadsden Treaty" (9:206).

Filibusters

9:212 Bridges, C. A. "The Knights of the Golden Circle: A Filibustering Fantasy." *Southwestern Historical Quarterly* 44:3 (1941), 287–302. The knights were an ultraexpansionist southern organization (1855–1865) focused on expansion into Mexico.

Brown, C. H. *Agents of Manifest Destiny: The Lives and Times of the Filibusters* (7:123) is an uneven study of the filibusters, devoting by far the most space to William Walker, and less useful than J. A. Stout, Jr., *The Liberators* (9:221), which is not cited. Three chapters are allotted to Mexico.

Carr, A. Z. *The World and William Walker* [1848–1860] (7:124).

9:213 Chamberlin, Eugene K. "Baja California after Walker: The Zerman Enterprise." *Hispanic American Historical Review* 34:2 (1954), 175–89. Chamberlin concludes that Zerman (1855–1868) was not a filibuster but was viewed as such because of Walker's earlier invasion.

9:214 Clarke, James M. "Antonio Meléndrez: Nemesis of William Walker in Baja California." *California Historical Society Quarterly* 12:4 (1933), 318–22. This essay, based on newspapers and a few letters, relates to the years 1853 to 1854.

9:215 Dunn, Roy S. "The KGC in Texas, 1860–1861." *Southwestern Historical Quarterly* 70:4 (1967), 543–73. This essay focuses on the strength and activities of the filibustering Knights of the Golden Circle in the principal Texas areas of settlement.

9:216 Fornell, Earl W. "Texans and Filibusters in the 1850's." *Southwestern Historical Quarterly* 59:4 (1956), 411–28. Fornell comes to much the same conclusions as other writers about filibusters' motives: money and adventure. He adds the desire for cheap labor and the slave trade.

Scroggs, W. O. *Filibusters and Financiers: The Story of William Walker and His Associates* (7:128) has two chapters which deal with Walker's expedition into Lower California.

9:217 Shearer, Ernest C. "The Callahan Expedition, 1855." *Southwestern Historical Quarterly* 54:4 (1951), 430–51. Discussed here is one of the filibustering expeditions in northern Mexico.

9:218 Shearer, Ernest C. "The Carvajal Disturbances." *Southwestern Historical Quarterly* 55:2 (1951), 201–30. A filibustering episode in 1850 to 1852.

9:219 Southerland, James M. "John Forsyth and the Frustrated 1857 Mexican Loan and Land Grab." *West Georgia College Studies in the Social Sciences* 11 (1972), 18–25. This account argues that John Forsyth, American minister to Mexico (1856–1858), was an early advocate of American commercial exploitation of Mexico and that he broke with the Buchanan administration's territorial acquisition policy.

9:220 Stout, Joe A., Jr. "Henry A. Crabb: Filibuster or Colonizer? The Story of an Ill-Starred Gringo Entrada." *American West* 8:3 (1971), 4–9. Crabb entered Sonora (1857) believing he was invited by the leading citizens to colonize the area. All but one of his party were massacred after only a few weeks there. Controversy still exists over whether this was done on the order of those Mexicans who had invited him to Sonora. Also see Robert H. Forbes, *Crabb's Filibustering Expedition into Sonora, 1857* (Tucson: Arizona Silhouettes, 1952).

9:221 Stout, Joe A., Jr. *The Liberators: Filibustering Expeditions into Mexico, 1848–1862, and the Last Thrust of Manifest Destiny.* Los Angeles: Westernlore, 1973. This is a good synthesis on filibustering, both American and French, from California into Mexico. Stout argues that filibusters were motivated by the desire for adventure and for economic gain, and shows the efforts of the U.S. government to intercept filibusters.

9:222 Wyllys, Rufus K. *The French in Sonora (1850–1854): The Story of French Adventures from California into Mexico.* Berkeley: University of California Press, 1929. While mostly focused on Raousset de Boulbon and other French filibusters, the book devotes some attention to Walker as well. Extensive bibliography.

9:223 Wyllys, Rufus K. "Henry A. Crabb: A Tragedy of the Sonora Frontier." *Pacific Historical Review* 9:2 (1940), 183–94. This 1857 episode discouraged the California sport of filibustering until long after the Civil War and created a nationalistic legend for the people of the Sonoran borderlands.

9:224 Wyllys, Rufus K. "The Republic of Lower California, 1853–1854." *Pacific Historical Review* 2:2 (1933), 194–213. This account examines William Walker's abortive effort to detach Baja California from Mexico.

10

Canadian-American Boundary, 1783–1872

Contributing Editor

HOWARD JONES
University of Alabama

Contents

Introduction

Much has been written on the history of the Canadian-American boundary, yet few writers have given adequate attention to its relationship to the international history of North America. The stakes were higher than the mere acquisition of land; they involved questions of national honor and the future control of the continent.

Kenneth Bourne, *Britain and the Balance of Power in North America, 1815–1908* (8:55), has focused on part of the issue by emphasizing British efforts during the nineteenth century to contain American expansion. His work, however, deals only lightly with the United States' side of the question. Bradford Perkins, *Prologue to War: England and the United States, 1805–1812* (6:11), has demonstrated that a major theme in America's early foreign policy was the attempt to gain Great Britain's admission that the United States was, indeed, a sovereign nation worthy of respect in international relations. Howard Jones, *To the Webster-Ashburton Treaty: A Study in Anglo-American Relations, 1783–1843* (10:31), also has attempted to establish this search for mutual trust in his work relating the treaty to the international history of North America. In a real sense, the history of the Canadian-American boundary question following the Treaty of Paris of 1783 linked closely to the long international struggle for the continent which traced back to the colonial wars.

To bring order to this period, many historians have discerned a growing Anglo-American rapprochement. Yet for contemporaries who could not know the outcome by the turn of the twentieth century, there was little reason for optimism. Many issues hampered the growth of what Frank Thistlethwaite, *The Anglo-American Connection in the Early Nineteenth Century* (8:63), has called the "Atlantic community." At bottom was a mutual suspicion which raised questions about almost every event that affected both nations. This bitterness became obvious in what observers might mistakenly dismiss as dry, meaningless boundary disagreements. Why, one might ask, should so many people become upset over a border matter in distant Maine? Or in Oregon? And in the waters off the Pacific Northwest coast? The point is that although there were social, political, and economic forces pulling the Atlantic nations together, there were specific issues and events driving them apart. "Ambivalence," David M. Pletcher, *The Diplomacy of Annexation: Texas, Oregon, and the Mexican War* (9:13), has argued, characterized the Anglo-American relationship throughout the nineteenth century. As far as Americans were concerned, the issue of national honor permeated much of the common history of the two English-speaking peoples. The responsibility of the administrations in London and Washington was to smooth these problems and encourage the feeling of rapprochement that mutual need eventually achieved by the end of the century.

Several countries were involved in the North American boundary question, but none were so important as Great Britain and the United States. For Anglo-American affairs during this period, one must turn first to the works of Samuel Flagg Bemis and Bradford Perkins. Bemis's studies of the late eighteenth century are standards, while his two-volume biography of John Quincy Adams, *John Quincy Adams and the Foundations of American Foreign Policy* (6:16) and *John Quincy Adams and the Union* (8:7), already has taken its place as a classic. Perkins's superbly researched trilogy of Anglo-American relations from the 1790s through the early 1820s, *The First Rapprochement: England and the United States, 1795–1805* (6:10); *Prologue to War* (6:11); and *Castlereagh and Adams: England and the United States, 1812–1823* (6:12), has developed major themes which give form and substance to the period. Howard Jones has related a series of seemingly disparate events from 1783 to 1843 to the North American boundary question in his book-length study of the Webster-Ashburton Treaty (10:31). On the Oregon question, no one has managed to synthesize the great mass of materials available on the controversy into a single volume. Frederick Merk, the most productive scholar on the issue, has pioneered extensive inquiries into the matter. His work on Oregon consists of numerous articles and collections of edited materials, some of which he has incorporated into *The Oregon Question: Essays in Anglo-American Diplomacy and*

Politics (10:68). The vast number of works already published on the Oregon controversy makes one wonder if there can be anything new to say on the matter, but it would be useful to have a study which brings together the previous work into a single volume. Such a task would be formidable, for the writer would have to focus on the origins of the question, highlight the crisis of 1845–1846, and trace it to the final settlement of 1872, when the German arbitration award provided by the Treaty of Washington resolved ownership of the San Juan Islands.

Despite many fine works already published on this period, there remains the need for more studies showing the interrelationship between domestic and foreign affairs in both England and the United States. Some historians allude to the effect that internal politics had on the development of foreign policy, while fewer still have attempted to show their intricate and direct relationship. There is no way to understand the Canadian-American boundary problem without considering the domestic situation in both New Brunswick and Maine, as well as in England and the United States. The same holds true during the long Oregon dispute. The internal problems facing the Peel ministry in London surely affected its decision to compromise in 1846, while the belligerent nature of the Polk administration was in part the product of a desire to reflect the expansionist attitudes prevailing among many Americans of the decade. Manifest destiny might have been the idealistic banner of the 1840s, but beneath it stood a people interested in immediate and realistic goals. A comprehensive and ambitious study of the intertwined nature of domestic and foreign factors would be welcome.

Several topics need further exploration by historians. It would be useful to see a broadly based study of expansionism and manifest destiny which included the movement for the annexation of Canada, as well as the usual account of American migration west. A new synthesis of American-British-Canadian relations would update the older work of John B. Brebner's *North Atlantic Triangle: The Interplay of Canada, the United States and Great Britain* (2:233). The important involvement of France in Anglo-American affairs, especially by the 1840s, also deserves greater attention. Maritime matters involving Britain and the United States need more research. The *Chesapeake-Leopard* affair of 1807 and the Embargo Act of that same year have not received adequate attention, and someone might explore more fully the reasons for Britain's decision to repeal the Orders in Council in 1811–1812. There should be more focus on the Rush-Bagot agreement of 1817 and ensuing Great Lakes armaments problems, and it would be helpful to have a full-length study of the Convention of 1818 with England. The extensive questions surrounding Anglo-American relations and the African slave trade require more work, while the Atlantic nations' problems over impressment need further exploration and analysis. In a general sense, there is need for more studies based upon British materials. Only then can we talk confidently about themes and trends characterizing the Atlantic nations' mutual history during the nineteenth century.

Until such works appear, the familiar themes will have to suffice. Manifest destiny and mission certainly influenced many Americans' expansionist interests during the early nineteenth century, yet, as Norman A. Graebner, *Empire on the Pacific: A Study in American Continental Expansion* (9:12), and others have shown, there were other factors as well. Maritime considerations—the Asiatic market in trade—attracted the interest of American merchants from the East Coast who probably thought little of idealistic principles allegedly running through the nation's expansionist thrust. Graebner's commercial interpretation lends balance to the idealistic viewpoints which often leave little room for the realities of economic pursuits. While many Americans moved west for adventure or for farmland, others were engaged in a race for empire in North America that would spread northward as well as westward.

Thus the motives behind the country's expansionism along all sectors of the Canadian-American border were diverse, complex, and in many cases purely individual; but the more important point is that the efforts by Great Britain and the United States to resolve the North American boundary question sometimes led to international problems which had potential for war. The issues beneath the surface disagreements were real: national honor, economic primacy, military and strategic maneuvering for control of a continent. The long struggle over the Canadian-American boundary deserves more attention because capable diplomats and responsible leaders in Washington and London took the most difficult course in resolving the question: they refused to go to war.

Resources and Overviews

RESEARCH AIDS

While pertinent bibliographies and other reference aids are listed here, there are more extensive lists in Chapter 1.

Bibliographies

Bemis, S. F., and Griffin, G. G., eds. *A Guide to the Diplomatic History of the United States, 1775–1921* (1:57) has relevant pages on U.S. relations with Britain and Canada in chapters 2, 4, 5, 9, 11, 13 and 16.

Billington, R. A., ed. *The American Frontier* (1:70) includes annotated citations on the Oregon question.

Brown, L. M., and Christie, I. R., eds. *Bibliography of British History, 1789–1851* (6:1).

Fehrenbacher, D. E., ed. *Manifest Destiny and the Coming of the Civil War* (1:71) contains unannotated lists of secondary materials relating to manifest destiny and the Oregon controversy.

Hasse, A. R., ed. *Index to United States Documents Relating to Foreign Affairs, 1828–1861* (1:304) provides references to many published documents, papers, and correspondence which relate to U.S.-Canada relations.

Paul, R. W., and Etulain, R. W., comps. *The Frontier and the American West* (1:74) lists materials on all aspects of U.S. westward expansion including such themes as manifest destiny.

Poore, B. P., ed. *A Descriptive Catalogue of the Government Publications of the United States, September 5, 1774–March 4, 1881* (1:309) briefly describes the contents of documents contained in the "Serial Set."

Winther, O. O., and Van Orman, R. A., comps. *A Classified Bibliography of the Periodical Literature of*

the *Trans-Mississippi West, 1811–1967* (1:77) is useful on the Oregon controversy.

Document Collections

More general collections are listed in Chapter 1, and other collections may be found in "Personalities," below.

American State Papers, Foreign Relations (1:349) has, in volume six, a list of books, maps, surveys, and manuscripts relating to the northeastern boundary dispute; it also shows the disagreements between British and American boundary commissioners through the 1820s.

Great Britain. *British and Foreign State Papers* (1:363) includes correspondence between Britain and the United States since 1812.

10:1 Irish University Press Series on British Parliamentary Papers. *Canada/Canadian Boundary*. 36 vols. Shannon: Irish University Press, 1968–1975. Canadian issues appearing in 19th-century British sessional papers have been collected into two ts: 33 volumes deal with Canadian affairs generally, and 3 volumes specifically relate to Canadian boundary questions.

Manning, W. R., ed. *Diplomatic Correspondence of the United States: Canadian Relations, 1784–1860* (1:343) includes communications with Britain relating to Canadian affairs; volume 3, covering 1836 to 1848, is especially helpful on the northeastern boundary, the *Caroline* affair, American involvement in the Canadian rebellion, and the Oregon controversy. The volumes are indexed by correspondent, topic, and names discussed.

Miller, D. H., ed. *Treaties and Other International Acts of the United States of America, 1776–1863* (1:376) includes, in volume 4, correspondence between Secretary of State Daniel Webster and British special minister Lord Ashburton, a lengthy analysis of the articles contained in their treaty of 1842, and numerous documents relating to the background and negotiation of the pact. Volume 5 contains an extensive discussion of the Oregon negotiations, as well as maps, diplomatic correspondence (1845–1846), and other documents; additionally it has an account of the San Juan Islands controversy.

Moore, J. B., ed. *History and Digest of the International Arbitrations to Which the United States Has Been a Party: Modern Series* (16:11) examines the legal issues of the northeastern boundary controversies, including the proceedings leading to the arbitration award of 1831 by the king of the Netherlands. Moore also discusses issues involving that segment of the North American boundary extending from the Rocky Mountains westward, and provides an account of the German emperor's award of 1872 relating to the San Juan Islands controversy.

Moore, J. B., ed. *International Adjudications, Ancient and Modern: History and Documents: Modern Series* (16:12) has fully documented reports of judicial decisions of international questions not recorded in the law reports. The volumes contain the most complete coverage of the St. Croix boundary commission's findings, a detailed discussion of attempts to arbitrate the Passamaquoddy Bay and Bay of Fundy issues, resolved by the Treaty of Ghent, and documents relating to the northeastern boundary issue.

Wharton, F., ed. *The Revolutionary Diplomatic Correspondence of the United States* (4:24) contains materials on the origins of the northeast boundary question.

OVERVIEWS

Allen, H. C. *Conflict and Concord: The Anglo-American Relationship since 1783* (2:231) shows that social, political, and economic factors contributed to an "Anglo-American cordiality" shortly after 1814.

Allen, H. C. *Great Britain and the United States: A History of Anglo-American Relations (1783–1952)* (2:232) emphasizes a similar theme.

10:2 Billington, Ray A. *The Far Western Frontier, 1830–1860*. New York: Harper, 1956. Billington traces the background of the Oregon controversy, and shows how propagandists tried unsuccessfully to promote mass American settlement. Though missionaries had made inroads into the Oregon Country by the late 1820s, it was not until the early 1840s that the Willamette Valley attracted Americans hit by depression and "Oregon fever." Extensive bibliography.

Bourne, K. *Britain and the Balance of Power in North America, 1815–1908* (8:55) uses British sources to show the military and naval aspects of Canadian-American border problems. From the War of 1812 through the early twentieth century, the British re-

mained apprehensive of an American assault on Canada.

Brebner, J. B. *North Atlantic Triangle: The Interplay of Canada, the United States and Great Britain* (2:233) is helpful on Canadian-American border problems.

Callahan, J. M. *American Foreign Policy in Canadian Relations* (2:218) includes accounts of America's involvement in the Canadian rebellion of 1837–1838, the Webster-Ashburton Treaty of 1842, and the negotiation of the Treaty of Washington of 1871.

Campbell, C. S., Jr. *From Revolution to Rapprochement: The United States and Great Britain, 1783–1900* (2:234) emphasizes Anglo-American rapprochement during this period.

Corbett, P. E. *The Settlement of Canadian-American Disputes: A Critical Study of Methods and Results* (16:122).

Craig, G. M. *The United States and Canada* [1600s–1960s] (2:219).

Deener, D. R., ed. *Canada–United States Treaty Relations* [1780–1960] (2:220).

Goetzmann, W. H. *When the Eagle Screamed: The Romantic Horizon in American Diplomacy, 1800–1860* (9:11).

McInnis, E. W. *The Unguarded Frontier: A History of American-Canadian Relations* [1790s–1940s] (2:222).

Reeves, J. S. *American Diplomacy under Tyler and Polk* (9:47) is a general, but dated, introduction to the northeastern boundary dispute (1783–1842), and the Oregon question (1803–1846).

10:3 Smith, Joe P. "The Republican Expansionists of the Early Reconstruction Era." Ph.D. diss., University of Chicago, 1933. This brief dissertation pays particular attention to interest in Canada (1849–1877). Bibliography.

Thistlethwaite, F. *The Anglo-American Connection in the Early Nineteenth Century* (8:63) examines the social, political, and economic factors—including the antislavery connection—between England and the United States (1790–1850), which helped to override numerous divisive issues and promote the "Atlantic community." Thistlethwaite also shows the calming effect of Anglo-American peace advocates during the Oregon crisis of 1846.

Varg, P. A. *United States Foreign Relations, 1820–1860* (8:6).

Personalities

Additional references to data on individuals may be found in Chapter 1, "Biography."

AMERICAN

John Quincy Adams
See Chapters 6 and 7, "Personalities," for additional references.

Bemis, S. F. *John Quincy Adams and the Foundations of American Foreign Policy* (6:16) discusses the northeastern boundary dispute from 1782 to 1831. Bemis also explains that although the Convention of 1818 provided for the 49th parallel as the Canadian-American boundary from the Lake of the Woods to the Rocky Mountains, it did not complete the line to the Pacific, thus leaving a section in the Northwest which later became the focal point of Anglo-American rivalry.

Bemis, S. F. *John Quincy Adams and the Union* (8:7) includes material on the *Caroline*- McLeod crises, the northeastern boundary and the Webster-Ashburton Treaty, and the Oregon question.

Thomas Hart Benton
10:4   Benton, Thomas H. *Thirty Years' View: Or, a History of the American Government for Thirty Years from 1820 to 1850.* 2 vols. New York: Appleton, 1856. The Missouri senator opposed the Webster-Ashburton Treaty. On the Oregon crisis, Benton wrote that he had suggested to President Polk that the treaty's terms be submitted to the Senate, and that he, Benton, would guide their passage by exhorting the Whigs to defeat the Democrats favoring the 54°40' line.

10:5   Chambers, William N. *Old Bullion Benton: Senator from the New West.* Boston: Little, Brown,

1956. Benton cooperated with Polk in persuading the Senate to accept the British proposal of the 49th parallel as the boundary in Oregon. Though Chambers does not attribute primary credit to Benton for the Senate's approval of the Treaty of 1846, the Missourian's withdrawal of his longtime call for the 49th parallel doubtless encouraged such a settlement. Bibliography.

James Buchanan
See Chapter 8, "Personalities," for additional references.

Klein, P. S. *President James Buchanan: A Biography* (8:9) discusses American reaction to the Oregon crisis, and shows that even though Secretary of State Buchanan continually opposed Polk's stand during the negotiations, he eventually received praise in England for the treaty.

10:6   Sioussat, St. George L. "James Buchanan." In Samuel Flagg Bemis, ed., *American Secretaries of State and Their Diplomacy.* New York: Knopf, 1928, vol. 5, pp. 237–336. The author examines the actions taken during the Oregon controversy by Polk's secretary of state, Buchanan.

Albert Gallatin
See Chapter 6, "Personalities," for additional references.

10:7   Merk, Frederick. *Albert Gallatin and the Oregon Problem: A Study in Anglo-American Diplomacy.* Cambridge: Harvard University Press, 1950. Gallatin was most responsible for easing the situation (1826–1827); but he could not reconcile the nationalist desires of Englishmen like George Canning and Americans like John Quincy Adams. Reprinted in Merk (10:68).

Walters, R., Jr. *Albert Gallatin: Jeffersonian Financier and Diplomat* (6:24) traces Gallatin's long involvement in the northeastern boundary controversy from the 1820s to 1843.

James K. Polk
McCormac, E. I. *James K. Polk: A Political Biography* (9:43) argues that Polk remained consistent throughout the Oregon crisis by always leaving the way open for compromise.

McCoy, C. A. *Polk and the Presidency* (9:44) argues that although the 1844 Democratic platform prompted Polk's tough stand on Oregon, he was always amenable to negotiation. Moreover, Polk showed political astuteness by submitting the compromise to the Senate and allowing that body to bear responsibility for the final decision.

Polk, J. K. *The Diary of James K. Polk during His Presidency, 1845 to 1849* (9:46) is useful on Polk's actions during the attempt to impeach Daniel Webster and on the Oregon crisis. Polk's candor reveals his own inconsistency in foreign affairs.

Sellers, C. G. *James K. Polk: Continentalist, 1843– 1846* (9:48) shows Polk's threats on Oregon to be bluffs aimed at forcing Britain to relinquish its demand for the Columbia River boundary; however, Polk did run the risk of two wars—against Mexico and Britain.

Richard Rush

Powell, J. H. *Richard Rush, Republican Diplomat, 1780–1859* (7:22) notes briefly Rush's participation, as America's minister to England, in Anglo-American discussions of the 1820s over the northeast boundary and Russian involvement in Oregon.

Rush, R. *Memoranda of a Residency at the Court of London, 1819–1825* (7:23) contains material on the early phases of Anglo-American negotiations over the northeast boundary.

Winfield Scott

Elliott, C. W. *Winfield Scott: The Soldier and the Man* (9:50) briefly notes Scott's "soldier-diplomat" role during the Canadian-American border troubles in the "Aroostook War" in Maine, the Alexander McLeod trial in New York, and the San Juan Islands dispute in Oregon Territory in late 1859.

10:8 Scott, Winfield. *Memoirs of Lieut.-General Scott, LL.D., Written by Himself.* 2 vols. New York: Sheldon, 1864. Scott makes some revealing comments on the Canadian border controversies.

John Tyler

See Chapter 8, "Personalities," for additional references.

10:9 Chitwood, Oliver P. *John Tyler: Champion of the Old South.* New York: Appleton-Century, 1939. Reprint 1964. Although outdated, this volume remains the only scholarly, political biography of Tyler and his career.

10:10 Morgan, Robert J. *A Whig Embattled: The Presidency under John Tyler.* Lincoln: University of

Nebraska Press, 1954. Morgan deals primarily with Tyler's theory and practice in the executive office, but presents some useful material on the Anglo-American controversies. Like Chitwood, he praises the president for encouraging Webster and Ashburton to reach a settlement in 1842. Bibliography.

10:11 Seager, Robert, II. *And Tyler Too: A Biography of John and Julia Gardiner Tyler.* New York: McGraw-Hill, 1963. The president carefully supervised the drafts of Webster's correspondence with Ashburton during their negotiations in 1842, and managed to keep the British minister negotiating when tempers became short. Bibliography.

Daniel Webster

See Chapter 8, "Personalities," for additional references.

Bartlett, I. H. *Daniel Webster* (8:25) is a new biography.

10:12 Current, Richard N. *Daniel Webster and the Rise of National Conservatism.* Boston: Little, Brown, 1955. Current argues that Webster's work on the treaty with England in 1842 was a notable contribution, but questions his use of the president's secret-service fund and unsigned newspaper editorials in bringing it about. Current includes a brief account of the attempt to impeach the former secretary of state in 1846. Bibliography.

10:13 Curtis, George T. *Life of Daniel Webster.* 2 vols. New York: Appleton, 1870. The collection includes letters from the 1820s showing Webster's acquaintance with influential Englishmen, and goes on to explain his role in the making of the treaty with England in 1842.

10:14 Duniway, Clyde A. "Daniel Webster." In Samuel Flagg Bemis, ed., *American Secretaries of State and Their Diplomacy.* New York: Knopf, 1928, vol. 5, pp. 3–64. Duniway explains Webster's role in bringing about the Webster-Ashburton Treaty. Bibliography.

10:15 Duniway, Clyde A. "Daniel Webster and the West." *Minnesota History* 9:1 (1928), 3–15. Webster did not support manifest destiny in the 1840s because he believed that republican institutions depended upon local governments working together in a cohesive national system. Yet Webster accepted the establishment of the final boundaries and the acquisition of Pacific coastal ports because such moves did not result from the conquest of territories large enough to become states.

10:16 Fuess, Claude M. *Daniel Webster*. 2 vols. Boston: Little, Brown, 1930. A judicious and favorable assessment of the secretary of state's role in securing the Webster-Ashburton Treaty of 1842. Bibliography.

10:17 McIntyre, James M., ed. *The Writings and Speeches of Daniel Webster*. 18 vols. Boston: Little, Brown, 1903. Volumes 16–18 print Webster's letters, while volume 14 contains his defense of the Webster-Ashburton Treaty before Congress (1846). Volume 11 includes Webster's diplomatic correspondence and papers. Charles M. Wiltse's microfilm edition (41 reels) of the *Daniel Webster Papers* (Ann Arbor, Mich.: University Microfilms, 1971) includes many of the same papers, but also contains a huge collection of dispatches from Edward Everett, American minister in London (1841–1845), often enclosing communications with Lord Aberdeen. There is a guide and index to the microfilm edition.

10:18 Wiltse, Charles M. "Daniel Webster and the British Experience." *Proceedings of the Massachusetts Historical Society* 85:3 (1973), 58–77. Wiltse argues that Webster was an Anglophile, and that this feeling affected his favorable actions toward the British.

Marcus Whitman

10:19 Bourne, Edward G. "The Legend of Marcus Whitman." *American Historical Review* 6:2 (1901), 276–300. Whitman's purpose was to promote the spread of Protestant missions in Oregon as a counter to those immigrants becoming Catholic, rather than to extend U.S. territorial borders.

10:20 Drury, Clifford M. *Marcus and Narcissa Whitman and the Opening of Old Oregon*. 2 vols. Glendale, Calif.: A. H. Clark, 1973. Although Whitman's primary responsibility was to evangelize and civilize the Indians, he became involved in the political future of the Oregon Territory. He greatly stimulated emigration of Americans resulting in the numerical superiority of Americans over British citizens which helped establish the border at 49°. Drury published an earlier account, *Marcus Whitman, M.D.: Pioneer and Martyr* (Caldwell, Idaho: Caxton, 1937).

Others

10:21 Adams, Herbert B. *The Life and Writings of Jared Sparks: Comprising Selections from His Journals and Correspondence*. 2 vols. Boston: Houghton Mifflin, 1893. This study includes an account of Sparks's relations with Webster on the red-line map controversy.

Chapin, J. B. "Hamilton Fish and American Expansion" (12:40) reveals Fish as a subtle, conscious expansionist of the Grant era, especially toward Canada.

Curtis, J. C. *The Fox at Bay: Martin Van Buren and the Presidency, 1837–1841* (8:28) praises Van Buren's efforts to maintain peace with Britain during the Canadian revolt, without alienating Americans who openly favored the rebels' ideals.

Duckett, A. L. *John Forsyth: Political Tactician* (8:29) contains details of the secretary of state's attempts to implement Van Buren's foreign policy during the Canadian border crises of the late 1830s.

Ernst, R. *Rufus King* (6:37) contains an account of the King-Hawkesbury talks (1803) over the northeast boundary, but because of other more pressing matters in Europe the British had little interest in resolving the issue.

CANADIAN AND BRITISH

William Lyon Mackenzie

10:22 Kilbourn, William. *The Firebrand: William Lyon Mackenzie and the Rebellion in Upper Canada*. Toronto: Clarke, Irwin, 1956. Mackenzie led Upper Canada during the rebellion against the British crown in 1837–1838. Bibliography.

10:23 MacKay, R. A. "The Political Ideals of William Lyon Mackenzie." *Canadian Journal of Economics and Political Science* 3:1 (1937), 1–22. Mackenzie's fiery leadership ability and belief in democratic ideals attracted more Americans to the rebellion in Upper Canada than to the one in Lower Canada. MacKay suggests that Mackenzie drew many of his ideas on popular government from America's own revolution, especially those on natural rights and the social contract theory.

Lord Palmerston

See Chapter 8, "Personalities," for additional references.

10:24 Bell, Herbert C. F. *Lord Palmerston*. 2 vols. London: Longmans, Green, 1936. This is the biography of the principal high British official involved in the northeastern boundary negotiations with the United States before 1841. Bell includes an explanation of Palmerston's stands in the attempt at arbitration in 1831, the *Caroline*-McLeod crises, and the settlements contained in the Webster-Ashburton Treaty of 1842.

Ridley, J. *Lord Palmerston* (8:45) reveals Palmerston's support for settlement of the northeastern boundary dispute by arbitration in 1831, efforts to calm the border situation above Maine in the late 1830s, warning of war over the McLeod affair, and strong opposition to the Webster-Ashburton Treaty.

Others

10:25 Brightfield, Myron F. *John Wilson Croker*. Berkeley: University of California Press, 1940. Ashburton at times confided in Croker, one of his closest acquaintances, on public matters more than with either Aberdeen or Peel. Croker advocated compromise on both the Maine and Oregon boundary questions.

10:26 Gash, Norman. *Sir Robert Peel: The Life of Sir Robert Peel after 1830*. London: Longmans, 1972. This study sheds light on British relations with the United States during the 1840s, but shows the Peel ministry's interest in keeping the peace during the Maine and Oregon boundary controversies. Bibliography.

10:27 Gray, Edward. "Ward Chipman, Loyalist." *Maine Historical Society Proceedings* 44 (1922), 331–53. This is a brief portrait of the British Loyalist who moved to New Brunswick and then served as crown counsel during the St. Croix boundary settlement of 1797 and again as commission member authorized by the Treaty of Ghent to resolve ownership of the islands in Passamaquoddy Bay.

10:28 Montgomery, Richard G. *The White-Headed Eagle: John McLaughlin, Builder of an Empire*. New York: Macmillan, 1935. As chief factor of the Hudson's Bay Company for many years, McLaughlin was a leading figure in the development of the Oregon Territory. He ruled his "empire" with an iron hand for the twin purposes of trading with the Indians and holding the territory for England. However, he did befriend the missionaries, which eventually opened the way to American emigration.

10:29 New, Chester W. *Lord Durham: A Biography of John George Lambton, First Earl of Durham*. Oxford: Clarendon Press, 1929. Even though Durham was indiscreet in his show of pomp during the hard times of the Canadian rebellion, he managed to institute a plan—the Durham Report—which allowed the Canadians self-government after the crisis had passed.

Northeast Boundary Settlement

See "Personalities," especially Albert Gallatin and Lord Palmerston.

10:30 Corey, Albert B. *The Crisis of 1830–1842 in Canadian-American Relations*. New Haven, Conn.: Carnegie Endowment for International Peace, 1941. This is a detailed survey of the Canadian rebellion and America's involvement in it. During the *Caroline* and Alexander McLeod crises, Lord Durham and General Scott helped to avert an Anglo-American war. The Webster-Ashburton Treaty resulted from both nations' realization of their common interests, and from the statesmanship of the two negotiators. Bibliography.

10:31 Jones, Howard. *To the Webster-Ashburton Treaty: A Study in Anglo-American Relations, 1783–1843*. Chapel Hill: University of North Carolina Press, 1977. Jones traces the origins of the northeastern boundary dispute from the vague provisions of the Treaty of Paris of 1783 through the various Anglo-American attempts of ensuing decades to effect a settlement. Besides noting the diplomatic aspects of the question, Jones emphasizes how American domestic politics and deep-rooted Anglophobia continually defeated the negotiators' efforts to mark the North American boundary. Bibliography.

BACKGROUND, 1783–1830s

See "Personalities," especially John Quincy Adams, Richard Rush, and John Tyler.

Negotiations, 1783–1815

10:32 Bemis, Samuel Flagg. "Canada and the Peace Settlement of 1782–3." *Canadian Historical Review* 14:3 (1933), 265–84. The United States did not gain more of Canada during the Paris discussions because Britain knew that both Spain and France opposed America's expansion west, and because Americans placed more value on the Mississippi Valley.

Bemis, S. F. *The Diplomacy of the American Revolution* (4:26) shows how the Mitchell map used in the boundary discussions at Paris (1782–1783) caused long-lasting difficulties in negotiating the U.S.-Canadian border.

Bemis, S. F. *Jay's Treaty* (5:193) contains information on the ensuing St. Croix boundary commission.

10:33 Bemis, Samuel Flagg. "Jay's Treaty and the Northwest Boundary Gap." *American Historical Review* 27:3 (1922), 465–84. During the Anglo-American talks in 1794, John Jay's opposition to British attempts to drop the boundary to the navigable waters of the Mississippi probably saved a considerable amount of land for the United States. America's northern border, Bemis argues, could have been at the 45th parallel instead of the 49th.

10:34 Brown, George W. "The St. Lawrence in the Boundary Settlement of 1783." *Canadian Historical Review* 9:3 (1928), 223–38. American diplomats in Paris failed to secure free navigation of the St. Lawrence River because no one questioned British control of the waterway. Thus the talks centered on Britain's use of the river's tributaries and its commercial access to American possessions.

Burt, A. L. *The United States, Great Britain and British North America from the Revolution to the Establishment of Peace after the War of 1812* (6:5) discusses American-British-Canadian relations from 1775 to 1820, including the origins of the Canadian boundary dispute (Paris 1782–1783), Jay's Treaty and the St. Croix boundary settlement of the 1790s, the abortive King-Hawkesbury Convention of 1803, the Monroe-Pinkney Convention of 1807 and the United States' refusal to approve it, and the Ghent boundary commissions, which tried to set the border from the Bay of Fundy to the Rocky Mountains.

Dangerfield, G. *The Era of Good Feelings* [1817–1825] (6:173) provides a sprightly account of the Ghent negotiations, with helpful insights on the Canadian boundary question. Dangerfield also briefly includes Richard Rush's talks (1824) with Stratford Canning and William Huskisson in London.

Engelman, F. L. *The Peace of Christmas Eve* (6:174) describes the Ghent negotiations of 1814 and the problems concerning ownership of the islands in Passamaquoddy Bay.

Morris, R. B. *The Peacemakers* (4:175) discusses the Canadian-American boundary talks in Paris (1782–1783), which revealed the problems in marking the border from Nova Scotia and the province of Maine to the Lake of the Woods.

Perkins, B. *Castlereagh and Adams . . . , 1812–1823* (6:12) examines the attempts by the Ghent boundary commissions to mark the Canadian-American line. Perkins holds that the arguments over the border were vital because many in London believed the Americans wanted Canada as the first major thrust toward ending British influence in North America.

Perkins, B. *The First Rapprochement . . . , 1795–1805* (6:10) incorporates a useful account of the arbitration settlement reached by the St. Croix boundary commission, and gives attention to the King-Hawkesbury talks concerning the boundary gaps between the Lake of the Woods and the Mississippi River, and the waters in Passamaquoddy Bay.

Perkins, B. *Prologue to War . . . , 1805–1812* (6:11) examines several critical issues—national pride, emotions, chance—which affected progress on the Canadian boundary settlement. Perkins also shows America's belief that the Indian problem in the Northwest (between the Great Lakes and the Mississippi River) resulted, at least in part, from the British presence in Canada.

Steel, A. "Impressment in the Monroe-Pinkney Negotiations, 1806–1807" (6:119) illustrates how this issue wrecked negotiations on various other matters, including the northeastern boundary.

King William's Award

10:35 Merk, Frederick. *Fruits of Propaganda in the Tyler Administration.* Cambridge: Harvard University Press, 1971. In this account of the arbitration award by the king of the Netherlands in 1831 and the reaction to it in Britain and the United States, Merk argues that the

U.S. Senate rejected the decision because of opposition in Maine.

10:36 Miller, Hunter. "An Annotated Dashiell's Map." *American Historical Review* 38:1 (1932), 70–73. During the arbitral proceedings, King William worked with what the Treaty of Ghent referred to as "Map A," which was published in 1830 by S. L. Dashiell and bore the title, "Map of the Northern Part of the State of Maine and of the adjacent British Provinces."

BORDER TROUBLES

See "Personalities," especially Martin Van Buren (under "Others"), William Lyon Mackenzie, and Winfield Scott.

Bourne, K. *Britain and the Balance of Power in North America, 1815–1908* (8:55) argues that Britain came dangerously close to war with the United States over border issues.

10:37 Creighton, D. G. "The Economic Background of the Rebellions of Eighteen Thirty-Seven." *Canadian Journal of Economics and Political Science* 3:3 (1937), 322–34. Creighton shows the effect of the depression on commercial and agricultural interests in the Canadas, and concludes that the economic crisis encouraged the resort to force by dissidents.

10:38 Dent, John C. *The Story of the Upper Canadian Rebellion: Largely Derived from Original Sources and Documents.* 2 vols. Toronto: Robinson, 1885. A journalistic account.

10:39 Guillet, Edwin C. *The Lives and Times of the Patriots: An Account of the Rebellion in Upper Canada, 1837–38, and of the Patriot Agitation in the United States, 1837–1842.* Toronto: University of Toronto Press, 1938. This account includes a narrative of the *Caroline* affair.

10:40 Hand, Augustus N. "Local Incidents of the Papineau Rebellion." *New York History* 15:4 (1934), 376–87. Concentrating on Louis Joseph Papineau as leader of the rebellion in Lower Canada, Hand contends that the movement (1837–1838) succeeded because the desired social and political reforms were not radical. The essay is useful in understanding American interest in the Canadian rebellion.

10:41 Kinchen, Oscar A. *The Rise and Fall of the Patriot Hunters.* New York: Bookman Associates,

1956. Some members of the Hunters' Lodges in both the United States and Canada were opportunists and adventurers, but most were people with character who sought only Canada's freedom from British rule during the rebellion of 1837–1838. Bibliography.

10:42 Longley, R. S. "Emigration and the Crisis of 1837 in Upper Canada." *Canadian Historical Review* 17:1 (1936), 29–40. The decision by Canadian bankers to call in loans during the depression drove several thousand Canadians into the United States to seek employment.

10:43 New, Chester W. "The Rebellion of 1837 in Its Larger Setting." *Canadian Historical Association Annual Report* (1937), 5–17. The goals of the American Revolution and the images of popular democracy which arose during the Jacksonian era provided much of the pattern for the social, political, and constitutional forces culminating in Lower Canada's insurrection.

The Caroline Affair, 1837

See also "The McLeod Trial," below.

10:44 Jones, Howard. "The *Caroline* Affair." *Historian* 38:3 (1976), 485–502. During the Canadian rebellion, British destruction of this American steamboat in December 1837 inflamed Americans along the New York-Canada border. According to many observers, the British decision to enter American waters and burn the vessel (one American dying in the scuffle) stimulated talk of a third Anglo-American war.

10:45 Shortridge, Wilson P. "The Canadian-American Frontier during the Rebellion of 1837–1838." *Canadian Historical Review* 7:1 (1926), 13–26. Shortridge shows that Americans, primarily along the border, expressed sympathy for the Canadians—especially after the *Caroline*'s destruction. Only the desire for peace in both London and Washington, he concludes, was able to overcome the forces and events seemingly leading to another war between England and the United States.

10:46 Tiffany, Orrin E. "The Relations of the United States to the Canadian Rebellion of 1837–38." *Buffalo Historical Society Publications* 8 (1905), 1–147. President Martin Van Buren's policies during the *Caroline* crisis are discussed.

The "Aroostook War," 1839

10:47 Burrage, Henry S. *Maine in the Northeastern Boundary Controversy.* Portland, Maine: Marks, 1919. Detailed and greatly favorable to Maine, the work convincingly argues that the government in Washington left the state alone to resist Britain's unfounded claims in the disputed territory and thus helped bring on the Aroostook crisis.

10:48 Jones, Howard. "Anglophobia and the Aroostook War." *New England Quarterly* 48:4 (1975), 519–39. Jones uses American, British, and Canadian archival materials to examine the complex issues of the northeast boundary, the rampant Anglophobia among Americans in Maine, and states' rights advocates who would brook no federal interference in their border concerns with New Brunswick.

10:49 LeDuc, Thomas. "The Maine Frontier and the Northeastern Boundary Controversy." *American Historical Review* 53:1 (1947), 30–41. On the Aroostook crisis of February 1839, LeDuc argues that the causes of that comic-opera "war" centered on Maine's interest in the rich limestone soil of the river valley, and on the British realization in 1837–1838 that they needed railroads to aid in the defense of the Canadas. LeDuc credits General Scott with resolving the uneasy situation by securing bipartisan support in Maine for the mutual withdrawal of British troops and state militiamen from the disputed area.

10:50 Lowenthal, David. "The Maine Press and the Aroostook War." *Canadian Historical Review* 32:4 (1951), 315–36. Lowenthal argues that Maine's newspapers and politicians were more warlike than its people, and shows that even though the Whig party initiated the crisis by ordering a state agent to halt trespassing along the Aroostook River, the Democrats did not consider the possible consequences of the provocative action.

10:51 Martin, Ged. *The Durham Report and British Policy: A Critical Essay.* Cambridge: At the University Press, 1972. Martin raises doubt about the influence of the Durham Report on Britain's colonial policy.

The McLeod Trial

10:52 Bonham, Milledge L. "Alexander McLeod: Bone of Contention." *New York History* 18:2 (1937),

189–217. McLeod, a Canadian sheriff and Loyalist, was arrested in New York for allegedly taking part in the *Caroline*'s destruction. Bonham shows that for more than a year the McLeod case was a source of controversy in Canada, England, the United States, and even France. The episode threatened Anglo-American relations, hurt the Whig party in New York, led to a federal law designed to prevent similar incidents, and affected later New York Supreme Court decisions.

10:53 Corey, Albert B. "Public Opinion and the McLeod Case." *Canadian Historical Association Annual Report* (1936), 53–64. Corey examines the effect of the McLeod case on legislators in Washington and Albany and on public opinion at large. Though newspapers enhanced the issues, Corey explains, excitement died as time for the trial approached because many Americans believed that McLeod's arrest and trial satisfied honor.

Jones, W. D. *The American Problem in British Diplomacy, 1841–1861* (8:59) uses British materials to argue that London moved close to war with the United States over the McLeod case.

10:54 Parks, Joseph H. *John Bell of Tennessee.* Baton Rouge: Louisiana State University Press, 1950. Secretary of War Bell's defense precautions taken during the McLeod crisis. Extensive bibliography.

10:55 Watt, Alastair. "The Case of Alexander McLeod." *Canadian Historical Review* 12:2 (1931), 145–67. Watt dispels many of the myths about the *Caroline*-McLeod crises. Watt explains the complicated jurisdictional problems between the state and federal governments during the McLeod case, and concludes that there is no evidence that Secretary of State Daniel Webster tried to influence the courts in New York. The Tyler administration did everything it legally could to secure McLeod's release but failed; only the defendant's alibi resolved the situation.

WEBSTER-ASHBURTON TREATY, 1842

See "Personalities," especially John Forsyth (under "Others"), John Tyler, and Daniel Webster. A major issue which greatly affected negotiations centered on the British slave trade patrol; see Jones (10:31) for a discussion, and Chapter 8, "Suppression of the Slave Trade," for additional references.

10:56 Adams, Ephraim D. "Lord Ashburton and the Treaty of Washington." *American Historical Review* 17:4 (1912), 764–82. Presenting the British side of the boundary problem, Adams focuses on how Ashburton's instructions from Aberdeen at first were general but soon became specific—especially the alteration which emphasized the necessity of acquiring land for a military road. In view of the problems Ashburton faced from his government in London, Adams argues that the special minister accomplished much during the negotiations.

10:57 Baldwin, J. R. "The Ashburton-Webster Boundary Settlement." *Canadian Historical Association Annual Report* (1938), 121–33. Baldwin shows the problems the Tyler administration encountered in persuading Maine to accept a compromise boundary, and accuses Ashburton of using secret British funds to influence Maine's decision. Baldwin concludes that Ashburton's open and conciliatory approach to the negotiations allowed Webster to outmaneuver him on the boundary question.

10:58 Current, Richard N. "Webster's Propaganda and the Ashburton Treaty." *Mississippi Valley Historical Review* 34:2 (1947), 187–200. Webster's victory in the northeastern boundary controversy lay more in shaping public opinion than in the realm of diplomacy. Through a newspaper campaign which started in Maine and spread into other parts of the nation, he created the "illusion," Current claims, that Americans favored a compromise with Britain. The president's secret-service fund permitted Webster to employ secret agents like Francis O. J. Smith to persuade the people of Maine to compromise their extreme demands on the boundary.

Fladeland, B. *Men and Brothers* (8:69) discusses how abolitionists in both Britain and the United States feared that the extradition provision of the Webster-Ashburton treaty would lead to the return of fugitive slaves in Canada. Ashburton, Fladeland shows, assured the abolitionists that extradition did not apply to runaway slaves.

10:59 Gill, George J. "Edward Everett and the Northeastern Boundary Controversy." *New England* *Quarterly* 42:2 (1969), 201–13. Gill defends the validity of the Oswald map by relying almost exclusively on the Everett manuscripts. Though America had legitimate claim to all of the disputed territory, he admits that, as Everett agreed with Webster, the British ministry could not accept the claim and that compromise therefore was essential.

Hidy, R. W. *The House of Baring in American Trade and Finance* (8:155) explains the Baring family's keeping Webster on retainer as legal adviser during the Anglo-American controversy of the 1830s over the United States' defaulting of British bonds.

10:60 Jones, Howard. "The Attempt to Impeach Daniel Webster." *Capitol Studies* 3:1 (1975), 31–44. The abortive attempt by Democratic Representative Charles Ingersoll of Pennsylvania to bring about the retroactive impeachment of Webster in 1846 was politically inspired. Jones shows that President Tyler gave Webster prior approval to use the secret-service fund in hiring Francis O. J. Smith, Jared Sparks, and others as secret agents to help resolve the Maine boundary dispute.

Jones, W. D. *The American Problem in British Diplomacy, 1841–1861* (8:59) treats the Webster-Ashburton Treaty within the broad context of Anglo-American relations.

Jones, W. D. *Lord Aberdeen and the Americas* (8:60) argues that Aberdeen considered Maine primarily a "pine swamp" and therefore was willing to settle the boundary on almost any basis that would safeguard Canada and satisfy Parliament.

10:61 Jones, Wilbur D. "The Influence of Slavery on the Webster-Ashburton Negotiations." *Journal of Southern History* 22:1 (1956), 48–58. In addition to the African slave-trade and right-of-search controversies, Ashburton lamented that his "great plague" during the Washington talks was the *Creole* affair. Jones shows that the pact did not fulfill the British emissary's hopes for a definitive Anglo-American settlement to lay the "groundwork of a more cordial general conciliation than has ever existed since the revolutionary war."

10:62 Jones, Wilbur D. "Lord Ashburton and the Maine Boundary Negotiations." *Mississippi Valley Historical Review* 40:3 (1953), 477–90. Britain's primary interest in the negotiations with America was

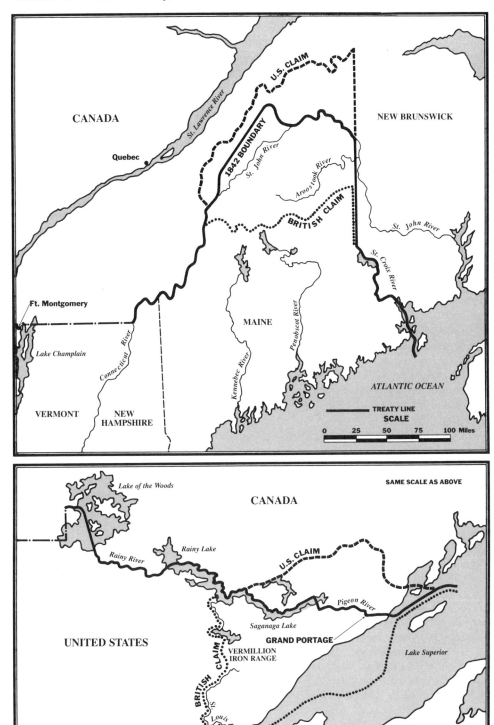

The Webster-Ashburton Treaty Boundary, 1842

to secure enough land to construct a military road between New Brunswick and Quebec. Though a chief reason for settlement was the conciliatory mood of the Peel government, Jones believes more credit should go to Ashburton for maintaining a friendly spirit during the talks.

LeDuc, T. "The Maine Frontier and the Northeastern Boundary Controversy"(10:49) demonstrates that Maine politics was the vital obstacle to the northeast boundary settlement of 1842, but Webster persuaded Maine (and Massachusetts) to accept a compromise. LeDuc also points out that when Maine declared that the concession of Rouse's Point was not enough, the Peel ministry granted the state free navigation of the St. John River in exchange for the territory it needed for a military road.

10:63   LeDuc, Thomas. "The Webster-Ashburton Treaty and the Minnesota Iron Ranges." *Journal of American History* 51:3 (1964), 476–81. Le Duc refutes the claim that the two negotiators knew in 1842 that there were rich iron deposits in the land secured by the United States in the northwest boundary settlement. In fact, LeDuc argues, their unawareness of the mineral deposits doubtless contributed to the success of the Anglo-American agreement in 1842.

10:64   Martin, Lawrence, and Bemis, Samuel Flagg. "Franklin's Red-Line Map Was a Mitchell." *New England Quarterly* 10:1 (1937), 105–11. Benjamin Franklin's map used in Paris (1782–1783) was produced by cartographer John Mitchell in 1755, and historian Jared Sparks's map discovery in the Paris archives was a d'Anville. The authors conclude that Sparks's interference in the boundary controversy in February 1842 caused the United States to give up a legitimate claim to all of the territory in dispute.

Merk, F. *Fruits of Propaganda in the Tyler Administration* (10:35) argues that Webster used the president's contingency fund to influence public opinion in Maine, and concludes that, even though its use is subject to criticism, the results were beneficial to both countries. Merk believes that both Americans and Britons in 1842 were aware of the existence of minerals in the Lake Superior-Rainy Lake regions, but that no one suspected its riches.

10:65   Merk, Frederick. "The Oregon Question in the Webster-Ashburton Negotiations." *Mississippi Valley Historical Review* 43:3 (1956), 379–404. The

Peel government's hastily prepared, uninformed, and imperialist-spirited instructions to Ashburton in 1842 impeded the Oregon negotiations with Webster in Washington, and consequently the situation was allowed to drift from an atmosphere of goodwill to crisis four years later. Reprinted in Merk (10:68).

10:66   Mills, Dudley A. "British Diplomacy and Canada: The Ashburton Treaty." *United Empire: The Royal Colonial Institute Journal* n.s. 2 (1911), 683–712. Mills discusses the northeastern boundary controversy from 1783 to 1842 and includes facsimiles of the various maps involved. This British writer concludes that the Treaty of Paris of 1783 did not entitle his country to the territory acquired during the negotiations, and therefore exonerates Ashburton of the charge of "capitulation" to the United States.

10:67   Zorn, Roman J. "Criminal Extradition Menaces the Canadian Haven for Fugitive Slaves, 1841–1861." *Canadian Historical Review* 38:4 (1957), 284–94. Zorn argues that because the British government, despite the extradition provision in the Webster-Ashburton Treaty, eventually adopted narrowly defined extradition procedures, the abolitionists were mollified, and Canada remained a haven for escaped slaves until the American Civil War.

The Oregon Treaty and Aftermath

Galbraith, J. S. *The Hudson's Bay Company as an Imperial Factor, 1821–1869* (8:154).

Goetzmann, W. H. *Exploration and Empire: The Explorer and the Scientist in the Winning of the American West* (10:71).

10:68   Merk, Frederick. *The Oregon Question: Essays in Anglo-American Diplomacy and Politics.* Cambridge: Harvard University Press, 1967. This collection of the author's previously published works traces the Oregon question from the late 18th century through its six sets of negotiations to 1846. The United

States rejected arbitration in 1846 mainly because it believed the arbiters would have divided the land involved in the triangle-shaped disputed area and thereby fail to provide America with a satisfactory seaport in the Northwest. Careful diplomacy and domestic politics in both the United States and England were more important in bringing about the final agreement.

10:69 Schafer, Joseph. "The British Attitude Toward the Oregon Question, 1815–1846." *American Historical Review* 16:2 (1911), 273–99. The author uses British Foreign Office correspondence to show that after 1815 both Britain and the United States had legitimate interests in Oregon and that the only solution was compromise.

10:70 Van Alstyne, Richard W. "International Rivalries in the Pacific Northwest." *Oregon Historical Quarterly* 46:3 (1945), 185–218. Tracing the beginnings of the international rivalries over Oregon and its adjoining waters from the 18th to 20th century, Van Alstyne shows how the initial commercial concerns changed to territorial ones by the 1820s, and how Secretary of State Daniel Webster's tripartite plan of 1842–1843 fit in with his goal of establishing American control over San Francisco as the vital connection with trade in the Far East.

MANIFEST DESTINY

See Chapter 9, "American Expansionism," which deals with the same theme as related to Texas and California.

Brack, G. M. *Mexico Views Manifest Destiny, 1821–1846* (9:142).

Goetzmann, W. H. *When the Eagle Screamed: The Romantic Horizon in American Diplomacy, 1800–1860* (9:11).

10:71 Goetzmann, William H. *Exploration and Empire: The Explorer and the Scientist in the Winning of the American West*. New York: Knopf, 1966. Goetzmann adds dimension to the study of the Oregon question by showing how the federal government sponsored much of the work of the explorer and scientist in the American west during the 19th century. Goetzmann regards John C. Frémont and Charles Wilkes as the first of the "explorer-diplomats" of the

1840s who were integrally involved in America's winning of Oregon. His work also contains a thorough essay on sources.

Graebner, N. A. *Empire on the Pacific* [1820–1848] (9:12) emphasizes the maritime factors involved in the Oregon question, especially the harbors.

10:72 Graebner, Norman A., ed. *Manifest Destiny*. Indianapolis: Bobbs-Merrill, 1968. This analogy of representative statements (1844–1860) by proponents and critics of manifest destiny shows the ideology which Americans used to justify the acquisition of Texas, California, the Southwest, and Oregon. It also beckoned to envision "all of Mexico, Cuba, Central America and beyond."

Merk, F., with Merk, L. B. *Manifest Destiny and Mission in American History: A Reinterpretation* [1830–1898] (2:52) uses the Oregon issue and Mexican War to show that manifest destiny was the sordid side of American expansionism.

Merk, F., with Merk, L. B. *The Monroe Doctrine and American Expansionism, 1843–1849* (7:154) shows that Americans believed that British involvement in Oregon violated the Monroe Doctrine and hence interfered with their manifest destiny.

10:73 Pratt, Julius W. "John L. O'Sullivan and Manifest Destiny." *New York History* 14:3 (1933), 213–34. Pratt explores O'Sullivan's efforts to express the contemporary excitement over democracy and mission felt in the United States during the 1840s.

10:74 Pratt, Julius W. "The Origin of 'Manifest Destiny.'" *American Historical Review* 32:4 (1927), 795–98. Even though the first reference in Congress to the term *manifest destiny* came in Massachusetts representative Robert C. Winthrop's speech of January 3, 1846, its initial appearance on the national scene was in a July–August 1845 editorial by John L. O'Sullivan in the *Democratic Review* which related it to the Oregon controversy.

10:75 Tuveson, Ernest L. *Redeemer Nation: The Idea of America's Millennial Role*. Chicago: University of Chicago Press, 1968. America's believed role as "redeemer nation" developed from a religious doctrine which included the concepts of chosen people, "millennial-utopian destiny" for man, mission, and an ongoing battle between good and evil. These ideas, he concludes, related to America's westward expansion by providing a rationale for the manifest destiny of the 1840s. Bibliography.

Van Alstyne, R. W. *The Rising American Empire* (2:96) traces Oregon events in the development of the American empire.

10:76 Vevier, Charles. "American Continentalism: An Idea of Expansion, 1845–1910." *American Historical Review* 65:2 (1960), 323–35. Vevier examines the intellectual bases of American expansionism, and argues that the concept of continentalism embodied both the nation's domestic accomplishments and its foreign affairs aims. The United States' national and imperial borders were continental, and its goal was to spread a distinct political society built upon the virtuous ideas contained in the doctrine of manifest destiny.

Weinberg, A. K. *Manifest Destiny: A Study of Nationalist Expansionism in American History* [1775–1935] (2:55) argues that in the case of Oregon as well as others, America's moral ideology was genuine; however, Weinberg says America's claims in Oregon resulted from a "defiant antilegalism" that ended in the compromise of 1846 because of the serious Mexican-American crisis.

Williams, W. A. *The Roots of the Modern American Empire: A Study of the Growth and Shaping of Social Consciousness in a Marketplace Society* (2:98).

BACKGROUND OF OREGON QUESTION, 1818–1840s

See "Personalities," especially Briton John McLaughlin (under "Others") and Marcus Whitman, an American.

10:77 Blue, George V. "The Oregon Question, 1818–1828: A Study of Dr. John Floyd's Efforts in Congress to Secure the Oregon Country." *Oregon Historical Quarterly* 23:3 (1922), 193–219. The Virginia representative's influence on America's growing interest in Oregon is examined.

10:78 Bourne, Edward G. "Aspects of Oregon History before 1840." *Oregon Historical Quarterly* 6:3 (1906), 255–75. Bourne examines the role of Virginia representative John Floyd, who in the early 1820s, with representative Francis Baylies, Massachusetts, realized the commercial prospects of Oregon's con-

nection with the Orient and called for American occupation of the Columbia River.

10:79 Bright, Verne. "The Folklore and History of the 'Oregon Fever.'" *Oregon Historical Quarterly* 52:4 (1951), 241–53. The lure of Oregon's rich land and the promises of the Linn bill then before the Senate captured the imagination of people hit by depression, and helped cause the Great Migration of 1843.

10:80 Cleland, Robert G. "Asiatic Trade and the American Occupation of the Pacific Coast." In the Annual Report of the American Historical Association for the Year 1914. Washington, D.C.: G.P.O., 1916, vol. 1, pp. 283–89. Cleland demonstrates that America's interest in the trade of the Orient was the primary motive for wanting Oregon.

10:81 DeVoto, Bernard. *Across the Wide Missouri*. Boston: Houghton Mifflin, 1947. Though DeVoto focuses on the events from 1832 through 1838, his narrative furnishes a background of the issues over Oregon which faced Britain and the United States by the following decade. He also discusses how missionaries served as the "advance guard" of the growing American empire. Bibliography.

10:82 DeVoto, Bernard. *The Course of Empire*. Boston: Houghton Mifflin, 1952. This volume follows the movement west up to 1806. DeVoto's account includes a brief explanation of the origins of interest in the *Ouragan* (Columbia) River in the 1760s (Indian name later changed to *Ourigan* before becoming *Oregon* in 1778).

10:83 Elliott, T.C. "An Event of One Hundred Years Ago." *Oregon Historical Quarterly* 19:3 (1918), 181–87. Elliott suggests that Secretary of State John Quincy Adams might have influenced President Monroe in 1817 to send the *Ontario,* under Captain James Biddle and with a State Department official on board, to lay American claim to the Columbia River region the following year. See A. L. Burt (6:5) for more on the *Ontario* affair.

10:84 Elliott, T. C. "The Surrender at Astoria in 1818." *Oregon Historical Quarterly* 19:4 (1918), 271–82. The British gave up Astoria under the provisions of the Treaty of Ghent, and thereby allowed the United States to raise its flag over the Columbia River basin.

10:85 Husband, Michael B. "Senator Lewis F. Linn and the Oregon Question." *Missouri Historical Review 66:1 (1971), 1–19. Linn worked from 1837 until his death in 1843 to acquire Oregon. The author concludes that Linn's work greatly publicized the Northwest and therefore aroused congressional and public interest.

10:86   Judson, Katharine B. "The British Side of the Restoration of Fort Astoria." *Oregon Historical Quarterly* 20:3/4 (1919), 243–60; 305–30. Judson uses British archival materials to establish that the restoration (1818) did not result from a victory of American ingenuity over British maneuvering.

10:87   Merk, Frederick. "The Genesis of the Oregon Question." *Mississippi Valley Historical Review* 36:4 (1950), 583–612. Merk discusses the origins of the Oregon question from the Pacific Northwest voyages of 1792 by British Captain Vancouver and American Captain Gray through the Anglo-American negotiations of 1826–1827. Reprinted in Merk (10:68).

10:88   Merk, Frederick. "The Ghost River Caledonia in the Oregon Negotiations of 1818." *American Historical Review* 55:3 (1950), 530–51. When the North West Company's Simon M'Gillivray in 1817 published the map in London showing the "ghost river Caledonia" (a distorted representation of the Skagit River south of the 49th parallel), he probably sought to influence the boundary decision from the Lake of the Woods to the Pacific Ocean. Reprinted in Merk (10:68).

10:89   Merk, Frederick. "Snake Country Expedition, 1824–25: An Episode of Fur Trade and Empire." *Mississippi Valley Historical Review* 21:1 (1934), 49–62. The Hudson's Bay Company sought to safeguard the Oregon fur trade from Americans by dominating the areas south and east of the Columbia River, and along the upper waters of the Missouri River. Reprinted in Merk (10:68).

Morison, S. E. *The Maritime History of Massachusetts, 1783–1860* (8:143) contains an informative account of how Boston merchants tried to determine whether the furs of the Northwest Coast would be sufficient to stimulate trade with China.

10:90   Rich, Edwin E. *Hudson's Bay Company, 1670–1870.* 3 vols. New York: Macmillan, 1961. Rich discusses the competition over Oregon in this classic study. Bibliography.

10:91   Ross, Frank E. "The Retreat of the Hudson's Bay Company in the Pacific North-West." *Canadian*

Historical Review 18:3 (1937), 262–80. American migration into Oregon, beginning in the 1830s, threatened Britain's Hudson's Bay Company fur-trading interests. By 1869, after years of controversy, a joint Anglo-American commission awarded the company $450,000 to withdraw its business from American soil.

10:92   Shippee, Lester B. "The Federal Relations of Oregon." *Oregon Historical Quarterly* 19:2–4 (1918), 89–133, 189–230, 283–331. This series of essays traces Oregon's relationship with the federal government (1819–1844). Shippee argues that the Oregon question had become a national concern by 1819, and examines the roles of John Floyd, John Quincy Adams, Hall J. Kelley, and Lewis F. Linn.

10:93   Winther, Oscar O. *The Great Northwest: A History.* New York: Knopf, 1947. Winther discusses the broad background of the Oregon issue. Bibliography.

THE OREGON TREATY, 1846

American Expansionism and Politics

See "Personalities," especially James K. Polk.

10:94   DeVoto, Bernard. *The Year of Decision, 1846.* Boston: Houghton Mifflin, 1942. The final volume in his trilogy (see also 10:81, 10:82) describes the spread of America's institutions and culture and the gradual development of the concept of federal union. DeVoto illustrates the effect pioneers had on the acquisition of Oregon by 1846 and carries the story to the fall of Mexico City (1847). Bibliography.

10:95   Franklin, John H. "The Southern Expansionists of 1846." *Journal of Southern History* 25:3 (1959), 323–38. Southern expansionists sought to uphold national honor by demanding all of Oregon as far north as the 54°40′ line.

Graebner, N. A. *Empire on the Pacific* [1820–1848] (9:12) argues that maritime goals drove Americans toward the harbors of the Pacific coast and a "commercial empire." Graebner maintains that the move for an Oregon compromise had to come from congressional Whigs and the metropolitan press. The loss of Vancouver Island became acceptable to Polk once the

American claim to harbors south of the Strait of Juan de Fuca was secure.

10:96 Graebner, Norman A. "Maritime Factors in the Oregon Compromise." *Pacific Historical Review* 20:4 (1951), 331–45. America's commercial interests in Asia deflated the move for 54°40' as much as the dangers of war with England or Mexico. The so-called compromise treaty of 1846 resulted from agreement between Aberdeen and Polk over a fair division of land and waterways in Oregon *before* the crisis developed in 1846. Their task was to convince both publics to accept the 49th parallel as the boundary.

10:97 Graebner, Norman A. "Politics and the Oregon Compromise." *Pacific Northwest Quarterly* 52:1 (1961), 7–14. By 1844 the Atlantic nations virtually had decided to draw the boundary at the 49th parallel, but American politics unnecessarily confused, an issue already being reduced in intensity by careful diplomacy.

10:98 Graebner, Norman A. "Polk, Politics, and Oregon." *East Tennessee Historical Society's Publications,* no. 24 (1952), 11–25. Even though Polk doubted the wisdom of the "whole of Oregon" platform, he entered the presidency determined to carry out his pledge. His compromise offer (49th parallel) in July 1845 was presented with no real hope of success, but it achieved the president's goal of making the British responsible for failure.

10:99 Howe, Daniel W. "The Mississippi Valley in the Movement for Fifty-Four Forty or Fight." *Proceedings of the Mississippi Valley Historical Association* (1912), 99–116. The debates in Congress showed that congressmen gradually came to question America's claim to all of Oregon. Besides, if the United States went to war, it might lose all of Oregon—especially if Britain and Mexico formed an alliance.

10:100 Merk, Frederick. "The Oregon Pioneers and the Boundary." *American Historical Review* 29:4 (1924), 681–99. Oregon pioneers affected the final location of the boundary by influencing the Hudson's Bay Company to move its headquarters from the Columbia River to Vancouver Island. Surrender of the Columbia, Merk continues, indicated that London did not regard the river as vital to British interests. Reprinted in Merk (10:68).

10:101 Merk, Frederick. "Presidential Fevers." *Mississippi Valley Historical Review* 47:1 (1960),

3–33. Polk's pledge of a single-term presidency unleashed a furious drive for the office which colored the Oregon debates of 1846. At the same time his move revealed the questionable nature of America's claim and suggested the possibility of war with the British unless a boundary compromise resulted. Reprinted in Merk (10:68).

10:102 Miles, Edwin A. " 'Fifty-four Forty or Fight'—An American Political Legend." *Mississippi Valley Historical Review* 44:2 (1957), 291–309. Despite the colorful accounts found in many writings on the period, this slogan did not appear in the presidential campaign of 1844. In fact, Miles continues, it came on the national scene nearly a year after Polk's inauguration.

Pletcher, D. M. *The Diplomacy of Annexation* (9:13) places the Oregon question within the broad context of Anglo-American relations, manifest destiny, and the problems with Mexico. Pletcher argues that Polk's threatening policy unnecessarily brought the Atlantic nations close to war over Oregon, and thus required traditional diplomacy to escape the perilous situation largely of his creation.

10:103 Sage, Walter N. "The Oregon Treaty of 1846." *Canadian Historical Review* 27:4 (1946), 349–67. Sage discusses the background of the Oregon question from the earliest explorations of the Northwest Coast to the signing of the treaty, and calls it a defeat for President Polk.

10:104 Schafer, Joseph. "Oregon Pioneers and American Diplomacy." In Guy Stanton Ford, ed., *Essays in American History Dedicated to Frederick Jackson Turner.* New York: Holt, 1910, pp. 35–55. By January 1843 the Peel ministry was aware of the Hudson's Bay Company's concern that American (and French) settlers in the Willamette Valley threatened its commercial life in the region. This development, Schafer concludes, created the atmosphere necessary for America's eventual diplomatic victory in 1846.

10:105 Schuyler, Robert L. "Polk and the Oregon Compromise of 1846." *Political Science Quarterly* 26:3 (1911), 443–61. The new president probably was sincere in his inaugural address when he declared that America's claim to all of Oregon was "clear and unquestionable." But his offer to compromise at the 49th parallel was also genuine, for the president believed the area north of the line was ill-suited for farming and thus good only for the fur trade.

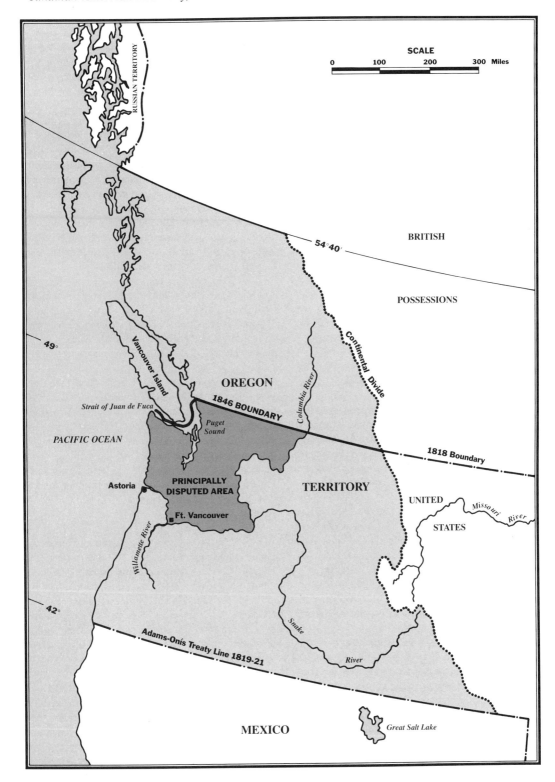

Oregon Territory Boundary Disputes and Settlements, 1846

10:106 Scott, Leslie M. "Influence of American Settlement upon the Oregon Boundary Treaty of 1846." *Oregon Historical Quarterly* 29:1 (1928), 1–19. London's interest in the area was small, it wanted peace and American trade, and it recognized that the increasing number of immigrants in the area endangered British subjects already there.

10:107 Soward, F. H. "President Polk and the Canadian Frontier." *Canadian Historical Association Annual Report* (1930), 71–80. Polk's expansionist goals dictated his actions during the Oregon crisis, and only Britain's willingness to compromise kept the peace. The president, Soward concludes, did not sacrifice the national interest in 1846 because of pressure from slaveowners, as several writers have declared.

Sprout, H., and Sprout, M. *The Rise of American Naval Power, 1776–1918* (40:117) dismisses the claim that the United States made preparations for war with Britain during the Oregon crisis of 1845–1846.

British Politics and Trade

Bourne, K. *Britain and the Balance of Power in North America, 1815–1908* (8:55) shows how the cautious military preparations taken by Peel and Aberdeen during the Oregon crisis calmed Britons who wanted war with the United States, and thereby secured wide support for the 1846 boundary compromise.

10:108 Commager, Henry S. "England and the Oregon Treaty of 1846." *Oregon Historical Quarterly* 28:1 (1927), 18–38. The United States' diplomatic triumph in 1846 largely resulted from London's distance from Oregon and relative lack of interest in the area; growing unpopularity in England of the Hudson's Bay Company; British troubles over the tariff; and the drive for peace led by Peel and Aberdeen.

10:109 Cramer, Richard S. "British Magazines and the Oregon Question." *Pacific Historical Review* 32:4 (1963), 369–82. In the two and one-half decades prior to the 1846 settlement, the major British magazines supported their government's claim for the disputed triangle above the Columbia River. Yet two journals—the *Edinburgh* in 1845 and the *Quarterly* in 1846—showed that key members of both the Whig and Tory parties were ready for compromise.

Jones, W. D. *Lord Aberdeen and the Americas* (8:60) argues that the Oregon dispute centered on Vancouver Island, the use of the Columbia River, and various other matters, and not simply on the area bounded by the Columbia and the 54°40′ line, nor even on the triangular sector outlined by the Columbia River and the 49th parallel itself.

10:110 Jones, Wilbur D., and Vinson, J. Chal. "British Preparedness and the Oregon Settlement." *Pacific Historical Review* 22:4 (1953), 353–64. The authors concentrate on Aberdeen's adept use of diplomacy and military readiness in upholding his country's prestige during the Oregon crisis. The key element in resolving the dispute was a mid-March dispatch sent from London by American minister Louis McLane which warned of specific naval preparations taken by the British to safeguard Canada and launch an attack on the United States.

Martin, T. P. "Cotton and Wheat in Anglo-American Trade and Politics, 1846–1852" (8:157) finds that Britain's interest in peace during the Oregon crisis was shown by its free-trade advocates who wanted to increase imports of American cotton and wheat.

10:111 Martin, Thomas P. "Free Trade and the Oregon Question, 1842–1846." In *Facts and Factors in Economic History: Articles by Former Students of Edwin Francis Gay.* Cambridge: Harvard University Press, 1932, pp. 470–91. America's free-trade advocates called for British repeal of the Corn Laws to placate southern and western low tariff Democrats. Britain's poor harvest in 1845 and the need for American grain, Martin argues, caused London to compromise on Oregon.

10:112 McCabe, James O. "Arbitration and the Oregon Question." *Canadian Historical Review* 41:4 (1960) 308–27. Oregon's "pine swamps" seemed unimportant to the British government, and it favored arbitration as long as there was no compromise of the Hudson's Bay Company's interests in the region and the nation's honor remained intact. The United States, however, opposed arbitration because it could not gamble on the possibility of failing to receive Pacific Ocean frontage.

10:113 Merk, Frederick. "The British Corn Crisis of 1845–46 and the Oregon Treaty." *Agricultural History* 8:3 (1934), 95–123. The "corn crisis" was not the principal factor in Britain's decision to accept the Oregon Treaty, for it was not dependent on American foodstuffs. The crucial factor, Merk concludes, was the free-trade movement in England. Reprinted in Merk (10:68).

10:114 Merk, Frederick. "British Government Propaganda and the Oregon Treaty." *American Historical Review* 40:1 (1934), 38–62. The Peel government, still wary from the charges of "capitulation" during the Webster-Ashburton negouiations, used an extensive propaganda campaign conducted by Aberdeen to persuade the British populace that settlement was no violation of national honor. Reprinted in Merk (10:68).

10:115 Merk, Frederick. "British Party Politics and the Oregon Treaty." *American Historical Review* 37:4 (1932), 653–77. The Oregon Treaty of 1846 is viewed as a British surrender which necessitated careful political maneuvering by the Peel government to withstand assaults from the Whig opposition. Reprinted in Merk (10:68).

10:116 Paullin, Charles O. "The Early Choice of the Forty-Ninth Parallel as a Boundary Line." *Canadian Historical Review* 4:2 (1923), 127–31. In 1712, at the end of Queen Anne's War, the Hudson's Bay Company wanted to limit French influence around Hudson Bay to the area below the 49th parallel. When England instructed its commissioners at Utrecht in 1713 to secure that boundary, it weakened its later claims and influenced the Oregon negotiations of 1818 and 1846.

10:117 Pratt, Julius W. "James K. Polk and John Bull." *Canadian Historical Review* 24:4 (1943), 341–49. In February 1846 Louis McLane, American minister to London, wrote Polk that Aberdeen was irritated at Secretary of State Buchanan's rejection of arbitration, the warlike tone of the congressional debate, and Polk's uncompromising stance, and hinted that Britain would not concede territory above the 49th parallel without a fight. Polk became convinced that the only solution to the boundary problem was compromise, and avoided the sting of retreat by allowing the Senate to approve such a step.

Schafer, J. "The British Attitude toward the Oregon Question, 1815–1846" (10:69) reveals that Aberdeen became convinced that his problem was to persuade Parliament and the British people that the only alternative to war was to abandon the Columbia River boundary. With the election of Polk, the British foreign secretary accepted the new executive's unofficial offer to draw the line at the 49th parallel.

10:118 Stacey, C. P. "The Hudson's Bay Company and Anglo-American Military Rivalries during the Oregon Dispute." *Canadian Historical Review* 18:3 (1937), 281–300. The anxiety felt by the British fur company during the Oregon crisis of 1845–1846 caused its owners to pressure the government in London to adopt military steps to safeguard the territory from Americans.

France and the Oregon Dispute

10:119 Blue, George V. "France and the Oregon Question." *Oregon Historical Quarterly* 34:1 (1933), 39–59; 144–63. This article contains copies of France's official correspondence (1830s–1840s) showing that the French minister in the United States (1842–1848), Alphonse Pageot, believed that southern Whigs and Democrats were convinced that war with Britain over Oregon was probable. Pageot suggested that Polk's firm stance perhaps necessitated mediation by a third power.

Blumenthal, H. *A Reappraisal of Franco-American Relations, 1830–1871* (8:82) emphasizes how France's "premature neutrality" during the Oregon crisis alienated both Britain and the United States, and caused political division at home as well. French foreign minister François Guizot based his policy upon maintaining a balance of power in North America.

10:120 Galbraith, John S. "France as a Factor in the Oregon Negotiations." *Pacific Northwest Quarterly* 44:2 (1953), 69–73. Aberdeen's concern over good relations with France determined much of his diplomacy during the Oregon crisis. Peel worried that even though the French government had no interests in that area of the world, it might cooperate with the United States in the event of an Anglo-American conflict over Oregon.

SAN JUAN ISLANDS SETTLEMENT

Clark, R. C. "The Diplomatic Mission of Sir John Rose, 1871" (14:81) argues that Rose was responsible for the establishment of the joint high commission which brought about the Treaty of Washington that settled the Canadian-American dispute over the San Juan Islands.

Cook, A. *The Alabama Claims, American Politics and Anglo-American Relations, 1865–1872* (14:82) includes the major aspects of the San Juan boundary controversy and Anglo-American relations.

10:121 DeRosier, Arthur H., Jr. "The Settlement of the San Juan Controversy." *Southern Quarterly* 4:1 (1965), 74–88. The author traces the dispute from its origins in the Oregon Treaty of 1846 through its settlement by German arbitration in 1872. DeRosier shows that this was the only United States boundary matter ever resolved by a disinterested party, and argues that it signified the growth of Anglo-American friendship and an increased sense of maturity in the Department of State.

10:122 Fish, Andrew. "The Last Phase of the Oregon Boundary Question: The Struggle for San Juan Island." *Oregon Historical Quarterly* 22:3 (1921), 161–224. The history of this controversy from its beginnings to the arbitration settlement under the Treaty of Washington of 1871.

10:123 Gough, Barry M. "British Policy in the San Juan Boundary Dispute, 1854–72." *Pacific Northwest Quarterly* 62:2 (1971), 59–68. Policies adopted by the British Foreign Office and carried out by the Royal Navy helped maintain the peace during this controversy. Though San Juan Island had strategic importance, British restraint, Gough argues, resulted from the general feeling of military and economic security enjoyed by Victorian society.

10:124 Long, John W., Jr. "The Origin and Development of the San Juan Island Water Boundary Controversy." *Pacific Northwest Quarterly* 43:3 (1952), 187–213. The controversy developed because the Oregon Treaty of 1846 did not mention the San Juan Archipelago lying between the 49th parallel and the Strait of Juan de Fuca. Long's essay traces the controversy through 1860.

10:125 Mason, Edwin C. "How We Won the San Juan Archipelago." *Collections of the Minnesota Historical Sociey* 9 (1901), 35–54. Mason, then inspector general of the Military Department of the Columbia, declares that only the measures taken by General Winfield Scott and other military officers preserved the peace.

10:126 McCabe, James O. *The San Juan Water Boundary Question.* Toronto: University of Toronto Press, 1964. British officials in the Washington negotiations unnecessarily sacrificed a strong Canadian claim by agreeing to exclude from the discussions the "Middle Channel," an area which could have been brought in because of the ambiguity of the Oregon Treaty of 1846. Bibliography.

10:127 Miller, Hunter, ed. *Northwest Water Boundary: Report of the Experts Summoned by the German Emperor as Arbitrator under Articles 34–42 of the Treaty of Washington of May 8, 1871, Preliminary to His Award Dated October 21, 1872.* University of Washington Publications in the Social Sciences, vol. 13, no. 1. Seattle: University of Washington Press, 1942. The official report of the arbitration award of 1872 refers to the Canadian-American boundary running through the Strait of Juan de Fuca.

10:128 Miller, Hunter. *San Juan Archipelago: Study of the Joint Occupation of San Juan Island.* Bellows Falls, Vt.: Windham, 1943. Controversy arose out of the Oregon Treaty of 1846 over which of the two channels jutting into the Strait of Juan de Fuca was the correct boundary. A minor episode (the "Pig War") in 1859 on the San Juan Islands lying between the channels was temporarily resolved by joint military occupation (1846–1872).

10:129 Murray, Keith A. *The Pig War.* Tacoma: Washington State Historical Society, 1968. A Pacific Northwest historical pamphlet, it includes illustrations and maps and discusses the San Juan Islands and the northwest boundary of the United States.

Nevins, A. *Hamilton Fish: The Inner History of the Grant Administration* (12:41) touches upon parts of the San Juan boundary controversy from 1870 through the German arbitration award of 1872.

10:130 Sage, Walter N. *Sir James Douglas and British Columbia.* Toronto: University of Toronto Press, 1930. Vancouver Island's longtime governor claimed throughout the 1850s that the San Juan Islands belonged to Britain.

Shippee, L. B. *Canadian-American Relations, 1849–1874* (14:80) includes an account of the San Juan boundary controversy from its origins in the Oregon Treaty of 1846 through its settlement by arbitration in 1872.

10:131 Tunem, Alfred. "The Dispute over the San Juan Water Boundary." *Washington Historical Quarterly* 23 (1932), 38–46, 133–37, 196–204, 286–300. Tumen uses printed documents to survey the controversy between the United States and Britain which centered around the location of the boundary line separating Vancouver Island from the mainland of the Washington Territory.

Civil War and More Border Troubles

U.S. CIVIL WAR, 1861–1865

10:132 Creighton, Donald G. "The United States and Canadian Confederation." *Canadian Historical Review* 39:3 (1958), 209–22. America's Civil War encouraged the movement toward a Canadian confederation. The matter of a federal union of British North America doubtless became urgent when the United States announced abrogation of the Reciprocity Treaty and warned that it would suspend the Rush-Bagot disarmament agreement affecting the Great Lakes.

10:133 MacDonald, Helen G. *Canadian Public Opinion on the American Civil War.* New York: Columbia University Press, 1926. Canadians generally split along party lines in reacting to the American Civil War as Liberals favored the North, while Conservatives supported the South. Most Canadians, however, wanted no conflict between Britain and the United States because Canada would be the battlefield. The Civil War therefore underlined the importance of the confederation movement as another way of preventing an Anglo-American war.

10:134 MacLean, Guy. "The *Georgian* Affair: An Incident of the American Civil War." *Canadian Historical Review* 42:2 (1961), 133–44. The Canadian government seized the *Georgian,* a vessel owned by a British citizen, because it suspected that it was being readied for Confederate privateering. Though the episode was minor, it suggests the existence of clandestine Confederate activities in Canada.

10:135 Néant, Hubert. "Le Canada et la guerre de secession (1860–1865)" [Canada and the war of secession (1860–1865)]. *Revue d'Histoire Diplomatique* 77 (1963), 342–61. Reports by the French consul general in Quebec, Baron Gauldrée Boilleau, claim the Canadians were pro-North during the American Civil War and feared that an Anglo-American war could grow out of the crisis.

10:136 Winks, Robin W. *Canada and the United States: The Civil War Years.* Baltimore: Johns Hopkins Press, 1960. Few people in Canada sympathized with the North during the American Civil War, especially after the *Trent* affair and after President Lincoln announced that the goal of the war was to preserve the Union. Canadians, Winks explains, were wary of further American attempts to annex them. He also shows the problems involved in persuading Americans to respect Canada's rights as a neutral during the war.

10:137 Winks, Robin W. "The Creation of a Myth: 'Canadian' Enlistments in the Northern Armies during the American Civil War." *Canadian Historical Review* 39:1 (1958), 24–40. Winks declares that the long-held claim that thousands of Canadians served with the Northern armies doubtless is a myth. He believes that Canadian public opinion probably was "more anti-Northern than anti-Southern" and that the bulk of the British North American press opposed the North.

FENIAN RAIDS, 1866–1871

See "Personalities," especially Hamilton Fish (under "Others").

10:138 D'Arcy, William. *The Fenian Movement in the United States, 1858–1886.* Washington, D.C.: Catholic University of America Press, 1947. This is a thorough account of the Irish-Americans' involvement in the secret Fenian movement which had as its principal goal the independence of Ireland from Great Britain. Bibliography.

10:139 Davis, Harold A. "The Fenian Raid on New Brunswick." *Canadian Historical Review* 36:4 (1955), 316–34. The attempt in late 1865 by two opposing factions within the Fenian Brotherhood, the American part of the Irish Revolutionary Brotherhood, to push for invasion of Canada and win control over the organization. The abortive raid encouraged the confederation movement in Canada, even though it had little impact on Maine-New Brunswick relations.

10:140 DeRosier, Arthur H., Jr. "Importance in Failure: The Fenian Raids of 1866–1871." *Southern Quarterly* 3:3 (1965), 181–97. During the late 1860s Fenian activities in Canada increased problems for those trying to resolve the *Alabama* claims dispute, fisheries' matter, San Juan question, and Manitoba-Dakota boundary issue. Also, the Fenians stirred up

Canadian annexationists in the United States, which ironically heightened Canadian nationalism.

10:141 Jenkins, Brian. *Fenians and Anglo-American Relations during Reconstruction.* Ithaca, N.Y.: Cornell University Press, 1969. The British government thought the United States should do more to restrain the Irish "Dynamiters"—especially when many of the Fenians' plots seemed to have been formulated in New York. Despite heightened emotions, both nations' determination to avert war with each other prevailed. Bibliography.

10:142 Neidhardt, W. S. "The Fenian Trials in the Province of Canada, 1866-7: A Case Study of Law and Politics in Action." *Ontario History* 66:1 (1974), 23ff. Fenian leaders in the United States did not favor the commutation of sentences dealt to the persons taken prisoner in the Fenian raids in Canada during the 1860s.

10:143 Neidhardt, W. S. " 'We've Nothing Else to Do': The Fenian Invasions of Canada, 1866." *Canada: An Historical Magazine* 1:2 (1973), 1–20. The Fenians caused an upsurge of national feeling in Canada that encouraged the confederation movement with their invasions. They hoped this "terrorist" activity would further the independence of Ireland from Great Britain.

10:144 Pritchett, John P. "The Origin of the So-Called Fenian Raid on Manitoba in 1871." *Canadian Historical Review* 10:1 (1929), 23–42. Pritchett draws from a letter from William. B. O'Donoghue to Jay Cooke of March 29, 1871, to show that the raid was a private filibustering attempt.

10:145 Senior, Hereward. "Quebec and the Fenians." *Canadian Historical Review* 48:1 (1967), 26–44. The Fenians hoped to use the United States as a base for invading British North America and, by exploiting harsh Anglo-American feelings remaining from the Civil War, perhaps bring on war. They failed in Quebec and elsewhere because of the indifference of Irish Catholics and French Canadians to their cause.

10:146 Stouffer, Allen P. "Canadian-American Relations in the Shadow of the Civil War." *Dalhousie Review* 57:2 (1977), 332–46. On the basis of American, British, and Canadian materials, Stouffer argues that Canadian-American relations improved after the 1866 Fenian raid.

RIEL REBELLIONS, 1869–1870, 1885

10:147 Gluek, Alvin C., Jr. *Minnesota and the Manifest Destiny of the Canadian Northwest: A Study in Canadian-American Relations.* Toronto: University of Toronto Press, 1965. This regional study focuses on the Red River Valley as the economic and physical link between the two nations (1821–1870).

10:148 Gluek, Alvin C., Jr. "The Riel Rebellion and Canadian-American Relations." *Canadian Historical Review* 36:3 (1955), 199–221. Canada's problems with the Riel rebellion in Rupert's Land offered American expansionists the possibility of establishing a continental republic. The uprising, however, was not indicative of widespread dissatisfaction with British North American rule—as President Grant and other Americans hoped.

10:149 Stanley, George F. G. *The Birth of Western Canada: A History of the Riel Rebellions.* London: Longmans, Green, 1936. Under the leadership of Louis Riel, the French Metis (half-breeds) and Indian tribes rose against Canadian intrusion and the imposition of an alien culture. The rebellions in 1869–1870 and in 1885 affected politics and emotions on both sides of the border. Bibliographical notes.

10:150 Warner, Donald F. "Drang Nach Norden: The United States and the Riel Rebellion." *Mississippi Valley Historical Review* 39:4 (1953), 693–712. Warner shows that America's manifest destiny aimed north toward British America as well as west and southwest, and concludes that the United States' annexation efforts during the Riel rebellion hurried the union of the Red River settlement with the Dominion of Canada.

U.S.-Canadian Military Relations

MILITARY ISSUES

Bourne, K. *Britain and the Balance of Power in North America, 1815–1908* (8:55) emphasizes the military aspects of the Canadian-American boundary question. Bourne discusses the principal strategic locations involved in Britain's concern over the northeast border after 1815. When the British began withdrawing their forces in the late 1860s and early 1870s, they did so because of a renewal of confidence in their military ability to withstand any future American threats on Canada or on their Atlantic trade.

10:151　Corey, Albert B. "Canadian Border Defence Problems after 1814 to Their Culmination in the Forties." *Canadian Historical Association Annual Report* (1938), 111–20. Corey shows that even though war had ended between Great Britain and the United States in 1814, the Canadian-American border did not stand unguarded. Not until the early 1830s had both Britain and the United States begun to implement the naval disarmament provisions contained in the Rush-Bagot agreement of 1817. The settlement of various Anglo-American difficulties by the 1840s encouraged the spread of demilitarization.

10:152　Hitsman, J. M. *Safeguarding Canada, 1763–1871.* Toronto: University of Toronto Press, 1968. A study of British plans to defend Canada against possible U.S. invasion, and the extent to which they were actually implemented. Hitsman's account, based largely on manuscript sources, is helpful on the Rush-Bagot agreement.

10:153　Stacey, C. P. "The Myth of the Unguarded Frontier, 1815–1871." *American Historical Review* 56:1 (1950), 1–18. Even though the Rush-Bagot agreement of 1817 was a major step toward promoting Anglo-American harmony, it did not provide full mutual disarmament on the Great Lakes. Small armed craft from both sides continued to regulate revenue flow, while the settlement itself had no effect on land defenses.

RUSH-BAGOT AGREEMENT, 1817

10:154　Callahan, James M. "Agreement of 1817: Reduction of Naval Forces upon the American Lakes." In the Annual Report of the American Historical Association for the Year 1895. Washington, D.C.: G.P.O., 1896, pp. 369–92. Callahan traces the origins of interest in disarming the Great Lakes from the 1790s through the Rush-Bagot agreement of 1817, and evaluates its effectiveness in the years afterward.

10:155　Callahan, James M. *The Neutrality of the American Great Lakes and Anglo-American Relations.* Baltimore: Johns Hopkins Press, 1898. Chapter 7 discusses Anglo-American problems from 1861–1896, including the continuation of the Rush-Bagot agreement of 1817.

10:156　Falk, Stanley L. "Disarmament on the Great Lakes: Myth or Reality?" *U.S. Naval Institute Proceedings* 87:12 (1961), 69–73. The Rush-Bagot agreement of 1817 did not demilitarize the Great Lakes, but it tried, and largely failed, to place limitations on naval forces. The Anglo-American nations did not end armaments along the Canadian-American frontier until they signed the Treaty of Washington in 1871.

10:157　Knaplund, Paul. "The Armaments on the Great Lakes, 1844." *American Historical Review* 40:3 (1935), 473–76. Two letters exchanged between Lord Stanley and Sir Robert Peel in 1844 about an Anglo-American dispute over armaments on the Great Lakes. Both Stanley and the American government doubted that the Rush-Bagot agreement of 1817 extended to steam-driven vessels.

Perkins, B. *Castlereagh and Adams . . . , 1812–1823* (6:12) describes the making of the Rush-Bagot agreement.

11

Civil War Diplomacy

Contributing Editor

FRANK J. MERLI
Queens College—City University of New York

Contents

Introduction

The literature of the diplomacy of the American Civil War has a number of distinct features. For one thing, the war impinged directly upon two of the major diplomatic controversies of the mid-nineteenth century—French intervention in Mexico and the postwar arbitration of the *Alabama* claims (both of which are treated in other chapters). For another, it should also be noted that much of the diplomacy of the war centered around the South's search for sea power, and while the special combination of circumstances that surrounded that search is unlikely to reappear, few episodes in our maritime experience provide more opportunities for speculation about the interrelatedness of naval power and national security.

More important, perhaps, Civil War historiography is unusually rich in "classic" accounts, works that have held up remarkably well over a long span of time. In this category, E. D. Adams's *Great Britain and the American Civil War* (11:31) and F. L. Owsley's *King Cotton Diplomacy* (11:24) are best known, though there are many others: J. P. Baxter, *Introduction of the Ironclad Warship* (11:191), C. W. Ramsdell, *Behind the Lines in the Southern Confederacy* (11:159), J. G. Randall and D. Donald, *Civil War and Reconstruction* (11:26), J. T. Scharf, *History of the Confederate States Navy . . .* (11:194), and J. C. Schwab, *The Confederate States of America, 1861–65* (11:160), to cite only a few still useful contributions. But in addition to those books that have stood the test of time, the subject has been directly enriched by an impressive number of newer works that seem destined to remain required reading for some time to come. Allan Nevins's monumental *War for the Union* (11:23) is one such study. Few would deny accolades to the mature scholarship of L. Case and W. Spencer, *The United States and France: Civil War Diplomacy* (11:34), or to A. J. and K. A. Hanna, *Napoleon III and Mexico* (15:60). Stuart Bernath's small study of the prize cases and diplomacy, *Squall across the Atlantic* (11:227), has rightly been called a model monograph, and R. Winks's more detailed *Canada and the United States:*

The Civil War Years (10:136) has been widely acclaimed. Indeed, one might say that the past decades have witnessed a virtual renaissance of Civil War diplomatic studies.

Does that mean, then, that the period is closed to further research, that there are no topics to tempt the scholar or student? A review of the literature suggests areas that need new work, fresh perspectives, updated methodology, or just more multiarchival digging. Putting the war in its proper international context is a subject that could benefit from a more sophisticated approach and a wider perspective—an "Atlantic history," as D. P. Crook calls it. If the war's impact abroad is to be properly appreciated, it is essential to understand the cultural, economic, and political links between America and Europe in the decades before the war, and to know something about the politics and personalities of those who confronted the problems raised by the war. This transnational approach, with its emphasis on a richly textured comparative history, remains in its infancy, but Robert Kelley's magnificent study in the genre, *Transatlantic Persuasion* (8:61), demonstrates what an untapped vein is awaiting the historian of proper temperament and training who will look at this subject with a fresh eye and a wider perspective. Putting the war in its proper international context is not easy, but some progress has been made. But how many American historians, if asked to name "the best one-volume history of the war," would answer as Emory Thomas and David Donald have done?

And what of the impact of the war on the world? While several works listed below touch on the theme of world aspects of the war, these have left many readers dissatisfied—and for good reason. Some work that seeks a wider dimension is currently underway, as several fine articles by Kinley Brauer have demonstrated, but more remains to be done before historians will be able to speak authoritatively about the European or the world response to the war.

Given the fascination that economic forces have for the current generation of historians, one of the oddest aspects of Civil War historiography is the lack of good studies of the war's economic impact overseas. With one or two notable exceptions, scholars have been chasing themselves in circles around the Erlanger loan and the corn versus cotton controversy without significantly advancing our understanding of international economics and diplomacy. True, a number of authors, following Owsley, have stressed the primacy of economic factors in conditioning foreign responses, but few of them make much effort to exploit the sophisticated methodologies currently available that have yielded such impressive results in other areas of study. The Gentry article (11:178) on the "success" of the Erlanger loan hints at the immense value of using new tools on old topics.

Another problem of some international importance—the blockade—also has been inadequately represented in the literature. Despite extensive treatment of that general subject (much of it centering on the romance of the runners), there is surprisingly little of substantial scholarly worth. Only a few works have begun to fill in the gaps in our knowledge of the mechanics, economics, or, even, the effectiveness of that weapon as a factor in Confederate defeat. Strange to say, there is no adequate treatment of that important subject, and J. R. Soley's venerable little book, *The Navy in the Civil War: The Blockade and Cruisers* (11:195), remains the best there is.

And what of biographies, a category well represented in recent literature? Students of the war have yearned for a modern biography of Lord Lyons, the British minister to America during the war. One hopes that someone will do for him what Daniel Carroll did so brilliantly for Henri Mercier and what John Niven did so beautifully for Gideon Welles. Neither of the Confederate commissioners to Europe has been afforded adequate biographical attention. J. M. Mason scarcely exists; for all practical purposes, he is a nonperson. The neglect of J. Slidell is more puzzling, for he seemingly possessed that elusive quality of mystery that should attract attention. Few would argue that Mason and Slidell are major figures, but each played an important part in the diplomatic history of their times. And there are others in the lower ranks who would repay the effort needed to rescue them from obscurity; such accounts might yield valuable insights.

The literature of the war's international dimension poses yet another problem. Should students accept recent works as the last work on vexing historiographical problems? Is the case of the *Trent* closed by Norman Ferris's *The Trent Affair: A Diplomatic Crisis* (11:121), as one historian has asserted? Or, to take another random example, has Mary Ellison's *Support for Secession* (11:108) "put to rest" the thorny question of the attitude of British workers toward the war? So provocative an assessment should touch off debate, not close it. As Kevin Logan has suggested in his "The Bee-Hive Newspaper and British Working Class Attitudes toward the American Civil War" (11:115), the special circumstances of Lancashire might not apply to other regions of England. Detailed investigations would be required to validate Ellison's sweeping generalizations about one of the war's most intractable controversies. One suspects that the final verdict is not yet in.

To date, no one has taken up the challenge that Frank Owsley issued nearly fifty years ago—to write a diplomatic history of the United States for the Civil War era. "And what a history it might be," Owsley speculated in his preface to the original edition of *King Cotton Diplomacy,* if some scholar were "willing to spend ten years or more in its preparation." Strange to say, more than a century after Appomattox, the great work on Civil War diplomacy remains unwritten.

_____

I wish to thank the many people who reviewed sections of this chapter and whose comments have enhanced its value.

Resources and Overviews

RESEARCH AIDS

While pertinent bibliographies and reference aids are listed here, there are more extensive lists in Chapter 1.

Bibliographies

Bemis, S. F. and Griffin, G. G., eds. *A Guide to the Diplomatic History of the United States, 1775–1921* (1:57), pp. 316–59, retains a certain utility for measuring the content of more recent works, particularly at putting the Civil War in a wider context.

11:1 Ferris, Norman B. "Diplomacy." In A. Nevins; J. Robertson, Jr.; and B. Wiley, eds., *Civil War Books: A Critical Bibliography.* 2 vols. Baton Rouge: Louisiana State University Press, 1967, vol. 1, pp. 241–78. The compiler has here selected and annotated nearly 400 items dealing with international aspects of the American Civil War. The list contains good samples of the literature, including German, Austrian, and French works. In some cases the comments are helpful; in others they are misleading or too opinionated.

Hanham, H. J., ed. *Bibliography of British History, 1851–1914* (8:1) contains a good, though brief, section on Anglo-American relations during the Civil War years.

Higham, R., ed. *A Guide to the Sources of United States Military History* (1:47) has materials in chapters 7–9 which relate to the Civil War era.

11:2 Nevins, Allan; Robertson, James, Jr.; and Wiley, Bell, eds. *Civil War Books: A Critical Bibliography.* 2 vols. Baton Rouge: Louisiana State University Press, 1967–1969. In addition to its entries for the domestic aspects of the war, this set contains a section entitled "The Navies," by Thomas Wells (vol. 1, pp. 217–39). Of the estimated 50,000 to 60,000 items relating to the Civil War, the Nevins bibliography attempts to evaluate some 5,000 to 6,000.

11:3 Smith, Myron J., Jr. *American Civil War Navies: A Bibliography.* Metuchen, N.J.: Scarecrow, 1972. This work, essentially an alphabetical listing of nearly 4,000 items in Union and Confederate naval history, has provided "a tool of enduring value" to historians. Beginning students might easily underrate the utility of this work, but after one has become familiar with its content and arrangement, it provides many research clues, even for advanced students.

11:4 Stoflet, Ada M., and Rogers, Earl M., comps. "A Bibliography of Civil War Articles, 1972." *Civil War History* 19:3 (1973), 238–76. Bibliographical essays such as this one appear annually in *Civil War History,* and provide the best way of keeping abreast of current scholarship. These essays range from general topics and antebellum government and politics to Reconstruction; also included are sections on foreign affairs, naval and military matters.

11:5 U.S. Department of the Navy. *Civil War Naval Chronology, 1861–1865.* Washington, D.C.: Department of Navy, Naval History Division, 1971. Though, strictly speaking, this chronology is not a bibliography, it is a day-by-day summary of naval activity, and it is filled with interesting illustrative material: battle scenes, extracts from letters, and contemporary paintings and drawings.

Document Collections

Other, more general collections of documents have been collected in Chapter 1.

11:6 France. Ministère des Affaires Etrangères. *Documents diplomatique (livres jaunes)* [Diplomatic documents (blue books)]. 13 vols. Paris: Imprimerie Impériale, 1860–1869. For other references to sources for continental and French materials, see the extensive bibliography in Case and Spencer's *The United States and France* (11:34) and Carroll's biography of Mercier (11:93), as well as the section on diplomacy by Ferris (11:1).

11:7 Richardson, James D., ed. *The Messages and Papers of Jefferson Davis and the Confederacy Including Diplomatic Correspondence, 1861–1865.* 2 vols. New York: Chelsea House; Bowker (1905), 1966. Allan Nevins's comprehensive introduction to this new edition ("The Embattled Confederacy: Its Tasks and Its Leadership") reminds us of the valuable place that this collection retains in Civil War historiography. Volume 1 contains the papers of Davis, while volume 2 has the diplomatic correspondence. The set should be used in conjunction with other collections, especially the *Official Records* (11:8).

11:8 U.S. Army. *The War of the Rebellion: Official Records of the Union and Confederate Armies.* 130 vols. Washington, D.C.: G.P.O., 1882–1900. This much tapped mother lode of material remains, as Emory Thomas noted, the sine qua non of works on the military history of the war. Though much exploited by generations of historians, its utility has not been exhausted.

U.S. Congress. *Congressional Globe: 23rd Congress to 42nd Congress, 2 December 1833–3 March 1873* (1:353).

U.S. Department of State. *Correspondence Concerning Claims against Great Britain* (14:7) offers, if one learns the knack of using this collection, a great deal of information about Civil War diplomacy.

U.S. Department of State. *Foreign Relations of the United States* (1:358) includes the usual diplomatic reports. The 19 volumes for the years 1861 to 1868 contain much material that was enclosed in dispatches from representatives abroad. The first sequences of volumes in this set remain an impressive monument to William H. Seward.

11:9 U.S. Department of the Navy. *Official Records of the Union and Confederate Navies in the War of the Rebellion.* 30 vols. Washington, D.C.: G.P.O., 1894–1927. The *ORN*, as this set is commonly called, is a valuable source of naval affairs during the war. In addition to day-to-day naval operations, the set contains large amounts of diplomatic correspondence. The *ORN* should be used in conjunction with its more ponderous companion set, the *ORA*, the official records of the Union and Confederate armies (11:8).

Indexes and Guides

11:10 Aimone, Alan C. "Official Data Gold Mine: The Official Records of the Civil War." *Lincoln Herald* 74:4 (1972), 192–202. This bibliographic essay or guide to one of the major resources of Civil War history provides a much needed service. The author traces the history of the set, points out some of the difficulties of using it, suggests remedies for them, and mentions some recent reference aids.

11:11 Beers, Henry P. *Guide to the Archives of the Government of the Confederate States of America.* Washington, D.C.: National Archives and Records Service, 1968. This volume is a companion to *Guide to Federal Archives Relating to the Civil War,* published by the National Archives in 1962 (11:13). In addition to describing archival materials, the editor provides in each section "bibliographical references, notations of finding aids, documentary publications, and other pertinent information." The *Guide* is a treasure trove of research material, with the sections on the Navy and State Departments most useful.

11:12 Jones, Robert H. "The American Civil War in the British Sessional Papers: Catalog and Commentary." *Proceedings of the American Philosophical Society* 107:5 (1963), 415–26. The author provides a much needed commentary on the uses of one of the great source collections for Civil War history. The author's first footnotes discuss the availability of the microprint edition of this valuable source; in note no. 20 he provides some hints on the sometimes confusing indexes and cross references. Also included is an index to American materials appearing in the yearly volumes.

11:13 Munden, Kenneth W., and Beers, Henry P., eds. *Guide to Federal Archives Relating to the Civil War.* Washington, D.C.: National Archives and Records Service, 1962. Although primarily a guide to documentary sources, this work, like its companion volume on Confederate archives (11:11), contains a

useful commentary on the literature. The sections on the State Department and naval affairs will perhaps have most utility for students of diplomacy. The editors have not restricted themselves to the war years but have included material on claims and other matters that stretched into the postwar years.

11:14 U.S. Department of Navy. *Official Records of the Union and Confederate Navies in the War of the Rebellion: General Index.* New York: Antiquarian Press (1927), 1961. This new edition is an exact photocopy of the 1927 volume. In addition, Philip Van Doren Stern has furnished an introduction that gives a capsule history of the publication of these volumes, offers advice on their use, and summarizes material in the *ORN* volumes (11:9).

OVERVIEWS

North, South, and Civil War

11:15 Barker, Alan. *The Civil War in America.* Garden City, N.Y.: Doubleday, 1961. This brief book provides an introduction (1861–1865) for both the general reader and the college student. Written by an Englishman, it has a number of useful comments and possesses the advantage of a foreign perspective.

11:16 Blumenthal, Henry. "Confederate Diplomacy: Popular Notions and International Realities." *Journal of Southern History* 32:2 (1966), 151–71. A seminal article, it looks at the critical importance of foreign responses to the South's bid for independence. Impressively researched, cogently argued, and required reading, it is a refreshing contrast to most standard views.

11:17 Brogan, Denis W. "A Fresh Appraisal of the Civil War." In his *American Aspects.* New York: Harper & Row, 1964, pp. 22–51. From his perspective as a European student of American affairs, Sir Denis's perceptive comments are noteworthy for their sympathetic view of both sides and for their fairminded assessments of the war.

11:18 Callahan, James M. *Diplomatic History of the Southern Confederacy.* Baltimore: John Hopkins Press, 1901. This work includes an account of the acquisition of the so-called Pickett Papers, a major collection of documents on diplomatic and naval affairs in the South.

11:19 Coulter, E. Merton. *The Confederate States of America, 1861–1865*. Baton Rouge: Louisiana State University Press, 1950. This still useful study is rather heavier on fact than upon interpretation. Chapter 9, "Diplomacy," is an adequate summary, though much outdated. This book might be compared to Thomas's *The Confederate Nation* (11:29) to measure the progress of historical scholarship in a generation. Bibliography.

11:20 Donald, David, ed. *Why the North Won the Civil War*. Baton Rouge: Louisiana State University Press, 1960. In every way a superior set of essays, this collection might have been more descriptively titled *Why the South Lost*. The essays represent the mature views of a number of eminent scholars.

11:21 Eaton, Clement. *A History of the Southern Confederacy*. New York: Macmillan, 1954. This work is generally regarded as one of the best modern surveys; it certainly gets a lot into a little space, while at the same time managing to provide a number of provocative assessments. The chapter on foreign relations, though dated, is a good resume.

11:22 Jones, Robert H. *Disrupted Decades: The Civil War and Reconstruction Years*. New York: Scribner's, 1973. This work, essentially a text for college courses, treats foreign affairs in brief compass (1850–1876).

11:23 Nevins, Allan. *The War for the Union*. 4 vols. New York: Scribner's, 1959–1971. This work of a master historian sums up for his generation the history of the Civil War era; it has rightly been acclaimed a "landmark in our historical literature." It may be consulted on military, technical, and political aspects of the war. Extensive bibliography.

11:24 Owsley, Frank L. *King Cotton Diplomacy: Foreign Relations of the Confederate States of America*. 2d ed. Chicago: University of Chicago Press, 1959. A pioneering work of research and synthesis, it is sympathetic to the South and stresses the economic factors prompting British responses. Although some of its assumptions and conclusions have been questioned, it remains a basic source for the study of the international dimension of the American Civil War. Extensive bibliography.

11:25 Potter, David M. *The South and the Sectional Conflict*. Baton Rouge: Louisiana State University Press, 1968. This collection of essays contains some of the author's best efforts to grapple with the enigmas of southern history (1800–1865). Readers of this *Guide* may wish to start with the two final essays, "Jefferson Davis and the Political Factors in Confederate Defeat" and "The Civil War in the History of the Modern World: A Comparative View."

11:26 Randall, James G. and Donald, David. *The Civil War and Reconstruction*. 2d rev. ed. Boston: Heath (1937), 1969. In many ways this book may still be the best way to get into the subject of Civil War history. Extensive bibliography.

11:27 Rhodes, James F. *History of the United States from the Compromise of 1850 to 1877*. 7 vols. New York: Harper; Macmillan, 1893–1906. This work is a representative example of the older multivolume histories of the war period. More contemporary studies of the war have still found it useful; but it has been replaced by Nevins (11:23).

11:28 Rhodes, James F. *Lectures on the American Civil War Delivered before the University of Oxford in Easter and Trinity Terms, 1912*. New York: Macmillan, 1913. The third lecture has a summary of foreign affairs during the war. Those remarks, up-to-date and accurate for their time and place, are now perhaps more useful for intellectual history than they are for the study of diplomacy.

11:29 Thomas, Emory M. *The Confederate Nation*. New York: Harper & Row, 1979. The chapter, "Foreign Relations of a Nascent Nation" is a gem of compression and sensible commentary. The notes and extensive bibliography are studded with provocative assessments.

11:30 Vandiver, Frank E. *Their Tattered Flags: The Epic of the Confederacy*. New York: Harper & Row, 1970. Generally, and rightly, regarded as "the best general reader's history," it contains some challenging opinions about the Confederacy and the reputation of its president.

Civil War and Foreign States

11:31 Adams, Ephraim D. *Great Britain and the American Civil War*. 2 vols. New York: Longmans, Green, 1925. Though a bit dated, it has aged remarkably well and, if one makes allowances for its pro-British stance, it remains the starting place for all students of the British response to the war.

Allen, H. C. *Great Britain and the United States: A History of Anglo-American Relations (1783–1952).* (2:232) has much to say on the Civil War era and, though based mostly on printed works, Allen's commentary is marked by discernment and comprehensive knowledge of the war issues and their impact on British society.

11:32 Beloff, Max. "Historical Revision No. CXVIII: Great Britain and the American Civil War." *History* 37 (1952), 40–48. This suggestive, thought-provoking article ranks with the essay by Norman Graebner's "Northern Diplomacy and European Neutrality (11:36), as a starting point for reassessments of the European response to the Civil War.

11:33 Burn, W. L. *The Age of Equipoise: A Study of the Mid-Victorian Generation.* London: Allen & Unwin, 1964. This work captures, as few books do, the mood of a generation (1852–1867). While the author plays down political history, he is very astute about the ways in which the political milieu circumscribed governmental initiatives.

11:34 Case, Lynn M., and Spencer, Warren F. *The United States and France: Civil War Diplomacy.* Philadelphia: University of Pennsylvania Press, 1970. A superior work of scholarship, it is based on a solid foundation of sources, uses rare private documents to flesh out the official records, and is fair minded in its conclusions. For students of Civil War diplomacy this volume is a mine of new information. And it is in the book's favor that it has a European orientation, rather than the traditional view from London or Washington.

11:35 Crook, David P. *The North, the South, and the Powers, 1861–1865.* New York: Wiley, 1974. Crook's work is "the best summary and interpretation of the diplomacy of the war era." It is, indeed, a remarkable work of synthesis, pregnant with critical and fair-minded observations. Extensive bibliography.

11:36 Graebner, Norman. "Northern Diplomacy and European Neutrality." In David Donald, ed. *Why the North Won the Civil War.* Baton Rouge: Louisiana State University Press, 1960, pp. 49–75. The essay is far-ranging, incisive, fair minded, and it gives off intellectual sparks, as well as demonstrating the author's mastery of theme and sources. The piece remains required reading, for there is no better place to begin an orientation to a complex subject.

11:37 Hyman, Harold, ed. *Heard Round the World: The Impact Abroad of the Civil War.* New York: Knopf, 1969. The essays trace the impact of the war on Britain, France, central Europe, Russia, Canada, and Latin America. They are an early attempt to widen the scope of scholarship on the international dimensions of the war. The notes give a good introduction to the literature as of 1969.

11:38 Jenkins, Brian. *Britain and the War for the Union* [1860–1862]. Montreal: McGill–Queen's University Press, 1974. This is a two-volume treatment of the entire Anglo-American Civil War experience. Reviewers have raised a number of questions about the style, emphasis, "occasionally erroneous interpretation of Union policy," and methodology.

11:39 Jones, Robert H. "Anglo-American Relations, 1861–1865: Reconsidered." *Mid-America* 45:1 (1963), 36–49. This article has a particular virtue for students: based largely on the British *Sessional Papers* (1:364), it thus provides access to primary material that students may evaluate for themselves.

11:40 Jordan, Donaldson, and Pratt, Edwin J. *Europe and the American Civil War.* Boston: Houghton Mifflin, 1931. A pioneering and influential study of European public opinion and the war, it helped create the view that British bourgeois and nonconformist opinion strongly supported the Union. While that view has been challenged recently, the authors' array of evidence still commands respect, and their concluding chapter is still worth reading.

11:41 Nevins, Allan. "Britain, France, and the War Issues." In his *The War for the Union: War Becomes Revolution, 1862–1863.* New York: Scribner's, 1960, pp. 242–74. This chapter merits special mention because of its superior summation of the war's issues in their international dimension; it should be required reading for all students of Civil War diplomacy. Extensive bibliography.

11:42 Sideman, Belle B., and Friedman, Lillian, eds. *Europe Looks at the Civil War.* New York: Orion, 1960. The editors have sought in this far-ranging set of excerpts from published materials to capture the human interest appeal and a sense of excitement. For American students, perhaps the most useful portions of the work are those that provide translations from contemporary French writings on the Civil War.

11:43 Stern, Philip Van Doren. *When the Guns Roared: World Aspects of the American Civil War.*

Garden City, N.Y.: Doubleday, 1965. Much of this work focuses on England and France. Though this work is a "popular" history, the author has done an impressive amount of work in out-of-the-way archives. The book, however, has a kaleidoscopic quality that many many find disturbing.

Winks, R. W. *Canada and the United States* (10:136) is a pioneering and definitive work in an area of Civil War history too often neglected. The "Note on Sources" and evaluations contained therein serve as a model for what annotation can do to improve the utility of a bibliography.

Personalities

UNION

Charles Francis Adams

11:44   Adams, Charles Francis, Jr. *Charles Francis Adams*. Boston: Houghton Mifflin, 1900. This work, long outdated, retains its utility for an Adams's-eye view of Civil War diplomacy. Today, no one would read it without comparing it to Duberman's superb treatment.

11:45   Adams, Charles Francis. *A Cycle of Adams Letters, 1861–1865*. 2 vols. Ed. by Worthington C. Ford. Boston: Houghton Mifflin, 1920. Filled with astute and often biting comment on a wide variety of subjects, the volumes bear the imprint of their famous correspondents.

11:46   Duberman, Martin B. *Charles Francis Adams, 1807–1886*. Boston: Houghton Mifflin, 1961. This biography was an early entry into the renaissance of scholarly revision of the international dimension of the Civil War. The work is balanced, judicious, and represents the virtues that a new generation of scholars are bringing to the study of Civil War diplomacy. Extensive bibliography.

John Bigelow

Bigelow, J. *France and the Confederate Navy, 1862–1865* (11:132).

11:47   Bigelow, John. *Retrospections of An Active Life*. 5 vols. New York: Baker & Taylor, 1909–1913.

These autobiographical volumes (1817–1911) constitute a mine of information about the American consul and minister in Paris during the war. They retain the imprint of their author's personality and strong opinions.

11:48   Clapp, Margaret. *Forgotten First Citizen: John Bigelow*. Boston: Little, Brown, 1947. Clapp's good, brief account of an important Civil War figure could have been improved by the use of French sources. Still, it provides a good starting place for a look at Bigelow's role.

Abraham Lincoln

Borit, G. S. "Lincoln's Opposition to the Mexican War" (9:173).

11:49   Lincoln, Abraham. *The Collected Works of Abraham Lincoln*. 9 vols. Ed. by Roy P. Basler, et al. New Brunswick, N.J.: Rutgers University Press, 1953. Among the many uses of this collection is its utility in helping one to weigh the relative influence of the president and secretary of state in the formulation and implementation of foreign policy.

11:50   Monaghan, Jay. *Diplomat in Carpet Slippers: Abraham Lincoln Deals with Foreign Affairs*. Indianapolis: Bobbs-Merrill, 1945. A sprightly account, it perhaps exaggerates the role of the president in the handling of foreign affairs. Critics have dubbed it "lightweight," but it merits very high marks for readability.

11:51   Randall, J. G. *Lincoln the President*. 4 vols. New York: Dodd, Mead, 1945–1955. This detailed life touches only lightly on foreign affairs (mostly in volume 3), but it has some perceptive comments on the war's international dimension. Extensive bibliography.

11:52   Thomas, Benjamin. *Abraham Lincoln: A Biography*. New York: Knopf, 1952. This work, perhaps the best of the one-volume lives of Lincoln (1809–1865), was designed primarily for the reading general public and beginning students. While it has little of value on foreign affairs, it may serve as a prelude to more detailed treatments of the Civil War president.

William H. Seward

11:53   Brauer, Kinley J. "Seward's 'Foreign War Panacea': An Interpretation." *New York History* 55:2 (1974), 133–57. This article seeks to correct the impression of Seward's famous foreign war panacea

(1861) as a flight of madness. The author sees the threats implied in that document as part of a consistent policy to thwart foreign influence in American affairs. The article should be compared with Ferris (11:102) and with Patrick Sowle's "A Reappraisal of Seward's Memorandum of April 1, 1861, to Lincoln," *Journal of Southern History* 33:2 (May 1967), pp. 234–39.

Ferris, N. B. *Desperate Diplomacy: William H. Seward's Foreign Policy, 1861* (11:102).

Paolino, E. N. *The Foundations of the American Empire: William Henry Seward and U.S. Foreign Policy* (15:18) omits the diplomacy of the Civil War to concentrate on American expansion. Provocative though it is, it perhaps raises more questions than it answers.

11:54 Seward, William H. *William H. Seward: An Autobiography, with a Memoir of His Life, and Selections from His Letters.* 3 vols. Ed. by Frederick Seward. New York: Derby & Miller, 1877. For a variant of this citation see Owsley (11:24); and for another variation on the theme, see Ferris (11:102). The title provides the annotation.

11:55 Seward, William H. *The Works of William H. Seward.* 5 vols. Ed. by George E. Baker. Boston: Houghton Mifflin, 1884. The fifth volume in this set is sometimes cited separately as *The Diplomatic History of the War for the Union.*

11:56 Sharrow, Walter G. "William Henry Seward and the Basis for American Empire, 1850–1860." *Pacific Historical Review* 36:4 (1967), 325–42. The article explores an important facet of Seward's prewar ideology. The balance of vision and reality merits "the title of statesman" for Seward.

11:57 Van Deusen, Glyndon G. *William Henry Seward.* New York: Oxford University Press, 1967. This volume is the standard work on Seward (1801–1872), if not the final word. It is comprehensive, thoroughly researched, and fair in its appraisal of Lincoln's secretary of state, who surely was significant in American Civil War diplomacy.

11:58 Warren, Gordon H. "Imperial Dreamer: William Henry Seward and American Destiny." In Frank J. Merli and Theodore A. Wilson, eds. *Makers of American Diplomacy from Benjamin Franklin to Henry Kissinger.* 2 vols. New York: Scribner's, 1974, vol. 1, pp. 195–221. This essay is a good place for the student to begin wrestling with the many faceted man who was guiding Union diplomacy. For while stress-

ing the work of the statesman and diplomat, Warren does not neglect Seward the expansionist and politician—indeed, he even finds room for Seward the dreamer.

Charles Sumner

Cohen, V. H. "Charles Sumner and the *Trent* Affair" (11:119).

11:59 Donald, David H. *Charles Sumner and the Rights of Man.* New York: Knopf, 1970. This magisterial study stresses Sumner's impact on foreign affairs (1861–1871), his role in the Senate Foreign Relations Committee, his attitudes toward England, and his part in the resolution of the *Trent* affair.

Sumner, C. *Memoirs and Letters of Charles Sumner* (12:70).

Gideon Welles

11:60 Niven, John. *Gideon Welles: Lincoln's Secretary of the Navy.* New York: Oxford University Press, 1973. This work provides a detailed, analytical assessment of the Union navy's role in thwarting southern aspirations toward independence and of Welles's key role in implementing the strategy that helped strangle the South. Bibliography.

11:61 Welles, Gideon. *Diary of Gideon Welles.* Ed. by Howard K. Beale. 3 vols. Rev. ed. New York: Norton, 1960. As John Niven has recently remarked, the Civil War and Reconstruction diaries of Welles "make up the most vivid and certainly the fullest inside account we have of those trying times." But he further notes that the *Diary* (1862–1867) has "misled generations of historians" who have used it improperly. Beale's editing is a model of careful scholarship and this edition makes the 1911 one of John T. Morse very nearly obsolete.

Charles Wilkes

11:62 Henderson, Daniel. *The Hidden Coasts: A Biography of Admiral Charles Wilkes.* New York: Sloane, 1953. Henderson's work is marred by excessive veneration of its subject (1798–1877), becoming as one critic put it "an exercise in hagiography." This work should be compared to the essay by Geoffrey Smith on Wilkes (11:66).

11:63 Jeffries, William. "The Civil War Career of Charles Wilkes." *Journal of Southern History* 11:3 (1945), 324–48. This article was one of the first modern reexaminations of the role of Wilkes in the events of the Civil War, and the author assesses that role carefully and perceptively.

11:64 Long, John S. "Glory-Hunting off Havana: Wilkes and the *Trent* Affair." *Civil War History* 9:2 (1963), 133–44. Long attempts to evaluate the "motives and justifications" of the man who brought on the most famous incident (1861–1862) in Civil War diplomacy. Wilkes was very much his own man, one who followed his own star and one who had an "insatiable thirst for naval glory."

11:65 Morgan, Williams J., et al., eds. *Autobiography of Rear Admiral Charles Wilkes: U.S. Navy, 1798–1877.* Washington, D.C.: Department of Navy, Naval History Division, 1978. A major source for the study of Wilkes's career is now made available for a wider public, and this work offers fascinating comments on politics, naval affairs, and 19th-century science. The manuscript autobiography revealed its author's "driving ambition, egotism, and atrocious penmanship."

11:66 Smith, Geoffrey S. "Charles Wilkes and the Growth of American Naval Diplomacy." In Frank J. Merli and Theodore A. Wilson, eds., *Makers of American Diplomacy from Benjamin Franklin to Henry Kissinger.* 2 vols. New York: Scribner's, 1974, vol. 1, pp. 135–63. The career of Wilkes—and it included more than the *Trent* imbroglio—demonstrates the way in which naval officers were in fact "the sharp cutting edge of diplomacy." Bibliographical essay.

Others

11:67 Dyer, Brainerd. "Thomas H. Dudley." *Civil War History* 1:4 (1955), 401–13. This unfootnoted article provides a good starting place for a study of Dudley (1819–1893), a man whose efforts to thwart Confederate shipbuilding in England are relatively unknown. A more detailed biographical sketch is printed with documents in the *American Philosophical Society Transactions* 34:147 (May 1895); also see "Three Critical Periods in our Relations with England during the Late War: Personal Recollections of Thomas H. Dudley, the Late United States Consul at Liverpool," *Pennsylvania Magazine of History and Biography* 17 (1893), 34–54.

11:68 Fox, Gustavus Vasa. *Confidential Correspondence of Gustavus Vasa Fox, Assistant Secretary of the Navy, 1861–1865.* 2 vols. Ed. by Robert M. Thompson and Richard Wainwright. New York: Naval History Society, 1918–1919. Though this set is disappointing on foreign affairs, it is extremely good on matters of technological innovation in naval war. And Fox's role in Civil War naval matters must take into account the appraisal of Niven's biography of Gideon Welles (11:60).

Kaplan, L. S. "The Brahmin as Diplomat in Nineteenth Century America: Everett, Bancroft, Motley, Lowell" (8:20) manages to weave into his analysis of a quartet of 19th-century diplomats (1840–1870) an impressive number of acute observations about the nature of Anglo-American relations in the 1860s.

11:69 Moran, Benjamin. *The Journal of Benjamin Moran, 1857–1865.* 2 vols. Ed. by Sarah A. Wallace and Frances E. Gillespie. Chicago: University of Chicago Press, 1948. This invaluable source provides an inside view of Civil War diplomacy as seen by the secretary of the American legation in London. Moran was a shrewd and waspish commentator. Not only is this work a tool for diplomatic history, it is a mine of social history as well.

11:70 Owsley, Harriet Chappell. "Henry Shelton Sanford and Federal Surveillance Abroad, 1861–1865." *Mississippi Valley Historical Review* 48:2 (1961), 211–28. This article adds a new dimension to an understanding of the Union's overseas intelligence network. The author suggests that Federal surveillance abroad played an important—and underrated—part in Union success.

11:71 Seward, Frederick. *Reminiscences of a Wartime Statesman and Diplomat, 1830–1915.* New York: Putnam's, 1916. Seward's account contains some useful and interesting commentary on wartime Washington, and is perhaps best in its private appraisals of men and events.

Thomas, B. P., and Hyman, H. M. *Stanton: The Life and Times of Lincoln's Secretary of War* (40:94).

CONFEDERATE

Also see "Confederate Purchasing Abroad," below, for various commercial agents.

James D. Bulloch

11:72 Roberts, William P. "James Dunwoody Bulloch and the Confederate Navy." *North Carolina Historical Review* 24:3 (1947), 315–66. An article that shows some appreciation for Bulloch's work (1861–

1865), but it lacks the sophistication of more modern treatments.

11:73 Willis, Virginia Bullock. "James Dunwoody Bulloch." *Sewanee Review* 34:4 (1926), 386–401. Willis's short piece is noteworthy for the genealogical material it contains about the chief Confederate naval agent in England.

Jefferson Davis

11:74 Davis, Jefferson. *Jefferson Davis, Constitutionalist: His Letters, Papers, and Speeches.* 10 vols. Ed. by Dunbar Roland. Jackson: Mississippi Department of Archives and History, 1923. Long the standard collection cited in works on the Civil War, this set will soon be replaced by the Monroe and McIntosh edition (11:75).

11:75 Davis, Jefferson. *The Papers of Jefferson Davis.* 2 vols. to date. Ed. by Haskell Monroe and James T. McIntosh. Baton Rouge: Louisiana State University Press, 1971. This series promises to be definitive.

11:76 Eaton, Clement. *Jefferson Davis.* New York: Free Press, 1977. Jefferson Davis (1808–1889) seems to defeat his biographers. This present volume has left critics dissatisfied. Until a better one appears, students may rely upon this work, which contains a good chapter on Davis and diplomacy, as well as an intriguing speculation on the Sphinx of the South.

11:77 McWhiney, Grady. "Jefferson Davis and the Art of War." *Civil War History* 21:2 (1975), 101–12. McWhiney makes one or two comments about one of the problems of Civil War diplomacy: to what extent did Davis's view of the navy impede the achievement of southern objectives abroad?

11:78 Patrick, Rembert W. *Jefferson Davis and His Cabinet.* Baton Rouge: Louisiana State University Press, 1944. The author has provided ministudies of the men who comprised the Confederate cabinet. Readers of this *Guide* will perhaps find the sketches of Mallory, Toombs, Hunter, and Benjamin most useful. In many respects the work is outdated; the Mallory profile was drawn before the appearance of Durkin's biography (11:81), but the author's observations still merit attention.

11:79 Vandiver, Frank E. *Jefferson Davis and the Confederate State: An Inaugural Lecture Delivered before the University of Oxford on 26 February 1964.* Oxford: Clarendon Press, 1964. This lecture, filled with many keen observations of Davis as diplomat, provides a provocative assessment of the Confederate president and his work. But the author's sympathy for his subject may carry the unwary reader farther than it is prudent to go.

11:80 Whitridge, Arnold. "Jefferson Davis and the Collapse of the Confederacy." *History Today* 11:2 (1961), 79–89. This popular piece by a distinguished British journalist-historian is critical of Davis. (The article is one of several *History Today* published on the general topic of Britain and the American Civil War during its centennial.)

Stephen R. Mallory

11:81 Durkin, Joseph T. *Stephen R. Mallory: Confederate Navy Chief.* Chapel Hill: University of North Carolina Press, 1954. This is a major source for the study of southern naval strategy (1861–1865) and Mallory's part in it. Durkin's work is fair minded, sympathetic, and researched in a wide variety of sources. Bibliography.

11:82 Melvin, Philip. "Steven Russell Mallory: Southern Naval Statesman." *Journal of Southern History* 10:2 (1944), 137–60. This is an early attempt to give Mallory some of the recognition he deserves. Its sources are limited mostly to printed records.

James M. Mason

11:83 Mason, Virginia. *The Public Life and Diplomatic Correspondence of James M. Mason: With Some Personal History by His Daughter.* Roanoke, Va.: Stone Printing, 1903. Mason (1798–1871) has fared even less well than Slidell in the historical literature. One suspects that the minister's pompous personality would try the patience of any biographer.

11:84 Sears, Louis M. "A Confederate Diplomat at the Court of Napoleon III." *American Historical Review* 26:2 (1921), 255–81. Based almost exclusively on the J. M. Mason Papers in the Library of Congress, this is an adequate assessment for its time and place; it should be compared to the more recent appraisal contained in Case and Spencer (11:34).

John Slidell

11:85 Sears, Louis M. *John Slidell.* Durham, N.C.: Duke University Press, 1925. A work of modest proportions, heavier on Slidell's (1793–1871) domestic than on his international activities (the Civil War mission receives scant attention though the author has an article on that subject). Oddly, the Confederate commissioners to Europe have not attracted biographers.

11:86 Willson, Beckles. *John Slidell and the Confederates in Paris.* New York: Minton, Balch, 1932. A lively book in which gossip is mixed with good secondary accounts to concoct a tale of intrigue at the highest level of international diplomacy and finance (1862–1865). Careful readers will recognize some of the quotations.

Others

11:87 Meade, Robert D. *Judah P. Benjamin and the American Civil War.* New York: Oxford University Press, 1943. This work provides one of the few satisfactory treatments of a major Confederate personality. Benjamin (1811–1884) was sometimes called the "brains of the Confederacy"; he is often described as the ablest man to emerge during the war; and certainly he was the best secretary of state the South ever had.

11:88 Oates, Stephen. "Henry Hotze: Confederate Agent Abroad." *Historian* 27:2 (1965), 131–54. Written from largely American published and secondary sources (and Hotze's papers), the piece lacks that all-important element of multiarchival research. One would like to know which British leaders were in fact influenced by Hotze's Confederate propaganda in Europe.

11:89 Williams, Frances L. *Matthew Fontaine Maury: Scientist of the Sea.* New Brunswick, N.J.: Rutgers University Press, 1963. This is a solid biography (1806–1873) of one of the South's internationally recognized citizens. While few question the importance of Maury's scientific work in oceanography, some critics have reservations about his performance as a purchasing agent for the Confederate navy. Bibliography.

EUROPEAN

William E. Gladstone

See Chapter 14, "Personalities," for additional references.

11:90 Collyer, C. "Gladstone and the American Civil War." *Philosophical and Literary Society Proceedings* 6:8 (1951), 583–94. Collyer provides a minor assessment of the role of the war on British politics and politicians, and especially of Gladstone's ambivalent reactions to transatlantic affairs.

Malament, B. C. "W. E. Gladstone: An Other Victorian?" (14:63) tells much about a man whose response to the American Civil War has baffled more than one diplomatic historian.

Morley, J. *The Life of William Ewart Gladstone* (14:64) is the standard work on Gladstone's life, but it is becoming obsolete with the publication of his diaries.

11:91 Reid, Robert L., ed. "William E. Gladstone's 'Insincere Neutrality' during the Civil War." *Civil War History* 15:4 (1969), 293–307. If, as Joseph Hernon has argued, Gladstone "is probably the key to interpreting British opinion on the Civil War," this documentary defense of his wartime views is required reading and much more important than his often-quoted 1896 confession of error.

Stansky, P. *Gladstone: A Progress in Politics* (14:65) provides students of the Civil War with Gladstone's views on slavery and the place of moral principles in foreign policy.

Lord Palmerston

Ashley, A. E. M. *The Life of Henry John Temple, Viscount Palmerston, 1846–1865* (8:41) has become much dated and, aside from its documents, has little to offer modern students.

Bell, H. C. F. *Lord Palmerston* (10:24) is generally considered the most satisfactory biography (1784–1865), has more material on the Civil War years than more recent works.

Connell, B., ed. *Regina v. Palmerston: The Correspondence between Queen Victoria and Her Foreign and Prime Minister, 1837–1865* (8:43) reveals the royal alterations in the *Trent* dispatches.

11:92 Cook, Edward. *Delane of the Times.* London: Constable, 1915. Though this work probably credits the editor of the London *Times* too much for creating the public image of Palmerston, it hints at an important truth about public relations in the Age of Palmerston. Students who denigrate the prime minister's keen awareness of public opinion miss an important dimension of his response to crisis diplomacy.

Guedalla, P. *Palmerston* (8:44) tells us much of the man and the era.

Ridley, J. *Lord Palmerston* (8:45) while laudable and readable, it is much dated and out of focus on the subject of the American Civil War.

Webster, C. *The Foreign Policy of Palmerston, 1830–1841* (8:47) is required reading for any consideration of Palmerstonian statecraft. There is little reason to assume that as prime minister in 1861 to 1865, he approached international affairs any differently than he did in his earlier years.

Lord John Russell

Russell, J. *The Later Correspondence of Lord John Russell, 1840–1878* (8:48) has a good, representative selection of the British foreign secretary's views during the Civil War.

Walpole, S. *The Life of Lord John Russell* (8:49) has, in volume 2, a good chapter on the Civil War, with copious extracts from contemporary documents.

Others

Argyll, George Douglas Campbell, 8th Duke of. *George Douglas Eighth Duke of Argyll (1823–1900)* (8:50) shows that Argyll stood foremost among the North's supporters in the British government; the second volume of his memoir has a useful chapter on the Civil War years, particularly his attitude toward Russell's recognition policy and the *Trent* affair, to mention but two episodes.

11:93   Carroll, Daniel B. *Henri Mercier and the American Civil War.* Princeton, N.J.: Princeton University Press, 1971. A work of many virtues, this book "treats with admirable understanding the French minister's relationship with Seward and his [Mercier's] opinion of the Union." Carroll also exonerates the French minister of excessive partisanship for the South; indeed he is "scrupulously just" in appraising Mercier's diplomatic ventures.

11:94   Curtis, George W., ed. *The Correspondence of John Lothrop Motley.* 2 vols. London: John Murray, 1889. A collection filled with many good things (including a nice observation of the law of the *Trent*), these volumes and the subject they treat deserve wider appreciation. And certainly Motley (1814–1877) was a unique diplomat in a special place at an important time, whose career if properly studied might shed more light on a neglected aspect of Civil War diplomacy.

11:95   Fitzmaurice, Lord Edmond. *The Life of Granville George Leveson Gower: Second Earl Granville, K.G., 1815–1891.* London: Longmans, Green, 1905. Although the first volume of this set has little to do with American affairs, its chapter "Foreign Affairs, 1862–1864" has some interesting comments on dis-

cussions of British mediation in the American Civil War. The author has included the usual long extracts from the documents and papers of the participants.

Maxwell, Sir H. E. *The Life and Letters of George William Frederick, Fourth Earl of Clarendon* (8:52) shows that Lord Clarendon had considerable, if muted, influence on mid-19th-century Anglo-American affairs.

11:96   Newton, Thomas L. W. *Lord Lyons: A Record of British Diplomacy.* 2 vols. London: Arnold, 1913. Although a too laudatory view of its subject, it has the value of very extended extracts from the private papers of the British minister to Washington. Three chapters in volume 1 are useful for a British view of the war. A biography of Lyons to rank with Carroll's on Mercier (11:93) and Duberman's on Adams (11:46) is badly needed.

11:97   Woodham-Smith, Cecil. *Queen Victoria: From Her Birth to the Death of the Prince Consort.* New York: Knopf, 1972. American affairs do not loom large in this work, but it contains a vivid account of the death of the prince at the time of the *Trent* crisis. The author's masterly control of the materials permits comment on the sources that historians have used in reconstructing the account of the prince's role in drafting the British note to America at the time of that crisis.

Britain Confronts the War

GENERAL BACKGROUND

Also see "Personalities" for Charles Francis Adams, Benjamin Moran (under "Union," "Others"), William E. Gladstone, Lord Palmerston, Lord John Russell.

Best, G. *Mid-Victorian Britain, 1851–1875* (8:54) captures a sense of being alive in the period when Britain enjoyed a preeminence rarely achieved in world affairs.

11:98 Bonham, Milledge L. *The British Consuls in the Confederacy.* New York: Columbia University Press, 1911. This work remains virtually the only treatment of its special subject. The difficulties of the consuls (1861–1863) are well handled, as is rising southern sentiment for their expulsion.

Bourne, K. *Britain and the Balance of Power in North America, 1815–1908* (8:55) contains only two chapters on the Civil War years but is required reading (especially on the *Trent* crisis of 1861) for an astute evaluation of British military and strategic considerations should an Anglo-American war break out in North America.

Bourne, K. *The Foreign Policy of Victorian England, 1830–1902* (8:56) devotes only a small portion of its pages to the Civil War, but the author's mastery of all facets of British diplomacy allows him to stress the interconnectedness of American and European affairs.

Jones, W. D. *The American Problem in British Diplomacy, 1841–1861* (8:59) is especially good in his appraisal of Lord Palmerston.

PROCLAMATION OF 1861

11:99 Adams, Charles Francis, Jr. "The British Proclamation of May, 1861."*Proceedings of the Massachusetts Historical Society* 48 (1915), 190–241. This much criticized article is useful as a guide to the evolution of Civil War historiography, for the author was a frequent contributor to historical journals near the turn of the century, and he had access to sources denied to other historians for some years thereafter.

11:100 Adams, Charles Francis, Jr. "The Negotiations of 1861 Relating to the Declaration of Paris of 1856." *Proceedings of the Massachusetts Historical Society* 46 (1913–1914), 23–84. Adams regards these negotiations as ill-considered, and thinks that Seward's policy in the first three months of the war was based on a "misapprehension" of affairs in America, Europe, and the South. See William H. Trescot's "The Confederacy and the Declaration of Paris," *American Historical Review* 23 (July 1918), 826–35, which discusses the negotiations from the perspective of a participant. This particular negotiation has not been properly studied.

11:101 Adams, Henry. "The Declaration of Paris, 1861." In George Hochfield, ed., *The Great Secession Winter of 1860–61 and Other Essays by Henry Adams.*

New York: Sagamore, 1958, pp. 361–90. Henry Adams was fascinated all his life by the duel he had witnessed between his father and the British foreign secretary during the years he served as his father's secretary in London. All readers of the *Education of Henry Adams* know of Henry's exposure to the "double-dyed rascality and duplicity of Lord Russell." Careful readers will take such comments with a grain of salt.

11:102 Ferris, Norman B. *Desperate Diplomacy: William H. Seward's Foreign Policy, 1861.* Knoxville: University of Tennessee Press, 1976. This detailed account seeks to enhance the reputation of Seward. The stress is more on England than on the Continent; and many will question the author's evaluation of the British minister, though his summary of the "legalism" of the British response to the war is suggestive, while his treatment of British "arrogance" is less so. Extensive bibliography.

SLAVERY AND THE SLAVE TRADE

See Chapter 7, "Slavery and Expansion," for American interests in Cuba and for American filibustering activities in the Caribbean; and Chapter 8, "Suppression of the Slave Trade," for background to 1862 treaty.

11:103 Brauer, Kinley J. "The Slavery Problem in the Diplomacy of the American Civil War." *Pacific Historical Review* 46:3 (1977), 439–69. The author's thesis—that slavery "had far more significance as a 'realistic' issue in the international history of the Civil War than scholars have previously granted it"—is beautifully buttressed with a wide array of evidence, both domestic and international.

Mathieson, W. L. *Great Britain and the Slave Trade, 1839–1865* (8:71) analyzes British attempts to stamp out the slave trade and to induce other nations, especially the United States, to cooperate. This study refers incidentally to events of the Civil War era and to the Lyons-Seward Treaty of 1862 for suppression of the trade.

11:104 Milne, A. Taylor. "The Lyons-Seward Treaty of 1862." *American Historical Review* 38:3 (1932), 511–25. While the student interested in the slave trade will still have to consult the papers in the Public Record Office in London used by Milne in the preparation of this article, a good bit of the preliminary work on that subject can be done by consulting the Irish University Press edition of the Parliamentary Papers (8:3).

11:105 Weinberg, Adelaide. *John Elliot Cairnes and the American Civil War: A Study in Anglo-American Relations*. London: Kingswood, 1968. This little known work addresses a major problem of the British response to the Civil War—the relationship of slavery to the disruption of the Union. Cairnes wrote an influential antislavery book which is generally credited with educating and shaping British public opinion toward the North.

OPINIONS: PUBLIC AND PRIVATE

Also see "Personalities," for Confederate agent Henry Hotze (under "Others").

11:106 Crook, D. P. "Portents of War: English Opinion on Secession." *Journal of American Studies* 4:2 (1971), 163–79. This bold essay in social history cautions against seeing British responses to the war in simplistic terms. D. G. Wright has a follow up to this theme, based on an evaluation of the views of the provincial press (*JAS* 5:2 [1971], 151–54).

11:107 Cullop, Charles P. *Confederate Propaganda in Europe, 1861–1865*. Coral Gables, Fla.: University of Miami Press, 1969. As a study of propaganda this small book leaves much to be desired, for it largely takes Hotze, the chief Confederate agent, at face value, and there is no extensive analysis of the impact of the South's message on leaders of British public opinion.

11:108 Ellison, Mary. *Support for Secession: Lancashire and the American Civil War*. Chicago: University of Chicago Press, 1972. This slim study provides a provocative reexamination of one of the Civil War's more intractable myths: the supposed pro-North sympathies of the British workers. Ellison concludes that Britain's cotton interests were united in supporting an independent South, a conclusion that would—if accepted—stand a century of historiography on its head.

11:109 Harrison, Royden. "British Labour and American Slavery." In his *Before the Socialists:*

Studies in Labour and Politics, 1861–1881. London: Routledge & Kegan Paul, 1965, pp. 40–69. Harrison modifies the old orthodoxy that the working class supported the northern cause during the war. Although many politically conscious workers were pro-Union, many leaders of the labor movement and much of its press expressed hostility to the North. Bibliography.

11:110 Harrison, Royden. "British Labour and the Confederacy." *International Review of Social History* 2:1 (1957), 78–105. An important assessment of opinions in the British labor movement by a master of the literature of social history. The notes provide frequent correctives to taken-for-granted views.

11:111 Hernon, Joseph M., Jr. "British Sympathies in the American Civil War: A Reconsideration." *Journal of Southern History* 33:3 (1967), 356–67. This important article challenges the oversimplified interpretation of the British response to the Civil War that has gained credence in a number of diplomatic studies of the war.

11:112 Hernon, Joseph M., Jr. *Celts, Catholics and Copperheads: Ireland Views the American Civil War*. Columbus: Ohio State University Press, 1968. The author, in a pioneering book, relates the struggle for independence in the American south to the question of home rule in Ireland. It is a study in what he calls "the texture of opinion." He handles his various themes with a sure hand and a firm knowledge of the key issues of Irish public opinion. Bibliography.

11:113 Jones, Wilbur D. "The British Conservatives and the American Civil War." *American Historical Review* 58:3 (1953), 527–43. In one of the best articles on the British response to the war, the author concludes, among other things, that in Conservative circles sympathy for the South was far less than commonly believed.

11:114 Kiger, John H. "Federal Governmental Propaganda in Great Britain during the American Civil War." *Historical Outlook* 19:5 (1928), 204–09. This early study could probably be updated with profit.

11:115 Logan, Kevin J. "The Bee-Hive Newspaper and British Working Class Attitudes toward the American Civil War." *Civil War History* 22:4 (1976), 337–48. Logan's piece demonstrates how a narrow focus and detailed research can challenge sweeping generalization about "attitudes" of the British workers. He hints that opinion in Lancashire might be due to special circumstances that did not apply elsewhere. Should be read in conjunction with Ellison (11:108).

11:116 Park, Joseph H. "The English Workingmen and the American Civil War." *Political Science Quarterly* 39:3 (1924), 432–57. An early attempt to get at the intriguing problem of the attitude of the English workers toward the American Civil War. The piece should be compared to more recent works, especially Ellison (11:108) and Harrison (11:109 and 11:110).

THE TRENT AFFAIR, 1861–1862

Also see "Personalities," especially John Lothrop Motley and the Duke of Argyll (under "European," "Others"), Confederates James M. Mason and John Slidell, and Union leaders Charles Sumner, Gideon Welles, and Charles Wilkes.

11:117 Adams, Charles Francis, Jr. "The *Trent* Affair." *Proceedings of the Massachusetts Historical Society* 45 (1911–1912), 35–148. The minister's son was one of the first to begin exploiting the papers of his father, and this early assessment of the *Trent* was a prime example of what might come from that marvelous source. The same issue of the *Proceedings* contains a piece by R. H. Dana, "The *Trent* Affair: An Aftermath," pp. 508–22, and a rejoinder by Adams, pp. 522–30.

11:118 Bourne, Kenneth. "British Preparations for War with the North, 1861–1862." *English Historical Review* 76:301 (1961), 600–632. This definitive article demonstrates the interconnection of military and diplomatic affairs. The sources are nearly as impressive as the arguments. The section on the *Trent* nicely illustrates the ways in which an old topic can be approached in new ways.

11:119 Cohen, V. H. "Charles Sumner and the *Trent* Affair." *Journal of Southern History* 22:2 (1956), 205–19. This article evaluates a key participant's role as peacekeeper. It should be compared to Donald's treatment in his biography of Sumner (11:59), and O'Rourke's article (11:123).

11:120 Drake, F. C. "The Cuban Background of the *Trent* Affair." *Civil War History* 19:1 (1973), 29–49. This article adds a new dimension to the context of this much studied diplomatic crisis. The emphasis here is on the role of the American consul in Cuba, Robert W.

Shufeldt, in the events preceding the capture of Mason and Slidell.

11:121 Ferris, Norman B. *The Trent Affair: A Diplomatic Crisis.* Knoxville: University of Tennessee Press, 1977. This detailed study of a famous Civil War crisis, "currently the best thing in print," has a number of virtues and some defects. Despite the author's avowed intent to explain why an essentially trivial incident escalated into a major confrontation, the book "loses the incident's larger significance in a welter of detail." Extensive bibliography.

11:122 Harris, Thomas L. *The Trent Affair, Including a Review of English and American Relations at the Beginning of the Civil War.* Indianapolis: Bobbs-Merrill, 1896. Though long outdated this work, which remained "the best work on its special subject" for three-quarters of a century, ought not to be dismissed cavalierly. It will continue useful as a period piece and as an exponent of particular views no longer fashionable in academic circles, and it must be said that the work definitely bears the impress of the author's biases.

11:123 O'Rourke, Alice. "The Law Officers of the Crown and the *Trent* Affair." *Mid-America* 54:3 (1972), 157–71. This article traces the evolution of the views of British legal advisers about the law of the *Trent,* and concludes that Seward's defense—or apology—had been substantially foreshadowed. The law of the *Trent* is highly complex; its ramifications can best be traced in the Baxter article (11:231) and documents in the *American Historical Review* 34 (October 1928) and in the Warren dissertation (11:125) on the *Trent.*

11:124 [Simpson], Evan John. *Atlantic Impact, 1861.* New York: Putnam's, 1952. This work looks at the affair through a series of vivid biographical sketches of leading (and peripheral) characters in the events of 1861–1862. Simpson captures mood and motive better than some more recent authors on the subject, but his cavalier disregard for evidence requires comparison to the more detailed accounts of Harris, Ferris, and Warren.

11:125 Warren, Gordon H. *Fountain of Discontent: The Trent Affair and Freedom of the Seas.* Boston: Northeastern University Press, 1981. The study provides an interesting comparison for the Ferris work on the same topic (11:121), and it is exceedingly good on the law of the *Trent,* a subject seldom treated properly. While the author is clearly in command of the sources, primary and secondary, he has the advantage of a clear and vigorous writing style. Extensive bibliography.

11:126   Wheeler-Bennett, J. "The *Trent* Affair: How the Prince Consort Saved the U.S." *History Today* 11:12 (1961), 805–16. A popular account of a famous incident that is noteworthy for its inclusion of rare archival materials.

THE MEDIATION CRISIS, 1862

Also see "Personalities" for Lord Granville (under "Others").

11:127   Adams, Charles Francis, Jr. "A Crisis in Downing Street." *Proceedings of the Massachusetts Historical Society* 47 (1914), 372–424. Adams overstresses the role of the Emancipation Proclamation as a factor in European diplomacy. The article should be compared to some of the more recent writings on the subject of European intervention in the war.

11:128   Brauer, Kinley J. "British Mediation and the American Civil War: A Reconsideration." *Journal of Southern History* 38:1 (1972), 49–64. A challenging reassessment of the intervention crisis in the fall of 1862, which also points up the way in which political conditions colored diplomatic actions.

11:129   Ellsworth, E. W. "Anglo-American Affairs in October of 1862." *Lincoln Herald* 66:2 (1964), 89–96. This piece should be compared to others on the mediation crisis of 1862, for example, Graebner, Brauer, Merli/Wilson, and with the articles that "reconsider" the European response, especially Beloff and Blumenthal.

11:130   Graebner, Norman A. "European Interventionism and the Crisis of 1862." *Journal of the Illinois State Historical Society* 69:1 (1976), 35–45. This article describes some of the tensions that developed in diplomatic circles on the subjects of military stalemate, slavery, Confederacy sympathies, and European distrust of the Lincoln administration.

11:131   Merli, Frank J., and Wilson, Theodore A. "The British Cabinet and the Confederacy, Autumn, 1862." *Maryland Historical Magazine* 65:3 (1970), 239–62. This article evaluates the possibilities of British intervention in American affairs in the fall of 1862. The authors conclude that such a course was narrowly averted; that the British prime minister, Lord

Palmerston, was less bellicose than usually depicted; and that George C. Lewis's contribution ought to be better appreciated.

The Continent Confronts the War

FRANCE

Also see "Personalities" for Union leader John Bigelow and French minister Henri Mercier (under "Others").

Barker, N. N. *Distaff Diplomacy: The Empress Eugénie and the Foreign Policy of the Second Empire* (8:81).

11:132   Bigelow, John. *France and the Confederate Navy, 1862–1865.* New York: Harper, 1888. Reprint 1968. This book provides an interesting look into the confused French response to the war. The information that Bigelow received of Confederate naval construction in France enabled the Americans to impede and finally to stop such activity.

Blumenthal, H. *France and the United States: Their Diplomatic Relations, 1789–1914* (2:224) compresses a mass of material and learning into two fine chapters on the 1860s.

Case, L. M., comp. and ed. *French Opinion on the United States and Mexico, 1860–1867: Extracts from the Reports of the Procureurs Généraux* (15:64) is an early, and still useful, attempt to understand French public opinion and the American Civil War. It has been updated by Case and Spencer's *The United States and France: Civil War Diplomacy* (11:34).

Evans, E. A. P. "Napoleon III and the American Civil War" (15:49) emphasizes the primacy of Mexico in Napoleonic diplomacy.

11:133   Ferri-Pisani, Camille. *Prince Napoleon in America, 1861: Letters from His Aide-de-Camp.* Trans. by Georges J. Joyaux. Bloomington: Indiana University Press, 1959. These letters, originally published in 1862, provide a unique view of the United States in the early months of the Civil War. The letters come close to a word-picture of men and events in a critical period, and they have been nicely edited.

11:134   Gavronsky, Serge. *The French Liberal Opposition and the American Civil War.* New York: Humanities Press, 1968. To establish the impact of the American Civil War on the daily affairs of Frenchmen, the author has exploited an impressive array of sources. His purpose is to show how the American war—a foreign event of the first magnitude—impinged on the policies of French liberalism. Biographical appendix and bibliography.

11:135   Pecquet du Bellet, Paul. *The Diplomacy of the Confederate Cabinet of Richmond and Its Agents Abroad: Being Memorandum Notes Taken in Paris during the Rebellion of the Southern States from 1861 to 1865.* Ed. by W. Stanley Hoole. Tuscaloosa, Ala.: Confederate Publishers, 1963. Of all the sources for a study of Civil War diplomacy, this is one of the strangest. It has been nicely edited.

11:136   Spencer, Warren. "The Jewett-Greeley Affair: A Private Scheme for French Mediation in the American Civil War." *New York History* 51:3 (1970), 238–68. The bizarre William Cornell "Colorado" Jewett and the eccentric Horace Greeley engaged in personal diplomacy in support of French mediation maneuvers in early 1863. There are also accounts of the incident in Case and Spencer (11:34) and in Carroll (11:93).

11:137   Wellesley, F. A., ed. *The Paris Embassy during the Second Empire: Selections from the Papers of Henry Richard Charles Wellesley, 1st Earl Cowley, Ambassador at Paris, 1852–1867.* London: Thornton Butterworth, 1928. Although only a very small portion of this work treats American affairs, the book is filled with references to British mistrust of France and the fear of unsettled conditions on the Continent, factors that did much to shape Britain's response to war in America. Even when the emperor supported England, as he did in the *Trent* affair, British officials were suspicious of his motives.

11:138   West, W. R. *Contemporary French Opinion of the Civil War.* Baltimore: Johns Hopkins Press, 1924. This early work forms a part of the historians' attempt to evaluate the controversy and propaganda during the war. For a more extended survey of the literature see the bibliographical listing in Owsley (11:24), pp. 564–66.

Maximilian's Mexican Venture

See Chapter 15, "The French in Mexico, 1861–1867."

RUSSIA

11:139   Adomov, E. A. "Russia and the United States at the Time of the Civil War." *Journal of Modern History* 2:4 (1930), 586–602. This article apparently was written without consulting Frank Golder's pioneering piece (*American Historical Review* 20 [1915], 801–12) on the Russian fleet or his other works on Russo-American relations during the Civil War (*AHR* 26 [1921], 454–63) and at the time of the Crimean War. The article was translated by R. P. Churchill and it is followed by "Documents Relating to Russian Policy during the American Civil War," pp. 603–11.

11:140   Kushner, Howard I. "The Russian Fleet and the American Civil War: Another View." *Historian* 34:4 (1972), 633–49. This article makes the interesting case that the Lincoln administration was aware of the practical purposes behind the visit of the Russian fleet (1863) and that the president and secretary of state skillfully exploited the situation for Union purposes.

Thomas, B. P. *Russo-American Relations, 1815–1867* (8:90).

11:141   Woldman, Albert A. *Lincoln and the Russians.* Cleveland: World, 1952. This not entirely satisfactory work provides mostly extracts from the papers and dispatches of the Russian minister in Washington. It is not very helpful or detailed on Russo-American relations.

SPAIN

11:142   Brauer, Kinley J. "The Appointment of Carl Schurz as Minister to Spain." *Mid-America* 56:2 (1974), 75–84. This is an evaluation of efforts to head off crisis in Spanish-American relations (1861) over the appointment of the "revolutionary" Schurz. Brauer has some useful things to say of the role of Cuba in the efforts of the South.

11:143   Brauer, Kinley J. "Gabriel García y Tassara and the American Civil War: A Spanish Perspective." *Civil War History* 21:1 (1975) 5–27. Brauer's article, virtually the only study on its special subject, uses sources in Madrid to trace Spain's response to the war, a reaction the author calls "a strange combination of daring new ventures and excessive caution."

11:144 Fischer, Leroy H., and Chandler, J. "United States–Spanish Relations during the American Civil War." *Lincoln Herald* 75:4 (1973), 134–47. This article has been faulted for its excessive dependence upon American sources, and it should be read in conjunction with Brauer's two studies immediately above.

OTHER NATIONS

11:145 Fragasso, Philip. "Giuseppe Garibaldi and the Civil War." *Civil War Times Illustrated* 16:7 (1977), 5–8, 42–44. This piece of popular history should be compared with two more scholarly approaches: the Forbes-Beckwith letter edited by H. Zettl (11:149), and R. J. Amundson's "Sanford and Garibaldi," *Civil War History* 14:1 (1968). The problem of who invited the famous Italian (1861) apparently has not yet been solved.

11:146 Kutolowski, J. "The Effect of the Polish Insurrection of 1863 on American Civil War Diplomacy." *Historian* 27:4 (1965), 560–77. This essay examines the interrelationship of the American Civil War and continental affairs in the 1860s. It is especially good on the ways in which the Polish uprising of 1863 impinged on the fortunes of the Confederates and Unionists in Europe.

11:147 Orzell, Laurence J. "A 'Favorable Interval': The Polish Insurrection in Civil War Diplomacy, 1863." *Civil War History* 24:4 (1978), 332–50. The author's demonstration of the relationship between European crises (1862–1864) and the waning of interest in American affairs is exceedingly good, and he knows the literature and uses it with sensitivity.

11:148 Tyrner-Tyrnauer, A. R. *Lincoln and the Emperors.* New York: Harcourt, Brace & World, 1962. An amateurish and unsophisticated attempt to bring new material (that in the Austrian State Archives) to bear on the impact of the Civil War in central Europe. It is difficult to imagine that Lincoln took as much interest in the emperors as the author does.

11:149 Zettl, Herbert, ed. "Garibaldi and the American Civil War." *Civil War History* 22:1 (1976), 70–76. The document (1861) provides a unusual view of an unusual man confronting a most unusual pro-

posal. The prospect of Garibaldi in command of the Union armed forces, empowered "to declare emancipation if he judged it necessary," conjures up strange visions indeed.

Some Economic Aspects of the War

Also see Chapter 8, "Commercial Relations," and Chapter 10, "British Politics and Trade," for more general materials.

GENERAL ASSESSMENTS: DOMESTIC AND INTERNATIONAL

11:150 Andreano, Ralph L. "A Theory of Confederate Finance." *Civil War History* 2:4 (1956), 21–28. This able, analytical article contains an extensive footnote review of the literature on its technical subject; see also Andreano's edited *The Economic Impact of the American Civil War* (Cambridge, Mass.: Schenkman, 1962) for a wider view of that special topic. For southern fiscal policy and economic affairs consult the bibliography in Thomas (11:29), pp. 351, 353–55.

11:151 Dalzell, George W. *The Flight from the Flag.* Chapel Hill: University of North Carolina Press, 1940. This nicely written book deals inadequately with an important subject—the destruction of the American merchant marine by the Confederate cruisers.

11:152 Futrell, Robert. "Federal Trade with the Confederate States, 1861–1865." Ph.D. diss., Vanderbilt University, 1950. A work that provides a useful starting point for study of an interesting aspect of wartime economic affairs. It should be used in conjunction with the more up-to-date works, especially those by Ludwell Johnson (11:155 and 11:156).

11:153 Hammond, Bray. *Banks and Politics in America: From the Revolution to the Civil War.* Princeton, N.J.: Princeton University Press, 1957. A prize-winning treatment of a complex subject, this work (1776–1865) treats the Civil War years in relatively small space, though many of the author's comments are perceptive. Extensive bibliography.

11:154 Hammond, Bray. "The North's Empty Purse, 1861–1862."*American Historical Review* 67:1 (1961), 1–18. The author provides a detailed evaluation of the congressional response to the "wild and wicked" proposal to finance the war with greenbacks, and he points out that the expedients adopted as war measures took on a much different history in the postwar era.

11:155 Johnson, Ludwell H. "Contraband Trade during the Last Year of the Civil War." *Mississippi Valley Historical Review* 49:4 (1963), 635–52. Johnson's sound study on the lucrative business of trading with the enemy uses a wide variety of sources in imaginative ways to get at some of the thornier problems of Civil War economic (and political) history.

11:156 Johnson, Ludwell H. "Trading with the Union: The Evolution of Confederate Policy." *Virginia Magazine of History and Biography* 78:3 (1970), 308–25. A piece regarded as definitive for its special subject; it may be read in conjunction with the author's previous article. Here the author stresses that the realities of the southern supply system made a mockery of efforts to halt trade with the North.

11:157 Khasigian, Amos. "Economic Factors and British Neutrality, 1861–1865." *Historian* 25:4 (1963), 451–65. This piece, a prize-winning student essay, demonstrates a nice command of the secondary literature, but it contains no very sophisticated analysis of "economic factors." The economic dimensions of the impact of the Civil War in Europe have received surprisingly little attention. This article should be read in conjunction with others on the same subject cited under "Corn versus Cotton," below.

11:158 Luraghi, Raimondo. "The Civil War and the Modernization of American Society: Social Structure and Industrial Revolution in the Old South before and during the War." *Civil War History* 18:3 (1972), 230–50. This innovative article by an Italian military historian provides intriguing insights about the Civil War by its use of comparative history. It has a number of hints about possible directions for studies of the Confederate south, and it offers an interesting case study of economic planning there.

11:159 Ramsdell, Charles W. *Behind the Lines in the Southern Confederacy.* Baton Rouge: Louisiana State University Press, 1944. Ramsdell's work has aged remarkably well; it can still be described as the best overview of the southern economy during wartime.

11:160 Schwab, John C. *The Confederate States of America, 1861–65: A Financial and Industrial History of the South during the Civil War.* New York: Scribner's, 1901. This work, which a recent student of Confederate finance has described as "a most important and original work . . . probably the finest Confederate economic history of the war," retains its usefulness and is a basic starting point on the subject of Confederate economic history.

11:161 Wright, D. G. "Bradford and the American Civil War." *Journal of British Studies* 8:2 (1969), 69–85. By a detailed analysis of the economic impact of the Civil War on one industrial city, the author calls into question some conclusions of Owsley's (11:24). This is a pioneering work and many more such detailed studies are needed.

CONFEDERATE PURCHASING ABROAD

Also see "Personalities" for James D. Bulloch, John Slidell, and, under "Others," Henry Hotze.

11:162 Davis, Charles S. *Colin J. McRae: Confederate Financial Agent.* Tuscaloosa, Ala.: Confederate Publishers, 1961. This brief work provides a fascinating introduction to the problems of financing southern operations overseas. Here, one sees in microcosm the long odds against which the Confederacy struggled, and the myriad difficulties that hovered over southern agents.

11:163 Delaney, Robert W. "Matamoros, Port for Texas during the Civil War."*Southwestern Historical Quarterly* 58:4 (1955), 473–87. Matamoros was a center for smuggling from Mexico into the Confederacy (1861–1865) to avoid the Union blockade.

11:164 Diamond, William. "Imports of the Confederate Government from Europe and Mexico."*Journal of Southern History* 6:4 (1940), 470–503. Based on official records of the Union and Confederate armies, this essay details not only the trade routes used but also considerable data on kinds and quantities of products introduced into the Confederacy.

11:165 Fenner, Judith. "Confederate Finances Abroad." Ph.D. diss., Rice University, 1969. Fenner's work provides a detailed analysis of Confederate financial affairs in Europe. The author concludes that lack of funds was an impediment to southern purchasing efforts in Europe. Extensive bibliography.

11:166 Huse, Caleb. *The Supplies for the Confederate Army: How They Were Obtained and How Paid For, A Fragment of History.* Boston: Marvin, 1904. This work, a sketchy, personal reminiscence, occupies a special place in the Civil War literature. Of all the servants of the South, Huse was one of the most determined, successful, and interesting; yet he has been ill served in history.

11:167 Lester, Richard I. *Confederate Finance and Purchasing in Great Britain.* Charlottesville: University of Virginia Press, 1975. A detailed analysis of a very complex subject, it contains a useful amount of technical data on shipbuilding, finance, and ordnance. Students will find its appendixes a mine of information. Extensive bibliography.

11:168 Robbins, Peggy. "Caleb Huse: Confederate Agent." *Civil War Times Illustrated* 17:5 (1978), 30–40. Robbin's piece furnishes a fascinating view of the difficulties of Confederate agents in Europe. The author estimates that nearly 90 percent of the small arms used by Southerners in the first two years of the war came from abroad and that Huse was personally responsible for the importation of some 100,000 Enfield rifles.

11:169 Thompson, Samuel B. *Confederate Purchasing Operations Abroad.* Chapel Hill: University of North Carolina Press, 1935. While a useful and critical work, it suffers from lack of research in foreign archives. It is good on imports into the Confederacy, but it should be used in conjunction with the more impressively researched Lester book (11:167).

THE DIPLOMACY OF COTTON

Also see above "Opinions: Public and Private" for attitudes of the British working class toward the Civil War.

King Cotton

11:170 Brady, Eugene A. "A Reconsideration of the Lancashire 'Cotton Famine.' " *Agricultural History* 37:3 (1963), 156–62. This revisionist article remains required reading for students of the King Cotton theory. Brady concludes that "the traditional view of the Lancashire Depression (1861–1862) as a product of a 'Cotton Famine' rests upon a warped, if not incorrect, view of the causal relationship."

11:171 Earle, Edward Mead. "Egyptian Cotton and the American Civil War." *Political Science Quarterly* 41:4 (1926), 520–45. Civil War in America led to increased cotton production in Egypt to compensate for loss of southern cotton exports to Britain. Britain's increased reliance on Egyptian production may have influenced the British decision to occupy Egypt.

11:172 Henderson, W. O. *The Lancashire Cotton Famine, 1861–1865.* Manchester: Manchester University Press, 1934. This standard work remains "authoritative and valuable"; but it should be read in conjunction with more recent studies, especially Brady's article (11:170).

11:173 Warren, Gordon H. "The King Cotton Theory." In Alexander DeConde, ed., *Encyclopedia of American Foreign Policy.* New York: Scribner's, 1978, vol. 2, pp. 515–20. Warren provides an up-to-date evaluation of the South's reliance on the potential coercive power of cotton to achieve its diplomatic ends. This short article is filled with astute observations and provides a useful point of departure.

11:174 Woodman, Harold D. *King Cotton and His Retainers: Financing and Marketing the Cotton Crop of the South, 1800–1925.* Lexington: University of Kentucky Press, 1968. A detailed examination of cotton culture and its place in the world economic system, this work includes a good section on the South's frantic scramble to market its crop on the eve of the Civil War and during the course of the war.

Corn versus Cotton

11:175 Crook, D. P. "A Dead Cock in the Pit." In his *The North, the South, and the Powers.* New York: Wiley, 1974, pp. 257–82. In a few pages, Crook evaluates the King Corn versus King Cotton controversy; he has some interesting things to say about the economics of British neutrality, and he cuts through a lot of the chaff about corn (wheat) and cotton. Crook is acute in appraising Louis Schmidt (*Iowa Journal of History and Politics* [1918]); Eli Ginzburg (*Agricultural History* [1936]) and the article by R. H. Jones (11:176). These works may be said to define the parameters of the controversy.

Jones, R. H. *Disrupted Decades: The Civil War and Reconstruction Years* (11:22) conveniently summarizes one of the more arcane topics of Civil War historiography, the Corn versus Cotton controversy (that Britain needed corn [wheat] more than she needed cotton and was therefore unable to help the South).

11:176 Jones, Robert H. "Long Live the King?" *Agricultural History* 37:4 (1963), 166–71. Jones attempts to define the parameters of the conflict between corn (wheat) and cotton as factors in shaping the British response to the war. Jones relies on the British Sessional Papers for his statistics.

Martin, T. P. "Cotton and Wheat in Anglo-American Trade and Politics, 1846–1852" (8:157).

Owsley, F. L. *King Cotton Diplomacy* (11:24) has a number of acute observations on the cotton versus corn controversy, and he gives a concise appraisal of the argument in his concluding chapter. In addition, one must consult his chapters on cotton as the foundation of Confederate diplomacy and on the cotton famine for authoritative statements on those subjects.

11:177 Potter, J. "Atlantic Economy, 1815–1860: The U.S.A. and the Industrial Revolution in Britain." In A. W. Coats and R. M. Robertson, eds., *Essays in American Economic History*. New York: Barnes & Noble, 1970, pp. 14–48. In addition to making a useful contribution to transatlantic history and to the economic history of the Anglo-American world, the author provides an evaluation of the place of corn (wheat) and cotton in the British economy in the middle years of the 19th century.

The Erlanger Loan, 1863

11:178 Gentry, Judith F. "A Confederate Success in Europe: The Erlanger Loan." *Journal of Southern History* 36:2 (1970), 157–88. This extremely important work calls into question the traditional "failure" of the South's cotton loan. If Gentry is right—and there is reason to think she is—there will be many a reputation revised downward.

11:179 Lester, Richard I. "An Aspect of Confederate Finance during the American Civil War: The Erlanger Loan and the Plan of 1864." *Business History*

16:2 (1974), 130–44. This piece should be read in conjunction with the Gentry article on the "success" of the Erlanger loan.

Naval and Military Affairs

See "Bibliographies" and "Document Collections" for additional materials.

STRATEGY AND TECHNOLOGY

Connelly, T. L., and Jones, A. *The Politics of Command: Factions and Ideas in Confederate Strategy* (40:153).

11:180 Reed, Rowena. *Combined Operations in the Civil War*. Annapolis, Md.: Naval Institute Press, 1978. Oddly, no study of combined military and naval operations in the Civil War had been made until the appearance of this book. Reed has produced a provocative, innovative piece of research and reminds us that "the first six months of the Civil War might be regarded, from the standpoint of strategy and operations, as a continuation in greatly expanded proportion of the Mexican War." Extensive bibliography.

Military Dimensions

See also "Document Collections" for *The War of the Rebellion: Official Records of the Union and Confederate Armies.* (11:8).

11:181 Catton, Bruce. *The Centennial History of the Civil War*. 3 vols. Garden City, N.Y.: Doubleday, 1961–1965. Catton has written one of the best of the general accounts of the war; certainly it is one of the best starting places for an appreciation of the war's impact.

Esposito, V. J., ed. *The West Point Atlas of American Wars* Vol. I: *1689–1900* (1:158) is devoted to the Civil War, and the maps and commentary are clear and informative, providing a good introduction to the complexities of the military history of the war. List of readings.

11:182   Foote, Shelby. *The Civil War: A Narrative*. 3 vols. New York: Random House, 1958–1974. Foote's work provides a novelist's—one might say, an artist's—view of the war that ''accepts the historian's standards without his paraphernalia.'' The volumes are noteworthy for vivid style, effective use of sources, sustained narrative, and for their balanced treatment of the war in all its human and geographical dimensions.

11:183   Freeman, Douglas S. *R. E. Lee: A Biography*. 4 vols. New York: Scribner's, 1949. Freeman's work, a monument of loving scholarship, retains its place as the best biography of the Confederate general.

11:184   Fuller, J. F. C. *Grant and Lee*. London: Eyre & Spottiswoode, 1933. This is a provocative book by a prominent British military historian who considered Grant the superior of his adversary.

11:185   Henderson, George F. R. *Stonewall Jackson and the American Civil War*. London: Longmans, Green (1898), 1936. A classic military biography that has led generations of readers to an appreciation of the history of the American Civil War.

11:186   Luraghi, Raimondo. *Storia della guerra civile americana* [History of the American Civil War]. Turin, It.: Einaudi Editore, 1966. This work, by an Italian military historian, has been ranked by Emory Thomas and David Donald as one of the best one-volume histories of the war, though Donald stresses its ''over-emphasis'' on military affairs. It provides an unusual perspective.

11:187   Shannon, Fred A. *The Organization and Administration of the Union Army, 1861–1865*. 2 vols. Cleveland: A. H. Clark, 1928. Shannon's study is an early and still useful foray into the realm of administrative history.

11:188   Wiley, Bell I. *The Life of Johnny Reb*. Indianapolis: Bobbs-Merrill, 1943. A pioneering attempt in the social history of the war; it should be read in conjunction with the author's companion volume, *The Life of Billy Yank* (1952).

11:189   Williams, Kenneth P. *Lincoln Finds a General*. 5 vols. New York: Macmillan, 1949–1956. This work provides an interesting example of the proper utilization of the *ORA* series (11:8), and it should be read in conjunction with Freeman's work (11:183) on Lee and his lieutenants.

Naval Dimensions

See ''Personalities,'' especially Jefferson Davis, Stephen R. Mallory, Gideon Welles, and, under ''Others,'' Matthew F. Maury.

11:190   Anderson, Bern. *By Sea and By River: The Naval History of the Civil War*. New York: Knopf, 1962. This work perhaps overestimates the effectiveness of the blockade. Anderson suggests that the success of the blockade runners has been exaggerated—but we still do not know if Anderson comes any closer than Frank Owsley to the truth.

11:191   Baxter, James P., III. *The Introduction of the Ironclad Warship*. Cambridge: Harvard University Press, 1933. This work remains a masterwork; it is a classic of its genre, as useful today as the day it was published. Far in advance of its time, it pioneered new directions in the study of technology and naval affairs (1850s–1870), and retains its status as a model study.

11:192   Jones, Virgil C. *The Civil War at Sea*. 3 vols. New York: Holt, Rinehart & Winston, 1960. Though primarily aimed at the general reader, it has a good treatment of the blockade and is full on the subject of the southern commerce raiders.

11:193   Nash, Howard P., Jr. *A Naval History of the Civil War*. South Brunswick, N.J.: Barnes, 1972. The latest attempt to synthesize the wide-ranging naval dimensions of the war. It should be compared to Merli (11:211), Anderson (11:190), and the Jones (11:192) trilogy above.

11:194   Scharf, J. Thomas. *History of the Confederate States Navy from Its Organization to the Surrender of Its Last Vessel*. New York: Rogers & Sherwood, 1887. A ponderous book which is the only detailed history of the Confederate navy, and though long out of date it retains a certain utility.

11:195   Soley, J. Russell. *The Navy in the Civil War: The Blockade and the Cruisers*. New York: Scribner's, 1883. Though it mirrors those virtues and vices of late 19th-century naval historiography, the work retains a considerable usefulness. Modern students may find it more convenient to consult the paperback edition put out by Jack Brussel (New York, n.d.).

11:196 Still, William N., Jr. "Confederate Naval Policy and the Ironclad." *Civil War History* 9:2 (1963), 145–56. Though the stress of this article is on domestic naval affairs, it demonstrates the centrality of ironclads to southern naval policy. Students will wish to consult Still's other works on Civil War naval technology.

11:197 Still, William N., Jr. "Technology Afloat." *Civil War Times Illustrated* 14:7 (1975), 4–9, 40–47. This article provides an excellent example of the virtues of popular or general history. In small space and without scholarly apparatus—and with a keen appreciation of readability—a master of his subject reminds readers that many of the so-called innovations of the war were, in fact, invented years before 1861.

11:198 Wells, Tom H. *The Confederate Navy: A Study in Organization.* University: University of Alabama Press, 1971. A small prize-winning book that has a chapter on naval administration in Europe. The work represents an all too rare excursion into more innovative approaches to the Confederate navy, and its appendixes furnish useful information not available elsewhere.

11:199 West, Richard S., Jr. *Mr. Lincoln's Navy.* New York: Longmans, Green, 1957. Though relying primarily upon printed sources, this work includes chapters on the blockade and the war on the high seas, as well as one on Wilkes and the *Trent* affair. It is a good introduction to Union naval strategy and to Welles's part in formulating it.

11:200 Wilson, Herbert W. *Ironclads in Action: A Sketch of Naval Warfare from 1855 to 1895, with Some Account of the Development of the Battleship in England.* 2 vols. London: Sampson, Low, Marston, 1896. Though rarely cited in the literature of the American Civil War, this work provides a unique history of the war's naval aspects. Nine of the fifteen chapters in the first volume are devoted to the Civil War, and the tenth contains an account of the 1866 Battle of Lissa, the only real test of the ramming principle revived by the application of steam to naval war.

FOREIGN NAVY OF THE CONFEDERACY

Also see "Personalities" for Union leaders John Bigelow and, under "Others," Thomas H. Dudley and Benjamin Moran, and Confederates James D. Bulloch and Stephen R. Mallory.

11:201 Adams, Brooks. "The Seizure of the Laird Rams." *Proceedings of the Massachusetts Historical Society* 45 (1911–1912), 243–333. This overlong, weepy account of the Laird rams is chiefly useful as another of those odd Adams's-eye views of Civil War diplomacy. Lord Russell's decision (1863) to detain the rams came pretty much without pressure from Charles Francis Adams.

11:202 Boykin, Edward. *Sea Devil of the Confederacy: The Story of the Florida and Her Captain, John Newland Maffitt.* New York: Funk & Wagnalls, 1959. A sprightly account (1862–1865), focusing on the career of the famous blockade runner and cruiser commander, this volume is unfootnoted and a bit overwritten. Based on standard secondary sources, it should be contrasted with F. L. Owsley, Jr., *The C.S.S. Florida.* (11:213).

11:203 Bulloch, James Dunwoody. *The Secret Service of the Confederate States in Europe: Or How the Confederate Cruisers Were Equipped.* 2 vols. New York: Franklin (1883), 1972. This is the best account of southern efforts to compensate for their lack of naval power, and Bulloch's account is well told—lively, accurate, and fair. It contains extensive extracts from his official correspondence.

11:204 Delaney, Norman C. *John McIntosh Kell of the Raider Alabama.* University: University of Alabama Press, 1973. Among the many virtues of this study of the career of J. M. Kell (first mate on the *Alabama*) is a superb reconstruction of the duel of the *Alabama* and *Kearsarge* in the English Channel off Cherbourg in June 1864.

11:205 Harrison, Lowell H. "The CSS *Shenandoah.*" *Civil War Times Illustrated* 15:4 (1976), 4–9, 44–47. The author provides an accurate, up-to-date survey (1863–1865) of the last Confederate cruiser. For an extended treatment of the raider's strange career, Harrison recommends Stanley F. Horn's *Gallant Rebel: The Fabulous Cruise of the C.S.S.*

Shenandoah (New Brunswick, N.J.: Rutgers University Press, 1947).

11:206 Hoole, William Stanley, ed. *Four Years in the Confederate Navy: The Career of Captain John Low.* Athens: University of Georgia Press, 1964. In addition to its contribution to our knowledge of Confederate naval affairs, this work has some useful hints on the techniques and fascinations of historical research. Bibliography.

11:207 Jones, Wilbur D. *The Confederate Rams at Birkenhead: A Chapter in Anglo-American Relations.* Tuscaloosa, Ala.: Confederate Publishers, 1961. Among the many special features of this study is the detailed analysis of British policy in the decision to seize the Laird rams in 1863. Equally impressive is the author's careful investigation of efforts to build a case against those inconvenient vessels.

11:208 Krein, David F. "Russell's Decision to Detain the Laird Rams." *Civil War History* 22:2 (1976), 158–63. The author uses the papers of the British undersecretary of state, Austin H. Layard, to trace the evolution of the British decision (1863) to detain the rams. He adds important information to the works of Jones (11:207) and Merli (11:211) on that subject, and provides added reason to play down that much misunderstood note of C. F. Adams to Lord Russell on September 5, 1863.

11:209 Maynard, Douglas H. "The Confederacy's Super-*Alabama*." *Civil War History* 5:1 (1959), 80–95. This article provides a good introduction to one of the South's lesser known warships (1862–1864). The work is one of several articles by the author on the general topic of southern naval affairs in Europe.

11:210 Maynard, Douglas H. "The Forbes-Aspinwall Mission." *Mississippi Valley Historical Review* 45:1 (1958), 67–89. Though this northern "intelligence" operation was not immediately achieved because the agents were unable to purchase the Laird rams to keep them out of Confederate hands or to secure British government pledges to prevent their departure, the Forbes-Aspinwall mission (1863) played an important part in beefing up Union counterefforts to Confederate activity in foreign shipyards.

11:211 Merli, Frank J. *Great Britain and the Confederate Navy, 1861–1865.* Bloomington: Indiana University Press, 1970. By focusing on the narrow theme of Confederate naval construction in Great Brit-

ain, the author illuminates many aspects of the larger dimensions of Britain's response to the American Civil War. Extensive, critical bibliography.

11:212 Merli, Frank J. "The Confederate Navy, 1861–1865." In Kenneth J. Hagan, ed., *In Peace and War: Interpretations of American Naval History, 1775–1978.* Westport, Conn: Greenwood, 1978, pp. 126–44. The author attempts an assessment of the unique circumstances of Confederate naval affairs and tries to relate those experiences to the larger experience of American naval history.

11:213 Owsley, Frank L., Jr. *The C.S.S. Florida: Her Building and Operation.* Philadelphia: University of Pennsylvania Press, 1965. This work provides a detailed, scholarly history (1862–1864) of the career of one of the most famous Confederate raiders.

11:214 Semmes, Raphael. *Service Afloat or the Remarkable Career of the Confederate Cruisers Sumter and Alabama during the War between the States* New York: P. J. Kennedy, 1869(?). This citation to Semmes's famous memoir is the one used by Frank Owsley in *King Cotton Diplomacy* (11:24) (and repeated by Owsley, Jr., in *The C.S.S. Florida*). William Stanley Hoole, in his edition of *Four Years in the Confederate Navy* (11:206), lists six variants of the title, dating from 1864 to 1887. Philip Van Doren Stern has abridged the 1869 edition of *Memoirs of Service Afloat during the War between the States* for the Indiana University Press under the title, *The Confederate Raider Alabama* (1962).

11:215 Summersell, Charles G. *The Cruise of C.S.S. Sumter.* Tuscaloosa, Ala.: Confederate Publishers, 1965. A work useful for the early career of Raphael Semmes, and one that illustrates the difficulties the Confederacy had in creating a navy.

NORTHERN BLOCKADE

Also see "Personalities" for Union leaders Gustavus Vasa Fox (under "Others"), Gideon Welles, Charles Wilkes.

11:216 Courtemanche, Regis A. *No Need of Glory: The British Navy in American Waters, 1860–1864.* Annapolis, Md.: Naval Institute Press, 1977. Largely based on the private papers of Vice Admiral Sir Alexander Milne, the British commander of the Royal Navy's North American and West Indian station, this small monograph shows how carefully Britain monitored events in America, particularly Union enforcement of the blockade of the Confederate coast. Bibliography.

11:217 Hanna, Kathryn. "Incidents of the Confederate Blockade." *Journal of Southern History* 11:2 (1945), 253–75. This highly regarded piece should be read in connection with Bernath's *Squall across the Atlantic* (11:227).

11:218 Hefferman, John B. "The Blockade of the Southern Confederacy, 1861–1865." *Smithsonian Journal of History* 2:4 (1967–1968), 24–44. One of a slowly growing number of solid studies of the blockade, this piece provides an in-depth analysis of the mechanics of the blockade and of Union efforts to close the major Confederate ports. It pays some attention to the evolution of the European response to those efforts.

11:219 Johnson, Robert E. "Investment by Sea: The Civil War Blockade." *American Neptune* 32:1 (1972), 45–57. The author argues that the blockade did not mark new departures in warfare but was an extension of well-established principles of naval war to the special circumstances of the Civil War in America. He stresses the unprecedented extent of its limits and the unusual feature of the use of this weapon in a "domestic disturbance."

11:220 Payne, Peter, and Merli, Frank J., eds. "A Blockade-Running Charter: Spring, 1862." *American Neptune* 26:2 (1966), 134–37. This document provides a rare glimpse at the technical and legal underpinnings of the lucrative trade in ships and goods between Europe and the South. The introduction hints at the value of research in Scottish business records and the private papers of American diplomats.

11:221 Price, Marcus W. "Masters and Pilots Who Tested the Blockade of the Confederate Ports, 1861–1865." *American Neptune* 21:2 (1961), 81–106. This piece may serve as a representative example of the kind of detailed research needed to prepare the way for a solid, substantial, and accurate study of blockade running.

11:222 Symonds, Craig, ed. *Charleston Blockade: The Journals of John B. Marchand, U.S. Navy, 1861–1862.* Newport, R.I.: Naval War College Press, 1976. This volume provides an all-too-rare glimpse at the humdrum monotony of blockade duty. It has been edited with meticulous attention to detail and the

commentary woven through the notes calls attention to related matters.

11:223 Taylor, Thomas E. *Running the Blockade: A Personal Narrative of Adventures, Risks, and Escapes during the American Civil War.* 2d ed. London: John Murray, 1896. A first-hand account of blockade running by a participant in the events he describes: "he was the chief organizer of a great and systematised attack on the Northern blockade. . . ." Moreover, he has interesting things to say about the attitudes of Englishmen to the intricate technicalities of the blockade.

11:224 Vandiver, Frank E., ed. *Confederate Blockade Running through Bermuda, 1861–1865: Letters and Cargo Manifests.* Austin: University of Texas Press, 1947. Reprint 1970. The documents contained in this slim volume are important sources for the activities of southern commercial interests in Bermuda. The editor's introduction is a mine of information, and not only on blockade running.

11:225 Wade, Norman. "We Are on the Blockading Again: Letters from a Nova Scotian in the Union Navy." *Civil War Times Illustrated* 15:10 (1977), 28–36. These letters, as the subtitle suggests, provide an unusual perspective on the war and one of its principal occupations. The last letter in the collection, "a poignant tribute to a fallen comrade," reminds us of the danger of the trade (Wade fell to his death from his lookout perch aloft) and of the ways in which the American Civil War affected the lives of foreigners.

The War and International Law

Books

Albion, R. G., and Pope, J. B. *Sea Lanes in Wartime: The American Experience, 1775–1942* (40:107) offers a handy introduction to the complexities of the American position on neutral trade in wartime.

11:226 Bernard, Mountague. *A Historical Account of the Neutrality of Great Britain.* London: Longmans, Green, Reader, & Dyer, 1870. A necessary work for understanding the British defense (1861–1870) of their actions during the Civil War, but one that should be used with caution, for, despite the author's "objectivity," it often seems as if he is offering an interpretation slanted toward Whitehall.

11:227 Bernath, Stuart L. *Squall across the Atlantic: American Civil War Prize Cases and Diplomacy.* Berkeley: University of California Press, 1970. This book, a model monograph, illuminates large questions by detailed analysis of a highly technical topic, and it points up the intricate relationship between international law and national self-interest. Its superb bibliography demonstrates the value of an interdisciplinary approach to diplomatic history. Students of legal aspects of the war will pay particular attention to the works of authorities on international maritime law listed on pp. 209–10, especially those by R. Phillimore, F. H. Upton, C. C. Hyde, H. W. Briggs, and T. Baty.

11:228 Freidel, Frank. *Francis Lieber: Nineteenth-Century Liberal.* Baton Route: Louisiana State University Press, 1947. This work contains an assessment of Lieber's key role in codifying the rules of land warfare during the Civil War, as well as some commentary on his interest in international law.

Moore, J. B. *A Digest of International Law* (1:372) retains its usefulness as a source for many of the legal and diplomatic problems raised by the war. Students will find added utility in this work if they use it in conjunction with J. P. Baxter's article ("Some British Opinions as to Neutral Rights, 1861–1865" [11:233]). Both of these works provide useful correctives to some of Frank Owsley's observations on "freedom of the seas."

11:229 O'Rourke, Mary M. "The Diplomacy of William H. Seward: His Policies as Related to International Law." Ph.D. diss., University of California, Berkeley, 1963. Stuart Bernath has accurately described this work as "especially useful for its detailed analysis of the diplomacy and legal evolution of the Union blockade." Extensive bibliography.

11:230 Palmer, Roundell, Earl of Selborne. *Memorials Part I: Family and Personal, 1776–1865.* 2 vols. London: Macmillan, 1896. Palmer was Queen Victoria's solicitor general for the Civil War years, and his signature appears on nearly all of the legal opinions given to the government during the war. Volume 2 of the *Memorials* contains a number of useful chapters on international law, belligerent rights, the *Trent,* the cruisers, the rams, and the curious case of the *Alexandra.*

Savage, C. *Policy of the United States toward Maritime Commerce in War* (40:116) includes, in volume 1, some twenty documents, naval orders, executive proclamations, diplomatic exchanges, and three Supreme Court decisions, for the Civil War years.

Essays

11:231 Baxter, James P., III. "The British Government and Neutral Rights, 1861–1865." *American Historical Review* 34:3 (1928), 9–29. This pioneer article retains its usefulness. Based on British and American sources, it is carefully argued and contains extensive quotes from its sources.

11:232 Baxter, James P., III. "Papers Relating to Belligerent and Neutral Rights, 1861–1865." *American Historical Review* 34:3 (1928), 77–91. This piece assembles a number of key documents from Washington, London, and Paris, and is essentially an appendix to the author's article on the British government and neutral rights which appeared in the same issue of the *Review.*

11:233 Baxter, James P., III. "Some British Opinions as to Neutral Rights, 1861–1865." *American Journal of International Law* 23:3 (1929), 517–37. This piece contains a fine review of the legal literature on the war. Many of the highly technical points can be traced in Moore's *Digest of International Law* (1:372). It would be well to compare this account with the more modern assessments in the DeConde *Encyclopedia of American Foreign Policy,* especially those by Merli/ Ferrell and Rappaport.

11:234 Bernath, Stuart L. "British Neutrality and the Civil War Prize Cases." *Civil War History* 15:4 (1969), 320–31. In a concise and comprehensive survey of British mercantile press reactions to American interpretations of maritime law, the author surveys the attitudes (and motives) of parliamentary critics of government policy, and he traces the implementation of that policy by the British minister in Washington and by the commander of Royal Naval units in American waters.

11:235 Bernath, Stuart L. "Squall across the Atlantic: The *Peterhoff* Episode." *Journal of Southern History* 34:3 (1968), 382–401. This article contains a fine summary of the complexities of the doctrine of continuous voyage in maritime law that was such a point of contention between England and the United States during the Civil War.

11:236 Jarvis, Rupert C. "The *Alabama* and the Law." *Transactions of the Historic Society of Lancashire and Cheshire* 111 (1959), 181–98. The author argues that at the time of departure from England the *Alabama* was a bona fide neutral vessel and that the law, as it then was, prevented any governmental interference with her departure. The author skillfully exploits an unusual source for much of his evidence.

Mallison, S. V., and Mallison, T. W., Jr. "A Survey of the International Law of Naval Blockade [1776–1976]" (16:147). Points up the enormous difficulty involved in working out a definition of blockade that would be effective against the South and not too provocative to Britain.

11:237 Merli, Frank J. "Crown versus Cruiser: The Curious Case of the *Alexandra*." *Civil War History* 9:2 (1963), 167–77. Based on a wide variety of British sources, this work points up the legal difficulties facing the British government as it attempted to define the limits of neutrality.

Merli, F. J., and Ferrell, R. H. "Blockades and Quarantines" (16:148). Relates the Civil War blockade experiences to the larger dimensions in the evolution of American concepts on the theory and practice of blockade.

11:238 Owsley, Frank L., Jr. "America and the Freedom of the Seas, 1861–65." In Avery Craven, ed., *Essays in Honor of William E. Dodd*. Chicago: University of Chicago Press, 1935, pp. 194–256. This essay was an early attempt to trace the American shift in position on the subject of neutral rights in war time. The author stresses the surrender of principle for expediency. Compare with A. Rappaport "Freedom of the Seas" (16:149).

Pratt, J. W. "The British Blockade and American Precedent" (19:148) seeks to demonstrate that Great Britain looked to American examples during the Civil War for the precedents of her practice in 1914 to 1918. And Pratt argues convincingly that the North's policy in 1861 to 1865 "presented to Great Britain the best possible example of a blockade of the sort desired." Should be compared to the relevent articles in DeConde's *Encyclopedia of American Foreign Policy* (1:164).

12

Expansionist Efforts after the Civil War, 1865–1898

Contributing Editor
PAUL S. HOLBO
University of Oregon

Contributors
Ronald J. Jensen
George Mason University

Arthur Ned Newberry III
University of Oregon

Barry R. Rigby
Takoma Park, Maryland

Contents

Introduction

The end of the Civil War and the beginning of the war with Spain in 1898 define, perhaps too neatly, the chronological limits of an era in American history. In domestic affairs, this was the Gilded Age—originally Mark Twain's satirical description for the mid-1870s but later a label applied to the several decades after 1865. Prior to the Second World War, a generation of "progressive" historians saw the politicians of the Gilded Age—the likes of Ulysses S. Grant, James G. Blaine, and William McKinley—as unimportant, probably corrupt, and weak figures, who allegedly devoted themselves to meaningless debates over the tariff and the money question while they served the interests of big business. More recent scholars restored some of these men to important roles, recognized the significance of the issues of their day, and placed them in the context of an age when the United States was becoming an industrial, urban nation.

For many years the popular interpretation of late-nineteenth-century foreign relations has been that a gradual evolution occurred from the disinterest of the post–Civil War generation (except for the purchase of Alaska) to a display of national power and expansion at the end of the century. Grant, Blaine, McKinley, and other political figures were not, until recently, accorded important positions in the American pantheon in foreign policy.

Historians' accounts of American foreign relations from 1865 to 1898 diverge widely, however, and major differences in perspective remain. Much of this diversity in interpretation has ideological origins; the best of it is the result of imaginative historical research. The result, in any event, is that this period in American foreign relations has been the subject of lively controversies and is a rich field for study.

A basic issue is the complex question of imperialism, to which the best introduction is David Healy, *Modern Imperialism* (12:3). The word *imperialism,* first used to describe the policies of Napoleon III, was applied to the colonial expansion of the major European powers in the late nineteenth century.

Some contemporary European diplomatists argued that colonies were essential for new markets. Critics of expansion answered in kind. The liberal English journalist John A. Hobson, who was influenced by Marxist ideas, contended in *Imperialism: A Study* (1902) that capitalism directly fostered imperialism in order to find markets for overproduction but that the policy was mistaken and that colonies were costly and led to wars. Later Marxist writers explained imperialism in purely economic terms but differed among themselves about causes and meaning. The classic essay by V. I. Lenin, *Imperialism, the Highest Stage of Capitalism* (1916), established the orthodox Marxist line that imperialism is an inevitable stage in the advanced development of capitalism. Non-Marxists responded with equally powerful arguments: that imperialism antedated capitalism, that imperialism used capitalism, that factors such as security and power were more important than economics, and that there was little correspondence between the areas of European trade and investment and the areas where colonies were acquired.

The debate over European imperialism has greatly affected the study of American foreign policy after 1865. Progressive historians believed that big business dominated politics in the Gilded Age. It seemed plausible to them that economic interests determined foreign policy as well. By far the most persuasive of the many books that took this view in the years after the First World War was Charles and Mary Beard, *The Rise of American Civilization* (12:83). The Beards, who were influenced by Marxist ideas, the progressive movement, and their own distaste for a business-oriented society, asserted a dominant influence on historical study during the late 1920s and 1930s. Their work is highly economic-determinist in focus, but it is rich in detail and merits reading.

At the high tide of influence of the economic-determinist interpretation in the mid-1930s, Julius W. Pratt offered a stiff challenge with *Expansionists of 1898* (12:82). Skillfully blending intellectual with diplomatic history, Pratt downgraded economic factors and reasoned that the ideas of preachers, professors, and editors were far more influential in shaping foreign policy.

The prestige of the economic-determinists, many of whom were isolationists, received a sharp blow when

Japan attacked Pearl Harbor. American foreign policy was seen in a more positive light during the war—and for almost two decades after 1945. Vestiges remained, however, of the older, critical view of the Gilded Age. The new, dominant school of realism was comparatively uninterested in this era and found little to admire in its statesmen, who seemed to compare unfavorably with their successors such as Theodore Roosevelt and Woodrow Wilson. A few textbooks still mentioned economic interests as a factor in the development of policy during the 1890s, moreover, although the ideas of social Darwinian intellectuals (now commonly including navalists such as Alfred T. Mahan) were generally considered more important in the rise of the United States to world power.

Scholarly perceptions of the era and its major figures gradually changed. One step was the publication in 1963 of H. Wayne Morgan's *William McKinley and His America* (12:67), a perceptive biography that initiated the revival of that president's reputation without attempting to fit him into the realist mold. Many excellent biographies subsequently appeared on Gilded Age statesmen from William H. Seward to John Hay, and in most cases the result has been enhanced appreciation. Meanwhile, the multifaceted book by John A. S. Grenville and George Berkeley Young, *Politics, Strategy and American Diplomacy* (12:93), developed a more complex outlook than much of the currently popular work of the realist school.

During the same years, there occurred a revival of the economic-determinist perspective, which ebbs and then flows again in modern American history. The seminal volume was William. Appleman Williams, *The Tragedy of American Diplomacy* (2:99), itself heavily influenced by the views of Charles A. Beard; it emphasized ideas somewhat more than Beard had done and was much less specific in detail but clearly of a piece with the older work. Largely ignored for a half-dozen years, Williams's book gradually spawned a series of largely derivative monographs, such as Walter LaFeber's *The New Empire* (12:84) and Thomas McCormick's *China Market* (17:237), that took the view that United States foreign policy was determined by the search for foreign markets—the open door abroad. The so-called New Left school established a considerable following during the Vietnam War.

Some scholars who were skeptical about the revived economic thesis attempted to accommodate it within an enlarged spectrum of interpretations. Ernest R. May, in *American Imperialism: A Speculative Essay* (2:94), imaginatively used concepts from the behavioral sciences and employed an international perspective to suggest that the European example of imperialism momentarily had affected the views of an American elite. Other historians directly challenged the evidence, arguments, and assumptions of the new economic-determinist school. A sharp debate ensued, as many citations in the following chapter demonstrate.

There also appeared broad new interpretations transcending the economic argument. Robert L. Beisner, *From the Old Diplomacy to the New* (12:6), held that altered perceptions and behavior after 1889 decisively changed American foreign policy. The more comprehensive, thoughtful survey by Charles S. Campbell, *The Transformation of American Foreign Relations* (12:7), likewise discounted the importance of economic influences and incorporated the findings of the numerous specialized scholarly books and articles on Gilded Age foreign policy that have been published in the past fifteen years.

Many opportunities remain for further research. There is a particular need for the examination of specific diplomats, secretaries of state, and second-level bureaucrats; for careful analyses of patterns of foreign trade and of the tariff; for study of specific expansionist episodes and the reasons for their failure; and especially for thoughtful reflections upon the political and emotional responses of Americans to the world of the late nineteenth century.

Resources and Overviews

RESEARCH AIDS

While pertinent bibliographies and reference aids are listed here, there are more extensive lists in Chapter 1.

Bibliographies

12:1 Braisted, William R. "The Navy in the Early Twentieth Century, 1890–1941." In Robin Higham, ed. *A Guide to the Sources of United States Military History.* Hamden, Conn.: Shoe String Press, 1975, pp. 344–77. While focusing largely on naval affairs, it does provide many references useful to diplomatic historians, including the rationale for the new navy.

12:2   De Santis, Vincent P. *The Gilded Age, 1877–1896*. Arlington Heights, Ill.: AHM, 1973. This bibliography includes chapters on politics and foreign affairs.

Golder, F. A. *Guide to Materials for American History in Russian Archives* [1781–1917] (1:292).

12:3   Healy, David. *Modern Imperialism: Changing Styles in Historical Interpretation*. Washington, D.C.: American Historical Association, 1967. This masterful historiographical essay emphasizes the late 19th century. The work is both interpretive and an essential guide to further inquiry.

Holbo, P. S. "Perspectives on American Foreign Policy, 1890–1916 . . . " (13:2) conveniently summarizes various interpretations of America's rise to world power.

Smith, D. M. "Rise to Great World Power, 1865–1918" (13:4) reviews recent historical interpretation.

12:4   Smith, Myron J., Jr., ed. *The American Navy, 1865–1918: A Bibliography*. Metuchen, N.J.: Scarecrow Press, 1974. While it focuses on naval matters, it lists many references of value for the diplomatic historian.

Document Collections

General collections are listed in Chapter 1 and other collections may be found in "Personalities," below.

12:5   U.S. National Archives and Record Service. *Records of the Russian-American Company, 1802–67*. M-11, 77 rolls. Washington, D.C., n.d. These records of the Russian-American Company, which had economic and political control over Alaska before the U.S. purchase in 1867, are in Russian longhand.

OVERVIEWS

12:6   Beisner, Robert L. *From the Old Diplomacy to the New, 1865–1900*. New York: Crowell, 1975. This imaginative volume assesses scholarly views of the period, identifies the chief issues, and offers a credible new reconciling interpretation. Instead of economic influences or an evolution toward imperialism, there was a substantial shift in the 1890s from a passive, reactive "old diplomacy" to a more deliberative "new paradigm." Extensive bibliography.

12:7   Campbell, Charles S., Jr. *The Transformation of American Foreign Relations, 1865–1900*. New York: Harper & Row, 1976. This comprehensive, balanced, up-to-date survey is an essential volume and best point of departure for the study of American foreign relations after 1865. It focuses on the transformation of America's international position and on changes in Anglo-American relations. It deemphasizes the importance of open door imperialism. Extensive bibliography.

12:8   Dobson, John M. *America's Ascent: The United States Becomes a Great Power, 1880–1914*. De Kalb: Northern Illinois University Press, 1978. Dobson contends that efforts to expand commerce, obtain colonies and later protectorates, and assert American moral superiority underlay the appearance of the United States as a world power. The book is a tendentious synthesis of revisionist and other interpretations. Bibliography.

12:9   Dozer, Donald M. "Anti-Expansionism during the Johnson Administration." *Pacific Historical Review* 12:3 (1943), 253–75. Dozer sketches expansionist efforts (1865–1869), measuring their strength by the reactions of Congress and the press. The article is eclectic and descriptive, but does not probe deeply into political factors.

12:10   Dulles, Foster Rhea. *Prelude to World Power: American Diplomatic History, 1860–1900*. New York: Macmillan, 1965. Dulles portrays American policy as active until 1867 and at low ebb through the 1880s as Americans were absorbed in domestic activities. Intellectual, journalistic, commercial, and naval influences caused the nation to look outward and led to revived nationalism, war, and empire. Bibliography.

12:11   Healy, David. *U.S. Expansionism: The Imperialist Urge in the 1890s*. Madison: University of Wisconsin Press, 1970. This book looks at the background and consequences of expansion in the 1890s. It takes a fresh look at the thinking that lay behind foreign policy as manifested in both secondary and major political figures. The treatment of American interest in Canada and Cuba is particularly sophisticated, as is the recognition of the duality of expediency and morality in expansionist thought. Bibliography.

Holt, W. S. *Treaties Defeated by the Senate: A Study of the Struggle between President and Senate over the Conduct of Foreign Relations* (2:150) devotes two chapters to the period from 1865 to 1900, and contains descriptions of many treaties and their fate at the hands of the Senate.

Perkins, D. *The Monroe Doctrine, 1867–1907* (15:52) finds no foreign threats, few territorial issues, and little American use before 1895 of the doctrine; nevertheless, the no-transfer principle grew quietly as a result of the diplomacy of the Grant administration.

12:12   Plesur, Milton. *America's Outward Thrust: Approaches to Foreign Affairs, 1865–1890.* De Kalb: Northern Illinois University, 1971. This sprightly, undogmatic book is an eclectic introductory survey of American international contacts in the Gilded Age. The author quarrels with the tired assumption that the era was one of doldrums. The chapters on cultural and popular interactions between the United States and other lands are the most interesting, though their importance for policy remains unclear. Extensive bibliography.

12:13   Schuyler, Eugene. *American Diplomacy and the Furtherance of Commerce.* New York: Scribner's, 1886. The first work to examine American diplomacy after 1865, it is still valuable because of its scholarliness, emphasis on commercial issues, and sharp commentaries on current diplomatic practices, the power of Congress over appropriations, and the need for consular reform (1865–1884).

12:14   Smith, Theodore C. "Expansion after the Civil War, 1865–71." *Political Science Quarterly* 16:3 (1901), 412–36. This pioneering and still useful study recognizes the extent of latent expansionism and some of the forces frustrating postwar expansionist schemes.

Van Alstyne, R. W. *The Rising American Empire* (2:96) describes the main forces in the Gilded Age as industrial and financial capitalism.

Political, Social, and Cultural Factors

12:15   Dobson, John M. *Politics in the Gilded Age: A New Perspective on Reform.* New York: Praeger, 1972. This is an even-handed comparison of the morals and motives of politicians and reformers, focusing on the election of 1884. The importance of the tariff is underplayed, and foreign policy receives scant attention. Bibliography.

12:16   Faulkner, Harold U. *Politics, Reform and Expansion, 1890–1900.* New York: Harper, 1959. The 1890s appear as a time of new intellectual awareness about changes in American life—the frontier, expansion, the city, immigration—and economic developments. The author often minimizes the impact of economic influences on foreign policy. Extensive bibliography.

12:17   Jensen, Richard. *The Winning of the Midwest: Social and Political Conflict, 1888–1896.* Chicago: University of Chicago Press, 1971. Jensen stresses the importance of religious values and party loyalty rather than economics for the political system in the Gilded Age. There are, however, many references to the tariff issue in politics and useful portrayals of the views of immigrant groups. Extensive bibliography.

12:18   Keller, Morton. *Affairs of State: Public Life in Late Nineteenth Century America.* Cambridge: Harvard University Press, 1977. Keller's massive study describes with impressive sophistication the values and organizational patterns of American public life. The author treats foreign policy within the context of the changes and tensions resulting from industrial polities, but he allows for the importance of variability and ambivalence.

12:19   Kleppner, Paul. *The Cross of Culture: A Social Analysis of Midwestern Politics, 1850–1900.* New York: Free Press, 1970. A quantitative, value-oriented political history, it stresses religious values rather than economic forces in the transformation of the Republican party to a party of prosperity. The broad political analysis is useful, as is the study of the tariff in its symbolic use. Bibliography.

12:20   Kleppner, Paul. *The Third Electoral System, 1853–1892: Parties, Voters, and Political Cultures.* Chapel Hill: North Carolina University Press, 1979. Combining quantitative and verbal analysis with documentary study, this volume emphasizes ethnoreligious perspectives in shaping national politics and challenges the liberal-rational analysis of political behavior.

12:21   Morgan, H. Wayne. *From Hayes to McKinley: National Party Politics, 1877–1896.* Syracuse, N.Y.: Syracuse University Press, 1969. Morgan successfully evokes the spirit of party politics in the Gilded Age. The forging of a national party system was led by forward-looking Republicans, and these developments had great significance for foreign policy. Extensive bibliography.

12:22　Morgan, H. Wayne, ed. *The Gilded Age.* Rev. ed. Syracuse, N.Y.: Syracuse University Press, 1970. This multiauthor work is the best overall study of American society in the late 19th century.

12:23　Morgan, H. Wayne. *Unity and Culture: The United States, 1877–1900.* Baltimore: Penguin, 1971. This concise volume is a good introduction to the patterns of politics, economic growth, art and literature, and foreign policy in the late 19th century. Extensive bibliography.

12:24　Nichols, Jeannette P. "The United States Congress and Imperialism, 1861–1897." *The Journal of Economic History* 21:4 (1961), 526–38. Nichols stresses negative reference groups on imperialism, centering on domestic politics, costs and wealth, and negative attitudes toward foreigners, especially the British. She found changes in the 1880s, but concludes that the period 1861 to 1897 was erratic.

Werking, R. H. *The Master Architects: Building the United States Foreign Service, 1890–1913.* (2:180) analyzes the bureaucratic determinants of American foreign policy, especially trade expansion.

12:25　Wiebe, Robert H. *The Search for Order, 1877–1920.* New York: Hill & Wang, 1967. Wiebe argues that America was transformed from a splintered society with small-town values to a unified society with new values of management and middle-class rationality. The impact on foreign policy is not clear. Bibliography.

12:26　Williams, R. Hal. *Years of Decision: American Politics in the 1890s.* New York: Wiley, 1978. This study of national politics synthesizes recent research on election patterns and presents the Republicans as activists who governed and the Democrats as negative. The treatment of foreign policy is thin. Bibliography.

Economic Factors

12:27　Davies, Robert B. " 'Peacefully Working to Conquer the World': The Singer Manufacturing Company in Foreign Markets, 1854–1889." *Business History Review* 43:3 (1969), 299–325. Singer was not affected by domestic business cycles and built an international sales and marketing organization without the aid of the government.

Doenecke, J. D. "The Most-Favored-Nation Principle" (39:48) contains a brief but useful section on controversial trade cases and the negative effects of the American conditional use of this principle after 1865.

Gould, L. L. "Diplomats in the Lobby: Franco-American Relations and the Dingley Tariff of 1897" (14:111) demonstrates that there was a connection between bimetallism and tariff making. There were intense negotiations between French diplomats and American senators, who used reciprocity to obtain French cooperation on bimetallism. A search for foreign markets was only a secondary factor behind reciprocity in 1897.

Holbo, P. S. "Trade and Commerce" (39:49) includes a detailed analysis of trends after 1865.

Nichols, J. P. "Silver Diplomacy [1876–1933]" (39:94) is a detailed study of international currency issues and negotiations.

Porter, G. *The Rise of Big Business, 1860–1910* (39:20) is the best brief introduction to issues in American business history after 1865, focusing on the technology of production, the system of distribution, and markets.

12:28　Stanwood, Edward. *American Tariff Controversies in the Nineteenth Century.* 2 vols. Boston: Houghton Mifflin, 1903. Stanwood, who favored the protective tariff, also supported the reciprocity program of Blaine. These volumes, while moderate in their treatment of Cleveland, provide a detailed political analysis from Blaine's point of view.

12:29　Tarbell, Ida M. *The Tariff in Our Times.* New York: Macmillan, 1911. Tarbell believed that protective tariffs in the late 19th century controverted the public will and involved unprincipled bargaining. This volume contains a number of revelations designed to support this view and to stress the importance of the tariff issue.

Taussig, F. W. *Free Trade: The Tariff and Reciprocity* (39:85) contains chapters analyzing the effects of Hawaiian reciprocity and the McKinley tariff from the low-tariff viewpoint.

Taussig, F. W. *The Tariff History of the United States* (39:86).

12:30 Taussig, Frank W. *Some Aspects of the Tariff Question.* Cambridge: Harvard University Press, 1915. Taussig analyzes tariffs according to the product, such as sugar, wool, and copper.

Wilkins, M. *The Emergence of Multinational Enterprise: American Business Abroad from the Colonial Era to 1914* (39:134) is a wide-ranging, balanced, and comprehensive study.

Personalities

Additional references on individuals may be found in Chapter 1, "Biographical Data."

Brooks Adams

Vevier, C. "Brooks Adams and the Ambivalence of American Foreign Policy" (2:54).

12:31 Williams, William A. "Brooks Adams and American Expansion." *New England Quarterly* 25:2 (1952), 217–32. An analysis of Adams's views on expansionism and of America's international role chiefly as related to Asia. Adams supposedly exerted considerable influence on the proponents of the "large policy" during the Spanish-American war.

Chester A. Arthur

Pletcher, David M. *The Awkward Years: American Foreign Relations under Garfield and Arthur* (12:46) argues that the foreign policy of the Garfield and Arthur administrations foreshadowed later expansionism.

12:31a Reeves, Thomas C. *Gentleman Boss: The Life of Chester Alan Arthur.* New York: Knopf, 1975. This is the definitive political biography of Arthur.

James G. Blaine

See Chapter 15, "Personalities," for additional references.

12:32 Blaine, James G. *Twenty Years of Congress: From Lincoln to Garfield.* 2 vols. Norwich, Conn.: Henry Bill, 1886. This politically motivated commentary on Congress must be used with care, but its characterizations of members are of considerable value. Blaine also made clear his views on such issues

as Alaska, Santo Domingo, Chinese immigration, and foreign trade.

Harrison, Benjamin. *The Correspondence between Benjamin Harrison and James G. Blaine, 1882–1893* (12:56).

Langley, L. D. "James Gillespie Blaine: The Ideologue as Diplomatist" (15:6) is the most satisfactory study of Blaine. The author weighs conflicting interpretations.

12:33 Spetter, Allan. "Harrison and Blaine: Foreign Policy, 1889–1893." *Indiana Magazine of History* 65:3 (1969), 215–27. The author argues convincingly that Harrison was determined to assume charge of foreign policy and that Blaine's frequent illnesses in 1890 diminished his influence. Harrison not only was aggressive, utilizing naval power, but supported a "large policy."

12:34 Tyler, Alice Felt. *The Foreign Policy of James G. Blaine.* Minneapolis: University of Minnesota Press, 1927. Tyler's thesis is that Blaine's stance was transitional between Seward's expansionism and later economic penetration, and that he had greater grasp and vision than any other secretary of his era. Fair-minded if in need of updating, the book provides a good introduction to Blaine. Bibliography.

Grover Cleveland

12:35 Dulebohn, George R. *Principles of Foreign Policy under the Cleveland Administrations.* Philadelphia, 1941. This work treats Cleveland (1885–1889, 1893–1897) as a conservative in foreign policy who meant to preserve national security, avoid entanglement in power politics, and settle disputes by peaceful means. The author argues that Cleveland was an archfoe of imperialism.

12:36 Merrill, Horace S. *Bourbon Leader: Grover Cleveland.* Boston: Little, Brown, 1957. Merrill treats Cleveland as an honest but plodding, conservative, and generally inactive president. The brief sections on foreign policy emphasize the influence of Olney and, unconvincingly, Cleveland's political isolation and irritability.

12:37 Nevins, Allan. *Grover Cleveland: A Study in Courage.* New York: Dodd, Mead, 1932. This admiring biography treats Cleveland as careful, honest, patient, and an unyielding opponent of imperialism. The major focus in foreign policy is on Venezuela, where Cleveland's unfortunate message awakened the public to accept the Monroe Doctrine, and Hawaii, where policy went awry.

Sanford B. Dole

12:38 Damon, Ethel M. *Sanford Ballard Dole and His Hawaii.* Palo Alto, Calif.: Pacific Books, 1957. Dole, long an important member of the Hawaiian government, became the first president of the provisional government established after the revolution of 1893 and retained that post after the formation of the Republic of Hawaii in 1894. Dole later became the first territorial governor after annexation of the Islands to the United States.

12:39 Dole, Sanford B. *Memoirs of the Hawaiian Revolution.* Ed. by Andrew Farrell. Honolulu: Advertiser Publishing, 1936. The personal account of the Hawaiian Revolution of 1893 by one of Hawaii's most important figures. Dole argued that the revolution would not have happened in 1893 but for the knowledge that U.S. Minister to Hawaii J. L. Stevens was in sympathy with it.

William M. Evarts

Barrows, C.L. *William M. Evarts: Lawyer, Diplomat, Statesman* (15:12) is fuller and more analytical than Dyer's biography. Barrows sees Evarts as less serious than Fish and less spectacular than Blaine. An old-fashioned diplomat, he was never hurried or flustered, or bored by routine; a lawyer by mentality, he was not interested in seeking out new issues. The coverage is fairly comprehensive, except for Caribbean issues.

Dyer, B. *The Public Career of William M. Evarts* (15:13) is generally factual and dispassionate. Dyer notes Evarts's procrastination and criticizes his Latin American policies—marked by aggressiveness (but not personal profiteering) and reversals regarding Mexico, by the use of amateur diplomats, and by failure to consummate a canal treaty. Dyer praises the promotion of commerce and improvement of relations with Japan.

Hamilton Fish

See also Chapter 17, "Personalities."

12:40 Chapin, James B. "Hamilton Fish and American Expansion." In Frank J. Merli and Theodore A. Wilson, eds. *Makers of American Diplomacy from Benjamin Franklin to Henry Kissinger.* New York: Scribner's, 1974, vol. 1, pp. 223–51. This is a tendentious but provocative essay, notable for its sharply critical view. Fish appears here as a wealthy, upper-class conservative who survived in the Grant administration by shifting allegiance to the Stalwarts, and as a subtle, conscious expansionist who believed in protectorates and "informal empire." Bibliography.

12:41 Nevins, Allan. *Hamilton Fish: The Inner History of the Grant Administration.* New York: Dodd, Mead, 1936. This famous biography must be used with care because of the protective treatment of Fish and hostile view of other members of the Grant administration. Some quoted statements are fictitious, but the narrative is dramatic and the interpretation worthy of note.

John W. Foster

12:42 Devine, Michael J. "John W. Foster and the Struggle for the Annexation of Hawaii." *Pacific Historical Review* 46:1 (1977) 29–50. A good account of Secretary of State John Foster's efforts to secure Hawaiian annexation. Devine demonstrates Foster's determination and sense of mission regarding annexation, and also describes some of the political machinations in Honolulu and Washington, D.C.

12:43 Foster, John W. *Diplomatic Memoirs.* 2 vols. Boston: Houghton Mifflin, 1909. These anecdotal volumes, which do not follow strict chronological order, contain useful details on Foster's important diplomatic service, notably his several foreign missions, negotiations for reciprocity, and work for other governments. Foster also offers many candid comments on presidents, secretaries of state, and foreign envoys.

James A. Garfield

12:44 Garfield, James A. *The Diary of James A. Garfield.* 3 vols. to date. Ed. by Harry J. Brown and Frederick D. Williams. East Lansing: Michigan State University Press, 1967– . This carefully edited series, now in three volumes, may become of value for the study of foreign affairs as it approaches the time of Garfield's presidency.

12:45 Peskin, Allan. *Garfield.* Kent, Ohio: Kent State University Press, 1978. Filled with observations on personalities and politics, this lengthy biography devotes a few pages to foreign policy, in which Garfield is credited for the major ventures of his short-lived administration. Extensive bibliography.

12:46 Pletcher, David M. *The Awkward Years: American Foreign Relations under Garfield and Arthur.* Columbia: University of Missouri Press, 1962. This carefully researched study of a neglected period stresses the confusion and frustration of policy, yet contends that the Garfield and Arthur administrations (1881–1885) foreshadowed and prepared for later expansionism. The analysis of the motives of politicians and businessmen is sophisticated. Bibliography.

Ulysses S. Grant

12:47 Badeau, Adam. *Grant in Peace: From Appomattox to Mount McGregor*. Hartford, Conn.: Scranton, 1887. Badeau, a close associate of Grant, provides much personal material (1865–1877).

12:48 Carpenter, John A. *Ulysses S. Grant*. New York: Twayne, 1970. The chief value of this concise biography is the accurate depiction of Grant's developing relationship with and dependence on Fish, who is described as fully informed about and supportive of the Dominican annexation plan. Cuba, arbitration, and Santo Domingo are linked as well.

12:49 Coolidge, Louis A. *Ulysses S. Grant*. Boston: Houghton Mifflin, 1917. This friendly but careful biography provides a coherent view of Grant's character, stressing his determination and honesty. The chapters on arbitration and Santo Domingo remain useful.

12:50 Grant, Ulysses S. *The Papers of Ulysses S. Grant*. 8 vols. to date. Ed. by John Y. Simon. Carbondale: Southern Illinois University Press, 1967–. This carefully edited collection, whose first eight volumes cover the period through 1863, should be of considerable value for the study of foreign relations when it reaches the presidential years.

12:51 Hesseltine, William B. *U.S. Grant: Politician*. New York: Dodd, Mead, 1935. Hesseltine refutes charges that Grant (1869–1877) was stupid or corrupt but accuses him of ignorance of the Constitution and of a lack of vision. Hesseltine treats Fish as the restraining force in foreign affairs, especially regarding Cuba, and finds unscrupulous persons behind Dominican policy. Bibliography.

Walter Q. Gresham

Calhoun, C. W. "American Policy toward the Brazilian Naval Revolt of 1893–94: A Reexamination" (15:206) analyzes the contention that Secretary of State Gresham intervened in this revolt to expand American markets, and finds this was not so.

12:52 Calhoun, Charles W. " 'The Ragged Edge of Anxiety': A Political Biography of Walter Q. Gresham." Ph.D. diss., Columbia University, 1977. This dissertation, almost half of which deals with

Gresham as secretary of state (1893–1895), not only reflects the renewed interest in the subject but corrects exaggerated revisionist interpretations. Extensive research and bibliography.

12:53 Gresham, Matilda. *Life of Walter Quintin Gresham*. 2 vols. Chicago: Rand, McNally, 1919. Five chapters in volume two deal with Gresham's service as secretary of state, including the Bering Sea arbitrations, Hawaii, and Latin America. The book's chief virtues are its vignettes and anecdotes, the clues to political alignments, and its revelations of Gresham's moral values.

William M. Gwin

12:54 McPherson, Hallie M. "The Interest of William McKendree Gwin in the Purchase of Alaska, 1854–1861." *Pacific Historical Review* 3:1 (1934), 28–38. Gwin was the "advance agent" who saw Alaska as one element in a vast Pacific commercial empire. As Buchanan's representative, Gwin conducted unofficial and inconclusive negotiations with Russia's minister in Washington during the 1850s.

12:55 Steele, Robert V. *Between Two Empires: The Life Story of California's First Senator, William McKendree Gwin*. Boston: Houghton Mifflin, 1969. This biography outlines the career of one of the earliest advocates of Pacific expansion. The account is not documented.

Benjamin Harrison

Baker, G. W., Jr. "Benjamin Harrison and Hawaiian Annexation: A Reinterpretation" (12:171).

12:56 Harrison, Benjamin. *The Correspondence between Benjamin Harrison and James G. Blaine, 1883–1893*. Ed. by Albert T. Volwiler. Memoirs, vol. 14. Philadelphia: American Philosophical Society, 1940. This extensive set of letters is suggestive of the relationship and ideas of the two men, and it contains useful details.

12:57 Sievers, Harry J. *Benjamin Harrison, Hoosier President: The White House and After*. Indianapolis: Bobbs-Merrill, 1968. The contention is that Harrison set foreign policy and that his goals were national strength and noninterference. The treatment of the important Hawaiian episode is brief and not analytical. Extensive bibliography.

Spetter, A. "Harrison and Blaine: Foreign Policy, 1889–1893" (12:33).

John Hay
See Chapters 13 and 14, "Personalities," for additional references.

12:58 Clymer, Kenton J. *John Hay: The Gentleman as Diplomat.* Ann Arbor: University of Michigan Press, 1975. This volume contains valuable information about diplomatic appointments during the McKinley administration and about the evolution of Hay's foreign policy views from ardent young Republican to unsentimental Anglo-American. Extensive bibliography.

Rutherford B. Hayes
12:59 Barnard, Harry. *Rutherford B. Hayes and His America.* Indianapolis: Bobbs-Merrill, 1954. Information on Hayes's foreign policy views toward Mexico and on his hostile relations with Blaine are scattered through this volume.

12:60 Davison, Kenneth E. *The Presidency of Rutherford B. Hayes.* Westport, Conn.: Greenwood, 1972. This balanced study of the Hayes-Evarts administration considers promotion of trade, by better consular reporting, their foremost achievement. Davison credits circumstances for improved relations with Mexico but argues that Hayes extended the Monroe Doctrine to Panama. Policy toward Europe and Canada was less successful. Extensive bibliography.

12:61 Hayes, Rutherford B. *Hayes: The Diary of a President, 1875–1881.* Ed. by T. Harry Williams. New York: McKay, 1964. The diary focuses heavily on ceremonial life and domestic politics, but it contains passing references to policy toward Mexico, an isthmian canal, Chinese immigration, and diplomatic appointments.

George F. Hoar
12:62 Hoar, George F. *Autobiography of Seventy Years.* 2 vols. New York: Scribner's, 1903. The chief value of this book is the author's expression of his strong opposition to discriminatory treatment of Chinese immigrants. Also available are sections on the Treaty of Washington and on the fisheries question.

12:63 Welch, Richard E., Jr. *George Frisbie Hoar and the Half-Breed Republicans.* Cambridge: Harvard University Press, 1971. This intelligent biography (1868–1900) portrays Senator Hoar as a highly partisan Free Soil and Half-Breed Republican who was an ardent protectionist, advocate of increasing trade, supporter of executive power in foreign affairs (except by Cleveland), and opponent of expansion. Extensive bibliography.

Queen Liliuokalani
12:64 Hodges, William C., Jr. *The Passing of Liliuokalani.* Honolulu: Honolulu Star-Bulletin, 1918. A short biography of the last monarch of Hawaii, which covers the life of the queen from her childhood, her overthrow in the revolution of 1893, the annexation of the Islands in 1898.

12:65 Liliuokalani. *Hawaii's Story by Hawaii's Queen.* Boston: Lee & Shepard, 1898. Reprint 1964. Queen Liliuokalani's rebuttal to the charges made by the revolutionaries and American expansionists regarding the corruption of her government and attempted usurpation of power. Liliuokalani explains why her forces surrendered after the American minister in the Islands recognized the provisional government established by the revolutionaries.

Alfred T. Mahan
See Chapter 41, "Personalities," for additional references.

LaFeber, W. "A Note on the 'Mercantilistic Imperialism' of Alfred Thayer Mahan" (14:39).

Seager, R., II. *Alfred Thayer Mahan: The Man and His Letters* (40:80) is intentionally traditional in form and eschews both New Left and behavioral perspectives, but is comprehensive and analytical. There is a helpful appraisal of Mahan's distinct and developing views on Hawaii and other expansionist issues.

William McKinley
See Chapter 13, "Personalities," for additional references.

12:66 Coletta, Paolo. "Prologue: William McKinley and the Conduct of United States Foreign Relations." In Paolo Coletta, ed., *Threshold to American Internationalism: Essays on the Foreign Policies of William McKinley.* New York: Exposition, 1970, pp. 11–33. An eclectic interpretation, this chapter contains both an older, more critical view and a newer, more favorable view of McKinley as politician and statesman.

12:67 Morgan, H. W. *William McKinley and His America.* Syracuse, N.Y.: Syracuse University Press, 1963. A ground-breaking book, this solidly researched biography led to recognition of McKinley as a shrewd politician and strong president. Bibliography.

William H. Seward

See Chapter 11, "Personalities," for additional references.

Paolino, E. N. *The Foundations of the American Empire: William Henry Seward and U.S. Foreign Policy* (15:18).

Van Deusen, G. G. *William Henry Seward* (11:57) stresses Seward's expansionist vision and concludes that he favored the acquisition of Alaska primarily for its strategic location.

Warren, G. H. "Imperial Dreamer: William Henry Seward and American Destiny" (11:58) evaluates Seward as an expansionist, a preserver of earlier hemispheric aims, and though generally unlucky himself, a precursor of later imperialists.

Claus Spreckels

12:68 Adler, Jacob. *Claus Spreckels: The Sugar King of Hawaii.* Honolulu: University of Hawaii Press, 1966. Adler argues that Spreckels dominated the Hawaiian sugar industry. Spreckels was involved in Hawaiian politics (1876–1908) first with his dealing with King Kalakaua and later when he attempted to restore Queen Liliuokalani following the revolution of 1893.

12:69 Adler, Jacob. *Claus Spreckels' Rise and Fall in Hawaii with Emphasis on London Loan of 1886.* Hawaiian Historical Society, 67th annual report. Honolulu: Hawaiian Historical Society, 1959. Spreckels became the head of the California sugar trust and also gained a strong voice in the affairs of Hawaii under King Kalakaua. The London Loan marked the end of Spreckels's power.

Charles Sumner

See Chapter 11, "Personalities," for additional references.

Donald, D. H. *Charles Sumner and the Rights of Man* (11:59) provides a penetrating examination of Sumner's personality and political practices, and contains a wealth of information about issues of foreign policy under Johnson and Grant (1865–1874).

12:70 Sumner, Charles. *Memoirs and Letters of Charles Sumner.* 4 vols. Boston: Lee & Shepard, 1877–1893. Volume 4 of this collection concerns the Alaska cession (1867–1868) and includes Sumner's Senate address on behalf of the treaty.

Others

Armstrong, W. M. *E. L. Godkin and American Foreign Policy, 1865–1900* (14:55).

Bemis, S. F., ed. *The American Secretaries of State and Their Diplomacy* (2:166) contains, in volumes 7 and 8, studies of the secretaries of state from Seward through Olney. There are biographical sketches and comprehensive descriptions emphasizing formal diplomacy. All of the studies remain of value. The two-part appraisal of Blaine by Joseph B. Lockey is particularly noteworthy. Bibliographies.

12:71 Boutwell, George S. *Reminiscences of Sixty Years in Public Affairs.* 2 vols. New York: McClure, Phillips, 1902. This celebrated memoir offers only cursory and somewhat inaccurate comments on such issues as Santo Domingo and arbitration.

DeNovo, J. A. "The Enigmatic Alvey A. Adee and American Foreign Relations, 1870–1924" (14:57) provides references and details about the contributions of this skilled draftsman of dispatches and treaties, faithful and witty bureaucrat, and tutor of young officials and new administrations.

12:72 Eggert, Gerald G. *Richard Olney: Evolution of a Statesman.* University Park: Pennsylvania State Press, 1974. This extensively researched biography graphically reveals Olney's harsh personality and his generally responsible positions in foreign policy. The author also refutes the theories of open door imperialism as applied to the second Cleveland administration (1893–1897). There is a valuable discussion of arbitration. Bibliography.

12:73 Foulke, William D. *Life of Oliver P. Morton, Including His Important Speeches.* 2 vols. Indianapolis: Bobbs-Merrill, 1899. This old biography remains useful because it makes clear Morton's attitude in the controversy over Santo Domingo. Bibliography.

12:74 Harrington, Fred H. *Fighting Politician: Major General N. P. Banks.* Philadelphia: University of Pennsylvania Press, 1948. This biography is valuable because of the extended treatment of Banks's important role (1865–1891) in shaping foreign policy and pressing for expansion. The scattered Banks manuscripts were consolidated following publication of this book, but it remains a fundamental source. Bibliography.

Niven, J. *Gideon Welles: Lincoln's Secretary of the Navy* (11:60) provides useful background for an understanding of the policies of the Johnson-Seward administration (1865–1869).

12:75 Richardson, Leon B. *William E. Chandler, Republican*. New York: Dodd, Mead, 1940. This is a balanced account of the previously inexperienced but energetic Chandler's management of complex naval politics and patronage (1882–1885), and of his oversight of the first development of the new navy. A lively discussion of political disputes over the first steel ships during the subsequent Cleveland administration is offered.

12:76 Shenton, James P. *Robert J. Walker: A Politician from Jackson to Lincoln*. New York: Columbia University Press, 1961. Shenton's biography traces Walker's expansionist beliefs (1850–1870), his association with other promoters of the cession, and his lobbying activities on behalf of the Alaska appropriation. Bibliography.

12:77 Tansill, Charles C. *The Foreign Policy of Thomas F. Bayard, 1885–1897*. New York: Fordham University Press, 1940. This massive, immensely detailed, exhaustively researched, and partisan biographical study focuses entirely on Bayard's diplomatic service, especially as secretary of state. The author praises Bayard's concern for good relations with England, and criticizes Olney, Cleveland, and Blaine, and most Republicans.

12:78 Van Deusen, Glyndon G. *Thurlow Weed: Wizard of the Lobby*. Boston: Little, Brown, 1947. Good detail about organizational and factional politics enhance this biography, which also contains information (as on Alta Vela) relevant to foreign policy (1865–1870). Bibliography.

Younger, E. *John A. Kasson: Politics and Diplomacy from Lincoln to McKinley* (14:62) is a biography of an Iowa Republican politician who served as Harrison's Samoan commissioner and McKinley's minister to negotiate reciprocity treaties. The biography's major value is its description of political factors and of details and disputes during the Congo and Samoan negotiations.

Ideas and Pressures of Expansionism

MANIFEST DESTINY AND SOCIAL DARWINISM

See Chapter 9, "American Expansionism," and Chapter 10, "Manifest Destiny"; also Chapter 2, "Philanthropy and Missionaries."

Hofstadter, R. "Manifest Destiny and the Philippines" (13:91) accounts for American foreign policy at century's end by describing "the psychic crisis of the 1890's" with its sources in political, social, economic, and psychological considerations.

12:79 Hofstadter, Richard. *Social Darwinism in American Thought, 1860–1915*. Rev. ed. New York: Braziller (1945), 1959. This is a brilliant exposition of the development and influence of Darwinism in American intellectual and political life and in foreign affairs. Bibliography.

12:80 May, Ernest R. *Imperial Democracy: The Emergence of America as a Great Power*. New York: Harcourt Brace Jovanovich, 1961. This broad-ranging study (1880–1890) takes the older view that Americans were concerned with domestic events, that their leadership was weak, and that world power was thrust on the United States. The value of this volume is its portrayal of the perception and reaction by foreign powers to America's emergence. Also see his *American Imperialism* (2:94).

Merk, F., with Merk, L. B. *Manifest Destiny and Mission in American History: A Reinterpretation* [1830–1898] (2:52) compares the Mexican War with the Spanish-American War to show the difference between *mission* and *manifest destiny*.

12:81 Muller, Dorothea R. "Josiah Strong and American Nationalism: A Reevaluation." *Journal of American History* 53:3 (1966), 487–503. This article corrects earlier arguments that Strong was a Darwinian, advocate of Anglo-Saxon supremacy, and territorial expansionist before 1898.

12:82 Pratt, Julius W. *Expansionists of 1898: The Acquisition of Hawaii and the Spanish Islands*. Baltimore: Johns Hopkins Press, 1936. This imaginative, long-influential work boldly challenges the economic interpretation of American policy and blends the study of intellectual and diplomatic history. The author stresses Darwinian ideas and gives considerable attention to public opinion. Bibliography.

Weinberg, A. K. *Manifest Destiny: A Study of Nationalist Expansionism in American History* (2:55) attempts to apply the study of the history of ideas to an analysis of American foreign policy. Emphasis is on the role of moral ideology in expansion, with attention to changing rationalizations and to an overall transformation from internal expansion to imperialism.

ECONOMIC INFLUENCES

See Chapter 2, "Imperialism," Chapter 13, "Progressive and Foreign Policy," and Chapter 17, "Spheres and the Open Door," for additional references.

Early/Economic Interpretations

12:83   Beard, Charles A., and Beard, Mary R. *The Rise of American Civilization.* 2 vols. New York: Macmillan, 1927. Lively and clearly written, volume 2 of this classic history established the basis for the economic-determinist interpretation by depicting the development of American imperialism during the Gilded Age.

12:84   LaFeber, Walter. *The New Empire: An Interpretation of American Expansion, 1860–1898.* Ithaca, N.Y.: Cornell University Press, 1963. This book, whose arguments and evidence have been debated extensively, is the most comprehensive of the economic-determinist interpretations. It holds that American expansionism resulted from the aggressive efforts of politicians, intellectuals, navalists, and business interests to obtain overseas markets and investments as a consequence of the industrial revolution and especially the depression after 1893. Bibliography.

Paolino, E. N. *The Foundations of the American Empire: William Henry Seward and U.S. Foreign Policy* (15:18) argues that Seward envisioned a global commercial empire, including depots, systems of communication and currency, and an open door in Asia; that he anticipated the expansionists of 1898; and that there is essential continuity in policy.

12:85   Schonberger, Howard B. *Transportation to the Seaboard: The "Communication Revolution" and American Foreign Policy, 1860–1900.* Westport, Conn.: Greenwood, 1971. The author, who adopts the view that domestic economic and ideological factors shaped American foreign policy after 1865 and that the events of the 1890s were merely the culmination of this economic nationalism, argues that farmers, shippers, and railroad men recognized the "transportation revolution" and wanted foreign markets. Bibliography.

Sklar, M. J. "The NAM and Foreign Markets on the Eve of the Spanish-American War" (13:100).

12:86   Terrill, Tom E. *The Tariff, Politics, and American Foreign Policy, 1874–1901.* Westport, Conn.: Greenwood, 1973. The thesis, drawn from the controversial economic-determinist argument, is that the tariff was an instrument for overseas economic expansion. The author treats the Harrison-Blaine administration as an important prelude and finds the two parties thereafter differing merely over tactics. There is an abbreviated discussion of reciprocity and its fate. Bibliography.

Williams, W. A. *The Roots of the Modern American Empire: A Study of the Growth and Shaping of Social Consciousness in a Marketplace Society* (2:98) develops the author's much debated thesis about the American frontier and overseas economic expansion in detail for the years after 1865, with new emphasis on the outlook of American agriculturists as the primary motivating force behind this economic imperialism.

Williams, W. A. *The Tragedy of American Diplomacy* (2:99) advances the controversial thesis that the economic depression of the 1890s created a consensus among political, intellectual, and business leaders that overseas economic expansion was essential for recovery and to avert domestic crisis.

Responses

12:87   Becker, William H. "American Manufacturers and Foreign Markets, 1870–1900: Business Historians and the 'New Economic Determinists.' " *Business History Review* 47:4 (1973), 466–81. This article draws from economic history to refute the thesis about overproduction and a business consensus on the need for foreign markets. Most producers with excess capacity created pools and trusts, and limited output by mergers. Those who sought foreign trade did not suffer overproduction but were rather innovative (such as Eastman and Singer), had economic advantages, and possessed effective sales organizations. Foreign demand and prices were important.

12:88 Becker, William H. ''An Exchange of Opinion: Foreign Markets for Iron and Steel, 1893–1913: A New Perspective on the Williams School of Diplomatic History.'' *Pacific Historical Review* 44:2 (1975), 233–62. This article challenges the open door thesis with attention to the pivotal iron and steel industry. The author asserts that steel men addressed their problems by action at home, not by seeking foreign markets with government aid. A useful exchange of opinion between Howard Schonberger and the author follows.

Beisner, R. L. *From the Old Diplomacy to the New, 1865–1900* (12:6).

Campbell, C. S., Jr. *The Transformation of American Foreign Relations, 1865–1900* (12:7).

Field, J. A., Jr. *America and the Mediterranean World, 1776–1882* (18:6) carefully examines the postwar climax and subsequent decline of mission spirit and activity, education, navalism, and commerce. The focus on the eastern Mediterranean casts light on different patterns elsewhere.

Field, J. A., Jr. ''American Imperialism: The Worst Chapter in Almost Any Book'' (2:101) poses a new technological explanation for imperialism based on the communication revolution, and stresses the role of historical accident.

12:89 Holbo, Paul S. ''Economics, Emotion, and Expansion: An Emerging Foreign Policy.'' In H. Wayne Morgan, ed., *The Gilded Age.* Rev. ed. Syracuse, N.Y.: Syracuse University Press, 1970, pp. 199–221, 315–19. This essay criticizes the arguments and evidence of earlier interpretations, especially those stressing foreign markets, social Darwinism, and foreign example, and brings out emotional and irrational elements, but contends that McKinley basically conducted policy firmly and conservatively.

12:90 Thompson, J. A. ''William Appleman Williams and the 'American Empire.' '' *Journal of American Studies* [Great Britain] 7:1 (1973), 91–104. This theoretical appraisal of the Williams school criticizes the loose use of words such as ''expansion'' and ''empire,'' the elusiveness of some arguments, the lack of evidence for influence of interest groups, the assumption of the primacy of economic ideas, the

emphasis on consensus, and the conception of trade as inherently imperialistic.

NAVAL INFLUENCES

See ''Personalities'' for William E. Chandler (under ''Others''), Alfred T. Mahan; also Chapter 17, ''Naval and Strategic Issues.''

12:91 Buhl, Lance C. ''Maintaining 'An American Navy,' 1865–1889.'' In Kenneth J. Hagan, ed., *In Peace and War: Interpretations of American Naval History, 1775–1978.* Westport, Conn.: Greenwood, 1978, pp. 145–73. The postwar navy, third rate but more suitable than pro-navy historians have admitted, was adequate for its defensive continental mission and for its traditional mission of advancing commerce. Focusing narrowly on naval bills, the author demonstrates that Congress wanted an American rather than European standard and justifiably placed the navy toward the bottom of national priorities. Bibliography.

12:92 Cooling, B. Franklin, III. *Benjamin Franklin Tracy: Father of the Modern American Fighting Navy.* Hamden, Conn.: Shoe String Press, 1973. This study is more balanced than Herrick's account (12:95) of a naval revolution under Tracy (1889–1893). One of a series of strong secretaries, Tracy espoused the idea of sea power, nickel armor, and a balanced battle fleet, was a skilled politician, revived the Naval War College, and introduced the merit system in the navy yards. But he failed to obtain coaling stations and, while expansionist (though not for economic reasons) and aggressive (When Blaine's steady hand was missing), always pulled back in the end. Extensive bibliography.

12:93 Grenville, John A. S., and Young, George B. *Politics, Strategy, and American Diplomacy: Studies in Foreign Policy, 1873–1917.* New Haven, Conn.: Yale University Press, 1967. The chapters of this book are sharply etched and skillfully connected studies of navalists, politicians, lobbyists, and statesmen. The essays on Luce, Harrison, Cleveland, and Lodge are noteworthy interpretations. Specific diplomatic episodes and naval development are intelligently analyzed.

12:94 Hagan, Kenneth J. *American Gunboat Diplomacy and the Old Navy, 1877–1889.* Westport, Conn.: Greenwood, 1973. The author posits a well-established naval policy from the late 1870s of global gunboat diplomacy with a navy consisting of commerce raiders, for the purpose of expanding commerce as an index of national greatness. There are useful descriptions of technical issues and the ideas of officers such as Luce, Porter, and Shufeldt. Bibliography.

12:95 Herrick, Walter R., Jr. *The American Naval Revolution.* Baton Rouge: Louisiana State University Press, 1966. This is a largely traditional account, laudatory in its conclusions. A revolution in naval doctrine and administration occurred around 1890, after the appearance of the steel cruisers, which by 1898 transformed the weak postwar navy into a unified battle fleet. The author emphasizes the stewardship of Benjamin Tracy and his continuing influence. Bibliography.

Karsten, P. *The Naval Aristocracy: The Golden Age of Annapolis and the Emergence of Modern American Navalism* (40:35) identifies American naval officers by their background, education, social position, and values.

12:96 Karsten, Peter. "The Nature of 'Influence': Roosevelt, Mahan, and the Concept of Sea Power." *American Quarterly* 23:4 (1971), 585–600. This careful analysis successfully challenges the accepted notion that Alfred T. Mahan significantly influenced Theodore Roosevelt. Roosevelt's writings advocating naval preparedness antedated Mahan's, Roosevelt "used" Mahan, and each had a role to fulfill. The Young Turk navalists championed Mahan's work because it supported their views. Ideas of naval development were in the air.

Livermore, S. W. "American Naval-Base Policy in the Far East, 1850–1914" (40:172) describes the acquisition of naval and coaling stations in Pago Pago, Hawaii, and Lower California.

12:97 Seager, Robert, II. "Ten Years before Mahan: The Unofficial Case for the New Navy, 1880–1890." *Mississippi Valley Historical Review* 40:3 (1953), 491–512. This notable article expounds the ideological concepts and contemporary political arguments used to remedy the navy's extreme weakness. It also describes efforts as early as the Hayes and Arthur administrations for naval development. The author did not probe the navalists' motivations but reached the important conclusion that Mahan had a "thought reservoir."

12:98 Spector, Ronald. "The Triumph of Professional Ideology: The U.S. Navy in the 1890s." In Kenneth J. Hagan, ed., *In Peace and War: Interpreta-*

tions of American Naval History, 1775–1978. Westport, Conn.: Greenwood, 1978, pp. 174–85. The 1890s was a time of vindication for advocates of the battleship and command-of-the-sea strategy. The author discusses concisely the impact of the ideas of Tracy, Luce, and Mahan, and of the new British battleship and a possible canal. Navy planners focused on defense against Britain to mid-1897. Spain (with an attack on the Philippines a matter of dispute) and Japan also received attention. Bibliography.

Sprout, H., and Sprout, M. *The Rise of American Naval Power, 1776–1918* (40:117) deals capably with the beginnings of the new navy. There is detailed analysis of the political setting, especially of the situation in Congress. A third chapter puts Mahan in the context of manifest destiny, now a controversial theme.

The Alaska Purchase, 1854–1867

See "Personalities," especially James G. Blaine, William M. Gwin, William H. Seward, Charles Sumner; also "Document Collections."

U.S.-RUSSIAN RELATIONS

See Chapter 7, "The Monroe Doctrine, to 1861," "The Russian-American Dimension," and Chapter 8, "Russia: Northwest America" and Chapter 14, "Alaskan Boundary Settlement."

12:99 Chevigny, Hector. *Lord of Alaska: Baranon and the Russian Adventure.* New York: Viking, 1942. Baranon was responsible for Russia's hold on Alaska. He was interested in John Jacob Astor's proposed alliance regarding trade as well as Schoffer's adventure in Hawaii.

12:100 Chevigny, Hector. *Russian America: The Great Alaska Venture, 1741–1867.* New York: Viking, 1965. Reprint 1979. This history surveys the exploration and settlement of Alaska. It centers on the political and economic development of the Russian-American Company and concludes with an analysis of Russian motives for ceding the territory. Bibliography.

Gaddis, J. L. *Russia, the Soviet Union and the United States: An Interpretive History* (2:248) places the cession negotiation in the context of Russian-American cordiality, but stresses geopolitical reasons for concluding the treaty.

Kushner, H. I. *Conflict on the Northwest Coast . . . , 1790–1867* (8:92) examines the conflict over fishing privileges in Alaskan waters prior to the purchase. It emphasizes the role of New England whalers and commercial expansionists in Washington as promoters of the cession and contends that Russia ceded the territory to prevent American seizure.

Laserson, M. M. *The American Impact on Russia: Diplomatic and Ideological, 1784–1917* (2:250).

12:101 Mazour, Anatole G. ''The Prelude to Russia's Departure from America.'' *Pacific Historical Review* 10:3 (1941), 311–19. This interpretive essay emphasizes Russia's interest in devoting more attention to continental Asia as a prime factor in the decision to cede Alaska.

Okun, S. B. *The Russian-American Company* (5:155) is the most complete Soviet work on Russian America, and is based on a wide assortment of government archives. Okun details the financial plight of the Russian-American Company, but also recognizes the influence of political considerations in the decision for cession.

Thomas, B. P. *Russo-American Relations, 1815–1867* (8:90) surveys the relationship between Russia and the United States through its most cordial phase. His conclusion, based upon State Department records, stresses mutual enmity toward Britain as the magnet that drew the two powers together.

Williams, W. A. *American-Russian Relations, 1781–1947* (2:256) stresses economic desires as the prime motive for cession.

THE PURCHASE, 1854–1867

12:102 Farrar, Victor J. *Annexation of Russian America.* Washington, D.C.: Roberts, 1937. Farrar describes the negotiation process (1854–1868) that resulted in the Alaska cession by narrating events rather than analyzing the motives of the negotiators or examining the diplomatic background. Bibliography.

12:103 Golder, Frank A. ''The Purchase of Alaska.'' *American Historical Review* 25:3 (1920), 411–25. In this, the first history of the purchase (1854–1868) based on Russian archival sources, Golder concludes that cordial Russian-American relations prior to 1867 greatly influenced the negotiation for Alaska.

12:104 Jensen, Ronald J. *The Alaska Purchase and Russian-American Relations.* Seattle: University of Washington Press, 1975. This extensively researched study examines cession negotiations from their tentative beginnings in 1854 through the congressional appropriation debate of 1868. Jensen analyzes the motives of both powers in the context of mid-19th-century diplomacy and concludes that strategic interests in China and the North Pacific determined the actions of policymakers in Russia and the United States. Extensive bibliography.

12:105 Narochnitskii, A. L. *Kolonialnaia politika kapitalisticheskikh derzhav na Dal'nem Vostoke, 1860–1895 gg* [Colonial politics of the capitalist powers in the Far East, 1860–1895]. Moscow: Akademii nauk USSR, 1956. This thorough statement of the Soviet interpretation of the cession concludes that the interest of American capitalists in the Pacific produced the purchase agreement, and that Seward acted as agent for those forces. Bibliography.

12:106 Shiels, Archie W. *The Purchase of Alaska.* College: University of Alaska Press, 1967. The excerpts from documents, newspaper articles, and journals contained in this volume are loosely connected by the compiler's commentary.

12:107 Sverdlov, N. V. ''Kistorii Russko-Amerikanskikh otnoshenii na Tikhom okean i Dal'nego Vostoka v XIX-nachale XX v'' [Toward a history of Russian-American relations in the Pacific Ocean and Far East from the nineteenth to the beginning of the twentieth century]. In *Sornik statei po istorii Dal'nego Vostoka.* Moscow: Akademii nauk USSR, 1958. This chapter stresses that the purchase was an expression of American imperialism in the Pacific area.

12:108 U.S. House. *Correspondence in Relation to Russian-America.* House Executive Document 177. Ser. 1339. Washington, D.C.: G.P.O., 1867. This collection of American documents (1867) includes the text of the treaty, Senator Sumner's speech advocating approval of the treaty, and a selection of newspaper editorials and other comments on the treaty.

Politics and Economics

12:109   Bailey, Thomas A. "Why the United States Purchased Alaska." *Pacific Historical Review* 3:1 (1934), 39–49. Bailey's analysis, resting on a survey of newspapers and congressional speeches, asserts that Americans felt a sense of obligation to Russia for support during the Civil War which aided passage of the Alaska treaty.

12:110   Batueva, T. M. "Prokhozhdenie dogovora o pokupke Aliaski v kongresse SShA v 1867–1868 gg" [Passing the treaty on the purchase of Alaska in the U.S. Congress in 1867–1868]. *Novaia i Noveishaia Istoriia* 4 (1971), 117–24. The author relies on contemporary newspaper accounts and congressional speeches in an effort to prove that Congress approved the treaty because of economic motives.

12:111   Dunning, William A. "Paying for Alaska." *Political Science Quarterly* 27:3 (1912), 385–98. Dunning reopened speculation regarding the use of bribery to facilitate the Alaska appropriation. Dunning based his article on the Andrew Johnson Papers.

12:112   Keithahn, Edward L. "Alaska Ice, Inc." *Pacific Northwest Quarterly* 36:2 (1945), 121–31. Keithahn outlines the activities of the American Russian Commercial Company of San Francisco (1850–1869) and concludes that its profitable ice contracts with the Russians contributed to the pressure for cession in California.

12:113   Luthin, Reinhard H. "The Sale of Alaska." *Slavonic and East European Review* 16:46 (1937), 168–82. Luthin traces the congressional appropriation for Alaska, rather than the cession itself, and gives special attention to the lobbying efforts of Robert J. Walker and to rumors of bribery.

12:114   Sherwood, Morgan B. "George Davidson and the Acquisition of Alaska." *Pacific Historical Review* 28:2 (1959), 141–54. Davidson explored Alaska for the U.S. government immediately after the treaty was signed (1867–1868). Although his report was intended to influence Congress to pass the Alaska appropriation, the author concludes that its impact was limited.

12:115   Vevier, Charles. "The Collins Overland Line and American Continentalism." *Pacific Historical Review* 27:3 (1959), 237–53. Vevier describes the efforts of Perry McDonough Collins to establish a telegraph line between the United States and Russia via Russian America. The line failed but the enterprise called American attention to the strategic value of Alaska as a commercial link to Asia.

U.S.-Russian Opinion

12:116   Miller, David H. "Russian Opinion on the Cession of Alaska." *American Historical Review* 48:3 (1943), 521–31. This document, translated from the Russian archives, consists of a memorandum from a foreign ministry official (1866) recommending that Russia retain Alaska.

12:117   Reid, Virginia Hancock. *The Purchase of Alaska: Contemporary Opinion*. Long Beach, Calif., 1940. Reid surveys public opinion, primarily as expressed in contemporary American newspapers, and concludes that the purchase of Alaska was popular at the time despite the well-publicized references to "Seward's Folly." Bibliography.

12:118   Welch, Richard E., Jr. "American Public Opinion and the Purchase of Russian America." *American Slavic and East European Review* 17 (1958), 481–94. Welch surveys 48 newspapers published between April 1867 and July 1868 from across the United States. He concludes that press opinion supported the cession and largely for economic reasons.

ALASKAN HISTORIES

12:119   Bancroft, Hubert H. *History of Alaska, 1730–1885*. San Francisco: Bancroft, 1886. Bancroft explores the colonial history of Alaska, its resources, the role of the Russian-American Company, and American settlement, but devotes only one chapter to the cession period. The author asserts that fear of a British takeover precipitated the Russian decision to cede the territory.

12:120   Hinckley, Ted C. *The Americanization of Alaska, 1867–1897*. Palo Alto, Calif.: Pacific Books, 1972. The author traces the settlement of Alaska from the arrival of Americans in 1867 to the gold rush. Bibliography.

12:121 Sherwood, Morgan B., ed. *Alaska and Its History*. Seattle: University of Washington Press, 1967. This collection of 25 previously published journal articles includes eight on the annexation period, as well as articles on the era of Russian occupation and American settlement (1741–1935). Bibliography.

12:122 Tompkins, Stuart R. *Alaska: Promyshlenik and Sourdough*. Norman: University of Oklahoma Press, 1945. Tompkins's history of Alaska describes Russian and American efforts to exploit the resources of the territory. The short chapter on purchase negotiations stresses mutual economic advantages that the treaty would bring to both nations. Extensive bibliography.

U.S. and Samoa

See "Personalities," especially Thomas F. Bayard, James G. Blaine, and John A. Kasson; also see Chapter 14, "Samoan Triangle, 1878–1900," and Chapter 32, "Central Pacific."

12:123 Anderson, Stuart. " 'Pacific Destiny' and American Policy in Samoa, 1872–1899." *Hawaiian Journal of History* 12 (1978), 45–60. This overview stresses the persistent interest of the United States in Samoa derived from the idea of American destiny in the Pacific.

12:124 Brookes, Jean I. *International Rivalry in the Pacific Islands, 1800–1875*. Berkeley: University of California Press, 1941. Brookes's general narrative account of the emergence of the Pacific as an arena of international rivalry devotes one chapter to the Steinberger episode in Samoa. Bibliography.

12:125 Davidson, James W., and Scarr, Deryck, eds. *Pacific Island Portraits*. Canberra: Australian National University Press, 1970. The essay by James W. Davidson on Lauaki is an important analysis of a Samoan opponent of foreign political control. Extensive bibliography.

12:126 Gray, John A. C. *America Samoa: A History of American Samoa and Its United States Naval Administration*. Annapolis, Md.: Naval Institute Press, 1960. This is the official naval history of American Samoa with material on the background to annexation, including a chapter on the 1889 crisis. Bibliography.

Ryden, G. H. *The Foreign Policy of the United States in Relation to Samoa* (14:129) is a highly detailed, meticulously researched account of the United States Samoa policy during the 19th century.

U.S., BRITAIN, AND GERMANY, 1878–1889

See Chapter 14, "Samoan Triangle, 1878–1900" for U.S.-German relations.

12:127 Bates, George H. "Some Aspects of the Samoan Question." *Century Magazine* 37:6 (1889), 945–49. Bates was a U.S. commissioner to Samoa in 1886 and a delegate to the Berlin Conference in 1889.

12:128 Churchward, William B. *My Consulate in Samoa*. London: Bentley, 1887. This is a firsthand description of international rivalry in Samoa during the late 1870s and early 1880s by the British consul. Bibliography.

12:129 Ellison, James W. "The Partition of Samoa: A Study in Imperialism and Diplomacy." *Pacific Historical Review* 8:3 (1939), 259–88. Ellison's account deals with the way in which competing American, German, and British claims to Samoa were settled in 1899.

12:130 Ellison, Joseph W. *The Opening and Penetration of Foreign Influence in Samoa to 1880*. Corvallis: Oregon State College Press, 1938. This is a brief outline of the beginnings of international rivalry in Samoa. Bibliography.

12:131 Hoyt, Edwin P. *The Typhoon That Stopped a War*. New York: McKay, 1968. Hoyt's narrative account of the 1889 crisis neglects much of the Samoan background for the drama. Bibliography.

12:132 Ide, Henry C. "The Imbroglio in Samoa." *North American Review* 168:511 (1899), 679–93. A personal account of the Samoan tangle by an American who served as an official of the tripartite administration during the 1890s.

Kennedy, P. M. *The Samoan Tangle: A Study in Anglo-German-American Relations, 1878–1900*

(14:128) details the conflicting policies of the great powers toward Samoa.

12:133 Masterman, Sylvia R. *The Origins of International Rivalry in Samoa, 1845–1884*. London: Allen & Unwin, 1934. This brief outline shows how the United States, Britain, and Germany became involved in Samoa. Bibliography.

McIntyre, W. D. *The Imperial Frontier in the Tropics, 1865–1875* . . . (32:158) concludes that suspected American designs on Samoa influenced the British decision to annex neighboring Fiji in 1874.

12:134 Steinberger, Albert B. *Report on Samoa or Navigator's Island*. Washington, D.C.: G.P.O., 1874. This brief account of the troubled situation in Samoa was designed to win the sympathy of Congress for extending American influence over the islands.

12:135 Stevenson, Robert L. *Footnote to History: Eight Years of Trouble in Samoa*. New York: Scribner's, 1892. An elegant narrative that includes some vivid personal sketches and an especially memorable description of the 1889 crisis.

12:136 Torodash, Martin. "Albert B. Steinberger: Some Biographical Notes." *Pacific Northwest Quarterly* 68:2 (1977), 49–59. This essay contains valuable information on the personal background and performance of a highly controversial figure.

ECONOMIC INFLUENCES

12:137 Churchward, L. G. "American Enterprise: The Foundations of the Pacific Mail Service." *Historical Studies* 3:11 (1947), 217–24. Churchward outlines the American attempt to win control over Pacific commerce through government subsidies and a Samoan coaling station.

12:138 Cooper, H. Stonehewer. *Coral Lands*. London: Bentley, 1880. This is a contemporary account of American activities in Samoa in the 1870s.

12:139 Rigby, Barry R. "Private Interests and the Origins of American Involvement in Samoa 1872–1877." *Journal of Pacific History* 8 (1973), 75–87. This brief analysis focuses on the importance of backstairs influence and land speculation in establishing the American stake in Samoa in the 1870s.

SAMOAN HISTORIES

Davidson, J. W. *Samoa Mo Samoa: The Emergence of the Independent State of Western Samoa* (32:164) is largely devoted to the 20th-century Samoan independence movement, but this account has a concise summary of the 19th-century international rivalry.

12:140 Gilson, Richard P. *Samoa 1830–1900: The Politics of a Multi-cultural Community*. Melbourne: Oxford University Press, 1970. The author's anthropological training together with his painstaking historical research makes this work indispensable for any student of American relations with Samoa. Extensive bibliography.

12:141 Keesing, Felix M. *Modern Samoa: Its Government and Changing Life*. London: Allen & Unwin, 1934. The Institute of Pacific Relations commissioned this early systematic study of the Western impact of Samoa. Bibliography.

U.S. Annexation of Hawaii, 1898

See "Personalities," especially Grover Cleveland, Sanford B. Dole, Hamilton Fish, Walter Q. Gresham, Benjamin Harrison, Queen Liliuokalani, and Claus Spreckels.

12:142 Armstrong, William N. *Around the World with a King*. Tokyo: Tuttle, 1977. Armstrong, a member of Kalakaua's cabinet, accompanied the last king on his circumnavigation of the world in 1881. The final chapter of the work included a study of the last days of the monarchy, the growth of American influence in the Islands, and annexation to the United States.

12:143 Bradley, Harold W. *The American Frontier in Hawaii: The Pioneers, 1789–1843*. Stanford, Calif.: Stanford University Press, 1942. Although Bradley emphasizes the narrowly "commercial" nature of early contacts, he sees them as "the harbinger of permanent ties to follow." This study is well footnoted, but from English-language sources only.

12:144   Daws, A. Gavan. *Shoal of Time: A History of the Hawaiian Islands.* Honolulu: University Press of Hawaii, 1968. This is a detailed, well-documented history of the Hawaiian Islands. The growth of American influence and the Oriental immigration, the end of the monarchy, and annexation are covered in a thorough and unbiased manner. Extensive bibliography.

12:145   Day, A. Grove. *Hawaii and Its People.* Rev. ed. New York: Duell, Sloan & Pearce, 1960. Reprint 1968. Day's work covers Hawaiian history from the arrival of Captain Cook in 1778 to statehood in 1959. Although the study is oriented more toward a study of life in the Islands, there is information concerning the growth of American influence in the Hawaiian Islands and the annexation of 1898.

12:146   Joesting, Edward. *Hawaii: An Uncommon History.* New York: Norton, 1972. Focusing on selected episodes, the author has written a very human history. The instances covered include the effect of the gold rush, the impact of meddling by American, French, and British consuls, the problems of the monarchy, and the revolution of 1893. Extensive bibliography.

12:147   Kuykendall, Ralph S., and Day, A. Grove. *Hawaii: A History from Polynesian Kingdom to American Commonwealth.* Rev. ed. New York: Prentice-Hall (1948), 1961. Although the authors chose not to be too detailed, they provide much important information on the U.S.-Hawaiian reciprocity treaties, the revolution of 1893, and the annexation of the Hawaiian Islands in 1898.

12:148   Pierce, Richard A. *Russia's Hawaiian Adventure, 1815–1817.* Berkeley: University of California Press, 1965. The attempt by the German surgeon and adventurer, George Anton Schoffer, to engineer Russian annexation of the Hawaiian Islands. Bibliography.

Pratt, J. W. *Expansionists of 1898: The Acquisition of Hawaii and the Spanish Islands* (12:82).

12:149   Tate, Merze. *The United States and the Hawaiian Kingdom.* New Haven, Conn.: Yale University Press, 1965. A thorough study of American influence in the Islands from the missionary beginnings to annexation in 1898. Tate argues that the U.S. minister encouraged the rebels who ousted the queen in 1893, and that the revolution of 1893 was caused by

the determination of the propertied class (mostly American) to control the government. Bibliography.

ECONOMIC INFLUENCES

12:150   Appel, John C. "American Labor and the Annexation of Hawaii: A Study in Logic and Economic Interest." *Pacific Historical Review* 23:1 (1954), 1–18. American labor was opposed to the annexation of the Hawaiian Islands, believing the move was designed to save the purses of the upper class and was imperialistic. Skilled labor saw few openings in the agriculturally based Hawaiian economy, and feared that Oriental labor in Hawaii might come to the United States to compete for jobs.

12:151   Canario, Lucille de Silva. "Destination Sandwich Islands." *Hawaiian Journal of History* 4 (1970), 3–52. Account of the trip made in 1887–1888 by 400 Portuguese to Hawaii; the Portuguese became an important labor force until the Asian migration.

12:152   Conroy, Francis H. *The Japanese Frontier in Hawaii, 1868–1898.* Berkeley: University of California Press, 1953. A scholarly study based largely on Hawaiian archival materials, which considers the diplomatic problems arising from Japanese immigration.

12:153   Davis, Eleanor H. *The Norse Migration: Norwegian Labor in Hawaii.* Hawaiian Historical Society, 71st annual report. Honolulu: Hawaiian Historical Society, 1962. In 1881 the first shipload of Norwegian contract laborers arrived in Hawaii to work the sugar fields. Conditions were not as good as the immigrants had expected, and many demanded improvements or release from their contracts. Eventually the plantation owners turned to what was hoped would be docile Asian labor.

12:154   Lasker, Bruno. *Filipino Immigration to Continental United States and to Hawaii.* Chicago: University of Chicago Press, 1931. Reprint 1969. An old study which still commands attention on the subject of Filipino immigration.

12:155   Russ, William A., Jr. "Hawaiian Labor and Immigration Problems before Annexation." *Journal of Modern History* 15:3 (1943), 207–22. Russ explains the massive labor shortage that faced Hawaiian industry during the 1850s and 1860s. The native Hawaiian population was decimated from repeated battles with disease; therefore it became necessary to import labor from Europe and areas of the Pacific. Russ supplies data on the relative importation costs that sugar planters faced in bringing various ethnic groups to the Islands.

12:156   Russ, William A., Jr. "The Role of Sugar in Hawaiian Annexation." *Pacific Historical Review* 12:4 (1943), 339–50. Although Russ demonstrated that Spreckels was opposed to annexation, as were many other prominent sugar men, sugar did have a role in the revolution of 1893 in that the sugar industry created the need for cheap Oriental labor in Hawaii.

12:157   Spreckels, Claus. "The Future of the Sandwich Islands." *North American Review* 152:412 (1891), 287–91. The leader of the sugar industry in Hawaii and an important figure in Hawaiian history, Spreckels argued that the native population was weak. Spreckels advocated reciprocity but continued to oppose annexation of the Islands by the United States. In 1893 it would be charged that he backed annexation for the economic gain of the sugar trust.

12:158   Weigle, Richard D. "Sugar and the Hawaiian Revolution." *Pacific Historical Review* 16:1 (1947), 41–58. Spreckels opposed annexation of Hawaii to the United States since it might cut off the flow of cheap Oriental labor to the Islands. The revolutionists, however, were more concerned with security. Weigle's thesis counters the view that the revolution of 1893 was brought about by the sugar industry so as to get the benefits secured by American producers.

Reciprocity Treaties

12:159   Dozer, Donald M. "The Opposition to Hawaiian Reciprocity, 1876–1888." *Pacific Historical Review* 14:2 (1945), 157–83. Dozer describes the major opponents of the reciprocity treaties between the United States and Hawaii. The treaties were opposed by American sugar cane and beet sugar producers and by those who believed the treaties were unjust since they conferred one-sided benefits on Hawaii. The anti-imperialist wing of the Democratic party opposed the Pearl Harbor amendment.

12:160   Hooley, Osborne E. "Hawaiian Negotiation for Reciprocity, 1855–1857." *Pacific Historical Review* 7:2 (1938), 128–46. The Hawaiian government was turned down in its 1848 and 1852 attempts to attain reciprocity, but renewed its efforts in 1855. Congress

failed to ratify the treaty as the Louisiana sugar interests rallied their supporters in the Senate.

12:161   Patterson, John. "The United States and Hawaiian Reciprocity, 1867–1870." *Pacific Historical Review* 7:1 (1938), 14–26. Patterson focuses on the unsuccessful effort in 1867 to obtain a reciprocity treaty. Political motives were mixed; some opponents feared reciprocity would prevent annexation.

12:162   Tate, Merze. *Hawaii: Reciprocity or Annexation.* East Lansing: Michigan State University Press, 1968. Tate concentrates on the arguments that surrounded the issue of reciprocity treaties between the United States and Hawaii, and supplies an in-depth account of the motivations of Americans and Hawaiians during the discussions for the 1876 treaty. The author discusses the important issue of the Pearl Harbor clause of the 1887 treaty. Bibliography.

HAWAIIAN REVOLUTION, 1893

12:163   Davies, Theophilus H. "The Hawaiian Situation." *North American Review* 156:438 (1893), 605–10. One of the first condemnations of the actions of the revolutionists by a resident of Hawaii. Davies argues that most native Hawaiians were averse to annexation, and he implies a conspiracy between the revolutionists and the American minister in the Islands.

12:164   Hammett, Hugh B. "The Cleveland Administration and Anglo-American Naval Friction in Hawaii, 1893–1894." *Military Affairs* 40:1 (1976), 27–31. The Cleveland administration was opposed to annexation but still wished to block foreign moves into the Islands. However, actions of American naval officers in Honolulu complicated Cleveland's task by appearing to back the provisional government, or by offending British naval officers or officials.

12:165   Lanier, Osmos, Jr. "Paramount Blount: Special Commissioner to Investigate the Hawaiian Coup, 1893." *West Georgia College Studies in the Social Sciences* 11 (1972), 45–55. Blount went to Hawaii at the request of President Cleveland, who was interested in the role played by the American forces. Blount's report led directly to Cleveland's attempted restoration of Hawaiian Queen Liliuokalani in December 1893.

12:166   Loomis, Albertine. *For Whom Are the Stars?* Honolulu: University of Hawaii Press, 1976. Although the author is more concerned with the events that occurred after the revolution of 1893, the Republic of Hawaii and the 1895 counterrevolution, the revolution and James Blount's special mission to the Islands are described. Extensive bibliography.

12:167   Russ, William A., Jr. *The Hawaiian Revolution (1893–1894).* Selinsgrove, Pa.: Susquehanna University Press, 1959. Russ finds that Minister Stevens made it clear to the revolutionaries that he was in sympathy with them before they acted. The author further argues that the greater menace in the minds of the revolutionaries was not the monarchy but the Japanese and Japanese-Hawaiians. Russ contends that the landing of American troops by Stevens made it impossible for the monarchy to defend itself. Extensive bibliography.

12:168   Russ, William A., Jr. *The Hawaiian Republic (1894–1898).* Selinsgrove, Pa.: Susquehanna University Press, 1961. The Spanish-American War finally made annexation of Hawaii possible. In 1893, the Islands were not needed, but in 1898 they were wanted. Annexation of Hawaii to the United States was seen by many in the Islands as the only way to be saved from the Oriental threat or economic ruin if further Asian immigration were stopped. Extensive bibliography.

12:169   Thurston, Lorrin A. *Memoirs of the Hawaiian Revolution.* Ed. by Andrew Farrell. Honolulu: Advertiser Publishing, 1936. Thurston, son of a missionary couple, was instrumental in carrying off the Hawaiian Revolution of 1893 and opening the way for American annexation. Thurston argues that the actions of Minister Stevens were not the deciding factor in the success of the action.

U.S. ANNEXATION, 1898

12:170   Bailey, Thomas A. "The United States and Hawaii during the Spanish-American War." *American Historical Review* 36:3 (1931), 552–60. Hawaii was not neutral during the Spanish-American War; rather, the Hawaiian government aided the American war effort even before Dewey's victory at Manila. The author argues that Hawaii was not needed for successful prosecution of the war.

12:171   Baker, George W., Jr. "Benjamin Harrison and Hawaiian Annexation: A Reinterpretation." *Pacific Historical Review* 33:3 (1964), 295–309. Harrison, unlike Blaine, was not an expansionist until 1893 and then was cautious, inward-looking, and determined to be proper and to avoid imputations of imperialism.

12:172   Beardslee, L. A. "Pilikias." *North American Review* 167:503 (1898), 473–80. There was much apprehension on the part of Hawaiians concerning American annexation. The author felt that the natives would follow the former queen and, therefore, the United States must get Liliuokalani on its side.

12:173   Foster, Burnside. "Leprosy and the Hawaiian Annexation." *North American Review* 167: 502 (1898), 300–305. This subject has received little attention by historians. Foster makes clear that there was no evidence that the problem would come to the United States if Hawaii were annexed.

12:174   Osborne, Thomas J. "The Main Reason for Hawaiian Annexation in July 1898." *Oregon Historical Quarterly* 71:2 (1970), 161–78. Osborne argues that the main reason for the annexation of Hawaii in 1898 was the lure of commercial interests in Asia.

12:175   Pearce, George. "Assessing Public Opinion: Editorial Comment and the Annexation of Hawaii: A Case Study." *Pacific Historical Review* 43:3 (1974), 324–41. Pearce argues that accounts of a massive wave of public opinion backing annexation of Hawaii are myths. Moreover, public opinion had little if any influence on decisionmakers.

12:176   Stevens, John L. "A Plea for Annexation." *North American Review* 157:445 (1893), 736–45. Stevens, former U.S. minister to Hawaii, brushed aside any argument as to the legality of his landing American troops in Honolulu during the revolution of 1893. Stevens argued that Hawaii was American and that the United States would suffer in both prestige and interest if it did not annex the island chain.

12:177   Stevens, Sylvester K. *American Expansion in Hawaii, 1842–1898.* Harrisburg, Pa.: Archives Publishing, 1945. A standard account of the steady growth and influence of the United States in Hawaii up to the time of annexation. Bibliography.

12:178   Thurston, Lorrin A. "The Sandwich Islands: The Advantages of Annexation." *North American Re-*

view 156:436 (1893), 265–81. Lorrin A. Thurston was one of the prime movers of the Hawaiian Revolution of 1893, and stressed the traditional interest of the United States in Hawaii as well as its strategic and economic importance to Americans.

OTHER NATIONS' ATTITUDES

12:179 Bailey, Thomas A. "Japan's Protest against the Annexation of Hawaii." *Journal of Modern History* 3:1 (1931), 46–61. Hawaiian efforts to stem Japanese immigration provoked a controversy, and Japan's protest added impetus to the annexation of Hawaii.

12:180 Tate, Merze. "British Opposition to the Cession of Pearl Harbor." *Pacific Historical Review* 29:4 (1960), 381–94. The British Admiralty believed that the harbor was the only suitable one in case of war. The 1887 revolution in Hawaii cleared the way for American ownership of Pearl Harbor; but by that year the British government was no longer concerned with the matter.

12:181 Tate, Merze. "Canada's Interest in the Trade and Sovereignty of Hawaii." *Canadian Historical Review* 44:1 (1963), 20–42. The Islands were an ideal link, with the completion of the Canadian Pacific Railroad, in a Liverpool to Australia route. Also, Hawaii would serve as a good landing area for a cable between the two regions.

12:182 Tate, Merze. "Great Britain and the Sovereignty of Hawaii." *Pacific Historical Review* 31:4 (1962), 327–48. In 1854 the official British policy was to stop annexation, and in 1873 Britain was opposed to the cession of Pearl Harbor to the United States. By 1893, Great Britain showed no concern over the possibility of annexation, while Russia desired American control of the Islands and Japan looked to three-party control of the strategic area. By 1898, Britain desired American ownership to stop German moves.

12:183 Tate, Merze. "Hawaii: A Symbol of Anglo-American Rapprochement." *Political Science Quarterly* 79:4 (1964), 555–75. This is primarily a study of changing British views over a half-century. The British were interested in some type of position in the Hawaiian Islands in the 1850s but gradually reduced their interest until in the 1890s they were urging the United States to annex the islands.

12:184 Tate, Merze. "The Myth of Hawaii's Swing toward Australasia and Canada." *Pacific Historical Review* 33:3 (1964), 273–93. Tate argues that Hawaiian politicians often used the threat of a swing toward Australia and Canada as a prod to the American Congress to get a reciprocity treaty passed. However, such a move in reality was impossible for the markets needed by the Hawaiian sugar industry could only be found in the United States.

12:185 Tate, Merze. "Twisting the Lion's Tail over Hawaii." *Pacific Historical Review* 36:1 (1967), 27–46. The study covers the changes in British policy toward American annexation of Hawaii from 1854 to 1898. British control of the Islands would have been a threat to the United States in light of the coming isthmian canal. Tate contends that by 1898 London no longer opposed American ownership of Hawaii, an indication of an Anglo-American rapprochement.

Other U.S. Activities

EFFORT TO ANNEX SANTO DOMINGO

See "Personalities," especially James G. Blaine, Ulysses S. Grant, Oliver P. Morton (under "Others"), William H. Seward, and Charles Sumner; also, Chapter 15, "Santo Domingo (Dominican Republic)."

12:186 MacMichael, David C. "The United States and the Dominican Republic, 1871–1940: A Cycle in Caribbean Diplomacy." Ph.D. diss., University of Oregon, 1964. The first six chapters of this massive study deal with the United States policy of correct relations and of hands off during the period after 1871. It supersedes all earlier works. Extensive bibliography.

Tansill, C. C. *The United States and Santo Domingo, 1798–1873* (5:123) concentrates on the post–Civil War period. The author relies almost exclusively on U.S. sources.

Welles, S. *Naboth's Vineyard: The Dominican Republic, 1844–1924* (2:323) is much more critical of the 19th-century involvement than of 20th-century policies.

Annexation Proposal

12:187   Garcia, José G. *A Brief Refutal of the Report of the Santo Domingo Commissioners*. New York: Zarzamendi, 1871. The case against annexation presented by a prominent member of the Cabral government of 1866 to 1868, which had committed itself to defending Dominican independence.

12:188   Hazard, Samuel. *Santo Domingo: Past and Present, with a Glance at Hayti*. New York: Low, Marston, Low & Searle, 1873. This is a biased account of the Dominican economic and political situation by a journalist in favor of annexation.

12:189   Howe, Samuel G. *Letters on the Proposed Annexation of Santo Domingo*. Boston: Wright & Potter, 1871. A vigorous defense of the annexation of the Dominican Republic is offered by a member of the 1871 U.S. commission there.

12:190   Pinkett, H. T. "Efforts to Annex the Dominican Republic to the United States 1866–1871." *Journal of Negro History* 26:1 (1941), 12–45.

This narrative of successive attempts to annex the Dominican Republic is based on secondary sources.

PURCHASE OF DANISH WEST INDIES

12:191   Koht, Halvdan. "The Origin of Seward's Plan to Purchase the Danish West Indies." *American Historical Review* 50:4 (1945), 762–67. There are two interesting themes in this brief article. The first is the contention that Seward's West Indies policies, often thought expansionist, were actually defensive. The related theme is that, after Germany defeated Denmark, Austria became interested in acquiring the islands as a connection to Maximilian's Mexico. There also were rumors and soundings about a swap with Germany for part of Schleswig. The idea behind Seward's policy (1864–1869) came from the U.S. consul in Denmark.

12:192   Tansill, Charles C. *The Purchase of the Danish West Indies*. Baltimore: Johns Hopkins Press, 1932. Reprint 1968. This is a detailed and definitive study, based on multiarchival research.

13

The Spanish-American War, 1898–1900

Contributing Editor
ARMIN RAPPAPORT
University of California, San Diego

Contributor
John Offner
Shippenburg State College

Contents

Introduction

The most useful observation which may be made about the literature of the Spanish-American War is that there is no single-volume general history. There is no book to which a reader may be directed which covers all phases and aspects of the subject: conditions in Cuba and Spanish policy toward them; the American response to Spain's policies; the causes of American intervention; the interests of other powers; the conduct of the war; the peace negotiations; the great debate on the acquisition of overseas territories; and the fighting to subdue the rebels in the Philippines. Such a study would not only present a complete narrative of events but would include the points of disagreement and controversy in the interpretation of those events among historians.

However, an introduction to the subject is offered by a number of works which cover a broader period of time and subject matter but which include the war, such as Robert L. Beisner, *From the Old Diplomacy to the New, 1865–1900* (12:6); Samuel F. Bemis, *The Latin American Policy of the United States* (2:260); Charles Campbell, *The Transformation of American Foreign Relations, 1865–1900* (12:7); and A. L. P. Denis, *Adventures in American Diplomacy, 1896–1906* (13:7). The reader will find in each of these books a general account of the events leading to the outbreak of the war—and from varying points of view. It would be well to balance Bemis, who justifies American intervention, with Beisner, who is critical of America's role, or with Dennis, who considers the war needless.

Of all the aspects of the war upon which historians have disagreed, none is more controversial than the character and policies of President McKinley. The controversy may best be expressed as questions: Was he a strong or weak leader? Was he pressured by Congress, the public, the press, the party to fight or did he lead the country to war when it became clear to him that Cuba could not be freed peacefully? Did he exhaust all the possibilities of settling differences with Spain by diplomacy or did he cut off Spain's efforts to settle the problems? An excellent starting point for a lucid historiographical treatment of the McKinley questions and for an understanding of the issues is Joseph Fry's essay "William McKinley and the Coming of the Spanish-American War: A Study in the Besmirching and Redemption of an Historical Image" (13:50). Fry leads the reader from the early view of McKinley as weak and irresolute by James Ford Rhodes in *The McKinley and Roosevelt Administrations, 1897–1909* to the more recent position taken by Margaret Leech in her *In the Days of McKinley* (13:52), which depicts the president as strong, firm, and principled. Seeing McKinley as helpless and feckless is not the province alone of older works. In *Imperial Democracy* (12:80), Ernest R. May takes that position.

Opinion differs widely, too, among scholars on what factors persuaded the United States to intervene in the Spanish-Cuban conflict. There are those who maintain that economic factors lay behind the decision for war and for acquiring colonies overseas. They claim it was to provide a market for surplus industrial and agricultural products, and opportunities for capital investment that led the country to fight. The so-called Wisconsin school, whose founder and leading figure is William Appleman Williams, stands preeminent in this camp. William's *The Tragedy of American Diplomacy* (2:99) and *The Roots of the Modern American Empire: A Study of the Growth and Shaping of Social Consciousness in a Marketplace Society* (2:98) are classic expressions of the theme. Equally impressive in this category is *The New Empire: An Interpretation of American Expansion, 1860–1898* (12:84) by Walter LaFeber, a student of Williams. As expected, the same position is adopted by Marxist historians such as Philip Foner, whose *The Spanish-Cuban-American War and the Birth of American Imperialism, 1895–1902* (13:21) stands as an example.

Other scholars have challenged the economic interpretation and have adduced evidence to show that the financial, business, and commercial communities opposed the war at least up to the end of March 1898. They suggest that ideological factors underlay the decision for war. Certain clergymen, historians, political scientists, and political leaders—social Darwinists all—convinced of Anglo-Saxon racial and cultural superiority, sought to extend the beneficent civilization to less fortunate people by conquest, if necessary. War with Spain, they believed, would lead to acquiring overseas territory where the American mission could be carried out. The political leaders, joined by navalists, were also motivated by nationalism and patriotism, wishing to extend American power in the world and join in the scramble for land and peoples and prestige then in vogue among the European powers. Julius Pratt in *Expansionists of 1898: The Acquisition of Hawaii and the Spanish Islands* (12:82), and in several articles, notably "The 'Large Policy' of 1898" (13:98) is the most significant contributor to this theme. Important, too, are Richard Hofstadter, *Social Darwinism in American Thought, 1860–1915* (12:79), and E. R. May, *American Imperialism: A Speculative Essay* (2:94).

Then there are those who saw the war's origin in the state of the public mind—the popular passion to fight Spain—best described by Walter Millis in *The Martial Spirit* (13:29) and in the influence of the press—"yellow journalism"—in maintaining the popular passion in a high state. Biographies such as W. A. Swanberg's *Citizen Hearst* (13:42) and *Pulitzer* (13:69) deal with the publishers of the *Journal* and the *World*, respectively, while books by Marcus Wilkerson, *Public Opinion and the Spanish-American War: A Study in War Propaganda* (13:110), and Joseph Wisan, *The Cuban Crisis as Reflected in the New York Press* (13:111), treat the role of the press in general. Not to be overlooked is Richard Hofstadter's important and suggestive thesis that the popular demand for war stemmed from the need for an outlet for domestic frustration to be found in his article "Manifest Destiny and the Philippines" (13:91).

An important, though not anticipated, consequence of the war was the acquisition of overseas possessions—principally, the Philippine Islands. That aspect of the conflict generated a lively and controversial literature. One element of disagreement was the reason for the failure of a sizable opposition to annexation to frustrate the plans of the annexationists. One of the earliest and most significant contributions to the controversy was Fred H. Harrington's seminal article, "The Anti-Imperialist Movement in the United States, 1898–1900" (13:199), in which he ascribes the failure of the anti-imperialist movement to the disparate and clashing nature of its adherents. Two other works on the subject ought to be considered—Robert L. Beisner, *Twelve against Empire: The Anti-Imperialists, 1898–1900* (13:197), which describes the views of key opponents of annexation, and Christopher Lasch, "The Anti-Imperialists, the Philippines, and the Inequality of Man" (13:200), which destroyed the popularly held myth that the anti-imperialists were less racist than the imperialists.

Expansionism and annexation stirred yet another dispute among scholars: the role of the Progressives in the imperial adventure. It began with a path-breaking article by William Leuchtenberg, "Progressionism and Imperialism: The Progressive Movement and American Foreign Policy, 1898–1916" (13:14), which argued that the Progressives favored imperialism although their domestic concerns may have seemed more consistent with opposition to expansionism. A number of replies to Leuchtenberg soon appeared in the journals, the best of which is Barton Bernstein and F. A. Leib, "Progressive Republican Senators and American Imperialism, 1898–1916: A Re-Appraisal" (13:12), which supports the opposite position.

There are additionally several dissertations—some old, some new—of such importance as to merit a listing here: John C. Appel, "The Relationship of American Labor to United States Imperialism" (Wisconsin, 1950); Thomas H. Baker, Jr., "Imperial Finale: Crisis, Decolonization, and War in Spain" (Princeton, 1976); James K. Eyre, "The Philippines, the Powers, and the Spanish-American War" (Michigan, 1940); John H. McMinn, "The Attitude of the English Press Toward the United States during the Spanish-American War" (Ohio State, 1939); Richard H. Miller, "The Peace of Paris, 1898: A Case Study of the Dilemmas of Imperialism" (Georgetown, 1969); John L. Offner, "President McKinley and the Origins of the Spanish-American War" (Pennsylvania State, 1957); William A. Karraker, "The American Churches and the Spanish-American War" (Chicago-Divinity School); Philip L. Snyder, "Mission, Empire, or Force of Circumstances? A Study of the American Decision to Annex the Philippine Islands" (Stanford, 1972); Cornelius Vahle, "Congress, the President, and Overseas Expansion, 1897–1901" (Georgetown, 1967); Richard D. Weigle, "The Sugar Interests and American Diplomacy in Hawaii and Cuba, 1893–1903" (Yale, 1939).

As of this time, there is no evidence that a much-to-be-desired single volume on the war is in progress, but it may be that the experience of the Vietnam War will be seen as similar in some respects to the Philippine insurrection and lead to a study analyzing the entire matter of the war against Spain and the Philippine annexation that followed.

Resources and Overviews

RESEARCH AIDS

While pertinent bibliographies and reference aids are listed here, there are more extensive lists in Chapter 1.

Bibliographies

Braisted, W. R. "The Navy in the Early Twentieth Century, 1890–1941" (12:1) lists important references for the Spanish-American War, both in the Caribbean and the Pacific.

Cortada, J. W., ed. *A Bibliographical Guide to Spanish Diplomatic History, 1460–1977* (1:90).

De Santis, V. P. *The Gilded Age, 1877–1896* (12:2) has bibliographical chapters on politics and foreign affairs.

13:1 Ellis, Richard N. "Civil-Military Relations, Operations, and the Army, 1865–1917." In Robin Higham, ed., *A Guide to the Sources of United States Military History*. Hamden, Conn.: Shoe String Press, 1975, pp. 247–68. Ellis provides references to military-diplomatic episodes during the Spanish-American War both in the Caribbean and the Philippines.

Healy, D. *Modern Imperialism: Changing Styles in Historical Interpretation* (12:3).

13:2 Holbo, Paul S. "Perspectives on American Foreign Policy, 1890–1916: Expansion and World Power." *Social Studies* 58:6 (1967), 246–56. Holbo presents various interpretations of the reasons and causes for America's rise to world power. A convenient and perceptive summary of the historiography of the problem.

13:3 May, Ernest R. "Emergence to World Power." In John Higham, ed., *The Reinterpretation of American History*. New York: Humanities Press, 1962, pp. 180–196. Although less useful than some of the other essays, it does consider some of the important books on this era.

13:4 Smith, Daniel M. "Rise to Great World Power, 1865–1918." In William H. Cartwright and Richard L. Watson, eds., *The Reinterpretation of American History and Culture*. Washington, D.C.: National Council for Social Studies, 1973, pp. 443–64. This is a good overview of recent and important literature.

Smith, M. J., Jr., ed. *The American Navy, 1865–1918: A Bibliography* (12:4) contains references to U.S. Navy activities during and after the Spanish-American War.

Trask, D. F.; Meyer, M. C.; and Trask, R. R., eds. *A Bibliography of United States–Latin American Relations since 1810* (1:120) is particularly strong on Cuban documents, memoirs, and histories; see chapter 5, "The Spanish-American War, 1895–1900," pp. 98–107. Meyer (1:119) updates the original volume.

Document Collections

General collections are listed in Chapter 1, and other collections may be found in "Personalities," below.

13:5 U.S. National Archives and Record Service. "History of the Philippine Insurrection against the United States 1899–1903; and Documents Relating to the War Department Project for Publishing the History." M-719, 9 rolls. Washington, D.C.: n.d. These nine rolls of microfilm are identified in the *List of National Archives Microfilm Publications*.

13:6 U.S. National Archives and Record Service. "Philippine Insurgent Records, 1896–1901; with Associated Records of the U.S. War Department, 1900–1906." M-254, 643 rolls. Washington, D.C.: n.d. These microfilm records are of value to the student of Philippine nationalism, and the political and military aspects of the insurrection against U.S. Army rule after the Spanish-American War. The captured insurgents records are in Spanish, although frequently there are translations. Rolls 1–82 contain materials considered to be especially valuable. Finding aids are included.

OVERVIEWS

Beisner, R. L. *From the Old Diplomacy to the New, 1865–1900* (12:6) provides an excellent account in chapter 5 of the coming of the war with Spain; McKinley is portrayed as a strong leader, resourceful and in control of the situation.

Bemis, S. F. *The Latin American Policy of the United States* [1776–1942] (2:260) justifies America's Cuban intervention.

Campbell, C. S., Jr. *The Transformation of American Foreign Relations, 1865–1900* (12:7) contains a clear account of Cuban conditions, the road to war, and debate on the acquisition of colonies after the war. It is a convenient summary which includes the most recent scholarship and argues that the president was not stampeded by the press, public, or Congress but asked for war after sober reflection.

13:7 Denis, Alfred L. P. *Adventures in American Diplomacy, 1896–1906.* New York: Dutton, 1928. Denis's old account concludes that the war was unnecessary, that given time Spain would have capitulated to American demands for a free Cuba, but that war was inevitable given the state of public passion, domestic politics, economic interests, and the pressure of the press.

Dobson, J. M. *America's Ascent: The United States Becomes a Great Power, 1880–1914* (12:8) is written from a wide variety of sources; its thesis is that the roots of American interest in expansion and imperialism go back to the 1880s.

13:8 Dulles, Foster Rhea. *The Imperial Years.* New York: Crowell, 1956. Reprint 1966. Dulles portrays McKinley as pushed into the war and into acquiring the Philippines by the pressures of Congress, the public, the press, and the proponents of the "large policy" (Lodge, Beveridge, Roosevelt, Mahan, etc.).

Field, J. A., Jr. "American Imperialism: The Worst Chapter in Almost Any Book" (2:101) reviews the literature and interpretations of American imperialism, and calls for a rethinking of traditional viewpoints.

Grenville, J. A. S., and Young, G. B. *Politics, Strategy, and American Diplomacy: Studies in Foreign Policy, 1873–1917* (12:93) is a searching examination of American policy which concludes that McKinley was consistent in his policy toward Spain, that he was patient and worked for a peaceful solution to the problem of Cuba, and that he went to war when it appeared that only war would bring Cuba independence. Bibliography.

LaFeber, W. *The New Empire: An Interpretation of American Expansion, 1860–1898* (12:84) provides a corrective to Pratt's theory on the role of the business community. LaFeber argues that business interests were not monolithic in opposing the war; some were for war.

13:9 Langer, William L. *The Diplomacy of Imperialism, 1890–1902.* 2d ed. New York: Knopf (1935), 1968. The classic account of the diplomacy of the European powers is indispensable as a backdrop to America's role in the period of the war with Spain. Extensive bibliography.

Langley, L. D. *Struggle for the American Mediterranean: United States–European Rivalry in the Gulf-Caribbean, 1776–1904* (2:308) deals with American interests in the Caribbean, the interests of the European powers, and Cuba's position in terms of American security.

May, E. R. *American Imperialism: A Speculative Essay* (2:94) describes the impact of imperialism abroad on the small and sophisticated American establishment that provided the leadership in determining American foreign policy and in molding American opinion.

May, E. R. *Imperial Democracy: The Emergence of America as a Great Power* (12:80) is the most complete study of European attitudes toward American imperialism. The American people apparently were solidly behind the drive for world power, while McKinley emerges as subject to the pressures of the public hysteria for war.

Merk, F., with Merk, L. B. *Manifest Destiny and Mission in American History: A Reinterpretation* [1830–1898] (2:52) compares the Mexican War with the Spanish-American War.

Perkins, D. *The Monroe Doctrine, 1867–1907* (15:52) treats the Cuban question in terms of the Monroe Doctrine. Perkins regards the intervention in Cuban affairs as inconsistent with, but not justified by, the doctrine.

Pratt, J. W. *Expansionists of 1898: The Acquisition of Hawaii and the Spanish Islands* (12:82) argues that the impetus to war was ideological not economic. Clergymen, historians, political scientists, and other social Darwinists called upon the United States to assume its proper place worthy of its Anglo-Saxon qualities.

13:10 Pratt, Julius W. *America's Colonial Experiment: How the U.S. Gained, Governed and in Part Gave Away a Colonial Empire.* New York: Prentice-Hall, 1950. The first two chapters cover the background and success of expansionism.

Williams, W. A. *The Roots of the Modern American Empire: A Study of the Growth and Shaping of Social Consciousness in a Marketplace Society* (2:98) sees the reason for the war in the demands and pressures of the agricultural interests for foreign markets; those interests played, he claims, a "primary causal role."

Williams, W. A. *The Tragedy of American Diplomacy* (2:99) is a brilliant and original and controversial interpretation of American diplomacy in the 20th century whose principal thesis is the quest for an open door worldwide as a market for the surplus products of farm and factory. The early chapters deal with the war with Spain and interpret its coming in terms of the open door.

Progressivism and Foreign Policy

See "The Debate on Imperialism," below; also Chapter 12, "Economic Influences," and Chapter 17, "Spheres and the Open Door" for additional materials on the theme of U.S. imperialism.

13:11 Baron, Harold. "Anti-Imperialism and the Democrats." *Science and Society* 21:3 (1957), 222–39. Although considered the party of anti-imperialism, the Democrats were in reality not homogeneous on this issue. There was considerable divergence of opinion and, indeed, by 1906, the party showed little interest in imperialism.

13:12 Bernstein, Barton J., and Leib, Franklin A. "Progressive Republican Senators and American Imperialism, 1898–1916: A Re-Appraisal." *Mid-America* 50:3 (1968), 163–205. In a reply to William Leuchtenberg's article (13:14), the authors point out that most progressive Republican senators opposed aggressive expansionism.

13:13 Cooper, John M., Jr. "Progressivism and American Foreign Policy: A Reconsideration." *Mid-America* 51:4 (1969), 260–77. Cooper analyzes the importance of foreign policy to three groups of Progressives: the Roosevelt-Lodge "Imperialist Progressives," the Bryanite "Agrarian Isolationists," and the Wilsonian "Liberal Internationalists." He concludes that some Progressives, who were strong on reform but ambivalent to diplomatic concerns during the pre-Wilson period, later became "internationalists." Others, such as the Bryanites and non-reform oriented Progressives (e.g., Lodge), became isolationists.

Israel, J. *Progressivism and the Open Door: America and China, 1905–1921* (17:236).

13:14 Leuchtenberg, William E. "Progressivism and Imperialism: The Progressive Movement and American Foreign Policy, 1898–1916." *Mississippi Valley Historical Review* 39:3 (1952), 483–504. This landmark study argues that Progressives, despite their primary concern for domestic reform, favored imperialism. This thesis has stimulated considerable historical controversy.

13:15 Markowitz, Gerald W. "Progressivism and Imperialism: A Return to First Principles." *Historian* 37:2 (1975), 257–75. Supporting the Leuchtenberg thesis, Markowitz claims that between 1898 and 1917 Progressives were expansionists because they believed new markets were needed to avoid depression, social strife, and class warfare. If those conditions were present in America, there could be no social reform which was the Progressive's dream.

13:16 Siracusa, Joseph M. "Progressivism, Imperialism, and the Leuchtenberg Thesis, 1952–1974." *Australian Journal of Politics and History* 20:3 (1974), 312–25. Siracusa traces the course, impact and validity of the Leuchtenberg thesis as judged by historical writings between 1952 and 1974, with reference to methodology and causation. It is a useful historiographical essay essentially sympathetic to Leuchtenberg's thesis.

Wiebe, R. H. *The Search for Order, 1877–1920* (12:25) relates the forces of progressivism to American foreign policy.

U.S.-Spanish-Cuban Relations from 1868

See Chapter 15 for U.S.-Cuban relations after 1899.

13:17 Bartlett, C. J. "British Reaction to the Cuban Insurrection of 1868–1878." *Hispanic American His-*

torical *Review* 37:3 (1957), 296–312. The British at first wished to see Cuba retained by Spain but gradually came to support American possession of the island.

Becker, J. *Historia de las relaciones exteriores de la España durante el siglo xix* [History of the foreign relations of Spain during the nineteenth century] (7:9) is a thoroughly documented account of 19th-century Spanish foreign relations by the archivist of the Spanish foreign office.

13:18 Benjamin, Jules R. *The United States and Cuba: Hegemony and Dependent Development, 1880–1934*. Pittsburgh: University of Pittsburgh Press, 1974. Chapter 1 deals with the origins of American hegemony on the island until 1902 and serves as a useful backdrop to understanding American interest in the revolution on the island which began in 1895. Bibliography.

13:19 Chapman, Charles E. *A History of the Cuban Republic: A Study in Hispanic-American Politics*. New York: Macmillan, 1927. A standard and thorough account of the situation in Cuba (1868–1900), useful for an understanding of events in the island leading up to American intervention. Bibliography.

13:20 Foner, Philip S. *A History of Cuba and Its Relations with the United States*. 2 vols. New York: International Publishers, 1962–1963. Volume 2 discusses the Cuban Revolution and provides a useful, if economic-determinist, background (1845–1895) to U.S. interests in Cuba. Overall, Foner indicts American policy. Bibliography.

13:21 Foner, Philip S. *The Spanish-Cuban-American War and the Birth of American Imperialism, 1895–1902*. 2 vols. New York: Monthly Review Press, 1972. Foner concludes that American intervention was not necessary to secure Cuban independence, and when it came it was counterrevolutionary. Not surprisingly, he considers American motives to be entirely economic. Volume 2 examines the American occupation of Cuba leading up to the Platt Amendment; see Chapter 15 of the *Guide*. Bibliographies.

13:22 Guerra y Sanchez, Ramiro. *Guerra de los Diez Años, 1868–1878* [The ten years war, 1868–1878]. 2 vols. Havana: Editorial de Ciencias Sociales, 1972. This is the most complete and thorough study of the Ten Years War.

13:23 Portell Vilá, Hermínio. *História de Cuba en sus relaciones con los Estados Unidos y España* [The history of Cuba in its relations with the United States and Spain]. 4 vols. Havana: Montero, 1938–1941. The author, writing from a strong Cuban and republican point of view, is critical of U.S. expansionism but also accuses the United States of indifference to Cuban problems on numerous occasions.

13:24 Portell Vilá, Hermínio. *Historia de la Guerra de Cuba y los Estados Unidos contra España* [A history of the war by Cuba and the United States against Spain.]. Havana: Municipio de la Habana, 1949. This work by one of Cuba's foremost historians plays down the role of the United States in securing Cuban independence.

13:25 Roig de Leuchsenring, Emilio. *Cuba no se su independencia a los Estados Unidos* [Cuba does not owe its independence to the United States]. 2d ed. Buenos Aires: Editorial Hemisferico, 1965. The author argues that the Cuban people won their independence solely by their own efforts and that the United States was always the enemy of Cuban independence.

Thomas, H. *Cuba: The Pursuit of Freedom* (2:315) is a lengthy, stirring account of Cuban history popularly written but based on sound sources. For the period of the war with Spain, his theme is that American people, press, and Congress wanted war.

13:26 Varona Guerrero, Miguel. *La Guerra de Independencia de Cuba, 1895–1898* [The Cuban war of independence, 1895–1898]. 3 vols. Havana: Editorial Lex, 1946. This is a history of the military campaigns of the second, and final, war for independence by a Cuban officer and aide to General Gomez.

Assessing the War

13:27 Keller, Allan. *The Spanish-American War: A Compact History*. New York: Hawthorne, 1969. A brief but spirited journalistic account of the coming of the war and of the war, it depicts the ineptitude of the U.S. military establishment and its mismanagement of the war, and argues that our intervention was needless.

13:28 Linderman, Gerald F. *The Mirror of War: American Society and the Spanish-American War*. Ann Arbor: University of Michigan Press, 1974. The book is an account of what the war meant to various people and groups, such as President McKinley, Theodore Roosevelt, and small-town America. Bibliography.

13:29 Millis, Walter. *The Martial Spirit: A Study of Our War with Spain.* Boston: Houghton Mifflin, 1931. Possessing the antiwar bias of the 1930s, it is a well-written account of national sentiment on the eve of the war. Millis's thesis is that the country was passionate for war and that the administration could not resist the public pressures thus forcing the president to ask Congress for a declaration of war.

13:30 Morgan, H. Wayne. *America's Road to Empire: The War with Spain and Overseas Expansion.* New York: Wiley, 1965. Morgan contends that U.S. intervention was provoked by Spain's refusal to make reforms in Cuba, and that McKinley decided on war when it appeared that Cuba's problems could not be solved peacefully. The subsequent expansion was a conscious exercise of America's new power. Bibliography.

Personalities

Additional references on individuals may be found in Chapter 1, "Biographical Data."

AMERICAN

13:31 Pier, Arthur S. *American Apostles to the Philippines.* Boston: Beacon, 1950. Reprint 1971. Pier's book consists of 12 short biographies (Dewey, Funston, Taft, Wood, Leech, Pershing, etc.) of those who supervised the takeover and administration of the Philippines. It is a condescending account that assumes the Filipinos were uncivilized.

Civilian Leaders

Albert J. Beveridge
13:32 Bowers, Claude. *Beveridge and the Progressive Era.* Boston: Houghton Mifflin, 1932. A dated account, it is still a useful biography of one of the

leaders of the "large policy" and an influential member of the Republican party.

13:33 Braeman, John. *Albert J. Beveridge: American Nationalist.* Chicago: University of Chicago Press, 1971. This is the most recent and best of the biographies of an important political leader at the turn of the century—a domestic progressive and expansionist.

William Jennings Bryan
See Chapters 15, 16, "Personalities," for additional references.

13:34 Coletta, Paolo E. *William Jennings Bryan.* 3 vols. Lincoln: University of Nebraska Press, 1964–1969. A standard biography of the Great Commoner and leader of the Democratic party who spearheaded the opposition to imperialism in 1899–1900. Bibliography.

13:35 Glad, Paul W. *The Trumpet Soundeth: William Jennings Bryan and His Democracy, 1896–1912.* Lincoln: University of Nebraska Press, 1960. This work contains only one brief chapter on America's entry into the Spanish-American War and the imperialism that followed.

13:36 Koenig, Louis W. *Bryan: A Political Biography of William Jennings Bryan.* New York: Putnam's, 1971. This is an acceptable life of the Democratic party leader. Bibliography.

Grover Cleveland
See Chapter 12, "Personalities," for additional references.

Nevins, A. *Grover Cleveland: A Study in Courage* (12:37) gives Cleveland favorable treatment in the handling of the Cuban issue.

William R. Day
13:37 McLean, Joseph E. *William Rufus Day: Supreme Court Justice from Ohio.* Baltimore: Johns Hopkins Press, 1946. McLean believes that McKinley and Day, rather than Sherman, handled the details and policy of the Department of State, including the Spanish negotiations. He sees public and congressional pressure being stronger than Day or McKinley could contain.

13:38 Shippee, Lester B., and Way, Royal B. "William Rufus Day." In Samuel Flagg Bemis, ed., *The*

American Secretaries of State and Their Diplomacy. New York: Knopf, 1929, vol. 9, pp. 27–112. Briefly in office and close confidant of McKinley, Day loyally carried out the president's wishes. Skeptical of Spanish actions in Cuba, he turned earlier than McKinley to intervention in Cuba. He also supported retention of the Philippine Islands.

John Hay

See Chapters 12, 14, "Personalities," for additional references.

Clymer, K. J. *John Hay: The Gentleman as Diplomat* (12:58) views Hay as calm and moderate in his approach to questions of foreign policy, but for war when he thought war inevitable and saw the war as an opportunity for an Anglo-American rapprochement.

13:39 Dennett, Tyler. *John Hay: From Poetry to Politics.* New York: Dodd, Mead, 1933. An old account of Theodore Roosevelt's secretary of state and McKinley's ambassador to Great Britain, but it remains the best source on Hay's life. The biography is short on analysis but complete in narrating the events.

13:40 Hay, John. *The Life and Letters of John Hay.* 2 vols. Ed. by Roscoe R. Thayer. Boston: Houghton Mifflin, 1915. This is an old but excellent life, with letters, of a friend and confidant of the leaders of the "large policy."

13:41 Kushner, Howard I., and Sherrill, Anne H. *John Milton Hay: The Union of Poetry and Politics.* New York: Twayne, 1977. A moderately successful effort to interpret Hay's career, it concentrates on his childhood, youth, and relationship with Abraham Lincoln. Bibliography.

William Randolph Hearst

13:42 Swanberg, W. A. *Citizen Hearst: A Biography of William Randolph Hearst.* New York: Scribner's, 1961. A stimulating, prize-winning biography of the newspaper magnate whose New York *Journal* was locked in a battle for circulation with Pulitzer's *World.* Their use of the Spanish-Cuban rebellion to promote sales gave rise to the phrase "yellow journalism."

13:43 Winkler, John K. *William Randolph Hearst: A New Appraisal.* New York: Hastings House, 1955. An interesting and perceptive account of the newspaper magnate whose *Journal* exerted a significant influence on policy decisions in the months preceding the declaration of war. Bibliography.

George F. Hoar

See also Chapter 12, "Personalities."

Welch, R. E., Jr. *George Frisbie Hoar and the Half-Breed Republicans* (12:63) claims that the source of his anti-imperialism was his fear that expansionism would adversely affect American institutions.

13:44 Welch, Richard E., Jr. "Opponents and Colleagues: George Frisbie Hoar and Henry Cabot Lodge, 1898–1904." *New England Quarterly* 39:2 (1966), 182–209. Although opponents on the issue of expansionism, they avoided a rupture in their private lives.

13:45 Welch, Richard E., Jr. "Senator George Frisbie Hoar and the Defeat of Anti-Imperialism, 1898–1900." *Historian* 26:3 (1964), 362–80. This is an interesting analysis of the failure of a plan by Hoar and Carl Schurz to establish a protectorate over the Philippines caused by a division among the anti-imperialists.

Henry Cabot Lodge

See also Chapter 19, "Personalities."

13:46 Garraty, John A. *Henry Cabot Lodge: A Biography.* New York: Knopf, 1953. The standard biography of one of the leading expansionists, it is an astute and sympathetic appraisal of the senator. Without an understanding of Lodge's views and role in policymaking, one cannot fully comprehend the political climate of the late 1890s.

Welch, R. E., Jr. "Opponents and Colleagues: George Frisbie Hoar and Henry Cabot Lodge, 1898–1904" (13:44).

Werking, R. H. "Senator Henry Cabot Lodge and the Philippines: A Note on American Territorial Expansion" (13:217).

John D. Long

13:47 Garrett, Wendell D. "John Davis Long, Secretary of the Navy, 1898–1902: A Study in Changing Political Alignments." *New England Quarterly* 31:1 (1958), 291–311. Long emerges from this study as a firm and able administrator who was by no means a jingoist but who was concerned about bringing the navy to combat strength and efficiency.

13:48 Long, John D. *America Yesterday: As Reflected in the Journal of John D. Long.* Ed. by L. S. Mayo. Boston: Atlantic, 1923. The journal of McKinley's secretary of navy provides a day-by-day account of cabinet meetings and reaction to events; compare with G. W. Allen, ed. *The Papers of John Davis Long, 1897–1904* (Boston: Massachusetts Historical Society, 1939).

William McKinley

See Chapter 12, "Personalities."

13:49   Coletta, Paolo, ed. *Threshold to American Internationalism: Essays on the Foreign Policy of William McKinley.* New York: Exposition, 1970. Four essays deal with our subjects: McKinley's conduct of foreign affairs, the coming of the war, the peace treaty, and the president as commander in chief. Except for the last essay (by David Healy), the book adds little to what is known; however, it is a convenient summary of events and policies.

13:50   Fry, Joseph A. "William McKinley and the Coming of the Spanish-American War: A Study in the Besmirching and Redemption of an Historical Image." *Diplomatic History* 3:1 (1979), 77–98. A convenient and intelligent survey of the treatment by historians of McKinley. Fry's own view is that the president was neither as weak as portrayed by some scholars nor as strong as depicted by others; he was, rather, complex and mediocre and lacking in imagination; he lacked the capacity for shaping events and for seeking alternatives to war.

13:51   Holbo, Paul. "Presidential Leadership in Foreign Affairs: William McKinley and the Turpie-Foraker Amendment." *American Historical Review* 72:4 (1967), 1321–35. In a story of strong presidential leadership, Holbo argues that McKinley prevented Congress from recognizing Cuban belligerency. A convincing argument is made in a closely reasoned essay.

13:52   Leech, Margaret. *In the Days of McKinley.* New York: Harper, 1959. Leech's prize-winning reinterpretation of McKinley provides a corrective to the previously held views that the president was weak and pressured into action by others. Leech presents a portrait of a firm, principled leader who was completely in command of the situation and knew exactly what he was doing.

13:53   McDonald, Timothy G. "McKinley and the Coming of War with Spain." *Midwest Quarterly* 7:3 (1966), 225–39. The author explores the possibility that McKinley went to war to gain the Philippines, but the argument is not very convincing. The president is charged with delaying the outbreak of the war until the USS *Baltimore* vacated Hong Kong and was prepared for battle in Manila Bay.

Morgan, H. W. *William McKinley and His America* (12:67) views McKinley as an effective president, neither intimidated nor cowed by Congress, or the press, or the public. In opting for war, he took the only course possible.

13:54   Morgan, H. Wayne. "William McKinley as a Political Leader." *Review of Politics* 28:4 (1966), 417–32. Morgan provides a shrewd and perceptive analysis of McKinley's political acumen and tactics in party affairs. Morgan is interesting on McKinley's views of politics and party in the system of American government.

13:55   Olcott, Charles. *The Life of William McKinley.* 2 vols. Boston: Houghton Mifflin, 1916. One of the earliest lives of the president, it is nonetheless useful and worth consulting. Olcott portrays the president as a strong leader.

13:56   Spielman, William C. *William McKinley: Stalwart Republican.* New York: Exposition, 1954. This is an uneven biography that treats the coming of the war, the war itself, and the treaty ending the war. McKinley emerges as reluctant for war but pushed into it by Congress and the public.

Whitelaw Reid

13:57   Cortissoz, Royal. *The Life of Whitelaw Reid.* 2 vols. New York: Scribner's, 1921. This is an old but reliable life of a central figure of the times and a member of the commission to negotiate the peace. Reid was a power in the Republican party and owner of one of the most important New York newspapers.

Duncan, B. *Whitelaw Reid: Journalist, Politician, Diplomat* (14:43) supersedes all others in terms of interpretation, coverage, completeness, and thoroughness.

Reid, Whitelaw. *Making Peace with Spain: The Diary of Whitelaw Reid, September–December, 1898* (13:159).

Frederic Remington

13:58   Allen, Douglas. *Frederic Remington and the Spanish-American War.* New York: Crown, 1971. It contains reports, illustrations, and pictures of the famous war correspondent and artist in Cuba.

13:59 Vorpahl, Ben M. "A Splendid Little War: Frederic Remington's Reaction to the 1898 Cuban Crisis as Revealed through his Letters to Owen Wister." *American West* 9:2 (1972), 25–35. A noted correspondent and artist in Cuba who saw the war as an exciting adventure much like the winning of the West; subsequently, he came to view the war from a broader perspective—that of the historian.

Theodore Roosevelt

See Chapters 14, 15, 17, and 19, "Personalities," for additional references.

13:60 Harbaugh, William H. *Power and Responsibility: The Life and Times of Theodore Roosevelt*. New York: Farrar, Straus & Cudahy, 1961. An intelligent examination of Roosevelt's thoughts and actions, it is perhaps the best one-volume biography of TR.

13:61 Roosevelt, Theodore. *The Rough Riders*. New York: New American Library (1899), 1961. A straight-forward account that vividly recounts the brief and bloody engagements in Cuba, and sharply criticizes the army's bungling during the campaign. The narrative demonstrates TR's gifts as a writer and reveals much about his personality. See also V. C. Jones, *Roosevelt's Rough Riders* (Garden City, N.Y.: Doubleday, 1971).

Others

13:62 Beer, Thomas. *Hanna*. New York: Knopf, 1929. A standard account of a leading senator who, although a close friend of McKinley's, does not appear to have played an important part in setting U.S. diplomatic policy.

13:63 Coolidge, Louis A. *An Old-Fashioned Senator: Orville H. Platt, of Connecticut*. New York: Putnam's, 1910. Platt was one of the influential senators close to the administration during the Cuban crisis.

13:64 Dawes, Charles G. *A Journal of the McKinley Years*. Ed. by Bascom N. Timmons. New York: Lakeside, 1950. This account contains perceptive comments and observations by McKinley's comptroller of the currency on the administration and the president himself. Dawes was a shrewd politician who subsequently became a vice-president of the United States.

Eggert, G. G. *Richard Olney: Evolution of a Statesman* (12:72) is a thoughtful, scholarly account of

Cleveland's secretary of state, who tried to resolve the frustrating problems created by the Cuban Revolution.

13:65 Merrill, Horace S., and Merrill, Marian G. *The Republican Command, 1897–1913*. Lexington: University of Kentucky Press, 1971. An account of important Republican political leaders, such as Senators William B. Allison, Stephen Elkins, Orville Platt, and John Spooner, who exerted an influence on McKinley. Bibliography.

13:66 Meyerhuber, Carl I., Jr. "Henry Lee Higginson and the New Imperialism, 1890–1900." *Mid-America* 56:3 (1974), 182–99. This article, as much about Henry Cabot Lodge as Higginson, is a useful account of Higginson's transformation from an opponent of the war and expansionism to a supporter of colonial acquisition. Higginson was a Boston "brahmin" and banker, and his experience was not untypical of his group.

Nevins, A. *Henry White: Thirty Years of American Diplomacy* (14:60) is particularly good for the background of Anglo-American relations. A confidant of John Hay, White worked hard to keep U.S. relations with England running smoothly.

13:67 Robinson, William A. *Thomas B. Reed, Parliamentarian*. New York: Dodd, Mead, 1930. Though Speaker of the House and a leading Republican, Reed was out of harmony with the party on going to war and annexation of new territories.

13:68 Sage, Leland L. *William Boyd Allison: A Study in Practical Politics*. Iowa City: State Historical Society of Iowa, 1956. Allison was one of the leaders in the Senate during the Cuban crisis.

13:69 Swanberg, W. A. *Pulitzer*. New York: Scribner's, 1967. An excellent biography of the newspaper magnate, Joseph Pulitzer, whose New York *World* both reflected the public excitement against Spain and provoked it with fiery articles, editorials, and pictures.

Naval and Military Leaders

George Dewey

13:70 Dewey, George. *Autobiography of George Dewey: The Admiral of the Navy*. New York: Scribner's, 1913. The distinguished victor of Manila Bay tells his story, which provides a useful comparison of men and events.

13:71 Healy, Laurin, and Kutner, Luis. *The Admiral*. New York: Ziff-Davis, 1944. A comprehensive life of Dewey in which his service in the war and at Manila is thoroughly covered.

13:72 Nicholson, Philip Y. "George Dewey and the Expansionists of 1898." *Vermont History* 42:3 (1974), 214–27. A portrayal of Dewey as an expansionist and the development of the theory that his appointment to command the Asiatic squadron was engineered by the expansionists Theodore Roosevelt and Mahan.

13:73 Spector, Ronald. *Admiral of the New Empire*. Baton Rouge: Louisiana State University Press, 1975. The most recent and the best life of Dewey which is based on solid research. Bibliography.

Alfred T. Mahan

See Chapter 40, "Personalities," for additional materials.

LaFeber, W. "A Note on the 'Mercantilistic Imperialism' of Alfred Thayer Mahan." (14:39) finds that Mahan differed from earlier mercantilists in that he supported the acquisition of colonies not for sources of bullion or raw materials or for places to sell goods but as coaling stations and naval bases to protect and facilitate international commerce.

13:74 Mahan, Alfred T. *Lessons of the War with Spain and Other Articles*. Boston: Little, Brown, 1899. Mahan reviews the strategic and tactical naval decisions of the Atlantic war.

Seager, R., II. *Alfred Thayer Mahan: The Man and His Letters* (40:80) recounts Mahan's minor role in the war which was mainly advising the government on certain matters of strategy.

John J. Pershing

See Chapter 19, "Personalities," for additional references.

Smythe, D. *Guerrilla Warrior: The Early Life of John J. Pershing* (19:103) discusses Pershing's role in the bitter Philippine insurrection.

13:75 Smythe, Donald. "Pershing in the Spanish-American War." *Military Affairs* 30:1 (1966), 25–53. This is an interesting account of the future commander of the American Expeditionary Force in France during the Spanish War. He compiled an excellent record as a quartermaster and at San Juan Hill.

Others

13:76 Hagedorn, Herman. *Leonard Wood: A Biography*. 2 vols. New York: Harper, 1931. An account of the role in the war of an important military leader who subsequently became governor-general of Cuba during the occupation.

Morison, E. E. *Admiral Sims and the Modern American Navy* (40:86) contains an account of Sims, as military attaché in Paris, who sent the Navy Department extremely valuable reports on the Spanish navy.

Palmer, F. *Bliss, Peacemaker: The Life and Letters of General Tasker Howard Bliss* (19:99) includes Bliss's observations on Spanish policy. He was military attaché in Madrid (1897–1898), and served in the field in Puerto Rico.

13:77 West, Richard S., Jr. *Admirals of the American Empire*. Indianapolis: Bobbs-Merrill, 1948. Included here are biographies of several career naval officers in the Spanish-American War: Schley, Sampson, Dewey, Mahan. The accounts are scholarly but popularly written by an expert in naval history. Bibliography.

CUBAN AND SPANISH

José Martí

13:78 Gray, R. B. *José Martí: Cuban Patriot*. Gainesville: University of Florida Press, 1962. Gray's account of the life and times of the notable Cuban patriot is an excellent one. Bibliography.

13:79 Lizaso, Felix. *José Martí: Martyr of Cuban Independence*. Trans. by E. E. Shuler. Albuquerque: University of New Mexico Press, 1953. This is a life of the Cuban patriot and hero. Bibliography.

13:80 Mañach, Jorge. *Martí: Apostle of Freedom*. Trans. by Coley Taylor. New York: Devin-Adair, 1950. A life of the Cubans' great national hero and patriot with a preface by Gabriele Mistrol.

13:81 Martí, José. *Our America: Writings on Latin America and the Struggle for Independence*. Ed. by Philip S. Foner. Trans. by Elinor Randall. New York: Monthly Review Press, 1977. A major portion of Martí's writings call for the independence of Cuba, and Puerto Rico. The lengthy introduction by Foner is useful.

José Rizal

13:82 Craig, Austin. *Lineage, Life and Labors of José Rizal, the Philippine Patriot: A Study of the Growth of Free Ideas in the Trans-Pacific American Territory.* Manila: Philippine Education Co., 1913. This is an old but still very useful biography of the great patriot of the Philippine war for independence.

13:83 Pascual, Ricardo R. *The Philosophy of Rizal.* Manila: Ayudo, 1962. The writings of José Rizal laid the foundation of Philippine nationalism.

13:84 Russell, Charles E., and Rodriquez, E. B. *The Hero of the Philippines.* London: Allen & Unwin, 1924. The authors tell the story of José Rizal, poet, patriot, martyr, and the great national hero of the Philippines who fought for freedom for his people against the Spanish. His writings later inspired Filipinos to continue the fight against the U.S.

Others

13:85 Comellas Garcia-Lleva, José Luis. *Cánovas.* Madrid: Ediciones Cid, 1965. A good biography of Cánovas, it includes an account of his dealings with the Cleveland administration. Bibliographical notes.

13:86 Foner, Philip S. *Antonio Maceo: The "Bronze Titan" of Cuba's Struggle for Independence.* New York: Monthly Review Press, 1970. A Cuban mulatto, Maceo symbolized the hopes of black Cubans as he fought for racial equality as well as Cuban independence.

13:87 Weyler, Valeriano. *Mi Mando en Cuba* [My mandate in Cuba]. 5 vols. Madrid: Gonzalez Rojas, 1910. The Spanish commander in Cuba and the creator of the "reconcentration" order justifies his policies and actions.

The Prelude to War

CAUSES OF AMERICAN INTERVENTION

See Chapter 12, "Ideas and Pressures of Expansionism."

Economic and Political Factors

13:88 Casellas, Salvador E. "Causas y Antecedentes diplomaticos de la Guerra Hispano-americana" [Diplomatic causes and antecedents of the Spanish-American War]. *Revista de Ciencias Sociales* 9:1 (1965), 55–75. The author finds that the financial and commercial interests in the United States caused the United States to intervene in Cuba and go to war with Spain.

13:89 Foner, Philip S. "Why the United States Went to War with Spain in 1898." *Science and Society* 32:1 (1968), 39–65. Foner, an economic-determinist, reviews literature dealing with the question of whether the war was one of economic imperialism. American intervention in Cuba, he concludes, was caused by the need for new markets and was instigated by Wall Street and by the trusts.

13:90 Hacker, Louis M. "The Holy War of 1898." *American Mercury* 21:83 (1930), 316–26. Although an economic historian, Hacker believes that the war was a Republican party maneuver perpetrated to help the party succeed in elections. The party leaders took advantage of, and capitalized on, the nation's passion for war.

13:91 Hofstadter, Richard. "Manifest Destiny and the Philippines." In Daniel Aaron, ed., *America in Crisis: Fourteen Crucial Episodes in American History.* New York: Knopf, 1952, pp. 173–203. Hofstadter views the outbreak of the war and expansionism in terms of social history, depicting a "psychic crisis of the 1890's." The war served as an outlet for aggressive impulses, while it began as a humanitarian crusade. Reprinted in his *The Paranoid Style in American Politics* (New York: Vintage, 1967), pp. 147–87.

13:92 Holbo, Paul. "The Convergence of Moods and the Cuban Bond 'Conspiracy' of 1898." *Journal of American History* 55:1 (1968), 54–72. Politicians, particularly Populists and Democrats, who distrusted bankers and who wanted war against Spain and the freeing of Cuba, accused the president of resisting because of the pressure of holders of Cuban bonds issued by Spain which would be worthless were Cuba to be free.

13:93 LaFeber, Walter. "That 'Splendid Little War' in Historical Perspective." *Texas Quarterly* 11:4 (1968), 89–98. The author argues that the war came as a result of the "collision of two or more independent chains of causes" of which there were three in 1898: the economic crisis, opportunities in Asia and the Caribbean and the Pacific for markets, and the growing partnership between business and government.

13:94 McCormick, Thomas J. "Insular Imperialism and the Open Door: The China Market and the Spanish-American War." *Pacific Historical Review* 32:2 (1963), 155–69. The author sees war and expansionism not for the economic usefulness of the possessions or for manifest destiny, or for the "large policy," but rather as stepping stones (e.g., coaling and cable stations and naval bases) to penetrate the China market.

13:95 McWilliams, Tennant. "Petition for Expansion: Mobile Businessmen and the Cuban Crisis, 1898." *Alabama Review* 28:1 (1975), 58–63. It appears, from evidence drawn from newspapers and business records, that businessmen favored peace in Cuba to safeguard their markets.

13:96 O'Connor, Nancy L. "The Spanish-American War: A Re-evaluation of Its Causes." *Science and Society* 22:2 (1958), 129–43. This article challenges Pratt's thesis that the business community did not support intervention.

13:97 Pratt, Julius. "American Business and the Spanish-American War." *Hispanic American Historical Review* 14:2 (1934), 163–201. An examination of business and commercial newspapers and periodicals leads Pratt to conclude that the financial and commercial interests did not want war. They feared the effects of war—disruption of the normal channels of trade, weakening of the currency, etc.—on their economic well-being.

13:98 Pratt, Julius W. "The 'Large Policy' of 1898." *Mississippi Valley Historical Review* 19:2 (1932), 219–42. By the "large policy," Pratt means the expansionist ambitions of certain leading Americans, who wished, for reasons quite divorced from economic considerations, to enlarge the area of American power and influence. He considers Beveridge, Brooks Adams, Henry Cabot Lodge, Theodore Roosevelt imperialists.

13:99 Rippy, J. Fred. "Enthusiasms of 1898." *South Atlantic Quarterly* 37:2 (1938), 139–49. Rippy defines "inevitable destiny" and the white man's burden, and uses them to explain American expansionism.

13:100 Sklar, Martin J. "The NAM and Foreign Markets on the Eve of the Spanish-American War." *Science and Society* 23:2 (1959), 133–62. There is no attempt to refute Julius Pratt's thesis that business interests opposed the war (13:97). Still, Sklar analyzes the objectives of the National Association of Manufacturers on the eve of the war and finds them deeply involved in securing overseas markets. Citing this evidence, the author suggests a reappraisal of the Pratt thesis.

Vevier, C. "American Continentalism: An Idea of Expansion, 1845–1910" (10:76) ties expansionism in the Spanish-American War period to historic continentalism of the pre–Civil War period. The later expansionism was not an aberration but was "the adjustment of new ideological justifications of the 1890's to an older nationalistic expansionist base."

Influence of the Press

See "Personalities," especially William Randolph Hearst, Frederic Remington, and, under "Others," Joseph Pulitzer.

13:101 Auxier, George W. "Middle Western Newspapers and the Spanish-American War." *Mississippi Valley Historical Review* 26:4 (1940), 523–34. An important study which shows, from a sampling of 40 journals—Democratic, Republican, and independent—that the press did influence the course to war, not because of its sensationalist approach but rather because it emphasized those issues which were in dispute between the United States and Spain, and which led to war.

13:102 Berg, Meredith W., and Berg, David M. "The Rhetoric of War Preparation: The New York Press in 1898." *Journalism Quarterly* 45:4 (1968), 655–60. The authors examine the treatment by the *World, Journal,* and *Times* of the events of 1898.

13:103 Boles, David C. "Editorial Opinion in Oklahoma and Indian Territory on the Cuban Insurrection, 1895–98." *Chronicles of Oklahoma* 47:3 (1969), 258–67. The press was lukewarm concerning the situation in Cuba until the *Maine* was sunk, after which it supported intervention and annexation of Cuba.

Brown, C. H. *The Correspondents' War: Journalists in the Spanish American War* (13:152) describes

American newspaper tycoons, journalists, and correspondents from 1895 to 1898.

13:104 Fry, Joseph A. "Silver and Sentiment: The Nevada Press and the Coming of the Spanish-American War." *Nevada Historical Society Quarterly* 20:4 (1977), 222–39. Fry analyzes editorials about Cuban affairs in 25 Nevada newspapers before the Spanish-American War. All papers criticized Spanish rule in Cuba and most disagreed with Cuban policies of President William McKinley (1843–1901). Papers supporting free silver resorted to yellow journalism and advocated war with Spain to improve Nevada's economy.

13:105 Gullason, Thomas A. "Stephen Crane's Private War on Yellow Journalism." *Huntington Library Quarterly* 22:3 (1959), 201–08. Crane, a correspondent in Cuba, attacked the unscrupulous demands by editors and newspaper owners for sensational news.

13:106 Rosenberg, Morton M., and Ruff, Thomas P. *Indiana and the Coming of the Spanish-American War.* Muncie, Ind.: Ball State University, 1976. A short monograph, it develops press opinion toward the issues leading up to the war.

13:107 Schellings, William J. "Florida and the Cuban Revolution, 1895–1898." *Florida Historical Quarterly* 39:2 (1960), 175–86. Florida was the only state in which all the important newspapers opposed war. Opposition was based on the danger to the state of an attack by the Spanish fleet and of the threat to business. After the passage of the Teller Amendment, opposition diminished because the amendment seemed to give the state relief from the possibility of competition from Cuba.

13:108 Shankman, Arnold M. "Southern Methodist Newspapers and the Coming of the Spanish-American War: A Research Note." *Journal of Southern History* 39:1 (1973), 93–96. The press opposed the war and supported McKinley's efforts to liberate Cuba peacefully. Once war began, the newspapers backed the administration, but with misgivings.

13:109 Sylvester, Harold J. "The Kansas Press and the Coming of the Spanish-American War." *Historian* 31:2 (1969), 251–67. The press supported war after McKinley declared it necessary.

13:110 Wilkerson, Marcus. *Public Opinion and the Spanish-American War: A Study in War Propaganda.*

Baton Rouge: Louisiana State University Press, 1932. A useful book that contains a compilation of newspaper quotations; but it lacks analysis. Bibliography.

13:111 Wisan, Joseph. *The Cuban Crisis as Reflected in the New York Press, 1895–1898.* New York: Columbia University Press, 1934. An account, chiefly using the *World* and the *Journal,* of how the press saw the events leading to the war. The book was widely cited in part because of its implication that the two newspapers played a major role in the decision for war. Bibliography.

Public Opinion and the Cuban Crisis

13:112 Appel, John C. "The Unionization of Florida Cigar Makers and the Coming of the War with Spain." *Hispanic American Historical Review* 36:1 (1956), 38–49. Labor favored war against Spain; its sympathies were with the Cubans, many of whom were cigar makers and unionists.

Armstrong, W. N. *E. L. Godkin and American Foreign Policy, 1865–1900* (14:55) analyzes Godkin's opposition to the war with Spain and the acquisition of colonies.

13:113 Davis, Michelle B., and Quimby, Robin W. "Senator Proctor's Cuban Speech: Speculations on a Cause of the Spanish-American War." *Quarterly Journal of Speech* 55:2 (1969), 131–41. An analysis of the famous speech which had a significant effect on American public opinion—its language, arguments, and structure. It reinforced the prevailing view on conditions in Cuba, and the observations were made by a man known as honest and moderate.

13:114 Gatewood, Willard B., Jr. "Black Americans and the Quest for Empire, 1893–1903." *Journal of Southern History* 38:4 (1972), 545–66. Blacks did not have a consistent attitude on the war and on imperialism chiefly because they found racists on both sides of the issues.

13:115 Gianakos, Perry E. "The Spanish-American War and the Double Paradox of the Negro American." *Phylon* 26:1 (1965), 34–50. The paradox, according to the author, is that while there was sympathy in the United States for the mistreatment of Cubans, there was no sympathy for the plight of American blacks.

Hofstadter, R. *Social Darwinism in American Thought, 1860–1915* (12:79) suggests the influence of Darwinism in shaping American foreign affairs.

13:116   Johnke, James. "Kansas Mennonites during the Spanish-American War." *Mennonite Life* 26:2 (1971), 70–82. Mennonites supported the war but turned against it when it became expansionist. They did not strongly support Bryan and his peace efforts in 1900, although they opposed the Republican expansionism; during the war they acted in noncombatant capacities.

13:117   King, G. Wayne. "Conservative Attitudes in the United States toward Cuba." *Proceedings of the South Carolina Historical Association* (1973), 94–104. Conservative business and congressional leaders and press opposed propaganda that might involve the United States in the war. The author believes that their views and influence delayed American intervention.

13:118   Leuchtenberg, William E. "The Needless War with Spain." *American Heritage* 8:2 (1957), 35–95. A popularly written, yet scholarly essay, which examines the events leading to war and concludes that McKinley surrendered to public opinion against his own inclinations and the counsel of his party.

13:119   McNeil, W. D. "'We'll Make the Spanish Grunt': Popular Songs about the Sinking of the 'Maine.'" *Journal of Popular Culture* 2:4 (1968), 537–51. Some 40 songs about the sinking of the *Maine,* which aroused considerable sentiment for war in that they blamed Spain for the disaster and sought revenge.

Muller, D. R. "Josiah Strong and American Nationalism" (12:81) sees Strong not as an aggressive nationalist—he did not wish to extend Anglo-Saxon Protestant Christianity by force and conquest, but by example, by exporting American institutions.

13:120   Quinn, D. Michael. "The Mormon Church and the Spanish-American War: An End to Selective Pacifism." *Pacific Historical Review* 43:3 (1974), 342–66. Brigham Young, Jr., opposed intervention and war, but other Mormon leaders supported the war because they deemed it a duty to support national policy.

13:121   Quint, Howard H. "American Socialists and the Spanish-American War." *American Quarterly* 10:2 (1958), 132–54. Humanitarianism and hysteria broke the solidarity of the ranks of Socialists; thus although the party opposed the war, some individuals succumbed to passion and supported the war. As for expansionism, the party was solidly opposed.

13:122   Zobrist, Benedict K. "How Victor Lawson's Newspapers Covered the Cuban War of 1898." *Journalism Quarterly* 38:3 (1961), 323–31. Lawson's Chicago papers, the *Record* and the *Daily News,* were among those newspapers that refrained from sensational reporting. Both papers' correspondents in Cuba sent dispatches that were models of factual reporting.

U.S.-SPANISH DIPLOMACY, 1895–1898

See "Personalities," especially Grover Cleveland, William R. Day, William McKinley, Richard Olney (under "Others"), Valeriano Weyler (under "Cuban and Spanish," "Others").

Benton, E. J. *Diplomacy of the Spanish-American War* (16:150).

13:123   Benton, Elbert J. *International Law and Diplomacy of the Spanish-American War.* Baltimore: Johns Hopkins Press, 1908. A straightforward account of American policy from 1895 to the signing of the peace treaty, based upon American sources. It is a typical example of old fashioned diplomatic history in that it tells only of official policy and has nothing on the forces at home which shaped those policies.

Chadwick, F. E. *The Relations of the United States and Spain: Diplomacy* (8:107) is a defense of American policy and an indictment of Spain. There are racist overtones in that the author implies that the American position was correct because of inherent superior humanistic qualities.

13:124   Díaz-Plaja, Fernando. *1898.* Madrid: Editorial Nacional, 1976. This book is largely a collection of quotations from various sources, such as newspapers, which gives a sense of Spanish reaction to the events of 1898. Much of the material focuses on internal political development.

13:125   Eggert, Gerald G. "Our Man in Havana: Fitzhugh Lee." *Hispanic American Historical Review* 47:4 (1967), 463–85. Lee, American consul in Havana, strongly urged intervention in Cuba and its annexation to the United States. It was he who urged the administration to send the *Maine* to Havana.

13:126 Farrell, John T. "Archbishop Ireland and Manifest Destiny." *Catholic Historical Review* 33:3 (1947), 269–301. Pope Leo XIII used Ireland at the end of March 1898 to attempt to head off a war through mediation, but this last-minute foreign intervention failed.

13:127 Ferrara, Orestes. *The Last Spanish War: Revelations in "Diplomacy."* Trans. by William E. Shea. New York: Paisley, 1937. Efforts by Spain to get Germany, Austria, and Great Britain to intervene in Cuba lest the island's loss mean the end of the Spanish monarchy.

13:128 Flack, Horace E. *Spanish-American Relations Preceding the War of 1898.* Baltimore: Johns Hopkins Press, 1906. An old study of the status of Cuba during the insurrection, of the causes of U.S. intervention, which Flack finds unjustifiable, and of the efforts by Spain to avoid war.

13:129 Morgan, H. Wayne. "The De Lôme Letter: A New Appraisal." *Historian* 26:1 (1963), 36–49. The author's thesis is that the importance of the De Lôme letter was that it destroyed American confidence in Spain's honesty. De Lôme was the Spanish minister to Washington.

The Maine Incident

13:130 Esteves, Herman R. "The United States, Spain, and the *Maine,* or the Diplomacy of Frustration." *Revista Interamericana* 2:4 (1972), 549–58. The author finds the *Maine* the immediate cause for the outbreak of the war. Spain believed itself innocent of any wrongdoing and on this issue acted above reproach. Failure to keep the peace, therefore, rests with the United States.

13:131 Rickover, Hyman. *How the Battleship Maine Was Destroyed.* Washington, D.C.: U.S. Department of Navy, Naval History Division, 1976. An analysis of the conclusions of the Board of Inquiry and of the Joint Army-Navy Board. Bibliography.

13:132 Weems, John E. *The Fate of the Maine.* New York: Holt, 1958. A popular and engaging history of the famous battleship from its commissioning to its destruction two and one-half years later. Bibliography.

Cuban Rebels in the U.S.

13:133 Auxier, George W. "The Propaganda Activities of the Cuban Junta in Precipitating the Spanish-American War, 1895–1898." *Hispanic American Historical Review* 19:3 (1939), 286–305. This is a useful analysis of the organization, purpose, and methods of the junta which did, in fact, exert considerable pressure on American opinion and helped to mold it in favor of war—as reflected in editorials in 40 midwestern newspapers.

13:134 Detter, Raymond A. "The Cuban Junta and Michigan, 1895–1898." *Michigan History* 48:1 (1964), 35–46. Detter writes of interference in American politics by Cuban exiles, using Michigan as an example.

13:135 Proctor, Samuel. "Filibustering Aboard the 'Three Friends.'" *Mid-America* 38:2 (1956), 84–100. This is an account of efforts by Americans in 1895–1896 to ship arms and other supplies to the Cuban rebels.

13:136 Rubens, Horatio S. *Liberty: The Story of Cuba.* New York: AMS Press (1932), 1970. Rubens served as the legal adviser to the Cuban junta.

Conduct of the War

See "Personalities," especially George Dewey, John D. Long, Alfred T. Mahan, John J. Pershing, Theodore Roosevelt, and naval leader Leonard Wood, under "Others"; also "Bibliographies" for Braisted, Ellis, and Smith.

13:137 Braisted, William R. "The Philippine Naval Base Problem, 1898–1909." *Mississippi Valley Historical Review* 41:1 (1954), 21–40. Braisted recounts the long debate over whether to construct a major naval base at Subic Bay, a base the navy wanted but one that the army said could not be defended from the landward side. See also his *The United States Navy in the Pacific, 1897–1909* (17:226).

13:138 Chadwick, French E. *The Relations of the United States and Spain: The Spanish-American War.* 2 vols. New York: Scribner's, 1911. Reprint 1968. A detailed, highly professional description of the war on land and on the seas by a naval officer who was also an excellent historian. The tone is partisan in spirit—nationalist and patriotic.

13:139 Cosmas, Graham A. *An Army for Empire: The United States Army in the Spanish-American War, 1898–1899.* Columbia: University of Missouri Press, 1971. The structure, composition, and administration of the army and of the War Department; the author concludes that the policymakers were not responsible for the army's poor performance. Bibliography. George J. Tanham, "Service Relations Sixty Years Ago," *Military Affairs* 23:3 (1959), 139–48 discusses interservice rivalries.

13:140 Freidel, Frank. *The Splendid Little War.* Boston: Little, Brown, 1958. This study paints a picture of the toll on the fighting forces and on the land on which they fought, emphasizing the commonplace aspects of the conflict. Bibliography.

13:141 Grenville, John A. S. "Diplomacy and War Plans in the United States, 1890–1917." *Transactions of the Royal Historical Society* 8:11 (1961), 1–21. Expansionists in the United States were not responsible for the attack on Manila; it was conceived by an officer in the Navy Department as a means of diverting Spain in East Asia. Also see his "American Naval Preparations for War with Spain, 1896–1898," *Journal of American Studies* 2:1 (1968), 33–47.

13:142 Leckie, Robert. *The Wars of America.* 2 vols. New York: Harper, 1968. Part 6 is on the Spanish-American War. The description of land and sea operations is good, but the author's comments on diplomatic events do not take into account the most recent scholarship.

13:143 Shaffer, Ralph E. "The Race of the *Oregon.*" *Oregon Historical Quarterly* 76:3 (1975), 269–98. A description of the *Oregon*'s voyage from the U.S. west coast to the Caribbean, a ten-week trip which demonstrated the need for an isthmus canal. See also Sanford Sternlicht's *McKinley's Bulldog: The Battleship Oregon* (Chicago: Nelson-Hall, 1977).

13:144 Spector, Ronald. "Who Planned the Attack on Manila Bay?" *Mid-America* 53:2 (1971), 94–102. Spector provides a corrective to the view held by some that Assistant Secretary of the Navy Theodore Roosevelt, during the absence of the secretary, ordered Dewey to attack the capital of the Philippines. Actually, naval officers in the department drew up

plans for the attack as early as June 1896; see also Grenville (13:141).

Sprout, H., and Sprout, M. *The Rise of American Naval Power, 1776–1918* (40:117) provides an excellent account of the Spanish War for an understanding of the navy's testing.

NAVAL AND LAND BATTLES

13:145 Crouch, Thomas W. *A Yankee Guerrilla: Frederick Funston and the Cuban Insurrection, 1896–1897.* Memphis: Memphis State University Press, 1975. Frederick Funston of Kansas was one of a score or so of Americans who voluntarily went to Cuba to fight as guerrillas.

13:146 Dierks, Jack C. *A Leap to Arms: The Cuban Campaign of 1898.* Philadelphia: Lippincott, 1970. Dierks analyzes the military and naval operations at Santiago de Cuba. Bibliography.

13:147 Gatewood, Willard B., Jr., ed. *"Smoked Yankees" and the Struggle for Empire: Letters from Negro Soldiers, 1898–1902.* Urbana: University of Illinois Press, 1971. These letters appeared in newspapers and revealed the experiences and attitudes of black servicemen in Cuba, the Philippines, and the United States—the story is not a heartening one.

13:148 Risco, Alberto. *La Escuadra del almirante Cervera* [The squadron of Admiral Cervera]. Madrid: Jiménez y Molina, 1920. This is a scholarly account of the battle of Santiago from the Spanish perspective. The work contains 43 pages of documents in the appendixes. Extensive bibliography.

13:149 Sargent, Herbert H. *The Campaign of Santiago de Cuba.* 3 vols. Chicago: McClure, 1907. This is an old, but very useful, account of the key campaign on land of the war.

13:150 Saum, Lewis O. "The Western Volunteer and the 'New Empire.'" *Pacific Northwest Quarterly* 57:1 (1966), 18–27. Western soldiers, the author concludes, fought not for economic motives but for moral and patriotic reasons. He finds that they did not like the Filipinos whom they fought.

13:151 Walker, Leslie W. "Guam's Seizure by the United States in 1898." *Pacific Historical Review* 14:1 (1945), 1–12. A military history of the U.S. Navy's taking of Guam.

CORRESPONDENTS/FOREIGN OBSERVERS

See "Personalities," especially Frederic Remington.

13:152 Brown, Charles H. *The Correspondents' War: Journalists in the Spanish-American War.* New York: Scribner's, 1967. A study of the role of numerous, audacious, conspicuous, and daring, correspondents in the war. They were censored but yet they had considerable freedom from their editors and from the military leaders. Bibliography.

13:153 Brown, Charles H. "Press Censorship in the Spanish-American War." *Journalism Quarterly* 42:4 (1965), 581–90. This essay describes the extensive and effective censorship of the press in the field.

13:154 Davis, Richard Harding. *The Cuban and Porto Rico Campaigns.* New York: Scribner's, 1898. An eyewitness account by one of the first war correspondents.

13:155 Ransom, Edward. "Baronet on the Battlefield: Sir Bryan Leighton in Cuba." *Journal of American Studies* 9:1 (1975), 3–20. A report by a British officer on the American army which is critical of the ineptitude, incompetence, and indecision of the officers.

13:156 Ransom, Edward. "British Military and Naval Observers in the Spanish-American War." *Journal of American Studies* 3:1 (1969), 33–56. At Santiago; the observations were not as complimentary as they were critical of the chaotic conditions.

Peace Treaty and Annexation

TREATY NEGOTIATIONS

See "Personalities," especially William R. Day, William McKinley, Whitelaw Reid.

13:157 Coletta, Paolo. "McKinley, the Peace Negotiations, and the Acquisition of the Philippines." *Pacific Historical Review* 30:4 (1961), 341–50. The author claims that McKinley knew exactly what he wanted; he was determined to secure the islands for the United States.

13:158 Hill, Charles E. *Leading American Treaties.* New York: Macmillan, 1922. Hill provides a factual account of the historical setting and the provisions of the Treaty of Paris. It is a convenient place to get the facts but little else.

13:159 Reid, Whitelaw. *Making Peace with Spain: The Diary of Whitelaw Reid, September-December, 1898.* Ed. by H. Wayne Morgan. Austin: University of Texas Press, 1965. An invaluable insider's view of the conference, with shrewd observations of men and of events. The peace commission consisted of men of varying views on several questions, and Reid notes the clashes among them.

13:160 Reuter, Frank T. *Catholic Influence on American Colonial Policies, 1898–1904.* Austin: University of Texas Press, 1967. Reuter examines some of the church-state problems in the new American empire, and observes Catholic reaction in the United States to these problems—in Cuba, Puerto Rico, Guam, and the Philippines. Bibliography.

PUERTO RICO

13:161 Berbusse, Edward J. *The United States in Puerto Rico, 1898–1900.* Chapel Hill: University of North Carolina Press, 1966. This account of the development of Puerto Rico from its autonomous state under Spanish rule to civil government under American law describes the social, religious, cultural, and educational changes. It provides an excellent background for understanding the conflict between the Spanish heritage and new Anglo-Saxonism.

13:162 Chiles, Paul N. *The Puerto Rican Press Reaction to the United States, 1888–1898.* New York: Arno (1942), 1975. Puerto Rican press reaction, both liberal and conservative, to the United States during this period fell into three main fields: economic, political, and cultural. All carried influence; American political theories were used by the liberals. Bibliography.

PHILIPPINE ANNEXATION/INSURRECTION

See Chapter 17, "U.S. Rule, 1899–1913."

13:163   Achutegui, Pedro S. de, S.J., and Bernard, Miguel A., S.J. *Religious Revolution in the Philippines.* 3 vols. Manila: Ateneo de Manila, 1960–1971. The religious revolution, concomitant with the political, aimed at replacing Spanish bishops and parish priests with Filipinos. Volume 3 has documents on the religious successes of 1898 to 1901.

Alfonson, O. M. *Theodore Roosevelt and the Philippines, 1897–1909* (17:287) seeks to discover why Roosevelt opposed the extension of self-government to the Philippines.

13:164   Bolton, Grania. "Military Diplomacy and National Liberation: Insurgent-American Relations after the Fall of Manila." *Military Affairs* 36:3 (1972), 99–104. A story of the lack of direction from Washington which accounted for the deterioration of relations between Aguinaldo, the rebel leader, and the American army.

13:165   Graff, Henry F., ed. *American Imperialism and the Philippine Insurrection.* Boston: Little, Brown, 1969. At the behest of Senator George Frisbie Hoar, hearings were held in 1902 on affairs in the Philippines. This volume offers excerpts from the Senate hearings as well as an introduction and brief biographical sketches of the participants.

13:166   Pomeroy, William J. *American Neo-Colonialism: Its Emergence in the Philippines and Asia.* New York: International Publishers, 1970. An interesting thesis is presented—that the acquisition of the Philippines destroyed "an indigenous agrarian revolution" to obtain a base for the China trade. Bibliography.

Stanley, P. W. *A Nation in the Making: The Philippines and the United States, 1899–1921* (2:356).

13:167   Welch, Richard E., Jr. *Response to Imperialism: The United States and the Philippine-American War, 1899–1902.* Chapel Hill: University of North Carolina Press, 1978. An excellent account of the impact of the insurrection on American society and politics, the response of American public opinion, and the official American response to the war. Extensive bibliography.

Military Operations

See "Personalities," especially John J. Pershing.

13:168   Gates, John M. *Schoolbooks and Krags: The United States Army in the Philippines, 1898–1902.* Westport, Conn.: Greenwood, 1973. A useful corrective to Wolff (13:171) and Cosmas (13:139), this is a favorable view of the army in the islands and its role in establishing schools, improving public health, organizing municipal government, and generally improving the quality of life in the Philippines. Bibliography.

13:169   Robinson, Michael C., and Schubert, Frank N. "David Fagen: An African-American Rebel in the Philippines, 1899–1901." *Pacific Historical Review* 44:1 (1975), 68–83. A curious story of black American soldiers in the Philippines who defected to the rebels as a consequence of disillusionment with their treatment by their own country. Fagen was their leader.

13:170   Tomblin, Barbara B. "The United States Navy and the Philippine Insurrection." *American Neptune* 35:3 (1975), 183–96. Tomblin provides a useful account of the role of the navy in the capture of the islands and in supporting the land forces.

13:171   Wolff, Leon. *Little Brown Brother.* Garden City, N.Y.: Doubleday, 1961. Reprint 1970. This is one of the harshest indictments of American conduct in the Philippine insurrection.

American Public Opinion

13:172   Freidel, Frank. "Dissent in the Spanish-American War and the Philippine Insurrection." *Proceedings of the Massachusetts Historical Society* 81 (1969), 167–84. While there was little dissent during the war against Spain, there was a great deal of dissent against the war in the Philippines. The focal point was in New England and was based chiefly on reports of the horrors of the war.

13:173   Gates, John M. "Philippine Guerrillas, American Anti-imperialism, and the Election of 1900." *Pacific Historical Review* 46:1 (1977), 51–64. Anti-imperialism in the United States encouraged Philippine guerrilla resistance, and Filipino nationalists hoped the 1900 election would lead to

Bryan's election and the reversal of McKinley's policies.

13:174 Hendrickson, Kenneth E., Jr. "Reluctant Expansionist: Jacob Gould Schurman and the Philippine Question." *Pacific Historical Review* 36:4 (1967), 405–21. Schurman headed a commission to assess conditions in the Philippines, but he fell out with the commission because he favored direct negotiations with Aguinaldo and temporary rule of the islands, not permanent ownership.

13:175 Welch, Richard E., Jr. "American Atrocities in the Philippines: The Indictment and the Response." *Pacific Historical Review* 43:2 (1974), 233–53. The author finds, surprisingly, not much outrage in the United States over reports of atrocities because of patriotism, racism, and the idea of the American mission.

13:176 Welch, Richard E., Jr. "Organized Religion and the Philippine-American War, 1899–1902." *Mid-America* 55:3 (1973), 184–206. Catholics and Protestants found their churches divided on questions affecting the Philippines, such as independence for the islands, the conduct of the war.

13:177 Welch, Richard E., Jr. "The Philippine Insurrection and the American Press." *Historian* 36:1 (1973), 35–41. A study of 180 newspapers divided into 122 for annexation and 58 against. The arguments presented by each side centered on matters such as the good faith of the nation, America's mission—all emotional and nonmaterial.

International Reaction

See Chapter 14 for general accounts of European diplomacy during this period.

GREAT BRITAIN

See "Personalities," especially John Hay.

13:178 Blake, Nelson M. "England and the United States, 1897–1899." In Dwight E. Lee and G. E. McReynolds, eds., *Essays in History and Interna-* *tional Relations in Honor of George Hubbard Blakeslee.* Worcester, Mass: Clark University Press, 1949, pp. 257–83. Blake's essay describes the origins of Anglo-American cordiality and cooperation during the war with Spain.

13:179 Campbell, Alex E. *Great Britain and the United States, 1895–1903.* London: Longmans, 1960. The story, by a British author, of growing Anglo-American cordiality in these crucial years. The period of the war demonstrated British sympathy for American problems. Bibliography. See also his *Anglo-American Understanding, 1893–1903* (Baltimore: Johns Hopkins Press, 1957).

13:180 Neale, R. G. *Great Britain and United States Expansion, 1898–1900.* East Lansing: Michigan State University Press, 1966. The author claims that the Anglo-American rapprochement has been exaggerated and that it was not significant in heading off mediation by the European powers. Yet, during this period, the British did support the United States. Bibliography.

13:181 Reuter, Bertha A. *Anglo-American Relations during the Spanish-American War.* New York: Macmillan, 1924. An older work, it is still useful for the story of the move between the two powers from hostility to friendship and its fruition at the time of the Spanish war. Bibliography.

13:182 Seed, Geoffrey. "British Reactions to American Imperialism Reflected in Journals of Opinion, 1898–1900." *Political Science Quarterly* 73:1 (1958), 254–72. British opinion supported American expansionism because of racial affinity, the idea of the white man's burden, and American support for the British in China.

13:183 Seed, Geoffrey. "British Views of American Policy in the Philippines as Reflected in Journals of Opinion, 1898–1907." *Journal of American Studies* 2:1 (1968), 49–64. British journals approved of the American acquisition but were critical of American mismanagement of the islands.

GERMANY

13:184 Bailey, Thomas A. "Dewey and the Germans at Manila Bay." *American Historical Review* 45:1 (1939), 59–81. A recounting of the difficulties between Dewey and the Germans at the time of the American assault on Manila. Dewey believed the

Germans deliberately sought to hinder American operations and to obstruct his blockade of the city, but Bailey finds no evidence to support these suspicions.

13:185 Quinn, Pearle E. "Diplomatic Struggle for the Carolines, 1898." *Pacific Historical Review* 14:3 (1945), 290–302. This article discusses German-American diplomatic wrangling over the Carolines following the Spanish-American War. Acceding to the terms of a "secret" treaty between Germany and Spain during the war, the United States allowed Germany to gain control over an important commercial and strategic site.

13:186 Rippy, J. Fred. "The European Powers and the Spanish-American War." *James Sprunt Historical Studies* 19 (1927), 12–52. Rippy is primarily concerned with German actions during the Spanish-American War. Intent on supporting monarchical supremacy in Spain, Rippy argues, Germany at the same time did not wish to antagonize the United States, feeling that this would only rebound to Britain's favor.

13:187 Shippee, Lester B. "Germany and the Spanish-American War." *American Historical Review* 30:4 (1925), 754–77. Germany coveted the Philippines, and possibly would have gotten them if the United States had not.

OTHER NATIONS

13:188 Brown, R. C. "Goldwin Smith and Anti-Imperialism." *Canadian Historical Review* 43:2 (1962), 93–101. Using a Canadian history professor's views, the author concludes that Canadians supported the Americans in the war and in the expansion that followed it.

13:189 Eyre, James K., Jr. "Japan and the American Acquisition of the Philippines." *Pacific Historical Review* 11:1 (1942), 55–71. The Japanese, fearful that the Germans would get the islands otherwise, wanted the United States to have them. Japan's role was to make the United States aware of the dangers of European rivalry for the islands if the United States did not take them.

13:190 Eyre, James K., Jr. "Russia and the American Acquisition of the Philippines." *Mississippi Valley Historical Review* 28:4 (1942), 539–62. It appears that Russia's interest in acquiring the islands (as well

as the interest of other powers) spurred the American decision to acquire them.

13:191 Gilmore, N. Ray. "Mexico and the Spanish-American War." *Hispanic American Historical Review* 43:4 (1963), 511–25. Mexico remained neutral in the struggle but her sympathies were with Spain. The war served as an impetus to the growing Pan-Hispanism movement which brought Spain closer to her former American colonies both culturally and economically.

13:192 Leynseele, H. Va. "Leopold II et les Philippines en 1898" [Leopold II and the Philippines in 1898]. *Bulletin des Séances l'Académie Royale des Sciences Coloniales* 2:6 (1956), 923–37. When the United States seemed undecided about the islands, Leopold evinced a keen interest in acquiring them.

13:193 Sears, Louis M. "French Opinion of the Spanish-American War." *Hispanic American Historical Review* 7:1 (1927), 25–44. Despite some minor errors of fact, the article emphasizes the sharply critical response of French opinion toward American policy relative to origins of the Spanish-American War.

13:194 Shelby, Charmion C. "Mexico and the Spanish-American War: Some Contemporary Expressions of Opinion." In Thomas E. Cotner and Carlos E. Castañeda, eds., *Essays in Mexican History*. Austin: University of Texas Press, 1958, pp. 209–28. Mexico was sympathetic to Spain but neutral in the conflict because of a fear of U.S. invasion and its dependency on the United States for economic well-being.

The Debate on Imperialism, 1898–1900

See also "Progressivism and Foreign Policy," above.

13:195 Beisner, Robert L. "1898 and 1968: The Anti-Imperialists and the Doves." *Political Science Quarterly* 85:2 (1970), 186–216. Beisner provides an interesting and suggestive comparison of the two anti-movements as to who the protestors were, what they did, and why they did it.

13:196 Marks, George P., ed. *The Black Press Views American Imperialism*. New York: Arno, 1971. It is made up of excerpts from the Black press.

ANTI-IMPERIALIST MOVEMENT

See "Personalities," especially William Jennings Bryan, George F. Hoar.

13:197 Beisner, Robert L. *Twelve against Empire: The Anti-Imperialists, 1898–1900*. New York: McGraw-Hill, 1968. The failure of the Republican opponents of expansion to frustrate the acquisition of colonies after the war was rooted in the fact that the Republicans were aged, divided, and hobbled by the historic position of their party on expansion.

13:198 Gatewood, Willard B., Jr. *Black Americans and the White Man's Burden, 1898–1903*. Urbana: University of Illinois Press, 1975. Blacks were ambivalent toward imperialism; their attitude was conditioned by their views on racism. Bibliography.

13:199 Harrington, Fred H. "The Anti-Imperialist Movement in the United States, 1898–1900." *Mississippi Valley Historical Review* 22:1 (1935), 211–30. An article that has become the standard account of the movement; it is most valuable for its analysis of the Anti-Imperialist League.

13:200 Lasch, Christopher. "The Anti-Imperialists, the Philippines, and the Inequality of Man." *Journal of Southern History* 24:3 (1958), 319–31. Lasch's study brands the anti-imperialists as racist and imperialists. The opponents of the acquisition of the Philippines did not want inferior races in the American empire.

13:201 Rollins, John W. "The Anti-Imperialists and Twentieth Century American Foreign Policy." *Studies on the Left* 3:1 (1962), 9–24. The anti-imperialists were not opposed to economic expansion overseas; they opposed only old-style colonialism—military conquest, and ruling a free people by coercion.

13:202 Schirmer, Daniel B. *Republic or Empire: American Resistance to the Philippine War*. Cambridge, Mass.: Schenkman, 1972. This is an account

of anti-imperialism in Boston—a struggle of old mercantile elite families in Boston against the imperialist bankers. G. Markowitz, "A Note on the Anti-Imperialist Movement of the 1890's," *Science and Society* 37:3 (1973), 342–45, critiques this study.

13:203 Tompkins, E. Berkeley. *Anti-Imperialism in the United States: The Great Debate, 1890–1920*. Philadelphia: University of Pennsylvania Press, 1970. The anti-imperialists, according to the author, had deep roots in a variety of political and ethical concepts. They made a contribution by alerting the American people to the dangers of overseas empire.

13:204 Tompkins, E. Berkeley. "The Old Guard: A Study of the Anti-Imperialist Leadership." *Historian* 30:3 (1968), 366–88. This is a useful analysis of the leadership in terms of age, profession, etc.

13:205 Welch, Richard E., Jr. "Motives and Policy Objectives of Anti-Imperialists, 1898." *Mid-America* 51:2 (1969), 119–29. This important analysis of 25 anti-imperialist leaders during the debate in 1898 on the Philippines finds that they believed in white superiority but accepted people of other color as capable. They favored economic penetration of the islands but not political control.

13:206 Zimmerman, James A. "Who Were the Anti-Imperialists and the Expansionists of 1893 and 1899: A Chicago Perspective." *Pacific Historical Review* 46:4 (1977), 589–601. This is a useful corrective to the views of Beisner (13:197) and Tompkins (13:203), who described the anti-imperialists as aged and conservative. The author finds the Chicago leadership to be from many ideological backgrounds and not any older than the expansionists; in fact, many were younger.

Literary Figures

13:207 Beisner, Robert L. "Thirty Years before Manila: E. L. Godkin, Carl Schurz, and Anti-Imperialism in the Gilded Age." *Historian* 30:4 (1968), 561–77. The two opposed expansionism for thirty years before 1898.

13:208 Gatewood, Willard B., Jr. "A Negro Editor on Imperialism: John Mitchell, 1898–1901." *Journalism Quarterly* 49:1 (1972), 43–50. An analysis of Mitchell's writings finds that he strongly opposed imperialism.

13:209 Gibson, William. "Mark Twain and Howells: Anti-Imperialists." *New England Quarterly* 20:1 (1947), 435–70. A contrast of the two authors' approaches to imperialism and the war: Howells was opposed from the first; Twain came to it later, when he realized the adverse effect of expansionism in American democracy. Compare with Samuel Stillen, "Dooley, Twain, and Imperialism," *Masses and Mainstream* 1:10 (1948), 6–13; and F. H. Harrington, "Literary Aspects of Anti-Imperialism," *New England Quarterly* 10:4 (1937), 650–67.

Gompers and Labor

13:210 Radosh, Ronald. "American Labor and the Anti-Imperialist Movement." *Science and Society* 28:1 (1964), 91–100. Gompers and the AFL did not oppose economic expansionism; they opposed old-style colonialism involving conquest of territories and large armies of occupation and colonial administrators. Horace B. Davis, "American Labor," ibid. 27:1 (1963), 70–76, believes labor feared competition of native workers.

13:211 Whittaker, William G. "Samuel Gompers: Anti-Imperialist." *Pacific Historical Review* 38:4 (1969), 429–45. Gompers was uneasy about the transformation of American policy from freeing Cuba to acquiring the Philippines. He believed that imperialism threatened the American worker. He helped found the Anti-Imperialist League in 1899. See also, D. L. McKee's "Samuel Gompers, the A.F. of L., and Imperialism, 1895–1900," *Historian* 21:2 (1959), 187–99.

PROPONENTS OF EXPANSIONISM

See "Personalities," especially Albert J. Beveridge, John Hay, Henry Cabot Lodge, Theodore Roosevelt.

13:212 Burnette, O. Laurence, Jr. "John Tyler Morgan and Expansionist Sentiment in the New South." *Alabama Review* 18:3 (1965), 163–82. A powerful southern Democrat, member of the Senate Foreign Relations Committee (1879–1907), Morgan was a proponent of expansionism motivated by the frustrations of domestic problems.

13:213 Gatewood, Willard B., Jr. "Black Editor on American Imperialism: Edward E. Cooper of the *Col-*

ored American, 1898–1901." *Mid-America* 57:1 (1975), 3–19. Cooper supported McKinley, the Republican party, and imperialism in the hopes of strengthening the federal government, thus weakening the power of the states and diminishing their ability to enforce segregation.

13:214 Kennedy, P. C. "La Follette's Imperialist Flirtation." *Pacific Historical Review* 29:1 (1960), 131–44. Although generally viewed as a pacifist and isolationist, La Follette ardently supported the war in 1898 and territorial expansion.

13:215 Loy, Edward H. "Editorial Opinion and American Imperialism: Two Northwest Newspapers." *Oregon Historical Quarterly* 72:3 (1971), 209–24. An examination of two newspapers reveals that interest in acquisition of territory declined rapidly after 1899, until it practically disappeared by 1903.

13:216 MacKenzie, Kenneth M. *The Robe and the Sword: The Methodist Church and the Rise of American Imperialism.* Washington, D.C.: Public Affairs Press, 1961. The church itself did not propagate imperialism, but it did help to develop a *rationale* which would make imperialism more palatable to those who might have been critical. Bibliography.

13:217 Werking, Richard H. "Senator Henry Cabot Lodge and the Philippines: A Note on American Territorial Expansion." *Pacific Historical Review* 42:2 (1973), 234–40. A letter from Lodge to Secretary of State Day places Lodge squarely in the expansionist camp, thus refuting the views of some scholars (Holbo, Grenville) that Lodge was not greatly interested in colonialism.

IMPERIALISM AND RACISM

13:218 Kennedy, Philip W. "Race and American Expansion in Cuba and Puerto Rico, 1895–1905." *Journal of Black Studies* 1:3 (1971), 306–16. Racial attitudes—Latin inferiority and Anglo-Saxon superiority—were elements in American expansionism and in the acquisition and governance of colonies.

13:219 Shenton, James P. "Imperialism and Racism." In D. Sheehan and H. C. Syrett, eds. *Essays in American Historiography.* New York: Columbia University Press, 1960, pp. 230–50. The author contends that the imperialism at the end of the century is a continuation of earlier imperialism and that racism in both instances was a prominent characteristic.

THE ELECTION OF 1900

13:220 Bailey, Thomas A. "Was the Presidential Election of 1900 a Mandate on Imperialism?" *Mississippi Valley Historical Review* 24:1 (1937), 43–52. The answer is no. The issues were too numerous and confusing to single out one of them as the chief question. Nonetheless, some of the political leaders took the outcome as though the issue were imperialism.

Baron, H. "Anti-Imperialism and the Democrats" (13:11) finds that the Democratic party was not united on the question of imperialism in the congressional or state campaigns in 1898. By 1900, however, anti-imperialism became the paramount issue led by Bryan.

13:221 Coletta, Paolo. "Bryan, McKinley, and the Treaty of Paris." *Pacific Historical Review* 26:1 (1957), 131–46. Bryan supported the treaty to get the Spanish out of the way and leave the way clear for Congress to give the Philippines their independence, thus permitting Bryan to concentrate on domestic matters. He did not press for ratification in order to make Philippine annexation an issue in the 1900 election.

13:222 Kennedy, Philip W. "The Racial Overtones of Imperialism as a Campaign Issue, 1900." *Mid-America* 48:3 (1966), 196–205. Democrats opposed taking on a race problem in the Philippines; while Republicans, who had liberated the black slaves, now sought to enslave the brown man.

13:223 Rystad, Goran. *Ambiguous Imperialism: American Foreign Policy and Domestic Politics at the Turn of the Century.* Stockholm: Esselte Studium, 1975. It contains a historiography of American expansionism and an analysis of the interaction of politics and foreign affairs as reflected in the election of 1900. Bibliography.

13:224 Schlup, Leonard. "Reluctant Expansionist: Adlai E. Stevenson and the Campaign against Imperialism in 1900." *Indiana Social Studies Quarterly* 29:1 (1976), 32–42. This is a description of the attitude of the Democratic vice-presidential candidate toward the Philippine acquisition.

13:225 Tompkins, E. Berkeley. "Scylla and Charybdis: The Anti-Imperialist Dilemma in the Election of 1900." *Pacific Historical Review* 36:2 (1967), 143–61. Anti-imperialists were unhappy with their association with Bryan's financial policies. They did not regard the outcome of the election as a defeat for their cause.

14

The United States and Europe, 1867–1914

Contributing Editors

LAWRENCE E. GELFAND
University of Iowa

SCOTT R. HALL
University of Iowa

Contributor

Wilton Fowler
University of Washington

Contents

Introduction

Although few contemporary scholars of American diplomatic history any longer interpret the decades between the American Civil War and the Spanish-American conflict as the "nadir" of American foreign policy, historians have yet to establish an overarching, general synthesis which explains America's relationship to the great European powers during these years. The same lack of a general synthesis exists for American relations with Europe between the Spanish-American War and World War I.

Recent scholarship argues that the decades of the 1870s and 1880s were a prelude to American overseas expansion. These years saw the rapid growth of foreign commerce based on a favorable balance of trade, which the United States achieved in the mid-1870s; the beginnings of the modern American navy; the development of a closer cultural and diplomatic relationship with the British empire; and a determination to maintain the western hemisphere free from political dependence on Europe. Reassertion of the Monroe Doctrine under a somewhat altered guise also tended to have a profound effect on those European powers holding territorial interests in the Americas.

The absence of a general synthesis should not imply that recent scholarship has ignored the European connections. An impressive spate of studies have investigated specific problems. Charles S. Campbell, *The Transformation of American Foreign Relations, 1865–1900* (12:7), and J. B. Brebner, *North Atlantic Triangle: The Interplay of Canada, the United States and Great Britain* (2:233), discuss the maturing relations among the English-speaking peoples. Henry Blumenthal's *France and the United States: Their Diplomatic Relations, 1789–1914* (2:224) is a fine survey of this relationship.

Europe, including the United Kingdom, was clearly the central concern of American foreign relations between the 1860s and 1914. Many reasons justified such high priority. Millions of Europeans migrated to the United States, their cultural as well as familial ties perpetuating a powerful, informal interest within the American body politic. In way of reaction, several organized movements to restrict immigration surfaced during these years. Related to immigration were the many complications involving naturalization, dual citizenship, and the unwillingness of several European countries to acknowledge the prerogative of individuals to change voluntarily their national allegiance. In the opposite direction, an increasing tide of American tourists took advantage of educational and other cultural opportunities to visit European countries for varying lengths of time. J. P. Shalloo, "United States Immigration Policy, 1882–1948" (14:31), and Carl Wittke, "Immigration Policy Prior to World War I" (14:32), provide an introduction to immigration laws and policies.

Statistics on American trade demonstrate the heavy dependence of the United States on both exports to, and imports from, Europe. Both American agriculture and industry shared in this dependence upon European markets. Large amounts of European capital were invested in the United States due to the limited risks and the expected high yields. Walter LaFeber's *The New Empire: An Interpretation of American Expansion, 1860–1898* (12:84), is a well-read introduction to economic dimensions of American foreign relations; while Mira Wilkins's *The Emergence of Multinational Enterprise: American Business Abroad from the Colonial Era to 1914* (39:134) provides yet another survey of economic issues.

World politics during the nineteenth century continued to be dominated by European powers. With the political unification of the Italian and German nation states under respective central monarchies and the consolidation of French power under the Third Republic and the modernization of economic institutions in czarist Russia, British supremacy in world affairs encountered serious challenges. Historians have yet to mine the vast European and American archival documentation to learn how American leaders and diplomats were perceiving these dynamic thrusts to the European balance of power. Were negotiations of the Triple Alliance and the Dual Alliance matters of little consequence to the United States? How were these negotiations reported to Washington? In their quest to form new coalitions of power, did European statesmen fail to take the United States into account?

We do know that certain leaders in the United

States, naval officers like Stephen Luce and Alfred T. Mahan and political leaders like Henry Cabot Lodge and Theodore Roosevelt, were cognizant of the changes taking place in European politics and their potential ramifications for American interests. Howard K. Beale's *Theodore Roosevelt and the Rise of America to World Power* (14:8) and Raymond A. Esthus's *Theodore Roosevelt and International Rivalries* (14:47) reveal this growing awareness of America's arrival as a major power.

Certain modifications were made in the American diplomatic service. Beginning in the 1890s, the American Congress made statutory provisions for the establishment of embassies in certain European countries, with these to be presided over for the first time by ambassadors. Embassies, legations, and consulates were instructed to assist American businessmen more actively than before in seeking markets for the increasing surpluses of American industrial and agricultural commodities. R. H. Werking, *The Master Architects: Building the United States Foreign Service, 1890–1913* (2:180), is a fine introduction to the changes.

Though still adhering at least officially to President Washington's venerable "Great Rule" of 1796, which spurned American participation in European political affairs, the U.S. government did send a delegation to the Madrid Conference of 1880, did host the Portsmouth Peace Conference of 1905, and was represented at the Algeciras Conference of 1906, whose agendas were exclusively concerned with European and Asian politics. Equally important, the United States sent delegations to participate in a succession of international conferences, some legal and humanitarian and others strictly commercial in design, but all of which addressed varied nonpolitical subjects: the treatment of prisoners and the wounded in wartime (1868); the first International Postal Congress (1874); adoption of a bureau of weights and measures (1875); the protection of industrial property (1883); protection of submarine cables (1884); repression of the African slave trade (1890); publication of customs tariffs (1890); the Red Cross (1898); and the Hague Peace Conference of 1899.

Increasingly close ties with Great Britain proved a persistent tendency during these decades. In some recent literature, there has been a serious attempt to push back into the 1870s the "Great Rapprochement" that was to reach a climax on the eve of world war in 1914. Work of the Joint High Commission and the subsequent Geneva arbitration awards that settled the *Alabama* claims dispute and certain other controversies arising from the American Civil War, settlement of the San Juan Islands boundary, and completion of a naturalization treaty marked the early stages of the

relationship. Britain's acquiescence to American pressures led to the arbitration of the Venezuelan boundary dispute of the 1890s, to revisions in the Hay-Pauncefote Treaty of 1900 and to the creation of the Joint High Commission for settling the Alaskan boundary dispute in 1903 without tangible quid pro quo. Other manifestations of British-American understanding are to be found in Britain's hands-off policy toward the United States during the Cuban crisis and the ensuing Spanish-American War. British-American collaboration in the pronouncement of the open door for China; diplomacy leading to the Algeciras Conference of 1906; and the arbitration of the long-standing North Atlantic fisheries dispute.

Source materials for research on U.S. relations with Europe are abundant and in recent years have become increasingly accessible as the National Archives and other repositories have provided whole series of documentation on microfilm. Treasures that await scholars amidst these vast microfilm series are almost beyond description. Records of the American consulates, legations, and embassies have been microfilmed and can be read at many university libraries, the regional Federal Records Centers throughout the United States, and at the Center for Research Libraries in Chicago. These rolls of microfilm can ordinarily be borrowed on requests through institutional loans. Also of real value to historians are the sizeable collections of microfilmed State Department records pertaining to the internal affairs of countries where the United States maintained legations and embassies. Such records hold much value for students of European history as well as for students of American foreign affairs.

Resources and Overviews

RESEARCH AIDS

While pertinent bibliographies and reference aids are listed here, there are more extensive lists in Chapter 1.

Bibliographies

Cortada, J. W., ed. *A Bibliographical Guide to Spanish Diplomatic History, 1460–1977* (1:90) includes many choice items, in chapters 17–19, relevant to U.S. relations during the half-century before the First World War.

Hanham, H. J., ed. *Bibliography of British History, 1851–1914* (8:1) includes, pages 303–09, an annotated listing of general bibliographical works, guides to manuscript collections in Britain and Ireland, as well as selected historiography pertaining to British-American relations. Also included is a section on materials concerning U.S. envoys to the United Kingdom. Other sections offer references to literature and sources treating British immigration, British investments, the Episcopal church, Ireland, U.S. investments in the United Kingdom, and Canadian relations with the United States.

Munden, K. W., and Beers, H. P., eds. *Guide to Federal Archives Relating to the Civil War* (11:13) have sorted out the various official publications that grew out of the *Alabama* claims and the Treaty of Washington. Chapter 5 is valuable for locating archival and certain private manuscript collections dealing with the many diplomatic complications arising from the American Civil War.

Smith, M. J., Jr., ed. *The American Navy, 1865–1918: A Bibliography* (12:4).

Document Collections

More general collections are listed in Chapter 1, and other collections may be found in "Personalities," below.

14:1   Cooke, William H., and Stickney, Edith P., eds. *Readings in European International Relations since 1879.* New York: Harper, 1931. A dated but still valuable collection of documents that shaped European international politics during the generation before the First World War, this work remains a standard reference work.

14:2   Dugdale, E. T. S., ed. *German Diplomatic Documents, 1871–1914.* 4 vols. New York: Harper, 1928–1931. These four volumes draw largely from documents earlier published in *Die Grosse Politik der Europäischen Kabinette 1871–1914*, edited by J. Lepsius, A. Mendelsohn Bartholdy, and Frederich Thimme (17:17). They contain a good many references to the United States.

14:3   France. Ministère des Affaires Etrangères. *Documents diplomatiques français (1871–1914)* [French diplomatic documents (1871–1914)]. 41 vols. Paris: Imprimerie Nationale, 1929–1959. The documents in this basic French collection are arranged chronologically, but each volume has a list of documents arranged by subject. Many of the volumes were published soon after the events described.

Germany. Auswärtiges Amt. *Die Grosse Politik der Europäischen Kabinette, 1871–1914* (17:17).

14:4   Great Britain. Foreign Office. *British Documents on the Origins of the War, 1898–1914.* Ed. by G. P. Gooch and Harold Temperley. 11 vols. London: H.M.S.O., 1926–1938. This British collection, like its German and French counterparts, focuses primarily on European international rivalries, but it does contain materials relating to U.S. diplomacy.

14:5   Irish University Press Series on British Parliamentary Papers. *Russia.* 38 vols. Shannon: Irish University Press, n.d. This collection of 19th-century papers and reports focuses on issues that join with Russo-American concerns. For instance, volumes 35–36 deal with trade, volume 37 with Turkish affairs, volume 33 with Napoleonic wars, and volume 31 with the Hague Conference of 1899.

Irish University Press Series on British Parliamentary Papers. *United States of America* (1:366) collects, in volume 50, papers and reports dealing with the U.S.-British-German diplomatic crisis over Samoa. Volumes 56–59 contain materials related to the Treaty of Washington.

14:6   Irish University Press Series on British Parliamentary Papers. *United States of America.* Vol. 15: *Correspondence Respecting American and British Affairs in Central America and South America, 1850–1896.* Dublin: Irish University Press, n.d. This volume contains data on the Venezuelan boundary question with British Guiana, correspondence (1896), and proposals for arbitration (1896).

14:7   U.S. Department of State. *Correspondence Concerning Claims against Great Britain.* 7 vols. Washington, D.C.: G.P.O., 1869–1871. The official publications relating to the postwar *Alabama* claims are thoroughly confusing; for a summary of the various sets of documents consult the Munden and Beers *Guide to Federal Archives Relating to the Civil War* (11:13), especially pp. 162ff. To compound confusion, there are equivalent British sets of documents and summaries presented to the Geneva court of arbitration. Also see official documents (14:87).

U.S. Department of State. "General Records of the Department of State, RG 59 and RG 84" (1:359) contains the "Diplomatic Despatches," one of several collections from Record Group 59, which consists of U.S. diplomatic personnel's reports to the Department of State. These reports are arranged by country from 1789 to 1906 (the "Decimal File, 1910–29" carries the collections further). See the most recent edition of the National Archives' *List of National Archives Microfilm Publications* for descriptions of the collections.

OVERVIEWS

14:8 Beale, Howard K. *Theodore Roosevelt and the Rise of America to World Power.* Baltimore: Johns Hopkins Press, 1956. Beale is mainly concerned here with Roosevelt's efforts to establish an American presence in world politics. There is much emphasis on American relations with European powers over Morocco, Latin America, China, the Philippines, and the Hague Conference of 1907.

Beisner, R. L. *From the Old Diplomacy to the New, 1865–1900* (12:6) seeks a common ground among conflicting historical interpretations of late-19th-century American diplomacy. Beisner's approach is most valuable to those wishing an introduction to the literature of the period. Although Beisner concentrates on Latin America and Asia, his coverage of American and European diplomacy sets the major themes in proper perspective.

Challener, R. D. *Admirals, Generals, and American Foreign Policy 1898–1914* (17:229) offers an analysis of how America's military and naval officers perceived and influenced the nation's foreign policy between the Spanish American War and the First World War. There is extensive treatment of the Venezuelan debts controversy of 1902. Additionally, Challener considers American apprehensions of Germany and Russia.

14:9 Coolidge, Archibald C. *The United States as a World Power.* New York: Macmillan, 1908. Although Coolidge's book dates from the very early 20th century, it offers some interesting and still valuable information on German-American, Russian-American, Franco-American, and British-American relations during the late 19th century.

Cooper, J. M., Jr. "Progressivism and American Foreign Policy: A Reconsideration" (13:13) analyzes the importance of foreign policy to three groups of Progressives: the Roosevelt-Lodge "Imperialist Progressives," the Bryanite "Agrarian Isolationists," and the Wilsonian "Liberal Internationalists."

Curti, M. E. *American Philanthropy Abroad: A History* (2:72) is a pioneering survey of American assistance to various benevolent causes overseas; it covers, in chapters 4–8, U.S.-European relations between the 1860s and the First World War.

14:10 Denis, Alfred L. P. *Adventures in American Diplomacy, 1896–1906.* New York: Dutton, 1928. Reprint 1969. This early work contains some still valuable chapters on the Venezuelan boundary dispute, the Spanish-American War, Hawaii and Samoa, Anglo-American relations, the isthmian question, East Asia, including the Russo-Japanese War, the Jewish question in eastern Europe, African concerns, the Hague conferences and the Algeciras Conference. A final chapter on the U.S. diplomatic service is most insightful.

Dobson, J. M. *America's Ascent: The United States Becomes a Great Power, 1880–1914* (12:8).

Esthus, R. A. "Isolationism and World Power" (2:67) finds that although the United States had become a "world power" in 1898, isolationism still dominated its foreign policy until World War I.

Field, J. A., Jr. *America and the Mediterranean World, 1776–1882* (18:6) is an excellent introduction to American involvement in the Mediterranean region, American response to the unification of Italy, and relations with the Turkish Near East.

14:11 Gardner, Lloyd C. "American Foreign Policy, 1900–1921: A Second Look at the Realist Critique of American Diplomacy." In Barton J. Bernstein, ed., *Towards a New Past: Dissenting Essays in American History.* New York: Pantheon, 1968, pp. 202–32. Gardner's article takes a hard look at George Kennan's "realistic" critique of the legalistic-moralistic approach to American foreign policy applied to the first two decades of the 20th century.

Grenville, J. A. S., and Young, G. B. *Politics, Strategy and American Diplomacy: Studies in Foreign*

Policy, 1873–1917 (12:93) contains eleven essays which bear heavily on America's rising influence in world affairs, overseas expansion, and military-naval planning.

14:12 Hart, Robert A. *The Great White Fleet: Its Voyage around the World, 1907–1909.* Boston: Little, Brown, 1965. This account of Theodore Roosevelt's sending of the American fleet on a global tour reflects America's growing power in world affairs.

Hilderbrand, R. C. *Power and the People: Executive Management of Public Opinion in Foreign Affairs, 1869–1921* (2:208).

Langer, W. L. *The Diplomacy of Imperialism, 1890–1902* (13:9) describes European diplomacy during the last decade of the 19th century, including consideration of German-American and British-American relations.

14:13 Langer, William L. *European Alliances and Alignments, 1871–1890.* 2d ed. New York: Knopf (1931), 1966. A standard account of European politics during the 1870s and 1880s. Students of international history will find this work very useful for background information.

Leopold, R. W. "The Mississippi Valley and American Foreign Policy, 1890–1941: An Assessment and an Appeal" (2:209) is a historiographical appraisal of scholarship bearing on midwestern sectionalism and world affairs, and is filled with suggestions for further research.

May, E. R. *American Imperialism: A Speculative Essay* (2:94) suggests the influence of the British imperial "model" on American policymakers.

May, E. R. *Imperial Democracy: The Emergence of America as a Great Power* (12:80) remains among the best general studies of American foreign relations during the critical 1890s.

Perkins, D. *The Monroe Doctrine, 1867–1907* (15:52) emphasizes the extent of the European governments' involvement in affairs of the western hemisphere during 1867 to 1907.

Plesur, M. *America's Outward Thrust: Approaches to Foreign Affairs, 1865–1890* (12:12) traces the growing recognition by Americans that they were reaching world power status. Toward Europe, Americans were ambivalent, wishing to avoid rivalries and war or succumbing to the problems afflicting Europe.

14:14 Plesur, Milton. "America Looking Outward: Hayes to Harrison." *Historian* 22:3 (1960), 280–95. Plesur seeks to reverse historical evaluation of 1887 to 1889 as the "nadir in American diplomacy." He argues that industrial expansion and commercial opportunities overseas created interest in consular reform, naval rehabilitation, and participation in world affairs. These activities prefaced America's debut as a world power after 1898.

14:15 Shaw, Albert. *International Bearings of American Policy.* Baltimore: Johns Hopkins Press, 1943. Topical chapters treat such subjects as American interest in the Mediterranean region, German militarism, and rivalries. This work extends from late 19th century until 1933.

14:16 Tarlton, Charles D. "The Styles of American International Thought: Mahan, Bryan, and Lippmann." *World Politics* 17:4 (1965), 584–614. An analysis of three styles of American political thought which expanded during 1898 to 1914 to include international politics: 1) deterministic, pessimistic, and realistic, as revealed in the writings of Alfred T. Mahan; 2) utopian, optimistic, and moralistic, as found in the pronouncements of William Jennings Bryan; and 3) pragmatic, sociological, and almost scientific, as illustrated by Walter Lippmann's *A Preface to Politics* and *The Stakes of Diplomacy.*

14:17 Taylor, A. J. P. *The Struggle for Mastery in Europe, 1848–1918.* Oxford: Clarendon Press, 1954. Taylor's international history of 19th- and early-20th-century Europe discusses several American connections.

Werking, R. H. *The Master Architects: Building the United States Foreign Service, 1890–1913* (2:180) is the story of reforms and reformers of the American foreign policy establishment. Werking considers the consular and diplomatic services as well as the bureaucratic operations of the Department of Commerce.

Economic and Commercial Factors

See especially Chapter 12, "Economic Factors," and Chapter 13, "Progressivism and Foreign Policy" and "Economic and Political Factors."

14:18 Becker, William H. "Foreign Markets for Iron and Steel, 1893–1913: A New Perspective on the Williams School of Diplomatic History." *Pacific Historical Review* 44:2 (1975), 233–48. Becker questions the validity of the thesis that trade expansion was a necessary condition for the economic well-being of the United States from the 1890s to World War I. Readers are directed to the rejoinder in the same issue (pp. 245–55) by Howard Schonberger, "William H. Becker and the New Left Revisionists: A Rebuttal."

Davies, R. B. "'Peacefully Working to Conquer the World': The Singer Manufacturing Company in Foreign Markets, 1854–1889" (12:27).

14:19 Gignilliat, John L. "Pigs, Politics and Protection: The European Boycott of American Pork, 1879–1891." *Agricultural History* 35:1 (1961), 3–12. The fear in Europe that American pork products were infected with trichinae triggered a general European boycott of American pork, approximately 10 percent of America's export trade. By 1890, the United States countered these boycotts through retaliation, raising U.S. tariffs, and by ordering government inspections of pork exports.

14:20 Goodhart, C. A. E. *The New York Money Market and the Finance of Trade, 1900–1913*. Cambridge: Harvard University Press, 1969. In a technical book dealing with the relationship between capital flows and foreign trade, Goodhart describes how offsetting capital flows prior to the inception of the Federal Reserve System kept the American economy more stable. If Goodhart is right, and he admits that the data on capital flows are inconclusive, then seasonal fluctuations in agricultural trade were not as economically disruptive as previously believed. He concludes that the New York money market was prepared to manage the nation's monetary policy after 1913. Bibliography.

Holbo, P. S. "Economics, Emotion and Expansion: An Emerging Foreign Policy" (12:89) questions some of the prevalent theories about economic influences on American expansionism during the late 19th century.

14:21 Kaufman, Burton I. "The Organizational Dimension of United States Economic Foreign Policy, 1900–1920." *Business History Review* 46:1 (1972), 17–44. U.S. foreign trade and investment in 1900 to 1920 brought together business and banking interests with the federal government to promote expansion. What emerged, Kaufman concludes, was an integrated, efficient organizational structure which facilitated commercial and financial expansion, especially through modification of the nation's antitrust laws.

LaFeber, W. *The New Empire: An Interpretation of American Expansion, 1860–1898* (12:84) is basically an economic interpretation of American foreign relations which emphasizes the role of American business in the 1890s. It contains a valuable section on the Venezuela boundary dispute, one on relations with Brazil, and another on economic rivalry with Britain.

14:22 Paterson, Thomas G. "American Businessmen and Consular Service Reform, 1890's to 1906." *Business History Review* 40:1 (1966), 77–97. Paterson emphasizes the domestic pressures of businessmen on foreign policy. He argues that the need to recover from the Depression of 1893 and the lure of growing United States economic power impelled reform.

14:23 Perkins, Edwin J. "The Emergence of a Futures Market for Foreign Exchange in the United States." *Explorations in Economic History* 11:3 (1974), 193–211. Perkins argues that a forward market in foreign currencies developed in the late 1870s, and analyzes three possible explanations: increasing economies of scale; the adoption of European financial technology; and the resumption of specie payments by American banks.

Porter, G. *The Rise of Big Business, 1860–1910* (39:20).

14:24 Pursell, Carroll W., Jr. "Tariff and Technology: The Foundation and Development of the American Tin-Plate Industry, 1872–1900." *Technology and Culture* 3:3 (1962), 267–84. Pursell describes early, but unsuccessful, American efforts to start a domestic tin plate industry, the ensuing debate over a tariff to protect the infant American industry, and the surge in American production after the McKinley tariff of 1890.

14:25 Sandarajan, V. "The Impact of the Tariff on Some Selected Products of the U.S. Iron and Steel Industry, 1870–1914." *Quarterly Journal of Economics* 84:4 (1970), 590–610. In the early years of the pig iron industry and in the industry near the seacoast, protective duties affected growth. In the period as a whole, however, other factors were dominant.

Schuyler, E. *American Diplomacy and the Furtherance of Commerce* [1865–1884] (12:13) was one of the earliest manuals of the American diplomatic service.

Separate chapters describe the U.S. consular and diplomatic services.

14:26 Simon, Matthew, and Novack, David. "Some Dimensions of the American Commercial Invasion of Europe, 1871–1914: An Introductory Essay." *Journal of Economic History* 24:4 (1964), 591–605. This article contends that the European market, though important, fell continuously between 1871 and 1914. The authors outline the composition of American export trade to Europe and delineate several "stages" of the trade.

14:27 Terrill, Tom E. "David A. Wells, the Democracy, and Tariff Reduction, 1877–1894." *Journal of American History* 56:3 (1969), 540–55. This article discusses Wells's arguments that lowered tariffs would increase trade and American prosperity, and provides the example of an American economic expansionist alive to concerns of economic competition with Europe.

Wilkins, M. *The Emergence of Multinational Enterprise: American Business Abroad from the Colonial Era to 1914* (39:134) presents especially vital information on how American companies challenged European corporations abroad. No other work on American corporations in foreign economic matters has its scope or depth.

14:28 Wilkins, Mira. "An American Enterprise Abroad: American Radiator Company in Europe, 1895–1914." *Business History Review* 43:3 (1969), 326–46. This was not a typical case. The company, spurred by domestic conditions, developed gradually, without planning. It only sought government aid on one occasion, and that for information.

Immigration Policies and Problems

14:29 Jones, Maldwyn A. "Immigrants, Steamships and Governments: The Steerage Problem in Transatlantic Diplomacy, 1868–74." In H. C. Allen and Roger Thompson, eds., *Contrast and Connection: Bicentennial Essays in Anglo-American History*. London: Bell, 1976, pp. 178–209. Though both the British and American governments wanted to help steerage passengers, they could not agree on an international solution, partly because the *Alabama* claims and Fenian raids poisoned the atmosphere.

14:30 Kuznets, Simon. "Immigration of Russian Jews to the United States: Background and Structure." *Perspectives in American History* 9 (1975), 35–124. From 1881 to 1914, 1.5 million Russian Jews emigrated to the United States, motivated by the pressures of industrialization and new technology, and the dislocation of people from the land.

14:31 Shalloo, J. P. "United States Immigration Policy, 1882–1948." In Dwight E. Lee, and George E. McReynolds, eds. *Essays in History and International Relations in Honor of George Hubbard Blakeslee.* Worcester, Mass.: Clark University Press, 1949, pp. 126–52. Reprint 1969. This is a useful summary of key legislation.

14:32 Wittke, Carl. "Immigration Policy Prior to World War I." *Annals of the American Academy of Political and Social Science* 262 (1949), 5–14. In this overview of immigration laws and politics, especially since the Civil War, Wittke notes the development of immigration restrictions from state statutes in the 1830s through the first federal restrictions beginning in 1882.

Personalities

Additional references on individuals may be found in Chapter 1, "Biographical Data."

AMERICAN

Charles Francis Adams
See Chapter 11, "Personalities," for additional references.

Duberman, M. B. *Charles Francis Adams, 1807–1886* (11:46) is very full on Adams's term as minister to Britain, but sketchy about his work as the American arbitrator at Geneva, 1872.

James G. Blaine
See Chapters 12 and 15, "Personalities," for additional references.

Tyler, A. F. *The Foreign Policy of James G. Blaine* (12:34) considers American policies toward Latin

America, Samoa, East Asia, and immigration, all concerns of James Blaine as secretary of state.

14:33 Volwiler, Albert T. "Harrison, Blaine, and American Foreign Policy, 1889–1893." *Proceedings of the American Philosophical Society* 79:4 (1938), 637–48. This address, which claims to be derived from State Department documents and Blaine's and Harrison's papers, is of special interest regarding the Bering Sea controversy.

Grover Cleveland

See Chapter 12, "Personalities," for additional references.

14:34 LaFeber, Walter. "The Background of Cleveland's Venezuelan Policy: A Reinterpretation." *American Historical Review* 66:4 (1961), 947–67. LaFeber emphasizes the "economic influence on the shaping of Cleveland's policy."

Hamilton Fish

See Chapter 12, "Personalities."

14:35 Davis, J. C. Bancroft. *Mr. Fish and the Alabama Claims: A Chapter in Diplomatic History.* Boston: Houghton Mifflin, 1893. Davis was an assistant secretary of state under Hamilton Fish during the *Alabama* negotiations.

Nevins, A. *Hamilton Fish: The Inner History of the Grant Administration* (12:41) contains some analysis of European relations with the United States, particularly during the 1870s: chapter 17 contains an American perspective on the Franco-Prussian War. This is still valuable for the treatment of the *Alabama* claims and Treaty of Washington.

John W. Foster

14:36 Devine, Michael J. *John W. Foster: Politics and Diplomacy in the Imperial Era, 1873–1917.* Athens: Ohio University Press, 1980. Foster was known to his contemporaries as "America's first professional diplomat," who early advocated an enlarged American presence abroad. This is the first full-scale treatment of his role in formulating U.S. foreign policy.

Foster, J. W. *Diplomatic Memoirs* (12:43) is possibly the most valuable set of memoirs written by an American actively involved in foreign affairs during the late 19th century. Chapters 12–17 discuss Foster's activities in Russia; chapters 18–24, his activities in

Spain; and volume 2 mainly considers arbitration, Asian matters, and some magnificent recollective comments about personalities and procedures in U.S. diplomacy.

James A. Garfield

See also Chapter 12, "Personalities."

Pletcher, D. M. *The Awkward Years: American Foreign Relations under Garfield and Arthur* (12:46) discusses several topics of U.S. relations with Europe, while explaining American expansionism during the early 1880s. Of particular interest is chapter 17, relative to the Berlin Congo Conference.

John Hay

See Chapter 13, "Personalities," for additional references.

Clymer, K. J. *John Hay: The Gentleman as Diplomat* (12:58) is a stimulating consideration of Hay's social (especially racial) attitudes upon his diplomacy.

Dennett, T. *John Hay: From Poetry to Politics* (13:39) is still the most readable biography of Hay, although it is dated on topics such as the Panama Canal and the Boer War.

14:37 Dulles, Foster Rhea. "John Hay 1898–1905." In Norman A. Graebner, ed., *An Uncertain Tradition: American Secretaries of State in the Twentieth Century.* New York: McGraw-Hill, 1961, pp. 22–39. This is a critical appreciation of Hay as secretary of state. Bibliography.

14:38 Sears, Louis M. "John Hay in London, 1897–1898." *Ohio Historical Quarterly* 65 (1956), 356–75. Sears describes John Hay's year as ambassador.

George F. Hoar

See also Chapter 12, "Personalities."

Hoar, G. F. *Autobiography of Seventy Years* [1876–1900] (12:62) has sections on the Treaty of Washington and the fisheries questions.

Alfred T. Mahan

See Chapter 40, "Personalities," for additional references.

14:39 LaFeber, Walter. "A Note on the 'Mercantilistic Imperialism' of Alfred Thayer Mahan." *Jour-*

nal of American History 48:4 (1962), 674–85. This article considers the philosophic basis of Mahan's writings and concludes that Mahan's views differed from traditional (17th- and 18th-century) mercantilism in several important ways: Mahan believed in commercial imperialism rather than landed imperialism; he emphasized the need for a strong navy but not necessarily a strong merchant marine; and he advocated an open door approach rather than the formation of a colonial empire. LaFeber argues that Mahan, therefore, adapted his mercantilistic views to the needs of the day.

George von Lengerke Meyer

Howe, M. A. DeW. *George von Lengerke Meyer: His Life and Public Services* [1858–1918] (17:53) emphasizes his career as American ambassador to Italy and Russia during Theodore Roosevelt's presidency and his service as postmaster general and secretary of the navy between 1907 and 1913.

14:40 Trani, Eugene P. "Russia in 1905: The View from the American Embassy." *Review of Politics* 31:1 (1969), 48–63. Trani describes the diplomatic reporting provided by the U.S. ambassador, Meyer, pertaining to the abortive revolution of 1905 and the Russo-Japanese peace moves. He concludes that much of Meyer's reporting was distorted, missing the essence of Russian political discontent due to Meyer's limited, upper-class Russian sources. The ambassador, however, is given credit for his diplomatic representations to the czar with respect to the Russian plans for peace.

14:41 Wiegand, Wayne A. "Ambassador in Absentia: George Meyer, William II and Theodore Roosevelt." *Mid-America* 56:1 (1974), 3–15. The article describes the close personal relationship existing between Kaiser William II and Meyer. The author states: "Few men shared the experience of being an audience for William's innermost thoughts on international affairs as frequently and intimately as Meyer." Presumably, Meyer's relationship proved influential during the Russo-Japanese War in 1905.

Richard Olney

Eggert, G. G. *Richard Olney: Evolution of a Statesman* (12:72) is a cogent analysis of Olney's diplomacy, especially of his part in the Venezuela boundary crisis. Extensive bibliography.

Young, G. B. "Intervention under the Monroe Doctrine: The Olney Corollary" (14:95).

Whitelaw Reid

See also Chapter 13, "Personalities."

Cortissoz, R. *The Life of Whitelaw Reid* (13:57) while useful on some points, is corrected and expanded by Duncan's study.

14:42 Duncan, Bingham. "Protectionism and Pork: Whitelaw Reid as Diplomat, 1889–1891." *Agricultural History* 33:4 (1959), 190–95. Efforts of American ambassador Whitelaw Reid and his *New York Tribune* to terminate the French government's boycott of American pork products provides the theme of this article. Duncan relates the termination to the modifications and liberal interpretations of the McKinley tariff of 1890.

14:43 Duncan, Bingham. *Whitelaw Reid: Journalist, Politician, Diplomat*. Athens: University of Georgia Press, 1975. About one-third of the book is devoted to Reid's diplomatic career as the minister to France, a member of the America's Commission to Negotiate Peace after the Spanish-American War, and as the minister to Great Britain (1905–1912). The author recounts Reid's activities as a talented diplomat with perhaps more European experience than any other appointee of the late 19th and 20th centuries.

Theodore Roosevelt

See also Chapters 15, 16, and 17, "Personalities."

Beale, Howard K. *Theodore Roosevelt and the Rise of America to World Power* (14:8).

14:44 Blake, Nelson M. "Ambassadors at the Court of Theodore Roosevelt." *Mississippi Valley Historical Review* 42:2 (1955), 179–206. Blake discusses how Roosevelt's relations with German, French, and British ambassadors to Washington helped to determine his outlook on several pressing questions in Latin America, Asia, and at the Algeciras Conference. Blake also notes how Roosevelt's reaction to various ambassadors foreshadowed America's "uneven neutrality" of the First World War.

14:45 Burton, David H. "Theodore Roosevelt: Confident Imperialism." *Review of Politics* 23:3 (1961), 356–77. TR firmly believed in the supremacy of the white race and particularly of the Anglo-Saxons. His attitudes with respect to the Philippines, Cuba, and other areas of East Asia and Latin America, the Boer War and World War I, are examined in the light of his basic philosophy.

14:46 Chessman, G. Wallace. *Theodore Roosevelt and the Politics of Power.* Boston: Little, Brown, 1969. Chapters 4, 5, 7, 8 of this interpretive biography deal with aspects of Roosevelt's diplomacy. Relying primarily on published sources, the author takes a positive view of Roosevelt's handling of American diplomacy, emphasizing in chapter 5 Roosevelt's outlook as a "just man armed."

14:47 Esthus, Raymond A. *Theodore Roosevelt and International Rivalries.* Waltham, Mass.: Ginn-Blaisdell, 1970. Esthus concentrates on Roosevelt's role as the first American president to resolutely venture into the tangled great power rivalries in Europe and Asia. Of particular interest to European affairs is the coverage of the Moroccan crisis and the Algeciras Conference, which helped lead Roosevelt to a more favorable view of the Anglo-French entente vis-à-vis Germany.

Harbaugh, William H. *Power and Responsibility: The Life and Times of Theodore Roosevelt* (13:60) does not primarily focus on Roosevelt's concerns with foreign policy, but it does describe several pertinent episodes involving American relations with the European powers.

14:48 Marks, Frederick W., III. "Morality as a Drive Wheel in the Diplomacy of Theodore Roosevelt." *Diplomatic History* 2:1 (1978), 43–62. The quest for virtue was a major motivating force in Theodore Roosevelt's life (1858–1919). His idea of virtue was a very personal one, conditioned by "the spirit of the age," but his convictions were strong and genuine. Nearly all the major diplomatic conflicts in which he was involved derived from what he perceived as a betrayal of his trust by other parties. In this light, such big stick incidents as the Panama Canal Zone acquisition, the Alaska boundary dispute, and the dispatch of the Great White Fleet take on a different hue.

14:49 Marks, Frederick W., III. *Velvet on Iron: The Diplomacy of Theodore Roosevelt.* Lincoln: University of Nebraska Press, 1980. Marks seeks to correct the myths and misconceptions that have arisen concerning Roosevelt's seemingly contradictory personality and policies. Bibliography.

14:50 Roosevelt, Nicholas. *Theodore Roosevelt: The Man as I Knew Him.* New York: Dodd, Mead, 1967. Chapter 13 of this memoir contains insights into Roosevelt's views of world politics.

Elihu Root
See also Chapter 16, "Personalities."

Jessup, P. C. *Elihu Root* (17:41) provides much valuable information on Root's public career as secretary of war beginning in 1899, his years as secretary of state under Theodore Roosevelt, and his later, numerous activities in American foreign affairs. This standard biography remains valuable even though the research was not extensive.

Charles Sumner
See Chapters 11 and 12, "Personalities," for additional references.

14:51 Davis, J. C. Bancroft. *Mr. Sumner, the Alabama Claims and Their Settlement: A Letter to the New York Herald.* New York: Taylor, 1878. This is a contemporary memoir by the assistant secretary of state under Hamilton Fish.

Donald, D. H. *Charles Sumner and the Rights of Man* (11:59) is the definitive study of the senator so loudly opposed to an easy settlement of the *Alabama* claims.

William Howard Taft
See Chapters 15 and 17, "Personalities," for additional references.

Minger, R. E. *William Howard Taft and United States Foreign Policy: The Apprenticeship Years, 1900–1908* (17:43) includes a valuable section on Taft's negotiations with the Vatican over Philippine church lands.

14:52 Pringle, Henry F. *The Life and Times of William Howard Taft.* 2 vols. New York: Holt, Rinehart, 1939. Reprint 1964. This broadly descriptive biography of an American leader deals at length with foreign affairs during the first three decades of the 20th century.

Andrew D. White
Altschuler, G. C. *Andrew D. White: Educator, Historian, Diplomat* (16:74).

14:53 White, Andrew D. *Autobiography of Andrew Dickson White.* 2 vols. New York: Century, 1905. An historian by training and profession, White served on several diplomatic missions beginning in the 1870s, when he went to Paris (1878), then to Berlin as American minister to Germany (1879–1881), minister to

Russia (1882–1884); a member of the Venezuelan Commission (1895–1896); ambassador to Germany (1897–1903); and chairman of the U.S. delegation to the Hague Conference (1899).

Hugh R. Wilson

See Chapters 20 and 21, "Personalities," for additional references.

14:54   Wilson, Hugh R. *The Education of a Diplomat*. New York: Longmans, 1938. These are Wilson's memories and impressions covering the early phase of his diplomatic career beginning with his days in Lisbon and ending with the U.S. entry into World War I.

Others

14:55   Armstrong, William M. *E. L. Godkin and American Foreign Policy, 1865–1900*. New York: Bookman, 1957. Godkin, born in Britain, was editor of *The Nation* from 1865 and also of the *New York Evening Post* after 1881. Anglo-American relations received his editorial commentary frequently, as did U.S. relations with other European nations. Bibliography.

Atkinson, H. A. *Theodore Marburg: The Man and His Work* (16:75) reports, uncritically, on his role as U.S. minister to Belgium (1912–1914).

14:56   Campbell, Charles S., Jr. "Edward J. Phelps and Anglo-American Relations." In H. C. Allen and Roger Thompson, eds., *Contrast and Connection: Bicentennial Essays in Anglo-American History*. London: Bell, 1976, pp. 210–24. Phelps, a Yale law professor, was minister to Britain (1885–1889). Campbell concludes that he was guilty of bad reporting and faulty understanding in the matter of Sackville's recall and in the fur seal controversy. Bibliography.

14:57   DeNovo, John A. "The Enigmatic Alvey A. Adee and American Foreign Relations, 1870–1924." *Prologue* 7:2 (1975), 69–80. Alvey Adee, who served in important capacities in the Department of State for more than forty years, had an encyclopedic knowledge of American diplomatic practices and precedents and international law. The author has provided references and details about the contributions of this skilled draftsman of dispatches and treaties, faithful and witty bureaucrat, and tutor of young officials and new administrations. Adee was particularly influential around the turn of the century.

14:58   Einstein, Lewis. *A Diplomat Looks Back*. Ed. by Lawrence Gelfand. New Haven, Conn.: Yale University Press, 1968. A memoir written toward the end of his career by a highly perceptive and active American observer whose experiences in diplomacy extended from the Algeciras Conference to Turkey, China, Costa Rica, and the Balkans prior to 1915. The memoirs extend in time through the Second World War.

Graebner, N. A., ed. *An Uncertain Tradition: American Secretaries of State in the Twentieth Century* (2:168) has essays on John Hay, Elihu Root, and Philander C. Knox.

Kaplan, L. S. "The Brahmin as Diplomat in Nineteenth Century America: Everett, Bancroft, Motley, Lowell" (8:20) questions why these intellectuals as a group were not more significant and successful as diplomats. Perhaps the answer to this dilemma is to be found in the statement drawn from Lowell on behalf of the literati, when he "identified foreign missions with reward[s] for eminence."

14:59   Mott, T. Bentley. *Myron T. Herrick: Friend of France*. Garden City, N.Y.: Doubleday, Doran, 1930. This sympathetic biography of the Cleveland banker who served as President Taft's ambassador to France, remaining in Paris until the onset of the European war in 1914, contains several chapters of interest to students of U.S.-European relations. Chapter 13 briefly considers Herrick's views of the controversy over the Panama Canal; chapters 15 and 17–26 consider his activities as ambassador through 1914.

14:60   Nevins, Allan. *Henry White: Thirty Years of American Diplomacy*. New York: Harper, 1930. This biography of probably America's premier diplomat between the Civil War and the First World War, considers American relations with the principal European states. Although the research was limited mainly to the White collection, the volume merits a careful reading.

Parkman, A. *David Jayne Hill and the Problem of World Peace* (16:81) describes Hill's role as assistant secretary of state under John Hay, his part in the creation of the Hague Convention, terms as ambassador to Switzerland, minister to the Second Hague Conference, and ambassador to Germany. In addition, the author discusses Hill's political life and analyzes his roles in the fight against the League of Nations and at the Washington Conference (1921–1922).

14:61 Rohrs, Richard C. "George Bancroft and American Foreign Relations." Ph.D. diss., University of Nebraska, 1977. Rohrs concentrates on Bancroft's public service, when he was secretary of the navy during the Polk administration, minister to England (1846–1849); minister to Prussia (1867–1874). This work considers Bancroft's activities, ideas, responses to the political dynamics in Europe, and broad questions of American foreign policy.

Tansill, C.C. *The Foreign Policy of Thomas F. Bayard, 1885–1897* (12:77) is a lengthy study of the man who was secretary of state (1885–1889), and minister to Britain (1893–1897). Largely valuable for the long quotations from Bayard's papers.

Wilson, H. L. *Diplomatic Episodes in Mexico, Belgium and Chile* (15:24).

14:62 Younger, Edward. *John A. Kasson: Politics and Diplomacy from Lincoln to McKinley.* Iowa City: State Historical Society of Iowa, 1955. This biography of the Iowa politician who served as U.S. minister to Austria-Hungary (1877–1881) and to Germany (1884–1885), and who gained esteem for his negotiating several international postal agreements offers some interesting and useful information for the European relations of the United States.

EUROPEAN

William E. Gladstone

14:63 Malament, Barbara C. "W. E. Gladstone: An Other Victorian?" *British Studies Monitor* 3:1 (1978), 22–38. This article furnishes an excellent illustration of how new information can illuminate old problems. Here the author uses the newly published Gladstone diaries (edited by M. R. D. Foot) to come to grips with the person of Gladstone. Though not diplomatic history, nor quite psychohistory, it is a fascinating peek into the realm of social and sexual history, and it tells us much about a man who has baffled more than one diplomatic historian.

14:64 Morley, John. *The Life of William Ewart Gladstone.* 2 vols. London: Macmillan, 1905. Long the standard life, but publication of the Gladstone diaries is rapidly making this biography obsolete; for as Barbara Malament has suggested, there were many things that Morley "either would not or could not see."

14:65 Stansky, Peter. *Gladstone: A Progress in Politics.* Boston: Little, Brown, 1979. The work relies primarily on the public record of the grand old man, the "colossus of modern British politics." Though the work focuses on British history, students may find some utility in Gladstone's views of slavery and his assessment of the place of moral principles in foreign policy.

Napoleon III

See also Chapter 15, "Personalities."

14:66 Casper, Henry W. *American Attitudes toward the Rise of Napoleon III.* Washington, D.C.: Catholic University of America Press, 1947. Examined here are the views of selected eastern press opinion, U.S. diplomats, and other observers; based on these rather meager sources, the author found considerable American hostility toward Louis Napoleon's regime.

Hanna, A. J., and Hanna, K. A. *Napoleon III and Mexico: American Triumph over Monarchy* [1861–1867] (15:60) is a study of triangular relations of the United States and France over conflicting policies on Mexico from the early 1850s to the demise of the Maximilian regime in Mexico in 1867.

Lord John Rose

Clark, R. C. "The Diplomatic Mission of Sir John Rose, 1871" (14:81) is an account of an unofficial British emissary to the Washington Treaty negotiations.

14:67 Long, Morden H. "Sir John Rose and the Informal Beginnings of the Canadian High Commissionership." *Canadian Historical Review* 12:1 (1931), 23–43. Long uses Canadian manuscripts in summarizing Rose's preliminary work before the Treaty of Washington negotiations of 1871.

Lord John Russell

Russell, Lord J. *The Later Correspondence of Lord John Russell, 1840–1878* (8:48).

Walpole, S. *The Life of Lord John Russell* (8:49).

Others

14:68 Campbell, Charles S., Jr. "The Dismissal of Lord Sackville." *Mississippi Valley Historical Review* 44:4 (1958), 635–48. Thorough study of the decision by Cleveland's administration to dismiss the British minister in 1888. Campbell finds the hastiness of the dismissal discreditable and blames the American minister in London, Phelps, for it.

Fitzmaurice, Lord E. *The Life of Granville George Leveson Gower: Second Earl Granville, K.G., 1815–1891* (11:95) contains a good chapter, in volume 2 on the Geneva arbitration (1871–1874).

14:69 Grenville, John A. S. *Lord Salisbury and Foreign Policy: The Close of the Nineteenth Century.* London: University of London, Athlone Press, 1964. Definitively researched, mature study of the man who was both prime minister and foreign minister of Britain during the Venezuela boundary crisis and subsequent episodes of the 1890s. Bibliography.

14:70 Gwynn, Stephen, ed. *The Letters and Friendships of Sir Cecil Spring Rice: A Record.* 2 vols. London: Constable, 1929. Correspondence with Woodrow Wilson, Henry Adams, Theodore Roosevelt, Lord Grey, and Balfour is provided in this annotated collection of letters of the British ambassador to America.

Maxwell, Sir H. E. *The Life and Letters of George William Frederick, Fourth Earl of Clarendon* (8:52) contains material on the abortive Johnson-Clarendon Treaty on the *Alabama* claims.

14:71 Watt, Donald C. "America and the British Foreign-Policy-Making Elite, from Joseph Chamberlain to Anthony Eden, 1895–1956." In Donald C. Watt, *Personalities and Policies: Studies in the Formulation of British Foreign Policy in the Twentieth Century.* Notre Dame, Ind.: University of Notre Dame Press, 1965, pp. 19–52. A suggestive rather than definitive consideration of elites in policy formulation, Watt's hypothesis is that rapprochement of 1898 to 1906 rested "very much" on the accident that policymakers in both countries belonged to social groups of similar outlooks.

Best, G. *Mid-Victorian Britain, 1851–1875* (8:54) captures a sense of the period when Britain enjoyed a preeminence in world affairs.

Bourne, K. *Britain and the Balance of Power in North America, 1815–1908* (8:55) devotes over one-third of his very impressive book to the period 1861 to 1908, when Britain was reducing its military influence in North America and when the role of the United States was changing from that of likely enemy to that of useful friend.

Bourne, K. *The Foreign Policy of Victorian England, 1830–1902* (8:56) succeeds in placing Anglo-American relations in context in the overall diplomacy of Britain.

Brebner, J. B. *North Atlantic Triangle: The Interplay of Canada, the United States and Great Britain* (2:233) is one of the basic studies of the relations of the United States, Canada, and Great Britain. Boundaries, fisheries, commerce, railroads, and many other Canadian-American problems receive careful attention.

Campbell, C. S., Jr. *From Revolution to Rapprochement: The United States and Great Britain, 1783–1900* (2:234) is the single best available treatment of British-American relations (1867–1899), it should be read in conjunction with the author's *The Transformation of American Foreign Relations* (12:7), where the critical importance of British-American relations to the overall diplomacy of the United States is argued.

Campbell, C. S., Jr. *The Transformation of American Foreign Relations, 1865–1900* (12:7) is the mature work of the leading scholar on British-American relations in the second half of the 19th century. He stresses overseas expansion and the relationship with Britain as the two principal themes of American diplomacy in the period and explains the evolution of British-American relations from hostility to rapprochement.

Anglo-Canadian-American Relations

Allen, H. C. *Great Britain and the United States: A History of Anglo-American Relations (1783–1952)* (2:232) is probably the best synthesis for the entire period ever written.

ANGLO-AMERICAN ECONOMICS

14:72 Adler, Dorothy R. *British Investment in American Railways, 1834–1898.* Charlottesville: University Press of Virginia, 1970. This study contains valuable data from business records, but there is virtually no relation of the data to any aspect of public policy. Bibliography.

14:73 Crapol, Edward. *America for Americans: Economic Nationalism and Anglophobia in the Late Nineteenth Century*. Westport, Conn.: Greenwood, 1973. Crapol focuses on American resentment of British investments, Anglo-American competition for markets, and the silver-gold controversy of 1896. Contemporary newspaper and magazine opinion (1870s–1890s) is relied upon heavily, supplemented by some use of private papers and government publications. Bibliography.

14:74 Edelstein, Michael. "The Determinants of U.K. Investment Abroad, 1870–1913: The U.S. Case." *Journal of Economic History* 34:4 (1974), 980–1007. Calculations of supply and demand elasticities show that the United States was among several beneficiaries of a demand for high-return, medium-risk assets that accompanied the growth of wealth in Great Britain. "Pull" forces strengthened during 1895 to 1913, but "push" forces dominated British investment in American railway securities.

14:75 Paul, Rodman W. "The Wheat Trade between California and the United Kingdom." *Mississippi Valley History Review* 45:3 (1958), 391–412. For a period of 35 years, from the end of the Civil War to the turn of the century, wheat grown in California, Oregon, and Washington was the second or third largest source of this cereal for Britain, wheat shipped from the U.S. Atlantic ports having been first.

14:76 Perren, Richard. "The North American Beef and Cattle Trade with Great Britain, 1870–1914." *Economic History Review* 24:3 (1971), 430–44. The shipment of live cattle from North America to the United Kingdom began in 1868 and became important about 1875. Despite restrictions imposed on American cattle by the Contagious Disease Animals Act in 1878, and on Canadian cattle in 1893, and despite humane legislation regulating conditions of transportation, it expanded until about 1900.

14:77 Rothstein, Morton. "America in the International Rivalry for the British Wheat Market, 1860–1914." *Mississippi Valley Historical Review* 47:3 (1960), 401–18. Following repeal of the English corn laws (1846), American wheat production became dependent upon the English market. Conversely, Great Britain came to regard the United States as her most dependable source of breadstuffs. By 1900, as rivals adopted American farming and marketing techniques, the United States lost its leadership in the wheat export trade, with disastrous results in the 1920s.

U.S.-CANADIAN RELATIONS

See Chapter 10 for 18th- and early-19th-century relations.

14:78 Brown, Robert C. *Canada's National Policy 1883–1900: A Study in Canadian-American Relations*. Princeton, N.J.: Princeton University Press, 1964. The fisheries, pelagic sealing, and Alaska boundary disputes are thoroughly canvased in this study, which rests on exhaustive investigation of archives and printed documents. Brown finds that Canadian nationalism matured during this period of British-American negotiation over Canadian questions. Extensive bibliography.

Corbett, P. E. *The Settlement of Canadian-American Disputes: A Critical Study of Methods and Results* (16:122) is an essential book for the arbitral and legal settlement of the problems of the boundaries and fisheries in Canadian-American relations.

Deener, D. R., ed. *Canada-United States Treaty Relations* [1780–1960] (2:220) is an important book for all scholars concerned with the many legal relationships between the United States and Canada.

Glazebrook, G. P. De T. *A History of Canadian External Relations* (2:221) contains, in chapter 7, especially pertinent materials on the legal relations of the United States and Canada during the last half of the 19th century.

14:79 Keenleyside, Hugh L. *Canada and the United States: Some Aspects of Their Historical Relations*. New York: Knopf, 1952. This study is important for boundary and fishing controversies. Bibliography.

14:80 Shippee, Lester B. *Canadian-American Relations, 1849–1874*. New Haven, Conn.: Yale University Press, 1939. This is one of the basic scholarly studies of Canadian-American relations. It contains comprehensive accounts of the Treaty of Washington, reciprocity, and what Shippee called "The Everlasting Fisheries Question."

HOSTILITY

See Chapter 10, "Civil War and More Border Troubles," for the Fenian raids (1866–1871) and Riel rebellions (1869–1870, 1885).

Alabama Claims

See, under "Personalities," Charles Francis Adams, Hamilton Fish, Lord John Rose, Lord John Russell, Charles Sumner; also see Chapter 11, "Foreign Navy of the Confederacy," for materials on Confederate commerce raiders, especially the *Alabama*; Chapter 10, "San Juan Islands Settlement," deals with the San Juan boundary dispute.

14:81 Clark, Robert C. "The Diplomatic Mission of Sir John Rose, 1871." *Pacific Northwest Quarterly* 27:3 (1936), 227–42. An account of the unofficial British emissary to the Washington negotiations of 1871 who tried to set up "modes" for resolving the questions facing the Anglo-American nations. Clark argues that Rose was responsible for the establishment of the joint high commission which brought about the Treaty of Washington and, among other accomplishments, settled the San Juan boundary.

14:82 Cook, Adrian. *The Alabama Claims, American Politics and Anglo-American Relations, 1865–1872*. Ithaca, N.Y.: Cornell University Press, 1975. Cook emphasizes the broad range of questions relating to the *Alabama* claims issue, including the major aspects of the San Juan boundary controversy during this period. The author concludes that there was no real danger of war between the Atlantic nations from 1865 to 1872. Bibliography.

14:83 Dashew, Doris W. "The Story of an Illusion: The Plan to Trade the *Alabama* Claims for Canada." *Civil War History* 15:4 (1969), 332–48. Dashew discusses the relationship between the *Alabama* claims question and American territorial expansion (1871).

Jarvis, R. C. "The *Alabama* and the Law" (11:236) argues that at its departure the *Alabama* was a bona fide neutral vessel.

14:84 Smith, Goldwin. *The Treaty of Washington 1871: A Study in Imperial History*. Ithaca, N.Y.: Cornell University Press, 1941. A scholarly study, especially useful for British and Canadian viewpoints on the treaty. Arbitration, reciprocity, boundaries, and fisheries all receive full treatment. Extensive bibliography.

14:85 Stacey, C. P. "Britain's Withdrawal from North America, 1864–1871." *Canadian Historical Review* 36:3 (1955), 185–98. Britain's European problems caused its government to settle differences with the United States in the Treaty of Washington and the arbitration which followed.

14:86 Tansill, Charles C. *Canadian-American Relations, 1875–1911*. New Haven, Conn.: Yale University Press, 1943. A study of large importance for many topics involving international law. Boundaries and fisheries are dealt with in detail. Arbitral tribunals and commissions are described carefully.

14:87 U.S. Department of State. *Papers Relating to the Foreign Relations of the United States, 1872: Part II, Papers Relating to the Treaty of Washington*. Washington, D.C.: G.P.O., 1872–1873. The most complete record of the official diplomatic correspondence (five volumes in ten parts) relating to the Treaty of Washington of 1871: see also U.S. Department of State, *Correspondence Concerning Claims against Great Britain* (14:7).

Alaskan Boundary Settlement

See "Personalities," especially George F. Hoar.

Bailey, T. A. "Theodore Roosevelt and the Alaska Boundary Settlement" (16:126).

14:88 Penlington, Norman. *The Alaska Boundary Dispute: A Critical Reappraisal*. Toronto: McGraw-Hill Ryerson, 1972. A bitter Canadian perspective of the Alaskan boundary dispute between the United States and Canada between 1896 and 1903. As background, the author discusses the Ukase of 1821 and the Anglo-Russian Treaty of 1825.

Fisheries and Furseals

See "Personalities," especially James G. Blaine.

Bailey, T. A. "The North Pacific Sealing Convention of 1911" (16:123).

14:89 Campbell, Charles S., Jr. "American Tariff Interests and the Northeastern Fisheries, 1883–1888." *Canadian Historical Review* 45:3 (1964), 212–28. Campbell analyzes Cleveland's mixed success in his fight with Congress over the related matters of imports from Canada and American claims to rights in the northeastern fisheries.

14:90 Campbell, Charles S., Jr. "The Anglo-American Crisis in the Bering Sea, 1890–1891." *Mississippi Valley Historical Review* 48:3 (1961), 393–414. In this analysis of the steps to the modus vivendi reached by Blaine and Salisbury in 1891, the influence of Henry W. Elliott, American naturalist, is emphasized.

Innis, H. A. *The Cod Fisheries: The History of an International Economy* [1497–1936] (16:124) is a comprehensive history of the fisheries off Newfoundland and the diplomatic issues involving them; a solid background to Canadian-American questions over fishing rights.

Longley, R. S. "Peter Mitchell: Guardian of the North Atlantic Fisheries, 1867–1871" (16:125).

DÉTENTE

See "Personalities," especially Grover Cleveland, Richard Olney, and, under "Others," Thomas F. Bayard, Edward J. Phelps.

Campbell, C. S., Jr. "The Dismissal of Lord Sackville" (14:68) is an examination of the incidents surrounding the Cleveland administration's abrupt dismissal, on the eve of the presidential election of 1888, of Lord Sackville, British minister to Washington.

14:91 Tulloch, H. A. "Changing British Attitudes towards the United States in the 1880's." *Historical Journal* 20:4 (1977), 825–40. British views of America changed in the late 19th century so that America began to be seen as an extension of England rather than as a land linked more closely to the radicalism of revolutionary France.

Venezuelan Boundary Dispute, 1895–1896

14:92 Boyle, T. "The Venezuela Crisis and the Liberal Opposition, 1895–96." *Journal of Modern History* 50:3 (1978), iii. Boyle discusses Anglo-American relations during the Venezuelan crisis, when the British Liberal party manifested pro-Americanism while British world power was ebbing.

14:93 Mathews, Joseph J. "Informal Diplomacy in the Venezuelan Crisis of 1896." *Mississippi Valley Historical Review* 50:2 (1963), 195–212. This essay

places heavy and fruitful reliance on the private papers of Chamberlain, Olney, and Salisbury.

14:94 Sloan, Jennie A. "Anglo-American Relations and the Venezuelan Boundary Dispute." *Hispanic American Historical Review* 18:4 (1938), 486–506. A pioneer effort that is still useful for its reflection of contemporary periodical opinion.

14:95 Young, George B. "Intervention under the Monroe Doctrine: The Olney Corollary." *Political Science Quarterly* 57:2 (1942), 247–80. Young has provided a cogent analysis of the implications of Olney's "20-inch" message to Salisbury.

Olney-Pauncefote Treaty, 1897

Blake, N. M. "The Olney-Pauncefote Treaty of 1897" (16:127) discusses the ill-fated general arbitration treaty between Britain and America.

RAPPROCHEMENT

See "Personalities," especially John Hay, Whitelaw Reid.

14:96 Campbell, Charles S., Jr. *Anglo-American Understanding, 1898–1903*. Baltimore: Johns Hopkins Press, 1957. A painstaking investigation of the diplomatic negotiations over an isthmian canal and the Alaska boundary during John Hay's tenure as secretary of state, it makes exhaustive use of State Department and Foreign Office archives. Extensive bibliography.

14:97 Campbell, Charles S., Jr. "Anglo-American Relations, 1897–1901." In Paolo E. Coletta, ed., *Threshold to American Internationalism: Essays on the Foreign Policies of William McKinley*. New York: Exposition, 1970, pp. 221–51. Campbell emphasizes the fragile or "hothouse" quality of the Anglo-American rapprochement.

14:98 Gelber, Lionel M. *The Rise of Anglo-American Friendship: A Study in World Politics, 1898–1906*. New York: Oxford University Press, 1938. A pioneer essay, it is still perhaps the most stylish, but is largely superseded by Charles S. Campbell's *Anglo-American Understanding* (14:96).

14:99 Heindel, Richard H. *The American Impact on Great Britain, 1898–1914: A Study of the United States in World History.* Philadelphia: University of Pennsylvania Press, 1940. A pioneer study of the relations between the two powers as they moved from hostility to friendship and understanding. For the period of the Spanish War, Heindel maintains that Britain supported the United States in the war and encouraged the taking of the Philippines. Bibliography.

Monger, G. *The End of Isolation: British Foreign Policy, 1900–1907* (17:247).

14:100 Perkins, Bradford. *The Great Rapprochement: England and the United States, 1895–1914.* New York: Atheneum, 1968. A graceful account of the efforts by the two governments to bring the countries closer together. The story is a familiar one but Perkins adds much detail to the already-known outline. Bibliography.

U.S. and the Boer War

14:101 Anderson, Stuart. "Racial Anglo-Saxonism and the American Response to the Boer War." *Diplomatic History* 2:3 (1978), 219–36. The important members of the American foreign policymaking community were too devoted to Anglo-Saxonism to give attentive hearing to the opinions of the Boers' supporters. Consequently, the budding Anglo-American rapprochement survived.

14:102 Ferguson, John H. *American Diplomacy and the Boer War.* Philadelphia: University of Pennsylvania Press, 1939. Although Ferguson feels that the U.S. consular service in South Africa was inadequate and incompetent, he believes that the American government successfully asserted and protected its rights and interests—while remaining neutral. He also concludes that the Boer attempt to enlist support in the United States was counterproductive. Bibliography.

14:103 Gatewood, Willard B., Jr. "Black Americans and the Boer War, 1899–1902." *South Atlantic Quarterly* 75:2 (1976), 226–44. Many American blacks lent support to the British cause during the war, only to discover the racial settlement resembled the conditions of blacks in the American south.

14:104 Hammond, John Hays. *The Autobiography of John Hays Hammond.* 2 vols. New York: Farrar & Rinehart, 1935. An account by an American engineer-capitalist who was on the ground in South Africa and who attempted to define and defend American interests in the Boer conflict.

14:105 Kruger, Rayne. *Good-Bye Dolly Gray: The Story of the Boer War.* Philadelphia: Lippincott, 1960. Kruger offers a detailed account, supplemented by a large number of photographs and some maps of the main battles.

14:106 Noer, Thomas J. *Briton, Boer, and Yankee: The United States and South Africa 1870–1914.* Kent, Ohio: Kent State University Press, 1978. A well-researched study of the role of South Africa in Anglo-American relations. Noer emphasizes the Boer War as a "British war for American interests." Bibliography.

14:107 Penlington, Norman. *Canada and Imperialism, 1896–1899.* Toronto: University of Toronto Press, 1965. A detailed analysis of relations between Canada and Britain from the Venezuela incident to the Canadian decision to participate in the Boer War.

14:108 Sands, W. H. "The American and African Civil Wars." *Contemporary Review* 79:5 (1901), 664–70. An interesting comparative examination of the American and Boer conflicts, separated by a generation in time and by the Atlantic Ocean. Sands concludes: "... on no account shall we allow British bayonets to be used to maintain the rule of the carpetbagger and the scalawag."

Franco-American Relations

See "Personalities," especially Hamilton Fish, Whitelaw Reid, Theodore Roosevelt, and, under "Others," Myron T. Herrick.

Barker, N. N. *Distaff Diplomacy: The Empress Eugénie and the Foreign Policy of the Second Empire* (8:81) traces the influence of Empress Eugénie, wife of Napoleon III, on French foreign policy. Her counsel, with reference to France's intervention in

Mexican politics during the 1860s, provides valuable insights for students of American foreign relations.

Blumenthal, H. *France and the United States: Their Diplomatic Relations, 1789–1914* (2:224) is the most comprehensive work on Franco-American relations for this period. As in his earlier work, Blumenthal stresses the potential for conflict between France and America, especially as it relates to the "blunders" of France under monarchical government; but, at the same time, Blumenthal tempers his analysis by acknowledging how the French and Americans repeatedly found a common ground to work out their differences. For the period after 1867, Blumenthal's coverage of French views on American colonial expansion, Franco-American economic relations, and Franco-American diplomacy in Africa and Asia is especially good.

Blumenthal, H. *A Reappraisal of Franco-American Relations, 1830–1871* (8:82) represents the first comprehensive study of Franco-American relations in the 19th century. The author's main purpose in writing this book is to strike down the myth of amicable Franco-American relations. Instead, he describes events, conflicting interests, and cultural differences which led the two nations repeatedly to the brink of war.

14:109 Blumenthal, Henry. *American and French Culture, 1800–1900: Interchange in Art, Science, Literature and Society.* Baton Rouge: Louisiana State University Press, 1975. Blumenthal designed this book as a complement to his work on Franco-American diplomatic relations. Covering French and American cultural exchanges from philosophy to painting, the volume emphasizes how French and American individuals, through their work, art, and thought, broke through political obstacles separating the two countries. Extensive bibliography.

14:110 Clifford, Dale. "Elihu Benjamin Washburne: An American Diplomat in Paris, 1870–1871." *Prologue* 2:3 (1970), 161–74. This article investigates the efforts of the ambassador to France, Benjamin Washburne, during a volatile period of French history. Washburne wanted the French post primarily because of its lack of activity. In this, he was disappointed. The Franco-Prussian War and the Paris Commune of 1871 both interfered with a leisurely ambassadorship. The article relates Washburne's pro-German sentiment, his general success in protecting American citizens and property,

and his inability to analyze the French political environment.

Curtis, E. N. "American Opinion of the French Nineteenth Century Revolutions" (8:84) includes the revolution of 1870.

14:111 Gould, Lewis L. "Diplomats in the Lobby: Franco-American Relations and the Dingley Tariff of 1897."*Historian* 39:4 (1977), 659–80. This masterful article, based on multiarchival research, demonstrates that there was a connection between bimetallism and tariff making. There were intense negotiations between French diplomats and American senators, who used reciprocity to obtain French cooperation on bimetallism. A search for foreign markets was only a secondary factor behind reciprocity in 1897. The author also finds considerable French interest and involvement in the McKinley and Wilson-Gorman tariffs.

14:112 Lewis, Tom T. "Franco-American Diplomatic Relations 1898–1907." Ph.D. diss., University of Oklahoma, 1971. A comprehensive survey of Franco-American relations with emphasis placed on the participatory diplomats, economic questions, imperial aspirations, cultural relations. The work is based mainly on American documentation and focuses on the convergence of Franco-American relations in such areas as China, Liberia, Venezuela, and at the Algeciras Conference of 1906.

The First Moroccan Crisis, 1904–1906

See Chapter 18, "Roosevelt and the Algeciras Crisis, 1904–1906."

Anderson, E. N. *The First Moroccan Crisis, 1904–1906* (18:110) provides a detailed account of the episode from a European perspective.

Beale, H. K. *Theodore Roosevelt and the Rise of America to World Power* (14:8) claims Roosevelt's intervention prevented a major war.

Lewis, T. T. "Franco-American Relations during the First Moroccan Crisis" (18:115) finds Roosevelt supportive.

U.S., Germany, and the Austro-Hungarian Empire

See "Personalities," especially Lewis Einstein, James A. Garfield, John A. Kasson, Andrew D. White; see also Chapter 18, "The Congo Question, 1884–1885" for the Berlin Conference on West Africa.

14:113 Cassedy, James H. "Applied Microscopy and American Pork Diplomacy: Charles Wardel Stiles in Germany, 1898–1899." *Isis* 62:1 (1971), 5–20. A fascinating description of Charles W. Stiles's contribution to terminating the German-American controversy over American exports of pork—alleged by the Germans to contain trichinae. Stiles not only debunked the German claims, but gained the respect of the German scientific community.

Dugdale, E. T. S., ed. *German Diplomatic Documents, 1871–1914* (14:2).

14:114 Fisk, George M. "German-American Diplomatic and Commercial Relations, Historically Considered." *Review of Reviews* 25 (1902), 323–28. This article remains of value because of its description of commercial, naturalization, extradition treaties, industrial relations, and the Samoan question that contributed to German-American relations during the mid and late 19th century.

14:115 Foner, Philip S. "Protests in the United States against Bismarck's Anti-Socialist Law." *International Review of Social History* 21:1 (1976), 30–50. Foner examines the American response to the German chancellor's anti-Socialist law of 1878 (forbidding political activities), as renewed in 1880. Although certain American newspapers were favorably disposed, there was much editorial criticism. Foner emphasizes the protest rallies and opposition that mounted especially in New York, Chicago, and Boston.

Gazley, J. G. *American Opinion of German Unification, 1848–1871* (8:95) is an early effort at evaluating public opinion that maintains American opinion of German unification was quite favorable. The author also argues that antagonistic feelings on the part of Americans toward Austria and France enhanced their favorable opinion of Germany.

14:116 Hall, Luella J. "The Abortive German-American-Chinese Entente of 1907–08." *Journal of Modern History* 1:2 (1929), 219–35. The author provides an account of Germany's attempt to force an American-German-Chinese entente in the face of increasingly strong British and French opposition in East Asia. Hall maintains that Roosevelt rejected the entente after a year of negotiations because he realized that the American position, even with the support of Germany, was untenable in China vis-à-vis Japan.

14:117 Keim, Jeannette. *Forty Years of German-American Political Relations*. Philadelphia: Dornan, 1919. This comprehensive analysis of U.S.-German relations puts its emphasis on their friendly status in 1870—arrangements governing naturalization, commercial relations, interests in Samoa, the Spanish-American War, the open door in China and the Monroe Doctrine.

14:118 Kreider, John K. "Diplomatic Relations between Germany and the United States 1906–1913." Ph.D. diss., Pennsylvania State University, 1969. The study focuses on the Algeciras Conference, tariff arrangements and trade, and converging interests of the two nations in Africa and Asia. The author emphasizes the cleavage between a pro-British Washington and the anti-British policies in Berlin.

14:119 McClure, Wallace. "German-American Commercial Relations." *American Journal of International Law* 19:4 (1925), 689–701. This article traces the history of the American most-favored-nation clause in treaties with the German states to the Treaty of 1923. The author distinguishes between *conditional* and *unconditional* clauses in relating the evolution in American policy toward the acceptance of an open door commercial arrangement.

14:120 Meyer, Luciana R-W. "German-American Migration and the Bancroft Naturalization Treaties 1868–1910." Ph.D. diss., City University of New York, 1970. This study describes several agreements between the United States and the several German states. It emphasizes the difficulties in administering these treaties (1868–1910), particularly in demonstrating the right of a person to change nationality voluntarily and then return to his/her country of origin.

14:121 O'Grady, Joseph P. "Religion and American Diplomacy: An Incident in Austro-American Relations." *American Jewish Historical Quarterly* 59:4 (1970), 407–23. This article examines the controversy over appointment of Anthony M. Kieley to Austria in 1885 as envoy extraordinary. The Cleveland administration fought to retain Kieley when Austria rejected him because his wife was Jewish. The author, noting this case as a precedent in American relations with the Arab nations, concludes that the Kieley case is complex, as Kieley had made intemperate remarks about the Italian government in 1871.

14:122 Schieber, Clara E. *The Transformation of American Sentiment toward Germany 1870–1914.* Boston: Cornhill, 1923. Schieber maintains that the U.S. government and American public opinion were sympathetic toward Germany during the Franco-Prussian conflict. This monograph seeks to show how this sympathy in 1870–1871 changed to hostility by 1914 to 1917.

14:123 Shippee, Lester B. "German-American Relations, 1890–1914." *Journal of Modern History* 8:4 (1936), 479–88. This review article provides an excellent summary of Alfred Vagts's larger study, *Deutschland und die Vereinigte Staaten in der Weltpolitik* (14:126), and is recommended especially for those unable to read Vagts's German text.

14:124 Sterne, Margaret. "The Presidents of the United States in the Eyes of Austro-Hungarian Diplomats: 1901–1913." *Austrian History Yearbook* 2 (1966), 153–71. These observations of Austrian diplomats, especially Baron Ladislaus Henjenmuller von Hengervar, cover a variety of topics.

14:125 Stolberg-Wernigerode, Otto. *Germany and the United States of America during the Era of Bismarck.* Trans. by Otto E. Lessing. Reading, Pa.: Henry Janssen Foundation, 1937. This survey reconstructs German-American relations during their rise as world powers. It supplements Alfred Vagts's *Deutschland und die Vereinigte Staaten in der Weltpolitik* (14:126), which covers the years following Bismarck's demise. Most important, this survey covers the genesis of conflict between the two powers due to economic expansion.

14:126 Vagts, Alfred. *Deutschland und die Vereinigte Staaten in der Weltpolitik* [Germany and the United States in world politics]. 2 vols. New York: Macmillan, 1935. This remains the standard treatment of German-American relations from the late 19th cen-

tury into the early 20th century. It is based in large measure on a careful canvas of documents pertaining to the United States in the German archives.

14:127 Vagts, Alfred. "Hopes and Fears of an American-German War, 1870–1915." *Political Science Quarterly* 54:4 (1939), 514–35; 55:1 (1940), 53–76. This extended essay is an illuminating discussion of naval leaders' thoughts on both sides of the Atlantic.

Samoan Triangle, 1878–1900

See "Personalities," especially Thomas A. Bayard (under "Others"), James G. Blaine; also see Chapter 12, "U.S. and Samoa."

Ellison, J. W. "The Partition of Samoa: A Study in Imperialism and Diplomacy (12:129) focuses on Anglo-German negotiations, the author describes how the United States exited gracefully from the dangers of foreign entanglements while at the same time obtaining the port of Pago Pago. Britain received from Germany Tonga, Solomon Islands, West Africa, and an agreement that Germany would not intervene in South Africa.

14:128 Kennedy, Paul M. *The Samoan Tangle: A Study in Anglo-German-American Relations, 1878–1900.* New York: Barnes & Noble, 1974. Kennedy takes up where Masterman (12:133) quits, and discusses Samoa in relation to broader questions of Anglo-German-American diplomacy and politics. In its scope and depth, this book is a first-rate international history, required for an assessment of the changing relations of the great powers in the late 19th century.

Masterman, S. R. *The Origins of International Rivalry in Samoa, 1845–1884* (12:133) is, despite its age, the most important monograph on the origins of the partition of Samoa. Masterman clearly outlines the differences in strategic significance of Samoa for the United States, Britain, and Germany, and labels the inability of Samoans to assert their autonomy as fundamental to the ensuing tripartite control.

14:129 Ryden, George H. *The Foreign Policy of the United States in Relation to Samoa.* New Haven, Conn.: Yale University Press, 1933. In this comprehensive treatment of American interest in Samoa to 1900, Ryden emphasizes America's relations with both Britain and Germany while also devoting attention to the Washington Conference of 1887, the Berlin Conference of 1889, the nature of the condominium, and the eventual partition of the islands by the powers.

Vagts, A. *Deutschland und die Vereinigte Staaten in der Weltpolitik* (14:126) contains a 300-page chapter on Samoa.

14:130 Wehler, Hans Ulrich. *Der Aufsteig des amerikanischen Imperialismus: Studien zur Entwicklung des Imperium Americanum* [The rise of American imperialism: studies in the development of the American empire]. Gottingen: Vandenhoeck & Ruprecht, 1974. Although concentrating on the broad sweep of American expansion, there is an important section on Samoa and a remarkable 58-page bibliography.

14:131 Wehler, Hans Ulrich. "1889: Wendepunkt der amerikanische Aussenpolitik: Die Anfange des modernen Panamericanismus-Die Samoakrise" [1889: the turning point of American foreign policy: the beginning of modern Pan-Americanism: the Samoa crisis]. *Historische Zeitschrift* 201 (1965), 57–109. The author, one of Germany's prominent historians, argues that the 1889 Samoa crisis was a crucial turning point in U.S. foreign policy.

The Spanish-American War, 1898

Bailey, T. A. "Dewey and the Germans at Manila Bay" (13:184) disparages arguments that American naval forces under Dewey and German naval forces under Admiral Diedrichs almost entered into combat. Even though friction existed and the German-American rivalry in the Philippines raised animosities to the surface, relations were controlled and proper. Bailey contends that writers commenting on the Manila Bay operations in 1898 distorted historical reality and contributed to anti-German sentiments in 1914.

Shippee, L. B. "Germany and the Spanish-American War" (13:187) is primarily concerned with the German government's attempt to gain control of the Philippines in 1898.

The Venezuelan Controversy, 1902–1903

See Chapter 15, "Venezuelan Crisis, 1902–1903."

Clifford, J. G. "Admiral Dewey and the Germans, 1903: A New Perspective" (15:117).

14:132 Parsons, Edward B. "The German-American Crisis of 1902–1903." *Historian* 33:4 (1971), 436–52. Parsons maintains that Roosevelt's earlier published accounts of his actions in the controversy were essentially correct. Roosevelt did, then, play the major role in forcing the kaiser's hand and preserving the expanding role of the Monroe Doctrine. The author not only recounts Roosevelt's actions, but recounts the historiography of the controversy.

14:133 Small, Melvin. "The United States and the German 'Threat' to the Hemisphere, 1905–1914." *The Americas* 28:3 (1972), 252–70. Small argues that the Germans posed no military or political threat to Latin America after the Venezuela controversy of 1902–1903; rather, the treat was perceived as a product of aggressive German economic policies. The Germans after 1903 fully recognized the American Monroe Doctrine and its corollaries, and would not seek to contravene them, nor could they, since events in the Old World were commanding their full attention.

U.S., Russia, and Eastern Europe

See "Personalities," especially John W. Foster (under "Others"), Andrew D. White.

Bailey, T. A. *America Faces Russia: Russian-American Relations from Early Times to Our Day* [1776–1950] (2:245) focuses on American public opinion of Russia. Any conditions of amity, Bailey concludes, were based on the lack of common interests. In those cases where the United States and Russia did share a common interest in the 19th century, harsh relations ensued, pointing to the later conflicts of the 20th century.

14:134 Carstensen, Frederick V. "American Multinational Corporations in Imperial Russia: Chapters in Foreign Enterprise and Russian Economic Development." Ph.D. diss., Yale University, 1976. This work is based on detailed investigations into the archives of the International Harvester Company, whose subsidiaries were the largest companies, domestic or foreign, operating in Russia as of 1914. This study provides two microanalytical case histories of foreign enterprise in prewar Russia.

14:135 Challener, Richard D. "Montenegro and the United States: A Balkan Fantasy." *Journal of Central European Affairs* 17:3 (1957), 236–42. Challener discusses the curious offers made in 1909 and 1911 to the United States by the Montenegrin government of naval bases at Val di Noce and Dulcigno. On the first occasion, the U.S. minister to Greece and Montenegro, Richmond Pearson, was enthusiastic about the offer, in contrast to the Navy and State departments, and President Taft.

14:136 Dyrud, Keith P. "The Rusin Question in Eastern Europe and in America 1890–World War I." Ph.D. diss., University of Minnesota, 1976. This study considers the ethnic group known as Rusins within the Austro-Hungarian empire after 1890, when significant numbers of Rusins migrated to the United States and encountered difficulties in adjustment.

Gaddis, J. L. *Russia, the Soviet Union and the United States* (2:248) provides, in chapter 2, a useful survey of diplomatic issues.

Laserson, M. M. *The American Impact on Russia: Diplomatic and Ideological, 1784–1917* (2:250) treats those "contacts and repercussions" of American and Russian diplomacy, politics, law, economics, and social organization. Thus, it seeks to contribute to an understanding of the cultural and social relations at the base of Russian-American diplomatic relations.

14:137 Marinescu, Beatrice, and Radulescu-Zoner, Serban. "American Consular Reports about Romania's Struggle to Win Independence." *East European Quarterly* 12:3 (1978), 349–58. The authors discuss the reactions of official representatives stationed in Bucharest during Romania's struggle for independence (1877), especially U.S. reaction and the reports of the U.S. vice-consul, Adolph Stern.

14:138 Owen, Gail L. "Dollar Diplomacy in Default: The Economics of Russian-American Relations, 1910–1917." *Historical Journal* 13:2 (1970), 251–72. Efforts to apply dollar diplomacy to the imperial Russian domain were initially blocked in Manchuria and Persia by czarist obstruction (1910–1911) and in Russia proper by the Jewish-inspired U.S. denunciation of the Russian-American trade agreement (1911–1913).

World War I, however, forced the Russians to turn primarily to the United States for needed materiel.

Sivachev, N. V., and Yakovlev, N. N. *Russia and the United States: U.S.-Soviet Relations from the Soviet Point of View* (2:253) provides, in chapter 1, a lucid introduction to Russian-American relations prior to the 1917 revolutions. Written from the Soviet perspective, this brief chapter is well worth reading.

14:139 Strakhovsky, Leonid I. "Russia's Privateering Projects of 1878: A Page in the History of Russian-American Relations." *Journal of Modern History* 7:1 (1935), 22–40. This article maintains that the U.S. government decided not to test Russia's goodwill after Britain had charged the United States with allowing Russia to solicit privateers in American waters. Such was a measure of Russian-American friendship. This article demonstrates certain diplomatic uses of international law.

14:140 Szajkowski, Zosa. "The European Aspect of the American-Russian Passport Question." *Publications of the American Jewish Historical Society* 46:2 (1956), 86–100. Russian mistreatment of American Jews while they visited relatives in Russia provides the central theme of this article. Russia followed discriminatory policies against all aliens of Jewish background residing in Russia. This article considers the passport question as it was confronted in France, Germany, and Britain during the years 1864 to 1911.

14:141 Wallace, William S. "Looking at Russia through the American Press: 1850–1891." *Historia* [Puerto Rico] 6:1 (1956), 49–58. An attempt is made here to judge American opinion toward Russia on the basis of press opinion. The author argues that opinion, with the exception of the Perkins claim case, was overwhelmingly favorable until after 1879, when Russian pogroms increased in intensity and were more widely recognized.

14:142 Wallace, William S. "A Montanan in Russo-American Relations: The Case of John Ginzberg." *Pacific Northwest Quarterly* 40:1 (1949), 35–43. The "right of expatriation" is the subject of this case study of John Ginzberg. The article shows how a Russian-American controversy arose over the detention by the Russians of a naturalized American who returned to his native Russia in 1884 and was there imprisoned.

14:143 Wallace, William S. "A Russian Incident, 1894–1897." *Publications of the American Jewish*

Historical Society 39:1 (1949), 67–86. This short "note" discusses the diplomacy of the John Ginzberg case which concerned the detention of Ginzberg, a naturalized American citizen, by Russia. Appended to the note are several pieces of correspondence by Ginzberg, Clifton R. Breckinridge, the American minister to St. Petersburg, and Richard Olney, secretary of state.

14:144 Wish, Harvey. "Getting Along with the Romanovs." *South Atlantic Quarterly* 48:3 (1949), 341–59. Wish strives to show the basis for understanding between the two countries during a time of great tension. He contends that the basis for agreement was greater than that for discord, although the United States never reconciled itself to Russian authoritarian characteristics.

Abrogation of the Treaty of 1832

14:145 Cohen, Naomi W. "The Abrogation of the Russo-American Treaty of 1832." *Jewish Social Studies* 25:1 (1963), 3–41. The Russian-American Commercial Treaty of 1832 was abrogated in 1911. Much of the credit for treaty abrogation was due the activities of the American Jewish Committee. Outlining the tactics of the committee, the author reveals that for the first time in its history, the American Jewish community appealed to public opinion to end foreign discriminatory policies.

14:146 Egan, Clifford L. "Pressure Groups, the Department of State and the Abrogation of the Russian-American Treaty of 1832." *Proceedings of the American Philosophical Society* 115:1 (1971), 328–34. This essay seeks to explain the recommendation from the Department of State opposing abrogation in 1911 of the Russian-American Treaty of 1832. Eventually, President Taft yielded to mounting pressures from Jewish-American organizations and resisted advice from his own State Department. Egan concludes that abrogation had no noticeable effect on Russian treatment of the Jews and did not lead to any improvement in Russian-American relations.

14:147 Shankman, Arnold. "Brothers across the Sea: Afro-Americans on the Persecution of Russian Jews, 1881–1917." *Jewish Social Studies* 37:2 (1975), 114–21. During 1881 to 1917, Afro-Americans joined European and American liberals in attacking Russian anti-Semitism. Unlike other protesters, however, American Negroes emphasized the parallel between czarist oppressions of the Jews and white America's persecution of blacks.

14:148 Stults, Taylor. "Roosevelt, Russian Persecution of Jews, and American Public Opinion." *Jewish Social Studies* 33:1 (1971), 13–22. Stults traces reaction by the U.S. Jewish community to the pogrom of 1903 in Kishinev, Russia. In addition to holding protest meetings, Jews tried to obtain an official statement from the government. Correspondence took place between President Theodore Roosevelt and Secretary of State John Hay on the matter.

Szajkowski, Zosa. "The European Aspect of the American-Russian Passport Question" (14:140) deals with Russian mistreatment of American Jews while they visited relatives in Russia. Russia was following discriminatory policies against all aliens of Jewish background residing in Russia.

American Relief Efforts, 1891–1892

14:149 Queen, George S. "American Relief in the Russian Famine of 1891–1892." *Russian Review* 14:2 (1956), 140–50. This revisionist interpretation argues that American aid to victims of the Russian famine was inconsequential and that American gifts were not needed in Russia. There was no serious shortage of grain, but there was a lack of transport. American benevolence was essentially symbolic of American willingness to alleviate distress abroad.

14:150 Simms, James Y., Jr. "Impact of Russian Famine, 1891–1892, upon the United States." *Mid-America* 60:3 (1978), 171–84. During 1891–1892, Russia suffered from one of the severest famines in its history. It had a major impact on American life: 1) it led to a major American relief movement for aid to Russia, 2) it eliminated Russia temporarily as a grain exporter and aided the U.S. grain growers in opening markets, and 3) it enhanced the reputation and economic clout of the Farmers Alliance movement and the Populist party in the United States by showing the importance of American farmers in the international grain crisis.

14:151 Smith, Harold F. "Bread for the Russians: William C. Edgar and the Relief Campaign of 1892." *Minnesota History* 42:1 (1970), 54–62. This article summarizes voluntary American assistance to victims of the Russian famine of 1891–1892. William Edgar, editor of a trade journal in Minneapolis, organized the assistance program. American agriculture enjoyed a bumper grain crop. American farmers who had earlier experienced famine themselves responded warmly to the Russians' need.

14:152   Spetter, Allan. "The United States, the Russian Jews and the Russian Famine of 1891–1892." *American Jewish Historical Quarterly* 64:3 (1975), 236–44. American assistance and sympathy expressed to Jews oppressed in czarist Russia during 1891–1892 were modified by the general support given to the czarist regime during those famine years. Concern for the mistreated Jewish minority was largely lost sight of when the American government and people, particularly in the Midwest, contributed grains and otherwise assisted Russians suffering from the famine.

Russo-Japanese War, 1904–1905

See "Personalities," especially George von Lengerke Meyer, Theodore Roosevelt; also see Chapter 17, "Russo-Japanese War, 1904–1905."

14:153   Best, Gary D. "Financing a Foreign War: Jacob H. Schiff and Japan, 1904–05." *American Jewish Historical Quarterly* 61:4 (1972), 313–24. Close to 25 percent of the total foreign loans raised by Japan during its war against Russia was raised in the United States. Jacob Henry Schiff (1847–1920) took a leading part in these successful efforts. He gave as his motive for aiding Japan the desire to undermine Russian autocracy.

14:154   Johnson, Paul W. "The Journalist as Diplomat: E. J. Dillon and the Portsmouth Peace Conference." *Journalism Quarterly* 53:4 (1976), 689–93. Dr. Emile Joseph Dillon (1854–1953), the St. Petersburg correspondent for the London *Daily Telegraph* during the Russo-Japanese War (1904–1905), led the public relations campaign with the American press on behalf of the Russian minister of finance, Sergei Witte.

14:155   Parsons, Edward B. "Roosevelt's Containment of the Russo-Japanese War." *Pacific Historical Review* 38:1 (1969), 21–44. This article examines Roosevelt's claim that he cautioned Germany not to align itself with Russia against Japan in 1904–1905. Parsons concludes that Roosevelt did indeed warn the

Germans to back off. The article includes a historiographical treatment of Roosevelt's attempt to use Japan as the lever for an open door in China.

14:156   Thorson, Winston B. "American Public Opinion and the Portsmouth Peace Conference." *American Historical Review* 53:3 (1948), 439–64. This article seeks to overturn the notion that Japan's supposedly harsh peace terms made Americans more cognizant of growing Japanese domination in East Asia. The author concludes that the peace of Portsmouth did not sway American opinion away from Japan, and cannot be noted as a significant turning point in American-Japanese relations.

14:157   Trani, Eugene P. *The Treaty of Portsmouth: An Adventure in American Diplomacy.* Lexington: University of Kentucky Press, 1969. This book gives Roosevelt the greater share of credit for ending the Russo-Japanese War. Roosevelt, sensitive to the need for stability in Asia and the threat of European intervention, persuaded the Japanese to limit their demands on the Russians, while at the same time convincing the Russians to cut their losses. Bibliography.

U.S. and Other Nations

ITALY AND THE PAPAL STATES

DeConde, A. *Half Bitter, Half Sweet: An Excursion into Italian-American History* (8:101) contains little on diplomatic affairs for 1867 to 1914.

14:158   Farrell, John T. "Background of the Taft Mission to Rome." *Catholic Historical Review* 37:1 (1951), 1–22. This article, including certain relevant documents, explains how the negotiations for the American purchase of the Friar lands in the Philippines occurred.

14:159   Fogarty, Gerald P., S.J. *The Vatican and the Americanist Crisis: Denis J. O'Connell, American Agent in Rome, 1885–1903.* Rome: Università Gregoriana Editrice, 1974. Denis O'Connell, protégé of Archbishop James Gibbons and rector of the American College in Rome, became an important political strategist for liberal Catholic causes during the late

19th century, while representing them at the Vatican. This monograph emphasizes how the American Catholic hierarchy related to the Vatican when confronting several internal crises during these years.

14:160   Humphreys, Sexson E. "United States Recognition of the Kingdom of Italy." *Historian* 21:3 (1959), 296–312. Almost simultaneous with the onset of the American Civil War, Italy achieved political unification under the monarchy of Victor Emmanuel II. This article explains how certain temporary confusion affected the American political response to the rapid flow of events in Italy. Recognition was extended by the Lincoln administration in April 1861.

14:161   Karlin, J. Alexander. "The Italo-American Incident of 1891 and the Road to Reunion." *Journal of Southern History* 8:2 (1942), 242–46. After eleven persons, including at least three Italian nationals, were exonerated by a New Orleans court on charges of murdering the city's police chief, an angry mob proceeded to lynch the eleven. Reacting to the vigilante action and the apparent disregard by the U.S. government for the protection of these residents, the Italian government recalled its minister. Public response to the recall in the United States was swift, as Americans in all parts of the country, North and South, showed their willingness to take up arms against Italy.

14:162   Marraro, Howard R. "The Closing of the American Diplomatic Mission to the Vatican and Efforts to Revive It, 1868–1870." *Catholic Historical Review* 33:4 (1948), 423–47. Marraro has written a fascinating account of the closing of the U.S. legation in 1868 and the domestic pressures in the United States that swarmed over the reopening of the legation. Even many prominent American Catholics opposed the reopening of the legation on grounds of continual separation of church and state in the United States. This article covers U.S. diplomatic relations with the Papacy from 1848 until the severance of relations in 1868.

14:163   Trauth, Mary P. "The Bancroft Dispatches on the Vatican Council and the *Kulturkampf.*" *Catholic Historical Review* 40:2 (1954), 178–90. Ambassador George Bancroft's vehemently anti-Catholic sentiment led to his approval of German actions which bordered on "tyranny." Sister Trauth notes that Bancroft's less than objective reporting on German politics endeared him to Bismarck and solidified relations between the United States and Germany; all this, however, resulted from Bancroft's discrimination against the Catholic church.

SCANDINAVIA

See Chapter 12, "Purchase of Danish West Indies."

Fogdall, S. J. M. P. *Danish-American Diplomacy, 1776–1920* (2:242) manages to cover many topics of interest, including trade and tariff matters, the status of the Danish West Indies, extradition arrangements, and arbitration conventions.

Hovde, B. J. *Diplomatic Relations of the United States with Sweden and Norway, 1814–1905* (8:106) has only one chapter on the post-1865 period, covering such topics as extradition and naturalization treaties.

Scott, F. D. *Scandinavia* (2:243).

Tansill, C. C. *The Purchase of the Danish West Indies* (12:192) treats the long and tortuous debate over the purchase of the Danish Antilles leading up to the treaty of August 4, 1916. What little is to be learned of Danish-American relations in the late 19th and early 20th centuries is to be had from this book.

14:164   Tilberg, Frederick. *The Development of Commerce between the United States and Sweden, 1870–1925.* Moline, Ill.: Ransom, 1928. Tracing the origins of American-Swedish trade back to the late 18th century, this work emphasizes the half-century after 1870. Tilberg treats the treaties, tariffs, and other relations affecting trade, but he is equally concerned with the changing nature of trading commodities.

SPAIN

Becker, J. *Historia de las relaciones exteriores de la España durante el siglo xix* (7:9).

Chadwick, F. E. *The Relations of the United States and Spain: Diplomacy* (8:107) covers the revolts in Cuba during the 1860s and the 1870s as well as the 1890s; internal problems afflicting Spain; the development of tensions between the United States and Spain leading to military conflict in 1898.

Cortada, J. W. "Diplomatic Rivalry between Spain and the United States over Chile and Peru, 1864–1871" (15:199) suggests that Spain was seeking to maintain a definable global balance of power effective on both sides of the Atlantic.

14:165   Jackson, Shirley Fulton. "The United States and Spain 1898–1918." Ph.D. diss., Florida State University, 1967. This account considers Spanish-American relations during the two decades following the military struggle of 1898. Problems considered include the American indemnity claims against Spain; negotiation of a supplementary treaty for cession of two overlooked islands in the Philippines, and reopening of the investigation into the *Maine* disaster. Commercial relations were important in these years, as were concerns over the events accompanying the Mexican Revolution.

Schuyler, E. *American Diplomacy and the Furtherance of Commerce* [1865–1884] (12:13) contains the best available account of the Spanish commercial treaty.

OTHER STATES

14:166   May, A. J. "Crete and the United States, 1866–1869." *Journal of Modern History* 16:4 (1944), 286–93. This short article concerns the American response to the insurrection in Crete (against Turkish rule). The author finds no evidence to support widespread beliefs at the time that the United States was seeking a base of operations in the Mediterranean.

Meier, H. K. *Friendship under Stress: U.S.-Swiss Relations, 1900–1950* (2:257) covers, in the first chapter, the beginning of the 20th century.

Meier, H. K. *The United States and Switzerland in the Nineteenth Century* (2:258) is the latest and most complete monograph on Swiss-American relations. Its coverage includes chapters on emigration, trade, diplomatic representatives, and diplomatic agreements.

14:167   Xydis, Stephen G. "Diplomatic Relations between the United States and Greece, 1868–1878." *Balkan Studies* 5:1 (1964), 47–62. This article highlights important aspects of American-Greek relations during the Grant administration. Though little attempt at interpretation is made, the author does conclude that American policy was sympathetic to Greece, but not to the point of abandoning the American tradition of noninvolvement in European affairs.

15

The United States and Latin America, 1861–1919

Contributing Editor
ROGER R. TRASK
Department of Defense

Contributor
Thomas Schoonover
University of Southwestern Louisiana

Contents

Introduction

The period from 1861 to 1919 was perhaps the most formative in the long history of relations between the United States and Latin America. The Monroe Doctrine, pronounced in 1823, adorned with several corollaries and much broadened in meaning, became the core of the Latin American policy of the United States. The Latin American area, in a sense, became the proving ground in the late nineteenth century and the early twentieth century for a more worldly and aggressive foreign policy of a nation undergoing industrialization and political maturation. The time-honored policy of political aloofness (isolationism), still generally applied by the United States before 1914, had no relevance when it came to Latin America. During the sixty years covered in this chapter, the United States vastly expanded its political and economic interests in Latin America, especially in Mexico, Central America, and the Caribbean nations. Partly as a result of this often heavy-handed expansion, the United States found itself very unpopular in Latin America by the end of World War I.

Good introductions to the 1861 to 1919 period can be found in Samuel F. Bemis, *The Latin American Policy of the United States* (2:260), and Dexter Perkins, *A History of the Monroe Doctrine* (2:273). From there the student must proceed to more specialized works—bilateral, topical, and period studies as well as journal articles. The same interpretive differences that one finds in the literature of other areas of U.S. diplomatic history exist in this field. There are the traditionalist interpretations, which see U.S. policy based on a variety of motives, especially concern for hemispheric security. An example is Dana G. Munro, *Intervention and Dollar Diplomacy in the Caribbean, 1900–1921* (15:97). There are the more critical revisionist works which emphasize U.S. imperialism, resistance to socioeconomic change in Latin America (especially in the twentieth century), and primary economic motivations. Robert F. Smith, *The United States and Revolutionary Nationalism in Mexico, 1916–1932* (15:174), is representative of this school of

thought. Some of the best research and most penetrating interpretations can be found in journal articles, most conspicuously in those published over the years in the *Hispanic American Historical Review*. Some Latin American historians, a few of whose works are listed in this chapter, have studied aspects of U.S. policy in their countries. The great majority of these writers are nationalistically motivated and supercritical of the United States. An obvious exception is Daniel Cosío Villegas, the eminent Mexican historian, whose writings on U.S.-Mexican relations, while critical of the United States, are solidly based on a variety of Mexican and American sources. Cosío Villegas's *Historia moderna de México: El Porfiriato, la vida política exterior* (15:172), is the best example.

Historians have devoted considerable attention to this era in U.S.-Latin American relations, but their research efforts have been uneven. Some countries and topics have attracted little attention while others have been examined meticulously. Although the entries in this chapter are not exhaustive, they do reflect accurately what historians of U.S.-Latin American relations have done. Some nations, especially the smaller ones in South America, like Uruguay and Paraguay, have received comparatively little attention. In contrast, Mexico has been studied extensively—especially the period of French intervention in the 1860s and the Mexican Revolution beginning in 1910. Theodore Roosevelt's big stick, William Howard Taft's dollar diplomacy, and Woodrow Wilson's missionary diplomacy in Latin America have also been worked over extensively.

The many gaps in the published history of U.S.-Latin American relations for 1861 to 1919 provide important research opportunities. One area of North American activity in Latin America that has been neglected is the work of various U.S. interest groups, like educators, archaeologists, missionaries, and others. While some scholars have studied the penetration of U.S. economic interests into various countries, such as David M. Pletcher in his work on Mexico during the Porfiriato, *Rails, Mines, and Progress: Seven American Promoters in Mexico, 1867–1911* (15:181), much remains to be done in this area. There is also need for new bilateral studies. The several volumes of this kind published by the Duke University Press during the interwar period are still useful, but they tend to be factual surveys which are limited in research and they do not cover the last half-century or so. The more recent series of bilateral studies included in the American Foreign Policy Library of Harvard University Press, are not exclusively histories of U.S. relations with the countries concerned; in some cases they are essentially national histories, with much less attention to relations with the United States. An example is Frederick B. Pike, *The United States and the Andean Republics: Peru, Bolivia, and Ecuador* (2:267). A new, thoroughly documented volume on the relations of the United States and Uruguay, to cite just one example, would be welcome. While we know much about U.S. relationships with major countries like Mexico and Argentina, what about Ecuador, or Honduras?

A further area of research that would prove fruitful involves the State Department and its representatives in Latin America. How were Latin American affairs handled by the State Department, in terms of its internal organization? How knowledgeable about and attentive to Latin American policy were the secretaries of state between 1861 and 1919? What kind of men were sent to represent the United States in Latin America, what were their major objectives, and how effective were they?

Finally, studies of how the Latin American policy of the United States related to the general foreign policy of the nation would be useful. Was Latin America handled as a special sphere, or was policy for the region to the south consciously integrated with the total foreign policy of the United States?

Further research needs will be revealed by a careful study of the items listed in this chapter. The listing is designed to be not only a guide to existing published materials but also a demonstration of the opportunities for new research.

Resources and Overviews

RESEARCH AIDS

While pertinent bibliographies and reference aids are listed here, there are more extensive lists in Chapter 1.

Bibliographies

Deal, C. W., ed. *Latin America and the Caribbean: A Dissertation Bibliography* (1:249).

Ellis, R. N. "Civil-Military Relations, Operations, and the Army, 1865–1917" (13:1) has references to U.S. Army operations in Mexico during the Wilson administration.

Griffin, C. C., ed. *Latin America: A Guide to the Historical Literature* [1776–1970] (1:118).

Healy, D. *Modern Imperialism: Changing Styles in Historical Interpretation* (12:3).

15:1 Hitchman, James H. "The Platt Amendment Revisited: A Bibliographical Survey." *Americas* 23:4 (1967), 343–69. A useful survey (1901–1967) of the views of Cuban and U.S. writers on the Platt Amendment since its formulation.

Holbo, P. S. "Perspectives on American Foreign Policy, 1890–1916 . . ." (13:2).

15:2 Quirate, Martín. *Historiografía sobre el Imperio Maximiliano* [Historiography of Maximilian's empire]. Mexico, D.F.: Universidad Nacional Autónoma de México, 1970. An extensive, thoughtful, and expansive historiographical essay which deals with all aspects of Maximilian's empire (1863–1867), including the international.

Smith, D. M. "Rise to Great World Power, 1865–1918" (13:4) reviews recent historical interpretation.

Smith, M. J., Jr., ed. *The American Navy, 1865–1918: A Bibliography* (12:4) is useful for naval activities in the Caribbean and Latin America.

Trask, D. F; M. C. Meyer; and R. R. Trask, eds. *A Bibliography of United States–Latin American Relations since 1810* (1:120) is organized chronologically and topically, with four chapters devoted directly to the 1861 to 1919 period, plus sections for the period in each of the country chapters. Meyer (1:119) updates the original volume.

Trask, R. R. "Inter-American Relations" (1:121) cites 142 works written since 1945.

U.S. Library of Congress. Hispanic Division. *Handbook of Latin American Studies* (1:123) provides references to current materials; an excellent source for updating Griffin's guide.

Document Collections

More general collections are listed in Chapter 1, and other collections may be found in "Personalities," below.

Gantenbein, J. W., ed. *The Evolution of Our Latin American Policy: A Documentary Record* [1776–1949] (2:262).

15:3 Irish University Press Series on British Parliamentary Papers. *Central and South America, 1800–1899.* Shannon: Irish University Press, 1974. This microfiche collection of 33,000 pages includes reports and documents covering, among other topics, commerce and economic development. Also see (14:6) for printed documents.

Karnes, T. L., ed. *Readings in the Latin American Policy of the United States* [1776–1972] (2:264) is a useful collection with about half covering the 1861 to 1919 period.

15:4 Monroy Huitrón, Guadaloupe, ed. *Archivo histórico de Matías Romero: Catálogo descriptivo* [Historical archives of Matías Romero: descriptive catalog]. Vol. 1: *Correspondencia recibido, 1837–1862* [Correspondence received, 1837–1862]. Vol. 2: *Correspondencia recibido, 1872–1884* [Correspondence received, 1872–1884]. Mexico, D.F.: Banco de México, 1965–1970. This catalog lists over 32,000 items in the personal archives of Matías Romero, Mexican lawyer and diplomat. He was minister to the United States (1863–1868, 1882–1892, 1892–1898).

15:5 Romero, Matías, comp. *Correspondencia de la Legación Mexicana en Washington durante la Intervención extranjera* [Correspondence of the Mexican legation in Washington during the foreign (i.e., French) intervention]. 10 vols. Mexico, D.F.: Imprento del Gobierno, 1892. Romero was both author and compiler of much of these volumes. As minister to the United States for the government of Benito Juárez, he reported at great length on his efforts to obtain aid from the U.S. government.

U.S. Department of State. "General Records of the Department of State, RG 59 and RG 84" (1:359) includes, in Record Group 59, the records to 1906 of diplomatic instructions to and diplomatic dispatches from Argentina, Bolivia, Brazil, Central America, Chile, Colombia, Cuba, Dominican Republic, Ecuador, Haiti, Mexico, Panama, Paraguay and Uruguay, Peru, and Venezuela. It also includes consular instructions to and dispatches from many posts in these nations. Record Group 84 includes records of foreign service posts to the year 1912.

OVERVIEWS

See Chapter 12, "Overviews" and "Ideas and Pressures of Expansionism," and Chapter 13, "Progressivism and Foreign Policy," for background.

Bemis, S. F. *The Latin American Policy of the United States: An Historical Interpretation* [1776–1942] (2:260) is dated, but useful as more than a fourth provides detailed coverage of the 1861 to 1919 era.

Challener, R. D. *Admirals, Generals, and American Foreign Policy, 1898–1914* (17:229) focuses especially on Latin America and East Asia.

Connell-Smith, G. *The United States and Latin America: An Historical Analysis of Inter-American Relations* [1776–1974] (2:261) in general critical of U.S. policy; about half of the volume covers the period through World War I.

Langley, L. D. *Struggle for the American Mediterranean: United States–European Rivalry in the Gulf-Caribbean, 1776–1904* (2:308) points to the competition of nations over the idea of constructing a canal connecting the Atlantic and Pacific oceans in the area.

Mecham, J. L. *The United States and Inter-American Security, 1889–1960* (2:283) emphasizes the development of the Monroe Doctrine and the inter-American system. The author, a prominent Latin Americanist, is not overly critical of U.S. policy, and sees security concerns as important in the development of U.S. policy.

Stuart, G. H., and Tigner, J. L. *Latin America and the United States* [1776–1975] (2:268) is a comprehensive textbook, arranged by topics and by countries, and useful for facts and information.

Personalities

Additional references on individuals may be found in Chapter 1, "Biographical Data."

AMERICAN

James G. Blaine

See Chapter 12, "Personalities," for additional references.

Bostert, R. H. "A New Approach to the Origins of Blaine's Pan American Policy" (15:88).

15:6 Langley, Lester D. "James Gillespie Blaine: The Ideologue as Diplomatist." In Frank J. Merli and Theodore A. Wilson, eds., *Makers of American Diplomacy from Benjamin Franklin to Henry Kissinger.* New York: Scribner's, 1974, vol. 1, pp. 253–78. This essay is the most satisfactory study of Blaine, who is assessed as both creative thinker and influential practitioner. The author weighed conflicting interpretations. Stressing Latin American policy, he found that Blaine was a sincere (if sometimes meddling) peacemaker, feared foreign intervention, had higher ethical standards than many contemporaries, and was a transitional, imaginative statesman. Bibliography.

15:7 Muzzey, David S. *James G. Blaine: A Political Idol of Other Days.* New York: Dodd, Mead, 1934. This biography treats Blaine's original Pan-American imbroglio as an effort to discredit him and views his second tenure as spirited, but increasingly moderate and protective, rather than provocative. There is an extensive, sound discussion of the tariff and reciprocity questions (1881–1892).

15:8 Wilgus, A. Curtis. "James G. Blaine and the Pan-American Movement." *Hispanic American Historical Review* 5:4 (1922), 662–708. A good description of the origins of the first Pan-American conference in 1889 and the proceedings of the conference itself. The author suggests that Blaine did not originate the movement, but does note his interest in the expansion of trade between the United States and Latin America.

William Jennings Bryan

See Chapters 13, 19, "Personalities," for additional references.

15:9 Adler, Selig. "Bryan and Wilsonian Caribbean Penetration." *Hispanic American Historical Review* 20:2 (1940), 198–226. Although opposed to previous U.S. policy in the Caribbean, Bryan, affected by economic interests, concern about the Monroe Doctrine, and determination to extend Wilsonian democracy, followed traditional patterns during his term as secretary of state (1913–1915).

15:10 Coletta, Paolo E. "Bryan, Anti-Imperialism and Missionary Diplomacy." *Nebraska History* 44:3 (1963), 167–87. Coletta explains why Bryan, an anti-imperialist, used the methods of the big stick and dollar diplomacy to extend U.S. power into Central America and the Caribbean (1913–1915). Coletta argues that the strongest factor influencing Bryan was his desire to aid the people of the countries involved; he was not motivated by security concerns or economic expansion.

15:11 Coletta, Paolo. "William Jennings Bryan and the United States–Colombian Impasse, 1903–1921." *Hispanic American Historical Review* 47:4 (1967), 486–501. Coletta discusses the negotiation and ratification fight of the Thomson-Urrutia Treaty (August 1914) to compensate Colombia for the loss of Panama in 1903. Bryan consistently supported, as secretary of state in 1914 and later as a private citizen, Colombia's point of view.

William M. Evarts

15:12 Barrows, Chester L. *William M. Evarts: Lawyer, Diplomat, Statesman.* Chapel Hill: University of North Carolina Press, 1941. This is fuller and more analytical than Dyer's biography. Barrows saw Secretary of State Evarts as less serious than Fish and less spectacular than Blaine. An old-fashioned diplomat (1877–1881), he was never hurried, flustered, or bored by routine. The most useful section is on the Monroe Doctrine and the isthmian canal. Bibliography.

15:13 Dyer, Brainerd. *The Public Career of William M. Evarts.* Berkeley: University of California Press, 1933. Two chapters of this biography deal with Evart's term as secretary of state. Dyer notes Evart's procrastination and criticizes his Latin American policies—marked by aggressiveness (but not personal profiteering) and reversals regarding Mexico, by the use of amateur diplomats, and by failure to consummate a canal treaty.

Ulysses S. Grant

See Chapter 12, "Personalities," for additional references.

Carpenter, J. A. *Ulysses S. Grant* (12:48) contains material on the U.S. plan for Dominican annexation.

Walter Q. Gresham

See also Chapter 12, "Personalities."

Gresham, M. *Life of Walter Quintin Gresham* (12:53) discusses Gresham's term as secretary of state (1893–1895), and such topics as Latin America.

Benjamin Harrison

See Chapter 12, "Personalities," for additional references.

Spetter, A. "Harrison and Blaine: Foreign Policy, 1889–1893" (12:33) covers, superficially, the Chilean crisis of 1891–1892.

Rutherford B. Hayes

See Chapter 12, "Personalities," for additional references.

Hayes, R. B. *Hayes: The Diary of a President, 1875–1881* (12:61) refers to U.S. policy toward Mexico and an isthmian canal.

Theodore Roosevelt

See Chapters 14 and 17, "Personalities," for additional references.

15:14 Burton, David. *Theodore Roosevelt: Confident Imperialist.* Philadelphia: University of Pennsylvania Press, 1969. An original and perceptive study of the sources of Roosevelt's views on all sorts of matters but chiefly on war and imperialism. Burton sees him as the epitome of the social Darwinist in America.

15:15 Burton, David. "Theodore Roosevelt's Social Darwinism and Views on Imperialism." *Journal of the History of Ideas* 26:1 (1965), 103–18. The author traces Roosevelt's views on imperialism, his belief in Anglo-Saxon superiority, and his estimate of the place of America in the world, to his acceptance of the theories of social Darwinism.

15:16 Friedlander, Robert A. "A Reassessment of

Roosevelt's Role in the Panamanian Revolution of 1903." *Western Political Quarterly* 14:2 (1961), 535–43. Roosevelt's actions before and during the Panamanian Revolution were not inconsistent with national honor, but rather were morally straightforward and legally justified. Roosevelt's impetuous statements frequently obscured the more carefully chartered course of actions.

Livermore, S. W. "Theodore Roosevelt, the American Navy, and the Venezuelan Crisis of 1902–1903" (15:120).

15:17 Roosevelt, Theodore. "How the United States Acquired the Right to Dig the Panama Canal." *Outlook* 99 (Oct. 7, 1911), 314–18. TR's account of his policy and action during the U.S. acquisition of the Canal Zone (1901–1903), the most "honorable chapter" in the history of the United States.

William H. Seward

See Chapter 11, "Personalities," for additional references.

15:18 Paolino, Ernest N. *The Foundations of the American Empire: William Henry Seward and U.S. Foreign Policy.* Ithaca, N.Y.: Cornell University Press, 1973. This study focuses on Seward the commercial hegemonist (1861–1869), and it omits the diplomacy of the American Civil War; consequently, it perhaps raises more questions than it answers. The author has a strong command of the literature, and he has some extremely interesting things to say about America's Caribbean diplomacy. Bibliography.

Van Deusen, G. G. *William Henry Seward* (11:57). Has one chapter devoted to Mexico.

William Howard Taft

See Chapters 14 and 17, "Personalities," for additional references.

15:19 Minger, Ralph E. "Panama, the Canal Zone, and Titular Sovereignty." *Western Political Quarterly* 14:2 (1961), 544–64. Taft made two trips to Panama in 1904 and 1908 as a troubleshooter for President Roosevelt, and this is an analysis of Taft's reports.

15:20 Minger, Ralph E. "William H. Taft and the United States Intervention in Cuba in 1906." *Hispanic American Historical Review* 41:1 (1961), 75–89. Sent to Cuba by President Roosevelt after a revolt there in 1906, Taft took control as temporary governor, based on the Platt Amendment. Although the revolt had ended by the time Taft left after several weeks in Cuba, he was not optimistic about Cuba's future.

Henry Lane Wilson

15:21   Blaisdell, Lowell L. "Henry Lane Wilson and the Overthrow of Madero." *Southwestern Social Science Quarterly* 43:2 (1962), 126–35. In 1913 a military conspiracy headed by Huerta overthrew the democratic government of Madero. The U.S. ambassador was implicated in Madero's downfall and accused of blatant interference in the internal affairs of Mexico.

15:22   Cosío Villegas, Daniel. "Sobre Henry Lane Wilson" [About Henry Lane Wilson]. *Memoria del Colegio Nacional* 4:4 (1961), 39–55. A critical account of Ambassador Wilson's role (1913–1914) by one of Mexico's most distinguished contemporary historians.

15:23   Pride, Ramón. *La culpa de Lane Wilson, embajada de los E.U.A. en la tragedia Mexicana de 1913* [The culpability of Lane Wilson, U.S. ambassador, in the Mexican tragedy of 1913]. Mexico, D.F.: Ediciones Botas, 1962. The story of Wilson's role in the downfall of Madero is told from the Mexican point of view.

15:24   Wilson, Henry Lane. *Diplomatic Episodes in Mexico, Belgium and Chile.* Garden City, N.Y.: Doubleday, 1927. This memoir covers Wilson's experiences from 1897 to 1914, and contains much on his role during the Madero period.

Woodrow Wilson

See Chapter 19, "Personalities," for additional references.

Gilderhus, M. T. *Diplomacy and Revolution: U.S-Mexican Relations under Wilson and Carranza* (15:131).

15:25   Goodell, Stephen. "Woodrow Wilson in Latin America: Interpretations." *Historian* 28:1 (1965), 96–127. A useful historiographical survey of writers from Wilson's own times to 1965; the writers are categorized as missionary diplomatists, antiimperialists, and expansionists.

Haley, P. E. *Revolution and Intervention: The Diplomacy of Taft and Wilson with Mexico, 1910–1917* (15:132).

Quirk, R. E. *An Affair of Honor: Woodrow Wilson and the Occupation of Veracruz* [1914] (15:143).

Teitelbaum, L. M. *Woodrow Wilson and the Mexican Revolution (1913–1916): A History of United States–Mexican Relations from the Murder of Madero until Villa's Provocation across the Border* (15:137).

15:26   Trask, Roger R. "Missionary Diplomacy." In Alexander DeConde, ed., *Encyclopedia of American Foreign Policy.* New York: Scribner's, 1978, vol. 2, pp. 575–83. This is an analysis of Woodrow Wilson's policy of intervention in Mexico, Central America, and the Caribbean nations; it is critical of Wilson's motives and methods. Bibliography.

Leonard Wood

See also Chapter 40, "Personalities."

15:27   Hitchman, James H. *Leonard Wood and Cuban Independence, 1898–1902.* The Hague: Nijhoff, 1971. Presenting a traditional interpretation, the author argues that Cuba had to be prepared for independence and that no nation other than the United States could have done it; the U.S. occupation is justified on this basis.

Lane, J. C. *Armed Progressive: General Leonard Wood* (40:64).

Others

15:28   Atkins, Edwin F. *Sixty Years in Cuba: Reminiscences of Edwin F. Atkins.* Cambridge, Mass.: Riverside Press, 1926. Atkins, son of an American sugar merchant, came into the ownership of a sizeable plantation in 1880 and remained active in its operation until 1909. Atkins includes a firsthand impression of the insurrection of the 1890s, the subsequent U.S. intervention, and the occupation. He relates how he helped General Wood rig the early Cuban elections.

Coolidge, L. A. *An Old-Fashioned Senator: Orville H. Platt of Connecticut* (13:63) is a laudatory biography of the author of the Platt Amendment affecting Cuba.

Einstein, L. *A Diplomat Looks Back* (14:58) recalls his experiences in Costa Rica.

15:29   Peterson, Harold F. *Diplomat of the Americas: A Biography of William I. Buchanan, 1825–1909.* Albany: State University of New York

Press, 1977. Buchanan was a diplomatic trouble-shooter from 1894 to 1909 in Panama and Venezuela.

15:30   Prisco, Salvatore, III. *John Barrett, Progressive Era Diplomat: A Study of a Commercial Expansionist, 1887–1920.* University: University of Alabama Press, 1973. A resident of Oregon in the 1890s, John Barrett entered the diplomatic service of the United States in 1894 as U.S. minister to Siam. For the next three decades, while serving on diplomatic assignments and as director general of the Pan American Union (1907–1920), Barrett sought to publicize and influence American commercial expansionism.

15:31   Stewart, Watt. *Henry Meiggs, Yankee Pizarro.* Durham, N.C.: Duke University Press, 1946. Meiggs was a famous American railroad builder in Peru and Chile in the late 19th century.

Tansill, C. C. *The Foreign Policy of Thomas F. Bayard, 1885–1897* (12:77) relates U.S. policy toward Mexico.

LATIN AMERICAN

Venustiano Carranza

15:32   Breceda, Alfredo. *Don Venustiano Carranza: Rasgas Biográficos* [Don Venustiano Carranza: biographical traits]. Mexico, D.F.: Talleres Gráficas de la Nación, 1930. A good biography of President Carranza written by a participant in the revolution.

15:33   Meno Brito, Bernandino. *Carranza: Sus Amigos, sus enemigos* [Carranza: His Friends, his enemies]. Mexico, D.F.: Ediciones Botas, 1935. The author covers events of the Carranza-Huerta period with heavy use of documentation.

Porfirio Díaz

15:34   Beals, Carleton. *Porfirio Díaz: Dictator of Mexico.* Philadelphia: Lippincott, 1932. Although it is dated, this is a colorful and devastatingly critical biography of Díaz.

15:35   Tweedie, E. H. *The Maker of Modern Mexico: Porfirio Díaz.* New York: Lane, 1906. A popularly written biography based on personal interviews and Díaz's diaries.

Victoriano Huerta

15:36   Grieb, Kenneth J. *The United States and Huerta.* Lincoln: University of Nebraska Press, 1969.

A well-documented book which portrays Huerta as a typical *caudillo* who might have accomplished much for Mexico if Woodrow Wilson had left him alone. The author sees Wilson's policy as based on moral principles, and his acts as violating these principles.

Hinckley, T. C. "Wilson, Huerta, and the Twenty-One Gun Salute" (15:141).

15:37   Meyer, Michael C. *Huerta: A Political Portrait.* Lincoln: University of Nebraska Press, 1972. This study contains a chapter on Huerta and Wilson.

Benito Juárez

Fuentes Mares, J. *Juárez y los Estados Unidos* [Juárez and the United States] (9:198) focuses on Juárez and different phases of Mexican history, examines critically the impact of the U.S. doctrine of manifest destiny on Mexico's internal struggles and focuses on Juárez and the McLane-Ocampo Treaty.

15:38   Roeder, Ralph. *Juárez and His Mexico: A Biographical History.* 2 vols. New York: Viking, 1947. A thoroughly researched biography which is set within the historical events, including U.S.-Mexican relations.

Francisco I. Madero

15:39   Blasier, Cole, "The United States and Madero." *Journal of Latin American Studies* 4:2 (1972), 207–31. This is a well-documented account of the activities against Mexico's President Madero by Ambassador Henry Lane Wilson, concluding that while Wilson did not reflect the policies of Woodrow Wilson, whom he represented, the United States still was responsible for his reprehensible actions.

15:40   Cumberland, Charles C. *Mexican Revolution: Genesis under Madero.* Austin: University of Texas Press, 1952. A monographic study of the Madero phase of the Mexican Revolution.

15:41   Ross, Stanley R. *Francisco I. Madero: Apostle of Mexican Democracy.* New York: Columbia University Press, 1955. A biographical study based on extensive use of public and private collections, including Madero's papers.

Matías Romero

See "Document Collections," above.

Goldwert, M. "Matías Romero and Congressional Opposition to Seward's Policy toward the French Intervention in Mexico" [1861–1867] (15:58).

Miller, R. R. "Matías Romero: Mexican Minister to the United States during the Juárez-Maximilian Era" (15:61).

Domingo Faustino Sarmiento

15:42 Bunkley, Allison W. *The Life of Sarmiento*. Princeton, N.J.: Princeton University Press, 1952. This is an important, though not definitive, biography which stresses Sarmiento's experiences and intellectual formation prior to 1852.

15:43 Scobie, James R. "Evocación de la Personalidad Sarmiento y de sus Visitas a los EE. UU." [Evocation of Sarmiento's personality and of his visits to the United States]. *Humanidades* [Argentina] 37:1 (1961), 289–304.

15:44 Stewart, Watt. "The Influence of Horace Mann on the Educational Ideas of Domingo Faustino Sarmiento." *Hispanic American Historical Review* 20:1 (1940), 12–31. Sarmiento visited Mann in Boston in the late 1840s and came under the influence of his educational ideas. When he was president of Argentina, Sarmiento used Mann's ideas in the early foundation of the Argentine public school system.

Others

15:45 Clements, Kendrick A. "Emissary from a Revolution: Luis Cabrera and Woodrow Wilson." *Americas* 35:3 (1979), 353–71. Clements argues that Cabrera, sent by Carranza to persuade President Wilson to lift the ban on U.S. arms and munitions to Mexico early in 1914, played an important role in Wilson's subsequent decision to rescind the embargo.

Clendenen, C. C. *The United States and Pancho Villa: A Study in Unconventional Diplomacy* [1910–1917] (15:147).

EUROPEAN

Philippe Bunau-Varilla

Ameringer, C. D. "Philippe Bunau-Varilla: New Light on the Panama Canal Treaty [1903] (15:107).

15:46 Ameringer, Charles D. "The Panama Canal Lobby of Philippe Bunau-Varilla and William Nelson Cromwell." *American Historical Review* 68:2 (1963), 346–63. This essay clearly establishes the close col-

laboration between Bunau-Varilla and Cromwell (1903) in convincing U.S. leaders to select the Panama canal route, persuading the New French Panama Canal Company to sell its concession to the United States, and arranging the draft treaty with Colombia sanctioning this sale.

15:47 Bunau-Varilla, Philippe. *Panama: The Creation, Destruction, and Resurrection*. London: Constable, 1913. This is Bunau-Varilla's personal account of the Panama affair.

Maximilian

15:48 Corti, Count Egon C. *Maximilian and Charlotte of Mexico*. 2 vols. New York: Knopf, 1928. For many years an important work on the French intervention in Mexico (1861–1867), this work has been superseded by the work of the Hannas (15:60), though students may still find it appealing for its somewhat romantic treatment of its two tragic principals.

Frazer, R. W. "Maximilian's Propaganda Activities in the United States, 1865–1866" (15:66).

Napoleon III

15:49 Evans, Elliot A. P. "Napoleon III and the American Civil War." Ph.D. diss., Stanford University, 1940. A study that emphasizes the primacy of Mexico in Napoleonic diplomacy toward the New World. The work is updated by Case and Spencer (11:34), Blumenthal (8:82), and the Hannas (15:60).

Hanna, A. J., and Hanna, K. A. *Napoleon III and Mexico: American Triumph over Monarchy* [1861–1867] (15:60).

The Monroe Doctrine, 1861–1919

See also Chapter 2, "Monroe Doctrine," for general references.

Alvarez, A., ed. *The Monroe Doctrine: Its Importance in the International Life of the States of the New World* [1823–1923] (7:130) is a collection of essays by eminent Latin Americans and Americans which assesses the Monroe Doctrine.

Bailey, T. A. "The Lodge Corollary to the Monroe Doctrine" (17:266) argues that there was no serious Japanese threat at Magdalena Bay in 1912 and that the Lodge Corollary was meant to be an addition to the Monroe Doctrine.

Bingham, H. *The Monroe Doctrine: An Obsolete Shibboleth* (7:150) argues that the Monroe Doctrine was an instrument of U.S. imperialism and should be scrapped.

Dozer, D. M., ed. *The Monroe Doctrine: Its Modern Significance* [1823–1963] (2:271) contains reprints of twenty-six selections on the Monroe Doctrine, representing American and Latin American views. The editor provides an introductory essay to the material.

15:50 [The Evolution of the Monroe Doctrine, 1823–1914]. *American Society of International Law Proceedings* 8 (1914), 1–230. The 8th annual meeting of the society featured a series of papers by scholars and diplomats dealing with the evolution of the Monroe Doctrine. The topics dealt with included various interpretations of the doctrine, who benefited from the doctrine, Latin American and European attitudes toward the doctrine.

15:51 Karnes, Thomas L. "Hiram Bingham and His Obsolete Shibboleth." *Diplomatic History* 3:1 (1979), 39–57. After examining Bingham's 1913 article and book, *The Monroe Doctrine: An Obsolete Shibboleth,* and the response to them (pro and con), Karnes points out that after World War I, Bingham recanted on his indictment of U.S. policy and argued that the Monroe Doctrine was still necessary.

Logan, J. A. *No Transfer: An American Security Principle* [1760–1945] (2:272) argues that Americans have opposed the transfer of colonial possessions in this hemisphere from one European power to another (and stronger) one, and this principle has been closely allied to the Monroe Doctrine although not at first formally connected with it.

15:52 Perkins, Dexter. *The Monroe Doctrine, 1867–1907.* Baltimore: Johns Hopkins Press, 1937. Perkins finds no foreign threats, few territorial issues, and little American use before 1895 of the Monroe Doctrine. The no-transfer principle grew quietly as the result of diplomacy and the activities of the Grant administration. This was a ground-breaking book, but the subject merits new consideration.

THE FRENCH IN MEXICO, 1861–1867

See "Personalities" for Maximilian, Napoleon III, Matías Romero, William H. Seward.

15:53 Barker, Nancy Nichols. "France, Austria, and the Mexican Venture, 1861–1864." *French Historical Studies* 3:2 (1963), 224–45. This able study stresses the interconnectedness of European politics and the Mexican adventure of Louis Napoleon. Barker relates his American plans to his Austrian ones.

15:54 Belenki, A. B. *La Intervención extranjera en México, 1861–1867* [Foreign intervention in Mexico, 1861—1867]. Mexico, D.F.: Fondo de Cultura Popular, n.d. This translation of a Russian original, published in 1959, is popular, interpretive, and Marxist. Notes indicate fairly wide use of printed primary and secondary sources from Europe (including Russia), Mexico, and the United States.

15:55 Blumberg, Arnold. "The Diplomacy of the Mexican Empire, 1863–1867." *Transactions of the American Philosophical Society* 61:8 (1971), 1–152. It is somewhat more oriented toward European power politics than the Hannas' work (15:60), but contains a good discussion of Seward's policies. Extensive bibliography.

15:56 Bock, Carl H. *Prelude to Tragedy: The Negotiation and Breakdown of the Tripartite Convention of London, October 31, 1861.* Philadelphia: University of Pennsylvania Press, 1966. This mammoth work traces in great detail and with considerable skill the opening movements in the making of the French grand design for Mexico. Its title is aptly descriptive, and it is authoritative.

Curtis, G. W., ed. *The Correspondence of John Lothrop Motley* (11:94) suggests some of the repercussions of Maximilian's Mexican adventure beyond France, America, and Mexico.

15:57 Fabela, Isidro. "La Doctrina Monroe y la segunda Intervención Francesa en México" [The Monroe Doctrine and the second French intervention in Mexico]. *Cuadernos Americanos* 16:5 (1957), 201–14. Fabela argues, rhetorically, that the United States refused to enforce the Monroe Doctrine in any way during the 1860s French intervention and the period when Maximilian ruled Mexico.

15:58 Goldwert, Marvin. "Matías Romero and Congressional Opposition to Seward's Policy toward the French Intervention in Mexico." *Americas* 22:1 (1965), 22–40. Congress was more vigorous than the secretary of state in supporting the Monroe Doctrine against French intervention. Matías Romero, representing the Juárez government, was a powerful force behind congressional pressures on Secretary of State Seward.

15:59 Gordon, Leonard. "Lincoln and Juárez: A Brief Reassessment of Their Relationship." *Hispanic American Historical Review* 48:1 (1968), 75–80. The author dismisses the contention that Lincoln and Juárez corresponded, and that Lincoln promised U.S. assistance in the struggle against the French.

15:60 Hanna, Alfred J., and Hanna, Kathryn A. *Napoleon III and Mexico: American Triumph over Monarchy.* Chapel Hill: University of North Carolina Press, 1971. The first part of the book deals with the French background of the intervention, the second with Seward's diplomacy leading to the French departure from Mexico. The thesis is traditional, with Napoleon III portrayed as an exporter of monarchy and an opponent of U.S. expansionism. Bibliography.

15:61 Miller, Robert R. "Matías Romero: Mexican Minister to the United States during the Juárez-Maximilian Era." *Hispanic American Historical Review* 45:2 (1965), 228–45. Matías Romero worked effectively in the 1861 to 1867 period as a propagandist, fund raiser, and procurer of arms and munitions for his country. He is credited with paving the way for a new and friendly era in U.S.-Mexican relations.

Perkins, D. *The Monroe Doctrine, 1826–1867* (7:132) devotes about two-fifths of his book to U.S.-Mexican relations, with special emphasis on William H. Seward's policies.

15:62 Robertson, William S. "The Tripartite Treaty of London." *Hispanic American Historical Review* 20:2 (1940), 167–89. Although this work would be updated by consulting Bock (15:56) and the Hannas (15:60) on the subject of French intervention, Robertson has some interesting things to say about the evolution of the grand design of Napoleon.

U.S., Maximilian, and Mexico

15:63 Auer, John J. "Lincoln's Minister to Mexico." *Ohio Archeological and Historical Quar-*

terly 59:2 (1950), 115–28. This is an account of the mission of Thomas Corwin and his unsuccessful loan treaty.

Blumenthal, H. *A Reappraisal of Franco-American Relations, 1830–1871* (8:82) deals with the French intervention, in Chapter 6.

15:64 Case, Lynn M., comp. and ed. *French Opinion on the United States and Mexico, 1860–1867: Extracts from the Reports of the Procureurs Généraux.* New York: Appleton-Century, 1936. An early and still useful attempt to get at the tricky problem of French public opinion during the American Civil War. The author's long and detailed study of French diplomacy in the mid-19th century has borne rich fruit with *The United States and France: Civil War Diplomacy* (11:34), written with Warren Spencer, a work that has every promise of remaining *the* definitive work on its subject.

15:65 Ferris, Nathan L. "The Relations of the United States with South America during the American Civil War." *Hispanic American Historical Review* 21:1 (1941), 51–78. While relations with South America were poor before the war started, Secretary Seward worked hard to improve them, with conspicuous success. A good summary of major diplomatic problems during the Civil War as they affected relations with South America.

15:66 Frazer, Robert W. "Maximilian's Propaganda Activities in the United States, 1865–1866." *Hispanic American Historical Review* 24:1 (1944), 4–29. In the face of opposition from President Andrew Johnson and others, Maximilian mounted a vigorous propaganda campaign in the United States, using the press, money, and other methods to influence public opinion. The author concludes that the effort was another example of Maximilian's blundering.

15:67 Frazer, Robert W. "The Ochoa Bond Negotiations of 1865–1867." *Pacific Historical Review* 11:4 (1942), 397–414. This was one of the leading *Juarista* efforts to obtain munitions in the United States.

15:68 Frazer, Robert W. "The United States, European and West Virginia Land and Mining Company." *Pacific Historical Review* 13:1 (1944), 28–40. This fraudulent mining company was tied in with projects for getting arms and men to the *Juaristas.*

15:69 Fuentes Mares, José. *Juárez y la Intervención* [Juárez and the intervention]. Mexico, D.F.: Editorial

Jus, 1962. Fuentes Mares examines Juárez's relations with the Tripartite Intervention of 1861, using Mexican, American, and European sources to set forth Confederate and Union responses to foreign intervention in Mexico.

15:70　Fuentes Mares, José. *Juárez y el Imperio* [Juárez and the empire]. Mexico, D.F.: Editorial Jus, 1963. This account of Juárez's relations with Maximilian and the French (1862–1867) devotes considerable space to the negative reaction of the United States to the empire.

15:71　Fuentes Mares, José. "Washington, Paris y el Imperio Mexicano" [Washington, Paris, and the Mexican empire]. *Historia Mexicana* 13:2 (1963–1964), 244–71. Fuentes Mares develops U.S.-French-Mexican relations concerning the effort to bring about French withdrawal from Mexico.

15:72　McCornack, Richard B. "Juárez y la Armada Norteamericana" [Juárez and American naval forces]. *Historia Mexicana* 6:4 (1957), 493–509. The author discusses two brief interventions of U.S. naval forces to help foil a conservative attack on Veracruz in 1860, and to prevent Santa Anna from landing at Veracruz in 1867.

15:73　Miller, Robert R. "Arms across the Border: United States Aid to Juárez during the French Intervention in Mexico." *Transactions of the American Philosophical Society* 63:6 (1973), 1–68. Miller has developed many parts of his narrative in more detailed articles, which are listed in his extensive bibliography. Also see Robert Brown, "Guns across the Border: American Aid to the Juárez Government during the French Intervention" (Ph.D. diss., University of Michigan, 1951).

15:74　Schoonover, Thomas D. *Dollars over Dominion: The Triumph of Liberalism in Mexican-United States Relations, 1861–1867.* Baton Rouge: Louisiana State University Press, 1978. In this analytical study of the Civil War years and beyond, the author argues that Union Republicans and Mexican liberals shared the ideology of laissez faire liberalism and collaborated in the U.S. economic penetration of Mexico during the 1860s and 1870s. Bibliography. These views are distilled in his essay in *Pacific Historical Review* 45:1 (1976), 23–45.

15:75　Schoonover, Thomas D. "Mexican Cotton and the American Civil War." *Americas* 30:4 (1974), 429–47. Cotton provided a basis for the expansion of

trade connections between the Juárez and Lincoln governments.

15:76　Schultz, G. A. "Lew Wallace's Mexican Project." *Civil War Times Illustrated* 14:7 (1975), 20–31. Wallace was a Union general and later governor of New Mexico who tried to give military aid to the *Juaristas.*

Confederacy and Mexico

15:77　Hanna, Alfred J. "A Confederate Newspaper in Mexico." *Journal of Southern History* 12:1 (1946), 67–83. This newspaper, called the *Mexican Times,* exercised little influence.

15:78　Hanna, Kathryn A. "The Roles of the South in the French Intervention in Mexico." *Journal of Southern History* 20:1 (1954), 3–21. A well-documented article describing the interrelationships of the diplomacy of the United States, France, Mexico, and the Confederacy during the French intervention.

15:79　Larios, Avila. "Brownsville-Matamoros: Confederate Lifeline." *Mid-America* 40:2 (1958), 67–89.

Owsley, F. L. *King Cotton Diplomacy* (11:24) contains two chapters on missions to Mexico and other efforts to obtain recognition by Maximilian.

15:80　Smith, Mitchell. "The 'Neutral' Matamoros Trade, 1861–1865." *Southwest Review* 37:4 (1952), 319–24. This is the first published of three similar articles on Mexican-Confederate trade.

15:81　Tyler, Ronnie C. *Santiago Vidaurri and the Southern Confederacy.* Austin: Texas State Historical Association, 1973. Vidaurri, a regional *caudillo* in northern Mexico, allied with the Confederates against both Washington and Mexico City. This well-written biography emphasizes international aspects of Vidaurri's activities. Extensive bibliography.

Confederate Colonists

15:82　Ellison, S. J. "An Anglo-American Plan for the Colonization of Mexico." *Southwestern Social Science Quarterly* 16:2 (1935), 42–52. Detailed here is William Gwin's plan during the Civil War for a

Confederate colony; see also Hallie M. McPherson's account in *Pacific Historical Review* 2:4 (1933), 357–86.

15:83 Frazer, Robert W. "Trade between California and the Belligerent Powers during the French Intervention in Mexico." *Pacific Historical Review* 15:4 (1946), 390–99. A story of actions and complaints of French and Mexican agents of U.S. federal officers regarding purchases of arms, munitions, and other goods; the United States proposed strict neutrality but tended to favor France.

15:84 Harmon, George D. "Confederate Migration to Mexico." *Hispanic American Historical Review* 17:4 (1937), 458–87. This shorter account considerably overlaps Rolle's extensive study (15:87).

15:85 Knapp, F. A., Jr. "A New Source on the Confederate Exodus to Mexico: The Two Republics." *Journal of Southern History* 19:3 (1953), 364–73. Knapp discusses a newspaper founded in Mexico in 1867 by a former Confederate.

15:86 Rister, Carl C. "Carlota: A Confederate Colony in Mexico." *Journal of Southern History* 11:1 (1945), 33–50. Rister comments on the attempts of Confederates, civilian and ex-military, to settle in Mexico; they were initially encouraged by the French, but as the *Juaristas* gained power Mexican hostility forced most settlers back to the United States.

15:87 Rolle, Andrew F. *The Lost Cause: The Confederate Exodus to Mexico.* Norman: University of Oklahoma Press, 1965. This fascinating study examines one of the more curious aspects of the American Civil War: The postwar exodus of Confederates to various foreign havens, Brazil, Egypt, Canada, and, most numerous, to Mexico. Students of diplomacy and naval matters will be attracted to the role of M. F. Maury in Mexico and the councils of Maximilian, but there are many other intriguing subjects as well. Extensive bibliography.

VENEZUELA BOUNDARY DISPUTE, 1895–1896

See Chapter 14 for references.

The Pan-American Movement

See Chapter 7 for earliest developments, and Chapter 2, "Pan-Americanism and Hemispheric Security," for general accounts.

Bernstein, H. *Making an Inter-American Mind* (7:87).

Inman, S. G. *Inter-American Conferences, 1826–1954: History and Problems* (2:280).

Scott, J. B. *The International Conferences of American States, 1889–1928* (16:14) collects the conventions, treaties, resolutions, protocols, recommendations, and reports adopted at the international conferences of American states.

Whitaker, A. P. *The Western Hemisphere Idea: Its Rise and Decline* [1600–1950] (2:284) examines the bases, real and imaginary, for unity among the countries of the western hemisphere, by a prominent Latin Americanist in the United States.

WASHINGTON CONFERENCE, 1889

See "Personalities," especially James G. Blaine.

15:88 Bostert, Russell H. "A New Approach to the Origins of Blaine's Pan American Policy." *Hispanic American Historical Review* 39:2 (1959), 375–412. Blaine called the first inter-American conference in 1881 in order to promote peace in the hemisphere and because of his fear that local wars might invite European intervention. The author minimizes economic motives as influential in Blaine's policy.

15:89 Bostert, Russell H. "Diplomatic Reversal: Frelinghuysen's Opposition to Blaine's Pan American Policy in 1882." *Mississippi Valley Historical Review* 42:4 (1956), 653–71. The author notes that Frelinghuysen favored a less active policy than Blaine, and that a factor in the cancellation of the Pan-American conference was its identification with Blaine's interest in increasing trade between the United States and Latin America.

15:90   Casey, Clifford B. "The Creation and Development of the Pan American Union." *Hispanic American Historical Review* 13:4 (1933), 437–56. Casey traces the history of the Pan American Union from its creation at the First Conference of American Republics at Washington (1889) through the Fourth Conference in 1910, and outlines the influence the United States wielded in the early years of the organization.

15:91   McGann, Thomas F. "Argentina at the First Pan American Conference." *Inter-American Economic Affairs* 1:2 (1947), 21–53. The author discusses the four main issues at the conference: problems of organization and procedure, a monetary union, an arbitration agreement, and a customs union. He concludes that Argentina's consistent differences with the United States meant that the new Pan American Union "was born with a South as well as a North Pole."

LATER PAN-AMERICAN CONFERENCES

15:92   Wilgus, A. Curtis. "The Second International American Conference at Mexico City." *Hispanic American Historical Review* 11:1 (1931), 27–68. Wilgus discusses the origins, proceedings, and results of the 1901 conference.

15:93   Wilgus, A. Curtis. "The Third International American Conference at Rio de Janeiro, 1906." *Hispanic American Historical Review* 12:4 (1932), 420–56. This essay discusses the origins and proceedings of the conference and the nature of U.S. participation; it was attended by Secretary of State Elihu Root.

Intervention Diplomacy and World War I, 1898–1919

15:94   Callcott, Wilfrid H. *The Caribbean Policy of the United States, 1890–1920.* Baltimore: Johns Hopkins Press, 1942. This old but still useful survey presents a traditionalist interpretation of U.S. policy.

15:95   Hudson, Manley O. "The Central American Court of Justice." *American Journal of International Law* 26:4 (1932), 759–86. This is a factual account of the origins, organization, work, and death of the court (1907–1919).

15:96   Kneer, Warren G. *Great Britain and the Caribbean, 1901–1913: A Study in Anglo-American Relations.* East Lansing: Michigan State University Press, 1975. The author argues that Great Britain conceded political hegemony to the United States in the Caribbean area after the Spanish-Cuban-American War, but insisted on an economic open door and equal opportunity in financial and commercial matters.

15:97   Munro, Dana G. *Intervention and Dollar Diplomacy in the Caribbean, 1900–1921.* Princeton, N.J.: Princeton University Press, 1964. A well-documented, comprehensive book which argues that U.S. motives were basically political rather than economic. The United States wanted to end political instability in the area to eliminate potential danger to U.S. security.

THE CUBAN QUESTION

See "Personalities," especially Theodore Roosevelt, William Howard Taft, Leonard Wood.

15:98   Cosmas, Graham A. "Securing the Fruits of Victory: The United States Army Occupies Cuba, 1898–1899." *Military Affairs* 38:3 (1974), 85–91. The author lauds the army of occupation as well organized, well administered, and working for Cuba's improvement.

15:99   Gillette, Howard, Jr. "The Military Occupation of Cuba, 1899–1902: Workshop for American Progressivism." *American Quarterly* 25:4 (1973), 410–25. Cuban occupation is seen as an initial attempt at administrative leadership to reform society through education, business-type efficiency, and responsible executive leadership. Success in Cuba stimulated the growing progressive reform movement in the United States.

15:100   Healy, David F. *The United States in Cuba, 1898–1902: Generals, Politicians, and the Search for Policy.* Madison: University of Wisconsin Press, 1963. Discusses the different views of Americans during the occupation period on the U.S. role in Cuba and the island's future; ultimately, U.S. policy was established by the Platt Amendment and the Reciprocity Treaty of 1902. Healy argues that the decisions were made by soldiers, politicians, and civil servants rather than by businessmen. Bibliography.

Hitchman, J. H. *Leonard Wood and Cuban Independence, 1898–1902* (15:27).

15:101　Millett, Allan R. *The Politics of Intervention: The Military Occupation of Cuba, 1906–1909.* Columbus: Ohio State University Press, 1968. A well-documented account of American policy, from the Cuban and U.S. perspectives; not especially critical of U.S. policy.

15:102　Pérez, Louis A., Jr. "Supervision of a Protectorate: The United States and the Cuban Army, 1898–1908." *Hispanic American Historical Review* 52:2 (1972), 250–71. It is an account of the changing role of the Cuban army. The army became a rural guard assisting in the establishment of order and the success of American occupation.

15:103　Smith, Robert F. "Cuba: Laboratory for Dollar Diplomacy, 1898–1917." *Historian* 28:4 (1966), 586–609. The author discusses Cuba as a laboratory for the tactical development of dollar diplomacy, the basic tactics of which were first implemented in Cuba. U.S. policy, according to the author, contributed to Cuban instability and intense Yankeephobia.

PLATT AMENDMENT

See "Personalities," especially Orville H. Platt (under "Others").

15:104　Cummins, Lejeune. "The Formulation of the 'Platt' Amendment." *Americas* 23:4 (1967), 370–89. Elihu Root and Leonard Wood were the principal authors of the amendment, and Senator Orville Platt had little to do with it. The sole purpose of the amendment, Cummins argues, was strategic.

Hitchman, J. H. "Platt Amendment Revisited: A Bibliographical Survey" (15:1) is an excellent review of the literature on the Platt Amendment seen from both the Cuban and U.S. perspectives.

15:105　Roig de Leuchsenring, Emilio. *Historia de la Enmienda Platt* [History of the Platt Amendment]. 2 vols. Havana: Cultural, S.A., 1935. This is a critical account of the history of the Platt Amendment (1901–1935) by a prominent Cuban scholar.

15:106　Roig de Leuchsenring, Emilio. "La Enmienda Platt, su interpretación primitiva y sus applicaciones posteriores" [The Platt Amendment, its initial interpretation and its later applications]. *Anuario de la Sociedad Cubana de Derecho Internacional* 5 (1922), 323–462. A critical account.

THE PANAMA CANAL QUESTION

See "Personalities," especially Philippe Bunau-Varilla, Theodore Roosevelt; also see Chapter 7, "Isthmian Diplomacy."

15:107　Ameringer, Charles D. "Philippe Bunau-Varilla: New Light on the Panama Canal Treaty." *Hispanic American Historical Review* 46:1 (1966), 28–52. Ameringer argues that Bunau-Varilla played a central role in fomenting the Panamanian Revolution of 1903 and influencing U.S. policy before and during the revolt. The author concludes that Bunau-Varilla got a bad treaty for Panama and adversely complicated the future of Panamanian-U.S. relations after 1903.

Arciniegas, G. *Caribbean: Sea of the New World* [1492–1900] (7:8) is good on 19th-century isthmian canal ventures.

15:108　Arosemena G., Diogenes A., comp. *Documentary Diplomatic History of the Panama Canal.* Panama: 1961. This volume includes documents from the early 19th century to 1955, both private and official; a Spanish edition is *Historia documentado del Canal de Panama* (Panama: Universidad de Panamá, 1962).

15:109　Crowell, Jackson. "The United States and a Central American Canal, 1869–1877." *Hispanic American Historical Review* 49:1 (1969), 27–52. Crowell discusses the efforts of the United States during the Grant administration to secure exclusive control of a canal route in Central America, particularly in Panama and Nicaragua. An 1870 Colombia-U.S. treaty granting a route in Panama, to which the British objected, was not approved by the Senate.

15:110　DuVal, Miles P. *Cadiz to Cathay: The Story of the Long Diplomatic Struggle for the Panama Canal.* 2d ed. Stanford, Calif.: Stanford University Press, 1947. An older but still useful account, narrative rather than analytical, tracing the canal idea from 1502 to 1902. DuVal examines 19th-century canal plans and ventures in detail; a sixty-four-page appendix contains canal treaties from 1846 to 1903.

Ealy, L. O. *Yanqui Politics and the Isthmian Canal* (2:326).

LaFeber, W. *The Panama Canal: The Crisis in Historical Perspective* (2:327) begins by describing pre-1903 Panamanian nationalism, and then discusses the 1903 Panamanian Revolution and subsequent U.S.-Panama relations.

Mack, G. *The Land Divided: A History of the Panama Canal and Other Isthmian Canal Projects* [1513–1944] (2:329).

15:111 McCullough, David. *The Path between the Seas: The Creation of the Panama Canal, 1870–1914.* New York: Simon & Schuster, 1977. A popular yet well-researched and authoritative study which provides a valuable synthesis. Bibliography.

15:112 Mellander, G. A. *The United States in Panamanian Politics: The Intriguing Formative Years.* Danville, Ill.: Interstate, 1967. Bunau-Varilla is credited with organizing the 1903 Panamanian revolt. The author also shows how U.S. interest in and control of the canal zone influenced Panamanian politics (1903–1908).

15:113 Miner, Dwight C. *The Fight for the Panama Route: The Story of the Spooner Act and the Hay-Herrán Treaty.* New York: Columbia University Press, 1940. A good analysis, it focuses on the politics of the canal route selection in the United States between 1901 and 1903.

15:114 Patterson, John. "Latin American Reactions to the Panama Revolution of 1903." *Hispanic American Historical Review* 24:2 (1944), 342–51. The author argues that opinion in Latin America on the Panama Revolution varied widely from country to country; contrary to the standard interpretation, there was no unanimity in Latin America of criticism of the United States.

Williams, M. W. *Anglo-American Isthmian Diplomacy, 1815–1915* (2:330).

THE ROOSEVELT COROLLARY

15:115 Rippy, J. Fred. "Antecedents of the Roosevelt Corollary of the Monroe Doctrine." *Pacific*

Historical Review 9:3 (1940), 267–79. A historical survey of the financial problems of Latin American countries and European pressures on them prior to 1904, beginning with European intervention in Mexico in the 1860s.

15:116 Rippy, J. Fred. "The Initiation of the Customs Receivership in the Dominican Republic." *Hispanic American Historical Review* 17:4 (1937), 419–57. Theodore Roosevelt's motives included the desire to protect lives and economic interests, fear of European intervention, willingness to cater to expansionists, and desire to aid the citizens of the Dominican Republic.

Venezuelan Crisis, 1902–1903

See Chapter 14, "The Venezuelan Controversy, 1902–1903."

15:117 Clifford, J. Garry. "Admiral Dewey and the Germans, 1903: A New Perspective." *Mid-America* 49:3 (1967), 214–20. Clifford explores the German threat to Venezuela in 1903.

15:118 Hendrickson, Embert J. "Roosevelt's Second Venezuelan Controversy." *Hispanic American Historical Review* 50:3 (1970), 482–98. This essay covers the years 1904 to 1908, when U.S. claims against Venezuela went unsettled because of the opposition of President Cipriano Castro. Roosevelt's pressure contributed to Castro's unseating in 1908, after which U.S.-Venezuelan problems were solved.

15:119 Holbo, Paul S. "Perilous Obscurity: Public Diplomacy and the Press in the Venezuelan Crisis, 1902–1903." *Historian* 32:2 (1970), 428–48. Holbo discusses the views of various historians on whether Roosevelt issued an ultimatum to Germany in 1902, and concludes that evidence is not available to completely resolve the question. He assesses Roosevelt's use of the press in this crisis as an effective instrument of U.S. "public diplomacy."

15:120 Livermore, Seward W. "Theodore Roosevelt, the American Navy, and the Venezuelan Crisis of 1902–1903." *American Historical Review* 51:3 (1946), 452–71. After an examination of U.S. naval movements in the Caribbean during the crisis, the author concludes that Roosevelt's account of his ultimatum to the Germans, although embellished, is essentially correct.

15:121 Platt, D. C. M. "The Allied Coercion of Venezuela, 1902–1903: A Reassessment." *Inter-American Economic Affairs* 15:4 (1962), 3–28. Platt refutes the argument that the English, German, and Italian intervention was on behalf of their bondholders; rather, it was the usual contemporary response of nations whose interests had been harmed.

15:122 Rippy, J. Fred. "The Venezuelan Claims Settlements of 1903–1905." *Inter-American Economic Affairs* 7:4 (1954), 65–77. This essay reviews the claims presented to the Mixed Claims Commission.

TAFT AND DOLLAR DIPLOMACY, 1909–1913

See "Personalities," especially William Howard Taft.

15:123 Dinwoodie, D. H. "Dollar Diplomacy in Light of the Guatemalan Loan Project, 1909–1913." *Americas* 26:3 (1970), 237–53. The essay examines one of Secretary of State Philander Knox's loan projects—the Guatemalan refunding scheme.

15:124 Munro, Dana G. "Dollar Diplomacy in Nicaragua, 1909–1913." *Hispanic American Historical Review* 38:2 (1958), 209–34. This is a detailed account of a classic example of dollar diplomacy during the Taft administration.

15:125 Scholes, Walter V. "Los Estados Unidos, México, y América Central en 1909" [The United States, Mexico, and Central America in 1909]. *Historia Mexicana* 10:4 (1961), 613–27. An account of U.S.-Mexican negotiations on the neutralization of Nicaragua and the elimination of the dictator Zelaya in 1909; it emphasizes divergence of the two nations' approaches and the fact that the United States had no partners in active intervention in Central America during this period.

15:126 Scholes, Walter V., and Scholes, Marie V. "The United States and Ecuador, 1909–1913." *Americas* 19:3 (1963), 276–90. The authors deal with U.S. interest in Ecuador's Galapagos Islands and other matters; they describe the "hard-sell" approach of the Taft administration's dollar diplomacy in Ecuador.

Smith, R. F. "Cuba: Laboratory for Dollar Diplomacy, 1898–1917" (15:103).

THE WILSON ADMINISTRATION

See "Personalities," especially Venusiano Carranza, Victoriano Huerta, Francisco I. Madero, Henry Lane Wilson, and Woodrow Wilson.

The Mexican Revolution to 1919

15:127 Blaisdell, Lowell L. *The Desert Revolution: Baja California, 1911.* Madison: University of Wisconsin Press, 1962. Blaisdell discusses activities of the Mexican revolutionary Ricardo Flores Magón in Baja California, and their effects on Mexican-American relations in the early 20th century.

15:128 Calvert, Peter. *The Mexican Revolution, 1910–1914: The Diplomacy of Anglo-American Conflict.* Cambridge: At the University Press, 1968. This excellently documented book examines Anglo-American conflict and eventual agreement of Mexican policy. The relationship between British and American oil companies in Mexico and how this relationship affected British and U.S. diplomatic action is given some emphasis. Bibliography.

15:129 Fabela, Isidro. *Historia diplomática de la Revolución Mexicana* [Diplomatic history of the Mexican Revolution]. 2 vols. Mexico, D.F.: Fondo de Cultura Económica, 1959. This is an authoritative account (1910–1918), critical of the United States, by a prominent Mexican historian and official who participated in some of the events he describes. Volume 2 covers U.S.-Mexican relations during the Wilson administration.

15:130 Gerhard, Peter. "The Socialist Invasion of Baja California, 1911." *Pacific Historical Review* 15:3 (1946), 295–304. The Flores Magón brothers attempted to invade northern Baja with a filibuster band, but were defeated. Those who fled back to the United States were tried in Los Angeles for violation of U.S. neutrality laws.

15:131 Gilderhus, Mark T. *Diplomacy and Revolution: U.S.-Mexican Relations under Wilson and Carranza.* Tucson: University of Arizona Press, 1977. This book analyzes Wilson's policy in Mexico (1915–1921). The author argues that Wilson wanted to restrain the Mexican Revolution within the confines of liberal capitalism, while Carranza worked to maintain Mexico's national self-determination. Extensive bibliography.

15:132　Haley, P. Edward. *Revolution and Intervention: The Diplomacy of Taft and Wilson with Mexico, 1910–1917.* Cambridge, Mass.: MIT Press, 1970. This account surveys U.S. policy during the early years of the Mexican Revolution.

15:133　Hill, Larry D. *Emissaries to a Revolution: Woodrow Wilson's Executive Agents in Mexico.* Baton Rouge: Louisiana State University Press, 1973. A well-researched and well-written book which deals with the ten executive agents and several unofficial agents Wilson sent to Mexico (1913–1921) to deliver messages (ultimata or threats) and report on the Mexican reactions.

15:134　Pletcher, David M. "An American Mining Company in the Mexican Revolutions of 1911–1920." *Journal of Modern History* 20:1 (1948), 19–26. Using the example of the Chicago Exploration Company, involved in silver-copper operations in northern Mexico, Pletcher demonstrates the disastrous effects of the revolution on some foreign enterprises.

15:135　Raat, William D. "The Diplomacy of Suppression: *Los Revoltosos,* Mexico, and the United States, 1906–1911." *Hispanic American Historical Review* 56:4 (1976), 529–50. Raat describes the efforts of the Roosevelt and Taft administrations to neutralize the *Revoltoso* (revolutionary) activities in the United States. The author puts some stress on the interest of the U.S. government in protecting American investments in Mexico.

15:136　Rosenberg, Emily S. "Economic Pressures in Anglo-American Diplomacy in Mexico, 1917–1918." *Journal of Interamerican Studies and World Affairs* 17:2 (1975), 123–52. The United States and Britain undertook efforts (not always cooperative) to get Carranza to end threats to oil fields and other investments in Mexico. The author argues that U.S. and British policy was not dictated by their oil interests.

15:137　Teitelbaum, Louis M. *Woodrow Wilson and the Mexican Revolution (1913–1916): A History of United States–Mexican Relations from the Murder of Madero until Villa's Provocation across the Border.* New York: Exposition, 1967. The author's uncle played a role in the events described; Wilson's policy is critically evaluated, but Teitelbaum notes that war

was avoided and the results could have been worse than they were.

15:138　Turner, Frederick C. "Anti-Americanism in Mexico, 1910–1913." *Hispanic American Historical Review* 47:4 (1967), 502–18. Anti-American sentiment during the early years of the Mexican Revolution was stimulated by personal animosity against American revolutionary fighters and attempts of Mexican factions to win support through appeals to xenophobic nationalism.

Tampico and Veracruz, 1913–1914

15:139　Baecker, Thomas. "The Arms of the *'Ypiranga'*: The German Side." *Americas* 30:1 (1973), 1–17. The Hamburg-American Line's *Ypiranga* sailed from Hamburg in March 1914, for Veracruz, Mexico, with an arms shipment of mixed origin. Transportation was "the only German role" in the transaction, and when U.S. forces seized Veracruz to prevent arms from reaching the Mexican government of Victoriano Huerta, the German government did not at first realize they were the cause.

15:140　Fabela, Isidro. *Documentos históricos de la Revolución Mexicana: Revolución y Regimen Constitucionalistica: Vol. III: Carranza, Wilson y el ABC* [Historical documents of the Mexican Revolution: the constitutionalist revolution and regime: Vol. III: Carranza, Wilson, and the ABC]. Mexico, D.F.: Fondo de Cultura Económica, 1962. Fabela, Carranza's foreign minister, concludes, in his editorial comments in this volume of over one hundred documents for the April-October 1914 period, that Carranza won a diplomatic victory over the United States in 1914.

15:141　Hinckley, Ted C. "Wilson, Huerta, and the Twenty-One Gun Salute." *Historian* 22:2 (1960), 197–206. This is a useful short account of the Tampico and Veracruz incidents of April 1914. The author concludes that Wilson's opposition to Huerta accounted for his stubbornness during these events.

Lutzker, M. A. "Can the Peace Movement Prevent War? The U.S.-Mexican Crisis of April 1914" (16:103).

15:142　Meyer, Michael C. "The Arms of the *Ypiranga.*" *Hispanic American Historical Review* 50:3 (1970), 543–56. It is argued that the arms carried to Mexico by the *Ypiranga* in April 1914, creating the Veracruz incident, had been purchased in the United States by German agents for Mexico, and that the arms provided Woodrow Wilson with an excuse for the final effort to oust Huerta.

15:143   Quirk, Robert E. *An Affair of Honor: Woodrow Wilson and the Occupation of Veracruz.* Lexington: University of Kentucky Press, 1962. An important account that argues that poor communications and rumors contributed to Wilson's decision to occupy Veracruz in 1914.

15:144   Scholes, Walter V., and Scholes, Marie V. "Wilson, Grey, and Huerta." *Pacific Historical Review* 37:2 (1968), 151–58. Using British documents, the authors show that Sir Edward Grey thought Wilson's policy in Mexico was unwise and tried to change Wilson's attitudes toward Huerta.

15:145   Ulloa, Berta. *La Revolución intervenida: Relaciones diplomáticas entre México y Estados Unidos, 1910–1914* [The intervening revolution: diplomatic relations between Mexico and the United States, 1910–1914]. Mexico, D.F.: El Colegio de México, 1971. A well-documented, multiarchival study emphasizing the period from February 1913 through June 1914, it is pro-Mexican but not polemical. The author argues that the United States precipitated the Tampico incident as a pretext for intervention in Mexico. Appendix.

Villa and the Columbus Raid, 1916

15:146   Braddy, Haldeen. *Pancho Villa at Columbus: The Raid of 1916.* El Paso: Texas Western Press, 1965. This brief monograph deals with the various factual and historiographical controversies about the raid, and concludes that it was a product of Villa's resentment and desire for booty.

15:147   Clendenen, Clarence C. *The United States and Pancho Villa: A Study in Unconventional Diplomacy.* Ithaca, N.Y.: Cornell University Press, 1961. This is a detailed account of Villa's activities (1910–1917) which led to the Pershing expedition of 1916–1917.

15:148   Katz, Friedrich. "Pancho-Villa and the Attack on Columbus, New Mexico." *American Historical Review* 83:1 (1978), 101–30. Katz discusses the reasons for the attack and the results: the attack did much to imperil Mexico's precarious independence, but the Pershing expedition failure to capture Villa did much to repair the damage.

15:149   Sandos, James A. "German Involvement in Northern Mexico, 1915–1916: A New Look at the Columbus Raid." *Hispanic American Historical Review* 50:1 (1970), 70–88. Sandos suggests that Villa might have been influenced indirectly by German interests when he decided to raid Columbus, New Mexico, in March 1916.

U.S. and Recognition of Carranza, 1915–1919

15:150   Gilderhus, Mark T. "The United States and Carranza, 1917: The Question of *de jure* Recognition." *Americas* 29:2 (1972), 214–31. Gilderhus discusses German influence in Mexico and its role in influencing the United States to recognize the Carranza government in August 1917.

15:151   Harris, Charles H., III, and Sadler, Louis R. "The Plan of San Diego and the Mexican–United States War Crisis of 1916: A Reexamination." *Hispanic American Historical Review* 58:3 (1978), 381–408. The plan of San Diego (1915) called for a general uprising to gain independence for Texas, New Mexico, Arizona, California, and Colorado. This article describes the plan and Carranza's interest in it: as a threat to get diplomatic recognition from the United States in 1915, and a way of trying to persuade Pershing's intervention forces to withdraw in 1916.

15:152   Kahle, Louis G. "Robert Lansing and the Recognition of Venustiano Carranza." *Hispanic American Historical Review* 38:3 (1958), 353–72. Secretary of State Lansing promoted U.S. recognition of the Carranza government because of his concern with relations between the United States and European countries (especially Germany).

15:153   Meyer, Michael C. "The Mexican-German Conspiracy of 1915." *Americas* 23:1 (1966), 76–89. Meyer discusses German activity in Mexico and its role in the decision of the United States to recognize Carranza in 1915.

15:154   Trow, Clifford W. "Woodrow Wilson and the Mexican Interventionist Movement of 1919." *Journal of American History* 58:1 (1971), 46–72. Anti-Mexican elements in the United States sought to force U.S. intervention and oust Carranza in 1919. Senators Albert Fall and Henry Cabot Lodge and Secretary of State Lansing cooperated with the interventionists whose plans President Wilson resisted.

Intervention in Central America/Caribbean

15:155 Baker, George W., Jr. "Ideas and Realities in the Wilson Administration's Relations with Honduras." *Americas* 21:1 (1964), 3–19. Wilson's Honduran relations (1913–1921) provide an excellent case study of the evolution of his Latin American policy from its idealistic conception to its realistic climax.

15:156 Baker, George W., Jr. "The Wilson Administration and Cuba, 1913–1921." *Mid-America* 46:1 (1964), 48–63. Wilson, like his predecessors, believed America had to play a paternal role until Cuba was ready for complete independence. His hope of implementing his idealistic policies toward Cuba never were realized.

15:157 Baker, George W., Jr. "The Wilson Administration and Nicaragua, 1913–1921." *Americas* 22:4 (1966), 339–76. Baker describes the Wilson efforts to solve Nicaragua's financial problems, the negotiation of the Bryan-Chamorro Treaty, and other events. The author, seeing Wilson's policy as interventionist, argues that the central objective was the financial and political stabilization of Nicaragua.

15:158 Baker, George W., Jr. "The Wilson Administration and Panama, 1913–1921." *Journal of Inter-American Studies* 8:2 (1966), 279–93. This is a detailed account of U.S. pressure on canal issues, economic and financial questions, and military intervention.

15:159 Baker, George W., Jr. "The Woodrow Wilson Administration and Guatemalan Relations." *Historian* 27:2 (1965), 155–69. An account of relations during the dictatorship of Manuel Estrada Cabrera in Guatemala which concludes that the Wilson administration accomplished little during this period.

15:160 Baker, George W., Jr. "Woodrow Wilson's Use of the Non-Recognition Policy in Costa Rica." *Americas* 22:1 (1965), 3–21. The application of Wilson's nonrecognition policy during the Tinoco regime (1917–1919), the author believes, was ill conceived and harmed U.S. interests in Costa Rica.

15:161 Calder, Bruce J. "Caudillos and Gavilleros versus the United States Marines: Guerrilla Insurgency during the Dominican Intervention, 1916–1924." *Hispanic American Historical Review* 58:4 (1978), 649–75. Calder discusses in detail the war between U.S. marines and Dominican guerrillas between 1917 and 1922. The guerrillas had some political motives, but also opposed the marines because of the U.S. intervention, the commission of atrocities, and racial discrimination.

15:162 Coker, William S. "The Panama Canal Tolls Controversy: A Different Perspective." *Journal of American History* 55:3 (1968), 555–64. Coker discusses the canal tolls controversy within the context of the terms of the Anglo-American arbitration treaty of 1908 and the British desire to submit the dispute to arbitration. After this treaty was renewed in 1914, Wilson pushed for repeal of the discriminatory tolls law.

15:163 Healy, David. *Gunboat Diplomacy in the Wilson Era: The U.S. Navy in Haiti, 1915–1916.* Madison: University of Wisconsin Press, 1976. The author sees the Caribbean policy of the United States as a mixture of strategic considerations, financial interests, and ideological and racial assumptions. He examines Admiral Caperton's rule in Haiti in detail, and sees U.S. policy as having been improvised by military officials in Haiti.

15:164 Meyer, Leo J. "The United States and the Cuban Revolution of 1917." *Hispanic American Historical Review* 10:2 (1930), 138–66. The United States supported the Menocal government in Cuba, opposed by Liberals led by Alberto Zayas. U.S. marines intervened when the sugar cane fields were threatened by the Liberal revolutionaries.

15:165 Posner, Walter H. "American Marines in Haiti, 1915–1922." *Americas* 20:3 (1964), 231–66. In this detailed account of the problems leading to U.S. intervention in 1915 and of U.S. control to 1922, the author finds many factors motivating the United States.

15:166 Smith, Daniel M. "Bainbridge Colby and the Good Neighbor Policy, 1920–1921." *Mississippi Valley Historical Review* 50:1 (1963), 56–78. Secretary of State Colby made a considerable effort to improve relations with Latin America during the last year of the Wilson administration; hence Smith argues that Colby was one of the initiators of the good neighbor policy.

Latin America and World War I

15:167 Mock, James R. "The Creel Committee in Latin America." *Hispanic American Historical Review* 22:2 (1942), 262–79. Mock concludes that U.S. propaganda activities to combat German interests in Latin America during World War I succeeded.

15:168 Rosenberg, Emily S. "Anglo-American Economic Rivalry in Brazil during World War I." *Diplomatic History* 2:2 (1978), 131–52. World War I began the trend toward lessened British economic influence and increased U.S. influence in Brazil, particularly in areas like meatpacking, wireless telegraphy, banking, and shipping lines.

15:169 Rosenberg, Emily S. "World War I and 'Continental Solidarity.'" *Americas* 31:3 (1975), 313–34. The author examines the emergence during the war of a Mexico-Argentina bloc to challenge the leadership of the U.S.-Brazil bloc, and the disunity in the hemisphere that followed. Ultimately the military and economic power of the United States subdued the Argentine-Mexican challenge.

15:170 Tulchin, Joseph S. *The Aftermath of War: World War I and U.S. Policy toward Latin America.* New York: New York University Press, 1971. Concentrating mostly on the post–World War I period, the author suggests that at this time the United States resolved to abstain from economic and political policies that would lead to military intervention and also that the United States supported its citizens' economic expansion in the area of Latin America. Nonintervention and dollar diplomacy were common in U.S. policy.

Relations with Individual Nations

MEXICO

See Chapter 9, "U.S.-Mexican Diplomatic Relations"; also see "The Mexican Revolution to 1919," above.

15:171 Anderson (Relyea), Pauline S. *Diplomatic Relations between the United States and Mexico under*

Porfirio Diaz, 1876–1910. Northampton, Mass.: Smith College Studies in History, 1924. A survey which provides the details of the major problems of the period.

Carreño, A. M. *La diplomacía extraordinaria entre México y Estados Unidos* (9:16).

Cline, H. F. *The United States and Mexico* (2:299) deals largely with the post-1910 era.

15:172 Cosío Villegas, Daniel. *Historia moderna de México: El Porfiriato, la vida política exterior* [Modern history of Mexico: the foreign policy of the Porfiriato]. 2 vols. Mexico, D.F.: Editorial Hermes, 1960–1963. Volume 2 includes a detailed account, based on Mexican and U.S. sources, of relationships between 1876 and 1910. The author, a prominent Mexican historian, gives the Mexican perspective, but maintains relative objectivity.

15:173 Cosío Villegas, Daniel. *The United States versus Porfirio Díaz.* Trans. by Nettie Lee Benson. Lincoln: University of Nebraska Press, 1964. A well-documented, interesting account of the two-year struggle (1876–1878) of the Díaz government for recognition by the United States.

Schmitt, K. M. *Mexico and the United States, 1821–1973: Conflict and Coexistence* (2:301) provides a recent survey, with two chapters on the period 1850 to 1920.

15:174 Smith, Robert F. *The United States and Revolutionary Nationalism in Mexico, 1916–1932.* Chicago: University of Chicago Press, 1972. A well-researched account of the reaction of the U.S. government and private economic interests to the Mexican Revolution in the period just before and subsequent to the adoption of the Mexican Constitution of 1917. The author sees Mexico as the model for socioeconomic revolutions in the hemisphere during the 20th century.

Zorrilla, L. G. *Historia de las relaciones entre México y los Estados Unidos de América, 1800–1958* (2:302) provides a comprehensive account from the Mexican point of view.

Special Studies

15:175 Clendenen, Clarence C. *Blood on the Border: The United States Army and the Mexican Irregulars.* London: Macmillan, 1969. This account focuses on a little emphasized, but important, aspect of U.S.-Mexican relations (1850–1930). Extensive bibliography.

15:176 Gregg, Robert D. *The Influence of Border Troubles on Relations between the United States and Mexico, 1876–1910.* Baltimore: Johns Hopkins Press, 1937. A specialized study, it focuses on one of the most durable and irritating problems between the two nations during the Porfiriato.

15:177 Hundley, Norris, Jr. *Dividing the Waters: A Century of Controversy between the United States and Mexico.* Berkeley: University of California Press, 1966. Concentrating on the period between 1906 and 1944, the author discusses the complicated questions of the division of waters from the Rio Grande, Colorado, and Tijuana rivers, more or less settled by a treaty in 1944. Extensive bibliography.

15:178 Kearney, Ruth E. "The Magdalena Bubble." *Pacific Historical Review* 4:1 (1935), 25–38. This was an abortive project for developing Lower California during the 1860s.

15:179 Knapp, Frank A., Jr. "Precursors of American Investment in Mexican Railroads." *Pacific Historical Review* 21:1 (1952), 43–64. Most of the article treats the period from 1867 to 1873.

Liss, S. B. *A Century of Disagreement: The Chamizal Conflict, 1864–1964* (35:175) is a concise review of a long-standing problem in U.S.-Mexican relations.

15:180 Pletcher, David M. "The Fall of Silver in Mexico, 1870–1910, and Its Effects on American Investments." *Journal of Economic History* 18:1 (1958), 33–55. While Mexico was a tempting field for U.S. investors in the late 19th century, the Mexican economic situation, and especially the decline in the value of silver, caused some of the investments, especially in railroads, to be unprofitable.

15:181 Pletcher, David M. *Rails, Mines, and Progress: Seven American Promoters in Mexico, 1867–1911.* Ithaca, N.Y.: Cornell University Press, 1958. Pletcher considers the work of William Rosecrans, Ulysses S. Grant, Edward L. Plumb, and others; he describes the expansion of U.S. economic influence in Mexico during the late 19th century.

15:182 Weber, Francis J. "The Pious Fund of the Californias." *Hispanic American Historical Review* 43:1 (1963), 78–94. Weber provides the details of the

lengthy U.S.-Mexican controversy over a fund established in the late 1690s to support Jesuit missions in the Californias.

CENTRAL AMERICA AND THE CARIBBEAN

See "Taft and Dollar Diplomacy, 1909–1913" and "The Wilson Administration," above.

Cuba

See "The Cuban Question," above.

15:183 Fitzgibbon, Russell H. *Cuba and the United States, 1900–1935.* Menasha, Wis.: Banta, 1935. An older but still useful account for the period it covers.

Foner, P. S. *A History of Cuba and Its Relations with the United States* (13:20) is a left revisionist account critical of the United States. Volume 2 covers 1845 to 1895.

Langley, L. D. *The Cuban Policy of the United States: A Brief History* [1776–1962] (2:314) argues that the Cuban policy of the United States differed from the nation's general Latin American policy and helped pave the way for Fidel Castro's rise to power. Three-quarters of the book deals with the period up to 1919.

Portell Vila, H. *História de Cuba en sus relaciones con los Estados Unidos y España* (13:23) is a well-documented, well-balanced work by a prominent Cuban historian, critical of both Cuba and the United States in its analysis.

Thomas, H. *Cuba: The Pursuit of Freedom* [1762–1968] (2:315).

Santo Domingo (Dominican Republic)

See Chapter 5, "The Haitian Revolution, 1789–1804," and Chapter 12, "Effort to Annex Santo Domingo."

15:184 Knight, Melvin M. *The Americans in Santo Domingo.* New York: Vanguard, 1928. A general his-

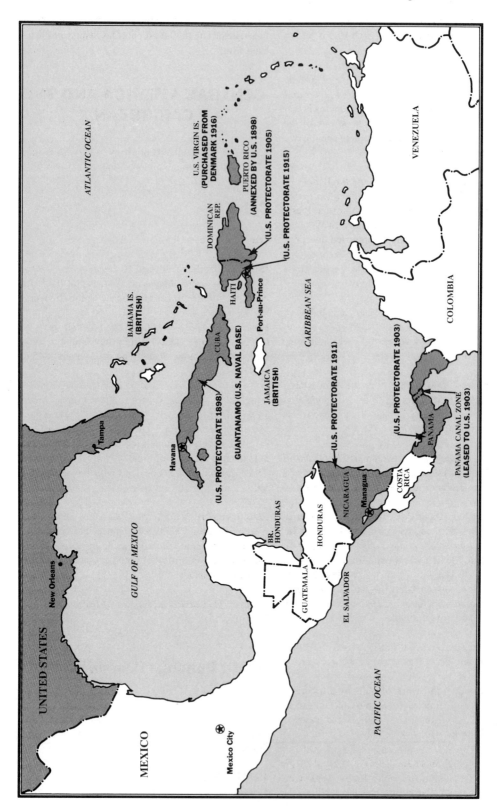

The United States in the Caribbean Area

ATLANTIC OCEAN

U.S. VIRGIN IS.
(PURCHASED FROM
DENMARK 1916)

PUERTO RICO
(ANNEXED BY U.S. 1898)

(U.S. PROTECTORATE 1905)

(U.S. PROTECTORATE 1915)

DOMINICAN
REP.

HAITI

Port-au-Prince

BAHAMA IS.
(BRITISH)

CUBA

CARIBBEAN SEA

GUANTANAMO (U.S. NAVAL BASE)

JAMAICA
(BRITISH)

(U.S. PROTECTORATE 1898)

(U.S. PROTECTORATE 1911)

(U.S. PROTECTORATE 1903)

Havana

Tampa

GULF OF MEXICO

New Orleans

UNITED STATES

MEXICO

Mexico City

BR.
HONDURAS

HONDURAS

GUATEMALA

EL SALVADOR

NICARAGUA

Managua

COSTA
RICA

PANAMA

PANAMA CANAL ZONE
(LEASED TO U.S. 1903)

COLOMBIA

VENEZUELA

PACIFIC OCEAN

424

tory, with good detail on the period of American influence in the early 20th century.

MacMichael, D. C. "The United States and the Dominican Republic, 1871–1940: A Cycle in Caribbean Diplomacy" (12:186).

15:185 Schoenrich, Otto. *Santo Domingo: A Country with a Future.* New York: Macmillan, 1918. This account contains a sketchy history of 19th-century American involvement in the Dominican Republic.

Tansill, C. C. *The United States and Santo Domingo, 1798–1873* (5:123) traces the development of American interest in Hispaniola and especially the lure of the West Indian commercial market.

Welles, S. *Naboth's Vineyard: The Dominican Republic, 1844–1924* (2:323) is a comprehensive account of U.S.-Dominican relations.

Haiti

See "The Wilson Administration," above; also Chapter 5, "The Haitian Revolution, 1789–1804."

Logan, R. W. *The Diplomatic Relations of the United States with Haiti, 1776–1891* (5:121) is the fullest account of Haiti-U.S. diplomatic relations. Logan finds little evidence of interest by Seward but more by Fish in "the Mole" or in a protectorate, and he argues that Haiti helped her neighbor remain independent.

15:186 Millspaugh, Arthur C. *Haiti under American Control, 1915–1930.* Boston: World Peace Foundation, 1931. The author, an economist and financial expert, served in Haiti for part of the period studied.

15:187 Montague, Ludwell L. *Haiti and the United States, 1714–1938.* Durham, N.C.: Duke University Press, 1940. This is a concise, analytical book in which the sections on Haiti remain valuable. There is a penetrating discussion of the quiet twenty years after 1871, with valuable appraisals of the differing stances of Seward, Fish, Evarts, and Frelinghuysen. Bibliography.

15:188 Schmidt, Hans. *The United States Occupation of Haiti, 1915–1934.* New Brunswick, N.J.: Rutgers University Press, 1971. The author argues that U.S. intervention in 1915 continued a pattern of expansionism that began in the 19th century. Although there were economic motives, he sees the 1915 inter-vention as a strategic move to prevent Germany from gaining influence in the Caribbean area.

15:189 Sears, Louis M. "Frederick Douglass and the Mission to Haiti, 1889–1891."*Hispanic American Historical Review* 21:2 (1941), 222–38. In his attempts to secure a naval base site at Mole St. Nicolas, Minister Douglass supported the political opposition to the Haitian president. Ultimately his mission ended in failure.

Central America

15:190 Bailey, Thomas A. "Interest in a Nicaragua Canal, 1903–1931." *Hispanic American Historical Review* 16:1 (1936), 2–28. Bailey provides details on the negotiation of the Bryan-Chamorro Treaty of 1914 and the U.S. intervention in Nicaragua in the 1920s.

15:191 Baylen, J. O. "American Intervention in Nicaragua, 1909–33: An Appraisal of Objectives and Results."*Southwestern Social Science Quarterly* 35:3 (1954), 128–54. This analysis of American policy combines self-interest and idealism in pursuit of certain objectives: the protection of American lives and property, and the strategic security of the approaches to the Panama Canal.

15:192 Cox, Isaac J. *Nicaragua and the United States, 1909–1927.* Boston: World Peace Foundation, 1927. Cox has written a scholarly and critical study which concludes with cautious and moderate observations.

Ealy, L. O. *The Republic of Panama in World Affairs, 1903–1957* (2:324) is a perceptive survey of Panamanian foreign policy, with emphasis on relations with the United States.

15:193 Hill, Roscoe R. "The Nicaraguan Canal Idea to 1913." *Hispanic American Historical Review* 28:2 (1948), 197–211. This essay traces the history of U.S. interest in a Nicaraguan canal route from the late 18th century to 1913; it is especially useful for background to the Bryan-Chamorro Treaty of 1914.

15:194 McCain, William D. *The United States and the Republic of Panama.* Durham, N.C.: Duke University Press, 1937. This comprehensive account covers the details of the 1903 to 1936 period.

15:195 Rippy, J. Fred. "Relations of the United States and Costa Rica during the Guardia Era."*Bulle-*

tin of the Pan American Union 77:2 (1943), 61–68. Rippy traces the economic development of Costa Rica (1870–1885), with special reference to the work of Minor C. Keith.

15:196 Rippy, J. Fred. "Relations of the United States and Guatemala during the Epoch of Justo Rufino Barrios." *Hispanic American Historical Review* 22:4 (1942), 595–605. Rufino Barrios ruled in Guatemala from 1873 to 1885; in hopes of U.S. aid in the modernization of Guatemala and in implementation of his plan to unite Central America, Rufino Barrios encouraged American investment in Guatemala.

15:197 Scheips, Paul J. "United States Commercial Pressures for a Nicaragua Canal in the 1890's." *Americas* 20:4 (1964), 333–58. Public and private interest in the United States in the Nicaraguan route was strong before the Panama Revolution of 1903.

15:198 Stewart, Watt. *Keith and Costa Rica: A Biographical Study of Minor Cooper Keith*. Albuquerque: University of New Mexico Press, 1964. Keith, an American, built the Costa Rica Railway in the 1870s and later was cofounder of the United Fruit Company. This is a model study of an American entrepreneur in Latin America.

Woodward, R. L. *Central America: A Nation Divided* (2:312).

SOUTH AMERICA

15:199 Cortada, James W. "Diplomatic Rivalry between Spain and the United States over Chile and Peru, 1864–1871." *Inter-American Economic Affairs* 27:4 (1974), 47–57. Cortada argues against the traditional interpretation that Spain's motives were imperialistic. Rather, the author suggests that Spain was interested in maintaining a definable global balance of power effective on both sides of the Atlantic. The United States, led by Secretary of State Seward, worried about the threat to the Monroe Doctrine.

Whitaker, A. P. *The United States and South America: The Northern Republics* (2:269).

Whitaker, A. P., ed. *The United States and the Southern Cone: Argentina, Chile, and Uruguay* (2:270).

Argentina

15:200 Dickens, Paul D. "Argentina Arbitrations and Mediations with Reference to United States Participation Therein." *Hispanic American Historical Review* 11:4 (1931), 464–84. Dickens discusses the Chaco arbitration (1878), the Andean boundary arbitration (1899), Misiones arbitration (1892–1895), and the ABC mediation (1914–1915).

15:201 Haring, Clarence H. *Argentina and the United States*. Boston: World Peace Foundation, 1941. A useful short survey of pre–World War II relations.

15:202 McGann, Thomas F. *Argentina, the United States, and the Inter-American System, 1880–1914*. Cambridge: Harvard University Press, 1957. The author studies Argentina's European orientation beginning in the 1880s and U.S.-Argentine competition for hemispheric leadership.

Peterson, H. F. *Argentina and the United States, 1810–1960* (2:287) details the major problems in the relations of two nations which competed for hemispheric leadership.

15:203 Rippy, J. Fred. "Yankee Teachers and the Founding of Argentina's Elementary School System." *Hispanic American Historical Review* 24:1 (1944), 166–69. Deals with the period 1868 to 1886, during which Argentina's public school system was established. President Sarmiento, much influenced by Horace Mann and his successors, brought many American teachers, mainly women, to teach in the normal schools of Argentina.

Whitaker, A. P. *The United States and Argentina* (2:288) stresses Argentine history as well as relations with the United States.

Brazil

15:204 Abranches, C. D. de. *Rio Branco e a politica exterior do Brasil, 1902–1912* [Rio Branco and the foreign policy of Brazil, 1902–1912]. 2 vols. Rio de Janeiro: Of. graf. Jornal do Brasil, 1945. This detailed account is from a Brazilian point of view.

15:205 Burns, E. Bradford. *The Unwritten Alliance: Rio Branco and Brazilian-American Relations*. New York: Columbia University Press, 1966. Burns concentrates on the initiation, execution, and implications of the shift of Brazil's diplomatic axis from England to the United States (1902–1912). Extensive bibliography.

15:206 Calhoun, Charles W. "American Policy toward the Brazilian Naval Revolt of 1893–94: A Reexamination." *Diplomatic History* 4:1 (1980), 39–56. This is a detailed analysis of the contention that Secretary Walter Q. Gresham intervened in the Brazilian Revolution to expand American markets. The author found that Gresham was not an economic expansionist but was a cautious secretary who pursued a narrow, nonaggressive policy based on traditional American diplomatic practices and international law.

Hill, L. F. *Diplomatic Relations between the United States and Brazil* (2:292) is a standard account on the subject.

15:207 LaFeber, Walter. "United States Depression Diplomacy and the Brazilian Revolution, 1893–1894." *Hispanic American Historical Review* 40:1 (1960), 107–18. The author argues that Secretary of State Walter Gresham decided that the United States should support the legitimate government of Brazil against its revolutionary opponents because of the assumed adverse effects on American economic interests of a rebel victory in Brazil.

15:208 Sensabaugh, Leon F. "The Coffee-Trust Question in United States–Brazilian Relations, 1912–1913." *Hispanic American Historical Review* 26:4 (1946), 480–96. The United States sought during the Taft administration to bring a suit against a group accused of monopolizing the Brazilian coffee market in the United States. After Wilson became president the suit was dropped, perhaps because of the Mexican problem and U.S. need for general support from Latin America.

Chile

Evans, H. C., Jr. *Chile and Its Relations with the United States* [1820–1927] (2:293).

15:209 Hardy, Osgood. "The Itata Incident." *Hispanic American Historical Review* 5:2 (1922), 195–226. A detailed account of a serious incident between Chile and the United States in 1891, involving the U.S. seizure of a Chilean ship. Hardy sees the affair as a

serious factor in developing anti-U.S. sentiment in Chile.

15:210 Hardy, Osgood. "Was Patrick Egan a 'Blundering Minister'?" *Hispanic American Historical Review* 8:1 (1928), 65–81. Egan was U.S. minister in Chile during the civil war in 1891; the author answers his title question in the negative, arguing that opposition to Egan in the United States was because he was a political appointee.

15:211 Kiernan, V. G. "Foreign Interests in the War of the Pacific." *Hispanic American Historical Review* 35:1 (1955), 14–36. This account, based on records of the British Foreign Office, emphasizes European, especially England's, interest in the war between Chile, Bolivia, and Peru (1879–1883). The United States considered England's motivations in the war as violations of the Monroe Doctrine.

15:212 Millington, H. *American Diplomacy and the War of the Pacific.* New York: Columbia University Press, 1948. U.S. policy during the war (1879–1883) is examined regarding Chile, Bolivia, and Peru.

Pike, F. B. *Chile and the United States, 1880–1962: The Emergence of Chile's Social Crisis and the Challenge to United States Diplomacy* (2:295) is a detailed analysis of the development of social problems in Chile and their effects on relations with the United States.

15:213 Vergara, Mario. *El Imperialismo Yankee en Chile: Resumen histórico del incidente del U.S.S. "Baltimore."* [Yankee imperialism in Chile: historical summary of the *U.S.S. Baltimore* incident]. Santiago: 1945. This account is severely critical of U.S. acts during the *Baltimore* incident.

Other Nations

Carey, J. C. *Peru and the United States, 1900–1962* (2:303) emphasizes economic relationships.

15:214 Dahl, Victor C. "Uruguay under Juan Idiarte Borda: An American Diplomat's Observations." *Hispanic American Historical Review* 46:1 (1966), 66–77. This account deals with the activities and reports of the U.S. minister, Granville Stuart (1894–1898), during a revolutionary period in Uruguay.

15:215 Frankel, Benjamin A. *Venezuela y los Estados Unidos, 1810–1888* [Venezuela and the United States, 1810–1888]. Caracas: Ediciones de la Fundación John Boulton, 1977. A well-documented and balanced account of diplomatic, commercial, financial, and cultural relations during the 19th century. The author pictures U.S. policy and action as very self-interested.

Parks, E. T. *Colombia and the United States, 1765–1934* (2:297) is a well-documented, comprehensive treatment.

15:216 Peterson, Harold F. "Efforts of the United States to Mediate in the Paraguayan War." *Hispanic American Historical Review* 12:1 (1932), 2–17. This interpretive essay focuses on the role and motives of the United States during the war of Brazil, Uruguay, and Argentina versus Paraguay (1865–1870).

Pike, F. B. *The United States and the Andean Republics: Peru, Bolivia, and Ecuador* [18th c.–1977]

(2:267) is an excellently documented, interpretive history of the three nations and their relations with the United States. More than one-third of the book covers relations through 1920.

15:217 Rippy, J. Fred. *The Capitalists and Colombia*. New York: Vanguard, 1931. Rippy deals mainly with the period after 1903, and emphasizes U.S. investments in Colombia.

15:218 Rosenberg, Emily S. "Dollar Diplomacy under Wilson: An Ecuadorian Case." *Inter-American Economic Affairs* 25:2 (1971), 47–53. President Wilson's reluctance to support American economic interests in Mexico was not typical of his policy elsewhere in Latin America. This article details the Wilson administration's pressures on Ecuador on behalf of U.S. and English railroad bondholders in that country.

16

Peace, Arbitration, and Internationalist Movements to 1914

Contributing Editor
WARREN F. KUEHL
University of Akron

Contributors
Calvin D. Davis
Duke University

David C. Lawson
University of New Mexico

Michael Lutzker
New York University

Contents

Introduction

Pacifists and internationalists constitute two pressure groups which have been exceptionally active in seeking to influence foreign affairs. They have sought to ameliorate warlike policies and attitudes, protested against involvement in wars, injected religious and moral values into debates over issues, worked to build support for the idea of a functional international community, and suggested constructive alternatives to alleviate crises and resolve disputes peacefully. They have labored in various ways, showing increasing adeptness and imagination with the passage of time.

Bemis and Griffin (1:57) devote a chapter to their efforts entitled "Miscellaneous International Conferences and Multilateral Treaties 1864–1914," which focuses on congresses, official and unofficial. The works cited primarily reflect what Sondra Herman, *Eleven against War: Studies in American Internationalist Thought, 1898–1921* (16:33), has characterized as the community internationalists because of a concern with universal standards of weights and measures, postal rates, monetary exchange, communications, and humane matters associated with the Red Cross, the treatment of prisoners of war, white slavery, opium, health, and the slave trade. A few politically related topics appear in sections on the Congo and Algeciras conferences. Bemis and Griffin cover the Hague conferences in a separate chapter on "International Arbitration and the Peace Movement."

Even a neophyte studying American foreign relations can quickly perceive how sparse scholarship was prior to the 1920s on these and related subjects. One reason lies in the immediacy to events, but the more practical explanation can be found in the limited range of U.S. interests prior to 1914. Historians of the time could see little relevance to the slow current moving their nation into the mainstream of international life with its attendant complexities and commitments. Also, in that earlier era, wars seemed less threatening to the nation's political, social, moral, and diplomatic life.

Not until the late 1920s and early 1930s, beginning with the pioneer works of Merle Curti, *The American Peace Crusade, 1815–1860* (16:85) and *Peace or War: The American Struggle, 1636–1936* (16:23), and Christina Phelps, *The Anglo-American Peace Movement in the Mid-Nineteenth Century* (16:89), did professional historians reflect a growing awareness of subjects of emerging importance. In the late 1930s and early 1940s a few other writers appeared, including Merze Tate, *The Disarmament Illusion: The Movement for a Limitation of Armaments to 1907* (16:162). Not until two decades later, however, did a new generation of scholars emerge. Sensitive to the extensive role of the United States in world affairs, aware of growing international obligations, and responsive to contemporary peace concerns, they sought to examine and record the ideas and efforts of a wide variety of earlier groups, individuals, and movements.

The formation of the Conference on Peace Research in History in 1963 reflected this interest, with several dissertations and significant books appearing in the 1960s. These works are marked by a wide diversity of approaches and perspectives. Some have concentrated on intellectual aspects and ideas; others have explored social attitudes and cultural phenomena which influenced the leaders of movements or diplomats; while several have been more traditional in describing events and the efforts of individuals and groups to influence policymakers. No agreement exists over terminology, which means students must wrestle with what each scholar means when he or she uses *pacifist*, *peace leader*, *liberal* or *conservative*, or *internationalist*, etc. Likewise, there is little agreement over what the dominant theme should be for various periods. Charles DeBenedetti's *The Peace Reform in American History* (16:26) attempts to provide one large umbrella concept to tie together highly varied movements.

Most of the literature for the period prior to 1914 has emphasized peace movements and ideas, considering international organization incidental to the thinking of peace leaders or the aims of societies. American internationalist thought and activity as a separate field of scholarly study, related yet distinctive from that of peace research, is of recent origin. It is marked by the 1969 works of Warren F. Kuehl, *Seeking World Order: The United States and International Organization to*

1920 (16:35), and Sondra R. Herman, *Eleven against War*.

The years from 1890 to 1914 have been most fully covered in both peace and internationalist literature, so that chronologically, taking recent dissertations into consideration, the middle to late nineteenth century is the only period yet in need of work. Topically, however, significant subjects still need treatment. There has been little concentrated effort to document the direct impact of either pacifists or internationalists on the formulation of policies. An institution-oriented study of peace societies and foundations which examines objectives in relation to achieved goals would go far to remedy this lack. There is no collective study of congressmen, senators, diplomats, or presidents of the peace persuasion, although biographies offer insights on an individual basis. One of the most influential groups, international lawyers, has not been explored as an entity, yet many of them held prominent positions in the State Department prior to 1914. Likewise, historians have virtually ignored the subject of international law, with no concentrated attention to the evolution of thought in the United States, why certain citizens responded so enthusiastically, what contribution they made to legal theory or codification, or what impact they had on foreign policy. Existing works merely describe developments without particular focus. There is as yet no history of the American Society of International Law, founded in 1907, despite its excellent *American Journal of International Law* published since 1907.

Although scholars have shown increasing interest in women's history, only a few studies have appeared on their role or efforts either as pacifists or internationalists, despite their prominence in both movements. Debate over whether the Department of State, historically speaking, has been a department of peace, would be worthy of analysis. The gap between performance and profession has often been noted, but no one has sought to determine whether American statesmen have pursued the peaceful settlement of disputes as an established policy, whether that has been merely a public profession, or whether it has varied over the years.

Other specific topics still merit consideration. Arbitration has been reasonably well covered (see especially Chapters 4 and 14 for the Jay Treaty and the *Alabama* claims), but conciliation, mediation, and good offices appear only as themes in several articles and books with as yet no comprehensive treatment on them either collectively or separately. Thus, despite an extensive body of literature discussing peace and internationalist effort, opportunities still exist for a new generation of scholars. There is now available extensive material once difficult if not impossible to obtain in the Garland Library of reprints (16:4) and in the Clearwater Publishing Company's microfiche Library of World Peace Studies (16:2), which consists of peace and internationalist journals, proceedings of peace congresses, and reports on conferences.

No effort has been made in this chapter to duplicate the many references in Bemis and Griffin to documents, reports, and other primary materials. Most of these, related to international conferences of the nineteenth and early twentieth centuries, were available when that *Guide* appeared. See also Chapter 15 for materials on the Pan-American movement, which contemporaries associated closely with peace and internationalist thought, and Chapter 12, which discusses expansionism and anti-imperialism.

Resources and Overviews

RESEARCH AIDS

While pertinent bibliographies and references aids are listed here, there are more extensive lists in Chapter 1.

Bibliographies

16:1 Atherton, Alexine L., comp. *International Organizations: A Guide to Information Sources*. Detroit: Gale, 1976. This guide is heavily based on a survey of book reviews in the major journals on international affairs. It contains a useful bibliographical essay, and entries are annotated. There are chapters on bibliographies, periodicals, yearbooks, document collections, library resources, historical background, the League of Nations and United Nations, collective security, and cooperative programs, both political and nonpolitical. It contains minor errors in titles and other data. There is an author, title, and subject index.

Boehm, E. H., ed. *Bibliographies on International Relations and World Affairs: An Annotated Directory* (1:136).

16:2 "Card Catalogue of the Peace Palace at The Hague [1800–1970]." New York: Clearwater, 1980.

This microfiche edition of approximately 600,000 catalogued holdings of the Library of the Peace Palace is especially useful because of the arrangement of its periodicals reference guide. This lists all articles in all serials in the library in many languages, arranged by subject, with each topic arranged chronologically. It is thus easy to follow the development of movements and ideas. The universal bibliography catalogue contains over 350,000 entries for books, pamphlets, and correspondence. These, too, have the unusual chronological arrangement. An introduction by Warren F. Kuehl is provided.

16:3   Boulding, Elise; Passmore, J. Robert; and Gassler, Robert S. *Bibliography on World Conflict and Peace: Second Edition.* Boulder, Colo.: Westview, 1979. The editors include over 1,000 entries in 26 categories, including references to other bibliographies and to abstracts, annuals, serials, and collections. With an interdisciplinary perspective, they focus on the structures of the international system and processes of peacemaking and conflict resolution.

Cook, B. W., ed. *Bibliography on Peace Research in History* (1:28) is a comprehensive list.

16:4   *The Garland Library of War and Peace.* New York: Garland, 1971. Although not designed as a bibliography, this extensive promotional book, with references and annotations to 360 titles, is an excellent guide to peace and internationalist literature. It contains an author index and is organized into 17 subject chapters by the editors of the Garland Library, Blanche Wiesen Cook, Charles Chatfield, and Sandi Cooper.

Haas, M., comp. *International Organization: An Interdisciplinary Bibliography* (1:37) is very useful for the early history of international organizations.

Hannigan, J. A., comp. *Publications of the Carnegie Endowment for International Peace, 1910–1967, Including International Conciliation, 1924–1967* (1:17) lists the endowment's pamphlet series and monographs from its sponsored research that contains information on peace activities and international law.

Holler, F. L., ed. *Information Sources of Political Science* (1:7).

Johnson, H. S., and Singh, B., comps. *International Organization: A Classified Bibliography* (1:38).

16:5   Kuehl, Warren F., comp. *Internationalism.* Los Angeles: California State University, Center for the Study of Armament and Disarmament, 1975. A listing of 260 works representative of the history of internationalism, this pamphlet contains sections on plans for the political organization of the world, community internationalists, the peaceful resolution of disputes, and stability based on an imposed peace.

16:6   Speeckaert, Georges P., comp. *Select Bibliography on International Organization, 1885–1964.* Brussels: Union of International Associations, 1965. This unannotated compilation includes journals and pamphlets, and covers private as well as public organizations.

Document Collections

More general collections are listed in Chapter 1, and other collections may be found in "Personalities," below; see also Chapter 38, "Document Collections."

16:7   Bridgman, Raymond L. *The First Book of World Law: A Compilation of the International Conventions to Which the Principal Nations are Signatory. . . .* Boston: Ginn, 1911. Reprint 1972. An early work tracing the development of international cooperation (1864–1911), it includes the texts of early conventions on the Universal Postal Union, Hague conferences, navigation (1899), sanitation (1881), submarine cables (1884), slave trade (1890), white slavery (1904), Red Cross (1864), telegraphy (1906), and weights and measures (1875). A 1972 (Garland) reprint contains a nine-page introduction by Warren F. Kuehl.

Chambers, J. W., II, ed. *The Eagle and the Dove: The American Peace Movement and United States Foreign Policy, 1900–1922* (16:96) brings together a valuable collection of documents, some not readily available elsewhere.

Deák, F., ed. *American International Law Cases, 1783–1968* (1:369) contains, in its 19 volumes, a full and complete compilation of cases arranged under the general categories of international law.

Friedman, L., comp. *The Law of War: A Documentary History* (1:370) consists of two volumes, which range (1600–1972) from reprinting Hugo Grotius's *The Law of War and Peace* to including documents from the courts-martial of William L. Calley, Jr., and

Ernest Medina. The introduction provides a useful survey of international law.

Hackworth, G. H., ed. *Digest of International Law* [1789–1940] (1:371) contains portions of diplomatic exchanges, rulings, treaties, and other data on recognition, expansion, neutrality, intervention, the Monroe Doctrine, extradition, nationality, and diplomatic codes. It supplements and updates John Bassett Moore's *Digest* (1:372).

16:8 Higgins, A. Pearce. *The Hague Peace Conference and Other International Conferences Concerning the Laws and Usages of War, Texts of Conventions with Commentaries*. Cambridge: At the University Press, 1909. A scholarly, detailed analysis that has great value to students of the history of international law.

16:9 Lake Mohonk Conference on International Arbitration. *Report of Annual Meeting*. 22 vols. Philadelphia and Lake Mohonk, N.Y., 1895–1916. Prospects for international arbitration and peace as seen by ex-diplomats, jurists, businessmen, educators, and other members of the elite invited to these gatherings (1895–1916). Speeches and discussion (printed verbatim) reflect the optimism of the pre-1914 era. The microfiche edition by Clearwater Publishing contains an introduction by Laurence M. Hauptman.

16:10 Manning, William R. *Arbitration Treaties among the American Nations to the Close of the Year 1910*. New York: Oxford University Press, 1924. This is a chronological compilation of accords and arbitral provisions in other treaties signed and ratified between or among American states prior to 1910. Contains a table giving the date of signature, names of signatory states, and the nature of each arbitration.

Moore, J. B. *Digest of International Law* (1:372) is a massive work of first importance (published as House Document 551, 56th Cong., 2d Sess.). It covers law as revealed in discussions, treaties, awards, precedents, and policies enunciated by government officials.

16:11 Moore, John Bassett, ed. *History and Digest of the International Arbitrations to Which the United States Has Been a Party: Modern Series*. 6 vols. Washington, D.C.: G.P.O., 1898. This is a thorough compilation of the arbitral settlements of the United States to 1898 by an established authority (published as House Misc. Document 212, 53d Cong., 2d Sess.). It contains texts of hearings, briefs, and related docu-

ments covering the Saint Croix River, Spanish spoliation claims of 1795, French indemnities of 1803 and 1831, and settlements under the Jay Treaty and the Treaty of Ghent. Moore's essay, "Historical and Legal Notes," contains valuable information on terminology, the development of arbitration, and its relationship to international law.

16:12 Moore, John B., ed. *International Adjudications, Ancient and Modern: History and Documents: Modern Series*. 6 vols. New York: Oxford University Press, 1929–1933. This collection contains fully documented reports of judicial decisions of international questions not recorded in the law reports.

16:13 Scott, James Brown, ed. *The Declaration of London, February 26, 1909*. New York: Oxford University Press, 1919. A collection of documents which includes an address by Elihu Root, "The Real Significance of the Declaration of London," which he gave at the sixth annual meeting of the American Society of International Law, April 25, 1912.

16:14 Scott, James Brown. *The International Conferences of American States, 1889–1928*. New York: Carnegie Endowment for International Peace, 1931. This is a collection of conventions, treaties, resolutions, protocols, recommendations, and reports adopted at the international conferences of American states. It includes a bibliography for each conference treated, an index of persons, and a subject index. In 1940 a first supplement was published under the same title, covering the period 1933 to 1940; it also contains an index of persons and a subject index.

Contemporary Periodicals

Each of the following periodicals is also available on microfiche from Clearwater Publishing.

16:15 *The Advocate of Peace*. Boston and Washington, D.C.: American Peace Society, 1837–1932. It conveys the growing stability of the peace movement and the American Peace Society and reveals continuing problems regarding auxiliary and independent groups. Early volumes reveal the disruptive impact of the debate over the justifiability of defensive war, and later ones of the problem of sanctions. The concept of a congress of nations disappeared by the mid-nineteenth century but reappeared in the 1890s as a paramount objective. The organ advanced stipulated arbitration, condemned the Mexican War, repeated warnings of the disaster inherent in growing sectional animosities, detailed accounts of the international peace congresses of 1843, 1848 to 1851, and 1890 to 1914, and revealed varying stands during the Civil War, Spanish-American War, and World War I. Introduction by David S. Patterson and Warren F. Kuehl.

16:16   *American Advocate of Peace.* Hartford: Connecticut Peace Society, 1834–1836. The organ of the Connecticut Peace Society and later of the beleaguered American Peace Society. It marked a distinct change of approach in comparison to preceding peace journals, with substantial feature-length articles, often by recognized scholars with an appeal to the intelligentsia. Still, it is clearly indicative of the intellectual foundations characteristic of earlier periodicals.

16:17   *The Calumet.* New York: American Peace Society, 1831–1834. Successor to the *Harbinger of Peace* (16:19), this journal is indicative of the near-chaotic disarray of the American Peace Society during the early 1830s. Ironically, it also reveals a growing sophistication in delineating the causes of war, thought on a congress of nations, the justifiability of defensive war, and the central role of the federal union in the future of the American nation.

16:18   *Friend of Peace.* Boston: Massachusetts Peace Society, 1815–1828. The world's first journal devoted exclusively to peace, it established a coherent body of principles and tenets followed by succeeding peace periodicals prior to 1860. Provides information on funding, membership, officers, and organizational structure of the Massachusetts Peace Society, its network of auxiliaries, and independent state and local peace societies. Reflective of the early peace movement's emotional efforts to convince an indifferent populace of the existential reality of war.

16:19   *The Harbinger of Peace.* New York: American Peace Society, 1828–1831. This organ of the American Peace Society, the first national body, sought to expand the geographic base of the peace movement. It also mirrored the movement's fundamental financial and institutional weaknesses. It contained the first serious discussions of a congress of nations and the justifiability of defensive war, and it printed lively exchanges of viewpoints reflecting the opinions of committed reformers and sympathetic observers. Useful in gauging the magnitude and makeup of the peace effort.

16:20   *Peacemaker and Court of Arbitration.* Philadelphia: Universal Peace Union, 1882–1913.

Reflective of the views of Alfred H. Love and his Philadelphia Universal Peace Union, this journal covers peace movements and pacifist ideologies. The *Peacemaker* espoused free trade, anti-imperialism, anticolonialism, and friendly relations with Great Britain. Its pages are full on arbitration efforts between 1890 and 1913. Introduction by David S. Patterson.

OVERVIEWS

Peace

16:21   Beales, A. C. F. *The History of Peace: A Short Account of the Organized Movements for International Peace.* New York: Dial, 1931. Reprint 1971. Largely devoted to late-19th- and early-20th-century peace efforts, this work offers a general survey of worldwide peace movements. It emphasizes the legalistic strain of both American and British efforts toward the codification of international law, disarmament, the establishment of a congress of nations, and the principle of stipulated arbitration.

16:22   Chatfield, Charles. "More Than Dovish: Movements and Ideals of Peace in the United States." In Ken Booth and Moorhead Wright, eds., *American Thinking about Peace and War: New Essays on American Thought and Attitudes.* New York: Barnes & Noble, 1978, pp. 111–34. Chatfield briefly reviews organizations and movements, noting diversities of goals and approaches (1815–1976), with a commentary on basic features despite differences.

16:23   Curti, Merle E. *Peace or War: The American Struggle, 1636–1936.* New York: Norton, 1936. Reprint 1971. Later monographs have expanded on many of the subjects Curti covers, but this work still remains a standard history of the broad peace movement in the United States prior to 1936. The focus is on pressure groups and their efforts to influence foreign policies. The reprint (Garland) contains a new introduction by Curti.

16:24   Davis, Harold E. "One Hundred and Fifty Years of the American Peace Society." *World Affairs* 141:2 (1978), 93–103. Davis emphasizes basic objectives, leaders, publications, and responses to wars in an uncritical appraisal.

16:25   Davison, Roderic H. "The Records of the American Peace Society." *World Affairs* 141:2 (1978), 177–82. Davison reviews society publications, monographs describing its work, and various depositories with records pertinent to its history.

16:26 DeBenedetti, Charles. *The Peace Reform in American History.* Bloomington: Indiana University Press, 1980. This interpretive study brings peace activity into focus with separate chapters entitled "Sectarian Reform" (1620–1763), "Revolutionary Reform" (1763–1816), "Humanitarian Reform" (1815–1865), "Cosmopolitan Reform" (1865–1901), "Practical Reform" (1901–1914), "Necessary Reform" (1914–1941), "Subversive Reform" (1941–1961), and "Deferred Reform" (1961–1980).

16:27 Ferrell, Robert H. "Peace Movements." In Alexander DeConde, ed., *Encyclopedia of American Foreign Policy.* New York: Scribner's, 1978, vol. 3, pp. 752–62. A brief but useful summary of movements, objectives, and tactics of peace workers and their relation to foreign policies (1815–1978). Bibliography.

16:28 Kelleher, Catherine McArdle. "In Peace and War: The Institutional Balance Reappraised." In Ken Booth and Moorehead Wright, eds. *American Thinking about Peace and War: New Essays on American Thought and Attitudes.* New York: Barnes & Noble, 1978, pp. 189–209. This analysis of congressional-executive decisionmaking notes the trends of nearly 200 years which have focused war and peace powers in the hands of the presidents. Emotionalism, limited congressional criticism or interest, its ineffective structure, and an unwillingness to challenge the executive have resulted in only limited and periodic efforts to crub the increasing power of the president to make war.

16:29 Lawson, David C., and Kuehl, Warren F. "Journals of the American Peace Society: *Advocate of Peace* (1837–1932)." *World Affairs* 140:2 (1978), 183–94. A description and analysis of peace aims and movements as seen through the journals of the American Peace Society, with a focus on objectives and leaders in relation to time and circumstances.

16:30 Whitney, Edson L. *The American Peace Society: A Centennial History.* Washington, D.C.: American Peace Society, 1928. Reprint 1972. A comprehensive but uncritical institutional history, it focuses on leadership, intellectual foundations, petition campaigns regarding specific threatened or actual armed conflicts, the struggle for a congress of nations, and official publications. Whitney offers a balanced account of William Ladd's contributions and is an effective counterpoise to works which explicitly or implicitly discredit early leaders of the society. The work contains valuable lists of officers, editors, and directors. Extensive bibliography.

Internationalism

16:31 Bolce, Harold. *The New Internationalism.* New York: Appleton, 1907. An early exposition on economic interdependence and an analysis of United States trade policy which strongly advocated reciprocity treaties.

Claude, I. L., Jr. "International Organization" (2:57) emphasizes conceptual developments rather than concrete bodies, showing the tendency of the United States (1776–1978) to be supportive of ideas and organizations despite isolationist tendencies.

Current, R. N. "The United States and 'Collective Security': Notes on the History of an Idea" [1900–1957]" (20:90) contains a thoughtful and somewhat critical review of pre-1930 ideas and their subsequent impact on foreign policy.

16:32 Faries, John C. *The Rise of Internationalism.* New York: Gray, 1915. This is one of the earliest efforts to record the evolution of internationalism by tracing the development of private and public agencies and societies.

16:33 Herman, Sondra R. *Eleven against War: Studies in American Internationalist Thought, 1898–1921.* Stanford, Calif.: Hoover Institution Press, 1969. An intellectual history which examines eleven leading thinkers, dividing them into those politically aware, the "polity" advocates, and those sensitive to human relationships, the "community" proponents. It covers Elihu Root, Nicholas Murray Butler, Hamilton Holt, Josiah Royce, Jane Addams, Thorstein Veblen, Woodrow Wilson, Theodore Marburg, John Bates Clark, A. Lawrence Lowell, and Franklin H. Giddings. Bibliography.

16:34 Hicks, Frederick C. *The New World Order: International Organization, International Law, International Cooperation.* Garden City, N.Y.: Doubleday, Page, 1920. A sound treatise by the law librarian of Columbia University on the development of the League of Nations, international law, arbitration, and the growth of international cooperation. It includes the texts of related treaties. The annotated bibliography is still useful.

Kuehl, W. F. "Internationalism" (2:59) provides a succinct summary of ideas and efforts by individuals and groups, from colonial times to the 1970s, to move the United States toward a more internationalist perspective.

16:35   Kuehl, Warren F. *Seeking World Order: The United States and International Organization to 1920.* Nashville: Vanderbilt University Press, 1969. The standard history of early American efforts to achieve a world organization. It shows the interrelations between peace and arbitration movements, international law, and diplomacy in the evolution of an idea culminating in the League of Nations. Extensive bibliography.

16:36   Kuehl, Warren F. "The World Federation League: A Neglected Chapter in the History of a Movement." *World Affairs Quarterly* 30:4 (1960), 349–64. This is a revealing account of an imaginative effort in 1910 of internationalists to commit Congress to the idea of a world organization through the Bennet bill, passed by both houses.

Mangone, G. J. *The Idea and Practice of World Government* (2:60) notes the impact of the American federal system on those thinkers structuring a model world government.

Osgood, R.E. *Ideals and Self-Interest in America's Foreign Relations* [1789–1953] (2:87) analyzes peace movements, internationalism, and the growing responsibility of the United States as a world power. The idealism of both the 1890s expansionists and the anti-imperialists was transmuted into the internationalism of the early 20th century, with the United States seen as leading the world to peace.

16:37   Reinsch, Paul S. *Public International Unions: Their Work and Organization: A Study in International Administrative Law.* Boston: Ginn, 1911. This is a pioneer effort to list and analyze the growth of international agencies as evidence of a changing world. It covers over 150 public and private organizations, with a focus on scientific, economic, and humanitarian concerns. Reinsch also discusses the evolution of administrative bodies and processes related to these developments.

Shafer, B. C. "Webs of Common Interests: Nationalism, Internationalism, and Peace" [1600–1970] (2:61) examines the growth of internationalist thought over nearly four centuries, including U.S. contributions.

16:38   Sohn, Louis B. "The Growth of the Science of International Organizations." In Karl Deutsch and Stanley Hoffman, eds., *The Relevance of International Law.* Cambridge, Mass.: Schenkman, 1968, pp. 251–69. Sohn reviews the evolution of the study of international organization in an historiographical essay. In reviewing the literature, he analyzes many American authors, their assumptions, and approaches. The footnotes provide an excellent bibliography.

16:39   Taylor, Arnold H. *American Diplomacy and the Narcotics Traffic, 1900–1939: A Study in International Humanitarian Reform.* Durham, N.C.: Duke University Press, 1969. Beginning with early concerns over the "opium problem," Taylor traces U.S. involvement in prewar conferences and commissions through cooperation with the League of Nations in efforts to curb production and traffic. Extensive bibliography.

Personalities

Additional references on individuals may be found in Chapter 1, "Biographical Data."

Jane Addams

16:40   Davis, Allen F. *American Heroine: The Life and Legend of Jane Addams.* New York: Oxford University Press, 1973. An analytical study of Addams (1860–1935) as a symbol of her times, in which important contrasts are drawn between her highly positive prewar image and the assaults on this image when she assumed a leadership role in the peace movement after 1914. Extensive bibliography.

16:41   Farrell, John C. *Beloved Lady: A History of Jane Addams' Ideas on Reform and Peace.* Baltimore: Johns Hopkins Press, 1967. This complete and well-researched life delves deeply into the motives that impelled Addams in her reform and peace endeavors. The latter encompasses approximately one-third of the work. The 514-item bibliography of Addams's writings is especially useful.

16:42   Herman, S. R. "Jane Addams: The Community as a Neighborhood." In her *Eleven against War: Studies in American International Thought, 1898–*

1921. Stanford, Calif.: Hoover Institution Press, 1969, pp. 114–49.

William Jennings Bryan

See Chapters 14 and 15, "Personalities," for additional references.

16:43   Coletta, Paolo E. "William Jennings Bryan's Plans for World Peace." *Nebraska History* 58:2 (1977), 193–217. Ethical and idealistic ideas are seen as the motivations behind Bryan's commitment to the peaceful resolution of conflict. The essay focuses on his conciliation accords (1905–1914), providing information on their background, responses, and the difficulties in implementing them when crises arose.

16:44   Smith, Willard H. "The Pacifist Thought of William Jennings Bryan." *Mennonite Quarterly Review* 45:1 (1971), 33–81; 45:2 (1971), 152–81. The origins of Bryan's pacifist views are noted by an examination of the impact of the Spanish-American War, his Christian beliefs, international travels and friends, especially Tolstoy, and his growing faith in the pacific settlement of disputes which culminated in his conciliation treaties.

Elihu Burritt

16:45   Burritt, Elihu. *The Learned Blacksmith: The Letters and Journals of Elihu Burritt.* Ed. by Merle E. Curti. New York: Wilson-Erickson, 1937. Reprint 1971. This account contains considerable background on crusades for arbitration and a congress of nations, led by the most prominent peace leader of the mid-19th century. The Garland reprint contains a new ten-page introduction by Curti plus three of Burritt's essays delivered at international peace congresses.

16:46   Tolis, Peter. *Elihu Burritt: Crusader for Brotherhood.* Hamden, Conn.: Shoe String Press, 1968. A detailed analysis of Burritt's thought, this study examines his views on the brotherhood of man, the cosmology of peace, and peace arguments. It emphasizes Burritt's role on the international scene, especially his campaign of "Friendly Addresses," the founding of the League of Universal Brotherhood, the publication of the *Bond of Brotherhood,* and the ensuing olive leaf and ocean penny postage efforts. A balanced perspective, it separates fact from myth but exaggerates the impact of nonresistance and underestimates the role of the American Peace Society in supporting related reform efforts. Extensive bibliography.

Nicholas Murray Butler

16:47   Butler, Nicholas Murray. *Across the Busy Years: Recollections and Reflections.* 2 vols. New York: Scribner's, 1939–1940. Butler's informal and rambling memoirs provide insight into his perspective and how he saw his role in politics, diplomacy, and peace efforts (1900–1947).

16:48   Chatfield, Charles, ed. *Before the War: Last Voices of Arbitration.* New York: Garland, 1972. Chatfield includes Nicholas Murray Butler's *The International Mind: An Argument for the Judicial Settlement of International Disputes* (1912), and John Haynes Holmes, *The International Mind* (1916). Both men saw the solution to war not in rigid legal systems but in promoting a willingness to understand and tolerate differences, although each sought different ways of attaining this. A thoughtful essay by Chatfield introduces their works.

16:49   Marrin, Albert. *Nicholas Murray Butler.* Boston: Twayne, 1976. Pages 137–188 of this intellectual study place Butler's thinking on peace, internationalism, and diplomacy into the perspective of his time and summarize Butler's goals and work. Bibliography.

Andrew Carnegie

16:50   Patterson, David S. "Andrew Carnegie's Quest for World Peace." *Proceedings of the American Philosophical Society* 114:5 (1970), 371–83. A brief but thorough examination (1890–1919) of the origins of Carnegie's pacifism and how it influenced his thinking on imperialism, wars, internationalism, his personal diplomacy, peace societies, and the creation of the Endowment for International Peace.

16:51   Wall, Joseph F. *Andrew Carnegie.* New York: Oxford University Press, 1970. Wall's lengthy account contains a useful discussion of Carnegie's peace philanthropy and his efforts at informal diplomacy among statesmen. Wall tends to downplay or ignore the issues that divided peace advocates. Bibliography.

Hamilton Holt

16:52   Kuehl, Warren F. *A Bibliography of the Writings of Hamilton Holt.* Winter Park, Fla.: Rollins College, 1959. This pamphlet contains 628 references to the writings of Holt, a leading internationalist and editor of *The Independent* magazine. It is indexed by subjects.

16:53 Kuehl, Warren F. *Hamilton Holt: Journalist, Internationalist, Educator.* Gainesville: University of Florida Press, 1960. Kuehl provides a valuable study of a prominent journalist who was a leading internationalist and peace advocate. Bibliography.

David Starr Jordan

16:54 Abrahamson, James L. "David Starr Jordan and American Antimilitarism." *Pacific Northwest Quarterly* 67:2 (1976), 76–87. This is a survey of the historiographical debate over American pacifist movements before World War I, and offers a new dimension to the debate by examining David Starr Jordan.

16:55 Burns, Edward McNall. *David Starr Jordan, Prophet Of Freedom.* Stanford, Calif.: Stanford University Press, 1953. A perceptive study of a leading peace advocate and internationalist who was the first director of the World Peace Foundation.

16:56 Hansen, Ralph W.; Palmer, Patricia J.; and Stein, Connie. *Guide to the Microfilm Editions of the David Starr Jordan Papers, 1861–1964.* Stanford, Calif., n.d. A biographical sketch, a description of various series, a roll identification, and a partial list of correspondents, plus a catalog of Jordan materials in other repositories that provide data on a prominent peace leader. Jordan was involved in the Bering Sea commission and served as the chief director of the World Peace Foundation after its founding in 1910. The collection also includes the G. A. Clark Papers covering 1890 to 1918 on the fur seals questions, and Alice N. Hayes, *David Starr Jordan: A Bibliography of His Writings.* (Stanford, Calif.: Stanford University Press, 1952). There are 184 reels of microfilm.

16:57 Jordan, David Starr. *The Days of A Man.* 2 vols. New York: World, 1922. Jordan's (1851–1931) role in arbitral, peace, and internationalist efforts are described as well as his conversion to pacifism and anti-imperialism. His position as president of Stanford University and his prestige as a scientist gave him stature and prominence in the peace movement.

William Ladd

16:58 Hemmenway, John. *The Apostle of Peace: Memoir of William Ladd.* Boston: American Peace Society, 1872. Reprint 1972. This collection of letters and reminiscences portrays Ladd as more of a strict pacifist than his published works. It fills a conspicuous void in the history of Ladd's peace testimonial but

must be viewed with respect to the total range of positions enumerated in his published materials. The letters in this volume (1819–1841) indicate that Ladd believed in the moral correctness of pacifism but was too prudent to irrevocably intertwine pacifism with peace activism.

16:59 Ladd, William. *The Essays of Philanthropos in Peace and War.* New York: Garland (1827), 1971. Ladd published his early peace essays (1820–1827) under the title *Philanthropos,* and these have been reproduced with an introduction by Peter Brock.

16:60 Ladd, William, ed. *Prize Essays on a Congress of Nations.* Boston: Whipple & Damrell, 1840. These six essays capped a decade's effort by the American Peace Society to formulate a definitive statement on the intellectual, moral, historical, and legal foundations of a congress of nations. Climaxed by Ladd's eclectic yet original essay, this work is the most comprehensive account available of the American internationalist's views of the proposed congress's organizational structure, inner workings, fundamental policies, and guiding precepts. A pioneering effort, it reveals Americans to be far ahead of British and European thinkers. Virtually ignored for years, it had its greatest impact upon internationalist efforts during the late 19th and early 20th centuries.

16:61 Schwarzenberger, Georg. *William Ladd: An Examination of an American Proposal for an International Equity Tribunal.* 2d ed. London: Constable, 1936. Primarily concerned with the proposals of Ladd and the American Peace Society, this work follows the development of the historical precedents of a congress, and renders a comprehensive analysis of the component judicial and executive elements of the proposed organization. It relates this agency to the structure and operation of subsequent international bodies and offers a limited biographical sketch of Ladd; but it does not treat all the approaches envisioned by Ladd. Bibliography.

16:62 Scott, James Brown. "Introduction." In William Ladd, *An Essay on a Congress of Nations....* New York: Oxford University Press, 1916. Scott's 40-page introduction to this edition of Ladd's 1840 treatise places Ladd's ideas in historical perspective.

John Bassett Moore

16:63 Megargee, Richard. "The Diplomacy of John Bassett Moore: Realism in American Foreign Policy." Ph.D. diss., Northwestern University, 1963. This is an interpretive study of Moore's influence on foreign policy through his position in the State Department; as a member of the Permanent Court of Arbitration (1912–1938); a judge on the Permanent Court of International Justice (1921–1928); and as teacher, writer, and adviser. It assesses his type of internationalism, neutrality policy, and role as a realistic exponent and critic of policies and positions.

16:64   Moore, John Bassett. *The Collected Papers of John Bassett Moore*. 7 vols. New Haven, Conn.: Yale University Press, 1944. This vast collection contains items of lasting value for students of international affairs. Especially noteworthy for the history of international law are "International Arbitration: Historical Notes and Projects," vol. 2, pp. 27–83, reprinted from *The American Conference on International Arbitration, April 22 and 23, 1896* (New York, 1896), and "Fifty Years of International Peace and the American Society for International Law," vol. 7, pp. 89–136, originally published in the *Harvard Law Review* 50:3 (1937).

Theodore Roosevelt

See Chapters 15 and 17, "Personalities," for additional references.

16:65   Olson, William C. "Theodore Roosevelt's Conception of an International League." *World Affairs Quarterly* 29:4 (1959), 329–53. Olson notes Roosevelt's support, both public and private, for a world organization, with only limited references to other contemporary ideas and attitudes.

Elihu Root

See Chapters 17 and 19, "Personalities," for additional references.

16:66   Bacon, Robert, and Scott, James Brown, eds. *Addresses on International Subjects by Elihu Root*. Cambridge: Harvard University Press, 1916. This collection of speeches (1907–1916), primarily to the American Society of International Law, shows Root's belief in the importance of the peaceful resolution of disputes, legal procedures, and an international court of justice.

16:67   Herman, S. R. "Elihu Root and Nicholas Murray Butler: The Polity as International Judiciary." In her *Eleven against War: Studies in American International Thought, 1898–1921*. Stanford, Calif.: Hoover Institution Press, 1969, pp. 24–54.

Jessup, P. C. *Elihu Root* (17:41) the second volume of this biography (1890–1937) is of great importance to students of diplomacy and international law, for it deals with Root's role in the Pan-American movement and the Hague conferences, and it includes an account of Root's work as the senior American counsel in the arbitration of the North Atlantic Coast fisheries dispute by the Permanent Court of Arbitration.

16:68   Scott, James Brown. "Elihu Root, Secretary of State, July 7, 1905–January 27, 1909." In Samuel Flagg Bemis, ed., *The American Secretaries of State and Their Diplomacy*. New York: Knopf, 1928, vol. 9, pp. 193–282. This old account is still a useful survey of Root's activities as secretary of state.

James Brown Scott

16:69   Finch, George A. "James Brown Scott, 1866–1943." *American Journal of International Law* 38:2 (1944), 183–217. This is a brief biography of one of the most influential international lawyers of the 20th century.

16:70   Nurnberger, Ralph D. "James Brown Scott: Peace through Justice." Ph.D. diss., Georgetown University, 1975. This is the only study of Scott who was the "Dean" of international lawyers. It examines his writings, his work for the Carnegie Endowment for International Peace and the American Society for International Law, his diplomatic missions, and his efforts to establish an international court of justice. Unfortunately, it covers only to 1920.

Oscar S. Straus

See also Chapter 18, "Personalities."

16:71   Cohen, Naomi W. *A Dual Heritage: The Public Career of Oscar S. Straus*. Philadelphia: Jewish Publication Society of America, 1969. Straus (1850–1926) was an experienced diplomat who played a major role in peace organizations prior to World War I; during the war he became a leader of the League to Enforce Peace. Extensive bibliography.

Straus, O. S. *Under Four Administrations: From Cleveland to Taft* (18:48) includes in his reminiscences references to conversations with European peace leaders and to his work as president of the New York Peace Society, which brought him into contact with the prewar peace movements.

Charles Sumner

See Chapters 11 and 12, "Personalities," for additional references.

16:72 Sumner, Charles. *Addresses on War*. New York: Garland, 1972. This reprint contains "The True Grandeur of Nations" (1845), in which Sumner sought to allay rumors of war with Britain over Oregon and with Mexico by developing the theme that the greatness of any nation rested in a policy of peace, while exactly the reverse was true of a militaristic state. The volume also contains other essays by Sumner on war, correspondence with his contemporaries, and an introduction by Ralph E. Weber.

William Howard Taft

See Chapters 14, 15, and 17, "Personalities," for additional references.

Campbell, J. P. "Taft, Roosevelt, and the Arbitration Treaties of 1911" (16:128).

16:73 Taft, William H. *The United States and Peace*. New York: Scribner's, 1914. Reprint 1971. A valuable source for Taft's views on the Monroe Doctrine, immigration, his model arbitration treaties, world organization, and an international court of justice, all from the perspective of historical background and contemporary events.

Andrew D. White

16:74 Altschuler, Glenn C. *Andrew D. White: Educator, Historian, Diplomat*. Ithaca, N.Y.: Cornell University Press, 1979. This thoughtful biography covers White's ambassadorship to Germany, his participation at the Hague Peace Conference of 1899, his role in the Venezuelan Boundary Commission, and his reaction to the Great War. Bibliography.

White, A. D. *Autobiography of Andrew Dickson White* (14:53).

Others

16:75 Atkinson, Henry A. *Theodore Marburg: The Man and His Work*. New York: Littman, 1951. An uncritical study useful in capturing the spirit and chronicling the work of a significant internationalist and U.S. minister to Belgium (1912–1914).

16:76 Baker, Adelaide N. "Planetary New Englander." *New England Galaxy* 13:1 (1971), 46–52. This uncritical review of the peace work of Emily G. Balch relates her ideas to social concerns, movements, and peace organizations.

16:77 Baker, Elizabeth F. *Henry Wheaton, 1785–1848*. Philadelphia: University of Pennsylvania Press, 1937. A biography of the American diplomat and

scholar who wrote the first major American treatise on international law.

16:78 Bartholdt, Richard. *From Steerage to Congress: Reminiscences and Reflections*. Philadelphia: Dorrance, 1930. This autobiography of a leading member of the American group of the Interparliamentary Union is useful in its comments and anecdotes covering his congressional career (1893–1915). The passages on World War I reflect the position of a German-American torn between loyalties to his peace position and his native country.

16:79 Doherty, Robert W. "Alfred H. Love and the Universal Peace Union." Ph.D. diss., University of Pennsylvania, 1962. This study of a doctrinaire pacifist covers Love's work and ideas, noting his attachment to religion, to peace, to other reforms, and to arbitration. It is somewhat critical of Love's limited perspective and ideological intolerance.

Freidel, F. *Francis Lieber: Nineteenth-Century Liberal* (11:228) includes a chapter entitled "Codifying the Rules of War," which is a basic reference for that topic in connection with the Civil War.

16:80 Levermore, Charles H. *Samuel Train Dutton: A Biography*. New York: Macmillan, 1922. This relatively unknown biography provides rich information because Dutton served as an administrator (1890–1920) in several peace societies which advanced ideas of international law and organization.

16:81 Parkman, Aubrey. *David Jayne Hill and the Problem of World Peace*. Cranberry, N.J.: Bucknell University Press, 1975. Hill (1850–1932) established his reputation as an educator, diplomat, delegate to the First Hague Conference, and an ardent advocate of arbitration and international law. He nonetheless displayed nationalistic qualities which led him to oppose membership in the League of Nations and the World Court. Parkman covers all aspects of Hill's career in an objective and thorough appraisal. Bibliography.

16:82 Trueblood, Benjamin F. *The Development of the Peace Idea, and Other Essays*. New York: Garland (1932), 1972. This compilation of essays compiled posthumously by friends consists of essays on Christian pacifism, arbitration, the Hague conferences, and other leaders. Most appeared in *Advocate of Peace*, which Trueblood edited (1892–1915). An introduction by Edwin D. Mead examines Trueblood in relation to the prewar peace movement; the reprint contains an introductory essay by Michael Lutzker.

American Pacifism and Peace Activity

PEACE MOVEMENTS TO 1890

See "Personalities," especially Elihu Burritt, William Ladd, and Charles Sumner.

16:83 Allen, Devere. *The Fight for Peace.* New York: Macmillan, 1930. Reprint 1971. In tracing themes of the peace ideology from 1815 into the 1920s, Allen examines the emergence of the early peace movement but overstates the pacifist sentiments of many of its leaders as well as the role played by Elihu Burritt. Written from the perspective of a radical pacifist this work offers stimulating challenges to more established appraisals but in doing so it underestimates the contributions of those nonpacifists labeled as moderates or conservatives. The reprint, in two volumes, contains an introduction by Charles Chatfield. Extensive bibliography.

16:84 Brock, Peter. *Pacifism in the United States: From the Colonial Era to the First World War.* Princeton, N.J.: Princeton University Press, 1968. This is an exceedingly detailed and thorough examination of sectarian pacifism through the Civil War, with some attention to nonsectarian concerns. The treatment of post–Civil War developments covers only 81 pages. Extensive bibliography.

Curti, M. E. "Pacifist Propaganda and the Treaty of Guadalupe Hidalgo" (9:177).

16:85 Curti, Merle E. *The American Peace Crusade, 1815–1860.* Durham, N.C.: Duke University Press, 1929. Reprint 1971. Curti emphasizes the growing coalescence of peace sentiments in the United States and abroad, and cooperation between the American and British peace movements on mutual concerns, such as stipulated arbitration, international peace congresses, and diplomacy associated with several international crises. He evaluates the realism and sense of mission of the American reformers and accurately identifies public apathy as the peace movement's most severe problem, but he overstates the significance of the New England Nonresistance Society and underestimates the intellectual contributions and organizational continuity of the American Peace

Society. The reprint contains a new introduction by Curti. Bibliography.

16:86 Galpin, Freeman W. *Pioneering for Peace: A Study of American Peace Efforts to 1846.* Syracuse, N.Y.: Bardeen, 1933. Galpin covers several early significant local peace societies (1815–1846) and their leadership. The work contains an invaluable narrative of press opposition to peace efforts and sees the early movement as an expression of the vitality of American humanism and a precursor of later efforts, especially with respect to the formulation of a structured peace ideology and strategy. Termination at 1846 precludes treatment of antebellum peace thought, particularly on stipulated arbitration, the Civil War, and international cooperation among peace organizations. Bibliography.

16:87 Lawson, David C. "Swords into Plowshares, Spears into Pruninghooks: The Intellectual Foundations of the First American Peace Movement, 1815–1865." Ph.D. diss., University of New Mexico, 1975. Lawson finds the Massachusetts Peace Society and American Peace Society dominant and significant in the antebellum peace crusade, and he gives less credit to the more pacifist-oriented New England Nonresistance Society and League of Universal Brotherhood. He focuses on attitudes regarding the nature and causes of war and recommendations for peace by tracing the evolution of specific concepts and tactics, and perceives efforts as more of a total involvement with peace, rather than an antiwar campaign.

16:88 MacDonald, Clyde W., Jr. "The Massachusetts Peace Society 1815–1828: A Study in Evangelical Reform." Ph.D. diss., University of Maine, 1973. Through a study of reform ideology associated with religion, the Enlightenment, and Federalist and Jeffersonian influences, MacDonald explains the emergence of the society. He also analyzes its leaders, motives, and work.

Merk, F. "Dissent in the Mexican War" (9:186).

16:89 Phelps, Christina. *The Anglo-American Peace Movement in the Mid-Nineteenth Century.* New York: Columbia University Press, 1930. Phelps focuses on international dimensions of the peace movement (1835–1854), with primary emphasis upon the efforts of reformers of the London Peace Society, and discusses the factors which influenced the international congresses of 1843 and 1848 to 1851. She covers attempts to establish a congress of nations and to promote the codification of international law, arbitration, and disarmament; included is a useful comparison between the 1840 proposal for a congress of nations and the Covenant of the League of Nations. Bibliography.

Schroeder, J. H. *Mr. Polk's War: American Opposition and Dissent, 1846–1848* (9:187) examines political parties and leaders as well as peace and religious groups, abolitionists, and literary figures.

Contemporary Writings

16:90 Beckwith, George C., ed. *The Book of Peace.* Boston: American Peace Society, 1845. These essays and broadsides admirably fulfill their intended objective as a sourcebook on the nature and causes of war and means to peace by the most important peace advocate of the later antebellum period.

16:91 Beckwith, George C., ed. *The Peace Manual: Or War and Its Remedies.* Boston: American Peace Society, 1847. Reprint 1971. A solid reflection of peace ideology and methods of persuasion. The reprint contains an introduction by Alice K. Harris.

16:92 *The First American Peace Movement.* New York: Garland (1815), 1972. This work contains Noah Worcester's widely distributed essay, "A Solemn Review of the Custom of War" (1815). It presented a wide variety of soon-to-be accepted doctrines, with considerable emphasis on the causes of war and human passions underlying violence. Worcester also discussed a federation of nations to adjudicate international disputes. David Low Dodge's influential "War Inconsistent with the Religion of Jesus Christ" (1815), and James Mott's "The Lawfulness of War for Christians Examined" are also reproduced. They reveal the strong religious appeal of the time to religious sensibilities. The introduction is by Peter Brock.

16:93 Jay, John. *A Review of the Causes and Consequences of the Mexican War.* Philadelphia: Hunt, 1849. An eminent jurist, reformer, and peace advocate indicts the legal justifications for expansion into Texas and the Mexican War (1846–1848). Jay found no legal or moral foundations for declaring war. It could have been avoided, and it represented an attempt to expand slavery and assuage national honor. The American Peace Society enthusiastically endorsed Jay's conclusions.

16:94 Livermore, Abiel A. *The War with Mexico Reviewed.* Boston: American Peace Society, 1850. Livermore applies a broad range of standard antiwar doctrines to the Mexican War in highlighting its moral and rational absurdity and the suffering on both sides. Thus, he denies the validity of American territorial claims, criticizes demands for retribution, and emphasizes the failure of America's political, religious, intellectual, and journalistic communities to prevent an unjustified tragedy.

16:95 Upham, Thomas C. *The Manual of Peace.* New York: Leavitt, Lord, 1836. This work by one of 19th-century America's most respected moral philosophers and peace theoreticians gave breadth and depth to the peace movement's analysis of the moral and rational nature of man, the legal and political foundations of a congress of nations, and the role of peace in world history. It is reflective of the peace reformers' implicit faith in progress and the essential goodness and rationality of man.

THE "PRACTICAL" PEACE MOVEMENTS, 1890–1914

See "Personalities," especially Jane Addams, Nicholas Murray Butler, Andrew Carnegie, David Starr Jordan, Oscar S. Straus, and, under "Others," Benjamin F. Trueblood.

16:96 Chambers, John W., II, ed. *The Eagle and the Dove: The American Peace Movement and United States Foreign Policy, 1900–1922.* New York: Garland, 1976. Chambers has compiled 85 "essays" representing a wide variety of peace advocacy. The views of major activists are included, with divisions for 1900 to 1914, 1914 to 1917, 1917 to 1918, and 1919 to 1922. Chambers's 83-page introduction is a composite analysis of ideas, their relationship to movements, and of attempts to influence foreign policies. Bibliography.

16:97 Chatfield, Charles, ed. *Peace Movements in America.* New York: Schocken, 1973. Chatfield's 22-page introduction thoughtfully analyzes peace movements in relation to political processes, social reform groups, values, assumptions, ideas, objectives, and problems, while the essays by established scholars cover 1890 to 1973.

16:98 Ershkowitz, Herbert. *The Attitude of Business toward American Foreign Policy, 1900–1916.*

Pennsylvania State University Studies, no. 21. University Park: Pennsylvania State University Press, 1967. The author uses business sources to show that many businessmen equated peace with growth of trade and war with its disruption. There was little evidence that the American business community favored United States entry into World War I. Bibliography.

16:99 Filene, Peter. "The World Peace Foundation and Progressivism, 1910–1918." *New England Quarterly* 36:4 (1963), 478–501. Filene sets peace activity within the context of progressivism and its characteristic assumptions. (See also Chapter 13, "Progressivism and Foreign Policy.")

16:100 Gianakos, Perry E. "Ernest Howard Crosby: A Forgotten Tolstoyan Anti-militarist and Anti-imperialist." In Charles Chatfield, ed., *Peace Movements in America*. New York: Schocken, 1973, pp. 1–19. This is an account of a poet and satirist (1856–1907) of the martial values.

16:101 Holcombe, Arthur N. "Edwin Ginn's Vision of World Peace," and "Edwin Ginn's Commitment to World Government." *International Conciliation* 19:1 (1965), 1–19; 20:2 (1966), 419–29. Ginn's views (1890–1910) on peace and world government are described from the perspective of developments to 1965.

16:102 Kraft, Barbara S. "Peacemaking in the Progressive Era: A Prestigious and Proper Calling." *Maryland Historian* 1:2 (1970), 121–44. This is a concise summary essay, primarily descriptive of the peace movement (1898–1915), which shows its diversity of goals and varied methods. Recent secondary literature was largely ignored.

16:103 Lutzker, Michael A. "Can the Peace Movement Prevent War? The U.S.-Mexican Crisis of April 1914." In Solomon Wank, ed., *Doves and Diplomats: Foreign Offices and Peace Movements in Europe and America in the Twentieth Century*. Westport, Conn.: Greenwood, 1978, pp. 127–53. Peace leaders preferred private mediation efforts rather than public opposition to Wilsonian policies, but were ineffective when war threatened. Lutzker suggests that presidential leadership played the crucial role in shaping public opinion during the crisis of 1912 to 1914.

16:104 Lutzker, Michael A. "The Formation of the Carnegie Endowment for International Peace: A Study of the Establishment Centered Peace Movement, 1910–1914." In Jerry Israel, ed., *Building the Organizational Society*. New York: Free Press, 1972, pp. 143–62. This essay stresses the ideas of the founders of the endowment and the importance of its role within the peace movement.

16:105 Lutzker, Michael A. "The Pacifist as Militarist: A Critique of the American Peace Movement, 1898–1914." *Societas* 5:2 (1975), 87–104. There was a consensus between many important leaders of the peace movement and those generally perceived as having a more military orientation.

16:106 Marchand, Charles Roland. *The American Peace Movement and Social Reform, 1898–1918*. Princeton, N.J.: Princeton University Press, 1972. This is a major study showing the special relationship of the peace movement to other reform efforts; it is particularly valuable for its analysis of the drastic changes the movement underwent in response to World War I. See also Chapter 13, "Progressivism and Foreign Policy." Extensive bibliography.

16:107 Martin, James P. "The American Peace Movement and the Progressive Era 1910–1917." 2 vols. Ph.D. diss., Rice University, 1975. This study relates peace efforts to other contemporary reforms through a study of leaders and organizations. It notes the transformation of the peace movement (1914–1917), with the emergence of new groups opposed to preparedness and intervention. Protection of progressive reforms motivated the new leaders. See also Chapter 13, "Progressivism and Foreign Policy."

16:108 Moritzen, Julius. *The Peace Movement of America*. New York: Putnam's, 1912. Reprint 1971. A contemporary study (1890–1912) of the strength of the peace movement and its impact on foreign policy issues, including arbitration, the yellow peril, the Interparliamentary Union, and the Pan-American movement. The reprint contains an introduction by Barbara S. Kraft.

16:109 Patterson, David S. "An Interpretation of the American Peace Movement, 1898–1914." In Charles Chatfield, ed., *Peace Movements in America*. New York: Schocken, 1973, pp. 20–38. Patterson explores the nature of peace leadership by examining the educational background, values, assumptions, tactics, and positions of persons prominent in prewar efforts. The essay supports other studies showing the elitist quality of individuals and movements.

16:110 Patterson, David S. *Toward a Warless World: The Travail of the American Peace Movement, 1887–1914.* Bloomington: Indiana University Press, 1976. An important work, broad in scope, carefully researched, that probes attitudes that underlay the rhetoric of peace advocates, and demonstrates their diverse reactions to major issues and their attempts to influence foreign policies. Bibliography.

Contemporary Writings

16:111 Bridgman, Raymond L. *World Organization.* Boston: Ginn, 1905. Reprint 1972. A collection of the writings of a Boston journalist who was especially influential in New England in advancing the idea of periodic international congresses. An appendix contains petitions and other documents on the background of the Second Hague Peace Conference. The reprint contains an introductory essay by Warren F. Kuehl.

16:112 Davis, Hayne, ed. *Among the World's Peacemakers: An Epitome of the Interparliamentary Union.* New York: Progressive, 1907. Reprint 1972. This compilation illustrates the extensive popular pressures aroused in the United States in support of the Second Hague Conference, especially the work of the Interparliamentary Union. The photographs are valuable as is a 17-page introduction by Michael A. Lutzker in the reprint.

16:113 James, William. "The Moral Equivalent of War." In Gay Wilson Allen, ed., *A William James Reader.* Boston: Houghton Mifflin, 1971, pp. 211–21. This widely quoted and incisive essay, written in 1910, urges antimilitarists to find peaceful substitutes for the idealism, self-sacrifice, and sense of discipline that war has often inspired.

16:114 Mead, Lucia Ames. *Patriotism and the New Internationalism.* Boston: Ginn, 1906. This volume is representative of attempts to introduce both the teaching of peace and internationalism into the schools.

16:115 Nock, Albert J. "Peace the Aristocrat." *Atlantic Monthly* 115:5 (1915), 593–99. Nock provides a perceptive discussion of the peace movement's appeal to the upper economic strata and its apparent lack of relevance to the poor.

Arbitration and International Law

ARBITRATION AND PEACEFUL RESOLUTION OF CONFLICTS

See "Personalities," especially William Jennings Bryan, Nicholas Murray Butler, David Starr Jordan, William Howard Taft.

16:116 Cory, Helen M. *Compulsory Arbitration of International Disputes.* New York: Columbia University Press, 1932. This work, based on sound scholarship, remains a fundamental study of its topic. Bibliography.

16:117 Hudson, Manley O. "The Permanent Court of Arbitration." *American Journal of International Law* 27:3 (1933), 440–60. Hudson reviews the origins of the court, its structure and operation, and reviews cases before tribunals (1902–1933). These included the Pious Fund (1902), fisheries (1910), Orinoco (1910), Norway-U.S. ships (1922), Palmas (1928), and SS *Kronprins Gustaf Adolf* and SS *Pacific* (1932) settlements, all of which involved the United States.

16:118 Myers, Denys P. "Arbitration and the United States." *World Peace Foundation Pamphlets: League of Nations Series* 10 (1927), 447–607. This still stands as an excellent summary and guide to arbitration treaties, settlements, and efforts to promote the peaceful settlement of disputes. It is especially full on the arbitral pacts of 1897, 1905, and 1911–1912, and the Bryan accords. An appendix lists all U.S. agreements by countries plus all arbitration treaties negotiated worldwide (1828–1926), in force in 1926.

16:119 *National Arbitration and Peace Congresses, 1907, 1909, 1911, 1913, 1915.* New York: Clearwater, 1978. These five assemblies represent a wide range of thought in the American peace movement. Sessions were held in New York, Chicago, Baltimore, St. Louis, and San Francisco, at which virtually every important movement figure spoke, including Taft, while president. Originally published separately under various titles, this microfiche edition contains an introduction by Warren F. Kuehl.

16:120 Ralston, Jackson H. *International Arbitration from Athens to Locarno.* Stanford, Calif.: Stanford University Press, 1929. Reprint 1972. This is a summary and analysis of principles in relation to conventions, settlements, and cases before the Hague Permanent Court of Arbitration. Valuable as a reference tool, the appendix has a list of "arbitral and judicial tribunals, 1794–1926." The reprint contains an introduction by Warren F. Kuehl.

16:121 Stuyt, Alexander M. *Survey of International Arbitration, 1794–1970.* Rev. ed. Dobbs Ferry, N.Y.: Oceana, 1972. A general listing of arbitral settlements with a brief summary of the issues and results. It includes over 100 references to U.S. involvement. The index listing by countries shows the dramatic decline in the use of arbitration by the United States since 1920.

Canadian-American Settlements

See Chapter 14 for full account.

Brown, R. C. *Canada's National Policy, 1883–1900: A Study in Canadian-American Relations* (14:78) contains much important information about arbitration settlements.

16:122 Corbett, Percy E. *The Settlement of Canadian-American Disputes: A Critical Study of Methods and Results.* New Haven, Conn.: Yale University Press, 1937. This is an essential book for the arbitral and legal settlement of the problems of the boundaries and fisheries in Canadian-American relations (1789–1937).

Shippee, L. B. *Canadian-American Relations, 1849–1874* (14:80) contains a comprehensive account of the Treaty of Washington and the settlement of other issues.

Tansill, C. C. *Canadian-American Relations, 1875–1911* (14:86) deals at length with boundaries and fisheries issues; arbitral tribunals and commissions are carefully described.

Fisheries and Sealing

16:123 Bailey, Thomas A. "The North Pacific Sealing Convention of 1911." *Pacific Historical Review* 4:1 (1935), 1–14. Bailey studies a successful attempt to regulate by convention a serious conservation problem in the open seas.

16:124 Innis, Harold A. *The Cod Fisheries: The History of an International Economy.* Rev. ed. Toronto: University of Toronto Press, 1954. A comprehensive scholarly history of the fisheries of Newfoundland from the late 15th century to the 1930s, it gives careful consideration to the diplomatic importance of the fisheries throughout their history.

16:125 Longley, R. S. "Peter Mitchell: Guardian of the North Atlantic Fisheries, 1867–1871." *Canadian Historical Review* 22:4 (1941), 389–402. This is an account of critical decisions in regards to the fisheries, which were of considerable significance in Canadian-American relations.

Other Episodes

16:126 Bailey, Thomas A. "Theodore Roosevelt and the Alaska Boundary Settlement." *Canadian Historical Review* 18:2 (1937), 123–35. This essay explains clearly the limits of the Theodore Roosevelt administration's devotion to international arbitration in 1903.

16:127 Blake, Nelson M. "The Olney-Pauncefote Treaty of 1897." *American Historical Review* 50:2 (1945), 228–43. This essay, which describes a general arbitration treaty between Britain and America, has an important place in the historiography of arbitration.

16:128 Campbell, John P. "Taft, Roosevelt, and the Arbitration Treaties of 1911." *Journal of American History* 53:2 (1966), 279–98. This study focuses on the politics behind the defeat of the treaties.

Cook, A. *The Alabama Claims, American Politics and Anglo-American Relations, 1865–1872* (14:82) is an important account of the negotiations of a treaty of large significance for Anglo-American relations, the arbitration movement, Canadian-American boundaries, and the fisheries problem.

Dickens, P. D. "Argentina Arbitrations and Mediations with Reference to United States Participation Therein" (15:200).

INTERNATIONAL LAW

See "Personalities," especially John Bassett Moore, Elihu Root, James Brown Scott, and, under "Others," Samuel T. Dutton, Henry Wheaton; also see Chapter 11, "The War and International Law."

16:129 Abrams, Irwin. "The Emergence of the International Law Societies." *Review of Politics* 19:3 (1957), 361–80. Abrams examines developments from 1860 to 1880 and the formation of the Institute for International Law and the Association for the Reform and Codification of the Law of Nations. The essay includes treatment of Americans James B. Miles, Francis Lieber, and David Dudley Field.

16:130 Balch, Thomas W. *A World Court in the Light of the United States Supreme Court.* Philadelphia: Allan, Lane & Scott, 1918. This is an early treatise by a Philadelphia lawyer which links domestic principles of law to international ones, with special emphasis on arbitration.

16:131 Bozeman, Adda B. "International Law." In Alexander DeConde, ed., *Encyclopedia of American Foreign Policy.* New York: Scribner's, 1978, vol. 2, pp. 455–72. A concise exposition of the roots and evolution of international law and U.S. responses in relation to foreign policy objectives, this essay also discusses leading American exponents. Bibliography.

16:132 Corbett, Percy E. *Law in Diplomacy.* Princeton, N.J.: Princeton University Press, 1959. A collection of interpretative essays which deal with major topics in the history of international law (1776–1959) and emphasize the relationship of national policies to law. Corbett is especially concerned with the approaches of Great Britain, the United States, and the Soviet Union to international law.

16:133 Finch, George A. "The American Society of International Law, 1906–1956." *American Journal of International Law* 50:2 (1956), 293–312. Finch, the second editor in chief of the *American Journal of International Law,* discusses the society's attitudes toward major developments in international law and organization during fifty years of its history.

16:134 Gross, Leo, ed. *International Law in the Twentieth Century.* New York: Appleton-Century-Crofts, 1969. This compilation from the *American Journal of International Law* (1907–1965), does

much to reveal attitudes, ideas, and contributions of Americans on a wide variety of subjects, including sanctions, recognition, courts and their jurisdiction, treaties, world organization, and the theory and practice of international law.

Henkin, L. *Foreign Affairs and the Constitution* [1789–1972] (2:138) is also important for its discussion of the American approach to international law and tribunals.

16:135 Hudson, Manley O. *International Tribunals: Past and Future.* Washington, D.C.: Brookings Institution and Carnegie Endowment, 1944. The Hague conventions, early arbitral settlements, and the Permanent Court of Arbitration are examined by Hudson, who also provides information on procedures, jurisdiction, administration, and personnel of various tribunals (1794–1943). Hudson also includes data on the Central American, Inter-American, and Permanent Court of International Justice. Bibliography.

16:136 Hyde, Charles C. *International Law, Chiefly as Interpreted and Applied by the United States.* 3 vols. 2d ed. Boston: Little, Brown, 1945. This widely acclaimed work, first published in 1922, traces by reference to hearings, treaties, settlements and agreements the degree of involvement of the United States in the formulation of international law and also how fully the United States has adhered to principles of justice in its dealings with other countries. The historical evolution (1789–1941) of concepts, doctrines, subjects, and processes is especially useful.

16:137 Myers, Denys P. "Law and the Peace Society." *World Affairs* 127:4 (1965), 231–37. Myers traces the efforts of the American Peace Society, from its founding in 1828, to support international law and advance a code, arbitration, and an international court of justice.

16:138 Nadelmann, Kurt H. "International Law at America's Centennial: The International Code Committee's Centennial Celebration and the Centenary of Field's International Code." *American Journal of International Law* 70:3 (1976), 519–29. David Dudley Field's preeminent position in the movement to codify international law is seen in this description of honors accorded to him in the 1870s. It also reveals the enthusiasm of other American advocates.

16:139 Nussbaum, Arthur. *A Concise History of the Law of Nations.* Rev. ed. New York: Macmillan,

1954. The best brief history of international law from ancient to modern times emphasizes theory rather than practice. Its discussion of international law in the 20th century is, however, inadequate. Bibliography.

16:140 Piscatori, James P. "Law, Peace, and War in American International Legal Thought." In Ken Booth and Moorhead Wright, eds., *American Thinking about Peace and War: New Essays on American Thought and Attitudes.* New York: Barnes & Noble, 1978, pp. 135–57. The assumptions of legal specialists have reflected the American political-legal system, a belief in open trade, and cultural values. Scholars since the 1860s have emphasized laws of war on the regulation of conflict on one hand and outlawry on the other. One accepts the legality of war; the other challenges it.

16:141 Wheaton, Henry. *History of the Law of Nations in Europe and America from the Earliest Times to the Treaty of Washington, 1842.* New York: Gould, Banks, 1845. Reprint 1973. This treatise was reprinted with an introduction by Warren F. Kuehl which reviews ideas on international law in relation to Wheaton's writings.

16:142 Ziegler, Benjamin M. *The International Law of John Marshall.* Chapel Hill: University of North Carolina Press, 1939. This account is essential for the American approach to international law in the early 19th century. Bibliography.

Neutrality

See Chapter 19 for World War I experiences.

16:143 Borchard, Edwin M., and Lage, William P. *Neutrality for the United States.* 2d ed. New Haven, Conn.: Yale University Press, 1940. Reprint 1973. While usually associated with the neutrality policy debate of the 1930s, this study contains important historical background data in two chapters, "The Conception and the Rules of Neutrality" and "The United States and Neutrality."

16:144 Coogan, John W. "The End of Neutrality: The United States, Britain, and Neutral Rights, 1899–1915." Ph.D. diss., Yale University, 1976. This is a provocative study of questions of international law in Anglo-American relations, especially in connection with American policy toward the European war in 1914 and 1915. Extensive bibliography.

16:145 *Neutrality: Its History, Economics and Law.* 4 vols. New York: Columbia University Press, 1935–36. Vol. 1: *The Origins,* by Philip C. Jessup and Francis Deák. Vol. 2: *The Napoleonic Period,* by W. A. Phillips and A. H. Reede. Vol. 3: *The World War Period,* by Edgar Turlington. Vol. 4: *Today and Tomorrow,* by Philip C. Jessup. The four volumes in this series are authoritative, scholarly histories of the international law of neutrality.

Freedom of the Seas

16:146 Baylen, Joseph O. "The United States and the London Naval Conference of 1908–1909: A Study in Anglo-American Amity." *Historia* [Puerto Rico] 5:1 (1955), 62–90. This is a detailed study of negotiations leading up to the International Prize Court Convention and the Declaration of London.

16:147 Mallison, Sally V., and Mallison, Thomas W., Jr. "A Survey of the International Law of Naval Blockade." *U.S. Naval Institute Proceedings* 102:2 (1976), 44–53. This essay (1776–1976) ranges over an impressive array of the literature of its subject. Students will be led to a realization of the differences in approach between law and diplomacy.

16:148 Merli, Frank J., and Ferrell, Robert H. "Blockades and Quarantines." In Alexander DeConde, ed., *Encyclopedia of American Foreign Policy.* 3 vols. New York: Scribner's, 1978, vol. 1, pp. 90–103. The authors attempt to relate the Civil War blockade experiences to the larger dimensions of the evolution of American concepts on the theory and practice of blockade. Students are urged to read the related articles in the *Encyclopedia,* "Economic Foreign Policy," "Freedom of the Seas," "Neutrality," and "International Law," for a comprehensive overview of the complexity of neutral trade in wartime.

Owsley, F. L., Jr. "America and the Freedom of the Seas, 1861–65" (11:238).

16:149 Rappaport, Armin. "Freedom of the Seas." In Alexander DeConde, ed., *Encyclopedia of American Foreign Policy.* New York: Scribner's, 1978, vol. 2, pp. 387–97. A masterly attempt to put this important question into historical perspective.

Special Studies

16:150 Benton, Elbert J. *Diplomacy of the Spanish-American War*. Baltimore: Johns Hopkins Press, 1908. This book's discussions of the international legal problems of the war (1898) still possess considerable scholarly merit.

Bernath, S. L. *Squall across the Atlantic: American Civil War Prize Cases and Diplomacy* (11:227) is one of the most important recent studies of the history of international law.

16:151 Bourguignon, Henry J. *The First Federal Court: The Federal Appellate Prize Court of the American Revolution, 1775–1787*. Philadelphia: American Philosophical Society, 1977. This is the first satisfactory study of American prize courts during the Revolution, and it is deserving of an important place in the historiography of international law. Extensive bibliography.

16:152 Hershey, Amos S. *The International Law and Diplomacy of the Russo-Japanese War*. New York: Macmillan, 1906. Although this work was completed soon after the war, it remains an important study of the development of international law. The book itself was of importance in the framing of the Hague conventions relative to the international law of the sea in 1907.

Hinckley, F. E. *American Consular Jurisdiction in the Orient* (18:12) describes the rights of 19th-century American citizens with respect to trials, extradition, expulsion, mixed tribunals, and missionary protections.

Jones, F. C. *Extraterritoriality in Japan and the Diplomatic Relations Resulting in Its Abolition, 1853–1899* (17:150).

16:153 Lint, Gregg L. "The Law of Nations and the American Revolution." *Diplomatic History* 1:1 (1977), 20–34. This is a very useful assessment of the American interest in the law of nations during the Revolution (1776–1783).

16:154 Pares, Richard. *Colonial Blockade and Neutral Rights 1739–1763*. Oxford: Oxford University Press, 1938. This is a major work of scholarship on the law of the sea in the 18th century.

Ubbelohde, C. *The Vice-Admiralty Courts and the American Revolution* (3:195) is a most important study of British vice-admiralty courts before the Revolution and is helpful for understanding the development of prize law. Extensive bibliography.

The Hague Conferences

See "Personalities," especially David Jayne Hill (under "Others"), Andrew D. White.

16:155 Davis, Calvin D. *The United States and the First Hague Peace Conference*. Ithaca, N.Y.: Cornell University Press, 1962. This study is concerned with all three of the major topics of the conference—limitation of armaments, the laws of war, and arbitration. It gives particular emphasis to the founding of the Permanent Court of Arbitration. Extensive bibliography.

16:156 Davis, Calvin D. *The United States and the Second Hague Peace Conference: American Diplomacy and International Organization, 1899–1914*. Durham, N.C.: Duke University Press, 1976. Based upon extensive research in American and British archival material, this book emphasizes the development of the Hague conferences and the Permanent Court of Arbitration into a world organization and explains the connections between the Hague system and the later League of Nations and World Court. It also discusses the changes and innovations made by the Hague conferences and the London Naval Conferences in international law and treats fully pressure groups and influences of individuals. Extensive bibliography.

16:157 Hull, William I. *The New Peace Movement*. Boston: World Peace Foundation, 1912. Both an historian and a pacifist, Hull reviews the achievements of the Hague conferences, focusing on the role of the United States. A 24-page essay, "The Latest Literature of the Peace Movement," provides a perspective on contemporary books, journals, and pamphlets.

16:158 Robinson, Margaret. *Arbitration and the Hague Peace Conferences 1899 and 1907*. Dissertation Collection, vol. 75, no. 1. Philadelphia: University of Pennsylvania, 1936. This was the first serious attempt to deal with the diplomacy of arbitration at the two conferences. Bibliography.

16:159   Scott, James Brown. *The Hague Peace Conferences of 1899 and 1907.* 2 vols. Baltimore: Johns Hopkins Press, 1909. Reprint 1971. The first volume of this work is an account of the Hague conferences by a leading American international lawyer who was solicitor of the State Department and a technical delegate to the 1907 conference. While it reveals little about actual negotiations at the conferences, it is of value for its analysis of the Hague conventions. The second volume is a collection of documents pertaining to the conferences.

DISARMAMENT EFFORTS

16:160   Berthrong, Merrill G. "Disarmament in European Diplomacy, 1816–1870." Ph D. diss., University of Pennsylvania, 1958. The year 1816 marks the initial appearance of disarmament as a subject of diplomatic negotiations among the major European powers. The author believes that, although disarmament was ostensibly the reason for calling the First Hague Conference, all hopes for its accomplishment had been abandoned after the Prussian victory over France in 1870.

16:161   Hosono, Gunji. *International Disarmament.* New York: Columbia University Press, 1926. This is one of the few attempts to present a historical account of disarmament. The first nine chapters contains a discussion of early disarmament techniques and episodes; chapters 7 and 8 deal with the two Hague Conferences. This volume was also published as *Histoire du désarmament* (Paris: Pedone, 1930).

16:162   Tate, Merze. *The Disarmament Illusion: The Movement for a Limitation of Armaments to 1907.* New York: Macmillan, 1942. A clear-eyed discussion of the issue based upon multiarchival research. It considers disarmament a political not a moral or mathematical problem, and is of special interest for its discussion of proposals for arms limitation at the First Hague Conference. Extensive bibliography.

17

United States and East and Southeast Asia to 1913

Contributing Editor

RAYMOND A. ESTHUS
Tulane University

Contributors

David L. Anderson
Sam Houston State University

John Chay
Pembroke State University

Mary V. Kuebel
Central Intelligence Agency

Ronald H. Spector
*Department of the Army,
Center of Military History*

Sandra C. Taylor
University of Utah

Contents

Introduction

The literature on United States–Asian relations in the pre–World War I period is extensive. This is not surprising considering the long and significant American involvement in Asia. In the years and decades that followed the voyage of the *Empress of China* to Canton in 1784, American merchants, diplomats, and missionaries created an American presence in Asia that was second only to that of the British; and in the overall picture of American foreign relations, Asia loomed large. Many scholars of history, therefore, have found the subject of American-Asian relations both important and fascinating. Moreover, as the bicentennial of that first voyage to China draws near, books and articles on U.S.-Asian relations continue to appear in impressive numbers.

Because of the large volume of literature that must be surveyed, it has been necessary to omit two categories: doctoral dissertations, and studies on Asians in the United States. Readers, nevertheless, can gain ready access to these materials. Many lists of doctoral dissertations on Asia have been compiled, and these have been included in the bibliographical section below. In these publications are listed hundreds of dissertations on, or relating to, U.S.-Asian relations. For the literature on Asians in the United States, the reader should begin by checking two special series on that topic that have recently been inaugurated, one by Arno Press and one by American Bibliographical Center–Clio Press. The publications in the Arno series include reprints as well as newly written studies. Two bibliographies are also helpful in gaining access to some of this literature: James M. McCutcheon, *China and America: A Bibliography of Interactions, Foreign and Domestic* (Honolulu: University Press of Hawaii, 1972), and Mitsugu Matsuda, *The Japanese in Hawaii: An Annotated Bibliography of Japanese Americans* (Honolulu: University of Hawaii, Social Science Research Institute, 1975).

The literature on America's relations with East and Southeast Asia is such that it is difficult to divide it into categories for presentation as bibliography. The sections and subsections of this chapter, therefore, are of necessity somewhat arbitrary. The reader may need to look in several sections to find all the material on a given person, subject, or period. For instance, literature relating to persons such as Samuel Wells Williams and Peter Parker—who were diplomats as well as missionaries—might be found in several sections. The intertwining of the stories of merchants, missionaries, and diplomats and the interlocking of the histories of nations such as China, Korea, and Japan dictate that the reader cast a wide net in seeking bibliographical information.

The future directions of historical scholarship on U.S.-Asian relations are reasonably clear. Much of the existing literature deals primarily with official diplomacy. Tyler Dennett's *Americans in Eastern Asia* (17:27) and A. Whitney Griswold's *The Far Eastern Policy of the United States* (17:220), which have long dominated the field, reflect this narrowly defined diplomatic approach. They also reflect the weakness of using only Western-language materials and the limitations of Western perceptions of Eastern cultures. Many aspects of the diplomatic story require revision based on a broader definition of diplomacy, a greater use of Asian-language sources, and a better understanding of cultural differences and their impact on East-West relations. The future success of this undertaking will depend largely on how well scholars surmount the formidable barriers of language and differing cultural perceptions.

In addition to new diplomatic studies, there is great need for studies on trade, missionaries, and mutual cultural impacts. Scholars who have studied with John K. Fairbank at Harvard University have made a very impressive beginning in the study of American missionaries and American merchant houses in China. Akira Iriye, who studied with Fairbank, has broken new ground in the understanding of American-Asian cultural interactions in his book *Across the Pacific: An Inner History of American–East Asian Relations* (2:332). On the Japan side, Robert Schwantes, in his *Japanese and Americans: A Century of Cultural Relations* (17:174), and a number of other scholars have pointed the way to a better understanding of Japanese-American cultural relations. Much still remains to be done. The role of Americans in late Tokugawa and Meiji Japan, for instance, is a subject of great interest to the Japanese even today, and it merits a more important place in the historical literature.

U.S. relations with Southeast Asia constitutes another significant opportunity for historians. A few scholars have made an important start in this area, but much more can be done. Unlike East Asia, where historical records abound, Southeast Asia presents serious problems in finding source materials. This is less true, of course, in the case of British held areas. But even given the difficulties of identifying indigenous records, American diplomatic, business, and missionary records permit much more historical work on America's relations with Southeast Asia.

In the coming years the study of American-Asian relations will present scholars with great challenges and important opportunities. The level of quality that is presently being achieved in this field and the new frontiers that are coming under exploration give promise that scholars will successfully meet the challenges as well as be attracted by the opportunities.

Finally, a word about the rendering of Asian names in this chapter. The style used in Asia has been followed in most cases. Family name is given first. Exceptions have been made where the individuals themselves have adopted the Western style.

Resources and Overviews

RESEARCH AIDS

While pertinent bibliographies and reference aids are listed here, there are more extensive lists in Chapter 1.

Bibliographies

17:1   Cordier, Henri. *Bibliotheca Sinica: Dictionnaire bibliographiques des ouvrages relatifs à l'empire chinois* [Bibliography of China: bibliographical dictionary of the foreign relations of the Chinese Empire]. 4 vols. Rev. ed. Paris: Guilmoto, 1904–1908. Cordier's classic work is the most extensive bibliography of China's foreign relations. A supplement was published by Paul Geuthner in 1924 in Paris.

Ellis, R. N. "Civil-Military Relations, Operations, and the Army, 1865–1917" (13:1) lists references to the army's operations in the Philippines and the China Relief Expedition.

Healy, D. *Modern Imperialism: Changing Styles in Historical Interpretations* (12:3).

Holbo, P. S. "Perspectives on American Foreign Policy, 1890–1916" (13:2).

Hucker, C. O. *China: A Critical Bibliography* (1:97) is useful for background material.

17:2   Irick, Robert L.; Yu Ying-shih; and Liu Kwang-ching. *American-Chinese Relations, 1784–1941: A Survey of Chinese-Language Materials at Harvard.* Cambridge: Harvard University Press, 1960. This listing includes entries on reference works, document collections, libraries and archives in the United States and East Asia, economic and cultural relations, Christian missions, education, social reform, immigration, and diplomatic relations.

17:3   Liu Kwang-ching. *Americans and Chinese: A Historical Essay and a Bibliography.* Cambridge: Harvard University Press, 1963. Liu's introductory essay discusses Sino-American contacts, American merchants, missionaries, and Chinese immigrants and outlines the problems of assessing the impact of such contacts on the development of Sino-American relations. The bibliography is a detailed list of manuscript collections, primary materials, and reference works, each category organized according to special groups such as merchants, missionaries, travelers, diplomats.

17:4   Lust, John *Index Sinicus: A Catalogue of Articles Relating to China in Periodicals and Other Collective Publications, 1920–1955.* Cambridge, Eng.: Heffer, 1964. This supplements Cordier's bibliography (17:1) and complements Yuan's list of monographs (17:6). It lists 19,734 items from 830 periodicals and 137 collective works that were published during 1920 to 1955.

May, E. R., and Thomson, J. C., Jr., eds. *American-East Asian Relations: A Survey* (2:334) includes bibliographical essays. The most valuable essays on the pre–World War I period include those by Edward D. Graham on early American–East Asian relations, John K. Fairbank on American relations with China in the mid-19th century, Liu Kwang-Ching on American relations with China in the late 19th century, and Robert S. Schwantes on American relations with Japan (1853–1895).

Morley, J. W., ed. *Japan's Foreign Policy, 1868–1941: A Research Guide* (1:100) includes four bibliographical essays which are important for U.S.-Japan relations: "Japan's Military Foreign Policies," by James B. Crowley; "Japan's Economic Foreign Policies, 1868–1893," by Arthur E. Tiedmann; "Japan's Cultural Foreign Policies," by Robert S. Schwantes; and "Japan's Policies toward the United States," by Akira Iriye. There is an appended list of standard works and also a list of recent works.

17:5 Rabe, Valentin H. *American-Chinese Relations, 1784–1941: Books and Pamphlets Extracted from the Shelf Lists of Widener Library.* Cambridge: Harvard University Press, 1960. This brief volume list contains over 1,000 items in the Widener Library, plus materials in other Harvard University libraries.

Silberman, B. S. *Japan and Korea: A Critical Bibliography* (1:101) is excellent for background material.

Smith, D. M. "Rise to Great World Power, 1865–1918" (13:4) reviews recent historical interpretation.

17:6 Yuan Tung-li. *China in Western Literature: A Continuation of Cordier's Bibliotheca Sinica.* New Haven, Conn.: Yale University Press, 1958. This large volume lists about fifteen thousand books in English, French, and German published between 1921 and 1957.

Indexes to Doctoral Dissertations

17:7 Gordon, Leonard H. D., and Shulman, Frank J., comps. *Doctoral Dissertations on China: A Bibliography of Studies in Western Languages, 1945–1970.* Seattle: University of Washington Press, 1972. This compilation includes 47 entries on missionaries in China, 34 on general studies of China's foreign relations, 51 on China's foreign relations during 1800 to 1880, and 94 on China's foreign relations during 1880 to 1914.

Shulman, F. J., comp. *Doctoral Dissertations on Asia: An Annotated Bibliographical Journal of Current International Research* (1:247) is a semiannual compilation beginning in 1975.

17:8 Shulman, Frank J., comp. *Doctoral Dissertations on Japan and Korea, 1969–1974: A Classified Bibliographical Listing of International Research.* Ann Arbor, Mich.: University Microfilms International, 1976. This is an update of Shulman's earlier compilation on the 1877 to 1969 period. It includes 19 entries on U.S.-Japan relations to 1937, 20 on Japan's image abroad, and 23 on Japanese cultural influence abroad. The listings on Korea include 19 entries on domestic affairs and foreign relations to 1910.

17:9 Shulman, Frank J., comp. *Japan and Korea: An Annotated Bibliography of Doctoral Dissertations in Western Languages, 1877–1969.* Chicago: American Library Association, 1970. This annotated bibliography includes 28 entries on U.S.-Japan relations in the period 1800 to 1914, 32 on Japanese immigration to the United States and Japanese in the United States, 24 on the influence of Japanese culture abroad, and 50 on Korean foreign relations to 1905.

Stucki, C. W., comp. *American Doctoral Dissertations on Asia, 1933–June 1966* (1:248) includes many dissertations on U.S.-Asian relations.

17:10 The, Lian, and Veur, Paul W. van der, comps. *Treasures and Trivia: Doctoral Dissertations on Southeast Asia Accepted by Universities in the United States.* Athens: Ohio University, Center for International Studies, 1968. The dissertations are listed by country. The few entries on relations between the United States and these countries are listed under "History." This publication includes some items which are not listed in Stucki's compilation.

Document Collections

More general collections are listed in Chapter 2, and other collections may be found in subsections below.

17:11 American Diplomatic and Public Papers: The United States and China. Series I: *The Treaty System and the Taiping Rebellion, 1842–1860.* Ed. by Jules Davids. 21 vols. Wilmington, Del.: Scholarly Resources, 1973.

17:12 American Diplomatic and Public Papers: The United States and China. Series II: *The U.S., China, and Imperial Rivalries, 1861–1893.* Ed. by Jules Davids. 18 vols. Wilmington, Del.: Scholarly Resources, 1979. These two compilations of basic documents include diplomatic correspondence, private letters, congressional and presidential papers, and treaties. Davids provides historical and biographical sketches. (Series 3, covering 1894 to 1905, is projected for 1981.)

Beasley, W. G., ed. and trans. *Selected Documents on Japanese Foreign Policy, 1853–1868* (17:110).

17:13 China Palace Museum. *Ch'ou-pan i-wu shih-mo* [The complete account of our management of barbarian affairs]. Peiping: Palace Museum, 1929–1931. This is the basic Chinese source on Sino-Western relations during 1836 to 1874. It includes 80 *chüan* (chapters) on the Tao-kuang period (1836–1850), 80 *chüan* on the Hsien-feng period (1851–1861), and 100 *chüan* on the T'ung-chih period (1861–1874). Earl Swisher, in his *China's Management of the American Barbarians* (17:68), has translated some of the documents relating to the United States in the 1841 to 1861 period.

17:14 Clyde, Paul H., ed. *United States Policy toward China: Diplomatic and Public Documents, 1839–1939*. Durham, N.C.: Duke University Press, 1940. Reprint 1964. This collection of 128 documents, primarily treaties and diplomatic correspondence, serves as a reference work and as a documentary history of the first century of official U.S.-China relations. Clyde's brief introductions place the items in context and includes a list of American diplomatic representatives in China.

17:15 Daigaku Shiryō Hensankakari [Tokyo University, Institute for the Compilation of Historical Documents]. *Dai Nihon Komonjo: Bakumatsu Gaikoku Kankei Monjo* [Sources of Japanese history: documents on foreign relations in the last days of the Tokugawa shogunate]. 37 vols. and 7 suppls. to date. Tokyo: Tokyo University, 1910–. This is the basic Japanese document collection on late Tokugawa foreign relations (1853–1868); some of these documents, for 1853 to 1859, appear in William G. Beasley's *Selected Documents on Japanese Foreign Policy, 1853–1868* (17:110). Subsequent to Beasley's publication, additional volumes of this basic source were published covering the period to 1868.

17:16 Fairbank, John K. *Ch'ing Documents: An Introductory Syllabus*. 2 vols. 2d ed. Cambridge: Harvard University Press, 1959. Volume 1 is a study-aid for American scholars who wish to do research in late Ch'ing documents, particularly documents relating to China's foreign relations. It deals with problems of translation and lists reference works and major collec-

tions of documents. Volume 1 also contains notes on selected documents. Volume 2 consists of the Chinese texts of these documents.

France. Ministère des Affaires Etrangères. *Documents diplomatiques français (1871–1914)* [French diplomatic documents (1871–1914)] (14:3) is a basic French collection of documents arranged chronologically, but each volume has a list of documents arranged by subject. Records relating to East Asian international relations can be easily located by these subject lists.

17:17 Germany. Auswärtiges Amt. *Die Grosse Politik der Europäischen Kabinette, 1871–1914* [The great politics of the European Cabinets, 1871–1914]. 40 vols. Berlin: Deutsche verlagsgesellschaft für politik und geschichte, 1922–1927. This collection of German diplomatic records includes many documents relating to the policies of the Western powers in East Asia; see especially volumes 14, 16, 17, 19, 25, and 32.

Great Britain. Foreign Office. *British Documents on the Origins of the War, 1898–1914* (14:4) contains many documents relating to East Asian diplomacy of the major powers, including the United States. See especially volumes 1, 2, 4, and 8.

17:18 Great Britain. Foreign Office. "FO 17: Foreign Office, General Correspondence before 1906, China 1815–1905." Microfilm. Millwood, N.J.: KTO Microfilm, n.d. The microfilmed material issued thus far in this continuing project includes 465 reels on 1815 to 1878 and 103 reels on 1879 to 1885.

17:19 Great Britain. Foreign Office. "Japan Correspondence, 1856–1940." Microfilm. Wilmington, Del.: Scholarly Resources, n.d. This microfilm material from Foreign Office collections No. 46 and No. 371 includes 50 reels on 1856 to 1867, 176 reels on 1868 to 1890, 148 reels on 1891 to 1905, and 66 reels on 1930 to 1940.

17:20 Irish University Press Series on British Parliamentary Papers. *China and Japan*. 52 vols. Shannon: Irish University Press, 1971. This convenient collection of 19th-century published British papers and reports devotes 42 volumes, arranged topically, to China and 10 to Japan.

17:21 Japan. Gaimushō [Foreign Ministry]. "Japanese Ministry of Foreign Affairs Archives, 1868–1945." Microfilm. Washington, D.C.: Library of Congress, 1949–1951. These films of over two million pages (2,116 reels) can be purchased or borrowed on interlibrary loan from the Library of Congress. An index was published by the Library of Congress (1954), *Checklist of Archives in the Japanese Ministry of Foreign Affairs, Tokyo, Japan, 1868–1945*, compiled by Cecil H. Uyehara. Especially valuable is the Telegram Series listed on pages 155–56 of this checklist.

17:22 Japan. Gaimushō [Foreign Ministry]. *Nihon Gaikō Bunsho: Meiji Nenkan* [Documents on Japanese foreign relations: Meiji period]. 45 vols. and suppls. Tokyo: Nihon Kokusai Rengō Kyōkai, 1936–1963. This is the basic Japanese document source; supplementary volumes have been published on specific topics, including three on the Boxer Rebellion [*Hokushin Jihen*], five on the Russo-Japanese War [*Nichiro Sensō*], one on the Chinese Revolution of 1911 [*Shinkoku Jihen-Shingai Kakumei*], and eight on treaty revision [*Jōyaku Kaisei Kankei*]. For a full listing of the treaty revision volumes, see "Treaty Revision" in the section on Meiji Japan, below.

17:23 *Korean-American Relations: Documents Pertaining to the Far Eastern Diplomacy of the United States.* 2 vols. Berkeley: University of California Press, 1951–1963. These documents, drawn from Department of State records, have been divided into volume 1: *The Initial Period, 1883–1886*, ed. by George M. McCune and John A. Harrison; and volume 2: *The Period of Growing Influence, 1887–1895*, ed. by Spencer J. Palmer.

Swisher, E. *China's Management of the American Barbarians: A Study of Sino-American Relations, 1841–1861, with Documents* (17:68) contains 700 pages of translated Chinese documents.

17:24 Teng Ssü-yu, and Fairbank, John K. *China's Response to the West: A Documentary Survey, 1839–1923.* Cambridge: Harvard University Press, 1954. Reprint 1966. This collection reveals the efforts of Chinese leaders to understand the alien Western civilization and to respond to it in a way that would preserve their own culture and institutions. It includes writings by such Chinese leaders as Lin Tse-Hsü, Ch'i-ying, Feng Kuei-fen, Tseng Kuo-fan, Li Hung-chang, Chang Chih-tung, K'ang Yu-wei, Liang Ch'i-ch'ao, and Yüan Shih-k'ai. A companion volume, *A Research Guide for China's Response to the West*, was published separately. It contains reference notes, a discussion of sources, and a bibliography of Western, Chinese, and Japanese works.

U.S. Department of State. "General Records of the Department of State, RG 59 and RG 84" (1:359) includes, in Record Group 59, the records to 1906 of diplomatic instructions to and diplomatic dispatches from China, Japan, Korea, and Siam, and notes from the legations of China, Japan, and Korea. It also includes consular instructions to and consular dispatches from posts in China, Japan, Korea, and also those at Bangkok, Batavia, Brunei, Manila, Padang, Saigon, and Singapore. Record Group 84 includes the records of foreign service posts in Japan and Bangkok to the year 1912. For reel numbers, see the latest edition of *List of National Archives Microfilm Publications*.

17:25 Wang Yen-wei, and Wang Liang, eds. *Chi'ing-chi wai-chiao shih-liao* [Historical material on foreign relations in the latter part of the Ch'ing Dynasty]. Peiping, 1932–1935. Reprint 1962. This is the basic documentary source on China's foreign relations in the period 1875 to 1911. It includes 218 *chüan* (chapters) on the Kuang-hsü period (1875–1908) and 24 *chüan* on the Hsuan-t'ung period (1908–1911).

OVERVIEWS

See Chapter 12, "Overviews" and "Ideas and Pressures of Expansionism," and Chapter 13, "Progressivism and Foreign Policy," for background studies.

17:26 Borg, Dorothy, comp. *Historians and American Far Eastern Policy.* New York: Columbia University Press, 1966. This consists of brief essays by leading authorities, including analyses of the work of Tyler Dennett (17:27) and A. Whitney Griswold (17:220) and a survey of Asian scholarship on U.S. East Asian policy.

Cohen, W. I. *America's Response to China: An Interpretive History of Sino-American Relations* [1839–1970] (2:340).

17:27 Dennett, Tyler. *Americans in Eastern Asia: A Critical Study of the Policy of the United States with Reference to China, Japan and Korea in the 19th Century.* New York: Macmillan, 1922. This classic work has been the standard work on 19th-century U.S. East Asian policy. Dennett contends that the United States avoided an isolated policy in China and sought to preserve its most-favored-nation status through cooperation with the other Western nations. Bibliographical essay and appendix listing American diplomatic representatives.

Dulles, F. R. *China and America: The Story of Their Relations since 1784* (2:342) is a critical and colorful survey.

17:28 Dulles, Foster Rhea. *Yankees and Samurai: America's Role in the Emergence of Modern Japan, 1791–1900.* New York: Harper & Row, 1965. This is probably Dulles's best book. America's role in the emergence of modern Japan is broadly examined. The emphasis is not upon trade and diplomacy but rather on all the important cultural relations—the experiment in development in Hokkaido, Ernest Fenollosa, Lafcadio Hearn, William Eliot Griffis, American visitors to Japan, etc. The focus is on individuals, both Americans and Japanese, who provided a bridge between the two cultures. Extensive bibliography.

Fairbank, J. K. *The United States and China* (2:344) provides a thoughtful commentary on 19th- and 20th-century U.S.-China relations.

17:29 Fairbank, John K. "'American China Policy' to 1898: A Misconception." *Pacific Historical Review* 39:4 (1970), 409–20. Fairbank argues that because of East-West cultural conflict and an interlocking treaty system, the idea of an "American" policy in 19th-century China is meaningless. Britain made the substantive decisions and the United States chose only how and when to say "me too."

17:30 Fairbank, John K., ed. *The Chinese World Order: Traditional China's Foreign Relations.* Cambridge: Harvard University Press, 1968. This volume is important primarily as background material for the study of Sino-American relations. It includes an essay by Fairbank on the early treaty system with the Western powers, while the other essays are valuable for an understanding of China's traditional foreign relations, a subject vital to understanding China's later relations with the Western nations. Extensive bibliography.

Iriye, A. *Across the Pacific: An Inner History of American–East Asian Relations* [1780–1963] (2:332) probes the role of images and stereotypes in shaping American, Chinese, and Japanese policies.

Neu, C. E. *The Troubled Encounter: The United States and Japan* [1853–1972] (2:348) covers the pre-1914 era briefly and interpretively.

Neumann, W. L. *America Encounters Japan: From Perry to MacArthur* (2:349).

Paullin, C. O. *Diplomatic Negotiations of American Naval Officers, 1778–1883* (2:177) deals with negotiations with Asian countries, including China during 1783 to 1846, Japan during 1797 to 1854, and Korea during 1866 to 1883. The text is largely narrative, with little analysis or interpretation.

17:31 Sansom, Sir George B. *The Western World and Japan.* New York: Knopf, 1950. This massive yet sketchy book deals with the Western impact (1542–1894) on Japan's politics and government, literature, intellectual currents, economic thought, law, education, and religion.

17:32 Treat, Payson J. *Diplomatic Relations between the United States and Japan 1853–1905.* 3 vols. Stanford, Calif.: Stanford University Press, 1932. Reprint 1963. Written by the pioneer scholar of Japanese-American diplomatic relations, the first two volumes, covering the period 1853 to 1895, are the more valuable. All three volumes focus exclusively on diplomatic relations, recounting in detail even minor diplomatic issues.

Personalities

Additional references on individuals may be found in Chapter 1, "Biographical Data."

AMERICAN

Anson Burlingame

17:33 Anderson, David L. "Anson Burlingame: American Architect of the Cooperative Policy in China, 1861–1871." *Diplomatic History* 1:3 (1977), 239–55. Burlingame, U.S. minister to China, endeavored to replace coercive Western policies in China with a more conciliatory and cooperative approach toward the Chinese government.

17:34 Williams, Frederick W. *Anson Burlingame and the First Chinese Mission to Foreign Powers.* New York: Scribner's, 1912. Reprint 1972. This is a sympathetic study of an idealistic American who served both as his country's first resident minister in Peking and the first official Chinese envoy to the Western nations. It details several major episodes in the interaction of the Chinese and Western civilizations in the 1860s. Bibliography.

Caleb Cushing

Kuo, Pin Chia. "Caleb Cushing and the Treaty of Wanghia, 1844" (17:81).

Welch, R. E., Jr. "Caleb Cushing's Chinese Mission and the Treaty of Wanghia: A Review: (17:84).

Hamilton Fish

See also Chapter 12, "Personalities."

Mayo, M. J. "A Catechism of Western Diplomacy: The Japanese and Hamilton Fish, 1872" (17:152).

Walter Q. Gresham

See also Chapter 12, "Personalities."

Paulsen, G. E. "Secretary Gresham, Senator Lodge, and American Good Offices in China, 1894" (17:232).

Townsend Harris

17:35 Consenza, Mario E., ed. *The Complete Journal of Townsend Harris: First American Consul General and Minister to Japan.* 2d rev. ed. Garden City, N.Y.: Doubleday, Doran, 1959. This is the major published source on Townsend Harris. The journal covers the period to June 18, 1858, and thus does not extend into the period when Harris served as minister at Edo.

17:36 Crow, Carl. *He Opened the Door of Japan: Townsend Harris and the Story of His Amazing Adventures in Establishing American Relations with the Far East.* New York: Harper, 1939. Reprint 1974. This laudatory account (1854–1861) is based primarily on the journal and papers of Harris. Bibliography.

John Hay

See Chapters 13 and 14, "Personalities," for additional references.

Dennett, T. *John Hay: From Poetry to Politics* (13:39) has been largely superseded by later studies, but is still valuable for an understanding of Hay himself.

Humphrey Marshall

Bain, C. A. "Commodore Matthew Perry, Humphrey Marshall, and the Taiping Rebellion" (17:85).

17:37 Schneider, Laurence A. "Humphrey Marshall, Commissioner to China, 1853–1854." *Kentucky Historical Society Register* 63:2 (1965), 97–120. A narrative of Marshall's role as commissioner to China based primarily on the records contained in House Executive Document 123, 33d Cong., 1st Sess., 1854.

U.S. House. *Correspondence between the State Department and the Late Commissioner to China* (17:92) contains the diplomatic correspondence of Humphrey Marshall, U.S. commissioner to China in 1852 to 1854.

Peter Parker

17:38 Gulick, Edward V. *Peter Parker and the Opening of China.* Cambridge: Harvard University Press, 1973. This biography, based on missionary and diplomatic records, traces Parker's career as missionary doctor at Canton and then U.S. commissioner to China (1855–1857). The author finds that Parker's achievements as a pioneer medical missionary in China greatly exceeded his accomplishments as a diplomat.

U.S. Senate. *Correspondence of the Late Commissioners in China* (17:93) contains the diplomatic correspondence of Peter Parker.

Matthew C. Perry

Morison, S. E. *"Old Bruin": Commodore Matthew Calbraith Perry, 1794–1858* (40:81) is the definitive study of Perry. Almost half the volume is devoted to the expedition to Japan.

17:39 Pineau, Roger, ed. *The Japan Expedition, 1852–1854: The Personal Journal of Commodore Matthew C. Perry.* Washington, D.C.: Smithsonian Institution Press, 1968. Perry dictated this journal during the voyage. It was the most significant source for the official narrative, but Hawks (17:121) did not include everything from it. Bibliography.

Swisher, E. "Commodore Perry's Imperialism in Relation to America's Present-Day Position in the Pacific [1853–1854]" (17:126).

William W. Rockhill

Pressman, H. "Hay, Rockhill and China's Integrity: A Reappraisal" (17:238).

Varg, P. A. "William Woodville Rockhill and the Open Door Notes" (17:239).

17:40 Varg, Paul A. *Open Door Diplomat: The Life of W. W. Rockhill.* Urbana: University of Illinois Press, 1952. This biography relates the Rockhill story (1853–1914) primarily as it is revealed in the Rockhill Papers and the State Department archives. In addition to recounting Rockhill's role as adviser to John Hay and later as minister at Peking, the study tells much about Rockhill as an individual and a scholar.

Theodore Roosevelt

See Chapters 13 and 15, "Personalities," for additional references.

Alfonson, O. M. *Theodore Roosevelt and the Philippines, 1897–1909* (17:287).

Bailey, T. A. *Theodore Roosevelt and the Japanese-American Crises* (17:258).

Beale, H. K. *Theodore Roosevelt and the Rise of America to World Power* (14:8) criticizes what he considers Roosevelt's bellicose handling of the Chinese boycott and Roosevelt's failure to formulate a policy that would have helped solve China's basic problems.

Esthus, R. A. *Theodore Roosevelt and Japan* (17:246).

Neu, C. E. *An Uncertain Friendship: Theodore Roosevelt and Japan, 1906–1909* (17:261).

Ro, K. H., and Smith, R. T. "Theodore Roosevelt and the Korean Intervention Question: An Analysis of a President's Defense" (17:193).

Elihu Root

See Chapters 16 and 19, "Personalities," for additional references.

17:41 Jessup, Philip C. *Elihu Root.* 2 vols. New York: Dodd, Mead, 1938. In this extensive biography, eleven chapters are given to Root's service as secretary of state during 1905 to 1908; two of these (27 and 28) are on East Asian policy. Before Root's death in 1937, Jessup interviewed him, and Root's own observations add important information to the historical record.

Willard Straight

See Chapter 39, "Personalities."

17:42 Croly, Herbert. *Willard Straight.* New York: Macmillan, 1924. Croly draws information almost exclusively from the colorful material in Straight's letters and journal. Straight's extraordinary career (1880–1918) included service as war correspondent in the Russo-Japanese War, vice-consul at Seoul, consul general at Mukden, Manchuria, acting chief of the State Department's Far Eastern Division, and agent of the American banking group in China during the days of dollar diplomacy.

Kahn, H. D. "Willard D. Straight and the Great Game of Empire" (39:41) concentrates on Straight's efforts (1906–1913) to give substance to the open door policy by promoting a tangible American financial stake in China. Kahn explores the differences between the dollar diplomacy of TR and that of Taft.

Scheiber, H. N. "World War I as Entrepreneurial Opportunity: Willard Straight and the American International Corporation" (39:42) details Straight's activities as American International Corporation vice-president (1915–1917), as well as the former diplomat's expansive thinking about America's role in the postwar international economy.

Vevier, C. *The United States and China, 1906–1913: A Study of Finance and Diplomacy* (17:265) focuses on the activities of Willard Straight.

William Howard Taft

See Chapters 14 and 15, "Personalities," for additional references.

17:43 Minger, Ralph E. *William Howard Taft and United States Foreign Policy: The Apprenticeship Years, 1900–1908.* Urbana: University of Illinois Press, 1975. Chapter 3 presents a credible account of Taft's negotiations with the Vatican for the acquisition of the Friar lands in the Philippines.

17:44 Scholes, Walter V., and Scholes, Marie V. *The Foreign Policies of the Taft Administration.* Columbia: University of Missouri Press, 1970. More than half of this work is devoted to East Asian policy. It is based on exhaustive research in American and British records, but it takes little from Japanese sources and nothing from Chinese sources. The authors see Taft's dollar diplomacy (1909–1913) as high-minded but inept. Extensive bibliography.

Samuel Wells Williams

17:45 Williams, Frederick Wells, ed. "The Journal of S. Wells Williams." *Journal of the North China Branch of the Royal Asiatic Society* 42 (1911), 3–232. This journal is a major source on the missions of

William B. Reed and John E. Ward to China in the period 1857 to 1860. Williams served as secretary to legation and interpreter under both these American ministers.

17:46   Williams, Frederick Wells. *The Life and Letters of Samuel Wells Williams, LL.D.: Missionary, Diplomatist, Sinologue.* New York: Putnam's, 1889. Reprint 1972. Samuel Wells Williams's career in Asia began in the 1830s and spanned over forty years. His book, *The Middle Kingdom,* was the standard 19th-century American work on China. He served as interpreter for Perry in Japan and for the American negotiator of the Treaty of Tientsin. He was legation secretary and frequently chargé d'affaires in Peking until 1876.

Others

17:47   Clyde, Paul H. "Attitudes and Policies of George F. Seward, American Minister at Peking, 1876–1880: Some Phases of the Cooperative Policy." *Pacific Historical Review* 2:4 (1933), 387–404. Clyde does not rank Seward high among American diplomats in 19th-century China, but Seward's lengthy dispatches to Washington contain much information on questions of treaty revision and interpretation, especially on judicial proceedings, extraterritoriality, and taxation of foreign goods.

17:48   Clyde, Paul H. "The China Policy of J. Ross Browne, American Minister to Peking, 1868–1869." *Pacific Historical Review* 1:3 (1932), 312–33. According to Clyde, Browne was accurate when he described his predecessor, Burlingame, as a sentimentalist who refused to acknowledge the antagonism of Chinese officials toward foreigners. Browne contended that the only realistic Western policy was to force China to obey the treaties, especially the commercial provisions.

17:49   Clyde, Paul H. "Frederick F. Low and the Tientsin Massacre." *Pacific Historical Review* 2:1 (1933), 100–08. Low served as U.S. minister in Peking from 1870 to 1874. Clyde characterizes Low as a "careful observer" and provides numerous excerpts from Low's reports to Washington on the diplomatically troublesome issues occasioned by Western missionary activity in China.

17:50   Denby, Charles. *China and Her People: Being the Observations, Reminiscences, and Conclusions of an American Diplomat.* 2 vols. Boston: Page, 1906. Charles Denby served as U.S. minister

plenipotentiary in Peking from 1885 to 1898, longer than any other American in the 19th century. His memoir, which is indexed, is liberally sprinkled with candid insights into the practices of Western diplomacy in China, especially about the ever-present tension between force and forbearance in American and other Western policies.

Dorwart, J. M. "The Independent Minister: John M. B. Sill and the Struggle against Japanese Expansion in Korea, 1894–1897" (17:188).

Eggert, G. G. *Richard Olney: Evolution of a Statesman* (12:72) defends Cleveland and Olney's policies concerning China.

Einstein, L. *A Diplomat Looks Back* (14:58) recalls his experiences in China.

Foster, J. W. *Diplomatic Memoirs* (12:43) gives extensive coverage of the role of Foster in peacemaking in 1895, when he served as adviser to the Chinese negotiators at Shimonoseki.

17:51   Griscom, Lloyd C. *Diplomatically Speaking.* New York: Literary Guild of America, 1940. Griscom devotes four of the thirty-six chapters of his memoirs to his service as minister to Japan during 1903 to 1905. Included are accounts of revealing conversations with Foreign Minister Komura preceding and during the Russo-Japanese War.

17:52   Harrington, Fred H. *God, Mammon and the Japanese: Dr. Horace N. Allen and Korean-American Relations, 1884–1905.* Madison: University of Wisconsin Press, 1961. Although this book centers around Horace N. Allen, the most important person to American-Korean relations until 1905, it is still the most comprehensive and readable work on the subject of American-Korean relations for the pre–World War I period. It provides a balanced account of the diplomatic, commercial, and missionary relationships between the two nations. Extensive bibliography.

Hoar, G. F. *Autobiography of Seventy Years* [1876–1900] (12:62) strongly opposed discriminatory treatment of Chinese immigrants.

17:53   Howe, M. A. DeWolfe. *George von Lengerke Meyer: His Life and Public Services.* New York: Dodd, Mead, 1920. This biography consists largely of quotations from the journal and letters of Meyer. More than two hundred pages are devoted to his service as ambassador to Russia in 1905–1906, service that included a major role in Roosevelt's peacemaking endeavor in 1905.

17:54 Phillips, William. *Ventures in Diplomacy.* Boston: Beacon, 1952. The diplomatic career of Phillips spanned the period from Theodore Roosevelt to Franklin Roosevelt. His principal role in East Asian matters came with his appointment as chief of the newly created Division of Far Eastern Affairs in 1908.

Prisco, S., III. *John Barrett, Progressive Era Diplomat: A Study of a Commercial Expansionist, 1887– 1920* (15:30) describes Barrett's service as U.S. minister to Siam beginning in 1894.

17:55 Quincy, Josiah. *The Journals of Major Samuel Shaw: The First American Consul at Canton.* Boston: Crosby & Nichols, 1847. Shaw served as the U.S. consul at Canton during 1786 to 1794, though he was often on voyages elsewhere during those years. Quincy has provided a 129-page biography of Shaw in addition to the consul's journals. Shaw's role as a powerless consul indicates the curiosity but lack of concern that characterized the U.S. government's view of Sino-American relations in the early years.

17:56 Roberts, Edmund. *An Embassy to the Eastern Courts of Cochin-China, Siam and Muscat.* New York: Harper, 1837. Roberts was one of the pioneer American diplomats in Southeast Asia. He negotiated the first American treaty with Siam in 1833, and unsuccessfully attempted to negotiate a treaty with Cochin-China (Vietnam).

Seaberg, C., and Paterson, S. *Merchant Prince of Boston: Colonel T. H. Perkins, 1764–1854* (8:148) focuses on the patriarch and his numerous descendents whose success in the early American China trade largely predetermined the course of its development to the Opium War. Although the authors concentrate on analyzing the business factors of this commercial success, they also discuss contacts between Perkins family members in China and local Chinese.

Spence, J. *The China Helpers: Western Advisers in China, 1620–1960* (2:347) analyzes the activities of Americans Peter Parker, Frederick T. Ward, W. A. P. Martin, Edward Hume, and O. J. Todd.

Tansill, C. C. *The Foreign Policy of Thomas F. Bayard, 1885–1897* (12:77) relates U.S. policy toward East Asia, especially Korea.

17:57 Wilson, F. M. Huntington. *Memoirs of an Ex-Diplomat.* Boston: Humphries, 1945. Huntington Wilson went to Tokyo in 1897 as second secretary of legation. His subsequent career—as first secretary (1900–1906), third assistant secretary of state (1906–1908), and first assistant secretary of state (1909–1913)—was devoted largely to East Asian affairs. His anti-Japanese inclinations had some impact on policy during the Roosevelt period but far greater impact in the Taft administration. His memoirs are filled with candid information about people and events.

ASIAN

Manjiro

17:58 Kaneko Hisakazu. *The Man Who Discovered America.* Boston: Houghton Mifflin, 1956. This is the story of the shipwrecked Japanese fisherman, Manjiro, who was educated in New England and returned to Japan in 1850. The shogun's government questioned him at length about the United States, gave him Samurai status with the surname Nakahama, but prevented him from having contact with the Perry expedition because he was in favor of opening Japan.

17:59 Warinner, Emily V. *Voyager to Destiny: The Amazing Adventure of Manjiro, the Man Who Changed Worlds Twice.* Indianapolis: Bobbs-Merrill, 1956. A popular, entertaining, but thoroughly researched account of the Japanese fisherman who was shipwrecked, rescued by an American ship, and educated in New England, and who returned to Japan in 1850.

Others

Chang, Hsin-pao. *Commissioner Lin and the Opium War* (17:80) focuses on the leading Chinese official who precipitated the Opium War.

17:60 Muragaki Awaji-no-kami. *Kokai Nikki: The Diary of the First Japanese Embassy to the United States of America.* Trans. by Helen M. Uno. Tokyo: Foreign Affairs Association of Japan, 1958. Muragaki was one of the two highest ranking envoys. His diary was also published as a series in *Contemporary Japan* in 1953 to 1955.

17:61 Satoh, Henry. *Agitated Japan: The Life of Baron Ii Kamon-no-kami Naosuke.* New York: Appleton, 1896. As the shogun's regent, Ii dealt with Harris when he served as the first American minister in Edo.

Satoh wrongly translates some dates from the Japanese calendar.

17:62 Satoh, Henry. *Lord Hotta, the Pioneer Diplomat of Japan*. 2d ed. Tokyo: Hakubunkan, 1908. Hotta was the leading official of the shogun's government when Harris negotiated the treaty of 1858.

17:63 Worthy, Edmund H. "Yung Wing in America." *Pacific Historical Review* 34:1 (1965), 265–87. This is the story of a Chinese diplomat who tried to bridge the cultures of China and America and ended up being accepted by neither. Born in China and educated at Yale (1850–1854), he became a naturalized U.S. citizen. In 1875 he was associate minister at Washington when Ch'en Lan-pin was named minister. Returning to China, he became involved in the Hundred Days Reform of 1898 and had to flee when that collapsed; meanwhile his American citizenship had been invalidated, and he had to secretly reenter the United States, where he died in 1912.

U.S. and China, to 1894

U.S.-CHINA, 1783–1857

17:64 Danton, George H. *The Culture Contacts of the United States and China: The Earliest Sino-American Culture Contacts, 1784–1844*. New York: Columbia University Press, 1931. This book draws attention to a facet of Sino-American relations which emerged along with commercial contacts. Especially valuable is the author's discussion of the philanthropic societies at Canton aimed at aiding the Chinese through education, medicine, etc. Bibliography.

17:65 Goldstein, Jonathan. *Philadelphia and the China Trade, 1682–1846: Commercial, Cultural, and Attitudinal Effects*. University Park: Pennsylvania State University Press, 1978. Philadelphia controlled about one-third of America's China trade during 1783 to 1846. The author seeks to analyze this trade, the role of the trade in stimulating the economy of Philadelphia, and the cultural impact of China on Philadelphia. He argues that Philadelphians had a generally positive image of China and its merchants.

17:66 Li Pao-hung. *Chung-mei wai-chiao kuan-hsi* [Sino-American diplomatic relations]. Taipei, 1972. This book offers a detailed history of Sino-American relations during and after the Opium War. The author concludes that many Chinese officials perceived a distinction between Americans and Englishmen in terms of both attitudes and interests. This book, through Chinese documents quoted and expanded footnotes, provides a useful guide to Chinese sources concerning the inauguration of Sino-American diplomatic relations. Bibliography.

17:67 Li Ting-i. *Chung-mei wai-chiao shih* [The history of Sino-American relations]. Taipei, 1960. Written by a Nationalist Chinese historian, this book stresses the friendship which characterized Sino-American relations from the beginning, a contrast to Maoist Chinese historians. This book is most valuable in its tracing of earliest Chinese awareness of America. The author carefully analyzes the Treaty of Wanghia to prove his thesis. Notes.

17:68 Swisher, Earl. *China's Management of the American Barbarians: A Study of Sino-American Relations, 1841–1861, with Documents*. New Haven, Conn.: Yale University Press, 1953. The author analyzes official Chinese attitudes and policies toward foreigners in general and Americans in particular. Seven hundred pages of translated documents support the author's argument that the Chinese perceived all Westerners as similar and thus based their relations with Americans on precedents set by Sino-English contacts. Extensive bibliography and a glossary of Chinese names and places.

The Old China Trade

See "Personalities," especially Samuel Shaw (under "Others").

17:69 Dermigny, Louis. *La Chine et l'occident: Le Commerce à Canton au XVIIIe Siècle, 1719–1833* [China and the West: the commerce at Canton in the eighteenth century, 1719–1833]. 4 vols. Paris: S.E.V.P.E.N., 1964. This massive work is a valuable repository of carefully collected evidence from British, French, Swiss, and German records. Much material was drawn from the India Office records at London and from nineteen French departmental archives. No American collections and few Chinese sources were used. Volume 4 contains maps, charts, prints, and drawings.

17:70 Downs, Jacques M. "American Merchants and the China Opium Trade, 1800–1840." *Business History Review* 42:4 (1968), 418–42. This article argues that the opium trade was significant to the commercial success of many Americans in the China trade. The author has synthesized earlier material and added new evidence to offer the most thorough account yet of American participation in the illegal trade.

17:71 Dulles, Foster Rhea. *The Old China Trade.* New York: Houghton Mifflin, 1930. This is a well-written description of Yankee traders and merchants, their adventures on the high seas and at Canton during the early decades of the China trade. This book has a precise bibliography of manuscript collections, journals, ships' logs, etc., important to research in the period 1784 to 1844.

17:72 Hunter, William C. *The ''Fan Kwae'' at Canton before Treaty Days, 1825–1844.* London: Kegan Paul, Trench, 1882. This reminiscence of an American merchant describes the life style and business operations imposed on foreigners in China and lends insight into the personal and business relations between Americans and Chinese.

17:73 Latourette, Kenneth S. "The Story of Early Relations between the United States and China, 1784–1844." *Transactions of the Connecticut Academy of Arts and Sciences* 22 (1917), 1–209. Reprint 1964. The earliest in-depth account of the development of Sino-American relations, this study traces the change from private trading to complex mercantile enterprise. Extensive bibliography.

17:74 Miller, Stuart C. "The American Trader's Image of China, 1785–1840." *Pacific Historical Review* 36:4 (1967), 375–95. This article argues that from the beginning of America's trade with China, Americans had negative attitudes and opinions about the Chinese. Compare with Goldstein (17:65).

17:75 Morse, Hosea B. *The Chronicles of the East India Company Trading to China, 1635–1834.* 3 vols. Oxford: Oxford University Press, 1926. This study offers much information concerning the early American experiences at Canton, including American merchants and their trade, their contacts with the Chinese, and their relations with the English merchants. The author also presents numerous tables of American trade statistics, often in comparison with those for the English.

17:76 Ross, Frank E. "American Adventures in the Early Marine Fur Trade with China." *Chinese Social and Political Science Review* 21:2 (1937), 221–67. Based on journal accounts, this article details the early encounters (1787–1812) between American fur traders and their Spanish and Russian counterparts on the Pacific coast.

17:77 Stelle, Charles C. "American Trade in Opium to China Prior to 1820." *Pacific Historical Review* 9:4 (1940), 425–44. The first recorded participation of Americans in the opium trade came two decades after the opening of trade in 1784. Prohibited by the English from trading with India, the drug's major source, they developed a profitable and competitive trade in Turkish opium.

17:78 Stelle, Charles C. "American Trade in Opium to China, 1821–1839." *Pacific Historical Review* 10:1 (1941), 57–74. This article discusses the innovations American merchants used to monopolize the trade in Turkish opium. The Americans were able to increase their profits from the drug even though their major competitors, the English, possessed all the advantages of a vast and powerful commercial empire.

17:79 Ver Steeg, Clarence L. "Financing and Outfitting the First United States Ship to China." *Pacific Historical Review* 22:1 (1953), 1–12. Concentrating on the Americans involved in the voyage of the *Empress of China,* the author offers information of the vessel's investors, their problems in preparing the ship and cargo, and the voyage to China itself (1783–1785).

The Opium War and Treaty of Wanghia

See "Personalities," especially Caleb Cushing.

17:80 Chang, Hsin-pao. *Commissioner Lin and the Opium War.* Cambridge: Harvard University Press, 1964. This book focuses on the leading Chinese official (1754–1840) who precipitated the Opium War and on the English with whom he had to deal; it sees other Westerners in this crisis as merely subordinates of the English, a perception derived from research in Chinese sources. Extensive bibliography.

Fay, P. W. "The Protestant Mission and the Opium War" (17:197).

17:81 Kuo, Pin Chia. "Caleb Cushing and the Treaty of Wanghia, 1844." *Journal of Modern History* 5:1 (1933), 34–54. The author concludes that Cushing's success in negotiating the Treaty of Wanghia was due less to Cushing's ability than to Chinese inexperience. The Chinese were bewildered by Western concepts of foreign relations and distracted by other problems.

17:82 U.S. Senate. *Correspondence between the Commander of the East India Squadron and Foreign Powers.* Senate Document 139. 29th Cong., 1st Sess., 1846. This document includes the exchange between Lawrence Kearny and the governor at Canton concerning American trading privileges in China.

17:83 U.S. Senate. [Correspondence Relating to the Treaty with the Ta Tsing Empire]. Senate Documents 58 and 67. 28th Cong., 2d Sess., 1845. The Senate document includes almost all of the diplomatic correspondence relative to the Cushing mission.

17:84 Welch, Richard E., Jr. "Caleb Cushing's Chinese Mission and the Treaty of Wanghia: A Review." *Oregon Historical Quarterly* 58:4 (1957), 328–57. Welch discusses Cushing's attitudes, his negotiations with the Chinese, and the final Sino-American treaty. The article not only lauds Cushing's mission as a protection of American interests in China but argues that mercantile interests were as crucial a component of manifest destiny as were agrarian interests.

The First Treaty Era and Taiping Rebellion

See "Personalities," especially Humphrey Marshall, Peter Parker, and, under "Others," T. H. Perkins.

17:85 Bain, Chester A. "Commodore Matthew Perry, Humphrey Marshall, and the Taiping Rebellion." *Far Eastern Quarterly* 10:3 (1951), 258–70. This article details the controversy (1853–1854) between Perry and Marshall that resulted from Perry's refusal to make warships available to Marshall for the commissioner's transportation to North China and for the protection of American lives and property threatened by the Taiping rebels.

17:86 Fairbank, John K. *Trade and Diplomacy on the China Coast: The Opening of the Treaty Ports, 1842–1858.* Cambridge: Harvard University Press, 1953. The author argues that national distinctions among Westerners are an ineffective means of understanding this period, since the Chinese viewed all Westerners as similar in attitude and behavior. Thus Sino-American relations became merely a subordinate facet of overall Sino-Western relations, which were determined by the powerful English. Extensive bibliography.

17:87 Griffin, Eldon. *Clippers and Consuls: American Consular and Commercial Relations, 1845–1860.* Ann Arbor, Mich.: Edwards, 1938. A digest rather than an analysis, this book offers a wealth of information concerning American consuls in China as well as American shipping in the treaty ports.

17:88 Henson, Curtis T., Jr. "The U.S. Navy and the Taiping Rebellion." *American Neptune* 38:1 (1978), 28–40. Henson narrates the activities of the American East India squadron on the China coast (1850–1861) and analyzes the problems resulting from the lack of cooperation between American naval and diplomatic officials during the Taiping Rebellion.

17:89 Langley, Harold D. "Gideon Nye and the Formosa Annexation Scheme." *Pacific Historical Review* 34:4 (1965), 397–420. The American merchant, Gideon Nye, played an energetic role in 1857 in urging the U.S. government to seize Formosa and in giving encouragement to Peter Parker, who was also pressing the scheme on Washington.

17:90 Teng, Ssü-yu. *The Taiping Rebellion and the Western Powers: A Comprehensive Survey.* Oxford: Clarendon Press, 1971. In this survey of all Western nations regarding the Taiping rebels, the author suggests that American policy, nominally one of neutrality, followed the whims of various individuals from attempted intervention to passive nonaction—yet, whatever its course, the United States did not follow English leadership. Extensive bibliography.

17:91 Tong, Te-kong. *United States Diplomacy in China, 1844–60.* Seattle: University of Washington Press, 1964. The author perceives the 1840s and 1850s as a period of flux in which the Chinese and the Americans adjusted to the new treaty system. He argues that American diplomats concluded that the only feasible American policy was that which later became known as the open door principle. Extensive bibliography.

17:92 U.S. House. *Correspondence between the State Department and the Late Commissioner to*

China. House Executive Document 123. 33d Cong., 1st Sess., 1854. This document contains the diplomatic correspondence of Humphrey Marshall, U.S. commissioner to China in 1852 to 1854.

17:93 U.S. Senate. *Correspondence of the Late Commissioners in China.* 2 vols. Senate Executive Document 22. 35th Cong., 2d Sess., 1859. These volumes contain the diplomatic correspondence of Commissioners Robert McLane and Peter Parker during 1854 to 1857

U.S.-CHINA, 1857-1894

See "Personalities," especially Anson Burlingame, Samuel Wells Williams, and, under "Others," J. Ross Browne, Charles Denby, Frederick F. Low, George F. Seward, and, under "Asian," "Others," Yung Wing.

17:94 Curti, Merle, and Stalker, John. " 'The Flowery Flag Devils'—The American Image in China 1840–1900." *Proceedings of the American Philosophical Society* 96:6 (1952), 663–90. Americans attempted to present to the Chinese an image of the United States as a peaceful, commercial nation with qualities that distinguished it from Europe. The Chinese accepted this impression but remained skeptical; by the end of the 19th century the Chinese viewed Americans with a mixture of fear and admiration.

17:95 Drake, Fred W. "A Nineteenth-Century View of the United States of America from Hsu Chi-yu's *Ying-huan chih-lueh.*" *Papers on China* 19 (1965), 30–54. Hsü Chi-yü was governor of Fukien. In 1848 he published *Ying-huan chih-lüeh* [Brief description of the oceans roundabout], which served as a guide for China's 19th-century new-style diplomats. The material on America, mostly descriptive, was favorable and naive.

17:96 Wright, Mary C. *The Last Stand of Chinese Conservatism: The T'ung-Chih Restoration, 1862–1874.* Stanford, Calif: Stanford University Press, 1957. Reprint 1966. Wright deemphasizes the American role in the cooperative policy and concludes that foreign cooperation with the Chinese government in the 1860s was mainly the work of Englishmen such as Frederick Bruce, Rutherford Alcock, and Robert Hart.

Diplomacy

17:97 Banno, Masataka. *China and the West, 1858–1861: The Origins of the Tsungli Yamen.* Cambridge: Harvard University Press, 1964. This monograph describes the creation and explains the methods of China's first modern foreign office. Based upon Chinese sources, it helps clarify the Chinese side of Sino-Western relations. Extensive bibliography.

17:98 Biggerstaff, Knight. "The Official Chinese Attitude toward the Burlingame Mission." *American Historical Review* 41:4 (1936), 682–702. Biggerstaff argues that the Chinese government was satisfied with Anson Burlingame's performance of his mission as China's first diplomatic envoy to the West in 1868 to 1870.

17:99 Cordier, Henri. *Histoire des relations de la Chine avec les puissances occidentales, 1860–1900* [History of China's relations with the western powers, 1860–1900]. 3 vols. Paris: Félix Alcan, 1901–1902. This is a detailed survey of all the major diplomatic episodes between China and the United States, France, Britain, and Russia from the Peking Convention of 1860 to the Boxer Rebellion. Cordier includes the texts of several key documents and biographical information on numerous Western diplomats.

17:100 Hsü, Immanuel, C. Y. *China's Entrance into the Family of Nations: The Diplomatic Phase, 1858–1880.* Cambridge: Harvard University Press, 1960. With the Treaties of Tientsin, Chinese diplomacy began a metamorphosis from the traditional Sinocentric world order to the Western system of coequal states. Hsü traces this transformation through the creation of foreign legations in Peking, the study of international law, and the establishment of Chinese legations abroad. Bibliography.

17:101 U.S. Senate. *Instructions to and Dispatches from the Late and Present Ministers in China.* Senate Executive Document 30. 36th Cong., 1st Sess., 1860. This volume contains the diplomatic correspondence of Minister William B. Reed and Minister John E. Ward during 1857 to 1859, the period that included the negotiation and ratification of the Treaty of Tientsin.

Business

17:102 Liu, Kwang-ching. *Anglo-American Steamship Rivalry in China, 1862–1874.* Cambridge: Harvard University Press, 1962. Liu argues that Western commercial enterprises had good, as well as bad, effects on China. Anglo-American competition for the internal Chinese carrying trade benefited Chinese commerce by providing needed transportation and by stimulating the creation of a Chinese steamship company. Bibliography.

17:103 Lockwood, Stephen C. *Augustine Heard and Company, 1858–1862: American Merchants in China.* Cambridge: Harvard University Press, 1970. Along with Russell and Company, Augustine Heard and Company was one of the biggest American commission houses on the China coast. The company's development reached its peak in 1858 to 1862.

Immigration

17:104 Barth, Gunther P. *Bitter Strength: A History of the Chinese in the United States, 1850–1870.* Cambridge: Harvard University Press, 1964. The early Chinese arrivals were sojourners intent upon making money and returning to China; hence they resisted assimilation and aroused the suspicions of Americans. This image remained even after the sojourners became immigrants seeking a place in American society. Bibliography.

17:105 Coolidge, Mary R. *Chinese Immigration.* New York: Holt, 1909. Reprint 1969. Coolidge's account is a highly detailed description and analysis of the Chinese immigration issue in all its aspects—diplomatic, legal, political, and social. She provides several statistical tables and a selected bibliography.

17:106 Miller, Stuart C. *The Unwelcome Immigrant: The American Image of the Chinese, 1785–1882.* Berkeley: University of California Press, 1969. Miller argues that an unfavorable image of the Chinese existed throughout all sections of the United States before 1882 and was not a view confined to the West Coast.

17:107 Paulsen, George E. "The Gresham-Yang Treaty." *Pacific Historical Review* 37:3 (1968), 281–97. The Sino-American treaty of 1894 suspended immigration of Chinese laborers for a period of ten years, an arrangement that was acceptable to China only because the alternative was even harsher U.S. restrictions. Also see his "The Abrogation of the Gresham-Yang Treaty," ibid. 40:4 (1971), 457–77.

17:108 Saxton, Alexander. *The Indispensable Enemy: Labor and the Anti-Chinese Movement in California.* Berkeley: University of California Press, 1971. Saxton elaborates the psychological and ideological complexities of the racism and class consciousness behind the hostility of the non-Chinese labor force in California toward the Chinese immigrants (1860–1910).

17:109 Zo, Kil Young. *Chinese Emigration into the United States, 1850–1880.* New York: Arno, 1979. This is a thorough account of the earliest decades of Chinese immigration to the United States.

U.S. and Japan, to 1894

TOKUGAWA JAPAN

17:110 Beasley, William G., ed. and trans. *Selected Documents on Japanese Foreign Policy, 1853–1868.* London: Oxford University Press, 1955. This is a translation of documents on the Perry treaty of 1854, the Harris treaty of 1858, the expulsion order of 1863, the Shimonoseki indemnity issue of 1863–1864, the imperial ratification of the treaties in 1865, and the opening of Hyogo in 1867. At the time Beasley published this book, the documents in the *Dai Nihon Komonjo: Bakumatsu Gaikoku Kankei Monjo* reached only to 1859; he draws the documents for 1860 to 1868 from other Japanese sources. Extensive bibliography.

17:111 Chang, Richard T. *From Prejudice to Tolerance: A Study of the Japanese Image of the West, 1826–1864.* Tokyo: Sophia University Press, 1970. Chang analyzes the changing image of the West held by two leading intellectuals of the late Tokugawa period, Fujita Tōko (1806–1855) and Sakuma Shōzan (1811–1864). Bibliography.

17:112 Jones, H. J. "Bakumatsu Foreign Employees." *Monumenta Nipponica* 29:3 (1974), 305–27. The article discusses some two hundred foreign employees who were in Japan in the late Tokugawa period. Among the small number of Americans were Samuel R. Brown and Guido F. Verbeck, who taught English, Thomas Hoag, who worked in a customs house, and Phipps Blake and Raphael Pumpelly, two mining engineers.

17:113 Paske-Smith, Montague. *Western Barbarians in Japan and Formosa in Tokugawa Days, 1603–1868.* Kobe: Thompson, 1930. Reprint 1968. The author, British consul at Osaka, bases his account on English East India Company records and the archives of the British consulates at Nagasaki and Osaka.

17:114 Paullin, Charles O. *American Voyages to the Orient, 1690–1865: An Account of Merchant and Naval Activities in China, Japan, and the Various Pacific Islands.* Annapolis, Md.: Naval Institute Press, 1971. This material was first serialized in the *U.S. Naval Institute Proceedings* in 1910–1911. It includes accounts of voyages to Japan in 1846, 1849, and 1851 to 1854.

17:115 Sakamaki Shunzo. *Japan and the United States, 1790–1853: A Study of Japanese Contacts with and Conceptions of the United States and Its People Prior to the American Expedition of 1853–54.* Tokyo, 1940. Reprint 1973. This study, based on Japanese- and English-language sources, is especially useful for information on American voyages to Japan in the 1830s and 1840s.

17:116 Wildes, Harry E. *Aliens in the East: A New History of Japan's Foreign Intercourse.* Philadelphia: University of Pennsylvania Press, 1937. Reprint 1973. Wildes includes extensive coverage of early contacts (1543–1868) of the Portuguese, Dutch, Russians, English, and Americans with Japan.

The Perry Mission, 1853–1854

See "Personalities," especially Manjiro, Matthew C. Perry.

17:117 Cole, Allan B., ed. *A Scientist with Perry in Japan: The Journal of Dr. James Morrow.* Chapel Hill: University of North Carolina Press, 1947. As agriculturalist with the Perry mission, Morrow spent more time on shore and met more Japanese than any other member of the expedition.

17:118 Cole, Allan B., ed. *With Perry in Japan: The Diary of Edward Yorke McCauley.* Princeton, N.J.: Princeton University Press, 1942. McCauley was an acting master's mate on the *Powhatan.* His diary recounts Perry's second voyage to Japan.

17:119 Cole, Allan B., ed. *Yankee Surveyors in the Shogun's Seas: Records of the U.S. Surveying Expedition to the North Pacific Ocean, 1853–56.* Princeton, N.J.: Princeton University Press, 1947. Reprint 1968. This is the report of a brash young naval officer who landed armed men at will along the coast of Japan and surveyed Japan's inland waters in violation of the Perry treaty.

17:120 . Graff, Henry F., ed. *Bluejackets with Perry in Japan.* New York: New York Public Library, 1952. This is a day-by-day account of Master's Mate John R. C. Lewis of the *Macedonian* and Cabin Boy William B. Allen of the *Vandalia.*

17:121 Hawks, Francis L. *Narrative of the Expedition of an American Squadron to the China Seas and Japan Performed in the Years 1852, 1853, and 1854 under the Command of Commodore M. C. Perry, United States Navy.* 3 vols. Washington, D.C.: Nicholson, 1856–1858. Reprint 1967. Volume 1 of this detailed official narrative report is based primarily on the journal of Commodore Perry, but it also incorporates material from the journals and reports of Fleet Captain Henry A. Adams, Flag Lieutenants Silas Bent and John Contee, Captain Joel Abbot, Commander Franklin Buchanan, Surgeons Daniel S. Green and Charles F. Fahs, Chaplain George Jones, Bayard Taylor, and others. Volume 2 contains various scientific reports, and volume 3 is a report on zodiacal light observations.

17:122 Hayashi Daigaku-no-kami. "Diary of an Official of the Bakufu." *Transactions of the Asiatic Society of Japan* 2d ser. 7 (1930), 98–119. This is a Japanese record of the negotiations between Perry and Hayashi, lord rector of the university. This diary was also published in *Contemporary Japan* in 1953 (nos. 1–3, pp. 73–96).

17:123 Preble, George H. *The Opening of Japan: A Diary of Discovery in the Far East, 1853–1856.* Ed. by Boleslaw Szczesniak. Norman: University of Oklahoma Press, 1962. As a lieutenant on the *Macedonian,* Preble was a close observer of events, including the negotiations at Kanagawa. Like many others, he refused to obey Perry's order to turn over his diary to the navy for use in compiling the official narrative.

17:124 Sakanishi Shio, ed. *A Private Journal of John Glendy Sproston.* Tokyo: Sophia University Press, 1940. Reprint 1968. This journal by a midshipman on the *Macedonian* was not used by Hawks in compiling the official narrative. The writer went with Perry's second visit to Japan.

17:125 Spalding, J. Willett. *The Japan Expedition: Japan and Around the World.* New York: Redfield, 1855. The author was the captain's clerk on the *Mississippi,* the flag ship of the squadron. Though he states that he did not keep a journal—which by Perry's order he would have been required to surrender to the navy—he gives a detailed day-by-day account of both voyages of Perry to Japan.

17:126 Swisher, Earl. "Commodore Perry's Imperialism in Relation to America's Present-Day Position in the Pacific." *Pacific Historical Review* (16:1 (1947), 30–40. Swisher discusses Perry's proposal for U.S. control of Hawaii, the Bonin Islands, Okinawa, and Formosa.

17:127 U.S. Senate. *Correspondence Relative to the Naval Expedition to Japan.* Senate Executive Document 34. 33d Cong., 2d Sess., 1855. This collection includes correspondence between Perry and the Navy Department and records of the negotiations at Kanagawa.

17:128 Vernon, Manfred C. "The Dutch and the Opening of Japan by the United States." *Pacific Historical Review* 28:1 (1959), 39–48. Though the Dutch were uneasy about the Perry expedition and expected it to fail, the governor general of Java sent instructions to the Dutch foreman at Nagasaki to give support to the objective of opening Japan.

17:129 Wallach, Sidney, ed. *Narrative of the Expedition of an American Squadron to the China Seas and Japan under the Command of Commodore M. C. Perry.* New York: Coward-McCann, 1952. This abridgment of the official narrative focuses on the diplomatic and political aspects of the mission.

17:130 Walworth, Arthur C. *Black Ships off Japan: The Study of Commodore Perry's Expedition.* New York: Knopf, 1946. Reprint 1966. Walworth was the first writer to use sources, such as the records of Williams, Spalding, and Preble, that were not incorporated in the official narrative.

17:131 Williams, S. Wells. "A Journal of the Perry Expedition to Japan (1853–1854)." *Transactions of the Asiatic Society of Japan* 1st ser. 37 (1910), 1–259. Williams's journal was not used by Hawks in compiling the official narrative. It gives the most extensive coverage of any of the private journals.

Townsend Harris, 1856–1861

See "Personalities," especially Townsend Harris, and Asians Baron Ii Kamon-no-kami Naosuke, Lord Hotta (under "Others").

17:132 Black, John R. *Young Japan: Yokohama and Yedo, 1858–79.* 2 vols. London: Trubner, 1880–1881. Reprint 1968. Black, the former editor of the *Japan Herald* and the *Japan Gazette,* gives a detailed first-hand description.

17:133 Heusken, Henry. *Japan Journal, 1855–1861.* Trans. by Jeanette C. van der Corput and Robert A. Wilson. New Brunswick, N.J.: Rutgers University Press, 1964. This is the journal of Harris's Dutch secretary and interpreter. Heusken recorded the events from October 1855 to June 1858. He resumed the journal in January 1861 just two weeks before he was assassinated by an antiforeign Japanese ronin.

17:134 McMaster, John. "Alcock and Harris: Foreign Diplomacy in Bakumatsu Japan." *Monumenta Nipponica* 22:3/4 (1967), 305–367. This article treats the diplomatic activities of Harris and British minister Rutherford Alcock in the period following the conclusion of the treaties of 1858.

17:135 Sakanishi Shio, ed. *Some Unpublished Letters of Townsend Harris.* New York: Japan Reference Library, 1941. Most of these long, descriptive letters from Harris in Japan were written to Caterine Ann Drinker, a young girl in a family that Harris met in Hong Kong.

17:136 Statler, Oliver. *Shimoda Story.* New York: Random House, 1969. The book is written with literary grace and, as the author states, with some liberty in filling out events where the evidence is scanty. The bulk of the volume relates to the experiences of Harris in Shimoda. Two final chapters relate the negotiations at Edo in 1858 and the subsequent residence of Harris in Edo. Extensive bibliography.

17:137 "Translations of 12 Interviews of Harris with Inouye Shinano no Kami and Iwase Higo no Kami." In David Hunter Miller, ed., *Treaties and Other International Acts of the United States of America, 1776–1863.* Washington, D.C.: G.P.O., 1942, vol. 7, pp. 638–48, 1089–170. Provided here are the Japanese minutes of the talks between Harris and Japanese officials during the negotiations for the 1858 treaty.

17:138 Wood, William M. *Fankwei: Or, the San Jacinto in the Seas of India, China, and Japan.* New York: Harper, 1859. This long account, written by the surgeon of the fleet, covers the voyage of Harris to Siam, China, and Japan and the landing of Harris at Shimoda.

Japanese Mission to U.S., 1860

See "Personalities," especially Muragaki Awaji-no-kami (under "Others").

17:139 Bush, Lewis W. *77 Samurai: Japan's First Embassy to America.* Tokyo: Kodansha International, 1968. This account is based on *Shichijushichinin no Samurai* by Hattori Itsurō, who used the journal of his great-grandfather Muragaki Awaji-no-kami.

17:140 Cole, Allan B. "Japan's First Embassy to the United States, 1860." *Pacific Northwest Quarterly* 32:2 (1941), 130–66. This is a thorough account of the mission.

17:141 Johnston, James D. *China and Japan: Being a Narrative of the Cruise of the U.S. Steam Frigate Powhatan, in the Years 1857, '58, '59, and '60, including an Account of the Japanese Embassy to the United States.* Philadelphia: Charles Desilver, 1860. The author was executive officer of the *Powhatan.* He accompanied the Japanese embassy in the United States.

17:142 Miyoshi, Masao. *As We Saw Them: The First Japanese Embassy to the United States (1860).* Berkeley: University of California Press, 1979. Written by a specialist in comparative literature, this book examines the diaries kept by members of the 1860 Japanese mission to the United States, describing the ways in which these first visitors to America reacted to new situations and comparing them with the diary of Townsend Harris.

17:143 Mori Masatoshi, ed. *The First Japanese Mission to the United States (1860).* Trans. by Fukuyama Junichi and Roderick H. Jackson. Kobe: Thompson, 1937. Reprint 1973. This is the diary of Yanagawa Masakiyo, the chief retainer of Niimi Masaoki who headed the embassy.

17:144 Nichi-Bei Shūko Tsūsho Hyakunen Kinen Gyōji Un'eikai, ed. *Man-en Gannen Kem-Bei Shisetsu Shiryō Shūsei* [Historical materials on the

1860 mission to the United States]. 7 vols. Tokyo: Kazama Shobō, 1960–1961. This is the major documentary source for the 1860 mission. It includes nine Japanese diaries, newspaper clippings, the diary of Captain John Mercer, and various official documents.

17:145 Yanaga, Chitoshi. "The First Japanese Embassy to the United States." *Pacific Historical Review* 9:2 (1940), 113–38. His account is based mostly on English-language sources.

MEIJI JAPAN, TO 1894

17:146 Kamikawa Hikomatsu, ed. *Japan-American Diplomatic Relations in the Meiji-Taisho Era.* Trans. by Kimuro Michiko. Tokyo: Pan-Pacific Press, 1958. This is a translation of volume 1 of *Nichibei Bunka Kōshō Shi* [History of Japanese-American cultural relations]. It includes 109 pages by Hanabusa Nagamichi on the period 1868 to 1895; much is revealed from Japanese sources.

17:147 Ohara Keishi, ed. *Japanese Trade and Industry in the Meiji-Taisho Era.* Trans. by Ōkata Tamotsu. Tokyo: Ōbunsha, 1957. Despite the general title, this volume deals only with U.S.-Japanese relations (1853–1926). It is volume 2 of *Nichibei Bunka Kōshō Shi* [History of Japanese-American cultural relations], which covers financial relations, the introduction of American industrial and agricultural technology, and trade in tea, silk, and cotton goods.

Treaty Revision

17:148 Hubbard, Richard B. *The United States in the Far East: Or, Modern Japan and the Orient.* Richmond, Va.: Johnson, 1899. The author was minister to Japan during 1885 to 1890. The account is mostly descriptive of Japan, but it includes two chapters on treaty revision.

17:149 Japan. Gaimushō [Foreign Ministry]. *Jōyaku Kaisei Kankei Nihon Gaikō Bunsho* [Japanese diplomatic documents on treaty revision]. 4 vols. and 4 suppls. Tokyo: Nihon Gakujutsu Shinkōkai, 1941–1953. This is the basic Japanese document collection on treaty revision. The supplementary volumes have titles as follows: *Jōyaku Kaisei Kankei Nihon Gaikō Bunsho, Kaigiroku* [Japanese diplomatic documents on treaty revision, minutes]; *Jōyaku Kaisei Keika Gaiyō* [A summary of the development of treaty revision]; *Tsūshō Jōyaku to Tsūshō Seisaku no Hensen* [Changes in trade treaties and trade policy]; *Jōyaku Kaisei Kankei Nihon Gaikō Bunsho, Tsuiho* [Japanese diplomatic documents on treaty revision, supplement].

17:150   Jones, Francis C. *Extraterritoriality in Japan and the Diplomatic Relations Resulting in Its Abolition, 1853–1899.* New Haven, Conn.: Yale University Press, 1931. Reprint 1970. This study is based primarily on published English-language sources. It emphasizes the British side, but gives some coverage of the U.S. side.

17:151   Kume Kunitake, ed. *Tokumei Zenken Taishi Bei-Ō Kairan Jikki* [Journal of the ambassador extraordinary and plenipotentiary's travels through America and Europe]. 5 vols. Tokyo: Hakubunsha, 1878. This is a major documentary source on the Iwakura mission of 1872–1873.

17:152   Mayo, Marlene J. "A Catechism of Western Diplomacy: The Japanese and Hamilton Fish, 1872." *Journal of Asian Studies* 26:3 (1967), 389–410. A detailed analysis of the negotiations on possible treaty revision between Secretary of State Fish and the envoys of the Iwakura mission.

17:153   Mayo, Marlene J. "Rationality in the Meiji Restoration: The Iwakura Embassy." In Bernard S. Silberman and H. D. Harootunian, eds., *Modern Japanese Leadership: Transition and Change.* Tucson: University of Arizona Press, 1966, pp. 323–70. An analysis of the decisionmaking by Japanese leaders in 1869 to 1871 resulting in the sending of the Iwakura mission to America and Europe.

17:154   Shimomura Fujio. *Meiji Shonen Jōyaku Kaisei Shi no Kenkyū* [Studies in the history of treaty revision during the early years of Meiji]. Tokyo: Yoshikawa Kōbunkan, 1962. This is the best study of treaty revision by a Japanese scholar.

17:155   Soviak, Eugene. "On the Nature of Western Progress: The Journal of the Iwakura Embassy." In Donald H. Shively, ed., *Tradition and Modernization in Japanese Culture.* Princeton, N.J.: Princeton University Press, 1971, pp. 7–34. This is an analysis of the nature and content of the five-volume journal of the Iwakura mission of 1872–1873 (the *Tokumei Zenken Taishi Bei-Ō Kairen Jikki*).

Visit of General Grant, 1879

17:156   Chang, Richard T. "General Grant's 1879 Visit to Japan." *Monumenta Nipponica* 24:4 (1969), 373–92. This detailed account focuses on the social aspects of the visit and Grant's role in the Ryukyu Islands controversy between Japan and China.

17:157   *Guranto Shōgun to no Go-taiwa Hikki* [Notes of His Majesty's interview with General Grant]. Tokyo: Kokumin Seishin Bunka Kenkyūjo, 1937. Records the two-hour informal talk that Grant had with the emperor on August 10, 1879, in which they discussed treaty revision, the Ryukyu question, parliamentary government, and foreign indebtedness.

17:158   Young, John R. *Around the World with General Grant.* 2 vols. New York: American News, 1879. The author, a correspondent of the New York *Herald*, includes a forty-page account of the visit to Japan that is mostly descriptive but includes summaries of Grant's talks with the emperor and Japanese officials.

Employment of Foreigners

17:159   Jones, Hazel J. "The Formulation of the Meiji Government Policy toward the Employment of Foreigners." *Monumenta Nipponica* 23:1/2 (1968), 9–30. Gives a detailed analysis of policy formulation during 1868 to 1870 relating to employment of foreigners and a brief account of modifications of policy in the 1870s and 1880s.

17:160   Jones, Hazel J. *Live Machines: Hired Foreigners and Meiji Japan.* Vancouver: University of British Columbia Press, 1980. The author examines the overall significance and extent of Japan's policy in hiring foreign experts; the changing emphasis from more general advisers to specialists; the regulatory machinery developed to deal with the sometimes recalcitrant Europeans and Americans; the image these employees had of their own value; and their worth in the eyes of their Japanese employers.

17:161   Umetani Noboru. *The Role of Foreign Employees in the Meiji Era in Japan.* Tokyo: Institute of Developing Economies, 1971. An extensive analysis which includes descriptions of the activities of Guido F. Verbeck, Henry W. Denison, David Murray, Edward Morse, and Ernest F. Fenollosa.

Cultural Relations and Perceptions

17:162 Anthony, David F. "Cultural Unity and Resilience in Japan's Encounter with the West." *Journal of World History* 9:1 (1965), 91–103. An interpretive essay on how the Japanese have been able to absorb much from other cultures and yet retain their unique identity and strength.

17:163 Beauchamp, Edward R. *An American Teacher in Early Meiji Japan.* Honolulu: University Press of Hawaii, 1976. This narrowly focused biographical study of William Elliot Griffis deals with his role as a teacher of physics and chemistry in Fukui during 1870 to 1872 and in Tokyo during 1872 to 1874. A concluding chapter deals with Griffis as interpreter and historian of Japan after his return to the United States in 1874. Griffis's experiences in Japan and his contacts with Japan served as the basis for eighteen books, including *The Mikado's Empire.*

17:164 Chisolm, Lawrence W. *Fenollosa: The Far East and American Culture.* New Haven, Conn.: Yale University Press, 1963. A study of an American professor of philosophy at Tokyo University who became the foremost interpreter of Japanese art to the Western world and as imperial commissioner of fine arts was an instructor to the Japanese concerning the great worth of their historic paintings and sculpture. Extensive bibliography.

17:165 Harris, Neil. "All the World a Melting Pot? Japan at American Fairs, 1874–1904." In Akira Iriye, ed., *Mutual Images: Essays in American-Japanese Relations.* Cambridge: Harvard University Press, 1975, pp. 24–54. Harris describes the favorable American opinion of both traditional and modern Japan that was elicited by Japanese exhibits at American fairs.

17:166 Kaikoku Hyakunen Kinen Bunka Jigyokai, ed. *Nichi-Bei Bunka Kōsho Shi* [History of Japanese-American cultural relations]. 6 vols. Tokyo: Yōyōsha, 1954–1956. Three of these volumes have been translated and are listed separately. They are volume 1, Kamikawa's book on Japanese-American diplomatic relations; volume 2, Ohara's book on Japan's trade and industry; volume 4, Kimura's book on literature, manners, and customs (17:168). The volumes that have not been translated are volume 3, a study of religion and education by Kishimoto Hideo; volume 5, a study of immigration to the United States by Nagai Matsuzō; and volume 6, an index.

17:167 Kamei, Shunsuke. "The Sacred Land of Liberty: Images of America in Nineteenth Century Japan." In Akira Iriye, ed., *Mutual Images: Essays in American-Japanese Relations.* Cambridge: Harvard University Press, 1975, pp. 55–72. The author finds that throughout most of the period 1853 to 1900 Japanese intellectuals were unstinting in their praise of the United States but that by the end of the century a more realistic and less romantic view emerged.

17:168 Kimura Ki. *Japanese Literature: Manners and Customs in the Meiji-Taisho Era.* Trans. by Philip Yampolsky. Tokyo: Ōbunsha, 1957. This is an informative, digressive, and rather subjective account of American-Japanese literary relations (1868–1926). It is one of the volumes of the *Nichi-Bei Bunka Kōsho Shi* [History of Japanese-American cultural relations] (17:166).

17:169 Lancaster, Clay. *The Japanese Influence in America.* New York: Rawls, 1963. This illustrated study analyzes the influence of Japanese art and architecture in America.

17:170 Lehmann, Jean-Pierre. *The Image of Japan: A Changing Society, 1850–1905.* Winchester, Mass.: Allen & Unwin, 1978. This work is thematic and deals with the images of Westerners visiting or residing in Japan concerning Japanese politics, industry, society, and the Russo-Japanese War. Bibliography.

17:171 Miner, Earl. *Japanese Traditions in British and American Literature.* Princeton, N.J.: Princeton University Press, 1958. A study of the impact on the West of Japanese literature and drama (1549–1956), an impact felt by such American writers as Ernest Fenollosa, Lafcadio Hearn, Amy Lowell, Ezra Pound, James Whistler, and Walt Whitman. Bibliography.

17:172 Nagai, Michio. "Westernization and Japanization: The Early Meiji Transformation of Education." In Donald H. Shively, ed., *Tradition and Modernization in Japanese Culture.* Princeton, N.J.: Princeton University Press, 1971, pp. 35–76. Traces the course of the westernization of Japanese education (1872–1890) as it changed from the French type to the American and then to the Prussian while preserving significant elements that were Japanese.

17:173 Nitobe Inazō. *The Intercourse between the United States and Japan: An Historical Sketch.* Baltimore: Johns Hopkins Press, 1891. Reprint 1973. The portions of this book that deal with diplomatic relations have been long outdated, but chapter 4, on American influences in Japan (1850–1880), is still of interest.

17:174 Schwantes, Robert S. *Japanese and Americans: A Century of Cultural Relations.* New York: Harper, 1955. Deals with the whole range of U.S.-Japanese cultural relations (1853–1953), but especially emphasizes American influence on the educational system of Meiji Japan. Extensive bibliography.

17:175 Stevenson, Elizabeth. *Lafcadio Hearn.* New York: Macmillan, 1961. This is the best biography of Hearn (1850–1904).

U.S. and Korea, to 1905

17:176 Mun Il-P'yŏng. *Hanmi Oshipnyun Sa* [Fifty years of history of American-Korean relations]. Seoul: Cho Kwang Sa, 1945. This general, interpretative work is a good introduction to the subject of American-Korean relations (1866–1905). The notable scholarship and excellent prose style of the author make the work a minor classic in Korean history.

17:177 Nelson, M. Frederick. *Korea and the Old Orders in East Asia.* New York: Russell & Russell, 1945. Nelson successfully treats American-Korean relations (1593–1910) within the frameworks of both Western diplomacy and the Oriental international system based on Confucianism. Attention to the cultural dimension of diplomatic relations makes the study unique and valuable. Bibliography.

THE OPENING OF KOREA

See "Document Collections" for *Korean-American Relations* (17:23).

17:178 Chien, Frederick Foo. *The Opening of Korea: A Study of Chinese Diplomacy, 1876–1885.* Hamden, Conn.: Shoe String Press, 1967. Only one chapter is devoted to the making of the American-Korean Treaty of 1882; the remainder is useful background material. Bibliography.

17:179 Coble, E. M. "United States–Korean Relations 1866–1871." *Transactions of the Korea Branch of the Royal Asiatic Society* 28 (1938), 1–229. This is a narrative of the 1866 *General Sherman* incident and of the 1871 Admiral Rogers expedition to Korean waters. It includes many documents from the U.S. State Department archives and translations of Korean official records. Bibliography.

17:180 Deuchler, Martina. *Confucian Gentlemen and Barbarian Envoys: The Opening of Korea, 1875–1885.* Seattle: University of Washington Press, 1977. Based on multiarchival research, this book deals with Korea's political, intellectual, and economic changes as well as its diplomatic developments. Especially valuable are the insights into Korean leadership during this period when crucial decisions were made on diplomatic questions.

17:181 Kim, Key-Hiuk. *The Last Phase of the East Asian World Order: Korea, Japan, and the Chinese Empire, 1860–1882.* Berkeley: University of California Press, 1979. The author examines how Korea, Japan, and China altered their traditional relations in response to the intrusion of the Western powers in East Asia.

17:182 Lee Bo-Un. "Shufeldt Tsedokkwa 1880 Nyunwi Cho-Mi Kyosup [Commodore Schufeldt and the Korean-American negotiation in 1880]." *Sahak Bo* 15:4 (1961), 61–91. In this well-documented article Lee argues that Commodore Shufeldt's efforts to open Korea in 1880 were frustrated by China's reluctance to allow the Western powers, with the assistance of Japan, to open Korea.

17:183 Lee, Yur-Bok. *Diplomatic Relations between the United States and Korea, 1866–1887.* New York: Humanities Press, 1970. With a concentration on the first five years of formal diplomatic relations between the two nations beginning in 1883, this scholarly work considers 12 years of American-Korean relations through 1887. The book is well-balanced and is the most useful work for the period covered. Extensive bibliography.

17:184 Noble, Harold J. "The Korean Mission to the United States in 1883." *Transactions of the Korea Branch of the Royal Asiatic Society* 18 (1929), 1–21.

Noble presents a detailed description of the first special Korean mission to the United States in 1883. The mission provided a great learning experience for the leaders of Korea, which had just opened its door to the Western world.

17:185 Pak Il-Gŏn. *Kundae Hanmi Oegyosa* [Diplomatic relations between Korea and the United States in the modern era]. Seoul: Pak U Sa, 1968. This is a descriptive study of American-Korean relations through 1888. The author, a Korean scholar with training in Korean and Chinese universities, used Korean and Chinese materials extensively.

17:186 Sunwoo, Hak-Won. "A Study of the U.S.-Korean Treaty of 1882 (Korea Opened to Western Powers)." *Korea Review* 2:1 (1949), 25–44. This article discloses some new information from the Korean side of the treaty-making process in 1881 and 1882.

THE MID-1880s AND AFTER

See "Personalities," especially Horace N. Allen (under "Others") and Willard Straight; also see "Document Collections" for *Korean-American Relations* (17:23).

17:187 Chay, Jongsuk. "The Taft-Katsura Memorandum Reconsidered." *Pacific Historical Review* 27:3 (1968), 321–26. Chay argues that the memorandum (1905) constituted an understanding between the United States and Japan regarding Korea that was more than a mere exchange of views.

17:188 Dorwart, Jeffrey M. "The Independent Minister: John M. B. Sill and the Struggle against Japanese Expansion in Korea, 1894–1897." *Pacific Historical Review* 44:4 (1975), 485–502. This recounts the American minister's unsuccessful attempts to curb the Japanese and to change the Washington government's view, a view that Sill regarded as too pro-Japanese.

17:189 Esthus, Raymond A. "The Taft-Katsura Agreement—Reality or Myth?" *Journal of Modern History* 31:1 (1959), 46–51. Esthus argues that the Taft-Katsura Agreed Memorandum (1905) was not an agreement or bargain involving Korea but only an honest exchange of views.

17:190 Lee Bae-Yong. "Kuhanmal Mikukwi Unsan Kumkwang Chaekulkwŭn Hwaektuke Taehayŭ [On

the acquisition of the mining rights of the Unsan Gold Mine by the United States at the end of the Yi Dynasty]." *Yŏksa Hakbo* 50–51:9 (1971), 43–111. Lee details the acquisition of the Unsan Gold Mine concession by American businessmen in 1896 and its operation to 1939. He argues that the Unsan Gold Mine was a "bonanza" for the Americans, bringing a net profit of $15 million in its 44-year operation, but it brought few benefits to the Koreans.

17:191 Lee Kwang-Rin. *Hankuk Kaehwasa Yŏnku* [A study on enlightenment in Korea]. Seoul: Ilchyo Kak, 1969. Several Americans occupied key positions in the modernization of Korea toward the end of the 19th century. This study, which emphasizes the 1880s, is valuable for an understanding of the roles played by these Americans. The book has a summary in English.

17:192 Noble, Harold J. "The United States and Sino-Korean Relations, 1885–1887." *Pacific Historical Review* 2:3 (1933), 292–304. Noble gives a concise account of the role of Lt. George C. Foulk in Seoul. Foulk ably executed the American policy of treating Korea as an independent nation in opposition to the efforts of his Chinese antagonist, Yüan Shih-k'ai, who endeavored to reinstate Korea's dependency on China.

17:193 Ro, Kwang Hae, and Smith, Robert T. "Theodore Roosevelt and the Korean Intervention Question: An Analysis of a President's Defense." *Koreana Quarterly* 11:3 (1969), 84–92. The authors undertake to refute Theodore Roosevelt's later (1916) explanation for his earlier policy of nonintervention on behalf of Korea during his presidency. Roosevelt claimed to have based that policy on 1) the lack of an opportunity for intervention, and 2) the absence of an obligation or justification for intervention.

U.S. Missionaries

See Chapter 2, "Philanthropy and Missionaries," for additional references.

Phillips, C. J. *Protestant America and the Pagan World: The First Half Century of the American Board of Commissioners for Foreign Missions, 1810–1860*

(2:80) recounts activities in the Middle East, Africa, South Asia, East Asia, and the Pacific.

CHINA

See "Personalities," especially Peter Parker, Samuel Wells Williams.

17:194 Boardman, Eugene P. *Christian Influence upon the Ideology of the Taiping Rebellion, 1851– 1864*. Madison: University of Wisconsin Press, 1952. This study focuses on the Taiping ideology as it existed in 1851 to 1854, the first three years of the rebellion. It discusses what the Taipings took, and failed to take, from Christianity and evaluates the role the Christian element played in the final outcome of the rebellion. Extensive bibliography.

17:195 Carlson, Ellsworth C. *The Foochow Missionaries, 1847–1880*. Cambridge: Harvard University Press, 1974. This study is based on British and American diplomatic records, Chinese sources, and missionary records. It is particularly valuable for its analysis of Chinese efforts to curtail the missionaries. Bibliography.

17:196 Cohen, Paul A. *China and Christianity: The Missionary Movement and the Growth of Chinese Anti-Foreignism, 1860–1870*. Cambridge: Harvard University Press, 1963. This study deals primarily with China's handling of British and French cases resulting from the opposition of the officials and the gentry to Christianity. Extensive bibliography.

Fairbank, J. K., ed. *The Missionary Enterprise in China and America* [1834–1935] (2:77) contains a collection of essays dealing with many aspects of missionary activities.

17:197 Fay, Peter W. "The Protestant Mission and the Opium War." *Pacific Historical Review* 40:2 (1971), 145–61. This relates the views of Protestant missionaries toward the Chinese and toward the Opium War (1834–1842). American missionaries in China at this time included Coleman Bridgman, Ira Tracy, David Abeel, Peter Parker, I. J. Roberts, J. Lewis, and Samuel R. Brown.

17:198 Forsythe, Sidney A. *An American Missionary Community in China, 1895–1905*. Cambridge: Harvard University Press, 1971. Written by a sociologist, this study analyzes the attitudes of 103 American Protestant missionaries in North China during the decade following the Sino-Japanese War. The author finds that missionaries were poor observers of the China scene, that they suffered from isolation, partly imposed and partly self-imposed, and that they had a negative or derogatory view of the Chinese. Bibliography.

17:199 Hyatt, Irwin T. *Our Ordered Lives Confess: Three Nineteenth-Century American Missionaries in East Shantung*. Cambridge: Harvard University Press, 1976. The three missionaries dealt with are T. P. Crawford, a Southern Baptist who opposed social and education work, Lottie Moon, who was interested in the plight of Chinese women, and Calvin Mateer, who worked with his wife in the school she founded (Christian College, Tengchow). The study touches on all the broad aspects of missionary activity and is especially valuable for the role of women in the missionary movement.

17:200 Latourette, Kenneth Scott. *A History of Christian Missions in China*. New York: Macmillan, 1929. Reprint 1967. An extensive survey that is still an indispensable source of information. Bibliography.

17:201 Liu, Kwang-Ching. *American Missionaries in China*. Cambridge: Harvard University Press, 1966. This is a collection of seven articles previously printed in Harvard's annual *Papers on China*. Among them are papers dealing with W. A. P. Martin, Devello Z. Sheffield, the founding of Hsiang-Ya Medical School, and the undertaking by missionaries of social services. An appendix lists all papers on missionary subjects published in *Papers on China* during 1950 to 1965.

17:202 Liu, Kwang-ching. "Early Christian Colleges in China." *Journal of Asian Studies* 20:1 (1960), 71–78. This brief article evaluates the objectives and influence of Shantung Christian University, Peking University, North China College at Tengchow, and St. John's College at Shanghai (1882–1911).

Lutz, J. G. *China and the Christian Colleges, 1850– 1950* (2:79).

17:203 Paulsen, George E. "The Szechwan Riots of 1895 and American Missionary Diplomacy." *Journal of Asian Studies* 28:2 (1969), 285–98. Paulsen examines American policy dealing with antimissionary riots in Chengtu and Kutien. He concludes that though America's strong stand and close cooperation with the British brought the degradation of the Szechwan viceroy, the policy failed to prevent new outrages in the subsequent years.

17:204 Rabe, Valentin H. *The Home Base of American China Missions, 1880–1920.* Cambridge: Harvard University Press, 1978. Rabe examines the growth of elaborate home base boards and interdenominational societies in which wealthy laymen used their skills in organization, money raising, and advertising. Extensive bibliography.

17:205 Teng, Yuan Chung. "Reverand Issachar Jacox Roberts and the Taiping Rebellion." *Journal of Asian Studies* 23:1 (1963), 55–67. Teng analyzes the influence of Roberts (1837–1862) on the future leader of the Taiping rebels, Hung Hsiu-ch'üan, as a result of Hung's study with him in Canton. He also recounts the later visits of Roberts to the Taiping capital and his final assessment of Hung as a "crazy man."

17:206 Varg, Paul A. *Missionaries, Chinese, and Diplomats: The American Protestant Missionary Movement in China, 1890–1952.* Princeton, N.J.: Princeton University Press, 1958. The coverage of the pre–World War I period is brief and analytical. It describes the shifting emphases in missionary programs toward humanitarian and educational concerns, and it analyzes the relationship of the missionary endeavor to American nationalism and imperialism.

JAPAN

17:207 Best, Ernest E. *Christian Faith and Cultural Crisis: The Japanese Case.* Leiden: Brill, 1966. The author uses sociological methodology to analyze the relationship between Protestant Christianity and the political/economic life of Meiji Japan (1859–1911). He concludes that Christianity did not have a profound impact, and the benefits usually attributed to its influence resulted more from Japan's desire to remove the unequal treaties by appearing "civilized" to the West. Bibliography.

17:208 Cary, Otis. *A History of Christianity in Japan.* 2 vols. New York: Revell, 1909. Reprint 1970. This work is basic and reliable. The first volume covers Catholic and Greek Orthodox missions; the second is a history of Protestant missions (1859–1908). The focus is Christian and the emphasis is on

the missionaries and their work rather than on the converts; it is especially valuable on Protestant missions. Bibliography.

17:209 Drummond, Richard H. *A History of Christianity in Japan.* Grand Rapids, Mich.: Eerdmans, 1971. The missionary author synthesized Japanese and Western scholarship, organizing his efforts around the theme of the tension between the Christian obligation to serve God rather than man, and the traditional tendency of Japanese political leadership to make loyalty to the state a religion surpassing all others. Extensive bibliography.

17:210 Howes, John F. "Japanese Christians and American Missionaries." In Marius Jansen, ed., *Changing Japanese Attitudes towards Modernization.* Princeton, N.J.: Princeton University Press, 1965, pp. 337–68. Howes concludes that the converts (1859–1912) underwent self-abasement due to Japan's humiliation at being unable to resist the West, they were then "spiritually reborn," and soon outgrew the missionaries as faith enabled them to raise their self-esteem and perceive their country in a new light. Extensive bibliography.

17:211 Iglehart, Charles W. *A Century of Protestant Christianity in Japan.* Rutland, Vt.: Tuttle, 1959. Interweaving the Christian story with an account of Japan's modern century, this work is not analytical but does summarize the phases of the expansion of Christianity and brings the story to the present.

17:212 Laures, Johannes. *The Catholic Church in Japan.* Rutland, Vt.: Tuttle, 1959. Reprint 1962. This work, based on primary sources, is one of few books on Catholicism in Japan (1549–1941). Most of the work deals with Catholicism prior to the ban imposed on Christianity by Tokugawa Ieyasu in the early 17th century.

17:213 Scheiner, Irwin. *Christian Converts and Social Protest in Meiji Japan.* Berkeley: University of California Press, 1970. Scheiner recounts how young samurai (1868–1912) who were alienated by the Meiji restoration accepted Christianity, choosing a new value system and legitimizing the choice by finding in it parallels with the Confucian world order. Extensive bibliography.

17:214 Thomas, Winburn T. *Protestant Beginnings in Japan: The First Three Decades, 1859–1889.* Rutland, Vt.: Tuttle, 1959. This work recounts the course of the movement from inauguration through rapid growth and into decline. The evaluation of the significance of Protestantism in Japan is typical of the missionary perspective. Extensive bibliography.

17:215 Thomson (Taylor), Sandra C. "Meiji Japan through Missionary Eyes: The American Protestant Experience." *Journal of Religious History* 7:3 (1973), 248–59. American Protestant missionaries promoted an image of Meiji Japan that helped shape popular and official attitudes. At first viewing it as pagan and vice ridden, they soon recognized it as progressive and enlightened.

17:216 Yamamori, Tetsunao. *Church Growth in Japan: A Study in the Development of Eight Denominations, 1859–1939.* So. Pasadena, Calif.: Wm. Carey Library, 1974. The work analyzes eight American-based Protestant churches in Japan; it is very useful for its evaluation of what factors particular to each faith accounted for its appeal or its decline, given the nature of Japanese society. Bibliography.

KOREA

See "Personalities," especially Horace N. Allen (under "Others").

17:217 Lee Nung Hwa. *Chosun Kitokgyo kup Oegyosa* [A history of Christianity and diplomacy in Korea]. Seoul: Hakwŏn Kak, 1968. Extensive use of the Korean material (1520–1902) by one of the most important traditional Korean scholars makes this book a valuable publication.

17:218 Paik, L. George. *The History of Protestant Missions in Korea, 1832–1910.* Pyongyang: Union Christian College Press, 1929. This pioneering study retains its usefulness. Because American missionaries were responsible for the majority of the two-nation cultural relations in Korea, the book occupies an important position in the field. Extensive bibliography.

17:219 Rhodes, Harry A., ed. *History of the Korean Mission: Presbyterian Church in the U.S.A., Vol. 1: 1884–1934.* Seoul: Christian Mission Presbyterian Church, 1934. The discussion of the initiation, organization, and operation of the Presbyterian church in Korea is useful for an understanding of American-Korean cultural relations. Bibliography.

U.S. and East Asia, 1894–1913

Denis, A. L. P. *Adventures in American Diplomacy, 1896–1906* (13:7) has four chapters dealing with East Asian policy, covering the period from the open door notes through the Portsmouth Peace Conference. The author's most valuable contribution is his exhaustive use of German records in *Die Grosse Politik.*

17:220 Griswold, A. Whitney. *The Far Eastern Policy of the United States.* New York: Harcourt, Brace & World, 1938. Reprint 1962. This work, which covers 1898 to 1937, long dominated the field of U.S.-East Asian relations, but has been largely superseded. The overall interpretive structure that Griswold gave to the McKinley and Taft periods generally has remained intact; the interpretation of the Theodore Roosevelt period has faired less well.

17:221 Hunt, Michael H. *Frontier Defense and the Open Door: Manchuria in Chinese-American Relations, 1895–1911.* New Haven, Conn.: Yale University Press, 1973. In looking at American-Chinese relations from the vantage point of the Chinese side, Hunt provides significant new insights into the nature of U.S. policy. Extensive bibliography.

17:222 Iriye, Akira. *Pacific Estrangement: Japanese and American Expansion, 1897–1911.* Cambridge: Harvard University Press, 1972. Based on a wide range of materials—cultural, intellectual, diplomatic, and economic—this study examines the confrontation and interaction of American and Japanese expansionist ideas and policies. The insights into Japanese thoughts in this period are especially valuable for American scholars. Extensive bibliography.

17:223 McClellan, Robert. *The Heathen Chinee: A Study of American Attitudes toward China, 1890–1905.* Columbus: Ohio State University Press, 1971. This study evaluates public thought as manifested in periodical literature. The author finds American opinion ambivalent with a sympathetic interest in Chinese culture coupled with a strong antipathy to Chinese immigration. Bibliography.

17:224 Varg, Paul A. *The Making of a Myth: The United States and China, 1897–1912.* East Lansing: Michigan State University Press, 1968. In this study official diplomacy and nonofficial American attitudes are treated in alternating chapters. In analyzing American images of China, the author draws on such publications as *The Journal of Commerce and Commercial Bulletin, The Review of Reviews, The Outlook,* and *The Missionary Review of the World.*

17:225 Zabriskie, Edward H. *American-Russian Rivalry in the Far East: A Study in Diplomacy and Power Politics, 1895–1914.* Philadelphia: University of Pennsylvania Press, 1946. Reprint 1973. The author utilizes the limited available Russian sources. The use of many long quotations ties the account very closely to the diplomatic documents.

NAVAL AND STRATEGIC ISSUES

See Chapter 12, "Naval Influences," for additional references.

17:226 Braisted, William R. *The United States Navy in the Pacific, 1897–1909.* Austin: University of Texas Press, 1958. The author has researched American diplomatic records as extensively as Navy and War Department records. His study is therefore not a narrow naval history, but rather a broad analysis of the United States' East Asia policy, with a major focus on the navy. See also his "The Philippine Naval Base Problem, 1898–1909" (13:137).

17:227 Braisted, William R. *The United States Navy in the Pacific, 1909–1922.* Austin: University of Texas Press, 1971. In this sequel, Braisted analyzes the interlocking of U.S. naval policy and East Asian diplomacy. Topics treated in the Taft period include the 1911 Orange Plan, the building of shore support in the eastern and western Pacific, the attempt to sell warships and provide naval personnel to China, and the contradictions that plagued the Taft administration during the Chinese Revolution of 1911–1912. Extensive bibliography.

17:228 Braisted, William R. "The United States Navy's Dilemma in the Pacific, 1906–1909." *Pacific Historical Review* 26:3 (1957), 235–44. This analyzes the navy's dilemma over how to protect the nation from both Germany and Japan with a one-ocean navy.

17:229 Challener, Richard D. *Admirals, Generals, and American Foreign Policy, 1898–1914.* Princeton, N.J.: Princeton University Press, 1973. This extensive study of civil-military relations in American foreign policy treats such topics as the search for bases, the Boxer Rebellion, Pacific war plans, the war scare of 1907, the Magdalena Bay question, and concern over the 1911 revolution in China. Bibliography.

Livermore, S. W. "American Naval-Base Policy in the Far East, 1850–1914" (40:172) discusses the various proposals for securing an American navy base on the coast of China or Korea.

SINO-JAPANESE WAR, 1894–1895

See "Personalities," especially John W. Foster (under "Others").

17:230 Dorwart, Jeffrey M. *The Pigtail War: American Involvement in the Sino-Japanese War of 1894–1895.* Amherst: University of Massachusetts Press, 1975. A straightforward account based on English-language sources, including State and Navy Department documents, private papers, and missionary records. Bibliography.

17:231 Hammersmith, Jack. "The Sino-Japanese War, 1894–95: American Predictions Reassessed." *Asian Forum* 4:1 (1972), 48–58. Americans were divided on who would win the war. A substantial number expected a Japanese victory from the beginning. Many who expected the Chinese to win did so only because of China's larger population and more abundant resources.

17:232 Paulsen, George E. "Secretary Gresham, Senator Lodge, and American Good Offices in China, 1894." *Pacific Historical Review* 36:2 (1967), 123–42. During the Sino-Japanese War, the American consul at Shanghai turned over to China two alleged Japanese spies who were quickly executed by Chinese authorities; the consul's action drew sharp criticism from Senator Henry Cabot Lodge.

SPHERES AND THE OPEN DOOR

See "Personalities," especially John Hay, William W. Rockhill.

Braisted, W. R. "China, the United States Navy, and the Bethlehem Steel Company, 1909–1920" (39:52) illuminates important differences between the open door policy of Secretary Hay and the dollar diplomacy of the Taft administration.

17:233 Campbell, Charles S., Jr. *Special Business Interests and the Open Door Policy.* New Haven, Conn.: Yale University Press, 1951. This analysis focuses on the influence of American business interests, such as the American Asiatic Association, on the formulation of the open door policy.

17:234 Eggert, Gerald G. "Li Hung-chang's Mission to America, 1896." *Midwest Quarterly* 18:3 (1977), 240–57. The author discounts the theory that the visit had an impact on U.S. policy, and he asserts that American men of finance were self-deceived in thinking the visit had importance for their investment hopes and plans.

17:235 Esthus, Raymond A. "The Changing Concept of the Open Door, 1899–1910." *Mississippi Valley Historical Review* 46:3 (1959), 435–54. This analyzes the influence of Willard Straight and Francis Huntington Wilson on the evolution of the open door policy.

Hunt, M. H. "Americans in the China Market: Economic Opportunities and Economic Nationalism, 1890s–1931" (39:54).

17:236 Israel, Jerry. *Progressivism and the Open Door: America and China, 1905–1921.* Pittsburgh: University of Pittsburgh Press, 1971. American policy is viewed as vacillating between competitive and cooperative efforts with other powers, shifts that reflected the domestic struggle between those favoring laissez faire and those favoring rationalized cooperation. The study sees cultural imperialism as well as economic imperialism in the open door policy. Bibliography.

Kennan, G. F. *American Diplomacy, 1900–1950* (2:111) theorizes that in drafting the open door, Hippisley was motivated by the interests of the Chinese Imperial Maritime Customs rather than by those of the British government.

Langer, W. L. *The Diplomacy of Imperialism, 1890–1902* (13:9) still gives the most definitive coverage of the acquisition of spheres of influence and navy bases in China.

17:237 McCormick, Thomas J. *China Market: America's Quest for Informal Empire, 1893–1901.* Chicago: Quadrangle, 1967. The author stresses the McKinley administration's commitment to marketplace expansionism, a policy that had an inner logic and thrust. The open door, he argues, was no new departure; it was the continuation of the program which envisaged the United States, the most advanced and competitive industrial nation, gaining the lion's share of the China market.

McCormick, T. J. "Insular Imperialism and the Open Door: The China Market and the Spanish-American War" (13:94) concludes that the China market was the dominant influence on America's Philippine policy in 1898.

17:238 Pressman, Harvey. "Hay, Rockhill and China's Integrity: A Reappraisal." *Papers on China* 13 (1959), 61–79. Pressman concludes that Rockhill had little influence on the drafting of the open door notes but great influence on the formulation of the integrity of China policy, a policy designed to serve America's expansionist needs.

17:239 Varg, Paul A. "William Woodville Rockhill and the Open Door Notes." *Journal of Modern History* 24:4 (1952), 375–80. Varg argues that Rockhill, having little interest in promoting American business interests, was motivated primarily by the desire to save China from partition.

Williams, W. A. *The Tragedy of American Diplomacy* (2:99) develops and enlarges the open door concept.

17:240 Young, Marilyn B. "American Expansion, 1870–1900: The Far East." In Barton J. Bernstein, ed., *Towards a New Past: Dissenting Essays in American History.* New York: Pantheon, 1968, pp. 176–201. Young asserts that economic arguments used by the imperialists were an integral part of a larger complex of nationalistic ideas and that national policies were clothed in jingoistic garb in order to make them attractive to the public.

17:241 Young, Marilyn B. *The Rhetoric of Empire: American China Policy, 1895–1901.* Cambridge: Harvard University Press, 1968. This is the most thorough account of U.S. policy for this important period. The author sees the era not in terms of economic motivations alone, but in the larger context of contradictions in policy springing from the period's confused nationalism and accompanying rhetoric. Extensive bibliography.

Boxer Rebellion

Hunt, M. H. "The American Remission of the Boxer Indemnity: A Reappraisal" (17:254).

17:242   Kelly, John S. *A Forgotten Conference: The Negotiations at Peking, 1900–1901*. Paris: Minard, 1963. This study of the negotiations ending the Boxer troubles is based primarily on printed sources.

17:243   Purcell, Victor. *The Boxer Uprising: A Background Study*. Cambridge: At the University Press, 1963. Purcell researched in the British Foreign Office records, the Salisbury Papers, missionary records, and Chinese sources. The study is especially strong on the origins and beliefs of the Boxers. Extensive bibliography.

17:244   Tan, Chester C. *The Boxer Catastrophe*. New York: Columbia University Press, 1955. This is the best study of the Boxer Rebellion (1898–1901). Though it deals with the involvement of the foreign powers, it contains only a limited amount of material on U.S. policy. Extensive bibliography.

17:245   Varg, Paul A. "William Woodville Rockhill's Influence on the Boxer Negotiations." *Pacific Historical Review* 18:3 (1949), 369–80. Rockhill sought to scale down the harsh demands of the European powers in the 1901 Boxer negotiations.

ROOSEVELT AND TAFT

See "Personalities," especially Theodore Roosevelt, Elihu Root, Willard Straight, William Howard Taft, and, under "Others," William Phillips, F. M. Huntington Wilson.

Cohen, W. I. *The Chinese Connection: Roger S. Greene, Thomas W. Lamont, George E. Sokolsky, and American–East Asian Relations* (2:341) relates the career of Roger S. Greene, who was a very capable consular officer at Nagasaki, Vladivostok, Dairen, Harbin, and Hankow during 1904 to 1914.

17:246   Esthus, Raymond A. *Theodore Roosevelt and Japan*. Seattle: University of Washington Press, 1966. This study is especially useful for its analysis of the policy of the Roosevelt administration (1901–1909) regarding Japan's interests on the Asian continent. Bibliography.

17:247   Monger, George. *The End of Isolation: British Foreign Policy 1900–1907*. London: Nelson, 1963. This study contains much valuable information on Anglo-American relations concerning East Asia. Extensive bibliography.

17:248   Uhalley, Stephen, Jr. "The Wai-wu-pu, the Chinese Foreign Office from 1901 to 1911." *Journal of the China Society* 5 (1967), 9–27. Uhalley finds that though the foreign office, headed by the old, wily, corrupt, and inefficient Prince Ch'ing, had a number of capable members, it was poorly informed and indecisive.

Russo-Japanese War, 1904–1905

See "Personalities," especially, under "Others," Lloyd C. Griscom, George von Lengerke Meyer; see also Chapter 14, "Russo-Japanese War."

17:249   Dennett, Tyler. *Roosevelt and the Russo-Japanese War*. Garden City, N.Y.: Doubleday, Page, 1925. This has serious factual errors but is useful for extensive quotations from the Roosevelt Papers and for the texts of letters and documents contained in the long appendix.

17:250   Esthus, Raymond A. "Roosevelt, Russia, and Peacemaking 1905." In Jules Davids, ed., *Perspectives in American Diplomacy*. New York: Arno, 1976, pp. 2–29. This essay analyzes Roosevelt's dealing with Sergi Witte and Czar Nicholas before and during the Portsmouth Peace Conference.

Hershey, A. S. *The International Law and Diplomacy of the Russo-Japanese War* (16:152).

17:251   Okamoto, Shumpei. *The Japanese Oligarchy and the Russo-Japanese War*. New York: Columbia University Press, 1970. This is one of the finest studies of Japan's foreign policy. It is indispensable for an understanding of the diplomacy of the Russo-Japanese War, including Roosevelt's peacemaking endeavor. Extensive bibliography.

Trani, E. P. *The Treaty of Portsmouth: An Adventure in American Diplomacy* (14:157) gives a thorough and colorful account of Roosevelt's role in the Portsmouth Peace Conference.

Roosevelt and China

17:252 Braisted, William R. "The United States and the American China Development Company." *Far Eastern Quarterly* 11:2 (1952), 147–65. A detailed account of the American China Development Company's endeavor to construct a Canton-Hankow railway line—an enterprise that was abandoned in 1905 because of the company's dispute with China over the participation of Belgian interests in the company.

17:253 Field, Margaret. "The Chinese Boycott of 1905." *Papers on China* 11 (1957), 63–98. Field finds that though students and merchants supported the boycott movement, it had no distinguishable organization structure, and though the Chinese government sympathized with the boycott, it avoided giving it overt support.

17:254 Hunt, Michael H. "The American Remission of the Boxer Indemnity: A Reappraisal." *Journal of Asian Studies* 31:3 (1972), 539–59. The author debunks the idea that the United States displayed magnanimity in returning yearly to China a portion of the Boxer indemnity payment (1901–1908).

17:255 Iriye, Akira. "Public Opinion and Foreign Policy: The Case of Late Chi'ing China." In Albert Feuerwerker, Rhoads Murphey, and Mary C. Wright, eds., *Approaches to Modern Chinese History*. Berkeley: University of California Press, 1967, pp. 216–38. A significant part of this essay deals with the role of Chinese public opinion in the anti-American boycott of 1905. The author concludes that the boycott itself was far less important than the experience it gave the Chinese in asserting their right to influence policymaking.

17:256 McKee, Delber L. *Chinese Exclusion versus the Open Door Policy, 1900–1906: Clashes over China Policy in the Roosevelt Era*. Detroit: Wayne State University Press, 1977. This study analyzes the Chinese exclusion policy and the resulting Chinese boycott against American products in 1905. McKee believes that the commissioners general of immigration, Terence V. Powderly and Frank P. Sargent, made overzealous interpretations of immigration laws that caused great harassment of Chinese merchants, tourists, and students. Bibliography.

17:257 Rhoads, Edward J. M. "Nationalism and Xenophobia in Kwantung (1905–1906): The Canton

Anti-American Boycott and the Lienchow Anti-Missionary Uprising." *Papers on China* 16 (1962), 154–97. This paper examines the boycott at Canton, the attack on the American Presbyterian mission station at Lienchow, and the relationship between the two events.

Immigration and the Crises with Japan

17:258 Bailey, Thomas A. *Theodore Roosevelt and the Japanese-American Crises*. Stanford, Calif.: Stanford University Press, 1934. Reprint 1964. This study is still useful for the wealth of information in American private papers and State Department files on TR's crises with Japan and the world cruise of the U.S. fleet (1905–1909).

Braisted, W. R. "The United States Navy's Dilemma in the Pacific, 1906–1909" (17:228).

17:259 Daniels, Roger. *The Politics of Prejudice: The Anti-Japanese Movement in California and the Struggle for Japanese Exclusion*. Berkeley: University of California Press, 1962. The author presents in detail the story of California's struggle for Japanese exclusion (1888–1924) and examines it as one of the antidemocratic threads in the fabric of America's national heritage. Extensive bibliography.

17:260 Kachi, Teruko Okada. *The Treaty of 1911 and the Immigration and Alien Land Law Issue between the United States and Japan, 1911–1913*. New York: Arno, 1979. Based on both American and Japanese records, this study examines the negotiations leading to the Treaty of 1911 and the largely unforeseen consequences of the treaty regarding immigration and land tenure.

17:261 Neu, Charles E. *An Uncertain Friendship: Theodore Roosevelt and Japan, 1906–1909*. Cambridge: Harvard University Press, 1967. This is a detailed study of the Japanese immigration issue and discrimination against the Japanese. It is particularly strong on the relationship between the troubles with Japan and the development of Roosevelt's naval policy. Extensive bibliography.

17:262 Neu, Charles E. "Theodore Roosevelt and American Involvement in the Far East, 1901–1909." *Pacific Historical Review* 35:4 (1966), 433–49. Neu argues that following the Russo-Japanese War Roosevelt consciously decided to work with Japan and to avoid any real commitment in support of the open door and the integrity of China.

Dollar Diplomacy in China

See "Personalities," especially Willard Straight, William Howard Taft, and, under "Others," F. M. Huntington Wilson.

17:263 Edwards, E. W. "Great Britain and the Manchurian Railways Question, 1909–1910." *English Historical Review* 81:321 (1966), 740–69. A detailed account, based on Foreign Office records, of the controversy over the Chinchow-Aigun railway project.

Field, F. V. *American Participation in the China Consortiums* (39:53).

17:264 Irick, Robert L. "The Chinchow-Aigun Railroad and the Knox Neutralization Plan in Ch'ing Diplomacy." *Papers on China* 13 (1959), 80–112. This paper gives a detailed analysis of the handling of the Chin-Ai project by Ch'ing officials. The author concludes that the project was from beginning to end (1906–1910) a political device to reassert Chinese sovereignty in Manchuria.

Scholes, W. V., and Scholes, M. V. *The Foreign Policies of the Taft Administration* (17:44) sees Taft's dollar diplomacy (1909–1913) as high-minded but inept.

17:265 Vevier, Charles. *The United States and China, 1906–1913: A Study of Finance and Diplomacy.* New Brunswick, N.J.: Rutgers University Press, 1955. This study, based on American sources, focuses especially on the activities of Willard Straight.

Japanese and Magdalena Bay, 1911–1912

17:266 Bailey, Thomas A. "The Lodge Corollary to the Monroe Doctrine." *Political Science Quarterly* 48:2 (1933), 220–39. Responding to rumors that the Japanese were interested in Magdalena Bay in 1912, the U.S. Senate passed the Lodge Resolution, which expressed its concern about foreign control (governmental or private) of harbors critical to U.S. security. Bailey argues that there was no serious Japanese

threat at the time, and that the Lodge Corollary was meant to be an addition to the Monroe Doctrine.

17:267 Chamberlin, Eugene K. "The Japanese Scare at Magdalena Bay" [1911–1912]. *Pacific Historical Review* 24:4 (1955), 345–59. A detailed account of the developments leading up to the scare over a possible Japanese base at Magdalena Bay in Baja California.

Chinese Revolution

17:268 Chong, Key Ray. "The Abortive American-Chinese Project for Chinese Revolution, 1908–1911." *Pacific Historical Review* 41:1 (1972), 54–70. Homer Lea, Charles Boothe, and W. W. Allen schemed to raise capital in the United States for the revolutionary activities of K'ang Yu-wei and Sun Yat-sen.

17:269 Metallo, Michael V. "American Missionaries, Sun Yat-sen, and the Chinese Revolution." *Pacific Historical Review* 47:2 (1978), 261–82. The author finds that the missionaries held Sun in high esteem before 1913, but thereafter tended toward skepticism and caution in their assessments.

U.S. and Southeast Asia

17:270 Gould, James W. "American Imperialism in Southeast Asia before 1898." *Journal of Southeast Asian Studies* 3:2 (1972), 306–14. Gould divides American activity in Southeast Asia before 1898 into three main periods: 1784 to 1831, 1832 to 1871, 1872 to 1898. Although all three periods are marked by intense activity, only the middle period, according to Gould, can be described as imperialistic.

17:271 Livermore, Seward W. "Early Commercial and Consular Relations with the East Indies." *Pacific Historical Review* 15:1 (1946), 31–58. This recounts early consular appointments to Batavia, Bombay, Calcutta, Manila, Rangoon, and Singapore and the largely unsuccessful efforts to secure recognition of consuls in colonial ports (1784–1856).

17:272 Snyder, James W., Jr. "American Trade in Eastern Seas: A Brief Survey of Its Early Years, 1783–1815." *Americana* 32:4 (1938), 621–38. The author analyzes the difficulties which earlier historians encountered in their efforts to determine the scope and nature of the East Asia trade. Using available statistics, the author generalizes about early voyages, the kinds of goods traded, and the various political and economic factors which affected commerce.

17:273 Spector, Ronald H. "The American Image of Southeast Asia, 1790–1865: A Preliminary Assessment." *Journal of Southeast Asian Studies* 3:2 (1972), 299–305. Spector concludes that Americans saw the people of the area as backward, treacherous, and rapacious and believed that Christianity and Western civilization would be immensely beneficial to the Asians.

U.S.-BURMA

17:274 Christian, John L. "American Diplomatic Interest in Burma." *Pacific Historical Review* 8:2 (1939), 139–47. This brief account treats American commercial and missionary as well as diplomatic activities in Burma (1784–1886).

17:275 Christian, John L. "Americans in the First Anglo-Burmese War." *Pacific Historical Review* 5:4 (1936), 312–24. This article outlines the role played by American missionaries in Burma, notably Jonathan Price and Adoniram Judson, as interpreters and mediators between the British and the Burmese during the first Anglo-Burmese war (1824–1826).

17:276 Trager, Helen Gibson. *Burma through Alien Eyes: Missionary Views of the Burmese in the 19th Century*. New York: Praeger, 1966. A study of American missionaries in Burma, including an analysis of the factors that contributed to the biased and inaccurate view of Burma that they transmitted to their countrymen at home. Bibliography.

U.S., EAST INDIES AND MALAYA

17:277 Ahmat, Sharom. "American Trade with Singapore, 1819–65." *Journal of the Malaysian Branch Royal Asiatic Society* 38 (1965), 241–57. This article discusses the growth of the American trade with

Singapore and details the ways in which the barriers to it were gradually overcome.

17:278 Ahmat, Sharom. "Some Problems of Rhode Island Traders in Java, 1799–1836." *Journal of Southeast Asian History* 6:1 (1965), 94–107. Rhode Island merchants enjoyed a brief period of prosperity trading in Javanese coffee. Jefferson's embargo hurt the trade badly, and after 1817, the Rhode Islanders faced British and Dutch commercial restrictions as well as the threat of piracy.

17:279 Gould, James W. *Americans in Sumatra*. The Hague: Nijhoff, 1961. A continuation of Gould's earlier article, this book traces the development of American commercial, scientific, humanitarian, and political activities in Sumatra from the Atjeh War in 1873 to 1940. Of special interest is the discussion of the role of Americans in the development of the oil and rubber industries. Bibliography.

17:280 Gould, James W. "Sumatra—America's Pepperpot, 1784–1873." *Essex Institute Historical Collections* 92 (1956), 83–153, 203–52, 295–349. A thorough account which throws light on American activities in the rest of Southeast Asia as well. Gould demonstrates that Americans had a substantial impact on the economic life of Sumatra and also influenced the policies of European powers.

17:281 Long, David F. "'Martial Thunder': The First Official American Armed Intervention in Asia." *Pacific Historical Review* 42:2 (1973), 143–62. This is an account of the attack on the Sumatran town of Quala Batu by the U.S. frigate *Potomac* in 1832 in reprisal for the robbery of the Salem merchant ship *Friendship*. The *Potomac*'s action raised a national argument over the wisdom of the attack and a constitutional debate over the right of the president to commit the nation to hostilities without a declaration of war.

17:282 Reed, Peter M. "Standard Oil in Indonesia, 1898–1928." *Business History Review* 32:1 (1958), 311–37. The principal focus is on the 1920s when the Department of State vigorously supported Standard Oil in its efforts to expand its interests in the East Indies.

17:283 Taylor, Fitch W. *The Flagship: Or a Voyage around the World in the United States Frigate Columbia*. 2 vols. New York: Appleton, 1840. Taylor sailed in the *Columbia* on its punitive expedition to the north coast of Sumatra to punish a local raja for the robbery of the American ship *Eclipse* in 1838. (Much of the cargo stolen was apparently opium.)

17:284 Tregonning, K. G. "American Activity in North Borneo, 1865–1881." *Pacific Historical Review* 23:4 (1954), 357–72. The attempt by two American adventurers, Claude Lee Moses and Joseph Torrey, to establish an American colony in North Borneo failed, but it started the chain of events that led to the founding of the British North Borneo Company.

U.S.-THE PHILIPPINES

The Spanish Era

17:285 Legarda, Benito. "American Entrepreneurs in the Nineteenth Century Philippines." *Explorations in Entrepreneurial History* 1st ser. 9 (1957), 142–60. American trading houses (1790–1880) in the Philippines like Peele, Hubbell and Russell, and Sturgis helped to transform the Philippine economy from one of subsistence to that of an agricultural export economy trading staples like coffee, sugar, abaca, and tobacco.

17:286 McHale, Thomas R., and McHale, Mary C., eds. *Early American-Philippine Trade: The Journal of Nathaniel Bowditch in Manila, 1796.* New Haven, Conn.: Yale University Press, 1962. Bowditch adds to the fragmentary knowledge of the Manila trade after the end of the annual Acapulco-Manila galleon trade in the 1780s. The editors' introduction sketches the Philippine economy from the Spanish conquest to the early 19th century.

U.S. Occupation and Insurrection

See Chapter 13, "Philippine Annexation/Insurrection."

Welch, R. E., Jr. *Response to Imperialism: The United States and the Philippine-American War, 1899–1902* (13:167) evaluates the response of American public opinion to the Filipino insurrection and analyzes official and popular responses in the light of the values and anxieties of the American people.

U.S. Rule, 1899–1913

See "Personalities," especially Theodore Roosevelt, William Howard Taft.

17:287 Alfonson, Oscar M. *Theodore Roosevelt and the Philippines, 1897–1909.* Quezon City: University of the Philippines Press, 1970. Reprint 1974. An interesting analysis, by a Filipino, of Roosevelt's views of the islands, which seeks to understand why Roosevelt ruled out Philippine self-government.

17:288 Clymer, Kenton J. "Humanitarian Imperialism: David Prescott Barrows and the White Man's Burden in the Philippines." *Pacific Historical Review* 45:4 (1976), 495–519. This article traces the career of a middle-level official who served in a variety of posts in the Philippines between 1900 and 1909. Clymer contends that for men like Barrows "humanitarian paternalism" or the white man's burden was a genuine motivation, not just hypocrisy masking baser motives.

17:289 May, Glenn A. "Social Engineering in the Philippines: The Aims and Execution of American Educational Policy, 1900–1913." *Philippine Studies* 24:2 (1976), 135–84. May contends that despite the great amounts of money and energy devoted to it, the American educational program in the Philippines "prepared the Filipinos neither for citizenship nor for productive labor."

17:290 McHale, Thomas R. "The Development of American Policy toward the Philippines." *Philippine Studies* 9:1 (1961), 47–71. An instructive review of American policy from the late 19th century to after independence.

Owen, N. G., ed. *Compadre Colonialism: Studies on the Philippines under American Rule* [1899–1935] (2:355).

17:291 Salamanca, Bonifacia S. *The Filipino Reaction to American Rule, 1901–1913.* Hamden, Conn.: Shoe String Press, 1968. The conservative Filipino elite influenced and limited the United States in its choice of policy. The author concludes that the impact of American rule was "greatest in the educational and religious field, less in democratization of politics and weakest in economic and social aspects of Filipino life."

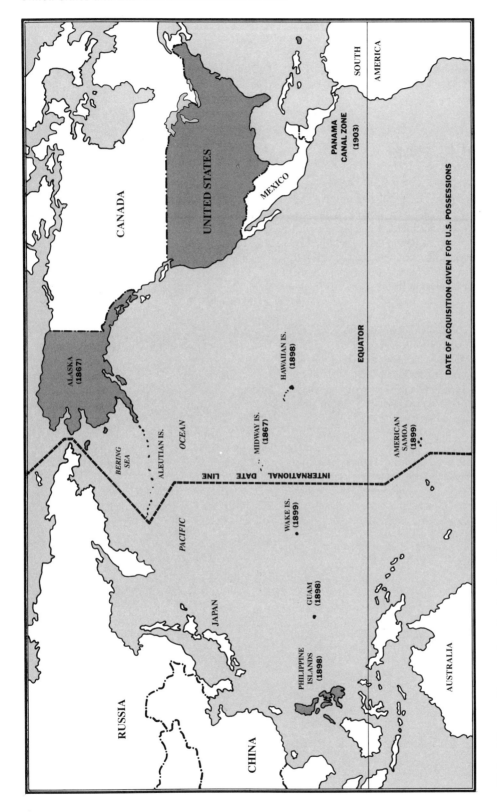

United States Expansion in the Pacific, 1905

Stanley, P. W. *A Nation in the Making: The Philippines and the United States, 1899–1921* (2:356) concludes that through its policy of "attraction" the United States was able to detach the Filipino elite from the insurrection and thus establish American control.

U.S.-SIAM

17:292   Batson, Benjamin A. "American Diplomats in Southeast Asia in the Nineteenth Century: The Case of Siam." *Journal of the Siam Society* 64:2 (1976), 39–112. A collective biographical account of American diplomatic representation in Siam and of the usually inexperienced, often quarrelsome, occasionally corrupt, but always colorful men who held the post of consul and later minister in Bangkok from 1856 until 1912.

17:293   Lord, Donald C. "Missionaries, Thai, and Diplomats." *Pacific Historical Review* 35:4 (1966), 413–31. Lord recounts the role of American missionaries in Siam as advisers to both the Thai government and American diplomats during the reigns of Nang Klao (1824–1851) and Mongkut (1851–1868).

17:294   Lord, Donald C. *Mo Bradley and Thailand.* Grand Rapids, Mich.: Eerdmans, 1969. Bradley (1828–1910) was a close friend, adviser, and physician to King Mongkut. He made few converts but introduced surgery, the printing press, vaccination, and modern obstetrics to Siam. Lord notes that American missionaries played a constructive role as advisers and interpreters for the Siamese government. Bibliography.

17:295   Moffat, Abbot L. *Mongkut, the King of Siam.* Ithaca, N.Y.: Cornell University Press, 1961. Chapter 5 of this biography of the Thai monarch has an excellent account of the negotiation of the Siamese-American treaty of 1856 by Townsend Harris.

17:296   Ruschenberger, W. S. W. *A Voyage Round the World Including an Embassy to Siam and Muscat.* Philadelphia: Carey, Lea & Blanchard, 1838. Ruschenberger, a naval surgeon, accompanied Edmund Roberts on his second mission to Southeast Asia in 1835–1836 to exchange ratifications of the treaty with Siam and make another attempt at negotiations with Annam (Vietnam).

Young, K. T. "The Special Role of American Advisers in Thailand, 1902–1949" (30:133).

U.S.-VIETNAM

See "Personalities," especially Edmund Roberts (under "Others").

17:297   Hammersmith, Jack L. "American Attempts to Prevent a War over 'Vietnam': The Experience of John Russell Young, 1882–1885." *Historian* 38:2 (1976), 253–67. American minister to China, John Russell Young, and the State Department sought to mediate the Sino-French dispute over Tonkin which led to the Black Flags war and the French conquest of northern Vietnam.

18

United States, Turkey, Middle East, and Africa to 1939

Contributing Editor
Thomas A. Bryson
West Georgia College

Contributor
Edward W. Chester
University of Texas at Arlington

Contents

Introduction

Historians of American diplomatic relations have largely neglected the study of this country's diplomatic experience in the Middle East and Africa. Frederick Jackson Turner's concern with the westward thrust of pioneers to settle the continental limits of the United States, and later historians' treatment of the American thrust across the Pacific Ocean to realize the aims of commerce and empire have resulted in the Middle East and Africa being shunted into the historical background. This is all the more distressing, for even before the inception of the American republic, Yankee merchant ships plied the blue waters of the Mediterranean in search of trade with Arabs, Turks, Africans, and others.

Following American independence and in the early years of the nineteenth century, a host of Americans ventured into the Middle East. Merchants, missionaries, mariners, ship constructors, archaeologists, scholars, naval officers, and diplomats established early contact with the people of the Levant and the Mediterranean world. It has been suggested that this nation had no comprehensive Middle Eastern policy beyond those traditional basic guiding principles which have directed diplomats since the early days of the nation. But an examination of the diplomatic record discloses that American diplomatists pursued the goals of the aforementioned interest groups. To that extent it can be said that the United States possessed a Middle Eastern policy.

During the period which this chapter covers, the diplomatic record indicates American missionaries constituted an important determinant of policymaking. Indeed, they mounted an important lobby that continued to operate very effectively in Washington until the outbreak of World War II. But commercial interests also vied to shape policy that would open Middle Eastern trading opportunities and access to the region's oil resources. During World War II, American oil interests began to achieve a primary position in shaping the nation's policy in the Middle East, where the region's oil resources would come to play an increasingly important role in this country's foreign policy considerations.

Although a few scholars turned their attention to the role of the United States in the Middle East prior to World War II—Harry N. Howard, Leland James Gordon, and Edward Mead Earle were the pioneers—it has only been since the war that there has been growing concern and increased scholarly output on this country's Middle East experience.

In the past fifteen years a number of books have appeared that greatly broadened our knowledge of American diplomatic activities in the Middle East and Africa prior to World War II. James A. Field, Jr., has written *America and the Mediterranean World, 1776–1882* (18:6). This is a monumental work that contains an excellent bibliography and discusses not only American diplomatic negotiations in the period between the days of the Barbary pirates to the British occupation of Egypt in 1882, but also treats the activities of American missionaries, mariners, merchants, and a host of others whose informal activities constituted a major portion of America's Middle Eastern interests.

A companion book to that of Field is the significant study by David H. Finnie, whose *Pioneers East: The Early American Experience in the Middle East* (18:7) also provides an outstanding bibliography and covers the activities of the American pioneers in the remote Middle East to the 1840s. What Field's work does for the nineteenth century, John A. DeNovo's does for the twentieth. His *American Interests and Policies in the Middle East, 1900–1939* (18:5) provides substantial treatment of this nation's diplomatic negotiations with the Middle East during the crucial period when the Ottoman empire was falling apart. As a preliminary step to writing this book, DeNovo prepared an excellent bibliographic essay, "American Relations with the Middle East: Some Unfinished Business" (18:2). Subsequently, DeNovo prepared a second essay entitled "Researching American Relations with the Middle East: The State of the Art, 1970" (1:106), which continues the search for material related to this field of study, and it will benefit the student whose primary concern is in the period prior to 1939.

Those individuals desiring an introduction to the United States in the Middle East may find Bryson's *American Diplomatic Relations with the Middle East,*

1784–1975: A Survey (2:359) useful. Also of significance is Bryson's *United States–Middle East Diplomatic Relations, 1784–1978: An Annotated Bibliography* (1:105). This annotated bibliographic guide provides students, librarians, and scholars with a working, annotated list of books, articles, and dissertations that relate to the study of American–Middle Eastern relations. It also suggests numerous other bibliographic guides which should prove helpful, and it points out document collections that treat the American role in the Middle East.

Concerning the African phase of this topic, the student may wish to examine Edward W. Chester's *Clash of Titans: Africa and U.S. Foreign Policy* (2:336), a good one-volume survey. Well over one-half of this study treats North and Sub-Saharan Africa during the period prior to World War II. It contains an excellent bibliography of articles, government publications, books, doctoral dissertations, and pamphlets. For Arab North Africa, see Charles F. Gallagher's *The United States and North Africa: Morocco, Algeria and Tunisia* (18:8). Unfortunately the title is misleading, for little of the study is devoted to U.S. diplomacy, but it does provide a useful background.

Paralleling developments in the Middle East, merchants and missionaries played a major role in opening up Africa to the United States. Unlike the Middle East, though, there was no overriding issue—such as oil or a national Jewish state—which called for the development of an American diplomatic policy prior to World War II. Instead, the quest for extraterritorial rights, or capitulations, provided a rather low-key basis for the highly fragmented policy which the U.S. government followed toward Africa. Against this background, isolated episodes such as the Berlin Conference on the Congo (1884–1885) and the Algeciras Conference on Morocco (1906) might briefly hold American attention. The only African nation to arouse any sustained interest in the United States was Liberia, set up during the early nineteenth century as a haven for free American blacks. Despite its widespread copying of American institutions, Liberia achieved at most modest success as a colonization venture.

Until recent years the relatively few books, articles, doctoral dissertations, and master's theses dealing with Africa concentrated on a half-dozen different nations: Egypt, Morocco, Liberia, Ethiopia, the Congo, and South Africa. North of the Sahara Desert the era of the Barbary pirates generated considerable scholarly writing, while south of it historians paid some attention to the colonization movement and the slave trade. Among those individuals who wrote classical works prior to 1945 on some phase of American relations with Africa were W. E. B. Du Bois, Early L.

Fox, Henry Sherwood, James Padgett, Robert Skinner, and George Beer.

Since World War II, however, the civil rights movement in the United States, together with Sub-Saharan African states becoming independent, has created increasing interest among historians toward Africa. As a result, there has been an increasing amount of materials published in America on black studies and Pan-Africanism, a number of them either directly or indirectly treating U.S.-African topics. Yet these books, articles, and dissertations written since 1945 frequently make a crusading search for a usable African past. Thus, despite the many first-rate scholarly works appearing in recent years, the reader should develop a critical approach.

Opportunities for future research abound in all of these areas. For the Middle East, one should consult the aforementioned essay by DeNovo, "Researching American Relations with the Middle East: The State of the Art, 1970," for nearly half of this essay suggests unexhausted research topics. Sub-Saharan Africa offers even more opportunities but fewer suggestions as to specific topics. However, the U.S. Department of State's microfilmed "General Records of the Department of State, RG 59" (1:359) may be helpful.

Resources and Overviews

RESEARCH AIDS

While pertinent bibliographies and reference aids are listed here, there are more extensive lists in Chapter 1.

Bibliographies

Bryson, T. A. *United States-Middle East Diplomatic Relations, 1784–1978: An Annotated Bibliography* (1:105). Provides an annotated list of books, articles, dissertations, document collections and treaty collections.

18:1 Clements, Frank A., comp. *The Emerging of Arab Nationalism from the Nineteenth Century to 1921.* Wilmington, Del.: Scholarly Resources, 1976. An excellent, well-annotated bibliography arranged under three major sections, with a short introductory essay: 1) struggle between the Arabs and the Turks; 2) peace settlement and its consequences; 3) the Fertile Crescent under the mandate system.

DeNovo, J. A. "Researching American Relations with the Middle East: The State of the Art, 1970" (1:106).

18:2 DeNovo, John A. "American Relations with the Middle East: Some Unfinished Business." In George L. Anderson, ed., *Issues and Conflicts: Studies in Twentieth Century American Diplomacy*. Lawrence: University of Kansas Press, 1959, pp. 63–98. This essay introduces the reader to many of the American interest groups that have influenced the shaping of American Middle Eastern policy, with an appended list of footnotes that points to bibliographic guides, primary, and secondary sources.

Duignan, P., ed. *Guide to Research and Reference Works on Sub-Saharan Africa* (1:112) will lead the serious researcher to materials which provide a background to U.S. activities in Africa. Particularly relevant are accounts of British and French colonial possessions.

Littlefield, D. W. *The Islamic Near East and North Africa: An Annotated Guide to Books in English for Non-Specialists* (1:107) provides background materials.

Selim, G. D., comp. *American Doctoral Dissertations on the Arab World, 1883–1974* (1:251).

Simon, R. S. *The Modern Middle East: A Guide to Research Tools in the Social Sciences* (1:109) emphasizes pertinent reference aids. Its primary focus is on modern history, political science, sociology, and anthropology.

Tamkoç, M. *A Bibliography on the Foreign Relations of the Republic of Turkey, 1919–1967: And Brief Biographies of Turkish Statesmen* (33:18).

Document Collections

More general collections are listed in Chapter 1, and other collections may be found in "Personalities," below.

18:3 Hurewitz, Jacob C., ed. *The Middle East and North Africa in World Politics: A Documentary Rec-*

ord. 3 vols., 2d rev. ed. New Haven, Conn.: Yale University Press (1956), 1979. The documents are arranged chronologically. The first volume covers the period of European expansion from 1535 to 1914, while the second covers the period of British and French supremacy during the years 1914 to 1945. Extensive bibliography.

Irish University Press Series on British Parliamentary Papers. *Slave Trade* (8:3) contains a great deal of material on Anglo-American clashes over the issue of joint antislavery patrols.

18:4 Knox, Dudley W., ed. *Naval Documents Related to the United States Wars with the Barbary Powers*. 6 vols. Washington, D.C.: Office of Naval Records and Library, 1939–1944. An excellent collection related to the American naval and diplomatic relations with the Barbary powers (1794–1817).

U.S. Department of State. "General Records of the Department of State, RG 59 and RG 84" (1:359) includes the "Diplomatic Despatches" to and from Liberia (1863–1906), Morocco (1905–1906), Persia (1838–1906), and Turkey (1818–1906). The "Decimal File, 1910–1929" includes microfilmed reports and dispatches from British Africa, Egypt, Ethiopia, and Morocco. Additionally, there are "Consular Despatches" available from these areas which deal with economic, political, and social conditions.

U.S. Senate. Committee on Foreign Relations. *A Select Chronology and Background Documents Relating to the Middle East* (33:30) contains some materials for the pre-World War II period.

OVERVIEWS

U.S. and the Middle East

Adler, C., and Margolith, A. M. *With Firmness in the Right: American Diplomatic Action Affecting Jews, 1840–1945* (2:358).

Bryson, T. A. *American Diplomatic Relations with the Middle East, 1784–1975: A Survey* (2:359) surveys early U.S. relations with Middle Eastern states and discusses the growth of commercial intercourse and missionary activities in shaping U.S. policy.

Bryson, T. A. *Tars, Turks, and Tankers: The Role of the U.S. Navy in the Middle East, 1800–1979* (2:360).

Has a brief chapter that treats American naval policy during the Barbary wars as an adjunct of American diplomacy.

Davison, R. H. "Where Is the Middle East?" (2:361) traces the use of the terms *Near East* and *Middle East*.

18:5   DeNovo, John A. *American Interests and Policies in the Middle East, 1900–1939*. Minneapolis: University of Minnesota Press, 1963. This is the best single treatment of U.S.-Middle East relations during the interwar era. It covers a wide range of problems in U.S.-Turkish negotiations, the quest for oil in Iraq, Saudi Arabia, Persia, and Bahrein, the rights of Americans in the mandates, trade expansion, and the problems of philanthropists and missionaries. Extensive bibliography.

18:6   Field, James A., Jr. *America and the Mediterranean World, 1776–1882*. Princeton, N.J.: Princeton University Press, 1969. This elegantly written account treats the American missionary and educational efforts and their consequences for modernization and Arab nationalism, the problems of missionary protection, and the naval and diplomatic responses. Also included are brief treatments of the naval exploration of the Dead Sea and the Koszta affair; the beginnings of Palestinian archeology; early American Zionism and Palestinian settlements; and the efforts of technicians and merchants. Extensive bibliography.

18:7   Finnie, David H. *Pioneers East: The Early American Experience in the Middle East*. Cambridge: Harvard University Press, 1967. This book treats a number of Americans who resided in Egypt, Mesopotamia [Iraq], Persia [Iran], Palestine, Syria, and Turkey in the early 19th century. It discusses the multiplicity of their goals, asserting that while these Americans were not official instruments of policy, they did influence the formulation of policy through the missionary lobby. The extensive bibliography includes many travel and resident accounts by early Americans who ventured to the Middle East.

18:8   Gallagher, Charles F. *The United States and North Africa: Morocco, Algeria and Tunisia*. Cambridge: Harvard University Press, 1963. A useful and succinct analysis of North Africa's prehistory and history, as well as the best overview of U.S.-North African relations (1784–1963) by a perceptive and often sympathetic observer. Bibliography.

18:9   Gordon, Leland J. *American Relations with Turkey, 1830–1930: An Economic Interpretation*.

Philadelphia: University of Pennsylvania Press, 1932. This is the most important single study of U.S.-Turkish relations, as well as one of the pioneer studies in U.S.-Middle East relations. While it concentrates on economic relations, it recognizes the missionary influence on policymaking.

18:10   Hall, Luella J. *The United States and Morocco, 1776–1956*. Metuchen, N.J.: Scarecrow, 1971. The author posits that America's relations with Morocco were more extensive than is commonly realized, and that this relationship should be viewed against a growing Moroccan nationalism. Extensive bibliography.

18:11   Helseth, William A. "The United States and Turkey: Their Relations from 1784 to 1962." Ph.D. diss., Fletcher School of Law and Diplomacy, 1962. This survey briefly sketches its subject during the 19th century and concentrates on missionary efforts to influence policymaking during the war years and the period of the Paris Peace Conference, when the Big Four was disposing of the defunct Ottoman empire. Bibliography.

18:12   Hinckley, Frank E. *American Consular Jurisdiction in the Orient*. Washington, D.C.: Lowdermilk, 1906. This work describes consular practice in 19th-century Turkey and Egypt and demonstrates the manner in which the U.S. government represented the interests of American citizens with respect to trials, extradition, expulsion, mixed tribunals, and missionary rights. Bibliography.

18:13   Kearney, Helen McCready. "American Images of the Middle East, 1824–1924: A Century of Antipathy." Ph.D. diss., University of Rochester, 1976. This dissertation focuses on popular American images of Turks, Armenians, and Arabs, relying on reports made by missionaries and diplomats. This image perceived the Turk as a barbarian, the Armenian as a servile person, and the Arab as only somewhat less barbaric and fanatical than the Turk. Bibliography.

Schuyler, E. *American Diplomacy and the Furtherance of Commerce* (12:13). This early history (1785–1815) suggests that shipping and agricultural interests supported an aggressive American policy in the Middle East.

18:14   Sousa, Nasim. *The Capitulatory Regime of Turkey: Its History, Origins, and Nature*. Baltimore: Johns Hopkins Press, 1933. Sousa claims that the

Chester Concession was a factor in U.S. participation at the Lausanne Conference, and discusses the demise of the capitulatory regime. Bibliography.

Stookey, R. W. *America and the Arab States: An Uneasy Encounter* (33:36) treats briefly the American confrontation with Barbary, the advent of Protestant missionaries, the growth of secular interests, and the U.S. role during and after World War I and in the interwar period.

18:15   Thomas, Lewis V., and Frye, Richard N. *The United States and Turkey and Iran.* Cambridge: Harvard University Press, 1951. This work concentrates on cultural and historical development in Turkey and Iran (1800–1950), with one brief chapter on U.S.-Turkish and U.S.-Persian relations.

18:16   Yeselson, Abraham. *United States–Persian Diplomatic Relations, 1883–1921.* New Brunswick, N.J.: Rutgers University Press, 1950. This is the only treatment of U.S.-Persian relations. Early American interests in Persia centered around the missionaries, although some 19th-century American diplomats did attempt to expand U.S. commercial interests. The United States had little interest in Persia and was reluctant to become entangled in the Anglo-Russian power struggle. After World War I, the U.S. prevented ratification of the Anglo-Persian treaty which would have made Persia a client state of Britain. Extensive bibliography.

U.S. Missionaries and Arab Nationalism

Anderson, R. *History of the Missions of the American Board of Commissioners for Foreign Missions to the Oriental Churches* [19th century] (2:75).

18:17   Antonius, George. *The Arab Awakening: The Story of the Arab National Movement.* New York: Putnam's, 1946. A classic account of the Arab intellectual awakening emerging in the 1840s. The author traces the awakening, which he believes to be the foundation of 20th-century Arab nationalism, to the influences of American missionaries. He reflects Arab resentment of secret Allied wartime treaties (and the assent of Woodrow Wilson) which divided the defunct Ottoman empire and undermined Arab nationalism. Bibliography.

18:18   Arpee, Leon. *The Armenian Awakening: A History of the Armenian Church, 1820–1860.* Chicago: University of Chicago Press, 1909. Arpee discusses the religious and cultural awakening in Armenia and relates this to the role of American missionaries working among the Armenians. These views may also be found in his *History of Armenian Christianity from the Beginning to Our Own Time* (New York, 1946).

Daniel, R. L. *American Philanthropy in the Near East, 1820–1960* (2:74) concentrates on early efforts by American missionaries to educate Mideast peoples through their schools and colleges, and covers the activities of Near East Relief, which expended $100 million on relief in the aftermath of World War I.

18:19   Earle, Edward Mead. "American Missions in the Near East." *Foreign Affairs* 7:3 (1929), 398–417. Earle claims that the missionary activity in East Asia outstripped all other American activities up to the 1920s and asserts that the missionaries had an important role in arousing nationalism among the subject peoples of the Ottoman empire.

18:20   Grabill, Joseph L. *Protestant Diplomacy and the Near East: Missionary Influence on American Policy, 1810–1927.* Minneapolis: University of Minnesota Press, 1971. While Grabill does introduce the missionary lobby in early American–Middle Eastern relations, his major focus is on the lobby's influence during the Woodrow Wilson era. Extensive bibliography.

18:21   Hatoor Al-Khalidi, Muyhee A. "A Century of American Contribution to Arab Nationalism, 1820–1920." Ph.D. diss., Vanderbilt University, 1959. This study focuses on the American contribution to the Arab intellectual awakening, and its emergence as a vital force in early Arab nationalism. Bibliography. (For more, see "U.S.-Syrian Relations," below.)

18:22   Heggoy, Willy N. "Fifty Years of Evangelical Missionary Movement in North Africa, 1881–1931." Ph.D. diss., Hartford Seminary, 1960. Heggoy discusses the efforts of missionaries in North Africa during the peak period of imperialism, and traces the history of the first fifty years of Protestant missionaries in North Africa with special reference to the Muslims.

18:23   Nordman, Bernard F. "American Missionary Work among Armenians in Turkey, 1830–1923." Ph.D. diss., University of Illinois, 1927. Nordman discusses the arrival of American missionaries in Turkey and assesses their accomplishments. Bibliography.

Phillips, C. J. *Protestant America and the Pagan World: The First Half Century of the American Board of Commissioners for Foreign Missions, 1810–1860* (2:80) devotes one chapter to the Middle East, which points out that U.S. diplomatic and naval support in Syria was very limited.

18:24   Phillips, Dennis H. "The American Missionary in Morocco." *Muslim World* 65:1 (1975), 1–20. These early missionaries enjoyed little real success even though they had the support of American diplomats. They did not see themselves as the servants of American imperial interests or as extensions of American culture.

18:25   Raleigh, Edward A. "An Inquiry into the Influences of American Democracy on the Arab Middle East, 1819–1958." Ph.D. diss., College of the Pacific, 1960. The author examines American political influence on Arab peoples of the Middle East during the period when the Ottoman empire was rapidly declining in strength. At the same time, American missionaries and educators exercised considerable influence on the cultural and political aspirations of the people of the emerging Middle East states. Bibliography.

18:26   Richter, Julius. *A History of Protestant Missions in the Near East.* New York: Revell, 1910. Richter discusses the work of the American Board and the other mission efforts and demonstrates that American missionaries largely predominated in the Middle East.

18:27   Rowden, Paul D. "A Century of American Protestantism in the Middle East, 1820–1920." Ph.D. diss., Dropsie University, 1959. Rowden emphasizes the impact of American Protestant missionaries on Syria, with solid treatment of their educational and intellectual role. Bibliography.

18:28   Sarton, George. *The Incubation of Western Culture in the Middle East.* Washington, D.C.: Library of Congress, 1951. Sarton focuses on the impact which American educators had on the Arab cultural revival in mid-19th century.

18:29   Shaw, Plato E. *American Contacts with the Eastern Churches, 1820–1870.* Chicago: American Society of Church History, 1937. This account relates early contacts between missionaries of American

Protestant churches with the Eastern churches. Bibliography.

18:30   Smith, Eli. *Researches of the Rev. E. Smith and Rev. H. G. O. Dwight in Armenia Including a Trip through Asia Minor, Georgia, and Persia.* 2 vols. Boston: Crocker & Brewster, 1833. Smith discusses the work of American missionaries among Armenians and Nestorians in the first decades of the 19th century.

Personalities

Additional references on individuals may be found in Chapter 1, "Biographical Data."

Mark L. Bristol

18:31   Bryson, Thomas A. "Admiral Mark Lambert Bristol: An Open Door Diplomat in Turkey." *International Journal of Middle East Studies* 5:4 (1974), 450–567. Bristol opposed the Armenian mandate and sought to achieve American economic parity with the British and French in post–World War I Turkey.

18:32   Buzanski, Peter M. "Admiral Mark L. Bristol and Turkish-American Relations, 1919–1922." Ph.D. diss., University of California, Berkeley, 1960. A well-written account that reviews the role of the U.S. high commissioner in Turkey, who in the 1920s worked to enable American commercial interests to expand and American philanthropic interests to continue their operations. Extensive bibliography.

Joseph C. Grew

See also Chapter 21, "Personalities."

18:33   Grew, Joseph C. *Turbulent Era: A Diplomatic Record of Forty Years, 1904–1945.* 2 vols. London: Hammond, 1953. This American diplomat's memoirs give extensive treatment to U.S. participation at the Lausanne Conference and to American relations with Turkey during his tenure as U.S. ambassador at Istanbul.

Heinrichs, W. H., Jr. *American Ambassador: Joseph C. Grew and the Development of the United States Diplomatic Tradition* (21:26) contains three chapters on American-Turkish relations during the time of Grew's tenure as U.S. ambassador to Turkey (1927–1932) and discusses his representation of missionary interests and his aid in laying the groundwork for better American-Turkish relations.

Cyrus Hamlin

18:34 Hamlin, Cyrus. *Among the Turks*. New York: Carter, 1878. Hamlin, an early missionary and founder of Robert College, provides many interesting sketches of life in Turkey during the 19th century, including the impact of the American missionaries on life in Turkey.

18:35 Hamlin, Cyrus. *My Life and Times*. Chicago: Congregational Publishing Society, 1893. This autobiographical account of Hamlin's life is set against the background of important development in 19th-century Turkey.

Henry Morgenthau, Jr.

See also Chapter 21, "Personalities."

18:36 Morgenthau, Henry, Jr. *All in a Lifetime*. Garden City, N.Y.: Doubleday, Page, 1922. Morgenthau asserts that American interests in Turkey were almost wholly altruistic and that he devoted much of his time guarding the property of the Christian missions. Also included is his role at the Paris Peace Conference.

18:37 Morgenthau, Henry, Jr. *Ambassador Morgenthau's Story*. Garden City, N.Y.: Doubleday, Page, 1919. This memoir discusses the author's intervention with the Turks on behalf of the Armenians at the time of the Turkish deportations in World War I, and explains his influence on the men who later formed a relief organization to aid the Armenians.

18:38 Tuchman, Barbara W. "The Assimilationist Dilemma: Ambassador Morgenthau's Story." *Commentary* 63:5 (1977), 58–62. In 1914 Henry Morgenthau, Jr., then U.S. ambassador to Turkey, arranged for financial aid to the Jewish colony in Palestine. Yet in 1921, he wrote an article stating his strong opposition to Zionism.

Yale, W. "Ambassador Henry Morgenthau's Special Mission of 1917" (18:128).

Mary Mills Patrick

18:39 Patrick, Mary Mills. *A Bosporus Adventure: Istanbul Woman's College, 1871–1924*. Stanford,

Calif.: Stanford University Press, 1934. Patrick provides a discussion of the growth and development of an important American educational institution in the Middle East during the declining years of the Ottoman empire.

18:40 Patrick, Mary Mills. *Under Five Sultans*. New York: Century, 1929. This autobiographical account of fifty years of work with the Constantinople Woman's College provides the reader with numerous details relating to diplomatic efforts on behalf of an American educational institution.

David Porter

18:41 Long, David F. *Nothing Too Daring: A Biography of Commodore David Porter, 1780–1843*. Annapolis: Md.: Naval Institute Press, 1970. This is the best biography of the first U.S. diplomatic representative to Turkey. It treats the commodore's role as chargé d'affaires at Constantinople and exposes the practice of nepotism in the consular service during the Age of Jackson. Bibliography.

18:42 Porter, David. *Constantinople and Its Environs*. 2 vols. New York: Harper, 1835. This memoir provides interesting background information for Commodore Porter's tenure as American diplomatic representative in Constantinople from 1831 to 1843.

Theodore Roosevelt

See Chapters 14, 15, and 17, "Personalities," for additional references.

18:43 Bishop, Joseph B. *Theodore Roosevelt and His Time: Shown in His Own Letters*. 2 vols. New York: Scribner's, 1920. This biography discusses Roosevelt's dealing with the Perdicaris telegram and his influence on the Algeciras Conference, where it asserts that he acted to avoid war between Britain and France and Germany. Bibliography.

William Shaler

Nichols, R. F. *Advance Agents of American Destiny* (7:24) contains two interesting chapters which focus on the role of William Shaler, American consul at Algiers from 1815 to 1828, who maintained an intense scholarly interest in Middle East language and culture, and contributed to American knowledge of that region.

18:44 Nichols, Roy F. "Diplomacy in Barbary." *Pennsylvania Magazine of History and Biography* 74:1 (1950), 113–41. This is an early presentation of the portion of Nichols's book, *Advance Agents of American Destiny,* which deals with the life of William Shaler.

Jan Smuts

18:45 Hancock, William K. *Smuts.* 2 vols. Cambridge: At the University Press, 1962–1968. These volumes provide a detailed and favorable biography of the South African leader.

18:46 Smuts, Jan. *Selections from the Smuts Papers.* 7 vols. Ed. by W. K. Hancock and Jean van der Poel. Cambridge: At the University Press, 1966–1973. This collection is most helpful for an under-standing of Smuts's role at the Paris Peace Conference after World War I, and especially his contributions to the formation of the League of Nations and the mandate system for German colonies. It is also useful in assessing South Africa's foreign policy in the period from unification to the Nationalist triumph in 1945.

Oscar S. Straus

18:47 Cohen, Naomi W. "Ambassador Straus in Turkey, 1909–1910: A Note on Dollar Diplomacy." *Mississippi Valley Historical Review* 45:4 (1959), 632–42. Straus did not conform to the pattern of other "dollar" diplomats. He felt that he should champion the cause of American missionary rights in Turkey, but opposed any action that might involve the United States in Europe's diplomatic tangles with Turkey. He viewed dollar diplomacy as a ploy that would involve the United States in the web of intrigue in Europe, and he thus earned the displeasure of Secretary of State Knox, who recommended that he not be retained in the diplomatic service.

18:48 Straus, Oscar S. *Under Four Administrations: From Cleveland to Taft.* Boston: Houghton Mifflin, 1922. The missionary lobby was powerful in directing late-19th-century American-Turkish relations; but during the period of dollar diplomacy, in the Taft era, commercial interests took precedence.

Others

18:49 Bryson, Thomas A. *A Biography of an American Consular Officer in the Middle East in the Age of Jackson: William Brown Hodgson, 1801–1871.* Atlanta: Resurgens, 1979. Hodgson was an American consular official in Turkey, Egypt, Algiers, and Tunis who had an interest in Middle Eastern languages and who sought positions with the consular service. Bibliography.

18:50 Conn, Cary C. "John Porter Brown, Father of Turkish-American Relations: An Ohioan at the Sublime Porte, 1832–1872." Ph.D. diss., Ohio State University, 1973. Conn treats the career of an early American consular official at Constantinople, focusing on his effort to acquire Oriental languages and knowledge of diplomatic practice and customs. He also emphasizes the need of 19th-century American consular officials for proper political connections to maintain a position in the service. Bibliography.

DeLeon, E. *Thirty Years of My Life on Three Continents* (18:81) provides the memoir of an American consular official in Egypt during the period 1853 to 1861.

18:51 Gates, Caleb F. *Not to Me Only.* Princeton, N.J.: Princeton University Press, 1940. This memoir covers the World War I years in Constantinople and shows the influence that American missionary-educators had on the shaping of U.S. policy vis-à-vis the Middle East during and after the war.

Griscom, L. C. *Diplomatically Speaking* (17:51) demonstrates the importance of missionaries in shaping U.S.-Turkish relations, through pressure on the State Department. For example, he sought to obtain redress for destruction of property by the Turks during the Armenian massacres of the 1890s.

18:52 McKee, Irving. *"Ben-Hur" Wallace: The Life of General Lew Wallace.* Berkeley: University of California Press, 1947. This is an interesting biography of the personal relations between diplomat Lew Wallace and the sultan of Turkey. It discusses Wallace's efforts to mediate the dispute between Britain and the sultan which led to the British occupation of Egypt in 1882. Bibliography.

18:53 Stephens, John L. *Incidents of Travel in Egypt, Arabia, Petraea, and the Holy Land.* 2 vols. New York: Harper, 1837. This is one of the major travel accounts of early American adventures with the Middle East. Stephens made an extensive excursion through the Middle East (1835–1836) and leaves a colorful account.

18:54 Washburn, George. *Fifty Years in Constantinople and Recollections of Robert College.* Boston: Houghton Mifflin, 1909. The second president of Robert College gives details of diplomatic crises between the United States and Turkey, such as the Turkish massacre of the Bulgarians in 1876 and the massacre of the Armenians in the 1890s.

Wilson, F. M. H. *Memoirs of an Ex-Diplomat* (17:57) suggests that the author influenced Turkey's policymaking during the Italo-Turkish War and the negotiations on the Chester Concession (1900–1914).

U.S. and the Barbary States

THE BARBARY WARS, TO 1817

See "Document Collections" for Knox (18:4).

18:55   Allen, Gardner W. *Our Navy and the Barbary Corsairs*. Cambridge: Harvard University Press, 1905. This is the earliest extensive treatment of American relations with the Barbary States (1784–1817). Its detailed narrative, with little interpretation, deals largely with naval operations. Bibliography.

18:56   Anderson, Roger C. *Naval Wars in the Levant, 1559–1853*. Princeton, N.J.: Princeton University Press, 1952. Anderson provides an excellent, if brief, account of the war with Tripoli set against the background of the larger struggle between the European powers with the Barbary pirates. Bibliography.

18:57   Barnby, H. G. *The Prisoners of Algiers: An Account of the Forgotten American-Algerian War, 1785–1797*. New York: Oxford University Press, 1966. This is easily the best account of the war with Algiers. It is rendered in good narrative style, with interpretative analysis that relates domestic and foreign policy, demonstrates the force of the Boston shipping lobby in shaping policy, and criticizes American diplomacy. Barnby also includes material on Joe Barlow, David Humphreys, James Cathcart and Richard O'Brien—consular officers. Bibliography.

18:58   Cantor, Milton. "Joel Barlow's Mission to Algiers." *Historian* 25:2 (1963), 172–94. During his Paris mission (1796–1797), James Monroe asked Joel Barlow to go to Algiers to expedite the release of American seamen. Cantor details Barlow's expensive but ultimately successful ransoming efforts, and depicts Barlow as the most skillful of several American diplomats engaged in this long drawn out negotiation.

The author also examines Barlow's treaty dealings with Tunis and Tripoli.

18:59   Carr, James A. "John Adams and the Barbary Problem: The Myth and the Record." *American Neptune* 26:4 (1966), 231–57. The "myth" which the author finds repeated is that John Adams, unlike Thomas Jefferson, preferred paying tribute to taking naval action. Carr maintains that Adams was less unwilling than unable to take strong action, hindered as he was by anti-navy Republicans in Congress and preoccupied with using what navy he had to prosecute the quasi-war with France.

Field, J. A., Jr. *America and the Mediterranean World, 1776–1882* (18:6) includes a chapter on the U.S. wars with the Barbary States which demonstrates the internal forces working in U.S. diplomacy.

Hall, L. J. *The United States and Morocco, 1776–1956* (18:10) contains, in chapter 2, a detailed narrative of American encounters with the Barbary States in the Confederation-Federalist era.

18:60   Irwin, Ray W. *The Diplomatic Relations of the United States with the Barbary Powers, 1776–1816*. Chapel Hill: University of North Carolina Press, 1931. Still useful to the scholar, this early study of U.S. relations with Morocco, Algiers, Tunis, and Tripoli is drawn largely from U.S. consular correspondence and published works. Bibliography.

18:61   MacLeod, Julia H. "Jefferson and the Navy: A Defense." *Huntington Library Quarterly* 8:2 (1945), 153–84. MacLeod seeks to correct the thesis that Jefferson was entirely hostile to the development of the U.S. Navy. Jefferson did advocate the use of force against the Barbary pirates, believing it less costly than the payment of tribute, but he opposed an untimely naval expansion before the country's economic resources could support it.

Paullin, C. O. *Diplomatic Negotiations of American Naval Officers, 1778–1883* (2:177) presents three uncritical chapters relating to the efforts of American naval officers to negotiate treaties with the Barbary States.

18:62   Ross, Frank E. "The Mission of Joseph Donaldson, Jr., to Algiers, 1795–97." *Journal of Modern History* 7:4 (1935), 422–33. Ross recounts the treaty and ransom negotiations which Donaldson began and Joel Barlow completed. The author finds Donaldson "unsuited to the task" but nonetheless successful because he was known to be honest and was willing to take advice from other, more effective American officials.

18:63 Wright, Louis B., and MacLeod, Julia H. *The First Americans in North Africa: William Eaton's Struggle for a Vigorous Policy against the Barbary Pirates, 1799–1805.* Princeton, N.J.: Princeton University Press, 1945. This critical study of early American diplomatic efforts with the Barbary States focuses on the career of William Eaton. The authors relate American Barbary policy with the Boston shipping lobby that favored an aggressive commercial policy in the Mediterranean. Timothy Pickering is portrayed as a staunch advocate of an aggressive policy toward Barbary. Bibliography.

U.S. AND THE BARBARY STATES, 1817–1900

18:64 Cruickshank, Earl F. "Morocco at the Parting of the Ways: A Study of an Attempt to Reform the System of Native Protection." Ph.D. diss., University of Pennsylvania, 1932. The author describes the protégé system which caused American consular officials in Morocco considerable difficulty. Bibliography.

18:65 Field, James A., Jr. "A Scheme in Regard to Cyrenaica." *Mississippi Valley Historical Review* 44:3 (1957), 445–68. A detailed treatment of the schemes of Michel Vidal, consul at Tripoli, and of the diplomatic crisis and show of naval force that resulted in the 1870s.

Hall, L. J. *The United States and Morocco, 1776–1956* (18:10) asserts that Roosevelt was motivated by a desire to support the Anglo-French entente at the Algeciras Conference.

18:66 Phillips, Dennis H. "The American Presence in Morocco, 1880–1904." Ph.D. diss., University of Wisconsin, 1972. Phillips argues that U.S. consuls abused the protégé system by the sale of protection to compensate for low salaries and concludes that American-Moroccan tensions were due to the cultural gap between the two peoples. Extensive bibliography.

19th-Century U.S.-Middle East Relations

U.S.-OTTOMAN RELATIONS

See "Personalities," especially Cyrus Hamlin, Mary Mills Patrick; also for U.S. and Greek Revolution, see Chapter 8.

18:67 Braden, Jean H. "The Eagle and the Crescent: American Interests in the Ottoman Empire, 1861–1870." Ph.D. diss., Ohio State University, 1973. American diplomacy was facilitated by the missionaries, who maintained a constant flow of information to the United States. The founding of Robert College at Constantinople heralded a new era in U.S.-Turkish relations. Bibliography.

18:68 DeKay, James E. *Sketches of Turkey in 1831 and 1832: By an American.* New York: Harper, 1833. DeKay provides the reader with interesting vignettes of Americans in Turkey during the months immediately following the Turko-American treaty.

Downs, J. M. "American Merchants and the China Opium Trade, 1800–1840" (17:70) discusses the growth of the American opium trade with the Ottomans and the connection between American Middle Eastern policy and East Asian interests.

18:69 Gimelli, Louis B. "Luther Bradish, 1783–1863." Ph.D. diss., New York University, 1964. This biography discusses Bradish's secret mission of 1820–1821 to investigate the possibility of negotiating a commercial treaty with the Ottomans. The author concludes that Bradish's mission demonstrated the advantage of direct conversations with Turks to achieve a treaty. Bibliography.

18:70 Greenwood, Keith M. "Robert College: The American Founders." Ph.D. diss., Johns Hopkins University, 1965. Greenwood treats the diplomatic negotiations among the U.S., Turkish, and British governments necessary to the establishment of the college. Bibliography.

18:71 Klay, Andor. *Daring Diplomacy: The Case of the First American Ultimatum*. Minneapolis: University of Minnesota Press, 1957. This book provides an account of the Martin Koszta affair in Smyrna, Turkey, in 1853.

18:72 Langley, Lester D. "Jacksonian America and the Ottoman Empire." *Muslim World* 68:1 (1978), 46–56. The Jackson administration defined American interests in the Ottoman empire primarily in terms of commercial expansion.

18:73 Lewis, Charles L. "The Old Navy at Constantinople." *U.S. Naval Institute Proceedings* 59:10 (1933), 1442–56. Lewis discusses, briefly, the role of the U.S. Navy in supporting American diplomacy with Turkey between 1800 and 1914.

18:74 Moore, John H. "America Looks at Turkey, 1876–1909." Ph.D. diss., University of Virginia, 1961. This study treats the Balkan wars, the personality of Abdul Hamid II, the American Protestant missionary effort, and the quest for trade expansion. Bibliography.

18:75 Morison, Samuel Eliot. "Forcing the Dardanelles in 1810: With Some Account of the Early Levant Trade of Massachusetts." *New England Quarterly* 1:2 (1928), 208–25. After establishing that the Boston-Smyrna trade extended back into the colonial era, Morison finds Bostonian merchants critical of Congress's pro-Greek sentiments during the Greek revolt (1820s) because American intervention would threaten the Boston-Smyrna trade.

18:76 Prime, E. D. G. *Forty Years in the Turkish Empire*. New York: Carter, 1876. An elegant account by an American missionary long on the scene during the declining years of the Ottoman empire. Prime provides insights into some of the problems facing American diplomats and gives the reader interesting vignettes of some American diplomatic agents.

Sousa, N. *The Capitulatory Regime of Turkey: Its History, Origins, and Nature* (18:14) studies all Frank's, including American, treaty rights in such areas as commerce, extradition, the tariff, property rights, extraterritoriality, missionary rights, and the naturalization-expatriation question. Bibliography.

18:77 Wright, W. Livingston. "American Relations with Turkey to 1831." Ph.D. diss., Princeton University, 1928. This account provides a thorough treatment

of the early American negotiations to obtain a commercial treaty with Turkey. Bibliography.

U.S.-EGYPTIAN RELATIONS

Bergquist, H. E. Jr. "Russo-American Economic Relations in the 1820's: Henry Middleton as a Protector of American Interests in Russia and Turkey" (8:134) reveals that Middleton played an important role in negotiating the 1830 treaty with Turkey.

18:78 Brinton, Jasper Y. *The American Effort in Egypt: A Chapter in Diplomatic History of the Nineteenth Century*. Alexandria, Egypt, 1972. An American judge, resident in Egypt for many years, provides an interesting survey of American diplomatic, missionary, and commercial ties with Egypt from 1784 to the end of the 19th century.

18:79 Brinton, Jasper Y. *The Mixed Courts of Egypt*. New Haven, Conn.: Yale University Press, 1930. An American judge on the mixed tribunal presents a sketch of the history of the mixed courts of Egypt (1870s-1930s) and a description of U.S. participation. Bibliography.

18:80 DeLeon, Edwin. *The Khedive's Egypt*. New York: Harper, 1878. An American diplomat expresses his opposition to the mixed courts system, believing that it jeopardized American rights in Egypt. He also discusses the problems besetting Egypt at a time (1854–1861) when the European powers were considering territorial acquisition in the Middle East.

18:81 DeLeon, Edwin. *Thirty Years of My Life on Three Continents*. 2 vols. London: Ward, Downey, 1890. The memoir depicts the efforts of an early American consul general in Egypt to defend the rights of American missionaries in Palestine.

18:82 Dye, William M. *Moslem Egypt and Christian Abyssinia: Or Military Service with the Khedive*. New York: Atkins & Prout, 1880. This study, by an American foreign service officer who served in Egypt, follows the rise of Egyptian nationalism.

18:83 Farman, Elbert E. *Egypt and Its Betrayal*. New York: Grafton, 1908. This is an excellent history of Egypt in the late 19th century by an American consul and judge.

18:84 Harrison, Thomas S. *The Homely Diary of a Diplomat in the East, 1897–1899*. Boston: Houghton Mifflin, 1917. An interesting memoir of an American diplomat, in Egypt during the height of British supremacy, which sheds some light on Middle Eastern customs and diplomatic practice.

18:85 Penfield, Frederick C. *Present Day Egypt*. New York: Century, 1899. This work briefly describes trade with Egypt at the turn of the century, and American use of the Suez Canal during the Spanish-American War, when U.S. Navy ships passed through the canal en route to the Philippines.

18:86 Serpell, David R. "American Consular Activities in Egypt, 1849–1863." *Journal of Modern History* 10:3 (1938), 344–63. American consuls exercised influence out of proportion to American trade to Egypt. They also engaged in the corrupt practice of selling protection to Egyptians in order to compensate for the lack of financial reward in the consular service.

18:87 Watson, Andrew. *The American Mission in Egypt, 1854–1896*. 2d ed. Pittsburgh: United Presbyterian Board of Publications (1898), 1904. A lengthy treatment of American missionary work in Egypt from earliest days to the end of the century, which describes American schools as an instrument of modernity in Egyptian life.

18:88 Watson, Charles R. *Egypt and the Christian Crusade*. Philadelphia: United Presbyterian Church, 1907. A sketch of American missionary work in Egypt, which emphasizes the activities of the Presbyterian church.

18:89 Watson, Charles R. *In the Valley of the Nile: A Survey of the Missionary Movement in Egypt*. New York: Revell, 1908. The author concentrates on the work of the United Presbyterian Church of North America, showing the role that American schools played in the intellectual awakening in Egypt.

18:90 Wright, Lenoir C. *United States Policy Toward Egypt, 1831–1914*. New York: Exposition, 1969. This is the only extended treatment of American-Egyptian relations in the 19th century. It covers diplomatic and commercial ties, and devotes considerable space to American impact on Egypt during and after the Civil War. Extensive bibliography.

Foreign Military Advisers

18:91 Chaillé-Long, Charles. *My Life on Four Continents*. 2 vols. London: Hutchinson, 1912. One of the participants provides interesting details of the reorganization of the Egyptian army during the post–Civil War period by former Union and Confederate officers.

18:92 Cox, Frederick J. "The American Naval Mission in Egypt." *Journal of Modern History* 26:2 (1954), 173–78. The author describes the work of American military advisers, in the 1870s, to the Egyptian navy. The advisers sought to improve Egyptian ordnance, particularly the use of such weapons as mines, torpedoes, and the like.

18:93 Crabitès, Pierre. *Americans in the Egyptian Army*. London: Routledge, 1938. The author describes the effort of American military advisers in Egypt following the Civil War and notes that they did not represent the U.S. government. The advisers led numerous scientific and military expeditions for the Khedive.

18:94 Hesseltine, William, and Wolf, Hazel C. *The Blue and the Gray on the Nile*. Chicago: University of Chicago Press, 1961. A narrative account of American Union and Confederate soldiers of fortune who served in Egypt after the Civil War, which denies that there was any official connection between the U.S. government and the military advisers. The authors describe the numerous activities in which these advisers were engaged. Bibliography.

18:95 Loring, William W. *A Confederate Soldier in Egypt*. New York: Dodd, Mead, 1884. A former Confederate officer relates his personal and military activities in Egypt while an adviser to the Egyptian army.

U.S.-PERSIAN RELATIONS

18:96 Benjamin, Samuel G. W. *Persia and the Persians*. Boston: Tichnor, 1887. Written by an American minister to Persia, this work contains brief comments on U.S. diplomatic and commercial interests in Persia. Mainly it is a history of the country.

18:97 Kazemzadeh, Firuz. *Russia and Britain in Persia, 1864–1914: A Study in Imperialism*. New Haven, Conn.: Yale University Press, 1968. While this study contains only a few brief references to the U.S. role in Persia during the 19th century, it does describe the Anglo-Russian struggle in Persia that fed the Persians' desire to use the United States as a makeweight. Bibliography.

18:98   Laurie, Thomas. *Dr. Grant and the Mountain Nestorians*. Boston: Gould & Lincoln, 1853. This is a memoir of the first U.S medical missionary to the Middle East, with extensive treatment of his work in the remote parts of Persia.

18:99   Perkins, Justin. *A Residence of Eight Years in Persia among the Nestorian Christians*. New York: Dodd, 1843. This early American missionary to the Nestorian Christians gives a good account of the hardships in Persia that accompanied his work during the 1830s.

U.S.-SYRIAN RELATIONS

18:100   Bashshur, Munir A. "The Role of Two Western Universities in the National Life of Lebanon and the Middle East: A Comparative Study of the American University of Beirut and the University of Saint-Joseph." Ph.D. diss., University of Chicago, 1964. A comparative history of two universities, one founded by American Protestants and the other by French Jesuits, which played large roles in the modernization of the Middle East. Bibliography.

18:101   Bliss, Daniel. *The Reminiscences of Daniel Bliss*. New York: Revell, 1920. A missionary-teacher and founder of Syrian Protestant College describes his work in Syria when American missionaries had an enormous impact on the local cultural life.

18:102   Davis, Harold. "The Jaffa Colonists from Downeast." *American Quarterly* 3:4 (1951), 344–56. A colony of Americans was established in Palestine during the 1860s. These religiously motivated Americans attempted to set up a model farm, employing the latest agricultural machinery, but it failed.

18:103   Dodge, Bayard. *The American University of Beirut: A Brief History of the University and the Lands Which It Serves*. Beirut: Khayats, 1958. A history of an American university that has had a pervasive impact on Lebanon and the Middle East.

18:104   Efimenco, N. Marbury. "American Impact upon Middle East Leadership." *Political Science*

Quarterly 69:2 (1954), 202–18. The author demonstrates the role of American schools as a factor in the Arab cultural revival (1830–1850). He argues that the schools introduced political ideas which stimulated Arab political nationalism and liberal reform.

18:105   Hitti, Philip K. *The Syrians in America*. New York: Doran, 1924. Hitti discusses the immigration of Syrians to America in the 19th and early 20th centuries.

18:106   Lynch, William F. *Narrative of the United States' Expedition to the River Jordan and the Dead Sea*. Philadelphia: Lea & Blanchard, 1849. This is a lengthy account by an American naval officer of a voyage down the River Jordan to the Dead Sea, with brief sketches of the peoples met along the way.

18:107   Penrose, Stephen B. L. *That They May Have Life: The Story of the American University of Beirut, 1866–1941*. New York: Trustees of the American University of Beirut, 1941. This university, which had an important impact on the development of Syria and Lebanon, contributed to the modernization of the entire Middle East.

18:108   Taylor, Alan R. "The American Protestant Mission and the Awakening of Modern Syria, 1820–1870." Ph.D. diss., Georgetown University, 1958. Taylor discusses the impact of American Protestants on the rise of Syrian nationalism in the 19th century. Bibliography.

18:109   Tibawi, A. L. *American Interests in Syria, 1800–1901: A Study of Educational, Literary and Religious Work*. Oxford: Oxford University Press, 1966. Tibawi contends that there is no evidence that the American missionaries were responsible for the Arab revival of the 19th century, but agrees that the missionaries did encourage the Muslim Arabs to retain their cultural identity. Extensive bibliography.

Pre–World War I Diplomacy, 1900–1914

See "Personalities," especially Theodore Roosevelt, Oscar Straus.

ROOSEVELT AND THE ALGECIRAS CRISIS, 1904–1906

18:110 Anderson, Eugene N. *The First Moroccan Crisis, 1904–1906*. Chicago: University of Chicago Press, 1930. Slighting, for the most part, the American contribution to the settlement at Algeciras, this work covers the details of the Franco-German rivalry over Morocco. It emphasizes the alignment of the entente powers against what would become the Axis nations, in the First World War. The book is valuable because of its detailed treatment of the Moroccan crisis from the perspective of the European powers.

Beale, H. K. *Theodore Roosevelt and the Rise of America to World Power* (14:8) claims Roosevelt acted in order to prevent a major war.

18:111 Collins, George W. "United States–Moroccan Relations, 1904–1912." Ph.D. diss., University of Colorado, 1965. Collins asserts that Roosevelt's actions at Algeciras were primarily motivated by the desire to preserve world peace, but that commercial expansion was also a factor and that the missionary influence in Morocco was noteworthy. Bibliography.

18:112 Davis, Harold E. "The Citizenship of Jon Perdicaris." *Journal of Modern History* 13:4 (1941), 517–26. Davis believes that Roosevelt reacted to the Perdicaris affair as he did to support the French position in Morocco.

Denis, A. L. P. *Adventures in American Diplomacy, 1896–1906* (13:7) discusses the kidnapping of Perdicaris, and the U.S. role in the Algeciras Conference.

Einstein, L. *A Diplomat Looks Back* (14:58) contends Roosevelt took a pro-French stand at Algeciras because of his sympathy with French ambition in Morocco.

18:113 Hourihan, William J. "Roosevelt and the Sultans: The United States Navy in the Mediterranean, 1904." Ph.D. diss., University of Massachusetts, 1975. This study examines Roosevelt's deployment of the U.S. Navy in the Mediterranean during the Moroccan crisis to ensure that America would be treated as an equal by the European powers. Bibliography.

18:114 Hourihan, William J. "Marlinspike Diplomacy: The Navy in the Mediterranean, 1904." *U.S. Naval Institute Proceedings* 105:1 (1979), 42–51. This article, based on his dissertation, presents a concise description of the employment of naval power to support American diplomatic efforts in Tangier and Constantinople in 1904.

18:115 Lewis, Tom T. "Franco-American Relations during the First Moroccan Crisis." *Mid-America* 55:1 (1973), 21–36. The author asserts that Roosevelt's support of the French at the Algeciras Conference was limited and based on the wish to prevent war and promote the open door policy.

CHESTER CONCESSION IN TURKEY, 1908–1913

See "Personalities" for F. M. Huntington Wilson (under "Others").

18:116 Askew, William C., and Rippy, J. Fred. "The United States and Europe's Strife, 1908–1913." *Journal of Politics* 4:1 (1942), 68–79. The authors show the relationship between the proposed U.S. mediation effort in the Balkan War of 1911–1912 and the U.S. desire for Turkish approval of the Chester Concession.

18:117 DeNovo, John A. "A Railroad for Turkey: The Chester Project of 1908–1913." *Business History Review* 33:3 (1959), 300–29. This essay treats U.S. involvement in Admiral Chester's quest for an economic concession from the Turks just prior to World War I.

Varg, P. *Open Door Diplomat: The Life of W. W. Rockhill* (17:40) quotes W. W. Rockhill as attributing the defeat of the Chester Concession to German influence in Turkey.

SHUSTER MISSION TO PERSIA, 1911

Curti, M., and Birr, K. *Prelude to Point Four: American Technical Missions Overseas, 1838–1930* (2:73) gives some attention to the Shuster mission.

Kazemzadeh, F. *Russia and Britain in Persia, 1864–1914: A Study in Imperialism* (18:97) examines Morgan Shuster's mission to Persia, and concludes that corrupt Persian politicians were responsible for the termination of the economic mission. Bibliography.

18:118 McDaniel, Robert A. *The Shuster Mission and the Persian Constitutional Revolution.* Minneapolis: Biblioteca Islamica, 1974. The author reviews Persian internal politics and finds that Persian politicians opposed the Shuster mission; this, coupled with Russian resistance, led to its ultimate termination. He is critical of Shuster's inability to maintain adequate communication with British and Russian diplomats. Bibliography.

18:119 Shuster, William M. *The Strangling of Persia: Story of the European Diplomacy and Oriental Intrigue that Resulted in the Denationalization of Twelve Million Mohammedans: A Personal Narrative.* New York: Century, 1912. The leader of an American financial mission to Persia sets forth the obstacles confronting his efforts to reform Persian finances. He concludes that political intrigue and the machinations of Britain and Russia prevented the completion of his objectives.

Yeselson, A. *United States–Persian Diplomatic Relations, 1883–1921* (18:16) provides a synopsis of the Shuster mission which he relates to Taft's dollar diplomacy.

From World War I to World War II, 1914–1939

See "Personalities," especially Mark L. Bristol, Joseph C. Grew, Henry Morgenthau.

18:120 Abbott, Freeland K. "American Policy in the Middle East: A Study of the Attitudes of the United States towards the Middle East, Especially during the Period 1919–1936." Ph.D. diss., Fletcher School of Law and Diplomacy, 1952. This study examines U.S. negotiations at the Paris Peace Conference on such matters as the Armenian question, the application of the open door to Middle Eastern oil fields, the Chester Concession, and the question of mandates. Addition-

ally, it discusses U.S. participation at the Lausanne and Montreux conferences. Bibliography.

18:121 Adler, Selig. "The United States and the Middle Eastern Dilemma, 1917–1939." *Maryland Historian* 7:1 (1976), 1–17. If FDR had put more pressure on Britain in regard to Palestine, many Jews might have been saved from the Holocaust. However, several factors combined to inhibit the administration, including isolationism, Anglophobia, the State Department's hostility to Zionism, Arab propaganda, and pressure from American oil companies concerned with maintaining friendly relations with the Arab majority in the Middle East.

Baram, P. J. *The Department of State in the Middle East, 1919–1945* (33:82). Discusses in detail the various foreign service officers responsible for the shaping of American policy vis-à-vis the Middle East.

18:122 Barton, James L. *The Story of Near East Relief, 1915–1930: An Interpretation.* New York: Macmillan, 1930. Barton discusses the inception of Near East Relief, its scope, history, and aims. He claims that the organization did not try in any way to influence the formulation of U.S. Middle East policy.

18:123 Bryson, Thomas A. "A Note on Near East Relief: Walter George Smith, Cardinal Gibbons and the Question of Discrimination against Catholics." *Muslim World* 61:3 (1971), 202–09. Smith persuaded Gibbons that no discrimination was being practiced (1919–1920), and that the cardinal and American Catholics should support Near East Relief.

Curti, M. E. *American Philanthropy Abroad: A History* (2:72) claims American efforts reached a high point in the Middle East during and after World War I.

Curti, M. and Birr, K. *Prelude to Point Four: American Technical Missions Overseas, 1838–1930* (2:73) touches on technical assistance efforts, and the King-Crane and Harbord missions.

18:124 Grabill, Joseph L. "Missionary Influence on American Relations with the Near East, 1914–1923." *Muslim World* 58:2 (1968), 141–54. The author seeks to estimate the amount of influence that missionaries brought to bear on the course of U.S.-Turkish relations during the interwar era, particularly the Armenian question.

18:125 Latourette, Kenneth Scott. "Colonialism and Missions: Progressive Separation." *Journal of*

Church and State 7:3 (1965), 330–49. The author briefly discusses missionary influence on diplomacy (1914–1920) and argues that missionaries did not represent official American policy in the Middle East or serve as instruments of imperial aspiration.

18:126 Sachar, Howard M. *The Emergence of the Middle East, 1914–1924*. New York: Knopf, 1969. The author examines the complex negotiations between the European powers that led to the partition of the Ottoman empire. He deals with the postwar negotiations in the region at the time that President Wilson tried to impose his principles upon a Middle Eastern settlement at the Paris Peace Conference. The failure of the Wilsonian settlement led to the Lausanne settlement. Bibliography.

18:127 Sachar, Howard M. *Europe Leaves the Middle East, 1936–1954*. New York: Knopf, 1972. This book devotes considerable space to the U.S. reaction to the Zionist question during the latter part of this period. It also treats British and French Middle Eastern problems during World War II, when the subject peoples proved restive and began to desire the right of self-determination. Extensive bibliography.

18:128 Yale, William. "Ambassador Henry Morgenthau's Special Mission of 1917." *World Politics* 1:1 (1949), 308–20. Henry Morgenthau sought to arrange a separate peace between the Allies and Turkey during World War I, only to have prominent American Zionists frustrate his mission because Zionist goals in Palestine could be realized only if Turkey remained at war.

PARIS PEACE CONFERENCE

See Chapter 19 for general references.

18:129 Beer, George Louis. *African Questions at the Paris Peace Conference: With Papers on Egypt, Mesopotamia, and the Colonial Settlement*. Ed. by Louis H. Gray. New York: Macmillan, 1923. Beer reviews some of the problems involved in the mandate territories awarded to Britain and France at the peace conference.

18:130 Buzanski, Peter M. "The Inter-Allied Investigation of the Greek Invasion of Smyrna, 1919." *Historian* 25:3 (1963), 325–43. This essay examines the role of an American naval officer serving on an inter-Allied commission to investigate the Greek landings at Smyrna.

Gelfand, L. E. *The Inquiry: American Preparations for Peace, 1917–1919* (19:283) analyzes American preparations for the postwar settlement of problems associated with the demise of the Ottoman empire.

18:131 Helmreich, Paul C. *From Paris to Sèvres: The Partition of the Ottoman Empire at the Peace Conference, 1919–1920*. Columbus: Ohio State University Press, 1974. This comprehensive account examines the protracted negotiations leading up to the partition of the Ottoman empire and the American efforts to gain a settlement that would accommodate the conflicting imperial aspirations of the powers and the nationalistic aspirations of the subject peoples of the old Ottoman empire. Bibliography.

18:132 Howard, Harry N. *The King-Crane Commission: An American Inquiry into the Middle East*. Beirut: Khayats, 1963. This study describes the investigation conducted in 1919 by the American section of the Inter-Allied Commission on the Middle East authorized by the peace conference. The report, officially published only in 1947, opposed establishment of a Zionist state in Palestine, warned against French control in Syria, favored a British mandate for Mesopotamia and Palestine, proposed an American mandate for Armenia and the internationalizing of Constantinople. Bibliography.

18:133 Howard, Harry N. *The Partition of Turkey: A Diplomatic History, 1913–1923*. Norman: University of Oklahoma Press, 1931. The author discusses the partition of the Ottoman empire and provides a background to America's Turkish policy during the war and at the Paris Peace Conference. Extensive bibliography.

Patrick, M. M. *A. Bosporus Adventure: Istanbul Woman's College, 1871–1924* (18:39) sheds light on the decisionmaking process at the Paris Peace Conference and on the lower echelon individuals who influenced Middle Eastern decisions at the conference.

THE PALESTINE QUESTION

18:134 Adler, Selig. "The Palestine Question in the Wilson Era." *Journal of Jewish Social Studies* 10:4 (1948), 303–34. The author asserts that Justice Brandeis persuaded President Wilson to support the Balfour Declaration and that this endorsement improved the Zionists' position.

18:135 Feinstein, Marnin. "The First Twenty-five Years of Zionism in the United States, 1882–1906" Ph.D. diss., Columbia University, 1963. Early American proponents of Zionist goals provoked intense arguments among the country's Jewish leaders. Bibliography.

18:136 Friedrich, Carl J. *American Policy toward Palestine*. Washington, D.C.: Public Affairs Press, 1944. This summary of interwar governmental policies on Zionism also contains a collection of pertinent documents.

18:137 Knee, Stuart E. "The King-Crane Commission of 1919: The Articulation of Political Anti-Zionism." *American Jewish Archives* 29:1 (1977), 22–52. The author claims that the members of the King-Crane Commission were anti-Zionist, therefore the commission's report opposed Zionist goals in Palestine.

18:138 Lebow, Richard N. "Woodrow Wilson and the Balfour Declaration." *Journal of Modern History* 40:4 (1968), 500–23. Lebow argues that President Wilson delayed endorsement of the Balfour Declaration in order not to arouse Turkish antipathy toward American missionary interests.

18:139 Lipstadt, Deborah E. "The Zionist Cause of Louis Lipsky, 1900–1921." Ph.D. diss., Brandeis University, 1977. This study treats the career of an early American Zionist whose influence was overshadowed by that of Justice Brandeis. Bibliography.

18:140 Manuel, Frank E. *The Realities of American-Palestine Relations*. Washington, D.C.: Public Affairs Press, 1949. Manuel examines American official reaction to the Jewish question during World War I, treats Zionist influence on Woodrow Wilson after the war, and shows that Americans considered the Palestine question to be a British problem during the interwar years. Bibliography.

18:141 Meyer, Isidore S., ed. *Early History of Zionism in America*. New York: American Jewish Historical Society, 1958. This series of essays explores the early history of Zionism in America.

18:142 Oder, Irwin. "The United States and the Palestine Mandate, 1920–1948: A Study of the Impact of Interest Groups on Foreign Policy." Ph.D. diss., Columbia University, 1956. Although American Zionists pressed Congress to pass a 1922 resolution endorsing the creation of a Jewish national home in Palestine, the government had no desire to be drawn into an Arab-Jewish-British controversy. Bibliography.

18:143 Parzen, Herbert. "Brandeis and the Balfour Declaration." *Herzl Yearbook* 5 (1963), 309–50. Parzen believes that Wilson favorably considered the Balfour Declaration because of a growing pro-Zionist sentiment among his top advisers.

18:144 Plesur, Milton. "The Relations between the United States and Palestine. (1917–1945)." *Judaism* 3:4 (1954), 469–79. Plesur surveys American policy from Woodrow Wilson's reaction to the Balfour Declaration to President Roosevelt's handling of the Palestine question during World War II.

18:145 Stein, Leonard. *The Balfour Declaration*. New York: Simon & Schuster, 1961. This is an exhaustive study of the Balfour Declaration, which ultimately received the endorsement of President Woodrow Wilson. Bibliography.

LAUSANNE (1923) AND MONTREUX (1936) CONFERENCES

Burns, R. D. *Arms Control and Disarmament: A Bibliography* (1:25) lists books, essays, and dissertations relating to the Lausanne and Montreux conferences (pp. 369–72).

18:146 Davison, Roderic H. "Turkish Diplomacy from Mudros to Lausanne." In Gordon A. Craig, and Felix Gilbert, eds., *The Diplomats, 1919–1939*. New York: Atheneum (1953), 1963, vol. 1, pp. 179–202. In addition to dealing with postwar Turkish diplomacy, this essay treats the development of Turkish negotiations with the Allies up to and including the Lausanne Conference.

18:147 DeLuca, Anthony R. "Montreux and Collective Security." *Historian* 38:1 (1975), 1–20. At the Montreux Conference of 1936, the demilitarized zones at the Turkish Straits were abolished, new rules of passage were adopted, and the international administrative commission was eliminated.

DeNovo, J. A. *American Interests and Policies in the Middle East, 1900–1939* (18:5) provides an interesting chapter on the American participation at this conference. DeNovo concludes that American participants were able to ignore the "terrible Turk" image and to support a reasonable treaty with Turkey.

Grew, J. C. *Turbulent Era: A Diplomatic Record of Forty Years, 1904–1945* (18:33) gives extensive treatment to U.S. participation at the Lausanne Conference.

18:148   Grew, Joseph C. "The Peace Conference of Lausanne, 1922–1923." *Proceedings of the American Philosophical Society* 98:1 (1954), 1–10. Although Grew goes into much greater detail in *Turbulent Era,* this article is valuable for the "pen sketches" of such delegates as Benito Mussolini, Raymond Poincaré, Lord Curzon, Eleutherios Venizelos, Ismet Pasha, and George Chicherin.

Howard, H. N. *Turkey, the Straits and U.S. Policy* (2:362) develops American-Turkish relations from the Treaty of 1830 through World War I and the Paris Peace Conference, and the Lausanne Conference of 1922–1923, when the initial postwar straits regime was adopted.

18:149   Howard, Harry N. "The United States and the Problem of the Turkish Straits." *Middle East Journal* 1:1 (1947), 59–72. This reference article covers, in brief, the Lausanne Conference, the Montreux Convention, and the period immediately following World War II.

18:150   Nicolson, Harold G. *Curzon: The Last Phase, 1919–1925: A Study in Post-War Diplomacy.* New York: Harcourt, Brace, 1934. This biography treats the Lausanne Conference from the point of view of a British diplomat.

American goods might freely enter the Egyptian marketplace.

Beard, C. A., and Smith, G. H. E. *The Idea of National Interest: An Analytical Study in American Foreign Relations* (2:123) describes Admiral Mark Bristol's efforts to achieve American parity with Britain in the Turkish economy.

18:152   Horton, George. *The Blight of Asia.* New York: Bobbs-Merrill, 1927. A consular official who served in Turkey (1920–1927) asserts that the U.S. government did not assist the American missionaries in the post–World War I era, but rather compromised their interests in favor of commercial activity.

18:153   Issa, Mahmoud K. "Trade between Egypt and the United States." Ph.D. diss., University of Minnesota, 1953. Commercial relations between the U.S. and Egypt during the interwar period are examined. Bibliography.

18:154   Kazdal, Mustafa N. "Trade Relations between the United States and Turkey, 1919–1944." Ph.D. diss., Indiana University, 1946. This study concentrates on commercial relations between United States and Turkey during the interwar era. Bibliography.

18:155   Trask, Roger R. "The United States and Turkish Nationalism: Investments and Technical Aid during the Ataturk Era." *Business History Review* 38:1 (1964), 58–77. American commercial and technical assistance activities in Turkey are reviewed.

ECONOMIC INFLUENCES

Baram, P. J. *The Department of State in the Middle East, 1919–1945* (33:82) examines the organization of the Department of State's Near East section and the outlook of its personnel. Baram argues that the United States worked to dismantle the imperial structures in the Middle East so as to further American commerce in the region.

18:151   Baram, Phillip J. "Undermining the British: Department of State Policies in Egypt and the Suez Canal before and during World War II." *Historian* 40:4 (1978), 631–49. Baram asserts that the State Department sought to dismantle the British privileged position in the Egyptian economy in order that

The Quest for Oil

See Chapter 33, "The U.S. and Middle Eastern Oil."

DeNovo, J. A. *American Interests and Policies in the Middle East, 1900–1939* (18:5) treats in detail U.S. diplomatic efforts with European powers to obtain equal access to the oil fields; he deals specifically with American interests in Iraq, Iran, Saudi Arabia, Bahrein, and Kuwait.

18:156   DeNovo, John A. "The Movement for an Aggressive American Oil Policy Abroad, 1918–1920." *American Historical Review* 61:4 (1956), 854–76. This essay treats the American anticipation of a postwar oil shortage and the aggressive effort of government and oil men to formulate a comprehensive policy to find new sources.

18:157 DeNovo, John A. "Petroleum and the United States Navy before World War I." *Mississippi Valley Historical Review* 41:4 (1955), 641–56. During the Taft administration the State Department began formulating an American oil policy that would eventually encompass the Middle East.

18:158 Earle, Edward Mead. "The Turkish Petroleum Company—A Study in Oleaginous Diplomacy." *Political Science Quarterly* 39:2 (1924), 265–77. This essay criticizes the State Department's effort (1920–1927) to assist American oil companies in their bid for new sources of petroleum in the Middle East, and asserts that such action was inconsistent with the Monroe Doctrine.

18:159 Finnie, David H. *Desert Enterprise: Middle East Oil Industry in Its Local Environment.* Cambridge: Harvard University Press, 1958. Finnie examines the origins of American oil concessions in the Middle East, the problems faced by the oil companies in dealing with the host countries and with the U.S. government, and the impact of the companies on the peoples of the Middle East (1920–1939).

Gibb, G. S., and Knowlton, E. H. *The Resurgent Years, 1911–1927.* Vol. 2 in *History of Standard Oil* (39:136) includes an excellent treatment of the State Department's use of the open door policy to support the effort of Standard Oil of New Jersey to gain access to Middle East oil in the 1920s.

18:160 Lenczowski, George. *Oil and State in the Middle East.* Ithaca, N.Y.: Cornell University Press, 1960. This study considers the relations between American oil companies and their host countries in the Middle East (1920–1960), with special emphasis on the national aspirations of the latter and the legal rights of the former. Bibliography.

18:161 Mosley, Leonard. *Power Play: Oil in the Middle East.* New York: Random House, 1973. The author presents a readable account (1920–1972) of U.S. governmental support for American oil men during the interwar period, concentrating on efforts in Iraq, Bahrein, and Saudi Arabia.

18:162 Nash, Gerald D. *United States Oil Policy, 1890–1964.* Pittsburgh: University of Pittsburgh Press, 1968. This study focuses on the relationship between the U.S. government and oil interests, and on the latter's quest for Middle East oil concessions. Nash asserts that the government, from Wilson on, continued to support Americans in the interwar era in Iraq, Bahrein, and Saudi Arabia. Bibliography.

18:163 O'Brien, Dennis J. "The Oil Crisis and the Foreign Policy of the Wilson Administration, 1917–1921." Ph.D. diss., University of Missouri, 1974. This study describes how, during World War I, American leaders perceived an American oil crisis, and how, in conjunction with oil executives, these leaders sought to alleviate that crisis by an overseas quest for new sources. The Middle East was viewed as an ideal hunting ground. Bibliography.

Shwadran, B. *The Middle East, Oil and the Great Powers* (33:152) demonstrates the manner in which the U.S. government and the American oil industry worked during the interwar period to obtain oil concessions in the Middle East.

18:164 Stocking, George W. *Middle East Oil: A Study in Political and Economic Controversy.* Nashville: Vanderbilt University Press, 1970. This work surveys American oil diplomacy from the 1920s to 1970, and argues that the State Department initiated an aggressive Middle Eastern oil policy during the Wilson administration. Stocking treats in detail an American quest for Middle East oil in the period following World War I. Bibliography.

18:165 Wall, Bennett H., and Gibb, George S. *Teagle of Jersey Standard.* New Orleans: Tulane University Press, 1974. This very readable biography discusses Teagle's efforts to secure Jersey Standard's entry into the Iraq international oil consortium in the 1920s. Bibliography.

NATIONAL DIMENSIONS

See "Overviews," above, for general surveys relating to the Middle East.

Iran (Persia)

Lenczowski, G. *Russia and the West in Iran, 1918–1948: A Study of Big-Power Rivalry* (33:171) is more concerned with the U.S. role in Iranian-Russian-British relations during World War II and the aftermath than with its role in the earlier period.

18:166 Millspaugh, Arthur C. *The American Task in Persia.* New York: Century, 1924. This American economist discusses the efforts of his first mission to Iran in the 1920s to modernize the Iranian government so that it might better meet the needs of its people and withstand the pressures of Britain and Russia.

18:167 Mojdehi, Hassan. "Arthur C. Millspaugh's Two Missions to Iran and Their Impact on American-Iranian Relations." Ph.D. diss., Ball State University, 1975. This account examines Millspaugh's role in Iranian affairs during 1922 to 1927, when his economic mission attempted to reform the Iranian system of taxation and government. It includes the reaction of the U.S. government to this important, informal mission. The second half of the work deals with Millspaugh's mission to Iran during World War II. Bibliography.

Ramazani, R. K. *The Foreign Policy of Iran, 1500 – 1941* (2:364) treats the Millspaugh mission to Iran in the 1920s, when the Iranians sought to assert their nationalistic aspirations in the face of British and Russian opposition. Included as well is a brief treatment of the Shuster mission.

18:168 Smith, Douglas L. "The Millspaugh Mission and American Corporate Diplomacy in Persia, 1922 – 1927." *Southern Quarterly* 14:2 (1976), 151 – 72. Reza Khan Pahlevi appointed Millspaugh to be director-general of Persian finances because he perceived the United States as a disinterested power with exportable capital and technology. This sort of activity appealed to the State Department, which hoped to secure concessions for private companies from Persia's anti-Soviet regime.

Saudi Arabia

18:169 al-Jazairi, Mohamed Zayyan. "Saudi Arabia: A Diplomatic History, 1924 – 1964." Ph.D. diss., University of Utah, 1971. A detailed account of Saudi Arabia's diplomatic history from 1924 to 1964, coupled with an historical sketch of the establishment and rise of the Saudi dynasty. Bibliography.

18:170 Twitchell, Karl S. *Saudi Arabia: With an Account of the Development of Its Natural Resources.* Princeton, N.J.: Princeton University Press, 1958. This book treats the author's early efforts to find oil in Saudi Arabia and his success in locating an American oil company (local) to develop the rich petroleum resources in that country. He brings the story down to

the postwar era, when Saudi oil assumed a larger role in American diplomacy.

18:171 Walt, Joseph W. "Saudi Arabia and the Americans, 1928 – 1951." Ph.D. diss., Northwestern University, 1960. Walt's excellent account treats the American quest for Arabian oil in the 1930s, when oil was first found in marketable quantities. Bibliography.

Turkey

18:172 Daniel, Robert L. "The United States and the Turkish Republic before World War II: The Cultural Dimension." *Middle East Journal* 21:1 (1967), 52 – 63. This essay argues that the missionary lobby created the "terrible Turk" image in the United States during the time that the Armenian question was paramount in U.S.-Turkish relations.

18:173 Evans, Laurence. *United States Policy and the Partition of Turkey, 1914 – 1924.* Baltimore: Johns Hopkins Press, 1965. Evans considers the multiplicity of problems associated with American-Turkish relations, such as the questions related to Armenians and Palestinians, American neutral rights, and others. It also traces the development of an American policy vis-à-vis Turkey at the Paris Peace Conference. Bibliography.

18:174 Johnson, Hugh S. "The American Schools in the Republic of Turkey, 1923 – 1933: A Case Study of Missionary Problems in International Relations." Ph.D. diss., American University, 1975. Missionary schools declined during this decade, when nationalism, secularism, and xenophobia determined Turkish reaction to foreign missionaries. Bibliography.

18:175 Kinross, John P. D. B., 3d Baron. *Atatürk: A Biography of Mustafa Kemal, Father of Modern Turkey.* New York: Morrow, 1965. This is the best biography in English of Kemal Ataturk, the key figure in modern Turkish history who consolidated the Muslim "sick man of Europe" into a viable secular republic. Kinross sees Ataturk as a flawed visionary determined to save his country from European and Russian domination while presiding over an ambitious program of social and economic modernization. Bibliography.

18:176 Trask, Roger R. "The Terrible Turk and Turkish-American Relations in the Interwar Period." *Historian* 33:1 (1970), 40 – 53. Trask discusses the rise of the "terrible Turk" image in the U.S. during the 1920s, as well as the effort of other Americans to correct this image and so pave the way for Turkish-American rapprochement in later years.

18:177   Trask, Roger R. "Turco-American Rapprochement, 1927–1932." In Sidney D. Brown, ed., *Studies on Asia*. Lincoln: University of Nebraska Press, 1967, pp. 139–70. American diplomats were finally able to persuade the various American interest groups in Turkey to accommodate Turkish nationalism, thus establishing goodwill toward the United States and paving the way for closer relations. Bibliography.

18:178   Trask, Roger R. *The United States Response to Turkish Nationalism and Reform, 1914–1939*. Minneapolis: University of Minnesota Press, 1971. Trask examines American interests in Turkey and American response to Turkish nationalism. He gives considerable space to missionary work, trade expansion, and the negotiation of the treaty that normalized relations between the two countries. Bibliography.

18:179   Trask, Roger R. "Unnamed Christianity in Turkey during the Ataturk Era." *Muslim World* 55:1 (1965), 66–76. Turkish authorities curtailed the teaching of Christian ethics in American schools, and the missionaries responded with a program of "unnamed Christianity" designed to replace the formal Christian teachings removed from the curricula.

U.S. and the Armenian Question, 1890–1927

18:180   Cook, Ralph E. "The United States and the Armenian Question, 1894–1924." Ph.D. diss., Fletcher School of Law and Diplomacy, 1957. Cook surveys the role of the Armenian question in American diplomacy and its impact on American-Turkish relations. He relates the pressure of American Armenophiles to assist American missionaries to the Armenians in the 1890s, and the American government's concern from the early massacres beyond the Paris Peace Conference. Bibliography.

18:181   Hovannisian, Richard G. *Armenia on the Road to Independence, 1918*. Berkeley: University of California Press, 1969. The author analyzes the rise of the Armenian Republic, which played a role in American-Turkish relations during and after the Paris Peace Conference. Extensive bibliography.

18:182   Hovannisian, Richard G. *The Republic of Armenia: The First Years, 1918–1919*. Berkeley: University of California Press, 1971. This volume provides further material on the Armenian Republic and continues the development of events in the Transcaucasus which so concerned the U.S. government in the post–World War I era. Extensive bibliography.

18:183   Kazemzadeh, Firuz. *The Struggle for Transcaucasia, 1917–21*. New York: Philosophical Library, 1951. The writer discusses in detail the situation in the Transcaucasus during and after World War I. He describes the events that gave rise to the Armenian Republic, and the Turkish and Russian reaction thereto. Bibliography.

18:184   Mirak, Robert. "Armenian Emigration to the United States to 1915: Leaving the Old Country." *Journal of Armenian Studies* 1:1 (1975), 5–42. Based on his dissertation (see next entry), this article describes Armenian migration to the United States. It supplies much data about an important ethnic pressure group that has influenced U.S.-Turkish relations.

18:185   Mirak, Robert. "The Armenians in the United States, 1890–1915." Ph.D. diss., Harvard University, 1965. This work describes an important ethnic pressure group which had much influence on U.S.-Turkish relations (1894–1927). Bibliography.

THE EARLY MASSACRES, 1890s

18:186   Edwards, Rosaline D. "Relations between the United States and Turkey, 1893–1897." Ph.D. diss., Fordham University, 1952. This account addresses the role of the United States in the diplomatic imbroglio that grew out of the Armenian massacres in the 1890s. It covers American-Turkish negotiations concerning the massacres and the right of Armenians to expatriate. Bibliography.

May, E. R. *Imperial Democracy: The Emergence of America as a Great Power* (12:80) has a brief section on American involvement in the Armenian question.

Great Britain hoped to achieve an Anglo-American rapprochement to effect a naval demonstration in Turkish waters, but American concern for Cuba outweighed interest in Armenia.

18:187 McDonough, George P. "American Relations with Turkey, 1898–1901." Ph.D. diss., Georgetown University, 1951. This is a detailed study of the Armenian question both from the standpoint of European diplomacy and in the context of U.S.-Turkish relations. It discusses the Armenian massacres of the 1890s and the U.S. reaction. Bibliography.

WORLD WAR I AND THE MANDATE ISSUE

18:188 Bierstadt, Edward H. *The Great Betrayal.* New York: McBride, 1924. The author concludes that the United States compromised efforts to salvage an independent Armenia in deference to the aspirations of American commercial interests in Turkey.

18:189 Brown, Philip M. "The Mandate over Armenia." *American Journal of International Law* 14:1 (1920), 396–406. Senate opposition to the Armenian mandate was based on the premise that U.S. acceptance of this obligation was tantamount to adherence to the League of Nations Covenant.

18:190 Bryson, Thomas A. "Mark Lambert Bristol, U.S. Navy, Admiral-Diplomat: His Influence on the Armenian Mandate Question." *Armenian Review* 21:4 (1968), 3–22. Bristol's influence was important in the Senate's rejection of President Wilson's proposed mandate for Armenia.

18:191 Bryson, Thomas A. "The Armenia-America Society: A Factor in American-Turkish Relations, 1919–1924." *Records of the American Catholic Historical Society* 82:2 (1971), 83–105. This essay demonstrates the manner in which an ethnic lobby tried to shape U.S. policy on the Armenian question in the postwar era.

18:192 Bryson, Thomas A. "Woodrow Wilson and the Armenian Mandate: A Reassessment." *Armenian Review* 21:3 (1968), 10–28. This essay appraises Wilson's handling of the Armenian question during and after the Paris Peace Conference, and examines some

conflicting historical interpretations. See also Bryson, "An American Mandate for Armenia: A Link in British Near Eastern Policy," ibid. 21:2 (1968), 23–41; and his "John Sharp Williams: An Advocate for the Armenian Mandate, 1919–1920," ibid. 26:3 (1973), 23–42.

18:193 Bryson, Thomas A. *Walter George Smith.* Washington, D.C.: Catholic University Press, 1977. Smith was an Armenophile who worked to achieve goals for the Americans at the Paris Peace Conference.

18:194 Daniel, Robert L. "The Armenian Question and American-Turkish Relations, 1914–1927." *Mississippi Valley Historical Review* 46:2 (1959), 252–75. Daniel contends that America's concern for Armenian rights and the question of self-determination aggravated relations between the United States and Turkey. Harsh treatment of Armenians by the Turks created an unstable diplomatic environment, but the American policymakers never considered the Armenian question seriously enough to warrant the use of force.

18:195 Daniel, Robert L. "The Friendship of Woodrow Wilson and Cleveland Dodge." *Mid-America* 43:3 (1961), 182–96. Daniel describes the close relationship between two men whose interest in the Armenian question developed from Dodge's lay family connection with the Near Eastern missionary and educational effort.

18:196 Gidney, James B. *A Mandate for Armenia.* Kent, Ohio: Kent State University Press, 1967. This is a good one-volume treatment of the American involvement in the Armenian question from 1915 to 1927. It gives broad analytical treatment to American policy on the Armenian mandate question at the Paris Peace Conference and to the Senate's consideration of the matter in 1919–1920. See also Thomas A. Bryson, "Woodrow Wilson, the Senate, Public Opinion, and the Armenian Mandate, 1919–1920," Ph.D. diss., University of Georgia, 1965. Both have extensive bibliographies.

18:197 Housepian, Marjorie. *The Smyrna Affair.* New York: Harcourt Brace Jovanovich, 1971. The author concentrates on the Smyrna fire and criticizes American diplomacy for compromising Armenian goals in favor of the Turks. Housepian is very critical of the U.S. high commissioner to Turkey, Admiral Mark Bristol. Bibliography.

Nevins, A. *Henry White: Thirty Years of American Diplomacy* (14:60) provides correspondence between White and Senator Lodge which is valuable to an understanding of U.S. consideration of the Armenian question at the Paris Peace Conference, 1919.

18:198   Westermann, William L. "The Armenian Problem and the Disruption of Turkey." In E. M. House, and Charles Seymour, eds., *What Really Happened at Paris: The Story of the Peace Conference*. New York: Scribner's, 1921, pp. 176–203. Westermann examines Wilson's consideration of the Armenian question and his qualified acceptance of the mandate at the Paris Peace Conference.

U.S. and Sub-Saharan Africa, to 1939

Chester, E. W. *Clash of Titans: Africa and U.S. Foreign Policy* [1783–1974] (2:336) is one of the few comprehensive surveys, covering both North and South Africa, with the bulk of the narrative dealing with those years between the American Revolution and World War II. It touches on economic, religious, and cultural contacts, as well as political affairs, relying heavily on the Foreign Relations series.

18:199   Clendenen, Clarence C., and Duignan, Peter. *Americans in Black Africa up to 1865*. Stanford, Calif.: Hoover Institution, 1964. The three major sections of this brief monograph deal with American traders, missionaries and colonization societies, and explorers and frontiersmen. Bibliography.

18:200   Clendenen, Clarence C.; Collins, Robert; and Duignan, Peter. *Americans in Africa 1865–1900*. Stanford, Calif.: Hoover Institution, 1966. This broad survey of American contacts with Africa focuses on diplomatic support for weak Liberia and participation in conferences on the Congo. Individual Americans in Africa included famous and little-known explorers, merchants, prospectors, soldiers, engineers, and farmers, who ranged from Egypt to Southern Africa. Bibliography.

18:201   Coupland, Reginald, *East Africa and Its Invaders: From the Earliest Times to the Death of Seyyid Said in 1856*. New York: Russell & Russell (1938), 1965. This book incorporates exhaustive research at the Public Record Office and the India Office. Chapter 12 examines "Traders from America and Germany."

18:202   Hammond, Harold E. "American Interest in the Exploration of the Dark Continent." *Historian* 18:2 (1956), 202–29. This article emphasizes the activities of the American Geographical Society (1850–1900), and features such explorers as Paul Du Chaillu, Henry Stanley, Alan Southworth, and Mrs. French-Sheldon.

Howe, R. W. *Along the African Shore* [1766–1973] (2:339) surveys African affairs, with more emphasis on the last several than Chester's study (2:336).

18:203   Jacobs, Sylvia M. *The African Nexus: Black American Perspectives on European Partitioning of Africa, 1880–1920*. Westport, Conn.: Greenwood, 1981. Jacobs focuses on the attitude of American black intellectuals toward the European dismemberment of Africa. The black protest to European imperialism, according to the author, nurtured Pan-Africanism in America and movement toward black cultural nationalism. Bibliography.

18:204   Ralston, Richard D. "A Second Middle Passage: African Student Sojourns in the United States during the Colonial Period and Their Influence upon the Character of African Leadership." Ph.D. diss., University of California, Los Angeles, 1972. American missionaries introduced these students to the American experience. Those students educated in a noncolonial environment were more likely to embrace egalitarian ideologies and to engage in anticolonial political agitation. The presence of these students in the United States also facilitated the growth of the Pan-African movement.

18:205   Rosenthal, Eric. *Stars and Stripes in Africa*. London: Routledge, 1938. Rosenthal describes his rather disorganized work as ". . . a History of American Achievements in Africa by Explorers, Missionaries, Pirates, Adventurers, Hunters, Miners, Merchants, Scientists, Soldiers, Showmen, Engineers and others, with some account of Africans who have played a part in American affairs." There is a series of short chapters, mostly on Southern Africa, but also on Liberia and Ethiopia. Bibliography.

AMERICAN MERCHANTS AND COMMERCE

18:206 Albion, Robert G. *Seaports South of Sahara: The Achievements of an American Steamship Service.* New York: Appleton-Century-Crofts, 1959. The Farrell Lines (1914–1959) had commercial contacts with South, East, and West Africa. They cooperated by making their archives available and granting interviews, resulting in an objective study.

18:207 Bennett, Norman R., and Brooks, George E., Jr., eds. *New England Merchants in Africa: A History through Documents 1802 to 1865.* Boston: Boston University Press, 1965. The documents in this collection—which were selected primarily for the light which they throw on the African scene—have been drawn from a wide variety of sources.

18:208 Brooks, George E., Jr., and Talbot, Frances K. "The Providence Exploring and Trading Company's Expedition to the Niger River in 1832–1833." *American Neptune* 35:2 (1975), 77–96. This attempt by Rhode Islanders to explore the Niger, carry on trade, and collect live animal specimens ended in failure. Not only was the lower Niger inhospitable to navigation, but an earlier British expedition had alienated the delta traders, and malaria eventually killed more than half of the members of the expedition.

18:209 Brooks, George E., Jr. *Yankee Traders, Old Coasters, and African Middlemen: A History of American Legitimate Trade with West Africa in the Nineteenth Century.* African Research Studies, no. 11. Boston: Boston University Press, 1970. This monograph seeks to describe the growth and organization of legitimate American trade with West Africa from the 1790s until the 1870s, and to relate American commerce to that of European, African, and Eurafrican traders. Extensive bibliography.

18:210 Haywood, Carl N. "American Whalers and Africa." Ph.D. diss., Boston University, 1967. The first American whalers to appear in African ports arrived at the Gulf of Guinea in 1763. Haywood examines the activities of U.S. whalemen at those ports, as well as their subsequent visits to East and West Africa.

18:211 Howard, Lawrence C. "A Note on New England Whaling and Africa before 1860." *Negro History Bulletin* 22:11 (1958), 13–16. A short, informative piece which spans two centuries of American whaling

from the Cape Verdes to the Gulf of Aden, by way of the Cape of Good Hope. Notes.

THE SLAVE TRADE

See Chapter 8 and 11 for Anglo-American diplomatic impasse over Britain's efforts (1814–1862) to halt the illicit trade.

18:212 Bernstein, Barton J. "Southern Politics and Attempts to Reopen the African Slave Trade." *Journal of Negro History* 51:1 (1966), 16–35. Bernstein points out that in no state did a majority of the citizens favor reopening the trade, so that the Confederate Constitution ban was not unexpected.

18:213 Curtin, Philip D. *The Atlantic Slave Trade: A Census.* Madison: University of Wisconsin Press, 1969. Curtin seeks to measure and describe the slave trade, and to synthesize existing information. Because of poor statistics, Curtin believes that his figures are probably within 20 percent of the actual totals. He concludes that approximately 10 million slaves were imported into the Americas between 1451 and 1870. Extensive bibliography.

Du Bois, W. E. B. *The Suppression of the African Slave-Trade to the United States of America, 1638–1870* (8:66) examines each colony and then surveys U.S. history from 1774 to 1870. The author includes two lengthy appendixes on legislation, footnotes, index, and a bibliography. In an apologia written over 60 years later, Du Bois regrets not placing more emphasis on the ideas of Freud and, especially, Marx.

Duignan, P., and Clendenen, C. *The United States and the African Slave Trade, 1619–1862* (8:67) attempts to demonstrate the economic and cultural impact of the illegal traffic on the United States, and its relations with Great Britain and the remainder of Europe.

Howard, W. S. *American Slavers and the Federal Law, 1837–1862* (8:70) portrays the U.S. government's efforts to crush the slave trade as ineffectual, and attempts to explain its impotence.

18:214 Mannix, Daniel P., with Cowley, Malcolm. *Black Cargoes: A History of the Atlantic Slave Trade, 1518–1865.* New York: Viking, 1962. A well-written account based upon Mannix's researches in London and East Africa, including the memoirs of smugglers and of the naval officers who tried to capture them. This volume does not treat the parliamentary and congressional struggles over the illegal traffic. Bibliography.

18:215   Pope-Hennessy, James. *Sins of the Fathers: A Study of the Atlantic Slave Traders, 1441–1807.* New York: Knopf, 1968. This study of the Atlantic slave traders is carried to the abolition of the slave trade by the British in 1807. Bibliography.

Soulsby, H. G. *The Right of Search and the Slave Trade in Anglo-American Relations, 1814–1862* (8:73) stresses the differences of opinion between the American and British governments, which prevented an early termination of the slave trade.

18:216   Takaki, Ronald. "The Movement to Reopen the African Slave Trade in South Carolina." *South Carolina Historical Magazine* 66:1 (1965), 38–54. Takaki shows that the advocates of reopening the slave trade could not even win over a majority in the state legislature during the 1850s.

18:217   Wax, Darold D. "Thomas Rogers and the Rhode Island Slave Trade." *American Neptune* 35:4 (1975), 289–301. Thomas Rogers sailed between Newport, Rhode Island, and West Africa on seven occasions between 1756 and 1773.

FROM COLONIZATION SOCIETY TO PAN-AFRICANISM

18:218   Harlan, Louis R. "Booker T. Washington and the White Man's Burden." *American Historical Review* 71:2 (1966), 441–67. Washington's major biographer tries to demonstrate that the black leader's involvement in African affairs was rather extensive. This interest, however, reflected his essential conservatism, since he felt that black people overseas should seek to better themselves within the existing political and racial order.

18:219   Hill, Adelaide Cromwell, and Kilson, Martin. *Apropos of Africa: Sentiments of Negro American Leaders on Africa from the 1800's to the 1950's.* London: Cass, 1969. This document collection includes selections from Paul Cuffe, Martin Delany, Henry M. Turner, Marcus Garvey, Booker T. Washington, and W. E. B. Du Bois. Bibliography.

18:220   Howard, Thomas C. "West Africa and the American South: Notes on James E. K. Aggrey and

the Idea of a University for West Africa." *Journal of African Studies* 2:4 (1975–1976), 445–66. A critical study of the idea of a university for Africans as promoted by Aggrey of the Gold Coast and North Carolina, foremost African educator, and founder in 1924 of the Prince of Wales College at Achimota in the Gold Coast.

18:221   King, Kenneth J. "Africa and the Southern States of the U.S.A.: Notes on J. H. Oldham and American Negro Education for Africans." *Journal of African History* 10:4 (1969), 659–77. King examines the conflict between the philosophy of W. E. B. Du Bois and that of J. H. Oldham and T. Jesse Jones.

18:222   Shepperson, George. "The American Negro and Africa." *British Association for American Studies Bulletin* N.S., no. 8 (1964), 3–20. This paper investigates the interaction of the American Negroes and African nationalists. Shepperson finds four perspectives for 1880 to 1918: Africans in America, the ideas of Booker T. Washington, Pan-Africanism, and the black history movement. He then discusses Marcus Garvey and the interwar period, before carrying the story to the present.

18:223   Shepperson, George. "Notes on Negro American Influences on the Emergence of African Nationalism." *Journal of African History* 1:2 (1960), 299–312. Shepperson concludes that American Negro leaders such as Marcus Garvey, W. E. B. Du Bois, and Booker T. Washington, helped to shape African nationalism.

18:224   Weisbord, Robert G. *Ebony Kinship: Africa, Africans, and the Afro-American.* Westport, Conn.: Greenwood, 1973. This work extends from the founding of the American Colonization Society in 1816 to the 1970s. There are chapters on Marcus Garvey, the Italo-Ethiopian War, and those entitled "The View from Africa" and "Afro-American's African Renaissance." Extensive bibliography.

American Colonization Society, 1816–1865

18:225   Boyd, Willis D. "The American Colonization Society and the Slave Recaptives of 1860–1861: An Early Example." *Journal of Negro History* 47:2 (1962), 108–26. A study which explores the work of the American Colonization Society in suppressing the African slave trade. Lincoln may have come to favor western hemisphere colonization sites as a result of the problems involved in the resettlement of several thousand slave recaptives in Liberia.

18:226 Campbell, Penelope. "Maryland in Africa: The Maryland State Colonization Society, 1831–1857." Ph.D. diss., Ohio State University, 1967. After 1832 the Maryland State Colonization Society, gaining the financial backing of the state legislature, became disenchanted with conditions at Monrovia, and established an independent settlement at Cape Palmas. In tracing its quarter-century of growth, Campbell examines the activities of James Hall, John Brown Russwurm, and others. Following a series of triumphs and tribulations, Cape Palmas became a part of Liberia in 1857.

18:227 Fox, Early L. *The American Colonization Society, 1817–1840*. Baltimore: Johns Hopkins Press, 1919. This dated monograph interprets the society's achievements in basically positive terms: the establishment of a model West African republic for Africans; and the salvation of many thousands of natives from slave ships.

18:228 Kirk-Greene, A. H. M. "America in the Niger Valley: A Colonization Centenary." *Phylon* 23:3 (1962), 225–39. Kirk-Greene considers this abortive scheme bold and imaginative, being the only example (aside from the British Niger expedition of 1841) to colonize Nigeria. After providing some biographical data on Martin Delany, the author focuses on the 1850s.

18:229 Sherwood, Henry N. "Paul Cuffe." *Journal of Negro History* 7:2 (1923), 153–229. Stressing his industry, religion, and education, Sherwood concludes that Cuffe's life is a tribute to both American democracy and the Quakers; he also portrays him as an important pioneer in African colonization.

18:230 Sherwood, Henry N. "Paul Cuffe and His Contributions to the American Colonization Society." *Proceedings of the Mississippi Valley Historical Society* 6 (1912–1913), 370–402. Sherwood offers Cuffe in a most favorable light, stressing that he was the first person to transport emigrants from the United States to Africa.

18:231 Staudenraus, P. J. *The African Colonization Movement, 1816–1865*. New York: Columbia University Press, 1961. Staudenraus declares that the issue of race was more important than that of chattel slavery.

This volume covers a half-century of colonization activity with great thoroughness, and includes a short bibliographical essay.

Back-to-Africa Movements, 1880s–1929

18:232 Bittle, William E., and Geis, Gilbert L. "Alfred Charles Sam and an African Return: A Case Study in Negro Despair." *Phylon* 23:2 (1962), 178–94. Half of the article deals with the historical place of the Negro in Oklahoma history, half with the abortive attempt by Chief Sam to settle blacks in the Gold Coast during World War I. Although admitting that Sam may have been a charlatan, a liar, and a cheat, Bittle and Geis nevertheless regard the Gold Coast scheme as a grand experiment.

18:233 Cronon, E. David. *Black Moses: The Story of Marcus Garvey and the Universal Negro Improvement Association*. Madison: University of Wisconsin Press, 1969. In this first full-length biography of Garvey (1887–1940), Cronon is "sympathetic without being adulatory or patronizing." Extensive bibliography.

18:234 Redkey, Edwin S. "Bishop Turner's African Dream." *Journal of American History* 54:2 (1967), 271–90. Turner is portrayed as an anti-American black nationalist who in the 1880s and 1890s desired neither integration nor accommodation.

18:235 Redkey, Edwin S. *Black Exodus: Black Nationalist and Back-to-Africa Movements, 1890–1910*. New Haven, Conn.: Yale University Press, 1969. This volume covers the American Colonization Society and the International Migration Society, and Henry M. Turner, Edward W. Blyden, and Benjamin Gaston. Redkey links the American Colonization Society and the Garvey movement; the story which he seeks to tell is that of lower-class blacks. Bibliography.

18:236 Weisbord, Robert G. "The Back-to-Africa Idea." *History Today* 18:1 (1968), 30–37. This brief popular account discusses such figures as Paul Cuffe, Henry Highland Garnet, Martin R. Delany, Benjamin Singleton, Henry M. Turner, J. Albert Thorne, Alfred Charles Sam, and Marcus Garvey.

Pan-Africanism

18:237 American Society of African Culture, eds. *Pan-Africanism Reconsidered*. Berkeley: University of California Press, 1962. The most significant paper in terms of pre-1945 historical background, in this report of the third annual Conference of the American Society of African Culture (1960), is the one by Rayford Logan. Unfortunately, there is neither bibliography nor index.

18:238 Geiss, Imanuel. *The Pan-African Movement: A History of Pan-Africanism in America, Europe, and Africa*. Trans. by Ann Keep. New York: Africana (1968), 1974. Geiss states that "Pan-Africanism is probably one of the most complex phenomena in modern history." In tracing its development, he demonstrates that it became a political movement after 1900, being more religious and cultural in nature prior to that date. Extensive bibliography.

18:239 Heiting, Thomas J. "W. E. B. Du Bois and the Development of Pan-Africanism, 1900–1930." Ph.D. diss., Texas Tech University, 1969. Covering the middle third of Du Bois's life, the author examines the Pan-African conferences and finds that Du Bois eventually became disenchanted with this cause. Heiting also traces Du Bois's relationship with such prominent figures as Booker T. Washington, Woodrow Wilson, and Marcus Garvey.

18:240 Legum, Colin. *Pan-Africanism: A Short Political Guide*. New York: Praeger, 1962. The first half of this volume is a narrative, the second a collection of documents. The period from 1900 through World War II is covered in the first two chapters.

18:241 Moses, Wilson J. *The Golden Age of Black Nationalism, 1850–1925*. Hamden, Conn.: Shoe String Press, 1978. In the opinion of Moses, black nationalism is practically indistinguishable as an intellectual movement from Pan-Africanism. The author treats his subject as a conservative rather than a radical ideology. Chapter 3 deals with the "civilizing missionary," Alexander Crummell, while chapter 10 discusses Pan-Africanism at the turn of the 20th century. Extensive bibliography.

18:242 Rogers, Ben F. "William E. B. Du Bois, Marcus Garvey and Pan-Africa." *Journal of Negro History* 40:2 (1955), 154–65. Rogers concludes that in the 1920s, Du Bois had intellect and ability, but lacked

appeal in the eyes of American Negroes; while the charismatic Garvey was a poor organizer and perhaps even an outright charlatan.

18:243 Scruggs, Otey M. "Carter G. Woodson, the Negro History Movement, and Africa." *Pan-African Journal* 7:1 (1974), 39–50. Scruggs begins his account in 1916, when Woodson began publishing the *Journal of Negro History*. In the opinion of Woodson, the task of the Negro scholar was ". . . to 'prove' the humanity of black people and to instill in them a healthy race pride by presenting the truth of the African-American past." He believed, along with Melville Herskovits, that African cultural elements survived among New World Negroes.

U.S.-AFRICAN AFFAIRS, 1880–1939

18:244 Downum, Garland. "The Madagascan Mission to the United States in 1883: Diplomacy and Public Relations." *Historian* 39:3 (1977), 472–89. The visit ostensibly was to ratify a commercial treaty, but actually it sought to line up American support against French efforts to seize Madagascar. The chief accomplishment was the awakening of the United States to Malagasy problems.

18:245 Fendall, Lonny W. "Theodore Roosevelt and Africa: Deliberate Non-Involvement in the Scramble for Territory and Influence." Ph.D. diss., University of Oregon, 1972. Fendall concentrates on Southern Africa, the Congo, and Liberia, and portrays TR as being aloof, rather than being an imperialist or kingmaker. He frequently deferred to Great Britain rather than have the United States act in Africa.

18:246 McKinley, Edward H. *The Lure of Africa: American Interests in Tropical Africa, 1919–1939*. Indianapolis: Bobbs-Merrill, 1974. After devoting an introduction to the pre–World War I years and a chapter to Europeans in Africa, the author concentrates on the variegated African activities of Americans. Rather than focusing on the diplomatic, McKinley explores a wide variety of topics, including the search for animals. Extensive bibliography.

18:247 Scott, Clifford H. "American Images of Sub-Sahara Africa, 1900–1939." Ph.D. diss., University of Iowa, 1968. According to Scott, with few exceptions "most conceptualizations of Africans fit patterned images of the Negro consistent with American racial folklore.'' The most common images were those of exotic savage, noble savage, faithful servant, exploited laborer, and estranged "white" Negro. Both racists and nonracists were little affected in their perceptions by contemporary intellectual debate.

18:248 Shepperson, George, and Price, Thomas. *Independent African: John Chilembwe and the Origins, Setting and Significance of the Nyasaland Native Rising of 1915*. Edinburgh: University Press, 1958. This massive study also investigates the activities of Joseph Booth, carrying the story back to 1892. The authors conclude the ". . . the Rising failed because it was too closely identified with Chilembwe as an individual." Bibliography.

18:249 Woods, Randall B. "Black America's Challenge to European Colonialism: The Waller Affair, 1891–1895." *Journal of Black Studies* 7:1 (1976), 57–77. John Waller, a black American consul and land developer, was arrested in March 1895—a year before absolute French hegemony in Madagascar was proclaimed—and sentenced to twenty years in jail as an alleged Hova spy. He was released only after the Cleveland administration threatened to break relations with France.

18:250 Woods, Randall B. "The Black American Press and the New Manifest Destiny: The Waller Affair." *Phylon* 38:1 (1977), 24–34. John L. Waller, a black U.S. consul at Madagascar, challenged French imperialism on that island and was imprisoned in 1895. The American black press criticized Waller's treatment and the U.S government for failing to secure his release.

The Congo Question, 1884–1885

18:251 Crowe, Sybil E. *The Berlin West African Conference, 1884–1885*. London: Longmans, Green, 1942. This detailed study of the important Berlin Conference focuses on Anglo-German relations, with American participants treated as active, verbose, ill-advised, utopian, and ultimately unimportant, since the United States did not finally ratify the agreement. Bibliography.

18:252 Kasson, John A. "The Congo Conference and the President's Message." *North American Review* 142:351 (1886), 119–33. This article, by an active participant in the Congo Conference, examines its various resolutions. Kasson summarizes President Grover Cleveland's opposition: "The only grounds upon which the President is made to rest his objections to the work of the Conference *do not exist.* "

18:253 McStallworth, Paul. "The United States and the Congo Question, 1884–1914." Ph.D. diss., Ohio State University, 1954. The leading personalities to emerge in this study include John Adam Kasson and King Leopold II. The Arthur administration's interest in the Congo is contrasted with the hands-off attitude of the Cleveland administrations; however, popular interest in the Congo continued to grow.

Pletcher, D. M. *The Awkward Years: American Foreign Relations under Garfield and Arthur* (12:46) discusses, in chapter 17, the Berlin Congo Conference.

18:254 Sanford, Henry S. "American Interests in Africa." *Forum* 9:4 (1890), 409–29. This article by a participant in the Berlin Conference examines the scramble in Africa for protectorates and possessions (1876–1890). It begins with the completion of the organizing of the American Geographical Society, and closes with an evaluation of the Congo Free State.

18:255 Sternstein, Jerome. "King Leopold II, Senator Nelson W. Aldrich, and the Strange Beginnings of American Economic Penetration of the Congo." *African Historical Studies* 2:2 (1969), 189–204. This essay examines the 1906 agreement between King Leopold II of Belgium, Senator Nelson W. Aldrich, and Thomas Fortune to grant to an American syndicate, of which the latter two men were a part, a mineral and rubber concession in the Congo.

Younger, E. *John A. Kasson: Politics and Diplomacy from Lincoln to McKinley* (14:62) discusses his ambassadorship to Germany during the Congo negotiations.

U.S., Africa, and Peace Conference, 1919

Beer, G. L. *African Questions at the Paris Peace Conference: With Papers on Egypt, Mesopotamia, and the Colonial Settlement* (18:129) provides lucid, thoughtful articles concerning the German colonies in Africa, Middle Africa, Egyptian problems and the future of Mesopotamia, which were written when

Beer was a member of the inquiry. The views expressed reflect his analysis of the colonial problems that would confront the peace conference.

18:256   Contee, Clarence G. "Du Bois, the NAACP, and the Pan-African Congress of 1919." *Journal of Negro History* 57:1 (1972), 13–28. Contee discusses the efforts of Du Bois and others on behalf of Pan-Africanism at Paris in 1919, and the success Du Bois had in establishing the Pan-African Conference. Du Bois encountered difficulties because of the reluctance of U.S. delegates to the Paris Peace Conference to support his actions.

18:257   Louis, William R. "The United States and the African Peace Settlement of 1919: The Pilgrimage of George Louis Beer." *Journal of African History* 4:3 (1963), 413–23. Louis presents an exhaustive but narrow analysis of the mandate controversy. Not only did Beer fail to acquire a mandate for the United States, he was powerless to block the Ruanda-Urundi agreement.

U.S.-Ethiopia (Abyssinia)

See Chapter 21, "Ethiopian Crisis, 1935–1937," for additional references.

18:258   Manheim, Frank J. "The United States and Ethiopia: A Study in American Imperialism." *Journal of Negro History* 17:2 (1932), 141–55. Although there is some coverage of the years since 1904, the main emphasis here is on the activities of Robert Skinner on behalf of U.S. trade with Ethopia (1903–1904).

18:259   Robbins, Jerrold. "The Americans in Ethiopia." *American Mercury* 29:113 (1933), 63–69. A contemporary assessment written on the eve of the Italo-Ethiopian War discusses conditions there in general. The article suggests that the Americans have an "inside track" among the whites to win an ascendant position.

18:260   Scott, William R. "A Study of Afro-American and Ethiopian Relations: 1896–1941." Ph.D. diss., Princeton University, 1971. This account attempts to disprove the widespread belief that the Ethiopians were hostile to the American blacks. Scott shows how the alleged contempt by Haile Selassie for U.S. Negroes kept the latter from supporting him wholeheartedly at the time of the Italo-Ethiopian War.

18:261   Skinner, Robert P. *Abyssinia of Today.* New York: Longmans, Green, 1906. This is an account of the first mission sent by the U.S. government to the court of the king of Ethiopia. First-hand accounts by diplomatic participants in American-African relations are a rarity, especially for these early years.

18:262   Weisbord, Robert G. "Black America and the Italian-Ethiopian Crisis: An Episode in Pan-Negroism." *Historian* 34:2 (1972), 230–41. Weisbord's article treats not only the Italo-Ethiopian War itself, but black American interest in Ethiopia. Weisbord concludes that "it is abundantly clear that Afro-Americans at a critical moment made a strong racial identification with their beleaguered 'brothers' in Ethiopia."

U.S.-Liberia

18:263   Anderson, R. Earle. *Liberia: America's African Friend.* Chapel Hill: University of North Carolina Press, 1952. The author visited Liberia, toured the Firestone rubber plantation, and interviewed several presidents of the republic. Anderson feels that America has neglected Liberia at times, but that the ties between the two nations nevertheless have grown stronger over the years.

18:264   Beecher, Lloyd N. "The State Department and Liberia, 1908–1941: A Heterogeneous Record." Ph.D. diss., University of Georgia, 1971. Beecher concludes that there is no evidence that State Department policy or diplomacy toward Liberia has been determined by such pressure groups as the black community, philanthropic organizations, or Firestone. He is of the opinion that the State Department's idealism or morality was at times a mere convenience, a substitute for force.

18:265   Bixler, Raymond W. *The Foreign Policy of the United States in Liberia.* New York: Pageant, 1957. This short volume portrays the American government as the great protector of Liberia against British and European imperialism, providing diplomatic, financial, military, and technical assistance to that nation. Over two-thirds of the book deals with the period after World War I. Bibliography.

18:266   Buell, Raymond Leslie. *The Native Problem in Africa.* 2 vols. Hamden, Conn.: Shoe String Press (1928), 1965. This account is based upon Buell's trip to Africa in 1925–1926. It emphasizes French,

British, and Belgian Africa. Two chapters stress American activities in Liberia: "The Firestone Agreement" and "The Loan That Succeeded." Bibliography.

18:267 Padgett, James A. "Ministers to Liberia and Their Diplomacy." *Journal of Negro History* 22:1 (1937), 50–92. A long essay which includes a considerable amount of biographical material for the years from 1863 to 1931. Padgett concludes: "Perhaps in no small country, especially in an out of the way backward country, has the ministerial and consular work been carried on in a more satisfactory manner than in this little Republic."

18:268 Schuyler, George S. "Uncle Sam's Black Step-Child." *American Mercury* 29:114 (1933), 147–56. Schuyler's article is highly critical of Liberia, whose government he portrays as being totally incompetent, and even barbarically cruel.

18:269 Wesley, Charles H. "The Struggle for the Recognition of Haiti and Liberia as Independent Republics." *Journal of Negro History* 2:4 (1917), 369–83. The first part of this essay deals with Haiti—whose struggle for recognition was more protracted—and the second part with Liberia. Wesley makes the claim that "the recognition of these republics as independent powers form one of the great landmarks in the Negro's progress toward democracy and justice."

League and Slavery Issue, 1929–1935
18:270 Du Bois, William E. B. "Liberia, the League and the United States." *Foreign Affairs* 11:4 (1933), 682–95. The author focuses on the League of Nations investigation of alleged slave trading there. Du Bois concludes relative to Liberia that "her chief crime is to be black and poor in a rich, white world."

18:271 Jones, R. L. "American Opposition to Slavery in Africa." *Journal of Negro History* 16:3 (1931), 266–86. A historical study (1876–1931) which demonstrates that U.S. opposition to slavery in Liberia was merely an extension of a historically defined policy.

18:272 Norris, Parthenia E. "United States and Liberia: The Slavery Crisis, 1929–1935." Ph.D. diss., Indiana University, 1961. Norris maintains that American-Liberian relations were more tangled during the years 1929 to 1935 than they were at any other time. The key issues were finances and involuntary servitude.

U.S.-South Africa

See Chapter 14, "U.S. and the Boer War."

18:273 Booth, Alan R. *The United States Experience in South Africa, 1784–1870.* Cape Town: Balkema, 1976. Commercial relations with the United States did not become significant until the 1830s and 1840s. As for the missionaries, they had to overcome a number of obstacles. Many Cape Europeans, too, were fearful and suspicious of the Americans.

18:274 Goldstein, Myra S. "The Genesis of Modern American Relations with South Africa, 1895–1914." Ph.D. diss., State University of New York at Buffalo, 1972. U.S. involvement in South Africa expanded during the last part of the 19th century, but not as a result of a search for overseas markets or investment. Instead, the growing contacts were the result of gold and diamonds, and of technical assistance. During the Boer War the United States remained neutral, but American supplies and war loans still played a role.

18:275 Keto, Clement T. "American Involvement in South Africa 1870–1915: The Role of Americans in the Creation of Modern South Africa." Ph.D. diss., Georgetown University, 1972. American missionaries arrived in South Africa as early as 1833, while discovery of minerals led to an influx of Americans involved in transportation and mining. The missionaries from the United States helped to create an educated elite which believed in racial equality. As a result, they were held partly responsible for the Zulu Rebellion of 1906. The black missionaries apparently were treated better by the British than by the Boers. Having set forth this background, the author in closing examines the Jameson raid and the Boer War.

18:276 Moolman, H. M. "Archival Research in the United States: A South African's Mission." *American Archivist* 17:2 (1954), 135–40. Details the investigations beginning in 1951 of South African historian C. F. J. Muller into American archives in search of material dealing with South Africa. The main focus of his research was on the Boer War.

Noer, T. J. *Briton, Boer and Yankee: The United States and South Africa, 1870–1914* (14:106) demonstrates that during these years Americans wished to trade with South Africa, while "uplifting" the black natives. There was widespread suspicion of the Boers in the United States prior to the Boer War, however. Following that conflict American relations with South Africa worsened, hurting commerce.

18:277   Ralston, Richard D. "American Episodes in the Making of an African Leader: A Case Study of Alfred B. Xuma (1893–1962)." *International Journal of African Historical Studies* 6:1 (1973), 72–93. Alfred B. Xuma of South Africa spent 1914 to 1926 acquiring a comprehensive education in the United States. The author compares Xuma's historical importance with that of James Aggrey and Nnamdi Azikiwe, while admitting that his experiences in the United States were not typical of the average African student.

18:278   Walshe, A. P. "Black American Thought and African Political Attitudes in South Africa." *Review of Politics* 32:1 (1970), 51–77. This study examines the impact of a number of key American blacks on South Africa, including Booker T. Washington, W. E. B. Du Bois, and Marcus Garvey. The most frequently cited African is Dr. A. B. Xuma. In the final section Walshe investigates Pan-Africanism.

19

World War I and Peace Settlement, 1914–1920

Contributing Editors

LAWRENCE E. GELFAND
University of Iowa

SCOTT R. HALL
University of Iowa

Contents

Introduction

The world war of 1914 to 1918 was a titanic military struggle fought between rival coalitions of national states. It unleashed cataclysmic forces that brought on violent revolutions in Russia, liquidation of the venerable Hapsburg empire in Austria-Hungary and the Ottoman empire, and a surge of nationalist fervor extending from East Central Europe to such disparate locations as Ireland, Egypt, Korea, India, and Turkey. The war markedly altered the normative structure of international politics that had dominated world affairs during the century following the Congress of Vienna.

Even before August 1914, the relatively stable political order as characterized by the predominance of Great Britain and France appeared threatened by the recently unified and challenging interests of the Italian and German nation-states. Elsewhere, the growing interests of Japan and the United States were threatening the prevailing European leadership. Such prewar trends were greatly accelerated during four years of protracted hostilities and the subsequent Paris Peace Conference. Clearly, one important consequence of the world war was the rapid ascendancy of the United States to positions of influence, authority, and leadership in the world political community. Arthur S. Link's *Woodrow Wilson: Revolution, War, and Peace* (19:121) provides a solid general introduction to the basic issues.

It is no exaggeration that the news of military hostilities in Europe was received with the shock of incredulity by Americans generally, no less so by officials at the State Department in Washington. At the very moment when war was imminent, the organized peace movement on both sides of the Atlantic was riding its highest crest of popularity. Yet, the familiar formula for preventing conflict, namely, the submission of international disputes to judicial arbitration appears never to have been given serious attention by the belligerent governments.

President Wilson quickly announced the American government's intention to maintain a policy of strict neutrality, which at first was interpreted to mean impartiality between and among the warring coalitions. A proclamation of neutrality was a simple expedient; implementation of this policy on a broad, national scale proved to be far more complicated. Allied propaganda emphasized alleged German atrocities committed against Belgian and French civilians. This was compounded by the German U-boat campaigns, resulting in the sinking of Allied and eventually American vessels, with attendant losses of American lives and property causing the executive and congressional branches in Washington to consider countermeasures. T. A. Bailey and P. B. Ryan have reassessed the most famous incident in their *The Lusitania Disaster: An Episode in Modern Warfare and Diplomacy* (19:152), while K. E. Birnbaum's *Peace Moves and U-Boat Warfare: Germany's Policy toward the United States, April 18, 1916–January 9, 1917* (19:144) reviews Germany's wavering policy. Despite a variety of controversies with the Allied governments, the Wilson administration demonstrated serious concern lest the Central Powers manage to achieve military victory. Moreover, the maritime ability of the British in particular to transport American goods, including munitions, coupled with the need of the Allies for loans, caused the American government to reassess the whole question of the legal rights of neutrals. By 1915, Wilson and the State Department concluded that American neutrality would not be compromised by allowing private sales and loans to the belligerents, most of which benefitted the British and their allies, not the Central Powers.

Some commentators have observed that American impartiality and an imposition of a commercial embargo would, practically speaking, have denied assistance only to the British and their cobelligerents, for the Germans and Austrians lacked the maritime capacity to transport goods purchased in the United States. Any embargo would thus have aided indirectly the Central Powers.

Historiography covering Wilsonian statecraft is replete with accounts of the president's efforts in seeking mediation. Regular initiatives to London, Paris, and Berlin undertaken by special envoy Edward M. House invariably proved inopportune, as did similar overtures to the respective ambassadors from the belligerent states in Washington. Neither the German government nor the British and French seemed willing to settle for less than military victory. By 1916, the president embarked upon a domestic campaign aimed at winning popular support for American military preparedness as well as his evolving programs laying the foundation for a just and permanent peace. Scholars need to examine the various strands of Wilsonian strategy to learn how they related to the creation of an eventual new international order following the termination of hostilities.

Throughout his presidency, Woodrow Wilson managed to be a centrist on matters of foreign policy, drawing early fire from both the interventionists like Theodore Roosevelt and from those Americans who accused him of war mongering. Later, his centrist positions during the peace negotiations drew hostile reactions from both the political right and left in the United States. Students of political strategy would do well to examine how Wilson sought to win support for his programs both in the United States and overseas. His use of speechmaking and public interviews with correspondents, and his relations with the Congress offer subjects meriting further investigation. Specifically, scholars might look at the process by which Wilson sought to win public approval for the League of Nations and for an American universalism well beyond the confines of the western hemisphere.

During recent years, scholars have become interested in the bureaucratic organization and administration of the American government during wartime. In this regard, we need to learn more about the numerous departments and independent agencies of government which became involved in the rapidly expanded programs of foreign affairs. A useful example of what can be done is B. I. Kaufman's study, *Efficiency and Expansion: Foreign Trade Organization in the Wilson Administration, 1913–1921* (19:129). A need for studies of various American embassies, legations, and consulates during wartime would seem reasonable. But historians ought to look beyond the operations of the State Department, to the War and Navy departments, the Treasury, Justice, Commerce, and Agriculture departments, all of which became deeply involved in important aspects of foreign affairs. And the numerous special wartime agencies, like Hoover's Food Administration and Baruch's War Industries Board, exercised substantial roles both before the armistice and later at the Paris Peace Conference.

Despite some excellent monographs that focus on the American response to Bolshevism—see, for example, A. J. Mayer's *Politics and Diplomacy at Peacemaking: Containment and Counterrevolution at Versailles 1918–1919* (19:226)—and the sending of American military forces to North Russia and Siberia beginning in the summer of 1918, there remains a need for comparative analyses of the several American responses to nationalist and revolutionary activism arising in Africa, the Middle East, and East Asia during the war and immediately after the armistice. Postwar reconstruction remains a broad subject awaiting additional investigations. The recognized need for international protection of ethnic minorities, especially in East Central and Southeastern Europe, ought to attract scholarly attention. And the large issues involved in regionalist versus universalist views of postwar U.S. policies could occupy a scholar profitably.

The existing historiography covering American policies during the war, the peace settlement, and the subsequent controversy over ratification of the Treaty of Versailles and its Covenant of the League of Nations is already impressively large and promises to grow rapidly as a new generation of scholars launches into research posing fresh questions. Source materials in the form of private manuscript collections like the Woodrow Wilson Papers and the State Department's archival series for this period are enormous in volume but have in recent years been made increasingly accessible thanks to microfilms available in many university and public libraries. From the numerous memoirs and diaries extant, both published and unpublished, one may infer that the importance of the wartime experience and participation in the peace negotiations was not lost even on relatively minor bureaucrats. Still, serious researchers must continue to undertake expeditions to the main repositories. So profuse in fact are the records that it is difficult to realize that this scholarly bounty became available almost entirely during the years since the early 1950s. In addition, students of this period should not overlook the many foreign repositories, especially those in the United Kingdom, Canada, France, Germany, Italy, and Japan, where collections of real value are to be found in national libraries and archives.

In many respects, the period of the world war and the Peace Conference of 1919 constituted the first exercise of America's leadership among the great powers in world affairs. If the exercise failed, as some historians have contended, the reasons would seem to be far more complicated than has heretofore been suggested. And what lessons have later generations of American statesmen derived from the American experience in the war and the peacemaking?

Resources and Overviews

RESEARCH AIDS

While pertinent bibliographies and reference aids are listed here, there are more extensive lists in Chapter 1.

Bibliographies

19:1   Almond, Nina, and Lutz, Ralph H. *An Introduction to a Bibliography of the Paris Peace Conference.* Stanford, Calif.: Stanford University Press, 1935. This early bibliography is especially concerned with materials housed at the Hoover Institution, Stanford, California. It remains a useful introduction to materials available before 1935.

19:2   Bayliss, Gwyn. *Bibliographical Guide to the Two World Wars: An Annotated Survey of English-Language Reference Materials.* London: Bowker, 1977. This is a valuable, recently compiled bibliography.

Birdsall, P. "The Second Decade of Peace Conference History" (19:221) notes published, document collections, etc., after 1929.

19:3   Braisted, William R. "The Navy in the Early Twentieth Century, 1890–1941." In Robin Higham, ed., *A Guide to the Sources of United States Military History.* Hamden, Conn.: Shoe String Press, 1975, pp. 344–77. This essay and list of 300-odd sources relates to the U.S. Navy in World War I, the naval limitation treaties of the 1920s and 1930s, and navy activities generally in the interwar era.

19:4   Ellis, Richard N. "Civil-Military Relations, Operations, and the Army, 1865–1917." In Robin Higham, ed., *A Guide to the Sources of United States Military History.* Hamden, Conn.: Shoe String Press, 1975, pp. 247–68.

19:5   Gilbert, Martin. *The First World War Atlas.* New York: Macmillan, 1971. This valuable atlas is an important tool for students of World War I.

Higham, R., ed. *Official Histories: Essays and Bibliographies from All Over the World* (23:5) includes a country-by-country survey of World War I national histories.

Morley, J. W., ed. *Japan's Foreign Policy, 1868–1941: A Research Guide* (1:100).

Rabe, V. H. *American-Chinese Relations, 1784–1941: Books and Pamphlets Extracted from the Shelf Lists of Widener Library* (17:5).

19:6   Schaffer, Ronald. *The United States in World War I: A Selected Bibliography.* War/Peace Bibliography Series, no. 7. Santa Barbara, Calif.: ABC-Clio, 1978. Although this bibliography does not emphasize foreign relations, it includes references to bureaucratic organization, military affairs, popular attitudes toward the war, demobilization, and postwar organization.

Smith, D. M. "National Interest and American Intervention, 1917: An Historiographical Appraisal" (19:162).

19:7   Swigger, Boyd K., comp. *A Guide to Resources for the Study of Recent History of the United States in the Libraries of the University of Iowa, State Historical Society of Iowa, and the Hoover Presidential Library.* Iowa City: University of Iowa Libraries, 1977. This is an excellent guide to printed and manuscript resources found at three important libraries.

19:8   Toscano, Mario, ed. *The History of Treaties and International Politics.* Baltimore: Johns Hopkins Press, 1966. An extensive listing of memoirs and documentary material relating to World War I is provided, along with insightful comments on the value of specific materials and collections.

Wells, S. F., Jr. "New Perspectives of Wilsonian Diplomacy: The Secular Evangelism of American Political Economy" (19:126).

Document Collections

More general collections are listed in Chapter 1, and other collections may be found in "Personalities," below.

19:9   Golder, Frank A., ed. *Documents of Russian History, 1914–1917.* Trans. by Emanuel Aronsberg. New York: Century, 1927. Reprint 1964. This collection of documents contains a few items of direct interest to the student of American foreign relations: Wilson's message to Russia on June 9, 1917, and the Russian comments thereon; Root's address to the Council of Ministers of June 15, 1917, and Wilson's address welcoming the ambassador of the provisional government to Washington (July 5, 1917).

Great Britain. Foreign Office. *British Documents on the Origins of the War, 1889–1898* (14:4) remains the most important source of published British documents on the origins of the war.

19:10   Miller, David Hunter. *My Diary at the Conference at Paris.* 21 vols. New York: Privately printed by Appeal Printing, 1924. Although the diary and collected documents are no longer as important for historians as they were when published, they should still be consulted. Volume 21 contains an excellent index. Microfilm copies are available.

19:11   *The Treaties of Peace, 1919–1923.* 2 vols. New York: Carnegie Endowment for International Peace, 1924. This is a most convenient compilation of the peace treaties concluded at the Paris Peace Conference.

19:12   U.S. Department of State. *Records of the Department of State Relating to World War I and Its Termination.* Microfilm. M-367, 518 rolls. Washington, D.C.: National Archives Microfilm Publications, n.d. This vast collection consists of records from the Department of State concerning American participation in the World War, but *not* the proceedings of the Paris Peace Conference, or the wartime records of other government departments and bureaus.

19:13   U.S. Department of State. *General Records of the American Commission to Negotiate Peace, 1919–1931 Microfilm Publication M820.* Microfilm. M-820, 563 rolls. Washington, D.C.: National Archives and Records Service, n.d. This collection covers virtually all the U.S. documentation pertaining to the work of the American Commission to Negotiate Peace at the Paris Peace Conference.

19:14   U.S. Department of State. *Papers Relating to the Foreign Relations of the United States: The Paris Peace Conference, 1919.* 13 vols. Washington, D.C.: G.P.O., 1942–1947. This supplement on the Paris Peace Conference is notable for its publication of whole series of records rather than excerpts. It is a basic source for the peace conference.

19:15   U.S. Department of State. *Papers Relating to the Foreign Relations of the United States, Russia,*

1918. 3 vols. Washington, D.C.: G.P.O., 1931–1932. This series, along with the companion volume for 1919, provides a useful selection from the basic U.S. documents relevant to Russian affairs and the Russian Civil War.

19:16   U.S. Department of State. *Papers Relating to the Foreign Relations of the United States, Russia, 1919.* Washington, D.C.: G.P.O., 1937.

Indexes to Documents

19:17   Rangel, Sandra K., comp. *Records of the American Commission to Negotiate Peace.* Washington, D.C.: National Archives and Records Service, 1974. This is an indispensable finding aid to the collection of records of the American Commission to Negotiate Peace at the Paris Peace Conference of 1919. This aid will facilitate use of Record Group 256 at the National Archives and also of National Archives and Records Service Microfilm Publication M820. Unfortunately, it does not indicate which documents are available on microfilm.

19:18   U.S. Department of State. *Index to Papers Relating to the Foreign Relations of the United States, 1900–1918.* Washington, D.C.: G.P.O., 1941. This is an important aid to finding the documents assembled in this published collection of records.

OVERVIEWS

Anderson, G. L., ed. *Issues and Conflicts: Studies in Twentieth Century American Diplomacy* (2:8) has three articles on crucial issues for the Wilson era: Roland N. Stromberg, "The Riddle of Collective Security" (pp. 147–70); Louis L. Gerson, "Immigrant Groups and American Foreign Policy" (pp. 171–92); and Robert H. Ferrell, "Woodrow Wilson and Open Diplomacy" (pp. 193–209).

19:19   Crozier, Emmet. *American Reporters on the Western Front, 1914–1918.* New York: Oxford University Press, 1959. Crozier recounts the experiences of American reporters assigned to Europe during the war.

Curti, M. E. *American Philanthropy Abroad: A History* (2:72) considers, in chapters 8–10, the philanthropic activities directed toward the overseas war effort, war relief, and programs for peace.

19:20 Duroselle, Jean-Baptiste. *From Wilson to Roosevelt: Foreign Policy of the United States, 1913–1945.* Trans. by Nancy Lyman Roelker. Cambridge: Harvard University Press, 1963. The first six chapters of this work cover the years 1913 to 1921, and attempt to explain why the United States rejected the role of world leadership that the international situation seemed to require. Duroselle finds Wilson's leadership to have been inadequate.

Gardner, L. C. "American Foreign Policy, 1900–1921: A Second Look at the Realist Critique of American Diplomacy" (14:11).

Langer, W. L. *The Diplomacy of Imperialism, 1890–1902* (13:9) describes how economic expansion and the need for foreign markets forced the European powers to compete for enlarged colonial empires before World War I.

19:21 Livermore, Seward W. " 'Deserving Democrats': The Foreign Service under Woodrow Wilson." *South Atlantic Quarterly* 69:1 (1970), 144–60. This article examines Wilson's use of patronage to fill positions in the foreign service.

Osgood, R. E. *Ideals and Self Interest in America's Foreign Relations: The Great Transformation of the Twentieth Century* (2:87) argues that although Wilson clearly understood American interests, his decision to defend American foreign policy on idealistic and moral grounds and his inadequate handling of public opinion had disastrous long-term effects.

19:22 Paxson, Frederick L. *American Democracy and the World War.* 3 vols. Boston: Houghton Mifflin, 1936–1948. These volumes provide a comprehensive though somewhat outdated survey of the years 1913 to 1923. The author's contention is that American democracy adapted to the crisis presented by World War I.

19:23 Seymour, Charles. *American Diplomacy during the World War.* Baltimore: Johns Hopkins Press, 1934. Reprint 1964. Although various aspects of Seymour's work have been revised, it holds up well, especially as it relates the president's position on neutrality and his reasons for intervention.

19:24 Smith, Daniel M. *Great Departure: United States and World War I, 1914–1920.* New York: Wiley, 1965. Smith aims his narrative at two questions: why did the United States repudiate its neutrality and go to war; and why, after it had committed itself to war, did the United States abandon the product of

victory by rejecting the Versailles Treaty? Biographical essay.

Taylor, A. J. P. *The Struggle for Mastery in Europe, 1848–1918* (14:17) is a brilliant if eccentric treatise on the origins of World War I which examines the decline of the European balance of power and the lack of suitable alternatives for perpetuating peace.

Origins of the War

19:25 Albertini, Luigi. *The Origins of the War of 1914.* 3 vols. Trans. by Isabella M. Massey. New York: Oxford University Press, 1952–1957. Although this massive history did not, as its author intended, end debate on the question of who was responsible for the war, it is the most complete survey on the subject.

19:26 Fischer, Fritz. *Germany's Aims in the First World War.* New York: Norton, 1967. In the most controversial revisionist work on the origins of World War I of the last 35 years, Fischer lays the blame for war squarely on Germany. Emphasis is on German-Austrian relations on the eve of the war, and on Germany's plans for a Prussian-dominated *MittelEuropa.*

19:27 Gordon, Michael R. "Domestic Conflict and the Origins of the First World War: The British and the German Cases." *Journal of Modern History* 46:2 (1974), 191–226. Gordon analyzes the effect of domestic conflict in both countries, through the interpretations of Fritz Fischer, and Arno Mayer and Peter Loewenberg.

19:28 Lafore, Laurence. *The Long Fuse: An Interpretation of the Origins of World War I.* Philadelphia: Lippincott, 1965. This synthetic reinterpretation is especially strong in its coverage of central and eastern European political and social developments before the war.

19:29 Lee, Dwight E. *Europe's Crucial Years: The Diplomatic Background of World War I, 1902–1914.* Hanover, N.H.: University Press of New England, 1974. The author disparages recent revisionist interpretations and concludes that balance of power politics and an insoluble Serbian situation made war inevitable. Extensive bibliographic essay.

19:30 Moses, John A. *The Politics of Illusion: The Fischer Controversy in German Historiography.* New York: Barnes & Noble, 1975. The author's intent is to present a detailed review of Fischer's controversial work combined with an overview of German historical scholarship on the origins of World War I for American scholars.

Personalities

Additional references on individuals may be found in Chapter 1, "Biographical Data."

AMERICAN

Civilian

Newton D. Baker

19:31 Baker, Newton D. *Why We Went To War.* New York: Harper, 1936. This work, part memoir, contains revealing comments by the wartime secretary of war—it is still worth reading.

19:32 Beaver, Daniel R. *Newton D. Baker and the American War Effort, 1917–1919.* Lincoln: University of Nebraska Press, 1967. This monograph describes the operations of the War Department and has some especially valuable sections showing how Secretary Baker related to his general officers, particularly General John Pershing.

William E. Borah

See Chapter 20, "Personalities," for additional references.

19:33 Maddox, Robert J. *William E. Borah and American Foreign Policy.* Baton Rouge: Louisiana State University Press, 1969. The first three chapters of this book describe Borah's leadership of the Senate irreconcilables and his position on the American intervention in Russia.

19:34 McKenna, Marian C. *Borah.* Ann Arbor: University of Michigan Press, 1961. In this sympathetic biography concerning American participation in the World War and the League of Nations, McKenna argues that Borah and Wilson differed not on principles but on "methods." Bibliography.

William Jennings Bryan

See Chapters 13, 15, and 16, "Personalities," for additional references.

Coletta, P. E. *William Jennings Bryan* (13:34) covers, in volumes 2 and 3 (*Progressive Politician and Moral Statesman, 1909–1915* and *Political Puritan, 1915–1925*), Bryan's tenure as secretary of state and his activities to keep the United States out of war after his resignation from office.

19:35 Coletta, Paolo E., ed. "Bryan Briefs Lansing." *Pacific Historical Review* 27:4 (1958), 383–96. This lengthy memorandum, written by Bryan after he submitted his resignation as secretary of state, was intended to inform his successor, Robert Lansing, of the status of U.S. foreign affairs. Especially revealing are such matters as the "cooling-off" treaties, conditions in Central America and the Caribbean, and Sino-Japanese relations.

William C. Bullitt

See Chapter 21, "Personalities," for additional references.

Farnsworth, B. *William C. Bullitt and the Soviet Union* (21:18) covers the intermingling of William C. Bullitt's career with Soviet and U.S. relations, his mission to Russia in 1919, and his denunciation of the Versailles Treaty to Lodge.

Josephus Daniels

See Chapter 21, "Personalities," for additional references.

19:36 Daniels, Josephus. *The Cabinet Diaries of Josephus Daniels: 1913–1921.* Ed. by E. David Cronon. Lincoln: University of Nebraska Press, 1963. Although diaries for 1914 and 1916 are missing, this collection of the secretary of the navy's observations on strategic and diplomatic considerations provides an important record of the war and armistice periods.

19:37 Daniels, Josephus. *The Wilson Era: Years of Peace, 1910–1917.* Chapel Hill: University of North Carolina Press, 1944. Daniels gives his view of the neutrality years as well as the early years of the president's political career. As might be expected, the sections on the development of the U.S. Navy are of most value.

Charles G. Dawes

See Chapters 20 and 21, "Personalities," for additional references.

19:38 Dawes, Charles G. *A Journal of the Great War.* 2 vols. Boston: Houghton Mifflin, 1921. A record of Dawes's activities as general purchasing agent for the American Expeditionary Force, this journal also has interesting comments on interallied cooperation, and the lack thereof, European politics, and military strategy.

John Dewey

See Chapter 20, "Personalities," for additional references.

19:39 Farrell, John C. "John Dewey and World War I: Armageddon Tests A Liberal's Faith." *Perspectives in American History* 9 (1975), 299–340. At first, Dewey supported American intervention in World War I because he thought that through such means the undesirable Old Order could be made over by extending the American model of government. After the peace negotiations, he became an isolationist.

Howlett, C. F. *Troubled Philosopher: John Dewey and the Struggle for World Peace* (20:33) finds Dewey's later pacifist views were greatly influenced by his experiences during the war, which tested some of his pragmatic assumptions.

Joseph C. Grew

See Chapter 21, "Personalities," for additional references.

Grew, J. C. *Turbulent Era: A Diplomatic Record of Forty Years, 1904–1945* (18:33) recounts, in the second part of this important memoir, his diplomatic activities in Berlin, Washington, and later Paris as a member of the American Commission to Negotiate Peace.

Herbert C. Hoover

See Chapters 20 and 21, "Personalities," for additional references.

19:40 Gelfand, Lawrence E., ed. *Herbert Hoover: The Great War and Its Aftermath, 1914–1923.* Iowa City: University of Iowa Press, 1979. This collection of essays includes Hoover's views on organizing the wartime government, on the Versailles Treaty and the Russian Revolution, and on international economics, including the use of food in diplomacy.

Hoover, H. C. *Memoirs* (20:42) covers, in volume 1, his services as head of the U.S. Food Administration, director of the Belgian relief, and member of the American peace commission.

19:41 Hoover, Herbert C. *An American Epic: Famine in Forty-Five Nations: The Battle on the Front Line, 1914–1923.* 3 vols. Chicago: Regnery, 1961. Part memoir, part history, this work depicts how Hoover and the American government attempted to cope with the worldwide dilemma of hunger and privation. Volumes 2 and 3 consider famine, organization behind the front, 1914 to 1923. Documents.

Edward M. House

19:42 Floto, Inga. *Colonel House in Paris: A Study of American Policy at the Paris Peace Conference, 1919.* Trans. by Pauline B. Katborg. Copenhagen: Universitets Forlaget Aarhaus, 1973. This critique of Colonel House's activities by a Danish historian is a valuable study of Wilsonian foreign policy and the peace negotiations of 1919. Floto stresses that House's loyalty to Wilson was less than complete.

George, A. L., and George, J. L. *Woodrow Wilson and Colonel House: A Personality Study* (19:73) describes how House came to understand Wilson's personality.

19:43 House, Edward M., and Seymour, Charles, eds. *What Really Happened at Paris: The Story of the Peace Conference.* New York: Scribner's, 1921. This collection of lectures delivered by former members of the Inquiry and the American mission at the peace conference endeavors to explain the evolution of important provisions of the treaties.

19:44 Seymour, Charles. *The Intimate Papers of Colonel House Arranged as a Narrative.* 4 vols. Boston: Houghton Mifflin, 1926–1928. Though this narrative somewhat exaggerates House's influence, it remains the best source on the colonel's activities and thoughts. Volumes 2–4 provide material on the war and the peace settlement.

Hiram W. Johnson

19:45 DeWitt, Howard A. "Hiram W. Johnson and Economic Opposition to Wilsonian Diplomacy: A Note." *Pacific Historian* 19:1 (1975), 15–23. Johnson opposed Wilson's foreign policy, especially U.S. participation in the League of Nations, because he feared a conspiracy of bankers and businessmen who stood to profit from American international involvement.

19:46 Lower, Richard C. "Hiram Johnson: The Making of an Irreconcilable." *Pacific Historical Review* 41:4 (1972), 505–26. Johnson's opposition to U.S. entrance into the League of Nations was based not so much on political ambition or adherence to isolationism as to progressive reform and democracy.

19:47 Olin, Spencer C., Jr. *California's Prodigal Sons: Hiram Johnson and the Progressives, 1911–1917*. Berkeley: University of California Press, 1968. The major focus of this book is on Johnson's personality and gubernatorial administration; there is very little on foreign relations.

Robert M. La Follette

Kennedy, P. C. "La Follette's Imperialist Flirtation" (13:214) discusses his support of the 1898 war and territorial expansion.

19:48 La Follette, Belle C., and La Follette, Fola. *Robert M. La Follette, June 4, 1855–June 18, 1925*. 2 vols. New York: Macmillan, 1953. Several chapters of this official biography are devoted to exploring the opposition of the Progressive senator from Wisconsin to Wilson's war and peace programs.

Robert Lansing

Beers, B. F. *Vain Endeavor: Robert Lansing's Attempts to End the American-Japanese Rivalry* (19:206).

19:49 Lansing, Robert. *The Big Four and Others of the Peace Conference*. Boston: Houghton Mifflin, 1921. These essays focus attention upon the principals at the peace conference: Orlando, Lloyd George, Clemenceau, Wilson, and also Venizelos, Feisal, Botha, Paderewski.

19:50 Lansing, Robert. *The Peace Negotiations, a Personal Narrative*. Boston: Houghton Mifflin, 1921. Reprint 1969. Lansing provides justifications for his actions and opinions at the peace conference and attempts to set the record straight.

19:51 Lansing, Robert. *War Memoirs of Robert Lansing, Secretary of State*. Indianapolis: Bobbs-Merrill, 1935. This is Lansing's posthumously published evaluation of his activities as secretary of state during the war years.

Smith, D. M. *Robert Lansing and American Neutrality, 1914–1917* (19:137).

19:52 U.S. Department of State. *Papers Relating to the Foreign Relations of the United States: The Lansing Papers, 1914–1920*. 2 vols. Washington, D.C.: G.P.O., 1939–1940. These volumes contain important selections from the correspondence, memoranda, and other documents of Lansing.

19:53 Williams, Joyce G. "The Resignation of Secretary of State Robert Lansing." *Diplomatic History* 3:3 (1979), 337–44. A reprint of Rear Admiral James E. Helm's "Report of Conversations Concerning the Resignation of Secretary Lansing," dated February 18, 1920.

Henry Cabot Lodge

See Chapters 13 and 20 for additional references.

Garraty, J. A. *Henry Cabot Lodge: A Biography* (13:46) details the wranglings of Lodge and Wilson for control over American foreign policy during the war and armistice period.

Lodge, H. C. *The Senate and the League of Nations* (19:314).

19:54 Mervin, David. "Henry Cabot Lodge and the League of Nations." *Journal of American Studies* 4:2 (1971), 201–16. A study of the metamorphosis of Senator Lodge's opposition to the League of Nations.

Henry Morgenthau, Jr.

See Chapters 18, 21, and 22, "Personalities," for additional references.

Morgenthau, H. *Ambassador Morgenthau's Story* (18:37) recounts the German subversion of and subsequent alliance with Turkey. Morgenthau was American ambassador to Turkey (1913–1916).

Walter Hines Page

19:55 Cooper, John M., Jr. *Walter Hines Page: The Southerner as American, 1855–1918*. Chapel Hill: University of North Carolina Press, 1977. Complementing Ross Gregory's biography, this complete study of the ambassador to London reveals how he transferred his passion for promoting a New South to a desire of fostering an enduring Anglo-American cooperation. Bibliography.

19:56 Gregory, Ross. *Walter Hines Page: Ambassador to the Court of St. James*. Lexington: University of Kentucky Press, 1970. This biography of a dedicated Wilsonian provides a fine example of how Wilson chose to ignore his diplomatic appointees, thereby causing confusion and difficulties at an important post. Bibliography.

19:57   Hendrick, Burton J. *The Life and Letters of Walter Hines Page.* 3 vols. Garden City, N.Y.: Doubleday, 1924–1926. These volumes contain many of Page's more important letters from London and extol the ambassador's rather naive acceptance of Britain's point of view.

Paul S. Reinsch

Pugach, N. "Making the Open Door Work: Paul S. Reinsch in China, 1913–1919" (39:37) describes the efforts of Paul Samuel Reinsch, as minister to China, to maintain the open door policy by strengthening economic ties between the United States and China.

19:58   Reinsch, Paul S. *An American Diplomat in China.* Garden City, N.Y.: Doubleday, 1922. Reinsch, American minister to China (1913–1919), includes material on the American response to Japan's Twenty-One Demands, the Lansing-Ishii notes, and the efforts of the United States to preserve Chinese territorial integrity.

Elihu Root

See Chapter 16, "Personalities," for additional references.

Dubin, M. D. "Elihu Root and the Advocacy of a League of Nations, 1914–1917" (19:306).

Jessup, P. C. *Elihu Root* (17:41) deals with the Lodge reservationists in the second volume.

19:59   Leopold, Richard W. *Elihu Root and the Conservative Tradition.* Boston: Little, Brown, 1954. Chapters 5 and 6 of this biography examine the conservative legal theorist's conception of Wilsonian diplomacy and the peace settlement.

Charles Seymour

See also "Edward M. House," above.

19:60   Seymour, Charles. *Letters from the Paris Peace Conference.* Ed. by Harold B. Whiteman. New Haven, Conn.: Yale University Press, 1965. These often revealing letters written in 1919 by Charles Seymour to his wife provide a fascinating record of events at the peace conference.

James T. Shotwell

See Chapter 20, "Personalities," for additional references.

19:61   Josephson, Harold. *James T. Shotwell and the Rise of Internationalism in America.* Rutherford, N.J.: Fairleigh Dickinson University Press, 1975. Chapters 3–5 of this biography cover the activities of Shotwell, a leading internationalist, during the war and at the Paris Peace Conference.

19:62   Shotwell, James T. *At the Paris Peace Conference.* New York: Macmillan, 1937. This diary of personal activities by an American adviser and negotiator at the peace conference is especially informative of events leading to the formation of the International Labor Organization. Shotwell's observations cover a multitude of subjects concerned with the peace negotiations.

Oswald Garrison Villard

19:63   Villard, Oswald G. *Fighting Years: Memoirs of a Liberal Editor.* New York: Harcourt, Brace, 1939. The "liberal's liberal," the editor of *The Nation* gives his scalding opinions here of Wilson's attempts to subvert the American liberal tradition.

19:64   Wrezin, Michael. *Oswald Garrison Villard: Pacifist at War.* Bloomington: Indiana University Press, 1965. This is the story of Villard's attempts as an editor and an individual to reconcile pacifism with the American liberal tradition.

Brand Whitlock

19:65   Davidson, John W. "Brand Whitlock and the Diplomacy of Belgian Relief." *Prologue* 2:3 (1970), 145–60. Treats the activities of Whitlock, minister and ambassador to Belgium (1914–1921), with regard to the relief operations in Belgium before and during the German occupation during World War I.

19:66   Whitlock, Brand. *The Letters and Journal of Brand Whitlock.* 2 vols. Ed. by Allan Nevins. New York: Appleton-Century, 1936. These letters and the journal refer to Whitlock's assignment as ambassador to Belgium.

Woodrow Wilson

19:67   Ambrosius, Lloyd E. "The Orthodoxy of Revisionism: Woodrow Wilson and the New Left." *Diplomatic History* 1:3 (1977), 199–214. In the New Left's revisionism there is an orthodoxy that affirmed many of the tenets of Wilson's liberal internationalism, but the New Left fails to understand his progressive vision of a new world order. For another criticism, see A. L. Seltzer, "Woodrow Wilson as 'Corporate Liberal': Toward a Reconsideration of Left Revisionist Historiography" (2:103).

19:68 Baker, Ray S. *Woodrow Wilson: Life and Letters.* 8 vols. Garden City, N.Y.: Doubleday, Doran, 1927. Baker's multivolume, incomplete biography of Wilson is drawn almost entirely from Baker's reading of the Wilson Papers. The letters are connected by a loose narrative.

19:69 Baker, Ray S. *Woodrow Wilson and the World Settlement.* 3 vols. Garden City, N.Y.: Doubleday, Page, 1922. This was the first extensive history of the peace conference from the perspective of a Wilsonian. The first two volumes contain a narrative account partly drawn from Baker's recollections; volume 3 presents many documents.

19:70 Bell, H. C. F. *Woodrow Wilson and the People.* Garden City, N.Y.: Doubleday, Doran, 1945. Examined here are Wilson's determined attempts to obtain a popular mandate for his policies.

19:71 Cooper, John M., Jr. "'An Irony of Fate': Woodrow Wilson's Pre–World War I Diplomacy." *Diplomatic History* 3:4 (1979), 425–38. After reviewing volumes 27–30 of Link's *The Papers of Woodrow Wilson,* Cooper concludes that Wilson was well experienced in foreign affairs by September 1914.

19:72 Diamond, William. *The Economic Thought of Woodrow Wilson.* Baltimore: Johns Hopkins Press, 1943. Reflecting the influence of Charles A. Beard, this early work on Wilson's economic philosophy devotes two chapters to Wilsonian foreign economic policy. Much of the more recent revisionist writing bears a similarity to the chapter entitled "The New World Order."

19:73 George, Alexander L., and George, Juliette L. *Woodrow Wilson and Colonel House: A Personality Study.* New York: Day, 1956. A "developmental biography," this work intends to describe how Wilson's personality affected his decisionmaking. The authors depict the manner in which House came to understand Wilson's personality and how this understanding contributed to the directions taken by Wilsonian politics and diplomacy.

19:74 Hoover, Herbert C. *The Ordeal of Woodrow Wilson.* New York: McGraw-Hill, 1958. Based on Hoover recollections as well as his later review of documents, this is a subjective but respected and by no means uncritical interpretation of the Wilsonian pursuit of permanent peace.

Link, A. S. *Woodrow Wilson: Revolution, War, and Peace* (19:121) is a revised version of his *Wilson the Diplomatist* (1957).

19:75 Link, Arthur S. *The Higher Realism of Woodrow Wilson and Other Essays.* Nashville, Tenn.: Vanderbilt University Press, 1971. Provided here are 24 of Link's essays or addresses (1944–1969). While various aspects of Wilson's character, philosophies, and politics are discussed, the unifying theme, as the title suggests, is Wilson's development of a "higher realism" in his politics and diplomacy.

19:76 Link, Arthur S. *Wilson.* 5 vols. to date. Princeton, N.J.: Princeton University Press, 1947–. This is the definitive, yet unfinished, biography of Woodrow Wilson, Volumes 3–5 deal with the period of neutrality and close with the declaration of war on Germany. Each volume not only provides insight into Wilson the individual, but relates the president's actions, philosophy, and policies to historical situations in "a considerable admixture of history with biography."

Osgood, R. E. "Woodrow Wilson, Collective Security, and the Lessons of History" (38:126).

19:77 Seymour, Charles. "The Paris Education of Woodrow Wilson." *Virginia Quarterly Review* 32:4 (1956), 578–93.

19:78 Turnbull, L. S., ed. *Woodrow Wilson: A Selected Bibliography.* Princeton, N.J.: Princeton University Press, 1948. Chapter 5, "Books in the Woodrow Wilson Field," is thoroughly outdated, but the remaining four chapters provide a useful bibliography of Wilson's publications, utterances, and addresses.

19:79 Walworth, Arthur. *Woodrow Wilson.* 2 vols. Boston: Houghton Mifflin, 1965. The second volume of this biography covers the period of the war and the peace settlement. Walworth's identification of Wilson as "the prophet" gives some idea of the mold in which Wilson is cast.

19:80 Weinstein, Edwin A. "Woodrow Wilson's Neurological Illness." *Journal of American History* 57:2 (1970), 324–51. Weinstein, a professor of neurology, presents evidence in this article relating to Wilson's change in behavior at the Paris Peace Conference and during the debates over ratification of the Versailles Treaty.

19:81 Wilson, Woodrow. *The Public Papers of Woodrow Wilson.* 33 vols. to date. Ed. by Arthur S. Link, et al. Princeton, N.J.: Princeton University Press, 1967– . Contemplated as a forty-five volume project, the series now covers Wilson's life to September 1914. Thus, a solid basis exists for examining Wilson's preparation for the direction of American foreign policy during the war years.

19:82 Wilson, Woodrow. *The Public Papers of Woodrow Wilson.* 6 vols. Ed. by Ray Stannard Baker and William E. Dodd, Jr. New York: Harper, 1925–1927. The last two volumes, entitled *War and Peace,* are the single most adequate published source of Wilson's addresses, messages, and public papers for events related to World War I diplomacy and foreign policy.

Others

19:83 Arnett, Alex M. *Claude Kitchin and the Wilson War Policies.* Boston: Little, Brown, 1937. This is an important biography of the House majority leader during the war. Kitchin criticized Wilsonian neutrality policies, regarding them as unneutral.

Baruch, B. M. *Baruch: The Public Years* (26:37) discusses his career of public service, and his recollections are still the best reading on the subject.

19:84 Bonsal, Stephen. *Unfinished Business.* Garden City, N.Y.: Doubleday, Doran, 1944. This is the diary of Colonel Stephen Bonsal, who served as an adviser and interpreter to Colonel House and President Wilson in the secret negotiations at the peace conference.

19:85 Briggs, Mitchell P. *George D. Herron and the European Settlement.* Stanford, Calif.: Stanford University Press, 1932. This monograph remains, after nearly a half-century, a valuable account of George Herron's mission in Switzerland during and after the World War to confer with various leaders from the Central Powers.

Coolidge, H. J., and Lord, R. H. *Archibald Cary Coolidge: Life and Letters* (20:67) is a collection of Coolidge's letters which contains information on his missions in Archangel, Vienna, and the peace conference.

19:86 Crane, Katharine. *Mr. Carr of State: Forty-Seven Years in the Department of State.* New York: St. Martin's Press, 1960. Chapters 18–25 treat the American consular service under the direction of Wilbur Carr. In addition to Carr's activities during the war, such issues as the relief of Americans stranded in Europe, refugee and prisoner of war management, and American ownership of foreign properties are discussed.

19:87 Creel, George. *The War, the World and Wilson.* New York: Harper, 1920. Creel was director of the Committee for Public Information. This recollection of the war and the battle for an honorable peace is the jeremiad of an irreconcilable Wilsonian.

Einstein, L. *A Diplomat Looks Back* (14:58) covers his years at Constantinople and Sofia, and provides shrewd insights into the meaning of the war for the United States.

19:88 Eulau, Heinz. "Wilsonian Idealist: Walter Lippman Goes to War." *Antioch Review* 14:1 (1954), 87–108. This article argues that Lippmann's participation in the war as a member of the Department of War, his trip to Paris in 1919, and his disappointment with the Versailles Treaty led him to abandon Wilsonian idealism.

19:89 Fortenberry, Joseph E. "James Kimble Vardaman and American Foreign Policy, 1913–1919." *Journal of Mississippi History* 35:2 (1973), 127–40. Vardaman (1861–1930), senator from Mississippi (1913–1919), criticized pro-British neutralism, preparedness, military or other aid to European nations, and intervention in Europe during World War I.

19:90 Francis, David R. *Russia from the American Embassy, April 1916–November, 1918.* New York: Scribner's, 1921. The American ambassador to Russia, David R. Francis, gives his account of the Bolshevik Revolution as being sponsored by the Germans and tells of his efforts to depose the Bolshevik government. Included are several interesting pieces of correspondence on the Russian Revolution and Soviet policies.

19:91 Gerard, James W. *My Four Years in Germany.* New York: Doran, 1917. Gerard, American ambassador to Germany (1914–1917), describes the German military establishment and the futile negotiations preceding the American declaration of war.

Graebner, N. A., ed. *An Uncertain Tradition: American Secretaries of State in the Twentieth Century* (2:168) includes essays on William Jennings Bryan and Robert Lansing.

Hammond, J. H. *The Autobiography of John Hays Hammond* (14:104) contains, in the second volume of this autobiography, information on the World Court League, of which Hammond was president, the League to Enforce Peace, preparedness measures, and the League of Nations movement.

19:92 Lamont, Thomas W. *Across World Frontiers.* New York: Harcourt, Brace, 1951. Lamont, a partner in J. P. Morgan and Company, represented the U.S. Treasury Department at the Paris Peace Conference. He was closely involved with reparations. This memoir includes some discussion of Morgan's firm in financing the Allied war effort and the second China Consortium. Although ignoring Anglo-American economic rivalries, he provides an authoritative overview of debates on German economic problems.

19:93 Meiburger, Anne Vincent. *Efforts of Raymond Robins toward the Recognition of Soviet Russia and the Outlawry of War, 1917–1933.* Washington, D.C.: Catholic University of America Press, 1958. A study of Robins and his activities between 1917 and 1933, which covers Robins's efforts in regard to recognition of the Soviet Union and the outlawing of war. A sympathetic account that points to Robins's idealism as a leading influence in his activities. At the same time, he was heavily involved in Republican politics of the era.

19:94 Mitchell, Kell F., Jr. "Frank L. Polk and Continued American Participation in the Paris Peace Conference, 1919." *North Dakota Quarterly* 41:1 (1973), 50–61. Frank Polk took charge of the American Commission to Negotiate Peace during midsummer of 1919 and continued at the helm until the commission terminated its activities in Paris on December 9, 1919.

Nevins, A. *Henry White: Thirty Years of American Diplomacy* (14:60) is an authorized biography which relates the story of the sole Republican member of the American Commission to Negotiate Peace.

19:95 Sharp, William G. *The War Memoirs of William Graves Sharp, American Ambassador to France, 1914–1919.* Ed. by Warrington Dawson. London: Constable, 1931. In the absence of existing manuscript papers from Ambassador Sharp, this memoir portrays the activities of the lawyer from Elyria, Ohio, who assumed important responsibilities at the outset of the European war.

19:96 Smith, Daniel M. *Aftermath of War: Bainbridge Colby and Wilsonian Diplomacy, 1920–1921.* Philadelphia: American Philosophical Society, 1970. Though he became Wilson's secretary of state, Colby remains of little importance.

Stimson, H. L., and Bundy, M. *On Active Service in Peace and War* (23:72) reveals, in chapters 4 and 5, Stimson's involvement with the preparedness program and the League of Nations controversy.

19:97 Thompson, J. A. "An Imperialist and the First World War: The Case of Albert L. Beveridge." *Journal of American Studies* 5:2 (1971), 133–50. After representing the views of ardent imperialists and extreme nationalists during the Spanish-American War, Beveridge came out in favor of isolationism from 1914 to 1917.

19:98 Vopicka, Charles J. *Secrets of the Balkans: Seven Years of a Diplomat's Life in the Storm Center of Europe.* Chicago: Rand-McNally, 1921. This memoir of the U.S. minister to Rumania, Serbia, and Bulgaria (1913–1920), traces the impact of the war on the Balkan nations, particularly Rumania. One interesting emphasis is Vopicka's attention to eastern European royalty.

Naval and Military

Tasker H. Bliss

19:99 Palmer, Frederick. *Bliss, Peacemaker: The Life and Letters of General Tasker Howard Bliss.* New York: Dodd, Mead, 1934. These letters reveal Bliss's critical view of the Paris negotiations.

19:100 Trask, David F. *General Tasker Howard Bliss and the "Sessions of the World" 1919.* Philadelphia: American Philosophical Society, 1966. This monograph explains Bliss's role at the peace conference and reveals many of his thoughts and frustrations as reflected in his numerous letters written at the time to his wife and to Secretary of War Newton Baker. Bliss's concern with disarmament is emphasized.

John J. Pershing

19:101 Lowry, Bullitt. "Pershing and the Armistice." *Journal of American History* 55:2 (1968), 281–91. A controversy arose between General Pershing and the White House over the kind of armistice to be imposed on Germany. Pershing's adoption of a hard line toward Germany was effectively quashed by the president but not before Pershing came perilously close to provoking a reprimand from the War Department.

19:102 Pershing, John J. *My Experiences in the World War*. 2 vols. New York: Stokes, 1921. The value of this memoir of the head of the American Expeditionary Force lies in its exposition of the difficulties of interallied military cooperation and in Pershing's interpretation of Wilson's policies.

19:103 Smythe, Donald. *Guerrilla Warrior: The Early Life of John J. Pershing*. New York: Scribner's, 1973. Pershing was the commander of the American Expeditionary Forces in World War I, and the punitive expedition in Mexico. Smythe's is a more dispassionate, critical biography than Frank Vandiver's. A second volume to include the World War I years is in preparation. Bibliography.

19:104 Vandiver, Frank E. *Black Jack: The Life and Times of John J. Pershing*. 2 vols. College Station: Texas A&M University Press, 1977. As leader of the 1917 Punitive Expedition into Mexico as well as commander of the American Expeditionary Forces in 1917–1918, Pershing was often the diplomat and even the maker of foreign policy as well as the soldier. This admiring biography ought to be supplemented by Smythe's still incomplete work. Bibliography.

Others

Coffman, E. M. *The Hilt of the Sword: The Career of Peyton C. March* (40:66) includes material on March's tenure as chief of staff of the army during World War I and a description of his jurisdictional disputes with Pershing and others in the war bureaucracy.

Lane, J. C. *Armed Progressive: General Leonard Wood* (40:64) contains material on Wood's service as Wilson's Chief of Staff.

Morison, E. E. *Admiral Sims and the Modern American Navy* (40:86).

EUROPEAN

See "Bibliographies," especially Toscano (19:8) for memoirs of European diplomats.

Count Johann H. von Bernstorff

19:105 Bernstorff, Johann H. von. *Memoirs of Count Bernstorff*. Trans. by Eric Sutton. New York: Random House, 1936. The chapter concerning Bernstorff's appointment as ambassador to the United States reveals his frustrated efforts to keep the United States from entering the war on the side of the Allies.

19:106 Bernstorff, Johann H. von. *My Three Years in America*. New York: Scribner's, 1920. These are memoirs of the ineffectual German ambassador to the United States from 1911 to 1917. Like other wartime memoirs, this account should be read critically.

Lord Edward Grey

Boothe, L. E. "A Fettered Envoy: Lord Grey's Mission to the United States, 1919–1920" (19:244).

19:107 Grey of Fallodon, Edward, Viscount. *Twenty-Five Years, 1892–1916*. 2 vols. London: Hodder & Stoughton, 1925. The memoirs of Lord Grey, under secretary (1892–1895) and foreign minister (1905–1916), continue to provide insight into the author's personality and aid in interpreting his policies.

David Lloyd George

19:108 Lloyd George, David. *The Truth about the Peace Treaties*. 2 vols. London: Gollancz, 1938. A heated, critical account, based on documents, which often rebuts André Tardieu's—*La Paix* (Paris: Payot, 1922)—criticisms of British policies.

19:109 Lloyd George, David. *War Memoirs*. 6 vols. London: Nicholson & Watson, 1933–1936. Although references are made to diplomacy, the emphasis is on military events. These volumes contain inaccuracies.

19:110 Rowland, Peter. *David Lloyd George: A Biography*. New York: Macmillan, 1975. For all of his faults, the British leader used his extraordinary sense of ingenuity to lay the foundation of Britain's welfare state, to negotiate peace with Germany, and to forge a settlement with Ireland.

Jan Smuts

Hancock, W. K. *Smuts* (18:45) is a detailed and favorable biography of the South African leader.

Smuts, J. *Selections from the Smuts Papers* (18:46) is especially useful for understanding Smuts's role at the Paris Peace Conference and his contributions to the formation of the League of Nations and the mandate system.

Others

19:111   Buchanan, Sir George. *My Mission to Russia and Other Diplomatic Memories.* 2 vols. London: Cassell, 1923. Buchanan was the British ambassador to St. Petersburg from 1910 to 1917.

19:112   Churchill, Winston. *The World Crisis, 1911–1918.* 4 vols. London: Butterworth, 1923–1927. Churchill's critical examination of the conduct of military operations reveals the evolution of the idea he applied during World War II: the authority of the government must prevail over that of the military in the conduct of war. A sequel (*The World Crisis: The Aftermath, 1918–1922*) appeared in 1929.

19:113   Fisher, Herbert A. L. *James Bryce: Viscount Bryce of Dechmont O.M.* 2 vols. New York: Macmillan, 1927. The second volume of Bryce's biography considers his attachments to the United States and his efforts on behalf of the League of Nations.

19:114   Fowler, Wilton B. *British-American Relations, 1917–1918: The Role of Sir William Wiseman.* Princeton, N.J.: Princeton University Press, 1969. Strained Anglo-American relations did not end with the American declaration of war. Sir William Wiseman, the head of British Intelligence in America, obtained the confidence of House and Wilson. Fowler describes how Wiseman's work became essential to the maintenance of Anglo-American cooperation during the war.

Gwynn, S., ed. *The Letters and Friendships of Sir Cecil Spring Rice: A Record* (14:70).

19:115   Papen, Franz von. *Memoirs.* New York: Dutton, 1952. Von Papen's activities as German military attaché in Washington are described.

19:116   Watson, David R. *Georges Clemenceau: A Political Biography.* London: Eyre Methuen, 1974. Watson sees "the Tiger" as the only politician who could have brought France through the final year of the war with the full constitutional system intact. By the time of the Versailles Conference, Clemenceau had become "a master of political tactics" and his skills are reflected in the final agreement. Extensive bibliography.

Wilsonian Leadership: Diplomacy and War

See "Personalities" for Woodrow Wilson.

19:117   Buehrig, Edward H., ed. *Wilson's Foreign Policy in Perspective.* Bloomington: Indiana University Press, 1957. This compilation of essays covers Wilson's relationship with Colonel Edward M. House, his assessment of collective security, his East Asian and Latin American policies, and an interpretation of the British view of Wilsonian diplomacy.

19:118   Buehrig, Edward H. *Woodrow Wilson and the Balance of Power.* Bloomington: Indiana University Press, 1955. An early example of works stressing the realistic aspects of Wilson's diplomacy, this book notes Wilson's appreciation of the relationship between American security and the European balance of power which influenced Wilson's decision to commit the United States to war.

19:119   Huthmacher, J. Joseph, and Susman, Warren I., eds. *Wilson's Diplomacy: An International Symposium.* Cambridge, Mass.: Schenkman, 1973. This collection of essays discusses Wilson's conception of the role of the president in foreign affairs (Arthur Link); French responses to Wilsonian diplomacy (Jean-Baptiste Duroselle); the varieties of "German anti-Wilsonism" (Ernst Frankel); and Wilson's intentions at the Paris Peace Conference (H. G. Nicholas).

19:120   Levin, Norman Gordon, Jr. *Woodrow Wilson and World Politics: America's Response to War and Revolution.* New York: Oxford University Press, 1968. This important work concentrates on the attempt of Wilsonian diplomacy to steer a course between revolution and war by achieving the acceptance of a program of liberal international capitalism. Extensive bibliography.

19:121   Link, Arthur S. *Woodrow Wilson: Revolution, War, and Peace.* Arlington Heights, Ill.: AHM, 1979. This substantially revised version of the author's *Wilson the Diplomatist: A Look at His Major Foreign Policies* (Baltimore: Johns Hopkins Press, 1957) concentrates on the main features of Wilsonian foreign policy, including problems of neutrality, the decision for war, the program for peace, and the struggle for the League of Nations. Extensive bibliography.

19:122   Martin, Laurence W. *Peace without Victory: Wilson and the British Liberals.* New Haven, Conn.: Yale University Press, 1958. This monograph is an important contribution to our knowledge of Wilson's concern with British and European liberal opinion in his quest for a just and permanent peace.

19:123   Mayer, Arno J. *Political Origins of the New Diplomacy, 1917–1918.* New Haven, Conn.: Yale University Press, 1959. Mayer examines the war aims and the interaction of domestic politics and foreign policy of the major belligerent nations. Contrasting the struggle between the advocates of the "old" diplomacy and those of the "new" diplomacy, it is a fine example of comparative history.

19:124   Notter, Harley. *The Origins of the Foreign Policy of Woodrow Wilson.* Baltimore: Johns Hopkins Press, 1937. This work contends that Wilson had formed the essential outlines of his foreign policy before he became president.

19:125   Parsons, Edward B. *Wilsonian Diplomacy: Allied-American Rivalries in War and Peace.* St. Louis: Forum, 1978. The author argues that Wilson's postwar economic and territorial objectives led him to overturn proposals announced in 1915–1916 by the time of the peace conference.

19:126   Wells, Samuel F., Jr. "New Perspectives of Wilsonian Diplomacy: The Secular Evangelism of American Political Economy." *Perspectives in American History* 6 (1972), 389–419. In this important review essay, Wells points out the new areas of endeavor, concentrating especially on such themes as the continuity between the Wilson-Harding eras, the economic and strategic objectives of Wilsonian diplomacy, and the growing acceptance of Wilson as a realistic diplomatist.

ECONOMIC FACTORS

Abrahams, P. P. "American Bankers and the Economic Tactics of Peace, 1919" (20:186).

Cooper, J. M., Jr. "The Command of Gold Reversed: American Loans to Britain, 1915–1917" (39:99).

19:127   Cuff, Robert D. "Woodrow Wilson and Business-Government Relations during World War I."

Review of Politics 31:3 (1969), 385–407. Wilson sought to ingratiate his administration with the nation's business groups. He invited businessmen to cooperate in Bernard M. Baruch's idea for a businessmen's commission which could begin planning for economic mobilization.

19:128   Dayer, Roberta A. "Strange Bedfellows: J. P. Morgan & Co., Whitehall and the Wilson Administration during World War I." *Business History* 18:2 (1976), 127–51. At the beginning of World War I, U.S. Treasury Secretary William McAdoo and others were suspicious of J. P. Morgan and Company's role as British purchasing and banking agent; but when the United States entered the war, this gave way to close collaboration.

DeNovo, J. A. "The Movement for an Aggressive American Oil Policy Abroad, 1918–1920" (18:156) shows that World War I caused U.S. officials to connect diplomacy, national security, and access to adequate petroleum reserves. However, this new understanding did not immediately result in a coherent national petroleum policy.

Hogan, M. J. *Informal Entente: The Private Structure of Cooperation in Anglo-American Economic Diplomacy, 1918–1928* (20:191).

Kaufman, B. I. "Organization for Foreign Trade Expansion in the Mississippi Valley, 1900–1920" (39:29).

19:129   Kaufman, Burton I. *Efficiency and Expansion: Foreign Trade Organization in the Wilson Administration, 1913–1921.* Westport, Conn.: Greenwood, 1974. During World War I, American opportunities in the area of foreign trade expansion increased dramatically. Kaufman describes how the Wilson administration moved to exploit these opportunities. Extensive bibliography.

19:130   Parrini, Carl P. *Heir to Empire: United States Economic Diplomacy, 1916–1923.* Pittsburgh: Pittsburgh University Press, 1969. Parrini is concerned with financial relations between the United States and the Allies during the war and its immediate aftermath.

Safford, J. J. "Edward Hurley and American Shipping Policy: An Elaboration on Wilsonian Diplomacy, 1918–1919" (39:45).

Safford, J. J. *Wilsonian Maritime Diplomacy, 1913–1921* (19:149).

Van Alstyne, R. W. "Private American Loans to the Allies, 1914–1916" (39:102).

AMERICAN NEUTRALITY, 1914–1917

See "Personalities" for Josephus Daniels, Robert Lansing, Henry Cabot Lodge, Walter Hines Page, and "Others" for James W. Gerard.

19:131   Devlin, Patrick. *Too Proud to Fight: Woodrow Wilson's Neutrality.* New York: Oxford University Press, 1975. Partly a biography of Wilson, partly a history of Wilsonian diplomacy (1914—1917), this book gives extensive treatment to the legal problems of neutrality.

Dignan, D. K. "The Hindu Conspiracy in Anglo-American Relations during World War I" (37:99) argues that the so-called Hindu conspiracy, which involved Indian revolutionary nationalists using the United States as a base of operations, was a more significant incident than is commonly acknowledged.

19:132   Kihl, Mary R. "A Failure in Ambassadorial Diplomacy." *Journal of American History* 57:3 (1970), 636–53. By the fall of 1916 neither Walter Hines Page, U.S. ambassador to Britain, nor Sir Cecil Spring-Rice, his British counterpart, were able to function effectively with the Wilson administration. Page was regarded as too hopelessly pro-British to serve Wilson's policy of neutrality, and Spring-Rice was regarded by Colonel House as overly suspicious of German intrigue.

19:133   May, Ernest R. *World War and American Isolation, 1914–1917.* Cambridge: Harvard University Press, 1959. By focusing attention on the alternatives considered and decisions made by Germany and Britain, May places Wilson's policy into an international perspective, thus allowing the reader to judge whether Wilson's actions were properly directed.

19:134   McDiarmid, Alice Morrisey. "The Neutrality Board and Armed Merchantmen, 1914–1917." *American Journal of International Law* 69:2 (1975), 374–81. After pondering the proper role of a neutral, the Joint State and Navy Neutrality Board affirmed the

right of merchant ships to be armed for defensive purposes.

19:135   Sarkissian, A. O. *Studies in Diplomatic History and Historiography in Honour of G. P. Gooch.* London: Longmans, Green, 1961. This Festschrift contains two important essays relating to American participation in World War I: Charles Seymour, "The House-Bernstorff Conservations in Perspective," and Bernadotte E. Schmitt, "The Relation of Public Opinion and Foreign Affairs before and during the First World War."

19:136   Schmitt, Bernadotte E. "American Neutrality, 1914–1917." *Journal of Modern History* 8:2 (1936), 200–211. This review article focuses on volume 5 of Baker's *Woodrow Wilson: Life and Letters,* and contrasts Baker's assessment of Wilson's neutrality policies with those in works by Charles Seymour, Walter Millis, and others.

19:137   Smith, Daniel M. *Robert Lansing and American Neutrality, 1914–1917.* Berkeley: University of California Press, 1958. This major study argues that Lansing's outlook emanated from a blend of strategic and ideological factors leading him to believe that German-American differences were irreconcilable and that Britain and America had, within limits, important parallel interests. Bibliography.

19:138   West, Rachel. *The Department of State on the Eve of the First World War.* Athens: University of Georgia Press, 1979. This book conveys a careful picture of the Department of State during the first two years of the Wilson administration.

Wilson's Mediation Efforts

See "Personalities" for Edward M. House, Lord Edward Grey.

19:139   Cooper, John M., Jr. "The British Response to the House-Grey Memorandum: New Evidence and New Questions." *Journal of American History* 59:4 (1973), 958–71. Recently opened documents repudiate David Lloyd George's assertion that Lord Grey alone torpedoed American mediation efforts.

19:140   Kernek, Sterling. "The British Government's Reactions to President Wilson's 'Peace' Note of December 1916." *Historical Journal* 13:4 (1970), 721–66. Lloyd George's attitude has been misunderstood; in reality he considered peace negotiations a danger to be avoided and a reason for more efficient warfare.

19:141 Patterson, David S. "Woodrow Wilson and the Mediation Movement, 1914–1917." *Historian* 33:4 (1971), 535–56. This article describes the efforts of various groups in the American peace movement to gain approval from President Wilson for their mediation plans. Patterson suggests that Wilson's declaration of war and his ultimate scorn for pacifists led those in the mediation movement to withhold their support for the president's peace program.

19:142 Zivojinović, Dragan. "Robert Lansing's Comments on the Pontifical Peace Note of August 1, 1917." *Journal of American History* 56:3 (1969), 556–71. Secretary of State Lansing recommended that Pope Benedict XV's peace note be rejected as a basis for negotiation. He saw the papal pronouncement emanating from a fear that socialism might undermine respect for Catholicism.

Maritime Issues

19:143 Bailey, Thomas A. "The United States and the Blacklist during the Great War." *Journal of Modern History* 6:1 (1934), 14–35. Bailey contends that blacklisting from this time on (June 1916) became a recognized instrument of organized warfare and that it placed added strains on America's benevolent neutrality toward Britain before April 1917.

19:144 Birnbaum, Karl E. *Peace Moves and U-Boat Warfare: Germany's Policy toward the United States, April 18, 1916–January 9, 1917*. Stockholm: Almquist & Wiksell, 1958. Germany's wavering policy between peace moves and submarine war is the theme of this book. Failure of communication and understanding of each other's purposes were responsible for the break between the United States and Germany.

19:145 Herwig, Holger H. *Politics of Frustration: The United States in German Naval Planning, 1889–1941*. Boston: Little, Brown, 1976. In an important work, the author examines the basis for an impending German-American naval war through the eyes of German naval planners. Bibliography.

19:146 Hurt, R. Douglas. "The Settlement of Anglo-American Claims Resulting from World War I." *American Neptune* 34:3 (1974), 155–73. Although

a formula was achieved to obtain compensation for Britain's seizure of American ships and property, the negotiations were impeded by London's fear of having to make a large payment and to modify its naval blockade policy.

19:147 Lundeberg, Philip K. "The German Naval Critique of the U-Boat Campaign, 1915–1918." *Military Affairs* 27:3 (1963), 105–18. German naval authorities disagreed on the importance of U-boat campaigns to the war effort. Lundeberg evaluates the arguments, notably those of Bauer, Tirpitz, and Spindler.

19:148 Pratt, Julius W. "The British Blockade and American Precedent." *U.S. Naval Institute Proceedings* 46:11 (1920), 1789–1802. The author seeks to demonstrate that British blockade operations in World War I were "an almost inevitable outgrowth of earlier practice" and that Great Britain looked to American examples during the Civil War for the precedents and justification of her practice in 1914 to 1918.

19:149 Safford, Jeffrey J. *Wilsonian Maritime Diplomacy, 1913–1921*. New Brunswick, N.J.: Rutgers University Press, 1978. Safford examines Wilson's merchant shipping policies and concludes that Wilsonian maritime policy was conducted during the neutrality and war years with the postwar foreign trade position of the United States clearly in mind. Extensive bibliography.

Savage, C. *Policy of the United States toward Maritime Commerce in War* (40:116) treats, in volume 2 (*1914–1918*), contraband, trade restrictions, loans and credits, control of exports, armed merchant ships, and enemy trading lists.

19:150 Siney, Marion C. *Allied Blockade of Germany, 1914–1916*. Ann Arbor: University of Michigan Press, 1957. Primarily concerned with Allied efforts to block northern European neutral trade with Germany, this book also contains information on American business with European neutrals.

19:151 Smith, Gaddis. *Britain's Clandestine Submarines, 1914–1915*. New Haven, Conn.: Yale University Press, 1964. This monograph focuses on Bethlehem Steel Corporation's building submarines for the British and raises some important questions concerning American neutral rights.

The Lusitania Sinking

19:152 Bailey, Thomas A., and Ryan, Paul B. *The Lusitania Disaster: An Episode in Modern Warfare and Diplomacy*. New York: Free Press, 1975. In the most balanced account of the *Lusitania* disaster available, Bailey and Ryan rebut the conspiracy theories of authors such as Colin Simpson, and assess the impact of the *Lusitania* sinking on American neutrality. Bibliography.

19:153 Simpson, Colin. *The Lusitania*. Boston: Little, Brown, 1973. Simpson agrees here with German claims that a British conspiracy existed to have the *Lusitania* sunk. He also argues that the *Lusitania* was armed and carrying dangerous contraband.

The Zimmermann Telegram

19:154 Bridges, Lamar W. "Zimmermann Telegram: Reaction of Southern, Southwestern Newspapers." *Journalism Quarterly* 46:1 (1969), 81–86. The reaction to the news of the Zimmermann telegram was mostly anger, as danger of a Mexican attack was considered remote, but the telegram had a unifying effect on the American people.

19:155 Tuchman, Barbara. *The Zimmermann Telegram*. New York: Viking, 1958. Tuchman traces the progress of the Zimmermann telegram from Room 40 (the British Admiralty Intelligence Bureau) to President Wilson. The final chapter argues that the telegram aided in confirming Wilson's decision to intervene.

AMERICA'S DECISION TO INTERVENE

See above, "Origins of the War."

19:156 Birdsall, Paul. "Neutrality and Economic Pressures, 1914–1917." *Science and Society* 3:2 (1939), 217–28. This early effort seeks to revise the historical consensus that German U-boat policy led the United States into war. Birdsall notes that American economic ties to the Allies gradually dissolved any hope of continued neutrality.

19:157 Buchanan, A. Russell. "American Editors Examine American War Aims and Plans in April, 1917." *Pacific Historical Review* 9:3 (1940), 253–65.

A celebrated article exhibiting the rather dated techniques of public opinion sampling through textual analysis of newspaper editorials. The editorials examined cover such questions as the assignment of guilt for the war, overwhelmingly anti-German; the reasons for American participation; and the plans America should make.

Cooper, J. M., Jr. "The Command of Gold Reversed: American Loans to Britain, 1915–1917" (39:99) is a reexamination of economic considerations in the relationship of the United States to the Allied side in World War I prior to 1917, and as a factor in intervention in 1917.

19:158 Doerries, Reinhard R. "Imperial Berlin and Washington: New Light on Germany's Foreign Policy and America's Entry into World War I." *Central European History* 11:1 (1978), 23–49. Doerries concludes that the Germans refused mediation by the American president, even when it appeared highly improbable that they could win the war.

19:159 Gregory, Ross. *The Origins of American Intervention in the First World War*. New York: Norton, 1971. Written primarily for undergraduates, this book emphasizes Wilson's perception of the role of the United States as a world power and the requirements of an expanding American economy. Bibliographic essay.

19:160 Leopold, Richard W. "The Problem of American Intervention, 1917: An Historical Retrospect." *World Politics* 2:3 (1950), 405–25. By focusing on several of the important works written during the 1930s, Leopold notes that such subjects as the war congress, strategic planning, and public opinion have been almost entirely neglected.

19:161 Seymour, Charles. *American Neutrality, 1914–1917: Essays on the Causes of American Intervention in the World War*. New Haven, Conn.: Yale University Press, 1935. In this series of essays Seymour underscores the importance of the German submarine campaign as the most compelling cause for American intervention in World War I.

19:162 Smith, Daniel M. "National Interest and American Intervention, 1917: An Historiographical Appraisal." *Journal of American History* 52:1 (1965), 5–24. Smith reviews the works of Buehrig, Link, Osgood, May, and others on the issue of national interest and intervention in World War I. Recent authors have stressed Wilson's acceptance of realistic diplomacy and balance of power politics as the primary motivations for his decision to intervene.

Van Alstyne, R. W. "Private American Loans to the Allies, 1914–1916." (39:102) recounts how Americans initially resented the offer of loans to belligerents; however, anti-German sentiment and economic necessity altered American opinion.

Dissenting Views

See, under "Personalities," Hiram W. Johnson, Robert M. La Follette, Oswald Garrison Villard; also see Chapter 16, "The 'Practical' Peace Movements, 1890–1914."

19:163 Bolt, Ernest C., Jr. *Ballots before Bullets: The War Referendum Approach to Peace in America, 1914–1941*. Charlottesville: University of Virginia Press, 1977. Choosing for war or peace on the basis of a public referendum is, at least in part, an experiment in making foreign policy subject to democratic traditions. See also Chapter 20, "The Ludlow Amendment."

Chambers, J. W., II, ed. *The Eagle and the Dove: The American Peace Movement and United States Foreign Policy, 1900–1922* (16:96).

19:164 Chatfield, Charles. *For Peace and Justice: Pacifism in America, 1914–1941*. Knoxville: University of Tennessee Press, 1971. Chatfield defines the place of pacifists, who refused to sanction any rationale for war, in the American peace movement. The first three chapters describe the activities of pacifist individuals, groups, and organizations during World War I.

19:165 Chatfield, Charles. "World War I and the Liberal Pacifist in the United States." *American Historical Review* 75:7 (1970), 1920–37. The modern American peace movement acquired much of its aggressive, political, and in some respects radical base during World War I.

19:166 Cook, Blanche W. "Democracy in Wartime: Antimilitarism in England and the United States, 1914–1918." *American Studies* 13:1 (1972), 51–68. Cook notes emergence of organizations in both countries that sought to preserve political liberty in wartime.

19:167 DeBenedetti, Charles. *Origins of the Modern American Peace Movement, 1915–1929*. Millwood, N.Y.: KTO, 1978. This revisionist work traces the development of the modern American peace movement from its origins during World War I as a coalition of internationalists, legalists, and social progressives to its development as a middle-class movement. Extensive bibliographical essay.

19:168 Duram, James C. "In Defense of Conscience: Norman Thomas as an Exponent of Christian Pacifism during World War I." *Journal of Presbyterian History* 52:1 (1974), 19–32. The early writings of Norman Thomas reflect his defense of conscientious objection (1915–1918) as a tenet of Christianity and pacifism in the face of universal conscription.

Herman, S. R. *Eleven against War: Studies in American Internationalist Thought, 1898–1921* (16:33) examines American internationalist thought through the activities and ideas of several active proponents: Jane Addams, Josiah Royce, Woodrow Wilson, Thorstein Veblen, Elihu Root, Nicholas Murray Butler, Hamilton Holt, Theodore Marburg, A. Lawrence Lowell, John Bates Clark, and Franklin H. Giddings.

19:169 Kraft, Barbara. *The Peace Ship: Henry Ford's Pacifist Adventure in the First World War*. New York: Macmillan, 1978. The attempt by peace workers to promote continuous mediation by neutral governments is fully revealed in this study of the *Oscar II*.

Marchand, C. R. *The American Peace Movement and Social Reform, 1898–1918* (16:106) argues that the peace movement was not dominated by pacifists, but made up mostly of individuals involved in a broad range of social reform organizations.

19:170 Peterson, Horace C., and Fite, Gilbert C. *Opponents of War, 1917–1918*. Madison: University of Wisconsin Press, 1957. In the standard treatment of American opposition to World War I, Peterson and Fite identify the most important groups and individuals opposed to the war and analyze the reasons for opposition.

19:171 Weinstein, James. "Anti-War Sentiment and the Socialist Party, 1917–1918." *Political Science Quarterly* 74:2 (1959), 215–39. The article maintains that the Socialist party represented the opinions of many Americans in its opposition to the war, and that this helps to explain why the Socialists did so well at the polls.

Revisionist Views

19:172 Barnes, Harry Elmer. *The Genesis of the World War: An Introduction to the Problem of War Guilt.* New York: Knopf, 1926. One of the first major revisionists to argue that the cause of the war lay with the Allies rather than Germany.

Cohen, W. I. *The American Revisionists: The Lessons of Intervention in World War I* (20:124) examines the utterances, publications, and thought of C. Hartley Grattan, Walter Millis, Charles Callan Tansill, Harry Elmer Barnes, and Charles Austin Beard in an attempt to ascertain the impact of World War I on leading revisionist thinkers.

19:173 Tansill, Charles C. *America Goes to War.* Boston: Little, Brown, 1938. Tansill focuses on public opinion, domestic economic troubles, and Wilson's pro-British advisers to reveal why, in his opinion, war with Germany was inevitable for the United States.

AMERICAN BELLIGERENCY, 1917–1918

19:174 Bailey, Thomas A. *The Policy of the United States toward Neutrals: 1917–1918.* Baltimore: Johns Hopkins Press, 1942. Reprint 1966. Bailey concludes that the United States recognized the rights of neutrals under international law and sought to adhere to principles it advocated during 1914 to 1917.

The Home Front

See, under "Personalities," Bernard M. Baruch, Herbert C. Hoover, Claude Kitchin; also see Schaffer (19:6) for bibliography.

19:175 Clarkson, G. B. *Industrial America in World War.* Boston: Houghton Mifflin, 1923. Written by the official historian of the War Industries Board, this book is an important source of information on the men, business, and policies of that organization.

19:176 Cuff, Robert D. *The War Industries Board: Business-Government Relations during World War I.* Baltimore: Johns Hopkins Press, 1973. Among its more important themes are those of the development of a wartime planning structure connecting business government and the military, and an evaluation of the defense planning bureaucracy. Extensive bibliography.

19:177 Gompers, Samuel. *American Labor and the War.* New York: Doran, 1919. The president of the American Federation of Labor assesses labor's contribution to the war and labor's opinion of Wilson's diplomatic objectives.

19:178 Koistinen, Paul A. C. "The 'Industrial-Military Complex' in Historical Perspective: World War I." *Business History Review* 41:4 (1967), 378–403. As part of the growing literature portraying World War I as a "watershed" in the organizational development of American business, this article traces the emerging interdependence of modern business and the military.

19:179 Larson, Simeon. *Labor and Foreign Policy: Gompers, the AFL, and the First World War, 1914–1918.* Cranbury, N.J.: Fairleigh Dickinson University Press, 1975. World War I drew union policy, for the first time, to foreign affairs. Samuel Gompers abandoned pacifism and favored military preparedness: the war became a "wonderful crusade."

19:180 Mock, James R., and Thurber, Evangeline. *Report on Demobilization.* Norman: University of Oklahoma Press, 1944. This is a bureaucratic history of World War I which attempts to show what postwar planning operations were undertaken and why they failed.

19:181 Mullendore, William C. *History of the United States Food Administration.* Stanford, Calif.: Stanford University Press, 1941. The official history of the U.S. Food Administration describes its organization, Herbert Hoover's role as director, and its contribution.

The Military Dimension

See "Personalities" for Newton D. Baker, Josephus Daniels, and "Naval and Military"; also see "Bibliographies" for Braisted (19:3), Ellis (19:4) and Gilbert (19:5).

19:182 Barbeau, Arthur E., and Henri, Florette. *The Unknown Soldiers: Black American Troops in World War I.* Philadelphia: Temple University Press, 1974. Detailed here are the attempts of black citizens to overcome the racist policies of the U.S. government and the American armed forces during World War I.

This is a revision of earlier works that disparaged the black contribution to the war effort.

Braisted, W. R. *The United States Navy in the Pacific, 1909–1922* (17:227) considers the relationship between American foreign and naval policies during World War I and the peace settlement.

19:183 Coffman, Edward M. *The War to End All Wars: The American Military Experience in World War I*. New York: Oxford University Press, 1968. This solid military history details the organization, planning, administration, and deployment of the American Expeditionary Force in World War I. Extensive bibliographic essay.

19:184 De Weerd, Harvey A. *President Wilson Fights His War: World War I and the American Intervention*. New York: Macmillan, 1968. A comprehensive military history of the war with an American emphasis. Excellent maps.

Earle, E. M., ed. *Makers of Modern Strategy: Military Thought from Machiavelli to Hitler* (40:20) deals with World War I (chapters 12–14) and with concepts of sea and air power strategy (chapters 17–20).

19:185 Hankey, Maurice P. A. *The Supreme Command, 1914–1918*. 2 vols. London: Allen & Unwin, 1961. Hankey, secretary to the Committee of Imperial Defense and later involved with the Supreme War Council and the Paris Peace Conference, writes from the British insider's point of view.

Lundeberg, P. K. "The German Naval Critique of the U-Boat Campaign, 1915–1918" (19:147).

19:186 Parsons, Edward B. "Why the British Reduced the Flow of American Troops to Europe in August–October 1918." *Canadian Journal of History* 12:2 (1977), 173–91. Great Britain reduced the flow of American troops to Europe to regain export markets lost to the United States during the war, to weaken the American challenge to British maritime supremacy, and to weaken Wilson's potential control of armistice and peace terms.

Sprout, H., and Sprout, M. *The Rise of American Naval Power, 1776–1918* (40:117) discusses American naval preparations during World War I.

19:187 Trask, David F. *Captains and Cabinets: Anglo-American Naval Relations, 1917–1918*. Columbia: University of Missouri Press, 1973. Trask blends a discussion of naval planning operations with that of British-American foreign policy, emphasizing how both Britain and the United States sought to protect their postwar positions while cooperating against the Germans. Extensive bibliography.

19:188 Trask, David F. *The United States in the Supreme War Council: American War Aims and Inter-Allied Strategy, 1917–1918*. Middletown, Conn.: Wesleyan University Press, 1961. Trask illuminates American war aims and the relationship between President Wilson's wartime preparations and his plans for the peace. Bibliography.

PUBLIC OPINION AND POLITICS

See "Dissenting Views," above.

19:189 Adler, Selig. "The Congressional Election of 1918." *South Atlantic Quarterly* 36:4 (1937), 447–65. Adler places this congressional election within the context of America's move to "splendid isolation" and examines the importance of a Republican majority in the Senate.

19:190 Allen, Howard W. "Republican Reformers and Foreign Policy, 1913–1917." *Mid-America* 44:2 (1962), 222–29. This article analyzes William E. Leuchtenberg's contention that progressive reformers who agreed on domestic programs usually agreed on foreign policy questions. By looking at the roll call votes of 17 Republican senators, Allen concludes that little unanimity on questions of foreign policy existed. See Chapter 13, "Progressive and Foreign Policy."

19:191 Cooper, John M., Jr. *The Vanity of Power: American Isolationism and the First World War, 1914–1917*. Westport, Conn.: Greenwood, 1969. Cooper argues that isolationism emerged during World War I as a coherent and enduring political philosophy. He discusses the divergent views separating such groups as ultranationalists, idealists, internationalists, and isolationists. Extensive bibliography.

19:192 Cuddy, Edward. "Pro-Germanism and American Catholicism, 1914–1917." *Catholic Historical Review* 54:4 (1968), 427–54. The article refutes the assertion of Arthur Link and others that the Catholic church was practically uniform in its pro-German sympathy, and concludes that there was great diversity of opinion in the Catholic church between 1914 and 1917.

Gerson, L. L. *The Hyphenate in Recent American Politics and Diplomacy* (2:203) examines (chapters 3–6) the influence of immigrant Americans on Wilsonian diplomacy and their response to Wilson's ideal of self-determination.

Hilderbrand, R. C. *Power and the People: Executive Management of Public Opinion in Foreign Affairs, 1869–1921* (2:208).

19:193 Livermore, Seward W. *Politics Is Adjourned: Wilson and the War Congress, 1916–1918.* Middletown, Conn.: Wesleyan University Press, 1966. Described here are the factional squabbles, ineffective presidential and party leadership, and Republican party opportunism which ousted the Democrats from control of the Congress in 1918. Bibliography.

19:194 McDonald, Timothy G. "The Gore-McLemore Resolution: Democratic Revolt against Wilson's Submarine Policy." *Historian* 26:1 (1963), 50–74. The author finds, contrary to conventional historical opinion, that Democratic congressmen recognized the president as the head of their party and followed his lead in foreign affairs.

Rappaport, A. *The Navy League of the United States* (2:212) argues that the Navy League promoted the opinions of naval planners on the grounds of patriotism and preparedness.

19:195 Thompson, J. A. "American Progressive Publicists and the First World War, 1914–1917." *Journal of American History* 58:2 (1971), 364–83. Thompson reviews the relationship between domestic attitudes and foreign policy found in an analysis of 20 prominent Progressive publicists: former muckrakers, editors, and free-lance writers. The study shows a divergence in attitudes toward belligerent powers before U.S. entry, but there was agreement that the war should result in a lasting peace guaranteed by some international organization.

19:196 Ward, Robert D. "The Origins and Activities of the National Security League, 1914–1919." *Mississippi Valley Historical Review* 47:1 (1960), 51–65. Ward describes how this organization became a political force which emphasized compulsory military training, promoted belligerency status for the United States, and eventually became known for its antidemocratic tactics.

Propagandizing the American People

See "Personalities" for George Creel (under "Others").

19:197 Blakey, George T. *Historians on the Homefront: American Propagandists for War.* Lexington: University of Kentucky Press, 1970. This book concerns the mobilization of historians in nonmilitary service in the U.S. government at home. These historians were apologists—supporters of the war effort.

19:198 Bonadio, Felice A. "The Failure of German Propaganda in the United States, 1914–1917." *Mid-America* 41:1 (1959), 40–57. Bonadio finds that German propaganda failed because of the conservative attachments of immigrants to political institutions and because of the ability of most immigrants to assimilate into the melting pot of American society.

19:199 Gruber, Carol S. *Mars and Minerva: World War I and the Uses of Higher Learning in America.* Baton Rouge: Louisiana State University Press, 1976. By focusing on the work of scholars in such organizations as the Committee on Public Information and the Inquiry, Gruber reveals the internal and external pressures placed on scholars who possessed divided loyalties for their country and for the truth.

19:200 Lasswell, Harold D. *Propaganda Technique in the World War.* London: Kegan Paul, 1938. Lasswell discusses several topics relating to the management of public opinion through propaganda, including the formation of propaganda organizations, civil versus military requirements of propaganda, and the demoralization of the enemy through propaganda.

19:201 Peterson, Horace C. *Propaganda for War: The Campaign against American Neutrality, 1914–1917.* Norman: University of Oklahoma Press, 1939. The author concludes that Britain helped push the United States to war by adroitly advertising Anglo-American ties, revealing German duplicity, and altering American consciousness.

19:202 Read, James M. *Atrocity Propaganda, 1914–1919.* New Haven, Conn.: Yale University Press, 1941. According to Read, atrocity stories published as propaganda fed the public's appetite for a Carthaginian peace, and thereby limited the flexibility of negotiators at the peace conference. Bibliography.

19:203 Sanders, M. L. "Wellington House and British Propaganda during the First World War." *Historical Journal* 18:1 (1975), 119–46. This essay traces Britain's attempt to counteract German propaganda.

WARTIME RELATIONS

19:204 Noer, Thomas J. "The American Government and the Irish Question during World War I." *South Atlantic Quarterly* 72:1 (1973), 95–114. This article examines Wilson's dealings with Irish nationalists, focusing on the attempts of Irish leaders to capitalize on the Wilsonian principle of self-determination and Wilson's efforts to curb such militant Irish organizations as the Sinn Fein.

19:205 Zivojinović, Dragan R. "The Vatican, Woodrow Wilson, and the Dissolution of the Hapsburg Monarchy 1914–1918." *East European Quarterly* 3:1 (1969), 31–70. The author clarifies certain problems of Vatican diplomacy during 1914 to 1918, and explains President Woodrow Wilson's policies and attitudes toward the Vatican during the same period.

East Asia

See "Personalities," especially Thomas W. Lamont (under "Others"), Robert Lansing.

19:206 Beers, Burton F. *Vain Endeavor: Robert Lansing's Attempt to End the American-Japanese Rivalry.* Durham, N.C.: Duke University Press, 1962. Beers demonstrates Lansing's independent position on the subject of Japanese-American relations and indicates how the secretary of state diverged from Wilson's intentions during important negotiations.

19:207 Howlett, Charles. "Democracy's Ambassador to the Far East: John Dewey's Quest for World Peace." *Pacific History* 20:4 (1976), 388–406. John Dewey's visit to East Asia at the conclusion of World War I had a two-fold significance: he was the first major American intellectual to recognize the importance of East Asia in American policy, and he became the symbol of American democracy.

Israel, J. *Progressivism and the Open Door: America and China, 1905–1921* (17:236).

19:208 Li Tien-yi. *Woodrow Wilson's China Policy, 1913–1917.* Kansas City: University of Kansas Press, 1952. This study omits consideration of the Shantung question, but it provides solid information on the American withdrawal from the China Consortium and on the American response to Japan's Twenty-One Demands.

19:209 May, Ernest R. "American Policy and Japan's Entrance into World War I." *Mississippi Valley Historical Review* 40:2 (1953), 279–90. May suggests that Bryan's attempt to revive former Secretary of State Hay's method of diplomacy and the reluctance of the State Department to assume new responsibilities allowed Japan to capitalize on the war.

Mazuzan, G. T. "'Our New Gold Goes Adventuring': The American International Corporation in China" (39:55).

19:210 Pugach, Noel H. "Standard Oil and Petroleum Development in Early Republican China." *Business History Review* 45:4 (1971), 452–73. In 1914 the Standard Oil Company of New York (Socony) attempted to enter into an oil exploration partnership with the new republican government of China. Despite diplomatic support from the Wilson administration, the project was abandoned.

Safford, J. J. "Experiment in Containment: The United States Steel Embargo and Japan, 1917–1918" (39:56).

19:211 Trani, Eugene P. "Woodrow Wilson, China, and the Missionaries, 1913–1921." *Journal of Presbyterian History* 49:4 (1971), 328–51. Wilson viewed Christianity as a unifying force in the world and the Chinese Revolution of 1911 as the first step toward the spread of Christianity and democracy for China.

Latin America

For additional references on Wilson's Latin American policies, see Chapter 15.

19:212 Clements, Kendrick A. "'A Kindness to Carranza': William Jennings Bryan, International Harvester, and Intervention in Yucatán." *Nebraska History* 57:4 (1976), 479–90. Secretary of State William Jennings Bryan endorsed a plan for military intervention in Yucatán (1913–1915) which would have benefited the International Harvester Corporation.

19:213 Clements, Kendrick A. "Woodrow Wilson's Mexican Policy, 1913–1915." *Diplomatic History* 4:2

(1980), 113–36. This study offers a corrective to those critics who have viewed Wilson as either naive or as a devious imperialist. The author argues that Wilson achieved a balance between a policy of intervention and one of nonintervention to deal fairly with a weaker neighbor.

Harris, C. H., III, and Sadler, L. R. "The Plan of San Diego and the Mexican–United States War Crisis of 1916: A Reexamination" (15:151) examine a plan which called for a Mexican-American rebellion and the establishment of an independent republic in the Southwest. Guerrilla raids on Anglos in south Texas followed (February 1915–July 1916). There is no solid evidence of German involvement.

19:214 Healy, David. "Admiral William B. Caperton and United States Naval Diplomacy in South America, 1917–1919." *Journal of Latin American Studies* 8:2 (1976), 297–323. Caperton's attempts to get Brazil, Uruguay, and Argentina into World War I against Germany were impressive but not successful; only Brazil eventually declared war on Germany, Uruguay was already pro-Allied, and Argentina stayed neutral and ambivalent.

19:215 Kaufman, Burton I. "United States Trade and Latin America: The Wilson Years." *Journal of American History* 58:2 (1971), 342–63. The Wilson administration urged expansion of U.S. exports through the Underwood tariff (1913); the Federal Reserve Act (1913), which was designed in part to facilitate the participation of U.S. banks in foreign credit operations; and the reorganization of the Commerce Department to encourage foreign trade.

19:216 Machado, Manuel A., Jr., and Judge, James T. "Tempest in a Teapot? The Mexican–United States Intervention Crisis of 1919." *Southwestern Historical Quarterly* 74:1 (1970), 1–23. This essay examines the factors in the 1919 crisis. President Venustiano Carranza had proven unable to protect American citizens and business interests from Mexican revolutionaries.

19:217 Martin, Percy. *Latin America and the War.* Baltimore: Johns Hopkins Press, 1925. Though dated, this work remains valuable. Subjects receiving special attention are the relationship between the United States and Latin American neutrals and the importance of Brazil as a belligerent.

Rosenberg, E. S. "Economic Pressures in Anglo-American Diplomacy in Mexico, 1917–1918" (15:136) reviews the United States' efforts to force

Mexico to moderate its revolutionary program in 1917–1918 by offering loans and food shipments. The Mexicans refused and instead opened discussion with Britain and other Latin American countries.

19:218 Rosenberg, Emily S. "The Exercise of Emergency Controls over Foreign Commerce: Economic Pressure on Latin America." *Inter-American Economic Affairs* 31:4 (1978), 81–96. Rosenberg surveys the growth of U.S. executive power over international trade and discusses the use of this power in dealing with Ecuador, Mexico, Honduras, and Brazil during World War I.

The Armistice and Peace Conference

See, under "Personalities," "American," Joseph C. Grew, Herbert C. Hoover, Edward M. House, Robert Lansing, Henry Cabot Lodge, Henry Morgenthau, Elihu Root; "Others," Stephan Bonsal, George D. Herron.

19:219 Bailey, Thomas A. *Woodrow Wilson and the Lost Peace.* New York: Macmillan, 1944. This volume describes certain fundamental dilemmas experienced by President Wilson during the peace negotiations of 1919. Implicit is the hope that the United States would avoid the errors of 1919 when reaching a settlement of World War II.

19:220 Benns, F. Lee. "The Two Paris Peace Conferences of the Twentieth Century." In Dwight E. Lee and George E. McReynolds, eds., *Essays in History and International Relations in Honor of George Hubbard Blakeslee.* Worcester, Mass.: Clark University Press, 1949, pp. 153–70. This essay comparing the two peace conferences following the two world wars will be of particular interest to students concerned with comparative history. Benns expresses some provocative judgments.

19:221 Birdsall, Paul. "The Second Decade of Peace Conference History." *Journal of Modern History* 11:3 (1939), 362–78. This important historiographical essay notes the continued concern with "principles and personalities." Birdsall also suggests that the published documents on the peace conference allow scholars to begin an examination of national policies and policymaking.

19:222   Hankey, Maurice P. *The Supreme Control at the Paris Peace Conference 1919: A Commentary.* London: Allen & Unwin, 1963. This last substantial writing from Sir Maurice Hankey, British secretary of various commissions during and after the World War, is especially useful to scholars anxious to understand the administrative procedures and organization of the peace conference.

19:223   Lauren, Paul G. "Human Rights in History: Diplomacy and Racial Equality at the Paris Peace Conference." *Diplomatic History* 2:3 (1978), 257–78. The peacemakers not only refused to adopt the principle of racial equality, despite Japanese pleadings, but even refused to recognize that this issue was of intense concern to many peoples.

19:224   Mantoux, Paul. *Paris Peace Conference: Proceedings of the Council of Four, March 24–April 18.* Geneva: Libraire Droz, 1964. This English translation of the minutes of the Council of Four meetings as recorded by the French secretary, Paul Mantoux, contains material that the historian will not find in the British minutes.

19:225   Marston, Frank S. *The Peace Conference of 1919.* London: Oxford University Press, 1944. This is a basic description of the organization and procedures used at the peace conference. Students will find Marston's work useful in understanding how the conference functioned.

19:226   Mayer, Arno J. *Politics and Diplomacy at Peacemaking: Containment and Counterrevolution at Versailles 1918–1919.* New York: Knopf, 1967. This large study shows the interrelationships of domestic to foreign policy considerations in the participating nations during the course of the peace conference. Mayer is concerned with how the conference responded to the threat of revolution from the Left and counterrevolution from the political Right.

19:227   Nicolson, Harold. *Peacemaking, 1919: Being Reminiscences of the Paris Peace Conference.* Boston: Houghton Mifflin, 1933. This memoir by an able British diplomatist offers a valuable view of the atmosphere in which negotiations were conducted.

19:228   Startt, James D. "Wilson's Mission to Paris: The Making of a Decision." *Historian* 30:4 (1968),

599–616. Describes the autumn 1918 argument in the press, among his advisers, and in Congress, about the question of sending a U.S. delegation headed by President Wilson to the Paris Peace Conference.

19:229   Temperley, H. W. V., ed. *A History of the Peace Conference of Paris.* 6 vols. London: Frowde, Hodder & Stoughton, 1920–1924. This work combines narrative description with selected documentary appendixes. The many authors of individual chapters were, in most instances, participants in the British or American delegations.

19:230   Thompson, Charles T. *The Peace Conference Day by Day.* New York: Brentano, 1920. The value of this volume is that it provides students with an easy chronological guide to the activities of the peace conference of 1919.

NATIONS AND INTERESTS

For evaluations of foreign diplomats' memoirs, see Toscano (19:8).

19:231   Duff, John B. "The Versailles Treaty and the Irish-Americans." *Journal of American History* 55:3 (1968), 582–98. In 1917–1918, Irish Americans supported President Wilson prior to his departure for Paris; by the summer of 1919, however, the president's relationship with influential Irish-American leaders had cooled.

19:232   Dumin, Frederick. "Self-Determination: The United States and Austria in 1919." *Research Studies* 40:3 (1972), 176–94. Dumin discusses the proposed Austro-German Anschluss of November 1918 and the reasons why the American delegation ultimately rejected the idea at the Paris Peace Conference.

19:233   Kahn, Robert, et al., eds. *The Habsburg Empire in World War I: Essays on the Intellectual, Military, Political and Economic Aspects of the Hapsburg War Effort.* Boulder, Colo.: East European Quarterly, 1977. This collection of essays examines various institutions and sources of conflict which ultimately led to the dissolution of the Hapsburg empire. For American historians, perhaps the most relevant essay is that of Paula S. Fichtner, entitled, "Americans and the Disintegration of the Hapsburg Monarchy: The Shaping of a Historiographical Model."

19:234   Mamatey, Victor S. *The United States and East Central Europe, 1914–1918: A Study in Wilsonian Diplomacy and Propaganda*. Princeton, N.J.: Princeton University Press, 1957. Mamatey describes the evolution of American policies toward the Austro-Hungarian empire and ultimately the dismemberment of that empire prior to the commencement of the Paris Peace Conference in January 1919.

19:235   Pomerance, Michla. "The United States and Self-Determination: Perspectives on the Wilsonian Conception." *American Journal of International Law* 70:1 (1976), 1–27. Idealists blame Woodrow Wilson for the failure of the principle of self-determination; realists consider it an impractical moralistic slogan; radicals believe it is a disguise for economic imperialism. Actually, the principle is ambiguous.

France

19:236   Andrew, C. M., and Kanya-Forstner, A. S. "The French Colonial Party and French Colonial War Aims, 1914–1918." *Historical Journal* 17:1 (1974), 79–106. The French colonialists claimed for France a zone from the Tarsus Mountains to the Sinai; but they got only the northern part, in the Sykes-Picot deal. Continuing to dominate French imperial policy, the colonialists won Cameroon in Africa, and beat back Italian claims there and in Asia Minor.

19:237   McCrum, Robert. "French Rhineland Policy at the Paris Peace Conference, 1919." *Historical Journal* 21:3 (1978), 623–48. French military efforts to help the separatists establish an independent Rhineland failed for lack of public support in the affected areas, while Allied opposition led Clemenceau to accept Allied economic and strategic guarantees of French national security.

19:238   Yates, Louis A. R. *The United States and French Security, 1917–1921: A Study in American Diplomatic History*. New York: Twayne, 1957. This study of the American guarantee treaty of French security remains valuable for its broad coverage of this important question.

Germany

19:239   Bane, Suda L. *The Blockade of Germany after the Armistice, 1918–1919*. Stanford, Calif.: Stanford University Press, 1942. Insofar as the United States is here treated, relevant topics among the many documents include the delivery methods and value of relief shipped from America to the Allies, neutrals, and Germany, and the resumption of trade with Germany.

19:240   Nelson, Harold. *Land and Power: British and Allied Policy on Germany's Frontiers, 1916–1919*. London: Routledge & Kegan Paul, 1963. This work examines the negotiations of the German territorial settlement at the Paris Peace Conference. The British viewpoint and Anglo-American cooperation are stressed.

19:241   Schwabe, Klaus. *Deutsche Revolution und Wilson-Frieden: Die Amerikanische und Deutsche Friedens-strategie Zwischen Ideologie und Macht-politik, 1918–1919*. [German revolution and Wilsonian peace: the American and German peace strategy between ideology and power politics, 1918–1919]. Düsseldorf: Droste, 1971. An important study based on German and American source materials for understanding the American-German relationship and the various negotiations undertaken during the critical months immediately following the war and during the peace conference.

19:242   Schwabe, Klaus. "Woodrow Wilson and Germany's Membership in the League of Nations, 1918–19." *Central European History* 8 (1975), 3–22. Wilson first believed that Germany should be a member, then that she should not, then that she should only be admitted to the league when she disarmed.

19:243   Schwarzschild, Leopold. *World in Trance: From Versailles to Pearl Harbor*. New York: Fischer, 1942. In the first part of this work, Schwarzschild is concerned with Germany's strategy toward the armistice and toward the peace settlement.

Great Britain

See, under "Personalities," "Foreign," David Lloyd George.

19:244   Boothe, Leon E. "A Fettered Envoy: Lord Grey's Mission to the United States, 1919–1920." *Review of Politics* 33:1 (1971), 78–94. Grey, a former foreign secretary, seemed a likely candidate for the vacant position of British ambassador to the United States. Instead, he was commissioned a special envoy and charged with solving all outstanding problems between the two countries.

19:245 Tillman, Seth P. *Anglo-American Relations at the Paris Peace Conference of 1919*. Princeton, N.J.: Princeton University Press, 1961. This volume offers the most comprehensive treatment of the American participation at the peace conference of 1919, extending beyond the signing of the Versailles Treaty in late June.

Hungary

See, under "Personalities," Herbert C. Hoover.

19:246 Hopkins, George W. "The Politics of Food: United States and Soviet Hungary, March–August, 1919." *Mid-America* 55:4 (1973), 245–70. The Allies chose Herbert Hoover's food blockade policy rather than Marshal Foch's policy of force to bring down the coalition government of Hungary's Bolshevik leader Bela Kun.

19:247 Pastor, Peter. "The Hungarian Revolution's Road from Wilsonianism to Leninism, 1918–19." *East Central Europe* 3:2 (1976), 210–19. Pastor challenges Arno Mayer's (19:226) contention that the Károlyi government in Hungary, 1918, had little or no ideological basis. He asserts that Mihály Károlyi embraced Wilsonianism as a revolutionary ideology because he felt it would radically change the country's antiquated social, political, and economic structure.

19:248 Smallwood, James. "Banquo's Ghost at the Paris Peace Conference: The United States and the Hungarian Question." *East European Quarterly* 12:3 (1978), 289–307. The author describes the reactions of American advisers to Bela Kun's communist takeover in Hungary. Woodrow Wilson understood the causes of bolshevism better than his advisers, but a number of factors limited his policy.

Italy and Yugoslavia

19:249 Albrecht-Carrié, René. *Italy at the Peace Conference*. New York: Columbia University Press, 1938. Italian ambitions, objectives, and claims formed an imposing problem at the peace conference. Though narrowly constructed, limited primarily to the negotiations at the conference, this work is the major study of Italy's contest with Wilsonian diplomacy.

19:250 Lederer, Ivo J. *Yugoslavia at the Paris Peace Conference: A Study in Frontier Making*. New Haven, Conn.: Yale University Press, 1963. This monograph offers a careful analysis of the controversies between the new Yugoslav state and Italy over the status of Fiume and Istria.

19:251 Page, Thomas N. *Italy and the World War*. New York: Scribner's, 1920. The American ambassador to Italy (1913–1919) provides a very sympathetic history of Italy, Italian war aims, and the Italian people.

19:252 Zivojinović, Dragan R. *America, Italy, and the Birth of Yugoslavia (1917–1919)*. New York: Columbia University Press, 1972. This comprehensive history focuses on American-Italian relations during the war and the peace conference.

19:253 Zivojinović, Dragan R. "The Emergence of American Policy in the Adriatic: December 1917–April 1919." *East European Quarterly* 1:3 (1967), 173–215. Zivojinović traces the change of American policy in the Italian-Yugoslav dispute over Adriatic territory following World War I. The basic question was the disposition of the former Adriatic territories of Austria-Hungary.

Soviet Union

See, under "Personalities," William C. Bullitt, and, under "Others," David R. Francis.

19:254 Fike, Claude E. "The United States and Russian Territorial Problems, 1917–1920." *Historian* 24:3 (1962), 331–46. President Wilson's vow to support national self-determination is analyzed in this article with regard to the Russian regions of the Ukraine, Georgia, and Turkestan.

19:255 Filene, Peter G. *Americans and the Soviet Experiment, 1917–1933*. Cambridge: Harvard University Press, 1967. In the first two chapters, the author traces the abrupt shift from a favorable attitude toward the Russian Revolution of March 1917, to a hostile attitude after the Bolsheviks came to power in November 1917.

19:256 Fry, Michael G. "Britain, the Allies, and the Problem of Russia, 1918–1919." *Canadian Journal of History* 2:1 (1967), 62–84. The author delineates the different British views on Allied intervention in Russia and demonstrates how these differences contributed to the difficulties of Allied planning.

19:257 Kennan, George F. "Russia and the Versailles Conference." *American Scholar* 30:1 (1960/1961), 13–42. Kennan describes Wilson's illness, the Hoover relief program, and the important effects that leaving Russia out of the peace conference had on future international developments.

19:258 Kennan, George F. *Soviet-American Relations, 1917–1920.* 2 vols. Princeton, N.J.: Princeton University Press, 1956–1958. Various aspects of this monumental study have been reinterpreted and elaborated upon, but it remains the most comprehensive narrative of Soviet-American relations from 1917 to 1920. Bibliography.

19:259 Lasch, Christopher. *American Liberals and the Russian Revolution.* New York: Columbia University Press, 1962. This work describes how the Russian Revolution exacerbated differences in outlook between two groups of American liberals, the "war liberals" and the "anti-imperialists." American foreign policy failed because the anti-imperialists declined to challenge directly the principles of the war liberals.

19:260 Thompson, John M. *Russia, Bolshevism, and the Versailles Peace.* Princeton, N.J.: Princeton University Press, 1967. This study thoroughly examines Allied and American planning on Russian recognition and the containment of Bolshevik expansion at the Paris Peace Conference. Extensive bibliography.

19:261 Ullman, Richard H. *Anglo-Soviet Relations, 1917–1921.* 2 vols. Princeton, N.J.: Princeton University Press, 1961–1968. The two volumes are subtitled *Intervention and the War* and *Britain and the Russian Civil War.* American policy toward Russia is treated here as dependent on British aims and evaluations. This is the most comprehensive work available on British policy toward Russia for the years 1918 through 1921. See Woodward (19:276).

Allied Intervention, 1917–1920

19:262 Bradley, John. *Allied Intervention in Russia.* New York: Basic Books, 1968. Useful as a single-volume survey of the Allied intervention in Russia, this book adds little to the historiographical debate. Bibliography.

19:263 Davis, Donald E., and Trani, Eugene P. "The American YMCA and the Russian Revolution." *Slavic Review* 33:3 (1974), 469–91. As the Communists tightened the screws of repression, YMCA

personnel retaliated by aiding the regime's opponents, primarily in Siberia.

19:264 Dupuy, Richard E. *Perish by the Sword: The Czechoslovakian Anabasis and Our Supporting Campaigns in North Russia and Siberia, 1918–1920.* Harrisburg, Pa.: Military Service Publishing, 1939. In a severely critical work, the author describes how Allied and American military policy in north Russia and Siberia made for a disastrous campaign. Blame is laid upon the State Department.

19:265 Graves, William S. *America's Siberian Adventure, 1918–1920.* New York: Cape & Smith, 1931. The commander of the American forces in Siberia criticizes sharply the efforts of the State Department, foreign governments, and Allied military commanders to embroil American forces in the Russian Civil War.

19:266 Guins, George C. "The Siberian Intervention, 1918–1919." *Russian Review* 28:4 (1969), 428–40. This article provides a brief description of the military and political situation existing in Siberia at the time of the Allied intervention.

19:267 Kennan, George F. "Soviet Historiography and America's Role in the Intervention." *American Historical Review* 65:2 (1960), 302–22. Kennan denounces the lack of objectivity in Soviet historical writing and points out that such work contributes little to international scholarly debate.

19:268 Lasch, Christopher. "American Intervention in Siberia: Reinterpretation." *Political Science Quarterly* 77:2 (1962), 205–23. Lasch concludes that current American opinion regarding Germany prompted Wilson's decision.

19:269 Maddox, Robert J. *The Unknown War with Russia: Wilson's Siberian Intervention.* San Rafael, Calif.: Presidio Press, 1977. This work concludes that Wilson embraced the decision to intervene in Siberia to assure the success of his plan for world peace.

19:270 Morley, James W. *The Japanese Thrust into Siberia, 1918.* New York: Columbia University Press, 1957. The author discusses the Japanese policymaking process, the split between Asia-first and West-first cliques, and the importance the Japanese attached to cooperative relations with Americans in East Asia.

19:271 Strakhovsky, Leonid I. *Intervention at Archangel: The Story of Allied Intervention and Russian*

Counter-Revolution in North Russia, 1918–1920. Princeton, N.J.: Princeton University Press, 1944. This study is a broader, more detailed sequel to his earlier work *The Origins of American Intervention in North Russia, 1918.* It is dated but still worth reading.

19:272 Trani, Eugene P. "Woodrow Wilson and the Decision to Intervene in Russia: A Reconsideration." *Journal of Modern History* 48:3 (1976), 440–61. It was Allied pressure for intervention, emanating especially from the British, that became the most important factor in the president's decision to send American troops to Russia.

19:273 Unterberger, Betty M. *America's Siberian Expedition, 1918–1920.* New York: Greenwood (1956), 1969. A good starting point for the historiography of the American intervention into north Russia and Siberia, this book is a balanced account of American motives and of the international complications and reactions aroused by the Russia Revolution.

19:274 White, John A. *The Siberian Intervention.* Princeton, N.J.: Princeton University Press, 1950. Primary emphasis is given to the Russian-Japanese rivalry for control over Siberia. The American intervention, the author argues, was meant to block Japan from absorbing Siberia.

19:275 Williams, William A. "The American Intervention in Russia, 1917–1920." *Studies on the Left* 3:4 (1963), 24–48. In a reply to George Kennan and other postwar writers, Williams asserts that Wilson's anti-Bolshevik sentiments led him to agree to join the Allied intervention in Siberia.

19:276 Woodward, David R. "The British Government and Japanese Intervention in Russia during World War One." *Journal of Modern History* 46:4 (1974), 663–85. New source material on the British point of view requires modification of Richard Ullman's *Intervention and the War* (19:261).

Africa and Pan-Africanism

See Chapter 18, "U.S., Africa, and the Peace Conference, 1919."

Middle Eastern Affairs

See Chapter 18, "Paris Peace Conference."

SPECIAL STUDIES

19:277 Binkley, Robert C. *Selected Papers of Robert C. Binkley.* Cambridge: Harvard University Press, 1948. Binkley was America's first historian to write critically about the peace conference of 1919. The three articles reprinted here were first published in the 1920s and early 1930s, but their insights remain of value to present scholars.

19:278 Birdsall, Paul. *Versailles Twenty Years After.* New York: Reynal & Hitchcock, 1941. Reprint 1962. Basically sympathetic to Wilson's diplomacy at the peace conference, this work tries to explain why the Versailles Treaty turned out as it did. The book still has considerable value.

19:279 Seymour, Charles. *Geography, Justice, and Politics at The Peace Conference of 1919.* New York: American Geographical Society, 1951. In this brief monograph, Seymour explains the relation of political geography to the European settlement, largely through the activities of Isaiah Bowman.

19:280 Sprout, Harold, and Sprout, Margaret. *Toward a New Order of Sea Power: American Naval Policy and the World Scene, 1918–1922.* Princeton, N.J.: Princeton University Press, 1940. Chapter 5 is especially important, as it bears on the relation between the League of Nations and naval power.

The Armistice

19:281 Rudin, Harry R. *Armistice, 1918.* Hamden, Conn.: Shoe String Press (1944), 1967. This work focuses attention on the negotiations leading to the German armistice; unfortunately, it was published prior to the opening of the belligerents' archives. Still, it offers an excellent introduction to the subject.

19:282 Walworth, Arthur. *America's Moment: 1918, American Diplomacy at the End of World War I.* New York: Norton, 1977. Walworth focuses attention on the period between the conclusion of military hostilities and the beginnings of the peace conference of 1919.

The Inquiry

19:283 Gelfand, Lawrence E. *The Inquiry: American Preparations for Peace, 1917–1919.* New Haven,

Conn.: Yale University Press, 1963. Reprint 1976. This is an administrative study of the independent bureau established by Wilson in September 1917 to develop an American peace program. Gelfand draws comparisons between the Inquiry's recommendations and the actual terms found in the treaties.

19:284 Haskins, C. H., and Lord, R. H. *Some Problems of the Paris Peace Conference.* Cambridge: Harvard University Press, 1920. Haskins was chief of the Western European Division of the Inquiry and Lord, who was instrumental in arrangements leading to the establishment of the new Polish state, was chief of the Eastern European Division. Both men were members of the American peace commission at Paris.

Reparations Issue

See "Personalities," especially (under "Others") Thomas W. Lamont; also Chapter 20, "German Reparations (Dawes Plan)."

19:285 Baruch, Bernard M. *Making the Reparations and Economic Sections of the Treaty.* New York: Harper, 1920. Baruch was economic adviser to the American Commission to Negotiate Peace and a member of every important economic and reparations committee at Paris. These recollections form an important part of the record concerning American intentions for reparations.

19:286 Bunselmeyer, Robert E. *The Cost of the War, 1914–1919: British Economic War Aims and the Origins of Reparation.* Hamden, Conn.: Shoe String Press, 1975. This is a reinterpretation of the concept and practice of assigning and assessing reparation as a part of the peace settlement.

19:287 Burnett, Philip M. *Reparation at the Paris Peace Conference from the Standpoint of the American Delegation.* 2 vols. New York: Columbia University Press, 1940. This work remains the standard, comprehensive treatment of the reparations question. The first volume consists of a narrative; the second is a valuable compilation of relevant documentation.

19:288 Keynes, John Maynard. *The Economic Consequences of the Peace.* New York: Harcourt, Brace & Howe, 1920. An early, devastating critique of Wilsonian statesmanship at the peace conference by the British economist, who served in the British delegation at Paris.

19:289 Mantoux, Étiene. *The Carthaginian Peace: Or, the Economic Consequences of Mr. Keynes.* New York: Scribner's, 1952. In an antidote to Keynes's *Economic Consequences of the Peace,* Mantoux argues that the reparations forced upon defeated Germany after the war were not excessive.

19:290 Pruessen, Ronald W. "John Foster Dulles and Reparations at the Paris Peace Conference, 1919: Early Patterns of Life." *Perspectives in American History* 8 (1974), 381–410. Dulles played a significant part as legal adviser in settling questions on reparations. He helped force the Allies to exclude war costs from the total German obligation.

Public Response

Adler, S. "The War-Guilt Question and American Disillusionment, 1918–1928" (21:129) argues that during the postwar decade, American disillusionment arose as publicists and revisionist historians cast doubt upon the motives of American leaders (1917–1919) in seeking American involvement in the war, in seeking national aggrandizement, and in forcing a vindictive settlement on Germany.

19:291 Duff, John B. "German-Americans and the Peace, 1918–1920." *American Jewish Historical Quarterly* 59:4 (1970), 424–44. This article describes German-American opinion of Wilson's peace initiatives and seeks to explain the German-American denunciation of Wilson in the 1920 elections.

19:292 Gerson, Louis L. *Woodrow Wilson and the Rebirth of Poland, 1914–1920: A Study in the Influence on American Policy of Minority Groups of Foreign Origin.* New Haven, Conn.: Yale University Press, 1953. This monograph emphasizes the activities of pressure groups in the United States on behalf of the formation of a postwar, independent Polish national state.

19:293 Noble, George B. *Policies and Opinions at Paris, 1919: Wilsonian Diplomacy, the Versailles Peace and French Public Opinion.* New York: Macmillan, 1935. This work derives from Noble's assumption that the ills of the mid-1930s "can in large measure be ascribed to the devastation and dislocation of the World War and to the failure of the peace makers of 1919 to establish a viable international order."

19:294 O'Grady, Joseph P., ed. *The Immigrants' Influence on Wilson's Peace Policies.* Lexington:

University of Kentucky Press, 1967. This collection of essays focuses on the efforts of eleven immigrant groups to influence President Wilson's peace program.

19:295   Startt, James D. "The Uneasy Partnership: Wilson and the Press at Paris." *Mid-America* 52:1 (1970), 55–69. During the war, Wilson was rather distant in dealing with newsmen, but on the eve of his departure for the peace conference he made efforts to assure less strained relations.

THE LEAGUE OF NATIONS

See, under "Personalities," Hiram W. Johnson, Henry Cabot Lodge, Elihu Root, James T. Shotwell.

19:296   Bartlett, Ruhl J. *The League to Enforce Peace.* Chapel Hill: University of North Carolina Press, 1944. This history of the League to Enforce Peace describes the activities, policies, and philosophies of the league, and its efforts to muster popular support for the League of Nations movement.

19:297   Boothe, Leon E. "Anglo-American Pro-League Groups Lead Wilson 1915–1918." *Mid-America* 51:1 (1969), 92–107. Exasperation in both countries heightened as Wilson's vagueness persisted. In the United States it retarded efforts to educate the general public on a postwar league concept; conversely, in England opinion had been developed carefully to support such a program by late 1918.

Coudert, F. R. *A Half-Century of International Problems: A Lawyer's View* (20:10), in sections 5 and 6 of this book, deals with the legal dimensions of World War I and comments on American participation in international organizations.

19:298   Egerton, George W. *Great Britain and the League of Nations: Strategy, Politics and International Organization, 1914–1919.* Chapel Hill: University of North Carolina Press, 1978. This study examines the development of the League of Nations idea in Britain and the effects of the "new" diplomacy and the League of Nations movement on Britain's strategic position.

19:299   Fleming, Denna F. *The United States and the League of Nations, 1918–1920.* New York: Putnam's, 1932. This study remains one of the standard works on the League of Nations controversy in the United States

as Wilson battled to gain public acceptance of the league in the Senate.

Fosdick, R. B. *Letters on the League of Nations: From the Files of Raymond B. Fosdick* (20:85) contains the correspondence of Fosdick, appointed by Wilson as undersecretary general of the League of Nations (1919–1920). These materials focus on the attitudes of American liberals toward the league.

Kuehl, W. F. *Seeking World Order: The United States and International Organization to 1920* (16:35) sees the years 1890 to 1920 as the crucial, formative years of American internationalist thought, and the fight for the League of Nations as the climax of more than a century of American internationalist agitation.

19:300   Marburg, Theodore. *Development of the League of Nations Idea: Documents and Correspondence of Theodore Marburg.* 2 vols. Ed. by John H. Latane. New York: Macmillan, 1932. Marburg, along with John Hays Hammond, James T. Shotwell, and others was a leading internationalist of the Wilson era.

19:301   Marburg, Theodore, and Flack, Horace E., eds. *Taft Papers on League of Nations.* New York: Macmillan, 1920. As president of the League to Enforce Peace, Taft's position among advocates of a League of Nations was preeminent.

19:302   Walters, Francis P. *A History of the League of Nations.* 2 vols. London: Oxford University Press, 1952. This is the standard history of the League of Nations. Volume 1 covers the origins of the league idea, its development during the war, and the drafting of the covenant.

Drafting the League Covenant

See Miller (19:10) for documents.

19:303   Curry, George W. "Woodrow Wilson, Jan Smuts, and the Versailles Settlement." *American Historical Review* 66:4 (1961), 968–86. Curry comments on the influence that Jan Christian Smuts of South Africa had on Wilson's thinking about the peace settlement and the unpopularity and eventual failure of the Smuts-Wilson approach.

19:304   Doty, Madeleine Z. *The Central Organisation for a Durable Peace (1915–1919).* Geneva: Institute Universitaire de hautes études internationales,

1945. American ideas and planners are brought into perspective in this description of a worldwide study group.

19:305 Dubin, Martin D. "The Carnegie Endowment for International Peace and the Advocacy of a League of Nations, 1914–1918." *Proceedings of the American Philosophical Society* 123:6 (1979), 344–68. Dubin focuses on the leaders of the endowment, Elihu Root, Nicholas Murray Butler, and James Brown Scott, showing how their legalistic and "voluntarist" approach to international cooperation differed from other views.

19:306 Dubin, Martin D. "Elihu Root and the Advocacy of a League of Nations, 1914–1917." *Western Political Quarterly* 19:3 (1966), 439–55. This article attempts to understand how Root could both advocate the league and, at the same time, help "to mastermind the Republican attack on the covenant." Root refused to believe that "paper arrangements" could be consistently or effectively applied.

19:307 Dubin, Martin D. "Toward the Concept of Collective Security: The Bryce Group's 'Proposals for the Avoidance of War,' 1914–1917." *International Organization* 24:2 (1970), 288–318. The proposals of Lord Bryce and his supporters for collective security and an international peacekeeping organization formed the basis for articles 12 to 17 of the covenant of the League of Nations.

19:308 Miller, David Hunter. *The Drafting of the Covenant.* 2 vols. New York: Putnam's, 1928. This is the standard, detailed account of the formulation of the League of Nations Covenant at the Paris Peace Conference by an important member of the American commission. Volume 1 is a narrative description; volume 2 contains the critically important documents.

Olson, W. C. "Theodore Roosevelt's Conception of an International League" (16:65) discusses the plans of 1914 and 1915 as well as Roosevelt's views (1917–1919).

19:309 Patterson, David S. "The United States and the Origins of the World Court." *Political Science Quarterly* 91:2 (1976), 259–77. After providing historical background (1890–1914), this essay concentrates on the impact of the war on international law assumptions and how thinkers responded. It also examines Wilson's opposition and notes how the covenant reflected a variety of views on the subject of a court.

Ratification Controversy

19:310 Abbott, Frank. "The Texas Press and the Covenant." *Red River Valley Historical Review* 4:1 (1979), 32–41. This survey of newspapers shows journalists generally praising Wilson, with considerable pro-league support, a broad moderate spectrum, and some nationalist but not isolationist views.

19:311 Egerton, George W. "Britain and the 'Great Betrayal': Anglo-American Relations and the Struggle for United States Ratification of the Treaty of Versailles." *Historical Journal* 21:4 (1978), 885–911. Egerton examines the attitudes and role of the British government (1919–1920) with regard to the fate of the Treaty of Versailles in the United States, and reassesses the efforts of Viscount Grey to gain U.S. ratification.

19:312 Fleming, Denna F. *The Treaty Veto of the American Senate.* New York: Putnam's, 1930. The interpretations of this book are dated, but it remains the preeminent narrative of the Senate debates on the Versailles Treaty.

19:313 Hewes, James E., Jr. "Henry Cabot Lodge and the League of Nations." *Proceedings of the American Philosophical Society* 114:4 (1970), 245–55. In a review of Lodge's senatorial position (1896–1920), the author finds him consistent in opposing universal commitments, yet not unreasonable in seeking some responsible position during the treaty fight.

Holt, W. S. *Treaties Defeated by the Senate: A Study of the Struggle between President and Senate over the Conduct of Foreign Relations* (2:150) examines the Senate's treatment of the Versailles Treaty, and breaks down the votes for the fifteen reservations and for the two attempts to obtain ratification without reservation.

19:314 Lodge, Henry Cabot. *The Senate and the League of Nations.* New York: Scribner's, 1925. This is Lodge's version of the Senate's handling of the League of Nations issue, along with his own opinions on the league.

19:315 Logan, Rayford W. *The Senate and the Versailles Mandate System.* Washington, D.C.: Minorities Publishers, 1945. Devoted exclusively to the Senate's consideration of article 22 of the League of Nations Covenant, the mandate question is considered within the context of the general debates on the

Treaty of Versailles, with the African and Armenian mandates receiving special attention.

19:316   Merritt, Richard L. "Woodrow Wilson and the 'Great and Solemn Referendum,' 1920." *Review of Politics* 27:1 (1965), 78–104. Based largely on the House diary and the collection of Wilson's papers edited by Ray Stannard Baker, this article describes Wilson's attempt to take the League of Nations issue to the American people.

Redmond, K. G. "Henry L. Stimson and the Question of League Membership" (20:88) reflects the sincere concern of international lawyers alarmed over article 10 and the disregard of evolutionary processes and legal procedures.

19:317   Rosenberger, Homer T. "The American Peace Society's Reaction to the Covenant of the League of Nations." *World Affairs* 141:2 (1978), 139–52. Rosenberger describes policies of the American Peace Society and its mixed reactions to the Paris Peace Conference and the drafting of the League of Nations Covenant.

19:318   Stern, Sheldon M. "American Nationalism vs. the League of Nations: The Correspondence of Albert J. Beveridge and Louis A. Coolidge, 1918–1920." *Indiana Magazine of History* 72:2 (1976), 138–58. This is a record of the correspondence between Albert J. Beveridge (Indiana) and Louis A. Coolidge (Massachusetts) during 1918 to 1920; both were expansionists and nationalists, and denounced Wilson's League of Nations proposal.

19:319   Stone, Ralph A. *The Irreconcilables: The Fight against the League of Nations.* Lexington: University of Kentucky Press, 1970. Stone explores the politics, philosophies, and tactics of the sixteen "irreconcilable" senators, revealing the diversity of their views and the uniformity of their resistance.

19:320   Vinson, John Chalmers. *Referendum for Isolation: The Defeat of Article Ten of the League of Nations Covenant.* Athens: University of Georgia Press, 1961. Vinson argues that the defeat of the League of Nations Covenant indicated the public's desire for an isolationist foreign policy.

19:321   Wimer, Kurt. "Woodrow Wilson and a Third Nomination." *Pennsylvania History* 29:2 (1963), 193–211. Wilson, according to the author, was serious about pursuing a third term and intent on making his campaign a referendum for the League of Nations.

19:322   Wimer, Kurt. "Woodrow Wilson Tries Conciliation: An Effort That Failed." *Historian* 25:4 (1963), 419–38. Wimer contends that Wilson was more flexible in his relations with the Senate over the league question than is usually contended.

19:323   Wimer, Kurt. "Woodrow Wilson's Plan for a Vote of Confidence." *Pennsylvania History* 28:3 (1961), 279–93. As the final element in his strategy, Wilson proposed during late 1919–1920 a solemn referendum allowing voters the opportunity to decide the issue.

19:324   Wimer, Kurt. "Woodrow Wilson's Plans to Enter the League of Nations through an Executive Agreement." *Western Political Quarterly* 11:4 (1958), 800–12. Wimer makes a plausible case for believing that Wilson sought to have the United States enter the league through an executive agreement, but Wilson gave up this plan when his legal advisers indicated it would be contrary to the American Constitution.

20

Internationalism, Isolationism, Disarmament, and Economics, 1920–1937

Contributing Editor

ROBERT H. FERRELL
Indiana University

Ross Gregory
Western Michigan University

Contributors

Peter Buckingham
Southwest Texas State University

Robert A. Hart
University of Massachusetts

John Garry Clifford
University of Connecticut

William Kamman
North Texas State University

Charles DeBenedetti
University of Toledo

Carl P. Parrini
Northern Illinois University

Justus D. Doenecke
University of South Florida

Roland N. Stromberg
University of Wisconsin at Milwaukee

Contents

Introduction

The dismal period in American foreign relations from 1920 to 1937 marks clearly a time when the great republic of the New World retreated from involvement in affairs everywhere—political affairs, that is—and Americans hoped that having made the world safe for democracy, they could enjoy their own country and other peoples could enjoy theirs. In view of what came afterward, in view of the disintegration of world peace and the coming of a second world war, there was every reason for the people of the United States to have taken the keenest interest in the politics of Europe and the other continents. Instead the wish became father to the thought, and the policy of isolation led to disaster.

Some people might argue now, and many people argued at the time, that there was no reason for Americans to have intervened anywhere, that the world was capable of ordering itself without American intervention. Strictly speaking, in terms of the military power and the political experience possessed by the governments of Great Britain and France, the two triumphant European democracies in World War I, enough power and political ability was at hand, had it been engaged for good ends, that is, for European and world peace. But the failures of other countries should not, so most observers now would say, excuse the failure of Americans during a seedtime of disaster.

The long title of this chapter pinpoints the diplomatic threads, the major ideas, the principles of the era 1920 to 1937, and the failure of American policy is easy to discern from considering these. Internationalism should have been the course of American diplomacy, but was not. It had been laid down as a principle by President Woodrow Wilson, whose settlement of the European war (as Americans were careful to call the World War by 1920) was apparently a recognized failure by 1920. Internationalism was dead before the presidential election of 1920, when two small-town Ohio newspapermen, James Cox of Dayton and Warren Harding of Marion, competed for the presidency. Cox came out for the League of Nations, trying his best to support the ailing Wilson, but Cox never had a chance. The movement away from internationalism was almost glacial in its proportions. Harding carefully came out for an association of nations, as he described his international hopes, but the word *association* meant nothing to the Marion candidate and he quickly forgot it after the election. The result was that the most powerful country economically in the world, and potentially the greatest military power in the world, chose not to participate politically in world affairs. The result was, as Selig Adler relates in the title of one of his books, *The Uncertain Giant* (20:8), a country that would not wield its own power.

The policy of isolationism seemed expressive of the purposes of almost everyone in the United States, and there was no real argument over it. Historian Raymond J. Sontag many years later could describe the world after 1918 as *A Broken World* (21:16), but Americans did not see international affairs that way, and chose to believe that plenty of military power and political knowhow were available if governments elsewhere, notably in Europe, chose to order world affairs. Isolationism went so far in the early 1930s that an Indiana congressman named Louis Ludlow called for a national referendum before the nation could again go to war, so that no internationalist-minded Woodrow Wilson would be able to fool the country into war. Ernest C. Bolt, Jr., set out this fantasy in his *Ballots before Bullets: The War Referendum Approach to Peace in America, 1914–1941* (19:163). An even more activist approach to isolationism had been taken some years earlier, in 1928, when most of the nations of the world collectively pledged to renounce war as an instrument of national policy (Robert H. Ferrell, *Peace in Their Time* [20:116]), and after this sort of pledge, war seemed impossible. And so, Americans thought, why offer the Europeans any help, since Americans already had banished war, or at least taken European promises not to go to war?

The United States government, with enthusiastic agreement from Atlantic to Pacific, did endorse one idea in favor of international peace, and that was disarmament. Early in the 1920s, Viscount Grey published his memoirs of the era before the World War, and said that the level of armaments was an exact indication of the warlike or peaceful tendencies of nation-states—that arms were like a thermometer of international trouble—and that great armaments caused great wars. This remarkable opinion from the man who had helped construct Britain's secret agreements with the government of France, agreements that more than anything else helped involve Britain in World War I, seemed believable after the war, when memories must have been dulled, and Americans certainly considered Grey a seer. Americans had their own reasons for favoring disarmament, mainly naval reasons; the American navy was taking a large part of the national budget, and it seemed redundant that the three largest post-1918 navies were the British, the American, and the Japanese, all nations on the victorious side. The result in the 1920s and early 1930s was a series of naval conferences, notably the conference of 1921–1922, described by Thomas H. Buckley, *The United States and the Washington Conference* (20:152). Raymond G. O'Connor set out the result of the London Naval Conference of 1930 with the uncertain title, *Perilous Equilibrium* (20:162). Despite the signs by 1930 that naval disarmament was not working well, belief in it lingered well into the mid-1930s, until the second London Conference, of 1935–1936, failed. Meanwhile the League of nations was trying to arrange for disarmament on land, and that effort failed at the Geneva World Disarmament Conference of 1932–1934.

By the mid-1930s, close to the end of the era of isolationism, only economics was left for American policy, and an old Wilsonian, Franklin D. Roosevelt's secretary of state, Cordell Hull of Tennessee, tried to bring world peace through economics with the Reciprocal Trade Agreements Act of 1934. The effort was ill-fated, for it dealt of course only with American policy, and individual agreements by each nation, perhaps sixty or seventy by that time, with every other nation, a sum of several thousand agreements, would have been necessary before world trade could open up through reciprocity. Other efforts to arrange international trade more easily, through settling the war debts-reparations tangle, the Dawes Plan and the Young Plan of the 1920s, the Hoover moratorium of the early 1930s, the negotiations in Washington early in 1933, came to naught as the Great Depression caught up Europe, the United States, and the industrialized parts of the world in so enormous an economic slowdown that some countries turned to dictatorships, and war came at the end of the decade.

In considering the principal diplomatic ideas of the 1920s, a modest debate has arisen over the meaning of American isolationism, and it deserves a short explanation. William Appleman Williams, the leader in cold war and other revisionism in the 1960s and 1970s, argues in a much cited article—"The Legend of Isolationism in the 1920's" (20:130)—that the decade and maybe later years was one of "express and extended involvement with—and intervention in the affairs of—other nations of the world." It was not therefore, he contends, an era of isolationism. But critics point out that since the United States government abstained during this era from political interference abroad, notably in Europe where the politics of the Continent were in disarray and leading to disaster, the country really was isolationist in the only area that counted. Individual readers must make up their minds about this issue.

In the years after World War II, the U.S. State Department opened its records for the 1920s and 1930s, and many books and articles were written therefrom; amendments to these books and articles became possible when the British government opened its records somewhat later. But is there more that scholars can do for the era? In recent years books have appeared on non–State Department activities—peace groups, internationalist organizations, personalities who affected foreign affairs, such movements as the Ludlow Amendment idea of the early 1930s. Students of the State Department itself have examined the elites of the department, and the ways in which decisions were made. Research possibilities still exist for the period 1920 to 1937 in the area of bringing together the facetlike investigations, of generalizing from the research done during the past third of a century, or else from looking at the United States from the vantage of Europeans, or of Asians. It is possible also to examine more thoroughly the economics of the period, looking in greater detail at war debts, or the patterns of trade, or trade associations, or the sorts of businesses that traded, and asking about the effect on political relations, that is, on diplomatic relations. There also has been perhaps too much crude labeling of purposes during the 1920s and early 1930s, of Republican policy or Democratic policy, or presidential labeling of Harding, Coolidge, Hoover, etc., diplomacy. The labels should come off. In such ways are research opportunities open to students who desire to see how in the later 1930s the nations of Europe and the world, with the United States almost standing by until the spring of 1941, again could go to war.

Resources and Overviews

RESEARCH AIDS

While pertinent bibliographies and reference aids are listed here, there are more extensive lists in Chapter 1.

Bibliographies

Braisted, W. R. "The Navy in the Early Twentieth Century, 1890–1941" (19:3) contains material which relates to the naval limitation treaties of the 1920s and 1930s, and navy plans and activities generally in the interwar era.

Burns, R. D. *Arms Control and Disarmament: A Bibliography* (1:25) offers many references to interwar arms control efforts, including the armistice (1918) and Versailles Treaty, pp. 143–49; naval treaties, beginning p. 149; and League of Nations, pp. 71–79.

Dexter, B., ed. *The Foreign Affairs Fifty-Year Bibliography: New Evaluation of Significant Books on International Relations, 1920–1970* (1:14) is a very useful condensation and new evaluation of books listed in the *Foreign Affairs Bibliographies* (1:15).

Doenecke, J. D., ed. *The Literature of Isolationism: A Guide to Non-Interventionist Scholarship, 1930–1972* (1:24).

20:1   Field, Norman S., ed. *League of Nations and United Nations Monthly List of Selected Articles: Cumulative 1920–1970.* 6 vols. Dobbs Ferry, N.Y.: Oceana, 1971. These articles are organized alphabetically by country.

Foreign Affairs Bibliography: A Selected and Annotated List of Books on International Relations (1:15) is issued at ten-year intervals, and each volume has three parts: "General International Relations"; "The World since 1914"; and "The World by Regions." Useful aid.

20:2   Stewart, William J., ed. *The Era of Franklin D. Roosevelt: A Selected Bibliography of Periodical, Essay, and Dissertation Literature, 1945–1971.* 2d

ed. Hyde Park, N.Y.: Franklin D. Roosevelt Library, 1974. This nicely annotated bibliography contains works on other subjects than diplomacy, but it is a handy reference to articles and dissertations about the Roosevelt era (1933–1945).

Yearbooks and Other Aids

Survey of International Affairs (1:146) covers the international relations of the world, with detailed attention to Europe during the interwar decades.

United States in World Affairs (1:147) is an annual survey of American foreign relations from 1931, under varying authorship. It is valuable for contemporary viewpoints.

Document Collections

More general collections are listed in Chapter 1, and other collections may be found in "Personalities," below.

20:3   Degras, Jane, ed. *Soviet Documents on Foreign Policy.* 3 vols. London: Oxford University Press, 1951–1952. Volume 1 covers 1917 to 1924; volume 2, 1925 to 1932; volume 3, 1933 to 1941. This useful collection on Soviet interwar diplomacy contains items from the commissariat for foreign affairs—interviews, speeches, dispatches, treaties not in the League of Nations series, and Communist party papers. Bibliography.

Documents on International Affairs (1:340) covers international affairs throughout the world, but is rich on European affairs and broadly representative of American diplomacy toward the Continent.

20:4   Great Britain. Foreign Office. *Documents on British Foreign Policy, 1919–1939.* London: H.M.S.O., 1946–. The British government has been generous in publication of public papers; and the above collection, still in process, is of enormous value to the student of diplomacy—not only for coverage of Anglo-American relations but also for documents on disarmament, East Asia, and other topics of interest to the United States.

Hackworth, G. H., ed. *Digest of International Law* [1789–1940] (1:371) contains portions of diplomatic exchanges, rulings, treaties, and other data on recognition, expansion, neutrality, intervention, the

Monroe Doctrine, extradition, nationality, and diplomatic codes. It supplements and updates John Bassett Moore's *Digest of International Law* (1:372).

20:5 League of Nations. "League of Nations Documents and Serial Publications, 1919–1946." Microfilm. New Haven, Conn.: Research Publications, n.d. This microfilm edition of the League of Nations documents is accompanied by E. A. Reno's descriptive guide.

U.S. Department of State. *Foreign Relations of the United States* (1:358) deals with the full scope of foreign policy. This remarkable collection includes annual volumes for years 1920 to 1937 devoted to such topics as East Asia, the American republics, and the British Commonwealth. Of course only a small number of the Department of State's massive archival holdings are printed.

U.S. Department of State. "General Records of the Department of State, RG 59 and RG 84" (1:359) includes the "Decimal File, 1910–1929" for diplomatic and consular dispatches. The *List of National Archives Microfilm Publications* identifies available collections and describes difficulties in using the microfilms.

U.S. Department of State. *Press Conferences of the Secretaries of State, 1922–1974* (1:360).

U.S. Department of State. *Press Releases* (1:361) carries information (1929–1939) about contemporary foreign policy. Weekly.

Indexes to Documents

20:6 Aufricht, Hans. *Guide to League of Nations Publications: A Bibliographical Survey of the Work of the League, 1920–1947.* New York: Columbia University Press, 1951. This guide selectively lists and describes by subject the publications of the league and its agencies. It should be used in conjunction with E. A. Reno's *League of Nations Documents* and V. Y. and C. Ghébali's *A Repertoire of League of Nations Serial Documents* (1:325).

20:7 Reno, Edward A., Jr., ed. *League of Nations Documents, 1919–1946: A Descriptive Guide and Key to the Microfilm Collection.* 3 vols. New Haven, Conn.: Research Publications, 1973–1975. This annotated guide is valuable in searching for league materi-

als, both serial publications and documents. These include the *Official Journal, Treaty Series, Statistical Yearbooks, World Trade, Money and Banking, World Economic Surveys, Annual Epidemiological Reports, International Health Yearbooks, Armaments Yearbooks,* and numbered documents.

OVERVIEWS

20:8 Adler, Selig. *The Uncertain Giant, 1921–1941: American Foreign Policy between the Wars.* New York: Macmillan, 1965. This synthesis of secondary works on the interwar era focuses on policy hesitations that resulted from the general public's uncertain response to Hitler. Isolationists who desired peace via lip service to internationalism, not realistic cooperation with other nations, increased in influence as world disorders worsened, their importance waning only with Pearl Harbor. Extensive bibliography.

20:9 Cooper, Russell M. *American Consultation in World Affairs for the Preservation of Peace.* New York: Macmillan, 1934. This study reviews relations with the League of Nations, Latin American and Manchurian tensions, and general efforts of the United States to stabilize the world between 1919 and 1934.

20:10 Coudert, Frederic R. *A Half-Century of International Problems: A Lawyer's View.* New York: Columbia University Press, 1954. These selections of writings and speeches are by a prominent international lawyer and ardent advocate of League of Nations membership.

Duroselle, J.-B. *From Wilson to Roosevelt: Foreign Policy of the United States, 1913–1945* (19:20) seeks to explain the moods of American foreign policy and how the Americans finally came to accept international responsibility. Bibliography.

20:11 Ellis, L. Ethan. *Republican Foreign Policy, 1921–1933.* New Brunswick, N.J.: Rutgers University Press, 1968. This broad survey, with its brisk style, is friendly to Secretary of State Hughes, and not so friendly to Secretary Kellogg. It is an authoritative review of developments during the decade, especially during the Kellogg years, and a careful analysis of the Stimson era. Bibliography.

20:12 Nevins, Allan. *The United States in a Chaotic World, 1918–1933.* New Haven, Conn.: Yale University Press, 1950. This work is still sound, despite the scholarship of later decades. It has the same internationalist view that characterized most works on the era. Bibliography.

20:13 Nevins, Allan. *The New Deal in World Affairs, 1933–1945.* New Haven, Conn.: Yale University Press, 1950. This volume is favorable to the New Deal and President Franklin D. Roosevelt. It is written from a distinctly internationalist view of the era. Bibliography.

O'Connor, R. G. *Force and Diplomacy: Essays Military and Diplomatic* (40:25) includes essays on disarmament between the wars.

Osgood, R. E. *Ideals and Self-Interest in America's Foreign Relations: The Great Transformation of the Twentieth Century* (2:87).

20:14 Rappard, William E. *The Quest for Peace since the World War.* Cambridge: Harvard University Press, 1940. A Swiss scholar, with remarkable connections to statesmen of the interwar years, reviews interwar efforts to maintain peace, by focusing on arbitration, disarmament, and collective security. His comments on U.S. involvements are direct but not critical.

20:15 Schlesinger, Arthur M., Jr. *The Crisis of the Old Order: 1919–1933.* Vol. 1 in *Age of Roosevelt.* Boston: Houghton Mifflin, 1957. This first volume of a multivolume work is marked by broad research, a lively style, and strong Democratic bias.

20:16 Shotwell, James T., and Salvin, Marina. *Lessons on Security and Disarmament from the History of the League of Nations.* New York: King's Crown, 1949. A retrospective account by a leading official of the Carnegie Endowment for International Peace who was a member of the American delegation to the Paris Peace Conference of 1919. Shotwell reviews interwar treaty efforts and actions to strengthen the security system. Nearly half of the book is devoted to the text of the treaties of 1924, 1928, and 1931.

20:17 Smith, Robert Freeman. "Republican Policy and the *Pax Americana,* 1921–1932." In William A. Williams, ed., *From Colony to Empire: Essays in the History of American Foreign Relations.* New York: Wiley, 1972, pp. 253–92. Smith reassesses the Republican decade for its economic diplomacy.

20:18 Wecter, Dixon. *The Age of the Great Depression: 1929–1941.* New York: Macmillan, 1948. A broad survey, this volume is useful for analysis of economic trends. Bibliography.

20:19 Wiltz, John E. *From Isolation to War, 1931–1941.* New York: Crowell, 1968. Although this little book was designed as a survey of the background to war, the author is a specialist on the Nye Committee hearings and devotes much attention to the 1930s. The book is almost a bibliography, for Wiltz offers textual discussion of important publications.

Public Opinion

Baker, R. *The American Legion and American Foreign Policy* (2:202) opposed disarmament programs (1920–1950) and endorsed isolationist policies until the late 1930s.

20:20 Butler, Harold T. "Partisan Positions on Isolationism vs. Internationalism, 1918–1933." Ph.D. diss., Syracuse University, 1963. This analysis of congressional votes, political campaigns, party platforms, press, and the partisanship of pressure groups concludes that neither party was more isolationist than the other. It affirms recent scholarship that sees the Middle West as not peculiarly isolationist.

20:21 Culbert, David H. *News for Everyman: Radio and Foreign Affairs in Thirties America.* Westport, Conn.: Greenwood, 1976. This volume focuses on Boake Carter, Elmer Davis, H. V. Kaltenborn, Fulton Lewis, Jr., Edward R. Murrow, and Raymond Gram Swing, all of whom expressed views on foreign policy issues. Extensive bibliography.

20:22 Edwards, Jerome E. *The Foreign Policy of Col. McCormick's Tribune, 1929–1941.* Reno: University of Nevada Press, 1971. Edwards examines the views on foreign policy of the publisher of the leading isolationist newspaper in the Midwest in the 1920s and 1930s, Robert R. McCormick of the *Chicago Tribune.* Especially detailed is McCormick's opposition to FDR's diplomacy between 1937 and 1941.

20:23 Guinsburg, Thomas N. "Senatorial Isolationism in America, 1919–1941." Ph.D. diss., Columbia University, 1969. The author concludes that senatorial isolationists helped prevent a more internationalist foreign policy. The Middle West was not more isolationist than other sections. A determined minority of senators wielded power and influence far out of proportion to their numbers. Bibliography.

Hero, A. O., Jr. *The Southerner and World Affairs* (2:207) examines the internationalism of the South during the 1930s.

20:24   Kuehl, Warren F. "Midwestern Newspapers and Isolationist Sentiment." *Diplomatic History* 3:3 (1979), 283–306. In a thorough examination of the editorial views of thirty newspapers in the heart of the Middle West, the author notes a greater internationalist sentiment than that of isolationism between 1919 and 1935. Tables show the commitment to isolationism or internationalism.

20:25   Perkins, Dexter. "The Department of State and American Public Opinion." In Gordon A. Craig and Felix Gilbert, eds. *The Diplomats, 1919–1939.* New York: Atheneum (1953), 1963, vol. 1, pp. 282–308. Perkins reflects on the role of public opinion in American foreign policy during the 1920s. He reviews four themes (collective security, the outlawry of war, relations with the league, and economic issues) and seeks to demonstrate how they were affected by public opinion.

Stuhler, B. *Ten Men of Minnesota and American Foreign Policy, 1898–1968* (2:213) shows again the dangers of stereotyping foreign policy attitudes in the Middle West.

Personalities

Additional references on individuals may be found in Chapter 1, "Biographical Data."

William E. Borah

Maddox, R. J. *William E. Borah and American Foreign Policy* (19:33) is a well-done portrait of a leading senator and his views on foreign affairs in the 1920s and 1930s. Especially powerful in the Harding and Coolidge years, Borah gave much attention to Russia, the League of Nations, the peace plans of the 1920s, neutrality in the 1930s. The author treats these events in detail.

McKenna, M. C. *Borah* (19:34) reveals how inadequately Borah understood the world problems he tried to solve.

20:26   Vinson, John Chalmers. *William E. Borah and the Outlawry of War.* Athens: University of Georgia Press, 1957. This is an analysis of Borah's influence on the peace movement between 1917 and 1931. Especially detailed on the Kellogg-Briand Pact, this study demonstrates the political base the peace movement was able to build in the 1920s.

Calvin Coolidge

20:27   McCoy, Donald R. *Calvin Coolidge: The Quiet President.* New York: Macmillan, 1967. McCoy provides a generally sympathetic account of Coolidge and the problems of the White House between 1923 and 1929. In this carefully researched volume, the author analyzes in particular Coolidge's diplomacy regarding Europe, Latin America, the World Court, and the movement for the outlawry of war.

20:28   Quint, Howard H., and Ferrell, Robert H., eds. *The Talkative President: The Off-the-Record Press Conferences of Calvin Coolidge.* Amherst: University of Massachusetts Press, 1964. Coolidge's press conferences never were reported verbatim, and the verbatim transcribed account seemed to have been lost, until it turned up in an unopened box at the Forbes Library in Northampton, Massachusetts. The editors condensed the transcripts and grouped the material according to topics.

Charles G. Dawes

See Chapters 13 and 19, under "Personalities."

20:29   Dawes, Charles G. *Journal as Ambassador to Great Britain.* Westport, Conn.: Greenwood (1939), 1970. Dawes's diary of his tenure as ambassador (1929–1931) is the only such published embassy diary during the interwar years of Anglo-American relations. Colorful, colloquial, often candid, the diary is bowdlerized from the manuscript version in the Northwestern University library.

20:30   Dawes, Charles G. *A Journal of Reparations.* New York: Macmillan, 1939. Dawes chaired one of two committees assigned to recommend revisions in the German reparations settlement. In this book, not always faithful to his diary, Dawes makes clear the large part which fellow committeeman Owen D. Young and Secretary of State Hughes played in the Dawes Plan.

Dorothy Detzer

20:31 Detzer, Dorothy. *Appointment on the Hill.* New York: Holt, 1948. This is a personal account of Detzer's 20 years as executive secretary and lobbyist for the Women's International League for Peace and Freedom. She helped in persuading legislators to withdraw U.S. Marines from Nicaragua, and promoted the inquiry into the munitions industry.

20:32 Rainbolt, Rosemary. "Women and War in the United States: The Case of Dorothy Detzer, National Secretary, Women's International League for Peace and Freedom." *Peace and Change* 4:3 (1977), 18–22. Rainbolt reviews Detzer's role in the Women's International League for Peace and Freedom (1920–1934), and her effect as a lobbyist and political analyst. Included is a look at her involvement in the Nye munitions investigation of 1934.

John Dewey

Howlett, C. F. "John Dewey and the Crusade to Outlaw War" (20:118).

20:33 Howlett, Charles F. *Troubled Philosopher: John Dewey and the Struggle for World Peace.* Port Washington, N.Y.: Kennikat, 1977. Dewey's interest in the peace movement after World War I has until recently received little attention. This account examines his change from an outspoken supporter of America's war aims to interest in educational peace research during the 1920s and 1930s.

Winterrle, J. "John Dewey and the League of Nations" (20:81).

Warren G. Harding

See also Chapter 21, "Personalities."

20:34 DeWitt, Howard A. "The 'New' Harding and American Foreign Policy: Warren G. Harding, Hiram W. Johnson, and Pragmatic Diplomacy." *Ohio History* 86:2 (1977), 96–114. DeWitt focuses on Hiram Johnson to show that Harding skillfully neutralized the Republican party's progressive-isolationist wing. Harding asked for Johnson's advice on foreign policy in order to preempt his influence inside the party and to massage the Californian's ego. This revisionist account emphasizes President Harding's "adroit manipulation of public attitudes and his pragmatic politics."

20:35 Jennings, David H. "President Harding and International Organization." *Ohio History* 75:2

(1966), 149–65; 75:3 (1966), 192–95. Reassessing Harding, Jennings finds him more manipulative than previously assumed in hedging on the League of Nations and World Court issues and in assuaging both internationalist and isolationist factions to maintain party harmony.

20:36 Murray, Robert K. *The Harding Era: Warren G. Harding and His Administration.* Minneapolis: University of Minnesota Press, 1969. A reinterpretation of the Harding administration that suggests that Harding himself was a factor in events between 1921 and 1923. The "new Harding" is perhaps overdrawn; nonetheless, this is a soundly researched treatment and it devotes attention to the diplomacy of the United States during the era.

20:37 Potts, Louis W. "Who Was Warren G. Harding?" *Historian* 36:4 (1974), 621–45. A study of the diverse evaluations of Warren G. Harding, it balances the generally accepted low estimates of Harding as a man, leader, and politician with the revisionism of recent years.

20:38 Trani, Eugene P., and Wilson, David L. *The Presidency of Warren G. Harding.* Lawrence: Regents Press of Kansas, 1977. This volume analyzes the diplomacy of the Harding administration in detail, with emphasis on the powerful role of Secretary of Commerce Hoover in the making of Harding diplomacy.

David Jayne Hill

20:39 Hill, David Jayne. *The Problem of a World Court: The Story of an Unrealized American Dream.* New York: Longmans, Green, 1927. After a survey of the beginnings of the World Court idea, the author deals with the attitude of the United States toward the court and reasons why the United States did not join.

Parkman, A. *David Jayne Hill and the Problem of World Peace* (16:81) examines Hill's opposition to U.S. membership in the League of Nations and the World Court.

Herbert C. Hoover

See Chapters 19 and 21 under "Personalities," for additional references.

20:40 Brandes, Joseph. *Herbert Hoover and Economic Diplomacy: Department of Commerce Policy, 1921–1928.* Pittsburgh: University of Pittsburgh Press, 1962. This is a fine treatment of Hoover's tenure as secretary of commerce, during which he built the department into an influential bureau and involved it in diplomacy. Brandes's view has come to be accepted by most students, who see the 1920s as the time in which economics came to be a major factor in American diplomacy.

20:41 Fausold, Martin L., and Mazuzan, George T., eds. *The Hoover Presidency: A Reappraisal.* Albany: State University of New York Press, 1974. A collection of essays on the Hoover years which includes several new interpretations of the Hoover presidency.

20:42 Hoover, Herbert C. *Memoirs.* 3 vols. New York: Macmillan, 1951–1952. The first volume is *The Years of Adventure* (1874–1920); the second, *The Cabinet and the Presidency* (1920–1933); the third, *The Great Depression* (1929–1941). The author's bitterness intrudes—a bitterness both against his successor, Roosevelt, and against the nations of Europe which, Hoover believed, caused the Great Depression.

20:43 Hoover, Herbert C. *The State Papers and Other Public Writings of Herbert Hoover.* 2 vols. Ed. by William Starr Myers. Garden City, N.Y.: Doubleday, Doran, 1934. The documents are in chronological order, with brief introductions. This collection is the equivalent of later collections, beginning with the papers of President Truman, published by the Government Printing Office.

Lyons, E. *Herbert Hoover* (21:31) is the fullest biography, updated from an earlier version published in 1948, but with only brief attention to Hoover's role as a critic of postwar U.S. foreign policy.

20:44 Myers, William Starr. *The Foreign Policies of Herbert Hoover, 1929–1933.* New York: Scribner's, 1940. The author sympathetically surveys the Hoover policies, as Hoover formulated them and strove to carry them out.

20:45 Tracey, Kathleen H., comp. *Herbert Hoover—A Bibliography: His Writings and Addresses.* Stanford, Calif.: Hoover Institution Press, 1977. The material listed here covers the period from Hoover's engineering career at the turn of the century to his postpresidential years, excluding much of his presidential papers since they are available elsewhere.

20:46 Wilson, Joan Hoff. *Herbert Hoover: Forgotten Progressive.* Boston: Little, Brown, 1975. This study is probably the best general treatment of Hoover's career, showing that Hoover was a progressive and not the reactionary he has been drawn. Wilson devotes a good deal of attention to Hoover's diplomatic ideas and activities.

Charles Evans Hughes

20:47 Danelski, David J., and Tulchin, Joseph S., eds. *The Autobiographical Notes of Charles Evans Hughes.* Cambridge: Harvard University Press, 1973. In the preface, Hughes described his efforts as "a body of facts for reference" and not an autobiography. The editors have supplemented Hughes's notes with materials from the U.S. Foreign Relations series, the Hughes Papers, and other sources.

20:48 Glad, Betty. *Charles Evans Hughes and the Illusions of Innocence: A Study in American Diplomacy.* Urbana: University of Illinois Press, 1966. A detailed treatment of Hughes as secretary of state (1921–1925), which argues that Hughes's background as a lawyer, which limited his vision, heavily influenced his diplomacy. This harsh critique is not convincing.

20:49 Hyde, Charles C. "Charles Evans Hughes." In Samuel Flagg Bemis, ed., *The American Secretaries of State and Their Diplomacy.* New York: Knopf, 1928, vol. 10, pp. 221–463. This semiofficial biography of Hughes, written by a former State Department official, is still valuable. In 1933, Hughes engaged Henry C. Beerits to prepare memoranda on key aspects of the former secretary's career, summaries which Hughes and his biographer, Merlo J. Pusey, subsequently used as major sources. Beerits, however, had relied heavily on Hyde's account.

20:50 Perkins, Dexter. *Charles Evans Hughes and American Democratic Statesmanship.* Boston: Little, Brown, 1956. This brief biography of Hughes devotes one long chapter to Hughes's term as secretary of state between 1921 and 1925, while treating Hughes's activities regarding the fight over the League of Nations. Very sympathetic to Hughes, Perkins suggests that Hughes was one of the most successful secretaries.

20:51 Pusey, Merlo J. *Charles Evans Hughes.* 2 vols. New York: Macmillan, 1951. This sympathetic two-volume study is the standard work on the diplomacy of Hughes. Traditional in approach, it deals in detail with such topics as Herbert Hoover's emerging influence in diplomacy between 1921 and 1925.

20:52 Vinson, John Chalmers. "Charles Evans Hughes." In Norman A. Graebner, ed., *An Uncertain*

Tradition: American Secretaries of State in the Twentieth Century. New York: McGraw-Hill, 1961, pp. 128–48. Presidents Harding and Coolidge gave Hughes almost complete freedom of action, but the Senate provided a challenge to the secretary, who chose to avoid conflict whenever possible. Hughes preferred logic to intuition, which made him "masterful in executing ideas, mediocre in producing them."

Hiram W. Johnson

See Chapter 19, "Personalities," for additional references.

20:53   Boyle, Peter G. "The Roots of Isolationism: A Case Study." *Journal of American Studies* 6:1 (1972), 41–50. An account of the isolationist stance which Senator Hiram Warren Johnson (1866–1945) adopted toward American foreign policy during the 1930s.

20:54   DeWitt, Howard A. "Hiram Johnson and Early New Deal Diplomacy, 1933–1934." *California Historical Quarterly* 53:4 (1974), 377–86. DeWitt assesses Hiram Johnson's influence in directing American foreign policy toward isolationism in the 1930s. He sponsored legislation banning loans to nations that defaulted on their war debts and pressed for an arms embargo that would apply impartially to all belligerents.

20:55   Greenbaum, Fred. "Hiram Johnson and the New Deal." *Pacific Historian* 18:3 (1974), 20–35. This essay discusses Hiram Johnson's endorsement of Franklin D. Roosevelt for president in 1932, his silence in 1936, and his opposition to Roosevelt's third term in 1940. It reviews Johnson's support of New Deal domestic and foreign policy matters.

Frank B. Kellogg

20:56   Ellis, L. Ethan. *Frank B. Kellogg and American Foreign Relations, 1925–1929.* New Brunswick, N.J.: Rutgers University Press, 1961. This carefully researched, standard account of Kellogg as secretary of state (1925–1929) demonstrates that Kellogg lost control of Mexican policy to Dwight Morrow and of Nicaraguan policy to Henry L. Stimson, but remained in control of policy toward China and the negotiations that resulted in the Kellogg-Briand Pact.

20:57   Ellis, L. Ethan. "Frank B. Kellogg." In Norman A. Graebner, ed., *An Uncertain Tradition: American Secretaries of State in the Twentieth Century.* New York: McGraw-Hill, 1961, pp. 149–67. Ellis describes Kellogg's secretaryship as "workman-

like but unimpressive." Kellogg often delegated policy to diplomats on the scene, as he did with Stimson in Nicaragua and Morrow in Mexico.

20:58   Ferrell, Robert H. *Frank B. Kellogg and Henry L. Stimson.* Vol. 2 in *The American Secretaries of State and Their Diplomacy,* ed. by Samuel Flagg Bemis and Robert Ferrell. New series. New York: Cooper Square, 1963. This study contends that each of the two secretaries, for different reasons, proved unsuccessful in reforming the nations of Europe and Asia. Bibliography.

George F. Kennan

See Chapters 24 and 25, "Personalities," for additional references.

Kennan, G. F. *Memoirs, 1925–1950* (24:124) is, in view of Kennan's influence in government and especially out, essential reading. It surveys the author's professional and intellectual development and discusses many of the trying issues in which he took part.

Henry Cabot Lodge

See Chapter 19, "Personalities," for additional references.

20:59   Carroll, John M. "Henry Cabot Lodge's Contributions to the Shaping of Republican European Diplomacy, 1920–1924." *Capitol Studies* 3:1 (1975), 153–65. Lodge may have led the fight against Wilsonian internationalism, but he played a key role in constructing a new policy of cooperation with Europe under Harding. The Senate majority leader also defended executive prerogatives in foreign affairs several times against attacks from "irreconcilables" such as Borah and Johnson.

Franklin D. Roosevelt

See Chapters 21, 22, and 23, "Personalities," for additional references.

Bullitt, O. H., ed. *"For the President—Personal and Secret": Correspondence between Franklin D. Roosevelt and William C. Bullitt* [1921–1937] (21:17).

Dallek, R. *Franklin D. Roosevelt and American Foreign Policy, 1932–1945* (21:51) is the most recent broad interpretative study.

20:60   Range, Willard. *Franklin D. Roosevelt's World Order.* Athens: University of Georgia Press, 1959. Looking beyond League of Nations and World Court involvement, Range examines Roosevelt's broader internationalist outlook from the perspective of the good neighbor policy, disarmament, world economic policy, and collective security. He finds Roosevelt generally consistent in his assumptions but unable to fit the world into them.

Roosevelt, F. D. *Complete Presidential Press Conferences of Franklin D. Roosevelt, 1933–1945* (21:54).

Rosenman, S. I., ed. *Public Papers and Addresses of Franklin Delano Roosevelt* (21:55).

James T. Shotwell

See Chapters 19 and 38, "Personalities," for additional references.

20:61   DeBenedetti, Charles. "James T. Shotwell and the Science of International Politics." *Political Science Quarterly* 89:2 (1974), 379–95. This essay focuses on Shotwell's internationalist belief that "experts" could master world problems and that scientific and systematic efforts could bring order to international affairs.

Josephson, H. *James T. Shotwell and the Rise of Internationalism in America* (19:61) details the activities of this antiwar publicist, informal diplomat, and occasional state department adviser, who retired as president of the Carnegie Endowment for International Peace in 1962, although it was much earlier that he exerted his principal influence.

Henry L. Stimson

See Chapters 21, 22, and 23, "Personalities," for additional references.

Ostrower, G. B. "Secretary of State Stimson and the League" (20:87).

Redmond, K. G. "Henry L. Stimson and the Question of League Membership" (20:88).

Hugh R. Wilson

See Chapters 14 and 21, "Personalities," for additional references.

20:62   Downing, Marvin L. "Hugh R. Wilson and American Relations with the League of Nations, 1927–1937." Ph.D. diss., University of Oklahoma, 1970. Wilson is portrayed as a capable if colorless

diplomat who served as the U.S. "observer" at a number of league conferences while he was minister to Switzerland. These conferences were mainly concerned with disarmament questions, but covered a number of lesser issues.

20:63   Wilson, Hugh R. *Diplomat between the Wars.* New York: Longmans, Green, 1941. This account is especially valuable for remembrance of the Geneva Disarmament Conference (1932–1934).

20:64   Wilson, Hugh R., Jr. *Disarmament and the Cold War in the Thirties.* New York: Vantage, 1963. Wilson covers his father's role in the negotiations of the early 1930s. Based on his father's files, the book discovers the failure of Hoover's diplomacy to be rooted in the intransigence of French and British leaders—a considerable simplification which, among other aspects, ignores nearly a decade of lukewarm American support for league efforts.

Others

See also Chapter 21, "Personalities," for "Others."

20:65   Bellush, Bernard. *He Walked Alone: A Biography of John Gilbert Winant.* The Hague: Mouton, 1968. Bellush presents a sympathetic portrait of Winant as governor of New Hampshire, New Deal administrator, the first American director of the International Labor Organization, and wartime ambassador to Britain.

20:66   Cole, Wayne S. *Senator Gerald P. Nye and American Foreign Relations.* Minneapolis: University of Minnesota Press, 1962. A well-researched study of Nye's influence on foreign policy. Especially well done is Nye's chairmanship of the Senate committee investigating the munitions industry and Nye's attempts to preserve neutrality as the United States moved toward participation in World War II.

20:67   Coolidge, Harold J., and Lord, Robert H. *Archibald Cary Coolidge: Life and Letters.* Boston: Houghton Mifflin, 1932. This is a biography of the editor of *Foreign Affairs* and an authority on American foreign relations.

20:68   Eddy, Sherwood. *Eight Adventurous Years: An Autobiography.* New York: Harper, 1955. The remembrances of a former secretary for Asia of the YMCA, missionary and evangelist, and prolific writer, who was concerned with social justice throughout the world.

20:69   Fisher, Irving N. *A Bibliography of the Writings of Irving Fisher*. New Haven, Conn.: Yale University Press, 1961. This is a bibliography of an economist who enthusiastically supported the League of Nations and endorsed the outlawry of war. For these purposes, the work emphasizes 1920 to 1924.

Graebner, N. A., ed. *An Uncertain Tradition: American Secretaries of State in the Twentieth Century* (2:168) has essays on Charles Evans Hughes, Frank B. Kellogg, Henry L. Stimson, and Cordell Hull.

20:70   Hooker, Nancy H., ed. *The Moffat Papers: Selections from the Diplomatic Journals of Jay Pierrepont Moffat, 1919–1943*. Cambridge: Harvard University Press, 1956. This compilation contains valuable comments by Moffat on his contacts with the league (1927–1931), and as chief of the State Department's Division of Western European Affairs (1932–1935) and of the Division of European Affairs (1937–1940). The diaries are an excellent source for the early diplomacy of the New Deal, especially the London Economic Conference.

20:71   Johnpoll, Bernard K. *Pacifist's Progress: Norman Thomas and the Decline of American Socialism*. Chicago: Quadrangle, 1970. This is not a biography of Thomas, but an account of Thomas as a political actor. Extensive bibliography.

20:71a   Jones, Kenneth P., ed. *U.S. Diplomats in Europe, 1919–1941*. Santa Barbara: ABC-Clio, 1981. These original essays are useful for materials dealing with second-level American diplomats such as Thomas W. Lamont, Alanson B. Houghton, and Owen D. Young. Bibliography and useful subject index.

Kuehl, W. F. *Hamilton Holt: Journalist, Internationalist, Educator* (16:53) is a well-researched treatment of this journalist, internationalist, educator, who throughout the 1920s labored for some form of association of the nations for the world. It is especially detailed in treatment of Holt's activities concerning the fight over the League of Nations. This sympathetic account shows the frustration Holt suffered in his quest for peace.

20:72   Page, Kirby. *Kirby Page, Social Evangelist: The Autobiography of a 20th Century Prophet for Peace*. Ed. by Harold E. Fey. Nyack, N.Y.: Fellowship, 1975. A prolific writer, Page was the most in-fluential American pacifist of his time, especially during the interwar period.

Phillips, W. *Ventures in Diplomacy* (17:54) contains a brief description of Phillips's duty as the United States' first minister to Canada, and notes that the Smoot-Hawley tariff was an important reason for his decision to resign.

20:73   Warner, Hoyt L. *The Life of Mr. Justice Clarke: A Testament to the Power of Liberal Dissent in America*. Cleveland, Ohio: Western Reserve University Press, 1959. Clarke's presidency of the League of Nations Non-Partisan Association and his internationalist convictions are fully portrayed in this biography, which also provides insight into ideas, movements, and strains among pro-league advocates in the 1920s.

Wheeler, G. E. *Admiral William Veazie Pratt, U.S. Navy: A Sailor s Life* (40:88) describes Pratt's service as a naval adviser at the Washington (1921–1922) and London (1930) naval conferences.

Internationalism

See "Personalities" for John Dewey, Franklin D. Roosevelt, James T. Shotwell, and, under "Others," Sherwood Eddy, Hamilton Holt.

20:74   Accinelli, Robert D. "Militant Internationalists: The League of Nations Association, the Peace Movement, and U.S. Foreign Policy, 1934–38." *Diplomatic History* 4:1 (1980), 19–38. In an analysis of leaders, groups, and programs, the author notes the difficulties encountered in seeking agreement on relations with the League of Nations, membership in the World Court, isolationist sentiment, and neutrality. Differing goals created tension between peace and internationalist advocates.

20:75   Kenny, James T. "Manley O. Hudson and the Harvard Research in International Law." *International Lawyer* 11:2 (1977), 319–29. Hudson's efforts to advance the study of teaching of international law and the compilation of conventions are described. Includes works on neutrality.

Kuehl, W. F. "Internationalism" (2:59).

LEAGUE OF NATIONS

See Chapter 19 for the origins of the league; also see "Document Collections" for Reno (20:7).

20:76 Barros, James. *Betrayal from Within: Joseph Avenol, Secretary-General of the League of Nations, 1933–1940*. New Haven, Conn.: Yale University Press, 1969. Barros holds Avenol responsible for the league's inability to respond to the crises of the 1930s. A chronological survey of these crises is useful. Bibliography.

20:77 Bendiner, Elmer. *A Time for Angels: The Tragicomic History of the League of Nations*. New York: Knopf, 1975. This account by a journalist is surprisingly thorough, which reflects his work with basic documents. It is perceptive in its analysis of characters. Relations of the United States with the league are reasonably well covered.

20:78 Burks, David D. "The United States and the Geneva Protocol of 1924: 'A New Holy Alliance'?" *American Historical Review* 64:4 (1959), 891–905. American fears that the Geneva protocol, if ratified, might bring a European concert for intervention in western hemisphere affairs reinforced the British opposition to the protocol which ultimately killed it.

20:79 Rappard, William E. *International Relations as Viewed from Geneva*. New Haven, Conn.: Yale University Press, 1925. An early book of analysis, by a scholar of Swiss background who knew President Woodrow Wilson and was fascinated by the league experiment.

Walters, F. P. *A History of the League of Nations* (19:302) remains the most thorough study of the league yet published. It benefits from the author's career with the league, ending with his service as deputy secretary-general. Where relevant, U.S. contacts are evaluated.

20:80 Williams, Bruce. *State Security and the League of Nations*. Baltimore: Johns Hopkins Press, 1927. An early work of analysis, from a scholarly point of view, it is interesting for its view of American international problems during the 1920s.

20:81 Winterrle, John. "John Dewey and the League of Nations." *North Dakota Quarterly* 34:3 (1966), 75–88. The liberal disillusionment with

peacemaking in 1919 is confirmed in this study of Dewey, who rejected the League of Nations because of its political orientation and its reliance on military sanctions.

U.S. and the League

See "Personalities," especially William E. Borah, Warren G. Harding, David Jayne Hill.

20:82 Carman, Harry J. *The Cooperation of the United States with the League of Nations*. New York: The League of Nations Association, 1930. This pamphlet typifies the many pro-league accounts designed to convince the American public that contact with the league was beneficial and not dangerous. Ursula P. Hubbard, *The Cooperation of the United States with the League of Nations, 1931–1936*, continued the effort in *International Conciliation*, no. 329 (1937).

20:83 Donnelly, J. B. "Prentiss Gilbert's Mission to the League of Nations Council, October 1931." *Diplomatic History* 4:2 (1978), 373–87. Gilbert as American consul in Geneva played a key role in discussions over Manchuria, which are concisely summarized in this article. It emphasizes that decisions by Stimson, Dawes, and Hoover fluctuated, thus limiting Gilbert's effectiveness.

20:84 Fleming, Denna F. *The United States and World Organization: 1920–1933*. New York: Columbia University Press, 1938. Reprint 1966. A pioneering account, now largely superseded, it is interesting for its analysis so close to the era.

20:85 Fosdick, Raymond B. *Letters on the League of Nations: From the Files of Raymond B. Fosdick*. Princeton, N.J.: Princeton University Press, 1966. As the first undersecretary general of the league, Fosdick had extensive contacts with European and American internationalists which are revealed in his letters. The work is especially full on the creation of the league, the first International Labor Organization meeting in Washington in 1919, and European responses to refusals to join the league.

20:86 Ostrower, Gary B. "The American Decision to Join the International Labor Organization." *Labor History* 16:4 (1975), 495–504. This is a thorough review (1933–1934) of the pros and cons of the decision of the Roosevelt administration to join the ILO.

20:87   Ostrower, Gary B. "Secretary of State Stimson and the League." *Historian* 41:4 (1979), 467–82. Ostrower sees Stimson as an important transition figure in the interwar period, moving from a position of supporting international cooperation and a reluctance to become involved during the Manchurian crisis to a late espousal of collective security.

20:88   Redmond, Kent G. "Henry L. Stimson and the Question of League Membership." *Historian* 25:2 (1963), 200–212. Stimson advocated U.S. membership in the League of Nations despite some reservations about the covenant. This essay surveys Stimson's recorded opinions from the 1920s to the 1940s.

Taylor, A. H. *American Diplomacy and the Narcotics Traffic, 1900–1939: A Study in International Humanitarian Reform* (16:39) concentrates on relations with League of Nations commissions, showing contacts, policies, and the unusual cooperation on a nonpolitical subject.

20:89   Wimer, Kurt. "The Harding Administration, the League of Nations, and the Separate Peace Treaty." *Review of Politics* 29:1 (1967), 13–24. Wimer examines Harding's ambivalent position toward the league, his views on an association of nations, and developments in the early twenties which led to the separate treaty. Internationalists failed to influence events.

Collective Security

See Chapter 38, "Collective Security."

20:90   Current, Richard N. "The United States and 'Collective Security': Notes on the History of an Idea." In Alexander DeConde, ed., *Isolation and Security: Ideas and Interests in Twentieth-Century American Foreign Policy.* Durham, N.C.: Duke University Press, 1957, pp. 33–55. A thoughtful and critical review of pre-1930s ideas and their effect on foreign policy. Comments on the origin of the phrase "collective security" are especially noteworthy.

20:91   Divine, Robert A. "Franklin D. Roosevelt and Collective Security, 1933." *Mississippi Valley Historical Review* 48:1 (1961), 42–59. Divine suggests that the 1933 controversy over the arms embargo showed Roosevelt had not yet been converted to collective security. He does argue that Secretary of State Cordell Hull and Ambassador Norman Davis advocated such a policy.

20:92   Jonas, Manfred. "The United States and the Failure of Collective Security in the 1930s." In John Braeman, Robert H. Bremner, and David Brody, eds., *Twentieth-Century American Foreign Policy.* Columbus: Ohio State University Press, 1971, pp. 241–93. The American consensus in favor of collective security after Pearl Harbor represented a watershed in American foreign policy. In turning down the League of Nations, the Senate and the American people rejected that principle. Advocates of collective security suffered further setbacks with the passage of the neutrality acts.

20:93   Ostrower, Gary B. *Collective Insecurity: The United States and the League of Nations during the Early Thirties.* Lewisburg, Pa.: Bucknell University Press, 1979. After a brief review of isolationist-internationalist activities in the 1920s, Ostrower focuses on the Manchurian crisis, its origins, responses, and U.S. involvement in league discussions. Growing contacts with the league resulting in membership in the ILO represented a continuing erratic behavior by the United States which helped only to render the league a less effective agency. Bibliography.

20:94   Stromberg, Roland N. *Collective Security and American Foreign Policy: From the League of Nations to NATO.* New York: Praeger, 1963. A masterful analysis of the intellectual poverty in the idea of collective security, and especially the weakness of the Wilsonian view. Wilson, the author relates, did not think out the power implications, as well as the intellectual basis, of his principal contribution to international affairs. Extensive bibliography.

20:95   Stromberg, Roland N. "The Idea of Collective Security." *Journal of the History of Ideas* 17:2 (1956), 250–63. Collective security came from "the people" as a response to the senseless slaughter of the Great War. Unfortunately, this element in the search for peace has not been very helpful because most often the formula is too narrow to allow patient diplomacy and realistic analysis.

20:96   Wright, Quincy, ed. *Neutrality and Collective Security.* Chicago: University of Chicago Press, 1936. From a symposium of the 1930s, it shows the color of the times. Wright was an expert in international law and its connection with the institutions of war, and his contributors emphasize a political science approach to international affairs.

WORLD COURT

See "Personalities," especially Calvin Coolidge and David Jayne Hill.

20:97   Accinelli, Robert D. "The Hoover Administration and the World Court." *Peace and Change* 4:3 (1977), 28–36. Accinelli weaves together popular interest in membership, congressional attitudes, and the ideas of Hoover and Stimson, especially Stimson. Reasons for failure can be traced not only to anti-court efforts but the vacillation of the administration and the effect of the depression.

20:98   Accinelli, Robert D. "The Roosevelt Administration and the World Court Defeat, 1935." *Historian* 40:3 (1978), 463–78. On January 29, 1935, the Senate voted against joining the World Court. Among the several reasons contributing to the defeat was, the author believes, the Roosevelt administration's failure to present a strong case in favor of U.S. membership.

20:99   Accinelli, Robert D. "Was There a 'New' Harding? Warren G. Harding and the World Court Issue." *Ohio History* 84:4 (1975), 168–81. Harding took charge of the proposal for U.S. membership in the World Court. He was evidently prepared to make "major concessions to the anti-Court faction in order to keep the party together." The author finds "old Harding" at work, displaying little of the initiative and determination that revisionist writers have seen.

20:100   Fleming, Denna F. *The United States and the World Court, 1920–1966.* Rev. ed. New York: Russell & Russell (1945), 1968. Although this study concentrates on American participation in the World Court after 1920, it stresses the League of Nations' failure in the Senate as an important precedent.

20:101   Jessup, Philip C. *The United States and the World Court . . . with Related Essays.* New York: Garland (1929), 1972. This reprint contains additional essays by Jessup and European scholars of international law. Jessup's original presentation, made shortly after his return with Elihu Root from a European meeting to arrange a formula for U.S. membership, is valuable for its review of developments (1920–1929).

20:102   Kahn, Gilbert N. "Presidential Passivity on a Nonsalient Issue: President Franklin D. Roosevelt and the 1935 World Court Fight." *Diplomatic History* 4:2 (1980), 137–60. The author analyzes the reasons

why Roosevelt did not press the Senate for consent to joining the World Court.

20:103   Margulies, Herbert F. "The Senate and the World Court." *Capitol Studies* 4:2 (1976), 37–52. Calvin Coolidge was unsuccessful in his efforts to develop support in the Senate for American membership in the World Court (1923–1924).

AMERICAN PEACE MOVEMENT

See "Personalities," especially Dorothy Detzer.

Chatfield, C. *For Peace and Justice: Pacifism in America, 1914–1941* (19:164) discusses the multifaceted movement for world peace, which flourished in the United States far more than it did elsewhere, perhaps because of the refusal of the American government to join the League of Nations.

Chatfield, C., ed. *Peace Movements in America* [1890–1973] (16:97) includes Chatfield's "Alternative Antiwar Strategies of the Thirties."

DeBenedetti, C. *Origins of the Modern American Peace Movement: 1915–1929* (19:167) is an authoritative account of the peace movement, which fits the peace workers into the diplomacy of the time.

DeBenedetti, C. *The Peace Reform in American History* (16:26) surveys voluntary citizen peace activism (1550–1975).

20:104   DeBenedetti, Charles. "Alternative Strategies in the American Peace Movement in the 1920's." *American Studies* 13:1 (1972), 69–79. The preoccupation of the American peace movement in these years was to redefine America's role in European affairs. Three strategies emerged: legalist, reformist, functionalist. Reprinted in Chatfield's *Peace Movements in America* (16:97).

20:105   DeBenedetti, Charles. "The American Peace Movement and the State Department in the Era of Locarno." In Solomon Wank, ed., *Doves and Diplomats.* Westport, Conn.: Greenwood, 1978, pp. 201–16. This essay demonstrates how the State Department deferred in the 1920s to the conservative legalist peace leaders (such as Elihu Root), avoided pro-League of Nations internationalists (such as James T. Shotwell), and ignored the great majority of clergy, women, and pacifists who supported post-1918 peace activism.

20:106 DeBenedetti, Charles. "The $100,000 American Peace Award of 1924." *Pennsylvania Magazine of History and Biography* 98:2 (1974), 224–49. Edward R. Bok's offer of a $100,000 prize for the best plan for connecting America to the maintenance of world peace attracted an outpouring of plans. This essay reviews them and the controversial process of award.

20:107 Ferrell, Robert H. "The Peace Movement." In Alexander DeConde, ed., *Isolation and Security: Ideas and Interests in Twentieth-Century American Foreign Policy*. Durham, N.C.: Duke University Press, 1957, pp. 82–106. Ferrell analyzes the movement for peace between the two world wars, dividing peace groups into conservative and liberal, and concludes that neither group understood international affairs during the era.

20:108 Jones, Mary H. *Swords into Plowshares: An Account of the American Friends Service Committee, 1917–1937*. New York: Macmillan, 1937. A history of the Quakers in times of crisis, at home and abroad. A lengthy appendix lists their activities, month by month.

20:109 MacCarthy, Esther. "Catholic Women and the War: The National Council of Catholic Women, 1919–1946." *Peace and Change* 5:1 (1978), 23–32. MacCarthy examines the attitudes of Catholic women in the council, which actively participated in the peace movement.

20:110 Macfarland, Charles S. *Pioneers for Peace through Religion based on the Records of the Church Peace Union... 1914–1945*. New York: Revell, 1946. Because of the Church Peace Union's outreach, this is an account of organized religion's interest and activity, especially of the World Alliance for International Friendship through the Churches. There are insights into personalities and responses to both world wars.

20:111 Miller, Robert M. "The Attitudes of the Major Protestant Churches in America toward War and Peace, 1919–1929." *Historian* 19:1 (1956/1957), 13–38. This is a detailed account of the responses of Protestant denominations and their leaders to cam-

paigns for League of Nations membership or cooperation, disarmament, and other internationalist goals.

20:112 Nelson, John K. *The Peace Prophets: American Pacifist Thought, 1919–1941*. Chapel Hill: University of North Carolina Press, 1967. An unrevised master's thesis that focuses on peace positions and ideas expressed by religious leaders and journals during the interwar years.

20:113 Richey, Susan. "Comment on the Political Strategy of Christian Pacifists: A. J. Muste, Norman Thomas, and Reinhold Niebuhr." *Towson State Journal of International Affairs* 11:2 (1977), 111–19. Richey reviews the interwar (1919–1939) writings of these three pacifists and analyzes their politics and philosophical perspectives.

KELLOGG-BRIAND PACT

See "Personalities," especially William E. Borah, Calvin Coolidge, Frank B. Kellogg.

20:114 Current, Richard N. "Consequences of the Kellogg Pact." In George L. Anderson, ed., *Issues and Conflicts: Studies in Twentieth Century American Diplomacy*. Lawrence: University of Kansas Press, 1959, pp. 210–29. This study offers insight into interwar responses to the Pact of Paris and consultative pacts, appeals, embargoes, and pronouncements.

20:115 DeBenedetti, Charles. "Borah and the Kellogg-Briand Pact." *Pacific Northwest Quarterly* 73:1 (1972), 22–29. This article contends that Borah used the idea of the outlawry of war and the 1928 Kellogg-Briand Pact to undercut those internationalists interested in tying the United States to the League of Nations and the Versailles Treaty.

20:116 Ferrell, Robert H. *Peace in Their Time: The Origins of the Kellogg-Briand Pact*. New Haven, Conn.: Yale University Press, 1952. Ferrell discusses the peace movement and the purposes of French diplomacy in Europe, which resulted in a grand demarche in 1927 that Secretary of State Kellogg parried and turned into a largely useless multilateral treaty. Bibliography.

20:117 Hefley, J. Theodore. "War Outlawed: 'The Christian Century' and the Kellogg Peace Pact." *Journalism Quarterly* 48:1 (1971), 26–32. Through the *Christian Century,* Charles Clayton Morrison spoke for the movement to outlaw war which resulted in the Kellogg-Briand Pact of 1928. Morrison supported the movement from 1924 until 1933, when he realized the pact was dead.

20:118   Howlett, Charles F. "John Dewey and the Crusade to Outlaw War." *World Affairs* 138:4 (1976), 336–55. Howlett discusses John Dewey's pacifism, idealism, and campaign to outlaw war in U.S. foreign policy (1918–1932).

20:119   Josephson, Harold. "Outlawing War: Internationalism and the Pact of Paris." *Diplomatic History* 3:4 (1979), 377–90. This essay shows the diverse ways internationalists moved to strengthen the Pact of Paris by working for arms embargo legislation, cooperation with the League of Nations, acceptance of the nonrecognition doctrine, and discretionary neutrality acts. They also sought to embody its principles in international law and to reconcile them with the covenant to provide collective security in the late 1930s.

Meiburger, A. V. *Efforts of Raymond Robins toward the Recognition of Soviet Russia and the Outlawry of War, 1917–1933* (19:93).

20:120   Stoner, John E. *S. O. Levinson and the Pact of Paris: A Study in the Techniques of Influence.* Chicago: University of Chicago Press, 1943. This biography of the champion of the outlawry of war shows why the Chicago publicist believed that "Outlawry" (he always wrote it with a capital "O") must be the starting point for all efforts at permanent peace. For ten years Levinson devoted much of his time and money to recruiting backers.

Isolationism

See "Personalities," especially Warren G. Harding, Hiram W. Johnson; see "Bibliographies" for Doenecke; and see Chapter 2, "Isolationism."

20:121   Adler, Selig. *The Isolationist Impulse: Its Twentieth Century Reaction.* New York: Abelard-Schuman, 1957. Although this book develops isolationist attitudes over a broad period, the focus

is on the 1920s. The author describes ethnic factors, economic pressures, and other forces that discouraged American entanglement in world affairs. Bibliography.

Beard, C. A., and Smith, G. H. E. *The Idea of National Interest: An Analytical Study in American Foreign Relations* (2:123) is a long and detailed account of isolationism, historically considered, written in the depths of the Great Depression by the leading American historian of his day, and expressive of a profound dissatisfaction with intervention by the United States in Europe and Asia and Latin America.

Billington, R. A. "The Origins of Middle Western Isolationism" [1890–1941] (2:65).

20:122   Carleton, William G. "Isolationism and the Middle West." *Mississippi Valley Historical Review* 33:3 (1946), 377–90. While isolationism may be stronger here than elsewhere, that strength is often exaggerated. In the middle and late 1930s isolationism was often anti–New Deal, rather than a protest against Democratic party foreign policy.

20:123   Carlisle, Rodney. "The Foreign Policy Views of an Isolationist Press Lord: W. R. Hearst and the International Crisis, 1936–41." *Journal of Contemporary History* 9:3 (1974), 217–27. Hearst's readership represented 12–14 percent of the total for daily newspapers in the United States during the mid-1930s. Hearst believed the United States should establish a deterrent armed force, not threaten Germany, nor make moves on the European continent in support of the Versailles Treaty or the League of Nations, give no encouragement to Britain or France, and watch Japan and the Soviet Union.

20:124   Cohen, Warren I. *The American Revisionists: The Lessons of Intervention in World War I.* Chicago: University of Chicago Press, 1967. According to the author, the contemporary historians who questioned Germany's 1914 war guilt contributed to the isolationist sentiment of the 1930s.

DeConde, A. "On Twentieth-Century Isolationism" (2:66).

20:125   DeConde, Alexander. "The South and Isolationism." *Journal of Southern History* 24:3 (1958), 332–46. The author questions the argument that Southerners are less isolationistic and more internationalistic than other regional groups. DeConde concedes that the South was definitely less isolationist in the year immediately prior to World War II but argues that this was because of special circumstances.

20:126 Jonas, Manfred. *Isolationism in America, 1935–41.* Ithaca, N.Y.: Cornell University Press, 1966. A careful analysis of the isolationist mood of America in the later 1930s, it includes the isolationist neutrality acts and the official moves toward involvement and, as events revealed, war.

20:127 Maddox, Robert J. "Another Look at the Legend of Isolationism in the 1920's." *Mid-America* 53:1 (1971), 35–43. Maddox is critical of the thesis of the Wisconsin school that the U.S. government was deeply involved, economically, in international affairs in the 1920s.

20:128 Papachristou, Judith. "An Exercise in Anti-Imperialism: The Thirties." *American Studies* 15:1 (1974), 61–77. Critics of President Roosevelt's foreign policy in the 1930s were not isolationists or pacifists but anti-imperialists.

20:129 Paterson, Thomas G. "Isolationism Revisited." *Nation* 209:6 (1969), 166–69. A survey of isolationism during the 1930s that concludes that social democracy will have trouble in the United States if Americans have to foster it abroad by force rather than by precept; argues that historians and politicians have distorted isolationism and confused a useful heritage.

20:130 Williams, William Appleman. "The Legend of Isolationism in the 1920's." In *History as a Way of Learning.* New York: New Viewpoints, 1973, pp. 117–34. The Republican era of 1921 to 1933 was one of "express and extended involvement with—and intervention in the affairs of—other nations of the world." Hughes, Hoover, and Stimson were apostles of a new corporatism designed to expand American power through the "internationalization of business." A reprint of his original essay in *Science and Society* 18 (1954), 1–20.

SENATE MUNITIONS INQUIRY

See, under "Personalities," "Others," Gerald P. Nye.

20:131 Engelbrecht, Helmuth C., and Hanighen, Frank C. *Merchants of Death.* New York: Garland (1934), 1972. A widely read, popular account that had some influence in prompting the Nye Com-

mittee's investigation into the activities of armament manufacturers.

Koistinen, P. A. C. "The 'Industrial Military Complex' in Historical Perspective: The Interwar Years" (19:178) argues that the present military-industrial complex originated in the close relations and support that the military and their suppliers established in the interwar period, and President Roosevelt's War Resources Board gave additional impetus to such a long-term trend.

20:132 Wiltz, John E. *In Search of Peace: The Senate Munitions Inquiry, 1934–36.* Baton Rouge: Louisiana State University Press, 1963. Offering a revisionist interpretation, Wiltz relates that the Nye Committee investigation debunked the "merchants of death" thesis, established the National Munitions Control Board, and provided information that the government found useful during World War II. He explains that the investigation probably bore only minor responsibility in passage of the neutrality acts of the latter 1930s.

LUDLOW AMENDMENT

Bolt, E. C., Jr. *Ballots before Bullets: The War Referendum Approach to Peace in America, 1914–1941* (19:163) provides an expanded view of the peace movement in the 1930s and the attendant war referendum proposal which had a longer past and more persistent support than most historians have recorded. The nature of Roosevelt's battle against the isolationists and this manifestation of the peace movement is clearly documented.

20:133 Burns, Richard Dean, and Dixon, W. Addams. "Foreign Policy and the 'Democratic Myth': The Debate on the Ludlow Amendment." *Mid-America* 47:4 (1965), 288–306. The authors seek to analyze the arguments used in the House during the crucial debate on the Ludlow Amendment. Of the several contemporary arguments, there was considerable discussion over the merits of a "pure" democracy versus a representative form of government.

20:134 Griffin, Walter R. "Louis Ludlow and the War Referendum Crusade, 1935–1941." *Indiana Magazine of History* 64:4 (1968), 267–88. Ludlow (1873–1950) was nearly successful in amending the Constitution to provide for a national referendum before a declaration of war.

NEUTRALITY ACTS

See Chapter 22, "Aid to Allies, 1938–1941."

Borchard, E. M., and Lage, W. P. *Neutrality for the United States* (16:143).

Cole, W. S. "Senator Key Pittman and American Neutrality Policies, 1933–1940" (22:31) reveals that although the chairman of the Foreign Relations Committee generally sought a middle course between isolationists and interventionists, he played a significant part in passage of the 1935 mandatory arms embargo act.

Divine, R. A. *The Illusion of Neutrality* (22:11) reviews the forces behind the neutrality legislation of the 1930s. Divine considers public attitudes as responsible for this dubious policy as any other factor, but he also finds President Roosevelt negligent in leadership. Bibliography.

20:135 Jablon, Howard. "The State Department and Collective Security." *Historian* 33:2 (1971), 248–63. Jablon disagrees with Robert A. Divine's assessment (22:11) that Secretary of State Hull and Norman Davis were strong advocates of collective action during the arms embargo dispute in 1933.

20:136 Jessup, Philip C. *Neutrality: Its History, Economics and Law.* Vol. 4 in *Today and Tomorrow.* New York: Columbia University Press, 1936. This fourth volume of a remarkable series was occasioned by the Nye Committee investigation of the mid-1930s and the general interest in neutral rights prior to the outbreak of a second world war.

20:137 Weiss, Stuart L. "American Foreign Policy and Presidential Power: The Neutrality Act of 1935." *Journal of Politics* 30:3 (1968), 672–95. The Neutrality Act of 1935, which narrowly restricted the power of the president in the conduct of foreign policy, was undesirable and might have been avoided had President Roosevelt taken the initiative in 1933.

20:138 Wiltz, John E. "The Nye Committee Revisited." *Historian* 23:2 (1961), 211–33. The author concludes that even without Nye, neutrality legislation would have come from Congress. Nye's intemperate speeches not only gave the Nye Committee a poor public image, but probably contributed to historians' giving Nye more credit than he deserved.

Disarmament and Arms Control

20:139 Atwater, Elton. *American Regulation of Arms Exports.* New York: Columbia University Press, 1941. Atwater sketches the arms traffic before regulation, and discusses in detail regulation of shipments to promote stability and discourage revolution in such areas as the Dominican Republic, Mexico, China, Cuba, Honduras, Nicaragua, and Brazil. He treats arms embargoes, which he sees as grossly exaggerated as a means of staying out of war. Shipping food and other supplies is more dangerous for neutrality, he asserts, than the sending of goods clearly categorized as absolute contraband.

20:140 Burns, Richard Dean, and Urquidi, Donald. *Disarmament in Perspective: An Analysis of Selected Arms Control and Disarmament Agreements between the World Wars, 1919–1939.* ACDA Rpt. RS-55. 4 vols. Washington, D.C.: G.P.O., 1968. The authors identify the characteristics of success and failure of 17 interwar treaties: volume 1, disarmament and the peace conference; volume 2, demilitarization of frontiers, islands, and straits; volume 3, limitation of sea power; volume 4, conclusions.

20:141 Burns, Richard Dean, and Urquidi, Donald. "Woodrow Wilson and Disarmament: Ideas vs Realities." *Aerospace Historian* 18:4 (1971), 186–94. In reviewing Woodrow Wilson's efforts toward world disarmament, the authors find that disarmament was only a theory during most of World War I, with low priority at the peace conference.

Farago, Ladislas. *The Broken Seal: The Story of "Operation Magic" and the Pearl Harbor Disaster* (22:264) relates that experts in the Office of Naval Intelligence provided American delegates at the Washington Conference with inside knowledge of Japanese tactics. Soon, however, Secretary of State Stimson told the codebreakers that "gentlemen do not read each other's mail." He discouraged use of decoding devices and other spy techniques.

20:142 Tate, Merze. *The United States and Armaments.* Cambridge: Harvard University Press, 1948. Tate surveys the interwar disarmament efforts and draws conclusions from them. This account is useful as an overview but it has been superseded by other studies including various dissertations which have used documents not then available.

NAVAL LIMITATION

20:143 Burns, Richard Dean. "Inspection of the Mandates, 1919–1941." *Pacific Historical Review* 37:4 (1968), 445–62. As a result of the peace settlement of 1919, the Japanese received the former German island groups—the Marianas, the Carolines, the Marshalls. U.S. authorities were long convinced that the Japanese were violating their promise not to construct military installations, although Japan did not begin outright military construction until 1940.

20:144 Burns, Richard Dean. "Regulating Submarine Warfare, 1921–41: A Case Study in Arms Control and Limited War." *Military Affairs* 35:2 (1971), 56–62. The essay discusses efforts to regulate submarine warfare, culminating in the submarine protocol of 1936. Although the major powers agreed to regulation, the arrangements were forgotten as soon as hostilities were underway in 1939 to 1941.

20:145 Doyle, Michael K. "The United States Navy—Strategy and Far Eastern Foreign Policy, 1931–1941." *Naval War College Review* 29:3 (1977), 52–60. Between the two world wars the national interest of the United States in East Asia exceeded America's capacity to defend it by force of arms. One possible resolution of the problem was the Washington agreements of 1921–1922. Navy officers disagreed with the ideas underlying this arrangement, which did not survive Japanese naval expansion in the 1930s.

20:146 Gibbs, Norman. "The Naval Conferences of the Interwar Years: A Study in Anglo-American Relations." *Naval War College Review* 30:1 (1977), 50–63. After years of differences between the two major naval powers, they realized that common interests and realities called for plans for common action against enemies. This essay traces the first steps in building an alliance between Washington and London.

Ito, M. *The End of the Imperial Japanese Navy* (23:190) includes chapters describing Japanese construction programs and battle strategies against the U.S. Navy. For nearly two decades Japanese admirals prepared to ambush American fleets which they believed would push into the western Pacific because of the audacious Orange Plan.

Morison, E. E. *Admiral Sims and the Modern American Navy* (40:86) shows the American phase of a battle fought in the admiralties of Britain, Japan, and other naval powers. Most navy professionals of the 1920s and 1930s continued to believe that sea power should be measured by battleships and the size and range of their guns. Sims and other forward-looking officers fought for recognition of carriers and submarines, bombs and torpedoes. The Westerners were not listening, and so the Japanese profited from this advice, yet paradoxically continued to invest too large a percentage of their funds in old-fashioned dreadnoughts.

20:147 Morton, Louis. "War Plan Orange: Evolution of a Strategy." *World Politics* 11:2 (1959), 221–50. The U.S. Navy maintained a contingency plan for war until the late 1930s, the Orange Plan, which envisioned fleet battles in the western Pacific. Such a plan was considered necessary for defense of the Philippines.

Rappaport, A. *The Navy League of the United States* (2:212) denies that the league was a front for shipbuilding lobbies.

20:148 Roskill, Stephen W. *Naval Policy between the Wars.* 2 vols. London: Collins, 1968–1976. The official historian for British naval policy during World War II undertook to fill in the period between his own studies and Arthur Marder's work on World War I. There is much material on Anglo-American rivalry in the 1920s, including details on the hesitant efforts at cooperation under Franklin D. Roosevelt and a great deal on the timidity of British naval planners in Europe and the Mediterranean during the appeasement years. Extensive bibliography.

Wheeler, G. E. *Prelude to Pearl Harbor: The United States Navy and the Far East, 1921–1931* (40:181) reviews the navy's response to the limitation treaties.

Washington Naval Conference, 1921–1922

See "Personalities," especially Charles Evans Hughes, and, under "Others," William V. Pratt; see also Chapter 21, "Abrogation of the Anglo-Japanese Alliance," and Chapter 32, "Washington Conference, 1921–1922."

20:149 Andrade, Ernest O., Jr. "The United States Navy and the Washington Conference." *Historian*

31:3 (1969), 345–63. The erosion of American naval power following the conference was rooted in the fact that auxiliary warships had not been restricted. This omission turned out to be crucial, for a stingy Congress, supported by public opinion, refused to provide funds to build cruisers, destroyers, and submarines in nearly the numbers constructed by the Japanese.

20:150 Asada Sadao. "Japan's 'Special Interests' and the Washington Conference, 1921–22." *American Historical Review* 67:1 (1961–1962), 62–70. In consenting to cancel the Lansing-Ishii agreement, the Japanese government believed that its special interests continued and that it reserved freedom of action in Manchuria. The ambiguity of the agreement was perpetuated in the "security" clause of the Nine-Power Pact.

20:151 Birn, Donald S. "Open Diplomacy at the Washington Conference of 1921–2: The British and French Experience." *Comparative Studies in Society and History* 12:3 (1970), 297–319. The Washington Conference, Birn claims, came as close to open diplomacy as any conference of the interwar era. Public opinion not only helped determine the policy of each nation, but it played a more direct role in day-to-day tactics. For a critique, see J. David Singer, "Popular Diplomacy and Policy Effectiveness: A Note on the Mechanisms and Consequences," ibid., pp. 320–26.

Braisted, W. R. *The United States Navy in the Pacific, 1909–1922* (17:227).

20:152 Buckley, Thomas H. *The United States and the Washington Conference, 1921–1922*. Knoxville: University of Tennessee Press, 1970. The bulk of the book deals with issues and events of the conference, and Buckley finds the Five-Power Treaty, the Four-Power Treaty, the Nine-Power Treaty, and the other results of the conference all largely satisfactory, for they accommodated the interests of American diplomats.

20:153 Dingman, Roger. *Power in the Pacific: The Origins of Naval Arms Limitation, 1914–1922*. Chicago: University of Chicago Press, 1976. Historians have attributed the desire to disarm to mutual understandings of respective strategic and economic capabilities, but Dingman stresses domestic political factors and the desire of statesmen to appear well at home. A brief but impressive comparison of bureaucratic politics in London, Washington, and Tokyo. Bibliography.

20:154 Hoag, C. Leonard. *Preface to Preparedness: The Washington Disarmament Conference and Public Opinion*. Washington, D.C.: American Council on Public Affairs, 1941. This book offers a detailed study of the public opinion campaign waged in the United States on behalf of disarmament, and captures the mood of the early 1920s. The author finds women's groups particularly important in the disarmament crusade.

20:155 Ichihashi Yamato. *The Washington Conference and After*. Palo Alto, Calif.: Stanford University Press, 1928. A summary—not a memoir—of the Washington Conference, by an individual attached to the Japanese delegation, later a historian at Stanford University.

Sprout, H., and Sprout, M. *Toward a New Order of Sea Power: American Naval Policy and the World Scene, 1918–1922*. (19:280) found that the Washington Naval Conference reflected a widespread revolt against navalism, with delegates discovering that it was easier to agree on limitation of capital ships than smaller fighting craft. Arguments revolved around cruisers, submarines, and airships. With the U.S. Navy gaining parity with Britain's as a result of the battleship agreement, a foundation was laid for Anglo-American cooperation on a much wider scale.

20:156 Van Meter, Robert H., Jr. "The Washington Conference of 1921–1922: A New Look." *Pacific Historical Review* 46:4 (1977), 603–24. Historians have ignored the influence of the depression of 1920–1921 on American policy at the Washington Conference. Secretary of Commerce Hoover and other Harding administration officials were convinced that disarmament would promote economic stabilization and recovery in Europe, which would help restore American prosperity by increasing overseas markets.

20:157 Vinson, John Chalmers. "The Problem of Australian Representation at the Washington Conference for the Limitation of Naval Armament." *Australian Journal of Politics and History* 4:2 (1958), 155–64. Australia desired direct representation at the Washington Conference (1921–1922), as it worried about Japanese naval power and sought the national prestige of participation. Secretary of State Hughes blocked this ambition.

20:158 Vinson, John Chalmers. *The Parchment Peace: The United States Senate and the Washington Conference, 1921–1922*. Athens: University of Georgia Press, 1955. Vinson traces the role of the Senate in helping bring about the Washington Naval Conference, analyzes views of members toward disarmament and East Asian policy, and discusses the debate over approval of the treaties. There is special coverage of the Senate's reaction to the Four-Power Pact.

Coolidge Conference, 1927

See "Personalities," especially Calvin Coolidge, Frank B. Kellogg.

20:159 Carlton, David. "Great Britain and the Coolidge Naval Disarmament Conference of 1927." *Political Science Quarterly* 83:4 (1968), 573–98. The conference failed because the statesmen were unable to overrule pessimists among their naval advisers. Anglo-American relations suffered as a result.

20:160 Dubay, Robert W. "The Geneva Naval Conference of 1927: A Study of Battleship Diplomacy." *Southern Quarterly* 8:2 (1970), 177–99. Although the Washington Conference had established an international ratio for capital ship construction among the leading world naval powers, lesser categories of vessels were not regulated. President Coolidge called for a conference in 1927 to negotiate a treaty to limit ships of less than 10,000 tons displacement.

London Naval Conference, 1930

See "Personalities," especially Charles G. Dawes, Herbert C. Hoover, Henry L. Stimson.

20:161 Mayer-Oakes, Thomas F. *Fragile Victory: Prince Saionji and the 1930 London Treaty Issue. . . .* Detroit, Mich.: Wayne State University Press, 1968. This view of the Japanese side of the 1930 London naval negotiations consists of an extended introduction and a translation of the first volume of Baron Harada Kumao's memoirs.

20:162 O'Connor, Raymond G. *Perilous Equilibrium: The United States and the London Disarmament Conference of 1930.* Lawrence: University of Kansas Press, 1962. Reprint 1969. The 1930 treaty extended the Washington Treaty by restricting ships under 10,000 tons, revising ratios, and including an escalator clause. O'Connor states that the London Conference in some ways strengthened the disarmament system and in some ways weakened it.

London Naval Conference, 1935–1936

20:163 Asada Sadao. "The Japanese Navy and the United States." In Dorothy Borg, Shumpei Okamoto, and Dale K. A. Finlayson, eds., *Pearl Harbor as History: Japanese-American Relations, 1931–1941.* New York: Columbia University Press, 1973, pp. 225–60. This valuable essay surveys the importance of naval limitation in the politicizing of Japanese naval officers from the London Conference of 1930 to the conference of 1935.

20:164 Berg, Meredith W. "Admiral William H. Standley and the Second London Naval Treaty, 1934–1936." *Historian* 33:2 (1971), 215–36. As chief of naval operations and a representative on the U.S. delegation to the conference, Standley kept alive the idea of naval limitation. Through all discouragements in negotiations from 1934 to 1936, he never lost sight of the need for an agreement, no matter how tentative or restricted.

20:165 Pelz, Stephen E. *Race to Pearl Harbor: The Failure of the Second London Naval Conference and the Onset of World War II.* Cambridge: Harvard University Press, 1974. This study of naval limitation (1921–1935) concentrates on the general staff of the Japanese navy. There is detailed commentary on both American and Japanese strategists as they adjusted their planning to rules produced by the disarmament conferences. Pelz shows how Japanese naval factions sought parity to force changes in the limitation system or else destroy it.

LEAGUE OF NATIONS EFFORTS

See "Personalities," especially Hugh R. Wilson.

20:166 Burns, Richard Dean. "International Arms Inspection Policies between World Wars, 1919–1934." *Historian* 31:4 (1969), 583–603. This essay, based on printed sources, seeks to identify the policies of the major powers negotiating a league-sponsored conferences. Interestingly, the United States at first opposed inspection, while the Soviet Union endorsed it.

20:167 Temperley, A. C. *The Whispering Gallery of Europe.* London: Collins, 1938. A military adviser to the British delegation at Geneva for some 15 years, the author assesses the league's disarmament endeavors.

20:168 Wheeler-Bennett, John W. *Disarmament and Security since Locarno, 1925–1931.* New York: Macmillan, 1932. The author appears to have had inside information from the British Foreign Office, and discusses league efforts to resolve disarmament issues. An earlier volume, *Information on the Reduction of Armaments* (London: Allen & Unwin, 1925), deals with the league's first years.

20:169 Wheeler-Bennett, John W. *The Pipe Dream of Peace: The Story of the Collapse of Disarmament.* New York: Morrow, 1935. The author discusses the general disarmament conference at Geneva that opened in 1932 and closed in 1934 without achieving its objectives. He also covers events in Europe, especially the rise of Hitler in Germany.

20:170 Winkler, Fred H. "Disarmament and Security: The American Policy at Geneva, 1926–1935." *North Dakota Quarterly* 39:4 (1971), 21–33. The Geneva Disarmament Conference of 1932 to 1934 marked the high point of America's cooperation in international security during the interwar years, and yet even here the American government attempted to block any proposal at the conference that might interfere with its military affairs or entangle it in European affairs.

20:171 Winkler, Fred H. "The War Department and Disarmament, 1926–1935." *Historian* 28:3 (1966), 426–46. Winkler comments on the professional soldiers' views of their role in foreign policy as well as on issues at hand. He finds that the War Department was willing to cooperate in disarmament as long as restrictions were to apply only to tangible forces and equipment, not the nation's potential for mobilization.

Economic Policies and Diplomacy

20:172 Adams, Frederick C. *Economic Diplomacy: The Export-Import Bank and American Foreign Policy, 1934–1939.* Columbia: University of Missouri Press, 1976. Adams finds the bank's activities instrumental in promoting economic outreach, involving the United States internationally in ways that would have been impossible prior to the bank's creation in 1934. The focus is on Latin America and East Asia. Extensive bibliography.

20:173 Allen, James B. "The Great Protectionist, Sen. Reed Smoot of Utah." *Utah Historical Quarterly* 45:4 (1977), 325–45. Reed Smoot (1862–1941), Utah senator (1903–1933), was an ardent spokesman for the protective tariff. He was convinced that American prosperity and self-sufficiency related directly to the tariff. His Senate years culminated in the ill-timed Smoot-Hawley tariff of 1930.

Brandes, J. *Herbert Hoover and Economic Diplomacy: Department of Commerce Policy, 1921–1928* (20:40).

20:174 Chalk, Frank R. "The United States and the International Struggle for Rubber, 1914–1941." Ph.D. diss., University of Wisconsin, 1970. During the 1920s, U.S. dependence upon rubber as a raw material for industrialization markedly increased. Chalk shows how Great Britain tried to combat American economic power by restricting production early in the 1920s. The endeavor merely delayed greater American control of world rubber supplies.

Chandler, L. V. *Benjamin Strong: Central Banker* (39:43) shows that Strong and the Federal Reserve Bank of New York cooperated with other central bankers, especially Montagu Norman and the Bank of England, in a way that presaged public foreign aid after World War II.

20:175 Costigliola, Frank C. "The Other Side of Isolationism: The Establishment of the First World Bank, 1929–1930." *Journal of American History* 59:3 (1972), 602–20. The Bank for International Settlements was established by a group of prominent New York bankers because of their belief that settlement of exchange rates and payment of reparations out of expanded German exports was essential to the economic expansion of the United States.

20:176 Dollar, Charles M. "The South and the Fordney-McCumber Tariff of 1922: A Study in Regional Politics." *Journal of Southern History* 39:1 (1973), 45–67. This article maintains that the southern congressional sentiment for tariff protection is not a recent phenomenon, and as early as 1922 there was support for a high tariff among Southerners in both houses of Congress.

20:177 Falkus, M. E. "United States Economic Policy and the 'Dollar Gap' of the 1920's." *Economic History Review* 24:4 (1971), 599–623. American policy in the 1920s is often judged by comparisons with Britain's role before 1914. It is doubtful if American tariff adjustments could have produced the desired effect on the U.S. balance.

20:178 Feis, Herbert. *The Diplomacy of the Dollar, 1919–1932.* New York: Norton (1950), 1966. Feis deals with a private effort, using private capital, but guided by the State Department toward investments which, it was hoped, would advance U.S. national interest.

Gardner, L. C. *Economic Aspects of New Deal Diplomacy* (21:12) argues that in pursuit of economic objectives, summarized in the idea of the open door, the U.S. government failed to obtain a compromise with Japan in 1941. In similar fashion the open door has led to most of America's difficulties since World War II.

Kaufman, B. I. *Efficiency and Expansion: Foreign Trade Organization in the Wilson Administration, 1913–1921* (19:129).

20:179 Keynes, John Maynard. "National Self-Sufficiency." *Yale Review* 22:4 (1933), 755–69. Keynes reverses his neoclassical position to advocate autarchic and isolationist policies of recovery from the depression—a reversal that may have had an unfortunate influence on New Deal policymakers.

20:180 Kindleberger, Charles P. *The World in Depression, 1929–1939.* Berkeley: University of California Press, 1973. Another argument that the world crisis of the 1930s issued from the fact that the United States after the war did not act as the British had acted from 1814 to 1914. Implicitly the book argues that industrial capitalism as a world system must have one general manager, so as to create international political, economic, and social stability. An international community of roughly equal capitalist powers is, according to the author, impossible.

20:181 Lauderbaugh, Richard A. "Business, Labor, and Foreign Policy: U.S. Steel, the International Steel Cartel, and Recognition of the Steel Workers Organizing Committee." *Politics and Society* 6:4 (1976), 433–57. The U.S. Steel Corporation's collective bargaining agreement with the Steel Workers Organizing Committee in early 1937 depended upon a verbal commitment to join the Entente Internationale de L'Acier (International Steel Cartel): In contravention of New Deal policies and the antitrust laws, the agreement included import restrictions, controlling competition in the international steel market, and protecting the U.S. market.

Lawrence, J. C. *The World's Struggle with Rubber, 1905–1931* (39:51) is still useful for the international history of rubber in the 1920s; this work has been largely supplanted by Chalk's dissertation (20:174).

Lewis, C. *America's Stake in International Investments* (39:92) is an indispensable introductory study of U.S. foreign economic policy in the 1920s and 1930s. No summary can do it justice; the book is a gold mine.

20:182 Moore, James R. "Sources of New Deal Economic Policy: The International Dimension." *Journal of American History* 61:3 (1974), 728–44. Roosevelt and his advisers advocated schemes for global public works backed by continued American loans, stabilization of currency exchange rates at devalued levels, a tariff "truce," and settlement of the war debts issue. But Congress, bent on inflationary policies, together with Britain and France's lack of cooperation, turned FDR to a nationalistic economic policy.

Ostrower, G. B. "The American Decision to Join the International Labor Organization" (20:86) finds that support for U.S. membership in the International Labor Organization arose from the Department of Labor under Frances Perkins. With the support of the Department of State and President Roosevelt, opposition from isolationists and financial conservatives was overcome by 1934.

Parrini, C. P. *Heir to Empire: United States Economic Diplomacy, 1916–1923* (19:130) describes how the United States, subsequent to the 1916 Paris Economic Conference, sought to create a world community of opinion on investments, raw material allocations, and matters of war debts, tariffs, and reparations. To do so the U.S. government, along with business and financial interests, opposed the closed door economic system advocated at Paris.

Safford, J. J. *Wilsonian Maritime Diplomacy, 1913–1921* (19:149) has a chapter devoted to the important Merchant Marine Act of 1920.

20:183 Schoepperle, Victor. "The Future of International Investment: Private vs. Public Lending."

American Economic Review 31:1, suppl. pt. 2 (1943), 336–41. A history of foreign investment in the 1920s and 1930s which includes a contention that such investment will have to be resumed, but that much of it will have to be undertaken by the U.S. government, either when the risks are too great for private capital or when the payoff is too far into the future to justify private investment.

20:184   Schumpeter, Joseph A. *Business Cycles: A Theoretical Historical and Statistical Analysis of the Capitalist Process.* New York: McGraw-Hill, 1964. Schumpeter disposes of much nonsense parading as fact among historians, economists, and political scientists. He shows that the so-called failure of the United States to accept a creditor status after World War I had little to do with the economic crisis in 1929, and that statesmen were familiar with fiscal policy as a stabilization technique long before Keynes published the *General Theory* in the mid-1930s.

20:185   Wilson, Joan Hoff. *American Business and Foreign Policy, 1920–1933.* Lexington: University of Kentucky Press, 1971. Wilson sketches a complex relationship between business and government, and argues that business opinion was too divided to allow a system of business management of foreign policy.

EUROPEAN RECOVERY

See Chapter 21, "U.S. and the Western Hemisphere" and "U.S. and East Asia," for economic policies.

20:186   Abrahams, Paul P. "American Bankers and the Economic Tactics of Peace, 1919." *Journal of American History* 56:3 (1969), 572–83. The U.S. Treasury Department prevented any sort of public or public-guaranteed loans for European reconstruction, despite a more sympathetic view by bankers. For this reason, American capital was not available to Europe until the Dawes Plan in 1924.

20:187   Leffler, Melvyn P. "American Policy Making and European Stability, 1921–1933." *Pacific Historical Review* 46:2 (1977), 207–28. This is a wide-ranging summary of U.S. diplomacy with respect to European stability and a refinement of W. A. Williams's perception of the 1920s as an era of international activism. Leffler views European stability as having been important to American interests but not, Washington thought, necessary to American capitalism nor to national security.

20:188   Leffler, Melvyn P. "Political Isolationism, Economic Expansionism, or Diplomatic Realism: American Policy toward Western Europe, 1921–1933." *Perspectives in American History* 8 (1974), 413–61. Americans sought to bring Germany into the international order in the 1920s by achieving a reparations agreement, stabilizing the mark, and deterring French military adventures. Americans, more than the French, believed the German government conciliatory and supported German claims to equality of rights under the Treaty of Versailles and claims to territorial adjustments in the east.

20:189   Rosen, Elliot A. "Intranationalism vs. Internationalism: The Interregnum Struggle for the Sanctity of the New Deal." *Political Science Quarterly* 81:2 (1966), 274–97. Rosen demonstrates that President Roosevelt decided to bring about domestic economic recovery without attempting to cooperate with other industrial states, and thus arrange for recovery implicitly at the expense of other nations.

Anglo-American Economics

See also "War Debts," below.

Costigliola, F. C. "Anglo-American Financial Rivalry in the 1920s" (39:110) argues that both the United States and Britain sought throughout the 1920s to rebuild a world capitalist economy, albeit in different ways, and that the United States won the struggle and thereafter pursued a stabilization policy that reflected its selfish "deflationary" interests.

20:190   Goldberg, Michael D. "Anglo-American Economic Competition 1920–1930." *Economy and History* 16 (1973), 15–36. Goldberg examines the factors that enabled the United States to enjoy prosperity in the decade after World War I while Britain suffered depression. He focuses on the role of Hoover as secretary of commerce in building overseas trade.

20:191   Hogan, Michael J. *Informal Entente: The Private Structure of Cooperation in Anglo-American Economic Diplomacy, 1918–1928.* Columbia: University of Missouri Press, 1977. Hogan focuses on Anglo-American economic programs for the postwar order and emphasizes cooperation rather than rivalry following the war. He suggests that continuity rather than discontinuity marked the change from Wilsonian leadership to that of Harding and Coolidge. The book is organized by such topics as petroleum, European reconstruction, cables and radio. Extensive bibliography.

Franco-American Economics

See also "War Debts," below.

Leffler, M. P. *The Elusive Quest: America's Pursuit of European Stability and French Security, 1919–1933* (21:102) offers insight into bankers' diplomacy to strengthen the French economy.

Schuker, S. A. *The End of French Predominance in Europe: The Financial Crisis of 1924 and the Adoption of the Dawes Plan* (39:115).

German-American Economics

See also "German Reparations (Dawes Plan)," below.

Bennett, E. W. *Germany and the Diplomacy of the Financial Crisis, 1931* (39:107) examines the efforts of Anglo-American statesmen to deal with this crisis.

20:192 Burke, Bernard V. "American Economic Diplomacy and the Weimar Republic." *Mid-America* 54:4 (1972), 211–33. When the German government came into deep political trouble because of the Great Depression and the gains of the Nazis in the elections of 1930, the Hoover administration virtually ignored Ambassador Frederic M. Sackett's call to encourage loans to Germany and sponsor a conference to resolve the war debts-reparations tangle.

20:193 Costigliola, Frank. "The United States and the Reconstruction of Germany in the 1920's." *Business History Review* 50:4 (1976), 477–502. Republican government officials and businessmen sought to maximize American economic expansion and minimize political commitment by a prosperous and peaceful European order, which meant bringing the German economy into that of the capitalist West. American strategy involved solving the reparations problem with the Dawes Plan.

20:194 Etzold, Thomas H. *Why America Fought Germany in World War II.* St. Louis: Forum, 1973. The Great Depression shattered American-German economic relations of the 1920s, and thereafter American officials were unresponsive to Germany's

economic problems—the foreign exchange crisis, the need to reduce or eliminate reparations and service of the Dawes and Young plan debts, and the need to redress the unfavorable trade balance with the United States. U.S. failure to negotiate a new trade treaty in 1935 led to the virtual end of trade. The economic confrontation of the mid-1930s was transformed into the political confrontation of 1941.

20:195 Falkus, M. E. "The German Business Cycle in the 1920's." *Economic History Review* 28:3 (1975), 451–65. Falkus argues that "exogenous" declines in foreign investment, for the most part by American capital, preceded the 1929 downturn in the German business cycle, and hence were partly the cause of the stockmarket collapse in the United States—as President Hoover believed.

20:196 Kolko, Gabriel. "American Business and Germany, 1930–1941." *Western Political Quarterly* 15:4 (1962), 713–28. Although the business press displayed strong anti-Nazi views during the 1930s, American corporate leaders operated within the autarchic economic framework of the Third Reich, despite knowledge of German war preparations, and of restrictions on currency convertibility and repatriation of profits. Businessmen believed they would get their profits ultimately.

20:197 Link, Werner. *Die Amerikanische Stabilisierungspolitik im Deutschland, 1921–32* [The politics of American stabilization measures in Germany, 1921–1932]. Düsseldorf: Droste, 1970. A massive study of American-German relations, which considers the connection between political ideology and economic interests, foreign and domestic politics, and argues that Americans, public and private, sought to maintain moderate governments, to foster trade, to assist between Germany and its erstwhile enemies, to weaken German-Russian relations.

Offner, Arnold A. "Appeasement Revisited: The United States, Great Britain, and Germany, 1933–1940" (22:116) attacks the New Left view that the United States went to war with Nazi Germany because "the German autarchic policy challenged the Open Door policy in Eastern Europe and Latin America and the American conception of a world political economy." This view, he contends, failed to take into account American efforts to appease Germany from 1933 to 1940.

20:198 Peterson, Edward N. *Hjalmar Schacht: For and Against Hitler: A Political-Economic Study of*

Germany, 1923–1945. Boston: Christopher House, 1954. Peterson examines Schacht's role in Germany's politics and economy beginning with issues arising out of the Dawes Plan, reparations, Young Plan, rearmament and trade policies. Bibliography.

Repko, A. F. "The Failure of Reciprocal Trade: United States–German Commercial Rivalry in Brazil, 1934–1940" (20:235).

20:199 Schröder, Hans-Jürgen. *Deutschland und die Vereinigten Staaten, 1933–1939: Wirtschaft und Politik in der Entwicklung des Deutsch-Amerikanischen Gegensatzes* [Germany and the United States, 1933–1939: economics and politics in the development of German-American hostility]. Wiesbaden: Franz Steiner, 1970. The conflict between America's economic open door and Germany's policy of autarchy set the steadily deteriorating course of American-German relations. U.S. officials saw Germany's blocked currencies, bilateral trade policies and barter agreements, the inroads to Latin American markets, the domination of the Balkans economically, as threats to the sort of free economic relations they desired. Economic conflict underlay the coming war.

Weinberg, G. L. *The Foreign Policy of Hitler's Germany: Diplomatic Revolution in Europe, 1933–1936* (21:128) suggests that Hitler did not consider the proposed 1935 trade treaty essential to his purposes. This study also contains material on German economic relations with Latin America.

20:200 Weinberg, Gerhard L. "Schachts Besuch in den USA im Jahre 1933" [Schacht's visit to the United States of America in the year 1933]. *Vierteljahrshefte für Zeitgeschichte* 11 (1963), 166–80. Roosevelt invited Hitler to Washington for talks concerning the World Economic Conference and the World Disarmament Conference, and Hitler sent Hjalmar Schacht, president of the Reichsbank, who demanded equality of arms and revision of debts and a moratorium on transfer of interest and amortization payments. The trip led only to an impasse and continued American-German disagreement about finance, trade, and disarmament.

Soviet-American Economics

See also Chapter 21, "Nonrecognition/Recognition."

20:201 Condoide, Mikhail V. *Russian-American Trade*. Columbus: Ohio State University Press, 1946.

This careful study of the "Soviet foreign trade monopoly" was one of the first postwar efforts to assess the history of Soviet-American economic relations with a view to what might be expected in the future. It contains much information on trade before World War II.

20:202 Gillette, Philip S. "Conditions of American-Soviet Commerce: The Beginning of Direct Cotton Trade, 1923–1924." *Soviet Union* 1:1 (1974), 74–93. The cotton trade resulted from Viktor P. Nogin's visit to the United States, and is an underappreciated turning point in U.S.-Soviet trade.

20:203 Gillette, Philip S. "American Capital in the Contest for Soviet Oil, 1920–23." *Soviet Studies* 24:4 (1973), 477–90. During these years there was a possibility of U.S. companies acquiring concessionary rights to Russian oil. Gillette reviews the oil situation before 1917, and analyzes the relationships among the Soviet government, the American government, and American oil companies in 1920 to 1923.

Smith, G. A. *Soviet Foreign Trade: Organization, Operation, and Policy, 1918–1971* (39:80).

20:204 Sutton, Antony C. *Western Technology and Soviet Economic Development, 1917–1965*. 3 vols. Stanford, Calif.: Hoover Institution Press, 1968–1973. A detailed, sophisticated work that is essential to understanding Soviet development. Sutton argues that Western aid was the sine qua non of Soviet progress. Elsewhere the author has advocated an end to this sort of assistance, remarking that it is "national suicide" for the United States to continue assistance in the present international era.

Wilson, J. H. *Ideology and Economics: U.S. Relations with the Soviet Union, 1918–1933* (21:177) analyzes the relative importance of ideological, economic, and organizational influences on policy toward Soviet Russia. The author has much to say about Soviet-American commercial relations and the role of market considerations.

LATIN AMERICA

Hilton, S. E. *Brazil and the Great Powers, 1930–1939: The Politics of Trade Rivalry* (39:62) reveals interesting aspects of American, British, and German policies to extend trade and influence in South America during the 1930s. Washington's efforts to push Hull's trade views ran counter to Brazil's interest in maintaining a bilateral trade arrangement with Germany.

20:205 Kane, N. Stephen. "Corporate Power and Foreign Policy: Efforts of American Oil Companies to Influence United States Relations with Mexico, 1921–1928." *Diplomatic History* 1:2 (1977), 170–98. Kane concludes that the oil lobby failed to gain aid from the State Department to curb Mexico's new petroleum laws. While the State Department defended the principle of nonretroactivity, it insisted that the oil companies deal with a willing Mexican government.

20:206 Klein, Herbert S. "American Oil Companies in Latin America: The Bolivian Experience." *Inter-American Economic Affairs* 18:1 (1964), 47–72. In the first expropriation of a foreign oil company in Latin America, the Bolivian government confiscated the Standard Oil Company of Bolivia on March 13, 1937. Klein examines the details of the seizure and the 1942 settlement.

20:207 Normano, J. F. *The Struggle for South America: Economy and Ideology.* London: Allen & Unwin, 1931. Covering approximately the first quarter of the 20th century, Normano's book describes the competition between European powers and the United States for influence in the economic future of South America.

20:208 Rabe, Stephen G. "Anglo-American Rivalry for Venezuelan Oil, 1919–1929." *Mid-America* 58:2 (1976), 97–110. Great Britain responded first to Venezuelan encouragement for foreign development of its oil, and the United States followed. After 1921, America and England cooperated in oil development in the Middle East and Venezuela.

20:209 Randall, Stephen J. "The International Corporation and American Foreign Policy: The United States and Colombian Petroleum, 1920–1940." *Canadian Journal of History* 9:2 (1974), 179–96. The petroleum industry was one of America's most significant areas of foreign investments during these years. Randall examines the virtual monopoly these companies acquired in Colombia.

20:210 Seidel, Robert N. "Progressive Pan Americanism: Development and United States Policy toward South America, 1906–1931." Ph.D. diss., Cornell University, 1973. Seidel charts the course of a policy he terms progressive Pan-Americanism, under which the growth of institutions in the United States

led to greater U.S. trade, investment, and development assistance to South America. By the time of the depression, limitations in the assistance program curtailed its effectiveness. Extensive bibliography.

Varg, P. A. "The Economic Side of the Good Neighbor Policy: The Reciprocal Trade Program and South America" (39:63) points out that only three of the ten South American republics entered into reciprocal trade agreements during 1934 to 1939, and at least two of those three nations (Brazil and Colombia) did so for political rather than economic reasons.

20:211 Wilkins, Mira. "Multinational Oil Companies in South America in the 1920's." *Business Historical Review* 48:3 (1974), 414–46. Wilkins considers foreign oil development in South America during the decade following World War I. Fears of a world oil shortage stimulated exploration and development. Certain nations encouraged these activities; others discouraged them, and Chile banned them.

20:212 Williams, William Appleman. "Latin America: Laboratory of American Foreign Policy in the Nineteen-Twenties." *Inter-American Economic Affairs* 11:1 (1957), 3–30. Latin American markets and raw materials and capital invested south of the Rio Grande, along with security interests in Panama, required new or modified policies that were generalized to the world at large. With the burgeoning domestic economy of the 1920s and reduced international competition, American officials such as Hughes and Hoover encouraged economic expansion and the open door, and were willing to provide support and protection when businessmen encountered difficulties.

20:213 Winkler, Max. *Investments of United States Capital in Latin America.* Boston: World Peace Foundation, 1929. This volume has introductory chapters on economic life in Latin America and on international investment, followed by a nation-by-nation survey of foreign investment. Charts on investment, trade, and economic activity are included.

EPISODES IN ECONOMIC DIPLOMACY

War Debts

See "Personalities," especially Hiram W. Johnson.

20:214   Dayer, Roberta Albert. "The British War Debts to the United States and the Anglo-Japanese Alliance, 1920–1923." *Pacific Historical Review* 45:4 (1976), 569–95. Recently opened British records show the relation between war debts and East Asian issues in British postwar policy. Whitehall believed that cooperation with Washington in East Asia might lead either to outright cancellation or, at the least, to a scaling down of war debts to the United States.

20:215   Flesig, Heywood. "War-Related Debts and the Great Depression." *American Economic Review* 66:2 (1976), 52–58. Because history is an uncontrolled experiment, it is questionable what would have happened to the war-related debts without the depression. In any event, they were "destined" for default.

20:216   Leffler, Melvyn P. "The Origins of Republican War Debt Policy, 1921–1923: A Case Study in the Applicability of the Open Door Interpretation." *Journal of American History* 59:3 (1972), 585–601. Public opinion and concern for domestic fiscal conditions responded to the desire for foreign markets, and thus the Republican party arranged its ideas about policy in regard to the war debts—that is, the party leaders decided that the debts should be collected.

Moulton, H. G., and Pasvolsky, L. *War Debts and World Prosperity* (39:113) trace the breakdown of efforts for a settlement early in the depression.

20:217   Pullen, William G. "World War Debts and United States Foreign Policy." Ph.D. diss., University of Georgia, 1972. This account explores the political and economic realities and misunderstandings which eventually led to an impasse in financial relations. Bibliography.

20:218   Rhodes, Benjamin D. "Herbert Hoover and the War Debts, 1919–33." *Prologue* 6:2 (1974), 130–44. Settlement of World War I war debts revolved about the person of Herbert Hoover, who first favored a conciliatory approach but was forced by political considerations to change course.

20:219   Rhodes, Benjamin D. "The Origins of Finnish-American Friendship, 1919–1941." *Mid-America* 54:1 (1972), 3–19. Rhodes provides details of the funding of the Finnish "war debt," from the agreement of May 1922 to August 1949, when Congress, recognizing the cold war implications of the debt, authorized that remaining payments fund a joint educational program.

20:220   Rhodes, Benjamin D. "Reassessing 'Uncle Shylock': The United States and the French War Debt, 1917–1929." *Journal of American History* 55:4 (1969), 787–803. The United States does not deserve the reputation of "Uncle Shylock" with regard to insistence on payment of the World War I debt. Policy was shortsighted rather than grasping.

20:221   Vinson, John Chalmers. "War Debts and Peace Legislation: The Johnson Act of 1934." *Mid-America* 50:3 (1968), 206–22. The two years preceding the Johnson Act (1934) represented a congressional attack against war debts defaulters, led by Senator Hiram Johnson.

German Reparations (Dawes Plan)

See "Personalities," especially Charles G. Dawes; also see "German-American Economics," above.

20:222   Bergmann, Carl. *The History of Reparations.* Boston: Houghton Mifflin, 1927. Bergmann, a German financial expert intimately involved in the reparations tangle, presents the German side of the question in detail, from 1918 to 1925, with attention to the role of the United States.

20:223   Etzold, Thomas H. "Fiscal Diplomacy: The House of Morgan, the State Department, and the Reparation Loans." *Peace and Change* 3:2/3 (1975), 109–12. Etzold describes the positions of the State Department and the Morgan Guaranty Trust Company with regard to reparations in the 1930s.

Hughes, B. A. "Owen D. Young and American Foreign Policy, 1919–1929" (39:44) explores Young's role in the German reparations question and his efforts to stabilize the German economy.

20:224   Jones, Kenneth P. "Discord and Collaboration: Choosing an Agent General for Reparations." *Diplomatic History* 1:2 (1977), 118–39. Disputes between the Coolidge administration, J. P. Morgan and Company, and the Bank of England over choosing an agent general to administer German reparations under the Dawes Plan provide a case study of American economic diplomacy. They point up the discord between government officials and private financiers over how to guarantee repayment of loans to American creditors and to depoliticize reparations.

Keynes, J. M. *The Economic Consequences of the Peace* (19:288) argues that the reparations forced upon Germany (c. $32 billion) were more than three times Germany's capacity to pay. Although this point later was disproved, his description of the economic consequences of the peace had a large readership and was one of the factors that persuaded many Americans to avoid the economic problems of Europe in the postwar era.

Lamont, T. W. *Across World Frontiers* (19:92) provides an authoritative overview of debates on the German economy regarding reparations.

Link, W. *Die Amerikanische Stabilisierungspolitik im Deutschland, 1921–32* (20:197) emphasizes reparations and their effect on politics, economics, and military issues.

20:225 Marks, Sally. "The Myths of Reparations." *Central European History* 11:3 (1978), 231–55. The amount of reparations required of Germany and its allies after World War I was not the 132 billion marks cited in the London Schedule of 1921 but the 50 million marks stipulated in the A and B bonds. Germany paid very little, and most of that was out of loans from Western bankers.

20:226 Schmidt, Royal J. *Versailles and the Ruhr: Seedbed of World War II*. The Hague: Nijhoff, 1968. Schmidt examines the Ruhr controversy and the Dawes Plan, from the French, British, German, and American viewpoints. The chapters on Wilson and Hughes provide an overview of U.S. policy. Bibliography.

Schuker, S. A. *The End of French Predominance in Europe: The Financial Crisis of 1924 and the Adoption of the Dawes Plan* (39:115) examines the economic weaknesses behind France's decline as a great power in the 1920s. Abandoned by Britain and the United States, the French resorted to force in collecting reparations from Germany as part of their quest to maintain the 1919 peace settlement, although in 1924 they agreed to a modification of the economic terms of the peace.

20:227 Trachtenberg, Marc. *Reparations in World Politics: France and European Economic Diplomacy, 1916–1923*. New York: Columbia University Press, 1980. An interpretative study of European diplomacy which sealed the fate of the Versailles system, it is most useful for background information regarding U.S. economic policies involving German reparations.

20:228 Wandel, Eckhard. *Die Bedeutung der Vereinigten Staaten von Amerika für das Deutsche Reparationsproblem, 1924–1929* [The meaning of the United States of America for the German reparations problem, 1924–1929]. Tübingen: J. C. B. Mohr, Paul Siebeck, 1971. Americans saw that a solution to reparations was necessary to obtain repayment of the war debts by the Allies and to produce a European economy able to absorb American capital and manufactures. But the Americans failed to give formal recognition to the essential link between reparations and war debts, between American and European affairs.

London Economic Conference, 1933

See "Personalities," especially Jay Pierrepont Moffat (under "Others"), Franklin D. Roosevelt.

20:229 Brown, William Adams, Jr. *The International Gold Standard Reinterpreted: 1914–1934*. New York: National Bureau of Economic Research, 1940. An excellent survey of the workings of the international gold standard, with a powerful analytical argument critical of the effort to restore it at the conclusion of World War I.

20:230 Feis, Herbert. *1933: Characters in Crisis*. Boston: Little, Brown, 1966. Feis was the State Department's economic adviser and he reconstructs the international dimensions of the depression. He focuses on the London Economic Conference and other efforts at international economic stabilization.

Nichols, J. "Roosevelt's Monetary Diplomacy in 1933" (39:39).

Wicker, E. R. "Roosevelt's 1933 Monetary Experiment" (39:40).

Reciprocal Trade Agreements

See "Personalities," especially Cordell Hull (under "Others"); also see Chapter 39, "Reciprocal Trade Agreements."

20:231 Allen, William R. "Cordell Hull and the Defense of the Trade Agreements Program, 1934–1940." In Alexander DeConde, ed., *Isolation and Security: Ideas and Interests in Twentieth-Century American Foreign Policy.* Durham, N.C.: Duke University Press, 1957, pp. 107–32. Allen examines Hull's trade philosophy and elucidates some of the deficiencies in Hull's thinking. Yet he emphasizes the important transition that the reciprocity program represented in commercial policy. He believes that the trade agreements program may not have been "the best that we could have hoped for, but it probably comes close to being the best that we could reasonably have expected."

20:232 Beckett, Grace L. *The Reciprocal Trade Agreement Program.* New York: Columbia University Press, 1941. Reprint 1972. Using materials published by the Departments of State, Commerce, and Agriculture, and by the tariff commission, Beckett discusses the considerations and precedents leading to this program.

20:233 Beckett, Grace L. "The Effect of the Reciprocal Trade Agreements upon the Foreign Trade of the United States." *Quarterly Journal of Economics* 54:1 (1940), 80–94. The Hull-Roosevelt Reciprocal Trade Agreements Act of 1934 did not increase exports in any large way, but it was important for preventing trade losses resulting from possible foreign commercial discrimination.

Hilton, S. E. *Brazil and the Great Powers, 1930–1939: The Politics of Trade Rivalry* (39:62) studies the use of the reciprocal trade program to combat Germany's bilateralism.

20:234 Kottman, Richard N. *Reciprocity and the North Atlantic Triangle, 1932–1938.* Ithaca, N.Y.: Cornell University Press, 1968. Kottman balances the primacy of economics in the international perceptions of Hull with the *Realpolitik* views in Britain and the dominions during the 1930s. The focus is the negotiation for the reciprocal trade agreement with Canada in 1935 and the British-American agreement of 1938. Until 1938, Kottman sees "only a modicum of cooperation between London and Washington." Bibliography.

20:235 Repko, Allan F. "The Failure of Reciprocal Trade: United States – German Commercial Rivalry in Brazil, 1934–1940." *Mid-America* 60 (1978), 3–20. The reciprocal trade program sought to block German economic and political penetration of Latin America, especially of Brazil, in belief that tariff reduction and unconditional most-favored-nation status for American-German trade would reverse the gains of the Germans. When this policy failed to curb the competitive Germans, the Americans turned to a more aggressive procedure, Export-Import Bank credits.

Schatz, A. W. "The Anglo-American Trade Agreement and Cordell Hull's Search for Peace, 1936–1938" (39:59) examines Hull's attempt to forge an Anglo-American commercial alliance for freer trade and to restore political stability, but the secretary of state failed to deal with the noneconomic factors underlying instability. Hull's effort was visibly a failure by 1938.

20:236 Schatz, Arthur W. "The Reciprocal Trade Agreements Program and the 'Farm Vote,' 1934–1940." *Agricultural History* 46:4 (1972), 498–514. Schatz concludes that from 1934 to 1936 the farm states were willing to give the program a chance to prove itself. After that, however, farm opposition increased, based on traditional protectionist attitudes, fear of eastern exploitation, and concern over the agreements' apparently undemocratic nature.

20:237 Steward, Dick. *Trade and Hemisphere: The Good Neighbor Policy and Reciprocal Trade.* Columbia: University of Missouri Press, 1975. A mostly country-by-country analysis, this study examines Hull's trade agreements program in Latin America. The author believes that American economic diplomacy enhanced U.S. self-interest while it did not promote economic recovery in Latin America. Hull plays an important part in the story, and Steward suggests that the secretary's role in New Deal diplomacy needs thorough revision. Extensive bibliography.

Wilkinson, J. R. *Politics and Trade Policy* (39:61) is a brief account of the Reciprocal Trade Agreements Act from the 1930s to the mid-1950s.

21

Interwar Diplomacy, 1920–1937

Contributing Editor

ROBERT H. FERRELL
Indiana University

Contributors

Peter Buckingham
Southwest Texas State University

John Garry Clifford
University of Connecticut

Thomas H. Etzold
Naval War College

Robert A. Hart
University of Massachusetts

William Kamman
North Texas State University

Arnold A. Offner
Boston University

Carl P. Parrini
Northern Illinois University

Gary M. Ross
Loma Linda University

Eugene P. Trani
University of Missouri at Kansas City

Contents

Introduction

The introduction to the preceding chapter set out the principles of American diplomacy during the interwar era, and it remains here to look closely at the diplomacy of the United States toward the more important countries and areas of the world. Diplomacy, one must add, was not "dynamic" toward Europe during this period, but the basis of selection of items for Europe and for other areas has been two-fold, namely, to show whatever interest or disinterest that Americans manifested, and (in the case of Europe and particularly the Soviet Union and Eastern Europe) to highlight the background of issues arising during World War II and the subsequent cold war.

The most important country for U.S. diplomacy in the 1920s and 1930s was, of course, Germany—the Germany of the Weimar Republic until January 1933, and thereafter the Germany of Adolf Hitler. Americans and other peoples so hoped for peace that they overlooked, first of all, the fragile nature of the Weimar Republic, a democratic government born out of defeat in 1918, and afterward hoped that the initial Nazi excesses, such as persecution of the Jews within Germany, and the active sponsorship within the United States of the German-American Bund, were only reactions by the Germans to the Treaty of Versailles. In retrospect it might have been better if the Allies after 1918 had agreed upon a single German policy, either lenient or severe. Arnold Offner's *American Appeasement* (21:124) shows the peculiar amalgam of standoffishness and of feelings of guilt that constituted American policy in the 1920s and especially the 1930s, which if taken in combination with the vacillating policies of Britain and France almost ensured a second world war.

If American policy toward Germany was mistaken, so was policy toward Soviet Russia. At the outset, after the excesses of the Bolshevik Revolution, the Americans were almost as irritated with the Soviets as were the British and French. But the deplorable condi-tion of the Russian people, with their terrible losses in the war and actual starvation due to the war's dislocations, persuaded Americans to look to relief for the Russian people. Herbert Hoover, the savior of Belgium during the early part of the war, later president of the United States, was the principal actor in the drama of saving the Russians. After relief came the question of American recognition, and Beatrice Farnsworth's succinct analysis, *William C. Bullitt and the Soviet Union* (21:18) is one of several good accounts of this issue. The reader will also want to consult the works of George F. Kennan, *Memoirs: 1925–1950* (24:124) and *Russia and the West under Lenin and Stalin* (21:158), for an overview of Soviet-American relations.

Among the events of the early and mid-1930s that roused Americans was the war that broke out in 1935 between a minor dictatorship of Europe, Mussolini's Italy, and the primitive country of Ethiopia. The emperor of Ethiopia went before the League of Nations and pleaded with the West to protect him from the rapacity of the Italians. It was an embarrassing occasion, and more so for the government of the United States, as shown by George W. Baer, *Test Case: Italy, Ethiopia, and the League of Nations* (21:110).

The first stage of aggression in East Asia had begun during World War I, when in 1915 the Japanese placed the Twenty-One Demands upon the Chinese. In the 1920s the Americans and British forced the Japanese to back down on some of these issues by combining them with naval disarmament (see Chapter 20). Akira Iriye's *After Imperialism: The Search for a New Order in the Far East, 1921–1931* (21:182) captures the moods of this crucial decade. In the mid-1920s the U.S. Senate refused to allow a few Japanese to enter the United States under an annual quota, and the so-called Exclusion Act of that era became a very sore point in American-Japanese relations.

By the end of the decade the Japanese army's leaders in the leased territory and the railway zone in Manchuria, areas that the Chinese had allowed to the Japanese, were becoming unhappy with the assertions of Chinese nationalism. Dorothy Borg surveys this era in her superb *The United States and the Far Eastern Crisis of 1933–1938* (21:188). Against this expansionism, carried out under the Japanese belief that

Japan, with a huge population and a few small islands, must expand or die, the American government offered nothing more serious than a doctrine of nonrecognition. Armin Rappaport, *Henry L. Stimson and Japan* (21:59) aptly describes the errors of this approach.

Fortunately, in the western hemisphere the U.S. government showed more clarity of thought. Admittedly there was a lag in analysis that lasted through most of the 1920s, for the approach of Theodore Roosevelt was not easily abandoned. But as the years passed it became evident that, as Roosevelt sometimes described his methods, "sound chastisement" was hardly the way to behave toward the increasingly proud peoples of Central America and the Caribbean. By the end of the 1920s the marine interventions were either ended or coming rapidly to an end, and officials in Washington were stressing their concern for Pan-American, rather than unilateral goals.

When in the early 1930s revolutions changed the regimes in many Latin American countries, the State Department did little or nothing, and without exception recognized the revolutionaries. Even in Cuba, always a concern of Washington officials, there was no serious thought of intervention in the early 1930s, when the regime of one dictator gave way to another. William Kamman, *A Search for Stability* (21:276), characterizes American policy toward Nicaragua. In the case of Mexico the treatment of Catholics by the revolutionary governments beginning in 1910 had been a large issue for Catholics north of the Rio Grande, but even this concern was treated carefully—for which see Robert E. Quirk, *The Mexican Revolution and the Catholic Church, 1910–1929* (21:256). Alton Frye, *Nazi Germany and the American Hemisphere: 1933–1941* (21:120), shows the second reason why American policy changed to the good neighbor, namely, that in addition to the rise of local nationalism there was new concern for German imperialism in the mid- and late 1930s.

How can students improve upon the literature of U.S. relations with individual countries and with areas of the world during the interwar years? Increasing scholarship by non-Americans—Germans, Russians, Italians, Chinese and Japanese, Latin Americans— has brought the need to know foreign languages in order to understand more about U.S. foreign relations, and in this, the hitherto monolinguistic approach to American international affairs, improvements need to be made. And as mentioned in the preceding chapter, there is need to understand economic relations, to generalize from monographs, and especially to get away from the political labeling of U.S. foreign policy into Republican policy or Democratic policy.

Resources and Overviews

RESEARCH AIDS

While pertinent bibliographies and reference aids are listed here, there are more extensive lists in Chapter 1.

Bibliographies

Bloomberg, M., and Weber, H. H. *World War II and Its Origins: A Selected Annotated Bibliography of Books in English* (23:2) lists some 400 books in chapter 2, "Pre-War Years, 1919–1939."

Braisted, W. R. "The Navy in the Early Twentieth Century, 1890–1941" (19:3) contains references to materials on the U.S. Navy's interwar activities and plans.

Dexter, B., ed. *The Foreign Affairs Fifty-Year Bibliography: New Evaluation of Significant Books on International Relations, 1920–1970* (1:14) is a very useful condensation and new evalution of books listed in the *Foreign Affairs Bibliographies* (1:15). *Foreign Affairs Bibliography: A Selected and Annotated List of Books on International Relations* (1:15) is issued at ten-year intervals, and each volume has three parts: "General International Relations"; "The World since 1914"; and "The World by Regions." Useful aid.

Irick, R. L., Yu Y., and Liu K. *American-Chinese Relations, 1784–1941: A Survey of Chinese-Language Materials at Harvard* (17:2) lists Chinese-language materials.

Morley, J. W., ed. *Japan's Foreign Policy, 1868–1941: A Research Guide* (1:100).

Rabe, V. H. *American-Chinese Relations, 1784–1941: Books and Pamphlets Extracted from the Shelf Lists of Widener Library* (17:5).

21:1 Stachura, Peter D., ed. *The Weimar Era and Hitler, 1918–1933: A Critical Bibliography.* Santa Barbara, Calif.: ABC-Clio, 1977. This comprehensive and critically annotated bibliography includes more than 3,000 citations to secondary literature published from 1945 to 1975 in English, French, and German.

Stewart, W. J., ed. *The Era of Franklin D. Roosevelt: A Selected Bibliography of Periodical, Essay, and Dissertation Literature, 1945–1971* (20:2) contains annotated, indexed materials on FDR's diplomacy (1933–1945).

Trask, D. F.; Meyer, M. C.; and Trask, R. R., eds. *A Bibliography of United States–Latin American Relations since 1810* (1:120) is a comprehensive guide, supplemented by Meyer (1:119).

Yearbooks and Other Aids

Keesing's Contemporary Archives: Weekly Diary of World Events (1:152) covers international events from 1931.

Political Handbook and Atlas of the World (1:144) is a valuable reference, annually from 1927.

Survey of International Affairs (1:146) covers international affairs, especially European, during the interwar years.

The United States in World Affairs (1:147) begins with 1931, and except for the years 1934 and 1935, which were combined into a single volume, is an annual survey. Walter Lippmann frequently was the author of the Council on American Foreign Relations' earlier volumes.

Document Collections

More general collections are listed in Chapter 1 and other collections may be found in "Personalities," below.

Clissold, S. *Soviet Relations with Latin America, 1918–1967: A Documentary Survey* (35:116).

21:2   Conference of Ambassadors. Paris. *Processed Minutes, No. 1–327, January 26, 1920–January 21, 1931.* 99 rolls. Stanford, Calif.: Hoover Institution Microfilms, n.d. This microfilm collection is extremely valuable for reviewing issues arising out of World War I peace treaties.

Degras, J., ed. *Soviet Documents on Foreign Policy* (20:3).

21:3   Eudin, Xenia J., and Fisher, Harold H. *Soviet Russia and the West, 1920–1927.* Stanford, Calif.: Stanford University Press, 1957.

21:4   Eudin, Xenia J., and North, Robert C. *Soviet Russia and the East, 1920–1927.* Stanford, Calif.: Stanford University Press, 1957. These two volumes contain the texts of 185 documents useful for understanding Soviet foreign policy.

21:5   Eudin, Xenia J., and Slusser, Robert M. *Soviet Foreign Policy, 1928–1934.* 2 vols. University Park: Pennsylvania State University Press, 1966–1967. These volumes contain seven chapters of narrative summary as well as 146 documents on a crucial era in Soviet history. Documents include speeches, articles from *Pravda, Izvestiia,* and *Bol'shevik,* and papers from the Communist party and the Comintern. Extensive bibliography.

21:6   France. Commission de Publication des Documents Relatifs aux origines de la Guerre 1939–1945. *Documents diplomatiques français, 1932–1939.* Paris: Imprimerie Nationale, 1963. This reconstructed collection, retrieved from war-damaged archives, is arranged by country. See Gadrat and Renouvin, below.

21:7   Gadrat, F., and Renouvin, P. "Les Documents diplomatiques français (1932–1939)" [French diplomatic documents, 1932–1939]. *Revue d'Histoire de la Deuxième Guerre Mondiale* 18:71 (1968), 1–11. The editors describe French diplomatic papers which had been delayed owing to damage sustained by the archives during the war. The first series (July 1932–March 1933) begins with the Lausanne Conference and ends with Mussolini's "new politics." The second series (January 1931–November 1936) covers Germany's reoccupation of the Rhine and the outbreak of the Spanish Civil War in 1936.

21:8   Germany. Auswärtiges Amt. *Akten zur Deutschen Auswärtigen Politik, 1918–1945* [Documents on German Foreign Policy, 1918–1945]. Göttingen: Vanderhock und Rupprecht, 1966–1978. The West German government has supplemented the U.S. collection of *Documents on German Foreign Policy: 1918–1945* (21:9) with the above collection, which is in 12 volumes for the pre-Hitler years (1925–1933). This work offers rich material for researchers of German-American relations.

Great Britain. Foreign Office. *Documents on British Foreign Policy, 1919–1939* (20:4).

Ssü-yü Teng and Fairbank, J. K. *China's Response to the West: A Documentary Survey, 1839–1923* (17:24).

21:9 U.S. Department of State. *Documents on German Foreign Policy, 1918–1945*. Washington, D.C.: G.P.O., 1957–1966. Series C, in five volumes, deals with the years 1933 to 1937 (series D, in thirteen volumes, carries the story well into the war). The West German government has supplemented this project with *Akten zur Deutschen Auswärtigen Politik, 1918–1945* (21:8).

U.S. Department of State. *Foreign Relations of the United States* (1:358) have 50-plus volumes for the years 1921 to 1937, including special collections on Japan (1931–1941) and the Soviet Union (1933–1939).

21:10 U.S. Department of State. *Peace and War: United States Foreign Policy, 1931–1941*. Washington, D.C.: G.P.O., 1943. This volume prints, in chronological order, a large number of diplomatic messages, speeches, and official documents relating to warnings of German and Japanese aggressive intentions.

U.S. Department of State. *Press Conferences of the Secretaries of State, 1922–1974* (1:360).

U.S. Department of State. *Press Releases* (1:361) carried information (1929–1939) about current policy, including major speeches by the president and secretary of state. Weekly.

OVERVIEWS

Adler, S. *The Uncertain Giant, 1921–1941: American Foreign Policy between the Wars* (20:8) focuses on policy hesitations that resulted from the public's uncertain response to Hitler.

Beard, C. A. *American Foreign Policy in the Making, 1932–1940: A Study in Responsibilities* (22:10) attempts to prove that Roosevelt led the nation into war.

Duroselle, J.-B. *From Wilson to Roosevelt: Foreign Policy of the United States, 1913–1945* (19:20) is critical of internationalist presidents, notably Wilson and Roosevelt.

Ellis, L. E. *Republican Foreign Policy, 1921–1933* (20:11).

21:11 Feis, Herbert. *Seen from E.A.: Three International Episodes*. New York: Norton (1946), 1966. Feis deals with episodes in which he played a part and that focus on the search for national security prior to World War II: 1) stockpiling of rubber prior to Pearl Harbor; 2) the search for oil from the Middle East; and 3) talk of embargoing oil to Italy during the Ethiopian crisis.

21:12 Gardner, Lloyd C. *Economic Aspects of New Deal Diplomacy*. Madison: University of Wisconsin Press, 1964. Economics are asserted to be the dominant influence in New Deal diplomacy. Gardner provides some useful corrections to works ignoring economic motives, but often stretches credulity. Bibliographical essay.

21:13 Leuchtenburg, William E. *Franklin D. Roosevelt and the New Deal, 1932–1940*. New York: Harper & Row, 1963. This book is probably the best survey of political attitudes and policies during the 1930s. The volume suggests why foreign problems were secondary to economic concerns, at least until 1938. Bibliography.

O'Connor, R. G. *Force and Diplomacy: Essays Military and Diplomatic* (40:25) includes essays on naval strategy, nonrecognition and use of sanctions.

Offner, A. A. *The Origins of the Second World War: American Foreign Policy and World Politics, 1914–1941* (22:16).

21:14 Payne, Howard C.; Callahan, Raymond; and Bennett, Edward M. *As Storm Clouds Gathered: European Perceptions of American Foreign Policy in the 1930s*. Durham, N.C.: Moore, 1979. Payne focuses on French-British-American "triangular tensions" as France contemplated its security dilemma after collapse of the Anglo-American guarantee. Callahan explores the lack of substance behind the special relationship supposed to have existed between Britain and the United States. Bennett examines the Soviet Union's frustrating attempt to discover the "real" American attitude toward Germany and Japan.

Schwarzschild, Leopold. *World in Trance: From Versailles to Pearl Harbor* (19:243).

21:15 Smith, Robert Freeman. "American Foreign Relations, 1920–1942." In Barton J. Bernstein, ed., *Towards a New Past: Dissenting Essays in American*

History. New York: Pantheon, 1968, pp. 232–62. Rejecting both the realist and traditionalist schools of diplomatic history, the author emphasizes the primacy of economics. Smith views the period from 1920 to 1942 as an era when American leaders experimented with neocolonialism.

21:16 Sontag, Raymond J. *A Broken World, 1919–1939*. New York: Harper & Row, 1971. This survey provides an outstanding introduction to European foreign affairs during the interwar years. Sontag argues that World War I's destruction of the 19th-century system gave rise to the issues that led to World War II. Bibliography.

Personalities

Additional references on individuals may be found in Chapter 1, "Biographical Data."

AMERICAN

William C. Bullitt

21:17 Bullitt, Orville H., ed. *"For the President—Personal and Secret": Correspondence between Franklin D. Roosevelt and William C. Bullitt*. Boston: Houghton Mifflin, 1972. These letters present details of Soviet-American relations in 1933 to 1936, along with Bullitt's often shrewd judgments.

21:18 Farnsworth, Beatrice. *William C. Bullitt and the Soviet Union*. Bloomington: Indiana University Press, 1967. This exemplary diplomatic biography discusses Bullitt's long involvement in Soviet-American affairs—especially in 1919 at Paris and in the mid-1930s in Moscow and Washington—with wit, sympathy, and insight. Bullitt favored recognition in the early 1930s, quickly became disillusioned, and spent the rest of his years warning of Soviet imperialism.

Josephus Daniels

See Chapter 19, "Personalities," for additional references.

21:19 Cronon, E. David. *Josephus Daniels in Mexico*. Madison: University of Wisconsin Press, 1960. In this detailed account of Daniels in Mexico as ambassador (1933–1941), Cronon views Daniels's service as the high-water mark of good neighbor diplomacy. Daniels was, he believes, one of the leading practitioners of that policy.

21:20 Daniels, Josephus. *Shirt-Sleeve Diplomat*. Chapel Hill: University of North Carolina Press, 1947. The portions of the author's autobiography dealing with President Lazaro Cardenas and the climactic episodes of the Mexican Revolution are important for the good neighbor policy, although the reader will have to wade through anecdotes and asides.

William E. Dodd

21:21 Dallek, Robert. "Beyond Tradition: The Diplomatic Careers of William E. Dodd and George S. Messersmith, 1933–1938." *South Atlantic Quarterly* 66:2 (1967), 233–44. Dodd and Messersmith were astute analysts and early opponents of the Nazi regime, who warned that Hitler was expansionist and urged American officials to organize domestic and foreign opposition. Dallek judges Messersmith more effective because he worked within diplomatic traditions, whereas Dodd was outspoken and deplored the ways of diplomats.

21:22 Dallek, Robert. *Democrat and Diplomat: The Life of William E. Dodd*. New York: Oxford University Press, 1968. This careful account of the University of Chicago historian and ambassador to Germany (1933–1937) examines Dodd's service in detail, showing perceptive predictions about Hitler and Nazi Germany. The author believes that Dodd was more successful than he has been judged.

21:23 Dodd, William E., Jr., and Dodd, Martha, eds. *Ambassador Dodd's Diary, 1933–1938*. New York: Harcourt, 1941. One of FDR's shrewdest diplomatic observers, Dodd loathed nazism in general and Hitler in particular, and warned again and again that the Germans would march if unchecked.

21:24 Offner, Arnold A. "William E. Dodd: Romantic Historian and Diplomatic Cassandra." *Historian* 24:4 (1962), 451–69. Offner argues that Dodd was quicker than most diplomats to see the strengths and weaknesses of national socialism and the way Hitler used German grievances to support an expansive policy. Dodd urged President Roosevelt to align with the British and French, so as to contain Germany.

Joseph C. Grew

Grew, J. C. *Turbulent Era: A Diplomatic Record of Forty Years, 1904–1945* (18:33).

21:25 Grew, Joseph C. *Ten Years in Japan.* New York: Simon & Schuster, 1944. This is an important contemporary record, notable for conveying the tenacity of Grew's efforts toward peace and for supplementing his *Report from Tokyo* by emphasizing the country and its people rather than the narrower phenomenon of Japanese militarism.

21:26 Heinrichs, Waldo H., Jr. *American Ambassador: Joseph C. Grew and the Development of the United States Diplomatic Tradition.* Boston: Little, Brown, 1966. A majestic treatment of Grew and his role in the U.S. diplomatic tradition, Heinrichs's account covers Grew's ambassadorships in Turkey (1927–1932) and Japan (1932–1941). The author covers a good deal more than Grew. Bibliography.

Warren G. Harding

See Chapter 20, "Personalities," for additional references.

21:27 Grieb, Kenneth J. *The Latin American Policy of Warren G. Harding.* Forth Worth: Texas Christian University Press, 1977. The author concludes that the Harding administration retreated from force and moralism while emphasizing cooperation in promoting stability and trade. President Harding made personal contributions in liquidating grievances, such as in the Colombian treaty and settlement of the Isle of Pines controversy.

Herbert C. Hoover

See Chapters 19, 20, and 22, "Personalities," for additional references.

21:28 DeConde, Alexander. *Herbert Hoover's Latin American Policy.* Stanford, Calif.: Stanford University Press, 1951. In this account of Hoover's views and activities toward Latin America with emphasis on the years he was president (1929–1933), DeConde argues that Hoover's Latin American policy was the beginning of the good neighbor policy normally attributed to FDR.

21:29 Ferrell, Robert H. *American Diplomacy in the Great Depression: Hoover-Stimson Foreign Policy, 1929–1933.* New Haven, Conn.: Yale University Press, 1957. A harsh view of Secretary Stimson's diplomacy, and similarly harsh judgment of Hoover. Ferrell's thesis is that the Great Depression forced

diplomats to avoid trouble, and in the hiatus of diplomacy during the depression the dictators and aggressive nations obtained their chance. Bibliography.

Hoover, H. C. *An American Epic: Famine in Forty-Five Nations: The Battle on the Front Line, 1914–1923* (19:41).

21:30 Hoover, Herbert C. *Addresses upon the American Road, 1933–1938.* New York: Scribner's, 1938. This is a collection of ex-President Hoover's speeches on American economic problems and the increasing difficulties in foreign relations, especially with the nations of Europe.

21:31 Lyons, Eugene. *Herbert Hoover.* Rev. ed. Garden City, N.Y.: Doubleday, 1964. This is the fullest biography of Hoover, updated from an earlier version.

Weissman, B. *Herbert Hoover and Famine Relief to Soviet Russia, 1921–1923* (21:163).

Stanley K. Hornbeck

21:32 Burns, Richard Dean. "Stanley K. Hornbeck: The Diplomacy of the Open Door." In Richard Dean Burns and Edward M. Bennett, eds., *Diplomats in Crisis: United States-Chinese-Japanese Relations, 1919–1941.* Santa Barbara, Calif.: ABC-Clio, 1974, pp. 91–117. This essay seeks to identify Hornbeck's political philosophy and approach to foreign policy issues. He was influential in shaping America's East Asian policies up to Pearl Harbor.

21:33 McCarty, Kenneth G., Jr. "Stanley K. Hornbeck and the Manchurian Crisis." *Southern Quarterly* 10:4 (1972), 305–24. Hornbeck, chief of the Division of Far Eastern Affairs in the State Department, advised Secretary Stimson to let the league handle the Manchurian problem, arguing that invocation of the Kellogg-Briand Pact would be ineffective. He advocated legal action against Japan, not condemnation based on morality.

Charles Evans Hughes

See Chapter 20, "Personalities," for additional references.

21:34 Trani, Eugene P. "Charles Evans Hughes: The First Good Neighbor." *Northwest Ohio Quarterly* 40:2 (1968), 138–52. This article analyzes the policy followed by Hughes toward Latin America and suggests that much of what later came to be known as the good neighbor policy had its origin with Hughes.

Cordell Hull

See Chapter 22, "Personalities," for additional references.

21:35 Drummond, Donald F. "Cordell Hull." In Norman Graebner, ed., *An Uncertain Tradition: American Secretaries of State in the Twentieth Century.* New York: McGraw-Hill, 1961, pp. 184–209. Drummond argues that Hull exercised considerable influence on FDR, but he never comprehended the ideas and international politics of the 20th century.

21:36 Hull, Cordell. *Memoirs.* 2 vols. New York: Macmillan, 1948. The memoirs are not exciting and they certainly reveal Hull's intense prejudices, but they are detailed and reward careful reading.

21:37 Jablon, Howard. "Cordell Hull, His 'Associates,' and Relations with Japan, 1933–1936." *Mid-America* 56:3 (1974), 160–74. Hull followed Stimson's "demonstrably bankrupt policy" because of an excessive reliance on advisers, especially Hornbeck, who believed in the nonrecognition doctrine and the open door.

Pratt, J. W. *Cordell Hull, 1933–1944* (22:24) is excellent in detailing such topics as the good neighbor policy, the Spanish Civil War, the coming of World War II, and Hull's role during the war.

Nelson T. Johnson

21:38 Buhite, Russell D. *Nelson T. Johnson and American Policy toward China, 1925–1941.* East Lansing: Michigan State University Press, 1968. Chief of the Division of Far Eastern Affairs, assistant secretary, and minister and ambassador to China, Johnson exerted a considerable influence on China policy between 1925 and 1941.

21:39 Wood, Herbert J. "Nelson Trusler Johnson: The Diplomacy of Benevolent Pragmatism." In Richard Dean Burns and Edward M. Bennett, eds., *Diplomats in Crisis: United States-Chinese-Japanese Relations, 1919–1941.* Santa Barbara, Calif.: ABC-Clio, 1974, pp. 7–26. Minister, later ambassador, to China and State Department expert on China, Johnson influenced U.S. policy toward East Asia in the 1920s and 1930s.

George S. Messersmith

21:40 Adams, D. K. "Messersmith's Appointment to Vienna in 1934: Presidential Patronage or Career Promotion?" *Delaware History* 18:1 (1978), 17–27. The records indicate that there was both patronage and careerism in the promotion.

Dallek, R. "Beyond Tradition: The Diplomatic Careers of William E. Dodd and George S. Messersmith, 1933–1938" (21:21) judges Messersmith as more effective because he worked within diplomatic traditions, whereas Dodd was outspoken and deplored the ways of diplomats.

21:41 Moss, Kenneth. "George S. Messersmith: An American Diplomat and Nazi Germany." *Delaware History* 17:4 (1977), 236–49. Messersmith, particularly in 1933 to 1940, helped shape American attitudes toward Nazi Germany. Messersmith believed in the balance of power and in an international economy and open trade; he wanted economic pressure against Nazi Germany.

21:42 Shafir, Shlomo. "George S. Messersmith: An Anti-Nazi Diplomat's View of the German-Jewish Crisis." *Jewish Social Studies* 35:1 (1973), 32–41. Messersmith (1883–1960) was an early, resolute opponent of Hitler's anti-Semitic policies, but never suggested any proposals for the rescue of Jews because he regarded the humanitarian issue as minor.

Henry Morgenthau, Jr.

See Chapter 22, "Personalities," for additional references.

21:43 Blum, John Morton. *From the Morgenthau Diaries.* Vol. 1: *Years of Crisis, 1928–1938.* Boston: Houghton Mifflin, 1959. In the first in a three-volume political biography of FDR's secretary of the treasury, Blum emphasizes Morgenthau's activities at the Treasury and his unique relationship with the president. Chapter 10 deals with such episodes of economic foreign policy as loans to Chiang Kai-shek, aid to France, trade with the Soviet Union, relations with Mexico, and disagreements with Secretary of State Hull.

Dwight Morrow

21:44 Ellis, L. Ethan. "Dwight Morrow and the Church-State Controversy in Mexico." *Hispanic American Historical Review* 38:4 (1958), 482–505. This article, friendly to Morrow, traces the intricate negotiations temporarily ending the religious controversy that suspended services in Mexico's Catholic churches. Ellis sees the episode as symptomatic of broader Mexican-American relations of this time, an era when Coolidge and Kellogg "virtually abdicated in Morrow's favor."

21:45 Nicolson, Harold G. *Dwight Morrow*. New York: Harcourt, Brace, 1935. Published a few years after its subject's death, this biography glances across some of the details of Morrow's eventful life but is remarkably keen in its judgments.

21:46 Ross, Stanley R. "Dwight W. Morrow, Ambassador to Mexico." *Americas* 14:3 (1958), 273–89. The Morrow mission (1927–1930) was sympathetic and undogmatic, and brought a relaxation of tension and foreshadowed the good neighbor policy.

21:47 Ross, Stanley R. "Dwight Morrow and the Mexican Revolution." *Hispanic American Historical Review* 38:4 (1958), 506–28. In a detailed review of Morrow's success as ambassador to Mexico, Ross argues that Morrow was a predecessor of the good neighbor policy.

Key Pittman

See also Chapter 22, "Personalities."

21:48 Israel, Fred L. *Nevada's Key Pittman*. Lincoln: University of Nebraska Press, 1963. This is a careful account of the man who served as chairman of the Senate Foreign Relations Committee (1933–1940). A hard-drinking man, Pittman frequently embarrassed Roosevelt by his conduct and his views.

21:49 Libby, Justin H. "The Irreconcilable Conflict: Key Pittman and Japan during the Interwar Years." *Nevada Historical Society Quarterly* 18:3 (1975), 128–39. Libby analyzes the anti-Japanese views of Pittman, who worked unsuccessfully during the 1930s for stronger American resistance to Japanese aggression in East Asia.

Franklin D. Roosevelt

See also Chapters 20, 22, and 23, "Personalities," for additional references.

21:50 Burns, James M. *Roosevelt: The Lion and the Fox*. New York: Harcourt, Brace, 1956. The first volume of a now completed biography—for volume 2, see 23:63—through the election of 1940, is a gracefully written account. Burns is an admirer of Roosevelt, and covers diplomacy between 1933 and 1940.

21:51 Dallek, Robert. *Franklin D. Roosevelt and American Foreign Policy, 1932–1945*. New York: Oxford University Press, 1979. This most recent scholarly study of FDR's foreign policy finds Roosevelt farseeing and purposeful. There are shrewd

observations on the London Economic Conference of 1933 and Roosevelt's secret efforts to secure Anglo-American cooperation in Asia after the Quarantine Speech (1937).

Gellman, I. F. *Roosevelt and Batista: Good Neighbor Diplomacy in Cuba, 1933–1945* (21:265).

21:52 Neumann, William L. "Franklin D. Roosevelt and Japan, 1913–1933." *Pacific Historical Review* 22:2 (1953), 143–53. Neumann suggests that Roosevelt's family commercial ties to China made him pro-Chinese and anti-Japanese, notwithstanding his efforts to recognize Japan's role in East Asia in the 1920s.

21:53 Roosevelt, Franklin D. *Franklin D. Roosevelt and Foreign Affairs*. 3 vols. Ed. by Edgar B. Nixon. Cambridge: Harvard University Press, 1969. A massive documentary record of the international correspondence of Roosevelt (1933–1937), the collection is arranged chronologically and indexed.

21:54 Roosevelt, Franklin D. *Complete Presidential Press Conferences of Franklin D. Roosevelt, 1933–1945*. 12 vols. New York: Da Capo, 1972. Also available in microfilm from the Franklin D. Roosevelt Library, Roosevelt's press conferences provide an excellent illustration of how FDR dealt with foreign policy subjects on and off the record. They are sometimes most valuable for the things he avoided in response to questions from hostile reporters.

21:55 Rosenman, Samuel I., ed. *Public Papers and Addresses of Franklin Delano Roosevelt*. 13 vols. New York: Random House, 1938–1950. A compilation by a close adviser of Franklin D. Roosevelt, this collection is equivalent to the public papers of other presidents later printed by the Government Printing Office.

Sherwood, R. E. *Roosevelt and Hopkins: An Intimate History* (22:23) is a classic account by the famous playwright and FDR's speechwriter, which draws from the Hopkins Papers.

Henry L. Stimson

See Chapters 22 and 23, "Personalities," for additional references.

21:56 Current, Richard N. "Henry L. Stimson." In Norman A. Graebner, ed., *An Uncertain Tradition: American Secretaries of State in the Twentieth Century*. New York: McGraw-Hill, 1961, pp. 168–83.

Stimson and Hoover were "basically incompatible" and the president soon lost faith in his secretary. Hoover thought of the Stimson Doctrine as a complete measure in and of itself, while Stimson viewed nonrecognition as a first step toward confrontation with Japan.

21:57 Current, Richard N. *Secretary Stimson: A Study in Statecraft.* New Brunswick, N.J.: Rutgers University Press, 1954. Current believes that Stimson misread the future during his service in both the Hoover and Roosevelt administrations. Especially critical concerning the conduct of Japanese-American affairs, Current argues that Stimson frequently changed his opinion without good reason.

Ferrell, R. H. *American Diplomacy in the Great Depression: Hoover-Stimson Foreign Policy, 1929– 1933* (21:29) presents a harsh view of Secretary Stimson's diplomacy, and a similarly harsh judgment of Hoover.

Ferrell, R. H. *Frank B. Kellogg and Henry L. Stimson* (20:58).

21:58 Morison, Elting E. *Turmoil and Tradition: The Life and Times of Henry L. Stimson.* Boston: Houghton Mifflin, 1960. This beautifully written "official" biography is fuller on the years before 1940, and has shrewd, sympathetic analysis of Stimson's attitudes toward naval limitation, war debts, the Manchurian crisis, and Anglo-American relations in general. Bibliography.

21:59 Rappaport, Armin. *Henry L. Stimson and Japan, 1931–1933.* Chicago: University of Chicago Press, 1963. Stimson's stubbornness, self-righteousness, and legalism were not important, the author concludes, for the United States lacked the ability to change events in Manchuria, even if its policies had been more practical.

21:60 Stimson, Henry L. *The Far Eastern Crisis: Recollections and Observations.* New York: Harper, 1936. Stimson does not regret so much his mistakes, or Japanese militarism, as the inability of peace-seeking nations to work together. Aggression succeeded because of failures in international law, the League of Nations, systems of mutual security, and Anglo-American relations.

Arthur H. Vandenberg

See Chapter 24, "Personalities," for additional references.

Tompkins, C. D. *Senator Arthur H. Vandenberg: The Evolution of a Modern Republican, 1884–1945* (22:37).

Sumner Welles

See Chapter 22, under "Personalities," for additional references.

Welles, S. *The Time for Decision* (22:39) uses a chapter in this survey of interwar diplomacy to discuss the good neighbor policy. Welles justified FDR's role in Cuba and was sympathetic toward the position of Argentina when that nation often seemed at odds with U.S. goals.

Hugh R. Wilson

See Chapters 14 and 20, "Personalities," for additional references.

21:61 Wilson, Hugh R., Jr. *A Career Diplomat: The Third Chapter: The Third Reich.* Westport, Conn.: Greenwood, 1973. The son of the last prewar American ambassador to Berlin edited his father's unpublished reports to Washington along with excerpts from Wilson's diary. This "third chapter" is more valuable than the first two—*The Education of a Diplomat* (14:54) and *Diplomat between the Wars* (20:63), which reach to 1937.

Others

See Chapter 20, "Others," for additional references.

21:62 Armstrong, Hamilton Fish. *Peace and Counterpeace: From Wilson to Hitler: Memoirs of Hamilton Fish Armstrong.* New York: Harper & Row, 1971. The author's account includes his early life from Princeton University, before World War I, through postwar experiences as military attaché in Berlin and as correspondent for the *New York Evening Post*, to his editorship of *Foreign Affairs.*

Bohlen, C. E. *Witness to History: 1929–1969* (24:98) illuminates the perennial contest in American policy between hard and soft lines toward the Soviet Union. It also conveys some of the effects on American observers of the Soviet purges and terrors of the 1930s.

Burns, R. D., and Bennett, E. M., eds. *Diplomats in Crisis: United States-Chinese-Japanese Relations, 1919–1941* (22:42) contains essays on John V. A. MacMurray, and W. Cameron Forbes.

21:63 Child, Richard. *A Diplomat Looks at Europe.* New York: Duffield, 1925. These reminiscences im-part the depth of America's disillusion with the politics of Europe in the 1920s. Child served as chief American observer at the Genoa and Lausanne conferences as well as ambassador to Italy.

Cohen, W. I. *The Chinese Connection: Roger S. Greene, Thomas W. Lamont, George E. Sokolsky, and American–East Asian Relations* (2:341).

DeNovo, J. A. "The Enigmatic Alvey A. Adee and American Foreign Relations, 1870–1924" (14:57) provides references and details about the contributions of this skilled draftsman of dispatches and treaties, faithful and witty bureaucrat, and tutor of young officials and new administrations.

Hooker, N. H., ed. *The Moffat Papers: Selections from the Diplomatic Journals of Jay Pierrepont Moffat, 1919–1943* (20:70) instructive on Anglo-American relations in view of Moffat's experiences in Washington, Australia, and Canada.

Petrov, V. *A Study in Diplomacy: The Story of Arthur Bliss Lane* (26:52).

Phillips, W. *Ventures in Diplomacy* (17:54) contains, in chapter 10, a brief description of Phillips's work as Washington's first minister to Canada. Phillips notes that an important reason for his decision to end his service in Canada was the Smoot-Hawley tariff.

21:64   Swanberg, W. A. *Luce and His Empire*. New York: Scribner's, 1972. A biography of magazine publisher Henry R. Luce, who had much to do with American opinion and with China. Born in China, Luce was a tireless supporter of Chiang Kai-shek, and brought pressure on the Hoover and Roosevelt administrations to protect China.

EUROPEAN

Winston S. Churchill
See Chapters 22, 23, and 25, "Personalities," for additional references.

21:65   Gilbert, Martin. *Winston S. Churchill*. Vol. 5: *The Prophet of Truth, 1922–1939*. Boston: Houghton Mifflin, 1977. Volume 5 of Gilbert's massive biography covers Churchill's five years as chancellor of the exchequer in the 1920s and the "wilderness years" of the 1930s. Gilbert quotes at length from letters, diaries, recollections, and speeches.

Adolf Hitler
See Chapters 22 and 23, "Personalities," for additional references.

21:66   Bullock, Alan. *Hitler: A Study in Tyranny*. New York: Harper & Row, 1964. In this, the best of many biographies of Hitler, Bullock portrays the German dictator as the indispensable man of the Nazi movement, a leader with remarkable abilities, yet one whose genius, poisonous egotism, and moral bankruptcy combined to create a revolution of nihilism. Bibliography.

21:67   Hitler, Adolf. *The Speeches of Adolf Hitler, April 1922–August 1939: An English Translation of Representative Passages*. 2 vols. New York: Oxford University Press, 1942. These volumes provide important insights into Hitler's thoughts. Volume 2 deals with foreign policy.

21:68   Maser, Werner. *Hitler's Mein Kampf: An Analysis*. London: Faber & Faber, 1970. Maser has divided his fine study into two parts: the first develops the origins of *Mein Kampf*; and the second is devoted to its more important ideas.

21:69   Weinberg, Gerhard L. "Hitler's Image of the United States." *American Historical Review* 69:4 (1964), 1006–21. Hitler's contradictory racial and sociopolitical ideas led him in the 1920s to admire American productive, technical, and financial capabilities and to see America in the 1930s as politically and economically effete. These failings, combined with the neutrality acts, led the führer to disregard the United States as an effective military force.

Ramsay MacDonald
21:70   Carlton, David. *MacDonald vs. Henderson: The Foreign Policy of the Second Labour Government*. London: Macmillan, 1970. This study sheds light on the unfortunate personal and working relations between Prime Minister MacDonald and Foreign Secretary Henderson. It surveys British relations with Germany and France over reparations, frontiers, disarmament, arbitration, and national security. Bibliography.

21:71   Marquand, David. *Ramsay MacDonald*. London: Cape, 1976. A massive, favorable biography of the British Labour party leader which emphasizes domestic politics rather than foreign policies, although there are interesting snippets dealing with Anglo-American relations. Bibliography.

Benito Mussolini

21:72 Diggins, John P. "Mussolini and America: Hero-Worship, Charisma, and the 'Vulgar Talent.'" *Historian* 28:4 (1966), 559–85. Mussolini's considerable popularity in the United States during the 1920s and early 1930s was due in part to favorable coverage by such magazines as *Saturday Evening Post, Fortune,* and *New Republic.*

21:73 Felice, Renzo de. *Mussolini.* 4 vols. to date. Turin: Einaudi, 1965–. In this massive, yet to be completed, biography in Italian, Felice breaks Mussolini's life down into four parts: the revolutionary, 1883 to 1920, (volume 1); the fascist, 1921 to 1929 (volumes 2 and 3); the Duce, 1929 to 1939 (volume 4); and the ally, 1939 to 1945. The author all but ignores Mussolini's life while analyzing the phenomenon of fascism.

21:74 Kirkpatrick, Ivone. *Mussolini.* New York: Hawthorn, 1964. A lengthy biography that examines Mussolini's rise to power, his policies during the 1920s and 1930s, and Italy's involvement in World War II.

21:75 Smyth, Denis. "'Duce Diplomatico' [Diplomatic leader]." *Historical Journal* 21:4 (1978), 981–1000. This is a review article that analyzes Mussolini's foreign policy in an attempt to resolve disagreements about the internal consistency of that policy, and its inspiration.

Joseph V. Stalin

See Chapter 25, "Personalities," for additional references.

21:76 Stalin, Joseph V. *Collected Works.* 14 vols. London: Red Star Press (1952–1955), 1975. This paperback reprint of the Soviet edition covers events up to 1940, including important foreign policy pronouncements. H. Bruce Franklin has condensed Stalin's works in *The Essential Stalin: Major Theoretical Writings, 1905–52* (New York: Doubleday, 1972).

21:77 Tucker, Robert C. *Stalin as Revolutionary, 1879–1929.* New York: Norton, 1973. In this fascinating psychobiography, Tucker contends that power did not interest Stalin as much as the desire to be another Lenin. Stalin projected an earthy charismatic leadership and a conservative plan of "socialism in one country" supported by frequent allusions to Lenin. Bibliography.

21:78 Ulam, Adam B. *Stalin: The Man and His Era.* New York: Viking, 1973. Following Stalin's life from cradle to grave, Ulam presents the Soviet leader as an able man, but one with a completely amoral approach to power. Stalin's conduct of foreign affairs is cast as the epitome of "the communist mind at its most realistic and its most suspicious."

Others

Bernstorff, J.H. von *Memoirs of Count Bernstorff* (19:105) has revealing chapters that treat the League of Nations in its early years and the disarmament movement in the 1920s. A number of Bernstorff's letters are here reproduced.

21:79 Colton, Joel G. *Léon Blum: Humanist in Politics.* New York: Knopf, 1966. This biography includes chapters relating to Blum's political activities during the 1930s.

21:80 Craig, Gordon A., and Gilbert, Felix, eds. *The Diplomats, 1919–1939.* 2 vols. New York: Atheneum (1953), 1963. This is an extraordinarily able analysis of mostly European diplomats of the interwar years. Although dated, it has appraisals that have held up.

Dalton, H. *The Fateful Years: Memoirs, 1931–1945* (23:92).

21:81 Eden, Anthony. *The Eden Memoirs: Facing the Dictators.* Boston: Houghton Mifflin, 1962. Eden's memoirs for the period when he was foreign secretary in the Baldwin and Chamberlain cabinets reveal his views toward the United States in the 1930s. Eden believed that an opportunity was lost in the winter of 1937–1938. Bibliography.

21:82 Laue, Theodore H. von. "Soviet Diplomacy: G. V. Chicherin, People's Commissar for Foreign Affairs, 1918–1930." In Gordon A. Craig and Felix Gilbert, eds., *The Diplomats, 1919–1939.* New York: Atheneum (1953), 1963, vol. 1, pp. 234–81. This essay organizes Chicherin's role in Soviet foreign affairs, which dealt with diplomacy and revolution.

21:83 Lipski, Jósef. *Diplomat in Berlin, 1933–1939: Papers and Memoirs of Jósef Lipski, Ambassador of Poland.* Ed. by Waclaw Jedrzejewicz. New York: Columbia University Press, 1968. The documents are chiefly dispatches from Lipski to the Polish foreign minister, covering conversations with Hitler, Göring, Neurath, and Ribbentrop. The subjects covered include the Polish-German nonaggression pact, Danzig, Anschluss, the Czechoslovak crisis, and the outbreak of war. Bibliography.

21:84 Litvinov, Maxim. *Notes for a Journal.* London: Deutsch, 1955. The reliability of this memoir is doubtful. The book shows the author's disenchantment with the Soviet system.

21:85 Lukasiewicz, Juliusz. *Diplomat in Paris, 1936–1939: Papers and Memoirs of Juliusz Lukasiewicz.* Ed. by Waclaw Jedrzejewicz. New York: Columbia University Press, 1970. While not as valuable as Lipski's papers, this volume covers the stresses and strains of the Franco-Polish alliance and the events of 1938–1939.

21:86 Middlemas, Keith, and Barnes, John. *Baldwin: A Biography.* New York: Macmillan, 1970. This is a massive rehabilitation of Baldwin. It seeks to rescue Baldwin's diplomatic reputation in the 1930s by underscoring his efforts to rearm after 1935. It is a starting point for British politics in the 1920s and 1930s. Bibliography.

Nicolson, Harold G. *Curzon: The Last Phase, 1919–1925* (18:150) is a kindly account of the British foreign secretary during the years after World War I.

21:87 Warner, Geoffrey. *Pierre Laval and the Eclipse of France.* New York: Macmillan, 1968. This political biography concentrates on his activities from January 1931 to August 1944.

Willson, B. *Friendly Relations: A Narrative of Britain's Ministers and Ambassadors to America (1791–1930).* (2:239).

EAST ASIAN

Chiang Kai-shek

See Chapters 22 and 27, "Personalities," for additional references.

21:88 Loh, Pichon P. Y. *The Early Chiang Kai-shek: A Study of His Personality and Politics, 1887–1924.* New York: Columbia University Press, 1971. This is a valuable account which provides the basis for a better understanding of Chiang's subsequent policies.

Others

Burns, R. D., and Bennett, E. M., eds. *Diplomats in Crisis: United States-Chinese-Japanese Relations,* *1919–1941* (22:42) contains essays on Wellington Koo, Hu Shih, Shidehara, Hirota, and Shigemitsu.

Moore, F. *With Japan's Leaders: An Intimate Record of Fourteen Years as Counsellor to the Japanese Government* (21:191).

Mosley, L. *Hirohito: Emperor of Japan* (22:68).

Peattie, M. R. *Ishiwara Kanji and Japan's Confrontation with the West* (22:77) is an analytical biography of the visionary general of the Imperial Japanese Army which throws light on Japan's political landscape in the 1930s and, more particularly, on the philosophical grounds of anti-Western nationalism.

Shigemitsu, M. *Japan and Her Destiny: My Struggle for Peace* (22:79).

U.S. and Europe

See "Personalities," especially Herbert C. Hoover, Cordell Hull, Henry Morgenthau, Franklin D. Roosevelt, and, under "Others," Jay Pierrepont Moffat.

21:89 DeBenedetti, Charles. "The First Detente: America and Locarno." *South Atlantic Quarterly* 75:4 (1976), 407–23. The five treaties concluded in Italy in 1925 are analogous to Henry Kissinger's détente of the 1970s. Both occasions seemed to inaugurate periods of international relaxation of tensions. Both depended on the personalities of foreign ministers (Kissinger, Briand, and Stresemann).

21:90 Jacobson, Jon. *Locarno Diplomacy: Germany and the West, 1925–1929.* Princeton, N.J.: Princeton University Press, 1972. This study examines the issues and personalities involved in the Locarno treaties, an effort at détente in the 1920s.

21:91 Tarulis, Albert N. *American-Baltic Relations, 1918–1922: The Struggle over Recognition.* Washington, D.C.: Catholic University Press, 1965. This study reviews the attitudes of the Wilson and Harding administrations toward the Baltic states, and describes those states' efforts to obtain de jure recognition from Washington.

GREAT BRITAIN

See "Personalities," especially Anthony Eden (under "Others"), Ramsay MacDonald.

21:92 Fry, Michael G. *Illusion of Security: North Atlantic Diplomacy, 1918–22.* Toronto: University of Toronto Press, 1972. This work discusses such Atlanticists as Lord Milner, Arthur Balfour, and Philip Kerr, who saw peace as depending on Anglo-American cooperation. Ottawa, they believed, would serve as a mediator between Washington and London. Their hopes failed.

21:93 Hachey, Thomas E. "Winning Friends and Influencing Policy: British Strategy to Woo America in 1937." *Wisconsin Magazine of History* 55:2 (1971/1972), 120–29. Hachey introduces and reprints Ambassador Ronald Lindsay's 1937 dispatch analyzing American policies and politics, and recommending ways in which London might win American support. It is a shrewd commentary.

21:94 Northedge, F. S. *The Troubled Giant: Britain among the Great Powers, 1916–1939.* New York: Praeger, 1966. The increasing irrelevance of the British navy to the balance of power, economic strains, and disunity in commonwealth and empire all contributed to Britain's decline, but the author ranks the failure to adjust to new ideas as the leading cause.

21:95 Taylor, A. J. P. *English History, 1914–1945.* New York: Oxford University Press, 1965. This account replaces C. L. Mowat's earlier *Britain between Wars, 1918–1940* (1955). Taylor's thesis on the origins of World War II figures prominently in his analysis of British diplomacy in the 1930s. Bibliography.

21:96 Watt, Donald C. *Personalities and Policies: Studies in the Formulation of British Foreign Policy in the Twentieth Century.* Notre Dame, Ind.: Notre Dame University Press, 1965. An excellent book written before the British gave up their fifty-year rule. There are now fuller accounts of this period, but Watt's analysis is still a benchmark. Bibliography.

Abrogation of the Anglo-Japanese Alliance

See Chapter 20, "Washington Naval Conference, 1921–1922."

21:97 Galbraith, John S. "The Imperial Conference of 1921 and the Washington Conference." *Canadian Historical Review* 29:2 (1948), 143–52. Canadians came to the sessions of 1921–1922 as members of a British delegation, and found their country's vital interests in the Pacific ignored by their British colleagues.

21:98 Klein, Ira. "Whitehall, Washington, and the Anglo-Japanese Alliance, 1919–1921." *Pacific Historical Review* 46:4 (1972), 460–83. Contrary to myth, the dominion leaders did not determine British foreign policy at the imperial conference. London decided to strengthen the North Atlantic triangle at the expense of the Anglo-Japanese alliance.

21:99 Spinks, C. N. "The Termination of the Anglo-Japanese Alliance." *Pacific Historical Review* 6:4 (1937), 321–40. The abrogation in 1921 of a treaty that had existed since 1902 resulted from assorted motives: American opposition to the alliance, strong Canadian support of the American position, postwar British desire to cut commitments.

FRANCE

See "Personalities," especially, under "Others," Léon Blum, Pierre Laval.

21:100 Carroll, John M. "A Pennsylvanian in Paris: James A. Logan, Jr., Unofficial Diplomat 1919–1925." *Pennsylvania History* 45:1 (1978), 3–18. During 1923 to 1925, Logan was the chief unofficial observer on the reparations commission and did much to make possible the Dawes Plan.

21:101 Dreifort, John E. "The French Popular Front and the Franco-Soviet Pact, 1936–1937: A Dilemma in Foreign Policy." *Journal of Contemporary History* 11:213 (1976), 217–36. The rightist Laval government signed the pact with the expectation that when in June 1936 a Popular Front coalition came to power under Léon Blum, the pact would become a military agreement. It did not. The French feared that in a Nazi-Soviet showdown France would lose no matter who won.

Duroselle, J.-B. *France and the United States: From the Beginnings to the Present* (2:226).

Furnia, A. H. *The Diplomacy of Appeasement: Anglo-French Relations and the Prelude to World*

War II, 1931–1938 (22:121) attempts to analyze the diverse Anglo-French policies that sought to preserve peace during Hitler's first years.

21:102 Leffler, Melvyn P. *The Elusive Quest: America's Pursuit of European Stability and French Security, 1919–1933*. Chapel Hill: University of North Carolina Press, 1979. To promote American exports while reconstructing Germany and stabilizing Europe, policymakers recognized the need for involvement in European affairs, although domestic matters usually took priority. In an era of isolationism, Republican leaders used bankers whenever possible, while making the Europeans bear the burden of stabilization. Extensive bibliography.

21:103 Strauss, David. *Menace in the West: The Rise of French Anti-Americanism in Modern Times.* Westport, Conn.: Greenwood, 1978. The author identifies the sources of modern anti-Americanism in France by concentrating on 1917 to 1932. He is good on intellectual differences.

21:104 Wandycz, Piotr S. *France and Her Eastern Allies, 1919–1925: French-Czechoslovak-Polish Relations from the Paris Peace Conference to Locarno.* Minneapolis: University of Minnesota Press, 1962. This study focuses on the Western effort to create an eastern barrier which, by keeping Germany and Russia apart, would guarantee European peace and security.

Zahniser, M. R. *Uncertain Friendship: American-French Relations through the Cold War* (2:228) includes a chapter on Franco-American relations during the interwar years, when the United States "sowed a harvest of resentments," first by allowing Germany to escape retribution after the Great War and then by refusing to confront the dictators in the 1930s.

French Security Guarantee, 1919

21:105 Ambrosius, Lloyd E. "Wilson, the Republicans and French Security after World War I." *Journal of American History* 59:2 (1972), 341–52. The 1919 security treaty shows the "irreconcilables" willing to guarantee France's security, but unwilling to involve the United States in President Wilson's "utopian plan for permanent peace," thus making the irreconcilables the precursors of post–World War II "realists."

Yates, L. A. R. *The United States and French Security, 1917–1921: A Study in American Diplomatic History* (19:238).

ITALY

See "Personalities," especially Benito Mussolini.

21:106 Cannistraro, Philip V., and Kovaleff, Theodore P. "Father Coughlin and Mussolini: Impossible Allies." *Journal of Church and State* 13:3 (1971), 427–43. Mussolini was aware that American public opinion must be cultivated. Coughlin was quite outspoken, and his policies were in agreement with those of Mussolini, but Mussolini hesitated to press such views on Americans.

21:107 Diggins, John P. "The Italo-American Antifascist Opposition." *Journal of American History* 54:3 (1967), 579–98. The author calls attention to an antifascist movement originating in the radical Italo-American labor movement and supported later by intellectuals who left Italy for America.

21:108 Diggins, John P. *Mussolini and Fascism: The View from America.* Princeton, N.J.: Princeton University Press, 1972. Diggins analyzes American attitudes toward Italian fascism from the early 1920s through World War II. Many Americans believed that Mussolini's regime would become more democratic once the Italian economy improved. After the Ethiopian War, America began to group Hitler with Mussolini. Extensive bibliography.

Ethiopian Crisis, 1935–1937

See Chapter 18, "U.S.-Ethiopia," for background.

21:109 Baer, George W. "Sanctions and Security: The League of Nations and the Italian-Ethiopian War, 1935–1936." *International Organization* 27:2 (1973), 165–80. League officials believed that limited sanctions could uphold the covenant and encourage collective security, but unexpected political events and the collapse of Ethiopian resistance ended their hopes.

21:110 Baer, George W. *Test Case: Italy, Ethiopia, and the League of Nations.* Stanford, Calif.: Hoover Institution Press, 1976. While focusing on Italy, Germany, Britain, and France, Baer does not neglect America. Ethiopia became a test case which discredited collective security, convinced British and French leaders that appeasement worked, and showed Hitler that the West was indecisive. Bibliography.

21:111 Braddick, Henderson B. "A New Look at American Policy during the Italo-Ethiopian Crisis, 1935–1936." *Journal of Modern History* 34:1 (1962), 64–73. Braddick argues that Secretary of State Hull supported the British against Italy because he hoped such a position would promote British cooperation in East Asia.

Feis, H. *Seen from E.A.: Three International Episodes* (21:11) includes a review of the suggestion to embargo oil to Italy during the Ethiopian crisis.

21:112 Friedlander, Robert A. "New Light on the Anglo-American Reaction to the Ethiopian War, 1935–1936." *Mid-America* 45:2 (1963), 115–25. The author argues that Ambassador Breckinridge Long's opposition to a stand against Italy greatly influenced the final policy. Breckinridge feared Italy might go to war with the United States.

21:113 Harris, Brice, Jr. *The United States and the Italo-Ethiopian Crisis.* Stanford, Calif.: Stanford University Press, 1964. Harris assigns blame to Britain and France for allowing Mussolini to conquer Ethiopia. He portrays FDR and Hull as prisoners of isolationist public opinion, and preoccupied with domestic concerns. Bibliography.

21:114 Norman, John. "Influence of Pro-Fascist Propaganda on American Neutrality, 1935–1936." In Dwight E. Lee and George E. McReynolds, eds., *Essays in History and International Relations in Honor of George Hubbard Blakeslee.* Worcester, Mass.: Clark University Press, 1949, pp. 193–214. This is an early effort to gauge the propaganda appeal of Italian-American publications during the Ethiopian War.

21:115 Parker, R. A. C. "Great Britain, France, and the Ethiopian Crisis, 1935–1936." *English Historical Review* 89:351 (1974), 293–332. Fear of an internal social revolution prevented the French from opposing Mussolini. Britain feared that if Italy attacked the British Mediterranean fleet, France would do nothing.

21:116 Richardson, Charles O. "The Rome Accords of January 1935 and the Coming of the Italian-Ethiopian War." *Historian* 41:1 (1978), 41–58. The misunderstandings arising from these records are

analyzed, as are the consequences of the Italian-Ethiopian War, which sabotaged Laval's European policy and drove Mussolini into joining the Axis.

21:117 Robertson, James C. "The Hoare-Laval Plan." *Journal of Contemporary History* 10:3 (1975), 433–64. Close examination of the Hoare-Laval Plan (1935) for dismemberment of Ethiopia confirms the suspicions of contemporaries who saw it as an endeavor to evade league commitments and to sacrifice Ethiopia for European security.

GERMANY

See under "Personalities" for William E. Dodd, Adolf Hitler, George S. Messersmith, Henry Morgenthau, Hugh R. Wilson.

21:118 Enssle, Manfred J. "Stresemann's Diplomacy Fifty Years after Locarno: Some Recent Perspectives." *Historical Journal* 20:4 (1977), 937–48. Gustav Stresemann contributed to the international equilibrium of Locarno and to its demise. He was simultaneously cooperative and revisionist on Germany's frontier problem.

21:119 Etzold, Thomas H. "The (F)utility Factor: German Information Gathering in the United States, 1933–1941." *Military Affairs* 39:2 (1975), 77–82. German intelligence operations in the United States (1933–1941), in spite of their volume, were not effective.

21:120 Frye, Alton. *Nazi Germany and the American Hemisphere, 1933–1941.* New Haven, Conn.: Yale University Press, 1967. The Germans spent a good deal on propaganda, concluded profitable barter agreements with Latin American countries and a few exchanges of military personnel, sought to persuade Argentina, Brazil, and Chile to join the Anti-Comintern Pact, and funneled money to political opponents of President Roosevelt.

21:121 Gottlieb, Moshe. "The Anti-Nazi Boycott Movement in the United States: An Ideological and Sociological Appreciation." *Jewish Social Studies* 35:3/4 (1973), 198–227. In 1933 the Jews organized a boycott and continued it until 1941. The boycott failed because of a lack of unity among U.S. Jews and failure to make its purpose appear universalistic and humanitarian.

21:122 Gottwald, Robert. *Die Deutsch-Ämerikanischen Beziehungen in der Ara Stresemann* [German-American relations in the Stresemann era]. Berlin: Colloquium, 1965. German diplomats encouraged Americans to mediate the reparations tangle and invest in Germany, and persuaded American opinion that fear of militarism was unfounded, that the Weimar Republic was a stable, liberal, middle-class polity. German-American friendship was at its height when Stresemann died in 1929.

21:123 McKale, Donald M. *The Swastika Outside Germany*. Kent, Ohio: Kent State University Press, 1977. This account details the activities of the Nazi Foreign Organization and its efforts to spread Nazi doctrine among groups abroad.

Offner, A. A. "Appeasement Revisited: The United States, Great Britain, and Germany, 1933–1940" (22:116) argues that American historians have believed that economic similarities made the United States and Britain natural allies, and antagonists of Germany. Yet during 1936 to 1940, German and American trade increased, as did American investments in Germany.

21:124 Offner, Arnold A. *American Appeasement: United States Foreign Policy and Germany, 1933–1938*. Cambridge: Harvard University Press, 1969. Offner is mindful of foreign and domestic constraints upon American diplomats, but critical of the Roosevelt administration's failure to cooperate with the British, either to appease or to oppose Germany.

21:125 Radkau, Joachim. *Die deutsche Emigration in den USA: Ihr Einfluss auf die amerikanische Europapolitik, 1933–1945* [German immigration to the United States: its influence on America's European policies, 1933–1945]. Düsseldorf: Bertelsmann Universitätsverlag, 1971. The author discusses German immigration to the United States, particularly during the 1920s and 1930s, and its influence on American policies toward Germany. Extensive bibliography.

21:126 Seabury, Paul. *The Wilhelmstrasse: A Study of German Diplomats under the Nazi Regime*. Berkeley: University of California Press, 1954. Seabury details the attempts to democratize the foreign office during the Weimar period. Hitler regarded the foreign office as "an intellectual garbage dump," and created alternative instruments of diplomacy responsible directly to him.

21:127 Spencer, Frank. "The United States and Germany in the Aftermath of War, 1918–1929." *International Affairs* [London] 43:4 (1967), 693–703. The United States came to the financial rescue of Europe twice, first with the Dawes Plan and then with the Young Plan, but Germany used American loans to reorganize heavy industry, the basis for eventual rearmament.

21:128 Weinberg, Gerhard L. *The Foreign Policy of Hitler's Germany: Diplomatic Revolution in Europe, 1933–1936*. Chicago: University of Chicago Press, 1972. This study argues that Hitler first consolidated his domestic position and built an industrial-military machine for the wars he intended to wage, as he moved cautiously in foreign affairs. Germany's foreign exchange shortage resulted from rearmament expenditures and subsidizing overseas propaganda and special political operations. Bibliography.

Versailles Treaty Era

21:129 Adler, Selig. "The War-Guilt Question and American Disillusionment, 1918–1928." *Journal of Modern History* 23:1 (1951), 1–28. By 1929 the war guilt question had made a deep impression upon the American mind, Germany enjoyed "a decent respect in the opinion of mankind," and as war clouds gathered over the next decade, Americans would strive not to be "taken in" again.

21:130 Bandholtz, Harry H. *An Undiplomatic Diary by the American Member of the Inter-Allied Military Mission to Hungary, 1919–1920*. Ed. by Fritz-Konrad Krüger. New York: Columbia University Press, 1933. This diary, covering the period from August 7, 1919, to February 7, 1920, recounts an American general's experiences in, and views of, the tumultuous events in Hungary at the end of the World War and the onset of the Horthy regime.

21:131 Evans, Ellen L., and Baylen, Joseph O. "History as Propaganda: The German Foreign Office and the 'Enlightenment' of American Historians on the War Guilt Question, 1930–1933." *Canadian Journal of History* 10:2 (1975), 185–208. The authors examine the campaign of the *Kriegsschuldreferat*, a subdivision of the German foreign office, and especially the work of the editor of the office's journal, Alfred Von Wegerer, in publicizing the writings of American revisionist historians.

21:132   Gatzke, Hans W. *Stresemann and the Rearmament of Germany*. Baltimore: Johns Hopkins Press, 1954. According to Gatzke, Stresemann's favorable attitude toward German rearmament was forced upon him by political circumstances. Bibliography.

21:133   Girard, Jolyon P. "American Diplomacy and the Ruhr Crisis of 1920." *Military Affairs* 39:2 (1975), 59–61. In 1920 communist workers in the Ruhr district began civil disturbances. The Weimar government retaliated by sending in troops. The Ruhr crisis of 1920 tested the diplomacy of the commander of the U.S. Occupation Army, Major General Henry T. Allen, who safeguarded U.S. interests and averted danger and entanglement.

21:134   Girard, Jolyon P. "Congress and Presidential Military Policy: The Occupation of Germany, 1919–1923." *Mid-America* 56:4 (1974), 211–20. Although Congress was unwilling to cut off funds for the U.S. Army of Occupation in Germany after World War I, it exerted pressure on Presidents Wilson and Harding to withdraw the troops.

21:135   Mueller, Gordon H. "Rapallo Reexamined: A New Look at Germany's Secret Military Collaboration with Russia in 1922." *Military Affairs* 40:3 (1976), 109–17. The Rapallo Treaty was closely related to secret military and political objectives. Germany's military relations with Russia were far more extensive and important than previously thought. See Bloomberg and Weber (23:2), p. 62, for other works on this relationship.

21:136   Nelson, Keith L. *Victors Divided: America and the Allies in Germany, 1918–1923*. Berkeley: University of California Press, 1975. An exhaustive account that details American policy toward the occupation of Germany, this book finds that President Harding and Secretary Hughes gave more thought to European affairs than previously believed. Extensive bibliography.

Wimer, K. "The Harding Administration, the League of Nations, and the Separate Peace Treaty" (20:89) discusses the Harding administration's separate peace with Germany—a strategy that Wilson tried, and failed, to prevent.

Persecution of Jews

See Chapter 18, "The Palestine Question," and Chapter 22, "U.S. and War Refugees."

21:137   Genizi, Haim. "James G. McDonald: High Commissioner for Refugees, 1933–1935." *Wiener Library Bulletin* [Great Britain] 30:43–144 (1977), 40–52. The League of Nations instituted a high commission for refugees. Headed by an American, the commission contended with American and world apathy.

21:138   Gottlieb, Moshe. "The Berlin Riots of 1935 and Their Repercussions in America." *American Jewish Historical Quarterly* 59:3 (1970), 302–31. The Berlin riots of 1935, which culminated in the Nuremberg laws, dramatized the helplessness of German Jewry, as well as the disinclination of the U.S. government to get involved.

21:139   Shafir, Shlomo. "Taylor and McDonald: Two Diverging Views on Zionism and the Emerging Jewish State." *Jewish Social Studies* 39:4 (1977), 323–46. Myron Taylor and James G. McDonald were public-spirited citizens involved in Roosevelt's pre–World War II effort to help the persecuted European Jews.

21:140   Sherman, A. J. *Island Refuge: Britain and Refugees from the Third Reich, 1933–1939*. Berkeley: University of California Press, 1973. This account describes Britain's response to the plight of German refugees, and is concerned primarily with the evolution of government policy.

21:141   Singer, David G. "The Prelude to Nazism: The German-American Press and the Jews 1919–1933." *American Jewish Historical Quarterly* 61:3 (1977), 417–31. Singer analyzes the German-American press, particularly that of the Midwest, during 1919 to 1933. He shows that attitudes toward Jews changed from support to unfriendliness.

21:142   Spear, Sheldon. "The United States and the Persecution of the Jews in Germany: 1933–1939." *Jewish Social Studies* 30:4 (1968), 215–42. Roosevelt and the State Department refused to protest German persecution of the Jews, urged Congress to avoid condemnatory resolutions, remained aloof from private trade boycotts, worried that the Germans might apply the Nuremberg laws to American citizens in Germany, and apologized in 1937 for Mayor LaGuardia's public denunciation of Hitler.

21:143   Szajkowski, Zosa. "The Attitude of American Jews to Refugees from Germany in the 1930's." *American Jewish Historical Quarterly* 51:2 (1971), 101–43. Against the background of American reluctance to admit additional immigrants, the attitude of American Jews to refugees from Germany was ambiguous.

Propaganda and the German-American Bund

21:144   Bell, Leland V. "The Failure of Nazism in America: The German-American Bund, 1936–1941." *Political Science Quarterly* 85:4 (1970), 585–99. Although the bund, during its short existence, received much attention and dispensed propaganda, the attempt to relate Nazi ideology to America failed.

21:145   Bell, Leland V. *In Hitler's Shadow: The Anatomy of American Nazism.* Port Washington, N.Y.: Kennikat, 1973. During the mid-1930s there was an attempt to nazify German Americans by appealing to Pan-Germanism. Despite initial successes the movement failed.

21:146   Diamond, Sander A. *The Nazi Movement in the United States, 1924–1941.* Ithaca, N.Y.: Cornell University Press, 1974. This study is not only a history of the Nazi movement in the United States, but also an examination of Germany's evolving views concerning Americans of German ancestry.

21:147   Johnson, Ronald W. "The German-American Bund and Nazi Germany, 1936–1941." *Studies in History and Society* 6:2 (1975), 31–45. The German-American Bund, directed by Fritz Kuhn, attempted to organize support for Hitler's government. Kuhn's leadership embarrassed the German foreign ministry as well as German Americans who opposed the Nazi regime.

21:148   Kipphan, Klaus. *Deutsche Propaganda in den Vereinigten Staaten, 1933–1941* [German propaganda in the United States, 1933–1941]. Heidelberg: Carl Winter Universitätsverlag, 1971. The Volksbund für das Deutschtum im Ausland, founded in 1880, and the Deutsches Ausland-Institut, founded in 1917, as well as the Freunde des Neuen Deutschland, founded in 1933 (the German-American Bund), sought favorable American responses to German policy. The propaganda largely failed.

21:149   Remak, Joachim. "'Friends of the New Germany': The Bund and German-American Relations." *Journal of Modern History* 29:1 (1957), 38–41. Fritz Kuhn, leader of the German-American

Bund, and a few Nazi party officials hoped to influence Americans, but State Department protests led Hitler to prohibit party members from propagandizing. Bund membership never exceeded about 6,000.

21:150   Ribuffo, Leo. "Fascists, Nazis and American Minds: Perceptions and Preconceptions." *American Quarterly* 26:4 (1974), 417–32. This is a review essay of several monographs on the American reaction during the New Deal era to Italian fascism, German nazism and the German-American Bund, Father Charles Coughlin's homegrown brand of extremism, and the United States and countersubversives on the eve of World War II.

21:151   Smith, Arthur L., Jr. *The Deutschtum of Nazi Germany and the United States.* The Hague: Nijhoff, 1965. This is a history of the relationship of German Americans to the rise of nazism in Germany, and the efforts by Hitler to win their support.

21:152   Smith, Arthur L., Jr. "The Kameradschaft USA." *Journal of Modern History* 34:4 (1962), 398–408. The German-American Bund never posed a great threat to American security. Bundists returning to Germany before the war could have been a source of intelligence, but Hitler's chaotic chain of command prevented any systematic exploitation of them.

POLAND

21:153   Costigliola, Frank C. "American Foreign Policy in the 'Nutcracker': The United States and Poland in the 1920's." *Pacific Historical Review* 48:1 (1979), 85–105. American efforts to stabilize the Polish economy failed because of massive and intertwined economic and political problems. U.S. policy had sought to rebuild postwar European economics in order to protect its markets, prevent the spread of communism, and reduce the possibility of war and revolution.

21:154   Debicki, Roman. *Foreign Policy of Poland, 1919–39: From the Rebirth of the Polish Republic to World War II.* New York: Praeger, 1962. The veteran Polish diplomat surveys his country's search for a "policy of equilibrium" to avoid falling under the domination of Germany and Russia. Bibliography.

21:155   Poland, Republic of. Ministry for Foreign Affairs. *Official Documents Concerning Polish-German and Polish-Soviet Relations, 1933–1939.* London: Hutchinson, 1941. The Polish government-in-exile presents documents and brief essays to show that "Poland was sincerely seeking to act as a factor for peace and equilibrium in Eastern Europe" in the 1930s before the Nazi-Soviet Pact.

21:156   Riekhoff, Harald von. *German-Polish Relations, 1918–1933*. Baltimore: Johns Hopkins Press, 1971. This account discusses how Locarno, the Rhineland evacuation, adoption of the Young Plan, and the subsequent Hoover moratorium all helped aggravate relations between Germany and Poland.

SOVIET UNION

See "Personalities," especially Charles E. Bohlen (under "American," "Others"), G. V. Chicherin (under "European," "Others"), and Joseph V. Stalin.

Bailey, T. A. *America Faces Russia: Russian-American Relations from Early Times to Our Day* [1776–1950] (2:245) bears the Bailey trademark— skillful use of anecdotes as an aid to insight. It is a well-done analysis.

Dulles, F. R. *The Road to Teheran: The Story of Russia and America, 1781–1943* (2:247) is marked by the wartime perspective from which it was prepared.

Filene, P. G. *Americans and the Soviet Experiment, 1917–1933* (19:255) traces shifts and tries to identify their causes. Americans favored the 1917 revolution, fell into disagreement when Russia left the war in 1918, but felt reassured by the New Economic Policy. The depression stirred American interest in economic planning and trade with the Soviet Union.

Gaddis, J. L. *Russia, the Soviet Union and the United States: An Interpretive History* (2:248) is a fine account of Soviet-American relations. The Soviet Union showed more ability to overcome ideological strictures in the 1920s and 1930s than did the American government. But the Soviets, Gaddis writes, did not live up to the promises they made in the recognition agreement.

21:157   Grant, Natalie. "The Russian Section: A Window on the Soviet Union." *Diplomatic History* 2:1 (1978), 107–15. After the Russian Revolution, American contacts with and information about the U.S.S.R. were limited. To remedy the situation, the State Department established a center for the study of Soviet affairs in the office of the Commissioner of the

United States for the Baltic Provinces of Russia, located in Riga, Latvia.

21:158   Kennan, George F. *Russia and the West under Lenin and Stalin*. Boston: Little, Brown, 1960. In part an apologia for American policy, especially the intervention in Siberia after World War I, this book was an important attempt to bring the essentials of Russian experience and outlook to a popular audience.

21:159   Kennan, George F. *Soviet Foreign Policy, 1917–1941*. Princeton, N.J.: Princeton University Press, 1960. A careful if brief analysis, which argues for accepting the world and especially Russia as it is, for looking to American interests when negotiating with the Soviets, for appreciating ideology and economic realities in Soviet behavior.

21:160   Langer, John D. "The 'Red General': Philip R. Faymonville and the Soviet Union, 1917–52." *Prologue* 8:4 (1976), 209–21. Brigadier General Faymonville's long absorption in Soviet affairs brought him into a position of influence when the United States granted diplomatic recognition to the U.S.S.R. in 1933. As military attaché in Moscow (1933–1938), he gained a reputation as a pro-Soviet observer, in spite of his often unfavorable opinion of Soviet actions.

21:161   Maddux, Thomas R. "Watching Stalin Maneuver between Hitler and the West: American Diplomats and Soviet Diplomacy, 1934–1939." *Diplomatic History* 1:2 (1977), 140–54. American diplomats such as George Kennan, Charles Bohlen, and Loy Henderson underestimated Stalin's overtures to the West. Consequently, the State Department discouraged FDR from making efforts at even limited cooperation with Stalin.

Ulam, A. B. *Expansion and Coexistence: Soviet Foreign Policy, 1917–1973* (2:254) finds that the United States was not important to Soviet policy in the 1920s; after U.S. recognition, the Soviets lost interest when the United States indicated it would do little to prevent Japanese expansionism.

Williams, W. A. *American-Russian Relations, 1781–1947* (2:256).

American Relief Operations, 1919–1923

See "Personalities," especially Herbert C. Hoover.

21:162 Fisher, Harold H. *The Famine in Soviet Russia, 1919–1923: The Operations of the American Relief Administration.* New York: Macmillan, 1927. This is a remarkable contemporary account of the American effort, led by Herbert Hoover, to alleviate the Russian famine. The book details the accomplishments of Hoover and his associates, and sets them in the context of the problems of Soviet government.

21:163 Weissman, Benjamin. *Herbert Hoover and Famine Relief to Soviet Russia, 1921–1923.* Stanford, Calif.: Hoover Institution Press, 1974. This is a detailed treatment of the American Relief Administration, headed by Secretary of Commerce Hoover. Weissman analyzes the apparent contradiction of Hoover the staunch anticommunist assisting the Soviet government.

21:164 Weissman, Benjamin M. "Herbert Hoover's 'Treaty' with Soviet Russia: August 20, 1921." *Slavic Review* 28:2 (1969), 276–88. Weissman describes the negotiations leading to the American Relief Administration's agreement with the Soviet Union on the distribution of food during the famine.

War Scare of 1927

21:165 Meyer, Alfred G. "The War Scare of 1927." *Soviet Union* 5:1 (1978), 1–25. The war scare of 1927 originated as a concern of Nikolai Bukharin, although it quickly became an object of political manipulation by Stalin and an opposition faction.

21:166 Sontag, John P. "The Soviet War Scare of 1926–27." *Russian Review* 34:1 (1975), 66–77. Events did give plausibility to a war as Britain talked of giving Danzig to Germany and compensating Poland with Lithuania; Chiang Kai-shek began persecuting Communists; Great Britain broke relations with the U.S.S.R.; the Soviet minister in Warsaw was assassinated; and Franco-Soviet relations broke down.

Nonrecognition/Recognition

See "Personalities," especially Franklin D. Roosevelt.

21:167 Bennett, Edward M. *Recognition of Russia: An American Foreign Policy Dilemma.* Waltham, Mass.: Blaisdell, 1970. Bennett argues that FDR decided to recognize Russia for a realistic reason—the ineffectiveness of nonrecognition. But by inflating

American expectations, Roosevelt introduced a fatal flaw into Soviet-American relations. Bibliography.

21:168 Bishop, Donald G. *The Roosevelt-Litvinov Agreements: The American View.* Syracuse, N.Y.: Syracuse University Press, 1965. Despite shortcomings in carrying out the Roosevelt-Litvinov agreements, recognition was an advantageous move. No other government did better than the United States in compelling the Russians to honor their promises.

21:169 Bowers, Robert E. "American Diplomacy, the 1933 Wheat Conference, and Recognition of the Soviet Union." *Agricultural History* 11:1 (1966), 39–52. This article discusses the bearing of commodity prices and depression economics on the recognition issue. Federal officials concerned with agricultural prices came to favor relations with the Soviet Union, which may have influenced Roosevelt.

21:170 Bowers, Robert E. "Hull, Russian Subversion in Cuba, and Recognition of the USSR." *Journal of American History* 53:3 (1966), 542–54. The author suggests that Secretary of State Cordell Hull's opposition to recognition derived partly from concern over communist efforts in Cuba. But Hull did not influence FDR on this matter.

21:171 Briley, Ronald F. "Smith W. Brookhart and Russia." *Annals of Iowa* 42:7 (1975), 541–56. In 1923 Senator Brookhart toured Europe to study the cooperative movement, and was particularly impressed with Scandinavia and the U.S.S.R. He campaigned for diplomatic recognition of Russia, and shocked the American public by praising the Communist regime.

21:172 Browder, Robert P. *The Origins of Soviet-American Diplomacy.* Princeton, N.J.: Princeton University Press, 1953. Browder concludes that in the late 1920s the Soviet leaders tried for recognition because of economic need, prestige, and fear of Japan. The delay in recognition, from 1917 to 1933, led to exaggerated hopes on both sides, virtually ensuring disappointment.

21:173 Kneeshaw, Stephen J. "The Kellogg-Briand Pact and American Recognition of the Soviet Union." *Mid-America* 56:1 (1974), 16–31. Kellogg contended that the pact did not extend recognition to the Soviet government, while the Soviets hoped that the pact might smooth the way for a rapprochement.

21:174 Libby, James K. *Alexander Gumberg and Soviet-American Relations, 1917–1933.* Lexington:

University Press of Kentucky, 1977. A Russian-born American businessman with sympathy for the Soviet experiment, Gumberg worked for recognition and for good relations. Libby sees people-to-people relations as dominating relations between the two countries.

Meiburger, A. V. *Efforts of Raymond Robins toward the Recognition of Soviet Russia and the Outlawry of War, 1917–1933* (19:93).

21:175   Schuman, Frederick L. *American Policy toward Russia since 1917: A Study of Diplomatic History, International Law and Public Opinion*. New York: International Publishers, 1928. The author criticizes American nonrecognition, not because of legal or political flaws but because it failed to serve American interests. He advocates abandonment of any hope of "bringing about the overthrow of the Soviet regime," arguing that peaceful, profitable relations with the Soviet Union were possible.

21:176   Wilson, Joan Hoff. "American Business and Recognition of the Soviet Union." *Social Science Quarterly* 52:2 (1971), 349–68. The article stresses the extent to which businessmen divided over recognition, resulting in less business influence on the decision than has been assumed.

21:177   Wilson, Joan Hoff. *Ideology and Economics: U.S. Relations with the Soviet Union, 1918–1933*. Columbia: University of Missouri Press, 1974. This important book argues that nonrecognition caused a lack of coordination between American economic foreign policy and "political" foreign policy because the growing foreign affairs bureaucracy became hardline anticommunists and opponents of recognition.

Uneasy Rapprochement

See "Personalities," especially William C. Bullitt.

21:178   Libby, James K. "Liberal Journals and the Moscow Trials of 1936–38." *Journalism Quarterly* 52:1 (1975), 85–92. American liberals were disenchanted with the U.S.S.R. prior to the Nazi-Soviet Pact of 1939. Commentary in *The Nation* and *New Republic* shows that liberals were progressively disturbed by the Moscow trials.

21:179   Maddux, Thomas R. "American Diplomats and the Soviet Experiment: The View from the Moscow Embassy, 1934–1939." *South Atlantic Quarterly* 74:4 (1975), 468–87. Despite differences of views,

the embassy representatives understood Stalin and the U.S.S.R. rather well. Events such as the purges, the new constitution, war preparations, and economic advances were studied, analyzed, and the conclusions passed on to Washington.

21:180   Uldricks, Teddy J. "The Impact of the Great Purges on the People's Commissariat of Foreign Affairs." *Slavic Review* 36:2 (1977), 187–204. This is a study of a portion of the great purge of the 1930s so as to assess the relationship, if any, between the purges and the evolution of Soviet foreign policy in the 1930s.

U.S. and East Asia

See Chapter 20, "Naval Limitation."

21:181   Clyde, Paul H. *International Rivalries in Manchuria, 1689–1922*. Columbus: Ohio State University Press, 1926. This is a history of international controversies over Manchuria from the 1890s to the Washington Conference (1921–1922).

21:182   Iriye, Akira. *After Imperialism: The Search for a New Order in the Far East, 1921–1931*. Cambridge: Harvard University Press, 1965. A theme in America's East Asian policy during the 1920s was containment of Japan and support for China, observable at the Washington Conference, in dealings with Chinese nationalism, in trade policies, and in other matters. Iriye believes the Americans sought harmony and balance, but drifted to policies that were merely habitual.

21:183   Louis, W. Roger. *British Strategy in the Far East, 1919–1939*. Oxford: Clarendon Press, 1971. This is a subtle overview of British foreign policy toward East Asia in the interwar period, especially 1919 to 1935. The focus is economic and racial troubles, with Sir Victor Wellesley and Sir John Pratt appearing as typical policymakers. Foreign Office distrust of American motives runs throughout. Extensive bibliography.

21:184   Tompkins, Pauline. *American-Russian Relations in the Far East*. New York: Macmillan, 1949. This book retains interest for its discussion, from the perspective of Soviet-American relations, of great power rivalries and revolution in China in the 1920s and 1930s.

21:185   Trotter, Ann. *Britain and East Asia, 1933–1937*. New York: Cambridge University Press, 1975. This first-rate study deals occasionally with Anglo-American relations. Trotter sees British policy attempting ineffectively to preserve trade with China while maintaining imperial defense.

21:186   Tuleja, Thaddeus V. *Statesmen and Admirals: Quest for a Far Eastern Naval Policy*. New York: Norton, 1973. In this account of American naval policy in the Pacific during the Hoover and Roosevelt administrations, Tuleja shows conflicting positions within the naval service. Disarmament policies in the 1920s reduced the possibility of using the navy to support East Asian policy.

Wheeler, G. E. *Prelude to Pearl Harbor: The United States Navy and the Far East, 1921–1931* (40:181).

Wilkins, M. "The Role of U.S. Business" (22:97) argues that American business groups in East Asia had little influence on U.S. foreign policy.

21:187   Williams, William Appleman. "China and Japan: A Challenge and a Choice of the 1920s." *Pacific Historical Review* 26:3 (1957), 259–79. American diplomats sought economic expansion in China and yet wished to avoid military involvement, but these goals were threatened both by the Chinese Revolution and by the increasing intervention of Japan.

JAPAN

See "Personalities," especially Joseph C. Grew, Stanley K. Hornbeck, Cordell Hull, Key Pittman, Henry L. Stimson; see also Chapter 20, "Naval Limitation."

Anderson, I. H., Jr. *The Standard-Vacuum Oil Company and United States East Asian Policy, 1933–1941* (22:235) discusses the intricate role of Stanvac in American East Asian policies.

Blaker, M. *Japanese International Negotiating Style* (22:207) sees a peculiarly Japanese bargaining style in pre–Pearl Harbor negotiations and other case histories. This style included domestic preoccupations and nationalism.

Borg, D., and Okamoto, S., eds. *Pearl Harbor as History: Japanese-American Relations, 1931–1941* (22:195) emphasize decisions within the respective foreign-policy elites, presses, and private organizations interested in foreign affairs.

21:188   Borg, Dorothy. *The United States and the Far Eastern Crisis of 1933–1938: From the Manchurian Incident through the Initial Stage of the Undeclared Sino-Japanese War*. Cambridge: Harvard University Press, 1964. Congress, the press, and public opinion generally disapproved of Japanese policy because of the Manchurian episode and the breakdown of naval disarmament in 1935; far more influential, however, were such isolationist forces as the Great Depression, the Nye investigation, and fear of war, as expressed by the neutrality acts.

21:189   Crowley, James B. *Japan's Quest for Autonomy: National Security and Foreign Policy, 1930–1938*. Princeton, N.J.: Princeton University Press, 1966. This book is noteworthy for the provocative theory that responsible civilian leaders deliberating the requirements of national security and economic well-being favored an East Asia hegemony. This theory opposes the usual conclusion that military ultraists seized power and launched the program of expansionism. Extensive bibliography.

21:190   Maxon, Yale C. *Control of Japanese Foreign Policy: A Study of Civil-Military Rivalry, 1930–1945*. Berkeley: University of California Press, 1957. This is a sophisticated account of Japanese civil-military relations during years of prolonged crisis. The author stresses the extraconstitutional coordinating mechanisms that became instruments of de facto military control over foreign policy. Extensive bibliography.

21:191   Moore, Frederick. *With Japan's Leaders: An Intimate Record of Fourteen Years as Counsellor to the Japanese Government, Ending December 7, 1941*. New York: Scribner's, 1942. An adviser on international affairs in the Japanese foreign office and in the Japanese embassy in Washington, the author describes chronologically and anecdotally the diplomacy that failed.

21:192   Moore, Jamie W. "Economic Interests and American-Japanese Relations: The Petroleum Controversy." *Historian* 35:4 (1973), 551–67. In March 1934 the Japanese Diet took the nation's oil industry out of the hands of foreigners. During these years of diplomatic controversy the United States avoided deference to a single corporate interest while defending the right of Americans to trade in East Asia.

Neu, C. E. *The Troubled Encounter: The United States and Japan* [1853–1972] (2:348) is an exemplary synthesis of secondary works, stressing America's ethnocentric desire for Japan's transformation and the haphazard process of decisionmaking.

21:193 Storry, Richard. *The Double Patriots: A Study of Japanese Nationalism.* Westport, Conn.: Greenwood (1957), 1973. The author surveys the political ideas, events, and tendencies of Japanese nationalist organizations between 1931 and 1941. He finds these organizations disproportionately influential because of Japan's collective leadership. Bibliography.

21:194 Wheeler, Gerald E. "Isolated Japan: Anglo-American Diplomatic Cooperation, 1927–1936." *Pacific Historical Review* 20:3 (1961), 165–78. Wheeler examines Anglo-American diplomatic cooperation, first with the idea of preventing Japanese naval parity and then, after Japan in 1934 abrogated the Washington naval treaty, drawing the English-speaking nations together on Asian affairs.

The Immigration Issue

21:195 Daniels, Roger. *The Politics of Prejudice: The Anti-Japanese Movement in California and the Struggle for Japanese Exclusion.* Berkeley: University of California Press, 1962. Daniels reinforces the argument that the 1924 legislation was a blow to Japanese pride and one of several factors that led to hostilities. This study concerns the scene in America.

21:196 Hellwig, David J. "Afro-American Reactions to the Japanese and the Anti-Japanese Movement, 1906–1924." *Phylon* 38:1 (1977), 93–104. Most black Americans agreed that some restrictions were probably needed, but were concerned that the Japanese were singled out for unfair treatment. By the late 1920s, Blacks came to identify with whites rather than the newcomers.

21:197 Mitchell, Kell F., Jr. "Diplomacy and Prejudice: The Morris-Shidehara Negotiations, 1920–1921." *Pacific Historical Review* 39:1 (1970), 85–104. The negotiations sought to coerce Japan under the guise of solving the difficulties of discrimination and restriction of Japanese immigration, problems that were secondary to larger East Asian policy.

21:198 Paul, Rodman W. *The Abrogation of the Gentlemen's Agreement.* Cambridge: Harvard University Press, 1936. The Immigration Act of 1924 was a turning point in Japanese-American relations, for it challenged Japanese self-esteem and produced long-remembered bitterness. If there had been no "grand disillusionment," Paul contends, Japanese officials might have been in a stronger position to resist anti-democratic pressures.

21:199 Rhee, T. C. "A Postscript on the Japanese-American Immigration Dispute, 1868–1924: A Diplomatic Tinderbox." *Asia Quarterly* [Belgium] 2 (1973), 131–55. It was the general climate of the time, aggravated by radical philosophies on both sides, that gradually propelled the immigration issue to the forefront of conflict.

Manchurian Crisis, 1931–1932

See "Personalities," especially Stanley K. Hornbeck, Henry L. Stimson.

21:200 Clauss, Errol M. "The Roosevelt Administration and Manchukuo, 1933–1941." *Historian* 32:4 (1970), 595–611. The fact that Roosevelt inherited both the Japanese fait accompli in Manchuria and the Hoover-Stimson policy did not forestall accommodation. America restrained its diplomatic representatives in the area and yet at the same time urged them to seek fair treatment of business concerns.

21:201 Doenecke, Justus D. "The Debate over Coercion: The Dilemma of American Pacifists and the Manchurian Crisis." *Peace and Change* 2:1 (1974), 47–52. The American peace movement gained a more realistic understanding of the barbarous world, recognized Japan's legitimate needs in Manchuria, and assumed partial responsiblity for Japan's actions. The dispute within the peace movement over sanctions shows a pondering of means and ends.

Donnelly, J. B. "Prentiss Gilbert's Mission to the League of Nations Council, October 1931" (20:83) points out that, aside from a brief moment of drama when the American took his seat at the council table, Gilbert contributed little to the deliberations.

21:202 Ferrell, Robert H. "The Mukden Incident: September 18–19, 1931." *Journal of Modern History* 27:1 (1955), 66–72. Colonel Seishiro Itagaki of the Kwantung army and several fellow officers instigated the Mukden incident in Manchuria much to the surprise and chagrin of civilian authorities in Tokyo.

21:203 Ogata, Sadako N. *Defiance in Manchuria: The Making of Japanese Foreign Policy, 1931–1932.* Berkeley: University of California Press, 1964. American disapproval was an enjoyable experience for many Japanese who resented U.S. policies on immigration, trade, and Chinese matters. Yet defiance of Washington was only incidental to the purposes of Japanese nationalists, who through action in Manchuria sought to defy the presumed timidity of their own government.

21:204 Pearson, Alden B., Jr. "A Christian Moralist Responds to War: Charles C. Morrison, *The Christian Century* and the Manchurian Crisis, 1931–33." *World Affairs* 139:4 (1977), 296–307. Morrison and *Christian Century* were the most outspoken of the Christian periodicals during the Japanese-provoked crisis. Morrison helped shape American's response.

21:205 Roberts, Stephen S. "The Decline of the Overseas Station Fleets: The United States Asiatic Fleet and the Shanghai Crisis, 1932." *American Neptune* 37:3 (1977), 185–202. The Japanese assault on Shanghai (January 1932) marked the decline of European and U.S. naval influence in China.

21:206 Smith, Sara R. *The Manchurian Crisis, 1931–1932: A Tragedy in International Relations.* New York: Columbia University Press, 1948. Smith sees Manchuria as one of many tragedies that resulted from failure of the United States to join the League of Nations, to cooperate with Britain, and to live up to the obligations of the Washington treaties and the Kellogg-Briand Pact.

21:207 Thorne, Christopher. *The Limits of Foreign Policy: The West, the League and the Far Eastern Crisis of 1931–1933.* New York: Putnam's, 1972. Thorne is critical of both British and American diplomacy during the Manchurian affair and after; he criticizes tactics and perceptions. He does not see World War II as having begun in 1931. Bibliography.

21:208 Yoshihashi, Takehiko. *Conspiracy at Mukden: The Rise of the Japanese Military.* New Haven, Conn.: Yale University Press, 1963. This is a discussion of the events leading up to, and during, the Mukden incident (1931–1933). It focuses on the seizure of power in Manchuria by the Japanese militarists. Bibliography.

Stimson-Hoover Doctrine

21:209 Current, Richard N. "The Stimson Doctrine and the Hoover Doctrine." *American Historical Review* 59:2 (1954), 513–42. Hoover was content with nonrecognition as a simple statement of American disapproval, whereas Stimson wanted to use the policy as a first step toward stronger statements and perhaps sanctions.

21:210 Hecht, Robert A. "Great Britain and the Stimson Note of January 7, 1932." *Pacific Historical Review* 38:2 (1969), 177–91. Foreign Secretary Sir John Simon rejected Stimson's nonrecognition strategy in belief that for economic, political, and strategic reasons his government could not afford to antagonize Japan.

21:211 Langer, Robert. *Seizure of Territory: The Stimson Doctrine and Related Principles in Legal Theory and Diplomatic Practice.* Princeton, N.J.: Princeton University Press, 1947. Long on historical background, the details of conferences of the 1930s, and evaluation of the Stimson Doctrine, this study anticipated a better result in international law than the Stimson statement.

21:212 Sternsher, Bernard. "The Stimson Doctrine: FDR 'versus' Moley and Tugwell." *Pacific Historical Review* 31:3 (1962), 281–89. These key members of FDR's "brain trust" tried unsuccessfully to convince the president-elect to break with the Hoover-Stimson East Asian policies.

CHINA

See "Personalities," especially Chiang Kai-shek, Nelson T. Johnson, Henry Morgenthau, and, under "Others," Henry R. Luce.

21:213 Abend, Hallett. *My Life in China: 1926–1941.* New York: Harcourt, Brace, 1943. These reminiscences of a *New York Times* correspondent portray the gradual development of the Chinese Nationalist regime and the expansion of Japanese power at China's expense.

21:214 Borg, Dorothy. *American Policy and the Chinese Revolution, 1925–1928.* New York: Macmillan, 1947. Secretary of State Kellogg's positive responses to Chiang Kai-shek helped the victory of the Nationalist party. Kellogg was a moderate whose diplomacy encouraged the Nationalists to avoid political extremes.

21:215 Clubb, O. Edmund. *Communism in China, as Reported from Hankow in 1932.* New York: Columbia University Press, 1968. This is a reprint of a report Clubb wrote while serving as vice-consul at Hankow. This is still an impressive piece of contemporary research into the origins of the communist movement from its split with the Kuomintang in 1927.

21:216 Cohen, Warren I. "The Development of Chinese Communist Policy toward the United States, 1922–1933." *Orbis* 11:1 (1967), 219–37. The Chinese Communist party concentrated its propaganda against Japan and England, the two powers with the greatest political, economic, and military stakes in China, rather than the United States. In late 1932, the CCP began to separate the United States from the other foreign powers as part of Stalin's search for allies against Japan.

21:217 Duke, David C. "Anna Louise Strong and the Search for a Good Cause." *Pacific Northwest Quarterly* 66:3 (1975), 123–37. This essay pictures Strong as a social activist who found in the Russian and Chinese revolutions causes equal to her energy and enthusiasm.

21:218 George, Brian T. "The State Department and Sun Yat-sen: American Policy and the Revolutionary Disintegration of China, 1920–1924." *Pacific Historical Review* 46:3 (1977), 387–408. Makers of American foreign policy came to see Sun not as a revolutionary and a nationalist, but as a troublemaker who retarded China's peaceful unification and political reform.

21:219 Hoyt, Frederick B. "Protection Implies Intervention: The U.S. Catholic Mission at Kanchow." *Historian* 38:4 (1976), 709–27. In 1928, as the Communists advanced on Kanchow, the missionaries remained, seeking American diplomatic help, which forced the Nationalists to protect them.

21:220 Hoyt, Frederick B. "The Summer of '30: American Policy and Chinese Communism." *Pacific Historical Review* 46:2 (1977), 229–49. During the summer the Chinese Communists attacked major cities, threatening the lives and property of Americans. Hoyt argues that these events convinced American diplomats that the Chinese Communists were "organized brigands."

21:221 Hunt, Michael H. "Pearl Buck—Popular Expert on China, 1931–1949." *Modern China* 3:1 (1977), 33–64. An examination of a China expert with an influence over popular understanding rather than policy. The author traces Buck's reaction to China and analyzes the nature and limits of her knowledge. References include a full listing of Buck's writings on China.

21:222 Israel, Jerry. "Mao's 'Mr. America': Edgar Snow's Images of China." *Pacific Historical Review* 47:1 (1978), 107–22. Snow (1905–1972) hoped to see America's democratic doctrines spread in China by American aid, trade, and education. He feared Japanese domination of China and searched for an alternative—a search that led him to see the Communists in an increasingly sympathetic light.

21:223 Leary, William M., Jr. "Wings for China: The Jouett Mission, 1932–1935." *Pacific Historical Review* 38:4 (1969), 447–62. Japanese bombing of China's cities in 1932 prompted the Chinese to seek aid in training its air force. While the Departments of State and War would not help, Commerce sent Colonel John H. Jouett, who trained 300 cadets and provided China with the nucleus of a modern air force.

21:224 Pugach, Noel H. "Anglo-American Aircraft Competition and the China Arms Embargo, 1919–1921." *Diplomatic History* 2:4 (1978), 351–72. Aircraft competition constituted only one of the many challenges to the well-intentioned embargo. Additionally, it reveals another area of Anglo-American disagreement.

21:225 Thomson, James C., Jr. *While China Faced West: American Responses in Nationalist China, 1928–1937.* Cambridge: Harvard University Press, 1969. Nanking announced the need for "relevant reforms," and the call was answered by American specialists in education, monetary policy, bureaucratic management, flood control, bridge building. There were improvements, but Thomson says that cultural difference brought many failures.

21:226 Walsh, Billie K. "The German Military Mission in China, 1928–38." *Journal of Modern History* 46:3 (1974), 502–13. This essay reviews the origins and activities of the German military mission.

Shantung Question, 1921–1922

See Chapter 20, "Washington Naval Conference, 1921–1922."

21:227 Fifield, Russell H. "Secretary Hughes and the Shantung Question." *Pacific Historical Review* 23:4 (1954), 375–85. Secretary of State Hughes skillfully conducted informal negotiations with British, Japanese, and Chinese representatives that resolved the question largely because there was no desire to embarrass Japan.

21:228 Pugach, Noel H. "American Friendship for China and the Shantung Question at the Washington Conference." *Journal of American History* 64:1 (1977), 67–86. Pugach assesses the role of American mediation in the Shantung dispute which resulted from the 1914 Japanese occupation of Shantung.

Economic Relations

Field, F. V. *American Participation in the China Consortiums,* [1909–1924] (39:53) has a clear chronology of European-American participation in the China Consortium.

21:229 Ghosh, Partha Sarathy. "Passage of the Silver Purchase Act of 1934: The China Lobby and the Issue of China Trade." *Indian Journal of American Studies* 6:1/2 (1976), 18–29. The China lobby pushed through this act over the opposition of Roosevelt and Secretary of the Treasury Morgenthau. The silver purchase program enriched the act's promoters but neither stabilized the Chinese currency nor revitalized U.S.-Chinese trade.

Hunt, M. H. "Americans in the China Market: Economic Opportunities and Economic Nationalism, 1890s–1931" (39:54) finds that governmental support was of little value, and the successful companies learned how to accommodate themselves to Chinese business practices, preferences, and nationalism.

21:230 Sewall, Arthur F. "Key Pittman and the Quest for the China Market, 1933–1940." *Pacific Historical Review* 44:3 (1975), 351–71. Senator Pittman used the argument that overseas economic expansion was the best means of economic recovery as a tactical device to raise the domestic price of silver, and his argument triumphed at the World Economic and Monetary Conference in 1933 and in the Silver Purchase Act of 1934.

21:231 Wilson, David A. "Principles and Profits: Standard Oil Responds to Chinese Nationalism, 1925–1927." *Pacific Historical Review* 46:4 (1977), 625–47. In March 1925 the Kuomintang (Nationalist) government in Kwantung imposed a tax on imported kerosene. The oil companies imposed an embargo. Support from workers in Kwantung and Hong Kong, and oil from the Soviet Union, circumvented the embargo.

THE PHILIPPINES

21:232 Friend, Theodore W. *Between Two Empires: The Ordeal of the Philippines, 1929–1946.* New Haven, Conn.: Yale University Press, 1965. The author focuses on political independence for the Filipinos, but gives attention to the commonwealth status between the wars and to the excitement caused by this short-term arrangement among Japanese and Southeast Asian nationalists. The New Order, beginning in late 1941 and early 1942, is also discussed.

21:233 Friend, Theodore W. "The Philippine Sugar Industry and the Politics of Independence, 1929–1935." *Journal of Asian Studies* 22:2 (1963), 179–92. Friend examines the Philippines' place in the American sugar market, and the role of sugar in the Philippine political economy.

Grunder, G. A., and Livezey, W. E. *The Philippines and the United States* (2:353) is a dated but still useful summary.

21:234 Hayden, John R. *The Philippines: A Study in National Development.* New York: Macmillan, 1942. Here is a careful analysis of conditions, promising and discouraging, in regard to Filipino capabilities for self-rule at the time of the Tydings-McDuffie Act of 1934. Hayden was vice-governor of the islands from 1933 to 1935.

21:235 Kirk, Grayson L. *Philippine Independence: Motives, Problems, and Prospects.* New York: Farrar & Rinehart, 1936. Kirk's argument is that the islands were not ready for independence. The author was spokesman for a Filipino faction that included Manuel Quezon, which sought to delay American retirement from the islands.

Lansang, J. A. "The Philippine-American Experiment: A Filipino View" [1898–1950] (2:354).

U.S. and the Western Hemisphere

LATIN AMERICA

21:236   Beaulac, Willard L. *Career Ambassador.* New York: Macmillan, 1951. This diplomatic memoir traces Beaulac's career from vice-consul in Tampico to ambassador in Colombia. There is much in Beaulac's story that is interesting—his encounters with revolutionaries and despots, and his presence in Haiti and Nicaragua during U.S. interventions.

Bemis, S. F. *The Latin American Policy of the United States: An Historical Interpretation* [1776–1942] (2:260) surveys U.S.–Latin American relations and concludes that Washington's policy was generally benevolent, even during periods of intervention.

21:237   Grieb, Kenneth J. "The United States and the Fifth Pan American Conference." *Inter-American Review of Bibliography* 20:2 (1970), 157–68. President Harding and Secretary of State Hughes tried to improve U.S.–Latin American relations through diplomatic persuasion rather than intervention.

21:238   Haring, Clarence H. *South America Looks at the United States.* New York: Macmillan, 1928. This volume, a product of a year's residence in South America (1925–1926), notes sources of suspicion and misunderstanding in racial and cultural barriers, in increasing commercial and financial penetration, and in political policies.

Scott, J. B. *The International Conferences of American States, 1889–1928* (16:14) contains the conventions, treaties, resolutions, protocols, recommendations, and reports adopted at the conferences. In 1940 the *First Supplement* was published, for 1933 to 1940.

21:239   Tulchin, Joseph. *The Aftermath of War: World War I and U.S. Policy toward Latin America.* New York: New York University Press, 1971. Tulchin's study extends through 1925 and demonstrates how World War I provided an opportunity for the United States to expand its political and economic influence in Latin America. Tulchin emphasizes the

service to the State Department afforded by oil, capital markets, and cables. Bibliographical essay.

Good Neighbor Policy/Monroe Doctrine

See "Personalities," especially Warren G. Harding, Herbert C. Hoover, Charles Evans Hughes, Franklin D. Roosevelt, Sumner Welles.

Cuevas Cancino, F. M. *Roosevelt y la Buena Vecindad* [1933–1945] (35:84) is laudatory of the good neighbor policy.

21:240   Dozer, Donald M. *Are We Good Neighbors? Three Decades of Inter-American Relations, 1930–1960.* Gainesville: University of Florida Press, 1959. Dozer combines his State Department experience with his training as an historian to demonstrate that to achieve its wartime objectives the United States overrode the essential nonintervention element of the good neighbor policy. Extensive bibliography.

21:241   Ferrell, Robert H. "Repudiation of a Repudiation." *Journal of American History* 51:4 (1965), 669–73. Ferrell attempts to untangle the historical confusion surrounding the Clark memorandum. After publication of the memorandum in 1930 the State Department exerted considerable effort to avoid endorsing it. Hoover's reluctance to endorse the memorandum carried over to the Roosevelt administration.

21:242   Gellman, Irwin F. *Good Neighbor Diplomacy: United States Policies in Latin America, 1933–1945.* Baltimore: Johns Hopkins University Press, 1979. This study examines the relationship of FDR's Latin American diplomacy to his global strategies. Gellman concludes that good neighbor diplomacy was as much the product of personality as policy.

21:243   Green, David. *The Containment of Latin America: A History of the Myths and Realities of the Good Neighbor Policy.* Chicago: Quadrangle, 1971. A study of FDR's good neighbor policy and how it seemed to reinforce U.S. domination of Latin America. Green argues that while the policy succeeded in strengthening America's economic position, it in fact led the United States to support of dictatorships.

21:244 Guerrant, Edward O. *Roosevelt's Good Neighbor Policy.* Albuquerque: University of New Mexico Press, 1950. Guerrant has chapters on abandonment of intervention, recognition policy, commerce, cultural and scientific relations, and the quest for law. He believes that Roosevelt consistently followed a hands-off policy, has strong reservations about the effectiveness of nonrecognition, and believes Hull's trade program was fundamentally sound but had limitations.

Perkins, D. *A History of the Monroe Doctrine* (2:273) summarizes the author's detailed studies of the Monroe Doctrine and extends those studies beyond the two world wars. Debate on the League of Nations, World Court, and the Kellogg Pact raised the issue of the Monroe Doctrine when many senators appended reservations to prove their loyalty to the great American dogma.

21:245 [----]ons, Gene A. "The Clark Memorandum Myth." *Americas* 34:1 (1977), 40–58. The memorandum on the Monroe Doctrine drawn up by J. Reuben Clark for Secretary of State Kellogg in 1928 depicted the doctrine as an expression of U.S. self-defense and did not explicitly renounce the right of intervention in Latin America, as often stated.

Steward, D. *Trade and Hemisphere: The Good Neighbor Policy and Reciprocal Trade* (20:237) presents a revisionist view which contends that Roosevelt's economic policies were a guise for imperialism.

21:246 Wood, Bryce. *The Making of the Good Neighbor Policy.* New York: Columbia University Press, 1961. This account of the making of a good neighbor policy reveals its gradual construction and lack of blueprint or doctrine. Ingredients were nonintervention and noninterference, pacific protection, and reciprocity. Wood is concerned with continuity when individuals and issues change, for much depended on Welles, Duggan, Hull, and Roosevelt. Bibliography.

MEXICO

See "Personalities," especially Josephus Daniels, Henry Morgenthau, Dwight Morrow.

21:247 Dulles, John W. F. *Yesterday in Mexico: A Chronicle of the Revolution, 1919–1936.* Austin: University of Texas Press, 1961. Dulles describes the domestic events between the Mexican presidential campaign of 1919 and the early days of the Cardenas regime, concentrating on Obregón, Huerta, and Calles. Extensive bibliography.

21:248 Horn, James J. "U.S. Diplomacy and the 'Specter of Bolshevism' in Mexico (1924–1927)." *Americas* 32:1 (1975), 31–45. Horn discusses the U.S. fear of Mexican bolshevism, a manifestation of a strong Mexico for Mexicans movement which incorporated nationalism and contributed to deterioration of diplomatic relations between Mexico and the United States.

21:249 Ignasias, C. Dennis. "Propaganda and Public Opinion in Harding's Foreign Affairs: The Case for Mexican Recognition." *Journalism Quarterly* 48:1 (1971), 41–52. The author describes the Mexican government's propaganda to influence the U.S. public, and the pressure by private American citizens upon the Harding administration (1920–1923) to recognize Obregón's government.

21:250 Kane, N. Stephen. "American Businessmen and Foreign Policy: The Recognition of Mexico, 1920–1923." *Political Science Quarterly* 90:2 (1975), 293–313. Kane presents a case study of business influence on recognition of the Obregón regime. He concludes that businessmen had little influence.

21:251 Kane, N. Stephen. "Bankers and Diplomats: The Diplomacy of the Dollar in Mexico, 1921–1924." *Business History Review* 47:3 (1973), 335–52. Kane examines the cooperative relations between American bankers, the State Department, and Mexico, illustrating the interdependence of the dollar and diplomacy in the 1920s.

21:252 Levenstein, H. A. "The AFL and Mexican Immigration in the 1920's: An Experiment in Labor Diplomacy." *Hispanic American Historical Review* 48:2 (1968), 206–19. The AFL sought to restrict Mexican immigration in the 1920s by persuading the Conferación Regional Obrera Mexicana (CROM) to press the Mexican government to enact restrictions. This plan failed when the CROM lost influence.

Smith, R.F. *The United States and Revolutionary Nationalism in Mexico, 1916–1932* (15:174) suggests that Harding and Hughes bettered relations when they abandoned some demands, but this lesson had to be relearned.

21:253   Smith, Robert Freeman. "The Morrow Mission and the International Committee of Bankers on Mexico: The Interaction of Finance Diplomacy and the New Mexican Elite." *Journal of Latin American Studies* 1:2 (1969), 149–66. Mexican officials recognized that the appointment of Morrow as ambassador lessened the possiblity of intervention. The Mexicans respected the International Committee of Bankers on Mexico, with which Morrow had been associated.

21:254   Trani, Eugene P. "Harding Administration and Recognition of Mexico." *Ohio History* 75:2/3 (1966), 137–48. Mexico refused to sign a treaty of amity and commerce as a condition of American diplomatic recognition. Acutely aware of mounting public pressures, Harding circumvented Hughes's legalistic approach and gave in.

The Religious Issue

21:255   Cronon, E. David. "American Catholics and Mexican Anticlericalism, 1933–1936." *Mississippi Valley Historical Review* 45:2 (1959), 201–30. Reacting to the anticlericalism of the Mexican Revolution, American Catholics launched a campaign of economic, political, and military pressure. The campaign improved religious conditions in Mexico.

21:256   Quirk, Robert E. *The Mexican Revolution and the Catholic Church, 1910–1929.* Bloomington: Indiana University Press, 1973. Religion constituted a bond between the United States and Mexico in the years before and after World War I. One outcome of the revolution of 1910, as it tried to reject the past, was a confrontation with the church. Dwight Morrow's achievement was to diminish church-state tensions within Mexico, and ease U.S.-Mexican hostilities.

21:257   Rice, M. Elizabeth Ann. *The Diplomatic Relations between the United States and Mexico, as Affected by the Struggle for Religious Liberty in Mexico, 1925–1929.* Washington, D.C.: Catholic University of America Press, 1959. The author attributes much of the success in mediation between the Calles regime and the Catholic church to Dwight W. Morrow's ability and prestige. The apparent progress in U.S.-Mexican relations during Morrow's service in Mexico did not prevent recurrence of problems in the next decade.

The Oil Issue

See Chapter 39, "Oil Operations."

Meyer, L. *Mexico and the United States in the Oil Controversy, 1917–1942* (39:144) believes the State Department exerted extensive economic pressure on the Cardenas government in 1938 and that Ambassador Daniels's moderating influence was less than sometimes thought.

Silva Herzog, J. *Historia de la expropiación de las empresas petroleras* (39:192) is one of the best studies on the subject.

CARIBBEAN

21:258   Grieb, Kenneth J. "The United States and the Rise of General Maximiliano Hernández Martínez." *Journal of Latin American Studies* 3:2 (1971), 151–72. The military coup which installed Hernández Martínez in power in El Salvador (1931) offered the first major test of the 1923 treaty. The treaty stipulated that Central American nations would withhold diplomatic recognition from "illegal" regimes.

21:259   Langley, Lester D. "Negotiating New Treaties with Panama, 1936." *Hispanic American Historical Review* 48:2 (1968), 220–33. The good neighbor policy encountered opposition in Panama because of U.S. security arguments. Langley details discussions leading to new treaties covering U.S. intervention in Panama, commissary rights, transit across the Canal Zone, transportation across the isthmus, and Panamanian radio transmission.

21:260   Millett, Richard. "The State Department's Navy: A History of the Special Service Squadron, 1920–1940." *American Neptune* 35:2 (1975), 118–38. The Special Service Squadron, organized after World War I, allowed U.S. naval forces to be deployed more efficiently in the Mexico–Central America area.

21:261   Munro, Dana G. *The United States and the Caribbean Republics, 1921–1933.* Princeton, N.J.: Princeton University Press, 1974. Munro, a former State Department official and diplomat in Latin America, is convinced that the policy of intervention gradually changed during the "Republican restoration" and that much of the groundwork for the New Deal's good neighbor policy was laid before 1933.

Cuba

21:262 Aguilar, Luis E. *Cuba 1933: Prologue to Revolution*. Ithaca: N.Y.: Cornell University Press, 1972. Aguilar describes the social, economic, and political forces behind Cuban nationalism to show that ideas and programs that seemed to originate with Castro's revolution actually began in 1933. He explores the early influence of the Communist party, and the U.S. interventionist role.

Benjamin, J. R. *The United States and Cuba: Hegemony and Dependent Development, 1880–1934* (13:18) is an investigation of the "hegemonic element in the relations between the United States and Cuba in the years leading up to the Cuban revolution of 1933."

21:263 Benjamin, Jules R. "The New Deal, Cuba, and the Rise of a Global Foreign Economic Policy." *Business History Review* 51:1 (1977), 57–78. Roosevelt's involvement in Cuban affairs helped to establish the global outlook of American foreign policy in the 1940s. Especially visible was the use of the Reconstruction Finance Corporation and the Export-Import Bank.

21:264 Cronon, E. David. "Interpreting the New Good Neighbor Policy: The Cuban Crisis of 1933." *Hispanic American Historical Review* 39:4 (1959), 538–67. At root in this crisis was what constitutes a good neighbor. Sumner Welles argued that the doctrine permitted armed intervention, while Hull and Daniels refused to accept that idea. Roosevelt sided with Hull and Daniels.

Fitzgibbon, R. H. *Cuba and the United States, 1900–1935* (15:183).

21:265 Gellman, Irwin F. *Roosevelt and Batista: Good Neighbor Diplomacy in Cuba, 1933–1945*. Albuquerque: University of New Mexico Press, 1973. FDR's avoidance of military intervention brought praise for the administration's success in hemispheric relations, but stability and expanded commercial relations between the island and its northern neighbor continued to be the goals; only the tactics changed. Bibliography.

21:266 Pérez, Louis A., Jr. "Capital, Bureaucrats, and Policy: The Economic Contours of United States–Cuban Relations, 1916–1921." *Inter-American Economic Affairs* 29:1 (1975), 65–80. Pérez links the expansion of U.S. intervention to investment of American capital. Cuban businessmen successfully exploited conflicts among U.S. interests.

21:267 Smith, Robert Freeman. *The United States and Cuba: Business and Diplomacy, 1917–1960*. New York: Bookman, 1962. Smith details the relations between economic and political factors in Cuban dependence on the United States.

21:268 Wright, Theodore P., Jr. "United States Electoral Intervention in Cuba." *Inter-American Economic Affairs* 13:3 (1959), 50–71. The author traces U.S. involvement in Cuban electoral legislation and practice from independence to the abrogation of the Platt Amendment in 1934.

Dominican Republic

See under "Personalities" for Warren G. Harding.

Calder, B. J. "Caudillos and Gavilleros versus the United States Marines: Guerrilla Insurgency during the Dominican Intervention, 1916–1924" (15:161) discusses a series of revolutionary incidents that led to the occupation by the U.S. Marines in 1916. The marines considered themselves racially superior to the Dominicans, and their abuse of peasants created more insurgents. The guerrillas surrendered in 1922 and shortly thereafter the marines left.

21:269 Grieb, Kenneth J. "Warren G. Harding and the Dominican Republic: U.S. Withdrawal, 1921–1923." *Journal of Inter-American Studies* 11:3 (1969), 425–40. Harding's administration began withdrawing American forces from the Caribbean, thus helping to pave the way for the good neighbor policy. The president dispatched Sumner Welles to the Dominican Republic to arrange an amicable settlement.

21:270 Juarez, J. R. "United States Withdrawal from Santo Domingo." *Hispanic American Historical Review* 42:2 (1962), 152–90. A discussion of the end of the U.S. occupation of Santo Domingo in 1924, stressing the period after World War I.

Guatemala

21:271 Grieb, Kenneth J. "Negotiating a Reciprocal Trade Agreement with an Underdeveloped Country: Guatemala as a Case Study." *Prologue* 5:1 (1973), 22–29. Grieb surveys the negotiations between the

United States and Guatemala (1933–1936) based on the Reciprocal Trade Agreements Act of 1934.

21:272 Grieb, Kenneth J. "The United States and General Jorge Ubico's Retention of Power." *Revista de Historia de América* 71 (1971), 119–35. General Jorge Ubico Castañeda (1878–1946) not only tacitly accepted U.S. policy in the Caribbean but praised it in the strongest terms. He placed American diplomats in an awkward position when in 1935 he sought to extend his term of office unconstitutionally.

Haiti

21:273 Hauptman, Laurence M. "Utah Anti-Imperialist: Senator William H. King and Haiti, 1921–34." *Utah Historical Quarterly* 41:2 (1973), 116–27. King was the only member of the inquiry into American occupation and administration of Haiti not to sign its favorable report. He argued for the practical advantages of Haitian independence.

Schmidt, H. *The United States Occupation of Haiti, 1915–1934* (15:188) argues that the decision to intervene resulted from a long-term U.S. hegemony in the Caribbean and that occupation was a departure from the principles of liberal internationalism.

21:274 Spector, Robert M. "W. Cameron Forbes in Haiti: Additional Light on the Genesis of the "Good Neighbor' Policy." *Caribbean Studies* 6:2 (1966), 28–45. Forbes headed the commission sent to Haiti by Hoover in 1930. The author details the settlement by Forbes, which permitted withdrawal of the U.S. Marines.

Welles, S. *Naboth's Vineyard: The Dominican Republic, 1844–1924* (2:323) remains a classic account.

Nicaragua

21:275 Greer, Virginia L. "State Department Policy in Regard to the Nicaraguan Election of 1924." *Hispanic American Historical Review* 34:4 (1954), 445–67. Secretary of State Hughes failed to oppose immediately the constitutionally questionable candidacy of Bartolome Martínez to succeed himself as president. When Hughes finally asserted his opposition, the Nicaraguan president retaliated by refusing to permit U.S. supervision of the election.

21:276 Kamman, William. *A Search for Stability: United States Diplomacy toward Nicaragua, 1925–1933.* Notre Dame, Ind.: University of Notre Dame Press, 1968. This account of the second marine intervention in Nicaragua reveals the unexpected complexities of military interference. Washington's desire for peace and stability involved the United States in supervised elections, creation of a national guard, and a difficult guerrilla war.

21:277 Macaulay, Neill. *The Sandino Affair.* Chicago: Quadrangle, 1967. Washington's attempts to restore peace in Nicaragua in 1926–1927 aroused opposition from a young Nicaraguan nationalist, Augusto C. Sandino. Macaulay describes the Sandino affair as a precursor of modern revolutionary guerrilla warfare.

21:278 Salisbury, Richard V. "United States Intervention in Nicaragua: The Costa Rican Role." *Prologue* 9:4 (1977), 209–17. President Ricardo Jiménez of Costa Rica secretly supported U.S. intervention during the Nicaraguan crises of 1912 and 1925 to 1927. Jiménez believed that the United States should either keep entirely out of Central American affairs, or, given the need to protect the Panama Canal, guarantee peace and stability in no uncertain manner.

21:279 Tierney, John J., Jr. "U.S. Intervention in Nicaragua, 1927–1933: Lessons for Today." *Orbis* 14:4 (1971), 1012–28. Tierney comments on three "sublimited" engagements made by the United States: The Vietnam War, the Philippine insurrection, and the Nicaragua intervention (1927–1933)—and studies the last in detail.

SOUTH AMERICA

Peterson, H. F. *Argentina and the United States: 1810–1960* (2:287). Includes two chapters for the 1920s and 1930s. Peterson recounts the ups and downs of Argentine-American trade, with difficulties arising from protective tariffs and sanitary restrictions.

21:280 Snyder, J. Richard. "William S. Culbertson in Chile: Opening the Door to a Good Neighbor, 1928–1933." *Inter-American Economic Affairs* 26:1 (1972), 81–96. William S. Culbertson, U.S. ambassador to Chile, improved foreign relations with an early attempt at the good neighbor policy.

Chaco War, 1928–1935

21:281 Gillette, Michael L. "Huey Long and the Chaco War." *Louisiana History* 11:3 (1970), 293–311. Long, in May 1934, accused the Standard Oil Company of New Jersey of aiding Bolivia against Paraguay in their war (1928–1935). He helped to defeat the ratification of the World Court by linking the court to Standard Oil and the league embargo against Paraguay.

21:282 Rout, Leslie B., Jr. *Politics of the Chaco Peace Conference, 1935–1939*. Austin: University of Texas Press, 1970. This multiarchival study traces the difficult attempts to bring peace between Bolivia and Paraguay. Washington encountered League of Nations involvement and Argentine rivalry. The author concludes that the peace settlement was not moral or impartial, but brought peace.

21:283 Wood, Bryce. *The United States and Latin America Wars: 1932–1942*. New York: Columbia University Press, 1966. The Chaco War, the Leticia dispute, and the Marañon conflict revealed weaknesses in the inter-American system for peaceful settlement of disputes and indicated the inability of Washington to prevent war in South America.

Brazil

21:284 McCann, Frank D., Jr. *The Brazilian-American Alliance, 1937–1945*. Princeton, N.J.: Princeton University Press, 1974. McCann discusses the events during the Vargas regime which brought about a close alliance between Brazil and the United States, and resulted in Brazil's dependence upon its new ally. He emphasizes the internal dynamics of Brazilian politics. Bibliography.

Repko, A. F. "The Failure of Reciprocal Trade: United States–German Commercial Rivalry in Brazil, 1934–1940" (20:235) discusses the effort to block German economic and political penetration of Latin America, especially of Brazil. The State Department followed a pragmatic policy, in belief that tariff reduction and unconditional most-favored-nation status for American-German trade would reverse the gains of the Germans.

Colombia

21:285 Bushnell, David. *Eduardo Santos and the Good Neighbor, 1938–1942*. Gainesville: University Presses of Florida, 1967. This brief monograph provides a useful account of U.S.-Colombia relations during Santos's presidency.

21:286 Randall, Stephen J. "Colombia, the United States, and Interamerican Aviation Rivalry, 1927–1940." *Journal of Interamerican Studies and World Affairs* 14:3 (1972), 297–324. Randall examines Washington's policy toward the Colombian airline, Scadta, and suggests that while strategic factors were present by 1940, one should not overlook the earlier commercial context from which the strategic factors originated. He concludes that Pan American Airways was an instrument of U.S. imperialism in Latin America.

21:287 Randall, Stephen J. *The Diplomacy of Modernization: Colombian-American Relations, 1920–1940*. Toronto: University of Toronto Press, 1977. While claiming to seek only an open door, equal access for trade and investment, and hemispheric security, American officials attempted to exclude foreign competitors from key sectors of the Colombian economy, especially petroleum and aviation. Bibliography.

Peru

Carey, J. C. *Peru and the United States, 1900–1962* (2:303) emphasizes economic relations.

21:288 St. John, Ronald B. "The End of Innocence: Peruvian Foreign Policy and the United States, 1919–1942." *Journal of Latin American Studies* 8:2 (1976), 325–44. Peru's foreign policy problems can be traced to Augusto B. Leguia's (1863–1932) "ill-advised dependency on the U.S. government, coupled with his tendency to promise territorial resolutions totally beyond the capacity" of Peru to achieve.

CANADA

See "Personalities," especially, under "Others," Jay Pierrepont Moffat, William Phillips.

Kottman, R. N. *Reciprocity and the North Atlantic Triangle, 1932–1938* (20:234) treats the evolution of economic solidarity which strengthened the bonds of the three countries. The author believes Canada made important contributions to Anglo-American détente.

21:289 Kottman, Richard N. "Herbert Hoover and the Smoot-Hawley Tariff: Canada, a Case Study." *Journal of American History* 62:3 (1975), 609–35. This article reviews Hoover's personal knowledge of Canada and how Canadian-American relations might be affected by the Smoot-Hawley tariff. Kottman is critical of Hoover, who according to him deserves no credit for being a good neighbor to Canada.

21:290 Kottman, Richard N. "Hoover and Canada: Diplomatic Appointments." *Canadian Historical Review* 51:3 (1970), 292–309. Hoover had little interest in Canada, except the St. Lawrence Seaway, and the president's diplomatic appointments to Canada were indications of this indifference.

Willoughby, W. R. *The St. Lawrence Waterway: A Study in Politics and Diplomacy* (2:223) has five chapters concerned with issues of the 1920s and 1930s covering the waterway, American tariff, and Canadian fear and suspicion of U.S. intentions.

22

Prelude to World War II, 1936–1941

Contributing Editors

EDWARD M. BENNETT
Washington State University

GARY M. ROSS
Loma Linda University

Contributor

Peter H. Buckingham
Southwest Texas State University

Contents

Introduction

Scholars who began as either defenders or challengers of Franklin Delano Roosevelt's foreign policy relating to the period 1937 to 1941 have given way in more recent years to those attempting to uncover the American role as perceived by administration spokesmen and the effects of United States policy on the developing war. Samples of the "court historians'" works—such as B. Rauch, *Roosevelt from Munich to Pearl Harbor* (22:34); R. E. Sherwood, *Roosevelt and Hopkins* (22:23)—are included to illustrate how far we have come in pursuing the historians' mission to uncover reality. The same is true of the inclusion of revisionist works—such as C. A. Beard, *President Roosevelt and the Coming of the War* (22:61); C. C. Tansill, *Back Door to War* (22:272)—and New Left histories—G. Kolko, *The Politics of War* (25:19); L. C. Gardner, *Economic Aspects of New Deal Diplomacy* (21:12)—many of which begin with preconceptions intended to be "proved" by the research which follows.

The more realistic assessments of American foreign policy in this crucial era—such as R. A. Divine, *The Illusion of Neutrality* (22:11) and D. Borg and S. Okamoto, eds., *Pearl Harbor as History* (22:195)—have chipped away at the evidence and let credit for failures and successes fall where it may. But most historians would agree with some of the conclusions of the revisionists and New Left writers that American policy was not covered with glory in pursuing the basic objectives of all foreign policies—pursuit of the national interest, defense of basic ideals, and defense of national security, which is a part of, but not the whole of, pursuing the national interest.

The Roosevelt administration had to deal with three main problems in making foreign policy in the 1930s: the isolationist mood of the nation and the Congress, which was in part related to the depression; threats to its interests and security coming from both Europe and Asia; and its own indecision concerning the best course to pursue in meeting the above problems. Most perplexing was the realization that to deal with threats to the peace in both Europe and Asia, it was necessary if possible to keep the powers creating the threat separated from one another. Thus the major thrust of Roosevelt's policy was toward making sure that the armed and aggressively inclined nations did not form a coalition, while convincing Americans that they would not be directly involved in any forthcoming war.

After Munich, President Roosevelt and his advisers became almost fatalistically convinced that the world was headed for war, and despite efforts of the president and Secretary of State Cordell Hull to appeal for peace, they had little hope for success. Roosevelt and Hull tried to think of ways they could ensure Allied victory without U.S. involvement, while not fully convinced that this would be feasible. This meant that they had to try to circumvent the neutrality legislation which hampered aid to the democracies, Russia and China, while keeping a close watch over the deepening Asian crisis. They paid close attention to the "test" war going on inside the civil war in Spain, which terminated in 1939, and to the Russo-Finnish War, which followed close on the heels of the Spanish struggle.

Sides formed in the United States supporting or opposing some forms of intervention to divert the growing crises in Europe and Asia or to aid the Allied side once the war began. Roosevelt followed this struggle of internal forces checking and sometimes commissioning public opinion polls and privately encouraging the interventionists in their struggle against the isolationists. This was a very slow process which did not keep pace with the rapid moves of the aggressors.

Probably the real turning point in both the president's attitude to the European war and in the complacency of the American people concerning a possible stalemate in Europe came with the fall of France on June 22, 1940. In the late summer Congress authorized accelerated rearmament, expansion of the U.S. Army and the U.S. Navy, and emergency measures to prepare for the possibility of war. In early September Congress approved FDR's destroyer-bases deal and by March 11, 1941, enacted the proposal he made in a fireside chat of December 29, 1940, the Lend-Lease Act, which undercut the Neutrality Act of 1939. Also in 1941 FDR approved the escort of convoys in the "neutral" zone, which he progressively moved farther out into the Atlantic as the United States occupied Greenland and Iceland. Incidents involving three American destroyers, the *Greer,* the *Kearny,* and the *Reuben James,* moved the United States closer to belligerency.

After 1937 the United States became more and more identified with the Chinese resistance, condemning Japan less for nullifying the post-Versailles settlement than for threatening an ally in the burgeoning struggle against totalitarianism. Most significant of all, the United States in 1939, 1940, and 1941 undertook in a graduated manner the imposition of economic sanctions and countermoves against Japan that counterproductively increased Japanese desperation for alternative resources such as those of Southeast Asia. Meanwhile formal and informal diplomatic negotiations proceeded apace but deadlocked over what each side perceived as excessive demands by the other. In some sense of the overused word, war between America and Japan became "inevitable," the only surprise being that Oahu, Hawaii, not some point considerably to the west, provided the setting. Thereupon, with only nominal hesitations on Hitler's part, the theaters were linked and war encompassed the world.

Accounts that record the foregoing, together with seemingly endless nuances, qualifiers, and details, are rich because of the archival bonanza that the loss of sovereignty by Germany and Japan gave the West and because of the ardor for data generated by the congressional investigation of Pearl Harbor (22:8) and the records of the International Military Tribunal for the Far East (IMTFE) (27:12). But by no means have all questions been foreclosed. Many scholars have challenged either the timidity or direction of the Roosevelt-Hull policies dealing with the coming of war in Europe, some asserting that FDR saw the "inevitability" of war as early as 1935, but did nothing but wait and see if the problems might not solve themselves, or else responded with "typical" American moralistic behavior suggesting that others closer to the problems should bear the burden of solving them. How accurate this assessment was, has been part of the debate among Roosevelt scholars.

Some scholars have examined U.S. foreign policy in an attempt to find the major themes relating to the development of the war in either American initiatives to the crises in Europe and Asia or the lack of them.

They have asked questions concerning American economic motives, perceptions of security needs, attempts to uphold a Wilsonian commitment to international law and treaty obligations, and have wondered if the selfishness and war weariness and disillusionment at the failure to make the world safe for democracy and to end war forever in 1919 did not create the climate for World War II.

Some questions concerning the coming of the war focus more specifically on Japan. Does the charge that militarism accounts for Japan's course beg the question and fail to deal with other domestic pressures such as the nationalist groups? Was the turn southward in Japan's program for conquest solely a military decision or was it face-saving in the light of the failure to subdue China proper? May it not also have been connected to the perception of Pan-Asianism? To what extent was the American response to Japan related to pressures from the navy, the oil companies, and other commercial entities? How was the response affected by the British, the Australians, and well-meaning amateur American diplomats? How much cross-cultural misunderstanding was there and how much has been learned from Pearl Harbor concerning misperception of intelligence?

There is the convergence of those sides as described in the binational conference papers edited and published by Dorothy Borg and Shumpei Okamoto in *Pearl Harbor as History.* Attesting that one-sided views inevitably oversimplify, this book demonstrates how both parties can be juxtiposed in studying any facet of the diplomatic relationship, particularly where there are comparable institutions to focus upon. The net effect of this has been that the shadow of wartime passions no longer clouds the investigation of wartime events, and in this we find evidence for recent historiography relating to both the European and Pacific phases of the war.

As is implied by including the foreign policy relating to the origins of World War II in Europe and Asia in a single chapter, there is one final subject to bring to the attention of the interested student and researcher. Is it possible really to separate American policy concerning these two areas? Does not the major task of future researchers lie in integrating the crises in Europe and the Pacific more completely in their attempts to assess the inhibitions apparent in the formulation of American policy as it attempted to deal with the coming of World War II?

Resources and Overviews

RESEARCH AIDS

While pertinent bibliographies and reference aids are listed here, there are more extensive lists in Chapter 1.

Bibliographies

Bloomberg, M., and Weber, H. H. *World War II and Its Origins: A Selected Annotated Bibliography of Books in English* (23:2) contains many references, in Chapter 2, to relations among nations during the 1930s.

Braisted, William R. "The Navy in the Early Twentieth Century, 1890–1941" (19:3) contains materials relating to the U.S. Navy and diplomacy as World War II loomed.

Dexter, B., ed. *The Foreign Affairs Fifty-Year Bibliography: New Evaluation of Significant Books on International Relations, 1920–1970* (1:14) is a very useful condensation and new evaluation of books listed in the *Foreign Affairs Bibliography* (1:15).

Doenecke, J. D., ed. *The Literature of Isolationism: A Guide to Non-Interventionist Scholarship, 1930–1972* (1:24).

Foreign Affairs Bibliography: A Selected and Annotated List of Books on International Relations (1:15) is issued at ten-year intervals, and each volume has three parts: "General International Relations"; "The World since 1914"; and "The World by Regions." Useful aid.

Funk, A. L., et al. *A Select Bibliography of Books on the Second World War* (23:4).

Morley, J. W., ed. *Japan's Foreign Policy, 1868–1941: A Research Guide* (1:100).

Rabe, V. H. *American-Chinese Relations, 1784–1941: Books and Pamphlets Extracted from the Shelf Lists of Widener Library* (17:5).

Stewart, W. J., ed. *The Era of Franklin D. Roosevelt: A Selected Bibliography of Periodical, Essay, and Dissertation Literature, 1945–1971* (20:2) contains annotated, indexed materials on FDR's diplomacy (1933–1945).

Ziegler, J., ed. *World War II: Books in English, 1945–1965* (23:9) eases the task of the researcher considerably because the section on diplomacy is quite exhaustive, excluding very little of importance published in the first twenty years after the war.

Historiographical Essays

22:1 Cole, Wayne S. "American Entry into World War II: A Historiographical Appraisal." *Mississippi Valley Historical Review* 43:4 (1957), 595–617. Cole provides a summary of the internationalist and revisionist perspectives, with some attention to the climate of opinion in which they developed, the problem of "court history," and certain historiographical deficiencies.

22:2 Doenecke, Justus D. "Beyond Polemics: An Historiography Re-Appraisal of American Entry into World War II." *History Teacher* 12:2 (1979), 217–51. This survey by an expert on American isolationism supplements but does not replace the older surveys. It examines the impact of the depression on all the major powers and the influence of unexplored areas of American domestic life.

22:3 Ikuhiko, Hata. "Japanese Historical Writing on the Origins and Progress of the Pacific War." In David Sissons, ed., *Papers on Modern Japan.* Canberra: Australian National University, 1968, pp. 79–90. Although this article takes note of the friendly reception in Japan to American revisionist studies of the war's origins, it recounts the rise of a positivist standpoint that uses in a relatively value-free, objective manner the documents that escaped the wholesale burnings during the surrender.

22:4 Morton, Louis. "1937–1941." In Ernest R. May and James C. Thomson, Jr., eds., *American–East Asian Relations: A Survey.* Cambridge: Harvard University Press, 1972, pp. 260–90. This historiographical essay covers the archival material and memoir literature of both sides, samples secondary works of American revisionists and internationalists, and identifies fresh lines of inquiry among newer, often bilingual scholars of the sixties.

22:5 Robertson, Esmonde M., comp. *Origins of the Second World War: Historical Interpretations.* London: Macmillan, 1971. These essays, prompted by A. J. P. Taylor's *The Origins of the Second World War* (22:106), examine not only Germany's policies but those of Italy and Japan. The materials then available are surveyed, and research areas suggested. Bibliography.

Yearbooks and Other Aids

Keesing's Contemporary Archives: Weekly Diary of World Events (1:152) covers international events, from 1931.

Political Handbook and Atlas of the World (1:144) is valuable for listing officials in power, from 1927. Annual.

Survey of International Affairs (1:146) is especially valuable for its contemporary view.

The United States in World Affairs (1:147) is an indispensable annual review since 1931.

Document Collections

More general collections are listed in Chapter 1, and other collections may be found in "Personalities," below.

Australia. Department of Foreign Affairs. *Documents on Australian Foreign Policy, 1937–1949* (32:9, 32:10) is a new series which covers, to date, 1937 to 1939.

Degras, J., ed. *Soviet Documents on Foreign Policy* [1917–1941] (20:3).

France. Commission de Publication des Documents Relatifs aux origines de la Guerre 1939–1945. *Documents diplomatiques française, 1932–1939* (21:6) covers, in the second series, Germany's reoccupation of the Rhineland (March 1936) and the outbreak of the Spanish Civil War (July 1936).

22:6 France. Foreign Office. *The French Yellow Book.* New York: Reynal & Hitchcock, 1940. This collection of documents from 1938–1939, originally published to justify the policy of appeasement, focuses on Franco-German relations, but the book also has much to say about Anglo-French diplomacy and

the abortive negotiations with the Soviet Union for an alliance against Hitler.

Great Britain. Foreign Office. *Documents on British Foreign Policy, 1919–1939* (20:4).

International Military Tribunal, *Trial of the Major War Criminals before the International Military Tribunal, Nuremberg, 14 November 1945–1 October 1946* (28:90) contains many documents relating to prewar events, volumes 23 and 24 are an index to the set.

International Military Tribunal for the Far East. *Record of the Proceedings* (27:12) is a valuable source of research materials on Japanese domestic affairs and diplomacy during 1928 to 1945. Brown (27:4), and Dull and Umemura (27:18) assist in using these materials.

Lebra, J. C., ed. *Japan's Greater East Asia Co-Prosperity Sphere in World War II: Selected Readings and Documents* (22:214).

U.S.S.R. Ministry of Foreign Affairs. *Correspondence between the Chairman of the Council of Ministers of the U.S.S.R. and the Presidents of the U.S.A. and the Prime Ministers of Great Britain during the Great Patriotic War of 1941–1945* (23:19) is of interest (volume 1) concerning the origins of World War II. Some of the later correspondence reflects back on the origins of the war and illustrates a jockeying for position by the Allies which solidifies one's understanding of the war's origins.

22:7 U.S.S.R. Ministry for Foreign Affairs. *Soviet Peace Efforts on the Eve of World War II.* 2 vols. Moscow: Novosti Press, 1973. This collection of 449 documents (September 29, 1938, to September 1, 1939) includes items from official American, British, German, Italian, and Polish publications available elsewhere, but most of the material from the Soviet archives is new.

22:8 U.S. Congress. Joint Committee on the Investigation of the Pearl Harbor Attack. *Pearl Harbor Attack: Hearings before the Joint Committee on the Investigation of the Pearl Harbor Attack.* 39 pts. 79th Cong., 1st Sess., 1946. This massive compilation of documents and testimony also includes the wartime investigations of the Roberts Commission, the Hart inquiry, the Navy Board of Inquiry, Clarke investigation, Clausen investigation, and the Hewitt inquiry.

22:9 U.S. Congress. Joint Committee on the Investigation of the Pearl Harbor Attack. Report; *Investigation of the Pearl Harbor Attack*. 79th Cong., 1st Sess., 1946. This one-volume summary of the 39 parts takes the so-called internationalist position that primary responsibility lay with the military clique dominating Japan in 1941 but that secondary responsibility lay with American military and naval area commanders who without dereliction of duty committed seven specified errors of judgment. A minority report is appended.

U.S. Department of State. *Documents on German Foreign Policy, 1918–1945* (21:9) contains, in series D, 13 volumes which cover the years 1937 to 1941.

U.S. Department of State. *Foreign Relations of the United States* (1:358) is of major interest to the student searching out the sources of American policy leading toward involvement in the European war (1937–1941).

U.S. Department of State. *Press Conferences of the Secretaries of State, 1922–1974* (1:360).

U.S. Department of State. *Press Releases* (1:361).

OVERVIEWS

Adler, S. *The Uncertain Giant, 1921–1941: American Foreign Policy between the Wars* (20:8) gives considerable attention to the effects of domestic problems on foreign policy.

22:10 Beard, Charles A. *American Foreign Policy in the Making, 1932–1940: A Study in Responsibilities*. New Haven, Conn.: Yale University Press, 1946. A revisionist work that uses available documents to "prove" that Roosevelt deserted the liberal tradition and deliberately led the nation into war.

22:11 Divine, Robert A. *The Illusion of Neutrality*. Chicago: University of Chicago Press, 1962. This work traces the internationalization of FDR circa 1939 and his struggle thereafter to lead toward intervention without appearing to do so. Especially useful is the careful identification of three groups in Congress, the administration, and the Department of State which were attempting to define the United States' interests and direction: traditionalists, internationalists, and isolationists. Extensive bibliography.

22:12 Divine, Robert A. *The Reluctant Belligerent: American Entry into World War II*. New York: Wiley, 1965. A readable, balanced, and brief general account, this book chronicles American, European, and East Asian diplomacy for purposes of showing, without condemning Roosevelt, that the initiatives surrendered to Germany and Japan nearly permitted an Axis victory.

Dozer, D. M. *Are We Good Neighbors? Three Decades of Inter-American Relations, 1930–1960* (21:240) emphasizes the danger of German penetration of Latin America. The development of wartime cooperation and the strategy involved make this volume pertinent to the study of American foreign policy and the European war (1939–1941).

22:13 Drummond, Donald F. *The Passing of American Neutrality, 1937–1941*. Ann Arbor: University of Michigan Press, 1955. This account parallels Langer and Gleason (22:15) in its topics and sympathies as it analyzes the demise of isolationism in American thought. Bibliography.

Duroselle, J.-B. *From Wilson to Roosevelt: Foreign Policy of the United States, 1913–1945* (19:20).

22:14 Fehrenbach, T. R. *F.D.R.'s Undeclared War, 1939–1941*. New York: McKay, 1967. Although there is little new in this volume, it does treat the problems FDR faced in developing a foreign policy and campaigning to gain support for it. The focus is on public opinion as an obstacle to what the author considers to be a sound foreign policy. Bibliography.

Gardner, L. C. *Economic Aspects of New Deal Diplomacy* (21:12) asserts that economics dominated New Deal diplomacy.

Greenfield, K. R. *American Strategy in World War II: A Reconsideration* (23:155) is a brief, but important, study which graphically illustrates the relationship of military and diplomatic decisions and the subordination of the latter to the former. The Germany-first decision in American policy receives special attention.

Greenfield, K. R., ed. *Command Decisions* (23:156) places the events leading to Pearl Harbor in the genre of command decisions by field officers and high-level officials. Louis Morton's essay takes the traditional view of Japan's army-culpability and analyzes the Germany-first strategy.

22:15 Langer, William L., and Gleason, S. Everett. *The Challenge to Isolation: The World Crisis of 1937–1940 and American Foreign Policy.* 2 vols. New York: Harper & Row, 1952. Reprint 1964. This was a pioneer study in the assessment of American foreign policy during the Roosevelt administration's struggle to escape from isolationism. Based on original sources long before they were available to the general researcher, the authenticity of the scholarship and the value of the criticism remain viable.

22:16 Offner, Arnold A. *The Origins of the Second World War: American Foreign Policy and World Politics, 1914–1941.* New York: Praeger, 1975. Offner sets the scene of American foreign policy at the beginning of World War II in the broader context of the European and Asian struggle for power and visualizes Roosevelt as playing against the stream of movement by other powers, but not solely as a victim of circumstances. Bibliography.

22:17 Russett, Bruce M. *No Clear and Present Danger: A Skeptical View of the United States Entry into World War II.* New York: Harper & Row, 1972. A revisionist study, prepared at the height of the Vietnam antiwar movement, which argues that Britain and Russia probably could have held off Germany without U.S. belligerency. Japan presumably could have been dissuaded, with concessions, from its drive for territory.

Snell, J. L. *Illusion and Necessity: The Diplomacy of Global War, 1939–1945* (23:39).

22:18 Watson, Mark Skinner. *Chief of Staff: Prewar Plans and Preparations.* Washington, D.C.: G.P.O., 1950. One of the volumes in the *United States Army in World War II,* this book treats General Marshall's response to America's unreadiness for war during the 1930s to 1941. It is useful on changes in American policy with respect to the defense of the Philippines, and the appointment of MacArthur to the Far Eastern command.

22:19 Watt, Donald C. *Too Serious a Business: European Armed Forces and the Approach of the Second World War.* Berkeley: University of California Press, 1975. This work is primarily a synthesis of published research. Watt argues that the war in these stages was primarily a civil war and that Allied military leadership was too cautious to perform its assigned role. The result was the dissolution of the European order. Bibliography.

Personalities

Additional references on individuals may be found in Chapter 1, "Biographical Data."

AMERICAN

William C. Bullitt

See also Chapter 21, "Personalities."

Bullitt, O. H., ed. *"For the President—Personal and Secret": Correspondence between Franklin D. Roosevelt and William C. Bullitt* (21:17) illustrates in the communiqués the vacillation between commitments and inaction which bedeviled American policy. Bullitt remained isolationist until the full blast of war set Hitler loose on a Europe which few knew or loved more completely than this strange man.

Joseph E. Davies

22:20 Davies, Joseph E. *Mission to Moscow, 1936–1938.* New York: Simon & Schuster, 1941. A very friendly and almost roseate view of the Soviet Union, written in the glow of the rapprochement that occurred in its year of publication.

22:21 Ullman, Richard H. "The Davies Mission and United States–Soviet Relations, 1937–1941." *World Politics* 9:2 (1957), 220–39. Davies constantly misread Soviet affairs during his tenure as American ambassador. However he proved to be correct, for the wrong reasons, in his prediction that the Russians could withstand the Hitler juggernaut, whereas State Department experts were wrong for the right reasons.

Joseph C. Grew

Grew, J. C. *Ten Years in Japan* (21:25) comprises selected diary entries of Grew's decade in Japan that ended with Pearl Harbor. Notable above all for conveying the tenacity of his peacekeeping efforts and for supplementing his *Report from Tokyo* by emphasizing the country and its people rather than Japanese militarism.

Grew, J. C. *Turbulent Era: A Diplomatic Record of Forty Years, 1904–1945* (18:33) recounts, in volume 2, events on the eve of Pearl Harbor. The work includes Grew's "certainties" about prewar courses of action, particularly his abortive 1941 recommendation of summitry as a means for avoiding war.

Heinrichs, W. H., Jr. *American Ambassador: Joseph C. Grew and the Development of the United States Diplomatic Tradition* (21:26) studies Grew for the way his life illustrated the nature of American professional diplomacy and only secondarily for roles played in the developing 1941 crisis. Grew emerges in the latter regard, however, as a person of admirable tact who was inhibited by traditional outlook and overdependence on intuition.

Herbert C. Hoover
See Chapters 20 and 21, "Personalities."

Hoover, H. C. *Addresses upon the American Road, 1933–1938* (21:30).

22:22 Hoover, Herbert C. *Further Addresses upon the American Road, 1938–1940.* Freeport, N.Y.: Books for Libraries Press (1940), 1972. Part 2 of this volume deals with Hoover's public addresses on American foreign policy from 1938 to 1940, during which time he became a major spokesman for antiinterventionist, isolationist groups. He expressed the more extreme anti-Roosevelt positions and was in the forefront of the movement to block intervention in "another European war."

Harry Hopkins
Adams, H. H. *Harry Hopkins* (23:59) provides a complete picture of Hopkins's personal contribution to U.S. wartime diplomacy.

22:23 Sherwood, Robert E. *Roosevelt and Hopkins: An Intimate History.* Rev. ed. New York: Harper, 1950. This remains the most thorough and reliable study touching Harry Hopkins's role in American foreign policy, which began tentatively in 1940 and became crucial as he provided the liaison between the United States and England and Russia in 1941.

Cordell Hull
See Chapter 21, under "Personalities."

Brune, L. H. "Considerations of Force in Cordell Hull's Diplomacy, July 26 to November 26, 1941" (22:246).

Hull, C. *Memoirs* (21:36) is a necessary source for an understanding of American policy leading up to World War II. Volume 2 covers the period when Hull was still largely in control of many aspects of American policy (1937–1941).

22:24 Pratt, Julius W. *Cordell Hull, 1933–1944.* 2 vols. New York: Cooper Square, 1964. This is perhaps the most important biography concerning American diplomacy in the decade before Pearl Harbor. It is also an indispensable supplement to Hull's own memoirs, for although Pratt sympathizes with the secretary (acknowledging, for example, the eclipse of the State Department during his tenure), he rebukes the inflexible moralism that accompanied and perhaps caused the breakdown of relations with Japan. Bibliography.

Nelson T. Johnson
See Chapter 21, "Personalities."

Buhite, R. D. *Nelson T. Johnson and American Policy toward China, 1925–1941* (21:38) illustrates how Americans in China responded to Japanese depredations. In Johnson's case, the advocacy of increasingly firm steps against Japan and in behalf of China flowed from a high regard for the latter that sometimes lacked profundity and imagination.

George F. Kennan
See Chapter 24, "Personalities," for additional references.

Kennan, G. F. *Memoirs, 1925–1950* (24:124) provides, in volume 1, the professional diplomat's view of his nation's policy and the development of the European war from 1939 to 1941.

22:25 Kennan, George F. *From Prague after Munich: Diplomatic Papers, 1938–1940.* Princeton, N.J.: Princeton University Press, 1968. Kennan wrote this series of 36 documents as secretary of legation and then "caretaker" of the Prague legation from the Munich crisis until after the outbreak of war in Europe. The documents are valuable not only for what they reveal about young Kennan's thought processes, but for a remarkably objective portrait of the dismemberment of Czechoslovakia.

Joseph P. Kennedy
22:26 Beschloss, Michael R. *Kennedy and Roosevelt: The Uneasy Alliance.* New York: Norton, 1980. The author analyzes the relationship between these two strong-willed men, and presents a fine study of the problems of leadership. Extensive bibliography.

22:27 Koskoff, David. *Joseph P. Kennedy: A Life and Times.* Englewood Cliffs, N.J.: Prentice-Hall, 1974. This biography of an American businessman who also served in various foreign service positions discusses his gradual shift to an isolationist orientation after negotiating trade agreements with Great Britain in 1938.

Charles A. Lindbergh

Cole, W. S. *Charles A. Lindbergh and the Battle against American Intervention in World War II* (22:84).

22:28 Lindbergh, Charles A. *The Wartime Journals of Charles A. Lindbergh.* New York: Harcourt Brace Jovanovich, 1970. There is no better way to get at the mind of the isolationist who advocated a Fortress America than reading this book. Lindbergh and many who agreed with him were willing to let the decadent Europeans stew in their own juice and perhaps not lament the prospect of a Nazi victory if it weakened control of the Jews and the communists in the world.

Douglas MacArthur

See Chapter 40, "Personalities," for additional references.

James, D. C. *The Years of MacArthur* [1880–1945] (23:107) is the first volume of a two-volume life-and-times biography, invoked but not superseded by Manchester in his more recent study. Although emphasizing MacArthur's role as administrator rather than as warrior, it is nevertheless useful for accenting his part in the belated program to defend the Philippines with a Far Eastern command despite the primacy of the Atlantic and the widespread view of the archipelago as an unprotectable pawn.

Manchester, W. *American Caesar: Douglas MacArthur, 1880–1964* (24:139) is a lively account which must be checked against James.

Henry Morgenthau, Jr.

See Chapter 21, "Personalities," for additional references.

22:29 Blum, John Morton. *From the Morgenthau Diaries.* Vol. 2: *Years of Urgency, 1938–1941.* Boston: Houghton Mifflin, 1965. This volume finds the treasury secretary and personal friend of Roosevelt leading the advocacy of economic assistance to the anti-Nazi powers, condoning provisions for China despite the corruption of her government, and proposing earlier and more ardently than anyone else the use of sanctions against the Japanese. See volume 1, *Years of Crisis, 1928–1938* (21:43), for the *Panay* incident and Munich.

22:30 U.S. Senate. Committee on the Judiciary. Report; *Morgenthau Diary* (China). 2 vols. 89th Cong. 1st Sess., Feb. 5, 1965. These entries from the massive Morgenthau diary at the Roosevelt Library, Hyde Park, N.Y., were selected and printed in an attempt to "prove" that Harry Dexter White had helped to undermine Chiang Kai-shek's government. The documents beginning in 1939 contain useful information.

Key Pittman

See also Chapter 21, "Personalities."

22:31 Cole, Wayne S. "Senator Key Pittman and American Neutrality Policies, 1933–1940." *Mississippi Valley Historical Review* 46:4 (1960), 644–62. Reasons for the Roosevelt administration's difficulties in advancing its interventionist position in 1939–1940 rested in part on the lukewarm support provided by the Democratic chairman of the Senate Foreign Relations Committee, Key Pittman. He was far more willing to take an aggressive stand against Japan than against Germany, and like Hull was frightened of public opinion.

Israel, F. L. *Nevada's Key Pittman* (21:48) shows that during the crucial period (1939–1940) FDR was forced to be more circumspect than he thought events called for, in part because he had to deal with a hostile, irascible chairman of the Foreign Relations Committee, which judged the president's foreign policy in the Senate.

Franklin D. Roosevelt

See Chapters 20, 21, and 23, "Personalities," for additional references.

22:32 Barron, Gloria J. *Leadership in Crisis: F.D.R. and the Path to Intervention.* Port Washington, N.Y.: Kennikat, 1973. This study analyzes the restraints of public opinion on Roosevelt and documents his strategy (consistent except for the Quarantine Speech) of leading public opinion by lagging behind it. FDR encouraged others to speak out to "goad" him into action. Bibliography.

Burns, J. M. *Roosevelt: The Soldier of Freedom, 1940–1945* (23:63) treats, in his first five chapters,

FDR's diplomacy and preparation for war and forcefully explains the Europe-first strategy which FDR developed after 1938 for both the diplomatic and military focus of his policy.

Dallek, R. *Franklin D. Roosevelt and American Foreign Policy, 1932–1945* (21:51) gives generous attention to Japan, arguing that its China policy was so linked in American minds with fascism that both had to be opposed by Roosevelt at the same time.

Divine, R. A. *Roosevelt and World War II* (23:65) discusses Roosevelt's conversion from quasi-isolationism to active opponent of Hitlerism. The slow, painful process of realization that the only way to prevent a Nazi world order was for the United States to enter a world war, is briefly but cogently expressed.

Kimball, W. F., ed. *Franklin D. Roosevelt and the World Crisis, 1937–1945* (23:67).

Lash, J. P. *Roosevelt and Churchill, 1939–1941: The Partnership that Saved the West* (22:108).

22:33 Leutze, James. "The Secret of the Churchill-Roosevelt Correspondence September 1939–May 1940." *Journal of Contemporary History* 10:3 (1975), 465–91. A careful examination of the Roosevelt-Churchill file does not disclose a plot on the American side to get the United States in the war to help Britain. The revelations of the letters do include the spy case of Tyler Gatewood Kent, a code clerk in the American embassy, who had hundreds of classified documents when he was arrested and convicted in London in 1940.

Range, W. *Franklin D. Roosevelt's World Order* (20:60) provides some perception of what Roosevelt hoped to accomplish by intervention in World War II.

22:34 Rauch, Basil. *Roosevelt from Munich to Pearl Harbor: A Study in the Creation of a Foreign Policy.* New York: Creative Age Press, 1950. Rauch defends, usually uncritically, Roosevelt's foreign policy and explains the policy leading to war by focusing on 1938 to 1941. He corrects much of Charles A. Beard's selective evidence.

22:35 Roosevelt, Elliott, and Lash, Joseph P., eds. *F.D.R.: His Personal Letters, 1928–1945.* 2 vols. New York: Duell, Sloan & Pearce, 1950. Volume 3 (1928–1945) is the most relevant for foreign affairs.

Roosevelt, F. D. *Complete Presidential Press Conferences of Franklin D. Roosevelt, 1933–1945* (21:54).

Roosevelt, F. D. *The Public Papers and Addresses of Franklin D. Roosevelt* (21:55) is useful in discerning the optimistic and often idealistic front Roosevelt presented to the public while denying any intent to entangle the United States in dangerous commitments, until he began to move away from this position in 1937.

22:36 [Roosevelt, Franklin D.] *Franklin D. Roosevelt and Foreign Affairs, January 1937–August 1939.* 11 vols. Ed. by Donald B. Schewe. New York: Garland, 1979–1980. These ten volumes of documents, reproduced in facsimile, continue the set begun by E. B. Nixon (21:53). The eleventh volume is a name and subject index.

Sherwood, R. E. *Roosevelt and Hopkins: An Intimate History* (22:23).

Henry L. Stimson

See Chapters 20, 21, and 23, "Personalities," for additional references.

Burtness, P. S., and Ober, W. U. "Secretary Stimson and the First Pearl Harbor Investigation" (22:262).

Current, R. N. "How Stimson Meant to 'Maneuver' the Japanese" (22:263).

Morison, E. E. *Turmoil and Tradition: The Life and Times of Henry L. Stimson* (21:58) takes a sympathetic attitude and devotes about one-third of the book to the years when Stimson counseled firmness against the Japanese.

Stimson, H. L., and Bundy, M. *On Active Service in Peace and War* (23:72) has become one of the classic American autobiographies. Not least among many significant aspects are its insights into army-navy clashes, elaboration of the administration's disdain for the area commanders in Hawaii, and disclosure of differences between Roosevelt and the liberal Republican on such matters as embargoes against Japan and the removal of the fleet to the Atlantic.

Arthur H. Vandenberg

See also Chapter 24, "Personalities."

22:37 Tompkins, C. David. *Senator Arthur H. Vandenberg: The Evolution of a Modern Republican, 1884–1945*. Lansing: Michigan State University Press, 1970. Written before all relevant papers were available, this is primarily an account of Vandenberg's career prior to World War II.

Sumner Welles

22:38 Hilton, Stanley E. "The Welles Mission to Europe, February–March 1940: Illusion or Realism?" *Journal of American History* 58:1 (1971), 93–120. This article challenges Langer and Gleason's assumption (22:15) that illusion persisted in Washington regarding Allied war aims. FDR realistically foresaw the desperate straits the Allies would find themselves in and attempted to stall the Nazi offensive.

22:39 Welles, Sumner. *The Time for Decision*. New York: Harper, 1944. Under Secretary of State Welles was a friend and confidant of FDR who survived Cordell Hull's jealousy and anger until 1943. His view of New Deal diplomacy is useful, and his perception of the events which led to war are particularly valuable as they often contradict Hull's memoirs.

John G. Winant

Bellush, B. *He Walked Alone: A Biography of John Gilbert Winant* (20:65).

22:40 Winant, John Gilbert. *Letter from Grosvenor Square: An Account of a Stewardship*. Boston: Houghton Mifflin, 1947. These memoirs by the U.S. ambassador to Britain from early 1941 through the duration of World War II are limited in scope and content. Chronology is limited to events before Pearl Harbor. Even within this short time period, Winant's detailed knowledge is sharply limited.

Others

Bohlen, C. E. *Witness to History: 1929–1969* (24:98) has only a small portion of his memoir devoted to the origins of World War II and American policy therein, but it adds information on how Bohlen learned of the pending Nazi-Soviet Pact.

22:41 Bowers, Claude G. *My Mission to Spain: Watching the Rehearsal for World War II*. New York: Simon & Schuster, 1954. The American ambassador to Spain (1933–1939) makes no pretense of being objective. His strong distaste for Franco, Hitler, and the appeasers shines through in this memoir. Bowers argued that the Spanish Republic was basically democratic with socialist leanings which would have dropped away if given a chance to evolve.

22:42 Burns, Richard Dean, and Bennett, Edward M., eds. *Diplomats in Crisis: United States-Chinese-Japanese Relations, 1919–1941*. Santa Barbara, Calif.: ABC-Clio, 1974. Vignettes of thirteen transnationally selected diplomats of varying influence, including Grew, Matsuoka, Nomura, Hu Shih, and Johnson, whose failures presaged Pearl Harbor.

Cohen, W. I. *The Chinese Connection: Roger S. Greene, Thomas W. Lamont, George E. Sokolsky, and American–East Asian Relations* (2:341) is a pioneering study of American public opinion (1914–1950) about developments in China and Japan. It is based on selected individuals who are examined both for their ideas and for their access to governmental decisionmakers.

Hooker, N. H., ed. *The Moffat Papers: Selections from the Diplomatic Journals of Jay Pierrepont Moffat, 1919–1943* (20:70) finds Moffat serving in the European Division of the Department of State as events began snowballing toward war.

22:43 Ickes, Harold L. *The Secret Diary of Harold L. Ickes: The Lowering Clouds, 1939–1941*. New York: Simon & Schuster, 1954. Ickes, secretary of the interior and curmudgeon of the Roosevelt cabinet, is ascerbic in his comments on his cabinet colleagues and others. An isolationist until Hitler's aggressive design was obvious, Ickes became one of the most vocal supporters of aid to the Allies.

22:44 Langer, William L. *In and Out of the Ivory Tower: The Autobiography of Willian L. Langer*. New York: Watson, 1977. Langer, referred to by some revisionists as a "court historian," seeks to correct what he thought was becoming a distorted record. Langer's evaluation of the evidence concerning the origins of American participation in World War II is important.

22:45 Leahy, William D. *I Was There*. New York: Whittlesay House, 1950. Ambassador to Vichy France, Leahy explains the administration's Vichy policy as he understood it. He also provides good quotes on and from key individuals touching American foreign policy (1940–1941).

Lee, R. E. *The London Journal of General Raymond E. Lee, 1940–1941* (23:75) is a fascinating, first-hand account of Anglo-American relations during a crucial period.

22:46 McFarland, Keith D. *Harry H. Woodring: A Political Biography of F.D.R.'s Controversial Secretary of War*. Lawrence: University of Kansas Press, 1975. Woodring's dismissal as secretary of war is marked as the point when FDR determined to go forward with all-out aid to the Allies and a military preparedness program. With people like Woodring, and Key Pittman chairing the Senate Foreign Relations Committee, the president had little choice but secrecy if he was to pursue his foreign policy program in 1939 and 1940.

Pogue, F. C. *George C. Marshall*. Vol. 2: *Ordeal and Hope, 1939–1942* (23:108) is an authorized, somewhat critical, study of America's reluctant, uncoordinated prewar planning. The Europe-first strategy (combined with the fortification of the Philippines) is analyzed, and Marshall's criticisms of General Short are explained and clarified.

Potter, E. B. *Nimitz* (23:119) is especially useful for describing responses by the civilian and military bureaucracies in Washington and Honolulu to the Pearl Harbor attack.

22:47 Viet, Jane K. "The Donkey and the Lion: The Ambassadorship of Joseph P. Kennedy at the Court of St. James, 1938–1940." *Michigan Academician* 10:3 (1978), 273–82. Viet discusses the ambassadorship of Kennedy, highlighting the strained relations between him and Winston Churchill, and outlining the foreign policy of the Roosevelt administration (1938–1940).

EUROPEAN

Eduard Beneš

22:48 Beneš, Eduard. *Memoirs: From Munich to New War and New Victory*. Trans. by Godfrey Lias. New York: Arno (1954), 1972. Beneš skips over the Munich crisis itself, having written a separate volume on the dismemberment of his country (*Mnichovske dny: Pameti*, Prague: Svoboda, 1968). However, he does lay the blame for Munich squarely on France and Britain out of the conviction that Stalin stood ready to fulfill Soviet obligations to the Czechs if the French had kept theirs.

22:49 Hudec, Karel, ed. *Edward Beneš in His Own Words: Threescore Years of a Statesman, Builder and*

Philosopher. New York: Grady, 1944. The Czech-American National Alliance compiled this set of useful quotations selected from Beneš's speeches, documents, and interviews on such subjects as Europe, Germany, Russia, and the United States.

Neville Chamberlain

22:50 Douglas, Roy. "Chamberlain and Eden, 1937–38." *Journal of Contemporary History* 13:1 (1978), 97–116. Neville Chamberlain became Prime Minister on May 28, 1937, with Anthony Eden as inherited foreign secretary. Almost from the first, the two were on a collision course.

22:51 Feiling, Keith. *The Life of Neville Chamberlain*. New York: Macmillan, 1946. Reprint 1970. Only the last third of the book deals with Chamberlain's prime ministership (1937–1940). Feiling recognizes Chamberlain's shortcomings and examines his views on America's European role, but ignores the Chamberlain-Kennedy relationship. The account of the prime minister's attitude toward Roosevelt and American policy make the book worth reading. Bibliography.

22:52 Macleod, Iain. *Neville Chamberlain*. New York: Atheneum, 1962. In an attempt to refute the myths surrounding Chamberlain, the study focuses on his early political career. This friendly account credits Chamberlain with more political wisdom than American historians usually do.

22:53 Scott, W. E. "Neville Chamberlain and Munich: Two Aspects of Power." In L. Krieger and F. Stern, eds., *The Responsibility of Power*. New York: Doubleday, 1967, pp. 353–69. Scott argues that the Munich "symbol" has incorrectly prejudged Chamberlain as a weak, weary old man. Chamberlain's error was not weakness, but miscalculation.

Winston S. Churchill

See Chapters 21, 23, and 25, "Personalities," for additional references.

Churchill, W. S. *The Second World War* (23:79) reviews American policy (1939–1941) as the British perceived it. In volumes 2 and 3, FDR becomes both a personality and an ally in Churchill's plans to defeat Hitler. It is of special importance to trace the evolution of British and American plans, as perceived by Churchill, to break down the American barrier of isolationism.

22:54 Churchill, Winston S. *Blood, Sweat, and Tears*. New York: Putnam's, 1941. This collection of Churchill's major defense and foreign policy speeches for the period 1938 to early 1941 includes the more familiar from the Battle of Britain.

Gilbert, M. *Winston S. Churchill*. Vol. 5: *The Prophet of Truth, 1922–1939* (21:65) details Churchill's critique of appeasement.

22:55 James, Robert R. *Churchill: A Study in Failure, 1900–1939*. New York: World, 1970. This critical review of Churchill's career, beginning with his election to Parliament, examines his personality and values. While vain and arrogant, Churchill was also courageous and principled. James presents material on Churchill's views on rearmament and appeasement.

Jonas, M.; Langley, H. D.; and Loewenheim, F. L., eds. *Roosevelt and Churchill: Their Secret Wartime Correspondence* (25:30) examines the path to intervention.

Lash, J. P. *Roosevelt and Churchill, 1939–1941: The Partnership that Saved the West* (22:108).

Charles de Gaulle

See Chapter 23, "Personalities," for additional references.

22:56 De Gaulle, Charles. *The Call to Honour* [1940–1942]. Vol. 1 in *The Complete War Memoirs*. Trans. by Jonathan Green. New York: Simon & Schuster, 1955. This volume deals with the attempt on de Gaulle's part to establish himself as the leader whose destiny was to restore France to greatness. His impatience with the Americans, and FDR in particular, and his anger at American policy, which continued to recognize the Vichy government, approaches contempt, a feeling which was reciprocated by Roosevelt. For the three-volume collection, see (23:82).

Hans Heinrich Dieckhoff

22:57 Jonas, Manfred. "Prophet without Honor: Hans Heinrich Dieckhoff's Reports from Washington." *Mid-America* 47:3 (1965), 222–33. The German ambassador warned that Germany should not count on future American neutrality. Dieckhoff's recall to Germany in late 1938 deprived the Reich of a most prescient observer.

22:58 Kimball, Warren F. "Dieckhoff and America: A German's View of German-American Relations,

1937–1941." *Historian* 27:2 (1965), 218–43. Keenly aware of American sensitivity about foreign interference in U.S. domestic affairs, Dieckhoff urged his government to distance itself from the German-American Bund. But he did not speak out emphatically against the anti-Semitic and anti-Catholic excesses of the Hitler government.

22:59 Remak, Joachim. "Two German Views of the United States: Hitler and his Diplomats." *World Affairs Quarterly* 28:1 (1957), 25–35. Dieckhoff, German ambassador in Washington after 1937, warned repeatedly and unmistakably that the United States would not remain neutral. The warnings were accepted by the German foreign office (especially Baron Ernst von Weizsacker) but not by Hitler.

Lord Halifax

See Chapter 23, "Personalities," for additional references.

Birkenhead, Earl of. *Halifax: The Life of Lord Halifax* (23:84) makes clear the way in which Halifax was blinded to the true nature of Hitler while he was foreign secretary (1938–1940).

Adolf Hitler

See Chapters 21 and 23, "Personalities," for additional references.

22:60 Compton, James V. *The Swastika and the Eagle: Hitler, the United States and the Origins of World War II*. Boston: Houghton Mifflin, 1967. Compton concludes that German policy toward, and Hitler's perception of, the United States were so contradictory and confused that America was largely discounted except by some of the professional German diplomats. The author does not believe Hitler had a plan for the United States when the war began. Bibliography.

Weinberg, G. L. "Hitler's Image of the United States" (21:69) finds that in the late 1920s Hitler admired America for its resources and vast domestic market, yet feared it as a threat to potential German predominance. In the 1930s he dismissed the United States as racially degenerate and hopelessly weak.

Benito Mussolini

See Chapters 21 and 23, "Personalities," for references.

Joseph V. Stalin
See Chapters 21 and 25, "Personalities," for references.

Others
22:61 Bonnet, Georges. *Defense de la Paix.* Vol. 1: *De Washington au Quai d'Orsay;* Vol. 2: *Fin d'une Europe* [Defending peace. Vol. 1: From Washington to the Quai d'Orsay; Vol. 2: The end of one Europe]. Geneva: Les Editions du Cheval Aile, 1946–1948. The memoirs of the French ambassador to Washington and minister of foreign affairs from April 1938 to September 1939. Bonnet is not above distorting key events and even documents to make his case stronger, so use with caution.

Cadogan, A. *The Diaries of Sir Alexander Cadogan, 1939–1945* (23:90) is invaluable for the British view of American policy at the outbreak of World War II. They shed much light on the Roosevelt-Churchill relationship.

Casey, R. G. *Personal Experience, 1939–1946* (32:62) is a rather thin memoir of the Australian minister to the United States (1940–1942) which belies the role he played in Anglo-American collaboration prior to World War II.

22:62 Ciano, Galeazzo. *The Ciano Diaries, 1936–1943.* Ed. by Hugh Gibson. Garden City, N.Y.: Doubleday, 1946. Count Ciano, the cynical and realistic minister of foreign affairs for Mussolini, recorded the objectives of the United States as he understood them, the objectives of Italian policy vis-à-vis the United States, and the Italian perception of American policy.

22:63 Colvin, Ian G. *The Chamberlain Cabinet.* New York: Taplinger, 1971. Using newly opened cabinet papers, Colvin supplements details to the appeasement policy.

22:64 Craige, Robert L. *Behind the Japanese Mask.* London: Hutchinson, 1945. British ambassador to Japan (September 1937–December 1941), Craige comments about prominent Japanese leaders and laments that Western concessions to Japan had not been forthcoming—they might have prevented war.

22:65 Dirksen, Herbert von. *Moscow, Tokyo, London: Twenty Years of German Foreign Policy.* Norman: University of Oklahoma Press, 1952. The aristocratic diplomat details his service in the German foreign office (1918–1928), and as ambassador to the Soviet Union (1928–1933), Japan (1933–1938), and Britain (1938–1939). The Soviets had already published the papers which von Dirksen collected for his own use (see volume 2 of *Documents and Materials Relating to the Eve of the Second World War,* Moscow, 1948).

22:66 Hardy, Oliver. *The Diplomatic Diaries of Oliver Hardy, 1937–1940.* Ed. by John Harvey. London: Collins, 1970. Hardy, Anthony Eden's private secretary when Eden headed the Foreign Office, kept a detailed diary, full of candid comment about personalities and policy. This volume contains interesting commentary on FDR's conversations with Ambassador Ronald Lindsay in the aftermath of the Quarantine Speech of 1937.

Ismay, H. *The Memoirs of General Lord Ismay* (23:139) relates British foreign policy strategy, Anglo-American diplomacy, and the Anglo-American military relationship. His acquaintance with Harry Hopkins, Joseph Kennedy, and John G. Winant when Kennedy and Winant were the U.S. ambassadors to Britain, make the memoir useful.

Lipski, Jósef. *Diplomat in Berlin, 1933–1939: Papers and Memoirs of Jósef Lipski, Ambassador of Poland* (21:83).

Lukasiewicz, Juliusz. *Diplomat in Paris, 1936–1939: Papers and Memoirs of Juliusz Lukasiewicz* (21:85).

Maisky, I. M. *Memoirs of a Soviet Ambassador: The War, 1939–43* (23:95) has plenty to say about American policy and especially about FDR and his representatives to Great Britain.

Stacey, C. P. *Mackenzie King and the Atlantic Triangle* (36:39) accentuates the role King played in acting as honest broker between Churchill and Roosevelt. The study, much extracted from *A Very Double Life: The Private World of Mackenzie King,* focuses on American policy from the Canadian perspective, as FDR prepared for war.

EAST ASIAN

Emperor Hirohito
22:67 Bergamini, David. *Japan's Imperial Conspiracy.* New York: Morrow, 1971. A controversial indictment of Hirohito calling him far more than a cere-

monial innocent victimized by military cliques: he was the initiator of diplomatic-military decisions, including the Pearl Harbor attack. To be read alongside Shillony's more recent study of the Japanese military in 1936. Extensive bibliography.

22:68   Mosley, Leonard. *Hirohito: Emperor of Japan.* Englewood Cliffs, N.J.: Prentice-Hall, 1966. This first full-length biography presents the emperor as a man of peace who courageously prevailed over fanatics to end the war but who, due to passive advisers, constitutional restraints, and his own retiring personality, had been unable earlier to avert the war. Bibliography.

Chiang Kai-shek

See Chapters 21 and 27, "Personalities," for additional references.

22:69   Chiang Kai-shek. *Resistance and Reconstruction: Messages during China's Six Years of War, 1937–1943.* New York: Harper, 1943. This collection of 60 speeches and messages, aimed at the Chinese people, offers a view of internal and external issues.

Hirota Kōki

22:70   Farnsworth, Lee. "Hirota Kōki: The Diplomacy of Expansionism." In Richard Dean Burns and Edward M. Bennett, eds., *Diplomats in Crisis: United States-Chinese-Japanese Relations, 1919–1941.* Santa Barbara, Calif.: ABC-Clio, 1974, pp. 227–50. Foreign minister (1933–1936, 1937–1938) and prime minister (1936–1937), Hirota found his "diplomacy of conciliation" overwhelmed by the military's demands for more aggressive policies.

22:71   Shiroyama, Saburo. *War Criminal: The Life and Death of Hirota Kōki.* Trans. by John Bester. Tokyo: Kodansha International, 1977. Hirota was the only Japanese civilian official to be executed as a war criminal. In this sympathetic portrayal, the author argues that Hirota hardly deserved his fate because the civilian governments of the 1930s were virtually powerless against the military.

Matsuoka Yōsuke

22:72   Huizenga, John. "Yōsuke Matsuoka and the Japanese-German Alliance." In Gordon A. Craig and Felix Gilbert, eds., *The Diplomats: 1919–1939.* Princeton, N.J.: Princeton University Press, 1953, vol. 2, pp. 615–48. An evaluation of the foreign minister's eventful year in office (July 22, 1940–July 16, 1941), stressing the contrast between the govern-

ment's negotiating the Tripartite Pact (and the hard line against America) and renouncing its presuppositions when Barbarossa invited the overthrow of bolshevism.

22:73   Teters, Barbara. "Matsuoka Yōsuke: The Diplomacy of Bluff and Gesture." In Richard Dean Burns and Edward M. Bennett, eds., *Diplomats in Crisis: United States-Chinese-Japanese Relations, 1919–1941.* Santa Barbara, Calif.: ABC-Clio, ,1974, pp. 275–96. Teters suggests that the talkative and ambitious Matsuoka, who directed the negotiation of the Tripartite Alliance (1940), may have been mentally unstable during his term in office.

Tōjō Hideki

22:74   Browne, Courtney. *Tōjō: The Last Banzai.* New York: Holt, Rinehart & Winston, 1967. Browne uses Tōjō's career to focus on the rise of Japanese militarism and the actions of the military during the war. Bibliography.

22:75   Butow, Robert J. C. *Tōjō and the Coming of the War.* Princeton, N.J.: Princeton University Press, 1961. This renowned book is both a biography of Japan's premier at the time of Pearl Harbor and a history of political events and diplomatic issues. Primarily, however, it is the latter. Butow argues that Tōjō and the ranking military people were reduced from leaders to "robots of their subordinates." Extensive bibliography.

Others

22:76   Kase, Toshikazu. *Journey to the Missouri.* New Haven, Conn.: Yale University Press, 1950. This memoir reaches back before Pearl Harbor and includes materials on wartime Japanese peace efforts. It is useful for absolving the emperor of war guilt, for identifying prominent antiwar elements before 1941, and for tracing the rise of militarism back to the Meiji Constitution.

Moore, F. *With Japan's Leaders: An Intimate Record of Fourteen Years as Counsellor to the Japanese Government, Ending December 7, 1941* (21:191) describes chronologically and anecdotally the diplomacy that failed, and offers an opinionated defense of Nomura.

22:77   Peattie, Mark R. *Ishiwara Kanji and Japan's Confrontation with the West.* Princeton, N.J.: Princeton University Press, 1975. An important corrective for the stereotyping of militarism, this analytical biography of the visionary general officer of the Imperial

Japanese Army throws light on Japan's political landscape in the 1930s and, more particularly, on the philosophical grounds of anti-Western nationalism. Bibliography.

22:78 Potter, John D. *Yamamoto: The Man Who Menaced America.* New York: Viking, 1965. A popular biography of the man who planned (though did not execute) the Pearl Harbor attack and who later failed to capture Midway Island.

22:79 Shigemitsu Mamoru. *Japan and Her Destiny: My Struggle for Peace.* New York: Dutton, 1958. This memoir from prison, to which the moderate foreign minister had been sentenced by the War Crimes Tribunal, covers the familiar ground of Showa-era diplomacy, especially that of Japan in China. It sheds new light, however, on naval machinations and on the confusion that reigned in Japanese government circles after 1931.

22:80 Tōgō Shigenori. *The Cause of Japan.* New York: Simon & Schuster, 1956. In a prison memoir the foreign minister of Japan, at the time of Pearl Harbor and again at the end of the war, chronicles the negotiations of the Tōjō cabinet with America, including his efforts, and argues that military officers rather than civilian officials initiated and supervised the war.

Isolation and Intervention

Borchard, E. M., and Lage, W. P. *Neutrality for the United States* (16:143) is worth examining for a contemporary view of two scholars who opposed *any* departure from traditional American neutrality, and for its obvious efforts to influence the election of 1940.

Culbert, D. H. *News for Everyman: Radio and Foreign Affairs in Thirties America* (20:21) sees more influence by the men he selects than perhaps there was, especially on government officials, and he pays less attention than he might to the influence of FDR on some of the newscasters. This is a valuable source on public opinion.

Divine, R. A. *Foreign Policy and U.S. Presidential Elections, 1940–1960* (2:141) focuses on the domestic political impact of foreign policy and argues that foreign policy may enter the political process without substantively affecting it. Bibliography.

Edwards, J. E. *The Foreign Policy of Col. McCormick's Tribune, 1929–1941* (20:22).

22:81 Flynn, George Q. *Roosevelt and Romanism: Catholics and American Diplomacy, 1937–1945.* Westport, Conn.: Greenwood, 1976. Roosevelt made a concerted effort to win Catholic support for his foreign policies. The extent of that effort in pursuing his battle against isolationism and in favor of neutrality law revision is carefully chronicled here. Flynn does not overemphasize the importance of Catholic support for foreign policy, especially in large urban centers and on Catholic politicians in the 1930s. Bibliography.

Gerson, L. L. *The Hyphenate in Recent American Politics and Diplomacy* (2:203) is one of the few volumes covering nearly all significant sources on the hyphenate Americans and their attitude toward Roosevelt's policy. The alterations in FDR's approach to foreign policy after the invasion of Poland and Norway are clearly drawn.

22:82 Steele, Richard W. "Preparing the Public for War: Efforts to Establish a National Propaganda Agency, 1940–41." *American Historical Review* 85:6 (1970), 1640–53. Steele has gone into every possible record to discover the development of the Bureau (subsequently the Office) of Facts and Figures, and who supported and opposed its creation. He concludes FDR was never more than a lukewarm supporter of the idea and gave lip service to it, which satisfied his interventionist supporters that something was being done to win public support.

ISOLATIONISTS

See "Personalities," especially Herbert C. Hoover, Charles A. Lindbergh; see also Chapters 2 and 20, "Isolationism."

Adler, S. *The Isolationist Impulse: Its Twentieth Century Reaction* (20:121) is the pioneer study of American isolationism. It ties domestic concerns to foreign policy. It is, however, partly polemic against the isolationists and their "ism."

Billington, R. A. "The Origins of Middle Western Isolationism" [1890–1941] (2:65).

Chatfield, C. *For Peace and Justice: Pacifism in America, 1914–1941* (19:164) shows that pacifists played an important role in promoting American isolationism in the interwar years. This comprehensive study illustrates the degree of that influence on the foreign policy process in the early stages of World War II.

22:83 Cole, Wayne. *America First: The Battle against Intervention, 1940–1941.* Madison: University of Wisconsin Press, 1953. A careful, analytical account of the primary organization whose goal it was to keep the United States out of war. This is an admirable discussion, in every way.

22:84 Cole, Wayne S. *Charles A. Lindbergh and the Battle against American Intervention in World War II.* New York: Harcourt Brace Jovanovich, 1974. Cole elucidates Lindbergh's motivation and influence in the America First movement's struggle against intervention in the European war. Those individuals favoring Fortress America and other forms of isolationism related to Lindbergh's efforts are also treated. Bibliography.

22:85 Doenecke, Justus D. "Non-Intervention of the Left: The Keep America Out of the War Congress, 1938–41." *Journal of Contemporary History* 12:2 (1977), 221–36. The Keep America Out of War Congress was founded in New York on March 6, 1938, under veteran pacifist reformer Oswald Garrison Villard. The KAOWC was a makeshift coalition of left-wing pacifist groups that urged jobs at home rather than abroad, anti-Asian involvement, neutrality, food not guns, etc.

Jonas, M. *Isolationism in America, 1935–41* (20:126) points out that the neutrality legislation was not aimed at neutrality so much as interdiction of any contaminatory contact with Europe; similarily, revision of the legislation was not intended to support neutrality.

22:86 Orser, Edward W. "World War II and the Pacifist Controversy in the Major Protestant Churches." *American Studies* 14:2 (1973), 5–24. Pacifism dominated the consciousness of the Protestant churches after the late 1930s, although none endorsed the absolutist position. By 1941, this sentiment had eroded considerably.

22:87 Walker, Samuel. "Communists and Isolationism: The American Peace Mobilization, 1940–1941." *Maryland Historian* 4:1 (1973), 1–12. The short-lived American Peace Mobilization was dominated by the Communist Party USA. The history of the APM exemplifies the decline of noninterventionism in America and illustrates the problems of the American Communist movement after the signing of the Russo-German nonaggression pact.

22:88 Zeitzer, Glen. "The Fellowship of Reconciliation on the Eve of the Second World War: A Peace Organization Prepares." *Peace and Change* 3:2/3 (1975), 46–51. The Fellowship of Reconciliation prepared a program of nonviolent resistance during 1940–1941 and tried to find ways to end World War II.

INTERVENTIONISTS

See "Personalities," especially Franklin D. Roosevelt; also see "Aid to the Allies, 1938–1941," below.

22:89 Chadwin, Mark L. *The War Hawks of World War II.* Chapel Hill: University of North Carolina Press, 1968. This work focuses exclusively on the role of the Century Club Group and the Fight for Freedom Committee in clearing the obstructions in the way of FDR's expanding aid program. The author explains the motives of those backing intervention. Bibliography.

22:90 Garlid, George W. "Minneapolis Unit of the Committee to Defend America by Aiding the Allies." *Minnesota History* 41:6 (1969), 267–83. Garlid reveals the conditions and tactics that contributed to the success of Minnesota internationalists in establishing a consensus that supported United States responsibility in world affairs.

22:91 Johnson, Walter. *The Battle against Isolation.* Chicago: University of Chicago Press, 1944. This is an early effort to examine the struggle between the isolationist and interventionist forces. William Allen White's role in forming the Committee to Defend America by Aiding the Allies, and the battle between this group and the America First organization, provide the framework for the internal struggle for public support.

22:92 Sniegoski, Stephen J. "Unified Democracy: An Aspect of American World War II Interventionist

Thought, 1939–1941." *Maryland Historian* 9:1 (1978), 33–48. This essay describes the arguments introduced by interventionists such as Lewis Mumford, Harold Ickes, Max Lerner, and Dorothy Thompson in support of American intervention against fascism.

22:93 Thompson, Dean K. "World War II, Interventionism, and Henry Pitney Van Dussen." *Journal of Presbyterian History* 55:4 (1977), 327–45. Henry Pitney Van Dussen (1897–1975) played a significant role in America's interventionist movement before its involvement in World War II.

22:94 Tuttle, William M., Jr. "Aid to the Allies Short-of-War versus American Intervention, 1940: A Reappraisal of William Allen White's Leadership." *Journal of American History* 56:4 (1970), 840–58. This is an excellent account of the infighting which plagued the interventionist groups in 1940—the Committee to Defend America by Aiding the Allies and the Century Club Group. These were important organizations for the development of the administration's foreign policy.

BUSINESS AND PROSPECTS OF WAR

See also "Embargoes and Sanctions," below.

22:95 Hoffer, Peter C. "American Businessmen and the Japan Trade, 1931–1941: A Case Study of Attitude Formation." *Pacific Historical Review* 41:2 (1972), 189–205. Until well into 1941, economic leaders and business journals supported U.S. neutrality, arguing that the maintenance of contact with Japanese businessmen was a contribution to future peace as well as essential to the American economy.

Kolko, G. "American Business and Germany: 1930–1941" (20:196) argues that, although the business press displayed strong anti-Nazi views during the 1930s, American corporate leaders operated within the autarchic economic framework of the Third Reich.

22:96 Stromberg, Roland N. "American Business and the Approach of War, 1935–1941." *Journal of Economic History* 13:1 (1953), 58–78. In the drift toward war, Stromberg writes, business played no independent role. It was "dragged along in the wake

of circumstance." Until the fall of France, the business community was probably more isolationist than other groups.

22:97 Wilkins, Mira. "The Role of U.S. Business." In Dorothy Borg and Shumpei Okamoto, eds., *Pearl Harbor as History: Japanese-American Relations, 1931–1941*. New York: Columbia University Press, 1973, pp. 341–76. American businessmen's thoughts and action apropos Japanese-American relations (1931–1941) are deduced from the study of six different types of businesses. All disdained the Far Eastern war, influenced the course of events only minimally, and lost profits even before Pearl Harbor.

U.S. and Europe, 1936–1941

See Chapters 20 and 21 for overlapping issues and events of the 1930s.

22:98 Adler, Les K., and Paterson, Thomas G. "Red Fascism: The Merger of Nazi Germany and Soviet Russia in the American Image of Totalitarianism, 1930's–1950's" *American Historical Review* 75:4 (1970), 1046–1064. Beginning in the 1930s, many Americans articulated similarities between Nazi Germany and Soviet Russia, between their ideologies, foreign policies, authoritarian controls, trade practices, and dictatorial leaders.

22:99 Maddux, Thomas R. "Red Fascism, Brown Bolshevism: American Image of Totalitarianism in the 1930's." *Historian* 40:1 (1977), 85–103. Maddux reevaluates the origins of the idea of "red fascism" as described by Adler and Paterson. He disputes their contention that such an identification between the two regimes came primarily during 1939 to 1941, and argues instead that the American press had much earlier reached a widespread consensus on the essential similarities.

Payne, H. C.; Callahan, R.; and Bennett, E. M. *As the Storm Clouds Gathered: European Perceptions of*

American Foreign Policy in the 1930s (21:14) relates a desperate reliance by France and Russia and to a lesser degree Great Britain on an aroused United States to forestall a devastating European war.

22:100 Pešelj, Branko M. "Serbo-Croatian Agreement of 1939 and American Foreign Policy." *Journal of Croatian Studies* 11–12 (1970–1971), 3–82. This essay examines the political and constitutional character of the agreement of August 26, 1939, and demonstrates the posture of the United States toward the agreement.

22:101 Schuman, Frederick L. *Europe on the Eve.* New York: Knopf, 1939. This skeptical study was prescient in its assessments of the need for collective security and its analysis of the reasons for the rapid rise of the aggressor states.

ORIGINS OF WORLD WAR II (EUROPE)

22:102 Dray, W. H. "Concepts of Causation in A. J. P. Taylor's Account of the Origins of the Second World War." *History and Theory* 17:2 (1978), 149–74. Dray examines the judgments of A. J. P. Taylor and his critics, particularly Hugh Trevor-Roper and F. H. Hinsley, about World War II as an exercise in the historiography of causation.

22:103 Lafore, Laurence D. *The End of Glory: An Interpretation of the Origins of World War II.* Philadelphia: Lippincott, 1972. Lafore views French indecision and the institutional collapse of the European state system as more significant than German aggression in causing World War II.

22:104 Mosley, Leonard. *On Borrowed Time: How World War II Began.* New York: Random House, 1969. The chief correspondent of the *London Sunday Times* describes the failure of the Western powers, from Munich to the opening of hostilities, to act wisely. Mosely places a good deal of the blame on the appeasement policies of France and Britain.

22:105 Robertson, James C. "The Outbreak of the Second World War." *Historical Journal* 21:4 (1978), 1001–07. David Hoggan's thesis of British blame for the outbreak of war over Poland is questioned and partially substantiated on the basis of four monographs. Hoggan argued that Britain was following a

traditional policy of upholding the European balance of power against any single power that threatened to dominate the Continent.

22:106 Taylor, A. J. P. *The Origins of the Second World War.* New York: Atheneum, 1962. This study is significant for the benign view it takes of Hitler, classifying him as a traditional European statesman merely defending legitimate German interests and regaining territories either vital to German security or belonging to Germany culturally and ethnically. Great Britain is blamed for the war, with a reluctant France tied to her policy. The American role is that of an interested onlooker who judged the Europeans as either wrongheaded or evil.

BRITAIN AND FRANCE

See "Personalities," especially Winston S. Churchill, Charles de Gaulle, John Winant.

Britain

22:107 Colvin, Ian G. *None So Blind: A British Diplomatic View of the Origins of World War II.* New York: Harcourt, Brace & World, 1963. Employing the papers of Sir Robert Vansittart, permanent under secretary of state for foreign affairs (1930–1938), Colvin describes the involved European diplomacy during the late 1930s. Vansittart's opinions had little effect on policy.

22:108 Lash, Joseph P. *Roosevelt and Churchill, 1939–1941: The Partnership that Saved the West.* New York: Norton, 1976. Very few scholars have gotten inside Roosevelt's mind to the degree that Lash does, but then no others lived in the White House with FDR as Lash did. Lash puts together a fascinating if not altogether convincing picture of the president consciously leading the nation to intervention. He traces the evolution of Anglo-American cooperation from hesitant beginnings to firm alliance.

22:109 Leutze, James R. *Bargaining for Supremacy: Anglo-American Naval Collaboration, 1937–1941.* Chapel Hill: University of North Carolina Press, 1977. Leutze presents the perspective that the Europe-first strategy of FDR was aimed at supplanting Britain as the major Atlantic power with a U.S. navy "second to none." Bibliography.

22:110 Leutze, James R. "Technology and Bargaining in Anglo-American Naval Relations, 1938–1946." *U.S. Naval Institute Proceedings* 103:6 (1977), 50–66. Between 1938 and 1946, the United States and Britain exchanged a great deal of technical information, although there were people on both sides who did not fully accept the arrangements. It was not until early 1941, when President Roosevelt signed the Lend-Lease Act, that there began a more open and extensive exchange of technical and scientific information.

22:111 Manne, Robert. "The British Decision for Alliance with Russia, May, 1939." *Journal of Contemporary History* 9:3 (1974), 3–26. During the latter half of March 1939, Neville Chamberlain's cabinet deliberately chose Poland rather than the U.S.S.R. as Britain's key Eastern European ally despite the advice of the chiefs of staff. By late May 1939, however, the cabinet was converted to accept the necessity of an alliance with the Soviet Union.

22:112 Rhodes, Benjamin D. "The British Royal Visit of 1939 and the 'Psychological Approach' to the United States." *Diplomatic History* 2:2 (1978), 197–211. There was much more to the royal visit than the famed hot dogs and strawberry shortcake picnic with FDR. The trip, which began as a purely social one, evolved into an appeal to American emotions and strengthened the atmosphere of American goodwill toward Britain on the eve of World War II.

Woodward, L. *History of the Second World War: British Foreign Policy in the Second World War* (23:40) is the official British history of Foreign Office operations during World War II. Suspicious of American motives and disgusted with what the Foreign Office personnel perceived as American cupidity and naiveté, they usually were forced to give ground to Churchill's way of doing things.

Appeasement/Rearmament

22:113 Dunbabin, J. P. D. "British Rearmament in the 1930s: A Chronology and Review." *Historical Journal* 18:3 (1975), 587–609. Dunbabin joins the debate on British rearmament by recounting the sequence of events and showing the complex interaction of economic and political factors in rearming.

22:114 Jones, R. J. Barry. "The Study of 'Appeasement' and the Study of International Relations." *British Journal of International Studies* 1:1 (1975), 68–76. Jones examines 20th-century historiography.

22:115 Lukowitz, David C. "British Pacifists and Appeasement: The Peace Union Pledge." *Journal of Contemporary History* 9:1 (1974), 115–28. A study of the organization and influence of the Peace Pledge Union.

22:116 Offner, Arnold A. "Appeasement Revisited: The United States, Great Britain, and Germany, 1933–1940." *Journal of American History* 64:2 (1977), 373–93. A refutation of the view that competing economic systems and declining trade relations were the basic causes of American-German conflict in the 1930s. The drift toward war came because of worsening political problems, and the deterioration in the military situation.

22:117 Rowse, A. L. *Appeasement: A Study in Political Decline, 1933–39.* New York: Norton, 1961. A bitter criticism of Britain's leaders who followed the policy of appeasing Hitler.

22:118 Shay, Robert P., Jr. *British Rearmament in the Thirties: Politics and Profits.* Princeton, N.J.: Princeton University Press, 1977. This is a comprehensive analysis of rearmament under the Baldwin and Chamberlain governments. It reveals the primary determinants of events and provides the principal considerations underlying Britain's appeasement policy. Extensive bibliography.

22:119 Wallace, William V. "Roosevelt and British Appeasement, 1938." *British Association for American Studies Bulletin* 5 (1962), 4–30. Early in 1938 Roosevelt suggested to Neville Chamberlain an international conference. Chamberlain did not reject the offer outright, but tried to stave it off while he negotiated with Hitler. Roosevelt did not want to be involved in bargaining with Hitler, and decided to put the offer in abeyance.

22:120 Watt, Donald C. "Roosevelt and Chamberlain: Two Appeasers." *International Journal* 28:1 (1972/1973), 185–204. A model article comparing the different styles and yet similar policies toward Germany followed by President Roosevelt and Prime Minister Chamberlain in the 1930s. The aftermath of the Quarantine Speech (1937) is central to Watt's analysis.

France

See "Personalities," especially American William D. Leahy (under "Others").

22:121 Furnia, Arthur H. *The Diplomacy of Appeasement: Anglo-French Relations and the Prelude to World War II, 1931–1938*. Washington, D.C.: University Press of Washington, D.C., 1960. This is an attempt to analyze the diverse Anglo-French policies aimed at preserving peace as the political status of Germany changed. Bibliography.

22:122 Haight, John McVickar, Jr. "France's Search for American Military Aircraft: Before the Munich Crisis." *Aerospace Historian* 25:3 (1978), 141–52. Baron Amaury de la Grange, an old friend of President Roosevelt's, and Air Minister Guy la Chambre spearheaded a drive to make up for France's aerial deficiency with purchases from America. La Grange and la Chambre faced significant domestic opposition as well as an isolationist public in America.

Langer, W. L. *Our Vichy Gamble* (23:228).

Paxton, R. O. *Vichy France: Old Guard and New Order, 1940–44* (23:229).

22:123 Young, Robert J. "The Aftermath of Munich: The Course of French Diplomacy, October 1938 to March 1939." *French Historical Studies* 8:2 (1973), 305–22. Young reviews the Munich agreement and France's foreign policy toward Eastern Europe.

GERMANY AND ITALY

See "Personalities," especially Herbert von Dirksen and Count Ciano (under "Others"), Hans Heinrich Dieckhoff, Adolf Hitler.

22:124 Cliadakis, Harry. "Neutrality and War in Italian Policy 1939–1940." *Journal of Contemporary History* 9:3 (1974), 171–90. Italian diplomacy between September 1939 and October 1940 aimed for a negotiated peace in which a balance of power between fascism and democracy would endure. On June 10, 1940, Italy declared war on France and England from the conviction that intervention would mean automatic Italian domination of the Mediterranean.

Compton, J. V. *The Swastika and the Eagle: Hitler, the United States and the Origins of World War II* (22:60) argues that there is no evidence of German planning for an attack on the United States, although Compton believes that Hitler's ambition would have led to it.

Frye, A. *Nazi Germany and the American Hemisphere, 1933–1941* (21:120).

22:125 Gottlieb, Moshe. "In the Shadow of War: The American Anti-Nazi Boycott Movement in 1939–1941." *American Jewish Historical Quarterly* 62:2 (1972), 146–61. This essay describes the U.S. Jewish organizational efforts to suppress the smuggling of diamonds, an industry largely in Jewish hands, to send food packages to occupied Europe, and to counter German inroads in trade with Latin America.

22:126 Miller, James E. "A Question of Loyalty: American Liberals, Propaganda, and the Italian-American Community, 1939–1940." *Maryland Historian* 9:1 (1978), 49–71. Miller examines the efforts of the Roosevelt administration to counter Fascist support among the Italian Americans. Despite these efforts, conservative Italians remained in control of media and Italian fraternal organizations; but the fear of fifth column activity was baseless.

Offner, A. A. *American Appeasement: United States Foreign Policy and Germany, 1933–1938* (21:124). See also Offner (22:116).

Seabury, Paul. *The Wilhelmstrasse: A Study of German Diplomats under the Nazi Regime* (21:126) demonstrates Hitler's distrust of career diplomats, a phenomenon not unique to Germany.

U.S., Germany, and War Refugees

See Chapter 21, "Persecution of Jews."

22:127 Brody, David. "American Jewry, the Refugees and Immigration Restriction (1932–1942)." *Publications of the American Jewish Historical Society* 45:4 (1955/1956), 219–47. When the Immigration Act of 1924 effectively restricted the inflow of additional immigrants, American Jewry agreed with this policy. This position underwent a decisive change after 1933, when Nazi persecutions in Europe forced an increased exodus of European Jews.

22:128 Feingold, Henry L. *The Politics of Rescue: The Roosevelt Administration and the Holocaust, 1938–1945*. New Brunswick, N.J.: Rutgers University Press, 1970. Insensitivity, apathy, fear of domestic and foreign reactions, and many other responses are tabulated as causes for the United States not taking the lead in fomenting a policy of rescuing Europe's Jews. The book reveals that many Americans, including the personnel of the Department of State, refused to believe what was happening in Germany.

22:129   Feingold, Henry L. "Roosevelt and the Holocaust: Reflections on New Deal Humanitarianism." *Judaism* 18:3 (1969), 259–76. The Roosevelt administration had neither the will nor the ability to make a large-scale commitment to rescue Europe's Jews. State Department obstructionism, Roosevelt's sensitivity to charges of a "Jew Deal," and the inability of Jews to exert unified pressure were among the factors limiting administration initiatives. Even had all impediments been overcome, mass rescue might not have occurred.

22:130   Gellman, Irwin F. "The *St. Louis* Tragedy." *American Jewish Historical Quarterly* 5:2 (1971), 144–56. In June 1939, more than 900 Jewish refugees aboard the Hamburg-American Liner *St. Louis* sought to obtain entry into Cuba but were barred. The U.S. government did nothing to assist despite pleas for help.

22:131   Wyman, David S. *Paper Walls: America and the Refugee Crisis, 1938–1941.* Amherst: University of Massachusetts Press, 1968. The author traces the combination of fear and cupidity which marred refugee assistance particularly by Breckenridge Long, who, ironically, was put in charge of the refugee section of the State Department. Wyman stresses the excessive fear of rocking the boat or doing anything to upset American public opinion when the war became more expansive in Europe. Bibliography.

SOVIET UNION

See "Personalities," especially William C. Bullitt, Joseph P. Davies.

22:132   Dewey, Donald O. "America and Russia, 1939–1941: The Views of the *New York Times.*" *Journalism Quarterly* 44:1 (1967), 62–70. Dewey summarizes the *Times* editorials and finds that the Nazi-Soviet Pact and the Soviet invasion of Finland prompted the outraged editors to label Soviet officials as "assassins" and "super-paranoiacs."

Gaddis, J. L. *Russia, the Soviet Union and the United States* (2:248) contends that Roosevelt attempted to keep the Russians inside a framework in which the Nazi-Soviet Pact could be forgotten if the opportunity arose to wean the Russians away from Hitler. After January 1941, FDR focused on ways to assist Russia when the forecast Nazi attack came and to warn Stalin of this impending action.

Grant, N. "The Russian Section: A Window on the Soviet Union" [1922–1939] (21:157) examines the State Department's center for the study of Soviet affairs in Riga, Latvia. When the United States recognized Latvia (1922), the center became the Russian section of the U.S. legation and remained in operation until 1939.

22:133   Hayter, William. *The Kremlin and the Embassy.* New York: Macmillan, 1967. Hayter discusses British policy toward the Soviet Union, beginning in 1935.

Kennan, G. F. *Soviet Foreign Policy, 1917–1941* (21:159).

Levering, R. B. *American Opinion and the Russian Alliance, 1939–1945* (25:123) explores the animosity which Americans felt toward the Soviet Union prior to the Nazi attack. The author's intent was to discover what effect this opinion had on the Roosevelt administration and vice versa.

Maddux, T. R. "American Diplomats and the Soviet Experiment: The View from the Moscow Embassy, 1934–1939" (21:179).

22:134   Maddux, Thomas R. "United States–Soviet Naval Relations in the 1930's: The Soviet Union's Efforts to Purchase Naval Vessels." *Naval War College Review* 29:2 (1976), 28–37. Stalin's decision in 1936 to purchase American naval vessels coincided with FDR's desire to cooperate with the Soviets in Europe and East Asia. Senior American naval officers, opposed to doing business with the Soviet Union on ideological and national security grounds, used obstructionist tactics to block the sales.

22:135   Tucker, Robert C. "The Emergence of Stalin's Foreign Policy." *Slavic Review* 36:4 (1977), 563–89. The goals of Stalinist foreign policy in the 1930s were for the Soviet Union to survive in a hostile international environment in which war was inevitable, to remain neutral in any conflict while building up a commanding position of strength, and to step in at the opportune moment and take territories to which

Russia had an historical claim or in which Stalin could promote a Soviet-guided revolution.

Ulam, A. B. *Expansion and Coexistence: Soviet Foreign Policy, 1917–1973* (2:254) is a reliable, important study of Soviet foreign policy.

Diplomacy and War in Europe, 1936–1941

See "Personalities," especially Cordell Hull, Key Pittman, Franklin D. Roosevelt, Sumner Welles.

22:136 Gehl, Jurgen. *Austria, Germany and Anschluss, 1931–38.* New York: Oxford University Press, 1963. While the United States did not figure directly in this event, it was another of those significant episodes that shape American policymakers' view of Hitler's Germany.

22:137 Loewenheim, Francis L. "An Illusion That Shaped History: New Light on the History and Historiography of American Peace Efforts before Munich." In Daniel R. Beaver, ed., *Some Pathways in Twentieth-Century History: Essays in Honor of Reginald Charles McGrane.* Detroit: Wayne State University Press, 1969, pp. 177–220. This essay traces the exploratory efforts and soundings of diplomats of foreign countries, inspired mainly by Roosevelt and Under Secretary of State Welles, to set up an international conference. It failed because of the domestic politics, Anglo-American distrust, hostile feelings between Welles and Secretary of State Hull, and the disinterest in foreign capitals, especially Berlin.

THE RHINELAND CRISIS, 1936

22:138 Emmerson, James T. *The Rhineland Crisis, 7 March 1936: A Study in Multilateral Diplomacy.* Ames: Iowa State University Press, 1977. This study examines Hitler's decision to remilitarize the Rhineland, and the military and political weakness of both France and Britain.

22:139 Robertson, Esmonde. "Hitler and Sanctions: Mussolini and the Rhineland." *European Studies Review* 7:4 (1977), 409–35. Mussolini flirted with France during the Laval Plan negotiations (1935), but Hitler's bold action in the Rhineland crisis won Mussolini's respect despite Italy's initial anger at the invasion. The failure of France and Britain to act increased the community of interest between the two dictators.

22:140 Thorson, Winston B. "The American Press and the Rhineland Crisis of 1936." *Research Studies of the State College of Washington* 15:4 (1947), 233–57. Public opinion, as reflected in the editorials of leading newspapers and magazines, did not view the Rhineland crisis as a threat to America. Many people, especially in the South and Middle West, became more cynical about European diplomacy and pessimistic concerning the prospects for peace.

SPANISH CIVIL WAR, 1936–1939

See "Personalities," especially American Claude G. Bowers (under "Others").

22:141 Crosby, Donald F. "Boston's Catholics and the Spanish Civil War, 1936–1939." *New England Quarterly* 44:1 (1971), 82–100. The Catholics of Boston feared and hated communism, and they believed that Spanish Communists were persecuting their church. Franco deserved their support because he would end the communist threat.

22:142 Guttmann, Allen. *The Wound in the Heart: America and the Spanish Civil War.* New York: Free Press, 1962. The American interest in the Spanish Civil War was "one more manifestation of the liberal tradition" which saw Spain as the last hope of democracy in Europe. The influence of Britain, domestic isolationism, and the Roman Catholic church combined to stay the hand of Roosevelt. Extensive bibliography.

22:143 Rosenstone, Robert A. "American Commissars in Spain." *South Atlantic Quarterly* 67:4 (1968), 688–702. American commissars in the International Brigades had wider ranging functions than the Soviet handbooks had anticipated. Men like Steve Nelson worked to improve the morale of American troops, to discipline the unruly, and to raise the political consciousness of soldiers.

22:144 Rosenstone, Robert A. "The Men of the Abraham Lincoln Battalion." *Journal of American History* 54:2 (1967), 327–38. An analysis of the backgrounds of 1,804 known volunteers, of the 3,000 Americans who served, shows that they were largely in their twenties, familiar with labor unrest, politically radical, and apathetic toward formal religion.

22:145 Singerman, Robert. "American-Jewish Reactions to the Spanish Civil War." *Journal of Church and State* 19:2 (1977), 261–78. This essay examines the American Jewish press's reaction to the treatment of Jews during the war.

22:146 Taylor, F. Jay. *The United States and the Spanish Civil War, 1936–1939.* New York: Bookman, 1956. The Spanish Civil War played a significant part in the struggle over revision of the American neutrality laws. The caution and frustration which seemed to characterize official policy toward Spain is elucidated in this study. Accepting a fait accompli in 1939 was difficult for FDR, but Hull's political caution convinced the president to acknowledge Franco's victory.

22:147 Traina, Richard P. *American Diplomacy and the Spanish Civil War.* Bloomington: Indiana University Press, 1968. This account of the subjugation of FDR's sympathies for the loyalists to the dictates of perceived internal political pressures for the rebels illustrates the halting reaction of the administration to a crisis which FDR and Hull foresaw as possibly leading to a general war. Bibliography.

22:148 Valaik, J. David. "American Catholics and the Second Spanish Republic, 1911–1936." *Journal of Church and State* 10:1 (1968), 13–28. American Catholics had been well prepared to accept Franco as the savior from communism and atheism. The more rational Catholic publications and leaders correctly assessed the Spanish church's reactionary past and its regressive social policies.

22:149 Whealey, Robert. "How Franco Financed His War—Reconsidered." *Journal of Contemporary History* 12:1 (1977), 133–52. The Nationalists drew aid and succour from capitalist companies, whether in Axis nations or the democracies. Although some corporations in the democracies undoubtedly traded with the Republicans, most of the major international corporate leaders backed the Nationalists.

FDR'S QUARANTINE SPEECH, 1937

22:150 Borg, Dorothy. "Notes on Roosevelt's 'Quarantine' Speech." *Political Science Quarterly* 72:3 (1957), 405–33. A detailed examination of the background of Roosevelt's famous foreign policy speech of 1937 which suggests that the speech was not meant to be a drastic departure from previous foreign policy, but rather part of a groping and intermittent effort.

22:151 Haight, John McVickar, Jr. "France and the Aftermath of Roosevelt's 'Quarantine' Speech." *World Politics* 14:2 (1962), 283–306. French leaders, especially Yvon Delbos and Léon Blum, who advocated a policy of resistance to the dictators, welcomed FDR's speech, but American conduct at the Brussels Conference (November 1937) proved disappointing when the administration refused to take positive action.

22:152 Haight, John McVickar, Jr. "Franklin D. Roosevelt and a Naval Quarantine of Japan." *Pacific Historical Review* 40:2 (1971), 203–26. This article refutes the notion advanced by Borg and others that Roosevelt relinquished his sense of firmness against aggression when the isolationists protested his Quarantine Speech. Spurred on by the *Panay* outrage a few weeks later, he explored more intensely the plans already in existence for a naval blockade of Japan.

22:153 Haight, John McVickar, Jr. "Roosevelt and the Aftermath of the Quarantine Speech." *Review of Politics* 24:2 (1962), 233–59. Haight attempts to clarify the uncertainty as to how Roosevelt meant to implement his Quarantine Speech (October 5, 1937) by demonstrating the president's regard for the Nine-Power Conference at Brussels (November 1937) as an opportunity for initiating positive action in East Asia.

22:154 Jacobs, Travis B. "Roosevelt's 'Quarantine Speech.'" *Historian* 24:4 (1962), 483–502. This article shows that public response was mixed if not slightly favorable. Roosevelt's problem was that he was caught without a specific plan.

MUNICH CRISIS, 1938

See "Personalities," especially Eduard Beneš, Neville Chamberlain.

22:155 Bruegel, J. W. "Dr. Beneš on the Soviet 'Offer of Help' in 1938." *East Central Europe* 4:1 (1977), 56–59. In a 1946 interview, Beneš noted that he had received various assurances from the U.S.S.R. in 1938, but the Soviets never specified the nature of the assistance. Furthermore, Beneš believed that Rumania and Poland likely would not allow Russian troop movements through their territories.

22:156 Crozier, Andrew. "Prelude to Munich: British Foreign Policy and Germany, 1935–8." *European Studies Review* 6:3 (1976), 357–81. The Munich agreement of September 1938 was the outcome of a policy initiated shortly before Chamberlain became prime minister in May 1937. Members of both the Foreign Office and the cabinet had agreed that peace with Germany could only be achieved with concessions to Germany.

22:157 Eatwell, Roger. "Munich, Public Opinion, and Popular Front." *Journal of Contemporary History* 6:4 (1971), 122–39. The Munich agreement was supposed to have been received with great rejoicing by Britons, but in a series of seven local elections (October–November 1938) foreign policy played a major role and the Conservatives suffered defeats.

22:158 Haight, John McVickar, Jr. "France, the United States, and the Munich Crisis." *Journal of Modern History* 32:4 (1960), 340–58. American rhetoric led the French to think that FDR would back the democracies against Hitler. But FDR's cautious statements only convinced the Daladier government that France could not count on the Americans. In essence, the United States helped to push Bonnett toward concessions.

22:159 Haslam, Jonathan. "The Soviet Union and the Czechoslovakian Crisis of 1938." *Journal of Contemporary History* 14:4 (1979), 441–61. Haslam examines two conflicting tendencies in Soviet foreign policy during the Munich crisis: Litvinov's broad commitment to collective security and Potemkin's narrower interpretation of his country's international interests.

22:160 Lammers, Donald N. "The May Crisis of 1938: The Soviet Version Considered." *South Atlantic Quarterly* 69:4 (1970), 480–503. Soviet historians have labored diligently to prove that only their country was faithful to Czechoslovakia during the May crisis while ignoring all evidence to the contrary. Thus far no completely satisfactory reconstruction of the complex chain of events has been presented.

22:161 Lewandowski, Richard B. "The Phantom Government: The United States and the Recognition of the Czechoslovak Republic, 1939–1943." *Southern Quarterly* 11:4 (1973), 369–88. The decision by the United States not to recognize the Munich agreement and the occupation of Czechoslovakia led to the creation of a government-in-exile by the Czechs.

22:162 Maisky, I. *The Munich Drama.* Moscow: Novosti Press, 1972. The Soviet ambassador to Britain (1932–1943) examines the Czech crisis, and criticizes Chamberlain, American ambassadors Joseph P. Kennedy, Hugh R. Wilson, and William C. Bullitt as appeasers.

22:163 Roman, Eric. "Munich and Hungary: And Overview of Hungarian Diplomacy during the Sudeten Crisis." *East European Quarterly* 8:1 (1974), 71–97. Only Germany would help Hungary but that assistance decreased Hungary's independence.

22:164 Schroeder, Paul W. "Munich and the British Tradition." *Historical Journal* 19:1 (1976), 223–43. The Munich agreement conformed to Great Britain's "standard nineteenth century approach to Central and East European problems." It was a plan to avoid war and maintain the balance of power in Europe.

22:165 Taylor, Telford. *Munich: The Price of Peace.* Garden City, N.Y.: Doubleday, 1979. The former Nuremberg prosecutor uses Munich as a centerpiece for analyzing European diplomacy and military affairs between the wars. Although this may be the best book yet produced on Munich, the author might have paid more attention to the Soviet Union and the United States.

22:166 Thorson, Winston B. "The American Press and the Munich Crisis in 1938." *Research Studies of the State College of Washington* 18:1 (1950), 40–68. In this study of 50 newspapers and 12 periodicals, Thorson concludes that Munich made the public more aware of the dangers to peace, although the editorials reveal uncertainty about America's role in the growing world crisis.

22:167 Toepfer, Marcia Lynn. "The Soviet Role in the Munich Crisis: An Historiographical Debate." *Diplomatic History* 1:4 (1977), 341–57. Orthodox historians emphasize Stalin's purge of the armed forces and the lack of transit routes to Czechoslovakia to account for Soviet inaction during the Munich crisis. Revisionists, as well as Soviet and Czech historians, stress Russian diplomatic activity on behalf of the Czechs and Western paranoia about cooperating with Spain.

22:168 Vnuk, F. "Munich and the Soviet Union." *Journal of Central European Affairs* 21:3 (1961), 285–304. Vnuk critiques *New Documents on the History of Munich* (Prague, 1968), claiming that the editors have revealed only part of the story. These documents do not prove that the Soviets offered the Czechs military aid.

NAZI-SOVIET PACT, 1939

22:169 Hilger, Gustav, and Meyer, Alfred G. *The Incompatible Allies: A Memoir-History of German-Soviet Relations, 1918–1941*. New York: Macmillan, 1953, p. 350. Hilger, who served German diplomatic interests in Russia during the interwar era, views the Nazi-Soviet Pact as the logical culmination of the Rapallo agreement of 1922. Stalin's rise to absolute power in the late 1930s and his de-emphasis of Marxist ideology made the nonaggression treaty possible.

22:170 Kaslas, Bronis J. "The Lithuanian Strip in Soviet-German Secret Diplomacy, 1939–1941." *Journal of Baltic Studies* 4:3 (1973), 211–25. A secret protocol (September 28, 1939) revised the Russo-German nonaggression pact (August 23, 1939). One provision transferred Lithuania from the German to the Soviet sphere of interest, excepting a strip of territory along Lithuania's southwest frontier. In compensation Germany accepted 7.5 million gold dollars, paid by the U.S.S.R. in February-April 1941.

22:171 Petrov, Vladimir. "The Nazi-Soviet Pact: A Missing Page in Soviet Historiography." *Problems of Communism* 17:1 (1968), 42–50. The author discusses A. M. Nekrich's *1941, 22 iiunia* (Moscow, 1965) which portrays Stalin as a schizophrenic incompetent who made a foolish deal with Hitler and then refused to see that Germany was preparing to invade the Soviet Union.

22:172 Petrov, Vladimir. "A Missing Page in Soviet Historiography: The Nazi-Soviet Partnership." *Orbis* 11:4 (1968), 1113–37. The partnership's direct antecedent was the Treaty of Rapallo and the common desire to overturn the status quo established by the Treaty of Versailles. It broke down because of the clash of German and Soviet interest in Eastern Europe and the Balkans.

22:173 Rossi, Angelo [Angelo Tasca]. *The Russo-German Alliance, August 1939–June 1941*. Boston: Beacon, 1951. The former Italian Communist labors to present the Nazi-Soviet Pact as a cynical act of Soviet imperialism.

22:174 Sontag, Raymond J., and Beddie, James S., eds. *Nazi-Soviet Relations, 1939–1941: Documents from the Archives of the German Foreign Office*. Washington, D.C.: G.P.O., 1948. Although the collection is useful, the editors ignore the whole historical background of the Nazi-Soviet Pact, choosing to begin their documentary history in the spring of 1939.

22:175 Watt, D. C. "The Initiation of the Negotiations Leading to the Nazi-Soviet Pact: A Historical Problem." In C. Abramsky, ed. *Essays in Honour of E. H. Carr*. London: Macmillan, 1974, pp. 152–70. Watt examines some of the unanswered questions regarding the negotiations, and suggests that Soviet enthusiasm for the pact resulted in providing Hitler a license to make war on the West. Extensive bibliography.

22:176 Weinberg, Gerhard L. *Germany and the Soviet Union, 1939–1941*. Leiden: Brill (1954), 1972. In this account of the origins of the Nazi-Soviet Pact and the subsequent 22-month alliance of convenience, the author gives the impression "of two great powers plodding fitfully along the path of expediency."

RUSSO-FINNISH WAR, 1939–1940

22:177 Engle, Eloise, and Paananen, Lauri. *The Winter War: The Russo-Finnish Conflict, 1939–40*. New York: Scribner's, 1973. Written from secondary sources, this book provides a useful survey of the important but little understood conflict between Russia and Finland. This account provides little analysis. Bibliography.

22:178 Schwartz, Andrew J. *America and the Russo-Finnish War*. Washington, D.C.: Public Affairs Press, 1960. Schwartz credits American friendship with assisting Finnish efforts during the "Winter War."

22:179 Sobel, Robert. *The Origins of Interventionism: The United States and the Russo-Finnish War*. New York: Bookman, 1960. The volume is divided between the Roosevelt administration's struggle to alter the neutrality legislation and American policy in the Russo-Finnish War.

AID TO THE ALLIES, 1938–1941

22:180 Haight, John McVickar, Jr. *American Aid to France, 1938–1940.* New York: Atheneum, 1970. This study provides a good account of the domestic political process of diplomatic negotiation in both nations. The Roosevelt-Morgenthau policy helped to prepare the American aircraft industry for later years. Bibliography.

22:181 Porter, David L. "Ohio Representative John M. Vorys and the Arms Embargo in 1939." *Ohio History* 83:2 (1974), 103–13. Freshman representative Vorys assisted in preventing the repeal of the arms embargo in 1939. Vorys rallied bipartisan support for an amendment to the Bloom bill restoring the arms embargo.

22:182 Ray, Deborah Wing. "The Takoradi Route: Roosevelt's Prewar Venture beyond the Western Hemisphere." *Journal of American History* 62:2 (1975), 340–58. Roosevelt, Hopkins, and Pan American Airways circumvented lend-lease and neutrality restrictions to set in operation an air route across the South Atlantic Ocean to West Africa and on to Cairo in 1941.

The "Destroyer Deal," 1940

22:183 Goodhart, Philip. *Fifty Ships that Saved the World: The Foundation of the Anglo-American Alliance.* Garden City, N.Y.: Doubleday, 1965. FDR transferred fifty aging destroyers to Britain in return for the lease of bases in the Caribbean and Newfoundland. Churchill overestimated the importance of the ships and Roosevelt oversold the significance of the bases.

22:184 Greenberg, Daniel S. "U.S. Destroyers for British Bases—Fifty Old Ships Go to War." *U.S. Naval Institute Proceedings* 88:11 (1962), 70–83. Greenberg shows that the 1940 trade of obsolete destroyers for bases marked a distinct change in American policy toward the European war.

22:185 Langenberg, William H. "Destroyers for Naval Bases: Highlights of an Unprecedented Trade." *Naval War College Review* 22:9 (1970), 80–92. Langenberg traces the maneuvers and actions of Roosevelt and Churchill during the summer of 1940 in the trade of fifty American overage destroyers for British bases.

Origins of Lend-Lease

See also Chapter 23 and Chapter 25, "Lend-Lease."

22:186 Bruchy, Stuart. "Beard on Foreign Policy." *American Historical Review* 73:3 (1968), 759–60. Before the Senate Foreign Relations Committee (February 1941), Charles A. Beard opposed the lend-lease bill on the grounds that it was sweeping and imprecise, that it would involve surrender of congressional powers to the executive, and that it would expend American wealth and possibly lives for unattainable objectives.

22:187 Dawson, Raymond H. *The Decision to Aid Russia, 1941: Foreign Policy and Domestic Politics.* Chapel Hill: University of North Carolina Press, 1959. Roosevelt believed that the existing military situation warranted support for the Russians if attacked. Dawson examines the tactics used by the administration to gain approval from Congress and the public.

22:188 Kimball, Warren F. "Lend-Lease and the Open Door: The Temptation of British Opulence, 1937–1942." *Political Science Quarterly* 86:2 (1971), 232–59. Kimball discusses the negotiation of the Lend-Lease Consideration Agreement (1941–1942) against the background of earlier U.S. foreign economic policy, and argues that the agreement represented the triumph of Hull's plans for peace and prosperity, including the abandonment of British Imperial Preference.

22:189 Kimball, Warren F. *The Most Unsordid Act: Lend-Lease, 1939–1941.* Baltimore: Johns Hopkins Press, 1969. This first-rate account of the origins of lend-lease shows FDR at his best as politician and diplomatist without sparing criticism of the president's tactics. Extensive bibliography.

22:190 Lukas, Richard C. "The Impact of 'Barbarossa' on the Soviet Air Force and the Resulting Commitment of the United States Aircraft, June–October, 1941." *Historian* 29:1 (1966), 60–80. U.S. efforts to meet Soviet requests for military aircraft reveal the disagreement between the president, who favored a stopgap shipment, and War Department officials, who opposed any offering given security needs.

U.S. and East Asia, 1937–1941

UNDECLARED ATLANTIC NAVAL HOSTILITIES

22:191 Ryan, Paul B., and Bailey, Thomas A. *Hitler vs. Roosevelt: Undeclared Naval War.* New York: Free Press, 1979. This account of quasi hostilities (1939–1941) focuses on Roosevelt's efforts to assist the British in the delivery of supplies through the Nazi submarine blockade. The authors cast a wide net, but do discuss the *Greer* and *Reuban James* episodes.

22:192 Trefousse, Hans L. *Germany and American Neutrality, 1939–1941.* New York: Octagon (1951), 1969. Trefousse has no doubt that Hitler planned to ultimately dominate the United States, but a neutral timetable was more suitable until he was ready to bring the Americans to submission. FDR would not be cajoled or frightened, and Hitler was forced to move his timetable forward in the attempted subjugation of America. Bibliography.

ATLANTIC CHARTER, 1941

See "Personalities," especially Winston S. Churchill, Franklin D. Roosevelt.

22:193 Lindley, William R. "The Atlantic Charter: Press Release or Historic Document?" *Journalism Quarterly* 41:3 (1964), 375–79, 394. This essay explores how a press release became "one of the important declarations of modern political history."

22:194 Wilson, Theodore A. *The First Summit: Roosevelt and Churchill at Placentia Bay 1941.* Boston: Houghton Mifflin, 1969. This is a thorough account of the first meeting between Churchill and Roosevelt. Roosevelt promised Churchill extensive aid but refused to face the possibility of American entry into the war. Churchill supported the Atlantic Charter, a statement of war aims and postwar plans. Bibliography.

See also Chapter 21 for overlapping issues and episodes.

Barclay, G. St. J. "Australia Looks to America: The Wartime Relationship, 1939–42" (32:115) describes the beginning of the extraordinary relationship.

22:195 Borg, Dorothy, and Okamoto, Shumpei, eds. *Pearl Harbor as History: Japanese-American Relations, 1931–1941.* New York: Columbia University Press, 1973. The emphasis of these essays is on decisionmaking processes within the respective foreign-policy elites and on other comparable institutions, such as the press and private agencies.

Clauss, E. M. "The Roosevelt Administration and Manchukuo, 1933–1941" (21:200) finds that Roosevelt inherited a Hoover-Stimson nonrecognition policy (see Chapter 21). The administration adhered officially to this policy while doing all possible to preserve American commercial interests in China and Manchuria.

22:196 Clifford, Nicholas R. "Britain, America, and the Far East, 1937–1940: A Failure in Cooperation." *Journal of British Studies* 3:1 (1963), 137–54. Washington's reticence during the Sino-Japanese War is well known. Nonparticipation by the United States in a joint scheme against Japan proposed by the otherwise-appeasing Chamberlain was intended to undermine Britain's effort to secure American protection of the empire.

22:197 Dreifort, John E. "France, the Powers, and the Far Eastern Crisis, 1937–1939." *Historian* 39:4 (1977), 733–53. This essay examines the neglected role of France in the Sino-Japanese War. France's main concern was the potential Japanese threat to its possessions in East Asia.

22:198 Herzog, James H. *Closing the Open Door: American-Japanese Diplomatic Relations, 1936–1941.* Annapolis, Md.: Naval Institute Press, 1973. Here is a description of American naval influence in foreign affairs. Admiral Stark refused to condone naval reinforcements and embargoes against Japan, while Admiral Yarnell desired these sanctions.

22:199   Lowe, Peter. *Great Britain and the Origins of the Pacific War: A Study of British Policy in East Asia, 1937–1941*. Oxford: Clarendon Press, 1977. This study examines British policy toward the approach of war in the Pacific. However, it contains much information about the common Anglo-American underestimation of Japan and preoccupation with Europe, and about Britain's reliance on the United States (except where appeasement of Japan seemed likely) to save its empire. Bibliography.

22:200   Morison, Samuel Eliot. *The Rising Sun in the Pacific, 1931–April 1942*. Boston: Little, Brown, 1948. This volume of the well-known multivolume *History of United States Naval Operations in World War II* (23:147) provides general information about the American-Japanese naval rivalry before December 7, 1941.

Neu, C. E. *The Troubled Encounter: The United States and Japan* [1853–1972] (2:348) is an exemplary synthesis of works on U.S.-Japanese relations (1890–1941), with insights into the haphazard decisionmaking that "troubled" relationships.

22:201   Pratt, Lawrence. "The Anglo-American Naval Conversations on the Far East of January 1938." *International Affairs* [London] 47:4 (1971), 745–63. Although unwilling to make general commitments to Britain for joint action against Japan, FDR saw the need for joint planning with the British navy in case of a two-ocean war.

22:202   Saburō Ienaga. *The Pacific War: World War II and the Japanese, 1931–1945*. Trans. by Frank Baldwin. New York: Pantheon, 1978. This is an idiosyncratic work of merit by an aggrieved but astute civil libertarian in Japan who indicts himself, his country, and the economic expansionism of the United States. Its central contention is an antiwar, antimilitary message which nevertheless provides rare insight into Japanese military activities. Bibliography.

22:203   *Taiheiyō sensō e no michi: kaisen gaikō-shi* [The road to the Pacific war: a diplomatic history before the war]. 7 vols. Tokyo: Asahi Shimbun Sha, 1962–1963. Fourteen Japanese historians using sources not heretofore available have recounted the foreign policies of Japan and the Japanese policies of other powers, with emphasis on military affairs and

decisionmaking. See Iriye's review (22:210). Excerpts from these volumes have been selected and translated under the editorship of James W. Morley, and published by Columbia University Press in five unnumbered volumes under the general title of *Japan's Road to the Pacific War*. The specific titles are: 1) *Japan Erupts: The London Naval Conference and the Manchurian Incident, 1928–1932*; 2) *The China Quagmire: Japan's Expansion on the Asian Continent, 1933–1941*; 3) *Deterrent Diplomacy: Japan, Germany, and the U.S.S.R., 1935–1940*; 4) *The Fateful Choice: Japan's Advance into Southeast Asia, 1939–1941*; and 5) *The Final Confrontation: Japan's Negotiations with the United States, 1941*.

22:204   Toland, John. *The Rising Sun: The Decline and Fall of the Japanese Empire, 1936–1945*. 2 vols. New York: Random House, 1970. Volume 1 is a most successful reconstruction of the enemy's mentality as disclosed in interviews with 500 Japanese military and civilian leaders. Pro-Japanese postures and exaggerated faultfinding with America are offset by an impressive philological analysis of Magic intercepts. Extensive bibliography.

22:205   Wheeler, Gerald E. "The United States Navy and War in the Pacific, 1919–1941." *World Affairs Quarterly* 30:3 (1959), 199–225. This article reviews the vicissitudes of American naval construction between the wars. The main contributions, however, are its elaboration of naval strategy toward the Philippines and Hawaii, and its estimate of naval influence upon American East Asian policy.

BASES OF JAPAN'S POLICY

22:206   Ballantine, Joseph W. "Mukden to Pearl Harbor: The Foreign Policies of Japan." *Foreign Affairs* 27:4 (1949), 651–64. This article by a former State Department official contributes a useful structuring or phasing of Japanese expansionism into extragovernmental policy, then governmental policy with reservations, and, finally, unequivocal governmental policy.

22:207   Blaker, Michael. *Japanese International Negotiating Style*. New York: Columbia University Press, 1977. This work in political science is valuable for having deduced a peculiarly Japanese bargaining style from the pre–Pearl Harbor negotiations and seventeen other case histories. This style included domestic preoccupations, studied perfidy, and the commitment to nationalism. Bibliography.

Crowley, J. B. *Japan's Quest for Autonomy: National Security and Foreign Policy, 1930–1938* (21:189) is noteworthy for the provocative theory that responsible civilian leaders rationally deliberating the requirements of national security and economic well-being spawned the goal of East Asia hegemony.

22:208 Hosoya, Chihiro. "Retrogression in Japan's Foreign Policy Decision-Making Process." In James W. Morley, ed., *Dilemmas of Growth in Prewar Japan*. Princeton, N.J.: Princeton University Press, 1971, pp. 81–105. This is an attempt to put Japan's foreign policy decisionmaking crisis of the 1930s into the context of modernization. Hosoya finds political modernization was retrogressing at the very time that social and economic modernization advanced.

22:209 Iriye, Akira. "The Failure of Military Expansionism." In James W. Morley, ed., *Dilemmas of Growth in Prewar Japan*. Princeton, N.J.: Princeton University Press, 1971, pp 107–38. In a trenchant examination of Japan's post-Manchurian militarism from the standpoint of ideology or rationale, Iriye reveals that the Japanese collectively perceived the 1920s as a decade of diplomatic futility and substituted the new and fateful assumption that the world of the 1930s was tending toward Pan-Asian and other regionalisms.

22:210 Iriye, Akira. "Japanese Imperialism and Aggression." *Journal of Asian Studies* 23:1 (1963), 103–13. In his English-language description, Iriye finds the multivolume *Taiheiyō sensō e no michi* (22:203) to have greater merit when dealing with Japan's foreign policy than when dealing with other powers' policies toward Japan. He applauds its treatment of Japan's southward advance as the most important contribution.

22:211 Iriye, Akira. "Japan's Foreign Policies between the Wars—Sources and Interpretations." *Journal of Asian Studies* 26:4 (1967), 677–82. This English-language description of the seven-volume collection of Japanese source materials published in 1964 to 1966 as *Gendaishi shiryō* [Documents on contemporary history] illustrates its relevance to U.S.-Japanese diplomacy in the 1930s.

22:212 Jones, F. C. *Japan's New Order in East Asia: Its Rise and Fall, 1937–45*. New York: Oxford

University Press, 1954. This is a critical, though non-conspiratorial, work on Japan's abortive quest for hegemony of East Asia. Jones argues that no master plan existed for expansionism, each forward move deriving instead from circumstances. Bibliography.

22:213 Kutakov, Leonid N. *Japanese Foreign Policy on the Eve of the Pacific War: A Soviet View*. Tallahassee, Fla.: Diplomatic Press, 1972. This Russian historian utilizes Soviet and People's Republic of China archives to reconstruct his country's views of Germany, Britain, Japan, and the United States from the late 1930s to Pearl Harbor. He advances the view that Western appeasement aimed to pit Germany and Japan against the U.S.S.R.

22:214 Lebra, Joyce C., ed. *Japan's Greater East Asia Co-Prosperity Sphere in World War II: Selected Readings and Documents*. New York: Oxford University Press, 1975. This collection of Japanese writings and documents deals with the rationale, implementation, and ex post facto evaluation of expansionism toward China and Southeast Asia in the 1930s. It is intended to update F. C. Jones (22:212), accentuate idealism, and suggest a revisionist notion of the sphere as more than imperialism. Extensive bibliography.

Maxon, Y. C. *Control of Japanese Foreign Policy: A Study of Civil-Military Rivalry, 1930–1945* (21:190) is a sophisticated account of Japanese civil-military relations during 15 years of crisis, including an upsurge of variously defined irrationalism. The extraconstitutional coordinating mechanisms became instruments of de facto military control over foreign policy when the more legal arbiter, the emperor, failed to intervene.

Moore, F. *With Japan's Leaders: An Intimate Record of Fourteen Years as Counsellor to the Japanese Government, Ending December 7, 1941* (21:191).

Storry, R. *The Double Patriots: A Study of Japanese Nationalism* (21:193) is a book whose title refers not to divided loyalties but to conditions of ultrapatriotism. Storry finds Japanese nationalist organizations disproportionately influential upon government because of Japan's collective leadership.

22:215 Willoughby, Westel W. *Japan's Case Examined*. Baltimore: Johns Hopkins Press, 1940. This contemporary book by an American Sinophile describes Japan's China policy and (more briefly) her Southeast Asia policy from the standpoint of aims and justifications. The book concludes with unequivocal repudiations based on international law and the multilateralizing of the Monroe Doctrine.

BASES OF CHINA'S POLICY

Tuchman, B. W. *Stilwell and the American Experience in China, 1911–1945* (23:112) has 150 pages on Stilwell's career in China in the 1920s and 1930s, a colorful day-by-day depiction of small units of the U.S. Army caught up in the confusion of civil war, politics among rival warlords, and the process of unification brought about by Chiang Kai-shek.

Young, A. N. *China and the Helping Hand, 1937–1945* (23:226) is a sample of the controversial literature surrounding China's fall to communism, written by an American financial adviser to the Nationalist government. It argues that U.S. foreign aid before December 1941 was perceived on the mainland as inadequate.

SINO-JAPANESE WAR, 1937–1945

See "Personalities," especially Joseph C. Grew, Cordell Hull, Nelson T. Johnson, Hirota Kōki, Henry Morgenthau.

22:216 Adams, Frederick C. "The Road to Pearl Harbor: A Reexamination of American Far Eastern Policy, July 1937–December 1938." *Journal of American History* 58:1 (1971), 73–92. America's response to the China incident is shown to have anticipated subsequent policies toward Japan after July 1941. The United States moved for the first time to preserve the open door, the Export-Import Bank provided credit to China, and armed intervention was contemplated.

Borg, D. *The United States and the Far Eastern Crisis of 1933–1938: From the Manchurian Incident through the Initial Stage of the Undeclared Sino-Japanese War* (21:188) is noteworthy for showing the continuity of American passivity toward changing Japanese tactics and for showing and explaining the American stance during the *Panay* incident.

22:217 Boyle, John H. *China and Japan at War, 1937–1945: The Politics of Collaboration*. Stanford,

Calif.: Stanford University Press, 1972. This volume is unique in focusing on the noncommunists who peopled Japan's mainland regimes and took the road to appeasement. Boyle finds in the use of proxies a residual rationalism among the Imperial Army and, by highlighting the failures of the noncommunist collaborators to attract allegiances and overcome hatreds, helps explain why Japan made the push southward. Extensive bibliography.

22:218 Chan, Lau Kit Ching. "Britain and the Sino-Japanese War: Arms Traffic to China through Hong Kong, 1937–1941." *Asia Quarterly* 3 (1977), 175–202. The transport of war materiel from Britain to China through Hong Kong was the most important cause of friction between Britain and Japan during 1937 to 1941.

22:219 Lee, Bradford A. *Britain and the Sino-Japanese War, 1937–1939*. Stanford, Calif.: Stanford University Press, 1973. This ambitious study of British policy toward the Sino-Japanese War compares and explains East Asian policy with respect to appeasement in Europe. Lee's conclusion that England made "no systematic attempt to wean Japan from forcible expansion" highlights American reluctance to cooperate with Whitehall as a factor in British policymaking. Extensive bibliography.

22:220 Schaller, Michael. "American Air Strategy in China, 1939–1941: The Origins of Clandestine Air Warfare." *American Quarterly* 28:1 (1976), 3–19. Influential American officials, with individuals and groups associated with the Chinese Nationalist regime, developed at least two plans for clandestine military attacks on Japan. These schemes, using private American aircraft and pilots, were developed outside of the State and War Departments.

22:221 Smylie, Robert F. "John Leighton Stuart: A Missionary in the Sino-Japanese Conflict, 1937–1941." *Journal of Presbyterian History* 53:3 (1975), 256–76. President of Yenching University John Leighton Stuart's unique outlook on China made him an intermediary among the varying forces striving for dominance in China. But because he was not a diplomat, he received little sympathy from Roosevelt.

The Panay Incident, 1937

22:222 Coox, Alvin D. *Year of the Tiger*. Philadelphia: Orient/West, 1964. This is a journalistic reconstruction of Japanese domestic and foreign (especially Chinese) episodes during 1938. Coox's analysis of the *Panay* crisis concludes the government bore no responsibility and the navy little guilt, given the intelligence equipment that was part of the ship's cargo.

22:223 Dennett, Tyler. "Alternative American Policies in the Far East." *Foreign Affairs* 16:3 (1938), 388–400. Writing in response to the *Panay* incident to warn the Japanese against overestimating the permanence of American isolationism, the author weighs the relative merits of pacifist and coercive measures by the United States, and advocates the graduated use of force.

22:224 Koginos, Manny T. *The Panay Incident: Prelude to War.* Lafayette, Ind.: Purdue University Press, 1967. More analytical than Perry's work (22:226), this volume moves beyond the episode's details—including questions of context, motive, and responsibility—to its overall significance as the driving force behind Roosevelt's program of naval expansion and as a factor in the denouncement of pacifism. Bibliography.

22:225 Okumiya, Masatake. "How the *Panay* was Sunk." *U.S. Naval Institute Proceedings* 79:6 (1953), 587–96. Okumiya led the dive bomber squadron that attacked the *Panay* while pursuing the Chinese. He emphasizes, as the Japanese government did, the unintentional guilt of his country, and attributes mistakes to explainable delays in announcing the victim's change of location.

22:226 Perry, Hamilton D. *The Panay Incident: Prelude to Pearl Harbor.* New York: Macmillan, 1969. The author's discussions with crew members of the vessel, together with interviews conducted in Japan, reinforce this detailed narrative of the episode and of Tokyo's subsequent apologies, payments, scapegoating, and rationalizing.

22:227 Swanson, Harlan J. "The *Panay* Incident: Prelude to Pearl Harbor." *U.S. Naval Institute Proceedings* 93:12 (1967), 26–37. This article's importance is that it confronts the disappearance of the incident from American thought and explains this with reference to an isolationist mood that precluded strong action.

THE TRIPARTITE ALLIANCE, 1940

See "Personalities," especially Matsuoka Yōsuke.

22:228 Iklé, Frank W. *German-Japanese Relations, 1936–1940.* New York: Bookman, 1956. This study of the rapprochement as it developed from the Anti-Comintern Pact to the Tripartite Pact overlooks weaknesses in the alliance and takes the dated view that anti-Americanism motivated the Japanese. It remains useful for showing how internal and international realities contributed to, and in turn were affected by, the alliance. Bibliography.

22:229 Lu, David J. *From the Marco Polo Bridge to Pearl Harbor: Japan's Entry into World War II.* Washington, D.C.: Public Affairs Press, 1961. This older work on Japanese expansionism is important for portraying Matsuoka as a consistent moderate and for anticipating the more recent investigators' belief in the anti-Soviet rather than anti-American nature of the Tripartite Pact. Bibliography.

22:230 Meskill, Johanna Menzel. *Hitler and Japan: The Hollow Alliance.* New York: Atherton, 1966. Until this book's appearance, literature on the Tripartite Pact had slighted the content and significance of secret addenda to the pact that diluted its automatic character and rendered it hollow from the beginning.

22:231 Morley, James W., ed. *Deterrent Diplomacy: Japan, Germany, and the USSR, 1935–1940.* New York: Columbia University Press, 1976. These excerpts from the *Taiheiyō sensō e no michi* [The road to the Pacific war] deal with Japan's use of alliance diplomacy (1935–1940) to clear Germany and the Soviet Union from the field. One essay on the Tripartite Pact sees the Japanese desiring to deter war but mistakenly strengthening the forces for aggression and stiffening the resolve of the Americans. Bibliography.

22:232 Presseisen, Ernst L. *Germany and Japan: A Study in Totalitarian Diplomacy, 1933–1941.* The Hague: Nijhoff, 1958. Probably the best analysis of the pact's origins, this book links the origins to the contemporary destroyer-bases deal, by portraying Japan as motivated by fears of both Russia and America, and by discerning commonalities that have often been obscured—League of Nations antipathies and the sense of material deprivation. Extensive bibliography.

22:233 Schroeder, Paul W. *The Axis Alliance and Japanese-American Relations, 1941.* Ithaca, N.Y.: Cornell University Press, 1958. Schroeder examines the role played by the Tripartite Alliance in Japanese-American negotiations, including the misunderstood "fact" that Japan hoped by it to avoid war and have a free hand in Asia. America's tactics after July 1941 are indicted in the realist vein for having overlooked Japan's willingness to retreat from Southern Indochina. Bibliography.

22:234 Trefousse, H. L. "Germany and Pearl Harbor." *Far Eastern Quarterly* 11:1 (1951), 35–50. This early account of Hitler's expectations shows that, rather than pushing Japan to attack the United States, he desired the latter's continued nonbelligerency. When Japan decided to move against Pearl Harbor, Hitler, to save an alliance, gave his approval.

EMBARGOES AND SANCTIONS

See "Personalities," especially Cordell Hull, Stanley K. Hornbeck, Key Pittman.

22:235 Anderson, Irvine H., Jr. *The Standard-Vacuum Oil Company and United States East Asian Policy, 1933–1941.* Princeton, N.J.: Princeton University Press, 1975. The role of Stanvac in the formation and execution of American policy toward Japan—the company found its supplies in the Netherlands East Indies and markets in China and Japan—is shown to have fluctuated. But on the eve of Pearl Harbor, Stanvac actively supported Roosevelt's oil embargo. Extensive bibliography.

22:236 Anderson, Irvine H., Jr. "The 1941 De Facto Embargo on Oil to Japan: A Bureaucratic Reflex." *Pacific Historical Review* 44:2 (1975), 201–31. Notable for its insights into the background of Pearl Harbor and the dynamics of federal bureaucracy, this article finds the July 1941 freeze of Japanese assets compatible with continued oil shipments until a month-long administrative tangle turned the freeze into a total embargo.

22:237 Crowley, James B. "A New Asian Order: Some Notes on Prewar Japanese Nationalism." In Bernard S. Silberman and H. D. Harootunian, eds., *Japan in Crisis: Essays on Taishō Democracy.* Princeton, N.J.: Princeton University Press, 1974, pp. 270–98. By championing the liberation of all Asian colonies, which was facilitated by the Nazi-Soviet Pact and the Axis alliance and in no wise forced by American embargoes, Japan distanced herself from Western-style imperialism in Chinese eyes.

22:238 Friedman, Donald J. *The Road from Isolation: The Campaign of the American Committee for Non-Participation in Japanese Aggression, 1938–1941.* Cambridge: Harvard University, East Asian Research Center, 1968. Friedman traces the efforts of the committee to convince the American public that the United States ought to take stronger measures, such as economic sanctions, to halt Japanese expansion. Bibliography.

22:239 Herzog, James H. "Influence of the United States Navy in the Embargo of Oil to Japan, 1940–1941." *Pacific Historical Review* 35:3 (1966), 317–28. The irony of Japanese aircraft and carriers during the Pearl Harbor attack operating on imported American fuel resulted because high-ranking navy personnel such as Admiral Stark, feeling unprepared for the war in the Pacific, had counseled against embargoes.

22:240 Libby, Justin H. "Anti-Japanese Sentiment in the Pacific Northwest: Senator Schwellenbach and Congressman Coffee Attempt to Embargo Japan." *Mid-America* 58:3 (1976), 167–74. Libby analyzes the efforts in the 1930s of Lewis B. Schwellenbach and John M. Coffee to enact an American embargo of Japan which they believed would protect the fishing interests of Washington State and keep the United States out of a war with Japan.

22:241 Masland, John W. "Commercial Influence upon Far Eastern Policy, 1937–1941." *Pacific Historical Review* 11:3 (1942), 281–99. A significant early analysis of East Asian trade groups in America which concludes that their influence was nominal: pursuing business as usual even while decrying Japan's political ambitions, they condoned restrictions no earlier than 1941.

22:242 Utley, Jonathan G. "Diplomacy in a Democracy: The United States and Japan, 1937–1941." *World Affairs* 193:2 (1976), 130–40. The State Department's reluctance and the American public's desire to embargo Japan are contrasted from the standpoint of respective expectations. Official fears of inciting the Japanese were overcome but the "democratic achievement" evaporates as ulterior purposes of the embargoes are noted.

22:243 Utley, Jonathan G. "Upstairs, Downstairs at Foggy Bottom: Oil Exports and Japan, 1940–41." *Prologue* 8:1 (1976), 17–28. Irvine Anderson, Jr.'s pioneering work is developed, and a situation described in which oil strategy was adopted at one government echelon but implemented at a lower, less moderate one. The numerous lower-level agencies are charged with weakening the State Department's hand and helping lead the nation into war.

The Decision for War, 1941

FINAL NEGOTIATIONS

See "Personalities," especially Cordell Hull, Joseph C. Grew, Franklin D. Roosevelt.

22:244 Ben-Zvi, Abraham. "American Preconceptions and Policies toward Japan, 1940–1941: A Case Study in Misperception." *International Studies Quarterly* 19:2 (1975), 228–48. This essay proposes a departure from revisionist-internationalist simplicities toward a typology of American policymakers based on belief systems: the globalist-realists (Stimson, Morgenthau, Hornbeck), the globalist-idealists (Hull), and, favored herein, the nationalist-pragmatists (Roosevelt, Grew, and the military).

22:245 Boyle, John H. "The Drought-Walsh Mission to Japan." *Pacific Historical Review* 34:2 (1965), 141–61. This intriguing essay recounts amateur diplomatic efforts in late 1940 and early 1941 by two American priests, briefly taken seriously in Konoye and Roosevelt circles, who through optimism or deceit misinterpreted official policy on both sides. Should be read in conjunction with Butow (22:247).

22:246 Brune, Lester H. "Considerations of Force in Cordell Hull's Diplomacy, July 26 to November 26, 1941." *Diplomatic History* 2:4 (1978), 389–405. The argument is made that by rejecting proposal B on November 26, Hull assumed a hard line against Japan that contradicted the belated decision to rearm and defend the Philippines.

22:247 Butow, R. J. C. "Backdoor Diplomacy in the Pacific: The Proposal for a Konoye-Roosevelt Meeting, 1941." *Journal of American History* 59:1 (1972), 48–72. The controversial idea of Japanese-American summitry is said to have foundered through bad timing and the realities of Japanese militarism, but mainly (though unbeknown to Grew and Konoye) through contamination by association with amateur diplomats (see Boyle [22:245], and Butow, *The John Doe Associates* [1974]).

22:248 Butow, R. J. C. "The Hull-Nomura Conversations: A Fundamental Misconception." *American Historical Review* 65:4 (1960), 822–36. This article focuses on the quiet diplomatic dialogue in Washington that commenced in March 1941 on the basis of a draft understanding whose private origins and qualified acceptance were not conveyed to the Japanese government.

22:249 Esthus, Raymond A. "President Roosevelt's Commitment to Britain to Intervene in a Pacific War." *Mississippi Valley Historical Review* 50:1 (1963), 28–38. This article clarifies American assurances to Britain on December 1, 1941, regarding joint military action against Japan in cases not involving American territory. Roosevelt's generosities hedged on preventive moves by Britain and assumed the necessity of prior congressional consent.

22:250 Feis, Herbert. *The Road to Pearl Harbor: The Coming of the War between the United States and Japan.* Princeton, N.J.: Princeton University Press, 1950. This moderately pro-Roosevelt volume perceives a progression of separation, hostility, enmity, and war; delineates the motives of Japan's Southeast Asia program; and argues that the abortive summit, not subsequent "demands," terminated the era of talk.

22:251 Hill, Norman. "Was There an Ultimatum before Pearl Harbor?" *American Journal of International Law* 42:2 (1948), 355–67. The Japanese note of November 20, 1941, and the American note of November 26, 1941, are compared to other historic ultimata. Neither constituted an ultimatum as used in international law, a communication threatening war.

22:252 Hsü, Immanuel C. Y. "Kurusu's Mission to the United States and the Abortive *Modus Vivendi.*" *Journal of Modern History* 24:3 (1952), 301–07. This article repudiates the popular view of the special envoy's last-minute dispatch to Washington as a camouflage for military preparations. These were already completed.

22:253　LaPlante, John B. "The Evolution of Pacific Policy and Strategic Planning: June 1940–July 1941." *Naval War College Review* 25:5 (1973), 57–72. Compatibilities between U.S. policy and strategy in late 1941, on which the ensuing four years' war effort was to be based, did not represent a careful integration of political and military processes, though they were not coincidental either.

Minear, R. H. *Victors' Justice: The Tokyo War Crimes Trial* (27:116) appears more useful for the later period because it focuses on the legal and procedural matters. However, its historical reflections expand Schroeder's thesis (22:233) into an argument that, technically speaking, prewar Japanese leaders did not qualify as aggressors in December 1941.

JAPAN'S DECISION FOR WAR

See "Personalities," especially Emperor Hirohito, Tōjō Hideki.

22:254　*Japan's Decision for War: Records of the 1941 Policy Conferences.* Trans. and ed. by Nobutaka Ike. Stanford, Calif.: Stanford University Press, 1967. This translation of Japanese Liaison and Imperial Conference notes by the Japanese army's chief of staff discloses unanimity regarding the New Order, extreme rigidity, and the risk taking that thwarted deterrence strategies.

22:255　Morton, Louis. "The Japanese Decision for War." *U.S. Naval Institute Proceedings* 80:12 (1954), 1325–35. This article is a careful effort to reconstruct the Japanese rationale for decisions made in the fall of 1941. It portrays Japanese leaders as assuming that the United States would negotiate for peace rather than pursue a long and costly war in East Asia.

PEARL HARBOR ATTACK, 1941

22:256　Hoehling, A. A. *The Week before Pearl Harbor.* New York: Norton, 1963. This volume is one of the handiest recitals and syntheses of testimony by the principals. Apathy in the War and Navy Departments and White House, criticized but not explained, emerges as the predominating theme.

22:257　Lord, Walter. *Day of Infamy.* New York: Holt, Rinehart & Winston, 1957. This book recreates a multiple perspective on the two hours of the Pearl Harbor attack. Bibliography.

22:258　Millis, Walter. *This Is Pearl: The United States and Japan, 1941.* New York: Morrow, 1947. Here is a stirring, contemporary, human-interest account of the failure of diplomacy and the origins of war. The author assigns major responsibility for military surprises to the field commanders and absolves Roosevelt.

22:259　Morton, Louis. "Pearl Harbor in Perspective: A Bibliographical Survey." *U.S. Naval Institute Proceedings* 81:4 (1955), 461–68. This is a handy review of the literature up to the mid-1950s, occasioned by publication of Admiral Kimmel's self-justifying memoir.

22:260　Ward, Robert E. "The Inside Story of the Pearl Harbor Plan." *U.S. Naval Institute Proceedings* 77:11 (1951), 1271–83. One of the few to look at Pearl Harbor as the technical feat that it was.

Responsibility for the Disaster

22:261　Beard, Charles A. *President Roosevelt and the Coming of the War, 1941: A Study in Appearances and Realities.* New Haven, Conn.: Yale University Press, 1948. This, if not Tansill's (22:272), is the paradigmatic revisionist work on Roosevelt and the Pacific war. The thesis is that the president vitiated democracy and violated his own pledges when he "maneuvered" the nation into war.

22:262　Burtness, Paul S., and Ober, Warren U. "Secretary Stimson and the First Pearl Harbor Investigation." *Australian Journal of Politics and History* 14:1 (1968), 24–36. This article reviews the activities of Stimson before, during, and after the Roberts Commission's hearings, and finds him influencing the outcome that minimized army responsibility.

22:263　Current, Richard N. "How Stimson Meant to 'Maneuver' the Japanese." *Mississippi Valley Historical Review* 40:1 (1953), 67–74. Stimson's troublesome November 25, 1941, diary entry ("the question was how we should maneuver them into the position of firing the first shot") is placed in the context of marshalling American support for resistance to Japanese moves in Southeast Asia.

22:264 Farago, Ladislas. *The Broken Seal: The Story of "Operation Magic" and the Pearl Harbor Disaster.* New York: Random House, 1967. The question of how a nation having rich intelligence sources could fail to anticipate its enemy's blow is confronted in this necessary if overdramatized account of American and Japanese code breaking operations between 1921 and 1941.

22:265 Ferrell, Robert H. "Pearl Harbor and the Revisionists." *Historian* 17:2 (1955), 215–33. This considered response to the revisionism as summarized in *Perpetual War for Perpetual Peace: A Critical Examination of the Foreign Policy of Franklin D. Roosevelt and Its Aftermath* (Caldwell, 1953), edited by Harry Elmer Barnes, concludes that military errors, while not matters of deliberate diplomatic planning, abounded at Pearl Harbor.

22:266 Kimmel, Husband E. *Admiral Kimmel's Story.* Chicago: Regnery, 1955. This self-exoneration, written in the vogue of revisionist literature, emphasizes the withholding of Magic intercepts from the area commanders by the administration.

22:267 McKechney, John. "The Pearl Harbor Controversy: A Debate among Historians." *Monumenta Nipponica* 18:1 (1963), 45–88. This author discovers a synthesis or eclecticism by portraying Roosevelt as one who, while not in any sense provoking Japan's attack, welcomed the opportunities it provided for silencing isolationist sentiment.

22:268 Melosi, Martin V. "National Security Misused: The Aftermath of Pearl Harbor." *Prologue* 9:2 (1977), 75–89. To preserve national security, especially intelligence operations, the administration attempted to end growing public interest in the bombing of Pearl Harbor by casting all blame upon the military commanders on the scene.

22:269 Melosi, Martin V. *The Shadow of Pearl Harbor: Political Controversy over the Surprise Attack, 1941–1946.* College Station: Texas A&M University Press, 1977. This study analyzes the domestic political repercussions of the Pearl Harbor attack during and immediately after World War II. The issue became the focus of excessive partisanship by both parties, and that the Democratic administration attempted a "mutated cover-up." Bibliography.

22:270 Morgenstern, George. *Pearl Harbor: The Story of the Secret War.* New York: Devin-Adair, 1947. This is an early major critique of the congressional investigation.

22:271 Richardson, James O., with Dyer, George C. *On the Treadmill to Pearl Harbor.* Washington, D.C.: G.P.O., 1973. Of overriding interest in the memoir is Admiral Richardson's argument that the fleet, for practical rather than strategic reasons, should be retained on the Pacific Coast rather than deployed to Pearl Harbor.

22:272 Tansill, Charles C. *Back Door to War: The Roosevelt Foreign Policy, 1933–1941.* Chicago: Regnery, 1952. Tansill, in a work second only to Beard's (22:261) as the classic example of revisionist, antiadministration accounts of America's entry into World War II, claims intervention served to cloak domestic political failures.

22:273 Theobald, Robert A. *The Final Secret of Pearl Harbor: The Washington Contribution to the Japanese Attack.* New York: Devin-Adair, 1954. This memoir of a senior officer at Pearl Harbor is significant as a revisionist source. It emphasizes Washington's failure to disclose to area commanders the hardening of its relations with Japan.

22:274 Wohlstetter, Roberta. *Pearl Harbor: Warning and Decision.* Stanford, Calif.: Stanford University Press, 1962. This prize-winning examination of the American failure to predict the Pearl Harbor attack emphasizes the limits of intelligence operations in terms of perception and communication. This work remains a definitive study on the limits of intelligence operations at Pearl Harbor and in general. Bibliography.

23

Wartime Diplomacy, 1941-1945

Contributing Editor

Forrest C. Pogue
Eisenhower Institute,
Smithsonian Institution

Contributors

James R. Leutze
University of North Carolina,
Chapel Hill

Mark M. Lowenthal
Library of Congress

Mark A. Stoler
University of Vermont

Contents

Introduction

Before the United States entered the war, President Roosevelt and many Americans favored an Allied victory over the Axis. We had given aid to China, Great Britain, and the Soviet Union, and had informally assured the British that if we became involved in war on the side of Britain on two fronts, we would follow a Europe-first strategy. Japan's attack stirred demands for a greater effort in the Pacific, but in a meeting between Roosevelt and Churchill and their advisers in Washington in late December 1941 and early January 1942, the United States reaffirmed the Europe-first strategy and accepted in the main the British strategic outline for conducting the coalition war.

Aside from the Europe-first commitment and the general principles of the Atlantic Charter issued after the Argentina Conference in 1941, there were no detailed provisions agreed on for a final peace treaty with members of the Axis. As the war progressed, the formula of unconditional surrender was set forth, plans for partition of Germany surfaced, and matters such as the levying of reparations were discussed. Much was left to be decided in the postwar period.

Pressure from commanders in the Pacific and from American opinion to step up the war against Japan increased the American desire to win the war in Europe as quickly as possible. For the military services, this meant a direct approach to the Continent rather uhan the peripheral strategy proposed by the British. In addition, surviving America-first feeling opposed any move to the eastern Mediterranean that would not serve basic American interests. A reluctance to get involved in the French factional fights led Roosevelt to shun recognition of General de Gaulle's French Committee. The belief that Soviet military assistance would be needed for the final defeat of Japan to reduce American casualties led the United States to avoid actions that appeared to challenge the Soviet Union in central Europe. In East Asia the president continued to favor a policy of building China into a great power, a policy with which neither Churchill nor Stalin agreed.

Early accounts on American policy and strategy in World War II appear in such books as Henry L. Stimson and McGeorge Bundy's *On Active Service* (23:72) and Robert Sherwood's *Roosevelt and Hopkins* (22:23). Chester Wilmot's *Struggle for Europe* (23:31) was one of the first strong statements questioning the U.S. strategy and policy in the war. Wilmot attacked American stress on a military rather than a political approach to the war, the insistence on unconditional surrender, the failure to favor a Balkan approach to counter Soviet advances in the Balkans and central Europe, and the failure to take Berlin and Prague. Shortly afterward, these views were backed by the various volumes of Churchill's memoirs (23:79) and by Sir Arthur Bryant's *The Turn of the Tide* (23:121) and *Triumph in the West* (23:122), based on the wartime diaries of Field Marshal Alan Brooke, the wartime chief of the Imperial General Staff.

As many of the wartime documents were cleared for study, the American case was bolstered by Maurice Matloff's *Strategic Planning for Coalition Warfare, 1943–1945* (23:159) and Herbert Feis's *Churchill, Roosevelt, Stalin* (25:8). The views of Brooke's American opposite number are presented in Forrest C. Pogue's volumes on General Marshall, *Ordeal and Hope* (23:108), *Organizer of Victory* (23:109). John Ehrman in volumes 5 and 6 of the British official volumes *Grand Strategy* (23:153) well outlines the British positions for strategy in northwest Europe, while Michael Howard in volume 4 (23:153) of the same series gives a carefully balanced account on Mediterranean strategy.

The most extreme revisionist statement on U.S. policy during the war appeared in Gabriel Kolko's *The Politics of War: The World and United States Foreign Policy, 1943–1945* (25:19). The United States, Kolko declares, used its military and economic power to prepare the way for American postwar global expansion. Seeing the Soviet Union as its chief antagonist, the United States sought to throw much of the burden of the war on the Soviet Union and to deny that country fruits of its victory. By refusing to see that the Russians were concerned mainly to secure their borders against future aggression and to gain reparations to repair the losses of war, the United States took actions which were responsible for the cold war. A more balanced statement came later in John L. Gaddis's *The United States and the Origins of the Cold War, 1941– 1947,* (25:16). A more recent volume, *Franklin D. Roosevelt and American Foreign Policy, 1932–1945* (21:51), by Robert Dallek, presents a comprehensive study and defense of Roosevelt's views.

General Douglas MacArthur in his *Reminiscences* (40:55), seconded by books by members of his staff and close admirers, attacked the policies of the president, the Joint Chiefs of Staff, the American navy, and Great Britain for failing to concentrate on winning the war in the Pacific first. Contrary arguments may be found in Louis Morton's *Strategy and Command: The First Two Years* (23:185) and in volume 2 of D. Clayton James's *The Years of MacArthur* (23:107).

The claims of General Joseph Stilwell in his diaries that Chiang Kai-shek was more interested in strengthening the hold of the Nationalist government than in defeating the Japanese has been supported in detail in the studies by Charles Romanus and Riley Sunderland, *Stilwell's Mission to China* (23:195), and *Stilwell's Command Problems* (23:194). Volume 1 of Tang Tsou's *America's Failure in China* (27:67) contains criticisms of Chiang Kai-shek's weaknesses and the United States' mistake in allowing him to believe that he would receive military and financial backing even if he did not reform his regime.

The various volumes of the U.S. Foreign Relations series dealing with the great conferences at Washington, Casablanca, Quebec, Cairo and Teheran, Yalta and Potsdam reflect the developments of American strategy and policy in political and military deliberations (see Chapter 25). The other Allies have not approached the United States in the number of documents published dealing with policy, although Britain has now opened papers for the World War II period at the Public Record Office and has printed a five-volume history, *History of the Second World War: British Foreign Policy in the Second World War,* by Sir L. Woodward (23:40).

Excellent biographies exist or are in progress on many of the key political and military figures of the war. A biography is lacking on Lord Portal, one of the ablest leaders of the war. More authoritative volumes are needed on Eden, Attlee, Mountbatten, Ismay, Lord Wilson of Libya, Air Marshal Harris, and Admiral Leahy. Books are in preparation on Arnold, Bradley, Devers, and Clark.

Despite excellent studies on aid to de Gaulle and the problems of cooperation with the French factions, a complete overall volume on U.S. relations with the French during the war is still lacking. Although infor-

mative studies have been made on unconditional surrender, the so-called Balkan strategy, the decision of the Americans to stop at the Elbe, more study is needed in German documents to see if a different course would have changed the political situation. Authoritative studies of many of these questions await the opening of Soviet archives.

Some questions deserve more exhaustive study than they have received: Would a stronger effort in northeast Italy in the summer and fall of 1944 have changed the balance of power in central Europe and the Balkans? Would concentration of U.S. efforts in the Pacific in 1942 and 1943 have shortened the war and forestalled Soviet gains in East Asia? Would the adoption of a more aggressive policy toward the Soviet Union by the fall of 1944 have changed the course of postwar history?

Resources and Overviews

RESEARCH AIDS

While pertinent bibliographies and reference aids are listed here, there are more extensive lists in Chapter 1.

Bibliographies

23:1 Barnard, Roy; Burns, William; and Ryan, Duane. *The Era of World War II: General and Reference Works. Biography.* Carlisle Barracks, Pa.: U.S. Military History Institute, 1977. This reference aid contains 21 pages on general works, 10 pages on reference, 152 pages on biography and personal accounts.

Bayliss, G. *Bibliographical Guide to the Two World Wars: An Annotated Survey of English-Language Reference Materials* (19:2) annotates listed reference works.

23:2 Bloomberg, Marty, and Weber, Hans H. *World War II and Its Origins: A Selected Annotated Bibliography of Books in English.* Littleton, Colo.: Libraries Unlimited, 1975. This annotated bibliography of books is a most valuable guide for diplomatic historians. It actually begins with the 1920s and 1930s, and emphasizes the political dimension.

Cronon, E. D., and Rosenof, T. D., comps. *The Second World War and the Atomic Age, 1940–1973* (24:1) lists diplomatic, military, political, economic, and social materials.

Dexter, B., ed. *The Foreign Affairs Fifty-Year Bibliography: New Evaluation of Significant Books on International Relations, 1920–1970* (1:14) contains excellent evaluations of books on international relations. There are 40 pages on World War II generally, but one should also consult sections on Europe, the western hemisphere, the Middle East, and Asia and the Pacific for the war period.

23:3 Enser, A. G. S. *A Subject Bibliography of the Second World War: Books in English, 1939–1974.* Boulder, Colo.: Westview, 1972. This is a useful, but curiously arranged, list of books on World War II.

Foreign Affairs Bibliography: A Selected and Annotated List of Books on International Relations (1:15) is issued at ten-year intervals, and each volume has three parts: "General International Relations"; "The World since 1914"; and "The World by Regions." Useful aid.

23:4 Funk, Arthur L., et al. *A Select Bibliography of Books on the Second World War.* 2d ed. San Francisco: American Committee on the History of the Second World War, 1975. This bibliography on books on World War II is issued periodically. See the committee's quarterly newsletter.

Higham, R., ed. *A Guide to the Sources of British Military History* (1:46) contains at least four chapters (pp. 470–566) bearing on the military-diplomatic history of World War II.

Higham, R., ed. *A Guide to the Sources of United States Military History* (1:47) contains at least three chapters of interest: R. W. Coakley's "The United States Army in World War II"; R. F. Futrell's "The U.S. Air Corps and the United States Air Force, 1909–1973"; and D. C. Allard's "The Navy, 1941–1973."

23:5 Higham, Robin, ed. *Official Histories: Essays and Bibliographies from All Over the World.* Manhattan: Kansas State University Library, 1970. This country-by-country survey covering both world wars

is uneven, but it does introduce most of the important national series.

23:6 International Commission for the Teaching of History. *The Two World Wars: Selective Bibliography.* Oxford: Pergamon, 1964. This dated bibliography (in French and English) has three parts: "World War I"; "Origins of World War II"; and "World War II." The section on World War II, by Henri Michel and Jean-Marie d'Hoop has been brought up to 1975 in Michel's *The Second World War* (23:30).

Lewis, J. R. *Uncertain Judgment: A Bibliography of War Crimes Trials* (1:39) has the most recent list of references regarding the Nuremberg trials, together with other German war crimes trials, and the International Military Tribunal, Far East.

23:7 Messick, Frederic M. "Spanish Neutrality in World War II: A Select Bibliography of Published Materials." *Iberian Studies* 6:1 (1977), 17–23. This essay lists important published materials relating to Spain's neutrality during World War II.

Miller, S. D., comp. *An Aerospace Bibliography* (1:50) deals with World War II (pp. 42–68), with the major emphasis on military and technical affairs.

23:8 Smith, Myron J., Jr. *World War II at Sea: A Bibliography of Sources in English.* 3 vols. Metuchen, N.J.: Scarecrow, 1976. This three-volume set (volume 3 is in two parts) provides comprehensive coverage of the sea forces of all nations engaged in World War II. The approximately 10,500 entries cover materials published between 1939 and December 1973—books, essays, documents, dissertations, etc.

Stewart, W. J., ed. *The Era of Franklin D. Roosevelt: A Selected Bibliography of Periodical, Essay, and Dissertation Literature, 1945–1971* (20:2).

23:9 Ziegler, Janet, ed. *World War II: Books in English, 1945–1965.* Stanford, Calif.: Hoover Institution Press, 1971. This extensive list of books on the war at all levels still is of considerable value. It also has a valuable introduction on bibliographies of foreign sources. Ziegler has updated part of this collection in Funk et al. (23:4).

Historiographical Essays

See Chapter 22 for essays on the origins of the European and Pacific wars.

Ikuhiko, H. "Japanese Historical Writing on the Origins and Progress of the Pacific War." (22:3).

23:10 Jacobsen, Hans-Adolf. *Konzeption einer Geschichte des Zweiten Weltkrieges, 1939–1945* [A historical conception of World War II, 1939–1945]. Frankfurt: Droeste, 1964. This extended essay discusses methods of treating the history of World War II, and contains an extensive bibliography and a description of selected archives.

23:11 Morton, Louis. *Writings on World War II.* Service Center for Teachers of History, no. 66. Washington, D.C.: American Historical Association, 1967. This pamphlet contains a long bibliographical essay analyzing interpretations and significant writings on World War II, and a selected bibliography. Both the essay and the bibliography are divided by topic, and remain quite valuable. They should be supplemented, however, with Morton's "World War II: A Survey of Recent Writings," *American Historical Review* 75 (Dec. 1970), 1987–2008.

23:12 Neumann, William L. "Allied Diplomacy in World War II: A Bibliographical Survey." *U.S. Naval Institute Proceedings* 81:7 (1955), 829–34. This essay offers an early appraisal of the emerging historical controversies on the issues involved as well as a solid review of the documents, memoirs, and histories then available.

Other Research Aids

23:13 Baudot, Marcel, et al., eds. *The Historical Encyclopedia of World War II.* New York: Facts on File, 1980. This volume offers a lengthy introduction suggesting the causes of the war; a chronology of events, from 1931 to 1947; and a concluding essay which seeks to describe the immediate and long-term effects of the war. Charts and maps.

23:14 *Revue d'Histoire de la Deuxième Guerre Mondiale.* Paris: Presses Universitaires de France, 1950– . A quarterly publication in French with the fourth issue being a monograph on a special subject; each issue contains book reviews and a lengthy bibliography of current publications.

Guides to Documents

Great Britain. Public Record Office. *The Second World War: A Guide to Documents in the Public* *Records Office* (25:6) consists largely of lists of documents and brief summaries of the wartime responsibilities of various ministries. An invaluable aid for those beginning work in the British archives.

23:15 O'Neill, James E., and Krauskopf, Robert W., eds. *World War II: An Account of Its Documents.* Washington, D.C.: Howard University Press, 1976. In addition to papers by American historians and archivists about collections in the United States, reports on documents in Great Britain, France, and the Soviet Union are provided by representatives of these countries.

23:16 U.S. National Archives and Records Service. General Services Administration. *Federal Records of World War II.* 2 vols. Washington, D.C.: G.P.O., 1950–1951. This was the initial effort to describe the archival materials created by civilian and military agencies during World War II. Volume 1 contains 54 pages on the Department of State (691–745), while volume 2 deals with military agencies.

Document Collections

More general collections are listed in Chapter 2, and other collections may be found in "Personalities," below.

Official Collections

Documents relating to the wartime conferences are listed below, "Summit Meetings," and in Chapter 25, "Wartime Conferences"; for guides to World War II archives, see Chapter 1.

23:17 "Intercepted Japanese Messages: The Documents of MAGIC, 1938–1945." Microfilm. Wilmington, Del.: Glazier, n.d. These 15 rolls of microfilm contain the daily intelligence summaries, prepared by U.S. Army cryptanalysts, from radio traffic between the Tokyo foreign office and Japanese officials in Berlin, Rome, Moscow, and elsewhere. The summaries from Berlin (Baron Oshima) provided valuable information regarding Hitler's European intentions.

International Military Tribunal. *Trial of the Major War Criminals before the International Military Tribunal, Nuremberg, 14 November 1945–1 October 1946* (28:90) contains many documents which relate to political and strategic issues.

International Military Tribunal for the Far East. *Record of the Proceedings* (27:12) has many documents relating to political and diplomatic issues.

23:18 "The Ultra Documents." Microfilm. New York: Clearwater, 1979. The British Public Record Office has assembled some 52,000 documents, extracted from the main series of military signals, which have been microfilmed on 104 reels.

23:19 U.S.S.R. Ministry of Foreign Affairs. *Correspondence between the Chairman of the Council of Ministers of the U.S.S.R. and the Presidents of the U.S.A. and the Prime Ministers of Great Britain during the Great Patriotic War of 1941–1945.* 2 vols. Moscow: Foreign Languages Publishing House, 1957. This collection claims to be Stalin's complete and unedited correspondence with Roosevelt, Churchill, Truman and Attlee. Differences will be found between some messages in these volumes and versions published elsewhere. It includes only messages sent.

U.S. Congress. Joint Committee on the Investigation of the Pearl Harbor Attack. Report; *Investigation of the Pearl Harbor Attack* (22:9) is a massive collection—eleven volumes of congressional hearings, nine volumes of documentary exhibits, and seventeen volumes of prior investigations and hearings on the Pearl Harbor attack.

U.S. Department of State. *Documents on German Foreign Policy, 1918–1945* (21:9).

U.S. Department of State. *Foreign Relations of the United States* (1:358) includes several valuable volumes for the years 1941 to 1945.

23:20 U.S. Senate. Committee on Foreign Relations. *A Decade of American Foreign Policy: Basic Documents, 1941–1949.* Sen. Doc. 123. 81st Cong. 1st Sess., 1959. This collection of 313 items reproduces public documents, treaties, reports, etc., that deal with the interallied negotiations.

23:21 *War in Asia and the Pacific, 1937–1949: Japanese and Chinese Studies and Documents.* 15 vols. Ed. by Donald S. Detwiler and Charles B. Burdick. New York: Garland, 1979–1980. The volumes contain 66 contemporary documents reproduced in facsimile from a large number of studies located at the army's Center for Military History, the Library of Congress, or the National Archives.

23:22 *World War II German Military Studies.* Ed. by Donald S. Detwiler, Charles B. Burdick, and Juergen Rohwer. 24 vols. New York: Garland, 1977–1978. These facsimile reproductions include 213 special reports prepared for the U.S. Army by former officers of the Wehrmacht.

Unofficial Collections

23:23 Buchanan, A. Russell, ed. *The United States and World War II: Military and Diplomatic Documents.* Columbia: University of South Carolina Press, 1972. This is an uneven collection of documents, intended to give the reader a taste of diplomatic cable traffic, war planning, policy planning, and combat accounts.

23:24 Jacobsen, Hans-Adolf, and Smith, Arthur L., Jr., eds. *World War II: Policy and Strategy: Selected Documents with Commentary.* Santa Barbara, Calif.: ABC-Clio, 1979. These well-organized documents reveal the growing momentum of Mussolini's rise and his inevitable eclipse by Adolf Hitler, the formation of the Axis triumvirate, Japan's entrance into the war, and the ultimate Allied victory. Chronology, index.

23:25 Langsam, Walter C., ed. *Historic Documents of World War II.* Princeton, N.J.: Van Nostrand, 1958. This is a useful collection of 47 military and political documents from 1938 and 1955. Each document is preceded by a short paragraph placing it in historical context.

Lebra, J. C., ed. *Japan's Greater East Asia Co-Prosperity Sphere in World War II: Selected Readings and Documents* (22:214).

23:26 Wilson, Theodore A., ed. *WW 2: Readings on Critical Issues.* New York: Scribner's, 1974. This collection provides an excellent introduction to the variety of primary and secondary material available on World War II. Topics covered include causes and legacies of the war, grand strategy, wartime diplomacy, strategic bombing, total war, and war crimes.

OVERVIEWS

23:27 Calvocoressi, Peter, and Wint, Guy. *Total War: The Story of World War II.* New York: Pantheon, 1972. This is an excellent general background of World War II, its strategy and operations, and with thoughtful considerations of its meaning for the future. Bibliography.

23:28 Divine, Robert A., ed. *Causes and Consequences of World War II.* Chicago: Quadrangle, 1969. This collection of excerpts from secondary works covers numerous historical controversies associated with U.S. entry into World War II, wartime diplomacy, and diplomatic consequences of the war. Extensive historiographical essay.

23:29 Howe, Quincy. *Ashes of Victory: World War II and Its Aftermath.* New York: Simon & Schuster, 1972. Howe set himself the task of describing and appraising the events of the war years and of showing "the War's continuing impact on the world we live in." Bibliography.

23:30 Michel, Henri. *The Second World War.* Trans. by Douglas Parmei. 2 vols. New York: Praeger, 1975. This general history of World War II gives special attention to German occupation and national resistance movements, and emphasizes global strategy and diplomatic planning. Extensive bibliography.

23:31 Wilmot, Chester. *The Struggle for Europe.* New York: Harper, 1952. This early military and diplomatic history of the war in Europe is sharply critical of Roosevelt and his advisers for naively subordinating political ends to military means during World War II, and for thereby making inevitable the extension of Soviet power. Bibliography.

23:32 Wright, Gordon. *The Ordeal of Total War, 1939–1945.* New York: Harper & Row, 1968. This volume is a brilliant analysis of the history and impact of World War II in Europe. The author emphasizes the economic, psychological, scientific and cultural, as well as the more traditional military, political, and diplomatic aspects of the war. Extensive bibliography.

Diplomatic and Political Dimensions

See Chapter 22 for references on the origins of the European and Pacific wars.

Beitzell, R. *Uneasy Alliance: America, Britain and Russia, 1941–1943* (25:7) emphasizes the disputes and compromises that developed in Allied relations.

Chamberlin, W. H. *America's Second Crusade* (25:15) is an interpretative history that covers U.S. entry into, as well as diplomacy during, World War II. It accuses Roosevelt of manipulating the United States into a needless war and of appeasing Stalin.

23:33 Darilek, Richard E. *A Loyal Opposition in Time of War: The Republican Party and the Politics of Foreign Policy from Pearl Harbor to Yalta.* Westport, Conn.: Greenwood, 1976. This volume analyzes the origins and evolution of Republican party attitudes toward foreign policy during World War II. It finds the Republican "loyal opposition" and bipartisan approach part of a strategy designed to maintain party unity, rather than part of any "conversion" in foreign policy beliefs. Bibliography.

Duroselle, J.-B. *From Wilson to Roosevelt: Foreign Policy of the United States, 1913–1945* (19:20).

Feis, H. *Churchill, Roosevelt, Stalin: The War They Waged and the Peace They Sought* (25:8) traces the history of the Grand Alliance through the big three leaders. It remains one of the most comprehensive and detailed histories of Allied wartime diplomacy.

23:34 Hachey, Thomas E. "American Profiles on Capitol Hill: A Confidential Study for the British Foreign Office in 1943." *Wisconsin Magazine of History* 57:2 (1973/1974), 141–53. This is a reproduction of, and commentary on, an April 1943 memorandum written by Isaiah Berlin of the British embassy in Washington, concerning the Senate Foreign Relations Committee and the House Foreign Affairs Committee. It analyzes the beliefs and personalities of each Senate and Congress member.

Kolko, G. *The Politics of War: The World and United States Foreign Policy, 1943–1945* (25:19) is the most comprehensive, detailed, and controversial of the New Left reinterpretations of U.S. World War II diplomacy.

23:35 Leonard, Thomas M. "The United States and World War II: Conflicting Views of American Diplomacy." *Towson State Journal of International Affairs* 7:1 (1972), 25–30. This brief historiographical essay identifies four interpretations of U.S. diplomacy during World War II, and discusses one representative work for each school.

23:36 McNeill, William H. *American, Britain and Russia: Their Cooperation and Conflict, 1941–1946.*

New York: Oxford University Press, 1953. This pioneering work is in many ways still the best general history of the Grand Alliance. Placing that alliance in the broad context of world history, McNeill explains the conflicting aims, methods, and world views of each member which, while successfully compromised during the war, ultimately led to dissolution.

23:37 Misse, Frederick B. "Roosevelt et le Département d'État" [Roosevelt and the Department of State]. *Revue d'Histoire de la Deuxième Guerre Mondiale* 82:1 (1971), 1–26. The inconsequential role assigned the State Department in World War II is attributed to attitudes which FDR developed in years before the war.

Neumann, W. L. *After Victory: Churchill, Roosevelt, Stalin and the Making of the Peace* (25:11).

Robertson, W. R. *Tito, Mihailovic and the Allies, 1941–45* (23:251) finds Allied political interest in Yugoslavia largely unfocused until near the end of the war.

Rostow, W. W. *The United States in the World Arena: An Essay in Recent History* (24:48).

23:38 Smith, Gaddis. *American Diplomacy during the Second World War, 1941–1945.* New York: Wiley, 1965. A thoughtful early sketch of wartime diplomacy and some of the main problems confronted by American leaders. A useful corrective to some more recent studies that work backward from the cold war to find motives of which wartime participants were not aware.

23:39 Snell, John L. *Illusion and Necessity: The Diplomacy of Global War, 1939–1945.* Boston: Houghton Mifflin, 1963. This is an excellent traditional attempt to give a compact and well-rounded overview of global diplomacy between the outbreak and close of World War II. Bibliography.

Ulam, A. B. *Expansion and Coexistence: Soviet Foreign Policy, 1917–1973* (2:254).

23:40 Woodward, Sir Llewellyn. *History of the Second World War: British Foreign Policy in the Second World War.* 5 vols. London: H.M.S.O., 1970–1976. These volumes are a straightforward, chronologically ordered narration of British foreign policy (1939–1945) as conducted by the Foreign Office. Woodward selected his evidence mainly from the Foreign Office papers and even with the opening of the Foreign Office records, this is an invaluable work. Although it rigorously avoids criticism of British policy, this work is a starting point for research in the British records concerning Anglo-American relations and postwar planning.

Refugees/Holocaust Issues

See also Chapter 21, "Persecution of Jews" and Chapter 22, "U.S., Germany, and War Refugees."

23:41 Adler, Selig. "The United States and the Holocaust." *American Jewish Historical Quarterly* 64:1 (1974), 14–23. The U.S. government did less to mitigate the catastrophe that befell European Jews than it could have because: 1) Washington initially made incorrect assumptions concerning the extent of the holocaust; 2) possible measures had a low priority on the war timetable; and 3) measures taken came too late to save many victims.

Feingold, H. L. *The Politics of Rescue: The Roosevelt Administration and the Holocaust, 1938–1945* (22:128).

23:42 Mashberg, Michael. "Documents Concerning the American State Department and the Stateless European Jews, 1942–1944." *Jewish Social Studies* 39:1/2 (1977), 163–82. A collection of documents from the papers of Secretary of the Treasury Morgenthau shows Treasury's efforts to bring to the president's attention the State Department's negation of tangible efforts to rescue European Jewry.

23:43 Morse, Arthur D. *While Six Million Died: A Chronicle of American Apathy.* New York: Random House, 1968. This is a journalist's indictment of U.S. and British bureaucratic lethargy toward the so-called Jewish problem.

23:44 Szajkowski, Zosa. "Relief for German Jewry: Problems of American Involvement." *American Jewish Historical Quarterly* 62:2 (1972), 111–45. This essay illustrates Jewish disunity (Zionist versus anti-Zionist philosophies) and governmental foot-dragging, which together made consistent, massive assistance impossible.

23:45 Willson, John P. "Carlton J. H. Hayes, Spain, and the Refugee Crisis, 1942–1945." *American Jewish Historical Quarterly* 62:2 (1972), 99–110. Willson describes the efforts of Hayes, wartime U.S. ambassador to Spain, to organize and expedite relief efforts for Jewish refugees moving through Spain, and analyzes his conflict with the U.S. War Refugee Board.

Military Dimensions

23:46 Fuller, J. F. C. *The Second World War, 1939–1945*. London: Eyre & Spottiswoode, 1948. Fuller is bitterly critical of Allied leaders, especially Churchill, for the political and moral bankruptcy he believes inherent in their waging of total war without any limitations or consideration to real political objectives. Fuller's distrust of civilian leadership and near sympathy for a nonmaterialistic fascistic philosophy taints many valuable judgments.

23:47 Hoyle, Martha Byrd. *A World in Flames*. New York: Atheneum, 1970. A straightforward narrative, given a chronological treatment so as to blend activities in various theaters, this combat narrative is designed to be the framework for further reading and research. Bibliography.

23:48 Liddell Hart, Basil H. *History of the Second World War*. New York: Putnam's, 1970. The author emphasizes British and Anglo-American operations, and supports British strategic concepts and criticisms of American wartime ideas and decisions. Although primarily concerned with military affairs, the work includes diplomatic-strategic issues. Bibliography.

23:49 MacDonald, Charles B. *The Mighty Endeavor: American Armed Forces in the European Theater in World War II*. New York: Oxford University Press, 1969. This is a highly readable general work on American forces in Europe in World War II by an official army historian of the war. Bibliography.

23:50 Parkinson, Roger. *Blood, Toil, Tears and Sweat*. New York: McKay, 1973. The second volume of a narrative history based on the British War Cabinet papers and further fleshed out with diaries and official histories, it is useful on how Britain organized for and dealt with the war, and how the war was perceived in London. Bibliography.

23:51 Parkinson, Roger. *A Day's March Nearer Home*. New York: McKay, 1974. The third volume deals with the campaigns in Italy and Northern Europe. Bibliography.

Stacey, C. P. *Arms, Men and Governments* (36:57) is the fullest account on Canadian-American relations during World War II.

The Home Front

23:52 Blum, John. *V Was for Victory: Politics and Culture during World War II*. New York: Harcourt Brace Jovanovich, 1976. Blum provides a most useful analysis of factors affecting domestic life during the war.

Divine, R. A. *Foreign Policy and U.S. Presidential Elections, 1940–1960* (2:141).

Flynn, G. Q. *Roosevelt and Romanism: Catholics and American Diplomacy, 1937–1945* (22:81).

23:53 Lingeman, Richard R. *Don't You Know There's a War On? The American Home Front, 1941–1945*. New York: Putnam's, 1970. Lingeman recounts the frustrations at home emerging from social, economic, and political events. Bibliography.

23:54 Myer, Dillon S. *Uprooted Americans: The Japanese Americans and the War Relocation Authority during World War II*. Tucson: University of Arizona Press, 1971. This is one of several accounts about the internment of Japanese Americans who were caught between public hysteria and political expediency. Bibliography.

Orser, E. W. "World War II and the Pacifist Controversy in the Major Protestant Churches" (22:86) shows that pacifists had trouble defining their role during the war. Orser also suggests the pacifists' wartime role has been neglected by historians.

23:55 Polenberg, Richard. *War and Society: The United States, 1941–1945*. Philadelphia: Lippincott, 1972. This study delineates the changes that took place in American society. It focuses on the modernization and concentration of agriculture, industry, and government. Bibliography.

23:56 Ross, Davis R. *Preparing for Ulysses: Politics and Veterans during World War II*. New York: Columbia University Press, 1969. Ross analyzes the origins, enactment, and implementation of legislation (GI bill) designed to ease the burdens of the returning veterans. Bibliography.

Personalities

Additional references on individuals may be found in Chapter 1, "Biographical Data."

POLITICAL

American

Also see Chapters 22 and 25 for additional references, especially see "Others."

James F. Byrnes
See Chapter 24, "Personalities," for additional references.

Byrnes, J. F. *All in One Lifetime* (24:100).

W. Averell Harriman
See Chapters 24 and 25, "Personalities," for additional references.

Harriman, W. A., and Abel, E. *Special Envoy to Churchill and Stalin, 1941–1946* (25:28) describes Harriman's service as Roosevelt's special emissary to Churchill and Stalin (1941–1943), and as ambassador to the Soviet Union (1943–1946). Harriman's intimate knowledge of the Allied leaders, and of the major wartime conferences and issues, is clearly revealed in these memoirs.

Carlton J. H. Hayes
23:57 Halstead, Charles R. "Historians in Politics: Carlton J. H. Hayes as an American Ambassador to Spain, 1942–45." *Journal of Contemporary History* 10:3 (1975), 383–405. Hayes, an eminent historian, was instructed to keep Spain from allying with the Axis powers, to dissuade Spanish authorities from cooperating with the enemy against the Allies and to try to obtain facilities for the American war effort.

23:58 Hayes, Carlton J. H. *Wartime Mission in Spain, 1942–45*. New York: Macmillan, 1945. Hayes stresses the nonbelligerency status of Spain and notes that Franco moved in the direction of benevolent neutrality toward the United States before the Allies had made significant gains in northwest Europe.

Willson, J. P. "Carlton J. H. Hayes, Spain, and the Refugee Crisis, 1942–1945" (23:45).

Harry Hopkins
23:59 Adams, Henry H. *Harry Hopkins*. New York: Putnam's, 1977. Drawing on memoirs which have appeared since Sherwood's account and on collections of papers opened in recent years, Adams gives us a more complete picture of Hopkins's personal contribution to the winning of the war than has hitherto appeared.

Sherwood, R. E. *Roosevelt and Hopkins: An Intimate History* (22:23) is a highly sympathetic dual biography which provides a detailed history of U.S. wartime diplomacy as seen through the personalities of the president and his closest adviser. It remains valuable for its insights into key individuals, and for its reproduction of a large number of high-level wartime letters, memoranda, and documents.

Cordell Hull
See Chapters 21 and 22, "Personalities," for additional references.

Hull, C. *Memoirs* (21:36) discusses his foreign policy decisions especially concerning Vichy, Franco's Spain, and Latin America. While Roosevelt made most of the war policy decisions without Hull's advice, this book is an essential aid to understanding America's wartime foreign policy.

Pratt, J. W. *Cordell Hull, 1933–1944* (22:24) is useful for the careful tracing of the inner-workings of the Roosevelt cabinet and Hull's maneuvers therein as he worked with and against other cabinet officers and subordinates. There are corrections of some of Hull's lapses of memory in his own memoirs.

Patrick J. Hurley
23:60 Buhite, Russell D. *Patrick J. Hurley and American Foreign Policy*. Ithaca, N.Y.: Cornell University Press, 1973. A balanced work that notes Hurley's strong points but also spells out his failures as a diplomat. The author notes how Hurley made Chiang Kai-shek's case his own, his role in the recall of General Stilwell, and his confusing testimony before the congressional hearings on the Far Eastern crisis. Extensive bibliography.

23:61 Lohbeck, Don. *Patrick J. Hurley*. Chicago: Regnery, 1956. This authorized biography reflects the extremely unfriendly view of Stilwell that Hurley developed in the Far Eastern hearings. This volume, like Stilwell's, should be checked carefully against other sources.

Henry Morgenthau, Jr.

See Chapters 18, 19, 21, 22, "Personalities," for additional references.

23:62 Blum, John Morton. *From the Morgenthau Diaries.* Vol. 3: *Years of War, 1941–1945.* Boston: Houghton Mifflin, 1967. This account gives valuable material on administration policy in this period as seen by Secretary of Treasury Morgenthau, a close personal friend and neighbor of President Roosevelt, who relied heavily on the secretary for advice on many matters besides purely Treasury matters.

U.S. Senate. Committee on the Judiciary. Report; *Morgenthau Diary (China)* (22:30).

Franklin D. Roosevelt

See Chapters 20, 21, 22, and 25, "Personalities," for additional references.

23:63 Burns, James MacGregor. *Roosevelt: The Soldier of Freedom, 1940–1945.* New York: Harcourt Brace Jovanovich, 1970. In this second volume, as in the first (21:50), the central theme is the gap between Roosevelt as the courageous lion in the realm of ideas and as the cautious and wily fox in the realm of implementation. FDR's refusal to match ends and means led to serious negative repercussions. Bibliography.

Dallek, R. *Franklin D. Roosevelt and American Foreign Policy, 1932–1945* (21:51) is the most comprehensive study of Roosevelt's diplomacy and the ablest defense of his policies. Dallek emphasizes the constraints under which Roosevelt was forced to work and overall finds his policies fully justified.

23:64 Dallek, Robert. "Franklin Roosevelt as World Leader: A Review Article." *American Historical Review* 76:5 (1971), 1503–13. This assessment uses James MacGregor Burns's *Roosevelt: The Soldier of Freedom* (23:63) and Henry Feingold's *The Politics of Rescue: The Roosevelt Administration and the Holocaust, 1938–1945* (22:128) as backdrops to examine the evolution of American scholarship of FDR as a foreign policy leader since the revisionist and "court" histories of the 1940s and 1950s.

23:65 Divine, Robert A. *Roosevelt and World War II.* Baltimore: Johns Hopkins Press, 1969. This major reinterpretation of Roosevelt's World War II diplomacy challenges the traditional interpretation of Roosevelt as an idealistic internationalist, and emphasizes instead the isolationism, pragmatism, and realism which characterized his foreign policies from 1933 through 1945.

23:66 Emerson, William. "Franklin D. Roosevelt as Commander-in-Chief in World War II." *Military Affairs* 22:4 (1958), 181–207. This reassessment of Roosevelt as military leader argues that he was very sensitive to the political aspects of war, that he controlled his military advisers rather than vice versa, and that he planned wartime strategy on the basis of political, albeit negative, motives.

Jonas, M.; Langley, H. D.; and Loewenheim, F. L., eds. *Roosevelt and Churchill: Their Secret Wartime Correspondence* (25:30).

23:67 Kimball, Warren F., ed. *Franklin D. Roosevelt and the World Crisis, 1937–1945.* Lexington, Mass.: Heath, 1973. A collection of articles, essays, and excerpts offering varying interpretations of Roosevelt's foreign policy leadership (1937–1945), with selections concentrating on Roosevelt himself, his goals and methods. The introduction summarizes the major schools of thought and interpretations of Roosevelt. Bibliography.

23:68 Kimball, Warren F. "Churchill and Roosevelt: The Personal Equation." *Prologue* 6:3 (1974), 169–82. Kimball reviews the personal correspondence between President Roosevelt and Prime Minister Churchill. Their relations were generally amicable, but the few disagreements were of a fundamental nature.

23:69 Matloff, Maurice. "Franklin Delano Roosevelt as War Leader." In Harry L. Coles, ed., *Total War and Cold War: Problems in Civilian Control of the Military.* Columbus: Ohio State University Press, 1962, pp. 42–65. This essay offers a balanced assessment which justifies most of Roosevelt's policies, most notably unconditional surrender, but which criticizes the president for holding rigidly to policies after they had outlived their usefulness, for underestimating Soviet ambitions, and for ignoring the postwar repercussions of wartime military actions.

Roosevelt, E. and Lash, J. P., eds. *F.D.R.: His Personal Letters, 1928–1945* (22:35) is a valuable early selection of Roosevelt's personal correspondence with excellent explanatory notes. Volume 2 covers the war years.

Sherwood, R. E. *Roosevelt and Hopkins: An Intimate History* (22:23) is actually the classic, contemporary portrait of Roosevelt's wartime ideas and policies.

23:70 Taylor, Myron C. *Wartime Correspondence between President Roosevelt and Pope Pius XII.* New York: Macmillan, 1947. The notes by Taylor, President Roosevelt's personal representative to the Vatican, often tell more than the letters. Most interesting is his effort to convince the Pope that the Russians were weakening in their opposition to religious freedom.

Warner, G. "From Tehran to Yalta: Reflections on FDR's Foreign Policy" (25:35).

John S. Service

See also Chapter 27, "Personalities."

23:71 Service, John S. *Lost Chance in China: The World War II Despatches of John S. Service.* Ed. by Joseph W. Esherick. New York: Random House, 1974. While these selected dispatches (1941–1945) by Service from China do not replace the official files, they give a useful compendium.

Edward R. Stettinius, Jr.

See Chapter 25, "Personalities," for additional references.

Stettinius, E. R., Jr. *The Diaries of Edward R. Stettinius, Jr., 1943–1946* (24:150) is valuable on the Dumbarton Oaks Conference, the Yalta Conference, the Mexico City Conference, and the San Francisco Conference, which launched the United Nations.

Stettinius, E. R., Jr. *Lend Lease: Weapon for Victory* (23:223).

Walker, R. L. "E. R. Stettinius, Jr." (24:151).

Henry L. Stimson

See also Chapters 20, 21, and 22, "Personalities."

Morison, E. E. *Turmoil and Tradition: The Life and Times of Henry L. Stimson* (21:58) covers Stimson's service as secretary of war from 1940 to 1945, but does not emphasize this aspect of Stimson's career. Less than 100 pages are devoted to the period of actual U.S. belligerency during World War II.

23:72 Stimson, Henry L., and Bundy, McGeorge. *On Active Service in Peace and War.* New York: Harper, 1949. This combination memoir and biography covers the years 1905 to 1945, with over half of the volume devoted to Stimson's experiences as secretary of war from 1940 to 1945. Diary excerpts provide an excellent, first-hand account of the War Department during these years, with special emphasis on wartime mobilization, grand strategy, postwar planning, and the atomic bomb decision.

Myron C. Taylor

23:73 Conway, John S. "Myron C. Taylor's Mission to the Vatican 1940–50." *Church History* 44:1 (1975), 85–99. The mission of Taylor, personal representative of Roosevelt and Truman to Pope Pius XII remains an anomaly in U.S. foreign relations. Since the United States maintained no formal mission to the Vatican, Taylor was the main link between the papacy and Washington.

23:74 Flynn, George Q. "Franklin Roosevelt and the Vatican: The Myron Taylor Appointment." *Catholic Historical Review* 58:2 (1972), 171–94. Roosevelt appointed Taylor as a special representative to the Vatican on December 24, 1939, culminating years of negotiating with leading American Catholics.

Taylor, M. C. *Wartime Correspondence between President Roosevelt and Pope Pius XII* (23:70).

Sumner Welles

See Chapter 22, "Personalities," for additional references.

Welles, S. *The Time for Decision* (22:39) was written in defense of Roosevelt's policies. Welles understates his own role in many of the more questionable initiatives, and belies the overall level of influence he had and the problems this caused with Hull.

Others

Bellush, B. *He Walked Alone: A Biography of John Gilbert Winant* (20:65) deals with Winant's experiences as wartime ambassador to Britain.

Bohlen, C. E. *Witness to History: 1929–1969* (24:98).

Forrestal, J. *The Forrestal Diaries* (26:46) consists of informal notes dictated by Forrestal while he was secretary of navy and secretary of defense (1944–1949), plus pertinent documents and memoranda.

Kennan, G. F. *Memoirs, 1925–1950* (24:124) covers his wartime service in Germany, Portugal, Britain, and Russia, and offers insights into such issues as the negotiations for American bases in the Azores, the work on the European Advisory Commission, and the lack of military-diplomatic coordination in U.S. policy.

23:75   Lee, Raymond E. *The London Journal of General Raymond E. Lee, 1940–1941.* Ed. by James Leutze. Boston: Little, Brown, 1971. Lee was U.S. military attaché in London during 1940 and 1941. His letters and journals offer a fascinating, first-hand account of Britain and of Anglo-American relations by a perceptive observer during a crucial period.

23:76   Long, Breckinridge. *The War Diary of Breckinridge Long: Selections from the Years, 1939–1944.* Ed. by Fred L. Israel. Lincoln: University of Nebraska Press, 1966. This edited diary provides a glimpse inside the Roosevelt administration. Long had special entree into two camps, the conservative southern Democratic group and the official State Department organization. Both had their differences with the president and his advisers, and in candidly recounting his views and reactions, Long makes a significant contribution.

23:77   Murphy, Robert D. *Diplomat among Warriors.* Garden City, N.Y.: Doubleday, 1964. As a representative of Roosevelt in North Africa (1942—1943), and political adviser to Eisenhower in the Mediterranean and northwest Europe, Murphy was involved in many momentous, sometimes controversial, events during World War II. It appears that Murphy's actions were based primarily on opportunity or preconception.

23:78   Standley, William H., and Ageton, Arthur A. *Admiral Ambassador to Russia.* Chicago: Regnery, 1955. Admiral Standley, ambassador to Russia (1942–1943), was critical of Roosevelt's policy of giving aid to the Soviets without demanding a quid pro quo. He particularly faults the lend-lease activities of Harry Hopkins and Brigadier General Faymonville and visits to Russian officials by representatives of Roosevelt such as former Ambassador Joseph Davies and by Wendell Wilkie.

Foreign

Eduard Beneš
See also Chapter 22, "Personalities."

Beneš, E. *Memoirs: From Munich to New War and New Victory* (22:48) explains what Beneš tried to do, while the Czechs were under Nazi rule, to neutralize the effects of Munich.

Winston S. Churchill
See Chapters 21, 22, and 25, "Personalities," for additional references.

23:79   Churchill, Winston S. *The Second World War.* 6 vols. Boston: Houghton Mifflin, 1948–1953. For many years these volumes (*The Gathering Storm, Their Finest Hour, The Grand Alliance, The Hinge of Fate, Closing the Ring,* and *Triumph and Tragedy*) constituted an essential source for anyone interested in Allied strategy and diplomacy during World War II. They remain a significant source and the finest memoir by any major World War II figure.

23:80   Churchill, Winston S. *The War Speeches of the Rt. Hon. Winston S. Churchill.* Ed. by Charles Eade. 3 vols. Boston: Houghton Mifflin, 1953. This is a complete collection of Churchill's wartime statements, made both in Parliament and elsewhere. Each speech is prefaced by a short narrative to place it in context, and each volume also has a detailed index and a chronology.

Higgins, T. *Winston Churchill and the Second Front* (23:164).

Jonas, M.; Langley, H. D.; and Loewenheim, F. L., eds. *Roosevelt and Churchill: Their Secret Wartime Correspondence* (25:30).

23:81   Moran, Charles M. Wilson, Lord. *Churchill: Taken from the Diaries of Lord Moran: The Struggle for Survival, 1940–1965.* Boston: Houghton Mifflin, 1966. The prime minister's physician was present during many historic moments during and after World War II and privy to many secrets, state as well as private. Churchill appears here in his strength and his weakness, as he wanted to appear and as he was, as he acted and as he thought. Moran did not always understand the inside story.

Charles de Gaulle
See Chapter 28, "Personalities," for additional references.

23:82   De Gaulle, Charles. *The Complete War Memoirs of Charles De Gaulle.* Trans. by Jonathan Green and Richard Howard. 3 vols. New York: Simon & Schuster, 1955–1960. The three volumes, *The Call* *to Honour* (1940–1942), *Unity* (1942–1944), *Salvation* (1944–1946), cover de Gaulle's call for resistance to the enemy after the fall of France to his establishment of a provisional French government in liberated France and relations with the Allies after the war.

23:83 Funk, Arthur L. *Charles De Gaulle: The Crucial Years, 1943–1944*. Norman: University of Oklahoma Press, 1959. This volume shows de Gaulle's efforts to establish France's position vis-à-vis Great Britain, the Soviet Union, and the United States. His role at the Casablanca Conference is made clear.

Viorst, M. *Hostile Allies: FDR and Charles de Gaulle* (23:231).

White, D. S. *Seeds of Discord: De Gaulle, Free France, and the Allies* (23:232).

Lord Halifax
23:84 Birkenhead, Frederick W. F. Smith, 2d Earl of. *Halifax: The Life of Lord Halifax*. Boston: Houghton Mifflin, 1966. The best life of Halifax yet to appear devotes more than half of its pages to his career before he became foreign secretary in 1938. It is valuable for the description of Halifax's service as ambassador to the United States (1940–1946).

23:85 Halifax, Edmund F. L. Wood, 1st Earl. *Fulness of Days*. London: Collins, 1957. Halifax was British foreign secretary (1938–1940) and ambassador to the United States (1940–1946). The volume is disappointingly thin, as the author offers little information on foreign relations.

Emperor Hirohito
See Chapter 22, "Personalities," for references.

Adolf Hitler
See Chapters 21 and 22 for additional references.

Deakin, F. W. *The Brutal Friendship* (23:177) is a thorough study of the relationship of Hitler and Mussolini.

23:86 Strawson, John. *Hitler's Battles for Europe*. New York: Scribner's, 1971. This book examines Hitler's role in shaping German military strategy; it also measures Hitler as a military leader. Bibliography.

Weinberg, G. L. "Hitler's Image of the United States" (21:69).

23:87 Woerden, A. V. N. "Hitler Faces England: Theories, Images and Policies." *Acta Historiae Neerlandica* 3 (1968), 141–59. Before 1923 Hitler thought Britain the natural enemy of Germany; but by the late 1920s he rejected that "very erroneous" conclusion. Subsequently, he favored close cooperation and friendship between the two nations.

Benito Mussolini
See Chapter 21, "Personalities," for additional references.

Deakin, F. W. *The Brutal Friendship* (23:177) is a thorough study of the relationships of Mussolini and Hitler.

23:88 Hibbert, Christopher. *Il Duce: The Life of Benito Mussolini*. Boston: Little, Brown, 1962. Most of the volume deals with Mussolini's activities from 1940 to 1945.

Joseph V. Stalin
See Chapters 21 and 25, "Personalities," for references.

Josip Broz-Tito
See also Chapter 24, "Personalities."

Robertson, W. R. *Tito, Mihailovic and the Allies, 1941–45* (23:251).

Others
23:89 Attlee, Clement R., 1st Earl. *As It Happened*. New York: Viking, 1954. This is an unusually candid memoir by the leader of the Opposition, lord privy seal, and deputy prime minister during World War II. Attlee does not reveal much that is not already known except his reactions to events. His successes and possibly his failures are now more understandable.

23:90 Cadogan, Sir Alexander. *The Diaries of Sir Alexander Cadogan, 1939–45*. Ed. by David Dilks. London: Cassell, 1971. This is one of the best inside looks at the British Foreign Office during World War II. As permanent under secretary of the Foreign Office, Cadogan could see and judge events. The diaries contain much valuable information about decisions, people, and the passing scene. Bibliography.

Casey, R. G. *Personal Experience, 1939–1946* (32:62) covers Casey's experiences as Australian minister to the United States (1940–1942), and subsequently as British minister of state for the Middle East and governor of Bengal.

Ciano, G. *The Ciano Diaries, 1936–1943* (22:62) —Mussolini's son-in-law and Italian foreign minister records the Italian perception of U.S. policy.

23:91 Ciechanowski, Jan. *Defeat in Victory*. Garden City, N.Y.: Doubleday, 1947. Ciechanowski was the ambassador to the United States from the Polish government-in-exile in London (1941–1945). These memoirs, while highly biased and critical of Roosevelt, offer numerous insights into Polish-American relations during the war.

23:92 Dalton, Hugh. *The Fateful Years: Memoirs, 1931–1945*. London: Muller, 1957. A sometimes indiscreet autobiography of a Labour party leader who became a senior British official during World War II and in the Attlee government. The most important sections deal with the Labour party's approach to the war and Dalton's service as minister of economic warfare and director of the Special Operations Executive (1940–1942).

23:93 Eden, Anthony. *The Memoirs of Anthony Eden, Earl of Avon: The Reckoning*. Boston: Houghton Mifflin, 1965. Although beginning with his resignation from the Chamberlain cabinet in 1938, two-thirds of this autobiography deals with Eden's experiences as British foreign secretary (1941–mid-1945). It offers exceptional insights into and explanations of the men and events dominating Allied diplomacy during the war. Bibliography.

Kase, T. *Journey to the Missouri* (22:76).

23:94 Macmillan, Harold. *The Blast of War, 1939–45*. New York: Harper & Row, 1968. This memoir of Britain's chief political adviser in the Mediterranean area provides important information on decisions and actions from Africa to Italy. Naturally defending British policy and most of Churchill's views, Macmillan takes the Americans to task for supporting Giraud, Operation Anvil, and opposition to the monarchy in Greece.

23:95 Maisky, Ivan M. *Memoirs of a Soviet Ambassador: The War, 1939–43*. Trans. by Andrew Rothstein. New York: Scribner's, 1967. These memoirs by the Soviet ambassador to Britain (1932–1943), covering the years 1939 to 1943, should be read with caution as he almost manages to conceal the fact that the Soviet Union attacked Poland in 1939. He is highly critical of Churchill for delaying a second front.

23:96 Mannerheim, Carl Gustav Emil von, Baron. *The Memoirs of Marshal Mannerheim*. Trans. by Eric Lewenhaupt. New York: Dutton, 1954. An account of his long career by the Finnish leader who helped gain Finland's independence from Russia, served as regent of the new government, and then led Finnish forces in the "Winter War" against the Soviets. He served as president from 1944 to 1946.

23:97 Nicolson, Harold. *The War Years, 1939–45*. Vol. 2 in *The Diaries and Letters of Harold Nicolson*. New York: Atheneum, 1967. This volume contains comment on political and military leaders and developments of the war.

Shigemitsu, M. *Japan and Her Destiny: My Struggle for Peace* [1931–1945] (22:79).

Tōgō, S. *The Cause of Japan* (22:80).

Warner, G. *Pierre Laval and the Eclipse of France* [1931–1944] (21:87).

MILITARY

American

Henry H. Arnold

23:98 Arnold, Henry H. *Global Mission*. New York: Harper, 1949. Although a memoir covering his entire military career and the early history of army air power, over half of this work deals with "Hap" Arnold's experiences as chief of staff of the U. S. Army Air Corps and member of the Joint Chiefs of Staff (1942–1945). Valuable insights are offered into the issues, individuals, and conferences involved in the formulation of Allied strategy, with special emphasis placed on the development of air power during the war. Must be read with caution on dates and sequence.

23:99 Parrish, N. F. "Hap Arnold and the Historians." *Aerospace Historian* 20:3 (1973), 113–15. General Arnold sought the aid of a committee of historians to help him with strategic discussions during World War II.

Claire L. Chennault

23:100 Chennault, Claire L. *Way of a Fighter: The Memoirs of Claire L. Chennault*. New York: Putnams's, 1949. This volume consists of a bitter attack on General Stilwell and to some extent on Marshall and others in the War Department who supported Stilwell. Chennault's views on Stilwell are highly colored by the generalissimo's views and by strong disagreements with Stilwell on the air strategy.

Spence, J. *The China Helpers: Western Advisers in China, 1620–1960* (2:347) contains two sections which contrast the careers of Joseph Stilwell and his rival, Chennault.

Dwight D. Eisenhower

See Chapter 24, "Personalities," for additional references.

Allied Expeditionary Forces, Supreme Headquarters [SHAEF]. *Report by the Supreme Commander to the Combined Chiefs of Staff on the Operations in Europe of the Allied Expeditionary Forces, 6 June 1944 to 8 May 1945* (40:54).

Ambrose, S. E. *Eisenhower and Berlin, 1945: The Decision to Halt at the Elbe* (23:163).

23:101 Ambrose, Stephen E. *The Supreme Commander: The War Years of General Dwight D. Eisenhower.* Garden City, N.Y.: Doubleday, 1969. This biography covers Eisenhower from his assignment to the War Plans Division of the Army General Staff (December 1941) through his acceptance of German surrender as commander of SHAEF (May 1945). The author, involved in the editing of Eisenhower's wartime papers, relies upon those papers in this biography. He defends Eisenhower's decisions in the numerous political-military conflicts in which he was involved.

23:102 Eisenhower, Dwight D. *Crusade in Europe.* Garden City, N. Y.: Doubleday, 1948. Eisenhower's memoirs of his wartime experiences from Army General Staff planner to commander of SHAEF cover a host of important diplomatic as well as military issues and offer some valuable insights. Overall, however, the volume is very bland.

23:103 Eisenhower, Dwight D. *Dear General: Eisenhower's Wartime Letters to Marshall.* Ed. by Joseph P. Hobbs. Baltimore: Johns Hopkins Press, 1971. This collection is enhanced by Hobbs's introductory chapters, which highlight recurring themes. The letters and commentary help place in perspective Eisenhower's problems and growth as Supreme Commander. Bibliography.

23:104 Eisenhower, Dwight D. *The Papers of Dwight David Eisenhower: The War Years.* Ed. by Alfred D. Chandler. 5 vols. Baltimore: Johns Hopkins Press, 1970. This collection is made up of previously classified memoranda, notes, telegrams, and letters written or dictated by Eisenhower as a member of General Marshall's planning staff in Washington (1941–1942) and as American and Allied commander in North Africa and Europe (1942–1945). Bibliography.

Ernest J. King

23:105 Buell, Thomas B. *Master of Sea Power: A Biography of Fleet Admiral Ernest J. King.* Boston: Little, Brown, 1980. This biography is the most complete study of Admiral King as chief of naval operations during World War II. It emphasizes King's role in U.S. strategy and naval operations.

23:106 King, Ernest J., and Whitehill, Walter M. *Fleet Admiral King: A Naval Record.* New York: Norton, 1952. This volume is a combination memoir and biography of the chief of naval operations and commander in chief of the U.S. Fleet during World War II. Less than half of the book deals with his World War II experiences, and those sections reveal little new information.

Douglas MacArthur

See also Chapters 23 and 40, "Personalities."

23:107 James, D. Clayton. *The Years of MacArthur* [1880–1945]. 2 vols. to date. Boston: Houghton Mifflin, 1970– . Incomparable study of MacArthur in World War II. Volume 1 covers MacArthur's life up to the time of the Pearl Harbor attack. It is particularly good on the clash between MacArthur and his superiors in Washington, his bitter fight against the Europe-first strategy, his disputes with the navy, and his plans for island hopping. Extensive bibliography.

MacArthur, D. *Reminiscences* (40:55) is a spirited memoir and defense of MacArthur's decisions and opinions over a long career. Apparently, from his perspective he was seldom if ever wrong, while his opponents within the U.S. military hierarchy were habitually beset by shortsightedness or worse. Must reading for defense of the Asia-first doctrine, the New Guinea-Mindanao axis, as well as his side of the MacArthur versus Washington and the MacArthur versus the navy dispute.

Manchester, W. *American Caesar: Douglas Mac-Arthur, 1880–1964* (24:139) is a lively and sometimes eloquent account of the U.S. commander in the Philippines, and Southwest Pacific theater of operations. Manchester draws on many sources but often neglects many official collections and official histories in favor of highly biased accounts. The work must be used with care and checked against James (23:107).

George C. Marshall

See Chapter 24 and 27, "Personalities," for additional references.

23:108 Pogue, Forrest C. *George C. Marshall.* Vol. 2: *Ordeal and Hope 1939–1942.* New York: Viking, 1966. This volume is the definitive account of Marshall from his installation in 1939 as U.S. Army chief of staff through the successful invasion of North Africa in late 1942. Important issues discussed here include prewar planning, Anglo-American strategic disputes and conferences, and the North Africa invasion. Extensive bibliography.

23:109 Pogue, Forrest C. *George C. Marshall.* Vol. 3: *Organizer of Victory, 1943–1945.* New York: Viking, 1973. This volume is very useful for an understanding of Allied decisionmaking, U.S. civil-military relations, as well as the central role Marshall played in shaping U.S. forces and the Allied victory. Extensive bibliography.

Joseph W. Stilwell

See also Chapter 27, "Personalities."

Liang Chin-tung. *General Stilwell in China, 1942–1944: The Full Story* (27:72) presents the Chinese case against Stilwell's policies and against the policy of the United States.

Romanus, C., and Sunderland, R. *Stilwell's Mission to China* (23:195).

23:110 Stilwell, Joseph W. *The Stilwell Papers.* Ed. by Theodore H. White. New York: Sloan, 1948. This volume is composed of selections from General Stilwell's personal command journal, longer essays and analyses, and letters to his wife (December 1941–October 1944). The result is a very colorful and caustic first-hand account of the major characters and issues in the China-Burma-India theater and of high-level strategic planning at the conferences Stilwell attended.

23:111 Stilwell, Joseph W. *Stilwell's Personal File: China, Burma, India, 1942–1944.* Ed. by Riley Sunderland and Charles F. Romanus. 5 vols. Wilmington, Del.: Scholarly Resources, 1976. This collection documents the diplomatic and military organizational plans and controversies surrounding Stilwell's Asian mission. It includes letters and documents, as well as Stilwell's own abridged version of the report of his CBI operation which he submitted to the War Department.

23:112 Tuchman, Barbara W. *Stilwell and the American Experience in China, 1911–1945.* New York: Macmillan, 1970. This highly readable biography examines Sino-American relations, with heavy emphasis on 1942 to 1944, through the career of General Stilwell. While highly favorable toward Stilwell, the work emphasizes American misconceptions of and inability to achieve objectives in Asia. Extensive bibliography.

23:113 Young, Kenneth R. "The Stilwell Controversy: A Bibliographical Review." *Military Affairs* 39:2 (1975), 66–68. Young reviews Stilwell's career in Asia and examines the controversy over Stilwell's effectiveness as the China-India-Burma theater commander (1942–1944). Young summarizes the different viewpoints and concludes that Stilwell's mission to China was doomed from the start.

Others

23:114 Bradley, Omar N. *A Soldier's Story.* New York: Holt, 1951. In these modest memoirs, General Bradley, one of the most successful Allied commanders, provides interesting insights on other leaders.

23:115 Brereton, Lewis H. *The Brereton Diaries, 3 October 1940–8 May 1945.* New York: Morrow, 1946. These diaries by a senior air officer were obviously written with an eye to later publication. Their value lies in the firsthand account of incidents such as the Japanese attack on MacArthur's air force in the Philippines and operations in the Mediterranean and England. A devotee of tactical air, Brereton knew all the senior officers and comments on many.

23:116 Butcher, Harry C. *My Three Years with Eisenhower.* New York: Simon & Schuster, 1946. Butcher, Eisenhower's naval aide, was directed to keep a diary of the general's activities. The actual diary is detailed, but must be used carefully, as it is chatty and opinionated concerning personalities and military operations and strategy, about which Butcher is often out of his depth. (The complete diary with supporting papers is in the Eisenhower Library.)

23:117 Clark, Mark W. *Calculated Risk.* New York: Harper, 1950. A story of the Mediterranean campaign by U.S. commander of the Fifth Army and 15th Army Group, Clark focuses primarily on the Italian action, defending the concept of using Italy as a magnet to draw German troops from the French and Russian fronts. He also argues that the attack should have been continued into the Balkans, thus saving them from communist domination.

23:118 Groves, Leslie R. *Now It Can Be Told: The Story of the Manhattan Project.* New York: Harper & Row, 1962. This personal story of General Groves, who supervised the building of the first atomic bombs, is in some sense an administrative history of the problems and triumphs of this ambitious project. The developments are described against a background of anxiety about security, the German program, and progress of the war. Valuable information is also included about military/civilian and Allied technological cooperation.

Leahy, W. D. *I Was There* (22:45) the account of the U.S. ambassador to Vichy and chief of staff to Roosevelt is of some use, but disappointing in that it stresses personalities more than events. The sections dealing with the wartime conferences are drawn from Leahy's diaries and are of the greatest value.

23:119 Potter, E. B. *Nimitz.* Annapolis, Md.: Naval Institute Press, 1976. As the authorized biographer of the chief U.S. naval commander in the Pacific in World War II, Potter was in a position to deal authoritatively with his subject. The work is valuable on naval strategy in the Pacific and on relations with army commanders in that area. Bibliography.

23:120 Wedemeyer, Albert C. *Wedemeyer Reports!* New York: Holt, 1958. The general takes the position that the politicians had imprecise war aims, underestimated the communists in Europe and in Asia and squandered the hard-won peace. He holds that a 1943 cross-channel attack would have succeeded. Although he praises Marshall for his advocacy of the cross-channel attack, he is sharply critical of the postwar mission to China.

Foreign

Field Marshal Alanbrooke (Alan Francis Brooke)

23:121 Bryant, Sir Arthur. *The Turn of the Tide: A History of the War Years Based on the Diaries of Field Marshal Lord Alanbrooke, Chief of the Imperial General Staff.* Garden City, N.Y.: Doubleday, 1957.

23:122 Bryant, Sir Arthur. *Triumph in the West: A History of the War Years Based on the Diaries of Field-Marshal Lord Alanbrooke, Chief of the Imperial General Staff.* Garden City, N.Y.: Doubleday, 1959. The two volumes provide the British view of the war. In addition to revealing British and Allied strategic differences and planning, volume 2 clearly shows the declining British ability to direct or influence Allied strategy. Both volumes are highly critical of Churchill and the Americans.

Field Marshal Harold Rupert L. G. Alexander

23:123 Alexander, Harold Rupert L. G., 1st Earl. *The Alexander Memoirs, 1940–1945.* Ed. by John North. New York: McGraw-Hill, 1962. Alexander was one of Britain's top commanders during the war, and is best known for his North African and Mediterranean campaigns. This volume, an edited collection of his reflections, is disappointingly thin and disjointed.

23:124 Nicolson, Nigel. *Alex: The Life of Field Marshal Earl Alexander of Tunis.* New York: Atheneum, 1973. A competent, sometimes chatty, biography of the Supreme Allied Commander in the Mediterranean, it helps bring out the qualities and limitations of this self-effacing and personally elusive leader, but adds little to discussions of Allied strategy and coordination.

Field Marshal Bernard Law Montgomery

23:125 Montgomery, Bernard Law, 1st Viscount. *The Memoirs of Field-Marshal the Viscount Montgomery of Alamein.* New York: World, 1958. Montgomery continues to argue strongly in favor of positions he took during the war, and on his overall role. This book makes heavy use of messages, speeches, etc. reprinted in full, and has less detail and analysis of major operations than his memoirs, *El Alamein to the River Sangro* (1948), and *Normandy to the Baltic* (1948). This volume should be used cautiously.

23:126 Thompson, Reginald W. *Montgomery, the Field Marshal: The Campaign in North-West Europe, 1944–45.* New York: Scribner's, 1970. While this is primarily a history of the British army in Northwest Europe from the Normandy landing to German surrender, it is also one of the better critical studies of Montgomery.

Sir Frederick E. Morgan

23:127 Morgan, Sir Frederick E. *Overture to Overlord.* Garden City, N.Y.: Doubleday, 1950. Morgan headed the Anglo-American planning staff for cross-channel operations (1943) and became deputy chief of staff under Eisenhower in SHAEF (1944). His memoirs offer valuable insights into the original planning for a cross-channel invasion of Europe, and into the origins and development of plans for military occupation of, and civil affairs in, Germany and the rest of Europe.

23:128 Morgan, Sir Frederick E. *Peace and War.* London: Hodder & Stoughton, 1961. The memoirs of Sir Frederick E. Morgan, whose role during World War II is described immediately above. While Morgan touches on many of the major issues, he does so briefly and without much coherence.

Field Marshal William J. Slim

23:129 Lewin, Ronald. *Slim, the Swordbearer.* Hamden, Conn.: Shoe String Press, 1976. A well-written biography of Field Marshal Slim, who led Allied troops to victory in Burma, this is a valuable study of operations and of matters of Allied strategy and command.

23:130 Slim, William J., 1st Viscount. *Defeat into Victory.* New York: McKay, 1961. This volume, one of the best personal accounts by a high-level commander in World War II, recounts how victory in Burma was brought out of earlier defeat. It is valuable for depicting the command problems in that area involving Chinese, Indian, and British forces and, especially, General Stilwell as commander of Chinese forces that owed allegiance to Mountbatten and Chiang Kai-shek.

Others

23:131 Bialer, Seweryn, ed. *Stalin and His Generals: Soviet Military Memoirs of World War II.* New York: Pegasus, 1969. These 45 autobiographical sketches of major Soviet military leaders provide useful insights into Russian military thinking. Bibliography.

23:132 Chuikov, Vasilii I. *The Battle for Stalingrad.* Trans. by Harold Silver. New York: Holt, Rinehart & Winston, 1964. An account by one of the chief Soviet marshals of the defense of Stalingrad, a pivotal action in the war between Germany and the Soviet Union. Although affected by Soviet policy censorship and unfair to men like Zhukov, it gives the main outline of one of the key actions in the defeat of Hitler.

23:133 Connell, John. *Wavell: Scholar and Soldier.* New York: Harcourt, Brace & World, 1965. This is a sympathetic biography of a complex and controversial military commander. Wavell is presented here as a genius who cannot win all his battles or the confidence of his prime minister. A strong narrative keeps this account moving; it ends in 1941, when Wavell is sent from Egypt to India.

23:134 Cunningham, Andrew Browne, Viscount Cunningham of Hyndhope. *A Sailor's Odyssey.* New York: Dutton, 1951. Since Cunningham was central to the naval war in the Mediterranean from 1940 to 1943, this autobiography is essential reading for anyone interested in those actions; but Cunningham also succeeded Dudley Pound as first sea lord, so there is much on allied strategy making here as well.

23:135 De Guingand, Francis. *Operation Victory.* New York: Scribner's, 1947. De Guingand, Montgomery's chief of staff, largely supports Montgomery's positions in the major controversies of Allied strategy, with the notable exception of the single thrust versus broad front issue. These memoirs are more judiciously phrased than Montgomery's.

23:136 Dönitz, Karl. *Memoirs: Ten Years and Twenty Days.* Trans. by R. H. Stevens. Cleveland: World, 1959. The memoirs of the admiral who built the German U-boat force after 1935 and who succeeded Admiral Raeder (January 1943) as head of the German navy are valuable for his views on U.S. breaches of neutrality in the North Atlantic, for his criticisms of Hitler, the Italian navy, and German strategy. He gives detail on his succession to Hitler in 1945.

23:137 Halder, Franz. *The Halder Diaries.* 7 vols. Washington, D.C.: Infantry Journal, 1950. These diary entries, by the German chief of the General Staff (August 14, 1939–September 24, 1942) are valuable for insights into German strategic planning in the Polish, Norwegian, French, and Eastern European campaigns.

23:138 Harris, Sir Arthur. *Bomber Offensive.* London: Collins, 1947. These personal recollections by the chief of Bomber Command during most of the World War II discuss air strategy and operations against Germany.

23:139 Ismay, Lord. *The Memoirs of General Lord Ismay.* New York: Viking, 1960. Although these memoirs cover Ismay's entire career, over half are devoted to his experiences as Churchill's chief of staff and personal representative on the British Chiefs of Staff Committee during World War II. Like Alanbrooke, Ismay offers an excellent, firsthand account of British and Allied strategic planning, conferences and disputes, with emphasis on the disagreements which separated Churchill from his military advisers.

23:140 Kennedy, Sir John. *The Business of War: The War Narrative of Major-General Sir John Kennedy.* Ed. by Bernard Fergusson. London: Hutchinson, 1957. As director of military operations, Kennedy was one of Alanbrooke's, and England's, chief strategic planners during World War II. These memoirs resulted from a narrative which he wrote on the basis of his wartime notes. Kennedy emphasizes the numerous clashes between Churchill and his military advisers.

23:141 Kesselring, Albert. *Kesselring: A Soldier's Record.* New York: Morrow, 1954. Kesselring held high commands in almost every one of Germany's European campaigns, including commander in chief in Italy.

Mountbatten, L., 1st Earl. *Report to the Combined Chiefs of Staff of the Supreme Allied Commander South East Asia, 1941–1945* (23:148).

Potter, J. D. *Yamamoto: The Man Who Menaced America* (22:78).

23:142 Strong, Kenneth. *Intelligence at the Top.* Garden City, N.Y.: Doubleday, 1969. The memoirs of Eisenhower's (British) chief of intelligence, while largely narrative, provide useful insights regarding the operations of Supreme Headquarters, Anglo-American coordination, the role and use of intelligence, and especially the disputes between Eisenhower and Montgomery.

23:143 Wilson, Sir Henry Maitland. *Eight Years Overseas, 1939–47.* London: Hutchins, 1950. These memoirs are useful for the years Wilson spent as British commander in chief in the Middle East, as Supreme Allied Commander in the Mediterranean and as head of the British staff mission to Washington. Wilson gives valuable background on Allied planning and disagreements.

23:144 Zhukov, Georgi K. *The Memoirs of Marshal Zhukov.* Trans. by Theodore Shabad. New York: Delacorte, 1971. Chief of staff of the Soviet High Command when Germany attacked the Red Forces in June 1941, Zhukov later commanded several army groups and ultimately became deputy supreme commander, second only to Stalin. Partisanship marks the volume but it gives some idea of Zhukov's key role in World War II and important information on the high command.

Strategy/Operations

See "Personalities," especially Winston S. Churchill, Franklin D. Roosevelt, Henry L. Stimson; also see "Bibliographies," especially Higham (23:5).

23:145 Craven, Wesley Frank, and Cate, James Lea, eds. *The Army Air Forces in World War II.* 7 vols. Chicago: University of Chicago Press, 1948–1958. This official history consists of both the organizational and operational aspects of the U.S. Army Air Forces during World War II. Separate volumes cover early plans and operations (1939–mid-1942), the European theater, the Pacific theater, the home front, and worldwide services.

23:146 Marshall, George C.; Arnold, H. H.; and King, Ernest J. *The War Reports of General Marshall, General Arnold and Admiral King.* Philadelphia: Lippincott, 1947. The official war reports of the three service members of the Joint Chiefs of Staff, offering a wealth of detailed information on the planning, logistics, and execution of global war. The volume is enhanced by a detailed index. These reports were published separately by the Government Printing Office.

23:147 Morison, Samuel Eliot. *History of United States Naval Operations in World War II.* 15 vols. Boston: Little, Brown, 1947–1962. This series combines details on naval strategy, high-level planning, and operational details of naval activity throughout the world. Morison's *The Two-Ocean War* (1963) is a one-volume summary.

23:148 Mountbatten, Louis, 1st Earl. *Report to the Combined Chiefs of Staff of the Supreme Allied Commander South East Asia, 1941–1945.* London: H.M.S.O., 1951. This is an official report on strategy, command, and operations in the South East Asia Command (1943–1945).

23:149 Roskill, Stephen W. *The War at Sea, 1939–1945.* 3 vols. London: H.M.S.O., 1954–1961. Although these volumes deal mostly with operations, they are also valuable for the development of British maritime strategy in the 1939 to 1945 period.

23:150 U.S. Department of the Army. Center of Military History. *Publications of the U.S. Center of Military History, 1977–1978.* Washington, D.C.: G.P.O., 1979. This guide includes the various operational and technical volumes produced in the U.S. Army in World War II series. In addition to the volumes specifically dealing with strategy and high-level command, the operational volumes and logistical volumes contain information on high-level planning.

GLOBAL STRATEGY

See "Personalities," especially George C. Marshall.

23:151 Ambrose, Stephen E. "Applied Strategy of World War II." *Naval War College Review* 22:9 (1970), 62–70. Ambrose attacks the myth of a purely military and nonpolitical strategy by the United States as compared to Britain, and points out that at war's end America occupied, controlled, or exerted the major influence in four of the five major industrial areas of the world.

23:152 Baldwin, Hanson W. *Great Mistakes of the War.* New York: Harper, 1950. Relying on hindsight, the author, a leading military critic, somewhat simplistically points up the failure of U.S. officials to keep political objectives in mind. Aside from suggesting that our grand strategy was flawed, he argues against the unconditional surrender doctrine and the dropping of the atomic bomb.

23:153 Butler, James R. M., ed. *Grand Strategy.* 6 vols. In *History of the Second World War: United Kingdom Military Series.* London: H.M.S.O.,

1956–1976. Volume 1 (*1919–1 September 1939,* by Norman H. Gibbs) covers British military planning and policies during the interwar years.

Volume 2 (*2 September 1939–June 1941,* by J. R. M. Butler) covers British and Allied strategic planning from the outbreak of the war to the German invasion of Russia. It includes sections on the exploratory staff talks with the United States (1940–1941), combined policy in the Atlantic, and strategy in the Pacific.

Volume 3 (*June 1941–August 1942,* by J. M. A. Gwyer and J. R. M. Butler) covers British and Allied strategic planning from Germany's attack on Russia through the decision to invade North Africa. Emphasis is on the formation of the Grand Alliance, aid to Russia, the cross-channel versus North Africa controversy of 1942, and the numerous conferences associated with these issues.

Volume 4 (*August 1942–September 1943,* by Michael Howard) covers the period of critical Anglo-American conferences, debates and decisions on cross-channel versus Mediterranean strategy, and a host of related issues. It contains an extended introduction which summarizes and updates available information on the Anglo-American strategic debate prior to August of 1942.

Volume 5 (*August 1943–September 1944,* by John Ehrman) analyzes the strategic debates of 1943–1944, most notably over the invasions of northern and southern France, and the numerous conferences which determined final strategy, the most important at Cairo and Teheran.

Volume 6 (*October 1944–August 1945,* by John Ehrman) analyzes Allied planning and conferences from the second Quebec Conference of 1944 through the Japanese surrender, and deals with the numerous diplomatic as well as military issues which arose during this time period.

23:154 Davis, Vernon E. *The History of the Joint Chiefs of Staff in World War II: Organizational Development.* 2 vols. Washington, D.C.: G.P.O., 1972. Volume 1, *Origin of the Joint and Combined Chiefs of Staff,* is an extremely useful history of the formation of the Joint Chiefs of Staff and early Allied planning and coordination through mid-1942, including two excellent chapters on U.S. and British defense organizational development prior to the war. Good on the relationship between the growth and development of JCS and collaboration with Britain and the overall course of the war.

Volume 2, *Development of the JCS Committee Structure,* concentrates on the internal development of the Joint Chiefs as it carried out its role in U.S. and Allied planning.

23:155 Greenfield, Kent Roberts. *American Strategy in World War II: A Reconsideration*. Baltimore: Johns Hopkins Press, 1963. The former chief historian of the U.S. Army summarizes some of the controversy regarding American World War II strategy, and discusses and reinterprets the basic elements of U.S.-Allied strategy, the Anglo-American strategic dispute, Roosevelt's role as commander in chief, and the role of air power.

23:156 Greenfield, Kent Roberts, ed. *Command Decisions*. Washington, D.C.: G.P.O., 1960. These twenty-three essays analyze decisions at various levels on both sides in World War II, and cover a number of types of decisions—diplomatic, political, logistical, grand strategic, and strategic. The selection is somewhat eclectic. (An abridged version has appeared in a trade edition.)

23:157 Henrikson, Alan K. "The Map as an 'Idea': The Role of Cartographic Imagery during the Second World War." *American Cartographer* 10:3 (1973), 19–53. The author maintains that a "revolution" occurred during World War II. This revolution, involving a shift from the sea-land Mercator view to the air view of a North Pole–centered azimuthal projection, helped to promote a new, global outlook which played a major role in shaping American conduct of the war and planning for the peace.

23:158 Kingston McLoughry, E. J. *The Direction of War: A Critique of the Political Direction and High Command in War*. New York: Praeger, 1955. This is an early attempt to show the lessons taught by World Wars I and II and the great need to unite military and political command. A valuable and provocative reappraisal of the British position, it argues the necessity of rethinking Allies' problems of World War II.

23:159 Matloff, Maurice. *Strategic Planning for Coalition Warfare, 1943–1944*. In *United States Army in World War II: The War Department*. Washington, D.C.: G.P.O., 1959.

23:160 Matloff, Maurice, and Snell, Edwin M. *Strategic Planning for Coalition Warfare, 1941–1942*. In *United States Army in World War II: The War Department*. Washington, D.C.: G.P.O., 1953. These two volumes trace American strategic planning within the context of the Grand Alliance and the numerous

Allied wartime conferences. Both volumes are rich in detail, well organized, and indexed. Bibliographies, glossaries, and notes.

23:161 Morison, Samuel Eliot. *Strategy and Compromise*. Boston: Little, Brown, 1958. This is a brisk but flawed review of Allied strategy during the war. Morison tends to stress strategic differences, with Churchill and Alanbrooke emerging as the main villains. However, he finds no suitable alternative to that strategy.

23:162 Wright, Monte D., and Paszek, Lawrence J., eds. *Soldiers and Statesmen*. Proceedings of the 4th Military History Symposium United States Air Force Academy, October 22–23, 1970. Washington, D.C.: G.P.O., 1973. The second session was devoted to the topic "The Wartime Chiefs of Staff and the President." Also included are written commentaries by Major General Haywood S. Hansell and Brigadier General George A. Lincoln, who worked with the Joint Chiefs of Staff on wartime plans.

EUROPEAN STRATEGY/OPERATIONS

See "Personalities," especially Field Marshal Alanbrooke, Dwight D. Eisenhower, Sir Frederick E. Morgan, Field Marshal Bernard Law Montgomery, and, under "American," "Others," Robert D. Murphy.

23:163 Ambrose, Stephen E. *Eisenhower and Berlin, 1945: The Decision to Halt at the Elbe*. New York: Norton, 1967. British leaders believed that it was important for later dealings with the Russians to enter Berlin first, but Eisenhower, concerned about casualties and the fact that his forces would withdraw shortly after the war ended to agreed upon occupation zones, would not drive for Berlin unless he was so ordered. The American chiefs of staff left the decision to him.

23:164 Higgins, Trumbull. *Winston Churchill and the Second Front*. New York: Oxford University Press, 1957. This work examines British strategic concepts for the European theater and the ensuing Anglo-American strategic debate over cross-channel versus North African/Mediterranean operations (1939–early 1943). It is highly critical of Churchill and the entire British approach, as well as of the compromise strategy which emerged. Bibliography.

23:165 Hinsley, Francis H. *Hitler's Strategy*. Cambridge: Cambridge University Press, 1951. This is a study of German naval strategy, not operations, and how it was coordinated with and influenced Hitler's other military decisions. The naval conflict with Britain is central in this study. It provides a valuable synthesis of major decisions such as Operations Sealion and Barbarossa, the Battle of the Atlantic, and war in the Far East.

23:166 Lattre de Tassigny, Jean de. *The History of the First French Army*. Trans. by Malcolm Barnes. London: Allen & Unwin, 1952. This is largely the operational story of the French army in France and Germany (1944–1945), covering the landings in the south, drive up the Rhône Valley, the fight in the Vosges, the crossing of the Rhine, and the drive into Germany.

23:167 Leighton, Richard M. "OVERLORD Revisited: An Interpretation of American Strategy in the European War, 1942–1944." *American Historical Review* 68:4 (1963), 919–37. This major reinterpretation of U.S. World War II strategy in Europe argues that the American approach was not fundamentally different from that of Britain. Despite perceptions to the contrary, both national strategies were pragmatic, flexible, and peripheral.

23:168 Pogue, Forrest C. "Political Problems of a Coalition Command." In Harry L. Coles, ed., *Total War and Cold War: Problems in Civilian Control of the Military*. Columbus: Ohio State University Press, 1962, pp. 108–28. Eisenhower's contribution as Supreme Commander has been underestimated. His job was complicated by conflicting Allied political interests and national pride.

23:169 Pogue, Forrest C. *The Supreme Command*. In *United States Army in World War II: The European Theater of Operations*. Washington, D.C.: G.P.O., 1954. This volume is a detailed study of the organization and activities of Supreme Headquarters, Allied Expeditionary Forces. One-third of the volume is devoted to planning and organization prior to the Normandy invasion; the remainder covers events and issues through the German surrender. Index and bibliography.

23:170 Stacey, Charles P. *The Victory Campaign: The Operations in North-West Europe, 1944–45*. Vol. 3 in *Official History of the Canadian Army in the Second World War*. Ottawa: Queen's Printer, 1960.

Although intended to give the story of Canadian activities, the volume is valuable for a Canadian view of differences between British and U.S. viewpoints on strategy. It is also excellent on problems between Canadian commanders and Montgomery.

23:171 Steele, Richard W. *The First Offensive, 1942: Roosevelt, Marshall and the Making of American Strategy*. Bloomington: Indiana University Press, 1973. Steele examines the 1942 Allied debate over European strategy within American ranks, as well as between the United States and Britain. He argues that all participants were motivated by political, rather than strategic factors, and finds Marshall's 1942 cross-channel plan a militarily unsound attempt to accommodate Roosevelt's politico-military demands. Bibliography.

Stoler, M. A. *The Politics of the Second Front: American Military Planning and Diplomacy in Coalition Warfare, 1941–1943* (25:129) argues effectively against the view that American military leaders ignored political factors in World War II planning. The United States wanted to defeat Germany, but did not want other national interests to suffer in the process.

Strawson, J. *Hitler's Battles for Europe* (23:86) deals with Hitler as a military leader and as a strategist.

North African Operations, 1942

23:172 Funk, Arthur L. *The Politics of TORCH: The Allied Landings and the Algiers Putsch, 1942*. Lawrence: University Press of Kansas, 1974. This is the first study to examine the political aspects of the Anglo-American invasion and occupation of North Africa from the French as well as the American and British points of view. The result is an excellent synthesis, with emphasis on Algiers and the Darlan affair. Extensive bibliography.

23:173 Howe, George F. *North Africa: Seizing the Initiative in the West*. In *United States Army in World War II: The Mediterranean Theater of Operations*. Washington, D.C.: G.P.O., 1957. This volume covers Anglo-American planning and operations in North Africa from 1941 through 1943, with major emphasis on the period from the Torch landings (November 1942) to the German surrender in Tunisia (May 1943). It includes detailed information also on the diplomatic negotiations and political issues which arose in this theater regarding French military forces, government, and leadership. Bibliography.

Cross-Channel Attack, 1944

23:174 Eisenhower Foundation. *D-Day: The Normandy Invasion in Retrospect.* Lawrence: University Press of Kansas, 1971. This volume consists of an edited collection of papers and commentaries to celebrate the 25th anniversary of the Normandy invasion. Politico-diplomatic and historical controversies associated with the invasion are discussed, along with strategic and tactical issues and personal recollections.

23:175 Harrison, Gordon A. *Cross-Channel Attack.* Washington, D.C.: G.P.O., 1951. Harrison covers planning for the cross-channel attack and the operations in Normandy until the beachhead was established. Approximately one-half of the book consists of strategy and Allied preparations for the invasion. Bibliography.

23:176 Villa, Brian L. "The Atomic Bomb and the Normandy Invasion." *Perspectives in American History* 11 (1977–1978), 461–502. The author maintains that Roosevelt in August 1943 exploited Winston Churchill's desire for an Anglo-American partnership in atomic energy to win British agreement to a 1944 cross-channel attack with an American commander.

Italy and the Mediterranean

See "Personalities," especially Field Marshal Harold Rupert L. G. Alexander, American Mark W. Clark (under "Others"), Benito Mussolini.

23:177 Deakin, F. W. *The Brutal Friendship.* New York: Harper & Row, 1962. This is a thorough study of the relationship between Mussolini and Hitler with particular reference to 1942-1943, when the Italian fascist government was collapsing. It carefully analyzes how military disaster caused the destruction of Mussolini's regime, drawing the Nazis and the Allies into the Italian quagmire.

23:178 Higgins, Trumbull. "The Anglo-American Historians' War in the Mediterranean, 1942–1945." *Military Affairs* 34:3 (1970), 84–88. This historiographical essay examines the dispute between British

and American historians, and among historians within each country, over the wisdom of the British Mediterranean approach to victory as opposed to the American cross-channel concept. The author offers a balanced and comprehensive overview of the debate.

23:179 Higgins, Trumbull. *Soft Underbelly: The Anglo-American Controversy over the Italian Campaign, 1939–1945.* New York: Macmillan, 1968. Higgins evaluates British aims and methods in the Italian campaign and the strategic disputes over the Mediterranean versus cross-channel approach to victory in Europe. The work complements his *Winston Churchill and the Second Front* (23:164) and retains the intense criticism of Churchill and the entire British approach. Bibliography.

23:180 Howard, Michael. *The Mediterranean Strategy in the Second World War.* New York: Praeger, 1968. Howard sees the Mediterranean strategy not as a fundamentally differing strategic concept, but as the opportunistic exploitation of an available theater when the Allies were unready to do anything else and could not afford to sit idle.

The Eastern Front

See "Personalities," especially Vasilii I. Chuikov and Georgi K. Zhukov (under "Others").

23:181 Clark, Alan. *Barbarossa: The Russian-German Conflict, 1941–45.* New York: Morrow, 1965. Breaking with the common pattern, the author defends Hitler's direction of the conflict, often siding with him against the generals. Colorfully written and satisfactory on strategy, this popular synthesis tells an exciting tale of combat operations well.

23:182 Schmidt, Paul K. (Paul Carell, pseud.) *Hitler Moves East, 1941–1943.* Boston: Little, Brown, 1965. Primarily relying on German records, but presenting both views, this account emphasizes front-line combat.

23:183 Schmidt, Paul K. (Paul Carell, pseud.) *Scorched Earth: The Russian-German War, 1943–1944.* Boston: Little, Brown, 1970. This sequel continues the story from the Battle of Kursk to the 1944 Soviet offensive.

PACIFIC
STRATEGY/OPERATIONS

See "Personalities," especially Emperor Hirohito, Ernest J. King, Jr., Douglas MacArthur, Field Marshal William J. Slim, Joseph W. Stilwell; see also Chapter 22, "The Decision for War, 1941."

Barclay, G. St. J. "Australia Looks to America: The Wartime Relationship, 1939–42" (32:115).

Boyle, J. H. *China and Japan at War, 1937–1945: The Politics of Collaboration* (22:217).

23:184   Collier, Basil. *The War in the Far East, 1941–1945: A Military History.* New York: Morrow, 1969. Collier's account provides a fine introduction to the Pacific war. Tables, maps, and bibliography.

23:185   Morton, Louis. *Strategy and Command: The First Two Years.* In *United States Army in World War II: The War in the Pacific.* Washington, D.C.: G.P.O., 1962. This volume concentrates on Allied and Japanese grand strategy in the Pacific from antecedents and prewar plans to the end of 1943. Appendixes include a number of useful primary documents from both sides. Bibliography.

Saburō Ienaga. *The Pacific War: World War II and the Japanese, 1931–1945* (22:202) provides rare insight into Japanese military activities and the military's role in plunging Japan into war. Its use of materials from ordinary soldiers, refugees, and housewives makes it a useful social, political, and intellectual study.

23:186   Stoler, Mark. "The Pacific First Alternative in American World War II Strategy." *International History Review* 2:3 (1980), 432–52. Stoler says that the U.S. Chiefs of Staff seriously considered turning American forces to the Pacific Theater in 1942 unless the British agreed to cross-channel operations for 1943. A strong stand by Roosevelt prevented this action.

23:187   Thorne, Christopher. *Allies of a Kind: The United States, Britain and the War against Japan, 1941–1945.* New York: Oxford University Press, 1978. This detailed and comprehensive volume is a major synthesis and reinterpretation of Anglo-American relations with regard to the war against Japan. It covers political as well as military issues and postwar planning for East Asia, and emphasizes the sharp differences which marked the Anglo-American alliance in these areas. Extensive bibliography.

Toland, J. *The Rising Sun: The Decline and Fall of the Japanese Empire, 1936–1945* (22:204) provides, in volume 1, a very readable survey of Japan in the Pacific war.

Military Operations

23:188   Hayashi, Saburo, and Coox, Alvin D. *Kogun: The Japanese Army in the Pacific War.* Quantico, Va.: Marine Corps Association, 1959. This is one of the better accounts; it discusses Japanese strategy and campaigns. It also contains some 90 biographical sketches of Japanese leaders.

23:189   Isely, Jeter A., and Crowl, Philip A. *The U.S. Marines and Amphibious War: Its Theory, and Its Practice in the Pacific.* Princeton, N.J.: Princeton University Press, 1951. This is an analytical study of the development of U.S. Marine Corps amphibious doctrine prior to 1941, and its application between 1942 and 1945.

23:190   Ito, Masanori. *The End of the Imperial Japanese Navy.* Trans. by A. Kuroda and R. Pineau. New York: Norton, 1962. For nearly two decades Japan planned to ambush American fleets, which they believed would push into the western Pacific because of the audacious Orange Plan. Ito regrets that all strategies were changed by events of 1940–1941, when the Americans entered World War II.

23:191   Kirby, S. Woodburn. *The War against Japan.* 5 vols. London: H.M.S.O., 1957–1969. The official account of British operations in East Asia consists of a narrative of operations, supply activities, and valuable material on high-level planning and cooperation with American political and military leaders.

Morison, S.E. *The Rising Sun in the Pacific, 1931–April 1942* (22:200) describes the near collapse of the U.S. Navy during the first five months of the Pacific war.

23:192   Sunderland, Riley. "The Secret Embargo." *Pacific Historical Review* 29:1 (1960), 75–80. This brief essay is a perceptive comment on Chiang Kai-shek's wartime practice of conserving his own forces while sacrificing the troops of rival Nationalist commanders and blaming the losses on General Stilwell. Warren I. Cohen provides more evidence on this same point in "Who Fought the Japanese in Hunan? Some Views of China's War Effort," *Journal of Asian Studies* 27 (Nov. 1967), 111–15.

China-Burma-India Operations

See "Personalities," especially Claire L. Chennault, Joseph W. Stilwell; also see Chapter 22, "Sino-Japanese War, 1937–1945"; and "China," below.

Caldwell, O. J. *A Secret War: Americans in China, 1944–45* (27:69).

Dorn, F. *Walkout with Stilwell in Burma* (27:70).

Liang Chin-tung. *General Stilwell in China, 1942–1944: The Full Story* (27:72).

23:193 Miles, Milton E. *A Different Kind of War: The Unknown Story of the U.S. Navy's Guerrilla Forces in World War II, China: Prepared from the Original Manuscript by Hawthorne Daniel.* Garden City, N.Y.: Doubleday, 1967. Miles presents one side of a bitter controversy about a naval mission's attempt to train guerrillas in China. The OSS, War Department, General Wedemeyer, and the State Department each found reasons for opposing this single-handed venture.

23:194 Romanus, Charles, and Sunderland, Riley. *Stilwell's Command Problems.* In *United States Army in World War II: The China-Burma-India Theater.* Washington, D.C.: G.P.O., 1956. This volume deals with the complicated command structure in that area, preparations for a Burma campaign, controversies among the British, Americans, and Chinese on priorities. It is informative on the Stilwell effort to get pressure exerted on Chiang Kai-shek to move against the Japanese. Bibliography.

23:195 Romanus, Charles, and Sunderland, Riley. *Stilwell's Mission to China.* In *United States Army in World War II: The China-Burma-India Theater.* Washington, D.C.: G.P.O., 1953. Romanus and Sunderland deal with the establishment of the Stilwell mission to China, the defeat in Burma, Stilwell's role as a trainer of troops, his clash with Chennault, and the beginnings of trouble with Chiang Kai-shek. Bibliography.

23:196 Romanus, Charles, and Sunderland, Riley. *Time Runs Out in CBI.* In *United States Army in World War II: The China-Burma-India Theater.* Washington, D.C.: G.P.O., 1959. This volume deals with the reorganization of the China theater under General Wedemeyer, with plans for air attacks from China, with completion of communications begun by Stilwell, with serious Japanese attacks which threatened air bases, and the end of Japanese control in China.

U.S., Soviet Union, and Japan

23:197 Dubinsky, A. M. *The Far East in the Second World War: An Outline History of International Relations and National Liberation Struggle in East and South-east Asia.* Moscow: Nauka, 1972. Using the Marxist-Leninist methodology, this book depreciates the "liberating mission" claimed by Japan and the United States in World War II and enlarges Russia's wartime roles beyond the antifascist and pro-Chinese ones usually emphasized.

23:198 Lensen, George. *A Strange Neutrality: Soviet-Japanese Relations during the Second World War, 1941–45.* Tallahassee, Fla.: Diplomatic Press, 1972. While the volume concentrates on Soviet-Japanese relationships in World War II, it necessarily deals with the way in which Soviet attempts to maintain neutrality affected its relations with the United States. A special appendix on Soviet treatment of U.S. fliers and the entry of the Soviet Union into the war against Japan are important parts of this work. Extensive bibliography.

23:199 May, Ernest R. "The United States, the Soviet Union and the Far Eastern War, 1941–1945." *Pacific Historical Review* 24:2 (1955), 153–74. The vain U.S. pleas for Soviet participation in the war against Japan ceased only after 1942, when the German debacle at Stalingrad quieted Allied fears of a Russian collapse in Europe. Roosevelt's interest in Soviet collaboration against Japan reappeared with Allied uncertainty toward the final battle for Japan.

23:200 Morton, Louis. "Soviet Intervention in the War against Japan." *Foreign Affairs* 40:4 (1962), 653–62. This article traces the history of U.S. policy toward Soviet intervention in the Pacific war, and concludes that this policy was based on the subordination of political to military considerations.

23:201 U.S. Department of Defense. *The Entry of the Soviet Union into the War against Japan: Military Plans, 1941–1945*. Washington, D.C.: G.P.O., 1955. A straightforward and convenient collection of documents, accompanied by narrative, concerning U.S. military advice on the question of Soviet participation in the war against Japan from 1941 to 1945.

STRATEGIC BOMBING

See "Personalities," especially Henry H. Arnold, Sir Arthur Harris (under "Others"); see also "Atomic Bomb and Japan's Surrender," below.

23:202 Cary, Otis. "The Sparing of Kyoto: Mr. Stimson's 'Pet City.' " *Japan Quarterly* 22:4 (1975), 337–47. Cary examines the stories as to why the city of Kyoto was not heavily bombed by U.S. air forces during World War II and why the city was spared from nuclear attack.

23:203 Helmreich, Jonathan A. "The Diplomacy of Apology: U.S. Bombings of Switzerland during World War II." *Air University Review* 28:4 (1977), 19–37. This essay discusses the problems caused by the inadvertent bombing of Swiss territory in 1943, 1944, and 1945 by elements of the Eighth Air Force. The most serious damage was inflicted in the cities of Schaffhausen, Zurich, and Basel. U.S. efforts to solve the problem and handle the diplomatic situation are examined in detail.

23:204 Hopkins, George E. "Bombing and the American Conscience during World War II." *Historian* 28:3 (1966), 451–73. The consensus favored the strategic bombing of German and Japanese cities. Americans ignored ethical distinctions between weapons because they were constantly reminded that they were engaged in "a total war."

23:205 MacIsaac, David. *Strategic Bombing in World War II: The Story of the United States Bombing Survey*. New York: Garland, 1976. This study provides an account of the organization and operation of USSBS and of the findings and conclusions, to help readers evaluate the extensive studies. The book also reviews the development of the strategic bombing doctrine.

23:206 MacIsaac, David, ed. *The United States Strategic Bombing Survey*. 10 vols. New York: Garland, 1976. The Strategic Bombing Survey staff produced 321 reports on various aspects of strategic bombing during World War II. Thirty of the more important reports are included in these volumes, 11 for the first time.

23:207 Rumpf, Hans. *The Bombing of Germany*. Trans. by Edward Fitzgerald. New York: Holt, Rinehart & Winston, 1963. This German view is critical of Allied bombing of Germany and especially of Douhet's theories. Rumpf holds that bombing strengthens the victims' will and does not remove the necessity of ground efforts. Bibliography.

23:208 Smith, Melden J. "The Strategic Bombing Debate: The Second World War and Vietnam." *Journal of Contemporary History* 12:1 (1977), 175–91. This article draws on Smith's dissertation on the bombing of Dresden in World War II and on studies by British and American authors of the effectiveness of World War II bombing to analyze contradictory views on bombing in Vietnam.

23:209 Verrier, Anthony. *The Bomber Offensive*. New York: Macmillan, 1968. This general account of the American and British strategic bomber offensive against Germany (1939–1945) questions the effectiveness of strategic bombing.

23:210 Webster, Sir Charles, and Frankland, Noble. *The Strategic Air Offensive against Germany, 1939–1945*. 4 vols. London: H.M.S.O., 1961. Much is given on British planning and early planning and operations, and the volumes cover the Combined Bomber Offensive, disagreement between British and American commanders on types of bombing, preparations for Overlord, high-level air command arrangements, and the like. The last volume consists of appendixes, documents, and statistics.

INTELLIGENCE OPERATIONS

See "Personalities," especially British officer Kenneth Strong (under "Others"); see also Chapter 40, "Intelligence Services."

23:211 Brown, Anthony C. *Bodyguard of Lies*. New York: Harper & Row, 1975. Brown weaves together the organization and operations of the British intelligence services, focusing on preparation for D-day. This account should be checked against later works based on declassified sources.

23:212   Clark, Ronald. *The Man Who Broke Purple: The Life of Colonel William F. Friedman, Who Deciphered the Japanese Code in World War II*. Boston: Little, Brown, 1977. By focusing on Friedman's career, Clark provides a fascinating glimpse into the art of cryptography. The account discusses military intelligence in World War I (briefly), surveys the interwar years, and concentrates on World War II.

23:213   Holmes, W. J. *Double Edged Secrets*. Annapolis, Md.: Naval Institute Press, 1979. The role of communications intelligence in the Pacific war is described by a former Pearl Harbor field officer of the navy's secret COMINT organization. Strategic intelligence, especially from submarines, together with the breaking of Japanese codes and ciphers, provided advance knowledge of adversary actions.

23:214   Hyde, H. Montgomery. *Room 3603: The Story of the British Intelligence Center in New York during World War II*. New York: Farrar, Straus, 1963. This is a narrative account of the sub-rosa activities of William Stephenson (Intrepid) and his British Security Coordination office in the United States during the war, by a member of his staff. While marred by incoherent organization, this should be used in preference to William Stephenson's *A Man Called Intrepid*.

23:215   Lewin, Ronald. *Ultra Goes to War: The First Account of World War II's Greatest Secret Based on Official Documents*. New York: McGraw-Hill, 1978. Lewin discusses the means (Ultra) by which the Allies intercepted and decoded German secret messages. He attempts to show how this information influenced combat decisions. Bibliography.

23:216   Smith, Richard H. *OSS: The Secret History of America's First Central Intelligence Agency*. Berkeley: University of California Press, 1972. This is a valuable guide to the organization, bureaucratic struggles, and operations of the OSS during World War II. Extensive bibliography.

23:217   Trefousse, Hans L. "The Failure of German Intelligence in the United States, 1935–1945." *Mississippi Valley Historical Review* 42:1 (1955), 84–100. This essay documents the ineptness of German espionage efforts, and shows how intelligence was rejected or misused by Hitler and his staff.

Interaction of Allies

SUMMIT MEETINGS

See Chapter 22, "Atlantic Charter, 1941," and Chapter 25 for Teheran, Yalta, and Potsdam conferences.

Beitzell, R. *The Uneasy Alliance: America, Britain and Russia, 1941–1943* (25:7) gives primary attention to four conferences: Quebec, Moscow, Cairo, and Teheran.

23:218   U.S. Department of State. *Foreign Relations of the United States: The Conferences at Washington, 1941–1942, and Casablanca, 1943*. Washington, D.C.: G.P.O., 1968. Major issues at these conferences included the formation of the United Nations alliance and the Combined Chiefs of Staff, Anglo-American strategic planning and arguments, North Africa and French leadership, and the unconditional surrender formula. Bibliography.

23:219   U.S. Department of State. *Foreign Relations of the United States: The Conferences at Washington and Quebec, 1943*. Washington, D.C.: G.P.O., 1970. Although the emphasis at both conferences was on Anglo-American strategic plans and disputes, much documentation is included on Italian surrender, atomic energy, and numerous postwar issues. Bibliography.

U.S. Department of State. *Foreign Relations of the United States, Diplomatic Papers: The Conferences at Cairo and Teheran, 1943* (25:58) includes documents from the first Cairo Conference, between Churchill, Roosevelt, and Chiang Kai-shek, and the second Cairo Conference, between Churchill and Roosevelt. Strategic issues dominated these conferences.

LEND-LEASE

See "Personalities," especially Edward R. Stettinius, Jr.; also Chapter 22, "Origins of Lend-Lease," and Chapter 25, "Lend-Lease" for consequences of termination.

23:220   Haltom, Margaret S. "Discrepancies in the Lend-Lease Program." *Southern Quarterly* 4:4

(1966), 446–68. This is a catalog of sins committed by the Lend-Lease Administration.

23:221 Langer, John D. "The Harriman-Beaverbrook Mission and the Debate over Unconditional Aid for the Soviet Union, 1941." *Journal of Contemporary History* 14:3 (1979), 463–82. Three months after German armies invaded the Soviet Union, British and American delegations in Moscow promised Stalin a long-range, large-scale aid program, "the First Soviet Supply Protocol." This generous unilateral commitment provoked high-level dissent within both British and American governments and touched off a debate that persisted.

23:222 Motter, T. H. Vail. *The Persian Corridor and Aid to Russia.* In *United States Army in World War II: The Middle East Theater.* Washington, D.C.: G.P.O., 1952. This is an official account of the development of a lend-lease supply route to Russia (1941–1945). It is replete with the difficulties of Allied cooperation.

23:223 Stettinius, Edward R., Jr. *Lend Lease: Weapon for Victory.* New York: Macmillan, 1944. A firsthand account of the lend-lease program by its administrator, it is interesting primarily for the attitudes and motivations of one of the program's primary advocates. Stettinius's view that the value of lend-lease must be monetarily balanced against our Allies' contribution in the front lines is valuable.

CHINA

See "Personalities," especially Claire L. Chennault, Patrick J. Hurley, George C. Marshal, John S. Service, Joseph W. Stilwell, Albert C. Wedemeyer (under "Military," "Others"); see also Chapter 27, "Wartime Relations with the Nationalists" and "U.S. and Chinese Communists."

Barrett, David D. *Dixie Mission: The United States Army Observer Group in Yenan, 1944* (27:89) describes the "Dixie mission" sent by Stilwell to the Chinese Communists in Yenan to open channels for intelligence on the Japanese.

23:224 Chan, K. C. "The Abrogation of British Extraterritoriality in China, 1942–43: A Study of Anglo-American-Chinese Relations." *Modern Asian Studies* 1:2 (1977), 257–91. The Nationalist government announced in 1929 its intention of terminating extraterritoriality in China. Anglo-American negotiations with China during the war resulted in both countries agreeing to new treaty relationships.

Davies, J. P., Jr. *Dragon by the Tail: American, British, Japanese, and Russian Encounters with China and with One Another* (27:39) while not favorable to the Nationalists nor to General Hurley and others, it adds considerably to the understanding of these critical years.

Feis, H. *The China Tangle: The American Effort in China from Pearl Harbor to the Marshall Mission* (27:64).

Tsou, T. *America's Failure in China, 1940–1941* (27:67) traces relations from the beginning of American aid to China against Japan to the conquest of the mainland by the Chinese Communists.

23:225 White, Theodore H. *In Search of History.* New York: Harper & Row, 1978. These recollections by an outstanding journalist are of value to historians for informed comments on wartime China and for his descriptions of General Stilwell, Chiang Kai-shek, Mao Tse-tung and Chou En-lai.

23:226 Young, Arthur N. *China and the Helping Hand, 1937–1945.* Cambridge: Harvard University Press, 1963. Young, an American financial adviser to China (1929–1947), attempts to give a balanced picture of foreign aid—particularly American—to Nationalist China. While stressing the positive side of Nationalist China's efforts, he does indicate factors within China that interferred with reform efforts.

FRANCE

See "Personalities," especially Charles de Gaulle, and U.S. Ambassador William D. Leahy (under "Military," "Others").

23:227 Funk, Arthur L. "Negotiating the 'Deal with Darlan.'" *Journal of Contemporary History* 8:2 (1973), 81–117. French cooperation with the Allies' invasion of North Africa in November 1942 was obtained at the price of recognizing Admiral Jean Darlan as high commissioner in Morocco and Algeria, despite his earlier pro-German record.

23:228 Langer, William L. *Our Vichy Gamble.* New York: Knopf, 1947. This is a good explanation of why the Roosevelt administration pursued its opportunistic policy vis-à-vis the collaborationist Vichy government, but the examination of alternatives is neither exhaustive nor totally convincing.

23:229 Paxton, Robert O. *Vichy France: Old Guard and New Order, 1940–44.* New York: Norton, 1972. An excellent volume on French collaboration with Germany, showing the part played by conservative and right-wing fears of social disorder, by French anti-Semitism, and by divisions between elements of French society. Extensive bibliography.

23:230 Vigneras, Marcel. *Rearming the French.* Washington, D.C.: G.P.O., 1957. Vigneras outlines the discussions between Roosevelt and Giraud at Casablanca concerning arms, and the later negotiations between French representatives and the War Department. Bibliography.

23:231 Viorst, Milton. *Hostile Allies: FDR and Charles de Gaulle.* New York: Macmillan, 1965. This is a sympathetic treatment of de Gaulle in his disagreements with Roosevelt and Churchill during World War II. Viorst is careful to note that the Roosevelt-de Gaulle incompatibility rested on differing national interests of the United States and France more than on personal characteristics. Bibliography.

23:232 White, Dorothy S. *Seeds of Discord: De Gaulle, Free France, and the Allies.* Syracuse, N.Y.: Syracuse University Press, 1964. This book is primarily a synthesis of the complex diplomatic developments that occurred while de Gaulle was trying to establish his legitimacy as leader of the non-Vichy French. De Gaulle comes off far better than blundering U.S. officials. Bibliography.

GREAT BRITAIN

See "Personalities," especially Winston S. Churchill and American John G. Winant (under "Others"); also see Chapter 25 for postwar planning.

23:233 Auty, Phyllis, and Clogg, Richard, eds. *British Policy towards Wartime Resistance in Yugoslavia and Greece.* New York: Barnes & Noble, 1975. This series of papers and recollections reconsiders British policy toward Yugoslav and Greek resistance movements. Specific topics covered include the activities of the Special Operations Executive, and the

"myth" of British plans for an Allied invasion of the Balkans.

Barker, E. *British Policy in South-East Europe in the Second World War* (25:97) outlines carefully the differences in attitudes and policies of Britain and the United States.

Leutze, J. R. "Technology and Bargaining in Anglo-American Naval Relations, 1938–1946" (22:110).

Louis, W. R. *Imperialism at Bay: The United States and the Decolonization of the British Empire, 1941–1945* (25:119) analyzes the wartime debate between the United States and Britain over the future of European colonies in general and the British empire in particular.

Smith, A. L., Jr. *Churchill's German Army: Wartime Strategy and Cold War Politics, 1943–1947* (25:22).

SOVIET UNION

See "Personalities," especially W. Averell Harriman, Harry Hopkins, and, under "Others," Charles E. Bohlen, William H. Standley.

23:234 Beardsley, E. H. "No Help Wanted: Medical Research Exchange between Russia and the West during the Second World War." *Medical History* 22:4 (1978), 365–77. Anglo-American efforts to establish a medical research exchange, which would have benefitted both sides, was rebuffed causing ill-feelings in the West.

23:235 Beardsley, E. H. "Secrets between Friends: Applied Science Exchange between the Western Allies and the Soviet Union during World War II." *Social Studies of Science* 7:4 ˙(1977), 447–74. Beardsley describes the inability of the United States and Britain to agree on scientific information exchange with the Soviet Union during World War II.

Dennett, R., and Johnson, J. E., eds. *Negotiating with the Russians* (25:73).

23:236 Infield, Glenn B. *The Poltava Affair: A Russian Warning, an American Tragedy.* New York: Macmillan, 1973. A little-known story of the establishment of three American air fields in Russia, which were destroyed by German air strikes. The Russians assisted the Germans, Infield believes, making this one of the first incidents of the cold war.

Levering, R. B. *American Opinion and the Russian Alliance, 1939–1945* (25:123) emphasizes the shifting nature of public opinion of Russia, and the ability of key "opinion makers" to influence public attitudes.

23:237 Lukas, Richard C. *Eagles East: The Army Air Forces and the Soviet Union, 1941–1945*. Tallahassee: Florida State University Press, 1970. Special attention is given to the issues of lend-lease, attempted military collaboration, and the ill-fated 1942 plan to send an Anglo-American air force to the eastern front; see *Military Affairs* 28:3 (1964), 145–62. Bibliography.

Mastny, V. *Russia's Road to the Cold War: Diplomacy, Warfare, and the Politics of Communism, 1941–1945* (25:24).

Small, M. "How We Learned to Love the Russians: American Media and the Soviet Union during World War II" (25:125) finds a drastic shift from a very negative 1939 image to a very positive 1944 view, but notes that the media simplistically and incorrectly emphasized Soviet-American similarities and a "new" Russia rather than explaining the real differences between the two nations.

Interactions with Other Nations

23:238 Alvarez, David J. "The Vatican and the War in the Far East, 1941–1943." *Historian* 40:3 (1978), 508–23. This essay examines the role of the Vatican, especially papal diplomacy, in East Asia (1941–1943) and analyzes the responses of the United States and Britain to the diplomatic meetings between the Holy See and Japan.

23:239 Jensdóttir Hardarson, Sólrún B. " 'Republic of Iceland' 1940–1944: Anglo-American Attitudes and Influences." *Journal of Contemporary History* 9:4 (1974), 27–56. Neither Britain nor the United States

had Danish-Icelandic relations in mind when undertaking to guarantee the absolute independence of Iceland, although the Icelanders adopted the interpretation.

Meier, H. K. *Friendship under Stress: U.S.-Swiss Relations, 1900–1950* (2:257) focuses on economic relations and Switzerland's importance as a neutral nation during World War II.

Hemispheric Defense

23:240 Anglin, Douglas G. *The St. Pierre and Miquelon Affairs of 1941: A Study in Diplomacy in the North Atlantic Quadrangle*. Toronto: University of Toronto Press, 1966. Cordell Hull's careful policy toward Vichy France caused him to be very circumspect in the disposition of these two French West Indian Islands and to be infuriated by de Gaulle's "invasion" of them. This volume reveals much about the Hull-Roosevelt relationship, about the administration's "hemispheric" preparation for World War II, and about the mistrust of de Gaulle. Bibliography.

23:241 Conn, Stetson; Engelman, Rose C.; and Fairchild, Byron. *Guarding the United States and Its Outposts*. In *United States Army in World War II: The Western Hemisphere*. Washington, D.C.: G.P.O., 1964. This study describes the army's "basic and primary concern"—the defense of the continental United States and its principal outposts, Hawaii, the Caribbean, Alaska, Greenland, and Iceland. Bibliography.

23:242 Conn, Stetson, and Fairchild, Byron. *The Framework of Hemispheric Defense*. In *United States Army in World War II: The Western Hemisphere*. Washington, D.C.: G.P.O., 1960. This volume analyzes American military planning (1939–1942) for and with other nations in the hemisphere, and includes much information on diplomatic as well as military relations with those nations—including Brazil, Mexico, and Canada. Bibliography.

23:243 Dziuban, Stanley W. *Military Relations between the United States and Canada, 1939–1945*. In *United States Army in World War II: Special Studies*. Washington, D.C.: G.P.O., 1959. Dziuban analyzes military-related political issues and uses manuscript collections as well as army files, but not Canadian records.

Frye, A. *Nazi Germany and the American Hemisphere, 1933–1941* (21:120) argues that while Nazi efforts did not pose a direct threat to hemispheric and U.S. interests, the overall opportunistic and hegemonial thrust of Hitler's policy, coupled with possible success in Europe, did justify Roosevelt's reactions. Bibliography.

EAST ASIA

See also Chapter 30, "Thailand in World War II."

23:244 Benda, Harry J. *The Crescent and the Rising Sun: Indonesian Islam under the Japanese Occupation, 1942–1945.* The Hague: Van Hoeve, 1958. Benda sees Japanese occupation as stimulating Indonesian nationalism, an issue in postwar affairs.

Friend, T. W. *Between Two Empires: The Ordeal of the Philippines, 1929–1946* (21:232) is valuable on the World War II period.

Gordon, L. "American Planning for Taiwan, 1942–1945" (27:87).

Martin, J. V. "Thai-American Relations in World War II" (30:135) describes the cooperation between the United States and the Free Thai movement and Siamese underground in the face of the official pro-Japanese stand of the Songgram government.

McMahon, R. J. "Anglo-American Diplomacy and the Reoccupation of the Netherlands East Indies" (30:96) discusses the British forces' arrival in the Dutch East Indies in 1945 to receive the surrender of the Japanese and turn the islands back to the Dutch. They encountered a strong nationalist movement already functioning as an independent government.

LATIN AMERICA

See also Chapter 35, "World War II, 1941–1945."

23:245 Blasier, Cole. "The United States, Germany, and the Bolivian Revolutionaries (1941–1946)." *Hispanic American History Review* 52:1 (1972), 26–54. Blasier examines the U.S. campaign against Nazi fascism in Bolivia involving three interrelated episodes: the Nazi putsch of 1941; the initial refusal of the United States to recognize the Villarroel

government in 1944; and the 1946 publication of the blue book against Juan Perón.

Dozer, D. M. *Are We Good Neighbors? Three Decades of Inter-American Relations, 1930–1960* (21:240).

Francis, M. J. *The Limits of Hegemony: United States Relations with Argentina and Chile during World War II* (35:91) explores the course of U.S. diplomacy dealing with Argentina's and Chile's nationalism and recalcitrance.

23:246 Francis, Michael J. "The United States and Chile during the Second World War: The Diplomacy of Misunderstanding." *Journal of Latin American Studies* 9:1 (1977), 91–113. The U.S. government felt that all American nations were morally obligated to fight the Axis, but the Chilean government felt that the war was beyond Chile's influence.

Gellman, I. F. *Roosevelt and Batista: Good Neighbor Diplomacy in Cuba, 1933–1945* (21:265) focuses on the U.S. ambassador as a major influence on political decisions, through his ability to influence economic actions.

23:247 Haines, Gerald K. "Under the Eagle's Wing: The Franklin Roosevelt Administration Forges an American Hemisphere." *Diplomatic History* 1:4 (1977), 373–88. During the late 1930s and early 1940s, the Roosevelt administration desired stable political conditions in its own "backyard." Thus involved in a worldwide struggle, these policymakers sought to create a stable, orderly hemisphere.

Hilton, S. E. "Brazilian Diplomacy and the Washington-Rio de Janeiro 'Axis' during the World War II Era" (35:87).

McCann, F. D., Jr. *The Brazilian-American Alliance, 1937–1945* (21:284).

23:248 Tulchin, J. S. "The Argentine Proposal for Non-Belligerency, April 1940." *Journal of Inter-American Studies* 11:4 (1969), 571–604. Tulchin analyzes the reasons why the United States brushed aside Argentina's friendly overture (when Roosevelt called for nonbelligerency two months later), and explains the impact on the Argentine government.

Woods, R. B. *The Roosevelt Foreign-Policy Establishment and the "Good Neighbor": The United States and Argentina, 1941–1945* (35:94) contends that during World War II the good neighbor policy was undermined by Argentina's refusal to join the war against the Axis.

SPAIN

See "Personalities," especially Carlton J. H. Hayes.

23:249   Cortada, James W. "Spain and the Second World War." *Journal of Contemporary History* 5:4 (1970), 65–75. In 1943–1944, the United States and Britain tried to persuade Franco to embargo the sale of wolfram to Germany. Meantime, Franco seemed to have recognized Japan's puppet government in the Philippines. Washington embargoed fuel (February 1944) to Spain before Franco agreed to an embargo on wolfram to Germany.

23:250   Feis, Herbert. *The Spanish Story: Franco and the Nations at War.* New York: Knopf, 1948. Feis's interpretive narration of the U.S. relationship to Franco's Spain (1939–1941) emphasizes how crucial the dealings with Spain were in keeping Hitler from access to the Mediterranean Sea at Gibraltar.

YUGOSLAVIA

23:251   Robertson, Walter R. *Tito, Mihailovic and the Allies, 1941–45.* New Brunswick, N.J.: Rutgers University Press, 1973. This volume shows British and American differences toward Yugoslav warring factions and the ultimate decisions to aid Tito. Robertson holds that Tito's independent attitude toward the U.S.S.R. was based in part on his cordial relations with the Western liaison officers. Bibliography.

23:252   Wheeler, Mark C. *Britain and the War for Yugoslavia, 1940–1943.* New York: Columbia University Press, 1980. Using recently declassified British documents, Wheeler provides a clear development of British wartime policy.

Surrender

23:253   Kecskemeti, Paul. *Strategic Surrender: The Politics of Victory and Defeat.* Stanford, Calif.: Stan-

ford University Press, 1958. Four case studies—the surrender of France, Italy, Germany, and Japan—were undertaken to find the point at which it was clear that the war had been lost.

23:254   Steele, Richard W. "American Popular Opinion and the War against Germany: The Issue of a Negotiated Peace, 1942." *Journal of American History* 65:3 (1978), 704–23. The author emphasizes administration fears of a negotiated peace movement led by prewar isolationist opponents of Roosevelt, and the president's efforts to counter this threat.

UNCONDITIONAL SURRENDER

23:255   Armstrong, Anne. *Unconditional Surrender: The Impact of the Casablanca Policy upon World War.* New Brunswick, N.J.: Rutgers University Press, 1961. The author concludes that the unconditional surrender formula arose because of a failure to separate ends from means or military strategy from political goals. The decision undoubtedly reflected the U.S. view of war as a crusade, but conclusions regarding its effect are more tentative. Bibliography.

23:256   Glennon, John P. "This Time Germany Is a Defeated Nation: The Doctrine of Unconditional Surrender and Some Unsuccessful Attempts to Alter It, 1934–1944." In Gerald N. Grob, ed., *Statesmen and Statecraft of the Modern West.* Barre, Mass.: Barre Publishers, 1967, pp. 109–51. This is a valuable summary of the background of the unconditional surrender formula.

23:257   O'Connor, Raymond G. *Diplomacy for Victory: FDR and Unconditional Surrender.* New York: Norton, 1971. O'Connor examines, and ultimately rejects, the leading revisionist arguments. He traces the origins of unconditional surrender to Roosevelt's World War I experience, and sees the doctrine as a convenient way of avoiding internal and Allied disharmony over political issues, while successfully prosecuting the war. Extensive bibliography.

ITALIAN SURRENDER

See "Personalities," especially Mark W. Clark (under "Others").

Dulles, A. *The Secret Surrender* (25:138) is a personal account of the negotiations which led to the surrender of German forces in Italy to British and American commanders in northern Italy before the capitulation of Germany.

Kogan, N. *Italy and the Allies* (28:148) surveys Italy's relations from surrender in 1943 through the peace settlement.

23:258 Smith, Bradley F., and Agarossi, Elena. *Operation Sunrise: The Secret Surrender*. New York: Basic Books, 1979. The newest and most complete study of the negotiations leading to the 1945 surrender of German forces in Italy. Bibliography.

GERMAN SURRENDER

See "Personalities," especially Karl Dönitz (under "Military," "Others"); see also Chapter 25, "Germany," for planning for postwar occupation.

23:259 Steinert, Marlis G. *Twenty-three Days: The Final Collapse of Nazi Germany*. Trans. by Richard Barry. New York: Walker, 1969. This is the story of the Dönitz government, its capitulation, and the immediate post-surrender period. Primary value derives from the uniquely German perspective and good portraits of Dönitz, Jodl, and von Krosigk.

ATOMIC BOMB AND JAPAN'S SURRENDER

See "Personalities," especially Emperor Hirohito and American Leslie Groves (under "Military," "Others"); see also Chapter 25, "Atomic Diplomacy."

23:260 Bernstein, Barton J. "The Perils and Politics of Surrender: Ending the War with Japan and Avoiding the Third Atomic Bomb." *Pacific Historical Review* 46:1 (1977), 1–27. The ambiguous American response to Japan's August 10, 1945, surrender offer strengthened the militarists in Japan and nearly prolonged the war. Americans were concerned about domestic political effects if the emperor were retained; therefore, they were considering a third atomic bomb or mounting a costly invasion.

23:261 Butow, Robert J. C. *Japan's Decision to Surrender*. Stanford, Calif.: Stanford University Press, 1954. Butow, as always, writes with great knowledge and appreciation of the subtleties and intricacies of the Japanese political process. The focus

throughout is on the situation in and as seen from Tokyo. Bibliography.

23:262 Feis, Herbert. *Japan Subdued: The Atomic Bomb and the End of the War in the Pacific*. Princeton, N.J.: Princeton University Press, 1961. The volume is partly a rebuttal of the charge that the atomic bomb was used to influence the Soviets. Feis notes that use of the bomb may have spared both the United States and Japan heavy casualties. The revised edition is titled *The Atomic Bomb and the End of World War II* (1966).

23:263 Giovannitti, Len, and Freed, Fred. *The Decision to Drop the Bomb*. New York: Coward-McCann, 1965. Giovannitti and Freed take into account the reasons and alternatives for the use of the bomb, and conclude that it was a well-calculated military decision, with underlying political reasons as well, designed to end the war quickly. Bibliography.

Hewlett, R. G., and Anderson, O. E., Jr. *The New World, 1939–1946*. Vol. 1 in *A History of the United States Atomic Energy Commission* (26:200) is a detailed official history of the development of the bomb (1938–1945) and American policy toward it (1945–1947).

23:264 Schoenberger, Walter S. *Decision of Destiny*. Athens: University of Ohio Press, 1969. A detailed examination of the development of the atomic bomb and the thinking about its use which developed as the war and the bomb progressed. Truman's decision to use the bomb was the logical outgrowth of the earliest assumption about its use. Extensive bibliography.

23:265 Sherwin, Martin J. *A World Destroyed: The Atomic Bomb and the Grand Alliance*. New York: Knopf, 1975. This study is a major analysis and reinterpretation of U.S. nuclear policy during World War II. Sherwin argues that such "atomic diplomacy" originated with Roosevelt rather than Truman, and that it constituted one of many political and military motives involved in nuclear policy and the decision to bomb Hiroshima. Extensive bibliography.

23:266 Sigal, Leon V. "Bureaucratic Politics and Tactical Use of Committees: The Interim Committee and the Decision to Drop the Atomic Bomb." *Polity* 10:3 (1978), 326–64. Working within the bureaucratic politics framework, Sigal shows how various types of committees forged interagency agreement on and secured compliance by governmental agencies to drop the atomic bomb.

23:267   Steiner, Arthur. "Baptism of the Atomic Scientists." *Bulletin of the Atomic Scientists* 31:2 (1975), 21–28. Steiner traces the fate of the Franck Report to illuminate one aspect of scientists' participation in national policymaking. James Franck, a Nobel laureate in physics, issued a committee report on June 11, 1945, calling for a "non-lethal demonstration of the soon-to-be-ready atomic bomb."

23:268   Villa, Brian L. "The U.S. Army, Unconditional Surrender, and the Potsdam Declaration." *Journal of American History* 63:1 (1976), 66–92. This administrative study analyzes the debate over possible modification of the unconditional surrender formula, most notably in regard to Japan, which took place within and between the War and State departments.

Yavenditti, M. J. "John Hersey and the American Conscience: The Reception of 'Hiroshima' " (27:146) analyzes motives and methods Hersey used in writing one of the most influential American accounts of the bombing.

24

U.S. Cold War Diplomacy: Overviews, Historiography, and Personalities

Contributing Editor

JOHN LEWIS GADDIS
Ohio University

Contents

Introduction

One subject has dominated both the conduct of United States foreign policy since 1945 and historical writing about it: that protracted, multifaceted, and (so far) mostly nonviolent rivalry between the United States and the Soviet Union known as the cold war. Just as it has proven virtually impossible for American diplomats to act anywhere in the world without reference to this question, so too historians, political scientists, journalists, and writers of memoirs have found it difficult to discuss any aspect of postwar international relations apart from the context of Soviet-American competition. The cold war, in one form or another, then, will be the subject of all the chapters that follow in this bibliography. This chapter is intended merely to introduce the subject by concentrating on general works not limited to particular topics or regions. Succeeding chapters will deal in greater detail with specific aspects of the cold war.

Some attention should be paid at the outset, though, to the three unusually distinct phases through which historical writing on the cold war has gone—the "orthodox," "revisionist," and "post-revisionist" schools of thought. Historians have disagreed with one another more strongly on the question of how the cold war began than on any other single issue in recent writing about American diplomatic history. An awareness of the general outlines of this controversy is essential, therefore, to an understanding of this rapidly growing body of historical literature.

The "orthodox" phase. Most Western accounts of the cold war written between the late 1940s and the mid-1960s fall into this category. They have in common a tendency to hold the Soviet Union primarily responsible for the breakdown of Allied cooperation after World War II, although there was disagreement among "orthodox" historians as to whether Moscow's postwar policies grew out of an excessive preoccupation with security or an ideologically-based determination to dominate the world. The United States, in these accounts, reacted only after repeated provocation, allowing itself reluctantly to be drawn

into global responsibilities, chiefly at the invitation of other countries concerned about the Russians. Most "orthodox" analyses were written before official documents became available for research; they tended to reflect, as a consequence, either the public positions taken by the U.S. government and its allies, or the personal memories of participants in the events described. The voluminous works of Herbert Feis (cited in the following chapters), provide the best detailed guide to the "orthodox" interpretation; for more succinct accounts, see W. W. Rostow, *The United States in the World Arena* (24:48), or the early editions of John W. Spanier, *American Foreign Policy since World War II* (24:50).

The "revisionist" phase. This interpretation became dominant between the mid-1960s and the mid-1970s, although it reflected the strong influence of two earlier works, William A. Williams's *The Tragedy of American Diplomacy* (2:99) and D. F. Fleming's *The Cold War and Its Origins* (24:9). "Revisionism" coincided with the first significant opening of government documents on the cold war period, and also with the outbreak of domestic opposition to the American role in Vietnam. From these perspectives, its exponents tended to view the United States as primarily responsible at least for the way in which the cold war developed, if not for the cold war itself. The Soviet Union, to the extent that its role was discussed at all, was generally seen as a more or less innocent victim. Explanations for American behavior varied, but they usually reflected in one form or another the argument that American domestic institutions, especially the demands of a capitalist economy, required the constant expansion of influence overseas, thus making conflict with other countries inevitable. Representative revisionist accounts include Gar Alperovitz, *Atomic Diplomacy* (25:157), David Horowitz, *Free World Colossus* (24:39), Joyce and Gabriel Kolko, *The Limits of Power* (24:40), and, among more moderate advocates of this point of view, Walter LaFeber, *America, Russia, and the Cold War* (24:18), Lloyd C. Gardner, *Architects of Illusion* (25:17), and Thomas G. Paterson, *Soviet-American Confrontation* (26:12).

The "post-revisionist" phase. Since the mid-1970s, most writing about the cold war has reflected a position somewhere between the "orthodox" and "revisionist" camps: both the Soviet Union and the

United States are acknowledged to have shared responsibility for the cold war, though both are generally viewed as having acted for what they perceived to be defensive reasons. There has been a deemphasis on the economic component of American foreign policy (an implied rejection of "revisionism"), but as well a deemphasis on the ideological component of Soviet foreign policy (an implied rejection of "orthodoxy"). "Post-revisionist" historians have stressed the careful use of archival materials and the importance of personalities (two characteristics often cited as missing in "revisionist" accounts), without at the same time losing sight of "revisionist" insights into the frequently self-interested nature of American cold war policies (a point usually missed in "orthodox" accounts). A representative sampling of books in the "post-revisionist" school would include Martin J. Sherwin, *A World Destroyed* (23:265), George C. Herring, Jr., *Aid to Russia* (25:144), Alonzo L. Hamby, *Beyond the New Deal* (26:58), John Lewis Gaddis, *The United States and the Origins of the Cold War* (25:16), Daniel Yergin, *Shattered Peace* (26:22), Bruce Kuniholm, *The Origins of the Cold War in the Near East* (33:89), and Geir Lundestad, *The American Non-Policy towards Eastern Europe* (26:113).

Other accounts falling into the "orthodox," "revisionist," and "post-revisionist" categories, as well as many books and articles that fit easily into none of them, are cited in this and the following chapters.

Despite the great volume of material that has been written on the cold war and is reflected in this *Guide*, many opportunities for further research remain. The following is a brief (but by no means exhaustive) list of general problems still unresolved by cold war scholars; it should be supplemented by lists included in the more specialized cold war chapters as well.

1. The nature of U.S. relations with countries outside the Soviet bloc, with special reference to the question of whether the expansion of American influence in the world after 1945 occurred by imposition or by invitation.

2. Related to the above, utilization of foreign archival materials that will increasingly become available in years to come.

3. The American perception of the communist world: to what extent, and for how long, was it seen as a monolith; to what extent, and with what success, were efforts made to exploit divisions within it?

4. The question of means: how did the perception of resources available shape the conduct of U.S. foreign and national security policy from administration to administration?

5. The influence of bureaucracies: to what extent

did they take on an institutional life of their own, apart from national policy? What were the results?

6. The role of the intelligence community, both as a source of information in policymaking and as an instrument for implementing policy.

7. The interaction of foreign and national security policy with domestic politics—an oddly neglected subject on which abundant sources are available.

8. The role of ideas—for example, "containment," "national security," "deterrence," "coexistence," "détente"—in shaping postwar American foreign policy.

9. Elites, interest groups, and foreign policy: what groups stood to benefit from what policies, and why?

10. The debate over the origins of the cold war and its subsequent influence, if any, on national policy.

Resources and Overviews

RESEARCH AIDS

While pertinent bibliographies and reference aids are listed here, there are more extensive lists in Chapter 1.

Bibliographies

Bibliographies dealing with specific cold war themes may be found in the relevant chapters.

Albrecht, Ulrich, et al. *A Short Research Guide on Arms and Armed Forces* (40:1) lists seven different categories of informational aids, including those to U.S. and Soviet forces.

Burt, R., comp. and ed., and Kemp, G., ed. *Congressional Hearings on American Defense Policy, 1947–1971: An Annotated Bibliography* (1:44) provides a list of hearings held on foreign policy and national defense issues for the 80th through the 92d Congresses, and includes a list of those testifying and brief summaries of subjects dealt with; but does not cover executive session testimony.

24:1   Cronon, E. David, and Rosenof, Theodore D., comps. *The Second World War and the Atomic Age, 1940–1973.* Northbrook, Ill.: AHM, 1975. Section 3 lists works (articles, books, and dissertations) for Europe, Russia, and the cold war and section 4 covers national defense and military policy. Not annotated.

Dexter, B., ed. *The Foreign Affairs Fifty-Year Bibliography: New Evaluation of Significant Books on International Relations, 1920–1970* (1:14) is a very useful condensation and new evaluation of books listed in the *Foreign Affairs Bibliography* (1:15).

Foreign Affairs Bibliography: A Selected and Annotated List of Books on International Relations (1:15) is the most thorough, annotated bibliography of books on all aspects of international affairs, with good coverage of foreign-language titles. Five volumes published to date, covering 1919 to 1932, 1932 to 1942, 1942 to 1952, 1952 to 1962, and 1962 to 1972; they are based on the book notes in each issue of *Foreign Affairs,* which provide a convenient supplement for the post-1972 period.

Grant, S. A. *Scholar's Guide to Washington, D.C. for Russian/Soviet Studies* (1:271).

Greenwood, J., comp. *American Defense Policy since 1945: A Preliminary Bibliography* (1:45) is a "preliminary" bibliography of books, articles, and government documents dealing with U.S. postwar defense policy. Includes sections on bibliographies, data and descriptive material, strategic thought and military doctrine, the defense policymaking process, defense output, weapons systems, and military programs, and the domestic effects of defense policies.

Hammond, T. T., comp. and ed. *Soviet Foreign Relations and World Communism: A Selected, Annotated Bibliography of 7,000 Books in Thirty Languages* (1:83) is the most thorough English-language bibliography of primary and secondary works on Soviet foreign policy and international communism from 1917 to 1961, with some items through 1964. Valuable for its critical annotations.

Jones, D. L. *Books in English on the Soviet Union, 1917–73: A Bibliography* (1:86) gives considerable attention to Soviet foreign relations—including those with the United States. Unannotated.

Meckler, A. M., and McMullin, R. *Oral History Collections* (1:254) includes numerous interviews of prominent American diplomats who have been engaged in cold war policymaking.

24:2   Okinshevich, Leo, comp. *United States History and Historiography in Postwar Soviet Writings, 1945–1970: A Bibliography.* Santa Barbara, Calif.: ABC-Clio, 1976. This bibliography covers books and articles dealing with all aspects of U.S. history published in the Soviet Union (1945–1970), with pp. 218–76 covering U.S. history since 1945.

Saran, V. *Sino-Soviet Schism: A Bibliography, 1956–1964* (31:4).

Seidman, J., comp. *Communism in the United States: A Bibliography* (1:75) is a thorough, annotated bibliography of some 7,000 books and articles dealing with communism in the United States (1919–1959). This is an updated and expanded version of the Fund for the Republic's *Bibliography on the Communist Problem in the United States* (1955).

Yearbooks and Other Aids

Columbia Broadcasting System. *Face the Nation: The Collected Transcripts from the CBS Radio and Television Broadcasts, 1954–1971* (1:347) provides transcripts of the weekly CBS television interview program. Indexed.

Current Digest of the Soviet Press (29:4) presents English translations of current articles from Soviet publications.

Facts on File: A Weekly Digest with Cumulative Index (1:151) is a convenient weekly summary of major news events, domestic and foreign, with cumulative indexes.

Florinsky, M. T., ed. *McGraw-Hill Encyclopedia of Russia and the Soviet Union* (1:166) is a useful reference for biographies of Soviet leaders, descriptions of treaties, etc.

Gallup, G. H. *The Gallup Poll: Public Opinion, 1935–1971* (1:348) includes data from some 7,000 polls dealing with all aspects of national life, with considerable attention paid to foreign affairs. Arranged chronologically; indexed.

Keesing's Contemporary Archives: Weekly Diary of World Events (1:152) is the British equivalent of *Facts on File,* also weekly with cumulative indexing. It is somewhat stronger in its coverage of international events than its American counterpart.

Political Handbook and Atlas of the World (1:144) is a valuable annual reference guide to world governments, listing officials in power, political parties, names of major newspapers, summaries of the year's events, and, since 1963, maps.

Prokhorov, A. M., ed. *Great Soviet Encyclopedia* (1:170) is an English translation of the multivolume Soviet publication, which contains a wealth of information about the U.S.S.R. and its leaders.

The Statesman's Year Book: Statistical and Historical Annual of the States of the World (1:145) provides basic factual information on countries of the world and major international organizations, published in Great Britain since 1864. It provides more factual and statistical information than its American counterpart, the *Political Handbook and Atlas of the World* (1:144), but lacks the latter's review of recent events in each country.

Survey of International Affairs [1920–1963] (1:146) is a distinguished series of essays—sometimes whole volumes—on specific aspects of international affairs. They provide a valuable, detailed narrative of international diplomacy through 1963. Intended to be used with its accompanying documentary series, *Documents on International Affairs* (1:340); useful also in conjunction with its American counterpart, *The United States in World Affairs.*

The United States in World Affairs (1:147) is an indispensable annual review of American foreign policy; containing excellent chronologies and bibliographies. Unfortunately, publication is now suspended—the last volume published was for 1970, and the years 1968 and 1969 have yet to be covered. In 1979, the Council on Foreign Relations did begin publishing as a fifth issue of its quarterly, *Foreign Affairs,* a review of the events of the preceding year, which, though different in format, will to an extent fulfill the functions of the suspended *United States in World Affairs* volumes.

Vital Speeches of the Day (1:153) is a biweekly publication reprinting, usually in full, major addresses of note by public figures.

Wieczynski, J. L., ed. *The Modern Encyclopedia of Russian and Soviet History* (1:171) is an ongoing,

multivolume project, beginning in 1976 with "A." It includes references to and entries on key Soviet diplomatic personalities and events.

24:3 *The Year Book of World Affairs* London: Publisher varies, 1947–. These annual volumes contain essays on a variety of topics, many of them central to U.S.-U.S.S.R. relations.

Yearbook on International Communist Affairs (1:148) is an annual from 1967 providing country-by-country profiles of communist parties, together with information on international communist activities.

Document Collections

More general collections have been listed in Chapter 1, and other collections are found in "Personalities," below.

24:4 *Declassified Documents Quarterly.* Washington, D.C.: Carrollton, 1975–. This is a quarterly guide to recently declassified government documents, cumulatively indexed and keyed to microfiche copies of the documents.

Documents on American Foreign Relations (1:339) is a compilation of major public documents on American foreign policy, intended to accompany the *United States in World Affairs* (1:147). In 1971, the title became *American Foreign Relations, 19–: A Documentary Record.*

Documents on International Affairs [1928–1963] (1:340) is the best source for the official documents and public statements of foreign leaders. Published as a supplement to the *Survey of International Affairs* (1:146).

Gruliow, L., ed. *Current Soviet Policies* (29:5) constitutes the translated documentary record of the 19th (1952), 20th (1956), 21st (1959), and 22d (1961) Communist party congresses. Although many of the documents (speeches, resolutions, reports, discussions) center on domestic Soviet issues, some, such as Khrushchev's secret 1956 de-Stalinization speech and several references to the relationship between internal and external politics, do address cold war topics. Index.

24:5 Hanak, H., ed. *Soviet Foreign Policy since the Death of Stalin.* London: Routledge & Kegan Paul,

1972. A collection of Soviet documents—speeches, treaties, interviews, newspaper articles, diplomatic notes—illustrating Moscow's policies toward capitalist, socialist, and Third World nations. An introduction places these sources in their historical setting.

24:6   Schlesinger, Arthur M., Jr., ed. *The Dynamics of World Power: A Documentary History of United States Foreign Policy, 1945–1973*. 5 vols. New York: Chelsea House, 1973. The most extensive documentary history of postwar American foreign policy, this work contains sections on Western Europe by Robert Dallek, Eastern Europe and the Soviet Union by Walter LaFeber, Latin America by Robert Burr, the Far East by Russell D. Buhite, the United Nations by Richard C. Hottelet, and Sub-Saharan Africa by Jean Herskovits.

Stockholm International Peace Research Institute. *SIPRI Yearbook of World Armaments and Disarmament* (40:9) a detailed annual study (1968–) of developments in armaments, weapon technology, and arms control negotiations; emphasis on Soviet-American nuclear competition and agreements. Includes documents, chronology, charts, and index.

[U.S.S.R.]. *Milestones of Soviet Foreign Policy, 1917–1967* (1:368) contains 73 important documents.

U.S. Department of State. *American Foreign Policy: Current Documents, 1956–1967* (1:356) is an official compendium. See also its predecessor, *American Foreign Policy, 1950–1955: Basic Documents* (1957). (1:355).

U.S. Senate. Committee on Foreign Relations. *A Decade of American Foreign Policy: Basic Documents, 1941–1949* (23:20).

U.S. Department of State. *Press Conferences of the Secretaries of State, 1922–1974* (1:360) is a microfilm of the typescript, verbatim record of these conferences. An important source for research on the views of such officials as John Foster Dulles, Dean Rusk, and Henry A. Kissinger.

U.S. President. *Public Papers of the Presidents of the United States* [1945–] (1:362) begins with the presidency of Harry S. Truman. These volumes constitute an official compilation of the presidents' public messages, speeches, and statements.

Cold War Histories

OVERVIEWS

Bailey, T. A. *America Faces Russia: Russian-American Relations from Early Times to Our Day* (2:245) is a dated but still useful survey of Russian-American relations. Bailey's main concern is with American attitudes toward Russia and how those attitudes were often shaped by stereotypes.

24:7   Brzezinski, Zbigniew. "How the Cold War Was Played." *Foreign Affairs* 51:1 (1972), 181–209. An attempt to identify the major phases of the cold war, the diplomatic, economic, military, and domestic political standing of the United States and the U.S.S.R. during each phase, and the extent to which assertive or reactive policies resulted.

24:8   Donnelly, Desmond. *Struggle for the World: The Cold War, 1917–1965*. New York: St. Martin's Press, 1965. This British account of the cold war argues that the phenomenon can only be understood by going back to the Bolshevik Revolution. As a consequence, only the last half of the book deals with events since 1945. Donnelly suggests that Mao's revolution succeeded where Lenin's failed, and hence poses at least as great a threat to the West.

24:9   Fleming, D. F. *The Cold War and Its Origins, 1917–1960*. 2 vols. Garden City, N.Y.: Doubleday, 1961. A massive account of the cold war which anticipated revisionism, though not from an economic perspective, the book is a sustained indictment of the United States as having primary responsibility for the cold war. Heavily based on journalistic sources.

24:10   Fontaine, Andre. *History of the Cold War: From the October Revolution to the Korean War, 1917–1950*. 2 vol. Trans. by Renaud Bruce. New York: Random House, 1968–1969. In this comprehensive history of the cold war (1917–1963), Fontaine, foreign editor of *Le Monde*, brings a high degree of objectivity and balance to his analysis, which emphasizes the ideological roots of the cold war. Includes a chronology of events and brief biographical sketches of major figures.

Gaddis, J. L. *Russia, the Soviet Union, and the United States* (2:248) is a concise but comprehensive survey of Russian-American relations (1781–1976), with emphasis on 1917 to 1976. Combining synthesis and original research, Gaddis describes how the interplay of interests and ideologies caused relations between the two countries to pass from conditions of relative harmony to those of conflict and ultimately big power confrontation.

24:11   Gaddis, John Lewis. *Strategies of Containment: A Critical Appraisal of Postwar United States National Security Policy.* New York: Oxford University Press, 1982. A reassessment of postwar national security policy in terms of "symmetrical" and "asymmetrical" approaches to containment—the first involves countering challenges to the balance of power at the time, in the place, and at the same level that they occur, the second involves doing so at times and in places of one's own choosing. Gaddis suggests that "symmetrical" containment is associated with the perception of expandable means; "asymmetrical" containment with the perception of fixed means.

24:12   Gamson, William, and Modigliani, Andre. *Untangling the Cold War: A Strategy for Testing Rival Theories.* Boston: Little, Brown, 1971. An attempt to apply the techniques of quantification and content analysis to the study of the cold war as a whole, the book identifies some 125 "interaction units" in Soviet-American relations (1946–1963). The major finding is that both sides viewed themselves as "consolidationist," but perceived each other as "expansive." Contains an extensive set of "data appendices," a glossary of terms, and a bibliography.

24:13   Halle, Louis J. *The Cold War as History.* New York: Harper & Row, 1967. This is an eloquent account of the cold war (1944–1962) by a former State Department official. The cold war was not, Halle argues, "a case of the wicked against the virtuous. Fundamentally, it is like the case of the scorpion and the tarantula in the bottle...." Bibliography.

24:14   Higgins, Hugh. *The Cold War.* New York: Barnes & Noble, 1974. A short British history of the cold war, generally sympathetic to the arguments of the American revisionists. It argues that the cold war ended with the development of the Sino-Soviet split, but that American anticommunism persisted.

24:15   Hudson, G. F. *The Hard and Bitter Peace: World Politics since 1945.* New York: Praeger, 1967.

A British scholar's analysis (1945–1966) which emphasizes the emergence of an uneasy stability in the relations of the super powers, threatened, however, by the opportunities and dangers of instability in the Third World. Bibliographical essay and chronology.

24:16   Ingram, Kenneth. *History of the Cold War.* New York: Philosophical Library, 1955. This is an early but evenhanded and bland account of the first ten years of the cold war.

Kennan, G. F. *Russia and the West under Lenin and Stalin* (21:158).

24:17   Knapp, Wilfrid. *A History of War and Peace, 1939–1965.* New York: Oxford University Press, 1967. A massive history of international diplomacy that mixes interpretation and analysis; it is generally sympathetic to the U.S. position on the origins of the cold war.

24:18   LaFeber, Walter. *America, Russia, and the Cold War, 1945–1975.* 3d ed. New York: Wiley (1967), 1976. A comprehensive history of American foreign policy in the cold war, written from a mildly revisionist perspective, it stresses the importance of economic influences. This edition has been substantially rewritten to incorporate recent scholarship. Extensive bibliographical essay and maps.

Larson, T. B. *Soviet-American Rivalry* (29:7) is a topical analysis of Soviet-American relations since the end of World War II. It concludes that the United States remains well ahead of the Soviet Union in all areas of competition except the military.

24:19   Lerche, Charles O., Jr. *The Cold War ... and After.* Englewood Cliffs, N.J.: Prentice-Hall, 1965. A brief survey of the cold war, it emphasizes the national strategies and conceptual assumptions of both sides. Lerche argues that the conflict was an abnormal phase in the history of international relations.

24:20   Luard, Evan, ed. *The Cold War: A Reappraisal.* New York: Praeger, 1964. These essays by British scholars reassessing the cold war (1945–1963) are organized primarily by regions of the world. Chronology.

24:21   Lukacs, John. *A New History of the Cold War.* 3d ed. Garden City, N.Y.: Doubleday (1961), 1966. An analytical history of the cold war (1945–1965), the last half of which is a broadly focused interpretation of Soviet-American rivalry in terms of societies, political theories, national interests, and national characters.

24:22 McLellan, David S. *The Cold War in Transition.* New York: Macmillan, 1966. This survey (1945–1965) concludes cautiously that "a foreign policy which is not defined with respect for universal values or at least those of a civilization transcending that of the nation itself is not in the national interest."

24:23 Rapoport, Anatol. *The Big Two: Soviet-American Perceptions of Foreign Policy.* New York: Pegasus, 1971. This interpretation of the Soviet-American rivalry by a prominent mathematician and game theorist argues that while the means of warfare have changed, through the development of nuclear weapons, perceptions of warfare and the functions it serves have not.

24:24 Rees, David. *The Age of Containment: The Cold War, 1945–1965.* New York: St. Martin's Press, 1967. This brief overview by a British author emphasizes the ideological roots of confrontation, with the Soviet Union viewed as primarily responsible. Bibliography and chronology.

24:25 Schuman, Frederick L. *The Cold War: Retrospect and Prospect.* 2d ed. Baton Rouge: Louisiana State University Press, 1967. A series of lectures (1961), together with a postscript (1967), which views the roots of Soviet behavior as influenced more by Russian history than by communist ideology.

24:26 Schurmann, Franz. *The Logic of World Power: An Inquiry into the Origins, Currents, and Contradictions of World Politics.* New York: Pantheon, 1974. A history of the triangular relationship between Washington, Moscow, and Peking (1945–1973), its approach is reminiscent of other revisionist accounts of the American "empire," but it differs from its counterparts in the attention it gives to Soviet and Chinese foreign policy.

24:27 Seabury, Paul. *The Rise and Decline of the Cold War.* New York: Basic Books, 1967. A compact essay on the origins, nature, and evolution of the cold war, it is strong on the intellectual origins of containment. The "classic" cold war ended, Seabury thinks, in the early 1960s.

24:28 Shulman, Marshall D. *Beyond the Cold War.* New Haven, Conn.: Yale University Press, 1966.

These lectures on the nature and evolution of the cold war (1945–1965) conclude that the conflict has been transformed and merged into a larger setting, and thus no longer provides an adequate framework for thinking about international relations.

Sivachev, N. V., and Yakovlev, N. N. *Russia and the United States: U.S.-Soviet Relations from the Soviet Point of View* (2:253) is a Soviet history of Russian-American relations written specifically for an American audience. The authors see American policy (but not that of the U.S.S.R.) as imperialistic and narrowly self-interested.

24:29 Ulam, Adam B. *The Rivals: America and Russia since World War II.* New York: Viking, 1971. A detailed analysis of Soviet-American relations (1945–1970), the book is a sustained critique of American diplomacy, particularly its lack of knowledge of the Soviet Union and its persistent overestimation of Soviet strength and self-confidence.

Williams, W. A. *American-Russian Relations, 1781–1947* (2:256) views U.S.-Russian relations as determined by an interplay of three factors: territorial and economic expansion and balance of power considerations (complicated after 1917 by America's reaction to the Russian Revolution). The book is dated and uneven, but many of its arguments have been elaborated by subsequent revisionist writers.

U.S. FOREIGN POLICY

24:30 Ambrose, Stephen E. *Rise to Globalism: American Foreign Policy since 1938.* Baltimore: Penguin, 1971. Ambrose's critical survey of American foreign policy argues that the United States shifted during the period covered from nonentanglement to a futile drive for global hegemony, motivated by both military insecurity and economic desperation. Bibliographical essay.

24:31 Aron, Raymond. *The Imperial Republic: The United States and the World, 1945–1973.* Trans. by Frank Jellinek. Englewood Cliffs, N.J.: Prentice-Hall, 1974. This critical analysis of postwar American foreign policy by a distinguished French political scientist stresses the evolution of containment from a doctrine of balancing power to one of indiscriminately projecting it. Aron also devotes attention to the United States in the world marketplace.

24:32 Barnet, Richard J. *Roots of War: The Men and Institutions behind U.S. Foreign Policy.* New York: Atheneum, 1972. An indictment of the American foreign policy apparatus, this book argues that since 1940 the United States has been engaged in a form of "permanent war," the causes of which can be found in American society.

24:33 Brown, Seyom. *The Faces of Power: Constancy and Change in United States Foreign Policy from Truman to Johnson.* New York: Columbia University Press, 1968. An analytical overview that stresses the multifaceted nature of power in the contemporary international environment and views differences between the administrations largely in terms of their varying perceptions of power.

24:34 Carleton, William G. *The Revolution in American Foreign Policy: Its Global Range.* 2d ed. New York: Random House, 1967. The "revolution" is the American emergence as a global power following World War II; this interpretive survey pays less attention to the causes of that phenomenon than to its manifestations. Bibliography.

24:35 Goldman, Eric F. *The Crucial Decade—And After: America, 1945–1960.* New York: Random House, 1960. A lively survey that has influenced many subsequent and more detailed accounts, its emphasis is on foreign policy, especially 1945 to 1950.

24:36 Graebner, Norman A. *Cold War Diplomacy: American Foreign Policy, 1945–1975.* 2d ed. New York: Van Nostrand (1962), 1977. This succinct account argues that the transition from the perception of the Soviet Union to the perception of international communism as the enemy "weakened the traditional restraints of American conservatism and propelled the nation into objectives that it could not achieve." Bibliography and documents.

24:37 Hamby, Alonzo L. *The Imperial Years: The U.S. since 1939.* New York: Weybright & Talley, 1976. This thorough overview of U.S. foreign and domestic policies since 1939 is written from a post-revisionist "liberal" perspective. Hamby argues that the problem of defending distinctive ideals at home without sacrificing vital interests in a chaotic world has "forced the United States to preside over an empire its citizens did not want." Valuable bibliographical essay.

24:38 Hammond, Paul Y. *Cold War and Detente: The American Foreign Policy Process since 1945.* 2d ed. New York: Harcourt Brace Jovanovich, 1975. This analytical survey of postwar American foreign policy stresses the domestic political and institutional roots of diplomacy. Bibliographical essay and maps.

24:39 Horowitz, David. *Free World Colossus: A Critique of American Foreign Policy in the Cold War.* Rev. ed. New York: Hill & Wang (1965), 1971. This critique of postwar American foreign policy generally follows the arguments of Fleming (24:9) and Williams (2:99), noting that its disparity of strategic power gave the United States greater opportunities to shape the competition.

24:40 Kolko, Joyce, and Kolko, Gabriel. *The Limits of Power: The World and United States Foreign Policy, 1945–1954.* New York: Harper & Row, 1972. The most massive and thoroughly researched revisionist account of the first postwar decade, but one written from an uncompromising perspective of economic determinism. The theme is the cold war as a confrontation between the United States and the rest of the world, not just the Soviet Union or the international communist movement.

24:41 Miller, Lynn H., and Pruessen, Ronald W., eds. *Reflections on the Cold War: A Quarter Century of American Foreign Policy.* Philadelphia: Temple University Press, 1974. This collection includes essays by Barton J. Bernstein on the Cuban missile crisis, Richard J. Barnet on the arms race, Lynn H. Miller on the UN and the cold war, and Richard A. Falk on U.S. and U.S.S.R. efforts to preserve their respective empires.

Morgenthau, H. J. *Truth and Power: Essays of a Decade, 1960–1970* (28:13).

24:42 Morgenthau, Hans J. *A New Foreign Policy for the United States.* New York: Praeger, 1969. A critique of postwar American foreign policy in the light of the Vietnam War which calls for a return to first principles, efforts to restrain the nuclear arms race, and an "ideological decontamination" of American foreign policy.

24:43 Morgenthau, Hans J. *In Defense of the National Interest.* New York: Knopf, 1951. This book by one of the foremost proponents of the "realist" school combines a critique of postwar American foreign policy with an appeal to approach the cold war as an exercise in traditional power politics. Morgenthau condemns policy erected upon moral principles and buttressed by utopianism, legalism, sentimentalism, and neoisolationism.

24:44 Nathan, James A., and Oliver, James K. *United States Foreign Policy and World Order*. 2d ed. Boston: Little, Brown, 1981. This detailed reassessment of postwar American foreign policy, written from a mildly revisionist perspective, sees as the underlying theme of the period efforts by U.S. officials to maintain global order through the use or threatened use of force.

24:45 Osgood, Robert E., et al. *America and the World: From the Truman Doctrine to Vietnam*. Baltimore: Johns Hopkins Press, 1970. A perceptive set of essays on postwar American foreign policy which includes articles on domestic politics, military and economic issues, together with relations with the Soviet Union, Europe, and the Third World.

24:46 Paterson, Thomas G., ed. *Containment and the Cold War: American Foreign Policy since 1945*. Reading, Mass.: Addison-Wesley, 1973. Using documents and interpretive essays, this anthology provides an historical and analytical overview of the American containment doctrine—its meaning and its impact on Soviet-American relations. Extensive bibliography.

24:47 Perkins, Dexter. *The Diplomacy of a New Age: Major Issues in U.S. Policy since 1945*. Bloomington: Indiana University Press, 1967. These lectures assess the cold war in terms of Soviet challenges and American responses; concludes that despite the fact that the United States became a world power reluctantly, it has not, on the whole, wielded its power unwisely.

24:48 Rostow, W. W. *The United States in the World Arena: An Essay in Recent History*. New York: Harper, 1960. This is an attempt to identify both the American national "style" and national "interest" in foreign policy (1941–1958), and to link these with the author's earlier theories on the stages of economic growth. The book is also a sustained explication of the orthodox interpretation of the origins of the cold war.

24:49 Serfaty, Simon. *The Elusive Enemy: American Foreign Policy since World War II*. Boston: Little, Brown, 1972. This balanced account concludes that many of the foreign policy successes of postwar administrations "were achieved outside the guidelines

set by their respective doctrines and designs; many of their failures were met on the basis of their doctrines and designs."

24:50 Spanier, John W. *American Foreign Policy since World War II*. 7th ed. New York: Praeger, 1977. A treatment of the cold war from a generally orthodox perspective; it reflects the "realist" tradition. In line with recent trends in that school of thought, though, the book has become progressively more critical of American foreign policy in successive editions. Annotated bibliography.

Williams, W. A. *The Tragedy of American Diplomacy* (2:99) is one of the most influential single volumes to be written on American diplomatic history during the past two decades. Its thesis, that prosperity at home required economic expansion overseas, became one of the central arguments of cold war revisionism.

24:51 Wittner, Lawrence S. *Cold War America: From Hiroshima to Watergate*. New York: Praeger, 1974. A revisionist history of the United States since World War II; half of the book is devoted to foreign policy. The thesis is that "as an integral part of their defense of corporate power, U.S. policy-makers drove the nation to the point of crisis, invading other countries, neglecting the needs of American society, and finally, in fear of their own citizens, leading an assault on free institutions." Extensive bibliographical essay.

Cold War Historiography

Books

24:52 Compton, James V., ed. *America and the Origins of the Cold War*. Boston: Houghton Mifflin, 1972. This is a useful early sampling of revisionist and orthodox perspectives on the origins of the cold war. Bibliographical essay.

24:53 Crabb, Cecil V. *Policy-Makers and Their Critics: Conflicting Theories of American Foreign Policy*. New York: Praeger, 1976. An analysis of postwar American foreign policy in terms of its critics. Among the schools of thought represented are liberal humanitarianism, realism, internationalism, and neoisolationism of both the liberal and conservative varieties. The argument is that critics of foreign policy should be subjected to the same standards of scrutiny to which they subject policymakers.

24:54 Gardner, Lloyd C.; Schlesinger, Arthur M., Jr.; and Morgenthau, Hans J. *The Origins of the Cold War*. Waltham, Mass.: Ginn, 1970. These three essays were written from different perspectives on the origins of the cold war (Gardner's and Morgenthau's are original; Schlesinger's is his 1967 *Foreign Affairs* article), together with rejoinders.

24:55 Hess, Gary R., ed. *America and Russia: From Cold War to Coexistence*. New York: Crowell, 1973. These historical essays are intended to illustrate conflicting perspectives on both the origins and evolution of the cold war (1945–1963). Bibliographical essay.

24:56 Horowitz, David, ed. *Containment and Revolution*. Boston: Beacon, 1967. This is a representative sampling of early revisionist essays, mostly focusing on the origins of the cold war.

24:57 Maddox, Robert James. *The New Left and the Origins of the Cold War*. Princeton, N.J.: Princeton University Press, 1973. A biting critique of seven revisionist accounts of the origins of the cold war (Williams, Fleming, Alperovitz, Horowitz, Kolko, Clemens, and Gardner) on the grounds that their scholarship reflects "pervasive misusages of the source materials." The book itself set off a controversy regarding its own methods of analysis.

24:58 Paterson, Thomas G., ed. *The Origins of the Cold War*. 2d ed. Lexington, Mass.: Heath, 1974. This convenient guide to the debate over the origins of the cold war includes both primary and secondary materials. Extensive bibliographical essay.

24:59 Siracusa, Joseph M. *New Left Diplomatic Histories and Historians: The American Revisionists*. Port Washington, N.Y.: Kennikat, 1973. A survey of trends in New Left writing on American diplomatic history, with special emphasis on the views of William Appleman Williams and on the debate over the origins of the cold war. It concludes with a series of observations on New Left historiography by several prominent "traditional" historians.

24:60 Tucker, Robert W. *The Radical Left and American Foreign Policy*. Baltimore: Johns Hopkins Press, 1971. A critique of New Left accounts based not on the revisionists' use of sources, as is Maddox's *The New Left and the Origins of the Cold War* (24:57), but on their logic. Tucker argues that the revisionists showed the United States to have behaved in a self-interested manner characteristic of most great powers in history, but that they provided little evidence that this behavior stemmed from unique internal socioeconomic causes.

Welch, W. *American Images of Soviet Foreign Policy: An Inquiry in Recent Appraisals from the Academic Community* (29:14) is an analytical review of influential American studies of Soviet diplomacy.

Essays

24:61 Bernstein, Barton J. "Les États-Unis et les origines de la guerre froide" [The United States and the origins of the cold war]. *Revue d'histoire de la deuxième guerre mondiale* 26:103 (1976), 51–72. This is a review of historiographical trends on the origins of the cold war, together with a thorough critique of "rejuvenated orthodoxy," which the author sees manifested primarily in John Lewis Gaddis's *The United States and the Origins of the Cold War* (25:16). A briefer English-language version of this article appeared in *Reviews in American History* 1:4 (1973), 453–62.

24:62 Bernstein, Barton J. "American Foreign Policy and the Origins of the Cold War." In Barton J. Bernstein, ed., *Politics and Policies of the Truman Administration*. Chicago: Quadrangle, 1970, pp. 15–77. Bernstein argues that American policy in the period 1945 to 1947 was neither innocent nor devoid of ideological content. By overextending itself, and by ignoring legitimate Soviet security interests, the United States contributed to the development of the cold war.

24:63 Brozan, Hugh. "America and the Cold War: Today and Yesterday." *Round Table* 62:245 (1972), 119–27. A British scholar unsympathetically assesses revisionist historiography on the origins of the cold war. Brozan concentrates especially on Gardner's *Architects of Illusion* (25:17) and the essays in Bernstein's *Politics and Policies of the Truman Administration* (24:192).

24:64 Graebner, Norman A. "Cold War Origins and the Continuing Debate." *Journal of Conflict Resolution* 13:1 (1969), 123–32. This balanced summary of the orthodox and revisionist positions calls for further research, particularly on why the Western democracies were prepared to acquiesce in the German domination of Eastern Europe in the late 1930s, but not in Soviet domination after World War II.

24:65 Hoffmann, Stanley. "Revisionism Revisited." In Lynn H. Miller and Ronald W. Pruessen, eds., *Reflections on the Cold War: A Quarter Century of American Foreign Policy.* Philadelphia: Temple University Press, 1974, pp. 3–26. Hoffmann applauds revisionist historians for their treatment of Soviet intentions following World War II. Where the revisionists err, he contends, is in their depiction of U.S. foreign policy: they ignore the contradictions of everyday life, the complexity of motivation, and the fact that U.S. policy was reformist, not conservative or revolutionary.

24:66 Holsti, Ole R. "The Study of International Politics Makes Strange Bedfellows: Theories of the Radical Right and the Radical Left." *American Political Science Review* 68:1 (1974), 217–42. This comparison of assumptions about international politics held by right-wing critics of Soviet foreign policy and left-wing critics of American foreign policy finds similarities, among other things, in the extent of reliance on theory, the dismissal of accident, the insistence on a Manichean view of the world, the perception of conflict as abnormal, and the absence of distinctions between foreign and domestic policies.

24:67 Horowitz, David. "Historians and the Cold War." *Ramparts* 12:2 (1973), 36–40, 58–62. A revisionist historian's account of the origins of cold war revisionism providing some analysis of its intellectual roots in the writings of Charles Beard.

24:68 Jaffe, Philip J. "The Cold War Revisionists and What They Omit." *Survey* 19:4 (1973), 123–43. Jaffe argues that revisionist historians disregard or distort many points which do not support their thesis.

24:69 Kennedy, Thomas L. "Shifting Perspectives on the Origins of the Cold War." *Towson State Journal of International Affairs* 4:2 (1970), 121–28. A careful assessment, with attention to the revisionists on the right in the 1950s, it concludes that revisionism in moderation advances the cause of history, but becomes self-destructive when carried to extremes.

24:70 Kimball, Warren F. "The Cold War Warmed

Over." *American Historical Review* 79:4 (1974), 1119–36. A review essay dealing with the Kolkos' *The Limits of Power* (24:40), Gaddis's *The United States and the Origins of the Cold War* (25:16), and Maddox's *The New Left and the Origins of the Cold War* (24:57), but concentrating primarily on the last.

24:71 Krueger, Thomas A. "The Social Origins of Recent American Foreign Policy." *Journal of Social History* 7:1 (1973), 93–101. A succinct and sympathetic statement of the arguments revisionist historians have advanced regarding elite influences over the conduct of American foreign policy.

24:72 Laqueur, Walter. "Rewriting History." *Commentary* 55:3 (1973), 53–69. A substantial critique of revisionist writing on Nazi Germany, World War II, and the origins of the cold war. Laqueur faults revisionists for concentrating on U.S. policies alone.

24:73 Lasch, Christopher. "The Cold War, Revisited and Revisioned." *New York Times Magazine* (January 14, 1968), 26ff. A reasonably balanced account of the controversy over the origins of the cold war, it concentrates on the writings of Williams, Alperovitz, and Oglesby.

24:74 Leigh, Michael. "Is There a Revisionist Thesis on the Origins of the Cold War?" *Political Science Quarterly* 89:1 (1974), 101–16. The author argues that the positions taken by six prominent revisionist historians on the nature of the Roosevelt-Truman transition, the decision to drop the atomic bomb, and the question of spheres of influence in Eastern Europe suggest there is no common revisionist thesis on the origins of the cold war.

24:75 Maier, Charles S. "Revisionism and the Interpretation of Cold War Origins." *Perspectives in American History* 4 (1970), 313–47. A careful analysis of the cold war revisionists, sensitive to the differences in their interpretations, but critical of their logical inconsistencies and lack of methodological sophistication.

24:76 Melanson, Richard A. "Revisionism Subdued? Robert James Maddox and the Origins of the Cold War." *Political Science Reviewer* 7 (1977), 229–71. A substantial analysis of the entire historiographical debate over the origins of the cold war, with particular attention to the controversy surrounding Maddox's book (24:57), which the author criticizes for its "surfeit of innuendo" and "brittle literal mindedness."

24:77 Pachter, Henry. "Revisionist Historians and the Cold War." In Irving Howe, ed., *Beyond the New Left.* New York: McCall, 1970, pp. 166–91. An early critique, it questions the revisionists' use of evidence, their neglect of external influences, and their insensitivity to the contexts in which events took place. An earlier version appeared in *Dissent* 15:6 (1968), 505–18.

24:78 Patterson, David S. "Recent Literature on Cold War Origins: An Essay Review." *Wisconsin Magazine of History* 55:4 (1972), 320–29. In this critique of works by the Kolkos, Clemens, Gardner, Feis and Paterson, the author argues that while the revisionists' specific interpretations remain open to question, they have demonstrated that Washington's broad definition of postwar security requirements unnecessarily provoked the Soviet Union.

24:79 Richardson, J. L. "Cold War Revisionism: A Critique." *World Politics* 24:4 (1972), 579–612. This lengthy analysis of the works of several major revisionists—notably Kolko, Alperovitz, and Horowitz is critical of the revisionists' use of evidence, their lack of a concept of the international order, and their insensitivity to context.

24:80 Schlesinger, Arthur M., Jr. "Origins of the Cold War." *Foreign Affairs* 46:1 (1967), 22–52. An ambivalent reassessment of the origins of the cold war, it criticizes revisionism for leaving out of its calculations "the intransigence of Leninist ideology, the sinister dynamics of a totalitarian society and the madness of Stalin."

24:81 Schulzinger, Robert D. "Moderation in Pursuit of Truth Is No Virtue; Extremism in Defense of Moderation Is a Vice." *American Quarterly* 27:2 (1975), 222–36. This is a witty and sometimes pungent critique of the revisionists' critics—notably Gaddis, Herring, Maddox, Wheeler-Bennett, and Tucker.

24:82 Seabury, Paul. "Cold War Origins, I." *Journal of Contemporary History* 3:1 (1968), 169–82. This is a thoughtful analysis of several of the early revisionist writers on the cold war. Seabury recalls a

revisionism of the right regarding cold war origins during the early 1950s, critical of American foreign policy for appeasement, not toughness.

24:83 Sellen, Robert W. "Origins of the Cold War: An Historiographical Survey." *West Georgia College Studies in the Social Sciences* 9 (1970), 57–98. This review of the literature through 1969 is useful for the attention paid to memoir material and to the early "orthodox" accounts of the origins of the cold war.

24:84 Shapiro, Edward S. "Responsibility for the Cold War: A Bibliographical Review." *Intercollegiate Review* 12:2 (1976/1977), 113–20. An overview aimed at readers unfamiliar with the topic, it pays particular attention to the Maddox controversy.

24:85 Stover, Robert. "Responsibility for the Cold War—A Case Study in Historical Responsibility." *History and Theory* 11:2 (1972), 145–78. This philosophical analysis of how 16 scholars have dealt with assigning responsibility for the cold war concludes that standards established depend on the purpose the historian has in undertaking the investigation.

24:86 Thomas, Brian. "Cold War Origins, II." *Journal of Contemporary History* 3:1 (1968), 183–98. Thomas's sympathetic early assessment of revisionism pays attention to its roots in the works of P. M. S. Blackett (26:204) and K. Zilliacus.

24:87 Ulam, Adam B. "On Modern History: Rereading the Cold War." *Interplay* 2 (1969), 51–57. One of the few evaluations of the revisionist argument by a specialist on Soviet foreign policy, it concludes that American diplomats were not sinister, but gullible.

24:88 Wilensky, Norman M. "Was the Cold War Necessary? The Revisionist Challenge to Consensus History." *American Studies* 13:1 (1972), 177–87. A sympathetic account, it seeks to identify the forces behind the revisionist position. The author considers them to be "the Vietnam war, the youth of critics, [and] the new faith in history as a tool for change."

24:89 Williams, William Appleman. "Confessions of an Intransigent Revisionist." *Studies on the Left* 3:5 (1973), 87–98. The most prominent of the revisionists states his purposes as a historian, replies to critics, and remains (mostly) unrepentant.

Personalities

Additional references on individuals may be found in Chapter 1, "Biographical Data"; also see "Presidential Administrations" below.

Dean Acheson

Acheson, D. *Power and Diplomacy* (28:18).

24:90 Acheson, Dean. *Present at the Creation: My Years in the State Department*. New York: Norton, 1969. Acheson emphasizes his years as secretary of state. His account is essential for an understanding of the man and his policies (1941–1953), although as one might expect, few self-doubts or second thoughts are expressed. Highly complimentary of Truman, it is less so of other major administration figures.

24:91 Acheson, Dean. *Sketches from Lives of Men I Have Known*. New York: Harper, 1961. This lively, informal series of portraits includes those statesmen Acheson dealt with during the 1940s and 1950s.

24:92 Bundy, McGeorge, ed. *The Pattern of Responsibility*. Boston: Houghton Mifflin, 1952. These excerpts from Acheson's public statements (1949–1951) are a useful guide to Acheson's official pronouncements as secretary of state, both prepared and extemporaneous.

24:93 Graebner, Norman A. "Dean G. Acheson, 1949–1953." In Norman A. Graebner, ed., *An Uncertain Tradition: American Secretaries of State in the Twentieth Century*. New York: McGraw-Hill, 1961, pp. 267–88. This early, sympathetic assessment stresses the radical right's attack on Acheson's policies.

LaFeber, W. "Kissinger and Acheson: The Secretary of State and the Cold War" (24:134).

24:94 McLellan, David S. *Dean Acheson: The State Department Years*. New York: Dodd, Mead, 1976. The most complete biography, it emphasizes Acheson's "realistic" view of international relations, his faith in action, and his impatience with self-doubt. It views him as having succeeded in mastering the bureaucracy, solidifying alliances, educating the public and Congress, but as having failed to maintain the larger strategic perspective.

24:95 Smith, Gaddis. *Dean Acheson*. Vol. 16 in *The American Secretaries of State and Their Diplomacy*, ed. by Samuel Flagg Bemis and Robert Ferrell. New series. New York: Cooper Square, 1972. In this balanced account of Acheson's tenure as secretary of state, Smith interprets Acheson's views in terms of a "great cycle" theory of threats to the balance of power, of which the Soviet Union was the third in the century; American efforts under Acheson's leadership were directed to seeing that the United States did not neglect this threat as it had the previous two until too late to avoid war. Bibliography.

George W. Ball

See also Chapter 28, "Personalities."

Ball, G. W. "Top Secret: The Prophecy the President Rejected" (30:30) prints Ball's dissenting view toward U.S. military intervention in Vietnam.

24:96 Ball, George W. *Diplomacy for a Crowded World: An American Foreign Policy*. Boston: Little, Brown, 1976. The former under secretary of state discusses the Nixon-Kissinger foreign policy, how it cured some past aberrations, and created new ones. He concludes: "to exercise effective leadership we must once again come to believe in ourselves, in our uniqueness as a nation, and in our special mission."

Adolf A. Berle, Jr.

See Chapter 35, "Personalities," for additional references.

24:97 Berle, Adolf A., Jr. *Navigating the Rapids, 1918–1971: From the Papers of Adolf A. Berle*. Ed. by Beatrice Bishop Berle and Travis B. Jacobs. New York: Harcourt Brace Jovanovich, 1973. The diaries and correspondence of a former Roosevelt "brains truster" and assistant secretary of state focus on World War II, but the last third of the book covers the postwar years, during which Berle kept in touch with foreign affairs, especially Latin American matters.

Charles E. Bohlen

See Chapters 26 and 29, "Personalities," for additional references.

24:98 Bohlen, Charles E. *Witness to History: 1929–1969*. New York: Norton, 1973. A memoir of fundamental importance for an understanding of the early cold war because of the author's vantage points as career Soviet expert, interpreter for Roosevelt and Truman, key State Department adviser, and ambassador to the Soviet Union, the Philippines, and France.

Ruddy, T. M. "Realist versus Realist: Bohlen, Kennan and the Inception of the Cold War" (26:40).

Chester Bowles
See Chapter 37, "Personalities," for additional references.

24:99   Bowles, Chester. *Promises to Keep: My Years in Public Life, 1941–1969.* New York: Harper & Row, 1971. These memoirs of the under secretary of state and ambassador to India during the Kennedy and Johnson administrations are important for an understanding of U.S. policies toward the Third World.

James F. Byrnes
24:100   Byrnes, James F. *All in One Lifetime.* New York: Harper, 1958. *All in One Lifetime,* a full autobiography, covers the same material as *Speaking Frankly,* in less detail but with greater candor.

24:101   Byrnes, James F. *Speaking Frankly.* New York: Harper, 1947. Byrnes began as an adviser to Roosevelt on domestic questions but gradually took Hopkins's place as a foreign policy adviser and became Truman's secretary of state. This work covers exclusively his diplomatic career.

24:102   Curry, George. "James F. Byrnes." In *The American Secretaries of State and Their Diplomacy,* ed. by Samuel Flagg Bemis and Robert Ferrell. New series. New York: Cooper Square, 1965, vol. 14, pp. 87–396. A balanced and informative assessment of Byrnes's career as secretary of state, it is based in part on Byrnes's papers and on interviews with him. Bibliography.

Ward, P. D. *The Threat of Peace: James F. Byrnes and the Council of Foreign Ministers, 1945–46* (25:82).

Allen W. Dulles
Dulles, A. *The Secret Surrender* (25:138).

24:103   Dulles, Allen W. *The Craft of Intelligence.* New York: Harper & Row, 1963. Not a full memoir, it is rather a discreet and anecdotal account of the role of intelligence in the postwar world by a former CIA director.

24:104   Mosley, Leonard. *Dulles: A Biography of Eleanor, Allen and John Foster Dulles and Their Family Network.* New York: Dial, 1978. This is a somewhat superficial and not entirely reliable account of the involvement of the Dulles family in the conduct of American foreign policy. The book's greatest interest lies in its discussion of Allen Dulles and the CIA.

John Foster Dulles
See Chapter 27, "Personalities," for additional references.

24:105   Berding, Andrew. *Dulles on Diplomacy.* Princeton, N.J.: Van Nostrand, 1965. These informal observations by Dulles on major foreign policy issues were transcribed at the time by the author, who served as assistant secretary of state under Dulles. The account is important for an understanding of Dulles's views.

24:106   Drummond, Roscoe, and Coblentz, Gaston. *Duel at the Brink: John Foster Dulles' Command of American Power.* Garden City, N.Y.: Doubleday, 1960. This volume, based largely on unattributed oral interviews with statesmen and others who dealt with Dulles, presents the secretary as a formidable and controversial figure.

Dulles, J. F. *War or Peace* (26:45) presents Dulles's 1950 views on postwar issues.

24:107   Dulles, John Foster. *War, Peace and Change.* New York: Garland, (1939) 1971. This account is useful for comparing Dulles's prewar with his post–World War II views.

24:108   Gerson, Louis L. *John Foster Dulles.* Vol. 17 in *The American Secretaries of State and Their Diplomacy,* ed. by Samuel Flagg Bemis and Robert Ferrell. New series. New York: Cooper Square, 1968. A somewhat bland but sympathetic biography, it is based on interviews with Dulles's associates and the Dulles Papers. Bibliographical essay.

24:109   Goold-Adams, Richard. *John Foster Dulles: A Reappraisal.* New York: Appleton-Century-Crofts, 1962. This perceptive and balanced British assessment concludes that Dulles was both "a man of tremendous principle and courage" and the possessor of "a devious and tortuous nature which could neither be relied upon nor easily understood."

24:110   Guhin, Michael A. *John Foster Dulles: A Statesman and His Times.* New York: Columbia University Press, 1972. An intellectual biography of Dulles, it emphasizes the evolution of his thought prior to his becoming secretary of state. The effort is to understand Dulles rather than to judge him. Extensive bibliography.

24:111   Holsti, Ole R. "Will the Real Dulles Please Stand Up." *International Journal* 30:1 (1974–1975), 34–44. This assessment of recent literature on Dulles, particularly Hoopes's *The Devil and John Foster Dulles,* makes some comparisons between Dulles and Kissinger. See also Holsti's "The 'Operational Code' Approach to the Study of Political Leaders: John Foster Dulles' Philosophical and Instrumental Beliefs," *Canadian Journal of Political Science* 3:1 (1970), 123–57.

24:112   Hoopes, Townsend. *The Devil and John Foster Dulles.* Boston: Little, Brown, 1973. Despite the lurid title, this is the most thorough biography of Dulles. Critical of the secretary of state's moralism but sensitive to his complexities, Hoopes provides a perceptive analysis of the foreign policies of both the Truman and Eisenhower administrations.

Dwight D. Eisenhower

See also Chapter 23, "Personalities."

24:113   Eisenhower, Dwight D. *At Ease: Stories I Tell to Friends.* Garden City, N.Y.: Doubleday, 1967. This book contains informal recollections, mostly of Eisenhower's early career. The volume provides little of historical significance, but it is more revealing of the man than are his memoirs.

24:114   Eisenhower, Dwight D. *The White House Years.* 2 vols. Garden City, N.Y.: Doubleday, 1963–1965. The voluminous but dry memoirs of his two terms in office by the former president contain much information on foreign and national security policy not available elsewhere.

24:115   Lyon, Peter. *Eisenhower: Portrait of the Hero.* Boston: Little, Brown, 1974. A full but somewhat casually written biography, the last third of which deals with the presidential years. Sympathetic to Eisenhower for showing restraint during the foreign policy crises of his administration, Lyon is critical of him for not doing more to end the cold war.

J. William Fulbright

24:116   Fulbright, J. William. *Fulbright of Arkansas.* Ed. by Karl E. Meyer. New York: Harper & Row,

1966. This is a useful collection of Fulbright's public speeches on foreign and domestic issues.

24:117   Fulbright, J. William. *Prospects for the West.* Cambridge: Harvard University Press, 1963. These lectures focus on U.S.-Soviet relations and the United States and its allies. Also see his *Old Myths and New Realities* (New York: Random House, 1964); *The Arrogance of Power* (30:31); *The Role of Congress in Foreign Policy* (2:154); and *The Pentagon Propaganda Machine* (New York: Liveright, 1970).

24:118   Johnson, Haynes, and Gwertzman, Bernard M. *Fulbright: The Dissenter.* Garden City, N.Y.: Doubleday, 1968. The most adequate biography to date of the longtime chairman of the Senate Foreign Relations Committee (1959–1974), covering his career through 1967. It is generally sympathetic, though not uncritical.

W. Averell Harriman

Harriman, W. A., and Abel, E. *Special Envoy to Churchill and Stalin, 1941–1946* (25:28) covers the issues that led to the disintegration of the Grand Alliance at war's end. Harriman records his assessment of Stalin and other Soviet leaders. Also see his *Peace with Russia?* (New York: Simon & Schuster, 1959).

24:119   Harriman, W. Averell. *America and Russia in a Changing World: A Half Century of Personal Observation.* Garden City, N.Y.: Doubleday, 1971. This is a participant's observations of the United States' often difficult relations with the Soviet Union. Harriman is willing to criticize specific Western decisions, but lauds JFK's maturing abilities to deal effectively with the Soviets.

Lyndon B. Johnson

24:120   Johnson, Lyndon B. *The Vantage Point: Perspectives on the Presidency, 1963–1969.* New York: Holt, Rinehart & Winston, 1971. Like most presidential memoirs, Johnson's are bland and self-exculpating, but important for the information they contain which is not otherwise available.

24:121   Kearns, Doris. *Lyndon Johnson and the American Dream.* New York: Harper & Row, 1976. This biography of Johnson contains a postscript evaluating Johnson's personality in psychohistorical and institutional terms.

24:122   Steinberg, Alfred. *Sam Johnson's Boy: A Close-Up of the President from Texas.* New York:

Macmillan, 1968. A massive, critical journalistic biography, this book covers Johnson's career up to his decision not to seek reelection in 1968.

George F. Kennan

See Chapters 22 and 29, under "Personalities," for additional references; also see Chapter 26, "Defining Containment."

Coffey, J. W. "George Kennan and the Ambiguities of Realism" (26:48) analyzes the basic themes in Kennan's famous article (signed "Mr. X.") in *Foreign Affairs*. Coffey argues that the concept of realism is not fruitful as a clue to Kennan's own thinking or a theory of foreign policy.

24:123   Herz, Martin F., ed. *Decline of the West? George F. Kennan and His Critics*. Washington, D.C.: Georgetown University Ethics and Public Policy Center, 1978. A useful sampling of Kennan's views on current policy issues, it includes the reactions of some of his critics and sympathizers.

24:124   Kennan, George F. *Memoirs, 1925–1963*. 2 vols. Boston: Little, Brown, 1967, 1972. These volumes cover Kennan's career from his entry into the State Department in 1925 through his retirement as ambassador to Yugoslavia in 1963. Their primary importance, though, lies in the early cold war years, when Kennan was articulating the concept of containment. They also are essential for an understanding of both American foreign policy in the cold war, and the dilemmas of the intellectual in government.

24:125   Knight, Jonathan. "George Frost Kennan and the Study of American Foreign Policy: Some Critical Comments." *Western Political Quarterly* 20:1 (1967), 149–60. Knight critically examines Kennan's writings on international relations and American foreign policy since 1947.

John F. Kennedy

See also Chapters 29 and 30, "Personalities."

24:126   Burns, James MacGregor. *John Kennedy: A Political Profile*. New York: Harcourt, 1960. A campaign biography of unusual quality, it is useful for Kennedy's pre-presidential career.

24:127   Kennedy, John F. *The Strategy of Peace*. Ed. by Allan Nevins. New York: Harper & Row, 1960. This is a useful collection of Kennedy's major pre-

presidential pronouncements on foreign and national security policy.

Nunnerly, D. *President Kennedy and Britain* (28:20).

Paterson, T. G. "Bearing the Burden: A Critical Look at JFK's Foreign Policy" (29:33) is an overview of Kennedy's foreign policy which emphasizes the influences of historical lessons, personality and style, and theories of nation-building. Considerable attention is given to Soviet-American relations and the Cuban missile crisis.

24:128   Sorensen, Theodore C. *Kennedy*. New York: Harper & Row, 1965. A lengthy and admiring biography-memoir by the president's speech-writer, it is distorted by the author's perspective, but well written. The last quarter of the book concentrates on foreign policy.

Henry A. Kissinger

See Chapters 30 and 37, "Personalities," for additional references.

24:129   Graubard, Stephen. *Kissinger: Portrait of a Mind*. New York: Norton, 1973. A careful analysis of Kissinger's writings prior to his entry into the government, it is essential for an understanding of his views on foreign policy.

24:130   Hoffmann, Stanley. *Primacy or World Order: American Foreign Policy since the Cold War*. New York: McGraw-Hill, 1978. This book is simultaneously a brief overview of American foreign policy during the cold war, a critique of the ideas of Henry Kissinger, an analysis of the problems of world order, and a set of recommendations for the future. The critique of Kissinger is of greatest value for the historian.

24:131   Kalb, Marvin, and Kalb, Bernard. *Kissinger*. Boston: Little, Brown, 1974. A thorough but interim journalistic biography, it concentrates on the years 1969 to 1973 and is generally sympathetic to its subject.

Kissinger, H. A. *Nuclear Weapons and Foreign Policy* (28:74).

24:132   Kissinger, Henry A. *American Foreign Policy*. 3d ed. New York: Norton, 1977. This is a convenient compilation of Kissinger's major public addresses as secretary of state between 1973 and 1977, together with two essays, written during the late 1960s, dealing with "domestic structure" and "central issues" in American foreign policy.

24:133 Kissinger, Henry A. *White House Years.* Boston: Little, Brown, 1979. A massive memoir of fundamental importance, covering the author's service as national security adviser in the first Nixon administration (1969–1973), this is an unusually thoughtful if at times defensive account. It is strong in its striking portraits of personalities, ingenious in its rationales for controversial policies, eloquent in its philosophical musings, spread throughout the book, on the nature of statesmanship in the modern world. In tone, though not in size, the closest contemporary analogue to Machiavelli's *The Prince.*

24:134 LaFeber, Walter. "Kissinger and Acheson: The Secretary of State and the Cold War." *Political Science Quarterly* 92:2 (1977), 189–97. Both Dean Acheson and Henry A. Kissinger attempted to translate their personal world views into a new global order. Despite their similar grounding in 19th-century European diplomacy, their legacy might well be their policies toward non-Western, revolutionary areas.

24:135 Landau, David. *Kissinger: The Uses of Power.* Boston: Houghton Mifflin, 1972. An early biography-critique, it concentrates on Kissinger's pre-1969 background and on his handling of the Vietnam War.

Morris, R. *An Uncertain Greatness: Henry Kissinger and American Foreign Policy* (24:223).

24:136 Stoessinger, John G. *Henry Kissinger: The Anguish of Power.* New York: Norton, 1976. A sympathetic analysis of Kissinger's scholarly and diplomatic achievements by a longtime friend, it emphasizes Kissinger's view of leadership as a matter of choosing between unpalatable alternatives.

Foy D. Kohler

See Chapter 29, "Personalities," for additional references.

Kohler, F. D., and Harvey, M. L., eds. *The Soviet Union: Yesterday, Today, Tomorrow: A Colloquy of American Long Timers in Moscow* (29:36) is a verbatim record of a panel discussion with former ambassadors to Russia George F. Kennan, Foy D. Kohler, and Jacob L. Bean and others with diplomatic service

in the U.S.S.R., such as Elbridge Durbrow, Loy W. Henderson, and Thomas P. Whitney.

Henry Cabot Lodge, Jr.

24:137 Lodge, Henry Cabot, Jr. *The Storm Has Many Eyes: A Personal Narrative.* New York: Norton, 1973. A brief memoir, with special attention to the author's role in drafting Eisenhower for president in 1952, his service as U.S. ambassador to the United Nations under Eisenhower, and the Khrushchev visit to the United States in 1959.

24:138 Miller, William J. *Henry Cabot Lodge.* New York: Heineman, 1967. This is an admiring biography of the former Massachusetts senator, U.S. ambassador to the United Nations, 1960 vice-presidential candidate, and two-time ambassador to South Vietnam.

Douglas MacArthur

See Chapter 40, "Personalities," for additional references.

James, D. C. *The Years of MacArthur* (23:107) is a balanced and carefully researched multivolume work which, when complete, will be the definitive life of MacArthur.

24:139 Manchester, William. *American Caesar: Douglas MacArthur, 1880–1964.* Boston: Little, Brown, 1978. At present the most satisfactory complete biography, colorfully written, it is sensitive to the many complexities of its subject.

George C. Marshall

See Chapters 23 and 27, "Personalities," for additional references.

24:140 Ferrell, Robert H. *George C. Marshall.* Vol. 15 in *The American Secretaries of State and Their Diplomacy,* ed. by Samuel Flagg Bemis and Robert Ferrell. New series. New York: Cooper Square, 1966. The most complete assessment to date of Marshall's contribution as secretary of state, but it was composed before State Department documents became available. Also see Alexander DeConde, "George Catlett Marshall, 1947–1949," in N. A. Graebner, ed., *An Uncertain Tradition: American Secretaries of State in the Twentieth Century* (2:168) pp. 245–66.

Pogue, F. C. *George C. Marshall* (40:58) when completed, promises to be the definitive biography of

Marshall. The three volumes published to date carry their subject through World War II.

Joseph McCarthy

See Chapter 26, "Personalities," for additional references.

24:141   Cook, Fred J. *The Nightmare Decade: The Life and Times of Senator Joe McCarthy.* New York: Random House, 1971. The most adequate biography to date, but it is journalistic and anecdotal. Cook views McCarthy more as the product of his times than as the instigator of them.

24:142   Reeves, Thomas C. "McCarthyism: Interpretations since Hofstadter." *Wisconsin Magazine of History* 60:1 (1976), 42–54. This carefully documented review of the literature—scholarly and unscholarly—on McCarthy and his influence concludes that there has been too little scholarly work.

24:143   Thomas, Lately. *When Even Angels Wept: The Senator Joseph McCarthy Affair: A Story without a Hero.* New York: Morrow, 1973. A lively but undocumented life of the Wisconsin senator, it begins with the premise that McCarthy was a "pirate" but then seeks to recount his career "without the slightest attempt to convert or condemn."

Richard M. Nixon

24:144   Gardner, Lloyd C., comp. *The Great Nixon Turnabout: America's New Foreign Policy in the Post-Liberal Era (How a Cold Warrior Climbed Clean Out of His Skin).* New York: New Viewpoints, 1973. This is a collection of documents and articles on Nixon's foreign policy during his first term.

24:145   Nixon, Richard M. *RN: The Memoirs of Richard Nixon.* New York: Grosset & Dunlap, 1978. A lengthy and revealing memoir, it is essential for an understanding of Nixon's foreign policy. It is unusually candid for a presidential memoir, but also at times evasive and self-justifying.

24:146   Nixon, Richard M. *Six Crises.* Garden City, N.Y.: Doubleday, 1962. This partial autobiography, written during Nixon's political "eclipse," reveals his attitudes toward political leadership. The six crises discussed are the Alger Hiss case, the "Nixon fund" crisis during the 1952 election, Eisenhower's heart attack, the 1958 South American trip, the Khrushchev "kitchen debate," and the 1960 election.

24:147   Wills, Garry. *Nixon Agonistes: The Crisis of the Self-Made Man.* Boston: Houghton Mifflin, 1970. This lengthy and influential book argues, not unsympathetically, that Nixon was his own worst enemy. It includes a perceptive portrait of Eisenhower as well.

Dean Rusk

24:148   Cohen, Warren I. *Dean Rusk.* Vol. 19 in *The American Secretaries of State and Their Diplomacy,* ed. by Samuel Flagg Bemis and Robert Ferrell. New series. Totowa, N.J.: Cooper Square, 1980. The only adequate biography of Kennedy and Johnson's secretary of state, it is based on personal interviews with him.

24:149   Rusk, Dean. *Winds of Freedom.* Boston: Beacon, 1963. This is a collection of former Secretary of State Rusk's speeches (1961–1962).

Edward R. Stettinius, Jr.

See also Chapter 25, "Personalities."

Campbell, T. M. *Masquerade Peace: America's UN Policy, 1944–1945* (38:158).

24:150   Stettinius, Edward R., Jr. *The Diaries of Edward R. Stettinius, Jr., 1943–1946.* Ed. by Thomas M. Campbell and George C. Herring, Jr. New York: New Viewpoints, 1975. Diaries, calendar notes, and memoranda of conversations from the papers of an inconspicuous secretary of state and the first U.S. representative to the United Nations make up this useful volume.

24:151   Walker, Richard L. "E. R. Stettinius, Jr." In *The American Secretaries of State and Their Diplomacy,* ed. by Samuel Flagg Bemis and Robert Ferrell. New series. New York: Cooper Square, 1965, vol. 14, pp. 1–87. A brief but workmanlike biography, it should be supplemented with the Campbell-Herring edition of the Stettinius diaries (24:150).

Adlai E. Stevenson

See Chapter 38, "Personalities," for additional references.

24:152   Martin, John Bartlow. *The Life of Adlai E. Stevenson.* 2 vols. Garden City, N.Y.: Doubleday, 1976–1977. This is a massive, sympathetic, but candid biography by a close associate.

24:153   Stevenson, Adlai E. *The Papers of Adlai E. Stevenson.* 8 vols. Ed. by Walter Johnson. Boston:

Little, Brown, 1972–1979. These volumes contain letters, speeches, and fragmentary diaries of the 1952 and 1956 Democratic presidential nominee, and ambassador to the United Nations under Kennedy and Johnson. The last five volumes (1952–1965) are of greatest importance for foreign affairs.

Robert A. Taft

See Chapter 26, "Personalities," for additional references.

24:154 Patterson, James T. *Mr. Republican: A Biography of Robert A. Taft*. Boston: Houghton Mifflin, 1972. This biography treats Taft's career in the Senate during the Truman years, and includes an analysis of Taft's differences with the White House on foreign policy issues. Patterson corrects a number of misconceptions concerning Taft's "isolationist" views on foreign policy. Extensive bibliography.

Harry S. Truman

See also Chapters 26 and 27, "Personalities."

24:155 Ferrell, Robert H., ed. *Off the Record: The Private Papers of Harry S. Truman*. New York: Harper & Row, 1980. This is a gracefully edited selection from Truman's personal papers, released only after his death. It includes diary entries, memoranda, and private letters (often unsent): as one might expect, the opinions recorded are, like the man, pungent and direct.

24:156 Hillman, William. *Mr. President*. New York: Farrar, Straus & Young, 1952. This collection includes selections from the president's personal diaries and his private letters. The picture presented of Truman is uncritical, but it offers insights into his character and thinking.

24:157 Kirkendall, Richard S. "Harry Truman." In Morton Borden, ed., *America's Eleven Greatest Presidents*. Chicago: Rand-McNally, 1971, pp. 255–88. The author argues that Truman's personality, not his hunger for power, was the basis of his success in politics.

24:158 Miller, Merle. *Plain Speaking: An Oral Biography of Harry S. Truman*. New York: Berkely, 1973. These pungent tape-recorded reminiscences by the former president were made in 1961–1962. Like many oral histories, they were unreliable as to facts and dates but suggestive as to personality.

Miscamble, W. D. "The Evolution of an Internationalist: Harry S. Truman and American Foreign Policy" (38:52) is an assessment of Truman's prepresidential career. The author argues that Truman, as a senator, became an advocate of U.S. preparedness and a strong proponent of U.S. membership in the United Nations.

24:159 Steinberg, Alfred. *The Man from Missouri: The Life and Times of Harry S. Truman*. New York: Putnam's, 1962. This is a popular biography and history of the Truman administration.

24:160 Truman, Harry S. *Memoirs*. 2 vols. Garden City, N.Y.: Doubleday, 1955–1956. This lengthy set of memoirs, especially thorough on the events of 1945, which occupy the entire first volume, should be used with more than usual care regarding facts and dates.

24:161 Truman, Margaret. *Harry S. Truman*. New York: Morrow, 1973. An admiring biography, it is evocative and insightful in its portrayal of its subject and important for excerpts from Truman's correspondence not published elsewhere.

Arthur H. Vandenberg

See Chapter 25, 26, and 28, "Personalities," for additional references.

Fetzer, J. A. "Senator Vandenberg and the American Commitment to China, 1945–1950" (27:45).

Gregg, R. G. "A Rhetorical Re-Examination of Arthur Vandenberg's 'Dramatic Conversion,' January 10, 1945" (25:38) argues that Vandenberg's speech announcing his conversion to internationalism was designed to induce Franklin D. Roosevelt to delineate clearly his foreign policy.

Hill, T. M. "Senator Arthur H. Vandenberg, the Politics of Bipartisanship, and the Origins of Anti-Soviet Consensus, 1941–1946" (26:60).

Tompkins, C. D. *Senator Arthur H. Vandenberg: The Evolution of a Modern Republican, 1884–1945* (22:37) is an account of Vandenberg's career through World War II, with two chapters dealing with Vandenberg's opinion, approach, and leadership of the Republican party regarding the United Nations, the Soviet Union, and postwar isolationism.

24:162 Vandenberg, Arthur H., Jr., ed. *The Private Papers of Senator Vandenberg.* Boston: Houghton Mifflin, 1952. These excerpts from the diary and correspondence of a key Republican senator during the early cold war years are vital for an understanding of the development and limits of bipartisanship, and of the decline of isolationism within the Republican party.

Henry A. Wallace

See Chapter 26, "Personalities," for additional references.

24:163 Markowitz, Norman D. *The Rise and Fall of the People's Century: Henry A. Wallace and American Liberalism, 1941–1948.* New York: Free Press, 1973. A sympathetic account of Wallace's public career during World War II and the early cold war years, it concludes that Wallace's foreign policy program, as articulated during the Progressive party campaign of 1948, was farsighted.

24:164 Schapsmeier, Edward L., and Schapsmeier, Frederich H. *Prophet in Politics: Henry A. Wallace and the War Years, 1940–1965.* Ames: Iowa State University Press, 1970. The second volume of a full-length biography of Wallace, this is a sympathetic treatment emphasizing Wallace's strong religious faith, though it is not uncritical of his role in the 1948 presidential campaign.

24:165 Walker, J. Samuel. *Henry A. Wallace and American Foreign Policy.* Westport, Conn.: Greenwood, 1976. This is a brief but balanced account of Wallace's views on foreign policy, with more attention than usual paid to his pre-1941 views.

24:166 Wallace, Henry A. *The Price of Vision: The Diary of Henry A. Wallace, 1942–1946.* Ed. by John Morton Blum. Boston: Houghton Mifflin, 1973. Probably the most remarkable diary to emerge from World War II and the early cold war years, it is filled with observations on people and events. It illustrates Wallace's weaknesses as well as his strengths. The editor, in his introductory essay, stresses the latter. The diary is essential for an understanding of Wallace's views on the Soviet Union and the cold war.

Walton, R. J. *Henry Wallace, Harry Truman, and the Cold War* (26:64).

Others

24:167 Allison, John M. *Ambassador from the Prairie, or, Allison Wonderland.* Boston: Houghton

Mifflin, 1973. The anecdotal memoir of a career foreign service officer who served as assistant secretary of state for Far Eastern affairs under Truman, and as ambassador to Japan, Indonesia, and Czechoslovakia under Eisenhower.

Beam, J. D. *Multiple Exposure: An American Ambassador's Unique Perspective on East-West Issues* (29:38).

24:168 Briggs, Ellis O. *Farewell to Foggy Bottom.* New York: McKay, 1964. These memoirs, mostly anecdotal, are by a career foreign service officer with postwar experience in Uruguay, Czechoslovakia, Korea, Peru, Brazil, Greece, and Spain.

24:169 Clayton, William L. *Selected Papers of Will Clayton.* Ed. by Frederick J. Dobney. Baltimore: Johns Hopkins Press, 1971. This volume includes selections from Clayton's papers from his service as assistant secretary of state for economic affairs (1944–1946) and under secretary of state for economic affairs (1946–1947). An introductory essay sets forth Clayton's economic philosophy.

24:170 Conant, James B. *My Several Lives: Memoirs of a Social Inventor.* New York: Harper & Row, 1970. These memoirs of a prominent scientist, educator, and diplomat who served as U.S. high commissioner for Germany during the Eisenhower administration contain material of importance on atomic energy, McCarthyism, German affairs, national security policy, and the formation, in 1950, of the original Committee on the Present Danger.

24:171 Connally, Tom, with Steinberg, Alfred. *My Name is Tom Connally.* New York: Crowell, 1954. The last third of this thin and anecdotal autobiography deals with the author's chairmanship of the Senate Foreign Relations Committee (1941–1947, 1949–1953), with emphasis on his contribution to bipartisanship.

24:172 Ford, Gerald R. *A Time to Heal.* New York: Harper & Row, 1979. These bland, anecdotal memoirs contain some insights into the former president's views on foreign policy.

24:173 Griffis, Stanton. *Lying in State.* Garden City, N.Y.: Doubleday, 1952. These are the anecdotal reminiscences by a former ambassador to Poland, Egypt, Argentina, and Spain during the Truman administration.

24:174 Jessup, Philip C. *The Birth of Nations*. New York: Columbia University Press, 1973. Not a full memoir, it is rather retrospective essays on the author's involvement in diplomacy concerning Korea, Indonesia, Morocco and Tunisia, Indochina, Israel, and the United Nations during the late 1940s and early 1950s.

24:175 Krock, Arthur. *Memoirs: Sixty Years on the Firing Line*. New York: Funk & Wagnalls, 1968. A memoir by a longtime *New York Times* reporter and columnist, it contains considerable material on postwar foreign policy, mainly from a presidential perspective.

Lash, J. P. *Eleanor: The Years Alone* (38:49) provides a sympathetic account of Eleanor Roosevelt's service on the U.S. delegation to the United Nations between 1946 and 1952, and of her progressive disillusionment with the policies of the Soviet Union.

24:176 Lilienthal, David E. *The Journals of David E. Lilienthal*. 6 vols. New York: Harper & Row, 1964–. This is probably the most thorough of all published postwar diaries. Lilienthal was the first chairman of the Tennessee Valley Authority, the first chairman of the Atomic Energy Commission, and since 1950 was in private business. Volume 2 (1945–1950) is especially important for its coverage of U.S. policy on atomic energy.

Murphy, R. D. *Diplomat among Warriors* (23:77) is the memoir of a career foreign service officer with an unusually varied record of service. The last third of the book contains important information on Germany and the Berlin blockade, Japan, the Korean armistice, and the Lebanon crisis.

24:177 Noble, G. Bernard. *Christian A. Herter*. Vol. 18 in *The American Secretaries of State and Their Diplomacy*, ed. by Samuel Flagg Bemis and Robert Ferrell. New series. New York: Cooper Square, 1970. A sympathetic biography of Dulles's successor as secretary of state during the final two years of the Eisenhower administration, it stresses Herter's personal qualities, but documents few changes from the policies of his predecessor.

24:178 Paterson, Thomas G., ed. *Cold War Critics: Alternatives to American Foreign Policy in the Truman Years*. Chicago: Quadrangle, 1971. This book contains essays on critics of the early cold war: Walter Lippmann, James P. Warburg, Senator Claude Pepper, Senator Glen Taylor, Senator Robert A. Taft,

black critics of American foreign policy, and I. F. Stone.

24:179 Pearson, Drew. *Drew Pearson Diaries, 1949–1959*. Ed. by Tyler Abell. New York: Holt, Rinehart & Winston, 1974. These confidential diaries of the controversial Washington columnist have considerable material of interest on foreign affairs.

24:180 Radosh, Ronald. *Prophets on the Right: Profiles of Conservative Critics of American Globalism*. New York: Simon & Schuster, 1975. These essays on Charles A. Beard, Oswald Garrison Villard, Robert A. Taft, John T. Flynn, and Lawrence Dennis find parallels between their critique of the American "empire" from the perspective of the Right, and the more recent New Left critique, to which the author is sympathetic.

24:181 Rostow, W. W. *The Diffusion of Power: An Essay in Recent History*. New York: Macmillan, 1972. A sequel to the author's earlier *The United States in the World Arena* (24:48), this volume is both a history of American foreign policy (1957–1969) and a memoir of the author's service as a key State Department and White House adviser in the Kennedy and Johnson administrations.

24:182 Steel, Ronald. *Walter Lippmann and the American Century*. Boston: Little, Brown, 1980. The definitive biography of the most influential American journalist of the century, it provides considerable new information on American foreign policy.

24:183 Strauss, Lewis L. *Men and Decisions*. Garden City, N.Y.: Doubleday, 1962. These memoirs, by Eisenhower's chairman of the Atomic Energy Commission (1953–1958) and a key member of that body under Truman, are important for the development of the hydrogen bomb, as well as security and disarmament issues in the late 1940s and the 1950s.

24:184 Sulzberger, Cyrus L. *A Long Row of Candles: Memoirs and Diaries, 1934–1954, and the Last of the Giants*. New York: Macmillan, 1969–1970. These excerpts from a voluminous diary of a foreign correspondent and columnist for the *New York Times* are candid, gossipy, usually revealing. This is especially true of the portrayals of Eisenhower and de Gaulle.

White, T. H. *In Search of History* (23:225) is a massive personal evaluation of the 1940s to 1963 by a distinguished journalist and author. It emphasizes the fall of Chiang Kai-shek, the achievements of the Marshall Plan, and Kennedy's presidency.

Presidential Administrations

THE TRUMAN YEARS

See, under "Personalities," Dean Acheson, John M. Allison (under "Others"), Charles E. Bohlen, James F. Brynes, Will Clayton (under "Others"), James B. Conant (under "Others"), Allen W. Dulles, John Foster Dulles, W. Averell Harriman, George F. Kennan, Douglas MacArthur, George C. Marshall, Joseph McCarthy, Robert D. Murphy (under "Others"), Edward R. Stettinius, Jr., Robert A. Taft, Harry S. Truman, Arthur H. Vandenberg, Henry A. Wallace.

Bibliographies and Documents

24:185 Bernstein, Barton J., and Matusow, Allen J., eds. *The Truman Administration: A Documentary History.* New York: Harper & Row, 1966. A collection of major documents, mostly public, which deals with the foreign and domestic policies of the Truman administration. Editorial comments and bibliography.

24:186 Stapleton, Margaret L. *The Truman and Eisenhower Years, 1945–1960: A Selective Bibliography.* Metuchen, N.J.: Scarecrow, 1973. This comprehensive but unannotated bibliography of some 1,000 books and articles provides good coverage of foreign affairs. Author and title index.

U.S. President. *Public Papers of the Presidents of the United States* [1945–] (1:362) includes Harry S. Truman's public papers.

Historiography

24:187 Ferrell, Robert H. "Truman Foreign Policy: A Traditionalist View." In Richard S. Kirkendall, ed., *The Truman Period as a Research Field: A Reappraisal, 1972.* Columbia: University of Missouri

Press, 1974, pp. 11–45. This critique of revisionist writings on the foreign policy of the Truman administration concludes that "the revisionists have not proved a single one of their points." The volume includes commentaries on this essay by Barton J. Bernstein and David S. McLellan.

24:188 Gardner, Lloyd C. "Truman Era Foreign Policy: Recent Historical Trends." In Richard S. Kirkendall, ed., *The Truman Period as a Research Field: A Reappraisal, 1972.* Columbia: University of Missouri Press, 1974, pp. 47–74. A sympathetic survey of revisionist writings on the foreign policies of the Truman administration which concludes that the revisionists have done more than their critics to take advantage of new source materials.

24:189 Griffith, Robert. "Truman and the Historians: The Reconstruction of Postwar American History." *Wisconsin Magazine of History* 59:1 (1975), 20–50. A thorough review of recent literature on the Truman administration's foreign and domestic policies, it contains a comprehensive bibliographical note.

24:190 McLellan, David S., and Reuss, John W. "Foreign and Military Policies." In Richard S. Kirkendall, ed., *The Truman Period as a Research Field.* Columbia: University of Missouri Press, 1967, pp. 15–86. This essay is dated now regarding sources, but it is still a valuable discussion of major foreign policy issues and research problems relating to the Truman administration.

24:191 Smith, Geoffrey. "'Harry, We Hardly Know You': Revisionism, Politics and Diplomacy, 1945–1954." *American Political Science Review* 70:2 (1976), 560–82. This thorough review of contemporary scholarship on the foreign and domestic policies of the Truman administration detects the emergence of a new "eclectic" synthesis, combining elements of the revisionist and orthodox points of view.

Surveys

24:192 Bernstein, Barton J., ed. *Politics and Policies of the Truman Administration.* Chicago: Quadrangle, 1970. Writing from a revisionist perspective, with primary emphasis on foreign policy, the contributors focus on the origins of the cold war, the Marshall Plan, the German question, Latin America, internal security, the loyalty program, and civil rights.

24:193   Cochran, Bert. *Harry Truman and the Crisis Presidency*. New York: Funk & Wagnalls, 1973. A critical history of the Truman administration, it advances the thesis that the administration came to rely on and indeed to welcome foreign policy crises as a means of implementing its program.

24:194   Donovan, Robert J. *Conflict and Crisis: The Presidency of Harry S. Truman, 1945–1948*. New York: Norton, 1977. This is the fullest and most satisfactory treatment of Truman's first term, based on recently opened archival materials. Donovan is generally sympathetic, though critical on specific episodes.

Hamby, A. L. *Beyond the New Deal: Harry S. Truman and American Liberalism* (26:58) describes how the liberal position on Soviet-American relations evolved after World War II and how Truman's management of containment policies came to be supported by the liberal movement.

Haynes, R. F. *The Awesome Power: Harry S. Truman as Commander in Chief* (40:91) describes the impact of the cold war on the president's authority as commander in chief.

Paterson, T. G., ed. *Cold War Critics: Alternatives to American Foreign Policy in the Truman Years* (24:178) has essays, written from a revisionist perspective, on critics of the Truman administration's foreign policies.

24:195   Phillips, Cabell. *The Truman Presidency: The History of a Triumphant Succession*. New York: Macmillan, 1966. Still the most comprehensive history of the entire administration, though written before most archival sources became available, it is strongly sympathetic to Truman.

24:196   Stone, I. F. *The Truman Era*. New York: Vintage, 1973. This collection of articles by a radical journalist offers a penetrating critique of the Truman administration's foreign and domestic policies.

THE EISENHOWER YEARS

See, under "Personalities," John M. Allison (under "Others"), Allen W. Dulles, John Foster Dulles, Dwight D. Eisenhower, Christian A. Herter (under "Others"), George F. Kennan, Henry Cabot Lodge, Jr., Joseph McCarthy, Robert D. Murphy (under "Others"), Richard M. Nixon, Lewis L. Strauss (under "Others").

Bibliographies and Documents

24:197   Branyan, Robert L., and Larsen, Lawrence H., eds. *The Eisenhower Administration, 1953–1961: A Documentary History*. 2 vols. New York: Random House, 1971. This is a voluminous and carefully annotated collection of documents, some not previously published, relating to Eisenhower's foreign and domestic policies.

Stapleton, M. L. *The Truman and Eisenhower Years, 1945–1960: A Selected Bibliography* (24:186).

U.S. President. *Public Papers of the Presidents of the United States* [1945–] (1:362) includes Eisenhower's public papers.

Historiography

24:198   Bernstein, Barton J. "Foreign Policy in the Eisenhower Administration." *Foreign Service Journal* 50:5 (1973), 17–20, 29, 30. This appraisal of the revisionist literature on Eisenhower divides accounts into "radical," "left-liberal," and "tactical" categories.

24:199   De Santis, Vincent P. "Eisenhower Revisionism." *Review of Politics* 38:2 (1976), 190–207. A full appraisal of historical writing on the Eisenhower administration, this article traces in detail the rising reputation of the 34th president in the wake of Vietnam and Watergate.

Surveys

24:200   Adams, Sherman. *Firsthand Report: The Story of the Eisenhower Administration*. New York: Harper, 1961. This is an early but useful inside account of the Eisenhower administration, with some attention to foreign policy matters, written by the assistant to the president (1953–1958).

24:201   Alexander, Charles C. *Holding the Line: The Eisenhower Era, 1952–1961*. Bloomington: Indiana University Press, 1975. In a balanced overview of the Eisenhower administration's foreign and domestic policies, Alexander concludes that while Eisenhower was "not one to inspire his countrymen to try for the unattainable," he did, nonetheless, "serve them with a degree of common sense not generally displayed by other Presidents in the years since World War II." Extensive bibliographical essay.

24:202 Capitanchik, David. *The Eisenhower Presidency and American Foreign Policy.* London: Routledge & Kegan Paul, 1969. This brief, insightful essay by a British political scientist on Eisenhower's personal contribution to the foreign policy of his administration concludes that Eisenhower "seems nearly always to have been able to ensure that United States policy as a whole conformed to the essential premises he had laid down."

24:203 Donovan, Robert J. *Eisenhower: The Inside Story.* New York: Harper, 1956. This journalistic account of Eisenhower's first term is of more than usual significance because it was based on interviews and White House documents. It provides a good picture of the formative period of Eisenhower's foreign policy.

24:204 Hughes, Emmet John. *The Ordeal of Power: A Political Memoir of the Eisenhower Years.* New York: Atheneum, 1963. A well-written if acerbic and disillusioned account by a former Eisenhower speech-writer that did much to set the view that Dulles dominated the administration's foreign policy.

Killian, J. R., Jr. *Sputnik, Scientists, and Eisenhower: A Memoir of the First Special Assistant to the President for Science and Technology* (29:129) notes the shock waves set loose by Sputnik and the advice leading scientists were giving Eisenhower in the early years of the Soviet-American missile race. Killian headed the President's Science Advisory Committee (1957–1959).

Kinnard, D. *President Eisenhower and Strategy Management: A Study in Defense Politics* (40:211) argues that Eisenhower dominated the making of national security policy.

Kistiakowsky, G. B. *A Scientist at the White House: The Private Diary of President Eisenhower's Special Assistant for Science and Technology* (29:130) gives an inside view of the Eisenhower administration's concern over the nuclear arms race, disarmament, the U-2 crisis, and summit diplomacy (1959–1960).

24:205 Parmet, Herbert S. *Eisenhower and the American Crusades.* New York: Macmillan, 1972. In a major political history of the Eisenhower administration, with heavy emphasis on the 1952 campaign and the first term, Parmet views Eisenhower's foreign policy as largely successful, directed toward containing both the Russians and the isolationist wing of the Republican party.

24:206 Reichard, Gary W. "Divisions and Dissent: Democrats and Foreign Policy, 1952–1956." *Political Science Quarterly* 93:1 (1978), 51–72. Reichard questions whether foreign policy bipartisanship was reestablished during Eisenhower's first term, citing Democratic opposition on such issues as foreign aid, Hungary, and Suez.

THE KENNEDY YEARS

See, under "Personalities," Charles E. Bohlen, Chester Bowles, Allen W. Dulles, J. William Fulbright, W. Averell Harriman, George F. Kennan, John F. Kennedy, W. W. Rostow (under "Others"), Dean Rusk, Adlai E. Stevenson.

Documents and Historiography

24:207 Beck, Kent M. "The Kennedy Image: Politics, Camelot, and Vietnam." *Wisconsin Magazine of History* 58:1 (1974), 45–53. A brief review of the literature on Kennedy, much of it journalistic, which concludes that assessments of JFK have been much influenced by subsequent events.

24:208 LaFeber, Walter. "Kennedy, Johnson and the Revisionists." *Foreign Service Journal* 50:5 (1973), 31–33, 39. One of the few assessments to date on the historiography of the Kennedy and Johnson administrations, it demonstrates that the emerging generally critical view cuts across conventional ideological persuasions.

U.S. President. *Public Papers of the Presidents of the United States* [1945–] (1:362) includes Kennedy's public papers.

Surveys

24:209 Fairlie, Henry. *The Kennedy Promise: The Politics of Expectation.* Garden City, N.Y.: Doubleday, 1973. This is a British journalist's critique of the Kennedy administration's foreign and domestic policies. The problem, he argues, was hyperactivity, and the confusion of it with substantive goals, substantive achievements.

24:210 FitzSimons, Louise. *The Kennedy Doctrine.* New York: Random House, 1972. In this revisionist critique of Kennedy's foreign policy, the author asserts that his alleged elitism led to "a foreign policy of overcommitment" and an economy dependent on the military-industrial complex.

Galbraith, J. K. *Ambassador's Journal: A Personal Account of the Kennedy Years* (30:39).

24:211 Gromyko, Anatolii A. *Through Russian Eyes: President Kennedy's 1036 Days.* Ed. by Philip A. Garon. Washington, D.C.: International Library, 1973. This is a Soviet account of the Kennedy administration, published in Russian (1968) by a prominent Soviet diplomat (the son of Foreign Minister Andrei Gromyko). For a critical review, see Nelson W. Polsby, "JFK through Russian Eyes," *Political Science Quarterly* 90:1 (1975), 117–26.

Halberstam, D. *The Best and the Brightest* (30:144) provides vivid portraits of policymakers in the Kennedy administration.

24:212 Heath, Jim F. *Decade of Disillusionment: The Kennedy-Johnson Years.* Bloomington: Indiana University Press, 1975. The only comprehensive overview of both the Kennedy and Johnson administrations, this account stresses the unfulfilled promises of the two Democratic administrations in both the foreign and domestic spheres. Extensive bibliographical essay.

24:213 Hilsman, Roger. *To Move a Nation: The Politics of Foreign Policy in the Administration of John F. Kennedy.* Garden City, NY: Doubleday, 1967. This is an extensive account of Kennedy's foreign policies by a political scientist who served as director of the Bureau of Intelligence and Research and as assistant secretary of state in Kennedy's State Department. Hilsman praises Kennedy's sense of strategy and statecraft.

24:214 Miroff, Bruce. *Pragmatic Illusions: The Presidential Politics of John F. Kennedy.* New York: McKay, 1976. A radical critique of Kennedy's foreign and domestic policies and a reinterpretation of the presidency as an institution. It concludes that Kennedy fueled rather than dampened down the cold war in Cuba, Berlin, and Southeast Asia.

Schlesinger, A. M., Jr. *Robert Kennedy and His Times* (29:34) is a partisan, but useful biography which includes several chapters on foreign policy.

24:215 Schlesinger, Arthur M., Jr. *A Thousand Days: John F. Kennedy in the White House.* Boston: Houghton Mifflin, 1965. A detailed personal memoir of the Kennedy administration, this account is strongly sympathetic to Kennedy, less so to his associates. Schlesinger provides much of importance on the administration's foreign policies, especially the Alliance for Progress, with which he was directly concerned.

24:216 Walton, Richard J. *Cold War and Counterrevolution: The Foreign Policy of John F. Kennedy.* New York: Viking, 1972. The first sustained revisionist critique of the Kennedy administration's foreign policies, this book argues that Kennedy's policies were those of classic cold war liberalism; that while Kennedy called, near the end of his life, for a reexamination of attitudes toward the cold war, he himself failed to understand the true nature of that conflict.

THE JOHNSON YEARS

See, under "Personalities," George W. Ball, Charles E. Bohlen, Chester Bowles, J. William Fulbright, Lyndon B. Johnson, W. W. Rostow (under "Others"), Dean Rusk, Adlai E. Stevenson.

Documents

U.S. President. *Public Papers of the Presidents of the United States* [1945–] (1:362) collects the public papers of the Johnson administration.

Surveys

24:217 Geyelin, Philip L. *Lyndon B. Johnson and the World.* New York: Praeger, 1966. An early, but uneasy assessment by a Washington journalist which argues that Johnson's tendency (and weakness) was to try to apply to foreign policy the same methods he had found successful in domestic politics.

24:218 Goldman, Eric F. *The Tragedy of Lyndon Johnson.* New York: Knopf, 1969. A prominent historian, disillusioned by his service as a special consultant to President Johnson, concludes that Johnson was both able and intelligent but poorly educated.

Halberstam, D. *The Best and the Brightest* (30:144) provides biographical sketches of the policymakers of the Johnson administrations. While centering on Vietnam, there is also useful material on relations with Europe.

Heath, J. F. *Decade of Disillusionment: The Kennedy-Johnson Years* (24:212).

Schandler, H. Y. *The Unmaking of a President: Lyndon Johnson and Vietnam* (30:222).

THE NIXON-FORD YEARS

See, under "Personalities," Gerald R. Ford (under "Others"), J. William Fulbright, Henry A. Kissinger, Richard M. Nixon.

Documents

U.S. President. *Public Papers of the President of the United States* [1945–] (1:362) collects the public papers of the Nixon-Ford administrations.

Surveys

24:219 Bell, Coral. *The Diplomacy of Detente: The Kissinger Era.* New York: St. Martin's Press, 1977. Bell analyzes Kissinger's diplomacy, with special emphasis on problems lying outside the immediate range of Soviet-American relations, notably Southeast Asia, Cyprus, Portugal and Southern Africa, and, as a case study in the "range of middle-power manoeuvre," Australia.

24:220 Brandon, Henry. *The Retreat of American Power.* Garden City, N.Y.: Doubleday, 1973. In a sympathetic account of the foreign policies of the Nixon administration (1969–1972), Brandon, a British journalist, focuses on the American withdrawal from overextended positions, and the implications of this for future U.S. foreign policy.

24:221 Hartmann, Robert T. *Palace Politics: An Inside Account of the Ford Years.* New York: McGraw-Hill, 1980. A personal aide to the president evaluates the politics and personalities of the Ford administration.

24:222 Liska, George. *Beyond Kissinger: Ways of Conservative Statecraft.* Baltimore: Johns Hopkins University Press, 1975. In an early critique of Kissinger, Liska argues that Kissinger shifted from a

"Bismarckian" strategy of balancing adversaries off against each other to a "Metternichian" one of accommodation with the major adversary to preserve an aging empire.

24:223 Morris, Roger. *Uncertain Greatness: Henry Kissinger and American Foreign Policy.* New York: Harper & Row, 1977. This is a sophisticated but emotional appraisal of Kissinger's contribution. Morris concludes that Kissinger was necessary to break through bureaucratic inertia, that his handling of Sino-Soviet diplomacy was generally successful, but that his diplomatic style was unsuited to dealings with the rest of the world.

24:224 Osgood, Robert E., et al. *Retreat from Empire? The First Nixon Administration.* Baltimore: Johns Hopkins University Press, 1973. These thoughtful essays deal with the diplomatic, military and economic policies of the first Nixon administration.

24:225 Safire, William. *Before the Fall: An Inside View of the Pre-Watergate White House.* Garden City, N.Y.: Doubleday, 1975. This account of Nixon's first term was prepared by a former speech-writer. Safire's treatment of Nixon's foreign policy is sympathetic, but he was on the periphery of many of the foreign policy decisions of this period.

Schell, J. *The Time of Illusion* (24:242) is a bitter indictment of the Nixon administration, which argues that Vietnam and Watergate were inextricably linked.

24:226 Szulc, Tad. *The Illusion of Peace: Foreign Policy in the Nixon-Kissinger Years.* New York: Viking, 1978. A thorough but hostile account of Nixon and Kissinger's foreign policies, it concludes that while the conceptual framework of the administration's policies was correct, its manner of execution was cynical, amoral, and ultimately destructive of the larger ends sought.

Special Topics

24:227 Barnet, Richard J. *Intervention and Revolution: The United States in the Third World.* Cleveland: World, 1968. Barnet argues that "national security managers" have cast the U.S. in the counterrevolutionary role of world policeman. The book includes case studies on the Truman Doctrine and Greece, Lebanon, the Dominican Republic, Vietnam, and covert intervention.

24:228   Bell, Coral. *Negotiation from Strength: A Study in the Politics of Power.* New York: Knopf, 1963. This book analyzes the assumption, shared by American statesmen from Acheson through Kennedy, that the United States should never negotiate with the Russians until it could do so from a position of strength. The results of this policy, the author concludes, were neither negotiations nor strength. Bibliography.

24:229   Donelan, Michael. *The Ideas of American Foreign Policy.* London: Chapman, 1963. An oddly neglected study of major ideas in American foreign policy from 1945 through the Cuban missile crisis by an informed British observer, this book gives special attention to "one world," communism, containment, collective security, and coexistence. Donelan finds that outmoded ideas are retained because there is insufficient time for reappraisal.

24:230   Donovan, John C. *The Cold Warriors: A Policy-Making Elite.* Lexington, Mass.: Heath, 1974. This study of decisionmaking immediately below the presidential level (1945–1973) concludes that U.S. strategic policy has been dominated "by a distinct policy elite" with its own set of priorities and objectives.

24:231   Gati, Charles, ed. *Caging the Bear: Containment and the Cold War.* Indianapolis: Bobbs-Merrill, 1974. These useful essays on the evolving meaning of containment include original studies by William Zimmerman, on Soviet policy, Donald Zagoria, on China, John Spanier, on the "revisionist" views of Zimmerman and Zagoria, and a brief bibliographical discussion of the debate over the origins of the cold war by Toby Trister.

24:232   Graebner, Norman A. *The New Isolationism: A Study in Politics and Foreign Policy since 1950.* New York: Ronald, 1956. The "new isolationists" are right-wing Asia-first elements, mostly in the Republican party, chiefly motivated, the author argues, by their own political interests.

24:233   Gurtov, Melvin. *The United States against the Third World: Antinationalism and Intervention.* New York: Praeger, 1974. Gurtov attempts to generalize about motives for and patterns of U.S. intervention in Third World areas, with individual case studies on Eisenhower in the Middle East, Kennedy in Africa, Johnson in Latin America, and Nixon in Asia.

24:234   Hoffmann, Stanley. *Gulliver's Troubles: Or the Setting of American Foreign Policy.* New York: McGraw-Hill, 1968. This detailed analysis of the American "style" in postwar foreign policy, and of the constraints imposed by American institutions, is intended as a backdrop to a study of U.S. relations with NATO.

24:235   Houghton, N. D., ed. *Struggle against History: U.S. Foreign Policy in an Age of Revolution.* New York: Simon & Schuster, 1968. This series of essays reconsiders American cold war policies in the light of Vietnam. The general theme is the United States as a counterrevolutionary power.

24:236   Julien, Claude. *America's Empire.* Trans. by Renaud Bruce. New York: Pantheon, 1971. In a strident French critique of American foreign policy, with emphasis on the cold war period, Julien argues that American domestic interests require exploitation of the underdeveloped world's resources.

24:237   Kaplan, Morton A. *The Life and Death of the Cold War: Selected Studies in Postwar Statecraft.* Chicago: Nelson-Hall, 1977. These essays on the early cold war, written in 1954 and 1955 and not updated since, cover such themes as Soviet policy, the atomic bomb, China, Yugoslavia, Czechoslovakia, Korea, and NATO.

24:238   Kertesz, Stephen D., ed. *American Diplomacy in a New Era.* Notre Dame, Ind.: University of Notre Dame Press, 1961. These essays deal with both historical and organizational aspects of postwar American foreign policy. The historical articles cover NATO, containment, disarmament, the western hemisphere, South and Southeast Asia, Japan, Sub-Saharan Africa, the Middle East, and the communist satellites.

24:239   Kiernan, Barnard P. *The United States, Communism, and the Emergent World.* Bloomington: Indiana University Press, 1972. Primarily an analysis of the appeal of communism in the Third World, this study concludes that American efforts to "contain" it have been a "formula for frustration." Extensive bibliographical essay.

Miller, L. H., and Pruessen, R. W., eds. *Reflections on the Cold War: A Quarter Century of American*

Foreign Policy (24:41) includes original essays on various aspects of the cold war, such as the United Nations, the objectives of American foreign policy, revisionism, the cold war in Asia, the decision to cross the 38th parallel, the Asian boundaries of coexistence, the Cuban missile crisis, the arms race, and counter-revolution.

24:240 Morris, Bernard S. *International Communism and American Policy.* New York: Atherton, 1966. A former State Department official's succinct history of the progressive fragmentation of the international communist "monolith" and of the American response to it, which, in the author's view, has been one of myopic neglect.

24:241 Nash, Henry T. *American Foreign Policy: Response to a Sense of Threat.* Homewood, Ill.: Dorsey, 1973. An analysis of how the executive agencies of the U.S. government—the military, the State Department, presidential advisers, the intelligence and arms control communities—have responded to the perceived threat of communism.

24:242 Schell, Jonathan. *The Time of Illusion.* New York: Knopf, 1976. This provocative account attempts to locate the roots of Vietnam and Watergate in the dilemmas of nuclear strategy that arose in the 1950s. Schell argues that in each of these cases a willingness to act had to be demonstrated in order to avoid self-induced fears of being unable to act at all.

24:243 Siracusa, Joseph M., and Barclay, Glen St. John, eds. *The Impact of the Cold War: Reconsiderations.* Port Washington, N.Y.: Kennikat, 1977. These useful original essays on the impact of the cold war outside the arena of Soviet-American competition review U.S. policies in Indochina, Australia, Italy, Belgium, Germany, Nigeria, Argentina, Yugoslavia, and China.

24:244 Solberg, Carl. *Riding High: America in the Cold War.* New York: Mason & Lipscomb, 1973. In a lively account of the impact of the cold war on American society, Solberg argues that in their zeal to expand the nation's influence overseas while protecting it against exaggerated dangers, successive postwar ad-

ministrations undermined the nation's domestic institutions. Bibliographical essay.

24:245 Steel, Ronald. *Pax Americana.* Rev. ed. New York: Viking, 1970. An influential critique of postwar American foreign policy, it argues that the United States had, by the mid-1960s, become an imperial power, intervening massively in the affairs of other states. Steel maintains that this happened inadvertently, and with the best of intentions.

24:246 Stillman, Edmund, and Pfaff, William. *Power and Impotence: The Failure of America's Foreign Policy.* New York: Random House, 1966. This volume analyzes and critiques the assumptions underlying American "globalism." It is based largely on the public statements of government officials.

24:247 Stoessinger, John G. *Nations in Darkness: China, Russia, and America.* 3d ed. New York: Random House (1971), 1978. An eloquent analysis of how misperceptions have affected relations between the United States, China, and Russia, which gives special attention to case studies from the post-1945 period.

24:248 Swomley, John M. *American Empire: The Political Ethics of Twentieth Century Conquest.* New York: Macmillan, 1970. This is an analysis of selected episodes in postwar American foreign policy—among them the origins of the cold war, Korea, Cuba, Vietnam—and a critique of the philosophy of "political realism" that the author thinks lies behind them.

24:249 Tugwell, Rexford G. *Off Course: From Truman to Nixon.* New York: Praeger, 1971. A former Roosevelt "brain truster's" argument that if only FDR had lived, the cold war might have been avoided; that only with the advent of Nixon and Kissinger was there a return to the "Rooseveltian wisdom" of nonideological coexistence.

24:250 Warburg, James P. *The United States in the Postwar World: A Critical Appraisal.* New York: Atheneum, 1966. A longtime critic of American foreign policy surveys its performance during the cold war and finds it to have been distorted by excessive fears of communism.

25

Anglo-American-Soviet Diplomacy for the Postwar World, 1941-1945

Contributing Editor
WARREN F. KIMBALL
Newark College
Rutgers University

Contributors
Louise Sieminski
Newark College
Rutgers University

David Reynolds
Cambridge University

Contents

Introduction

World War II not only marked the start of an era where the United States government and, apparently, the bulk of the American public accepted a global political role for the nation, but it also marked the beginning of the "paper explosion," which has rapidly filled our public and private archives almost to overflowing. Since historical research tends to concentrate both where the records are and where major events occur, the outpouring of printed sources and secondary studies on American foreign policy and diplomacy in World War II has been staggering. Largely because of that volume, the editors of this *Guide* have somewhat artificially carved the wartime period up into smaller, more digestible chunks. Nevertheless, users of this *Guide* are strongly cautioned to consult all of the chapters which deal with wartime diplomacy, including those chapters which are organized along topical or geographic lines. Because most of the published materials treat both wartime and postwar foreign policy together, there is considerable overlap between Chapters 22, 23, 25, and 26. The focus of each of those chapters is, however, different and will direct the user toward different end points. The editors have added numerous cross-references, but only a careful perusal by each reader will guarantee that the *Guide* is used to best advantage.

When President Franklin Roosevelt announced that he was no longer "Dr. New Deal" but had switched to "Dr. Win-the-War," and Secretary of State Cordell Hull told Secretary of War Henry Stimson, just before the Japanese attack on Pearl Harbor, that the matters were "in the hands of . . . the Army and the Navy," they seemed to be adjourning diplomacy for the duration of the war—and a good many critics made that interpretation. Without doubt, the serious military crisis the United States faced early in 1942—Pearl Harbor, German occupation of Western Europe and advances deep into the Soviet Union, the fall of Tobruk in North Africa and of Singapore in Southeast Asia, and Allied inability to control German submarine warfare in the Atlantic—preoccupied Ameri-

can leaders. There the war was in doubt. But that did not mean that concern about postwar foreign policy and diplomacy came to a halt. The Department of State quickly established internal committees to study such issues, as recounted in Harley Notter, *Postwar Foreign Policy Preparation, 1939–1945* (25:74).

From the very beginning of the war, even before the United States formally became a belligerent, questions of Anglo-Soviet-American relations in the postwar world cropped up. Starting with the Atlantic Conference in August 1941, such concerns increased until they came to dominate the bilateral and trilateral relations between the three great powers. Perhaps the best way to gain familiarity with those issues is to examine the literature on the major wartime conferences, beginning with Theodore Wilson's *The First Summit* (22:194), on through Diane Clemens's *Yalta* (25:59) and Charles Mee's *Meeting at Potsdam* (25:69). A broader pair of guides might be Herbert Feis's *Churchill, Roosevelt, Stalin: The War They Waged and the Peace They Sought* (25:8) and William McNeill's *America, Britain and Russia* (23:36). Unfortunately, those valuable works were written before the British opened their files for the wartime period, and must be supplemented (and occasionally supplanted) by the many articles and monographs which have used the British records and which began to appear during the mid-1970s.

Once familiar with the broad outlines of diplomacy for the postwar world, the many official histories and printed documentary collections become invaluable. The British official series *History of the Second World War* made use of the documents before they were opened to the public, and such subseries as *Grand Strategy* (23:153) and Sir Llewellyn Woodward's *History of the Second World War: British Foreign Policy in the Second World War* (23:40) consistently point to issues that other studies could not investigate until after 1972. The most illuminating single documentary collection is the volumes for 1941 to 1945 in the U.S. Department of State series, *Foreign Relations of the United States* (1:358). It may be impractical to try to read any or all of those volumes from cover to cover, for they are intended as research tools not narratives, but a careful sampling of *Foreign Relations of the United States (World War II Conference Series)* (25:55) is indispensable to any broad understanding of the development of American postwar policy. The opening of U.S. records for the war, also largely in 1972, has allowed scholars to investigate questions which the editors of the series chose not to include. Changes in interpretations have caused historians to focus on many questions which seemed less important when the volumes were compiled, but they still present the broad outlines of American diplomacy for the postwar world.

The varying interpretive approaches taken by historians to these issues have generated a great deal of heat and, fortunately, a great deal of light as well. Anti-Roosevelt revisionism, typified by those studies which bitterly attacked the American "surrender" to the Soviets at the Yalta Conference and summarized in Athan Theoharis, *The Yalta Myths* (25:65), were answered by scholars given special access to State Department records, particularly Herbert Feis. During the 1950s and into the 1960s, such defenses of American foreign policy—occasionally laced with mild criticisms of Roosevelt's lack of "realism"—became the standard interpretation found in almost every textbook. Then, led by William A. Williams's *The Tragedy of American Diplomacy* (2:99), there appeared a number of studies which argued that the United States had at least helped stimulate the cold war by threatening important Soviet interests. These critics, lumped under the rubric New Left, asserted that the United States shaped its postwar planning to preserve American economic and political influence while denying such influence to the Soviet Union. Such critiques vary from the mild approach in Lloyd Gardner, *Architects of Illusion* (25:17), to the avowedly radical attack on American capitalism and Soviet conservatism in Gabriel Kolko, *The Politics of War* (25:19). The initial response by those defending what had become the conventional view was sharp and, sometimes under the influence of the contemporary pressures of the Vietnam War, even bitter. But, in time, a new synthesis about the wartime origins of the postwar world began to emerge. Some, like Robert Dallek, *Franklin D. Roosevelt and American Foreign Policy, 1932–1945* (21:51), used the newly available documentation to restate the conventional position, while others, like George Herring, *Aid to Russia, 1941–1946* (25:144), took a stance somewhere between the two factions. And more studies continue to appear.

Meanwhile, another group of scholars, also using the newly opened records, began a reexamination of Anglo-American relations and postwar planning. Instead of emphasizing the remarkable cooperation between the two allies during the war, people like Christopher Thorne, *Allies of a Kind* (23:187), William

Roger Louis, *Imperialism at Bay* (25:119), and Warren F. Kimball, "Lend-Lease and the Open Door" (22:188), found areas where competition for postwar economic and political power characterized Anglo-American relations.

The historiographical parameters of Anglo-American-Soviet diplomacy for the postwar world seem to have been established, at least for the next decade or so. Geopoliticians like Bruce Kuniholm, *The Origins of the Cold War in the Near East* (33:89), and Lynn Davis, *The Cold War Begins* (25:98), will continue to emphasize Soviet aggressiveness, while those who focus on the motives and goals of American foreign policy, like Thomas Paterson, *Soviet-American Confrontation* (26:12), will find U.S. global expansion one of the root causes of wartime and postwar conflict between the three great powers. Meanwhile, scholars will continue to mine the now-available British and American records to turn out monographs which will eventually stimulate new syntheses. Interpretive arguments will persist, as they do in every field of history, but in the area of World War II, given the lack of documents about Roosevelt's thinking and the unlikelihood of access to Soviet records, those disputes seem likely to be intense.

Resources and Overviews

RESEARCH AIDS

While pertinent bibliographies and reference aids are listed here, there are more extensive lists in Chapter 1.

Bibliographies

See Chapter 24, "Bibliographies" and "Cold War Historiography" for additional references on the cold war.

Barnard, R.; Burns, W.; and Ryan, D. *The Era of World War II: General and Reference Works* (23:1).

Bayliss, G. *Bibliographical Guide to the Two World Wars: An Annotated Survey of English-Language Reference Materials* (19:2) annotates reference works.

Bloomberg, M., and Weber, H. H. *World War II and Its Origins: A Selected Annotated Bibliography of Books in English* (23:2) is a valuable guide to books on World War II, including U.S.-Soviet issues.

Cronon, E. D., and Rosenof, T. D., comps. *The Second World War and the Atomic Age, 1940–1973* (24:1).

Dexter, B., ed. *The Foreign Affairs Fifty-Year Bibliography: New Evaluation of Significant Books on International Relations, 1920–1970* (1:14) has some 40 pages dealing with World War II.

Foreign Affairs Bibliography: A Selected and Annotated List of Books on International Relations (1:15) is issued at ten-year intervals, and each volume has three parts: "General International Relations"; "The World since 1914"; and "The World by Regions." Useful aid.

Funk, A. L., et al. *A Select Bibliography of Books on the Second World War* (23:4).

Neumann, W. L. "Allied Diplomacy in World War II: A Bibliographical Survey" (23:12) offers an early (1955) appraisal of emerging historical controversies.

Stewart, W. J., ed. *The Era of Franklin D. Roosevelt: A Selected Bibliography of Periodical, Essay, and Dissertation Literature, 1945–1971* (20:2).

Ziegler, J., ed. *World War II: Books in English, 1945–1965* (23:9).

Yearbooks and Other Aids

The Annual Register of World Events: A Review of the Year (1:142) is especially useful for Britain and Commonwealth countries.

DeConde, A., ed. *Encyclopedia of American Foreign Policy* (1:164) includes essays which cover a range of subjects from alliances to unconditional surrender, each by a scholar who originally researched the subject.

Gallup, G. H. *The Gallup Poll: Public Opinion, 1935–1971* (1:348) pays considerable attention to foreign policy issues.

Maxwell, R., ed. and comp. *Information U.S.S.R.: An Authoritative Encyclopedia about the Union of Soviet Socialist Republics* (1:168).

Survey of International Affairs (1:146) is useful for specific issues.

The United States in World Affairs (1:147) is an annual review of American foreign policy.

Document Collections

More general collections are listed in Chapter 1, and other collections may be found under "Personalities," below; for conference documents, see "Wartime Conferences," below.

Documents on American Foreign Relations (1:339) is an annual intended to accompany the *United States in World Affairs* volumes.

Documents on International Affairs (1:340) is a good source for official documents and public statements of foreign leaders.

25:1   Great Britain. Royal Institute of International Affairs. *Review of the Foreign Press, 1939–1945*. 27 vols. Millwood, N.Y.: Kraus-Thomson, n.d. These ten series have been reprinted in ten volumes, and cover all geographical areas.

25:2   Leiss, Amelia C., with Dennett, Raymond. *European Peace Treaties after World War II*. Boston: World Peace Foundation, 1954. This is a convenient collection of negotiations and texts of treaties with Italy, Bulgaria, Hungary, Rumania, and Finland.

25:3   Molotov, V. M. *Problems of Foreign Policy: Speeches and Statements, April 1945–November 1948*. Moscow: Foreign Languages Publishing House, 1949. The first few documents in this volume pertain to Soviet postwar plans as the war in Europe came to an end. These works were designed for public consumption but may prove valuable to scholars working with other sources.

U.S.S.R. Ministry of Foreign Affairs. *Correspondence between the Chairman of the Council of Ministers of the U.S.S.R. and the Presidents of the U.S.A. and the Prime Ministers of Great Britain during the Great Patriotic War of 1941–1945* (23:19) contains the correspondence between the heads of the governments of the Soviet Union, Great Britain, and the United States for the war period. They are presented without additions or alternations; however, only the messages sent are included. For Soviet documents on big three wartime conferences, see (25:54).

U.S. Department of State. *Foreign Relations of the United States* (1:358) is a valuable source; for *World War II Conference Series,* see (25:55).

25:4 U.S. House. Committee on Foreign Affairs. *World War II International Agreements and Understandings: Entered into during Secret Conferences Concerning Other People.* Washington, D.C.: G.P.O., 1953. Collected here are the texts of various arguments entered into by the United States, with notes on background of negotiations and status of agreements. Special attention is given to violations by the Soviet Union.

U.S. Senate. Committee on Foreign Relations. *A Decade of American Foreign Policy: Basic Documents, 1941–49* (23:20) collects a number of previously published documents valuable for the years 1941 to 1945.

Indexes to Documents
25:5 *The Cumulated Index to the U.S. Department of State Papers Relating to the Foreign Relations of the United States, 1939–1945.* 2 vols. Millwood, N.Y.: Kraus-Thomson, 1980. These volumes organize the separate indexes in the 57 volumes into one alphabetical arrangement.

25:6 Great Britain. Public Record Office. *The Second World War: A Guide to Documents in the Public Record Office.* London: H.M.S.O., 1972. This guide was prepared to accompany the release, in January 1970, of previously closed papers relating to World War II. It consists largely of lists of documents and brief summaries of the wartime responsibilities of various ministries. An invaluable work for those beginning work in the British archives.

OVERVIEWS

See Chapter 23, "Overviews," for general works on World War II; also see Chapter 24, "Overviews."

25:7 Beitzell, Robert. *An Uneasy Alliance: America, Britain and Russia, 1941–1943.* New York: Knopf, 1972. The author describes the tensions between Roosevelt, Churchill, and Stalin during the initial two years of the Grand Alliance as emanating from diverse ideological positions and, in Stalin's mind, broken promises and false dealings.

25:8 Feis, Herbert. *Churchill, Roosevelt, Stalin: The War They Waged and the Peace They Sought.*

Princeton, N.J.: Princeton University Press, 1957. This early study of World War II diplomacy was, for many years, the standard work. Because it focuses on the three leaders, it remains a useful source of information on their thought, particularly as they expressed themselves during the major wartime conferences. Although it needs revision in the light of new sources and ideas, it still provides a good summary of tripartite diplomacy, particularly as the end of war approached.

Fleming, D. F. *The Cold War and Its Origins, 1917–1960* (24:9) is one of the first works to trace the origins of the cold war tensions to the Russian Revolution. It is, however, dated.

25:9 Herz, Martin F. *Beginnings of the Cold War.* Bloomington: Indiana University Press, 1966. A longtime foreign service officer, the author examines issues such as Poland, spheres of influence, lend-lease and shows their roles in beginning the cold war. Aiming primarily at students, he gives a balanced account without attempting any final conclusions. Bibliography.

25:10 King, F. P. *The New Internationalism: Allied Policy and the European Peace, 1939–1945.* Hamden, Conn.: Shoe String Press, 1973. In this survey the author views the war as an opportunity for internationalism, i.e., international cooperation as opposed to the isolationist sentiments of the 1930s. King claims that while cooperation was mandated by the war, the Allies continued to work together through the Yalta Conference. Bibliography.

McNeill, W. H. *America, Britain and Russia: Their Cooperation and Conflict, 1941–1946* (23:36) is a thorough though dated study of the Grand Alliance. McNeill argues that deep differences separated the Allies but that the war necessitated cooperation. Once the common enemy was defeated, the Grant Alliance fell apart.

25:11 Neumann, William L. *After Victory: Churchill, Roosevelt, Stalin and the Making of the Peace.* New York: Harper & Row, 1967. This is a balanced analysis of the conflicting war aims of the major powers in World War II. The way the war was waged, rather than diplomatic blunders, was the major factor in dictating the peace, argues the author.

25:12 Reynolds, David. "Competitive Co-Operation: Anglo-American Relations in World War Two." *Historical Journal* 23:1 (1980), 233–45. In a review article dealing with six recently published books on

Anglo-American wartime relations, Reynolds argues that opposition to Hitler's Germany never made British and American policymakers forget other, more national objectives.

Thorne, C. *Allies of a Kind: The United States, Britain and the War against Japan, 1941–1945* (23:187) is particularly concerned with the development of postwar policy. This is the starting point for research on Anglo-American relations in Asia.

25:13   Toynbee, Arnold J., and Toynbee, Veronica M., eds. *The Realignment of Europe*. New York: Oxford University Press, 1955. This volume in the Survey of International Affairs series for the war years (1939–1946) deals with events in Europe following the collapse of German power: the first steps toward economic rehabilitation under UNRRA, the expansion of Soviet control in the states of Eastern Europe, and the hectic resurrection of political life in Greece, Italy, and Western Europe.

25:14   Wheeler-Bennett, Sir John, and Nicholls, Anthony. *The Semblance of Peace: The Political Settlement after the Second World War*. London: Macmillan, 1972. This general study, though dated by the opening of the British archives, spans the entire wartime era with the emphasis on wartime planning for the peace. The authors place the blame for the breakdown in wartime cooperation and the subsequent cold war on Russia's ambitions for European and Asian expansion and American wartime appeasement of the Soviet Union. Extensive bibliography and documents.

Wilmot, C. *The Struggle for Europe* (23:31) is critical of Roosevelt and his advisers for subordinating political ends to military means, and thus allowing the postwar Soviet expansion.

American Policies

Alexander, C.C. *Nationalism in American Thought, 1930–1945* (2:30) covers many aspects of nationalism, including its effect upon Americans' views of themselves and the external world.

25:15   Chamberlin, William H. *America's Second Crusade*. Chicago: Regnery, 1950. Written from the prewar anti-interventionist point of view, it is highly critical of Roosevelt for manipulating the United States into a needless war, for appeasing Stalin during the conflict, and for thereby creating a new Soviet menace at least as dangerous as the defeated Axis.

Although dated, it constitutes an excellent example of the immediate postwar revisionist critique of FDR. Bibliography.

Fontaine, A. *History of the Cold War: From the October Revolution to the Korean War, 1917–1950* (24:10) traces the roots of the cold war back to American intervention in the Russian Revolution, the occasion of the first head-on clash between the forces of Wilsonianism and Leninism. Fontaine devotes nearly two-thirds of his book to subsequent Soviet-Western encounters up to 1945, the year that the United States and Russia renewed their confrontation in what quickly became "an unprecedented duel."

25:16   Gaddis, John Lewis. *The United States and the Origins of the Cold War, 1941–1947*. New York: Columbia University Press, 1972. This monograph deals exclusively with the origins of the cold war and excludes other aspects of tripartite diplomacy during the war. It traces the development of Soviet-American relations during the war and in the immediate post-war period, finding that the responsibility for the cold war lies primarily with the Soviets, although Roosevelt's policies frequently contributed to the growing tension. Gaddis emphasizes the role played by American public opinion. Bibliography.

Gardner, L. C. *Economic Aspects of New Deal Diplomacy* (21:12) stresses the importance of New Deal economic goals for Franklin Roosevelt's foreign policy.

25:17   Gardner, Lloyd C. *Architects of Illusion: Men and Ideas in American Foreign Policy, 1941–1949*. Chicago: Quadrangle, 1970. Gardner argues that the cold war was shaped by American officials who, in determined adherence to their "illusions" regarding the nature of the postwar world, missed opportunities for accommodation with the Soviet Union. Bibliography.

25:18   Graebner, Norman. "The Limits of Victory." *Studies in Modern European History and Culture* 3 (1977), 75–93. The United States entered World War II with high-minded goals, but during the war, cooperation with the Soviet Union was necessary. Yet the postwar situation cannot be blamed on American policy, but on geography and military strategy.

25:19   Kolko, Gabriel. *The Politics of War: The World and United States Foreign Policy, 1943–1945*. New York: Random House, 1968. The author claims that American foreign policy had three basic goals:

suppression of the Left wherever it appeared, the maintenance of the open door for American trade and influence in Eastern Europe, and economic expansion at the expense of the British empire. The Soviet Union's policies were essentially conservative, trying to control or suppress the Left.

Lippmann, W. *U.S. Foreign Policy: Shield of the Republic* (2:48) urges postwar U.S. concentration on a defense of the "Atlantic Community."

25:20   Rose, Lisle A. *After Yalta*. New York: Scribner's, 1973. This monograph maintains that U.S. foreign policy during the first months of the Truman administration was characterized by vacillation and confusion on the part of American policymakers in the face of Soviet belligerence. Rose sees the atomic bomb, especially, as the primary cause of the Soviet-American break, but denies that Washington officials devised a coherent strategy of atomic diplomacy for the purpose of challenging the Russians. Bibliography.

25:21   Rose, Lisle A. *The Coming of the American Age, 1945–1946*. Vol. 1: *Dubious Victory: The United States and the End of World War II*. Kent, Ohio: Kent State University Press, 1973. A narrative of Soviet-American relations from Truman's succession to the presidency to Hiroshima, this book elaborates certain points put forth in *After Yalta*. Attention is given to the influence of Congress and public opinion on American policy, to the Truman administration's diplomatic and military calculations regarding Europe and to its preoccupation with the war in the Far East, and to how American acquisition and use of the atomic bomb dissipated what small amount of trust existed between the United States and the Soviet Union.

Rostow, W. W. *The United States in the World Arena: An Essay in Recent History* (24:48) examines the diplomatic and military policies of the United States (1941–1959) with an eye to the interplay of domestic and foreign affairs, especially to the way policy was shaped by the interaction of national style, national interest, and stages of economic growth.

Smith, G. *American Diplomacy during the Second World War, 1941–1945* (23:38) criticizes the American attempt to create a cooperative relationship with the Soviet Union as based upon a foolishly optimistic belief that the Russians would be reasonable and cooperative. The work is outdated by new documents.

Yergin, D. *Shattered Peace: The Origins of the Cold War and the National Security State* (26:22) divides America's makers of Soviet foreign policy into two groups, maintaining that Roosevelt followed the "Yalta Axioms," or a coexistence-oriented wartime diplomacy. Truman instead pursued diplomacy based on the "Riga Axioms," or a hardline policy promoted by State Department officials who maintained that the Soviet Union sought world domination through revolution. Yergin argues that Truman's policy led to the cold war.

British Policies

Butler, J. R. M., ed. *Grand Strategy*. Vol 6: *History of the Second World War, October 1944–August 1945* by J. Ehrman (23:153) is not primarily concerned with postwar planning, but it provides a key to understanding British thinking about strategy late in the war as related to postwar issues. For example, the role of the British in the war against Japan, the problems of command in South East Asia, and British concern about its postwar military and political position in the Mediterranean. Also see volume 4 (by Michael Howard) and volume 5 (by J. Ehrman).

25:22   Smith, Arthur L., Jr. *Churchill's German Army: Wartime Strategy and Cold War Politics, 1943–1947*. Beverly Hills, Calif.: Sage, 1977. It is Smith's thesis that Britain initiated the cold war against the Soviet Union and did so before World War II ended. Churchill allowed German army units, which should have surrendered to the Soviets, to surrender to the British and to keep their units intact so as to be available in the event of a confrontation with the Soviets. Furthermore, the British kept a sizable portion of the units long after the war was over.

Woodward, L. *History of the Second World War: British Foreign Policy in the Second World War* (23:40) focuses on Anglo-British relations and postwar planning. Also see below for postwar economic planning.

Soviet Policies

25:23   Fischer, Louis. *The Road to Yalta: Soviet Foreign Relations, 1941–45*. New York: Harper & Row, 1972. In the author's view the cold war grew out of naive Allied responses to ruthless Stalinistic expansion, expansion envisaged by the Soviet leader as early as 1939.

Kennan, G. F. *Russia and the West under Lenin and Stalin* (21:158) combines narrative, analysis, and personal observation in this study of the dynamics of Soviet foreign policy, the personalities of those responsible for its conduct, and the uncertainty, misunderstanding, and occasional blundering on both sides. This book provides background useful for understanding the triangular diplomacy during World War II.

25:24 Mastny, Vojtech. *Russia's Road to the Cold War: Diplomacy, Warfare, and the Politics of Communism, 1941–1945*. New York: Columbia University Press, 1979. This book is a thorough, scholarly account of Russian war aims, postwar aims, and Allied diplomatic interaction from the Soviet perspective. Extensive bibliography.

Sivachev, N. V., and Yakolev, N. N. *Russia and the United States: U.S.-Soviet Relations from the Soviet Point of View* (2:253) finds two Soviet historians contrasting Russia's commitment to peaceful coexistence to America's imperialistic policies.

Triska, J. F., and Finley, D. D. *Soviet Foreign Policy* [1917–1968] (29:25) is a useful starting point for studying the fundamental issues in the study of Soviet diplomatic behavior.

Ulam, A. B. *Expansion and Coexistence: Soviet Foreign Policy, 1917–1973* (2:254).

Ulam, A. B. *The Rivals: America and Russia since World War II* (24:29).

Personalities

Additional references on individuals may be found in Chapter 1, "Biographical Data"; also see Chapter 24, "Personalities" and "Presidential Administrations."

AMERICAN

Dean Acheson
See Chapter 24, "Personalities," for additional references.

Acheson, D. *Present at the Creation: My Years in the State Department* (24:90) presents material on the wartime years.

25:25 Perlmutter, Oscar. "Acheson and the Diplomacy of World War II." *Western Political Quarterly* 14:4 (1961), 896–911. This essay dismisses as "fanciful legend" the notion that Acheson was the architect, or even the architect's assist, of American diplomatic policy during World War II. Rebuts the charge that Acheson was the leader of a pro-Russian clique, that he protected Alger Hiss, and that he was responsible for controversial China and Yalta policies.

Charles E. Bohlen
See Chapters 26 and 29, "Personalities," for additional references.

Bohlen, C. E. *Witness to History: 1929–1969* (24:98) portrays Roosevelt as trying to balance domestic political considerations and maintain Allied unity through realistic compromises at the same time. Ultimately, Bohlen contends, breakup of the Allied coalition was inevitable since there was never any hope that the Soviets would cooperate in the postwar world.

Mark, E. "Charles E. Bohlen and the Acceptable Limits of Soviet Hegemony in Eastern Europe: A Memorandum of 18 October 1945" (25:101) claims that the idea of spheres of influence was acceptable to most Washington policymakers. However, a distinction was made between "open" spheres for culture and economic activity, and "exclusive" spheres for military/political activity.

James F. Byrnes
See also Chapter 24, "Personalities."

Byrnes, J. F. *All in One Lifetime* (24:100) deals with the whole of Governor Byrnes's long political career, but it has valuable material on his years as secretary of state.

Byrnes, J. F. *Speaking Frankly* (24:101) is a personal account of U.S./Soviet diplomacy in the later years of the war and the immediate postwar period—valuable as a record of the negotiations at Yalta and Potsdam, for the breakdown of those agreements and for the start of the cold war.

Ward, P. D. *The Threat of Peace: James F. Byrnes and the Council of Foreign Ministers, 1945–46* (25:82) sees Byrnes as partly responsible for heating up the cold war. Compare with Robert L. Messer's *The End of an Alliance: James F. Byrnes, Roosevelt, Truman and the Origins of the Cold War* (see at [25:82]).

Joseph E. Davies

See Chapter 22, "Personalities," for additional references.

25:26 MacLean, Elizabeth Kimball. "Joseph E. Davies and Soviet-American Relations, 1941–1943." *Diplomatic History* 4:1 (1980), 73–93. This is an account of Davies's mission to Moscow in 1943 to persuade Stalin to meet with Roosevelt (minus Churchill) as well as an overview of Davies's role as Roosevelt's personal liaison with the Soviets in 1941–1942. MacLean argues that Davies and Roosevelt held similar views concerning the desirability of a close wartime-postwar relationship with the U.S.S.R., and that Roosevelt's death and the Truman presidency upset the delicate balance in Soviet-American relations.

James Forrestal

See Chapter 26, "Personalities," for additional references.

Forrestal, J. *The Forrestal Diaries* (26:46) is formed by memoranda Forrestal made concerning issues and people he dealt with as undersecretary of the navy, secretary of the navy, and secretary of defense. Most interesting are the accounts of cabinet meetings and the development of the Morgenthau Plan for postwar Germany.

W. Averell Harriman

25:27 Bland, Larry I. "Averell Harriman, the Russians and the Origins of the Cold War in Europe, 1943–45." *Australian Journal of Politics and History* 23:3 (1977), 403–16. Bland portrays Averell Harriman, Roosevelt's lend-lease expediter in London, and later ambassador in Moscow, as representative of "the best in the American diplomatic tradition." By 1943 he urged hard reciprocal bargaining with the Russians. His optimism about Soviet postwar intentions was shaken in 1945 by the fate of Poland and the prisoners of war issue.

Harriman, W. A. *America and Russia in a Changing World: A Half Century of Personal Observation* (24:119) consists of lectures, pronouncements, and statements on past and future aspects of the Soviet-American relationship by a veteran diplomat. Not a full memoir.

25:28 Harriman, W. Averell, and Abel, Elie. *Special Envoy to Churchill and Stalin, 1941–1946.* New York: Random House, 1975. Harriman was Roosevelt's lend-lease representative in London from 1941 to 1943 and ambassador to the Soviet Union from 1943 to 1946. This book is part memoir, part biography; it contains some new material, but rarely offers insights into policymaking.

Harry Hopkins

See Chapter 23, "Personalities," for references.

Cordell Hull

See Chapters 21 and 22, "Personalities," for additional references.

Hull, C. *Memoirs* (21:36) is more useful for the years preceding the war, especially the negotiations with Japan, than for the waging of the war itself, when the State Department was largely excluded from many major strategic and military decisions.

George F. Kennan

See Chapters 22, 24, 26, and 29, under "Personalities," for additional references.

Kennan, G. F. *Memoirs, 1925–1950* (24:124) offers many insights into American diplomacy during World War II, especially into our alliance with the Soviet Union. While minimizing American alliance problems with Britain, Kennan claims that Roosevelt's emphasis on victory and placating the Soviet Union led to difficulties in postwar planning, i.e., the Soviets refused to cooperate politically even before the war ended.

George C. Marshall

See also Chapters 23, 24, and 27.

Pogue, F. C. *George C. Marshall.* Vol. 3: *Organizer of Victory, 1943–1945* (23:109) is a first-rate account of the last two years of the war from the perspective of Army Chief of Staff Marshall. A model of research, this work is primarily valuable for wartime strategy, although there are insights into postwar planning.

Henry Morgenthau, Jr.

See Chapters 21 and 22 for additional references.

Blum, J. M. *From the Morgenthau Diaries.* Vol. 3: *Years of War, 1941–1945* (23:62).

25:29 U.S. Senate. Committee on the Judiciary. *Morgenthau Diary (Germany): Selected Excerpts on*

Post-War Plans for Germany. 2 vols. Washington, D.C.: G.P.O., 1967. Selected from the diaries and attached papers of Henry Morgenthau, the excerpts together with an accompanying introduction by Anthony Kubek, conclude that the true architect of the Morgenthau Plan was Harry Dexter White, assistant secretary of treasury. (The stated purpose of these volumes was to prove that White had been an agent of Soviet espionage.) See Kimball, *Swords and Plowshares?* (25:94), for the Morgenthau Plan.

Franklin D. Roosevelt

See Chapters 20, 21, 22, and 23, "Personalities," for additional references.

Bullitt, O. H., ed. *"For the President:—Personal and Secret": Correspondence between Franklin D. Roosevelt and William C. Bullitt* (21:17) was compiled by Bullitt's brother from previously closed family papers. Bullitt's correspondence with Roosevelt, as ambassador to the Soviet Union and later to France, is useful for understanding Bullitt's viewpoints, although there are occasional insights into Roosevelt's thinking.

Burns, J. M. *Roosevelt: The Soldier of Freedom, 1940–1945* (23:63) stresses Roosevelt's influence in foreign affairs, but Roosevelt the thinker and politician is also portrayed. Burns views the president as a man torn between idealism and realism, with many of Roosevelt's idealistic goals ruined by political expediency. Despite praise for his subject, Burns is critical of Roosevelt.

Dallek, R. *Franklin D. Roosevelt and American Foreign Policy, 1932–1945* (21:51) deals in part with Franklin Roosevelt's political and military strategies during World War II. This book is an excellent starting point for any work on American foreign policy during World War II, although because of its scope it cannot go into detail on any single issue.

Dallek, R. "Franklin Roosevelt as World Leader: A Review Article" (23:64) examines the evolution of American scholarship of FDR as a foreign policy leader.

Divine, R. A. *Roosevelt and World War II* (23:65) argues that the president capably conducted diplomacy contributing to the Axis powers' defeat, however, the president committed serious tactical errors in dealing with the Soviet Union even as he sought Stalin's cooperation. For these failures Roosevelt must

share responsibility for the cold war, even though Stalin's intransigence was the underlying cause.

Dulles, F. R., and Ridinger, G. E. "The Anti-Colonial Policies of Franklin D. Roosevelt" (25:118) argues that Roosevelt was fervently opposed to colonialism on philosophical grounds and that he actively and consistently worked to eliminate it even over the objections of the British.

25:30 Jonas, Manfred; Langley, Harold D.; and Loewenheim, Francis L., eds. *Roosevelt and Churchill: Their Secret Wartime Correspondence* New York: Saturday Review Press, 1975. This volume prints 548 of the nearly 2,000 pieces of correspondence exchanged by Churchill and Roosevelt (1939–1945). Although many of the messages pertain to military matters, the collection includes important selections which relate to postwar affairs. The list of published sources is quite extensive. In spite of some technical errors, this is a useful collection.

25:31 Kimball, Warren F., ed. *Churchill and Roosevelt: "A Righteous Comradeship": Their Complete Correspondence, 1939–1945*. Princeton, N.J.: Princeton University Press, 1981. This work is a complete compilation of the Churchill-Roosevelt correspondence. While all issues appear throughout their messages, postwar issues, after mid-1943, came to dominate the discussions. Includes extensive headnotes and some interpretative essays.

25:32 McNeal, Robert H. "Roosevelt through Stalin's Spectacles." *International Journal* 18:2 (1963), 194–206. The Soviet leader's Marxist-Leninist preconceptions of imperialist behavior led him to suspect Roosevelt of wrongdoing at every turn in regard to China, the disposition of colonies, the United Nations, and the revival of Germany.

25:33 Neumann, William L. "Roosevelt's Foreign Policy Decisions, 1940–1945." *Modern Age* 19:3 (1975), 272–84. Neumann describes Roosevelt as an American politician who was out of depth in foreign affairs. Furthermore, Roosevelt is presented as an evasive liar who betrayed his responsibility and caused many of the problems of the postwar world through sheer incompetence.

Range, W. *Franklin D. Roosevelt's World Order* (20:60) presents Roosevelt as an international idealist and a man concerned not with power politics but with personalities. Roosevelt's emphasis on personalities and his erroneous belief that everyone held American values of liberty and democracy were in part responsible for the breakdown of cooperation in the postwar world.

25:34 Roosevelt, Elliott. *As He Saw It*. New York: Duell, Sloan & Pearce, 1946. This is a highly personal memoir by the president's son, who was present at all of the wartime conferences except Yalta. Roosevelt claims that his father was very interested in economic postwar planning and that he believed that the European colonial powers threatened the future peace of the world more than the Soviet Union. There appears to be a number of historical inaccuracies here, but the book is a useful source for FDR's postwar aims.

25:35 Warner, Geoffrey. "From Tehran to Yalta: Reflections on FDR's Foreign Policy." *International Affairs* 43:3 (1967), 530–36. The author challenges the notion that Roosevelt was naive regarding Soviet-American relations.

Edward R. Stettinius, Jr.

See Chapter 24, "Personalities," for additional references.

Stettinius, E. R., Jr. *The Diaries of Edward R. Stettinius, Jr., 1943–1946* (24:150). Records Stettinius's thoughts during the time he was under secretary of state (1943) and secretary of state (1944–1945). Stettinius's role in postwar planning at Yalta, the Dumbarton Oaks Conference, Latin American relations, and the formation of the UN are highlighted.

25:36 Stettinius, Edward R., Jr. *Roosevelt and the Russians: The Yalta Conference*. Garden City, N.Y.: Doubleday, 1949. As Roosevelt's secretary of state Stettinius took meticulous notes of each day's events at Yalta. These notes present a chronological account of the meeting which is the basis of this book. Stettinius defends Roosevelt's actions at Yalta.

Henry L. Stimson

See Chapters 20, 21, 22, and 23, "Personalities," for additional references.

Stimson, H. L., and Bundy, M. *On Active Service in Peace and War* (23:72) concentrates on military planning but touches on postwar planning, including a firsthand account of the atomic bomb decision.

Harry S. Truman

See Chapters 24 and 26, "Personalities," for additional references.

Miscamble, W. D. "The Evolution of an Internationalist: Harry S. Truman and American Foreign Policy" (38:52) looks at Truman's pre-presidential career as a senator in order to examine the development and nature of Truman's commitment to the internationalist cause. As a senator, Truman overcame his uncertainty on foreign policy issues to become an advocate of U.S. preparedness and a strong proponent of U.S. membership in a new international organization.

Arthur H. Vandenberg

See Chapters 24 and 26, "Personalities," for additional references.

25:37 Cable, John N. "Vandenberg: The Polish Question and Polish Americans, 1944–1948." *Michigan History* 57:4 (1973), 296–310. Michigan's Republican senator Arthur H. Vandenberg, best remembered for his strong bipartisanship as World War II ended and the cold war began, was only moderately bipartisan on the Polish issue. Responding sympathetically to his anticommunist, Polish American constituency, Vandenberg articulated and championed the Polish cause at the national level.

25:38 Gregg, Richard G. "A Rhetorical Re-Examination of Arthur Vandenberg's 'Dramatic Conversion,' January 10, 1945." *Quarterly Journal of Speech* 6:2 (1975), 154–68. Gregg argues that Vandenberg's speech announcing his conversion to internationalism was designed to induce Franklin D. Roosevelt to delineate clearly his foreign policy.

Hill, T. M. "Senator Arthur H. Vandenberg, the Politics of Bipartisanship, and the Origins of Anti-Soviet Consensus, 1941–1946" (26:60).

Vandenberg, A. H., Jr. *The Private Papers of Senator Vandenberg* (24:162) contains excerpts from the Vandenberg Papers (1940–1951), which are valuable on his apparent shift from isolationism to global views, and on his cooperation with the Democratic administration on wartime and postwar policy.

Henry A. Wallace

See Chapters 24 and 26, "Personalities," for additional references.

Walker, J. S. *Henry A. Wallace and American Foreign Policy* (24:165) examines Wallace's views on foreign affairs throughout his career. Roughly one-fourth of the book deals with Wallace's wartime opinions and his role in postwar planning.

Wallace, H. A. *The Price of Vision: The Diary of Henry A. Wallace, 1942–1946* (24:166) portrays Wallace as a progressive, an idealist, and an economic internationalist. Wallace consistently worked on postwar plans: to him the war was a vehicle for practical idealism, the end of the war would be the end of artifical trade restraints.

Sumner Welles

See Chapter 22, "Personalities," for additional references.

25:39 Welles, Sumner. *Where Are We Heading?* New York: Harper, 1946. Welles assesses various American officials and their actions during World War II, and provides an insider's view of the Atlantic Charter meeting. Welles advocates strong support for the infant United Nations. He states that Roosevelt, prior to his death, had taken the first steps in seeking a cooperative relationship with the system of Russian communism.

Others

Berle, A. A., Jr. *Navigating the Rapids, 1918–1971: From the Papers of Adolf A. Berle* (24:97) presents a small portion of Berle's papers. As assistant secretary of state (1938–1944), Berle worked extensively on postwar plans, especially in the areas of civil aviation, the United Nations, and Latin America. Also, Berle's accounts of the State Department infighting, his hatred of British mercantilism, and his acceptance of the Soviet sphere of influence in Eastern Europe make this work a valuable source.

Bowles, C. *Promises to Keep: My Years in Public Life, 1941–1969* (24:99) discusses Bowles's role as head of the Office of Price Administration, which was involved in postwar domestic economic planning.

25:40 Deane, John R. *The Strange Alliance: The Story of Our Efforts at Wartime Co-operation with Russia.* New York: Viking, 1947. Deane, the U.S. secretary of the Combined Chiefs of Staff and the head of a military mission to the Soviet Union in 1943, contends that the Soviets never had any intentions of cooperating in the postwar world and that Roosevelt was duped by the Soviets into believing that they would.

Grew, J. C. *Turbulent Era: A Diplomatic Record of Forty Years, 1904–1945* (18:33) is a collection of diary excerpts, letters, and dispatches selected by Grew from his papers. Although Grew had been director of the Office of Far Eastern Affairs, a member of the U.S. delegation to the Dumbarton Oaks Conference, and under secretary of state, this work offers few insights into postwar planning.

25:41 Iatrides, John O., ed. *Ambassador MacVeagh Reports: Greece, 1933–1947.* Princeton, N.J.: Princeton University Press, 1980. This volume contains letters and telegrams to President Roosevelt from Lincoln MacVeagh, the U.S. ambassador in Athens. A large portion of the correspondence relates to Anglo-American arguments and policy regarding postwar Greece.

Leahy, W. D. *I Was There* (22:45) offers useful insight into the thinking of one of Roosevelt's key foreign policy advisers, although details are frequently vague. Leahy was privy to all secret matters, and attended most of the big three conferences. Leahy's account of the Yalta Conference is interesting.

Murphy, R. D. *Diplomat among Warriors* (23:77) contains Murphy's firsthand account of his wartime activities in Italy and North Africa, especially as political adviser to Eisenhower. Murphy is critical of Roosevelt's supposed naiveté and tendency toward personal diplomacy.

Standley, W. H., and Ageton, A. A. *Admiral Ambassador to Russia* (23:78) is based on diaries and notes of Admiral Standley, who was ambassador to Russia (1942–1943). Critical of Roosevelt's policy of giving all out aid to the Soviet Union without demanding a quid pro quo, he particularly faults the lend-lease activities of Harry Hopkins and Brigadier General Faymonville and visits to Russian officials by representatives of Roosevelt such as former Ambassador Joseph Davies and Wendell Willkie.

Wedemeyer, A. C. *Wedemeyer Reports!* (23:120) argues that the politicians had imprecise war aims, underestimated the communists in Europe and Asia, and otherwise squandered the hard-won peace. The general believes that a 1943 cross-channel attack would have been successful.

EUROPEAN

Winston S. Churchill

See chapters 21, 22, and 23, "Personalities," for additional references.

Churchill, W. S. *The Second World War* (23:79) provided the framework for the study of the politics of strategy in World War II until the opening of the British files on World War II in 1972. This work remains crucial to any understanding of Churchill's thoughts and actions despite certain inaccuracies.

Higgins, T. *Winston Churchill and the Second Front* (23:164) examines Anglo-American debate over cross-channel versus North African/Mediterranean operations (1939–1943).

Kimball, W. F. "Churchill and Roosevelt: The Personal Equation" (23:68) finds their relations were generally amicable, but the few disagreements were of a fundamental nature. Churchill resented playing a secondary role and was very distrustful of Soviet motives. It is doubtful if their relationship could have withstood the rigors of postwar problems.

Moran, Lord [C. M. Wilson]. *Churchill: Taken from the Diaries of Lord Moran: The Struggle for Survival, 1940–1965* (23:81) contains material on Churchill's thoughts and observations about the postwar world. The comments Moran relates are all too frequently without context and never fully developed, but they are valuable nonetheless. The accompanying narrative reflects Moran's personal observations as well as those of Churchill and other British leaders.

25:42 Taylor, A. J. P., et al. *Churchill Revised: A Critical Assessment.* New York: Dial, 1969. The five essays in this book examine Churchill as a statesman, politician, author, military leader, and as a private individual. This is a thoughtful study which presents Churchill's view of the world in which he lived and of the world he hoped to create in the postwar era.

Charles de Gaulle

See Chapters 23 and 28, "Personalities," for additional references.

25:43 DePorte, A. W. *De Gaulle's Foreign Policy, 1944–1946.* Cambridge: Harvard University Press, 1968. The author argues that de Gaulle's short rule (1944–1946) foreshadowed in most ways the pursuit of foreign policies that he was to follow twelve years later when he returned to power. DePorte emphasizes the conflict between the General and Roosevelt over France's great power status.

Viorst, M. *Hostile Allies: FDR and Charles de Gaulle* (23:231) posits the political and personal incompatibility of Roosevelt and de Gaulle. *Hostile Allies* provides useful insights into the Allied problems with wartime

and postwar France, but has been dated by the release of new documents.

White, D. S. *Seeds of Discord: De Gaulle, Free France, and the Allies* (23:232) is dated, but still useful; it examines early Allied dealings with the Free French and planning for postwar France.

Joseph V. Stalin

See Chapters 21 and 22 under "Personalities," for references.

25:44 Bychowski, Gustav. "Joseph V. Stalin: The Dictatorship of the Proletariat." In Benjamin B. Wolman, ed., *The Psychoanalytic Interpretation of History.* New York: Basic Books, 1971, pp. 115–49. The author probes the psychological roots of Stalin's personality and then examines how that personality affected the nature and practice of dictatorship inside the Soviet Union.

25:45 Deutscher, Isaac. *Stalin: A Political Biography.* 2d ed. New York: Oxford University Press, 1966. This comprehensive study remains an insightful, valuable work. Deutscher writes that traditional and revolutionary elements intertwined in Stalin's postwar foreign policies, with the former holding sway over the latter. Bibliography.

Djilas, M. *Conversations with Stalin* (26:69) discusses Djilas's visit, in his capacity as a high Communist party functionary, to Moscow as part of a Yugoslav military mission in 1944. Largely anecdotal, this work offers insights into Stalin's nonofficial attitude toward the West.

25:46 Fischer, Louis. *The Life and Death of Stalin.* New York: Harper, 1952. The author discusses isolationism and expansionism as the twin themes of Stalinist foreign policy.

25:47 Hingley, Ronald. *Joseph Stalin: Man and Legend.* London: Hutchinson, 1974. Hingley's biography is valuable for the connections it makes between Stalin's political motivation and his private personality. Bibliography.

25:48 Tucker, Robert C. *The Soviet Political Mind: Stalinism and Post-Stalin Change.* New York: Norton, 1971. This work elaborates how the psychopathological aspects of Stalin's personality shaped his domestic and foreign policies.

Ulam, A. B. *Stalin: The Man and His Era* (21:78) examines the life and character of the Soviet dictator within the broader historical context of "the movement and society in which his fantastic career unfolded and which he then succeeded in molding in his image."

25:49   Warth, Robert D. *Joseph Stalin*. New York: Twayne, 1969. Without his "malignant presence," Soviet-Western relations would have degenerated to the level that prevailed during his declining years. Yet, the underlying cause of the Cold War was the West's refusal to recognize Soviet preponderance in Eastern Europe.

Josip Broz-Tito

See also Chapter 25, "Personalities."

Auty, P. *Tito: A Biography* (26:73) is a scholarly biography.

Others

25:50   Birse, A. H. *Memoirs of an Interpreter*. New York: Coward-McCann, 1967. These memoirs give the reader some insights into the problems faced by the Allies. As the translator at Teheran and Yalta, Birse's account of Roosevelt's off the record remarks to Stalin concerning British colonialism are particularly interesting.

Cadogan, A. *The Diaries of Sir Alexander Cadogan, 1939–45* (23:90) is a remarkably frank and rather critical (of the United States) diary by a leading official of the British Foreign Office, eventually permanent under secretary; it sheds light on a great many postwar issues, although much of the material is sketchy.

Dönitz, K. *Memoirs: Ten Years and Twenty Days* (23:136) underlines his effort in 1945 to stop hostilities on the Western front while continuing the fight against the Soviet Union.

Eden, A. *The Memoirs of Anthony Eden, Earl of Avon: The Reckoning* (23:93) uses Eden's dispatches, wartime diary, and personal recollections to construct a narrative of the war. Interesting are Eden's candid statements that, despite Britain's desire to hold on to its empire, military needs determined political policy and that the war itself determined that the United States and the Soviet Union would rule the postwar world. He suggests that Roosevelt was duped by Stalin.

Macmillan, H. *The Blast of War, 1939–45* (23:94) deals with the settlements in North Africa, Italy, and Greece.

Maisky, I. M. *Memoirs of a Soviet Ambassador: The War, 1939–43* (23:95) presents a cautious, selective account of Soviet wartime policy. Less anecdotal than most memoirs, Maisky, Soviet ambassador to the United Kingdom, indicates Soviet distrust for her allies. He is particularly critical of Churchill for delaying the second front. Must be used with other sources.

25:51   Strang, Lord. *Home and Abroad*. London: Deutsch, 1956. Lord Strang was the permanent under secretary of state for foreign affairs. Of especial interest to scholars working on postwar planning is Strang's chapter on his role as Britain's representative on the European Advisory Board.

Wartime Conferences

See "Personalities" for A. H. Birse (under "European," "Others"), Charles E. Bohlen, Franklin D. Roosevelt.

Eubank, K. *The Summit Conferences, 1919–1960* (29:57) surveys the reasons for and accomplishments of summit meetings, including Yalta and Potsdam.

25:52   Franklin, William M. "Yalta Viewed from Tehran." In Daniel R. Beaver, ed., *Some Pathways in Twentieth-Century History: Essays in Honor of Reginald Charles McGrane*. Detroit: Wayne State University Press, 1969, pp. 253–61. Franklin argues that many of the most important decisions written out at Yalta were actually reached in general fashion at Tehran. He recommends that Tehran be studied more extensively. Bibliography.

25:53   Mastny, Vojtech. "Soviet War Aims at the Moscow and Teheran Conferences of 1943." *Journal of Modern History* 47:3 (1975), 481–504. Mastny sees a discrepancy between Soviet war aims and those of the Western Allies during the Moscow and Teheran conferences. While the Soviet desire to end the war by creating a second front remained constant, other Soviet aims—the breakup of Germany, the decolonization of France, and the territorial shift of Poland— began to emerge when the second front did not seem forthcoming. Mastny blames the carelessness of Churchill and Roosevelt for encouraging Stalin to embark upon these policies.

25:54 U.S.S.R. Ministry of Foreign Affairs. *The Teheran, Yalta, and Potsdam Conferences.* Moscow: Progress, 1968. This book contains the Soviet records of these big three conferences. While less complete than the Western records, due possibly to translation problems, there are no substantive differences.

25:55 U.S. Department of State. *Foreign Relations of the United States: World War II Conference Series.* Washington, D.C.: G.P.O., 1955–1972. In addition to the regular volumes for each year in the series *Foreign Relations of the United States,* the State Department has published *The Conferences at Washington, 1941–1942, and Casablanca, 1943* (23:218); *The Conferences at Washington and Quebec, 1943* (23:219); *The Conferences at Cairo and Teheran, 1943* (25:58); *The Conference of Quebec, 1944*; *The Conferences at Malta and Yalta, 1945*; and *The Conference of Berlin (Potsdam).* These invaluable volumes include documents from many non–State Department sources, including the Joint Chiefs of Staff, and are remarkably extensive. Postwar issues were a major topic of conversation at the conferences.

TEHERAN, 1943

25:56 Misse, M. "Le Rôle des États-Unis dans les Conferences du Caire et de Téhéran" [The role of the United States in the Cairo and Teheran conferences]. *Revue d'Histoire de la Deuxième Guerre Mondiale* 18:71 (1968), 13–30. Misse examines the policy followed by the American delegation at the Cairo and Teheran summit conferences (November–December 1943). He focuses on the relationship between Roosevelt and Stalin, and concludes that the decisions made at Teheran had greater effects on postwar Europe than those made at Yalta.

25:57 Sharp, Tony. "The Origins of the 'Teheran Formula' on Polish Frontiers." *Journal of Contemporary History* 12:2 (1977), 381–93. On the eve of the Teheran Conference (December 1, 1943) Churchill proposed the adjustment of the Polish frontier to the

Oder River and the Curzon Line. Stalin agreed as long as Russia got the Konigsberg area of East Prussia. This "Teheran formula" was accepted on the premise that British and American influence in the negotiated area would not be great.

25:58 U.S. Department of State. *Foreign Relations of the United States, Diplomatic Papers: The Conferences at Cairo and Teheran, 1943.* Washington, D.C.: G.P.O., 1961. This volume of documents covers the three continuous yet separate conferences of November–December 1943: the first Cairo Conference, between Churchill, Roosevelt, and Chiang Kai-shek; the Teheran Conference, between Churchill, Roosevelt, and Stalin; and the second Cairo Conference, between Churchill and Roosevelt. Strategic arguments and agreements dominated all three conferences, although numerous postwar political issues were also discussed.

YALTA, 1945

See under "Personalities," especially Edward R. Stettinius, Jr., and, under "Others," William D. Leahy, William H. Standley.

25:59 Clemens, Diane Shaver. *Yalta.* New York: Oxford University Press, 1970. This book treats Yalta as a conference marked by compromise by all parties, not a triumph by the Soviet Union nor a retreat by the West. The author analyzes the advantages held by each of the major participants and concludes that reasonable adjustments were made in the face of differing national interests. Instead of the start or a prelude to the cold war, Yalta was an alternative. Bibliography.

25:60 Fenno, Richard F., Jr., ed. *The Yalta Conference.* 2d ed. Lexington, Mass.: Heath (1955), 1972. The second, expanded edition adds important reinterpretations which have appeared in recent years, most notably from the revisionist school on the origins of the cold war, and a revised introduction by Fenno. Extensive bibliography.

25:61 Schulzinger, Robert D. "*Yalta* by Diane Shaver Clemens and *The Yalta Myths: An Issue in U.S. Politics, 1945–1955* by Athan G. Theoharis." *History and Theory* 12:1 (1973), 146–62. This review essay points out the shortcomings of these and other recent works on U.S. World War II diplomacy.

Specifically, the author believes that more emphasis is needed on Yalta as an important issue in the battle between the advocates of the "new" and the defenders of the "old" diplomacy.

25:62 Snell, John L., et al. *The Meaning of Yalta: Big Three Diplomacy and the Balance of Power.* Baton Rouge: Louisiana State University Press, 1956. This is an early study of the last of the big three meetings by Snell, Forrest C. Pogue, Charles F. Delzell, and George A. Lensen. Each historian takes one of the four major issues discussed at Yalta: the fates of Germany, Central-Eastern Europe, the Far East, and the creation of the United Nations.

Stettinius, E. R., Jr. *Roosevelt and the Russians: The Yalta Conference* (25:36).

25:63 Theoharis, Athan. "The Origins of the Cold War: A Revisionist Interpretation." *Peace and Change* 4:1 (1976), 3–11. This essay considers President Franklin D. Roosevelt's vagueness at the Yalta Conference (1945) as a source of the cold war.

25:64 Theoharis, Athan. "Roosevelt and Truman on Yalta: The Origins of the Cold War." *Political Science Quarterly* 87:2 (1972), 210–41. Inexperienced in foreign affairs and receiving advice from State Department hardliners, Truman attempted to "undo" the commitments made by Roosevelt at Yalta. This manifestation of Truman's presidential leadership contributed to the deterioration in U.S.-Soviet relations.

25:65 Theoharis, Athan G. *The Yalta Myths: An Issue in U.S. Politics, 1945–1955.* Columbia: University of Missouri Press, 1970. This study examines conservative attacks on Roosevelt's diplomacy and the Democrats' defense.

25:66 Vloyantes, John P. "The Significance of Pre-Yalta Policies Regarding Liberated Countries in Europe." *Western Political Quarterly* 11:2 (1958), 209–28. This early account concludes that big three policies in the period before Yalta combined with military developments to determine the fate of the liberated countries, particularly those in the Balkans and Eastern-Central Europe.

POTSDAM, 1945

See "Personalities," especially Harry S. Truman.

25:67 Feis, Herbert. *Between War and Peace: The Potsdam Conference.* Princeton, N.J.: Princeton University Press, 1960. A fact-laden narrative of Allied diplomacy during the period between the German and Japanese surrenders, it focuses on the intricate negotiations at Potsdam. Feis places his highly detailed account of big three discussions within the broader context of the mutual distrust and suspicion then eroding the wartime coalition.

25:68 Mark, Eduard. " 'Today Has Been a Historical One': Harry S. Truman's Diary of the Potsdam Conference." *Diplomatic History* 4:3 (1980), 317–26. Mark reprints Truman's impressions of persons and events at Potsdam. There is little sign here of the "somewhat bumptious confidence so often ascribed to the thirty-third president."

25:69 Mee, Charles L., Jr. *Meeting at Potsdam.* New York: Evans, 1975. Mee blames the cold war on all sides: the United States, Britain, and the Soviet Union were distrustful, aggressive, and provocative. All three leaders appear as opportunists in this work. The loss of the common foe led the leaders to the inevitable clash of the politically and economically different victors. Extensive bibliography.

25:70 Paterson, Thomas G. "Potsdam, the Atomic Bomb, and the Cold War: A Discussion with James P. Byrnes." *Pacific Historical Review* 41:2 (1972), 225–30. Paterson presents and comments on a memorandum by Senator Warren R. Austin concerning a conversation with Secretary of State James F. Byrnes (August 20, 1945). The document sheds light on Soviet-American diplomacy at the Potsdam Conference and includes information about the relationship between the dropping of the atomic bomb and Russian participation in the war against Japan.

25:71 Strang, Lord, et al. "Potsdam after Twenty-Five Years." *International Affairs* [London] 46:3 (1970), 441–89. Lord Strang assesses the diplomatic background to the Potsdam Conference; Robert Cecil examines the Potsdam decisions and how the conference became a part of Soviet and American cold war mythology; Andre Fontaine analyzes French objections to a united Germany; and Walter Clemens sees the failure to reach agreement on Germany as a constant factor and the central problem in the Soviet Union's relations with the West.

Postwar Planning and Emerging Issues

See James F. Byrnes, W. Averell Harriman, Harry Hopkins, Arthur H. Vandenberg; also see "Bretton Woods, 1944," below; for the development of the United Nations, see Chapter 38.

Armstrong, A. *Unconditional Surrender: The Impact of the Casablanca Policy upon World War* (23:255) is a study of the doctrine of unconditional surrender as it affected Germany. The author implies that the doctrine prolonged the war by unifying Germany. While this work uses German sources, recent Britsh documents date the book.

25:72　Beaumont, Joan. "A Question of Diplomacy: British Military Mission 1941–45." *Journal of the Royal United Services Institute for Defense Studies* 118:3 (1973), 74–77. This is a detailed examination of the work of the British military mission to Moscow (1941–1945). Russian hostility and suspicion rendered the success of the mission hopeless; in defiance of Foreign Office instructions to practice conciliation, the members of the mission restored to bargaining and confrontation, but found this equally unrewarding.

25:73　Dennett, Raymond, and Johnson, Joseph E., eds. *Negotiating with the Russians*. Boston: World Peace Foundation, 1951. Of special interest are articles on negotiations relating to military assistance, lend-lease, Nuremberg trial arguments, Bretton Woods, the establishment of the Far Eastern Commission, and an agreement on refugees and displaced persons. Philip E. Mosely's final chapter, on Soviet techniques of negotiations, sums up the basic problems as perceived by the diplomats of the era of World War II.

25:74　Notter, Harley A. *Postwar Foreign Policy Preparation, 1939–1945*. Washington, D.C.: G.P.O., 1949. This is an indispensable source on middle-level State Department thinking about almost every conceivable postwar issue. Although much of the book is concerned with bureaucratic and organization matters, it offers valuable insights into the development of department thinking, even though the recommendations of the various committees were rarely inplemented.

25:75　Poole, Walter S. "From Conciliation to Containment: The Joint Chiefs of Staff and the Coming of the Cold War, 1945–1946." *Military Affairs* 42:1 (1978), 12–16. At first the JCS saw the United States simply mediating Anglo-Soviet quarrels, but gradually the wheel turned full circle and they saw the United States as the prime mover in stopping Soviet aggression. By late 1945, the author places the JCS into cold war historiography, arguing that their recommendations were defensive reactions and not offensive threats.

25:76　Riste, Olav. "Frce Ports in North Norway: A Contribution to the Study of FDR's Wartime Policy towards the USSR." *Journal of Contemporary History* 5:4 (1970), 77–95. Riste investigates the origin and response to FDR's visionary proposal of 1941 that a postwar network of free ports under international trusteeship would help foster peace. The president reasoned that easy access to several internationalized warm water ports might serve to slake Russia's territorial appetite.

25:77　Warner, Geoffrey. "The United States and the Origins of the Cold War." *International Affairs* [London] 46:3 (1970), 529–44. This review of the *Foreign Relations of the United States* (1:358) for 1945 provides a useful introduction to the series. It examines the beginnings of Russo-American antagonism over policy, primarily in Europe, but also in Asia and Latin America.

EUROPEAN ADVISORY COMMISSION

King, F. P. *The New Internationalism: Allied Policy and the European Peace, 1939–1945* (25:10).

25:78　Kuklick, Bruce. "The Genesis of the European Advisory Commission." *Journal of Contemporary History* 4:4 (1969), 189–201. EAC was established in 1943 to provide planning for the last phases of the war and thereafter. This study is important because negotiations for its organization clearly revealed the distrust between Russia and the West and bared the long-range objectives of each of the big three.

25:79　Mosely, Philip E. *The Kremlin and World Politics: Studies in Soviet Policy and Action*. New York: Vintage, 1960. This volume contains an inside account of the European Advisory Commission, and is useful for that purpose.

25:80 Nelson, Daniel J. *Wartime Origins of the Berlin Dilemma*. University: University of Alabama Press, 1978. This important book traces the wartime negotiations that led to situations that resulted in the series of confrontations over Berlin in later years. Basically a history of the European Advisory Commission, it demonstrates that the big four shackled the commission's work. Bibliography.

LONDON COUNCIL OF FOREIGN MINISTERS, 1945

25:81 Knight, Jonathan. "Russia's Search for Peace: The London Council of Foreign Ministers, 1945." *Journal of Contemporary Hisory* 13:1 (1978), 137–63. Russian foreign policy in 1945 hoped to refurbish the ideological armory of communism, to bring friendly governments into power on the Soviet periphery and to resume a central role in European politics. Also, the Soviets unsuccessfully pursued a trusteeship over an Italian colony, especially one on the Mediterranean.

25:82 Ward, Patricia Dawson. *The Threat of Peace: James F. Byrnes and the Council of Foreign Ministers, 1945–46*. Kent, Ohio: Kent State University Press, 1979. Ward focuses on U.S. diplomacy and Secretary of State James F. Byrnes at the Council of Foreign Ministers meetings that drafted the peace treaties. Byrnes is seen as partly responsible for heating up the cold war with his anti-Soviet rhetoric. Bibliography. Compare with Robert L. Messer's *The End of an Alliance: James F. Byrnes, Roosevelt, Truman and the Origins of the Cold War* (Chapel Hill: University of North Carolina Press, 1982), which views Byrnes as a transitional figure from wartime to postwar policies.

THE GERMAN QUESTION

See also Chapter 26, "U.S. and Germany."

25:83 Backer, John H. *The Decision to Divide Germany: American Foreign Policy in Transition*. Durham, N.C.: Duke University Press, 1978. American-Soviet cooperation in Germany failed not because of Soviet aggression or American capitalist imperialism but because of a multiplicity of factors: failure of leadership, American public desire to end the war and leave Europe, and mistrust and intransigence on both sides. This is the most complete scholarly treatment of the subject. See also R. Harrison

Wagner, "The Decision to Divide Germany and the Origins of the Cold War," *International Studies Quarterly* 24:2 (1980), 155–90. Extensive bibliography.

25:84 Dorn, Walter L. "The Debate over American Occupation Policy in Germany in 1944–45." *Political Science Quarterly* 72:4 (1957), 481–501. A detailed study of the background of JCS 1067, the Joint Chiefs of Staff directive guiding initial American occupation policy in Germany.

25:85 Gimbel, John. "Cold War: German Front." *Maryland Historian* 2:1 (1971), 41–55. This review essay takes issue with the revisionist theses of Gardner (26:85) and Schlauch (25:90).

25:86 Kimball, Warren F. "The Ghost in the Attic: The Soviet Union as a Factor in Wartime Postwar Planning for Germany." In A. Funk, ed., *Politics and Strategy in the Second World War*. Manhattan, Kans.: Military Affairs/Aerospace Historian, 1976. Kimball argues that fear of the Soviet Union did not play a major role in the Anglo-American postwar plans for Germany which were developed during World War II.

25:87 Kuklick, Bruce. "A Historian's Perspective: American Appeasement of Germany, 1941–51." *Prologue* 8:4 (1976), 237–40. The actual policy of the United States during this decade, and before, had been to integrate Germany into the European economic community, on the premise that an economically strong Germany was vital to the good health of the continent. This policy, begun during the Weimar Republic, was continued following World War II.

25:88 Mosely, Philip E. "Dismemberment of Germany: The Allied Negotiations from Yalta to Potsdam." *Foreign Affairs* 28:1 (1950), 487–98. An early account of Allied discussions on the dismemberment of Germany, it is still valuable because the author served on a State Department planning staff and then with the U.S. delegation on the European Advisory Commission (1944–1945). His account of the terms of the armistice at Reims has been revised somewhat by William Franklin (25:95).

25:89 Mosely, Philip E. "The Occupation of Germany: New Light on How the Zones Were Drawn." *Foreign Affairs* 28:4 (1950), 580–604. As a member of the working Security Committee, an interdepartmental committee of the State, War and Navy departments, established to coordinate U.S. members of the European Advisory Commission and, later, as political adviser designated by the State Department to be U.S. member of the European Advisory Commission, Mosely gives a valuable account, with personal insight, on the drawing of lines of occupation. His account is less complete than William Franklin's article (25:95).

25:90   Schlauch, Wolfgang. "American Policy towards Germany, 1945." *Journal of Contemporary History* 5:4 (1970), 113–28. Certain American leaders came to the conclusion during the war that the restoration of a stable Europe, potent enough to prevent communism from spreading into Western Europe, depended largely on the rapid rehabilitation of Germany.

25:91   Sharp, Tony. *The Wartime Alliance and the Zonal Division of Germany.* Oxford: Clarendon Press, 1975. Sharp claims that Allied discussions were directly affected by Western and Soviet images of each other's power and perceived objectives for the postwar political order combined with military strategy. The main contribution is the addition of data from British sources. Bibliography.

25:92   Snell, John L. *Wartime Origins of the East-West Dilemma over Germany.* New Orleans: Hauser, 1959. Snell views the international dilemma over Germany as stemming from the wartime policy of postponement. Germany became the focal point of several non-related problems: nationalism vs. internationalism, Soviet territorial expansion vs. American economic and cultural expansion. Bibliography.

The Morgenthau Plan

See under "Personalities," especially James Forrestal, Henry Morgenthau, Jr.

25:93   Allen, Diane M. "Development of Postwar Policy in Germany." *Western Political Quarterly* 17:1 (1964), 109–16. Hull and Stimson offered a moderate postwar policy for Germany; Morgenthau's projected program was harshly vindictive. A "hasty compromise" was reached with Truman's endorsement of JCS 1067, a supposedly definitive directive. Truman did not approve Morgenthau's ideas, but was unable to prevent their inclusion in JCS 1067 (later discarded).

25:94   Kimball, Warren. *Swords and Plowshares? The Morgenthau Plan for Defeated Nazi Germany 1943–1946.* New York: Lippincott, 1976. In a long essay, combined with documents, on the Morgenthau plan for Germany, Kimball argues that in throwing out the plan, the United States also tossed out the possi-

bility of a neutral, disengaged Germany that might have eliminated a major source of cold war tension. Bibliography.

Access to Berlin

25:95   Franklin, William M. "Zonal Boundaries and Access to Berlin." *World Politics* 16:1 (1963), 1–31. This painstaking study of Allied plans deals with the political-military problem of the occupation of Berlin. Franklin emphasizes the deep divisions between the president and the State Department and the Americans and the British rather than any Anglo-American-Soviet problem. He argues that access to Berlin for the Allies was understood by all sides.

25:96   Kuby, Eric. *The Russians and Berlin, 1945.* London: Heinemann, 1965. This work concentrates on German reaction to the Soviet occupation of Berlin at the close of the war. However, the brief scenes of Allied interaction may be useful to those working in the area of Allied postwar planning for Germany. Bibliography.

Nelson, D. J. *Wartime Origins of the Berlin Dilemma* (25:80) concentrates on the planning for postwar Germany as a major problem of wartime alliance diplomacy. Nelson's detailed account of the workings of the European Advisory Commission is particularly useful.

EASTERN EUROPE

See "Personalities," especially Charles E. Bohlen.

Auty, P., and Clogg, R., eds. *British Policy towards Wartime Resistance in Yugoslavia and Greece* (23:233) reconsiders British policy toward Yugoslav and Greek resistance movements in light of recently declassified British Foreign Office papers. Specific topics covered include the activities of the Special Operations Executive, the "myth" of British plans for an Allied invasion of the Balkans, and different aspects of British policies.

25:97   Barker, Elizabeth. *British Policy in South-East Europe in the Second World War.* New York: Harper & Row, 1976. Although this volume concentrates on British policy, it outlines the differences in attitudes and policies of Great Britain and the United States. Bibliography.

Occupation Zones in Germany and Austria, 1945–46

25:98 Davis, Lynn Etheridge. *The Cold War Begins: Soviet-American Conflict over Eastern Europe.* Princeton, N.J.: Princeton University Press, 1974. Soviet-American differences (1941–1945) over the area are held to be the single most important cause of the cold war. Focusing on the State Department, Davis concludes that American policies were neither devious nor especially coherent, but rather unrealistic in that they sought to implement the principles of the Atlantic Charter while failing to take into account how that might threaten vital Soviet security interests. Bibliography.

25:99 Hammett, Hugh B. "America's Non-Policy in Eastern Europe and the Origins of the Cold War." *Survey* 19:4 (1973), 144–62. Roosevelt had a "puzzling" yet "well-intentioned idealism" but never a policy, accounting for his behavior at Teheran and Yalta. Truman never reversed Roosevelt's conciliatory policy, he just made the decisions.

25:100 Kovrig, Bennett. *The Myth of Liberation: East-Central Europe in U.S. Diplomacy and Politics since 1941.* Baltimore: Johns Hopkins University Press, 1973. Since 1941, U.S. policies toward East-Central Europe have had as a common denominator an interest in (but not necessarily a commitment to) liberation of the area. At no time, though, has the United States been able to translate its declarations in favor of liberation into operational policies. Bibliography.

Lundestad, G. *The American Non-Policy towards Eastern Europe, 1943–1947: Universalism in an Area Not of Essential Interest to the United States* (26:113) systematically treats American policy in each of the Eastern European countries.

25:101 Mark, Eduard. "Charles E. Bohlen and the Acceptable Limits of Soviet Hegemony in Eastern Europe: A Memorandum of 18 October 1945." *Diplomatic History* 3:2 (1979), 201–13. As outlined by Bohlen and proclaimed by Secretary of State Byrnes in October 1945, the U.S. position on spheres of influence in Eastern Europe at the end of World War II was by no means inflexible. U.S. officials made a distinction between "open" spheres for cultural and economic activities, and "exclusive" spheres for military and political activities.

25:102 Resis, Albert. "The Churchill-Stalin Secret Percentages Agreement on the Balkans, Moscow, October, 1944." *American Historical Review* 83:2 (1978), 368–87. Working from memoirs and British documents, particularly the British records of the

Moscow Conference (codenamed TOLSTOY), Resis concludes that the spheres of influence doctrine in the Balkans was only part of the British and Soviet agreement: the larger plan of Britain regarding her empire in the Far East and Soviet aspirations of territorial gains in Eastern Europe were silently acknowledged.

Robertson, W. R. *Tito, Mihailovic and the Allies, 1941–45* (23:251) is a study of the Allies' attitudes toward the Yugoslav factions during World War II. Interest in Yugoslavia was unfocused until the end of the war, at which time political considerations came to the fore. Soviet disinterest in Yugoslavia's problems is viewed as having immense significance for postwar Southern Europe.

25:103 Siracusa, Joseph M. "The Meaning of Tolstoy: Churchill, Stalin, and the Balkans; Moscow, October 1944." *Diplomatic History* 3:4 (1979), 443–63. The author presents the record of the October 1944 meetings at the Kremlin between Churchill and Stalin with little comment or interpretation of those highly important discussions on the makeup of postwar Eastern Europe.

The Polish Issue

See "Personalities," especially W. Averell Harriman, Harry S Truman, Arthur H. Vandenberg.

25:104 Hammersmith, Jack L. "Franklin Roosevelt, the Polish Question, and the Election of 1944." *Mid-America* 59:1 (1977), 5–17. Since the Republicans made major gains in the 1942 congressional elections, in part by concentrating on ethnic minorities, FDR and the Democrats took special care in 1944 to woo the Polish Americans. Roosevelt avoided the Polish-Russian question and successfully appealed to Polish Americans' special interests.

25:105 Hammersmith, Jack L. "The U.S. Office of War Information (OWI) and the Polish Question, 1943–1945." *Polish Review* 19:1 (1974), 67–76. This essay shows how the Office of War Information's overseas branch disseminated propaganda while trying to avoid creating friction between Poland and the U.S.S.R.

Irons, P. H. " 'The Test Is Poland': Polish Americans and the Origins of the Cold War" (26:115) documents Polish American efforts to influence U.S. policy toward Poland and the Soviet Union during and shortly after World War II. The Polish Americans failed to exert any lasting influence, even though the Roosevelt and Truman administrations rendered some rhetorical support.

25:106 Mikolajczyk, Stanislaw. *The Rape of Poland: Pattern of Soviet Aggression.* New York: Whittlesey House, 1948. The prime minister of the Polish government in London (1943–1945) gives the Polish view of the Polish problem in the last years of the war. Mikolajczyk criticizes Roosevelt for misleading the Polish leaders and praises Churchill for attempting to aid them. He believes that the Western Allies sold out Poland at Yalta.

25:107 Miscamble, Wilson D. "Anthony Eden and the Truman-Molotov Conversations of April, 1945." *Diplomatic History* 2:2 (1978), 167–80. The Truman-Molotov conversation of April 23, 1945, did not indicate a reversal of America's wartime policy of cooperation with the U.S.S.R. At Eden's instigation, President Truman, who had discussed questions of general policy with Molotov in the scheduled meeting the previous day, intended the famous "dressing down" to refer to the Polish question only.

25:108 Orzell, Laurence. "Poland and Russia, July 1941–April 1943: The 'Impossible' Alliance." *Polish Review* 21:4 (1976), 35–58. Orzell examines World War II foreign relations between Poland and the U.S.S.R. (1941–1943), their tenuous diplomatic ties, and acts of Soviet aggression which led to the termination of diplomatic relations in 1943.

25:109 Orzell, Laurence J. "A 'Painful Problem': Poland in Allied Diplomacy, February–July, 1945." *Mid-America* 59:3 (1977), 147–70. The future of Poland seriously affected Allied diplomacy in the winter and spring of 1945; differences among the United States, Britain, and the U.S.S.R. eventually were to lead to the cold war. In 1945, two different Polish governments existed and territorial questions created problems.

25:110 Rozek, Edward J. *Allied Wartime Diplomacy: A Pattern in Poland.* New York: Wiley, 1958. This dated work examines British and American diplomatic maneuvering (1939–1947) and subsequent agreements with the Soviet Union concerning postwar Poland. Rozek claims that the unwillingness of the Allies to look beyond the defeat of Germany and general diplomatic bungling led to the sacrifice of Poland. Bibliography.

25:111 Sadler, Charles. "Pro-Soviet Polish-Americans: Oskar Lange and Russia's Friends in the Polonia, 1941–1945." *Polish Review* 22:4 (1977), 25–39. Lange emerged from the pro-Soviet faction of American Poles to become an articulate statesman of its beliefs. Later he renounced the U.S. citizenship he had received in 1943, to become the first ambassador to the United States from the postwar Polish government.

Sharp, T. "The Origins of the 'Teheran Formula' on Polish Frontiers" (25:57).

25:112 Terry, Sarah Meiklejohn. "The Oder-Neisse Line Revisited: Sikorski's Program for Poland's Postwar Western Boundary, 1939–42." *East Central Europe* 5:1 (1978), 39–68. General Wladyslaw Sikorski's memorandum of December 4, 1942, to President Roosevelt, giving his views about postwar Poland, refutes the conventional wisdom that the Oder-Neisse line was the invention of the Communists.

25:113 Thackrah, J. R. "Aspects of American and British Policy towards Poland from the Yalta to the Potsdam Conference, 1945." *Polish Review* 21:4 (1976), 3–34. This essay examines the foreign policy of the United States and Britain with regard to Poland and the attempts both countries made to secure a democratic state for the Polish people in the first six months of 1945.

The Greek Crisis

See "Personalities," especially Harold Macmillan (under "European," "Others"), Lincoln MacVeagh (under "American," "Others"); see also Chapter 26, "The Greek Civil War."

Auty, P., and Clogg, R., eds. *British Policy towards Wartime Resistance in Yugoslavia and Greece* (23:233) reviews British policy toward the Greek resistance movements.

25:114 Iatrides, John O. *Revolt in Athens: The Greek Communist "Second Round," 1944–1945.* Princeton, N.J.: Princeton University Press, 1972. This book provides a balanced account of the bloody military conflict that flared up between the Greek resistance forces and British troops in the winter of 1944–1945. The fighting did not result from an attempted Communist coup, but from the disagreements and suspicions that emerged in the crucible of wartime unrest. The book provides a background to the American 1947 decision to intervene. Extensive bibliography.

McNeill, W. H. *The Greek Dilemma: War and Aftermath* (26:141) is a firsthand account.

25:115 Wittner, Lawrence S. "American Policy toward Greece during World War II." *Diplomatic History* 3:2 (1979), 129–49. In this overview of America's Greek policy during World War II, the author contends that, despite the State Department protests, Roosevelt supported Britain's policy of containing the Greek Left and maintaining the status quo.

25:116 Woodhouse, Christopher M. *The Struggle for Greece, 1941–1949.* London: Hart-Davis, Mac-Gibbon, 1976. A distillation of much recent scholarship as well as the author's personal experience as the top British agent in wartime Greece, this work represents the emergence of a new and important synthesis on the Greek civil war and its international dimensions. Extensive bibliography.

25:117 Xydis, Stephen G. "America, Britain and the USSR in the Greek Arena, 1944–47." *Political Science Quarterly* 78:4 (1963), 581–96. The progression of events that led the United States toward the decision to assist Greece. The author states that Greece served as a testing ground for Allied cooperation and experiments.

U.S. AND DECOLONIZATION

See "Personalities," especially Franklin D. Roosevelt; also see Chapters 30 and 37 for Indochina and India.

25:118 Dulles, Foster Rhea, and Ridinger, Gerald E. "The Anti-Colonial Policies of Franklin D. Roosevelt." *Political Science Quarterly* 70:1 (1955), 1–18. The authors claim that Roosevelt was fervently opposed to colonialism on philosophical grounds and that he actively and consistently worked to eliminate it. Dulles and Ridinger portray Roosevelt as a visionary, desirous of a postwar world in which people chose their own form of government and those unable to govern themselves were placed under international trusteeship. This work is dated.

Hess, G. R. "Franklin D. Roosevelt and Indochina" (30:37) analyzes American wartime policy and postwar plans in regard to Indochina. The author praises Roosevelt's trusteeship idea, but criticizes the president for his characteristic failure to develop any systematic plans to achieve this goal.

LaFeber, W. "Roosevelt, Churchill and Indochina 1942–1945" (30:38) argues that Roosevelt created the plan of replacing colonial rule with a UN trusteeship to undermine the British and French empires. In Indochina Roosevelt wanted the United States and China to replace the Europeans; the United States would be the stronger partner and would have access to all the raw materials of that area.

25:119 Louis, William R. *Imperialism at Bay: The United States and the Decolonization of the British Empire 1941–1945.* New York: Oxford University Press, 1978. This book deals with British and American wartime planning for the future of the colonial world. It is a solid work which explores the historic and wartime antagonism between Britain's imperial colonial system and America's informal, liberal, democratic one embodied in the trusteeship concept. Extensive bibliography.

Thorne, C. "Indochina and Anglo-American Relations, 1942–1945" (30:161) presents Roosevelt's anticolonialism as stemming from his desire for a postwar political and security system in the Far East, and for access to markets and raw materials.

25:120 Watt, D. C. "American Anti-Colonial Policies and the End of the European Colonial Empire 1941–1962." In his *Contagious Conflict.* The Hague: Brill, 1973, pp. 93–125. The author claims that the anticolonial policies of the United States failed not because the United States abandoned them in order to gain European support to counterbalance Soviet influence, but because these policies were reflective of narrow and rigid American political thought.

25:121 Williams, J. E. "The Joint Declaration on the Colonies: An Issue in Anglo-American Relations, 1942–1944." *British Journal of International Studies* 2:3 (1976), 267–92. Williams compares British and American attitudes toward colonialism and imperialism in regard to British colonies in Southeast Asia (1942–1944) and examines the Roosevelt administration's unsuccessful attempt to form a joint declaration toward the colonies.

Divisive Wartime Issues

See "Personalities," especially George F. Kennan, Joseph V. Stalin, and American John R. Deane (under "Others").

SOVIETS IN AMERICAN PUBLIC OPINION

Adler, L. K., and Paterson, T. G. "Red Fascism: The Merger of Nazi Germany and Soviet Russia in the American Image of Totalitarianism, 1930's–1950's" (22:98).

25:122   Buckley, Gary J. "American Public Opinion and the Origins of the Cold War: A Speculative Assessment." *Mid-America* 60:1 (1978), 35–42. A case study of American public opinion regarding the U.S.S.R. during and shortly after World War II which argues that at no time did American public opinion show more than a 55 percent (February 1945) and 54 percent (August 1945) positive attitude.

Doenecke, J. D. *Not to the Swift: The Old Isolationists in the Cold War Era* [1943–1954] (26:34) shows the "old" isolationists' dissatisfaction with FDR's internationalism, and concern about the new inroads of "communism."

25:123   Levering, Ralph B. *American Opinion and the Russian Alliance, 1939–1945.* Chapel Hill: University of North Carolina, 1976. The author explores the wartime climate of public opinion which he perceives as being schizophrenic: friendliness toward the Soviet Union grew but so did fear of communism. Levering finds no intense animosity present during the war, but public opinion opposed to the Soviet Union increased sharply following the war's end. Extensive bibliography.

25:124   Small, Melvin. "Buffoons and Brave Hearts: Hollywood Portrays the Russians, 1939–1944." *California Historical Quarterly* 52:4 (1973), 326–37. Before the German invasion of the U.S.S.R. (1941) the films caricatured the Russians as buffoons (as in "Ninotchka"), but after the U.S.S.R. joined the fight against the Nazis and U.S. entry, Hollywood portrayed the Russian people as defending freedom against tyranny ("Mission to Moscow," "North Star").

25:125   Small, Melvin. "How We Learned to Love the Russians: American Media and the Soviet Union during World War II." *Historian* 36:3 (1974), 455–78. Public opinion polls reveal that people changed their minds about the U.S.S.R. during World War II. Media presentations regarding Russia during the same periods also made a decided favorable shift. The rapidity with which America later again became anticommunist suggests reservations as to the media's permanent effectiveness.

POLITICAL ISSUES

The Second Front

See "Personalities," especially Winston S. Churchill, Ivan Maisky (under "European," "Others"), Albert C. Wedemeyer (under "American," "Others").

25:126   Grigg, John. *1943: The Victory That Never Was.* New York: Hill & Wang, 1980. This work revives the old thesis that a cross-channel invasion was possible in 1943. Grigg contends that it was not Churchill who opposed the 1943 invasion but Sir Alan Brooke, the chief of the Imperial Staff, and argues that such an invasion would have shortened the war and placed the Western powers in a better bargaining position with the Soviet Union.

25:127   Sekistov, V. "Why the Second Front Was Not Opened in 1943." *Soviet Military Review,* no. 8 (1972), 50–52. This brief essay repeats a frequent Soviet allegation that the United States and Britain had sufficient men and materiel to launch a cross-channel attack in 1942, but their leaders hoped that Nazi Germany and Soviet Russia would destroy each other.

25:128   Stoler, Mark A. "The 'Second Front' and American Fear of Soviet Expansion, 1941–1943." *Military Affairs* 39:3 (1975), 136–41. American political and military leaders in World War II did consider the danger of Soviet expansionism in planning strategy for victory over Germany. In 1943 Washington acted to insure the presence of American forces in

Germany, and three *Rankin* plans were contingencies in the event of Germany's weakening.

25:129 Stoler, Mark A. *The Politics of the Second Front: American Military Planning and Diplomacy in Coalition Warfare, 1941–1943.* Westport, Conn.: Greenwood, 1977. The dispute between the United States and Britain over when and where to establish a second front, according to Stoler, was created by the differing current and future necessities of each country: Roosevelt's domestic situation demanded that the war shift to the East as soon as possible, the British wanted to secure the Middle East and Mediterranean for future economic reasons. Bibliography.

The Katyn Massacre

25:130 Zawodny, J. K. *Death in the Forest: The Story of the Katyn Forest Massacre.* Notre Dame, Ind.: University of Notre Dame Press, 1962, p. 219. A thorough study of the Katyn Woods murders, it emphasizes the diplomatic problem of having the Poles as "inconvenient allies." Bibliography.

Warsaw Uprising, 1944

25:131 Chandler, Harriette L. "The Transition to Cold Warrior: The Evolution of W. Averell Harriman's Assessment of the U.S.S.R.'s Polish Policy, October 1943–Warsaw Uprising." *East European Quarterly* 10:2 (1976), 229–45. Although Harriman helped develop the philosophical foundations of the containment policy, he approached his job as ambassador to the U.S.S.R. with considerable understanding and acceptance of the goals of Soviet foreign policy. His position was generally conciliatory toward the Soviets until their refusal to aid the beleaguered Poles in the Warsaw uprising.

25:132 King, Frank P. "British Policy and the Warsaw Rising." *Journal of European Studies* 4:1 (1974), 1–18. King surveys the changes in relations during World War II between the great powers occasioned by the Warsaw uprising in the autumn of 1944.

25:133 Lukas, Richard C. "The Big Three and the Warsaw Uprising." *Military Affairs* 39:3 (1975), 129–34. Lukas discusses the impact of the 1944 Warsaw uprising on the big three and analyzes the policies each power pursued during the crisis. It nearly ruptured the Allied alliance and may well have been the starting point of the cold war.

The Separate Peace Issue

See Chapter 23, "Unconditional Surrender," and "The German Question," above.

25:134 Fieldhouse, Noel. "The Anglo-German War of 1939–42: Some Movements to End It by a Negotiated Peace." *Transactions of the Royal Society of Canada,* no. 9 (1971), 285–312. A review of efforts by British individuals and groups to secure a negotiated peace. These people argued that Germany had indeed been wronged, and that Britain could no longer enforce its will in Eastern Europe.

Villa, B. L. "The U.S. Army, Unconditional Surrender, and the Potsdam Declaration" (23:268) concentrates on the divisions within the U.S. government over the official Allied surrender policy—unconditional surrender. The army generally opposed that concept and partially, and at times totally, circumvented it in the Italian, German, and Japanese surrenders.

The Soviets
25:135 Koch, H. W. "The Spectre of a Separate Peace in the East: Russo-German 'Peace Feelers,' 1942–1944." *Journal of Contemporary History* 10:3 (1975), 531–49. A series of meetings took place during 1942 to 1944 involving Germany's Dr. Peter Kleist, a specialist in international law and honorary member of the SS, and a certain Edgar Clauss, a middleman for the U.S.S.R.

25:136 Mastny, Vojtech. "Stalin and the Prospects of a Separate Peace in World War II." *American Historical Review* 77:5 (1972), 1365–88. Mastny uses German documents to suggest that Stalin was ready to conclude a separate peace in 1943 but was unable to obtain a satisfactory territorial settlement from Germany. Mastny further contends that British and American efforts to placate the Soviet Union for their failure to provide a second front led Stalin to seek more ambitious territorial gains.

The Americans
25:137 Chandler, Harriette L. "Another View of Operation Crossword: A Revision of Kolko." *Military Affairs* 42:2 (1978), 68–74. Operation Crossword was the preliminary effort to secure a surrender on the northern Italian front in the spring of 1945. The Anglo-American decision to deny Soviet participation in the negotiations prompted Gabriel Kolko to suggest that the move was politically motivated. However,

recently declassified material confirms that the decision was based solely on military considerations.

25:138 Dulles, Allen. *The Secret Surrender*. New York: Harper & Row, 1966. Personal account by the future head of the Central Intelligence Agency of the negotiations which led to the surrender of German forces in Italy to British and American commanders in northern Italy before the final capitulation in Germany.

Smith, B. F., and Agarossi, E. *Operation Sunrise: The Secret Surrender* (23:258) is the newest and most complete study of the negotiations leading to the surrender of German forces in Italy. Bibliography.

Forced Repatriation

25:139 Buhite, Russell D. "Soviet-American Relations and the Repatriation of Prisoners of War." *Historian* 35:3 (1973), 384–97. The author summarizes the prisoner of war issue of 1945, claiming that it was a major factor in the breakdown of Soviet-American relations. This work documents the lack of planning in the prisoner of war problem and the serious consequences that arose as a result.

25:140 Elliot, Mark. "The United States and Forced Repatriation of Soviet Citizens, 1944–47." *Political Science Quarterly* 88:2 (1973), 253–75. Elliot looks at how Soviet negotiating tactics, the ineptitude of U.S. military officials, and U.S. concern for American POWs in Soviet-occupied territory contributed to an agreement which resulted in the forced repatriation of Soviet citizens at the end of World War II.

ECONOMIC ISSUES

25:141 Eckes, Alfred E., Jr. "Open Door Expansionism Reconsidered: The World War II Experience." *Journal of American History* 59:4 (1973), 909–24. Eckes criticizes the analyses of Williams and Kolko of U.S. postwar economic planning and argues that domestic market generally was seen as more important than foreign trade, and that multilateralism was framed to include U.S.S.R. and was generally welcomed abroad, by for example Britain, as beneficial economic internationalism.

25:142 Paterson, Thomas G. "The Abortive Loan to Russia and the Origins of the Cold War, 1943–1946." *Journal of American History* 56:1 (1969), 70–92.

Paterson traces the evolution of U.S. policy and diplomacy with respect to postwar reconstruction aid to the Soviet Union. From 1944 to 1946, the United States used the possibility of a postwar loan to Russia as a bargaining lever with which to influence Soviet behavior. The failure to arrange a loan exacerbated tensions between the two countries.

Lend-Lease

See "Personalities," especially W. Averell Harriman, and, under "Others," John R. Deane, William H. Standley; also see Chapters 22, "Origins of Lend-Lease," and 23, "Lend-Lease."

25:143 Coakley, Robert W. "Roosevelt et le Pret-Bail" [Roosevelt and lend-lease]. *Revue d'Histoire de la Deuxième Guerre Mondiale* 82:1 (1971), 73–96. This study of lend-lease focuses on FDR's personal interest in the program, particularly with regard to aid to Russia.

Dawson, R. H. *The Decision to Aid Russia, 1941: Foreign Policy and Domestic Politics* (22:187).

25:144 Herring, George C., Jr. *Aid to Russia, 1941–1946: Strategy, Diplomacy, the Origins of the Cold War*. New York: Columbia University Press, 1973. Herring describes Roosevelt's policy of unconditional aid to the Soviet Union, which had virtually no limitations as FDR sought to reassure Stalin of Allied intentions. As the war drew to a close, Roosevelt refused to modify the aid program, whereas Truman accepted the advice of Harriman and others by taking a tougher stand. Truman did not intend to use lend-lease as an instrument of coercion but did assume that the Soviets would accept political compromises in return for postwar aid. Extensive bibliography.

25:145 Herring, George C., Jr. "Lend-Lease to Russia and the Origins of the Cold War, 1944–1945." *Journal of American History* 56:1 (1969), 93–114. The abrupt reduction of lend-lease assistance to Russia in May 1945 was not an attempt to coerce the Soviet Union. Lend-lease to all countries was being reduced, but termination of Roosevelt's liberal policy of aid to Russia and an initially overzealous interpretation of the new policy did hurt the Russians economically.

Kimball, W. F. "Lend-Lease and the Open Door: The Temptation of British Opulence, 1937–1942" (22:188).

Langer, J. D. "The 'Red General': Philip R. Faymonville and the Soviet Union, 1917–52" (21:160) discusses Faymonville's appointment by Harry Hopkins as a military representative on the Russian end of the lend-lease program. An unfavorable and biased report on his loyalty and credibility, coupled with Roosevelt's failure to support him, caused the termination of the general's role in Soviet-American affairs.

Lukas, R. C. *Eagles East: The Army Air Forces and the Soviet Union, 1941–1945* (23:237) discusses issues involving lend-lease.

25:146   Martel, Leon. *Lend-Lease, Loans, and the Coming of the Cold War: A Study of the Implementation of Foreign Policy.* Boulder, Colo.: Westview, 1979. Primarily concerned with decisionmaking within the U.S. government, the book concentrates on four economic decisions, made near the end of World War II, which related to U.S.-U.S.S.R. relations: the curtailment of lend-lease; the cessation of lend-lease to the U.S.S.R.; U.S. responses to a Soviet loan request; and U.S. handling of a second Soviet loan request. Extensive bibliography.

Motter, T. H. V. *The Persian Corridor and Aid to Russia* (23:222) discusses the problems of Allied cooperation.

German Reparations Question

See Chapter 26, "Reparations Issue."

25:147   Kuklick, Bruce. *American Policy and the Division of Germany: The Clash with Russia over Reparations.* Ithaca, N.Y.: Cornell University Press, 1972. This is a carefully reasoned account of the issue that may indeed be at the heart of the origins of the cold war—German reparations payments. The book also offers the best analysis to date of multilateralism as the key to the economic origins of American-Soviet antagonisms in the mid-1940s, and of the internecine struggle among the State, War and Treasury departments which contributed to the partition of Germany and the subsequent hostile division of Europe. Extensive bibliography.

Ratchford, B. U., and Ross, W. D. *Berlin Reparations Assignment: Round One of the German Peace Settlement* (26:106) is a firsthand account of the issue as it flared up between September 1945 and March 1946.

Bretton Woods, 1944

Eckes, A. E., Jr. *A Search for Solvency: Bretton Woods and the International Monetary System, 1941–1971* (39:123) is a thorough study of the Treasury Department's plans for a new postwar monetary order as expressed at the international conference held in the summer of 1944. Bibliography.

25:148   Gardner, Richard N. *Sterling-Dollar Diplomacy: The Origins and Prospects of Our International Economic Order.* Rev. ed. New York: McGraw-Hill (1956), 1969. Gardner's study depicts American efforts to reconstruct the international monetary system and revive world commerce along multilateral lines. He focuses on the Bretton Woods accords, the Anglo-American Financial Agreement, and the General Agreement on Tariffs and Trade. This expanded edition contains a new introductory chapter putting the accomplishments of postwar policymakers in a much more favorable perspective than did the first edition.

25:149   Oliver, Robert W. *International Economic Cooperation and the World Bank.* London: Macmillan, 1975. Oliver traces the development of the World Bank. He examines American foreign economic policy in the interwar era in order to explain the origins and purposes of the new institution. Focusing on Harry Dexter White's role, Oliver analyzes American plans for the International Bank for Reconstruction and Development. Extensive bibliography.

25:150   Rowland, Benjamin M. "Preparing the American Ascendancy: The Transfer of Economic Power from Britain to the United States, 1933–1944." In Benjamin M. Rowland, ed., *Balance of Power or Hegemony: The Interwar Monetary System.* New York: New York University Press, 1976, pp. 193–224. Rowland examines the origins of the Bretton Woods system, arguing that the extent of dollar hegemony was an accident of war and that Britain did have an alternative in the form of the sterling area. But in the hope of U.S. political and military support, Britain accepted the covert nationalism of the multilateral trade and monetary policies of State and Treasury.

25:151   Sayers, R. S. *Financial Policy, 1939–1945.* London: H.M.S.O., 1956. This volume in the official British *History of the Second World War* (Civil Series) deals learnedly and extensively with wartime planning for finance in the postwar world. It is the starting point for any study of Anglo-American financial relations.

25:152 Van Dormael, Armand. *Bretton Woods: Birth of a Monetary System.* London: Macmillan, 1978. This account complements Gardner's *Sterling-Dollar Diplomacy* (25:148). It studies official British and U.S. plans for a postwar monetary system, centering on the Bretton Woods Conference and the implementation of the agreements reached there.

Britain's Economic Decline

25:153 Balogh, Thomas. *Unequal Partners.* Oxford: Basil Blackwell, 1963, vol. 2. This memoir-analysis of war economics and postwar economic planning is written by an economist who was involved with J. M. Keynes in that planning. Balogh, who opposed the Bretton Woods agreement, views the problems of the peace as being caused by the failure of postwar economic planning.

25:154 Herring, George C., Jr. "The United States and British Bankruptcy, 1944–1945: Responsibilities Deferred." *Political Science Quarterly* 86:2 (1971), 260–80. The author places the blame for British financial problems at the close of the war on the fact that Americans had not perceived the extent to which the war had weakened British power. Americans were suspicious and antagonistic toward the British, who were considered dangerous postwar competitors.

Kimball, W. F. "Lend-Lease and the Open Door: The Temptation of British Opulence, 1937–1942" (22:188).

25:155 Opie, Redvers. "Anglo-American Economic Relations in War-Time." *Oxford Economic Papers* n.s. 9:2 (1957), 115–51. The author was economic adviser to the British embassy in Washington during the war. He draws on his own experiences to survey negotiations to formulate and then implement article 7 of the Lend-Lease Consideration Agreement, which committed the United States and Britain to agree on steps leading to the elimination of economic discrimination.

25:156 Penrose, E. F. *Economic Planning for the Peace.* Princeton, N.J.: Princeton University Press, 1953. In this book, which is part memoir and part economic theory, Penrose, economic adviser to John Gilbert Winant, traces the development of postwar economic plans from 1941 through 1946. Penrose contends that errors of the peace were caused by faulty planning in the areas of postwar international economic recovery and permanent international economic stability.

ATOMIC DIPLOMACY

See under "Personalities," especially Henry L. Stimson; also see Chapter 23, "Atomic Bomb and Japan's Surrender."

25:157 Alperovitz, Gar. *Atomic Diplomacy: Hiroshima and Potsdam.* New York: Vintage, 1967. Alperovitz's controversial thesis is that the bomb provided Truman with what he thought would be the diplomatic and military punch he needed to reverse Roosevelt's policy of accommodation with the Soviet Union and to compel Soviet acquiescence in American postwar plans for Central and Eastern Europe. Bibliography.

25:158 Bernstein, Barton J., ed. *The Atomic Bomb: The Critical Issues.* Boston: Little, Brown, 1976. By 1975 analysts still had not agreed on the causes of the cold war or on the major issues raised nearly three decades earlier about the atom bomb and American foreign policy. These essays, many reprinted, provide useful introduction to these critical issues. Bibliography.

25:159 Bernstein, Barton J. "Roosevelt, Truman, and the Atomic Bomb, 1941–1945: A Reinterpretation." *Political Science Quarterly* 90:1 (1975), 23–69. Roosevelt defined the relationship between the atomic bomb and American diplomacy. When Truman became president, he was restricted politically, psychologically, and institutionally from critically reassessing this legacy. Truman accepted the bomb as a legitimate weapon of war, and he fully appreciated that its power would be a factor in U.S. diplomacy. Possession of the bomb reduced the incentives for compromise and stiffened American demands vis-à-vis the Soviet Union, and thus contributed to the onset of the cold war.

25:160 Bernstein, Barton J. "Shatterer of Worlds: Hiroshima and Nagasaki." *Bulletin of the Atomic Scientists* 31:10 (1975), 12–22. U.S. policymakers in the Roosevelt and Truman administrations had little doubt about the desirability of using atomic weapons both for ending the war in the Pacific and for intimidating the U.S.S.R.

25:161 Bernstein, Barton J. "The Uneasy Alliance: Roosevelt, Churchill, and the Atomic Bomb, 1940–1945." *Western Political Quarterly* 29:2 (1976), 202–30. Bernstein reinterprets the wartime Anglo-American relationship on atomic energy, defined primarily by Roosevelt and Churchill. A postwar Anglo-American entente could be constructed on the atomic bomb.

25:162 Hammond, Thomas T. "'Atomic Diplomacy' Revisited." *Orbis* 19:4 (1976), 1403–28. The theses of Gar Alperovitz in his *Atomic Diplomacy: Hiroshima and Potsdam* (25:157) "are either implausible, exaggerated or unsupported by the evidence" and do not stand up under careful analysis.

25:163 Maddox, Robert James. *"Atomic Diplomacy:* A Study in Creative Writing." *Journal of American History* 59:4 (1973), 925–34. Maddox criticizes Alperovitz's *Atomic Diplomacy* (25:157) for severe distortions and misrepresentations of the evidence, and the historical profession in general for its uncritical acceptance of this work. For a more detailed and comprehensive critique by Maddox of New Left

histories in general, see his *The New Left and the Origins of the Cold War* (24:57).

25:164 Morton, Louis. "The Decision to Use the Atom Bomb." *Foreign Affairs* 35:2 (1957), 334–53. The author disagrees with the notion that the bomb was used to forestall Russian intervention, though there were undoubtedly some people who favored this course.

Sherwin, M. J. *A World Destroyed: The Atomic Bomb and the Grand Alliance* (23:265).

25:165 Sherwin, Martin J. "The Atomic Bomb and the Origins of the Cold War: U.S. Atomic Energy Policy and Diplomacy, 1941–1945." *American Historical Review* 78:4 (1973), 945–68. President Roosevelt left no definitive statement on the postwar role of the atomic bomb. Among his alternatives he considered were international control, advocated by his science advisers, and an Anglo-American postwar monopoly, urged by Churchill, indicates that the potential postwar diplomatic value of the bomb began to shape his atomic energy policies as early as 1943.

26

United States and the Soviet Union, 1946–1953

Contributing Editor
MARTIN J. SHERWIN
Tufts University

Contributors
Carolyn Eisenberg
New York City

Robert Griffith
University of Massachusetts,
Amherst

Robert Messer
University of Illinois,
Chicago Circle

Lawrence A. Yates
Command and General Staff College,
Fort Leavenworth

Contents

Introduction

The early cold war was an age of strong leadership on both sides: of Truman versus Stalin. The ideas, actions, and interactions of these leaders and their foreign policy advisers were central to the relations between the United States and the Soviet Union during this period. It also was a time of seminal, even revolutionary policy thinking and action; of global containment, the Truman Doctrine, and the Marshall Plan; of entangling alliances such as NATO; and of peacetime mobilization such as that called for in NSC-68. It was a time of direct and indirect confrontation between the world's military giants in Eastern Europe, in Iran, in Greece and Turkey, in Berlin.

On one side of this bipolar world, the Soviet Union maintained the world's largest army. On the other side, the United States clung to its atomic monopoly and overwhelming economic superiority. In this crisis atmosphere of worldwide confrontation, efforts at international arms control failed. The news of the first Soviet atomic bomb was soon followed by the American commitment to build the hydrogen bomb.

Other factors impinging upon U.S.-Soviet relations during these years were newer in form than in substance. Domestic politics and public opinion continued to exert a limiting if not formative influence over foreign policy. Unlike Stalin, Truman faced opposition to his continuing in office after 1948. Soon after that upset victory the political opposition came increasingly, but inaccurately, to be called McCarthyism. The re-emergence of what Richard Hofstadter termed the paranoid style in American history, grew into a force that no politician could ignore.

These and other elements of U.S.-Soviet relations are treated in this chapter. They by no means exhaust the list of relevant topics. Any comprehensive inquiry must take into account that during this period virtually any crisis anywhere in the world was interpreted in terms of the global U.S.-Soviet rivalry. Examples of important topics not included in this chapter are the civil war in China, the limited war in Korea, and the beginnings of American involvement in Indochina. For these topics, consult Chapters 27 and 30.

The emergence of the postwar U.S.-Soviet rivalry is necessarily complex and relative. The multisided, interconnected process of change called the origins of the cold war contains few agreed upon or simple truths. (For a discussion of the contending schools of cold war historiography see Chapter 24.) However, one central fact is clear from the historical literature. Although we certainly do not know everything, we know a great deal more about the U.S. side of the cold war equation than we are ever likely to know about the Soviet side. Historians, East and West, have benefitted greatly from the availability of masses of material in government and private archives in the United States and Great Britain. This deluge of evidence from Western sources contrasts to the trickle of published Soviet official documents and memoirs of former officials.

As can be seen from the subheadings in this chapter, the questions raised and issues debated in the historical literature reflect the enormous imbalance in the evidence available to scholars. This imbalance is apparent in the literature on the opposing doctrines of capitalist encirclement versus containment of Soviet expansion. The debate over containment began almost immediately after the not-so-mysterious Mr. "X" (George Kennan) (26:49) first publicly proclaimed it as "the main element of any United States policy toward the Soviet Union. . . ." Discussion of the original meaning, interpretation and subsequent application or misapplication of Kennan's ideas has generated a considerable body of scholarly literature (26:123–29). Research connected with this ongoing debate has cast light on the larger process of American foreign policy formulation. As a result, we know more about the internal dynamics of the American side of U.S.-Soviet relations.

By contrast the Soviet policymaking process remains in relative darkness. Comparable evidence, either in quantity or quality, simply is not available for analysis and debate. The student of U.S.-Soviet relations is faced with trying to recreate the inner workings of a complex mechanism with only some of the parts, most of which are American-made.

A researcher new to the subject might begin by

comparing two recent overviews of American-Russian and Soviet relations—John Gaddis, *Russia, the Soviet Union, and the United States* (2:248) and Nikolai Sivachev and Nikolai Yakovlev, *Russia and the United States* (2:253). Gaddis, an American historian, and Sivachev and Yakovlev, Soviet scholars writing for an American audience, arrive at fundamentally different conclusions about the origins of the cold war. Their use of evidence and writing styles also demonstrates the differences between Western and Soviet historical scholarship.

Insights into postwar U.S.-Soviet relations provided by the "orthodox" approach are offered by Adam Ulam, *The Rivals* (24:29); "revisionist" history is presented by Walter LaFeber, *America, Russia and the Cold War* (24:18). A representative sample of works concentrating on the early cold war period includes Herbert Feis, *From Trust to Terror* (26:8), by a former State Department official and representative of the orthodox view; the influential "soft" revisionist treatment by Daniel Yergin, *Shattered Peace* (26:22); the more radical analysis of Gabriel and Joyce Kolko's *The Limits of Power* (24:40); and the recent "eclectic" synthesis by Thomas Paterson, *On Every Front* (26:11), which includes an excellent bibliographic essay.

An introductory list of works, like the fuller bibliography that follows, is necessarily selective and incomplete, as U.S.-Soviet cold war relations is an open-ended course of study. Recently opened British government files are only beginning to be mined by historians. This new perspective on U.S.-Soviet relations has yet to be incorporated into the literature. Unfortunately, new British material only further tips the balance in favor of Western sources. In all probability, comparable Soviet sources, if they exist, will remain beyond the scrutiny of scholars for the foreseeable future, leaving cold war historiography growing but congenitally impaired.

Resources and Overviews

RESEARCH AIDS

While pertinent bibliographies and reference aids are listed here, there are more extensive lists in Chapter 1.

Bibliographies

See Chapter 24, "Bibliographies" and "Cold War Historiography," for additional references on the cold war.

Cronon, E. D., and Rosenof, T. D., comps. *The Second World War and the Atomic Age, 1940–1973* (24:1).

Dexter, B., ed. *The Foreign Affairs Fifty-Year Bibliography: New Evaluations of Significant Books on International Relations, 1920–1970* (1:14) is useful on the postwar period.

Ferrell, R. H. "Truman Foreign Policy: A Traditionalist View" (24:187) upholds Truman's record in foreign policy as a "good one," and criticizes revisionist writers for their methods and their interpretations. Looking at the cold war from 1945 through 1947, he offers a point-by-point refutation of revisionist arguments.

Foreign Affairs Bibliography: A Selected and Annotated List of Books on International Relations (1:15) is issued at ten-year intervals, and each volume has three parts: "General International Relations"; "The World since 1914"; and "The World by Regions." Useful aid.

Gardner, L. C. "Truman Era Foreign Policy: Recent Historical Trends" (24:188) discusses orthodox, realist, and revisionist approaches to the early cold war, and concludes that of the three groups, the revisionists have led the way in the serious treatment of newly opened archival material.

Griffith, R. "Truman and the Historians: The Reconstruction of Postwar American History" (24:189).

26:1 Hutson, Susan Hoffman. *McCarthy and the Anti-Communist Crusade: A Selected Bibliography.* Political Issues Series, 5:2. Los Angeles: California State University, Center for the Study of Armament and Disarmament, 1979. Hutson provides references to many of the various issues that arose from 1945 to 1954. Introductory essay.

Okinshevich, L., comp. *United States History and Historiography in Postwar Soviet Writings, 1945–1970* (24:2).

Seidman, J., comp. *Communism in the United States: A Bibliography* (1:75) provides many references for these years.

U.S. Department of State. *Point Four: Near East and Africa: A Selected Bibliography on Economically Underdeveloped Countries* (1:110) lists mostly economic studies published in the 1940s which were collected to assist in developing the Point Four program.

Yearbooks and Other Aids

26:2 Brookings Institution, International Studies Group. *Major Problems of United States Foreign Policy, 1947; 1948–1949; 1949–1950; 1950–1951; 1951–1952.* Washington, D.C.: Brookings Institution, 1947–1951. Each volume in this annual survey provides an overview of America's position and interests in world affairs, a review of major foreign policy problems confronting the United States, and at least one paper offering a detailed analysis of a selected problem as that problem would be perceived and addressed by American policymakers. Extensive bibliography.

DeConde, A., ed. *Encyclopedia of American Foreign Policy* (1:164) contains several essays on different themes regarding the cold war.

Gallup, G. H. *The Gallup Poll: Public Opinion, 1935–1971* (1:348) pays considerable attention to foreign policy issues.

Keesing's Contemporary Archives: Weekly Diary of World Events (1:152) has good coverage of foreign affairs events.

Maxwell, R., ed. and comp. *Information U.S.S.R.: An Authoritative Encyclopedia about the Union of Soviet Socialist Republics* (1:168).

Survey of International Affairs [1920–1963] (1:146) is useful for specific issues.

The United States in World Affairs (1:147) is an annual review or book-length summary of American foreign policy. Indexed.

Document Collections

More general collections are listed in Chapter 1, and other collections may be found under "Personalities," below.

Documents on American Foreign Relations (1:339) is an annual intended to accompany the *United States in World Affairs* (1:147) volumes.

Documents on International Affairs (1:340) is a good source for official documents and public statements by foreign leaders.

26:3 Etzold, Thomas H., and Gaddis, John Lewis, eds. *Containment: Documents on American Policy and Strategy, 1945–1950.* New York: Columbia University Press, 1978. A collection of recently declassified documents on national security policy from the period 1945 to 1950, that includes some previously unpublished contingency plans for war with the Soviet Union. It also contains introductory essays: Etzold, "American Organization for National Security, 1945–1950"; and Gaddis, "The Strategy of Containment."

26:4 LaFeber, Walter, ed. *Eastern Europe and the Soviet Union.* Vol. 2 in *The Dynamics of World Power: A Documentary History of United States Foreign Policy, 1945–1973.* New York: Chelsea House, 1973. The first half of this collection provides American and Soviet speeches, press conferences, and other documents.

Leiss, A. C., with Dennett, R. *European Peace Treaties after World War II* (25:2) is a convenient collection of negotiations and texts of treaties with Italy, Bulgaria, Hungary, Rumania, and Finland.

Molotov, V. M. *Problems of Foreign Policy: Speeches and Statements, April 1945–November 1948* (25:3).

U.S. Department of State. *Foreign Relations of the United States* (1:358) is a valuable source, now covering most of this period.

U.S. Department of State. *Press Conferences of the Secretaries of State, 1922–1974* (1:360) is a microfilm of the verbatim record. An important source for record of officials.

U.S. House. Committee on Foreign Affairs. *World War II International Agreements and Understandings: Entered into during Secret Conferences Concerning Other People* (25:4) contains the texts of various agreements entered into by the United States, with notes on background of negotiations and status of agreements. Special attention is given to violations by the Soviet Union.

U.S. President. *Public Papers of the Presidents of the United States* [1945–] (1:362) begins with Harry S. Truman's public papers.

U.S. Senate. Committee on Foreign Relations. *A Decade of American Foreign Policy: Basic Documents, 1941–49* (23:20) is a useful collection of official statements and documents.

26:5 U.S. Senate. Committee on Foreign Relations. *Executive Sessions of the Senate Foreign Relations Committee.* Historical Series. 5 vols. Washington, D.C.: G.P.O., 1976. These volumes contain important material on U.S. foreign policy during the late 1940s and early 1950s, especially regarding the Korean War, security agreements, foreign aid, etc.

OVERVIEWS

See Chapter 24, "Overviews," for surveys of American foreign affairs since World War II.

Brzezinski, Z. "How the Cold War Was Played" (24:7) identifies several phases of the cold war since 1945 and the Soviet-American interaction in each period, comparing the economic and military power, the "international standing," and the "domestic policy base" of the two major competitors.

26:6 Carr, Albert Z. *Truman, Stalin, and the Peace.* Garden City, N.Y.: Doubleday, 1950. An American liberal and occasional Washington insider evaluates Truman's efforts to establish a lasting peace. Carr himself prescribes a long-range U.S. commitment to foreign aid, support for popular leaders and democratic parties throughout the world, and a willingness to negotiate with the Russians, coupled with a determination to resist aggression.

26:7 Deutscher, Isaac. "Twenty Years of Cold War." In his *Ironies of History: Essays on Contemporary Communism.* Berkeley, Calif.: Ramparts, 1966, pp. 147–63. Western assumptions regarding the political and military intentions of the Soviet Union at the end of World War II were unreal. Russia was in no condition at war's end to pose a military threat to the West. Also, Stalin did not use communist parties in the West to promote world revolution; indeed, he often acted to retard revolutionary activity. The goal of the United States may have been to contain communism, but Stalin did a better job of it than anyone else.

26:8 Feis, Herbert. *From Trust to Terror: The Onset of the Cold War, 1945–1950.* New York: Norton, 1970. This book treats "the more crucial situations and actions" which affected the decline of mutual trust between the United States and the Soviet Union after World War II. The narrative, at times disjointed and incomplete, emphasizes Soviet-American differences over Europe (especially Germany) and the control of atomic energy. Bibliography.

Fleming, D. F. *The Cold War and Its Origins, 1917–1960* (24:9) is one of the first revisions of orthodox cold war history. Fleming, an unreconstructed Wilsonian, accuses Truman of inviting the postwar Soviet-American confrontation by reversing Roosevelt's policy of accommodation with the Russians.

Fontaine, A. *History of the Cold War: From the October Revolution to the Korean War, 1917–1950* (24:10) focuses on the European aspects of the cold war.

26:9 Graebner, Norman A., ed. *The Cold War: A Conflict of Ideology and Power.* 2d ed. Lexington, Mass.: Heath, 1976. Most of the pieces in this cold war anthology are concerned with the nature of Soviet foreign policy. Special attention is given to the question of whether the Soviet Union is simply a powerful nation pursuing traditional policies or a fanatic society seeking world revolution. Extensive bibliography.

26:10 Halle, Louis, et al. "The Cold War and Beyond." *International Journal* 23:3 (1968), 335–455. Articles in this issue treat such topics as cold war revisionism, the Marshall Plan, the UN, and the Berlin blockade.

Kolko, J., and Kolko, G. *The Limits of Power: The World and United States Foreign Policy, 1945–1954* (24:40) is a massive, radical critique of American foreign policy in the postwar decade. This book analyzes Soviet-American relations in the context of America's attempt to restructure a stable system of international capitalism in a world beset by violence and repression, revolutionary upheaval, and counterrevolution—the dominant themes of the postwar era.

The style is turgid, but the presentation detailed and comprehensive. Extensive bibliography.

26:11 Paterson, Thomas G. *On Every Front: The Making of the Cold War*. New York: Norton, 1979. In a concise, topical essay on Soviet-American relations during the first years of the cold war, Paterson analyzes the manner in which "systemic, fundamental, and tactical factors" caused American and Soviet leaders to abandon the quest for world community and, in pursuit of their own perceived interests, to erect instead competing spheres of influence. Extensive bibliography.

26:12 Paterson, Thomas G. *Soviet-American Confrontation: Postwar Reconstruction and the Origins of the Cold War*. Baltimore: Johns Hopkins University Press, 1973. While acknowledging that the causes of the cold war can be reduced to no single determinant, Paterson focuses on how the United States, in pursuit of "peace and prosperity," sought to use its economic power to compel Russia (and Great Britain) to accept American plans for postwar economic reconstruction. Extensive bibliography.

Perkins, D. *The Diplomacy of a New Age: Major Issues in U.S. Policy since 1945* (24:47) finds much that is praiseworthy in the American approach to the Marshall Plan and NATO.

26:13 Seton-Watson, Hugh. *Neither War Nor Peace: The Struggle for Power in the Postwar World*. New York: Praeger, 1960. This British account of international relations (1945–1959) is unusual in its emphasis on Europe and the Third World and its relative neglect of Soviet-American relations. The approach is analytical rather than chronological. The decisive forces of the postwar years have been totalitarianism (primarily the communist variety), and "anti-European nationalism."

Smith, A. L., Jr. *Churchill's German Army: Wartime Strategy and Cold War Politics, 1943–1947* (25:22) suggests that Britain's cold war policies began before the war ended.

Wheeler-Bennett, J., and Nicholls, A. *The Semblance of Peace: The Political Settlement after the Second World War* (25:14) is a prodigious study of Allied war aims during World War II and the peace negotiations and settlements that followed. Roosevelt, the authors argue, desired a Soviet-American postwar alliance at the expense of England and France, but Russia's efforts to extend the area of its political and ideological

domination caused the Western powers to unite in opposition to the Soviet challenge.

American Policies

Ambrose, S. E. *Rise to Globalism: American Foreign Policy since 1938* (24:30) examines the "revolution in attitudes, policies, and methods" which accompanied the transformation of the United States from a hemispheric to a global power, responsible for the maintenance and protection of a widespread empire.

Aron, R. *The Imperial Republic: The United States and the World, 1945–1973* (24:31) seeks to present American foreign policy "as it was." His conclusions are often challenging and thought provoking, even for those who do not share the author's "realist," antirevisionist orientation.

Brown, S. *The Faces of Power: Constancy and Change in United States Foreign Policy from Truman to Johnson* (24:33) analyzes the way in which four U.S. administrations (1945–1968) have sought through a shifting emphasis on military, economic, and idealistic means to achieve and maintain a global balance of power. The book offers a clear evaluation of the relationship between American power and foreign policy in the cold war.

26:14 Druks, Herbert M. *Harry S. Truman and the Russians, 1945–1953*. New York: Speller, 1966. An early, uncritical narrative which praises Truman for standing up to the Soviet menace, this work is noteworthy today primarily because it is one of the few book-length accounts of Soviet-American relations during the entire Truman administration.

Freymond, J. *De Roosevelt à Eisenhower: La Politique étrangère americaine, 1945–1952* (28:9) is a discerning appraisal of U.S. foreign policy by a prominent French scholar.

Gaddis, J. L. *The United States and the Origins of the Cold War, 1941–1947* (25:16) is a thorough and balanced synthesis utilizing both traditionalist and revisionist arguments. The book gives special attention to the constraints imposed on American officials by public opinion, domestic politics, and bureaucratic inertia, and to the impact of personality and perception on the formulation of policy.

Gardner, L. C. *Architects of Illusion: Men and Ideas in American Foreign Policy, 1941–1949* (25:17).

26:15 Lippmann, Walter. *The Cold War*. New York: Harper & Row (1947), 1972. This book comprises Lippmann's critique of the assumptions underlying America's containment policy as articulated by George F. Kennan in his famous "X" article. His prophetic book stands as an early milestone in the debate over U.S. cold war policies.

May, E. R. *"Lessons" of the Past: The Use and Misuse of History in American Foreign Policy* (2:22) demonstrates how the lessons of the 1930s—totalitarian aggression, Western appeasement, and world war—helped shape the Truman administration's attitudes, and thus its policies, toward the Soviet Union.

26:16 May, Ernest R. "The Cold War." In C. Vann Woodward, ed., *The Comparative Approach to American History*. New York: Basic Books, 1968, pp. 328–45. May reviews the first twenty years of the cold war, emphasizing the Truman period. He also draws parallels and contrasts between the American postwar experience and the experience of imperial nations of the past.

26:17 Neal, Fred Warner. "The Cold War in Europe, 1945–1967." In N. D. Houghton, ed., *Struggle against History: U.S. Foreign Policy in an Age of Revolution*. New York: Simon & Schuster, 1968, pp. 20–40. Focusing on the Truman years, Neal argues that a key factor in American policy was an obsession that the United States confronted a pressing Soviet military threat. Neal reexamines communist ideology, the Soviet takeover of Eastern Europe, postwar events in Greece and Turkey, and conflict over Germany, and concludes that the danger of Soviet military aggression never existed.

Paterson, T. G., ed. *Cold War Critics: Alternatives to American Foreign Policy in the Truman Years* (24:178) sheds light on the current scholarly debate over postwar foreign policy. The critics—ranging from Henry Wallace to Walter Lippmann to Robert Taft—came from diverse backgrounds and reflected different political orientations.

Paterson, T. G., ed. *Containment and the Cold War: American Foreign Policy since 1945* [1945–1972] (24:46).

26:18 Pruessen, Ronald W. "The Objectives of American Foreign Policy and the Nature of the Cold War." In Lynn H. Miller and Ronald W. Pruessen, eds., *Reflections on the Cold War: A Quarter Century*

of American Foreign Policy. Philadelphia: Temple University Press, 1974, pp. 27–55. Pruessen focuses on U.S. policy toward Europe and the Near East in the first half of 1947. The United States responded to economic stagnation on the basis of concerns about world trade and prosperity that predated the cold war. The shrill cold war rhetoric that accompanied America's response was employed to elicit congressional and public support for traditional political-economic objectives.

26:19 Reitzel, William; Kaplan, Morton A.; and Coblentz, Constance G. *United States Foreign Policy, 1945–1955*. Washington, D.C.: Brookings Institution, 1956. An early but careful history and critique of the first decade of postwar American foreign policy that suggests that while U.S. military and economic power increased during the period in question, overall influence in the world declined, though more from changes in the nature of the international system than from the actions of the Soviet Union. Bibliography.

Rose, L. A. *After Yalta* (25:20) maintains that the initial months found the Truman administration mired in vacillation and confusion. Rose regards the atomic bomb issue as the primary cause of the Soviet-American break.

Rostow, W. W. *The United States in the World Arena: An Essay in Recent History* (24:48) examines the interplay of domestic and foreign policies during the early cold war years.

26:20 Sander, Alfred D. "Truman and the National Security Council, 1945–1947." *Journal of American History* 59:2 (1972), 369–88. Truman, backed by the apprehensions of the White House Staff and the Bureau of the Budget, feared the council might encroach on the prerogatives of his office and give undue military weight to policy decisions. The council was made statutory by Congress in 1947, but Truman considered its actions as strictly advisory.

26:21 Tadashi, Amuga. "The United States and the Cold War: The Cold War Era in American History." In Yōnosuke Nagai and Akira Iriye, eds., *The Origins of the Cold War in Asia*. New York: Columbia University Press, 1977, pp. 66–88. The author sees the cold war as the last phase in a long first period of American history in which Americans combined simplistic images of the world with moral self-righteousness.

26:22 Yergin, Daniel. *Shattered Peace: The Origins of the Cold War and the National Security State*.

Boston: Houghton Mifflin, 1977. This elegantly written study of Soviet-American relations (1945–1948) is primarily concerned with big power diplomacy and the linkage between perception and behavior. Yergin places the burden of responsibility for the cold war on American officials who failed to understand Soviet intentions. Extensive bibliography. Compare with Hugh DeSantis's *Diplomacy of Silence: The American Foreign Service, the Soviet Union and the Cold War, 1933–1947* (2:164).

Soviet Policies

26:23 Brzezinski, Zbigniew K. *The Soviet Bloc: Unity and Conflict.* Rev. ed. Cambridge: Harvard University Press, 1971. This analysis of the origins and evolution of the Soviet empire in Eastern Europe examines five historical phases, treating the interplay of power and ideology in the relationships among communist states, and tracing the transformation of the bloc into an alliance system.

26:24 Dallin, Alexander, ed. *Soviet Conduct in World Affairs.* New York: Columbia University Press, 1960. These essays interpret the wellsprings of Soviet foreign policy, especially during the Stalinist period. The emphasis is on motive and intention.

26:25 Lederer, Ivo J., ed. *Russian Foreign Policy: Essays in Historical Perspective.* New Haven, Conn.: Yale University Press, 1962. The theme of these essays is the continuity between czarist and Soviet foreign policy. Topics covered include objectives, motivation, methods, and the formation and implementation of foreign policy; some authors emphasize the similarities, others the differences between the two systems. The essays are of uniformly high quality and provide an indispensable historical perspective on Soviet relations during the cold war period.

26:26 Mackintosh, J. M. *Strategy and Tactics of Soviet Foreign Policy.* New York: Oxford University Press, 1963. Mackintosh maintains that the goals of Soviet strategy since World War II have been communist world revolution, the quest for which was revived at the end of the war, and protection of the Soviet home base.

Mosely, P. E. *The Kremlin and World Politics: Studies in Soviet Policy and Action* (25:79) contains essays ranging from Soviet negotiating techniques to general aspects of Soviet expansion to Soviet and American policies in East Central Europe.

26:27 Ponomaryov, B., with Gromyko, A., and Khvostov, V., eds. *History of Soviet Foreign Policy, 1945–1970.* Moscow: Progress Publishers, 1974. This volume, the second in a history of Soviet foreign policy since the Bolshevik Revolution, provides the most comprehensive account available in English of the cold war from the Soviet point of view.

26:28 Seton-Watson, Hugh. *From Lenin to Khrushchev: The History of World Communism.* New York: Praeger, 1960. In this comparative analysis of communist movements, the author asserts that, between 1918 and 1953, international communism passed through seven distinct phases, each closely tied to a phase in the development of the Soviet Union.

Sivachev, N. V., and Yakovlev, N. N. *Russia and the United States: U.S.-Soviet Relations from the Soviet Point of View* (2:253) is written from the Soviet perspective.

26:29 Tucker, Robert, et al. "Postwar Soviet Foreign Policy: A World Perspective." *Journal of International Affairs* 8:1 (1954), 5–113. Robert Tucker, Philip Mosely, J. B. Hoptner, and others offer a contemporary yet sophisticated assessment of Soviet foreign policy after World War II.

Ulam, A. B. *Expansion and Coexistence: Soviet Foreign Policy, 1917–1973* (2:254) is an extensive study of the motives and workings of Soviet diplomacy since the Bolshevik Revolution, with emphasis on relations with the West.

26:30 U.S. House. Committee on Foreign Affairs. Staff Report; *Soviet Diplomacy and Negotiating Behavior: Emerging New Context for U.S. Diplomacy.* Washington, D.C.: G.P.O., 1979. This work studies Soviet negotiating behavior from the post–World War I period through SALT II. The authors argue that Russian diplomats have been obsessed with security, controlled by rigid bureaucratic instructions, and motivated by their revolutionary belief that the bargaining process is war by political means.

Welch, W. *American Images of Soviet Foreign Policy: An Inquiry in Recent Appraisals from the Academic Community* (29:14) undertakes a critical evaluation of American literature on Soviet foreign policy, examining the contents and scholarly merits of twenty-two books on the subject by prominent experts on Soviet affairs. The books are classified according to the image they project of Soviet policy—the Great Beast, the Mellowing Tiger, the Neurotic Bear.

26:31 Werth, Alexander. *Russia: The Postwar Years*. New York: Taplinger, 1971. This work seeks to examine the early cold war years (1945–1948) from a Soviet perspective. Emphasis is not just on the collapse of the wartime coalition but also on the creation of Stalin's empire in Eastern Europe. Stalin responded to Western provocations that were unnecessary and which would not have occurred but for Roosevelt's death.

26:32 Wesson, Robert G. *Soviet Foreign Policy in Perspective*. Homewood, Ill.: Dorsey, 1969. The duality of Soviet foreign policy, i.e., expansion and coexistence, and the influence of domestic requirements on that policy, are the underlying themes of this survey. Bibliography.

Special Studies

Dennett, R., and Johnson, J. E., eds. *Negotiating with the Russians* (25:73) focuses more on the technique and process of negotiating than on substantive issues. Most of the contributors agree that Soviet-American negotiations are rarely productive unless the international political climate is favorable.

26:33 Wright, Theodore P., Jr. "The Origins of the Free Elections Dispute in the Cold War." *Western Political Quarterly* 14:4 (1961), 850–64. Wright traces the roots of the "free elections" issue between the United States and the Soviet Union and shows how it developed into the most persistent and publicized Western demand in the cold war.

Politics and Public Opinion

See also "Politics, Anticommunism, and Foreign Policy," below.

Adler, L. K., and Paterson, T. G. "Red Fascism: The Merger of Nazi Germany and Soviet Russia in the American Image of Totalitarianism, 1930's–1950's" (22:98) finds that many Americans both before and after World War II drew an analogy between Nazi Germany and the Soviet Union. The analogy derived from the seeming similarities between the two systems and failed to consider differences in origins, ideologies, goals, and practices. The result significantly shaped American perceptions of world events during the cold war.

Buckley, G. J. "American Public Opinion and the Origins of the Cold War: A Speculative Assessment" (25:122) argues that much of the prewar hostility toward "Red Russia" persisted in the minds of many Americans, causing them to temper their hopes for cooperation with a suspicion and fear of Soviet intentions. These mixed emotions created a "permissive" atmosphere in which U.S. policymakers could "get tough" with the Russians.

26:34 Doenecke, Justus D. *Not to the Swift: The Old Isolationists in the Cold War Era*. Lewisburg, Pa.: Bucknell University Press, 1979. This account traces the isolationists (1943–1954) from their refusal to accept wartime "internationalism" to Eisenhower's election, the defeat of the Bricker amendment, the censure of McCarthy. Extensive bibliography.

Gerson, L. L. *The Hyphenate in Recent American Politics and Diplomacy* (2:203) treats the election of 1948, the Soviet Union and Slavic Americans, and the debate over liberation and containment in the context of "The Cold War and the Hyphenate Consensus."

26:35 LaFeber, Walter. "American Policy-Makers, Public Opinion, and the Outbreak of the Cold War, 1945–1950." In Yōnosuke Nagi and Akira Iriye, eds., *The Origins of the Cold War in Asia*. New York: Columbia University Press, 1977, pp. 43–65. Between 1945 and 1950, the cold war orientation of American foreign policy was determined by a small number of executive branch officials who, in pursuit of their objectives, encountered little in the way of resistance from Congress or from an at first indifferent, then supportive, public.

26:36 Rourke, John T. "Congress and the Cold War." *World Affairs* 139:4 (1977), 259–77. Rourke examines the role of Congress in the formulation of foreign policy (1945–1948). Using the British loan, the Truman Doctrine, and the Marshall Plan as illustrations, he concludes that the administration had to resort to hyperbolic rhetoric to gain congressional support for necessary programs. This in turn led to U.S. excesses and diplomatic rigidity.

Westerfield, H. B. *Foreign Policy and Party Politics: Pearl Harbor to Korea* (2:155) examines three ways to achieve democratic control of foreign policy: partisanship, bipartisanship, and extrapartisanship. Among the specific subjects dealt with in this perspective are U.S. programs for postwar Europe and the decline in Soviet-American relations.

East-West Trade

Holzman, F. D. *International Trade under Communism: Politics and Economics* [1945–1975] (39:78).

Mikesell, R. F., and Behrman, J. N. *Financing Free World Trade with the Sino-Soviet Bloc* [1945–1958] (36:79) argues that the post-1945 era was marked by a growing multilateralism of trade and the devising of new means to pay for it. Tables.

Sutton, A. C. *Western Technology and Soviet Economic Development, 1917–1965* (20:204) argues, in volume 3, that Western assistance has been vital to Soviet progress.

Uren, P. E., ed. *East-West Trade: A Symposium* [1945–1966] (29:171) is valuable as a Canadian viewpoint. The volume discusses broad issues such as the effects of state bureaucracy, state purchases, and legal restraints. After a general overview of relations since 1945, Uren contributes an important paper on strategic aspects of East-West trade.

Wilczynski, J. *The Economics and Politics of East-West Trade* (29:172) provides a rather technical discussion of exchange rates, socialist theory of trade, dumping, the politics of grain trade, strategic export controls, and arbitration arrangements.

Personalities

Additional references on individuals may be found in Chapter 1, "Biographical Data"; also see Chapter 24, "Personalities" and "Presidential Administrations."

AMERICAN

Dean Acheson

See Chapter 24, "Personalities," for additional references.

Acheson, D. *Present at the Creation: My Years in the State Department* (24:90) is essential for an understanding of the man and his policies.

Smith, G. *Dean Acheson* (24:95) is a thoughtful account of Acheson's tenure as secretary of state (1949–1953).

Bernard Baruch

26:37 Baruch, Bernard M. *Baruch*. 2 vols. New York: Holt, Rinehart & Winston, 1957–1960. These are the memoirs of the U.S. representative on the United Nations Atomic Energy Commission (1946–1947), and perennial "adviser to Presidents." The second volume, composed when Baruch was 90, covers his career from World War I through the cold war, but adds little to Coit's account of his post-1945 role.

26:38 Coit, Margaret L. *Mr. Baruch*. Boston: Houghton Mifflin, 1957. Coit concludes that Baruch became the victim of his own self-cultivated image; that he would have had greater influence had he been willing to risk failure by assuming public responsibilities.

Charles E. Bohlen

See Chapter 29, "Personalities," for additional references.

Bohlen, C. E. *Witness to History: 1929–1969* (24:98) covers Bohlen's involvement in American-Russian relations over a period of three decades. His treatment of the Truman period looks at Potsdam and the foreign ministers' conferences, the Berlin blockade, and the Korean War. Interspersed with his insights into Soviet policy are vivid character portraits of such cold war personages as Truman, Stalin, Marshall, Byrnes, and Acheson.

26:39 Harrington, Daniel F. "Kennan, Bohlen, and the Riga Axioms." *Diplomatic History* 2:4 (1978), 423–37. Harrington challenges Daniel Yergin's assertion (26:22) that Kennan and Bohlen were leading proponents of the Riga axioms (i.e., the Soviet Union as a revolutionary state bent on world domination). Neither Kennan nor Bohlen viewed communist ideology as the determinant of Soviet foreign policy, saw Russia as having a "grand design" for world conquest, or believed negotiations with Soviet leaders pointless.

Mark, E. "Charles E. Bohlen and the Acceptable Limits of Soviet Hegemony in Eastern Europe: A Memorandum of 18 October 1945" (25:101).

26:40 Ruddy, T. Michael. "Realist versus Realist: Bohlen, Kennan and the Inception of the Cold War." *Midwest Quarterly* 17:2 (1976), 122–41. George F.

Kennan and Charles E. Bohlen held similar beliefs concerning Soviet ideas and actions after World War II. However, Kennan "was a theorist and a pessimist," while Bohlen "was an optimist and a man of action."

James F. Byrnes

See Chapter 24, "Personalities," for additional references.

Curry, G. *James F. Byrnes* (24:102) is a balanced assessment of Byrnes's career as secretary of state (1945–1947). For another treatment, see Robert L. Messer's *The End of an Alliance: James F. Byrnes, Roosevelt, Truman and the Origins of the Cold War* (Chapel Hill: University of North Carolina Press, 1982). Messer views Byrnes as a transition figure, a sensitive indicator of shifting opinion with the American foreign policy hierarchy.

26:41 Gormly, James L. "Secretary of State James F. Byrnes, an Initial British Evalutation." *South Carolina Historical Magazine* 79:3 (1978), 198–205. This account reproduces the report of Lord Halifax, British ambassador to the United States, concerning James F. Byrnes, and discusses British estimates of his competence (1945–1946).

Lucius D. Clay

See also Chapter 27, "Personalities."

26:42 Clay, Lucius D. *Decision in Germany*. Garden City, N.Y.: Doubleday, 1950. A history of the American occupation, this book is written by the former U.S. military governor. The account is less interesting than the published collection of Clay's papers and also diverges from them in significant respects. This is a most important book, which casts light on interpretive questions.

26:43 Clay, Lucius D. *The Papers of General Lucius D. Clay: Germany, 1945–1949*. 2 vols. Ed. by Jean Edward Smith. Bloomington: Indiana University Press, 1974. This collection of General Clay's papers is important for Clay's analysis of French actions, his differences with the State Department, and his interpretation of Soviet intentions.

John Foster Dulles

See Chapters 24 and 27, "Personalities," for additional references.

26:44 Dulles, John Foster. "Thoughts on Soviet Foreign Policy and What to Do About It." *Life*

Magazine 20:22/23 (1946), 113–26, 118–30. Dulles was one of the first American statesmen to go public with an analysis of postwar Soviet foreign policy and a prescription for how the United States should respond to it.

26:45 Dulles, John Foster. *War or Peace*. New York: Macmillan, 1950. Dulles describes the Soviet threat in ideological terms, and assesses the strengths and weaknesses of postwar American policies designed to counter communist expansion and revolution. The book was written for a popular audience; nevertheless, it offers illuminating details on Dulles's early activities as a diplomat and supporter of bipartisanship.

James Forrestal

26:46 Forrestal, James. *The Forrestal Diaries*. Ed. by Walter Millis. New York: Viking, 1951. The diaries (1944–1949) contain accounts of cabinet meetings, high-level deliberations, informal conversations, etc. The hard-line anticommunism which guided Forrestal's policy recommendations as secretary of the navy and secretary of defense colors the discussion of issues and events.

26:47 Rogow, Arnold A. *James Forrestal: A Study of Personality, Politics, and Policy*. New York: Macmillan, 1963. An early, but still the most complete, biography of the first secretary of defense. Emphasis is on the events leading up to Forrestal's suicide in 1949.

W. Averell Harriman

See Chapters 24 and 25, "Personalities," for references.

George F. Kennan

See Chapters 22, 24, and 29, "Personalities," for additional references; see also "Defining Containment," below.

26:48 Coffey, John W. "George Kennan and the Ambiguities of Realism." *South Atlantic Quarterly* 73:2 (1974), 184–98. Kennan was not consistent in his writings about the meaning of containment or the fundamental nature of the cold war. The inconsistency stemmed not from his inability to communicate his ideas effectively but from the ambiguity of the doctrine of realism to which he subscribed. Realism, Coffey argues, offers no clear and consistent explanation of international developments.

Harrington, D. F. "Kennan, Bohlen, and the Riga Axioms" (26:39).

Kennan, G. F. *Memoirs* (24:124) offers thoughtful observations on such topics as his "Long Telegram" from Moscow, the Truman Doctrine and the Marshall Plan, his "X" article, Germany, and NATO. He laments that the policy of limited, political containment of Soviet expansionism which he advocated became under Truman and his successors an over-militarized, overextended, unduly rigid doctrine, with all too often disastrous consequences for U.S. foreign policy.

26:49 "X" [George F. Kennan]. "The Sources of Soviet Conduct." *Foreign Affairs* 25:4 (1947), 566–82. In this widely read, controversial article, Kennan analyzes the psychological, institutional, historical, and ideological roots of the "political personality of Soviet power." That power, Kennan argues, would expand wherever it was permitted to do so; free societies could contain the Soviet threat to their institutions "by the adroit and vigilant application of counter-force at a series of constantly shifting geographical and political points. . . ." The "X" article was received by the American public as the basic premises underlying the Truman administration's Russian policies.

Arthur Bliss Lane

26:50 Cable, J. N. "Arthur Bliss Lane: Cold Warrior in Warsaw, 1945–1947." *Polish American Studies* 30:2 (1973), 66–82. The U.S. ambassador to Poland, Lane had compassion for the Polish people and a desire to save them from communism. But his thinly veiled hatred of the communist Lublin regime only made a difficult situation worse, and his anti-Soviet rhetoric circumscribed opportunities for the United States to influence events in Poland.

26:51 Lane, Arthur Bliss. *I Saw Poland Betrayed.* Indianapolis: Bobbs-Merrill, 1948. Bliss was U.S. ambassador to Poland (1945–1947), and writes of the communist takeover that occurred there. He is critical of American and Allied policies.

26:52 Petrov, Vladimir. *A Study in Diplomacy: The Story of Arthur Bliss Lane.* Chicago: Regnery, 1971. A detailed account of a career diplomat who served in Nicaragua (1933–1936), Yugoslavia, and Poland. Lane, disillusioned by events in Poland after World War II, resigned so he could protest publicly the course of events in that country. This is an interesting

study of the relations between a diplomat and the Department of State.

George C. Marshall
See Chapters 23, 24, and 27, "Personalities," for additional references.

Ferrell, R. H. *George C. Marshall* (24:140) is the complete assessment to date of Marshall's term as secretary of state.

Joseph McCarthy
See Chapter 24, "Personalities," for additional references.

26:53 Cohn, Roy. *McCarthy.* New York: New American Library, 1968. A former associate's ambivalent assessment, it concludes that while not without fault, "McCarthy used the best methods available to him to fight a battle that needed to be fought."

26:54 Matusow, Allen J., ed. *Joseph R. McCarthy.* Englewood Cliffs, N.J.: Prentice-Hall, 1970. An edited collection of writings by and about McCarthy, it provides a useful introduction and bibliographical note.

Reeves, T. C. "McCarthyism: Interpretations since Hofstadter" (24:142) is a careful review of the literature.

26:55 Rovere, Richard. *Senator Joe McCarthy.* Cleveland: World, 1959. In this early but influential biography, an experienced journalist concludes that McCarthy was "a species of nihilist; he was an essentially destructive force, a revolutionist without any revolutionary vision, a rebel without a cause."

Robert A. Taft
See also Chapters 24 and 25, "Personalities."

26:56 Armstrong, John P. "The Enigma of Senator Taft and Foreign Policy." *Review of Politics* 17:2 (1955), 206–31. Taft believed that an active foreign policy would endanger a sound domestic policy, but according to the author Taft failed to understand that domestic liberty had as its prior condition national security.

26:57 Berger, Henry W. "Senator Robert A. Taft Dissents from Military Escalation." In Thomas G. Paterson, ed., *Cold War Critics: Alternatives to American Foreign Policy in the Truman Years.* Chicago: Quadrangle, 1971, pp. 167–204. Berger develops Taft's objections to the Truman administration's strategy and tactics toward overseas objectives. Taft objected to actions which could limit America's freedom of choice abroad and involve the United States in war, and might compromise basic American values.

Patterson, J. T. *Mr. Republican: A Biography of Robert A. Taft* 24:154) is a carefully argued biography of a prominent conservative critic.

Harry S. Truman

See Chapter 24, "Personalities," and "The Truman Years," for additional references.

Cochran, B. *Harry Truman and the Crisis Presidency* (24:193) focuses on the major problems and events surrounding the Truman administration, and on Truman's political personality and leadership ability. Cochran faults Truman for failing to reach accommodation with the Soviet Union, to take serious steps toward arms control, to come to terms with independence movements in Asia, and to set up a workable economic relationship with the rest of the world.

Donovan, R. J. *Conflict and Crisis: The Presidency of Harry S. Truman, 1945–1948* (24:194) covers Truman's first term in the White House. Donovan's focal point is the White House, where consideration of foreign policy matters could not be insulated from the impingement of domestic crises or from the frenetic pace and myriad demands which characterized day-to-day life in the Oval Office.

Druks, H. M. *Harry S. Truman and the Russians, 1945–1953* (26:14).

Griffith, R. "Truman and the Historians: The Reconstruction of Postwar American History" (24:189) reviews the historical literature on President Truman's foreign policy, including changing interpretations and evaluations of the Marshall Plan, Truman Doctrine, Point Four, atomic diplomacy, the Korean War, containment, and the origins of the cold war.

26:58 Hamby, Alonzo L. *Beyond the New Deal: Harry S. Truman and American Liberalism.* New York: Columbia University Press, 1973. In a sympathetic account of the Truman presidency and of the impact of the cold war on American politics, Hamby praises Truman for defending the New Deal and adapting it to the altered circumstances of the postwar era.

26:59 Hensley, Carl W. "Harry S. Truman: Fundamental Americanism in Foreign Policy Speechmaking, 1945–1946." *Southern Speech Communication Journal* 40:2 (1975), 180–90. Hensley maintains that an analysis of Truman's speeches (1945–1946) indicates that the president sought to construct a foreign policy based on "fundamental Americanism," i.e., the belief in freedom as a natural right for all people. The rhetoric of Truman's early speeches provided the basis for the Truman Doctrine and subsequent cold war proclamations.

Miscamble, W. D. "The Evolution of an Internationalist: Harry S. Truman and American Foreign Policy" (38:52) looks at Truman's career as a senator in order to examine the development and nature of Truman's commitment to the internationalist cause. As a senator, Truman became an advocate of U.S. preparedness and a strong proponent of U.S. membership in the United Nations.

Arthur H. Vandenberg

See Chapters 24 and 25, "Personalities," for additional references.

Cable, J. N. "Vandenberg: The Polish Question and Polish Americans, 1944–1948" (25:37).

26:60 Hill, Thomas M. "Senator Arthur H. Vandenberg, The Politics of Bipartisanship, and the Origins of Anti-Soviet Consensus, 1941–1946." *World Affairs* 138:3 (1975–1976), 219–41. Hill analyzes Vandenberg's policy of bipartisanship, his isolationism followed by interventionism after Pearl Harbor, and the impact of these policies on the anti-Soviet consensus.

26:61 Hudson, Daryl J. "Vandenberg Reconsidered: Senate Resolution 239 and American Foreign Policy." *Diplomatic History* 1:1 (1977), 46–63. Hudson points to the private negotiations leading up to the Vandenberg resolution as evidence of Vandenberg's influence on the policymaking process and as support for the conclusion that the senator was a "major influence in determining American policy toward Europe and the United Nations in 1948."

Vandenberg, A. H., Jr., ed. *The Private Papers of Senator Vandenberg* (24:162) contains papers pertaining to the Truman years, covering Vandenberg's role as a practitioner of bipartisanship, his views on the communist threat, and his influence on the making of foreign policy.

Henry A. Wallace

See Chapter 24, "Personalities," for additional references.

26:62 Hamby, Alonzo L. "Henry A. Wallace, the Liberals, and Soviet-American Relations." *Review of Politics* 30:2 (1968), 153–69. A study of the relationship of Henry Agard Wallace (1888–1965) to the American liberal movement during and after World War II, it discusses the process by which Wallace moved from unquestioned leadership of the liberals in 1945 to a position on the fringe of liberal politics in 1948.

Markowitz, N. D. *The Rise and Fall of the People's Century: Henry A. Wallace and American Liberalism, 1941–1948* (24:163) is the first scholarly account of the unsuccessful Progressive party "peace campaign" of 1948. Henry Wallace had been long in disfavor among politicians and historians for his sharp criticism of the emerging cold war.

26:63 Wallace, Henry A. *Toward World Peace.* New York: Reynal & Hitchcock, 1948. This campaign publication sets forth Wallace's critique of Truman's cold war policies and presents a program for "peace without appeasement."

26:64 Walton, Richard J. *Henry Wallace, Harry Truman, and the Cold War.* New York: Viking, 1976. A favorable account of Wallace and the 1948 presidential campaign, it argues that the Progressive party platform anticipated most of the positions on domestic and foreign issues held by the liberal community in the late 1960s and early 1970s. "Henry Wallace was essentially right," the author concludes, "and Harry Truman was essentially and tragically wrong." Bibliography.

Others

Gardner, L. C. *Architects of Illusion: Men and Ideas in American Foreign Policy, 1941–1949* (25:17) looks into the activities of such leaders as Byrnes, Clayton, Acheson, Clay, Forrestal, and Kennan, who fashioned American policies toward Europe. Gardner concludes that their policies lacked wisdom.

26:65 Hughes, H. Stuart. "The Second Year of the Cold War: A Memoir and an Anticipation." *Commentary* 48:2 (1969), 27–32. Hughes observes that, while the revisionists have rightly attacked the cold war mentality of many American policy makers, "something of the feel and taste of the late 1940s has slipped into oblivion." Hughes recalls his own experience as a middle-level State Department official (1946–1947) during which time he and his colleagues sought a middle course between armed hostility and a cordial modus vivendi with the Soviet Union.

26:66 Jones, Joseph M. *The Fifteen Weeks.* New York: Viking, 1955. Jones was a State Department official (February–June 1947) when the Truman Doctrine was proclaimed, the policy of containment implemented, and the Marshall Plan formulated. His detailed narrative of those frenetic days captures the drama of the decisions and behind-the-scenes preparations.

Koskoff, D. *Joseph P. Kennedy: A Life and Times* (22:27) finds that Kennedy, by 1947, opposed both the Truman Doctrine and the Marshall Plan. The outbreak of war in Korea caused Kennedy to argue that U.S. "giveaway" programs had not "solved" anything.

Murphy, R. D. *Diplomat among Warriors* (23:77) covers his years as political adviser to General Clay during the occupation of Germany and the Berlin crisis.

Pearson, Drew. *Drew Pearson Diaries, 1949–1959* (24:179).

26:67 Smith, Walter Bedell. *My Three Years in Moscow.* Philadelphia: Lippincott, 1950. Smith, U.S. ambassador to the Soviet Union (1946–1949), offers his observations on life in the Soviet Union, on Soviet leaders, intentions, and policies, and on key cold war developments during his tenure of duty.

Strauss, L. L. *Men and Decisions* (24:183) is important for both the hydrogen bomb decision and the Oppenheimer case. Strauss was chairman of the Atomic Energy Commission.

EUROPEAN

Clement R. Attlee

See also Chapter 28, under "Personalities."

Attlee, C. R. *As It Happened* (23:89).

Joseph V. Stalin

See Chapters 21, 25, and 26, "Personalities," for additional references.

26:68 Diplomaticus. "Stalinist Theory and Soviet Foreign Policy." *Review of Politics* 14:4 (1952), 468–83. Provides a frame of reference which can be used to judge Soviet behavior. The author divides Stalinist theory into three categories, theses, strategy, and tactics, and shows the influence of each of Stalin's policies.

26:69 Djilas, Milovan. *Conversations with Stalin.* New York: Harcourt, Brace & World, 1962. Djilas, a Yugoslav communist official at the time of his three trips to Moscow (1944–1948), describes his disillusionment with the Soviet Union as a result of his encounter with "Soviet reality." Djilas's portrait of Stalin's personality and behavior, and his account of Stalin's pronouncements on world affairs, especially on Soviet-East European relations and on Soviet relations with the West, cannot be overlooked.

26:70 Historicus [George A. Morgan]. *Foreign Affairs* 27:2 (1949), 175–214. Morgan stresses the importance of theory as a determinant of Stalin's policies. Stalin's theory of revolution allowed for tactical retreat, but the Marxist doctrine of world revolution to which he was committed remained steadfast. World communism was Stalin's supreme aim; the power of the Soviet state was the instrument he used in pursuit of that objective.

26:71 Shulman, Marshall D. *Stalin's Foreign Policy Reappraised.* Cambridge: Harvard University Press, 1963. This book analyzes the dynamics of Soviet foreign policy during Stalin's last years. Shulman maintains that the "peaceful coexistence" theme associated with the post-Stalinist leadership actually had begun to take shape as early as 1949. The new "Right" policy did not, however, aim at permanent rapprochement with the West but sought to adapt Soviet policy to the historical circumstances of the period.

26:72 Warth, Robert D. "Stalin and the Cold War." *South Atlantic Quarterly* 59:1 (1960), 1–12. Stalin for all his defects was no romantic revolutionary but a skilled and cautious politician whose postwar strategy in Europe sought Soviet security by hobbling Germany and establishing a sphere of influence in Eastern Europe. Negotiations between the Soviet Union and the West might have been productive had the United States been more realistic in its position on the Soviet presence in Eastern Europe.

Josip Broz-Tito

26:73 Auty, Phyllis. *Tito: A Biography.* New York: McGraw-Hill, 1970. This is a substantial scholarly contribution by a British authority on Yugoslavian affairs.

Dedijer, V. *The Battle Stalin Lost: Memoirs of Yugoslavia, 1948–1953* (26:117).

26:74 Maclean, Fitzroy. *The Heretic: The Life and Times of Josip Broz-Tito.* New York: Harper, 1957. A biography that deals with Tito's politics through the break with Stalin.

Robertson, W. R. *Tito, Mihailovic and the Allies, 1941–1945* (23:251).

Others

26:75 Mastny, Vojtech. "The Cassandra in the Foreign Commissariat." *Foreign Affairs* 54:2 (1975), 366–76. Toward the end of his career Maxim Litvinov (1876–1951) tantalized foreigners by expressing dissent from his government's official line. However, there was no quarrel with Joseph Stalin about advancing the goals of the U.S.S.R. by whatever means necessary, but only about the fitness of the different means.

Williams, F. *Ernest Bevin: Portrait of a Great Englishman* (28:38).

General Diplomatic Issues

U.S. AND GERMANY

See "Personalities," especially James F. Byrnes, Lucius D. Clay, Robert D. Murphy (under "Others"); also see Chapter 25, "The German Question."

26:76 Grosser, Alfred. *The Colossus Again: Western Germany from Defeat to Rearmament.* Trans. by Richard Rees. New York: Praeger, 1955. This unusually even-handed discussion of the evolution of West Germany (1945–1954), written from a German perspective, emphasizes the role of the United States and the other occupying powers in shaping the social, economic, moral, and political conditions in postwar Germany.

26:77 Middleton, Drew. *The Struggle for Germany.* Indianapolis: Bobbs-Merrill, 1949. An important journalistic account of American activities in postwar Germany, this book analyzes U.S. economic and social policy, and chronicles the disintegration of the wartime alliance between the United States and the Soviet Union.

26:78 Warburg, James P. *Germany: Key to Peace.* Cambridge: Harvard University Press, 1953. Covering the period of U.S.-German relations from 1946 to 1953, Warburg concludes that American policies were wrong and that Truman's containment policy failed. Warburg was especially fearful of the consequences of rearming Germany. Bibliography.

Occupation Policies (Including Austria)

26:79 Bach, Julian, Jr. *America's Germany: An Account of the Occupation.* New York: Random House, 1946. Written by an American military correspondent in Germany (1945), these personal observations optimistically report that American occupation policies, in the first year, seemed to be working successfully. It is a good example of the early American idealism.

26:80 Backer, John. *Priming the German Economy: American Occupation Policies, 1945–48.* Durham, N.C.: Duke University Press, 1971. This is a detailed presentation of the U.S. effort to restore the German economy. The author, a former participant in military government, poses few critical questions about activities of American officials resurrecting the German industrial structure. Backer is valuable for the Joint Export-Import Agency.

26:81 Balabkins, Nicholas. *Germany under Direct Controls: Economic Aspects of Industrial Disarmament.* New Brunswick, N.J.: Rutgers University Press, 1964. This book examines the American and British program for the industrial disarmament of Germany and evaluates the impact of this program on the economic life of the two zones. Balabkins pays particular attention to controls on coal and steel production.

26:82 Balfour, Michael, and Main, John. *Four-Power Control in Germany and Austria, 1945–1946.* London: Oxford University Press, 1956. Written by British writers, this volume is based largely on the public record and personal involvements. It is volume 8 in the *Survey of International Affairs.*

26:83 Davidson, Eugene. *The Death and Life of Germany: An Account of the American Occupation.* New York: Knopf, 1959. The book discusses the American role in Germany (1945–1955). It follows its subject through to the mid-1950s, where most works end with the establishment of the Federal Republic in 1949. This study is wide in scope, but weak on interpretation. Bibliography.

26:84 Davis, Franklin M., Jr. *Come as a Conqueror: The United States Army's Occupation of Germany, 1945–1949.* New York: Macmillan, 1967. A good introduction to the U.S. Army's role in the German occupation by a former military officer, it is based largely on personal observation. It deals with the army, not the military government.

Feis, H. *From Trust to Terror: The Onset of the Cold War, 1945–50* (26:8) is specifically concerned with the German problem. The work contains one of the more sophisticated versions of the anti-Soviet analysis.

26:85 Gardner, Lloyd. "America and the German 'Problem,' 1945–49." In Barton J. Bernstein, ed., *Politics and Policies of the Truman Administration.* Chicago: Quadrangle, 1970, pp. 113–49. Gardner offers a relatively sympathetic, though brief discussion of the Soviet approach. He gives more attention than is usually paid to American apprehensions about the British, the French, and the German Socialists as potential adversaries of U.S. policy.

26:86 Gimbel, John. "American Military Government and the Education of a New Leadership." *Political Science Quarterly* 83:2 (1968), 248–67. This article explains the limitations of the American effort to create a democratic leadership in postwar Germany. Focusing on the American treatment of the German länderrat, Gimbel shows how other priorities superseded the American commitment to democratization.

26:87 Gimbel, John. *The American Occupation of Germany: Politics and the Military 1945–49.* Stanford, Calif.: Stanford University Press, 1968. Still the classic, this book is an unsurpassed discussion of the

American occupation. The author was given special access to military records. The book illuminates the relationship between the Americans and the Germans (1945–1949). Extensive bibliography.

26:88 Gimbel, John. "The Artificial Revolution in Germany." *Political Science Quarterly* 76:1 (1961), 88–104. Responding to Montgomery's *Forced to Be Free,* Gimbel probes the question of whether an outside power can produce a democratic revolution within another society. He bases his conclusions on data gathered for the German town of Marburg. This is an important, provocative article.

26:89 Gimbel, John. "On the Implementation of the Potsdam Agreement: An Essay on U.S. Postwar German Policy." *Political Science Quarterly* 87:2 (1972), 242–69. Gimbel examines Secretary of State James F. Byrnes's Stuttgart speech (September 6, 1946) to explain U.S. policy in Germany, Europe, and the cold war. This speech supports few of the conclusions that historians have drawn from it.

26:90 Herz, John H. "The Failure of De-Nazification in Germany." *Political Science Quarterly* 83:4 (1968), 569–94. A useful examination of the evolution of American denazification policy (May 1945–March 1948), the article provides a chronological description of the different stages of the American approach, and employs military government statistics to argue that the Americans failed to denazify their zone.

26:91 Kelly, M. A. "The Reconstruction of the German Trade Union Movement." *Political Science Quarterly* 64:1 (1949), 24–46. This article provides an overview of the role of the Allied governments in promoting the development of trade unions under the occupation. The essay is superficial, nevertheless, as one of the few sources in English, it is worth consulting.

26:92 Litchfield, Eduard, ed. *Governing Post-War Germany.* Ithaca, N.Y.: Cornell University Press, 1953. These essays exploring the political aspects of military government, edited by the former director of the Civil Affairs Division in Germany, discuss U.S. political aims and probe the effect of the occupation on the new West German political institutions.

26:93 Martin, James S. *All Honorable Men.* Boston: Little, Brown, 1950. Written by the former head of the decartelization branch of the Office of Military Government, this is a fine survey of the American decartelization program. This book offers insights into

U.S. economic policy for Germany, and the relationship between that policy and emerging difficulty on the Allied Control Council.

26:94 Merritt, Richard L. "American Influences in the Occupation of Germany." *Annals of the American Academy of Political and Social Science,* no. 428 (1976), 91–103. The author concludes that denazification was successfully carried out by the United States, but that democratization was neglected as the cold war made it necessary to strengthen Germany.

26:95 Montgomery, John D. *Forced to Be Free: The Artificial Revolution in Germany and Japan.* Chicago: University of Chicago Press, 1957. This account of the American democratization program in Germany and Japan contends that the program was ineffective in key respects. Since the author fails to locate the democratization effort within the wider framework of overall American objectives for Germany, his analysis is weak.

26:96 Peterson, Edward N. *The American Occupation of Germany: Retreat to Victory.* Detroit: Wayne State University Press, 1978. This critical study of the American occupation has a wide focus and ranges from a discussion of policy formation at the top of the military hierarchy to implementation at the local level. Bibliography.

26:97 Schmitt, Hans A., ed. *US Occupation in Europe after World War II.* Lawrence: Regents Press of Kansas, 1978. These uneven papers, by experts on the American occupation of Germany and Austria, include a summary of a round-table discussion among high-level participants in military government. Most has been presented elsewhere, but the volume does pinpoint some of the major historiographical disagreements.

26:98 Slusser, Robert, ed. *Soviet Economic Policy in Postwar Germany.* New York: Research Program on the U.S.S.R., 1953. These essays by former Soviet officials include discussions on confiscation and dismantling of German industry, the Soviet administration, agricultural policy, and the uranium mining activities in Saxony.

Toynbee, A. J., and Toynbee, V. M., eds. *The Realignment of Europe* (25:13) deals with events in Europe following the collapse of Germany (1945–1946). It describes the initial steps toward economic rehabilitation and the expansion of Soviet control over Eastern Europe.

26:99 Warburg, James P. *Germany: Bridge or Battleground?* New York: Harcourt, Brace, 1947. Warburg was a severe critic of American policy toward Germany and wrote in order to change it. Despite this overtly political intention, the book makes excellent use of the available sources and offers a clear, stimulating analysis of the interrelations of the occupying powers in postwar Germany.

26:100 deZayas, Alfred M. "The Legality of Mass Population Transfers: The German Experience 1945–48." *East European Quarterly* 12:1 (1978), 1–23; 12:2 (1978), 143–60. Although Churchill and Truman tried to limit expulsions, they acquiesced in the tragic transfer of millions, which resulted in, among other things, two million civilian deaths.

26:101 deZayas, Alfred M. *Nemesis at Potsdam: The Anglo-Americans and the Expulsion of the Germans*. Rev. ed. London: Routledge & Kegan Paul, 1979. In a bitter indictment of the United States, Britain, and the Soviet Union, the author recounts the forced transfer of some 15 million Germans (1945–1949), resulting in two million deaths, from eastern German provinces. Bibliography.

26:102 Ziemke, Earl F. *The U.S. Army in the Occupation of Germany, 1944–1946*. Washington, D.C.: Center of Military History, 1975. In this official military history, Ziemke examines the army's role in Germany during the war and in the early period of the occupation. A thorough work, it sidesteps major controversy. Bibliography.

26:103 Zink, Harold. *The United States in Germany, 1944–55*. Englewood Cliffs, N.J.: Van Nostrand, 1957. This comprehensive study of U.S. occupation policy in Germany, written by the first chief historian of the U.S. High Commission in Germany, presents new information on a variety of subjects. These include the organization and structure of military government, civil-military relations, and the functioning of OMGUS in the areas of politics, economics, and culture.

Reparations Issue

See Chapter 25, "German Reparations Question."

26:104 Gimbel, John. "The American Reparations Stop in Germany: An Essay on the Political Use of History." *Historian* 37:2 (1975), 276–96. Gimbel concludes that the suspension of reparations deliveries

from the American zone in Germany (May 3, 1946) was not an anti-Soviet act as such, but a reaction to French refusals to treat Germany as a single economic unit.

Kuklick, B. *American Policy and the Division of Germany: The Clash with Russia over Reparations* (25:147) is the only revisionist book devoted to U.S. policy in postwar Germany. The book is the preeminent work on the reparations dispute. Since the author's research is largely confined to this issue, his effort to provide an overall explanation for German disunity is less compelling. Bibliography.

26:105 Lasby, Clarence G. *Project Paperclip: German Scientists and the Cold War*. New York: Atheneum, 1971. This volume treats a much neglected aspect of the reparations question. It provides a fascinating account of the removal of German scientists and technicians to America for industrial and military use.

26:106 Ratchford, B. U., and Ross, William D. *Berlin Reparations Assignment: Round One of the German Peace Settlement*. Chapel Hill: University of North Carolina, 1947. This firsthand account of the development of the reparations issue (September 1945–March 1946) is a basic source. Certain of their ideas seem dated, yet the volume contains useful information.

Reunification Issue

See Chapter 25, "The German Question," for the decision to divide Germany into zones.

Backer, J. H. *The Decision to Divide Germany: American Foreign Policy in Transition* (25:83) is the most recent scholarly attempt to explore the sources of German partition. The author argues that U.S. policymakers misunderstood Soviet intentions. Backer's use of social science jargon detracts from this useful account.

26:107 Hartmann, Frederick H. *Germany between East and West: The Reunification Problem*. Englewood Cliffs, N.J.: Prentice-Hall, 1965. A conventional account of the reunification problem (1945–1963), it discusses the issue from the German as well as the great power perspective. The bibliography is inadequate.

26:108 Nehl, J. P. *The Eastern Zone and Soviet Policy in Germany, 1945–50.* New York: Oxford University Press, 1951. This early study argues that the development of the Soviet zone resulted from Soviet concerns with the German problem and from emerging cold war issues.

Snell, J. L. *Wartime Origins of the East-West Dilemma over Germany* (25:92) concentrates on American wartime planning for Germany. Snell attempts to link the dispute over a "harsh" versus "soft" peace to the subsequent breakdown of quadripartite cooperation. On the issue of German partition, this study is helpful.

OTHER EUROPEAN ISSUES

See Chapter 25, "Eastern Europe."

26:109 Brzezinski, Zbigniew. "U.S. Foreign Policy in East Central Europe: A Study in Contradiction." *Journal of International Affairs* 11:1 (1957), 60–71. From World War II to the mid-1950s, the United States had no meaningful policy toward East Central Europe. The "free but friendly" approach at Yalta later gave way to containment, which in turn gave way to liberation. These approaches were simply slogans masking the unarticulated and ineffective "real" policies.

Byrnes, R. F., ed. *The United States and Eastern Europe* (28:161) provides a brief but useful introduction to the history, society, politics, and economics of postwar Eastern Europe, as well as to the area's relationship to the communist world, on the one hand, and the West, on the other.

26:110 Holt, Robert T., and Van de Velde, Robert W. *Strategic Psychological Operations and American Foreign Policy.* Chicago: University of Chicago Press, 1960. The authors discuss the general framework of the psychological instrument of statecraft and then discuss American psychological operations during the 1948 Italian elections. They believe that American actions were a "major factor" in the outcome of the elections.

26:111 Juda, Lawrence. "United States' Nonrecognition of the Soviet Union's Annexation of the Baltic States: Politics and Law." *Journal of Baltic Studies* 6:4 (1975), 272–90. Juda discusses legal, political, and diplomatic aspects (1940–1970s) of U.S. policies.

26:112 Kertesz, Stephen D., ed. *The Fate of East Central Europe: Hopes and Failures of American Foreign Policy.* Notre Dame, Ind.: University of Notre Dame Press, 1956. These essays survey American foreign policy toward East Central Europe both in a long-range historical context and as a part of the cold war. For the post–World War II period, each country is examined in separate essays.

Kovrig, B. *The Myth of Liberation: East-Central Europe in U.S. Diplomacy and Politics since 1941* (25:100).

26:113 Lundestad, Geir. *The American Non-Policy towards Eastern Europe, 1943–1947: Universalism in an Area Not of Essential Interest to the United States.* New York: Humanities Press, 1975. In this multifaceted work, Lundestad conducts a country-by-country survey of American relations with Eastern Europe, examining how idealistic self-interest defined American aims in the region and how those aims were modified by objective conditions and higher priorities, the result being the lack of a consistent U.S. policy. Lundestad relates his conclusions to the historiography of cold war origins. Extensive bibliography.

26:114 Seton-Watson, Hugh. *The East European Revolution.* New York: Praeger, 1951. In this classic book the author expertly traces the history of the iron curtain states through the war and into the successive stages of Sovietization.

The Polish "Test Case"

See "Personalities," especially James F. Byrnes, Arthur Bliss Lane, Arthur H. Vandenberg; also see Chapter 25, "The Polish Issue."

Cable, J. N. "Arthur Bliss Lane: Cold Warrior in Warsaw, 1945–1947" (26:50) analyzes Poland's development (1945–1947) through the actions of U.S. Ambassador Lane. Lane's inability to reconcile himself to a Socialist government in Poland hurt the Polish cause.

Herz, M. F. *Beginnings of the Cold War* (25:9) gives special attention to the growing conflict over Poland and Eastern Europe.

26:115 Irons, Peter H. "'The Test is Poland': Polish Americans and the Origins of the Cold War." *Polish American Studies* 30:2 (1973), 5–63. The events and policies which led to the inclusion of Poland in the Soviet bloc are recounted from firsthand experience in this vitriolic chronicle by the American ambassador to postwar Poland.

Rozek, E. J. *Allied Wartime Diplomacy: A Pattern in Poland* [1939–1947] (25:110) is highly critical of Western wartime policies regarding Russo-Polish relations and boundaries, and attempts to defend the Polish government-in-exile against Churchill's charges of intransigence during the war.

Wright, T. P., Jr. "The Origins of the Free Elections Dispute in the Cold War" (26:33).

Tito-Stalin Split, 1948–1949

See "Personalities," especially Joseph V. Stalin, Josip Broz-Tito.

26:116   Armstrong, Hamilton Fish. *Tito and Goliath*. New York: Macmillan, 1951. This is an insightful, but often speculative, contemporary assessment of the Soviet-Yugoslav break. The book explores the causes of the split, the events surrounding it, and the impact of Tito's heresy on world communism and on Stalin's subsequent actions in Eastern Europe.

26:117   Dedijer, Vladimir. *The Battle Stalin Lost: Memoirs of Yugoslavia, 1948–1953*. New York: Viking, 1970. Dedijer was director of information in Yugoslavia at the time of the Stalin-Tito split. His personal, informative account of the schism, based solely on Yugoslav sources, provides fresh material on Stalin's unsuccessful efforts after 1948 to subjugate the Yugoslav government.

26:118   Johnson, A. Ross. *The Transformation of Communist Ideology: The Yugoslav Case, 1945–1953*. Cambridge, Mass.: MIT Press, 1972. This careful analysis discusses Yugoslavian affairs (1945–1948) with insights into the political undercurrents.

26:119   Kousoulas, D. George. "The Truman Doctrine and the Stalin-Tito Rift: A Reappraisal." *South Atlantic Quarterly* 72:3 (1973), 427–39. Prior to March 1947, Tito's support for communist guerrillas in Greece presented problems for Moscow with the Truman Doctrine. Stalin feared that the United States would enter Greece and use it as a base from which to check Soviet plans in Eastern Europe. It was Tito's provoking of the West, not his threat to Stalin's vanity

and power, that prompted the Soviet-Yugoslav split. The split forced Tito to curtail aid to the Greek communists.

26:120   Lees, Lorraine M. "The American Decision to Assist Tito, 1948–1949." *Diplomatic History* 2:4 (1978), 407–22. The reorientation of American policy toward Yugoslavia during the early months of the Stalin-Tito split was cautious, as U.S. policymakers wondered if the schism was permanent, and worried lest a positive U.S. response undermine Tito's position. In early 1949, the United States began extending economic aid to Yugoslavia.

26:121   Ulam, Adam B. *Titoism and the Cominform*. Cambridge: Harvard University Press, 1952. This study combines a factual account of the Soviet-Yugoslav schism with an analysis of Titoism and its significance in terms of world communism, Soviet policy, the relationship between communist power and ideology, and Yugoslavia'a own internal development and perceptions of the outside world.

Development of the Containment Policy

See "Personalities," especially Dean Acheson, Charles E. Bohlen, James Forrestal, George F. Kennan, Harry S. Truman.

Burnham, J., ed. *What Europe Thinks of America* (28:41) is a collection of essays by conservative Europeans who believe the United States needs a stronger European policy.

Paterson, T. G., ed. *Containment and the Cold War: American Foreign Policy since 1945* (24:46) contains readings on the history of containment (1945–1972), mostly excerpts from the writings of Kennan and his contemporary critics, but with historical analyses as well by William A. Williams, Lloyd C. Gardner, Eduard M. Mark, and David P. Monzingo.

26:122   Serfaty, Simon. "An International Anomaly: The United States and the Communist Parties in France and Italy, 1945–1947." *Studies in Compara-*

tive Communism 8:1/2 (1975), 123–46. In France, after 1945, American influence did not play a major role in the ouster of Communists from the Ramadier government. In Italy, U.S. influence was greater. De Gasperi was aware of the U.S. position, that substantial U.S. economic aid was contingent on the ouster of the Communists.

Defining Containment

26:123 Gaddis, John Lewis. "Containment: A Reassessment." *Foreign Affairs* 55:4 (1977), 873–87. Gaddis supports George Kennan's later disclaimer that the "X" article should not be taken as a definitive statement of what Kennan meant by *containment*. Gaddis concludes that Kennan sought to contain Soviet expansion by employing limited means and differentiating between vital and secondary American interests.

26:124 Gati, Charles. "'X' Plus 25: What Containment Meant." *Foreign Policy,* no. 7 (1972), 22–40. Gati analyzes Kennan's "The Sources of Soviet Conduct" and finds the relationship between communist ideology and Soviet foreign policy unsophisticated, the views on the Soviet system's vulnerability overoptimistic, and the linkage of domestic vulnerability to an aggressive expansionism unconvincing. Gati distinguishes between the "globalism" of Mr. "X" and the "limitationism" of Kennan's actual views.

26:125 Mark, Eduard M. "The Question of Containment: A Reply to John Lewis Gaddis." *Foreign Affairs* 56:2 (1978), 430–41. Kennan's reservations about a policy of global containment were undermined by his own analyses of the international situation. Kennan described the Soviet threat as to require a combined political and military response at any number of points along the periphery of the Soviet Union.

26:126 McLellan, David S. "Who Fathered Containment? A Discussion." *International Studies Quarterly* 17:2 (1973), 205–26. America's cold war policy of containing the U.S.S.R. resulted from State Department experience with aggressive Soviet behavior in Turkey and Iran during 1945–1946. This view has been substantiated by Kuniholm (33:89).

26:127 Messer, Robert L. "Paths Not Taken: The United States Department of State and Alternatives to Containment, 1945–1946." *Diplomatic History* 1:4 (1977), 297–319. Until Kennan's "Long Telegram"

arrived in February 1946, the debate among State Department officials over policy toward Russia was remarkably open. Messer examines two "soft" alternatives to Kennan's "hard" position, and explains why Kennan's analyses and recommendations were accepted.

26:128 Powers, Richard J. "Who Fathered Containment?" *International Studies Quarterly* 15:4 (1971), 526–43. Powers compares and contrasts Kennan's "Long Telegram" and Clark Clifford's 1946 report (26:130) to the president. Both Kennan and Clifford counseled resistance to Soviet expansion, but Clifford placed more emphasis on a Soviet military threat and the need for superior U.S. military force. Powers argues that Clifford's report had the greater influence on policy formulation.

26:129 Wright, C. Ben. "Mr. 'X' and Containment." *Slavic Review* 35:1 (1976), 1–36. Wright looks at four of Kennan's pieces (1944–1946) on Russia. He disputes Kennan's disclaimer that Mr. "X" did not have in mind the military containment of a military threat, and thus provided a blueprint for America's postwar global involvement. Kennan replies, pp. 32–36.

"X" [George F. Kennan]. "The Sources of Soviet Conduct" (26:49) is the controversial "X" article in which Kennan analyzes the roots of Soviet power. See Lippmann's prompt criticism (26:15).

THE TRUMAN DOCTRINE

26:130 [Clifford, Clark]. "American Relations with the Soviet Union: Report to the President by the Special Counsel to the President, September 24, 1946." In Arthur Krock, *Memoirs: Sixty Years on the Firing Line.* New York: Funk & Wagnalls, 1968, pp. 419–82. This report to President Truman by his special counsel, Clark Clifford, projected the image of a militant, expansionistic Soviet Union whose leaders believed that conflict between the U.S.S.R. and the capitalist West was inevitable. The United States must use "the language of military power" to prevent further Soviet aggression.

26:131 Freeland, Richard M. *The Truman Doctrine and the Origins of McCarthyism: Foreign Policy, Domestic Politics, and Internal Security, 1946–1948.* New York: Knopf, 1972. In a provocative thesis linking domestic politics and foreign policy, Freeland contends that America's cold war policies became rigidly anti-Soviet when the administration, in order to mobilize public support for its efforts to develop American economic and strategic interests in Europe, deliberately aroused anticommunist sentiment by inaccurately depicting international problems as the product of Soviet perfidy and aggression. Bibliography.

26:132 Gaddis, John Lewis. "Was the Truman Doctrine a Real Turning Point?" *Foreign Affairs* 52:2 (1974), 386–402. The Truman Doctrine of 1947 represented neither a radical reorientation of American foreign policy nor the assumption by the United States of worldwide commitments to contain communism. Truman's proclamation was in line with previously established precedents for dealing with shifts in the European balance of power, and the U.S. did not commit itself to global containment until 1950.

26:133 Kernell, Samuel. "The Truman Doctrine Speech: A Case Study of the Dynamics of Presidential Opinion Leadership." *Social Science History* 1:1 (1976), 20–44. The author found that the Truman speech, despite the inflammatory rhetoric involved, did not generate widespread anticommunist sentiment. Policy support was found to be related to party loyalty.

Kuniholm, B. R. *The Origins of the Cold War in the Near East: Great Power Conflict and Diplomacy in Iran, Turkey, and Greece* (33:89) concludes that the "policy of containment in the Near East was a realistic and pragmatic policy." This superb study focuses on events prior to 1947 to show how the traditional struggle for power along the Northern Tier was a major factor in the origins and development of the cold war.

Paterson, T. G. *Soviet-American Confrontation: Postwar Reconstruction and the Origins of the Cold War* [1945–1948] (26:12) sheds new light upon the Truman Doctrine. Paterson focuses upon the importance of postwar petroleum resources to American policymakers, who he argues turned naturally to a defense of the vast Anglo-American holdings in the Near and Middle East.

26:134 Ryan, Henry B., Jr. "The American Intellectual Tradition Reflected in the Truman Doctrine." *American Scholar* 42:2 (1972–1973), 294–307. Policymakers can initiate pragmatic solutions to specific problems only after paying homage to basic currents in America's intellectual heritage. As an example, Ryan cites the Truman Doctrine, which called upon the United States to undertake a moral

mission of salvation in a world gripped by a struggle between good and evil.

26:135 Warner, Geoffrey. "The Truman Doctrine and the Marshall Plan." *International Affairs* 50:1 (1974), 82–92. A review of several volumes in the Foreign Relations series and a narrative of American diplomacy with respect to the Soviet Union, Western Europe, and the Near East (1946–1947); the focus is on those events which led to the formulation of the Truman Doctrine and the Marshall Plan.

The Iranian Crisis

See Chapter 33, "The Iranian Crisis."

26:136 Hess, Gary R. "The Iranian Crisis of 1945–46 and the Cold War." *Political Science Quarterly* 89:1 (1974), 117–46. Hess examines one of the earliest Soviet-American confrontations of the cold war, that over Iran in 1945–1946. He sheds new light on how not only national security considerations but also powerful domestic pressures to demonstrate a strong stand against the Soviet Union shaped the vigorous American support for Iran.

26:137 Mark, Eduard M. "Allied Relations in Iran, 1941–1947: The Origins of a Cold War Crisis." *Wisconsin Magazine of History* 59:1 (1975), 51–63. A cold war crisis developed in Iran between the United States and Russia over differing policies of cooperation.

26:138 Thorpe, James A. "Truman's Ultimatum to Stalin on the 1946 Azerbaijan Crisis: The Making of a Myth." *Journal of Politics* 40:1 (1978), 188–95. The claim, first presented in 1952, that Harry S. Truman gave Joseph Stalin an ultimatum which forced the Russian evacuation of Azerbaijan (May 1946) is a myth created by Truman and perpetuated by scholars.

The Greek Civil War

See Chapter 25, "The Greek Crisis," and Chapter 28, "U.S. Aid to Greece."

26:139 Averoff-Tossizza, Evangelos. *By Fire and Axe: The Communist Party and the Civil War in Greece, 1944–1949*. Trans. by S. A. Rigos. New Rochelle, N.Y.: Caratzas, 1978. This study by a Greek scholar and government official provides a most useful background for understanding the civil war in political and military terms.

Iatrides, J. O., ed. *Ambassador MacVeagh Reports: Greece, 1933–1947* (25:41) is useful for the shaping of American policy.

26:140 Matthews, Kenneth. *Memories of a Mountain War: Greece, 1944–1949.* London: Longmans, 1972. This long and clear perspective, by a BBC correspondent, provides a solid background to the conflict.

26:141 McNeill, William H. *The Greek Dilemma: War and Aftermath.* London: Gollancz, 1947. This firsthand account of the background to the Greek crisis by an historian and former assistant U.S. military attaché in Athens, although sympathetic to American intervention, presents a mordant picture of the right-wing Athens government and its former British patrons.

26:142 O'Ballance, Edgar. *The Greek Civil War, 1944–49.* New York: Praeger, 1966. With his primary focus on military activities, O'Ballance recounts the story of the civil war which erupted intermittently.

26:143 Stavrianos, Leften S. *Greece: American Dilemma and Opportunity.* Chicago: Regnery, 1952. This is a perceptive study of the Greek civil war, American intervention, and their consequences. American policymakers, coached by the British and caught up in their own cold war concerns, misunderstood the nature of Greek political reality.

26:144 Wittner, Lawrence S. "The Truman Doctrine and the Defense of Freedom." *Diplomatic History* 4:2 (1980), 161–88. This study reviews American policies and actions in Greece (1947–1949) and concludes that officials repeatedly acquiesced in or encouraged police state measures contrary to American ideals.

Woodhouse, C. M. *The Struggle for Greece, 1941–1949* (25:116) is a new and important synthesis.

26:145 Xydis, Stephen G. *Greece and the Great Powers, 1944–1947: Prelude to the "Truman Doctrine."* Thessalonica: Institute for Balkan Studies, 1963. This is the best of the early works that deal with the international aspects of the Greek civil war. Its strength lies in its use of Greek government records, nevertheless, the book becomes dated as new materials appear relevant to American, British, and Soviet

policy. Bibliography. See also his essay (25:117), which summarizes his views.

The Turkish Straits

See Chapter 18, "Lausanne (1923) and Montreux (1936) Conferences," and Chapter 33, "Turkish Straits."

26:146 Alvarez, David J. "The *Missouri*'s Visit to Turkey: An Alternative Perspective on Cold War Diplomacy." *Balkan Studies* 15:2 (1974), 225–36. Focusing upon the interests and perceptions of principals in the State Department and Navy Department, the author concludes that containment of Russian ambitions was not the primary motive behind the *Missouri* mission.

Howard, H. N. *Turkey, the Straits and U.S. Policy* (2:362) is the standard reference on this topic.

Howard, H. N. "The United States and the Problem of the Turkish Straits" (18:149) covers the issue through the 1920s and 1930s to 1945–1946.

26:147 Knight, Jonathan. "American International Guarantees for the Straits: Prelude to the Truman Doctrine." *Middle Eastern Studies* 13:2 (1977), 241–50. Truman proposed internationalization of the Turkish Straits in 1945. The proposal failed because 1) Turkey doubted U.S. ability to prevent Russian control of the straits, 2) the U.S.S.R. opposed any arrangement which denied it strategic control of the straits, 3) State Department experts doubted that either the administration or the country was prepared to accept such obligations, and 4) the president was too preoccupied in 1945 to obtain support for his proposal.

26:148 Knight, Jonathan. "American Statecraft and the 1946 Black Sea Straits Controversy." *Political Science Quarterly* 90:3 (1975), 451–75. Knight explores American diplomacy during the 1946 Black Sea Straits controversy between Turkey and the Soviet Union. He argues that while the Truman administration bolstered Turkey's position, including the deployment of naval forces, it refrained from any direct military confrontation with the Soviets.

THE MARSHALL PLAN

See "Personalities," especially Joseph M. Jones (under "Others"), George C. Marshall.

26:149 Arkes, Hadley. *Bureaurcracy, the Marshall Plan, and the National Interest*. Princeton, N.J.: Princeton University Press, 1973. This case study of how national interest is defined looks at the interaction of the executive branch, congress, and the bureaucracy, and shows how the process of bureaucratic administration transformed the blend of national interest and generosity which prompted the Marshall Plan. Extensive bibliography.

26:150 Atwell, Mary W. "A Conservative Response to the Cold War: Senator James P. Kem and Foreign Aid." *Capitol Studies* 4:2 (1976), 53–66. A dissenting voice in the Senate (1945–1950), Kem objected to Truman's foreign policy.

26:151 Bailey, Thomas A. *The Marshall Plan Summer: An Eyewitness Report on Europe and the Russians in 1947*. Stanford, Calif.: Hoover Institution Press, 1977. Bailey toured Europe under the auspices of the National War College during the summer of 1947. This book, basically a diary of conditions and attitudes as he then saw them, tells us something of contemporary conditions and much of Bailey's perceptions.

Brown, W. A., Jr., and Opie, R. *American Foreign Assistance* (39:153) is a basic book on American assistance (1945–1952); it is especially good on aid to France.

26:152 Clayton, William L. "GATT, the Marshall Plan. and OECD." *Political Science Quarterly* 78:4 (1963), 493–503. This is the recollections of a key participant in the planning and development of the Marshall Plan with only passing reference to the Organization for European Economic Cooperation or the general trade agreement.

26:153 Eudin, Xenia J. "Moscow's Views of American Imperialism." *Russian Review* 13:4 (1954), 276–84. A parallel is drawn between the Soviet attitude toward the Marshall Plan and the proposed federation of Europe, and the Soviet interpretation of the Dawes Plan.

26:154 Gimbel, John. *The Origins of the Marshall Plan*. Stanford, Calif.: Stanford University Press, 1976. Gimbel holds that the Marshall Plan grew out of bureaucratic wrangling between the State Department and the War Department over policies affecting occupation of Germany. The War Department sought German economic recovery in order to end the occupation before it became too costly. It was hoped that the Marshall Plan, by promoting general European recovery, would make German recovery politically acceptable in the United States and Europe. Extensive bibliography.

26:155 Hitchens, Harold L. "Influences on the Congressional Decision to Pass the Marshall Plan." *Western Political Quarterly* 21:1 (1968), 51–68. This essay examines the 1948 congressional debate over the Marshall Plan (European recovery program). Among the numerous factors which resulted in passage of the plan were the growth of favorable public opinion, the impact of the 1948 general election, and a maze of pressure and interest groups.

26:156 Jackson, Scott. "Prologue to the Marshall Plan: The Origins of the American Commitment for a European Recovery Program." *Journal of American History* 65:4 (1979), 1043–68. Jackson uses an eclectic, chronological approach to pinpoint the dominant motivating factors at each step in the formulation of the program.

Kolko, J., and Kolko, G. *The Limits of Power: The World and United States Foreign Policy, 1945–1954* (24:40) is critical of the Marshall Plan as an act of American capitalism seeking immediate gains.

26:157 Mallalieu, William C. *British Reconstruction and American Policy, 1945–1955*. New York: Scarecrow, 1956. This concentrated analysis of British postwar economic reconstruction pays special attention to U.S. policy and the Marshall Plan.

26:158 Paterson, Thomas G. "The Quest for Peace and Prosperity: International Trade, Communism, and the Marshall Plan." In Barton J. Bernstein, ed., *Politics and Policies of the Truman Administration*. Chicago: Quadrangle, 1970, pp. 78–112. American officials viewed freedom, prosperity, and world trade as inseparable components of peace and stability. In an interdependent world, open, nondiscriminatory trade patterns were essential both for world and U.S. prosperity and for checking the threat to peace posed by revolutionary totalitarianism.

26:159 Price, Harry B. *The Marshall Plan and Its Meaning*. Ithaca, N.Y.: Cornell University Press, 1955. In writing this official history of the Marshall Plan, the author had access to all pertinent records and to key personnel. Price discusses the development and impact of the Marshall Plan and offers a comprehensive evaluation of the program.

Warner, G. "The Truman Doctrine and the Marshall Plan" (26:135).

White, T. H. *In Search of History* (23:225) has perceptive judgments on the men who administered the Marshall Plan and the effects of that plan on Europe.

26:160 Wilson, Theodore A. *The Marshall Plan, 1947–1951*. Headline Series, no. 236. New York: Foreign Policy Association, 1977. Wilson covers the variety of domestic and international factors which influenced the formulation, implementation, and ultimate success of the Marshall Plan. It restored European self-confidence, and in the process set the foundation for the complex social-political-economic structure that has since characterized relations between the world's industrially advanced countries.

FOUNDING OF NATO

See Chapter 36, "Canada and NATO."

26:161 Heindel, Richard H., et al. "The North Atlantic Treaty in the U.S. Senate." *American Journal of International Law* 43:4 (1949), 633–65. This contemporary series of articles examines the Senate debates over the compatibility of NATO obligations to the United States' traditional isolationism.

26:162 Henrikson, Alan K. "The Creation of the North Atlantic Alliance, 1948–1952." *Naval War College Review* 32:3 (1980), 4–39. This useful survey emphasizes the roles played by Britain's foreign secretary, Ernest Bevin, and certain American officials, especially Assistant Secretary of State John D. Hickerson.

26:163 Ireland, Timothy P. *Creating the Entangling Alliance: The Origins of the North Atlantic Treaty Organization*. Westport, Conn.: Greenwood, 1981. Ireland argues that the United States originally hoped that NATO would strengthen the independent, European nations as a balance to Soviet power and thus *reduce* the need for American involvement in Europe. Bibliography.

26:164 Ismay, Lionel [Lord Hastings]. *NATO: The First Five Years, 1949–1954*. Paris: NATO, 1955. This detailed, historical chronicle of the North Atlantic Treaty Organization also represents an analysis of the inner workings of the bureaucracy of the Atlantic Alliance.

26:165 Kaplan, Lawrence S. *A Community of Interests: NATO and the Military Assistance Program, 1948–1951*. Washington, D.C.: Office of Secretary of Defense, Historical Office, 1980. This book focuses on the role of the Department of Defense, together with the Department of State and other European-oriented agencies, in fashioning a military assistance program that would serve NATO members. The Korean War gave this undertaking a sense of urgency.

26:166 Kaplan, Lawrence S. "NATO and Its Commentators: The First Five Years." *International Organization* 8:4 (1954), 447–67. This short bibliographical essay covers NATO up to 1953.

26:167 Kaplan, Lawrence S. "Toward the Brussels Pact." *Prologue* 12:2 (1980), 73–86. The author reviews the origins of the NATO concept (1947–1948) as it emerged on both sides of the Atlantic. His focus on the roles of various individuals and organizations is most useful.

26:168 Kaplan, Lawrence S. "The United States and the Atlantic Alliance: The First Generation." In John Braeman, Robert H. Bremner, and David Brody, eds., *Twentieth-Century American Foreign Policy*. Columbus: Ohio State University Press, 1971, pp. 294–309. This broad survey discusses NATO's difficulties and its ability to adjust to changing times.

26:169 Kaplan, Lawrence S. "The United States and the Origins of NATO, 1946–1949." *Review of Politics* 31:2 (1969), 210–22. The origins of NATO are inextricably linked with the rediscovery of Europe by the United States.

26:170 Osgood, Robert. *NATO: The Entangling Alliance*. Chicago: University of Chicago Press, 1962. Osgood's analysis of the origins and early development of NATO stands as the benchmark for any further study of the Atlantic Alliance. Bibliography.

26:171 Reid, Escott M. *Time of Fear and Hope: The Making of the North Atlantic Treaty, 1947–1949*. Toronto: McClelland & Stewart, 1977. This impressive account—in part a memoir by a Canadian diplomat—provides the best study of how NATO was framed (1948–1949). Bibliography.

26:172 Vaern, Grethe. "The United States, Norway, and the Atlantic Pact, 1948–1949." *Scandinavian Studies* 50:2 (1978), 150–76. Vaern reviews the entry of Norway into NATO, concluding that there are grounds for varied interpretations as to how the Americans perceived the attitude of Norwegian Foreign Minister Halvard Lange.

POINT FOUR PROGRAM

26:173 Bingham, Jonathan B. *Shirt-Sleeve Diplomacy.* New York: Day, 1954. Bingham, deputy administrator of the Point Four program (1951–1953), discusses its rationale and administrative problems, and provides a number of examples of how the program worked. Also see Annette Baker, "President Truman's Fourth Point and the United Nations," *International Conciliation,* no. 452 (1949), 459–503.

26:174 Bose, Tarun C. "The Point Four Programme: A Critical Study." *International Studies* 7:1 (1965), 66–97. This is a useful survey of the Point Four program from its inception to its operation. Bose evaluates and reviews criticisms of the program.

26:175 Hutcheson, Harold H. "Government and Capital in Point Four." *Foreign Policy Reports* 25:6 (1949), 66–75. This essay has information pertaining to U.S./UN programs promoting the improvement and growth of underdeveloped areas.

26:176 Paterson, Thomas G. "Foreign and under Wraps: The Point Four Program." *Wisconsin Magazine of History* 56:2 (1972/1973), 119–26. The Truman administration could no longer assume that developing nations would side with the West in the cold war, so it proclaimed the Point Four program, which combined private investment and technical assistance to recipient nations.

Warne, W. E. *Mission for Peace: Point Four in Iran* [1951–1955] (33:182).

NSC-68

26:177 "NSC-68." *Naval War College Review* 26:6 (1975), 53–108. Reprinted here is the complete text of NSC-68, minus its "terms of reference," which established U.S. objectives. Also reprinted in Etzold and Gaddis (26:3) together with many other documents which place NSC-68 in context.

26:178 Siracusa, Joseph M. "NSC 68: A Reappraisal." *Naval War College Review* 33:6 (1980), 4–14. This examination of NSC-68 suggests that the basic American strategic position taken toward the U.S.S.R. in 1950 only restated, with minor modifications, a position adopted in the wake of the 1948 Berlin blockade crisis. The Truman administration did view the 1949 Soviet atomic test with sufficient alarm to decide to experiment with the thermonuclear weapon. Available evidence suggests that the case for a direct relationship between formulation of NSC-68 and the U.S. commitment to UN police action in Korea is, at best, tenuous. See Paul Y. Hammond, "NSC 68: Prologue to Rearmament," in Warner R. Schilling, Paul Y. Hammond, and Glenn H. Snyder, *Strategy, Politics, and Defense Budgets* (New York: Columbia University Press, 1962), for an early assessment.

26:179 Wells, Samuel F., Jr. "Sounding the Tocsin: NSC 68 and the Soviet Threat." *International Security* 4:2 (1979), 116–58. This is a careful analysis of the assumptions behind the formulation of NSC-68. The debate stirred by this essay is extended by the comments of John Lewis Gaddis and Paul Nitze, "NSC 68 and the Soviet Threat Reconsidered," *International Security* 4:4 (1980), 164–76. Gaddis employs George Kennan's perception of U.S. security requirements to criticize NSC-68, while Nitze, an architect of the document, is understandably defensive.

Soviet Responses

See "Personalities," especially American Walter Bedell Smith (under "Others") and Joseph V. Stalin.

26:180 Bagguley, John. "The World War and the Cold War." In David Horowitz, ed., *Containment and Revolution.* Boston: Beacon, 1967, pp. 76–124. Credit for engaging and defeating the German armies belongs to Russia, not Britain and the United States, whose military operations were restricted to secondary theaters. The discord that followed Yalta was a natural occurrence since England and America tried to deprive Russia of its share of the spoils of war.

SOVIETIZATION OF EASTERN EUROPE

26:181 Brannen, Barry. "The Soviet Conquest of Rumania." *Foreign Affairs* 30:3 (1952), 466–87.

Brannen, the U.S. naval representative on the Allied Control Council for Rumania (1944–1946), recites the series of events that led to the communization of that country.

26:182 Kertesz, Stephen D. "The Methods of Communist Conquest: Hungary, 1944–1947." *World Politics* 3:1 (1950), 20–54. Kertesz writes of how the Soviet Union, by using force and by taking advantage of favorable interpretations of the Hungarian armistice agreement, the Potsdam accords, and the Hungarian peace treaty, took control of Hungary.

26:183 McCauley, Martin, ed. *Communist Power in Europe, 1944–1949*. London: Macmillan, 1977. These essays can be divided into three general categories: case studies of countries in which communist parties took power either during or after World War II; those of countries in which the communists failed to take power; and miscellaneous topics.

Mikolajczyk, S. *The Rape of Poland: Pattern of Soviet Aggression* (25:106) provides a moving account of the events—of the "appeasement" and "betrayal," as he would have it—which led finally to the communization of Poland.

26:184 Rubinstein, Alvin Z. "The Sovietization of Eastern Europe." *Social Science* 30:2 (1955), 99–104. The author assesses Soviet intentions and describes how, during and after World War II, the Soviet Union moved to dominate Eastern Europe.

Seton-Watson, H. *The East European Revolution* [1941–1950] (26:114) represents an early endeavor to describe and analyze the establishment of communist power in Eastern Europe and the impact of sovietization on the area. The approach is comprehensive, examining the political, economic, social, and cultural transformations wrought by Stalin's revolution from above.

26:185 Seton-Watson, Hugh. "Soviet Occupation in Romania, Bulgaria, and Hungary." *Public Policy* 17:2 (1968), 145–63. The author looks at changes in Soviet occupation policies (1944–1947) and studies the methods, intentions, and achievements of those policies during the period of change.

Smith, G. A. *Soviet Foreign Trade: Organization, Operation, and Policy, 1918–1971* (39:80).

26:186 Wandycz, Piotr S. "The Soviet System of Alliances in East Central Europe." *Journal of Central European Affairs* 16:2 (1956), 177–86. Wandycz analyzes the four stages in which the Soviet Union constructed an alliance system in East Central Europe (1943–1950). The value of the treaties of alliance was primarily propagandistic, as the Soviet Union sought the appearance of legality.

THE CZECH COUP, 1948

26:187 Friedman, Otto. *The Break-up of Czech Democracy*. London: Gollancz, 1950. An anticommunist Czech, Friedman was in exile when he wrote this narrative of the coup d'état in Czechoslovakia. It is a surprisingly well-balanced account, although a bit too harsh on former President Beneš, whom Friedman holds responsible for failing to unite the democratic parties in opposition to the communists.

26:188 Steinitz, Mark S. "United States Economic Assistance Policy toward Czechoslovakia, 1946–1948." *Maryland History* 7:2 (1976), 21–46. The author argues that American inflexibility on economic aid directly undermined Czechoslovak moderates and thus helped contribute to the communist takeover.

26:189 Ullmann, Walter. "Czechoslovakia's Crucial Years, 1945–1948: An American View." *East European Quarterly* 1:3 (1967), 217–30. Using the papers of Lawrence A. Steinhardt, U.S. ambassador to Czechoslovakia, Ullman looks at the failure of U.S. diplomacy to prevent the communization of that country. The opportunities existed to do so, but balking at world leadership and still hoping to prevent an irrevocable break with the Soviet Union, the United States failed to capitalize on them.

26:190 Ullmann, Walter. "Some Aspects of American-Czechoslovak Relations, 1945–1947." *East European Quarterly* 10:1 (1976), 65–76. The author selects topics that he judges important; he finds that American diplomacy was well-meaning but lacked understanding and skill.

26:191 Ullmann, Walter. *The United States in Prague*. Boulder, Colo.: East European Quarterly Book, 1978. The book centers on the American embassy and Ambassador Steinhardt. Washington failed to give the embassy any direction and the result was the final communist takeover.

26:192 Zinner, Paul E. *Communist Strategy and Tactics in Czechoslovakia, 1918–1948*. New York:

Praeger, 1963. Zinner deemphasizes the role of external factors such as Soviet power, and focuses on the Czech Communist party. He examines the history of Czech communism, and concludes that from 1945 on, the Czech communists were in an advantageous position from which to seize power.

THE BERLIN BLOCKADE, 1948–1949

See, under "Personalities," Charles E. Bohlen, Lucius D. Clay; also see Chapter 25, "Access to Berlin," and Chapter 29, "The Powers and Berlin."

Clay, L. D. "Berlin" (29:72) provides a survey of the Berlin issue from the 1940s to 1961.

26:193   Davison, W. Phillips. *The Berlin Blockade: A Study in Cold War Politics.* Princeton, N.J.: Princeton University Press, 1958. The author contrasts Soviet activities, which he maintains were initiated after careful preparation, with the West's initial indecisiveness. In the end, however, the blockade represented a Soviet defeat, serving only to consolidate Allied influence in western Germany while heightening cold war tensions.

26:194   Gottlieb, Manuel F. *The German Peace Settlement and the Berlin Crisis.* New York: Paine-Whitman, 1960. This is a thoughtful exploration of the emerging quarrel between the United States and the Soviet Union in the German arena. Gottlieb is informative in his treatment of the American response to developments in the Russian zone, and in his discussion of the battle over currency reform. Bibliography.

26:195   Jessup, Philip C. "The Berlin Blockade and the Use of the United Nations." *Foreign Affairs* 50:1 (1971), 163–73. This brief review of events of 1948 shows the degree to which the United States relied on the UN in resolving the crisis. It contains references to Jessup's role at the time. See also his "Park Avenue Diplomacy: Ending the Berlin Blockade," *Political Science Quarterly* 87:3 (1972), 377–400.

26:196   Smith, Jean Edward. *The Defense of Berlin.* Baltimore: Johns Hopkins Press, 1963. The book traces East-West conflict over Berlin (1945–1962). It provides considerable information on the division of the city during the crisis of 1948–1949.

Nuclear Arms Competition and Control

See also Chapter 29, "Nuclear Arms Competition and Control," and Chapter 40, "Arms Control and Disarmament."

26:197   Bechhoefer, Bernhard G. *Postwar Negotiations for Arms Control.* Washington, D.C.: Brookings Institution, 1961. About three-quarters of this highly detailed study is devoted to nuclear arms control negotiations (1945–1960), some conducted under the auspices of the United Nations. American and Soviet positions are well outlined through numerous quotations from public documents. Bechhoefer himself participated in many of the talks as a State Department officer.

26:198   Brodie, Bernard, ed. *The Absolute Weapon: Atomic Power and World Order.* New York: Harcourt, Brace, 1946. Articles by Brodie, Frederick Dunn, Arnold Wolfers, William Fox, and Percy Corbett offer a contemporary assessment of the atomic bomb, the effect of the bomb on Soviet-American relations and on the UN, and the international control of atomic energy.

26:199   Herken, Gregg. *The Winning Weapon: The Atomic Bomb in the Cold War, 1945–1950.* New York: Knopf, 1980. Herken's three-part study treats the diplomatic, political, and military impact of atomic weapons on U.S. foreign policy. The focus is mainly on 1945 to 1947, except for the military dimension, which extends to 1950. The author is critical of such American leaders as Byrnes, Truman, and General Groves for myopic, opportunistic handling of the power they believed that they alone possessed. Extensive bibliography. Also see Herken's "'A Most Deadly Illusion': The Atomic Secret and American Nuclear Weapons Policy, 1945–1950," *Pacific Historical Review* 49:1 (1980), 51–76, for an overview of the book.

26:200   Hewlett, Richard G., and Anderson, Oscar E., Jr. *The New World, 1939–1946.* Vol. 1 in *A History of the United States Atomic Energy Commission.* University Park: Pennsylvania State University Press, 1962. This work, which relies on many documents still classified, is representative of the best "institutional" history. This volume explores the early engineering problems in creating the A-bomb, and the postwar political battles among politicians and scientists.

26:201 Hewlett, Richard G., and Duncan, Francis. *Atomic Shield, 1947–1952*. Vol. 2 in *A History of the United States Atomic Energy Commission*. University Park: Pennsylvania State University Press, 1969. This study develops U.S. nuclear policy as it related to Anglo-American and Soviet-American negotiations for arms control. The H-bomb decision is also detailed.

26:202 Nogee, Joseph L. *Soviet Policy towards the International Control of Atomic Energy*. Notre Dame, Ind.: University of Notre Dame Press, 1961. Nogee reconstructs Soviet policy on the control of atomic energy (1945–1953) as that policy was developed in response to U.S. initiatives. The Russians never viewed the issue of control with the same urgency as the West, he concludes; indeed, they viewed international control itself as a threat to the stability and survivability of the Soviet regime.

Parrish, N. F. *Behind the Sheltering Bomb* (40:192) remains the best survey of the early impact of atomic weapons on American military policy (1945–1950).

Quester, G. H. *Nuclear Diplomacy: The First Twenty-Five Years* [1945–1970] (40:229) is a chronological study that emphasizes the U.S.-Soviet nuclear arms race.

Roberts, C. M. *The Nuclear Years: The Arms Race and Arms Control, 1945–1970* (40:230) is a "primer" that surveys the nuclear race to the SALT negotiations.

BARUCH PLAN, 1946

See "Personalities," especially Dean Acheson, Bernard Baruch.

26:203 Bernstein, Barton J. "The Quest for Security: American Foreign Policy and International Control of Atomic Energy, 1942–1946." *Journal of American History* 60:4 (1974), 1003–44. Roosevelt made the initial decision to exclude the Soviet Union from knowledge about the development of the atomic bomb. Truman did not reverse this decision, but delayed telling Stalin about the bomb, and then only belatedly offered a plan for the international control of atomic energy. The plan was unsatisfactory to the

Russians just as Soviet counterproposals were unsatisfactory to the United States.

26:204 Blackett, P. M. S. *Fear, War and the Bomb: Military and Political Consequences of Atomic Energy*. New York: Whittlesey House, 1949. Revisionists of the 1960s and 1970s would develop and modify Blackett's thesis that the United States used the atomic bomb on Japan in order to end the war in the Pacific before the Russians could intervene, and that the Baruch Plan for the control of atomic energy posed a political and economic threat to the Soviet system.

26:205 Lieberman, Joseph I. *The Scorpion and the Tarantula: The Struggle to Control Atomic Weapons, 1945–1949*. Boston: Houghton Mifflin, 1970. Lieberman finds both the United States and the Soviet Union responsible for the failure to control atomic weapons.

26:206 Lilienthal, David E. *The Atomic Energy Years: 1945–1950*. Vol. 2 in *The Journals of David E. Lilienthal*. New York: Harper & Row, 1964. Lilienthal was chairman of the Atomic Energy Commission (1946–1950). His private papers for those years offer unique insights into the making of U.S. atomic energy policy during the period of America's atomic monopoly.

26:207 U.S. Department of State. *A Report on the International Control of Atomic Energy: Prepared for the Secretary of State's Committee on Atomic Energy by a Board of Consultants*. Dept. of State Pub. 2498. Washington, D.C.: G.P.O., 1946. This pamphlet contains the Acheson-Lilienthal report which formed the basis of the Baruch Plan of 1946. Reprinted frequently.

H-BOMB DECISION

26:208 Bellany, Ian. "The Origins of the Soviet Hydrogen Bomb: The York Hypothesis." *Journal of the Royal United Services Institute for Defence Studies* 122:1 (1977), 56–58. Most sources have hitherto agreed that the U.S.S.R. tested its first hydrogen bomb in August 1953. Now evidence suggests that such a test did not take place until November 1955.

26:209 Rosenberg, David A. "American Atomic Strategy and the Hydrogen Bomb Decision." *Journal of American History* 66:1 (1979), 62–87. Rosenberg has been among the first historians to examine documents declassified during the 1970s concerning post-World War II military policy. The present article reveals much about the making of national security policy and the state of American intelligence in the years just after World War II, in addition to illuminating the specific military considerations influencing the hydrogen bomb decision.

26:210 Schilling, Warner R. "The H-Bomb Decision: How to Decide without Choosing." *Political Science Quarterly* 76:1 (1961), 24–46. This early survey reviews opinions and recommendations of officials and bureaucracies during January–March 1950 regarding the decision to develop the H-bomb. It provides a useful background to the issues (or lack of them).

26:211 York, Herbert. *The Advisors: Oppenheimer, Teller, and the Superbomb*. San Francisco: Freeman, 1976. York discusses the origins of U.S. and U.S.S.R. H-bomb programs, and focuses on the technical side of the debate between Oppenheimer and Teller. Also see David Holloway, "Soviet Thermonuclear Development," *International Security* 4:3 (1979/1980), 193–97.

Politics, Anticommunism, and Foreign Policy

See "Personalities," especially Joseph McCarthy, Harry S. Truman, Henry A. Wallace.

26:212 McAuliffe, Mary Sperling. *Crisis on the Left: Cold War Politics and American Liberals, 1947–1954*. Amherst: University of Massachusetts Press, 1978. Focusing on Americans for Democratic Action, the American Civil Liberties Union, the American Committee for Cultural Freedom, and the Congress of Industrial Organization, this volume examines the impact of the cold war on the old, New Deal left and traces the emergence of a newer, "cold war" liberalism.

26:213 Shannon, David A. *The Decline of American Communism: A History of the Communist Party of the*

United States since 1945. New York: Harcourt, Brace & World, 1959. A history of the postwar American Communist party which concludes that the party failed primarily because of its unquestioning allegiance to the Soviet Union, which made it impossible to attract political support in the United States.

26:214 Starobin, Joseph R. *American Communism in Crisis, 1943–1957*. Cambridge: Harvard University Press, 1972. A thoughtful and carefully documented analysis of the decline of American communism during the cold war years concludes that the American communists' movement was "shattered" as much by their own behavior, their inability to choose between the antagonistic strains in their own movement and their impotence to change their course, as it was by the formidable power of their opposition.

ELECTION OF 1948

See "Personalities," especially Harry S. Truman, Henry A. Wallace.

Divine, R. A. *Foreign Policy and U.S. Presidential Elections, 1940–1960* (2:141) is a good general account of the role of foreign policy debate in presidential campaigns. See especially chapters 5–7 on the election of 1948, in which, Divine argues, contrary to conventional accounts, foreign policy played an important role in Truman's campaign for election.

26:215 Divine, Robert A. "The Cold War and the Election of 1948." *Journal of American History* 59:1 (1972), 90–110. Diplomacy played a more crucial role in the 1948 victory of Harry S Truman (1884–1972) than historians have generally believed. In the Czech crisis (February 1948), Truman's tough line and his challenge to Congress to pass the Marshall Plan and selective service undermined support for Wallace, assisting the identification of Wallace with communist support.

Markowitz, N. D. *The Rise and Fall of the People's Century: Henry A. Wallace and American Liberalism, 1941–1948* (24:163) is the first scholarly account of Wallace's unsuccessful Progressive party "peace campaign" of 1948.

Snetsinger, J. *Truman, the Jewish Vote, and the Creation of Israel* (33:94) has much on the election of 1948.

FROM ANTICOMMUNISM TO McCARTHYISM

See "Personalities," especially Joseph McCarthy.

26:216 Bell, Daniel, ed. *The New American Right.* New York: Criterion, 1955. In this important collection of essays, prominent historians and social scientists argue that McCarthyism represented a "radical right" attack on modern America and its elite-governed institutions. This collection remains of interest to contemporary scholars not just for its interpretation of McCarthyism, but also as a revealing example of postwar liberal thought. A revised and expanded version was published as *The Radical Right* (Garden City, N.Y.: Doubleday, 1963).

26:217 Belknap, Michael R. *Cold War Political Justice: The Smith Act, the Communist Party, and American Civil Liberties.* Westport, Conn.: Greenwood, 1977. Belknap traces the trials, convictions, and imprisonment of American Communists under the Smith Act, which forbade advocacy of the violent overthrow of the government.

26:218 Caute, David. *The Great Fear: The Anti-Communist Purge under Truman and Eisenhower.* New York: Simon & Schuster, 1978. *The Great Fear* attempts, not always successfully, to trace the sweeping impact of McCarthyism on American society. Its greatest value lies in its near encyclopedic recitation of repressive incidents.

26:219 Diggins, John P. *Up from Communism: Conservative Odysseys in American Intellectual History.* New York: Harper & Row, 1975. A provocative intellectual history of four American radicals—Max Eastman, John Dos Passos, Will Herberg, and James Burnham—who emerged in the 1950s as important spokesmen for American conservatism.

Freeland, R. M. *The Truman Doctrine and the Origins of McCarthyism: Foreign Policy, Domestic Politics, and Internal Security, 1946–1948* (26:131) contends that the Truman Doctrine was designed to "sell" the American people on a program of military and economic assistance to Europe. While crude anticommunism accomplished this task, it acquired a momentum of its own, launching the loyalty-security hysteria.

26:220 Goodman, Walter. *The Committee: The Extraordinary Career of the House Committee on Un-*

American Activities. New York: Farrar, Straus & Giroux, 1968. Impressionistic and superficially researched, this nevertheless remains the best general account of the stormy history of the House Committee on Un-American Activities.

26:221 Griffith, Robert. *The Politics of Fear: Joseph R. McCarthy and the Senate.* Lexington: University Press of Kentucky, 1970. Griffith argues that McCarthy's power and notoriety stemmed primarily from his association with the Communist issue, the support given him from Republicans in their quest for political power, the acquiescence of fearful Democrats, and the institutional inertia of the Senate itself. McCarthy was the product of the new politics of anticommunism.

26:222 Griffith, Robert, and Theoharis, Athan, eds. *The Specter: Original Essays on the Cold War and the Origins of McCarthyism.* New York: Franklin Watts, 1974. Most of the essays reject the notion that McCarthyism was a mass movement and explore instead the role various elites and established institutions played in creating the postwar politics of anticommunism.

26:223 Harper, Alan D. *The Politics of Loyalty: The White House and the Communist Issue, 1946–1952.* Westport, Conn.: Greenwood, 1969. A history of the politics surrounding the internal security programs of the Truman administration. Harper argues that Truman had a strong commitment to civil liberties but was compelled by conservative attacks to adopt repressive policies.

26:224 Latham, Earl. *The Communist Controversy in Washington: From the New Deal to McCarthy.* Cambridge: Harvard University Press, 1966. Latham critically reviews many of the "episodes" involving charges of communist conspiracies, and finds that they are unsupported by data. Bibliography.

26:225 Lens, Sidney. *The Futile Crusade: Anti-Communism as American Credo.* Chicago: Quadrangle, 1964. A strident critique of postwar American anticommunism, which the author sees as the product of the "military-industrial complex."

Purifoy, L. M. *Harry Truman's China Policy: McCarthyism and the Diplomacy of Hysteria 1947–1951* (27:82) is a forceful presentation of the argument that McCarthyism prevented American disengagement from China. Purifoy contends that public opinion demanded an anticommunist crusade and that the

Truman administration maintained its ties with Chiang Kai-shek to appease this sentiment.

26:226   Rogin, Michael P. *The Intellectuals and McCarthy: The Radical Specter*. Cambridge, Mass.: MIT Press, 1967. A brilliant critique of those who, like Daniel Bell and Richard Hofstadter, have insisted that McCarthyism represented a mass movement on the "radical right." McCarthyism, Rogen argues, was produced by the actions and inactions of elites, both Democratic and Republican, both liberal and conservative.

26:227   Theoharis, Athan. *Seeds of Repression: Harry S. Truman and the Origins of McCarthyism*. Chicago: Quadrangle, 1971. In this revisionist study Theoharis argues that the Truman administration, in its attempts to rally public support for containment, helped create the conditions out of which McCarthyism arose. For a study which argues the same theme even more explicitly, see Richard M. Freeland (26:131).

26:228   Weinstein, Allen. *Perjury: The Hiss-Chambers Case*. New York: Knopf, 1978. By far the best of all the books dealing with the Alger Hiss affair, it presents a powerful though not totally convincing case for Hiss's guilt. For a recent, though less successful attempt to prove Hiss's innocence, see John Chabot Smith, *Alger Hiss—The True Story* (New York: Holt, Rinehart & Winston, 1976).

27

United States and East Asia, 1941–1953

Contributing Editor

MICHAEL H. HUNT
University of North Carolina,
Chapel Hill

Contributors

Christopher Chipello
Johns Hopkins School of
Advanced International Studies

Bruce Cumings
University of Washington

Roger Dingman
University of Southern California

Steven I. Levine
American University

James Reardon-Anderson
Johns Hopkins School of
Advanced International Studies

Michael Schaller
University of Arizona

Nancy Bernkopf Tucker
Colgate University

Samuel F. Wells, Jr.
Woodrow Wilson International
Center for Scholars

Contents

Introduction

The 1940s and early 1950s was a critical period in United States relations with East Asia. A bare summary of the major developments in those years highlights the fact of a deepening American involvement with long-term consequences for both the region and the United States. Military occupations thrust the United States deep into the internal affairs of Korea and Japan. Postwar continuation of wartime support for the Chinese Nationalists exacerbated an already distant and suspicious relationship with the Communists. The Korean War, in turn, forged enduring American ties to ruling groups in South Korea, Japan, and Taiwan while setting the seal on the hostility between Washington and Peking.

Historians have already entered on a major reappraisal of these events, the earliest of which is less than forty years behind us, and in the process they are revising the ground-breaking studies done in the 1950s and 1960s. The impetus for this reappraisal, building over the last decade, has come in large measure from the appearance of a wide range of new source materials—the Asia-related volumes of the official documentary series *Foreign Relations of the United States* (1:358), the new historical series (26:5) prepared by the Senate Foreign Relations Committee, the records of the British foreign office, and a wide assortment of personal papers. Previously, only selected historians and policymakers enjoyed privileged access to the official record. They produced an impressively large body of works, as the entries below testify, many of them landmarks in the field. These works, however, provided only glimpses of the sources but not the full access essential to open historical inquiry, evaluation, and interchange. Only now with much of the political and military record opening for research has it become possible to subject the key interpretive issues to free, informed, and long overdue scrutiny and debate.

The eclipse of domestic political controversy over the loss of China and the conduct of the Korean War has also helped clear the way for the reappraisal now under way. Well into the 1960s, works on American Asian policy tended to reflect the terms of that controversy, with its broad acceptance of the existence of a communist "menace" in Asia and its disagreement over whether the Truman administration's response to it was sufficiently prompt or forceful. This interpretive tendency was as evident in 1963 studies—Tang Tsou's *America's Failure in China, 1941–1950* (27:67) and Anthony Kubek's *How the Far East Was Lost* (27:65)—as it had been in 1952 with the appearance of Kenneth Scott Latourette's *The American Record in the Far East, 1945–1951* (New York: Macmillan), and Harold M. Vinacke's *The U.S. and the Far East, 1945–1951* (New York: American Institute of Pacific Relations). As the Sino-Soviet split and the wrenching conflict in Indochina unsettled long-established American policy assumptions about Asian communism, historians began reexamining the roots of the Asian cold war. Some concluded that the United States had overreacted in the postwar years—a point made earlier in the works of Owen Lattimore, William Appleman Williams, and I. F. Stone, but generally neglected in scholarly works on Asian policy. The so-called New Left revisionists have done the most to give this new interpretive perspective bold and systematic treatment—with considerable attendant controversy.

The maturation of East Asian studies in the United States in the 1960s and 1970s has given a further fillip to the exploration of the cold war in Asia. The arrival on the scene of historians able to draw in the Asian perspective was remarkably long delayed. It was only in the 1930s, under the sponsorship of the American Council of Learned Societies, the Rockefeller Foundation, and the American Council of the Institute of Pacific Relations, that Asian studies in the United States began to establish its independence from missionary and European scholarship (the latter with its strong philological and pre-modern bent). World War II provided the stimulus to continued growth by putting an unprecedented number of Americans (a small but critical company of them to emerge as leaders in the postwar development of the field) in direct touch with contemporary Asian affairs. The postwar period witnessed the rise of major Asian studies centers at a half dozen universities and an increasing number of trained specialists, especially in the 1960s, as the Ford Foundation and the federal government pumped money into the field. The major organization devoted to scholarly work on Asia, the Association for Asian Studies (earlier known as the Far Eastern Association), grew from 600 at its inception in 1948–1949 to 4,700 by 1970.

Even so, these developments did not at first translate into work on U.S.–East Asian relations. Historians of Asia trained in the 1930s tended to channel their energies into the nineteenth century, a period for which there were both documentation and the pressing interpretive question about modernization (Asia's response to the West). The postwar crop of Asian specialists for their part either, in the case of historians, steered clear of events that could not be fully documented or, in the case of political scientists, devoted themselves to the long neglected internal dynamics of contemporary Asia. Not until the early 1960s did the first specialists with historical training begin to tackle the Asian side of U.S.–East Asian relations, and even then the cold war eluded serious attention. Only within the last decade have we seen the emergence of works which investigate the cold war in both Asian and American terms.

The agenda for future work must surely begin on the Asian side of the relationship, which has lagged—and will undoubtedly continue to lag—behind our grasp of the American side. However, this work (and the ideal of a full and balanced history of the Asian cold war) depends for its realization on overcoming a variety of obstacles arrayed before it. Chief among these are the small audience in the United States interested in and willing to support Asian studies, the difficulty of the prerequisite training, and finally the restrictions both on source materials and on contacts with historians in China and Korea. (Japan is the happy exception here. Archives are opening, scholars are making a vital contribution, and contact with American counterparts has become a matter of routine.) The foreign language entries in this chapter stand at the very least as a reminder that Asian actors—and scholars—stand prominently on the historical stage alongside Americans.

New studies should also give more attention to nongovernmental aspects of relations in this period. The roles of images and interest groups, to take one example, and the long-term social consequences of official policies, to take another, are general topics important both in themselves and in setting the role of policymakers in the United States and in East Asia in some broader historical perspective. Among the works that point in this direction are Kenneth Shewmaker's *Americans and Chinese Communists, 1927–1945* (27:90), Jessie Lutz's *China and the Christian Colleges, 1850–1950*, chapters 11 and 12 (2:79), and

Howard Schonberger's "American Labor's Cold War in Occupied Japan" (27:130). The Japanese and Korean occupations particularly cry out for a broad cultural rather than a narrow policy approach. Japan is likely to receive such treatment once the current explosion of research on the occupation runs its course and the results can be digested. In the case of Korea, historians have been slow to break new ground, so preoccupied have they been with the political and military questions arising directly from the outbreak and conduct of war on the peninsula. Bruce Cuming's *The Origins of the Korean War: Liberation and the Emergence of Separate Regimes, 1945–1947* (Princeton, N.J.: Princeton University Press, 1981) may redirect some of those older concerns.

Once we have a better, broader understanding of bilateral relations with Japan, China, and Korea, we should give thought to weaving them together into a comprehensive view of regional interaction and then exploring the links between East Asian developments and U.S. relations with other regions, most prominently Southeast Asia, Western Europe, and the Soviet Union. A beginning can be made now toward a synthesis, but it will be some time before the building blocks will be numerous enough and firmly enough in place to serve as a foundation for the writing of enduring and sophisticated works.

The historical reappraisal already under way has thrust forward some key questions, likely to command attention for some time to come. On the American side we need to know when and how cold war concerns intruded in American East Asian policy, shaping in particular the course of the Japanese occupation (was 1948 the turning point?), the response to the rise of Chinese Communism, and the decision first to intervene in Korea and then to march north across the thirty-eighth parallel. We also need to know more about the attitudes and assumptions guiding policymakers in their approach to Asia. Were their perceptions acute, were they uniformly held within the foreign policy establishment, and did they give rise to a coherent Asian policy? Those with an interest in possible "lost chances" for averting the Asian cold war will want to consider what alternative approaches were advanced and rejected or perhaps never advanced at all. How much were policy choices (as for example in relation to China in the late 1940s) narrowed by public alarm over communism and by partisan political calculations? Put differently, to what extent did policy mirror the values of the society and the interests of influential groups within it?

For Asia, swept by nationalism and disrupted by empire-building and war, the main task is to trace the impact of intruding Soviet and American military forces and the attendant political pressures exercised by these two increasingly antagonistic major powers. It would be helpful to have a clearer sense of the evolving relationship between Asian communists and the U.S.S.R. as well as of the sometimes uneasy collaboration with the United States followed by the Nationalists in China, the Rhee regime in Korea, and the conservative party in Japan. We need to know more about Asian leaders generally and about the links between their domestic bases of support and their foreign policies before we can make secure pronouncements about such issues as the origins of the Korean War or the receptivity of the Chinese Communists to some understanding with the United States.

In the meantime—pending the arrival of the historiographical millenium—the newcomer can make a good start with the article by Russell Buhite, " 'Major Interests': American Policy toward China, Taiwan, and Korea, 1945–1950" (27:21), the appropriate chapters in the two-volume survey by Joyce and Gabriel Kolko (24:40, 25:19), and the contributions to two recently published volumes, one edited by Nagai Yōnosuke and Akira Iriye (27:25) and the other by Dorothy Borg and Waldo Heinrichs (27:20). To make the acquaintance of the past as high-level policymakers recall it, begin with the memoirs of Dean Acheson, Harry Truman, and George Kennan, and then go on to the other first-person accounts more specifically devoted to the Asia scene that are listed under the appropriate topics below (though always staying alert to the tricks of memory, both defective and selective, that works of this sort are peculiarly prone to). But in the end it is to the primary sources that the novice, like the veteran, must turn in order to grasp the full historical challenge posed by the cold war in Asia.

Barton Bernstein, Dorothy Borg, Ray Moore, and Steven Pelz have been good enough to review the entries for this chapter and make a variety of helpful suggestions and additions.

Resources and Overviews

RESEARCH AIDS

While pertinent bibliographies and reference aids are listed here, there are more extensive lists in Chapter 1.

Bibliographies

27:1 Blanchard, Carroll H., Jr. *Korean War Bibliography and Maps of Korea.* Albany, N.Y.: Korean Conflict Research Foundation, 1964. This bibliography of Western-language materials (including both scholarly and general periodicals) is unique in its breadth and depth. Valuable on the course of the war, it is less useful on the origins.

Foreign Affairs Bibliography: A Selected and Annotated List of Books on International Relations (1:15) contains references to East Asia and to U.S.–East Asian relations which are useful for information concerning economic, cultural, and political issues.

Hutson, S. H. *McCarthy and the Anti-Communist Crusade: A Selected Bibliography* (26:1) lists references to the *Amerasia* case, the Institute of Pacific Relations hearings and the Owen Lattimore controversy.

Lewis, J. R. *Uncertain Judgment: A Bibliography of War Crimes Trials* (1:39) includes a comprehensive list of materials on the Tokyo trials.

Miller, S. D., comp. *An Aerospace Bibliography* (1:46) has a section (pp. 69–74) on the air war in Korea.

27:2 Sakamoto Yoshikazau, et al. *Nihon senryō bunken mokuroku* [A bibliography of the occupation of Japan]. Tokyo: Nihon Gakujutsu Shinkōkai, 1972. A thorough guide to Japanese-language books and articles published before 1972; the authors and titles appear in romanized Japanese. A supplement lists principal Japanese policymakers.

27:3 Ward, Robert E., and Shulman, Frank J. *The Allied Occupation of Japan, 1945–1952.* Chicago: American Library Association, 1974. This is the most comprehensive bibliography on American-Japanese relations for this period. While providing excellent coverage of secondary works, memoirs, and contemporary journals, it offers only sketchy treatment of archival materials. An appendix provides a valuable list of all occupation personnel.

Historiographical Essays

27:4 Brown, Delmer M. "Recent Japanese Political and Historical Materials." *American Political Science*

Review 43:5 (1949), 1010–17. Here an expert on Japanese nationalism makes the first attempt to survey and evaluate the materials assembled for the Tokyo war crimes trials. Because this article deals with materials found by the occupation teams but not offered or accepted as evidence, it is wider in scope than the Dull and Umemura *Index* (27:18). The two should nevertheless be used together.

27:5 Dallek, Robert. "The Truman Era." In Ernest R. May and James C. Thomson, Jr., eds., *American–East Asian Relations: A Survey*. Cambridge: Harvard University Press, 1972, pp. 356–76. A review of the state of the art, this essay also suggests a multitude of still unanswered questions on American–East Asian relations during the Truman administration. It is somewhat dated with regard to which documents remain classified and which have been published, and it looks exclusively at English-language books and archives.

27:6 Dower, John W. "Occupied Japan as History and Occupation History as Politics." *Journal of Asian Studies* 34:2 (1975), 485–504. This valuable historiographical essay by one of the few scholars who have examined both Japanese and American archival sources chastises American historians for their intellectual timidity in accepting the premise that occupation policy was a "success" and suggests new standards for assessing that policy.

27:7 Leopold, Richard W. "The Korean War: The Historian's Task." In Francis H. Heller, ed., *The Korean War: A Twenty-five Year Perspective*. Lawrence: Regents Press of Kansas, 1977, pp. 209–24. This useful guided tour through some of the major scholarly literature, official archives, and personal papers is capped by some proposals for further research on the American side.

27:8 Moore, Ray A. "Reflections on the Occupation of Japan." *Journal of Asian Studies* 38:4 (1979), 721–34. This comment on current occupation research offers suggestions on topics that need attention. The author contends that contradictions and inconsistencies of occupation policy go back to conflicting views of Japan, the war, and the surrender that were written into the basic policy document for the occupation.

27:9 Wubben, H. H. "American Prisoners of War in Korea: A Second Look at the 'Something New in History' Theme." *American Quarterly* 22:2 (1970), 3–19. In a summary of the literature on a neglected but fascinating topic, Wubben contends that critics of alleged prisoner misconduct have misread the evidence and that in comparative terms captured Americans behaved unexceptionally. For more on the subject of POWs—both American and Communist—see the works by sociologist Albert D. Biderman.

Yearbooks and Other Aids

China Yearbook (31:5).

Facts on File: A Weekly Digest with Cumulative Index (1:151) contains among its weekly summaries of contemporary events, episodes, and issues related to U.S.–East Asian affairs.

Herrman, A. *An Historical Atlas of China* (1:161).

Keesing's Contemporary Archives: Weekly Diary of World Events (1:152) is the British equivalent of *Facts on File*, but has somewhat stronger coverage of foreign affairs.

Political Handbook and Atlas of the World (1:144) is a valuable annual reference guide to all governments and their officials and political parties, including East Asian countries.

Survey of International Affairs [1920–1963] (1:146) provides a useful narrative of international diplomacy, including U.S.–East Asian affairs, prepared by scholars.

The United States in World Affairs (1:147) is a useful annual survey and analysis which covers up to 1970, with 1968 and 1969 yet to be printed.

Document Collections

More general collections are listed in Chapter 1, and other collections may be found in "Personalities," below.

27:10 Chung-kuo jen-min k'ang-Mei yüan-Ch'ao tsung-hui, hsüan-ch'uan pu [Chinese people's resist-America aid-Korea campaign committee, propaganda department]. *Wei-ta ti k'ang-Mei-yüan-Ch'ao yün-tung* [The great resist-America aid-Korea campaign]. Peking: Jen-min ch'u-pan she, 1954. This is the single most important, comprehensive collection of Chinese Communist documents on the Korean War. The truce talks receive special attention in another volume. Other collections (several in English) made available by the People's Republic offer commentary on the contemporary American role in Taiwan and Japan. For a full descriptive listing, see P. Berton and E. Wu, *Contemporary China: A Research Guide* (31:1), pp. 310–19.

27:11 Dutt, Vidya P., ed. *East Asia: China, Korea, Japan, 1947–1950.* New York: Oxford University Press, 1958. This useful reference contains documents organized by country and deals with domestic and foreign affairs.

Gallup, G. H. *The Gallup Poll: Public Opinion, 1935–1971* (1:348) pays considerable attention to foreign affairs, including American attitudes toward East Asian issues.

27:12 International Military Tribunal for the Far East. *Record of the Proceedings.* Microfilm. Washington, D.C.: Library of Congress, 1947. This collection of documents and testimony deals with the Tokyo war crimes trial of those allegedly most responsible for involving Japan in the war. It is a useful source on Japanese domestic life and diplomacy (1928–1945). For index see Dull and Umemura (27:18).

27:13 Kim Se-jin, ed. *Documents on Korean-American Relations, 1943–76.* Seoul: Research Center for Peace and Unification, 1976. This indexed volume brings together a large number of important documents. But like most of the South Korean literature on the period, it neglects once classified Korean and American documents. Anyone interested in digging deeper should see the relevant sections of the *Foreign Relations of the United States* (1:358), and such Korean-language collections as Kuksa p'yonch'an wiwonhoe [National History Compilation Committee], ed., *Taehan Min'guk-sa, Charyo* [History of the Republic of Korea, materials] 7 vols. (Seoul: Kuksa p'yonch'an wiwonhoe, 1970–1974).

27:14 [U.S.S.R.]. *The Soviet Union and the Korean Question.* London: Soviet News, 1950. This official record, which brings together in one convenient volume the public statements of the Soviet Union on Korean questions, contains few surprises. There are few Soviet studies of the period in Russian or in English to illuminate the Soviet perspective. The magazine *New Times* (1945–1950) is the most helpful in this regard.

U.S. Department of State. *Foreign Relations of the United States* (1:358) is an invaluable collection essen-

tial for research on U.S.–East Asian relations in this period. The relevant volumes deal with the major developments during the wartime and early cold war period and cover political, military, economic, and cultural interaction. The difficulties which its compilers have had in getting materials from the files of agencies outside the Department of State (especially the National Security Council) declassified has delayed publication and diminished its value as a comprehensive record.

27:15 U.S. Department of State. *United States Relations with China, with Special Reference to the Period 1944–49.* Washington, D.C.: G.P.O., 1949. Issued as a defense by the Truman administration against charges that it had lost China to the Communists, this collection includes Dean Acheson's letter of transmittal to President Truman and documents mainly from the period 1947–1948. It was reissued in 1967 by Stanford University Press as *The China White Paper, August 1949* (2 vols.). This new edition includes an introductory essay by Lyman P. Van Slyke, which describes the genesis of this controversial study and the impact it had on both Chinese and American politics. The new edition also contains a detailed index missing in the original.

U.S. Senate. Committee on Foreign Relations. *Executive Sessions of the Senate Foreign Relations Committee* (26:5) contains important material on U.S. East Asian policy in the late 1940s and early 1950s; it should be read with earlier published committee hearings.

27:16 U.S. Senate. Committee on Foreign Relations and Committee on Armed Services. Hearings; *Military Situation in the Far East.* 5 vols. Washington, D.C.: G.P.O., 1951. These hearings, held following President Truman's recall of General MacArthur, provided an opportunity for a public cross-examination of the chief architects of American foreign policy. Although repetitive, the testimony is essential to an understanding of the assumptions and decisions that shaped the conduct of the war. A useful discussion of the hearings is available in John Wiltz, "The MacArthur Inquiry, 1951," in Arthur M. Schlesinger, Jr., and Roger Burns, eds., *Congress Investigates* (New York, 1975), vol. 5, pp.3593–636.

27:17 U.S. Senate. Committee on the Judiciary. Hearings; *Institute of Pacific Relations.* 15 pts. 82d Cong., 1st and 2d Sess., 1951–1953. The committee's hunt for subversives, particularly those responsible for the "loss of China," led to the creation of this useful historical record.

Index to Documents

27:18 Dull, Paul S., and Umemura, Michael T. *The Tokyo Trials: A Functional Index to the Proceedings of the International Military Tribunal for the Far East.* Ann Arbor: University of Michigan Press, 1957. This is a 94-page index to the nearly fifty thousand pages of the *Proceedings* and hence an invaluable tool for the researcher. It is patterned after the subject index to the Nuremberg military tribunal (28:90).

OVERVIEWS

See Chapter 24, "Overviews," for surveys of American foreign affairs since World War II.

27:19 Beloff, Max. *Soviet Policy in the Far East, 1944–1951.* London: Oxford University Press, 1953. This account remains a good introduction to Soviet policy in East Asia and as such is relevant to Sino-American relations, although Beloff has almost nothing to say directly on U.S. policy.

27:20 Borg, Dorothy, and Heinrichs, Waldo H., Jr., eds. *Uncertain Years: Chinese-American Relations, 1947–1950.* New York: Columbia University Press, 1980. These essays develop key facets of Sino-American diplomatic relations down to the outbreak of the Korean War, including Dean Acheson's stand on China, the place of East Asia in U.S. strategic planning, and Chinese policies (both Communist and Nationalist) toward the United States. The collection is notable for its systematic use of recently released U.S. government documents and neglected Chinese Communist materials and for its inclusion of extensive scholarly commentary on the essays. Index and detailed chronology.

27:21 Buhite, Russell D. " 'Major Interests': American Policy toward China, Taiwan, and Korea, 1945–1950." *Pacific Historical Review* 47:3 (1978), 425–51. This article suggests that policymakers came to believe that there existed in Asia an intermediate zone of "major interests," and thereby seeks to explain the seeming anomaly of American expenditure of significant resources in an area which was not then seen as "vital" but could not be written off as "peripheral."

27:22 Etzold, Thomas H. "The Far East in American Strategy." In Thomas H. Etzold, ed., *Aspects of Sino-American Relations since 1784.* New York: New Viewpoints, 1978, pp. 102–26. The author argues that containment of communism motivated the U.S. policy in Asia between 1948 and 1951. Asian containment was at first based on a mainland-island strategy, but the Chinese civil war made this unworkable. The Korean War served to resurrect the old strategy, leading to unwanted commitments on the Asian continent.

27:23 Iriye, Akira. *The Cold War in Asia.* Englewood Cliffs, N.J.: Prentice-Hall, 1974. Iriye here applies his "systemic" analysis of international relations to postwar East Asia (1945–1950). He describes the "Yalta system," founded on an agreement between the United States and the Soviet Union to divide East Asia along lines of military control with China in the middle as a "gray area." The civil war in China led to the collapse of this agreement and the onset of the cold war. Critical bibliography.

27:24 Iriye, Akira. "Was There a Cold War in Asia?" In John Chay, ed., *The Problems and Prospects of American–East Asian Relations.* Boulder, Colo.: Westview, 1977, pp. 3–24. The author contends that, although the United States viewed postwar developments in Asia through a cold war perspective, it did not formulate a cold war strategy for the Pacific until late 1949–early 1950—after the Soviet Union exploded an A-bomb and Mao established the People's Republic of China. The new strategy was reflected in NSC-68 (see Chapter 26).

Kolko, G. *The Politics of War: The World and United States Foreign Policy, 1943–1945* (25:19).

Kolko, J., and Kolko, G. *The Limits of Power: The World and United States Foreign Policy, 1945–1954* (24:40)—these two works give detailed attention to East Asia. Written from a "left revisionist" perspective, both accounts stress American opposition to revolutionary change in Asia.

27:25 Nagai Yōnosuke, and Iriye, Akira, eds. *The Origins of the Cold War in Asia.* New York: Columbia University Press, 1977. This important set of essays by outstanding American, Japanese, and British specialists is notable for its use of a broad range of source materials and its wide-ranging coverage, including American public opinion, American-Japanese relations, origins of the Korean War, and British, Soviet, and Chinese Communist policies. Index.

27:26 Rose, Lisle A. *Roots of Tragedy: The United States and the Struggle for Asia, 1945–1954.* Westport, Conn.: Greenwood, 1976. This survey was written to answer the question of why American responses to "turbulence" in East and Southeast Asia were so tragically inappropriate. Rose rejects the search for economic advantage as a satisfactory answer and instead emphasizes the conservative social and political instincts that guided American policymakers.

27:27 Varg, Paul. *Closing the Open Door: Sino-American Relations, 1936–1946.* East Lansing: Michigan State University Press, 1973. This chronicle of U.S. policy toward China is primarily concerned with high-level policymakers and the formal implementation of decisions.

27:28 Zagoria, Donald S. "Choices in the Postwar World: Containment and China." In Charles Gati, ed., *Caging the Bear: Containment and the Cold War.* Indianapolis: Bobbs-Merrill, 1974, pp. 109–27. Zagoria contends that domestic politics and in ultimate terms a superficial conception of international politics prevented the United States from exploiting Sino-Soviet tensions and reaching an accommodation with Communist China.

Public Opinion and Politics

See "Personalities," especially Owen Lattimore (under "Others") and Arthur H. Vandenberg.

27:29 Chern, Kenneth S. "Politics of American China Policy, 1945: Roots of the Cold War in Asia." *Political Science Quarterly* 91:4 (1976/1977), 631–47. Chern reviews the first phase of the American debate over intervention in the Chinese civil war. The author sees "an incipient China lobby" locked in conflict with a Truman administration unable to articulate forcefully its own policy position.

27:30 Hedley, John H. "The Truman Administration and the 'Loss' of China: A Study of Public Attitudes and the President's Policies from the Marshall Mission to the Attack on Korea." Ph.D. diss., University of Missouri, 1964. This account is notable for its extensive use of White House and State Department Public Opinion Studies Staff materials. The author concludes that popular sentiment set virtually no boundaries on U.S. China policy and that later attacks on Truman were the effort of a minority.

Hohenberg, J. *Between Two Worlds: Policy, Press, and Public Opinion in Asian-American Relations* [1941–1960s] (31:25).

Hunt, M. H. "Pearl Buck—Popular Expert on China, 1931–1949" (21:221) is an examination of a China expert with an influence over popular perceptions rather than official policy. Using Buck's extensive work, the author traces her reaction to China in crisis and analyzes the nature and limits of her expertise.

Kahn, E. J., Jr. *The China Hands: America's Foreign Service Officers and What Befell Them* (27:49) is a study of 13 foreign service officers who served in wartime China and whose reports to Washington at the time might arguably have changed the course of Sino-American relations had they not been ignored. The author describes their experience after they left China and the damaging effects of the McCarthy era on their careers.

Latham, E. *The Communist Controversy in Washington: From the New Deal to McCarthy* (26:224) includes a discussion (pp. 239–316) of the impact of China policy on U.S. domestic politics. Latham rejects the conspiracy theory as unsupported by the data. Bibliography.

27:31 Roche, George C. "Public Opinion and the China Policy of the United States, 1941–1951." Ph.D. diss., University of Colorado, 1965. The author provides wide coverage of newspapers and magazines. Although this volume is short on interpretative analysis, it is a fine source of information. Extensive bibliography.

27:32 Thomas, John N. *The Institute of Pacific Relations: Asian Scholars and American Politics.* Seattle: University of Washington Press, 1974. This slim account describes the major private organization devoted to promoting study of Asia in the 1930s and 1940s and its demise under the weight of cold war controversy. The author is critical of IPR leaders for laying the organization open to attack by frequently taking a "partisan" position on Asian affairs. Bibliography and index.

Westerfield, H. B. *Foreign Policy and Party Politics: Pearl Harbor to Korea* (2:155) is an early and detailed examination of why China policy became a partisan issue. Coverage of China aid legislation is particularly good. The book is now dated by the release of transcripts of executive session hearings on foreign policy in Congress and by the cold war assumptions pervading the interpretation.

China Lobby

27:33 Keeley, Joseph. *The China Lobby Man: The Story of Alfred Kohlberg.* New Rochelle, N.Y.: Arlington House, 1969. Kohlberg, an importer of Chinese textiles, was an outspoken and persistent critic of U.S. China policy during the late 1940s and 1950s. He advised Senator McCarthy on China. This generally laudatory biography seeks to explain Kohlberg's interest in China.

27:34 Koen, Ross Y. *The China Lobby in American Politics.* New York: Harper & Row, 1974. This remains the only book to examine seriously the China Lobby—what it was, who belonged to it, and what effect it had on U.S. foreign policy. Although published in 1960 by Macmillan, the book was suppressed by the publisher in response to political pressure. Extensive bibliography.

27:35 Wertenbaker, Charles, and Horton, Philip. "The China Lobby." *Reporter* 6 (Apr. 15, 1952), 2–24; 6 (Apr. 29, 1952), 5–24. This exposé of the China Lobby attracted widespread attention and continues to be a good source of information. The authors concentrated on identifying the members of the pro–Chiang Kai-shek group.

Japan Lobby

Roberts, J. G. "The 'Japan Crowd' and the Zaibatsu Restoration" (27:129).

27:36 Schonberger, Howard. "The Japan Lobby in American Diplomacy, 1947–1952." *Pacific Historical Review* 46:3 (1977), 327–60. This study traces the efforts of former diplomats, businessmen, and journalists to turn U.S. Japan policy away from reform toward diplomatic and political alliance with Japanese conservatives.

Personalities

Additional references on individuals may be found in Chapter 1, "Biographical Data."

AMERICAN

See Chapter 24, "Personalities" and "Presidential Administrations," for additional references.

Dean Acheson

See Chapter 24, "Personalities," for additional references.

Acheson, D. *Present at the Creation: My Years in the State Department* (24:90) recalls his views on the Far East generally, and the Korean War in particular.

27:37 McLellan, David S. "Dean Acheson and the Korean War." *Political Science Quarterly* 83:1 (1968), 16–39. McLellan gives the secretary low marks for his insensitivity to the fears of the Chinese Communists and for his failure to oppose General MacArthur's military action north of the 38th parallel.

Claire L. Chennault

Chennault, C. L. *Way of a Fighter: The Memoirs of Claire L. Chennault* (23:100) is an unabashedly "pro-Chiang" memoir, which provides useful information about the exercise of American air power in Asia, Chennault's bitter conflict with General Stilwell, and the development of the so-called China Lobby.

Mark W. Clark

27:38 Clark, Mark W. *From the Danube to the Yalu.* New York: Harper, 1954. This autobiographical account includes treatment of the closing days of the Korean War, when the author was the commander of the UN forces. Clark paints some interesting, even revealing, portraits of Syngman Rhee (a close friend), MacArthur, General Hodge (commander of the occupation of Korea, 1945–1948), and others.

U.S. Department of Army, *United States Army in the Korean War* (27:188).

John P. Davies, Jr.

27:39 Davies, John P., Jr. *Dragon by the Tail: American, British, Japanese, and Russian Encounters with China and with One Another.* New York: Norton, 1972. Davies's book is both a memoir of his years as a foreign service officer in China (1937–1945) and an analysis of American and Soviet confrontations with Chinese nationalism. His account of political infighting in China and Washington makes compelling reading.

27:40 Fetzer, James A. "The Case of John Paton Davies, Jr." *Foreign Service Journal* 54:11 (1977), 15–22, 31–32. A foreign service officer caught in the McCarthy era purges of State Department personnel, John Paton Davies emerges in this article as an unlikely candidate for censure.

John Foster Dulles

See Chapter 24, "Personalities," for additional references.

Curtis, G. L. "The Dulles-Yoshida Negotiations on the San Francisco Peace Treaty" (27:135).

Patrick J. Hurley

Buhite, R. D. *Patrick J. Hurley and American Foreign Policy* (23:60) traces Hurley's career from its humble beginnings through the ranks of law, business, politics, and diplomacy. Buhite devotes a major portion of the study to Hurley's mission to China. Even though essentially sympathetic, this study shows Hurley as an often comic, sometimes even pathetic figure.

Lohbeck, D. *Patrick J. Hurley* (23:61) is an "authorized" biography describing Hurley's public attack on the Yalta agreement and early U.S. China policies.

C. Turner Joy

Joy, C. T. *How Communists Negotiate* (27:200).

27:41 Joy, C. Turner. *Negotiating While Fighting: The Diary of Admiral C. Turner Joy at the Korean Armistice Conference.* Ed. by Allan E. Goodman. Stanford, Calif.: Hoover Institution Press, 1978. This detailed diary covers Joy's activities from July 1951 to May 1952 as the chief of the UN delegation to the armistice talks. This is an essential source.

Douglas MacArthur

See Chapters 23 and 40, "Personalities," for additional references; also see "Truman-MacArthur Controversy," below.

MacArthur, D. *Reminiscences* (40:55) contains General MacArthur's view of his involvement in the Korean War (as commander of UN forces) as well as in the Japanese occupation (as American proconsul). The book remains important for the light it sheds on MacArthur's motives and character, but it must be checked against the documentary record.

Manchester, W. *American Caesar: Douglas MacArthur, 1880–1964* (24:139) is a complete biography.

Wittner, L. S. "MacArthur and the Missionaries: God and Man in Occupied Japan" (27:132).

George C. Marshall

See Chapters 23 and 24, "Personalities," for additional references.

Beal, J. R. *Marshall in China* (27:76) is a "memoir" by an adviser to the Chinese government during the period of the Marshall mission.

27:42 Marshall, George C. *Marshall's Mission to China: December 1945–January 1947.* 2 vols. Arlington, Va.: University Publications of America, 1976. As President Truman's special representative to China, Marshall was to arrange a cease-fire and form a coalition government which would include both Communists and Nationalists. This is Marshall's final report. All but 24 of the supporting documents included here also appear in the "China White Paper" (27:15) and the U.S. Foreign Relations series (1:358).

Henry Morgenthau, Jr.

See Chapters 18, 19, 21, and 22, "Personalities," for additional references.

U.S. Senate. Committee on the Judiciary. Report; *Morgenthau Diary (China)* (22:30) contains documents gathered to show the Roosevelt administration was "soft on communism." These two volumes contain almost all references in the diaries for 1938 through 1944.

John S. Service

Service, J. S. *Lost Chance in China: The World War II Despatches of John S. Service* (23:71) is a collection of 71 of Service's dispatches from China (1941–1945), including reports, assessments of Nationalist and Communist activities, and recommendations for changes in U.S. policy. Twenty-six of these documents have not been published previously.

27:43 Service, John S. *The Amerasia Papers: Some Problems in the History of U.S.-China Relations.* Berkeley: University of California, Center for Chinese Studies, 1971. Writing in response to continuing attacks upon his loyalty, the author describes his fateful entanglement in the Amerasia case, evaluates his own role in wartime China, and offers a critique of U.S. policy. Service argues that Mao's "non-ideological" foreign policy left room for accommodation with the United States and that Ambassador Hurley is to blame for the American failure to explore the chances for better relations.

27:44 U.S. Senate. Committee on the Judiciary. *The Amerasia Papers: A Clue to the Catastrophe of China.* 2 vols. Washington, D.C.: G.P.O., 1970. Reprinted here are 315 of the 1,700 U.S. government documents that were seized by the federal agents from the offices of *Amerasia* magazine on June 6, 1945, and that led to the arrest of John Service and five others. These documents deal with U.S.-China relations (1944–1945) and include many of Service's own dispatches.

Joseph W. Stilwell

See Chapter 23, "Personalities," for additional references.

Liang Chin-tung. *General Stilwell in China, 1942–1944: The Full Story* (27:72) was written in response to Barbara Tuchman's biography of Stilwell. (American edition: *To Change China: Western Advisers in China, 1620–1960.* 1980.)

Spence, J. *The China Helpers: Western Advisers in China, 1620–1960* (2:347) uses the careers of General Joseph W. Stilwell and his rival, General Claire L. Chennault, to explore the hopes and fantasies foreigners brought to China.

Stilwell, J. W. *The Stilwell Papers* (23:110) remains a starting point for anyone studying the conditions faced by Americans in wartime China. Stilwell makes Chiang and his associates into devils, while overlooking the general social and political conditions which sustained them. For a fuller collection of Stilwell materials, see *Stilwell's Personal File: China, Burma, India, 1942–1944* (23:111).

Tuchman, B. *Stilwell and the American Experience in China, 1911–1945* (23:112) is both exciting reading and a fine introduction to the politics of the U.S.-Nationalist alliance. Stilwell's life in the army, culminating with his command of all U.S. forces in China, serves as the medium for analyzing the military and political strategy pursued by Americans in China.

Harry S. Truman

See Chapters 24, 26, and 40, "Personalities," for additional references.

Haynes, R. F. *The Awesome Power: Harry S. Truman as Commander in Chief* (40:91) examines Truman's relationship to the military command structure and concludes that Truman was the first of the "new" presidents who would handle a succession of military

crises (including the Korean War) without congressional advice and consent.

Purifoy, L. M. *Harry Truman's China Policy: McCarthyism and the Diplomacy of Hysteria, 1947–1951* (27:82).

Arthur H. Vandenberg

See Chapters 24, 25, 26, and 38, "Personalities," for additional references.

27:45 Fetzer, James A. "Senator Vandenberg and the American Commitment to China, 1945–1950." *Historian* 36:2 (1974), 283–303. This study deals with the senator's attempt to play a mediatory role in the increasingly acrimonious congressional debate over the Truman administration's China policy.

Others

Allison, J. M. *Ambassador from the Prairies, or, Allison Wonderland* (24:167) details in chapter 8 his work, first as head of the Japan-Korean Division of the Department of State, then as aide to John Foster Dulles, drafting and negotiating the peace and security treaties of 1951.

27:46 Clubb, O. Edmund. *The Witness and I.* New York: Columbia University Press, 1974. Clubb, a China specialist, served as America's last consul general in Peking and subsequently, in 1950, director of the State Department's Office of Chinese Affairs. This book details his struggle against the vague charges and anonymous informants that forced him to leave the China service in 1952.

27:47 Collins, J. Lawton. *War in Peacetime: The History and Lessons of Korea.* Boston: Houghton Mifflin, 1969. Collins served as chief of staff of the army and hence as a member of the Joint Chiefs of Staff during the entire Korean War. His memoir describes events from the perspective of a senior military officer who supported the limited war strategy and President Truman's decision to recall General MacArthur.

27:48 Emmerson, John K. *The Japanese Thread: A Lifetime in the U.S. Foreign Service.* New York: Holt, Rinehart & Winston, 1978. The earlier chapters of this carefully crafted memoir by a distinguished American diplomat offer valuable commentary on the makers of U.S. East Asian policy. Chapters 9 and 10 are of special interest for their discussions of policy planning and the early phase of the Japanese occupation.

27:49   Kahn, E. J., Jr. *The China Hands: America's Foreign Service Officers and What Befell Them.* New York: Viking, 1972. This is a collective biography of the foreign service officers whose diplomatic careers were damaged or destroyed by the anticommunist witch-hunts of the early 1950s. Included are David D. Barnett, O. Edmund Clubb, John Paton Davies, Jr., Everett F. Drumright, John K. Emmerson, Fulton Freeman, Raymond P. Ludden, James K. Penfield, Edward E. Rice, Arthur R. Ringwalt, John S. Service, Philip D. Sprouse, and John Carter Vincent. Bibliography.

27:50   Lattimore, Owen. *Ordeal by Slander.* Boston: Little, Brown, 1950. In this book Owen Lattimore recounts his initial success at repelling charges of espionage lodged against him by McCarthy. In addition, the author discusses the important questions in Sino-American relations of that time, such as the problem of Taiwan.

27:51   May, Gary. *China Scapegoat: The Diplomatic Ordeal of John Carter Vincent.* Washington, D.C.: New Republic Books, 1979. This "life and times" biography covers Vincent's 28 years as a China expert and his ordeal at the hands of investigators between 1947 and his forced retirement in 1953.

27:52   Rankin, Karl L. *China Assignment.* Seattle: University of Washington Press, 1964. This book recounts developments in China and Taiwan from the perspective of a foreign service officer who served as consul general in Canton and Hong Kong and later as minister and ambassador to Taiwan.

27:53   Ridgway, Matthew B. *The Korean War: How We Met the Challenge: How All-out Asian War Was Averted: Why MacArthur Was Dismissed: Why Today's War Objectives Must Be Limited.* Garden City, N.Y.: Doubleday, 1967. This narrative history, written by the general who assumed command in Korea after MacArthur's recall, defends limited war and civilian control of the military. Ridgway charges MacArthur with serious military errors and political ineptitude and uses the Korean experience to argue against the value of heavy bombing in Vietnam.

27:54   Sebald, William J., and Russell, Brines. *With MacArthur in Japan: A Personal History of the Occupation.* New York: Norton, 1965. This account by MacArthur's principal diplomatic adviser contains valuable insights and commentary on the principal personages and events in American-Japanese relations.

27:55   Stuart, John Leighton. *Fifty Years in China.* New York: Random House, 1954. This book testifies above all to Stuart's devotion to the Chinese people and to a reformed China. By virtue of his position as American ambassador, Stuart participated in or was eyewitness to most of the important events of the 1946 to 1949 period. The final chapters of the volume, which were written by Stanley Hornbeck after Stuart suffered a debilitating stroke, take a strong anticommunist line inconsistent with the tenor of the rest of the book.

Wedemeyer, A. C. *Wedemeyer Reports!* (23:120) is an account by the successor to General Stilwell as U.S. commander in China. Wedemeyer seems here intent on strengthening his anticommunist credentials by emphasizing his support for the Nationalist regime.

27:56   Williams, Justin. *Japan's Political Revolution under MacArthur: A Participant's Account.* Athens: University of Georgia Press, 1979. A middle-ranking official of the Government Section recounts his role in "the daring and ambitious experiment in social engineering" in Japan under MacArthur. Sketches of MacArthur, Whitney, Kades, and other Government Section officials are uncritical. Williams's account of his own role in Diet reform reveals his low opinion of Japanese politics and politicians.

EAST ASIAN

Chiang Kai-shek

See also Chapter 21, "Personalities."

Chiang Kai-shek. *Resistance and Reconstruction: Messages during China's Six Years of War, 1937–1943* (22:69).

27:57   Chiang Kai-shek. *Soviet Russia in China: A Summing Up at Seventy.* New York: Farrar, Straus & Giroux, 1957. The leader of the Chinese Nationalists traces the declining fortunes of his forces from wartime cooperation with the United States, through the attempted American mediation, and on to the civil war against the Communists. He blames defeat on the tendency of Washington and Americans in China to fall victim to international communist propaganda.

Mao Tse-tung

27:58 Mao Tse-tung. *Selected Works of Mao Tse-tung*. Peking: Foreign Languages Press, 1961–1965, vols. 3 and 4. These two volumes reprint items ranging from significant essays, such as "On People's Democratic Dictatorship" and "The Present Situation and Our Task," to brief comments on land reform and the negotiations with the Nationalists. Especially notable in terms of Sino-American relations is the series of editorials denouncing the "China White Paper."

27:59 Schram, Stuart. *Mao Tse-tung.* New York: Simon & Schuster, 1966. This standard biography, though in need of revision in the wake of recent revelations and thin on relations with the United States, offers essential background.

Syngman Rhee

27:60 Bernstein, Barton J. "Syngman Rhee: The Pawn as Rook; The Struggle to End the Korean War." *Bulletin of Concerned Asian Scholars* 10:1 (1978), 38–47. The author traces attempts by Rhee, America's obstreperous but shrewd ally, to disrupt the American-led effort to secure an armistice. President Eisenhower reluctantly provided Rhee assurance of American support in the form of a mutual security pact.

27:61 Oliver, Robert T. *Syngman Rhee: The Man Behind the Myth.* Cornwall, N.Y.: Cornwall Press, 1955. Oliver, a close friend and adviser to Rhee, wrote this biography as a tribute. Even so, this account remains a source of fruitful leads and tidbits on the career of a most remarkable and influential Korean. Oliver today holds a collection of Rhee's papers and correspondence.

Yoshida Shigeru

27:62 Dower, John W. *Empire and Aftermath: Yoshida Shigeru and the Japanese Experience, 1868–1954.* Cambridge: Harvard University Press, 1979. This is the first English-language biography, based on Japanese and American archival materials, of the Japanese architect of postwar American-Japanese collaboration. Extensive bibliography.

27:63 Yoshida Shigeru. *The Yoshida Memoirs: The Story of Japan in Crisis.* Trans. by Yoshida Kenichi. Boston: Houghton Mifflin, 1962. This vital memoir by Japan's most important postwar leader is greatly abridged from the original four-volume Japanese edition.

U.S. and China, 1941–1953

See Chapter 23, "Pacific Strategy/Operations" and "China," for additional references related to World War II.

27:64 Feis, Herbert. *The China Tangle: The American Effort in China from Pearl Harbor to the Marshall Mission.* Princeton, N.J.: Princeton University Press, 1953. As Feis sees it, an essentially benign American policy was stymied by the incompetence of the Nationalists and the malevolence of the Chinese Communists. As a former ranking member of the State Department, Feis enjoyed access to official records, but the lack of attributions makes it difficult to evaluate the sources and conclusions.

27:65 Kubek, Anthony. *How the Far East Was Lost: American Policy and the Creation of Communist China, 1941–1949.* Chicago: Regnery, 1963. Kubek is the principal scholarly spokesman for the thesis that the United States "lost" China to the Communists through a combination of incompetence by Democratic officials and treason by professional bureaucrats. For a variant on this McCarthyite attack, see Freda Utley, *The China Story* (Chicago: Regnery, 1951).

27:66 Peck, Jim. "Americans and the Chinese Revolution, 1942–1946: An Interpretation." In Ernest R. May and James C. Thomson Jr., eds., *American–East Asian Relations: A Survey.* Cambridge: Harvard University Press, 1972, pp. 319–55. Peck argues that the Chinese Communists were not dogmatically anti-American and blames U.S. policy in the early postwar period for alienating the Communists. Peck has elaborated on the flawed American perception of the Chinese revolution in "The Roots of Rhetoric: The Professional Ideology of America's China Watchers," *Bulletin of Concerned Asian Scholars* 2 (Oct. 1969), 59–69.

27:67 Tsou, Tang. *America's Failure in China, 1941–1950.* 2 vols. Chicago: University of Chicago Press, 1963. The United States "failed," Tsou argues, because it first devoted inadequate support to its ambitious goal of making China a great power and then did not use sufficient military force to ensure the defeat of the Communists. Tsou's cold war preoccupations are evident in his charges that foreign service officers did not understand the true nature of Chinese Communism.

27:68 Warner, Geoffrey. "America, Russia, China and the Origins of the Cold War, 1945–1950." In Joseph M. Siracusa and Glen St. J. Barclay, eds., *The Impact of the Cold War: Reconsiderations*. Port Washington, N.Y.: Kennikat, 1977, pp. 144–62. This essay emphasizes Soviet flexibility versus American rigidity toward conditions in China. The latter is ascribed to U.S. domestic politics, public opinion, Congress, and the limited vision of America's leaders.

White, T. H. *In Search of History* (23:225) includes descriptions of Stilwell, Chiang Kai-shek, Mao Tse-tung and Chou En-lai. White was in China during the war years.

WARTIME RELATIONS WITH THE NATIONALISTS

See under "Personalities," especially Chiang Kai-shek, Claire L. Chennault, John P. Davies, Jr., Patrick J. Hurley, Henry Morgenthau, Joseph W. Stilwell.

27:69 Caldwell, Oliver J. *A Secret War: Americans in China, 1944–45*. Carbondale: Southern Illinois University Press, 1972. Caldwell here recalls his personal experience between 1941 and 1945 working for the U.S. Office of Strategic Services and cooperating with General Tai Li of the Nationalist secret police. The author is critical of both the Nationalists and the Communists. For the personal perspective of another American who worked with Tai Li, see M. E. Miles's *A Different Kind of War* (23:193).

27:70 Dorn, Frank. *Walkout with Stilwell in Burma*. New York: Crowell, 1971. Dorn not only describes his trek out of Burma with Stilwell in 1942, but goes on to recount their ensuing adventures in Chinese wartime politics and efforts to reform the Nationalist armies.

27:71 Fairbank, Wilma. *America's Cultural Experiment in China, 1942–1949*. Washington, D.C.: G.P.O., 1976. This is one of a series of monographs chronicling the work of the State Department's International Educational and Cultural Exchange Program. Fairbank, who participated in the China program from its inception in 1942 until 1947, records it with care and in detail.

LaFeber, W. "Roosevelt, Churchill and Indochina, 1942–1945" (30:38) demonstrates how Anglo-American policies in Southeast Asia were affected by military and political conditions in China. LaFeber offers a cogent analysis of FDR's attitudes toward his Chinese Nationalist ally.

27:72 Liang Chin-tung. *General Stilwell in China, 1942–1944: The Full Story*. New York: St. Johns University Press, 1972. The author repeats the McCarthyite attacks upon American foreign service officers for "losing China." The chief merit of Liang's book lies in the author's ability to communicate the sense of injured pride and trampled nationalism experienced by Nationalist leaders in their dealings with Stilwell and Roosevelt. Bibliography.

27:73 Liang Chin-tung. "The Sino-Soviet Treaty of Friendship and Alliance of 1945." In Paul K. T. Sih, ed., *Nationalist China during the Sino-Japanese War, 1937–1945*. Hicksville, N.Y.: Exposition, 1977, pp. 373–97, 405–08. A former official of the Chinese Nationalist government, Liang provides an insider's account of the negotiations for the treaty which Washington hoped would stabilize Soviet–Chinese Nationalist relations. Liang sees the U.S.S.R. as expansionist and untrustworthy and the United States as inept and overly conciliatory during this period.

Romanus, C. F., and Sunderland, R. *U.S. Army in World War II: The China-Burma-India Theater* (23:194, 23:196) is a remarkably thorough and analytical account of both the military and political dimensions of the Stilwell and Wedemeyer missions.

27:74 Schaller, Michael. *The U.S. Crusade in China, 1938–1945*. New York: Columbia University Press, 1979. This is an examination of the effort by which Franklin Roosevelt and Americans in China sought to forge a "liberal" China out of the cauldron of invasion, civil war, and great power rivalries. Here, as well as in articles in the *Pacific Historical Review* 44 (Nov. 1975) and the *American Quarterly* 28 (Spring 1976), Schaller sheds fresh light on American involvement in Chinese politics and in clandestine warfare. Extensive bibliography.

Sunderland, R. "The Secret Embargo" (23:192) provides a brief, perceptive comment on Chiang Kai-shek's wartime practice of conserving his own forces while sacrificing the troops of rival Nationalist commanders and blaming the losses on General Stilwell. Warren I. Cohen provides more evidence on this same point in "Who Fought the Japanese in Hunan? Some Views of China's War Effort," *Journal of Asian Studies* 27 (Nov. 1967), 111–15.

27:75 White, Theodore, and Jacoby, Annalee. *Thunder Out of China.* New York: Sloane, 1946. This wide-ranging account combines the best aspects of popular history and journalism. The authors, who witnessed much of what they describe, offer a panoramic view of China's wartime leaders, its politics, battles, famine, and diplomacy. Part of an extraordinary outpouring of reportage on China in the 1940s; authors of other notable accounts include Harrison Forman, Gunther Stein, Graham Peck, Robert Payne, and Jack Belden.

Young, A. N. *China and the Helping Hand, 1937– 1945* (23:226) offers insight on the American financial aid program to the Nationalist government, through which Young served for many years as a financial adviser. Young argues that U.S. financial and military aid to China was inadequate to meet the task at hand.

U.S. MEDIATION AND THE CHINESE CIVIL WAR

See "Personalities," especially George C. Marshall.

27:76 Beal, John R. *Marshall in China.* Garden City, N.Y.: Doubleday, 1970. John Beal, an American journalist, served as an adviser to the Chinese government during the period of the Marshall mission. His "memoir," narrative and anecdotal, is thus important as an account by an insider. Beal emphasizes the decay of the Nationalists and the unyielding determination of the Communists.

27:77 Englehardt, Tom. "Long Day's Journey: American Observers in China, 1948–1950." In Bruce Douglass and Ross Terrill, eds., *China and Ourselves.* Boston: Beacon, 1970, pp. 90–121. This article contends that Americans in China tended to be a self-centered and self-satisfied lot, without an understanding of China's revolutionary struggle or the resentment aroused by their exploitative activities.

27:78 Leary, William M., Jr. "Aircraft and Anti-Communists: CAT in Action, 1949–52." *China Quarterly,* no. 52 (1972), 654–69. An account of the "patriotic" effort by Claire Chennault and Whiting Willauer of Civil Air Transport (CAT) to keep Nationalist planes in Hong Kong out of the hands of the Communists. The author contends that the U.S. government provided the enterprise substantial help.

27:79 Levine, Steven I. "A New Look at American Mediation in the Chinese Civil War: The Marshall Mission and Manchuria." *Diplomatic History* 3:4 (1979), 349–75. This reappraisal, based on Chinese and Soviet as well as American sources, sets Marshall's effort in the context of both the early cold war and the Chinese civil war. Marshall's fundamental goal, the author argues, was not to unify China but to block the further spread of Soviet influence in China.

27:80 May, Ernest R. *The Truman Administration and China, 1945–1949.* Philadelphia: Lippincott, 1975. This volume serves primarily as a starting point for further discussion or research. Despite its claims, the volume does not cover 1949; both the narrative and the documents stop with Marshall's decision not to send troops to China. Bibliographic essay and source materials.

27:81 Melby, John F. *The Mandate of Heaven: Record of a Civil War; China, 1945–1949.* Toronto: University of Toronto Press, 1968. This is the diary of a foreign service officer who travelled widely in China between November 1945 and December 1948, and participated in the Marshall and Wedemeyer missions. It provides insights into the events of this critical period and the thinking of key figures, such as Marshall and Ambassador Stuart.

27:82 Purifoy, Lewis M. *Harry Truman's China Policy: McCarthyism and the Diplomacy of Hysteria, 1947–1951.* New York: New Viewpoints, 1976. Purifoy contends that McCarthyism compelled the Truman administration to maintain its ties with Chiang Kai-shek and take a hostile stance toward the Communists. The author, however, has not supported his views with archival research or public opinion poll data.

U.S. Forces in China, 1945–1946

27:83 Barbey, Daniel E. *MacArthur's Amphibious Navy: Seventh Amphibious Force Operations, 1943– 1945.* Annapolis: Md.: Naval Institute Press, 1969. Admiral Barbey was commander of the Seventh Amphibious Force in the western Pacific during and after World War II. The last two chapters of this book deal with naval operations off the coast of Manchuria and

North China during late 1945. Particularly interesting is the account of U.S. Marine landings in China.

27:84 Frank, Benis M., and Shaw, Henry, Jr. *Victory and Occupation*. Vol. 5 in *The History of U.S. Marine Corps Operations in World War II*. Washington, D.C.: G.P.O., 1968. This official history includes coverage of operations in China and the resulting contacts with Communst and Nationalist forces.

27:85 Shaw, Henry I., Jr. *The United States Marines in North China, 1945–1949*. Rev. ed. Washington, D.C.: G.P.O., 1962. This brief account of U.S. Marine operations in North China focuses primarily on late 1945 and early 1946.

Formosa [Taiwan]

27:86 Ballantine, Joseph W. *Formosa: A Problem for United States Foreign Policy*. Washington, D.C.: Brookings Institution, 1952. This study, intended as a guide for policymakers, offers summary treatment of Formosa's land and population, its history since the Ming dynasty (with emphasis on Japanese rule), the events which brought Chiang Kai-shek to Taiwan, and the development of the American position up to 1952 on aid and the island's future.

27:87 Gordon, Leonard. "American Planning for Taiwan, 1942–1945." *Pacific Historical Review* 37:2 (1968), 201–28. This article deals with Taiwan in U.S. wartime strategy in the Pacific, and in planning postwar occupations. American officials resisted Chinese Nationalists' claims to control the island, so Taiwan's legal status was still unresolved at the war's end.

27:88 Kerr, George H. *Formosa Betrayed*. Boston: Houghton Mifflin, 1965. This popular history of Formosa deals chiefly with the events of 1945 to 1947, which the author observed as a foreign service officer. The volume emphasizes Chinese Nationalist misrule and official American indifference. Not well footnoted.

U.S. AND CHINESE COMMUNISTS

See under "Personalities," especially Dean Acheson, John P. Davies, Jr., Mao Tse-tung, John S. Service, and under "Others," O. Edmund Clubb, Owen Lattimore.

27:89 Barrett, David D. *Dixie Mission: The United States Army Observer Group in Yenan, 1944*. Berkeley: University of California, Center for Chinese Studies, 1970. Colonel Barrett, a career officer with long experience in China, was head of the U.S. Army Observer Group in Yenan in 1944 and 1945, when he was dismissed for allegedly undermining U.S. policy by discussing military aid to the Communists. This account, rich in anecdote and revealing of the personalities involved, attempts to set the record straight. Photographs.

Borg, D., and Heinrichs, W. H., eds. *Uncertain Years: Chinese-American Relations, 1947–1950* (27:20).

Duke, D. C. "Anna Louise Strong and the Search for a Good Cause" (21:217) pictures Strong as a social activist who found in the Russian and Chinese revolutions causes equal to her energy and enthusiasm.

Lutz, J. G. *China and the Christian Colleges, 1850–1950* (2:79) includes two chapters (11 and 12) on student anti-Americanism in the late 1940s and the efforts of the People's Republic of China to control missionary schools. Two valuable case studies supplementing Lutz's account are Philip West, *Yenching University and Sino-Western Relations, 1916–1952* (Cambridge: Harvard University Press, 1976), chapter 7; and Mary E. Ferguson, *China Medical Board and Peking Union Medical College* (New York: China Medical Board of New York, 1970), chapters 9 and 10.

27:90 Shewmaker, Kenneth E. *Americans and Chinese Communists, 1927–1945: A Persuading Encounter*. Ithaca, N.Y.: Cornell University Press, 1971. In this wide-ranging study of "private" American diplomacy in China, Shewmaker chronicles the lives and activities of an impressive number of journalists, adventurers, and curiosity-seekers. He is particularly concerned with explaining the differing reactions of journalists to conditions in Nationalist and Communist areas. Bibliography.

27:91 Tozer, Warren. "The Foreign Correspondents' Visit to Yenan in 1944: A Reassessment." *Pacific Historical Review* 41:2 (1972), 207–24. Tozer concludes that contrary to McCarthy era charges, the correspondents' reports from the Chinese Communist headquarters had little effect on U.S. policy and were reasonably accurate.

27:92 Tozer, Warren W. "Last Bridge to China: The Shanghai Power Company, the Truman Administration and the Chinese Communists" *Diplomatic History* 1:1 (1977), 64–78. This article traces the response of an American-owned utility to the Communist takeover and to U.S. China policy. Especially notable is the author's use of the company's rich archives.

27:93 Tucker, Nancy Bernkopf. "An Unlikely Peace: American Missionaries and the Chinese Communists, 1948–1950." *Pacific Historical Review* 45:1 (1976), 97–116. This article demonstrates that a significant body of missionary opinion favored recognition as a pragmatic and realistic response to China's social revolution. Until the Korean War, Chinese Communist actions and pronouncements convinced many missionaries that their expertise was welcomed.

27:94 Vladimirov, Pyotr. *The Special Region of China, 1942–1945.* Garden City, N.Y.: Doubleday, 1975. A Soviet Comintern official once resident in Yenan, Vladimirov offers a view of Mao Tse-tung as a conniving, anti-Soviet figure eager to strike deals with American imperialism. This work should be used with caution since Vladimirov's notes and diary have probably been interlarded with post facto Soviet commentary.

27:95 Walsh, James P. "The Death of John Birch—Documented." *Wisconsin Magazine of History* 58:3 (1975), 209–18. Recent declassified documents reveal that Captain John M. Birch, son of missionary parents, imbibed a zealous patriotism that he carried into his intelligence work for the air force in China. His hostile attitude toward the Communists interrogating him accounted in part for his death.

Issue of Recognition

See "Personalities," especially Harry S. Truman; also see Chapter 31, "Recognizing Communist China."

Ronning, C. A. *A Memoir of China in War and Revolution* (36:51) is the memoirs of a Canadian diplomat stationed in China (1945–1951). It discusses the question of Canada's recognition of China.

27:96 U.S. Senate. Committee on Foreign Relations. *The United States and Communist China in 1949 and 1950: The Question of Rapprochement and Recognition,* prepared by Robert M. Blum. Washington, D.C.: G.P.O., 1973. This carefully researched pamphlet examines the issue of U.S. nonrecognition of the People's Republic of China. It contends that the Truman administration seriously considered opening

diplomatic relations with the new regime, but was repelled by Communist hostility from July 1949 onwards.

Origins of Chinese Communist Foreign Policy

27:97 Cohen, Warren. "The Development of Chinese Communist Policy toward the United States, 1933–1945." *Orbis* 11:2 (1967), 551–69. This second of a two-part study of Chinese Communist policy toward the United States between 1922 and 1945 is based on Communist sources. (For part 1, see [21:216]). Cohen argues that the Hurley mission was pivotal in arousing Communist mistrust of the United States.

Gittings, J. *The World and China, 1922–1972* (2:345) is an important introduction to Chinese Communist foreign policy.

27:98 Reardon-Anderson, James. *Yenan and the Great Powers: The Origins of Chinese Communist Foreign Policy, 1944–46.* New York: Columbia University Press, 1980. This is the first complete study of Chinese Communist policy toward the United States and the Soviet Union at the close of World War II. It relates that policy to domestic and intraparty politics and the changing situation on the battlefield. Bibliography.

U.S. and Japan, 1945–1953

See under "Personalities," especially, under "Others," John M. Allison, John K. Emmerson; see Chapter 24 for World War II issues and episodes.

27:99 Asahi Shimbun. *The Pacific Rivals: A Japanese View of Japanese-American Relations.* Trans. by Peter Grilli and Murakami Yoshio. New York: Weatherhill/Asahi, 1972. Part 3 presents thirty-two brief articles covering all aspects of Japanese-American relations during the occupation years. These onetime newspaper articles provide insights into Japanese responses to American policies.

27:100 Dower, John W. "Occupied Japan and the American Lake, 1945–1950." In Edward Friedman and Mark Selden, eds., *America's Asia: Dissenting Essays on Asian-American Relations*. New York: Pantheon, 1971, pp. 146–206. Dower argues here that American occupation policies emerged from Washington's geopolitical determination to dominate the Pacific.

27:101 Etō Jun. *Mō hitotsu no sengo shi* [Another postwar history]. Tokyo: Kodansha, 1978. The author offers excerpts from interviews with 12 Japanese leaders of the early postwar period as part of his effort to promote a reexamination of the standard interpretation of the occupation. This work includes (pp. 403–73) official Japanese records of Yoshida's September 20 and Konoe's October 4 meetings with MacArthur.

27:102 Feis, Herbert. *Contest over Japan.* New York: Norton, 1967. Feis examines the process by which Japan-related questions contributed to the growth of Soviet-American antagonisms in 1945. Both his data and hypotheses need to be checked against recently released American and British documents.

27:103 Goodman, Grant K., comp. *The American Occupation of Japan: A Retrospective View.* Lawrence: University of Kansas, Center for East Asian Studies, 1968. Robert Ward, Martin Bronfenbrenner, and Edward Norbeck here evaluate the political, social, and economic dimensions of American occupation policies.

27:104 Kawai Kazuo. *Japan's American Interlude.* Chicago: University of Chicago Press, 1960. This work by a former editor of the *Nippon Times* was the first attempt at a scholarly synthesis of Japanese-American relations during the occupation years. Bibliography.

27:105 Kosaka Masataka. *100 Million Japanese: The Postwar Experience.* Tokyo: Kodansha International, 1972. This broad impressionistic survey of postwar U.S.-Japan relations (1945–1971), based on the author's earlier study of Yoshida Shigeru, is useful primarily for its treatment of Japanese reactions to American policies.

27:106 Nakamura Takafusa, ed. *Senryōki Nihon no keizai to seiji* [Economics and politics during the Japanese occupation]. Tokyo: Tokyo daigaku shuppankai, 1979. These papers by leading Japanese scholars focus on occupation policy, the cold war and

George Kennan's influence, political parties, local government, agriculture, censorship, the emancipation of women, and labor policy to 1949. They are uneven in quantity and quality, but all are based on research in Japanese and American archives.

27:107 Ōkura shō zaisei shi shitsu hen [Finance Ministry. Historical Section]. *Shōwa zaisei shi: Shūsen kara kōwa made: Dai san kan Amerika no taiNichi senryō seisaku* [Financial history of the Showa era from the end of war to peace. Volume 3: American policy for the occupation of Japan]. Tokyo: Tōyō keizai shimpō sha, 1976. This is the most thorough study of American-Japanese relations for 1941 to 1952. It analyzes the planning and implementation of the major political and economic policies. Document, bibliographic, and biographical guides.

27:108 Ōmori Minoru. *Sengo hishi* [The secret history of postwar Japan]. 10 vols. Tokyo: Kodansha, 1969–1979. Each volume in this major popular account of the occupation has a different title: *The Red Flag and GHQ, The MacArthur Constitution,* etc. This collection is notable for provocative speculation. Bibliography and index.

27:109 Shisō no kagaku kenkyūkai hen [Science of Thought], ed. *Nihon senryō gun: Sono hikari to kage* [The occupation army: the light and the shadow]. 2 vols. Tokyo: Tokuma shōten, 1979. Topics range from reforms in labor and agriculture to censorship and the impact on the *buraku* people (outcasts), crime, prostitution, and other social problems not often treated in occupation research. This work includes a valuable bibliographic essay by Takemae Eiji.

27:110 Shūkan shinchō henshu bu [Editorial Section. Shincho Weekly]. *Makkasa no Nihon* [MacArthur's Japan]. Tokyo: Shinchō sha, 1970. These essays on all aspects of occupation policy (1945–1952) are based primarily on interviews with surviving American participants. The essays also touch on the Korean War and Japanese rearmament.

27:111 Sodei Rinjirō. *Makkasa no nisen nichi* [MacArthur's two thousand days]. Tokyo: Chūō Kōron sha, 1974. Here an American-trained political scientist offers interpretive essays on American occupation policies. Bibliography.

27:112 Suzuki Tadakatsu. *Shūsen kara kōwa made* [From war's end to peace]. Vol. 26 in *Nihon gaikō shi* [A history of Japanese diplomacy]. Tokyo: Kajima kenkyū jo shuppan kai, 1973. This is a comprehensive survey of U.S.-Japan relations during the occupation by a professional diplomat who served as principal liaison to the Eighth Army headquarters.

27:113   Takemae Eiji, et al. *Nihon senryō hisshi* [The secret history of the occupation of Japan]. 2 vols. Tokyo: Asahi shimbun sha, 1977. These essays on all aspects of U.S. occupation policy toward Japan are by younger Japanese scholars who have exploited both American and Japanese archival sources.

27:114   Ward, Robert E. "Reflections on the Allied Occupation and Planned Political Change in Japan." In Robert E. Ward, ed., *Political Development in Modern Japan*. Princeton, N.J.: Princeton University Press, 1968, pp. 477–535. In this broad review of the objectives, planning processes, and occupation control mechanisms, the author gives American policy high marks.

TOKYO WAR CRIMES TRIALS

27:115   Keenan, Joseph B., and Brown, Brendan F. *Crimes against International Law*. Washington, D.C.: Public Affairs Press, 1950. Both authors participated in the Tokyo trials and based this juridical discussion on their experiences.

27:116   Minear, Richard H. *Victors' Justice: The Tokyo War Crimes Trial*. Princeton, N.J.: Princeton University Press, 1971. Strongly colored by the Vietnam War controversy, this book stands as the first serious scholarly examination of the uses of legal process, international law, and history in the Tokyo trials. Bibliography.

27:117   Piccigallo, Philip R. *The Japanese on Trial: Allied War Crimes Operations in the East, 1945–1951*. Austin: University of Texas Press, 1979. This account reviews the role of each participating nation in the establishment, performance, and disposition of Far East war crimes trials.

27:118   U.S. Department of State. *Trial of Japanese War Criminals*. Washington, D.C.: G.P.O., 1946. This compilation contains only preliminary statements and information on the structure of the tribunal. Unlike the Nuremberg proceedings, those for the Tokyo trials were never published in full; however, they are available on microfilm (27:12).

SPECIAL ASPECTS OF THE OCCUPATION

27:119   Blakeslee, George H. *The Far Eastern Commission: A Study in International Cooperation: 1945 to 1952*. Washington, D.C.: G.P.O., 1953. This is a detailed evaluation of the role of the Far Eastern Commission in peacemaking with Japan. The author was a principal planner of occupation policies, a distinguished academic "Japan hand," and an adviser to the commission.

27:120   Borton, Hugh. *American Presurrender Planning for Postwar Japan*. New York: Columbia University, East Asian Institute, 1967. A scholar turned policy-planner here recalls the interagency struggle to develop coherent policies for Japan. Borton emphasizes the role played by the State Department in setting the initial course for the occupation.

27:121   Etō Jun. *Wasureta koto to wasuresaserareta koto* [What we forgot and what we were forced to forget]. Tokyo: Bungei shunjū, 1979. A well-known Japanese literary critic and historian explores how the occupation rewrote the history of the war and the surrender while suppressing opposing Japanese versions. This provocative analysis deserves attention.

27:122   Fearey, Robert T. *The Occupation of Japan, Second Phase: 1948–1950*. New York: Macmillan, 1950. This is a contemporary assessment of the effect of American-inspired changes on the Japanese people. The author, a key adviser to John Foster Dulles, discusses security as the principal problem in peacemaking.

27:123   Martin, Edwin W. *The Allied Occupation of Japan*. New York: American Institute of Pacific Relations, 1948. A key State Department official describes the intent and execution of American policy toward Japan from 1945 through 1947.

27:124   Morley, James W. "The First Seven Weeks." *Japan Interpreter* 6:2 (1970), 151–64. This is a valuable description of the reactions of Japanese leaders to initial American policies. Morley portrays them as shrewd political operatives with long-range goals that would determine the future course of American-Japanese relations.

27:125   Oppler, Alfred C. *Legal Reform in Occupied Japan: A Participant Looks Back*. Princeton, N.J.:

Princeton University Press, 1976. This uneven memoir offers insight into the workings of the Government Section and the processes by which American policies were translated into Japanese law.

Economic Reform

27:126 Dore, Ronald. *Land Reform in Japan*. London: Oxford University Press, 1959. This is a classic study of a major occupation reform by one of Britain's best Japanologists. While not based on extensive archival research, it nonetheless provides sound analysis of land reform discussions between MacArthur's headquarters and the Japanese government and between the United States and its allies.

27:127 Hadley, Eleanor M. *Antitrust in Japan*. Princeton, N.J.: Princeton University Press, 1970. This detailed study by an economist and former Government Section official describes efforts to restructure the Japanese economy and Japanese-American economic relations.

27:128 Hollerman, Leon. "International Economic Controls in Occupied Japan." *Journal of Asian Studies* 38:4 (1979), 707–19. The author argues that the occupation's economic policy, rather than promoting free trade, created a foreign exchange and foreign trade control system which in the hands of the Japanese government has proved to be a formidable weapon in Japan's fight to exclude foreign goods and capital.

Roberts, J. G. *Mitsui: Three Centuries of Japanese Business* (31:137) provides unusual insights, in chapters 25 and 26, into the Mitsui business empire's response to American antitrust policies. This study also offers a useful commentary on relations among business, the Japanese government, and MacArthur's headquarters.

27:129 Roberts, John G. "The 'Japan Crowd' and the Zaibatsu Restoration." *Japan Interpreter* 12:3/4 (1979), 383–415. An account of how *Newsweek*'s foreign editor, Harry F. Kern, and other members of the American Council on Japan "conspired" with Japanese conservatives to oppose MacArthur's breakup of the zaibatsu and worked to support George Kennan's proposed revisions of official occupation policy.

27:130 Schonberger, Howard. "American Labor's Cold War in Occupied Japan." *Diplomatic History* 3:3 (1979), 249–72. The author traces the effort between 1945 and 1952 to create an American-style labor movement in Japan and exclude Communist influence. The effort succeeded but at the price of leaving labor weak and divided.

Political Purges

27:131 Baerwald, Hans. *The Purge of Japanese Leaders under the Occupation*. Berkeley: University of California Press, 1959. This first detailed account of a major occupation reform effort was prepared by a former member of the Government Section.

Montgomery, J. D. *Forced to Be Free: The Artificial Revolution in Germany and Japan* (26:95) concentrates on denazification in Germany and the purge of Japanese leaders.

Religious Impact

27:132 Wittner, Lawrence S. "MacArthur and the Missionaries: God and Man in Occupied Japan." *Pacific Historical Review* 40:1 (1971), 77–98. This essay shows how the general, much to the chagrin of his subordinates, promoted Christianity. It concludes that MacArthur's efforts failed because of the gap between Christian principle and American practice and because of the firmly established place in Japanese life of Buddhism and Shinto.

27:133 Woodard, William P. *The Allied Occupation of Japan, 1945–1952, and Japanese Religions*. Leiden: Brill, 1972. This is a detailed account of occupation efforts to separate church and state, eliminate militarism, and undermine the religious standing of the emperor. The author was a member of the Religious Division, Civil Information and Education Section. Bibliography.

PEACE TREATY AND SECURITY ARRANGEMENTS

See under "Personalities," especially Dean Acheson, Yoshida Shigeru.

The Peace Treaty

27:134 Cohen, Bernard C. *The Political Process and Foreign Policy: The Making of the Japanese Peace Settlement.* Princeton, N.J.: Princeton University Press, 1957. This structural analysis of the domestic politics of peacemaking gives Dulles and Truman high marks. It provides detailed coverage of public opinion, special interest groups, and congressional behavior.

27:135 Curtis, Gerald L. "The Dulles-Yoshida Negotiations on the San Francisco Peace Treaty." In *Columbia Essays in International Affairs: The Dean's Papers, 1966.* New York: Columbia University Press, 1967, vol. 2, pp. 37–62. The author argues that the ambassador and the prime minister failed in 1950 and 1951 to resolve the problem of assuring Japan's security.

27:136 Dunn, Frederick S. *Peacemaking and the Settlement with Japan.* Princeton, N.J.: Princeton University Press, 1963. This early scholarly assessment treats the Japanese settlement as a case study in American adjustment to cold war conditions.

27:137 Nishimura Kumao. *San Furanshisuko heiwa jōyaku* [The San Francisco Peace Treaty]. Vol. 40 in *Nihon gaikō shi* [Diplomatic history of Japan]. Tokyo: Kajima kenkyū jo shuppan kai, 1971. This is the best Japanese treatment of peacemaking to date, written by the then head of the Foreign Ministry's Treaty Bureau. Its descriptions of preliminary peacemaking efforts (1946–1947) and insights into Prime Minister Yoshida's political style are especially valuable.

Mutual Security and Rearmament

See Chapter 31, "Mutual Security Treaties."

27:138 Auer, James E. *The Postwar Rearmament of Japanese Maritime Forces, 1945–1971.* New York: Praeger, 1973. This is a detailed description of the continuation of Japanese naval activities after 1945 and the formation of the Japanese Maritime Self-Defense Force. Extensive bibliography.

27:139 Dingman, Roger. "Reconsiderations: The U.S.-Japan Security Treaty." *Pacific Community* 7:4 (1976), 471–93. Dingman analyzes the American origins of the security treaty in terms of rational choice,

organizational processes, and bureaucratic politics. He argues that the treaty was not the only "logical" solution to Japan's security problem and identifies its subsequent negative impact on American-Japanese relations.

27:140 Hata Ikuhiko. *Shiroku: Nihon saigunbi* [The historical record: Japan's rearmament]. Tokyo: Bungei shunju, 1976. These valuable essays focus on the origins of the no-war provision of the Japanese constitution, the impact of the cold war and Korean War on the U.S.-Japan security relationship, and the formation of Japanese self-defense forces. Bibliography.

Osgood, R. E. *The Weary and the Wary: U.S. and Japanese Security Policies in Transition* [1945–1971] (31:128).

27:141 Sapin, Burton. "The Role of the Military in Formulating the Japanese Peace Treaty." In Gordon B. Turner, ed., *A History of Military Affairs in Western Society since the 19th Century.* Ann Arbor, Mich.: Edwards, 1952, pp. 1003–14. This pioneering effort analyzes the role of the Joint Chiefs of Staff in peacemaking, and concludes that while the military wanted bases in Japan it had little interest in extending a security commitment to Tokyo.

27:142 Weinstein, Martin E. *Japan's Postwar Defense Policy, 1947–1968.* New York: Columbia University Press, 1971. A political scientist uses interviews and published Japanese secondary literature to argue that Tokyo's leaders had a definite defense policy shaped at least as much by their perceived national needs as by American pressure for rearmament.

POPULAR IMAGES

27:143 Glazer, Nathan. "From Ruth Benedict to Herman Kahn: The Postwar Japanese Image in the American Mind." In Akira Iriye, ed., *Mutual Images: Essays in American-Japanese Relations.* Cambridge: Harvard University Press, 1975, pp. 138–68. This survey of public opinion, the major ideas of Japanologists, and the responses of literary figures finds a pervasive American view of Japan as alien, unstable, and unpredictable.

27:144 Iwasaki Akira. "The Occupied Screen." *Japan Quarterly* 25:3 (1978), 302–22. A rare "inside" Japanese view of the problems and misunderstandings that arose as occupation-period Japanese rewrote via film their nation's recent history.

27:145 Johnson, Sheila K. *American Attitudes toward Japan, 1941–1975.* Washington, D.C.: American Enterprise Institute, 1975. This is a pioneering examination of American images, attitudes, and stereotypes concerning Japan. Chapters 3–6 survey popular reactions to Hiroshima, the occupation, sex roles, and Japanese culture.

27:146 Yavenditti, Michael J. "John Hersey and the American Conscience: The Reception of 'Hiroshima.'" *Pacific Historical Review* 43:1 (1974), 24–49. This essay analyzes motives and methods in the writing of the most influential American account of the bombing, and argues that while the book failed to stir protests about the combat use of the atomic bomb, it did awaken American popular sympathy for and understanding of the Japanese. (See also Chapter 23, "Atomic Bomb and Japan's Surrender.")

U.S. and Korea, 1941–1953

See "Personalities," especially Syngman Rhee; also see Chapter 38, "Korean War, 1945–1953."

27:147 Baldwin, Frank, ed. *Without Parallel: The American-Korean Relationship since 1945.* New York: Pantheon, 1974. This collection surveys the "unprecedented American commitment and intervention in post-1945 Korea." Articles by Cumings, Halliday, and Simmons on American policy toward Korea (1945–1950) argue for the civil origins of the war and heavy American responsibility for the course of events in Korea during the period. Articles by Bix and Palais also touch on this period. Useful footnotes, chronology, and index.

27:148 Berger, Carl. *The Korea Knot: A Military-Political History.* Philadelphia: University of Pennsylvania Press, 1957. Long a standard account of Korean-American relations (1943–1953), this work faults the United States for not paying sufficient attention to Korean needs, while extolling Truman's good

sense in committing U.S. troops in 1950. Bibliography and index.

27:149 Cho Soon Sung. *Korea in World Politics, 1940–1950.* Berkeley: University of California Press, 1967. The author, who used the best sources then available, judges American policy largely ill-informed and ineffective. His suggestion that the United States should have done much more to promote Korean unification under southern auspices reflects South Korean nationalist biases. Extensive bibliography and index.

27:150 Goodrich, Leland M. *Korea: A Study of U.S. Policy in the United Nations.* New York: Council on Foreign Relations, 1956. Reprint 1979. This book presents a traditional American interpretation of UN policy toward Korea (September 1947–November 1950). Goodrich hails UN intervention as a proper response by the peace-loving nations, led by the United States, to a threat to their collective security. This work includes a useful compilation of UN resolutions.

27:151 Gordenker, Leon. *The United Nations and the Peaceful Unification of Korea: The Politics of Field Operations, 1947–1950.* The Hague: Nijhoff, 1959. This standard work covers the UN-sponsored 1948 elections in South Korea, the activities of the UN Temporary Commission on Korea, the UN resolutions on the Korean question after the war began, and other UN activities related to Korea. Bibliography.

27:152 Halliday, Jon. "What Happened in Korea? Rethinking Korean History, 1945–1953." *Bulletin of Concerned Asian Scholars* 5:3 (1973), 36–44. Halliday finds many questions and anomalies in the conventional view of Korea in these years, and provides suggestions for further research.

27:153 Henderson, Gregory. *Korea: The Politics of the Vortex.* Cambridge: Harvard University Press, 1968. The chapters on postwar Korea are excellent sources, both for the scholarship and the author's personal insight on many of the events he witnessed as a U.S. foreign service officer. The book argues that Korean society is subject to strong centripetal tendencies causing groups, classes, and political parties to fragment. Sources in Korean and English, with detailed annotation and indexing.

27:154 *History of the Just Fatherland Liberation War of the Korean People.* Pyongyang: Foreign Languages Press, 1957. This official North Korean account of the period leading up to the Korean War and the war itself emphasizes the revolution in the South and the quest for national liberation from American imperialism. The responsiblity for the outbreak of fighting is laid on Syngman Rhee, egged on by the Americans. The book remains useful as one of the few expositions in English of the northern view.

27:155   Kim Chum-kon. *The Korean War.* Seoul: Kwangmyong, 1973. This work articulates the standard South Korean view on the Korean War. The author, a professor with close government ties, insists on "the treacherous duplicity of the north Korean aggressors." The book incidentally provides some interesting insights on the communist and leftist efforts in the South, both before and during the war. Included are 400 pages of documentation that must be used with caution.

27:156   Scalapino, Robert, and Lee Chong-sik. *Communism in Korea.* 2 vols. Berkeley: University of California Press, 1972. This extensively documented account of Korean communism from 1918 to the 1970s includes important chapters on North Korea and the left wing in the South. The work is based on Korean-language sources. Excellent companions to this study are Dae-sook Suh, *The Korean Communist Movement, 1918–1948* (Princeton University Press, 1967), particularly the chapter on North Korea (1945–1948); a companion collection of documents (Princeton University Press, 1970); and Lee Chong-sik, *Materials on Korean Communism, 1945–1947* (Honolulu: University of Hawaii, Center for Korean Studies, 1977).

27:157   U.S. Department of State. *North Korea: A Case Study in the Techniques of Takeover.* Publ. no. 7118. Washington, D.C.: Department of State, 1961. This official study was based on captured North Korean materials and interviews with prisoners of war. Those Korean-language materials filling thousands of archival boxes have been declassified and are now available at the Federal Records Center, Suitland, Maryland. They are by far the best source on the North during the period 1947 to 1950.

THE OCCUPATION, 1945–1948

27:158   Friedrich, Carl, ed. *American Experiences in Military Government in World War II.* New York: Rinehart, 1948. This valuable collection includes two useful articles on the Korean experience. The

book assesses Americans as military governors, including various shortcomings that were obvious by 1948. Bibliography and index.

27:159   Gayn, Mark. *Japan Diary.* New York: Sloane, 1948. About 100 pages of this eyewitness account deal with the U.S. occupation of Korea. It offers unique coverage of the extensive civil disorders in the fall of 1946 in several southern provinces, and has some rare portraits of key figures. Long thought overly critical, the account has been borne out by declassified materials. Index.

27:160   Gordenker, Leon. "The United Nations, the United States Occupation, and the 1948 Election in Korea." *Political Science Quarterly* 73:3 (1958), 426–50. This early examination of U.S. influences in the occupation and politics of Korea deals with the UN commission in Korea.

27:161   Grey, Arthur L., Jr. "The Thirty-Eighth Parallel." *Foreign Affairs* 29:3 (1951), 482–87. This article on the division of Korea in August 1945 still makes for good reading, but it must be supplemented by newly released U.S. government documents.

27:162   Matray, James I. "An End to Indifference: America's Korean Policy during World War II." *Diplomatic History* 2:2 (1978), 181–96. This account traces the formulation of American plans for a Korean trusteeship and the reaction of Korean exile groups as well as the governments of China, Britain, and the U.S.S.R. to those plans. The author labels "realistic" Roosevelt's policy, with its commitment to protecting Korea from renewed international rivalry and to guiding its political development.

27:163   McCune, George. *Korea Today.* Cambridge: Harvard University Press, 1950. One of the best books in the field by one of the few Koreanists in the United States in the 1940s, this study treats the period 1945 to 1948 in all its complexity. McCune is often quite critical of the course of the American occupation—a point of view shared by many of the other East Asian experts who served with him in the government.

27:164   Meacham, Stewart. *Labor Report.* Seoul: U.S. Army Military Government in Korea, 1948. Meacham, labor adviser to the commanding general, develops in this report his criticisms of military government labor policies. This remains the best English-language account of labor conditions in South Korea in the late 1940s (available at the Library of Congress).

Another brief contemporary social survey—this one dealing with the agrarian situation and the land reform program—is *Final Report and History of the New Korea Company* (Seoul: National Land Administration, 1948). The author, C. Clyde Mitchell, has since prepared a dissertation on the same subject at Harvard University.

27:165   Meade, Edward G. *American Military Government in Korea*. New York: Columbia University Press, 1951. This is an excellent account (still the only one on the subject) by a former participant in the provincial military government. Limited in coverage to the southwestern Cholla provinces, the book provides interesting research leads and hypotheses. Index with notes as guides to archival materials.

27:166   Morris, William G. "The Korean Trusteeship, 1941–1947: The U.S., Russia, and the Cold War." Ph.D. diss., University of Texas, 1974. This outstanding dissertation, strongest on the period 1942 to 1949, uses State Department archival materials to trace the origins of State's Korea policy, and its tempestuous battles with Syngman Rhee and his allies.

[U.S.S.R.]. *The Soviet Union and the Korean Question* (27:14) brings together in one convenient volume the public statements of the Soviet Union on Korean questions.

27:167   U.S. Army. Twenty-Fourth Corps. Historical Section. *History of the U.S. Armed Forces in Korea*. 3 vols. Seoul and Tokyo: U.S. Armed Forces in Korea, 1947. This official history of the army's occupation of Korea is an important source, running to several thousand pages. The chapters vary greatly in quality. Other noteworthy accounts, also produced by army historians, are C. Leonard Hoag's draft manuscript, "American Military Government in Korea: War Policy and the First Year of Occupation, 1941–1946," and Richard D. Robinson's unpublished study of the first two years of occupation, "Betrayal of a Nation." Copies of both are available from the Korean-American Relations Documentations Center at the University of Washington.

THE KOREAN WAR, 1950–1953

See "Personalities," especially Dean Acheson, Harry S Truman; also see Chapter 36, "China and the Ko-

rean War," and Chapter 38, "Korean War, 1945–1953."

27:168   Chon-sa p'yonch'an wiwonhoe [War History Compilation Committee]. *Han'guk Chonjaengsa* [History of the Korean War]. 9 vols. Seoul: Kukpang-bu, 1967–1970.

27:169   Chon-sa p'yonch'an wiwonhoe. *History of the United Nations Forces in Korea*. 5 vols. Seoul: Kukpang-bu, 1967–1970. These two extraordinarily detailed, lengthy series, prepared under the auspices of the South Korean Defense Department are excellent sources on the war and the period leading up to it. The nine Korean volumes are much preferable to the five English-language ones, which leave much untranslated. Both versions must be used with the knowledge they reflect an officially approved line.

27:170   Guttmann, Allen, ed. *Korea: Cold War and Limited War*. 2d ed. Lexington, Mass.: Heath, 1972. This anthology is a useful introduction to the variety of perspectives from which American scholars have tried to analyze the conflict. Bibliography.

27:171   Heller, Francis H., ed. *The Korean War: A Twenty-Five Year Perspective*. Lawrence: Regents Press of Kansas, 1977. This volume emerged from a conference attended by some scholars of the Korean War and high-level American policymakers of the 1950s. It consists of the scholars' articles and the policymakers' responses. Extensive bibliography.

Osgood, R. E. *Limited War: The Challenge to American Strategy* (40:190) argues for the necessity of limited wars in the nuclear age and uses American intervention in Korea as proof that the United States can fight such a war successfully. The book played a major role in defining the "lessons" of Korea for later American policymakers. See also the relevant chapters in B. Brodie, *War and Politics* (40:19); Ernest R. May, *"Lessons" of the Past* (2:22); and A. L. George and R. Smoke, *Deterrence in American Foreign Policy* (40:200).

27:172   Rees, David. *Korea: The Limited War*. New York: St. Martin's Press, 1964. This book represents the first satisfactory overview of the Korean War, yet its analysis of the global strategic environment and the causes of the war are superficial. It emphasizes the importance of Korea in the evolution of American thinking about limited war in the nuclear age and covers both combat operations and the domestic political debate. Bibliography.

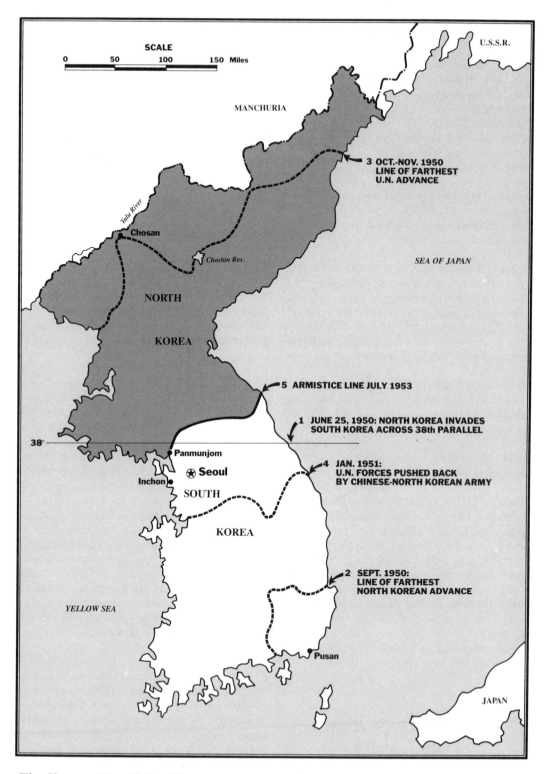

The following labels appear on the map:

SCALE
0   50   100   150 Miles

U.S.S.R.

MANCHURIA

3 OCT.-NOV. 1950 LINE OF FARTHEST U.N. ADVANCE

Yalu River

Chosan

Choshin Res.

SEA OF JAPAN

NORTH

KOREA

5 ARMISTICE LINE JULY 1953

1 JUNE 25, 1950: NORTH KOREA INVADES SOUTH KOREA ACROSS 38th PARALLEL

38°

Panmunjom

4 JAN. 1951: U.N. FORCES PUSHED BACK BY CHINESE-NORTH KOREAN ARMY

⊛ **Seoul**

Inchon

SOUTH

KOREA

2 SEPT. 1950: LINE OF FARTHEST NORTH KOREAN ADVANCE

YELLOW SEA

Pusan

JAPAN

The Korean War, 1950–53

27:173   Schnabel, James F., and Watson, Robert J. *The Korean War*. Pts. 1 and 2. Vol. 3 in *The History of the Joint Chiefs of Staff: The Joint Chiefs of Staff and National Policy*. Wilmington, Del.: Glazier, 1979. This recently declassified (1978), official, in-house history deals with the role of the Joint Chiefs (1950–1951) in political and military decisionmaking and in liaison between the administration and commanders in the field.

Stairs, D. *The Diplomacy of Constraint: Canada, the Korean War and the United States* (36:78) is a solid analysis.

27:174   Stone, I. F. *The Hidden History of the Korean War*. 2d ed. New York: Monthly Review Press, 1971. This polemic, first published in 1952, was the point of departure for revisionist interpretations of American involvement in the Korean War. While Stone's contention that the South Korean government, with secret American help, deliberately provoked attack from the North is dubious, many other central points have been supported by recent scholarship.

Origins of the War

Selections in the sections immediately above and below also embrace this issue.

27:175   Devillers, Philippe. "L'U.R.S.S., la Chine et les origines de la guerre de Corée" [The U.S.S.R., China, and the origins of the Korean War]. *Revue Française de Science Politique* 14 (Dec. 1964), 1179–94. Based on interviews (1950–1951) with anonymous diplomats and others, the author argues that the Soviet Union did not encourage the North Korean attack and once it began could not restrain it. He explains the decision for war in terms of maneuvering within the North Korean military and political elite. A provocative work, it is valuable for the testimony from diplomatic insiders.

27:176   Stueck, William; Kolko, Joyce; and Kolko, Gabriel. "An Exchange of Opinion." *Pacific Historical Review* 42:4 (1973), 537–75. This collection of two articles—a review essay by Stueck on the chapters on the Korean War in the Kolkos' book *The Limits of Power* and a reply by the Kolkos—and rejoinders by both sides serves the useful function of sharply focusing the debate on a highly controversial interpretation of the origins and outbreak of the war. The two sides agree that North Korea initiated hostilities, and disagree on virtually everything else.

Early Phase, June–November 1950

27:177   Bernstein, Barton J. "The Week We Went to War: American Intervention in the Korean Civil War" and "The Policy of Risk: Crossing the 38th Parallel and Marching to the Yalu." *Foreign Service Journal* 54:1 (1977), 6–9, 33–35; 54:2 (1977), 8–11, 33–34; 54:3 (1977), 16–22, 29. In review of the early, dramatic phases of the war, Bernstein confirms the conventional view that Truman and Acheson interpreted the North Korean attack as a Soviet test of American will. Washington failed, the author argues, to recognize that the conflict was a civil war, unwisely reversed its earlier judgment that Korea was not vital to American security, and then fully supported MacArthur in the ill-fated attempt to achieve unification by force despite the increasingly strong warnings coming from Peking.

27:178   Friedman, Edward. "Problems in Dealing with an Irrational Power: America Declares War on China." In Edward Friedman and Mark Selden, eds., *America's Asia: Dissenting Essays on Asian-American Relations*. New York: Pantheon, 1971, pp. 207–52. This revisionist account attempts to reconstruct the Sino-American collision in Korea from the Chinese perspective. The author argues that Peking sought to deter the United States by sending a set of carefully calculated and graduated signals, but that American policymakers refused to take at face value Peking's warnings that it would fight in defense of national interests.

27:179   LaFeber, Walter. "Crossing the 38th: The Cold War in Microcosm." In Lynn H. Miller and Ronald W. Pruessen, eds., *Reflections on the Cold War: A Quarter Century of American Foreign Policy*. Philadelphia: Temple University Press, 1974, pp. 71–90. Truman's decision to order American troops across the 38th parallel is treated here as a fundamental turning point in the history of American foreign policy since World War II. LaFeber argues that crossing the 38th parallel had a decisive impact on American policy toward East Asia, Indochina, and Europe, on the defense budget, and on the domestic political climate.

27:180   Lichterman, Martin. "To the Yalu and Back." In Harold Stein, ed., *American Civil-Military Decisions: A Book of Case Studies*. Birmingham: University of Alabama Press, 1963, pp. 569–642. This article presents the view of policymakers in Washington uneasy over MacArthur's conduct of the war north of the 38th parallel. Only after Chinese intervention forced them to limit the war did they move to confront the willful general. Lichterman suggests that MacArthur's handling of the war was not the main cause of Chinese intervention. Bibliography.

27:181 Matray, James I. "Truman's Plan for Victory: National Self-Determination and the Thirty-Eight Parallel Decision in Korea." *Journal of American History* 66:2 (1979), 314–33. This new look at the decision to cross the 38th parallel contends that the Truman administration acted out of a desire to unify Korea and to assure Korean reconstruction free of Soviet interference.

27:182 Noble, Harold J. *Embassy at War.* Ed. by Frank Baldwin. Seattle: University of Washington Press, 1975. Completed in 1952, this account by the first secretary of the American embassy in Seoul at the time of the North Korean invasion covers the first three months of the war. Noble's premature death prevented immediate publication of the manuscript. Noble, the only officer in the embassy to write an account of the war, offers valuable insights on tensions in the daily working relationship between Rhee and the Americans and on the panic and shock that the North Korean invasion created in Seoul.

27:183 Paige, Glenn D. *The Korean Decision, June 24–30, 1950.* New York: Free Press, 1968. Paige attempts to reconstruct in a narrative, hour-by-hour fashion the debates at the highest levels of the Truman administration about whether to intervene in Korea. In this manner he tests a model of foreign policy decision-making developed by Richard Snyder. His conclusion is that Truman reacted calmly and rationally in spite of the atmosphere of crisis. Bibliography. Paige looks back critically on his own work in *American Political Science Review* 71:4 (1977), 1603–09.

27:184 Simmons, Robert R. *The Strained Alliance: Peking, P'yŏngyang, Moscow and the Politics of the Korean Civil War.* New York: Free Press, 1975. Employing previously neglected U.S. Army intelligence reports and translations of Soviet, Chinese, and North Korean radio broadcasts, this work challenges the traditional interpretation that the Soviet Union controlled North Korean and Chinese behavior in the war. It analyzes the Korean struggle as a civil war, not as an episode in the Soviet-American global chess match, and stresses tensions between the three adjoining Communist states. Often speculative, this revisionist study will force rethinking of long-held assumptions. Bibliography. For a critical evaluation, see Steven I. Levine

in the *Bulletin of Concerned Asian Scholars* 8 (July-Sept. 1976), 62.

27:185 Whiting, Allen S. *China Crosses the Yalu: The Decision to Enter the Korean War.* Stanford, Calif.: Stanford University Press, 1960. The most promising substitute for archival records has been the textual analysis of speeches, articles, and broadcasts—a method applied to the Korean War by Allen Whiting. Among his conclusions are that China had foreknowledge of the North Korean invasion, but did not help in its preparation, and that China intervened because it saw a military threat from a Korea completely occupied by UN forces. Bibliography.

Military Operations

See "Personalities," Mark W. Clark, Douglas MacArthur, and, under "Others," J. Lawton Collins, Matthew B. Ridgway.

27:186 Field, James A., Jr. *History of United States Naval Operations: Korea.* Washington, D.C.: G.P.O., 1962. This official history makes clear the navy's importance in supply, amphibious operations, land bombardment, and air support. Of particular interest are sections dealing with the paucity of forces available to enforce the neutralization of the Formosa Straits and the rapid improvement of weapons technology between 1948 and 1951.

27:187 Futrell, Robert F. *The United States Air Force in Korea, 1950–1953.* New York: Duell, Sloan, & Pearce, 1961. This account, sponsored by the Air Force Historical Division, describes in detail the air war in Korea and provides some coverage of the dispute over air power in the war and the role of strategic bombing. The author contends that air power was of critical importance in the military successes achieved by UN forces.

27:188 U.S. Department of the Army. Office of the Chief of Military History. *United States Army in the Korean War.* 3 vols. Washington, D.C.: G.P.O., 1961–1972. The volumes in this official series on the army in the Korean War offer detailed but often guarded treatment of military decisions in Washington, combat operations in Korea, and the peace talks at Panmunjom. The major sources are the often still classified records of the Far East Command and the Department of the Army. Includes excellent maps. Authors of the individual volumes are James F.

Schnabel (1), Roy E. Appleman (2), and Walter G. Hermes (3).

Korean Forces

27:189 Sawyer, Robert K. *Military Advisors in Korea: KMAG in Peace and War*. Washington, D.C.: G.P.O., 1962. This official study is the place to begin on the topic of the Korean Military Advisory Group (set up at the end of the occupation in 1948) and the origins of the southern military. This generally excellent account makes use of documentation from military archives.

27:190 U.S. Far East Command, G-2 (Intelligence) Section. *History of the North Korean Army*. Tokyo: Far East Command, 1952. This formerly top-secret study is now available at the Office of the Chief of Military History. The only study of its kind now available, it is essential reading not only on the North Korean army but also on the weaknesses and biases of MacArthur's intelligence apparatus. It is particularly useful on the early years of the army, the extensive Korean participation in the Chinese civil war, and the North Korean army leaders. It must be used with care, and with full acquaintance with other literature on the North during the period.

Charges of "Germ Warfare"

27:191 Endicott, Stephen L. "Germ Warfare and 'Plausible Denial': The Korean War, 1952–1953." *Modern China* 5:1 (1979), 79–104. This new look at an old controversy is hampered by still incomplete evidence. The author sees some grounds for belief that the United States did indeed experiment with germ warfare.

Stockholm International Peace Research Institute. *The Problem of Chemical and Biological Warfare* (40:241) summarizes, in volume 4, pp. 196–221, and volume 5, pp. 238–58, the charges against the United States, and reviews the reports issued by the various commissions. "The evidence produced was considered unconvincing by the majority of UN members." See also D. Rees, *Korea: The Limited War* (27:172), pp. 347–63.

Truman-MacArthur Controversy

See under "Personalities," especially Douglas MacArthur, Harry S. Truman.

27:192 Higgins, Trumbull. *Korea and the Fall of MacArthur: A Précis in Limited War*. New York: Oxford University Press, 1960. This study concentrates on the debate between General MacArthur and the Truman administration over the conduct of the war. The author describes in detail the attitudes of both sides toward limited war. Bibliography.

27:193 Rovere, Richard H., and Schlesinger, Arthur M., Jr. *The General and the President, and the Future of American Foreign Policy*. New York: Farrar, Straus & Young, 1951. General MacArthur receives more attention than President Truman. The authors, writing during the recall uproar, stress MacArthur's failure to prepare for a Chinese counteroffensive in November 1951, and find his views on foreign policy unpersuasive. Documents.

27:194 Spanier, John W. *The Truman-MacArthur Controversy and the Korean War*. New York: Norton, 1965. While most scholarship sees the general's own headstrong and egotistical personality as the chief cause of the crisis, this book stresses the built-in potential for civil-military conflict in limited wars, a general problem exacerbated by the confusion about Korean policy within the Truman administration. Bibliography.

27:195 Wiltz, John E. "Truman and MacArthur: The Wake Island Meeting." *Military Affairs* 42:4 (1978), 169–76. Wiltz takes issue with the prevailing view that the Wake Island meeting arose from a desire to coordinate high policy. He instead characterizes the trip as a form of "presidential theater" undertaken to improve the domestic political standing of Truman and the Democrats on the eve of the November election.

Politics and Public Opinion

27:196 Caridi, Ronald J. *The Korean War and American Politics: The Republican Party as a Case Study*. Philadelphia: University of Pennsylvania Press, 1968. This study charts Republican senatorial policy toward the war. Caridi argues that fear of Republican political gains helped shape Truman's policy in such decisions as attempting to unify Korea, and that Republicans in the Senate were guided wholly by political expediency.

27:197 Lofgren, Charles A. "Mr. Truman's War: A Debate and Its Aftermath." *Review of Politics* 31:2

(1969), 223–41. This article explores the precedent-setting debate over the constitutional basis for American intervention in Korea. The Truman administration argued that it had committed troops to Korea under the aegis of the United Nations, a point Republicans in Congress hotly disputed, especially after the Chinese intervention.

27:198 Modigliani, Andre. "Hawks and Doves, Isolationism and Political Distrust: An Analysis of Public Opinion on Military Policy." *American Political Science Review* 66:3 (1972), 960–78. This quantitative analysis of public opinion during the Korean War, based on nine national samples taken by the National Opinion Research Center (April 1951–October 1952), finds both discontent with limited war and considerable "dovish" sentiment on the lower rungs of the socioeconomic ladder.

27:199 Mrozek, Donald J. "Progressive Dissenter: Herbert Hoover's Opposition to Truman's Overseas Military Policy." *Annals of Iowa* 43:4 (1976), 275–91. This article explores Hoover's attack on the Truman administration's defense policy. The author contends that Hoover called for limits to American military commitments to better insulate American society from costly foreign conflicts.

Mueller, J. E. *War, Presidents and Public Opinion* (30:211) analyzes the evolution of American public opinion toward both the Korean and Vietnam wars and toward the wartime presidents. It shows strong popular support for American action in Korea until the Chinese intervention, whereupon support dropped sharply and remained low.

Negotiating the Armistice

See "Personalities," especially C. Turner Joy.

27:200 Joy, C. Turner. *How Communists Negotiate.* New York: Macmillan, 1955. Admiral Joy, head of the UN delegation at the Korean armistice negotiations, reviews his experience dealing with the Chinese.

27:201 Vatcher, William H. *Panmunjom: The Story of the Korean Military Armistice Negotiations.* New York: Praeger, 1958. This is an account of the negotiations by the psychological warfare adviser for the UN command; worth reading but not a major effort.

28

United States and Europe after 1945

Contributing Editor
THOMAS H. BUCKLEY
University of Tulsa

Contributors
Edwin B. Strong
University of Tulsa

Mary K. Schenck
University of Tulsa

Fraser Harbutt
Emory University

Contents

Introduction

The period from 1945 to 1980 was a most difficult period in American relations with Europe. It began with a shattered Europe, devastated by the second war, and then grew into a divided Europe dominated by the United States in the West and the Soviet Union in the East. Western Europe under the American nuclear umbrella grew both more prosperous and restive with the passing of each decade. If policies appeared simple in conception and administration in the early years of the era, they were far more complex by the 1970s. American power waned. Individual European nations attempted to carve out independent policies as the two super powers went from cold war to détente to heightened antagonism. By the 1970s the United States no longer had an overall European policy but had a mosaic of relations with European nations that revealed little pattern or indication of final outcome. There were certainly those who yearned for the simplicities of the early cold war years, and hoped to restore them, but the world of 1980 in Europe was neither as simple nor as amenable to solution as that of 1945. The only certainty was to become uncertainty. This was to offer major challenges to both Americans and Europeans as they groped for solutions that would advance their national interests.

Any student who wishes to do research in American relations with Europe since 1945 will soon discover two major problems. First, relations with the Soviet Union, and the resultant cold war problems, have dominated research and writing to the exclusion of almost everything else. Major aspects of those problems are covered in other chapters of this guide and books listed there touch upon American relations with almost all the European nations in a broad, Europe-as-a-whole context rather than on an individual nation basis. And second, on some topics there is an abundance of information, such as on the Nuremberg war crimes trials, while on the other subjects, such as U.S. relations with Albania or Switzerland, little, if anything, of significance has been written.

The latter problem is the result of many influences, which range, in the case of Albania, from the existence of no official or even unofficial relations with the United States, to nations like Switzerland with which relations have been largely economic. Other obstacles have been that the Department of State papers are only open to approximately 1955 at this writing; language barriers and a lack of European primary materials to do multiarchival research aggravate the problem. Almost none of the European archives have materials open for this period. Finally, there still exists a belief among historians that the period from 1945 to 1980 is not yet history and thus they leave the era to journalists, memoir writers, and others who deal in contemporary history.

Among the best introductory works on conditions in Europe at the beginning of the era are Hajo Holborn's *The Political Collapse of Europe* (28:11) and Theodore White's *Fire in the Ashes* (28:17). Robert Osgood's *NATO: The Entangling Alliance* (26:170) discusses the problems surrounding the first military alliance in American history since the French alliance of 1778. Descriptions of major cracks in the Western alliance can best be found in Richard E. Neustadt, *Alliance Politics* (28:104), and Roy Macridis, *De Gaulle: Implacable Ally* (28:27).

Coral Bell's book *The Diplomacy of Detente* (24:219) and Henry Kissinger's *White House Years* (24:133) are important works on U.S. relations with Europe in the early 1970s and should be supplemented by Henry Brandon's *The Retreat of American Power* (24:220) and Robert Osgood's *Retreat from Empire? The First Nixon Administration* (24:224). A. W. DePorte's *Europe between the Superpowers* (28:8) surveys the end of the era.

This is an era, as indicated previously, that offers both an abundance of topics and problems for those wishing to do original research. It remains, according to the most recent (1980) *SHAFR Research and Roster Guide,* a neglected era and area; only 35 items out of 854 listed touch specifically on the subject of this chapter. Even a perusal of the recent *Dissertation Abstracts* reveals a meager number of projects underway. This hopefully will change as more primary materials become open with the passing of each year. Still, there are many topics that could be tackled now. Among these are U.S. relations with Albania, Belgium, Luxembourg, Sweden, Norway, Finland, Denmark, Switzerland, Netherlands, Spain, Portugal, and almost all the East European countries.

Resources and Overviews

RESEARCH AIDS

While pertinent bibliographies and reference aids are listed here, there are more extensive lists in Chapter 1.

Bibliographies

28:1 Cortada, James W. "Bibliographic Essay on Twentieth-Century Spanish Diplomacy." In James W. Cortada, ed., *Spain in the Twentieth-Century World: Essays on Spanish Diplomacy, 1898–1978.* Westport, Conn.: Greenwood, 1980, pp. 261–73. This essay is a useful listing of sources in English and Spanish languages, particularly books.

Dexter, B. *The Foreign Affairs Fifty-Year Bibliography: New Evaluation of Significant Books on International Relations, 1920–1970* (1:14).

Foreign Affairs Bibliography: A Selected and Annotated List of Books on International Relations (1:15) is issued at ten-year intervals, and each volume has three parts: "General International Relations"; "The World since 1914"; and "The World by Regions." Useful aid.

28:2 Hunter, Brian. *Soviet-Yugoslavia Relations, 1948–1972: A Bibliography of Soviet, Western and Yugoslav Comment and Analysis.* New York: Garland, 1976. Items in this volume are arranged according to the title's theme and include materials in Russian, Western, and Yugoslavian languages. The contents and arrangement, once understood, can be useful. Indexes.

Kanet, R. E. *Soviet and East European Foreign Policy: A Bibliography of English- and Russian-Language Publications, 1967–1971* (1:87) includes over 3,200 books, pamphlets, and articles from a wide list of journals. Items are listed by author, not subject.

Lewis, J. R. *Uncertain Judgment: A Bibliography of War Crimes Trials* (1:39) is far and away the best bibliography on all war crimes trials, including, of course, Nuremburg. It is unannotated, but is organized topically.

U.S. Department of the Army. *Nuclear Weapons and NATO:* [In] *Analytical Survey of Literature* (1:52).

28:3 Žekulin, N. G. "Canadian Publications on the Soviet Union and Eastern Europe for 1977." *Canadian Slavonic Papers* 20:4 (1978), 544–67. It lists approximately 300 bibliographies, monographs, articles, review articles, sections of books, and signed encyclopedia articles published in 1977 by Canadian scholars. This is the second annual bibliography.

Yearbooks and Other Aids

Facts on File: A Weekly Digest with Cumulative Index (1:151) is a convenient weekly summary of major news events.

Keesing's Contemporary Archives: Weekly Diary of World Events (1:152) is the British equivalent of *Facts on File,* which is somewhat stronger in its coverage of international events.

Political Handbook and Atlas of the World (1:144) is a valuable guide for officials in power, political parties, and summaries of the year's events.

The Statesman's Year Book: Statistical and Historical Annual of the States of the World (1:145).

The United States in World Affairs [1931–1970] (1:147).

Yearbook on International Communist Affairs (1:148) provides, from 1967 onwards, a country-by-country profile of communist parties and their activities.

Document Collections

More general collections are listed in Chapter 1, and other collections may be found in "Personalities," below.

Branyan, R. L., and Larsen, L. H., eds. *The Eisenhower Administration, 1953–1961: A Documentary History* (24:197).

28:4 Dallek, Robert, ed. *Western Europe*. Vol. 1 in *The Dynamics of World Power: A Documentary History of United States Foreign Policy, 1945–1973*. New York: Chelsea House, 1973. This volume, together with volume 2, *Eastern Europe and the Soviet Union* (26:4), edited by Walter LaFeber, are most useful collections of public documents.

Documents on American Foreign Relations (1:339) is a compilation of major public documents; beginning in 1971, the title changed to *American Foreign Relations, 19–: A Documentary Record*.

Documents on International Affairs [1928–1963] (1:340).

U.S. Department of State. *American Foreign Policy: Current Documents, 1956–1967* (1:356) is a continuation of *American Foreign Policy: Basic Documents* (1957), 2 vols.

U.S. Department of State. *Press Conferences of the Secretaries of State, 1922–1974* (1:360) is a microfilmed typescript of the verbatim record.

OVERVIEWS

See Chapter 24, "Overviews," for general accounts of the United States, the U.S.S.R., and the cold war.

Aron, R. *The Imperial Republic: The United States and the World, 1945–1973* (24:31) is a critical essay on the United States in the world and in the world market. Aron wonders whether the American republic will ever attain maturity and argues that there are permanent duties, limited rights, and no way to retreat from responsibilities.

Bell, C. *Negotiation from Strength: A Study in Politics of Power* (24:228) is a good description of U.S. relations with Europe against the U.S.S.R. The author concludes that the two competing alliances may be bound to the policy purposes of their most vulnerable members in Europe.

Brown, S. *The Faces of Power: Constancy and Change in United States Foreign Policy from Truman to Johnson* (24:33) considers the basic policy premises that underlie the international behavior of the United States, and argues that it has relied too heavily on physical coercion.

28:5 Brzezinski, Zbigniew. *Alternative to Partition: For a Broader Conception of America's Role in Europe*. New York: McGraw-Hill, 1965. This book, written for Eastern as well as Western European audiences, calls for Western and especially American leadership in ending the European stalemate; it also examines the Eastern European-Soviet relationship and role in future European development.

28:6 Calleo, David. *Europe's Future: The Grand Alternatives*. New York: Horizon, 1965. This study examines the concurrent development of nationalism and federalism in postwar Europe using de Gaulle's France as an example of nationalism and the Common Market as an example of federalism.

28:7 Czempiel, Ernste O., and Rustow, Dankwart A., eds. *The Euro-American System: Economic and Political Relations between North America and Western Europe*. Boulder, Colo.: Westview, 1976. This book is a series of essays by American and European experts exploring the Euro-American system; they found it sound but troubled.

28:8 DePorte, A. W. *Europe between the Superpowers: The Enduring Balance*. New Haven, Conn.: Yale University Press, 1979. This is an important essay on the decline and death of the classical European state system and the birth of a new bipolar system. The author concludes that there is much more permanence to the new system than diplomatic historians have been willing to recognize.

28:9 Freymond, Jacques. *De Roosevelt à Eisenhower: La Politique étrangère américaine, 1945–1952* [From Roosevelt to Eisenhower: American foreign policy, 1945–1952]. Geneva: Droz, 1953. A discerning appraisal of U.S. foreign policy (1945–1952) by a prominent French student of international affairs; this account presents a European perspective.

28:10 Gelber, Lionel. *Crisis in the West: American Leadership and the Global Balance*. London: Macmillan, 1975. This volume is a compilation of published articles (1937–1975) dealing with the rise and fall of American leadership. It is important for a view of the changing hopes over a long period of time by a consistent foreign observer of U.S. policies.

28:11 Holborn, Hajo. *The Political Collapse of Europe*. New York: Knopf, 1951. In this important book, the author argues that in World War II the "collapse of the traditional European system (1910–1950) became an irrevocable fact. What is commonly called the historic Europe is dead and beyond resurrection."

Julien, C. *America's Empire* (24:236) is a broad study of the growth of the American empire (1890–1970), bringing out "the simplicity of its objectives and the ambivalence of its actions." The French author has some penetrating insights.

Kertesz, S. D., ed. *American Diplomacy in a New Era* (24:238) has a most interesting essay by J.-B. Duroselle, a longtime French observer of the American scene, entitled "Virtues and Shortcomings of American Diplomacy."

Kolko, J., and Kolko, G. *The Limits of Power: The World and United States Foreign Policy, 1945–1954* (24:40) is a critical account of U.S. policies toward Europe, and elsewhere, arguing that American capitalism in order to save itself had to turn outward; the Marshall Plan was not an act of generosity but American capitalism seeking material gains.

28:12 Luce, Clare Booth. "Whatever Happened to the American Century." *Strategic Review* 3:3 (1975), 10–23. The former diplomat believes that American military power has declined so much that the communists will achieve their goal of world hegemony.

28:13 Morgenthau, Hans J. *Truth and Power: Essays of a Decade, 1960–70*. New York: Praeger, 1970. These essays on American foreign policy of the 1960s, written during that period by one of the leading academic realists, reveal much about the period and even more about the writer.

Osgood, R. E., et al. *America and the World: From the Truman Doctrine to Vietnam* (24:45) includes a chapter by Lawrence W. Martin which provides an excellent overview of U.S. policies toward Europe; several other chapters also have useful materials on economic and military aspects.

Perkins, D. *The Diplomacy of a New Age: Major Issues in U.S. Policy since 1945* (24:47) finds much that is praiseworthy in the American approach to the Marshall Plan and NATO.

28:14 Rosecrance, Richard, ed. *America as an Ordinary Country: U.S. Foreign Policy and the Future*. Ithaca, N.Y.: Cornell University Press, 1976. There are several good chapters in this collection, especially "Europe and Contradictions in American Policy" by

Pierre Hassner, and Peter Katzenstein's "West Germany's Place in American Foreign Policy."

28:15 Servan-Schreiber, Jean-Jacques. *The American Challenge*. Trans. by Ronald Steel. New York: Atheneum, 1968. Servan-Schreiber, in a controversial book, argues that Europe (1945–1967) was in decline. The economic invasion of Europe by the United States was of such magnitude that Europe was likely to become its subsidiary. Unlike de Gaulle, he suggested not a building of barriers but a selective Americanization.

Steel, R. *Imperialists and Other Heroes: A Chronicle of the American Empire* [1945–1970] (29:114) is critical of American imperialism. Steel finds great errors in the motivation and conduct of U.S. foreign policy.

28:16 Tucker, Robert W. *A New Isolationism: Threat or Promise?* New York: Universe, 1972. This most lively book argues in favor of a new isolationism. It would not result in a Fortress America, for American strategic power would remain, but American influence overseas would decline.

28:17 White, Theodore H. *Fire in the Ashes: Europe in Mid-Century*. New York: Sloane, 1953. Because of its insights and literary quality this book is still good reading, and a useful starting point for one trying to recapture the feeling of the time.

Personalities

Additional references on individuals may be found in Chapter 1, "Biographical Data."

AMERICAN

See Chapter 24, "Personalities" and "Presidential Administrations," for additional references.

Dean Acheson

See Chapter 24, "Personalities," for additional references.

Acheson, D. *Present at the Creation: My Years in the State Department* [1941–1953] (24:90) focuses on cold war episodes, but does mention developments related to Germany, Spain, Yugoslavia, NATO, the Schuman Plan, as well as European problems generally.

28:18 Acheson, Dean. *Power and Diplomacy.* Cambridge: Harvard University Press, 1958. These four lectures develop familiar themes in Acheson's thinking—the need for flexible military capabilities and the emphasis upon the NATO alliance. He did not favor the "neutralization" of Germany.

George W. Ball

Ball, G. W. *Diplomacy for a Crowded World: An American Foreign Policy* (24:96) discusses his critical perceptions of the Nixon-Kissinger foreign policy, including their European policies.

28:19 Ball, George W. *The Discipline of Power: Essentials of a Modern World Structure.* Boston: Little, Brown, 1968. This is not a memoir, but an argument on how to organize power in a rational way. Ball believes "we have mixed a vague and irrelevant universalism with a new and transitional pragmatism: improvised crusades and crusading improvisations." He calls for long-term planning and believes that priority must be given to northern temperate zones rather than elsewhere.

Charles E. Bohlen

See also Chapters 26 and 29, "Personalities."

Bohlen, C. E. *Witness to History: 1929–1969* (24:98) reviews his years as ambassador to France.

Lucius D. Clay

Clay, L. D. *Decision in Germany* (26:42) is certainly one of the most important books on U.S. policies toward Germany (1945–1949). It should be used in conjunction with the Clay Papers.

Clay, L. D. *The Papers of General Lucius D. Clay: Germany, 1945–1949* (26:43) is valuable for Clay's analysis of France's German policies.

John Foster Dulles

See Chpter 24, "Personalities," for additional references.

Drummond, R., and Coblentz, G. *Duel at the Brink: John Foster Dulles' Command of American Power* (24:106) presents the secretary of state as a formidable and controversial figure.

Hoopes, T. *The Devil and John Foster Dulles* (24:112) provides a perceptive analysis of the foreign policies of the Truman and Eisenhower administrations.

Dwight D. Eisenhower

See Chapter 24, "Personalities," for additional references.

Eisenhower, D. D. *The White House Years* (24:114) contains much information on foreign and national security policy.

Lyndon B. Johnson

See Chapter 24, "Personalities," for additional references.

Johnson, L. B. *The Vantage Point: Perspectives on the Presidency, 1963–1969* (24:120) is bland and self-justifying, yet it is important for information on foreign affairs.

George F. Kennan

See Chapters 24 and 29, "Personalities," for additional references.

Kennan, G. F. *Memoirs, 1925–1963* (24:124) includes, in the second volume, Kennan's account of his ambassadorial years to Yugoslavia (1961–1963).

John F. Kennedy

See also Chapters 24 and 29, "Personalities."

Fairlie, H. *The Kennedy Promise: The Politics of Expectation* (24:209) asserts that the Kennedy administration was the "last confident—almost braggart— assertion of the capacity of American positivism to fulfill the prophecy of American puritanism."

28:20 Nunnerly, David. *President Kennedy and Britain.* New York: St. Martin's Press, 1972. The author concludes that Kennedy developed a working partnership based on close personal ties that was most successful. Kennedy restored "decency to patriotism and revived some of the romance about America."

Schlesinger, A. M., Jr. *A Thousand Days: John F. Kennedy in the White House* (24:215) deals sympathetically with Kennedy's foreign policy.

Henry A. Kissinger

See Chapter 24, "Personalities," for additional references.

Kalb, M., and Kalb, B. *Kissinger* (24:131) concentrates on 1969 to 1973 and is generally sympathetic to its subject.

Kissinger, H. A. *Nuclear Weapons and Foreign Policy* (28:74).

Kissinger, H. A. *White House Years* (24:133) is interesting and controversial, and relates U.S. policies toward Europe (1968–1973).

28:21 Kissinger, Henry A. *The Troubled Partnership: A Re-appraisal of the Atlantic Alliance.* New York: McGraw-Hill, 1965. This book represents the author's point of view shortly before he became a policymaker. The ability of the Western alliance to hold its territory intact since World War II led to a resulting weakness of resolve within NATO. Kissinger provides a lucid critique of nuclear decision-making in the alliance.

Richard M. Nixon

See Chapter 24, "Personalities," for additional references.

Brandon, H. *The Retreat of American Power* (24:220) believes that Nixon and Kissinger changed U.S. foreign policy decisively, and for years to come.

Nixon, R. M. *RN: The Memoirs of Richard Nixon* (24:145) is a lengthy and revealing memoir, essential for understanding Nixon's foreign policy.

Osgood, R. E., et al. *Retreat from Empire? The First Nixon Administration* (24:224) has a chapter by Osgood entitled "The Diplomacy of Allied Relations" that suggests that the alliance will have difficulties in an era of negotiation.

Others

Beam, J. D. *Multiple Exposure: An American Ambassador's Unique Perspective on East-West Issues* (29:38) covers the period from 1947 to 1973, when the ambassador served in Warsaw, Prague, and finally Russia. Jacob Beam has good material on the China talks in Warsaw and on the Russian invasion of Czechoslovakia.

Gardner, L. C. *Architects of Illusion: Men and Ideas in American Foreign Policy, 1941–1949* (25:17) looks into the activities of Byrnes, Acheson, Clay, Forrestal, and Kennan, who fashioned U.S. policies toward Europe.

Lodge, H. C., Jr. *The Storm Has Many Eyes: A Personal Narrative* (24:137) of Lodge's diplomatic experiences at the UN, in Vietnam, and at the Vatican.

Steel, R. *Walter Lippmann and the American Century* (24:182) represents an important voice, not always listened to, on U.S. relations with Europe. Steel points out that Lippmann was unable to take a consistent approach to the issues he wrote about.

Tugwell, R. G. *Off Course: From Truman to Nixon* (24:249) provides blunt comments by an old New Dealer about Eisenhower, Kennedy, Johnson, and Nixon (1945–1970). Tugwell offers some sharp judgments about U.S. foreign relations.

EUROPEAN

Konrad Adenauer

28:22 Adenauer, Konrad. *Erinnerungen.* 4 vols. Stuttgart: Deutsche Verlags-Anstalt, 1965–1968. The memoirs of Chancellor Adenauer, for the years 1945 to 1963, are an important source for U.S.-German relations and the Atlantic community. The first volume has appeared in English as *Memoirs, 1945–1953* (Chicago: Regnery, 1966).

28:23 Prittie, Terence. *Konrad Adenauer, 1876–1967.* Chicago: Cowles, 1972. This is a critical but sympathetic biography. Other biographies include Rudolf Augstein's hostile *Konrad Adenauer* (London: Secker & Warburg, 1964) and Charles Wighton's *Adenauer: A Critical Biography* (New York: Coward-McCann, 1964).

Clement R. Attlee

Attlee, C. R. *As It Happened* (23:89) covers the 1945 to 1951 period, with a single chapter on foreign affairs. Attlee's irritation with the impact of American domestic politics upon the Anglo-American relationship is manifest, but he supported the pro-American policy of Bevin, who was clearly dominant in foreign affairs.

28:24 Attlee, Clement R., 1st Earl. *A Prime Minister Remembers: The War and Post-war Memoirs of the Right Honorable Earl Attlee.* Ed. by Francis Williams. London: Heinemann, 1961. A laudatory, uncritical biography, it emphasizes the years 1945 to 1951. There are many references to the Anglo-American relationship which Attlee saw as necessary and constructive, though he was resentful of the Truman administration's economic pressures on Britain and its Palestine policy.

Willy Brandt

See also Chapter 29, "Personalities."

Brandt, W. *People and Politics: The Years 1960–1975* (29:40) is a memoir of Berlin's precarious position in the Soviet-American confrontation.

Charles de Gaulle

See Chapter 23, "Personalities," for additional references.

28:25 Crawley, Adrian. *De Gaulle.* London: Collins, 1969. Written by an Englishman, this is a short, balanced biography. Extensive bibliography.

28:26 Crozier, Brian. *De Gaulle.* New York: Scribner's, 1973. This is perhaps the most readable of the many de Gaulle biographies. It is critical and supports the argument that de Gaulle was trying to emulate either Richelieu or Napoleon and failed. While there is little on U.S.-French relations, it is a good introduction to "le grand Charles." Bibliography.

28:27 Macridis, Roy C., ed. *De Gaulle: Implacable Ally.* New York: Harper & Row, 1966. A good introduction by Maurice Duverger argues that de Gaulle is a man of the 19th *or* 21st century and that his speeches were designed to disguise his thoughts rather than to clarify them. Macridis includes many useful documents and speeches.

28:28 Newhouse, John. *De Gaulle and the Anglo-Saxons.* New York: Viking, 1970. The primary focus of French foreign policy in the Gaullist era was the result of the desire by Charles de Gaulle to liberate France from the predominant influence of the Anglo-Saxons. Newhouse primarily examines the Gaullist era and the French point of view.

Harold Macmillan

28:29 Macmillan, Harold. [Memoirs]. 6 vols. New York: Harper & Row, 1966–1973. These well-written volumes, each separately titled, by Britain's former prime minister contain information on U.S.-British affairs. See his *Winds of Change, 1914–1939*; *The Blast of War, 1939–1945*; *Tides of Fortune, 1945–1955*; *Riding the Storm, 1956–1959*; *Pointing the Way, 1959–1961*; and *At the End of the Day, 1961–1963.* Bibliographical references.

28:30 Sampson, Anthony. *Macmillan: A Study in Ambiguity.* New York: Simon & Schuster, 1967. This study focuses on the career of Macmillan as a British statesman, and prime minister (1957–1963).

Josip Broz-Tito

See Chapter 25, "Personalities," for references.

Others

28:31 Crossman, Richard. *The Diaries of a Cabinet Minister.* 2 vols. New York: Holt, Rinehart & Winston, 1975–1976. These volumes describe, in fascinating detail, the prime ministership of Harold Wilson (1964–1968), and include many interesting comments on American relations.

28:32 Dalton, Hugh. *High Tide and After: Memoirs, 1945–1960.* London: Muller, 1962. The autobiography of the Labour chancellor of the exchequer (1945–1947) is mainly concerned with domestic politics, but offers an insider's view of such issues as the 1946 American loan, and the Palestine question.

28:33 Donoughue, Bernard, and James, G. W. *Herbert Morrison: Portrait of a Politician.* London: Weidenfeld & Nicolson, 1973. This comprehensive biography contains a brief chapter on Morrison's tenure as foreign secretary in 1951, and concludes that he "lacked the supreme qualities of vision and style, as well as luck" needed to succeed.

28:34 Monnet, Jean. *Memoirs.* Trans. by Richard Mayne. New York: Doubleday, 1978. By the chief architect of the European Community, and a Frenchman who influenced European policies for over fifty years, this is must reading.

28:35 Reed, Bruce, and Williams, Geoffrey. *Denis Healey and the Policies of Power.* London: Sidgwick & Jackson, 1971. This useful study reviews the career of a prominent Labour secretary of state for defense. Healey was involved in NATO planning and arms control policymaking.

28:36 Schmidt, Helmut. *Defence or Retaliation: A German Contribution to the Consideration of NATO's Strategic Problem.* New York: Praeger, 1962. From the West German perspective, Schmidt examines the history of German defense policy, the role of NATO and nuclear weapons in the defense of Europe, and concludes that a reappraisal of the NATO strategic doctrine is needed. He subsequently headed the West German government.

28:37 Stikker, Dirk U. *Men of Responsibility: A Memoir.* New York: Harper & Row, 1965. This memoir of a former secretary general of NATO (retired 1967), Dutch foreign minister and ambassador to London, details his participation in the important political, economic, and strategic issues of the Atlantic community since 1940. He describes the "men of responsibility" with whom he dealt during these years.

28:38 Williams, Francis. *Ernest Bevin: Portrait of a Great Englishman.* London: Hutchinson, 1952. A generally uncritical biography in which the pre-1945 domestic political context dominates. The author attempts no final assessment of Bevin's tenure as foreign secretary though his efforts against leftist opposition to secure good relations with the United States are approved.

28:39 Wilson, Harold. *A Personal Record: The Labour Government, 1964–1970.* Boston: Little, Brown, 1971. These memoirs of the British prime minister (1964–1970) contain a great deal of information on American-British relations. Wilson was critical of many U.S. policies.

U.S. and Europe: Special Issues

28:40 Aron, Raymond. *In Defense of Decadent Europe.* Trans. by Stephen Cox. South Bend, Ind.: Regnery/Gateway, 1979. This is a broad interpretation emphasizing the failures of the Soviet Union and the successes of Europe and the United States.

28:41 Burnham, James, ed. *What Europe Thinks of America.* New York: Day, 1953. This is a collection of essays by conservative European writers critical of U.S. foreign policies toward Europe as not being strong enough.

28:42 Chace, James, and Ravenal, Earl C., eds. *Atlantis Lost: U.S.-European Relations after the Cold War.* New York: New York University Press, 1976. Each essay attempts to predict the future of Euro-American relations, and each has a different vision of the future.

28:43 Freymond, Jacques. *Western Europe since the War: A Short Political History.* New York: Praeger, 1964. This study is one of the most readable examinations of the political evolution of Western Europe yet written. It is concise and yet complete. It represents the starting point for any analysis or study of postwar European politics.

28:44 Galantière, Lewis. *America and Mind of Europe.* London: Hamish Hamilton, 1951. Originally published as a special issue of *Saturday Review of Literature,* this small volume includes some perceptive insights into the problems of American leadership as viewed by a collection of largely European writers.

28:45 Grosser, Alfred. *The Western Alliance: European-American Relations since 1945.* Trans. by Michael Shaw. New York: Continuum, 1980. Written from a French point of view, this work explores the unresolved problems that have plagued the alliance since its inception.

28:46 Hilsman, Roger M., and Good, Robert C., eds. *Foreign Policy in the Sixties: The Issues and the Instruments: Essays in Honor of Arnold Wolfers.* Baltimore: Johns Hopkins Press, 1965. Among an excellent collection of articles, especially important for Europe are those of L. W. Martin on the future of the Grand Alliance, L. W. Pye on foreign aid, and P. C. Davis on the 1955 Geneva summit meeting.

28:47 Kaiser, Karl, and Schwarz, Hans-Peter, eds. *America and Western Europe: Problems and Prospects.* Lexington, Mass.: Lexington Books, 1978. These essays attempt to evaluate and project U.S.–Western European relations in the mid-1970s. Wagner's "The European's Image of America" is interesting reading, while most of the other essays focus on the health of the Western economic system, the vitality of security policies, and the impact of trilateral philosophy.

Kennan, G. F. *The Cloud of Danger: Current Realities of American Foreign Policy* (29:226) provides perceptive thoughts on American relations with Western and Eastern Europe, as well as the Soviet Union, which call for a paring down of alliance commitments by the United States.

U.S. AND EUROPEAN UNION

28:48   Beloff, Max. *The United States and the Unity of Europe.* Washington, D.C.: Brookings Institution, 1963. This treatise does an excellent job of tracing the genesis and early development of U.S. policy toward European integration. Beloff is successful in disentangling the many components of American policy in the immediate postwar period.

28:49   Beugel, Ernst H. van der. *From Marshall Aid to Atlantic Partnership: European Integration as a Concern of American Foreign Policy.* Amsterdam: Elsevier, 1966. This comprehensive book, with many documents in the text, traces the idea of integration and predicts more of it in the future. Bibliography.

28:50   Camps, Miriam. *European Unification in the Sixties: From the Veto to the Crisis.* New York: McGraw-Hill, 1966. Although this study covers only three years, it represents a penetrating examination of a major issue that threatened the cooperative spirit within Western Europe, and between Europe and the United States. The author demonstrates a sound understanding of the political realities of the European Community.

28:51   Haas, Ernst B. *The Uniting of Europe: Political, Social, and Economic Forces, 1950–1957.* London: Stevens, 1958. Haas concentrates on the European Coal and Steel Community as an example of how European integration might come about. He studies particular political groups and institutions and attempts to determine their impact. Bibliography.

28:52   Manderson-Jones, R. B. *The Special Relationship: Anglo-American Relations and Western European Unity, 1947–56.* London: Weidenfeld & Nicolson, 1972. This is an analytical account of the interplay between American and British policy during the quest for European unity. The author correctly points out that the United States did not always treat Britain in any special manner. Bibliography.

28:53   Northrop, Filmer S. C. *European Union and United States Foreign Policy: A Study in Sociological Jurisprudence.* New York: Macmillan, 1954. The author discusses the relationship (1948–1954) between law and the people of Europe as they are influenced by the United States to come together in a union. This is an unusual, interesting approach to history.

U.S. AND EUROPEAN COMMON MARKET

See "Personalities," especially Jean Monnet (under "Others"); also see Chapter 39, "Trade since 1945" and "GATT."

28:54   Hinshaw, Randall. *European Community and American Trade: A Study in Atlantic Economics and Policy.* New York: Praeger, 1964. This is a book about the Common Market and related developments in Western Europe from the standpoint of the United States. It is an economic study in the sense that it attempts to shed light on the impact of European integration on America, and more broadly, on Atlantic economic strength.

28:55   Humphrey, Don D. *The United States and the Common Market: A Background Study.* Rev. ed. New York: Praeger, 1964. The book is a brief history of the United States and the Common Market with an analysis of the impact of economic ties upon the various countries involved, particularly the United States.

28:56   Krause, Lawrence B. *European Economic Integration and the United States.* Washington, D.C.: Brookings Institution, 1968. Krause discusses the European Economic Community and the European Free Trade Association and their impact upon the United States. In 1968, the author did not find them threatening.

28:57   McCreary, Edward A. *The Americanization of Europe: The Impact of Americans and American Business on the Uncommon Market.* Garden City, N.Y.: Doubleday, 1964. This volume is a general, semitechnical introduction to the workings of American business in Europe based on over 300 interviews.

28:58   Moran, Theodore H. "Multinational Corporations and the Political Economy of U.S.-European Relations." *Journal of International Affairs* 30:1 (1976), 65–79. In an attempt to escape American hegemony, the countries of the European Economic Community have sought to avoid economic and technological dependence on the United States, as reflected in the activities of the multinational corporations.

THE ALLIANCE SYSTEM

See "Personalities," especially Dean Acheson, Charles de Gaulle.

28:59 Calleo, David P. "The European Coalition in a Fragmenting World." *Foreign Affairs* 54:1 (1975), 98–112. Were it not for the super powers, Europe would not need a confederation. Western Europe's dependence upon the United States has been relatively easy upon Europe's own economic and military interests, and little has had to be sacrificed.

Chace, J., and Ravenal, E. C., eds. *Atlantis Lost: U.S.-European Relations after the Cold War* (28:42) contains ten essays on the Atlantic alliance. It is thoughtful and at times speculative but lacks cohesion; nonetheless, a common theme is that a variety of forces will block closer relationships.

28:60 Hartley, Livingston. "The North Atlantic Assembly." *Atlantic Community Quarterly* 13:4 1975/1976), 486–91. Hartley discusses the work of the North Atlantic Assembly since the organization started in 1955 as the NATO Parliamentarians Conference.

28:61 Osgood, Robert E. *Alliances and American Foreign Policy*. Baltimore: Johns Hopkins Press, 1968. Osgood concludes that in 1967 the bipolar military balance in Europe was still the dominant fact of European life. He wonders whether such an arrangement might not break down into a much more pluralistic one.

28:62 Richardson, James L. *Germany and the Atlantic Alliance: The Interaction of Strategy and Politics*. Cambridge: Harvard University Press, 1966. Richardson concentrates on the political problems caused by strategic military choices.

28:63 Steel, Ronald. *The End of Alliance: America and the Future of Europe*. New York: Viking, 1964. The world has changed much since NATO was created, but the United States seems not to notice. Those in Europe, such as Charles de Gaulle, who called for modification are seen by the United States as contributing to the weakness of the alliance.

Stromberg, R. N. *Collective Security and American Foreign Policy: From the League of Nations to NATO* (20:94) is the basic book on the idea of collective security in American foreign policy (1914–1956). He points out both the strengths and weaknesses of that approach and suggests that the weaknesses may predominate.

28:64 Williams, Geoffrey. *The Permanent Alliance: The European-American Partnership, 1945–* *1974*. Leiden: Sijthoff, 1977. While touching on NATO, this book concentrates on a broader historical framework of political-military doctrines and their application. Williams argues for greater European autonomy on local issues and American leadership on global issues.

28:65 Wolfers, Arnold, ed. *Alliance Policy in the Cold War*. Baltimore: Johns Hopkins Press, 1959. This book largely revolves around NATO problems but deals on a broader plane with concepts of collective security. It remains a useful collection of essays.

U.S. AND NATO

See Chapter 26, "Founding of NATO"; see "German Rearmament," below; and also see Chapter 36, "Canada and NATO."

28:66 Bare, C. Gordon. "Burden-Sharing in NATO: The Economics of Alliance." *Orbis* 20:2 (1976), 417–36. During 1970 to 1974 the United States, feeling it was making "a disproportionate contribution both to NATO and to the international economic order of the industrialized democracies," sought some economic relief.

28:67 Barnet, Richard J., and Raskin, Marcus G. *After Twenty Years: The Decline of NATO and the Search for a New Policy in Europe*. New York: Random House, 1965. This tightly written treatise on the Atlantic alliance argues that the military aspects of NATO have outlived their usefulness. Continuation of the alliance in its present form will hinder détente.

28:68 Buchan, Alastair. *NATO in the 1960's*. New York: Praeger, 1960. Buchan examines the East-West antagonism and its impact on NATO. Buchan sees the conflict continuing and calls for NATO to seek a better capacity for limited war.

28:69 Buteux, Paul. "Theatre Nuclear Weapons and European Security." *Canadian Journal of Political Science* 10:4 (1977), 781–808. Buteux evaluates to what extent present arguments about the strategic and political function of nuclear armaments deployed by NATO are comparable to those made in the 1950s and 1960s.

28:70 Caudill, Orley B. "NATO: The Durable Alliance." *Southern Quarterly* 8:1 (1969), 1–35. Caudill reviews the first 20 years of NATO, ratified April 4, 1949. The strength of the alliance rests in article 5, in which "the Parties agree that an armed attack against one or more of them in Europe or North America shall be considered an attack on them all."

28:71 Dyer, Philip W. "Will Tactical Nuclear Weapons Ever Be Used?" *Political Science Quarterly* 88:2 (1973), 214–29. Dyer considers the origins and nature of tactical nuclear weapons and their relation to the problems of NATO. Arguing that scientists, not military men, provided the early initiative in their development, he concludes that the weapons have no conceivable role in future ground warfare.

28:72 Fox, William T. R., and Fox, Annette B. *NATO and the Range of American Choice.* New York: Columbia University Press, 1967. This well-written book constitutes a handbook of resources for the study of NATO as it concluded its second decade. The study of the problems of consultation in the alliance is its major contribution.

28:73 Fox, William T. R., and Shilling, Warner R., eds. *European Security and the Atlantic System.* New York: Columbia University Press, 1973. This collection of diverse critiques on the defense of Europe and the U.S. contribution thereto provides one of the few perspectives on NATO at the beginning of détente.

Kissinger, H. A. *The Troubled Partnership: A Reappraisal of the Atlantic Alliance* (28:21) critiques nuclear decisionmaking.

28:74 Kissinger, Henry A. *Nuclear Weapons and Foreign Policy.* New York: Harper, 1957. This book launched both Kissinger's public career and a continuing public debate over the use of nuclear weapons. Although the book deals with more than Europe, its primary focus is Western Europe, NATO, and potential U.S.-Soviet conflict. Kissinger's thesis is that a limited war using nuclear weapons ought to be among the policy options of the United States.

28:75 Knorr, Klauss, ed. *NATO and American Security.* Princeton, N.J.: Princeton University Press, 1959. Eleven distinguished contributors often disagree and overlap but come to one focal point: a joint arrangement is preferable to independent nuclear deterrents. The book emphasizes the military strategy of NATO.

28:76 Loeb, Larry M. "Jupiter Missiles in Europe: A Measure of Presidential Power." *World Affairs* 139:1 (1976), 27–39. Loeb discusses presidential influence in military strategy and NATO in the placing

of Jupiter missiles in Europe (1957–1963) by emphasizing the actions of Eisenhower and Kennedy.

Osgood, R. *NATO: The Entangling Alliance* [1945–1961] (26:170) is still a most useful survey of NATO's early years.

EUROCOMMUNISM

28:77 Kriegel, Annie. *Eurocommunism: A New Kind of Communism?* Trans. by Peter S. Stern. Stanford, Calif.: Hoover Institution, 1978. The author believes that while Eurocommunism offers Western European communist parties an escape from Stalinism, it is not a fundamental schism along the Sino-Russian line. The European communist parties continue to support almost all the goals of the Soviet Union.

28:78 McInnes, Neil. *Euro-Communism.* London: Sage, 1976. A good short introduction to what Eurocommunism is and where it might go. McInnes concludes that the Soviet Union might well face a third schism of the communist movement if the Eurocommunist parties develop along democratic lines.

28:79 Revel, Jean-François. *The Totalitarian Temptation.* Garden City, N.Y.: Doubleday, 1977. Although Revel deals with history with a very broad brush, his tough-minded evaluation of the role of Eurocommunism in the recent past is provocative.

U.S. and Major European Nations

See Chapters 26 and 29 for the United States and the Soviet Union.

GERMANY

See Chapters 25 and 26 for U.S.-German issues in the context of World War II and the early cold war years; Chapter 29 deals with the Berlin crisis of 1958 to 1961.

Alexander, C. C. *Holding the Line: The Eisenhower Era, 1952–1961* (24:201) provides information on the German unification issue.

28:80 Baras, Victor. "Stalin's German Policy after Stalin." *Slavic Review* 37:2 (1978), 259–67. The Soviet note of March 10, 1952, indicated that reunification of the Germanies was unlikely. The author examines Stalin's 1952 German policy, his reunification proposal, West German vulnerability, and the relationship between the reunification proposal and the June 1953 uprising in East Germany.

28:81 Baring, Arnulf. *Uprising in East Germany, June 17, 1953*. Ithaca, N.Y.: Cornell University Press, 1972. This study is an analysis of the reasons for the uprising and the results.

28:82 Dulles, Eleanor Lansing. *One Germany or Two: The Struggle at the Heart of Europe*. Stanford, Calif.: Hoover Institution Press, 1970. Dulles concludes that Germany is "the indispensable ally" for the United States in Europe and that American policy cannot hope to influence its future policies without concerted effort. Extensive bibliography.

28:83 Freund, Gerald. *Germany between Two Worlds*. New York: Harcourt, Brace, 1961. A German scholar reviews Germany's problems from 1945 to 1960 and deals with the American connection in some detail. The book is especially useful for public opinion trends in both countries.

Gatzke, H. W. *Germany and the United States: A "Special Relationship"?* (2:229) provides a good introduction to German-American issues, and argues that there was no special relationship.

28:84 Kellermann, Henry J. *Cultural Relations as an Instrument of U.S. Foreign Policy: The Educational Exchange Program between the United States and Germany, 1945–1954*. Washington, D.C.: G.P.O., 1978. The State Department official chiefly responsible for the program discusses its major changes. These changes clearly reflected the increasingly positive image of Germany and the role that it might play in the developing Western alliance.

28:85 Merkl, Peter M. *German Foreign Policies, West and East: On the Threshold of a New European Era*. Studies in International and Comparative Politics, no. 3. Santa Barbara, Calif.: ABC-Clio, 1974. This study analyzes the foreign policy postures of both Germanies against a 100-year background.

28:86 Morgan, Roger. *The United States and West Germany, 1945–1973: A Study in Alliance Politics*. London: Oxford University Press, 1974. The best short survey of American-German relations. This book should be the basic starting point for the interested student. Bibliography.

28:87 Treverton, Gregory F. *The Dollar Drain and American Forces in Germany: Managing the Political Economics of Alliance*. Athens: Ohio University Press, 1978. Treverton zeroes in on one aspect of American-German relations and gives an excellent description of the resultant problems. American offset-demands bore directly on Germany's basic political processes of spending and raising revenue, and were bound to cause trouble.

Warburg, J. P. *Germany: Key to Peace* [1946–1953] (26:78) is especially fearful of the consequences of German rearmament.

deZayas, A. M. *Nemesis at Potsdam: The Anglo-Americans and the Expulsion of the Germans* (26:101) is the little known story, quite tragic, of the often cruel expulsion of millions of Germans from Eastern Europe to the West in the waning days of World War II. Without controls or authoritative supervision, the promised "humane" conditions seldom existed.

Nuremberg Trials

See under "Bibliographies" for Lewis (1:39).

28:88 Blayney, Michael S. "Herbert Pell, War Crimes, and the Jews." *American Jewish Historical Quarterly* 65:4 (1976), 335–52. Pell was an early and vigorous denouncer of Nazi policies; his letters to the president stand in marked contrast to the restrained style and attitude of the State Department. His 1943 appointment to the UN War Crimes Commission led almost from the beginning to increased conflict with the State Department.

28:89 Bosch, William J. *Judgement on Nuremberg: American Attitudes toward the Major German War Crime Trials*. Chapel Hill: University of North Carolina Press, 1970. A public opinion study of policymakers, lawyers, congressmen, the clergy, historians, the military, the public, and behavioral scientists on the Nuremberg trials. Most agreed that preexisting assumptions, not the objective event, determined judgments on the tribunal. Extensive bibliography.

28:90   International Military Tribunal. *Trial of the Major War Criminals before the International Military Tribunal, Nuremberg, 14 November 1945 –1 October 1946.* 42 vols. Nuremberg: International Military Tribunal, 1947–1949. This set covers the trial of 24 persons (volumes 23 and 24 are indexes to the set). It can be supplemented by *Nazi Conspiracy and Aggression,* 8 vols. (1946), which includes documentary evidence gathered by the prosecuting staff, and by *Trials of War Criminals before the Nuremberg Military Tribunals under Control Law no. 10,* 15 vols. (1949–1953).

28:91   Smith, Bradley F. *Reaching Judgment at Nuremberg.* New York: Basic Books, 1977. Smith focuses on the eight judges who sat on the bench at Nuremberg. He finds that they had little guidance and thus functioned much like a traditional court. There are many fascinating insights in this basic work.

28:92   Taylor, Telford. *Nuremberg and Vietnam: An American Tragedy.* Chicago: Quadrangle, 1970. Taylor examines the concept of war crimes and trials from the perspective of two contrasting situations. While he argues firmly for principles of international law, his application of the crimes category to the United States in Vietnam stimulated debate.

German Rearmament

Grosser, A. *The Colossus Again: Western Germany from Defeat to Rearmament* (26:76).

28:93   Kelleher, Catherine McArdle. *Germany and the Politics of Nuclear Weapons.* New York: Columbia University Press, 1975. This study provides a detailed account of German policy on nuclear weapons (1945–1970) and of the NATO alliance relationship.

28:94   Martin, Lawrence W. "The American Decision to Re-arm Germany." In Harold Stein, ed., *American Civil-Military Decisions: A Book of Case Studies.* Birmingham: University of Alabama Press, 1963, pp. 645–60. This essay is a useful introduction to the problem of German rearmament. It is a carefully chronicled, detailed presentation of U.S. policymakers' decision to abandon their prior commitment to demilitarization and to accord the Germans an important role in the defense of Europe.

28:95   McGeehan, Robert. *The German Rearmament Question: American Diplomacy and European Defense after World War II.* Urbana: University of Illinois Press, 1971. McGeehan traces the steps whereby the United States, especially after Korea, sought to rearm Germany. He argues that despite the defeat of the EDC, largely due to the fears of France, American policies succeeded. Bibliography.

Schmidt, H. *Defense or Retaliation: A German Contribution to the Consideration of NATO's Strategic Problem* (28:36) examines the history of West Germany's defense policies.

28:96   Simpson, Benjamin M., III. "The Rearming of Germany, 1950–1954: A Linchpin in the Political Evolution of Europe." *Naval War College Review* 23:3 (1971), 76–90. A good short review of the main events on the way to a rearmed Germany.

GREAT BRITAIN AND IRELAND

See "Personalities," especially Clement R. Attlee, and under "Others," Hugh Dalton, Harold Wilson.

Akenson, D. H. *The United States and Ireland* (2:216) concentrates on the 20th century, and the 1960s in particular. It is a useful introduction to Irish-American issues.

28:97   Bell, Coral. *Debatable Alliances: An Essay in Anglo-American Relations.* New York: Oxford University Press, 1964. The author considers the Anglo-American relationship as an element in the central power balance. Bell points out that West Germany has become America's pivotal ally, and that Britain went from protagonist to attendant lord.

28:98   Dawson, Raymond, and Rosecrance, Richard. "Theory and Reality in the Anglo-American Alliance." *World Politics* 19:1 (1966), 21–51. The authors argue that the Anglo-American alliance in theory should have broken down over the Suez crisis, but did not. The theory of alliances fails to explain it, but policy must recognize that there are ties stronger than alliances.

28:99   Epstein, Leon. *Britain: Uneasy Ally.* Chicago: University of Chicago Press, 1954. The most comprehensive analysis of British responses to American foreign policy (1945–1952), this work is a useful complement to diplomatic histories. The main British concern in the early postwar period was uncertainty over an American commitment to defend Europe against Soviet aggression.

28:100 Ezell, Edward C. "Cracks in the Post-War Anglo-American Alliance: The Great Rifle Controversy, 1947–1957." *Military Affairs* 38:4 (1974), 138–41. After World War II, Britain desired to change its standard issue rifle, but adamant American refusal to accept a .280 caliber cartridge curtailed the project. This is a good case study of alliance problems.

28:101 Gelber, Lionel M. *The Alliance of Necessity: Britain's Crisis, the New Europe and American Interests.* New York: Stein & Day, 1966. Gelber argues that the United States, if she wants Britain as an ally, must help the British find an alternative to Europeanization. He is clearly against U.S. policy which he thinks will diminish, not strengthen, Britain's influence and power.

28:102 Gelber, Lionel M. *America in Britain's Place: The Leadership of the West and Anglo-American Unity.* New York: Praeger, 1961. Gelber discusses the problems of Anglo-American unity under the current international strains. Of interest are his chapters on "Who Speaks for 'America'?" and on the crisis in relations produced by the 1956 Suez episode.

Manderson-Jones, R. B. *The Special Relationship: Anglo-American Relations and Western European Unity, 1947–56* (28:52) argues that Britain sought, as its primary aim, leadership of an intergovernmental union of Western Europe, as opposed to full European unity or a junior partnership with the United States.

28:103 McInnis, Edgar W. *The Atlantic Triangle and the Cold War.* Toronto: University of Toronto Press, 1959. This volume concerns Canada, Britain, and the United States and accentuates the stability of the relationship and plays down the disharmonies.

28:104 Neustadt, Richard E. *Alliance Politics.* New York: Columbia University Press, 1970. Examining British-American relations during the Suez crisis (1956) and the Skybolt missile affair (1962), Neustadt concludes that there were many misperceptions between the two countries because both sides misread the interests pursued by the other.

Nicholas, H. G. *The United States and Britain* (2:237) is a broad introductory survey with about the last third concentrating on the period since 1945.

28:105 Nicholas, Herbert G. *Britain and the U.S.A.* Baltimore: Johns Hopkins Press, 1963. Nicholas concentrates on the period since 1945 and argues that the

vitality, unity, and creativeness of the 1947 to 1950 period had disappeared by the time of the Suez crisis. He places responsibility for the decline on both sides.

28:106 Northedge, Frederick S. *British Foreign Policy: The Process of Readjustment, 1945–1961.* London: Allen & Unwin, 1962. This work includes a perceptive discussion of the differences in the British and American approaches to foreign policy and of the contentious issues which tested but did not break the relationship. Bibliography.

Nunnerly, D. *President Kennedy and Britain* (28:20).

28:107 Roberts, Henry L., and Wilson, Paul A. *Britain and the United States: Problems in Cooperation.* New York: Harper, 1953. This is a broad survey covering the main problems as they developed since 1945. Still of some use for the outlook of the Council on Foreign Relations, which was interested in European unity.

28:108 Russett, Bruce M. *Community and Contention: Britain and America in the Twentieth Century.* Cambridge, Mass.: MIT Press, 1963. Rather than a straightforward historical approach (the title is misleading since much of the material deals with the post-1945 period), Russett discusses elites, mass communications, and effects of education. A stimulating and interesting book.

28:109 Wallace, William. "The Management of Foreign Economic Policy in Britain." *International Affairs* [London] 50:2 (1974), 251–67. International economic policy was relatively insulated from British foreign policy after 1945, when many economic factors were subordinated to strategic and other factors. This changed during the 1960s and had effects upon policymaking and priorities.

The British Left and Foreign Policy

28:110 Epstein, Leon S. "The British Labour Left and United States Foreign Policy." *American Political Science Review* 45:4 (1951), 974–95. This is an examination of left-wing Labour distrust of U.S. foreign policy since 1945. The author identifies 1945–1946 and the Korean War period as times when this mistrust, expressing itself through leftist hostility to power politics, rearmament, and capitalism, was particularly intense.

28:111 Fitzsimmons, M. A. "British Labour in Search of a Socialist Foreign Policy." *Review of Politics* 12:2 (1950), 197–214. This is a brief survey of left-wing Labour thought regarding foreign policy (1945–1950). The author suggests that much of the left-wing opposition to Bevin's pro-American policies came from frustrated utopians.

28:112 Fitzsimmons, M. A. *The Foreign Policy of the British Labour Government.* Notre Dame, Ind.: University of Notre Dame Press, 1953. Labour's foreign policy is represented as being inspired mainly by necessity and traditional British interests rather than party or ideological pressures. Labour adjusted to reality by collaborating with the United States along Churchillian lines.

Gordon, M. R. *Conflict and Consensus in Labour's Foreign Policy, 1914–1965* (2:235) argues that in 1945 the Attlee government repudiated the commitment to a distinctly socialist foreign policy in favor of Anglo-American collaboration.

28:113 Meehan, Eugene J. *The British Left Wing and Foreign Policy: A Study of the Influence of Ideology.* New Brunswick, N.J.: Rutgers University Press, 1960. This study of the influence of leftist ideology on British foreign policy concentrates on 1945 to 1951. It is conceived in theoretical terms but is a valuable compendium of the hostility to American capitalism. Bibliography.

Pelling, H. *America and the British Left: From Bright to Bevin* (2:238) has one chapter on the U.S. and British left since 1945, which stresses Labour's uneasiness over the McCarthy era of the early 1950s.

Windrich, E. *British Labour's Foreign Policy* (2:240).

Anglo-American Nuclear Policies

Dawson, R., and Rosecrance, R. "Theory and Reality in the Anglo-American Alliance" (28:98) concentrates on the issues of nuclear cooperation and concludes that history, tradition, and affinity, as much as self-interest, lay at the heart of the "special relationship."

28:114 Duncan, Francis. "Atomic Energy and Anglo-American Relations, 1946–1954." *Orbis* 12:4

(1969), 1188–207. The author concludes that, by the passage of the Atomic Energy Act of 1954, the Anglo-American partnership had become even fuller and closer than it had been in World War II.

28:115 Gowing, Margaret. *Independence and Deterrence: Britain and Atomic Energy, 1939–1952.* 2 vols. New York: St. Martin's Press, 1974. These volumes reflect Britain's skillful persuasion of a distrustful United States to share nuclear weapons information, to secure British independent nuclear status easily and cheaply within an American-dominated alliance. Bibliography.

28:116 Pierre, Andrew J. *Nuclear Politics: The British Experience with an Independent Strategic Force, 1939–1970.* London: Oxford University Press, 1972. This book is the basic study of British nuclear policies and the American influences on those policies. Bibliography.

28:117 Rosecrance, Richard N. *Defense of the Realm: British Strategy in the Nuclear Epoch.* New York: Columbia University Press, 1968. This account examines the evolution of British defense planning, with particular emphasis on the initial decade after World War II.

28:118 Snyder, William P. *The Politics of British Defense Policy, 1945–1962.* Columbus: Ohio State University Press, 1965. This useful survey clearly presents the dilemmas confronting Britain's planning and, by implication, its significance for the United States.

Suez Crisis, 1956

See "Personalities," especially John Foster Dulles; also see Chapter 33, "The 1956 Suez Crisis/The 1956 War," for additional references.

28:119 Bowie, Robert R. *Suez 1956.* International Crisis and the Role of Law Series. New York: Oxford University Press, 1974. This study of the 1956 Suez crisis attempts to explore what part international law, norms, or agencies played in the decisions and actions of the major protagonists.

Finer, H. *Dulles over Suez: The Theory and Practice of His Diplomacy* (33:101) is hostile to Dulles, and this long book sometimes turns into a harangue.

Neustadt, R. E. *Alliance Politics* (28:104) discusses Anglo-American misperceptions during the Suez crisis (1956).

28:120 Nutting, Anthony. *No End of a Lesson: The Inside Story of the Suez Crisis.* New York: Potter, 1967. This book reveals the sorry behavior of the British government under Sir Anthony Eden. The Suez episode brought on Nutting's resignation from Parliament and ended his political career.

Robertson, T. *Crisis: The Inside Story of the Suez Conspiracy* (36:73) deals with the impact on Canada of the Anglo-American conflict resulting from the episode.

28:121 Thomas, Hugh. *Suez.* New York: Harper, 1967. This book argues that Suez was the last gasp of an imperial country ending its "pretentions in comic style" and that the use of force was a most serious mistake. Thomas is also critical of American leaders.

FRANCE

See "Personalities," especially Charles E. Bohlen, Charles de Gaulle.

Brinton, C. C. *The Americans and the French* (2:225) is a general survey that concentrates on the post–World War II era.

Brown, W. A., Jr., and Opie, R. *American Foreign Assistance* (39:153) is particularly useful on aid to France under the Marshall Plan.

28:122 Carmor, Guy de. *The Foreign Policies of France, 1944–1968.* Trans. by Elaine P. Halperin. Chicago: University of Chicago Press, 1970. A detailed survey (1944–1968) which argues that, while French foreign policy has followed some unusual paths, the general direction has been clear: "opposition to American hegemony, refusal to form a federated Europe; the rebuttal of England."

Duroselle, J.-B. *France and the United States: From the Beginnings to the Present* (2:226) covers the period since 1945 in the last hundred pages. While some of his American sources are dated he does bring an important French perspective to his work.

28:123 Furniss, Edgar S., Jr. *France: Troubled Ally: De Gaulle's Heritage and Prospects.* New York:

Harper, 1960. This account represents one of the better attempts at analyzing French policy in the Fourth and Fifth republics. Furniss examines French foreign policy in the 15 years following World War II within the environment where it was shaped.

28:124 Kolodziej, Edward A. *French International Policy under De Gaulle and Pompidou: The Politics of Grandeur.* Ithaca, N.Y.: Cornell University Press, 1974. While the author discusses French foreign policy in its broadest context, he includes much useful material on Franco-American relations.

28:125 Lerner, Daniel, and Aron, Raymond, eds. *France Defeats EDC.* New York: Praeger, 1957. A series of essays, with a good introduction by Aron, which stresses the different outlooks from Paris and Washington from 1945 to 1956 on EDC.

28:126 McKay, Donald C. *The United States and France.* Cambridge: Harvard University Press, 1951. Though now dated, this summary of Franco-American relations and of the chief problems confronting the French Republic is useful for the period up to 1950.

28:127 Sabrosky, Alan N. "French Foreign Policy Alternatives." *Orbis* 19:4 (1976), 1429–47. Since the end of World War II, "France has occupied an ambiguous place in the international community," but it now seems ready to regain much of its status because of détente and the end of bipolarity.

Strauss, D. *Menace in the West: The Rise of French Anti-Americanism in Modern Times* (21:103) concentrates on 1917 to 1932, but has some interesting materials on the later periods.

Zahniser, M. R. *Uncertain Friendship: American-French Relations through the Cold War* (2:228) indicates that the problems of Germany and Charles de Gaulle were at the center of the Franco-American relationship. He believes France has "gradually defined her position toward the United States essentially as one of an uncommitted ally."

Franco-American Nuclear Policies

28:128 Kohl, Wilfrid L. *French Nuclear Diplomacy.* Princeton, N.J.: Princeton University Press,

1971. A good solid historical work, it covers the period from 1958 to 1970; chapter 3 details the American-French conflict. The volume emphasizes the great change in U.S. policies from Kennedy to Nixon. Bibliography.

28:129   Mendl, Wolfe. *Deterrence and Persuasion: French Nuclear Armament in the Context of National Policy, 1945–1969*. New York: Praeger, 1970. The author analyzes why France developed an independent nuclear force. For the origins of France's atomic policy, see Lawrence Scheinman's *Atomic Energy Policy in France under the Fourth Republic* (Princeton, N.J.: Princeton University Press, 1965).

28:130   Zoppo, Ciro E. "France as a Nuclear Power." In Richard N. Rosecrance, ed., *The Dispersion of Nuclear Weapons*. New York: Columbia University Press, 1964. Zoppo gives a good historical description of the growth of French nuclear capability and the failure of the United States to prevent that development.

First Indochina War, 1945–1954

See also Chapter 30, "U.S. and the First Indochina War, 1941–1954," for additional references.

Irving, R. E. M. *The First Indochina War: French and American Policy, 1945–1954* (30:157) is primarily a study of French policies, which finds each year the American indirect involvement becoming more prominent. Irving emphasizes the great reluctance of the United States to unreservedly commit itself to French goals or to the Vietnam government, but how it slowly but surely did both.

28:131   Kelly, George A. *Lost Soldiers: The French Army and Empire in Crisis, 1947–1962*. Cambridge, Mass.: MIT Press, 1965. This informative account reviews the problems of the French army in Indochina and Algeria.

Sullivan, M. P. *France's Vietnam Policy: A Study in French-American Relations* (30:147) covers a neglected area of Franco-American relations (1963–1973) in a judicious, short study.

U.S. and Southern, Central, and Northern Europe

28:132   Burgess, Philip M. *Elite Images and Foreign Policy Outcomes: A Study of Norway*. Columbus: Ohio State University Press, 1968. The author argues that the "strategic image" held by a country's "authoritative elite" affects subsequent policy choices. Burgess's example of this thesis is Norwegian foreign policy (1940–1949), which includes the prelude to NATO.

28:133   Erdman, Paul E. *Swiss-American Economic Relations, Their Evolution in an Era of Crisis*. Basel: Kyklos-Verlag, 1956. This is a comparative study of the basic positions of Switzerland and the United States in the world economy (1925–1955); the last third of the book deals with post–World War II U.S.-Swiss relations, financial conflict between the two states, and the implementation of the Washington accord.

28:134   Govaerts, Frans. "Belgium and the Cold War." In Joseph M. Siracusa and Glen St. J. Barclay, eds., *The Impact of the Cold War: Reconsiderations*. Port Washington, N.Y.: Kennikat, 1977, pp. 40–63. This essay deals with Belgium's foreign policy, internal development, foreign trade, and military policy.

28:135   Nuechterlein, Donald E. *Iceland: Reluctant Ally*. Ithaca, N.Y.: Cornell University Press, 1961. This volume discusses U.S.-Icelandic defense relations since 1940 and largely deals with some of the problems of having foreign troops based in another state. Iceland was the first NATO power to allow communists to participate in elections.

28:136   Pollis, Adamantia. "United States Foreign Policy towards Authoritarian Regimes in the Mediterranean." *Millennium: Journal of International Studies* 4:1 (1975), 28–51. Pollis examines U.S. foreign policy toward the regimes in Greece, Turkey, Spain, and Portugal in order to identify the determinants of U.S. policy in the postwar period and to relate these factors to the theoretical formulations used in international relations.

Scott, F. D. *Scandinavia* (2:243) is a good introduction to foreign policy issues.

GREECE

See Chapter 26, "The Greek Civil War."

28:137   Katris, John A. *Eyewitness in Greece: The Colonels Come to Power.* St. Louis: New Critics Press, 1971. A Greek journalist's statement on U.S. involvement in the 1967 coup, this volume is extremely critical of American policies in support of the colonels.

28:138   Kousoulas, Dimitrios G. *The Price of Freedom: Greece in World Affairs, 1939–53.* Syracuse, N.Y.: Syracuse University Press, 1953. A broad, general introduction by a native of Greece who was there during the time period covered. This is a useful starting point.

28:139   McNeill, William H. *The Metamorphosis of Greece since World War II.* Chicago: University of Chicago Press, 1978. While not specifically on U.S.-Greek relations, this volume by a historian who has observed and written on Greece for more than 35 years is an important starting point for anyone who wants to understand modern Greece.

Stavrianos, L. S. *Greece: American Dilemma and Opportunity* (26:143) reviews political development in Greece (1939–1951). Critical of British and American Greek policy in the past, Stavrianos is concerned with the danger that the United States might tie itself to the Greek government and lose the support of the Greek people.

U.S. Aid to Greece

28:140   McNeill, William H. *Greece: American Aid in Action, 1947–1956.* New York: Twentieth Century Fund, 1957. This volume describes the impact of U.S. aid on Greece from 1947 to 1956. McNeill concludes that both Greek and American efforts have made a difference over the ten-year period in raising the level of the Greek economy.

28:141   Munkman, C. A. *American Aid to Greece: A Report on the First Ten Years.* New York: Praeger, 1958. By a former member of the American Economic Mission to Greece, this offering is very critical of the manner in which U.S. aid was applied to Greece.

The Cyprus Issue, 1974

See Chapter 33, "Cyprus," for references.

28:142   Coufoudakis, Van. "U.S. Foreign Policy and the Cyprus Question: An Interpretation." *Millennium: Journal of International Studies* 5:3 (1976–1977), 245–68. To secure Cyprus's westward orientation, the United States tried to limit the independence of both Bishop Makarios and Cyprus, an effort seen in U.S. support of Greco-Turkish partition and during the 1974 Turkish invasion.

28:143   Couloumbis, Theodore A., and Hicks, Sallie M., eds. *U.S. Foreign Policy toward Greece and Cyprus: The Clash of Principle and Pragmatism.* Washington, D.C.: Center for Mediterranean Studies, 1975. Many candid and various opinions were expressed at a conference on the Cyprus issue and these are its proceedings. It is most useful for its bibliographical footnotes.

28:144   Polyviou, Polyvios G. *Cyprus: The Tragedy and the Challenge.* Washington, D.C.: American Hellenic Institute, 1975. Concentrating on the 1974 crisis, the author is much more critical of British policies than of American. The book is useful for its Greek viewpoint on international law and the United Nations.

28:145   Stern, Laurence. "Bitter Lessons: How We Failed in Cyprus." *Foreign Policy,* no. 19 (1975), 34–78. Concentrating on the Turkish invasion of Cyprus, the author argues that Kissinger badly mishandled almost the whole situation and appeared to favor Turkey in the dispute.

28:146   Stern, Laurence. *The Wrong Horse: The Politics of Intervention and the Failure of American Diplomacy.* New York: Time Books, 1977. Stern feels that U.S. policy toward Greece and Turkey played an integral part in the Cyprus crises. The U.S. support of Greece's military rulers and their covert desire for a partition of Cyprus conflicted with the U.S. public stance of supporting an independent government on Cyprus.

ITALY

DeConde, A. *Half Bitter Half Sweet: An Excursion into Italian-American History* (8:101) is a broad survey of Italian-American relations that includes much material on the period since 1945. It does not concentrate on diplomatic relations but has much material on it.

28:147 DeSantis, Vincent P. "Italy in the Cold War." In Joseph M. Siracusa and Glen St. J. Barclay, eds., *The Impact of the Cold War: Reconsiderations.* Port Washington, N.Y.: Kennikat, 1977, pp. 26–39. De Santis surveys Italy's political and economic recovery (1945–1970s) from World War II.

Hughes, H. S. *The United States and Italy* (2:241) is a good introduction to Italian-American relations.

28:148 Kogan, Norman. *Italy and the Allies.* Cambridge: Harvard University Press, 1956. Covering the period from 1944 to 1954, the author gives a general description of American-Italian problems. It is especially valuable for Italian internal politics.

28:149 Platt, Alan A., and Leonardi, Robert. "American Foreign Policy and the Postwar Italian Left." *Political Science Quarterly* 93:2 (1978), 197–215. The authors discuss three critical periods in Italy's postwar history: between 1945 and 1948, during Italy's socioeconomic reconstruction; between 1960 and 1963, when Italy prepared for the entrance of the Socialist party into a government coalition; and from 1970 to 1976, when Communists increasingly participated in Italian government.

28:150 Woolf, S. J., ed. *The Rebirth of Italy, 1943–1950.* New York: Humanities Press, 1972. In these essays the unifying theme is that the shape of present-day Italy developed largely during 1943 to 1950. The essays examine such topics as the resistance movement, the party system, and foreign policy. They are useful for background.

Trieste Issue

28:151 Novak, Bogdan C. "American Policy toward the Slovenes in Trieste, 1941–1974." *Papers in Slovene Studies* (1977), 1–25. U.S. foreign policy vis-à-vis the Slovenes in Trieste was detrimental during the 1945 to 1951 period, and the United States continued to favor Italian claims until 1954. Since 1954 the American position came closer to being neutral.

28:152 Novak, Bogdan C. *Trieste, 1941–1954: The Ethnic, Political, and Ideological Struggle.* Chicago: University of Chicago Press, 1970. This is an excellent book describing the struggle between Italy and Yugo-

slavia over the disposition of Trieste. In the process the author gives a lot of material on the American position. Bibliography.

PORTUGAL

See Chapter 37 for the Angolan Civil War.

28:153 Ebinger, Charles K. "External Intervention in Internal War: The Politics and Diplomacy of the Angolan Civil War." *Orbis* 20:3 (1976), 669–99. While describing the actions of all the interested parties, the author gives the United States significant attention and concludes that Kissinger made the wrong choices.

28:154 Szulc, Tad. "Lisbon and Washington: Behind Portugal's Revolution." *Foreign Policy,* no. 21 (1975), 3–62. This important article surveys what Szulc believes was a vacillating, inconsistent U.S. policy.

SPAIN

Cortada, J. W. *Two Nations over Time: Spain and the United States, 1776–1977* (2:244) is a good introduction to Spanish-American relations.

28:155 Cortada, James W., ed. *Spain in the Twentieth-Century World: Essays on Spanish Diplomacy, 1898–1978.* Westport, Conn.: Greenwood, 1980. This collection of essays provides an excellent background to U.S.-Spanish relations; it is particularly valuable for the Spanish-American War (1898), the Spanish Civil War (1936–1939), and Spain in NATO during the 1960s and 1970s. Extensive bibliography.

28:156 Hadian, Ron. "United States Foreign Policy toward Spain, 1953–1975." *Iberian Studies* 7:1 (1978), 3–13. Hadian examines negotiations between the United States and Spain (1953–1975) which reveal the surprising diplomatic success of Franco in securing substantial U.S. economic and military aid.

28:157 Halstead, Charles R. "Spanish Foreign Policy, 1936–1978." In James W. Cortada, ed., *Spain in the Twentieth-Century World: Essays on Spanish Diplomacy, 1898–1978.* Westport, Conn.: Greenwood, 1980, pp. 41–94. This essay cogently defines the objectives of Franco's foreign policies from the days of the Spanish Civil War (1936–1939). Although

Franco introduced major economic reforms in 1951, which saw a substantial influx of foreign capital, he continued to see himself as a foe of communism (and of his civil war opponents).

28:158 Hughes, Emmet John. *Report from Spain.* New York: Holt, 1947. Hughes was press attaché at the American embassy in Madrid from 1942 to 1946. This is an indictment of the Franco regime as a police state resting on the Falange, the army, and the church.

28:159 Watson, Will, et al. *Spain: Implications for United States Foreign Policy.* Stamford, Conn.: Graylock, 1976. This book has as its main point the fact that Spain was the only country in the world where the United States had significant military forces without a military alliance. The book attempts to examine that unwritten alliance and is critical of past U.S. policies.

28:160 Whitaker, Arthur P. *Spain and Defense of the West: Ally and Liability.* New York: Harper, 1961. Whitaker looks into the evolving relationship of the United States and Spain under the defense agreement made in 1953. His major conclusion is that because of a narrow military concept of strategy the United States assumed a heavy political and moral liability by its support of the Franco regime. Bibliography.

U.S. and Eastern Europe

See also Chapters 25 and 26 for early cold war implications.

Brzezinski, Z. K. *The Soviet Bloc: Unity and Conflict* (26:23) is thorough and detailed and serves as a handbook on the Eastern European nations of the Warsaw Pact.

28:161 Byrnes, Robert F., ed. *The United States and Eastern Europe.* Englewood Cliffs, N.J.: Prentice-Hall, 1967. This small volume, with chapters by various experts, provides a good introduction to foreign policy issues (1945–1966).

28:162 Byrnes, Robert F. "United States Policy toward Eastern Europe: Before and After Helsinki." *Review of Politics* 37:4 (1975), 435–63. By providing

the United States and its allies with greater access to Eastern Europe, and by an aggressive Western policy demonstrating the cultural, economic, and technical strengths, the West may be able to use politics and culture to gradually end the "Soviet Empire over Europe."

28:163 Caldwell, Lawrence T., and Miller, Steven E. "East European Integration and European Politics." *International Journal* 32:2 (1977), 352–85. The authors suggest a reassessment of American and Western attitudes toward political change in Europe in the light of alterations in Soviet–Eastern European relations.

28:164 Campbell, John C. *American Policy toward Communist Eastern Europe: The Choices Ahead.* Minneapolis: University of Minnesota Press, 1965. Campbell's book includes a good brief historical background of each country to 1965.

28:165 Gati, Charles. "The Forgotten Region." *Foreign Policy,* no. 19 (1975), 135–45. Gati traces the development of U.S. policy toward Eastern Europe from one of great concern in the 1950s to an almost total lack of interest by 1975.

28:166 Handlery, George. "Propaganda and Information: The Case of U.S. Broadcasts to Eastern Europe." *East European Quarterly* 8:4 (1975), 391–412, 499–501. Handlery makes a careful comparison of radio broadcasts from Western and Eastern Europe during 1973 to determine, among other things, whether or not Radio Free Europe is simply a relic of the cold war. Radio Free Europe was found relatively objective.

Kertesz, S. D., ed. *The Fate of East Central Europe: Hopes and Failures of American Foreign Policy* (26:112) is an old collection, but still useful for the viewpoints of 1945 to 1955.

Kovrig, B. *The Myth of Liberation: East-Central Europe in U.S. Diplomacy and Politics since 1941* (25:100) finds that there was a great difference between U.S. intentions for Eastern Europe (1941–1970) and its ability to carry them out. He finds few villains or heroes, and many limits to American power.

28:167 Lukaszewski, Jerzy. "The United States, the West, and the Future of Eastern Europe." *Journal of International Affairs* 22:1 (1968), 16–25. Since "liberation" in 1945, the U.S.S.R. has encouraged Eastern European nationalism in order to maintain a Soviet hegemony which is now fading with the generation of leaders who founded it.

28:168 Rachwald, Arthur R. "United States Policy in East Europe." *Current History* 74:436 (1978), 150–53. This is a good, short review of U.S. policies from 1968 to 1977.

28:169 Socor, Vladimir. "The Limits of National Independence in the Soviet Bloc: Rumania's Foreign Policy Reconsidered." *Orbis* 20:3 (1976), 701–32. To many in the West, Rumania's foreign policy initiatives during the past 10 to 15 years have smacked of independent action and seemingly have not always followed current interests and objectives pursued by the Soviet Union.

28:170 Wolff, Robert L. *The Balkans in Our Time.* Cambridge: Harvard University Press, 1956. This volume is the most inclusive single survey of the recent history of Yugoslavia, Rumania, Bulgaria, and Albania, but it is now badly dated. Bibliography.

AUSTRIA

28:171 Allard, Sven. *Russia and the Austrian State Treaty: A Case Study of Soviet Policy in Europe.* University Park: Pennsylvania State University Press, 1970. This detailed, detached account by Sweden's ambassador to Austria during the 1950s provides many insights on East-West diplomatic maneuvers.

28:172 Bader, William B. *Austria between East and West, 1945–1955.* Stanford, Calif.: Stanford University Press, 1966. While basically dealing with the relationship between Austria and the Soviet Union, there is some useful material on U.S. policies from the Austrian viewpoint. Bibliography.

28:173 Ferring, Robert L. "The Austrian State Treaty of 1955 and the Cold War." *Western Political Quarterly* 21:4 (1968), 651–67. Ferring argues that the Kremlin's acceptance of Austrian neutrality was based on cold, sober calculations by the Soviets to advance Russian interests.

28:174 Hiscocks, Richard. *The Rebirth of Austria.* New York: Oxford University Press, 1953. Written by a Canadian who was personally concerned with the Allied occupation of Austria, it is basically a history of Austria, but does include material on the U.S. role.

CZECHOSLOVAKIA

See Chapter 26, "The Czech Coup, 1948."

28:175 Paul, David W. "Soviet Foreign Policy and the Invasion of Czechoslovakia: A Theory and A Case Study." *International Studies Quarterly* 15:2 (1971), 159–201. Early Soviet hesitancy resulted from a lack of consensus within the Soviet elite. During the summer of 1968, however, Czech events convinced Soviet leadership that Czechoslovakia was a threat to Soviet security and that radical action was necessary.

28:176 Valenta, Jiri. *Soviet Intervention in Czechoslovakia, 1968: Anatomy of a Decision.* Baltimore: Johns Hopkins University Press, 1979. Based on a bureaucratic politics paradigm approach, it discusses the Czech problem in 1968.

28:177 Windsor, Philip. "Yugoslavia, 1951, and Czechoslovakia, 1968." In Barry M. Blechman and Stephen S. Kaplan, eds., *Force without War: U.S. Armed Forces as a Political Instrument.* Washington, D.C.: Brookings Institution, 1978, pp. 440–514. The first crisis resulted from Tito's split from the Soviet bloc, the second from internal Czech politics.

28:178 Wolfe, James H. "West Germany and Czechoslovakia: The Struggle for Reconciliation." *Orbis* 14:1 (1970), 154–79. The Warsaw Pact invasion of Czechoslovakia in 1968 represented a setback to the attempts by West Germany and Czechoslovakia to reconcile differences resulting from World War II.

HUNGARY

28:179 Lillich, Richard B. "The United States–Hungarian Claims Agreement of 1973." *American Journal of International Law* 69:3 (1975), 534–59. On March 6, 1973, the United States and Hungary signed an agreement requiring Hungary to pay almost $19 million for claims from war damage, nationalization of property, and financial debts.

The 1956 Uprising

Gaskill, G. "Timetable of a Failure" (38:178) reviews the UN in 1956, especially the Hungarian question.

28:180 Hedli, Douglas J. "United States Involvement or Non-Involvement in the Hungarian Revolution of 1956." *International Review of History and Political Science* 11:1 (1974), 72–78. This article argues that the United States acted out of ignorance and misperceptions in 1956 and offered the Hungarians absolutely nothing.

28:181 Király, Belak, and Jónás, Paul, eds. *The Hungarian Revolution of 1956 in Retrospect*. New York: Columbia University Press, 1978. A volume of essays that throws a great deal of light on the Hungarian Revolution of 1956, this book is a good basic starting point.

28:182 Radvanyi, Janos. *Hungary and the Superpowers: The 1956 Revolution and Realpolitik*. Stanford, Calif.: Hoover Institution Press, 1971. This book, by a participant in the events of 1956, states that Mao Tse-tung encouraged Khrushchev to intervene with force. Radvanyi also has some interesting material on the Cuban missile crisis. This is a useful book on U.S. policies from a Hungarian perspective.

POLAND

See Chapters 25 and 26 for early cold war issues.

Hayden, E. W. *Technology Transfer to East Europe: U.S. Corporate Experience* (29:195) demonstrates how U.S. firms are working out cooperative ventures inside the Soviet sphere, especially Poland.

Humphrey, H. H. *Observations on East-West Economic Relations: U.S.S.R. and Poland, a Trip Report* (29:182) argues that the West has little to fear from increased economic interchange with the Soviet bloc if policies are properly developed.

28:183 Kaplan, Stephen S. "United States Aid to Poland, 1957–1964: Concerns, Objectives and Obstacles." *Western Political Quarterly* 28:1 (1975), 147–66. After 1956 the United States sent substantial economic aid to Poland and granted her most-favored-nation status. The author argues that the Eisenhower administration was correct in changing its policy despite strong congressional opposition.

28:184 Pienkos, Donald. "Ethnic Orientations among Polish Americans." *International Migration Review* 11:3 (1977), 350–62. In a survey of 246 persons of Polish background in Milwaukee, the author discovered, not surprisingly, that those who were born in Poland had a much higher interest in U.S.

foreign policy toward Poland than those of the later generations.

28:185 Rachwald, Arthur R. "Poland between the Superpowers: Three Decades of Foreign Policy." *Orbis* 20:4 (1977), 1055–83. Poland's foreign policy goals—security, territorial integrity, recovery—have been formed more or less independently of the U.S.S.R.

Wandycz, P. *The United States and Poland* (2:217) provides a good introduction to post-1945 Polish-American relations.

YUGOSLAVIA

See Chapter 26, "Tito-Stalin Split, 1948–1949."

28:186 Auty, Phyllis. "Yugoslavia and the Cold War." In Joseph M. Siracusa and Glen St. J. Barclay, eds., *The Impact of the Cold War: Reconsiderations*. Port Washington, N.Y.: Kennikat, 1977, pp. 125–43. Auty reviews Yugoslavia's policies relative to the Soviet Union and the United States. This survey examines both domestic and foreign policy.

28:187 Campbell, John C. *Tito's Separate Road: America and Yugoslavia in World Politics*. New York: Harper & Row, 1967. The author carefully describes the main controversies in U.S.-Yugoslav relations and concludes that in general American policymakers have acted wisely.

28:188 Garrett, Stephen A. "On Dealing with National Communism: The Lessons of Yugoslavia." *Western Political Quarterly* 26:3 (1973), 529–49. Garrett analyzes U.S. foreign policy toward Yugoslavia following the expulsion of that communist country from the Cominform in 1948.

28:189 Larson, David L. *United States Foreign Policy toward Yugoslavia, 1943–1963*. Washington, D.C.: University Presses of America, 1979. Published in 1979, but completed in 1963, and thus badly dated in its sources, this volume can serve as an introduction until a more up-to-date book appears. Bibliography.

28:190 Markovich, Stephen C. "American Foreign Aid and Yugoslav Internal Policies." *East European Quarterly* 9:2 (1975), 185–95. This essay analyzes the relationship between U.S. foreign aid and Yugoslavia's economic development. It concludes that

American aid was without strings and that it "contributed to the speed" of Yugoslav economic development.

28:191 Remington, Robin Alison. "Yugoslavia and European Security." *Orbis* 17:1 (1973), 197–226. Remington discusses Yugoslavian nonalignment and European security from the 1940s to 1972.

28:192 Silberman, Laurence. "Titoism and Beyond." *Wilson Quarterly* 2:2 (1978), 96–102. The author believes that Yugoslavia is much more communist, more authoritarian, and more anti-American than the United States has recognized.

28:193 Silberman, Laurence. "Yugoslavia's 'Old' Communism: Europe's Fiddler on the Roof." *Foreign Policy,* no. 26 (1977), 3–27. This article argues that U.S. policy toward Yugoslavia is based on false assumptions and that the United States has mistakenly supported Yugoslavia without questioning what gains have been achieved.

29

United States
and the Soviet Union
after 1953

Contributing Editor
THOMAS G. PATERSON
University of Connecticut

Contributors
John Gimbel
California State University, Humboldt

Walter LaFeber
Cornell University

Jean-Donald Miller
*Virginia Polytechnic Institute and
State University*

James A. Nathan
University of Delaware

Contents

Introduction

Soviet Premier Joseph Stalin's death and Dwight D. Eisenhower's elevation to the U.S. presidency, both in 1953, began a marked shift in Soviet-American relations. Until that time the cold war was characterized by bitter rivalry, with negotiations secondary to propaganda wars, military buildups, and frightening crises. No summit conference had been held since that of Potsdam in 1945. Soviet and U.S. client states were still, in 1953, fighting in Korea. Soviet and American soldiers stared nervously at one another across barricades in the divided city of Berlin. A nuclear arms race was underway and neither side seemed willing to discuss serious controls. Trade was at a virtual standstill, and cultural contacts and academic exchanges were negligible.

Gradually Soviet-American relations moved from vituperative confrontation in the early 1950s to cautious and limited détente in the 1970s. The movement, as reflected in Thomas B. Larson's *Soviet-American Rivalry* (29:7), was slow and hardly smooth, rocked as it was so many times by crises, but the two great powers became convinced that bilateral negotiations and treaties served their separate interests in a world becoming multipolar. President Eisenhower himself signaled the shift in his speech of April 16, 1953, wherein he appealed for a new era in the Moscow-Washington relationship. He directed a blunt question to the Kremlin: "What is the Soviet Union ready to do?" As for the Soviets, they responded by espousing "peaceful coexistence" and helping to bring the Korean War to a negotiated conclusion. Thereafter, Soviet-American relations seemed to alternate between cold war "thaws" and "freezes."

All the while the two adversaries talked more and shouted less. In 1955 Premier Nikita Khrushchev met with Eisenhower at the Geneva summit. Other high level meetings followed. In 1963 the super powers signed the Test Ban Treaty, established a hot line between the two capitals for easier communication during crises, and signed a trade agreement for the sale of American wheat to Russia. Nineteen sixty-eight saw the Non-Proliferation Treaty. The Berlin issue was defused by a treaty in 1971 guaranteeing access rights. The following year the Strategic Arms Limitation Talks (SALT I) were completed, as recorded by John Newhouse in *Cold Dawn* (29:156), and a massive wheat deal was struck.

Interspersed with agreements, however, were crises. The catalog is familiar in the annals of the cold war: the Berlin crises of 1958 and 1961, the U-2 incident of 1960 that spoiled the Paris summit meeting, the inconclusive and frigid Vienna conference the following year, and the 1962 Cuban missile crisis. G. H. Quester (40:229) and A. L. George and R. Smoke (40:200) survey the saber-rattling episodes, while H. S. Dinerstein (29:101) and J. A. Nathan (29:110) debate President Kennedy's handling of the Cuban crisis. Differences over trade, Soviet and U.S. interventions abroad, competing policies toward the People's Republic of China, and the status of human rights in the Soviet Union also produced rancor.

Détente was the byword of Soviet-American relations in the 1970s. SALT II negotiations were completed. Trade relations were improving, as Marshall I. Goldman noted in his *Détente and Dollars* (29:180). Academic exchanges and joint scientific ventures were increasing. Less heard were dire warnings of nuclear war. The two giants continued to be competitors, of course. Communism and capitalism remained incompatible. Although the Soviet Union and the United States had signed arms control agreements, they had not endorsed disarmament and both maintained awesome nuclear arsenals. Both intervened in local conflicts far from their shores. Both continued to charge the other with meddling in weaker states. Both governments were served by huge intelligence agencies that monitored one another. And the American call for the observance of human rights in the repressive Soviet Union aroused Soviet cries of internal interference and countercharges that the United States was practicing a double standard because of its discriminatory practices toward its own black minority. Détente, in short, did not mean an ending of rivalry, but rather a series of steps along a continuum, dating from the early 1950s, toward peaceful competition.

The Soviet invasion of Afghanistan in 1980 and the angry American denunciation (including a boycott of the Moscow Olympic Games and a grain embargo) sent Soviet-American relations once again onto a cold war track with substantial obstacles.

The works listed in this chapter present the ups and downs of bilateral Soviet-American relations since 1953. This historiography has faced several difficulties. Because of the very recent vintage of events, historians have barely begun to write studies based upon archival research. Also, because American documents for the 1950s through the 1970s remain largely restricted and hence largely closed to research at the time of this publication, scholars have had to rely upon published materials. Worse still, Soviet archives are tightly closed, and published Soviet documents are minimal in number—whether in Russian or in English. Students of Soviet-American relations in the post-Stalin era have thus had to engage in a good deal of guessing about Soviet intentions, capabilities, and decisions. Speculation rather than certainty, incomplete rather than thorough research—these are the characteristics of the scholarly literature. Indeed, many of the works listed below were prepared, not by historians who have mined the rich holdings of archives or private manuscript collections, but by political scientists and foreign affairs analysts who have devised various theories to explain Soviet and American behavior. These writers are sometimes more interested in the formulation of policies for the future than in past developments. The scholarship on Soviet-American relations since 1953, in short, is at an infant stage and almost every topic listed in this chapter will profit from the declassification of documents, and the rethinking or revisionism that will grow out of new research.

Scholars have debated a number of general questions as they discuss categories of Soviet-American relations and major crises. Does Soviet diplomacy derive from internal imperatives such as totalitarianism and ideology which inexorably push the Soviet Union along an expansionist and obstructionist course, or does that diplomacy spring from a perceived foreign threat—as a reaction to American policies? What has been the American image of the Soviet Union? Have the various agreements and détente been advantageous or disadvantageous to U.S. interests? Has the United States missed opportunities to reduce cold war tensions by adhering to exaggerated fears of Soviet intentions? Why could not the Soviet Union and the United States settle their differences? What "power" has each adversary possessed to wage the cold war?

Addressing questions such as these, the scholarly literature has increasingly treated the Soviet-American relationship less as a morality play or as the story of an impending apocalypse and more as a con-

test between two strategic and economic giants with different ideologies, both of which must share responsibility for the acrimonious and vigorous competition they have visited upon a fearful world.

In the selections for this chapter, English-language works are favored over the sparse published Russian-language materials, in large part because few libraries hold the latter and some of the most useful Soviet-originated sources have been translated. General histories of U.S. foreign policy, unless they give predominant attention to *bilateral* Soviet-American relations, are not listed here but rather in Chapter 24. Historical studies are favored over theoretical works, but some of the latter, especially those that cite historical example to demonstrate conclusions, have been included. Few studies of the Soviet decisionmaking process have been listed, unless, again, historical treatment is evident. Biographies and autobiographies about or by people who specialized in some aspect of Soviet-American relations are listed, but others are located in Chapter 24, where biographical studies of the presidents and secretaries of state are especially included.

Resources and Overviews

RESEARCH AIDS

While pertinent bibliographies and reference aids are listed here, there are more extensive lists in Chapter 1.

Bibliographies

See Chapter 24, "Bibliographies" and "Cold War Historiography," for additional references on the cold war.

Albrecht, Ulrich U., et al. *A Short Research Guide on Arms and Armed Forces* (40:1) lists seven different categories of informational aids, including those to U.S. and Soviet forces.

Burns, R. D. *Arms Control and Disarmament: A Bibliography* (1:25) lists, under subject headings, various Soviet-American negotiations and treaties from the 1950s to 1970s.

29:1 Burns, Richard Dean, and Hutson, Susan Hoffman, comps. *The Salt Era: A Selected Bibliography*. Rev. ed. Los Angeles: California State University, Center for the Study of Armament and Disarmament, 1979. This pamphlet lists articles, books, and documents on the SALT negotiations and treaties.

Burt, R., comp. and ed., and Kemp, G., ed. *Congressional Hearings on American Defense Policy, 1947–1971: An Annotated Bibliography* (1:44).

Cronon, E. D., and Rosenof, T. D., eds. *The Second World War and the Atomic Age, 1940–1973* (24:1) includes articles, books, and dissertations in section 3, "Europe, Russia, and the Cold War," and in section 4, "National Defense and Military Policy."

Dexter, B. *The Foreign Affairs Fifty-Year Bibliography: New Evaluation of Significant Books on International Relations, 1920–1970* (1:14) is useful for new evaluations of books listed in the *Foreign Affairs Bibliography* (1:15).

29:2 Dossick, Jesse J. *Doctoral Research on Russia and the Soviet Union, 1960–1975*. New York: Garland, 1976. This is a list of American, Canadian, and British doctoral dissertations in various fields, including Soviet-American relations. Arranged by subject with no annotations, it is a companion volume to Dossick's 1960 publication with the same title.

Foreign Affairs Bibliography: A Selected and Annotated List of Books on International Relations (1:15) gives considerable attention to works on Soviet-American relations. A useful aid, briefly annotated.

29:3 Gillingham, Arthur, and Roseman, Barry, comps. *Cuban Missile Crisis: A Selected Bibliography*. Los Angeles: California State University, Center for the Study of Armament and Disarmament, 1976. A variety of viewpoints are represented in this pamphlet.

Grant, S. A. *Scholars' Guide to Washington, D.C. for Russian/Soviet Studies* (1:271) is a detailed listing of libraries, archives, manuscript and film collections, and government agencies.

Greenwood, J., comp. *American Defense Policy since 1945: A Preliminary Bibliography* (1:45).

Hammond, T. T., comp. and ed. *Soviet Foreign Relations and World Communism: A Selected, Annotated Bibliography of 7,000 Books in Thirty Languages* (1:83) covers Soviet relations with all parts of the world, including the United States, and Soviet policy toward such questions as disarmament and trade.

Jones, D. L. *Books in English on the Soviet Union, 1917–73* (1:86) gives considerable attention to U.S.-Soviet relations.

Kanet, R. E. *Soviet and East European Foreign Policy: A Bibliography of English- and Russian-Language Publications 1967–1971* (1:87) includes over 3,200 books, pamphlets, and articles from a wide list of journals, with numerous entries for Soviet-American relations.

Meckler, A. M., and McMullin, R. *Oral History Collections* (1:254) includes interviews of prominent American diplomats who have dealt with the Soviet Union, conducted under such auspices as the Eisenhower Administration Project (Columbia University) and the Dulles Oral History Project (Princeton University). These oral histories, as well as those at other institutions, including the presidential libraries, can be located through this guide.

Okinshevich, L., comp. *United States History and Historiography in Postwar Soviet Writings, 1945–1970* (24:2) is a guide to works *in Russian*.

Yearbooks and Other Aids

See also Chapter 24, "Yearbooks and Other Aids."

29:4 *Current Digest of the Soviet Press*. New York: Joint Committee on Slavic Studies, 1949– . This periodical presents English translations of current articles from Soviet publications like *Pravda* and *Izvestia* on a variety of topics. Useful for following Soviet attitudes.

DeConde, A., ed., *Encyclopedia of American Foreign Policy* (1:164) has essays on topics such as the cold war and summit conferences by distinguished historians and political scientists.

Florinsky, M. T., ed. *McGraw-Hill Encyclopedia of Russia and the Soviet Union* (1:166) is a useful reference for biographies of Soviet leaders, descriptions of treaties, etc.

Maxwell, R., ed. and comp. *Information U.S.S.R.: An Authoritative Encyclopedia about the Union of Soviet Socialist Republics* (1:168) is a translation of volume 5 of the *Great Soviet Encyclopedia*.

Prokhorov, A. M., ed. *Great Soviet Encyclopedia* (1:170) is an English translation of a multivolume Soviet publication which provides a wealth of information about the U.S.S.R. and its leaders.

Stockholm International Peace Research Institute. *World Armaments and Disarmament: SIPRI Yearbook* (40:9) is a detailed annual study, beginning in 1968–1969, of weapons technology and arms control negotiations, with emphasis on Soviet-American arms competition.

Survey of International Affairs (1:146) is an annual historical narrative of major events, including those in East-West relations.

The United States in World Affairs (1:147) is an annual review of American foreign policy. Indexed.

Wieczynski, J. L., ed. *The Modern Encyclopedia of Russian and Soviet History* (1:171) is an ongoing multivolume project, beginning in 1976 with "A." It includes references to and entries on key Soviet diplomats and events.

Yearbook on International Communist Affairs (1:148) is an annual, from 1967, which provides a country-by-country profile of communist parties and activities.

The Year Book of World Affairs (24:3) contains many essays central to U.S.-U.S.S.R. relations.

Document Collections

More general collections are listed in Chapter 2, and other collections may be found in "Personalities," below; also see Chapter 24, "Document Collections."

Branyan, R. L., and Larsen, L. H., eds. *The Eisenhower Administration, 1953–1961: A Documentary History* (24:197) is a collection of published and unpublished documents on the domestic and foreign policy issues of the Eisenhower years. It includes an appendix which lists the chief officers of the Eisenhower administration, a brief bibliographical essay, and an index.

Documents on American Foreign Relations (1:339) is a collection of major speeches, reports, and other documents. It is continued by *American Foreign Relations, 19–: A Documentary Record.*

Documents on International Affairs [1928–1963] (1:340) includes many Soviet and American materials.

29:5   Gruliow, Leo, ed. *Current Soviet Policies.* 4 vols. New York: Praeger; Columbia University Press, 1953–1962. These volumes constitute the translated documentary record of the 19th (1952), 20th (1956), 21st (1959), and 22d (1961) Communist party congresses. Khrushchev's secret 1956 de-Stalinization speech and several references to the relationship between internal and external politics address cold war topics. Index.

Hanak, H., ed. *Soviet Foreign Policy since the Death of Stalin* (24:5) contains speeches, treaties, interviews, newspaper articles, diplomatic notes illustrating Moscow's policies toward capitalist, socialist, and Third World nations.

LaFeber, W., ed. *Eastern Europe and the Soviet Union.* Vol. 2 in *The Dynamics of World Power: A Documentary History of United States Foreign Policy, 1945–1973* (26:4) is a collection of American and Soviet speeches, press conference transcripts, memoranda, testimonies, telegrams, and other documents, over half of which cover the period 1953 to 1973.

[U.S.S.R.]. *Milestones of Soviet Foreign Policy, 1917–1967* (1:368) includes 73 important documents.

U.S. Department of State. *American Foreign Policy: Current Documents, 1956–1967* (1:356).

U.S. Department of State. *Press Conferences of the Secretaries of State, 1922–1974* (1:360) is a microfilm of the typed verbatim record of these conferences. An important source for research on the views of such officials as John Foster Dulles, Dean Rusk, and Henry A. Kissinger.

Public Opinion

Columbia Broadcasting System. *Face the Nation: The Collected Transcripts from CBS Radio and Television Broadcasts, 1954–1971* (1:347) contains the unedited transcripts of the weekly CBS television and radio interview program. Indexed.

Gallup, G. H. *The Gallop Poll: Public Opinion, 1935–1971* (1:348) pays considerable attention to foreign affairs.

OVERVIEWS

See also Chapter 24, "Overviews," for additional general works.

Soviet-American Relations

See also Chapter 28, "Eurocommunism."

Bell, C. *Negotiation from Strength: A Study in the Politics of Power* (24:228) studies the American idea, dating from 1950, of "negotiation from strength" with the Russians. The various summit and near-summit talks are treated in this sometimes wandering work which finds the idea a detriment to diplomacy.

Brown, S. *The Faces of Power: Constancy and Change in United States Foreign Policy from Truman to Johnson* (24:33) argues that containment of international communism has been a constant objective; the debate at home has been over the means of implementing that policy.

Brzezinski, Z. "How the Cold War Was Played" (24:7) identifies several phases of the cold war since 1945 and the Soviet-American interaction in each period, comparing economic and military power, "international standing," and "domestic policy base."

29:6 Franck, Thomas M., and Weisband, Edward. *Word Politics: Verbal Strategy among the Superpowers.* New York: Oxford University Press, 1971. A comparison of the Brezhnev Doctrine and Johnson Doctrine, both of which seemed to justify great power intervention in their respective spheres: the U.S.S.R. in Eastern Europe and the United States in Latin America. Yet each rejects the doctrine of the other, using the same rhetoric. Bibliography.

Gaddis, J. L. *Russia, the Soviet Union and the United States: An Interpretive History* (2:248) treats the period since 1953 in the last two chapters. Gaddis sees the Cuban missile crisis as a turning point in the cold war. The cold war then moved from "confrontation to negotiation."

George, A. L., and Smoke, R. *Deterrence in American Foreign Policy: Theory and Practice* (40:200) shows deterrence at work (1945–1974) vis-à-vis the Soviet Union in a number of case studies, including the Berlin crisis and the Cuban missile crisis.

Gromyko, A. A. *Through Russian Eyes: President Kennedy's 1036 Days* (24:211) is highly partisan and flawed—the name of Khrushchev does not appear—but it reveals the Soviet perspective on the United States and its foreign policy. See critical review essay, Nelson W. Polsby, *Political Science Quarterly* 90:1 (1975), 117–26.

Halle, L. J. *The Cold War As History* (24:13) downplays the ideological components of the cold war to concentrate on power politics—especially the "self-interest of the Russian state." Halle finds an inevitability to the Soviet-American confrontation.

Kennan, G. F. "The United States and the Soviet Union, 1917–1976." (2:249) suggests that the Khrushchev era was a propitious time for improvement in relations.

29:7 Larson, Thomas B. *Soviet-American Rivalry.* New York: Norton, 1978. With the purpose of elucidating contemporary issues, Larson studies some of the divisive areas of Soviet-American relations since 1945: historical, economic, political, ideological, and military rivalries, as well as competition for influence in other nations. This book provides a useful overview of ways these two large powers with different social systems have competed for world leadership. Bibliography.

Lerche, C. O., Jr. *The Cold War . . . and After* (24:19) provides a brief, analytical overview of the cold war strategies of the United States and U.S.S.R., well-grounded in historical examples. The author portrays the Soviet Union as an expansionist "actor" to which the United States must react.

29:8 Lippmann, Walter. *The Coming Tests with Russia.* Boston: Little, Brown, 1961. Based on an April 1961 interview with Khrushchev, this short book surveys current issues in Soviet-American relations. Lippmann found the long interview "sobering": the U.S.S.R. was not contemplating war and desired to tame crises, but was determined to encourage revolutions in developing nations.

Lukacs, J. *A New History of the Cold War* (24:21) discusses the social, political, national, and ideological "tendencies" of the two competitors. Lukacs sees 1956 as the "crucial year" of the cold war, for the United States did not intervene in Hungary and the Soviet Union interpreted this restraint to mean the United States respected spheres of influence.

Miller, L. H., and Pruessen, R. W., eds. *Reflections on the Cold War: A Quarter Century of American Foreign Policy* (24:41) includes essays by B. J. Bernstein on the Cuban missile crisis, R. J. Barnet on the arms race, and R. A. Falk on the United States and U.S.S.R. as counterrevolutionaries.

29:9 Parker, William. *The Superpowers: The United States and the Soviet Union Compared.* New York: Wiley, 1972. This British scholar posits a geopolitical interpretation: the need for security outweighs ideological considerations, and the foreign policy of both nations is determined by the resources available within their boundaries. Tables.

Paterson, T. G., ed. *Containment and the Cold War: American Foreign Policy since 1945* (24:46) provides, with documents and interpretive essays, an historical and analytical overview of the American containment doctrine.

Rapoport, A. *The Big Two: Soviet-American Perceptions of Foreign Policy* (24:23) is an interpretive, rambling essay on the competition between the nuclear super powers and their "perceptions" of each other.

29:10 Roberts, Henry L. *Russia and America: Dangers and Prospects.* New York: Harper, 1956. Based upon discussions among distinguished public servants and scholars at the Council of Foreign Relations (1953–1955), Roberts's volume outlines the major problems in Soviet-American relations at the beginning of the post-Stalin era.

Rubinstein, A. Z., and Ginsburgs, G., eds. *Soviet and American Policies in the United Nations: A Twenty-Five-Year Perspective* (38:202) examines a wide variety of topics, including disarmament, decolonization, economic development, and peacekeeping.

Sivachev, N. V., and Yakovlev, N. N. *Russia and the United States: U.S.-Soviet Relations from the Soviet Point of View* (2:253) is critical of American policies which are seen as imperialistic and narrowly self-interested. Laudatory of détente in the 1970s.

29:11 Stone, I. F. *The Haunted Fifties.* New York: Random House, 1963. This collection of articles from *I. F. Stone's Weekly,* by the thoughtful and iconoclastic journalist, includes commentary on Soviet-American relations from the death of Stalin to the first months of the Kennedy administration. Stone is critical of America's distortion of Soviet intentions. See

also his two sequels: *In a Time of Torment* (1967), which includes a critique of Kennedy's handling of the Cuban missile crisis, and *Polemics and Prophecies* (1970).

29:12 Talbott, Strobe. "U.S.-Soviet Relations: From Bad to Worse." *Foreign Affairs* 58:3 (1980), 515–39. A veteran journalist surveys the Soviet-American relationship in 1979 and early 1980, concentrating on the divisive questions of SALT and Afghanistan.

Ulam, A. B. *The Rivals: America and Russia since World War II* (24:29) argues that the United States, lacking "realism," has exaggerated the Soviet threat, failing to negotiate with the U.S.S.R. at times when the United States was superior and could have made gains.

29:13 Ulam, Adam B. "U.S.-Soviet Relations: Unhappy Coexistence." *Foreign Affairs* 57:3 (1979), 555–71. In an overview of the Carter administration's Soviet policies for 1977–1978, Ulam highlights the deterioration of détente and America's playing of the "China card."

29:14 Welch, William. *American Images of Soviet Foreign Policy: An Inquiry in Recent Appraisals from the Academic Community.* New Haven, Conn.: Yale University Press, 1970. Through an analytical review of influential American studies of Soviet diplomacy, Welch identifies three images: "Great Beast" (represented, for example, by W. W. Kulski), "Mellowing Tiger" (George F. Kennan and Adam Ulam), and "Neurotic Bear" (Michael P. Gehlen and Louis J. Halle). Welch found that most American works saw Soviet conduct as militant rather than peaceable.

Soviet Foreign Policy

29:15 Byely, B., et al. *Marxism-Leninism on War and Army (A Soviet View).* Moscow: Progress Press, 1972. Reprint 1974. This reprint of a Soviet English-language edition designed for high-ranking Soviet military officers provides a summary of Marxist-Leninist teachings on war and its economic causes. Soviet views on varieties of wars (civil, bourgeois, anti-imperialist) and the behavior of "imperialist" states are outlined. Reprint published under the auspices of the U.S. Air Force.

29:16 Cohen, Stephen F.; Rabinowitch, Alexander; and Sharlet, Robert, eds. *The Soviet Union Since*

Stalin. Bloomington: Indiana University Press, 1980. Included in this collection of original essays is Charles Gati's "The Stalinist Legacy in Soviet Foreign Policy." Subsequent essays by R. E. Kanet, J. D. Robertson and A. Z. Rubinstein question Gati's emphasis on the continuity with Stalin's foreign policy of the last quarter-century of Russian diplomacy.

29:17 Dallin, David J. *Soviet Foreign Policy after Stalin.* Philadelphia: Lippincott, 1961. This volume treats Moscow's diplomacy toward a host of countries and issues with emphasis on unsuccessful attempts to extend the "Soviet empire" and on the successful strengthening of Soviet military power. Dallin argues that the United States, by protecting Western Europe, contributed to the "emancipation trends in the Eastern bloc."

29:18 Garthoff, Raymond L. *Soviet Strategy in the Nuclear Age.* Rev. ed. New York: Praeger, 1962. Garthoff outlines Soviet strategic thought about nuclear, as well as limited, war. Chapter 6 discusses "The Soviet Image of the Enemy"—the United States—and notes the Soviet emphasis on American air power. Bibliography.

29:19 Gehlen, Michael P. *The Politics of Coexistence: Soviet Methods and Motives.* Bloomington: Indiana University Press, 1967. A theoretical examination emphasizing "nonideological" or national interest influences on the Soviet policy of coexistence and the methods employed by the U.S.S.R. in pursuing that policy.

29:20 Kaplan, Stephen S., et al. *Diplomacy of Power: Soviet Armed Forces as a Political Instrument.* Washington, D.C.: Brookings Institution, 1981. The authors identify 190 instances, from armed intervention to threats, in this study of Soviet "coercive diplomacy." Soviet policies toward the Korean War, Cuban missile crisis, and the Vietnam War, among other topics, are discussed at length.

29:21 Kulski, W. W. *Peaceful Co-Existence: An Analysis of Soviet Foreign Policy.* Chicago: Regnery, 1959. Kulski provides a lengthy analysis of the "basic patterns, objectives, and means" of Soviet foreign policy since 1917. He detects no change in Moscow's long-term foreign policy objectives: domination of the world by Russia and the final victory of communism.

29:22 Kulski, W. W. *The Soviet Union in World Affairs: A Documented Analysis, 1964–1972.* Syracuse, N.Y.: Syracuse University Press, 1973. Kulski,

a former Polish diplomat, studies Soviet foreign policy as the pursuit of national interest rather than Marxist-Leninist ideology. For Soviet-American relations, a "pattern of competition-partnership" is discerned. Bibliography.

Lederer, I. J., ed. *Russian Foreign Policy: Essays in Historical Perspective* (26:25) treats the relationship between czarist and Soviet foreign policy, paying particular attention to the components of ideology and national interest. The essays cover most geographical areas, as well as Soviet goals and negotiating techniques.

Mosely, P. E. *The Kremlin and World Politics: Studies in Soviet Policy and Action* (25:79) stresses Soviet "bad manners" and "obstinacy," the flexibility of Soviet tactics, and consistent Soviet expansionist aims—all bespeaking continued cold war rivalry.

29:23 Nogee, Joseph L., and Donaldson, Robert H. *Soviet Foreign Policy since World War II.* New York: Pergamon, 1981. Pointing to such factors as polycentrism in the communist world, Soviet totalitarianism, and leadership, the authors present a critical assessment of Soviet foreign policy. After discussing the "Soviet approach to foreign policy," they trace chronologically the escalation of the cold war, ending with the decline of détente. Bibliography.

Ponomaryov, B., with Gromyko, A., and Khvostov, V., eds. *History of Soviet Foreign Policy, 1945–1970* (26:27) is a Soviet history of the cold war, applauding Moscow's peace efforts and global opposition to the United States. The work surveys "the steady shift of the balance of strength in favour of socialism...."

Sokolovskii, V. D. *Soviet Military Strategy* (40:195) details Soviet strategic concepts and presents a harsh critique of the strategies of "imperialist" or capitalist states, with special attention devoted to the United States.

29:24 Tatu, Michel. *Power in the Kremlin: From Khrushchev To Kosygin.* Trans. by Helen Katel. New York: Viking, 1969. Tatu surveys decisionmaking, maneuvering for power, and debate in the Kremlin during the U-2 affair, the Cuban missile crisis, and Khrushchev's political fall. Tatu details the pressures exerted on Khrushchev from doctrinaire Communists who opposed the premier's détente with the West. Chronology and brief biographies.

29:25 Triska, Jan F., and Finley, David D. *Soviet Foreign Policy.* New York: Macmillan, 1968. This analytical work on the making, administration, and doctrines of Soviet foreign policy concentrates on "how and why" questions and tests them through historical example. A useful starting point for the fundamental issues in the study of Soviet diplomatic behavior. Bibliography.

Ulam, A. B. *Expansion and Coexistence: Soviet Foreign Policy, 1917–1973* (2:254) discusses the motives and workings of Soviet diplomacy since the Bolshevik Revolution, with emphasis on relations with the West.

U.S. House. Committee on Foreign Affairs. Staff Report; *Soviet Diplomacy and Negotiating Behavior: Emerging New Context for U.S. Diplomacy* (26:30) argues that Russian diplomats have been obsessed with security, controlled by rigid bureaucratic instructions, and motivated by their revolutionary belief that the bargaining process is war by political means.

29:26 Wolfe, Thomas W. *Soviet Power and Europe, 1945–1970.* Baltimore: Johns Hopkins Press, 1970. Most of this book covers the post-1953 period and focuses on the centrality of Europe in the East-West confrontation. Different possible interpretations of Soviet policy are identified and discussed, but the author tends to take a dark view of Soviet intentions throughout.

29:27 Zimmerman, William. *Soviet Perspectives on International Relations, 1956–1967.* Princeton, N.J.: Princeton University Press, 1969. Zimmerman finds that Soviet views about American foreign policy changed from attributing decisions to Wall Street to emphasizing the power of the federal government in Washington. Extensive bibliography.

Personalities

Additional references on individuals may be found in Chapter 1, "Biographical Data."

AMERICAN

See Chapter 24, "Personalities" and "Presidential Administrations," for additional references.

Charles E. Bohlen

See Chapter 26, "Personalities," for additional references.

Bohlen, C. E. *Witness to History: 1929–1969* (24:98) recounts his long involvement in Soviet affairs. Bohlen served as ambassador to Moscow (1953–1957) and as an adviser to secretaries of state and presidents after that.

29:28 Rosenau, James N. *The Nomination of "Chip" Bohlen.* New York: McGraw-Hill, 1962. Rosenau studies the stormy politics surrounding the 1953 nomination of Charles E. Bohlen as ambassador to the Soviet Union. Bohlen's role at and later defense of Yalta created noisy but unsuccessful opposition, including that of Senator Joseph McCarthy.

John Foster Dulles

See Chapter 24, "Personalities" and "The Eisenhower Years," for additional references.

29:29 Dulles, John Foster. "A Policy of Boldness." *Life Magazine* 32:20 (1952), 146ff. Published prior to the 1952 presidential campaign, this article contains Dulles's critique of the Truman administration's foreign policies together with his brief for liberation and for what would later be called "massive retaliation."

Goold-Adams, R. *John Foster Dulles: A Reappraisal* (24:109) is a perceptive and balanced assessment.

Hoopes, T. *The Devil and John Foster Dulles* (24:112) is a critical but thorough biography which provides a searching analysis of Eisenhower's foreign policies.

Dwight D. Eisenhower

See Chapters 23 and 24, "Personalities" and "The Eisenhower Years," for additional references.

29:30 Divine, Robert A. *Eisenhower and the Cold War.* New York: Oxford University Press, 1981. This brief sketch of Eisenhower's foreign policy emphasizes American-Soviet relations in the 1950s. Divine treats Eisenhower as an activist, yet prudent, president who worked to end the cold war, but fell short.

Eisenhower, D. D. *The White House Years* (24:114) contains the president's views on foreign and national security policies.

W. Averell Harriman

See Chapter 24, "Personalities."

Harriman, W. A. *America and Russia in a Changing World: A Half Century of Personal Observation* (24:119) finds the former ambassador to Moscow and roving envoy recollecting moments in his diplomatic career.

Lyndon B. Johnson

See Chapter 24, "Personalities" and "The Johnson Years."

Johnson, L. B. *The Vantage Point: Perspectives on the Presidency, 1963–1969* (24:120) avoids self-criticism, but offers important information.

George F. Kennan

See Chapters 22 and 24, "Personalities," for additional references; also see Chapter 26, "Defining Containment."

Kennan, G. F. *The Cloud of Danger: Current Realities of American Foreign Policy* (29:226).

Kennan, G. F. *Memoirs, 1925–1963* (24:124) covers, in volume 2, the post-Stalin era and includes Kennan's account of his changing views toward the Soviet Union in the 1950s and his ambassadorship to Yugoslavia (1961–1963) during that period when the cold war heated up.

29:31 Kennan, George F. *On Dealing with the Communist World*. New York: Harper & Row, 1964. Fresh from Yugoslavia, Kennan assesses the state of American relations with the "Communist world." Noting the disintegration of Soviet power, he endorses "peaceful coexistence" and East-West trade.

29:32 Kennan, George F. *Russia, the Atom and the West*. New York: Harper, 1958. In Kennan's famous and controversial Reith lectures over British Broadcasting Corporation radio (November–December 1957) the former State Department official appealed for mutual "disengagement" of American and Soviet forces from the heart of Europe. In this work, also, Kennan looks at the changes in the Soviet Union which, for him, suggest new real possibilities for negotiations.

John F. Kennedy

See Chapters 24 and 30, "Personalities" and "The Kennedy Years," for additional references.

29:33 Paterson, Thomas G. "Bearing the Burden: A Critical Look at JFK's Foreign Policy." *Virginia Quarterly Review* 54:2 (1978), 193–212. In an overview of Kennedy's foreign policy, Paterson emphasizes the influences of historical lessons, personality and style, and theories of nation-building. Considerable attention is given to Soviet-American relations. Based in part upon memoirs and records in the Kennedy Library.

Schlesinger, A. M., Jr. *A Thousand Days: John F. Kennedy in the White House* (24:215) is a strongly sympathetic review of the administration's foreign policy.

Walton, R. J. *Cold War and Counterrevolution: The Foreign Policy of John F. Kennedy* (24:216) argues Kennedy's policies were those of cold war liberalism.

Robert F. Kennedy

See also Chapter 24, "The Kennedy Years."

Kennedy, R. F. *Thirteen Days: A Memoir of the Cuban Missile Crisis* (29:120).

29:34 Schlesinger, Arthur M., Jr. *Robert Kennedy and His Times*. Boston: Houghton Mifflin, 1978. This partisan biography by a Kennedy adviser includes several chapters on the foreign policy of the 1960s. The Cuban missile crisis is treated as a triumph of patience and diplomacy, revealing that Attorney General Robert Kennedy struck a personal deal with Ambassador Anatoly Dobrynin to withdraw American missiles from Turkey if the Soviets pulled theirs out of Cuba.

Henry A. Kissinger

See Chapter 24, "Personalities" and "The Nixon-Ford Years."

Hoffmann, S. *Primacy or World Order: American Foreign Policy since the Cold War* (24:130) provides an interim critique of Kissinger's ideas.

Kalb, M., and Kalb, B. *Kissinger* (24:131) is a contemporary biography focusing on 1969 to 1973.

Foy D. Kohler

29:35 Kohler, Foy D. *Understanding the Russians: A Citizen's Primer*. New York: Harper & Row, 1970. The American ambassador to the Soviet Union (1962–1966) writes a personalized and highly opinionated overview of Soviet history and "international Communism" since 1917. Kohler rather simply depicts a relentless, global Soviet/Communist thrust against the "free world."

29:36 Kohler, Foy D., and Harvey, Mose L., eds. *The Soviet Union: Yesterday, Today, Tomorrow: A Colloquy of American Long Timers in Moscow*. Miami: University of Miami, Center for Advanced International Studies, 1975. This is a verbatim record of a panel discussion with former ambassadors to the Soviet Union George F. Kennan, Foy D. Kohler, and Jacob L. Beam and others with diplomatic service in the U.S.S.R., such as Elbridge Durbrow, Loy W. Henderson, and Thomas P. Whitney. Wide-ranging and diffuse, but a useful accounting of the views of many American experts on Soviet affairs.

Richard M. Nixon

See also Chapter 24, "Personalities" and "The Nixon-Ford Years."

29:37 Gardner, Lloyd C., comp. *The Great Nixon Turnabout: America's New Foreign Policy in the Post-Liberal Era (How a Cold Warrior Climbed Clean Out of His Skin)*. New York: New Viewpoint, 1973. This collection of Nixon's speeches and articles by various authors on the president's policies is critical of the president's diplomatic conduct.

Nixon, R. M. *RN: The Memoirs of Richard Nixon* (24:145) provides Nixon's understanding of his foreign policy.

Szulc, T. *The Illusion of Peace: Foreign Policy in the Nixon-Kissinger Years* (24:226) is a critical study of the Nixon-Kissinger foreign policy (1969–1974) that provides what might be called an "insider's view" of secret diplomacy. The movement toward détente figures prominently in the work, and Szulc concludes that détente fell far short of Nixon's claims for it.

Adlai E. Stevenson

See also Chapter 24, "Personalities" and "The Kennedy Years."

Martin, J. B. *The Life of Adlai E. Stevenson* (24:152) is a sympathetic, yet candid account of Stevenson's views on foreign policy.

Others

29:38 Beam, Jacob D. *Multiple Exposure: An American Ambassador's Unique Perspective on East-West Issues*. New York: Norton, 1978. Beam was ambassador to Poland (1957–1961), Czechoslovakia (1966–1969), and the Soviet Union (1969–1973). His memoirs are guarded and thin, although there is some interesting reporting on the 1972 Nixon summit in Moscow.

Cohen, W. I. *Dean Rusk* (24:148) is the first scholarly study of the secretary of state who served from 1961 to 1969.

Killian, J. R., Jr. *Sputnik, Scientists, and Eisenhower: A Memoir of the First Special Assistant to the President for Science and Technology* [1957–1959] (29:129).

Kistiakowsky, G. B. *A Scientist at the White House: The Private Diary of President Eisenhower's Special Assistant for Science and Technology* [1959–1960] (29:130).

Lodge, H. C., Jr. *The Storm Has Many Eyes: A Personal Narrative* (24:137) is an autobiography by the former senator and ambassador which presents recollections of events in Soviet-American relations since the 1940s.

Noble, G. B. *Christian A. Herter* (24:177) is a sympathetic appraisal of Dulles's successor as secretary of state (1959–1960).

Rostow, W. W. *The Diffusion of Power: An Essay in Recent History* (24:181) is a sweeping and often personal survey of recent diplomatic history, which treats Soviet-American competition in the international community. Believing that "much of what has been written about me is inaccurate," Rostow also seeks to set the record straight about himself.

Strauss, L. L. *Men and Decisions* (24:183) is important for the disarmament issues of the Eisenhower administration.

EUROPEAN

Willy Brandt

29:39 Brandt, Willy. *The Ordeal of Coexistence.* Cambridge: Harvard University Press, 1963. The German political leader takes a skeptical view of Soviet professions of "peaceful coexistence." The work includes many references to Brandt's city of Berlin as a question in the cold war.

29:40 Brandt, Willy. *People and Politics: The Years 1960–1975.* Boston: Little, Brown, 1978. Elected mayor of Berlin in 1961, Brandt had already been a witness to that city's precarious place in the Soviet-American confrontation. This memoir gives his remembrances of such issues as the Berlin Wall.

Leonid I. Brezhnev

29:41 Brezhnev, Leonid I. *On the Policy of the Soviet Union and the International Situation.* Garden City, N.Y.: Doubleday, 1973. In this set of the Soviet general secretary's speeches there are numerous comments on the U.S.-U.S.S.R. relationship.

29:42 Brezhnev, Leonid I. *Peace, Détente, Cooperation.* New York: Consultants Bureau, 1981. This collection of speeches (1971–1980) addresses such issues as SALT, détente, the Middle East, Afghanistan, trade relations, and peaceful coexistence.

29:43 Brezhnev, Leonid I. *Peace, Détente, and Soviet-American Relations: Public Statements by Leonid Brezhnev.* New York: Harcourt Brace Jovanovich, 1979. This is a collection of Brezhnev's speeches, articles, and interviews on a variety of issues in Soviet-American relations in the 1970s.

29:44 U.S.S.R. Academy of Sciences. *Leonid I. Brezhnev: Pages from His Life.* New York: Simon & Schuster, 1978. This is a fawning biography of the Soviet leader with considerable attention given to détente in the 1970s. Excellent photographs.

Nikita S. Khrushchev

29:45 Crankshaw, Edward. *Khrushchev—A Career.* New York: Viking, 1966. Crankshaw provides a fast-paced biography of the Soviet leader who succeeded Stalin. It is a story of a personal struggle which ended in 1964, when his domestic critics scored him for, among other errors, moving too quickly toward an understanding with the United States.

29:46 Khrushchev, Nikita S. *For Victory in Peaceful Competition with Capitalism.* New York: Dutton, 1960. This collection of the Russian premier's speeches and statements of 1958 on international issues emphasizes the Soviet quest for "peaceful coexistence."

29:47 Khrushchev, Nikita S. *Khrushchev Remembers.* Trans. by Strobe Talbott, with commentary and notes by Edward Crankshaw. Boston: Little, Brown, 1970. Approximately half of the memoir is devoted to Khrushchev's coming to power after Stalin's death. Included are his accounts of the Geneva Conference and the Cuban missile crisis. The publisher's introductory note stresses the authenticity of the premier's words.

29:48 Khrushchev, Nikita S. *Khrushchev Remembers: The Last Testament.* Trans. and ed. by Strobe Talbott. Boston: Little, Brown, 1974. This companion volume to *Khrushchev Remembers* (1970), like its predecessor based on tape recordings of rambling reminiscences, includes material held back from the first book as well as new recollections. Recounted here are many of Khrushchev's diplomatic moments—trouble with Eastern Europe and China, his tour of the United States, the U-2 incident, and the Cuban missile crisis.

29:49 Khrushchev, Nikita S. *Khrushchev Speaks: Selected Speeches, Articles, and Press Conferences.* Ed. by Thomas P. Whitney. Ann Arbor: University of Michigan Press, 1963. Whitney provides commentary for these important documents.

29:50 Khrushchev, Nikita S. "On Peaceful Coexistence." *Foreign Affairs* 38:1 (1959), 1–18. The Soviet leader provides Moscow's perspective on "peaceful coexistence" or "peaceful competition" between states with different social systems. He outlines Soviet policy on a number of issues, criticizes Americans who advocate "rolling back" communism, and calls for improved trade relations.

29:51 Wedge, Bryant. "Khrushchev at a Distance—A Study of Public Personality." *Trans-Action* 5:10 (1968), 24–28. Invited by the Central Intelligence Agency (1960) to participate in a conference on the personality of Khrushchev, social psychiatrist Wedge also sent a report to President Kennedy just before the 1961 Vienna summit meeting. It is a revealing study of the Russian premier and of the implications for Soviet-American negotiations.

Eisenhower and Summit Diplomacy

See "Personalities," especially Charles E. Bohlen, John Foster Dulles, Dwight D. Eisenhower; also see Chapter 24, "The Eisenhower Years."

Alexander, C. C. *Holding the Line: The Eisenhower Era, 1952–1961* (24:201) provides a balanced overview of the Eisenhower administration's foreign and domestic policies.

29:52 Burnham, James. *Containment or Liberation: An Inquiry into the Aims of United States Foreign Policy.* New York: Day, 1952. A well-known conservative intellectual combines a contemporary critique of containment with a call for a policy of liberation aimed at eliminating or at least reducing the sphere of Soviet power.

KHRUSHCHEV'S AMERICAN VISIT, 1959

29:53 Kharlamov, M., and Vadeyev, O., eds. *Face to Face with America: The Story of N. S. Khrushchov's Visit to the U.S.A.* Moscow: Foreign Languages Publishing House, 1960. A detailed Soviet narration of the trip, effusive with praise for the premier's defense of Soviet communism in the United States. Many off-the-record comments are liberally quoted herein. Companion volume to *Let Us Live in Peace and Friendship* (1959).

29:54 *Let Us Live in Peace and Friendship: The Visit of N. S. Khrushchev to the U.S.A., September 15–27, 1959.* Moscow: Foreign Languages Publishing House, 1959. This documentary study includes the premier's major public statements while in the United States. An American edition appeared as *Khrushchev in America* (New York: Crosscurrents Press, 1960).

Lodge, H. C., Jr. *The Storm Has Many Eyes: A Personal Narrative* (24:137) has one chapter devoted to Khrushchev's visit. Lodge was his escort; he reconstructs conversations with the Soviet premier.

29:55 Windt, Theodore O., Jr. "The Rhetoric of Peaceful Coexistence: Khrushchev in America, 1959." *Quarterly Journal of Speech* 57:1 (1971), 11–22. Against a background of crisis in Berlin and power struggle in the Kremlin, Khrushchev came to the United States seeking "peaceful coexistence" and exploited his own personality and the curiosity of Americans about him to forward that goal.

SUMMIT DIPLOMACY

29:56 Davis, Paul C. "The New Diplomacy: The 1955 Geneva Summit Meeting." In Roger M. Hilsman and Robert C. Good, eds., *Foreign Policy in the Sixties: The Issues and the Instruments: Essays in Honor of Arnold Wolfers.* Baltimore: Johns Hopkins Press, 1965, pp. 159–90. In this overview of the goals, issues, and process of negotiations at Geneva, the author highlights the "interplay of propaganda and diplomacy" characteristic of the meeting.

29:57 Eubank, Keith. *The Summit Conferences, 1919–1960.* Norman: University of Oklahoma Press, 1966. Eubank surveys the reason for and accomplishments of summit meetings, including Geneva (1955) and the aborted Paris session (1960).

29:58 Plischke, Elmer. "Eisenhower's 'Correspondence Diplomacy' with the Kremlin—Case Study in Summit Diplomatics." *Journal of Politics* 30:1 (1968), 137–58. Open summit diplomacy, which necessarily involves publicity, can create exaggerated expectations and the possibility of disillusionment. Eisenhower used open "correspondence diplomacy" in sending 52 communications to the Kremlin (1955–1960).

29:59 Plischke, Elmer. "International Conferencing and the Summit: Macro-Analysis of Presidential Participation." *Orbis* 14:3 (1970), 673–713. Plischke discusses different kinds of summit conferences and the roles of "summit conferencing" by presenting a synthesis of how such conferences are used by American presidents.

29:60 Plischke, Elmer. *Summit Diplomacy: Personal Diplomacy of the President of the United States.* Westport, Conn.: Greenwood (1958), 1974. This brief book is concerned more with the way presidential "summit diplomacy" has been conducted than with its results. Plischke gives much of his attention to Eisenhower's relations with Soviet leaders (Geneva Conference) and finds summits to be fruitful diplomatic ventures, but not panaceas.

29:61 U.S. Department of State. *Background of Heads of Government Conference, 1960: Principal Documents, 1955–1959, with Narrative Summary.* Washington, D.C.: G.P.O., 1960. This is a collection of letters, statements, and communiqués from or about the Geneva Conference of 1955 and the 1959 summit in the United States, with other materials on foreign ministers meetings.

U-2 INCIDENT, 1960

29:62 Cook, Fred J. *The U-2 Incident, May, 1960: An American Spy Plane Downed over Russia Intensifies the Cold War.* New York: Watts, 1973. Cook describes Powers's flight in detail. He criticizes the CIA for becoming "a virtual law unto itself," treats Eisenhower as a dupe of governmental bureaucrats, and argues the incident spoiled U.S.-U.S.S.R. relations at a time of easing cold war tensions.

29:63 Nathan, James A. "A Fragile Detente: The U-2 Incident Reexamined." *Military Affairs* 39:3 (1975), 97–104. Nathan asserts that the official story regarding the flight seems at odds with known data concerning the performance of the U-2 and Soviet antimissile capability at the time. The argument is placed in the context of overall Soviet-American relations.

29:64 Powers, Francis Gary, with Gentry, Curt. *The Trial of the U2: Exclusive Authorized Account of the Court Proceedings of the Case of Francis Gary Powers Heard before the Military Division of the Supreme Court of U.S.S.R., Moscow, August 17, 18, 19, 1960.* Intro. by Harold J. Berman. Chicago: Translation World Publishers, 1960. This is a statement by Soviets on how they handled Powers and the downing of his U-2 plane. Berman's introduction provides background.

29:65 Gentry, Curt. *Operation Overflight: The U-2 Spy Pilot Tells His Story for the First Time.* New York: Holt, Rinehart & Winston, 1970. Powers's retelling of the U-2 incident, cleared by the CIA, is a good example of the official story, complete with the assertion that the real culprit was Lee Harvey Oswald.

Prouty, L. F. *The Secret Team: The CIA and Its Allies in Control of the United States and the World* (40:127) argues (chapter 20) that Powers's plane was sabotaged by the CIA's "Secret Team" so that a successful summit conference would not take place. Little documentation. See also Prouty's update article in *Gallery* 6:2 (1978), in which he uses new information from a Senate hearing declassified in 1975.

29:66 U.S. Senate. Committee on Foreign Relations. Hearings; *Events Incident to the Summit Conference.* 86th Cong. 2d Sess., 1960. A collection of unclassified testimony of the U.S. principles, insertions by congressmen made for the record, and appendixes of press releases and chronologies, among others.

29:67 U.S. Senate. Committee on Foreign Relations. Report; *Events Relating to the Summit Conference.* Rpt. no. 1761. 86th Cong., 2d Sess., 1960. Although they were knowledgeable about the U-2 programs, the president and appropriate cabinet officers "did not specifically approve the timing of a specific flight." The failure was "plain bad luck." A useful summary of the diplomatic background and basic questions.

29:68 Wise, David, and Ross, Thomas. *The U-2 Affair.* New York: Random House, 1962. This is an overview of events gleaned from numerous interviews with government officials and public sources.

Kennedy and Crisis Diplomacy

See "Personalities," especially Lyndon B. Johnson, John F. Kennedy, Nikita S. Khrushchev; also see Chapter 24, "The Kennedy Years" and "The Johnson Years."

THE POWERS AND BERLIN

See also Chapter 26, "The Berlin Blockade."

The Problem

See "Personalities," especially Willy Brandt.

29:69 Altschull, J. Herbert. "Khrushchev and the Berlin 'Ultimatum': The Jackal Syndrome and the Cold War." *Journalism Quarterly* 54:3 (1977), 545–

51, 565. In 1958, when Khrushchev issued a note complaining of the presence of West Berlin within U.S.S.R.-controlled territory, the American press generally and the *New York Times* (the "Lion") in particular interpreted the note as an ultimatum, and thereafter the historians (the "Jackals") have tended to perpetuate this view.

29:70 Bark, Dennis L. *Agreement on Berlin: A Study of the 1970–72 Quadripartite Negotiations.* Stanford, Calif.: Hoover Institution Press, 1974. This is a summary of the Berlin problem (1944–1969) followed by descriptions of the intra-German discussions (between Chancellor Willy Brandt and Chairman Willy Stoph) in Erfurt and Kassel in 1970 and the allied negotiations that produced the four-power agreement of September 3, 1971. The agreement and accompanying documents are appended. Bibliography.

29:71 Catudal, Honoré M., Jr. *The Diplomacy of the Quadripartite Agreement on Berlin: A New Era in East-West Politics.* Berlin: Berlin-Verlag, 1978. A description and analysis of the four-power negotiations that led to the treaty of September 3, 1971, on Berlin. It briefly describes two "secret protocols" to the 1971 agreement, one regarding neo-Nazi activity in Berlin and another on West German parliamentary activity in West Berlin. Bibliography.

29:72 Clay, Lucius D. "Berlin." *Foreign Affairs* 41:1 (1962), 47–58. This is a survey of the Berlin issue from its wartime origins through the building of the wall in August 1961 by the former American military governor of Germany.

29:73 Doeker, Gunther; Melsheimer, Klaus; and Schroder, Dieter. "Berlin and the Quadripartite Agreement of 1971." *American Journal of International Law* 67:1 (1973), 44–62. They discuss the Quadripartite Agreement (September 3, 1971) between France, the U.S.S.R., Britain, and the United States.

Smith, J. E. *The Defense of Berlin* (26:196) is an historical and analytical account, from the wartime agreements on Germany and Berlin through the crisis culminating in the construction of the Berlin Wall in 1961. Smith believes that the Kennedy administration should have taken a harder line in 1961. Maps, chronologies, and excerpts of documents.

Crisis of 1958–1961

29:74 Barker, Elizabeth. "The Berlin Crisis, 1958–1962." *International Affairs* [London] 39:1 (1963), 59–73. A BBC diplomatic correspondent's description and analysis of five phases of the developing crisis that culminated with the Kennedy-Khrushchev meeting in Vienna in June 1961 and the erection of the Berlin Wall in August 1961.

29:75 Camp, Glen D., Jr. *Berlin in the East-West Struggle, 1958–61.* New York: Facts on File, 1971. This detailed, day-by-day account of the Berlin crisis, which began in 1958, includes extensive quotations from documents.

29:76 Cate, Curtis. *The Ides of August: The Berlin Wall Crisis, 1961.* New York: Evans, 1978. Based in part on German sources and oral histories, this is an emotion-packed narrative of the events surrounding the erection of the Berlin Wall in August 1961. Bibliography.

29:77 Keller, John W. *Germany, the Wall and Berlin: Internal Politics during an International Crisis.* New York: Vantage, 1964. Using mostly press sources in Germany and the West, Keller reconstructs the atmosphere of 1961; it is most useful for public opinion.

29:78 Merritt, Richard L. "The Berlin Wall: What Was It All About?" *Midwest Journal of Political Science* 17:1 (1973), 189–95. Merritt examines recent writings dealing with the Berlin crisis (1958–1961) and discusses how certain cold war attitudes about the Berlin Wall have changed through the years.

29:79 Merritt, Richard L. "A Transformed Crisis: The Berlin Wall." In Roy C. Macridis, ed., *Modern European Governments: Cases in Comparative Policy Making.* Englewood Cliffs, N.J.: Prentice-Hall, 1968, pp. 140–73. This introduction to the continuing Berlin problem analyzes Walter Ulbricht's and the German Democratic Republic's policies and motives for building the wall and presents a day-by-day account of the 1961 crisis and the responses of the Western allies, the Kennedy administration, the German Federal Republic, and West Berliners.

29:80 Schick, Jack M. *The Berlin Crisis, 1958–1962.* Philadelphia: University of Pennsylvania, 1971. This account discusses the interrelationship of the

Soviet ultimatum on Berlin, the Geneva Conference of 1959, the U-2 incident and the Paris summit of 1960, the Kennedy-Khrushchev meeting in 1961, the Berlin Wall, and the Cuban missile crisis of 1962. Bibliography.

29:81 Shell, Kurt L. "Berlin and the German Problem." *World Politics* 16:1 (1963), 137–46. In a review essay of six contemporary books (three of them in German) dealing with the Berlin problem, Shell identifies three views on the Berlin crisis that began with the Soviet ultimatum of November 17, 1958: Berlin is a "vital bridgehead of freedom," a "bone in the throat of Soviet Russia," or a "potential bridge" between the conflicting powers.

29:82 Slusser, Robert M. "The Berlin Crises of 1958–59 and 1961." In Barry M. Blechman and Stephen S. Kaplan, eds., *Force without War: U.S. Armed Forces as a Political Instrument*. Washington, D.C.: Brookings Institution, 1978, pp. 343–439. Slusser reviews Presidents Eisenhower and Kennedy's efforts to deal with Soviet pressure on Berlin. The East German erection of the Berlin Wall ended the crisis.

29:83 Slusser, Robert M. *The Berlin Crisis of 1961: Soviet-American Relations and the Struggle for Power in the Kremlin, June–November 1961*. Baltimore: Johns Hopkins University Press, 1973. Slusser's chronological analysis of the Berlin crisis of 1961, emphasizes the Soviet Union's role and provides a detailed case study of Soviet policy formation during a time of internal power struggles. Bibliography and glossary.

29:84 Speier, Hans. *Divided Berlin: The Anatomy of Soviet Political Blackmail*. New York: Praeger, 1961. This study, beginning with the Soviet note of November 27, 1958, demanding a change in the four-power status of the city, ends with the June 1961 Kennedy-Khrushchev meeting in Vienna, before the wall was built.

29:85 Tanter, Raymond. *Modelling and Managing International Conflicts: The Berlin Crises*. Beverly Hills, Calif.: Sage, 1974. This study uses the Berlin crises of 1948–1949 and 1961 as subjects to construct a model for managing international conflicts. It contains brief historical summaries of the two crises and is heavily weighted with statistics, charts, and diagrams. Detailed chronologies.

29:86 Trivers, Howard. *Three Crises in American Foreign Affairs and a Continuing Revolution*. Carbondale: Southern Illinois University Press, 1972. Chapter 1 is a personal account of the Berlin Wall controversy of 1961, especially the October Friedrichstrasse confrontation between American and Soviet tanks.

29:87 Wright, Quincy. "Some Legal Aspects of the Berlin Crisis." *American Journal of International Law* 55:4 (1961), 959–65. Wright discusses the Soviet Union's right, under international law, to make a peace treaty with East Germany, the German Democratic Republic's rights to control its own territories, and the problem of Western access to divided Berlin.

MISSILE GAP ISSUE

29:88 Dick, James C. "The Strategic Arms Race, 1957–1961: Who Opened a Missile Gap?" *Journal of Politics* 34:4 (1972), 1062–110. There was no "missile gap" and "under Eisenhower's stewardship, America responded more than adequately to a perceived threat [from the U.S.S.R.] that proved in actuality to be more mythical than real." Dick is critical of Americans who exaggerated the Soviet threat.

29:89 Gray, Colin S. " 'Gap' Prediction and America's Defense: Arms Race Behavior in the Eisenhower Years." *Orbis* 16:1 (1972), 257–74. This is a survey of the "bomber gap" and "missile gap" controversies. Gray thinks the missile gap was a "plausible illusion" in the late 1950s, even though "Eisenhower bequeathed a comfortable margin of strategic superiority" to the Kennedy administration. Subsequent American claims of nuclear supremacy helped induce the Cuban missile crisis and the Soviet-American arms race of the 1960s.

29:90 Licklider, Roy E. "The Missile Gap Controversy." *Political Science Quarterly* 85:4 (1970), 600–15. Licklider examines the welter of confused claims of Soviet numerical superiority in intercontinental ballistic missiles (ICBMs), the extent of such assumed superiority, how the missile gap relates to a deterrence gap, and the U.S. response to such claims and counterclaims.

CUBAN MISSILE CRISIS, 1962

See "Personalities," especially John F. Kennedy, Robert F. Kennedy, Nikita S. Khrushchev, Adlai E. Stevenson; see also Chapter 34, "Missile Crisis, 1962," for Cuban views.

29:91 Abel, Elie. *The Missile Crisis.* Philadelphia: Lippincott, 1968. A narrative based on documents and the recollections of several dozen decisionmakers involved in the crisis, especially Robert Kennedy and Paul Nitze.

29:92 Adler, Stephen. "The Cuban Missile Crisis: Strategic Theory in Practice." In Andrew W. Cordier, ed., *Columbia Essays in International Affairs: The Dean's Papers, 1971.* New York: Columbia University Press, 1972, pp. 178–217. Adler surveys a variety of interpretations as to why the Soviets placed the missiles in Cuba and why the United States thought it necessary to get them out. He notes that each side abandoned its own strategic doctrines during the crisis. It was Soviet weakness, not a sense of advantage or a "probe," which was at the root of Moscow's motivation. Bibliography.

29:93 Allison, Graham T. *Essence of Decision: Explaining the Cuban Missile Crisis.* Boston: Little, Brown, 1971. A lengthier version of his *American Political Science Review* article (September 1969), this study suggests that three decisionmaking models can be applied to the missile crisis: the "rational actor model," the "organizational process model," and the "governmental politics model." It emphasizes the role of the bureaucracy. Bibliography.

29:94 Alsop, Stewart, and Bartlett, Charles. "In Times of Crisis." *Saturday Evening Post* 235:12 (1962), 16–20. This essay is famous for delineation of the terms "hawks" and "doves" and Rusk's expression that it was an "eyeball-to-eyeball" confrontation. The authors suggest further that Adlai Stevenson advocated "a Munich."

29:95 Bernstein, Barton J. "The Cuban Missile Crisis: Trading the Jupiters in Turkey?" *Political Science Quarterly* 95:1 (1980), 97–125. Bernstein uses newly available declassified evidence to make several points: that President Kennedy himself actually placed the Jupiter missiles in Turkey in 1961; that he never ordered their withdrawal, only a feasibility study in 1962; that during the Cuban missile crisis, the president toyed with the idea of a trade—missiles in Cuba

for missiles in Turkey; that he gave the Soviets a loose promise that the missiles in Turkey would be withdrawn in the future. Bernstein criticizes Kennedy for gambling on a private pledge when the Soviets sought a public pledge.

29:96 Bernstein, Barton J. "The Week We Almost Went to War." *Bulletin of the Atomic Scientists* 32:2 (1976), 13–21. Bernstein argues here and in "Their Finest Hour?" *Correspondent* 32 (Aug. 1964), 119–21, and in "The Cuban Missile Crisis," in Lynn Miller and Ronald Pruessen, eds., *Reflections on the Cold War* (24:41), pp. 108–42, that Kennedy sought confrontation rather than negotiation and that the crisis was unnecessary.

29:97 Caldwell, Dan. "A Research Note on the Quarantine of Cuba, October 1962." *International Studies Quarterly* 22:4 (1978), 625–33. In this examination of the logs of 11 of the 46 American ships that participated in the blockade of Cuba, Caldwell finds that the ships did pull back from 800 to 500 miles after the president's order to give the Soviets more time to decide how to respond to the blockade. This evidence refutes Allison's argument (29:93) that the navy disobeyed the president.

29:98 Crane, Robert D. "The Cuban Crisis: A Strategic Analysis of American and Soviet Policy." *Orbis* 6:4 (1963), 528–63. Crane concludes that the hardliners in the U.S.S.R. saw their action as a "limited probe." If successful they could have then "embarked safely on major expansionist policies." The "lessons" of the crisis drawn by American leaders: U.S. moderation will beget Soviet moderation and time is on the side of the United States both in Cuba and in the world at large.

29:99 Detzer, David. *The Brink: Cuban Missile Crisis, 1962.* New York: Crowell, 1979. A fast-paced narrative, heavy with anecdote, light on analysis, that depicts President Kennedy as tense, firm, and restrained. Bibliography.

29:100 Dewart, Leslie. "The Cuban Crisis Revisited." *Studies on the Left* 5:2 (1965), 15–40. Dewart argues that Khrushchev's goal was to force Kennedy to settle the cold war. The U.S., Dewart thinks, set a trap for the Russians. See Dewart's postscript in Divine, *The Cuban Missile Crisis* (29:102), pp. 189–90.

29:101 Dinerstein, Herbert S. *The Making of a Missile Crisis, October 1962.* Baltimore: Johns Hopkins

University Press, 1976. A reconstruction of Soviet beliefs about the international and, specifically, Latin American context of the crisis as well as the Cuban and American responses. "Neither Kennedy nor Khrushchev desired the crisis," but "they frightened each other and the rest of the world needlessly." Extensive bibliography.

29:102   Divine, Robert A., ed. *The Cuban Missile Crisis.* Chicago: Quadrangle, 1971. A collection of documents and articles that is one of the best places to start to get a sense of the issues and the literature on the crisis. Bibliography.

29:103   Garthoff, Raymond L. "American Reaction to Soviet Aircraft in Cuba, 1962 and 1978." *Political Science Quarterly* 95:3 (1980), 427–39. Garthoff places the 1978 issue over Soviet MIG-23 fighter-bombers in the context of the 1962 Soviet-American "understanding" that followed the Cuban missile crisis—a U.S. pledge not to invade Cuba and a Soviet promise not to place offensive weapons in Cuba. Noting that the "understanding" was not actually consummated until 1970, Garthoff argues that the 1962 equivalent of the MIG-23 was not then considered an offensive weapon and therefore should not have been labeled such in 1978.

FitzSimons, L. *The Kennedy Doctrine* (24:210) asks, in chapter 5, "Was the crisis necessary?" The author emphasizes that diplomacy was suspended when "unconditional surrender" was insisted upon.

29:104   George, Alexander L. "The Cuban Missile Crisis." In Alexander L. George, David K. Hall, and William E. Simons, eds., *The Limits of Coercive Diplomacy: Laos, Cuba, Vietnam.* Boston: Little, Brown, 1971, pp. 86–144. An analysis of the domestic stakes of the Kennedy administration in the crisis and a narrative of the events that emphasize the necessary ingredients of coercion. George emphasizes the relative uniqueness of the crisis and finds Kennedy's use of the "carrot and stick" to be "just right."

29:105   Gerberding, William P. "International Law and the Cuban Missile Crisis." In Lawrence Scheinman and David Wilkinson, eds., *International Law and Political Crisis: An Analytic Casebook.* Boston: Little, Brown, 1968, pp. 175–211. Disagreeing with Chayes (29:118), Gerberding argues that legal reasoning was used for its "utility as legal props for policy determined on other non-legal grounds."

29:106   Gromyko, Anatolii A. "The Caribbean Crisis." *Soviet Law and Government* 11:1 (1972), 3–53. Written by a Soviet historian and translated into English, this two-part essay concludes that the crisis was "contrived" by a Kennedy administration which rejected traditional diplomacy in favor of confrontation and desired to oust Castro.

29:107   Hafner, Donald L. "Bureaucratic Politics and 'Those Frigging Missiles': JFK, Cuba and U.S. Missiles in Turkey." *Orbis* 21:2 (1977), 307–33. Hafner argues, in a critique of Graham Allison's treatment (29:93), that the president's shock and surprise at the peak of the Cuban crisis, on discovering that the withdrawal of Jupiter missiles from Turkey had not been carried out as he had earlier ordered, is a "myth." The origin of the "myth" was Elie Abel's account (29:91).

29:108   Hagan, Roger. "Triumph or Tragedy." *Dissent* 10:1 (1963), 13–26. Hagan argues that the Cubans did have something to fear from the United States before the crisis and that the crisis vindicated the nascent McNamara Doctrine on uses of gradual response.

29:109   Horelick, Arnold L. "The Cuban Missile Crisis: An Analysis of Soviet Calculations and Behavior." *World Politics* 16:3 (1964), 363–89. This abridged RAND Corporation memorandum especially asks why the Soviets deployed the missiles. The answers: 1) to buttress the flagging worldwide position of the Soviets, and 2) to use the weapons as a lever in the Berlin question.

29:110   Nathan, James A. "The Missile Crisis: His Finest Hour Now." *World Politics* 27:2 (1975), 256–81. Nathan questions the interpretation that the Cuban missile crisis was a good example of "crisis management." He notes that luck and the "illusion of control" rather than "mastery" were evident, and that domestic problems may have governed Kennedy's handling of the crisis. Nathan concludes that the tragic lesson of the crisis—that "success in international crisis was largely a matter of national guts"—influenced an interventionist policy toward Vietnam.

29:111   Pachter, Henry M. *Collision Course: The Cuban Missile Crisis and Coexistence.* New York: Praeger, 1963. An early postcrisis chronicle which narrates events and presents some general conclusions about power conflict in the nuclear age. Documents and a chronology.

29:112   Paper, Lewis J. "The Moral Implications of the Cuban Missile Crisis." *American Scholar* 41:2 (1972), 276–83. Paper asserts that the United States responded rightly in the crisis to ensure its security. Yet the capacity of one individual to determine the fate of millions of others is morally questionable.

29:113   Pederson, John C. "Soviet Reporting of the Cuban Crisis." *U.S. Naval Institute Proceedings* 91:10 (1965), 54–63. An examination of the Soviet press's view of the Monroe Doctrine and U.S. policy toward Castro's Cuba before, during, and immediately after the missile crisis.

29:114   Steel, Ronald. *Imperialists and Other Heroes: A Chronicle of the American Empire.* New York: Random House, 1975. Steel's revisionist essay reviews Robert Kennedy's *Thirteen Days* (29:120) and argues that 1) diplomacy was suspended, 2) intelligence failed and no one really understood Soviet motives, and 3) the outcome may have resulted as much from luck as from skill.

29:115   U.S. Senate. Committee on Armed Services. *Interim Report by Preparedness Investigating Subcommittee . . . on Cuban Military Buildup.* 88th Cong., 1st Sess., 1963. This, the Stennis Report, argues that the American failure to detect the missiles was due to U.S. analysts who "were strongly influenced by their philosophical judgment that it would be contrary to Soviet interests to introduce strategic missiles into Cuba." This conclusion is disputed in Klaus Knorr, "Failures in National Intelligence Estimates: The Case of the Cuban Missile Crisis," *World Politics* 16:3 (1964), 455–67.

29:116   Wohlstetter, Roberta. "Cuba and Pearl Harbor: Hindsight and Foresight." *Foreign Affairs* 43:4 (1965), 691–707. Wohlstetter compares the Pearl Harbor attack with the placement of missiles in Cuba. She argues that the United States failed in both cases to make allowance for deception. The problem in intelligence is that the data never reveals all: it is ambiguous and incomplete.

Personal Accounts and Documents

29:117   Acheson, Dean. "Dean Acheson's Version of Robert Kennedy's Version of the Cuban Missile Affair." *Esquire* 71:2 (1969), 76ff. Acheson reflects on his role in the crisis and on Robert Kennedy's *Thirteen Days* (29:120). He considers the outcome "lucky," because the Executive Committee was "leaderless" and many of its members "had little knowledge in either the military or diplomatic field." Acheson favored an air strike against Cuba.

29:118   Chayes, Abram. *The Cuban Missile Crisis: International Crises and the Role of Law.* New York: Oxford University Press, 1974. Chayes was a legal adviser to the State Department at the time of the missile crisis and consulted with the Executive Committee. This book describes the use the committee made of his advice, especially on relations with the Organization of American States and the United Nations. Legal memoranda are included.

29:119   Hilsman, Roger, and Steel, Ronald. "An Exchange on the Missile Crisis." *New York Review of Books* 12 (May 8, 1969), 36–38. Hilsman, a State Department official during the missile crisis, disputes Ronald Steel, *New York Review of Books* (March 13, 1969) or *Imperialists and Other Heroes* (29:114), who argued that quiet diplomacy was possible. Steel replies.

29:120   Kennedy, Robert F. *Thirteen Days: A Memoir of the Cuban Missile Crisis.* New York: Norton, 1969. A memoir by the president's brother, who gives a moment-by-moment account of the decisions taken and the lessons drawn from the events. Robert Kennedy participated in the Executive Committee meetings. Appendix.

29:121   Larson, David L., ed., *The Cuban Crisis of 1962: Selected Documents and Chronology.* Boston: Houghton Mifflin, 1963. This is a collection of more than 100 documents, including interviews, editorials, press releases, treaties, and security council resolutions. It includes an excellent chronology. Bibliography.

29:122   LeMay, Curtis E. "Deterrence in Action." *Ordnance* 47:257 (1963), 526–30. A description of combat preparation and movement during the crisis by the then air force chief of staff. LeMay argues that a crisis-ready Strategic Air Command gave Kennedy the decisive edge in the confrontation.

29:123   "Messages Exchanged by President Kennedy and Chairman Khrushchev during the Cuban Missile Crisis of October 1962." *U.S. Department of State Bulletin* 69:1795 (1973), 635–55. Included are all the letters sent—five by Kennedy, five by Khrushchev—during the crisis, some of which were declassified and made public for the first time in 1973.

U Thant. *View from the UN* [1961–1970] (38:82) candidly discusses his role in trying to mediate the Cuban missile crisis (pp. 154–96).

Nuclear Arms Competition and Control

See "Missile Gap Issue," above; also see Chapter 26 for origins of nuclear arms negotiations, and Chapter 40 for additional references.

Bechhoefer, B. G. *Postwar Negotiations for Arms Control* (26:197) is still one of the fullest descriptions of arms control and disarmament negotiations to 1960.

29:124 Bernstein, Barton J. "The Challenges and Dangers of Nuclear Weapons: Foreign Policy and Strategy, 1941–1978." *Maryland Historian* 9:1 (1978), 73–99. Bernstein reviews U.S. nuclear policies since 1941. The arms race, founded upon mutual distrust, will continue, but nuclear war is unlikely unless an amoral technologist errs.

29:125 Gray, Colin S. *The Soviet-American Arms Race.* Westmead, Farnborough, Eng.: D.C. Heath, 1976. Gray argues that the arms race behavior of the super powers differs in intensity but not in kind from other powers, regardless of dissimilar ideological rationalizations.

29:126 Hayden, Eric W. "Soviet-American Arms Negotiations—1960–68: A Prelude to SALT." *Naval War College Review* 24:5 (1972), 65–82. In a general overview of arms control talks and agreements, the author notes that both American and Soviet proposals were often devised for their propaganda value.

29:127 Hollist, W. Ladd. "An Analysis of Arms Processes in the United States and the Soviet Union." *International Studies Quarterly* 21:3 (1977), 503–28. The United States (1948–1970) reacted more to changes in Soviet arms expenditures than to levels of Soviet arms, while the Soviet Union tended to react more to the level of U.S. arms. This research was based on computer simulation.

29:128 Kaplan, Fred M. *Dubious Specter: A Second Look at the "Soviet Threat."* Pamphlet no. 6. Washington, D.C.: Transnational Institute, 1977. With considerable data, the author attempts to explode the "myth" of the Soviet nuclear threat to the United States in the 1970s. He criticizes those who exaggerate Soviet forces in order to garner public and congressional support for new American strategic weapons systems.

29:129 Killian, James R., Jr. *Sputnik, Scientists, and Eisenhower: A Memoir of the First Special Assistant to the President for Science and Technology.* Cambridge, Mass.: MIT Press, 1977. Killian headed the President's Science Advisory Committee (1957–1959). His autobiography notes the shock waves set loose by Sputnik and the advice leading scientists were giving Eisenhower in the early years of the Soviet-American missile race. Bibliography.

29:130 Kistiakowsky, George B. *A Scientist at the White House: The Private Diary of President Eisenhower's Special Assistant for Science and Technology.* Cambridge: Harvard University Press, 1976. A missile expert hired by the White House, Kistiakowsky gives an inside view of the Eisenhower administration's concern over the nuclear arms race, disarmament, the U-2 crisis, and summit diplomacy (1959–1960).

Klass, P. J. *Secret Sentries in Space* (40:249) describes the American and Soviet reconnaissance satellite programs and their impact on arms control talks. With these "spy" satellites each side can detect the "secret" missiles of the other.

29:131 Moynihan, Daniel P. "Reflections: The SALT Process." *New Yorker* 55 (Nov. 19, 1979), 104ff. The senator from New York, critical of SALT II, probes the question of SALT I's effectiveness and SALT II's promises. It is a thoughtful discussion of American and Soviet strategic doctrine and practice.

Myrdal, A. *The Game of Disarmament: How the United States and Russia Run the Arms Race* (40:228) is a memoirlike "neutralist" study by a Swedish diplomat of Soviet-American efforts to reach disarmament.

29:132 Newhouse, John. "Reflections: The SALT Debate." *New Yorker* 55 (Dec. 17, 1979), 130 ff. Newhouse takes a sympathetic view of SALT II through a survey of pro-and-con arguments. He thinks that the "SALT agreements are not a reward for better

Soviet behavior but, rather, goals that embody hard-headed assessments of America's national interest."

O'Neill, R., ed. *The Strategic Nuclear Balance: An Australian Perspective* (32:149).

29:133   Payne, Samuel B., Jr. *The Soviet Union and SALT.* Cambridge, Mass.: MIT Press, 1980. Based on published Soviet statements and writings, this book studies the attitudes of both Soviet proponents and opponents of arms control since 1968.

Quester, G. H. *Nuclear Diplomacy: The First Twenty-Five Years* [1945–1970] (40:229) is a chronological study of the cold war that emphasizes the Soviet-American nuclear arms race.

Roberts, C. M. *The Nuclear Years: The Arms Race and Arms Control, 1945–1970* (40:230) is a "primer" that surveys the nuclear arms race from Hiroshima to SALT.

U.S. Arms Control and Disarmament Agency. *Arms Control and Disarmament Agreements: Texts and Histories of Negotiations* (40:223) includes the "hot line" agreement, Test Ban Treaty, Outer Space Treaty, and many others. Brief narratives place the agreements in historical context and note their status in 1980.

29:134   York, Herbert F. *Race to Oblivion: A Participant's View of the Arms Race.* New York: Simon & Schuster, 1970. This nuclear physicist, an adviser to Eisenhower (late 1950s) and a member of national advisory committees (the 1960s), presents an informative history of Soviet-American nuclear competition. Among other topics, he discusses the impact of Sputnik, the missile gap controversy, and the dangers of a "scientific-technological elite."

SOVIET POLICIES

See also "Overviews," above, for general accounts of Soviet military strategy.

29:135   Bloomfield, Lincoln P.; Clemens, Walter C., Jr.; and Griffiths, Franklyn. *Khrushchev and the Arms Race: Soviet Interests in Arms Control and Disarmament, 1954–1964.* Cambridge, Mass.: MIT Press, 1966. This study examines the Soviet movement toward a policy of limited arms control with the United States to preserve its strength and limit new American gains. Bibliography.

29:136   Cottrell, Alvin J. "Soviet Views of U.S. Overseas Bases." *Orbis* 7:1 (1963), 77–95. This defense analyst argues that the Soviets have viewed U.S. overseas bases as launching sites for a surprise attack, and for provocative U-2 flights. The Soviet objective is the dismantling or "disengagement" of these bases, especially in the NATO operational area.

29:137   Dallin, Alexander, et al. *The Soviet Union and Disarmament: An Appraisal of Soviet Attitudes and Intentions.* New York: Praeger, 1964. This volume, concentrating on the 1950s and early 1960s, finds a growing sincerity in Soviet intentions toward arms control, especially under Khrushchev, and outlines the variety of influences upon Soviet behavior. Bibliography.

29:138   Deane, Michael J. "The Soviet Assessment of the 'Correlation of World Forces': Implications for American Foreign Policy." *Orbis* 20:3 (1976), 625–36. The Soviets have used the concept of correlation of forces since prerevolutionary days. The concept can refer to "the relative alignment of two opposing forces or groups of forces" in domestic or international affairs, or to particular types of force, such as class forces, political forces, economic forces, or military forces.

29:139   Horelick, Arnold L., and Rush, Myron. *Strategic Power and Soviet Foreign Policy.* Chicago: University of Chicago Press, 1966. The authors argue that the U.S.S.R. attempted in the 1950s to "exploit strategic weapons politically" and then to deceive the United States about the scope of the Soviet ICBM program. The exposure of Soviet missile inferiority prompted Moscow to place missiles in Cuba. Chronology.

29:140   Jackson, William D. "The Soviets and Strategic Arms: Toward an Evaluation of the Record." *Political Science Quarterly* 94:2 (1979), 243–61. Jackson surveys the several different analyses of Soviet behavior in nuclear arms competition and the chronology of Soviet strategic power and policy, wherein 1961 is a major turning point.

29:141   Kolkowicz, Roman, et al. *The Soviet Union and Arms Control: A Superpower Dilemma.* Baltimore: Johns Hopkins Press, 1970. This is an analysis of the "perceptions, motivations, incentives, and constraints that shape Soviet policies on arms control."

29:142   Larson, Thomas B. *Disarmament and Soviet Policy, 1964–1968.* Englewood Cliffs, N.J.: Prentice-Hall, 1969. In this discussion of the specifics of U.S.-U.S.S.R. arms control negotiations, Larson concludes that the Sino-Soviet split might persuade the Soviets to shy away from disarmament pacts that would restrict their power vis-à-vis China. Bibliography.

TEST BAN TREATY, 1963

See "Personalities," especially W. Averell Harriman, Nikita S. Khrushchev.

29:143 Dean, Arthur H. *The Test Ban and Disarmament: The Path of Negotiation.* New York: Harper & Row, 1966. Dean served as chairman of the U.S. delegation at the disarmament meetings which led to the Test Ban Treaty. His book is part autobiographical, part political (explaining U.S. policies), and part prescriptive (appeals for continued negotiations with the U.S.S.R.).

29:144 Divine, Robert A. *Blowing on the Wind: The Nuclear Test Ban Debate, 1954–1960.* New York: Oxford University Press, 1978. Divine studies the divided response of Americans and their leaders to the dangers of fallout from atmospheric testing of nuclear devices. He provides a useful background to the conclusion of the Soviet-American test ban treaty of 1963. Bibliography.

29:145 Jacobson, Harold K., and Stein, Eric. *Diplomats, Scientists, and Politicians: The United States and the Nuclear Test Ban Negotiations.* Ann Arbor: University of Michigan Press, 1966. A detailed study of the background and negotiations leading to the 1963 Nuclear Test Ban Treaty. Bibliography.

29:146 Jönsson, Christer. *Soviet Bargaining Behavior: The Nuclear Test Ban Case.* New York: Columbia University Press, 1979. This Swedish political scientist uses the nuclear test ban negotiations (1958–1963) for a case study of Soviet negotiating behavior. Jönsson concludes that Soviet behavior was "more flexible and less propagandistic" than Western observers portrayed it. Extensive bibliography.

29:147 McBridge, James H. *The Test Ban Treaty: Military, Technological, and Political Implications.* Chicago: Regnery, 1967. This critical study of the 1963 Test Ban Treaty finds the treaty "prejudicial to the security of the United States" and an advantage for the Soviet Union in its quest to gain nuclear superiority.

29:148 York, Herbert F. "The Great Test-Ban Debate." *Scientific American* 227:5 (1972), 15–23. This essay judges the effects of the Test Ban Treaty after 1963 as a success. York also appeals for continued efforts to reach nuclear controls.

STRATEGIC ARMS LIMITATION TALKS (SALT)

See "Personalities," especially Henry A. Kissinger, Richard M. Nixon.

29:149 Bates, E. A., Jr. "The SALT Standing Consultative Commission: An American Analysis." *Millennium: Journal of International Studies* 4:2 (1975), 132–45. Bates examines the creation of the SALT Standing Consultative Commission, its functions, organization, and procedures, with particular reference to the Anti-Ballistic Missile System Treaty of 1972.

29:150 Bernstein, Barton J. "SALT: The Dangerous Illusion." *Inquiry* 1 (July 24, 1978), 16–19. The SALT I treaty and SALT II agreements have done little to curb the arms race, because they permitted both the U.S. and the U.S.S.R. to develop new weapons systems.

29:151 Burt, Richard, ed. *A Strategic Symposium: SALT and U.S. Defense Policy.* Edison, N.J.: Transaction, 1979. Several commentators have written brief essays on SALT and its impact on strategic stability and defense programs, with criticisms of SALT the most prominent. The articles first appeared in *Washington Quarterly* 2:1 (1979).

29:152 Foreign Policy Association. *SALT II: Toward Security or Danger?* New York: Foreign Policy Association, 1979. This balanced pamphlet reviews SALT I, the key issues over SALT II, and the debate over SALT in the United States. Tables and glossary.

29:153 Garthoff, Raymond L. "SALT I: An Evaluation." *World Politics* 31:1 (1978), 1–25. Garthoff helped negotiate SALT I, which he finds a positive achievement in mitigating arms competition. He also notes shortcomings, such as the failure to achieve a ban on MIRVs; see also Garthoff's "Negotiating with the Russians: Some Lessons from SALT," *International Security* 1 (1977), 3–24.

29:154 Gray, Colin S. "Détente, Arms Control and Strategy: Perspective on SALT." *American Political*

Science Review 70:4 (1976), 1242–56. This is a lengthy, analytical review of several books on the Soviet-American SALT negotiations (1969–1976).

29:155   Kintner, William R., and Pfaltzgraff, Robert L., Jr., eds. *SALT: Implications for Arms Control in the 1970s*. Pittsburgh: University of Pittsburgh Press, 1973. Among the topics covered in these essays are the impact of SALT on world politics, technological innovations, the arms control bargaining process, and SALT and American security. W. W. Rostow begins with a personal history of talks with the Soviets in the 1960s. Glossary.

29:156   Newhouse, John. *Cold Dawn: The Story of SALT*. New York: Holt, Rinehart & Winston, 1973. In this account of the background and conduct of the arms limitations talks leading to the Moscow agreements of 1972, Newhouse draws heavily on "private conversations" with public officials whose names he desires to keep secret.

29:157   Nitze, Paul H. "The Strategic Balance between Hope and Skepticism." *Foreign Policy,* no. 17 (1974–1975), 136–56. A leading critic of the SALT agreements and negotiating process, Nitze believes that the United States is signing agreements that favor the Soviets and cause the deterioration of "the present high quality of the U.S. deterrent posture ..."

29:158   Panofsky, W. K. H. *Arms Control and SALT II*. Seattle: University of Washington Press, 1979. Panofsky soberly endorses the SALT process as a necessary step toward the control of strategic weapons. He discounts the idea of Soviet nuclear superiority and first-strike capability. This brief account provides a succinct review of the subject by a scientist.

29:159   Payne, Samuel B., Jr. "The Soviet Debate on Strategic Arms Limitation, 1968–72." *Soviet Studies* 27:1 (1975), 27–45. Payne identifies a debate between Soviet "arms controllers" and "militarists," who differ over whether strategic arms limitation is desirable for the U.S.S.R. and whether the United States would abide by an agreement.

29:160   Talbott, Strobe. *Endgame: The Inside Story of SALT II*. New York: Harper & Row, 1979. This book based on interviews and secret sources studies the complicated negotiations which led to the SALT II treaty of 1979. Talbott concentrates on American bureaucratic infighting rather than on clashes of philosophy or strategic doctrine.

29:161   U.S. Senate. Committee on Foreign Relations. Hearings; *Strategic Arms Limitation Agreements. 92d Cong., 2d Sess., 1972.* Public hearings on SALT I, with testimony and exchanges with committee members. Officials, academics, and interest group representatives are included.

29:162   Willrich, Mason, and Rhinelander, John B., eds. *SALT: The Moscow Agreements and Beyond.* New York: Free Press, 1974. Chalmers Roberts, Marshall Shulman, and eight other specialists study the negotiating road leading to the 1972 agreements and analyze the agreements themselves. Appended are various documents relating to SALT and a glossary. Bibliography.

29:163   Wolfe, Thomas W. *The SALT Experience.* Cambridge, Mass.: Ballinger, 1979. Wolfe surveys the various interpretations of the SALT process. He concludes that by pursuing the idea of "mutual assured destruction" or MAD, the United States is leaving itself exposed to nuclear annihilation in order to reassure the Soviet Union.

Economic, Cultural, and Scientific Relations

ECONOMIC RELATIONS

See Chapter 39 for U.S. commercial policy.

29:164   Brada, Josef C., and King, Arthur E. "The Soviet-American Trade Agreements: Prospects for the Soviet Economy." *Russian Review* 32:4 (1973), 345–59. An examination of the "basic long-run strategies employed by the two nations since World War II" and the reason for their failure which, in turn, led to a change in trade policy.

29:165   Friesen, Connie M. *The Political Economy of East-West Trade.* New York: Praeger, 1976. In one of the best overviews of exchanges during the cold war, Friesen uses material from the Soviet as well as U.S. side, and emphasizes the role of politics in the development of economic exchanges. Bibliography.

29:166 Harvey, Mose L. *East-West Trade and United States Policy*. New York: National Association of Manufacturers, 1966. The study surveys East-West trade (especially the 1964 grain deal), argues that trade is a weapon and should be used with conscious purpose against the Soviet Union (although not necessarily against Yugoslavia), fears the United States does not understand the growing battle over the Third World, and concludes that détente is disadvantageous.

Mikesell, R. F., and Behrman, J. N. *Financing Free World Trade with the Sino-Soviet Bloc* (39:79) argues that the post-1945 era was marked by growing multilateralism of trade and the devising of new financial means to pay for it. The authors doubt, however, that Soviet bloc nations can move rapidly, or far, toward multilateralism.

29:167 Pisar, Samuel. *Coexistence and Commerce: Guidelines for Transactions between East and West*. New York: McGraw-Hill, 1970. Pisar extensively surveys East-West economic relations and argues that although coexistence is necessary, Soviet state-trading operations and increasing international barriers to trade will create critical problems. An often skeptical projection of capitalist-communist economic relations. Bibliography.

29:168 Rockefeller Brothers Fund. *Prospects for Peace: The Rockefeller Panel Reports*. Garden City, N.Y.: Doubleday, 1961. This volume provides a general understanding of the Kennedy administration's views, and how U.S. leaders defined the growing economic competition with the Soviets. Several of the essays focus on growing challenges from China and the newly emerging nations which must be met within the overall struggle with the Soviets.

Sutton, A. C. *Western Technology and Soviet Economic Development, 1945–1965* (20:204) in this, volume 3 of Sutton's detailed study, are examples of American trade with the Soviet Union which have contributed to that nation's economic growth—such as the "ball bearing case" of 1961 and the "Fiat deal" of 1968. Sutton is very critical of American shipments to the U.S.S.R. which could possibly be converted to military use. Bibliography.

29:169 U.S. Senate. Committee on Banking and Currency. Hearings; *East-West Trade*. 3 pts. 90th Cong., 2d Sess., 1968. These extensive hearings and documents include statements by businessmen, scholars, and politicians, and reprints of articles on the regulation of trade with communist countries. A use-ful compilation for studying U.S.-U.S.S.R. economic relations in the 1960s.

U.S. Senate. Committee on Foreign Relations. *A Background Study on East-West Trade Prepared . . . by the Legislative Reference Service of the Library of Congress* (39:81) is one of the best analyses of East-West trade from the 1930s until the mid-1960s. It deals with all aspects including Western controls, the role of China and Cuba, U.S. exporters' problems, and the Soviet bloc's ability to pay for purchases.

29:170 U.S. Senate. Committee on Foreign Relations. Hearings; *Background Documents on East-West Trade*. 89th Cong., 1st Sess., 1965. The committee considered these to be the most important documents that governed East-West trade (1949–1965). Some of the tariff material reaches back to 1930. Most of the documents are detailed and technical.

U.S. Senate. Committee on Foreign Relations. Hearings; *East-West Trade* [1960s] (39:82) evaluates an apparent thaw in East-West economic relations. State Department memoranda on Soviet bloc trade and the U.S. policy toward that trade are especially significant.

29:171 Uren, Philip E., ed. *East-West Trade: A Symposium*. Toronto: Canadian Institute of International Affairs, 1966. Valuable for a Canadian viewpoint, the volume discusses broad issues such as the effect of state bureaucracy, state purchases, and legal restraints. After a general overview of relations since 1945, Uren contributes an important paper on strategic aspects of East-West trade. A good account for the general reader.

29:172 Wilczynski, Jozef. *The Economics and Politics of East-West Trade*. New York: Praeger, 1969. In discussing post-1945 East-West trade trends, Wilczynski provides a technical discussion of exchange rates, socialist theory of trade, dumping, the politics of grain trade, strategic export controls, and arbitration arrangements. Relative advantages and disadvantages for both sides are analyzed. Bibliography.

Soviet Policies and Competition

29:173 Allen, Robert L. *Soviet Economic Warfare*. Washington, D.C.: Public Affairs Press, 1960. A detailed account which assumed that economic war would be waged between the two powers as well as over newly emerging nations, that China and other communist nations would help the Soviets, and that the Russian economy would grow rapidly. It has a good description of Soviet trade generally and with Asia, the Middle East, and Latin America. Bibliography.

29:174 Campbell, William H., et al. *U.S.-Soviet Trade: Facts for the Businessman's Appraisal: Structure, Trends, Procedures, Experiences.* Cleveland: Trade Research Associates, 1960. Written during the "Camp David thaw" of 1959–1960, this is a good overview of Soviet trade policies and economic potential. Recommendations are given to businessmen interested in East-West trade, and three case histories are presented of firms involved in the trade. Tables, graphs, maps.

Holzman, F. D. *International Trade under Communism: Politics and Economics* (39:78) traces post-1945 commercial policies, including the Yugoslav and de-Stalinization problems that appeared, notes the development of COMECON and the effect of the Brezhnev Doctrine, and relates these events to détente and Common Market policies in the West.

29:175 Kovner, Milton. *The Challenge of Coexistence: A Study of Soviet Economic Diplomacy.* Washington, D.C.: Public Affairs Press, 1961. An historical survey since the 1920s, the work analyzes U.S.S.R. economic relations with Finland, Israel, the Third World, and the United States, among others. Kovner argues that during coexistence periods economic replaces political-military rivalry. Bibliography.

Smith, G. A. *Soviet Foreign Trade: Organization, Operation, and Policy, 1918–1971* (39:80) compares the Lenin, Stalin, and Khrushchev policies and analyzes East-West as well as Soviet-satellite relationships.

29:176 U.S. House. Committee on Foreign Affairs. *Staff Memorandum on the Communist Economic Offensive.* Washington, D.C.: G.P.O., 1958. The pamphlet argues that the Soviet quest for self-sufficiency is giving way to economic warfare against the West. Using tables on trade growth, it discusses Soviet military assistance and foreign aid, comparing these with the U.S. counterparts.

Liberalization and Restrictions in the 1970s

29:177 Bazhenov, G. "U.S.S.R.-U.S.A.: Businesslike Cooperation." *International Affairs* [Moscow] 20:8 (1974), 15–21. Finding a "fantastic interest among U.S. businessmen" in developing trade with Russia, the Soviet author favorably surveys commercial cooperation in the early 1970s during the period of "normalization" of relations.

29:178 Costick, Miles M. *Economics of Détente and U.S.-Soviet Grain Trade.* Washington, D.C.: Heritage Foundation, 1976. A conservative criticism of U.S. policies which allowed Soviet purchases to upset the U.S. consumer market and aid an inefficient Russian system, the book analyzes Nixon-Ford grain deals and provides background on grain export policies and attendant speculation. Bibliography.

29:179 Finley, David D. "Détente and Soviet-American Trade; An Approach to a Political Balance Sheet." *Studies in Comparative Communism* 8:1/2 (1975), 66–97. Finley engages in a theoretical discussion of whether détente leads to entente, and includes a listing of the positive and negative effects trade has on East-West relations. There is a good table on the amount of materials involved.

29:180 Goldman, Marshall I. *Détente and Dollars: Doing Business with the Soviets.* New York: Basic Books, 1975. Goldman believes trade liberalization will not lead to internal Soviet liberalization and he notes growing Russian deficits in trade. Appendixes provide information on U.S. companies active in the U.S.S.R. Extensive bibliography.

29:181 Grossman, Gregory. "U.S.-Soviet Trade and Economic Relations: Problems and Prospects." *Association for Comparative Economic Studies Bulletin* 15:2 (1973), 3–22. U.S.-U.S.S.R. trade has not been so much affected by lack of most-favored-nation agreement as by failure of U.S. business to understand consumer tastes and problems of selling within Russia.

29:182 Humphrey, Hubert H. *Observations on East-West Economic Relations: U.S.S.R. and Poland, a Trip Report.* Washington, D.C.: G.P.O., 1973. A leading Democrat argues that mutual trade must replace military competition, supporting his argument with discussions of most-favored-nation status, technology transfers, cultural exchange programs, balance-of-payment problems, and the possibility of a vast natural gas deal with the Soviets.

29:183 Leites, Nathan. "The New Economic Togetherness: American and Soviet Reactions." *Studies in Comparative Communism* 7:3 (1974), 246–85. The Russians interpret U.S. efforts to develop trade as a result of American economic problems.

29:184 Mondale, Walter F. "Beyond Détente: Toward International Economic Security." *Foreign Affairs* 53:1 (1974), 1–23. Important partly because of the author (senator and later vice-president) and partly because it was written as East-West economic tensions increased. Mondale believes economic changes are modifying relations and making each bloc less insulated and therefore more vulnerable to economic pressures.

29:185 Sorensen, Theodore C. "Why We Should Trade with the Soviets." *Foreign Affairs* 46:3 (1968), 575–83. The former presidential aide to President Kennedy argues that the political objections to U.S.-U.S.S.R. trade should be set aside so that economic relations could smooth the path to peace and permit American businessmen an opportunity to exploit the Russian market.

29:186 Stern, Paula. *Water's Edge: Domestic Politics and the Making of American Foreign Policy.* Westport, Conn.: Greenwood, 1979. A history of the Jackson Amendment to the Trade Reform Act of 1974, which sought to deny Russia trade concessions until it relaxed its Jewish emigration policies. Stern, who was a congressional staff aide during the trade bill debates, concludes that Jackson's amendment was "good politics" but ineffective foreign policy. Bibliography.

29:187 Trager, James. *The Great Grain Robbery.* New York: Ballantine, 1975. A journalistic exposé arguing that the U.S.S.R. fooled American consumers and officials in the mammoth 1972 grain sales. Contains good information on the U.S. side, especially American agribusiness operations internationally. Bibliography.

29:188 "Trade, Technology, and Leverage." *Foreign Policy,* no. 32 (1978), 63–106. Several scholars debate Soviet-American economic relations, focusing on the question of whether American trade and technology can be used effectively as a lever to press

the U.S.S.R. into more cooperation in the era of détente.

29:189 U.S. Congress. Joint Economic Committee. *Issues in East-West Commercial Relations: A Compendium of Papers.* 95th Cong., 2d Sess., 1979. Eighteen essays which emphasize Western technology transfer, the financing of East-West trade, Soviet-American agricultural trade, and maritime practices. Chronology (1970s) of East-West commercial relations and statistical charts.

29:190 U.S. Congress. Joint Economic Committee. *Soviet Economic Prospects for the Seventies: A Compendium of Papers.* 93d Cong., 1st Sess., 1973. This collection of papers, with many tables, discusses U.S.-Soviet commercial relations since World War II, Soviet financing of trade, industrial cooperation, the 1972 agreements, and trade liberalization.

29:191 Vertrov, A. "Economic Ties between Socialist and Capitalist States." *International Affairs* [Moscow] 16:9 (1970), 7–11. A Soviet view of trade relaxation that urges moving beyond trade in commodities to increased scientific and technical cooperation, and lists the pioneering efforts taken in this regard in East-West relations. Also contains a warning to socialist states to avoid dependence on Western goods.

29:192 Wilczynski, Jozef. *The Multinationals and East-West Relations.* Boulder, Colo.: Westview, 1976. The author believes that not only U.S. multinationals, but Soviet and other East bloc multinationals will increasingly shape international trade until they meet in what he terms "transideological collaboration." List of multinationals involved.

29:193 Yergin, Daniel. "Politics and Soviet-American Trade: The Three Questions." *Foreign Affairs* 55:3 (1977), 517–38. Yergin gives a chronology of 1970s events, emphasizes the role of American politics, and argues that U.S. financing—not just the Jewish emigration question—killed the 1972 trade agreements.

Technology Transfer

29:194 Hanson, Philip. "Technology Transfer to the Soviet Union." *Survey* 23:2 (1977–1978), 73–104. Soviet importation of Western technology through negotiable channels remains small and has not increased dramatically relative to Soviet domestic investment. Negotiable technology transfer has been concentrated in a few industries and has significantly influenced the growth of those industries.

29:195 Hayden, Eric W. *Technology Transfer to East Europe: U.S. Corporate Experience*. New York: Praeger, 1976. Hayden demonstrates how U.S. firms are working out cooperative ventures inside the Soviet sphere. Especially good on Poland, it is a good survey of the entire sphere. Bibliography.

29:196 U.S. Senate. Committee on Governmental Affairs. Hearings; *Transfer of Technology to the Soviet Union and Eastern Europe*. 2 pts. 93d Cong., 2d Sess., 1974; and 95th Cong., 1st Sess., 1977. The 1974 hearings exposed and stopped the sale of equipment which the Soviets could have used for their secret police. Volume 2 contains 1977 testimony of the Texas Instruments' president who has opposed transfer of certain technology to the U.S.S.R.

CULTURAL AND SCIENTIFIC RELATIONS

29:197 Barghoorn, Frederick C. "Cultural Exchanges between Communist Countries and the United States." *Annals of the American Academy of Political and Social Science* 372 (1967), 113–23. Finding that cultural exchanges "reinforce existing tendencies toward rationality, permissiveness, and openness" in communist society, this political scientist and participant surveys exchanges and their difficulties in the 1950s and 1960s.

29:198 Barghoorn, Frederick C. *The Soviet Cultural Offensive: The Role of Cultural Diplomacy in Soviet Foreign Policy*. Princeton, N.J.: Princeton University Press, 1960. A study of the purposes and techniques of Soviet "cultural" diplomacy, which the author closely equates with messianic propaganda. Discussed are such topics as student exchanges, tourist travel, exhibitions, and historical research in the 1950s.

29:199 Byrnes, Robert F. *Soviet-American Academic Exchanges, 1958–1975*. Bloomington: Indiana University Press, 1976. Byrnes gives special attention to the Inter-University Committee and its administration of the principal Soviet-American exchange programs. Bibliography.

29:200 Koehler, Ludmila. "A Cultural Encounter: U.S. Students Visit the U.S.S.R." *Russian Review* 29:4 (1970), 433–43. In the 1960s the Soviets encouraged and helped arrange tours of the Soviet Union by American university students, who have benefited considerably from the cultural aspects of the program, despite limitations on their contact with Russians.

29:201 Seryogin, I. "The Present Stage of Soviet-American Scientific and Technical Cooperation." *International Affairs* [Moscow] 20:2 (1974), 73–78. The author thinks money will be saved, science expanded, and "normalization" of relations served through Soviet-American cooperation. He provides a brief overview of cooperation, including the agreement of 1972, in the areas of space, ocean exploration, stock-breeding, and trade in patents and licenses.

29:202 Twentieth Century Fund. *The Raised Curtain: Report of the Twentieth Century Fund Task Force on Soviet-American Scholarly and Cultural Exchanges*. New York: Twentieth Century Fund, 1977. An evaluation of Soviet-American scholarly and cultural exchanges since the agreement of 1958, this volume enumerates the benefits of the exchanges, but criticizes Soviet restrictions. Herbert Kupferberg's documented "Background Paper" notes that both the United States and U.S.S.R. have sought "political" rewards from the exchanges.

29:203 U.S. House. Committee on Science and Technology. Hearings; *Key Issues in U.S.-U.S.S.R. Scientific Exchanges and Technology Transfers*. 95 Cong., 2d Sess., 1979. Besides the testimony on the state of Soviet-American scientific exchanges at the end of the 1970s, this volume reprints useful articles and statements. Political ramifications, including freedom of inquiry ("human rights") for Soviet scientists, are discussed along with examples of benefits derived from exchanges in such fields as medicine, space, and engineering.

Cooperation in Space

29:204 Frutkin, Arnold W. *International Cooperation in Space*. Englewood Cliffs, N.J.: Prentice-Hall, 1965. This post-Sputnik appeal for scientific cooperation in the conquering of outer space gives special attention to U.S.-U.S.S.R. relations and the limited agreement of 1962.

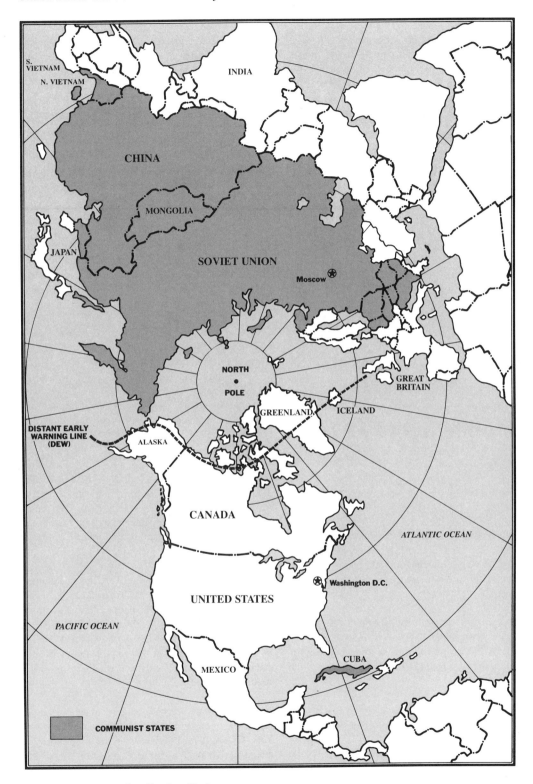

The U.S. Faces the Soviet Union

29:205   Harvey, Dodd L., and Ciccoritti, Linda C. *U.S.-Soviet Cooperation in Space*. Miami: University of Miami, Center for Advanced International Studies, 1974. The authors spell out both the positive and negative aspects of space cooperation (1955–1973), but they argue that the Soviets are self-interested and that the results of cooperative ventures are likely to be limited. Extensive bibliography.

29:206   Malloy, James A., Jr. "The Dryden-Blagonravov Era of Space Cooperation, 1962–1965." *Aerospace Historian* 24:1 (1977), 40–46. This period was one of a concentrated effort at Soviet-American cooperation. Dryden and Blagonravov established a few avenues of agreement, thus preparing the way for more serious collaboration.

29:207   Whelan, Joseph G. "The Press and Khrushchev's 'Withdrawal' from the Moon Race." *Public Opinion Quarterly* 32:2 (1968), 233–50. Since the lunar goal symbolized the whole space effort, this episode was crucial in subsequent U.S. legislative budget cuts.

Détente in the 1970s

For references on the human rights issue, see Chapter 38.

29:208   Barnet, Richard J. *The Giants: Russia and America*. New York: Simon & Schuster, 1977. Barnet discusses the onset of détente and the apparent Soviet imitation of American techniques for projecting global power in the 1970s.

29:209   Brown, Seyom. "A Cooling Off Period for U.S.-Soviet Relations." *Foreign Policy*, no. 28 (1977), 3–21. Brown studies the issues in Soviet-American relations for the 1970s and accounts for the decline of détente.

29:210   Gati, Charles, and Gati, Toby Trister. *The Debate over Détente*. Foreign Policy Association *Headlines Series*, no. 234 (1977), 1–63. This pamphlet provides a useful summary and discussion of the issues (strategic, economic, and political) in Soviet-American détente.

29:211   Gilbert, Stephen P., et al. *Soviet Images of America*. New York: Crane, Russak, 1977. Using published Soviet materials to delineate Soviet perceptions and misconceptions of the United States which have shaped Soviet decisions in world affairs, the authors stress Moscow's image of a weakening United States and the movement toward détente. Bibliography.

29:212   Hurwitz, Leon. "Watergate and Détente: A Content Analysis of Five Communist Newspapers." *Studies in Comparative Communism* 9:3 (1976), 244–56. *Pravda* and *Izvestia*, in contrast to Communist newspapers outside the U.S.S.R., were more favorable to Nixon during the Watergate affair.

29:213   Kraft, Joseph. "Letter from Moscow." *New Yorker* 54 (Oct. 16, 1978), 110ff. An American reporter surveys the troubled Soviet-American relations during the first 18 months of Carter's administration, but sets the story in the diplomacy of earlier years.

29:214   Petrov, Vladimir. *U.S.-Soviet Detente: Past and Future*. Washington, D.C.: American Enterprise Institute for Public Policy Research, 1975. This slim volume examines and appraises détente, especially as perceived by the Soviet Union. The Soviets will adhere to détente while expanding their economic and military strength and will avoid ideologically inspired crusades. The United States, on the other hand, must be alert to Soviet intentions.

29:215   Pranger, Robert J., ed. *Détente and Defense: A Reader*. Washington, D.C.: American Enterprise Institute for Public Policy Research, 1976. Containing numerous diplomatic documents and statements for and against détente, this anthology provides an extensive airing of the topic, including SALT.

29:216   Rubinstein, Alvin Z. "The Elusive Parameters of Détente." *Orbis* 19:4 (1976), 1344–58. Since 1968, détente for the United States has been a series of tactical responses to key problems. For the U.S.S.R., détente derives from the China problem, the desire for Western technology, recognition of the territorial status quo in Europe, and from stabilization of the strategic arms race.

29:217   Schwab, George, and Friedlander, Henry, eds. *Detente in Historical Perspective*. 2d ed. New York: Cyrco, 1978. Political scientists and historians, including Hans J. Morgenthau and Arthur M. Schlesinger, Jr., discuss the pros and cons of détente. Documents.

29:218 Schwartz, Morton. *Soviet Perceptions of the United States.* Berkeley: University of California Press, 1978. Schwartz argues that in the 1970s the Soviets took a more pragmatic and sophisticated view of the United States, displaying less doctrinal rigidity and more analytical flexibility, thereby serving détente. Bibliography.

29:219 Simes, Dimitri K. *Detente and Conflict: Soviet Foreign Policy, 1972–1977.* Beverly Hills, Calif.: Sage, 1977. This brief study of Moscow's détente diplomacy by a 1973 emigré Soviet scholar stresses domestic U.S.S.R. constraints which limit détente. Bibliography.

29:220 Sobel, Lester A., ed. *Kissinger and Detente.* New York: Facts on File, 1975. An almost day-by-day factual account of American relations with the U.S.S.R. and China (1968–1975). A handy reference aid.

29:221 Sonnenfeldt, Helmut. "Russia, America and Détente." *Foreign Affairs* 56:2 (1978), 275–94. The Carter administration hoped to deemphasize America's preoccupation with the U.S.S.R., yet Russia's steady accumulation of military strength dictated against it. Specific negotiations will have little effect on the Soviet compulsion to amass power.

29:222 U.S. Senate. Committee on Foreign Relations. Hearings; *Détente.* 93d Cong., 2d Sess., 1975. These informative 1974 hearings attracted an impressive group of witnesses (among them were Henry A. Kissinger, W. Averell Harriman, and Dean Rusk). An excellent place to begin to understand the objectives and criticisms of détente.

29:223 U.S. Senate. Committee on Foreign Relations. *Perceptions: Relations between the United States and the Soviet Union.* 95th Cong., 2d Sess., 1978. This large collection of essays probes Soviet interests, attitudes, objectives, and capabilities—and American responses—in the era of détente. It includes such questions as human rights, trade, cultural exchange, arms negotiations, and the domestic factors shaping Soviet diplomacy.

29:224 Urban, G. R., ed. *Détente.* New York: Universe Books, 1976. Printed here is a series of interviews conducted by Urban for broadcast over Radio Free Europe (1973–1975). Among the European, British, and American interviewees on the subject of détente and Nixon-Kissinger policy are George W.

Ball, Zbigniew Brzezinski, Alfred Grosser, Sir William Hayter, Dean Rusk, and Adam Ulam. Urban's questions are informed and the answers lengthy.

CASE FOR DÉTENTE

Bell, C. *The Diplomacy of Détente: The Kissinger Era* (24:219) defends détente and concludes: "Detente does not mean that the power contest has ended. It only proposes a mode by which it may be made less dangerous and pointed in a more creative direction."

29:225 Gromyko, Anatolii A. "The Future of Soviet-American Diplomacy." *Annals of the American Academy of Political and Social Science* 414 (1974), 27–40. Détente, as seen in the Soviet Union, is a process of relaxation of tension and peaceful coexistence. The scientific and technological revolution will have a profound impact on this process.

29:226 Kennan, George F. *The Cloud of Danger: Current Realities of American Foreign Policy.* Boston: Little, Brown, 1977. This veteran observer of Soviet-American relations takes a broad, critical look at American foreign policy, devoting considerable attention to the need for détente. He particularly attempts to refute alarmists who exaggerate the Soviet threat because they incorrectly view Soviet leaders as warmongers.

29:227 Neal, Fred Warner, ed. *Détente or Debacle: Common Sense in U.S.-Soviet Relations.* New York: Norton, 1979. This collection, with essays by George F. Kennan, John Kenneth Galbraith, G. B. Kistiakowsky, and Samuel Pisar, among others, deals with questions such as trade, human rights, and SALT and the arms race. A brief summary of the case for détente.

29:228 Nikolayev, Y. "A New Milestone in Soviet-American Relations." *International Affairs* [Moscow] 20:9 (1974), 3–15. This Soviet view of détente, revealing why Moscow sought accommodation with the United States, gives special attention to the June–July 1974 talks in Moscow.

29:229 Simes, Dimitri K. "The Anti-Soviet Brigade." *Foreign Policy,* no. 37 (1979–1980), 28–42. Simes identifies the foes of cooperation with the Soviet Union—the "anti-détente coalition"—and critically analyzes their complaints, faulting these "new cold warriors" for blaming the Soviets for America's own failures.

CRITICISMS OF DÉTENTE

29:230 Barghoorn, Frederick C. *Détente and the Democratic Movement in the USSR.* New York: Free Press, 1976. Barghoorn's thesis is that détente "is and will remain seriously flawed and limited as long as the Soviet rulers maintain an oppressive internal regime." An outspoken study of and identification with Soviet dissidents and a forceful statement on behalf of American demands for "human rights" in Russia.

29:231 Conquest, Robert. *Present Danger: Towards a Foreign Policy.* Stanford, Calif.: Hoover Institution Press, 1979. Conquest paints a gloomy picture of Soviet-American relations, with America's task being that of avoiding nuclear war and surrender to Soviet despotism.

29:232 Draper, Theodore. "Détente." *Commentary* 57:6 (1974), 25–47. This wide-ranging critical review of the Kissinger-Nixon foreign policy faults détente for being "a go-for-broke operation." Draper updates his criticism in "Appeasement and Détente," *Commentary* 61:2 (1976), 27–38, arguing that Americans were being "beguiled" by détente in the face of long-term Soviet "imperial pressures."

29:233 Institute for Contemporary Studies. *Defending America.* San Francisco: Basic Books, 1977. Seeing the Soviet Union as an unceasing menace, Theodore Draper, Paul Seabury, Robert Conquest, and others strongly attack détente.

29:234 Meany, George. "Détente and the Workingman." *Atlantic Community Quarterly* 14:1 (1976), 37–41. The president of the AFL-CIO, in vigorous cold war anticommunist language, angrily scores détente as appeasement of the "imperialist" Soviets, who suppress their workers and threaten world peace.

29:235 Pipes, Richard. "Détente: Moscow's View." In Richard Pipes, ed., *Soviet Strategy in Europe.* New York: Crane, Russak, 1976, pp. 3–44. A leading critic of détente, Pipes complains that it has largely favored the U.S.S.R., which he depicts as an expansionist state.

29:236 Pipes, Richard. *U.S.-Soviet Relations in the Era of Détente: A Tragedy of Errors.* Boulder, Colo.: Westview, 1981. Highly critical of détente, Pipes, who became an adviser to the Reagan administration in 1981, believes that the Soviets tried deceptively to use détente to outdistance the United States in weapons development. He argues that a "grand strategy" underlies Soviet foreign policy.

29:237 Solzhenitsyn, Aleksandr. *Détente: Prospects for Democracy and Dictatorship.* New Brunswick, N.J.: Transaction, 1976. One of the Soviet Union's most outspoken dissidents and exiles vigorously attacks the movement toward détente. Appended to Solzhenitsyn's comments are the critical reactions of several scholars.

29:238 Weeks, Albert L. *The Troubled Détente.* New York: New York University Press, 1976. Finding communist ideology the driving force in Soviet foreign policy, Weeks surveys Soviet ideas and negotiating behavior since Lenin. He concludes that détente is just another way for the Soviet Union "to control or at least strongly influence key areas of the globe while strengthening its economy...." Bibliography.

30

United States, Southeast Asia, and the Indochina Wars since 1941

Contributing Editor

GEORGE C. HERRING
University of Kentucky

Contents

Introduction

From 1941 to 1975, Southeast Asia assumed a central role in United States foreign policy, a position it had not occupied before and seems unlikely to regain in the foreseeable future. Before World War II, most of the region remained under European colonial control, and American influence was small. The Japanese conquest of Southeast Asia in 1941–1942 impressed upon Americans for the first time the economic and strategic importance of the region, leading to increased postwar involvement, and during the 1950s, Southeast Asia became a major battleground in the cold war.

The eruption of revolutions throughout the area, many of them assumed to be under communist control or subject to communist influence, aroused grave concern for the stability of a region deemed vital to the United States. The communist triumph in China in 1949 added a direct and ominous threat. To contain the perceived communist menace, the United States initiated large-scale economic and military assistance to the newly independent nations of Southeast Asia, the French in Indochina, and the British in Malaya. When a French defeat in 1954 appeared to endanger the region still further, the United States took the lead in creating the Southeast Asia Treaty Organization, a collective security arrangement through which it assumed defense commitments to a number of nations.

Containment of communism in Southeast Asia led to the dispatch of combat forces to Vietnam in 1965, eventually resulting in America's longest and most traumatic war. Following the end of the Vietnam War in 1975, however, many of the programs established in the 1950s languished, and Southeast Asia again receded into an area of secondary importance.

Despite the interest stirred by the Vietnam War, scholarly writing on U.S. relations with Southeast Asia remains limited in volume and fragmentary in coverage. Documentation from the American side is available only through 1951, and from the side of the former colonial powers and the Southeast Asian nations themselves is virtually nonexistent. Because of the specialized knowledge and linguistic skills required to deal with the diverse cultures of Southeast Asia, few scholars have studied the region intensively, and although area studies programs proliferated in American universities during the Vietnam War, the results thus far have been small. Most of the work has been done by a handful of journalists, political scientists, and area specialists, and much of it is ephemeral. There are few monographs dealing with specific topics. Only Russell Fifield has attempted a broad, up-to-date survey of American relations with Southeast Asia, and his work, *Americans in Southeast Asia: The Roots of Commitment* (30:62), stops in 1954.

Inasmuch as there has been historiographical debate, it has been an offshoot of the debate on Vietnam and the larger issue of U.S. relations with third world countries. Most Americans agreed during the heyday of the cold war that the United States had vital interests in Southeast Asia that required major increments of economic and military aid, collective security arrangements, even the commitment of military forces. While not questioning the premises upon which policy was based, some critics did challenge the methods employed. With particular reference to Vietnam, the journalists Robert Shaplen, in *The Lost Revolution* (30:160), and David Halberstam, in *The Making of a Quagmire* (30:162), argued that the United States was devoting too much attention to military assistance without doing enough to promote economic development and that it was supporting reactionary governments at the expense of political freedom. On a regional basis and in more restrained tones, Fifield's *Southeast Asia in United States Policy* (30:63) advanced many of the same criticisms.

By the late 1960s, the policy itself had come under heavy fire. Stating a position increasingly endorsed by liberals, David P. Mozingo's "Containment in Asia Reconsidered" (30:65) argued that the political stability and industrial base which had made containment workable in Europe did not exist in Southeast Asia and warned that a policy which sought to uphold the status quo in a region swept by revolutionary change was doomed to fail. Escalation of the Vietnam War produced a radical school of thought which went much deeper in its indictment. In *The Roots of American Foreign Policy* (2:93), Gabriel Kolko charged that

U.S. policy in Southeast Asia and Vietnam was characteristic of the American approach to the Third World. To maintain its vulnerable economy, the United States had imposed on Third World countries exploitative arrangements which gave it access to raw materials and markets for its finished products on favorable terms. To uphold these arrangements, the United States supported reactionary governments and used its military power unsparingly to subdue nationalist revolutions.

In contrast to Southeast Asia as a whole, the Vietnam War has produced a body of literature which is surprisingly large and varied given the nearness of the event. In its various phases, American involvement in Vietnam spanned a quarter of a century, and the length of the conflict alone perhaps ensured that it would be intensively studied while in progress. By the mid-1960s, moreover, the war had become the most controversial issue in recent American history, and the publication of the *Pentagon Papers* (30:18, 30:19) in 1971 made available to writers an unusually large quantity of documents at an early stage. The result is a sizeable body of writing, much of it of very good quality.

A noisy and frequently bitter debate erupted as soon as the United States escalated the war in 1965, continued for the duration of the conflict, and persisted in only slightly modified form and in more subdued tones after its end. Official spokesmen justified intervention on the grounds that the fall of Vietnam to communism would cause the loss of all of Southeast Asia, with disastrous political, economic, and strategic consequences for the United States. By the mid-1960s, the official rationale had come under attack from several quarters. Radicals such as Kolko charged that the American "ruling class" had intervened in Vietnam to demonstrate that revolution could not succeed, thereby perpetuating its domination of the world economy. Liberals, many of whom had supported American involvement in its early stages, argued that the United States had unwisely intervened in a civil Vietnamese conflict only remotely connected to the cold war and had staked its prestige in an area of marginal importance. In an early attempt to uncover the sources of American misperception, Arthur Schlesinger, Jr., advanced the so-called quagmire thesis, (30:146) the idea that overly optimistic advisers had misled reluctant presidents step by step into the quagmire of Vietnam. Former State Department official James Thomson's influential essay, "How Could Vietnam Happen? An Autopsy" (30:148), similarly traced the debacle to bureaucratic error and malfunctions. Synthesizing the liberal critique, Halberstam's best-seller, *The Best and the Brightest* (30:144), also blamed the hubris of the policymakers, particularly Lyndon Johnson, and accused them of deceiving an unwilling nation into an unwanted war.

As passions subsided and more documentation became available, scholars sought deeper explanations for American involvement. In *The Irony of Vietnam: The System Worked* (30:143), Leslie Gelb vigorously challenged the quagmire thesis and the bureaucratic argument, contending that presidents from Truman to Nixon, with full support from Congress and the public, had knowingly perpetuated a bloody stalemate in Vietnam to forestall, at least temporarily, the presumably catastrophic consequences of a communist victory. Gelb thus concluded that "the system worked"—the bureaucracy functioned as it was supposed to and the United States maintained a non-communist South Vietnam until domestic support evaporated. He also concluded that the policy failed, however, arguing that the doctrine of containment inevitably led to excessive commitments in peripheral areas.

In the aftermath of war, writers also vigorously debated the causes of American failure. Participants such as General William Westmoreland, *A Soldier Reports* (30:45), insisted that had the civilian leadership employed America's vast military power decisively, instead of hedging it about with restrictions, victory could have been attained. In his controversial study, *America in Vietnam* (30:184), political scientist Guenter Lewy upheld the necessity of American intervention, exonerated the United States from charges of war crimes, and argued that the nation could and should have prevailed. Lewy placed primary blame on the military, however, arguing that they foolishly attempted to apply conventional war strategies in a guerrilla war. The most recent survey of American involvement, George Herring's *America's Longest War* (30:24), takes issue with both points of view, concluding that the weakness of South Vietnam, the determination of North Vietnam, and the international and domestic constraints on American power, made failure inevitable. At this writing, there is no consensus on the major issues raised by the war, and the debate seems likely to continue.

Despite the profusion of writing on the war, U.S. involvement with Southeast Asia and Vietnam remains an underdeveloped area in terms of scholarship. There is a great need for broad synthetic overviews of American relations with the region and with individual nations. The American response to the Southeast Asian revolutions at the end of World War II is only beginning to be analyzed. Much work needs to be done in such broad areas as intercultural relations, the impact of U.S. military and economic aid, and the effects of American political involvement. Scholars have only scratched the surface in regard to the Vietnam War. The American decisionmaking process has been studied in depth, but the continuing availability of new documentation makes it a still profitable area of investigation. Very little work has been done on pacification, the economic and social effects of American escalation, U.S. involvement in South Vietnamese politics, and the diplomacy of the war. Lessons learned from Vietnam will likely have a profound effect on American policy for years to come. Despite the apparent waning of interest in Southeast Asia and the inherent difficulties in the subject, this topic offers an exciting and potentially vital area of investigation for diplomatic historians.

Resources and Overviews

RESEARCH AIDS

While the pertinent bibliographies and reference aids are listed here, there are more extensive lists in Chapter 1.

Bibliographies

30:1   Bixler, Paul. *Southeast Asia: Bibliographic Directions in a Complex Area*. Middletown, Conn.: Choice, 1974. This is a brief series of bibliographical essays dealing with the countries of the region as well as specific topics such as the overseas Chinese.

30:2   Burns, Richard Dean, and Leitenberg, Milton. *The Indochina Wars, 1941–1982*. Santa Barbara, Calif.: ABC-Clio, 1983. This expanded edition of Leitenberg and Burns, *The Vietnam Conflict* (1973), lists nearly 5,000 books, bibliographies, dissertations, documents, and articles related to the three Indochina wars. It concentrates on the Second Indochina War, and includes materials on Cambodia, Laos, and Thailand, in addition to U.S.-Vietnamese affairs.

30:3   Chen, John H. M. *Vietnam: A Comprehensive Bibliography*. Metuchen, N.J.: Scarecrow, 1973. Lists over 2,300 items, mainly books and documents, Vietnamese as well as Western.

Dexter, B., ed. *The Foreign Affairs Fifty-Year Bibliography: New Evaluation of Significant Books on International Relations, 1920–1970* (1:14) is a very useful condensation and new evaluation of books listed in the *Foreign Affairs Bibliographies*.

Foreign Affairs Bibliography: A Selected and Annotated List of Books on International Relations (1:15) is a useful annotated bibliography on all aspects of international affairs.

Hay, S. N., and Case, M. H. *Southeast Asian History: A Bibliographic Guide* (1:103) is a comprehensive, well-annotated bibliography.

30:4   Morrison, Gayle, comp.; Hay, Stephen, ed. *A Guide to Books on Southeast Asian History (1961–1966)*. Santa Barbara, Calif.: ABC-Clio, 1968. Updates Hay's *Southeast Asian History* (1:103) by including books published between 1961 and 1966, but it does not include articles and dissertations. The annotations are full and useful.

Onorato, M. P., ed. *Philippine Bibliography (1899–1946)* (1:95) is a useful, brief introduction to the Philippines.

Pelzer, K. J. *West Malaysia and Singapore: A Selected Bibliography* (1:104) is a comprehensive, unannotated bibliography.

30:5   Phan Tien Chau. *Vietnamese Communism: A Research Bibliography*. Westport, Conn.: Greenwood, 1975. A bibliography of 3,400 items in various languages, including English, it covers a broad range of subjects.

30:6   Thombley, Woodworth G., and Stiffin, William J. *Thailand: Politics, Economy, and Socio-Cultural Setting: A Selective Guide to the Literature*. Bloomington: Indiana University Press, 1972. A valuable introduction to the literature, listing dissertations, as well as articles and books, it includes brief annotations.

30:7   Trager, Frank N. *Burma: A Selected and Annotated Bibliography*. New Haven, Conn.: Human Relations Area Files Press, 1973. This is an exhaustive bibliography, containing more than 2,000 items.

30:8   Tregonning, Kennedy G. *Southeast Asia: A Critical Bibliography*. Tucson: University of Arizona Press, 1969. The most comprehensive bibliography on the subject, it lists over 2,000 items and includes articles as well as books on Southeast Asian history and culture, with brief annotations.

Historiographical Essays

30:9 Braestrup, Peter. "Vietnam as History." *Wilson Quarterly* 2:2 (1978), 178–87. A brief, but comprehensive and critical survey of the major works that have been published on Vietnam since 1968.

30:10 Dunn, Joe P. "In Search of Lessons: The Development of a Vietnam Historiography." *Parameters* 9:4 (1979), 28–40. This up-to-date survey of the literature on Vietnam attempts to highlight broad trends in interpretation and it includes a large listing of major works. Dunn emphasizes the recent emergence of a "mild revisionism," more restrained and balanced than the predominantly antiwar writings of the 1960s and early 1970s.

30:11 Siracusa, Joseph M. "The United States, Viet Nam, and the Cold War: A Reappraisal." *Journal of Southeast Asian Studies* 5:1 (1974), 82–101. A useful analysis of early writings on Vietnam, it argues that American intervention must be studied in the larger context of the cold war assumptions and "mind-sets" that took root during 1945 to 1950.

Atlases and Other Aids

30:12 *Atlas of Southeast Asia.* Intro. by D. G. E. Hall. London: Macmillan, 1964. The 23-page introduction by Hall emphasizes political and historical development; the photographs illustrate some important aspects, the countries and their peoples.

Facts on File: A Weekly Digest with Cumulative Index (1:151) is a convenient weekly summary of major news events, domestic and foreign.

Keesing's Contemporary Archives: Weekly Diary of World Events (1:152) is the British equivalent of *Facts on File.*

Stockholm International Peace Research Institute. *World Armaments and Disarmament: The SIPRI Yearbook* [1968–.] (40:9) contains materials on military operations during the Vietnam War.

Vital Speeches of the Day (1:153) reprints major addresses by public figures.

Document Collections

More general collections are listed in Chapter 1, and other collections may be found in "Personalities," below.

Columbia Broadcasting System. *Face the Nation: The Collected Transcripts from CBS Radio and Television Broadcasts, 1954–1971* (1:347).

Declassified Documents Quarterly (24:4) is a guide to recently declassified government documents. Indexed and keyed to microfiche copies of the documents.

30:13 Falk, Richard A., ed. *The Vietnam War and International Law.* 4 vols. Princeton, N.J.: Princeton University Press, 1967–1976. Falk's massive collection of articles, documents, and legal opinions covering the manifold legal questions raised by the war carries a distinctly antiwar tone, but various points of view are represented.

Gallup, G. H. *The Gallup Poll: Public Opinion, 1935–1971* (1:348) includes data from some 7,000 polls dealing with all aspects of national life, with considerable attention paid to foreign affairs.

30:14 Heath, G. Louis, ed. *Mutiny Does Not Happen Lightly: The Literature of the American Resistance to the Vietnam War.* Metuchen, N.J.: Scarecrow, 1976. Although poorly organized, these original materials constitute a comprehensive introduction to the primary sources of the anti-Vietnam War movement. Especially useful are the various ephemeral materials. Bibliography.

U.S. Department of State. *Press Conferences of the Secretaries of State, 1922–1974* (1:360) is a microfilmed typescript, verbatim record of these conferences.

30:15 *Vietnam: The Definitive Documentation of Human Decisions.* Ed. by Gareth Porter. 2 vols. Stanfordville, N.Y.: Coleman, 1979. This is a useful collection of materials, and includes some documents not printed elsewhere. Its major contribution lies in its collecting and translating of Vietnamese materials.

The Pentagon Papers

30:16 Kahin, George M. "The Pentagon Papers: A Critical Evaluation." *American Political Science Review* 69:2 (1975), 675–84. This indispensable, critical analysis compares the three editions of the *Pentagon*

Papers and assesses their value and shortcomings as a historical source. Bibliographic notes.

30:17   Sheehan, Neil, et al. *The Pentagon Papers as Published by the New York Times.* Chicago: Quadrangle, 1971. A brief, readable, and handy collection, this is a synopsis of the original Pentagon analyses written by the staff of the *New York Times* as well as a sampling of the major documents, some of which are not included in other editions.

30:18   U.S. Department of Defense. *The Pentagon Papers: The Defense Department History of United States Decision Making on Vietnam: The Senator Gravel Edition.* 5 vols. Boston: Beacon, 1971–1972. The most complete and orderly of the three editions of the *Pentagon Papers,* it contains most of the original historical analyses but fewer documents than the Department of Defense edition. Volume 5 includes an index and critical commentaries.

30:19   U.S. Department of Defense. *United States-Vietnam Relations, 1945–1967: Study.* 12 vols. Washington, D.C.: G.P.O., 1971. Although poorly printed and difficult to use, this edition (sometimes referred to as the Hebert edition) contains the most extensive collection of documents on American policymaking in Vietnam. When used in conjunction with the other editions, it is an indispensable source.

OVERVIEWS

See Chapter 24, "Overviews," for surveys of U.S. foreign affairs since World War II.

30:20   Clubb, Oliver E., Jr. *The United States and the Sino-Soviet Bloc in Southeast Asia.* Washington, D.C.: Brookings Institution, 1962. A brief, sparsely documented essay which surveys great power rivalry in Southeast Asia in the post–World War II era. Although dated, it is useful for the insights of the "experts" on the policy issues of the 1950s and early 1960s.

30:21   Colbert, Evelyn Speyer. *Southeast Asia in International Politics, 1941–1956.* Ithaca, N.Y.: Cornell University Press, 1977. In a broad narrative tracing the origins of great power rivalry in Southeast Asia, Colbert offers few conclusions, but she provides a valuable introduction to the subject. Bibliography.

30:22   Cooper, Chester L. *The Lost Crusade: America in Vietnam.* New York: Dodd, Mead, 1970. A comprehensive account from the end of World War II through the Johnson administration which stresses the futility of U.S. involvement. It remains one of the better studies of the subject. The author, who was involved in policymaking in the 1960s, provides valuable insights into policymaking and into the peace initiatives (1965–1967). Bibliography.

30:23   Fitzgerald, Frances. *Fire in the Lake: The Vietnamese and the Americans in Vietnam.* Boston: Little, Brown, 1972. In a passionate indictment of American involvement in Vietnam, the author stresses the legitimacy of the Vietminh revolution, which, she argues, had deep roots in Vietnamese political culture and which the Americans failed to comprehend. The argument is highly controversial, but the book is essential for understanding the Vietnamese side of the struggle. Bibliography.

30:24   Herring, George C. *America's Longest War: The United States and Vietnam, 1950–1975.* New York: Wiley, 1979. This is an up-to-date, comprehensive, and readable account which relies heavily on recently declassified documents, and provides the best overview of the subject. Extensive, critical bibliography.

30:25   Kahin, George M., and Lewis, John W. *The United States in Vietnam.* Rev. ed. New York: Delta, 1969. This was one of the first scholarly critiques of American policy in Vietnam and remains one of the best. Emphasizing the Vietnamese dimensions of the conflict, Kahin and Lewis argue that by opposing first the Vietminh and later the Vietcong and North Vietnam, the United States placed itself against the one viable political force in Vietnam, a force whose basic goals stemmed more from nationalism than from communist ideology. Bibliography.

30:26   Kendrick, Alexander. *The Wound within: America in the Vietnam Years, 1945–1974.* Boston: Little, Brown, 1974. A dramatic account which, although superficial on many questions, nevertheless provides a useful overview and gives good coverage to the domestic impact of the war. Bibliography.

30:27   Martin, Edwin W. *Southeast Asia and China: The End of Containment.* Boulder, Colo.: Westview, 1977. A brief analysis by a former foreign service officer of the realignment of power in Southeast Asia following the American withdrawal from Vietnam and its implications for U.S. policy.

30:28 Poole, Peter A. *Eight Presidents and Indochina.* Huntington, N.Y.: Krieger, 1978. Relying primarily on published documents, the former foreign service officer has put together a careful and balanced survey of American involvement with Indochina from the outbreak of World War II to late 1977. The book provides a useful overview of the subject.

30:29 Shaplen, Robert. *Time Out of Hand: Revolution and Reaction in Southeast Asia.* Rev. ed. New York: Harper & Row, 1970. This is a sweeping, frequently provocative survey of Southeast Asian politics in the 1960s.

Personalities

Additional references on individuals may be found in Chapter 1, "Biographical Data."

AMERICAN

See Chapter 24, "Personalities" and "Presidential Administrations," for additional references.

George W. Ball

See also Chapter 24, "Personalities."

30:30 Ball, George W. "Top Secret: The Prophecy the President Rejected." *Atlantic* 230 (June 1972), 35–49. Ball, the major dissenter to U.S. involvement within the State Department, prints a memorandum reflecting his mid-1960s views.

John Foster Dulles

See Chapter 24, "Personalities," for additional references.

Hoopes, T. *The Devil and John Foster Dulles* (24:112) reviews Dulles's activities during the 1950s, particularly during the First Indochina War.

Dwight D. Eisenhower

See Chapter 24, "Personalities," for additional references.

Eisenhower, D. D. *The White House Years* (24:114) contains in volume 1, *Mandate for Change, 1953–*

1956, the president's reluctance to intervene in the First Indochina War.

Parmet, H. *Eisenhower and the American Crusades* (24:205) revises the traditional view of the U.S. role in the Dien Bien Phu crisis.

J. William Fulbright

See Chapter 24, "Personalities," for additional references.

30:31 Fulbright, J. William. *The Arrogance of Power.* New York: Random House, 1966. This volume provides useful insights into Fulbright's rationale for shifting from supporting the Johnson administration to opposing it on Vietnam intervention.

Johnson, H., and Gwertzman, B. M. *Fulbright: The Dissenter* (24:118) is the most thorough biography of the longtime chairman of the Senate Foreign Relations Committee (1959–1974), through 1967.

W. Averell Harriman

See also Chapter 24, "Personalities."

Harriman, W. A. *America and Russia in a Changing World: A Half Century of Personal Observation* (24:119) suggests that, had Kennedy lived, the United States would not have gotten bogged down in Vietnam. He also includes interesting insights on the Paris peace talks.

Roger Hilsman

Hilsman, R. *To Move a Nation: The Politics of Foreign Policy in the Administration of John F. Kennedy* (24:213) is a memoir by a top adviser to Kennedy on counterinsurgency. Hilsman was intimately involved in the shaping of the strategic hamlet program and in the decisions that led to the overthrow of Ngo Dinh Diem.

30:32 Pelz, Stephen E. "'When Do I Have Time to Think?' John F. Kennedy, Roger Hilsman, and the Laotian Crisis of 1962." *Diplomatic History* 3:2 (1979), 215–29. Pelz publishes here, along with extended critical commentary, a lengthy document in which Hilsman recounts the administration's response to the Laotian crisis of 1962. Pelz concludes that policymaking in the Kennedy administration was "helter-skelter" rather than systematic and carefully calculated.

Lyndon B. Johnson

See Chapter 24, "Personalities," for additional references.

Johnson, L. B. *The Vantage Point: Perspectives on the Presidency, 1963–1969* (24:120) is dull and apologetic and reveals little of a colorful and dynamic personality, but it includes excerpts from many documents which remain classified and therefore provides an essential source for the study of the Vietnam conflict.

Kearns, D. *Lyndon Johnson and the American Dream* (24:121) is a psychobiography that is less than persuasive, but it provides some valuable insights into Johnson's personality and leadership style.

Schandler, H. Y. *The Unmaking of a President: Lyndon Johnson and Vietnam* (30:222).

John F. Kennedy

See Chapters 24 and 29, "Personalities," for additional references.

Hill, K. L. "President Kennedy and the Neutralization of Laos" (30:109) finds that of the policy alternatives for Laos available to President John F. Kennedy, none was really attractive. Kennedy questioned the wisdom of the Eisenhower administration's commitments and thought their implications were potentially dangerous.

30:33   Mahajani, Usha. "President Kennedy and United States Policy in Laos, 1961–1963." *Journal of Southeast Asian Studies* 2:2 (1971), 87–99. An appraisal which praises Kennedy for the Laos negotiations but concludes that his post-Geneva policies eventually undermined the 1962 settlement.

30:34   Patrick, Richard. "Presidential Leadership in Foreign Affairs Reexamined: Kennedy and Laos without Radical Revisionism." *World Affairs* 140:3 (1978), 245–58. Patrick attempts to rebut the revisionist stereotype of Kennedy as a cold warrior and to establish, through study of the Laotian crisis of 1961, a model for presidential leadership in foreign policy. His conclusions, provocative although overstated, are that Kennedy's commitment to neutralization of Laos fostered détente and that his methods of crisis management established a "prototype in need of development for the third century of American democracy."

Schlesinger, A. M., Jr. *A Thousand Days: John F. Kennedy in the White House* (24:215) is a highly sympathetic personal history which contains valuable insights into the policy debates on Vietnam and the president's thinking.

Henry A. Kissinger

See Chapter 24, "Personalities," for additional references.

Kalb, M., and Kalb, B. *Kissinger* (24:131) is an admiring volume which contains useful detail on Kissinger's role in the peace negotiations of 1972–1973. The book should be compared with the more critical accounts of Kissinger's policies by Shawcross (30:80), Morris (24:223), and Szulc (24:226).

Kissinger, H. A. *White House Years* (24:133) devotes more than one-third of this 1,500-page memoir of the first Nixon administration to Vietnam, arguing that the policies pursued were the only ones consistent with America's global interests. He quotes at length from internal documents and his own papers and diaries, making this an invaluable source.

30:35   Kissinger, Henry A. "The Vietnam Negotiations." *Foreign Affairs* 47:2 (1969), 211–34. Written before Kissinger was appointed Nixon's national security adviser, this essay contains an insightful critique of the Johnson strategy in Vietnam and anticipates the Nixon and Kissinger policies.

Morris, R. *Uncertain Greatness: Henry Kissinger and American Foreign Policy* (24:223) is highly critical of Kissinger's handling of Vietnam. The volume is valuable for its inside account of Kissinger's methods of operations and the formulation of the Nixon-Kissinger Vietnam policy in 1969–1970.

Henry Cabot Lodge, Jr.

See also Chapter 24, "Personalities."

Lodge, H. C., Jr. *The Storm Has Many Eyes: A Personal Narrative* (24:137) is a disappointing memoir, quite thin and very defensive on Lodge's service as ambassador to Vietnam and his role in the 1963 coup.

Richard M. Nixon

See Chapter 24, "Personalities," for additional references.

Nixon, R. M. *RN: The Memoirs of Richard Nixon* (24:145) is one of the more valuable presidential memoirs of recent years. Nixon frequently reveals more of himself than he intends. In regard to Vietnam, this volume is particularly valuable for the abortive peace effort of 1969 and for the 1972–1973 negotiations that led to American withdrawal.

30:36 Nixon, Richard M. "Asia after Vietnam." *Foreign Affairs* 46:1 (1967), 111–25. In this important essay written during his political comeback, Nixon reveals his keen personal interest in the future of Asia and hints at the outlines of his policies toward the Vietnam War and China.

Schell, J. *The Time of Illusion* (24:242) is a bitter indictment of the Nixon administration which argues that Vietnam and Watergate were inextricably linked as part of an obsessive effort by Nixon and his entourage to maintain their "credibility" in the face of threats real and imagined at home and abroad. Schell overstates his thesis, but demonstrates the links between foreign and domestic policy in the Nixon years.

Szulc, T. *The Illusion of Peace: Foreign Policy in the Nixon-Kissinger Years* (24:226) makes no attempt to hide his dislike for Nixon and Kissinger's policies and methods of operation. *The Illusion of Peace*, nevertheless, provides useful detail on such topics as the peace effort of 1969, the invasion of Cambodia, Nixon's response to the 1972 Easter Offensive, and the 1972–1973 peace negotiations.

Franklin D. Roosevelt
See Chapters 21, 22, and 23, "Personalities," for additional references.

30:37 Hess, Gary R. "Franklin D. Roosevelt and Indochina." *Journal of American History* 59:2 (1972), 353–68. A careful study which suggests that Roosevelt's trusteeship plan offered a possible alternative to thirty years of conflict in Indochina and "deserved more thoughtful consideration by the Allies and more vigorous advocacy by Roosevelt than it received."

30:38 LaFeber, Walter. "Roosevelt, Churchill and Indochina, 1942–1945." *American Historical Review* 80:5 (1975), 1277–95. A provocative analysis which argues that Roosevelt's trusteeship scheme was part of a larger U.S. plan to replace British influence in East Asia. The strategy—and the trusteeship plan with it—collapsed as a result of Roosevelt's inability to impose it on the British and French and because of the political weakness of Chiang Kai-shek.

Others
Allison, J. M. *Ambassador from the Prairie, or, Allison Wonderland* (24:167) is an informative memoir by a foreign service officer with one chapter on his tour as ambassador to Indonesia, 1957–1958.

Bohlen, C. E. *Witness to History: 1929–1969* (24:98) discusses his tour as ambassador to the Philippines.

Cohen, W. I. *Dean Rusk* (24:148) is an account of Presidents Kennedy and Johnson's secretary of state. Rusk's role in the U.S. decision to intervene in Vietnam is reviewed.

Colby, W. E., and Forbath, P. *Honorable Men: My Life in the CIA* (40:92) is defensive. Colby is tight-lipped about many of the agency's activities, but he does provide a useful discussion of such things as clandestine operations against North Vietnam, American involvement in the 1963 coup, and the Phoenix Program.

Ford, G. R. *A Time to Heal* (24:172) contains a brief discussion of the president's response to the fall of South Vietnam and the *Mayaguez* crisis.

30:39 Galbraith, John Kenneth. *Ambassador's Journal: A Personal Account of the Kennedy Years.* Boston: Houghton Mifflin, 1969. As ambassador to India, the noted economist was a close observer of events in Vietnam, and he was frequently skeptical of the direction of American policy there. His memoirs recall his visits to Saigon, and include a number of incisive letters to Kennedy commenting on Vietnam developments.

Hartmann, R. T. *Palace Politics: An Inside Account of the Ford Years* (24:221) recalls the *Mayaguez* incident and the fall of South Vietnam.

Jessup, P. C. *The Birth of Nations* (24:174) recounts Jessup's participation in the negotiations leading to the independence of Indonesia and later as ambassador-at-large. He played a major role in the decision to recognize the Bao Dai government. His personal recollections of these important events contain valuable insights into U.S. policy in Southeast Asia (1948–1951).

30:40 Jones, Howard P. *Indonesia: The Possible Dream.* New York: Harcourt Brace Jovanovich, 1971. Part memoir, part history of recent Indonesian politics and relations with the United States, this volume was written by a career diplomat who served in Indonesia (1954–1965) and admired the Indonesians and their charismatic leader Sukarno. It is particularly valuable for its account of the 1958 coup.

30:41 Lansdale, Edward G. *In the Midst of Wars.* New York: Harper & Row, 1972. Lansdale was a flamboyant CIA counterinsurgency expert who was sent to Vietnam after assisting with the suppression of the Huk rebellion in the Philippines. His account of his role as adviser to Ngo Dinh Diem (1954–1957) probably omits a great deal, but is nevertheless informative and valuable, and vividly depicts the intrigue and confusion in Saigon in the 1950s.

Lewis, D. L. *King: A Critical Biography* (38:69) relates Dr. Martin Luther King's opposition to the Vietnam War.

Rostow, W. W. *The Diffusion of Power: An Essay in Recent History* (24:181) is a massively detailed analysis of American foreign policy in the 1960s by a top adviser to Kennedy and Johnson. Rostow's study is not, strictly speaking, a memoir, but it nevertheless contains important insights into the attitudes of the policymakers.

Schlesinger, A. M., Jr. *Robert Kennedy and His Times* (29:34) is a detailed, sympathetic study of Robert Kennedy, based on materials not generally available to scholars, which contains a thorough and quite useful analysis of Vietnam policy in the administration of John Kennedy.

30:42 Sharp, U. S. Grant. *Strategy for Defeat.* San Rafael, Calif.: Presidio, 1978. Sharp's memoir focuses on the air war for which he, as commander in chief of Pacific forces, was responsible. His argument that air power would have worked had it not operated under emasculating restrictions is not persuasive.

30:43 Stanton, Edwin F. *In Brief Authority: Excursions of a Common Man in an Uncommon World.* New York: Harper's, 1956. This is an interesting memoir by the career diplomat and East Asia expert who became America's first ambassador to Thailand. Stanton's recollections of his contacts with king and court and of the beginnings of the American technical assistance program in Thailand are especially enlightening.

Steel, R. *Walter Lippmann and the American Century* (24:182) develops Lippmann's disillusionment with America's Vietnam policies.

Taylor, M. D. *Swords and Ploughshares* (40:60) is a detailed and valuable, if somewhat bland, memoir by a top adviser to Presidents Kennedy and Johnson who also spent two years as ambassador to South Vietnam.

30:44 Trewhitt, Henry L. *McNamara.* New York: Harper & Row, 1971. Trewhitt's sympathetic biography, based primarily on printed sources and interviews, is a solid work which clarifies McNamara's instrumental role in the escalation of the Vietnam War and his later disillusionment.

30:45 Westmoreland, William C. *A Soldier Reports.* Garden City, N.Y.: Doubleday, 1976. Westmoreland's account of his stewardship in Vietnam is defensive, blaming the civilians in Washington and the media for losing a war that was winnable. This bland memoir is valuable for its discussion of military operations and the U.S. role in South Vietnam and for its insights into the thinking of the man who conceived the ill-fated search and destroy strategy.

ASIAN

Ngo Dinh Diem

30:46 Bouscaren, Anthony T. *The Last of the Mandarins: Diem of Vietnam.* Pittsburgh: Duquesne University Press, 1965. The only English-language biography of Ngo Dinh Diem, this volume must be used with care. Bouscaren is a militant anticommunist, and his study is sketchy and uncritical.

30:47 Warner, Geoffrey. "The United States and the Fall of Diem." 2 pts. *Australian Outlook* 28:3 (1974), 245–58; 29:1 (1975), 3–17. Warner's sober and scholarly essay (part 1: "The Coup That Never Was") is the best account of the maneuvering that led to the abortive coup of August 1963. The essay on the November coup (part 2: "The Death of Diem") concludes that although the United States did not instigate the plot, it contributed decisively to its success.

Ho Chi Minh

30:48 Fall, Bernard B., ed. *Ho Chi Minh on Revolution: Selected Writings, 1920–1966.* New York: Praeger, 1967. This is a valuable compilation of Ho's writings, most of them for the period 1945 to 1965.

30:49 Lacouture, Jean. *Ho Chi Minh: A Political Biography.* Trans. by Peter Wiles. New York: Knopf, 1968. An immensely readable biography by a distinguished French journalist, which regards Ho as more a nationalist than a communist, and is highly critical of France and the United States for attempting to subdue the Vietminh revolution.

Norodom Sihanouk

30:50 Osborne, Milton. *Politics and Power in Cambodia: The Sihanouk Years.* New York: Longmans, 1974. A contemporary account which concludes that CIA involvement in Cambodia was secondary to Sihanouk's leadership failures as an explanation for the 1970 coup.

30:51 Sihanouk, Norodom. *My War with the CIA: The Memoirs of Prince Norodom Sihanouk.* New York: Pantheon, 1973. This passionate and frequently overstated memoir, written in exile, recounts in some detail the prince's conflicts with the United States from the mid-1950s to his deposition in 1970.

Achmed Sukarno

30:52 Legge, J. D. *Sukarno: A Political Biography.* New York: Praeger, 1972. A thoroughly researched and critical biography which gives good coverage to Sukarno's foreign policy and his stormy relationship with the United States.

30:53 Penders, C. L. M. *The Life and Times of Sukarno.* London: Sidgwick & Jackson, 1974. An excellent introduction to a complex and controversial figure, this biography is based on extensive research and captures the many dimensions of its subject.

30:54 Sukarno, Achmed. *Sukarno: An Autobiography as Told to Cindy Adams.* Indianapolis: Bobbs-Merrill, 1965. Unreliable on matters of detail, this autobiography nevertheless reveals much of the flamboyant and mercurial personality of Sukarno and of his attitudes toward the United States.

Others

30:55 Nguyen Cao Ky. *Twenty Years and Twenty Days.* New York: Stein & Day, 1976. As head of South Vietnam's air force, president, and then vice-president, Ky was near the center of power in Saigon for two decades. His memoir blames the United States and his colleague Nguyen Van Thieu for the debacle, and it is useful for observations on the workings of the Saigon government and its interaction with the United States.

30:56 Tran Van Don. *Our Endless War: Inside Vietnam.* San Rafael, Calif.: Presidio, 1978. A top South Vietnamese army officer, Tran Van Don, was involved in the plot to overthrow Diem and was at the center of South Vietnam's turbulent politics for the next twelve years. His memoirs describe the corruption and intrigue which paralyzed the Saigon government.

30:57 U Nu. *U Nu, Saturday's Son.* Trans. by U Law Yone. New Haven, Conn.: Yale University Press, 1977. This autobiography of Burma's prime minister (1948–1958) contains some references to dealings with the United States.

30:58 Van Tien Dung. *Our Great Spring Victory: An Account of the Liberation of South Vietnam.* Trans. by John Spraegens, Jr. New York: Monthly Review, 1977. A frankly exuberant memoir by the North Vietnamese chief of staff which recounts the planning for and events of the Ho Chi Minh campaign to "liberate" South Vietnam. The volume is interesting for the glimpses it provides into the strategic debates in Hanoi's politburo and for the calculations of possible American reactions to a large-scale offensive.

30:59 Wheeler, Gerald E. "Manual Quezon and the American Presidents." *Asian Studies* 2:2 (1964), 231–46. An informative essay, which argues that the personal relationship between Franklin Roosevelt and Quezon played a significant role in Philippine independence and postwar collaboration.

U.S. and Southeast Asia since 1941

30:60 Butwell, Richard. "The Nixon Doctrine in Southeast Asia." *Current History* 61:364 (1971), 321–26. A brief, contemporary appraisal which argues that U.S. policy in Southeast Asia did not change drastically as a result of the Nixon Doctrine.

30:61 Darling, Frank C. "United States Policy in Southeast Asia: Permanency and Change." *Asian Survey* 14:7 608–26. An early attempt to assess the impact of the American withdrawal from Vietnam on

Southeast Asia as a whole. The author argues that the United States has important interests in the region and must continue to play an active role there.

30:62 Fifield, Russell H. *Americans in Southeast Asia: The Roots of Commitment.* New York: Crowell, 1973. The best study of American policy (1941–1954), it is comprehensive in coverage, balanced, if somewhat bland in its conclusions—a basic source for anyone interested in the origins of American involvement in the region and in individual countries. Extensive bibliography.

30:63 Fifield, Russell H. *Southeast Asia in United States Policy.* New York: Praeger, 1963. A detailed analysis of U.S. policy in Southeast Asia in the late 1950s and early 1960s, topically organized, with extended treatment of such matters as SEATO and the American role in economic development. Dated but still useful. Extensive bibliography.

30:64 Henderson, William, ed. *Southeast Asia: Problems of United States Policy.* Cambridge, Mass.: MIT Press, 1964. Although the essays are dated, they reflect American attitudes toward Southeast Asia in the early 1960s on a variety of important topics, including foreign aid, SEATO, and Southeast Asian reactions to U.S. policy.

30:65 Mozingo, David P. "Containment in Asia Reconsidered." *World Politics* 19:3 (1967), 361–77. An early, perceptive critique which argues that the conditions which made containment successful in Europe do not exist in Asia and that by committing itself to a policy of containment in Asia the United States has undertaken an impossible task.

Nagai Y., and Iriye, A., eds. *The Origins of the Cold War in Asia* (27:25) is the best introduction to the transformation of U.S. East Asian policy (1949–1951). This collection of essays deals with various aspects of U.S. policy before and during the Korean War. Three of the essays are specifically devoted to Southeast Asia.

30:66 Weatherbee, Donald E. "U.S. Policy and the Two Southeast Asias." *Asian Survey* 18:4 (1978), 408–21. Weatherbee's essay expresses concern that the low priority given to Southeast Asia by the United States after 1975 and the human rights policy of the Carter administration may further weaken U.S. ties with the ASEAN nations at a time when they feel particularly vulnerable.

U.S. AID

30:67 Hayes, Samuel P., ed. *The Beginnings of American Aid to Southeast Asia: The Griffin Mission of 1950.* Lexington, Mass.: Lexington Books, 1971. This volume includes the original reports of the Griffin mission, which led to American economic assistance to Vietnam, Laos, and Cambodia, along with brief analyses of the mission and the programs which resulted from it.

30:68 Montgomery, John D. *The Politics of Foreign Aid: American Experience in Southeast Asia.* New York: Praeger, 1962. A comparative study of the administration of U.S. aid programs in Taiwan, Burma, Vietnam, and Thailand. The author, an aid official in Vietnam, pinpoints numerous problems. Although dated, the book provides a valuable discussion of the operation of American economic assistance programs in the 1950s.

30:69 Nichols, Jeannette P. "United States Aid to South and Southeast Asia, 1950–1960." *Pacific Historical Review* 32:2 (1963), 171–84. A sketchy survey of some of the major problems encountered in the administration of foreign aid programs in the Colombo Plan nations. The author stresses that conflict among the nations of the region has made a cooperative approach difficult.

30:70 Wolf, Charles, Jr. *Foreign Aid: Theory and Practice in Southern Asia.* Princeton, N.J.: Princeton University Press, 1960. A highly technical analysis of the foreign aid program (1951–1957) which seeks to frame models to improve the effectiveness of economic and military aid in the developing countries.

SEATO

See "Personalities," especially John Foster Dulles.

30:71 Eckel, Paul E. "SEATO: An Ailing Alliance." *World Affairs* 134:2 (1971), 97–114. Eckel traces the Southeast Asia Treaty Organization from its inception in 1954 and reviews the position taken by the nations of SEATO and how the organization dealt with the problems which beset its three protocol states (Laos, Cambodia, and South Vietnam).

30:72 Modelski, George A., ed. *SEATO: Six Studies.* Melbourne: Cheshire, 1962. The essays discuss the organization of the alliance and the relations of Australia and various Asian states with it. The U.S. role is not discussed in any depth, but the various essays provide useful commentary on it.

Ritharom, C. "The Making of the Thai-U.S. Military Alliance and the SEATO Treaty of 1954: A Study in Thai Decision-Making" (30:129).

30:73 Thomas, M. L. "A Critical Appraisal of SEATO." *Western Political Quarterly* 10:4 (1957), 926–36. An early critical analysis which concludes that SEATO's inherent weaknesses, especially the lack of unity among its members, make the realization of its objectives impossible.

BURMA

See "Personalities," especially U Nu (under "Others").

30:74 Cady, John F. *The United States and Burma.* Cambridge: Harvard University Press, 1976. More an interpretive essay on recent Burmese history and culture than a study of U.S. relations with Burma, this volume is the only work of substance on the topic. Extensive bibliography.

30:75 Johnstone, William C. *Burma's Foreign Policy: A Study in Neutralism.* Cambridge: Harvard University Press, 1963. A documented study of Burma's foreign policy during the cold war, with some consideration of relations with the United States, which concludes, much too pessimistically, that neutralism forced Burma into dependence on China.

CAMBODIA

See "Personalities," especially Norodom Sihanouk.

30:76 Burchett, Wilfred G. *The Second Indochina War: Cambodia and Laos.* New York: International Publishers, 1970. This outspoken account by an Australian journalist is chiefly valuable because the author maintained close contact with North Vietnam and with insurgent groups in Indochina and, although he is uncritical, he is able to shed important light on their attitudes and policies.

30:77 Caldwell, Malcolm, and Tan, Lek. *Cambodia in the Southeast Asian War.* New York: Monthly Review, 1973. This is a bitter indictment of U.S. policy.

30:78 Girling, J. L. S. "Crisis and Conflict in Cambodia." *Orbis* 14:2 (1970), 349–65. A detailed essay which concludes that no one wanted the Cambodian crisis—events simply got out of control—and that all parties gained from it except Cambodia.

30:79 Grant, Jonathan S., ed. *Cambodia: The Widening War in Indochina.* New York: Washington Square, 1971. This series of uneven but useful essays, by the Committee of Concerned Asian Scholars, covers a wide variety of topics related to the 1970 coup. Bibliography.

30:80 Shawcross, William. *Sideshow: Kissinger, Nixon and the Destruction of Cambodia.* New York: Simon & Schuster, 1979. A detailed, disturbing account by a British journalist who holds the United States primarily responsible for expansion of the war into Cambodia and for the devastation that followed. Shawcross provides a wealth of new information on the war in Cambodia and is unsparing in his criticism of Nixon and Kissinger.

30:81 Smith, Roger M. *Cambodia's Foreign Policy.* Ithaca, N.Y.: Cornell University Press, 1965. Smith provides a balanced study of Cambodia's relations with the major powers and its neighbors Vietnam and Thailand (1954–1964). Extensive bibliography.

The Mayaguez Incident, 1975

30:82 Head, Richard G.; Short, Frisco W.; and McFarlane, Robert E. *Crisis Resolution: Presidential Decision Making in the Mayaguez and Korean Confrontation.* Boulder, Colo.: Westview, 1978. The authors, affiliated with the National Defense University, argue that the administration's success gave the nation "moral uplift," restored faith in U.S. credibility, and demonstrated strategic resolve "worthy of a great power."

30:83 Rowan, Roy. *The Four Days of Mayaguez.* New York: Norton, 1975. This "instant history," based on interviews with President Ford and other participants, provides a colorful account of the incident itself, but does not consider the larger issues raised by the incident and the subsequent criticism of Ford's crisis management.

30:84 Zutz, Robert. "The Recapture of the S.S. *Mayaguez:* Failure of the Consultation Clause of the War Powers Resolution." *New York University Jour-*

nal of International Law and Politics 8:3 (1976), 457–78. Zutz examines the legality of President Ford's attempt to secure release of the S.S. *Mayaguez,* which the Cambodians seized on May 12, 1975, in light of section 3 of the War Powers Resolution.

INDONESIA/MALAYSIA

See "Personalities," especially, under "Others," John M. Allison, Howard P. Jones.

30:85   Bunnell, Frederick P. "The Central Intelligence Agency Deputy Directorate for Plans 1961 Secret Memorandum on Indonesia: A Study in the Politics of Policy Formulation in the Kennedy Administration." *Indonesia,* no.22 (1976), 131–70. This essay analyzes the struggle between those Kennedy advisers who wanted to accommodate Sukarno and those who wanted to take a hard line with him.

30:86   Bunnell, Frederick P. "The Kennedy Initiatives in Indonesia, 1962–1963." Ph.D. diss., Cornell University, 1969. A valuable study, much broader than the title implies, which analyzes the struggle between Kennedy advisers over U.S. policy toward Sukarno. Useful not only for U.S.-Indonesian relations but for insights into policymaking.

30:87   Colbert, Evelyn. "The Road Not Taken: Decolonization and Independence in Indonesia and Indochina." *Foreign Affairs* 51:3 (1973), 608–28. A comparison of the different approaches taken in resolving similar conflicts of the late 1940s. Colbert stresses international factors as the most important cause of the different outcomes, placing too little emphasis on the U.S. role.

Gould, J. W. *Americans in Sumatra* (17:279) is an overdramatized account which details the role of individuals and business and religious groups. The book contains chapters on trade and investment, missionaries and "scholar-adventurers," and the role of Americans in education and scholarship.

30:88   Gould, James W. *The United States and Malaysia.* Cambridge: Harvard University Press, 1969. This volume is primarily an introduction to Malaysian history and culture, but it does contain a useful chapter on relations with the United States since Malaysia attained independence. Bibliography.

30:89   Lew, Daniel S. "America, Indonesia, and the Rebellion of 1958." *United Asia* 17:4 (1965), 305–09.

Lew points out that the coolness of Indonesian-U.S. relations in the early 1960s stemmed from the encouragement that the United States gave to the 1958 rebels.

30:90   Masters, Edward E. "American Relations with Indonesia." *Asia,* no. 19 (1970), 78–93. This is a brief survey and defense of the post-1965 regime and of U.S. policy by a foreign service officer stationed in Indonesia during the 1965 coup.

30:91   Peritz, Rene. "American-Malaysian Relations: Substance and Shadow." *Orbis* 11:2 (1967), 532–50. This essay is a useful survey of contemporary problems in U.S.-Malaysian relations.

Rose, L. A. *Roots of Tragedy: The United States and the Struggle for Asia, 1945–1954* (27:26) reviews the evolution of U.S. East Asian policy between the end of World War II and the outbreak of the Korean War, with one chapter on the Indonesian revolution.

30:92   Van Der Kroef, Justus M. "The 1965 Coup in Indonesia: The C.I.A.'s Version." *Asian Affairs* 4:2 (1976), 117–31. A critical analysis of a CIA document assessing the 1965 coup, which is useful for its revelations of official U.S. attitudes toward the upheaval in Indonesia.

30:93   Weinstein, Franklin B. *Indonesian Foreign Policy and the Dilemma of Dependence.* Ithaca, N.Y.: Cornell University Press, 1976. This careful study of Indonesian foreign policy in the 1970s devotes considerable attention to relations with the United States.

U.S. and Indonesian Independence, 1944–1949

See "Personalities," especially Philip C. Jessup (under "Others").

30:94   Hornbeck, Stanley K. "The United States and the Netherlands East Indies." *Annals of the American Academy of Political and Social Science,* no. 255 (1948), 124–35. A brief survey by a career diplomat which is important for its revelations of official attitudes toward the colonialist-nationalist struggle in the immediate post–World War II era.

30:95   Leupold, Robert J. "The United States and Indonesian Independence, 1944–1947." Ph.D. diss., University of Kentucky, 1976. This dissertation is especially valuable for its thorough assessment of the economic, military, political, and personal factors which shaped U.S. policy toward Indonesian independence during and immediately after World War II.

30:96 McMahon, Robert J. "Anglo-American Diplomacy and the Reoccupation of the Netherlands East Indies." *Diplomatic History* 2:1 (1978), 1–24. This is an excellent analysis which sheds much light on great power reaction to the colonial question in the immediate aftermath of World War II.

30:97 McMahon, Robert J. "The United States and Decolonization in Southeast Asia: The Case of Indonesia." Ph.D. diss., University of Connecticut, 1977. McMahon's comprehensive study of the evolution of U.S. policy toward the Netherlands East Indies (1945–1949) concludes that direct American pressure forced the Dutch to extend independence and that U.S. policy was motivated by perceptions of the anticommunism and strength of the nationalist movement. Bibliography.

30:98 Taylor, Alastair M. *Indonesian Independence and the United Nations.* Ithaca, N.Y.: Cornell University Press, 1960. This standard account of an important problem by a member of the United Nations Secretariat during the negotiations concludes that resolution of this problem was the UN's "first definitive political achievement." Bibliography.

LAOS

30:99 Adams, Nina S., and McCoy, Alfred W., eds. *Laos: War and Revolution.* New York: Harper & Row, 1971. These essays cover topics such as Laotian culture and politics as well as various aspects of American involvement in Laos. Outspoken in their criticism of U.S. policy, they bring together a great deal of information not easily available elsewhere. Bibliography.

30:100 Goldstein, Martin E. *American Policy toward Laos.* Rutherford, N.J.: Fairleigh Dickinson University Press, 1973. In a careful analysis, Goldstein reviews America's role in Laos through the settlement of 1962. Bibliography.

30:101 Halpern, B., and Halpern, J. "Laos and America—A Retrospective View." *South Atlantic Quarterly* 63:2 (1964), 175–87. This is an informative critique of American policy in Laos, particularly the foreign aid program.

30:102 Stevenson, Charles A. *The End of Nowhere: American Policy toward Laos since 1954.* Boston: Beacon, 1972. Stevenson's well-documented study focuses on the American decisionmaking process and finds the sources of failure in the "obsessive anti-Communism" of the policymakers. Bibliography.

30:103 Thee, Marek. *Notes of a Witness: Laos and the Second Indochina War.* New York: Random House, 1973. A Polish diplomat and member of the international commission responsible for administering the Geneva agreements on Laos, Thee's eyewitness account of the crisis of 1961–1962 is harshly critical of the United States.

30:104 Young, Kenneth R. "The United States and Laos: The Kong Le Debacle." *Asian Forum* 4:1 (1972), 22–40. The coup d'etat of Captain Kong Le, who captured the capital city of Vientiane on August 9, 1960, demonstrates that American involvement in Laos suffered from mismanagement and lacked a firm philosophical commitment.

30:105 Zasloff, Joseph J. "Laos, 1972: The War, Politics, and Peace Negotiations." *Asian Survey* 13:1 (1973), 60–75. This is a brief and balanced survey of the major developments in Laos through 1972.

Neutralization of Laos, 1960–1962

See "Personalities," especially Roger Hilsman, John F. Kennedy.

30:106 Czyzak, J. J., and Salans, C. F. "International Conference on the Settlement of the Laotian Question and the Geneva Agreements of 1962." *Journal of Southeast Asian History* 7:2 (1966), 27–47. This straightforward account of the Geneva Conference of 1962, written by a legal adviser to the conference, describes the agreements and is much too optimistic in its conclusions.

30:107 Dommen, Arthur. *Conflict in Laos: The Politics of Neutralization.* Rev. ed. New York: Praeger, 1971. A detailed and balanced study, written by a knowledgeable journalist, which focuses on the period 1954 to 1970. Bibliography.

30:108 Fall, Bernard B. *Anatomy of a Crisis: The Laotian Crisis of 1960–1961.* Rev. ed. Garden City, N.Y.: Doubleday, 1969. Although dated, Fall's work remains the best analysis of the conflict in Laos between 1954 and 1961. A firm anticommunist himself, Fall nevertheless concludes that the Eisenhower-Dulles policy polarized politics in Laos and contributed to the growth of communist strength.

30:109 Hill, Kenneth L. "President Kennedy and the Neutralization of Laos." *Review of Politics* 31:3 (1969), 353–69. This critical study of Kennedy's policies in Southeast Asia argues that the policy of disengagement applied in Laos should also have been employed in Vietnam. It provides a good summary of the 1962 agreement on Laos and its implementation.

THE PHILIPPINES

See "Personalities," especially Charles E. Bohlen, Edward G. Lansdale (under "Others"), Manuel Quezon (under "Asian," "Others"); also see Chapter 21, "The Philippines."

30:110 Abueva, J. V. "Filipino Democracy and the American Legacy." *Annals of the American Academy of Political and Social Science,* no. 428 (1976), 114–33. Abueva's provocative study of intercultural relations concludes that the U.S. attempt to export democracy to the Philippines had "uniquely Filipino results—an authoritarian-democratic political culture."

30:111 Buss, Claude A. *The United States and the Philippines: Background for Policy.* Washington, D.C.: American Enterprise Institute, 1977. Buss provides a useful assessment of the deterioration of Philippine-U.S. relations during the Vietnam War (1965–1975).

Friend, T. W. *Between Two Empires: The Ordeal of the Philippines, 1929–1946* (21:232) is valuable as a background to Philippine-U.S. relations.

30:112 Golay, Frank H., ed. *The United States and the Philippines.* Englewood Cliffs, N.J.: Prentice-Hall, 1966. These informative essays, most of them covering the period after independence, deal with problems of decolonization, trade and investments, and mutual security.

Grunder, G. A., and Livezey, W. E. *The Philippines and the United States* (2:353) is a dated but still useful survey.

30:113 Hernando, Orlando M. "The United States and the Philippines, 1946–1975: A Study of a Small

Power in an Alliance." Ph.D. diss., University of Oklahoma, 1976. Hernando examines the Philippine-U.S. alliance (1946–1975) in the conceptual framework of small power alliance politics. He concludes that the Philippines entered the alliance to satisfy its needs for security, prestige, economic aid, and domestic stability, and argues that these needs continue to exist.

30:114 Jenkins, Shirley. *American Economic Policy toward the Philippines.* Stanford, Calif.: Stanford University Press, 1954. Jenkins's balanced treatment focuses on the post–World War II period. She is critical of the United States for failing to assist in the development of a strong economic basis for political independence.

30:115 Kim, Sung Yong. *United States–Philippine Relations, 1946–1956.* Washington, D.C.: Public Affairs Press, 1968. This is an overly optimistic assessment of the bases of Philippine-American "friendship" in the postindependence decade. Bibliography.

30:116 Kolko, Gabriel. "The United States and the Philippines: The Beginning of Another Vietnam?" *Journal of Contemporary Asia* 3:1 (1973), 70–84. As Marcos has pursued contradictory foreign and domestic policies for personal aggrandizement, he has lost control of the economy. Backing Marcos presents a dilemma for the United States, because his political future is uncertain.

Lansang, J. A. "The Philippine-American Experiment: A Filipino View" [1898–1950] (2:354) offers a critical assessment of American tutelage.

30:117 Meyer, Milton W. *A Diplomatic History of the Philippine Republic.* Honolulu: University of Hawaii Press, 1965. This meticulous study (1945–1961) emphasizes relations with the United States, and deals effectively with such major issues as trade and military bases, but it does not penetrate the intercultural dimensions of the relationship or the subsurface tensions.

30:118 Smith, Robert A. *Philippine Freedom, 1946–1958.* New York: Columbia University Press, 1958. Smith's uncritical account provides useful treatment of Filipino politics and diplomacy.

30:119 Taylor, George E. *The Philippines and the United States: Problems of Partnership.* New York: Praeger, 1964. This broad survey of the postwar period is dated in its approach and conclusions.

30:120 Thompson, W. Scott. *Unequal Partners: Philippine and Thai Relations with the United States.* Lexington, Mass.: Lexington Books, 1975. This topical analysis, emphasizing the period of the Vietnam War (1965–1973), concludes that Philippine interests were better served than those of Thailand by close alignment with the United States.

30:121 Ventura, Mamerto S. "Philippine Post-War Recovery and Reform: A Study of United States–Philippine Cooperation." *Philippine Journal of Public Administration* 12:1 (1968), 7–30. This is a careful, if uncritical, account of the programs launched by the Philippines with U.S. assistance at the conclusion of the Huk wars.

30:122 Wurfel, David. "Foreign Aid and Social Reform in Political Development: A Philippine Case Study." *American Political Science Review* 53:2 (1959), 456–82. Wurfel's detailed study of the implementation of the American aid program (1950–1957) argues that foreign aid, accompanied by strong pressures, can help promote social and political reform.

30:123 Youngblood, Robert L. "Philippine-American Relations under the New Society." *Pacific Affairs* 50:1 (1977), 45–63. This informative study (1973–1976) concludes that the Philippines has become more dependent on the United States while its desire for independence has become greater.

THAILAND

See "Personalities," especially Edwin F. Stanton (under "Others").

30:124 Bradley, William L., et al. *Thailand: Domino by Default: The 1976 Coup and Implications for U.S. Policy.* Athens: Ohio University Press, 1978. In a brief, pessimistic essay Bradley argues that unless the Thai government changes its policies the insurgency will gain in strength and most likely succeed.

30:125 Casella, Alessandro. "U.S.-Thai Relations." *World Today* 26:3 (1970), 118–24. Casella examines the secret 1965 agreement which permitted U.S. bases in Thailand in exchange for American defense commitments.

30:126 Darling, Frank C. "America and Thailand." *Asian Survey* 7:4 (1967), 213–25. This essay updates

the author's 1965 study in light of the escalation of the Vietnam War and the expanded U.S. role in Thailand.

30:127 Darling, Frank C. *Thailand and the United States.* Washington, D.C.: Public Affairs Press, 1965. Darling's informative survey of Thai-American relations focuses on the post–World War II period. Bibliography.

30:128 Marks, Thomas A. "Thai Security during the 'American Era,' 1960–1976." *Issues and Studies* 15:4 (1979), 61–88. Marks analyzes the rise of Thai-American collaboration in the 1960s and its decline in the 1970s, concluding that the crucial factor in both cases was the issue of national security as perceived by both sides. It is valuable for its assessment of the breakdown of cooperation toward the end of the Vietnam War.

30:129 Ritharom, Chatri. "The Making of the Thai-U.S. Military Alliance and the SEATO Treaty of 1954: A Study in Thai Decision-Making." Ph.D. diss., Claremont Graduate School, 1976. The author investigates Thailand's shift from neutrality to alliance with the West and finds the sources of the policy change in Thai domestic politics as well as cold war pressures.

30:130 Tanham, George K. *Trial in Thailand.* New York: Crane, Russak, 1974. A memoir by the counterinsurgency expert in Bangkok (1968–1970), it points up the difficulties of containing revolution either by repression or economic development. Overly optimistic, the book is nevertheless useful for the implementation of U.S. programs and the Thai response.

30:131 Viksnins, George. "United States Military Spending and the Economy of Thailand, 1967–1972." *Asian Survey* 13:5 (1973), 441–57. Viksnins's careful analysis, employing quantitative and macroeconomic methods, plays down the impact of U.S. military spending on the Thai economy.

30:132 Wilson, David A. *The United States and the Future of Thailand.* New York: Praeger, 1970. Wilson is convinced that Thailand will be able to sustain its national cohesiveness despite internal and external pressures. He believed that the United States and Thailand would be able to cooperate after the Vietnam War.

30:133 Young, Kenneth T. "The Special Role of American Advisers in Thailand, 1902–1949." *Asia,* no. 14 (1969), 1–31. This informative essay, written by a diplomat, recounts the role played by Americans in Thailand long before the United States attached any significance to that Southeast Asian nation.

Thailand in World War II

30:134   Fine, Herbert A. "The Liquidation of World War II in Thailand." *Pacific Historical Review* 34:1 (1965), 65–82. Fine's essay argues that the United States used its leverage to check British attempts to infringe on Thai sovereignty and independence, and reveals a rising American interest to Southeast Asia at the end of World War II.

30:135   Martin, James V. "Thai-American Relations in World War II." *Journal of Asian Studies* 22:4 (1963), 451–67. World War II introduced a "degree of complexity and intensity to Thai-American relations that contrasted sharply with their quiet uneventfulness in the era preceding it."

30:136   Niksch, Larry A. "United States Foreign Policy in Thailand's World War II Peace Settlements with Great Britain and France." Ph.D. diss., Georgetown University, 1976. The author contends that the United States took a strong stand in favor of Thailand's independence and used its influence with Britain effectively to secure a settlement favorable to Thailand.

30:137   Sethachuay, Vivat, "United States–Thailand Diplomatic Relations during World War II." Ph.D. diss., Brigham Young University, 1977. The author examines in detail the complex relationship between the United States and Thailand in World War II and concludes that U.S. policy enabled Thailand to remain independent.

U.S. and the Indochina Wars

See also "Cambodia" and "Laos," above; also Chapter 36, "The Vietnam War."

30:138   Charlton, Michael, and Moncrief, Anthony. *Many Reasons Why: The American Involvement in Vietnam.* New York: Hill & Wang, 1979. Based on a series of interviews with leading policymakers and participants conducted by the British Broadcasting Corporation, this volume provides a useful retrospective view of the causes of American involvement.

30:139   Ellsberg, Daniel. *Papers on the War.* New York: Simon & Schuster, 1972. The most important essay is based on Ellsberg's work in compiling the Defense Department study (the *Pentagon Papers*) and persuasively challenges the so-called quagmire thesis, the argument that the United States slipped unknowingly into the quagmire of Vietnam.

30:140   Fall, Bernard B. *Last Reflections on a War.* Garden City, N.Y.: Doubleday, 1967. Fall was one of the few Westerners with an intimate knowledge of Vietnamese history and culture, and these essays are valuable in placing the conflict in that larger context.

30:141   Fall, Bernard B. *The Two Vietnams: A Political and Military Analysis.* 2d ed. New York: Praeger, 1967. A careful study of the conflict in Vietnam from the end of World War II to 1965, it emphasizes the Vietnamese dimension of the struggle, but the American role in Vietnam is dealt with extensively. Fall, a firm anticommunist, is highly critical of U.S. policy.

30:142   Fifield, Russell H. "Vietnam: A Unique American Experience." *Yale Review* 68:2 (1979), 161–75. Fifield, a leading observer of Southeast Asia, attempts to put the Vietnam War in perspective. He provides a useful overview of the causes of U.S. involvement and the sources and consequences of failure, stressing the limited validity of its lessons.

30:143   Gelb, Leslie, with Betts, Richard K. *The Irony of Vietnam: The System Worked.* Washington, D.C.: Brookings Institution, 1979. The title is misleading—the authors are *critical* of U.S. policy—and the principal thesis, that American policymakers knowingly perpetuated a stalemate in Vietnam, is debatable, but *The Irony of Vietnam* is the best study available of the policy processes and the assumptions of the policymakers.

30:144   Halberstam, David. *The Best and the Brightest.* New York: Random House, 1972. A massive, rambling account which indicts the policymakers of the Kennedy-Johnson years for gross errors of judgment. Halberstam's sketches of the policymakers are vivid, frequently brilliant, but by blaming a handful of individuals he ignores the larger societal and institutional impulses.

30:145 Kolko, Gabriel. "The United States in Vietnam, 1944–1966: Origins and Objectives." In his *The Roots of American Foreign Policy*. Boston: Beacon, 1969, pp. 88–132. The best brief statement of the radical critique of U.S. involvement in Vietnam, Kolko's essay argues that the United States intervened to demonstrate its capacity to thwart Third World radical revolutions.

Ronning, C. A. *A Memoir of China in War and Revolution* (36:51) contains the reminiscences of a Canadian diplomat at the Geneva Conference of 1954, and his trips to Hanoi in the late 1960s.

30:146 Schlesinger, Arthur M., Jr. *The Bitter Heritage: Vietnam and American Democracy, 1941–1966*. Boston: Houghton Mifflin, 1966. An early liberal critique by a historian and former Kennedy adviser, it advances the "quagmire thesis"—the idea that overzealous foreign policy officials misled reluctant presidents step by step into the quagmire of Vietnam.

30:147 Sullivan, Marianna P. *France's Vietnam Policy: A Study in French-American Relations*. Westport, Conn.: Greenwood, 1978. In a careful study, the author traces Franco-American differences on Vietnam (1963–1973) to the very nature of the unstable alliance between an ascending superpower and a declining middle power, and argues that de Gaulle's Vietnam policy was shaped primarily by his determination to remain independent from the United States. Extensive bibliography.

30:148 Thomson, James C., Jr. "How Could Vietnam Happen? An Autopsy." *Atlantic* 221 (April 1968), 47–53. In this important analysis, former State Department official Thomson stresses the institutional sources of error in Vietnam policymaking.

U.S. AND THE FIRST INDOCHINA WAR, 1941–1954

See "Personalities," especially John Foster Dulles, Dwight D. Eisenhower, Franklin D. Roosevelt; also see Chapter 28, "First Indochina War, 1945–1954."

30:149 Bator, Viktor. *Vietnam: A Diplomatic Tragedy: Origins of United States' Involvement*. New York: Oceana, 1965. This early analysis of the roots of U.S. involvement in Vietnam holds the Eisenhower administration responsible for the crucial commitments.

30:150 Drachman, Edward R. *United States Policy toward Vietnam, 1940–1945*. Rutherford, N.J.: Fairleigh Dickinson University Press, 1970. Drachman's survey appeared before documents were available. Bibliography.

30:151 Fall, Bernard B. *Street without Joy*. Rev. ed. New York: Schocken, 1972. Fall's classic account of French military operations in Indochina (1950–1954), contains numerous insights into U.S. policies and French reaction to them.

30:152 Gurtov, Melvin. *The First Vietnam Crisis: Chinese Communist Strategy and United States Involvement*. New York: Columbia University Press, 1967. Gurtov's is a balanced study which places the Indochina crisis of 1953–1954 in a broad international context and criticizes the Eisenhower administration for misjudging the dynamics of the crisis. Bibliography.

30:153 Hammer, Ellen J. *The Struggle for Indochina, 1940–1955: Viet Nam and the French Experience*. Rev. ed. Stanford, Calif.: Stanford University Press, 1956. Hammer's detailed account of the First Indochina War remains in many respects the best study. The author integrates political and military developments and places the conflict in its larger international context. She is sharply critical of French and American policy.

30:154 Herring, George C. "The Truman Administration and the Restoration of French Sovereignty in Indochina." *Diplomatic History* 1:2 (1977), 97–117. Herring concludes that the Truman administration acquiesced in the return of France to Indochina primarily to ensure French support for its policy in Europe.

30:155 Hess, Gary R. "The First American Commitment in Indochina: The Acceptance of the Bao Dai Solution." *Diplomatic History* 2:4 (1978), 331–50. Hess concludes that many American policymakers were skeptical of French intentions and of Bao Dai's potential for success, but that they saw no alternative in view of the communist triumph in China and Ho Chi Minh's communist affiliations.

30:156 Hess, Gary R. "United States Policy and the Origins of the French-Vietminh War, 1945–46." *Peace and Change* 3:2 (1975), 21–33. Hess concludes that the United States missed an important opportunity to accommodate itself to the only viable nationalist force there because of its preoccupation with Ho Chi

Minh's communist background and the cold war in Europe.

30:157 Irving, Ronald E. M. *The First Indochina War: French and American Policy, 1945–1954.* London: Croom Helm, 1975. Political and diplomatic rather than military in focus, this brief study analyzes the impact of French politics on Indochina policy and the complex, unsatisfactory relationship between the United States and France. Bibliography.

30:158 Krog, Carl. "American Journals of Opinion and the Fall of Vietnam, 1954." *Asian Affairs* 6:5 (1979), 324–32. Krog finds a great diversity of opinion on such major 1954 questions as the consequences of the fall of Vietnam, defense arrangements needed to compensate for the anticipated Communist victory, and the necessity and desirability of U.S. military intervention in Indochina.

30:159 Randle, Robert F. *Geneva 1954: The Settlement of the Indochinese War.* Princeton, N.J.: Princeton University Press, 1969. The standard account of the Geneva Conference of 1954, massively detailed and carefully documented, it emphasizes the inherent unworkability of the settlement. Bibliography.

30:160 Shaplen, Robert. *The Lost Revolution: The U.S. in Vietnam, 1946–1966.* Rev. ed. New York: Harper & Row, 1966. This volume is excellent on the politics of the First Indochina War and on the interaction among the Americans, French, and Vietnamese.

30:161 Thorne, Christopher. "Indochina and Anglo-American Relations, 1942–1945." *Pacific Historical Review* 45:1 (1976), 73–96. Thorne emphasizes the great diversity of views on Indochina within the U.S. bureaucracy and concludes that Roosevelt lacked a coherent policy, and that Churchill also lacked a clearcut policy and was inclined to defer to the United States.

INSURGENCY AND COUNTERINSURGENCY, 1954–1964

U.S. and South Vietnam

See "Personalities," especially Ngo Dinh Diem, Henry Cabot Lodge, Jr., and, under "Others," Wil-

liam Colby, John Kenneth Galbraith, Nguyen Cao Ky, Edward G. Lansdale, Robert McNamara, W. W. Rostow, Maxwell D. Taylor.

30:162 Halberstam, David. *The Making of a Quagmire.* New York: Random House, 1964. A highly critical account of the dramatic developments in Vietnam (1962–1963), Halberstam's book remains invaluable for its detail and its depiction of the key personalities, Vietnamese and American.

30:163 Hooper, Edwin; Allard, Dean C.; and Fitzgerald, Oscar P. *The United States Navy and the Vietnam Conflict: The Setting of the Stage to 1959.* Washington, D.C.: G.P.O., 1976. With many useful maps and charts, this first volume of the navy's official history of the Vietnam War contains valuable information on naval aid to France in the First Indochina War and on the creation of the South Vietnamese Navy (1954–1959). Bibliography.

30:164 Mecklin, John. *Mission in Torment: An Intimate Account of the U.S. Role in Vietnam.* Garden City, N.Y.: Doubleday, 1965. An informative memoir by a former USIA official, it vividly describes the confusion and backbiting among American officials in Vietnam in the early 1960s.

30:165 Scigliano, Robert. *South Vietnam: Nation under Stress.* Boston: Houghton Mifflin, 1964. Although dated, Scigliano's work remains the most comprehensive study of South Vietnam in the 1950s and early 1960s, detailing economic and social problems that are scarcely touched on in most works. He also provides some valuable commentary on the American role in South Vietnam before the Kennedy buildup. Bibliography.

30:166 Scigliano, Robert, and Fox, Guy. *Technical Assistance in Vietnam: The Michigan State Experience.* New York: Praeger, 1965. A brief, but useful, summary of the Michigan State University advisory group's training of South Vietnamese police and public administrators, it is particularly valuable for its comments on the interaction between Americans and Vietnamese.

30:167 Tregaskis, Richard. *Vietnam Diary.* New York: Holt, Rinehart & Winston, 1963. An extremely valuable and frequently overlooked account by a veteran war correspondent, it chronicles in some detail the activities of American "advisers" in Vietnam in the Kennedy years.

North Vietnam and the Vietcong

See "Personalities," especially Ho Chi Minh.

30:168 Chen, King C. "Hanoi's Three Decisions and the Escalation of the Vietnam War." *Political Science Quarterly* 90:2 (1975), 239–59. Chen concludes that Diem's American-supported campaign against the Communists in South Vietnam compelled North Vietnam to commit itself to war. His discussion of secret negotiations between Diem and the Hanoi regime in 1963 is particularly interesting.

30:169 Pike, Douglas. *Viet Cong: National Liberation Front of South Vietnam*. Cambridge, Mass.: MIT Press, 1966. Pike provides a detailed and valuable study of Vietcong organization and techniques. His conclusions are debatable and should be compared with those of Frances Fitzgerald's *Fire in the Lake* (30:23).

ESCALATION AND WAR, 1964–1968

See "Personalities," especially Lyndon B. Johnson, Robert Kennedy, and, under "Others," William Colby, Robert McNamara, W. W. Rostow; also see Chapter 32, "The Vietnam War, 1964–1973."

Enthoven, A. C., and Smith, K. W. *How Much Is Enough? Shaping the Defense Program, 1961–1969* (40:185) provides the larger context in which many key Vietnam decisions were made.

30:170 Graff, Henry. *The Tuesday Cabinet*. Englewood Cliffs, N.J.: Prentice-Hall, 1970. Graff's records of his conversations with Dean Rusk, McGeorge Bundy, and the president himself (1965–1969) provide one of the most valuable available accounts of the official rationale for U.S. involvement in Vietnam.

30:171 Palmer, Gregory. *The McNamara Strategy and the Vietnam War: Program Budgeting in the Pentagon, 1960–1968*. Westport, Conn.: Greenwood, 1978. Palmer argues that U.S. failure in Vietnam stemmed from the attempt of McNamara and his civilian "whiz kids" to apply cost effectiveness budgeting methods to military problems. The thesis is overstated, but the study provides a useful critique of McNamara's management of the Pentagon and the war. Bibliography.

30:172 Thomson, James C., Jr. "Getting Out and Speaking Out." *Foreign Policy*, no. 13 (1973/1974), 49–69. This insightful essay explores the important question of why men who disagree with established policy to the point of resignation hesitate to speak out once they become private citizens.

Tonkin Gulf Incident, 1964

30:173 Austin, Anthony. *The President's War: The Story of the Tonkin Gulf Resolution and How the Nation Was Trapped in Vietnam*. Philadelphia: Lippincott, 1971.

30:174 Galloway, John. *The Gulf of Tonkin Resolution*. Rutherford, N.J.: Fairleigh Dickinson University Press, 1970.

30:175 Goulden, Joseph C. *Truth Is the First Casualty: The Gulf of Tonkin Affair—Illusion and Reality*. Chicago: Rand-McNally, 1969.

30:176 Windchy, Eugene C. *Tonkin Gulf*. Garden City, N.Y.: Doubleday, 1971. The four books listed above (30:173–30:176) differ very little in sources used, information revealed, tone, or conclusions. Each relies on the Senate hearings of 1967–1968 and on interviews with participants. Each tends toward the exposé, indicting the Johnson administration for deliberately deceiving the American public and Congress. All conclude that there was good reason to doubt whether a second attack had actually taken place in the Gulf of Tonkin. Of the four, Windchy's will remain the standard account until a more up-to-date scholarly study is available.

Military Operations

See "Personalities," especially, under "Others," U. S. Grant Sharp, William C. Westmoreland.

30:177 *Air War: Vietnam*. Intro. by Drew Middleton. Indianapolis: Bobbs-Merrill, 1978. Written by air force officers, these essays deal with such topics as the Linebacker I campaign of 1972, the air force's response to improving North Vietnamese air defenses, and the air force role in the *Mayaguez* incident. They provide a useful corrective to much of the negative reporting on the American use of air power in Vietnam and make clear the tactical importance of air power in the spring 1972 campaigns, but they do not deal with

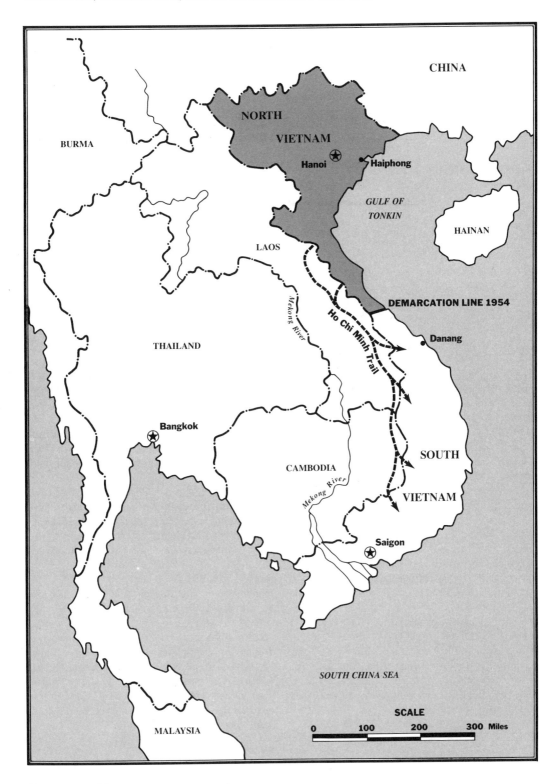

The War in Vietnam

the more vital issue of the strategic importance of the bombing.

30:178 Blaufarb, Douglas S. *The Counterinsurgency Era: U.S. Doctrine and Performance, 1950 to the Present*. New York: Free Press, 1977. A thorough analysis of U.S. counterinsurgency programs in the cold war era written by a former CIA official, it contains four chapters on Vietnam. Bibliography.

30:179 Caputo, Philip. *A Rumor of War*. New York: Holt, Rinehart & Winston, 1977. Caputo served in Vietnam as a marine lieutenant in 1965 and 1966. His memoir vividly depicts the nature of combat in I-Corps and the attitudes of the Americans involved in it.

30:180 Collins, James L., Jr. *The Development and Training of the South Vietnamese Army, 1950–1972*. Washington, D.C.: G.P.O., 1975. This official history of the army's training program in South Vietnam, based on documents and internal studies that remain classified, contains a full discussion of implementation of the Vietnamization policy.

30:181 Gallucci, Robert L. *Neither Peace Nor Honor: The Politics of American Military Policy in Vietnam*. Baltimore: Johns Hopkins University Press, 1975. Gallucci analyzes the decisions (1961–1967) to bomb North Vietnam and to commit troops to South Vietnam and the conduct of the air war, and finds military professionalism and a closed bureaucratic system responsible for strategies flawed in their assumptions and their methods. Bibliography.

30:182 Herr, Michael. *Dispatches*. New York: Knopf, 1977. A classic account by a youthful war correspondent, written in the lingo of the "grunt," which graphically describes the excitement and horrors of the war in 1968.

30:183 Kinnard, Douglas. *The War Managers*. Hanover, N.H.: University Press of New England, 1976. An army officer turned historian, Kinnard surveyed more than one hundred U.S. Army generals. His findings make clear that in retrospect, at least, there is no single military viewpoint as to what went wrong. Extensive bibliography.

30:184 Lewy, Guenter. *America in Vietnam*. New York: Oxford University Press, 1978. Lewy's book is based on extensive research in Department of Defense records and provides the best analysis to date of U.S. military operations (1965–1973), the Vietnamization

program, and the collapse of South Vietnam. Lewy is sharply critical of American strategists, who, he argues, failed to understand the dynamics of revolutionary war. His attempts to defend the war as necessary and to exonerate the United States from charges of war crimes and atrocities are tendentious.

30:185 Littauer, Raphael, and Uphoff, Norman. *The Air War in Indochina*. Rev. ed. Boston: Beacon, 1972. The best overall study of the air war (1964–1970), remarkably thorough and balanced, it is based on published U.S. documents. The volume includes extensive charts and tables as well as a full discussion of the effectiveness and legal and moral aspects of American air operations in Indochina. Bibliography.

30:186 O'Ballance, Edgar. *The Wars in Vietnam, 1954–1973*. New York: Hippocrene, 1976. This is a brief, competent military history, useful for details of operations but bland in its conclusions.

30:187 Palmer, Dave R. *Summons of the Trumpet: U.S.-Vietnam in Perspective*. San Rafael, Calif.: Presidio, 1978. This readable study by a former army officer is one of the better overall accounts of U.S. military operations in Vietnam. Palmer effectively challenges the popular myth of North Vietnamese omniscience and American and South Vietnamese ineptitude. He places primary responsiblity for the debacle on the civilians in Washington who made the proper use of U.S. military power impossible. Bibliography.

30:188 Schell, Jonathan. *The Village of Ben Suc*. New York: Knopf, 1967. A dramatic and moving eyewitness account which indicts the United States for the disruption and hardships caused the people of South Vietnam by large-scale search and destroy operations.

Smith, M. J. "The Strategic Bombing Debate: The Second World War and Vietnam" (23:208).

30:189 Thompson, James C. *Rolling Thunder: Understanding Policy and Program Failure*. Chapel Hill: University of North Carolina Press, 1980. The author assesses the reasons for the failure of the Rolling Thunder campaign, but focuses on the internal opposition to it, showing how opponents gradually gained enough strength to end it.

My Lai: War Crimes

30:190 Goldstein, Joseph; Marshall, Burke; and Schwartz, Jack. *The My Lai Massacre and Its Cover-Up: Beyond the Reach of Law?* New York: Free

Press, 1976. This volume contains the full report of the Peers Commission, which investigated the incident, as well as excerpts from the trials and from related legal opinions.

30:191　Peers, W. R. *The My Lai Inquiry.* New York: Norton, 1979. General Peers conducted the official investigation of the My Lai affair, and his account provides a judicious assessment of the inquiry as well as a valuable overall study of My Lai.

Taylor, T. *Nuremberg and Vietnam: An American Tragedy* (28:92).

South Vietnam: Pacification and Politics

See "Personalities," especially under "Others," Nguyen Cao Ky, Tran Van Don.

30:192　Goodman, Allan E. *Politics in War: The Bases of Political Community in South Vietnam.* Cambridge: Harvard University Press, 1973. Although technical in its methodology and optimistic in its conclusions, Goodman's study of South Vietnamese politics after the election of 1967 is the only scholarly analysis of the essential dilemma the United States faced in Vietnam.

30:193　Grinter, Lawrence E. "Bargaining between Saigon and Washington: Dilemmas of Linkage Politics during War." *Orbis* 18:3 (1974), 837–67. Grinter argues that American influence in South Vietnam declined as its commitment increased.

30:194　Grinter, Lawrence E. "South Vietnam: Pacification Denied." *South-East Asian Spectrum* 3 (July 1975), 49–76. A thorough appraisal of the various pacification programs conducted by the United States and South Vietnam (1954–1975), Grinter's essay concludes that pacification failed because the South Vietnamese leadership could never establish a sense of community with the rural population.

30:195　Kahin, George M. "Political Polarization in South Vietnam: U.S. Policy in the Post-Diem Period." *Pacific Affairs* 52:4 (1979/1980), 647–73. Kahin argues that the United States quickly came to oppose the Duong Van Minh group not only because it was perceived as ineffectual but also because it resisted U.S. direction, promoted reconciliation with the Vietcong, and was sympathetic to the neutralization of South Vietnam.

30:196　Lacouture, Jean. *Vietnam between Two Truces.* Trans. by Konrad Kellen and Joel Carmichael. New York: Knopf, 1966. An impressionistic account by a French journalist, it is chiefly valuable for its insights into South Vietnamese personalities and politics (1963–1966).

30:197　Shaplen, Robert. *The Road from War: Vietnam, 1965–1970.* New York: Harper & Row, 1970. This collection of Shaplen's "letters" to the *New Yorker* covers a variety of topics, and despite the lack of unity and coherence, it contains many astute observations. It is valuable for its discussion of South Vietnamese politics.

30:198　West, Francis, J., Jr. *The Village.* New York: Harper & Row, 1972. This narrative account by a former marine officer traces the impact over a period of years of the pacification programs on the village of Binh Nghia.

North Vietnam and Communist Powers

See "Personalities," especially Ho Chi Minh.

30:199　Funnell, V. C. "Vietnam and the Sino-Soviet Conflict, 1965–1976." *Studies in Comparative Communism* 11:1/2 (1978), 142–99. Funnell's essay offers few new insights, but it provides the most up-to-date and comprehensive analysis now available. The article also includes 28 pages of valuable documents.

30:200　McGarvey, Patrick J., ed. *Visions of Victory: Selected Vietnamese Communist Military Writings, 1964–1969.* Stanford, Calif.: Hoover Institution, 1969. A useful compilation of articles and broadcasts, most of them by North Vietnamese military leaders (1965–1968). The selections deal with such topics as ideology, military strategy and operations, and the role of the militia.

30:201　Popp, Daniel S. "The Soviet Perception of American Goals in Vietnam." *Soviet Union* 2:2 (1975), 145–61. A useful analysis of the official Soviet line on Vietnam, it argues that the Soviet buildup in North Vietnam was a response to the Johnson Doctrine and U.S. escalation of the war.

30:202　Van Dyke, Jon M. *North Vietnam's Strategy for Survival.* Palo Alto, Calif.: Pacific Books, 1972. Van Dyke provides the best available study of the

North Vietnamese war effort. Focusing on domestic mobilization rather than military strategy, he analyzes such things as adaptation to the bombing, mobilization of the population, and dispersal of industry and agriculture.

30:203 Zagoria, Donald. *Vietnam Triangle: Moscow, Peking, Hanoi*. New York: Pegasus, 1967. This study is dated, but Zagoria is an experienced, astute observer of communist politics, and his analysis of a complex and neglected topic is still of value.

Public Opinion and Domestic Impact

See "Personalities," especially J. William Fulbright; also see Chapter 38, "Peace Movements," "Since 1965."

30:204 Baskir, Lawrence M., and Strauss, William A. *Chance and Circumstance: The Draft, the War, and the Vietnam Generation*. New York: Knopf, 1978. The authors study those who did not fight in Vietnam: the evaders, avoiders, deserters, and exiles. They conclude that these individuals were deeply affected by the war and suggest that the full impact of the Vietnam War will not be felt until this generation attains political power. Bibliography.

Beisner, R. L. "1898 and 1968: The Anti-Imperialists and the Doves" (13:195) renders judgments on the anti-imperialists which are more profound than those on the doves, but Beisner provides a valuable comparison between two groups who became bitter critics of established policies.

30:205 Burstein, Paul, and Fredenburg, William. "Changing Public Policy: The Impact of Public Opinion, Antiwar Demonstrations, and War Costs on Senate Voting on Vietnam War Motions." *American Journal of Sociology* 84:1 (1978), 99–122. Their examination indicates that though each affected senatorial opinion (1964–1973), all were entangled so that individual effects are uninterpretable.

30:206 Converse, Philip, and Schumann, Howard. " 'Silent Majorities' and the Vietnam War." *Scientific American* 222:6 (1970), 17–25. This brief analysis is important for its assessment of a long-term trend in the public mood.

Foner, P. S. *American Labor and the Indochina War: The Growth of Union Opposition* (38:269).

30:207 Halstead, Fred. *Out Now! A Participant's Account of the American Movement against the Vietnam War*. New York: Monad, 1978. This comprehensive account is the best available study of the antiwar movement. Halstead makes no attempt to hide his biases, but his study has great value in its discussion of the internal workings of the movement and the frequently bitter informal debates on strategy and tactics.

30:208 Harris, Louis. *The Anguish of Change*. New York: Norton, 1973. A useful study by a leading public opinion analyst, it uses polling data to assess the turbulent politics and public mood of the late 1960s and early 1970s. Harris provides some enlightening commentary on public reaction to the war and the Johnson and Nixon administrations' response to public opinion.

30:209 Lubell, Samuel. *The Hidden Crisis in American Politics*. New York: Norton, 1971. Lubell devotes a chapter to public reactions to Vietnam and concludes that the public was neither hawk nor dove.

30:210 Lunch, William L., and Sperlich, Peter W. "American Public Opinion and the War in Vietnam." *Western Political Quarterly* 32:1 (1979), 21–44. They trace the shifts in public moods through four phases: innocence to rally round the flag; a permissive majority; escalation; and withdrawal. They confirm the findings of earlier students of the subject that young, white middle-class males were the most consistent supporters of the war and that blacks, females, and the lower classes were the most consistent opponents.

30:211 Mueller, John E. *War, Presidents and Public Opinion*. New York: Wiley, 1973. Mueller finds marked similarities in the public response to the wars in Korea and Vietnam and concludes that Vietnam was only slightly more unpopular than Korea. Bibliography.

30:212 Rosenberg, Milton; Verba, Sidney; and Converse, Philip. *Vietnam and the Silent Majority—The Dove's Guide*. New York: Harper & Row, 1970. Although written as a handbook for antiwar workers, this study contains some important observations on public opinion and Vietnam based on independent polling data.

30:213 Stevens, Robert W. *Vain Hopes, Grim Realities: The Economic Consequences of the Vietnam War*. New York: New Viewpoints, 1976. Stevens's detailed analysis of economic policymaking during the period of the Vietnam War stresses the central role of the war in bringing about the economic disorders of the 1970s.

30:214   Stoler, Mark A. "What Did He *Really* Say? The 'Aiken Formula' for Vietnam Revisited." *Vermont History* 46:2 (1978), 100–108. One of the first scholarly assessments of the varied positions assumed by congressional critics of Johnson's policies, it refutes the "myth" that George Aiken advocated the United States should declare itself victorious and get out of Vietnam. Stoler makes clear that the senator's views were much more complex and that he never endorsed withdrawal.

30:215   Verba, Sidney, et al. "Public Opinion and the War in Vietnam." *American Political Science Review* 61:2 (1967), 317–33. An important early analysis of public reaction to the war, it concludes that the public mood was ambivalent, permitting American leaders considerable leeway in making policy.

The Tet Offensive, 1967–1968

30:216   Braestrup, Peter. *Big Story: How the American Press and Television Reported and Interpreted the Crisis of Tet 1968 in Vietnam and Washington.* 2 vols. Boulder, Colo.: Westview, 1977. Braestrup compares media coverage of the events with what he feels are the more balanced historical judgments. He indicts the media for sensationalism, shallow reporting, and inaccuracy, and concludes that the journalists erred in interpreting Tet as a stunning U.S. defeat. Braestrup is cautious in assessing the impact of the media on policy. Extensive appendixes.

30:217   Brodie, Bernard. "The Tet Offensive." In Noble Frankland and Christopher Dowling, eds., *Decisive Battles of the Twentieth Century.* London: Sidgwick & Jackson, 1976, pp. 321–34. Brodie is among the most respected students of politics and military strategy, and his brief assessment of the Tet offensive is the most persuasive in print.

30:218   Clifford, Clark. "A Viet Nam Reappraisal." *Foreign Affairs* 47:4 (1969), 601–22. Clifford's account of his own disillusionment with the war after Tet and his role in the Johnson administration's policy changes of March 1968 is a valuable source for the policy debate of the period.

30:219   Henry, John B. "February, 1968." *Foreign Policy,* no. 4 (1971), 3–34. Henry concludes that the Joint Chiefs of Staff and Westmoreland attempted to use the crisis atmosphere of Tet to force mobilization of the reserves and escalation of the war. His essay does not carry through the March policy decisions, but it remains useful for the first stages of the reappraisal.

30:220   Hoopes, Townsend. *The Limits of Intervention: An Inside Account of How the Johnson Policy of Escalation in Vietnam Was Reversed.* New York: McKay, 1969. Only about half of this book deals with the policy decisions of February and March 1968. Under secretary of the air force (1967–1968), Hoopes recounts his disillusionment with the war and his role in the policy debates after Tet. His study provides a useful, if one-dimensional, look at the decisionmaking process.

30:221   Oberdorfer, Don. *Tet!* Garden City, N.Y.: Doubleday, 1971. This dramatic journalistic account of the Tet offensive and its impact in the United States is dated, but still it is the most comprehensive study available.

30:222   Schandler, Herbert Y. *The Unmaking of a President: Lyndon Johnson and Vietnam.* Princeton, N.J.: Princeton University Press, 1977. Schandler's exhaustive analysis of the decisionmaking process in 1968 draws heavily on personal interviews with many of the participants, and will not likely be superseded for many years. Extensive bibliography.

WITHDRAWAL AND AFTER, 1969–1980

See "Personalities," especially Henry A. Kissinger, Richard M. Nixon.

Peace Negotiations

See "Personalities," especially W. Averell Harriman.

30:223   Bloomfield, Lincoln P. *The U.N. and Vietnam.* New York: Carnegie Endowment, 1968. Bloomfield briefly reviews government contacts with United Nations officials regarding the Vietnam problem and suggests new approaches.

30:224   Goodman, Allan E. *The Lost Peace: America's Search for a Negotiated Settlement of the Vietnam War.* Stanford, Calif.: Hoover Institution, 1978. Goodman's study is the most comprehensive, up-to-date account of American peace negotiations between

1965 and 1973. He also includes a useful epilogue on implementation of the 1973 agreement.

30:225 Johnson, Walter. "The U Thant–Stevenson Peace Initiatives in Vietnam, 1964–1965." *Diplomatic History* 1:3 (1977), 285–95. This essay recounts the abortive efforts of Adlai Stevenson and UN Secretary General U Thant to bring about peace negotiations and suggests some of the reasons for their failure.

30:226 Kraslov, David, and Loory, Stuart H. *The Secret Search for Peace in Vietnam*. New York: Random House, 1968. An early account of the various peace initiatives (1965–1967), it purports to show how the Johnson administration bungled or sabotaged promising peace moves. It should be used with caution as recently declassified documents suggest that the authors are unreliable on major issues and that they overestimate the possibilities of productive peace negotiations.

30:227 Porter, Gareth. *A Peace Denied: The United States, Vietnam and the Paris Agreement*. Bloomington: Indiana University Press, 1975. Porter compiled a valuable account of the negotiation of the Paris agreement of 1973 and its nonimplementation by all sides. Although its North Vietnamese biases are obvious, this volume is indispensable for understanding the motives and attitudes of the Hanoi leadership.

30:228 Radvanyi, Janos. *Delusion and Reality: Gambits, Hoaxes and Diplomatic One-Upmanship in Vietnam*. South Bend, Ind.: Gateway, 1978. Part memoir, part scholarly analysis, this study by a former Hungarian diplomat of the peace initiatives (1965–1966) contains astute observations on the role of the Soviet Union and the Eastern European nations. The author minimizes the sincerity of the various Communist peace moves. Bibliography.

30:229 U Thant. "The Secret Search for Peace in Vietnam." In his *View from the UN*. Garden City, N.Y.: Doubleday, 1978, pp. 57–84. Noting the reluctance of any involved power to bring the Vietnam issue before the United Nations, U Thant discusses his personal search for a settlement.

Fall of South Vietnam, 1975

See "Personalities," especially, under "Others," Gerald Ford, Van Tien Dung.

30:230 Dawson, Alan. *Fifty-Five Days: The Fall of South Vietnam*. Englewood Cliffs, N.J.: Prentice-Hall, 1977. Dawson's dramatic account of the fall of South Vietnam vividly captures the confusion and human tragedy which marked the end of thirty years of war.

30:231 Parker, Maynard. "Vietnam: The War That Won't End." *Foreign Affairs* 53:2 (1975), 352–74. This essay is one of the few serious attempts to analyze developments in Vietnam after the U.S. withdrawal. Parker's conclusions are much too optimistic, but he nevertheless provides a useful discussion of what the Vietnamese called the "postwar war."

30:232 Snepp, Frank. *Decent Interval: An Insider's Account of Saigon's Indecent End*. New York: Random House, 1977. The CIA's strategy analyst in Vietnam during the last two months, Snepp recounts the confusion and ineptitude which characterized the American and South Vietnamese response to the North Vietnamese invasion. The book must be used with caution, but it provides a glimpse into the inner workings of the South Vietnamese government and the American mission in Saigon during the last days.

30:233 Terzani, Tiziano. *Giai Phong! The Fall and Liberation of Saigon*. Trans. by J. Shepley. New York: St. Martin's Press, 1976. An Italian journalist, Terzani had excellent contacts with Vietnamese on both sides, and his detailed account of the collapse of the old regime and the installation of the new is a valuable source for the climactic events of April to July 1975.

30:234 Thompson, W. Scott. "The Indochinese Debacle (1975) and the United States." *Orbis* 19:3 (1975), 990–1011. Thompson's essay is highly critical of the United States for its inaction, and pessimistic in its appraisal of the impact of the fall of South Vietnam on international relations and U.S. foreign policy.

Aftermath and "Lessons"

30:235 Holsti, Ole R., and Rosenau, James N. "The Meaning of Vietnam: Belief Systems of American Leaders." *International Journal* 32:3 (1977), 452–74. Using data from questionnaires submitted to a group of American "leaders," the authors find little more agreement on the lessons of Vietnam than existed on the war itself. They conclude that the persisting disagreement is rooted in the "belief systems" of the leaders, which are in turn related to their occupations and resistant to change, making the development of a new consensus on U.S. foreign policy unlikely in the immediate future.

30:236   Lake, Anthony, ed. *The Legacy of Vietnam.* New York: New York University Press, 1976. This collection of essays represents one of the first serious attempts to put the war into historical perspective and to assess its impact. Speculative rather than in-depth analyses, the essays are sober and balanced.

Osgood, R. E. *Limited War Revisited* (40:191) includes a provocative chapter on the military and political lessons of Vietnam.

30:237   Pfeffer, Richard M., ed. *No More Vietnams? The War and the Future of American Foreign Policy.* New York: Harper & Row, 1968. This volume contains the views of a number of scholars from different fields and with divergent positions on the sources of American frustration in Vietnam and the implications for U.S. foreign policy. The book reveals with clarity and force the dimensions of the scholarly debate on Vietnam.

30:238   Ravenal, Earl C. *Never Again: Learning from America's Foreign Policy Failures.* Philadelphia: Temple University Press, 1978. This provocative little volume contains the best available critique of the early postwar debate on Vietnam. Ravenal's analysis of the lessons learned thus far is consistently penetrating.

30:239   Roskin, Michael. "From Pearl Harbor to Vietnam: Shifting Generational Paradigms." *Political Science Quarterly* 89:3 (1974), 563–88. This early attempt to assess the impact of Vietnam on the foreign policy assumptions of Americans suggests that the full effects may not be felt until the Vietnam generation assumes influence. Roskin's comparison with the Pearl Harbor generation is insightful, although he

may overstate Vietnam-imbedded noninterventionist attitudes.

30:240   Siracusa, Joseph M. "Lessons of Viet Nam and the Future of American Foreign Policy." *Australian Outlook* 30:2 (1976), 227–37. Siracusa explores the reaction of politicians and foreign policy elites to the fall of South Vietnam and makes some interesting observations as to why the postwar debate was relatively subdued.

30:241   Thompson, W. Scott, and Frizzell, Donaldson D., eds. *The Lessons of Vietnam.* New York: Crane, Russak, 1977. This volume focuses on the reasons why the United States failed to achieve its objectives in Vietnam. It is rather narrowly construed, emphasizing methods employed rather than the larger assumptions of U.S. policy, but it contains a useful debate on such important topics as the use of air power, the search and destroy strategy, and pacification.

30:242   Zasloff, Joseph, and Brown, McAlister. *Communist Indochina and U.S. Foreign Policy.* Boulder, Colo.: Westview, 1978. This book contains three chapters on internal developments in Indochina and two on relations with the United States. The book is balanced in its assessments, but it is dated, since it was written before the Third Indochina War.

The Third Indochina War

30:243   Turley, William S., and Race, Jeffrey. "The Third Indochina War." *Foreign Policy,* no. 38 (1980), 92–116. This essay provides a careful appraisal of developments in Southeast Asia after the end of the Second Indochina War in 1975. The authors argue that the withdrawal of U.S. power from the region opened the way to a resumption of traditional ethnic and national conflicts—the Vietnamese-Cambodian and Sino-Vietnamese wars.

31

United States and East Asia after 1953

Contributing Editor
AKIRA IRIYE
University of Chicago

Contributor
Anthony Cheung
University of Chicago

Contents

Introduction

As the other chapters dealing with the post-1950 period reveal, the past thirty years are an historiographical terra incognita. Crucial documents have become available only recently, and those sporadically. Almost all foreign archives are still closed. Under the circumstances, virtually any topic one can think of can be viewed as a potential subject for monographic study by future historians.

Studying American relations with East Asia is especially complicated because we have few signposts to guide us. True, one can start with the Korean armistice of 1953 and trace the two off-shore island crises with the People's Republic of China in the 1950s, then note such events in the 1960s as the anti-American riots in Japan in 1960 and those in China during the Cultural Revolution (1966–1969), and conclude with the rapprochement between China and the United States that was effected during the 1970s. But such a list only skims the surface and says nothing about the dynamics of American-Japanese-Korean-Chinese (Nationalist and Communist) relations during the three decades, let alone puts them in the context of the global developments in U.S.-Soviet affairs. Domestically, too, these countries underwent profound change, economically as well as politically. How their respective transformations affected one another and the overall pattern of American-Asian relations cannot be examined until historians develop more sophisticated interpretive frameworks than are available today.

Finally, it may be pointed out that American–East Asian relations have been far more than geopolitics, alliances, and the like. When Henry Kissinger explained, in his *White House Years* (24:133), his decision to approach Peking as a geopolitical necessity, he put it in a context that both Americans and Chinese— and Russians and others, for that matter—understood.

At the same time, relations have had many nongeopolitical aspects. We should recall that in many ways the history of American-Asian relations has been a history of the Americanization of Asia. Americanization has involved the impact of America's material culture, technology, economic organization, political ideology, and the like upon other peoples, and Chinese, Japanese, and Koreans have been particularly attracted to and influenced by them. During the period 1953 to 1981, however, their receptivity to Americanization varied enormously, from Japan's almost complete submergence in American cultural influences to China's self-conscious rejection of them, which, however, was neither long-lasting nor entirely successful. In the meantime, in such areas as food, fashions, and consumer products, American life began to be transformed by the impact of Asian culture. That societies interact with one another as cultures, not simply as powers or economies, should always be kept in mind when discussing U.S. foreign affairs.

Few items in this chapter address these matters. Historians have only begun to write monographs on the last thirty years. A reliable overview is Barnett, *China and the Major Powers in East Asia* (31:10). Probably the most important work listed here is Kissinger's above-noted memoirs (24:133), which recount U.S. diplomacy in effecting a rapprochement with the People's Republic of China, and also contain insightful statements about policies toward Japan, the Korean peninsula, and Asia in general, as well as about the "Guam Doctrine" of 1969, which redefined the limits of American commitments in the region.

Most other works are more or less contemporary accounts and should be viewed as tentative statements, even as primary sources, rather than definitive scholarly treatments. Even so, they reveal the kinds of issues that have attracted scholarly attention. By the same token, they leave out much. Future researchers, therefore, may profitably study extensively any number of topics in American–East Asian relations since 1953.

Resources and Overviews

RESEARCH AIDS

While pertinent bibliographies and reference aids are listed here, there are more extensive lists in Chapter 1.

Bibliographies

31:1 Berton, Peter, and Wu, Eugene. *Contemporary China: A Research Guide*. Ed. by Howard Koch, Jr. Stanford, Calif.: Hoover Institution Press, 1967. The basic materials incorporated in this guide concern post-1949 mainland China and post-1945 Taiwan. Annotations.

Dial, R. *Studies on Chinese External Affairs: An Instructional Bibliography of Commonwealth and American Literature* (1:96).

Foreign Affairs Bibliography: A Selected and Annotated List of Books on International Relations (1:15) is issued at ten-year intervals, and each volume has three parts: "General International Relations"; "The World since 1914"; and "The World by Regions." Useful aid.

Gordon, L. H. D., and Shulman, F. J., comps. *Doctoral Dissertations on China: A Bibliography of Studies in Western Languages, 1945–1970* (17:7).

31:2 Lindbeck, John M. H. *Understanding China: An Assessment of American Scholarly Resources*. New York: Praeger, 1971. Lindbeck provides a qualitative and quantitative review of these resources.

McCutcheon, J. M., comp. *China and America: A Bibliography of Interactions, Foreign and Domestic* (1:98) is a highly selective bibliography of secondary literature in English covering the 1700s to the 1970s. It is arranged by subjects such as foreign policy, public opinion, and missionaries.

31:3 Nihon Kokusai Seiji Gakkai, ed. *Sengo Nihon no kokusai seijigaku* [Studies of international relations

in postwar Japan]. Tokyo: Yūhikaku, 1979. This is a compendium of representative works produced by Japanese scholars since 1945 that deal with diplomatic history, international relations, and area studies. There are good and useful sections on Japanese diplomatic history and U.S.-Japanese relations, past and present. Thousands of books and articles are listed, with brief introductions covering various subjects.

31:4 Saran, Vimla. *Sino-Soviet Schism: A Bibliography, 1956–1964*. New York: Asia Publishing House, 1971. A bibliography of both communist and noncommunist materials that have appeared in English.

Shulman, F. J., comp. *Doctoral Dissertations on Japan and Korea, 1969–1974: A Classified Bibliographical Listing of International Research* (17:8).

Shulman, F. J., comp. *Japan and Korea: An Annotated Bibliography of Doctoral Dissertations in Western Languages, 1877–1969* (17:9).

Yearbooks and Other Aids

31:5 *China Yearbook*. Taipei: China Publishing, 1951– . This is a valuable official reference work which contains information on both Taiwan and mainland China. Supersedes *China Handbook*.

Facts on File: A Weekly Digest with Cumulative Index (1:151).

Far Eastern Economic Review: Yearbook (1:143) has comprehensive coverage of China, Japan, and Korea.

Herrman, A. *An Historical Atlas of China* (1:161).

Keesing's Contemporary Archives: Weekly Diary of World Events (1:152) is the British equivalent of *Facts on File*, with cumulative index. It has somewhat stronger coverage of foreign affairs.

Political Handbook and Atlas of the World (1:144) is a valuable annual reference guide to world governments and their officials and political parties. It contains summaries of the year's events and, since 1963, maps.

The United States in World Affairs (1:147) is a useful annual survey and analysis which covers up to 1970, with 1968 and 1969 as yet to be printed.

Yearbook on International Communist Affairs (1:148) is an annual, from 1967, providing a country-by-country profile.

Document Collections

More general collections are listed in Chapter 1.

31:6 Ch'i-shih nien-tai yüeh-k'an [The Seventies Monthly], comp. *Chung-Mei kuan-hsi wen-chien hui-pien: 1940–1976* [A collection of documents on Sino-American relations, 1940–1976]. Hong Kong: Ch'i-shih nien-tai yüeh-k'an, 1977. This is a compilation of 106 official and semiofficial documents. The chronologically arranged documents, some of which are excerpts, include Chinese official statements, speeches and writings of Mao, editorials and commentaries of the *People's Daily,* and translated U.S. official statements. The volume also provides a 57-page chronology of major events in Sino-American relations (1784–1976).

Columbia Broadcasting System. *Face the Nation: The Collected Transcripts from CBS Radio and Television Broadcasts, 1954–1971* (1:347).

Gallup, G. H. *The Gallup Poll: Public Opinion, 1935–1971* (1:348) pays considerable attention to foreign affairs.

31:7 Ishikawa Tadao; Nakajima Mineo; and Ikei Masaru, eds. *Sengo shiryō: Nit-Chū kankei* [Postwar documents: Japanese-Chinese relations]. Tokyo: Nihon Hyōronsha, 1970. These documents deal with diplomatic and economic relations between Japan and the People's Republic of China. This is a convenient reference for any study of East Asian affairs during the 1950s and 1960s.

31:8 Jen-min ch'u-pan-she [People's Publishing House], comp. *Chung-Mei kuan-hsi (wen-chien he tzu-liao hsüan-pien)* [Sino-American relations (selected documents and sources)]. Peking: Jen-min ch'u-pan-she, 1971. This volume consists of several groups of selected documents on Sino-American relations (1940–1971). The two major groups provide over 60 official statements of Chou En-lai, the foreign and defense ministries; *People's Daily* editorials; and translated U.S. official documents. Others include quotations from Mao's speeches and writings, pre-1949 sources on the Taiwan issue, and key documents dealing with U.S.-Taiwan relations. A chronology of

major events in Sino-American relations (1784–1949) is also given.

31:9 Saitō Makoto; Nagai Yōnosuke; and Yamamoto Mitsuru. *Sengo shiryō: Nichi-Bei kankei* [Postwar documents: Japanese-American relations]. Tokyo: Nihon Hyōronsha, 1970. A very useful collection of documents dealing with political, economic, and ideological relations between Japan and the United States. Particularly valuable are the documents on peace movements and public opinion in Japan.

OVERVIEWS

See Chapter 24, "Overviews," for surveys of American foreign affairs since World War II.

31:10 Barnett, A. Doak. *China and the Major Powers in East Asia.* Washington, D.C.: Brookings Institution, 1977. In this analysis of international politics in East Asia, the author examines the history, factors, and problems in China's bilateral relations with the Soviet Union, Japan, and the United States. The complex four-power system in the region, China's active role in it, and the forces affecting equilibrium are discussed. Barnett finds that Peking takes the pragmatic approach where vital security interests are concerned.

31:11 Burnell, Elaine H., ed. *Asian Dilemma: United States, Japan and China.* Santa Barbara, Calif.: Center for the Study of Democratic Institutions, 1969. This volume is compiled from comments and discussions of a 1969 conference between Japanese and American government officials and scholars. It is topically arranged and deals with policy problems affecting the United States, Japan, and China. The isolation of China and the broader questions of security, stability, and prosperity in Asia are discussed.

31:12 Chay, John, ed. *The Problems and Prospects of American–East Asian Relations.* Boulder, Colo.: Westview, 1977. These research papers discuss American postwar and future relations with China, Japan, and Korea. Nine main chapters, preceded by an essay on the cold war in Asia, are grouped under the three Asian countries. Part 1 studies new perspectives in Sino-American relations, American perceptions of China, and relations with Taiwan; part 2 examines political, trade, and energy issues between the United States and Japan; part 3 deals with American-Korean relations, with discussions on security and economic issues.

31:13 Clough, Ralph N. *East Asia and U.S. Security.* Washington, D.C.: Brookings Institution, 1975. This study reassesses U.S. security interests and policy in East Asia with the end of American involvement in Vietnam. The author focuses on Japan, China, and the Soviet Union, which with the United States form a four-power system in the region. He emphasizes the need to maintain the vital alliance with a lightly armed and nonnuclear Japan and to improve relations with China and the Soviet Union.

31:14 Cowing, Cedric B., ed. *The American Revolution: Its Meaning to Asians and Americans.* Honolulu: East-West Center, 1978. An interesting collection of essays on the meaning of the American Revolution to contemporary Asian countries that are engaged in their own nation-building. The contributions, representing all Asian countries except the People's Republic of China, stress the differences involved in transmitting American ideas and practices to Asia.

31:15 Graebner, Norman A., ed. *Nationalism and Communism in Asia: The American Response.* Lexington, Mass.: Heath, 1977. These selected essays deal broadly with various points of view toward America's role in Asia. Bibliography.

31:16 Greene, Fred. *U.S. Policy and the Security of Asia.* New York: McGraw-Hill, 1968. In this defense of the assumptions, goals, and actions underlying U.S. policy toward Asia, the author considers regional balance of power essential to American security interests. He surveys the U.S. treaty system and military presence in Asia, and describes the communist threat and China's military strategy.

31:17 Hellmann, Donald C., ed. *China and Japan: A New Balance of Power.* Lexington, Mass.: Lexington Books, 1976. Three essays deal with Japan and the United States, including a discussion on domestic politics as a factor in Japanese foreign and security policies, an analysis of Japan's political economy, and a review of American economic policy toward Japan. The others deal with the economic constraints on China's global influence, the political and strategic aspects of Chinese foreign policy, and Sino-U.S. bilateral relations.

31:18 Jo, Yung-hwan, ed. *U.S. Foreign Policy in Asia: An Appraisal.* Santa Barbara, Calif.: ABC-Clio, 1978. This comprehensive overview of U.S. foreign

policy in Asia consists of documented scholarly contributions. These reports provide factual information and a number of differing viewpoints.

31:19 Lach, Donald F., and Wehrle, Edmund S. *International Politics in East Asia since World War II.* New York: Praeger, 1975. A survey of East Asian international relations since 1945, it examines the foreign policies of China, Japan, and, to a lesser extent, other countries.

May, E. R., and Thomson, J. C., Jr., eds. *American–East Asian Relations: A Survey* (2:334) consists of 17 essays organized under four periods: 18th and 19th centuries, 1900 to 1922, 1922 to 1941, and 1941 to 1969. This chronological survey of American diplomatic, commercial, and military relations with East Asia, with emphasis on China and Japan, is a notable effort. As a fundamental work, it provides a stimulating basis for further study and research in the field.

31:20 Scalapino, Robert A. *Asia and the Road Ahead: Issues for the Major Powers.* Berkeley: University of California Press, 1975. This book discusses the major problems and issues confronting the major powers in Pacific-Asia. The author focuses on six nations in the region: Japan, China, India, Indonesia, the Soviet Union, the United States, and contends that balanced interaction among them is vital.

31:21 Wu, Yuan-li. *U.S. Policy and Strategic Interests in the Western Pacific.* New York: Crane, Russak, 1975. This is a study of U.S. foreign and defense policy in the western Pacific during Nixon's presidency. The author discusses the new American posture in Pacific-Asia and analyzes the essence of the Nixon Doctrine, the factors underlying Sino-American rapprochement, and the perception-response of Japan, Korea, Taiwan, and other countries.

U.S., East and Southeast Asia

Funnell, V. C. "Vietnam and the Sino-Soviet Conflict, 1965–1976" (30:199) is an up-to-date, comprehensive account.

31:22 Gordon, Bernard K. "Japan, the United States, and Southeast Asia." *Foreign Affairs* 56:3 (1978), 579–600. No longer confident in America's military and economic commitments in Southeast Asia, Japan has decided to extend its influence unilaterally. It is essential to the interests of Japan and the United States that their close and interdependent relationship continue "in the East Asian rim areas."

Martin, E. W. *Southeast Asia and China: The End of Containment* (30:27) is a brief analysis of the realignment of power in Southeast Asia following the U.S. withdrawal from Vietnam.

Zagoria, D. *Vietnam Triangle: Moscow, Peking, Hanoi* (30:203).

Public Opinion, Politics, and Mutual Perceptions

31:23　Fairbank, John K. *China Perceived: Images and Policies in Chinese-American Relations.* New York: Knopf, 1974. This is a collection of previously published essays (1946–1972) that focus on perceptions and policies in Sino-American relations. Part 1 gives Fairbank's personal observations in China before and after the Chinese Revolution, in 1946 and 1972 respectively; part 2 discusses American and Chinese policies toward each other in the 19th and 20th centuries; part 3 deals with contact and mutual perceptions in the 1880s and 1970s; part 4 summarizes the Chinese life of five Americans; and the last part is on the study of American–East Asian relations.

31:24　Harrison, Selig S. *The Widening Gulf: Asian Nationalism and American Policy.* New York: Free Press, 1978. This is a study of the American encounter with Asian nationalism. Using selected countries and cases as illustrations, Harrison analyzes nationalism's interplay with communism and focuses on its relationship with American military and economic policy.

31:25　Hohenberg, John. *Between Two Worlds: Policy, Press, and Public Opinion in Asian-American Relations.* New York: Praeger, 1967. This is a study of the relationship between foreign correspondence and foreign policy from 1941 to the mid-1960s. The author finds that the exchange of news, ideas, and opinion between the United States and Asia is often political in character, involving governments and their struggle with the independent news media for control.

Isaacs, H. R. *Images of Asia: America Views of China and India* [1700s–1957] (2:333) is a valuable study of American images and ideas of China and India. The author describes the wide spectrum of impressions, attitudes, and feelings, tracing their sources within

individual experience as well as the related historical background.

31:26　Steele, A. T. *The American People and China.* New York: McGraw-Hill, 1966. In this study of American public opinion on China, the author relies primarily on his interviews with "opinion leaders" and public opinion polls, especially a 1964 national survey the results of which are included in an appendix. Steele discusses past and recent American attitudes toward China, the diversity of views among opinion leaders, the significance of public opinion and pressure groups, the roles of the news media and the educational system in shaping the public's knowledge, and finally he examines public opinion in relationship to policymaking at the government level.

Thomas, J. N. *The Institute of Pacific Relations: Asian Scholars and American Politics* (27:32) is an account of the major private organization devoted to promoting study of Asia in the 1930s and 1940s and its demise under the weight of cold war investigations and controversy.

31:27　Wu, Yuan-li. *As Peking Sees Us: "People's War" in the United States and Communist China's America Policy.* Stanford, Calif.: Hoover Institution Press, 1969. This is an interpretation of Peking's perception of America's internal unrest and disorder in the 1960s. It also examines the views of black militants in relation to Maoist revolutionary thought and analyzes the implications in China's policy toward the U.S.

Personalities

Additional references on individuals may be found in Chapter 1, "Biographical Data."

AMERICAN

See Chapter 24, "Personalities," and "Presidential Administrations," for additional references.

John Foster Dulles
See Chapters 24 and 27, "Personalities," for additional references.

Gerson, L. L. *John Foster Dulles* (24:108) contains material on the various Formosa Straits crises.

Dwight D. Eisenhower

See Chapter 24, "Personalities," for additional references.

Eisenhower, D. D. *The White House Years* (24:114) contains, in the first volume, *Mandate for Change,* information regarding his attitudes and policies toward East Asia. It is informative for the Formosa Straits crisis (1954–1955). Volume 2, *Waging Peace, 1956–1961,* has information on the Quemoy crisis (1958).

Henry A. Kissinger

See Chapters 24 and 30, "Personalities," for additional references.

Kissinger, H. A. *American Foreign Policy* (24:132) is a convenient compilation of Kissinger's major public addresses as secretary of state (1973–1977). These have frequent references to East Asia.

Kissinger, H. A. *White House Years* [1969–1973] (24:133) covers his secret trip to China and the historic summit meeting in Peking.

Richard M. Nixon

Nixon, R. M. "Asia after Vietnam" (30:36) reveals Nixon's keen interest in the future of Asia, particularly China, before his election to the presidency.

Nixon, R. M. *RN: The Memoirs of Richard Nixon* (24:145) contains information about Nixon's decision to reopen formal relations with China.

Others

Adams, S. *Firsthand Report: The Story of the Eisenhower Administration* (24:200) has some information about the Formosa Straits decisions.

Beam, J. D. *Multiple Exposure: An American Ambassador's Unique Perspective on East-West Issues* (29:38) has good material on the China talk in Warsaw.

Emmerson, J. K. *The Japanese Thread: A Lifetime in the U.S. Foreign Service* (27:48) is an autobiographical account of the author's career in the U.S. foreign service, marked by a strong personal bond to Japan, where he served beginning in prewar years and also ending there in the 1960s. He observes that the American approach to China and Japan had been too emotional in character, which contributed to the failure of diplomacy in Asia.

Kahn, E. J., Jr. *The China Hands: America's Foreign Service Officers and What Befell Them* (27:49) is a study of 13 former foreign service officers who served in wartime China and whose reports to Washington at the time could have significantly changed the course of Sino-American relations had they not been ignored. The author focuses on their experiences after they left China and on the damaging effects of the McCarthy era on their careers. The China hands include men such as Edmund Clubb, John Davies, and John Service.

Rankin, K. L. *China Assignment* (27:52) is a personal account, by the former U.S. ambassador to the Republic of China, written during his assignment in Canton, Hong Kong, and Taipei, where he served from 1949 to 1958. He closely describes the course of Sino-American relations as it appeared to him at the time, emphasizing that a strategy of active support to the Chinese Nationalists is in the United States' interests. He also shows the practical problems in coordinating diplomatic operations overseas.

EAST ASIAN

Chou En-lai

31:28   Hsu Kai-yu. *Chou En-lai: China's Gray Eminence.* New York: Doubleday, 1968. This biography traces the course of Chou's communist career that began in France, through the turmoil of revolutionary China in which he played an active role, building the Communist party and army, and mediating inside and outside the party for its final victory over China. His conduct of foreign policy as China's premier is also discussed.

31:29   Robinson, Thomas W. "Chou En-lai and the Biographic Study of Chinese Communism." *China Quarterly,* no. 79 (1979), 608–19. Robinson reviews four recent biographies of Chou En-lai. They are Jules Archer's *Chou En-lai* (N.Y.: Hawthorn, 1973), Hsu Kai-yu's *Chou En-lai* (31:28), Li Tien-min *Chou En-lai* (Taipei: Institute of International Relations, 1970), and John M. Roots's *Chou: An Informal Biography of China's Legendary Chou En-lai* (Garden City, N.Y.: Doubleday, 1978). Robinson concludes that, while there is enough data available, a thorough biography has yet to be written.

White, T. H. *In Search of History* (23:225) relates White's many meetings with Chou.

Mao Tse-tung

See also Chapter 27, under "Personalities."

Schram, S. *Mao Tse-tung* (27:59) is a biography of Mao Tse-tung's life from childhood to the time of the Cultural Revolution which focuses on the successive stages of his career as a revolutionary leader and thinker that has shaped the course of Chinese history. The author sees Mao as a strong believer in the capacity of the human will to transform man and society through thought reform and mass action, as reflected in China's policy since 1949.

31:30 Schram, Stuart, ed. *Chairman Mao Talks to the People: Talks and Letters, 1956–1971.* Trans. by John Chinnery and Tieyun. New York: Pantheon, 1975. This documentary volume consists of 26 translated and annotated speeches and statements of Mao Tse-tung on political, economic, and philosophical problems. It includes an introductory discussion on the key elements of his thinking on organization of the party, education and culture, dialectics of development, and foreign policy.

Park Chung-hee

31:31 Kim Chong-sin. *Seven Years with Korea's Park Chung-hee.* Seoul: Hollyn, 1967. This is a very sympathetic account of Park's political activities by a South Korean journalist.

31:32 Pak Chong-hui. *Major Speeches by Korea's Park Chung Hee.* Seoul: Hollyn, 1970. The South Korean leader seeks to explain his domestic and foreign policies.

Others

31:33 Klein, Donald W., and Clark, Anne B. *Biographic Dictionary of Chinese Communism, 1921–1965.* 2 vols. Cambridge: Harvard University Press, 1971. This is a valuable aid for identifying individuals.

31:34 Paek Pong. *Kim Il Sung: A Biography.* 3 vols. Tokyo: Miraishi, 1969–1970. This is an English translation of a very sympathetic biography of North Korea's leader.

31:35 *Who's Who in Communist China.* Hong Kong: Union Research Institute, 1969–1970. 2 vols. Rev. ed. These volumes cover over 3,000 leading important individuals in all aspects of Chinese life and politics.

U.S. and China

See "Personalities," especially Chou En-lai, Mao Tse-tung, Richard M. Nixon.

31:36 Barnds, William J., ed. *China and America: The Search for a New Relationship.* New York: New York University Press, 1977. Akira Iriye's essay analyzes Chinese perception of the United States since 1949. Economic relations, cultural exchange, and the Taiwan issue in the 1970s are respectively dealt with by Alexander Eckstein, Lucian Pye, and Ralph Clough. The concluding essay, by William Barnds, assesses China's role in U.S. policy.

31:37 Blum, Robert. *The United States and China in World Affairs.* Ed. by A. Doak Barnett. New York: McGraw-Hill, 1966. This book, prepared after the author's death, examines U.S.-China relations in the contemporary world. It describes Communist China's foreign affairs in general and policy toward the United States. It also reviews and appraises American policy toward China, and discusses the major problems in Sino-American relations.

Cohen, W. I. *America's Response to China: An Interpretative History of Sino-American Relations* (2:340) is a concise and imaginative interpretation of Sino-American relations (1800s–1960s) which focuses on American perceptions and responses to China that rest on fluctuating and unrealistic sentiments. In examining American attitudes toward the growth of communism, Cohen points out that obsessive fear of it and involvement in the Chinese civil war constitute the "great aberration."

31:38 Dulles, Foster Rhea. *American Policy toward Communist China, 1949–1969.* New York: Crowell, 1972. In this volume written for the general reader, Dulles describes Sino-American relations and their major problems in the two decades since the Chinese Communists came to power. In tracing their rivalry, he emphasizes American misconceptions of the new nation, anticommunist obsession, and the pursuit of an unrealistic policy of containment and isolation that led to confrontation. He concludes that no real resolution to the outstanding issues is in sight.

Etzold, T. H., ed. *Aspects of Sino-American Relations since 1784* (2:343) describes, in the last chapter,

America's relations with Chinese Communist leaders since the 1920s.

31:39 Fairbank, John K. *China: The People's Middle Kingdom and the U.S.A.* Cambridge: Harvard University Press, 1967. This introduction to contemporary China and its relations with the United States consists of eleven essays, of which three offer perspectives on the Chinese Revolution, two treat Taiwan, and six discuss other aspects of American policy toward Communist China.

Gittings, J. *The World and China, 1922–1972* (2:345) is a useful introduction to Chinese Communist foreign policy.

31:40 Hinton, Harold C. *China's Turbulent Quest: An Analysis of China's Foreign Relations Since 1949.* New York: Macmillan, 1972. Rev. ed. This reasoned appraisal of the many imponderables in China's foreign relations reviews that country's role as a nuclear power, the unclear results of the Cultural Revolution, the Sino-Soviet border disputes, and Nixon's China policy.

31:41 Irie Keishirō, and Andō Seishi, eds. *Gendai Chūgoku no kokusai kankei* [The foreign relations of contemporary China]. Tokyo: Nihon Kokusai Mondai Kenkyūjo, 1975. The book contains 18 essays, dealing with Communist China's relations with capitalist, socialist, and Third World countries since 1949. Particularly useful is Ota Katsuhiro's essay analyzing changing Chinese strategies in the context of domestic politics. The collection is representative of numerous Japanese studies of Chinese foreign policy.

31:42 Iriye, Akira, ed. *U.S. Policy toward China: Testimony Taken from the Senate Foreign Relations Committee Hearings, 1966.* Boston: Little, Brown, 1968. This volume is compiled largely from the statements and exchanges between China specialists and senators at the Senate hearings on China in March 1966, one of the most notable attempts at expanding the public's knowledge of China. The excerpts, which include important testimony from the preceding hearings on Vietnam, are arranged topically under historical background, nature of the Communist regime and its foreign policy, and American policy toward China.

31:43 MacFarquhar, Roderick, ed. *Sino-American Relations, 1949–1971.* New York: Praeger, 1972. This is mainly a documentary survey of major issues and developments in Sino-American relations from 1949 to the diplomatic breakthrough in 1971. Included are three short essays on the breakthrough, which discuss the causes of China's foreign policy shift and the implications of Nixon's China policy for the United States in Asia.

31:44 Moorsteen, Richard, and Abramowitz, Morton. *Remaking China Policy: U.S.-China Relations and Governmental Decision Making.* Cambridge: Harvard University Press, 1971. This study, which is intended for high-level policymakers and government specialists on China, deals with the complex problems of governmental decisionmaking and the development of long-term China policy. The authors propose organizational and procedural changes to improve sources of information on China, and to increase the policy relevance of information as well as exploratory policy moves toward Peking.

31:45 Oksenberg, Michel C., and Oxnam, Robert B., eds. *Dragon and Eagle: United States–China Relations, Past and Future.* New York: Basic Books, 1978. This volume of essays is arranged in six parts dealing with broad perspective; mutual perceptions; specific aspects of bilateral relations; the factors of Japan and the Soviet Union; interactions with Taiwan, Northeast and Southeast Asia; and the issue of international law. A very useful bibliographical guide is also included.

31:46 Simmonds, John D. *China's World: The Foreign Policy of a Developing State.* New York: Columbia University Press, 1971. China's foreign policy, as reviewed by an Australian writer, is seen as dictated by the internal need to find an external enemy.

31:47 Tsou, Tang, ed. *China's Policies in Asia and America's Alternatives.* Vol. 2 in *China in Crisis.* Chicago: University of Chicago Press, 1968. This volume analyzes Peking's foreign policy, military affairs, and relations with its neighbors. It also discusses the problems and alternative courses in U.S. policy toward China.

U.S., CHINA, AND THE SOVIET UNION

31:48 Chai, Trong R. "Chinese Policy toward the Third World and the Superpowers in the UN General Assembly, 1971–1977: A Voting Analysis." *International Organization* 33:3 (1979), 391–404. This analysis suggests that China has for the most part demonstrated its pro-Third World and anti-superpower position within the context of the UN, and judging by available evidence will continue to do so.

31:49 Gelber, Harry G. "The Sino-Soviet Relationship and the United States." *Orbis* 15:1 (1971), 118–33. Traces the course of Sino-Soviet relations in the 1960s, noting the withdrawal on both sides following the open border confrontation and conflict in 1969. The Sino-Soviet conflict was an important consideration in every U.S. policy in Asia in this period.

31:50 Griffith, William E. *Cold War and Coexistence: Russia, China and the United States.* Englewood Cliffs, N.J.: Prentice-Hall, 1971. This study focuses on the triangular relationship of the United States, Russia, and China. It first surveys American bilateral relations with Russia and China in modern times to World War II and then examines postwar international politics and crises which revolve around rivalries among the three powers.

31:51 Sergeichuk, S. *Through Russian Eyes: American-Chinese Relations.* Trans. by Elizabeth Cody-Rutter. Arlington, Va.: International Library, 1975. This outline of postwar U.S. policy toward China (1950s–1970s) is a translation of the revised 1973 Russian edition. The emerging Sino-American rapprochement is viewed as fundamentally opportunistic and anti-Soviet in character. This study, typical of Soviet criticism of the motives of China's leadership and American "reactionaries," provides a Soviet interpretation accessible to the non-Russian reader.

31:52 Wilcox, Francis O., ed. *China and the Great Powers: Relations with the United States, the Soviet Union, and Japan.* New York: Praeger, 1974. This slim volume consists of four essays that focus on China and its relations with the other three great powers in East Asia. One essay discusses Sino-Soviet relations and its prospects and another considers whether China and Japan are rivals or allies in the context of multilateral relations. The other two deal with Sino-American relations, particularly the steps the United States can probably take to improve relations with China.

Sino-Soviet Dispute

31:53 Gittings, John. *Survey of the Sino-Soviet Dispute: A Commentary and Extracts from the recent Polemics, 1963–1967.* New York: Columbia University Press, 1968. This survey extends Zagoria's ac-

count (31:59) and, additionally, provides over 100 selected Soviet and Chinese documents.

31:54 Griffith, William E. *The Sino-Soviet Rift.* Cambridge, Mass.: MIT Press, 1964.

31:55 Griffith, William E. *Sino-Soviet Relations, 1964–1965: Analyzed and Documented.* Cambridge, Mass.: MIT Press, 1967. These two volumes supplement Gittings (31:53) and Zagoria (31:59) as they discuss the conflict from 1962 to 1965.

31:56 Hinton, Harold C. *The Sino-Soviet Confrontation: Implications for the Future.* New York: Crane, Russak, 1976. This paper from the National Strategic Information Center traces the Sino-Soviet dispute from its origins to the mid-1970s and analyzes the key issues involved. It also assesses different possible directions of the dispute, particularly after leadership succession in each country, the implications for the United States, and the policy initiatives open to Washington.

31:57 Nakajima Mineo. *Chū-So tairitsu to gendai* [The Sino-Soviet antagonism and the contemporary world]. Tokyo: Chūōkōronsha, 1978. The best and most comprehensive account of Sino-Soviet relations during the 1950s that has been published in Japan. The author makes extensive use of sources in Chinese, Korean, Russian, and other languages to document the almost inevitable development of a serious rift between the two socialist countries.

31:58 Zablocki, Clement J., ed. *Sino-Societ Rivalry: Implications for U.S. Policy.* New York: Praeger, 1966. This collection of essays, presented to a U.S. House Committee on Foreign Affairs subcommittee, provides a variety of views.

31:59 Zagoria, Donald S. *The Sino-Soviet Conflict, 1956–1961.* New York: Atheneum, 1964. While dated, this study is still a standard work. It provides a useful discussion on how to interpret communist polemical writings.

U.S., CHINA, AND THE UN

31:60 Alpert, Eugene J., and Bernstein, Samuel J. "International Bargaining and Political Coalitions: U.S. Foreign Aid and China's Admission to the U.N." *Western Political Quarterly* 27:2 (1974), 314–27. The authors examine the nature of voting behavior and of coalition formation on the issue of

China's admission to the UN (1961–1968), using U.S. foreign aid as an independent variable in explaining voting patterns.

Appleton, S. *The Eternal Triangle? Communist China, the United States and the United Nations* (38:205) is a study of American policy on China's representation in the United Nations. The author treats the problem historically as well as from the legal and political points of view. One chapter provides a survey of American public opinion on the issue.

Bloomfield, L. P. "China, the United States, and the United Nations" (38:206) contains tables of votes and a review of issues and efforts to seat China.

Cheng, P. "Peking's Entry into the United Nations: Review and Retrospect" (38:207) discusses the history of UN involvement with the issue of representation for the People's Republic of China, and examines the changes in support for the People's Republic as revealed in voting on the issue in the General Assembly. Tables.

Erskine, H. "The Polls: Red China and the U.N." (38:208) traces the changing American public opinion on the seating of mainland China in the United Nations. In the 1950s only 7 percent of Americans favored such a move; by the 1970s the figure had risen to only 35 percent, yet only 20 percent would favor leaving the UN if China were seated.

Guhin, M. A. "The United States and the Chinese People's Republic: The Non-Recognition Policy Reviewed" (38:209) focuses on John Foster Dulles, reviewing his attitude toward China and communism beginning in 1917 and showing a complex set of circumstances in the decisionmaking process.

Weng, B. S. J. *Peking's UN Policy: Continuity and Change* (38:210) seeks to describe the various elements influencing China's policies toward the United Nations.

U.S.-CHINA:
CRISES AND ISSUES

31:61   Kalicki, J. H. *The Pattern of Sino-American Crises: Political-Military Interactions in the 1950s.* New York: Cambridge University Press, 1975. This is an analysis of how the "crisis behavior theory" operated between the United States and China in the 1950s.

The first of three parts studies the background of confrontation and the Korean War; the second discusses how confrontation elaborated to crises in Indochina (1954) and in the Taiwan Straits (1954–1955); the third studies the management of confrontation during the intercrises period and the Taiwan Straits crisis of 1958.

31:62   Lampton, David M. "The U.S. Image of Peking in Three International Crises." *Western Political Quarterly* 26:1 (1973), 28–50. Lampton analyzes the relationship between U.S. policy toward Communist China and the images of Communist China held by U.S. foreign policy during the crises in Korea (1950), Indochina (1954), and Laos (1961–1962).

31:63   Newman, Robert P. "Lethal Rhetoric: The Selling of the China Myths." *Quarterly Journal of Speech* 61:2 (1975), 113–28. Newman analyzes the effects of ideas about China on U.S. foreign policy and describes how these ideas became current.

Crisis in the Formosa Straits, 1950–1958

See "Personalities," especially John Foster Dulles, Dwight D. Eisenhower.

31:64   George, Alexander L., and Smoke, Richard. "The Quemoy Crisis, 1958." In their *Deterrence in American Foreign Policy: Theory and Practice.* New York: Columbia University Press, 1974, pp. 363–89. This essay examines the U.S. role in the minicrisis that arose during the Communist bombardment of the Nationalist islands of Quemoy and Matsu (August 23–September 4, 1958).

31:65   George, Alexander L., and Smoke, Richard. "The Taiwan Strait Crisis, 1954–1955." In their *Deterrence in American Foreign Policy: Theory and Practice.* New York: Columbia University Press, 1974, pp. 266–94. This episode began when mainland China responded to statements by Chiang Kai-shek and Syngman Rhee by bombarding the island of Quemoy and calling for the liberation of Formosa. Critics claim that Eisenhower and Dulles overreacted.

31:66   Halperin, M. H., and Tsou, Tang. "The 1958 Quemoy Crisis." In M. H. Halperin, ed., *Sino-Soviet Relations and Arms Control.* Cambridge, Mass.: MIT Press, 1967, pp. 265–303. The authors consider in detail Sino-Soviet relations during this crisis, and conclude that there may not have been any major disagreement about strategy.

31:67 Irish, Marian D. "Public Opinion and American Foreign Policy: The Quemoy Crisis of 1958." *Political Quarterly* 31:2 (1960), 151–62. Irish concludes that perhaps the American press was overexcited and the American people underinformed during the crisis.

31:68 Tsou, Tang. "Mao's Limited War in the Taiwan Strait." *Orbis* 3:3 (1959), 332–50.

31:69 Tsou, Tang. "The Quemoy Imbroglio: Chiang Kai-shek and the United States." *Western Political Quarterly* 12:4 (1959), 1075–91. These two contemporary essays assess the motives and objections of all parties' policies.

Two-China Dilemma

31:70 Kintner, William R., and Copper, John F. *A Matter of Two Chinas: The China-Taiwan Issue in U.S. Foreign Policy.* Philadelphia: Foreign Policy Research Institute, 1979. This slim book assesses the political-strategic, economic, legal, and human rights implications of U.S. recognition of the People's Republic of China, with a discussion on the future of Taiwan and America's role in assuring its prosperity and security.

31:71 Kubek, Anthony. *The Red China Papers: What Americans Deserve to Know about U.S.-Chinese Relations.* New Rochelle, N.Y.: Arlington House, 1975. This interpretation of Sino-American relations is sympathetic to the Chinese Nationalist regime. The author gives a brief survey of the modern history of China and its relations with the United States, and discusses the "pivotal" World War II period and the American role in China's fall to the Communists. Taiwan as an ally of the United States is described, and Nixon's shift in policy toward Peking is strongly criticized.

31:72 Myers, Ramon H., ed. *Two China States: U.S. Foreign Policy and Interests.* Stanford, Calif.: Hoover Institution Press, 1978. The four essays of this brief book, by William Whitson, Norma Schroder, Martin Wilbur, and Ramon Myers, discuss the political, military, economic, and human dimensions in Sino-U.S. relations, and the stabilizing role of the United States in East Asia.

China Lobby

See also Chapter 27, "China Lobby."

31:73 Backrack, Stanley D. *The Committee of One Million: The "China Lobby" and U.S. Policy, 1953–1971.* New York: Columbia University Press, 1976. The China Lobby sought to perpetuate an anti-Chinese Communist policy in the U.S. government. The author analyzes the origins of the China Lobby within the context of the Communist takeover in China and subsequent Korean War. He describes the organization of the committee and how it exerted pressure on successive administrations to prevent U.S. recognition of Peking and its admission to the UN. The congressional, financial, diplomatic, and other activities of the committee are treated in detail.

Keeley, J. *The China Lobby Man: The Story of Alfred Kohlberg* (27:33).

Koen, R. Y. *The China Lobby in American Politics* (27:34) is a systematic study of the role of the China Lobby in American politics and policymaking during the 1940s and 1950s. The author provides a background review to the phenomenon, identifies the China lobbyists, and discusses the major issues they exploited and the pattern of their wide acceptance. The specific effects of acceptance of the China Lobby outside and inside the government are closely examined, with an assessment of the negative impact on American policy.

Taiwan Problem

See also Chapter 27, "Formosa."

31:74 Bueler, William M. *U.S. China Policy and the Problem of Taiwan.* Boulder: Colorado Associated University Press, 1971. This is a survey of the Taiwan question in U.S. China policy and a case for the island's independence as a solution. The author shows how this problem evolved by tracing American policy from Truman to Nixon, and examines the underlying assumptions as well as existing realities in Taiwan.

31:75 Clough, Ralph N. *Island China.* Cambridge: Harvard University Press, 1978. This study analyzes the Taiwan problem in the context of U.S. policy in Asia and of the island's postwar political, economic, and international developments. It examines Taiwan's interaction with mainland China and Japan, and assesses the difficult alternatives in American normalization of relations with Peking.

31:76 Cohen, Jerome A., et al. *Taiwan and American Policy: The Dilemma in U.S.-China Relations.* New York: Praeger, 1971. This volume consists of six short papers and edited proceedings of a 1971 conference. Aspects of the Taiwan problem and options for U.S. policy are analyzed and discussed.

31:77 Jacoby, Neil H. *U.S. Aid to Taiwan: A Study of Foreign Aid, Self-Help and Development.* New York: Praeger, 1966. This study of American economic aid and its relationship to Taiwan's development (1951–1965) evaluates the successes and failures of foreign aid with criteria such as long-term GNP growth, sociopolitical development, economic effects, and impact on economic policies. The implications for U.S. economic aid policy are also assessed.

Recognizing Communist China

31:78 Chiu, Hungdah. "Normalizing Relations with China: Some Practical and Legal Problems." *Asian Affairs* 5:2 (1977), 67–87. This essay discusses important, inadequately analyzed problems concerning Republic of China–U.S.–mainland China relations: the 1972 Shanghai communiqué; the legal status of Taiwan as perceived by the participants and by international law and practice; the impact of normalization of relations; possible responses of Taiwan to U.S. moves toward normalization with mainland China.

31:79 Davis, Forrest, and Hunter, Robert A. *The Red China Lobby.* New York: Fleet, 1963. This book defends American containment and its nonrecognition policy toward Communist China. Following an account of Sino-American relations since 1844, it discusses the issue of recognition and attacks the "revisionists" inside and outside the U.S. government who support a change in policy toward Peking. It maintains that the Chinese and Russian Communists are firm allies and that the United States must pursue a policy of liberation.

31:80 Devane, Richard T. "The United States and China: Claims and Assets." *Asian Survey* 18:12 (1978), 1267–79. The claims issue began December 16, 1950, as one of the United States' responses to Chinese intervention in the Korean War.

31:81 Newman, Robert P. *Recognition of Communist China? A Study in Argument.* New York: Macmillan, 1961. In this book the author makes a case for the recognition of Communist China by presenting and analyzing the pros and cons in terms of moral, political, and legal issues, with the principle that arguments must be brought to a satisfactory relationship. Newman discusses at length the political issues, all of which he finds in favor of recognition. Moral arguments are ruled as not decisive, while the legal issues agree with the political. Extensive bibliography.

Sino-American Détente, the 1970s

31:82 Barnett, A. Doak. *China Policy: Old Problems and New Challenges.* Washington, D.C.: Brookings Institution, 1977. This book describes the state of U.S.-China relations in the 1970s and defines a basis for American policy in the future. The author argues that further steps be taken toward normalization of relations despite the 1972 Shanghai communiqué. He discusses immediate and long-term issues such as trade and economic relations, scientific and cultural exchanges; future U.S.-China security relations and arms control; and American policy in the context of Soviet and Japanese interests as well as areas of potential conflict such as Korea and Southeast Asia.

31:83 Barnett, A. Doak. *A New U.S. Policy toward China.* Washington, D.C.: Brookings Institution, 1971. This book presents a new China policy for the 1970s. The author gives a background review and discusses recent changes in American attitudes and posture toward China in a new Asian setting. He recommends gradual and mutual accommodation with China through the broadening of trade and contacts. The issues of UN representation, Taiwan, strategic and arms control policy are specially treated.

31:84 Barnett, A. Doak, and Reischauer, Edwin O., eds. *The United States and China: The Next Decade.* New York: Praeger, 1970. This book is arranged topically in six sections, each with corresponding speeches and discussions. The several dozen conference speakers discuss China's political trends, world security, economic development, and relations with the United States.

31:85 Fairbank, John K., ed. *Our China Prospects: A Symposium.* Philadelphia: American Philosophical Society, 1977. These are short papers for a 1976 symposium on Sino-American relations. The participants discuss topics such as American intervention and the Chinese Revolution, the origins of the Sino-American cold war, and current relations in economic, technological, and scholarly exchange.

31:86 Hinton, Harold C. *Peking-Washington: Chinese Foreign Policy and the United States*. Beverly Hills, Calif.: Sage, 1976. This study covers the development of Sino-American relations in the 1970s, with emphasis on China's foreign policy. The author examines the background to the new changes, China's approach to normalization of relations with the United States, the problems involved, the effects of détente, and future prospects.

31:87 Hsiao, Gene T., ed. *Sino-American Detente and Its Policy Implications*. New York: Praeger, 1974. This collection of scholarly essays assesses the implications of Sino-American détente over a year after Nixon's China trip and the signing of the Shanghai communiqué. Half of the essays evaluate America's role and strategic position in the Asia-Pacific region, trade and cultural relations with China, and China's participation in the UN. The rest examine the impact of the détente on other countries and Taiwan.

31:88 Sutter, Robert G. *China-Watch: Toward Sino-American Reconciliation*. Baltimore: Johns Hopkins University Press, 1978. This is a survey of U.S.-China relations with emphasis on the 1970s. The author reviews American wartime relations with the Chinese Communist party, containment policy and the Geneva talks in the 1950s, and discusses the underlying factors of reconciliation in the 1970s, including the Sino-Soviet conflict. Concerned with the lack of progress in normalization of relations, he finds Sino-American rapprochement narrowly based.

31:89 Terrill, Ross, ed. *The China Difference: A Portrait of Life Today Inside the Country of One Billion*. New York: Harper & Row, 1979. In this useful guide to China during the 1970s, 16 authorities examine aspects of Chinese politics, society, and culture through a comparative framework, stressing differences between China and America in such areas as self-expression, human rights, and the arts.

31:90 Terrill, Ross. *800,000,000: The Real China*. Boston: Little, Brown, 1972. This is an informative and perceptive account of a 1971 visit to China. The author reports on the social, political, and economic aspects of life observed, and describes his interviews and meetings with officials including Chou En-lai. He also focuses on key issues between China and America, Peking's foreign policy, and Chinese perceptions of the world.

SPECIAL STUDIES

Economic Relations

31:91 Eckstein, Alexander. "China's Trade Policy and Sino-American Relations." *Foreign Affairs* 54:1 (1975), 134–54. This essay examines fluctuating patterns of Sino-American trade and the foreign economic policy of the People's Republic of China. There was no trade during 1951 to 1971, after which trade consisted largely of agricultural exports from the United States to China. The economic conditions of the 1970s hurt China's exports to the United States, and the absence of most-favored-nation status for China has meant a full tariff levy on Chinese goods.

31:92 Eckstein, Alexander, ed. *China Trade Prospects and U.S. Policy*. New York: Praeger, 1971. There are three essays in this volume on U.S.-China trade issues and prospects. The book includes an analysis of the U.S. trade embargo, an examination of Chinese law in relation to trade with the United States, a projection on Sino-American trade prospects, and numerous statistical tables.

31:93 Leng, Shao-chuan, ed. *Post-Mao China and U.S.-China Trade*. Charlottesville: University Press of Virginia, 1977. This volume begins with a survey of China's current political development and economy, and examines China's foreign trade and trade prospects with the United States. Also treated is the political aspect of China's foreign trade, including its international impact and oil policy.

31:94 Li, Victor H. "Ups and Downs of Trade with China." *Columbia Journal of Transnational Law* 13:3 (1974), 371–80. Li discusses the rapid growth of U.S.-China trade (1970–1973) and predicts future volumes of trade with China.

31:95 Mah Feng-hwa. *The Foreign Trade of China*. Chicago: Aldine, Atherton, 1971. This detailed survey (1950–1967) is bolstered with statistical tables.

31:96 Neilan, Edward, and Smith, Charles R. *The Future of the China Market: Prospects for Sino-American Trade*. Washington, D.C.: American Enterprise Institute for Public Policy Research, 1974. This brief study is intended to stimulate interest on the subject of Sino-U.S. trade. The authors, who visited China, discuss China's economy, the factors affecting its foreign trade, its trade machinery, import and export, and prospects for trade with the United States.

Nuclear Weapons and Arms Control

See also Chapter 40, "Arms Control and Disarmament."

31:97   Clemens, Walter C., Jr. *The Arms Race and Sino-Soviet Relations*. Stanford, Calif.: Hoover Institution, 1968. Clemens examines the possible relationship between nuclear arms control and the Sino-Soviet dispute.

31:98   Clough, Ralph N., et al. *The United States, China, and Arms Control*. Washington, D.C.: Brookings Institution, 1975. This book analyzes China's nuclear arms policy and its effect on U.S. defense in East Asia and American-Soviet strategic balance. A number of possible approaches to arms control talks with China are suggested, with emphasis on a reciprocal pledge of "no-first-use" of nuclear weapons and reaching international agreements regarding Korea.

31:99   Halperin, Morton H. *China and the Bomb*. New York: Praeger, 1965. The author seeks the implications of China's testing its first atomic bomb.

31:100   Halperin, Morton H., and Perkins, Dwight H. *Communist China and Arms Control*. New York: Praeger, 1965. This venture seeks to identify the factors which determine China's arms control and disarmament policies.

31:101   Hsieh, Alice L. *Communist China's Strategy in the Nuclear Era*. Englewood Cliffs, N.J.: Prentice-Hall, 1962. Hsieh discusses the development of Communist China's military and strategic thinking, up to January 1960.

Negotiation Practice and Treaty Compliance

31:102   Chiu, Hungdah. *The People's Republic of China and the Law of Treaties*. Cambridge: Harvard University Press, 1972. The author argues that China's view of treaty law does not differ substantially from that of Western nations, except for its concept of "unequal treaties," which developed out of China's experience.

31:103   Lall, Arthur. *How Communist China Negotiates*. New York: Columbia University Press, 1968. A delegate to the 14-nation Foreign Ministers' Conference on Laos (1961–1962), Lall discusses the intricate negotiations and develops them in the context of a theory of Chinese international relations.

31:104   Lee, Luke T. *China and International Agreements: A Study in Compliance*. Durham, N.C.: Rule of Law Press, 1969. This well-researched study concludes that the Chinese respect treaty obligations much as do other nations. Compare with James Chieh Hsiung, *Law and Order in China's Foreign Relations* (New York: Columbia University Press, 1972).

31:105   Young, Kenneth T. *Negotiating with the Chinese Communists: The United States Experience, 1953–1967*. New York: McGraw-Hill, 1968. This study by the former U.S. ambassador to Thailand gives an account of the negotiations and contacts between the United States and Communist China. The author focuses on the course, style, and mechanism of the ambassadorial talks at Geneva and Warsaw. He recommends a moderate policy based on realistic thinking and understanding in order to improve relations with China.

U.S. and Japan

31:106   Barnds, William J., ed. *Japan and the United States: Challenges and Opportunities*. New York: New York University Press, 1979. These essays were originally papers on recent developments, key issues, and prospects of U.S.-Japanese relations in the 1980s. David MacEachron discusses the two countries' common interests and differences. The effects of Japan's domestic politics and defense needs on its foreign policy are respectively analyzed by Gerald Curtis and Martin Weinstein, while U.S.-Japanese economic and trade relations are dealt with by William Rapp, Robert Feldman, and I. M. Destler.

31:107   Chapin, Emerson, ed. *Japan and the United States in the 1970's*. New York: Japan Society, 1971. This volume is the record of discussions at a 1969 conference on the political, economic, and social aspects of U.S.-Japanese relations in the 1970s. Presentations by James Abegglen, Herman Kahn, and James

Morley stress the key developments in Japan and their external impact.

31:108 Clapp, Priscilla, and Halperin, Morton H., eds. *United States–Japanese Relations: The 1970's.* Cambridge: Harvard University Press, 1974. The 11 essays discuss the general outlook for American-Japanese relations, the factor of American domestic politics, trade prospects, influence on the Asian economy, the role of Sino-Japanese relations, and security issues.

31:109 Curtis, Gerald L., ed. *Japanese-American Relations in the 1970s.* Washington, D.C.: Columbia Books, 1970. The seven essays in this volume include discussions on the challenges and opportunities for Japan and the United States in the 1970s, the prospects for Japan's economic growth and involvement in Asia, China's role in Japanese-American relations, and American policy in Southeast Asia.

31:110 Destler, I. M.; Hideo Sato; Clapp, Priscilla; and Haruhiro Fukui. *Managing an Alliance: The Politics of U.S.-Japanese relations.* Washington, D.C.: Brookings Institution, 1976. This book examines the interplay of domestic politics and foreign policy in U.S.-Japanese relations, the effects of mutual misunderstanding, and the importance of the conduct of negotiations as illustrated by three cases—the security treaty revision, the Okinawa reversion, and the textile dispute. It also discusses political and bureaucratic institutions in foreign policy making and the interaction of national systems.

31:111 Georgetown University. Center for Strategic Studies. *United States–Japanese Political Relations: The Critical Issues Affecting Asia's Future.* Washington, D.C.: Georgetown University, Center for Strategic Studies, 1968. This is a panel report on topics such as Japan's role in Asia's stability and development, economic and security issues confronting the United States and Japan, and their relations with the communist countries. Included is a background paper which examines Japan's political, economic, security, and foreign affairs.

31:112 Gibney, Frank. *Japan: The Fragile Super Power.* New York: Norton, 1975. An excellent introduction to contemporary Japanese society and foreign relations by a man who participated in the occupation of the country and later returned to it as a publisher. U.S.-Japanese relations are discussed in terms of their cultural contrast as well as Japan's anomalous position

as an economic giant with an extremely precarious base.

31:113 Hellmann, Donald C. *Japan and East Asia: The New International Order.* New York: Praeger, 1972. This study of Japan's role in East Asia and the world examines a number of key issues in Japan's international relations, including East Asian regionalism, the influence of domestic politics on foreign policy, economic goals, and involvement in East Asia. The U.S.-Japanese alliance and Japan's evolving security problem are treated at great length.

31:114 Irie Michimasa. *Sengo Nihon gaikō-shi* [Postwar Japanese foreign policy]. Tokyo: Sagano Shoin, 1978. A survey of postwar Japanese foreign affairs, the book's main value resides in its document section, which reprints many important documents covering the years after the war.

31:115 Kajima Morinosuke. *Modern Japan's Foreign Policy.* Rutland, Vt.: Tuttle, 1969. The author, for 13 years the chairman of the Liberal Democratic party's Foreign Relations Research Committee and of the Foreign Affairs Committee of the Diet's House of Councillors, provides a Japanese perspective in this condensed English version of his 1965 book.

31:116 Kaplan, Morton A., and Kinhide, Mushakoji, eds. *Japan, America, and the Future World Order.* New York: Free Press, 1976. Arranged in four sections, these essays discuss the major aspects of U.S.-Japan relations in a bilateral, regional, and global context during the 1970s and beyond. The first section, which deals with external issues, puts their relations in global perspective and examines Japan's relations with China; the second studies internal decisionmaking processes, self and mutual perceptions; the third deals with economic relations; and the fourth is a shorter section on technological and environmental issues.

Kōsaka M. *100 Million Japanese: The Postwar Experience* (27:105) is an impressionistic survey (1945–1971) of U.S.-Japanese relations.

31:117 Passin, Herbert, ed. *The United States and Japan.* Englewood Cliffs, N.J.: Prentice-Hall, 1966. The essays, which focus on the immediate issues in U.S.-Japanese relations, include discussions on mutual perceptions, the legacy of the occupation, the political issues which are closely related to Japan's domestic politics, economic issues, Japanese views of the problems, and future prospects.

Reischauer, E. O. *The United States and Japan* (2:351) is an introductory work by the former U.S. ambassador to Japan which reviews U.S.-Japanese relations in the prewar, occupation, and postwar periods. Reischauer provides an overall view of the problem and a discussion of Japan's physical environment, prewar economy, and the characteristics of its people. The American occupation, its immediate effects, postwar developments, and the prospects for American-Japanese relations are carefully examined.

31:118   Reischauer, Edwin O. *The Japanese*. Cambridge: Harvard University Press, 1977. The best single-volume introduction to Japanese politics and society, it is a distillation by the world's foremost authority on Japan, and should provide a good starting point for any student interested in U.S. relations with that country.

31:119   Vogel, Ezra F. *Japan as No. 1: Lessons for America*. Cambridge: Harvard University Press, 1979. The author stresses those aspects of Japanese politics, society, and economic institutions that have contributed to the country's postwar achievements, and contrasts them to problems in the United States. The book is a good way to go beneath superficial discussions of the two countries' diplomatic and trade issues.

PUBLIC OPINION AND MUTUAL PERCEPTIONS

Asahi Shimbun. *The Pacific Rivals: A Japanese View of Japanese-American Relations* (27:99) is the English version of an interesting series of articles originally published in Japan's most influential newspaper, the *Asahi Shimbun*. The long series of short and anecdotal articles presents a Japanese view of Japanese-American relations (1854–1960s) which is characterized by mutual ignorance and misconceptions.

Glazer, N. "From Ruth Benedict to Herman Kahn: The Postwar Japanese Image in the American Mind" (27:143) is a broad review (1945–1970) of American public opinion shifts, major ideas of American scholars, and literary figures' responses to Japan. It uncovers shared feelings of alienness, paradoxicality, instability, and unpredictability.

Johnson, S. K. *American Attitudes toward Japan, 1941–1975* (27:145).

31:120   Rosovsky, Henry, ed. *Discord in the Pacific: Challenges to the Japanese-American Alliance*. Washington, D.C.: Columbia Books, 1972. The nine essays attempt to identify the major sources of discord in what is believed to be a transitional era between the United States and Japan by examining changes in domestic and world scenes, mutual misconceptions, and the intercultural communication gap.

SPECIAL STUDIES

31:121   Mendel, Douglas H., Jr. "American Policy on Okinawan Reversion." *Asian Forum* 4:1 (1972), 12–21. Mendel analyzes the changes in American foreign policy toward Okinawa from the decision to make the island the major U.S. base in East Asia in 1950 to the Nixon-Sato joint commiqué (November 21, 1969), which promised to return the island to Japan during 1972.

31:122   Morley, James W. *Japan and Korea: America's Allies in the Pacific*. New York: Walker, 1965. This is a short study of Japan and Korea in relation to the United States. The first of two parts consists of interpretive essays on contemporary politics in Japan, North and South Korea, their foreign relations, and the problems they pose for U.S. policy. Part 2 gives useful tabular reference material on their political, economic, and cultural affairs.

31:123   Park, Yung H. "The 'Anti-Hegemony' Controversy in Sino-Japanese Relations." *Pacific Affairs* 49:3 (1976), 476–90. Park examines the nature and development of the antihegemony controversy raised by China, with particular emphasis on domestic and foreign factors governing Japan's attitude during the thaw in U.S.-Chinese diplomacy (1972–1976).

31:124   Park, Yung H. "Japan's Perspectives and Expectations Regarding America's Role in Korea." *Orbis* 20:3 (1976), 761–84. Because of Richard Nixon's visit to mainland China in 1972 and the apparent thaw in Seoul-Pyongyang relations that same year, Japan's attitude toward North Korea changed and Japanese industry rushed to take advantage of this new market. But by 1974, business relations with North Korea had cooled.

31:125   Schmidhauser, John R., and Totten, George O., III, eds. *The Whaling Issue in U.S.-Japan Relations*. Boulder, Colo.: Westview, 1978. These essays review the history of the whaling controversy, the status of whaling international law, and the policy alternatives confronting Japan.

Mutual Security Treaties

See Chapter 27, "Mutual Security and Rearmament."

31:126 Greene, Fred. *Stresses in U.S.-Japanese Security Relations.* Washington, D.C.: Brookings Institution, 1975. This study examines the major aspects of the U.S.-Japanese security treaty and the problems that have arisen in the course of the changing domestic and international environment. The author discusses the Japanese debate on the treaty, the problems that emerged in its implementation since 1960, and Japan's own defense program.

31:127 Michael, Franz, and Sigur, Gaston J. *The Asian Alliance: Japan and United States Policy.* New York: National Strategy Information Center, 1972. This monograph surveys postwar Japan and its relations with the United States, with emphasis on contemporary development in the Asian context. The authors also assess the relevance of Japan's alignment with the United States and believe that greater independence within the security treaty arrangement is of mutual interest.

31:128 Osgood, Robert E. *The Weary and the Wary: U.S. and Japanese Security Policies in Transition.* Baltimore: Johns Hopkins University Press, 1972. This monograph examines the contemporary international environment and how it affects American and Japanese interests. The Nixon Doctrine, U.S.-Japanese security relations, and the nature of power and interests are discussed.

31:129 Packard, George R., III. *Protest in Tokyo: The Security Treaty Crisis of 1960.* Princeton, N.J.: Princeton University Press, 1966. This study examines the critical events of May-June 1960, when opposition to U.S.-Japanese security treaty revision erupted into demonstrations, riots, and Diet sit-ins in Tokyo, which eventually led to the cabinet's downfall and cancellation of President Eisenhower's visit. The author attempts to understand the Japanese political process as well as the nature of the U.S.-Japanese alliance. He finds that the crisis of 1960 was the result of both domestic and international forces.

Rearmament and Arms Control

See also Chapter 40, "Arms Control and Disarmament."

Auer, J. E. *The Postwar Rearmament of Japanese Maritime Forces, 1945–1971* (27:138) describes in detail the continuation of Japanese naval activities after 1945 and the formation of the Japanese Maritime Self-Defense Force.

31:130 Frankel, Joseph. "Domestic Politics of Japan's Foreign Policy: A Case Study of the Ratification of the Non-Proliferation Treaty." *British Journal of International Studies* 3:3 (1977), 254–68. Frankel examines the ratification of the nonproliferation treaty (January 1975–May 1976) as a case study in which differences in Japanese and Western foreign policy decisionmaking can be determined.

31:131 Maki, John M. "Japan's Rearmament: Progress and Problems." *Western Political Quarterly* 7:4 (1955), 545–68. This essay recounts the earliest rearmament efforts.

31:132 McNelly, Theodore. "The Renunciation of War in the Japanese Constitution." *Political Science Quarterly* 74:2 (1962), 350–78. The U.S. role in persuading the Japanese to keep article 9 in their constitution has been regretted by subsequent U.S. administrations. See also his "American Influence and Japan's No-War Constitution," ibid 67:4 (1952), 589–98.

31:133 Morley, James W., ed. *Forecast for Japan: Security in the 1970's.* Princeton, N.J.: Princeton University Press, 1972. The seven essays discuss the fiscal aspects of Japan's defense, Japan's strategic thinking, domestic politics, influential business groups, and confrontation of realpolitik abroad.

31:134 Weinstein, Franklin B., ed. *U.S.-Japan Relations and the Security of East Asia: The Next Decade.* Boulder, Colo.: Westview, 1978. The essays in this volume consider the nature of security policies and arms control, strategic and nuclear defense of Japan, Korea's prospects, and the strategic context in Asia.

Weinstein, M. E. *Japan's Postwar Defense Policy, 1947–1968* (27:142) gives a concise description of postwar Japanese thinking on national security matters which has deemphasized military strengthening and stressed economic expansion. The author finds a remarkable consistency in Japanese attitudes, assumptions, and tactics as they have sought to utilize an American alliance in Japan's interest. He argues that these basic principles can be traced back to 1947 and that the initiative came from the Japanese.

Economic Relations

Hollerman, L. "International Economic Controls in Occupied Japan" (27:128) argues that the initial foreign exchange and trade control system established under the occupation has been subsequently used by the Japanese government to exclude foreign goods and capital.

31:135 Hunsberger, Warren S. *Japan and the United States in World Trade*. New York: Harper & Row, 1964. A comprehensive review of Japan's trade with the United States, it also examines Japan's trading and balance-of-payments position in the world economy.

31:136 Ozaki, Robert S. *The Control of Imports and Foreign Capital in Japan*. New York: Praeger, 1972. This volume identifies Japanese policies and regulations which provide a success program of limited and strategic protectionisms.

31:137 Roberts, John G. *Mitsui: Three Centuries of Japanese Business*. New York: Weatherhill, 1973. Chapters 25 and 26 of this general history of one of Japan's greatest family business empires provide unusual insights into its leaders' responses to American antitrust policies. Extensive bibliography.

31:138 Yamamura, Kozo. *Economic Policy in Postwar Japan: Growth versus Economic Democracy*. Berkeley: University of California Press, 1967. This study examines the results of economic democratization attempted by the U.S. occupation.

U.S. and Korea

Baldwin, F., ed. *Without Parallel: The American-Korean Relationship since 1945* (27:147) surveys the "unprecedented American commitment and intervention in post-1945 Korea."

31:139 Bernstein, Barton J. "The Origins of America's Commitments in Korea." *Foreign Service Journal* 55:3 (1978), 10–13, 34. The author argues that U.S. presence in Korea (1950–1960) has stabilized the area and restrained Syngman Rhee's desire to unify Korea by whatever means.

31:140 Choi Chong-Ki. "Unification and Security on the Korean Peninsula." *Asia Quarterly* 2 (1976), 107–35. Choi describes the reunification policies of North and South Korea and the new tensions on the peninsula and examines the security policy of South Korea. Neither North or South is willing to risk unification at the sacrifice of its own political or economic system, and the wide gulf between the two systems makes it impossible to integrate them into a common framework.

31:141 Clough, Ralph N. *Deterrence and Defense in Korea: The Role of U.S. Forces*. Washington, D.C.: Brookings Institution, 1976. This is a brief analysis of the role of American forces in Korea. The author examines their military and political significance as viewed by the two Koreas, Russia, China, and Japan. Evaluating the courses of action open to the United States, he proposes a long-term strategy involving South Korea and Japan for the strengthening of the former's defense and the gradual withdrawal of American forces.

31:142 Clough, Ralph N., et al. "Arms Control in Korea." In their *The United States, China, and Arms Control*. Washington, D.C.: Brookings Institution, 1975, pp. 105–27. This chapter reviews the special U.S. responsibility in Korea since the armistice and examines proposals for reducing the risk of future military conflict.

SOUTH KOREA

31:143 Adelman, Irman, ed. *Practical Approaches to Development Planning: Korea's Second Five-Year Plan*. Baltimore: Johns Hopkins Press, 1969. Reviewing South Korea's 1967 to 1971 developmental plan, the Korean and American authors focus on the country's economic and political development.

31:144 Chung Kyung Cho. *Korea: The Third Republic*. New York: Macmillan, 1971. This account provides a well-organized review of South Korea's politics and political system.

31:145 Sunoo, Harold Hakwon. *America's Dilemma in Asia: The Case of South Korea.* Chicago: Nelson-Hall, 1979. This book uses the case of South Korea to illustrate the contradictions faced by the United States in Asia. According to the author, while the United States seeks economic development in Asian societies to ensure political stability, it underplays political and social development, which results in internal conflicts and tensions. American involvement in Korea since mid-20th century and its interaction with internal developments are discussed.

The Korean Armistice

31:146 Kreibel, P. Wesley. "Korea: The Military Armistice Commission 1965–1970." *Military Affairs* 36:3 (1972), 96–99. By 1965 the Military Armistice Commission (Korea) system had ceased to function as intended because of North Korean intransigence. The commission became, however, a useful channel of communication when the North Koreans chose to use it.

31:147 Strauss, William L. "The Military Armistice Commission: Deterrent of Conflict?" *Journal of Korean Affairs* 5:1 (1975), 24–46. Strauss evaluates the effectiveness of the Military Armistice Commission established in Korea at the end of the Korean War to enforce boundary lines along the 38th parallel (1953–1973).

NORTH KOREA

31:148 Koh Byung Chul. *The Foreign Policy of North Korea.* New York: Praeger, 1969. This is a study of the Pyongyang regime's role in world politics.

Scalapino, R., and Lee Chong-Sik. *Communism in Korea* (27:156) reviews the history and functioning of North Korea.

Pueblo Incident, 1968

31:149 Armbruster, Trevor. *A Matter of Accountability: The Study of the Pueblo Affair.* New York: Coward-McCann, 1970. The author reviews North Korea's seizure of the USS *Pueblo,* an intelligence-gathering ship, on January 3, 1968. He blames Washington military officials for the capture.

31:150 Armbruster, William A. "The Pueblo Crisis and Public Opinion." *Naval War College Review* 23:7 (1971), 84–110. Armbruster discusses the influence of public opinion on the handling of the capture of the *Pueblo* and its aftermath. The United States' reaction to the capture of the "spy ship" and to its crew after their release was largely a response to public outcry in America.

31:151 Bucher, Lloyd M., with Rascovich, Mark. *Bucher: Mystery.* Garden City, N.Y.: Doubleday, 1970. A memoir of the episode by the captain of the *Pueblo.* His actions are severely criticized by Edward R. Murphy, Jr., *Second in Command* (New York: Holt, Rinehart & Winston, 1971).

31:152 Simon, Sheldon W. "The *Pueblo* Incident and the South Korean 'Revolution' in North Korea's Foreign Policy: A Propaganda Analysis." *Asian Forum* 2:3 (1970), 201–14. Simon discusses the use of propaganda analysis as a technique for assessing foreign policy, specifically the manner in which North Korea created a foreign policy resource from its January 1968 capture of the U.S. intelligence ship, *Pueblo.*

32

The United States, Australia, New Zealand, and the Central Pacific

Contributing Editor
JOSEPH M. SIRACUSA
University of Queensland,
Australia

Contributors
Glen St. John Barclay
University of Queensland,
Australia

Richard Herr
University of Tasmania,
Australia

Henry S. Albinski
Pennsylvania State University

Contents

Introduction

United States interest in Australia and New Zealand has of necessity been far less intense and of far briefer duration than that of the Commonwealth countries in America. To be sure, as outlined in Gordon Greenwood's pioneering study, *Early American-Australian Relations* (32:90), there were many important commercial contacts in the earliest years of Australian colonization, from the first settlement in New South Wales in the 1790s to the time of the gold fever in Victoria in the 1830s. Yankee sailors, whalers, and explorers, furthermore, made their presence known for the next hundred years.

Australia did not begin to figure with any significance in United States strategic thinking, however, until late in 1939, when Great Britain made Admiral William D. Leahy aware that its East Asian empire would have to be defended, if at all, by American naval power should the United Kingdom become simultaneously involved in war with Japan as well as with the European Axis powers. By contrast, Australian defense planners had, since the days of Prime Minister Alfred Deakin in 1905, longingly looked to the United States as a protecting power against the Japanese nation emerging onto the world stage.

Washington did indeed fulfill this role after Pearl Harbor. The wartime alliance, the essence of which is captured in Roger Bell's felicitous title, *Unequal Allies* (32:106), was nonetheless seriously imbalanced. Australia was viewed by Washington as a critically important base for a counterattack against Japan, and New Zealand less so but convenient. From their own vantage points, Canberra and Wellington came to perceive the United States as in effect their sole defense against Japanese aggression. Australian–United States relations were also placed under stress by the Australian misconception of fundamental American strategy.

At another significant level, there can be little doubt that the shared wartime experience, which witnessed the presence of almost two million U.S. servicemen on Australian soil, initiated a new phase in American-Australian relations. Australians found it easy to assume the existence of cultural, political, and linguistic affinities with the United States that were sometimes more apparent than real. In turn, Americans found Australia an attractive place for investment and market penetration, as well as a congenial and reliable ally.

During the 1950s and 1960s successive administrations in Canberra sought to strengthen the newly found security relationship with the United States as much as possible. The Australian-New Zealand-U.S. Tripartite Security Treaty of 1952 (ANZUS), described at length in Trevor R. Reese's *Australia, New Zealand and the United States* (32:140), came to be regarded as the cornerstone of modern Australian foreign policy. The implications of ANZUS, together with the alliance's contribution to the "special relationship" that presumably exists between Canberra and Washington, have been intensively examined by Australian and American scholars alike. So, too, but with less enthusiasm, were the implications of growing American control over Australian economic developments.

The mood, if not the degree, of interest on the Australian side underwent a fundamental change during the post-Vietnam era, which coincided with the brief reemergence of the Australian Labor party in 1972. Techniques of American New Left revisionists were belatedly employed to stress the divergence of economic interests between Australia and the United States during World War II—see Bell's previously noted *Unequal Allies,* in particular—and severe criticism was aimed at what was seen as excessive regard paid to Washington's peculiar cold war concern in the region. Though this wave of historical writing may well have passed already with the political mood to which it was attuned, Australian analysts have increasingly concerned themselves with the relevance of the ANZUS alliance in a world in which circumstances have changed. Put another way, the perceived threats to the Australian external environment as envisaged in ANZUS have been replaced by others and in a way that may well be outside the scope of ANZUS. In fact, the best thinking on the subject has concluded, in the words of T. B. Millar's magisterial *Australia in Peace and War* (32:23), that "Australia has contributed substantially more to ANZUS than she received from it," the main benefit being an intangible one, "a sense of assurance of help in future danger."

The role of New Zealand in this web of Pacific relations is more difficult to define. Smaller, less significant economically and militarily and more isolated than its neighbor across the Tasman Sea, New Zealand has historically felt herself compelled to assert her independence from Australia in order to avoid the appearance of but an echo. Traditionally, New Zealand governments have seldom been in a position to challenge Australian foreign policy initiatives, nor, for that matter, to propose meaningful alternatives. Autonomy had been proclaimed in general by following the Australian lead but at a slower pace and in a slightly different direction. Nor have New Zealanders laid claim to the various affinities with Americans that Australians have been wont to emphasize. Still, Wellington followed Washington and Canberra into Vietnam, though with pronounced misgivings and proportionally far smaller forces.

In this sense the pattern of Australian–New Zealand disharmony and, by extension, the inner thinking of ANZUS since the late 1960s, has yet to be explored. More justice has been done to the more positive aspects of New Zealand's external relations. New Zealand is, for example, the principal homeland of the Polynesian race and, arguably, one of the most successfully functioning multiracial societies in the world today. This factor has ensured the development of New Zealand's special role as friend and guide of the South Pacific microstates. In any event, the emergence of New Zealand's special significance to the region is superbly documented in Angus Ross, *New Zealand Aspirations in the Pacific in the Nineteenth Century* (32:93) and *New Zealand's Record in the Pacific Islands in the Twentieth Century* (32:26). What this relationship involved, in practice, was that New Zealand supplied the microstates with economic aid and, in turn, absorbed their unemployed. One of the most interesting areas for prediction in South Pacific studies would be to determine how much longer New Zealand could provide these services and to what extent the special Polynesian relationship will be affected when they are stopped. These are questions that will vitally concern the performance of New Zealand as a partner in ANZUS and as a continuing source of stability in the Southwest Pacific.

Resources and Overviews

RESEARCH AIDS

While pertinent bibliographies and reference aids are listed here, there are more extensive lists in Chapter 1.

Bibliographies

Foreign Affairs Bibliography: A Selected and Annotated List of Books on International Relations (1:15) includes limited coverage of Australia and New Zealand in the five volumes published to date.

32:1 Hudson, W. J., ed. "Australia's External Relations: Towards a Bibliography of Journal Articles (Section I: Asia)." *Australian Outlook* 24:3 (1970), 328–45. The first of several efforts in this field, this is a selective bibliography of periodical literature on Australia's external relations chosen from material published from 1945 to 1970. Special emphasis is on Asia.

32:2 Hudson, W. J., ed. "Australia's External Relations: Towards a Bibliography of Journal Articles (Section II)." *Australian Outlook* 25:1 (1971), 69–93. This is the second part of a selective bibliography of periodical literature on Australia's external relations from 1945 to 1970. The emphasis here is on non-Asian matters.

32:3 Hudson, W. J. and Fisher, W. L., eds. "Australia's External Relations: Toward a Bibliography of Journal Articles, 1970–1975" (Part 1). *Australian Outlook* 30:3 (1976), 414–31. This is the first part of a comprehensive though unannotated bibliography of periodical literature on Australia's external relations selected from material published since mid-1970.

32:4 Hudson, W. J., ed. "Australia's External Relations: Toward a Bibliography of Journal Articles" (Part 2). *Australian Outlook* 31:1 (1977), 38–51. This is the second part of a comprehensive bibliography of periodical literature on Australia's external relations selected from material published since mid-1970.

32:5 Launitz-Schurer, Leopold, and Siracusa, Joseph M. "Some Recent Trends in the Study of United States History in Australia." *Australian Journal of Politics and History* 22:2 (1976), 179–86. A survey of recent developments in the study of U.S. history in Australia, this essay is full on the bibliography of Australian-American relations.

32:6 Launitz-Schurer, Leopold, and Siracusa, Joseph M. "The State of United States History in Australia." In John A. Moses, ed., *Historical Disciplines and Culture in Australasia: An Assessment*. St. Lucia: University of Queensland Press, 1979, pp. 239–52. A thorough survey of recent trends and developments in the study of U.S. history in Australia, this essay is full on the bibliography of Australian-American relations. Included is an appendix listing postgraduate thesis in U.S. history completed in Australian universities (1965–1975).

32:7 U.S. Department of the Army. Library. *Pacific Islands and Trust Territories: A Selected Bibliography*. Washington, D.C.: G.P.O., 1971. This is a useful reference which includes a supplement of maps.

Yearbooks and Other Aids

32:8 *Pacific Islands Yearbook and Who's Who.* Sydney: Melbourne Publishing, 1932–. This is a detailed reference work, published irregularly since 1932.

Document Collections

More general collections are listed in Chapter 1.

32:9 Australia. Department of Foreign Affairs. *Documents on Australian Foreign Policy, 1937–1949: Vol. I: 1937–38*. Canberra: Australian Government Publishing Service, 1975. This is the initial volume in the first series to be published of *Documents on Australian Foreign Policy*, which, it is hoped, will provide a full documentation of the evolution of Australian foreign policy since 1901. This volume covers the years from the preparation for the Imperial Conference held in London to the aftermath of the Munich agreement. This and subsequent volumes should become indispensable.

32:10 Australia. Department of Foreign Affairs. *Documents on Australian Foreign Policy, 1937–49: Vol. II: 1939*. Canberra: Australian Government Publishing Service, 1976. This volume is the second in a series of volumes of documents designed to cover the years 1937 to 1949. Volume 2 describes Australia's reactions to the spectre of war both in Europe and East Asia. Revealed throughout is the changing nature of the relationship between Canberra and London.

32:11 Barclay, Glen St. John, and Siracusa, Joseph M., eds. *Australian-American Relations since 1945*. Sydney: Holt, Rinehart & Winston, 1976. This is a convenient one-volume documentary history of modern Australian-American relations (1945–1976). The editors, while not ignoring the historical background of the relationship, pay particular attention to the origins of the United States–Australia–New Zealand Tripartite Security Treaty (ANZUS), the course of relations during the Indochina conflict and the emergence of the Labor government of Gough Whitlam.

32:12 Greenwood, Gordon, and Harper, Norman, eds. *Australia in World Affairs*. 4 vols. to date. Melbourne: Cheshire, 1957–. This work represents the first quinquennial survey of Australian foreign policy published for the Australian Institute of International Affairs. The essays by Fred Alexander, Gordon Greenwood, and Norman Harper are of particular value. Extensive bibliography.

32:13 Greenwood, Gordon, and Grimshaw, Charles, eds. *Documents on Australian International Affairs, 1901–1918*. Melbourne: Nelson, 1977. A useful introduction to the official series, which commences with the year 1937, this collection deals with the character and content of Australian foreign policy from federation in 1900 to 1918.

32:14 New Zealand. Ministry of Foreign Affairs. *New Zealand Foreign Policy: Statements and Documents, 1943–1957*. Wellington: Shearer, 1972. An indispensable collection of public documents on foreign policy at a time when New Zealand recognized "that the narrow perspectives of the past were no longer adequate to New Zealand's national needs."

U.S. Department of State. *Foreign Relations of the United States* (1:358) currently contains materials relating to U.S.–Australian–New Zealand relations to the early 1950s.

OVERVIEWS

See Chapter 24, "Overviews," for surveys of American foreign affairs since World War II.

32:15 Barclay, Glen St. John. *The Empire is Marching*. London: Weidenfeld & Nicolson, 1976. Barclay analyzes, with extensive documentation, the contribution made by the dominions to the British war effort in the South African War (1899–1902) and the two world wars. He criticizes the British failure to try to organize the resources of the empire and commonwealth into a genuine system of imperial defense. Extensive bibliography.

32:16 Beddie, D. B., ed. *Advance Australia: Where?* Melbourne: Oxford University Press, 1975. This work is, essentially, a collection of papers read at the annual conference of the Australian Institute of International Affairs (1974). Particularly noteworthy are the papers by Hedley Bull on the Whitlam government's external policy outlook, and Harry Gelber on Australia and the great powers.

32:17 Booker, Malcolm. *The Last Domino: Aspects of Australia's Foreign Relations*. Sydney: Collins, 1976. This is a selective and highly interpretive account of the future of Australian foreign policy by a seasoned Australian diplomat. The author pessimistically sees the end of the American alliance and the adoption of neutrality as the only alternative to disaster. Bibliography.

32:18 Gordon, Bernard K. *New Zealand Becomes a Pacific Power*. Chicago: University of Chicago Press, 1960. A scholarly and well-written assessment, it makes full use of evidence then available. Bibliography.

32:19 Greenwood, Gordon. *Approaches to Asia*. Sydney: McGraw-Hill, 1974. *Approaches to Asia* is a combination history/documentary of Australian postwar policies and attitudes toward Asia. It is a valuable source book. Extensive bibliography.

32:20 Hudson, W. J. *Australia and the Colonial Question at the United Nations*. Honolulu: East-West Center Press, 1970. Hudson examines Australia's struggle, in the United Nations, to remain on good terms with the anticolonial majority and still retain its interests in Papua and New Guinea. This is a valuable introductory work.

32:21 Hudson, W. J. *Australian Diplomacy*. Melbourne: Macmillan, 1970. This is a brief but solid introduction to the history of Australian diplomacy since federation (1900–1970). It especially concentrates on the post-1935 period, when External Affairs was reestablished as a separate commonwealth department. Bibliography.

32:22 Larkin, Thomas C. *New Zealand's External Relations*. Wellington: New Zealand Institute of Public Administration, 1962. This is an interesting survey by an officer of the New Zealand Department of Foreign Affairs.

32:23 Millar, T. B. *Australia in Peace and War: External Relations, 1788–1977*. New York: St. Martin's Press, 1978. This is a brilliant assessment of Australia's external relations from the colonial period to the present. Chapters 6 and 11, both dealing with various aspects of Australian-American relations, are of particular significance to students of U.S. diplomacy. Extensive bibliography.

32:24 Millar, T. B. *Foreign Policy: Some Australian Reflections*. Melbourne: Georgian House, 1972. T. B. Millar, one of the most respected scholars in the Australian international relations establishment, set out to define briefly the meaning and essence of Australia's foreign policy—past and present (1900–1970). In the main, he succeeded.

32:25 New Zealand. Institute of International Affairs. *New Zealand in World Affairs: Vol. 1*. Wellington: New Zealand Institute of International Affairs, 1977. This is a well-presented and documented account of postwar trends in New Zealand foreign policy, and of the origins and development of the New Zealand Department of Foreign Affairs.

32:26 Ross, Angus, ed. *New Zealand's Record in the Pacific Islands in the Twentieth Century*. Auckland, N.Z.: Longman Paul, 1969. A thorough, documented study which examines New Zealand's political and administrative responsibilities in the Cook Islands, Western Samoa, and the Tokelau Islands.

32:27 Watt, Sir Alan Stewart. *The Evolution of Australian Foreign Policy, 1938–1965*. New York: Cambridge University Press, 1967. This book is generally regarded as the best single historical introduction to Australian foreign policy as it has developed since 1938, the year of the Munich crisis. The author, a well-known diplomat, is judicious throughout. Extensive bibliography.

32:28   Wood, Frederick L. W. *New Zealand in the World*. Wellington: New Zealand, Department of Internal Affairs, 1940. Wood presents a brief, but also well-written, summary of New Zealand's external relations from the first European contacts to the outbreak of war in 1939. Bibliography.

National Histories

32:29   Alexander, Fred. *Australia since Federation*. Melbourne: Nelson, 1967. The aim of the book is to tell the story of Australia from the establishment of the commonwealth at the turn of this century to the 1960s. It is one of the best introductions to the subject available. Bibliography.

32:30   Barclay, Glen St. John. *A History of the Pacific*. London: Sidgwick & Jackson, 1978. This study provides a general overview of cultural and political developments in the Pacific region. Concentration is expressly upon the experience of the Pacific peoples themselves, rather than of the intruding powers. Bibliography.

32:31   Burdon, Randall M. *The New Dominion: A Social and Political History of New Zealand, 1918–39*. New York: Hillary House, 1965. This is the first detailed survey of New Zealand's development between the two world wars.

32:32   Clark, Manning H. *A Short History of Australia*. Rev. ed. London: Heinemann, 1969. Clark's *Short History* provides a scholarly review of the general history of Australia. The author is the doyen of Australianists.

32:33   Firkins, Peter. *The Australians in Nine Wars: Waikato to Long Tan*. New York: McGraw-Hill, 1972. An informative, journalistic history of Australian military achievements during the last 100 years, it emphasizes the Australian contribution to the world wars.

32:34   Greenwood, Gordon, ed. *Australia: A Social and Political History*. Sydney: Angus & Robertson, 1955. The aim of the editor was to produce, within a single volume, a political and social history of Australian society that shows the many-sided nature of its development. Essays on the modern era are especially useful in coming to grips with the Australian national character and its external outlook. The result is a pioneering work. Extensive bibliography.

32:35   Oliver, William H. *The Story of New Zealand*. London: Faber, 1963. Like Sinclair (32:37), this author is also a poet, and brings unusual perceptiveness and literary flair to this interpretative history, which includes worthwhile insights into New Zealand attitudes toward the world outside. Bibliography.

32:36   Preston, Richard, ed. *Contemporary Australia: Studies in History, Politics, and Economics*. Durham, N.C.: Duke University Press, 1969. This collection of essays resulted from a year-long program of seminars and lectures on Australia held at Duke University. The essays by Greenwood, Albinski, and Brash throw much light on the Australian-American connection. Extensive bibliography.

32:37   Sinclair, Keith. *A History of New Zealand*. Rev. ed. Harmondsworth, U.K.: Penguin, 1969. This is a well-written survey by a New Zealand historian who is also one of his country's leading poets. It is given added interest by the author's proto-Marxist approach to social and economic issues and cultural sensitivity.

32:38   Younger, Ronald M. *Australia and the Australians*. New York: Humanities Press, 1970. This is a massive survey of Australian history and contemporary political, demographic, economic, and social development.

Policymaking Process

32:39   Albinski, Henry S. "Australian External Policy, Federalism and the States." *Political Science* 28:1 (1976), 1–12. This essay, by an American leading specialist, examines the constraints on external policymaking and implementation derived from context of power distribution. He also reviews the effects of state-based activity and political pressure on public external policy.

32:40   Albinski, Henry S. "Foreign Policy." In Roy Forward, ed., *Public Policy in Australia*. Melbourne: Cheshire, 1974, pp. 15–24. Albinski provides an overview of structural, party-political, leadership, and electoral influences. He illustrates how such forces have affected policy outputs. Bibliography.

32:41 Australia. Department of Foreign Affairs. *Submission by the Department of Foreign Affairs to the Royal Commission on Australian Government Administration.* Canberra: Australian Government Publishing Service, 1974. This is a brief description of Department of Foreign Affairs organization and role, relationship to other departments, and recommendations for improvement in overall Australian foreign policy coordination/administration from the foreign affairs standpoint.

32:42 Ball, Desmond J. "Political Constraints on Defense and Foreign Policy Making." In Roger Scott and J. L. Richardson, comps., *The First Thousand Days of Labor.* Canberra: Canberra College of Advanced Education, 1975, pp. 266–86. This essay looks at the political, social, structural, and other inheritances that limited policy initiatives under the Labor government. Ball finds policy process a conservatizing force.

32:43 Collins, Hugh. "The 'Coombs Report': Bureaucracy, Diplomacy and Australian Foreign Policy." *Australian Outlook* 30:3 (1976), 387–413. This is an assessment of the value of recommendations of the Royal Commission on Government Administration regarding administration of foreign policy, especially in personnel features. Commentary extends to both the personnel and the coordinating aspects of the Department of Foreign Affairs.

32:44 Farran, Andrew. "Foreign Policy and Resources." In Roger Scott and J. L. Richardson, comps., *The First Thousand Days of Labor.* Canberra: Canberra College of Advanced Education, 1975, pp. 357–71. Farran examines ministerial and departmental behavior on energy policy as a reflection on interdepartmental conflict. His study has wide consequences for foreign policy involved in bureaucratic disputes.

32:45 Grant, Bruce. *The Crisis of Loyalty: A Study of Australian Foreign Policy.* Sydney: Angus & Robertson, 1972. In this extremely thoughtful work, Grant urges Australians to develop new concepts of national affairs that would recognize the fact that Australia is no longer a U.S. satellite.

32:46 Hocking, B. L. "Parliament, Parliamentarians and Foreign Affairs." *Australian Outlook* 30:2 (1976), 280–303. This study reviews foreign policy formation contributions of Parliament collectively, in committee, in relation to the executive; it also considers parliamentarians vis-à-vis parties, groups, and constituents.

32:47 Knight, John W. "Aspects of the Foreign Policy Decision-Making Process." In Roger Scott and J. L. Richardson, comps., *The First Thousand Days of Labor.* Canberra: Canberra College of Advanced Education, 1975, pp. 248–65. Foreign policy processes are seen here as interaction between policymaking and policy-reception stages. An important essay.

32:48 Millar, T. B. "The Making of Australian Foreign Policy." In D. B. Beddie, ed., *Advance Australia: Where?* Melbourne: Oxford University Press, 1975, pp. 146–65. Political leadership, personal ministerial advisers and bureaucratic personalities in influence roles are examined by Millar. He is concerned with the effects of the attentive public and outside groups on foreign policy.

Economic Relations

32:49 Bell, Roger. "Australian-American Relations and Reciprocal Wartime Economic Assistance, 1941–6: An Ambivalent Association." *Australian Economic History Review* 16:1 (1976), 23–49. This is an examination of both Australian and American attempts to exploit their wartime arrangements for their own national economic and trade benefit after the war. The arguments are less than persuasive, however.

Brash, D. T. *American Investment in Australian Industry* (39:87) is a useful survey and analysis of American corporate investment in Australian manufacturing and an evaluation of the benefits and costs Australia derives from such investment.

32:50 Brash, Donald T. "Australia as Host to the International Corporation." In Charles P. Kindleberger, ed., *The International Corporation.* Cambridge, Mass.: MIT Press, 1970, pp. 293–318. This is an excellent essay dealing with foreign investors in Australia, with particular emphasis on the Americans, by the leading specialist. The author concludes that Australia will continue to be an attractive investment for U.S. capital.

32:51 Churchward, L. G. "The American Influence on the Australian Labour Movement." *Historical Studies* 5:19 (1952), 258–77. The author examines American influences on the Australian labor movement—such as the social critics Henry George and Edward Bellamy and socialists like Daniel de Leon and Eugene Debs and the example of the Knights of Labor and the Industrial Workers of the World—from the 1880s to the 1920s. He argues that these influences have on occasion left their imprint on important sections of the Australian labor movement.

Churchward, L. G. "Rhode Island and the Australian Trade, 1792–1812" (5:131).

32:52 Crawford, Sir John Grenfell, et al. *Australian Trade Policy 1942–1966: A Documentary History.* Canberra: Australian National University Press, 1968. This collection of 14 key government decisions is arranged to explain the contrast between the prewar milieu, in which the Ottawa agreement dominated Australia's external economic relations, and the postwar developments.

32:53 Fox, Annette Baker. *The Politics of Attraction: Four Middle Powers and the United States.* New York: Columbia University Press, 1977. This work is, in the words of the author, "a study of interpretation and responsiveness between the United States and each of four friendly middle powers, two of the four being next-door neighbors to the superpower." Pairing and "comparing neighboring Canada and distant Australia... with neighboring Mexico and distant Brazil," Fox seeks to determine the extent and ways one country responded to the needs of the other, and how the policies of one country affect those of the other. The result is an impressive achievement. Extensive bibliography.

Levi, W. "The Earliest Relations between the United States of America and Australia" [1792–1812] (5:133).

32:54 McColl, G. D. *The Australian Balance of Payments: A Study of Post-War Developments.* New York: Cambridge University Press, 1965. An Australian scholar discusses problems in Australia's international economic transactions incurred by increased postwar import demands.

32:55 Megaw, M. Ruth. "Australia and the Anglo-American Trade Agreement, 1938." *Journal of Imperial and Commonwealth History* 3:2 (1975), 191–211. Though Australia desired to open trade relations with the United States on a mutual basis, lack of direct diplomatic ties and preference paid by the Americans to Britain caused Australia to forfeit favorable possibilities in the 1935 to 1938 trade agreement talks in order to assure British success.

32:56 Perkins, J. O. N. *The Pattern of Australia's International Payments.* Melbourne: Nelson, 1971. An introduction to Australia's transactions with the rest of the world, it is primarily concerned with the 1960s. The author explains the main features of Australia's trade with, and payments to and from, such nations as the United States.

Potts, E. D., and Potts, A. *Young America and Australian Gold: Americans and the Gold Rush of the 1850's* (8:122).

32:57 Potts, E. Daniel, and Potts, Annette. "Thomas Welton Stanford (1832–1918) and American-Australian Business and Cultural Relations." *Historical Studies* 17:67 (1976), 193–209. The authors discuss the career of Stanford, who immigrated to Australia from the United States in 1859 and became extremely wealthy. The essay reveals hitherto unknown details of his career, including his promotion of the Singer sewing machine and his efforts to develop cultural and educational exchanges between Australia and California.

32:58 Salmon, J. H. M. *History of Gold Mining in New Zealand.* Wellington: Government Printer, 1963. This is a substantial account of what was at the time (1850s) the major element giving New Zealand importance in the eyes of the world outside.

32:59 Snape, R. H. *International Trade and the Australian Economy.* Melbourne: Longmans, 1973. This theoretical discussion of international trade is followed by a discussion of Australia's trade policy, including its important trading relationship with the United States.

32:60 Tsokhas, Kosmas, and Simms, Marian. "The Political Economy of United States' Investment in Australia." *Politics* 13:1 (1978), 65–80. The major concerns of this article are conceptual ones, related to the nature of U.S. investment in Australia.

Personalities

Additional references on individuals may be found in Chapter 1, "Biographical Data."

AMERICAN

Dean Acheson

See Chapter 24, "Personalities," for additional references.

Acheson, D. *Present at the Creation: My Years in the State Department* (24:90) provides some details of the negotiation of the ANZUS Treaty and of the early meetings of the ANZUS Council, established in accord with the treaty.

Others

32:61 Siracusa, Joseph M. "Ambassador Marshall Green, America, and Australia." *World Review* 14:3 (1975), 17–25. An account of U.S. Ambassador Marshall Green's role in adjusting America's traditional relationship to the Labor government of Gough Whitlam, which came to power in late 1972. Within a period of two years, Green made it clear to Australians of all political persuasions that the United States no longer looked for a locked-step relationship.

AUSTRALIAN

Richard G. Casey

32:62 Casey, Richard G. *Personal Experience, 1939–1946.* New York: McKay, 1963. Casey was the first Australian minister to the United States (1940–1942), and subsequently British minister of state for the Middle East and then governor of Bengal. This volume is a narrative based on, and with excerpts from, his diary. It tends to skip around a lot, and certainly belies the role Casey played in Anglo-American collaboration prior to the United States entry into the war.

32:63 Millar, T. B., ed. *Australian Foreign Minister: The Diaries of R. G. Casey, 1951–1960.* London: Collins, 1972. This is a selection from the diaries of R. G. (Lord) Casey, Australian minister for external affairs from April 1951 to January 1960. The diary entries record Casey's impressions of the world of international politics during the 1950s.

Herbert V. Evatt

32:64 Edwards, Peter G. "Evatt and the Americans." *Historical Studies* 18:73 (1979), 546–60. Australian writers have generally argued that U.S. policymakers disliked H. V. Evatt, Australian minister for external affairs (1941–1949), because of either his policy positions or his abrasive diplomatic style.

This article argues that there was also a profound mistrust of Evatt's character and integrity and his role in domestic politics. This mistrust significantly affected American interpretations of Evatt's actions and therefore of Australian policy toward the United States.

32:65 Evatt, Herbert V. *Foreign Policy of Australia.* Sydney: Angus & Robertson, 1945. The foreign policy thoughts of Evatt, minister for external affairs in the Labor party's federal administration under Prime Ministers John Curtin and Ben Chifley (1941–1949) are contained in this volume. It is impossible to appreciate the nature of Australian-American wartime relations without first coming to grips with Evatt's policies.

32:66 Tennant, Kylie. *Evatt: Politics and Justice.* Sydney: Angus & Robertson, 1970. This is a sympathetic portrayal of the life of Australia's wartime and postwar foreign minister. It is particularly useful on Evatt's role in the framing of the United Nations Charter and his leadership of the smaller powers as well as on the Australian-American wartime relationship. Bibliography.

Peter Fraser

32:67 McIntosh, Alister. "Working with Peter Fraser in Wartime: Personal Reminiscences." *New Zealand Journal of History* 10:1 (1976), 3–20. This is a chatty memoir by a former permanent head of the New Zealand Department of Foreign Affairs, who was certainly one of the nation's most esteemed diplomats and public servants. He illuminates some of the attitudes toward the United States of New Zealand's most reticent prime minister.

32:68 Thorn, James. *Peter Fraser.* London: Odhams, 1952. This biography of New Zealand's World War II prime minister was prepared by his parliamentary under secretary.

Sir Robert G. Menzies

32:69 Menzies, Sir Robert Gordon. *Afternoon Light: Some Memories of Men and Events.* New York: Coward-McCann, 1968.

32:70 Menzies, Sir Robert Gordon. *The Measure of the Years.* London: Cassells, 1972. These two books are reminiscences by the Australian statesman who was prime minister (1939–1941, 1949–1966). Important sources.

32:71 Perkins, Kevin. *Menzies: Last of the Queen's Men.* London: Angus & Robertson, 1968. This is an anecdotal but informative study of a prime minister who dominated his country's politics for nearly 20 years.

Others

32:72 Edwards, Cecil. *Bruce of Melbourne: Man of Two Worlds.* London: Heinemann, 1966. This is a biography of a prominent Australian who was prime minister (1923–1929) and high commissioner to Great Britain (1933–1945).

32:73 Eggleston, Frederick W. *Reflections on Australian Foreign Policy.* New York: Institute of Pacific Relations, 1957. This book, the recollections of a diplomat and scholar, covers the long sweep of Australian external relations, dealing with what the author considers the basics of his nation's foreign policy. Among other things, Eggleston was the first Australian minister to China (1941–1944) and minister to the United States (1944–1946). Extensive bibliography.

32:74 Heyden, Peter R. *Quiet Decision: A Study of George Foster Pearce.* New York: Cambridge University Press, 1965. A former private secretary to Pearce uses his own personal recollections and private papers to discuss a man who influenced the Australian political scene. Sir George was a founder of the Labor party in Western Australia, senator (1901–1937), and defense minister during World War I.

32:75 Hughes, Colin A. *Mr. Prime Minister: Australian Prime Ministers, 1901–1972.* Melbourne: Oxford University Press, 1976. This work consists of a series of sketches of Australian prime ministers (1901–1972) from Edmund Barton to William McMahon. The author also suggests the various contributions each man made to the office. Bibliography.

32:76 Hughes, William M. *The Splendid Adventure.* London: Benn, 1929. These are the memoirs of the Australian prime minister (1915–1923) who served throughout World War I and led his country's delegates to the Paris Peace Conference. Hughes was a symbol of Australian nationalist sentiment, including the White Australia policy.

32:77 La Nauze, John A. *Alfred Deakin: A Biography.* 2 vols. New York: Cambridge University Press, 1965. Alfred Deakin (1856–1919) was a founder of the Australian Federation and three times prime minister. This is a significant work.

32:78 Rivett, Rohan. *Australian Citizen: Herbert Brooks, 1867–1963.* New York: Cambridge University Press, 1965. This is the biography of the first (and last) Australian commissioner-general to the United States. After eighteen months in New York, Brooks, who had previously represented his country at the League of Nations in Geneva, returned home.

32:79 Rodan, Paul. "The Prime Ministership of Harold Holt." Thesis, La Trobe University, 1976. The main emphasis is on the domestic policy and problems of Harold R. Holt, but the work contains useful information and commentary on the development of the Australian-American relationship during the critical years of Australia's commitment to the Vietnam War. Bibliography.

32:80 Ross, Lloyd. *John Curtin: A Biography.* Melbourne: Macmillan, 1977. This biography of Australia's prime minister during World War II pays significant attention to wartime Australian-American relations and to Curtin's dealings with Americans such as General Douglas MacArthur. Extensive bibliography.

32:81 Spender, Sir Percy C. *Exercises in Diplomacy.* Sydney: Sydney University Press, 1969. This indispensable source provides the first detailed account of the genesis of the ANZUS Treaty and the Colombo Plan by a participant. Spender served as the Australian minister for external affairs from 1949 to 1951.

32:82 Watt, Sir Alan S. *Australian Diplomat: Memoirs of Sir Alan Watt.* Sydney: Angus & Robertson, 1972. These reminiscences by a leading Australian diplomat who represented his country in the United States, the U.S.S.R., the Federal Republic of Germany, and Japan contain valuable insights.

Australian, New Zealand, and U.S. Relations

32:83 Edwards, Peter G., ed. *Australia through American Eyes, 1935–1945.* St. Lucia: University of

Queensland Press, 1979. A slim collection of ten documents—ranging from the views of J. Pierrepont Moffat to Nelson T. Johnson—this particular compendium examines how Australia appeared to a significant and highly trained group of U.S. diplomats in a most critical period. This is an ideal first book to turn to on the subject. Bibliography.

32:84 Fredman, Lionel E. *The United States Enters the Pacific.* Sydney: Angus & Robertson, 1969. In this brief sketch of American expansionism, Fredman, a well-known Australian Americanist, provides an excellent chapter in American-Australian relations, from the earliest beginnings to 1968. Not unlike many other commentators on the relationship, the author concludes the American alliance will continue to be a cardinal feature of Australian foreign policy. Bibliography.

32:85 Grattan, C. Hartley. *The United States and the Southwest Pacific.* Cambridge: Harvard University Press, 1961. In this study Grattan deals with American-Australian relations from the long-term historical perspective. This is a significant book by the former leading American Australianist. Bibliography.

32:86 Harper, Norman D., ed. *Australia and the United States.* Melbourne: Nelson, 1971. A compendium of documents and readings in Australian history, this collection brings together a number of diverse views on the impact of Australia and the United States on each other. Many of the essays address themselves to significant foreign policy issues.

32:87 Levi, Werner. *American-Australian Relations.* Minneapolis: University of Minnesota Press, 1947. In an early work on the subject, the author traces the growth and development of American-Australian relations from the late 18th century to the aftermath of World War II. Levi concludes that despite their differences, the United States and Australia will continue to be important to each other. Extensive bibliography.

32:88 Lissington, Margaret P. *New Zealand and the United States, 1840–1944.* Wellington: Government Printer, 1972. A cursory but very well-documented survey, this slim volume has the additional merit of being the only one of its kind. Extensive bibliography.

PRE-WORLD WAR I

32:89 Gordon, Donald C. "Roosevelt's 'Smart Yankee Trick.'" *Pacific Historical Review* 30:4

(1961), 351–58. In 1908, Theodore Roosevelt sought, informally, to involve Canada and Australia in a united front barring Japanese migration.

32:90 Greenwood, Gordon. *Early American-Australian Relations.* Melbourne: Melbourne University Press, 1944. In one of the earliest works on the subject, the author traces Australian-American relations (1792–1830) from the first settlement in New South Wales to the time of the gold fever in Victoria. The work also takes into consideration relations with South America. Bibliography.

Hart, R. A. *The Great White Fleet: Its Voyage around the World, 1907–1909* (14:12) is a boisterous and highly impressionistic but well-documented account of the naval exercise that first introduced Australia and New Zealand to the reality of U.S. sea power.

32:91 Meaney, Neville. "'A Proposition of the Highest International Importance': Alfred Deakin's Proposal and Its Significance for Australian Imperial Relations." *Journal of Commonwealth Political Studies* 5:3 (1967), 200–214. A seminal article that deals with the meaning of Australian Prime Minister Alfred Deakin's 1909 proposal to the colonial secretary with respect to proclaiming a "Monroe Doctrine" of the Pacific.

32:92 Meaney, Neville. *The Search for Security in the Pacific, 1901–14.* Vol. 1 in *A History of Australian Defence and Foreign Policy, 1901–23.* Sydney: Sydney University Press, 1976. Taking the so-called maximalist position, Meaney argues that Australia had a distinct foreign policy not only before 1942 but also before 1914. This is a well-documented volume that challenges many accepted beliefs.

32:93 Ross, Angus. *New Zealand Aspirations in the Pacific in the Nineteenth Century.* Oxford: Clarendon Press, 1964. This is a fascinating, documented study of an extraordinary aspect of colonial history—when New Zealanders really believed that their destiny was to become the Great Britain of the South Pacific, and when that was still a destiny to aspire to. Extensive bibliography.

32:94 Taylor, C. P. "New Zealand, the Anglo-Japanese Alliance and the 1908 Visit of the American Fleet." *Australian Journal of Politics and History* 15:1 (1969), 55–76. The visit of the Great White Fleet provided New Zealanders with their first vision of American sea power, and encouraged some national leaders to think seriously of the possibility of U.S. protection against a menace from Japan.

32:95 Wilkes, Charles. *Narrative of the United States Exploring Expeditions during the Years 1838, 1839, 1840, 1841, 1842.* 5 vols. and atlas. Philadelphia: Lee & Blanshard, 1845. Known as the *U.S. South Seas Surveying and Exploring Expedition,* these volumes cover the natural history, anthropology, geology, hydrology of the area as well as history and politics. Volumes 2 and 3 cover specifically Australia and New Zealand, the rest primarily Oceania (except half of volume 4, on the Northwest Coast).

WAR AND PEACE, 1914–1939

32:96 Megaw, M. Ruth. "Undiplomatic Channels: Australian Representation in the United States, 1918–39." *Historical Studies* 15:60 (1973), 610–30. Megaw examines Australian relations with the United States in the interwar years and traces Australian attitudes to foreign policy as represented by the changing view of official representation in the United States.

32:97 Milner, Ian F. G. *New Zealand's Interests and Policies in the Far East.* New York: Institute of Pacific Relations, 1939. This account is of historical interest as an overview from a pre–World War II perspective. Bibliography.

World War I

See "Personalities" for William M. Hughes (under "Others").

32:98 Boyd, Mary. "The Military Administration of Western Samoa, 1914–1919." *New Zealand Journal of History* 2:1 (1968), 148–64. Boyd discusses the New Zealand occupation of the former German colony during World War I; included are some references to relations with American Samoa.

32:99 Scott, Ernest. *Australia during the War.* Vol. 2 in *Official History of Australia in the War of 1914–1918.* Sydney: Angus & Robertson, 1936. This volume, which is part of the official Australian war history series, deals with the impact of World War I on Australian society: "It describes the background—political, social, industrial, economic—against which the war-effort of Australia was projected." Bibliography.

The Interwar Years

See "Personalities," especially, under "Others," Herbert Brooks, William M. Hughes.

32:100 Esthus, Raymond A. *From Enmity to Alliance: U.S.-Australian Relations, 1931–1941.* Melbourne: Melbourne University Press, 1965. In a brief but impressive book, Esthus, an American, describes and analyzes American-Australian relations from the Great Depression to Pearl Harbor. It is a good introduction to the period under consideration. Extensive bibliography.

32:101 McIntyre, William D. "New Zealand and the Singapore Base between the Wars." *Journal of Southeast Asian Studies* 11:1 (1971), 2–21. McIntyre discusses New Zealand's concern with imperial defense in the Pacific between the wars. It is an essential counterpart to the more readily available Australian studies.

32:102 Megaw, M. Ruth. "The Scramble for the Pacific: Anglo–United States Rivalry in the 1930s." *Historical Studies* 17:69 (1977), 458–73. This is a study of the dispute over the sovereignty of the Phoenix Islands and the Line Islands, when several small islands acquired a strategic importance in view of Pan American Airways' attempt to open routes between Hawaii and Australia and New Zealand. Agreement was finally reached in 1938 for joint sovereignty of Canton and Enderbury for 50 years.

Washington Conference, 1921–1922

See Chapter 20, "Washington Naval Conference, 1921–1922," for additional references.

Braisted, W. R. *The United States Navy in the Pacific, 1909–1922* (17:227) is valuable for the way in which it illuminates Australian and New Zealand attitudes toward the United States and Japan in the context of the Anglo-Japanese Alliance.

32:103 Thornton, Robert. "The Semblance of Security: Australia and the Washington Conference, 1921–22." *Australian Outlook* 32:1 (1978), 65–83. Examining the Washington Conference from a purely Australian point of view, the author concludes that "although in the long run the Washington treaties did not give Australians any real sense of safety, they nonetheless did provide them with at least a short-lived if somewhat illusory sense of security."

Vinson, J. C. "The Problem of Australian Representation at the Washington Conference for the Limitation of Naval Armament" (20:157) is the story of Australian efforts to gain direct representation at the Washington Conference in 1921. Failure to do so was held by Australia to be an unnecessary slight and unfortunate precedent.

WORLD WAR II

See "Personalities," especially Richard G. Casey, Herbert V. Evatt, Peter Fraser, and, under "Others," John Curtin, Frederick W. Eggleston.

Books

32:104   Baker, John V. T. *Official History of the New Zealand People in the Second World War, 1939–45: The New Zealand People at War: War Economy.* Wellington: New Zealand, Department of Internal Affairs, 1965. This detailed and comprehensive analysis, by a leading New Zealand statistician, is an important work.

32:105   Barclay, Glen St. John. *Their Finest Hour.* London: Barker, 1977. Barclay critically examines British strategic preoccupations as a result of which the eastern empire was left substantially to the protection of the United States during the period from the fall of France to Pearl Harbor. Extensive bibliography.

32:106   Bell, Roger J. *Unequal Allies: Australian-American Relations and the Pacific War.* Melbourne: Melbourne University Press, 1977. Bell, an Australian revisionist much influenced by the American New Left, undertakes a reexamination of the nature of Australian-American relations during the crucial period from 1941 to 1946. Not surprisingly, the author finds Australian influence on U.S. wartime policy peripheral and marginal. Bibliography.

32:107   Gillespie, Oliver A. *Official History of New Zealand in the Second World War, 1939–45: The Pacific.* Wellington: New Zealand, Department of Internal Affairs, 1952. New Zealand did not play a major part in the Pacific war. The book does however provide useful data on Australian–New Zealand defense planning in the Pacific before Pearl Harbor, and on the initial desperate responses to the Japanese thrust.

32:108   Hasluck, Paul. *Australia in the War of 1939–45 (Civil).* 2 vols. Canberra: Australian War Memorial, 1952–1970. Volume 1, *The Government*

and the People, 1939–1941, and volume 2, *The Government and the People, 1942–1945,* are indispensable studies of Australia's political and social history during the war.

32:109   Mansergh, Nicholas. *Survey of British Commonwealth Affairs, Problems of Wartime Co-operation and Post-War Change, 1939–1952.* London: Royal Institute of International Affairs, 1958. Essentially a commentary on public statements, it is strongly colored by the editor's belief in the merits and viability of the British Commonwealth.

32:110   McCarthy, Dudley. *South-West Pacific Area—First Year: Kokoda to Wau.* Canberra: Australian War Memorial, 1959. A detailed account of the campaign, it gives full expression to Australian views of U.S. assistance and of General Douglas MacArthur in particular. It is part of the Australian official war history series.

32:111   Milner, Samuel. *Victory in Papua.* In *United States Army in World War II: The War in the Pacific.* Washington, D.C.: G.P.O., 1957. This entertainingly written account of the New Guinea campaign provides an interesting comparison with McCarthy's far more detailed and often resentful Australian official version. Extensive bibliography.

32:112   New Zealand. Department of Internal Affairs. *Documents Relating to New Zealand's Participation in the Second World War, 1939–45.* 3 vols. Wellington: New Zealand, Department of Internal Affairs, 1949–1963. These volumes are indispensable to the study of the British Commonwealth at war (1939–1945).

32:113   Wigmore, Lionel. *The Japanese Thrust.* Canberra: Australian War Memorial, 1957. This is a detailed account of the origins and first stages of the campaign that found Australia and the United States fighting as allies in the South Pacific.

32:114   Wood, Frederick L. W. *Official History of New Zealand in the Second World War, 1939–45: The New Zealand People at War: Political and External Affairs.* Wellington: New Zealand, Department of Internal Affairs, 1958. This is an elegantly written and frequently illuminating account.

Essays

32:115   Barclay, Glen St. John. "Australia Looks to America: The Wartime Relationship, 1939–42." *Pacific Historical Review* 46:2 (1977), 251–71. Australian expectations of U.S. support in the first critical months of the Pacific war were based upon a serious misunderstanding of basic American strategic preoccupations, for which neither Washington nor Canberra were really to blame. The shock of discovery in mid-1942 was correspondingly intense if not necessarily damaging in its effects.

32:116 Barclay, Glen St. John. "Singapore Strategy: The Role of the United States in Imperial Defense." *Military Affairs* 39:2 (1975), 54–58. Barclay describes the process by which the British increasingly left to the United States the responsibility for the defense of the eastern empire in World War II, and the attempts by Australian and New Zealander defense planners to discover what plans were in fact being made for their protection in Washington and London.

32:117 Bell, Roger. "Australian-American Disagreement over the Peace Settlement with Japan, 1944–46." *Australian Outlook* 30:2 (1976), 238–62. Bell analyzes the disagreement over the peace settlement which was a continuation of friction over Allied strategic priorities precipitated by rapid Japanese advances in 1942. Australia opposed the Anglo-American policy of defeating Germany first; and after 1943, Australian criticism of America became more pronounced.

Bell, R. "Australian-American Relations and Reciprocal Wartime Economic Assistance, 1941–6: An Ambivalent Association" (32:49) finds that both the United States and Australia made sufficient contributions and concessions to ultimate victory over Japan, during World War II, but neither country was prepared seriously to compromise its immediate or long-term economic interests to further this end.

32:118 Edwards, P. G. "R. G. Menzies's Appeal to the United States, May–June 1940." *Australian Outlook* 28:1 (1974), 64–70. Prime Minister Robert Gordon Menzies's appeal to the United States in May and June 1940 for material aid for the British war effort indicated the growing realization that Australian security depended more on the United States than on Great Britain.

32:119 Thorne, Christopher. "MacArthur, Australia and the British, 1942–1943: The Secret Journal of MacArthur's Liaison Officer." *Australian Outlook* 29:1 (1975), 53–67; 29:2 (1975), 197–210. The entries in the journal suggest that while future relationship between Britain and the dominions was far from

clear, the United States had clearly established itself as an important factor in future Australian affairs.

POST–WORLD WAR II

See "Personalities," especially Richard G. Casey, Herbert V. Evatt.

32:120 Albinski, Henry S. *Australian External Policy under Labor*. St. Lucia: University of Queensland Press, 1977. Albinski analyzes Australian external policy under the first Labor party government (1972–1975) elected to federal office in nearly a quarter of a century. The result is a first-class study of Gough Whitlam's foreign policy, although much more than that is covered. Extensive bibliography.

32:121 Amicis, Jan de. "It Just Happened: The Transformation of American Migrants in Australia from Sojourners to Settlers." *Australian and New Zealand Journal of Sociology* 12:2 (1976), 136–44. The American immigrant population grew from 10,810 in 1961 to 30,035 in 1971. The author examines explanations for American immigration and the assimilation of Americans into Australian society, but deals less fully with the high return rate.

Bell, C. *The Diplomacy of Detente: The Kissinger Era* [1969–1977] (24:219) devotes an entire chapter to the significance of detente on Australian foreign policy. Bell concludes that detente widened the area of Australian diplomatic maneuver.

32:122 Bell, Roger. "Australian-American Discord: Negotiations for Post-War Bases and Security Arrangements in the Pacific 1944–1946." *Australian Outlook* 27:1 (1973), 12–33. By early 1944, Australia was no longer looking primarily to the United States for defense. It was prepared to foster U.S. involvement in the South Pacific by negotiating reciprocal base rights, a tripartite defense scheme, or a regional security arrangement, but was opposed to U.S. proposals for the unilateral use of Manus Island, and U.S. expansion in the southwest Pacific.

32:123 Boyd, Mary, ed. *Pacific Horizons: A Regional Role for New Zealand*. Wellington: New Zealand Institute of International Affairs, 1972. This slim collection of papers delivered by foreign service officials and academics examines some of the options available to New Zealand as a minipower in the South Pacific.

32:124 Cuddy, Dennis L. *The Yanks Are Coming: American Immigration to Australia.* San Francisco, Calif.: R&E Research Associates, 1977. Cuddy studies in great detail the motivations, satisfactions, complaints, and status of American migrants to Australia in recent years. The statistical data are impressive.

32:125 Fitzpatrick, John E. "Australian Relations with Britain and the United States, 1949–1956." Thesis, University of Queensland, 1975. Comparable with the McKinnon thesis (32:130) in its use of available published and unpublished sources, it is written with analytical and literary flair. Extensive bibliography.

32:126 Gelber, Henry C. *The Australian-American Alliance: Costs and Benefits.* Baltimore: Penguin, 1968. In this brief study, Gelber, a political scientist, attempts to understand why the U.S. alliance has become the main axis of Australian defense and security policies. On the basis of a cost/benefit assessment, the author concludes that for the United States the costs of defending Australia are less than Australia's usefulness to some of America's central purposes in the Indo-Pacific region. Bibliography.

32:127 Harper, Norman. "The American Alliance in the 1970s." In J. A. C. Mackie, ed., *Australia in the New World Order.* Melbourne: Nelson, 1976, pp. 217–46. This essay presents the Australian case for retaining the American alliance. Nonetheless, he concludes, Australia should develop as much freedom of action as possible within the alliance.

32:128 Harper, Norman D., ed. *Pacific Orbit: Australian-American Relations since 1942.* Melbourne: Cheshire, 1968. An uneven collection of essays, this work emphasizes various aspects of the relationship. Of particular value are the essays by Norman Harper, Bruce Grant, and Zelman Cowen.

32:129 Haupt, Margaret. "Australian Policy towards the West New Guinea Dispute, 1945–1962." Thesis, Australian National University, 1972. This is an exhaustive study of an issue which caused Australians to question the order of U.S. priorities in the South Pacific, and the exact nature of the cover provided by the ANZUS Treaty. While new U.S. documents are now available, the interpretation and conclusions are still tenable. Extensive bibliography.

32:130 McKinnon, Noela M. "Australian Foreign Policy, 1957–1965: A Study of Four Foreign Minis-

ters." Thesis, University of Queensland, 1975. When it was written, this study was the most comprehensive and perceptive study of Australian external relations during this period, with particular emphasis on the American relationship. Extensive bibliography.

32:131 Mediansky, F. A. "United States Interests in Australia." *Australian Outlook* 30:1 (1976), 136–54. Mediansky, in a fashion typical of defense critics in Australia, doubts that there is anything resembling a "special relationship" between Canberra and Washington. Moreover, he questions the costs of maintaining a U.S. presence in Australia in an age of strategic weapons.

32:132 Millar, T. B. *Australia's Foreign Policy.* Sydney: Angus & Robertson, 1968. The focus of Millar's study is the problems of Australian foreign policy as they appeared from the perspective of the 1950s and 1960s. Bibliography.

32:133 O'Neill, Robert. *Australia in the Korean War, 1950–53.* Vol. 1: *Strategy and Diplomacy.* Canberra: Australian War Memorial and Australian Government Publishing Service, 1981. Based on full access to the classified documents of the Australian government, and supplemented by the views of surviving ministers, senior public servants, and military officers, the study examines the causes of the Korean War, how and why Australia chose to participate, and the development of Allied strategy at the most intense period of the cold war. Bibliography.

32:134 Siracusa, Joseph M. "Further Reflections on United States Interests in Australia." *Australian Outlook* 30:3 (1976), 475–79. Siracusa makes a strong case for what he believes to be the "special relationship" that has animated Australian-American relations since World War II. He perceives America's traditional alliance with Australia to be in the continued best interest of both Americans and Australians.

32:135 Siracusa, Joseph M., and Barclay, Glen St. J. "Australia, the United States, and the Cold War, 1945–51: From V-J Day to ANZUS." *Diplomatic History* 5:1 (1981), 39–52. This essay examines and analyzes the origins of the United States, Australia, New Zealand Tripartite Security Treaty (ANZUS), which was signed at San Francisco on September 1, 1951. Australia wanted an alliance; the United States wanted cooperation. Neither got exactly what it wanted.

32:136 Vandenbosch, Amry, and Vandenbosch, Mary B. *Australia Faces Southeast Asia: The Emergence of a Foreign Policy.* Lexington: University of Kentucky Press, 1968. This is an account of the effect of British withdrawal from Asia on Australian foreign policies.

32:137 Weisbrod, Hanno. "Australia's Security Relations with the United States, 1957–1963." Thesis, Australian National University, 1972. This is an informative and illuminating account because of the author's access to sensitive material, some of which is in fact still restricted. Extensive bibliography.

ANZUS Treaty

See "Personalities," especially Dean Acheson, and, under "Australian," "Others," Percy Spender.

32:138 Albinski, Henry S. "American Perspectives on the ANZUS Alliance." *Australian Outlook* 32:2 (1978), 131–52. The author concludes that "on balance, the precedents of the tripartite relationship, the compatibility of outlooks and the perceived utility of ANZUS and its Pacific members to the United States are likely to combine to safeguard American receptivity."

32:139 Barclay, Glen St. John. "The Future of Australian-American Relations." *Australian Outlook* 30:3 (1976), 459–74. Traditionally, the ANZUS pact has been regarded by Australian spokesmen as the keystone of U.S.-Australian relations. The author argues that the most effective relations between Washington and Canberra have developed outside the ANZUS structure, and that the relevance of ANZUS itself depends almost totally upon Australia's capacity to act as a credible defense partner of the United States.

Gelber, H. C. *The Australian-American Alliance: Costs and Benefits* (32:126) is convinced that the American-Australian alliance "is the main axis of Australian defence and security policies" and "one of the vital determinants of Australian foreign policy."

32:140 Reese, Trevor R. *Australia, New Zealand and the United States: A Survey of International Relations, 1941–1968.* London: Oxford University Press, 1969. This is a broad survey of the conclusion and operation of the ANZUS Treaty, including the benefits for Australia and New Zealand. Reese's work is, in every respect, an important and scholarly contribution to the field. Bibliography.

32:141 Siracusa, Joseph M. "Australian-American Relations, 1980: A Historical Perspective." *Orbis* 24:2 (1980), 271–87. This article examines the various perceptions Australians and Americans have had of each other in the 20th century and the extent to which they have shaped national security considerations. The author, an American scholar, deals especially with the changed circumstances that led Canberra to look toward the United States in the post–World War II era. The conclusion is that Australian and U.S. foreign policies tend both to complement and parallel each other.

32:142 Starke, Joseph G. *The ANZUS Treaty Alliance.* Melbourne: Melbourne University Press, 1965. The Australian–New Zealand–United States alliance of 1951, which formalized Canberra's shift from London to Washington, is the central element of Australia's defense policy. Starke underscores the point that no matter which party is in power, Australian policymakers will continue to look to the United States for the nation's ultimate security.

32:143 Watt, Alan. "The ANZUS Treaty: Past, Present, and Future." *Australian Outlook* 24:1 (1970), 17–36. This is a penetrating analysis of the origin and meaning of the Australian–New Zealand–U.S. Security Treaty over the first two decades of its existence by an experienced diplomat.

The Vietnam War, 1964–1973

See "Personalities," especially Australian Harold Holt (under "Others"); see also Chapter 30.

32:144 Albinski, Henry S. *Politics and Foreign Policy in Australia: The Impact of Vietnam and Conscription.* Durham, N.C.: Duke University Press, 1970. The purpose of the author is "to adopt the Vietnam and conscription themes as vehicles for interpreting the interplay between external affairs and domestic politics in Australia." The result is an important work. Bibliography.

32:145 McDougall, Derek. "The Australian Press Coverage of the Vietnam War in 1965." *Australian Outlook* 20:3 (1966), 303–10. The author has made an assessment of the coverage of the Vietnam War during 1965 for three important Australian dailies. It is a useful insight and a valuable tool of comparison.

Defense and Nuclear Weapons

For more on nuclear issues, see Chapter 29, "Nuclear Arms Competition and Control."

32:146 Bellany, Ian. *Australia in the Nuclear Age.* Sydney: Sydney University Press, 1972. A study of Australia's contemporary defense systems in which the author argues for nuclear arms for Australia in case India and Japan have them and if the United States withdraws from Asia.

32:147 Millar, T. B. *Australia's Defence.* Melbourne: Melbourne University Press, 1965. In a careful statement of the Australian defense problem—with particular attention on China—as seen from the perspective of the mid-1960s, the author concludes that Australia's security will continue to depend, ultimately, on the support of its great and powerful friends. Millar has remained remarkably consistent over the years.

32:148 O'Neill, Robert, ed. *Insecurity! The Spread of Weapons in the Indian and Pacific Oceans.* Canberra: Australian National University Press, 1978. This collection of essays analyzes current and future trends in the proliferation of weaponry in and around the Indian and Pacific oceans. Bibliography.

32:149 O'Neill, Robert, ed. *The Strategic Nuclear Balance: An Australian Perspective.* Canberra: Australian National University Press, 1975. This deals, essentially, with trends in the strategic relations of the great powers (1945–1974). The papers are, with several exceptions, of a high quality and are a keen insight into Australia's thinking about its American ally.

Central and Western Pacific

See also Chapter 12, "U.S. Annexation of Hawaii, 1898."

Brookes, J. I. *International Rivalry in the Pacific Islands, 1800–1875* (12:124).

32:150 Coulter, John W. *The Pacific Dependencies of the United States.* New York: Macmillan, 1957. An anthropologist's assessment of postwar development in America's Pacific dependencies. Coulter is critical of traditional cultures in the islands, seeing them as impediments to rational economic progress. Nonetheless, he argues for training in anthropological techniques as a means of preparing American administrators for their duties in the Pacific. Chapter bibliographies.

Davidson, J. W., and Scarr, D., eds. *Pacific Island Portraits* [1800–1914] (12:125).

32:151 Dulles, Foster Rhea. *America in the Pacific: A Century of Expansion.* Boston: Houghton Mifflin, 1932. A survey of the historical background of U.S. interests in the Pacific, covering the western expansion of the continent, early relations with China and Japan and the acquisition of Samoa, Hawaii, and the Philippines. Bibliography.

32:152 Furnas, Joseph Chamberlain. *Anatomy of Paradise: Hawaii and the Islands of the South Seas.* New York: Sloane, 1948. *Anatomy of Paradise* must now be considered a classic in the field, for despite its popular appeal the book has qualities of enduring scholarship. It was written at the height of American postwar enthusiasm for the Pacific Islands and therefore serves as a benchmark against which the subsequent decline may be usefully measured. Extensive bibliography.

32:153 Grattan, C. Hartley. *The Southwest Pacific since 1900: A Modern History: Australia, New Zealand, the Islands, Antarctica.* Ann-Arbor: University of Michigan Press, 1963. Although Grattan's text extends to beyond the Pacific Islands, it is one of the few general histories available for the islands region. A companion volume to a smaller book which treats the history of the area to 1900, it is a massive undertaking. Grattan succeeds admirably in providing both general analysis and individual detail. Extensive annotated bibliography.

32:154 Grattan, C. Hartley. *The Southwest Pacific to 1900: A Modern History.* Ann Arbor: University of Michigan Press, 1963. This is a broad survey of Pacific history concentrating on international rivalry. Bibliography.

32:155 Great Britain. Admiralty. Naval Intelligence Division. *Pacific Islands.* Vol. 1: *General Survey.*

Vol. 2: *Eastern Pacific.* Vol. 3: *Western Pacific (Tonga to the Solomon Islands).* Vol. 4: *Western Pacific (New Guinea and Islands Northward).* Geographical Handbooks Series B.R. 519, 519a, 519b, 519c (restricted). London: H.M.S.O., 1943–1945. Without doubt the most complete and detailed compilation of facts about the Pacific Islands available to World War II. The series is labeled "restricted" because much of the information contained in it had to be used without permission from previous authors due to the exigencies of war. The attention to detail offers a mine of information for contemporary historians. Extensive bibliography.

32:156 Keesing, Felix M. *The South Seas in the Modern World.* New York: Day, 1941. This book by the well-known anthropologist of Oceanics surveys the island region of the Pacific and attempts to define comprehensively the political, strategic, and economic role these Oceanic islands play in the world today, and especially the modern experience and problems of the peoples native to them. Bibliography.

32:157 King, Frank P. *Oceania and Beyond: Essays on the Pacific since 1945.* Westport, Conn.: Greenwood, 1976. Its collection of articles on Micronesia is particularly noteworthy for their treatment of American influence in the trust territory. The various articles are critical of U.S. involvement. No less critical are two other papers which survey the postwar relations of the United States with the entire islands region generally. Bibliography.

32:158 McIntyre, W. David. *The Imperial Frontier in the Tropics 1865–1875: A Study of British Colonial Policy in West Africa, Malaya and the South Pacific in the Age of Gladstone and Disraeli.* New York: St. Martin's Press, 1967. The author points out that suspected American designs on Samoa influenced the British decision to annex neighboring Fiji in 1874. Extensive bibliography.

32:159 Oliver, Douglas L. *The Pacific Islands.* Rev. ed. Honolulu: University of Hawaii Press, 1961. Oliver's work is the most useful for the novice. It is relatively brief yet comprehensive. Since Oliver's background is that of an anthropologist, his book lacks the historical detail of Grattan's general volume. Bibliography.

32:160 Perkins, Whitney T. *Denial of Empire: The United States and Its Dependencies.* Leiden: Sythoff, 1962. Because this book encompasses the entire range of American acquisitions since 1867, it is only partially concerned with the three present American Pacific possessions. Despite its general scope Perkins's work does offer an insight into U.S. colonial practice, which has been "a denial of empire" even in the face of its reality. The continental procedures derived from the experience under the Northwest Ordinance has much to do with this development in the Pacific. Bibliography.

32:161 Scarr, Deryck. *Fragments of Empire: A History of the Western Pacific High Commission, 1877–1914.* Canberra: Australian National University Press, 1967. Although primarily concerned with British expansion in the South Pacific, the work contains numerous references to U.S. activities. Bibliography.

32:162 U.S. Department of State. *Trust Territory of the Pacific Islands.* Washington, D.C.: G.P.O., 1948–. This annual report of the United States to the United Nations for the Pacific trust area was prepared by the Department of Navy (1948–1951), by Interior (1952–1953), and since then by State. Title varies.

32:163 Viviani, Nancy. *Nauru: Phosphate and Political Progress.* Honolulu: University of Hawaii Press, 1970. A pioneering study of Nauru's development toward independence, with emphasis on Australia's economic interest in the island.

AMERICAN SAMOA

See also Chapter 12, "U.S. and Samoa."

32:164 Davidson, James W. *Samoa Mo Samoa: The Emergence of the Independent State of Western Samoa.* New York: Oxford University Press, 1967. A history of Western Samoa, the former German protectorate, that was administered by New Zealand from 1920 to 1961 and that became an independent state on January 1, 1962. The volume is also an autobiography of a leading champion of Western Samoan independence. Bibliography.

Gray, J. A. C. *American Samoa: A History of American Samoa and Its United States Naval Administration* (12:126) is a unique treatment of a little researched area of American Samoan history. The period of Navy Department administration was an extremely important one to American Samoa affecting particularly the traditional customs of the territory and its relations with German-, and then New Zealand-controlled Western Samoa.

Kennedy, P. M. *The Samoan Tangle: A Study in Anglo–German–American Relations* (14:128) has the advantage of access to later research and material than Masterman's similar but much earlier study. However, this advantage is partially offset by the wider interest of Kennedy's book. Rather than focusing primarily on the Samoan issue, Kennedy has cast his net wider to examine the implications of the Samoan settlement for the changing international relations of the period.

Masterman, S. R. *The Origins of International Rivalry in Samoa, 1845–1884* (12:133) is still perhaps the best available treatment of the tripartite struggle among Britain, Germany, and the United States for the Samoan Islands that ultimately resulted in their partition in 1899 between the United States and Germany.

32:165 West, Francis J., Jr. *Political Advancement in the South Pacific: A Comparative Study of Colonial Practice in Fiji, Tahiti and American Samoa.* Melbourne: Oxford University Press, 1961. There have been few works which have sought to examine the internal political developments of American Samoa by comparison with its non-American regional neighbors. Although the logic of the comparison is not always compelling, West's study does anticipate the cultural dilemma which faces contemporary Samoans. They are expected to defer to the American political experience and yet retain the qualities which make them Samoan.

TRUST TERRITORY (MICRONESIA)

32:166 Beardsley, Charles. *Guam: Past and Present*. Rutland, Vt.: Tuttle, 1964. A concise and informative handbook of the largest of the Mariana Islands that is administered as an unincorporated U.S. territory under the jurisdiction of the Department of the Interior.

32:167 Carano, Paul, and Sanchez, Pedro C. *A Complete History of Guam.* Rutland, Vt.: Tuttle, 1964. A pedestrian chronology of Guam's political history but nonetheless a valuable book given the dearth of historical literature about the island. The

work tends to focus on the impact of the intrusive Spanish, American, and Japanese conquerors, but fails to consider adequately Guam's role in the region. Extensive bibliography.

32:168 De Smith, Stanley A. *Microstates and Micronesia: Problems of America's Pacific Islands and Other Minute Territories.* New York: New York University Press, 1970. This book has become a classic study of the problems of contemporary microstates. It sympathetically examines the prospects for both Micronesia and the United States as each confronts the need to resolve the territory's future status, but its conclusions are not altogether optimistic. Bibliography.

32:169 Heine, Carl. *Micronesia at the Crossroads: A Reappraisal of the Micronesia Political Dilemma.* Canberra: Australian National University Press, 1974. Despite flaws in style, Heine's review of colonial activity in Micronesia under the Spanish, Germans, Japanese, and Americans is poignant and compelling. The book is particularly valuable for its analysis of the massive shift to westernization under the American administration. Bibliography.

32:170 Kahn, E. J., Jr. *A Reporter in Micronesia.* New York: Norton, 1966. A reporter's view of Micronesia in the years of growing American interest and involvement in the trust territory following the Solomon Report, Kahn's book, while sympathetic to the traditional culture of the Micronesians, depicts U.S. development efforts in a favorable light.

32:171 McHenry, Donald F. *Micronesia: Trust Betrayed: Altruism vs. Self-Interest in American Foreign Policy.* Washington, D.C.: Carnegie Endowment, 1975. This study perceives the American administration of Micronesia as at odds both with the U.S. historic commitment to decolonization and with its obligations to the United Nations. The book provides exceptional detail regarding the course of the future status negotiations which have been in progress since 1969. It is one of the few genuine foreign policy studies available on Micronesia. Bibliography.

32:172 Meller, Norman. *The Congress of Micronesia: Development of the Legislative Process in the Trust Territory of the Pacific Islands.* Honolulu: University of Hawaii Press, 1969. Meller served as a consultant for the development of the first territorywide legislature and the detail of this book reflects his intimate involvement. The emergence of the Congress of Micronesia both in form and practice is revealed even more convincingly by the depth of the U.S. impact on the political process of the trust territory.

32:173   Pomeroy, Earl S. *Pacific Outpost: American Strategy in Guam and Micronesia.* Stanford, Calif.: Stanford University Press, 1951. One of the first academic works to stress the need for a large military presence in Micronesia and on Guam, its main thrust centers on the failure to adequately fortify Guam prior to the outbreak of World War II. The book's historical approach makes it a useful contribution to the limited historiography of Guam. Extensive bibliography.

32:174   Price, Willard D. *America's Paradise Lost.* New York: Day, 1966. A firsthand report on the Trust Territory of the Pacific Islands, which the author contends has been shamefully neglected through low U.S. appropriations and inadequate staff.

32:175   Price, Willard. *Japan's Islands of Mystery.* London: Heinemann, 1944. Price's book manages to convey a sober survey of these islands under Japan prior to the outbreak of war. The book also offers some rare insights into U.S. relations with Micronesia and their logic, which were to determine the postwar connection.

32:176   Thompson, Laura. *Guam and Its People.* 3d ed. Princeton, N.J.: Princeton University Press (1942), 1947. In the first edition (1942) the focus was chiefly on the educational problems of Guam. Now the book is extended to cover the major issues which face administrators on the island, after several years of Japanese occupation and the succeeding years as a U.S. naval base.

32:177   Wiens, Herold J. *Pacific Island Bastions of the United States.* Princeton, N.J.: Van Nostrand, 1962. This is essentially a geographer's interpretation of the strategic value of the Micronesian islands for the United States. The work had its major impact as an apology for a substantial defense interest in the Trust Territory of the Pacific Islands. Bibliography.

New Guinea and Fiji (Melanesia)

32:178   Brookfield, H. C. *Colonialism, Development and Independence: The Case of the Melanesian Islands in the South Pacific.* New York: Cambridge University Press, 1972. A study of the complicated history of the Melanesian islands—ruled severally or successively by Holland, Germany, Britain, France, Australia, Japan, Indonesia, and the United States.

32:179   Coulter, John W. *The Drama of Fiji: A Contemporary History.* Rutland, Vt.: Tuttle, 1967. A geographer and former UN trusteeship official surveys the economic and political problems of the British colony that became independent with Dominican status in the commonwealth on October 19, 1970.

32:180   Hastings, Peter. *New Guinea: Problems and Prospects.* Melbourne: Cheshire, 1969. A journalist's survey of New Guinea, its political development, and its relations with its neighbors, especially with Australia, which underestimated the ease with which Western political and social institutions could be implanted in a Melanesian setting.

32:181   Mair, Lucy P. *Australia in New Guinea.* Rev. ed. Melbourne: Melbourne University Press, 1970. An updated edition of a classic study first published in 1948, it is an important source.

32:182   Thompson, Virginia McLean, and Adloff, Richard. *The French Pacific Islands: French Polynesia and New Caledonia.* Berkeley: University of California Press, 1971. The authors of this comprehensive and well-documented study state that their aim is "to examine the phenomenon responsible for the French islands' present transitional situation and to indicate the problems that their inhabitants will inevitably face when and if the islands' status is changed from a quasi-colonial to a sovereign one."

32:183   White, Osmar E. D. *Parliament of a Thousand Tribes: A Study of New Guinea.* London: Heinemann, 1966. A useful introduction to New Guinea by a writer who knows the country well, with a discussion of Indonesian and Australian interests in that region.

33

The United States and the Middle East since 1941

Contributing Editor
BRUCE KUNIHOLM
Duke University

Contributors
Bernard Reich
George Washington University

Rouhollah Ramazani
University of Virginia

Steven Dorr
Middle East Institute

George Harris
Department of State

Michael Hudson
Georgetown University

Ann M. Lesch
Ford Foundation

R. Hrair Dekmejian
*State University of New York,
Binghamton*

David Long
Department of State

Aaron Miller
Department of State

Michael Van Dusen
*Staff, Committee on Foreign Affairs
House of Representatives*

John C. Campbell
Council on Foreign Relations

John Duke Anthony
*School of Advanced International Studies
Johns Hopkins University*

Contents

Introduction

The study of U.S. policy toward the Middle East in the postwar world is perhaps more challenging than studying U.S. relations with any other region. A multiplicity of countries, cultures, religions, sects, linguistic families, ethnic groups, and tribes all have contributed to a long and rich history that the region's inhabitants continue to find relevant to their current differences. Further complicating matters is the region's strategic location, which for centuries has subjected it to the rivalries and interests of the great powers; and oil, which since the 1973 Arab-Israeli War has moved the Middle East to the center stage of great power politics. Oil has created unprecedented wealth (as well as financial power) and has generated vast economic, demographic, and social change. It also has turned the region into an armed camp where many conflicts—whether between tribes, sects, rival power elites, economic and social classes, or the great powers themselves—play themselves out under potentially explosive conditions.

As a consequence, critical assessments of American diplomacy require a firm grasp of the contexts within which U.S. policies are conceived and implemented. Indispensable to any analysis is a grounding in the complex problems of the Middle East, a feel for the various loyalties and alignments that structure its mores and politics, a sensitivity to the manner in which conflicts between the super powers interact with these factors, a familiarity with the key personalities involved, a sense of the structure and operation of the relevant foreign policy bureaucracies (including, of course, that of the United States), and an appreciation of the various pressure groups that affect their conduct.

The difficulty of acquiring such a background derives not only from linguistic and cultural barriers, and from the elements of secrecy that inevitably attend the conduct of foreign policy, but also from the ontological and epistemological distinctions traditionally drawn between the Occident and the Orient—distinctions which flow naturally, perhaps, from power imbalances inherent in the historical relationship between the two, and which have been canonized in much of the historical writing about the Middle East.

In short, a full appreciation of U.S. diplomacy in the Middle East since 1941 necessitates a much broader focus than that provided by historical interpretations whose perspectives are limited to particular events (e.g., the Arab-Israeli wars) or substantive issues (e.g., oil pricing and production policies or arms sales). What is required is a multidisciplinary approach that cuts through frequently held stereotypic assumptions about the region; that examines in depth not only the international, but also the relevant regional, national, and local dimensions of particular problems as well. For that reason, this chapter gives extensive coverage to regional, country, and substantive studies that complement the section on the United States and the Middle East.

A thoughtful assessment of U.S. policies toward Iran in the 1970s, for example, requires an understanding of very different but nonetheless related developments and issues: Iran's historical role as buffer between East and West; the role played by the West in exploiting, refining, and distributing the region's resources; Britain's crucial regional role up to 1968 (when Whitehall decided to withdraw from the Persian Gulf); circumstances in the international arena (e.g., Vietnam) and in the Middle East (e.g., Egypt and Iraq) that led the United States to promulgate the Nixon Doctrine and implement it in the Persian Gulf; the postwar history of Iran and Saudi Arabia (which for different reasons became the "twin pillars" of U.S. policy after British withdrawal from the gulf in 1971); the Arab-Israeli wars; the personality of the Shah; the thinking of Henry Kissinger and Zbigniew Brzezinski; bureaucratic conflicts within the U.S. government; the advent of OPEC; the international arms trade; international finance; Iran's difficulties with modernization, and the consequences of the Shah's failure to promote viable structures for political participation. Examination of the revolution in Iran and the fall of the Shah would require close scrutiny of many other—particularly domestic—factors (e.g., the role of religion in Iranian politics and the problems of identity confronted by many twentieth-century Iranians).

What should be stressed is that in a field as complex and important as the study of U.S. diplomacy in the

Middle East, narrow historiographical disagreements that dominate the study of other areas here are subsumed by broader differences over basic assumptions, matters of perception, or selective focus on one or another facet of more general problems. The major challenge is not to master historiographical quibbles, but to transcend them; to ask the right questions and define the relevant contexts for exploring answers to them.

This chapter attempts to provide a selective but comprehensive guide to the commencement of such an endeavor and to convey some sense of the kinds of resources that are available: extensive bibliographies such as George Atiyeh's *The Contemporary Middle East, 1948–1973* (33:3), major documentary collections such as J. C. Hurewitz's *The Middle East and North Africa in World Politics* (18:3), and broad general surveys such as George Lenczowski's *The Middle East in World Affairs* (33:32), or Michael Hudson's different but equally valuable *Arab Politics* (33:159); more narrowly focused works such as Bernard Reich's *Quest for Peace* (33:122) or Nadav Safran's *Israel: The Embattled Ally* (33:220) on the United States and Israel, George Harris's *Troubled Alliance* (33:186) on the United States and Turkey, or Aaron Miller's *Search for Security* (33:150) on the United States and Saudi Arabia; country studies such as Louis Dupree's *Afghanistan* (33:167) or Rouhollah Ramazani's *Iran's Foreign Policy, 1941–1973* (2:365); examinations of particular crises or problems that have led the United States to involve itself in the affairs of the Middle East, such as Bruce Kuniholm's *The Origins of the Cold War in the Near East* (33:89); and incisive analyses such as Amos Elon's *The Israelis: Founders and Sons* (33:38) and Fawaz Turki's *The Disinherited: Journal of a Palestinian Exile* (33:40), which in this case delineate important facets of the Israeli and Palestinian psyche respectively. Because the emphasis is on breadth, and because so many aspects of the Middle East mosaic are interrelated, readers will profit from glancing through the entire chapter before reading it.

An emphasis on breadth also imposes limitations on the number of citations that can be accorded different subjects. Since the best scholarly articles on relevant aspects of the Middle East are generally cited in the footnotes and more extensive bibliographies of the best books, this chapter gives preference to books over articles. Some articles, of course, are indispensable to the beginning scholar—in particular two surveys by John DeNovo: "American Relations with the Middle East: Some Unfinished Business" (18:2) and "Researching American Relations with the Middle East: The State of the Art, 1970" (1:106). Researchers should also be prepared to consult journals such as

Middle East Journal, International Journal of Middle East Studies, Jerusalem Quarterly, the *Journal of Palestine Studies, Diplomatic History, Foreign Affairs, Foreign Policy, Orbis,* and others which publish important articles on the Middle East and which in some cases have good indexes. The books and surveys cited in this chapter, however, are far more comprehensive than any single article could ever be and, as a result, have been selected because they generally constitute a better introduction to the basic literature and a better resource for those treading on unfamiliar territory.

Lack of detailed documentary evidence for the period after 1950 also necessitates a greater dependence on less reliable sources such as memoirs. For this reason, and because of the importance of personalities in Middle East politics, autobiographies and biographies of Middle East leaders are given considerable space. Those by and about American presidents, statesmen, and diplomats, on the other hand, are generally excluded or given only token reference (to remind one of the fact that they exist). In most cases these works contain only a chapter or two that is relevant to U.S. policy in the Middle East anyway, and the student—with judicious use of this and other chapters, particularly Chapter 24, in the bibliography—can easily discover what they are.

The foregoing should make clear that the scope for thoughtful studies of U.S. diplomacy in the Middle East is virtually unlimited. The U.S. government's rule for the declassification of public documents (20 years in theory, longer in practice) means essentially that U.S. diplomacy in the Middle East after 1950 has yet to be scrutinized in scholarly detail. Doctoral candidates looking for a topic can anticipate that the record block for 1950 to 1954 will become available in the National Archives in mid-1981, and that the record block for 1955 to 1959 will become available in 1983–1984. As a result, they can dig through the secondary and other literature on a particular problem that interests them (a very important condition) and time the commencement of their primary research to coincide with the availability of documents. Since no comparable studies will exist, thorough and thoughtful monographs on important problems should be publishable.

Students and teachers can benefit enormously from seminars on the Middle East that look at problems from a multidisciplinary perspective. A student interested in U.S. policy can team up with others who focus on insights offered by sociology or literature; economic issues; the role of ethnicity in determining alignments within a region or country; the influence of Islam, Pan-Turanism or Pan-Arabism; the policies of Britain, France, or the Soviet Union; domestic influences on American politics, etc. Important and complex problems, such as the Palestinian question, the Arab-Israeli wars, the Cyprus problem, the rise and fall of the Shah, and the special relationship between Saudi Arabia and the United States all lend themselves to such an approach.

Other colleagues have offered suggestions and provided entries, including William Cover, G. Neal Lendenmann, John Ruedy, Dennis Williams, Laurence Evans, Evan Wilson, Barbara Stowasser, and John DeNovo.

Resources and Overviews

RESEARCH AIDS

While pertinent bibliographies and reference aids are listed here, there are more extensive lists in Chapter 1.

Bibliographies

33:1 Alexander, Yonah. *Israel: Selected Annotated and Illustrated Bibliography.* Gilbertsville, N.Y.: Buday, 1968. Although annotations in this bibliography vary in completeness, the citations provide a comprehensive listing of all aspects of life in Israel. Some of the main headings include history, geography, archaeology, biography and autobiography, religion, philosophy, literature, and international relations.

33:2 "The Arab-Israeli Conflict in Periodical Literature." *Journal of Palestine Studies.* Vol. 1–. Beirut: Institute of Palestine Studies; Kuwait: University of Kuwait, 1971–. Published quarterly, this bibliography surveys 132 periodicals for articles and book reviews on Palestine and the Arab-Israeli conflict. Subjects covered include history, geography, politics, law, diplomacy, social and economic conditions, education, literature, biography, and bibliography. It provides an ongoing update for the Khalidi and Khadduri bibliography (33:10).

33:3 Atiyeh, George N., comp. *The Contemporary Middle East, 1948–1973: A Selective and Annotated Bibliography.* Boston: G. K. Hall, 1975. The author's annotations for the more than 6,000 entries add a valuable dimension to his comprehensive coverage of the issues. Articles and books are organized geographically and thereunder topically: general works, bibliographies, history, politics, social conditions, education, and economics. Citations on political conditions and the Middle East in world affairs are of particular interest. Indexes.

33:4 "Bibliography of Periodical Literature." *Middle East Journal.* Washington, D.C.: Middle East Institute, 1947–. Published quarterly, the bibliography surveys over 300 periodicals for social science materials on the Middle East since the rise of Islam. Focusing on the contemporary Middle East, entries are grouped according to such broad subject headings as documents, geography, history and politics, economic conditions, social conditions, law, biography, and book reviews. A separate subject/geographic listing of recent publications covers monographs and documents.

33:5 Bodurgil, Abraham, comp. *Turkey, Politics and Government: A Bibliography, 1938–1975.* Washington, D.C.: Library of Congress, 1978. A comprehensive bibliography on Turkey's political and social life. The 2,020 monographs and journal articles include 1,018 in Turkish, 731 in English and the remainder in other European languages. The bibliography is organized topically, covering, in part, history; politics; political ideologies, parties and leaders; and Turkey's foreign relations. Indexes.

Bryson, T. A. *United States–Middle East Diplomatic Relations, 1784–1978: An annotated Bibliography* (1:105) comprises 1,353 entries of books, articles, and selected dissertations. Organized according to important time periods or events, approximately half of the work covers the post-1941 period. Brief annotations are included; dissertations are collected in a separate listing at the end. Author index.

33:6 Centre d'Études pour le Monde Arabe Moderne. *Arab Culture and Society in Change.* Beirut: Université de St. Joseph, CEMAM Dar el-Mashreq Publishers, 1973. An excellent bibliography on the modern Arab world, it emphasizes social, economic, and political conditions. It is strong on periodical articles from magazines and journals in the region itself, particularly Lebanon.

33:7 Fatemi, Ali M. S.: Kokoropoulos, Panos; and Amirie, Abbas. *Political Economy of the Middle East:*

A Computerized Guide to the Literature. Akron, Ohio: University of Akron, 1970. A useful reference which contains some 2,600 listings of books and articles, most of which were published between 1958 and 1970. Sources listed include references to vital economic and political information, abstracts, bibliographies, dissertations, special studies, and articles related to economic development and trade in the Middle East. Indexes.

33:8   Hopwood, Derek, and Grimwood-Jones, Diana, eds. *Middle East and Islam: A Bibliographic Introduction.* Middle East Libraries Committee: Bibliotheca Asiatica, no. 9. Zug, Switz.: Inter Documentation, 1972. Provides a comprehensive listing of literature on the Middle East and Islam. Major subject sections include reference; Islamic studies (history, law, art, and religion); general subject studies (anthropology, geography, political science, recent economic history, official publications); regional (or country) studies; and Arabic literature and language. Each topic, prepared by a specialist, includes an introduction and occasional annotations.

33:9   Hussaini, Hatem I. *The Arab-Israeli Conflict: An Annotated Bibliography.* Detroit, Mich.: Association of Arab-American University Graduates, 1975. The editor, who heads the PLO Information Office in the United States, has chosen sources which present an Arab point of view on the Palestine problem as well as Western perspectives critical of Zionism. References deal with the problem's historical origins, the ensuing conflict, Israeli occupation policies, the Palestinian resistance movement, criticisms of Zionism, as well as other aspects.

International Monetary Fund and International Bank for Reconstruction and Development. Joint Library. *Economics and Finance: Index to Periodical Articles, 1947–1971* (39:5) has one volume dealing with Africa and the Middle East. It includes references on international relations, foreign aid, trade agreements, tariff policy, and foreign capital investment.

33:10   Khalidi, Walid, and Khadduri, Jill, eds. *Palestine and the Arab-Israeli Conflict: An Annotated Bibliography.* Beirut: Institute for Palestine Studies, 1974. This major bibliographic source covers the political dimensions of the Palestinian question. The organizational approach is largely chronological, with 4,580 entries (1880–1971). The editors cover demographic, social, and economic issues, as well as religious subjects cast in a social, economic, or political context. Contains English, Arabic, and Hebrew

sources, although other European-language materials are included. Index.

Littlefield, D. W. *The Islamic Near East and North Africa: An Annotated Guide to Books in English for Non-Specialists* (1:107) has much to interest the specialist as well. Overall, this work is a useful companion volume to Atiyeh's bibliography (33:3).

33:11   Pearson, J. D., comp. *Index Islamicus, 1906–1955: A Catalogue of Articles on Islamic Subjects in Periodicals and Other Collective Publications. Supplements: I, 1956–60; II, 1961–5; III, 1966–70; IV, 1971–5.* London: Mansell, 1958. Strongest in history, language, literature, religion, and philosophy, this bibliography is a valuable guide to an historical perspective on the Middle East as well as to the religious and philosophical values which help mold Middle Eastern attitudes. All volumes employ a subject/geographic arrangement. Kept up-to-date by supplements; see also *Quarterly Index Islamicus.*

33:12   al-Qazzaz, Ayad. *Women in the Middle East and North Africa: An Annotated Bibliography.* Middle East Monographs, no. 21. Austin: University of Texas, Center for Middle Eastern Studies, 1977. Approximately 300 published and unpublished entries, exclusively in English, are listed alphabetically by author. Two indexes, one by country and the other by topic, are the keys to this bibliography. The increasing importance of the role of women in Middle Eastern politics and society underscores the value of this work.

33:13   *Quarterly Index Islamicus.* London: Mansell, 1977– . This journal supplements the *Index Islamicus* and, additionally, surveys monographs. It is cumulated every five years.

33:14   Schulz, Ann. *International and Regional Politics in the Middle East and North Africa: A Guide to Information Sources.* Detroit, Mich.: Gale, 1977. An important reference for the diplomatic historian, its in-depth survey of the political scientist's periodical and monograph literature gives specific attention to the regional and international politics of the MIddle East. An introductory essay precedes the major divisions of the book, which include regional issues, foreign policies of the Middle Eastern states, external powers in the Middle East, the Arab-Israeli conflict, petroleum, reference materials, and serials. Indexes.

33:15   Selim, George D., comp. *American Doctoral Dissertations on the Arab World, 1883–1974.* 2d rev.

ed. Washington, D.C.: Library of Congress, 1976. The 1,825 American doctoral dissertations listed alphabetically by author provide a rich source of information on all aspects of the Arab world. To assist the user, there is an index based on the dissertation subject and key words in the title. Although often unpublished, these works provide valuable insights not always available elsewhere.

33:16   Sherman, John, ed. *The Arab-Israeli Conflict, 1945–1971: A Bibliography.* New York: Garland, 1978. Although not as balanced as some bibliographies on the topic, this work is useful for its chronological organization and its coverage of U.S. government publications, including the documents in the U.S. Department of State *Bulletin.* As entries are grouped on a year-by-year basis, a researcher may easily locate items contemporary with particular events.

Simon, R. S. *The Modern Middle East: A Guide to Research Tools in the Social Sciences* (1:109) emphasizes pertinent reference aids. Its primary focus is on modern history, political science, sociology and anthropology.

33:17   Sweet, Louise E., ed. *The Central Middle East: A Handbook of Anthropology and Published Research on the Nile Valley, the Arab Levant, Southern Mesopotamia, the Arabian Peninsula, and Israel.* New Haven, Conn.: Human Relations Area Files Press, 1971. Although dated, the annotated bibliographies appended to each chapter have not been superseded. This primary source for anthropological studies on the central Middle East is extremely useful for the period through 1967. See also John Gulick, "The Anthropology of the Middle East," *Middle East Studies Association Bulletin* 3:1 (1969), 1–14 (part 3 of MESA's State of the Art series), and Louise E. Sweet, "A Survey of Recent Middle Eastern Ethnology," *Middle East Journal* 23:2 (1969), 221–32.

33:18   Tamkoç, Metin. *A Bibliography on the Foreign Relations of the Republic of Turkey, 1919–1967: And Brief Biographies of Turkish Statesmen.* Publication 2. Ankara: Middle East Technical University, Faculty of Administrative Sciences, 1968. A bibliography of some 1,800 entries prepared primarily for English speakers, this unusually complete listing is divided into primary and secondary sources in Turkish, followed by works in other languages by Turkish officials and nationals. A final section contains non-Turkish sources and reflects holdings in major Western collections. Journal articles, dissertations, books, and documents are included.

33:19   U.S. Department of Army. *Middle East: The Strategic Hub: A Bibliographic Survey of the Literature.* Rev. ed. Washington, D.C.: G.P.O., 1978. This bibliography consists of annotated articles, books, and reports dealing with current affairs. Maps and "Background Notes" on each country.

U.S. Department of State. *Point Four: Near East and Africa: A Selected Bibliography on Economically Underdeveloped Countries.* (1:110) lists mostly economic studies published in the 1940s which were collected to assist in developing the Point Four program.

Atlases and Other Aids

33:20   Beaumont, Peter, et al. *The Middle East: A Geographical Study.* New York: Wiley, 1976. The authors examine such matters as geology, climate, resources, and population, and explore their relationship with politics, culture, and economics; the book also includes a number of country studies focused around selected themes, and an extensive bibliography of geographical subjects. Also see William B. Fisher, *The Middle East: A Physical, Social, and Regional Geography,* 6th ed. (London: Methuen, 1971).

33:21   Congressional Quarterly. *The Middle East: U.S. Policy, Israel, Oil and the Arabs.* 4th ed. Washington, D.C.: Congressional Quarterly, 1979. An excellent reference and summary of Middle East affairs; contains succinct country profiles, sections on a variety of issues and policies, statistics on oil and arms transfers, as well as brief capsule biographies and an extensive chronology of Middle East affairs (1945–1979). Tables, maps, and extensive bibliography.

33:22   Gilbert, Martin. *The Arab-Israel Conflict: Its History in Maps.* 2d ed. London: Weidenfeld & Nicolson, 1976. These maps trace the Arab-Israeli conflict from its origins to the mid-1970s and depict not only the wars and their outcomes, but also such themes as refugees, terrorism, arms supplies, and settlements in occupied territories. The author focuses on the history of the Jews (as opposed to the history of both parties to the conflict) and chooses to emphasize those interpretations that legitimize a pro-Israeli point of view.

International Institute for Strategic Studies. *The Military Balance* (40:8) is valuable for the Middle East, where rapid changes and new arms transfer agreements require constantly updated assessments of military capabilities. Also see the institute's other publications, including the annual *Strategic Survey* and the *Adelphi Papers*.

33:23 Kingsbury, Robert, and Pounds, Norman. *An Atlas of Middle Eastern Affairs*. New York: Praeger, 1963. This atlas illustrates the historical, geographic, demographic, political, and ethnic factors which shape the contemporary Middle East. While a new edition is clearly needed to account for changes since 1963, this slim volume provides a succinct view of geographical factors.

33:24 Legum, Colin, ed. *Middle East Contemporary Survey, 1976 – *. New York: Holmes & Meier, 1977 – . An annual record and analysis of political, economic, military, and international developments in the Middle East; it includes essays on a wide variety of subjects, and a country-by-country survey.

33:25 *The Middle East and North Africa*. London: Europa, 1948 – . This annual contains useful essays on regional and substantive issues. Part 1 includes general surveys of the Middle East and North Africa, the religions of the region, the Arab-Israeli confrontation, the Jerusalem issue, oil, and arms transfers. Part 2 provides detailed information on regional organizations, while parts 3 and 4 consist of country surveys and other reference material.

33:26 Shimoni, Yaacov, et al. *Political Dictionary of the Middle East in the 20th Century*. Rev. ed. New York: Quadrangle, 1974. Compiled by Israeli specialists, this concise political compendium of the present and recent past presents a generally accurate and objective picture of the Middle East. The dictionary covers a broad range of material, alphabetically arranged, on countries and peoples, national and political movements, parties and leaders, ideas and ideologies, disputes and wars, alliances and treaties.

Document Collections

More general collections are listed in Chapter 1, and other collections may be found in particular subsections below (e.g., "The 1956 Suez Crisis/The 1956 War").

Columbia Broadcasting System. *Face the Nation: The Collected Transcripts from CBS Radio and Television Broadcasts, 1954 – 1971* (1:347).

33:27 Davis, Helen M. *Constitutions, Electoral Laws, Treaties of the States in the Near and Middle East*. 2d ed. Durham, N.C.: Duke University Press, 1953. A documentary record of the constitutions, laws, and treaties that have embodied the hopes and aspirations of the countries of the Middle East. It does not include material after September 1950.

Gallup, G. H. *The Gallup Poll: Public Opinion, 1935 – 1971* (1:348).

Hurewitz, J. C., ed. *The Middle East and North Africa in World Politics: A Documentary Record* (18:3) examines, in volume 2 (*British-French Supremacy, 1914 – 1945*), the evolution of international politics and its interplay with regional politics. The editor includes 177 entries, each with a brief analytical introduction, and an excellent bibliography. When volume 3 (*British-French Withdrawal and Soviet-American Rivalry, 1945 – *) appears, this series of documents on the Middle East will be the most authoritative in the field.

33:28 *International Documents on Palestine, 1967 – *. Beirut: Institute for Palestine Studies, 1970 – . These annual volumes contain written and oral documentation of international policies and attitudes toward the Palestine question. Material includes treaties, joint communiqués, policy statements, speeches, parliamentary proceedings, interviews, and resolutions adopted by conferences and congresses, and reflects the editors' perceptions of this critical issue. The documents translated from Arabic and Hebrew, not easily obtainable in the United States, are valuable.

33:29 Moore, John Norton, ed. *The Arab-Israeli Conflict*. 3 vols. Princeton, N.J.: Princeton University Press, 1974. The first two volumes include selected readings on principal issues and alternatives for their settlement, while the last volume brings together the principal documents relating to the Arab-Israeli conflict. These volumes facilitate access to scholarly readings in the international legal literature. Extensive bibliography.

U.S. Department of State. *Foreign Relations of the United States* (1:358) is an indispensable starting point for research on U.S. foreign relations in the Middle East. The documents published are well selected, well indexed, and accompanied by useful file references and explanatory notes. The recent volumes on the Near East extend into the early 1950s.

33:30 U.S. Senate. Committee on Foreign Relations. *A Select Chronology and Background Docu-*

ments Relating to the Middle East. 2d rev. ed. Washington, D.C.: G.P.O., 1975. A chronology of developments in the Middle East from 1946 to 1974 is followed by documents relating to the major issues facing U.S. Middle East policy in the period since World War II.

OVERVIEWS

See Chapter 24, "Overviews," for surveys of American foreign affairs since World War II, as well as general listings under "Regional and Country Studies," below.

Davison, R. H. "Where Is the Middle East?" (2:361) traces the use of the terms "Near East" and "Middle East."

33:31 Hammond, Paul Y., and Alexander, Sidney S. *Political Dynamics in the Middle East.* New York: American Elsevier, 1972. Consisting of chapters by 16 experts in the field, this book is intended to contribute to sound policy judgments about the Middle East. Contents include regional politics, changing military perspectives, the internal politics and foreign policies of Israel, Palestinian refugees, and great power (European, U.S., and Soviet) policies.

33:32 Lenczowski, George. *The Middle East in World Affairs.* 4th ed. Ithaca, N.Y.: Cornell University Press, 1980. The author's objectivity, coupled with his capacity to synthesize enormous amounts of material, makes this edition the best general guide to the main themes of the postwar years in the Middle East. Extensive bibliography.

U.S. and the Middle East

See "Personalities" and various subheadings under "U.S. and the Middle East," below, especially for non-Arab countries.

33:33 Badeau, John S. *The American Approach to the Arab World.* New York: Harper & Row, 1968. This still useful "policy book" was written by the former president of the American University in Cairo and later U.S. ambassador to Egypt under President Kennedy. It discusses the American approach to the

Arab world, and examines American interests and the forces operating in the Arab world with which U.S. policy must contend.

33:34 Beling, Willard A., ed. *The Middle East: Quest for an American Policy.* Albany, N.Y.: State University of New York Press, 1973. These essays examine some of the main actors, the interactions of the Middle East states, their relations with the major powers, and the formation of U.S. policy toward the Middle East. The last section examines the roles that special interest groups, Congress, elite newspaper opinion, and the Christian church play in formulating U.S. policy.

Bryson, T. A. *American Diplomatic Relations with the Middle East, 1784–1975: A Survey* (2:359).

Bryson, T. A. *Tars, Turks, and Tankers: The Role of the U.S. Navy in the Middle East, 1800–1979* (2:360) treats the role of the navy in support of American foreign policy.

Daniel, R. L. *American Philanthropy in the Near East, 1820–1960* (2:74) treats the evolution of private American programs of public assistance.

33:35 Polk, William R. *The United States and the Arab World.* 3d ed. Cambridge: Harvard University Press, 1975. This first-rate introduction to an analysis of the Arab world, by a scholar and former member of the State Department Policy Planning Council, isolates those legacies crucial to contemporary Arab identity, and chronicles the development and independence of the Arab states. Polk then looks carefully at the contemporary Arab world and at its relations with the United States since World War II. Bibliography.

Safran, Nadav. *Israel: The Embattled Ally* (33:220) provides a detailed and comprehensive, though undocumented, analysis of U.S.-Israeli relations. See also Bernard Reich, *Quest for Peace* (33:122).

33:36 Stookey, Robert W. *America and the Arab States: An Uneasy Encounter.* New York: Wiley, 1975. A brief but comprehensive analysis of America's private and public interaction with the Arab states. Focusing on the post–World War II period, in part on the rise of Arab and Palestinian nationalism, and on the need for the United States and Israel to recognize its significance, the author, a longtime diplomat and historian, is especially good in his discussion of the economics and politics of oil. Bibliographical essay.

Arab-Israeli Conflict

See also "Personalities," various wars listed under "U.S. and the Middle East," and "The Confrontation States," below.

33:37 Dupuy, Trevor. *Elusive Victory: The Arab-Israeli Wars, 1947–1974.* New York: Harper & Row, 1978. This comprehensive account covers all the wars in detail, with extremely useful maps, diagrams and lists of the order of battle as well as casualties.

33:38 Elon, Amos. *The Israelis: Founders and Sons.* New York: Bantam, 1971. A sympathetic analysis of the Israeli psyche which explains the motivations, identity concerns, and problems of Israelis of Eastern European origin. The author provides an indispensable background for understanding the founders of Israel and the generation that succeeded them. Extensive bibliography.

33:39 Khouri, Fred J. *The Arab-Israeli Dilemma.* 2d ed. Syracuse, N.Y.: Syracuse University Press, 1977. Benefitting from conversations with many of the principals, the author has written a comprehensive, well-documented study of the Arab-Israeli conflict which places special emphasis on its United Nations context. The earlier edition's fine bibliography is eliminated.

33:40 Turki, Fawaz. *The Disinherited: Journal of a Palestinian Exile.* 2d ed. New York: Monthly Review, 1974. The memoir of a Palestinian writer born in 1940 near Haifa. His autobiography, which expresses the human dimension of the Palestine problem, depicts his flight to Lebanon in 1948 and his childhood in a refugee camp near Beirut. Turki describes his sense of alienation and his search for personal and national identity in the Palestinian diaspora. For insight into 1974 epilogue, see Joseph Ryan's "Refugees within Israel: The Case of the Villagers of Kafr Bir'im and Iqrit," *Journal of Palestine Studies* 2 (Summer 1973), 55–81.

Special Studies

See also "Regional and Country Studies," below.

33:41 Khadduri, Majid, ed. *Major Middle Eastern Problems in International Law.* Washington, D.C.: American Enterprise Institute for Public Policy Research, 1972. A survey that elucidates for the general reader, within the framework of international law, the juridical and diplomatic elements of major Middle East problems. The problems addressed include sovereignty, collective security, the Palestine conflict, Jerusalem, the occupied territories, refugees, passage through international waterways, and other territorial and jurisdictional issues. See also Ali El-Hakim, *The Middle Eastern States and the Law of the Sea* (Syracuse, N.Y.: Syracuse University Press, 1980), for a technical discussion of maritime law.

33:42 Livingston, Marius H. *International Terrorism in the Contemporary World.* Westport, Conn.: Greenwood, 1978. While the essays are uneven, and only a few deal specifically with the Middle East, it is useful for its broad coverage of terrorism. The book analyzes such topics as international terrorism's historical and psychological aspects, its political consequences, its legal problems, and the relationship between international terrorism and the military. Extensive bibliography.

Arab Nationalism

See Chapter 18, "U.S. Missionaries and Arab Nationalism"; and "Regional and Country Studies," especially Michael Hudson (33:246).

33:43 Ajami, Fouad. "The End of Pan-Arabism." *Foreign Affairs* 57:2 (1978/1979), 355–73. The author argues that pan-Arabism, which has dominated the political consciousness of modern Arabs, is nearing its end. In its wake, he sees a fragmentation of the Arab existential and political crisis, and a slow process whereby raison d'état is gaining ground. While the passing of pan-Arabism ends one set of troubles, normalization of the Arab state system brings another set.

33:44 MacDonald, Robert W. *The League of Arab States: A Study in the Dynamics of Regional Organization.* Princeton, N.J.: Princeton University Press, 1965. The author's focus on the Arab League's structural and operational aspects allows him to delineate its strengths and weaknesses, as well as to assess its efficiency in realizing its goals. He views the Arab League as useful for accommodating intraregional rivalries and national particularisms. Bibliography.

33:45 Sayegh, Fayez. *Arab Unity: Hope and Fulfillment.* New York: Devin-Adair, 1958. A revealing analysis of Arab nationalism by a Palestinian political scientist who in 1958 saw more hope and probability of fulfillment than subsequent years brought. Interesting on Nasser and the wellsprings of his popularity, the book is useful for its criticism of British and American Middle Eastern policy.

33:46 Sharabi, Hisham B. *Nationalism and Revolution in the Arab World*. Princeton, N.J.: Van Nostrand, 1966. An analysis of modern Arab political history by one of the Arab world's foremost intellectuals. The chapter on socialism and revolution, with its classification of the regimes of the early 1960s, and the chapter on the language of politics, with its definition of key terms, are worth studying. Part 2 contains a selection of political statements and speeches dealing with pan-Arabism, revolutionary ideologies, constitutions, and regime declarations. Bibliography.

Social and Cultural Determinants

See also particular countries under "Regional and Country Studies," below.

33:47 Beck, Lois, and Keddie, Nikki, eds. *Women in the Muslim World*. Cambridge: Harvard University Press, 1978. A useful collection of articles which attempts to account for the subordination of women and to explore how they may lessen the controls of a male-dominated society. The book is organized around such topics as legal and socioeconomic change; historical and religious roles; and case studies of nomadic, village, and urban life. Extensive bibliography.

33:48 Bell, Richard. *Introduction to the Qur'an*. Edinburgh: Edinburgh University Press, 1958. This book summarizes and eclipses 19th- and 20th-century Western scholarship in Koranic studies. After analyzing the historical situation in the Arabian Peninsula at the end of the 6th century A.D., and describing Muhammad's career, the author examines the origins of the Koran according to Islamic belief and Western critical study. He then analyzes the structure and main doctrines of the Holy Book as well as its indebtedness to Jewish and Christian teachings. Bibliography.

33:49 Berque, Jacques. *The Arabs: Their History and Future*. Trans. by Jean Stewart. London: Faber & Faber, 1964. One of the great Orientalists of our time, Berque writes with subtlety and insight about Arab society and culture under the impact of modernity. His categories and methodology defy Anglo-American empiricism, yet what he has to say about generational differences, political values, language and popular art, and economic development must be absorbed by anyone seriously interested in the Arabs today.

33:50 Gibb, Hamilton A. R. *Mohammedanism*. New York: New American Library (1949), 1958. Sir Hamilton Gibb's classic on Islam continues to be an authoritative introduction to its history and doctrines. The nature of the Koran, its doctrine and ritual, the Hadith (the tradition of the Prophet and his companions), and the Shari'a (revealed law) are discussed in the chapters on Sunni (orthodox) Islam. They are followed by an introduction to schismatic movements, in particular the Shi'a. Finally, the author analyzes Sufism (Islamic mysticism), and looks at its role in Islamic society. Bibliography. One should also consult Fazlur Rahman, *Islam* (New York: Holt, Rinehart & Winston, 1966).

33:51 Gulick, John. *The Middle East: An Anthropological Perspective*. Pacific Palisades, Calif.: Goodyear, 1976. The most comprehensive synthesis of anthropological studies of the Middle East, it consists of a discussion of the region's historical and ecological background; basic hypotheses about the region's people, society and culture; an examination of how people live; and a summary of the Middle East's major sociocultural aggregates. Extensive bibliography.

Personalities

Additional references on individuals may be found in Chapter 1, "Biographical Data."

AMERICAN

See Chapter 24, "Personalities" and "Presidential Administrations," for additional references.

Dean Acheson

See Chaper 24, "Personalities," and pertinent subsections under "U.S. and the Middle East," below, for additional references.

Acheson, D. *Present at the Creation: My Years in the State Department* (24:90) comments on U.S. recognition of Israel (ch. 20), the overthrow of Mossadeq (ch. 52), and other Middle East issues.

John Foster Dulles

See Chapter 24, "Personalities," for additional references, and "The Eisenhower Years, 1953–1960," below.

Hoopes, T. *The Devil and John Foster Dulles* (24:112) has a detailed and critical analysis of Dulles's role in the Suez and Lebanon (chs. 20–25, 27).

Dwight D. Eisenhower

See Chapters 23 and 24, "Personalities," and "The Eisenhower Years, 1953–1960," below.

Eisenhower, D. D. *The White House Years* (24:114) comments in volume 1, *Mandate for Change* on the overthrow of Mossadeq (ch. 6). *Waging Peace, 1956–1961*, volume 2, has an account of the 1956 Suez crisis (chs. 2–3) and the Lebanese crisis (chs. 7 and 11).

Lyndon B. Johnson

Johnson, L. B. *The Vantage Point: Perspectives on the Presidency, 1963–1969* (24:120) has an account of the 1967 war (ch. 13).

John F. Kennedy

See Chapter 24, "Personalities," for additional references.

33:52 Nurse, Ronald J. "Critic of Colonialism: JFK and Algerian Independence." *Historian* 39:2 (1977), 307–26. An examination of Kennedy's congressional record indicates that there was a steadfast Kennedy position: "the United States must ally itself with the new nationalism of Asia, Africa and the Middle East even at the expense of America's traditional allies in Western Europe."

Henry A. Kissinger

See also Chapter 24, "Personalities," and "The 1973 War," below.

Kissinger, H. A. *White House Years* (24:133) contains Kissinger's account (pp. 594–631) of the Jordanian crisis (1970–1971).

Richard M. Nixon

See also Chapter 24, "Personalities," and "The Nixon/Carter Years, the 1970s," below.

Nixon, R. M. *RN: The Memoirs of Richard Nixon* (24:145) contains Nixon's account of the 1970–1971 Jordanian crisis (pp. 483–85) and the 1973 war (pp. 920–43).

Harry S. Truman

See references under "The Truman Years, 1945–1952," below.

Truman, H. S. *Memoirs* (24:160) discusses in *Years of Trial and Hope* his policies toward Iran and Turkey (ch. 7), as well as his policies toward Palestine and his decision to recognize Israel (chs. 10–12).

Others

33:53 Alvarez, David J. "The Embassy of Laurence A. Steinhardt: Aspects of Allied-Turkish Relations, 1942–1945." *East European Quarterly* 9:1 (1975), 39–52. Steinhardt acted to restrain the United States from following Britain's attempts to force Turkey into World War II. Steinhardt argued that Turkey's fear of the Soviet Union make it reluctant to declare itself officially on the side of the Allies without firm British and American assurances that Turkey's territorial integrity would be respected.

Murphy, R. D. *Diplomat among Warriors* (23:77) contains information on the 1956 Suez crisis (ch. 26) and the Lebanese crisis (ch. 27).

MIDDLE EASTERN

King Abdullah

33:54 Abdullah, King of Jordan. *Memoirs of King Abdullah of Transjordan*. Trans. by G. Khuri; ed. by Philip P. Graves. London: Cape, 1950. A memoir by Jordan's first king, whose key recollections begin with his early days in the Hejaz and conclude with Transjordan's independence in 1946. The English translation is incomplete, although extensive notes and comments are added. The memoir reveals Abdullah's elite Muslim Arab traditionalism as well as his pragmatic Anglophile openness to notions of evolutionary progress in the modern world.

33:55 Abdullah, King of Jordan. *My Memoirs Completed*. Trans. by Harold W. Glidden. London: Longmans (1954), 1978. This personal memoir, republished with an introduction by King Hussein, was completed not long before Abdullah's assassination on July 20, 1951. It covers the period 1946 to 1951. Also see Hussein's reflections in *Middle East Journal* 32:1 (1978), 79–86.

Menachem Begin

33:56 Begin, Menachem. *The Revolt*. Rev. ed. Trans. by Samuel Katz. New York: Dell, 1978. A memoir of the Israeli prime minister's years as leader of the Irgun Zvai Leumi, in which he recounts his experience in the Jewish revolt against British mandatory rule in Palestine. The book provides important insights into the Irgun and the personality and views of Begin.

33:57 Haber, Eitan. *Menachem Begin: The Man and the Legend.* New York: Dell, 1979. A biography of the sixth prime minister of Israel, which begins with his childhood in Poland and concludes with an epilogue discussing his role in the peace process that led to the Camp David Accords of September 1978. The author, an Israeli journalist, considers Begin's role as an underground leader in the Palestine mandate and as a leader of the opposition in Israel's parliament for 29 years.

David Ben-Gurion

33:58 Bar-Zohar, Michael. *Ben-Gurion: A Biography.* Trans. by Peretz Kidron. New York: Delacorte, 1978. This translation of the longer three-volume work provides a comprehensive overview of Ben-Gurion's life and a useful introduction to the man whose role was crucial to the creation of Israel.

33:59 Pearlman, Moshe. *Ben Gurion Looks Back in Talks with Moshe Pearlman.* New York: Simon & Schuster, 1965. This book provides an account of the first prime minister, as well as profound insight into the people, events, and leaders with whom he came in contact. Topics include the effort to establish Israel as an independent state, and Israeli politics and foreign policy. Also consult David Ben-Gurion's own *Israel: Years of Challenge* (New York: Holt, Rinehart & Winston, 1963).

Moshe Dayan

33:60 Dayan, Moshe. *Moshe Dayan: Story of My Life.* New York: Morrow, 1976. This long autobiography has little material on his early life or about Dayan himself, but contains great detail on the four Arab-Israeli wars.

33:61 Teveth, Shabtai. *Moshe Dayan: The Soldier, the Man, the Legend.* Trans. by Leah and David Zinder. Boston: Houghton Mifflin, 1973. A biography of Moshe Dayan, who served as Israel's chief of staff, minister of defense, and minister of foreign affairs, based on extensive research and numerous interviews, not only with Dayan and his family, but with admirers and detractors.

Abba Eban

33:62 Eban, Abba. *Abba Eban: An Autobiography.* New York: Random House, 1977. One of the few really valuable memoirs by a statesman, this book chronicles Eban's life from his birth in South Africa and his successes as a Cambridge Orientalist, to his service as ambassador to the United States and finally as foreign minister of Israel. He dramatizes the differences within the Zionist movement over the issue of partition, both during the mandate period and after the creation of Israel. He clearly delineates Israel's dilemma in resolving the conflict between its desire for unilateralism and its dependence on the United States, and expresses his preference for political separation from, rather than rule over, the Palestinians.

33:63 St. John, Robert. *Eban.* New York: Dell, 1972. A detailed biography of Israel's former ambassador to Washington, and foreign minister, based on extensive interviews with Eban and his associates and on Eban's personal files and archives.

King Hussein

33:64 Hussein, King of Jordan. *Uneasy Lies the Head.* New York: Geis, 1962. The king's straightforward, popular style conveys his personality: his sense of duty, satisfactions, sorrows, and frequent loneliness. The work includes an account of Hussein's grandfather, King Abdullah; discussions of inter-Arab relations and the Palestinians; and descriptions of the dismissal of Glubb, as well as the crises of 1957 and 1958. Hussein's *My "War" with Israel* (New York, 1969) tells his side of the 1967 war.

33:65 Snow, Peter. *Hussein: A Biography.* Washington, D.C.: Luce, 1972. A sympathetic but objective biography of King Hussein by a British diplomatic correspondent who emphasizes the important influence of King Abdullah and the British on King Hussein. The author focuses on the dominant personality of Hussein in Jordan's internal and external relations, and includes a valuable section on the 1970–1971 civil war.

Gamal Abd el-Nasir [Nasser]

33:66 Lacouture, Jean. *Nasser.* Trans. by Daniel Hofstadter. New York: Knopf, 1973. One of the best biographies of Nasir, it contains an excellent account of Nasir's formative years and the factors shaping his policies as Egypt's leader. This intimate portrait of the Egyptian leader views him against the backdrop of crises that shaped his and Egypt's future. While the author's analysis is sympathetic to Nasir, it is sharply critical of his policies toward Israel and the West.

33:67 Nutting, Anthony. *Nasser*. New York: Dutton, 1972. A sympathetic and comprehensive account of the Nasir years by Britain's minister for foreign affairs in the Eden government. The author participated in Anglo-Egyptian negotiations during the fifties and subsequently maintained a close friendship with Nasir and other Egyptian leaders.

33:68 Vatikiotis, P. J. *Nasser and His Generation*. New York: St. Martin's Press, 1978. The author examines the impact of Nasir's personality on the course of events affecting Egypt, Israel, and the Arab world. The Nasirite phenomenon is viewed against the backdrop of the interwar crisis that shaped the personalities and perceptions of Nasir and his associates.

Shah Mohammed Reza Pahlavi

See also "The U.S. and the Fall of the Shah," below.

33:69 Bayne, E. A. *Persian Kingship in Transition*. New York: American University Field Staff, 1968. A useful volume on the shah's views and dreams, it includes extensive quotations from the shah's conversations with the author. It can be read beneficially with the shah's own autobiography as a means of probing the thinking of this Iranian ruler. Bibliography.

33:70 Pahlavi, Mohammed Reza, Shah. *Mission for My Country*. New York: McGraw-Hill, 1961. Although written as an autobiography, it is more an account of the shah's perspective on his country's history, politics, economics, and foreign policy. His abiding prejudice against the National Front as well as his hatred of communism and suspicion of the Russians permeates the volume. His predilection for military strength as the first prerequisite of Iran's economic, social, and political development reveals much about his massive military purchases. See also his *Answer to History* (33:133).

33:71 Saikal, Amin. *The Rise and Fall of the Shah*. Princeton, N.J.: Princeton University Press, 1980. This volume looks at the shah's geopolitical perspectives and his ill-fated efforts to transform Iran into a regional power.

Others

33:72 Chamoun, Camille Nimr. *Crise au Moyen-Orient* [Crisis in the Middle East]. Paris: Gallimard, 1963. The former president of Lebanon and subsequent leader of the Christian separatists describes his youth and entry into Lebanese and Arab politics. He dwells upon his troubled presidency (1952–1958) and the brief civil war that terminated it, and attacks Nasir for his designs on the entire area.

33:73 Chiha, Michel. *Politique intérieure* [Domestic politics]. Beirut: Éditions du Trident, 1964. These essays by one of the founding fathers of the modern Lebanese state were written during 1943 to 1954; they provide important insights into the thought and personality of the principal philosopher of Lebanese pluralism.

33:74 Furlonge, Sir Geoffrey. *Palestine Is My Country: The Story of Musa Alami*. New York: Praeger, 1969. This sympathetic portrait of the head of one of Jerusalem's great families covers the period from Alami's birth in Jerusalem in 1897 to the time of writing. The author combines an account of Alami's determined struggle to play a responsible role in behalf of fellow Palestinians with a general account of developments in Palestine.

33:75 De Gaury, Gerald. *Faisal: King of Saudi Arabia*. New York: Praeger, 1967. A useful and sympathetic biography of the late King Faisal by a British officer and diplomat with long years of experience in Saudi Arabia. The author, who draws on personal materials (particularly in discussing Faisal's formative years), has been criticized for skirting problems and paying more attention to the glitter rather than the substance of Faisal's life. Bibliography.

33:76 Meir, Golda. *My Life*. New York: Putnam's, 1975. The autobiography of Israel's minister of labor (1949–1956), minister of foreign affairs (1956–1966), and prime minister (1969–1974) is most enlightening in discussing her earlier life. The account of her later years, particularly of her service as prime minister, provides little insight.

33:77 Prittie, Terence. *Eshkol: The Man and the Nation*. New York: Pitman, 1969. A biography of Israel's third prime minister (as well as minister of defense and finance, among other posts) by an admiring British journalist, the study focuses on the history which Eshkol helped make. It is especially noteworthy for its well-balanced treatment of Eshkol's relationship with Ben-Gurion. Bibliography.

33:78 Rabin, Yitzhak. *The Rabin Memoirs*. Boston: Little, Brown, 1979. This personal memoir, although toned down from the original Hebrew edition, is interesting for the author's bitter criticism of his political rival, Shimon Peres, and is especially valuable for its description of U.S.-Israeli relations during his tenure as Israel's ambassador to the United States (1968–1973) and prime minister (1974–1977).

33:79 Rouleau, Eric. *Abou Iyad: Palestinien sans patrie* [Abu Iyad: Palestinian without a country]. Paris: Fayolle, 1978. A founder of the Fatah guerrilla movement and a prominent leader in the Palestine Liberation Organization analyzes the past twenty years of the Palestinian resistance, describing its mistakes along with its achievements. He provides a candid self-appraisal.

33:80 el-Sadat, Anwar. *In Search of Identity*. New York: Harper & Row, 1978. Sadat's memoirs provide a valuable resource for understanding the psychological makeup of the man and his perception of reality. Sadat reflects on many important events, including the June 1967 war, Israel, Presidents Johnson and Nixon, Brezhnev, Qaddafi and Nasir. Particularly important are the sections on Sadat's secret planning of the October 1973 war and his momentous peace mission to Israel.

33:81 Weizmann, Chaim. *Trial and Error: The Autobiography of Chaim Weizmann*. New York: Schocken, 1966. The autobiography of Israel's first president and one of the Zionist leaders instrumental in bringing about Israel's establishment. The book describes Weizmann's (and Israel's) experience, from his birth in the Jewish Pale of Settlement (1874) to the creation of Israel (1948).

U.S. and the Middle East

WORLD WAR II

See also "The Truman Years, 1945–1952," especially Kuniholm (33:89) and Wilson (33:95), and "The U.S. and Middle Eastern Oil," especially Miller (33:150) and Stoff (33:154).

33:82 Baram, Phillip J. *The Department of State in the Middle East, 1919–1945*. Philadelphia: University of Pennsylvania Press, 1978. Baram examines Department of State policies in the Middle East (defined as Iraq, Syria, Jordan, Lebanon, Israel, Egypt, and Saudi Arabia), with special emphasis on 1939 to 1945. The author argues that the homogeneity of the department's middle-level management led it to support principles that were self-serving, contradictory, and shortsighted; to encourage national self-determination through majority rule; and therefore to oppose Zionist aspirations as well as those of other minority groups such as Kurds, Assyrians, and Maronite Christians. While its assumptions require careful scrutiny, the book's detailed research and analysis make it a provocative and important reference.

33:83 DeNovo, John A. "The Culbertson Economic Mission and Anglo-American Tensions in the Middle East, 1944–1945." *Journal of American History* 63:4 (1976), 913–36. William S. Culbertson's special economic mission to the Middle East in 1944, to survey postwar business prospects, illustrates a deep-rooted American emphasis on free enterprise as a stabilizing political force.

33:84 Dougherty, James J. "Lend-Lease and the Opening of French North and West Africa to Private Trade." *Cahiers d'Études Africaines* 15:3 (1975), 481–500. With these French possessions separated from France by World War II, new mechanisms for supplying consumer goods had to be developed. The Americans favored government-to-government assistance (lend-lease), but toward the end of the war American companies pressed for a resumption of trade.

Howe, G. F. *North Africa: Seizing the Initiative in the West* (23:173) includes a brief but illuminating account of the political and strategic interests of the United States in the Mediterranean zone, including the Middle East as well as North Africa. It defines the importance of these areas both in their own right and as part of such larger issues as relations with the Soviet Union and Britain in the war against Germany.

33:85 Kirk, George E. *The Middle East in the War*. London: Oxford University Press, 1952. This volume analyzes political and economic conditions in the Middle East during World War II. While dated, the work's detailed character, together with its integration of contemporary sources (cited), give it a perspective that makes it a valuable reference.

Motter, T. H. V. *The Persian Corridor and Aid to Russia* (23:222) illustrates the limited interest of the United States in the Middle East during World War II. It also contains brief accounts of relations between the

United States, Britain, and the Soviet Union in Iranian affairs.

Sachar, H. M. *Europe Leaves the Middle East, 1936–1954* (18:127) is a comprehensive, objective, synthesis of the 18-year period during which Germany, France, and Britain gradually withdrew from their involvement in Middle East affairs. The author chronicles the West's equivocal efforts to meet the rising nationalist demands of the Middle East, to confront first Axis and then Soviet threats to strategic and economic interests.

33:86   Thorpe, James A. "The United States and the 1940–1941 Anglo-Iraqi Crisis: American Policy in Transition." *Middle East Journal* 25:1 (1971), 79–89. This essay delineates the steps by which the U.S. stance of nonintervention and acquiescence to British leadership shifted to a more active role as a result of Allied reverses and increasing Axis influence.

33:87   Wilmington, Martin W. *The Middle East Supply Centre.* Ed. by Laurence Evans. Albany, N.Y.: State University of New York Press, 1971. An account of the American role in the British-originated mechanism for wartime civilian supply in the Middle East during World War II, this work reveals the lack of direct American interests in the Middle East beyond the common war aims of the Allies. It also illustrates the secondary and supporting role played by the United States in the project. Extensive bibliography.

THE TRUMAN YEARS, 1945–1952

See "Personalities," especially Dean Acheson, Harry S. Truman; also see Chapter 24, "The Truman Years."

Beginning of the Cold War, 1945–1947

33:88   Gormly, James L. "Keeping the Door Open in Saudi Arabia: The United States and the Dhahran Airfield, 1945–46." *Diplomatic History* 4:2 (1980), 189–206. An account of Anglo-American sparring which ended with the United States achieving a larger role in Saudi affairs. See also "The U.S. and Middle Eastern Oil," especially under Miller (33:150).

33:89   Kuniholm, Bruce R. *The Origins of the Cold War in the Near East: Great Power Conflict and*

Diplomacy in Iran, Turkey, and Greece. Princeton, N.J.: Princeton University Press, 1980. The author carefully documents how the traditional great power struggle along the Middle East's Northern Tier was a major factor in the origins and development of the cold war. He argues that the trouble with the policy of containment was not so much its inception as its rationalization, the legacy of that rationalization, and the analogies engendered by the policy's early success in the Near East. Extensive bibliography.

33:90   Zingg, Paul J. "The Cold War in North Africa: American Foreign Policy and Postwar Muslim Nationalism, 1945–1962." *Historian* 39:1 (1976), 40–61. Those responsible for U.S. foreign policy saw North Africa as part of the East-West conflict. U.S. policymakers confused North African communism with genuine Muslim nationalism.

The Iranian Crisis

See also "Iran" below, especially Eagleton (33:170) and Ramazani (2:365).

Hess, G. R. "The Iranian Crisis of 1945–46 and the Cold War" (26:136).

Kuniholm, B. R. *The Origins of the Cold War in the Near East: Great Power Conflict and Diplomacy in Iran, Turkey, and Greece* (33:89) carefully examines all aspects of the Iranian crisis and assesses their significance for the development of U.S. policy toward the region during the early postwar years.

Mark, E. M. "Allied Relations in Iran, 1941–1947: The Origins of a Cold War Crisis" (26:137).

33:91   Pfau, Richard. "Containment in Iran, 1946: The Shift to an Active Policy." *Diplomatic History* 1:4 (1977), 359–72. Pfau emphasizes Ambassador George Allen's crucial role in the resolution of the Iranian crisis that dragged on until the end of 1946.

Thorpe, J. A. "Truman's Ultimatum to Stalin on the 1946 Azerbaijan Crisis: The Making of a Myth" (26:138).

The Turkish Straits

See Chapter 18, "Lausanne (1923) and Montreux (1936) Conferences," and Chapter 26, "The Turkish Straits."

33:92   De Luca, Anthony R. "Soviet-American Politics and the Turkish Straits." *Political Science Quarterly* 92:3 (1977), 503–24. De Luca analyzes the 1946 debate between the United States and the U.S.S.R. concerning revision of the Montreux Convention. Much of the debate involved an interpretation of Turkey's record as custodian of the straits during World War II.

Howard, H. N. *Turkey, the Straits and U.S. Policy* (2:362) provides a useful historical synthesis of the problem as well as of U.S. involvement in it. The author examines the detailed negotiations and clarifies the otherwise arcane issues which, however rooted in the past, have influenced great power conflicts over the straits. A primary reference on the straits question.

Knight, J. "American Statecraft and the 1946 Black Sea Straits Controversy" (26:148) argues that the administration's policy on the straits crisis was restrained.

Kuniholm, B. R. *The Origins of the Cold War in the Near East: Great Power Conflict and Diplomacy in Iran, Turkey, and Greece* (33:89) places the 1946 debate over the Turkish Straits in historical and geopolitical perspective.

U.S. Recognition of Israel, 1948

33:93   Mazuzan, George T. "United States Policy toward Palestine at the United Nations, 1947–48: An Essay." *Prologue* 7:3 (1975), 163–76. The State Department's support of a UN trusteeship, its support for partitioning Palestine, its reversal of that decision, and the final recognition of Israel are linked to American perceptions of Soviet strategy and to concurrent events in Palestine.

33:94   Snetsinger, John. *Truman, the Jewish Vote, and the Creation of Israel.* Stanford, Calif.: Hoover Institution, 1974. This indispensable analysis of the domestic politics of the Truman administration recounts the American Jews' successful effort to win the president to their cause: the creation of Israel. Snetsinger argues that Truman's administrative assistant David Niles and special counsel Clark Clifford were instrumental in persuading Truman to follow policies supportive of the Jewish state. Bibliography.

33:95   Wilson, Evan M. *Decision on Palestine: How the U.S. Came to Recognize Israel.* Stanford, Calif.: Hoover Institution, 1979. Drawing on extensive research, interviews, and his personal recollections while at the Department of State's Palestine desk, the author looks closely at the development of U.S. policy

toward Palestine (1942–1948). Truman's White House advisers successfully overrode the advice of the State Department and the military. See also Michael Cohen, "American Influence on British Policy in the Middle East during World War Two: First Attempts at Coordinating Allied Policy on Palestine," *American Jewish Historical Quarterly* 67:1 (1977), 50–70, which examines problems blocking an Anglo-American consensus on the Palestine question. Extensive bibliography.

The 1948–1949 War

See also "Israel/Palestine," below.

33:96   Bell, J. Bowyer. *The Long War: Israel and the Arabs since 1946.* Englewood Cliffs, N.J.: Prentice-Hall, 1969. A chronicle of the Arab-Israeli dispute (1946–1967) which puts the wars in perspective by viewing the conflict as a long war with quiet interludes of uneasy truces. The focus is on the 1948 and 1956 wars with a brief epilogue on the 1967 war. Extensive bibliography.

Collins, L. and Lapierre, D. *O Jerusalem!* (33:238).

33:97   Lorch, Netanel. *The Edge of the Sword: Israel's War of Independence, 1947–1949.* New York: Putnam's, 1961. A detailed military history of the 1948–1949 Arab-Israeli war by an Israeli officer who later became chief of the Military History Division of the Israeli General Staff. The author covers the military, naval, and air campaigns, as well as the strategies that lay behind them, although he is vague about relevant political questions. See also Edgar O'Ballance, *The Arab-Israeli War, 1948* (London: Faber & Faber, 1956).

THE EISENHOWER YEARS, 1953–1960

See "Personalities," especially John Foster Dulles, Dwight D. Eisenhower, Robert D. Murphy; also see Chapter 24, "The Eisenhower Years."

33:98   Campbell, John C. *Defense of the Middle East: Problems of American Policy.* New York: Praeger, 1960. A study of U.S. Middle East policy from World War II until the end of the Eisenhower administration. The author discusses various Middle East defense proposals, the Baghdad pact, the 1956 crisis, the Eisenhower Doctrine, and the Lebanese and Iraqi crises of 1958. He also attempts to define and analyze the region's political, economic, and military problems. Bibliography.

33:99 U.S. Senate. Committee on Foreign Relations. *Executive Sessions of the Senate Foreign Relations Committee* [84th Cong., 2d Sess., 1956]. Historical Series, vol. 8. Washington, D.C.: G.P.O., 1978. These secret hearings, made public in 1978, cover debate over the Aswan Dam, mutual security programs for the Middle East (as well as Africa, Asia, and Latin America), and the Mutual Security Act of 1956.

Overthrow of Mossadeq, 1953

See also "Iran," below.

Cottam, R. W. *Nationalism in Iran* (33:177) criticizes the U.S. role in the overthrow of the Mossadeq regime.

33:100 Roosevelt, Kermit, Jr. *Countercoup: Struggle for the Control of Iran.* New York: McGraw-Hill, 1979. Roosevelt was one of the principals in the countercoup against Mossadeq. The book was published in 1979, but withdrawn, and scheduled for release in 1980.

The 1956 Suez Crisis/ The 1956 War

See "Personalities," especially John Foster Dulles, Gamal Abd el-Nasir; also see Chapter 28, "Suez Crisis, 1956."

33:101 Finer, Herman. *Dulles over Suez: The Theory and Practice of His Diplomacy.* Chicago: Quadrangle, 1964. A detailed and critical study of U.S. policy during the Suez crisis of 1956, focusing on U.S. policy in general and on the role of Secretary of State John Foster Dulles in particular. Bibliography.

33:102 Love, Kennett. *Suez: The Twice-Fought War.* New York: McGraw-Hill, 1969. A former *New York Times* correspondent has written a detailed and comprehensive history of the origins and diplomatic activity of the Suez war (1956). He includes a discussion of the broader Arab-Israeli conflict and a brief chapter on the 1967 war.

Nutting, A. *No End of a Lesson: The Inside Story of the Suez Crisis* (28:120)

Robertson, T. *Crisis: The Inside Story of the Suez Conspiracy* (36:73).

33:103 U.S. Department of State. *The Suez Canal Problem: July 26–September 22, 1956: A Documentary Publication.* Washington, D.C.: G.P.O., 1956. Background material and documents covering the first two months of the controversy stemming from President Nasir's seizure of the Suez Canal. It includes texts of agreements and treaties bearing on the legal status of the Canal.

33:104 U.S. Department of State. *United States Policy in the Middle East: September 1956–June 1957, Documents.* Washington, D.C.: G.P.O., 1957. A collection of documents on the Suez crisis and war that covers September 1956 to June 1957. The documents include U.S. Middle East policy statements; reactions to developments in the region; and related policy issues (including Palestinian refugees and the Baghdad pact).

The Eisenhower Doctrine, 1957

33:105 DeNovo, John A. "The Eisenhower Doctrine." In Alexander DeConde, ed., *Encyclopedia of American Foreign Policy.* New York: Scribner's, 1978, vol. 1, pp. 292–301. This is an overview of the background and purpose of the doctrine. Bibliography.

33:106 Genco, Stephen J. "The Eisenhower Doctrine: Deterrence in the Middle East, 1957–1958." In Alexander George and Richard Smoke, *Deterrence in American Foreign Policy: Theory and Practice.* New York: Columbia University Press, 1974, pp. 309–62. This account provides a succinct conceptual as well as historical analysis of the Eisenhower Doctrine and U.S. policy during the crises of 1957–1958. Bibliography.

33:107 U.S. Senate. Committee on Foreign Relations. [Hearings on the Eisenhower Doctrine] *Executive Session of the Senate Foreign Relations Committee, together with Joint Session with the Senate Armed Services Committee.* [85th Cong., 1st Sess., 1957] Historical Series, vol. 9. Washington, D.C.: G.P.O., 1979. Among other issues, the Eisenhower Doctrine dominated congressional concern over foreign policy in 1957. This volume covers the hearings on Eisenhower's request to send troops to the Middle East, as well as such topics as the Mutual Security Act of 1957 (Middle East). Released to the public December 1979.

33:108 Yizhar, Michael. "Israel and the Eisenhower Doctrine." *Wiener Library Bulletin* 28:33/34 (1975), 58–64. Yizhar examines Israeli and American interpretations of the U.S. Middle East resolution (1957), known popularly as the Eisenhower Doctrine, which promised U.S. military forces to assist any Middle East nation against armed aggression from any country controlled by international communism.

The Lebanese Intervention, 1958

See also "Personalities," especially John Foster Dulles.

33:109 Agwami, M. S., ed. *The Lebanese Crisis: A Documentary Study.* Bombay: Asia Publishing House, 1965. A useful documentary collection which attempts to reconstruct the story of the crisis, as well as to explore its local, regional, and international ramifications. It will be a helpful adjunct to such collections as the U.S. Foreign Relations series, when the 1958 volume on the Middle East is published.

33:110 Quandt, William B. "Lebanon, 1958, and Jordan, 1970." In Barry M. Blechman and Stephen S. Kaplan, eds., *Force without War: U.S. Armed Forces as a Political Instrument.* Washington, D.C.: Brookings Institution, 1978, pp. 222–88.

33:111 Qubain, Fahim I. *Crisis in Lebanon.* Washington, D.C.: Middle East Institute, 1961. This is still the most informed account of what took place in 1958. The author attributes the crisis to a division in the soul of the Lebanese people. This division, he asserts, involves the concepts that the Lebanese holds of his identity, of the nature and function of his country, of his country's relation to its Arab neighbors and to the world at large. Diversely held by distinct goups within Lebanon's confessional system, these concepts, which condition the responses of groups to external and internal stimuli, precipitated the crisis in 1958. Also consult sources listed under "The Eisenhower Doctrine."

THE KENNEDY/JOHNSON YEARS, 1961–1968

See "Personalities," especially Lyndon B. Johnson, John F. Kennedy; see also Chapter 24, "The Kennedy Years" and "The Johnson Years."

33:112 Cooke, James J., and Heggory, Andrew A. "The American Periodical Press and Ahmed Ben Bella." *Muslim World* 61:4 (1971), 293–302. This survey of articles about Ahmed Ben Bella, Algeria's first premier (1962–1966), suggests that the American press did not understand the nationalistic leader and often misinterpreted him.

33:113 Kaplan, Stephen S. "United States Aid and Regime Maintenance in Jordan, 1957–1973." *Public Policy* 23:2 (1975), 189–217. Since 1957, Jordan's King Hussein has been maintained largely through U.S. diplomatic, military, and financial support. U.S. strategy has been to restrict pressure on Israel while retaining friendly relations with Arab oil producers.

33:114 Sutcliffe, Claud R. "Some Mistaken Assumptions of U.S. Foreign Policy: A Case Study of an A.I.D. Project in Jordan." *Comparative Political Studies* 6:1 (1973), 123–28. Sutcliffe examines the impact and implications of the East Ghor Canal irrigation project in Jordan (1961–1966).

The Arab-Israeli War, 1967

See also "Personalities."

33:115 Abu-Lughod, Ibrahim. *The Arab-Israeli Confrontation of June 1967: An Arab Perspective.* Evanston, Ill.: Northwestern University Press, 1970. A collection of essays by Arab scholars in Britain and the United States that are critical of Western and pro-Israeli views of the 1967 war. The essays include analyses of such subjects as media coverage of the war, the Arab world, and the UN context of Arab-Israeli relations. Bibliography.

33:116 Brecher, Michael. *Decisions in Crisis: Israel 1967 and 1973.* Berkeley: University of California, 1979. The author combines theoretical perspectives with a knowledge of detail to delineate the factors influencing Israel's decisions in the 1967 and 1973 wars.

33:117 Draper, Theodore. *Israel and World Politics: Roots of the Third Arab-Israeli War.* New York: Viking, 1968. Draper examines the factors which led to the 1967 war. Recommended more for its treatment of events immediately preceding the war than for its analysis of the historical context of those events, the study includes a substantial number of documents on the 1967 settlement and on the prewar crisis of May and June 1967. Also see Walter Laqueur, *The Road to War, 1967: The Origins of the Arab-Israeli Conflict* (London: Weidenfeld & Nicolson, 1968).

33:118 Ennes, James M. *Assault on the Liberty: The True Story of the Israeli Attack on an American Intelligence Ship.* New York: Random House, 1979. Ennes asserts that Israel's attack on the USS *Liberty* was premeditated, carried out to prevent discovery of Israel's intention to invade Syria, and that the truth of the matter has been withheld from the American people by successive administrations.

33:119 Howard, Michael, and Hunter, Robert. *Israel and the Arab World: The Crisis of 1967.* Adelphi Paper no. 41. London: International Institute for Strategic Studies, 1967. A brief overview of the 1967 conflict which looks at its historical and political background, immediate origins, and significance.

33:120 Rikhye, Indar Jit. *The Sinai Blunder.* London: Cass, 1980. This account provides the commander of the UNEF's assessment of the various mistakes that set the stage for the 1967 war.

THE NIXON/FORD/CARTER YEARS, THE 1970s

See "Personalities," especially Menachem Begin, Henry A. Kissinger, Richard M. Nixon, and, under "Others," Anwar el-Sadat; Chapter 24, "The Nixon Years"; and various titles under different countries listed under "Regional and Country Studies," below.

33:121 Quandt, William B. *Decade of Decisions: American Policy toward the Arab-Israeli Conflict, 1967–1976.* Berkeley: University of California Press, 1977. As a former member of the National Security Council staff, the author writes with a unique perspective on issues of American policymaking in the Middle East, including the June 1967 war, the Rogers initiatives of 1967 to 1970, the Jordan crisis of September 1970, the October 1973 war, and Kissinger's "step-by-step" diplomacy under Presidents Nixon and Ford. The author's "inside" view of the dramatic developments during the October war is valuable. Bibliography.

33:122 Reich, Bernard. *Quest for Peace: United States–Israel Relations and the Arab-Israeli Conflict.* New Brunswick, N.J.: Transaction, 1977. A detailed study of the special relationship between the U.S. and Israel which examines the larger context of U.S. Middle East interests and efforts to resolve the Arab-Israeli conflict. The book concentrates on the period after 1967—half of it is concerned with the period after the 1973 war—and provides an objective account of diplomatic negotiations. Extensive notes.

33:123 Stevens, Georgiana G. "1967–1977: America's Moment in the Middle East?" *Middle East Journal* 31:1 (1977), 1–15. Stevens argues that the overriding aim of U.S. policy in the Middle East since the June war of 1967 has been to prevent Soviet dominance.

The Jordan Crisis, 1970

See "Personalities," especially King Hussein, Henry A. Kissinger, Richard M. Nixon; see also citations under "The Nixon/Ford/Carter Years, the 1970s," "Israel/Palestine," and William Quandt, "Lebanon, 1958, and Jordan, 1970" (33:110).

The 1973 War

See "Personalities," especially Moshe Dayan, Richard M. Nixon, and, under "Others," Anwar el-Sadat; see other citations under "Overviews" and "The Nixon/Ford/Carter Years, the 1970s."

33:124 el Badri, Hassan; el-Magdoub, Taha; and Zohdy, Mohammed Diael-Din. *The Ramadan War, 1973.* Dunn Loring, Va.: Dupuy, 1978. An analysis of the 1973 October war by three senior Egyptian officers, who participated in its planning and execution. The emphasis is on military operations.

Brecher, Michael. *Decisions in Crisis: Israel 1967 and 1973* (33:116)

33:125 London Sunday Times. Insight Team. *Insight on the Middle East War.* London: Deutsch, 1974.

A study of the October war of 1973 which examines battlefield developments, and the decisions which affected them, as well as the diplomatic and intelligence failures which preceded the conflict. The initial postwar efforts to achieve a settlement are considered briefly.

33:126 O'Ballance, Edgar. *No Victor, No Vanquished: The Yom Kippur War.* San Rafael, Calif.: Presidio, 1978. O'Ballance presents an objective, detailed account of the military aspects of the war that broke the stultifying state of no peace, no war, and left no victor, no vanquished. The author also looks at the political background to the war, the preparation of both sides, and their armed forces and armaments.

33:127 Sheehan, Edward R. F. *The Arabs, Israelis, and Kissinger: A Secret History of American Diplomacy in the Middle East.* New York: Reader's Digest Press, 1976. This analysis of U.S. diplomacy carefully chronicles the diplomatic process that began with the October 1973 war and ended with the Sinai II accords in August 1975. The author, a distinguished journalist, delineates the success of Kissinger's tactics and criticizes the excessive caution of his overall strategy.

33:128 Whetten, Lawrence. *The Canal War: Four Power Conflict in the Middle East.* Cambridge, Mass.: MIT Press, 1974. The author looks at the military conduct of the Canal War and the political negotiations for its settlement (June 1967 to January 1974). Focusing on the interactions among the United States, the Soviet Union, Egypt, and Israel, he examines the impact of the changing military balance on efforts to negotiate a political solution. He concludes that great power negotiating positions must rest squarely on mutually acceptable estimates of their respective security interests. Bibliography.

33:129 Williams, Louis, ed. *Military Aspects of the Israeli-Arab Conflict.* Tel Aviv: University Publishing Projects, 1975. These proceedings of an international symposium held in Jerusalem focus on various aspects of the 1973 Arab-Israeli war, including the art of war, military reporting, superpower competition, military balance, and a review of the main battles and their lessons.

The Cyprus Crisis, 1974

See Chapter 28, "The Cyprus Issue, 1974," and "Cyprus," below.

The U.S. and the Arab Boycott of Israel

33:130 Dodell, Sue E. "United States Banks and the Arab Boycott of Israel." *Columbia Journal of Transnational Law* 17:1 (1978), 119–43. This brief history of the official Arab boycott of Israel (1951–1977) discusses the U.S. financial response to the boycott through legislation such as antitrust laws, antiboycott sections attached to the Tax Reform Act of 1976, and reporting requirements of the Securities and Exchange Commission.

33:131 Turck, Nancy. "The Arab Boycott of Israel." *Foreign Affairs* 55:3 (1977), 472–93. Turck reviews the nature of the Arab boycott of Israel and the wisdom of legislation proposed by the United States to combat the role of American business in it.

The U.S. and the Fall of the Shah

See also "Personalities," especially Shah Mohammed Reza Pahlavi, and "Iran," below.

33:132 Ledeen, Michael, and Lewis, William. "Carter and the Fall of the Shah: The Inside Story." *Washington Quarterly* 3:2 (1980), 3–40. While some of the analysis is flawed, it nonetheless provides a useful point of departure for the many books and articles that are sure to follow on this controversial subject.

33:133 Pahlavi, Mohammed Reza, Shah. *Answer to History.* New York: Stein & Day. 1980. The shah gives his version of how and why he was deposed.

33:134 Shaplen, Robert. "Eye of the Storm." *New Yorker* 80 (June 2, 9, 16, 1980). The author, with access to State Department records, paints a sympathetic portrait of Under Secretary David Newsom and provides insight into the problems and functioning of the Department of State—particularly in the Middle East, and especially the Iranian crisis.

33:135 Sullivan, William H. "Dateline Iran: The Road Not Taken." *Foreign Policy,* no. 40 (1980), 175–86. The U.S. ambassador gives his perception of the Iran crisis. He is critical of the NSC and National Security Adviser Brzezinski's handling of the whole affair.

Special Studies

SOVIETS IN THE MIDDLE EAST

33:136 Carrère d'Encausse, Hélène. *"La Politique sovietique au Moyen-Orient, 1955–1975* [Soviet policy in the Middle East, 1955–1975]. Paris: Presses de la Fondation Nationale des Sciences Politiques, 1975. The author is a specialist on the question of Islam within the U.S.S.R., an asset which gives an added dimension to the study of Soviet policy toward the Islamic countries. The book emphasizes the dilemmas faced by the Soviets in arming the Arab states and trying to control their decisions.

33:137 Laqueur, Walter Z. *The Soviet Union and the Middle East.* New York: Praeger, 1959. This pioneering work is enhanced by the author's special knowledge. The book can be supplemented by the author's earlier *Communism and Nationalism in the Middle East* (London: Routledge & Kegan Paul, 1956), which looks at the activities of communist and other revolutionary parties and movements. Notes.

33:138 Lederer, Ivo J., and Vucinich, Wayne S., eds. *The Soviet Union and the Middle East: The Post–World War II Era.* Stanford, Calif.: Hoover Institution Press, 1974. Essentially a country-by-country survey which analyzes the bilateral relations of the U.S.S.R. with Turkey, Iran, Syria, Lebanon, Jordan, Israel, Egypt, and the states of Maghreb. These essays tend to agree that the Soviets intended, after World War II, to minimize the influence of the West and to seize targets of opportunity when the risk was low. Lederer provides historical perspective, and Vucinich contributes a useful bibliographical essay.

33:139 Ro'i, Yaacov, ed. *The Limits to Power: Soviet Policy in the Middle East.* New York: St. Martin's Press, 1979. This book, written largely by Israeli scholars, provides more thorough and comprehensive information than any other available on Soviet policy during the October war and its aftermath. For earlier years, see Ro'i's *From Encroachment to Involvement: A Documentary Study of Soviet Policy in the Middle East, 1945–1973* (New York: Wiley, 1974), which is a convenient collection of Soviet documents with extensive commentary.

33:140 Smolansky, Oles M. *The Soviet Union and the Arab East under Khrushchev.* Lewisburg, Pa.: Bucknell University Press, 1974. Egypt, Syria, and Iraq were the principal targets of Khrushchev's diplomacy. The research leads to mixed conclusions as to the success of Soviet policy, with emphasis on the Soviet Union's inability to cope with Arab nationalism and the Middle East's complex local conflicts. Bibliography.

ARMS TRANSFERS

33:141 Glassman, Jon D. *Arms for the Arabs: The Soviet Union and War in the Middle East.* Baltimore: Johns Hopkins University Press, 1975. Examining carefully Soviet behavior before and during the 1956, 1967, and 1973 wars, this book delineates Soviet attempts to balance coexistence with revolution. While the Soviets withheld delivery of potentially decisive arms and avoided directly confronting the United States, they threatened military intervention at or near the conclusion of every conflict. If another war occurred in the Middle East, U.S.-U.S.S.R. relations would become acute. Bibliography.

33:142 Hurewitz, Jacob C. *Middle East Politics:The Military Dimension.* New York: Praeger, 1969. This is a comprehensive survey of military politics in the Middle East (excluding Cyprus and the PDRY) since 1945. The author shows how hypotheses (supported by "professional armers") about the relationship between military change on the one hand, and economic and social change on the other, do not stand up when examined in the context of the Middle East. He also argues that "professional disarmers" are unrealistic in their assertions that the investment of nonindustrial states in military equipment wastes resources. Extensive bibliography.

33:143 Jabber, Fuad Amin (Paul). *Not by War Alone: Security and Arms Control in the Middle East.* Berkeley: University of California Press, 1980. The author examines a past attempt at arms control in the Middle East as well as prospects for arms control in the aftermath of the 1973 war; he also provides a useful analysis of the basic requirements for effective and durable international accords.

33:144 Jabber, Fuad Amin (Paul). "The Politics of Arms Transfer and Control: The Case of the Middle East." Ph.D. diss., University of California, Los Angeles, 1974. Focusing on the years 1950 to 1955,

Jabber examines the Anglo–French–American declaration of May 1950, aimed at balancing armaments in the Middle East, and Nasser's subsequent purchase of Soviet bloc arms.

33:145 Sampson, Anthony. *The Arms Bazaar: From Lockheed to Lebanon*. New York: Viking, 1977. Although no comprehensive analysis of U.S. and European arms transfers exists, Sampson's journalistic account is useful and more balanced than its title implies.

THE U.S. AND MIDDLE EASTERN OIL

See also Chapter 18, "The Quest for Oil," and Chapter 39, "Oil Operations."

33:146 Blair, John M. *The Control of Oil*. New York: Pantheon, 1976. Blair provides a comprehensive analysis of the producing and marketing systems of the international petroleum industry. Although tracing the history of concessions and marketing agreements in Middle East oil (the "evolution of control"), the author focuses on the "mechanisms of control" through which the companies, supported by producing and consuming governments, control Middle East oil. Blair provides a background to U.S. oil diplomacy in the Middle East and sheds light on industry-government relationships. Bibliography.

33:147 Kaufman, Burton I. *The Oil Cartel Case: A Documentary Study of Antitrust Activity in the Cold War Era*. Westport, Conn.: Greenwood, 1978. The author provides valuable insights into the relationship between five American oil companies and the Departments of State and Defense, and the White House, and offers a new perspective on who influenced whom. The book traces the Justice Department's 1953 decision to bring suit, follows the Truman administration's decision not to pursue a criminal investigation in the interests of national security considerations, and concludes with the Eisenhower administration's policy of continuing to subordinate antitrust to cold war concerns. Bibliography.

33:148 Klebanoff, Shoshana. *Middle East Oil and U.S. Foreign Policy with Special Reference to the U.S. Energy Crisis*. New York: Praeger, 1974. Although focusing primarily on the U.S. role in international oil, with emphasis on production and marketing, it reviews American oil diplomacy in the Middle East from the 1920s to the 1973 oil embargo. The author delineates the development of Middle East oil from a desirable commercial interest into an intense strategic and political concern. Bibliography.

33:149 Longrigg, Stephen H. *Oil in the Middle East: Its Discovery and Development*. 3d ed. London: Oxford University Press, 1968. This book addresses the technical aspects of petroleum development in the Middle East in the context of great power involvement. The author, a former Iraq Petroleum Company executive and British civil servant, is sympathetic to the British companies and government. Bibliography.

33:150 Miller, Aaron D. *Search for Security: Saudi Arabian Oil and American Foreign Policy, 1939–1949*. Chapel Hill: University of North Carolina Press, 1980. Miller looks at the origins of the U.S.-Saudi "special relationship," and focuses on the development of Saudi Arabian oil during World War II and the immediate postwar years. The United States, to promote the Aramco concession and maintain the nation's stake in Saudi reserves, relied on economic, military, and diplomatic support. As the cold war evolved, State and Defense Department officials sought to consolidate and protect the nation's stake in Saudi Arabia against potential threats raised by Soviet expansion and the Palestine problem. See also Barry Rubin, "Anglo-American Relations in Saudi Arabia, 1941–1951," *Journal of Contemporary History* 14:2 (1979), 253–68. Extensive bibliography.

Mosley, L. *Power Play: Oil in the Middle East* [1920–1972] (18:161).

Nash, G. D. *United States Oil Policy, 1890–1964* (18:162) traces U.S. policy toward domestic and foreign oil, and explores the context in which official policy toward Middle East oil developed. European efforts to exclude the Americans from Middle East oil following World War I and the challenges of war and cold war, he concludes, forced the oilmen and government into closer cooperation. Bibliographical essay.

33:151 Sampson, Anthony. *The Seven Sisters: The Great Oil Companies and the World They Shaped*. New York: Viking, 1975. The author's analysis of the companies' power and control goes beyond anti-company stereotypes to examine the impact of personalities on the companies' relations with host governments and with each other. This work provides a useful and colorful account of the companies' efforts to stake out and maintain their claim to Middle East oil from the Red Line of the 1920s to the gas lines of the 1970s.

33:152 Shwadran, Benjamin. *The Middle East, Oil and the Great Powers.* 3d ed. New York: Wiley, 1973. This updated edition is the most comprehensive reference work on the history of oil concessions in the Middle East. Critical of the oil companies where Longrigg (33:149) is sympathetic, Shwadran provides a wealth of information on petroleum development and its impact on the region. Sections on U.S. oil diplomacy in Iran and Saudi Arabia during World War II and the immediate postwar years are particularly good. Extensive bibliography.

33:153 Stobaugh, Robert, and Yergin, Daniel, eds. *Energy Future.* New York: Random House, 1979. This comprehensive analysis of America's energy problem argues for conservation and solar energy as the only practical solution. Reduction of demand focuses on the domestic side of problems we tend to place in an international context, with the scapegoats appropriately designated as other than ourselves. This study outlines the practical realities of the problem and confronts us with the fact that the real problem begins, and can be resolved, at home.

33:154 Stoff, Michael. *Oil, War, and American Security: The Search for a National Policy on Foreign Oil, 1941–1947.* New Haven, Conn.: Yale University Press, 1980. This is a clear and analytical examination of disputes within the U.S. government over oil policy during and immediately after World War II.

INTEREST GROUPS

See also "The U.S. and Middle Eastern Oil," above.

33:155 Ismael, Jacqueline S., and Ismael, Tareq Y. "The Arab Americans and the Middle East." *Middle East Journal* 30:3 (1976), 390–405. The authors survey the social context of Arabs in America, the social and political interethnic rivalries affecting U.S. foreign policy in the Middle East, and the politicization of American Arabs over Middle East conflicts.

33:156 Lilienthal, Alfred M. *The Zionist Connection: What Price Peace?* New York: Dodd, Mead, 1978. While this polemical book lacks balance, it provides essential background, along with detailed documentation, of the Zionist influence in the United States.

33:157 Trice, Robert H. "Congress and the Arab-Israeli Conflict: Support for Israel in the U.S. Senate, 1970–1973." *Political Science Quarterly* 92:3 (1977), 443–63. Support was strongest in the Northeast, and it was equal between Democrats and Republicans. Three factors are commonly assumed to affect this support: ideological differences, the Jewish vote, and Jewish financial contributions. But analysis indicates that these three variables together can account for only about 16 percent of the variance in individual senators' support.

33:158 Trice, Robert H. *Interest Groups and the Foreign Policy Process: U.S. Policy in the Middle East.* Beverly Hills, Calif.: Sage, 1976. A brief but useful analysis, it outlines a conceptual framework for explaining why interest groups behave the way they do, and then applies it to domestic interest group activities related to the Arab-Israeli conflict (1966–1974). Bibliography. Also see Trice's "The American Elite Press and the Arab-Israeli Conflict," *Middle East Journal* 33 (Summer 1979), 304–25, for a careful analysis of editorial opinions and coverage (1967–1974).

Regional and Country Studies

See also "Special Studies" under "Overviews," above.

American University. Foreign Area Studies. Area Handbook Series (2:214) provides an extremely useful introduction to each country's history, traditions, values, and culture as well as data on economic, military, political, social, and institutional issues. The handbooks contain extensive bibliographies, maps, charts, and tables; they are frequently updated, and constitute a good starting point for one's first venture into the literature on any of the countries of the Middle East.

33:159 Hudson, Michael C. *Arab Politics: The Search for Legitimacy.* New Haven, Conn.: Yale University Press, 1977. Hudson provides a comparative analysis of politics in 18 Arab states and the Palestinian movement and an excellent general introduction to Middle East politics. The book initially deals with

Arab identity, Islam, cultural pluralism, the legacy of imperialism, the crisis of authority, and the consequences of modernization. The second part consists of comparative case studies of the struggle for legitimation in the monarchies and republics of the Arab world.

33:160　Lenczowski, George, ed. *Political Elites in the Middle East.* Washington, D.C.: American Enterprise Institute for Public Policy Research, 1975. These essays provide a useful description and analysis of political elites in Iran, Turkey, Egypt, Syria, Iraq, Lebanon, and Israel. The authors' approaches differ widely, but they share the view that the study of elites is instrumental to the understanding of political conditions.

33:161　Long, David E., and Reich, Bernard, eds. *The Government and Politics of the Middle East and North Africa.* Boulder, Colo.: Westview, 1980. The authors provide a current survey of national, regional, and great power economics, politics, and military perspectives.

33:162　al-Marayati, Abid A. *The Middle East: Its Government and Politics.* Belmont, Calif.: Duxbury, 1972. A useful collection, it utilizes varying approaches to present a balanced picture. The first group of essays examines the Middle East as a whole in the context of geographical, historical, economic, sociocultural, and political factors; a second group provides country analyses, while a third shows how external and regional forces affect change.

33:163　Sayigh, Yusif A. *The Economies of the Arab World: Development since 1945: The Determinants of Arab Economic Development.* London: Croom Helm, 1978. An extremely valuable reference, volume 1 takes a country approach which looks at basic economic and social indicators: national product, sectoral structure, education and manpower development, transformation in the socioeconomic (and political) system, and degree of seriousness of economic planning. Extensive notes. Volume 2 explores the main determinants and deterrents to development, both in the economic and noneconomic realms, and examines the main development issues.

THE NORTHERN TIER

33:164　Ramazani, Rouhollah K. *The Northern Tier: Afghanistan, Iran and Turkey.* New York: Van Nostrand, 1966. An introduction to three countries which

share many features: a degree of basic geographic unity, similar topography and climate, common geographic proximity to the Soviet Union, common Islamic civilization, and an imperial past.

Afghanistan

33:165　Adamec, Ludwig. *Afghanistan's Foreign Affairs to the Mid-Twentieth Century: Relations with the USSR, Germany, and Britain.* Tucson: University of Arizona Press, 1974. Adamec examines the history of Afghanistan to the end of World War II, with a brief chapter on the period from 1945 to 1973. He is especially good on the country's buffer-state politics in the geopolitical arena.

33:166　Dil, Shaheen F. "The Cabal in Kabul: Great-Power Interaction in Afghanistan." *American Political Science Review* 71:2 (1977), 468–76. The July 17, 1973, coup serves as a case study of the nature and extent of great power interest and involvement in Afghanistan.

33:167　Dupree, Louis. *Afghanistan.* Princeton, N.J.: Princeton University Press, 1978. The best single introduction to Afghanistan, this book is sweeping in scope and encyclopedic in its detail. Approximately two hundred pages cover the period from World War II to the present, in addition to two epilogues (written in 1973 and 1978). Many useful charts, illustrations, and an extensive bibliography. For recent assessments of Afghanistan, one should consult the author's many American University Field Staff Reports.

Iran

See "Personalities," especially Shah Mohammed Reza Pahlavi; see also under "United States and the Middle East," especially "Beginning of the Cold War, 1945–1947"; and see "The U.S. and the Fall of the Shah."

33:168　Avery, Peter. *Modern Iran.* New York: Praeger, 1965. This general account is unique in its treatment of intrigues, episodes, and rumors that shape Iranian political life. It treats social, political, and economic developments chronologically, beginning in 1813. The author's knowledge of Persian life and literature makes his account a useful contribution. Extensive bibliography.

Foreign Affairs

33:169 Chubin, Shahram, and Zabih, Sepehr. *The Foreign Relations of Iran: A Developing State in a Zone of Great-Power Conflict.* Berkeley: University of California Press, 1974. This volume's contribution lies in its detailed attention to Iran's regional policies, especially in the Persian Gulf (mid-1960s–mid-1970s). The treatment of Iran's relations with the superpowers is scanty, and the all-important relations with Britain during the government of Mossadeq are surprisingly overlooked. Extensive bibliography.

33:170 Eagleton, William, Jr. *The Kurdish Republic of 1946.* New York: Oxford University Press, 1963. This is the standard, though slender, work on the Kurdish Republic of Mahabad. For an analysis of the Kurdish nationalist movements, in the context of regional and international politics, see Chris Kutschera, *Le Mouvement national kurde* (Paris: Flammarion, 1979), and Edgar O'Ballance, *The Kurdish Revolt: 1961–1970* (London, Faber & Faber, 1973).

33:171 Lenczowski, George. *Russia and the West in Iran, 1918–1948: A Study in Big-Power Rivalry.* Ithaca, N.Y.: Cornell University Press, 1949. Reprint 1953. The contribution of this volume lies in its treatment of the role of the great powers in Iran during World War II and the early postwar period. It is also a valuable account of Iran's domestic politics (1942–1945). It was supplemented subsequently to cover events through 1952.

Ramazani, R. K. *Iran's Foreign Policy, 1941–1973: A Study of Foreign Policy in Modernizing Nations* (2:365) is the best single volume on Iran's foreign policy in the postwar era.

33:172 Ramazani, Rouhollah K. *The Persian Gulf: Iran's Role.* Charlottesville: University of Virginia Press, 1972. A concise account of Iranian interests in, and policies and actions toward, the Persian Gulf area as they appeared at the time of Britain's decision to terminate its longstanding special treaty relationship with nine states along the northern Arabian littoral. Appendixes deal with the resolution of the Iranian claim to the Bahrain archipelago and with the problem of Abu Musa Island and the two Tunbs Islands, which Iran occupied. Bibliography. Also see the author's *The Persian Gulf and the Strait of Hormuz* (33:264).

Politics and Economic Development

33:173 Amirie, Abbas, and Twitchell, Hamilton A., eds. *Iran in the 1980's.* Tehran: Institute for International Political and Economic Studies, 1978. The volume was prompted by the increasing criticism of the pace and scope of the shah's economic policies and especially military purchases. It aimed basically at establishing a dialogue between American and Iranian scholars and officials on future developments in Iran.

33:174 Amuzegar, Jahangir. *Iran: An Economic Profile.* Washington, D.C.: Middle East Institute, 1977. This volume's optimistic projection of Iran's future economic development has been overtaken by events. However, it is valuable as a descriptive account of the Iranian economy before 1978. The economic data are based on the files of the shah's government; they are not available in this form elsewhere. Bibliography.

33:175 Bill, James A. *The Politics of Iran: Groups, Classes and Modernization.* Columbus, Ohio: Merrill, 1972. The Halpernian influence is evident in the author's emphasis on the emergence of a new professional middle class and its relationship to other classes. The inevitability of the ascendance of this emerging class has not been borne out. The Iranian revolution was dominated by traditional religious leaders and initially supported by the lower classes. Bibliography.

33:176 Binder, Leonard. *Iran: Political Development in a Changing Society.* Berkeley: University of California Press, 1962. This is the first serious analysis of Iran's political system. The volume's shortcomings (conceptual ambiguities and social science jargon mar the first chapter) are compensated for by the author's perception of the dynamics of contemporary Iranian politics. On the whole it contributes to an understanding of political development in the changing society of Iran.

33:177 Cottam, Richard W. *Nationalism in Iran.* Pittsburgh: University of Pittsburgh Press, 1964. This is the only serious study of Iranian nationalism in English. Its contribution lies in examining the cultural, historical, and social bases of Iranian nationalism and the racial, ethnic, religious, and regional problems that it encounters. The author's criticism of the U.S. role in the overthrow of the Mossadeq regime in 1953 takes on added meaning in the context of Iran's revolution.

33:178 Graham, Robert. *Iran: The Illusion of Power.* London: Croom Helm, 1978. The author delineates a variety of interrelated issues, showing, for example, how Iranian politics contributed to the economic chaos that attended the country's development. This account portrays the country's dilemmas and economic difficulties, from its sudden acquisition of increased wealth in 1973 to the grave problems of 1977–1978. For insight into the thinking of Ayatollah Khomeini and Mehdi Bazargan, see Oriana Fallaci's brief but illuminating interviews in the *New York Times,* October 7, 28, 1979.

33:179   Jacqz, Jane W., ed. *Iran: Past, Present and Future: Aspen Institute/Persepolis Symposium.* New York: Aspen Institute for Humanistic Studies, 1976. An uneven volume, its best chapters concern Iran's economic problems and prospects. The superficial accounts on Iranian domestic politics show how little serious attention was paid to political development by Iranian political scientists during the shah's regime. Bibliography and index.

33:180   Keddie, Nikki R., ed. *Scholars, Saints, and Sufis: Muslim Religious Institutions since 1500.* Berkeley: University of California Press, 1972. The author of *Religion and Rebellion in Iran* includes two valuable chapters on Iran. The former study should now be read in the broader context of this new volume on Islam. The religiously dominated Iranian revolution with its regionwide implications makes this volume especially useful. For an examination of the nature of Iranian Shi'ism and its social and political contexts, see Michael Fischer, *Iran: From Religious Dispute to Revolution* (Cambridge: Harvard University Press, 1980), and Shahrough Akhavi, *Religion and Politics in Contemporary Iran: Clergy-State Relations in the Pahlavi Period* (Albany, N.Y.: State University of New York Press, 1980).

33:181   Lambton, Ann K. S. *The Persian Land Reform, 1962–1966.* London: Oxford University Press, 1969. Together with her previous study, *Landlord and Peasant in Persia: A Study of Land Tenure and Land Revenue Administration,* this volume provides the most detailed account of the subject. The deposed shah's controversial land reform program is objectively described and assessed. A postscript carries the account to 1968.

33:182   Warne, William E. *Mission for Peace: Point Four in Iran.* Indianapolis: Bobbs-Merrill, 1956. Initiated by President Truman's inaugural address in 1949, Point Four programs were intended to help countries help themselves. This book by the chief of the Point Four mission in Iran (1951–1955) is a personal account of the program's trials and tribulations.

33:183   Zabih, Sepehr. *The Communist Movement in Iran.* Berkeley: University of California Press, 1966. The only book on the communist movement in Iran in English, its emphasis is on the appeal of communism, the communist leadership and rank and file, and the relationship of communism to nationalism and Islam. The volume also deals with the evolution of communist doctrine in the East. The prospects of the revival of the Tudeh party in the wake of the shah's downfall enhances its interest. Extensive bibliography.

33:184   Zonis, Marvin. *The Political Elite of Iran.* Princeton, N.J.: Princeton University Press, 1971. This is the only study on the attitudes of Iran's political elite in the context of Iranian society and culture. Regardless of a methodological controversy over the volume, its contribution lies in the systematic examination of the behavior of the Iranian political elite and, to a lesser extent, counterelite during the shah's rule. Extensive bibliography.

Turkey

See "Personalities," especially, under "Others," Laurence A. Steinhardt.

33:185   Ahmad, Feroz. *The Turkish Experiment in Democracy, 1950–1975.* London: Hurst, 1977. This book interweaves historical analysis by decade with detailed inspection of major themes—the political parties, the economy, and the role of the military. It ends with a lengthy survey of foreign policy themes, including Turkey's new orientations in the mid-1970s. Extensive bibliography and index.

Foreign Affairs

33:186   Harris, George S. *Troubled Alliance: Turkish-American Problems in Historical Perspective, 1945–1971.* Washington, D.C.: American Enterprise Institute for Public Policy Research, 1972. This well-informed work surveys the factors that brought the partners together, the changes in Turkey's strategic position, and the emergence of strains in the alliance. It relates these troubles to domestic as well as foreign factors (especially the Cyprus issue). The analysis explains Turkish bargaining techniques, and offers a forecast of the alliance's future. Extensive bibliography, appendix, and index.

33:187   Karpat, Kemal H., et al. *Turkey's Foreign Policy in Transition, 1950–1974.* Leiden: Brill, 1975. Four experts on Turkish foreign policy stress political and economic relationships. They identify the Cyprus problem as a turning point for Turkey (and cover the phase of 1974 military intervention).

33:188 Mango, Andrew. *Turkey: A Delicately Poised Ally.* Beverly Hills, Calif.: Sage, 1975. A brief explanation of Turkey's domestic and foreign policy, especially from World War II to the early 1970s, this book places the Cyprus crisis in perspective as a domestic issue which greatly influences Turkey's relations abroad. Relations with the United States are treated, as is the problem of the Kurdish ethnic minority.

33:189 Váli, Ferenc A. *Bridge across the Bosporus: The Foreign Policy of Turkey.* Baltimore: Johns Hopkins Press, 1971. This study of Turkey's foreign policy (1945–1970) assesses relations with the United States and NATO, the Soviet Union, Greece and Cyprus, the Middle East, and economic ties with the West. The author is best in treating strategic concerns which he presents from a geopolitical point of view. Bibliography.

33:190 Weisband, Edward. *Turkish Foreign Policy, 1943–1945: Small State Diplomacy and Great Power Politics.* Princeton, N.J.: Princeton University Press, 1973. Focusing first on the domestic sources of Turkey's policies, the author provides an incisive analysis of Turkish foreign policy during a critical period in World War II. The author had access to private papers unavailable to the general public. Extensive bibliography.

33:191 White, John. *Pledged to Development: A Study of International Consortia and the Strategy of Aid.* London: Overseas Development Institute, 1967. This work, devoting about 80 pages to a case study of the Turkey consortium (1962–1965), is a blow-by-blow account of Turkey's relations with its creditors. Although the coverage is limited, its analysis provides useful background for subsequent international rescue operations.

Domestic Politics

33:192 Dodd, C. H. *Politics and Government in Turkey.* Berkeley: University of California Press, 1969. A survey (1960–1965) of politics, political organizations, and administrative institutions, this work is useful for its analysis of coalition dynamics and pressure groups, and for its identification of the left-right controversy. The author also reviews the role of the Cyprus issue in domestic politics. Bibliography.

33:193 Frey, Frederick W. *The Turkish Political Elite.* Cambridge, Mass.: MIT Press, 1956. An exhaustive analysis of the educational, occupational, and family characteristics of the Turkish parliamentarians of the First Republic (1920–1957), this study indicates trends in leadership positions and in the makeup of Parliament and the cabinet. It diagnoses Turkish intraelite conflict since World War II. Extensive bibliography.

33:194 Hershlag, Zvi Y. *Turkey: The Challenge of Growth.* Leiden: Brill, 1968. A study of Turkey's economic activities as well as of the evolution of the philosophy of development in the republican era, this comprehensive analysis challenges the conventional periodization of the development of the Turkish economy. Coverage of foreign assistance is limited. Bibliography and statistics.

33:195 Karpat, Kemal H. *Turkey's Politics: The Transition to a Multi-Party System.* Princeton, N.J.: Princeton University Press, 1959. Primarily a study of the years 1945 to 1950, when Turkey moved away from a one-party system, this work opens with a general history of the cultural-political and the economic-social transformation of the First Turkish Republic. Thereafter follows a more profound analysis of various cultural, political, economic, and social problems along such axes as nationalism, secularism, populism, and communism. Extensive bibliography.

33:196 Landau, Jacob M. *Radical Politics in Modern Turkey.* Leiden: Brill, 1974. Surveying the various political and religious movements on the extremities of the Turkish political right and left, the author analyzes the emergence of radical politics in the 1960s. He reviews the press, trade unions, and leftist and rightist political parties and their electoral performance, and notes the implications for the orientation of Turkey's foreign policy. Extensive bibliography.

33:197 Özbudun, Ergun. *Social Change and Political Participation in Turkey.* Princeton, N.J.: Princeton University Press, 1976. A study of the dynamics of voting in Turkey, this work considers how political orientations have been affected by economic and social modernization, especially from 1960 to 1970. The author examines the extent to which the dominant center-periphery cleavage is being gradually replaced by a functional cleavage. Extensive bibliography.

33:198 Robinson, Richard D. *The First Turkish Republic: A Case Study in National Development.* Cambridge: Harvard University Press, 1963. This study of the First Turkish Republic (1923–1960) covers economic growth, detailing the problems of rapid development under a democratic system. Turkey's geostrategic position receives stress as does the impact of military modernization. The author describes the military coup and points to the problems of making democracy work in the Second Republic. Notes.

Cyprus

See Chapter 28, "The Cyprus Issue, 1974."

33:199 Cranshaw, Nancy. *The Cyprus Revolt: An Account of the Struggle for Union with Greece*. London: Allen & Unwin, 1978. This is a detailed history of the Greek Cypriot revolt against Britain to 1960. The author sheds new light on the organization and tactics of the guerrilla forces under Colonel Grivas as well as on Archbishop Makarios's political use of force, and delineates carefully the international aspects of negotiations that led to the establishment of the republic. Bibliography.

33:200 Durrell, Lawrence. *Bitter Lemons*. New York: Dutton, 1957. This impressionistic study provides unique insight into the island's people and their daily lives as the Cyprus revolt was unfolding. One of its virtues is its illustration of individual rather than generalized opinions and attitudes.

33:201 Kyriakides, Stanley. *Cyprus: Constitutionalism and Crisis Government*. Philadelphia: University of Pennsylvania Press, 1968. The author analyzes the legal dimension of the Cyprus issue, emphasizing British attempts at self-government after World War II, the 1960 Constitution, and the problems of executing its provisions. The author views the rigid communalism in the 1960 Constitution, festering communal mistrust, and the involvement of external interests all as major factors leading to the breakdown of the political system. Bibliography.

33:202 Purcell, H. D. *Cyprus*. New York: Praeger, 1969. This general history of Cyprus from early times to the late 1960s includes a provocative account of the British period and of independent Cyprus. The introductory chapter provides a useful description of modern Cyprus: its land, people, and economy.

33:203 Salih, Halil Ibrahim. *Cyprus: The Impact of Diverse Nationalism on a State*. University : University of Alabama Press, 1978. This short, clear analysis by an author sympathetic with the Turkish Cypriots attempts to assess objectively the Cyprus problem, the 1974 war, and the aftermath of the war. The author concludes that the two Cypriot communities cannot coexist under the 1960 to 1963 system because Britain's refusal to act as peacemaker has resulted in irreconcilable differences between the two ethnic communities. The only solution, he believes, is double enosis (partition between Greece and Turkey) or domestic autonomy coupled with a unified foreign policy. Extensive bibliography and appendixes.

THE CONFRONTATION STATES

See above for "U.S. and the Middle East," "The Arab-Israeli War, 1967," "The Nixon/Ford/Carter Years, the 1970s," and "The 1973 War."

Egypt

See "Personalities," especially Gamal Abd el-Nasir [Nasser] and, under "Others," Anwar el-Sadat, and various wars under "U.S. and the Middle East."

33:204 Abdel-Malek, Anouar. *Egypt: Military Society, the Army Regime, the Left and Social Change under Nasser*. Trans. by Charles Lam Markmann. New York: Vintage, 1968. This critical analysis identifies the causal factors behind Nasir's successes and failures. Writing as a nationalist and as a Marxist, the author describes Egypt's prerevolutionary past and criticizes the regime's failure to institute a truly socialist revolution. This book provides an Egyptian view of developments from 1950 to Nasir's reemergence after the June 1967 defeat.

33:205 Baker, Raymond W. *Egypt's Uncertain Revolution under Nasser and Sadat*. Cambridge: Harvard University Press, 1978. This useful overview seeks to analyze the scope and depth of Egypt's transformation since 1952. The author views Egypt's domestic developments in the context of its foreign involvements and policies, showing how the two leaders used foreign policy to aid domestic reform. The failure of the two regimes is ultimately ascribed to a lack of organization and ideology. Extensive bibliography.

33:206 Binder, Leonard. *In a Moment of Enthusiasm: Political Power and the Second Stratum in*

Egypt. Chicago: University of Chicago Press, 1978. A painstaking study of the Egyptian rural middle class, which the author considers as being the pivotal segment of Egyptian society after the 1952 revolution. The members of this class dominated both the legislature and the party organization, and acted as the grass-roots mediators between the state and the people. Extensive bibliography.

33:207　Dekmejian, Richard H. *Egypt under Nasir: A Study in Political Dynamics.* Albany: State University of New York Press, 1971. A theoretical study of the Nasir period which attempts to explain Nasir's emergence as a Pan-Arab leader and to examine the ideological foundations of his movement. The author analyzes the period's historiography, takes a close look at the ministerial and party elites, and assesses the consequences of the June 1967 war for Nasir and for Egypt's foreign policy. Extensive bibliography.

33:208　Ismael, Tareq Y. *The U.A.R. in Africa: Egypt's Policy under Nasser.* Evanston, Ill.: Northwestern University Press, 1971. Aside from the Arab-Israeli confrontation, a major focus of Egyptian foreign involvement under Nasir was Africa, which exacerbated Egypt's conflict with the United States and the West. Ismael examines Egypt's role in the African continent in the context of Nasir's alignment with the neutralist bloc, and analyzes Egyptian relations with the Sudan and the Congo.

33:209　Kerr, Malcolm H. *The Arab Cold War: Gamal 'Abd al-Nasir and His Rivals, 1958–1970.* 3d ed. London: Oxford University Press, 1972. The best interpretive account of inter-Arab relations under Nasir, it focuses on Nasir's Pan-Arabist role in the context of the Syrian-Egyptian union, the union's breakup, and the abortive negotiations with Syrian Ba'th leaders to form a new union. Also included are Nasir's dealings with Iraq, Jordan, Saudi Arabia, and the Palestinian Liberation Organization.

33:210　Mitchell, Richard P. *The Society of the Muslim Brothers.* London: Oxford University Press, 1969. This careful study examines the history of the society in the context of Egyptian political culture from its founding in 1928 through its two major crises of 1948 and 1954. The book also examines the organization and structure of the society and explores its ideas and plans for bringing about a truly Islamic order. Extensive bibliography.

33:211　Rubinstein, Alvin Z. *Red Star on the Nile.* Princeton, N.J.: Princeton University Press, 1974. An authoritative study of Soviet-Egyptian relations after the June 1967 war, using the concept of "influence" as an analytical tool, and recounting the asymmetrical relationship which benefitted the Egyptians more than the Soviets. The author demonstrates that interaction and Soviet presence did not result in any abiding ideological or systematic influence in Egypt. Extensive bibliography.

Israel/Palestine

See "Personalities," especially Menachem Begin, David Ben-Gurion, Moshe Dayan, Abba Eban, Golda Meir (under "Others"); also see "Overviews" and subheadings under "U.S. and the Middle East."

33:212　Brecher, Michael. *Decisions in Israel's Foreign Policy.* New Haven, Conn.: Yale University Press, 1975. In this companion volume to his *Foreign Policy System of Israel,* the author explores seven major Israeli foreign policy decision areas: Jerusalem; German reparations; the Korean War and China; the Jordan waters; the Sinai campaign; the Six Day War; and the Rogers proposals. Extensive bibliography.

33:213　Brecher, Michael. *The Foreign Policy System of Israel: Setting, Images, Process.* New Haven, Conn.: Yale University Press, 1972. This detailed study of Israel's foreign policy system examines its operational psychological environments, as well as the policy process. The author carefully examines the personalities of government leaders and the images they hold as factors affecting their foreign policy choices. Bibliography.

Elon, A. *The Israelis: Founders and Sons* (33:38).

33:214　Eytan, Walter. *The First Ten Years: A Diplomatic History of Israel.* New York: Simon & Schuster, 1958. This survey of the major aspects of Israel's foreign relations (1948–1957) discusses Israel's relations with its neighbors, the great powers, and the states of Asia, as well as Israel's relationship with Jewish diaspora. A chapter is devoted to Israel's foreign service.

33:215　Fabian, Larry L., and Schiff, Ze'ev, eds. *Israelis Speak: About Themselves and the Palestinians.* Washington, D.C.: Carnegie Endowment for International Peace, 1977. This book focuses the opinions of a group of 13 Israelis on the relationship between Israel and the Palestinian Arabs. While there is a notable absence of Sephardic and Oriental perspectives, the book otherwise provides a fair sample of the internal debate on the Palestinian problem.

33:216 Fein, Leonard. *Israel: Politics and People.* Boston: Little, Brown, 1968. A revised edition of *Politics in Israel,* this work utilizes the concepts of political culture and political socialization to examine the Israeli political process. The author focuses on immigrant integration, its effects on Israeli society, and the problem of security.

33:217 Isaac, Rael J. *Israel Divided: Ideological Politics in the Jewish State.* Baltimore: Johns Hopkins University Press, 1976. The author argues that two movements born in the aftermath of the 1967 war—the Land of Israel movement, which sought to incorporate captured territory, and the peace movement, which sought to conciliate Israel's Arab neighbors—are essential to understanding Israel's politics. This volume suggests that these movements have offered the only viable policy alternatives open to Israel since 1967; by raising existential questions, the movements have also accelerated ideological polarization and created a challenge to the state's basic institutions. Extensive bibliography.

33:218 Laqueur, Walter. *A History of Zionism.* New York: Holt, Rinehart & Winston, 1972. This work surveys Zionism's European background and evaluates the movement's leading figures, as well as factions, up to the establishment of Israel. The best introduction to the complexity of the ideological underpinnings of the Jewish state. Extensive bibliography.

33:219 Luttwak, Edward, and Horowitz, Dan. *The Israeli Army.* New York: Harper & Row, 1975. This study focuses on the men and ideas that have shaped the Israeli Army's strategy and tactics. The author's critique of the military's development through each of the four major Arab-Israeli wars is supported by useful maps, charts, and diagrams.

33:220 Safran, Nadav. *Israel: The Embattled Ally.* Cambridge: Harvard University Press, 1978. A comprehensive though undocumented examination of Israel's evolution; the second half constitutes a thorough analysis of Israel's relations with the United States in the context of international politics. The author sees the 1967 war as a watershed, after which U.S. and Israeli interests corresponded almost entirely until October 1973, when their perceived real interests became more interdependent than identical.

The Palestine Mandate

See Chapter 18, "The Palestine Question"; see also "Personalities," "Overviews," and "U.S. and the Middle East," above.

33:221 Bell, J. Bowyer. *Terror Out of Zion: Irgun Zvai Leumi, LEHI, and the Palestine Underground, 1929–1949.* New York: St. Martin's Press, 1977. This book carefully examines the role of the underground and terror in the creation of the Israeli state. Bell argues that the Irgun-LEHI (the Stern Gang) played a more significant role in the emergence of the state of Israel than was previously thought. Bibliography.

33:222 Hurewitz, J. C. *The Struggle for Palestine.* New York: Schocken (1950), 1976. This study provides a balanced chronicle of political conflict in Palestine from the Arab revolt in 1936 until the departure of the British in 1948. The author outlines the conflicting demands of the Zionist movement, the Palestinian Arabs, and the British. Bibliography.

33:223 Sykes, Christopher. *Crossroads to Israel, 1917–1948.* Bloomington: Indiana University Press, 1965. This in-depth analysis of the factors which set the stage for the creation of Israel is a useful synthesis of many of the complex elements which contributed to the Palestine problem as it developed during the mandate years. The book, although dated, still provides important insight into the Arab-Israeli problem that evolved after 1948.

The Palestinians

See "Personalities," especially, under "Others," Musa Alami and Abu Iyad; see also "Overviews," especially Fawaz Turki (33:40).

33:224 el-Asmar, Fouzi. *To Be an Arab in Israel.* Beirut: Institute for Palestine Studies, 1975. The memoir of a Palestinian writer, born in Lydda in 1937, who remained with his family inside Israel after 1948. The author recounts his experiences as a member of an unwanted minority group and describes his personal and political struggles.

33:225 Cooley, John K. *Green March, Black September: The Story of the Palestinian Arabs.* London: Cass, 1973. This clear analysis of the Palestinian resistance movement depicts the hopes raised by the battle of Karameh in March 1968, deals with the crippling setback in the civil war in Jordan in September 1970, which spawned the indiscriminate violence of the Black September commandos, and describes the compromise articulated by Jordan's King Hussein in

March 1972. The book also describes the cultural and political dimensions of Palestinian nationalism.

33:226   Lesch, Ann M. *Political Aspirations of the Palestinians on the West Bank and the Gaza Strip.* Washington, D.C.: American Enterprise Institute for Public Policy Research, 1979. A unique chronicle of political life on the West Bank and the Gaza Strip under Israeli military occupation, the study emphasizes the Palestinians' critiques of self-rule plans proposed by Israeli politicians and outlines the kind of interim period that the Palestinians would accept as a prelude to independence.

33:227   Lustick, Ian. *Arabs in the Jewish State: A Study in the Control of a National Minority.* Austin: University of Texas Press, 1980. Exhaustively researched, this book examines Israeli policies calculated to control the Arab population and prevent the emergence of independent mass-based political groups. The author concludes that in the future the government will have to pay substantially higher costs if it is to maintain the same degree of control over the Arab population that it has in the past. He also sees a comprehensive peace settlement exacerbating rather than ameliorating Jewish-Arab conflict.

33:228   Mishal, Shaul. *West Bank/East Bank: The Palestinians in Jordan, 1949–1967.* New Haven, Conn.: Yale University Press, 1978. Based on Jordanian documents that were captured by Israel in the 1967 war, this careful study analyzes the complex relationships between the Jordan government and its Palestinian residents from 1949, when Jordan annexed the West Bank, until 1967, when it lost control to Israel.

33:229   Quandt, William B.; Jabber, Fuad; and Lesch, Ann M. *The Politics of Palestinian Nationalism.* Berkeley: University of California Press, 1973. Provides a dispassionate analysis of the political structure of the Palestine national movement until 1972. Lesch summarizes the dilemmas facing the Palestinian nationalists from 1917 to 1948. Quandt details the resistance movement's internal organization and ideology (1965–1972), and Jabber analyzes the effects on the movement of its dependence on the Arab states. Bibliography.

33:230   el-Rayyes, Riad, and Nahas, Dunia. *Guerrillas for Palestine.* London: Croom Helm, 1976. This slim volume is particularly useful for its description of the different guerrilla groups, the overall structure of the Palestine Liberation Organization, and the profiles of the major figures in the resistance movement. It includes material on the period after the October war.

33:231   Said, Edward. *The Question of Palestine.* New York: Times Books, 1979. Said asserts that the Palestinian question is a contest between two interpretations of reality: Palestinian and Israeli. The book constitutes an attempt to provide insight into the Palestinian view and to elucidate the biases implicit in our assumptions of it.

33:232   Sayigh, Rosemary. *Palestinians: From Peasants to Revolutionaries.* London: Zed, 1979. A sympathetic study of ordinary Palestinians living in Lebanese refugee camps which gives voice to the refugees' experiences since the 1940s. The main thesis is that they endured twenty years of humiliation from their reluctant Arab hosts until the birth of their own resistance movement provided a sense of identity and purpose.

Turki, Fawaz. *The Disinherited: Journal of a Palestinian Exile* (33:40).

33:233   Van Arkadie, Brian. *Benefits and Burdens: A Report on the West Bank and the Gaza Strip Economies since 1967.* Washington, D.C.: Carnegie Endowment for International Peace, 1977. This book describes the economic interdependence that has emerged between the West Bank, the Gaza Strip, and Israel. Van Arkadie analyzes the costs and benefits to the Palestinians in the different sectors of the economy and describes the ambiguous economic impact of the large-scale movement of Arab workers into Israel.

33:234   Waines, David. *A Sentence of Exile: The Palestine/Israel Conflict, 1897–1977.* Wilmette, Ill.: Medina, 1977. A useful survey of the conflict between Jewish and Arab nationalism which is especially valuable for its interpretation of Palestinian attitudes and perceptions of the conflict. Polemical, but also useful is David Hirst, *The Gun and the Olive Branch: The Roots of Violence in the Middle East* (London: Faber & Faber, 1977).

33:235   Zureik, Elia T. *The Palestinians in Israel: A Study in Internal Colonialism.* London: Routledge & Kegan Paul, 1979. Focused on the position of the Arab minority in Israel, this sociological analysis details the Arabs' transformation from peasantry to proletariat, and the patterns of land alienation that affected them. The author stresses the colonial nature of the relations between Arabs and Jews inside Israel and analyzes the politicization of the Israeli Arabs.

Jerusalem

33:236 Benvenisti, Meron. *Jerusalem: The Torn City*. Trans. by Peretz Kidron. Minneapolis: University of Minnesota Press, 1976. A former Israeli deputy mayor of Jerusalem looks at the Arab-Israeli conflict in Jerusalem and describes how it has affected the city's inhabitants—particularly the large Arab population. While it addresses the years between 1948 and 1967, most of the book emphasizes the period since 1967. A useful appendix.

33:237 Bovis, H. Eugene. *The Jerusalem Question*. Stanford, Calif.: Hoover Institution, 1971. This scholarly treatment of the Jerusalem question delineates the problem—sovereignty over the city, and administration of the Holy Places—and views it in the context of European and Arab-Israeli differences over its jurisdiction since World War I. Especially valuable is its careful documentation of attempts to implement plans for internationalization of the city. Extensive bibliography, maps and appendixes.

33:238 Collins, Larry, and Lapierre, Dominique. *O Jerusalem!* New York: Simon & Schuster, 1972. Based on research and interviews with participants in the 1948 fighting in and around Jerusalem, this book provides a dramatic account of the struggle for control of Jerusalem. While more sympathetic to the Jewish side, the authors convey a sense of the emotional intensity that existed on both sides. Bibliography.

33:239 Wilson, Evan M. *Jeruslaem: Key to Peace*. Washington, D.C.: Middle East Institute, 1970. This book examines the problem of Jerusalem and the Holy Places. The author provides personal insight into the problem, explores some of the wider issues involved, and advances his thoughts on alternative solutions to the problem.

Jordan

See "Personalities," especially King Abdullah, King Hussein, and under "The Kennedy/Johnson Years, 1961–1968."

33:240 Aruri, Naseer Hasan. *Jordan: A Study in Political Development (1921–1965)*. The Hague: Nijhoff, 1972. This book examines the political origins and growth of Jordan, and addresses such problems as leadership, governmental structure, economics, demography, external relations, and the cycles in inter-Arab relations. The author emphasizes the inter-

nal stresses between traditionalism and radicalism, the identity crisis of Transjordanians and Palestinians, and the government's pursuit of stability and security. Extensive bibliography.

33:241 Faddah, Mohammad I. *The Middle East in Transition: A Study of Jordan's Foreign Policy*. New York: Asia Publishing House, 1974. This book focuses on Jordanian foreign policy issues, interests, personalities, and decisionmaking (1919–1967). It includes major sections on Palestine, the 1948 war, relations with Britain, relations with the United States, and inter-Arab relations. The author concludes that Jordan's survival can be attributed to the personality, courage, and finesse of Kings Abdullah and Hussein. Extensive bibliography.

33:242 Glubb, John B. *A Soldier with the Arabs*. London: Hodder & Stoughton, 1957. This is Glubb's personal narrative of his experience in Jordan: as commander of Transjordan's Arab Legion during the war with Israel (1947–1948); through the assassination of Abdullah and the accession of King Hussein; concluding with the rise of new Arab nationalism leading to Glubb's sudden dismissal in March 1956. The author provides innumerable insights into policies and personalities in Jordanian and Middle East affairs. For Transjordan under the mandate and in World War II, see the author's *Story of the Arab Legion* (London: Hodder & Stoughton, 1948).

33:243 Sinai, Anne, and Pollack, Allen, eds. *The Hashemite Kingdom of Jordan and the West Bank: A Handbook*. New York: American Academic Association for Peace in the Middle East, 1977. This collection contains useful information and provides a convenient historical-political treatment of Jordan to early 1977, although it is marred by errors and oversimplifications. Robert Stookey's article on U.S.-Jordanian relations (1946–1976) is a superior contribution. Extensive bibliography.

Lebanon

See "Personalities," especially, under "Others," Camille Nimr Chamoun and Michel Chiha; also see above, "The Eisenhower Doctrine" and "The Lebanese Intervention, 1958."

33:244 Binder, Leonard, ed. *Politics in Lebanon*. New York: Wiley, 1966. This collection deals with political culture, integration, economic development, traditional conflict resolution, political institutions, party politics, decisionmaking, and regional relations.

33:245 Gordon, David C. *Lebanon: The Fragmented Nation*. Stanford, Calif.: Hoover Institution Press, 1980. A useful, thoughtful, and sympathetic synthesis of recent Lebanese history that includes chapters on Lebanese identities; the American University of Beirut; the Lebanese civil war; and the author's personal encounters with academicians and intellectuals in Lebanon.

33:246 Hudson, Michael C. *The Precarious Republic: Political Modernization in Lebanon*. New York: Random House, 1968. A comprehensive political analysis that forecasts future problems arising from Lebanon's rapid, uneven modernization and its rigid yet fragile political institutions. Emphasis is on "radical outsiders" who are excluded from the formal system, and upon the impact of regional instability. The author sees the institutionalized sectarian system as increasingly dysfunctional and perceives a need for more effective central government. Extensive bibliography.

33:247 Suleiman, Michael W. *Political Parties in Lebanon: The Challenge of a Fragmented Political Culture*. Ithaca, N.Y.: Cornell University Press, 1967. Lebanese political parties are usefully grouped into transnational parties (pan-Arab and non-pan-Arab), religious and ethnic organizations, and exclusively Lebanese parties. The comparative discussion of ideologies and structures throws light on Lebanon's subsequent troubles.

The Civil War of 1975–1976

33:248 Barakat, Halim I. *Lebanon in Strife: Student Preludes to the Civil War*. Austin: University of Texas Press, 1977. An Arab sociologist and novelist presents findings on student attitudes in Lebanon. He discusses the sources of radicalism and political alienation, traces the development of the student movement, and finds that Lebanon's "mosaic" society contributed to the Lebanese civil war of the 1970s. Bibliography.

33:249 Khalidi, Walid. *Conflict and Violence in Lebanon: Confrontation in the Middle East*. Cambridge: Harvard Center for International Affairs, 1980. This is the most recent and best analysis of the Lebanese civil war.

33:250 Salibi, Kamal Suleiman. *Crossroads to Civil War: Lebanon, 1958–1976*. Delmar, N.Y.: Caravan, 1976. This indispensable account of the first

part of the Lebanese civil war is essentially chronological. And although it ends in early 1976, at a point when the war was far from over, it still has great value. Salibi is remarkably evenhanded and is particularly good on the complex relations among the various coalition members.

33:251 Snider, Lewis, and Haley, P. Edward, eds. *Lebanon in Crisis: Participants and Issues*. Syracuse, N.Y.: Syracuse University Press, 1979. This collective effort assesses the causes and consequences of the Lebanese civil war of the 1970s. Empahsis is on the regional and international context of the problem, with particular attention to the Palestinian role in the conflict.

Syria

33:252 Dam, Nikolaos van. *The Struggle for Power in Syria*. New York: St. Martin's Press, 1979. Sectarian, regional, and tribal loyalties have played a critical role in the political and socioeconomic history of Syria since independence. The author lays stress on sectarian polarization in the armed forces and details the roles of the Druze and Alawi minorities in intra-armed force conflicts.

33:253 Devlin, John F. *The Ba'th Party: A History from Its Origins to 1966*. Stanford, Calif.: Hoover Institution, 1976. This study provides a critical history of the most important political organization to emerge during Syria's struggle for independence. The author looks at the ten year alliance between the Ba'th party and Hama politicians, the many personal, ideological, professional, and civil-military rivalries, and the disillusioning experiment in Arab unity. Bibliography.

33:254 Longrigg, Stephen H. *Syria and Lebanon under French Mandate*. London: Oxford University Press, 1958. The author provides a background to Syrian independence in 1946, analyzing the French role during the mandate period, and delineating the antagonisms between Syrian nationalists and French colonial officials as World War II arrived. The author examines Syrian developments during the war years and ends with the withdrawal of French troops. Bibliography.

33:255 Rabinovich, Itamar. *Syria under the Ba'th, 1963–1966: The Army-Party Symbiosis*. Jerusalem: Israel Universities Press, 1972. This study scrutinizes the Ba'th party's first three years and details the ideological, political, and personal rivalries which occurred between officers and civilian party officials, among rival officer groups, and between the Iraqi and Syrian branches of the party. This book provides a sequel to Seale's book and essential background to the Syrian role in Arab politics at the time of the 1967 war. Bibliography.

33:256 Seale, Patrick. *The Struggle for Syria: A Study of Post-War Arab Politics, 1954–1958.* New York: Oxford University Press, 1965. This study emphasizes the internal struggles among political parties, bickering politicians, and rival army officer groups in the context of external forces in the Arab world and the West. It offers an essential background to the formation of the United Arab Republic in 1958. Bibliography.

ARABIAN PENINSULA AND PERSIAN GULF

33:257 Albaharna, Husain M. *Arabian Gulf States: Their Legal and Political Status and Their International Problems.* 2d ed. Beirut: Librairie du Liban, 1975. This book by a longtime official of Bahrain examines the history of Great Britain's treaty relations with the Arab principalities of the Persian Gulf and traces the evolution of these states' international status. The author writes with authority on political development, constitutional structures, and conflicting boundary claims. This edition includes important developments that occurred since 1968, among them Iran's occupation of Abu Musa and the two Tunbs Islands. Extensive bibliography, texts of agreements, and maps.

33:258 Anthony, John D. *Arab States of the Lower Gulf: People, Politics, Petroleum.* Washington, D.C.: Middle East Institute, 1975. Anthony examines Bahrain, Qatar, and the United Arab Emirates for the changes that oil wealth has brought to their political and socioeconomic systems. The author looks at the governmental structures of the individual sheikdoms, and analyzes their internal political dynamics. Extensive bibliography.

33:259 Holden, David. *Farewell to Arabia.* London: Faber & Faber, 1966. Written in an elegant style, this book remains a favorite among students of the peninsula. Among its enduring contributions are the author's perceptive rendering of local color and his always thoughtful and provocative account of people

and politics at a decisive point in the peninsula's history.

33:260 Hopwood, Derek, ed. *The Arabian Peninsula: Society and Politics.* London: Allen & Unwin, 1972. This volume contains material pertinent to 20th-century developments in the area. Following a bibliographical survey, there are six papers on historical topics, three on political developments and international relations, three on sociology and culture, and two on economics.

33:261 Kelly, John B. *Eastern Arabian Frontiers.* New York: Praeger, 1964. A detailed study of the conflicting claims of Saudi Arabia, Abu Dhabi, and Oman to the "Buraimi Oasis" and other disputed areas in the eastern part of the Arabian Peninsula (to 1963). The author finds little merit in Saudi claims.

33:262 Long, David E. *The Persian Gulf: An Introduction to Its Peoples, Politics and Economics.* Rev. ed. Boulder, Colo.: Westview, 1978. Long sketches each of the gulf states, analyzes the role of each in regional affairs, and assesses the region's place in world affairs. Although the discussion on Iran is now obsolete, this book still provides a good introduction to the gulf. For a more recent, more general survey, see Alvin J. Cottrell, ed., *The Persian Gulf States: A General Survey* (Baltimore: Johns Hopkins University Press, 1980). Extensive bibliography.

33:263 Noyes, James H. *The Clouded Lens: Persian Gulf Security and U.S. Policy.* Stanford, Calif.: Hoover Institution, 1979. Analyzes the transition made by the Persian Gulf countries from colonial domination to independence. Essentially a discussion of U.S. foreign policy, the monograph focuses on military assistance and sales.

Ramazani, R. K. *The Persian Gulf: Iran's Role* (33:172).

33:264 Ramazani, Rouhollah K. *The Persian Gulf and the Strait of Hormuz.* The Netherlands: Sijthoff & Noordhoff, 1979. Clearly delineates complicating regional tensions as well as problems relating to the Strait of Hormuz.

33:265 Sadik, Muhammad T., and Snavely, William P. *Bahrain, Qatar, and the United Arab Emirates: Colonial Past, Present Problems, and Future Prospects.* Lexington, Mass.: Lexington Books, 1972. This book by two development specialists is of special value for those interested in administrative, social and economic change in the nine lower gulf sheikdoms which terminated their special treaty relationship with Great Britain in 1971. Bibliography, charts, and tables.

33:266 Washington Center for Strategic and International Studies. *The Gulf: Implications of British Withdrawal.* Washington, D.C.: Georgetown University Center for Strategic and International Studies, 1969. This is an alarmist assessment of the prospects for stability in the gulf as a result of the 1968 announcement by the British government of its intention to withdraw from the area by the end of 1971. It remains of value because it typifies the thinking of those who perceive the area as an object to be contested over by outside powers.

Bahrain

33:267 Belgrave, Charles D. *Personal Column.* London: Hutchinson, 1960. Reprinted 1972. This is an autobiographical account of the author's years (1926–1957) in Bahrain, during which, as the British political agent, he helped to lay the groundwork for modern Bahrain.

Iraq

33:268 Batatu, Hanna. *The Old Social Classes and the Revolutionary Movements of Iraq: A Study of Iraq's Old Landed and Commerical Classes and of Its Communists, Ba'thists and Free Officers.* Princeton, N.J.: Princeton University Press, 1978. The author examines in great depth social classes and class movements in Iraq. Part 1 examines the influential elites of prerepublican Iraq; part 2 the origins and evolution of the Communist party to the 1950s; and part 3 the movements of the Communists, Ba'thists, and Free Officers from the 1950s to 1978. The book is unrivaled in the depth of biographical data that is presented. Extensive bibliography and biographical data.

33:269 Dann, Uriel. *Iraq under Qassem: A Political History, 1958–1963.* New York: Praeger, 1969. The author, an Israeli scholar, examines the period in which 'Abd al-Karim Qassem held power in Iraq. The study is sympathetic to Qassem as an individual, although it notes the failure of his regime to realize its ambitions and is critical of his mishandling of the Kurdish situation.

33:270 Khadduri, Majid. *Independent Iraq, 1952–1958: A Study in Iraqi Politics.* 2d ed. London: Oxford University Press, 1960. A descriptive history of Iraq from independence (1932) to the revolution of 1958, which emphasizes the period before 1953. Appendixes, the most useful of which is a list of the prime ministers of Iraq (1921–1958) and their dates of office.

33:271 Khadduri, Majid. *Republican Iraq: A Study in Iraqi Politics since the Revolution of 1958.* London: Oxford University Press, 1969. In an analysis of the revolution of 1958 and of the succeeding ten-year struggle for power, the author examines competing ideological groups and contrasts the Nasirite and Ba'thist approaches to Arab socialism.

33:272 Khadduri, Majid. *Socialist Iraq: A Study in Iraqi Politics since 1968.* Washington, D.C.: Middle East Institute, 1978. Khadduri describes the assumption and consolidation of power by the Arab Socialist Ba'th party from 1968 to 1977. He also addresses social, economic, and foreign policy issues, as well as Iraq's Kurdish problem. Appendixes.

33:273 Penrose, Edith, and Penrose, E. F. *Iraq: International Relations and National Development.* Boulder, Colo.: Westview, 1978. This study examines the political and economic development of Iraq (1914–1977). The authors are particularly good in their treatment of economic matters, above all the evolution of petroleum policies. They are critical of Iraq's political development. Bibliography.

Kuwait

33:274 Freeth, Zahra, and Winstone, H. V. F. *Kuwait: Prospect and Reality.* London: Allen & Unwin, 1972. An industrial writer and the daughter of the late Colonel H. R. P. Dickson, renowned former adviser to the government of Kuwait, collaborated on this informative account. The volume offers insights into the role which oil has played in changing Kuwaiti society and in orienting the country's policies toward the outside world. See also M. W. Korija and P. G. Sadler, *The Economy of Kuwait: Development and Role in International Finance* (London: Macmillan, 1979).

Oman

33:275 Peterson, John. *Oman in the Twentieth Century: Political Foundation of an Emerging State.* London: Croom Helm, 1978. A political history which looks at the interplay of four themes in Omani politics: the sultans and the ruling family; administrative development; the exercise of tribal politics; and external influences. Extensive bibliography, appendixes, maps, and tables.

33:276　Townsend, John. *Oman: The Making of a Modern State.* London: Croom Helm, 1977. The book examines the emergence of Oman as a modern state under the reign of Sultan Qabus. It also includes a brief overview of Oman's geography and history, including a chapter on the reign of Qabus's father, Said bin Taymur (r. 1932–1970). Bibliography.

Qatar

33:277　el-Mallakh, Ragaei. *Qatar: Development of an Oil Economy.* London: Croom Helm, 1979. The author traces the development of the oil industry, looks closely at economic and agricultural development, and places his analysis in an international context. For a well-written series of interviews with people from all segments of Qatari society, see Graham Helga, *Arabian Time Machine: Self-Portrait of an Oil State* (London: Heinemann, 1978).

Saudi Arabia

See "Personalities," especially, under "Others," King Faisal; also see above, "The U.S. and Middle Eastern Oil," especially Aaron Miller (33:150).

33:278　Long, David E. *The Hajj Today: A Survey of the Contemporary Makkah Pilgrimage.* Albany: State University of New York Press, 1979. This book looks at the origins, rites, and administrative aspects of the Hajj and then analyzes the social, political, and economic impact on Saudi Arabia of the Great Pilgrimage to Mecca that 1,500,000 people make annually. The work contains considerable discussion of Saudi institutions found nowhere else in English. Extensive bibliography.

33:279　Long, David E. *Saudi Arabia.* Beverly Hills, Calif.: Sage, 1976. This brief monograph serves in the absence of a more definitive study as an introduction to Saudi Arabia. Peter Hobday, *Saudi Arabia Today: An Introduction to the Richest Oil Power* (New York: Macmillan, 1978), provides details on the recent past, while Fouad Al-Farsy, *Saudi Arabia: A Case Study in Development* (London: Stacey International,

1977), provides an examination of the kingdom's polity, administrative organization, and development. See also Norman Anderson et al., *The Kingdom of Saudi Arabia* (London: Stacey International, 1977), for helpful maps, charts, and articles.

33:280　Philby, Harry St. John B. *Arabian Jubilee.* New York: Day, 1953. No introduction to Saudi Arabia is complete without sampling one of the works of the British explorer, writer, and confidant of the late King Abd al-Aziz (Ibn Saud). It traces the development of modern Saudi Arabia, and contains genealogical charts of the royal family. See also his *Sa'udi Arabia* (1955).

United Arab Emirates

33:281　Mann, Clarence. *Abu Dhabi: Birth of an Oil Sheikhdom.* 2d ed. Beirut: Khayats, 1969. An account of Abu Dhabi's history from the 1800s to the mid-1960s. Among the interesting sections are those on the ruling family, the leading tribes, the "Buraimi Oasis crisis," the impact of oil wealth on the sheikdom, and the role of the British. Extensive bibliography, a genealogy of the Al Bu Falah ruling family, a chronology, texts of the treaties, and maps.

The Yemen

33:282　Bujra, Abdalla S. *The Politics of Stratification: A Study of Political Change in a South Arabian Town.* Oxford: Clarendon Press, 1971. This is a Kenyan anthropologist's comprehensive and pioneering study of the transformation of political attitudes and values in the Hadramawt region of the People's Democratic Republic of Yemen.

33:283　O'Ballance, Edgar. *The War in the Yemen.* Hamden, Conn.: Shoe String Press, 1971. O'Ballance provides the most comprehensive analysis of the 1960s civil war in Yemen. Recent events confirm the author's judgment that the confrontations there were not ideological, but endemic, and that they will continue as tribal coalitions, supported first by one and then another foreign power, acting out the heritage bestowed upon them by centuries of conflict.

33:284　Stookey, Robert W. *Yemen: The Politics of the Yemen Arab Republic.* Boulder, Colo.: Westview, 1978. The author traces the origins of the Y.A.R.'s distinguishing contemporary features. He delineates the cleavage between the Zaydi sect of Shi'a Islam and the Shafi'i rite of Sunni Islam, and then relates it to current Yemeni politics. Extensive bibliography.

33:285 Trevaskis, Sir Kennedy. *Shades of Amber: A South Arabian Episode.* London: Hutchinson, 1968. This is an authoritative account of the last days of British control in Aden and the attempt to create a South Arabian federation, by its chief designer. Also see Charles H. Johnston's *The View from Steamer Point: Three Crucial Years in South Arabia,* a personal account of the author's years (1960–1963) as British governor in Aden.

33:286 Wenner, Manfred W. *Modern Yemen, 1918–1966.* Baltimore: Johns Hopkins Press, 1967. A scholarly study of modern Yemen which examines Yemen's historical and cultural background, internal developments under Imams Yahya and Ahmad, and foreign policy. The research was completed in mid-1966, before the end of the Yemeni civil war and the reuniting of the warring republican and royalist factions. Extensive bibliography.

NORTH AFRICA
(THE MAGHREB)

Gallagher, C. F. *The United States And North Africa: Morocco, Algeria and Tunisia* (18:8) treats broadly the historical and cultural development of the peoples of North Africa, and provides an overview of U.S.–North African relations (1784–1963). A new and updated edition is much needed.

33:287 Julien, Charles-André. *L'Afrique du Nord en marche: Nationalismes musulmans et souveraineté française* [North Africa on the march: Moslem nationalism and French sovereignty]. 3d ed. Paris: Julliard, 1972. The first edition of this book was hastily written in the early 1950s and represented a sympathetic attempt to explain North African nationalist agitation. Surprisingly, it has stood, though flawed and incomplete, as the best overview of the Maghreb's march to independence. Extensive bibliography.

33:288 Laroui, Abdallah. *The History of the Maghrib: An Interpretive Essay.* Trans. by Ralph Manheim. Princeton, N.J.: Princeton University Press, 1977. In questioning standard notions of the Maghreb's "historical log," and the revolution which supposedly served as its conscious compensation, the author reconsiders what the attitude of a Maghrebi, concerned with his future, should be toward his past

The result is a provocative book which raises a number of questions and answers a few. Bibliography.

Algeria

Cooke, J. J., and Heggory, A. A. "The American Periodical Press and Ahmed Ben Bella" (33:112).

33:289 Horne, Alistair. *A Savage War of Peace: Algeria, 1954–1962.* London: Macmillan, 1977. A comprehensive account of the Algerian struggle for independence which emphasizes the role of the French in Algeria and the effects of the Algerian situation on French politics. The book is particularly good on the formation and organization of the FLN, although it has been criticized by some for failing to grasp the fundamental political and social issues of the rebellion.

33:290 Quandt, William B. *Revolution and Political Leadership: Algeria, 1954–1968.* Cambridge, Mass.: MIT Press, 1969. The author concludes that the sources of political conflicts among Algerian leaders lie primarily in various patterns of elite political socialization. This is the best of several good studies of the Algerian political system and the origins of contemporary Algeria. Excellent bibliography and useful appendixes.

Libya

33:291 First, Ruth. *Libya: The Elusive Revolution.* New York: Holmes & Meier, 1975. This book concentrates on the period since 1969 and explores such themes as revolution, oil, and Arab unity. The author attempts to understand Libya in its own context, not Europe's, and tries to measure its achievements against the need for revolutionary change. One should also consult the more recent analysis of Libya's politics and society under Qaddafi by Omar el-Fathaly and Monte Palmer, *Political Development and Social Change in Libya* (Lexington, Mass.: Lexington Books, 1980). Bibliography.

Morocco

33:292 Blair, Leon B. "The Impact of Franco-American Military Agreements on Moroccan Nationalism, 1940–1956." *Rocky Mountain Social Science Journal* 9:1 (1972), 61–68. Despite Franco-American military agreements, the American presence had an encouraging influence on Moroccan nationalism.

Hall, L. J. *The United States and Morocco, 1776 – 1956* (18:10).

33:293 Waterbury, John. *The Commander of the Faithful: The Moroccan Political Elite—A Study in Segmented Politics.* New York: Columbia University Press, 1970. This is the best analysis to date of Morocco's political system and how it has functioned since Morocco achieved independence in 1956. The author examines how the Moroccan regime has been influenced by, and seeks to sustain, patterns of behavior which are intricately related to the country's political culture and social structure.

Tunisia

33:294 Moore, Clement H. *Tunisia since Independence: The Dynamics of One-Party Government.* Berkeley: University of California Press, 1965. This monograph examines the political regime of Tunisia since independence in 1956. Because Tunisia's political system is at once democratic and authoritarian, with personal and historical factors more significant than ideology, the author's capacity to free himself from Western categories, and to address these factors, makes this book a solid study of independent Tunisia. Extensive bibliography.

34

United States, Caribbean, and Central America after 1941

Contributing Editor

THOMAS M. LEONARD
University of North Florida

Contents

Introduction

Since 1941, the United States has primarily sought political tranquility throughout the Caribbean and Central America. Regional calm was considered necessary for the security of the Panama Canal. During World War II and in the immediate postwar years, the United States accepted charges by local ruling elites that pressure by lower socioeconomic groups was communist inspired. For the most part, U.S. officials ignored the pleas for massive aid programs to correct the effects of economic dislocation. The situation was aggravated further by extensive private U.S. investment in the region, which, historically, had been protected by local ruling elites and U.S. policy. Until 1960 the United States was too busy conducting the cold war in Europe and Asia to give much attention to the Caribbean and Central America.

Fidel Castro's revolution in Cuba proved a turning point with both regional politics and U.S. policy. Castroism encouraged leaders of the underprivileged to militantly pressure for political and social change. The United States subsequently introduced aid programs to improve the quality of life, but in the process came to view most opposition leaders as Marxist oriented.

A survey of regional socioeconomic problems can be found in two anthologies. That edited by A. Curtis Wilgus, *The Caribbean* (34:19), deals with the pre-Castro years, while that edited by Richard Millett and W. Marvin Will, *The Restless Caribbean* (34:16), covers the contemporary period. Taken together, these works demonstrate the growing understanding in the United States of regional developmental needs. An excellent historical example analyzing one nation's social and economic structure is Wyatt McGaffey and Clifford Barnett's *Twentieth Century Cuba: The Background of the Castro Revolution* (34:90). However, such studies are not available for every regional country, leaving the reader to rely upon the writings of revolutionary leaders, whose works share the common characteristic of placing blame for their nation's plight upon U.S. economic imperialism.

U.S. policy toward the region, particularly since Castro, has produced economic and social aid programs, and more recently, a plea for human rights. The significance of this policy change has been illustrated by Raymond J. Barrett's "The United States and the Caribbean" (34:21) and Harold Molineu's "The Concept of the Caribbean in the Latin American Policy of the United States" (34:27). Barrett argues that the United States should continue an active role in regional development, otherwise groups opposed to its interests would come to power. Molineu maintains that regional political instability failed to threaten U.S. interests.

Historically, the Panama Canal had been primary to U.S. Central American policy. Although the so called "50 families" which ruled Panama enjoyed economic, social, and political prominence, the nation's masses failed to receive tangible benefits from the canal operation. Only after World War II did Panamanian nationalism, as expressed by its masses, come forward to demand ownership of the country's major resource. Treaty revision in 1955 failed to satisfy those demands, and Panamanian militancy continued. Subsequent to the 1964 riots, negotiations were renewed, resulting in the 1978 treaties providing for Panama's ultimate ownership of the canal. This story has been told best by Walter LaFeber, *The Panama Canal: The Crisis in Historical Perspective* (34:327). LaFeber's sympathy for the Panamanian case has been countered by J. Fred Rippy, "United States and Panama" (34:174), who argues that the United States should not have appeased Panamanian demands. Regarding the 1978 treaties, balanced arguments covering such issues as defense, economics, and legal rights can be found in Abraham Lowenthal and Milton Charlton's "The United States and Panama: Confrontation or Cooperation?" (34:185).

The first successful postwar challenge to regional traditional ruling elites came in 1948 in Costa Rica, where José Figueres headed a successful revolution. However, the United States gave little attention to the movement, largely because of the concern with European economic recovery and the apparent absence of communist influence. However, six years later, the United States intervened in Guatemala, assisting in the overthrow of Jacobo Arbenz Guzmán, whose administration was allegedly Marxist oriented. Like his predecessor, Juan José Areválo, Arbenz favored rural and urban labor groups. He directed the confiscation of some U.S.-owned properties, including that of the United Fruit Company, and redistribution to rural laborers. Frederick B. Pike's "Guatemala, the United States and Communism in the Americas" (34:193) illustrates the crosscurrents of self-interest: the U.S. concern with communism and the Latin concern with economic development. Furthermore, the United States' allegation that a Marxist government in Guatemala threatened its regional security interests has been refuted by Philip B. Taylor, Jr., "The Guatemalan Affair: A Critique of United States Foreign Policy" (34:202). While the intervention may not have been the major issue in John Foster Dulles's conduct of the cold war, it signaled a change in the U.S. policy of nonintervention in regional domestic affairs.

Fidel Castro's successful 1959 revolution in Cuba challenged all the elements characteristic to the region: political dictatorship, local socioeconomic deprivation, large U.S. investment, and U.S. concern for regional security. More literature has been produced regarding U.S. policy toward Castro's Cuba than any other country or topic. Theodore Draper's two volumes (34:95, 34:96) on Castro's revolution provide an excellent understanding and analysis of the movement and the communist influence. Once Castro was entrenched in power, the United States branded him a communist based on his activities, i.e., confiscation of U.S. properties, failure to provide for free elections, and subsequent ties to the Soviet Union.

As with Guatemala, the United States determined that a communist-leaning regime had to go, and therefore supported the ill-conceived Bay of Pigs invasion, a decision properly placed in the cold war framework by Richard Walton (24:216). The introduction of Soviet missiles in 1962 escalated Cuba from a regional to an international problem. No longer dealing only with a small nation, the United States had to consider Soviet intentions and options, all of which have been explored by Robert Divine, *The Cuban Missile Crisis* (29:102).

Since 1962, the issue of U.S.-Cuban rapprochement has been widely discussed. In his "The United States and Castro: Breaking the Deadlock" (34:116), Edward González suggests that the United States take the initiative. That Castro's continued uncompromising hard line, however, has been responsible for continued chilled relations is argued by Walter J. Raymond (34:113). And that these relations have been exacerbated by the Cuban extension into Africa is the thrust of G. J. Bender's essay "Angola, the Cubans, and American Anxieties" (37:200).

The United States believed that Castro instigated other regional revolts, such as the Dominican crisis in 1965. The overthrow of Donald Reid Cabral in April of that year resulted in the landing of American marines and President Lyndon B. Johnson's "doctrine" that the United States would intervene unilaterally in any Latin state to prevent a communist coup. This position has been defended by U.S. foreign service officer John Bartlow Martin (34:129), but the United States erroneously interpreted Castro's role in the Dominican revolt.

These issues were again raised with the 1979 overthrow of Nicaragua's Somoza regime by Sandinista rebels. There was concern with communist influence, the loss of U.S. economic interests, and a threat to regional security. However, by 1979 the United States developed a greater appreciation for the masses of those people left out of the socioeconomic mainstream. Reflective of this opinion, and sympathetic to the Sandinistas, is Alejandro Bendana's "Crisis in Nicaragua" (34:223).

An examination of the literature on U.S. policy toward the Caribbean and Central America reveals its crisis orientation. It has analyzed major events or topics within specific countries—Cuba, Dominican Republic, Guatemala, Nicaragua, and Panama. For the most part, this literature has been placed into the cold war framework. There remains a need for understanding local political leaders and parties, social and economic diversity, and the internal pressures for reform. Changing requirements since 1941 also require an analysis of U.S. defense needs vis-à-vis the Panama Canal and Guantanamo Bay. For the most part, the Caribbean and Central America continue as a virgin preserve for historical study.

Resources and Overviews

RESEARCH AIDS

While pertinent bibliographies and references aids are listed here, there are more extensive lists in Chapter 1.

Bibliographies

34:1 Baa, Enid M., comp. *Theses on Caribbean Topics.* San Juan, P.R.: University of Puerto Rico

Press, 1970. A list of doctoral dissertations and master's theses dating to the 19th century, it emphasizes the years 1945 to 1967. A broad range of topics—economics, history, politics, international relations—are located through an awkward country-subject index.

Bayitch, S. A. *Latin America and the Caribbean: A Bibliographical Guide to Works in English* (1:115) emphasizes the years since 1941 and has chapters for each country. Topics include history, foreign relations, government, natural resources, and population.

34:2   Bray, Wayne D. *Controversy over a New Canal Treaty between United States and Panama: Selective Annotated Bibliography of United States, Panamanian, Colombian, French, and International Organization Sources.* Washington, D.C.: Library of Congress, 1978. This is a valuable guide which contains extensive annotations of pertinent materials.

34:3   *Central America: A Bibliography.* 2d ed. Los Angeles: California State University, Latin American Studies Center, 1980. A list of general references, it includes nearly 2,000 items in both English and Spanish languages. Not annotated.

34:4   Comitas, Lambros. *The Complete Caribbeana, 1900–1975: A Bibliographical Guide to the Scholarly Literature.* 4 vols. Millwood, N.Y.: KTO Press, 1977. These volumes, updating the 1968 edition, contain over 17,000 references to former colonial areas: Surinam, French Guiana, Guyana in South America; Belize in Central America; and the Bahamas, Bermuda, and the Antilles in the Caribbean. Covers people, institutions, resources, and indexes (volume 4).

Deal, C. W., ed. *Latin America and the Caribbean: A Dissertation Bibliography* (1:249) lists 7,200 dissertations, mainly for the 1962 to 1977 period, which cover all disciplines from agriculture and anthropology to sociology and speech. The chapters on history and law and political science list many dissertations on U.S.–Latin American relations. All taken from *Dissertation Abstracts International,* but without annotations.

34:5   Fort, Giberto V. *The Cuban Revolution of Fidel Castro Viewed from Abroad.* Lawrence: University of Kansas Libraries, 1969. Fort covers all aspects of the revolution: opposition in exile, laws, religious persecution, education, fiction, and poetry. Also of interest are the sections on prerevolutionary Cuba, Fidel Castro, Cuba and international organizations, the Bay of

Pigs invasion, the missile crisis, and Cuba and the United States. Well annotated.

34:6   Highfield, Arnold R., with Bumgarner, Max, comp. and ed. *A Bibliography of Articles on the Danish West Indies and the United States Virgin Islands in the New York Times 1867–1975.* Gainesville: University Presses of Florida, 1978.

34:7   Kantor, Harry. *A Bibliography of Unpublished Doctoral Dissertations and Masters Theses Dealing with the Governments, Politics and International Relations of Latin America.* Gainesville: University of Florida Press, 1953. The entries date from 1911, but emphasize the years 1940 to 1952. This is an excellent source guide to university location of materials.

34:8   Pérez, Louis A., Jr. *The Cuban Revolutionary War, 1953–1958: A Bibliography.* Metuchen, N.J.: Scarecrow, 1976. This is an exhaustive listing of works, without annotations, on a range of topics, including U.S. policy; the preponderance of references are in Spanish. It concentrates on materials published during 1953 to 1975.

Trask, D. F.; Meyer, M. C.; and Trask, R. R., eds. *A Bibliography of United States–Latin America Relations since 1810: A Selected List of Eleven Thousand Published References* (1:120). Extremely helpful are the bibliography listings for each Central American nation. Meyer (1:119) supplements and updates this volume.

U.S. Department of the Army. *Latin America and the Caribbean: Analytic Survey of the Literature* [1975 ed.] (1:122) is useful for contemporary books and articles, plus "Background Notes" for each country and many maps.

U.S. Library of Congress. Hispanic Division. *Handbook of Latin American Studies* (1:123) is the most complete annual bibliography in English of current research and publications.

34:9   Váldes, Nelson P., and Lieuwen, Edwin. *The Cuban Revolution: A Research-Study Guide, 1959–1969.* Albuquerque: University of New Mexico Press, 1971. This is an indispensable bibliographical guide with detailed subject categories. U.S. libraries holding significant collections are indicated.

34:10   Véliz, Claudio, ed. *Latin America and the Caribbean: A Handbook.* New York: Praeger, 1968. A basic reference work, with essays which are encyclopedic in extent, supplemented by statistical and bibliographical materials. There is a lengthy chapter on inter-American relations.

Historiographical Essays

Ferguson, Y. H. "The Dominican Intervention of 1965: Recent Interpretations" (34:126) concludes that the Constitutionalists would have won had the United States not intervened.

Griffith, W. "The Historiography of Central America since 1830" (1:130) points to the large gaps in the field, including foreign policy.

34:11 Rey, J. A. "Revolution and Liberation: A review of Recent Literature on the Guatemalan Situation." *Hispanic American Historical Review* 38:2 (1958), 239–55. An excellent historiographical discussion of the overthrow of the Jacobo Arbenz government in 1954. It emphasizes the literature since 1954.

Snarr, D. N., and Brown, E. L. "An Analysis of Ph.D. Dissertations on Central America, 1960–1974" (1:250).

Yearbooks and Other Aids

See also Chapter 24, "Yearbooks and Other Aids."

Facts on File: A Weekly Digest with Cumulative Index (1:151).

Keesing's Contemporary Archives: Weekly Diary of World Events (1:152).

Political Handbook and Atlas of the World (1:144).

The Statesman's Year Book: Statistical and Historical Annual of the States of the World (1:145).

Document Collections

More general collections are listed in Chapter 1, and other collections may be found in "Personalities," below; also see Chapter 35, "Document Collections."

Burr, R., ed. *Latin America* [1945–1973] (35:15).

Mesa, R. Q., comp. *Latin American Serial Documents: A Holdings List* (35:18) provides a guide to the more accessible published documents of Latin American countries, most of which are held in U.S. libraries.

34:12 Preiswerk, Roy, ed. *Documents on International Relations in the Caribbean.* Rio Piedras: University of Puerto Rico, 1970. This is an invaluable documentary collection covering a broad range of topics; titles include "Extra Regional Economic Relations," "Regional Cooperation and Integration," "Defense," and "Conflicts and Disputes."

U.S. Department of State. *Foreign Relations of the United States* (1:358) contains annual volumes with selections of diplomatic correspondence between the United States and the Central American/Caribbean nations. The emphasis is upon economic and political relations.

U.S. Department of State. *Press Conferences of the Secretaries of State, 1922–1974* (1:360) is a microfilm of typescript verbatim record of these important conferences.

U.S. National Archives Microfilm Publications. *Purport Lists for the Department of State Decimal File, 1910–1944* (1:258) explains how to use diplomatic records in the National Archives. Although records are now available through 1954, the decimal system remains the same as described herein. Microfilm copies of the documents for each country are available for the years 1910 to 1944 from the National Archives.

U.S. President. *Public Papers of the Presidents of the United States* [1945–] (1:362).

34:13 Vivas, Rafael Leivas. *Los Tratados Internacionales de Honduras* [International treaties of Honduras]. Tegucigalpa: Universidad Nacional Autónoma de Honduras, 1971. This is an annotated listing of over 500 Honduran treaties for the years 1839 to 1969.

OVERVIEWS

See Chapter 24, "Overviews," for surveys of American foreign affairs since World War II.

34:14 Ameringer, Charles. *The Democratic Left in Exile: The Antidictatorial Struggle in the Caribbean, 1945–1959.* Coral Gables, Fla.: University of Miami Press, 1974. Ameringer examines the careers of Be-

tancourt, Figueres, Muñoz Marin, Bosch, Cuban Au-
tenticos and the Caribbean Legion movements. Extensive bibliography.

34:15   Bosch, Juan. *De Cristóbal Colón a Fidel Castro: El Caribe frontera imperial* [From Christopher
Columbus to Fidel Castro: the Caribbean imperial
front]. Madrid: Alfaguara, 1970. The former Dominican president presents a jaundiced view which
concludes that the region has been a victim of American, European, and communist imperialism.
Bibliography.

Davis, H. E., and Wilson, L. C., eds. *Latin American Foreign Policies: An Analysis* [1810–1974]
(35:22) examines the foreign policies of individual
states and, in the final chapter, offers conclusions
about Cuba and Panama.

Duggan, L. *The Americas: The Search for Hemisphere Security* [1823–1948] (2:279) treats wartime
and postwar relations, emphasizing the need for
socioeconomic reforms.

Karnes, T. L. *The Failure of Union: Central America,
1824–1960* (2:307) traces the attempts at union. Its
strength is the post-1871 period.

34:16   Millett, Richard, and Will, W. Marvin, eds.
*The Restless Caribbean: Changing Patterns of Inter-
national Relations.* New York: Praeger, 1979. An excellent collection of essays, it focuses on contemporary regional problems, including Cuba, Jamaica,
Trinidad and Tobago's foreign policies; influence of
oil; future canal prospects; population movements;
and Soviet influence.

34:17   Mitchell, Harold. "Islands of the Caribbean."
Current History 58:342 (1979), 107–10. Mitchell argues that contrary to the superpowers' interest in the
region, Caribbean states are overcoming obstacles to
regional cooperation.

34:18   Sherlock, Philip. "Prospects in the Caribbean." *Foreign Affairs* 41:4 (1963), 744–56. The
West Indian states desired U.S. aid for economic and
social development, but did not want to come under
her protective umbrella having just escaped British
colonialism.

34:19   Wilgus, A. Curtis, ed. *The Caribbean: Contemporary International Relations.* Gainesville: University of Florida Press, 1957. A wide-ranging collection of essays covering diplomatic relations, trade and
business, cultural cooperation, and the confederation
movements in the British and Dutch territories and
Central America.

Inter-American System

See Chapter 35, "Organization of American States."

Connell-Smith, G. *The Inter-American System*
[1889–1965] (2:277) is a critical review of U.S.
claims of success and, as such, provides a useful
contrast to Mecham's laudatory account.

Mecham, J. L. *The United States and Inter-American
Security, 1889–1960* (2:283) presents the orthodox
case for the system. Mecham argues that the system is
the best organized and most effective of all "regional
arrangements," and necessary for U.S. security.

34:20   Pan American Union. Division of Laws and
Treaties. *Applications of the Inter-American Treaty of
Reciprocal Assistance, 1948–1956.* Washington,
D.C.: Pan American Union, 1957. With documents
and commentary on the Rio Treaty, a summary of
OAS action is presented on several cases: Costa
Rica–Nicaragua disputes (1948–1949 and 1955);
Haiti (1949); Caribbean situation (1950); Guatemala,
1954.

U.S., Caribbean, and Central America

See Chapter 35, "Overviews," for general accounts of
U.S.-Latin American relations.

Aguilar Monteverde, A. *Pan Americanism from Monroe to the Present: A View from the Other Side*
[1821–1967] (2:259) presents a sweeping criticism of
U.S. policies toward Latin America.

34:21   Barrett, Raymond J. "The United States and
the Caribbean." *Air University Review* 22:4 (1971),
44–51. Central America is under diverse pressures for
change and the United States should guide this change
in a peaceful and constructive manner, within the
general U.S. objectives for this region.

Blasier, C. *The Hovering Giant: United States Responses to Revolutionary Change in Latin America*
[1910–1964] (35:26) examines U.S. response to social
revolution in Guatemala and Cuba.

34:22 Crassweller, Robert D. *The Caribbean Community: Changing Societies and U.S. Policy*. New York: Praeger, 1972. A businessman discusses the region's diversity in light of recent political events and recommends U.S. assistance programs, but not to the area's political leadership. Extensive bibliography.

34:23 Etchison, Don L. *The United States and Militarism in Central America*. New York: Praeger, 1975. This brief survey of Central America focuses on the military aspects of U.S. policy under the Kennedy, Johnson, and Nixon administrations.

34:24 Hardy, Osgood. "Rafael Leonidas Trujillo Malina: The United States' Postwar Attitude toward the Dictatorships." *Pacific Historical Review* 15:4 (1946), 409–16. The author suggests that the United States should not intervene militarily to bring down dictatorships, but rather permit the Latins to solve their own problems.

Langley, L. D. *The United States and the Caribbean, 1900–1970* (2:309) suggests that U.S. policy toward the Caribbean has been motivated more by political and cultural factors than economic considerations.

34:25 Martz, John D. *Central America: The Crisis and the Challenge*. Chapel Hill: University of North Carolina Press, 1959. Martz concentrates upon the domestic turmoil during the 1940s and 1950s and the inability of the United States to deal effectively with unrepresentative governments. Bibliography.

34:26 McLean, E. R. "The Caribbean: An American Lake." *U.S. Naval Institute Proceedings* 67:7 (1941), 947–60. World War II necessitated the development of Caribbean defense sites, fulfilling Alfred T. Mahan's prediction of an American lake.

34:27 Molineu, Harold. "The Concept of the Caribbean in the Latin American Policy of the United States." *Journal of Inter-American Studies and World Affairs* 15:3 (1973), 285–307. This essay concludes that political instability in the Caribbean poses no major threat to the United States.

34:28 Moran, C. "The Evolution of Caribbean Strategy." *U.S. Naval Institute Proceedings* 68:3 (1942), 365–73. The diversity of political and economic factors among the Caribbean nations contributed to the U.S. position as sole enforcer of the region's security.

Perkins, D. *The United States and the Caribbean* (2:311) emphasizes 20th-century U.S.-Caribbean relations, including U.S. economic interests. In the second edition, Perkins contends that altered conditions have made the maintenance of good relations more difficult.

34:29 Plank, John N. "The Caribbean: Intervention When and How." *Foreign Affairs* 44:1 (1965), 37–48. Plank warns that communist influence in the Caribbean could increase unless the United States actively encourages political democracy, economic well-being, and social justice.

34:30 Sáenz, Vincente. *Centro América en pie* [In support of Central America]. Mexico, D.F.: Liberacion, 1944. Sáenz criticizes the good neighbor policy of the United States for maintaining Central American dictators.

34:31 Saxe-Fernández, John. "The Central American Defense Council and Pax Americana." In Irving Louis Horowitz, Josue De Castro, and John Gerassi, eds., *Latin American Radicalism: A Documentary Report on Left and Nationalist Movements*. New York: Random House, 1969, pp. 75–101. This essay argues that the United States aims to train Central American armed forces to resist counterinsurgency in order to maintain the social stratified order.

34:32 Schreiber, Anna P. "Economic Coercion as an Instrument of Foreign Policy: U.S. Economic Measures against Cuba and the Dominican Republic." *World Politics* 25:3 (1973), 387–413. This essay traces the deterioration of U.S.-Cuban relations following the accession to power of Fidel Castro, and the subsequent U.S. economic retaliation against Cuba and all countries that traded with it.

Thomas, A. V. W., and Thomas, A. J., Jr. *Non-Intervention: The Law and Its Import in the Americas* [1500–1955] (2:274) seeks to clarify the meaning of intervention and nonintervention as related to U.S. relations with Latin America.

34:33 "U.S. Strategies for Central America." *Latin America and Empire Report* 8:5 (1973), 1–39. This account deals with three separate topics: the Central American Common Market, the Central American Defense Council, and U.S. investment in the region. The essays indict the United States for dominating Central American affairs.

34:34 Welles, Sumner. "Intervention and Interventions." *Foreign Affairs* 26:1 (1947), 116–33. Welles argues that when the United States abandoned its policy of intervention in Central America during the 1930s better relations followed. Based on this example, he calls for outlawing intervention by large states in the affairs of smaller states.

Wright, T. P., Jr. *American Support of Free Elections Abroad* (2:133) is a critical, although uneven, treatment of eight Central American and Caribbean countries, which questions the goals and techniques of U.S. policy.

Economic Relations

34:35 Arévalo, Juan José. *The Shark and the Sardines*. Trans. by June Cobb and Raul Osequeda. New York: Stuart (1956), 1961. Written by a former president of Guatemala, this is a classic polemic, highly critical of U.S. policies (1900–1954). Its value derives from being a heralded expression of Latin American opinion of the United States.

34:36 Axline, W. Andrew. *Caribbean Integration: The Politics of Regionalism*. New York: Nichols, 1979. Axline provides an excellent review of integration theory and its application to the Caribbean, with an explanation of those factors militating against integration.

34:37 Cochrane, James D. "U.S. Attitudes towards Central American Integration." *Inter-American Economic Affairs* 18:2 (1964), 713–91. Through its assistance programs, both bilateral and regional, the United States has established its interest in Central American integration.

34:38 Congreso Centroamericano de Estudiantes de Derecho Sobre Integración Política de Istmo. *Integración política de Centroamericano* [Political integration of Central America]. Guatemala City: Editorial Universitaria Centroamericana, 1966. This is a basic source for the study of the movement for Central American integration.

34:39 Landry, David M. "U.S. Policy and Lessons Learned from the Central American Economic Integration Experience." *Southern Quarterly* 11:4 (1973), 297–308. Landry describes the positions of Presidents Lyndon Johnson and Richard Nixon concerning a Latin American common market. Latin American economic integration should be encouraged, but the barriers raised in each country by special pressure groups impede cooperation.

34:40 May, Stacy, and Plaza, Galo. *The United Fruit Company in Latin America*. Washington, D.C.: National Planning Association, 1958. This is an analysis of the company's economic impact upon Latin America.

34:41 McCann, Thomas P. *An American Company: The Tragedy of United Fruit*. New York: Crown, 1976. Written by a former company official, this volume is critical of the company's relationship with the Latin Americans. It is especially valuable for the years after 1951.

34:42 Rosenblum, Jack J. "El Interés Norteamericano en la Integración Económica Centroamericano [North American interest in the economic integration of Central America]." *Foro Internacional* 13:42 (1972), 27–44. Rosenblum argues tht the United States supports the Central American Common Market because it contributes to continued U.S. hegemony in the region.

34:43 Schmitter, Philippe C. *Autonomy or Dependence as Regional Integration Outcomes: Central America*. Berkeley, Calif.: Institute of International Studies, 1972. Although the United States has promoted Central American integration, it has acted bilaterally to protect its economic interests in the region.

34:44 U.S. Agency for International Development. Regional Office for Central America and Panama. *Economic Integration Treaties of Central America*. Guatemala City, 1966. This pamphlet lists the six treaties providing for Central American economic integration (1959–1960).

34:45 Wionczek, Miguel S. "Change and the Role of Integration: The Latin American Free Trade Area and the Central American Common Market." In Richard B. Gray, ed., *Latin America and the United States in the 1970s*. Itasca, Ill.: Peacock, 1971, pp. 177–217. A critical analysis of U.S. foreign economic policy toward Latin America, which charges that idealism will result only in disillusionment.

Area Handbooks

Prepared by Foreign Area Studies of American University, each *Area Handbook* concentrates upon the post–World War II period, providing a basic understanding of the social, economic, political, and military institutions of each nation. Each volume usually includes an extensive bibliography.

34:46 Black, Jan Knippers, et al. *Area Handbook for Cuba.* Washington, D.C.: G.P.O., 1976.

34:47 Black, Jan Knippers, et al. *Area Handbook for Trinidad and Tobago.* Washington, D.C.: G.P.O., 1976.

34:48 Blutstein, Howard I., et al. *Area Handbook for Costa Rica.* Washington, D.C.: G.P.O., 1970.

34:49 Blutstein, Howard, et al. *Area Handbook for Honduras.* Washington, D.C.: G.P.O., 1971.

34:50 Blutstein, Howard, et al. *Area Handbook for El Salvador.* Rev. ed. Washington, D.C.: G.P.O., 1979.

34:51 Dombrowski, John, et al. *Area Handbook for Guatemala.* Washington, D.C.: G.P.O., 1970.

34:52 Kaplan, Irving, et al. *Area Handbook for Jamaica.* Washington, D.C.: G.P.O., 1976.

34:53 Ryan, John, et al. *Area Handbook for Nicaragua.* Washington, D.C.: G.P.O., 1970.

34:54 Weil, Thomas. *Area Handbook for the Dominican Republic.* Washington, D.C.: G.P.O., 1973.

34:55 Weil, Thomas, et al. *Area Handbook for Haiti.* Washington, D.C.: G.P.O., 1973.

34:56 Weil, Thomas, et al. *Area Handbook for Panama.* Washington, D.C.: G.P.O., 1972.

Personalities

Additional references on individuals may be found in Chapter 1, "Biographical Data."

AMERICAN

See Chapter 24, "Personalities" and "Presidential Administrations," for additional references.

Lyndon B. Johnson

See Chapter 24, "Personalities" and "The Johnson Years," for additional references.

34:57 Goldboom, Maurice. "Johnson So Far." *Commentary* 39:6 (1965), 47–65. A former foreign service officer indicts LBJ's foreign policy for being too greatly influenced by former Secretary of State Acheson's advocacy of power rather than morality. The Dominican Republic is given as one illustration.

Johnson, L. B. *The Vantage Point: Perspectives on the Presidency, 1963–1969* (24:120) is bland and defensive but does contain references to Caribbean affairs, especially the Dominican Republic episode (1965).

John F. Kennedy

See Chapter 24, "Personalities" and "The Kennedy Years," for additional references.

Paterson, T. G. "Bearing the Burden: A Critical Look at JFK's Foreign Policy" (29:33) contains a review of the Cuban missile crisis.

Schlesinger, A. M., Jr. *A Thousand Days: John F. Kennedy in the White House* (24:215) discusses the Bay of Pigs and Cuban missile crisis episodes. Chapters entitled "The Bay of Pigs" and "Ordeal by Fire" discuss the varied advice Kennedy received from his advisers.

Walton, R. J. *Cold War and Counterrevolution: The Foreign Policy of John F. Kennedy* (24:216) concludes that, despite rhetoric to the contrary, Kennedy's foreign policy was that of continuing the cold war. The failure of the Bay of Pigs invasion encouraged him to succeed, and the missile crisis gave him confidence of success in Vietnam.

Robert F. Kennedy

See also Chapter 24, "The Kennedy Years."

Kennedy, R. F. *Thirteen Days: A Memoir of the Cuban Missile Crisis* (29:120) is a day-by-day account of White House decisionmaking.

Schlesinger, A. M., Jr. *Robert Kennedy and His Times* (29:34) discusses the Cuban missile crisis.

Henry A. Kissinger

See also Chapter 24, "Personalities" and "The Nixon-Ford Years."

34:58 Kessler, Francis. "Kissinger's Legacy: A Latin American Policy." *Current History* 72:424 (1977), 76–78. After years of neglect, Kissinger successfully opened a new dialogue with Latin America based upon the U.S. need for natural resources. The Panama Canal Treaty negotiations illustrated the new dialogue.

John Bartlow Martin

Martin, J. B. *Overtaken by Events: The Dominican Crisis from the Fall of Trujillo to the Civil War* (34:129) is by a former ambassador to the Dominican Republic who later became President Johnson's personal envoy charged with resolving the political crisis.

34:59 Martin, John Bartlow. *United States Policy in the Caribbean*. Boulder, Colo.: Westview, 1978. Martin calls for a special U.S. relationship with the region, urging nonintervention but supporting a strong naval presence and military training assistance programs. Bibliography.

Franklin D. Roosevelt

See Chapters 20, 21, 22, and 23, "Personalities," for additional references.

Gellman, I. F. *Roosevelt and Batista: Good Neighbor Diplomacy in Cuba, 1933–1945* (21:265).

Others

34:60 Bonsal, Philip W. *Cuba, Castro and the United States*. Pittsburgh: University of Pittsburgh Press, 1971. Bonsal, U.S. ambassador to Cuba during Castro's ascent to power, provides a personal account of that period, and a criticism of U.S. influence.

Braden, S. *Diplomats and Demagogues: The Memoirs of Spruille Braden* (35:64) defends his conservative view of the Latin American political structure.

Briggs, E. O. *Farewell to Foggy Bottom* (24:168) is critical of constant rotation of the diplomatic corps and the politicizing of ambassadorial posts.

34:61 Sands, William F. *Our Jungle Diplomacy.* Chapel Hill: University of North Carolina Press, 1944. The experiences of an American diplomat to Central America, who is severely critical of the work of the State Department and organization of the diplomatic service.

Smith, E. E. T. *The Fourth Floor: An Account of the Castro Communist Revolution* (34:98) charges the Eisenhower administration with a pro-Castro attitude. By a former ambassador to Cuba.

CARIBBEAN AND CENTRAL AMERICAN

Fulgencio Batista

34:62 Batista, Fulgencio. *Cuba Betrayed.* New York: Vintage, 1962. Batista, writing in exile, attempts to defend his record. A great portion of the book answers Castro's charges against him.

34:63 Chester, Edmund. *A Sergeant Named Batista.* New York: Holt, 1954. This first full-length biography of Batista in English is favorably slanted toward the Cuban dictator.

Juan Bosch

Bosch, J. *De Cristóbal Colón a Fidel Castro: El Caribe frontera imperial* (34:15).

34:64 Bosch, Juan. *The Unfinished Experiment: Democracy in the Dominican Republic.* New York: Praeger, 1965. Bosch charges that Trujillo's continued influence prevents the development of a meaningful democracy—covers the post-Trujillo period, May 1961 to May 1964.

34:65 Bosch, Juan. *Pentagonism: A Substitute for Imperialism.* New York: Graves, 1968. A harsh criticism of U.S. policy in the Dominican Republic by ex-President Bosch. The original was published as *El Pentagonismo: Sustituto del imperialismo* (Mexico, D.F.: Siglo Veintiuno, 1968).

Fidel Castro

34:66 Bonachea, Rolando E. *A Briefly Annotated Bibliography of Fidel Castro's Works, 1959–1970.* Pittsburgh: University of Pittsburgh Center for International Studies, 1973. This pamphlet is an excellent guide to Castro's writings and speeches.

34:67 Castro, Fidel. *Revolutionary Struggle: Volume I (1947–1958) of the Selected Works of Fidel Castro.* Ed. by Rolando E. Bonachea and Nelson P. Valdés. Cambridge, Mass.: MIT Press, 1972. A useful, substantial collection of Castro's numerous communications, it is preceded by more than 100 pages of historical and biographical material. Extensive bibliography.

34:68 Clark, Joseph. "Thus Spake Fidel Castro." *Dissent* 17:11 (1970), 38–56. After examining Castro's speeches, Clark concludes that Castroism is an ideological maverick and that Castro's dictatorship could result in the same conditions that caused Batista's fall in 1959.

34:69 Matthews, Herbert L. *Fidel Castro.* New York: Simon & Schuster, 1969. Matthews sympathizes with Castro's goals and objectives, and argues for a change in the U.S. attitude toward Cuba.

François Duvalier

34:70 Diederich, Bernard, and Burt, Al. *Papa Doc: The Truth about Haiti Today.* New York: McGraw-Hill, 1969. Diederich had been a resident of Haiti for fourteen years prior to his expulsion in 1963. With fellow journalist Al Burt, he is very critical of Duvalier's rule in Haiti. A rather lurid story, but vivid and informal.

34:71 Gingras, Jean Pierre O. *Duvalier, Caribbean Cyclone: The History of Haiti and Its Present Government.* New York: Exposition, 1967. This is a critical evaluation of Duvalier's regime and an invitation to revolution.

José Figueres

34:72 Ameringer, Charles D. *Don Pepe: A Political Biography of José Figueres of Costa Rica.* Albuquerque: University of New Mexico Press, 1978. The author has written a laudatory biography of a prominent figure in Costa Rican politics. Figueres is presented as a champion of democracy and the lower classes, and one who looked to the United States for hemispheric leadership. Bibliography.

34:73 Kantor, Harry. *Bibliography of José Figueres.* Tempe: Arizona State University Press, 1972. This pamphlet is a list of works by and about one of Costa Rica's most significant political figures.

Ernesto "Ché" Guevara

34:74 Cambini, Hugo. *El Ché Guevara.* Buenos Aires: Paidás, 1968. A biography of Ché Guevara, it begins with his youth in Argentina and ends with his attempt to form a guerrilla movement in Bolivia.

34:75 Guevara, Ernesto. *Che: Selected Works of Ernesto Guevara.* Ed. by Rolando E. Bonachea and Nelson P. Valdés. Cambridge, Mass.: MIT Press, 1969. This is a collection of the writings, speeches, interviews, and letters of Ché Guevara. The Bolivian diary is not included.

34:76 James, Daniel. *Ché Guevara: A Biography.* New York: Stein & Day, 1969. A full-length study of the myth-enshrouded *guerrillero* whom the author sees as "more the apostle of violence than the maker of revolution, more the agent of destruction than the builder of a continent."

34:77 Sauvage, Leo. *Che Guevara: The Failures of a Revolutionary.* Englewood Cliffs, N.J.: Prentice-Hall, 1973. The author provides a description of Ché's inability to achieve any of his major aims, and doubts Ché's qualities of humanity and compassion.

Michael Manley

34:78 Hale, Bob. "Michael Manley: Jamaica's Born-Again Socialist." *Christian Century* 94:39 (1977), 1117–19. In this interview, Manley reaffirms his belief that socialism answers Jamaica's needs, and at the same time draws U.S. ire.

34:79 Manley, Michael. "Overcoming Insularity in Jamaica." *Foreign Affairs* 49:1 (1970), 100–10. At the time, Manley was leading opposition spokesman, advocating a foreign policy independent of the United States, and toward Caribbean regionalism.

Anastasio Somoza

34:80 Halftermeyer, Gratus. *El General Anastasio Somoza, su vida y su obra* [General Anastasio Somoza: his life and his work]. Managua: Nacional Imprenta, 1957. A government pamphlet which applauds Somoza's contributions to Nicaragua.

34:81 Lernoux, P. "Somozas of Nicaragua." *Nation* 225:3 (1977), 72–77. This is a brief, critical survey of the Somoza family's activities.

Rafael Leonidas Trujillo

34:82 Crassweller, Robert D. *Trujillo: Life and Times of a Caribbean Dictator.* New York: Macmillan, 1966. A comprehensive and well-balanced work, it is based upon a wide range of sources. Extensive bibliography.

34:83 Galindez, Jesus de. *La Era de Trujillo* [The Trujillo era]. Santiago, Chile: Editorial del Pacífico, 1956. This is one of the best studies of Trujillo's dictatorship. The footnotes provide leads to source material.

Hardy, O. "Rafael Leonidas Trujillo Malina: The United States' Postwar Attitude toward the Dictatorships" (34:24).

Others

Arévalo, J. J. *The Shark and the Sardines* (34:35) is an attack upon the United States and its business interests by a former Guatemalan president.

34:84 Pippin, Larry L. *The Remón Era: An Analysis of a Decade of Events in Panama, 1947–1957.* Stanford, Calif.: Institute of Hispanic American and Luso-Brazilian Studies, 1964. The author suggests that Remón represented Panama's lower socioeconomic classes, and sought to improve their lot by increasing Panama's share of canal benefits. Extensive bibliography.

Toriello, G. *La batalla de guatemala* (34:203) contains charges, by the former Guatemalan foreign minister, that U.S. actions in Guatemala during 1954 ended the good neighbor policy.

34:85 Williams, Eric E. *Inward Hunger: The Education of a Prime Minister.* Chicago: University of Chicago Press, 1971. This is the political biography of the Prime Minister of Trinidad and Tobago.

34:86 Ydígoras Fuentes, Miguel, with Rosenthal, Mario. *My War with Communism.* Englewood Cliffs, N.J.: Prentice-Hall, 1963. Ousted from power in Guatemala in a 1963 coup, General Ydígoras relates his activities against communist pressure and describes his years in office and the unceasing internal pressures from Castro's Cuba.

The Caribbean

CUBA

See under "Personalities" for Fidel Castro, Ché Guevara.

34:87 Halperin, Maurice. *The Rise and Decline of Fidel Castro: An Essay in Contemporary History.* Berkeley: University of California Press, 1972. Several chapters are devoted to the Cuban-Soviet-American triangle from the Cuban perspective. This narrative probes for Cuban motivations and reactions. Bibliography.

34:88 Johnson, Leland L. "U.S. Business Interests in Cuba and the Rise of Castro." *World Politics* 17:3 (1965), 440–59. Johnson discusses the role that U.S. investment in Cuba may have played in helping to shape political relations between the United States and Cuba during the early years (1959–1964) Fidel Castro was in power.

Langley, L. D. *The Cuban Policy of the United States: A Brief History* [1776–1962] (2:314) provides a good brief introduction to the issues arising from Castro's anti-American policies.

34:89 Maris, Gary L. "International Law and Guantanamo." *Journal of Politics* 29:2 (1967), 261–86. Maris examines the Permanent Treaty with Cuba (1903), under which the United States maintains a leasehold on the naval base at Guantánamo Bay, Cuba. Under the treaty, Cuban sovereignty is "real and basic," while American "control is complete."

34:90 McGaffey, Wyatt, and Barnett, Clifford. *Twentieth Century Cuba: The Background of the Castro Revolution.* Garden City, N.Y.: Doubleday, 1965. This is an important study for understanding Cuba's social, political, and economic structures, and their relationship to Castro's revolution. Extensive bibliography.

Thomas, H. *Cuba: The Pursuit of Freedom* [1762–1968] (2:315) is an excellent introduction.

Batista Regime to 1959

See "Personalities," especially Fulgencio Batista, Franklin D. Roosevelt.

Gellman, I. F. *Roosevelt and Batista: Good Neighbor Diplomacy in Cuba, 1933–1945* (21:265) is an excellent analysis of U.S. policy; although the good neighbor policy assisted in maintaining the status quo, the Cubans also contributed to their own stagnation.

Smith, R. F. *The United States and Cuba: Business and Diplomacy, 1917–1960* (21:267) charges that U.S. policy had been dictated by business interests which contributed to the status quo rather than the professed ideals of self-determination.

34:91 Suarez-Rivas, Eduardo. *Un Pueblo Crucificado* [A crucified nation]. Coral Gables, Fla.: Service Offset, 1964. A political study (1923–1959), it is supportive of Fulgencio Batista.

34:92　Thomas, Hugh. "Origins of the Cuban Revolution." *World Today* 19:10 (1963), 448–60. The Cuban revolt of 1959 was the culmination of a series of thwarted revolts, primarily caused by the sugar industry.

Rise of Castro, to 1961

See under "Personalities," especially Philip W. Bonsal (under "Others").

34:93　Benitez, Fernando. *La batalla de Cuba* [The battle for Cuba]. Mexico, D.F.: Ediciones Era, 1960. A laudatory view of Castro's movement, this account is critical of U.S. policy toward the revolution.

34:94　Cuba. Ministerio de Relaciones Exteriores [Ministry of Foreign Relations]. *A nueva diplomacia Cuba* [Cuba's new diplomacy]. Havana: Nacional Imprenta, 1959. This pamphlet contains an official statement of Cuba's foreign policy, expressing opposition to an inter-American police force, hostile dictatorships, and denials of Cuban threats to the security of other Caribbean states.

34:95　Draper, Theodore. *Castro's Revolution: Myths and Realities.* New York: Praeger, 1962. This analysis of Castro's revolution denies that peasant groups played a significant role, as pro-Castro supporters have argued.

34:96　Draper, Theodore. *Castroism: Theory and Practice.* New York: Praeger, 1965. Together with the volume above, this account presents a searching, critical analysis of Castro's Cuba and its peculiar relationship to the communist movement. Bibliographical footnotes.

34:97　Matthews, Herbert. *The Cuban Story.* New York: Braziller, 1961. In a sympathetic account of Castro's revolution, Matthews suggests that the United States should endeavor to shape nascent revolutionary forces into a democratic image.

34:98　Smith, Earl E. T. *The Fourth Floor: An Account of the Castro Communist Revolution.* New York: Random House, 1962. A former ambassador to Cuba charges that the Eisenhower administration and State Department officials had a pro-Castro attitude which permitted his coming to power.

34:99　Suárez, Andrés. *Cuba: Castroism and Communism, 1959–1960.* Cambridge, Mass.: MIT Press, 1967. A former Castro official portrays the Cuban dictator as a skillful politician in this carefully researched work. Excellent bibliographical footnotes.

34:100　Williams, William A. *The United States, Cuba and Castro: An Essay on the Dynamics of Revolution and the Dissolution of Empire.* New York: Monthly Review Press, 1962. The author contends that the United States is to blame for the extreme leftward movement of Castro.

Bay of Pigs Episode

See under "Personalities," especially John F. Kennedy.

34:101　Hunt, Howard. *Give Us This Day.* New York: Arlington House, 1973. A former CIA agent writes that the Bay of Pigs invasion was a justified attempt to overthrow Castro.

34:102　Johnson, Haynes B., et al. *The Bay of Pigs: The Leader's Story of Brigade 2500.* New York: Norton, 1964. Based primarily on interviews with Cuban exiles, the account reviews Washington's decisions as seen by leaders of the invasion force.

34:103　MacGerman, Joseph E. "Bay of Pigs Revisited." *Military Review* 57:4 (1971), 77–85. This essay argues that despite the invasion's failure and resulting humiliation of the United States, the training of exiles for counter-insurgency remained advantageous for the United States—mostly in terms of cost and low risk.

34:104　Szulc, Tad, and Meyer, K. E. *The Cuban Invasion: The Chronicle of a Disaster.* New York: Praeger, 1962. This journalistic account provides an overall picture and places the blame for the invasion's failure on the CIA and the Joint Chiefs of Staff.

34:105　Wyden, Peter. *Bay of Pigs: The Untold Story.* New York: Simon & Schuster, 1979. This is the most complete account to date of this ill-conceived plot; it rests heavily upon interviews with participants. Bibliography.

Missile Crisis, 1962

See Chapter 29, "Cuban Missile Crisis, 1962," for the U.S.-U.S.S.R. perspective; also see under "Personalities," especially John F. Kennedy, Robert F. Kennedy.

Abel, E. *The Missile Crisis* (29:91) is a journalistic chronology of the crisis based on this correspondent's personal experiences and conversations with several of the participants. Gives significance to the role of Robert F. Kennedy.

Allison, G. T. *Essence of Decision: Explaining the Cuban Missile Crisis* (29:93) presents the logic and assumptions used by most of the analysts who explain the crisis events.

34:106 Castro, Fidel. *Atlas Armas*. Havana: Gobierno Municipal Revolucionario, 1963. Castro reviews the missile crisis and conversations with U Thant.

Dinerstein, H. S. *The Making of a Missile Crisis, October 1962* (29:101) analyzes the crisis and choices before the administration.

Divine, R. A., ed. *The Cuban Missile Crisis* (29:102) is a well-balanced anthology, including interpretations of Soviet motivations and the continuing debates over President Kennedy's actions.

34:107 Seydon, G. Smith. "Public Diplomacy and the Missiles of October." *Naval War College Review* 24:2 (1971), 28–43. Seydon demonstrates Kennedy's orchestrated use of public statements to warn Russia of the seriousness of the U.S. purpose.

34:108 "U.S. Quarantine of Cuba, October 1962." *American Journal of International Law* 57:3 (1963), 515–65; 588–604. This is a collection of essays by legal scholars interpreting the legality of the quarantine.

Relations since 1962

34:109 Mesa-Lago, Carmelo. *Cuba in the Nineteen Seventies: Pragmatism and Institutionalization*. Rev. ed. Albuquerque: University of New Mexico Press, 1978. The author predicts that Soviet influence will remain, although Cuba will seek increased contacts with the outside world. End notes.

34:110 Petras, James F. "The U.S.-Cuban Policy Debate." *Monthly Review* 26:9 (1975), 22–33. Petras

examines the shift in views toward U.S. policy toward Cuba among significant congressmen.

34:111 Plank, John N., ed. *Cuba and the United States: Long Range Perspectives*. Washington, D.C.: Brookings Institution, 1967. Ten scholarly essays survey various aspects of U.S.-Cuban relations. They form valuable work for understanding the Cuban Revolution. Extensive bibliography.

34:112 Quester, George H. "Missiles in Cuba, 1970." *Foreign Affairs* 49:3 (1971), 493–506. Quester argues that a Soviet submarine base at Cienfuegos may be strategically desirable as a deterrent in the balance of terror.

34:113 Raymond, Walter J. "The Feasibility of Rapprochement between the Republic of Cuba and the United States: The Case of the Guantanamo Naval Base." *Caribbean Quarterly* 21:1/2 (1975), 35–46. Despite less sabre-rattling by the Ford-Kissinger team, Castro's uncompromising hard line caused the continuation of a cold war view between the two nations.

34:114 Viator. "Cuba Revisited after Ten Years of Castro." *Foreign Affairs* 48:2 (1970), 312–21. This essay argues that dependence on Russia must be broken and a return to the profit motive established if Cuba is to improve its economy.

U.S. Economic Embargo

34:115 Dent, David, and O'Brien, Carol. "The Politics of the U.S. Trade Embargo of Cuba, 1959–1977." *Towson State Journal of International Affairs* 12:1 (1977), 43–60. The authors examine the rationale and effectiveness of economic coercion, through embargo, of Cuba's exports to the United States (1959–1977).

34:116 González, Edward. "The United States and Castro: Breaking the Deadlock." *Foreign Affairs* 50:4 (1972), 722–37. González suggests that the United States should take the initiative in ending the Cuban boycott.

34:117 Volsky, George. "Cuba's Foreign Policy." *Current History* 70:2 (1976), 69–72. The United States was unsure of Cuba's international position and foreign trade needs, thus failed to respond to Castro's 1975 overtures for improved relations.

U.S., Cuba, and Africa

See Chapter 37, "Angolan Revolution, 1961–1975."

Bender, G. J. "Angola, the Cubans, and American Anxieties" (37:200) finds that the United States sees the Cuban presence in Angola as merely an extension of Soviet influence.

34:118 Dominguez, Jorge. "Cuban Foreign Policy." *Foreign Affairs* 57:1 (1978), 83–108. The author believes that the United States has no leverage to alter Cuban military presence in Africa.

34:119 Durch, William J. "The Cuban Military in Africa and the Middle East: From Algeria to Angola." *Studies in Comparative Communism* 11:1/2 (1978), 34–74. Cuba's military intervention in Angola follows the pattern of its past activities. Castro has developed over the past 15 years a policy of aiding colonial liberation movements. Cuba intervened with combat troops in Algeria, Syria, and Angola from 1961 to 1976 and sent training detachments to many African states.

34:120 Janke, Peter. "Marxism in Africa: The Cuban Connection." *Midstream* 24:7 (1978), 3–10. The Marxist-Leninist African states, Angola, Ethiopia, and Mozambique, are far from reaching their objectives but have depended since 1975 on the military forces or a small support staff of political commissars and media persons from Cuba and East Germany.

34:121 Levesque, Jacques. "La Guerre d'Angola et le role de Cuba en Afrique" [The Angola War and Cuba's role in Africa]. *Etudes Internationales* [Canada] 9:3 (1978), pp. 429–34. This essay reviews the position taken by Russia, China, and several South American and African states toward Cuba's military role in Angola in 1975.

DOMINICAN REPUBLIC

See under "Personalities," especially Juan Bosch, Lyndon B. Johnson, John Bartlow Martin, Rafael Leonidas Trujillo.

Atkins, G. P., and Wilson, L. C. *The United States and the Trujillo Regime* [1904–1960s] (2:316) provides a survey of these relations.

Fagg, J. E. *Cuba, Haiti and the Dominican Republic* [1750–1960] (2:318) is a useful introduction to the history of the Dominican Republic and its neighbors.

34:122 Plastrich, Stanley. "Bosch and Balaguer: Dominican Roulette, the Politics of Rival Caudillos." *Dissent* 17:6 (1970), 517–30. This examination of the Dominican political arena recommends that the United States not become involved.

Demise of Trujillo, 1960–1962

Schreiber, A. P. "Economic Coercion as an Instrument of Foreign Policy: U.S. Economic Measures against Cuba and the Dominican Republic" (34:32) discusses U.S. economic coercion (1960–1962) to bring down the Trujillo dictatorship.

34:123 Slater, Jerome. "The United States, the Organization of American States and the Dominican Republic (1961–1962)." *International Organization* 18:2 (1964), 268–91. Slater provides an excellent analysis of U.S. intervention in the context of inter-American diplomacy.

Crisis of 1965

See under "Personalities," especially Lyndon B. Johnson, John Bartlow Martin.

34:124 Draper, Theodore. "The Dominican Intervention Reconsidered." *Political Science Quarterly* 86:1 (1971), 1–36. Draper argues that the United States should have supported the pro-Bosch forces in 1965, rather than risk emergence and domination of Castroite leaders.

34:125 Draper, Theodore. *The Dominican Revolt: A Case Study in American Policy.* New York: Commentary, 1968. This is a perceptive analysis of the nature of U.S. intervention during the Dominican crisis, based largely on articles published in *Commentary*.

34:126 Ferguson, Yale H. "The Dominican Intervention of 1965: Recent Interpretations." *International Organization* 27:4 (1973), 517–48. Ferguson reviews current articles and books on the 1965 crisis, and concludes the Constitutionalists would have won if the United States had not intervened. From the beginning the United States was deeply suspicious of the rebels and saw the coup as possibly Communist- or Castro-oriented.

Franck, T. M., and Weisband, E. *Word Politics: Verbal Strategy among the Superpowers* (29:6) compares the Brezhnev Doctrine (Czechoslovakian intervention, 1968) and Johnson Doctrine (Dominican crisis, 1965), both of which seemed to justify great power intervention in their respective spheres: the U.S.S.R. in Eastern Europe and the U.S. in Latin America. Yet each rejects the doctrine of the other, while using the same rhetoric to explain their interventions.

34:127 Gleijeses, Piero. *The Dominican Crisis: The 1965 Constitutionalist Revolt.* Baltimore: Johns Hopkins University Press, 1978. Because the United States erroneously interpreted the revolt as Castro-oriented rather than a legitimate movement to end political oppression, the United States intervened. The action only further inflamed Latin opinion against the United States.

34:128 Lowenthal, Abraham F. *The Dominican Intervention.* Cambridge: Harvard University Press, 1972. This volume will stand for some time as the comprehensive account of U.S. intervention. It demonstrates the traditional patterns that influence U.S. decisions. Extensive bibliography.

34:129 Martin, John Bartlow. *Overtaken by Events: The Dominican Crisis from the Fall of Trujillo to the Civil War.* Garden City, N.Y.: Doubleday, 1966. President Lyndon Johnson's personal envoy charged with solving the 1965 crisis begins with the view that the Communists had taken over the revolution.

34:130 Odena, Isidoro, Jr. *La intervención ilegal en Santo Domingo* [The illegal intervention in Santo Domingo]. Buenos Aires: Desarvelo, 1965. An Argentine, severely critical of U.S. action in 1965, warns against the creation of a permanent inter-American peace force.

34:131 Parkinson, F. "Santo Domingo and After." *The Yearbook of World Affairs* 20 (1966), 143–68. This is a provocative review of the Dominican intervention in May 1965, and its hemispheric implications.

34:132 Slater, Jerome N. "The Dominican Republic, 1961–66." In Barry M. Blechman and Stephen S. Kaplan, eds., *Force without War: U.S. Armed Forces as a Political Instrument.* Washington, D.C.: Brookings Institution, 1978, pp. 289–342. This essay deals with the ouster of Trujillo in 1961 and focuses on the 1965 crisis which found U.S. military forces intervening in the Dominican civil strife.

34:133 Slater, Jerome N. *Intervention and Negotiation: The United States and the Dominican Revolution.* New York: Harper & Row, 1970. A well-documented work which refutes the State Department theory that the United States had to act quickly in order to prevent a communist takeover. Extensive bibliography.

34:134 Slater, Jerome N. "The Limits of Legitimization in International Organizations: The Organization of American States and the Dominican Crisis." *International Organization* 23:1 (1969), 48–72. Slater concludes that the use of the OAS was peripheral to American interests.

34:135 Szulc, Tad. *Dominican Diary.* New York: Delacorte, 1965. A firsthand account by a *New York Times* correspondent, it contends that American officials failed to understand the struggle, resulting in a policy that strengthened exremists, both left and right.

34:136 Thomas, Aaron J., Jr., and Thomas, Ann Van Wynen. *The Dominican Republic Crisis, 1965: Background Paper and Proceedings of the Ninth Hammarskjöld Forum.* Dobbs Ferry, N.Y.: Oceana, 1967. This essential work for any study of the Dominican crisis discusses legal and political issues. Extensive bibliography.

34:137 Wilson, Larman C. "La intervención de las Estados Unidos en el Caribe: La crisis de 1965 en las República Dominican" [United States intervention in the Caribbean: the 1965 crisis in the Dominican Republic]. *Revista de Política Internacional* 122:4 (1972), 37–82. The author concludes that U.S. intervention was an illegal and unilateral exercise of military force.

HAITI

See under "Personalities," especially François Duvalier.

34:138 Bellgegarde-Smith, Patrick. "Haiti, Perspectives of Foreign Policy: An Essay on the International Relations of a Small State." *Caribbean Quarterly* 20:3/4 (1974), 21–38. Haitian foreign policy sought to insure a wide latitude of domestic freedom in order to guarantee national survival. Within this framework, the Haitians understood the U.S. goal of Caribbean stability.

34:139　Charlus, Gerard P. "Haití: Otra vez los Marines?" [Haiti: again the marines?]. *Pensamiento Crítico* 32:9 (1969), 165–81. Claiming the Haitian government was propped by U.S. arms, the author predicts future domestic violence, resulting in American intervention.

34:140　Efron, Edith. "The 'New Movement' in Haiti." *Caribbean Quarterly* 4:1 (1955), 14–31. Efron argues that the struggle to overcome the impact of elite rule will take generations.

Heinl, R. D., and Heinl, N. G. *Written in Blood: The Story of the Haitian People, 1492–1971* (2:319) covers the political-military history of Haiti until Duvalier's death in 1971, but it fails to discuss the nation's socioeconomic aspects.

34:141　Joseph, Raymond A. "Haiti: Ripe for the Marines?" *Nation* 208:13 (1969), 392–97. As long as the State Department continues to condone Duvalier and his actions, the United States must bear some responsibility for the chaos that will follow his ouster.

34:142　Logan, Rayford W. "U.S. Colonial Experiment in Haiti." *World Today* 17:10 (1961), 435–46. The United States has done little to ameliorate Haiti's economic, social, and political stagnation, resulting in skepticism toward the Alliance for Progress.

34:143　Manigat, Leslie F. *Haiti of the Sixties: Object of International Concern.* Washington, D.C.: Center for Foreign Policy Research, 1964. These lectures by a Frenchman warn that Haiti, because of its political dictatorship, economic and social backwardness, is ripe for communism. Extensive bibliography.

34:144　Moore, O. Ernest. "Is Haiti Next?" *Yale Review* 51:2 (1961), 254–63. To save Haiti from following Cuba's path, Moore recommends an economic and social development program.

34:145　Rotberg, Robert I., with Clague, Christopher K. *Haiti: The Politics of Squalor.* Boston: Houghton Mifflin, 1971. The authors concentrate upon the social and economic history of Haiti. However, their bibliography includes several post-World War II references on foreign affairs.

JAMAICA

See under "Personalities," especially Michael Manley.

34:146　"Caribbean Conflict: Jamaica and the U.S." *NACLA Report on the Americas* 12:3 (1978). In an effort to control the island's bauxite reserves through multinational corporations, the United States was in conflict with Prime Minister Michael Manley's "Democratic Socialism."

34:147　O'Flaherty, J. D. "Finding Jamaica's Way." *Foreign Policy,* no. 31 (1978), 137–58. This is a critical assessment of Manley's socialistic programs at home and efforts to steer clear of the United States in pursuit of a Caribbean policy.

34:148　Phillips, James J. "Jamaica: A Repeat of the Chile Pattern?" *Christian Century* 93:30 (1976), 815–17. Because Jamaica's economy is closely linked to the United States, there exists the possibility that the United States might intervene in the island's turbulent domestic politics.

GRENADA, TRINIDAD, AND TOBAGO

34:149　Buckley, William F., Jr. "Meanwhile at Caribbean East." *National Review* 31:47 (1979), 1515. A charge that U.S. policy toward the Marxist-leaning state of Grenada is incoherent.

34:150　"Focus on Trinidad." *NACLA's Latin America and Empire Report* 10:8 (1976), 14–30. Trinidad's government has placed itself in consortium with the U.S. oil companies at the sacrifice of its own workers.

34:151　Matthews, Harry G. *Multinational Corporations and Black Power.* Cambridge, Mass.: Schenkman, 1976. Matthews analyzes the conflicting goals of multinationals and "black power" nationalists in Trinidad and Tobago.

34:152　Ryan, Selwyn D. "The Transition to Nationhood in Trinidad and Tobago, 1797–1962." 2 vols. Ph.D. diss., Cornell University, 1972. This study covers the nation's history, and provides an excellent bibliography.

34:153　Walker, Annette. "The New Jewel: Revolution in Grenada." *NACLA: Report on the Americas* 14:1 (1980), 40–43. Walker offers a favorable view of the 1979 coup engineered by Maurice Bishop and his development plans, which include Cuban assistance.

Central America

34:154   U.S. House. Committee on Foreign Affairs. Hearings; *Human Rights in Nicaragua, Guatemala, and El Salvador: Implications for U.S. Policy.* 94th Cong., 2d Sess., 1976. These hearings include testimony charging the Central American governments with gross violations of civil and political rights, and pleas for the United States to pressure for correction of such abuses.

PANAMA

34:155   Alfaro, Ricardo J. *Media Siglo de Relaciónes entre Panamá y los Estados Unidos* [A half-century of relations between Panama and the United States]. Panama: Secretaría de Información, 1959. This pamphlet is important for its explanation of Panamanian demands after World War II.

34:156   Cameron, Duncan H. "The Panama Canal Policy of the United States." *Midwest Quarterly* 11:2 (1970), 141–52. Cameron argues that the dangers to the Panama Canal come from Panama itself and the Americans in the zone.

34:157   Ealy, Lawrence O. "The Isthmanian Republic in World War II." In his *The Republic of Panama in World Affairs, 1903–1957.* Philadelphia: University of Pennsylvania Press, 1957, pp. 105–23. The Panamanian government fully cooperated with U.S. efforts to keep suspected belligerents from the canal. Extensive bibliography.

34:158   Georgetown University. Center for Strategic Studies. *Panama Canal Issues and Treaty Talks.* Washington, D.C.: Georgetown University, 1967. The majority at this symposium supports the need for new treaties, with greater benefits for Panama. The minority opinion is that surrender of the canal would result in loss of U.S. prestige and power in all Central America.

34:159   Langley, Lester. "U.S.-Panamanian Relations since 1941." *Journal of Inter-American Studies and World Affairs* 12:3 (1970), 339–66. This is an excellent discussion of Panama's pressure for increased authority in the zone, keying upon the crises of 1947, 1955, and 1964.

Liss, S. B. *The Canal: Aspects of United States–Panamanian Relations* (2:328) emphasizes the cold war years, with an analysis of communist influence in Panama.

34:160   Padelford, N. J. "Neutrality, Belligerency, and the Panama Canal." *American Journal of International Law* 35:1 (1941), 55–89. An explanation of how the United States preserved the canal's neutrality and provided exceptions to Panamanian and British ships during World War II.

34:161   Tate, M. D. "Panama Canal and Political Partnership." *Journal of Politics* 25:1 (1963), 119–38. To cool down Panamanian pressure and improve its canal benefits, the author suggests that Panamanians share in canal security, that Panama gear her military and agriculture to the zone's needs, and the United States raise the annuity and fly both flags in the zone.

34:162   Torrijos Herrera, Omar. *La Batalla de Panamá* [Panama's battle]. Buenos Aires: Editorial Universiteria de Buenos Aires, 1973. Responsibility for Panama's economic and social plight is placed upon its ruling elite and U.S. ownership of the canal.

34:163   U.S. Department of State. *United States and Panama.* Washington, D.C.: Department of State, 1952. A detailed account of canal and zone defense, based upon State Department documents, can be found in part 2—"The War Period," pp. 83–197.

34:164   Woolsey, L. H. "Executive Agreements Relating to Panama: Relation to the Treaty Making Power." *American Journal of International Law* 37:3 (1943), 482–89. This is a summary of the congressional debates over the 1942 executive agreements which transferred certain rights and property to Panama.

1955 Treaty

34:165   Ealy, Lawrence O. "Eisenhower and the Panamanian Questions." In his *Yanqui Politics and the Isthmian Canal.* University Park: Pennsylvania State University Press, 1971, pp. 109–19. Ealy finds that despite the 1955 treaty, the exclusive U.S. operation of the canal and control over the canal zone continued to increase Panamanian nationalism.

34:166   Fenwick, Charles G. "The Treaty of 1955 between the United States and Panama." *American Journal of International Law* 49:4 (1955), 543–47.

Although the treaty appears generous to Panama, U.S. interests were not sacrificed by the 1955 agreement.

34:167 LaFeber, Walter, "Arias, Remon and Eisenhower." In his *The Panama Canal: The Crisis in Historical Perspective.* New York: Oxford University Press, 1978, pp. 90–131. LaFeber sees the emergence of Panama's national guard as a political force and pressure from lower socioeconomic groups increasing Panama's demands for canal benefits.

34:168 U.S. Senate. Committee on Foreign Relations. Hearings; *Executive F, the Treaty of Neutral Understanding and Cooperation with the Republic of Panama.* Washington, D.C.: G.P.O., 1955. These hearings discuss the 1955 treaty's merits and demerits.

1964 Riots and Aftermath

34:169 Baxter, Richard R., et al. *The Panama Canal.* Hammarskjöld Forums. New York: New York City Bar Association, 1964. This pamphlet provides an excellent discussion of U.S. legal rights in the zone, which have protected U.S. interests but contributed to Panama's frustrations, as registered in the 1964 riots. Extensive bibliography.

34:170 Ealy, Lawrence O. "President Johnson Fails to End the Panama Problem." In his *Yanqui Politics and the Isthmian Canal.* University Park: Pennsylvania State University Press, 1971, pp. 120–37. Ealy shows that domestic problems in both Panama and the United States influenced the failure to conclude a new treaty (1967–1968).

34:171 Fenwick, Charles G. "Legal Aspects of the Panama Case." *American Journal of International Law* 58:2 (1964), 436–41. This is an explanation of Panama's legal rights under the Rio Treaty to call for a meeting of consultation regarding the 1964 riots, and charge the United States with aggression.

34:172 International Commission of Jurists. Investigating Committee. *Report on the Events in Panama, January 9–12, 1964.* Geneva: International Commission of Jurists, 1964. An examination of the riots, without charging a specific group with responsibility, it emphasizes U.S. dominant position as underlying cause of Panamanian discontent.

34:173 LaFeber, Walter. "Chiari, Johnson and Dobbs." In his *The Panama Canal: The Crisis in Historical Perspective.* New York: Oxford University

Press, 1978, pp. 132–59. LaFeber argues that Panama's oligarchical leaders failed to obtain canal benefits for lower socioeconomic groups, resulting in a military coup d'etat in 1968.

34:174 Rippy, J. Fred. "United States and Panama: The High Cost of Appeasement." *Inter-American Economic Affairs* 17:4 (1964), 87–94. A charge that continued U.S. generosity to Panama, in terms of canal benefits, has not relieved the republic's economic and social problems; nor would nationalization of the canal solve these problems.

Torrijos Regime

34:175 Burns, E. Bradford. "Panama's Struggle for Independence." *Current History* 66:389 (1974), 19–22. Panama's negotiating objective is to gain complete sovereignty over the canal, a position firmly entrenched in nationalism, a position which the State Department has failed to understand.

34:176 Flood, Daniel J. "U.S. Policy and Soviet Objectives in the Panama Canal." *East Europe* 20:9 (1971), 13–22. A longtime congressional defender of U.S. interests in the canal zone fears that Russia would benefit from the vacuum created by the United States acceding to Panama's demands.

34:177 Frank, Thomas, and Weisband, Edward. "Panama Paralysis." *Foreign Policy,* no. 21 (1975), 168–87. The U.S. loss of the canal would have minimal adverse effect upon the U.S. economy or security interests.

34:178 LaFeber, Walter. "Torrijos, Kissinger and Carter." In his *The Panama Canal: The Crisis in Historical Perspective.* New York: Oxford University Press, 1978, pp. 160–61. LaFeber finds that the Torrijos regime, responsive to the socioeconomic needs of the republic, successfully negotiated favorable canal treaties with the United States.

34:179 Maehling, Charles, Jr. "The Panama Canal: A Fresh Start." *Orbis* 20:4 (1977), 1007–23. Maehling suggests that internationalization of the canal would best serve U.S. economic and strategic interests.

34:180 Minor, Kent J. "The United States and Panamanian Relations, 1958–1973." Ph.D. diss., Case Western Reserve University, 1976. This is a detailed account of relations, illustrating the development of coercive efforts by Panama, particularly under Torrijos. Extensive bibliography.

34:181 Ropp, Steve C. "Military Reformism in Panama: New Directions or Old Inclinations." *Caribbean Studies* 12:3 (1972), 45–63. Despite the reform tendencies of General Omar Torrijos, Panama's national guard, like the deposed civilian aristocracy, may be less inclined toward social change.

34:182 Rosenfeld, Stephen S. "The Panama Negotiations—A Close Run Thing." *Foreign Affairs* 54:1 (1975), 1–13. Since 1968, General Torrijos turned the treaty negotiations into an international issue, as Secretary Kissinger attempted to conciliate Panamanian nationalism.

34:183 Ryan, Paul. "Canal Diplomacy and U.S. Interests." *U.S. Naval Institute Proceedings* 103:1 (1977), 43–53. Ryan argues that the canal should not be surrendered as long as it has strategic value to the United States.

1978 Treaty

34:184 Baldwin, Hanson W. "The Panama Canal: Sovereignty and Security." In *A New Treaty for Panama?* Washington, D.C.: American Enterprise Institute for Public Policy Research, 1977, pp. 12–34. A summary of arguments against the 1977 treaties which emphasizes Panama's inability to operate and maintain the canal, and the adverse effect the loss of the canal would have on U.S. economic and strategic interests.

34:185 Lowenthal, Abraham, and Charlton, Milton. "The United States and Panama: Confrontation or Cooperation?" In *A New Treaty for Panama?* Washington, D.C.: American Enterprise Institute for Public Policy Research, 1977, pp. 2–11. In this synthesis of arguments supporting and opposing the 1977 treaties, the authors debate whether turning over the canal to Panama is in the best interests of the United States.

34:186 McGee, Gale. "Why We Should Ratify Panama Canal Treaties." *Orbis* 21:3 (1978), 535–45. McGee, a former senator and current U.S. permanent representative to the OAS, argues for ratification of the canal treaties in order to improve the U.S. image in Latin America.

34:187 U.S. Department of State. *Selected Documents: Panama Canal Treaties.* Nos. 6A, 6B, 6C.

Washington, D.C.: G.P.O., 1977. These three pamphlets present excerpts of the treaties' most important clauses and the Carter administration's justification for accepting the treaties.

34:188 U.S. Senate. Committee on Foreign Relations. Hearings; *Panama Canal Treaties.* 4 vols. Washington, D.C.: G.P.O., 1977–1978. The committee's hearings contain pro and con arguments ranging from administrative supports to interest groups against the proposed treaties.

GUATEMALA

34:189 Castro, Jose Rafael. *Política internacional de Guatemala, 1944–1957* [Guatemalan international policy, 1944–1957]. Havana: Imprint "H.C.," 1957. This account argues that Guatemala continued to follow U.S. leadership in the early cold war years.

34:190 Catalón, J. Luis. *Solidaridad Americana* [American solidarity]. Guatemala City: Hispania, 1944. This pamphlet pays tribute to the ideals of the Atlantic Charter and Pan-Americanism.

34:191 Martins, Carlos D. *La conferencia de Bogotá y la posición de Guatemala* [The Bogota Conference and Guatemala's position]. Guatemala City: Departamento de Publicidad de la Presidencia de la Republic, 1948. Martins warns that continued American solidarity must not be allowed to degenerate into acceptance of U.S. domination.

34:192 Melville, Thomas. *Guatemala: The Politics of Land Ownership.* New York: Free Press, 1971. Emphasizing the period since 1945, Melville is concerned that land ownership by the few, including United Fruit Company, leaves the door open for revolution. Extensive bibliography.

34:193 Pike, Frederick B. "Guatemala, the United States and Communism in the Americas." *Review of Politics* 17:2 (1955), 232–61. Developments in Guatemala since 1944 demonstrate that the United States is concerned with communism while the Latin Americans have been more concerned with their own economic development.

34:194 Schneider, Ronald M. *Communism in Guatemala, 1944–1954.* New York: Praeger, 1958. This account places emphasis upon the years preceding the 1954 revolution.

34:195 U.S. Department of State. *Intervention of International Communism in Guatemala.* Washington, D.C.: G.P.O., 1954. This report emphasizes the growth of communism in Guatemala from 1944 until 1954.

1954 Intervention

See under "Personalities," especially, under "Others," Miguel Ydígoras Fuentes.

34:196 Chardkoff, Richard B. "Communist Toehold in the Americas." Ph.D. diss., Florida State University, 1967. This is an excellent survey of the communist role in the 1954 revolution.

34:197 Fenwick, Charles G. "Jurisdictional Questions Involved in the Guatemalan Revolution." *American Journal of International Law* 48:4 (1954), 597–602. Fenwick examines the U.S. legal position to protect rights of citizens, i.e., United Fruit Company, under international law.

34:198 Galich, Manuel. *Por que lucha Guatemala: Arévalo y Arbenz: des hombres contro un imperio* [The reasons for the Guatemalan struggle: Arévalo and Arbenz: two men against an empire]. Buenos Aires: Elmer, 1952. This is a responsibly written critique of U.S. intervention in 1954.

34:199 Gordon, Max. "A Case History of U.S. Subversion: Guatemala, 1954." *Science and Society* 35:2 (1971), 129–55. An examination of the Jacobo Arbenz Guzmán regime (1944–1954), it reviews the nature of U.S. investments in Guatemala and the cause of events leading to the overthrow of Arbenz.

34:200 Grant, Donald. "Guatemala and United States Foreign Policy." *Journal of International Affairs* 9:1 (1955), 64–72. U.S. intervention in 1954 might have been avoided had assistance been provided for the Arévalo government.

34:201 McDermott, Louis M. "Guatemala, 1954: Intervention or Aggression?" *Rocky Mountain Social Science Journal* 9:1 (1972), 79–88. McDermott analyzes U.S. interference in Guatemala during 1944 to 1954 in order to clarify the terms *intervention* and *aggression.* Neither U.S. fear of communism in Guatemala nor the Guatemalan expropriation of the United Fruit Company fit the limits of intervention in the traditional view.

34:202 Taylor, Philip B., Jr. "The Guatemalan Affair: A Critique of United States Foreign Policy." *American Political Science Review* 50:3 (1956), 787–807. Intervention in 1954 was unnecessary as a communist government in Guatemala would not have substantially threatened U.S. regional security.

34:203 Toriello, Guillermo. *La batalla de Guatemala* [The battle for Guatemala]. Mexico, D.F.: Cuadernos Americanos, 1955. The former Guatemalan foreign minister charges that U.S. actions in the 1954 intervention cancelled out what remained of the good neighbor policy.

U.S.-Guatemala Relations since 1955

34:204 Baver-Paiz, Alfonso. "The 'Third Government of the Revolution' and Imperialism in Guatemala." *Science and Society* 30:2 (1970), 146–65. This essay concludes that the Julio Cesar Mendez Montenegro government should be condemned for selling out to U.S. imperialism.

34:205 Crain, D. A. "Guatemalan Revolutionaries and Havana's Ideological Offensive of 1966–1968." *Journal of Inter-American Studies* 17:2 (1975), 175–205. Crain analyzes the change in Castro's relations with Guatemala's guerrillas. Notes and bibliography provide excellent references.

34:206 Jenkins, Brian, and Sereseres, Cesar D. "U.S. Military Assistance and the Guatemalan Armed Forces." *Armed Forces and Society* 3:4 (1977), 575–95. The U.S. provided Guatemala with military assistance loans and direct aid grants (1953–1973). Local guerrillas were the reason for the aid, but it produced a more modern and professional army that became politicized.

34:207 Sloan, John W. "Electoral Frauds and Social Change: The Guatemalan Example." *Science and Society* 34:1 (1970), 78–91. A combination of forces— the United States, the Catholic church, and land-owners—will never permit a genuine revolutionary government to emerge in Guatemala.

34:208 U.S. House. Committee on Foreign Affairs. *Report on the Special Study Mission to Guatemala.* Washington, D.C.: G.P.O., 1957. This report contains justification for continued aid to the government of Carlos Castillo Armas.

COSTA RICA

See under "Personalities," José Figueres.

34:209   Bell, John P. *Crisis in Costa Rica: The Revolution of 1948.* Austin: University of Texas Press, 1971. This analysis of the various groups in Costa Rica which supported José Figueres Ferrer in the 1948 revolution examines the effect of U.S. and Latin American foreign policies on the outcome of the revolt. Bibliography.

34:210   DeWitt, R. Peter, Jr. *The Inter-American Development Bank and Political Influence: With Special Reference to Costa Rica.* New York: Praeger, 1977. This account charges that the United States is using the Inter-American Development Bank to cause Costa Rican dependency upon the U.S. economy, a model that is applicable to all of Latin America.

34:211   English, Burt H. *Liberación Nacional in Costa Rica: The Development of a Political Party in a Transitional Society.* Gainesville: University of Florida Press, 1971. English studies Costa Rica's Liberal party and its policies, including those toward the United Fruit Company. Extensive bibliography.

34:212   Heath, Dwight B. "Costa Rica and Her Neighbors." *Current History* 58:2 (1970), 95–101. Despite the "white myth," which alleges Costa Rican superiority, that nation shares the same economic, social, and political problems as its Central American neighbors, including U.S. domination.

34:213   Kantor, Harry. *The Costa Rican Elections of 1953: A Case Study.* Gainesville: University of Florida Press, 1968. This pamphlet provides an excellent analysis of José Figueres's victory, illustrating the important role of Costa Rican Communists.

34:214   Saxe-Fernández, John. "The Militarization of Costa Rica." *Monthly Review* 24:1 (1972), 61–70. The author concludes, based upon U.S. public documents, that the Costa Rican police force had been converted into an anti-guerrilla army.

NICARAGUA

See under "Personalities," Anastasio Somoza.

34:215   Chamorro Cardenal, Pedro Joaquín. *Diario de un preso* [Diary of a prisoner]. Managua: Editorial

Nuevos Horizontes, 1963. A critic of the Somozas presents his views on politics and the corruption of the ruling regime, taken from notes he wrote in prison. He was later assassinated.

34:216   Chamorro Cardenal, Pedro Joaquín. *Estripe Sangrienta: Los Somoza* [Bloodstained stock: the Somozas]. Mexico, D.F.: Patria y Libertad, 1957. An exile attacks the Somoza family and its rule; he is also critical of U.S. policy for supporting the tyrannical rule.

34:217   Crawley, Eduardo. *Dictators Never Die: A Portrait of Nicaragua and the Somozas.* New York: St. Martin's Press, 1979. An Argentine journalist's chronicle of the struggle of unrest in Nicaragua.

34:218   Gámez, José D. *Historia Moderna de Nicaragua* [Modern history of Nicaragua]. Managua: Banco de America, 1975. This account points to economic and social accomplishments of Somoza, applauds his foreign policy, and plays down opposition pressure, including that from exiles abroad. Extensive bibliography.

34:219   [Koch, Edward]. "The Koch–State Department Correspondence on U.S. Relations with Nicaragua." *Inter-American Economic Affairs* 29:4 (1976), 85–93. The correspondence between Congressman Edward Koch and the State Department in 1976, where Koch is critical of the Somoza regime and continued U.S. military and economic aid to it.

34:220   Mendieta Alfaro, Róger. "Panorama política nicaraguense" [Nicaragua's political panorama]. *Combate* 3:15 (1961), 48–54. The author concludes that many Nicaraguans share Fidel Castro's anti-American feelings because of the close relationship between the United States and Somoza.

34:221   Millett, Richard. *Guardians of the Dynasty.* New York: Orbis Books, 1977. In a well-documented study of Nicaragua's national guard, the author demonstrates the U.S. role, which enabled the Somoza dictatorship to survive. Extensive bibliography.

34:222   Petersen, J. A. "Somoza vs. the Americas." *Nation* 168:1 (1949), 63–66. Somoza's support of the December 1948 Costa Rican incursion left him isolated from his American neighbors.

Overthrow of Somoza

34:223 Bendana, Alejandro. "Crisis in Nicaragua." *NACLA: Report on the Americas* 12:6 (1978), 1–42. The author is a Nicaraguan who sees the "rebels" as a legitimate movement to overthrow the elite-sponsored U.S. dictatorship in Nicaragua.

34:224 Pearson, Neale J. "Nicaragua in Crisis." *Current History* 76:44 (1979), 78–80. This essay provides a brief review of Somoza's final days in power.

HONDURAS

34:225 Clowand, Davis J. *Schools in Banana Land*. Boston: United Fruit Company, 1965. In this pamphlet a former United Fruit Company manager in Honduras reports on paternalistic company-sponsored projects there.

34:226 Martínez, Jose F. *Honduras Historica* [Historic Honduras]. Tegucigalpa: Imprenta Nacional, 1974. This account contains a survey of the nation's history, including statements on foreign policy principles.

34:227 Paredes, Lucas. *Liberalismo y nacionalismo: Transfugismo politico* [Liberalism and nationalism: political disaffection]. Tegucigalpa: Imprenta Honduras, 1963. Paredes provides an account heavily documented with newspaper articles from *El Dia,* organ of the Honduran Liberal party, covering the period between the 1930s and 1960s.

34:228 Ponce, Reynolds. *La United Fruit Co. y lo segunda republica* [The United Fruit Co. and the Second Republic]. Comayagua, Honduras: Bulnes, 1960. This is an attack against the United Fruit Company and a call to oust the company from Honduras.

34:229 Villeda Morales, Ramón. *La defensa de la democracia frente a la amenaza communista* [The defense of democracy against the communist

menace]. Tegucigalpa: Imprenta Nacional, 1969. A pamphlet of official government statements which stresses the extent of communist inroads, and the steps taken to overcome its influence.

34:230 Vivas, Rafael Leivas. *Honduras: Fuerzas Armadas* [Honduras: armed forces]. Tegucigalpa: Universidad Nacional Autonoma de Honduras, 1973. Vivas claims the armed forces have been upgraded to suppress internal and external challenges.

EL SALVADOR

34:231 Lemus, José Maria. *Pueblo Ejército y doctrina revolucionaria* [National army and revolutionary doctrine]. San Salvador: Ministeria del Intérior, 1952. President Lemus explains his use of the army as a tool for social revolution.

34:232 Lernoux, P. "El Salvador Suppresses Church." *Nation* 225:4 (1977), 100. This is an exposé of President Humberto Romero's attack upon the Catholic church for defending the rights of lower classes. It is important for understanding the dichotomy of El Salvador's society.

34:233 Marlos, Salvador R. *Centro-América en el conflicto* [Central America in conflict]. San Salvador: Cisneros, 1942. This pamphlet is an explanation of El Salvador's support for the Allied cause in World War II.

34:234 Mullin, Jay. "Military Affairs Abroad: Salvador-Honduras War, 1969." *Air University Review* 21:3 (1970), 87–92. U.S. refusal to give requested military aid contributed to a cessation of hostilities in this border conflict.

34:235 White, Alastair. *El Salvador*. New York: Praeger, 1973. A history of the country since its colonial days, it emphasizes contemporary politics, economics, social structure. International relations are covered both within the Central American framework and the world at large.

35

United States, Mexico, and South America since 1941

Contributing Editor
LARRY D. HILL
Texas A&M University

Contents

Introduction

United States policy toward Latin America since 1941 has been designed generally to make the western hemisphere a safe sphere of influence. Even so, policymakers in Washington did not consistently give high priority to relations with Latin America. Periods of intense official interest were followed by lapses into relative indifference. This waxing and waning was determined largely by considerations of national security, with economic and ideological factors also exerting considerable influence.

At the beginning of World War II, the United States, seeking to maintain a solid hemispheric front against Axis subversion and aggression, gave high priority to inter-American affairs. By the late war years, however, the United States became increasingly preoccupied with developments in other parts of the world, and early in the cold war, relations with Latin America were given low priority. Even the strengthening of the inter-American system, a process that culminated in 1948 with the creation of the Organization of American States, was entered into by the United States with the view of checking the influence of the Soviet Union and deterring the spread of communism in the western hemisphere.

Throughout the 1950s the United States continued to concentrate on waging cold war in Europe and Asia. As requests from Latin America for aid to match that being directed to other parts of the world were repeatedly ignored in Washington, hemispheric solidarity deteriorated. A series of shocks in the late fifties and early sixties caused the United States to again give high priority to Latin American affairs. Officials from the United States met with repeated and violent demonstrations in South America. Fidel Castro seized power in Cuba, became a proselytizer of social revolution, and aligned with the Soviet Union. In response the United States launched the Alliance for Progress, with the avowed purpose of fostering economic development, social uplift, and political democracy in Latin America. Results never matched aspirations, and by the late sixties, Washington was concentrating on military and political strategems to forestall communist penetration of the hemisphere.

As the government and people of the United States became preoccupied with domestic strife and the war in Southeast Asia, interest in Latin America again waned. Throughout the 1970s most initiatives to improve hemispheric relations came from Latin America. By 1980 it appeared that the United States did not have a Latin American policy.

Bilateral relations with Mexico and South American nations have also been marked by intermittent periods of tension and cordiality. Although the imperatives of national security have been a major factor, frequently economic considerations, especially those involving United States capital investments, have had an even greater impact on relations. Over the past forty years, the United States and Mexico have gradually developed a cordial but guarded relationship based on their ability to compromise on a variety of complex issues. In South America, the United States has enjoyed the most satisfactory relationship with Brazil; with Argentina, the least.

Just as World War II elevated Latin American affairs to a position of first priority, so it produced in this country a dramatic expansion of interest in Latin American studies. Indeed, most of the scholarly literature relating to inter-Armerican affairs published in the United States during the past forty years was produced by persons with extensive training in one or more fields of Latin American studies. Each year from 1941 to 1945 Arthur P. Whitaker published a volume of essays entitled *Inter-American Affairs* (35:85). These compilations kept not only academicians but all interested Americans abreast of developments in Latin America. During the war university-trained Latin Americanists, many with graduate degrees, served the Department of State and Office of the Coordinator of Inter-American Affairs. Some of these scholars later produced important historical works. Among those dealing with Latin American relations, Laurence Duggan's *The Americas: The Search for Hemisphere Security* (2:279) and Bryce Wood's *The Making of the Good Neighbor Policy* (21:246) were especially influential. Duggan and Wood maintained that the good neighbor and wartime policies produced positive benefits for both the United States and Latin America.

The Organization of American States and the Alliance for Progress were also analyzed by persons directly involved in their operation. John C. Dreier (35:122), a ten-year ambassador to OAS, and William Manger (35:125), formerly assistant secretary general of the organization, cataloged its successes and called for its strengthening. State Department officials Lincoln Gordon (35:150) and William D. Rogers (35:156) asserted that the Alliance for Progress represented a genuine U.S. effort to promote reform in Latin America.

These intimately involved authors contributed to the development of an orthodox, or "liberal," interpretation of United States–Latin American relations. So did university scholars. The proponents of this orthodox interpretation assumed that there was a basic compatibility of interests between the United States and Latin America. Difficulties in relations were explained as resulting from cultural differences, temporary conflicts between private and national interests, and periodic lapses into disinterest on the part of the United States. Good intentions were generally accorded to U.S. policymakers, even if their efforts did not always produce satisfactory results. During the 1950s and early 1960s the liberal interpretation dominated writings on inter-American affairs.

Critically analytical works were produced from this orthodox perspective. Two of the most perceptive were Jerome Slater, *The OAS and United States Foreign Policy* (35:129), and Jerome Levinson and Juan de Onis, *The Alliance That Lost Its Way: A Critical Report on the Alliance for Progress* (35:152). The liberal interpretation could also be found in studies of U.S. relations with specific Latin American nations. Howard F. Cline's *The United States and Mexico* (2:299) and Frederick B. Pike's *The United States and the Andean Republics: Peru, Bolivia, and Ecuador* (2:267), plus Arthur P. Whitaker's two studies, *The United States and Argentina* (2:288) and *The United States and South America: The Northern Republics* (2:269), all revealed an in-depth understanding of the special problems of the countries treated.

Some accounts following the liberal interpretation were quite critical of U.S. policy. After perusing hundreds of Latin American newspapers, magazines, and journals, Donald M. Dozer demonstrated in *Are We Good Neighbors? Three Decades of Inter-American Relations, 1930–1960* (21:240) that the people of Latin America had good reason to be critical of the intentions as well as the outcomes of U.S. policies. Actually Dozer's critique was preceded by several Latin American polemics. Widely read in Latin America, books by Juan J. Arévalo (34:35), Ramón Oliveres (35:34), and Genaro Carnero Checa (35:27)

viewed U.S. policy as imperialistic. Carnero Checa, especially, took a position that would be repeated in scholarly works—that United States capitalist penetration had impoverished Latin America and sustained reactionary governments.

The Castro revolution in Cuba, and the shock waves it sent throughout Latin America, provided, perhaps, the greatest stimulus to the study of inter-American relations. Much of the output was in the liberal vein. Indeed, J. Lloyd Mecham's *A Survey of United States–Latin American Relations* (2:265) became a highly influential orthodox synthesis. Robert N. Burr's *Our Troubled Hemisphere* (35:100) defended the inter-American system and called for its overhaul. Yet with increasing frequency scholarly writers took the position that United States acts abroad were essentially destructive. Adopting a "radical" interpretation, they insisted that U.S. policy was determined by the imperatives of expansive capitalism. Policymakers had deliberately and continuously promoted the interests of North American capitalists operating in Latin America. Radicals admitted no compatibility of interests between the United States and Latin America; instead, they saw conflict. As the United States strove to dominate, Latin Americans sought sovereignty over their own economies.

A seminal work from a radical perspective is David Green's *The Containment of Latin America* (21:243). He views the United States as exploitive in developing the good neighbor policy and wartime cordiality with Latin America. Postwar monopolistic practices are examined in Samuel L. Baily, *The United States and the Development of South America, 1945–1975* (35:131). As the title of his book *Dollar Diplomacy Modern Style* (35:151) suggests, Simon G. Hanson claims that North American businessmen were the main beneficiaries of the Alliance for Progress. James Petras and Morris Morely (35:227) attribute the 1973 overthrow of Chile's Marxist president Salvador Allende to U.S. imperialist machinations. A British historian, Gordon Connell-Smith, provides a synthesis of radical interpretations in *The United States and Latin America* (2:261).

Latin American social scientists contributed a radical interpretation of their own—dependency theory. The basic premise of this model is that the economic development of Latin America has been determined and limited by the needs of the world's highly developed capitalist nations. Hence, problems produced by Latin American underdevelopment stemmed directly and indirectly from foreign capitalist expansion. Again, the United States was singled out as the main exploiter. Dependency theory was quickly appropriated by North American social scientists. A seminal essay by a North American scholar is Suzanne J. Bodenheimer's "Dependency and Imperialism: The Roots of Latin American Underdevelopment" (35:44).

The popularity of radical interpretations should not obscure the persistence of more moderate treatments. Some of these writings revised earlier revisions. Two essays published in 1973, one by Stephen S. Kaplan and Norman C. Bonsor (35:213), the other by Eric N. Baklanoff (35:217), argued that U.S. aid and capital investments produced positive as well as negative results in Latin America. Even more recently, two books, Randall B. Woods's *The Roosevelt Foreign-Policy Establishment and the "Good Neighbor"* (35:94) and Irwin F. Gellman's *Good Neighbor Diplomacy* (21:242), apply more complex and balanced interpretations than those previously offered by liberals or radicals.

With increasing frequency, accounts have appeared which argue that United States influence is declining in the hemisphere or that it was never as great as previously supposed. Herbert Goldhamer's *The Foreign Powers in Latin America* (35:105) traces the decline of unilateral dominance of U.S. capital. Arthur P. Whitaker, in *The United States and the Southern Cone: Argentina, Chile, and Uruguay* (2:270), notes that North American ability to manipulate affairs in that area has been exaggerated. By the late seventies political scientists Abraham F. Lowenthal (35:108) and Jerome Slater (35:113) could argue that while United States influence persists in Latin America, nowhere is it strong enough to be considered imperialistic.

Despite the outpouring of writings on United States–Latin American relations, few of the works may be considered definitive. In recent years the output of political scientists and economists has been greater than that of historians. Inaccessibility of materials has retarded multiarchival historical research. Availability of sources has resulted in the World War II period receiving the most attention. Yet there is a need for additional study. For example, there is no in-depth treatment of the Office of the Coordinator of Inter-American Affairs. United States wartime relations with Mexico need greater consideration, as does the "special relationship" that developed between the two countries in the forty years after 1940. As regards South American nations, many of the surveys of bilateral relations have been in print at least twenty years. There are no specialized studies of the Latin American policies of specific presidential administrations after that of Franklin D. Roosevelt. Economic relationships, especially those involving trade and the activities of specific North American companies, de-

serve additional treatment. There are few scholarly analyses of the impact of the Alliance for Progress on separate countries. Nor are there adequate comparative studies. Inter-American cultural relations is a field just beginning to receive attention. If United States hegemony in the western hemisphere is at an end, the study of its decline may offer clues for improving future inter-American relations.

Resources and Overviews

RESEARCH AIDS

While pertinent bibliographies and reference aids are listed here, there are more extensive lists in Chapter 1.

Bibliographies

Bartley, R. H., and Wagner, S. L. *Latin America in Basic Historical Collections: A Working Guide* [1492–1970] (1:265) describes the contents of library holdings related to Latin America.

Bayitch, S. A. *Latin America and the Caribbean: A Bibliographical Guide to Works in English* (1:115) lists books, articles, and pamphlets relating to several disciplines; these are classified by general topics and countries.

35:1 Chaffee, Wilber A., Jr., and Griffin, Honor M. *Dissertations on Latin America by United States Historians, 1960–1970: A Bibliography*. Austin: University of Texas, Institute of Latin American Studies, 1973. Entries are grouped by countries and alphabetically by author within each group, plus information on whether available on interlibrary loan or microfilm, and if dissertation appears in *Dissertation Abstracts*.

35:2 Chilcote, Ronald H. *Revolution and Structural Change in Latin America: A Bibliography on Ideology, Development and the Radical Left, 1930–1965*. 2 vols. Stanford, Calif.: Hoover Institution, 1970. This exhaustive, classified, annotated bibliography contains 10,005 citations to articles and books mainly in Spanish, English, Portuguese, and French. Introductions to each section assess the usefulness and availability of items cited. Subject, author, and periodical indexes.

Cosío Villegas, D., comp. *Cuestiones Internacionales de México: Una Bibliografía* (1:133) is an important bibliography whose scope is broader than the title suggests. Three of the eight sections deal specifically with Mexico; the other sections list works in international relations, U.S.–Latin American relations, and intra-American affairs.

Deal, C. W., ed. *Latin America and the Caribbean: A Dissertation Bibliography* (1:249) emphasizes the 1962 to 1977 period, and covers all disciplines; material taken from *Dissertation Abstracts* but with no annotation.

35:3 Feigin de Roca, Elisabeth, and Gaer de Sabulsky, Alicia, comps. *Historiografía Argentina, 1930–1970* [Argentine historiography, 1930–1970]. 2 vols. Buenos Aires: Librería Piloto, 1972. This extensive listing (5,097 titles) of books and articles published in Argentina covers the history of Argentina up to 1970. It is arranged chronologically with subject subdivisions. A historiographical essay and author index add to its usefulness.

Foreign Affairs Bibliography: A Selected and Annotated List of Books on International Relations (1:15) is very valuable for the period since 1941.

35:4 Greenleaf, Richard E., and Meyer, Michael C., eds. *Research in Mexican History: Topics, Methodology, Sources and a Practical Guide to Field Research.* Lincoln: University of Nebraska Press, 1973. This collaborative field research guide is one of the best of its kind in any field of history. The historiographical essays and bibliographies alone would make it worthwhile, but the tips on research and descriptions of libraries and archives make it an indispensable aid for research in U.S.-Mexican relations.

Griffin, C. C., ed. *Latin America: A Guide to the Historical Literature* [1776–1970] (1:118) is the best one-volume annotated bibliography relating to Latin American history in its broadest sense. It is logically and chronologically arranged; part 7 covers international relations since 1930. Extensive index.

35:5 Harmon, Ronald M., and Chamberlain, Bobby J. *Brazil: A Working Bibliography in Literature, Linguistics, Humanities, and the Social Sciences.* Tempe: Arizona State University Press, 1975. This unanno-

tated bibliography emphasizes basic works available in the United States, especially those published since 1960. It is arranged by subject and includes an author index.

Kantor, H. *A Bibliography of Unpublished Dissertations and Masters Theses Dealing with the Governments, Politics and International Relations of Latin America* (34:7) has entries dating from 1911, but emphasizes the years 1940 to 1952.

35:6 Levine, Robert M., ed. *Brazil: Field Research Guide in the Social Sciences.* New York: Columbia University, Institute of Latin American Studies, 1966. This guide was produced by a generation of Brazilianists who wrote their chapters while in the midst of doctoral research. The early chapters give general hints of value, as does the chapter entitled "Foreign Relations," by Charles Daugherty. Bibliography.

35:7 Lombardi, John V.; Damas, German Carrera; and Adams, Roberta E., comps. *Venezuelan History: A Comprehensive Working Bibliography.* Boston: G. K. Hall, 1977. A logical starting place for the study of Venezuelan history, this bibliography lists over 4,000 items in English and Spanish. Emphasizing those works published since World War II, it includes books, articles, and dissertations. Within broad categories, the organization is by author and title.

Molineu, H., comp. *Multinational Corporations and International Investment in Latin America: A Selected and Annotated Bibliography . . .* (1:33).

35:8 Norris, Robert E. *Guía Bibliografiá para el Estudio de la Historia Ecuatoriana* [A bibliographic guide to the study of the history of Ecuador]. Austin: University of Texas Press, Institute of Latin American Studies, 1978. Listing mainly books, articles, and printed documents, this bibliography is organized by historical periods and by major historical themes. Subject and author indexes.

35:9 Sable, Martin H. *The Guerrilla Movement in Latin America since 1950: A Bibliography.* Milwaukee: University of Wisconsin, Center for Latin America, 1977. Material is subdivided by countries and includes U.S. government documents as well as books, articles, and dissertations.

Trask, D. F.; Meyer, M. C.; and Trask, R. R., eds. *A Bibliography of United States–Latin American Relations since 1810* (1:120) is the single most useful bibliography on the subject. Arranged topically and chronologically, then by bilateral relations, it includes a highly usable table of contents and an author index. Meyer (1:119) supplements the original bibliography to 1978.

Trask, R. R. "Inter-American Relations" (1:121) is a historiographical essay, dealing with writings on U.S.–Latin American relations written since 1945.

U.S. Department of the Army. *Latin America and the Caribbean: Analytic Survey of the Literature* (1:122) is useful for contemporary books and articles, as well as background material, plus maps, for each country.

U.S. Library of Congress. Hispanic Division. *Handbook of Latin American Studies* (1:123) is the most current and most extensive summary of research and publications on Latin America in all fields. Each volume includes an author index, and there is a cumulative author index for the years 1936 to 1966.

Watson, G. H. *Colombia, Ecuador, and Venezuela: An Annotated Guide to Reference Materials in Humanities and Social Sciences* [1498–1970] (1:135) provides a critical analysis of reference materials.

Wilgus, A. C. *Latin America, Spain and Portugal: A Selected and Annotated Bibliographical Guide to Books Published in the United States, 1954–1974* (1:125) is organized by region, and then by country, with such subsections as history, politics, foreign relations, biography, and bibliography.

Indexes to Periodicals and Newspapers

Charno, S. M., comp. *Latin American Newspapers in United States Libraries: A Union List* (1:229) lists some 5,500 titles from Latin America and Puerto Rico held in seventy U.S. libraries.

35:10 Cox [Vagt], Barbara G. *HAPI: Hispanic American Periodicals Index.* Los Angeles: University of California, Latin American Center, 1975–. Annual listing by subject and author of articles of interest to Latin Americanists which appear in more than 200 major journals published in Latin America, the Caribbean, the United States and Europe. Also contains list of main subject headings used both in Spanish and Portuguese and a list of journals indexed.

35:11 Information Services on Latin America. *ISLA: Information Sources on Latin America.* Orinda,

Calif.: ISLA, 1970–. ISLA Clipping Services provides monthly comprehensive coverage of Latin American political, economic, and social news as published in eight major newspapers (*Christian Science Monitor, Journal of Commerce, Le Monde/Manchester Guardian, Los Angeles Times, Miami Herald, New York Times, Wall Street Journal, Washington Post*). Material is arranged by country and has a semiannual index.

35:12 Pan American Union. Columbus Memorial Library. *Index to Latin American Periodical Literature, 1929–1960.* 10 vols. Boston: G. K. Hall, 1962–1968. This is a basic eight volumes (1962) plus a two-volume supplement (1968). The periodicals indexed are generally of Latin American origin, but many are from the United States and other countries. These are cited whenever the articles contain information about Latin America or are by Latin American authors. Superseded by *Indice General de Publicaciones Periódicas Latino-Americanas* (1960–1970) and the *Hispanic American Periodical Index* (1975–).

35:13 Pan American Union. Columbus Memorial Library. *Indice General de Publicaciones Periódicas Latino-Americanas: Humanidades y Ciencias Sociales. Index to Latin American Periodicals: Humanities and Social Sciences.* Washington, D.C.: Pan American Union, 1961–1970. A quarterly publication that is the supplement to *Index to Latin American Periodical Literature 1929–1960.* It has been superseded by the *Hispanic American Periodical Index* (1975–), which plans eventually to cover the years 1971 to 1974.

Yearbooks and Other Aids

See also Chapter 24, "Yearbooks and Other Aids."

35:14 Facts on File. *Latin America.* New York: Facts on File, 1972–. A comprehensive annual survey of news development in Latin America and the Caribbean, it contains most of the material originally published in *Facts on File.*

Facts on File: A Weekly Digest with Cumulative Index (1:151).

Keesing's Contemporary Archives: Weekly Diary of World Events (1:152).

Political Handbook and Atlas of the World (1:144).

Document Collections

More general collections are listed in Chapter 2, and other collections may be found in "Personalities," below.

35:15   Burr, Robert, ed. *Latin America*. In Arthur M. Schlesinger, Jr., Gen. ed. Vol. 3 in *The Dynamics of a World Power: A Documentary History of United States Foreign Policy, 1945–1973*. New York: Chelsea House, 1973. This collection of 196 documents assembles in convenient form the essential documents of U.S.–Latin American foreign policy. The 33-page introduction places specific documents in context. Analytical index.

U.S. Department of State. *American Foreign Policy, 1950–1955: Basic Documents* (1:355) is a supplement to *A Decade of American Foreign Policy*, with a section on the western hemisphere.

U.S. Department of State. *American Foreign Policy: Current Documents, 1956–1967* (1:356) has for each year a one-volume collection which includes principal messages, addresses, statements, reports, diplomatic notes, and treaties of a given calendar year which indicate the scope, goals, and implementation of foreign policy. Each volume includes a section on the western hemisphere.

U.S. Department of State. *Foreign Relations of the United States* (1:358) contains documents bearing upon all topics relating to inter-American affairs and U.S. bilateral relations with Latin American nations. For each year (1941–1950s) there is at least one volume, and frequently more, which treats specifically the American republics or western hemisphere. Each volume has an analytical index.

U.S. Department of State. *Press Conferences of the Secretaries of State, 1922–1974* (1:360) is a microfilm of the typescript verbatim record of the conferences. An important source.

U.S. National Archives Microfilm Publications. *Purport Lists for the Department of State Decimal File, 1910–1944* (1:258) shows the diplomatic records available on microfilm from the National Archives.

U.S. Senate. Committee on Foreign Relations. *A Decade of American Foreign Policy: Basic Documents, 1941–1949* (23:20) is a collection of principal messages, addresses, statements, reports, diplomatic notes, and treaties with a section dealing specifically with the western hemisphere.

U.S. President. *Public Papers of the Presidents of the United States* [1945–] (1:362).

Indexes and Guides to Documents

35:16   Fernández Esquivel, Rosa M. *La Publicaciones Oficiales de México: Guía de Publicaciones periódicas y seriadas, 1937–1967* [The official publications of Mexico: guide to the periodical and serial publications, 1937–1967]. Mexico, D.F.: Universidad Nacional Autónomo de México, 1967. Besides listing the periodical and serial documents of the national government of Mexico, this guide analyzes their importance, origin, and distribution. The latest name of an agency is used in cataloging, with antecedents listed. There is an index to titles and a bibliography of works dealing with government documents of other countries.

35:17   Lombardi, Mary. *Brazilian Serial Documents: A Selective and Annotated Guide*. Bloomington: Indiana University Press, 1974. This guide is organized by issuing agency; as a result the table of contents provides an authentic table of organization of the Brazilian national government. The index provides an alphabetical listing cataloged through 1971.

35:18   Mesa, Rosa Quintero, comp. *Latin American Serial Documents: A Holdings List*. 12 vols. to date. Ann Arbor, Mich.: University Microfilms, 1968–. This projected series of nineteen volumes provides a guide to the more accessible published documents of Latin American governments. A rather broad interpretation of documents is used. Each volume covers a separate country.

OVERVIEWS

See Chapter 24, "Overviews," for surveys of American foreign affairs since World War II.

35:19   Atkins, G. Pope. *Latin America in the International Political System*. New York: Free Press, 1977. A comprehensive text on the international relations of Latin America (1810–1976), this volume is basically descriptive, although the first chapter does advance a few concepts drawn from systems of theory.

Arranged topically by chapters, the organization is more effective than a standard chronological approach. Extensive bibliography.

35:20 Calvert, Peter. *Latin America: Internal Conflict and International Peace.* New York: St. Martin's Press, 1969. This is a succinct outline of the political and diplomatic history of Latin America, concentrating on the 20th century. The central theme focuses on Latin American diplomats seeking to construct stable international relations in spite of internal instability. They have been adept at making common cause against external threats and at maximizing their powers in international bodies.

35:21 Davis, Harold E.; Finian, John J.; Peck, F. Taylor. *Latin American Diplomatic History: An Introduction.* Baton Rouge: Louisiana State University Press, 1977. This account treats Latin American relations (1493–1975) with the United States, as well as non-American nations, and interregional relations, Pan Americanism, and the OAS. It presents history from a Latin American perspective and from the viewpoints of the separate nations. Extensive bibliography.

35:22 Davis, Harold E., and Wilson, Larman C., eds. *Latin American Foreign Policies: An Analysis.* Baltimore: Johns Hopkins University Press, 1975. These essays explore the foreign policies of Latin American nations and demonstrate that Latin American nations share many policy objectives. Yet the conclusion emerges that it would be inaccurate to refer to Latin America as a bloc. The final chapter offers conclusions relating to the most powerful nations— Argentina, Brazil, Chile, Cuba, Panama, and Mexico. Bibliographical notes.

Duggan, L. *The Americas: The Search for Hemisphere Security* [1823–1948] (2:279) treats wartime relations and postwar relations.

35:23 Hilton, Ronald, ed. *The Movement toward Latin American Unity.* New York: Praeger, 1969. This collection of articles covers almost every aspect of Latin American integration.

35:24 Plaza, Galo. *Latin America: Today and Tomorrow.* Washington, D.C.: Acropolis, 1971. A distinguished statesman speaks out for democratic processes and for a liberal, evolutionary approach to political, social, and economic problems.

35:25 Ronning, C. Neale. *Law and Politics in Inter-American Diplomacy.* New York: Wiley, 1963.

A study of contemporary interpretations of inter-American law caused by changing political, social, and economic conditions in the western hemisphere.

U.S. and Latin America

Aguilar Monteverde, A. *Pan Americanism from Monroe to the Present: A View from the Other Side* [1821–1967] (2:259) presents a sweeping criticism of U.S. Latin American policies.

Arévalo, J. J. *The Shark and the Sardines* [1900–1954] (34:35) is a classic polemic, highly critical of U.S. policies.

35:26 Blasier, Cole. *The Hovering Giant: United States Responses to Revolutionary Change in Latin America.* Pittsburgh: University of Pittsburgh Press, 1976. This work compares U.S. responses to social revolutions in Mexico, Bolivia, Guatemala, and Cuba (1910–1964). This integrated account is arranged by stages in the revolutionary process and U.S. responses to those stages. Major features of the interpretation involve the impact of revolutionary seizures of U.S. properties and U.S. global strategies toward Germany and the Soviet Union on responses to revolution in Latin America. Notes.

35:27 Carnero Checa, Genaro. *El Aguila Rampante: El Imperialismo Yanqui Sobre América Latina* [The eagle rampant: Yankee imperialism over Latin America]. Mexico, D.F.: Ediciones Semanario Peruano, 1956. Along with Ramón Oliveres's *El Imperialismo Yanqui en América* (35:34), this anti-American polemic was widely read in Latin America during the 1950s. The author claims that U.S. capitalist penetration had impoverished the masses, impeded the development of new industries, and aided reactionary governments in Latin America. It is a country-by-country treatment.

Connell-Smith, Cornell G. *The United States and Latin America: An Historical Analysis of Inter-American Relations* [1776–1974] (2:261) is a synthesis of revisionist interpretations. Connell-Smith sees the United States as projecting a "self-image" as a world power benevolent in dealings with its neighbors; in fact, its relations with Latin America have been similar to those between European powers and their client states. Compare with Mecham (2:265).

35:28 Cosío Villegas, Daniel. *American Extremes.* Trans. by Américo Paredes. Austin: University of

Texas Press, 1964. A notable Mexican historian and essayist believes that U.S. business interests and military leaders had an unchallenged influence in developing policy toward Latin America. No friend of the Alliance for Progress, he was suspicious of U.S.-sponsored reform in Latin America. But he freely acknowledges that problems in Latin America did not arise exclusively or even primarily from the actions of the United States.

35:29 Franco, Pablo. *La influencia de las Estados Unidos en América Latina* [United States influence in Latin America]. Montevideo: Ediciones Tauro, 1967. A critique of the U.S. cultural, political, and economic influence in Latin America.

35:30 Gil, Federico G. *Latin American–United States Relations.* New York: Harcourt Brace Jovanovich, 1971. This brief survey (1821–1970) perceives cycles in inter-American relations, with periods of rising U.S. interest in Latin America, followed by declining interest, conflict, and almost total disregard. Two of the high points were the good neighbor policy and the Alliance for Progress. Suggested readings.

35:31 Lieuwen, Edwin. *United States Policy in Latin America.* New York: Praeger, 1965. This is a brief summary and interpretation of U.S.–Latin American relations, with emphasis on recent events. The author finds a U.S. determination to make Latin America a sphere of influence. As a strategic expression, that was particularly true since World War II. Bibliography.

35:32 Lodge, George Cabot. *Engines of Change: United States Interests and Revolution in Latin America.* New York: Knopf, 1970. A plea for the alignment of the United States with the forces of nontotalitarian revolutionary change in politics, religion, and society, with proposals for new administrative techniques and structures.

Mecham, J. L. *A Survey of United States–Latin American Relations* [1810–1964] (2:265) is a basic orthodox survey. Mecham maintains that U.S. policy has consistently been motivated by its own national security. Compare with Connell-Smith (2:261).

35:33 Needler, Martin C. *The United States and the Latin American Revolution.* Rev. ed. Los Angeles: University of California, Latin American Center Publications, 1977. U.S. understanding of Latin American revolutions has been hampered by narrow preoc-cupation with private interests, with shibboleths about national security that shroud real conditions, and with ideological fixations left over from an earlier generation. Extensive bibliography.

35:34 Oliveres, Ramón. *El Imperialismo Yanqui en América: La Dominación Política y Económica del Continente* [Yankee imperialism in the Americas: the political and economic domination of the continent]. Buenos Aires, 1952. A prominent Buenos Aires newspaper editor denounces U.S. activities (1941–1951) in Mexico, Venezuela, Peru, Bolivia, Chile, Brazil, Uruguay, and, especially, Argentina. He views the United States as bent on world domination and as using World War II to further that drive. He is a well-informed polemicist.

35:35 Palmer, Thomas W. *Search for a Latin American Policy.* Gainesville: University of Florida Press, 1957. This sweeping survey of U.S. political and economic relations (1933–1956) concludes that Latin America was justified in its disillusionment by U.S. treatment. Palmer characterized the status of Latin America in the overall policy of the United States as one of "strange loneliness."

35:36 Pike, Frederick B. "Corporatism and Latin American–United States Relations." *Review of Politics* 36:1 (1974), 132–70. This unique interpretation suggests how a corporate social structure in Latin America has influenced relations with the United States (1900–1972). Pike focuses on how the ruling elites have utilized U.S. economic involvement to sustain their power and how that involvement has often threatened their position.

35:37 Ramírez Necochea, Herman. *Los Estados Unidos y América Latina, 1930–1965* [The United States and Latin America, 1930–1965]. Santiago de Chile: Editora Austral, 1965. A Chilean Marxist historian argues that the United States has historically spoken in favor of Latin America reform while discouraging fundamental change. The good neighbor policy grew out of labor influence and the conscience of a few intellectuals, but was motivated by fear of outside aggression. The U.S. appeals for wartime solidarity were a mask for defending capitalist imperialism, while the Alliance for Progress was a modern version of dollar diplomacy.

Inter-American System

See "Organization of American States," below.

Ball, M. M. *The Problem of Inter-American Organization* [1889–1944] (2:276) provides a concise introduction to the Pan American system and its various organs.

Connell-Smith, G. *The Inter-American System* [1889–1965] (2:277) is a critical review of U.S. claims of success and, as such, the work provides a useful contrast to Mecham's (2:283) laudatory account.

35:38 Gardner, Mary A. *The Inter-American Press Association: Its Fight for Freedom of the Press, 1926–1960*. Austin: University of Texas Press, 1967. This is a useful study of a neglected field of inter-American relations.

35:39 Gregg, Robert W. *International Organization in the Western Hemisphere*. Syracuse, N.Y.: Syracuse University Press, 1968. Gregg's thoughtful essays critically examine the inter-American system as well as the dominant role played by the United States in hemispheric relations.

35:40 Jose, James R. *An Inter-American Peace Force within the Framework of the Organization of American States*. Metuchen, N.J.: Scarecrow, 1970. The concept of the often-mooted peace force is examined from every angle. The author concludes that it is not likely to be conjured into early existence.

Martz, J. D., and Schoultz, L., eds. *Latin America, the United States, and the Inter-American System* (2:282) focuses on the recent changes in the hemisphere's political economy, the control exercised by the United States, and the issue of human rights.

Mecham, J. L. *The United States and Inter-American Security, 1889–1960* (2:283) presents the orthodox case for the inter-American system. Mecham maintains that the inter-American system is the best organized and most effective of all "regional arrangements" and concludes that it was necessary for U.S. security.

35:41 Veneroni, Horacio L. *Fuerza Militar interamericana* [Inter-American military force]. Buenos Aires, 1966. This is a criticism of the proposal to establish an inter-American peacekeeping force.

Good Neighbor Policy/ Monroe Doctrine

See Chapter 21, "Good Neighbor Policy/Monroe Doctrine."

Dozer, D. M. *Are We Good Neighbors? Three Decades of Inter-American Relations, 1930–1960* (21:240) demonstrates that to achieve its wartime objectives the United States exerted its preponderant power in the western hemisphere, thereby overriding the essential nonintervention element of the good neighbor policy. The long-term result was the disintegration of cordial relations with Latin America.

35:42 Fabela, Isidro. *Intervención* [Intervention]. Mexico, D.F.: Universidad Nacional Autónoma de México, Escuela Nacional de Ciencias Políticas y Sociales, 1959. The author discusses the law of intervention in an inter-American setting, presenting the opinions of legal scholars from Europe, Latin America, and the United States. He is critical of the U.S. role in the development of the concept (1865–1954). His effort reflects Mexico's preoccupation with nonintervention as a major precept of her foreign policy. Bibliography.

Gellman, I. F. *Good Neighbor Diplomacy: United States Policies in Latin America, 1933–1945* (21:242) is the newest synthesis available. Of particular value is the concentration on the variety of personalities who contributed to the success of the policy.

Green, D. *The Containment of Latin America: A History of the Myths and Realities of the Good Neighbor Policy* (21:243) views the good neighbor policy as merely a new instrument for pursuing a traditional U.S. aim—the containment of Latin America. By "contain" the author means dominate, monopolize, and exploit. The World War II years consolidated U.S. influence in Latin American economic development and convinced New Dealers to keep a closed hemisphere while seeking an open world elsewhere.

Guerrant, E. O. *Roosevelt's Good Neighbor Policy* (21:244) is still one of the standard works on the subject. It surveys the essential features of the good neighbor policy, including some developments after Roosevelt's death. Guerrant is critical of Truman's postwar policy of preoccupation with affairs outside the hemisphere.

Perkins, D. *A History of the Monroe Doctrine* (2:273) disagrees with those who claim that through the Act of Chapultepec, the UN Charter, and the OAS Charter, its principles were internationalized.

Thomas, A. V. W., and Thomas, A. J., Jr. *Non-Intervention: The Law and Its Import in the Americas* [1500–1955] (2:274) seeks to clarify the meaning of intervention and nonintervention as applied to U.S. relations with Latin America.

Dependency Theory

35:43   Bath, C. Richard, and James, Dilmus D. "Dependency Analysis of Latin America: Some Criticisms, Some Suggestions." *Latin American Research Review* 11:3 (1976), 3–54. This article evaluates the evolution of the dependency model as used by scholars in analyzing U.S.–Latin American economic relations. In demonstrating the diverse ways in which the model may be applied, Bath and James also subject it to a systematic critique. Extensive bibliography.

35:44   Bodenheimer, Susanne J. "Dependency and Imperialism: The Roots of Latin American Underdevelopment." *Politics and Society* 1:3 (1971), 327–57. This is a seminal article which effectively uses the early dependency writings of Latin American social scientists. Writing from a Marxist perspective, the author sees all problems of Latin American underdevelopment as stemming directly or indirectly from foreign capitalist expansion.

35:45   Cardoso, Hernando Henrique. "Consumption of Dependency Theory in the United States." *Latin American Research Review* 12:3 (1977), 7–24. The author points out that dependency theory became accepted because it explained the realities in Latin America better than other frameworks and revealed the inadequacies of modernization theory. Future research, Cardoso warns, must avoid simplistic abstract formulas which pose as syntheses.

35:46   Chilcote, Ronald H. "Dependency: A Critical Synthesis of the Literature." *Latin American Perspectives* 1:1 (1974), 4–29. After tracing the evolution and impact of dependency theory, the author draws some critical conclusions about its use by scholars in Latin America and the United States. The extensive bibliography alone makes this a valuable essay.

35:47   Chilcote, Ronald H., and Edelstein, Joel C., eds. *Latin America: The Struggle with Dependency*

and Beyond. Cambridge, Mass.: Schenkman, 1974. The first survey of Latin American history from the perspective of dependency theory, its introduction discusses "diffusion models," which suggest that development will come through outside influence and assistance, and "dependency models," which insist that foreign penetration causes underdevelopment. Extensive bibliography.

35:48   Dos Santos, Theotonio. "La Crisis de la Teoría de Desarrollo y las Relaciones de Dependencia en América Latina" [The theory of development and the accounts of dependency in Latin America]. In Helio Jaguaribe, et al., *La Dependéncia Político-Económico de América Latina.* Mexico, D.F.: Siglo Veintiuno Editores, 1969, pp. 147–87. This essay not only provides one of the most succinct expositions of dependency analysis but comments critically on other studies dealing with Latin American development.

35:49   Dos Santos, Theotonio. "The Structure of Dependence." *American Economics Review* 60:2 (1970), 231–36. This essay capsulizes the many writings of this noted Brazilian (at the time he was teaching in Chile) economist. This piece is more effective when read in conjunction with above essay by Bodenheimer (35:44).

35:50   Fernandez, Raúl A., and Ocampo, José F. "The Latin American Revolution: A Theory of Imperialism, Not Dependency." *Latin American Perspectives* 1:1 (1974), 30–61. The authors view dependency theory as a misguided revision of Marxism and call for a return to purer Marxist-Leninist-Maoist theories of imperialism for explaining Latin American underdevelopment.

35:51   Frank, André G. *Capitalism and Underdevelopment in Latin America: Historical Studies of Chile and Brazil.* New York: Monthly Review, 1967. This interpretation is directed as much against Latin American communists as U.S. imperialists. Within a Marxist analysis, he suggests a reinterpretation of Latin America's past (1500–1965) based on metropolis-satellite relationships. The book raises important questions that led to further study of Latin American revolutions and the U.S. role in their development.

35:52   Frank, André Gunder. "Dependence Is Dead, Long Live Dependence and the Class Struggle: An Answer to Critics." *Latin American Perspectives* 1:1 (1974), 87–106. A prominent progenitor of dependency theory reviews his own writings in light of the many criticisms he has received.

35:53 Gaspar, Edmund. *United States–Latin America: A Special Relationship?* Washington, D.C.: American Enterprise Institute for Public Policy Research, 1978. The author contends that an unmitigated race for wealth (1500–1977) has left Latin America economically and politically dependent upon the United States. Yet he rejects the cultural and social implications of dependency theories. He is perceptive to the pervasive emotional opposition of Latin Americans to U.S. hegemony, but defends U.S. primacy in the hemisphere.

35:54 Johnson, Dale L. "Dependence and the International System." In James D. Cockcroft, André Gunder Frank, and Dale L. Johnson, eds., *Dependence and Underdevelopment: Latin America's Political Economy.* Garden City, N.Y.: Doubleday, 1972, pp. 71–111. This lucid exposition of dependency theory maintains that the driving force behind U.S. foreign policy has always been the expansive need of private capitalism. In Latin America, U.S. private investment, aid programs, military assistance, and international agencies have been interwoven to maintain influence and control. The essay comments on other dependency literature.

35:55 Ray, David. "The Dependency Model of Latin American Underdevelopment: Three Basic Fallacies." *Journal of Interamerican Studies and World Affairs* 15:1 (1973), 4–20. In critiquing dependency writings, especially those of Dos Santos and Bodenheimer, the author maintains that they ignore more comprehensive explanations of Latin American underdevelopment and oversimplify realities.

Slater, J. "The United States and Latin America: The New Radical Orthodoxy" (35:113) is critical of dependency theory.

Personalities

Additional references on individuals may be found in Chapter 1, "Biographical Data."

AMERICAN

See Chapter 24, "Personalities" and "Presidential Administrations," for additional references.

Dean Acheson

See Chapter 24, under "Personalities," for additional references.

Acheson, D. *Present at the Creation: My Years in the State Department* (24:90) is valuable for the portraits of contemporaries with whom the author dealt. Latin American affairs are mentioned sparingly, but the author's positions, and those of the administrations he served, are made clear.

Willard L. Beaulac

Beaulac, W. L. *Career Ambassador* (21:236) was an early advocate of aid to Latin America. He also offers an excellent eyewitness account of the tumult *(Bogotázo)* at the Ninth International Conference of American States in Bogota in 1948.

35:56 Beaulac, Willard L. *A Diplomat Looks at Aid to Latin America.* Carbondale: Southern Illinois University Press, 1970. While offering little in the way of new information, these informal observations provide insights into one career diplomat's mind: how he thought, more than what he did. The tone is definitely paternalistic. He treats the period from 1958 to 1968.

Adolf A. Berle, Jr.

Berle, A. A., Jr. *Navigating the Rapids, 1918–1971: From the Papers of Adolf A. Berle* (24:97) includes Berle's descriptive analysis of his service as assistant secretary of state (1938–1945), ambassador to Brazil (1945–1946), and head of President John F. Kennedy's Task Force on Latin America (1961). Influential in formulating the good neighbor policy, Berle was an outspoken advocate of hemispheric unity as a deterrent to outside aggression. Analytical index.

35:57 Berle, Adolf A., Jr. *Latin America: Diplomacy and Reality.* New York: Harper & Row, 1962. Having recently headed President John F. Kennedy's Task Force on Latin America, the author discusses contemporary relations with Latin America. He proposes that in extending aid the United States should insist that Latin American countries protect human rights and refrain from serving as a base for hostilities toward the United States.

35:58 Berle, Adolf A., Jr. *Tides of Crisis.* New York: Reynal, 1957. This longtime promoter of the inter-American system viewed the success of the OAS as critical to U.S. position in world affairs. He also maintained that the United States needed to insure that Latin America received a fair share of the economic benefits from a better-integrated western hemisphere.

Dwight D. Eisenhower

See also Chapter 24, under "Personalities."

Eisenhower, D. D. *The White House Years* (24:114) gives the most attention to inter-American affairs of all the presidential memoirs. Volume 1 includes comments on brother Milton Eisenhower's factfinding tour and the Tenth International Conference of American States at Caracas in 1954. Volume 2 discusses relations with Mexico, Vice-President Richard Nixon's tumultuous 1958 tour of South America, the president's Latin American tour of 1960, the Bogotá conference of 1960, and the new economic policies growing out of that conference.

Milton S. Eisenhower

35:59 Eisenhower, Milton S. *The President Is Calling*. Garden City, N.Y.: Doubleday, 1974. Eisenhower maintains that during his brother's presidency, the United States reached a real turning point in relations with Latin America and that all President Kennedy had to do was give a snappy name—Alliance for Progress—to a policy that evolved between 1958 and 1960. Bibliography.

35:60 Eisenhower, Milton S. *The Wine Is Bitter: The United States and Latin America*. Garden City, N.Y.: Doubleday, 1963. Largely a summary of his missions to Central and South America on behalf of his brother, President Dwight D. Eisenhower, the author contended that all Latin American countries were going to undergo revolutions (some violent, some in democratic form) and that U.S. policy should evolve to aid rather than resist that trend.

Cordell Hull

See Chapter 21 and 22, under "Personalities," for additional references.

Hull, C. *Memoirs* (21:36) is a rich source (volume 2) for studying the personnel involved in and the nature of U.S.–Latin American relations in the years 1941 to 1944. Hull views the attitude of the Latin American republics during World War II, with the exception of Argentina, as a vindication of the good neighbor policy.

Pratt, J. W. *Cordell Hull, 1933–1944* (22:24) includes a lengthy section, in volume 2, "Good Neighbors in Wartime." This uncritical treatment includes other scattered references to inter-American relations, as well as the wartime conflict with Argentina.

35:61 Woods, Randall B. "Hull and Argentina: Wilsonian Diplomacy in the Age of Roosevelt." *Journal of Inter-American Studies and World Affairs* 16:3 (1974), 350–71. Secretary of State Cordell Hull's paradoxical 1943–1944 policy toward Argentina's government of General Pedro Ramírez can be understood better in the context of the Wilsonian tradition. Like Wilson, Hull viewed foreign policy matters in terms of right and wrong, "sin" and "salvation." As a result, Hull abetted the rise of an even more intransigent regime, that of Juan Perón.

Lyndon B. Johnson

See also Chapter 24, under "Personalities."

Johnson, L. B. *The Vantage Point: Perspectives on the Presidency, 1963–1969* (24:120) gives limited space to relations with Latin America, although the Alliance for Progress, the Punta del Este summit of 1967, the Latin American common market, and the presidential visit to Mexico in 1966 are discussed.

John F. Kennedy

See also Chapter 24, under "Personalities."

35:62 Maher, Theodore J. "The Kennedy-Johnson Responses to Latin American Coups d'Etat." *World Affairs* 131:3 (1968), 184–97. This article reveals why Kennedy insisted dogmatically that democracy must be enforced in Latin America, yet did not impose sanctions on all military regimes, and why Johnson adopted openly a more pragmatic approach of not distinguishing between constitutional governments and military juntas.

Schlesinger, A. M., Jr. *A Thousand Days: John F. Kennedy in the White House* (24:215) provides relations with Latin America with a lengthier treatment than any survey of the Kennedy years. It offers an account of the ideas behind the development of the Alliance for Progress. Bilateral relations with various countries are given extensive treatment.

Sorensen, T. C. *Kennedy* (24:128) confirms that John F. Kennedy had a deep concern for the quality of life in Latin America. There is great detail on the Alliance for Progress. The author was one of those advisers who helped name the program.

Richard M. Nixon

See Chapter 24, under "Personalities," for additional references.

Nixon, R. M. *RN: The Memoirs of Richard Nixon* (24:145) discusses the impact of revolution in Cuba at length, as well as his ill-fated trip to South America in 1958. Relations with Latin America during his presidency receive scant attention, except for commentary on Chilean Marxist President Salvador Allende.

Franklin D. Roosevelt

See Chapters 20, 22, and 23, under "Personalities," for additional references.

Cuevas Cancino, F. M. *Roosevelt y la Buena Vecindad* [1933–1945] (35:84) gives President Roosevelt high marks for the good neighbor policy.

Dallek, R. *Franklin D. Roosevelt and American Foreign Policy, 1932–1945* (21:51).

Roosevelt, F. D. *Public Papers and Addresses of Franklin Delano Roosevelt* (21:55) includes in the last four volumes addresses and statements to press conferences bearing mainly upon public policy. Relations with Latin America are mentioned in each of the four volumes. Analytical indexes.

Edward R. Stettinius, Jr.

See also Chapter 23, under "Personalities."

Stettinius, E. R., Jr. *The Diaries of Edward R. Stettinius, Jr., 1943–1946* (24:150) is valuable for his views on regional collective security agreements growing out of the Mexico City and San Francisco conferences of 1945. His comments on economic relations with Latin America anticipated future problems. Analytical index.

Harry S. Truman

See also Chapters 24 and 27, under "Personalities."

Truman, H. S. *Memoirs* (24:160) touches upon a great variety of topics bearing upon inter-American relations and upon bilateral relations with several Latin American nations.

Sumner Welles

Welles, S. *The Time for Decision* (22:39) is particularly critical of Secretary of State Cordell Hull's policy toward Argentina. The result of that policy, Welles claims, was to drive Argentina into virtual secession from the most advanced regional system ever evolved. He believed that the inter-American system would be the foundation of a future international organization. Index.

Welles, S. *Where Are We Heading?* (25:39) is an informed inventory of the leading problems then facing Secretary of State James F. Byrnes and includes a lengthy section on inter-American relations. Welles was particularly impatient with State Department moralists who were preoccupied with the nature of Argentina's government.

Others

35:63 Bowers, Claude. *Chile through Embassy Windows, 1939–1953.* New York: Simon & Schuster, 1958. This memoir of a writer-historian turned diplomat provides a detailed account of the intrigues and political developments in Chile during and after World War II. Chile's delay in breaking relations with the Axis is attributed to the cumbersomeness of that nation's existing democracy.

35:64 Braden, Spruille. *Diplomats and Demagogues: The Memoirs of Spruille Braden.* New Rochelle, N.Y.: Arlington House, 1971. What emerges from these memoirs is the political thinking of a business-oriented conservative. Having served as a mining engineer in Chile, ambassador to Colombia, Cuba, and Argentina, and assistant secretary of state for Latin American affairs, Braden leaves a fascinating record of personal and public diplomacy. Of particular interest is his vindication of his role in postwar relations with Argentina.

35:65 Morrison, De Lesseps. *Latin American Mission: An Adventure in Hemisphere Diplomacy.* New York: Simon & Schuster, 1965. A recollection of 26 months as President John F. Kennedy's representative to the OAS and roving ambassador in Latin America, this account reflects Morrison's reputation for impetuous behavior. He is critical of some of the president's advisers.

LATIN AMERICAN

Rómulo Betancourt

35:66 Alexander, Robert J. *The Venezuelan Democratic Revolution: A Profile of the Regime of Rómulo Betancourt.* New Brunswick, N.J.: Rutgers University Press, 1964. Alexander examines the "democratic left" in Venezuela and notes that agrarian reform has been the most fundamental economic and social change brought about by Betancourt's democratic revolution.

35:67 Betancourt, Rómulo. *La revolución democrática en Venezuela: Documentas del gobierno presidido par Rómulo Betancourt* [Democratic revolution in Venezuela: documents of the presidency of Rómulo Betancourt]. 4 vols. Caracas: Imprenta Nacional, 1968. Betancourt's speeches and other public statements made while he was president of Venezuela (1958–1964).

Juan D. Perón

35:68 Alexander, Robert J. *Juan Domingo Perón: A History.* Boulder, Colo.: Westview, 1979. More an interpretive history of Argentina (1943–1974) than a biography, this work by a prolific historian supplements his earlier *Perón Era.* The newer account retraces the early career of Argentina's charismatic leader, as well as his years in exile and return to power in the 1970s. Perón's impact, and that of Eva, on Argentine foreign policy is discussed.

35:69 Alexander, Robert J. *The Perón Era.* New York: Columbia University Press, 1951. Mainly an analysis of Peronismo, this volume deals with Argentina's foreign relations during the late 1940s. Alexander provides a balanced treatment of the developing cooperation between the United States and Argentina. Bibliography.

35:70 Blanksten, George I. *Perón's Argentina.* Chicago: University of Chicago Press, 1953. The author, a State Department official, knew many of the personalities about whom he writes. This study is a very detailed account of Juan Perón's rise to power and his political and foreign policy strategies. The work also treats World War II relations with the United States. Bibliography.

Others

35:71 Alexander, Robert J. *Prophets of Revolution: Profiles of Latin American Leaders.* New York: Macmillan, 1962. By analyzing the lives of twelve political leaders, the author reviews 20th-century Latin American revolutions. Among those included are Chile's Arturo Alessandri, Peru's Víctor Raúl Haya de la Torre, Venezuela's Rómulo Betancourt, Bolivia's Víctor Paz Estenssoro and Hernán Siles, Brazil's Getulio Vargas, and Argentina's Juan Perón. Extensive bibliography.

35:72 Alisky, Marvin, ed. *Who's Who in Mexican Government.* Tempe: Arizona State University, Center for Latin American Studies, 1969. It contains biographical data that are hard to get on major figures in Mexican political life. There is a selected bibliography and a glossary of Mexican political and governmental terms.

35:73 Andrade, Víctor. *My Missions for Revolutionary Bolivia, 1944–1962.* Ed. by Cole Blasier. Pittsburgh: University of Pittsburgh Press, 1976. The author served Bolivia in various top government posts, including foreign minister and ambassador to the United States. Before the revolution in 1952, he conceived as his task the securing of the highest price possible for his country's tin. Later he was obliged to defend the radical changes that transformed his country.

35:74 Barroni, Otelo, and Vacca, Roberto. *La Vida de Eva Perón* [The life of Eva Perón]. Buenos Aires: Editorial Galerma, 1971. This is a well-documented study of Eva Perón's role in Argentine life between 1946 and 1952.

35:75 Bourne, Richard. *Political Leaders of Latin America.* New York: Knopf, 1970. Bourne examines the lives and careers of Guevara, Stroessner, Frei, Kubitschek, Eva Perón, and Carlos Lacerdon.

35:76 Camp, Roderic Ai. *Mexican Political Biographies, 1935–1976.* Tucson: University of Arizona Press, 1976. Short biographies of individuals important to contemporary Mexican politics, living and deceased, from 1935 to early 1964. Bibliographic essay.

35:77 Dulles, John W. F. *Castello Branco: The Making of a Brazilian President.* College Station: Texas A&M University Press, 1978. Dulles provides a detailed account of political strongman Humberto de Alençar Castello Branco, who succeeded in unifying Brazil's divided military factions to overthrow the populist president João Goulart. The U.S. role in the rise of the military is discussed. Extensive bibliography.

35:78 Dulles, John W. F. *Vargas of Brazil: A Political Biography.* Austin: University of Texas Press, 1967. This is a narrow political biography of Getulio Vargas, who was dictator (1937–1945) and popularly elected president (1951–1954). The Brazilian-American alliance, as well as the personal Vargas-Roosevelt relationship, is treated in detail. Extensive bibliography.

Jagan, C. *The West on Trial: My Fight for Guyana's Freedom* (35:239) blames the United States for his problems.

35:79 Lleras Restrepo, Carlos. *Hacia la restauración democrática y el cambio social: Nuevo testimonio sobre la política colombiana* [Toward democratic restoration and social change: new testimony on Colombian politics]. 2 vols. Bogotá: Editiorial Agra, 1963. A collection of speeches and articles, written between 1955 and 1963, by a leader of the Liberal party, who subsequently became president of Colombia (1966–1970).

35:80 Lopez Michelson, Alfonso. *Colombia en la hora cero: Proceso y enjuiciamiento del frente nacional* [Colombia in the zero hour: process and judgment of the National Front]. 2 vols. Bogotá: Ediciones Tercer Mundo, 1963. A collection of papers and speeches by the leader of the leftist Movimiento Revolucionario Liberal who was president of Colombia (1974–1978).

35:81 Maraf, Tristán, pseud. (Gustavo Adolfo Navarro). *Victor Paz Estenssoro: Vida y trasfondo de la político boliviano* [Victor Paz Estenssoro: life and background of the Bolivian politician]. La Paz: Librería y Editorial Juventud, 1965. A socialist critique of the Movimiento Nacionalista Revolucionario government and of its leader Paz Estenssoro.

35:82 Shapira, Yoram. *Mexican Foreign Policy under Echeverria*. Beverly Hills, Calif.: Sage, 1978. This work concentrates on the relationship between the social upheaval in Mexico and Echeverria's subsequent development of a foreign policy (1970–1976). As he attempted to solve Mexico's internal development problems, he sought to make Mexico a leader in Third World affairs. Bibliography.

Tambs, L. A., et al., eds. *Latin American Government Leaders* (1:200) contains short biographical sketches.

World War II, 1941–1945

See "Personalities," especially Cordell Hull, Franklin D. Roosevelt; see also Chapter 21, "Good Neighbor Policy/Monroe Doctrine," and Chapter 23, "Latin America."

35:83 Callcott, Wilfrid H. *The Western Hemisphere: Its Influence on United States Policies to the End of World War II*. Austin: University of Texas Press, 1968. This account lauds President Roosevelt's hemispheric diplomacy as a success. The American president succeeded in guaranteeing the whole hemisphere against European aggression, he concludes. As a result American nations developed an essential unity in outlook and objectives. Extensive bibliography.

35:84 Cuevas Cancino, Francisco M. *Roosevelt y la Buena Vecindad* [Roosevelt and the good neighbor]. Mexico, D.F.: Fondo de Cultura Economica, 1954. Uncharacteristically, this Mexican account is laudatory of the good neighbor policy. The author contends that Roosevelt tried to apply the golden rule and Christian ethics in international politics.

35:85 Whitaker, Arthur P., ed. *Inter-American Affairs: An Annual Survey . . . 1941–1945*. 5 vols. New York: Columbia University Press, 1942–1946. These volumes are a gold mine of information on politics, diplomacy, economics and finance, cultural relations, and developments in social welfare, public health, and labor. In addition to appendixes incorporating a great variety of statistics, each volume concludes with an annotated chronology. Index.

Wood, B. *The Making of the Good Neighbor Policy* (21:246) is the most authoritative work on the subject. The focus for the early World War II period is on the consequences of U.S. abandonment of the use of force in its relations with Latin American countries.

ECONOMIC AND MILITARY COOPERATION

Conn, S.; Engelman, R. C.; and Fairchild, B. *Guarding the United States and Its Outposts* (23:241) discuss the uses of new bases in the Caribbean and South America.

Conn, S., and Fairchild, B. *The Framework of Hemispheric Defense* (23:242) deals with military relations with other American nations. The greatest concentration is on Brazil and Mexico. A detailed map of military-related activities is included.

35:86 Craig, Richard B. *The Bracero Program: Interest Groups and Foreign Policy*. Austin: University of Texas Press, 1971. Concentrating on interest group struggles at the international, national, and local levels that led to the inception and 22-year existence of the Mexican Contract Workers Program, this work demonstrates that the Mexican government had as much interest in maintaining the program as did U.S. farmers. Bibliography.

35:87 Hilton, Stanley E. "Brazilian Diplomacy and the Washington–Rio de Janeiro 'Axis' during the World War II Era." *Hispanic American Historical Review* 59:2 (1979), 200–229. Taking issue with Frank D. McCann (35:89), the author contends that the Brazil-U.S. relationship during World War II enabled Brazil to make great strides toward establishing industrial and military supremacy in South America. Brazilian leaders are viewed as opportunists, while the Roosevelt administration is depicted as eschewing efforts to control Brazilian policies.

35:88 Levenstein, Harvey A. *Labor Organization in the United States and Mexico: A History of Their Relations.* Westport, Conn.: Greenwood, 1971. Until the beginning of World War II, Mexican labor leaders sought to enlist their U.S. counterparts in an effort to promote reform (1913–1963). During the war both sides veered away from reform, turned anticommunist, and lost interest in an alliance. The author concludes that international labor policy was correlated with national foreign policy and that domestic political concerns were the primary factors. Bibliography.

McCann, F. D., Jr. *The Brazilian-American Alliance, 1937–1945* (21:284) focuses largely on the military aspects of the alliance. The author demonstrates that Brazil's agreements to secure arms from the United States, while designed to insure Brazilian strength and independence, resulted in her becoming more dependent upon the United States. The comparisons drawn between Getulio Vargas and Franklin D. Roosevelt are enlightening.

35:89 McCann, Frank D. "Brazil, the United States, and World War II: A Commentary." *Diplomatic History* 3:1 (1979), 59–76. Expanding upon a theme presented in his book, the author demonstrates that Brazilian leaders during World War II were well aware of their country's growing dependence on the United States. They did not perceive U.S. penetration as a threat, but as a means to achieve greater power. An image of dependency resulted, sowing seeds of present Brazilian anti-Americanism.

35:90 U.S. Inter-American Affairs Office. *History of the Office of Coordinator of Inter-American Affairs.*

Washington, D.C.: G.P.O., 1947. Created in 1940 for the purpose of strengthening hemispheric solidarity against Axis subversion and aggression, this agency was headed by Nelson A. Rockefeller. This official history details CIAA efforts in such areas as commerce, finance, economic development, transport, press, radio, motion pictures, and education.

HEMISPHERE UNITY

Blasier, C. "The United States, Germany, and the Bolivian Revolutionaries (1941–1946)" (23:245) reveals that tin mining and other interests used the spectre of Nazi subversion to influence the State Department. This article examines the U.S. campaign against fascism in Bolivia during World War II. Blasier contends that this effort aided traditional interests and hindered reformist opposition, thus hampering rather than promoting U.S. purposes.

Espinosa, J. M. *Inter-American Beginnings of U.S. Cultural Diplomacy, 1936–1948* (2:190) reviews the cultural programs and shows that such efforts originated as a result of the perceived Axis threat to the Americas.

35:91 Francis, Michael J. *The Limits of Hegemony: United States Relations with Argentina and Chile during World War II.* Notre Dame, Ind.: University of Notre Dame Press, 1977. This volume is valuable in relating diplomatic exchanges to internal political developments in Argentina and Chile. The author concludes that the public condemnations and experiments in economic deprivations resorted to by the United States accomplished little, while quiet secret diplomacy succeeded better. Extensive bibliography.

35:92 Francis, Michael J. "The United States at Rio, 1942: The Strains of Pan Americanism." *Journal of Latin American Studies* 6:1 (1974), 77–95. Focusing on the domestic and foreign policy aims of the representatives from Chile, Argentina, and Brazil, this article explains why at the Rio Conference (1942) a rupture of diplomatic relations with the Axis powers rather than a joint declaration of war or a unanimous break of relations with the Axis was recommended.

Frye, A. *Nazi Germany and the American Hemisphere, 1933–1941* (21:120) challenges the revisionist contention that the rise of Nazi Germany did not jeopardize the security of the United States and its Latin American neighbors. He concludes that military and political superiority over the western hemisphere formed a part of Hitler's global ambitions.

35:93 Woods, Randall B. "Decision-making in Diplomacy: The Rio Conference of 1942." *Social Science Quarterly* 55:4 (1975), 901–18. After formulating a construct to measure the motives and behavior of diplomats in policymaking situations, the author tests the construct in a specific historical context—the 1942 Rio de Janeiro Conference. This method sheds new light on the U.S.-Argentine confrontation immediately following U.S. entry into World War II.

The Argentine Problem

See "Personalities," especially Cordell Hull, Sumner Welles.

Bagú, S. *Argentina en el Mundo* (35:189).

35:94 Woods, Randall B. *The Roosevelt Foreign-Policy Establishment and the "Good Neighbor": The United States and Argentina, 1941–1945.* Lawrence: Regents Press of Kansas, 1979. The author demonstrates how U.S.-Argentine relations during World War II undermined the good neighbor policy. He takes issue with both orthodox and revisionist historians for ignoring the impact of bureaucracy on the making of foreign policy. He argues that U.S.-Argentine relations were affected by struggles between groups within the State Department and between the State Department and other cabinet-level offices and the many wartime agencies. Extensive bibliographical essay.

U.S., Latin America, and the UN

See, under "Personalities," Edward R. Stettinius, Jr.

35:95 Houston, John A. *Latin America in the United Nations.* New York: Carnegie Endowment for International Peace, 1956. This is a documented, detailed account of the significant role played in the United Nations by the countries of Latin America during 1945 to 1955. Of special interest is the foreword by Panamanian internationalist Dr. Ricardo J. Alfaro. Extensive bibliography.

Kolko, G. *The Politics of War: The World and United States Foreign Policy, 1943–1945* (25:19) treats the broad spectrum of U.S. wartime relations as a singular

effort to achieve world dominance. The United States attempted to use the western hemisphere to extend control through an American bloc in the United Nations General Assembly. The Act of Chapultepec and article 51 of the UN Charter were promoted by the United States as a means of creating such a bloc.

35:96 Tillapaugh, J. "Closed Hemisphere and Open Door? The Dispute over Regional Security at the U.N. Conference, 1945." *Diplomatic History* 2:1 (1978), 25–42. The author takes to task revisionists who claim that at the San Francisco Conference (1945) the United States supported regional security arrangements as a means of controlling the western hemisphere while holding the rest of the world open to American influence. The Latin American delegates forced the issue to perpetuate the terms of the Act of Chapultepec (1945) and to check U.S. interference in their affairs.

35:97 Woods, Randall B. "Conflict or Community? The United States and Argentina's Admission to the United Nations." *Pacific Historical Review* 46:3 (1977), 361–86. The author does not accept the revisionist view of U.S. support for Argentina's membership in the United Nations. Rather than seeking to build anticommunist strength in the UN, policymakers were motivated by a commitment to principles of nonintervention, internationalism, and respect for the sovereignty of all nations.

U.S. and Latin America since 1945

35:98 Adams, Richard N., et al. *Social Change in Latin America Today: Its Implications for United States Policy.* New York: Harper, 1960. Largely a sociological and anthropological study (1945–1959), this volume is a statement of social change and five country (Peru, Bolivia, Brazil, Guatemala, and Mexico) studies. The authors saw the Indian, Negro, and mestizo of the country, village, and city slum as the elements toward which the United States must direct policy. This study anticipated some of the goals of the Alliance for Progress.

35:99 Bailey, Norma A. *Latin America in World Politics.* New York: Walker, 1967. This survey concludes that Latin American countries for some time would be client states. Bailey maintains that the United States would not tolerate the Soviets acquiring more clients in the western hemisphere, and that Latin Americans will play upon that fear to increase their own foreign policy flexibility. Appendixes include treaties and other acts.

35:100 Burr, Robert N. *Our Troubled Hemisphere: Perspective on United States–Latin American Relations.* Washington, D.C.: Brookings Institution, 1967. In this historical study the author concludes that the solutions lie in a stronger OAS, a strengthened Alliance for Progress and a better understanding by the United States of its hemispheric neighbors.

35:101 Cochrane, James D. "U.S. Policy towards Recognition of Government and Promotion of Democracy in Latin America since 1963."*Journal of Latin American Studies* 4:2 (1972), 275–91. The policy of not recognizing or extending aid to Latin American regimes that seize power from constitutionally selected ones, which was inaugurated by the Kennedy administration, was shortly compromised by Kennedy, then abandoned by Johnson and Nixon.

35:102 Cotler, Julio, and Fagen, Richard R., eds. *Latin America and the United States: The Changing Political Realities.* Stanford, Calif.: Stanford University Press, 1974. This book consists of both North American and Latin American perspectives. When compared, the two perspectives illustrate the fundamental differences between U.S. scholarship and the approach of Latin American academics. The conclusions generally demonstrate that the United States dominates relations of Latin American nations. See Slater (35:113). Index.

Dávila, C. G. *We of the Americas* [1790–1948] (2:278) decries the failure of Pan Americanism. It is valuable for the post-1945 period.

35:103 Gerassi, John. *The Great Fear: The Reconquest of Latin America by Latin Americans.* New York: Macmillan, 1963. Written at the height of the Alliance for Progress, this volume is a devastating criticism of U.S. policy and Latin American oligarchs. The author offers little hope for piecemeal social reform and prophesies revolution. Bibliography.

35:104 Gil, Federico G. "United States–Latin American Relations in the Changing Mid-1970s." *SECOLAS Annals* 7 (1976), 5–19. The Nixon-Kissinger policy is not meeting Latin American challenges. They failed to deal with Latin American initiatives from the Consensus of Vina del Mar and failed to implement the recommendations of the Commission on United States–Latin American Relations (Linowitz Report). Congress is criticized for legislation discriminating against Latin American trade.

35:105 Goldhamer, Herbert. *The Foreign Powers in Latin America.* Princeton, N.J.: Princeton University Press, 1972. The major study of the decline of unilateral dominance of U.S. capital in Latin America (1945–1970), this volume describes the political, economic, and cultural activities of nonhemispheric nations and the United States in Latin America since World War II. Latin American nations are less concerned than the United States about threatening extrahemispheric powers.

35:106 Gómez Robledo, Antonio. *La Seguridad Colectiva en el Continente Americano* [Collective security in the Americas]. Mexico, D.F.: Universidad Nacional Autónoma de México, Escuela Nacional de Ciencias Políticas y Sociales, 1960. This scholarly study reviews the history of the idea and institutions of collective security in the western hemisphere (1945–1958). The author approves of the Rio Treaty of 1947 but opposes any extension of obligations which would make the inter-American system comparable to NATO.

35:107 Kane, William E. *Civil Strife in Latin America: A Legal History of U.S. Involvement.* Baltimore: Johns Hopkins Press, 1972. Despite the renunciation of interventionism in the OAS Charter, the perceived communist threat has caused the United States to intervene in Latin American internal affairs. In doing so the United States has sacrificed international law for national security.

35:108 Lowenthal, Abraham F. "The United States and Latin America: Ending the Hegemonic Presumption." *Foreign Affairs* 55:1 (1976), 199–213. This essay suggests that U.S. control of the western hemisphere can no longer be maintained. Cuba's success in removing herself from U.S. domination served as a symbol for other Latin American countries. Lowenthal believes that the first step toward improved Latin American policy should be to realize that we should not have a Latin American policy at all.

35:109 Pérez, Louis A., Jr. "International Dimensions of Inter-American Relations, 1944–1960." *Inter-American Economic Affairs* 27:1 (1973), 47–68. Pérez traces the decline of hemispheric solidarity following World War II (1944–1960) and attributes the trend largely to American preoccupation with external aggression. Indeed, Pérez maintains that until 1958 the framework within which the United States related to Latin America was determined largely by international currents.

35:110 Rippy, J. Fred. *Globe and Hemisphere: Latin America's Place in the Postwar Foreign Relations of the United States.* Chicago: Regnery, 1958. Rippy deals mainly with economic aspects of U.S.– Latin American relations, detailing the nature and value of U.S. private investment and government aid. The author views the Latin Americans as ungrateful recipients of U.S. largesse. Extensive bibliography.

35:111 Rockefeller, Nelson A. *The Rockefeller Report on the Americas: The Official Report of a United States Presidential Mission for the Western Hemisphere.* Chicago: Quadrangle, 1969. This is basically the report presented to President Nixon following a 1969 twenty-nation factfinding visit. Rockefeller recommended concessions in lending and trade policies.

35:112 Silvert, Kalman H., et al. *The Americas in a Changing World: A Report of the Commission on United States–Latin American Relations.* New York: Quadrangle, 1975. This book contains a collection of essays plus the report of the Commission on United States–Latin American Relations (Linowitz Commission). These are unified by a plea for a U.S. policy which can respond satisfactorily to fundamental changes in Latin America.

35:113 Slater, Jerome. "The United States and Latin America: The New Radical Orthodoxy." *Economic Development and Cultural Change* 25:4 (1977), 747–62. In a review of Cotler and Fagen's *Latin America and the United States* (35:102), Slater criticizes radical scholars, even those who break with dependency theory, for invariably succumbing to the position that U.S. policy toward Latin America is consciously imperialistic. He insists that while the United States has influence in Latin America, nowhere is it enough to justify the term "imperialism."

35:114 Stephansky, Ben S. "'New Dialogue' on Latin America: The Cost of Policy Neglect." In Ronald G. Hellman and H. Jon Rosenbaum, eds., *Latin America: The Search for a New International Role.* New York: Wiley, 1975, pp. 153–66. After five years of neglect, Secretary of State Henry Kissinger called for a "New Dialogue" between the United States and Latin America. This essay demonstrates

that missed opportunities during those five years of neglect are difficult to make up. The record of the Nixon years is surveyed and policy alternatives are outlined.

Wagner, R. H. *United States Policy toward Latin America: A Study in Domestic and International Politics* (39:168) analyzes the interaction between domestic politics and policies toward Latin America in the period from World War II to the Alliance for Progress. This work focuses on why aid programs failed to develop a domestic constituency while defense programs have. Extensive end notes and index.

U.S., THE COLD WAR, AND LATIN AMERICA

35:115 Alexander, Robert J. *Communism in Latin America.* New Brunswick, N.J.: Rutgers University Press, 1957. This volume reflects U.S. concern over communist penetration in Latin America during the 1950s. The author believes that the antidictator trend in Latin America was aiding the Communists, who were enjoying greater freedom of expression. Bibliography.

35:116 Clissold, Stephen. *Soviet Relations with Latin America, 1918–1967: A Documentary Survey.* London: Oxford University Press, 1968. The documents are drawn from a wide variety of sources. They are divided under three headings: "Antecedents"; "The Comintern Period"; and "War, Cold War, and Peaceful Coexistence."

35:117 Green, David. "The Cold War Comes to Latin America." In Barton J. Bernstein, ed., *Politics and Policies of the Truman Administration.* Chicago: Quadrangle, 1970, pp. 149–95. The author contends that President Truman sought to continue President Roosevelt's efforts to create an open door world. But in response to a perceived threat from the Soviet Union, he adopted political, economic, and military policies that created a U.S. sphere of influence in the western hemisphere.

35:118 Hulsey, R. H. "Cuban Revolution: Its Impact upon American Foreign Policy." *Journal of International Affairs* 14:2 (1960), 158–74. Castro's revolution forced the United States to upgrade Latin American affairs. Hulsey recommends that the United States, Western Europe, and Japan unite with a massive aid program for the region to save it from communism.

35:119   Parkinson, F. *Latin America, the Cold War, and the World Powers, 1945–1973*. Beverly Hills, Calif.: Sage, 1974. This study examines the different phases of the cold war as they affected Latin America (1945–1973). The author concludes that in the early stages Latin America was a pawn of the world powers, but by the late 1960s the cold war exerted little influence and intra-American relations took on new primacy. Extensive bibliography.

35:120   Trask, Roger R. "The Impact of the Cold War on United States–Latin American Relations, 1945–1949." *Diplomatic History* 1:3 (1977), 271–84. At the end of World War II, the United States was committed to an international organization which would include the Latin American republics. Under the impact of perceived Soviet and communist threats, the United States altered its policy in favor of a hemispheric defense system as a means of fighting the cold war in the Americas.

ORGANIZATION OF AMERICAN STATES (OAS)

35:121   Ball, Mary M. *The OAS in Transition*. Durham, N.C.: Duke University Press, 1969. This is a complete, documented handbook of the OAS organization (1947–1968). Although historical background and evolution of the OAS are treated, the book is mainly a description of the various organs and agencies of the inter-American system. Extensive bibliography.

35:122   Dreier, John C. *The Organization of American States and the Hemisphere Crisis*. New York: Harper & Row, 1962. This is a favorable resumé of the OAS from its beginnings as the Pan American Union to the second Punta del Este Conference (1962). The author, a ten-year U.S. ambassador to OAS, was optimistic about its future but recognized that any efforts to strengthen OAS powers would be viewed by Latin Americans as increasing U.S. political dominance.

35:123   Dreier, John C. "New Wine in Old Bottles: The Changing Inter-American System." *International Organization* 22:2 (1968), 477–93. Dreier examines the results to two 1967 inter-American conferences— the Third Special Inter-American Conference at Buenos Aires and the Meeting of American Chiefs of State at Punta del Este. The Punta del Este conferees urged a new course of fundamental importance for the hemisphere—the creation of a Latin American common market.

35:124   Fernández-Shaw, Felix G. *La Organización de los Estados Americanos (O.E.A.): Una nueva visión de América* [The Organization of American States (OAS): a new American vision]. 2d ed. Madrid: Ediciones Culturas Hispánicas, 1963. This updated edition, a comprehensive work on the history and functioning of the Organization of American States, contains many documents.

35:125   Manger, William. *Pan America in Crisis: The Future of the O.A.S.* Washington, D.C.: Public Affairs Press, 1961. Associated with the Pan American Union for 43 years, and formerly the assistant secretary general of the Organization of American States, the author is impatient with the complacency within the system. He is critical of the bureaucracy and its inefficiency.

35:126   Manger, William. "Reform of the OAS: The 1967 Buenos Aires Protocol of Amendment to the 1948 Charter of Bogota: An Appraisal." *Journal of Inter-American Studies* 10:1 (1968), 1–14. The author points out that the purpose of charter revision was to strengthen economic principles of the inter-American system, yet lessen authority of some OAS agencies and redistribute functions.

35:127   Meek, George. "U.S. Influence on the Organization of American States." *Journal of Inter-American Studies and World Affairs* 17:3 (1975), 311–25. Meek examines roll call votes of various OAS meetings, assemblies, and agencies to determine U.S. influence. He concludes that during the early years the United States exerted great influence, especially on issues of communist penetration. Since 1965 the Latin American delegations have become sensitive to interventionist issues, and the United States has had little success.

35:128   Sepúlveda, César. *El Sistema Interamericano: Génesis, Integración, Decadencia* [The inter-American system: origins, growth, decline]. 2d ed. Mexico, D.F.: Editorial Porrua, 1974. This is a description of the development of the Organization of American States. It serves as a sequel to Mary M. Ball's description of the organs and functions of the Pan American system. Almost one-half of the volume is appendixes, which include documents relating to the OAS. Bibliography.

35:129 Slater, Jerome. *The OAS and United States Foreign Policy.* Columbus: Ohio State University Press, 1967. This is the best treatment of U.S. relations with the OAS. Slater emphasizes that the United States perceives different roles for the OAS at different times in order to implement the policy of the day. He believes that the OAS has functioned effectively as a hemispheric security system, but has become a shaky alliance. Extensive bibliography.

35:130 Thomas, Ann Van Wynen, and Thomas, A. J., Jr. *The Organization of American States.* Dallas: Southern Methodist University Press, 1963. A detailed study of the historical background and principal functions of the OAS, it concentrates on its juridical aspects. It is an excellent view of the disputes that have arisen in the system. End notes provide an extensive bibliography.

ECONOMIC RELATIONS

35:131 Baily, Samuel L. *The United States and the Development of South America, 1945–1975.* New York: New Viewpoints, 1976. This work refutes traditional interpretations that the interests of the United States and those of South America are compatible. U.S. policy (1945–1975) has sought to direct economic growth by employing private capital and has been preoccupied with protecting U.S. security and economic interests. Extensive bibliography.

35:132 Baklanoff, Eric N. "The Expropriation of United States Investments in Latin America, 1959–1974: A Study of International Conflict and Accommodation." *SECOLAS Annals* 8 (1977), 48–60. In no area of the world have U.S. properties and business investments been more threatened with nationalization than in Latin America. Antipathy toward U.S. direct investments is shared by diverse groups in Latin America. Baklanoff recommends that U.S. policy should not encourage future U.S. direct investment in Latin America.

35:133 Dell, Sidney S. *The Inter-American Development Bank: A Study in Development Financing.* New York: Praeger, 1972. This book reviews the policies of the IDB in relation to the purpose for which it was founded and its role in Latin American development. The author acknowledges that the IDB cannot produce fundamental economic and social reform and structural change. It is the servant of the member governments and can only expand the overall flow of capital to Latin America.

35:134 Grunwald, Joseph; Wionczek, Miguel S.; and Carney, Martin. *Latin American Economic Integration and U.S. Policy.* Washington, D.C.: Brookings Institution, 1972. This is a study critical of U.S. policy in regard to Latin American economic integration from both U.S. and Latin American perspectives. The authors are critical of government officials for giving integration only verbal support and note U.S. bilateral economic relations is impeding the effort.

Ingram, G. M. *Expropriation of US Property in South America: Nationalization of Oil and Copper Companies in Peru, Bolivia and Chile* [1900–1973] (39:184) describes three cases of expropriation of American-owned industries.

35:135 Jiménez Lazcano, Mauro. *Integración económica e imperialismo* [Economic integration and imperialism]. Mexico, D.F.: Editorial Nuestro Tiempo, 1968. A study of Latin American economic integration which argues that integration will lead to increased foreign control rather than economic development.

35:136 Machado, Manuel A., Jr. *Aftosa: A Historical Survey of Foot-and-Mouth Disease and Inter-American Relations.* Albany: State University of New York Press, 1969. This is a brief account of the inter-American efforts, sponsored by the Pan American Health Organization, to control hoof-and-mouth disease (1946–1968). The author points out how political and ethnic diversity in the hemisphere complicated the attack on a common problem. Bibliography.

Pinelo, A. J. *The Mutlinational Corporation as a Force in Latin American Politics: A Case Study of the International Petroleum Company in Peru* [1914–1968] (39:146) traces the efforts by a Standard Oil subsidiary to survive. The IPC became a "whipping boy" in Peruvian politics.

35:137 Romualdi, Serafino. *Presidents and Peons: Recollections of a Labor Ambassador in Latin America.* New York: Funk & Wagnalls, 1967. The author, the representative of the AFL in Latin America (1946–1965), highlights "the activities and achievements of the U.S. labor movements in combating the attempts of Communists and other totalitarian forces to gain control of organized labor."

35:138 Smetherman, Bobbie B., and Smetherman, Robert M. *Territorial Seas and Inter-American Relations: With Case Studies of the Peruvian and U.S. Fishing Industries.* New York: Praeger, 1974. This is a summary of the 200-mile claim issue and analysis of its domestic implications. The authors note the similarity of Latin American nations' recent 200-mile claim to their earlier support of the principle of nonintervention, both of which, the United States claimed, contravene international law.

35:139 Spalding, Hobart A., Jr. "U.S. and Latin American Labor: The Dynamics of Imperialist Control." *Latin American Perspectives* 3:1 (1976), 45–69. Emphasizing the role of the American Institute for Free Labor Development, this article analyzes U.S. labor's involvement in Latin American labor movements. The institute has aided U.S. foreign policy by supporting Latin American unions which are procapitalist.

Swansbrough, R. H. *The Embattled Colossus: Economic Nationalism and the United States Investors in Latin America* [1789–1976] (39:95) examines the psychological and political roots of economic nationalism in Latin America and examines the tensions between the United States and Latin American nations because of their differing perceptions.

35:140 Swansbrough, Robert H. "The Mineral Crisis and U.S. Interest in Latin America." *Journal of Politics* 38:1 (1976), 2–24. Swansbrough examines the increasing U.S. dependence on foreign sources for vital raw materials. These national interests dictate that Washington assign a higher priority to relations with Latin America.

U.S. Aid

See, under "Personalities," William L. Beaulac.

35:141 Binning, William C. "The Nixon Foreign Aid Policy for Latin America." *Inter-American Economic Affairs* 25:1 (1971), 31–45. Nixon's "low profile" policy for Latin America was designed to move from paternalism to a "mature partnership." It concentrated on improving trade opportunities and channeling aid through multilateral agencies.

35:142 Kaplan, Stephen S. "The Distribution of Aid to Latin America: A Cross-National Aggregate Data and Time Series Analysis." *Journal of Developing Areas* 10:1 (1975), 37–60. Why over the years 1946 to 1973 was there an unequal distribution of U.S. aid to Latin American countries? The author finds that distribution was a function of population size; balance of payments was also important, as was military expendi-

ture. There was little or no relationship between aid and U.S. direct investment.

35:143 Petras, James F., and LaPorte, Robert, Jr. *Cultivating Revolution: The United States and Agrarian Reform in Latin America.* New York: Random House, 1971. Using reform movements in Peru and Chile during the 1950s and 1960s as case studies, the authors conclude that U.S. policy was apparently concerned with neither land reform nor production. It may have been directed at continuing cooperation with the ruling elite, for political rather than economic considerations.

35:144 Rabe, Stephen G. "The Elusive Conference: United States Economic Relations with Latin America, 1945–1952." *Diplomatic History* 2:3 (1978), 279–94. While formulating comprehensive aid programs for Europe and Asia, the United States repeatedly avoided the calling of a high-level conference to establish a similar program for Latin America. Instead, the United States preached self-help, technical cooperation, and private enterprise and investment to the Latin Americans.

Alliance for Progress

See "Personalities," especially Lyndon B. Johnson, John F. Kennedy.

35:145 Agudelo Villa, Hernando. *La Alianza para el Progreso: Esperanza y Frustración* [The Alliance for Progress: hope and frustration]. Bogotá: Ediciones Tercer Mundo, 1966. This Colombian believes that the Alliance for Progress lost sight of its original goals. Insufficient U.S. financial aid, lack of truly multilateral direction, and the tendency of the United States to use financial aid as an instrument of policy explains the decline. Agudelo Villa does not give sufficient weight to Latin American shortcomings.

35:146 Agudelo Villa, Hernando. *La Revolución de Desarrollo: Orígen y Evolución de la Alianza para el Progesso* [The revolution of development: the origins and evolution of the Alliance for Progress]. Mexico, D.F.: Editorial Roble, 1966. This is an account of the intentions and early plans of the alliance. The alliance is viewed as an authentic revolution, a genuine attempt to combine the efforts of the haves and have-nots for social progress. In a subsequent volume (above), he reverses his position.

35:147   Alba, Victor. *Alliance without Allies: The Mythology of Progress in Latin America.* Trans. by John Pearson. New York: Praeger, 1965. This polemic contends that the alliance did not reach 90 percent of Latin Americans. The alliance, Alba claims, was based on the premise that by aiding the middle class, democracy and progressive reform would be furthered.

35:148   Canelas O., Amado. *Radiografiá de la Alianza para el Atraso* [X-ray of the Alliance for "Backwardness"]. La Paz, Bol.: Libreria "Altiplano," 1963. This is a leftist analysis of the Alliance for Progress.

35:149   Dreier, John C., ed. *The Alliance for Progress: Problems and Perspectives.* Baltimore: Johns Hopkins Press, 1962. A collection of essays by persons directly involved appraises the first year of its operation.

35:150   Gordon, Lincoln. *A New Deal for Latin America: The Alliance For Progress.* Cambridge: Harvard University Press, 1963. This view of the alliance by a former Harvard economics professor, State Department official, and ambassador to Brazil expresses the view that genuine economic and social reform was central to the alliance, as was the U.S. aim to promote its security and private economic interests.

35:151   Hanson, Simon G. *Dollar Diplomacy Modern Style: Chapters in the Failure of the Alliance for Progress.* Washington, D.C.: Inter-American Affairs Press, 1970. President Kennedy inaugurated a policy for dealing with peoples about whom he knew nothing; Latin Americans weren't ready to cooperate. They just wanted the United States to drop money and go away. U.S. business interests emerged as the only beneficiaries.

35:152   Levinson, Jerome, and Onis, Juan de. *The Alliance That Lost Its Way: A Critical Report on the Alliance for Progress.* Chicago: Quadrangle, 1970. This work by a former alliance official and a journalist familiar with Latin America characterizes the alliance in 1961 as "a dramatic and fundamental reorientation of Washington's policy toward Latin America." Yet the authors admit that a decade of the alliance in operation has yielded "more shattered hopes than accomplishments" and "more disillusion than satisfaction."

35:153   Lowenthal, Abraham F. "United States Policy toward Latin America: 'Liberal,' 'Radical,' and 'Bureaucratic' Perspectives." *Latin American Research Review* 35:3 (1973), 3–26. Lowenthal suggests that "liberals," who view the alliance as a well-meant effort that hit short of the mark, and "radicals," who maintain that it was merely a new phase of U.S. imperialism that succeeded, have concentrated on goals and results. He suggests that attention should be given to the bureaucratic processes.

35:154   May, Herbert K. *Problems and Prospects of the Alliance for Progress: A Critical Examination.* New York: Praeger, 1968. The author sustains his enthusiasm for the alliance and maintains that it had a better record of achievement than was recognized. He called for a reorganization, a latinization of the alliance.

35:155   Perloff, Harvey S. *Alliance for Progress: A Social Innovation in the Making.* Baltimore: Johns Hopkins Press, 1969. Characterizing the alliance as "a truly magnificent concept . . . ," the author blames its shortcomings on execution rather than intent. He maintained that even after eight years of operation the alliance had future potential.

35:156   Rogers, William D. *The Twilight Struggle: The Alliance for Progress and the Politics of Development in Latin America.* New York: Random House, 1967. Formerly a deputy coordinator for the alliance, Rogers maintains that the United States did respond to the need for a social revolution in Latin America and that the alliance largely succeeded in providing one.

35:157   Schlesinger, Arthur M., Jr. "The Alliance for Progress: A Retrospective." In Ronald G. Hellman and H. Jon Rosenbaum, eds., *Latin America: The Search for a New International Role.* New York: Wiley, 1975, pp. 57–92. The author maintains that President Kennedy intended to promote substantive economic growth, structural change, and political democratization. He is critical of Kennedy's preoccupation with counterinsurgency and with the alliance for its cumbersome bureaucracy. He is most critical of President Johnson's reducing the commitment to structural change and political democratization.

MILITARY ASSISTANCE

35:158   Baines, John M. "U.S. Military Assistance to Latin America: An Assessment." *Journal of Inter-American Studies and World Affairs* 14:4 (1972), 469–86. The author notes that beginning in 1938, and increasingly during World War II, Latin America looked to the United States as the major arms supplier. U.S. policy gradually shifted from fostering hemispheric defense to promoting internal security; but military assistance programs have not been the direct cause of antidemocratic coups and militarism in Latin America.

35:159   Barber, Willard F., and Ronning, C. Neale. *Internal Security and Military Power: Counterinsurgency and Civic Action in Latin America.* Columbus: Ohio State University Press, 1966. The United States has sought to use the Latin American military to battle internal subversion and promote technical progress in the Americas. But the training and aid have put the military in the business of promoting social welfare. U.S. involvement with the Latin American military has often placed the Pentagon and State Department at cross-purposes. Bibliography.

35:160   Johnson, John J. *The Military and Society in Latin America.* Stanford, Calif.: Stanford University Press, 1964. In this thoughtful examination the author argues that the role of the military, increasingly influenced by the urban middle class, will continue to be important in unstable Latin American societies. Extensive bibliography.

35:161   Lieuwen, Edwin. *Arms and Politics in Latin America.* 2d ed. New York: Praeger, 1963. Besides developing the role of the military in the political and social developments in twelve countries since the 1930s, the author treats U.S. development of the Latin American military. He concluded that the military assistance programs have had unfortunate results for both the United States and Latin America. Extensive bibliography.

35:162   Lieuwen, Edwin. *Generals vs. Presidents: Neomilitarism in Latin America.* New York: Praeger, 1964. More or less a sequel to *Arms and Politics,* this work analyzes seven military coups between 1962 and 1964. The author relates the coups to the implementation of the Alliance for Progress and discusses the dilemma for U.S. recognition policies: how to strengthen security and, at the same time, promote democratic ideals. Bibliography.

ARMS CONTROL AND DISARMAMENT

See Chapter 40, "Arms Control and Disarmament," for general references.

35:163   Gall, Norman, "Nuclear Proliferation: Atoms for Brazil, Dangers for All." *Foreign Policy,* no. 23 (1976), 155–201. Despite President Carter's efforts, West Germany agreed to supply Brazil with the technology and equipment which could provide Brazil with a nuclear weapon capability.

35:164   Garcia Robles, Alfonso. *The Denuclearization of Latin America.* New York: Carnegie Endowment for International Peace, 1967. This is a discussion of a 1963 proposal for the creation of a nuclear free zone in Latin America. Spanish original: *La desnuclearización de la América Latina,* 2d rev. ed. (México, D.F.: Colegio de México, 1966).

35:165   Redick, John P. "The Politics of Denuclearization: A Study of the Treaty for the Prohibition of Nuclear Weapons in Latin America." Ph.D. diss., University of Virginia, 1970. This account provides the most extensive coverage of the Treaty of Tlatelolco in English. Also see his "Regional Nuclear Arms Control in Latin America," *International Organization* 29 (Spring 1975), 415–45.

35:166   Robinson, Davis R. "The Treaty of Tlatelolco and the United States: Latin American Nuclear Free Zone." *American Journal of International Law* 64:2 (1970), 282–309. This is a study of the historical development of the treaty designed to exclude nuclear weapons from Latin America. The United States did not sign Protocol I, which called upon outside countries to undertake treaty obligations with respect to their territories within the zone. The United States did adhere to Protocol II, which calls for nuclear powers not to contribute to violating the treaty and not to threaten use of or to use nuclear weapons against treaty members.

Relations of Individual States

35:167   Astiz, Carlos Alberto, ed., with McCarthy, Mary F. *Latin American International Politics: Ambitions, Capabilities, and the National Interest of Mexico, Brazil, and Argentina.* Notre Dame, Ind.: University of Notre Dame Press, 1969. These essays demonstrate that while most Latin American countries did not develop separate foreign policies, four—Cuba, Mexico, Brazil, and Argentina—have done so. Since Cuba is a special case, its foreign policy is excluded. The other three nations see themselves as not only playing a role in inter-American affairs, but in global politics as well.

MEXICO

See "Personalities," especially Luis Echeverria (under "Others").

Cline, H. F. *The United States and Mexico* (2:299) is as much an interdisciplinary survey as a history of bilateral relations. Half of the text covers the period 1941 to 1962.

35:168   Cline, Howard F. *Mexico: Revolution to Evolution, 1940–1960.* New York: Oxford University Press, 1963. This respected treatment of a critical period of Mexico's political and economic development includes a lengthy section on foreign relations. The author views Mexico's foreign policy as a continuation of President Lazaro Cardenas's, emphasizing nonintervention and self-determination. Extensive bibliography.

35:169   Corominas, Enrique V. *Mexico, Cuba, y la O.E.A.* [Mexico, Cuba, and the OAS]. Buenos Aires: Ediciones Política, Economía y Finanzas, 1965. An important analysis and defense of Mexico's foreign policies toward Cuba and other Latin American countries by a former Mexican delegate to the OAS.

35:170   Fabela, Isidro. *Buena y Mala Vecindad* [Good and bad neighbor]. Mexico, D.F.: Editorial América Nueva, 1958. A famous Mexican diplomat, jurist, and historian offers praise for President Roosevelt, but is critical of Truman and Eisenhower. There are essays on U.S.-Mexico bilateral relations, as well as U.S. relations with Latin America (1933–1954). Fabela indicts U.S. policy after 1945 on military, economic, and juridical grounds.

35:171   Fagen, Richard R. "The Realities of U.S.-Mexican Relations." *Foreign Affairs* 55:4 (1977), 685–700. Despite the fact that such issues as treatment of U.S. prisoners in Mexican jails, drug traffic, and Colorado River water salinity get the newsplay, the question that dominates U.S.-Mexican relations is economic linkage. The U.S. presence in the Mexican economy is enormous; but increasingly the United States is dependent on Mexico.

35:172   Ojeda, Mario. *Alcances y Limites de la Política Exterior de México* [The capacities and limits of Mexico's foreign policy]. México, D.F.: Colegio de México, 1976. This Mexican scholar argues that his nation's foreign policy, which emphasizes national sovereignty and independent choice, has been complicated by U.S.–Soviet Union rivalry. Mexico has been the most consistent of all Latin American countries in opposing U.S. initiatives, and during the presidency of Luis Echeverria (1970–1976) Mexico's foreign policy achieved a universal focus. Extensive bibliography.

35:173   Ross, Stanley R., ed. *Views across the Border: The United States and Mexico.* Albuquerque: University of New Mexico Press, 1978. These essays illustrate the complexity of issues presented when different cultures meet. The essays are divided into groups relating to culture, politics, economics, migration, health, ecology, and individual and social psychology. End notes provide an excellent bibliography.

Schmitt, K. M. *Mexico and the United States, 1821–1973: Conflict and Coexistence* (2:301) develops two main themes: the economic dependency of Mexico on the United States and the power differential between the two countries. During 1941 to 1973, the author argues, U.S.-Mexican relations provided an example of how a great power and a small power interact, and move from rivalry to grudging respect.

Zorrilla, L. G. *Historia de las relaciones entre México y los Estados Unidos de América, 1800–1958* (2:302) presents a Mexican perspective to contrast with those of U.S. scholars. The extensive bibliography at the beginning of volume 1 is valuable for Mexican sources (1821–1963).

Diplomatic Episodes

35:174   Gómez Robledo, Antonio. *México y el Arbitraje Internacional: El Fondo Piadoso de las Californias, La Isla de la Pasión, El Chamizal* [Mexico and international arbitration: the Pious Fund of the Californias, Passion Island, the Chamizal]. Mexico, D.F.: Editorial Porrúa, 1965. The author points out that Mexico has been more inclined to make an issue of these cases than has the United States. While the account is sometimes impassioned, it is generally a balanced appeal for the uniform application of international law. Documents.

Hundley, N., Jr. *Dividing the Waters: A Century of Controversy between the United States and Mexico* (15:177) is an account of the complicated division of waters from the Rio Grande, Colorado, and Tijuana rivers. It was designed to be a study from both sides of the border, but Mexico refused to open its records. Also discussed is the Colorado River water salinity in the Mexicali Valley.

35:175 Liss, Sheldon B. *A Century of Disagreement: The Chamizal Conflict, 1864–1964*. Washington, D.C.: University Press of America, 1965. This volume treats not only the boundary dispute (1864–1964) but the social and cultural atmosphere of the El Paso-Ciudad Juárez area. The controversy has been more of an emotional irritant than a major conflict. Extensive bibliography.

35:176 Sepúlveda, César. *La Frontera de México: Historia, Conflictos, 1762–1975* [The border of Mexico: history and conflicts, 1762–1975]. México, D.F.: Editorial Porrúa, 1976. A sober treatment by a Mexican scholar, it considers the Chamizal question, the division of international river waters, the salinity of the Colorado River, and the last boundary adjustments in 1970. Extensive bibliography.

35:177 Weber, Francis J. *The United States versus Mexico: The Final Settlement of the Pious Fund*. Los Angeles: Historical Society of Southern California, 1969. A minor issue between the United States and Mexico since 1848 resulted in Mexico paying a claim (1967) to the California Jesuits. The original claim, involving Spain and inherited by Mexico, dated from 1735. The settlement, along with the Chamizal settlement, during the Kennedy-Johnson administrations led to better relations with Mexico. Bibliography.

Oil and Other Economic Factors

See also Chapter 39.

35:178 Bermúdez, Antonio J. *La Política Petrolera Mexicana* [The politics of Mexican petroleum]. Mexico, D.F.: Editorial J. Mortiz, 1976. Largely a memoir of the former director general of Petróleos Mexicanos, Bermúdez insists that Mexico's oil reserves must not be used as the reserves for other countries.

35:179 Bermúdez, Antonio J. *The Mexican Petroleum Industry: A Case Study in Nationalism*. Stanford, Calif.: Stanford University, Institute of Hispanic American and Luso-Brazilian Studies, 1963. This detailed study traces the development of Petróleos Mexicanos (Pemex) during the period (1946–1958) when the author headed Mexico's nationalized oil industry.

35:180 Hansen, Roger D. *The Politics of Mexican Development*. Baltimore: Johns Hopkins Press, 1971. The author criticizes the Mexican Revolution for its failure to diminish the gap between rich and poor, and assigns the principal blame to 19th-century, self-seeking entrepreneurial attitudes of the traditional Mexican elite.

35:181 Machado, Manuel A., Jr. *An Industry in Crisis: Mexican–United States Cooperation in the Control of Foot-and-Mouth Disease*. Berkeley: University of California Press, 1968. The study details the crisis in Mexico (1946–1954) and how cooperation stamped out the disease. Anti-Americanism complicated early efforts, but the cooperative effort improved relations. Bibliography.

35:182 Williams, Edward J. *The Rebirth of the Mexican Petroleum Industry: Developments and Policy Implications*. Lexington, Mass.: Lexington Books, 1979. Although primarily an analysis of Mexico's potential for internal development, much of this study is concerned with foreign relations. The traditional "special relationship" between the two countries will intensify, but the power equation will change as the United States becomes dependent upon Mexican oil. Extensive bibliography.

35:183 Wionczek, Miguel S. *El Nacionalismo Mexicano y la inversión extranjera* [Mexican nationalism and foreign investments]. México, D.F.: Siglo Veintiuno Editores, 1967. "Mexicanization," the gradual absorption of foreign-owned industries by the government, is studied in historical perspective in the sugar, electric, and extractive industries.

35:184 Wright, Harry K. *Foreign Enterprise in Mexico*. Chapel Hill: University of North Carolina Press, 1971. A broad inquiry into legal, institutional, and social factors that constitute the environment for investment in Mexico.

Immigration and Labor

35:185 Corwin, Arthur F. "Causes of Mexican Emigration to the United States." *Perspectives in American History* 7 (1973), 557–635. The author cites economic deprivation, dislocation, and economic opportunity in the United States to explain Mexican emigration. He notes also that the common land frontier between the two countries is a "geo-social fact" that distinguishes Mexican migration from that of other nations.

35:186   Corwin, Arthur F. "Mexican Emigration History, 1900–1970." *Latin American Research Review* 8:2 (1973), 3–24. This essay reviews publications from both the United States and Mexico and outlines research opportunities. The sources are evaluated, and there is a list of bibliographical aids.

35:187   Corwin, Arthur F., ed. *Immigrants and Immigrants: Perspectives on Mexican Labor Migration to the United States*. Westport, Conn.: Greenwood, 1978. Thirteen chapters trace the historical evolution of Mexican immigration (1848–1976). The impact on Mexico and contributions to the U.S. economy, other than labor, are virtually ignored.

Craig, R. B. *The Bracero Program: Interest Groups and Foreign Policy* (35:86).

Levenstein, H. A. *Labor Organization in the United States and Mexico: A History of Their Relations* (35:88).

SOUTH AMERICA

Liss, S. B. *Diplomacy and Dependence: Venezuela, the United States and the Americas* [1810–1977] (2:306) emphasizes the bilateral relationship and argues that the United States has had considerable impact on Venezuela's economic growth, political liberalism, and maldistribution of wealth.

Pike, F. B. *The United States and the Andean Republics: Peru, Bolivia, and Ecuador* [1820–1976] (2:267) argues that U.S. leaders have never fully comprehended Andean culture, which emphasizes corporate (patron-client) value systems.

Whitaker, A. P. *The United States and South America: The Northern Republics* (2:269) is as much a comprehensive multidisciplinary survey as diplomatic history. After pointing out the common features of Venezuela, Peru, Colombia, Ecuador, and Bolivia, Whitaker concentrates on their relations with the United States during and after World War II. Bibliography.

Whitaker, A. P., ed. *The United States and the Southern Cone: Argentina, Chile, and Uruguay* (2:270) sees U.S. actions as an extension of the interventionist policy once limited to the Caribbean. But America's power to manipulate events in that region has been vastly overrated.

Argentina

See "Personalities," especially American Spruille Braden (under "Others"), and Juan D. Perón.

35:188   Alexander, Robert J. *An Introduction to Argentina*. New York: Praeger, 1969. A discussion of all aspects of the Argentine nation and people, past and present, which though dated is still a solid introduction to Argentina.

35:189   Bagú, Sergio. *Argentina en el Mundo* [Argentina in the world]. Vol. 3 in *La Realidad Argentina en el Siglo XX*. México, D.F.: Fondo de Cultura Económica, 1961. One of four volumes explaining why Argentina has not achieved political and cultural hegemony over South America, this study treats foreign relations. Although not dealing primarily with U.S.-Argentina relations, these bilateral relations are discussed at length.

35:190   Ciria, Alberto. *Estados Unidos nos mira* [The United States views us]. Buenos Aires: Ediciones La Bastilla, 1973. This defensive Peronist intellectual wrote a critical analysis of North Americans writing about Argentina (1935–1970). He includes monographs and articles, as well as memoirs and less scholarly items. The bibliographic citations alone make this a useful book.

35:191   Conil Paz, Alberto, and Ferrari, Gustavo. *Argentina's Foreign Policy, 1930–1962*. Trans. by John J. Kennedy. Notre Dame, Ind.: University of Notre Dame Press, 1966. Two nationalistic Argentine scholars examine such episodes as the lend-lease consultations, Secretary of State Cordell Hull's campaign of pressure during World War II, postwar relations with the United States and the UN, and Arturo Frondizi's relations with Fidel Castro. Extensive bibliography.

35:192   Goldwert, Marvin. *Democracy, Militarism and Nationalism in Argentina, 1930–1966*. Austin: University of Texas Press, 1972. The military, and its relationship to political and social life, are examined in an attempt to explain the course of Argentine history since the fall of Yrigoyen.

35:193 Kirkpatrick, Jeane J. *Leader and Vanguard in Mass Society: A Study of Peronist Argentina*. Cambridge, Mass.: MIT Press, 1971. This is a well-researched study.

Peterson, H. F. *Argentina and the United States, 1810–1960* (2:287) is intent on chronicling in detail the diplomatic and commercial relations. One theme pervades his account—a duel for continental leadership.

35:194 Potash, Robert A. *The Army and Politics in Argentina, 1928–1945: Yrigoyen to Peron*. Stanford, Calif.: Stanford University Press, 1969. This is a detailed and scholarly analysis of the political role of the Argentine military.

Whitaker, A. P. *The United States and Argentina* (2:288) is a sound introductory volume. Emphasis is given to the rise of Juan Perón and the strained relations between the two countries during and immediately following World War II.

35:195 Whitaker, Arthur P. *Argentine Upheaval: Peron's Fall and the New Regime*. New York: Praeger, 1956. This slim sequel (1946–1955) to the author's *United States and Argentina* deals with internal affairs, but is insightful of foreign policy issues. Whitaker concludes that Perón's growing closeness to the United States was a factor in his fall.

Bolivia

See, under "Personalities," Víctor Andrade (under "Others").

35:196 Barton, Robert. *A Short History of the Republic of Bolivia*. 2d ed. La Paz, Bol.: Los Amigos del Libro, 1968. An introductory study, it contains an appendix listing U.S. diplomatic agents who served in Bolivia from 1948 to 1968.

35:197 Blasier, Cole. "The United States and the Revolution." In James M. Malloy and Richard S. Thorn, eds., *Beyond the Revolution: Bolivia since 1952*. Pittsburgh: University of Pittsburgh Press, 1971, pp. 53–109. Blasier maintains that the Bolivian Revolution (1937–1964) is the only genuine social revolution the United States has supported. He believes that U.S. aid made the revolution work. Washington did so because of humanitarian considerations and a desire to deradicalize the revolution.

35:198 Céspedes, Augusto. *Imperialismo y Desarrollo* [Imperialism and development]. La Paz, Bol., 1963. The author, a moderate, criticizes the Bolivian government's relations with the United States. He insists that development in Bolivia (1952–1962) under the aegis of U.S. aid benefitted primarily the United States, which was increasing its share of control over manufacturing. He is also critical of AFL-CIO efforts to shape Andean labor into a North American mold.

35:199 Klein, Herbert S. *Parties and Political Change in Bolivia, 1880–1952*. New York: Cambridge University Press, 1970. The author traces in full the antecedent forces of the 1952 revolution.

35:200 Malloy, James M. *Bolivia: The Uncompleted Revolution*. Pittsburgh: University of Pittsburgh Press, 1970. The author believes that Bolivia has been continuously in a revolutionary situation since 1936. Political and economic events are traced to 1964.

35:201 Malloy, James M., and Thorn, Richard S., eds. *Beyond the Revolution: Bolivia since 1952*. Pittsburgh: University of Pittsburgh Press, 1971. This is a collection of studies on Bolivian political, economic, and social developments since 1952.

35:202 Sanders, G. Earl. "The Quiet Experiment in American Diplomacy: An Interpretative Essay on Aid to the Bolivian Revolution." *Americas* 33:1 (1976), 25–49. After years of distrust, the United States accepted Bolivia's Movimiento Nacionalisto Revolucionario (MNR). The State Department decided that MNR offered a chance for stability in 1952 and that U.S. aid could consolidate the party's "pragmatic center" against its labor-left wing. U.S. aid had a moderating effect.

35:203 Wilkie, James W. *The Bolivian Revolution and U.S. Aid since 1952: Financial Background and Context of Political Decisions*. Los Angeles: University of California, Latin American Center, 1969. U.S. aid contributed between one-fourth and one-third of the Bolivian operating budget in the late 1950s and early 1960s. Bolivian outlays for social needs overshadowed expenditures in basic economic development. Wilkie makes a case for using budgets and actual expenditures as a test for the ideology of political movements. Extensive bibliography.

35:204 Zovdag, Cornelius H. *The Bolivian Economy, 1952–65: The Revolution and Its Aftermath.* New York: Praeger, 1966. A former official of AID in Bolivia examines the social, economic, and political impact of the Bolivian Revolution.

Brazil

See "Personalities," especially, under "Others," Castello Branco, Getulio Vargas.

35:205 Black, Jan Knippers. *United States Penetration of Brazil.* Philadelphia: University of Pennsylvania Press, 1977. Although this study may exaggerate U.S. machinations in Brazil (1961–1964), it offers details on the roles of the U.S. Information Service, the American Institute for Free Labor Development, the Inter-American Police Academy, U.S. corporations, U.S. military, and Brazilian "linkage groups." The author demonstrates how extravagant U.S. policymakers have been in defining the imperatives of U.S. national security. Extensive bibliography.

Burns, E. B. *A History of Brazil* (2:289).

35:206 Dubnic, Vladimir R. de. *Political Trends in Brazil.* Washington, D.C.: Public Affairs Press, 1968. A knowledgeable account of contemporary Brazilian politics which centers upon the Quadras, Goulart, and Castello Branco regimes.

35:207 Dulles, John W. F. *Unrest in Brazil: Political-Military Crises, 1955–1964.* Austin: University of Texas Press, 1970. The author continues his chronicling of Brazil's recent political history by concentrating on personalities who held the presidency. He treats the presidencies of Juscelino Kubitschek and João Goulart, both of whom made a great impact on inter-American affairs and bilateral relations. Extensive bibliographies.

Fontaine, R. W. *Brazil and the United States: Toward a Maturing Relationship* [1808–1974] (2:291) examines the strains imposed upon the traditional relationship by Brazil's desire to become the "other major power" in the western hemisphere.

35:208 Parker, Phyllis R. *Brazil and the Quiet Intervention* [1961–1964]. Austin: University of Texas Press, 1979. Based primarily on interviews and materials in the Kennedy and Johnson libraries, this analysis of the U.S. role in the overthrow of Brazil's Goulart administration and rise of the Castello Branco regime views events largely through the eyes of American conspirators.

35:209 Schneider, Ronald M. *Brazil: Foreign Relations of a Future World Power.* Boulder, Colo.: Westview, 1976. Schneider demonstrates that since 1964 Brazil has achieved world power status. New economic alliances with Western Europe and Japan have supplanted strategic ones. The traditional U.S.-Brazil partnership, the author concludes, is dead.

35:210 Skidmore, Thomas E. *Politics in Brazil, 1930–1964: An Experiment in Democracy.* New York: Oxford University Press, 1967. Attempting to investigate the causes of the fall of President João Goulart in 1964, the author has written a detailed interpretation of what he regards "as the most important factors determining the trend of Brazilian politics since the Revolution of 1930." Extensive bibliography.

Economic Factors

35:211 Baer, Werner. *The Development of the Brazilian Steel Industry.* Nashville: Vanderbilt University Press, 1969. This is a well-documented review of the growth of the Brazilian steel industry, the largest in Latin America.

35:212 Ellis, Howard S., ed. *The Economy of Brazil.* Berkeley: University of California Press, 1969. Contributions by Brazilian and American economists on Brazil's post–World War II economic development.

35:213 Kaplan, Stephen S., and Bonsor, Norman C. "Did United States Aid Really Help Brazilian Development? The Perspective of a Quarter-Century." *Inter-American Economic Affairs* 27:3 (1973), 25–46. The authors argue that it may be an error to dismiss U.S. aid to Latin America as a failure. While aid has not led to a redistribution of wealth nor significantly improved the standard of living in Brazil, they maintain that it has fostered industrial growth and that may hold a potential for social welfare.

35:214 McMillan, Claude, Jr., and Gonzalez, Richard F. *International Enterprise in a Developing Economy: A Study of U.S. Business in Brazil.* East Lansing: Michigan State University, Bureau of Business and Economic Research, 1964. This study examines the nature, organization, and beneficial impact of North American corporate enterprise on the Brazilian economy.

35:215 Roett, Riordan. *The Politics of Foreign Aid in the Brazilian Northeast.* Nashville: Vanderbilt University Press, 1972. This work demonstrates that the Agency for International Development (AID) undermined original well-meant Alliance for Progress goals (1962–1970). Bypassing local social planners, AID officials, seeking an immediate political impact, channeled funds through the entrenched oligarchy, hampering modernization. Bibliography.

35:216 Wirth, John D. *The Politics of Brazilian Development, 1930–1954.* Stanford, Calif.: Stanford University Press, 1970. A study of the economic policymaking during the Vargas era, with particular reference to steel, petroleum, and foreign trade.

Chile

See "Personalities," especially Claude Bowers (under "Others"), Richard M. Nixon.

35:217 Baklanoff, Eric N. "The Expropriation of Anaconda in Chile: A Perspective on an Export Enclave." *SECOLAS Annals* 4 (1973), 16–38. This essay examines Anaconda Copper's postwar responses (1946–1972) to Chile's investment climate and the company's influence on the Chilean economy. The author concludes that Anaconda was economically beneficial to Chile and that Allende's charges of excess profits were baseless.

35:218 *Chile: A Critical Survey.* Santiago: Institute of General Studies, 1972. Allende's regime in Chile is convincingly depicted in these detailed and careful studies, whose combined scope covers the entire national life. The 16 authors are respected scholars and others prominent in public affairs.

35:219 Fagen, Richard R. "The United States and Chile: Roots and Branches." *Foreign Affairs* 53:2 (1975), 297–313. The author is critical of U.S. intervention in Chile before and after the election of Marxist President Salvador Allende. The U.S. response must be viewed as a product of cold war thinking, Fagen insists.

35:220 Gross, Leonard. *The Last, Best Hope: Eduardo Frei and Chilean Democracy.* New York: Random House, 1967. A journalistic survey of Eduardo Frei's regime.

35:221 Michaels, Albert L. "The Alliance for Progress and Chile's 'Revolution in Liberty,' 1964–1970."

Journal of Interamerican Studies and World Affairs 18:1 (1976), 74–99. The author demonstrates that while the alliance achieved some of its goals in Chile, it failed because economic development conflicted with other thrusts of American foreign policy, such as protecting markets and overseas investments.

Pike, F. B. *Chile and the United States, 1880–1962: The Emergence of Chile's Social Crisis and the Challenge to United States Diplomacy* (2:295) devoting much space to internal developments, Pike demonstrates that relations between the two countries have been affected since the 1930s by the social ferment in Chile.

35:222 Walpin, Miles D. *Cuban Foreign Policy and Chilean Politics.* Lexington, Mass.: Heath Lexington Books, 1972. In this study of recent Chilean political developments, the author argues that "great power infusions are of major importance to internal political conflicts and outcomes."

Allende Years

35:223 Debray, Régis. *The Chilean Revolution: Conversations with Allende.* New York: Pantheon, 1972. A well-known French leftist interviews President Allende on his regime and politics in Chile.

35:224 Gil, Federico G. "Socialist Chile and the United States." *Inter-American Economic Affairs* 27:2 (1973), 29–48. This article is an account of U.S.-Chile economic relations from the election to the fall of President Salvador Allende.

35:225 Gil, Federico G.; Lagos, Ricardo E.; and Landsberger, Henry A., eds. *Chile, 1970–1973: Lecciones de Una Experiencia* [Chile, 1970–1973: the lessons of an experience]. Madrid: Editorial Tecnos, 1977. This collection of essays by participants in a seminar on Chile's Popular Unity coalition proceed from the premise that the U.S. government and private corporations, with Chile's middle class, created unstable political and economic conditions, but were not the "determinant" in the fall of Salvador Allende's government.

35:226 Moss, Robert. *Chile's Marxist Experiment.* Newton Abbot: David & Charles, 1973. A British journalist debunks accounts which ascribe the fall of Salvador Allende to the machinations of the CIA and U.S.-based multinational corporations. He emphasizes the economic and social chaos in Chile. Bibliography.

35:227 Petras, James, and Morely, Morris. *The United States and Chile: Imperialism and the Overthrow of the Allende Government.* New York: Monthly Review Press, 1975. Blaming the Nixon administration's determination to protect American business and multinational corporations, the authors explain the fall of the Allende government. This narrow focus ignores the internal dynamics within Chile.

35:228 U.S. House. Committee on Foreign Affairs. Hearings; *The United States and Chile during the Allende Years, 1970–1973.* Washington, D.C.: G.P.O., 1975. For presenting a variety of points of view, this is the best single volume on the subject. It contains articles and letters, as well as prepared statements by Latin Americanists with a strong interest in Chile. Extensive bibliography and annotated chronology.

Colombia

35:229 Dix, Robert H. *Colombia: The Political Dimensions of Change.* New Haven, Conn.: Yale University Press, 1967. This is a solid study of the process of modernization—industrialization and urbanization—in Colombia.

35:230 Galbraith, W. O. *Colombia: A General Survey.* 2d ed. New York: Oxford University Press (1953), 1966. This revised edition contains updated material on political and economic developments. A useful introduction to contemporary Colombia.

35:231 Guzman Campas, German. *La violencia en Colombia: Parte descriptiva* [Violence in Colombia: descriptive part]. Cali: Ediciones Progreso, 1968. An expanded version of Guzman Campas's contribution to a multi-author study, *La violencia,* it was first published in 1962 and is recognized as a major work on Colombian history from 1948 to 1958.

35:232 Holt, Pat M. *Colombia Today—and Tomorrow.* New York: Praeger, 1964. Holt provides a brief survey of contemporary Colombia, touching upon, among other things, the politics of the National Front, the Peace Corps, coffee, and the "conservative" church.

35:233 Torres Restryso, Camillo. *Revolutionary Priest: The Complete Writings and Messages of Camillo Torres.* Ed. with an introduction by John Gerassi. Trans. by June de Cipriano Aloantara et al. New York: Random House, 1971. Included here are the speeches and writings by a well-known priest who was a revolutionary leader and a guerrilla fighter in Colombia. (He was later killed in the field.)

Ecuador

35:234 Bialek, Robert W. *Catholic Politics: A History Based on Ecuador.* New York: Vantage, 1963. Bialek provides a history of the relations between the Catholic church and state in Ecuador.

35:235 Salgado, Germanico. *Ecuador y la integración económica de América Latina* [Ecuador and Latin American economic integration]. Buenos Aires: Instituto para la Integración de América Latina, Banco Interamerican de Desarrollo, 1970. This is a careful investigation of the structure and development possibilities of the Ecuadorian economy, including a discussion of the significance for Ecuador, the Latin American Free Trade Association (LAFTA) and the Andean Pact.

Guiana (Guyana)

35:236 Burnham, Forbes. *A Destiny to Mould: Selected Speeches by the Prime Minister of Guyana.* Ed. by C. A. Nascimento and R. A. Burrowes. New York: Africana Publishing, 1970. This is a collection of speeches by a leading political figure of Guyana covering the period from 1955 to 1969.

35:237 Despres, Leo A. *Cultural Pluralism and Nationalist Politics in British Guyana.* Chicago: Rand-McNally, 1967. Despres has written a scholarly study of the impact which ethnic and cultural factors have had upon the political system of Guyana.

35:238 Irving, Brian, ed. *Guyana: A Composite Monograph.* Hato Rey, P.R.: Inter-American University Press, 1972. Irving's short chapters cover politics, economics, and social aspects.

35:239 Jagan, Cheddi. *The West on Trial: My Fight for Guyana's Freedom.* London: Joseph, 1967. In these personal reflections Guyana's first premier and the leader of the procommunist People's Progressive party blames big business, Britain, and the United States for his inability to stay in power.

35:240 Reno, Philip. *The Ordeal of British Guiana.* New York: Monthly Review Press, 1964. This eulogy of the Jagan regime depicts the Guyanese people as "determined to move ahead—in spite of British obstruction and U.S. intervention."

35:241 Simms, Peter. *Troubles in Guyana: An Account of People, Personalities and Politics as They Were in British Guiana.* London: Allen & Unwin, 1968. Political developments leading to Guyana's independence are thoroughly examined.

Peru

35:242 Belaúnde Terry, Fernando. *Peru's Own Conquest.* Lima: American Studies Press, 1965. In these provocative and revealing personal reflections, the former president of Peru writes of his country—its problems and his plans. Belaúnde Terry was again elected president of Peru in 1980.

Carey, J. C. *Peru and the United States, 1900–1962* (2:303) is a detailed account, emphasizing governmental and private economic relationships. It also provides an analysis of Nixon's 1958 misadventures in Lima.

Einhorn, J. P. *Expropriation Politics* (39:183) examines the Peruvian expropriation of the International Petroleum Company.

35:243 Kantor, Harry. *The Ideology and Program of the Peruvian Aprista Movement.* Berkeley: University of California Press, 1953. A history, generally favorable, of the Alianza Popular Revolucionaria Americana (APRA), intended for all Latin America, though of greatest political importance in Peru.

35:244 Olson, Richard S. "Economic Coercion in International Disputes: The United States and Peru in the IPC Expropriation Dispute of 1968–1971." *Journal of Developing Areas* 9:3 (1975), 395–413. The Velasco government conceived a strategy to deter application of the 1962 Hickenlooper Amendment (by which the United States could cut off aid to a country that expropriated American-owned property). The United States could not apply full sanctions for fear of threatening other U.S. properties in Peru.

35:245 Peterson, Harries-Clichy, and Unger, Tomás. *Petróleo: Hora cero* [Oil: zero hour]. Lima: Distribuidora Inca, 1964. This factual and statistical study, written by a Peruvian and a North American, concludes that political factors have outweighed economic considerations and have hindered the development of the oil industry in Peru.

Pike, F. B. *The Modern History of Peru* (2:304).

35:246 Sharp, Daniel A., ed. *United States Foreign Policy and Peru.* Austin: University of Texas Press, 1972. This symposium on the Peruvian revolution of 1968 was submitted to the Peruvian and U.S. governments for their consideration. Not a standard scholarly work, it was a deliberate effort to affect future U.S. policy.

Uruguay

35:247 Alisky, Marvin. *Uruguay: A Contemporary Survey.* New York: Praeger, 1969. This is a summary of all aspects of Uruguayan life, including its geographical basis, economy, politics, culture, and foreign relations.

35:248 Nunez, Carlos. *Las Tupamaros: Vanguardia armada in el Uruguay* [The Tupamaros: armed vanguard in Uruguay]. 3d ed. Montevideo: Provincias Unidas, 1969. Nunez analyzes the origins, actions, methods, and significance of the Tupamaro urban guerrilla movement.

Venezuela

Liss, S. B. *Diplomacy and Dependence: Venezuela, the United States and the Americas* [1810–1977] (2:306).

35:249 Luzardo, Radolfo. *Notas histórico-económicas, 1928–1963* [Historical-economic notes]. Caracas: Editorial Sucre, 1963. This is a detailed political history of Venezuela (1928–1963).

35:250 Martz, John D. *Acción Democrática: Evolution of a Modern Political Party in Venezuela.* Princeton, N.J.: Princeton University Press, 1966. Martz's factual and objective account traces the origins and rise to power of Venezuela's National Revolutionary party.

35:251 Pérez Alfonso, Juan Pablo. *Petróleo y dependencia* [Petroleum and dependency]. Caracas: Síntesis Dos Mil, 1971. This is an analysis of Venezuela's petroleum policy and its effects on the country's development. The author argues against granting concessions to foreign companies and for a cautious, long-range petroleum policy which will provide a solid basis for the economic development of Venezuela.

35:252 Sáder Pérez, Rubén. *Petróleum Nacional y Opinión Pública* [National petroleum and public opinion]. Caracas: Ediciones Ofidi, 1966. The Venezuelan State Oil Company and Venezuela's role in the Organization of Petroleum Exporting Countries (OPEC) are studied.

36

Canadian-American Relations since 1941

Contributing Editor

ROBERT S. BOTHWELL
University of Toronto

Contents

Introduction

Canada's prime minister, Pierre Elliott Trudeau, once compared the Canadian-American relationship to that between the mouse and the elephant. From the mouse's point of view, the elephant fills the horizon, and few if any important decisions may be taken without assessing their effect on this unpredictable beast. The view from the elephant is understandably different, and the discrepancy serves to illustrate the preponderance of Canadian sources in the chapter which follows.

The United States and Canada have been formal allies since 1940. The decisions taken in that year, and in the year following, formally confirmed and amplified the political and economic linkages between the two countries, based as they were on geography, economic convenience, and cultural similarity. Yet the sheer size and importance of the United States provoked a sense of political claustrophobia, emphasized by the continuous and rapid decline in the power and standing of Great Britain, Canada's transatlantic partner. Many Canadian nationalists, whether of a traditional or a Marxist variety, have seized on the Canadian-American relationship as the true source of Canadian ills, though their prescriptions have often seemed less precise than their complaints.

Much of the literature of Canadian-American relations, therefore, is taken up with the debate between Canadian nationalists and their opponents. Some of that debate is illustrated here, especially in the sections dealing with the nuclear weapons crisis of 1962–1963, American investment in Canada, Vietnam, and relations since 1968. Because so much of the literature in this category is polemical, it would be pointless to list it all, but because of its importance in its effect on Canadian-American relations it has been thought advisable to present a sample, even though much of it does not meet conventional scholarly criteria.

Most of the selections are, of course, conventionally academic, though historians will notice that works by historians peter out after about 1950 or 1955. There are relatively few professional historians engaged in contemporary foreign policy, and restrictions on the use of Canadian documents have made research difficult and inconclusive for the period after 1950. Because Canadian political science has a strong narrative tradition it has been possible to supplement the work of historians with that of the relatively few economists who can write literate English unencumbered with econometric jargon. Much work on Canadian-American economic relations has been done, particularly in the private sector, and especially for the Canadian-American Committee, an outgrowth of the National Planning Association and the C. D. Howe Research Institute.

Periodization has been relatively simple. World War II and its immediate aftermath are a natural unit in the history of Canadian foreign relations. The disappointment of the hopes and dreams of the wartime period was followed by a period of rethinking and recombining, which lasted from 1946 to 1950. By the latter date, all of the crucial policy decisions affecting Canadian postwar foreign policy were taken, and most of the international institutions that Canada would join were in place. Though there has been considerable debate about the nature of Canada's foreign policy, and of Canada's connection to the United States, there has never been any serious possibility that the decisions of 1946 to 1950 would be unmade. The thirty-three years after 1945 have been treated as a single subtheme, though the decade after 1968, the period of Pierre Elliott Trudeau's tenure in office, has been segregated from the rest. Even his attempt to redefine Canadian foreign policy came to little, and toward the end of the 1970s Canada was once again drawing closer to the United States after a period of estrangement.

Economic affairs are closely linked to political issues. Because there exists a gulf between the economic literature and the political analysis, however, economic matters occupy a separate section. Immigration and emigration are to be found nestling under economics. As with political matters, most of the analysts and commentators are Canadians, though often with transborder roots to their American graduate training.

Resources and Overviews

RESEARCH AIDS

While pertinent bibliographies and reference aids are listed here, there are more extensive lists in Chapter 1.

Bibliographies

Foreign Affairs Bibliography: A Selected and Annotated List of Books on International Relations (1:15) is issued at ten-year intervals, and each volume contains a section on the world by regions, which lists Canada.

36:1 Granatstein, J. L., and Stevens, Paul, eds. *Canada since 1867: A Bibliographical Guide*. Toronto: Hakkert, 1974. This bibliography, in essay form, covers national politics, foreign and defense policy, business and economic history, and social and intellectual history. Each chapter was prepared by a subject specialist.

36:2 Matuik, Laurence, and Grant, Madeline, eds. *A Reading Guide to Canada in World Affairs*. Toronto: Canadian Institute of International Affairs, 1972. A basic bibliography, it focuses on contemporary Canadian foreign affairs.

36:3 Page, Donald M. *A Bibliography of Works on Canadian Foreign Relations, 1945–1970*. Toronto: Canadian Institute of International Affairs, 1973. Page provides the most complete bibliography of Canadian foreign relations. He arranges unannotated items under a broad range of topics, including foreign countries. Appended are the "Chronological List of Statements and Speeches Issued by the Department of External Affairs," and "Cumulative Index to the Monthly Report on Canadian External Relations and International Canada, 1962–1970." Indexes.

36:4 Page, Donald M. *A Bibliography of Works on Canadian Foreign Relations, 1971–1975*. Toronto: Canadian Institute of International Affairs, 1977. This volume updates the initial bibliography (1945–1970), and it follows the same format. The Institute of International Affairs plans to continue five-year update volumes.

36:5 "Recent Publications Relating to Canada." *Canadian Historical Review* 1 (1920–). This quarterly includes recent publications on Canadian foreign relations.

36:6 Thibault, Claude. *Bibliographia Canadiana*. Don Mills, Ont.: Longmans, 1973. This bibliographic guide to historical literature has a detailed subject index that is arranged chronologically and topically.

36:7 Wright, Gerald, and Appel Molot, Maureen. "Selected Bibliography of Literature on Canadian-American Relations." *International Organization* 28:4 (1974), 1015–23. This bibliographical essay covers the period from 1900 to 1974.

Yearbooks

36:8 *Canada in World Affairs*. Toronto: Oxford University Press, 1941– . The yearbook surveys Canadian foreign relations, beginning in the late 1930s and continuing to 1965. Each volume is by a different scholar, and the several books vary greatly in quality. Especially useful are the volumes covering 1939 to 1946 and 1961 to 1963. After a hiatus of a decade, the series was resumed in 1980 with the publication of volume 13.

36:9 *The Canadian Annual Review of Politics and Public Affairs*. Ed. by John T. Saywell. Toronto: University of Toronto Press, 1961– . This annual survey of Canadian events includes a section on foreign relations; formerly the *Canadian Annual Review* (1961–1971).

Document Collections

36:10 Blanchette, Arthur E. *Canadian Foreign Policy, 1955–1965: Selected Speeches and Documents*. Toronto: McClelland & Stewart, 1977. Blanchette has collected the more important official pronouncements on Canadian foreign relations, including continental defense and Canadian-American relations. Bibliography.

36:11 Blanchette, Arthur E. *Canadian Foreign Policy, 1966–1976: Selected Speeches and Documents*. Toronto: Gage, 1980. This additional collection includes material on Vietnam, Canadian-American relations, and NATO. Bibliography is spotty and unhelpful.

36:12 Canada. Department of External Affairs. *Documents on Canadian External Relations.* Vols. 7 and 8 [1939–1941] Ottawa: Information Canada, 1975–1976. The first useful volumes in this official series, volumes 7 and 8, touch on Canadian-American disputes over St. Pierre and Miquelon and Greenland, as well as the conduct of diplomacy between the two countries.

36:13 Canada. Department of External Affairs. *Documents on Canadian External Relations.* Vol. 12, *1946.* Ottawa: Supply & Services Canada, 1977. A comprehensive and useful collection, it covers defense arrangements with the United States, the Paris Peace Conference of 1946, and atomic energy.

36:14 Canada. Department of External Affairs. *Documents on Relations between Canada and Newfoundland, 1935–1949.* Ottawa: Information Canada, 1974. Volume 1 contains much information on American bases in Newfoundland and on plans for the defense of North America during World War II.

36:15 MacKay, R. A. *Canadian Foreign Policy, 1945–1954: Selected Speeches and Documents.* Toronto: McClelland & Stewart, 1971. MacKay provides a useful collection of statements and speeches covering such subjects as NATO, continental defense, and the St. Lawrence Seaway.

36:16 Swanson, Roger F., ed. *Canadian-American Summit Diplomacy, 1923–1973: Selected Speeches and Documents.* Toronto: McClelland & Stewart, 1975. The documents and public statements collected here relate to meetings between Canadian prime ministers and American presidents. Not all meetings are covered, presumably because documentation was lacking.

OVERVIEWS

36:17 American Assembly. *The United States and Canada.* Englewood Cliffs, N.J.: Prentice-Hall, 1964. The three essays by Canadians and three by Americans explore such topics as the interlocking histories of countries, the sociological aspects of their connections, the issues which have caused controversy between them, and the relationship of their roles in NATO and in world affairs.

36:18 Bothwell, Robert; Drummond, Ian; and English, John. *Canada since 1945: Power, Politics and Provincialism.* Toronto: University of Toronto Press, 1981. A history of Canada since 1945, this account gives special attention to international trade and the interrelations of Canada and the United States. It is based on primary materials for the periods 1945 to 1957 and 1963 to 1967.

Brebner, J. B. *North Atlantic Triangle: The Interplay of Canada, the United States and Great Britain* (2:233) is the most important general work on Canadian-American relations (1500–1942).

36:19 Clark, Gerald. *Canada: The Uneasy Neighbor.* New York: McKay, 1965. A leading Canadian correspondent discusses two central areas of tension and anxiety—English Canada vis-à-vis French Canada and Canada as a whole vis-à-vis the United States.

36:20 Clarkson, Stephen, ed. *An Independent Foreign Policy for Canada?* Toronto: McClelland & Stewart, 1968. This is a balanced and comprehensive examination of Canadian foreign relations—especially those with the United States—by a group of academics whose views span the spectrum. It is representative of contemporary views.

Craig, G.M. *The United States and Canada* (2:219) is an introduction to Canadian-American relations (1600–1967) intended for undergraduates and the general public. The author argues that success in strengthening American-Canadian ties will depend on appreciation of differences as well as similarities between the two nations.

36:21 Creighton, Donald G. *The Forked Road: Canada, 1939–1957.* Toronto: McClelland & Stewart, 1976. This is a general history of Canada during the war and postwar years, which places special, disapproving, emphasis on Canadian relations with the United States. The book has been criticized by specialists because of its scanty primary research and doubtful claims.

Deener, D. R., ed. *Canada–United States Treaty Relations* (2:220) is a collection of essays, not always on treaty relations. It contains a useful essay on military relations and several on international law, as well as on power and gas exports and the Columbia River. It also contains a list of treaties and agreements between Canada and the United States.

36:22 Fraser, Blair. *The Search for Identity: Canada, 1945–1967.* Garden City, N.Y.: Doubleday,

1967. Fraser provides a fast-paced journalistic account of Canada's recent history.

Glazebrook, G. P. D. *A History of Canadian External Relations* (2:221) has been until recently the standard work on Canadian external relations (1840–1950).

36:23 Granatstein, J. L., ed. *Canadian Foreign Policy since 1945: Middle Power or Satellite?* 3d ed. Toronto: Copp Clark, 1973. A collection of readings designed for undergraduates (1945–1973), it deals with, among other matters, Canadian-American relations, and has a useful section on the defense crisis of 1962–1963. An introductory chapter covers pre-1945 Canadian foreign policy. Bibliography.

36:24 Holmes, John W. *The Better Part of Valour: Essays on Canadian Diplomacy.* Toronto: McClelland & Stewart, 1970. A wide-ranging collection of essays by a prominent ex-diplomat and foreign affairs commentator, it includes several accounts on the problems of Canadian-American relations (1960–1970), and Indochina.

36:25 Holmes, John W. *Canada: A Middle-Aged Power.* Toronto: McClelland & Stewart, 1976. A collection of essays by an ex-diplomat originally published as articles or delivered as speeches (1970–1975), this gracefully written volume includes a section on North America.

36:26 Keenleyside, Hugh L., and Brown, Gerald S. *Canada and the United States: Some Aspects of Their Historical Relations.* Rev. ed. New York: Knopf (1929), 1952. This account includes useful information (1783–1952) on economics, politics, immigration and emigration; however, it has become seriously dated.

36:27 Nish, C. "Canada and the American Dilemma: Realism versus Idealism, 1945–1964." In Charles A. Barker, ed., *Power and Law: American Dilemma in World Affairs.* Baltimore: Johns Hopkins Press, 1971, pp. 66–81. Nish examines Canadian and American roles in UN-related peacekeeping activities (Korea and Vietnam).

36:28 Preston, Richard A., ed. *The Influence of the United States on Canadian Development: Eleven Case Studies.* Durham, N.C.: Duke University Press, 1972. The essays, a potpourri ranging over the spectrum of Canadian-American relations (1900–1971), from cultural influences to labor history, vary widely in scholarship and merit.

36:29 Stacey, Charles P. *Canada and the Age of Conflict.* Toronto: University of Toronto Press, 1981, vol. 2. This volume (1921–1948) is particularly useful for the diplomacy of World War II and for the relationship between Prime Minister Mackenzie King and President Roosevelt.

Personalities

Additional references to data on individuals may be found in Chapter 1, "Biographical Data."

AMERICAN

See Chapter 24, under "Personalities" and "Presidential Administrations," for additional references.

Hooker, N. H., ed. *The Moffat Papers: Selections from the Diplomatic Journals of Jay Pierrepont Moffat, 1919–1943* (20:70) covers Moffat's service as American minister in Ottawa (1940–1943). It is not, however, a complete collection of Moffat's dispatches, and must be supplemented from the Moffat Papers and the State Department files.

CANADIAN

John G. Diefenbaker

36:30 Diefenbaker, John G. *One Canada: Memoirs of the Right Honourable John G. Diefenbaker.* 3 vols. Toronto: Macmillan, 1975–1977. These volumes, a tedious and frequently inaccurate reminiscence by Canada's prime minister from 1957 to 1963, testify to his bad relations with the Kennedy administration and provide a very one-sided version of the nuclear weapons controversy between Canada and the United States. These volumes should be used with caution.

Ghent, J. "Did He Fall or Was He Pushed? The Kennedy Administration and the Collapse of the Diefenbaker Government" (36:100).

36:31 Grant, George. *Lament for a Nation: The Defeat of Canadian Nationalism.* Toronto: McClelland & Stewart, 1965. Grant romanticizes the significance of Prime Minister Diefenbaker's struggles with the

United States in the early 1960s. This book enjoyed widespread Canadian popularity and went through several printings; it is important for its impact on Canadian academic opinion.

36:32   Lyon, Peyton V. *The Policy Question: A Critical Reappraisal of Canada's Role in World Affairs.* Toronto: McClelland & Stewart, 1963. In this polemical attack by an ex-diplomat on Prime Minister Diefenbaker's foreign policy, Lyon stresses Canada's poor relations with the United States.

36:33   Newman, Peter C. *Renegade In Power: The Diefenbaker Years.* Toronto: McClelland & Stewart, 1963. A well-informed journalist's account of the Diefenbaker government from 1957 to 1963, it deals with Canadian-American conflict over Cuba and nuclear weapons.

36:34   Sévigny, Pierre. *This Game of Politics.* Toronto: McClelland & Stewart, 1965. This is an account of Diefenbaker's political career as leader of the Progressive Conservative party and prime minister (1957–1963).

Walter L. Gordon

36:35   Gordon, Walter L. *A Political Memoir.* Toronto: McClelland & Stewart, 1977. The memoirs of Canada's minister of finance from 1963 to 1965 focus on his efforts toward creating distance between Canada and its southern neighbor. This book chronicles Gordon's lack of success.

36:36   Smith, Denis. *Gentle Patriot: A Political Biography of Walter Gordon.* Edmonton, Alta.: Hurtig, 1973. Smith provides a favorable account of the political career of Canada's finance minister. He deals with U.S. interest equalization tax, the *Reader's Digest–Time* affair, Vietnam, and the American investment generally.

William Lyon Mackenzie King

36:37   Mackenzie King, William Lyon. *The Mackenzie King Diaries, 1932–1949.* Toronto: University of Toronto Press, 1980. This microfiche edition of the Canadian prime minister's original diaries is perhaps the single most valuable source for Canadian external policy in the 1930s and 1940s. The diaries detail their author's relationship with President Roosevelt and describe the spy scandals of 1945–1946.

36:38   Pickersgill, John W., ed. *The Mackenzie King Record.* 4 vols. Toronto: University of Toronto Press, 1960–1970. These are the wartime and postwar diaries

of Canada's prime minister from 1935 to 1948. The first volume (1939–1944) was heavily edited; the remaining three faithfully present the most important topics in the original. The *Record* covers King's meetings with Roosevelt, Churchill, Attlee, and Truman, the two Quebec Conferences, the founding of the United Nations, the Paris Peace Conference, the postwar spy scandals.

36:39   Stacey, Charles P. *Mackenzie King and the Atlantic Triangle.* Toronto: Macmillan, 1976. A series of lectures delivered at the University of Western Ontario in 1976, the book presents a concise account of Mackenzie King's relations with the United States and Great Britain.

Lester B. Pearson

36:40   Barros, James. "Pearson or Lie: The Politics of the Secretary-General's Selection, 1946." *Canadian Journal of Political Science* 10:1 (1977), 65–92. Barros deals with the American suggestion that Lester Pearson become the UN's first secretary-general.

36:41   Pearson, Lester B. *Mike: The Memoirs of the Right Honourable Lester B. Pearson.* 3 vols. Toronto: University of Toronto Press, 1972–1975. Only the first volume was completed before Pearson's death. The second and third volumes are based on Pearson's diary, official papers, and preliminary drafts. The memoirs provide information on his service as Canadian ambassador in Washington, minister of external affairs (1948–1957), and prime minister (1963–1968), and are especially useful on the Korean War.

Louis St. Laurent

36:42   Pickersgill, John W. *My Years with Louis St. Laurent.* Toronto: University of Toronto Press, 1975. This study of the Canadian prime minister (1948–1957) is by his closest political associate. Largely centered on domestic affairs, the account takes note of St. Laurent's relationships with Presidents Truman and Eisenhower.

36:43   Thomson, Dale C. *Louis St. Laurent: Canadian.* Toronto: Macmillan, 1967. This biography of St. Laurent by his former private secretary includes material on the Suez crisis, the St. Lawrence Seaway, and the issue of American investment in Canada.

Pierre Trudeau

36:44   Dobell, Peter C. *Canada's Search for New Roles: Foreign Policy in the Trudeau Era.* Toronto: Oxford University Press, 1972. Dobell discusses Canadian foreign policy in the light of the Trudeau government's professed determination to reorient Canadian foreign policy around more contemporary themes. This is a well-informed but tentative exploration of Trudeau's (1968–1971) acquaintance with the United States and the world. Bibliography.

36:45 Stewart, Walter. *Trudeau in Power.* New York: Outerbridge & Dienstfrey, 1972. This is a critique of the Canadian prime minister's performance since his 1968 election.

36:46 Thordarson, Bruce. *Trudeau and Foreign Policy: A Study in Decision-Making.* Toronto: Oxford University Press, 1972. The author examines the attitudes of the Trudeau government toward Canada's traditional alliances, including that with the United States, and its early efforts to review and reorient Canadian foreign policy. Bibliography.

Others

36:47 Bothwell, Robert S., and Kilbourn, William M. *C. D. Howe: A Biography.* Toronto: McClelland & Stewart, 1979. This study of Canada's principal economic minister (1935–1957) is based on Canadian, American, and British archival sources. It deals with Canadian-American defense production and with American investment in Canada.

Burns, E. L. M. *A Seat at the Table* (36:101) discusses his experiences at international disarmament conferences (1960–1965).

36:48 Heeney, Arnold D. P. *The Things That Are Caesar's: The Memoirs of a Canadian Public Servant.* Toronto: University of Toronto Press, 1972. Heeney was for many years the secretary to the cabinet, and served twice as Canadian ambassador to the United States (1953–1957, 1959–1962). His memoirs, literally composed on his deathbed, are reliable for overall impressions but frequently inaccurate on details.

36:49 Pope, Maurice A. *Soldiers and Politicians: The Memoirs of Lt.-General Maurice A. Pope.* Toronto: University of Toronto Press, 1962. Pope served on the Canadian Joint Staff Mission in Washington during World War II, at the San Francisco Conference and in Berlin during the blockade. His memoirs, based on his diary, are carefully written and accurate.

Reid, E. M. *Time of Fear and Hope: The Making of the North Atlantic Treaty, 1947–1949* (26:171).

36:50 Ritchie, Charles S. A. *The Siren Years: A Canadian Diplomat Abroad, 1937–1945.* Toronto:

Macmillan, 1974. Ritchie served in the Canadian legation in Washington (1937–1939) and at the San Francisco Conference. This volume publishes his diaries for the war years; they are of high literary quality as well as politically perceptive.

36:51 Ronning, Chester A. *A Memoir of China in War and Revolution.* New York: Pantheon, 1974. These reminiscences of a Canadian diplomat stationed in China (1945–1951) cover the Geneva Conference of 1954, the question of Canadian recognition of China (and U.S. pressures against it), and the author's trips to Hanoi in the late 1960s. An impressionistic and somewhat imperceptive volume, it is based on material in the author's possession.

36:52 Roy, Reginald H. *For Most Conspicuous Bravery.* Vancouver: University of British Columbia Press, 1977. Roy's biography of a World War II general, subsequently minister of national defense (1957–1960), covers military relations on the Pacific coast during World War II, and defense relations with the United States (1957–1960).

36:53 Swettenham, John. *McNaughton.* 3 vols. Toronto: Ryerson, 1968–1969. This biography of Canada's delegate to the UN Atomic Energy Commission, later Canadian chairman of the International Joint Commission, contains material on the Baruch Plan and the Columbia River treaty, in volume 3 (1944–1964).

World War II

See, under "Personalities," William Lyon Mackenzie King, Charles S. A. Ritchie (under "Others").

MILITARY-POLITICAL RELATIONS

See "Personalities," especially, under "Others," Maurice A. Pope, Reginald H. Roy.

Anglin, D. G. *The St. Pierre and Miquelon Affairs of 1941: A Study in Diplomacy in the North Atlantic*

Quadrangle (23:240) is a readable and authoritative work, but it omits Canadian and American official papers.

36:54 Christian, William A., Jr. *Divided Island: Faction and Unity on Saint Pierre.* Cambridge: Harvard University Press, 1969. Christian concentrates on the history of Saint Pierre, with the invasion of 1941 as the high point. Bibliography.

Conn, S., and Fairchild, B. *The Framework of Hemispheric Defense* (23:242) is a survey of hemisphere defense which devotes two chapters to Canadian-American relations. It places Canadian-American planning in a larger context.

36:55 Diubaldo, Richard J. "The Canol Project in Canadian-American Relations." *Canadian Historical Association Historical Papers* (1977), 178–95. This essay concerns the construction by the U.S. Army of an impractical and expensive pipeline in the Canadian north.

Dziuban, S. W. *Military Relations between the United States and Canada, 1939–1945* (23:243) examines the role of American forces in Canada, the North-West Staging Route, defense planning, and military operations.

36:56 Keenleyside, Hugh, L. "The Canadian–United States Permanent Joint Board on Defence, 1940–45." *International Journal* 16:1 (1960), 50–77. A well-informed account of the first five years of the board, it is based on the author's personal experience as Canadian secretary. The essay is especially valuable for its perceptions of personalities and the details of the board's functioning.

36:57 Stacey, Charles P. *Arms, Men and Governments.* Ottawa: Queen's Printer, 1970. Stacey's book is the fullest account available of Canadian-American relations during World War II. It relies on American and British material as well as Canadian documents.

36:58 Stacey, Charles P. *Six Years of War: The Army in Canada, Britain and the Pacific.* Vol. 1 in *Official History of the Canadian Army in the Second World War.* Ottawa: Queen's Printer, 1955. It covers Canadian-American cooperation in the Aleutian campaign, 1943.

36:59 Tucker, Gilbert N. *The Naval Service of Canada.* Ottawa: King's Printer, 1952, vol. 2. This official history of the Royal Canadian Navy relies on Canadian documents and gives a very brief account of Canadian-American naval collaboration in the North Atlantic.

ECONOMIC RELATIONS

See "Personalities," especially C. D. Howe (under "Others").

36:60 Acheson, A. L. K.; Chant, J. F.; and Prachowny, M. F. J. *Bretton Woods Revisited.* Toronto: University of Toronto Press, 1972. This account includes reflections, on the 25th anniversary of Bretton Woods, by the surviving Canadian participants.

36:61 Bothwell, Robert S., and English, John R. "Canadian Trade Policy in the Age of American Dominance and British Decline, 1943–1947." *Canadian Review of American Studies* 8:1 (1977), 52–65. The article argues that Canadian trade policy after World War II alternated between the pursuit of multilateralism and the resigned acceptance of preference in the British or American market.

36:62 Granatstein, J. L. *Canada's War, 1939–1945.* Toronto: Oxford University Press, 1975. This is the best available account of the civilian side of the Canadian war effort. It covers Canadian-American relations in considerable detail and is useful for its examples and conclusions.

36:63 Granatstein, J. L. and Cuff, Robert D. "The Hyde Park Declaration 1941: Origins and Significance." *Canadian Historical Review* 55:1 (1974), 59–80. The authors present a generally sound account of the origins of the Hyde Park Declaration of 1941. They are weaker on its significance, and omit mention of the consequences.

36:64 James, R. Warren. *Wartime Economic Cooperation.* Toronto: Ryerson, 1949. James's comprehensive account of Canadian-American economic relations is solid and reliable, though difficult to read.

36:65 Pierce, Sidney, and Plumptre, A. F. W. "Canada's Relations with War-time Agencies in Washington." *Canadian Journal of Economics and Political Science* 1:3 (1945), 402–18. This is an authoritative account of Canadian dealings with the Office of Price Administration and the War Production Board during World War II by two ranking Canadian financial officials.

36:66 Plumptre, A. F. W. *Three Decades of Decision: Canada and the World Monetary System, 1944–75.* Toronto: McClelland & Stewart, 1977. Despite its title, the book gives considerable space to the wartime background of postwar economic arrangements.

Postwar Military-Political Issues

36:67 Minifie, James M. *Peacemaker or Powdermonkey: Canada's Role in a Revolutionary World.* Toronto: McClelland & Stewart, 1960. This book is a highly critical examination of Canadian alliances with the United States by a Canadian correspondent in Washington. It had considerable political impact and great importance in the debate over nuclear weapons in the early 1960s.

36:68 Reford, Robert W. *Canada and Three Crises.* Toronto: Canadian Institute of International Affairs, 1969. Reford discusses Canadian-American relations in the context of three international crises: the Formosa Straits crisis (1955), Suez (1956), and Cuba (1962).

36:69 Warnock, John W. *Partner to Behemoth: The Military Policy of a Satellite Canada.* Toronto: New Press, 1970. The author contends that Canadian foreign policy since 1945 has tended to be ever more subservient to the United States. The book has been criticized for its sweeping generalizations and assumptions. Bibliography.

THE COLD WAR

See "Personalities," especially William Lyon Mackenzie King, and, under "Others," Maurice A. Pope.

36:70 Holmes, John W. *The Shaping of Peace: Canada and the Search for World Order, 1943–1957.* Toronto: University of Toronto Press, 1979. This study covers the development of Canadian foreign policy and expresses a strong point of view, but it is dispassionate and remote.

McInnis, E. W. *The Atlantic Triangle and the Cold War* (28:103) surveys current strategic thinking on the performance and prospects of the North Atlantic Alliance.

36:71 Merchant, Livingston T., ed. *Neighbors Taken for Granted: Canada and the United States.* New York: Praeger, 1966. A collection of essays by American and Canadian authors who discuss various aspects of Canadian-American relations. Especially interesting is Dean Acheson's essay, "Stern Daughter of the Voice of God."

36:72 Page, Donald M., and Munton, Donald. "Canadian Images of the Cold War, 1946–7." *International Journal* 33:3 (1977), 577–604. Using the archives of the Canadian Department of External Affairs, the authors examine official perceptions of Soviet intentions and American responses at the onset of the cold war.

36:73 Robertson, Terence. *Crisis: The Inside Story of the Suez Conspiracy.* New York: Atheneum, 1965. Robertson deals with Canadian reaction to the breakdown in Anglo-American relations that accompanied the Suez crisis of 1956. Bibliography.

Canada and NATO

Eayrs, J. *In Defence of Canada* (36:89) provides, in volume 4, an excellent summary of Canada's role in the NATO negotiations of 1948–1949, and goes on to examine Canadian-American military relations in the context of NATO from 1949 to 1955. It also deals with the admission of Turkey, Greece, and West Germany to the alliance.

36:74 Miller, E. H. "Canada's Role in the Origin of NATO." In G. N. Grob, ed., *Statesmen and Statescraft of the Modern West.* Barre, Mass.: Barre Publishers, 1967, pp. 251–90. Canada, as a "middle power," contributed greatly to the founding of NATO and has played a leading role since. A dated analysis.

36:75 Pearson, Lester B. "Canada and the North Atlantic Alliance." *Foreign Affairs* 27:3 (1949), 369–76. Pearson, one of the leaders involved in founding NATO, explains why the alliance is necessary.

Reid, E. M. *Time of Fear and Hope: The Making of the North Atlantic Treaty, 1947–1949* (26:171) is an account by a participant in the negotiation of the North

Atlantic Treaty, which draws on his own recollections and on extensive archival research. This is one of the most complete accounts available.

China and the Korean War

See "Personalities," especially Lester B. Pearson, and, under "Others," Chester A. Ronning.

36:76 Angus, Henry F. *Canada and the Far East, 1940–1953.* Toronto: University of Toronto Press, 1953. This is a contemporary discussion of Canada's attempts to adjust its policy in the Far East to meet the requirements of an alliance with the United States.

36:77 Holmes, John W. "Canada and China: The Dilemmas of a Middle Power." In A. M. Halpern, ed., *Policies toward China: Views from Six Continents.* New York: McGraw-Hill, 1965, pp. 103–22. Holmes deals with the impact of American concerns and policy on Canadian recognition of China.

36:78 Stairs, Denis. *The Diplomacy of Constraint: Canada, the Korean War and the United States.* Toronto: University of Toronto Press, 1974. This is a brilliant analysis of Canadian-American relations in the context of the cold war and Korea. The author demonstrates that Canadian diplomacy aimed to contain both the spread of communism and the sometimes overhasty response of the United States. Most of the book's points have subsequently been confirmed by the release of government papers. Extensive bibliography.

36:79 Wood, Herbert F. *Strange Battleground: Official History of the Canadian Army in Korea.* Ottawa: Queen's Printer, 1966. Wood chronicles the detailed operations of the Canadian Special Service Brigade in Korea. Questions of policy are generally omitted.

The Vietnam War

See "Personalities," especially Walter L. Gordon.

36:80 Bridle, Paul. "Canada and the International Commissions in Indochina, 1954–1972." *Behind the Headlines* (Canadian Institute of International Affairs), 32:4 (1973), 1–28. Bridle, a diplomat who served on the International Control Commission, bases his account on personal experiences and Department of External Affairs files.

36:81 Culhane, Claire. *Why Is Canada in Vietnam? The Truth about Our Foreign Aid.* Toronto: NC Press, 1972. This attack on Canadian Vietnam policy argues Canadian-American complicity and suggests that the Canadian government suppressed or distorted relevant evidence.

36:82 Dobell, William M. "A 'Sow's Ear' in Vietnam." *International Journal* 29:3 (1974), 356–92. Dobell discusses Canada's brief role on the International Commission for Control and Supervision in Vietnam in 1973. He concentrates on foreign policy methodology.

36:83 Holmes, John W. "Canada and the Vietnam War." In J. L. Granatstein and R. D. Cuff, eds. *War and Society in North America.* Toronto: Nelson, 1971, pp. 184–99. The author, an ex-diplomat, comments on Canada's connection with the Vietnam War from the standpoint of personal experience.

36:84 Holmes, John W. "Geneva: 1954." *International Journal* 22:3 (1967), 457–83. Holmes was a member of the Canadian delegation to the Geneva Conference of 1954. He comments on Dulles's diplomacy, on Anglo-American relations, and on the origins of the International Control Commission for Vietnam.

36:85 Ross, Douglas. "In the Interests of Peace: Perception and Response in the History of Canadian Foreign Policy Decision-making Concerning the International Commission for Supervision and Control for Vietnam, 1954–1965." Ph.D. diss., University of Toronto, 1979. By far the most complete account of Canadian participation in the ICSC for Vietnam, this dissertation outlines and evaluates the divergences of policy inside the Canadian Department of External Affairs. Ross suggests that Canadian diplomats were divided into three camps: conservative, moderate and liberal-radical.

36:86 Taylor, Charles. *Snow Job: Canada, the United States and Vietnam.* Toronto: Anansi, 1974. Taylor argues Canadian subservience to and complicity in American aggression in Vietnam (1954–1973). He takes a somewhat simplistic approach to both Canadian diplomacy and American policy. Bibliography.

36:87 Williams, Roger N. *The New Exiles.* New York: Liveright, 1971. Williams discusses American exiles in Canada from a draft-evader's point of view.

MILITARY RELATIONS

See "Personalities," especially, under "Others," Reginald H. Roy.

36:88 Brewin, F. Andrew. *Stand on Guard: The Search for a Canadian Defence Policy.* Toronto: McClelland & Stewart, 1965. This critique of Canadian defense policy is by the parliamentary critic of the New Democratic party. Of special interest because of the author's membership on the Special Committee on Defence, it provides rare insight into the relation between Parliament and foreign and defense policy.

36:89 Eayrs, James. *In Defence of Canada.* 4 vols. to date. Toronto: University of Toronto Press, 1964–1980. Volume 3, *Peacemaking and Deterrence* (1972) is a somewhat disjointed account of Canadian defense policy between World War II and the Korean War, but it is useful as a general guide to Canadian policymaking. It covers continental defense planning and atomic cooperation; some of its assertions should be checked.

36:90 Eayrs, James. *Northern Approaches: Canada and the Search for Peace.* Toronto: Macmillan, 1961. This collection of essays, by a prominent scholar and commentator on foreign relations, treats such subjects as continental defense, NATO, and Cuba.

36:91 Gray, Colin S. *Canadian Defence Priorities: A Question of Relevance.* Toronto: Clarke, Irwin, 1972. This book reviews Canadian defense policy in the early 1970s, paying special attention to NATO and NORAD. Extensive bibliography.

36:92 Hertzman, Lewis; Warnock, John; and Hockin, Thomas. *Alliances and Illusions: Canada and the NATO-NORAD Question.* Edmonton, Alberta: Hurtig, 1969. The authors review Canadian military and political collaboration in NATO and the North American Air Defense Command, and recommend reducing or terminating Canadian commitments to both organizations.

36:93 Kirton, John J. "The Consequences of Integration: The Case of the Defence Production Sharing Agreements." In A. Axline et al., *Continental Community? Independence and Integration in North America.* Toronto: McClelland & Stewart, 1974, pp. 116–36. A useful resumé of the history of defense production sharing between the United States and

Canada, it refines and updates McLin's *Canada's Changing Defense Policy.*

36:94 McLin, Jon B. *Canada's Changing Defense Policy, 1957–1963: The Problems of a Middle Power in Alliance.* Baltimore: Johns Hopkins Press, 1967. This is a superb reconstruction of Canadian defense relationships with the United States during the Diefenbaker government. Though based on public documents supplemented by interviews, its judgments are authoritative. Extensive bibliography.

36:95 Sutherland, R. J. "Canada's Long-Term Strategic Situation." *International Journal* 17:3 (1962), 199–223. A strategic analyst working for the government presents an intelligent and authoritative summation of Canada's strategic interests. The author argues that geography and self-interest combine to bind Canada to the United States.

36:96 Wang, Eric B. "Sovereignty and Canada-US Co-operation in North American Defence." In R. St. J. Macdonald, Gerald R. Morris, and Douglas M. Johnston, eds., *Canadian Perspectives on International Law and Organization.* Toronto: University of Toronto Press, 1974, pp. 861–84. This account is based on a close study of the documentation of Canadian-American defense relations. Wang discusses forms, procedures, and arrangements for arbitration.

Atomic Energy: Early Issues

36:97 Eggleston, Wilfrid. *Canada's Nuclear Story.* Toronto: Clarke, Irwin, 1966. In a history of Canada's nuclear program, Eggleston discusses Anglo-American-Canadian World War II cooperation in atomic research. Bibliography.

Gowing, M. *Independence and Deterrence: Britain and Atomic Energy, 1939–1952.* (28:115) presents, in volume 1, *Policy Making* (1939–1945), and volume 2, *Public Execution* (1945–1952), a concise and balanced discussion of Anglo-American-Canadian atomic relations, research, and diplomacy.

36:98 Munro, John A., and Inglis, Alex I. "The Atomic Conference of 1945 and the Pearson Memoirs." *International Journal* 29:1 (1973–1974), 90–109. Pearson's summary of the tripartite conference on atomic matters, held in Washington in

November 1945, is useful in the absence of an American view.

Canadian-American Nuclear Debate, 1962–1963

See "Personalities," especially John G. Diefenbaker.

36:99 Conant, Melvin. *The Long Polar Watch: Canada and the Defense of North America.* New York: Harper, 1962. This is an examination of the Canadian nuclear weapons debate from an American perspective; it is useful for the contemporary information and viewpoints.

36:100 Ghent, Jocelyn. "Did He Fall or Was He Pushed? The Kennedy Administration and the Collapse of the Diefenbaker Government." *International History Review* 1:2 (1979), 246–70. Ghent's comprehensive and authoritative analysis of the Canadian-American nuclear crisis of 1962–1963 is based on Kennedy's papers.

Grant, G. *Lament for a Nation: The Defeat of Canadian Nationalism* (36:31).

Newman, P.C. *Renegade in Power: The Diefenbaker Years* (36:33).

Arms Control and Disarmament

See "Personalities," especially, under "Others," A. G. L. McNaughton.

36:101 Burns, E. L. M. *A Seat at the Table.* Toronto: Clarke, Irwin, 1972. Burns was a Canadian delegate to international disarmament conferences from 1960 to 1965. This is a well-researched and balanced treatment of a complicated subject. Bibliography.

36:102 Davy, Grant R. "Canada's Role in Disarmament Negotiations, 1946–1957." Ph.D. diss., Fletcher School of Law and Diplomacy, 1962. Using published materials, Davy traces Canada's efforts in negotiations which involved the large powers. Except in the case of the Baruch Plan (1946), Canada usually followed U.S. positions. Bibliography.

36:103 Gotlieb, Allan E. *Disarmament and International Law: A Study of the Role of Law in the*

Disarmament Process. Toronto: Canadian Institute of International Affairs, 1965. Gotlieb dissects the disarmament proposals and discussions between 1962 and 1964. Written by one of the members of the Canadian delegation, it is authoritative.

CANADIAN-AMERICAN RELATIONS SINCE 1968

See "Personalities," especially Pierre Trudeau.

Political and Diplomatic

36:104 Abrams, Matthew J. *The Canada–United States Interparliamentary Group.* Toronto: Canadian Institute for International Affairs, 1973. The book examines the performance of the Canada-U.S. Interparliamentary Group and issues pessimistic conclusions about the group's performance and utility.

36:105 Alper, D. K., and Monahan, R. L. "Bill C-58 and the American Congress: The Politics of Retaliation." *Canadian Public Policy* 4:2 (1978), 184–92. The article discusses the linkage in the U.S. Congress of the Canadian refusal to allow tax deductions on advertising in U.S. media (Bill C-58) with U.S. tax changes unfavorable to Canada.

36:106 Armstrong, Willis C. "The American Perspective." *Proceedings of the Academy of Political Science* 32:2 (1976), 1–13. This is a discussion of American attitudes toward Canada, by an ex-diplomat with considerable experience in Canadian-American affairs.

36:107 Canada. Standing Senate Committee on Foreign Affairs. *Canada–United States Relations: The Institutional Framework for the Relationship.* Ottawa: Queen's Printer, 1975. Based on testimony from a broad range of witnesses, the committee presented recommendations for a low-key, expanded relationship between Canada and the United States. It provides a useful summary of Canadian-American relations and institutions in the mid-1970s.

36:108 Dickey, John S. "The Relationship in Rhetoric and Reality: Merchant-Heeney Revisited." *International Journal* 27:2 (1972), 172–84. A prominent student of Canadian-American relations discusses the principles applied to the conduct of those relations.

36:109 Dobell, Peter C. "Negotiating with the United States." *International Journal* 36:1 (1981), 17–38. Dobell discusses the character of Canadian-American negotiations, noting the decline in American expertise on the subject of Canada. He concludes with the abortive Fisheries Treaty of 1979, and argues that in diplomatic dealings with the United States it is necessary to deal with Congress and the executive together.

36:110 Fox, Annette Baker; Hero, Alfred O., Jr.; and Nye, Joseph S., eds. *Canada and the United States: Transnational and Transgovernmental Relations.* New York: Columbia University Press, 1976. This collection of essays ranges over the period since 1960 and covers a wide variety of issues, from the Law of the Sea to Canadian-American political relations. It is useful especially on economic relations. Bibliography.

36:111 Lumsden, Ian, ed. *Close the 49th Parallel, etc.: The Americanization of Canada.* Toronto: University of Toronto Press, 1970. A collection of essays on Canadian-American relations published at the height of the Vietnam War, it reflects the passions of the moment. The essays vary greatly in quality.

36:112 Lyon, Peyton V., and Leyton-Brown, David. "Image and Policy Preference: Canadian Elite Views on Relations with the United States." *International Journal* 32:3 (1977), 640–71. This article, based on extensive interviews with Canadian bureaucratic, political, and business leaders, examines elite opinions of the United States and discovers a divergence between elite preferences and the government's ostensible policy.

36:113 Lyon, Peyton V., and Tomlin, Brian W. *Canada as an International Actor.* Toronto: Macmillan, 1979. Two chapters review recent developments in Canadian-American relations and provide useful information, but they are laden with jargon and marred by historical inaccuracies. Bibliography.

36:114 Redekop, John H. "A Reinterpretation of Canadian-American Relations." *Canadian Journal of Political Science* 9:2 (1976), 227–43. Redekop attempts to classify Canadian-American relations according to current international relations theory. It is interesting as a mode of analysis rather than as an account of events.

36:115 Resnick, Philip. *The Land of Cain: Class and Nationalism in English Canada, 1945–1975.* Vancouver: New Star Books, 1977. A Marxist analysis of Canadian society, it argues that the United States has exerted a consciously imperialistic influence on Canadian life since 1945 and that the Canadian elite has accommodated itself to U.S. demands. Though based on extensive research, many of the book's conclusions are speculative. Extensive bibliography.

36:116 Sharp, Mitchell W. "Canada-U.S. Relations: Options for the Future." *International Perspectives* (special issue) (1972), 1–24. This official, long-delayed statement of the Canadian government's policy toward the United States was composed as the result of a lengthy policy review inside the Department of External Affairs, and signed by the secretary of state for external affairs.

36:117 Sigler, John H., and Goresky, Dennis. "Public Opinion on Canadian-American Relations." *International Organization* 28:4 (1974), 637–68. The authors discuss fluctuations in Canadian popular perceptions of the United States and conclude that Vietnam and Watergate had a considerable impact.

36:118 Swanson, Roger F. "The Ford Interlude and the U.S.-Canadian Relationship." *American Review of Canadian Studies* 8:1 (1978), 3–17. A chronicle of events concentrating on summitry, it is a useful listing of dates and events.

36:119 Swanson, Roger F. *Intergovernmental Perspectives on the Canada–United States Relationship.* New York: New York University Press, 1978. Swanson discusses the decline in effectiveness of Canadian-American joint organizations.

36:120 Swanson, Roger F. "The United States Canadian Constellation, I: Washington, D.C." *International Journal* 27:2 (1972), 185–218. This is a comprehensive but arid survey of agencies in Washington dealing with Canada.

36:121 Swanson, Roger F. "The United States Canadian Constellation, II: Canada." *International Journal* 28:2 (1973), 325–67. This catalogue of the mechanics of American representation in Canada, including a brief history of American representation, focuses on American diplomatic and consular offices in 1972. It lists ministers and ambassadors, and includes a table showing consulates in Canada since 1833.

36:122 Thomson, Dale C., and Swanson, Roger F. *Canadian Foreign Policy: Options and Perspectives.* Toronto: McGraw-Hill/Ryerson, 1971. A primer on Canadian foreign policy, it concentrates on the period after 1968, but provides appropriate historical background. Somewhat dated.

36:123 Willoughby, William R. *The Joint Organizations of Canada and the United States.* Toronto: University of Toronto Press, 1980. This account summarizes the performance of Canadian-American joint organizations, such as the International Joint Commission.

36:124 Winham, Gilbert R. "Choice and Strategy in Continental Relations." In A. Axline et al., *Continental Community? Independence and Integration in North America.* Toronto: McClelland & Stewart, 1974. This is a general discussion of the dynamics of Canadian-American relations in the early 1970s.

Provincial Relations: Quebec

36:125 Atkey, Ronald G. "The Role of the Provinces in International Affairs." *International Journal* 26:1 (1970–1971), 249–73. In this history and analysis of the Canadian provinces in international relations, the author notes trans-border contacts between Canadian provinces and American states and discusses the legal position of the various provincial governments vis-à-vis other countries.

36:126 Feldman, Elliott J., and Nevitte, Neil, eds. *The Future of North America: Canada, the United States and Quebec Nationalism.* Cambridge: Harvard Center for International Affairs, 1979. A collection of papers that discuss the impact of Canadian federalism and Quebec nationalism on Canadian-American relations. Bibliography.

36:127 Latouche, Daniel. "Quebec and the North American Subsystem: One Possible Scenario." *International Organization* 28:4 (1974), 931–60. The author, a convinced Quebec separatist, argues that Quebec independence is probable and suggests that an independent Quebec would not be hostile to the United States, either politically or economically.

36:128 Painchaud, Paul, ed. *Le Canada et le Québec sur la scène internationale* [Canada and Quebec on the international scene]. Quebec: Centre québécois de relations internationales, 1977. This collection of essays, many translated from English, con-tains a short section on Quebec's relations with the outside world, and sections on Canadian-American and Quebec-American relations.

36:129 Thomson, Dale C. "Quebec and the Bicultural Dimension." *Proceedings of the Academy of Political Science* 32:2 (1976), 27–39. Thomson discusses Quebec's influence on Canada's international relations, and concludes that it has had a positive effect on Canadian-American affairs.

36:130 Tremblay, Rodrique. *Indépendance et Marché Commun: Québec-E.U.* [Independence and the Common Market: Quebec-U.S.]. Montreal: Éditions du Jour, 1970. An economist argues that, given the cost to Quebec of Canadian tariffs, the province would be better off in a customs union with the United States—whether the rest of Canada joined or not.

Economic Issues

See "Personalities," especially Walter L. Gordon.

36:131 Canadian-American Committee. *A Time of Difficult Transitions: Canadian-American Relations in 1976.* Montreal: Canadian-American Committee, 1976. This is a brief summary of Canadian-American relations at a time when economic policies of the two countries conflicted.

36:132 English, H. Edward. "The Role of Canadian-United States Relations in the Pursuit of Canada's National Objectives." *American Review of Canadian Studies* 6:1 (1976), 3–17. The author criticizes the Canadian government's professed policy of choosing between integration with the United States and other desiderata. He argues that Canada should optimize its existing integration with the American economy as a basis for other policy initiatives.

36:133 Johnson, Harry G. *The Canadian Quandary.* Toronto: McClelland & Stewart (1963), 1977. These essays by a prominent Canadian economist criticize Canadian nationalists' prescriptions for the Canadian economy, and take direct issue with their critique of Canadian-American economic relations.

TRADE AND INVESTMENT

36:134 Beigie, Carl E. *The Canada-U.S. Automotive Agreement: An Evaluation.* Montreal: Canadian-American Committee, 1970. This is an analysis of the first five years of the Canadian-American Automotive Agreement.

36:135 Canadian-American Committee. *Bilateral Relations in an Uncertain World Context: Canada-U.S. Relations in 1978.* Montreal: Canadian-American Committee, 1978. This review of developments in Canadian-American relations concentrates on trade and finance. A handy summary.

36:136 Drummond, Ian M. "The Implications of American Economic Nationalism." In Norman Hillmer and Garth Stevenson, eds., *Foremost Nation: Canadian Foreign Policy in a Changing World.* Toronto: McClelland & Stewart, 1977, pp. 3–23. This vigorous, controversial defense of the status quo in Canadian-American trading relations demolishes several ultranationalist arguments against American investments and trading policy. Bibliography.

36:137 English, H. Edward. "Canada's International Economic Policy." In T. N. Brewis, H. E. English, Anthony Scott, and Pauline Jewett, eds., *Canadian Economic Policy.* 2d ed. Toronto: Macmillan, 1965, pp. 146–79. English discusses Canadian trade policy, GATT, and attitudes toward American investment in the light of the revival of Europe and the formation of the European Common Market.

36:138 Kirton, John J. "The Politics of Bilateral Management: The Case of the Automotive Trade." *International Journal* 36:1 (1980–1981), 39–69. Kirton traces the history of Canadian-American automotive trading since the 1950s, and concentrates on governmental reactions. His useful examination of the Autopact of 1965 argues that it was linked to Canadian action over the Cyprus crisis.

36:139 Trezise, Philip H. "Interdependence and Its Problems." *International Journal* 29:4 (1974), 523–34. A former assistant secretary of state for economic affairs discusses trade and investment across the Canadian-American border, and the economic options facing the two countries.

U.S.-Canadian Trade

36:140 Canada Economic Council. *Looking Outward: A New Trade Strategy for Canada.* Ottawa: Information Canada, 1975. This analysis of Canada's trade dilemmas by a semi-public board of economic advisers examines free trade with the United States.

36:141 Cuff, Robert D., and Granatstein, Jack L. *American Dollars, Canadian Prosperity.* Toronto: Samuel-Stevens, 1978. A scholarly study of Canadian-American trade relations (1945–1950) that deals with such subjects as reciprocity and the Marshall Plan.

36:142 Lyon, Peyton V. *Canada–United States: Free Trade and Canadian Independence.* Ottawa: Information Canada for the Economic Council of Canada, 1975. This is an analysis of Canadian trade options which takes up free trade with the United States.

36:143 Lyon, Peyton V. "Second Thoughts on the Second Option." *International Journal* 30:4 (1975), 646–70. Lyon argues that the Canadian government should consider a free trade area with the United States, and criticizes the condemnation of this option by Canadian nationalists.

36:144 Pestieau, Caroline. *The Sector Approach to Trade Negotiations: Canadian and U.S. Interests.* Montreal: C. D. Howe Research Institute, 1976. This pamphlet discusses Canadian and American strategies in the Tokyo round of GATT, and the factors influencing each.

36:145 Pestieau, Caroline. *Subsidies and Countervailing Duties.* Montreal: C. D. Howe Research Institute, 1976. Pestieau's pamphlet discusses the implications for Canada's economic policy in the American imposition of countervailing duties to offset subsidies, an important issue in Canadian-American relations since 1968.

36:146 Reuber, Grant L. "What's New about Recent United States Foreign Economic Policy?" *International Journal* 27:2 (1972), 287–305. Reuber's review of Canada's place in American trade policy examines the impact of Nixon's economic shock of August 1971.

36:147 Stovel, John A. *Canada in the World Economy.* Cambridge: Harvard University Press, 1959.

This is a useful survey and study of the development of the Canadian economy (1840–1957) in the context of a larger Atlantic trading area.

36:148   Wonnacott, Ronald J., and Wonnacott, Gordon P. *Free Trade between the United States and Canada*. Cambridge: Harvard University Press, 1967. Now dated, this study is a representative argument of the case for Canadian-American free trade as perceived in the mid-1960s.

U.S. Investment in Canada

36:149   Aitken, Hugh G. J. *American Capital and Canadian Resources*. Cambridge: Harvard University Press, 1961. This examination of American imports of Canadian raw materials and American investment in Canada explains Canadian reaction to American investment. Extensive bibliography.

36:150   Brecher, Irving, and Reisman, S. S. *Canada–United States Economic Relations*. Ottawa: Queen's Printer, 1957. A useful discussion of Canadian-American economic relations after the war, it is a notable contrast to the report of the Royal Commission on Canada's Economic Prospects.

36:151   Brewster, Kingman. *Law and United States Business in Canada*. Montreal and Washington D.C.: Private Planning Association/National Planning Association, 1960. Brewster provides a very useful summary of the effect of American laws, especially tax and antitrust, on the Canadian operations of U.S. firms.

36:152   Canada. Task Force on the Structure of Canadian Industry. *Foreign Ownership and the Structure of Canadian Industry*. Ottawa: Queen's Printer, 1968. The product of a task force of economists with varying viewpoints, the report defines a drastic problem—heavy foreign investment—which it tries to reconcile with a high standard of living. Its recommendations are mild. Known as the Watkins Report, after the task force chairman, the document had a considerable impact in focusing nationalist resentment toward foreign investment.

36:153   Clement, Wallace A. *Continental Corporate Power: Economic Linkages between Canada and the United States*. Toronto: McClelland & Stewart, 1977. Based on a survey of businessmen, this analysis by an anticapitalist sociologist discusses linkages between the Canadian and American business worlds. It contains a brief historical section. Extensive bibliography.

36:154   Godfrey, Dave, and Watkins, Mel, eds. *From Gordon to Watkins to You*. Toronto: New Press, 1970. This is a choppy, episodic discussion and chronicle of developing Canadian attitudes toward foreign investment in the 1960s.

36:155   Kilbourn, William M. *Pipeline: Transcanada and the Great Debate: A History of Business and Politics*. Toronto: Clarke, Irwin, 1970. Kilbourn has written a very useful history of the most controversial American investment in Canada—trans-Canada pipelines. Bibliography.

Levitt, K. *Silent Surrender: The Multinational Corporation in Canada* (39:127) is a Marxist analysis of the consequences of multinational (American) investment in Canada. Levitt's material is interesting, occasionally compelling, but flawed by generalizations and assumptions.

36:156   Litvak, Isaiah, and Maule, Christopher J. *Alcan Aluminium Ltd.: A Case Study:* Ottawa: Canada, Department of Supply and Services, 1977. This rare study of an individual subsidiary of an American corporation discusses the gradual divorce between Alcan and its American parents.

36:157   Litvak, I. A., and Maule, C. J. *Cultural Sovereignty: The Time and Reader's Digest Case in Canada*. New York: Praeger, 1974. A complicated case of cultural politics, the *Time* and *Reader's Digest* affair lasted from the mid-1950s to the mid-1970s. This study provides a resumé of the first three-quarters of the affair's history; the culmination, however, came two years after this study was completed.

36:158   Litvak, I. A.; Maule, Christopher J.; and Robinson, R. D. *Dual Loyalty: Canada–United States Business Arrangements*. Toronto: McGraw-Hill, 1971. This valuable collection of case studies, with an appendix of relevant statutes and other documents, contains general chapters dealing with such issues as the extraterritorial application of American law.

36:159   Newman, Peter C. *The Distemper of Our Times*. Toronto: McClelland & Stewart, 1968. A political history of Canada (1963–1968), this book pays special attention to the issue of American investment in Canada and reprints useful documents on a quarrel between the Canadian government and the First National City Bank.

36:160 Safarian, A. E. *Foreign Ownership of Canadian Industry.* New York: McGraw-Hill, 1966. A reliable economic study, it is an exploration of the impact of foreign investment on the structure and performance of Canadian industry. Extensive bibliography.

Capital Flow

36:161 Brecher, Irving. *Capital Flows between Canada and the United States.* Montreal: Canadian-American Committee, 1965. Brecher covers direct investment, portfolio and short-term capital, exchange rates, and makes the point that since 1945 American capital inflows into Canada have been massive in size, and volatile in behavior.

36:162 *Canadian–United States Financial Relationships.* Boston: Federal Reserve Bank of Boston, 1971. These proceedings of a conference of American and Canadian economists and bankers deal with the integration of U.S.-Canadian capital markets, the balance of payments, and the role of the private sector.

36:163 Wonnacott, Paul. *The Canadian Dollar, 1948–1962.* Toronto: University of Toronto Press, 1965. This is a useful discussion of Canada's floating dollar, including an account of pre-1948 developments.

SPECIAL STUDIES

Agriculture

36:164 Britnell, George, and Fowke, Vernon C. *Canadian Agriculture in War and Peace.* Stanford, Calif.: Stanford University Press, 1962. One of the few scholarly studies of Canadian agricultural policies, it was written at a time when Canadian agricultural cooperation with the United States was a major factor in both countries' trade policies. It contains information on the Combined Food Board.

36:165 Heady, Earl O. *A North American Common Market.* Ames: Iowa State University Press, 1969. These proceedings of a conference of agricultural economists examine how a North American common market would affect agriculture.

36:166 Warley, T. K. *Agriculture in an Interdependent World: U.S. and Canadian Perspectives.* Montreal: Canadian-American Committee, 1977. This discussion, in historical perspective, of the problems and prospects facing North American agriculture includes bilateral trade problems, agricultural aid, and the possibilities of increasing supply.

36:167 Wilson, Charles F. *A Century of Canadian Grain: Government Policy to 1951.* Saskatoon, Sask.: Western Producer Prairie Books, 1978. Wilson's·encyclopedic history of Canada's grain trading policy draws on the author's own extensive experience and on government files. Material on the International Wheat Agreement of 1949 is also provided. Extensive bibliography.

Fisheries and Law of the Sea

36:168 Johnson, Barbara, and Zacher, Mark W., eds. *Canadian Foreign Policy and the Law of the Sea.* Vancouver: University of British Columbia Press, 1977. These essays detail Canadian-American negotiations over such issues as exploitation of the seabed, the 200-mile limit, maritime pollution, and the third Law of the Sea Conference. They concentrate more on policy than on law.

36:169 Mitchell, C. L. "The 200-Mile Limit: New Issues, Old Problems for Canada's East Coast Fisheries." *Canadian Public Policy* 4:2 (1978), 172–83. This essay dwells on the advantages which may be gleaned from an extension of Canada's jurisdiction to a 200-mile maritime limit. It urges a rational reform of the fishing industry. Bibliography.

Oil and Energy

36:170 Beigie, Carl, and Hero, Alfred O., Jr., eds. *Natural Resources in U.S.-Canadian Relations.* 2 vols. Boulder, Colo.: Westview, 1980. This is a superb collection of studies, both general and specific, on American-Canadian resource relations. The essays in volume 2, on iron ore and uranium, are particularly authoritative.

36:171 Erickson, E. W., and Waverman, L., eds. *The Energy Question: An International Failure of Policy.* 2 vols. Toronto: University of Toronto Press, 1974. Volume 2, *North America,* is a collection of essays by Canadian and American economists which examines both the history and the present state of Canadian and American energy supply. This is the best available short account of Canadian energy policy.

36:172   Gordon, Richard L. *Coal and Canada-U.S. Energy Relations.* Montreal: Canadian-American Committee, 1976. This controversial examination of the state of coal production in North America (1945–1976) warns of bleak possibilities ahead, including a possible coal embargo.

36:173   Gray, Earle. *The Great Canadian Oil Patch.* Toronto: Maclean-Hunter, 1970. This is a popular history of the Canada oil industry by the editor of a trade journal.

36:174   Maxwell, Judith. *Energy from the Arctic.* Montreal: Canadian-American Committee, 1973. Maxwell discusses the engineering, financial, and political problems involved in extracting gas in the Arctic and transporting it to southern Canada and the United States.

36:175   McIntyre, Hugh C. *Uranium, Nuclear Power and Canadian-U.S. Energy Relations.* Montreal: Canadian-American Committee, 1978. This analysis of the current state of American demand and Canadian supply of uranium recommends utilization policies for uranium resources.

36:176   Miller, John T., Jr. *Foreign Trade in Gas and Electricity in North America.* New York: Praeger, 1970. The most comprehensive account of energy imports and exports in North America since 1945, Miller's study is based on a close reading of the relevant Canadian and American documents. It has, in particular, a useful account of natural gas imports into the United States during the 1950s.

36:177   Perlgut, Mark. *Electricity across the Border: The Canadian-American Experience.* Montreal: Canadian-American Committee, 1978. A concise survey of Canadian electricity exports to the United States, it concentrates on the period since 1970. Bibliography.

36:178   Smith, Philip. *Brinco: The Story of Churchill Falls.* Toronto: McClelland & Stewart, 1975. This history of the Churchill Falls project, designed to bring electricity from Newfoundland to sell in the United States, is valuable for its insights into national, international, and provincial interests superimposed on a business enterprise.

Waterways and Pollution

36:179   Chevrier, Lionel. *The St. Lawrence Seaway.* Toronto: Macmillan, 1959. This brief history of the construction of the St. Lawrence Seaway, by the Canadian negotiator of the seaway agreement, and subsequent president of the Canadian St. Lawrence Seaway authority, includes maps and drawings.

36:180   Jordan, F. J. E. "The International Joint Commission and Canada–United States Boundary Relations." In R. St. J. Macdonald, Gerald R. Morris, and Douglas M. Johnston, eds., *Canadian Perspectives on International Law and Organization.* Toronto: University of Toronto Press, 1974, pp. 522–41. This useful summary of the career of the International Joint Commission (1909–1974) provides examples of the different problems to which it has turned its attention, including the Columbia River, fisheries, and navigation.

36:181   Logan, R. M. *Canada, the United States and the Law of the Sea Conference.* Montreal: Canadian-American Committee, 1974. Logan provides a comprehensive explanation of the complicated ramifications of the Canadian and American positions on the law of the sea. Glossary and extensive bibliography.

36:182   Piper, Don C. *The International Law of the Great Lakes: A Study of Canadian-American Cooperation.* Durham, N.C.: Duke University Press, 1967. This account seeks to "extract the conventional rules and customary principles of international law" that govern the two nations.

36:183   Sussman, Gennifer. *The St. Lawrence Seaway.* Montreal: C. D. Howe Research Institute and National Planning Association, 1978. Sussman surveys the history, construction, and utilization of the St. Lawrence Seaway. The author concentrates on the seaway's performance since its opening in 1959 and argues that hasty negotiations left a legacy of problems. Statistical tables and maps.

36:184   Swainson, Neil. *Conflict over the Columbia: The Canadian Background to an Historic Treaty.* Montreal: McGill-Queen's University Press, 1979. This is an accurate, reliable examination of the background of the Columbia River Treaty of 1961. Bibliography.

Willoughby, W. R. *The St. Lawrence Waterway: A Study in Politics and Diplomacy* (2:223) is a model study of an ancient and complex issue. It examines the background of the St. Lawrence Seaway and the successful conclusion of negotiations. Because the author did not have comparable access to Canadian documents, the book is fuller on the American side. Extensive bibliography.

Labor and Immigration

36:185   Abella, Irving M. *Nationalism, Communism and Canadian Labour*. Toronto: University of Toronto Press, 1973. Abella discusses the development of international unions in Canada (1935–1956), their connection with the CIO, and with the Canadian Congress of Labour, the impact of communism and the expulsion of Communists in tandem with the CIO. He argues that the purge of the Communists was unwise. Bibliography.

36:186   Corbett, David C. *Canada's Immigration Policy: A Critique*. Toronto: University of Toronto Press, 1957. Corbett's discussion of Canada's overall immigration policy pays some attention to immigration from the United States.

36:187   Crispo, John. *International Unionism: A Study in Canadian-American Relations*. Toronto: McGraw-Hill, 1967. The author gives a brief history of international unionism in Canada, and discusses relevant aspects in the 1960s: the Canadian role in international unions, relations between the Canadian Labour Congress and the AFL-CIO, the attitude of Canadian governments toward international unions. Bibliography.

36:188   Hawkins, Freda. *Canada and Immigration: Public Policy and Public Concern*. Quebec: McGill-Queen's University Press, 1972. This is a confused analysis of the immigration problems Canada has confronted since 1945, put in an international context. Corbett's discussion (36:186) is to be preferred.

36:189   Lines, Kenneth D. *British and Canadian Immigration to the United States since 1920*. San Francisco: R&E Research Associates, 1978. Valuable for its research, it is a disorganized discussion containing much fascinating information.

36:190   Norris, Thomas G. *Report of Industrial Inquiry Commission on the Disruption of Shipping*. 2 vols. Ottawa: Queen's Printer, 1963. This is a report of an inquiry into the Seamen's International Union and its Canadian director, Hal Banks. When faced with prosecution in Canada, Banks fled to his native United States and could not be extradited. The Norris inquiry, which includes excerpts from testimony, is a searching examination of one international union in Canada. Bibliography.

36:191   Parai, Louis. *Immigration and Emigration of Professional and Skilled Manpower during the Post-War Period*. Ottawa: Queen's Printer, 1965. A guide to the effects of Canadian immigration policies, it provides information on the "brain drain" of Canadian skilled and professional manpower to the United States. Charts and tables.

37

United States, South Asia, and Sub-Saharan Africa since 1941

Contributing Editors

GARY R. HESS
Bowling Green State University

THOMAS NOER
Carthage College

LOUIS WILSON
Claremont Men's College

Contents

Introduction

American diplomatic relations with both South Asia and Sub-Saharan Africa have become increasingly important since 1945. Yet as the past three and a half decades have witnessed a considerable expansion of American activity in these regions, coupled with much controversy at times, scholarly endeavor has generally been focused elsewhere.

United States relations with South Asia (India, Pakistan, Bangladesh, and Sri Lanka) has been the subject of a limited, but growing and increasingly sophisticated literature. Since official documents for the period since the area gained independence are only gradually becoming available, much of the work done by historians has been on American contacts with South Asia during the period of British control. Perhaps the most emphasis has been on the American response to Indian nationalism, especially during the two world wars.

The scholarship on the activities of Indian nationalists in America during World War I was initially dominated by a British perspective, which presented the Indians as revolutionaries engaged in an ill-conceived "Hindu conspiracy." Recent work, however, has paid greater attention to the attitudes and aspirations of the Indians and to the extent of Anglo-American collaboration in prosecuting the "conspirators."

The American official and popular response to the prolonged British-Indian crisis during World War II has been the subject of several studies. A major point of concern and difference within that literature has been whether the Roosevelt administration followed policies which served American interests; essentially, scholars have questioned whether the United States should have acted more forcefully on behalf of Indian nationalism, or whether the constraints imposed by the war limited American initiative to expressions of sympathy for the nationalist cause. In addition to the work on preindependence political relations, historians have also examined the development of cultural (including missionary activities, Indian immigrants in

America, Indo-American mutual perceptions) and economic relations.

Historians, political scientists, and journalists writing about developments since 1947 have been especially attracted to the American involvement in the prolonged Indo-Pakistani dispute. Much of this literature has been polemical; yet there are a considerable number of balanced studies which have examined, from differing perspectives, American attitudes toward India and Pakistan, the reasons for the generally pro-Pakistani position of the United States, and American strategic and economic objectives in South Asia.

While there is no single comprehensive, scholarly overview of Indo-American relations, readers seeking a basic introduction to the field might well begin with C. H. Heimsath and S. Mansingh, *A Diplomatic History of Modern India* (37:26); W. J. Barnds, *India, Pakistan, and the Great Powers* (37:18); and S. M. Burke, *Mainsprings of Indian and Pakistani Foreign Policies* (37:19). The development of India's foreign policy during the era of Jawaharlal Nehru (1947–1964), which was a period of strains and misunderstanding between New Delhi and Washington, can be very thoroughly explored, especially through the work of Michael Brecher. His studies of Nehru and Krishna Menon are thorough, balanced, and provocative—*Nehru: A Political Biography* (37:45); and *India and World Politics: Krishna Menon's View of the World* (37:43). Another important work on the same period is A. P. Rana, *The Imperatives of Nonalignment: A Conceptual Study of India's Foreign Policy Strategy in the Nehru Era* (37:138). The American alliance with Pakistan and its impact on Indo-American relations has been the subject of numerous works, but among the best, especially in terms of understanding changes evolving from the Bangladesh crisis of 1971, are B. K. Shrivastava, "Indo-American Relations: Retrospect and Prospect" (37:139); W. Wilcox, *The Emergence of Bangladesh: Problems and Opportunities for a Redefined American Policy in South Asia* (37:127).

On the development of American attitudes toward India and the nationalist movement during the period from World War I to the partition of the subcontinent in 1947, the following studies, taken together, form a useful overview: Joan M. Jensen, "The 'Hindu Conspiracy': A Reassessment" (37:100); Alan Raucher, "American Anti-Imperialists and the Pro-India Movement, 1900–32" (37:105); G. R. Hess, *America Encounters India, 1941–1947* (37:109); H. R. Isaacs, *Scratches on Our Minds: American Images of China and India* (37:74).

The field of American–South Asian relations has a large number of topics which should be examined by scholars as more official documents become available. The development of American relations with the newly independent states of India and Pakistan from 1947 to 1954 and the establishment of the Southeast Asia Treaty Organization and mutual defense agreement with Pakistan deserve serious study. Some American documents have been made available regarding the Indo-Pakistani crisis of 1971. The development of the American economic impact on India—including PL-480, economic and technical assistance, and private enterprise—has been studied only in limited ways. The shaping of American attitudes toward India and its leaders, especially Jawaharlal Nehru, Krishna Menon, and Indira Gandhi, warrants serious attention, as does the other side of the story, i.e., Indian and Pakistani perceptions of the United States, its culture, and leaders. The influence of American propaganda in South Asia, dating from the OWI in World War II to the Voice of America and the vast U.S. information services activities, should also be studied. Finally, examination of the work and influence of American diplomats in India, especially Chester Bowles, would be valuable additions to the literature.

Prior to World War II, black Africa was largely tangential to U.S. diplomacy. Except for Liberia, direct American economic interests in the continent were minimal and strategic considerations were virtually nonexistent. Given the relative powerlessness of black Americans, cultural contacts also were slight. Washington was an active observer and occasional critic of the European colonialization of Africa and supported British hegemony in South Africa, but by the early twentieth century both official and private American involvement in the continent had waned.

Three decisive events revived U.S. interest in Africa in the postwar period. Most significant was the rapid decolonialization of the continent in the period 1957 to 1963. Although the United States was at best a reluctant supporter of African freedom, it was forced to adapt its foreign policy in response to the end of European rule. The creation of the Bureau of African Affairs in 1958, although largely symbolic, did mark a recognition that an independent Africa demanded an independent African policy for the United States.

Coincidental with African independence was the reemergence of the racial issue within America. The civil rights and black power movements of the 1950s and 1960s had a major impact on U.S. relations with Africa. Black Americans raised the racial issue at home and also forced its consideration abroad. While blacks were rarely able to lobby effectively on specific policy issues, they did manage to increase official U.S. attention to independent Africa.

Along with decolonization and the domestic civil rights movement, the cold war rivalry between the United States and the Soviet Union shaped relations with Africa. Much of America's opposition to "premature independence" in Africa was based on its fears that the new nations would be too weak to resist communist penetration. The distrust of neutralism and attacks on nonalignment that characterized American diplomacy under Eisenhower and Dulles greatly damaged U.S. relations with the new African nations.

The Kennedy administration's verbal commitment to civil rights at home and to an "Africa-first" policy has led a number of historians to see a fundamental policy shift in 1961. They argue that Kennedy's appointments, personal courting of African leaders, and sympathy with the Third World completely revitalized America's African diplomacy. Other scholars contend that Kennedy's changes were largely cosmetic and there were few alterations of either the objectives or tactics of U.S. policy. Despite New Frontier rhetoric, America still responded to the continent in terms of cold war strategic considerations.

Despite the surge of U.S. interest in Africa after independence, direct American intervention has been rare. America did use covert activities during the Congo crisis of the early 1960s in support of the centralized government and against assumed radical leaders. The United States actively tried to defeat Marxist guerrillas in Angola in the 1970s. During the Biafran War of the late 1960s, the United States maintained neutrality, although private U.S. agencies were active on both sides of the struggle.

In the past decade U.S. diplomacy toward Africa has been dominated by the problems posed by the three remaining bastions of white resistance to black rule: the Portuguese colonies of Angola and Mozambique; Zimbabwe (Rhodesia); and South Africa. The United States was forced to transform its traditional commitments to self-determination, majority rule, and individual freedom into specific policies toward governments that denied all three. Sincere but abstract support of "freedom" clashed with immediate and concrete economic, strategic, and political interests.

Material on the recent era is of widely varying quality. Given the paucity of primary evidence available, most studies of U.S. relations with Africa have been heavily based on published sources and interviews. Much of it is highly polemical—either denouncing American policy as "racist" and "counterrevolutionary" or defending U.S. actions as "realistic" and "balanced." Journalists, former governmental officials, and political scientists, rather than historians, have dominated the field. Sources in the United States are widely scattered and many documents remain unclassified. As a result, what material exists on Africa is often less complete, sophisticated, and objective than on other areas of American diplomacy.

There are only two surveys of the history of U.S. relations with the entire continent: Edward Chester's *Clash of Titans: Africa and U.S. Foreign Policy* (2:336) is the most complete analysis of American involvement in Africa. A more lively but less balanced account is Russell Warren Howe, *Along the Africa Shore: An Historic Review of Two Centuries of U.S.-African Relations* (2:339). Howe's work is more interpretative and more effective on the recent period, but less complete and scholarly than Chester's.

The multiarchival monograph or innovative, interpretative essay that characterize the study of U.S. relations with nearly all other areas of the globe are almost nonexistent on Africa. The region offers one of the few remaining "underdeveloped" areas of American diplomatic history. Regardless of their ideology or methodology, scholars of U.S. foreign relations seeking new topics, a chance to test prevailing interpretations, or develop comparative studies, have near limitless opportunities through the study of U.S. involvement in black Africa.

Gary Hess prepared the sections dealing with the United States and South Asia; Thomas Noer and Louis Wilson developed the sections relating to the United States and Sub-Saharan Africa.

Resources and Overviews

RESEARCH AIDS

While pertinent bibliographies and reference aids are listed here, there are more extensive lists in Chapter 1.

Bibliographies

37:1 African Bibliographic Center. "Black Is Black? A Selected and Introductory Bibliographical Guide to Current Resources on Relations between the Black American and the African." *Current Bibliography on African Affairs* 1:5 (1968), 5–9. This list of material written during the decade of the early and mid-1960s reflects the changes in both African and black America and the interrelation between the two. The bibliographic items cited include Ruper Emerson's *Africa and U.S. Policy* (1967); John A. Davis, "The American Negro in Africa," in *Jewish Frontier* (1964); Thomas O. Echewa, "Africans vs. Afro-Americans," *Negro Digest* (Jan. 1965); and G. Horner, "America and Negro Africa: A Survey of Attitudes and Behavior," *Journal of American Scientific Affiliation* (June 1964).

37:2 Danaher, Kevin. *South Africa and the United States: An Annotated Bibliography.* Washington, D.C.: Institute for Policy Studies, 1979. This pamphlet lists 221 books and articles dealing with U.S. involvement in South Africa.

DeLancey, M. W. *Bibliography on African International Relations* (1:111) focuses on African states and organizations and briefly annotates books and articles that refer to them.

Duignan, P., ed. *Guide to Research and Reference Works on Sub-Saharan Africa* (1:112).

37:3 Forrester, Anne M. "Black American Views Africa: A Selected Bibliography of Perspectives." *A Current Bibliography on African Affairs* 1:6 (1968), 5–10. Recent events in U.S. history, the author notes, have resulted in much reflection and reassessment among a large number of black Americans as to their relationship with black Africa.

el-Khawas, M. A., and Kornegay, F. A., Jr., eds. *American-Southern African Relations: Bibliographic Essays* (1:113).

37:4 Mahar, J. Michael. *India: A Critical Bibliography.* Tucson: University of Arizona Press, 1964. This general, annotated bibliography is useful for background data.

37:5 Marcus, Harold C. *The Modern History of Ethiopia and the Horn of Africa: A Select and Annotated Bibliography.* Stanford, Calif.: Hoover Institution, 1972. This massive reference work is extremely useful.

37:6　Noer, Thomas. "Non-Benign Neglect: America and Africa in the Twentieth Century." In Gerald Haines and J. Samuel Walker, eds., *American Foreign Relations: Historiographic Review*. Westport, Conn.: Greenwood, 1980. This bibliographic essay reviews U.S.–Sub-Saharan Africa relations with special emphasis on policy developments during 1960 to 1969.

37:7　U.S. Department of State. *Africa: Problems and Prospects: A Bibliographic Survey*. Rev. ed. Washington, D.C.: G.P.O., 1977. This is an analytical survey, as well as an annotated review of the literature, that focuses on the various African nations. It also includes source materials such as atlases, encyclopedias, and yearbooks. Many maps are included.

U.S. Department of State. *Point Four: Near East and Africa: A Selected Bibliography on Economically Underdeveloped Countries* (1:110) lists mostly economic studies published in the 1940s which were collected to assist in developing the Point Four program.

Atlases and Other Aids

37:8　*African Abstracts*. London: International African Institute, 1950–1972. This quarterly review collected articles appearing in current periodicals and condensed them. Ceased publication (vols. 1–23).

African Recorder: A Fortnightly Record of African Events, with Index (1:149).

37:9　*African Research Bulletin*. Exeter, Eng.: African Research, 1964–.

Asian Recorder: A Weekly Digest of Asian Events with Index (1:150) is a weekly summary of events in all Asian countries, but contains much information on India.

37:10　McEvedy, Colin. *Atlas of African History*. New York: Facts on File, 1980. With 59 maps, the atlas offers an overview of developments on the African continent since prehistorical times.

Political Handbook and Atlas of the World (1:144) is a valuable annual reference guide to various national governments.

The Statesman's Year Book: Statistical and Historical Annual of the States of the World (1:145).

Yearbook on International Communist Affairs [1967–] (1:148) provides an annual, country-by-country profile of communist parties and activities.

Document Collections

More general collections are listed in Chapter 1.

Columbia Broadcasting System. *Face the Nation: The Collected Transcripts from CBS Radio and Television Broadcasts, 1954–1971* (1:347).

37:11　India. Lok Sabha Secretariat. *Foreign Policy of India: Texts of Documents, 1947–1964*. New Delhi: Lok Sabha Secretariat, 1966. This is a compilation of treaties, joint statements, and agreements entered into or issued by the government of India.

37:12　India. Ministry of External Affairs. *Foreign Affairs Record*. New Delhi, 1955–. The equivalent of the U.S. Department of State *Bulletin*, this is a monthly publication by the Ministry of External Affairs of the texts of statements, speeches, and agreements.

37:13　Jain, Rajendra, ed. *Soviet–South Asian Relations, 1947–1978*. 2 vols. Atlantic Highlands, N.J.: Humanities Press, 1978. These volumes are a compilation of official Soviet statements on developments in South Asia; an appendix includes detailed data on trade and general economic relations.

37:14　Kumar, Satish, ed. *Documents on India's Foreign Policy, 1972*. Delhi: Macmillan of India, 1975–. The first in a series of volumes produced to remedy the lack of any substantial annual compilation of foreign policy documents. This volume, like its successors, includes an introductory survey and a thorough compilation of official documents.

37:15　Pakistan. Ministry of Foreign Affairs. *Foreign Affairs Pakistan*. Islamabad, 1974–. Published monthly by the government of Pakistan, this series provides documents, statements, and other official releases pertaining to Pakistani foreign policy.

37:16　Pakistan. Ministry of Foreign Affairs. *Joint Communiqués, 1968–1973*. Islamabad: Ministry of Foreign Affairs, 1973. This is a useful compilation of official statements pertaining to Pakistani foreign policy.

37:17　Poplai, S. L., ed. *India 1947–50, Vol. 2: External Affairs*. London: Oxford University Press,

1959. A thorough compilation of communiqués and statements on Indian foreign policy, the documents center on India's major concerns of this era, i.e., Pakistan relations, especially the Kashmir dispute.

U.S. Department of State. *Foreign Relations of the United States* (1:358) contains documentary materials up to the early 1950s.

OVERVIEWS

See Chapter 24, "Overviews," for surveys of American foreign affairs since World War II.

South Asia

37:18 Barnds, William J. *India, Pakistan, and the Great Powers.* New York: Praeger, 1972. This is a basic introduction to the foreign policies of India and Pakistan and their relationship, as well as relations with China, the Soviet Union, and the United States. It contains detailed information on South Asian foreign economic aid, foreign trade, and defense expenditures. Bibliography.

37:19 Burke, S. M. *Mainsprings of Indian and Pakistani Foreign Policies.* Minneapolis: University of Minnesota Press, 1974. Burke traces Indian and Pakistani foreign policies to the religious foundations of the two nations, British policy, and the influence of Nehru. This is a thorough summary of Indo-Pakistani relations (1947–1974) and the influence of the United States, the Soviet Union, and China on South Asia. Extensive bibliography.

37:20 Choudhury, Golam W. *India, Pakistan, and the Major Powers.* New York: Free Press, 1975. A summary of American, Russian, and Chinese interests and policies in South Asia since 1947, it stresses the chronic instability of the region as a source of major power competition. Bibliography.

37:21 Lyon, Peter. "Strategy and South Asia: Twenty-Five Years On." *International Journal* 27:3 (1972), 333–56. The Lyon article provides a useful analysis of the strategic and political changes in South Asia from the end of Britain's imperial authority to the Indo-Pakistani war of 1971. India's status as the predominant regional power is discussed with respect to long-term stability.

37:22 Sherwani, Latif Ahmed. *India, China, and Pakistan.* Karachi: Council for Pakistan Studies, 1967. Written in the aftermath of the Indo-Pakistani crisis of 1965–1966, this is an expression of the Pakistani viewpoint on relations with India. It is noteworthy for its effort to explain, through Indian sources, the bases of Indian foreign policy. Bibliography.

37:23 Ziring, Lawrence, ed. *The Subcontinent in World Politics: India, Its Neighbors, and the Great Powers.* New York: Praeger, 1978. This useful overview contains five articles on Indian foreign policy, and one each on Pakistani policy, Soviet interests, and American interests in the region.

India

37:24 Appadorai, Angadipuram. *Essays in Politics and International Relations.* Bombay: Asia Publishing House, 1969. These essays were published between 1936 and 1966, many in journals not readily available. Appadorai was one of the principal scholar-analysts of Indian politics and foreign policy, and this collection includes, among several articles on Indian diplomacy since independence, essays on Nehru's ideology and the Bandung Conference.

37:25 Gupta, Karunakar. *India in World Politics: A Period of Transition, Fall 1956 to Spring 1960.* Calcutta: Scientific Book Agency, 1969. A detailed study of the impact on India of changing international relations, from the Suez crisis of 1956 to the abortive summit conference of 1960, it is critical of Nehru's policy toward China during this period. Bibliography.

37:26 Heimsath, Charles H., and Mansingh, Surjit. *A Diplomatic History of Modern India.* Calcutta: Allied, 1971. A comprehensive survey of India's international relations, this book provides the best single introduction to India's foreign policy and places the relationship with the United States within the context of India's general approach to world affairs. Extensive bibliography.

37:27 Prasad, Bimla. *The Origins of Indian Foreign Policy: The Indian National Congress and World Affairs, 1885–1947.* Calcutta: Bookland, 1960. This is a detailed examination of the positions taken by the Indian National Congress on world problems and its views of international developments from its founding until independence.

37:28 Sar Desai, D. R. *Indian Foreign Policy in Cambodia, Laos, and Vietnam, 1947–1964.* Berkeley: University of California Press, 1968. A thorough study of India's response to nationalism and communism in Indochina, it emphasizes the reasons for intermittent interest and the related lack of Indian knowledge about the region. India's role in the International Control Commission established in 1954 is also discussed. Extensive bibliography.

37:29 Singh, Baljit. *India's Foreign Policy: An Analysis*. London: Asia Publishing House, 1976. Singh relates Indian foreign policy to theories on international politics and evaluates its effectiveness in terms of political, security, and economic objectives. He includes chapters on India's relations with the major powers, Pakistan, and the Third World (includes the Vietnam War). Extensive bibliography.

Pakistan

37:30 Burke, S. M. *Pakistan's Foreign Policy: An Historical Analysis*. London: Oxford University Press, 1973. The most comprehensive, scholarly overview of Pakistan's foreign policy since 1947, it includes considerable material on the 1954 alliance with the United States. A brief postscript discusses the impact of the independence of Bangladesh on Pakistan's international relations. Extensive bibliography.

37:31 Jain, Jagelish. *China, Pakistan, and Bangladesh*. New Delhi: Radiant, 1974. Drawing upon Chinese-language sources, Jain summarizes Peking's view of Pakistan since 1950. Chinese anxiety resulting from evidence of increasing Soviet influence in the mid-1960s gave way to mutual interests and a strengthening of relations as a result of the Bangladesh crisis. Bibliography.

37:32 Singh, Sangat. *Pakistan's Foreign Policy: An Appraisal*. New York: Asia Publishing House, 1970. Singh provides a summary of the origins of Pakistan's foreign policy, especially the factor of India, and traces developments through 1970. Documents and bibliography.

37:33 Syed, Anwar. *China and Pakistan: Diplomacy of an Entente Cordiale*. Amherst: University of Massachusetts Press, 1974. Syed traces the development of Sino-Pakistani relations since 1950, and maintains that the "entente cordiale" had its origins in the relatively benign Chinese response to Pakistan's alliance with the United States. Mutual interests regarding India and the Soviet Union have been basic to the Chinese-Pakistani relationship. Includes data on Pakistan's international indebtedness and foreign aid.

Personalities

Additional references on individuals may be found in Chapter 1, "Biographical Data."

AMERICAN

See Chapter 24, under "Personalities" and "Presidential Administrations," for additional references.

George Ball
See also Chapter 24, under "Personalities."

Ball, G. W. *The Discipline of Power: Essentials of a Modern World Structure* (28:19) finds Kennedy's under secretary of state criticizing U.S. policy for being overly concerned with Africa at the expense of relations with Europe. He is critical of American efforts against South Africa and Rhodesia.

37:34 Ball, George W. *The Elements of Our Congo Policy*. Washington, D.C.: Department of State, 1961. Ball, then under secretary of state, outlines the basis of U.S. policy in the Congo. This pamphlet argues that the U.S. supported UN intervention in the Congo to establish stability in this central African nation, to protect lives and property, both African and European, and to impede Soviet or Chinese movement into the area.

Chester Bowles
Bowles, C. *Promises to Keep: My Years in Public Life, 1941–1969* (24:99) includes a detailed statement on his experiences as ambassador to India, especially the second of his missions to New Delhi (1963–1969). Bowles maintained his strong sympathy for India and remained critical of many aspects of American policy and diplomatic practice in Asia. He also discusses Kennedy's shift to a pro-African policy.

37:35 Bowles, Chester. *Africa's Challenge to America*. Berkeley: University of California Press, 1956. In the aftermath of World War II, the anticolonial activities of many subjected peoples increased. As early as 1942, Chester Bowles suggested that the Atlantic Charter include the colonial areas of Africa and Asia. This was not done. By 1951 independence for the Gold Coast was a certainty and the "winds of change" were evident in other parts of Africa. Bowles's account is an excellent statement of liberal frustrations with U.S. policies toward Africa in the 1950s.

37:36   Bowles, Chester. *Ambassador's Report.* New York: Harper & Row, 1954. While providing much information on India's political and economic development during the first few years after independence, the work's principal value is its insight into the thinking of Bowles at the end of his first tour as ambassador.

John F. Kennedy
See Chapter 24, under "Personalities," for additional references.

Schlesinger, A. M., Jr. *A Thousand Days: John F. Kennedy in the White House* (24:215) hails Kennedy's efforts in Africa as one of his major foreign policy triumphs, and emphasizes the sharp departure from the Eisenhower approach.

Henry A. Kissinger
See Chapters 24 and 30, under "Personalities," for additional references.

37:37   Kissinger, Henry A. "Southern Africa and the United States: An Agenda for Cooperation." In his *American Foreign Policy.* 3d ed. New York: Norton, 1977, pp. 365–81. In this April 27, 1967, speech in honor of President Kenneth Kaunda, Kissinger outlined the Ford administration's policies toward Zambia, Rhodesia, Namibia, and South Africa. Kissinger also stated that regional economic development would be a major focus of the Ford administration's Southern African policies. He concluded by noting that his "proposals" were not "a program made in America to be passively accepted by Africans . . . [but] they are an expression of common aspirations and an agenda of cooperation."

Morris, R. *Uncertain Greatness: Henry Kissinger and American Foreign Policy* (24:223) characterizes Kissinger policies toward Africa as those of "foresight and folly." The determinants for Kissinger were that Portugal was a NATO ally, and U.S. private investments in South Africa. Morris considered the "Tar Baby" policies, as they were called by the National Security Council, "a disaster, naive in concept and practically impossible for the government to execute."

Richard M. Nixon
See Chapter 24, under "Personalities," for additional references.

Nixon, R. M. *RN: The Memoirs of Richard Nixon* (24:145) discusses his position during the Indo-Pakistan War (1971).

Szulc, T. *The Illusion of Peace: Foreign Policy in the Nixon-Kissinger Years* (24:226) argues that the Third World occupied only a marginal position in the Nixon-Kissinger foreign policies (pp. 175–78; 219–25). Nixon's knowledge and understanding of the Nigerian civil war is criticized; he apparently was ready to recognize the Biafran state, but Kissinger convinced the president that nothing was to be gained by this action. The most telling and strongest attack on Nixon-Kissinger policies toward Africa is the NSSM 39 policies.

Others
37:38   Attwood, William. *The Reds and Blacks: A Personal Adventure.* New York: Harper & Row, 1967. Kennedy's ambassador to Guinea emphasizes Africa as an area of cold war competition between the United States and Soviet Union, and stresses the victories of the "New Frontier" in Africa.

37:39   Davis, Nathaniel. "The Angola Decision of 1975: A Personal Memoir." *Foreign Affairs* 57:1 (1978), 109–24. The author, assistant secretary of state for African affairs in 1975, gives a personal account of how the United States chose to intervene in Angola. He disagreed with Secretary Kissinger's policies and resigned.

Galbraith, J. K. *Ambassador's Journal: A Personal Account of the Kennedy Years* (30:39) is a detailed statement on Galbraith's experiences as ambassador to India (1961–1963) drawn from his daily notes. The text lacks analysis of Indo-American relations, but it contains insight into the thinking of Galbraith on India, its problems, and its leaders.

Kennan, G. F. *The Cloud of Danger: Current Realities of American Foreign Policy* (29:226) devotes the African section (pp. 68–79) almost entirely to Southern Africa. He argues that U.S. policy in Africa reflects a guilt complex and that the United States has no obligation to attempt to remedy the various inequities. Kissinger overreacted to the Soviets in Angola and because of the failures of Kissinger's policies in Angola he proposed the Anglo-American agreements for Rhodesia.

Phillips, W. *Ventures in Diplomacy* (17:54) is the memoir of the official whom Roosevelt sent to India as his personal representative in 1943. In the substantial chapter devoted to India, Phillips details his frustration in dealing with the British and provides the earliest publication of his reports to Roosevelt.

37:40 Williams, G. Mennen. *Africa for the Africans.* Grand Rapids, Mich.: Eerdmans, 1969. This memoir by Kennedy's flamboyant assistant secretary of state for Africa stresses the new directions of Kennedy's policy toward Africa. He also emphasizes the role of the domestic civil rights movement in influencing U.S. policy.

SOUTH ASIAN

Mohandas K. Gandhi

37:41 Fischer, Louis. *The Life of Mahatma Gandhi.* New York: Harper, 1950. This is a very sympathetic biography of Gandhi. It includes information on Gandhi's correspondence and conversations with Fischer and his efforts to gain American support during World War II.

37:42 Payne, Pierre S. R. *The Life and Death of Mahatma Gandhi.* New York: Dutton, 1969. A massive information biography, it is also useful for Gandhi's political views during India's struggle for independence.

Krishna Menon

37:43 Brecher, Michael. *India and World Politics: Krishna Menon's View of the World.* London: Oxford University Press, 1968. An important study of Menon and India's foreign policy, it provides the text of an extended taped dialogue between Menon and Brecher on the policy of nonalignment and other aspects of his diplomacy and offers a systematic analysis of his view of the world and its impact on the decisionmaking process in India. Also included is a content analysis of Menon's world view.

37:44 George, T. J. S. *Krishnan Menon: A Biography.* London: Cape, 1964. This study is a worthwhile introduction to Menon's career, especially in terms of understanding his attitudes toward the West. It traces his controversial career as an Indian representative at the United Nations and as minister of defense.

Jawaharlal Nehru

37:45 Brecher, Michael. *Nehru: A Political Biography.* London: Oxford University Press, 1959. Brecher's biography provides a detailed and authoritative study of Nehru's emergence as a nationalist leader

and the first several years of his leadership of independent India.

37:46 Moraes, Frank. *Jawaharlal Nehru: A Biography.* New York: Macmillan, 1956. A balanced and thorough biography of Nehru written at the height of his domestic and international influence, it is especially valuable in tracing the importance of his early career, his father, and Gandhi on Nehru's policies as prime minister. Bibliography.

37:47 Moraes, Frank. *Nehru: Sunlight and Shadow.* Bombay: Jaico Publishing House, 1964. A substantial biography of Nehru and his time, this work concentrates on Nehru's later years (1956–1964) and deals fully with the demise of Sino-Indian relations and its effect on Nehru's declining influence internationally and domestically.

37:48 Nehru, Jawaharlal. *India's Foreign Policy: Selected Speeches, September 1946 to April 1961.* Delhi: Government of India, 1961. This is the best single source of Nehru's statements on foreign policy, and for tracing the outlines of Indian diplomacy (1947–1961).

37:49 Nehru, Jawaharlal. *Selected Works of Jawaharlal Nehru.* 10 vols. to date. Ed. by S. Gopel et al. New Delhi: Orient Longman, 1972–. This is a major collection offering a thorough compilation of Nehru's letters and speeches. Volume 10 brings the record through 1940. The forthcoming volumes will be of major importance in tracing Indian foreign policy.

37:50 Norman, Dorothy, ed. *Nehru, the First Sixty Years.* 2 vols. New York: Day, 1965. A detailed compilation of the speeches, interviews, and other public statements of Nehru to 1950, this is a valuable guide to his thinking on India and world problems.

37:51 Range, Willard. *Jawaharlal Nehru's World View: A Theory of International Relations.* Athens: University of Georgia Press, 1961. Range's study brings coherence to Nehru's thinking on international relations. A major weakness in Nehru's assumptions is the failure to address realistically the means of attaining his objectives.

Rabindranath Tagore

37:52 Hay, Stephen N. "Rabindranath Tagore in America." *American Quarterly* 14:3 (1962), 439–63. A detailed analysis of Tagore's attitudes toward the

United States and of the reasons for his U.S. visits. The varying American reception to Tagore's five visits between 1912 and 1930 is examined within the context of internal and international changes.

37:53 Mukherjee, Sujit. *Passage to America: The Reception of Rabindranath Tagore in the United States, 1912–1941.* Calcutta: Bookland, 1964. This is a detailed examination of Tagore's visits to the United States, his reception, and his changing views of America.

Others

37:54 Brittain, Vera. *Envoy Extraordinary: A Study of Vijaya Lakshmi Pandit and Her Contribution to Modern India.* London: Allen, 1965. This sympathetic biography, based on interviews with Pandit and written with the cooperation of the government of India, provides a good introduction to her thinking, career, and influence. Bibliography.

37:55 Gandhi, Indira. *Speeches and Writings.* New York: Harper & Row, 1975. This book includes nearly all of Indira Gandhi's important speeches and statements on foreign policy. It includes a brief, but useful, introductory memoir which centers on her reminiscences of Jawaharlal Nehru and Mohandas Gandhi.

37:56 Shastri, Lal Bahadur. *Selected Speeches (June 11, 1964 to January 10, 1966).* New Delhi: Ministry of Information and Broadcasting, 1974. A useful compilation of Shastri's statements, mostly on foreign policy, during his brief tenure as prime minister, it includes much information on the crises with Pakistan in 1965 and the Tashkent Conference.

AFRICAN

Kwame Nkrumah

37:57 Davidson, Basil. *Black Star: A View of the Life and Times of Kwame Nkrumah.* New York: Praeger, 1973. Davidson, an admirer of Nkrumah, glosses over his ego, excesses, and eventual ouster. Still the book offers a good interpretation of Nkrumah's ideas about nonalignment and Pan-Africanism, and gives some attention to his often stormy relations with the United States.

37:58 Nkrumah, Kwame. *The Autobiography of Kwame Nkrumah.* Edinburgh: Nelson, 1957. Nkrumah led the first successful independence movement in Africa. His autobiography, written in the year

of Ghanian freedom, is self-serving but is important for its description of the tactics of anticolonialism used in Ghana, and copied by much of Africa in the next decade.

37:59 Nkrumah, Kwame. *Dark Days in Ghana.* New York: International Publishers, 1968. The president reviews the coup (February 1966) which deposed him and criticizes the military regime which followed.

37:60 Omari, T. Peter. *Kwame Nkrumah: The Anatomy of an African Dictatorship.* London: Hurst, 1970. This political biography seeks to evaluate the role of the controversial Ghanian leader within the context of contemporary African and Ghanian history.

Julius Nyerere

37:61 Nyerere, Julius. *Freedom and Unity: A Selection from Writings and Speeches, 1952–1967.* New York: Oxford University Press, 1967. Although much of Nyerere's rhetoric is for internal consumption, this volume is helpful in understanding the dynamics of the independence struggle, Nyerere's significance in inter-African diplomacy, and his views on African nonalignment in the cold war.

37:62 Smith, William. *We Must Run While They Walk: A Portrait of Africa's Julius Nyerere.* New York: Random House, 1971. This sympathetic biography of the Tanzanian leader provides a good summary of both the domestic and foreign policies of one of Africa's most influential statesmen.

Others

37:63 Colvin, Ian G. *The Rise and Fall of Moise Tshombe: A Biography.* London: Frewin, 1968. Colvin has written a sympathetic biography of the secessionist leader of Katanga, who was a major figure in the Congo crisis (1960–1964).

37:64 Dei-Anang, Michael. *The Administration of Ghana's Foreign Policy, 1957–1965: A Personal Memoir.* London: Athlone, 1975. This book deals with the problems of working with Nkrumah in the postindependence years. It does contain some documents on Ghanian foreign policy.

37:65 Hall, Richard. *Kaunda, Founder of Zambia.* London: Longmans, 1965. An adequate biography, it was published only a year after independence. The book contains little on economic or political problems.

37:66   Hatch, John. *Two African Statesmen: Kaunda of Zambia and Nyerere of Tanzania.* Chicago: Regnery, 1976. This is a brief summary of the struggle for independence, the problems of postindependence, and relations with Europe and America through the lives of two influential African leaders.

37:67   Kanza, Thomas. *Conflict in the Congo: The Rise and Fall of Lumumba.* Baltimore: Penguin, 1970. This is an account of Patrice Lumumba's short, turbulent career as prime minister of the new Republic of the Congo, as written by his minister for UN affairs.

37:68   Mosley, Leonard O. *Haile Selassie: The Conquering Lion.* Englewood Cliffs, N.J.: Prentice-Hall, 1965. This is a balanced, informed biography of the Ethiopian leader and supporter of U.S. policy on the Horn of Africa.

37:69   Murray-Brown, Jeremy. *Kenyatta.* New York: Dutton, 1973. A solid study of the leader of Kenya's independence movement and first president; however, there is little on foreign policy.

U.S. and South Asia

MUTUAL IMAGES AND PERCEPTIONS

37:70   Goodfriend, Arthur. *The Twisted Image.* New York: St. Martin's Press, 1963. This is a critique of American propaganda efforts in India, by an official of the U.S. Information Agency, based on his observations and experiences on assignment in India (1957–1960).

37:71   Heimsath, Charles. "American Images of India as Factors in U.S. Foreign Policy Making." *Asian Thought and Society* 2:3 (1977), 271–89. Heimsath discusses Americans' negative image of India since 1947 in literature, the media, and interviews of the informed and uninformed, and examines its effect on foreign policy decisionmaking.

37:72   Hess, Gary R. "The Forgotten Asian Americans: The East Indian Community in the United States." *Pacific Historical Review* 43:4 (1974), 576–96. This article focuses on the experience of Indian immigrants in the United States from the early 20th century to the influx since 1965. It relies on a number of sociological studies of East Indians in America.

37:73   Hess, Gary R. "The 'Hindu' in America: Immigration and Naturalization Policies and India, 1917–1946." *Pacific Historical Review* 38:1 (1969), 59–79. Hess traces the experience of Indian immigrants in the United States, with special attention to the restrictions on immigration and naturalization and the efforts of Indian groups in America to achieve a quota and citizenship rights.

37:74   Isaacs, Harold R. *Scratches on Our Minds: American Images of China and India.* New York: Day, 1958. This is a pioneering study of American popular perceptions of India—its people and culture. It emphasizes the extent to which India has been unknown, or at best "scratches on our minds" and subjected to distorted, stereotypical images. Reprinted (1972) as *Images of Asia: American Views of China and India* (2:333).

37:75   Jones, Dorothy B. *The Portrayal of China and India on the American Screen, 1896–1955: The Evolution of Chinese and Indian Themes, Locales, and Characters as Portrayed on the American Screen.* Cambridge, Mass.: MIT Press, 1955. This work supplements the Isaacs book. It details the image of India as depicted in American films. A few stock themes and characterizations dominated the portrayal of India.

37:76   Mukherjee, Sujit. "Early American Images of India." *India Quarterly* 20:1 (1964), 43–50. This is a useful, although sketchy, survey of the various American images of India and how India was depicted by influential writers of the 19th century.

37:77   Pathak, Sushil Mahhaua. *American Missionaries and Hinduism (A Story of Their Contacts from 1813 to 1910).* Delhi: Munshiram Manaharlal Oriental, 1967. This book provides a reasonably comprehensive survey of early Protestant missionary activity. It is based largely on mission records. Bibliography.

U.S. AND SOUTH ASIA: TRADE AND AID

37:78   Datar, Asha L. *India's Economic Relations with the USSR and Eastern Europe, 1953 to 1969.* New York: Cambridge University Press, 1972. Datar's carefully researched volume reviews the nature of Soviet aid and trade to India, and concludes it is not preferable to that of the West.

37:79 Kumar, Dharma. *Foreign Investments in India.* New York: Oxford University Press, 1965. Kumar not only examines the amount and distribution of foreign investment, but compares it to the situation prior to independence.

37:80 Ward, Barbara. *India and the West.* New York: Norton, 1961. This is an extensive summary of the problem confronting India's plans for modernization and the role of Western economic and technical assistance. The book includes important data on Indian development and foreign assistance.

Trade

37:81 Bhaghat, Goberdhan. *Americans in India: Commercial and Consular Relations, 1784–1860.* New York: New York University Press, 1951. This is a basic background study. It details the development of Indo-American diplomatic and commercial relations.

Furber, H. "The Beginnings of American Trade with India, 1784–1812" (5:132) details the development and importance of the India market.

Livermore, S. W. "Early Commercial and Consular Relations with the East Indies" (17:271) traces the American interest in developing trade with India and other parts of the colonial "East Indies" from 1784 to about 1850.

37:82 Misra, Panchananda. "Indo-American Trade Relations: The Period of Growth, 1784–1850." *Journal of Indian History* 42:3 (1964), 833–46. This is a useful summary of the development of Indo-American trade and of the activities of early American diplomats in India.

Price, J. M. "One Family's Empire: The Russell-Lee-Clerk Connection in Maryland, Britain, and India, 1707–1857" (8:159).

Aid

37:83 Baber, Sattar. *United States Aid to Pakistan: A Case Study of the Influence of the Donor Country on the Domestic and Foreign Policies of the Recipient.* Karachi: Pakistan Institute of International Affairs,

1974. This book is an important well-documented summary of American technical, economic, and military assistance to Pakistan. It reflects, however, the Pakistani disenchantment with the United States and thus is critical of American objectives and programs. Bibliography.

37:84 Brecher, Irving, and Abbas, S. A. *Foreign Aid and Industrial Development in Pakistan.* New York: Cambridge University Press, 1972. This account shows that foreign aid greatly contributed to Pakistan's industrial growth in the 1960s.

37:85 Chandrasekhar, Sripati. *American Aid and India's Economic Development.* New York: Praeger, 1965. After a thorough review of U.S. technical, economic, and educational assistance to India (1950–1965), Chandrasekhar concludes that American assistance was of significance in the steady improvement of the Indian economy. Extensive bibliography.

37:86 Dutta, Rani. "American Attitudes towards U.S. Technical and Economic Assistance to India, 1949–1953." *Indian Political Science Review* 3:3/4 (1969), 157–84. This article provides useful information on the attitudes of Congress, the press, and various interest groups toward the early Point Four program. India did not figure prominently in the consideration of economic assistance programs until about 1953, when criticisms of India's foreign policy became more significant.

37:87 Eldridge, Philip J. *The Politics of Foreign Aid in India.* New York: Schocken, 1970. This study examines the objectives of the aid donors and the political impact of the aid on India. It also reviews the economic characteristics of the aid.

37:88 Hess, Gary. "American Agricultural Missionaries and Efforts at Economic Improvement in India." *Agricultural History* 42:1 (1968), 23–33. This provides a survey of the leading American agricultural missionaries in India in the early 20th century and assesses their influence.

37:89 Hess, Gary. *Sam Higginbottom of Allahabad: Pioneer of Point Four to India.* Charlottesville: University Press of Virginia, 1967. This is a biography of an American agricultural missionary, and a history of the Allahabad Agricultural Institute, the school which he founded in 1910. Bibliography.

37:90 Lewis, John P. *Quiet Crisis in India: Economic Development and American Policy.* Washington, D.C.: Brookings Institution, 1962. This influential study includes a thorough discussion of the American economic aid program (1950–1962). Bibliography.

37:91 Loomba, Joanne F. "U.S. Aid to India, 1951–1967: A Study in Decision Making." *India Quarterly* 28:4 (1972), 304–31. This article provides detailed data on American economic assistance programs in India and of the objectives and expectations of policymakers and congressional leaders. It is observed that while self-interest is a major objective, American officials have shown little confidence that interests have been served by the assistance program.

37:92 Maheshwari, B. "Bokaro: The Politics of American Aid." *International Studies* 10:1/2 (1968), 163–80. Since Britain and the Soviet Union had already assisted India's industrial development through the construction of steel mills, India viewed the question of U.S. assistance to Bokaro as a test of American interest in India's development.

37:93 Shrivastava, B. K. "PL-480 Counterpart Funds and Inflation: Myth and Reality." *Asian Economic Review* 11:2 (1969), 145–59. A well-documented summary not only of the influence of American-owned funds, but of the complex procedures of the PL-480 program. Shrivastava concludes that, contrary to some economists and politicians, PL-480 was not a major source of Indian inflation.

37:94 Wolf, Charles, Jr. *Foreign Aid: Theory and Practice in Southern Asia.* Princeton, N.J.: Princeton University Press, 1960. Written by a former American diplomatic and technical assistance officer in Asia, this study is the most comprehensive work available on the development of American military and economic assistance programs in South and Southeast Asia. It is particularly useful for tracing the background, implementation, and problems of the mutual security program. Bibliography.

U.S. AND INDIAN NATIONALISM, 1900–1947

See under "Personalities," especially Mahatma Gandhi and American William Phillips (under "Others").

The Nationalist Movement, 1900–1940

37:95 Banerjee, Kalyan Kumar. "East Indian Immigration into America: Beginnings of Indian Revolutionary Activity." *Modern Review* [Calcutta] 116 (1964), 355–61. One of the first contributions by an Indian scholar to the literature, the Banerjee article served to broaden perspectives on the background of early Indian political activities in the United States.

37:96 Bose, Arun Coomer. "Indian Nationalist Agitators in the U.S.A. and Canada till the Arrival of Har Dayal in 1911." *Journal of Indian History* 43:1 (1965), 277–99. Bose traces in detail the early phases of the Indian nationalist activity in the United States, and relates its emergence to the partition of Bengal and the considerable increase of Indians, especially students, migrating to the United States.

37:97 Bose, Arun Coomer. *Indian Revolutionaries Abroad, 1905–1922.* Patna: Bharati Bhawan, 1971. The most thorough work available on the activities of Indian nationalists overseas in the early 20th century. The bulk of the book deals with the activities in the United States during World War I. Extensive bibliography.

37:98 Brown, Giles. "The Hindu Conspiracy, 1914–1917." *Pacific Historical Review* 17:3 (1948), 299–310. The earliest scholarly treatment of Indian political activity in the United States during World War I, it is now dated, but remains an important contribution.

37:99 Dignan, Don K. "The Hindu Conspiracy in Anglo-American Relations during World War I." *Pacific Historical Review* 10:1 (1941), 57–76. Dignan emphasizes the British concern with Indian political activities in the United States and pressure on American authorities to take action against the "revolutionaries."

37:100 Jensen, Joan M. "The 'Hindu Conspiracy': A Reassessment." *Pacific Historical Review* 48:1 (1979), 65–83. Jensen writes that the ready acceptance by American officials of the British concern about Indian political activity in the United States resulted in a questionable interpretation of the conspiracy statute when it was used against the Indians. The article includes a useful summary of scholarship on the "Hindu conspiracy."

37:101 Manchanda, Mohinder K. *India and America, Historical Links 1776–1920*. Chandrigarh: Young Men Harmilap Association, 1976. The author focuses on the early-20th-century Indian immigration and exclusion from the United States and Indian nationalist activity in America during World War I. Bibliography.

37:102 Mathur, L. P. *Indian Revolutionary Movement in the United States of America*. Delhi: Chand, 1970. In this thorough study of the Ghadar party's activities in the United States, Mathur writes from a nationalist perspective and is sympathetic, although not uncritical, toward the Ghadar movement. Bibliography.

37:103 Naidis, Mark. "Propaganda of the Gadar Party." *Pacific Historical Review* 20:3 (1951), 251–60. Naidis's article traces the propaganda techniques and style of the Ghadar (Revolution) party during World War I. It demonstrates how the Ghadar leaders attempted to exploit contemporary American movements and concerns as well as events in India, especially the Amritsar massacre.

37:104 Rathore, Naaen Gul. "Indian Nationalist Agitation in the United States: A Study of Lala Lajpat Rai and the India Home Rule League of America, 1914–1920." Ph.D. diss., Columbia University, 1965. This is the best study available on the moderate Indian political activity in the United States during World War I. It provides a thorough and critical examination of Rai's career. Bibliography.

37:105 Raucher, Alan. "American Anti-Imperialists and the Pro-India Movement, 1900–32." *Pacific Historical Review* 43:1 (1974), 83–110. In an examination of the attitudes of American liberal internationalists toward the Indian nationalist movement, Raucher pays particular attention to views and images of Gandhi.

37:106 Singh, Harnam. *Indian National Movement and American Opinion*. Delhi: Central Electric Press, 1962. It is based on extensive research in numerous periodicals and fourteen leading newspapers. It finds American opinion favorably disposed toward India's nationalist aspirations.

37:107 Spellman, John W. "The International Extensions of Political Conspiracy as Illustrated by the Ghadr Party." *Journal of Indian History* 37:1 (1959), 23–45. This study of the emergence of the Ghadar movement—its early activities in India, its extension outside India, and its legacy beyond World War I—includes a summary of the trials of the Ghadar leaders in the United States.

The Indian Crisis, 1941–1947

37:108 Collins, Larry, and Lapierre, Dominique. *Freedom at Midnight*. New York: Simon & Schuster, 1975. The authors have detailed the story of the last years of British India and the partition which involved an endless bloodbath of riots, civil war, and assassinations. The towering figures of Mountbatten, Nehru, Jinnah, and Gandhi and their interrelations are woven throughout this epic study. Bibliography.

37:109 Hess, Gary R. *America Encounters India, 1941–1947*. Baltimore: Johns Hopkins University Press, 1971. This study traces the American official and popular response to Indian nationalism during the political upheavals (1941–1947) and includes material on British and Indian propaganda activities in the United States. It is critical of the Roosevelt administration's handling of the Indian question during World War II. Bibliography.

37:110 Hope, A. G. *American and Swaraj: The U.S. Role in Indian Independence*. Washington, D.C.: Public Affairs Press, 1968. This study concentrates on the years 1941 to 1947. It is wholly favorable in its assessment of the American response to Indian nationalism.

37:111 Jauhri, R. C. *American Diplomacy and Independence for India*. Bombay: Vora, 1970. This book details the 1941 to 1947 period of Indo-American relations. It is critical of the Roosevelt administration's policy during the war.

37:112 Jauhri, R. C. "The American Effort to Avert the Impending Partition of India, 1946–47." *Indian Journal of American Studies* 8:2 (1978), 1–11. The Americans tried to avert the partition of the area into mutually hostile Hindu and Moslem countries. The United States gave up its mediatory efforts only after its representatives concluded that partition was inevitable.

37:113 Mullins, Frances Harper. "American Diplomacy and Indian Independence, 1941–1945." Ph.D. diss., Fletcher School of Diplomacy, 1971. This study provides insight into the policymaking process on the Indian question and into the development of Indo-American economic relations during World War II. Bibliography.

37:114 Muzumdar, Haridas Thakordas. *America's Contributions to India's Freedom*. Allahabad: Central Book Depot, 1962. This is a study, based on secondary sources as well as memory, by one of the major Indian political activists in the United States during the 1930 to 1947 period. It contains useful information on the operations of and rivalries among Indian nationalists in America.

37:115 Prasad, Yuvaraj Deva. "American Reaction to Gandhi's Arrest in 1942: The Conflict of Ideology and Necessity." *Journal of Indian History* 50:149 (1972), 611–18. In August 1942, when the Indian National Congress demanded that the British immediately "quit India," Gandhi and other Indian leaders were arrested. The need to preserve British-American cooperation in the war against Germany and Japan forestalled any official U.S. support for Indian independence.

37:116 Shaplen, Robert. "One Man Lobby." *New Yorker* (Mar. 24, 1951), 35–55. Shaplen provides a substantial account of the enterprising J. J. Singh, the head of the India League of America in the 1940s and the most important source of nationalist propaganda in the United States.

37:117 Venkataramani, M. S. "The Roosevelt Administration and the Great Indian Famine." *International Studies* 4:4 (1963), 241–64. This article is a critical examination of the Roosevelt administration's response to the war-caused Bengal famine of 1943.

37:118 Venkataramani, M. S., and Shrivastava, B. K. "America and the Indian Political Crisis, July–August 1942." *International Studies* 6:1 (1964), 1–48. This essay examines in detail American policy and is very critical of the Roosevelt administration, especially for its prolonged delay in replying to Gandhi's letter to Roosevelt.

37:119 Venkataramani, M. S., and Shrivastava, B. K. "The U.S. and the Cripps Mission." *India Quarterly* 19:3 (1963), 214–65. This essay details the work of Louis Johnson and is critical of the Roosevelt administration's response to the Cripps mission. Venkataramani and Shrivastava argue that the Roosevelt administration, in the person of Harry Hopkins, undermined Johnson's work as a mediator.

37:120 Venkataramani, M. S., and Shrivastava, B. K. "The United States and the 'Quit India' Demand." *India Quarterly* 20:2 (1964), 101–39. This article concludes the authors' three related articles on American policy during the critical spring and summer of 1942 and continues their criticism of the American response to Indian nationalism.

U.S. AND SOUTH ASIA SINCE 1947

37:121 Brown, W. Norman. *The United States, and India, Pakistan, and Bangladesh*. Cambridge: Harvard University Press, 1972. This book provides a brief summary of American–South Asian relations, but its principal purpose is to introduce Americans to South Asian culture, politics, and history, with special emphasis on developments since independence. Bibliography.

37:122 Gupta, Ramesh Chand. *U.S. Policy towards India and Pakistan*. Delhi: B.R. Publishing, 1977. This book provides a thorough summary of American policy during the Indo-Pakistani conflict over Bangladesh in 1971. It is an outgrowth of a dissertation completed at Jawaharlal Nehru University. Bibliography.

37:123 Kaul, K. K. *U.S.A. and the Hindustan Peninsula, 1952–1966*. Lucknow: Postak Kendra, 1977. This book is a detailed analysis of Indian, Pakistani, American, and Nepalese foreign policies. The author is generally sympathetic toward American objectives and policies with regard to India. Extensive bibliography.

37:124 Palmer, Norman D. *South Asia and United States Policy*. Boston: Houghton Mifflin, 1966. This major study emphasizes South Asia's importance to the United States within the context of the international system as it was seen in the early 1960s. It provides a firm background to an understanding of South Asian political and economic developments since independence. Extensive bibliography.

U Thant. *View from the UN* [1961–1970] (38:82) discusses U Thant's role in "Asian Subcontinent," including the Indo-Pakistani conflict and the birth of Bangladesh.

37:125 Ziring, Lawrence. "Pakistan and India: Politics, Personalities and Foreign Policy." *Asian Survey*

18:7 (1978), 706–30. This useful summary of contemporary developments in South Asia and their impact upon American interests stresses the influence of Bhutto and Indira Gandhi.

Bangladesh

37:126   Naik, J. A. *India, Russia, China and Bangladesh.* New Delhi: Chand, 1972. This account places much of the blame for the Bangladesh conflict on U.S. policies.

37:127   Wilcox, Wayne. *The Emergence of Bangladesh: Problems and Opportunities for a Redefined American Policy in South Asia.* Washington, D.C.: American Enterprise Institute, 1973. Wilcox surveys the collapse of the Pakistan political system, the civil war, and the Indian intervention which led to the establishment of Bangladesh. He provides a good summary of the influence of these developments on major powers' interests in South Asia.

37:128   Williams, L. F. R. *The East Pakistan Tragedy.* New York: Drake, 1972. This is a contemporary, pro-Pakistan account of the conflict that led to the creation of Bangladesh.

Ceylon

37:129   Karunatilake, H. N. S. *Economic Development in Ceylon.* New York: Praeger, 1971. This is a broad survey of Ceylon's economic conditions (1950–1970).

37:130   Olson, Richard S. "Expropriation and International Economic Coercion: Ceylon and the West 1961–65." *Journal of Developing Areas* 11:2 (1977), 205–26. In 1961 the Ceylonese nationalized American and British petroleum companies with assets of $11.6 million. When compensation could not be agreed upon, the United States in 1964 applied the Hickenlooper Amendment, which required the foreign aid suspension. Then the U.S.S.R. sold oil to Ceylon at 25 percent below world market price.

37:131   Pakeman, Sidney A. *Ceylon.* New York: Praeger, 1964. This general history surveys the era of British rule and the years since World War II.

India

37:132   Banerjee, Jyitirmay. "Security Through Regionalism: India's Foreign Policy in the 1970s." *Political Science Review* 17:1/2 (1978), 91–126. Banerjee maintains that India, despite its predominant regional position after the 1971 war, remained insecure as a result of hostility from the major powers. This resulted in giving priority to improving relations with China, Pakistan, Iran, and the Afro-Asian bloc.

37:133   Barnds, William J. "India and America at Odds." *International Affairs* [London] 49:3 (1973), 371–84. Barnds traces the persistent Indo-American inability to achieve a mutually acceptable relationship to a number of basic factors, including the ill-founded perceptions of one another.

37:134   Heimsath, Charles. "United States–Indian Relations: A Generation of Unfulfillment." *International Journal* 27:3 (1972), 469–79. This is a useful summary of the persistent antagonisms and disappointments in Indo-American relations from World War II to the Bangladesh crisis of 1971.

37:135   Kapur, Ashok. "Strategic Choices in India Foreign Policy." *International Journal* 27:3 (1972), 448–68. An important statement on Indo-American relations, the Kapur article discusses Indian foreign policy in two distinct phases, with 1962 as the dividing point. Central to India's diplomatic calculations after 1962 was reducing the American influence in South Asia and the assertion of its own paramount position.

37:136   Nanda, B. R., ed. *Indian Foreign Policy: The Nehru Years.* Honolulu: University Press of Hawaii, 1976. This collection of essays includes especially valuable chapters on India and the United States, and Nehru and nonalignment.

37:137   Nayar, Baldev Raj. *American Geopolitics and India.* New Delhi: Manohar, 1976. This book argues that the United States has sought to "contain" India. This policy is seen as beginning in the 1950s with the American alliance with Pakistan. The principal focus is on the Nixon administration's policies in South Asia and the resulting American threat to Indian security. Extensive bibliography.

37:138   Rana, A. P. *The Imperatives of Nonalignment: A Conceptual Study of India's Foreign Policy Strategy in the Nehru Era.* Delhi: Macmillan of India, 1976. A scholarly examination of Nehru's foreign policy, which argues, contrary to critics of that policy following the border war with China, that nonalignment was the appropriate course for India. It relates the policy of nonalignment to security, political culture, and the international system. Extensive bibliography.

37:139 Shrivastava, B. K. "Indo-American Relations: Retrospect and Prospect." *International Studies* 14:1 (1975), 21–38. This article analyzes Indo-American solutions (1945–1975) with principal emphasis on the extent to which the American military alliance with Pakistan hindered effectiveness in dealing with India. Following the 1971 war, the United States is seen as moving toward a more realistic South Asian policy and acknowledging India's status as a part of the global power structure.

37:140 Talbot, Phillips, and Poplai, S. L. *India and America: A Study of Their Relations.* New York: Harper & Row, 1958. This study provides a good introduction to Indo-American political, cultural, and economic relations during the first decade after independence.

37:141 Tewani, S. C. *Indo-U.S. Relations.* New Delhi: Radiant, 1977. This is a revised dissertation. A useful summary of Indo-American relations, it emphasizes the role of the United States in Indo-Pakistani disputes. Bibliography.

37:142 Venkataramani, M. S. "The U.S. Senate Committee on Foreign Relations and India, 1958–59." *India Quarterly* 16:1 (1960), 51–61. A detailed study of the Senate Foreign Relations Committee hearings on India in 1958–1959 considered against the background of the misunderstandings in Indo-American relations since 1947. A greater American appreciation of India's international objectives and internal problems was seen emerging in the hearings.

Border Dispute with China, 1954–1964

37:143 Eekelen, William F. van. *Indian Foreign Policy and the Border Dispute with China.* The Hague: Nijhoff, 1964. The work of a Netherlands diplomat who was stationed in New Delhi (1957–1960), this study traces the Panscheel concept in Sino-Indian relations and its collapse in the border war of 1962. Eekelen provides a detailed analysis of the political and legal aspects of the dispute. Extensive bibliography.

37:144 Lamb, Alastair. *The China-India Border: The Origins of the Disputed Boundaries.* New York: Oxford University Press, 1964. A scholarly survey of the Sino-India boundary controversy that erupted in 1962.

37:145 Maxwell, Neville. *India's China War.* New York: Pantheon, 1971. Maxwell draws together the military and diplomatic activities surrounding the Chinese expedition of 1962.

Pakistan

37:146 Barnds, William J. "China's Relations with Pakistan: Durability amidst Discontinuity." *China Quarterly,* no. 63 (1975), 463–89. The relatively stable Chinese relations with Pakistan derive from Pakistan's geographic location, its weakness, its role as a bridge to the Islamic states, and Peking's conviction that India is too closely linked with Moscow.

37:147 Chaudhri, Mohammed Ahsen. *Pakistan and the Great Powers.* Karachi: Council for Pakistan Studies, 1970. Good summary of Pakistani relations with the United States, Soviet Union, and China. The movement toward alignment with the United States in the 1950s and the shift toward nonalignment in the 1960s is detailed. Bibliography.

37:148 Hussain, Arif. *Pakistan: Its Ideology and Foreign Policy.* London: Cass, 1966. An important effort to relate Pakistan's foreign policy to Islamic ideology and national interest, this study has considerable material on relations with the United States, especially the basis of the 1954 military alliance. Bibliography.

37:149 Venkataramani, M. S., and Arya, Harish Chandra. "America's Military Alliance with Pakistan: The Evolution of an Uneasy Partnership." *International Studies* 8:1/2 (1966), 73–125. This article focuses on the international context of the early 1950s in which the American alliance with Pakistan was formulated. It also deals with increasing criticism in the United States of the pact, especially after Ayub Khan's seizure of power in 1958.

COLD WAR AND OTHER DIPLOMATIC ISSUES

U.S. and the Indian Ocean

37:150 Crocker, Chester A. "The African Dimension of Indian Ocean Policy." *Orbis* 20:3 (1976), 637–67. Among the areas discussed are 1) the recognition in London and Paris that their presence in Africa was limited by their colonial legacy; 2) the fact that the U.S.S.R. has been the more willing of the two superpowers to pay the price and take the risks of fostering military client relationships in Africa; and 3) that the United States has perceived fewer advantages and greater liabilities in African military ties. The essay concludes that the Angolan civil war of 1975–1976 has set in motion the profound rethinking of America's African policy since the outset of the 1960s.

37:151 Seth, S. P. "Indian Ocean and Indo-American Relations." *Asian Survey* 15:8 (1975), 645–55. A good introduction to the American decision to enhance its military presence in the Indian Ocean, particularly through expanding the Diego Garcia Base. The reasons for the adverse Indian reaction are also detailed.

37:152 Stoddard, Theodore L., et al. *Area Handbook for Indian Ocean Territories*. Washington, D.C.: G.P.O., 1971. This volume is useful for background information and general reference.

Nuclear Proliferation

37:153 Kapur, Ashok. *India's Nuclear Option: Atomic Diplomacy and Decision-Making*. New York: Praeger, 1976. A comprehensive study of India's external attitudes and activity on nuclear arms and of the relationship between domestic politics and foreign policy as evidenced in the 1974 nuclear test decision. It provides considerable material on nuclear testing and arms control as a factor in Indo-American relations. Extensive bibliography.

37:154 Khalilzad, Zalmay. "Pakistan: The Making of a Nuclear Power." *Asian Survey* 16:6 (1976), 580–92. This critique of Pakistan's justification for developing nuclear energy maintains that since India will be the dominant nuclear power in the region, Pakistan's strategic position cannot be enhanced by nuclear weapons.

37:155 Power, Paul F. "The Indo-American Nuclear Controversy." *Asian Survey* 19:6 (1979), 574–97. Power traces Indo-American differences over nonproliferation to the national interests, experiences, and perceptions of the two countries.

U.S. and the Indo-Pakistan War, 1971

See under "Personalities," especially Henry A. Kissinger, Richard M. Nixon.

37:156 Hall, David K. "The Indo-Pakistani War of 1971." In Barry M. Blechman and Stephen S. Kaplan, eds., *Force without War: U.S. Armed Forces as a Political Instrument*. Washington, D.C.: Brookings Institution, 1978, pp. 175–217. This essay (actually half of an essay) focuses on President Nixon's efforts to "tilt" U.S. policy from India to Pakistan during their 1971 conflict.

37:157 Kunhi Krishnan, T. U. *The Unfriendly Friends, India and America*. New Delhi: Indian Book Company, 1974. This is a highly critical examination of the Nixon administration's response to the Indo-Pakistani clash over Bangladesh. Bibliography.

37:158 Van Hollen, Christopher. "The Tilt Policy Revisited: Nixon-Kissinger Geopolitics and South Asia." *Asian Survey* 20:4 (1980), 339–61. A critique of Kissinger's defense of the "tilt" toward Pakistan during the 1971 conflict which argues that the United States should have worked to resolve the dispute within a South Asian context. Also see Michael Walter, "The U.S. Naval Demonstration in the Bay of Bengal during the 1971 Indo-Pakistan War," *World Affairs* 141:4 (1979), 293–306.

U.S. and Sub-Saharan Africa

Bohannan, P., and Curtin, P. D. *Africa and Africans* (2:335) is an essential aid in understanding the clash between the West and Africa.

Chester, E. W. *Clash of Titans: Africa and U.S. Foreign Policy* (2:336) is the best survey of American relations with black Africa to date. Chester stresses traditional economic and political interests.

Curtin, P. *African History* (2:337) is a good starting point for those interested in white contacts with the continent.

Fage, J. D., and Oliver, R., eds. *The Cambridge History of Africa* (2:338) is a detailed summary of African history incorporating the most recent scholarship.

Howe, R. W. *Along the Africa Shore: An Historic Review of Two Centuries of U.S.-African Relations* (2:339) is a well-written, but spotty summary of U.S. diplomacy in Africa by a veteran journalist. It is useful for the 1960s.

37:159   Whitaker, Jennifer Seymour, ed. *Africa and the United States: Vital Interests.* New York: New York University Press, 1978. A collection of articles on the economic and political relations between the United States and Africa which concentrates on the Anglophonic African countries. The strategic aspect of U.S. relations is also addressed, with the focus on the Indian Ocean and South Africa. Professor Legvold's article, "The Soviet Union's Strategic Stake in Africa," demonstrates the interrelation between U.S. policies in Africa and détente.

BLACK AMERICANS AND PAN-AFRICANISM

See Chapter 18, "Pan-Africanism."

37:160   Contee, Clarence. "The Emergence of Du Bois as an African Nationalist." *Journal of Negro History* 54:1 (1969), 48–63. This narrative develops Du Bois's growing interest in Africa and Pan-Africanism.

37:161   Davis, John A. "Black Americans and United States Policy toward Africa." *Journal of International Affairs* 23:2 (1969), 236–49. This essay reflects the lack of direct influence of blacks on America's policies toward Africa.

37:162   Helmreich, William B. *Afro-Americans and Africa: Black Nationalism at the Crossroads.*

Westport, Conn.: Greenwood, 1977. This account emphasizes the growing interest of American blacks in Africa during the 1960s.

37:163   Marable, W. Manning. "Booker T. Washington and African Nationalism." *Phylon* 35:4 (1974), 398–406. Early 20th-century South African black nationalists owe much to Booker T. Washington. Although Washington did not personally invest much effort in assisting black Africa, he did take an interest in black South Africans' efforts to organize and uplift themselves.

37:164   McCalman, Ian D. "Africa and Negro-American Nationalism: From Negritude to Black Revolution." *Australian National University Historical Journal* 7 (1970), 42–59. McCalman examines the idea that, through the medium of Africa, American Negroes could reassert their own distinctive nationalism, sense of nationhood, and unique national character. He emphasizes cultural, intellectual, and literary matters, rather than political or socioeconomic affairs.

37:165   Nzuwah, Mariyawanda, and King, William. "Afro-Americans and U.S. Policy towards Africa." *Journal of Southern African Affairs* 2:2 (1977), 235–44. U.S. relations with Africa point out that Afro-Americans have not historically had a role in the formulation of U.S. policy toward Africa. The lack of influence of Afro-Americans stands in contrast to other ethnic groups which, although comprising a smaller percentage of the population, exert considerable influence.

Ralston, R. D. "American Episodes in the Making of an African Leader: A Case Study of Alfred B. Xuma (1893–1962)" (18:277) illustrates the thesis that "the American experiences of African students were one of the important variables affecting developments in African leadership during the colonial period."

Shepperson, G. "Notes on Negro American Influences on the Emergence of African Nationalism" (18:223) is an informative survey of the major men who have contributed to a sense of African identity, beginning with Edward Blyden and ending with George Padmore and Thurgood Marshall. Marcus Garvey and Du Bois influenced early nationalist leaders in black Africa, and their ideas contributed to 20-century Pan-Africanism.

37:166   Tunteng, P. Kiven. "George Padmore's Impact on Africa: A Critical Appraisal." *Phylon* 35:1

(1974), 33–44. The author discusses his relation with Kwame Nkrumah, who had been his student in London, and who appointed Padmore his adviser on African affairs when he became prime minister of Ghana.

37:167 Watson, Denton L. "The NAACP and Africa: An Historical Profile." *Crisis* 84:4 (1977), 131–38. W. E. B. Du Bois encouraged the NAACP to finance the first two Pan-African congresses, and kept the NAACP actively interested in African affairs, especially as a pressure group during the formative years of the United Nations.

37:168 Weil, Martin. "Can the Blacks Do for Africa What the Jews Did for Israel?" *Foreign Policy,* no. 15 (1974), 109–30. Unlike Polish Catholics and Jews, black Americans have had little impact on U.S. policies toward Africa. This is because of a lack of an electoral threat, a lobbying apparatus, and the ability to appeal successfully to the symbols of American concepts of nationhood.

37:169 Wilkins, Roger. "What Africa Means to Blacks." *Foreign Policy,* no. 15 (1974), 130–42. For black Americans born in the 1930s and 1940s black Africa held little personal association. Their points of reference, with few exceptions, such as Du Bois and Malcolm X, traced their heritage to the South. In the early 1960s, African students were usually aloof from American blacks. By the late 1960s this relationship had shifted dramatically to one of mutual respect and often mutual support.

U.S. AFRICAN POLICIES

37:170 Baker, Ross K. "The 'Back Burner' Revisited: America's African Policy." *Orbis* 15:1 (1971), 428–47. American interest in Africa since the New Frontier enthusiasm of the early 1960s has receded to a pragmatic complacency.

Barnet, R. J. *Intervention and Revolution: The United States in the Third World* (24:227) provides a radical, New Left perspective which emphasizes America as a counterrevolutionary power interested in economic dominance of Africa.

37:171 Baum, Edward. "The United States, Self-Government, and Africa: An Examination of the Nature of the American Policy on Self-Determination with Reference to Africa in the Postwar Era." Ph.D. diss., University of California, Los Angeles, 1964.

This narrative reviews the adjustment of U.S. policy to the rapid emergence of independent black African nations.

37:172 Emerson, Rupert. *Africa and the United States' Policy.* Englewood Cliffs, N.J.: Prentice-Hall, 1967. This is an excellent summary of American policy toward Africa from Truman to Johnson. It is highly critical of the low priority American diplomacy has granted Africa.

37:173 Grundy, Kenneth W., and Falchi, John P. "The United States and Socialism in Africa." *Journal of Asian and African Studies* 4:4 (1969), 300–14. Though the American public and their leaders have biases against socialist enterprises, the nature of African domestic economic systems has had little influence on aid programs.

Gurtov, M. *The United States against the Third World: Antinationalism and Intervention* (24:233) contains a perspective similar to Barnet's (24:227); the section on Africa deals largely with President Kennedy.

37:174 Issacman, Allen, and Wiley, David, eds. "Southern Africa and United States Policy in the 1970's." *Issue* 5:3 (1975), 1–72. The general focus of each of the five sections is the nature of U.S. foreign policy in the respective areas. Contributors generally agreed with Willard Johnson's assessment that "the policies we have been pursuing are wrong—both morally and practically."

37:175 Johnson, Willard. "United States Foreign Policy towards Africa." *Africa Today* 20:1 (1973), 15–44. A policy statement issued by the task force on Africa for George S. McGovern's 1972 presidential campaign. It combines criticism of past "benign neglect" toward Africa with a nine-point recommendation for U.S. policy toward Africa.

37:176 McHenry, Donald F. "Captive of No Group." *Foreign Policy,* no. 15 (1974), 142–49. McHenry, the ambassador to the UN, argues that black Americans have no special responsibility to Africa or U.S. policy toward Africa. He surveys U.S. policy under Kennedy and Nixon.

37:177 Moss, James A. "United States and Africa: A Timely Reassessment." *Journal of Human Relations* 5:14 (1966), 287–93. U.S. policies in black Africa will provide an "acid test" of this government's commitment to civil and human rights. The author reviews U.S. support for nationalist movements from 1945 to 1958.

37:178   Nielsen, Waldemar. *The Great Powers and Africa.* New York: Praeger, 1969. This account includes a discussion of U.S. policies, with criticisms similar to those of Emerson (37:172). It is especially useful on Eisenhower's and Kennedy's policies.

37:179   Obichere, Boniface. "American Diplomacy in Africa: Problems and Prospects." *Pan-African Journal* 7:1 (1974), 67–80. Obichere analyzes U.S. policy toward Africa since 1787, with an emphasis on the post-1960 years. Among the aspects covered are AID (Agency for International Development) missions, consular offices, and millionaire ambassadors.

37:180   Segal, Aaron. "Africa and the United States Media." *Issue* 6:2/3 (1976), 49–56. Segal examines major newspapers and periodicals within the United States, and concludes that the coverage by the American media of African affairs was poor.

The Roosevelt-Truman Years, 1941–1952

See under "Personalities," especially Chester Bowles; also see Chapter 24 for "The Truman Years."

37:181   American Assembly. *The United States and Africa.* New York: Columbia University Press, 1958. Ghana had become the first black African nation to gain independence and other colonies were soon to follow. This report is the result of three days of discussions on the nature of U.S.-Africa relations to date, and the nature of problems facing various African societies. Statistical tables and maps.

37:182   Miller, Jean-Donald. "The United States and Sub-Saharan Africa, 1939–1950." Ph.D. diss., University of Connecticut, 1979. Miller concentrates on the development of independence movements in black Africa and the impact of the cold war on U.S. perceptions of its interests there.

37:183   Solomon, Mark. "Black Critics of Colonialism and the Cold War." In Thomas G. Paterson, ed., *Cold War Critics: Alternatives to American Foreign Policy in the Truman Years.* Chicago: Quadrangle, 1971, pp. 205–39. Solomon argues that "by the end of World War II, black American intellectuals were united in believing that the battle against white

racism in their own country could not be won without a larger international battle against colonial imperialism in Africa."

The Eisenhower-Kennedy-Johnson Years, 1953–1968

See under "Personalities," especially George Ball, John F. Kennedy, and, under "Others," William Attwood, G. Mennen Williams; also see Chapter 24, "Presidential Administrations."

37:184   Bartlett, Vernon. *Struggle for Africa.* New York: Praeger, 1953. This account is an attempt to awaken official U.S. interest in Africa on the eve of the independence struggle. It is useful for its 1950s perspectives.

37:185   Chukwumerije, Ibezim. "The New Frontier and Africa, 1961–1963." Ph.D. diss., State University of New York, Stony Brook, 1976. This is the most complete and balanced assessment so far of the changes in U.S. policy under Kennedy. The author acknowledges the symbolic and other alterations of Kennedy, but also points out the continuity in American goals from the Eisenhower years.

37:186   Shah, Harin. *The Great Abdication: American Foreign Policy in Asia and Africa.* New Delhi: Atma Ram, 1957. Shah is critical of the Eisenhower administration's objectives and tactics in Africa. He emphasizes U.S. unwillingness to accept black nationalism and nonalignment in the cold war.

37:187   Walters, Ronald. "The Formation of United States' Foreign Policy toward Africa, 1958–1963." Ph.D. diss., American University, 1971. Walters sees a major shift in U.S. policy toward recognizing the importance of Africa by the Kennedy administration.

37:188   Washington Task Force on African Affairs. *Congress and Africa.* Washington, D.C.: African Bibliographic Center, 1973. This account summarizes congressional interest and inattention to black Africa in the 1960s.

Congo Crisis, 1960–1964

See under "Personalities," especially, under "Others," Africans Patrice Lumumba, Moise Tshombe; see also Chapter 38, "Congo Crisis, 1960–1964."

37:189 Kaplan, Lawrence S. "The United States, Belgium, and the Congo Crisis of 1960." *Review of Politics* 29:2 (1967), 239–56. This interpretive essay assesses the U.S. role in the Congo, noting a "surprising consistency" in policy, U.S. commitments to Belgium through NATO, and attempts to reconcile goals with UN objectives. Belgian critics failed to appreciate the situation the United States faced, while Americans were less than sensitive to Belgian concerns.

37:190 Lefever, Ernest W. "The U.N. as a Foreign Policy Instrument: The Congo Crisis." In Roger M. Hilsman and Robert C. Good, eds., *Foreign Policy in the Sixties: The Issues and the Instruments: Essays in Honor of Arnold Wolfers.* Baltimore: Johns Hopkins Press, 1965, pp. 141–57. Lefever is somewhat critical in his analysis of U.S. motives and the role of the UN in the Congo.

37:191 O'Brien, Conor Cruise. *To Katanga and Back.* New York: Simon & Schuster, 1962. O'Brien commanded the United Nations' operation in the Congo during the initial phases (1960–1961); this is his account of affairs. Bibliography.

37:192 Simmonds, R. *Legal Problems Arising from the UN Military Operations in the Congo.* The Hague: Nijhoff, 1968. Simmonds traces the military operations during the Congo crisis and the legal problems connected with military activities (1960–1965). Bibliography.

37:193 Weissman, Stephen. *American Foreign Policy in the Congo, 1960–1964.* Ithaca, N.Y.: Cornell University Press, 1974. This is the most detailed and analytical work on American policy and the Congo crisis. Weissman is critical of U.S. involvement.

The Nixon-Ford Years, 1969–1976

See under "Personalities," especially Henry A. Kissinger, Richard M. Nixon.

37:194 Joiner, Harry M. *American Foreign Policy: The Kissinger Era.* Huntsville, Ala.: Strode, 1977. From 1966 to 1976 U.S. investments rose significantly but less than U.S. investment in Brazil; the United States trades less with Africa than any other region. Joiner concludes that since 1966 Africa has become a stable continent, one which the United States has

neglected and in which the Soviets have made significant political gains as a result of our politics.

37:195 el-Khawas, Mohamed A., and Cohen, Barry, eds. *The Kissinger Study of Southern Africa: National Security Study Memorandum 39 (SECRET).* Westport, Conn.: Lawrence Hill, 1976. National Security Study Memorandum 39, ordered by Kissinger in early 1970 was designed to help form U.S. policy toward Southern Africa. The result was a series of options based upon the premise that the minority Europeans in Southern Africa were there to stay and that U.S. economic and strategic interest, as defined by Nixon and Kissinger, and CIA Director Helms, was tied to these governments.

37:196 Lockwood, Edgar. "National Security Study Memorandum 39 and the Future of United States Policy toward Southern Africa." *Issue* 4:3 (1974), 59–72. Known as "Nissem," among Africanists, the Memorandum 39 of 1969 (NSSM 39) popularized Nixon's "tilt" toward Southern Africa's white regimes. The real significance to NSSM, according to Lockwood, is that it clearly demonstrates Kissinger's commitment to "*realpolitik* analysis."

37:197 U.S. House. Committee on Foreign Affairs. Hearings; *Policy toward Africa for the Seventies.* 91st Cong., 2d Sess., 1970. Among the scholars, diplomats, and military men testifying were Waldemar A. Nielsen, William Attwood, Joseph C. Satterthwaite, Elliott Skinner, and Ruth S. Morgenthau. Tables on U.S. trade (1960–1969) are included. Bibliography.

37:198 U.S. House. Committee on International Relations. *Report of Special Study Mission to Southern Africa, Aug. 10–30, 1969: Report No. 91–610.* 91st Cong., 1st Sess., 1969. Of special interest are the discussions of the political turmoil in Rhodesia, the leading liberation movements operating in southern Africa, the Arusha Declaration and the impact of this Tanzania position on Southern Africa, and affairs in South Africa. Included is the list of U.S. private companies and affiliates operating in South Africa in 1969.

Angolan Revolution, 1961–1975
See under "Personalities," especially Nathaniel Davis (under "Others"), Henry A. Kissinger.

37:199 Azevedo, Mario J. "Zambia, Zaire, and the Angolan Crisis Reconsidered: From Alvor to Shaba." *Journal of Southern African Affairs* 2:3 (1977), 275–93. In 1961 three Angolan groups began guerrilla warfare against Portugal: the Popular Movement for the

Liberation of Angola (MPLA), the National Front for the Liberation of Angola (FNLA), and the National Union for the Total Independence of Angola (UNITA). The United States supported the pro-Western FNLA/UNITA fronts, and the United States and South Africa began sending aid to Zambia and Zaire, together with assurances of help in solving the problem of Southern Africa, in exchange for support. The MPLA's victory led Zambia and Zaire to seek reconciliation.

37:200 Bender, Gerald J. "Angola, the Cubans, and American Anxieties." *Foreign Policy,* no. 31 (1978), 3–30. Globalists see the world mainly in terms of superpower politics, while regionalists insist on a foreign policy based on area realities and situations. Under the growing influence of Brzezinski's globalist outlook, the United States continues to see the Cuban presence in Angola as merely an extension of Soviet incursions into Southern Africa.

Ebinger, C. K. "External Intervention in Internal War: The Politics and Diplomacy of the Angolan Civil War" (28:153) discusses the activities of the Angolan Nationalists on the eve of the April 25, 1974, Portuguese coup, indicating the level of support from external forces such as Zaire to the three major liberation groups. In 1975, Kissinger supported the intervention of South African forces into Angola. This action resulted in a complete failure of U.S. policy toward Angola, and to some degree accounts for the pro-Soviet and anti-Western position of the present Angolan government.

37:201 Hallett, Robin. "The South African Intervention in Angola, 1975–76." *African Affairs* 77:308 (1978), 347–86. Interested in Angola for economic and strategic reasons, South Africa intervened in Angola to prevent a communist takeover. Failure to prevent the takeover was due primarily to faulty intelligence reports, including those furnished by the United States.

37:202 Hodges, Tony. "The Struggle for Angola: How the World Powers Entered A War in Africa." *Round Table,* no. 262 (1976), 173–84. Hodges describes the roles of the Soviet Union, Cuba, the United States, and South Africa in the Angolan war. Domestic American opposition to President Ford's Angolan policy and the backfiring of South African intervention forced the Western powers to pull back, allowing the MPLA to win, and the Soviet Union to score a major diplomatic triumph.

37:203 Klinghoffer, Arthur J. *The Angolan War: A Study in Soviet Policy in the Third World.* Boulder, Colo.: Westview, 1980. Using this local conflict as a case study, Klinghoffer discusses both the Soviet and Cuban roles in it. He also evaluates the questions raised by the Soviet venture on U.S.-U.S.S.R détente.

37:204 Livingston, Neil C., and Von Nordheim, Manfred. "The US Congress and the Angola Crisis." *Strategic Review* 5:2 (1977), 34–44. Interviews with members of Congress illustrate how Angola emerged as a new point of confrontation between the executive and the legislative branch over the making of foreign policy. The congressional decision to cut off aid to Angola raised doubts among America's allies as to whether the United States is abdicating its world role.

37:205 Marcum, John. *The Angolan Revolution.* 2 vols. Cambridge, Mass.: MIT Press, 1969–1978. These volumes comprise an exhaustive history of the independence movement in Angola, and provide considerable information on U.S. attitudes, activities, and official policy.

37:206 Stockwell, John. *In Search of Enemies: A CIA Story.* New York: Norton, 1978. This is an account by a former CIA operative in Angola of U.S. efforts to block a Marxist victory.

37:207 U.S. House. Committee on International Relations. Hearings; *United States–Angolan Relations.* 95th Cong., 2d Sess., 1978. This review was the result of the Carter administration's attempt to map out a new program toward Angola, and to a lesser extent toward Mozambique. Important to understanding the U.S. position toward Angola was the issue of the nature of U.S. relations with President Mobutu of Zaire, the importance of the Cuban presence in the region, and the future of the oil-rich fields in the Cabinda. Of particular interest is the role the CIA played in the region, as is evident from the testimony of John Stockwell.

37:208 Weissman, Stephen R. "CIA Covert Action in Zaire and Angola: Patterns and Consequences." *Political Science Quarterly* 94:2 (1979), 263–86. The case studies of CIA covert action in Zaire and Angola are used to describe the nature of CIA intervention in the Third World. Reasons for successes and failures are suggested.

Sahel (Sudan) Famine

37:209 Dow, Thomas E., Jr. "Famine in the Sahel: A Dilemma for United States Aid." *Current History*

68:405 (1975), 197–201. It seems clear that any effort that treats the Sahel food shortage as simply an emergency will only result in spreading the misery. Current U.S. policies in this way will only serve to maintain the problem.

37:210 Sheets, Hal, and Morris, Roger. "Disaster in the Desert." *Issue* 4:1 (1974), 24–43. This essay discusses the role of planning disaster relief and other dimensions of U.S. and UN response to the drought in the Sahel in West Africa.

The Carter Years, 1977–1980

37:211 Adelman, Kenneth L. "The Black Man's Burden." *Foreign Policy*, no. 28 (1977), 86–109. Some of the inconsistencies in and problems of the Carter administration's new African policy are analyzed. Human rights provides the public justification for the policy, yet in implementation the policy chastises only the white-ruled African states and ignores the fact that most black states also have a poor record on civil and political freedom.

37:212 Adelman, Kenneth L. "The Runner Gambles: Carter's Foreign Policy in the Year One." *Policy Review*, no. 3 (1978), 89–116. President Carter during his first year was often startled by seemingly predictable diplomatic events mostly of his own making. Examples include the vice-president's call for one-man, one-vote in South Africa. Mr. Carter should take pride in the fact that, unlike his predecessors, he is practicing preventive diplomacy.

37:213 Bienen, Henry. "U.S. Foreign Policy in a Changing Africa." *Political Science Quarterly* 93:3 (1978), 443–64. U.S. policymaking must be geared to international political and economic differences in Africa; a simple continental approach is not adequate. Carter administration responses to Zaire, Somalia, and Ethiopia herald possible changes in this regard.

37:214 Shepherd, George W., Jr. "The Struggle to a New Southern African Policy: The Carter Task." *Journal of Southern African Affairs* 2:1 (1977), 99–120. The United States must take a strong antiapartheid and pro-Africa, pro-human rights position. The revolutionary situation in Southern Africa and the dependency of the three white minority-ruled African societies are discussed as the basis for new directions in U.S. policy.

U.S., Soviet Union, and China

37:215 Brzezinski, Zbigniew, ed. *Africa and the Communist World*. Stanford, Calif.: Hoover Institution, 1963. These alarmist essays focus on the growth of Soviet, Chinese, and East European influence in black Africa.

37:216 Cohn, Helen Desfosses. "Soviet-American Relations and the African Arena." *Survey* 19:1 (1973), 147–64. The Soviet ideological and revolutionary policy changed after 1966 to become more conventional, and U.S. aid dropped off. When developmental plans of the early 1960s were not realized both superpowers shifted their attention elsewhere.

37:217 Kanet, Roger E. "The Cominterm and the 'Negro Question': Communist Policy in the United States and Africa, 1921–1941." *Survey* 19:4 (1973), 86–122. Kanet discusses Cominterm policy on the "Negro question" and reasons for the Communist failure to develop strong revolutionary movements among the black population in either Africa or the United States.

37:218 Larkin, Bruce D. *China and Africa, 1949–1970: The Foreign Policy of the People's Republic of China*. Berkeley: University of California Press, 1971. Larkin reviews Chinese activities, and concludes that these endeavors have not been greatly successful.

37:219 Legum, Colin. "The Soviet Union, China, and the West in Southern Africa." *Foreign Affairs* 54:4 (1976), 745–62. The Soviet intervention in Angola is usually seen as a gain for the Soviets and a loss for the West. While this interpretation might hold some truth, an important element is ignored—the Sino-Soviet rivalry.

37:220 Morris, Milton. "The Soviet Africa Institute and the Development of African Studies." *Journal of Modern African Studies* 11:2 (1973), 247–65. Morris traces the development of Soviet academic interest in Africa since World War II, and examines the writings of Soviet Africanists and their effect on Soviet policy toward Africa. Current Soviet research on Africa is sophisticated and addresses a wide array of issues.

37:221 Nyerere, Julius K. "America and Southern Africa." *Foreign Affairs* 55:4 (1977), 671–84. The author sees U.S. African policy in terms of traditional U.S. opposition to communism. This is considered the dominant element in postwar U.S. foreign policy. The communist countries have shown great interest in supplying African needs and, ironically, providing some legitimacy to the U.S. anticommunist crusade.

37:222 Park, Sang-seek. "Africa and Two Koreas: A Study of African Non-Alignment." *African Studies Review* 21:1 (1978), 73–88. A study of African foreign policy on cold war questions (1960–1975), particularly as they relate to diplomatic recognition of North and South Korea. African countries have exhibited different policies at different times.

37:223 Payne, Richard J. "The Soviet/Cuban Factor in the United States Policy toward Southern Africa." *Africa Today* 25:2 (1978), 7–26. Payne examines changes in foreign policy with special emphasis on Southern Africa, and concludes that changes since 1976 have been spurred by Russian/Cuban success in Angola. The new policy supports majority rule and protection of minority rights, and encourages African solutions to African problems.

37:224 Thom, William G. "Trends in Soviet Support for African Liberation." *Air University Review* 25:5 (1974), 36–43. Thom discusses the major trends in the U.S.S.R's support for African liberation movements since the late 1950s, and reviews the historical development and practicality of African liberation, the significance of Soviet aid, relations with individual movements, dangers of world power involvement, and Sino-Soviet competition in Africa.

37:225 Yu, George T. "China's Role in Africa." *Annals of the American Academy of Political and Social Science* 432 (1977), 96–109. Chinese involvement in Africa has fluctuated since 1955, when China began to seek recognition and support from African nations. Since 1970, China has again emerged as a major actor on the African continent. Chinese policy must be seen in the context of China's struggle against the superpowers.

U.S., Africa, and the UN

Beichman, A. *The "Other" State Department: The United States Mission to the United Nations* (38:197) provides a useful analysis of U.S. policy toward Africa in the UN and the conflict between the State Department and the UN delegation on African issues.

37:226 Nicol, Davidson. "Africa and the U.S.A. in the United Nations." *Journal of Modern African Studies* 16:3 (1978), 365–95. Tracing the widely swinging U.S. policy at the UN since 1960, the author

suggests that historically the United States has been favorable to Africa, but on account of more important international concerns the United States has disregarded the needs of Africa.

THE SUB-SAHARAN COUNTRIES

American University. Foreign Area Studies., Area Handbook Series (2:214) provides country studies which address such issues as history, traditions, culture, economy, and military and political institutions. For many sub-Sahara African nations, these handbooks may provide the best background.

37:227 Cohen, D. L. and Tribe, M. A. "Suppliers' Credits in Ghana and Uganda: An Aspect of the Imperialist System." *Journal of Modern African Studies* 10:4 (1972), 525–41. This is an analysis of the use of suppliers' credit to finance development projects as an aspect of imperialism in Uganda and Ghana. The concept of imperialism is defined in primary, secondary, and tertiary degreees.

37:228 Copson, Raymond W. "African International Politics: Underdevelopment and Conflict in the Seventies." *Orbis* 22:1 (1978), 227–45. Relations between the new states of Africa during the 1970s have been very unstable, marked by ethnic, territorial, ideological, and personal conflicts.

37:229 Rood, Leslie L. "Foreign Investment in African Manufacturing." *Journal of Modern African Studies* 13:1 (1975), 19–34. The host governments in the developing nations welcome foreign investment but are concerned about outside exploitation. The first comprehensive figures on private foreign direct investment in the developing world make possible this analysis.

Southern Africa

37:230 Dugard, John, ed. *The South West Africa/ Namibia Dispute: Documents and Scholarly Writings on the Controversy between South Africa and the United Nations*. Berkeley: University of California Press, 1973. This is a useful reference to an important, lengthy dispute.

37:231 Lemarchand, Rene, ed. *American Policy in Southern Africa: The Stakes and the Stance*. Washington, D.C.: University Press of America, 1978. The United States is faced with "critical choices" in Southern Africa, and these articles are designed to provide a "critical assessment of past U.S. policies toward specific [Southern African] territories ... [and] seeks to enhance our comprehension of current developments."

37:232   Ofuatey-Kodjoe, W. "The United States, Southern Africa and International Order." *Journal of Southern African Affairs* 1 (1976), 111–24. This essay sees inconsistency between U.S. policy and action in relation to Southern Africa, and examines its effect on the region and on international order.

37:233   Spencer, Leon. "The American Role in the South West Africa Question." Ph.D. diss., Indiana University, 1967. This account summarizes U.S. policy, with emphasis on UN diplomacy, toward the protracted dispute concerning South Africa's claim of control over the area.

37:234   Turner, James, and Gervasi, Sean. "The American Economic Future in Southern Africa: An Analysis of an Agency for International Development Study on Zimbabwe and Namibia." *Journal of Southern African Affairs* 3:1 (1978), 85–98. Prior to Angola's independence the United States, despite appeals for racial equality in the area, supported the minority regimes in Southern Africa. AID would influence change in the area through rapid economic development using the same institutions that had exploited the black majorities in the first place.

Zimbabwe (Southern Rhodesia)

37:235   Hayakawa, S. I. "Rhodesia." *Policy Review,* no. 11 (1980), 115–24. Senator Hayakawa sees the major problem within Rhodesia as "tribal" in nature and suggests that the United States should rely on the European minority for the present.

37:236   Lake, Anthony. *The "Tar Baby" Option: American Policy towards Southern Rhodesia.* New York: Columbia University Press, 1976. A former member of the National Security Council's staff summarizes the American response to the Rhodesian crisis (1965–1975). He offers an excellent review of internal debates over policy, congressional action (the Byrd Amendment), and the inability of blacks and liberals to influence U.S. policy.

37:237   Lobban, Richard. "American Mercenaries in Rhodesia." *Journal of Southern African Affairs* 3:3 (1978), 319–26. The author briefly describes the in-

formation he has compiled about American mercenaries serving in Rhodesia. He discusses their recruitment, salaries, general personal characteristics, and activities.

37:238   Marshall, Charles Burton. *Crisis over Rhodesia: A Skeptical View.* Baltimore: Johns Hopkins Press, 1967. Marshall is critical of American efforts against the minority Rhodesian government. He argues that U.S. actions are illegal, contrary to American interests, and will lead to increased racial violence.

37:239   Randolph, P. Sean. "The Byrd Amendment: A Postmortem." *World Affairs* 141:1 (1978), 57–70. The sources of the formulation of the Byrd Amendment of the 1977 Angola-American proposal for settling the Rhodesian problem is provided. Sithole argues against an interim administration prior to the introduction of majority rule.

37:240   Sithole, Masipula. "Rhodesia: An Assessment of the Viability of the Angola-American Proposals." *World Affairs* 141:1 (1978), 71–81. An assessment is provided of the 1977 Angola-American proposal for settling the Rhodesian problem. Sithole argues against an interim administration prior to the tion of majority rule.

37:241   U.S. House. Committee on Foreign Affairs. Hearings; *Economic Sanctions against Rhodesia.* 92d Cong., 1st Sess., 1971. Rhodesia declared independence from Great Britain (November 1965); soon thereafter economic sanctions were imposed against the Ian Smith government. By June 1971, under the Nixon administration, there was a growing mood that economic sanctions should be lifted from Rhodesia.

37:242   U.S. House. Committee on Foreign Affairs. Hearings; *Future Direction of U.S. Policy toward Southern Rhodesia.* 93d Cong., 1st Sess., 1973. These hearings comprise a comprehensive discussion of U.S.–Southern Rhodesian relations under the Nixon-Kissinger administration. One of the main issues discussed was the importance of continued violations of the UN economic sanctions against Southern Rhodesia by the purchasing of chrome by the Union Carbide Corporation.

37:243   U.S. House. Committee on Foreign Affairs. Hearings; *The Repeal of the Rhodesian Chrome Amendment.* 93d Cong., 1st Sess., 1973. After the passage of the so-called Byrd Amendment or Rhodesian chrome amendment (i.e., Military Procurement

Act of 1971, Sect. 503), opposition to the amendment increased. These hearings were called to discuss the evidence for and against the Rhodesian chrome amendment.

37:244 U.S. House. Committee on Foreign Affairs. Hearings; *Sanctions as an Instrumentality of the United Nations—Rhodesia as a Case Study.* 92d Cong., 2d Sess., 1972. During the first years of the Nixon administration, the economic and political sanctions imposed against Southern Rhodesia were not strictly adhered to, i.e., the Byrd Amendment permitted the importation of Rhodesian chrome. The function of these hearings was to answer the "broad question of whether or not sanctions can be an effective means for the United Nations to bring about peaceful political change."

37:245 U.S. House. Committee on International Relations. Hearings; *Political Developments in Southern Rhodesia, Fall 1977.* 95th Cong., 1st Sess., 1977. The hearings seek to find out why Southern Rhodesia had been able to withstand the economic boycott imposed by Great Britain and the United Nations. Most nations which supported the boycott against Southern Rhodesia also opposed the imposition of appropriate measures to insure the success of the boycott. U.S. corporations are identified as violating the boycott.

37:246 U.S. House. Committee on International Relations. Hearings; *Trade Sanctions against Rhodesia.* 96th Cong., 1st Sess., 1979. Despite pressure on the Carter administration to recognize the Rhodesian/Zimbabwe government of Abel Muzorewa, Secretary of State Vance outlined the basis for continued support of the economic and political sanctions against Rhodesia.

South Africa

37:247 Barber, James P. *South Africa's Foreign Policy, 1945–1970.* New York: Oxford University Press, 1971. An English scholar focuses on the internal influences upon South Africa's external policies.

37:248 Belfiglio, Valentine J. "United States Economic Relations with the Republic of South Africa." *Africa Today* 25:3 (1978), 57–68. Describing the extent of economic interdependence between the United States and the Republic of South Africa, the author concludes that, in seeking a viable foreign policy, the United States cannot ignore the fact that 41 percent of its African exports are to South Africa and that American foreign investments are over $1.5 billion.

37:249 Greenberg, Stanford. "U.S. Policy toward the Republic of South Africa, 1945–1964." Ph.D. diss., Harvard University, 1965. This is a narrative account of U.S. diplomacy, with little analysis.

37:250 el-Khawas, Mohamed A. "Partners in Apartheid: U.S. Economic and Military Linkages with South Africa." *Journal of Southern African Affairs* 2:3 (1977), 323–42. The author argues that American private and governmental activities help to sustain the system of apartheid in South Africa. Because South Africa is of economic and strategic importance, Washington has not translated its public condemnation of apartheid into actions that might force the white-minority regime to alter its racial policies.

37:251 Latour, Charles. "South Africa: NATO's Unwelcome Ally." *Military Review* 57:2 (1977), 84–93. Because of South Africa's strategic position, any communist threat to that nation is an equal threat to NATO. The most likely threat would be an invasion from the north by African troops aided by a major outside communist power. Existing guerrilla organizations that could become involved in such an invasion are discussed.

37:252 Murapa, Rududzo. "A Global Perspective of the Political Economy of U.S. Policy towards South Africa." *Journal of Southern African Affairs* 2:1 (1977), 77–98. Henry Kissinger's Southern African policy is viewed as part of a global strategy designed to protect American and other capitalist interests in the region. That strategy involves the United States equipping and protecting certain strategically located nations in return for their performing certain capitalist policing activities.

37:253 Nielsen, Waldemar. *African Battleline: American Policy Choices in Southern Africa.* New York: Harper & Row, 1965. In posing alternative policies toward apartheid, Nielsen advocates stronger U.S. efforts to force racial changes in South Africa.

37:254 Rotberg, Robert. *Suffer the Future: Policy Choices in South Africa.* Cambridge: Harvard University Press, 1980. Rotberg presents a balanced view of alternatives facing the United States in dealing with South Africa. He believes that the Afrikaners face no real threat from black guerrillas and, thus, the United States should continue modest pressure for gradual change.

37:255 Rubin, Leslie, ed. "South Africa 1948–1973: Apartheid after Twenty-Five Years." *Issue* 4:3

(1974), 2–42. Various authors discuss the various aspects of apartheid since 1948, and its impact on various aspects of black South African life.

37:256 Seidman, Ann. *South Africa and U.S. Multinational Corporations.* Westport, Conn.: Lawrence Hill, 1978. Seidman argues that American business connections with South Africa help to support apartheid.

37:257 U.S. House. Committee on Foreign Affairs. Hearings; *U.S.–South African Relations.* 89th Cong., 2d Sess., 1966. The testimonies of liberals, blacks, conservatives, business leaders, and government officials focus on past and future U.S. policies.

37:258 U.S. House. Committee on International Relations. Hearings; *United States–South Africa Relations: Nuclear Cooperation.* 95th Cong., 1st Sess., 1977. As a result of U.S., French, German (West), and British assistance, South Africa now has the technical capability "to build a nuclear bomb." Among the topics discussed by this committee were the legal basis for U.S.–South African nuclear cooperation; the status of South Africa's capability to develop nuclear weapons; the implication for Americans and Africans of South Africa's nuclear weapons capability; and, finally, the recommendations for U.S. policy. Central to this discussion was the role of Namibia both as a source of uranium and as a testing site.

37:259 U.S. Senate. Committee on Foreign Relations. Hearings; *South Africa—U.S. Policy and the Role of U.S. Corporations.* 94th Cong., 2d Sess., 1976. A massive collection of statements and studies of U.S. policies toward South Africa and the impact U.S. private businesses are having in that Southern African nation.

37:260 Vandenbosch, Amry. *South Africa and the World: The Foreign Policy of Apartheid.* Lexington: University Press of Kentucky, 1971. This thorough account of South African foreign policy (1910–1969) is useful for background information.

37:261 Western Massachusetts Association of Concerned African Scholars. *U.S. Military Involvement in Southern Africa.* Boston: South End Press, 1978. The United States, Britain, France, West Germany, and Japan have failed to impose effective and realistic arms embargoes on South Africa and Rhodesia. These essays are uneven and polemical, but they do suggest areas of research and provide clues to data.

37:262 Wouk, Jonathan. "U.S. Policy toward South Africa, 1960–1967." Ph.D. diss., Pittsburgh University, 1972. Wouk contends that American blacks and liberals were largely ineffective in pressuring Presidents Kennedy and Johnson to take an active policy against apartheid.

Central Africa

Burundi

37:263 Bowen, Michael; Freeman, Gary; and Miller, Kay. "No Samaritan: The U.S. and Burundi." *Africa Report* 18:4 (1973), 32–39. This brief essay discusses the civil disturbance, tribal genocide, and U.S. tardiness in forming a foreign policy, with a response from the State Department.

37:264 Morris, Roger, et al. "The United States and Burundi in 1972." *Foreign Service Journal* 50:11 (1973), 8–15, 29–30. A report tracing the reaction of the U.S. government to genocide in Burundi, and a reply by the State Department.

Zaire—Congo-Kinshasa

37:265 Kabwit, Ghislain C. "Zaire: The Roots of the Continuing Crisis." *Journal of Modern African Studies* 17:3 (1979), 381–407. Since coming to power in 1965, President Mobutu Sese Seko has managed to retain, indeed expand, his hold over the mineral-rich state of Zaire. He has been able to accomplish this because of his astute political moves and because of the support of the United States, Belgium, and to a lesser extent France.

37:266 Young, Crawford. "Zaire: The Unending Crisis." *Foreign Affairs* 57:1 (1978), 169–85. This article addresses two key questions regarding Zaire. The first deals with the economic and political instability of the Mobutu regime, which before the 1973 oil crises and the fall in copper prices promised to lead Zaire into prosperity and political order. The second deals with appropriate policy responses by the United States, given the internationalization of the situation and the Soviet and Cuban involvement in nearby Angola.

West Africa

37:267 Morrow, John H. *First American Ambassador to Guinea.* New Brunswick, N.J.: Rutgers University Press, 1968. This is the personal account of

Eisenhower's appointee, an academic, to Guinea (1959–1961).

37:268 Nicolson, I. F. "Nigeria: Wars Cold and Hot, and Lukewarm Ideas." In Joseph M. Siracusa and Glen St. J. Barclay, eds., *The Impact of the Cold War: Reconsiderations.* Port Washington, N.Y.: Kennikat, 1977, pp. 84–100. A former British colonial administrator, Nicolson seeks to sort out the impact of American and European, including Soviet, policies and ideas on Nigeria.

37:269 Ungar, Sanford J. "Dateline West Africa: Great Expectations." *Foreign Policy,* no. 32 (1978), 184–94. Ungar, the managing editor of *Foreign Policy,* visited three capital cities, in Cameroon, Nigeria, and Senegal, and comments on the West African views of the U.S.

Ghana

37:270 Austin, Dennis. *Politics in Ghana, 1946–1960.* New York: Oxford University Press, 1964. This useful account provides a post–World War II background and develops the initial years of Ghanian independence.

37:271 Thompson, Willard S. *Ghana's Foreign Policy, 1957–1966: Diplomacy, Ideology, and the New State.* Princeton, N.J.: Princeton University Press, 1969. An excellent study which examines Ghana's foreign policy goals and the means to achieve them within the context of the country's resources. Thompson faults Nkrumah for failing to grasp this elementary relationship of goals and means. Bibliography.

Nigeria

37:272 Akpan, Ntieyong U. *The Struggle for Secession, 1966–1970.* London: Cass, 1972. An opponent to Biafra's efforts at secession reviews the civil war.

37:273 Cronje, Suzanne. *The World and Nigeria: The Diplomatic History of the Biafran War, 1967–1970.* London: Sidgwick & Jackson, 1972. Despite the title, this is not a complete analysis of the international response to the war in Nigeria. It does, however, have some material dealing with both the public and private American efforts in the conflict.

37:274 De St. Jorre, John. *The Brother's War: Biafra and Nigeria.* Boston: Houghton Mifflin, 1972. The author combines a thorough account of the tragic civil war with an analysis of the principal issues.

37:275 Kirk-Greene, A. H. M. *Crisis and Conflict in Nigeria: A Documentary Sourcebook, 1966–1970.* 2 vols. New York: Oxford University Press, 1971. These primary documents, preceded by a very long introduction, provide a very useful source to events leading up to and including the Nigerian civil war.

37:276 Phillips, Claude S., Jr. *The Development of Nigerian Foreign Policy.* Evanston, Ill.: Northwestern University Press, 1964. Phillips analyzes the formative period (1959–1963) in the development of Nigeria's foreign policy.

37:277 Stremlay, John J. *Biafra: The International Politics of the Nigerian Civil War, 1967–1970.* Princeton, N.J.: Princeton University Press, 1971. A solid account of the origins and international effects of the Biafran revolt; it not only deals with the policies of the major powers but with the diplomacy of black Africa as well.

37:278 Uwechue, Raph. *Reflections on the Nigerian Civil War: Facing the Future.* New York: Africana, 1971. A moderate book which states the author's reasons for supporting the secessionist movement, and describes gradual disillusionment.

East Africa

37:279 Bailey, Martin. "Tanzania and China." *African Affairs* 74:294 (1975), 39–50. An analysis of why Tanzania has closer ties with China than with any other non-African nation. Relations began in 1961 and the countries have exchanged state visits.

37:280 Ullman, Richard H. "Human Rights and Economic Power: The United States versus Idi Amin." *Foreign Affairs* 56:3 (1978), 529–43. Over seven years, President Amin and his ubiquitous terror squads slaughtered 100,000 Ugandans. The United States and the international community could use its purchases of Ugandan coffee to influence Amin.

Mozambique

37:281 Issacman, Allen, and Davis, Jennifer. "United States Policy toward Mozambique since 1945: 'The Defense of Colonialism and Regional Stability.'" *Africa Today* 25:1 (1978), 29–55. U.S. foreign policy toward Mozambique since World War II was determined by U.S. desires for stability and by anticommunism. This largely polemical attack on

U.S. policy is useful for its review of American opposition to local nationalisms.

37:282 U.S. House. Committee on International Relations. Hearings; *Perspectives on Mozambique.* 95th Cong., 2d Sess., 1978. In June 1975 Mozambique became an independent African nation. However, because the United States views Mozambique as a communist satellite, AID assistance is prohibited. The purpose of these hearings was to reevaluate U.S.-Mozambique relations.

Horn of Africa:
Ethiopia and Somalia

37:283 Francis, Samuel T. "Conflict in the Horn of Africa." *Journal of Social and Political Studies* 2:3 (1977), 131–42. The conflict within the Horn of Africa affects both the internal stability of the regional nations and their external relationships. Failure by either the United States or Soviet Union to stabilize Somalia and Ethiopia relations might lead to war, with repercussions far beyond the nations of the area.

37:284 Schwab, Peter. "Cold War on the Horn of Africa." *African Affairs* 77:306 (1978), 6–20. An analysis of U.S. and Soviet military influence in northeast Africa (1930–1977), finds that the Soviets have gained influence in Ethiopia and other areas on the Horn. U.S. influence has increased in the states surrounding the Horn.

37:285 Shack, William A. "Ethiopia and Afro-Americans: Some Historical Notes, 1920–1970." *Phylon* 35:2 (1974), 142–55. Afro-Americans have generally focused their attention on West Africa, from which most of them originated, but independent Ethiopia also has played a role. Being Christian, Ethiopia was attractive to Back-to-Africa advocates.

37:286 Warren, Anita, and Warren, Herrick. "The U.S. Role in the Eritrean Conflict." *Africa Today* 23:2 (1976), 39–53. This essay provides a brief history of Eritrea from the Axumite empire to 1975, finds a distinct difference between Eritrea and the rest of Ethiopia, and concludes that U.S. foreign policy is in a no-win dilemma.

38

International Organization, Law, and Peace Movements since 1941

Contributing Editor
WARREN F. KUEHL
University of Akron

Contributors

Charles DeBenedetti
University of Toledo

Robert A. Divine
University of Texas

Gary B. Ostrower
Alfred University

Lawrence S. Wittner
*State University of New York
Albany*

Contents

Introduction

The relationship of international organization, law, and peace movements to U.S. foreign policy since 1941 is generally acknowledged. The United States led in planning for and creating the United Nations and in providing moral, political, and economic support in its early years. Membership clearly marked the abandonment of that significant policy of isolationism that had thwarted earlier efforts to join the League of Nations. Acceptance of the International Court of Justice in 1946 likewise reflected the culmination of decades of effort by citizens and policy leaders to advance the ideal of peace through law. Reservations attached to adherence, however, still revealed a strong desire to retain independence of action, and they did much to limit the effectiveness of the court.

Peace activists, organizations, and ideology have also grown in importance. In earlier decades the relationship of peace ideology and action may have been removed from foreign policy-making except in unusual instances. Since 1946 this has been less true. Nuclear pacifism has had an impact on treaties related to outer space, testing, free zones, and arms control and disarmament negotiations. Protest movements during the war in Vietnam altered government policies substantially. Criticisms of the Central Intelligence Agency's operations, coupled with demands for respect of human rights on a global scale, clearly affected that agency's range of overseas operations, and debate over peacetime conscription has imposed limits on foreign policy options.

Yet diplomatic historians have treated these significant changes in sporadic fashion. Internationalism has been especially neglected. Historians of the twenty-first century may well characterize the twentieth century as an age of internationalism as they ponder the emergence of the League of Nations, the United Nations, and thousands of agencies, societies, associations, both political and nonpolitical. Few followers of Clio yet seem to recognize that possibility. An examination of standard diplomatic textbooks verifies the general neglect. Authors refer to the UN in

passing, with emphasis primarily on its founding. They treat the UN peripherally and do not examine U.S.-UN relationships consistently enough even to ask whether the United States has ever formulated a UN foreign policy.

A few historians, notably Robert A. Divine, in his *Second Chance* (38:160), have examined the wartime planning and attitudes of citizens and policymakers which led to the creation of the United Nations. Subsequent years have been left largely to political scientists to explore, as the entries in this chapter amply reveal. Most of their books and articles contain some information historical in nature, but the treatment is usually analytic and interpretive rather than descriptive.

Even here the primary focus has been on the relationship of the United States to the UN in its political context. One interpretation dominates. It perceives the UN for over twenty years as the tool of the United States and as an organization caught in cold war rivalries. A corollary notes that with emerging nations, the growth in membership, and the creation of blocs, the United States lost its once dominant position. Yet this interpretation applies largely to the main organs of the United Nations. There have been virtually no published historical studies of the role of the United States in the many UN agencies and commissions to test the simple thesis of domination and to perceive more precisely what the relationship has been in such nonpolitical areas.

The reason for such neglect cannot lie in the absence of materials. Ample documentation is already available in the public records of the UN, in State Department compilations and reports, and in the Foreign Relations series carrying into the 1950s. Archival records related to the U.S. mission to the UN can also be consulted. A few biographies, as well as memoirs, have appeared, and diplomatic historians may also rely on oral history in an area rich in personalities.

It is thus easy to suggest topics open to researchers. Political scientists have already pointed the way with questions which historians must pursue. These involve the importance of the UN to policymakers, the formulation of UN policies, the impact of the cold war, and the influence the National Security Council or lesser agencies have had in determining positions taken. The attitude of Congress toward the UN merits special attention in respect to funding or its continuing concern about overinvolvement. A collective biography of U.S. ambassadors to the UN or an examination of the mission itself and any changing patterns would be useful. Individual studies are needed on relationships with specialized bodies in the world system. These include International Atomic Energy, Food and Agriculture, World Health, Universal Postal Union, International Telecommunications, World Meteorology, and disarmament.

Likewise, historical descriptions and assessments of the role of the United States in broad international activities are needed, such as refugees, drugs, education, culture, development, outer space, aviation, the oceans, population, and economic assistance. Finally, on the nonpolitical side, over three thousand international societies are representative of a burgeoning community transnationalism. This is a field ripe for exploration, either through collective studies or examinations of individual organizations.

The general neglect of international law by historians is also self-evident. No work treats developments since 1941 to show where Americans as individuals or societies fit into thought or action. Likewise, despite one limited study on the Connally reservation, little interest has appeared on the International Court of Justice or on Americans who have served as judges. The introduction to Chapter 15 notes earlier and general topics associated with international law still in need of work.

Propagandists and pressure groups favoring a more international commitment exist in large numbers, and many of them merit studies, including the United Nations Association, the Carnegie Endowment for International Peace, and the World Peace and Woodrow Wilson foundations. The names of Quincy Wright, Clyde Eagleton, and Clark Eichelberger provide illustrative examples of individuals worthy of examination as activists or scholars. Initial data is also available for intensive analyses of public opinion on international issues.

The subject of peace history has received more attention by historians than the previous two topics. Lawrence Wittner provides a general narrative of activities for 1941 to 1960 in *Rebels against War* (38:266), and Charles DeBenedetti's *The Peace Reform in American History* (16:26) includes material for 1941 to 1975. Yet biographies of leaders, studies of major peace groups, and solid appraisals of antiwar movements of the 1960s and 1970s are needed. Little effort has emerged to relate the moral indignation associated with the latter era to the debate over idealism and realism in American foreign policy.

Because much of the post-1941 era has not been fully explored in monographs, it is vital to consult articles in the key journals. These are *International Organization* (1947–), *International Conciliation* (1907–1972), *Vista* (formerly *Changing World*, 1965–), and *Foreign Affairs: An American Quarterly Review* (1922–). Developments in international law can be followed in the *American Journal of International Law* (1970–) and in the *Proceedings* of the American Society of International Law. The Conference on Peace Research in History publishes *Peace and Change* (1972–).

Documentary materials are also essential. The Department of State issues miscellaneous "series" publications that are exceedingly valuable for internationalism developments. These provide historical background and information not only on the United Nations and its related agencies but also on NATO and regional organizations. The first was the Arbitration Series followed by the discontinued Conference Series. The latter was replaced by the International Organization and Conference Series, with four subdivisions: 1) general, 2) regional, 3) United Nations, 4) specialized agencies of the United Nations. There were also United States–United Nations Information and United States and United Nations Report series, both discontinued. Many of these publications, often in small pamphlets, either provide documentation on topics under consideration or explain policy positions. The State Department's Foreign Policy Series also contains important expressions of policy. Two publications worth noting on international organization are "The United States and the United Nations: A Department of State Discussion Paper" (no. 8875, General Foreign Policy Series 302, 1976) and "United States Foreign Policy: An Overview" (no. 8814, General Foreign Policy Series 296, rev. January, 1976). Government document file S 1.70 should be consulted for these as well as for the larger and annual government publications cited in the listings of this chapter.

For developments in peace, international law, and internationalist movements prior to 1914, consult Chapter 16; for 1914 to 1920 see Chapter 19, and for the interwar years, Chapter 20. Information on monetary and banking developments appears in Chapter 40. Works on arms control and disarmament and global commitments associated with a doctrine of responsibility appear in Chapter 40. Regional international arrangements are covered in Chapters 35 (Latin America) and 29 (Europe). Additional titles on the Congo crisis can be found in Chapter 38 and on the Vietnam War in 31. The broad and specialized bibliographies cited in Chapter 16 are also valuable for later years. Those by Haas (1:37), Holler (1:7), and Atherton (16:1) are especially useful because of their full coverage and annotations.

Resources and Overviews

RESEARCH AIDS

While pertinent bibliographies and reference aids are listed here, there are more extensive lists in Chapter 1.

Bibliographies

"Card Catalogue of the Peace Palace at The Hague [1800–1970]" (16:2) is a microfiche edition of approximately 600,000 cataloged holdings which is especially useful because of the arrangement of its Periodical Reference Guide.

Foreign Affairs Bibliography: A Selected and Annotated List of Books on International Relations (1:15) provides additional materials on such topics as international law and international organization and government.

Grieves, F. L. *International Law, Organization, and the Environment: A Bibliography and Research Guide* (1:35) is valuable in revealing the range of research possibilities in the international field. Lacks any classification by nation, so U.S. policy is not easy to locate. Author index.

Hannigan, J. A., comp. *Publications of the Carnegie Endowment for International Peace, 1910–1967, Including International Conciliation, 1924–1967* (1:17) lists its pamphlet series and monographs from its sponsored research that contain information on peace activities and international law.

Holler, F. L., ed. *Information Sources of Political Science* (1:7).

38:1 Huxford, Marilyn, and Schelling, Sandra. *Perspectives on War and Peace in a Changing World: A Selected Bibliography.* St. Louis: St. Louis Univer-

sity Press, 1975. This extensive list of books on U.S. foreign relations (1945–1975) contains information on peace movements and on international organization developments.

LaBarr, D. F., and Singer, J. D. *The Study of International Politics: A Guide to the Sources for the Student, Teacher, and Researcher* (1:19) contains sections listing journals with titles of articles by volume and bibliographies. Lacks subject index.

38:2 Robinson, Jacob, comp. *International Law and Organization: General Sources of Information.* Leiden: Sijthoff, 1967. A comprehensive listing of journals, yearbooks, books, and guides, with the emphasis on legal subjects and bodies.

Disarmament and Peace Research

Burns, R. D. *Arms Control and Disarmament: A Bibliography* (1:25) lists materials related to UN disarmament efforts.

Cook, B. W., ed. *Bibliography on Peace Research in History* (1:28) is a comprehensive list.

38:3 Durkee, Kinde, comp. *Peace Research: Definitions and Objectives: A Bibliography.* Los Angeles: California State University, Center for the Study of Armament and Disarmament, 1976. The emphasis in this pamphlet is upon scientific peace research which is interdisciplinary and goal oriented. The five sections are entitled "Defining Peace Research," "Topics," Centers and Projects," "Analysis of Peace Research," and "Reference Materials."

Peace Research Abstracts Journal [1964–] (1:223) covers books and articles under a ten-heading classification system. Heads include "International Law, Economics, and Diplomacy," "International Institutions and Regional Alliances," "Ideology and Issues," "Nations and National Policies," "Limitation of Arms," and "Decision Making and Communications." Users must familiarize themselves with the coding index.

38:4 Pickus, Robert, and Woito, Robert. *To End War: An Introduction to the Ideas, Books, Organizations, Work. . . .* Berkeley: World without War Council, 1970. This guide to peace research contains annotations to books, periodicals, and groups. Chapters cover causes of war, disarmament, world development and organization, the draft and conscientious objection, nonviolence, international relations, and political processes. Author and title indexes.

United Nations. Dag Hammarskjöld Library. *Disarmament: A Select Bibliography* (1:29) is a useful compilation of English- and foreign-language books and articles dealing with contemporary issues. Four volumes (1962–1977) to date.

38:5 U.S. Arms Control and Disarmament Agency. *Arms Control and Disarmament: A Quarterly Bibliography with Abstracts and Annotations.* 9 vols. Washington, D.C.: U.S. Arms Control and Disarmament Agency, 1964–1973. A major abstract service which included sections on political and peace issues, ideas, and efforts, as well as articles and books on UN peacekeeping, security and strategies of international political organizations, and international law, including pacific settlement and adjudication. It covers books and 1,200 periodicals.

International Organizations

Atherton, A. L., comp. *International Organizations: A Guide to Information Sources* (16:1).

Haas, M., comp. *International Organization: An Interdisciplinary Bibliography* (1:37) contains sections on the League of Nations system and the UN, regional bodies, and nonpolitical organizations.

38:6 Hüfner, Klaus, and Naumann, Jens. *The United Nations System: International Bibliography.* 3 vols. Munich: Verlag Dokumentation, 1976–1979. This five-part selective listing of secondary literature on the UN includes monographs and articles from journals and "collective volumes" from French, English and German sources. Volume 1 covers 1945 to 1965; volume 2 (two parts), 1965 to 1970; and volume 3 (two parts), 1971 to 1975.

38:7 Johnsen, Julia E., comp. *Federal World Government.* Vol. 20, no. 5 in *The Reference Shelf.* New York: Wilson, 1948. This debater's handbook reflects the strong movement in the United States (1945–1948) to transform the UN or create a more effective international organization. The lists of references and compilation of essays reveal the diverse approaches.

38:8 Johnsen, Julia E., comp. *United Nations or World Government.* Vol. 19, no. 5 in *The Reference Shelf.* New York: Wilson, 1947. This debater's handbook is still a useful tool because of its many references, chronology, list of organizations and compilation of 12 articles and additional excerpts representative of postwar responses to the UN and to contemporary world government and federalist movements (1945–1947).

Johnson, H. S., and Singh, B., comps. *International Organization: A Classified Bibliography* (1:38).

38:9 Kay, David A. "United States National Security Policy and International Organization: A Critical View of the Literature." In Lawrence S. Finkelstein, ed., *The United States and International Organization: The Changing Setting.* Cambridge, Mass.: MIT Press, 1969, pp. 197–207. A review essay of major studies on United States–UN relations, it focuses on works by Ruth B. Russell and L. P. Bloomfield. It is critical of both their analyses and descriptive quality.

Speeckaert, G. P., comp. *Select Bibliography on International Organization, 1885–1964* (16:6).

38:10 Summers, Robert E., comp. *The United States and International Organizations.* Vol. 24, no. 5 in *The Reference Shelf.* New York: Wilson, 1952. Summers provides an especially valuable compilation of essays and references revealing of concerns and issues related to the election of 1952 and the war in Korea. World federalism appeared as a strong movement.

38:11 Winton, Harry N. M., ed. *Publications of the United Nations System: A Reference Guide.* New York: Bowker, 1972. Part 1 outlines the UN system, structure, agencies, and publications plus indexes, catalogues, and other finding aids. Part 2 covers reference materials under 29 subject headings. Part 3 describes about 300 periodicals. Materials since 1972 can be found in *International Bibliography: Information, Documentation* (New York: Bowker).

38:12 Yalem, Ronald J. "The Study of International Organization, 1920–1965: A Survey of the Literature." *Background* 10:1 (1966), 1–56. This review of significant works covers the literature chronologically and topically with some annotation. It is followed by a list of references. *Background* also listed annually articles and books on international affairs.

Yearbooks and Other Aids

38:13 *Annual Review of United States Affairs, 1949–*. New York: New York University Press, 1950–. Started in 1949 at New York University, this annual compilation contains brief summaries of developments, excerpts of speeches, and documents. It improved over the years both in content and indexing until 1974, when the latter was dropped. The 1974 volume contains a valuable guide supplement to documents and agencies.

38:14 Chamberlin, Waldo, et al. *A Chronology and Fact Book of the United Nations, 1941–1976*. Dobbs Ferry, N.Y.: Oceana, 1976. This guide, published periodically, contains standard data on countries, structure and procedure of the UN and the budget.

38:15 United Nations. *Yearbook of the United Nations*. New York: UN Office of Public Information, 1946–. Each annual volume summarizes developments arranged according to operating bodies, agencies, and topics. It includes a limited number of documents plus information on delegations, finances, and structure. The subject index and an index of names, beginning in 1961, provides access to information on the United States.

38:16 *United Nations Monthly Chronicle* [May 1964–]. New York: UN Office of Public Information, 1964–. This regular publication issued by the UN Office of Public Information summarizes activities each month, news items, lists of documents, scheduled meetings, and budget information. It was preceded by the *United Nations Bulletin* (August 1946–June 1954) and *United Nations Review* (July 1954–April 1964).

Document Collections

38:17 Cordier, Andrew W., and Foote, Wilder, eds. *Public Papers of the Secretaries-General of the United Nations*. 8 vols. New York: Columbia University Press, 1969–1978. A useful collection showing both the influences of the United States upon the secretaries-general and subsequent UN policies and the attitude of the UN leaders toward the United States.

Deák, F., ed. *American International Law Cases, 1783–1968* (1:369) contains, in its 19 volumes, a full and complete compilation of cases arranged under the general categories of international law.

Friedman, L., comp. *The Law of War: A Documentary History* (1:370) consists of two volumes which range from reprinting Hugo Grotius's *The Law of War and Peace* to including documents from the courts-martial of William L. Calley, Jr., and Ernest Medina.

38:18 United Nations. *United Nations Conference on International Organization, San Francisco, 1945*. 22 vols. New York: UN Information Organization, 1945–1955. This is the full documentary record with background introductions.

38:19 U.S. Department of State. *Country Reports on Human Rights Practices*. Washington, D.C.: G.P.O., 1961–. Under legislative requirements of the Foreign Assistance Act of 1961, the State Department every six months issues reports on worldwide violations of human rights to the House Sub-Committee on International Relations. Document series Y4. F76/1:H88 files these by year.

38:20 U.S. Department of State. *Digest of United States Practice in International Law*. Washington, D.C.: G.P.O., 1975–. This multivolume series beginning with 1974 provides annual digests of U.S. practice. It includes descriptive passages and selected documents by subjects.

U.S. Department of State. *Foreign Relations of the United States* (1:358) covers UN relations, arms control, regional alliances, trade policy, foreign assistance, and international atomic energy issues and often national security policy.

U.S. Department of State. *International Organization and Conference Series* (2:62) provides information on the history of each organization covered, its work, plans, and the nature of U.S. participation.

38:21 U.S. Department of State. *United States Contributions to International Organizations*. Washington, D.C.: G.P.O., 1951–. Under requirement set by the 81st Congress (1949–1950), the department lists annually by commission, bureau, agency, or organization U.S. contributions. Tables record all participating governments showing the dollar amount provided and the percentage of the total. Each volume contains cumulative tables of totals since 1945. Data covers regional organizations, including the OAS and NATO.

38:22 U.S. Department of State. *U.S. Participation in the UN (Report on the United Nations)*. Washington, D.C.: G.P.O., 1947–. This annual "Report by the President to the Congress," beginning with 1946, is a succinct description of participation with the UN and all its agencies. It is primarily descriptive with less delineation of U.S. policy positions than one might expect. The names of representatives to various commissions or posts are valuable. Title varies.

38:23 U.S. Senate. Committee on Foreign Relations. Hearings; *Review of the United Nations Charter.* 83d and 84th Congs., 1954–1955. 12 pts. Washington, D.C.: G.P.O., 1955. Private citizens and notables, including former President Truman, presented their views on charter revision and changes in the international peace and security system.

38:24 Whiteman, Marjorie M. *Digest of International Law.* 15 vols. Washington, D.C.: G.P.O., 1963–1973. This compilation, done under the auspices of the State Department, succeeds the Hackworth *Digest* (1:371), covering materials since 1940. It contains considerable historical background as it touches on many international matters—rivers, basins, harbors, canals, fisheries, the continental shelf and oceans, air and space, and territorial issues. Index is in volume 15.

Indexes to Documents

Brimmer, B., et al. *A Guide to the Use of United Nations Documents (Including Reference to the Specialized Agencies and Special U.N. Bodies)* (1:327) is, while somewhat dated, still useful because the documentation system and guides described remain the same.

38:25 Dimitrov, Th'eodore D., ed. *Documents of International Organisations: A Bibliographic Handbook. . . .* Chicago: American Library Association, 1973. These references cover documents for UN bodies and other intergovernmental organizations. It contains a useful guide plus indexes and some brief annotations. There is also an essay on how to use the documents.

38:26 Hajnal, Peter I. *Guide to United Nations Organization, Documentation and Publishing for Students, Researchers, Librarians.* Dobbs Ferry, N.Y.: Oceana, 1978. This guide, a successor to Brimmer (1:327), describes the UN organization, explains UN publications and documents, and provides an annotated bibliography of secondary literature.

OVERVIEWS

Internationalism

See also Chapters 16 and 20, "Internationalism."

Claude, I. L., Jr. "American Attitudes towards International Organization" [1920–1978] (2:56).

Claude, I. L., Jr. "International Organization" [1776–1978] (2:57).

38:27 Claude, Inis L., Jr. *Swords into Plowshares: The Problems and Progress of International Organization.* 4th ed. New York: Random House, 1971. Claude examines the international system from an "historical approach." Chapters treat antecedents of the UN, and the origins, problems, and future of the UN, as well as discuss collective security, regional organizations, trusteeships, and disarmament. Bibliography.

38:28 Finkelstein, Lawrence S., ed. *The United States and International Organization: The Changing Setting.* Cambridge, Mass.: MIT Press, 1969. Historical perspective appears in the essays by Finkelstein, "International Cooperation in a Changing World," Inis L. Claude, Jr., "The United Nations, the United States, and the Maintenance of Peace," and Joseph S. Nye, "United States Policy toward Regional Organization." All originally appeared in *International Organization* 23 (1969). Extensive bibliography.

38:29 Gardner, Richard N. *In Pursuit of World Order: U.S. Foreign Policy and International Organizations.* Rev. ed. New York: Praeger, 1966. Gardner focuses on financing the International Court of Justice, voting patterns, alliance systems, and responses to population growth, development, trade, monetary policy, space, and human rights.

38:30 Haas, Ernst B. *Tangle of Hopes: American Commitments and World Order.* Englewood Cliffs, N.J.: Prentice-Hall, 1969. Sections on public opinion, the cold war, alliances and regional organizations, and changes in trade and foreign aid have historical data, in an otherwise present- and future-oriented study.

38:31 Haas, Ernst B. *The Web of Interdependence: The United States and International Organizations.* Englewood Cliffs, N.J.: Prentice-Hall, 1970. This brief volume examines peacekeeping, decolonization, monetary systems, human rights, development, arms control and disarmament, trade, foreign aid, science and technology, and policies toward evolving international systems.

Hoffmann, Stanley. *Primacy or World Order: American Foreign Policy since the Cold War* (24:130) examines the trend of the United States to assume a greater role in world affairs and the resulting problems. He touches on political, economic, human, and military aspects in an analytical and thoughtful exposition.

Kuehl, W. F. "Internationalism" [1776–1978] (2:59).

Mangone, G. J. *The Idea and Practice of World Government* [ancient times to 1951] (2:60).

38:32 Wasson, Donald, comp. *American Agencies Interested in International Affairs.* 5th ed. New York: Praeger, 1964. This is a list of study, research, and educational organizations along with descriptions of activities and publications. There is a section on chambers of commerce. Subject index.

Wynner, E., and Lloyd, G. *Searchlight on Peace Plans: Choose Your Road to World Government* [ancient times to 1944] (2:64).

United Nations

38:33 Cheever, Daniel S., and Haviland, H. Field, Jr. *Organizing for Peace: International Organization in World Affairs.* Boston: Houghton Mifflin, 1954. This full review of developments focuses on the UN and contains many references to U.S. activities and policies. It is valuable for its overview of contacts with specialized agencies. Bibliography.

38:34 Goodrich, Leland M. "The Changing Role of United States in the United Nations." *India Quarterly Journal of International Affairs* 32:1 (1976), 46–67. This compact summary (1945–1975) examines the role of public opinion, the cold war, the changing nature of the UN and its agencies, and world shifts away from colonialism in noting the new conditions affecting U.S. policy.

38:35 Russell, Ruth B. *The United Nations and United States Security Policy.* Washington, D.C.: Brookings Institution, 1968. A policy study which argues in favor of détente rather than rivalry in the UN to achieve U.S. objectives. The work covers the Cuban crisis, nuclear concerns, arms control, peacekeeping operations, plus legal and diplomatic adjustments through the United Nations. Bibliography.

38:36 Weiler, Lawrence D., and Simons, Anne P. *The United States and the United Nations: The Search for International Peace and Security.* New York: Manhattan, 1967. It includes background on the origin of U.S. planning for the UN, attitudes toward, and impact of membership on policy; it also examines

questions in relation to security needs, with a focus on the UN's first decade.

Peace and Pacifism

38:37 Boulding, Kenneth E. "The Peace Research Movement in the United States." In Ted Dunn, ed., *Alternatives to War and Violence.* London: Clarke, 1963, pp. 40–51. This brief selection discusses the development of a peace research movement in the United States during 1945 to 1963.

38:38 Brock, Peter. *Twentieth Century Pacifism.* New York: Van Nostrand Reinhold, 1970. The author reviews American pacifism from the turn of the century to the late 1960s by chronicling movements ranging from Mennonite quietists, to socialist antimilitarists, to Gandhian *satyagrahis.*

38:39 Bussey, Gertrude, and Tims, Margaret. *Woman's International League for Peace and Freedom, 1915–1965: A Record of Fifty Years' Work.* London: Allen & Unwin, 1965. This is the story of that international organization in which the American section played a key role. This historical account draws upon the WIL's files and conference records to provide a picture of its efforts in behalf of peace, disarmament, and social justice. See also Randall (38:78).

38:40 Lynd, Staughton, ed. *Nonviolence in America: A Documentary History.* Indianapolis: Bobbs-Merrill, 1966. This collection of sources on nonviolent civil disobedience in America, ranging from colonial days to 1966, goes beyond pacifists to embrace a variety of groups, ranging from anarchists to activists for racial justice. The editor has contributed a lengthy introduction.

38:41 Schlissel, Lillian, comp. *Conscience in America: A Documentary History of Conscientious Objection in America, 1757–1967.* New York: Dutton, 1968. The editor brings together materials on the legislative and judicial history of conscientious objection, as well as personal statements opposed to conscription.

38:42 Sibley, Mulford Q., ed. *The Quiet Battle: Writings on the Theory and Practice of Non-Violent Resistance.* Boston: Beacon, 1968. Although nonviolent resistance is frequently linked by ideology and personalities to peace movements, sometimes it is not. This excellent collection draws upon writings exploring these two types of nonviolent resistance. The editor's introductory and concluding comments are particularly valuable.

38:43   Singer, J. David. "An Assessment of Peace Research." *International Security* 1:1 (1976), 118–37. Singer reviews approaches, methods, and concerns of peace researchers since the 1890s, noting the increasing diversity of approaches since 1945 and schisms which have evolved.

38:44   Weinberg, Arthur, and Weinberg, Lila, eds. *Instead of Violence.* Boston: Beacon, 1965. This excellent anthology of writings on nonviolence throughout history contains numerous selections by Americans.

Personalities

AMERICAN

Diplomats

Warren R. Austin

Mazuzan, G. T. "America's U.N. Commitment, 1945–1953" (38:182) traces the career of Warren R. Austin as America's first ambassador to the United Nations. Appointed by President Truman in June 1946, Austin discovered that his internationalism had to be reconciled with the unilateral policy that the United States often followed.

38:45   Mazuzan, George T. *Warren R. Austin at the U.N., 1946–1953.* Kent, Ohio: Kent State University Press, 1977. The author traces the career of the American ambassador during the UN's formative years. Austin is viewed as a moralist and a universalist during a period when the Truman administration moved toward a cold war posture. Bibliography.

Cordell Hull

Hull, C. *Memoirs* (21:36) contains, in volume 2, a detailed account of the secretary of state's contributions to the planning of the UN and the preliminary drafting of the charter. Hull stresses his determination to ensure congressional support and he describes the various steps he took to create a bipartisan approach.

38:46   Vandenbosch, Amry. "Cordell Hull: Father of the United Nations." *World Affairs* 136:2 (1973),

99–120. The author examines Hull's views on the League of Nations, the World Court, the good neighbor policy, and a postwar international organization. Hull's influence in Congress and in arousing popular support between 1943 and 1945 appear to be exaggerated.

Philip C. Jessup

Jessup, P. C. *The Birth of Nations* (24:174) recounts his service in many official posts, including judge on the International Court of Justice and deputy chief of the U.S. mission to the United Nations.

Jessup, P. C. *The United States and the World Court . . . with Related Essays* (20:101).

Daniel P. Moynihan

Moynihan, D. P. "The Politics of Human Rights" (38:238) puts this issue in a strategic frame of reference.

38:47   Moynihan, Daniel P. *A Dangerous Place.* Boston: Atlantic; Little, Brown, 1978. Moynihan offers his perspective on U.S.-UN policy from his eight-month experience as chief delegate. The work continues the controversy initiated by his blunt criticism of unrealistic policies.

Eleanor Roosevelt

38:48   Hareven, Tamara K. *Eleanor Roosevelt: An American Conscience.* Chicago: Quadrangle, 1968. Reprint 1975. Contains one chapter, entitled "The Crusade for Human Rights," which includes all references to the UN work of Eleanor Roosevelt.

38:49   Lash, Joseph P. *Eleanor: The Years Alone.* New York: Norton, 1972. Lash describes Eleanor Roosevelt's participation in UN work, especially the Human Rights Commission.

Edward R. Stettinius, Jr.

Campbell, T. M. *Masquerade Peace: America's UN Policy, 1944–1945* (38:158) focuses on the role played by Secretary of State Stettinius and provides a rare analysis of Washington's UN policy in the context of the emerging cold war. The author identifies six phases in the evolution of U.S. policy and concludes that international cooperation gave way to a view of the UN as an instrument in the U.S.-U.S.S.R. struggle. Bibliography.

Stettinius, E. R., Jr. *The Diaries of Edward R. Stettinius, Jr., 1943–1946* (24:150) focuses on the role

Stettinius played in organizing the UN from the conference at Dumbarton Oaks through the San Francisco Conference in the spring of 1945. This work shows how U.S. officials arrived at major decisions on how the UN could be integrated with overall American foreign policy objectives.

Walker, R. L. "E. R. Stettinius, Jr." (24:151).

Adlai E. Stevenson
Martin, J. B. *The Life of Adlai E. Stevenson* (24:152).

38:50   Prosser, Michael H., ed. *An Ethic for Survival: Adlai Stevenson Speaks on International Affairs, 1936–1965.* New York: Morrow, 1969. This volume contains the essential addresses of Stevenson on the UN and a broad range of international issues. Bibliography.

Stevenson, A. E. *The Papers of Adlai E. Stevenson* (24:153) contains (volume 2) considerable material on Stevenson's work to create the UN, his role as a delegate, and his attitudes toward agencies and policies (1945–1947). Volume 3 includes his views as a presidential candidate, 1952, and subsequent volumes have references to various UN developments.

38:51   Stevenson, Adlai E. *Looking Outward: Years of Crisis at the United Nations.* New York: Harper & Row, 1963. Stevenson includes addresses and speeches at the UN and other papers defending U.S. policy (1945–1963).

Harry S. Truman
See Chapter 24, under "Personalities," for additional references.

38:52   Miscamble, Wilson D. "The Evolution of an Internationalist: Harry S. Truman and American Foreign Policy." *Australian Journal of Politics and History* 23:2 (1977), 268–83. This review of Truman's thinking examines impressions and ideas that evolved from experiences in World War I, as a senator, and from extensive reading. His internationalist views as president had thus been set long before 1945.

Arthur H. Vandenberg
See Chapter 24, under "Personalities," for additional references.

38:53   Bradshaw, James S. "Senator Arthur H. Vandenberg and Article 51 of the United Nations Charter." *Mid-America* 57:3 (1975), 145–56. This article skillfully assesses the key role of Senator Vandenberg as author of article 51 permitting individual or collective self-defense. Bradshaw believes that article 51 helped avoid a congressional battle over UN membership, and that it laid the basis for a bipartisan foreign policy.

38:54   Briggs, Philip J. "Senator Vandenberg, Bipartisanship and the Origins of United Nations' Article 51." *Mid-America* 60:3 (1978), 163–69. Vandenberg played a key role in the decision to incorporate article 51 into the charter. This provision allowing regional defensive alliances was considered vital to western hemisphere accords, and Briggs argues that it opened the way for the NATO treaty.

38:55   Gazell, James A. "Arthur H. Vandenberg, Internationalism, and the United Nations." *Political Science Quarterly* 88:3 (1973), 375–94. The author perceptively traces the evolution of Vandenberg's views from the late 1920s to the Senator's participation at the San Francisco Conference in 1945. Vandenberg's conversion owed much to his belief that modern technology had rendered isolationism obsolete.

Tompkins, C. D. *Senator Arthur H. Vandenberg: The Evolution of a Modern Republican, 1884–1945* (22:37) traces Vandenberg's conversion from prewar isolationism to wartime internationalism and support for the UN through the senator's landmark speech in January 1945. The author emphasizes Vandenberg's cautious approach to bipartisan foreign policy.

Vandenberg, A. H., Jr., ed. *The Private Papers of Senator Vandenberg* (24:162) contains both diary passages and excerpts from letters that document the Michigan senator's role in working with the State Department before and during the San Francisco Conference.

Others
38:56   Buckley, William F., Jr. *United Nations Journal: A Delegate's Odyssey.* New York: Putnam's, 1974. Buckley recounts his experiences as a delegate in 1975 to the UN Human Rights Commission. He provides insight into personalities, procedures, and the history of human rights.

38:57   Clement, Lee. *Andrew Young at the United Nations.* Salisbury, N.C.: Documentary Publications, 1978. This account contains excerpts of speeches, photographs, a chronology, and an index, along with a superficial analysis.

38:58 Eichelberger, Clark M. *Organizing for Peace: A Personal History of the Founding of the United Nations.* New York: Harper & Row, 1977. The author, director of the League of Nations Association and its successor, the United Nations Association, describes his personal role in the formation of the United Nations. Chapters on the part his organizations played in mobilizing public opinion during World War II and on his conversations with Sumner Welles and Franklin D. Roosevelt are particularly informative.

38:59 Gildersleeve, Virginia. *Many A Good Crusade.* New York: Macmillan, 1954. These memoirs recount Gildersleeve's longtime interest in the movement for U.S. participation in an international organization. There is valuable material on her role as a delegate at the UN Conference on International Organization in 1945, particularly her interest in human rights.

Lodge, H. C., Jr. *The Storm Has Many Eyes: A Personal Narrative* (24:137) reviews his work at the UN (1953–1960) with an emphasis on personalities and policymaking. Lodge in a number of books has commented on his role in UN affairs.

38:60 Patterson, James T. "Alternatives to Globalism: Robert A. Taft and American Foreign Policy, 1939–1945." *Historian* 36:4 (1974), 670–88. Taft never made it clear how he reconciled his faith in a powerful world court with his insistence on the preservation of national sovereignty, nor how a world court could operate without an international police force.

38:61 Wadsworth, James J. *The Glass House: The United Nations in Action.* New York: Praeger, 1966. A realistic account of Wadsworth's eight years as a member of the U.S. mission. The emphasis is on nonpolitical relationships, specialized agencies, and day-to-day experiences.

Citizen Activists

Kenneth E. Boulding

Boulding, K. E. "The Peace Research Movement in the United States" (38:37).

38:62 Kerman, Cynthia. "Kenneth Boulding and the Peace Research Movement." In Charles Chatfield, ed., *Peace Movements in America.* New York: Schocken, 1973, pp. 133–49. This article sympathetically analyzes the life and career of Kenneth Boulding,

founder of the *Journal of Conflict Resolution* and a leader of the peace research movement. The author shows Boulding's consistent efforts to link social science methods with the struggle against war.

A. J. Muste

38:63 Hentoff, Nat, ed. *The Essays of A. J. Muste.* New York: Simon & Schuster, 1970. This excellent collection, drawn from American pacifist leader A. J. Muste's writings (1905–1966), contains a lengthy autobiographical account. Most of the influential writings deal with the major issues facing the American peace movement since 1941.

38:64 Hentoff, Nat. *Peace Agitator: The Story of A. J. Muste.* New York: Macmillan, 1963. Written in a lively fashion, this survey provides an account of the man who was probably the most important pacifist theorist and activist in modern American history. Muste's career, which fused radicalism and pacifism, is sympathetically described.

38:65 Robinson, Jo Ann. "A. J. Muste and Ways to Peace." In Charles Chatfield, ed., *Peace Movements in America.* New York: Schocken, 1973, pp. 81–94. Despite A. J. Muste's importance in the American peace movement, this is the only scholarly effort to examine Muste's life and career. The author demonstrates that despite Muste's participation in a variety of secular radical movements, he was driven by a religious faith which gave his writings and presence their extraordinary power.

James T. Shotwell

See Chapters 19 and 20, under "Personalities."

Josephson, H. *James T. Shotwell and the Rise of Internationalism in America* (19:61) includes a chapter on Shotwell's role as chairman of the Commission to Study the Organization of Peace, the major peace group working for the creation of a postwar world organization during World War II. The author details both the efforts to win public support for the future UN and Shotwell's contributions as the coordinator of the many peace groups represented at the San Francisco Conference.

38:66 Shotwell, James T. *The Autobiography of James T. Shotwell.* Indianapolis: Bobbs-Merrill, 1961. This is the autobiography of one of the leading American protagonists of internationalism and collective security.

Others

38:67   Bigelow, Albert. *The Voyage of the Golden Rule: An Experiment with Truth.* Garden City, N.Y.: Doubleday, 1959. As the opposition to nuclear weapons testing gathered momentum in the late 1950s, American pacifists began a series of civil disobedience campaigns. This book tells the story of four protestors who sailed their ship, the *Golden Rule,* into a U.S. nuclear testing zone in the Pacific and were arrested. Written by one of the participants, it is a firsthand account of resistance to preparations for nuclear war. See Reynolds (38:74).

38:68   Day, Dorothy. *Loaves and Fishes.* New York: Harper & Row, 1963. This is a personal account of the Catholic Worker movement, written by its founder. Established in 1933, the Catholic Worker movement combined urban Houses of Hospitality for the poor, rural farming communes, orthodox religion, and activist pacifism. After 1941, the Catholic Worker movement was a small but vigorous force against war.

Johnpoll, B. K. *Pacifist's Progress: Norman Thomas and the Decline of American Socialism* (20:71) shows how Socialist party leader Norman Thomas, even after he abandoned absolute pacifism, remained a key figure in the American peace movement. Although this biography concentrates on pre-1941 years, Thomas's later role as a critic of World War II and of the cold war is examined.

38:69   Lewis, David L. *King: A Critical Biography.* New York: Praeger, 1970. It is sometimes forgotten that Martin Luther King, Jr., was a leader not only of the struggle for racial justice but of the American peace movement. Indeed, he was a trenchant critic of the war in Vietnam and a recipient of the Nobel peace prize. The author takes a disdainful view of King's early religious emphasis but warms to his subject as King increasingly challenged the American government on behalf of the poor and the oppressed.

38:70   McSweeney, John P. "Chancellor Reuben Gustavson, Internationalism, and the Nebraska People." *Nebraska History* 57:3 (1976), 379–97. Gustavson's role as a grass-roots internationalist is described along with his efforts to raise support for the UN in Nebraska.

38:71   Peck, James. *We Who Would Not Kill.* New York: Stuart, 1958. This book provides an inside account of the experience of conscientious objectors in U.S. federal penitentiaries during World War II. Writ-ten by one of their number, it focuses upon resistance activities at Danbury prison and provides a glimpse of their postwar activities in the struggle for peace and social justice.

38:72   Pickett, Clarence E. *For More Than Bread.* Boston: Little, Brown, 1953. In this book, the former executive secretary of the American Friends Service Committee discusses his work with that organization (1929–1952). Although the AFSC was not exclusively a peace organization, it did contribute significantly to peace sentiment and activism.

38:73   Randall, Mercedes M. *Improper Bostonian: Emily Greene Balch.* New York: Twayne, 1964. Awarded the Nobel peace prize in 1946, Balch was an outstanding leader of the peace movement. Scholarly but sympathetic, this biography traces her lengthy career in the Women's International League for Peace and Freedom. Although Balch was an elder states-woman by the postwar era, her work, writings, and associations remained of considerable significance.

38:74   Reynolds, Earle L. *The Forbidden Voyage.* New York: McKay, 1961. Reprint 1975. After the pacifist crew of the *Golden Rule* was arrested for attempting to disrupt the U.S. nuclear testing program in the Pacific, an American anthropologist, Earle Reynolds, and his family continued their civil disobedience. Sailing his ship, the *Phoenix,* into the testing zone in July 1958, Reynolds was imprisoned. This book is his account of his motives and of the experience. See Bigelow (38:67).

38:75   Young, Wilmer J. *Visible Witness: A Testimony for Radical Peace Action.* Wallingford, Pa.: Pendle Hill, 1961. Written by a Quaker pacifist, this pamphlet tells the story of Omaha Action, a civil disobedience venture which entailed nonviolently trespassing upon a U.S. nuclear missile base in 1959.

UN OFFICIALS

Dag Hammarskjöld

38:76   Cordier, Andrew W., and Foote, Wilder, eds. *Dag Hammarskjöld* [1953–1961]. Vols. 2–5 in *Public Papers of the Secretaries-General of the United Nations.* New York: Columbia University Press, 1972–1975. Volume 2 (1953–1956) includes Hammarskjöld's mission to Peking, the Atoms for Peace Conference; volume 3 (1956–1957) provides material on the 1956 Suez crisis and creation of the UN

Emergency Force; volume 4 (1958–1960) includes the Lebanon affair, the 1959 Berlin crisis, and the neutralization of Laos; and volume 5 (1960–1961) includes materials on the Congo crisis.

38:77 Miller, Richard I. *Dag Hammarskjöld and Crisis Diplomacy.* Rev. ed. Dobbs Ferry, N.Y.: Oceana, 1961. A popularly written, but well-researched account, its chapters cover the China problem, Suez crisis, Hungary uprising, Lebanon, Southeast Asia, and the Congo, with considerable focus on U.S. actions (1953–1962).

Trygve Lie

38:78 Cordier, Andrew W., and Foote, Wilder, eds. *Trygve Lie* [1946–1953]. Vol. 1 in *Public Papers of the Secretaries-General of the United Nations.* New York: Columbia University Press, 1969. This volume includes such major events as the partition of Palestine and the creation of Israel, the Korean War, and the acceptance of the role of the secretary-general as spokesman for the goals of the charter.

38:79 Lie, Trygve. *In the Cause of Peace: Seven Years with the United Nations.* New York: Macmillan, 1954. The first secretary-general writes, with many passing references to the role of the United States in the UN during 1945 to 1952, with special attention to internal security concerns, the headquarters, personnel issues, and the Korean War.

U Thant

38:80 Cordier, Andrew W., and Foote, Wilder, eds. *U-Thant* [1961–1971]. Vols. 6–8 in *Public Papers of the Secretaries-General of the United Nations.* New York: Columbia University Press, 1975–1978. Volume 6 (1961–1964) includes the Cuban missile crisis, dispute over West Irian, UN mission to Yemen, UN fiscal problems, and UN intervention in Cyprus, volume 7 (1965–1967) deals with the Indian-Pakistani war, crisis over the Dominican Republic, and the Vietnam War; and volume 8 (1968–1971) sees the seating of the People's Republic of China and the wake of the Six Days War.

38:81 Saksena, K. P. "Secretary-General U Thant." *India Quarterly* 31:4 (1975), 342–61. Saksena analyzes the career of U Thant (b. 1909) as secretary-general of the UN and compares and contrasts the administrative style and effectiveness of U Thant and his predecessors Trygve Lie and Dag Hammarskjöld.

38:82 U Thant. *View from the UN.* Garden City, N.Y.: Doubleday, 1978. This memoir by the secretary-general of the United Nations (1961–1970) covers his very active role in international affairs. His candid observations about individuals and events make this volume worth reading.

The United Nations

38:83 *Everyman's United Nations: A Complete Handbook of the Activities and Evolution of the United Nations during its First Twenty Years, 1945–1965.* 8th ed. New York: UN Office of Public Information, 1968. These basic descriptive guides provide information on the structure and operation of the UN and include an examination of charges or complaints registered against the United States in the United Nations. Titles vary.

38:84 Fehrenbach, T. R. *This Kind of Peace.* New York: McKay, 1966. A sympathetic, popular account of the origins and first twenty years of the UN from the perspective of the major powers' roles. It is descriptive rather than analytic.

38:85 Goodrich, Leland M.; Hambro, Edvard V.; and Simons, Anne P., comps. *Charter of the United Nations: Commentary and Documents.* 3d ed. New York: Columbia University Press, 1969. This study contains considerable material on the relationships of the United States to the UN and international issues as these evolved.

38:86 Goodrich, Leland M., and Simons, Anne P. *The United Nations and the Maintenance of International Peace and Security.* Washington, D.C.: Brookings Institution, 1955. Reprint 1979. This work contains extensive references to U.S. responses to various UN issues and to policy positions. As a detailed analysis of the UN role as a peace agency, it covers collective security ideas and methods, arms control, and methods of resolving disputes.

38:87 Griffin, G. Edward. *The Fearful Master: A Second Look at the United Nations.* Boston: Western Islands, 1964. Griffin's polemic is representative of anti-UN concerns and highly critical of U.S. policies and involvements. It is strongly anticommunist in tone.

38:88   Gunter, Michael M. "The Problem of Ministate Membership in the United Nations System: Recent Attempts towards a Solution." *Columbia Journal of Transnational Law* 12:3 (1973), 464–86. Gunter discusses the attempts, made between 1965 and 1972 primarily by Britain and the United States, to solve the problem of granting small countries membership in the United Nations.

Houston, J. A. *Latin America in the United Nations* [1945–1955] (35:95) focuses on the significant role played by Latin American nations.

38:89   Jacobson, Harold K. "Structuring the Global System: American Contributions to International Organization." *Annals of the American Academy of Political and Social Science,* no. 428 (1976), 77–90. An overview—often superficial—of the way in which American ideals (limited government, consent of the governed, equality) influenced U.S. policy toward the formation of international organizations (such as the UN and NATO).

38:90   Rowe, Edward T. "Financial Support for the United Nations: The Evolution of Member Contributions, 1946–1969." *International Organization* 26:4 (1972), 619–57. This analysis concludes that the U.S. share in relation to its wealth has been less a burden on it than for states with limited economies. The trend has been to increase the responsibility for those least able to afford it. Extensive tables.

SECRETARY-GENERAL, SECURITY COUNCIL, AND GENERAL ASSEMBLY

See "UN Officials," under "Personalities," above.

Barros, James. "Pearson or Lie: The Politics of the Secretary-General's Selection, 1946" (36:40) examines the motives and methods of the United States, Britain, and the U.S.S.R. in the selection of the UN's first secretary-general.

38:91   Boyd, Andrew. *Fifteen Men on a Powder Keg: A History of the UN Security Council.* London: Methuen, 1971. This is a balanced, selective, but undocumented history (1945–1970) by a former secre-

tary of the British League of Nations Association. There is considerable focus on U.S. involvement and policy, covering individuals, the UN and the OAS, peacekeeping forces, and many crises and problems.

38:92   Finger, Seymour M., and Mugno, John F. "The Politics of Staffing the United Nations Secretariat." *Orbis* 19:1 (1975), 117–45. The authors discuss administrative problems and appointments in the bureaucracy of the UN Secretariat during the 1970s, emphasizing the influence of political pressures.

38:93   Gordenker, Leon. *The UN Secretary-General and the Maintenance of Peace.* New York: Columbia University Press, 1967. This account contains passing references to State Department planning toward the UN, especially on the appointments of Lie, Hammarskjöld, and Thant,. the Suez and Cuban crises, Korea, and the Congo.

38:94   Hiscocks, Richard. *The Security Council: A Study in Adolescence.* New York: Free Press, 1973. A scholarly assessment of the Security Council from an historical perspective by an Englishman, it places U.S. actions and decisions in a useful world setting. Extensive bibliography.

38:95   Keohane, Robert O. "Political Influence in the General Assembly." *International Conciliation,* no. 557 (1966), 1–64. Keohane notes changes in the General Assembly and explains the United States' declining influence.

38:96   Meron, Theodor. "Staff of the United Nations Secretariat: Problems and Directions." *American Journal of International Law* 70:4 (1976), 659–93. Contrary to the intention of the UN Charter, nationality and other political considerations have overshadowed the principle of merit in the recuitment and promotion of UN Secretariat staff.

38:97   Riggs, Robert E. *Politics in the United Nations: A Study of United States Influence in the General Assembly.* Urbana: University of Illinois Press, 1958. This work focuses on the partitioning of Palestine, the Korean War, colonialism, and organizational and structural questions. There is a singular emphasis on U.S. responses and policies. Extensive bibliography.

38:98   Rowe, Edward T. "The United States, the United Nations, and the Cold War." *International Organization* 25:1 (1971), 59–78. A statistical examination of votes in the General Assembly (1945–1971) on issues shows the extent of U.S. influence. Rowe concludes that until 1966 the U.S. could rally support for its positions.

38:99 Wilcox, Francis O. "Representation and Voting in the United Nations General Assembly." In Richard A. Falk and Saul H. Mendlovitz, eds., *The Strategy of World Order*. Vol. 3: *The United Nations*. New York: World Law Fund, 1966, pp. 272–94. Prepared as *Staff Study No. 4, Subcommittee on the United Nations Charter*, this study reviews voting practices and inequities and various proposals by Americans to change the system. These include suggestions by John Foster Dulles, Clark and Sohn, the Federal Union, and United World Federalists.

DISARMAMENT AND ARMS CONTROL

See Chapter 26, "Baruch Plan, 1946," and Chapter 40, "Arms Control and Disarmament."

Reports and Documents

See "Bibliographies, "Disarmament and Peace Research," above.

38:100 Keesing's Research Report. *Disarmament Negotiations and Treaties, 1946–1971*. New York: Scribner's, 1972. This is a descriptive and chronological account of efforts to curb the nuclear arms race. It is useful as a guide to UN reports, debates, resolutions, commissions, and accords (1946–1971).

Stockholm International Peace Research Institute. *Arms Control: A Survey and Appraisal of Multilateral Agreements* (40:222) includes texts of accords and summarizes UN resolutions and votes taken (1969–1977).

38:101 United Nations. *Basic Problems of Disarmament: Reports of the Secretary-General*. New York: UN Office of Public Information, 1970. This volume contains three reports, prepared during the 1960s, aimed at assessing the potential danger posed by weapons of mass destruction.

38:102 United Nations. *The United Nations Disarmament Yearbook* [1976–]. New York: UN Office of

Public Information, 1977– . This is an annual account of debates and negotiations within the UN system. These useful yearbooks supplement *The United Nations and Disarmament* [1945–1975], immediately below.

38:103 United Nations. *The United Nations and Disarmament, 1945–1970*. New York: UN Office of Public Information, 1970. With supplement (1970–1975), issued by the Secretariat, this work provides an account of debates and negotiations within the UN system. Covering attempts to control atomic energy and chemical, biological, conventional, and nuclear weapons and testing, the volumes provide a useful outside perspective on U.S.-Soviet positions. Appendixes include the texts of conventions.

Special Studies

38:104 Bargman, Abraham. "The United Nations, the Superpowers, and Proliferation." *Annals of the American Academy of Political and Social Science*, no. 430 (1977), 122–32. After examining nuclear tensions and debates, Bargman notes the limited involvement of the UN and suggests the creation of an international nuclear security planning group.

Bechhoefer, B. G. *Postwar Negotiations for Arms Control* [1945–1960] (26:197) is still one of the fullest descriptions of arms control and disarmament negotiations through UN channels.

Bernstein, B. J. "The Challenges and Dangers of Nuclear Weapons: Foreign Policy and Strategy, 1941–1978" (29:124).

38:105 Chamberlin, Waldo. "Arms Control and Limitation." In Franz B. Gross, ed., *The United States and the United Nations*. Norman: University of Oklahoma Press, 1965, pp. 65–86. This analysis of assumptions in 1945 and subsequent difficulties focuses on emerging suspicions between the United States and U.S.S.R., confrontations, crises, preparedness responses, continuing efforts at negotiations, and the mechanism created for discussions.

38:106 Cheever, Daniel S. "The UN and Disarmament." *International Organization* 19:3 (1965), 463–83. A full review of proposals, treaties, and negotiations, it is a negative assessment based on the super powers' lack of confidence in multilateral discussions and the structural limitations within the UN system which frustrate meaningful dialogue.

38:107 Cory, Robert H., Jr. "International Inspection: From Proposals to Realization." *International Organization* 13:4 (1959), 495–504. Cory concentrates on the late 1950s and proposals that the UN become involved in an international inspection system. Nationalistic concerns of the United States and the Soviet Union and administrative inadequacies hindered implementation.

38:108 Finkelstein, Lawrence S. "The United Nations and Organizations for the Control of Armaments." *International Organization* 16:1 (1962), 1–19. In a review of UN processes and concerns over nuclear testing and proliferation, the author is pessimistic that the UN can play a significant role given national positions and proposals.

Henkin, L. *Arms Control and Inspection in American Law* (40:248).

38:109 Kihss, Peter. "The Atom Bomb in the United Nations." *Foreign Policy Reports* 26:8 (1950), 85–89. This 1945 to 1949 review by a *New York Herald-Tribune* reporter focuses on proposals and debates in 1946 to outlaw or create a control system within the United Nations.

38:110 Lieberman, Joseph I. *The Scorpion and the Tarantula: The Struggle to Control Atomic Weapons, 1945–1949.* Boston: Houghton Mifflin, 1970. A thorough presentation of the nuclear problem from the origins of the bomb and efforts to impose limits through 1949. Bibliography.

38:111 Myrdal, Alva. "Disarmament and the United Nations." In Andrew W. Cordier and Wilder Foote, eds., *The Quest for Peace: The Dag Hammarskjöld Memorial Lectures.* New York: Columbia University Press, 1965, pp. 149–66. This is a useful explanation of where and how disarmament discussions fit into the UN system, with some comment on the Geneva Conference committee, issues, problems, and prospects.

38:112 Rubinstein, Alvin Z. "The United States, the Soviet Union, and Atoms for Peace: Background to the Establishment of the United Nations International Atomic Energy Agency." *World Affairs Quarterly* 30:1 (1959), 46–62. This essay reviews the background, policies, and concerns related to atomic development and control.

PEACEKEEPING, SANCTIONS, AND COLLECTIVE SECURITY

38:113 Blaisdell, Donald C. "Coordination of American Security Policy at the United Nations." *International Organization* 2:3 (1948), 469–77. The relationship of the U.S. defense structure to the UN Military Staff Committee is examined.

38:114 Bloomfield, Lincoln P. "The U.N. and National Security." In Harold K. Jacobson, ed., *America's Foreign Policy.* New York: Random House, 1960, pp. 695–709. Revised 1969. A general review of the development of the UN with special emphasis on security, peacekeeping, and conflict resolution activities, it contains a section entitled "Security Objectives of the United States." Reprinted from *Foreign Affairs* 36 (1958), 597–610.

38:115 Buchanan, William; Krugman, H. E.; and Van Wagenen, R. W. *An International Police Force and Public Opinion—Polled Opinion in the United States, 1939–1953.* Princeton, N.J.: Princeton University Press, 1954. This pamphlet contains a detailed analysis of polls.

38:116 Claude, Inis L., Jr. "The OAS, the UN, and the United States." *International Conciliation,* no. 547 (1964), 1–67. A thorough analysis of U.S. policy attitudes toward regional organizations, with the United States seeing them as instruments of national security.

38:117 Finkelstein, Lawrence S. "International Cooperation in a Changing World: A Challenge to United States Foreign Policy." *International Organization* 23:3 (1969), 559–88. This is a thoughtful assessment of the U.S. doctrine of responsibility through the UN, regional security organizations, economic aid, and development, and a review of pros and cons over the degree of involvement.

Russell, R. B. *The United Nations and United States Security Policy* (38:35) is a serious and insightful study of the security role of the United Nations. Although the author emphasizes UN activity during the 1960s, she includes informative material on such topics as the origin of the veto and the Korean War.

UN Peacekeeping

38:118 Adams, T. W., and Cottrell, Alvin J. "American Foreign Policy and the UN Peacekeeping Force in Cyprus." *Orbis* 12:1 (1968), 490–503. An analysis of the Cyprus problem (1964–1967) and the relationship of the UN peacekeeping force to U.S. objectives.

38:119 Bailey, Sydney D. "Cease-Fires, Truces, and Armistices in the Practice of the U.N. Security Council." *American Journal of International Law* 71:3 (1977), 461–73. Bailey distinguishes among cease-fire, truce, and armistice, using background from the Middle Ages, Hugo Grotius, and late 19th and early 20th centuries.

38:120 Rikhye, Indar Jit; Harbottle, Michael; and Egge, Bjorn. *The Thin Blue Line: International Peacekeeping and Its Future.* New Haven, Conn.: Yale University Press, 1974. This historical study contains extensive material on U.S.-UN relationships and is somewhat critical of the "big power complex" and intervention in areas like Indochina.

38:121 Rosner, Gabriella. *The United Nations Emergency Force.* New York: Columbia University Press, 1963. This broad study contains references to the attitude, policies, and role of the United States in the creation and operation of emergency forces between 1956 and 1962, with emphasis on the Middle East. Bibliography.

38:122 Stegenga, James A. "Peacekeeping: Post-Mortems or Previews?" *International Organization* 27:3 (1973), 373–85. This essay reviews James M. Boyd, *United Nations Peace-Keeping Operations: A Military and Political Appraisal* (New York: Praeger, 1971); Larry L. Fabian, *Soldiers without Enemies: Preparing the United Nations for Peacekeeping* (Washington, D.C.: Brookings Institution, 1971); Michael Harbottle, *The Blue Berets* (Harrisburg, Pa.: Stackpole, 1972); and Alan James, *The Politics of Peace-Keeping* (New York: Praeger, 1969).

38:123 Wainhouse, David W. *International Peace-keeping at the Crossroads: National Support–Experience and Prospects.* Baltimore: Johns Hopkins Press, 1973. This large study of UN experiences contains data on U.S. involvement in and support of peacekeeping operations and policies. It includes material on public opinion and the role of Congress, the Executive Office and the Defense Department.

Collective Security

See Chapter 20, "Collective Security."

38:124 Claude, Inis L., Jr. *Power and International Relations.* New York: Random House, 1962. An excellent bibliography reveals the historical perspective in this study, which focuses on balance of power and collective security concepts with some discussion of Wilsonian and U.S. policies and responses.

38:125 Hogan, Willard N. *International Conflict and Collective Security: The Principle of Concern in International Organization.* Lexington: University of Kentucky Press, 1955. A thoughtful examination of international trends toward the acceptance of the collective security idea with particular focus on the interwar years and the League of Nations, arbitration, and disarmament. U.S. responses are traced but not in a consistent way. Extensive bibliography.

38:126 Osgood, Robert E. "Woodrow Wilson, Collective Security, and the Lessons of History." In Earl Latham, ed., *The Philosophy and Policies of Woodrow Wilson.* Chicago: University of Chicago Press, 1958, pp. 187–98. Osgood places post-1945 concepts and programs of collective security into historical perspective, showing Wilson's ideological influence.

Stromberg, R. N. *Collective Security and American Foreign Policy: From the League of Nations to NATO* (20:94) focuses on the idea of collective security more than on the practice. He reviews proposals and thinking prior to 1939, and then traces the evolution of the concept during the war, culminating with NATO and the Suez crisis. Stromberg is analytic, thoughtful, and critical.

Special Topics

Korean War, 1945–1953
See Chapter 27, "U.S. and Korea, 1945–1953."

38:127 Acheson, Dean. "Review of U.N. and U.S. action to Restore Peace." *U.S. Department of State Bulletin* 23:575 (1950), 43–46. Acheson's address of June 29, 1950, on the Korean situation contains information on the decision to intervene.

38:128 Buehrig, Edward H. "The United States, the United Nations and Bi-Polar Politics." *International Organization* 4:4 (1950), 573–84. This essay perceives the UN as an effective agency for the U.S. objective of achieving a stable world. It has considerable material on Korea.

Goodrich, L. M. *Korea: A Study of U.S. Policy in the United Nations* (27:150) presents in detail U.S. efforts to involve the General Assembly and Security Council. A thoughtful conclusion summarizes the difficulties for both the United States and the United Nations.

38:129 Goodrich, Leland M. "Korea: Collective Measures against Aggression." *International Conciliation,* no. 494 (1953), 129–92. Goodrich covers the UN response in 1950, noting U.S. initiatives, and then reviews subsequent actions. The perspective is balanced and thorough for a contemporary study.

Gordenker, L. *The United Nations and the Peaceful Unification of Korea: The Politics of Field Operations, 1947–1950* (27:151) focuses on the decisions and actions of the UN; he provides insight into U.S. attitudes and policies prior to 1950, paying careful attention to relations with various commissions which sought to resolve problems and examines issues that frustrated solutions.

38:130 Hoyt, Edwin C. "The United States Reaction to the Korean Attack. . . ." *American Journal of International Law* 55:1 (1961), 45–76. Hoyt examines the applicable principles and declarations under international law, focusing on the UN Charter, which led to involvement in Korea and the decision to isolate Formosa. He reveals the attitudes of public and political leaders and is critical of the limited perspective given to international law.

38:131 Lyons, Gene M. "American Policy and the United Nations' Program for Korean Reconstruction." *International Organization* 12:2 (1958), 180–92. An historical review of UN programs and actions and U.S. responses, with a focus on 1951 to 1953, it contains an analysis of why the United States elected to channel its relief through the defense program.

Paige, G. D. *The Korean Decision, June 24–30, 1950* (27:183) includes the beliefs of policymakers that they were strengthening the UN and collective security principles, and analyzes and evaluates the decision-makers and their responses.

38:132 Truman, Harry S. "Communist Attack on Korea a Violation of U.N. Charter." *Vital Speeches of the Day* 16:20 (1950), 610–12. Truman's radio address

to the American people explains the reason for involvement in Korea.

Congo Crisis, 1960–1964

See "Personalities," especially Dag Hammarskjöld, U Thant; also see Chapter 37, "Congo Crisis, 1960–1964."

38:133 Gendebien, Paul-Henry. *L'Intervention des Nations Unies au Congo, 1960–1964* [The United Nations intervention in the Congo, 1960–1964]. Paris: Mouton, 1967. A Dutch scholar examines the UN's operations and finds that despite many difficulties the intervention did maintain the Congo's territorial integrity and limit the violence and chaos.

38:134 Lefever, Ernest W. "U.S. Policy: The UN and the Congo." *Orbis* 11:2 (1967), 394–413. Lefever expresses concern over U.S. involvement in an area usually regarded as outside the sphere of direct American interest.

U Thant. *View from the UN* (38:82) discusses his role in settling the Congo affair after the death of Dag Hammarskjöld (pp. 95–153).

Vietnam War, 1964–1972

See Chapter 30, "U.S. and the Indochina Wars."

Bloomfield, L. P. *The U.N. and Vietnam* (30:223).

Falk, R. A., ed. *The Vietnam War and International Law* (30:13) provides an overview of the various major positions American international legal scholars have taken on the character and consequences of American involvement on world order.

Johnson, W. "The U Thant-Stevenson Peace Initiatives in Vietnam, 1964–1965" (30:225) notes the frustrating experience faced by Stevenson, whose recommendations were largely ignored by the Johnson administration.

SPECIALIZED AGENCIES

38:135 Alcock, Antony E. *History of the International Labour Organisation.* London: Macmillan, 1971. This work by an English scholar touches on U.S.

relationships to the ILO, but it does not focus on American involvement. Bibliography.

38:136 De Capello, H. H. Krill. "The Creation of the United Nations Educational, Scientific and Cultural Organization." *International Organization* 24:1 (1970), 1–30. This article examines the Conference of Ministers of Education of the Allied Governments (1942–1945), and the 1945 Conference of the United Nations for the Establishment of an International Organization for Education and Culture. The author provides an informative account of the way in which American negotiators modified the proposals of their British and French counterparts.

38:137 Finger, Seymour M. "United States Policy toward International Institutions." *International Organization* 30:2 (1976), 347–60. Finger discusses the need for close cooperation with international institutions in U.S. foreign policy in the 1970s and considers the roles of NATO, the World Bank and other UN agencies, the International Monetary Fund, and the International Atomic Energy Agency.

38:138 Fox, Grace. "The Origins of UNRRA." *Political Science Quarterly* 65:4 (1950), 561–84. The development of the UNRRA agreement and the preliminary work of Herbert H. Lehman as director of foreign relief and rehabilitation operations.

38:139 Gardner, Richard N., and Millikan, Max F., eds. *The Global Partnership: International Agencies and Economic Development*. New York: Praeger, 1968. This account contains extensive data on the participation of the United States in a wide variety of international economic agencies, commissions, and banks, plus foreign aid, development, and lending policies. Extensive bibliography.

38:140 Lyons, Gene M.; Baldwin, David A.; and McNemar, Donald W. "The Politicization Issue in the UN Specialized Agencies." *Proceedings of the Academy of Political Science* 32:4 (1977), 81–92. In recent years the U.S. commitment to the specialized agencies of the UN has declined. Developing nations dominate these agencies and use them to seek support for their own national development and to promote a new world economic order.

38:141 Sewell, James P. *UNESCO and World Politics: Engaging in International Relations*. Princeton, N.J.: Princeton University Press, 1975. This general history provides background on UNESCO's origins, founding, and development. Luther Evans, director-

general (1953–1958), and other Americans who served as deputy director-generals are discussed along with U.S. policies in relation to UNESCO programs, budgets, and objectives.

38:142 Smithies, Arthur. "The U.S., the U.N. and the Underdeveloped World." *Orbis* 2:3 (1958), 337–55. The author sees U.S. military aid and alliances and cold war postures restrictive of efforts to extend aid through multilateral channels.

International Mandates and Trusteeships

38:143 Chowdhuri, Ramendra N. *International Mandates and Trusteeship Systems: A Comparative Study*. The Hague: Nijhoff, 1955. This comprehensive study contains an evaluation of the administration by the United States of its Pacific Islands under a trusteeship (1945–1955), with special insight into its origins. Bibliography.

De Smith, S. A. *Microstates and Micronesia: Problems of America's Pacific Islands and Other Minute Territories* (32:168) is a detailed assessment by an English scholar of the trust administration under the UN of Micronesia, including background, problems, and economy.

38:144 Murray, James N., Jr. *The United Nations Trusteeship System*. Urbana: University of Illinois Press, 1957. Murray briefly describes and analyzes U.S. attitudes toward mandates prior to 1945 and trusteeship arrangements in the Pacific under United Nations. Extensive bibliography.

U.S. and the United Nations

38:145 Barber, Hollis W. "The United States vs. the United Nations." *International Organization* 27:2 (1973), 139–63. A critical analysis of the gap between promise and performance which examines responses to the two Chinas, financial support, posture toward ministates, decolonization, and the ILO.

38:146   Bloomfield, Lincoln P. *The United Nations and U.S. Foreign Policy: A New Look at the National Interest.* 3d ed. London: University of London Press, 1969. Bloomfield describes the changing responses of the United States (1945–1967) on legal, economic, and human rights issues, and on armaments, colonialism, space, and peacekeeping. He includes valuable information on policy goals and strategies, with some perspective on developments.

38:147   Claude, Inis L., Jr. *The Changing United Nations.* New York: Random House, 1967. This short interpretive work contains observations on U.S. contacts, policies, and assumptions underlying relationships with the UN (1945–1967). One chapter describes UN cold war rivalries. Bibliography.

38:148   Graves, James A. "A Study of the Legal and Organizational Relationships of International Organizations and Their Host States: With Emphasis on the United Nations and the United States." Ph.D. diss., University of Kentucky, 1965. This account contains much that will interest historians who wish to examine the early years of the UN (1945–1954). The author covers such topics as the UN's legal jurisdiction, taxation powers, diplomatic immunity, and security maintenance.

38:149   Gross, Franz B., ed. *The United States and the United Nations.* Norman: University of Oklahoma Press, 1964. These essays examine the impact of the UN on U.S. policy and note changes in the UN and shifts in U.S. policy. Essays by H. K. Jacobson, "Economic and Social Matters," Waldo Chamberlin, "Arms Control and Limitation," and Franz B. Gross, "The United States National Interests and the United Nations," are historically oriented.

38:150   Haviland, H. Field, Jr. "The United States and the United Nations." *International Organization* 19:3 (1965), 643–65. This is a general outline of U.S.-UN contacts and of responses to issues, crises, and programs.

38:151   Hazzard, Shirley. *Defeat of an Ideal: A Study of the Self-Destruction of the United Nations.* Boston: Little, Brown, 1973. This is a critical review of the dominant role of the United States by a former staff member of the Secretariat.

38:152   Hula, Erich. "The United States and the United Nations." In Robert A. Goldwin, ed., *Beyond the Cold War: Essays on American Foreign Policy in a Changing World Environment.* Chicago: Rand-

McNally, 1965, pp. 216–35. This reappraisal of the UN and U.S. policy (1945–1963) is based on a general review of trends and problems.

38:153   Hyde, L. K., Jr. *The United States and the United Nations: Promoting the Public Welfare: Examples of American Co-operation, 1945–1955.* New York: Manhattan, 1960. This study, by a former member of the U.S. mission to the UN, analyzes the U.S. role in the UN (1945–1955) to indicate general trends or policies. It covers planning, formation, human rights, refugees, and the development of economic, social, and specialized agencies. Hyde generally avoids political issues.

38:154   Kuehl, Warren F. "The Principle of Responsibility for Peace and National Security, 1920–1973." *Peace and Change* 3:2/3 (1975), 84–93. An interpretive essay showing the evolution of an idea promoted by internationalists (1920–1945), which called for U.S. involvement to maintain peace. This principle of responsibility reached a logical culmination (1945–1973), marked by membership in the UN, alliance systems, containment, acceptance of a unilateral role as policeman of the world, and a general endorsement of the idea of collective security.

38:155   Riggs, Robert E. *US/UN: Foreign Policy and International Organization.* New York: Appleton-Century-Crofts, 1971. Concerned more with policy structure and objectives than with historical narrative, it contains considerable background information. The range of topics is impressive covering social, economic, political, intellectual, and general interrelationships on an international scale. Extensive bibliography.

38:156   Schiff, Martin. "The United States and the United Nations: On a Collision Course." *Orbis* 18:2 (1974), 553–81. This review of the declining influence of the United States in the UN (1955–1973) documents the growth of Third World countries and the Soviet bloc. It also notes efforts to alter the UN and to counter U.S. policies.

38:157   U.S. Senate. Committee on Foreign Relations. *Review of the United Nations Charter: A Collection of Documents.* Sen. Doc. 87. 83d Cong., 2d Sess., 1954. This report contains both UN and U.S. statements, resolutions, reports, communications, and other proposals used in considering possible charter changes one decade after the UN's founding. The Foreign Relations Committee also issues periodic reports which review the participation of the United States in the United Nations.

CREATING THE UN, 1941–1945

See "Personalities," especially Clark M. Eichelberger (under "Diplomats," "Others"), Cordell Hull, Edward R. Stettinius, Jr., Arthur H. Vandenberg.

38:158 Campbell, Thomas M. *Masquerade Peace: America's UN Policy, 1944–1945.* Tallahassee: Florida State University Press, 1973. Campbell focuses on efforts by policy leaders to develop a UN reflecting U.S. traditions and aspirations, showing how American actions to achieve a democratic and economically open world contributed to the origins of the cold war. Bibliography.

38:159 Campbell, Thomas M. "Nationalism in America's UN Policy, 1944–1945." *International Organization* 27:1 (1973), 25–44. An interpretive essay which finds the universalist ideas of Hull, supported by Roosevelt, were undermined by critics, especially from the military, because of concern over Soviet designs. This eroded the strength of the UN because Truman heeded nationalist voices.

38:160 Divine, Robert A. *Second Chance: The Triumph of Internationalism in America during World War II.* New York: Atheneum, 1967. Internationalists took advantage of the wartime reaction against prewar isolationism to mobilize public support for the future United Nations. This study focuses on both private groups and public leaders and reveals the ambivalent attitudes of Franklin Roosevelt toward international organization. Extensive bibliography.

38:161 Gross, Leo. "The Charter of the United Nations and the Lodge Reservations." *American Journal of International Law* 41:3 (1947), 531–54. Gross examines the Lodge Reservations and the fear that the British empire would possess six votes in the League of Nations compared to one for the United States. He finds no parallel concern over unequal voting strength for the U.S.S.R. in the UN in this comparison of the League of Nations and the United Nations.

Notter, H. A. *Postwar Foreign Policy Preparation, 1939–1945* (25:74) is the official history of State Department planning for the future peace. The book is most helpful in revealing the changing personnel and committees charged with postwar planning within the State Department.

38:162 Pasvolsky, Leo. "The United States and the United Nations." In Quincy Wright, ed., *A Foreign Policy for the United States.* Chicago: University of Chicago Press, 1947, pp. 75–88. This review by a key administrator of planning for the UN (1941–1945) within the State Department shows an awareness of broad issues. It reflects a sense of responsibility by administrative leaders at the time and for the future.

38:163 Russell, Ruth B., assisted by Muther, Jeannette E. *A History of the United Nations Charter: The Role of the United States, 1940–1945.* Washington, D.C.: Brookings Institution, 1958. This massive study of U.S. governmental planning for the UN, based on privileged access to State Department records, traces the major role played by American officials, notably Cordell Hull, Sumner Welles, and Leo Pasvolsky, in shaping the eventual UN Charter. Nearly half the book deals with the final drafting of the charter at San Francisco.

38:164 Sweetser, Arthur. "The United States, the United Nations and the League of Nations." *International Conciliation,* no. 418 (1946), 51–59. Sweetser reviews the reversal in policy (1939–1945), leading to membership in the UN and describes the role of the United States toward League agencies (1940–1945).

38:165 Tiwari, Shreesh C. *Genesis of the United Nations: A Study of the Development of the Policy of the United States of America in Respect of the Establishment of a General International Organization . . . , 1941–1945.* Varanasi, India: Naivedya Niketan, 1968. This study of U.S. involvement in the creation of the UN by an Indian scholar is of special interest because of its perspective. It contains insights into political attitudes and the internal formulation of policies.

Politics and Public Opinion

38:166 Culbertson, Ely. *Total Peace: What Makes Wars and How to Organize Peace.* Garden City, N.Y.: Doubleday, Doran, 1943. This widely discussed book helped develop favorable attitudes toward international organization during the war and the world federation movement in the late 1940s.

Darilek, R. E. *A Loyal Opposition in Time of War: The Republican Party and the Politics of Foreign*

Policy from Pearl Harbor to Yalta (23:33) examines the reasons why Republican leaders opted for bipartisanship on the UN issue during World War II, concluding that it was primarily a matter of political expediency. His analysis sustains in greater detail the broader study by Westerfield (2:155).

38:167 Riggs, Robert E. "Overselling the UN Charter—Fact or Myth." *International Organization* 14:2 (1960), 277–90. This analysis of the propaganda campaign (1944–1945) to persuade the American people to accept the UN dispels the myth that the promises and descriptions were starry-eyed. A realistic awareness pervaded speeches and literature.

38:168 Robins, Dorothy B. *Experiment in Democracy: The Story of U.S. Citizens' Organizations in Forging the Charter of the United Nations.* New York: Parkside, 1971. Despite this study's drawbacks, it contains useful information about the citizen organizations and, perhaps most important, includes an excellent 82-page appendix containing scores of documents bearing on the public campaign for the United Nations. Bibliography.

Westerfield, H. B. *Foreign Policy and Party Politics: Pearl Harbor to Korea* (2:155) traces the evolution of a bipartisan approach to foreign policy in the 1940s with emphasis on the UN issue. Westerfield pays special attention to the role of Republican leaders in striving to keep postwar world organization out of partisan politics.

38:169 Willkie, Wendell. *One World.* New York: Simon & Schuster, 1943. A ghost-written account by the 1940 presidential candidate of a wartime trip to Russia, China, and the Middle East which became an instantaneous best seller. Its popularity demonstrated the receptiveness of the American people to the vague, idealistic internationalism that Willkie preached.

San Francisco Conference, 1945

Louis, W. R. *Imperialism at Bay: The United States and the Decolonization of the British Empire, 1941–1945* (25:119) focuses on what later became the trusteeship system of the UN.

Ritchie, C. S. A. *The Siren Years: A Canadian Diplomat Abroad, 1937–1945* (36:50) covers his experiences at the San Francisco Conference.

Tillapaugh, J. "Closed Hemisphere and Open Door? The Dispute over Regional Security at the U.N. Conference, 1945" (35:96) argues that confusion over regional versus global security arrangements led Latin American nations, who saw in the Act of Chapultepec (1944) their protection from local aggression and U.S. interference, to force the issue. The dispute over regional security was not an attempt by the United States to control the western hemisphere.

38:170 U.S. Department of State. *Charter of the United Nations: Report to the President on the Results of the San Francisco Conference.* Washington, D.C.: G.P.O., 1945. This is the report of the U.S. delegation.

38:171 U.S. Department of State. *The United Nations Conference on International Organization: Selected Documents with Historical Background.* Conference Series 83, Publ. no. 2490. Washington, D.C.: G.P.O., 1946. Provides documentary material on U.S. positions and its role at the San Francisco Conference.

38:172 U.S. Senate. Committee on Foreign Relations. Hearings; *The Charter of the United Nations.* 79th Cong., 1st Sess., 1945.

Woods, R. B. "Conflict or Community? The United States and Argentina's Admission to the United Nations" (35:97) shows the pressures within the United States for favorable action and the Soviet Union's arguments against entry. The principles of nonintervention and sovereignty prevailed over resentments toward Argentina's wartime policy.

U.S. AND UN SINCE 1945

See "Personalities," especially Warren R. Austin, Daniel P. Moynihan, Adlai E. Stevenson, Harry S. Truman, and, under "Diplomats," "Others," William F. Buckley, Jr., Henry Cabot Lodge, Andrew Young, James L. Wadsworth.

38:173 Bloomfield, Lincoln P. "The United Nations in Crisis—The Role of the United Nations in United States Foreign Policy." *Daedalus* 91:4 (1962), 749–65. This is a full discussion of U.S.-UN policy (1960–1962) from the perspective of cold war rivalries, anticolonialism, alliance systems, and the Congo crisis.

38:174 Bloomfield, Lincoln P. "American Policy toward the UN—Some Bureaucratic Reflections." *International Organization* 12:1 (1958), 1–16. Bloomfield selected eight criteria to discuss policy: extravagant pronouncements, tests for official action, the U.S. mission and its relationship to the State Department, the assistant secretary of state for international organization affairs, specialists, funding, and policymaking processes.

38:175 Cohen, Benjamin V. "The Impact of the United Nations on United States Foreign Policy." *International Organization* 5:2 (1951), 274–81. This is a review of U.S. policies (1945–1951) toward former Italian colonies in Africa, Indonesia, Palestine, Iran, and Korea, and the impact of the UN on U.S. programs and perceptions.

38:176 "Five Goals of U.S. Foreign Policy [Transcript of Television Program Broadcast September 24, 1962]." *U.S. Department of State Bulletin* 47:1216 (1962), 547–58. A valuable document which shows the position and attitudes of Dean Rusk, Robert S. McNamara, George W. Ball, Fowler Hamilton, Adlai E. Stevenson, and W. W. Rostow toward the UN, foreign aid, international sanctions, and their relationship to cold war attitudes.

38:177 Fleming, Denna F. "The United States in the United Nations." *Annals of the American Academy of Political and Social Science,* no. 278 (1951), 73–82. Fleming examines the record of U.S. leadership in the UN, covering policies related to Iran, Berlin, Spain, and Korea. He also discusses the Acheson Plan.

38:178 Gaskill, Gordon. "Timetable of a Failure." *Virginia Quarterly Review* 34:2 (1958), 161–91. Issues within the UN in 1956, especially the Hungarian question, are analyzed from the perspective of the "failure" of Henry Cabot Lodge.

38:179 Gross, Franz B. "The U.S. National Interest and the UN." *Orbis* 7:2 (1963), 367–85. This essay reviews policies noting various dilemmas, the searches for an effective strategy, difficulties of decisionmaking, postures toward issues, and the problems faced by the United States (1945–1963) in shifting to multilateral diplomacy.

38:180 Higgins, Benjamin H. *United Nations and U.S. Foreign Economic Policy.* Homewood, Ill.: Irwin, 1962. Higgins reviews objectives and processes of U.S. economic policy and covers UN influences in determining such matters as foreign economic assistance, trade, development, banking, technical assistance, and all the related problems.

38:181 Mangone, Gerard J. "United States Foreign Policy and the United Nations." In Stephen K. Bailey, ed., *American Politics and Government: Essays in Essentials.* New York: Basic Books, 1965, pp. 239–50. This concise and useful summary of U.S. attitudes and policies covers 1945 to 1965.

38:182 Mazuzan, George T. "America's U.N. Commitment, 1945–1953." *Historian* 40:2 (1978), 309–30. A study of internationalist efforts and hopes through the work of Warren Austin, it is a useful summary of Mazuzan's biography and also covers the major issues that arose and U.S. responses.

38:183 McNemar, Donald W. "The United States and the United Nations." In David A. Baldwin, ed., *America in an Interdependent World: Problems of United States Foreign Policy.* Hanover, N.H.: University Press of New England, 1976, pp. 315–46. A general review of U.S.-UN relations (1974–1976), which focuses on the "utility of the U.N. for American foreign policy," the possibility of reform, and new strategies.

38:184 Rajan, M. S. "United States Attitude toward Domestic Jurisdiction in the United Nations." *International Organization* 13:1 (1959), 19–37. Rajan traces the origins of the domestic jurisdictional limitation in article 27 of the Charter to U.S. concerns as he discusses the problem of interpreting the article.

38:185 Van Wagenen, Richard W. "American Defense Officials' Views on the United Nations." *Western Political Quarterly* 14:1 (1961), 104–19. The author examines the relationships which 25 Department of Defense officials see between the UN and U.S. national interest, and how military objectives can be made compatible with the goals of each.

Politics and Public Opinion

38:186 Cory, Robert H., Jr. "The Role of Public Opinion in United States Policies toward the United Nations." *International Organization* 11:2 (1957), 220–27. Cory explores whether the U.S. public was informed or uninformed, and affirms a popular belief that the UN may be averting another world war.

38:187 Gardner, Richard N., ed. *Blueprint for Peace: Being the Proposals of Prominent Americans* to the White House Conference on International Cooperation. New York: McGraw-Hill, 1966. These proposals for UN policy positions, formulated November 29–December 1, 1965, cover international law, human rights, economic development, finance, trade, space, culture, science and technology, disarmament, population, food, cultural exchange, and weather, often with historical background.

38:188 Hero, Alfred O., Jr. "The American Public and the U.N., 1954–1966." In Maurice Waters, ed., *The United Nations International Organization and Administration.* New York: Macmillan, 1967, pp. 505–21. Reprinted from the *Journal of Conflict Resolution* 10:4 (1966), 436–75, it includes analytical tables which examine national survey data and related evidence of public opinion. Hero explores national distributions of opinion, the relationship of UN attitudes toward one another and other aspects of foreign policy, and patterns of opinion reflected in social and political groups. He covers the admission of China, emergency forces, the UN as a peace agency, and developmental aid.

38:189 Manly, Chesly. *The U.N. Record: Ten Fateful Years for America.* Chicago: Regnery, 1955. Manly, representing an anti-UN position, urges U.S. withdrawal.

38:190 Michalak, Stanley J., Jr. "The Senate and the United Nations: A Study of Changing Perception." Ph.D. diss., Princeton University, 1967. This account uses the U.S.-UN relationship as a vehicle to analyze congressional—especially senatorial—influence in the foreign policy area (1945–1954). Distinguishing many varieties of internationalist and isolationist opinion in the Senate, the author provides especially useful chapters on the Vandenberg Resolution and the Korean War.

38:191 Raith, Charles A. "The Anti-UN Coalition before the Senate Foreign Relations and the House Foreign Affairs Committees during the Years 1945–1955." Ph.D. diss., University of Pennsylvania, 1962. This provocative, but poorly written, account focuses on seven right-wing, anti-UN groups, small in numbers but possessing considerable public influence. The author argues that the members of these organizations are not so much opposed to the UN itself, as that they fear U.S.-UN cooperation would alter the American economic system. Bibliography.

38:192 Scott, William A., and Withey, Stephen B. *The United States and the United Nations: The Public*

View, 1945–1955. New York: Manhattan, 1958. A valuable study which both records and analyzes satisfaction and dissatisfaction in public opinion toward the UN and particular issues that arose. These included the seating of the People's Republic of China, Korea, membership, atomic energy, the veto, and revision of the charter.

38:193 Wilcox, Francis O. "The United States Accepts Compulsory Jurisdiction." *American Journal of International Law* 40:4 (1946), 699–719. There is considerable historical perspective on congressional debate, resolutions, and the Connally and Vandenberg amendments and a thoughtful analysis of their impact.

38:194 Wooley, Wesley T., Jr. "The Quest for Permanent Peace—American Supranationalism, 1945–1947." *Historian* 35:1 (1972), 18–31. The views of prominent citizens appear in an analysis of their world perspective. James Burnham, Ely Culbertson, Norman Cousins, Robert Hutchins, Emery Reves, Clarence Streit, Raymond Gram Swing, William B. Ziff, and several world federalist and world government groups revealed considerable dissatisfaction with the UN Charter as they called for a more effective agency.

U.S. and the Veto

38:195 Campbell, Thomas M. "U.S. Motives and the Veto Power." *International Organization* 28:3 (1974), 556–60. Responding to Nelson, Campbell asserts that the U.S. originally hoped to make the UN a universalist organization by limiting use of the great power veto, but that after Dumbarton Oaks, as American fears of Soviet ambitions increased, the State Department retreated.

38:196 Nelson, Charles G. "Revisionism and the Security Council Veto." *International Organization* 28:3 (1974), 539–55. Nelson claims that Campbell overstated American enthusiasm for a universalistic approach to international organization (which would have been symbolized by a Security Council in which powers could not veto measures directed against themselves). Nelson argues that Campbell overstated the importance of Pentagon opposition to the veto power.

U.S. Mission to UN

38:197 Beichman, Arnold. *The "Other" State Department: The United States Mission to the United*

Nations—Its Role in the Making of Foreign Policy. New York: Basic Books, 1968. A study which notes the distinctive features of the mission as an operating institution sharing powers and functions with the State Department (1946–1968).

38:198 Bloomfield, Lincoln P. "United States Participation in the United Nations." In Stephen D. Kertesz, ed., *American Diplomacy in a New Era.* Notre Dame, Ind.: University of Notre Dame Press, 1961, pp. 459–91. This essay concentrates on processes, showing the State Department's structure, "chain of command," and policy formulation. It also examines funding and political considerations.

38:199 Bloomfield, Lincoln P. "The Department of State and the United Nations." *International Organization* 4:3 (1950), 400–411. In a review of the structure and operation of the UN, Bloomfield lists the many federal agencies involved as he examines the role of the State Department as the coordinating agency of U.S. participation. There is a valuable description of various bureaus and offices.

38:200 Gareau, Frederick H. "Congressional Representatives to the UN General Assembly: Corruption by Foreign Gentry?" *Orbis* 21:3 (1977), 701–24. This statistical study, with tables on voting records, shows the responses of senators before and after their participation as representatives to the General Assembly. It should be read with Robert E. Riggs, "One Small Step for Functionalism: UN Participation and Congressional Attitude Change," *International Organization* 31:3 (1977), 515–39, which also notes an increasingly favorable attitude after serving.

38:201 Richardson, Channing B. "The United States Mission to the United Nations." *International Organization* 7:1 (1953), 22–34. A description of the mission's first seven years, with emphasis on origins, duties, and role in foreign policy formulation, it is critical of the argument that the UN was a tool of U.S. policy.

U.S., SOVIET UNION, AND UN

38:202 Rubinstein, Alvin Z., and Ginsburgs, George, eds. *Soviet and American Policies in the United Nations: A Twenty-Five-Year Perspective.* New York: New York University Press, 1971. This collection includes essays by Robert G. Wesson on world outlooks, Arthur Lall on disarmament, Harold K. Jacobson on decolonization, Daniel S. Cheever on

economic development and the sea bed, James P. Sewell on security concepts, and Edward McWhinney on law.

38:203 Stoessinger, John G. *The United Nations and the Superpowers: United States–Soviet Interaction at the United Nations.* 3d ed. New York: Random House, 1973. Stoessinger seeks "to study the dynamics of the United States–Soviet Union relationship at the UN." Nine examples illustrate the behavior of both powers. These include the Congo and Suez crises, membership policy, finances, the veto, the Secretariat, human rights, and atomic energy.

38:204 Wilcox, Francis O. "United States Policy in the United Nations." In Francis O. Wilcox and H. Field Haviland, Jr., eds., *The United States and the United Nations.* Baltimore: Johns Hopkins Press, 1961, pp. 151–78. This is a review of major problems faced in the UN by the United States and its responses to them (1945–1961). Reflects the time in which it was written by revealing a healthy suspicion and fear of the Soviet Union by a former assistant secretary of state of international organization affairs.

U.S., CHINA, AND UN

38:205 Appleton, Sheldon. *The Eternal Triangle? Communist China, the United States and the United Nations.* East Lansing: Michigan State University Press, 1961. A detailed history of the "two-China problem" in the UN which traces U.S. efforts to block the seating of the People's Republic of China. It contains interesting polls of public opinion and tables of UN votes on the issue. Extensive bibliography.

38:206 Bloomfield, Lincoln P. "China, the United States, and the United Nations." *International Organization* 20:4 (1966), 653–676. This essay contains tables of votes and a review of issues and efforts to seat China.

38:207 Cheng, Peter. "Peking's Entry into the United Nations: Review and Retrospect." *Asian Forum* 4:4 (1972), 16–29. Cheng discusses the history of UN involvement with the issue of representation for the People's Republic of China and examines the changes in support for the People's Republic as revealed in voting on the issue in the General Assembly. Tables.

38:208 Erskine, Hazel. "The Polls: Red China and the UN." *Public Opinion Quarterly* 35:1 (1971),

123–35. This essay traces the changing American public opinion on the seating of mainland China in the United Nations. In the 1950s only 7 percent of Americans favored such a move, by the 1970s the figure had risen to only 35 percent; yet only 20 percent would favor leaving the UN if China were seated.

38:209 Guhin, Michael A. "The United States and the Chinese People's Republic: The Non-Recognition Policy Reviewed." *International Affairs* 45:1 (1969), 44–63. Guhin focuses on John Foster Dulles, reviewing his attitudes toward China and communism beginning in 1917 and showing a complex set of circumstances in the decisionmaking process.

38:210 Weng, Bryon S. J. *Peking's UN Policy: Continuity and Change.* New York: Praeger, 1972. The author seeks to describe the various elements influencing China's policies toward the United Nations.

Optional Paths

INTERNATIONAL LAW

38:211 Bruce, William J. "The United States and the Law of Mankind: Some Inconsistencies in American Observance of the Rule of Law." In Charles A. Barker, ed., *Power and Law: American Dilemma in World Affairs.* Baltimore: Johns Hopkins Press, 1971, pp. 85–110. The impact of multilateral agreements and the emergence of Third World countries have revealed discrepancies between U.S. professions about the integrity of international law and actual practice. Bruce notes the difficulty of obtaining Senate approval of international conventions, or gaining removal of the Connally Amendment.

Chayes, A. *The Cuban Missile Crisis: International Crises and the Role of Law* (29:118).

38:212 Clark, Grenville, and Sohn, Louis B. *World Peace through World Law: Two Alternative Plans.* 3d ed. Cambridge: Harvard University Press, 1966. This significant volume promoted discussion about peace through law in American academic and legal circles. It includes specific suggestions to strengthen the United Nations.

38:213 Corbett, Percy E. *The Growth of World Law.* Princeton, N.J.: Princeton University Press, 1971. Corbett provides a useful survey of the development of international law since 1939.

Deák, F. "Neutrality Revisited" (2:58) reviews the changes in the international system (1930–1972).

38:214 Deutsch, Karl, and Hoffmann, Stanley, eds. *The Relevance of International Law.* Cambridge, Mass.: Schenkman, 1968. Reprint 1971. This collection of essays should command the attention of students of diplomatic history, political science, and international law.

Gross, L., ed. *International Law in the Twentieth Century* (16:134) is a compilation from the *American Journal of International Law* (1907–1965) which reveals American contributions on a wide variety of subjects.

Henkin, L. *Foreign Affairs and the Constitution* [1789–1972] (2:138) discusses the American approach to international law and tribunals.

38:215 Henkin, Louis. "International Organization and the Rule of Law." In Lawrence S. Finkelstein, ed., *The United States and International Organization: The Changing Society.* Cambridge, Mass.: MIT Press, 1969, pp. 98–124. A detailed discussion of the "making of law" through the work of international agencies and organizations, the significance of the new laws, and American attitudes.

38:216 McClure, Wallace. *World Legal Order: Possible Contributions by the People of the United States.* Chapel Hill: University of North Carolina, 1960. This study places in historical perspective (1789–1960) constitutional and treaty provisions, domestic court decisions, and policymaking processes to the development of international law. The focus is on developments since 1945. Bibliography.

Nussbaum, A. *A Concise History of the Law of Nations* [1600–1954] (16:139).

38:217 Wilson, Robert R. "The International Law Standard in Recent Treaties and Agreements of the United States." *American Journal of International Law* 66:3 (1972), 526–36. Wilson discusses examples of U.S. practice (1948–1971) regarding the specification of international law as a basic standard: 1) agreements which contain specific references to international law; 2) bilateral agreements; 3) multilateral agreements applying international law as a standard, without stating what the law is; and 4) the relevance of the above to the development of international law.

World Courts

See "Personalities," especially Philip C. Jessup.

Fleming, D. F. *The United States and the World Court, 1920–1966* (20:100) covers efforts of citizens to obtain approval of membership in the Permanent Court of International Justice and the International Court of Justice. It is critical of the United States as upholder of international law.

38:218   Kitchel, Denison. *Too Grave a Risk: The Connally Amendment Issue.* New York: Morrow, 1963. Surprisingly, this is the only book devoted to this controversial subject. A foreword by Barry Goldwater documents the tone in challenging the idea of peace through law for the United States.

38:219   Preuss, Lawrence. "The International Court of Justice, the Senate, and Matters of Domestic Jurisdiction." *American Journal of International Law* 40:4 (1946), 720–36. A careful review which provides background on discussions (1945–1946) on the reservations added to Senate approval of court membership, with an historical review of American concerns from 1910 to 1945.

38:220   U.S. Department of State. *The International Court of Justice: Selected Documents Relating to the Drafting of the Statute.* Conference Series 84, Pub. no. 2491. Washington, D.C.: G.P.O., 1946. This report contains the deliberations of a committee of jurists in Washington in April 1945 which drafted the statute for the court.

Genocide Treaty

38:221   Gayner, Jeffrey B. "The Genocide Treaty." *Journal of Social and Political Studies* 2:4 (1977), 235–45. Gayner outlines the provisions of the Convention on Presentation and Punishment of the Crime of Genocide, which was initiated in 1948 and remains to be ratified by the Congress.

WORLD FEDERALISM AND ALTERNATIVE MODELS

38:222   Commission to Study the Organization of Peace. *Building Peace: Reports of the Commission to Study the Organization of Peace, 1939–1972.* 2 vols. Metuchen, N.J.: Scarecrow, 1973. The commission, under the auspices of the United Nations Association of the United States, issued periodic study reports. These began in 1939 with proposals for a new world organization. Thereafter, scholarly teams addressed issues related to security, disarmament, regional arrangements, charter review and revision. They can also be found separately, issued by various publishers, under individual titles.

38:223   Committee to Frame a World Constitution. *Preliminary Draft of a World Constitution, as Proposed and Signed by Robert N. Hutchins, et al.* Chicago: University of Chicago Press, 1948. The work of a committee funded by Anita McCormick Blaine and representative of an ardent group of world government advocates headed by Hutchins and G. A. Borgese.

38:224   Corbett, Percy E. "Congress and Proposals for International Government." *International Organization* 4:3 (1950), 383–99. Corbett reviews various proposals for world federation or government or charter revision and the contemporary drive to promote these through congressional resolutions.

38:225   Douglas, William O. *Towards a Global Federalism.* New York: New York University Press, 1968. This volume by an associate justice of the Supreme Court examines in thoughtful fashion global problems from the perspective of international law, methods of resolving disputes peacefully, human rights, trade, and foreign aid and development as it calls for a rule of law.

38:226   Hennessy, Bernard. "A Case Study of Intra-Pressure Group Conflicts: The United World Federalists." *Journal of Politics* 16:1 (1954), 76–95. This study takes a critical look at the largest world government group of the postwar era, the United World Federalists. Founded in 1947, UWF underwent an immediate surge of growth and development, only to lose momentum in the 1950s. Part of this loss of momentum, the author maintains, was due to internal difficulties.

38:227 Lent, Ernest S. "The Development of United World Federalist Thought and Policy." *International Organization* 9:4 (1955), 486–501. Lent reviews and important movement through the perspective of organizations, leaders, strategies, ideas, and programs.

Radosh, R. *Prophets on the Right: Profiles of Conservative Critics of American Globalism* (24:180) shows how anti-imperialist thinking has at least some of its roots in the Old Right. The author examines the careers of Charles A. Beard, Lawrence Dennis, John T. Flynn, Robert A. Taft, and Oswald Garrison Villard. He does much to restore clarity to their positions, long obscured by proponents of the cold war.

Wooley, W. T., Jr. "The Quest for Permanent Peace—American Supranationalism, 1945–1947" (38:194) reviews and analyzes the world government-federation movement through an examination of leading writers and their ideas, especially Clarence Streit, William B. Ziff, Ely Culbertson, Raymond Gram Swing, Norman Cousins, Robert Hutchins, and James Burnham.

38:228 Yoder, Jon A. "The United World Federalists: Liberals for Law and Order." In Charles Chatfield, ed., *Peace Movements in America*. New York: Schocken, 1973, pp. 95–115. Yoder critically analyzes the world federalists' "liberal" emphasis upon effectiveness and pragmatism that led them to compromise with the very nationalism to which, in theory, they were opposed. The result, he contends, was the rapid demise of their movement.

REGIONALISM

See "Personalities," especially Arthur H. Vandenberg.

38:229 Gibson, Carlos. "American Regionalism and the United Nations." *Annals of the American Academy of Political and Social Science,* no. 360 (1965), 120–24. Gibson examines the Monroe Doctrine and the Pan American Union (1795–1965) in an analysis of regionalism. He notes the shift from unilateral enforcement to an equal partnership, with the resulting impact upon relations toward the UN by both the U.S. and Latin American governments, all supporting the principle of regionalism.

38:230 Nye, Joseph S. "United States Policy toward Regional Organization." *International Organization* 23:3 (1969), 719–40. This study reviews the OAS, NATO, and other defense agreements, showing U.S. support for regional common markets in Latin America and Europe. Reprinted in Paul A. Tharp, comp., *Regional International Organizations* (New York: St. Martin's Press, 1971, pp. 254–72).

38:231 Streit, Clarence K. *Union Now with Britain.* New York: Harper, 1941. This volume, along with Streit's *Union Now*, first published in 1939, set the stage for intensive public discussions on the nature of any effective international organization and what role the United States should play. It greatly influenced the strong world federalist movement of the late 1940s.

HUMAN RIGHTS

See "Personalities," especially Virginia Gildersleeve (under "Diplomats," "Others"), Eleanor Roosevelt.

38:232 Birnbaum, Karl E. "Human Rights and East-West Relations." *Foreign Affairs* 55:4 (1977), 783–99. A general survey of the Soviet handling of internal dissidents and Carter's "human rights" policy designed to press a more liberal treatment. The author notes the potential for conflict between Carter's stance and détente.

38:233 Grayson, George W. "The United States and Latin America: The Challenge of Human Rights." *Current History* 76:444 (1979), 45–53ff. The author argues that Carter's human rights policy has had little effect in Latin America despite the improvement of some political conditions. More important, the United States has received greater economic benefits because of the policy.

38:234 Holcombe, Arthur N. *Human Rights in the Modern World.* New York: New York University Press, 1948. An early examination of U.S. views and policies, it analyzes the reasons for nonratification of the convention.

38:235 Kommers, Donald, and Loescher, Gilbert, eds. *Human Rights and American Foreign Policy.* Notre Dame, Ind.: University of Notre Dame Press, 1979. The essays in this volume examine the foreign policy aspects of human rights concepts and agreements, including details on monitoring of violations, the Helsinki accords, decisionmaking, strategies, and priorities.

38:236 Mower, A. Glenn, Jr. "The American Convention on Human Rights: Will It Be Effective? *Orbis* 15:4 (1972), 1147–72. The adoption of the American Convention on Human Rights in 1969 represented an important step. Implementing this accord is a more difficult matter. Compulsory machinery is lacking; the doctrine of state sovereignty militates against outside intervention to enforce compliance.

38:237 Mower, A. Glenn, Jr. *The United States, the United Nations, and Human Rights: The Eleanor Roosevelt and Jimmy Carter Eras.* Westport, Conn.: Greenwood, 1979. Beginning with a review of the UN Charter, Mower describes the influence of Roosevelt on the drafting of the declaration and on U.S. policy at the time. Her departure brought a decline in emphasis by policy leaders concerned with stability and détente until Carter vigorously revived it.

38:238 Moynihan, Daniel P. "The Politics of Human Rights." *Commentary* 64:2 (1977), 19–26. Western makers of foreign policy have long ignored human rights as an element of tactical or strategic concern. Democratic nations, not totalitarian ones, opposed the U.S. 1975 proposal to the UN for worldwide amnesty for political prisoners. But the issue of human rights is precisely where antidemocratic regimes are the weakest.

38:239 Schlesinger, Arthur M., Jr. "Human Rights and the American Tradition." *Foreign Affairs* 57:3 (1979), 503–26. The Carter administration's efforts to make human rights a basic factor in the formulation of foreign policy has produced considerable confusion and misunderstanding here and abroad. Though human rights have long been a cherished part of the American tradition, we can best work for their universal application by setting a good example at home.

38:240 U.S. House. Committee on Foreign Affairs. Hearings; *Human Rights and U.S. Foreign Policy: A Review of the Administration's Record.* 95th Cong., 1st Sess., 1977. These hearings are valuable because of an appendix which contains Department of State written responses to subcommittee questions.

U.S. House. Committee on Foreign Affairs. Hearings; *Human Rights in Nicaragua, Guatemala, and El Salvador: Implications for U.S. Policy* (34:154) reports the House Subcommittee on International Organizations consideration of alleged violations of human and political rights in these countries. Similar hearings were held on North Korea, Namibia, Uruguay, and Paraguay in 1977. Document series Y4. F76/1:H88 includes additional *Country Reports on Human Rights Practices* for each year.

38:241 U.S. House. Committee on Foreign Affairs. Hearings; *International Protection of Human Rights: The Work of International Organizations and the Role of U.S. Foreign Policy.* 93d Cong., 1st Sess., 1973. These hearings before the Subcommittee on International Organizations and Movements include the testimony of a variety of individuals, including military figures, attorneys, internationalists, and women's and labor groups. The appendixes contain drafts of legislation, conventions, lists of violations of human rights, articles, letters, and Library of Congress staff reports which note U.S. responses to violations in 1973.

38:242 U.S. House. Committee on Foreign Affairs. Report; *Human Rights in the International Community and in U.S. Foreign Policy, 1945–76.* 95th Cong., 1st Sess., 1977. The subcommittee issued this summary compilation of U.S. positions and policy. It also includes congressional legislation in force in support of human rights abroad. There are more than 50 other subcommittee reports, including several with overviews beginning in 1945.

38:243 U.S. House. Committee on Foreign Affairs. Report; *Human Rights in the World Community: A Call for U.S. Leadership.* 93d Cong., 2d Sess., 1974. A report which shows that calls for action predated the Carter administration's emphasis on human rights. It provides background on human rights as a foreign policy, reviews various conventions and programs, and recommends a strong stand against violations abroad.

38:244 Van Dyke, Vernon. *Human Rights, the United States, and World Community.* New York: Oxford University Press, 1970. This account examines the scope, philosophy, and assumptions of human rights, and analyzes U.S. policy toward conventions and the declaration.

38:245 Verdoodt, Albert. *Naissance et Signification de la Déclaration Universelle Droits de l'Homme* [Origin and significance of the Universal Declaration of Human Rights]. Collection Université Catholique de Louvain, Collection de l'École des sciences politiques et sociales, no. 175. Louvain: Warny, 1964. This is the definitive monograph on the drafting of the Universal Declaration of Human Rights by the Nuclear Committee of ECOSOC (1947–1948), which Eleanor Roosevelt chaired. Bibliography.

PEACE MOVEMENTS

See "Overviews," "Peace and Pacifism," above; also see "Personalities," especially activists Emily Greene Balch (under "Others"), Kenneth E. Boulding, A. J. Muste.

Chatfield, C., ed. *Peace Movements in America* [1890–1973] (16:97).

38:246 Conlin, Joseph R., ed. *American Anti-War Movements.* Beverly Hills, Calif.: Glencoe, 1968. In this slim volume, the author has collected a variety of sources from three centuries of American peace activism (1650–1968), ranging from the Quakers to the movement against the Vietnam War.

DeBenedetti, C. *The Peace Reform in American History* (16:26) surveys voluntary citizen peace activism (1550–1975) and emphasizes pacifism, internationalism, antimilitarism, conscientious objection, and other forms of antiwar activism.

38:247 DeBenedetti, Charles. "The American Peace Movement and the National Security State, 1941–1971." *World Affairs* 141:2 (1978), 118–29. This analysis relates peace concerns to global security needs and notes the responses of pacifists to wars and military preparedness.

38:248 Mayer, Peter, ed. *The Pacifist Conscience.* Chicago: Regnery, 1967. This book consists of a broad range of pacifist writings throughout history. Among statements by Americans in the period since 1941 are those by A. J. Muste, Dorothy Day, Martin Luther King, Jr., and C. Wright Mills. Extensive bibliography.

38:249 Nathan, Otto, and Norden, Heinz, eds. *Einstein on Peace.* New York: Schocken, 1968. This edited collection of Albert Einstein's letters and published writings recalls the famed mathematician's role, for much of his life, as a staunch opponent of war. As the comments of the editors indicate, Einstein played an important part in the post–World War II peace movement, helping to spread an awareness of the threat to humanity posed by nuclear weapons.

38:250 Rapoport, Anatol. "Changing Conceptions of War in the United States." In Ken Booth and Moorehead Wright, eds., *American Thinking about Peace and War: New Essays on American Thought and Attitudes.* New York: Barnes & Noble, 1978, pp. 59–82. By looking at public attitudes, peace researchers, the "war establishment," and the peace movement, Rapoport concentrates on views since 1945 and finds little hope that peace voices will have much effect on "the globally instituted war system."

38:251 Weinstein, James. *Ambiguous Legacy: The Left in American Politics.* New York: Watts, 1975. In this ambitious work, the author analyzes the rise and fall of three radical political movements in twentieth century America: the Socialist party, the Communist party and the New Left. The sections on the Progressive party and the New Left are relevant to an understanding of the American peace movement in the cold war era.

38:252 Wilson, E. Raymond. *Uphill for Peace: Quaker Impact on Congress.* Richmond, Ind.: Friends United, 1975. This is the first history of the Friends Committee on National Legislation. Personal and encyclopedic, it is nevertheless valuable for understanding the interaction between "respectable" peace activists and American policymakers in the cold war era.

From 1941 to 1965

Divine, R. A. *Blowing on the Wind: The Nuclear Test Ban Debate, 1954–1960* (29:144) focuses upon the public debate over nuclear weapons testing in the United States during the 1950s.

Ekirch, A. A., Jr. *The Civilian and the Military* (40:32) emphasizes the increasing militarization of American life; the last two chapters, on World War II and the postwar era, contain considerable information on antimilitary currents as well.

38:253 Finn, James, ed. *Protest, Pacifism and Politics.* New York: Random House, 1967. This collection of interviews with 38 prominent peace activists and social critics, together with brief descriptions of their roles as opponents of war, provides an account of the movement against the Vietnam War in its early years.

38:254 Glazer, Nathan. "The Peace Movement in America, 1961." *Commentary* 31:4 (1961), 288–96.

The author, then a member of a moderate peace group, writes of the state of the American peace movement in 1961. Focusing upon the National Committee for a SANE Nuclear Policy, he discusses the rift within that organization caused by the issue of Communist membership.

38:255 Katz, Milton, and Katz, Neil. "Pragmatists and Visionaries in the Post World War II American Peace Movement: SANE and CNVA." In Solomon Wank, ed., *Doves and Diplomats: Foreign Offices and Peace Movements in Europe and America in the Twentieth Century.* Westport, Conn.: Greenwood, 1978, pp. 265–88. The National Committee for a SANE Nuclear Policy and the Committee for Nonviolent Action emerged in 1957. Although they directed their initial criticism at nuclear weapons testing, they differed in their approach to antiwar activism.

38:256 Mishler, Elliot G. "The Peace Movement and the Foreign Policy Process." In Roger D. Fisher, ed., *International Conflict and Behavioral Science: The Craigville Papers.* New York: Basic Books, 1964, pp. 257–65. This speculative discussion considers the targets of peace pressure groups, the intangible yet intuitive response of policymakers, conflicts of interests over policies, and the need for a reassessment of fundamental goals before the internal policymaking system can be altered.

38:257 Naeve, Virginia, ed. *Changeover: The Drive for Peace.* Denver: Swallow, 1963. This collection of statements, essays, poems, letters, and photographs provides the reader with a grass-roots picture of the American peace movement at the outset of the 1960s. It was a growing movement, concerned about the threats of nuclear testing and nuclear war.

38:258 Newfield, Jack. *A Prophetic Minority.* Rev. ed. New York: New American Library, 1970. This book, dealing with the development of the New Left in the United States in the early 1960s, is dated, but it recaptures much of the romanticism of the early movement against the Vietnam War.

Orser, E. W. "World War II and the Pacifist Controversy in the Major Protestant Churches" (22:86) examines the impact of the war on peace ideologies, efforts, and leaders. The strong pacifist sentiment of the 1930s in religious circles eroded when faced by a crisis. Leaders like Harry Emerson Fosdick and Ernest F. Tittle failed to rally the churches to a cohesive peace position.

38:259 Pauling, Linus. *No More War!* New York: Dodd, Mead, 1958. This book provides a trenchant analysis of the dangers posed by nuclear war, a first-hand account of the scientists' movement against it, and a powerful argument for altering the nature of American "defense" in the nuclear age.

38:260 Rotblat, Joseph. *Pugwash: The First Ten Years.* New York: Humanities Press, 1968. Related by the secretary general of the Pugwash Continuing Committee, this is the story of international scientific conferences designed to counter the preparations among the great powers for thermonuclear war. The extensive appendixes range from the 1955 Einstein-Russell Manifesto, which triggered the meetings, to the statement of the first South-East Asian Regional Pugwash Conference, 1967.

38:261 Russell, Bertrand. "The Early History of the Pugwash Movement." In Seymour Melman, ed., *Disarmament: Its Politics and Economics.* Boston: American Academy of Arts and Sciences, 1962, pp. 18–31. Thanks to a 1955 appeal, by Albert Einstein and Bertrand Russell, to spare mankind from nuclear destruction, the Pugwash conferences (1955–1962) among scientists from East and West began in 1957.

38:262 Sibley, Mulford Q., and Jacob, Philip E. *Conscription of Conscience: The American State and the Conscientious Objector, 1940–1947.* Ithaca, N.Y.: Cornell University Press, 1952. This study of conscientious objectors during World War II is particularly useful for clarifying the history of the provisions for conscientious objection in the Selective Service Act of 1940 and for describing the broad range of activities engaged in by pacifists during and immediately after the war.

38:263 Smith, Alice Kimball. *A Peril and a Hope: The Scientists' Movement in America, 1945–47.* Chicago: University of Chicago Press, 1965. The author traces the atomic scientists' movement from its wartime genesis to its postwar activism. The book shows how, in the postwar era, the scientists became a political force and influenced the further development of atomic energy.

38:264 Vickers, George R. *The Formation of the New Left: The Early Years.* Lexington, Mass.: Lexington Books, 1975. This monograph demonstrates the importance of peace concerns for the emerging New Left early in the 1960s. The Student Peace Union figured briefly as a significant political action arm.

38:265 Waskow, Arthur I. *The Worried Man's Guide to World Peace.* Garden City, N.Y.: Doubleday, 1963. A survey of the work of peace activists in the early 1960s. Although not historical, it does provide insights into the thoughts, politics, and modes of action of peace activists. It contains a list of the major peace-oriented organizations and journals of the time.

38:266 Wittner, Lawrence S. *Rebels against War: The American Peace Movement, 1941–1960.* New York: Columbia University Press, 1969. Beginning with the heyday of American pacifism in the period before World War II, this work elucidates the peace movement's wartime and postwar difficulties, as well as its gradual revival after the mid-1950s. The author contends that two trends were important in the movement's renaissance: the growth of "nuclear pacifism" and the development of nonviolent resistance. Extensive bibliography.

38:267 Zinn, Howard. *SNCC: The New Abolitionists.* 2d ed. Boston: Beacon, 1965. The author has compiled a sympathetic history of the Student Non-Violent Coordinating Committee during its early, pacifist years. He stresses the civil rights organization's multidimensional radicalism and its clash with a more contented liberalism.

Since 1965

See Chapter 30, "Public Opinion and Domestic Impact."

Baskir, L. M., and Strauss, W. A. *Chance and Circumstance: The Draft, the War, and the Vietnam Generation* (30:204) is a study of the interplay between U.S. manpower requirements and policies in wartime and the 53 million men and women who came of age in the years 1964 to 1973. Especially valuable are nine charts which detail the flow of the "Vietnam generation" through draft avoidance, evasion, and exile.

38:268 Ferber, Michael, and Lynd, Staughton. *The Resistance.* Boston: Beacon, 1971. This book tells of the draft resistance movement during the Vietnam War. Beginning with its origins in a brief flurry in 1947, the book progresses through the dramatic antiwar events of 1970.

38:269 Foner, Philip S. *American Labor and the Indochina War: The Growth of Union Opposition.* New York: International Publishers, 1971. This useful introduction to a much neglected topic is especially helpful in recounting the story of the Labor Assembly for Peace, the most important liberal-labor peace coalition in recent times.

Halstead, F. *Out Now! A Participant's Account of the American Movement against the Vietnam War* (30:207) is the best available study of interworkings of the antiwar movement.

38:270 Horowitz, Irving L. *The Struggle Is the Message: The Organization and Ideology of the Anti-War Movement.* Berkeley, Calif.: Glendessary, 1970. A preliminary but thoughtful analysis of the anti-Vietnam War movement as an exercise in social protest. The study overemphasizes the place of violence in the antiwar movement. Of special use is a series of tables which detail the date, place, size, sponsorship, and incidents of violence in antiwar demonstrations (1965–1968).

38:271 Mantell, David M. *True Americanism: Green Berets and War Resisters: A Study of Commitment.* New York: Teachers College Press of Columbia University, 1974. This is a psychological analysis of how personal development shaped the content of political decisionmaking in matters regarding war and peace in the American 1960s. This study highlights the importance of family relationships in affecting war/peace decisions. Bibliography.

38:272 O'Brien, James. "The Anti-War Movement and the War." *Radical America* 8:3 (1974), 53–86. An intelligent analysis and criticism from the Left of the sources, effectiveness, and historical significance of organized opposition to the Vietnam War.

38:273 Powers, Thomas. *The War at Home: Vietnam and the American People, 1964–1968.* New York: Grossman, 1973. Powers provides a reliable account of the emergence of widespread domestic opposition to the Vietnam War. Although he exaggerates the role of "the people," he shows the relationship between mounting public protest and the vagaries of official U.S. policymaking.

38:274 Sale, Kirkpatrick. *SDS.* New York: Random House, 1973. This massive book is a history of the short-lived Students for a Democratic Society, the major organizational expression of the New Left during the 1960s. Intertwined with the struggle against the Vietnam War, it notes the rise and fall of SDS.

38:275 Useem, Michael. *Conscription, Protest, and Social Conflict: The Life and Death of a Draft Resistance Movement.* New York: Wiley, 1973. A sociological analysis of organized anticonscription activism, which represented a major force in the anti–Vietnam War movement. Useem blends comprehensible sociological categories with the changing historical context. Extensive bibliography.

39

Economic Issues and Foreign Policy

Contributing Editor

JOAN HOFF WILSON
Indiana University

Contributors

Sharon L. Bollinger
University of Wyoming

Melvyn P. Leffler
Vanderbilt University

Robert H. Van Meter, Jr.
University Without Walls,
Skidmore College

William O. Walker III
Ohio Wesleyan University

Mira Wilkins
Florida International University

Contents

Introduction

Unlike their counterparts in related disciplines, diplomatic historians have only recently shown sustained scholarly interest in systemic policy analysis of macroeconomic models. Political scientists, who have traditionally dominated the study of international relations, primarily focused on the political dimension of U.S. diplomacy. However, the paradigms they developed to explain domestic and international decisionmaking do not lend themselves to the type of factual documentation normally employed by historians. Economists, the other dominant group writing about international relations, have been largely preoccupied with statistics and systems analysis. Neglect of politics made their work even less appealing to diplomatic historians than that of political scientists.

This division between political scientists and economists has artificially separated international (and domestic) politics from international (and domestic) economics. While each has produced a body of literature rich in theory and practice, there has been little systematic analysis of the relationship of economics *to* foreign policy. Similarly, no structure exists within the federal government for coordinating the two. The Council on International Economic Policy (CIEP), created in 1971 to provide a "unified perspective" by dealing with "all aspects of international economic policy" affecting the diplomacy of the United States, is now defunct.

For a variety of reasons, therefore, historians have been reluctant to apply their synthesizing skills and multinational research techniques to international economic policy. First, there is the highly compartmentalized and theoretical nature of the literature; second, governmental reform has failed to produce a unified decisionmaking framework for analysis; and third, historians have often been inadequately trained in economics. However, a new historiographical development is overcoming the traditional hesitancy of foreign policy specialists to enter the field of international economics.

The first generation of professional diplomatic historians of the 1920s largely ignored ideological, organizational, *and* economic concepts. Instead, most of them approached foreign relations almost exclusively through the use of formal communiqués between nations, interspersed with biographical material about presidents, secretaries of state, and highly placed foreign service personnel. Occasionally, some emphasis was also placed on the presumed impact of public opinion on U.S. foreign policy. Although a few pre–World War II revisionists like Charles C. Tansill, *America Goes to War* (19:173), attempted to explain American entrance into World War I in political and economic rather than patriotic terms, it was not until the 1940s and 1950s that a significant split developed among diplomatic historians about the relationship of the political economy of the United States to its foreign policies. Initially they divided simplistically into pro- and anti-capitalist camps, which has led to an acrimonious standoff between so-called liberal realists and radical revisionists. While the former are often critical of American foreign policy, they uniformly deny that systematic economic considerations have ever been central to its formulation. The latter generally assume that "diplomacy is essentially a response to forces generated by America's economic and social structure."

Liberal realists were originally influenced by the writing of diplomat-historians like George F. Kennan, *American Diplomacy, 1900–1950* (2:111), and Herbert Feis, *The Diplomacy of the Dollar, 1919–1932* (20:178), as well as by political scientist Hans J. Morgenthau. Their point of view has been well represented over the years by Lewis Mumford, Samuel Eliot Morison, Samuel Flagg Bemis, Dexter Perkins, Arthur M. Schlesinger, Jr., Norman A. Graebner, Robert Ferrell, Robert A. Divine, and Robert W. Tucker. Post–World War II radical revisionists first looked to Charles A. Beard, *President Roosevelt and the Coming of the War, 1941* (22:261), and William A. Williams, *The Tragedy of American Diplomacy* (2:99), for inspiration. In the 1960s their economic and ideological critique of U.S. foreign policy was present in the *right and left* of center writings of Murray H. Rothbard, Walter LaFeber, Lloyd C. Gardner, Gabriel Kolko, Robert Freeman, Richard H. Miller, Richard J. Barnet, Marilyn Blatt Young, Barton J. Bernstein, and Carl P. Parrini.

This debate has reached a point of diminishing historiographical returns, especially as it has focused largely on the nature of American expansionism in the late nineteenth century and on the origins of the cold war. What is now needed is a new synthesis which does not border on either the ideological chauvinism of the liberal realists or the economic reductionism of the radical revisionists. Such a new methodological approach appears to be taking shape among a younger generation of diplomatic historians who are productively examining the "complex impact of ideological *and* economic motivation as it is affected by structural relationships and role-playing within government agencies and business organizations." In particular, they have drawn from interdisciplinary socioeconomic, psycho-organizational theories first developed by postwar entrepreneurial historians like Allan Nevins, Fritz Redlich, Thomas C. Cochran, and Edward Chase Kirkland, and sociologists like C. Wright Mills, Arnold Rose, and G. William Domhoff. These theories were later refined by work conducted at the Research Seminar on Bureaucracy, Politics and Policy of the Institute of Government in the John F. Kennedy School of Government at Harvard, under the direction of Ernest R. May, Morton H. Halperin, and Richard E. Neustadt.

Using a corporatist theory to explain the interaction of domestic and international policies, many of this new group of diplomatic historians first wrote about World War I and the 1920s, while political scientists analyzed decisions made during certain cold war crises. Instead of relying on pluralist explanations so characteristic of liberal realists or Marxists-statist interpretations typical of the radical revisionists, these historians explain in detail the ideological, organizational, and economic aspects of American foreign policy by demonstrating (often through the prosopographical technique of collective biography) how public and private leaders at home and abroad have attempted for most of this century to build a multinational system of power-sharing, bureaucratic control based on informal collaboration.

No specific name has yet been assigned to this "corporatist" approach. Basically, however, its proponents view American and other Western societies as organized "around interdependent functional groups each collaborating with the other, each endowed with public authority, each led by supposedly 'enlightened' private elites, each tied bureaucratically to the government through a patchwork pattern of public-private committees, and each cooperating with the state to manage society's affairs." To varying degrees historians Ellis Hawley, Joseph Brandes, Robert Wiebe,

N. Gordon Levin, Joseph S. Tulchin, Joan Hoff-Wilson, Melvyn P. Leffler, Robert H. Van Meter, Burton I. Kaufman, Irvine H. Anderson, Robert Neal Seidel, Thomas G. Paterson, and Frank Costigliola can be considered part of this new school's attempt to explain domestic and foreign relations. Such methodology and interpretation can be found in Michael J. Hogan, *Informal Entente: The Private Structure of Cooperation in Anglo-American Economic Diplomacy* (20:191), and the essays in William H. Becker and Samuel F. Wells, Jr., eds., *Economics and American Diplomacy: An Assessment* (39:8).

Most important, this latest historiographical school clearly recognizes that aside from war and its prevention, foreign economics is what international relations is all about. Economic negotiations now constitute the most substantial and difficult component of global problems between nations. Yet economic policymaking, as related to bureaucratic politics, remains less investigated than defense decisionmaking or the closely related political-strategic field of foreign policymaking. With formal or self-taught training in economics and armed with theories about corporation, decisionmaking, and the functioning of elite groups, historians will increasingly find fruitful research into the domestic influences on international economic positions taken by nations. The essays edited by Peter J. Katzenstein in *Between Power and Plenty: Foreign Economic Policies of Advanced Industrial Nations* (39:15) indicate the usefulness of this approach.

Likewise, economic theories about worldwide allocation of scarce resources and political science theories about power relations at home and abroad are no longer studied as separate entities. Instead, interdisciplinary methodological approaches are developing systematic conceptual frameworks of analysis which permit a discussion of the global distribution of resources in relation to, not separate from, domestic and foreign power blocs. Graham Allison and Peter Szanton, *Remaking Foreign Policy* (39:26), I. M. Destler, *Making Foreign Economic Policy* (39:66), and Robert A. Pastor, *Congress and the Politics of U.S. Foreign Economic Policy, 1929–1976* (39:30), utilize some of these new models and techniques. Finally, organizational problems impeding the decisionmaking process and thwarting the coordination of American political and economic goals at the federal and international levels are more urgent subjects of research than ever before.

Turning from policymaking methodology to specific research topics, it becomes clear that major changes which occurred in the international money system in the early 1970s have encouraged scholars to turn from isolated case studies of U.S. economic foreign policy toward examining the general impact of the American political economy on the world in this century and especially since World War II. The breakdown in 1971 of the so-called liberal international economic system based on the 1944 Bretton Woods monetary agreement also threatened the other postwar pillar of international economics, the General Agreement on Tariffs and Trade. These developments, along with the commodity crisis of 1973–1974, dramatically highlighted a new sense of awareness about mutual dependency among both decisionmakers and researchers. Economic interdependence is not a new concept. It has been publicly debated since World War I. Until the 1970s, however, countries indulged in the practice of talking about interdependency without trying to reconcile it with repeated outbursts of national independence. No nation now has that luxury.

It also became increasingly evident in the 1970s that regional economic blocs represent the most significant change in geopolitics since World War II and prime topics of research for scholars. Pragmatic regionalism rather than ideological or idealistic internationalism is now the key to understanding geopolitical economic practices. The economic equality among the United States, the European Economic Community (EEC), and Japan is an example of a most significant regional configuration. Japan's attempts to establish regional hegemony through agreements with the ASEAN nations (Thailand, Malaysia, Singapore, the Philippines, and Indonesia) simply emulate early attempts by the EEC to establish preferential access to the ACP nations of Africa, the Caribbean, and the Pacific through the 1975 Lomé Agreement. Both are clear indications of economic regionalism as was the creation in 1978 of the European Monetary System, which plans to create a European currency unit by 1982. In addition to regional competition among the advanced industrial states, actions by OPEC and demands for a new economic order from less developed nations also highlight geographical considerations. Lastly, the deficiencies of what has been called the "macho factor" in the conduct of world affairs, particularly as it has impeded efforts to overcome poverty in less developed nations, constitutes an important new area of research.

The field of international economic policy clearly represents one of the most important research frontiers for diplomatic historians to explore in the last quarter of the twentieth century. Despite their late start in this field, diplomatic historians may use it as a methodological and interpretative vehicle for transcending the current stalemate between liberal realists

and radical revisionists to create a new post–cold war historiographical synthesis.

Resources and Overviews

RESEARCH AIDS

While pertinent bibliographies and reference aids are listed here, there are more extensive lists in Chapter 1.

Bibliographies

39:1 Amstutz, Mark R. *Economics and Foreign Policy: A Guide to Information Sources.* Detroit: Gale, 1977. This guide examines the most important information sources relating to economics and foreign policy rather than separating international economics from international politics. Amstutz annotates more than 750 books and articles and presents a brief introductory history of various schools of thought in this burgeoning new field.

Aufricht, H. *Guide to League of Nations Publications: A Bibliographical Survey of the Work of the League, 1920–1947* (20:6) has extensive financial and economic sections. It should be used in conjunction with Edward Reno's *League of Nations Documents, 1919–1946* (20:7).

39:2 Bivinic, Mayra. *Women and World Development: An Annotated Bibliography.* Washington, D.C.: American Association for the Advancement of Science, 1976. A companion volume to Tinker and Bramsen's collection of essays, *Women and World Development* (39:21), this is the only published annotated bibliography on the subject.

Conover, H. F. *A Guide to Bibliographical Tools for Research in Foreign Affairs* (1:3) includes specialized sources for regional studies, including early UN material. All items are annotated and many economic monographs and general economic reference sources are included.

39:3 Daniels, Lorna M. *Business Information Sources*. Berkeley: University of California Press, 1976. This annotated bibliography contains information on computerized sources and a separate chapter covering foreign economic statistics and foreign economic trends. It emphasizes recent material in the English language published in the United States.

Fatemi, A. M. S.; Kokoropoulos, P.; and Amirie, A. *Political Economy of the Middle East: A Computerized Guide to the Literature* (33:7) includes references to vital economic and political sources.

Field, Norman S. *League of Nations and United Nations Monthly List of Selected Articles: Cumulative, 1920–1970* (20:1) contains many references to international economic policy.

Foreign Affairs Bibliography: A Selected and Annotated List of Books on International Relations [1919–1972] (1:15) is not as useful on economic matters as most students and specialists now require. Although each volume has an "Economic Factors" section, most of them (with the exception of the last volume) were compiled before international economic policy became a major consideration of American historians of foreign policy.

Hernes, H. *The Multinational Corporation: A Guide to Information Sources* (1:31).

39:4 International Monetary Fund. *Catalogue of Publications 1946–71*. Washington, D.C.: International Monetary Fund, 1972. This catalogue lists all publications and documents issued by the fund for public use. The documents were originally prepared for use within the fund and are, therefore, particularly useful for those interested in the structural procedures as well as policy formulation. Most entries are in English.

39:5 International Monetary Fund and International Bank for Reconstruction and Development. Joint Library. *Economics and Finance: Index to Periodical Articles, 1947–1971*. 4 vols. *Supplementary Volume, 1972–1974*. Boston: G. K. Hall, 1972–1976. This excellent source reviews nearly 800 American and foreign journals on technology and economics. The individual volumes are arranged by geographical area, except for the first one which focuses on theoretical and descriptive economics, including special subjects such as gold, Eurodollars, and GATT. The subject classifications have been expanded in the first supplement.

Khawas, M. A. el-, and Kornegay, F. A., Jr., eds. *American-Southern Africa Relations: Bibliographic Essays* (1:113) contains a useful essay covering U.S. investments in the area.

Lall, S. *Foreign Private Manufacturing Investment and International Corporations: An Annotated Bibliography* (1:32).

Molineu, H., comp. *Multinational Corporations and International Investment in Latin America: A Selected and Annotated Bibliography. . . .* (1:33).

Schulz, A. *International and Regional Politics in the Middle East and North Africa: A Guide to Information Sources* (33:14) provides annotated references which deal with post–1945 foreign policy and economic issues, especially oil.

Wheeler, L. J. *International Business and Foreign Trade: Information Sources* (1:34).

Document Collections

More general collections are listed in Chapter 2.

Daniels, L. M. *Business Information Sources* (39:3) contains a separate chapter covering foreign economic statistics and foreign economic trends.

Ghébali, V. Y., and Ghébali, C. *A Repertoire of League of Nations Serial Documents, 1919–1947* (1:325) provides each section, including the financial and economic, with a selected bibliography. It is not an inventory of individual documents, but a survey of all the known *series* of documents. There is also a detailed introduction to classification systems used by the League of Nations.

39:6 International Monetary Fund. *Balances of Payments Yearbook, 1948–*. Washington, D.C.: International Monetary Fund, 1948–. These statistics are drawn largely from balance of payment statements sent to the fund by member countries subject to amendment by the fund staff in order to achieve greater intercountry comparability.

Reno, E. A., Jr., ed. *League of Nations Documents, 1919–1946: A Descriptive Guide and Key to the Microfilm Collection* (20:7) is a guide to documents, which includes extensive financial and economic sections, should be used in conjunction with Hans Aufricht's *Guide to League of Nations Publications* (20:6).

OVERVIEWS

39:7   Bauer, Robert A. *The Interaction of Economics and Foreign Policy*. Charlottesville: University of Virginia Press, 1975. Of particular interest is Richard J. Trethewey's essay on a theoretical framework to distinguish political and economic aspects of international relations; John R. Karlik's review of the economic factors influencing American foreign policy; and Fritz Bock's description of the impact of international economic factors on the conduct of foreign policy.

39:8   Becker, William H., and Wells, Samuel F., Jr., eds. *Economics and American Diplomacy: An Assessment*. New York: Columbia University Press, 1981. These eight essays span the period from 1789 to the present. The authors analyze the degree economic change at home and abroad has influenced American foreign policy at different times and examine such topics as America's place in the global economy, the relative importance of economic factors in shaping major diplomatic decisions, the economic assumptions and objectives of the policymakers, and the operation and influence of pressure groups.

39:9   Boulding, Elise. *Women: The Fifth World*. Headline Series, no. 248. New York: Foreign Policy Association, 1980. It is Boulding's contention that one of the major reasons that industrial powers have failed to overcome poverty in the less developed nations is that for decades male development planners "ignored the *fifth world,* that special set of spaces in every society where women carry out their productive roles."

39:10   Cohen, Benjamin J., ed. *American Foreign Economic Policy: Essays and Comments*. New York: Harper & Row, 1968. This collection contains some classic essays on a wide variety of economic issues facing foreign policy decisionmakers following World War II. In addition to Cohen's opening essay analyzing general principles, three specific problem areas are singled out: international finance; economic relations within the industrialized world; and U.S. economic policy toward communist and Third World countries. Bibliography.

39:11   Cohen, Stephen D. *The Making of United States International Economic Policy: Principles,* *Problems and Proposals for Reform*. New York: Praeger, 1977. This is an attempt to supply facts, concepts, and proposals to provide a constructive, effective, and consistent U.S. international economic policy through 1) understanding what this policy phenomenon is; 2) knowledge of the major variables and constants in the policymaking process; and 3) reorganizing the decisionmaking process.

Donovan, J. C. *The Cold Warriors: A Policy-Making Elite* (24:230).

39:12   Friedman, Irving S., and Garritsen, Margaret M. *Foreign Economic Problems of Postwar United States*. New York: American Institute of Pacific Relations, 1947. The authors, associated with the International Monetary Fund, present a general factual review of American economic foreign policy since 1929 and advocate the establishment of a multilateral system of trade once postwar reconstruction has taken place. They are very critical of the narrow commercial policies the United States pursued in the 1930s.

39:13   Harris, Seymour E., ed. *Foreign Economic Policy for the United States*. Cambridge: Harvard University Press, 1948. This volume contains sections covering policy and administration, individual country and area studies, international economic cooperation, the postwar European Recovery Program, and problems of international economic disequilibrium. It represents the best of "establishment" postwar thought on these complicated international economic questions.

39:14   Horowitz, David, ed. *Corporations and the Cold War*. New York: Monthly Review Press, 1969. The essays, written from a revisionist perspective, on the role of business in shaping American foreign policy, concentrate on the postwar period.

39:15   Katzenstein, Peter J., ed. *Between Power and Plenty: Foreign Economic Policies of Advanced Industrial States*. Madison: University of Wisconsin Press, 1978. This is a provocative collection based on research into domestic and foreign policies of the major industrial nations: the United States, Britain, West Germany, Italy, France, and Japan. All the essays point up the fact that "lack of action, or inappropriate action, taken in domestic politics often leads to serious consequences in the international political economy."

39:16   Kindleberger, Charles P. "U.S. Foreign Economic Policy, 1776–1976." *Foreign Affairs* 55:2

(1977), 395–417. A sweeping view of the American role in international economic affairs which concentrates on the period after 1920. Essentially an apolitical, conventional description which denies all revisionist interpretations of the past and suggestions for the future, it concludes that the internationalization of monetary policy is inevitable in an interdependent world and that the United States "must be prepared to contribute to the public good of management of the international economic system in the long run, and to respond to crises, applying different rules and standards to each, striving not to let the one corrupt the other."

LaFeber, W. *The New Empire: An Interpretation of American Expansion, 1860–1898* (12:84).

39:17　Maier, Charles S. "The Politics of Productivity: Foundations of American International Economic Policy after World War II." *International Organization* 31:4 (1977), 607–33. U.S. objectives are usually described in terms of enlightened idealism or capitalist expansionism. But much of the way policymakers envisaged international economic reconstruction derived from the ambivalent way in which domestic economic conflict had been resolved before and during the New Deal.

39:18　Millikan, Max F., and Rostow, W. W. *A Proposal-Key to an Effective Foreign Policy.* New York: Harper, 1957. A special adviser to the Economic Commission for Europe during the European recovery period, Rostow collaborated with a staff member, Milikan, from the committees of the Marshall Plan and other foreign economic policymaking bodies to construct a plan for American participation in the economic development of underdeveloped areas.

39:19　Monroe, Wilbur F. *The New Internationalism: Strategy and Initiatives for US Foreign Economic Policy.* Lexington, Mass.: Heath, 1976. Monroe states that a new comprehensive economic foreign policy is necessary for the United States to cope with future world challenges. Dealing with a broad spectrum of international economic issues, he suggests an integrated comprehensive set of solutions. Bibliography.

39:20　Porter, Glenn. *The Rise of Big Business, 1860–1910.* New York: Crowell, 1973. This is the best brief introduction to the literature on and issues in American business history after 1865. The author emphasizes the technology of production, the system of distribution, and the nature of markets rather than the

moral issues of industrial statesmen or robber barons. Extensive bibliography.

39:21　Tinker, Irene, and Bramsen, Michele B., eds. *Women and World Development.* Washington, D.C.: American Association for the Advancement of Science, 1976. This is a collection of essays on a topic that has generally been ignored by male policymakers in the field of development planning. Of particular importance is Tinker's "The Adverse Impact of Development on Women" and R. Blumberg's "Fairy Tales and Facts: Economy, Family Fertility, and the Female."

Varg, P. A. *Foreign Policies of the Founding Fathers* (5:15) remains the most comprehensive attempt to relate the early diplomacy of the U.S. from the War for Independence through the War of 1812 with economic theory and economic practices of revolutionary leaders.

Varg, P. A. *United States Foreign Relations, 1820–1860* (8:6) is a sequel to his *Foreign Policies of the Founding Fathers* relates American diplomacy to the tremendous economic expansion at home, to cultural ties with Europe, to the upheavals and rivalries of Europe, and the nature of Chinese and Japanese societies.

39:22　Varg, Paul A. "Foreign Policy: Past and Future." *Centennial Review* 21:3 (1977), 261–72. In a tightly reasoned summary of several of his books, Varg argues that a consistent theme in American foreign policy has been the determination to keep markets everywhere open to free competition. Now that other nations are able to compete with the United States for markets, limited global resources are forcing a reevaluation of this country's traditional "go-it-alone" practices.

39:23　Williams, Benjamin H. *Economic Foreign Policy of the United States.* New York: McGraw-Hill, 1929. This now classic volume has greatly influenced scholars of economic foreign policy. The presentation, in which Williams focuses upon the expansion of trade and investment as the United States began to assume its modern role in the world economy, is a relatively comprehensive inspection of the activities of business and government. Bibliography.

39:24　Wilson, Joan Hoff. "Economic Foreign Policy." In Alexander DeConde, ed., *Encyclopedia of American Foreign Policy.* New York: Scribner's,

1978, vol. 1, pp. 281–91. A general review of writing about U.S. economic relations since the colonial period, this essay explains the historiographical trends of such literature, defines the terminology it employs, and discusses in general the historical evolution of American economic diplomacy.

39:25 Woodruff, William. *America's Impact on the World: A Study of the Role of the United States in the World Economy, 1750–1970.* New York: Wiley, 1975. While generally eulogizing American influence all over the globe, this work is curiously critical of the understanding U.S. citizens have of political and economic foreign policy. The analysis is basically superficial, but many essential facts and approximately fifty pages of statistical tables are presented. Bibliography.

Organizing Foreign Economic Policymaking

39:26 Allison, Graham, and Szanton, Peter. *Remaking Foreign Policy: The Organizational Connection.* New York: Basic Books, 1976. Arguing that American foreign policy machinery has not adapted well to the shifting currents of international economics, these authors suggest how a determined president can achieve significant organizational reform through informal and subtle changes in governmental structure and emphasis. Both draw heavily upon consulting work they have performed for the government and employ a variety of examples from recent U.S. foreign policy decisions to illustrate their points.

39:27 Bergsten, C. Fred. "The Response to the Third World." *Foreign Policy,* no. 17 (1974/1976), 3–34. How should the United States respond to the economic challenges of the Third World? Bergsten suggests the United States negotiate multilateral nondiscriminatory trade treaties and help developing nations industrialize, while simultaneously taking economic defensive measures.

39:28 Bergsten, C. Fred. "The Threat from the Third World." *Foreign Policy,* no. 11 (1973), 102–24. Bergsten thinks that the Third World has the potential to seriously hurt or at least cause significant cost adjustments to Western economies. In this prescient article, he criticizes U.S. policy for neglecting the Third World.

Destler, I. M. *Making Foreign Economic Policy* (39:66).

Kaufman, B. I. *Efficiency and Expansion: Foreign Trade Organization in the Wilson Administration, 1913–1921* (19:129) argues that the Wilson administration, in search of efficiency in foreign trade, collaborated with business in trade expansion. As a result, the business-government liaison virtually transformed the nation's subsequent economic history.

39:29 Kaufman, Burton I. "Organization for Foreign Trade Expansion in the Mississippi Valley, 1900–1920." *Business History Review* 46:4 (1972), 444–65. Kaufman describes how regional trade expansion within the United States played a role in the larger pattern of foreign trade expansion of the period. Most of the nation's trade and financial activities remained eastern oriented, but the creation of the Mississippi Valley Association (1919) signaled the emergence of modern national economic interdependence.

39:30 Pastor, Robert A. *Congress and the Politics of U.S. Foreign Economic Policy, 1929–1976.* Berkeley: University of California Press, 1980. This book provides both a comprehensive description of American economic relations during the past 50 years, and a theoretical framework for explaining it by focusing on trade policy (1929–1976), foreign assistance policy (1945–1976), and foreign investment policy (1960–1976).

Paterson, T. G. "American Businessmen and Consular Service Reform, 1890s to 1906" (14:22) describes the movement for reform resulting from the depression of the 1890s. An informal coalition of business groups and interested government officials succeeded in bringing about many desired reforms through legislative and executive action in 1906.

Schuyler, E. *American Diplomacy and the Furtherance of Commerce* (12:13) is one of the earliest manuals of American diplomatic practice. Separate chapters describe the U.S. consular and diplomatic services and the organizational structure of the State Department as they functioned during the last decades of the 19th century.

39:31 U.S. Commission on the Organization of the Government for the Conduct of Foreign Policy. *Commission on the Organization of the Government for the Conduct of Foreign Policy: Appendices.* 7 vols. Washington, D.C.: G.P.O., 1975. The efforts of the Murphy Commission represents the most exhaustive study of the structure for conducting American diplomacy ever undertaken. Major policymakers going back to the Eisenhower years testified. Their verbatim testimony and most unedited reports can be found in the National Archives. Volume 3 contains detailed case studies on U.S. foreign economic policy, a series of essays on "routine" economic relations with Latin America, and several general essays on intelligence and personnel matters affecting the conduct of economic relations abroad.

39:32   U.S. House Committee on International Relations. Report; *The Coordination of United States International Economic Policy*. Washington, D.C.: G.P.O., 1977. Prepared by Stephen D. Cohen for the committee, which had jurisdiction over the Council on International Economic Policy (CIEP), this report details the structural components of U.S. international economic policy since World War II. In particular it discusses the rise and demise of the CIEP.

Werking, R. H. *The Master Architects: Building the United States Foreign Service, 1890–1913* (2:180) traces the structural and functional changes in the U.S. foreign service prior to 1913. The desire to expand foreign trade led to reorganization in the consular service, the diplomatic corps, and the Department of State.

39:33   Werking, Richard H. "Bureaucrats, Businessmen, and Foreign Trade: The Origins of the United States Chamber of Commerce." *Business History Review* 52:3 (1978), 321–41. Werking shows that the U.S. Chamber of Commerce at the time of its founding in 1912 did not want to exclude the federal government from participation in national economic growth. He argues that the Chamber of Commerce provided an institutional connection between the business community and government officials.

39:34   Werking, Richard H. "Selling the Foreign Service: Bureaucratic Rivalry and Foreign-Trade Promotion, 1903–1912." *Pacific Historical Review* 45:2 (1976), 185–207. Werking concludes, in seeming contrast to Burton I. Kaufman, that the federal government played an active role in the expansion of foreign trade early in the 20th century, even before the legislative assistance of the Wilson administration.

Personalities

Additional references on individuals may be found in Chapter 1, "Biographical Data."

AMERICAN, TO 1941

Herbert Feis

Feis, H. *The Diplomacy of the Dollar, 1919–1932* (20:178) was one of the first attempts to examine American loan policy in the 1920s. Feis examines the efforts of Republican officials to guide the outflow of private American capital. In a reflective concluding chapter, the former State Department official makes some comparisons between the post–World War I and World War II experiences.

Feis, H. *Europe: The World's Banker, 1870–1914* (39:90).

39:35   Healey, Maryanne F. "Witness, Participant, and Chronicler: The Role of Herbert Feis as Economic Adviser to the State Department, 1931–1943." Ph.D. diss., Georgetown University, 1973. This is a fine analysis of Feis's most productive years as a policymaker. Extensive bibliography.

Warren G. Harding

See also Chapters 20 and 21, under "Personalities."

Grieb, K. J. *The Latin American Policy of Warren G. Harding* (21:27) contends that although Harding continued to advocate the promotion of Yankee business interests in the hemisphere, he emphasized a more measured, pragmatic approach than his predecessors. He substituted diplomatic persuasion for military coercion without abandoning the notion of American hemispheric domination.

Herbert C. Hoover

See Chapters 19, 20, and 21, under "Personalities," for additional references.

Brandes, J. *Herbert Hoover and Economic Diplomacy: Department of Commerce Policy, 1921–1928* (20:40) remains a valuable contribution to the rehabilitation of Hoover's reputation as an advanced economic thinker, especially during the 1920s, when he served as secretary of commerce under both Harding and Coolidge.

Hoover, H. C. *The Ordeal of Woodrow Wilson* (19:74) contains often candid recollections of men and decisions at the Paris Peace Conference of 1919. It illuminates the anti-Bolshevik thrust of U.S. policy and provides an overview of the politics of the blockade and food relief.

Cordell Hull

See Chapters 20 and 21, under "Personalities," for additional references.

Hull, C. *Memoirs* (21:36) is especially good for understanding Hull's economic orientation and his emphasis on trade agreements.

Henry Morgenthau, Jr.

See Chapters 21 and 22, under "Personalities," for additional references.

39:36   Gardner, Lloyd. "The Role of the Commerce and Treasury Departments." In Dorothy Borg and Shumpei Okamoto, eds., *Pearl Harbor as History: Japanese-American Relations, 1931–1941.* New York: Columbia University Press, 1973, pp. 261–85. Gardner emphasizes the Commerce and Treasury departments' fears of Japanese attempts to integrate additional areas in East Asia into their "state-trading system." The author focuses on Secretary of the Treasury Henry Morgenthau's efforts to use silver policy and American credits to combat Japanese expansion. Gardner also stresses the common view among American policymakers that Axis aggression posed a "worldwide threat to liberal democracy."

Dwight Morrow

Nicolson, H. G. *Dwight Morrow* (21:45) is episodic rather than analytical, but it offers useful details, especially on efforts to reach some accommodation with the Mexican Revolution.

Paul Reinsch

See also Chapter 19, under "Personalities."

39:37   Pugach, Noel. "Making the Open Door Work: Paul S. Reinsch in China, 1913–1919." *Pacific Historical Review* 38:2 (1969), 157–75. This essay analyzes Reinsch's views on implementing the open door policy and explores relations between businessmen and government officials interested in expanding the American stake in China. The author emphasizes Reinsch's frustration at the timidity of American businessmen as well as the ambassador's opposition to the idea of supplanting the open door with a Japanese-American condominium.

Franklin D. Roosevelt

See also Chapters 20, 21, 22, and 23, under "Personalities," for additional references.

39:38   Freidel, Frank. *FDR: Launching the New Deal.* Boston: Little, Brown, 1973. This is a comprehensive account of Roosevelt's actions from the time of his election to July 1933. Freidel presents more information on Roosevelt's foreign policies during this period than has any other writer. As a result, the volume is indispensable for evaluating Roosevelt's decision to pursue an independent monetary policy regardless of its impact on the London Economic Conference.

Gardner, L. C. *Economic Aspects of New Deal Diplomacy* (21:12) is a pioneering but disjointed and inadequately documented work which requires supplementation by monographs dealing with specific topics, such as reciprocal trade and monetary policy.

39:39   Nichols, Jeannette. "Roosevelt's Monetary Diplomacy in 1933." *American Historical Review* 56:2 (1951), 295–317. An early effort to study the developments that led to Roosevelt's famous "bombshell address," breaking up the London Economic Conference. Nichols emphasizes the president's uncertain course in the months prior to the conference and his increasing desire to have maximum flexibility in his pursuit of internal recovery and a rise in domestic prices.

39:40   Wicker, Elmus R. "Roosevelt's 1933 Monetary Experiment." *Journal of American History* 57:4 (1971), 864–79. Wicker demonstrates how the president came into increasing conflict with his financial advisers who sympathized with Roosevelt's domestic problems but who also stressed the need for international monetary cooperation in order to expedite recovery.

Willard D. Straight

Also see Chapter 17, under "Personalities."

39:41   Kahn, Helen Dodson. "Willard D. Straight and the Great Game of Empire." In Frank J. Merli and Theodore A. Wilson, eds., *Makers of American Diplomacy from Benjamin Franklin to Henry Kissinger.* New York: Scribner's, 1974, vol. 2, pp. 29–54. Sometime consul general in Mukden, head of State Department Far Eastern Division, and Wall Street promoter, Straight helped shape E. H. Harriman's Manchurian railway scheme and negotiations for the Hukuang loan and First China Consortium. Based on the author's 1968 dissertation, this essay concentrates on Straight's efforts (1906–1913) to give substance to the open door policy by promoting a tangible American financial stake in China.

39:42 Scheiber, Harry N. "World War I as Entrepreneurial Opportunity: Willard Straight and the American International Corporation." *Political Science Quarterly* 84:3 (1969), 481–511. In detailing Straight's activities as AIC vice-president (1915–1917) as well as the former diplomat's expansive thinking about America's role in the postwar international economy, Scheiber stresses the continuity of U.S. economic expansion and the broad similarities between the Wilson administration's economic foreign policy and that of its predecessors and successors.

William Howard Taft

See Chapters 14, 15, and 17, under "Personalities," for additional references.

Scholes, W. V., and Scholes, M. V. *The Foreign Policies of the Taft Administration* (17:44) argues that the diplomacy of the Taft administration was primarily concerned with Asia and Latin America. The thrust of policy was to expand trade and investment. But contrary to some accounts of dollar diplomacy, the Scholeses argue that foreign policy under Taft should be seen less as an effort to dominate foreign countries than as a legitimate endeavor to increase trade, and occasionally as an exercise in moral interposition.

Woodrow Wilson

See also Chapter 19, under "Personalities," for references.

Levin, N. G., Jr. *Woodrow Wilson and World Politics: America's Response to War and Revolution* (19:120) remains the best interpretive account of Wilson's economic views and his attempts to translate them into a coherent foreign policy.

Others

39:43 Chandler, Lester V. *Benjamin Strong: Central Banker.* Washington, D.C.: Brookings Institution, 1958. This account of Strong's career as governor of the Federal Reserve Bank of New York focuses on his efforts to restore European monetary and financial stability after World War I. Chandler does a fine job describing Strong's relations with Montagu Norman, governor of the Bank of England. The author also depicts Strong's conflicts with the Federal Reserve Board as he endeavored to use new mechanisms to avoid inflation at home while contributing to monetary stability abroad.

Hammond, J. H. *The Autobiography of John Hays Hammond* (14:104) is, because of Hammond's longtime interest in Mexican mining properties and his easy access to American and Mexican leaders, valuable for Hammond's comments about the Mexican Revolution. His response to the revolution shed light on the shaping of American policy.

39:44 Hughes, Brady A. "Owen D. Young and American Foreign Policy, 1919–1929." Ph.D. diss., University of Wisconsin, 1969. Owen D. Young, president of the Radio Corporation of America and General Electric, helped to shape U.S. policy on two key economic questions: control of overseas wireless communications, and the financial reconstruction of Europe. This study analyzes Young's role in creating an international wireless consortium and in efforts to deal with reparations and stabilize the German economy. Bibliography.

39:45 Safford, Jeffrey J. "Edward Hurley and American Shipping Policy: An Elaboration on Wilsonian Diplomacy, 1918–1919." *Historian* 35:4 (1973), 568–86. A self-made millionaire, Illinois manufacturer Hurley headed the U.S. Shipping Board (1917–1919) and presided over the procurement and disposition of America's vast wartime merchant fleet. The essay examines the largely unsuccessful attempt to use U.S. maritime policy for bargaining at the Paris Peace Conference and explains how Hurley (and Wilson) reconciled a noticeably competitive attitude toward the British with the larger Wilsonian vision of a new international order.

39:46 Synder, J. Richard. "William S. Culbertson and the Formation of Modern American Commercial Policy, 1917–1925." *Kansas Historical Quarterly* 35:4 (1969), 369–410. A tariff expert and, from 1917 to 1925, member of the U.S. Tariff Commission, Culbertson sought to adapt America's commercial policy to its changed role in the world economy—major creditor and exporter of manufactured goods. This essay, based largely on the Culbertson and Harding papers, analyzes Culbertson's role in shaping the Tariff Act of 1922 and explores his unsuccessful efforts to effect tariff reductions through use of discretionary powers granted the president under that act.

Wilson, F. M. H. *Memoirs of an Ex-Diplomat* (17:57) is useful for its discussion of Knox's economic diplomacy, especially the First China Consortium, and for what it reveals about Wilson's own strong racial and ethnic biases.

AMERICAN, SINCE 1941

For the post–World War II era, see Chapter 24, under "Personalities" and "Presidential Administrations," for additional references.

Chester Bowles

See also Chapter 37, under "Personalities."

Bowles, C. *Promises to Keep: My Years in Public Life, 1941–1969* (24:99) argues that basic changes need to be made in American foreign policy, including new ideas on Europe's development and using foreign aid programs as an instrument for thwarting and deflecting the forces of feudalism and of communism. Foreign aid programs should be hinged to programs of social justice in developing nations.

John Foster Dulles

See Chapters 24 and 27, under "Personalities," for additional references.

Dulles, J. F. *War or Peace* (26:45) argues that U.S. economic foreign policy had succeeded in filling the economic vacuum in Europe following World War II. Dulles believed that total economic unity in Europe would not be possible until Germany became an integral part of the West. This genuine unity in Europe would include a domestic market with no internal trade barriers.

Guhin, M. A. *John Foster Dulles: A Statesman and His Times* (24:110) traces the development of a philosophy that guided Eisenhower's secretary of state. After the 1919 Paris Peace Conference, Dulles became convinced that political stability and economic well-being were closely intertwined. By the 1950s, Dulles believed that economic programs of foreign policy were as important as military programs. In defending the 1957 Mutual Security Program, Dulles warned that the United States had to combat isolationism and neutrality impulses within the country.

George F. Kennan

See also Chapters 22, 24, and 29, under "Personalities," for additional references.

Kennan, G. F. *The Cloud of Danger: Current Realities of American Foreign Policy* (29:226) advocates a "grand design" for American foreign policy. All of the old themes from his earlier publications are present, with a focus on bilateral relationships. Kennan advocates less emphasis on financial aid so that the United States doesn't become too extensively involved with others. Kennan states that unlimited U.S. foreign trade and external economic involvement will limit its freedom and hamper independent action.

Kennan, G. F. *Memoirs* (24:124) evaluates the formulation and implementation of certain plans, including the Marshall Plan. Kennan notes an American aversion to regional plans, such as the Marshall Plan. Kennan believes that European unification was not necessary for economic reasons but was necessary for solving the German problem. The proposal for a "world trading, maritime bloc" based on a single currency with common sovereignty failed due to the financial problems of the British, including devaluation of the pound sterling.

Dean Rusk

See also Chapter 24, under "Personalities."

Rusk, D. *Winds of Freedom* (24:149) contains excerpts from speeches (1961–1962) dealing with general foreign policy formulation as well as specific statements about the Alliance for Progress. Rusk viewed foreign aid in general as the joint responsibility of all industrial nations, not the United States alone.

Others

Adams, S. *Firsthand Report: The Story of the Eisenhower Administration* (24:200) discusses the 1958 efforts to design a policy of free foreign trade, stating that Eisenhower committed himself to assist underdeveloped countries with a long-term goal of building a permanent structure for peace by giving these countries a chance to build their own trade and commerce.

Barnet, R. J. *Roots of War: The Men and Institutions behind U.S. Foreign Policy* (24:32).

Clayton, W. L. *Selected Papers of Will Clayton* (24:169) discusses his participation in the Geneva Agreement on Tariffs and Trade (GATT) and as head of the U.S. delegation on the Committee for Economic Cooperation in Europe. He upheld liberal economic policies and participated in the planning and development of the Marshall Plan.

Donovan, J. C. *The Cold Warriors: A Policy-Making Elite* (24:230) is a provocative socioeconomic study of the military-industrial bureaucrats who were primarily responsible for designing post–World War II foreign policy. This remains the best of a number of collective biographical works about decisionmakers—many of whom played key roles in shaping the early economic aspects of U.S. cold war diplomacy.

Hughes, E. J. *The Ordeal of Power: A Political Memoir of the Eisenhower Years* (24:204) finds that by 1957, hostility in Congress to financial aid to India and Yugoslavia forced Eisenhower to appeal to the American voters for support. The president believed that to save money at the cost of allowing a communist conspiracy to succeed was "reckless." The cut in appropriations by Congress was viewed by Eisenhower as a personal defeat.

Koskoff, D. *Joseph P. Kennedy: A Life and Times* (22:27) discusses Kennedy's gradual shift to an isolationist orientation after negotiating trade agreements with Great Britain in 1938. By 1947, Kennedy opposed both the Truman Doctrine and the Marshall Plan, while suggesting a "Marshall Plan for the Americas," especially for defense purposes. The outbreak of hostilities in Korea caused Kennedy to argue that the United States giveaway programs had not "solved" anything.

39:47 Randall, Clarence B. *A Foreign Economic Policy for the United States.* Chicago: University of Chicago Press, 1954. Randall served as special consultant on foreign economic policy during the Eisenhower administration. He advocated a free trade policy with a gradual and selective reduction in tariff barriers with multilateral cooperation. Randall also believed that the government should encourage the investment of private American capital in the world economy.

Commercial Policy

39:48 Doenecke, Justus D. "The Most-Favored-Nation Principle." In Alexander DeConde, ed., *Encyclopedia of American Foreign Policy.* New York: Scribner's, 1978, vol. 2, pp. 603–09. This essay contains a brief but useful section on controversial trade cases and the negative effects of the American conditional most-favored-nation principle. Bibliography.

Savage, C. *Policy of the United States toward Maritime Commerce in War* (40:116) provides an excellent documentary survey of American commercial policy during times of war.

TRADE TO 1920

See "Personalities," especially William S. Culbertson, Edward Hurley, Herbert C. Hoover, Woodrow Wilson; also see the various chronological sections below.

Davies, R. B. " 'Peacefully Working to Conquer the World': The Singer Manufacturing Company in Foreign Markets, 1854–1889" (12:27).

Goodhart, C. A. E. *The New York Money Market and the Finance of Trade, 1900–1913* (14:20) describes how offsetting capital flows prior to the inception of the Federal Reserve System worked to keep the American economy more stable than it might otherwise have been.

39:49 Holbo, Paul S. "Trade and Commerce." In Alexander DeConde, ed., *Encyclopedia of American Foreign Policy.* New York: Scribner's, 1978, vol. 3, pp. 945–60. This is an interpretive survey of American commerce as related to foreign policy. It includes a detailed analysis of trends. Bibliography.

39:50 Hutchins, John G. B. *The American Maritime Industries and Public Policy, 1789–1914.* Cambridge: Harvard University Press, 1941. This extensively researched study traces the great changes which occurred in the organization and economic position of the American shipping and shipbuilding industries. The volume deals with the national state and maritime industries, the maritime industry and the wooden sailing ship, and the large-scale enterprise associated with the development of steam navigation. Extensive bibliography.

39:51 Lawrence, James C. *The World's Struggle with Rubber, 1905–1931.* New York: Harper, 1931. Lawrence's study, still useful in part for the international history of rubber in the 1920s, has been largely supplanted by Frank R. Chalk's dissertation (20:174).

Setser, V. G. *The Commercial Reciprocity Policy of the United States, 1774–1829* (4:150) traces the shaping of U.S. commercial reciprocity policy during this important period.

Woodman, H. D. *King Cotton and His Retainers: Financing and Marketing the Cotton Crop of the South, 1800–1925* (11:174).

East Asia

See "Personalities," especially Paul Reinsch, Willard D. Straight, William Howard Taft; also see Chapter 17, "Spheres and the Open Door" and the other subthemes.

39:52 Braisted, William R. "China, the United States Navy, and the Bethlehem Steel Company, 1909–1920." *Business History Review* 42:1 (1968), 50–66. Braisted's article illuminates important differences between the open door policy of Secretary of State John Hay and dollar diplomacy as practiced by the Taft administration. Moreover, the Bethlehem Steel Company's contract to sell warships to China bore little relationship to the strategic interests of the United States, disregarded the needs of China, and affected British-Japanese-American relations.

Esthus, R. A. "The Changing Concept of the Open Door, 1899–1910" (17:235) asserts that by 1910 the original concept of the open door had been altered substantially by the efforts of Willard Straight and F. M. Huntington-Wilson, among others. No longer would equality of commercial opportunity be the primary focus of the policy. The open door instead came to symbolize both an anti-Japanese attitude and fewer limitations on policy objectives in China.

39:53 Field, Frederick V. *American Participation in the China Consortiums.* Chicago: University of Chicago Press, 1931. Valuable for its description of the American consortium policy in China (1909–1924), this account argues that American participation in consortiums was a practical political as well as economic tool. While somewhat outdated, the book has a clear chronological development of European-American participation in China consortiums.

Hunt, M. H. *Frontier Defense and the Open Door: Manchuria in Chinese-American Relations, 1895–1911* (17:221) argues that neither China nor the United States understood the other's objectives in Manchuria during the period under consideration. Both countries saw the region as a valuable frontier, but American concern for Manchuria was not matched by a concomitant influx of capital. The U.S. government, along with business interests, failed to realize that the

Chinese, even in a period of domestic turmoil, viewed Manchuria as crucial to their future.

39:54 Hunt, Michael H. "Americans in the China Market: Economic Opportunities and Economic Nationalism, 1890s–1931." *Business History Review* 51:3 (1977), 277–307. Hunt looks beyond the contemporary rhetoric and the debate among historians to assess the reality of the China market. He argues that a strong market existed for kerosene and tobacco products, but less so for textiles in the period under consideration. Moreover, government support for trade expansion made little difference in the volume of trade. What did matter were local conditions in China and the domestic strength of the American manufacturer.

Israel, J. *Progressivism and the Open Door: America and China, 1905–1921* (17:236) asserts that a study of domestic politics and institutions is useful for understanding Sino-American relations between 1905 and 1921. Within this framework, he finds that Americans had difficulty resolving differences between competitive and cooperative attempts to achieve the objectives of the open door policy.

39:55 Mazuzan, George T. "'Our New Gold Goes Adventuring': The American International Corporation in China." *Pacific Historical Review* 43:2 (1974), 212–32. There existed numerous ways in which U.S. business interests sought to penetrate the putative China market during World War I. One endeavor was through the creation of the American International Corporation. The vicissitudes of Chinese politics and the demands of the war combined to minimize the effectiveness of the AIC. Consequently, as Mazuzan demonstrates, the open door remained as elusive as ever.

Pugach, N. H. "Anglo-American Aircraft Competition and the China Arms Embargo, 1919–1921" (21:224) finds Americans seeking to sell surplus war materiel, especially airplanes, to contending factions in China. Pugach describes how this activity, in violation of an arms embargo, briefly encouraged Anglo-American competition in the arms trade. It undercut emerging major power cooperation in China, the primary example of which was the second consortium loan.

Pugach, N. H. "Standard Oil and Petroleum Development in Early Republican China" (19:210) adds to our knowledge about the limitations of the open door policy.

39:56 Safford, Jeffrey J. "Experiment in Containment: The United States Steel Embargo and Japan, 1917–1918." *Pacific Historical Review* 39:4 (1970), 439–51. The United States tried various ways during World War I to limit Japan's commercial and territorial expansion in the Far East. One means which proved unavailing was the 1917–1918 embargo on steel. The embargo may have had a short-term effect, but it also taught the Japanese that economic difficulties would result from the denial of access to raw materials and industrial commodities.

Varg, P. A. *The Making of a Myth: The United States and China, 1897–1912* (17:224) contends that the lack of practical success in opening China to Western trade and influence produced an American policy, characterized by paternalism and benign sentimentality, which could not adequately mitigate the difficulties posed by internal chaos in China, competitive relations among the foreign powers there, and the commercial and financial ambitions of American citizens.

Vevier, C. *The United States and China, 1906–1913: A Study of Finance and Diplomacy* (17:265) describes U.S. involvement in railroad development projects in Manchuria, the creation of a bank in China, and the first consortium loan. American success was limited, due largely to the changing nature of relations with Japan, a fact often overlooked by businessmen and diplomats in China.

Latin America

See "Personalities," especially William Howard Taft; also see Chapter 15, "Taft and Dollar Diplomacy," as well as other subsections.

Kaufman, B. I. "United States Trade and Latin America: The Wilson Years" (19:215) argues that organizational and ideological changes in economic foreign policy made it possible for the United States to replace European countries as the most active trading partner of Latin American nations during World War I.

Munro, D. G. *Intervention and Dollar Diplomacy in the Caribbean, 1900–1921* (15:97) argues that U.S. motives were political rather than economic.

Rosenberg, E. S. "The Exercise of Emergency Controls over Foreign Commerce: Economic Pressure on Latin America" (19:218) surveys U.S. economic foreign policy toward Latin America during World War I, and shows how war-related commodity controls had a vast impact upon Latin American nations. Executive power increased to include responsibility for import-export management, supervision of capital flows, and blacklisting.

Smith, R. F. "Cuba: Laboratory for Dollar Diplomacy, 1898–1917" (15:103).

Middle East

See Chapter 18 for scattered references.

Cohen, N. W. "Ambassador Straus in Turkey, 1909–1910: A Note on Dollar Diplomacy" (18:47) finds that Straus opposed the idea of dollar diplomacy.

DeNovo, J. A. *American Interests and Policies in the Middle East, 1900–1939* (18:5) contains material on trade expansion.

Field, J. A., Jr. *America and the Mediterranean World, 1776–1882* (18:6) includes material on the activities of early American merchants.

Gordon, L. J. *American Relations with Turkey, 1830–1930: An Economic Interpretation* (18:9).

Wright, L. B., and MacLeod, J. H. *The First Americans in North Africa: William Eaton's Struggle for a Vigorous Policy against the Barbary Pirates, 1799–1805* (18:63).

TRADE, 1920–1945

See "Personalities," especially Herbert Feis, Cordell Hull, Franklin D. Roosevelt.

Chalk, F. R. "The United States and the International Struggle for Rubber, 1914–1941" (20:174).

Condoide, M. V. *Russian-American Trade* (20:201).

Etzold, T. H. *Why America Fought Germany in World War II* (20:194) stresses the U.S. failure to negotiate a new trade treaty in 1935 as a major factor in mounting political confrontations.

39:57 Kelly, William B., Jr. "Antecedents of Present Commercial Policy, 1922–1934." In William B. Kelly, Jr., ed., *Studies in United States Commercial Policy*. Chapel Hill: University of North Carolina Press, 1963, pp. 3–68. Kelly analyzes major aspects of Republican commercial policy in the 1920s. He focuses on the unconditional most-favored-nation clause, the flexibility formula, the retaliatory provision, and the high tariff duties. He argues that American commercial policy was not attuned to the new position that the United States had assumed in the world economy.

Kimball, W. F. "Lend-Lease and the Open Door: The Temptation of British Opulence, 1937–1942" (22:188) argues that after the passage of the Lend-Lease Act economic considerations assumed larger significance in determining U.S. policy. During the negotiations over the Lend-Lease Master Agreement, the State Department played a decisive role and sought to put an end to the British system of imperial preferences. In this way, the United States tried to capitalize upon British distress to establish a postwar economic order conducive to American interests and ideals.

Reciprocal Trade Agreements

See also Chapter 20, "Reciprocal Trade Agreements."

Kottman, R. N. *Reciprocity and the North Atlantic Triangle, 1932–1938* (20:234) explores the relationships between the United States, Britain, and Canada in the mid–1930s. Hull's belief that a new political order could be based on internationalist economic foundations was distrusted in London. The Canadians played a limited role in providing a channel of communication between the United States and Great Britain. Kottman's book helps to explicate the factors undermining Anglo-American cooperation in the mid–1930s. Bibliography.

39:58 McHale, James M. "National Planning and Reciprocal Trade: The New Deal Origins of Government Guarantees for Private Exporters." *Prologue* 6:3 (1974), 189–200. McHale briefly outlines the evolution of the Export-Import Bank and the role it was assigned to play in promoting recovery. According to the author, government planners during the New Deal "joined the tactics of the NRA to those of the trade agreements program by publicly underwriting the risks of some foreign buyers' insolvency while the Department of State worked to gain worldwide markets for America."

39:59 Schatz, Arthur W. "The Anglo-American Trade Agreement and Cordell Hull's Search for Peace,

1936–1938." *Journal of American History* 57:1 (1970), 85–103. This article emphasizes Secretary of State Hull's belief that freer trade, especially in the form of an Anglo-American commercial agreement, would revive the international economy and "slow the drift toward war." But at the same time the stress on commercial policy disregarded fundamental international political questions and accorded with the prevailing stream of political isolationism. Moreover, Hull's tough bargaining over concessions often revealed the narrow American self-interest that was one motivating force behind the reciprocity program.

39:60 Tasca, Henry J. *The Reciprocal Trade Policy of the United States: A Study in Trade Philosophy.* Philadelphia: University of Pennsylvania Press, 1938. This book is a sympathetic account of the evolution of the reciprocity program under the New Deal. Tasca discusses the legislative history of the Reciprocal Trade Act of 1934 and examines the efforts to administer the new commercial formula.

39:61 Wilkinson, Joe R. *Politics and Trade Policy.* Washington, D.C.: Public Affairs Press, 1960. Wilkinson presents a brief account of the evolution of the reciprocal trade agreements program from the mid–1930s through the mid–1950s. The author is primarily concerned with the interaction between politics and trade policy and with the shifting attitudes of the political parties toward the New Deal's commercial legislation.

East Asia

See "Personalities," especially Henry Morgenthau; see also Chapter 22, "Embargoes and Sanctions."

Anderson, I. H., Jr. *The Standard-Vacuum Oil Company and United States East Asian Policy, 1933–1941* (22:235).

Friend, T. W. "The Philippine Sugar Industry and the Politics of Independence, 1929–1935" (21:233).

Ghosh, P. S. "Passage of the Silver Purchase Act of 1934: The China Lobby and the Issue of China Trade" (21:229).

Moore, J. W. "Economic Interests and American-Japanese Relations: The Petroleum Controversy" [1934–1937] (21:192).

Sewall, A. F. "Key Pittman and the Quest for the China Market, 1933–1940" (21:230).

Latin America

See "Personalities," especially Warren G. Harding, Dwight Morrow.

39:62   Hilton, Stanley E. *Brazil and the Great Powers, 1930–1939: The Politics of Trade Rivalry.* Austin: University of Texas Press, 1975. Hilton has provided an analytic study of the commercial rivalry between the United States, Britain, and Germany in Brazil in the 1930s. He elucidates the New Deal's efforts to use the good neighbor policy and reciprocal trade program to combat Nazi Germany's bilateralism. Hilton skillfully demonstrates how Brazil exploited great power rivalries in its own self-interest. As do other recent accounts of the good neighbor policy, this volume questions the efficacy of Hull's efforts to improve relations between the United States and its southern neighbors. Useful bibliography.

Repko, A. F. "The Failure of Reciprocal Trade: United States–German Commercial Rivalry in Brazil, 1934–1940" (20:235) elucidates some of the major problems inherent in Hull's reciprocal trade program. The secretary of state was not inclined to make concessions that would benefit Brazil if these concessions endangered domestic interests. Brazil was not convinced that multilateral trade was more advantageous than bilateral agreements with Germany.

Steward, D. *Trade and Hemisphere: The Good Neighbor Policy and Reciprocal Trade* (20:237) focuses on the role of Cordell Hull and the State Department and incisively argues that the reciprocity program of the New Deal was motivated by a mixture of self-interest and idealism. Steward emphasizes, however, that the results of the program were the retardation of industrialization in Latin America, the encouragement of monocultures, and the incorporation of treaty nations within the trade orbit of the United States.

39:63   Varg, Paul A. "The Economic Side of the Good Neighbor Policy: The Reciprocal Trade Program and South America." *Pacific Historical Review* 45:1 (1976), 47–72. Like the recent volume by Dick Steward, this article contends that the reciprocal trade program of the good neighbor policy was a failure. Varg stresses the domestic opposition to Hull's program. This opposition circumscribed the State De-

partment's ability to offer South American nations relatively free access to the American market.

Middle East

Baram, P. J. *The Department of State in the Middle East, 1919–1945* (33:82) stresses the role of the State Department in breaking down preferential trade arrangements and, thereby, opening the way for American commerce.

Baram, P. J. "Undermining the British: Department of State Policies in Egypt and the Suez Canal before and during World War II" (18:151) finds the department dismantling Britain's privileged position in the Egyptian economy so American commerce could enter.

Bryson, T. A. "Admiral Mark Lambert Bristol: An Open Door Diplomat in Turkey" (18:31).

Horton, G. *The Blight of Asia* (18:152) argues that the U.S. government compromised missionaries' role in favor of commercial activity.

TRADE SINCE 1945

See "Personalities," especially Will Clayton (under "American, since 1941," "Others").

39:64   Bauer, Raymond; Pool, Ithiel de Sola; and Dexter, Lewis A. *American Business and Public Policy: The Politics of Foreign Trade.* New York: Atherton, 1963. These authors have written what remains a standard study of economic self-interest and its relation to U.S. commercial diplomacy (1930s–1950s). In keeping with the "entrepreneurial" school of historical thought, the work projects a pseudo-objective, value-free image of the actions of businessmen and corporations in their attempts to influence foreign policy.

39:65   Briscoe, Lynden. "The Growth and Structure of International Trade since the Second World War." *British Journal of International Studies* 1:3 (1975), 209–25. The distribution of natural resources and technological change have been of some importance, but governmental policy, reduced quotas, and tariff barriers, assisted by a stable monetary system in the United States, and encouragement of agricultural production throughout Western Europe also have led to a rapid growth in world trade (1945–1975).

39:66   Destler, I. M. *Making Foreign Economic Policy.* Washington, D.C.: Brookings Institution, 1980. This book explores the process by which U.S. foreign economic policy choices are made by presenting three case studies: grain sales to the Soviet Union in the 1970s; the soybean embargo of 1973; and the passage of the Trade Act of 1974. The author analyzes these events and then suggests ways for managing food and trade issues.

39:67   Grossack, Irvin. *The International Economy and the National Interest.* Bloomington: Indiana University Press, 1979. Grossack contends that conventional trade theory is incapable of explaining the actions of multinational corporations or the problems now facing the international economy. By redefining *exports* and *imports,* he constructs a theoretical model for integrating international trade and investment. Finally he is critical of the American government for encouraging foreign investment on the part of U.S. companies to contain communism abroad while neglecting the negative effect on the domestic economy.

39:68   Hultman, Charles W. "Access to Supplies: A New Concept in U.S. Commercial Policy." In Satish Raichur and Craig Liske, eds., *The Politics of Aid, Trade and Investment.* New York: Wiley, 1975, pp. 161–77. Hultman describes increased U.S. interest in access to supplies following the OPEC embargo and the terms of the Trade Reform Act of 1974, designed to insure an uninterrupted supply of commodities at reasonable prices.

39:69   Krauss, Melvyn B. *The New Protectionism: The Welfare State and International Trade.* New York: New York University Press, 1978. By "new protectionism," Krauss means the structural change in international trade due to the many welfare states belonging to the international community. He argues that the welfare state paradoxically depends on economic growth for support while supporting policies that impede and reduce economic growth.

39:70   Pearson, Frederic S., and Baumann, Robert. "Foreign Military Intervention and Changes in United States Business Activity." *Journal of Political and Military Sociology* 5:1 (1977), 79–97. "Neo-Leninist" and elitist theories of business influence on and benefits from U.S. military action (1948–1967) are investigated. There was no overall correlation between intervention and overseas business benefits, although in certain cases access to African raw materials increased, as did trade with Asia and the Middle East and capital flows to Asia.

39:71   Peterson, Peter G. *The United States in the Changing World Economy.* 2 vols. in 1. Washington, D.C.: G.P.O., 1971. These two slim volumes present both the theoretical and factual background for understanding Nixon's economic foreign policy initiatives of August 1971. The first one is especially useful because it outlines the rationale behind devaluation and other aspects of the new economic policy.

39:72   "United States Trade and Foreign Policy." *Current History* 76:447 (1979), 193–230. A valuable summary of American commercial policy, including one article by Edward W. Erickson and Thomas J. Grennes on arms, oil, and the dollar. Others deal with U.S. trade with Western Europe and Japan, the U.S.S.R., China, the developing world, and OPEC.

GATT

See "Personalities," especially William S. Culbertson (under "American, to 1941," "Others").

39:73   Cline, William R.; Noboru Kawanabe; Kronsjo, T. O. M.; and Williams, Thomas. *Trade Negotiations in the Tokyo Round: A Quantitative Assessment.* Washington, D.C.: Brookings Institution, 1978. Evaluating quantitatively the future effects of trade liberalization resulting from the Tokyo round, the authors conclude that the gains will easily outweigh the losses.

39:74   Evans, John. *The Kennedy Round in American Trade Policy: The Twilight of GATT.* Cambridge: Harvard University Press, 1971. In a review of the issues and policies pursued by the United States in the Kennedy round conferences, Evans is critical of America's past positions and pessimistic about future developments in international trade. Bibliography.

39:75   GATT [General Agreement on Tariffs and Trade], Director-General. *The Tokyo Round of Multilateral Trade Negotiations.* Geneva: GATT, 1979. This is a valuable, detailed account of the Tokyo round negotiations by the GATT secretariat.

39:76   Herter, Christian A. "U.S. Aims in the Kennedy Round." *Atlantic Community Quarterly* 2:2 (1964), 240–46. This discussion of the Kennedy round of negotiations conducted under the General Agreement on Tariffs and Trade (GATT) in 1963 emphasizes that the United States should strive for a 50 percent tariff cut on many industrial products. Herter, secretary of state during the Eisenhower administration, advocated minimum trade liberalization on agricultural products "taking into account the characteristic problems of the various categories of farm products."

39:77   Preeg, Ernest H. *Traders and Diplomats: An Analysis of the Kennedy Round of Negotiations under the General Agreement on Tariffs and Trade.* Washington, D.C.: Brookings Institution, 1970. A participant's account of the Kennedy round from 1963 to 1967, this volume is the basic book on the topic.

U.S. and European Common Market

See Chapter 28, "U.S. and European Common Market."

Hinshaw, R. *European Community and American Trade: A Study in Atlantic Economics and Policy* (28:54) is an account, from the U.S. standpoint, of the Common Market and related developments in Western Europe.

Krause, L. B. *European Economic Integration and the United States* (28:56) discusses the impact upon the United States of the European Economic Community and European Free Trade Association.

McCreary, E. A. *The Americanization of Europe: The Impact of Americans and American Business on the Uncommon Market* (28:57).

East-West Trade

See Chapter 29, "Economic Relations."

Allen, R. L. *Soviet Economic Warfare* (29:173) is a detailed account exemplifying cold war attitudes of the late 1950s, which assumed that economic war would be waged between the two powers as well as over newly emerging nations, that China and other communist nations would help the Soviets, and that the Russian economy would grow rapidly. Good description of Soviet trade generally and especially with Asia, Middle East, and Latin America.

Friesen, C. M. *The Political Economy of East-West Trade* (29:165) is one of the best overall surveys of exchanges during the cold war. Friesen uses important material from the Soviet as well as U.S. side, and

emphasizes the role of politics in the development of economic exchanges.

Harvey, M. L. *East-West Trade and United States Policy* (29:166) surveys East-West trade (especially the 1964 grain deal), argues that trade is a weapon and should be used with conscious purpose against Russia (although not necessarily against Yugoslavia), fears the United States does not understand the growing battle over the Third World, and concludes that détente is disadvantageous.

39:78   Holzman, Franklyn D. *International Trade under Communism: Politics and Economics.* New York: Basic Books, 1976. After discussing communist trade theory, Holzman traces post–1945 commercial policies, including the Yugoslav and de-Stalinization problems that appeared, notes the development of COMECON and the effect of the Brezhnev Doctrine, and relates these events to détente and Common Market policies in the West. He also includes good comparative statistics and analyzes the trade–foreign aid relationship. Bibliography.

Kovner, M. *The Challenge of Coexistence: A Study of Soviet Economic Diplomacy* (29:175) analyzes U.S.S.R. economic relations (1920s–1950s) with Finland, Israel, the Third World, and the United States, among others. Kovner argues that during coexistence periods economic replaces political-military rivalry and that the Soviets are skilled in using economic weapons.

Kuklick, B. *American Policy and the Division of Germany: The Clash with Russia over Reparations* (25:147) offers the best analysis to date of "multilateralism" as the key to the economic origins of American-Soviet antagonisms in the mid-1940s.

39:79   Mikesell, Raymond F., and Behrman, Jack N. *Financing Free World Trade with the Sino-Soviet Bloc.* Princeton, N.J.: Princeton University Press, 1958. The authors argue the post–1945 era was marked by growing multilateralism of trade and the devising of new financial means to pay for it. They doubt, however, that Soviet bloc nations can move rapidly, or far, toward multilateralism. The volume contains 150 pages of important tables on trade and payments between East and West. Note that the Soviet "bloc" still includes China in 1958. Bibliography.

39:80   Smith, Glen A. *Soviet Foreign Trade: Organization, Operation, and Policy, 1918–1971.* New York: Praeger, 1973. A survey, especially strong on the historical background, comparing the Lenin, Stalin, and Khrushchev policies, analyzes East-West as well as Soviet-satellite relationships. Extensive bibliography.

Sutton, A. C. *Western Technology and Soviet Economic Development, 1917–1965* (20:204) includes examples of American trade with Russia which have contributed to that nation's economic growth—such as the "ball bearing case" of 1961 and the Fiat deal of 1968. Sutton is very critical of American shipments to the U.S.S.R. which could possibly be converted to military use. He concludes that "we have created and continue to maintain what appears to be a first-order threat to the survival of Western civilization."

U.S. Senate. Committee on Banking and Currency. Hearings; *East-West Trade* (29:169) includes statements by businessmen, scholars, and politicians and reprints of articles on the regulation of trade with communist countries.

U.S. Senate. Committee on Foreign Relations Hearings; *Background Documents on East-West Trade* (29:170) are considered by the Foreign Relations Committee to be the most important documents that governed East-West trade. Most of the documents are post–1949, but some of the tariff material reaches back to 1930. Most of the documents are detailed and technical, but some—such as departmental responses to Senate requests for information—are more general in nature.

39:81 U.S. Senate. Committee on Foreign Relations. *A Background Study on East-West Trade Prepared . . . by the Legislative Reference Service of the Library of Congress.* 89th Cong., 1st. Sess., 1965. This is one of the best analyses of East-West trade from the 1930s until the mid-1960s. It deals with all aspects of the trade, including Western controls, the role of China and Cuba, U.S. exporters' problems, and the Soviet bloc's ability to pay for purchases. Detailed tables and extensive bibliography.

39:82 U.S. Senate. Committee on Foreign Relations. Hearings; *East-West Trade.* 2 pts. 88th Cong., 2d Sess., 1964–1965. Top government, business, and labor officials, along with academic experts, evaluate an apparent thaw in East-West economic relations. The wide-ranging hearings also produced important tables on the international commerce generated in this context by such nations as Cuba, Poland, Canada, and West Germany. State Department memoranda on

Soviet bloc trade and U.S. policy toward that trade are especially significant.

Wilczynski, J. *The Multinationals and East-West Relations* (29:192) believes that not only U.S. multinationals, but Soviet and other East bloc multinationals will increasingly shape international trade until they meet in what he terms "transideological collaboration." The work includes a long and helpful list of multinationals involved.

TARIFF POLICIES

See "Personalities," especially Cordell Hull, and, under "American, since 1941," "Others," Clarence B. Randall.

Allen, J. B. "The Great Protectionist, Sen. Reed Smoot of Utah" (20:173).

Dollar, C. M. "The South and the Fordney-McCumber Tariff of 1922: A Study in Regional Politics" (20:176).

Kottman, R. N. "Herbert Hoover and the Smoot-Hawley Tariff: Canada, a Case Study" (21:289) portrays Hoover as insensitive to Canadian needs during the process of tariff revision in 1929 and 1930. Preoccupied with the St. Lawrence seaway project, the president ignored Canadian warnings regarding the deleterious impact of higher tariffs. Kottman rejects the current revisionist view of Hoover and condemns the president's "indifference to the economic requirements of the nation's best customer."

39:83 Rom, Michael. *The Role of Tariff Quotas in Commercial Policy.* New York: Holmes & Meier, 1979. A tariff quota combines the characteristics of the tariff, which acts through the price mechanism to reduce trade, and the quota, which limits the amount of trade. Rom's study is the first to explore this hybrid method of trade control.

39:84 Schattschneider, Elmer E. *Politics, Pressures, and the Tariff: A Study of Free Private Enterprise in Pressure Politics, as Shown in the 1929–30 Revision of the Tariff.* New York: Prentice-Hall, 1935. Schattschneider analyzes the efforts of a variety of groups to influence the revision of the tariff during 1929 and 1930. He does a fine job examining the interaction between the institutional processes of tariff revision and the ability of well-organized groups to mold protective legislation in their own self-interest.

39:85 Taussig, Frank W. *Free Trade: The Tariff and Reciprocity*. New York: Macmillan, 1920. This volume is written from the low-tariff viewpoint.

39:86 Taussig, Frank W. *The Tariff History of the United States*. New York: Putnam's, 1931. This is a keen analysis of individual tariff acts and their effects, as seen from a low-tariff perspective.

Terrill, T. E. *The Tariff, Politics, and American Foreign Policy, 1874–1901* (12:86) analyzes the ideological, political, and foreign policy facets of the tariff issue. Little attention is given such issues as interest groups and their relation to congressional tariff-making, individual presidents, or specific tariff measures. The focus is almost entirely on the political and economic effects that American leaders thought the tariff had—not on the actual economic impact of the tariff on the American economy or abroad. Bibliography.

MONETARY AND FINANCIAL POLICY

39:87 Brash, Donald T. *American Investment in Australian Industry*. Cambridge: Harvard University Press, 1966. This is a careful study of American investment in Australia: why it was made, the ownership patterns and sources of funds, the management, technical benefits, the performance, the effects on trade. As in many studies of U.S. foreign investment, the *foreign policy* aspects are shortchanged. Bibliography.

39:88 Caves, Richard E. "International Corporations: The Industrial Economics of Foreign Investment." *Economica* 38:1 (1971), 1–27. The application of industrial organization theory to international business is well done in this short piece. Caves synthesizes much of the current thinking of economists on multinational corporations.

39:89 Dunning, John H., ed. *Studies in International Investment*. London: Allen & Unwin, 1970. Most of the articles in this collection were published between 1962 and 1969. The following topics are discussed: British investments in the United States from 1860 to 1913; the impact of American and British investments on European economic growth; the effects of American investment on British technological development; and inter-firm efficiency comparisons of American and British firms operating in the United Kingdom.

39:90 Feis, Herbert. *Europe: The World's Banker, 1870–1914*. New Haven, Conn.: Yale University Press, 1930. Feis presents the standard account of the connections between international finance and diplomacy prior to World War I. Simply put, the movement of capital abroad promised an increase in the volume of trade. Throughout the period (1870–1914), European capital remained in service to the investing state, although it had the additional effect of allowing industrializing nations such as the United States to compete profitably in the quest for markets.

39:91 Kindleberger, Charles P. "Origins of United States Direct Investment in France." *Business History Review* 48:3 (1974), 382–413. U.S. investments date back to the time of Napoleon; economic penetration proceeded rapidly until 1929, and not until the postwar era did a new spurt begin. Also the present-day American multinational firm is a natural and logical offspring of the 19th-century variety.

39:92 Lewis, Cleona. *America's Stake in International Investment*. Washington, D.C.: Brookings Institution, 1938. This basic early book on America's international economic commitments deals with U.S. foreign investments by sector. The book contains detailed statistical tables.

39:93 Lewis, W. Arthur. *Growth and Fluctuations, 1870–1913*. London: Allen & Unwin, 1978. In this technical work, Lewis contrasts, within the context of a Kondratiev swing in prices, the varying rates of industrial production in Germany, Great Britain, and the United States. The book assists an understanding of pre-1914 trade and monetary policies. Lewis casts doubt upon the proposition that industrializing nations necessarily must invest abroad.

39:94 Nichols, Jeannette P. "Silver Diplomacy." *Political Science Quarterly* 48:4 (1933), 565–88. This is a detailed study (1876–1933) of international currency issues and negotiations. There are some references to the connection of currency matters and the tariff, and to international attitudes.

39:95 Swansbrough, Robert H. *The Embattled Colossus: Economic Nationalism and the United States Investors in Latin America*. Gainesville: University of Florida Press, 1976. This study analyzes the psychological and political roots of economic nationalism in Latin America and examines the tensions that have developed between the United States and Latin American nations (1789–1976) because of their differing perceptions of the role of private enterprise in the development process. It also treats U.S. legislative efforts, such as the Hickenlooper Amendment, to secure investment guarantee agreements. Extensive bibliography.

FINANCIAL POLICY TO 1920

See also Chapter 18, "Chester Concession in Turkey, 1908–1913."

Abrahams, P. P. "American Bankers and the Economic Tactics of Peace, 1919" (20:186) explores the differing views of the federal government and American bankers over how to finance European reconstruction after World War I. Since the Treasury Department refused to support government-backed consortium loans, extensive reconstruction financing had to await developments in the 1920s.

39:96   Abrahams, Paul P. "The Foreign Expansion of American Finance and Its Relationship to the Foreign Economic Policies of the United States, 1907–1921." Ph.D. diss., University of Wisconsin, 1967. Abrahams describes the process by which banks and the federal government worked to expand American finance abroad. The Federal Reserve Act and subsequent legislation greatly aided the replacement of sterling with dollar exchange. Yet as the author shows, collaboration diminished after World War I, when the government encouraged private banks to assume the financial burdens of reconstruction. Bibliography.

39:97   Bloomfield, Arthur I. *Monetary Policy under the International Gold Standard, 1880–1914.* New York: Federal Reserve Bank, 1959. Prior to 1914 the international gold standard did not operate solely at the behest of the Bank of England. Monetary policies of various central banks provided greater management of the gold standard than scholars and financial experts formerly believed. The creation of the Federal Reserve System and considerable transfers of gold to the United States did not prevent international financial dislocation after World War I, despite America's economic strength.

39:98   de Cecco, Marcello. *Money and Empire: The International Gold Standard, 1890–1914.* Oxford: Blackwell, 1974. The author describes how the world monetary situation that accompanied economic growth in Great Britain, Germany, and the United States in the quarter century prior to World War I diminished the financial leadership of the Bank of England. The role of the U.S. Treasury, as de Cecco shows, was important because the treasury's hoarding of gold impeded the smooth working of monetary policy and significantly contributed to the instability prevalent in the international system by 1914.

39:99   Cooper, John M., Jr. "The Command of Gold Reversed: American Loans to Britain, 1915–1917." *Pacific Historical Review* 45:2 (1976), 209–30. World War I severely strained Britain's financial capabilities. As Cooper shows, U.S. bankers and the government used their increased gold reserves to replace Britain as the world's leading financial power. By means of loan policy the United States met with some success in utilizing its nascent financial strength to moderate Allied war aims prior to American entry into the war.

39:100   Hardach, Gerd. *The First World War, 1914–1918.* Berkeley: University of California Press, 1977. Hardach concludes that World War I offered few solutions for economic difficulties arising out of the prewar race for colonies, trade rivalry, and labor disputes in major countries. He develops the theme that expanded capital flows during wartime replaced gold movements as the mechanism crucial for maintaining partial balance of payments equilibrium internationally. Extensive bibliography.

39:101   Phelps, Clyde W. *The Foreign Expansion of American Banks: American Branch Banking Abroad.* New York: Ronald, 1927. Phelps details the rapid expansion of American branch banking into foreign countries from the passage of the Federal Reserve Act (1914) to the 1920s. The expansion of commercial and investment banks as well as private banking houses was largely successful until 1920, when organizational weaknesses within some banks forced a reduction in operations. Bibliography.

Trask, R. R. "The United States and Turkish Nationalism: Investments and Technical Aid during the Ataturk Era" (18:155).

39:102   Van Alstyne, Richard W. "Private American Loans to the Allies, 1914–1916." *Pacific Historical Review* 2:2 (1933), 180–93. Van Alstyne emphasizes the importance for the Allied war effort of the October 1915 loan to Great Britain and France. The loan enhanced American support for the Allies at a crucial time. An early study of wartime economic foreign policy, this article should be supplemented with more recent research.

East Asia

39:103 Hou Chi-ming. *Foreign Investment and Economic Development in China, 1840–1937*. Cambridge: Harvard University Press, 1965. This study challenges the view that foreign economic activities in China impeded China's economy and suppressed Chinese-owned enterprises.

39:104 Remer, C. F. *Foreign Investment in China*. New York: Macmillan, 1933. The best single study of foreign investment in China. The book is a classic.

Latin America

Calvert, P. *The Mexican Revolution, 1910–1914: The Diplomacy of Anglo-American Conflict* (15:128) finds the United States and Britain contended for predominant financial influence in Mexico. As Calvert demonstrates, the struggle did not have an immediate impact upon Mexico, with its near-subsistence economy. With the withdrawal of British capital from Mexico during World War I, U.S. influence grew.

Dinwoodie, D. H. "Dollar Diplomacy in Light of the Guatemalan Loan Project, 1909–1913" (15:123).

39:105 Mayer, Robert. "The Origins of the American Banking Empire in Latin America: Frank A. Vanderlip and the National City Bank." *Journal of Interamerican Studies and World Affairs* 15:1 (1973), 60–76. After the Federal Reserve Act took effect in 1914, National City Bank of New York under the presidency of Frank A. Vanderlip expanded its operations throughout the world, especially into South America. During World War I U.S. capital replaced European funding of commercial and financial ventures. The postwar years brought a reduction of the bank's operations, but the place of American banking abroad had been secured.

Munro, D. G. *Intervention and Dollar Diplomacy in the Caribbean, 1900–1921* (15:97) claims that U.S. policy in the Caribbean was dictated more by security considerations than by the desires of business and government to dominate the area economically. Intervention should therefore be seen as an impetus to political stability and financial responsibility.

Nearing, S., and Freeman, J. *Dollar Diplomacy: A Study in American Imperialism* (2:95) remains the most thorough and best-known indictment of U.S. economic penetration of Latin America in the early 20th century.

Pletcher, D. M. "An American Mining Company in the Mexican Revolutions of 1911–1920" (15:134) demonstrates the disastrous effects of revolutionary disorder on some foreign enterprises.

Pletcher, D. M. "The Fall of Silver in Mexico, 1870–1910, and Its Effects on American Investments" (15:180).

Pletcher, D. M. *Rails, Mines, and Progress: Seven American Promoters in Mexico, 1867–1911* (15:181) shows that U.S. trade and investment with Mexico were directly linked to that country's economic development during the rule of Porfirio Diaz. Especially in railroads and mining, where the majority of funds were invested, the hopes of American promoters for substantial profits were rarely realized.

Rippy, J. F. *The Capitalists and Colombia* (15:217) deals mainly with U.S. investments, especially after 1903.

Rosenberg, E. S. "Anglo-American Economic Rivalry in Brazil during World War I" (15:168) analyzes the deterioration of Great Britain's economic dominance of Brazil after 1914, and notes the inroads made by U.S. trade and capital. Important, too, in this process was the evolving preference in Brazil for American-made goods.

Rosenberg, E. S. "Dollar Diplomacy under Wilson: An Ecuadorian Case" (15:218) suggests that the Wilson administration, except in the case of Mexico, pursued its predecessor's policy of dollar diplomacy in Latin America. The author builds her case using debt default in Ecuador as an example.

Rosenberg, E. S. "Economic Pressures in Anglo-American Diplomacy in Mexico, 1917–1918" (15:136) contends that foreign and economic diplomatic pressures upon Carranza did not abate during World War I. Instead, dollar diplomacy, in the form of the International Bankers Committee on Mexico, continued apace. The United States employed the prospects of loans and other inducements to modify the radicalism of the revolution.

Sensabaugh, L. F. "The Coffee-Trust Question in United States–Brazilian Relations, 1912–1913" (15:208).

Smith, R. F. "Cuba: Laboratory for Dollar Diplomacy, 1898–1917" (15:103) views dollar diplomacy both as a tactic to achieve larger policy objectives and as congruent with the basic goal of advancing internationally U.S. economic interests. From 1898 to 1917, Cuba served as one area for the implementation of dollar diplomacy. Tactics employed there promoted stability and order through the promise of loans and investments.

Smith, R. F. *The United States and Revolutionary Nationalism in Mexico, 1916–1932* (15:174) focuses on the inherent tension between an industrial-creditor nation and a revolutionary nationalist state. By trying to assert control over its economy and effect internal reforms, Mexico threatened the interests of American investors, especially in petroleum. Largely supportive of the goals of businessmen, if not their tactics, Wilson's and subsequent administrations failed to turn Mexico toward an economy based upon liberal, private enterprise.

39:106 Smith, Robert Freeman. "The Formation and Development of the International Bankers Committee on Mexico." *Journal of Economic History* 23:4 (1963), 574–86. The Mexican Revolution threatened the expansion of American trade and capital there. With the prevalence of economic expansion as an important part of U.S. foreign policy, a way had to be found to minimize the potential conflict between revolutionary nationalism and foreign business interests. The International Bankers Committee on Mexico employed patience and persuasion rather than threats to reach partial agreements after World War I on bond indebtedness.

FINANCIAL POLICY, 1920–1945

See "Personalities," especially Franklin D. Roosevelt, and, under "American, to 1941," "Others," Benjamin Strong, Owen D. Young; see also Chapter 20, "Economic Policies," which also includes "German Reparations (Dawes Plan)," and "War Debts."

Adams, F. C. *Economic Diplomacy: The Export-Import Bank and American Foreign Policy, 1934–1939* (20:172) examines the role of the Export-Import Bank in New Deal foreign policy. The author rejects the idea that the United States was isolationist in the 1930s and argues that "the Export-Import Bank symbolized the continued belief of American statesmen that the nation had an important stake in the international economy." The author maintains that policymakers were influenced, but not controlled, by economic interest groups seeking immediate export outlets. Extensive bibliography.

39:107 Bennett, Edward W. *Germany and the Diplomacy of the Financial Crisis, 1931.* Cambridge: Harvard University Press, 1962. Bennett's study is a systematic account of the efforts of European and American statesmen to deal with the great financial crisis of 1931. The author does a very fine job weaving together the economic, financial, and political aspects of the crisis. Bennett is critical of America's failure to assume greater political responsibility to preserve the peace. Bibliographical essay.

39:108 Clarke, Stephen V. O. *Central Bank Cooperation, 1924–1931.* New York: Federal Reserve Bank of New York, 1967. This book analyzes the efforts of the Federal Reserve Bank of New York to cooperate with European central banks in an effort to restore monetary stability after World War I. Clarke clearly portrays the successes of the mid-1920s and incisively examines the domestic and international pressures that undermined central bank cooperation after 1927. The author does not attempt to explain how central bank efforts reflected larger cross-currents of American diplomacy in the 1920s.

39:109 Clarke, Stephen V. O. *Exchange-Rate Stabilization in the Mid-1930's: Negotiating the Tripartite Agreement.* Princeton, N.J.: Princeton University Press, 1977. Clarke provides a fine account of the attempts to reestablish monetary cooperation among the democracies in the mid-1930s. He demonstrates how suspicious Roosevelt was of any effort to restore the classical gold standard. Yet aware of the advantages that might ensue from exchange rate stabilization, the president agreed to open negotiations with the French and British so long as control over policy remained in the hands of his friend and treasury secretary, Henry Morgenthau.

39:110 Costigliola, F. C. "Anglo-American Financial Rivalry in the 1920s." *Journal of Economic History* 37:4 (1977), 911–34. Costigliola argues that during the 1920s both the United States and Britain "sought to rebuild a viable capitalist world economy." Yet their visions of how the international monetary system should function differed. The British wanted a flexible gold exchange standard while the Americans desired a "market-regulated gold standard" that would "give full vent to United States economic predominance." American financial power compelled the British to acquiesce.

Costigliola, F. C. "The Other Side of Isolationism: The Establishment of the First World Bank, 1929–1930" (20:175) analyzes the American role in the establishment of the Bank for International Settlements. Focusing on the efforts of Owen D. Young, J. Pierpont Morgan, Thomas W. Lamont, and a few additional prominent American financiers, the author urgues that the BIS was the result of the bankers' desire to institutionalize the processes of central bank cooperation and separate world politics from international economics.

Hogan, M. J. *Informal Entente: The Private Structure of Cooperation in Anglo-American Economic Diplomacy, 1918–1928* (20:191) examines, in the opening chapters, Anglo-American efforts to deal with postwar monetary and financial problems. The author emphasizes the American interest in European reconstruction efforts, analyzes the American orientation toward foreign loans, war debts, and reparations, and stresses the attempt of both Wilsonian and Republican officials to depoliticize postwar economic relations and establish a framework of cooperation with Great Britain.

39:111 Hogan, Michael J. "The United States and the Problem of International Economic Control: American Attitudes toward European Reconstruction, 1918–1920." *Pacific Historical Review* 44:1 (1975), 84–103. Hogan demonstrates that President Woodrow Wilson adhered almost rigidly to the principle of cooperative, privately financed reconstruction. At the same time Wilson rejected intergovernmental debt adjustment schemes or treasury loans.

Leffler, M. P. *The Elusive Quest: America's Pursuit of European Stability and French Security, 1919–1933* (21:102) explores a number of issues linking the interests of the United States, France, and Western Europe. Leffler analyzes in depth the efforts of American policymakers to stabilize financial affairs in Europe. The author depicts the complex relations between private financiers, central bankers, and American government officials. Extensive bibliography.

Leffler, M. P. "The Origins of Republican War Debt Policy, 1921–1923: A Case Study in the Applicability of the Open Door Interpretation" (20:216) demonstrates that in molding war debt policy Republican officials were well aware that a reduction of payments would contribute to European monetary stabilization and thereby increase American exports. Yet a variety of domestic fiscal and political pressures circumscribed Republican options. The author argues that domestic priorities often interfered with the pursuit of open door commercial aspirations.

Lewis, C. *America's Stake in International Investment* (39:92).

39:112 Meyer, Richard H. *Bankers' Diplomacy: Monetary Stabilization in the Twenties.* New York: Columbia University Press, 1970. This monograph describes central bank efforts to stabilize the currencies of Belgium, Italy, Poland, and Rumania in the mid-1920s. Meyer does a fine job analyzing the relationships among French, British, and American central bankers. He does not focus on the relationships between central bankers and government officials in the United States, Britain, or France. Bibliography.

Moore, J. R. "Sources of New Deal Economic Policy: The International Dimension" (20:182) argues that European nations rebuffed Roosevelt's initial attempts at cooperation and pushed the Democratic president toward monetary unilateralism and the breakup of the London Economic Conference. Attributing more coherence to Roosevelt's policies than many other writers, the author believes that the subsequent course of European and American economic history would have been different if European leaders had not spurned the president's initial offers.

39:113 Moulton, Harold G., and Pasvolsky, Leo. *War Debts and World Prosperity.* Washington, D.C.: Brookings Institution, 1932. This volume summarizes the evolution of most war debt and reparation agreements during the decade of the 1920s. The authors do a fine job tracing the breakdown of the settlements during the early years of the depression. Appendixes provide statistical data on war debt borrowing and postwar payments.

Rhodes, B. D. "Reassessing 'Uncle Shylock': The United States and the French War Debt, 1917–1929" (20:220) contends that the French government sought to revise its financial obligations to the United States even as additional indebtedness was being incurred.

Woodrow Wilson's administration, piqued by French intransigence, set a precedent in opposing debt cancellation. Both governments failed to recognize the complexity of the debt issue.

39:114 Rowland, Benjamin M., ed. *Balance of Power or Hegemony: The Interwar Monetary System.* New York: New York University Press, 1976. The six essays in this volume examine whether the international monetary system needs a dominating power to impose order and preserve stability. The contributors do not come up with a consensus. The volume contributes to our understanding of the functioning and breakdown of the international monetary system in the interwar era.

39:115 Schuker, Stephen A. *The End of French Predominance in Europe: The Financial Crisis of 1924 and the Adoption of the Dawes Plan.* Chapel Hill: University of North Carolina Press, 1976. Schuker demonstrates how French financial weakness compelled French leaders to make concessions to Germany that assured Germany's rise to preeminence. This masterful study examines American financial policies toward Europe and focuses on the leverage exerted by prominent financiers; it is essential for understanding the consequences of American monetary and financial policies. Extensive bibliography.

39:116 Southard, Frank A. *American Industry in Europe.* Boston: Houghton Mifflin, 1931. A descriptive work that deals with the expansion of, the extent of, and the rationale for American companies' investments in European industry. It shows how independent of the State Department the U.S. investments in Europe were. Bibliography.

39:117 Wicker, Elmus R. *Federal Reserve Monetary Policy, 1917–1933.* New York: Random House, 1966. Wicker examines the evolution of Federal Reserve policy and stresses the role played by treasury and Federal Reserve officials. He analyzes the economic goals as well as the financial acumen of influential policymakers. The book is important because it elucidates the national and international factors bearing upon Federal Reserve monetary policy. Bibliography.

Wilson, J. H. *American Business and Foreign Policy, 1920–1933* (20:185).

Latin America

See "Personalities," especially John Hays Hammond (under "American, to 1941," "Others").

Kane, N. S. "Bankers and Diplomats: The Diplomacy of the Dollar in Mexico, 1921–1924" (21:251) shows how American financial power could be used to secure political as well as economic concessions from Mexico. According to Kane, American bankers and State Department officials worked in an interdependent fashion to achieve common objectives.

Meyer, L. *Mexico and the United States in the Oil Controversy, 1917–1942* (39:144).

Pérez, L. A., Jr. "Capital, Bureaucrats, and Policy: The Economic Contours of United States–Cuban Relations, 1916–1921" (21:266) finds that U.S. business interests increased their investment in Cuban sugar during 1916 to 1921. This expansion was marked by a coalescence of interest between the Department of State and the business community.

39:118 Seidel, Robert N. "American Reformers Abroad: The Kemmerer Missions in South America, 1921–1931." *Journal of Economic History* 32:4 (June 1972), 520–45. Work of American economic advisers has been generally neglected, especially in relation to the study of U.S. foreign policy. Seidel focuses on the work of Edwin W. Kemmerer in five Andean countries (1923–1931) to illustrate some characteristics of U.S. economic foreign policy. Also see Seidel's *Progressive Pan Americanism: Development and United States Policy toward South America, 1906–1931,* Cornell University Latin American Studies Program, Dissertation Series, no. 45, 1973.

Winkler, M. *Investments of United States Capital in Latin America* (20:213) has introductory chapters on economic life in Latin America and on international investment are followed by a nation-by-nation survey of foreign investment. There are charts on investment, trade, and economic activity.

FINANCIAL POLICY SINCE 1945

See Chapter 26, "The Marshall Plan."

Gardner, R. N. *Sterling-Dollar Diplomacy: The Origins and Prospects of Our International Economic*

Order (25:148) focuses on the Bretton Woods accords, the Anglo-American Financial Agreement, and the General Agreement on Tariffs and Trade.

Kumar, D. *Foreign Investments in India* (37:79).

39:119 Sewell, John W. *The United States and World Development: Agenda 1977.* New York: Praeger, 1977. This fifth annual assessment by the Overseas Development Council of relationships between the United States and developing countries recommends drastic change in the economic, social, and political systems. Included are 50 pages of valuable statistics for 1965 to 1975.

39:120 "The Third World: Public Debt, Private Profit." *Foreign Policy,* no. 30 (1978), 132–69. In a special section devoted to the problem of Third World indebtedness, *Foreign Policy* printed articles of differing views. While the authors do not agree on solutions, they clarify the nature of the problem and its origins by reviewing the lending practices of the International Monetary Fund, the World Bank, and the private lending markets.

International Monetary System

39:121 Bernstein, Edward M. "The United States and the International Monetary Fund." *Public Policy,* no. 11 (1961), 281–93. This is a straightforward description of the system, the U.S. relationship to it, and requirements for future success.

39:122 Calleo, David P., and Rowland, Benjamin M. *America and the World Political Economy: Atlantic Dreams and National Realities.* Bloomington: Indiana University Press, 1973. The authors challenge American political and economic internationalist ideals. They conclude "an international economic system that does not make sufficient allowances for nationalism is thus doomed to failure." Extensive bibliography.

39:123 Eckes, Alfred E., Jr. *A Search for Solvency: Bretton Woods and the International Monetary System, 1941–71.* Austin: University of Texas Press, 1975. Eckes's volume reviews American wartime planning to restructure the postwar international monetary system. Focusing on the efforts of treasury officials, especially Henry Morgenthau and Harry Dexter White, he demonstrates how American policymakers sought to create a postwar economic order that would be conducive to peace and posterity.

39:124 Novak, Jeremiah. "The Geopolitics of the Dollar." *Worldview* 22:1 (1979), 23–26, 35–36. Novak views November 1, 1978, as a critical turning point in geopolitical history. On that day the United States announced massive borrowing from the International Monetary Fund to save the dollar and for the first time since 1893 the treasury began to issue bonds denominated in foreign currencies. With these acts, according to Novak, America forfeited the international economic supremacy it had enjoyed since 1915 and acknowledged that the European Economic Community (EEC) and Japan are its economic equals.

Van Dormael, A. *Bretton Woods: Birth of a Monetary System* (25:152) complements Gardner's study.

Multinationals

39:125 Bergsten, C. Fred; Horst, Thomas; and Moran, Theodore H. *American Multinationals and American Interests.* Washington, D.C.: Brookings Institution, 1978. Foreign policy issues are included in the range of American interests (employment, exports-imports, taxation) discussed. The book deals with various theories of multinational corporations and looks at the theories in the context of policy issues.

39:126 Gilpin, Robert. *U.S. Power and the Multinational Corporations: The Political Economy of Foreign Direct Investment.* New York: Basic Books, 1975. A thoughtful look at the multinational corporations from the viewpoint of national interest. The book considers the growth of the United States as a world power and its relationship to the growth of multinational corporations.

39:127 Levitt, Kari. *Silent Surrender: The Multinational Corporation in Canada.* Toronto: Macmillan, 1970. A polemic that argues that U.S. companies have so dominated the Canadian economy that Canada is truly a dependent nation. The book views Canada as though it were a less developed country.

Seidman, A. *South Africa and U.S. Multinational Corporations* (37:256).

Servan-Schreiber, Jean-Jacques. *The American Challenge* (28:15) claims American business was taking over Europe, because American multinationals had technological superiority.

39:128 "Special Issue on the Multinational Enterprise." *Business History Review* 48:3 (1974), 277–449. This collection of articles deals with the origins of direct multinational investment. The firms studied were for the most part chartered outside the United States. Detailed footnotes included.

39:129 Staley, Eugene. *Raw Materials in Peace and War.* New York: Council on Foreign Relations, 1937. A book about "international raw material problems" that deals with the United States as producer and consumer, multinational investments, and U.S. policies. In 1937, Staley was writing, "there is no escape from international raw material interdependence, given the demands of modern industrialism."

39:130 Stocking, George W., and Watkins, Myron W. *Cartels in Action.* New York: Twentieth Century Fund, 1946. A basic book on international cartels, which documents the involvement of many American multinational corporations. The first of a valuable three-volume series dealing with the problems of domestic monopolies and international cartels. Bibliography.

39:131 "Toward a Historical Understanding of the Multinational Corporation." *Peace and Change* [2 special issues] 3/4 (1976). A unique collection of essays on the activities of U.S. multinationals in various parts of the world, with suggestions for both understanding and controlling them.

39:132 Vernon, Raymond. *Sovereignty at Bay: The Multi-National Spread of U.S. Enterprises.* New York: Basic Books, 1971. Concentrating on the growth of American multinational enterprises, the author argues there is a great deal to worry about in their unrestrained activities.

39:133 Vernon, Raymond. *Storm over the Multinationals.* Cambridge: Harvard University Press, 1977. Topics include multinational enterprise as symbol; multinational enterprise, "a close up view"; strategies of enterprise; the strain on national objectives of industrial and developing countries; transnational processes and national goals. Raymond Vernon was director of the Harvard Business School Project on Multinational Corporations.

39:134 Wilkins, Mira. *The Emergence of Multinational Enterprise: American Business Abroad from the* *Colonial Era to 1914.* Cambridge: Harvard University Press, 1970. This volume covers the growth and development of U.S. multinational enterprise in the years before World War I. While the emphasis is on the multinational corporation, the author is concerned with the relationships between U.S. government policies and the role of U.S. business abroad. Extensive bibliography.

39:135 Wilkins, Mira. *The Maturing of Multinational Enterprise: American Business Abroad from 1914 to 1970.* Cambridge: Harvard University Press, 1974. The first comprehensive history of American business abroad from 1914 to 1970, this book is a sequel to the author's *The Emergence of Multinational Enterprise.* The book provides details on when, which, why, and how U.S. businesses went to foreign countries and their experiences once abroad. It includes data on the involvement (or lack of involvement) of the U.S. government. Extensive bibliography.

OIL OPERATIONS

Blair, J. M. *The Control of Oil* (33:146) provides a comprehensive analysis of the producing and marketing systems of the international petroleum industry.

DeNovo, J. A. "The Movement for an Aggressive American Oil Policy Abroad, 1918–1920" (18:156) shows that World War I made clear to U.S. officials the connection between diplomacy, national security, and access to adequate petroleum reserves. This connection did not immediately result in the formulation of a coherent national petroleum policy in the early postwar years.

39:136 Gibb, George S., and Knowlton, Evelyn H. *The Resurgent Years, 1911–1927.* Vol. 2 in *History of Standard Oil.* New York: Harper, 1956. In this volume of the authorized history of Standard Oil of New Jersey, Gibb and Knowlton show that increased consumer demand for petroleum products and structural changes within the company's organization led to the participation of Standard Oil in the international competition after World War I. The authors conclude that resistance to the company by the Taft and Wilson administrations probably delayed American access to foreign oil reserves longer than would have otherwise been the case.

39:137 Hidy, Ralph W., and Hidy, Muriel E. *Pioneering in Big Business, 1882–1911.* Vol. 1 in

History of Standard Oil. New York: Harper, 1955. This is the first of a three-volume scholarly business history of Standard Oil Company (New Jersey); it carries the story to the great antitrust case of 1911. It deals in detail with that multinational oil company's striving to reach foreign markets.

Kaufman, B. I. *The Oil Cartel Case: A Documentary Study of Antitrust Activity in the Cold War Era* (33:147) is a history of the U.S. government's 1953 civil antitrust suit against five major American oil companies which raise much broader issues.

39:138   Krasner, Stephen D. "Oil Is the Exception." *Foreign Policy*, no. 14 (1974), 68–84. An analytical argument, explaining why other commodity exporters will not be able to successfully imitate the OPEC cartel.

39:139   Larson, Henrietta M.; Knowlton, Evelyn H.; and Popple, Charles S. *New Horizons 1927–1950*. Vol. 3 in *History of Standard Oil*. New York: Harper & Row, 1971. This is the third and final volume of the scholarly history of Standard Oil Company (New Jersey), the predecessor of Exxon. It is a business history of a multinational enterprise, which covers the travails of this company in Venezuela, Europe, the Middle East, and other parts of the world.

39:140   Vernon, Raymond, ed. *The Oil Crisis*. New York: Norton, 1976. This deals with the oil crisis of 1973–1974. It is an integrated volume that considers the crisis from the vantage point of various actors, including the United States and the multinational oil companies.

39:141   Williamson, Harold F., et al. *The American Petroleum Industry: The Age of Energy, 1899–1959*. Evanston, Ill.: Northwestern University Press, 1963. As this account shows, 1900 to 1920 witnessed a substantial increase in domestic crude oil production, modernization of transportation and marketing techniques, and increased competition within the industry. The increase in consumption of petroleum products during World War I necessitated subsequent large-scale American access to foreign oil reserves.

Asia

Anderson, I. H., Jr. *The Standard-Vacuum Oil Company and United States East Asian Policy, 1933–1941* (22:235) is a study of a multinational oil company and U.S. diplomacy in the Far East in the years before

World War II. This book gives details of the interactions between the business requirements of the U.S. enterprise and political strategies of the U.S. government. It contains invaluable new information on the formulation and implementation of the U.S. oil embargo against Japan.

Moore, J. W. "Economic Interests and American-Japanese Relations: The Petroleum Controversy" [1934–1937] (21:192).

Pugach, N. H. "Standard Oil and Petroleum Development in Early Republican China" (19:210) argues that the failure of Standard Oil to discover and develop oil resources in China during the presidency of Woodrow Wilson adds to our knowledge of the limitations of the open door policy. Pugach shows that the most pronounced characteristics of the quest for oil in China were the questionable business practices of Standard Oil and the way in which China manipulated rival companies.

Reed, P. M. "Standard Oil in Indonesia, 1898–1928" (17:282) finds that Standard Oil was no more able to gain access to oil reserves in Indonesia than to other reserves in the Far East prior to 1920. Virtually excluded by Royal Dutch-Shell, Standard had to await the more successful entreaties of the Department of State in the 1920s. Yet even government assistance did not prompt a full revision of Dutch policy until 1928.

Latin America

39:142   Grieb, Kenneth J. "Standard Oil and the Financing of the Mexican Revolution." *California Historical Quarterly* 50:1 (1971), 59–71. In a necessarily speculative argument, because of the lack of direct evidence, Grieb makes a case for the involvement by Standard Oil of New Jersey on the side of the rebels in the Mexican Revolution. If for no other reasons, the desire to protect its own investment and to beat competitors would have induced company officials to consider seriously financial assistance.

39:143   Hoffmann, Fritz L. "Edward L. Doheny and the Beginnings of Petroleum Development in Mexico." *Mid-America* 13:2 (1942), 94–108. Hoffmann provides useful information on the origins of the petroleum industry in Mexico, the role of the Mexican government in development, and the genesis of subsequent disputes between revolutionary governments and the oil companies.

39:144 Meyer, Lorenzo. *Mexico and the United States in the Oil Controversy, 1917–1942*. 2d ed. Trans. by Muriel Vasconcellos. Austin: University of Texas Press, 1977. Meyer presents as a general theme the conflict between economic nationalism, U.S. strategic interests, and the rights of American investors in Mexican oil. Meyer equates the interests of the oil companies and the U.S. government, but his contribution in showing the tension between revolutionary forces and foreigners in Mexico is important for understanding the Mexican perspective on the revolutionary years. Extensive bibliography.

39:145 O'Brien, Dennis J. "Petroleo e Intervención—Relaciones entre los Estados Unidos y México—1917–1918" [Petroleum and intervention: relations between the United States and Mexico, 1917–1918]. *Historia Mexicana* 27:1 (1977), 103–40. Mexican oil was vital to the Allied war effort during World War I. As O'Brien amply shows, Mexican oil reached the Allies through a combination of oil company cooperation, effective diplomacy by the Department of State, good fortune, and the passive acquiescence of the Carranza government.

39:146 Pinelo, Adalberto J. *The Multinational Corporation as a Force in Latin American Politics: A Case Study of the International Petroleum Company in Peru*. New York: Praeger, 1973. This study traces the attempts by a Standard Oil subsidiary to survive against Peruvian government opposition. Unlike most other studies of the role of multinationals in Latin American affairs, this one concludes that IPC was not a "force" in Peruvian politics; it was a perfect whipping boy. Bibliography.

Wood, B. *The Making of the Good Neighbor Policy* (21:246) covers the problems of multinational oil companies in Mexico and Venezuela.

Middle East

See also Chapter 18, "The Quest for Oil," and Chapter 33, "The U.S. and Middle Eastern Oil."

39:147 Anderson, Irvine H., Jr. *Aramco, the United States, and Saudi Arabia: A Study in the Dynamics of Foreign Policy, 1933–1950*. Princeton, N.J.: Princeton University Press, 1980. Using Aramco as a case study, Anderson details the change in official attitudes when government planners discovered that the country would become a net importer of oil following World War II. After the attempt to establish a federal petroleum reserves corporation with a controlling interest in Aramco failed, the State Department futilely tried to achieve the same ends through an Anglo-American petroleum agreement which was defeated in the Senate, forcing the government to rely on the benign support of private enterprise to achieve its goals. Extensive bibliography.

DeNovo, J. A. *American Interests and Policies in the Middle East, 1900–1939* (18:5) demonstrates that until the 1920s access of American oil companies to the vast oil fields of the Middle East remained more elusive than real. Growing nationalism in the region altered that perception; after 1920 American companies began competing in earnest with European oil companies for access to oil reserves.

39:148 Kaufman, Burton I. "Mideast Multinational Oil, U.S. Foreign Policy, and Antitrust: The 1950's." *Journal of American History* 63:4 (1976), 937–59. Kaufman criticizes Truman's and Eisenhower's use of American-controlled multinational oil companies as instruments of foreign policy to ensure oil supplies and to hinder the spread of Soviet influence in the Third World. He maintains that this policy contradicted the U.S. stand against international cartels and may have contributed to the formation of OPEC.

OTHER OPERATIONS

39:149 Mikdashi, Zuhayr. "Collusion Could Work." *Foreign Policy,* no. 14 (1974), 57–68. Mikdashi believes mineral exporting countries have bright prospects in establishing cartels along the OPEC model. He suggests that either way, the developing nations will not lose, as a transfer of wealth is in their long-range interests.

39:150 Moran, Theodore H. *Multinational Corporations and the Politics of Dependence: Copper in Chile*. Princeton, N.J.: Princeton University Press, 1974. This is a splendid case study of the experiences of American copper companies in Chile. It deals with issues of economic nationalism, *dependencia,* and expropriation and the corporate responses. Bibliography.

39:151 Wilkins, Mira, and Hill, Frank E. *American Business Abroad: Ford on Six Continents*. Detroit: Wayne State University Press, 1964. This history of Ford Motor Company's foreign business deals with that multinational enterprise's business 1903 to 1963—a business whose operations spanned the globe and whose activities touched and were touched by most facets of 20th-century economic and political history—worldwide. Extensive bibliography.

Special Topics

FOREIGN AID

See "Personalities" (since 1941), especially Chester Bowles, John Foster Dulles, and, under "Others," Sherman Adams, John E. Hughes; see also Chapter 26, "The Marshall Plan" and "Point Four Program," and Chapter 35, "Alliance for Progress."

39:152 Baldwin, David A. *Economic Development and American Foreign Policy*. Chicago: University of Chicago Press, 1966. This is an analysis of the evaluation of "soft" lending (long-term dollar loans at no or low interest) in the American aid program. Baldwin compares the shifting attitudes toward various techniques of foreign aid and their relative effectiveness.

39:153 Brown, William A., Jr., and Opie, Redvers. *American Foreign Assistance*. Washington, D.C.: Brookings Institution, 1953. This is a basic book on American assistance (1945–1952); it is especially good on aid to France.

39:154 Deans, Robert H. "U.S. Foreign Assistance Programs: The Impact of Local Currencies in Economic Development." *Journal of Developing Areas* 5:4 (1971), 589–604. Deans analyzes U.S.-owned and counterpart funds provided other nations for military support, economic development, or payment of U.S. obligations under the Agency for International Development (AID) or the Agricultural Trade Development and Assistance Act of 1954 (PL 480) commodity programs.

Eldridge, P. J. *The Politics of Foreign Aid in India* (37:87).

39:155 Feis, Herbert. *Foreign Aid and Foreign Policy*. New York: St. Martin's Press, 1964. A thorough pragmatic and standard postwar analysis of Allied foreign aid and international politics, from the condescending perspective of the "have" and "have not" nations.

39:156 Franco, G. Robert. "Economic and Political Aspects of U.S. Multilateral Aid." In Satish Raichur and Craig Liske, eds., *The Politics of Aid, Trade and Investment*. New York: Wiley, 1975, pp. 123–59. Franco favors multilateral, "untied" aid to developing nations and notes that among the major developed countries the United States is the only one channelling a large portion of its foreign assistance in this manner. He admits that in a totally united foreign aid system, the United States would lose about $1 billion in export earnings a year.

39:157 Howe, James W., ed. *The U.S. and the Developing World: Agenda for Action*. New York: Praeger, 1974. A series of articles analyzing the trend of growing resource scarcity, and suggesting global solutions to alleviate the impending crisis. The study also considers trade, monetary reform, food, and ocean management. Statistical tables are included.

39:158 Kanet, Roger E. "Soviet and American Behaviour toward the Developing Countries: A Comparison." *Canadian Slavonic Papers* 15:4 (1973), 439–61. Both the Soviet Union and the United States employ the same general types of foreign policy when focused on particular areas. In the Middle East and South Asia both supply military and economic assistance.

39:159 Kaufman, Burton I. "The United States Response to the Soviet Economic Offensive of the 1950s." *Diplomatic History* 2:2 (1978), 153–65. Kaufman reviews the change in U.S. development programs toward the Third World as the Soviet foreign assistance increased (1955–1959).

39:160 Liska, George. *The New Statecraft: Foreign Aid in American Foreign Policy*. Chicago: University of Chicago Press, 1960. This book develops a comprehensive theory of the role of foreign aid as an instrument of foreign policy. Bibliography.

Loomba, J. F. "U.S. Aid to India, 1951–1967: A Study in Decision Making" (37:91).

39:161 Mason, Edward S. *Foreign Aid and Foreign Policy*. New York: Harper & Row, 1964. Mason discusses foreign aid as an instrument of foreign policy. He explains its characteristics, analyzes its rationale, and asks how foreign aid is to be shared equitably among the wealthier nations. A special look is taken at the Alliance for Progress. Bibliographical footnotes.

39:162   Mikesell, Raymond F. *The Economics of Foreign Aid*. Chicago: Aldine, 1968. Mikesell is concerned mainly with official foreign economic assistance to less developed countries. Although he examines familiar economic growth models, his study is for the most part policy oriented. Extensive bibliography.

Montgomery, J. D. *The Politics of Foreign Aid: American Experience in Southeast Asia* (30:68) argues that political theory about foreign aid has lagged behind its practice. Montgomery describes the process by which economic aid was provided to undeveloped countries through a number of case studies from the 1950s.

39:163   Nelson, Joan M. *Aid, Influence, and Foreign Policy*. New York: Macmillan, 1968. This is a brief, useful introduction to the rationale behind American foreign aid from the end of World War II to the late 1960s. Most of the material is based on unquestioned AID assumptions. It candidly outlines the short-run, as well as long-term, political purposes and the general "influence potential" of U.S. economic aid—over half of which in recent years has been administered by AID.

39:164   O'Leary, Michael K. *The Politics of American Foreign Aid*. New York: Atherton, 1967. This is a brief, but one of the first, attempts at a comprehensive analysis of how foreign aid appropriations are made. It includes an analysis of public opinion, the role of the executive, and U.S. objectives in world affairs. It is far from definitive, but does provide a starting point for scrutinizing the entire political process as it relates to American aid abroad following World War II. Bibliography.

39:165   Riselbach, Leroy N. "The Demography of the Congressional Vote on Foreign Aid, 1939–1958." *American Political Science Review* 58:3 (1964), 577–88. Riselbach reveals that the vote on the Arms Embargo Act of 1939 was along party lines, but two years later, with the passage of the Lend-Lease Act, the regional factor had become more relevant than party loyalty.

39:166   Rosenau, James N. *National Leadership and Foreign Policy: A Case Study in the Mobilization of Public Support*. Princeton, N.J.: Princeton University Press, 1963. This is a quantitative study of how the U.S. government sought to mobilize support for its foreign aid program in 1958 among the policy influencing elite of America.

39:167   Thorp, Willard L. *The Reality of Foreign Aid*. New York: Praeger, 1971. This is a sophisticated, favorable evaluation of past and present American foreign aid policies. It conveys no particular sense of urgency about, or new insights into, the poverty and population problems of less developed nations.

39:168   Wagner, Robert H. *United States Policy toward Latin America: A Study in Domestic and International Politics*. Stanford, Calif.: Stanford University Press, 1970. From an organizational perspective, Wagner analyzes the relationship between foreign policy goals and the political process in the United States in formulating decisions on assistance to Latin America.

Wolf, C., Jr. *Foreign Aid: Theory and Practice in Southern Asia* [1945–1960] (37:94) traces the background, implementation, and problems of the mutual security program.

Military Assistance

39:169   Hovey, Harold A. *United States Military Assistance: A Study of Policies and Practices*. New York: Praeger, 1965. This is a comprehensive recounting of U.S. military assistance programs.

39:170   Louscher, David J. "The Rise of Military Sales as U.S. Foreign Assistance Instrument." *Orbis* 20:4 (1977), 933–64. Until 1961, U.S. foreign aid policies depended on the military assistance program and on economic grants and loans. After 1961, according to Louscher, the Foreign Military Sales (FMS) program became this country's primary method of giving assistance to other nations.

39:171   "U.S. Arms and Foreign Aid." *Current History* 77:448 (1979), 1–38. This valuable article by David F. Gordon, summarizing how foreign aid became an institutionalized aspect of American foreign policy, introduces the other articles in this issue. Other authors discuss aid and arms in Africa, the Middle East, Latin America, South Asia, and Southeast Asia. There is a short bibliography on aid, arms, and trade.

Food Programs

39:172   Destler, I. M. "United States Food Policy 1972–1976: Reconciling Domestic and International Objectives." *International Organization* 32:3 (1978), 617–54. U.S. food policy results from four competing concerns: a strategy to best work with them is the acceptance of the day-to-day predominance of the Agriculture Department.

39:173 Foland, Ellen S. "A Cartel of One: The U.S. and the World Food Crisis." *Social Policy* 7:1 (1976), 32–35. Foland traces the development of Public Law 480, the Food for Peace Act (1954), and discusses the social, political, and economic costs and beneficiaries, both foreign and domestic, of our foreign aid program.

39:174 Hopkins, Raymond F., and Puchala, Donald J. *Global Food Interdependence: Challenge to American Foreign Policy.* New York: Columbia University Press, 1980. Throughout the 20th century, the United States has been the world's major exporter of food. The authors examine U.S. food policies in the areas of production, trade, and aid.

39:175 Kern, Clifford R. "Looking a Gift Horse in the Mouth: The Economics of Food Aid Programs." *Political Science Quarterly* 83:1 (1968), 59–75. Kern discusses U.S. food aid programs since the late-1950s, detailing some of the outcomes of selected programs.

39:176 Reinton, Per Olav. "The Development Perspective of the Green Revolution." *Bulletin of Peace Proposals* 4:2 (1973), 170–78. Reinton analyzes the political and social effects of the Green Revolution (1963–1967). It has created a relationship between the peasant producer and the petrochemical industry unique in the history of cereal production.

39:177 Stanley, Robert G. *Food for Peace: Hope and Reality of U.S. Food Aid.* New York: Gordon & Breach, 1973. A good factual review of U.S. food policies from the turn of the century through the 1960s. It includes a detailed discussion of how PL 480 operates and what it has accomplished.

BOYCOTTS AND ECONOMIC SANCTIONS

See also Chapter 22, "Embargoes and Sanctions," and Chapter 37, "Zimbabwe (Southern Rhodesia)."

39:178 Doxey, Margaret P. *Economic Sanctions and International Enforcement.* New York: Oxford University Press, 1971. This study draws heavily from historical examples of economic warfare and sanc-

tions to suggest a checklist of prerequisites necessary for successful economic sanctions. Bibliography.

39:179 Gold, Joseph. "The 'Sanctions' of the International Monetary Fund." *American Journal of International Law* 66:5 (1972), 737–62. This is a detailed analysis of the "contribution sanctions can make to respect for international law and the effectiveness of multilateral treaties." The original IMF Articles of Agreement were adopted at the Bretton Woods Conference in July 1944.

39:180 Losman, Donald L. *International Economic Sanctions: The Cases of Cuba, Israel and Rhodesia.* Albuquerque: University of New Mexico Press, 1979. Losman examines boycott activity against three dissimilar countries by the United States (Cuba), Arabs (Israel), and the UN (Rhodesia). He concludes that boycotts can be successful in the short run; however, their long-term political effectiveness is not guaranteed. Bibliography.

39:181 Losman, Donald L. "International Boycotts: An Appraisal." *Politico* 37:4 (1972), 648–72. Analyzes the impact and effectiveness of the U.S. boycott of Cuba, the Arab boycott of Israel, and UN sanctions against Rhodesia. The degree of economic importance of the import-export trade determines a boycott's effectiveness.

Randolph, P. S. "The Byrd Amendment: A Postmortem" (37:239) examines the now-circumvented Byrd Amendment (1971) to the Armed Forces Authorization of 1972, which exempted Rhodesian chrome imports from U.S. restrictions (and the UN boycott), inasmuch as the United States was importing much chrome from the U.S.S.R.

Expropriation

39:182 Baklanoff, Eric N. *Expropriation of US Investments in Cuba, Mexico, and Chile.* New York: Praeger, 1975. Expropriation is often motivated by a nationalistic need to generate self-esteem when sufficient natural resources are lacking. Baklanoff notes the result of uncompensated expropriation can be impoverishment due to alienation of foreign investment.

39:183 Einhorn, Jessica Pernitz. *Expropriation Politics.* Lexington, Mass.: Lexington Books, 1974. This examination of the Peruvian expropriation of the International Petroleum Company uses the bureaucratic politics model. Bibliography. See also A. J. Pinelo, *The Multinational Corporation as a Force in Latin American Politics* (39:146).

39:184 Ingram, George M. *Expropriation of US Property in South America: Nationalization of Oil and Copper Companies in Peru, Bolivia and Chile.* New York: Praeger, 1974. This is a thorough case study analysis of U.S. investment in Latin America. Ingram considers the history of U.S. investment, the reasons for expropriation, and its political and economic effects on both the United States and the host country. Extensive bibliography.

Klein, H. S. "American Oil Companies in Latin America: The Bolivian Experience" (20:206) examines the details surrounding the first expropriation of a foreign oil company in Latin America (1937).

39:185 Knudsen, Harold. *Expropriation of Foreign Private Investments in Latin America.* Bergen, Norway: Universitetsforlaget, 1974. Knudsen asks to what extent, and how much multinational–host country conflict resulting in expropriation is due to social economic variables. Extensive bibliography.

39:186 Kuhn, W. "The Hickenlooper Amendment as a Determinant of the Outcome of Expropriation Disputes." *Social Science Journal* 14:1 (1977), 71–81. Kuhn examines issues in international law regarding the status of U.S. foreign investments in Brazil, Ceylon, Indonesia, Zambia, Chile, Peru, Bolivia, and Venezuela, arguing that the Hickenlooper Amendment to the Foreign Assistance Act (1962) has not enhanced respect for U.S. property by host country governments (1962–1970s).

39:187 Lipson, Charles H. "Corporate Preferences and Public Policies: Foreign Aid Sanctions and Investment Protection." *World Politics* 28:3 (1976), 396–421. Since 1959, Congress has tried to protect U.S. direct foreign investments from expropriation by quite explicit amendments to various foreign assistance acts. Probably the most important of these legislative efforts, the Hickenlooper Amendment, the Gonzales Amendments, and the effective repeal of the Hickenlooper Amendment, are contradictory and have been applied only sporadically.

39:188 Lowenfeld, Andreas F. *Expropriation in the Americas: A Comparative Law Study.* New York: Dunellen, 1971. This is an objective, legal examination of expropriation in the major South American nations.

39:189 Olson, R. S. "Economic Coercion in World Politics: With a Focus on North-South Relations." *World Politics* 31:4 (1979), 471–95. In a theoretical examination, Olson argues that subtle forms of economic persuasion are more likely to induce compliance.

39:190 Sigmund, Paul E. *Multinationals in Latin America: The Politics of Nationalization.* Madison: University of Wisconsin Press, 1980. Sigmund argues that, in Latin America at least, most of the exposed enclaves of the extractive business that were the major targets of the economic nationalists have now been taken over, remaining the major irritants affecting the relation of Third World government with foreign investors. He examines five major cases in detail—Mexico, Cuba, Chile, Peru, and Venezuela.

39:191 Silva Herzog, Jesus, ed. *El Petróleo de México: Recopilación de documentos oficiales del conflicto de orden económico de la industria petrolera* [Petroleum industry: summary of official documents of the economic class struggle of the petroleum industry]. Mexico, D.F.: Gobierno de México, 1940. Reprint 1963. This is a summary of official documents pertaining to expropriation and the oil industry of Mexico.

39:192 Silva Herzog, Jesus. *Historia de la expropriación de las empresas petroleras* [History of the expropriation of the petroleum companies]. 3d ed. Mexico, D.F.: Instituto Mexicano de Investigaciones Economicas, 1964. In one of the best studies of the subject, Silva Herzog presents a panorama of the circumstances that prompted Mexican government action. Historical data on the industry and the role of foreign companies, texts of the laws, reports, etc., are included.

MILITARY-INDUSTRIAL COMPLEX

39:193 Cook, Fred J. *The Warfare State.* New York: Macmillan, 1962. In this early but influential critique of the military-industrial complex, written from a journalistic perspective, Cook anticipates many of the arguments of the cold war revisionists.

39:194 Cooling, B. Franklin, III. "The Formative Years of the Naval-Industrial Complex: Their Meaning for Studies of Institutions Today." *Naval War College Review* 27:5 (1975), 53–62. Faced with the demands of building a new steel navy, men like Secretary of the Navy B. F. Tracy forged the basic links between industry and government which proved beneficial to both, but which also led to the practices and expansive military budget with which we are all familiar.

39:195 Cooling, B. Franklin, III, ed. *War, Business, and American Society: Historical Perspectives on the Military-Industrial Complex.* Port Washington, N.Y.: Kennikat, 1977. This collection of essays by various authorities takes as its theme the deep historical roots of the military-industrial complex. The complex is not merely a recent phenomenon, Cooling argues in a strong introduction and the other writers tend to confirm with detailed evidence; in one way or another, the military-industrial complex has always been a part of American life and an influence upon American policymakers, at least since the early 19th century. Bibliography.

Koistinen, P. A. C. *The Hammer and the Sword* (40:38) is a solid work on the beginnings and development of American planning for economic mobilization (1920–1945).

39:196 Lee, William T. "The 'Politico-Military-Industrial Complex' of the U.S.S.R." *Journal of International Affairs* 26:1 (1972), 73–86. Despite Soviet denials, a politico-military-industrial complex does exist in the U.S.S.R.; it is distinguishable by its institutional structure and its influence on weapons development, military doctrine, and budget trends. After siring the Soviet research and development effort, the complex created an "economy within an economy."

39:197 Melman, Seymour. *The Permanent War Economy: American Capitalism in Decline.* New York: Simon & Schuster, 1974. By focusing on the technology and productivity, Melman argues that the cold war military economy (from 1946 to 1974 more than $1,500 billion) has eroded away industrial productivity, the foundation of every nation's economic growth. This volume evolved from his earlier studies *Our Depleted Society* (1965) and *Pentagon Capitalism* (1970).

39:198 Nardinelli, Clark, and Ackerman, Gary B. "Defense Expenditures and the Survival of American Capitalism: A Note." *Armed Forces and Society* 3:1 (1976), 13–17. To test the Marxist hypothesis that large defense spending by the national government was necessary for the growth and survival of the capitalistic economic system, a statistical analysis was

applied to the relationship between U.S. (real) gross national product and (real) defense expenditures during 1905 to 1973. Not only was the Marxian hypothesis incorrect, but defense expenditures crowded out private investment expenditures, especially for 1946 to 1973.

39:199 Pursell, Carroll W., Jr., ed. *The Military-Industrial Complex.* New York: Harper & Row, 1972. This is a collection of articles on the military-industrial complex by the major scholars and actors in the field. Documents and technical data are provided.

39:200 Russett, Bruce M., and Stepan, Alfred. *Military Force and American Society.* New York: Harper & Row, 1973. The authors are concerned with the enormous expansion of military forces and expenditures, together with an increase in the military's participation in activities previously reserved for civilians. Extensive bibliography.

OCEAN (SEABED) RESOURCES

39:201 Amacher, Ryan C., and Sweeney, Richard J. *The Law of the Sea: US Interests and Alternatives.* Washington, D.C.: American Institute for Public Policy Research, 1976. This series of articles reviews the proceeds of a conference on the law of the sea negotiations. These essays present diverse views and perceptions from lawyers, economists, and political scientists.

39:202 Barkenbus, Jack N. *Deep Seabed Resources.* New York: Free Press, 1979. Barkenbus provides both an historical and current analysis of the law of the sea negotiations, supplemented by legal and technical data. Bibliography.

39:203 Eckert, Ross D. *The Enclosure of Ocean Resources.* Stanford, Calif.: Hoover Institution, 1979. Eckert accepts the shift from narrowly defined territorial waters to a 200-mile limit for exploitation of ocean resources. However, he believes other aspects of the current Law of the Sea Conference are out of tune with economic realities. Extensive bibliography.

39:204 Johnson, Barbara, and Langdon, Frank. "Two Hundred Mile Zones: The Politics of North Pacific Fisheries." *Pacific Affairs* 49:1 (1976), 5–27. The authors analyze the history of maritime diplomacy leading to the third Law of the Sea Conference, and examine the political interplay among Canada, the

United States, the Soviet Union, and Japan regarding 200-mile zones and fisheries issues.

39:205 Richardson, Elliot L. "Power, Mobility and the Law of the Sea." *Foreign Affairs* 58:4 (1980), 902–19. The head of the U.S. delegation to the UN conference on the law of the sea describes the current state of negotiations regarding territorial sea limits and deep seabed mining. Richardson indicates that on the former, the United States is in agreement, while the latter category requires further negotiation.

39:206 Schachter, Oscar. *Sharing the World's Resources.* New York: Columbia University Press, 1977. A broad discussion of the poorer nations' demand for an equitable redistribution of world wealth. Schachter analyzes the philosophical and legal aspects, as well as the political, economic, and institutional factors affecting a solution to world poverty.

40

The Armed Forces, Strategy, and Foreign Policy

Contributing Editor
RUSSELL F. WEIGLEY
Temple University

Contributors
Richard Dean Burns
*California State University,
Los Angeles*

Richard H. Immerman
Princeton University

Contents

Introduction

Historians of American foreign relations have generally paid far less attention to the military as an instrument for the defense and advancement of national policy than have the historians of virtually any other great power. Since 1941, of course, the military dimensions of American policy have abruptly loomed so large that they often appear to dominate the scene, and historians of foreign relations have had to acquaint themselves with the historical forces that might explain the American military—or at least they should have done so. Two sets of circumstances, however, account for a prolonged neglect of the military aspects of the history of American foreign relations. One is inherent in the nature of American history, the other an incident of the ways in which American history happens to have been studied.

First, most obviously and fundamentally, throughout much of the history of American foreign relations, the military indeed played only a minor role. Through the long era of free security before the middle of the twentieth century, the United States neither depended upon its armed forces as the major reliance for the defense of the national territory nor developed vital interests overseas requiring military protection. Even the westward advance of the continental frontier against the Indians was accomplished less by applying military force than by the mere weight of the expansion of white population and settlement. To be sure, there were occasional brief moments when the ability to mobilize military power was critical to the nation's survival; the United States after all achieved its independence through war. But the moments when the military occupied stage center were exceedingly rare. For the most part, the army was merely a frontier constabulary. The navy impinged upon foreign relations somewhat more directly, by showing the flag and protecting American mercantile activity in foreign ports; but the interests defended by the navy were almost never vital national ones. Even after the United States became a world power, the assertion of its interests abroad was more often expressed through its economic than its military strength, at least until 1941.

Second, the study of American military history long remained peripheral to the study of American foreign relations also because of the manner in which military history was usually written. If historians whose special concern was directed elsewhere than toward the military paid still less attention to the military than they should have given the small role of the military, it was partly because the few historians who did specialize in the military past isolated themselves by taking the most narrowly military view of that past. They concentrated on battles and campaigns, on military tactics rather than on military strategy, let alone exploring the area where military strategy might have met national policy. They wrote almost nothing about the relationship of the American military to the civil state—except from time to time to condemn the interference of civilians in the mysteries of the conduct of war—let alone illuminating the social and cultural context of military institutions.

Even after the contribution of the military to American foreign policy became so abruptly anything but peripheral, the writing of American military history had to change, if studies of the subject were to become useful to anyone but the seeker of tactical lessons applicable on the battlefield. Fortunately, a broadening of the horizons of military history, naturally prompted in part by international events, had begun to appear just before the American plunge into World War II. Edward Mead Earle of the Institute for Advanced Study initiated in 1940 a seminar in military affairs participated in by members of the Princeton University faculty as well as members of the institute. Out of this seminar came Earle's pioneering collection of essays in the history of military thought, *Makers of Modern Strategy: Military Thought from Machiavelli to Hitler* (40:20). Out of association with Earle came Bernard Brodie's *Sea Power in the Machine Age* (40:168) and, more directly concerned with the history of the military in American foreign policy, Harold and Margaret Sprout's *The Rise of American Naval Power* (40:117). These three books are the first landmarks of the "new military history," a military history reaching beyond the battlefield to explore the social and political forces influencing the military, the military impact upon those forces in turn, and not least, the military role in foreign relations. Earlier military histories had occasionally dealt with these larger areas. Earle's influence, underwritten by the vast expansion of the military involvement in American policy during World War II, converted this broad approach to military history into the predominant style. Earle's book is still the most valuable single work for anyone seeking to understand strategic thought. Brodie went on to write numerous works on strategy and foreign policy, among which his *War and Politics* (40:19) may be the best, most basic introduction to current issues growing out of the convergence of those two fields.

Thus the works cited in this chapter disproportionately date from after 1940 not only for the usual reason that newly available evidence and new interpretations have superseded earlier studies, but more because, with few exceptions, older works in military history that tie the subject to foreign relations do not exist. Fortunately, the "new military history" emerging since 1940 has not confined its attention to the post-1940 events that sustained its growth. The new military historians have looked backward to resurvey the whole American military past, and their efforts to do so should certainly commend themselves to historians of American foreign relations. The American military may have been of only peripheral importance to the history of foreign relations before 1941; but the military institutions and attitudes that evolved during the century and a half of American independence before 1940, and even during the colonial era, go far to explain the nature of the military participation in foreign policy during and since World War II. Most notably, out of the more remote past there developed among the military as well as within the American nation generally a conviction that war is a phenomenon of absolutes, fought by unlimited means to achieve the adversary's unconditional surrender. No element in the American military system has been more troublesome than this conviction in the effort since 1945 to tailor American military means to rational calculations of the ends they might serve.

This chapter deals largely with overviews of the military past, those works that explore the long historical development of current military attitudes and policy, or those at least that sweep across the chronological boundaries of several of the other chapters of this guide. Military histories directly related to the history of foreign policy but confined to a more limited time span are listed in the appropriate chronological chapters.

The emphasis is on the "new military history," stressing the military role in society and particularly in foreign relations rather than battles and campaigns;

but the old military history of battles and campaigns has not been altogether rejected here because a knowledge of how the cutting edge of national policy actually cuts at the moment of application in battle remains central to understanding what the military can and cannot do in the service of national policy. Perhaps the most compelling problem in the writing of American military history today is to integrate the history of the application of military force in war—or even in deterrence—into the new military history which, eschewing drums and trumpets, has too often run toward the other extreme of excluding study of the use of force from examinations of the history of institutions whose reason for being is the management of force and violence.

The limitation of military forces through arms control and disarmament is currently a subject in need of definition and historical synthesis. Historians have focused their attentions on the pre-1939 period—particularly on naval limitation efforts during the interwar years—where archives are now open, leaving post-1945 events to journalists and theorists such as military strategists, economists, and political scientists. Only basic works are listed here, while sources dealing with specific negotiations and treaties are listed in the appropriate chronological chapters. To guide the researcher to the burgeoning literature of this topic, bibliographies are listed below. The most recent and comprehensive of these is Richard Dean Burns's *Arms Control and Disarmament* (1:25), the introduction of which "represents a minor study on classification, on arms control and disarmament measures, their incentives and outcomes."

Resources and Overviews

RESEARCH AIDS

While pertinent bibliographies and reference aids are listed here, there are more extensive lists in Chapter 1.

Bibliographies

Blackstock, P. W., and Schaf, F. L., Jr., eds. *Intelligence, Espionage, Counterespionage, and Covert*

Operations: A Guide to Information Sources (1:43) is a fine introduction to U.S. and U.S.S.R. operations.

Burns, R. D. *Arms Control and Disarmament: A Bibliography* (1:25) offers comprehensive coverage of post-1945 negotiations and agreements.

Burt, R., comp. and ed., and Kemp, G., ed. *Congressional Hearings on American Defense Policy, 1947– 1971: An Annotated Bibliography* (1:44) is a complete guide to the congressional hearings for its period.

Foreign Affairs Bibliography: A Selected and Annotated List of Books on International Relations (1:15) is published at ten-year intervals, and has a useful section, "War and Peace." Useful materials are also scattered through the volumes.

United Nations. Dag Hammarskjöld Library. *Disarmament: A Select Bibliography* (1:29) is a useful compilation of books and articles. Four volumes, covering 1962 to 1977, have been printed.

Military Topics

Albion, R. G. *Naval and Maritime History: An Annotated Bibliography* (1:41) is a thorough and well-organized bibliography.

40:1 Albrecht, Ulrich, et al. *A Short Research Guide on Arms and Armed Forces.* New York: Facts on File, 1979. A useful aid to researchers who seek current information about the characteristics of modern weapons systems (post-1945), who owns them and in what quantities. Covering seven different categories of informational aids, the guide concentrates on weapons and armed forces in Europe, the Third World, and the United States.

Anderson, M. *Conscription: A Select and Annotated Bibliography* (1:42) includes materials on all-volunteer military and universal military training.

Greenwood, J., comp. *American Defense Policy since 1945: A Preliminary Bibliography* (1:45) is a comprehensive, balanced introductory bibliography.

40:2 Greico, Joseph M., and Clarke, Duncan L. "National Security Affairs: A Selective Bibliography." *Policy Studies Journal* 7:1 (1978), 157–64. This is a bibliography of books, articles, and dissertations published during the 1960s and 1970s pertaining to national security.

40:3 Halperin, Morton H. *Limited War: An Essay on the Development of the Theory and an Annotated Bibliography.* Cambridge: Harvard University, Center for International Affairs, 1962. Halperin was among the "strategy intellectuals" who developed the concept of limited war. His summary of the evolution of the concept and his bibliography are equally valuable.

Higham, R., ed. *A Guide to the Sources of United States Military History* (1:47) is relevant for all periods; of particular interest is C. L. Christman's chapter, "The Department of Defense, Defense Policy and Diplomacy, 1945–73."

Jessup, J. E., Jr., and Coakley, R. W., eds. *A Guide to the Study and Use of Military History* (1:48) is an indispensable bibliography of world military history, with emphasis on the United States.

40:4 Larson, Arthur D. *Civil-Military Relations and Militarism: A Classified Bibliography Covering the United States and Other Nations of the World with Introductory Notes.* Manhattan: Kansas State University Library, 1971. A guide to the "new" military history and to related studies in other disciplines, it places military institutions in their political and social context. Its focus is mainly on the 20th century.

40:5 Larson, Arthur D. *National Security Affairs: A Guide to Information Sources.* Detroit: Gale, 1973. Larson is among the most expert bibliographers in the national security field. This bibliography more than most helps the researcher find his way to documentary as well as secondary material.

Miller, S. D., comp. *An Aerospace Bibliography* (1:50) covers air and space topics from early in the 20th century.

Millett, A. R., and Cooling, B. F., III, comps. *Doctoral Dissertations in Military Affairs: A Bibliography* (1:246) is a broadly conceived bibliography. It is updated annually in *Military Affairs.*

40:6 Smith, Myron J., Jr. *The Soviet Navy, 1941– 1978: A Guide to Sources in English.* Santa Barbara, Calif.: ABC-Clio, 1980. This volume includes not only books, articles, and documents on technical issues, but also contains references related to economic, arms control, political and strategic issues. It will be joined by volumes entitled *The Soviet Air and Strategic Rocket Forces, 1939–1980,* and *The Soviet Army.*

40:7 [U.S. Air Force. Air University.] *Air University Library Index to Military Periodicals*. Maxwell Air Force Base, Ala.: Air University Library, 1949–. The most complete annual guide to sources of information of a type that space limitations have compelled this chapter relatively to neglect. Although not annotated and without index, items are cross-referenced under an elaborate subject arrangement. Historical essays are listed.

U.S. Department of the Army. *Nuclear Weapons and NATO: [An] Analytical Survey of Literature* (1:52).

Yearbooks and Other Aids

Brassey's Annual: The Armed Forces Year-Book [1886–] (1:154) is useful for specific information about armies and weapons.

Esposito, V. J., ed. *The West Point Atlas of American Wars* (1:158).

40:8 International Institute for Strategic Studies. *The Military Balance*. London: IISS, 1962–. It contains a "quantitative assessment of the military power and defence expenditures of countries throughout the world," and lists characteristics of specific weapons systems. The IISS also publishes the *Strategic Survey* (1967–), which attempts to assess changes in military situations.

40:9 Stockholm International Peace Research Institute. *World Armament and Disarmament: The SIPRI Yearbook*. New York: Humanities Press, 1968–. This exceptionally informative annual survey provides a nongovernmental assessment of the year's military and disarmament issues. It contains a vast array of current statistics on world armaments drawn from a wide variety of sources.

United Nations. *The United Nations Disarmament Yearbook* [1976–] (38:102).

Document Collections

More general collections are listed in Chapter 1, and other collections may be found under "Personalities," below.

40:10 Cole, Alice C., et al., eds. *The Department of Defense: Documents on Establishment and Organization, 1944–1978*. Washington, D.C.: G.P.O., 1979. The editors are experienced official historians whose comprehensive knowledge of defense establishment documentation assures the selection of salient documents to illustrate both the interservice controversies about the appropriate shape of a defense department and the organizational evolution of the department.

40:11 Dupuy, Trevor N., and Hammerman, Gay M., eds. *A Documentary History of Arms Control and Disarmament*. New York: Bowker, 1973. This historical collection (546 B.C.–1973) is useful for providing a perspective on these issues, and for pulling together hard to locate items.

40:12 Kohn, Richard H., ed. *Military Laws of the United States from the Civil War through the War Powers Act of 1973*. New York: Arno, 1979. This basic military and naval legislation is reprinted from *The Public Statutes at Large of the United States of America*.

40:13 Millis, Walter, ed. *American Military Thought*. Indianapolis: Bobbs-Merrill, 1966. Millis has brought together the most convenient anthology of the basic documents of American military history. He defined military thought broadly, and included texts of basic laws and executive documents but relatively few unofficial expressions of military thought.

40:14 U.S. Arms Control and Disarmament Agency. *Documents on Disarmament*. Washington, D.C.: G.P.O., 1960–. This is an annual documentary publication continuing the U.S. Department of State publication of the same title, which began by printing the pertinent 1945 to 1960 documents. It is a most useful, basic collection.

40:15 U.S. Department of State. Historical Office. *Documents on Disarmament, 1945–1959*. 2 vols. Washington, D.C.: G.P.O., 1960. This publication of documentary texts has been continued since 1960 as *Documents on Disarmament*; see above.

40:16 U.S. Senate. Committee on Foreign Relations. Subcommittee on Disarmament. *Disarmament and Security: A Collection of Documents, 1919–1955*. Washington, D.C.: G.P.O., 1956. Included here is a selection of the principal treaties, agreements, and background documentation.

OVERVIEWS

Military Policy and Society

Barnet, R. J. *Roots of War: The Men and Institutions behind U.S. Foreign Policy* (24:32) is an analysis of the revisionist proposition that the internal character of American society has come to require an external policy of permanent violence. Barnet concludes that the proposition is valid, but for bureaucratic and domestic political as well as the economic reasons.

40:17 Bernardo, C. Joseph, and Bacon, Eugene H. *American Military Policy: Its Development since 1775.* 2d ed. Harrisburg, Pa.: Stackpole, 1961. The authors uncritically accept the military's institutional view of most issues, and they perpetuate the idea that civilians traditionally have been uninformed about and neglectful of the military. Despite this bias, it is the best introduction to the acts of Congress and official executive pronouncements affecting the armed forces. Bibliography.

40:18 Blechman, Barry M., and Kaplan, Stephen S., eds. *Force without War: U.S. Armed Forces as a Political Instrument.* Washington, D.C.: Brookings Institution, 1978. This collection of essays is tied to two broad objectives: to identify the incidents when the United States employed "its armed forces for political objectives"; and "to evaluate the effectiveness of the armed forces as a political instrument." Eight case studies are examined in depth. Bibliography.

40:19 Brodie, Bernard. *War and Politics.* New York: Macmillan, 1973. There has been no American Clausewitz, but Brodie's wide-ranging historical knowledge and questioning, philosophical bent of mind approaches such stature. Brodie explores why Americans went to war against Germany and Japan, the North Koreans and Communist Chinese, and the Viet Cong and North Vietnamese and continually offers new applications of Clausewitz's reflections on war. Bibliography.

40:20 Earle, Edward Mead, ed. *Makers of Modern Strategy: Military Thought from Machiavelli to Hitler.* Princeton, N.J.: Princeton University Press, 1943. This classic anthology (1469–1940) deals with a few American strategists: Alexander Hamilton and the economic basis of military power; Alfred Thayer Mahan; and Billy Mitchell and Alexander De Seversky. An understanding of U.S. military policy demands an acquaintance with the fundamental concepts of strategy developed by the Baron de Jomini, Karl von Clausewitz, Giulio Douhet, and the others. Extensive bibliography.

40:21 Hobbes, Richard. *The Myth of Victory: What is Victory in War?* Boulder, Colo.: Westview, 1979. As a retired army officer and professor, Hobbes challenges assumptions that the achievements of wars (1776–1979) outweigh their costs. He is especially critical of total war and total victory concepts and examines democratic processes which lead to wars and such illusory assumptions. Bibliography.

40:22 Matloff, Maurice, ed. *American Military History.* Washington, D.C.: G.P.O., 1969. This latest ROTC military history textbook (1607–1967) has achieved considerable independence of judgment. It is as good an introduction to the history of the army's battles and campaigns—its particular strong suit—as can be found. Extensive bibliographical essay.

40:23 Millis, Walter. *Arms and Men: A Study of American Military History.* New York: Putnam's, 1956. Although dated, this book remains the best all-around survey of American military history (1607–1956), linking together policy, strategy, technology, and their pay-off in the use of military force actively or through deterrence to attain military objectives. If one reads only a single book on American military history, this book should be it. Bibliography.

40:24 O'Connor, Raymond G., ed. *American Defense Policy in Perspective: From Colonial Times to the Present.* New York: Wiley, 1965. An anthology of both documents and historical writings (1607–1964) dealing with organization, strategy, and to a limited extent military operations as well as policy. Documents range from James Monroe's plan for a naval peace establishment following the War of 1812 to John Foster Dulles's massive retaliation speech.

40:25 O'Connor, Raymond G. *Force and Diplomacy: Essays Military and Diplomatic.* Coral Gables, Fla.: University of Miami Press, 1972. These essays cover disarmament, naval strategy, nonrecognition, and use of sanctions.

40:26 Shy, John W. "The American Military Experience: History and Learning [1607–1970]." *Journal of Interdisciplinary History* 1:2 (1971), 205–28. Shy sees in the bitter struggles with the Indians, for example, the roots of the American conception of war as an unlimited endeavor fought for the absolute defeat of the enemy. His efforts to incorporate into the analysis insights borrowed from psychology are less satisfactory.

40:27   Simpson, B. Mitchell, III, ed. *War, Strategy, and Maritime Power.* New Brunswick, N.J.: Rutgers University Press, 1977. These Naval War College lectures are useful because general works on American military history usually take the army's view. Essays include "The Origins of Maritime Strategy and the Development of Seapower," "The Evolution of American Nuclear Thought," and "The Decline and Fall of the Joint Chiefs of Staff." Bibliography.

40:28   Small, Melvin. *Was War Necessary? National Security and U.S. Entry into War.* Beverly Hills, Calif.: Sage, 1980. Small examines the U.S. wars against Britain in 1812, Mexico, Spain, Germany, the Axis powers, and North Korea and challenges the claim that American security was threatened in each instance. Even those who disagree with the conclusions will be forced to reconsider their thinking about the causes of America's wars.

40:29   Smith, Dale O. *U.S. Military Doctrine: A Study and Appraisal.* New York: Duell, Sloan & Pearce, 1955. This history, by an air force brigadier general, treats uncritically all opinions favoring strong military forces, particularly the ideas of strategic air power, and critically any viewpoint skeptical of large military expenditures. Bibliography.

40:30   Weigley, Russell F. *The American Way of War: A History of United States Military Strategy and Policy.* New York: Macmillan, 1973. This is a study of strategy intellectuals and military men. The book argues that Civil War strategies, aimed at annihilation of enemy armies and resources, have led to American commitment to unconditional surrender. Persisting through World War II, this strategic tradition has not well fitted the post-1945 world. Bibliography.

Military in American Society

See Chapter 39, "Military-Industrial Complex."

40:31   Ambrose, Stephen E., and Barber, James A., eds. *The Military and American Society.* New York: Free Press, 1972. These essays (1945–1971) cover such topics as the administration of the military, the

military-industrial complex, the military influence on foreign policy, the social effects of military service, the military and race relations, the question of conscription, the military and domestic order, and the ecological impact of military activities.

Cooling, B. F., III, ed. *War, Business, and American Society: Historical Perspectives on the Military-Industrial Complex* (39:195) takes as its theme the deep historical roots of the military-industrial complex (1789–1976). The complex is not merely a recent phenomenon, Cooling argues in a strong introduction and the other writers tend to confirm with detailed evidence.

40:32   Ekirch, Arthur A., Jr. *The Civilian and the Military.* New York: Oxford University Press, 1956. This book is a history of American antimilitarist thought, Ekirch distinguishing the antimilitarist from the pacifist as a person who "may accept war and armies as a sometimes necessary evil." The emphasis is on the 20th century and the antiwar movements of the years between the world wars.

40:33   Guttmann, Allen. "Conservatism and the Military Establishment." In his *The Conservative Tradition in America.* New York: Oxford University Press, 1967. Students of military influence on American policy have accepted Huntington's (40:44) argument that the officer corps subscribes to conservative values which are at odds with the liberal ethos of the American mainstream. Guttmann argues that American officers are Americans first and military professionals second, and that their values are essentially liberal ones shared with the American mainstream. Bibliography.

40:34   Janowitz, Morris. *The Professional Soldier: A Social and Political Portrait.* Glencoe, Ill.: Free Press, 1960. In a pioneer sociological study of the officer corps, Janowitz analyzes officers' careers in relation to their socioeconomic background. He early analyzed the implications of the displacement of the "heroic leader" by the military manager as the principal type of professional soldier. Bibliography.

40:35   Karsten, Peter. *The Naval Aristocracy: The Golden Age of Annapolis and the Emergence of Modern American Navalism.* New York: Free Press, 1972. This pathbreaking analysis identifies American naval officers (1840–1930) by their background, education, social position, values and motives (concern for country and careers). Extensive bibliography.

40:36 Karsten, Peter. *Soldiers and Society: The Effects of Military Service and War on American Life.* Westport, Conn.: Greenwood, 1978. The recruitment process, training, the tour of duty and combat, and homecoming are examined in their impacts not only upon the soldier but also upon his family, the economy, and social and political values (1607–1977).

40:37 Kemble, C. Robert. *The Image of the Army Officer in America: Background for Current Views.* Westport, Conn.: Greenwood, 1973. Kemble explores the depiction of the soldier in American literature, fiction and nonfiction, except poetry, to study the image of the professional soldier. The volume emphasizes the period through the Spanish-American War, with an epilogue linking historical attitudes to current conceptions. Bibliography.

40:38 Koistinen, Paul A. C. *The Hammer and the Sword.* New York: Arno, 1979. This is a photographic reproduction of a 1965 University of California, Berkeley, Ph.D. dissertation, whose subtitle was "Labor, the Military and Industrial Mobilization, 1920–1945." It is the best work on the beginnings and development of American planning for economic mobilization in war and on the application of that planning in World War II. Extensive bibliography.

40:39 Morton, Louis. "Civilians and Soldiers: Civil-Military Relations in the United States." In William H. Nelson, ed. *Theory and Practice in American Politics.* Chicago: University of Chicago Press, 1964, pp. 123–37. Valuable despite its brevity, the article develops the historical background of the military-industrial complex and garrison-state conceptions and takes a balanced, cautious stance on the question of whether military influence in American politics has become excessive. Bibliography.

40:40 Moskos, Charles C., Jr. *The American Enlisted Man: The Rank and File in Today's Military.* New York: Russell Sage Foundation, 1970. What Morris Janowitz, *The Professional Soldier* (40:34), is to the American officer corps, Moskos's *The American Enlisted Man* is to the rank and file. The termination of selective service has not reduced the book's usefulness. Bibliography.

Russett, B. M., and Stepan, A. *Military Force and American Society* (39:200).

Military and the Government

40:41 Albion, Robert G. "The Naval Affairs Committees, 1816–1947." *U.S. Naval Institute Proceedings* 78:11 (1952), 1226–37. An authority on the history of naval administration surveys the changing organization and influence of the congressional committees, the background of congressional members, the power of the chairmen, and the relationships of the committees with the Navy Department.

40:42 Bletz, Donald F. *The Role of the Military Professional in U.S. Foreign Policy.* New York: Praeger, 1972. A political scientist and career army officer insists that the military professional ought to play an important role in the making of foreign policy. Bibliography.

40:43 Hammond, Paul Y. *Organizing for Defense: The American Military Establishment in the Twentieth Century.* Princeton, N.J.: Princeton University Press, 1961. The most complete survey of the organization of the War, the Navy, and later the Defense Department (1900–1960), it is a detailed comparison of the army's Chief of Staff and General Staff system with the navy's Chief of Naval Operations, General Board, and bureau system. Bibliography.

40:44 Huntington, Samuel P. *The Soldier and the State: The Theory and Politics of Civil-Military Relations.* Cambridge: Harvard University Press, 1957. A survey of the political influence of the military profession (1700–1957), with emphasis on the American military since World War II. Bibliography.

40:45 May, Ernest R. "The Development of Political-Military Consultation in the United States." *Political Science Quarterly* 70:2 (1955), 161–80. This essay reviews the State-War-Navy Coordinating Committee and other early beginnings to the Eisenhower administration's efforts toward efficient staff work between the military and civil contributors to policy.

40:46 May, Ernest R., ed. *The Ultimate Decision: The President as Commander in Chief.* New York: Braziller, 1960. Wartime commanders-in-chief—Madison, Polk, Lincoln, McKinley, Wilson, Franklin D. Roosevelt, and Truman—are examined along with Washington and Eisenhower. Bibliography.

40:47 Millis, Walter; with Mansfield, Harvey C., and Stein, Harold. *Arms and the State: Civil-Military*

Elements in National Policy. New York: Twentieth Century Fund, 1958. These studies examine the changing organization and political and social impact of the military in World War II and the cold war. Though dated, the studies remain worthwhile. Bibliography.

Rappaport, A. *The Navy League of the United States* [1902–1952] (2:212) is a history of the Navy League's coalition of businessmen, academics, and even clergymen as a civilian lobbying organization. However, Rappaport demonstrates that the members of the Navy League were less wealthy and less strategically placed than might be expected.

40:48   Smith, Louis. *American Democracy and Military Power: A Study of Civil Control of the Military Power in the United States.* Chicago: University of Chicago Press, 1951. A thorough study of the relationships between the military and the president, the various executive departments, Congress, and the judiciary, it emphasizes the constitutional provisions regarding the military and the historical evolution of constitutional issues. Bibliography.

40:49   Stein, Harold, ed. *American Civil-Military Decisions: A Book of Case Studies.* Birmingham: University of Alabama Press, 1963. These essays cover the Far Eastern crisis of 1931–1932, the controversy over control of helium, the M-day (mobilization day) plans of the years between the world wars, aid to Russia in World War II, World War II naval strategy and diplomacy, the Italian armistice, directives for the occupation of Germany, the supercarrier and B-36 controversies, the decision to advance to the Yalu during the Korean War, the rearming of Germany, and American bases in Spain. Bibliography.

40:50   Vagts, Alfred. *Defense and Diplomacy: The Soldier and the Conduct of Foreign Relations.* New York: Columbia University Press, 1956. The most comprehensive study (1700–1955) of the military role in the making of foreign policy worldwide, deals with the origins and the halting of wars, with soldiers as diplomats as well as in relation to diplomats, and with such issues as intelligence, military missions and instructors, and the use of force in foreign policy short of war. Extensive bibliography.

40:51   White, Howard. *Executive Influence in Determining Military Policy in the United States.* Urbana: University of Illinois Press, 1924. This old standard is useful for its perspective in the era before the imperial presidency and an immense military budget and bureaucracy.

Personalities

Additional references on individuals may be found in Chapter 1, "Biographical Data."

MILITARY LEADERS

Also see under various chapters for wartime leaders.

Air Force

Henry H. Arnold

See Chapter 23, under "Personalities," for references.

William Mitchell

40:52   Hurley, Alfred F. *Billy Mitchell: Crusader for Air Power.* New ed. Bloomington: Indiana University Press, 1975. General Mitchell remained the principal source of the American conception of air power. This biography by a professional air force officer blends appropriate technical knowledge, sympathy for Mitchell, and detachment and criticism. Bibliography.

40:53   Mitchell, William. *Memoirs of World War I: "From Start to Finish of Our Greatest War."* New York: Random House, 1960. Billy Mitchell's posthumously published memoirs are important as the most readable statement of his theory of air power. Though evidently based on a diary kept by Mitchell during the war, the memoirs were obviously much revised during his later years.

Army

Mark W. Clark

Clark, M. W. *Calculated Risk* (23:117) is an account of the World War II Mediterranean campaign by the U.S. Commander of the Fifth Army and 15th Army Group.

Clark, M. W. *From the Danube to the Yalu* (27:38) is an autobiographical account that includes treatment of the Korean War. Clark commanded the UN forces during the closing days of the war.

Dwight D. Eisenhower

See Chapters 23 and 24, under "Personalities," for additional references.

40:54 Allied Expeditionary Forces. Supreme Headquarters [SHAEF]. *Report by the Supreme Commander to the Combined Chiefs of Staff on the Operations in Europe of the Allied Expeditionary Forces, 6 June 1944 to 8 May 1945*. Washington, D.C.: G.P.O., 1945. Eisenhower's official report as Supreme Commander on operations from D-day to V-E day is a narrative account of the campaign in northwest Europe as seen from the vantage point of the Supreme Commander. He glosses over the major areas of controversy. Other editions have appeared under various titles.

Ambrose, S. E. *The Supreme Commander: The War Years of General Dwight D. Eisenhower* (23:101) is a well-written biography (1941–1945).

Eisenhower, D. D. *The Papers of Dwight David Eisenhower: The War Years* (23:104) covers the years Eisenhower served on Marshall's planning staff (1941–1942), as American and Allied Commander in North Africa and Europe (1942–1945), as head of Occupation Forces (1945), and as the Chief of Staff.

Douglas MacArthur

See Chapters 23, 24, and 27, under "Personalities," for additional references.

James, D. C. *The Years of MacArthur* [1880–1945] (23:107) is incomparably best study of MacArthur. Volume 1 covers his life through 1941; volume 2 deals with his World War II experiences. Subsequent volumes are anticipated.

40:55 MacArthur, Douglas. *Reminiscences*. New York: McGraw-Hill, 1964. The general's memoirs, written shortly before his death, are terse, self-justifying, and revealing as to personality, but contain few new historical insights.

40:56 MacArthur, Douglas. *A Soldier Speaks*. New York: Praeger, 1965. This is a collection of MacArthur's speeches. Brief editorial comment is included.

40:57 Wittner, Lawrence S., ed. *MacArthur*. Englewood Cliffs, N.J.: Prentice-Hall, 1971. This is a useful collection of MacArthur's writings, together with representative appraisals of him by contemporaries and historians. Bibliography.

George C. Marshall

See Chapters 23, 24, and 27 under "Personalities," for additional references.

Ferrell, R. H. *George C. Marshall* [1945–1949] (24:140) assesses Marshall's contributions as secretary of state.

40:58 Pogue, Forrest C. *George C. Marshall*. 3 vols. to date. New York: Viking, 1963– . The principal biography of Marshall (1880–1959), the World War II Army Chief of Staff and post-1945 shaper of American foreign policy, is a major contribution to the history of American foreign relations. Pogue has used Marshall's career to explore the history of the 20th-century army. For descriptions of volumes 2 and 3, see 23:108, 23:109.

Matthew B. Ridgway

Ridgway, M. B. *The Korean War . . .* (27:53) argues against the value of heavy bombing in Vietnam, based on his Korean experience.

40:59 Ridgway, Matthew B., with Martin, Harold H. *Soldier: The Memoirs of Matthew B. Ridgway*. New York: Harper, 1956. The principal impact of this memoir was that of a treatise on limited war as an alternative to the doctrine of massive retaliation. General Ridgway rejected limited nuclear war as well as massive retaliation and regarded ready, versatile, limited-war forces as the only foundation of a usable military policy.

Winfield Scott

See Chapters 9 and 10, under "Personalities," for references.

Elliott, C. W. *Winfield Scott: The Soldier and the Man* (9:50) finds Winfield Scott (1786–1866) shaping the ethos, administration, and strategic and tactical thought of the army. Though not a West Point graduate, he became a professional soldier through self-education, and then he fostered the rise of professionalism throughout the officer corps.

Maxwell D. Taylor

40:60   Taylor, Maxwell D. *Swords and Plowshares.*
New York: Norton, 1972. Taylor's career as a soldier-
diplomat began as early as 1935, when he was assigned to the U.S. embassy in Tokyo to study
Japanese. This career flowered as commander of the
Eighth Army in Korea, military representative to the
president, and ambassador in Saigon, in addition to
service as Army Chief of Staff and chairman of the
Joint Chiefs of Staff.

40:61   Taylor, Maxwell D. *The Uncertain Trumpet.*
New York: Harper, 1960. Written after General
Taylor's retirement as Army Chief of Staff, this book
opposed massive retaliation, and argued for a strategy
of flexible response, which would be able to deter
limited as well as general war.

Emory Upton

40:62   Ambrose, Stephen E. *Upton and the Army.*
Baton Rouge: Louisiana State University Press, 1964.
Emory Upton's (1839–1881) *Military Policy of the
United States* and his other writings and influences
upon the army provided a mixed inheritance of dedica-
tion to professional, technical, and tactical excellence
and of military disdain for many aspects of civilian
control and even democracy. Bibliography.

40:63   Upton, Emory. *The Military Policy of the
United States.* Washington, D.C.: G.P.O., 1904. This
volume is the single most influential book in American
military history. Upton's hostility to the American
military system extended even to the principal of civilian control. This military history (1775–1862) written
in support of his proposals for change was the first
systematic U.S. military history to appear, and it has
influenced subsequent writing.

Leonard Wood

Hagedorn, H. *Leonard Wood: A Biography* (13:76) is
an admiring account of General Wood, who was as
much a politician as a soldier. In spite of himself,
however, Wood as Chief of Staff under Taft and Wilson did more than any other professional soldier to
ready the American army for major war overseas; and
his career touched on the army's role in international
politics in many other ways as well.

Hitchman, J. H. *Leonard Wood and Cuban Independence, 1898–1902* (15:27).

40:64   Lane, Jack C. *Armed Progressive: General
Leonard Wood.* San Rafael, Calif.: Presidio, 1978. As
Elihu Root was the principal civilian founder of the

modern army, so Leonard Wood (1860–1927) was the
principal professional contributor to the transformation. While Chief of Staff, he assured the ascendancy
of that office within the army, while also doing much
to ready the army for large-scale mobilization and
war. Bibliography.

Others

40:65   Ambrose, Stephen E. *Halleck: Lincoln's
Chief of Staff.* Baton Rouge: Louisiana State University Press, 1960. The beginnings of the modern command system of the army emerged during the Civil
War, particularly when U. S. Grant became General-
in-Chief of the army and H. W. Halleck moved from
that office to the post of Chief of Staff. Bibliography.

40:66   Coffman, Edward M. *The Hilt of the Sword:
The Career of Peyton C. March.* Madison: University
of Wisconsin Press, 1966. Sociologists studying the
modern military emphasize the displacement of the
heroic leader by the military manager; General March
(1864–1955) embodied this transition as the Chief of
Staff who assured the General Staff's ascendancy over
John J. Pershing, the very model of the heroic leader in
the field. Bibliography.

40:67   Deutrich, Mabel E. *Struggle for Supremacy:
The Career of Fred C. Ainsworth.* Washington, D.C.:
Public Affairs Press, 1962. Whether the American
army could effectively carry the burdens of world
power may well have depended on whether the Chief
of Staff could overcome the traditional autonomy of
the War Department administration bureaus. Ainsworth (1852–1934) as adjutant general fought—and
almost won—the last battle for the independence of
the bureaus against Chief of Staff Leonard Wood.
Bibliography.

40:68   Gavin, James M. *War and Peace in the Space
Age.* New York: Harper, 1958. After the massive retaliation policies of the Eisenhower administration
precipitated the retirement of General Gavin, he argued that America's neglect of its military was placing
it at the mercy of the Soviet Union in general nuclear
war as well as in limited war.

40:69   Liddell Hart, B. H. *Sherman: Soldier,
Realist, American.* New York: Praeger, 1958. Sherman's conceptions of strategy have influenced the
American army to the present, and as commanding
general of the army following the Civil War he was
instrumental in establishing the school system that
nurtured a professional officer corps. This biography
deals most satisfactorily with Sherman as strategist.

40:70 Millett, Allan R. *The General: Robert L. Bullard and Officership in the United States Army, 1861–1925*. Westport, Conn.: Greenwood, 1975. Bullard's career (1885–1919) spanned the transition from the Indian-fighting army to the army involved in colonial and international affairs. In diary, notebooks, and letters, he comments astutely on the changing army. Bibliography.

Navy

Ernest J. King

See Chapter 23, under "Personalities," for references.

King, E. J., and Whitehill, W. M. *Fleet Admiral King: A Naval Record* (23:106) is an account of the World War II chief of naval operations and commander-in-chief of the fleet, who was by no means also diplomatic, but whose position made him necessarily a sailor-diplomat. Enough of King's cantankerousness permeates his memoirs to reveal something of his limitations as well as his strengths.

Stephen B. Luce

40:71 Gleaves, Albert. *Life and Letters of Rear Admiral Stephen B. Luce, U.S. Navy, Founder of the Naval War College*. New York: Putnam's, 1925. Without Luce (1827–1917) to establish the Navy War College and seek out "a naval Jomini" to instruct in naval strategy and history, A. T. Mahan might never have become a premier naval strategist. Luce laid the foundation for many of Mahan's teachings in his own prolific writing and speaking. See also "The Admiral in Politics: Stephen B. Luce and the Foundation of the Modern American Navy," in John A. S. Grenville and George B. Young, *Politics, Strategy, and American Diplomacy, 1873–1917* (New Haven: Yale University Press, 1966).

40:72 Hayes, John D., and Hattendorf, John B., eds. *The Writings of Stephen B. Luce*. Newport, R.I.: Naval War College Press, 1975. Lacking a recent biography, Admiral Luce has suffered historians' neglect, notwithstanding contributions to naval thought rivaling Mahan's in importance. This anthology of Luce's writings begins to remedy the neglect; a brief biographical sketch precedes the selections from Luce. Bibliography.

Alfred T. Mahan

40:73 Hagan, Kenneth J. "Alfred Thayer Mahan: Turning America Back to the Sea." In Frank J. Merli and Theodore A. Wilson, eds., *Makers of American Diplomacy from Benjamin Franklin to Henry Kissinger*. New York: Scribner's, 1974, vol. 1, pp. 279–304. This derivative essay focuses on the thought of the much vaunted Mahan. The author identifies precursors for most of Mahan's ideas and concedes little influence on policy but asserts that he was a successful propagandist. Bibliography.

LaFeber, W. "A Note on the 'Mercantilistic Imperialism' of Alfred Thayer Mahan" (14:39) seeks to relate strategic thought to the ideas of civilian mercantilists and other civilian foreign policy intellectuals. This article is a slightly expanded version of the discussion of Mahan in LaFeber's *The New Empire: An Interpretation of American Expansion, 1860–1898* (12:84), pp. 85–101.

40:74 Livezey, William E. *Mahan on Sea Power*. Norman: University of Oklahoma Press, 1947. This summary and analysis of the ideas of the foremost American contributor to strategic thought not only provides a convenient introduction to Mahan (1840–1914) but also includes a bibliography of Mahan's numerous writings. The author believes Mahan to have been less influential with his peers than Luce or Sims. Bibliography.

Mahan, A. T. *Sea Power in Its Relations to the War of 1812* (6:9).

40:75 Mahan, Alfred T. *From Sail to Steam: Recollections of Naval Life*. New York: Harper, 1907. Mahan's memoirs offer a more convenient summation of his major strategic ideas than his most famous book, *The Influence of Sea Power upon History, 1660–1783* (2:43). The memoirs are also useful for Mahan's own account of the genesis of his thinking.

40:76 Mahan, Alfred T. *Letters and Papers of Alfred Thayer Mahan*. 3 vols. Ed. by Robert Seager II and Doris D. Maguire. Annapolis, Md.: Naval Institute Press, 1975. This collection is as comprehensive as the present generation of scholars is likely to obtain. The editors claim to have found no more than a quarter of Mahan's letters.

40:77 Pratt, Julius W. "Alfred Thayer Mahan." In William T. Hutchinson, ed., *The Marcus W. Jernegan Essays in American Historiography*. Chicago: University of Chicago Press, 1937, pp. 207–26. This remains the best essay on Mahan as an historian, but it is also valuable for the author's larger observations on Mahan as a successful propagandist (especially abroad) and a prophet.

40:78   Puleston, William D. *Mahan: The Life and Work of Captain Alfred Thayer Mahan.* New Haven, Conn.: Yale University Press, 1939. Puleston's biography may be displaced as the standard work by Seager's account (40:80), but it remains worthy of study as the work of a naval officer close enough to Mahan's time that he could convey a first-hand feeling for the setting.

40:79   Puleston, William D. "A Re-examination of Mahan's Concept of Sea Power." *U.S. Naval Institute Proceedings* 56:9 (1940), 1229–36. A major controversy concerning Mahan's strategic thought involves the extent to which he appreciated the impact of modern technology upon strategic principles. Puleston here argues that the admiral was cognizant of technological change.

40:80   Seager, Robert, II. *Alfred Thayer Mahan: The Man and His Letters.* Annapolis, Md.: Naval Institute Press, 1977. While seemingly delighting in a "warts and all" portrait of the man with emphasis on the warts, Seager is more respectful of Mahan's intellectual contributions than some other recent writers, notably Peter Karsten in *The Naval Aristocracy* (40:35). This work will be the standard biography of Mahan. Bibliography.

Matthew C. Perry

See also Chapter 17, under "Personalities."

40:81   Morison, Samuel Eliot. *"Old Bruin": Commodore Matthew Calbraith Perry, 1794–1858.* Boston: Little, Brown, 1967. Perry's role in the opening of Japan to American commerce makes him a conspicuous example of the military man involved in foreign policy. Perry was a sailor-diplomat not only in Japan but in Liberia, the West Indies, the Ottoman empire, and the Kingdom of the Two Sicilies. Bibliography.

Others

40:82   Coletta, Paolo E. *Admiral Bradley A. Fiske and the American Navy.* Lawrence: Regents Press of Kansas, 1979. Fiske (1854–1942) was an innovator of major importance in both naval technology and naval administration. He was largely responsible for creating the post of chief of naval operations, though personality clashes with Secretary Josephus Daniels denied him that post. This biography is indispensable to the student of 20th-century civil-military relations. Extensive bibliography.

40:83   Cummings, Damon E. *Admiral Richard Wainwright and the United States Fleet.* Washington, D.C.: G.P.O., 1962. Wainwright (1849–1926) was chief of naval intelligence shortly before the Spanish War, executive officer of the *Maine* when the ship blew up, a hero of the battle of Santiago, superintendent of the Naval Academy, and a member of the General Board. His career is one of the most helpful through which to follow the modernization of the navy. Bibliography.

40:84   Ferguson, Eugene S. *Truxtun of the Constellation: The Life of Commodore Thomas Truxtun, U.S. Navy, 1755–1822.* Baltimore: Johns Hopkins Press, 1956. Commanders of naval squadrons were perforce also diplomats from the first, often because of slow communications enjoying wider discretion than the most senior emissaries abroad in the 20th century. Truxtun commanded a squadron in the West Indies during the quasi-war with France. Bibliography.

40:85   McKee, Christopher. *Edward Preble: A Naval Biography, 1761–1807.* Annapolis, Md.: Naval Institute Press, 1972. Preble commanded the squadron that blockaded Tripoli (1803–1804). He was more important as a one-man naval academy, the teacher of many of the officers who led the navy during the War of 1812 and well into the 19th century. His biography serves as perhaps the best available history of the navy in his time. Bibliography.

40:86   Morison, Elting E. *Admiral Sims and the Modern American Navy.* Boston: Houghton Mifflin, 1941. Morison offers a model naval biography in the book's relating of the technical aspects of Sims's (1858–1936) career to his involvement in international relations and eventual command of U.S. Naval Forces in European Waters in 1918. Sims's reforms in gunnery and criticisms of ship design are crucial to an understanding of the navy's capacities in the early 20th century. Bibliography.

40:87   Paullin, Charles O. *Commodore John Rodgers: Captain, Commodore, and Senior Officer of the American Navy, 1773–1838.* Cleveland, Ohio: Clark, 1910. Rodgers commanded the blockading squadron off Tripoli and helped negotiate peace treaties with Tripoli, Morocco, and Tunis. He was the senior officer on active service during the War of 1812 and immediately thereafter. Bibliography.

40:88   Wheeler, Gerald E. *Admiral William Veazie Pratt, U.S. Navy: A Sailor's Life.* Washington, D.C.: G.P.O., 1974. Pratt was a naval adviser at both the Washington Naval Conference of 1921–1922 and the London Conference of 1930, as well as assistant chief of naval operations during World War I, president of the Naval War College, and chief of naval operations 1930 to 1933. Wheeler deals with the administrative, strategic, and diplomatic phases of Pratt's career. Bibliography.

CIVILIAN LEADERS

Newton D. Baker

See Chapter 19, under "Personalities," for additional references.

Beaver, D. R. *Newton D. Baker and the American War Effort, 1917–1919* (19:32) emphasizes the study of managerial and technological aspects of military history.

Robert S. McNamara

40:89 Roherty, James M. *Decisions of Robert S. McNamara: A Study of the Role of the Secretary of Defense.* Coral Gables, Fla.: University of Miami Press, 1970. Roherty contrasts McNamara, a "functionalist" secretary relying on managerial processes, with his "generalist" predecessors who relied for decisionmaking on political bargaining and conciliation. He argues that McNamara's methods so negated the political give-and-take essential to American government as to stultify the making and execution of policy. Bibliography.

Trewhitt, H. L. *McNamara* (30:44).

Theodore Roosevelt

See Chapters 13, 15, 16, and 17, under "Personalities," for additional references.

40:90 O'Gara, Gordon C. *Theodore Roosevelt and the Rise of the Modern American Navy.* Princeton, N.J.: Princeton University Press, 1943. An early product of the "new" military history that has tied military history with diplomatic and civil history, this book was excessively influenced by the navalists' and Roosevelt's values. See more recent studies of aspects of Roosevelt's relationship with the navy, such as Charles E. Neu, *An Uncertain Friendship: Theodore Roosevelt and Japan, 1906–1909* (17:261) on the cruise of the Great White Fleet. But this overview remains valuable. Bibliography.

Elihu Root

See Chapters 16 and 19, under "Personalities," for additional references.

Jessup, P. C. *Elihu Root* (17:41) sees Root as perhaps the single most influential American secretary of war; his "Root reforms" effected the major steps in the transformation of the army from a frontier constabulary to an instrument of world power. It should be supplemented by James E. Hewes, Jr., *From Root to McNamara* (40:96).

Harry S. Truman

See Chapters 24, 26, and 27, under "Personalities," for additional references.

40:91 Haynes, Richard F. *The Awesome Power: Harry S. Truman as Commander in Chief.* Baton Rouge: Louisiana State University Press, 1973. This is the only scholarly book-length study to focus on a single president's performance in the role of Commander in Chief. As such, it suggests wide implications for the study of presidential power. Bibliography.

Others

40:92 Colby, William E., and Forbath, Peter. *Honorable Men: My Life in the CIA.* New York: Simon & Schuster, 1978. Although circumspect and self-justifying, this memoir by a former director of the Central Intelligence Agency is probably the most useful "inside" account of the role of intelligence agencies in postwar American foreign policy.

Cooling, B. F., III. *Benjamin Franklin Tracy: Father of the Modern American Fighting Navy* (12:92) finds Tracy (1830–1915) presiding over the building of the first modern American battleships. Tracy borrowed arguments from Admiral Mahan to win congressional approval for his naval program. The contracting required that he become a key figure in the emerging military-industrial complex.

Dulles, A. W. *The Craft of Intelligence* (24:103) reviews the role of the CIA in Europe during the Truman period. Not only are personal narratives interspersed throughout the volume, but the former director also reveals his own opinions on how and why the United States must conduct intelligence operations against the Soviet Union.

Freidel, F. *Francis Lieber: Nineteenth-Century Liberal* (11:228) assesses his key role in codifying the rules of land warfare during the American Civil War.

Niven, J. *Gideon Welles: Lincoln's Secretary of the Navy* (11:60) is an account of civil rather than international war, when Welles directed the first major expansion of the navy. Few civilian heads of the military departments have been so fortunate in the quality of their biography.

40:93 Powers, Thomas. *The Man Who Kept Secrets: Richard Helms and the CIA*. New York: Knopf, 1979. A study of the CIA by an outsider, Powers's volume traces the CIA and its connection with U.S. foreign policy through the career of Richard Helms. Although sketchy on the Truman period, during which Helms was in Washington, it does raise important questions concerning the relationship of the CIA to the presidency. Bibliography.

40:94 Thomas, Benjamin P., and Hyman, Harold M. *Stanton: The Life and Times of Lincoln's Secretary of War*. New York: Knopf, 1962. Stanton ranks with John C. Calhoun and Elihu Root as one of the great administrators of the War Department. His conduct of the first large-scale American mobilization for war left few precedents; but an understanding of his stewardship is essential to the history of the evolution of the War Department. Bibliography.

Wiltse, C. M. *John C. Calhoun: Nationalist, 1782– 1828* (7:25) discusses Calhoun, James Monroe's secretary of war, who reorganized the administrative and logistical bureaus. The contrast between the military conduct of the War of 1812 and the Mexican War sprang largely from Calhoun's War Department reforms. See also the War Department sections of Leonard D. White, *The Jeffersonians: A Study in Administrative History, 1801–1829* (6:78).

The Armed Services

THE ARMY AND NATIONAL GUARD

See under "Personalities" for "Army," above.

40:95 Ganoe, William A. *History of the United States Army*. Rev. ed. New York: Appleton-Century, 1942. This detailed survey is somewhat old-fashioned, emphasizing battles and campaigns, but also contains a wealth of information on military legislation and administration. Bibliography.

40:96 Hewes, James E., Jr. *From Root to McNamara: Army Organization and Administration, 1900– 1963*. Washington, D.C.: G.P.O., 1975. This book is by far the most complete history of army administration from the birth of the modern army through the army's growing 20th-century involvement in considerations of world politics. Bibliography.

40:97 Huston, James A. *The Sinews of War: Army Logistics, 1775–1953*. Washington, D.C.: G.P.O., 1966. Military force can accomplish on behalf of foreign policy only what is logistically possible. Military historians have tended to neglect the unexciting logistical foundations of military power; but this book is a complete survey. Bibliography.

40:98 Kreidberg, Marvin A., and Henry, Merton G. *History of Military Mobilization in the United States Army, 1775–1945*. Washington, D.C.: G.P.O., 1955. The most complete survey of how manpower and the national economy were mobilized for American wars and afterwards demobilized. The chapters on 20th-century industrial mobilization and on the army's industrial mobilization planning between the world wars are strong. The volume also provides a history of American conscription. Bibliography.

40:99 Lewis, Emanuel R. *Seacoast Fortifications of the United States: An Introductory History*. Washington, D.C.: Smithsonian Institution Press, 1970. From the American Revolution and the presidency of George Washington to 1948—when nuclear weapons and the approach of the missile age made coastal fortifications obsolete—fortifying the coast was the most consistent, continuous theme of American military policy. This is the only comprehensive survey. Bibliography.

40:100 Palmer, John M. *America in Arms: The Experience of the United States with Military Organization*. New Haven, Conn.: Yale University Press, 1941. More than an historical survey of American military organization, this book is a polemic; the summing-up work of a soldier-historian who deplored the influence of Emory Upton upon the writing of American military history and, unlike Upton, believed that the only proper military reliance of a democracy is a citizen's army.

40:101 Robinson, Willard B. *American Forts: Architectural Form and Function*. Urbana: University of Illinois Press, 1977. Until the 20th century, the American army thought defensively about foreign affairs; it perceived its role as the defense of national territory against raids and invasions. Western frontier forts as well as coastal fortifications are included in this survey. Extensive bibliography.

40:102   Spaulding, Oliver L. *The United States Army in War and Peace.* New York: Putnam's, 1937. Spaulding's work is characterized by the focusing on operations, on battles and campaigns that shaped military history before World War II. There are useful details on army organization. Bibliography.

40:103   Weigley, Russell F. *History of the United States Army.* New York: Macmillan, 1967. The book deals less with the military on the battlefield than with civil-military relations, organization and administration, and military thought. Its theme is that the U.S. Army has consisted of two rival armies, the small professional regular army and the citizen-soldiers of the militia, the National Guard, and the wartime army expansions. Bibliography.

40:104   Weigley, Russell F. *Towards an American Army: Military Thought from Washington to Marshall.* New York: Columbia University Press, 1962. Although there are references to strategic thought, this work is concerned with controversies over the kind of military organization most appropriate to American democracy. George Washington at various times favored reliance on professional soldiers and reliance on a citizens' militia. These two conflicting lines of argument persisted in the nation's military thought, culminating in the writings of Emory Upton and John M. Palmer and summarized by Weigley. Bibliography.

National Guard

40:105   Derthick, Martha. *The National Guard in Politics.* Cambridge: Harvard University Press, 1965. Derthick focuses especially on the National Guard Association (1879–1964) as the political voice of the National Guard and on the National Guard Bureau, its beachhead within the military bureaucracy. The guard's attitudes and influence have had to be reckoned with in shaping foreign policy. Bibliography.

40:106   Hill, Jim Dan. *The Minute Man in Peace and War: A History of the National Guard.* Harrisburg, Pa.: Stackpole, 1964. Though flawed by a compulsion to defend the National Guard against all critics, this book is the most satisfactory history of the National Guard and its militia antecedents. Historically the

guard figured importantly in evaluations of American military power. Bibliography.

THE NAVY AND MARINE CORPS

See under "Personalities" for "Navy," above.

40:107   Albion, Robert G., and Pope, Jennie Barnes. *Sea Lanes in Wartime: The American Experience, 1775–1942.* New York: Norton, 1942. Though it reflects the time of its composition, when, as Churchill said, to lose the Atlantic sea lanes was to lose all, this book offers a handy introduction to the complexities of the American position on neutral trade in wartime.

40:108   Coletta, Paolo E. *The American Naval Heritage in Brief.* Washington, D.C.: University Press of America, 1978. An uneven and sometimes carelessly written book, it treats administration well, in addition to warships, strategy, and tactics. Despite its limitations this book may be the most useful survey of the naval dimensions of national policy. Extensive bibliography.

40:109   Davis, George T. *A Navy Second to None: The Development of Modern American Naval Policy.* New York: Harcourt, Brace, 1940. This is a general survey of U.S. naval policy. The "modern naval policy" was little more than recognition of the need for ships.

40:110   Davis, Vincent J. *The Admirals Lobby.* Chapel Hill: University of North Carolina Press, 1967. Though the book's emphasis is overwhelmingly on the 20th century, especially on World War II and after, its discussion of admirals' influence in politics is set in the context of the political history of the Navy Department. Bibliography.

40:111   Hagan, Kenneth J., ed. *In Peace and War: Interpretations of American Naval History, 1775–1978.* Westport, Conn.: Greenwood, 1978. These essays review the main issues of controversy. There is a nice balance between wartime strategy and campaigns and inquiries into peacetime organization, naval thought, and service to and influence upon American foreign policy. Bibliography.

40:112   Heinl, Robert D., Jr. *Soldiers of the Sea: The United States Marine Corps, 1775–1962.* Annapolis, Md.: U.S. Naval Institute, 1962. The Marine Corps has been a conspicuous adjunct of foreign policy, but there has been no history of the corps that escapes an emphasis on battles and beachheads for an analytical examination of the marines' contributions in, and influence upon foreign policy. This book has long been the standard survey. Bibliography.

40:113 Knox, Dudley W. *A History of the United States Navy*. Rev. ed. New York: Putnam's, 1948. The "new" military history which attempts to place armed forces into their larger political and social contexts has yet to produce a history of the navy. Knox's work, emphasizing combat and written uncritically by a naval officer, is despite its flaws the most comprehensive survey available.

Mallison, S. V., and Mallison, T. W., Jr. "A Survey of the International Law of Naval Blockade" (16:147).

Merli, F. J., and Ferrell, R. H. "Blockades and Quarantines" (16:148).

40:114 Millett, Allan R. *Semper Fidelis: The History of the United States Marine Corps*. New York: Macmillan, 1980. This study supersedes all previous works, especially in matters of administration, doctrine, and foreign intervention.

Paullin, C. O. *Diplomatic Negotiations of American Naval Officers, 1778–1883* (2:177) is a detailed account by the leading historian of the U.S. Navy of his time of the most direct involvement of the military in peacetime diplomacy. A modern reexamination of the topic would be useful. Bibliography.

40:115 Paullin, Charles O. *Paullin's History of Naval Administration, 1775–1911: A Collection of Articles from the U.S. Naval Institute Proceedings*. Annapolis, Md.: U.S. Naval Institute, 1968. Though narrowly focused on the internal workings of the navy, the work is unparalleled in the detail in which it portrays 19th-century naval administrative systems and methods. The navy's administrative bureaus became so complex a network of checks, balances, and jealousies that understanding them demands such detail.

40:116 Savage, Carlton. *Policy of the United States toward Maritime Commerce in War*. 2 vols. Washington, D.C.: G.P.O., 1934. Reprint 1969. The work is especially useful for tracing the evolution of America's position (1776–1914) and for making comparisons between time periods.

40:117 Sprout, Harold, and Sprout, Margaret. *The Rise of American Naval Power, 1776–1918*. Princeton, N.J.: Princeton University Press, 1939. Reprint 1966, 1980. Though it is concerned with naval policy and strategy at the places where the navy and the civilian executive and legislature intersect, rather than with the development of policy and strategy, this book remains the nearest approach to a satisfactory history of the navy. Bibliography.

AIR FORCE

See under "Personalities" for "Air Force," above.

Craven, W. F., and Cate, J. L., eds. *The Army Air Forces in World War II* (23:145) is a massive work which treats the service's evolution before World War II. Much of volume 1 deals with the evolution out of the Signal Corps into Army Air Service, Army Air Corps, and Army Air Forces; much of volume 6 deals with pre-1941 development of aircraft. The air force is so new as an independent service, or even as a major part of the army, that the lack of an adequate history is not surprising.

40:118 Goldberg, Alfred, ed. *A History of the United States Air Force, 1907–1957*. Princeton, N.J.: Van Nostrand, 1957. This book has the predictable virtues and shortcomings of a work sponsored by the Air Force Association to commemorate the fiftieth anniversary of American military aviation; but the virtues are more conspicuous than the shortcomings. Bibliography.

INTELLIGENCE SERVICES

See under "Personalities," under "Civilian Leaders," "Others," especially William E. Colby, Allen W. Dulles, Richard Helms; also see Chapter 23, "Intelligence Operations."

Clark, R. *The Man Who Broke Purple: The Life of Colonel William F. Friedman, Who Deciphered the Japanese Code in World War II*. (23:212) details the cryptographic career of William F. Friedman from World War I through World War II and provides insight into the military intelligence bureaucracy.

40:119 De Gramont, Sanche. *The Secret War: The Story of International Espionage since World War II*. Trans. by Ted Morgan. New York: Putnam's, 1962.

De Gramont's now dated volume describes the contests between the CIA and KGB following World War II. Unfortunately the author's fascination with the agents themselves often overshadows the events and the context. Nevertheless, it is a useful account.

40:120 Kahn, David. *The Codebreakers: The Story of Secret Writing*. New York: Macmillan, 1967. This is the only full-length history of cryptology, defined here as the science embracing cryptography (rendering messages unintelligible) and cryptanalysis (breaking codes and ciphers), other than Fletcher Pratt's outdated *Secret and Urgent* (1942). Bibliography.

Klass, P. J. *Secret Sentries in Space* (40:249) demonstrates the value of photography, communications, and electronic intelligence from spacecraft. This is the principal means of "national" verification of strategic arms limitations and general military activities.

40:121 Philby, Kim. *My Silent War*. New York: Grove, 1968. The fascinating and revealing memoirs by the man Allen Dulles called "the best spy the Russians ever had." While the various biographies of Philby contribute little to this period's literature on Europe, his personal account contains lengthy discussion of his actions in the context of the CIA, KGB, and British SIS.

40:122 Ransom, Harry H. *The Intelligence Establishment*. Cambridge: Harvard University Press, 1970. This is an expanded and updated version of his earlier *Central Intelligence and National Security* (1959). Both books deal with the basic political and bureaucratic aspects of U.S. intelligence services, including such topics as secrecy requirements and legislative oversight.

Smith, R. H. *OSS: The Secret History of America's First Central Intelligence Agency* (23:216) also covers the transition postwar period as the CIA emerged.

Central Intelligence Agency

40:123 Cline, Ray S. *Secrets, Spies and Scholars: Blueprint of the Essential CIA*. Washington, D.C.: Acropolis, 1976. The author, a member of the OSS, the CIA (1949–1969) and director of State Department intelligence (1969–1973), has drawn from his experiences to explain how the CIA evolved as it did.

40:124 Kirkpatrick, Lyman B., Jr. *The Real CIA*. New York: Macmillan, 1968. One of the earlier memoirs by a CIA official, Kirkpatrick's volume gives one of the best inside accounts of the CIA's organization.

40:125 Marchetti, Victor, and Marks, John D. *The CIA and the Cult of Intelligence*. New York: Knopf, 1974. This account discloses details about CIA political operations since the early 1950s by Marchetti, a 14-year CIA veteran, and by Marks, an ex-State Department intelligence analyst. Moreover, they develop a thesis about why the CIA changed its clandestine priorities from spying to covert activities.

40:126 "The Pike Papers: House Select Committee on Intelligence CIA Report." *Special Supplement to Village Voice* (Oct. 1976), 1–38. This weekly New York newspaper published excerpts of the secret final report by the House committee. It details U.S. intelligence activities during the Vietnam War, the Mid-East wars, the Soviet invasion of Czechoslovakia, and the India-Pakistan War.

40:127 Prouty, L. Fletcher. *The Secret Team: The CIA and Its Allies in Control of the United States and the World*. Englewood Cliffs, N.J.: Prentice-Hall, 1973. As the title implies, this memoir by another CIA insider emphasizes the role of U.S. intelligence operations in international diplomacy. While it concentrates on Allen Dulles and the post-Truman years, there is useful information concerning Walter Bedell Smith and early CIA operations in Europe and later events. Bibliography.

40:128 Rositzke, Harry. *The CIA's Secret Operations: Espionage, Counterespionage, and Their Covert Action*. New York: Reader's Digest Press, 1977. More balanced than de Silva's *Sub Rosa*, the book demonstrates the anti-Soviet thrust of U.S. intelligence policy in postwar Europe, especially in regard to espionage and propaganda. It also describes covert operations.

40:129 de Silva, Peer. *Sub Rosa: The CIA and the Uses of Intelligence*. New York: Times Books, 1978. Although the volume is short on analysis, and suffers from de Silva's unconcealed attempt to defend CIA activities, *Sub Rosa* nevertheless contributes to the literature.

40:130 U.S. Senate. Select Committee to Study Government Operations with Respect to Intelligence

Activities. Interim Report; *Alleged Assassination Plots Involving Foreign Leaders.* 94th Cong., 1st Sess., 1975. Contains information about alleged CIA involvement in plots to assassinate Fidel Castro of Cuba, Patrice Lumumba of the Congo, Rafael Trujillo of the Dominican Republic, General Rene Schneider of Chile, and Ngo Dinh Diem of South Vietnam. The report also provides considerable detail on covert operations in the five countries. Staff reports and other reports of this committee document many operations of the U.S. intelligence community.

Soviet Intelligence Service

40:131 Barron, John. *KGB: The Secret Work of Soviet Secret Agents.* Pleasantville, N.Y.: Reader's Digest Press, 1974. These selected stories and episodes of Soviet agents provide considerable insight into the Committee for State Security's (KGB) espionage and covert political activities. It is probably the most authoritative work on the Soviet espionage system.

40:132 Dallin, David J. *Soviet Espionage.* New Haven, Conn.: Yale University Press, 1955. Dallin's study is an early but still valuable volume on the Soviet intelligence apparatus. By a Soviet emigre, the account is particularly useful in following KGB activities following World War II in Europe.

MILITARY EDUCATION

40:133 Ambrose, Stephen E. *Duty, Honor, Country: A History of West Point.* Baltimore: Johns Hopkins Press, 1966. Through much of the 19th century, the U.S. Army educational system had only an undergraduate school, West Point. Notwithstanding the heavily engineering rather than military nature of the West Point curriculum, the Military Academy gave the army a firm basis for the development of professionalism. Ambrose's book is the best history of West Point. Extensive bibliography.

40:134 Ellis, Joseph, and Moore, Robert. *School for Soldiers: West Point and the Profession of Arms.* New York: Oxford University Press, 1974. This book concentrates on present-day West Point, but it is informed by historical perspective, and it offers the virtues of the view from inside. It is critical but not a polemic. Bibliography.

40:135 Fleming, Thomas J. *West Point: The Men and Times of the United States Military Academy.* New York: Morrow, 1969. In most respects Ambrose's *Duty, Honor, Country* (40:133) is superior to Fleming's history of West Point, but Fleming is worth consulting on the period from the Civil War to Douglas MacArthur's superintendency after World War I. West Point stagnated during this period, but several issues arose, including the arrival of the first black cadets. Bibliography.

40:136 Forman, Sidney. *West Point: A History of the United States Military Academy.* New York: Columbia University Press, 1950. This history of West Point is shorter and older than Ambrose's *Duty, Honor, Country* (40:133) and less a reflective history than a chronicle of persons and events. Nevertheless, it offers a valuable complement to Ambrose's book. Bibliography.

40:137 Lovell, John P. *Neither Athens nor Sparta? The American Service Academics in Transition.* Bloomington: Indiana University Press, 1979. A graduate of West Point and an instructor at the Naval Academy and the Army War College, Lovell blends an insider's sympathy with an academician's critical stance in examining the Military, Naval, Air Force, and Coast Guard academies. He emphasizes the changes since the 1950s under the impact of the increasingly complex role of military officers in forming national security policy. The question of the proper purpose of military education is at the heart of his book. Bibliography.

40:138 Lyons, Gene M., and Masland, John W. *Education and Military Leadership: A Study of the ROTC.* Princeton, N.J.: Princeton University Press, 1959. Following World War II, the ROTC became not only a major source of officers, but in the army, ROTC graduates also rose to important posts. Thus the history of the ROTC is an essential part of the history of the education of American officers. Bibliography.

40:139 Lyons, Gene M., and Morton, Louis. *Schools for Strategy: Education and Research in National Security Affairs.* New York: Praeger, 1965. The world of the "think tanks" studying military issues since World War II changes so rapidly that this survey is already dated. Nevertheless, the book is the best introduction to the history and nature of academic, campus-based programs in national security affairs and of government and private research programs and institutes such as the RAND Corporation. Bibliography.

40:140 Masland, John W., and Radway, Laurence I. *Soldiers and Scholars: Military Education and National Policy.* Princeton, N.J.: Princeton University Press, 1957. No professionals spend more time in schools than military officers. This book is the most comprehensive survey of American military education from the service academies and ROTC programs through the various levels of professional education to the war colleges. It is critical and analytical. Bibliography.

40:141 Nenninger, Timothy K. *The Leavenworth Schools and the Old Army: Education, Professionalism, and the Officer Corps of the United States Army, 1881–1918.* Westport, Conn.: Greenwood, 1978. Graduate professional education developed by several schools at Fort Leavenworth began with the School of Application for Infantry and Cavalry sponsored by General W. T. Sherman, and culminated in the modern Command and General Staff College. Nenninger presents a civilian scholar's critical study of the Leavenworth schools to the ascendancy of a "Leavenworth clique" in the World War I army. Bibliography.

40:142 Pappas, George S. *Prudens Futuri: The Army War College, 1901–1947.* Carlisle Barracks, Pa.: Alumni Association of the U.S. Army War College, 1967. Since its founding as part of the Elihu Root reforms intended to fit the army for the responsibilities of world power, the Army War College has been the capstone of its service's professional educational system. Yet the college has been plagued by uncertainties about its role. Bibliography.

40:143 Spector, Ronald. *Professors of War: The Naval War College and the Development of the Naval Profession.* Newport, R.I.: Naval War College Press, 1977. The Naval War College was not only the first American war college but one whose curriculum was closely related to diplomacy. Its early staff has never been excelled in any American military school: A. T. Mahan, among the world's influential strategic thinkers, shared a place there with the almost equally perspicacious Stephen B. Luce, founder of the college, and William McCarty Little, father of American war gaming. Bibliography.

Military Institutions and Foreign Policy to 1945

COLONIAL PERIOD

See Chapter 3 for references to specific conflicts.

40:144 Boorstin, Daniel J. "A Nation of Minute Men." In his *The Americans: The Colonial Experience.* New York: Random House, 1958, pp. 343–72. This essay (1607–1783) is indispensable to an understanding of the unique dimensions that the North American colonial and frontier experience developed in the American approach to military affairs. Though the citizen-soldier was not an American invention, he developed peculiarly American characteristics. Bibliography.

40:145 Buffinton, Arthur H. "The Puritan View of War." *Colonial Society of Massachusetts Publications, Transactions, 1930–33* 28 (1930–1933), 67–86. Just as histories of American thought must grapple with the Puritans, so the history of American military thought must also confront the Puritan reconciliation of harsh warfare with Christianity. This analysis has not yet been superseded.

Leach, D. E. *Arms for Empire: A Military History of the British Colonies in North America, 1607–1763* (3:32) is the best overview of the origins of American military institutions, attitudes, and practice in the colonial period. The coverage of campaigns is ample, but Leach's special strength lies in his relating of military affairs to colonial and British imperial politics.

40:146 Morton, Louis. "The Origins of American Military Policy." In Raymond G. O'Connor, ed., *American Defense Policy in Perspective: From Colonial Times to the Present.* New York: Wiley, 1965, pp. 9–15. This is the best brief discussion of the earliest American military legislation and organization, the formation of colonial militias out of which American military institutions grew. Reprinted from *Military Affairs* 22:1 (1958), 75–82.

Peckham, H. H. *The Colonial Wars, 1689–1762* (3:37) skillfully integrates into a survey of the clashes of European empires in North America discussions of the development of each major type of military organization involved and its implications for sub-sequent American military history, including militia, regulars, rangers, and naval forces.

Shy, J. W. *Toward Lexington: The Role of the British Army in the Coming of the American Revolution* (3:225) emphasizes American hostility to British standing forces as contributing to the coming of the American Revolution and to American attitudes toward military organization. Shy also includes much about the development of the colonial militias in counterpoint to the role of the British regular army.

AMERICAN REVOLUTION

See Chapter 4 for specific sections dealing with military affairs.

40:147 Gross, Robert A. *The Minutemen and Their World.* New York: Hill & Wang, 1976. Through its focus on Concord, Massachusetts, during the revolutionary era its emphasis is on the military dimensions of New England community organization. It interprets the Revolution itself as an effort not to pursue democratic individualism but to revitalize the sense of community. Bibliography.

40:148 Hatch, Louis C. *The Administration of the American Revolutionary Army.* New York: Longmans, Green, 1904. This institutional history has never been superseded as an account of the institutional structure of the first American army. The combination of borrowings from the British with native American developments shaped later American military organizations and attitudes.

Higginbotham, D. *The War of American Independence: Military Attitudes, Policies, and Practice, 1763–1789* (4:29) integrates the military history of the Revolution into its political, economic, social, and diplomatic aspects. Higginbotham reviews the role of the revolutionary militias and irregulars and suggests their contributions to subsequent American military history.

40:149 Higginbotham, Don, ed. *Reconsiderations on the Revolutionary War: Selected Essays.* Westport, Conn.: Greenwood, 1978. This collection is useful to the student of the military and foreign policy because the essays emphasize the international context and implications of the American War of Independence. Particularly representative are "The American War of Independence in World Perspective"; "British

Strategy: The Theory and Practice of Eighteenth-Century Warfare"; and "The Relationship between the Revolutionary War and European Military Thought and Practice in the Second Half of the Eighteenth Century." Bibliography.

40:150 Palmer, Dave R. *The Way of the Fox: American Strategy in the War for America, 1775–1783.* Westport, Conn.: Greenwood, 1975. Primarily a study of George Washington as a military strategist, this work reviews the history of the concept of strategy—a new concept in Washington's era—to place the Revolution and its American commander in chief into a proper context. Palmer accomplishes the latter task despite attempting to transform Washington into a more aggressive general than he really was. Bibliography.

40:151 Shy, John W. *A People Numerous and Armed: Reflections on the Military Struggle for American Independence.* New York: Oxford University Press, 1976. Shy has collected a number of his published essays which emphasize that the American Revolution was an unconventional war, the prototype of the war of national liberation, and the social origins of revolutionary soldiers together with the subsequent social impact of their military service. Bibliography.

40:152 Underdal, Stanley J., ed. *Military History of the American Revolution: Proceedings of the 6th Military History Symposium, United States Air Force Academy 10–11 October 1974.* Washington, D.C.: G.P.O., 1976. These papers emphasize the organization and the socioeconomic composition of the revolutionary forces—not so much in detailed expository pieces as in suggestions for further research. Bibliography.

TO THE CIVIL WAR, 1783–1865

See "Personalities," especially, under "Army," Winfield Scott, and "Others," H. W. Halleck, William T. Sherman; under "Navy," Matthew C. Perry, and "Others," Edward Preble, John Rodgers, Thomas Truxtun; and, under "Civilian Leaders," "Others," Gideon Welles; also see Chapters 5, 6, 9, and 11 for specific conflicts.

Bauer, K. J. *The Mexican War, 1846–1848* (9:148) is probably the most balanced, comprehensive survey of the Mexican War. It deals amply with the diplomatic as well as the military aspects of the war. Its special value lies, however, in its analysis of the state of the art of war in the early 19th century and of the evolution of American military institutions.

Baxter, J. P., III. *The Introduction of the Ironclad Warship* (11:191) emphasizes the United States and the *Monitor-Merrimack* duel and its implications. To understand the uses of modern navies, it is necessary to understand something of the complexities of the race between armor and armament introduced by the shell gun and the coming of iron.

40:153 Connelly, Thomas L., and Jones, Archer. *The Politics of Command: Factions and Ideas in Confederate Strategy*. Baton Rouge: Louisiana State University Press, 1973. This book merits consideration for its review of 19th-century European and American military thought as a background to the development of Confederate strategic ideas. It is a fine introduction to strategic thought under the influence of Napoleon and the early commentators on Napoleonic war. Bibliography.

Corey, A. B. "Canadian Border Defence Problems after 1814 to Their Culmination in the 'Forties" (10:151) discusses the possibility of war with Canada which presented the United States with much of such international military problems as it confronted. This article from the Canadian perspective illuminates a remote corner of the American military past.

40:154 Cunliffe, Marcus. *Soldiers and Civilians: The Martial Spirit in America, 1775–1865*. Boston: Little, Brown, 1968. Cunliffe, an English historian, permits us to see a major part of our military past as others see it. American distrust of professional soldiers notwithstanding, Cunliffe perceives Americans as fascinated by military affairs and the panoply of war. He sets the history of American professional and citizen-soldiers alike in a social and intellectual context. Bibliography.

Earle, E. M. "Adam Smith, Alexander Hamilton, and Friedrich List: The Economic Foundations of Military Power" (5:25) provides an analysis of Hamilton's "Report on Manufacturers." According to the author, Hamilton advocated diversified economy to ensure self-sufficiency which provides defensive military strength. He calls Hamilton "an American Colbert or Pitt or Bismarck."

40:155 Franklin, John Hope. *The Militant South, 1800–1861*. Cambridge: Harvard University Press, 1956. This book is the major statement of a thesis also emphasized by S. P. Huntington's *The Soldier and the State* (40:44): the American military tradition is largely a Southern regional tradition. The thesis has been challenged by Marcus Cunliffe in *Soldiers and Civilians* (40:154). Nevertheless, the thesis commands attention. Bibliography.

40:156 Halleck, H. Wager. *Elements of Military Art and Science*. 3d ed. New York: Appleton, 1862. This book is the first major treatise on warfare by an American professional soldier. It has been dismissed as a paraphrase of the Baron de Jomini; but the book includes observations on particular U.S. military problems.

40:157 Jacobs, James R. *The Beginning of the U.S. Army, 1783–1812*. Princeton, N.J.: Princeton University Press, 1947. Although largely concerned with Indian campaigns, this volume is the fullest history of the founding of the regular army. The evolution of tactical and administrative organization is well handled. Bibliography.

40:158 Kohn, Richard H. *Eagle and Sword: The Beginnings of the Military Establishment in America, 1783–1802*. New York: Free Press, 1975. If Alexander Hamilton had had his way, the U.S. Army might have become active in domestic politics and it would also have been designed for international adventures. Kohn's is the standard political-military history of the army's most politicized period. Extensive bibliography.

40:159 Langley, Harold D. *Social Reform in the United States Navy, 1798–1862*. Urbana: University of Illinois Press, 1967. This history of efforts to alleviate the harsh life of the seaman ties naval history to the currents of 19th-century reforms. It also provides details about the navy that showed the flag and guarded commerce in places as distant as Constantinople and the South China Sea. Extensive bibliography.

40:160 Prucha, Francis P. *The Sword of the Republic: The United States Army on the Frontier, 1783–1846*. New York: Macmillan, 1969. The army's role as an Indian-fighting constabulary reveals the roots of the future army. This comprehensive history emphasizes the army's nation-building role—its forts around which white civilization grew in the West—more than its battles. Extensive bibliography.

40:161 Smelser, Marshall. *The Congress Founds the Navy, 1787–1798*. Notre Dame, Ind.: University of Notre Dame Press, 1959. Smelser reviews the congressional debates about the navy and treats equally the congressional champions of naval power and those who viewed it with reluctance. Bibliography.

40:162   Utley, Robert M. *Frontiersmen in Blue: The United States Army and the Indian, 1848–1865.* New York: Macmillan, 1967. This work is useful not only for its discussions of military organization and administration whose patterns endured, but also for its detailing of the influence of the problem of defending the West upon early strategic thought. Extensive bibliography.

40:163   Ward, Harry M. *The Department of War, 1781–1795.* Pittsburgh, Pa.: University of Pittsburgh Press, 1962. The development of the War Department and the army under the Confederation progressed far enough, notwithstanding lack of funds, to lend some support to the thesis that the Confederation might in time have evolved into an effective government; the Washington administration built on an established foundation. For the tactical organization of the army, see J. R. Jacobs, *The Beginning of the U.S. Army, 1783–1812* (40:157).

TO WORLD WAR I, 1865–1914

See under "Personalities," especially Elihu Root, Theodore Roosevelt; also see Chapter 13 for the Spanish-American War.

Challener, R. D. *Admirals, Generals, and American Foreign Policy, 1898–1914* (17:229) is an immensely detailed analysis of military activities and attitudes in foreign policy. Chapter 1, "Ideas, Institutions, and Practices," has sections on the military "world view," principles and methods of American civil-military and interservice cooperation, channels of communication and shared assumptions between the military and civilians, and the differences between American and European practice in civil-military relations.

Grenville, J. A. S., and Young, G. B. *Politics, Strategy, and American Diplomacy: Studies in Foreign Policy, 1873–1917* (12:93) includes several essays that relate military and foreign policy with uncommon breadth of understanding: on Admiral Stephen B. Luce, the influence of naval strategy upon the acquisition of the Philippines, and Admiral Dewey's leadership of the General Board of the navy.

The second torpedoed forever the old notion that Assistant Secretary of the Navy Theodore Roosevelt had impulsively ordered Commodore Dewey's squadron to prepare to attack the Philippines.

40:164   Karsten, Peter. "Armed Progressives: The Military Reorganized for the American Century." In Jerry Israel, ed., *Building the Organizational Society.* New York: Free Press, 1972, pp. 197–232. The American military ethos at the opening of the 20th century was more closely akin to progressivism than historians have tended to acknowledge. The military reforms shared the Progressives' impulse to rationalize governmental organization by borrowing the managerial methods of the private corporation. Bibliography.

Quirk, R. E. *An Affair of Honor: Woodrow Wilson and the Occupation of Veracruz* (15:143) is a comprehensive account of the military as well as the diplomatic aspects of the occupation of Veracruz in 1914.

The Army

See under "Personalities," especially Emory Upton, Leonard Wood, and, under "Others," Fred C. Ainsworth, Robert L. Bullard.

Clendenen, C. C. *Blood on the Border: The United States Army and the Mexican Irregulars* (15:175) emphasizes 20th-century military friction between the United States and Mexico, especially the Pershing Punitive Expedition, but also develops lesser known military incursions, including American intervention in Mexican civil wars of the 19th century and Indian-fighting forays below the border. Here the army became a conspicuous instrument of foreign policy.

Cosmas, G. A. *An Army for Empire: The United States Army in the Spanish-American War, 1898–1899* (13:139) argues that the army's Elihu Root reforms of the early 20th century were anticipated during the 1890s, when the army began preparing for overseas expeditions before and in anticipation of the war with Spain. The revisionist account of the war with Spain emphasizes military achievements rather than shortcomings.

Gates, J. M. *Schoolbooks and Krags: The United States Army in the Philippines, 1898–1902* (13:168) suggests parallels with the Indochina War and raises intriguing questions about why the pacification of the

Filipino insurrectionists was relatively so easy. Gates suggests that one of the main themes in the Philippines was the extension of the Progressive era's idealism overseas.

Millett, A. R. *The Politics of Intervention: The Military Occupation of Cuba, 1906–1909* (15:101) discusses not only the politics leading to the intervention, but also the political disputes, often waged within the occupying army and between army officers and civilians, over extending the purposes to include more fundamental reforms in Cuban institutions.

40:165   Utley, Robert M. *Frontier Regulars: The United States Army and the Indian, 1866–1891.* New York: Macmillan, 1973. This volume is not only an administrative and organizational history of the army; it also emphasizes problems of developing a military doctrine to cope with irregular warfare, an issue with major implications for the 20th century and particularly the Indochina War. Extensive bibliography.

The Navy

See under "Personalities," especially Stephen B. Luce, Alfred T. Mahan, and, under "Others," Bradley A. Fiske, Richard Wainwright, and civilian Benjamin F. Tracy (under "Others"); also see Chapter 12, "Naval Influences," and Chapter 17, "Naval and Strategic Issues."

40:166   Alden, John D. *The American Steel Navy: A Photographic History of the U.S. Navy from the Introduction of the Steel Hull in 1883 to the Cruise of the Great White Fleet, 1907–1909.* Annapolis, Md.: Naval Institute Press, 1972. The text discussing the military implications of the naval architecture depicted by the photographs illuminates the capacities and limitations of the ships and thus of the ways in which the new steel navy could serve the purposes of American foreign policy. Bibliography.

40:167   Bennett, Frank M. *The Steam Navy of the United States: A History of the Growth of the Steam Vessel of War in the U.S. Navy and of the Naval Engineer Corps.* Pittsburgh: Warren, 1896. The steam warship obviously enhanced naval mobility, but it also limited it: where the sailing ship could cruise indefinitely, touching shore only to take on fresh water and provisions, the steam warship was limited by its capacity to carry coal. This durable standard details the technological foundations of the early modern navy.

Braisted, W. R. *The United States Navy in the Pacific, 1897–1909* (17:226) shows that the Pacific was the navy's special sphere of interest in American foreign relations. In this and his subsequent volume, *The United States Navy in the Pacific, 1909–1922* (17:227), Braisted reviews the navy's role in Pacific Ocean diplomacy and strategy. In this volume, the larger strategic and commercial issues revolve around the quest for adequate bases.

40:168   Brodie, Bernard. *Sea Power in the Machine Age.* Princeton, N.J.: Princeton University Press, 1941. This early work by a premier American strategy intellectual remains the best exposition of what navies could and could not accomplish from the close of the sailing era to the eve of the nuclear age. Particularly, it makes technological issues comprehensible and integrates them into the larger history of naval power. Bibliography.

Buhl, L. C. "Maintaining 'An American Navy,' 1865–1889" (12:91).

Hagan, K. J. *American Gunboat Diplomacy and the Old Navy, 1877–1889* (12:94) surveys both the underlying ideas and the activities of the navy in Latin American, African, and Asian waters during the years just before Mahan and the new steel navy. The navy's principal purpose was to develop markets for American goods and to protect those citizens who tried to develop the markets.

40:169   Hattendorf, John B. "Technology and Strategy: A Study in the Professional Thought of the U.S. Navy, 1900–1916." *Naval War College Review* 24:3 (1971), 25–48. Hattendorf's emphasis is on the Naval War College and the effort to develop a more systematic strategic thought than that of Mahan, with greater appreciation of the interplay of strategy, tactics, and technology. Hattendorf offers the best short analysis of William McCarty Little's development of the naval war game.

40:170   Herrick, Walter R., Jr. *The American Naval Revolution.* Baton Rouge: Louisiana State University Press, 1966. With emphasis on the administration of Secretary of the Navy B. F. Tracy—now supplemented by B. F. Cooling's biography of Tracy (12:92)—and to a lesser extent on the remainder of the 1890s, Herrick weaves together executive and congressional policy debates, concepts of strategy, issues of ship design, and efforts to organize ships into a fleet. Such related foreign policy issues as the search for bases and the Chilean war scare are integrated into this history. Bibliography.

Herwig, H. H. *Politics of Frustration: The United States in German Naval Planning, 1889–1941* (19:145) argues that the German government came to regard the United States as an inveterate partner of Britain and therefore an obstacle that must be overcome in Germany's rise to world power. The German navy, supporting and reinforcing this view, prepared its contingency plans accordingly.

40:171 Knox, Dudley W. "The Role of Doctrine in Naval Warfare." *U.S. Naval Institute Proceedings* 41:2 (1915), 325–54. Historians' preoccupation with A. T. Mahan obscured the contributions of other sailor-intellectuals. Knox was especially influential, and often a critic of Mahan. This article is representative of his thought, and is important in its call for conceptualization of the purposes of the navy.

40:172 Livermore, Seward W. "American Naval-Base Policy in the Far East, 1850–1914" *Pacific Historical Review* 13:2 (1944), 113–35. Portions of this article describe the acquisition of naval and coaling stations in Pago Pago, Hawaii, and Lower California, their general disuse, and controversies within the Department of the Navy on their utility.

Seager, R., II. "Ten Years Before Mahan: The Unofficial Case for the New Navy, 1880–1890" (12:97) demonstrates that Mahan's ideas were by no means a bolt from the blue, but that his thinking and influence proceeded logically from the work of earlier naval reformers.

THE WORLD WARS, 1914–1945

See Chapter 19 (World War I) and Chapter 23 (World War II) for additional references.

40:173 Collier, Basil. *The Lion and the Eagle: British and Anglo-American Strategy, 1900–1950.* New York: Putnam's, 1972. This is a discussion by a British military historian of the diplomatic and strategic background of Anglo-American relations, and the rising supremacy of the United States in that relationship.

40:174 Greene, Fred. "The Military View of American National Policy, 1904–1940." *American*

Historical Review 66:2 (1961), 354–77. Military leaders felt themselves lacking in guidance from civilian leaders regarding national policy and subordinate to the civilians. Yet their responsibilities compelled them to develop policies on hemispheric defense, Pacific Ocean defense, and army-navy cooperation.

Koistinen, P. A. C. "The 'Industrial-Military Complex' in Historical Perspective: The Interwar Years" (19:178) is a detailed examination of the antecedents of the post-1945 military-industrial complex.

40:175 Matloff, Maurice. "The American Approach to War, 1919–1945." In Michael Howard, ed., *The Theory and Practice of War: Essays Presented to B. H. Liddell Hart on His Seventieth Birthday.* New York: Praeger, 1966, pp. 213–43. The author addresses army and air corps planning with particular expertise, but he does full justice as well to the navy and to the rise of interservice planning. Bibliography.

Morton, L. "War Plan Orange: Evolution of a Strategy" (20:147) reflects the changing balance of sea power in the Pacific, under the impact of naval limitation treaties among other factors, and a struggle between realism and hope to determine whether American outposts might withstand Japanese attack in the western Pacific until the navy rallied.

Schmidt, H. *The United States Occupation of Haiti, 1915–1934* (15:188) examines an American use of military intervention to try to create a stable, friendly, and perhaps democratic government in a foreign country. The Haitian occupation presaged the problems of later, larger-scale interventions. Schmidt integrates military history into the diplomatic and economic history of the occupation.

The Army

See under "Personalities," especially Newton D. Baker, Mark W. Clark, Dwight D. Eisenhower, Douglas MacArthur, Peyton C. Marsh (under "Others"), George C. Marshall, Matthew B. Ridgway.

Coffman, E. M. *The War to End All Wars: The American Military Experience in World War I* (19:183) is the best overall survey of the American military participation in World War I. It relates the events of the war to subsequent developments in the American services, especially the army.

40:176 Nelson, Otto L., Jr. *National Security and the General Staff.* Washington, D.C.: Infantry Journal Press, 1946. There is no satisfactory history of the Army General Staff. Paul Y. Hammond, *Organizing for Defense* (40:43), and James E. Hewes, Jr. *From Root to McNamara* (40:96), both tell part of the story. Meanwhile Nelson's book has to suffice; its most useful feature is its reprinting of many pertinent documents. Bibliography.

Air Power

See under "Personalities," especially Henry H. Arnold, William Mitchell.

40:177 Hansell, Haywood S. *The Air Plan That Defeated Hitler.* Atlanta: MacArthur/Longino & Porter, 1972. A first-hand account, by a principal air planner just before and during World War II, of the designing of the American daylight bombing offensive against Germany and its wartime refinement. To cripple Germany by destroying critical points in the German economy, the air planners had to select targets with fine discernment.

40:178 Quester, George H. *Deterrence before Hiroshima: The Airpower Background of Modern Strategy.* New York: Wiley, 1966. Quester's cautionary theme is that post-1945 concepts of nuclear destructiveness do not offer a much more terrible vision of war than did pre-1940 notions of the potential horrors of aerial bombing. Yet the horrors failed to deter war or bombing. Quester offers a succinct history of ideas and practice in aerial war. Bibliography.

NAVY AND MARINE CORPS

See under "Personalities," especially Ernest J. King, William V. Pratt (under "Others").

Braisted, W. R. *The United States Navy in the Pacific, 1909–1922* (17:227) has a broader scope than the title suggests; naval relations with Britain in the Atlantic also figure importantly. However, it remains an exhaustive examination of American naval policy toward Japan, focusing on the effort to redress a Pacific balance of power.

40:179 Harrod, Frederick S. *Manning the New Navy: The Development of a Modern Naval Enlisted Force, 1899–1940.* Westport, Conn.: Greenwood, 1978. The navy of wooden sailing ships had been recruited in American and foreign seaports. The navy of the machine age demanded mechanical aptitude of its enlisted men; seeking also to fulfill a preference for old-stock white American sailors, the navy searched for recruits in the small towns of the U.S. interior. Bibliography.

Isely, J. A., and Crowl, P. A. *The U.S. Marines and Amphibious War: Its Theory, and Its Practice in the Pacific* (23:189) finds that seizing island bases from the Japanese by amphibious assault suggested a mission for the marines, who had never had a clear military purpose. Amphibious assaults, however, also raised problems that after Gallipoli might seem insurmountable; this book explores the doctrinal solutions to the problems.

40:180 Reynolds, Clark G. *The Fast Carriers: The Forging of an Air Navy.* 2d ed. Huntington, N.Y.: Krieger, 1978. There is no analysis of the impact of carriers and air power on naval strategy comparable to Bernard Brodie's dissection of earlier naval strategy and technology, *Sea Power in the Machine Age* (40:168). This history of the evolution of carrier doctrine and its application in World War II partially fills the void.

Tuleja, T. V. *Statesmen and Admirals: Quest for a Far Eastern Naval Policy* (21:186) surveys the frustrations involved in attempting to mesh American East Asian diplomacy with naval policy and naval limitations. It carries through the 1930s many of the issues developed in Gerald E. Wheeler's *Prelude to Pearl Harbor.* It deals with the tensions between traditional conceptions of sea power and the rise of carrier-based and other air power.

40:181 Wheeler, Gerald E. *Prelude to Pearl Harbor: The United States Navy and the Far East, 1921–1931.* Columbia: University of Missouri Press, 1963. Carrying forward the themes of William R. Braisted's volumes *The United States Navy in the Pacific, 1897–1909* and *1909–1922* (17:226; 17:227), Wheeler's book is less detailed in exploring the intricacies of naval policy where policy meets diplomacy, but it has greater detail on ships and naval organization. Wheeler is also supplemented for the later 1930s by Thaddeus V. Tuleja, *Statesmen and Admirals* (21:186). Bibliography.

The Cold War and After

40:182 Blechman, Barry M., and Kaplan, Stephen S. "The Use of the Armed Forces as a Political Instrument." *Naval War College Review* 30:4 (1978), 80–87. During 1946 to 1975 the United States used its armed forces for political purposes 215 times. Displays by the military have been effective, but they cannot adequately substitute for long-range policies or consistent goals.

40:183 Kende, Istvan. "Twenty-Five Years of Local Wars." *Journal of Peace Research* 8:1 (1971), 5–22. Dealing quantitatively with local wars since World War II, the wars are discussed both regionally and on a global level, and are classified according to a number of characteristics. The Third World is increasingly becoming the scene of local war.

THE "STRATEGY INTELLECTUALS"

Brodie, B., ed. *The Absolute Weapon: Atomic Power and World Order* (26:198) is the first major effort to explore the strategic implications of the atomic bomb. This anthology is useful to indicate the direction of thinking on the morrow of Hiroshima, and for its insights into what was to come. It is still worth reading.

40:184 Bush, Vannevar. *Modern Arms and Free Men: A Discussion of the Role of Science in Preserving Democracy.* New York: Simon & Schuster, 1949. The principal American coordinator of scientific contributions in World War II attempted one of the first forecasts of the impact of the atomic bomb and other devices such as guided missiles. Bush was confident of the bomb's deterrent powers and of civilization's capacity to survive an atomic war.

40:185 Enthoven, Alain C., and Smith, K. Wayne. *How Much Is Enough? Shaping the Defense Program, 1961–1969.* New York: Harper & Row, 1971. Part memoir, part history, the volume is a detailed study by two of McNamara's "whiz kids" which defends the secretary's management of national security policies in the 1960s.

40:186 Hitch, Charles J., and McKean, Roland N., eds. *The Economics of Defense in the Nuclear Age.* Cambridge: Harvard University Press, 1960. This volume on the cost-effectiveness and systems-analysis approaches to resolving issues of weapons procurement and national security policy outlines the direction the Department of Defense would take under the secretaryship of Robert S. McNamara. Bibliography.

40:187 Kahn, Herman. *On Thermonuclear War.* 2d ed. New York: Free Press, 1969. The first and best known of several books through which Kahn induced strategy intellectuals to contemplate the possible contingencies of nuclear war. To Kahn, nuclear war was not so horrible that it could never occur; rather, rational human beings should plan to salvage what they can from nuclear war.

40:188 Kaufmann, William W., ed. *Military Policy and National Security.* Princeton, N.J.: Princeton University Press, 1956. This symposium offered the strategy intellectuals' earliest reasoned, public rebuttals of the massive retaliation doctrine, most notably a reprinting of Kaufmann's own "The Requirements of Deterrence." Kaufmann doubts the credibility of massive nuclear deterrence as a barrier to limited wars and argues for a variety of deterrence systems. Bibliography.

Kissinger, H. A. *Nuclear Weapons and Foreign Policy* (28:74) was more effective in combatting the doctrine of massive retaliation than in persuading policymakers or public that tactical nuclear weapons could make limited war at tolerable cost.

40:189 Morgenstern, Oskar. *The Question of National Defense.* New York: Random House, 1959. While warning of the instability of the nuclear stalemate, Morgenstern called for American nuclear forces invulnerable to preemptive attack. This book perceives dangers lurking at every turn of nuclear strategy, but also expresses confidence in America's ability to employ military power advantageously.

40:190 Osgood, Robert E. *Limited War: The Challenge to American Strategy.* Chicago: University of Chicago Press, 1957. Though overshadowed in terms of mass readership by the almost simultaneous publication of Henry A. Kissinger's *Nuclear Weapons and Foreign Policy* (28:74), Osgood's *Limited War* is at least as persuasive a presentation for limited war as a rational and effective instrument of policy. He includes a useful historical survey of limitations upon war. Bibliography.

40:191 Osgood, Robert E. *Limited War Revisited.* Boulder, Colo.: Westview, 1979. This is a concise, critical review of the theory and practice of limited war by one of the leading creators of the 1950s version of the theory.

40:192 Parrish, Noel F. *Behind the Sheltering Bomb.* New York: Arno, 1979. This work, a photographic reproduction of a 1968 dissertation, whose subtitle was "Military Indecision from Alamogordo to Korea," remains the best survey of the early impact of atomic weapons on American military policy. Bibliography.

40:193 Salomon, Michael D. "New Concepts for Strategy Parity." *Survival* 19:6 (1977), 255–62. Strategic thought of the 1950s and 1960s, epitomized and formed by Bernard Brodie, Herman Kahn, and Thomas Schelling, incorporated the realization that military effectiveness and maintenance of national security were competing objectives, a key factor missing in current strategic thought.

40:194 Wohlstetter, Albert J. "The Delicate Balance of Terror." *Foreign Affairs* 37:1 (1959), 211–34. Denying the assumption that rival nuclear powers were like two scorpions in a bottle, Wohlstetter argued that small technical advances in nuclear weaponry could yield disproportionate strategic advantages and tempt one of the nuclear powers toward a preemptive strike.

The Soviet Challenge

Byely, B., et al. *Marxism-Leninism on War and Army* (29:15) is a reprint of a 1968 Soviet publication designed for high-ranking Soviet military officers which provides a summary of Marxist-Leninist teachings on war and its economic causes. Soviet views on varieties of wars (civil, bourgeois, anti-imperialist) and the behavior of "imperialist" states are outlined.

Garthoff, R. L. *Soviet Strategy in the Nuclear Age* (29:18) outlines Soviet strategic thought about nuclear, as well as limited, war.

Jackson, W. D. "The Soviets and Strategic Arms: Toward an Evaluation of the Record" [1953–1979] (29:140).

40:195 Sokolovskii, V. D. *Soviet Military Strategy.* 3d ed. Ed. with an analysis and commentary by Har-

riet Fast Scott. New York: Crane, Russak, 1975. This book details Soviet strategic concepts and presents a harsh critique of the strategies of "imperialist" or capitalist states, with special attention devoted to the United States. The translation includes passages from earlier editions, and the editor compares the various editions.

MILITARY POLICY AND STRATEGY

See under "Personalities," "Army," especially James M. Gavin (under "Others"), Matthew B. Ridgway, Maxwell D. Taylor; also see Chapter 26, "Origins of NATO," and Chapter 28, "U.S. and NATO."

40:196 Aron, Raymond. *The Great Debate: Theories of Nuclear Strategy.* Trans. by Ernst Pawel. Garden City, N.Y.: Doubleday, 1965. In this thought-provoking book, the noted French author provides a succinct evaluation of post-1945 events. He examines the great power competition and the offspring of that competition, thermonuclear weapons.

40:197 Betts, Richard K. *Soldiers, Statesmen, and Cold War Crises.* Cambridge: Harvard University Press, 1977. Reconstructing twenty cold war crises, Betts rejects alike the notion that military professionals have dominated decisions on the use of force, and the notion that military professionals have not possessed sufficient access to decisionmaking. The military have offered divided counsel, and their views have been at least as likely to accord with those of civilian policymakers as to be more aggressive.

Blaufarb, D. S. *The Counterinsurgency Era: U.S. Doctrine and Performance, 1950 to the Present* (30:178) is the most comprehensive effort thus far to summarize the intellectual roots of American policy toward communist insurgencies and to unite into a coherent whole analyses of counterinsurgency efforts in the Philippines, Thailand, and Indochina. Dealing with civilian as well as military approaches, Blaufarb delineates the dilemmas posed by counterinsurgency for America's conventional military forces.

40:198 Deitchman, Seymour. *Limited War and American Defense Policy.* Cambridge, Mass.: MIT Press, 1964. An early effort to gain historical perspective from the first two decades of limited war, the book remains a sound overview of theory and practice to the eve of the transition to an emphasis on unconventional war. Bibliography.

40:199 Freedman, Lawrence. *U.S. Intelligence and the Soviet Strategic Threat.* Boulder, Colo.: Westview, 1977. This book deals less narrowly with intelligence and more with military policy in general than the title might imply, for Freedman's concern is with the nature of perceptions of changes in Soviet strength that might diminish American strength. Using the McNamara policies and especially the IBM decisions as test cases, he is concerned with keeping intelligence estimates independent of the judgments of policymakers who have axes to grind. Bibliography.

40:200 George, Alexander L., and Smoke, Richard. *Deterrence in American Foreign Policy: Theory and Practice.* New York: Columbia University Press, 1974. The historian may conclude that the effort to use normatively an abstract deterrence model gets in the way of exploring such crises as the Berlin blockade, the Korean War, the Taiwan Straits Crisis, the Middle East crisis of 1957–1958, the Quemoy crisis, the various Berlin crises of 1958 through 1961, and the Cuban missile crisis. Nevertheless, these case studies are very useful. Bibliographies.

Hollist, W. L. "An Analysis of Arms Processes in the United States and the Soviet Union" (29:127) examines alternative explanations, or models, of arms buildups in the U.S.S.R. and the United States (1948–1970). The United States reacted more to changes in Soviet arms expenditures than to levels of Soviet arms, while the Soviet Union tended to react more to the level of U.S. arms than to changes.

40:201 Moulton, Harland B. *From Superiority to Parity: The United States and the Strategic Arms Race, 1961–1971.* Westport, Conn.: Greenwood, 1973. Moulton surveys the evolution of a strategy of deterrence and of controlled nuclear war if deterrence should fail, the "bomber gap" and "missile gap" controversies, and the McNamara strategy of gradual acceptance of nuclear parity and the consequent return to deterrence rather than waging war. Bibliography.

40:202 Paul, Roland A. *American Military Commitments Abroad.* New Brunswick, N.J.: Rutgers University Press, 1973. Despite becoming dated, this book is the best analysis of the varying categories into which American military commitments can be placed and of the principal examples and implications of each category.

40:203 Schwarz, Urs. *American Strategy: A New Perspective: The Growth of Politico-Military Thinking in the United States.* Garden City, N.Y.: Doubleday, 1966. Emphasizing the period since World War II, this overview offers a useful introduction for the beginning student of American strategic thought. Written by a Swiss journalist, it has the additional value of presenting an outsider's perspective on, to quote a chapter title, "A Peace-loving yet Military Republic."

40:204 Stubbs, Richard, and Ranger, Robin. "Mechanistic Assumptions and United States Strategy." *International Journal* 33:3 (1978), 557–72. Mechanistic images fostered by the social and intellectual climate and internationalized by American theorists have pushed arms control and military strategy along questionable lines.

40:205 Yarmolinsky, Adam. *The Military Establishment: Its Impacts on American Society.* New York: Harper & Row, 1971. Though Yarmolinsky describes the current American military establishment as "massive, powerful, and pervasive" and thus concludes that we stand in considerable danger of becoming "a militarized society," his book has nothing of the sensationalism that marred similar works of the Indochina War era. Bibliography.

Ziemke, E. F. *The U.S. Army in the Occupation of Germany, 1944–1946* (26:102) is an extremely detailed study that lifts one aspect of the history of American military government from the usual neglect of this subject. Planning and guiding concepts are dealt with as fully as practices.

Politics of Weapons Development

40:206 Armacost, Michael H. *The Politics of Weapons Innovation: The Thor-Jupiter Controversy.* New York: Columbia University Press, 1969. Armacost shows how weapons policies are influenced by the nature of the political processes through which decisions are made.

40:207 Sapolsky, Harvey M. *The Polaris System Development: Bureaucratic and Programmatic Success in Government.* Cambridge: Harvard University Press, 1972. This book is a case study of a rare government program that succeeded. It is valuable for students of bureaucratic politics, management techniques, weapons procurement, and arms control problems.

40:208   Yanarella, Ernest J. *The Missile Defense Controversy: Strategy, Technology, and Politics, 1955–1972.* Lexington: University Press of Kentucky, 1977. Yanarella offers the missile-defense controversy as a test case of the proposition that technology governs strategic-weapons policy, that what can be done technologically will be done. He does not wholly accept the proposition. His case study reviews how national security decisions are formulated. Bibliography.

THE MILITARY AND GOVERNMENT

The Executive

40:209   Clark, Keith C., and Legere, Laurence J. *The President and the Management of National Security.* New York: Praeger, 1969. This book details the organization and functioning of the White House national security staffs. Slightly less emphasis is given to the State and Defense Departments and their relationships with the White House. Bibliography.

40:210   Huntington, Samuel P. *The Common Defense: Strategic Programs in National Politics.* New York: Columbia University Press, 1961. For no other American administration do we have analyses of the interconnections of political, strategic, fiscal, and bureaucratic influences in forming national security policy comparable to this record of the Truman and Eisenhower administrations. Though the detail makes the work tedious, the whole is rendered persuasive by Huntington's theory of political-military relations, developed in his *The Soldier and the State* (40:44). Bibliography.

40:211   Kinnard, Douglas. *President Eisenhower and Strategy Management: A Study in Defense Politics.* Lexington: University Press of Kentucky, 1977. Kinnard argues that Eisenhower dominated the making of national security policy during his presidency, conceived the strategic policies of his administration, and used the National Security Council and the other agencies of bureaucracy to manage his policies. The book should be supplemented by Samuel P. Huntington, *The Common Defense,* above. Bibliography.

Mueller, J. E. *War, Presidents and Public Opinion* (30:211) surveys public opinion about wars (1939–1972). Mueller finds consistent patterns that no president has readily changed. Every war tends to become unpopular as it lengthens and as American casualties grow. Brief though its historical perspective is, this book cannot be avoided by anyone concerned with the dimensions of dissent during American wars.

40:212   Schilling, Warner R.; Hammond, Paul Y.; and Snyder, Glenn H. *Strategy, Politics, and Defense Budgets.* New York: Columbia University Press, 1962. Case studies of the preparation of the fiscal 1950 defense budget, of NSC-68, and of the Eisenhower administration's "New Look" illuminate defense policymaking processes and military strategy. Bibliography.

Department of Defense

See under "Personalities," especially Robert S. McNamara.

40:213   Caraley, Demetrios. *The Politics of Military Unification: A Study of Conflict and the Policy Process.* New York: Columbia University Press, 1966. The standard survey of the movement toward a federation (perhaps a more accurate term than "unification") of the armed forces in a Department of Defense, up to the initial establishment of that department. Bibliography.

40:214   Coletta, Paolo E. "The Defense Unification Battle, 1947–50: The Navy." *Prologue* 7:1 (1975), 6–17. From the passage of the National Security Act (1947) to the outbreak of the Korean War, the office of the secretary of defense grew at the expense of the navy, which had to scrap its plans for a supercarrier and drastically cut naval air power and the Marine Corps.

40:215   Davis, Vincent J. *Postwar Defense Policy and the U.S. Navy, 1943–1946.* Chapel Hill: University of North Carolina Press, 1966. While attempting to retain as much as possible of its wartime strength and interservice prestige, the navy also had to accommodate a revolution brought about by the rise of the aircraft carrier. The reader will find that postwar planning was hampered almost as much by disagreements within as by opponents of naval influence outside the navy.

40:216   Halperin, Morton H. "War Termination as a Problem in Civil-Military Relations." *Annals of the American Academy of Political and Social Science,* no. 392 (1970), 86–95. Part of a volume devoted to "How Wars End," the whole of which is worthy of attention for its exploration of a neglected problem. Halperin deals with American and foreign, particularly French, instances of civil-military problems arising out of efforts to end wars.

40:217   Haynes, Richard F. "The Defense Unification Battle, 1947–50: The Army." *Prologue* 7:1 (1975), 27–31. During the unification of defense (1947–1950) the War Department lost its aviation component but tried to maintain budgetary parity. This resulted in the army's becoming larger in size and smaller in prestige as an administrative subdivision of the Defense Department.

40:218   Korb, Lawrence J. *The Joint Chiefs of Staff: The First Twenty-Five Years.* Bloomington: Indiana University Press, 1976. Korb outlines the formal and informal responsibilities of the Joint Chiefs; presents descriptions of the career patterns of the twenty-eight officers who served as chiefs during the first twenty-five years; discusses the relationships of the Joint Chiefs with presidents, secretaries of defense, and Congress; and reviews the participation of the Joint Chiefs in foreign policy and military operations. Bibliography.

40:219   Ries, John C. *The Management of Defense: Organization and Control of the U.S. Armed Services.* Baltimore: Johns Hopkins Press, 1964. Ries offers both an historical overview of the evolution of the Department of Defense and a critical analysis of its effectiveness. Ries believes that effective civilian control will come only when the secretary of defense is recognized as primarily an adjudicator among differing military viewpoints. Bibliography.

40:220   Sherry, Michael S. *Preparing for the Next War: American Plans for Postwar Defense, 1941–45.* New Haven, Conn.: Yale University Press, 1977. Sherry argues that the sense of national insecurity created by the Axis threat generated a strong preparedness movement and a preoccupation with military strength that antedated the cold war.

40:221   Wolk, Herman S. "The Defense Unification Battle, 1947–50: The Air Force." *Prologue* 7:1 (1975), 18–26. From 1947 to 1950, the air force sought independence and the building of an "atomic" air

force. These objectives led to a fierce political-military struggle with the navy and resulted in the strengthening of the secretary of defense's powers.

Arms Control and Disarmament

See Chapter 16, "Disarmament Efforts," Chapter 20, "Disarmament and Arms Control," Chapter 29, "Nuclear Arms Competition and Control," and Chapter 38, "Disarmament and Arms Control."

Keesing's Research Report. *Disarmament Negotiations and Treaties, 1946–1971* (38:100) is a chronological and descriptive account of efforts to curb the nuclear arms race.

40:222   Stockholm International Peace Research Institute. *Arms Control: A Survey and Appraisal of Multilateral Agreements.* New York: Crane, Russak, 1978. This useful compilation lists and reviews various agreements (1959–1970), notes problems, and describes the international negotiating machinery available. It includes the texts of accords and summarizes UN resolutions and votes taken (1969–1977).

United Nations. *Basic Problems of Disarmament: Reports of the Secretary-General* (38:101) contains three reports, prepared during the 1960s.

United Nations. *The United Nations and Disarmament, 1945–1970* (38:103) together with supplement (1970–1975) provides a broad survey of debates and negotiations within the UN system. Annually updated by *United Nations Disarmament Yearbook* [1976–] (38:102).

40:223   U.S. Arms Control and Disarmament Agency. *Arms Control and Disarmament Agreements: Texts and Histories of Negotiations.* Washington, D.C., 1980. This periodically updated volume—three editions having previously appeared—presents the official view. The discussions of the basic terms and the lists of nations adhering to each treaty are especially useful.

POST-1945 NEGOTIATIONS

See Chapter 26, "Baruch Plan, 1946."

Bechhoefer, B. G. *Postwar Negotiations for Arms Control* (26:197) is still one of the fullest descriptions of arms control efforts and general disarmament negotiations for 1945 to 1960. There is ample material on U.S. proposals, negotiators, and policy positions and assumptions.

Bernstein, B. J. "The Challenges and Dangers of Nuclear Weapons: Foreign Policy and Strategy, 1941–1978" (29:124) examines the "options of 'atomic diplomacy'" and the responses of various administrations to changing conditions and challenges. Options are described, including massive retaliation, arms control, flexible options, and counterforce strategy.

40:224   Carolton, David, and Schaerf, Carlo, eds. *Arms Control and Technological Innovation.* New York: Wiley, 1976. These essays cover a much broader spectrum of topics than the title suggests; as such it provides a useful survey of the major postwar arms control issues.

Dallin, A., et al. *The Soviet Union and Disarmament: An Appraisal of Soviet Attitudes and Intentions* (29:137) concentrates on the 1950s and early 1960s. The authors find a growing sincerity in Soviet intentions toward arms control, especially under Khrushchev, and outline the variety of influences upon Soviet behavior.

40:225   Forbes, Henry W. *The Strategy of Disarmament.* Washington, D.C.: Public Affairs Press, 1962. There are no outstanding general introductions to arms control and disarmament issues which include the essential historical dimensions. Forbes's account is the best available survey of these problems with some insights into historical lessons.

40:226   Levine, Robert A. *The Arms Debate.* Cambridge: Harvard University Press, 1963. This volume seeks to delineate strategists and arms controllers into various "schools." Although dated, it does help to connect strategic arms concepts to arms control issues.

Lieberman, J. I. *The Scorpion and the Tarantula: The Struggle to Control Atomic Weapons, 1945–1949* (38:110).

40:227   Morray, Joseph P. *From Yalta to Disarmament: Cold War Debate.* New York: Monthly Review, 1961. A history of the cold war in terms of the public rhetoric of both U.S. and Soviet officials, it emphasizes disarmament and the international control of atomic energy.

40:228   Myrdal, Alva. *The Game of Disarmament: How the United States and Russia Run the Arms Race.* New York: Pantheon, 1976. A leading Swedish diplomat provides a memoirlike "neutralist" study of Soviet-American efforts to reach disarmament.

40:229   Quester, George H. *Nuclear Diplomacy: The First Twenty-Five Years.* New York: Dunellen, 1970. A chronological study of the cold war, it emphasizes the Soviet-American nuclear arms race.

40:230   Roberts, Chalmers M. *The Nuclear Years: The Arms Race and Arms Control, 1945–1970.* New York: Praeger, 1970. In this "primer," a *Washington Post* journalist surveys the nuclear arms race from Hiroshima to SALT.

Test Ban Treaty, 1963

See Chapter 29, "Test Ban Treaty."

Divine, R. A. *Blowing on the Wind: The Nuclear Test Ban Debate, 1954–1960* (29:144) emphasizes the tendency to sacrifice public security to the security of government officials in their offices and serves as an introduction to the domestic politics of arms control.

Jacobson, H. K., and Stein, E. *Diplomats, Scientists and Politicians: The United States and the Nuclear Test Ban Negotiations* (29:145) describes and analyzes negotiations, with some perspective on the international political system, showing the complex procedures, obstacles, and policies at work.

Nonproliferation Treaty, 1968

40:231   Camilleri, J. A. "The Myth of the Peaceful Atom." *Millennium* 6:2 (1977), 111–27. Agreements on nuclear safeguards, such as the Nonproliferation Treaty, have failed to provide meaningful barriers, especially with the increased application of nuclear technology in the world.

40:232   Greenwood, Ted; Feiveson, Harold A.; and Taylor, Theodore B. *Nuclear Proliferation: Motivations, Capabilities, and Strategies for Control.* New York: McGraw-Hill, 1977. These essays cover the major problems in a clear fashion, limiting the use of technical data to that necessary to understand the political dimensions of proliferation.

40:233   Epstein, William. *The Last Chance: Nuclear Proliferation and Arms Control.* New York: Free Press, 1976. This is a fine survey of a current issue by a man who was involved in United Nations disarmament activities for over twenty-five years.

40:234   Nye, Joseph S. "Nonproliferation: A Long-term Strategy." *Foreign Affairs* 56:3 (1978), 601–23. Nye reviews American nuclear nonproliferation efforts during the 1950s and 1970s. The development and diffusion of nuclear technology requires of all involved nations a commitment to caution and to shared benefits.

SALT, 1972–

See Chapter 29, "Strategic Arms Limitations Talks (SALT)."

Newhouse, J. *Cold Dawn: The Story of SALT* (29:156) is the best early effort by a single author to summarize and appraise the SALT I negotiations and agreements.

Talbott, S. *Endgame: The Inside Story of SALT II* (29:160) studies the complicated negotiations that led to the 1979 SALT II treaty.

Willrich, M., and Rhinelander, J. B., eds. *SALT: The Moscow Agreements and Beyond* (29:162).

Seabed Treaty, 1971

40:235   Ramberg, Bennett. *The Seabed Arms Control Negotiations: A Study of Multilateral Arms Control Conference Diplomacy.* Monograph Series in World Affairs, vol. 15, book 2. Denver, Colo.: Graduate School of International Studies, 1978. This is the fullest account of the negotiations of the Seabed Treaty. See also his "Tactical Advantages of Opening Positioning Strategies: Lessons from the Seabed Arms Control Talks, 1967–1970," *Journal of Conflict Resolution* 21:4 (1977), 685–700.

40:236   U.S. Arms Control and Disarmament Agency. *International Negotiations on the Seabed Arms Control Treaty.* Publication 68. Washington, D.C., 1973. Prepared by Robert W. Lambert and John W. Syphax of the agency, this uncritical account provides a useful summary of the negotiations from public documents.

ARMS TRANSFERS

40:237   Harkavy, Robert E. *The Arms Trade and International Systems.* Cambridge, Mass.: Ballinger, 1975. Written by a political scientist with a rare appreciation of historical data, this thoughtful volume provides the best introduction available to the very complicated issues involved in arms traffic. Extensive bibliography.

40:238   Hessing, Anne, et al. *Controlling Future Arms Trade.* New York: McGraw-Hill, 1977. Although this volume is designed to discuss future policy options, it does examine key issues in a post-1945 political context.

40:239   Stockholm International Peace Research Institute. *The Arms Trade with the Third World.* New York: Humanities Press, 1971. This massive volume presents post-1945 issues within an historical context. It is also valuable for its collecting of arms trade data. Tables. It is supplemented by a SIPRI monograph, *The Arms Trade Registers* (Cambridge, Mass.: MIT Press, 1975).

CHEMICAL/BIOLOGICAL RESTRAINTS

40:240   Brown, Frederic J. *Chemical Warfare: A Study in Restraints.* Princeton, N.J.: Princeton University Press, 1968. A comprehensive account of the Geneva Gas Protocol (1925) and its possible impact on World War II chemical warfare operations.

40:241   Stockholm International Peace Research Institute. *The Problem of Chemical and Biological Warfare.* 6 vols. New York: Humanities Press, 1971–1975. These volumes explore virtually all aspects of CB warfare; historical, technical, and political.

40:242   Thomas, Ann Van Wynen, and Thomas, A. J., Jr. *Legal Limits on the Use of Chemical and Biological Weapons: International Law, 1899–1970.*

Dallas: Southern Methodist University Press, 1970. This examination of the legal restraints to CB warfare is one of the fullest accounts available.

SPECIAL STUDIES

40:243 Allison, Graham T., and Morris, Frederic A. "Armaments and Arms Control: Exploring the Determinants of Military Weapons." *Daedalus* 104:3 (1975), 99–129. The emphasis in arms control is often on foreign relations, yet internal factors in both the United States and the Soviet Union are the predominant determinants of the weapons systems.

40:244 "Arms, Defense Policy, and Arms Control." *Daedalus* 104:3 (1975), 1–214. The most comprehensive survey of the issues of arms control as they appeared to authorities representing a variety of viewpoints from strategy intellectuals to proponents of disarmament. A companion volume to Donald G. Brennan, ed., *Arms Control, Disarmament, and National Security* (40:246), which began as an issue of *Daedalus* and largely framed the debate for the 1960s.

40:245 Barnet, Richard J., and Falk, Richard A., eds. *Security in Disarmament.* Princeton, N.J.: Princeton University Press, 1965. This excellent collection of essays focuses on the problems inherent in verifying and supervising arms control agreements. Quite readable, these essays were written while experts still viewed arms control as essentially a political issue.

40:246 Brennan, Donald G., ed. *Arms Control, Disarmament, and National Security.* New York: Braziller, 1961. This collection of essays by strategy intellectuals, political leaders, and journalists set the terms of arms control and disarmament discussion for the 1960s and first acquainted the public with the

issues. Despite its having been overtaken by events, it is indispensable to a survey of the history of thinking about arms control. Bibliography. Most of the essays first appeared in *Daedalus* 89:4 (1960).

40:247 Clarke, Duncan L. *Politics of Arms Control: The Role and Effectiveness of the U.S. Arms Control and Disarmament Agency.* New York: Free Press, 1979. The arms control agency, established in 1961, has had to struggle with competitors—the State and Defense departments and the White House—to influence U.S. policies. This account deals thematically with the agency's problems, but includes much information of value to the historian.

40:248 Henkin, Louis. *Arms Control and Inspection in American Law.* New York: Columbia University Press, 1958. Reprint 1974. This analysis covers operative treaty provisions, congressional and constitutional positions, and international administrative regulations as well as world court involvements. The author finds no major limitations in domestic law other than those self-imposed. Bibliography and valuable appendixes.

Hewlett, R. G., and Anderson, O. E., Jr. *The New World, 1939–1946* (26:200) is a detailed official history of the development of the atomic bomb.

40:249 Klass, Philip J. *Secret Sentries in Space.* New York: Random House, 1971. Klass develops the story of American and Soviet reconnaissance satellite programs. He focuses on their impact on arms control treaties. With these "spy" satellites each side can detect military build-ups of the other, including missiles.

York, H. F. *Race to Oblivion: A Participant's View of the Arms Race* (29:134).

Appendix I
Makers of American Foreign Policy

Presidents	Secretaries of State	Chairman of the Senate Foreign Relations Committee
George Washington (1789–1797)	Thomas Jefferson (1790–1794)	
	Edmund Randolph (1794–1795)	
	Timothy Pickering (1795–1800)	
John Adams (1797–1801)	Timothy Pickering (1795–1800)	
	John Marshall (1800–1801)	
Thomas Jefferson (1801–1809)	James Madison (1801–1809)	
James Madison (1809–1817)	Robert Smith (1809–1811)	James Barbour (1816–1818)
	James Monroe (1811–1817)	
James Monroe (1817–1825)	John Quincy Adams (1817–1825)	James Barbour (1816–1818)
		Nathaniel Macon (1818–1819)
		James Brown (1819–1820)
		James Barbour (1820–1821)
		Rufus King (1821–1822)
		James Barbour (1822–1825)
John Quincy Adams (1825–1829)	Henry Clay (1825–1829)	Nathaniel Macon (1825–1826)
		Nathan Sanford (1826–1827)
		Nathaniel Macon (1827–1828)
		Littleton W. Tazewell (1828–1832)
Andrew Jackson (1829–1837)	Martin Van Buren (1829–1831)	Littleton W. Tazewell (1828–1832)
	Edward Livingston (1831–1833)	John Forsyth (1832–1833)
	Louis McLane (1833–1834)	William Wilkins (1833–1834)
	John Forsyth (1834–1841)	Henry Clay (1834–1836)
		James Buchanan (1836–1841)
Martin Van Buren (1837–1841)	John Forsyth (1834–1841)	James Buchanan (1836–1841)
William H. Harrison (1841)	Daniel Webster (1841–1843)	William C. Rives (1841–1842)
John Tyler (1841–1845)	Daniel Webster (1841–1843)	William C. Rives (1841–1842)
	Abel P. Upshur (1843–1844)	William S. Archer (1842–1845)
	John C. Calhoun (1844–1845)	
James K. Polk (1845–1849)	James Buchanan (1845–1849)	William Allen (1845–1846)
		Ambrose H. Sevier (1846–1848)
		Edward A. Hannegan (1848–1849)
		Thomas H. Benton (1849)
Zachary Taylor (1849–1850)	John M. Clayton (1849–1850)	William R. King (1849–1850)
Millard Fillmore (1850–1853)	Daniel Webster (1850–1852)	Henry S. Foote (1850–1851)
	Edward Everett (1852–1853)	James M. Mason (1851–1861)
Franklin Pierce (1853–1857)	William L. Marcy (1853–1857)	James M. Mason (1851–1861)
James Buchanan (1857–1861)	Lewis Cass (1857–1860)	James M. Mason (1851–1861)
	Jeremiah S. Black (1860–1861)	
Abraham Lincoln (1861–1865)	William H. Seward (1861–1869)	Charles Sumner (1861–1871)
Andrew Johnson (1865–1869)	William H. Seward (1861–1869)	Charles Sumner (1861–1871)
Ulysses S. Grant (1869–1877)	Elihu B. Washburne (1869)	Charles Sumner (1861–1871)
	Hamilton Fish (1869–1877)	Simon Cameron (1871–1877)
Rutherford B. Hayes (1877–1881)	William M. Evarts (1877–1881)	Hannibal Hamlin (1877–1879)
		William W. Eaton (1879–1881)
James A. Garfield (1881)	James G. Blaine (1881)	Ambrose E. Burnside (1881)

From T. C. Paterson, J. G. Clifford and K. J. Hagan, *American Foreign Policy; A History,* 2d ed. Lexington, MA: Heath, 1982.

Presidents	Secretaries of State	Chairmen of the Senate Foreign Relations Committee
		George F. Edmunds (1881)
Chester A. Arthur (1881–1885)	Frederick T. Frelinghuysen (1881–1885)	William Windon (1881–1883) John F. Miller (1883–1887)
Grover Cleveland (1885–1889)	Thomas F. Bayard (1885–1889)	John F. Miller (1883–1887) John Sherman (1887–1893)
Benjamin Harrison (1889–1893)	James G. Blaine (1889–1892) John W. Foster (1892–1893)	John Sherman (1887–1893)
Grover Cleveland (1893–1897)	Walter Q. Gresham (1893–1895) Richard Olney (1895–1897)	John T. Morgan (1893–1895) John Sherman (1895–1897)
William McKinley (1897–1901)	John Sherman (1897–1898) William R. Day (1898) John Hay (1898–1905)	William P. Frye (1897) Cushman K. Davis (1897–1901)
Theodore Roosevelt (1901–1909)	John Hay (1898–1905) Elihu Root (1905–1909) Robert Bacon (1909)	William P. Frye (1901) Shelby M. Cullom (1901–1913)
William Howard Taft (1909–1913)	Philander C. Knox (1909–1913)	Shelby M. Cullom (1901–1913)
Woodrow Wilson (1913–1921)	William Jennings Bryan (1913–1915) Robert Lansing (1915–1920) Bainbridge Colby (1920–1921)	Augustus O. Bacon (1913–1915) William J. Stone (1915–1919) Henry Cabot Lodge (1919–1924)
Warren G. Harding (1921–1923)	Charles E. Hughes (1921–1925)	Henry Cabot Lodge (1919–1924)
Calvin Coolidge (1923–1929)	Charles E. Hughes (1921–1925) Frank B. Kellogg (1925–1929)	Henry Cabot Lodge (1919–1924) William E. Borah (1925–1933)
Herbert C. Hoover (1929–1933)	Henry L. Stimson (1929–1933)	William E. Borah (1925–1933)
Franklin D. Roosevelt (1933–1945)	Cordell Hull (1933–1944) Edward R. Stettinius, Jr. (1944–1945)	Key Pittman (1933–1941) Walter F. George (1941) Tom Connally (1941–1947)

Presidents	Secretaries of State	Chairmen of the Senate Foreign Relations Committee	Secretaries of Defense	Assistants to the President for National Security Affairs
Harry S. Truman (1945–1953)	Edward R. Stettinius, Jr. (1944–1945)	Tom Connally (1941–1947)	James V. Forrestal (1947–1949)	
	James F. Byrnes (1945–1947)	Arthur H. Vandenberg (1947–1949)	Louis A. Johnson (1949–1950)	
	George C. Marshall (1947–1949)	Tom Connally (1949–1953)	George C. Marshall (1950–1951)	
	Dean G. Acheson (1949–1953)		Robert A. Lovett (1951–1953)	
Dwight D. Eisenhower (1953–1961)	John F. Dulles (1953–1959)	Alexander Wiley (1953–1955)	Charles E. Wilson (1953–1957)	Robert Cutler (1953–1955; 1957–1958)
	Christian A. Herter (1959–1961)	Walter F. George (1955–1957)	Neil H. McElroy (1957–1959)	Dillon Anderson (1955–1956)
		Theodore F. Green (1957–1959)	Thomas S. Gates, Jr. (1959–1961)	William H. Jackson (1956)
		J. W. Fulbright (1959–1975)		Gordon Gray (1958–1961)
John F. Kennedy (1961–1963)	Dean Rusk (1961–1969)	J. W. Fulbright (1959–1975)	Robert S. McNamara (1961–1968)	McGeorge Bundy (1961–1966)
Lyndon B. Johnson (1963–1969)	Dean Rusk (1961–1969)	J. W. Fulbright (1959–1975)	Robert S. McNamara (1961–1968)	McGeorge Bundy (1961–1966)
			Clark M. Clifford (1968–1969)	Walt W. Rostow (1966–1969)
Richard M. Nixon (1969–1974)	William P. Rogers (1969–1973)	J. W. Fulbright (1959–1975)	Melvin R. Laird (1969–1973)	Henry A. Kissinger (1969–1976)
	Henry A. Kissinger (1973–1977)		Elliot L. Richardson (1973)	
			James R. Schlesinger (1973–1976)	
Gerald R. Ford (1974–1977)	Henry A. Kissinger (1973–1977)	J. W. Fulbright (1959–1975)	James R. Schlesinger (1973–1976)	Henry A. Kissinger (1969–1976)
		John Sparkman (1975–1979)	Donald Rumsfeld (1976–1977)	Brent Snowcroft (1976–1977)
Jimmy Carter (1977–1981)	Cyrus R. Vance (1977–1980)	John Sparkman (1975–1979)	Harold Brown (1977–1981)	Zbigniew Brzezinski (1977–1981)
	Edmund Muskie (1980–1981)	Frank Church (1979–1981)		
Ronald Reagan (1981–)	Alexander M. Haig, Jr. (1981–1982)	Charles Percy (1981–)	Casper Weinberger (1981–)	Richard Allen (1981)
	George P. Shultz (1982–)			William P. Clark, Jr. (1981–)

ROBERT R. LIVINGSTON was born in New York City, November 27, 1746; graduated from King's College (now Columbia) in 1765; married Mary Stevens in 1770; admitted to the bar the same year; member of the New York Provincial Convention 1775; delegate to the Continental Congress 1775–1776, 1779–1780, 1784–1785; served on several congressional committees, one being the committee to draft the Declaration of Independence; delegate to the New York State constitutional convention, 1777, and with Gouverneur Morris and John Jay drafted that state's constitution; helped secure New York's ratification of the Constitution in 1788; served as head of the Department of Foreign Affairs, the forerunner of the Department of State, 1781–1783; administered the presidential oath of office to George Washington in 1789; in 1801 became U.S. Minister to France; while there, helped effect the 1803 Louisiana Purchase; member of the New York Canal Commission in 1811; patron and partner of Robert Fulton; died at his estate in Clermont, New York, February 26, 1813.

JOHN JAY was born in New York City, December 12, 1745; graduated from King's College in 1764; admitted to the bar in 1768 and practiced law; married Sarah Van Brugh Livingston in 1774; member of the Continental Congress 1774–1779; as a member of the New York Provincial Congress in 1776–1777, aided in obtaining approval of the Declaration of Independence and in drafting the state constitution; Chief Justice of New York State 1777–1778; President of the Continental Congress 1778–1779; Minister to Spain 1779–1782; one of the Commissioners named in 1781 to negotiate peace with Great Britain, signed the treaties of 1782 and 1783; took office as Secretary for Foreign Affairs under the Continental Congress December 21, 1784, served until the establishment of government under the Constitution, and continued unofficially to superintend the Department until Jefferson took office as Secretary of State on March 22, 1790; during his tenure of office, treaties of commerce

Biographic information through 1977 is from U.S. Bureau of Public Affairs, Office of Public Communication. *The Secretaries of State; Portraits and Biographical Sketches*. Department of State Publication 8921. Department and Foreign Service Series 162. Washington: Government Printing Office, 1978.

with Prussia and Morocco and a consular convention with France were negotiated; Chief Justice of the United States 1789–1795; Minister to Great Britain 1794–1795, negotiated and signed Jay's Treaty; Governor of New York 1795–1801; retired to his farm at Bedford, near New York City, where he died May 17, 1829.

THOMAS JEFFERSON was born at "Shadwell," Goochland (now Albemarle) County, Virginia, April 13, 1743; graduated from the College of William and Mary in 1762; admitted to the bar and commenced practice in 1767; held various local public offices; member of the Virginia House of Burgesses 1769–1775; married Martha (Wayles) Skelton in 1772; member of the Continental Congress 1775–1776; prepared the first draft of the Declaration of Independence and signed the final Declaration; member of the Virginia House of Delegates 1776–1779; Governor of Virginia 1779–1781; again a member of the Continental Congress 1783–1784; one of three Ministers named in 1784 to negotiate treaties with European nations and the Barbary States; Minister to France 1785–1789; commissioned Secretary of State in President Washington's Cabinet September 26, 1789, entered upon his duties March 22, 1790, and served until December 31, 1793; as Secretary of State, successfully administered a policy of neutrality in the war between Great Britain and France; Vice President of the United States 1797–1801; President of the United States 1801–1809; retired to "Monticello," his estate in Virginia; engaged in literary, architectural, scientific, and agricultural pursuits; participated in the founding and served as rector of the University of Virginia; died at "Monticello," Albemarle County, Virginia, July 4, 1826.

EDMUND RANDOLPH was born at "Tazewell Hall," near Williamsburg, Virginia, August 10, 1753; attended the College of William and Mary; admitted to the bar and practiced in Williamsburg; appointed aide-de-camp to General Washington in 1775; member of the Virginia constitutional convention and Mayor of Williamsburg in 1776; married Elizabeth Nicholas the same year; Attorney General of Virginia 1776–1786; member of the Continental Congress 1779–1782;

Governor of Virginia 1786–1788; delegate to the Annapolis Convention of 1786 and to the federal constitutional convention of 1787, member of the Virginia convention of 1788 that ratified the Constitution; member of the State House of Delegates 1788–1789; Attorney General in President Washington's Cabinet 1789–1794; commissioned Secretary of State January 2, 1794, entered upon his duties the same day, and served until August 20, 1795; as Secretary of State, directed the negotiation of the treaty of 1795 with Spain; moved to Richmond and resumed the practice of law; senior counsel for Aaron Burr in the treason trial of 1807; died in Clarke County, Virginia, September 12, 1813.

TIMOTHY PICKERING was born in Salem, Massachusetts, July 17, 1745; graduated from Harvard College in 1763; admitted to the bar in 1768 and commenced practice in Salem; held various local public offices; entered the Revolutionary Army as a colonel in 1775; elected to the State Legislature in 1776; married Rebecca White the same year; appointed Adjutant General and elected by the Continental Congress as a member of the Board of War in 1777; Quartermaster General of the Army 1780–1785; entered mercantile business in Philadelphia in 1785; organized Luzerne County, Pennsylvania, and represented it in the convention of 1787 that ratified the federal Constitution and in the state constitutional convention of 1789–1790; Postmaster General 1791–1795; Secretary of War in President Washington's Cabinet in 1795; Secretary of State ad interim August 20–December 9, 1795; commissioned Secretary of State December 10, 1795, entered upon his duties the same day, and served until May 12, 1800, when he was dismissed from office; as Secretary of State, opposed the French in the "XYZ Affair" of 1797–1798 and entered into preparations for war; became Chief Justice of the Massachusetts Court of Common Pleas in 1802; Senator from Massachusetts 1803–1811; member of the State Executive Council 1812–1813; Representative from Massachusetts 1813–1817; died in Salem, January 29, 1829.

JOHN MARSHALL was born near Germantown, in what became Fauquier County, Virginia, September 24, 1755; privately educated; officer in the Revolution; studied law at the College of William and Mary, admitted to the bar in 1780, and began practice; member of the Virginia Assembly 1782–1791 and 1795–1797; member of the state Executive Council

1782–1784; married Mary Willis Ambler in 1783; member of the Virginia convention of 1788 that ratified the federal Constitution; one of the "XYZ" commissioners of 1797–1798 to adjust differences with France; Representative from Virginia 1799–1800; commissioned Secretary of State in President Adams' Cabinet May 13, 1800, entered upon his duties June 6, 1800, and served until February 4, 1801; as Secretary of State, directed the negotiation of the reconciliation convention of 1800 with France; commissioned Chief Justice of the United States January 31, 1801, and took office February 4, 1801; continued as Secretary of State ad interim February 4–March 4, 1801; member of the Virginia constitutional convention of 1829; author of a five-volume biography of George Washington; during thirty-four years as Chief Justice of the United States, established the authority and prestige of the Supreme Court; died in Philadelphia, Pennsylvania, July 6, 1835.

JAMES MADISON was born at Port Conway, Virginia, March 16, 1751; graduated from the College of New Jersey in 1771; studied law and was admitted to the bar; elected to the Virginia constitutional convention and member of the state Assembly in 1776; member of the state Executive Council 1778–1779; member of the Continental Congress 1780–1783 and 1786–1788; Virginia House of Delegates 1784–1786; delegate to the Annapolis convention of 1786 and to the federal convention of 1787, where he played a major part in the framing of the Constitution; cooperated with Hamilton and Jay on a series of essays later published as *The Federalist*; member of the Virginia convention of 1788 that ratified the Constitution; Representative from Virginia 1789–1797; married Dolly (Payne) Todd in 1794; again a member of the House of Delegates in 1799; served as presidential elector in 1800; commissioned Secretary of State in President Jefferson's Cabinet March 5, 1801, entered upon his duties May 2, 1801, and served until March 3, 1809; during his tenure of office France offered and the United States accepted the Louisiana Purchase; President of the United States 1809–1817; retired to "Montpellier" (now "Montpelier"), his estate in Virginia; became rector of the University of Virginia in 1826; member of the Virginia constitutional convention of 1829, died at "Montpellier," Orange County, Virginia, June 28, 1836.

ROBERT SMITH was born in Lancaster, Pennsylvania, November 3, 1757; moved with his parents to

Baltimore, Maryland, at an early age; graduated from the College of New Jersey in 1781; served briefly as a private in the Continental Army; studied law, admitted to the bar in Baltimore, and soon had a large admiralty practice; one of the presidential electors of Maryland in 1789; married Margaret Smith in 1790; member of the Maryland Senate 1793–1795, and of the House of Delegates 1796–1800; sat in the Baltimore city council 1798–1801; served as Secretary of the Navy in President Jefferson's Cabinet 1801–1809; nominated, confirmed, and commissioned Attorney General in 1805, but did not serve; commissioned Secretary of State in President Madison's Cabinet March 6, 1809, entered upon his duties the same day, and served until April 1, 1811; as Secretary of State, negotiated the Smith-Erskine Agreement of 1809, rejection of which by the British Government marked a turning point in the relations between the two countries; returned to Baltimore, where he filled offices in various private organizations; died in Baltimore, Maryland, November 26, 1842.

JAMES MONROE was born in Westmoreland County, Virginia, April 28, 1758; attended the College of William and Mary 1774–1776; officer in the Continental Army; studied law under Jefferson 1780–1783; member of the Virginia Assembly in 1782 and 1786; member of the Continental Congress 1783–1786; attended the Annapolis convention of 1786; married Eliza Kortright the same year; admitted to the bar and practiced in Fredericksburg; member of the state convention of 1788 that ratified the federal Constitution; Senator from Virginia 1790–1794; Minister to France 1794–1796; Governor of Virginia 1799–1802; again Minister to France in 1803; served as Minister to Great Britain 1803–1807; headed a diplomatic mission to Spain 1804–1805; again elected to the Virginia Assembly in 1810; again Governor of Virginia in 1811; commissioned Secretary of State in President Madison's Cabinet April 2, 1811, entered upon his duties April 6, 1811, and served until September 30, 1814; both Secretary of War and Secretary of State ad interim October 1, 1814–February 28, 1815; again commissioned Secretary of State February 28, 1815, entered upon his duties the same day, and served until March 3, 1817; during his tenure of office the War of 1812 was fought and the Treaty of Ghent, which restored peace, was negotiated; President of the United States 1817–1825; retired to his farm in Virginia; presiding officer of the Virginia constitutional convention of 1829; died in New York City, July 4, 1831.

JOHN QUINCY ADAMS was born in Braintree (now Quincy), Massachusetts, July 11, 1767; studied in France and the Netherlands; served briefly as private secretary to the American Minister in Russia in 1781; secretary to his father during the peace negotiations with Great Britain 1782–1783; graduated from Harvard University in 1787; admitted to the bar in 1790 and practiced in Boston; served as Minister Resident to the Netherlands 1794–1797; married Louisa Catherine Johnson in 1797; Minister to Prussia 1797–1801; elected to the Massachusetts Senate in 1802; Senator from Massachusetts 1803–1808; professor of rhetoric and oratory at Harvard 1806–1809; Minister to Russia 1809–1814; head of the commission that negotiated the Treaty of Ghent with Great Britain in 1814; Minister to Great Britain 1815–1817; commissioned Secretary of State in President Monroe's Cabinet March 5, 1817, entered upon his duties September 22, 1817, and served until March 3, 1825; as Secretary of State, negotiated the treaty of 1819 with Spain for the cession of the Floridas and collaborated with the President in the formulation of the Monroe Doctrine; President of the United States 1825–1829; Representative from Massachusetts 1831–1848; author of many writings and speeches and a notable diary covering half a century; died in Washington, D.C., February 23, 1848.

HENRY CLAY was born in Hanover County, Virginia, April 12, 1777; attended public school; studied law in Richmond, Virginia; admitted to the bar and commenced practice in Lexington, Kentucky, in 1797; married Lucretia Hart in 1799; served in the state House of Representatives 1803–1806; Senator from Kentucky 1806–1807; served again in the state House of Representatives 1807–1809; again Senator from Kentucky 1810–1811; Representative from Kentucky and Speaker of the House 1811–1814; one of the Commissioners who negotiated the Treaty of Ghent with Great Britain in 1814; again Representative from Kentucky 1815–1821 and 1823–1825, and Speaker of the House 1815–1820 and 1823–1825; unsuccessful candidate for the presidency in 1824; commissioned Secretary of State in President John Quincy Adams' Cabinet March 7, 1825, entered upon his duties the same day, and served until March 3, 1829; as Secretary of State, negotiated a number of commercial treaties and sought unsuccessfully to have the United States participate in the Inter-American Congress at Panama in 1826; again Senator from Kentucky 1831–1842; Whig candidate for the Presidency in 1832 and in

1844; in retirement 1845–1848; again Senator from Kentucky 1849–1852; died in Washington, D.C., June 29, 1852.

MARTIN VAN BUREN was born at Kinderhook, near Albany, New York, December 5, 1782; attended local schools; admitted to the bar and commenced practice in Kinderhook in 1803; married Hannah Hoes in 1807; moved to Hudson, New York, where he was surrogate 1808–1813; served in the state Senate 1812–1820; chosen regent of the University of New York in 1815; state Attorney General 1816–1819, residing in Albany; delegate to the state constitutional convention of 1821; Senator from New York 1821–1828; Governor of New York in 1829; commissioned Secretary of State in President Jackson's Cabinet March 6, 1829, entered upon his duties March 28, 1829, and served until May 23, 1831; as Secretary of State, settled a long-standing dispute with Great Britain over West Indian trade and obtained important treaties with Turkey and France; served as Minister to Great Britain 1831–1832 on a recess appointment that failed confirmation by the Senate; Vice-President of the United States 1833–1837; President of the United States 1837–1841; unsuccessful candidate for the presidency on the Democratic ticket in 1840 and on the Free-soil ticket in 1848; retired to "Lindenwald," his country home at Kinderhook, New York, where he died July 24, 1862.

EDWARD LIVINGSTON was born at "Clermont," Columbia County, New York, May 28, 1764; graduated from the College of New Jersey in 1781; admitted to the bar in 1785 and practiced in New York City; married Mary McEvers in 1788 (died 1801); Representative from New York 1795–1801; United States Attorney for the District of New York and Mayor of New York City 1801–1803; moved to New Orleans in 1804 and practiced law; married Louise Moreau de Lassey (née D'Avezac) in 1805; aide to General Jackson at the Battle of New Orleans; elected to the Louisiana House of Representatives in 1820; prepared a penal code for the state which, though not adopted, brought him fame; engaged in a protracted controversy with the federal government over title to land known as Batture Sainte Marie, which was finally decided in his favor; Representative from Louisiana 1823–1829; Senator from Louisiana 1829–1831; commissioned Secretary of State in President Jackson's Cabinet May 24, 1831, entered upon his duties the same day, and served until May 29, 1833; as

Secretary of State, drafted the celebrated Nullification Proclamation of 1832; Minister to France 1833–1835; died at "Montgomery Place," Dutchess County, New York, May 23, 1836.

LOUIS McLANE was born in Smyrna, Delaware, May 28, 1786; midshipman in the Navy 1798–1801; attended Newark Academy (now the University of Delaware); admitted to the bar in 1807 and commenced practice in Smyrna; married Catherine Mary Milligan in 1812; served in the War of 1812; Representative from Delaware 1817–1827; Senator from Delaware 1827–1829; Minister to Great Britain 1829–1831; Secretary of the Treasury in President Jackson's Cabinet 1831–1833; commissioned Secretary of State May 29, 1833, entered upon his duties the same day, and served until June 30, 1834; as Secretary of State, reorganized the Department, introducing systematic procedure into its operations; became president of the Morris Canal and Banking Company in New York City; moved to Baltimore, Maryland, where he was president of the Baltimore and Ohio Railroad Company 1837–1847; while holding the last-mentioned position, again Minister to Great Britain 1845–1846; delegate to the Maryland constitutional convention of 1850; died in Baltimore, October 7, 1857.

JOHN FORSYTH was born in Fredericksburg, Virginia, October 22, 1780; moved to Augusta, Georgia, with his parents; graduated from the College of New Jersey in 1799; admitted to the bar in 1802 and commenced practice in Augusta; married Clara Meigs in 1801 or 1802; became Attorney General of Georgia in 1808; Representative from Georgia 1813–1818; Senator from Georgia 1818–1819; Minister to Spain 1819–1823; again Representative from Georgia 1823–1827; Governor of Georgia 1827–1829; again Senator from Georgia 1829–1834; delegate to the anti-tariff convention at Milledgeville, Georgia, in 1832; earned the reputation of being one of the most powerful debaters of his time; commissioned Secretary of State in President Jackson's Cabinet June 27, 1834, entered upon his duties July 1, 1834, continued in office under President Van Buren, and served until March 3, 1841; as Secretary of State, brought to a successful conclusion a serious controversy with France regarding payment under the claims convention of 1831; died in Washington, D.C., October 21, 1841.

DANIEL WEBSTER was born in Salisbury, New Hampshire, January 18, 1782; graduated from Dartmouth College in 1801; taught school; admitted to the bar in 1805 and commenced practice in Boscawen, New Hampshire; moved to Portsmouth, New Hampshire, in 1807; married Grace Fletcher in 1808 (died 1828); Representative from New Hampshire 1813–1817; moved to Boston in 1816 and soon became known as one of the foremost lawyers and orators of his time; presidential elector in 1820; delegate to the Massachusetts constitutional convention of 1820–1821; member of the state House of Representatives in 1822; Representative from Massachusetts 1823–1827; Senator from Massachusetts 1827–1841; married Caroline Le Roy in 1829; was nominated by the state legislature for the presidency in 1836; commissioned Secretary of State in President Harrison's Cabinet March 5, 1841 entered upon his duties March 6, 1841, continued in office under President Tyler, and served until May 8, 1843; as Secretary of State, negotiated the famous Webster-Ashburton Treaty of 1842 with Great Britain; again Senator from Massachusetts 1845–1850; commissioned Secretary of State in President Fillmore's Cabinet July 22, 1850, entered upon his duties July 23, 1850, and served until his death in Marshfield, Massachusetts, October 24, 1852.

ABEL PARKER UPSHUR was born at "Vaucluse," Northampton County, Virginia, June 17, 1791; attended the College of New Jersey and Yale College; admitted to the bar in 1810 and practiced in Richmond; member of the Virginia House of Delegates 1812–1813 and 1825–1827; married Elizabeth Dennis, who died; married Elizabeth A. B. Upshur in 1826; judge of the General Court of Virginia 1826–1829; delegate to the state constitutional convention of 1829; judge of the reorganized General Court 1830–1841; Secretary of the Navy in President Tyler's Cabinet 1841–1843; served as Secretary of State ad interim June 24–July 23, 1843; commissioned Secretary of State July 24, 1843, entered upon his duties the same day, and served until his death; as Secretary of State, reopened negotiations for the annexation of Texas; killed by the explosion of a gun aboard the U.S. warship *Princeton* on the Potomac River about fifteen miles below Washington, D.C., February 28, 1844.

JOHN CALDWELL CALHOUN was born at "the Long Canes settlement," in what became Abbeville County, South Carolina, March 18, 1782; graduated from Yale College in 1804 and from Litch-field Law School in 1806; admitted to the bar in 1807 and commenced practice in Abbeville, South Carolina; married Floride Bonneau Colhoun in 1811; gave up the practice of law and established himself as a planter; member of the state House of Representatives 1808–1809; Representative from South Carolina 1811–1817; Secretary of War in President Monroe's Cabinet 1817–1825; Vice President of the United States 1825–1832, when he resigned; Senator from South Carolina 1832–1843; commissioned Secretary of State in President Tyler's Cabinet March 6, 1844, entered upon his duties April 1, 1844, and served until March 10, 1845; as Secretary of State, signed an abortive treaty for the annexation of Texas and aided in accomplishing annexation by joint resolution of Congress; delegate of South Carolina to, and presiding officer of, a railroad-and-waterway convention held in Memphis, Tennessee, in 1845; again Senator from South Carolina 1845–1850; author of voluminous writings and speeches; died in Washington, D.C., March 31, 1850.

JAMES BUCHANAN was born at Cove Gap, near Mercersburg, Pennsylvania, April 23, 1791; graduated from Dickinson College in 1809; admitted to the bar in 1812 and practiced in Lancaster, Pennsylvania; served in the defense of Baltimore in the War of 1812; member of the Pennsylvania House of Representatives 1814–1816; Representative from Pennsylvania 1821–1831; Minister to Russia 1832–1833; Senator from Pennsylvania 1834–1845; commissioned Secretary of State in President Polk's Cabinet March 6, 1845, entered upon his duties March 10, 1845, and served until March 7, 1849; as Secretary of State, negotiated and signed the Oregon Treaty of 1846 with Great Britain, directed the negotiation of the Treaty of Guadalupe Hidalgo of 1848 with Mexico, and sought unsuccessfully to purchase Cuba from Spain; unsuccessful candidate for the Democratic presidential nomination in 1852; served as Minister to Great Britain 1853–1856; one of three United States Ministers who drew up the "Ostend Manifesto" of 1854; President of the United States 1857–1861; retired to "Wheatland," his country estate near Lancaster; never married; died at "Wheatland" June 1, 1868.

JOHN MIDDLETON CLAYTON was born at Dagsboro, Sussex County, Delaware, July 24, 1796; graduated from Yale College in 1815; attended Litch-field Law School; admitted to the bar in 1819, commenced practice in Dover, Delaware, and won a reputation unrivaled in the state; married Sarah Ann Fisher in 1822; member of the state House of Representatives 1824–1826; Secretary of State of Delaware 1826–1828; Senator from Delaware 1829–1836; delegate to the state constitutional convention of 1831; Chief Justice of Delaware 1837–1839; engaged in scientific farming near New Castle, Delaware, and gained a wide reputation as an agriculturist; again Senator from Delaware 1845–1849; commissioned Secretary of State in President Taylor's Cabinet March 7, 1849, entered upon his duties March 8, 1849, and served until July 22, 1850; as Secretary of State, negotiated and signed the Clayton-Bulwer Treaty of 1850 with Great Britain; resumed his agricultural pursuits; again Senator from Delaware 1853–1856; died in Dover, November 9, 1856.

EDWARD EVERETT was born in Dorchester, Massachusetts, April 11, 1794; graduated from Harvard University in 1811; pursued theological studies and received his M.A. degree in 1814; became pastor of the Brattle Street Unitarian Church, Boston, in 1814; studied and traveled in Europe 1815–1819, receiving his Ph.D. degree at Göttingen in 1817; occupied the chair of Greek literature at Harvard 1819–1825; edited the *North American Review* 1820–1824; married Charlotte Gray Brooks in 1822; Representative from Massachusetts 1825–1835; Governor of Massachusetts 1836–1839; Minister to Great Britain 1841–1845; president of Harvard 1846–1849; commissioned Secretary of State in President Fillmore's Cabinet November 6, 1852, entered upon his duties the same day, and served until March 3, 1853; as Secretary of State, declined a proposal of France and Great Britain that the United States enter into a convention with them guaranteeing to Spain the possession of Cuba; Senator from Massachusetts 1853–1854; became known as one of the greatest orators of his day; unsuccessful candidate for the Vice-Presidency on the Constitutional Union ticket in 1860; presidential elector in 1864; died in Boston, January 15, 1865.

WILLIAM LEARNED MARCY was born in Sturbridge (now Southbridge), Massachusetts, December 12, 1786; graduated from Brown University in 1808; admitted to the bar in 1811 and commenced practice in Troy, New York; married Dolly Newell in 1812 (died 1821); served in the War of 1812; recorder of Troy 1816–1818 and 1821–1823; became adjutant General of New York in 1821; state Comptroller

1823–1829; married Cornelia Knower about 1825; Associate Justice of the state Supreme Court 1829–1831; Senator from New York 1831–1833; Governor of New York 1833–1838; member of the Mexican Claims Commission 1840–1842; Secretary of War in President Polk's Cabinet 1845–1849; resumed the practice of law; commissioned Secretary of State in President Pierce's Cabinet March 7, 1853, entered upon his duties March 8, 1853, and served until March 6, 1857; as Secretary of State, negotiated or directed the negotiation of numerous treaties, among them the Gadsden Treaty of 1853 with Mexico and the reciprocity treaty of 1854 with Great Britain, and settled various delicate problems of international relations, among them the Koszta case with Austria, the *Black Warrior* case with Spain, and the Patrice Dillon case with France; died at Ballston Spa, New York, July 4, 1857.

LEWIS CASS was born in Exeter, New Hampshire, October 9, 1782; attended Exeter Academy; went to the Northwest Territory in 1799; admitted to the bar in 1802 and practiced in Zanesville, Ohio; married Elizabeth Spencer in 1806; elected to the Ohio House of Representatives the same year; United States Marshal for the District of Ohio 1807–1812; served with distinction in the War of 1812, attaining the rank of brigadier general; Governor of Michigan Territory 1813–1831; Secretary of War in President Jackson's Cabinet 1831–1836; served as Minister to France 1836–1842; unsuccessful candidate for Democratic presidential nomination in 1844 and again in 1852; Senator from Michigan 1845–1848; was the Democratic candidate for the Presidency in 1848; again Senator from Michigan 1849–1857; commissioned Secretary of State in President Buchanan's Cabinet March 6, 1857; entered upon his duties the same day, and served until December 14, 1860; as Secretary of State, obtained British acceptance of the American construction of the Clayton-Bulwer Treaty and abandonment by Great Britain of its claim to a right to visit and search American vessels; returned to his home in Detroit, Michigan, and engaged in literary pursuits; died in Detroit, June 17, 1866.

JEREMIAH SULLIVAN BLACK was born near Stony Creek, Somerset County, Pennsylvania, January 10, 1810; attended public schools; admitted to the bar in 1830 and began the practice of law; appointed Deputy Attorney General of Somerset County in 1831; married Mary Forward in 1836; served as President

Judge of the Court of Common Pleas for the sixteenth judicial district 1842–1851; elected to the state Supreme Court in 1851 and was reelected in 1854, by lot serving the first three years as Chief Justice; served as Attorney General in President Buchanan's Cabinet 1857–1860; commissioned Secretary of State December 17, 1860, entered upon his duties the same day, and served until March 5, 1861; as Secretary of State, instructed the principal United States representatives in Europe to use their best efforts to prevent recognition of the Confederate States; appointed United States Supreme Court reporter in 1861 and prepared *Black's Reports*, in two volumes; moved to York, Pennsylvania, and resumed the practice of law; engaged in controversial writing, member of the Pennsylvania constitutional convention of 1872–1873; counsel for William Belknap in his impeachment trial in 1876 and for Samuel J. Tilden before the Electoral Commission in 1877; died in York, August 19, 1883.

WILLIAM HENRY SEWARD was born at Florida, Orange County, New York, May 16, 1801; graduated from Union College in 1820; admitted to the bar in 1822 and commenced practice in Auburn, New York, in 1823; married Frances Miller in 1824; member of the State Senate 1830–1834; Governor of New York 1838–1842; resumed the practice of law; Senator from New York 1849–1861; unsuccessful candidate for the Republican presidential nomination in 1860; commissioned Secretary of State in President Lincoln's Cabinet March 5, 1861, entered upon his duties March 6, 1861, continued in office under President Johnson, and served until March 4, 1869; as Secretary of State, handled with skill the delicate relations of the United States with foreign nations during the Civil War, and in 1867 negotiated and signed the treaty with Russia for the cession of Alaska to the United States; made a trip around the world 1870–1871 and was everywhere accorded an enthusiastic reception; retired to his home in Auburn in 1871, where he died October 10, 1872.

ELIHU BENJAMIN WASHBURNE was born in Livermore, Maine, September 23, 1816; attended the common schools; held an editorial position on the Augusta *Kennebec Journal*; attended Harvard Law School in 1839 and was admitted to the Massachusetts bar in 1840; moved to Galena, Illinois, later the same year and commenced the practice of law; delegate to the Whig National Conventions at Baltimore in 1844 and 1852; married Adèle Gratiot in 1845; Representa-

tive from Illinois 1853–1869; commissioned Secretary of State in President Grant's Cabinet March 5, 1869, entered upon his duties the same day, and served until March 16, 1869, a period of only twelve days; served as Minister to France 1869–1877 and was the only official representative of a foreign government to remain in Paris during the siege of 1870–1871 and the days of the Commune; on his return to the United States, settled in Chicago, Illinois, and engaged in historical and literary pursuits; unsuccessful candidate for the Republican presidential nomination in 1880; president of the Chicago Historical Society 1884–1887; died in Chicago October 22, 1887.

HAMILTON FISH was born in New York City, August 3, 1808; graduated from Columbia College in 1827; admitted to the bar in 1830 and practiced in New York City; married Julia Kean in 1836; Representative from New York 1843–1845; Lieutenant Governor of New York in 1848 and Governor 1849–1850; Senator from New York 1851–1857; president general of the Society of the Cincinnati 1854–1893; during the Civil War, on a Board of Commissioners of the federal government for the relief and exchange of prisoners; president of the New York Historical Society 1867–1869; commissioned Secretary of State in President Grant's Cabinet March 11, 1869, entered upon his duties March 17, 1869, and served until March 12, 1877; as Secretary of State, was one of the Commissioners of the United States who negotiated the Treaty of Washington of 1871 with Great Britain for the settlement of differences between the two countries, directed negotiations that resulted in the settlement of American claims against Spain, and signed the reciprocity treaty of 1875 with Hawaii; retired from public life; died at "Glen Clyffe," his estate near Garrison, New York, September 7, 1893.

WILLIAM MAXWELL EVARTS was born in Boston, Massachusetts, February 6, 1818; graduated from Yale College in 1837; attended Harvard Law School 1838–1839; admitted to the bar in 1841 and practiced in New York City; married Helen Minerva Wardner in 1843; Assistant United States Attorney for the Southern District of New York 1849–1853; chairman of the New York delegation to the Republican National Convention at Chicago in 1860; member of a government mission to Great Britain 1863–1864; delegate to the New York State constitutional convention of 1867–1868; chief counsel for President Johnson in the impeachment trial of 1868; Attorney General in

President Johnson's Cabinet 1868–1869; one of counsel for the United States before the tribunal of arbitration at Geneva 1871–1872; chief counsel for the Republican Party before the Electoral Commission in 1877; commissioned Secretary of State in President Hayes' Cabinet March 12, 1877, entered upon his duties the same day, and served until March 7, 1881; as Secretary of State, defined American policy with regard to an isthmian canal, took a strong stand toward Mexico in defense of American lives and property, and directed the negotiation of treaties with China relating to commerce and immigration; delegate to the International Monetary Conference at Paris in 1881; Senator from New York 1885–1891; died in New York City, February 28, 1901.

JAMES GILLESPIE BLAINE   was born in West Brownsville, Pennsylvania, January 31, 1830; graduated from Washington College in 1847; taught school in Kentucky; married Harriet Stanwood in 1850; taught school and studied law in Philadelphia 1852–1854; moved in 1854 to Maine, where he purchased an interest in the Augusta *Kennebec Journal* and served on the editorial staff of the Portland *Advertiser*; one of the founders of the Republican Party; member of the Maine House of Representatives 1859–1862 and Speaker of the House 1861–1862; served as chairman of the Republican State Committee 1859–1881; Representative from Maine 1863–1876 and Speaker of the House 1869–1875; Senator from Maine 1876–1881; unsuccessful candidate for the Republican presidential nomination of 1876 and again in 1880; commissioned Secretary of State in President Garfield's Cabinet March 5, 1881, entered upon his duties March 7, 1881, continued in office under President Arthur, and served until December 19, 1881; Republican candidate for the Presidency in 1884; commissioned Secretary of State in President Harrison's Cabinet March 5, 1889, entered upon his duties March 7, 1889, and served until June 4, 1892; as Secretary of State, convened and presided over the First Pan American Conference in 1889; died in Washington, D.C., January 27, 1893.

FREDERICK THEODORE FRELINGHUYSEN   was born in Millstone, New Jersey, August 4, 1817; graduated from Rutgers College in 1836; admitted to the bar in 1839 and practiced in Newark, New Jersey; married Matilde E. Griswold in 1842; city attorney of Newark in 1849 and a member of the city council in 1850; trustee of Rutgers College 1851–1885; representative of New Jersey at the peace congress held in Washington, D.C., early in 1861; Attorney General of New Jersey 1861–1866; Senator from New Jersey 1866–1869 and 1871–1877; member of the Electoral Commission of 1877 to decide the contested presidential election of 1876; resumed the practice of law; commissioned Secretary of State in President Arthur's Cabinet December 12, 1881, entered upon his duties December 19, 1881, and served until March 6, 1885; as Secretary of State, fostered commercial relations with Latin America, sent delegates to the Berlin Conference of 1884–1885 on the Congo, and opened treaty relations with Korea; died in Newark, May 20, 1885.

THOMAS FRANCIS BAYARD   was born in Wilmington, Delaware, October 29, 1828; attended private schools and an academy at Flushing, New York; studied law, was admitted to the bar in 1851, and commenced practice in Wilmington; United States District Attorney for Delaware 1853–1854; moved to Philadelphia, Pennsylvania, and practiced law there, returning to Wilmington in 1858; married Louise Lee in 1856 (died 1886); Senator from Delaware 1869–1885; member of the Electoral Commission of 1877 to decide the contested presidential election of 1876; unsuccessful candidate for the Democratic presidential nomination in 1876, in 1880, and again in 1884; commissioned Secretary of State in President Cleveland's Cabinet March 6, 1885, entered upon his duties March 7, 1885, and served until March 6, 1889; as Secretary of State, paved the way for settlement of the Samoan question with Great Britain and Germany, arranged a solution regarding fisheries that allayed difficulties with Canada, and upheld the special interest of the United States in the Hawaiian Islands; resumed the practice of law in Wilmington; married Mary W. Clymer in 1889; served as Ambassador to Great Britain 1893–1897; died in Dedham, Massachusetts, September 28, 1898.

JOHN WATSON FOSTER   was born in Pike County, Indiana, March 2, 1836; graduated from Indiana University in 1855 (A.M. 1858); attended Harvard Law School; admitted to the bar in 1857 and commenced practice in Evansville, Indiana; married Mary Parke McFerson in 1859; served in the Union Army, attaining the rank of brevet brigadier general; edited the Evansville *Daily Journal* 1865–1869 and postmaster of Evansville 1869–1873; chairman of the Republican State Committee in 1872; Minister to Mexico 1873–1880 and Minister to Russia 1880–1881; established an international law practice in

Washington, D.C.; Minister to Spain 1883–1885; special plenipotentiary to negotiate reciprocity agreements 1890–1891; agent of the United States in the Fur-seal Arbitration 1892–1893; commissioned Secretary of State in President Harrison's Cabinet June 29, 1892, entered upon his duties the same day, and served until February 23, 1893; as Secretary of State signed the abortive treaty of 1893 for the annexation of Hawaii; Commissioner for China in the negotiation of the treaty of peace of 1895 with Japan; Ambassador on special mission to Great Britain and Russia in 1897; agent of the United States before the Alaska Boundary Tribunal in 1903; represented China at the Second Hague Conference in 1907; author of numerous published writings; died in Washington, November 15, 1917.

WALTER QUINTIN GRESHAM was born near Lanesville, Harrison County, Indiana, March 17, 1832; attended Indiana University; admitted to the bar in 1854 and practiced in Corydon, Indiana; married Matilda McGrain in 1858; elected to the state Legislature in 1860; served in the Union Army, attaining the rank of brevet major general of volunteers; opened a law office in New Albany, Indiana, in 1865; financial agent of Indiana in New York City 1867–1869; delegate to the Republican National Convention at Chicago in 1868; United States Judge for the District of Indiana 1869–1883; Postmaster General in President Arthur's Cabinet 1883–1884 and Secretary of the Treasury briefly in 1884; United States Circuit Judge for the Seventh Judicial District 1884–1893; unsuccessful candidate for the Republican presidential nomination in 1888; went over to the Democratic Party in 1892; commissioned Secretary of State in President Cleveland's Cabinet March 6, 1893, entered upon his duties March 7, 1893, and served until his death; as Secretary of State, advised against resubmission to the Senate of the annexation treaty of 1893 with Hawaii, and brought about the settlement of a dispute between Great Britain and Nicaragua; died in Washington, D.C., May 28, 1895.

RICHARD OLNEY was born in Oxford, Massachusetts, September 15, 1835; graduated from Brown University in 1856 (A.M.) and from Harvard Law School in 1858; admitted to the bar in 1859 and commenced practice in Boston, Massachusetts; married Agnes Park Thomas in 1861; member of the Massachusetts House of Representatives in 1874; Attorney General in President Cleveland's Cabinet 1893–1895; commissioned Secretary of State June 8, 1895, entered

upon his duties June 10, 1895, and served until March 5, 1897; as Secretary of State, induced the British Government to submit to arbitration its dispute with Venezuela over the boundary between Venezuela and British Guiana, and insisted on the protection of American lives and property and on reparation for injuries in the disorders then prevailing in Cuba, China, and Turkey; resumed the practice of law; regent of the Smithsonian Institution 1900–1908; American member of the Permanent International Commission under the Bryan-Jusserand Treaty of 1914 with France 1915–1917; died in Boston, April 8, 1917.

JOHN SHERMAN was born in Lancaster, Ohio, May 10, 1823; attended a local academy; admitted to the bar in 1844 and practiced in Mansfield, Ohio; married Margaret Sarah Cecilia Stewart in 1848; delegate to the Whig National Conventions of 1848 and 1852; moved to Cleveland, Ohio, in 1853; chairman of the first Republican convention in Ohio in 1855 and participated in the organization of the national Republican Party; Representative from Ohio 1855–1861; Senator from Ohio 1861–1877; Secretary of the Treasury in President Hayes' Cabinet 1877–1881; again Senator from Ohio 1881–1897; authority on matters of federal finance; unsuccessful candidate for the Republican presidential nomination in 1880, in 1884, and again in 1888; commissioned Secretary of State in President McKinley's Cabinet March 5, 1897, entered upon his duties March 6, 1897, and served until April 27, 1898; as Secretary of State, supported the American interpretation of most-favored-nation treatment in matters relating to international trade; retired from public life; died in Washington, D.C., October 22, 1900.

WILLIAM RUFUS DAY was born in Ravenna, Ohio, April 17, 1849; graduated from the University of Michigan in 1870; admitted to the bar in 1872 and commenced practice in Canton, Ohio; married Mary Elizabeth Schaefer in 1875; Judge of the Court of Common Pleas 1886–1890; appointed United States Judge for the Northern District of Ohio in 1889, but because of ill health resigned before taking office; served as Assistant Secretary of State 1897–1898; commissioned Secretary of State in President McKinley's Cabinet April 26, 1898, entered upon his duties April 28, 1898, and served until September 16, 1898; as Secretary of State, secured the neutrality of the nations of western Europe in the Spanish-American War and signed the protocol of 1898 for the cessation of hostilities; chairman of the United States Commission that negotiated and signed the treaty of peace of 1898 with Spain; Judge of the United States Court of Appeals for the Sixth Circuit 1899–1903; Associate Justice of the United States Supreme Court 1903–1922; Umpire in the Mixed Claims Commission, United States and Germany, 1922–1923; died at his summer home at Mackinac Island, Michigan, July 9, 1923.

JOHN HAY   was born in Salem, Indiana, October 8, 1838; graduated from Brown University in 1858; admitted to the Illinois bar in 1861; private secretary to President Lincoln 1861–1865; Secretary of Legation at Paris 1865–1867, Chargé d'Affaires ad interim at Vienna 1867–1868, and Secretary of Legation at Madrid 1869–1870; journalist with the New York *Tribune* 1870–1875; engaged successfully in the writing of verse and fiction; married Clara Louise Stone in 1874; Assistant Secretary of State 1879–1881; made frequent trips to Europe 1881–1896; co-author with John G. Nicolay of *Abraham Lincoln: A History* (10 volumes, 1890); Ambassador to Great Britain 1897–1898; commissioned Secretary of State in President McKinley's Cabinet September 20, 1898, entered upon his duties September 30, 1898, continued in office under President Roosevelt, and served until his death; as Secretary of State, supported the "open door" policy in China, prevented the dissolution of the Chinese Empire in 1900, obtained settlement of the Alaska-Canada boundary controversy, acquired a clear title to Tutuila, and secured by treaty the right for the United States to construct and defend the Panama Canal; died at his summer home at Newbury, New Hampshire, July 1, 1905.

ELIHU ROOT   was born in Clinton, New York, February 15, 1845; graduated from Hamilton College in 1864 and from New York University Law School in 1867; admitted to the bar in 1867 and practiced in New York City; married Clara Frances Wales in 1878; United States Attorney for the Southern District of New York 1883–1885; delegate to the state constitutional convention of 1894; Secretary of War in the Cabinets of Presidents McKinley and Roosevelt 1899–1904; member of the Alaskan Boundary Tribunal in 1903; commissioned Secretary of State in President Roosevelt's Cabinet July 7, 1905, entered upon his duties July 19, 1905, and served until January 27, 1909; as Secretary of State, created the American-Canadian International Joint Commission and negotiated arbitration treaties with twenty-four

nations; Senator from New York 1909–1915; was counsel for the United States in the North Atlantic Coast Fisheries Arbitration in 1910; became a member of the Permanent Court of Arbitration the same year; president of the Carnegie Endowment for International Peace 1910–1925; president of the New York State constitutional convention of 1915; chief of a special mission to Russia in 1917; member of the committee of jurists which planned the Permanent Court of International Justice in 1920; delegate to the Washington Conference on Limitation of Armament 1921–1922; died in New York City, February 7, 1937.

ROBERT BACON   was born in Jamaica Plain, Massachusetts, July 5, 1860; graduated from Harvard University in 1880; after a trip around the world, commenced a business career with Lee, Higginson and Company of Boston in 1881; married Martha Waldron Cowdin in 1883; member of the firm of E. Rollins Morse and Brother of Boston 1883–1894; member of the New York firm of J. P. Morgan and Company 1894–1903; Assistant Secretary of State 1905–1909 and Acting Secretary while Elihu Root was in South America in 1906; commissioned Secretary of State in President Roosevelt's Cabinet January 27, 1909, entered upon his duties the same day, and served until March 5, 1909; as Secretary of State, obtained the advice and consent of the Senate to the canal treaties of 1909 with Colombia and Panama; Ambassador to France 1909–1912; became a Fellow of Harvard in 1912; made a journey to South America at the request of the Carnegie Endowment for International Peace in 1913; went to France in August 1914 and helped with the work of the "American Ambulance"; commissioned a major and detailed to General Pershing's staff in 1917; promoted to lieutenant colonel in 1918 and served as Chief of the American Military Mission at British General Headquarters; died in New York City, May 29, 1919.

PHILANDER CHASE KNOX   was born in Brownsville, Pennsylvania, May 6, 1853; graduated from Mount Union College in 1872; admitted to the bar in 1875 and practiced in Pittsburgh, Pennsylvania; Assistant United States Attorney for the Western District of Pennsylvania 1876–1877; married Lillie Smith in 1880; president of the Pennsylvania Bar Association in 1897; as counsel for the Carnegie Steel Company, took a prominent part in organizing the United States Steel Corporation in 1901; Attorney General in the Cabinets of Presidents McKinley and Roosevelt

1901–1904; Senator from Pennsylvania 1904–1909; unsuccessful candidate for the Republican presidential nomination in 1908; commissioned Secretary of State in President Taft's Cabinet March 5, 1909, entered upon his duties March 6, 1909, and served until March 5, 1913; as Secretary of State, reorganized the Department on a divisional basis, extended the merit system to the Diplomatic Service up to the grade of chief of mission, pursued a policy of encouraging and protecting American investments abroad, and accomplished the settlement of the Bering Sea controversy and the North Atlantic fisheries controversy; resumed the practice of law in Pittsburgh; again Senator from Pennsylvania 1917–1921; died in Washington, D.C., October 12, 1921.

WILLIAM JENNINGS BRYAN was born in Salem, Illinois, March 19, 1860; graduated from Illinois College in 1881 (A.M. 1884) and from Union College of Law in 1883; admitted to the bar in 1883 and practiced in Jacksonville, Illinois; married Mary Elizabeth Baird in 1884; moved to Lincoln, Nebraska, in 1887 and continued the practice of law; delegate to the Democratic state convention in 1888; Representative from Nebraska 1891–1895; edited the Omaha *World-Herald* 1894–1896; delegate to the Democratic national conventions in 1896, 1904, 1912, 1920, and 1924; Democratic candidate for the Presidency in 1896, in 1900, and again in 1908; raised a regiment of volunteer infantry in 1898 and was commissioned colonel; founded a weekly newspaper, *The Commoner*, in 1901; toured the world 1905–1906; engaged in editorial writing and delivering Chautauqua lectures; commissioned Secretary of State in President Wilson's Cabinet March 5, 1913, entered upon his duties the same day, and served until June 9, 1915; as Secretary of State, negotiated treaties "for the advancement of peace" with thirty nations; resumed his writing and lecturing; established his home in Miami, Florida, in 1921; opposed Clarence Darrow as counsel in the Scopes trial at Dayton, Tennessee, in 1925; died in Dayton, July 26, 1925.

ROBERT LANSING was born in Watertown, New York, October 17, 1864; graduated from Amherst College in 1886; admitted to the bar in 1889 and practiced in Watertown; married Eleanor Foster in 1890; associate counsel for the United States in the Bering Sea Arbitration 1892–1893; counsel for the Mexican and Chinese Legations in Washington 1894–1895 and 1900–1901; counsel for the United States before the Bering Sea Claims Commission 1896–1897, before the Alaskan Boundary Tribunal in 1903, in the North Atlantic Coast Fisheries Arbitration 1908–1910, and in the American and British Claims Arbitration in 1912; agent of the United States in the last-mentioned arbitration 1913–1914; instrumental in founding the American Society of International Law in 1906 and in establishing the *American Journal of International Law* in 1907; Counselor of the Department of State 1914–1915; Secretary of State ad interim June 9–23, 1915; commissioned Secretary of State in President Wilson's Cabinet June 23, 1915, entered upon his duties June 24, 1915, and served until February 13, 1920; as Secretary of State, protested against British blockade and contraband practices, and signed the treaty of 1916 for the purchase of the Danish West Indies and the Lansing-Ishii Agreement of 1917 with Japan; practiced international law in Washington, D.C.; died in Washington, D.C. October 30, 1928.

BAINBRIDGE COLBY was born in St. Louis, Missouri, December 22, 1869; graduated from Williams College in 1890 and from New York Law School in 1892; admitted to the bar and practiced in New York City; married Nathalie Sedgwick in 1895 (divorced 1929); member of the state Assembly 1901–1902; assisted in founding the Progressive Party and was a delegate to its conventions in 1912 and 1916; counsel for a joint committee of the New York Legislature in an investigation of the public-utility commissions and public-service corporations in 1916; special assistant to the United States Attorney General in antitrust proceedings in 1917; member of the American Mission to the Inter-Allied Conference at Paris the same year; member of the United States Shipping Board 1917–1919 and a trustee and vice-president of the Emergency Fleet Corporation in 1918; commissioned Secretary of State in President Wilson's Cabinet March 22, 1920, entered upon his duties March 23, 1920, and served until March 4, 1921; as Secretary of State, forcefully enunciated American policy toward Soviet Russia and toward the mandates over former German colonies; practiced law in partnership with Woodrow Wilson in New York City 1921–1923; continued the practice of law; married Anne (von Ahlstrand) Ely in 1929; died in Bemus Point, New York, April 11, 1950.

CHARLES EVANS HUGHES was born in Glens Falls, New York, April 11, 1862; graduated from Brown University in 1881 (A.M. 1884) and from Columbia Law School in 1884; admitted to the bar in 1884 and practiced in New York City; married Antoinette Carter in 1888; professor of law at Cornell University

1891–1893; counsel for committees of the New York Legislature 1905–1906; special assistant to the United States Attorney General in the coal investigation in 1906; Governor of New York 1907–1910; Associate Justice of the United States Supreme Court 1910–1916; Republican candidate for the presidency in 1916; commissioned Secretary of State in President Harding's Cabinet March 4, 1921, entered upon his duties March 5, 1921, continued in office under President Coolidge, and served until March 4, 1925; as Secretary of State, presided over the Washington Conference on Limitation of Armament 1921–1922; member of the Permanent Court of Arbitration 1926–1930; chairman of the United States delegation to the Sixth Pan American Conference in 1928 and delegate to the Pan American Conference on Arbitration and Conciliation 1928–1929; judge of the Permanent Court of International Justice 1928–1930; Chief Justice of the United States Supreme Court 1930–1941; died in Osterville, Massachusetts, August 27, 1948.

FRANK BILLINGS KELLOGG was born in Potsdam, New York, December 22, 1856; went to Minnesota with his parents 1865; attended public schools; admitted to the bar in 1877 and commenced practice in Rochester, Minnesota; City Attorney of Rochester 1878–1881 and Olmstead County attorney 1882–1887; married Clara Margaret Cook in 1886; moved to St. Paul, Minnesota, in 1887 and continued the practice of law; Government delegate to the Universal Congress of Lawyers and Jurists at St. Louis, Missouri, in 1904; member of the Republican National Committee 1904–1912 and a delegate to the Republican National Convention in 1904, 1908, and 1912; special counsel for the government to prosecute antitrust suits; president of the American Bar Association 1912–1913; Senator from Minnesota 1917–1923; delegate to the Fifth Pan American Conference in 1923; served as Ambassador to Great Britain 1923–1925; commissioned Secretary of State in President Coolidge's Cabinet February 16, 1925, entered upon his duties March 5, 1925, and served until March 28, 1929; as Secretary of State, was coauthor of the Kellogg-Briand Peace Pact of 1928; awarded the Nobel Peace Prize in 1929; resumed the practice of law in St. Paul; judge of the Permanent Court of International Justice 1930–1935; died in St. Paul, December 21, 1937.

HENRY LEWIS STIMSON was born in New York City, September 21, 1867; graduated from Yale University in 1888; attended Harvard University (A.M. 1889) and Harvard Law School 1889–1890; admitted to the bar in 1891 and practiced in New York City; married Mabel Wellington White in 1893; United States Attorney for the Southern District of New York 1906–1909; Secretary of War in President Taft's Cabinet 1911–1913; delegate at large to the New York State constitutional convention of 1915; served in the United States Army in France 1917–1918, attaining the rank of colonel; practiced law in New York City; special representative of the President to Nicaragua in 1927; Governor General of the Philippine Islands 1927–1929; commissioned Secretary of State in President Hoover's Cabinet March 5, 1929, entered upon his duties March 28, 1929, and served until March 4, 1933; as Secretary of State, was chairman of the American delegation to the London Naval Conference in 1930, and formulated the "Stimson Doctrine" with regard to Japanese activities in China; resumed the practice of law in New York City; Secretary of War in the Cabinets of Presidents Roosevelt and Truman 1940–1945; retired from public life; died at "Highhold," his estate in West Hills, Huntington Township, Long Island, October 20, 1950.

CORDELL HULL was born in Overton (now Pickett) County, Tennessee, October 2, 1871; attended National Normal University, Lebanon, Ohio, 1889–1890; delegate to the Tennessee Democratic convention in 1890; graduated from Cumberland University Law School in 1891; admitted to the bar the same year and practiced in Celina, Tennessee; member of the state House of Representatives 1893–1897; served in Cuba as captain, Fourth Regiment, Tennessee Volunteer Infantry, in 1898; resumed the practice of law; judge of the Fifth Judicial Circuit of Tennessee 1903–1907; Representative from Tennessee 1907–1921 and 1923–1931; married Rose Frances (Witz) Whitney in 1917; chairman of the Democratic National Committee 1921–1924; Senator from Tennessee 1931–1933; commissioned Secretary of State in President Roosevelt's Cabinet March 4, 1933, entered upon his duties the same day, and served until November 30, 1944; as Secretary of State, sponsored a reciprocal-trade program, was chairman of American delegations to numerous international conferences, and was United States delegate to the Moscow Conference in 1943; appointed a delegate to the United Nations Conference at San Francisco in 1945; awarded the Nobel Peace Prize the same year; retired from public life; died at the Naval Hospital, Bethesda, Maryland, July 23, 1955.

EDWARD REILLY STETTINIUS, Jr., was born in Chicago, Illinois, October 22, 1900; attended the University of Virginia 1919–1924; married Virginia Gordon Wallace in 1926; associated with General Motors Corporation 1926–1934, becoming a vice-president in 1931; associated with United States Steel Corporation 1934–1940, becoming chairman of the board of directors in 1938; chairman of the War Resources Board in 1939; member of the advisory committee to the Council of National Defense in 1940; chairman of the Priorities Board and director of the Priorities Division of the Office of Production Management in 1941; Lend-Lease Administrator, special assistant to the President, and a member of the Canadian-American Joint Defense Production Committee 1941–1943; member of the Board of Economic Warfare 1942–1943; Under Secretary of State 1943–1944; commissioned Secretary of State in President Roosevelt's Cabinet November 30, 1944, entered upon his duties December 1, 1944, continued in office under President Truman, and served until June 27, 1945; as Secretary of State, accompanied President Roosevelt to the Yalta Conference in 1945, and was chairman of the United States delegation to the United Nations Conference at San Francisco the same year; was United States representative to the United Nations 1945–1946; rector of the University of Virginia 1946–1949; died in Greenwich, Connecticut, October 31, 1949.

JAMES FRANCIS BYRNES was born in Charleston, South Carolina, May 2, 1879; attended public schools; official court reporter 1900–1908; admitted to the bar in 1903 and practiced in Aiken, South Carolina; editor of the Aiken *Journal and Review* 1903–1907; married Maude Perkins Busch in 1906; solicitor for the Second Circuit of the State 1908–1910; Representative from South Carolina 1911–1925; delegate to all the Democratic national conventions from 1920 to 1940; practiced law in Spartanburg, South Carolina, 1925–1931; Senator from South Carolina 1931–1941; Associate Justice of the United States Supreme Court 1941–1942; director of the Office of Economic Stabilization 1942–1943; director of the Office of War Mobilization and Reconversion 1943–1945; accompanied President Roosevelt to the Yalta Conference in 1945; commissioned Secretary of State in President Truman's Cabinet July 2, 1945, entered upon his duties July 3, 1945, and served until January 21, 1947; as Secretary of State, accompanied President Truman to the Potsdam Conference in 1945, was United States member of the Council of Foreign Ministers at London

in 1945 and at Paris and at New York City in 1946, and represented the United States at the Paris Peace Conference in 1946; practiced law in Washington, D.C., 1947–1950; Governor of South Carolina 1951–1955; died in Columbia, South Carolina, April 9, 1972.

GEORGE CATLETT MARSHALL was born in Uniontown, Pennsylvania, December 31, 1880; graduated from Virginia Military Institute in 1901; married Elizabeth Carter Coles in 1902 (died 1927); served in the United States Army 1901–1945, attaining the rank of general of the Army; saw overseas service in World War I; married Katherine Boyce (Tupper) Brown in 1930; Chief of Staff of the Army 1939–1945; participated in the various World War II conferences of President Roosevelt with Prime Minister Churchill and with Marshal Stalin and Generalissimo Chiang Kai-shek; accompanied President Truman to the Potsdam Conference in 1945; special representative of the President to China with the rank of Ambassador 1945–1947; commissioned Secretary of State in President Truman's Cabinet January 8, 1947, entered upon his duties January 21, 1947, and served until January 20, 1949; as Secretary of State, was United States member of the Council of Foreign Ministers at Moscow and at London in 1947, and put forward the "Marshall Plan" for European economic recovery the same year; president of the American National Red Cross 1949–1950; Secretary of Defense 1950–1951; retired from public life; died in Washington, D.C., October 16, 1959.

DEAN GOODERHAM ACHESON was born in Middletown, Connecticut, April 11, 1893; graduated from Yale University in 1915 and from Harvard Law School in 1918; married Alice Stanley in 1917; an ensign in the United States Navy 1918–1919; served as private secretary to Louis D. Brandeis, Associate Justice of the United States Supreme Court, 1919–1921; admitted to the bar and practiced in Washington, D.C., 1921–1933 and 1934–1941; Under Secretary of the Treasury in 1933; Assistant Secretary of State 1941–1945 and Under Secretary of State 1945–1947; resumed the practice of law; appointed by the President a member of the Commission on Organization of the Executive Branch of the Government in 1947; chairman of the American section of the Permanent Joint Defense Board 1947–1948; commissioned Secretary of State in President Truman's Cabinet January 19, 1949, entered upon his duties January 21, 1949, and served until January 20, 1953; as Secretary of

State, was the United States member of the Council of Foreign Ministers at Paris in 1949, participated in the negotiation and signing of the North Atlantic Treaty of 1949, and served as chairman of the third session of the North Atlantic Council at Washington in 1950; resumed the practice of law; died in Sandy Spring, Maryland, October 12, 1971.

JOHN FOSTER DULLES was born in Washington, D.C., February 25, 1888; graduated from Princeton University in 1908; attended the Sorbonne 1908–1909 and George Washington University Law School 1910–1911; practiced law in New York City 1911–1917; married Janet Pomeroy Avery in 1912; served in the United States Army 1917–1918, attaining the rank of major; resumed the practice of law; adviser to President Wilson at the Paris Peace Conference and a member of the Reparations Commission and Supreme Economic Council in 1919; delegate to the Berlin Debt Conferences in 1933, to the United Nations Conference at San Francisco in 1945, and to the United Nations General Assembly in 1946, 1947, 1948, and 1950; interim Senator from New York in 1949; consultant to the Secretary of State in 1950; special representative of the President, with the rank of Ambassador, to negotiate the Japanese peace treaty 1950–1951; commissioned Secretary of State in President Eisenhower's Cabinet January 21, 1953, entered upon his duties the same day, and served until April 22, 1959; during his six-year tenure he made some 60 foreign trips and journeyed a total of almost half a million miles; instrumental in expanding the free world alliance system; died in Washington, D.C., May 24, 1959.

CHRISTIAN ARCHIBALD HERTER was born in Paris, France, March 28, 1895; graduated from Harvard in 1915; attaché to U.S. Embassy in Berlin 1916–1917 and for two months in charge of U.S. legation in Brussels; married Mary Caroline Pratt in 1917; served in the Department of State from 1917–1919; secretary, U.S. Commission to Negotiate Peace, Paris 1918–1919; personal assistant to Secretary of Commerce Herbert Hoover 1919–1924; executive secretary of the European Relief Council 1920–1921; newspaper editor and associate editor 1924–1936; lecturer, Harvard University 1929–1930; served in the Massachusetts House of Representatives 1931–1943 and as Speaker of that body 1939–1943; Representative to the U.S. Congress 1943–1953 and head of a House select committee that helped pave the way for

the Marshall Plan; Governor of Massachusetts from 1953 to 1957; served as Under Secretary of State 1957–1959 and commissioned Secretary of State in President Eisenhower's Cabinet on April 21, 1959, entered upon his duties April 22, 1959, and served until January 20, 1961; served as a trade negotiator in the administrations of John F. Kennedy and Lyndon B. Johnson; died in Washington, D.C., December 30, 1966.

DEAN DAVID RUSK was born in Cherokee County, Georgia, February 9, 1909; graduated from Davidson College in 1931; as a Rhodes Scholar studied at St. John's College, Oxford University 1931–1934; from 1934 to 1940 on the faculty of Mills College, Oakland, California and appointed Dean of Faculty in 1938; married Virginia Foisie in 1937; attained the rank of colonel during World War II and served as the deputy chief of staff for the China-Burma-India theater; assistant chief of the Department of State's Division of International Security Affairs in 1946; special assistant to the Secretary of War 1946; from 1947 to 1949 served in the Department of State as director of the Office of Special Political Affairs which later became the Office of United Nations Affairs; in 1949 appointed Deputy Under Secretary of State; in 1950 appointed Assistant Secretary of State for Far Eastern Affairs; president of the Rockefeller Foundation 1952–1961; commissioned Secretary of State in President Kennedy's Cabinet on January 21, 1961, entered upon his duties the same day, continued in office under President Johnson, and served until January 20, 1969; helped deal with such problems as the Cuban Missile Crisis, the 1967 Arab-Israeli war, the Dominican Republic intervention, the "Pueblo" incident, the closure of the border between East and West Berlin, and especially the Vietnam war; professor of international law at the University of Georgia 1969 to the present.

WILLIAM PIERCE ROGERS was born in Norfolk, New York, on June 23, 1913; graduated from Colgate University in 1934 and earned a law degree from Cornell University in 1937; married Adele Langston in 1936; Assistant District Attorney of New York County 1938–1942 and 1946–1947; served in U.S. Navy 1942–1946; counsel and chief counsel to the U.S. Senate Special Committee to Investigate the National Defense Program 1947–1948; chief counsel to the Senate Investigations Subcommittee of the Executive Expenditures Committee 1948–1950; practiced law 1950–1953; Deputy Attorney General

1953–1957; Attorney General 1957–1961; served as member of the U.S. delegation to the U.N. 20th General Assembly in 1965; member of the President's National Commission on Law Enforcement and Administration of Justice 1965–1967; U.S. representative to the United Nations in 1967; commissioned Secretary of State in President Nixon's Cabinet on January 21, 1969, entered upon duties January 22, 1969, and served until September 3, 1973; promoted a cease-fire in the Middle East in 1970 which lasted until the 1973 war; dealt with problems of security and cooperation in Europe; signed the Vietnam peace agreement; returned to the practice of law; received the Presidential Medal of Freedom October 15, 1973.

HENRY ALFRED KISSINGER   was born in Fürth, Germany, on May 27, 1923; emigrated to the United States in 1938; served in the U.S. Army in World War II; married Anne Fleischer in 1949– divorced in 1964; married Nancy Maginnes in 1974; earned his B.A. in 1950, M.A. in 1952, and Ph.D. in 1954 at Harvard University and was a member of the faculty from 1954 to 1971; consultant on foreign policy in the Kennedy and Johnson administrations; adviser to Governor Nelson Rockefeller of New York; named Assistant for National Security Affairs by President Nixon in 1968; in this position his many activities included participation in the 1972 presidential visit to the People's Republic of China and in the negotiations leading to the Vietnam peace agreement; commissioned Secretary of State in President Nixon's Cabinet on September 21, 1973, entered upon duties on September 22, 1973, continued in office under President Ford, and served until January 20, 1977; among other accomplishments as Secretary of State, was instrumental in the signing of cease-fire agreements by Israel with Egypt and Syria in 1973; promoted policy of détente with Soviet Union, which included the signing of trade and arms agreements; dealt with problems of energy and economic cooperation; awarded Nobel Peace Prize in 1973; lecturer and consultant on foreign affairs.

CYRUS ROBERTS VANCE   was born in Clarkburg, West Virginia, on March 27, 1917; graduated from Yale University in 1939 and Yale University Law School in 1942; served in the U.S. Navy during World War II; married Grace Sloane in 1947; practiced law in New York City, 1947–1960 and 1967–1977; consulting counsel for the Senate Special Committee on Space and Astronautics in 1958; General Counsel for

the Department of Defense 1961–1962; Secretary of the Army 1962–1964 and Deputy Secretary of Defense 1964–1967; President's special representative investigating the Detroit civil disturbances in 1967; served as special representative of the President in the Cyprus crisis in 1967; in 1968 was special representative of the President in Korea; negotiator at the Paris Peace Conference on Vietnam 1968–1969; commissioned Secretary of State in President Carter's Cabinet on January 23, 1977, entered upon his duties the same day, and served until April, 1980; returned to the practice of law.

EDMUND SIXTUS MUSKIE   was born in Rumford, Maine, March 28, 1914; graduated from Bates College 1936 and from Cornell Law School 1939; admitted to Massachusetts Bar 1939, Maine Bar 1940, and United States District Court 1941; practiced law in Waterville, Maine 1940, 1945–1955; served in the United States Navy 1942–1945; member Maine House of Representatives 1947–1951, and Democratic floor leader of that body 1949–1951; married Jane Frances Gray in 1948; Governor of Maine 1955–1959; Senator from Maine 1959–1980; Democratic candidate for the vice-presidency in 1968; chairman of Senate Budget Committee 1974–1980; commissioned Secretary of State in President Carter's Cabinet in 1980, and served until January 20, 1981; as Secretary of State, dealt with the Iranian hostage crisis; senior partner in law firm of Chadbourne, Parke, Whiteside and Wolff 1981 to the present.

ALEXANDER MEIGGS HAIG, JR.   was born in Philadelphia, Pennsylvania, December 2, 1924; graduated from the United States Military Academy 1947, the Naval War College 1960, and Georgetown University 1961; joined the United States Army in 1947, rising to the rank of General in 1973; married Patricia Antoinette Fox in 1950; deputy special assistant to the Secretary and Deputy Secretary of Defense 1964–1965; battalion and brigade commander in the Republic of Vietnam 1966–1967; Regimental Commander and Deputy Commandant of the United States Military Academy 1967–1969; Senior Military Advisor to the Assistant to the President for National Security Affairs 1970–1973; Vice-Chief of Staff, United States Army 1973; special emissary to Vietnam 1973; retired from United States Army 1973; Assistant to the President and White House Chief of Staff under Presidents Nixon and Ford 1973–1974; recalled to active duty in the United States Army 1974;

appointed Commander-in-Chief, United States European Command 1974–1979; Supreme Allied Commander Europe, NATO 1979; President and Chief Operating Officer, United Technologies Corporation 1980–1981; commissioned Secretary of State in President Reagan's Cabinet in January, 1981, and served until June, 1982.

GEORGE PRATT SCHULTZ was born in New York City, December 13, 1920; graduated from Princeton University in 1942 and from the Massachusetts Institute of Technology in 1949; served in the United States Marine Corps 1942–1945, attaining the rank of major, saw overseas service in the Pacific in World War II; married Helena Maria O'Brien 1946; faculty, MIT 1948–1957; Senate staff economist, President's Council of Economic Advisors 1955–1956 (on leave, MIT); professor of industrial relations 1957–1962, then dean 1962–1969, Graduate School of Business, University of Chicago; Secretary of Labor 1969–1970; director, Office of Management and Budget 1970–1972; Secretary of the Treasury 1972–1974; professor of management and public policy, Graduate School of Business, Stanford University 1974; executive vice-president 1974–1975, then president 1975–1979, Bechtel Corporation; vice-chairman, The Bechtel Group 1980–1982; commissioned Secretary of State in President Reagan's Cabinet in July, 1982.

Author Index

For discussion of a particular author's philosophy and arguments, see under the author's name in the Subject Index.

Italic numbers indicate authors and editors cited secondarily: editors listed in addition to authors, editors of collected works that contain primary citations, and authors and editors of works cited only in annotations.

Aaron, Daniel, 13:91
Abbas, S. A., 37:84
Abbot, William W., 3:24
Abbott, Frank, 19:310
Abbott, Freeland K., 18:120
Abdel-Malek, Anouar, 33:204
Abdullah, King of Jordan, 33:54–55
Abel, Elie, 25:28, 29:91
Abell, Tyler, *24:179*
Abella, Irving M., 36:185
Abend, Hallett, 21:213
Abernethy, Thomas P., 4:152, 6:3, 6:19
Abrahams, Paul P., 20:186, 39:96
Abrahamson, James L., 16:54
Abramowitz, Morton, 31:44
Abrams, Irwin, 16:129
Abrams, Matthew J., 36:104
Abramsky, C., *22:175*
Abranches, C. D. de, 15:204
Abueva, J. V., 30:110
Abu-Lughod, Ibrahim, 33:115
Accinelli, Robert D., 20:74, 20:97–99
Acheson, A. L. K., 36:60
Acheson, Dean, 24:90–91, 28:18, 29:117, *36:71,* 38:127
Achutegui, Pedro S. de, S. J., 13:163
Ackerman, Gary B., 39:198
Acomb, Evelyn, *4:116*
Adamec, Ludwig, 33:165
Adams, Brooks, 11:201
Adams, Charles Francis, *5:16,* 11:45
Adams, Charles Francis, Jr., 11:44, 11:99–100, 11:117, 11:127
Adams, D. K., 21:40
Adams, Ephraim D., 9:92, 9:116, 10:56, 11:31
Adams, Frederick C., 20:172, 22:216
Adams, Henry, 6:4, *6:24,* 11:101
Adams, Henry H., 23:59
Adams, Henry M., 5:152, *6:24*
Adams, Herbert B., 10:21
Adams, James Truslow, 1:172
Adams, John, 3:67, 5:16
Adams, John Quincy, 6:14–15
Adams, Mary P., 6:91
Adams, Nina S., 30:99
Adams, Richard N., 35:98
Adams, Roberta E., 35:7

Adams, Samuel, 3:68
Adams, Sherman, 24:200
Adams, T. W., 38:118
Adams, Thomas R., 3:1
Adamson, Rolf, 8:131
Adelman, Irman, 31:143
Adelman, Kenneth L., 37:211–212
Adenauer, Konrad, 28:22
Adler, Cyrus, 2:358
Adler, Dorothy R., 14:72
Adler, Jacob, 12:68–69
Adler, Les K., 22:98
Adler, Selig, 15:9, 18:121, 18:134, 19:189, 20:8, 20:121, 21:129, 23:41
Adler, Stephen, 29:92
Adloff, Richard, 32:182
Adomov, E. A., 11:139
African Bibliographic Center, 37:1
Agarossi, Elena, 23:258
Ageton, Arthur A., 23:78
Agudelo Villa, Hernando, 35:145–146
Aguilar, Luis E., 21:262
Aguilar Monteverde, Alonso, 2:259
Agwami, M. S., 33:109
Ahmad, Feroz, 33:185
Ahmat, Sharom, 17:277–278
Aimone, Alan C., 11:10
Aitken, Hugh G. J., 36:149
Ajami, Fouad, 33:43
Akenson, Donald H., 2:216
Akhavi, Shahrough, *33:180*
Akpan, Ntieyong U., 37:272
Alba, Victor, 35:147
Albaharna, Husain M., 33:257
Alberts, Robert C., 4:70
Albinski, Henry S., 32:39–40, 32:120, 32:138, 32:144
Albion, Robert G., 1:41, 8:132–133, 18:206, 40:41, 40:107
Albrecht, Ulrich, 40:1
Albrecht-Carrié, René, 19:249
Alcaraz, Ramón, 9:132
Alcock, Antony E., 38:135
Alden, John D., 40:166
Alden, John R., 3:78
Aldridge, Alfred O., 4:47
Alessio Robles, Vito, 9:19
Alexander, Charles C., 2:30, 24:201
Alexander, Fred, *32:12,* 32:29
Alexander, Harold Rupert Leofric

George, 1st Earl, 23:123
Alexander, Robert J., 35:66, 35:68–69, 35:71, 35:115, 35:188
Alexander, Sidney S., 33:31
Alexander, Yonah, 33:1
Alfaro, Ricardo J., 34:155
Alfonson, Oscar M., 17:287
Alger, Chadwick F., 2:199
Alisky, Marvin, 35:72, 35:247
Allard, Dean C., 30:163
Allard, Sven, 28:171
Allen, Cyril, 7:101
Allen, Devere, 16:83
Allen, Diane M., 25:93
Allen, Douglas, 13:58
Allen, Gardner W., 4:163, 5:204
13:48, 18:55
Allen, Gay Wilson, *16:113*
Allen, Harry C., 2:231–232, *14:29*
Allen, Howard W., 19:190
Allen, James B., 20:173
Allen, Robert L., 29:173
Allen, William R., 20:231
Allied Expeditionary Forces, Supreme Headquarters [SHAEF], 40:54
Allison, Graham T., 29:93, 39:26, 40:243
Allison, John M., 24:167
Alman, Miriam, 1:291
Alméras, Henri d', 5:93
Almond, Gabriel A., 2:200
Almond, Nina, 19:1
Alper, D. K., 36:105
Alperovitz, Gar, 25:157
Alpert, Eugene J., 31:60
Alsop, Stewart, 29:94
Altschuler, Glenn C., 16:74
Altschull, J. Herbert, 29:69
Alvarez, D. Alejandro, 7:130
Alvarez, David J., 23:238, 26:146, 33:53
Alvord, Clarence W., 3:187
Amacher, Ryan C., 39:201
Ambacher, Bruce, 7:117
Ambrose, Stephen E., 23:101, 23:151, 23:163, 24:30, 40:31, 40:62, 40:65, 40:133
Ambrosius, Lloyd E., 19:67, 21:105
American Assembly, 36:17, 37:181
American Historical Association, 1:1, 1:64, 1:215

Subject Index

Topics This section lists nations, topics, themes, and selected episodes and formal programs. The expanded table of contents also offers a chronological subject index to many diplomatic events and issues.

Individuals   The individuals listed here, both American and foreign, appear in the "Personalities" sections of the various chapters, in the entry titles, or in the annotations. Since not all autobiographies or memoirs, or other published works, are included here, be sure to compare this list with the author index. For example, historians (such as Charles A. Beard) may be listed here if their interpretations have been subjected to critical review, however their published works may only be listed in the author index. Similarly, if a diplomat wrote only his memoirs and his name did not appear elsewhere in the *Guide*, he may only be listed in the author index.

    So for best results, always consult, and compare, both the "individuals" list and the author index.

Americans

Foreigners